The HarperCollins World Reader

Single Volume Edition

MARY ANN CAWS
Chief Editor
City University of New York

CHRISTOPHER PRENDERGAST
Editor
City University of New York

HarperCollins*CollegePublishers*

The section on Africa was initially developed by Richard Bjornson: It is dedicated to his memory.

Acquisitions Editor: Lisa Moore
Developmental Editor: Dawn Groundwater
Project Coordination, Text and Cover Design: York Production Services
Cover Illustration: Jacob Lawrence: The Library. 1960.
National Museum of American Art/Art Resource, New York.
Photo Researcher: Sandy Schneider
Production Manager: Willie Lane .
Compositor: York Production Services
Printer and Binder: R. R. Donnelley & Sons Company
Cover Printer: The Lehigh Press, Inc.

For permission to use copyrighted material. grateful acknowledgment is made to the copyright holders on pp. 2799–2820, which are hereby made part of this copyright page.

The HarperCollins World Reader: Single Volume Edition
Copyright © 1994 by Mary Ann Caws

Library of Congress Cataloging-in-Publication Data

The HarperCollins world reader.
    Includes bibliographical references and indexes. Contents: 1. Antiquity to the early modern world —   2. The modern world.
    1. Literature—Collections.   I. Caws, Mary Ann.   II. Prendergast, Christopher.
PN6014.H3125   1994
808.8   93-39305
    ISBN 0-06-501382-4 (v. 1)
    ISBN 0-06-501383-2 (v. 2)
    ISBN 0-06-500750-6 (SVE)

    94 95 96 97   8 7 6   5 4 3 2 1

S
A

Brief Contents

Detailed Contents

SECTION III
East Asia: Early and Middle Periods   600

SECTION XII
The Modern Middle East   1596

SECTION XIII
Modern Africa   1734

SECTION XVII
Oral Literature Today 2590

SECTION XVIII
Writing Across Boundaries   2656

Preface

The HarperCollins World Reader assembles in one place—within the limits imposed by length—the selections that all the various editors together have chosen to form the best grid through which to perceive interlocking and yet separate currents of world literatures. The editorial team comprises over forty regional editors, consultants, and essayists, each with specialized knowledge in particular areas, as well as hundreds of reviewers with extensive experience as instructors of world literature.

In bringing together this diversity of texts and presentations, we have tried to offer a sensible and sensitive balance of new and familiar material, considering not only what is most teachable, but also what is most readable at the present moment. Alongside the main currents of traditional literatures, we wanted to represent voices previously neglected, some quieter, some louder. *The Harper-Collins World Reader* seeks to promote interactive reading within a comparative perspective. While each regional section fits into the overall structure governed by a *world* perspective, we have made every attempt to retain the specific and often contrasting styles of the readings and commentaries. Since a "world reader" is not a just a selection of readings, but also the person reading the world through them, our diverse ways of seeing and constructing viewpoints proved essential to this complicated project.

The Organization:
A New Way of Thinking

The HarperCollins World Reader provides a great range of material from very old to very new, in a manageable number of pages. Our team of specialized editors has taken great care to stress the specific character of the particular regions for which they were responsible. The literary content and arrangement of the individual sections are determined by their own cultural context rather than by Western or Eurocentric preconceptions. The expertise of our editors provides *The HarperCollins World Reader* with a rich diversity in both selections and genres giving a variety that would not be available from a small number of specialists.

We begin with The Ancient Mediterranean World, which is built around three distinct phases in this period of civilization (heroes, cities, and empires)—phases that brought the ancient Near East and Greek cultures into contact with one another in a cross-fertilization we see elsewhere throughout Asia, the Middle East, and Africa. This multicultural perspective that opens the book prepares the way for the crossweave of material throughout. South Asia, East Asia, the Middle East, and Africa are approached in the light of their own literary chronology, so that the time periods with which we are most familiar, such as "the middle ages," "Renaissance" or the "Age of Enlightenment" become largely irrelevant for them. This approach enables instructors to teach what is most critical within a particular tradition, according to its own conceptions, following the intellectual and geographic currents or interrelations. This comparative perspective is further encouraged through a Comparative Table of Contents by Theme found at the end of the book.

Two sections of particular interest, Oral Literature Today and Writing Across Boundaries, bear witness to *The HarperCollins World Reader's* combined emphasis on regional particularity and cross-cultural connections as they extend into the contemporary world. Brought together by theme rather than region, the works within these two sections focus on oral traditions and writing across cultural borders, respectively. Oral Literature Today combines an international array of genres that have been orally transmitted throughout generations and generations of face-to-face performance, while Writing Across Boundaries focuses on the writing of contemporary authors who have crossed lateral borders, either through exile or self-exile, and who play an important role in the understanding of our modern literary heritage.

What Is So Exciting About
The HarperCollins World Reader?

Reading takes vitality, energy, imagining. "You have," said the French philosopher Gaston Bachelard, "to imagine too much in order to have enough." We have all had to imagine a great deal in order to present this much, knowing that we could not possibly represent everything we would have liked to. We are particularly proud of the special features we have been able to include in this text:

- A global perspective in selections taken from all regions of the world and an organization representative of new conceptions and ways of thinking about these literatures
- Marginal as well as mainstream voices in literature, particularly the inclusion of women's voices
- A wide range of genres: poems, short stories, tales, legends, essays, aphorisms, letters, journals, and plays
- Exceptional translations: many of the works are translated for the first time within these pages. In some cases, such as the Bible and Dante, different translations are used for different parts of the work, so that the original is seen from more than one point of view. The Bible, for example, is rendered in four different versions, each with its own particular style and relevance; the King James version, which has had such an influence on English-language literature, the New International Version, the Jerusalem Bible translation, and the Revised Standard Version
- Extensive pedagogical support in the teaching of this material, including introductions that guide students through the historical, cultural, geographic, linguistic, and literary background of each region, with special attention to gender relations. Most selections are also preceded by a headnote that provides a brief biographical background on the author as well as specific information on the importance of each selection in the literary history of its region and period
- Artwork from around the world in a four-color insert, as well as interior black-and-white images preceding each section and within text selections, are included to visually enhance and complement the literature selections
- An Afterword on translation by Jorge Luis Borges
- A comparative chronology of world cultures
- An alternate Comparative Table of Contents organized by theme
- An essay on how to read and write about world literature

Acknowledgments

All the many people who have given their time and effort to *The HarperCollins World Reader* join me in hoping that its readers will find their own world widened in these pages.

Throughout the intensive and lengthy work required here, all of us were encouraged by the hundreds of world literature instructors who responded to questionnaires and telephone surveys and/or reviewed the manuscript in various drafts — sharing with us their experience in teaching this subject and their hopes for its future. They have all guided our progress and helped us shape this text to meet the needs of the changing emphasis in such a vast field undergoing constant metamorphosis.

Sydney Aboul-Hosn, Pennsylvania State University

Michael Aishelman, University of Virginia

Stanley Alexander, Stephen F. Austin State University

Liahna Babener, Montana State University

Richard Badessa, University of Louisville

Lea Baechler, Columbia University

Robert Baggs, University of Massachusetts at Amherst

Christopher Baker, Lamar University

Sylvan Barnet, Tufts University

Tita Baumlin, Southwest Missouri State University

David Benson, University of Connecticut

Paula Berggren, Baruch College, City University of New York

Ronald Bogue, University of Georgia

Max Braffet, Southwest Texas State University

Ward Briggs, University of South Carolina

Michael Bright, Eastern Kentucky University

Steven Buccleugh, Auburn University

Arthur Buck, West Virginia University

Roland Bush, California State University — Long Beach

Davey Carozza, University of Wisconsin — Milwaukee

Gerome Coffee, Montana State University

Arthur Coffin, Montana State University

Linda Coleman, University of Maryland

John Coumes, Southeastern Louisiana State University

Robert O. Crespi, University of California — Santa Cruz

Thomas Dasher, Valdosta State College

Frank Day, Clemson University

Steward DeSchell, Boston University

Caroline Eckhardt, Pennsylvania State University

Beverly Freer, Western Oregon State College

Catherine Gannon, California State University — San Bernardino

Patricia Gardner, Utah State University

Pat Garret, Louisiana Tech University

Sharon Gravett, Valdosta State College

Donald Gray, Indiana University

Sue Greene, Towson State University

MaryJean Gross, Southwest Texas State University

Donald Haberman, Arizona State University

John Hagge, Iowa State University

Sarah Hansom, University of Rhode Island

Janice Harris, University of Wyoming

Donald Hassler, Kent State University

Walter Hesford, University of Idaho

E. W. Hirschberg, University of South Florida

Ruth Hoberman, Eastern Illinois University

Rebecca Hogan, University of Wisconsin—Whitewater

Phil Holcomb, Angelo State University

Gail Houston, Brigham Young University

Ann Howard, University of Nevada at Las Vegas

Chris Hudgins, University of Nevada at Las Vegas

Ilinka Johnstine, Indiana University

Steve Kaplan, University of Southern Colorado

George Kennedy, University North Carolina—Chapel Hill

Scott Kiserman, University of Maryland

Andy Knoedler, University of Colorado at Boulder

Sidney Knoles, North Carolina State University

Gene Koppel, University of Arizona

Eleni Kourduriotis, Columbia University

Tom Kovach, University of Alabama

Douglas Krienke, Sam Houston State University

Tom LaPointe, Rutgers University

Rick Leahy, Boise State University

John Leavey, University of Florida

Catherine Lederer, Southwest Missouri State University

Jae Lee, Portland State University

Joan Levine, Boston University

John Locke, University of Arkansas

Marilyn Malina, University of Rhode Island

Marilyn Manners, University of California at Los Angeles

Nicholas Margaritis, Western Washington University

Harriet Margolis, Oakland University

Joellen Masters, Boston University

Donovan McDonough, St. Michael's College

John McNamara, University of Houston

Ronald McReynolds, Central Missouri State University

John Mercer, Northeastern State University

Mona Oliver, Northeast Louisiana University

Lee Paterson, Duke University

Donald Pattow, University of Wisconsin—Stevens Point

Robert Philipson, New York University

Pamela Pittman, Central Oklahoma State University

Jeff Portnoy, University of Nevada at Las Vegas

William Potts, Oregon State University

Richard Priebe, Virginia Commonwealth University

Renee Ramsey, Indiana State University

Pete Richardson, University of North Texas

Frances Rippy, Ball State University

Jean Roberts, The American University

Gregory Sadlek, University of Nebraska at Omaha

Alfred Shivers, Stephen F. Austin State University

Conrad Shynaker, University of Central Arkansas

Rachel Skalitzky, University of Wisconsin—Milwaukee

Bob Skulachy, Columbia University

Bill Streipberger, University of Washington

Johnye Strickland, University of Arkansas

Paula Sunderman, Mississippi State University

John Tanner, Brigham Young University

Pat Taylor, Western Kentucky University

Cammy Thomas, Millsaps College

Paul Trout, Montana State University

Laura Tulley, State University of New York at Binghamton

William Ulmer, University of Alabama

Martin Wallen, Oklahoma State University

Steve Ward, North Dakota State University

Thomas Wheeler, University of Tennessee at Knoxville

Charles Whitney, University of Nevada at Las Vegas

Gary Williams, University of Idaho

Bruce Wilson, St. Mary's College

John Wilson, University of Maine, Orono

Elaine Wise, University of Louisville

Richard Wolf, Mississippi State University

Joe Zavadil, University of New Mexico

Many thanks to those whose counsel was essential at various stages in this project:

Haskell Block, SUNY, Binghamton

Richard Brod, Modern Language Association

E. Mason Cooley, College of Staten Island, CUNY

Patrick Cullen, College of Staten Island and Graduate School, CUNY

Manthia Diawara, New York University

Robert Enright, Border Crossings, Manitoba

Daniel Gerould, Graduate School, CUNY

David Gordon, Hunter College and the Graduate School, CUNY

Judy Goulding, Modern Language Association

Barbara Harlow, University of Texas

Carolyn Heilbrun, Graduate School, CUNY

Michael Holquist, Yale University

Gerhard Joseph, Lehman College and the Graduate School, CUNY

Amy Mandelker, Graduate School, CUNY

Nancy K. Miller, Lehman College and Graduate School, CUNY

Dan Miron, Columbia University

Stephen Nichols, Johns Hopkins University

Burton Pike, Graduate School, CUNY

Edward Said, Columbia University

Grace Schulman, Baruch College, CUNY

Brian Swann, Cooper Union

Special thanks go to our authors of the Instructor's Manual:

Madeline Aria, Columbia University

Olga M. Davidson, Brandeis University

Tita Baumlin, Southwest Missouri State University

Louise Forsyth

Eric Haralson, Hofstra University

Randall Huff, University of San Francisco

Martha S. Grise, Eastern Kentucky University

Sharon Gravett, Valdosta State University

David Buerher, Valdosta State University

My warmest gratitude to each of the regional editors, art editors, and essayists for their prompt and generous support through all the stages of this project, in which each of them played an integral part. I could not have imagined such enthusiastic cooperation before beginning, and now in ending, I can only wish them easier projects from now on. May their glory be as great as their patience has been.

Without the determination and perseverance of my editors at HarperCollins, this massive project would never have seen the light of day: I want to thank Laurie Likoff, Betty Slack, and in particular Lisa Moore for her confidence in the project and in me; Marian Wassner, whose imaginative zeal took it through the early development stage; and Dawn Groundwater for carrying it through. Thanks also to Clifford Browder, Jeff Brown, Tom Maeglin, and to Terry-lynn Grayson and Susan Bogle at York Production Services for their patience in overseeing the whole production.

I also want to thank the poet/translators Robert Fagles and C. W. Williams for their friendship and assistance; the Slatkin family for their welcome and their care; my students Angela Bargenda and Kiyoko Ishikawa, for helping out; Liangyan Ge for helping with the Chinese sections; and the Henri Peyre Institute for the Humanities for its support. Particular thanks to William Kurzyna for preparing the comparative cultures addition, and to Matthew Rorison Caws for his steadfastness in editing, in counseling on geography, and in preparing the comparative table of contents by theme (with a team consisting of Anna Gebbie, Amy Stein, and Laura Rabhan). It would be impossible for me to express sufficient gratitude, from all of us, to Mark Getlein, whose infinitely intelligent research and imaginative solutions are responsible for the Historical Background appended to the introductions to each section (a massive job in which he was aided by David Cantor, Tan Lin, and Gordon Tapper).

Finally, my special gratitude to Gloria Loomis for her encouragement and understanding; to Boyce Bennett, for his unfailing good humor; to Hilary and Jonathan Caws-Elwitt for their loving interest; to Christopher Prendergast for his ideas concerning the world, our readings of it, and the texts and essays selected; and to all my friends who moved from bewilderment at the scope of this undertaking to a guarded fascination with its outcome.

Mary Ann Caws
Chief Editor

PUBLISHER'S NOTE: *The HarperCollins World Reader* is available in three formats. For one-semester courses, it is available as a single volume edition (ISBN: 0-06-500750-6). For two-semester courses, *The HarperCollins World Reader* is available in split versions: *The HarperCollins World Reader,* Antiquity to the Early Modern World (which begins with Section 1, The Ancient Mediterranean World, and ends with Section VIII, The Early Americas) (ISBN: 0-06-501382-4), as well as *The HarperCollins World Reader,* The Modern World (which begins with Section IX, Modern South Asia, and ends with Section XVIII, Writing Across Boundaries) (ISBN: 0-06-501383-2).

In addition, HarperCollins has made available an extensive teaching resource package to support *The HarperCollins World Reader*. For more information on any of the following resources, please contact your HarperCollins representative or write to: English Literature Marketing Manager, HarperCollins College Publishers, 10 East 53rd Street, New York, NY 10022.

- *The Odyssey*, translated by Richmond Lattimore, can be packaged with *The HarperCollins World Reader*, Antiquity to the Early Modern World, at a 60% discount off the list price for *The Odyssey*.
- *100 Years of Solitude*, by Gabriel Garcia Marquez, can be packaged with *The HarperCollins World Reader*, The Modern World, at a 60% discount off the list price for *100 Years of Solitude*.
- *Issues in World Literature*, edited by Mary Ann Caws with Pat Laurence, City College, City University of New York, and Sarah Bird Wright, College of William and Mary. This book of essays was written specifically to accompany this text and can be packaged with *The HarperCollins World Reader* gratis for students. The essays include: "The World Reader and the Idea of World Literature" by Christopher Prendergast, City University of New York; "Reading a World" by Mary Ann Caws, City University of New York; "Whose Canon Is It Anyway?" by Barbara Christian, University of California at Berkeley; "Literature and Politics" by Susan Rubin Suleiman, Harvard University; "The Politics of Genre" by Stephen Heath, Jesus College, Cambridge University; "Speaking of Writing and Writing Speech: The Orality and Literacy of Literature" by Christopher Miller, Yale University; "Gender Reading" by Susan Gubar, Indiana University, Carolyn Heilbrun, City University of New York, bell hooks, City College, City University of New York, Mrya Jehlen, University of Pennsylvania, and Catharine R. Stimpson, Rutgers University; "Place, Exile, and Affiliation: Migrant and Global Literatures" by Shirley Geok-lin Lim, University of California at Santa Barbara; "Culturally Variable Ways of Seeing: Art and Literature" by Mary Beard, Newnham College, Cambridge University; "Periods and Ideologies" by Earl Miner, Princeton University; "Making Room for the Avant-Garde" by Marjorie Perloff, Stanford University.
- Comprehensive *Instructor's Manual*, by a team of experienced world literature instructors, provides in-depth coverage of each region and each selection from an historical, literary, and pedagogical perspective. The *Instructor's Manual* includes sample syllabi, a glossary of literary terms, and for each section of the text, an overview of the historical and literary issues of the region and period with a special focus on the role of women; a pronunciation guide; and classroom strategies, such as suggestions for making connections between texts across cultures and periods, ideas for using media in the classroom, discussion questions, topics for writing, and an extensive bibliography.
- *Writers on Writers* videotape, depicting Anton Chekhov's story "Enemies" (included in Section XIV: Modern Europe) through an original screenplay by Jamaica Kincaid and followed by an interview with Kincaid in which she reads from her work (including "Girl," in Section XV: The Caribbean) and discusses adapting works across cultures. This videotape is produced through an exclusive partnership among HarperCollins College Publishers, WGBH (Boston), and the British Broadcasting Corporation. It is only available through HarperCollins and is free to adopters of *The HarperCollins World Reader*. A library of other high-quality audio- and videotapes is also available to qualified adopters of *The HarperCollins World Reader*.

The
HarperCollins
World Reader

Back panel of a throne of Tutankhamen.
Egyptian, Eighteenth Dynasty
(fourteenth century B.C.E.).

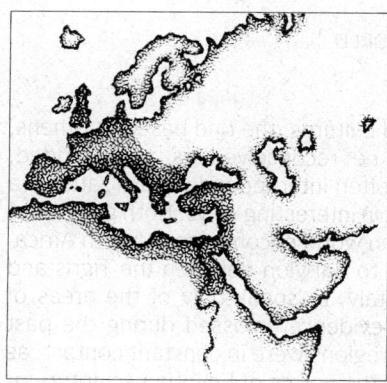

SECTION I
The Ancient Mediterranean World

This section brings together a number of ancient texts from Mesopotamia and the regions surrounding the Mediterranean Sea. The selections encompass a span of time ranging from the third millennium B.C.E. to the second century of the common era, and they are drawn from the civilizations of Sumer, Akkad, Babylonia, Egypt, Israel, Greece, and Rome.

In considering this broad arc of time and these diverse civilizations under a single heading, we are already making a significant and, we believe, long overdue departure from the conventional viewpoint, which has tended to oppose two great unities: "The Ancient Near East," comprising Mesopotamia, Egypt, and Israel, and "The Classical World" of Greece and Rome. In the ancient Near East (to reduce this notion of opposition to its essence), religion and mysticism were thought to dominate; in the classical world, humanism and rational inquiry were considered to have sprung into being in a moment of unprecedented cultural genius. This view adequately served the eighteenth- and nineteenth-century European scholars who formulated it, for it allowed them to concentrate on what they saw as the two most direct sources of their own culture: the religion of the Hebrews (including Jesus) and the humanism of Greece. But it could be maintained only through an oversimplification of both Greece and Israel and the wholesale exclusion of other bodies of material that archaeology and scholarship have steadily brought to light.

Antiquity can no longer be adequately described as a bipolar opposition of two unified cultures, the one based in Athens, the other in Jerusalem; rather, it should be reconceived as an extended, multipolar system of historically related and often interdependent civilizations, a region at once disunified and yet still coherent in interesting ways. Both geographically and culturally, the ancient Mediterranean world encompassed North Africa, Palestine and the Fertile Crescent stretching to Babylon between the Tigris and Euphrates rivers, Asia Minor, Greece, and Italy, to speak only of the areas of greatest literary production. Archaeological evidence amassed during the past two centuries has shown that these different regions were in constant contact, as is vividly evident in the Greek adaptations of the norms of Egyptian sculpture or the transmission of what eventually became the Roman alphabet from the Semites to the Greeks via the Phoenicians.

The ancient Mediterranean included literary cultures of great antiquity as well as those of later origin. The oldest writing systems in the world, Egyptian hieroglyphics and Sumerian cuneiform, were created early in the third millennium B.C.E., and many of the literary forms of later antiquity — lyric and epic poetry, historical texts, hymns and religious texts, and stories for pure enjoyment — were first explored by the Sumerians, their successors in Babylonia and Assyria, and the Egyptians. The literary production of most of these older cultures continued through the first millennium B.C.E., overlapping first with the Hebrews and a variety of other groups (Phoenicians, Minoans, Mycenaeans, Chaldeans, and Hittites, to name but a few), and then with the Greeks and Romans.

The literatures of the ancient Mediterranean share "family resemblances" in their exploration of questions about the construction of the cosmos and of human society within it, about the nature of mortality and the relationship of the gods to the mortal realm, and about human social relations, both individual and collective. The writers of antiquity were keenly aware of the degree to which their societies were responding to the other societies around them. Indeed, a recurrent theme in ancient literature is the definition of a culture in relation to its surroundings and in relation to its own past, a process that often involved either incorporating or purging elements transmitted from abroad. The wanderings of Odysseus in the *Odyssey*, for example, reinforce what it is to be Greek by looking at what is not Greek. The first writers of the Hebrew Bible adapted older polytheistic creation myths to serve their own belief in a single god; later writers revised some of their efforts, in all probability ridding them of residual traces of polytheism that were no longer acceptable. When empires were created through conquest, more complex moral and philosophical issues of cultural contact evolved. Seen in this light, for example, the Egyptian *Hymn to the Aten* shows a developed awareness of the diversity of the cultures under Egyptian rule.

The readings we have selected here emphasize the interrelations and overarching coherence of the ancient Mediterranean world. We have aimed not for a survey that represents each culture equally but instead for illuminating juxtapositions, progressions, and contrasts. To encourage a new approach, we have chosen not to isolate the selections by culture, nor to interweave them in a single, extended chronological sequence. Rather, we have grouped the readings under three headings: The World of Heroes, The World of the City, and The World of Empire. The headings are not thematic (though they can be used as a springboard for thematic discussion), but reflect three broad stages in a pattern of development largely shared by these civilizations. We propose them as a framework for considering the literature of the ancient Mediterranean in the light of changing perspectives through which its various peoples sought to understand their existence. Headnotes to the selections draw attention where appropriate to the diverse roles of literature in these societies and invite readers to make connections across cultures, across categories, and over time.

The surviving literature of the ancient world generally reflects the concerns and perspectives expressive of the male-dominated societies that produced it. There is little direct testimony that helps us to understand the experience and the viewpoint of women in these societies. In an effort to use what indirect evidence we have, we have made a point of including texts in which women figure prominently as heroines or goddesses. The *Hymn to Demeter,* though in all probability composed by a man, is particularly noteworthy in its representation of the institution of marriage from a female point of view, focusing on the separation of mother and daughter. The lyrics of the Greek poet Sappho included here are among the few surviving texts from a woman's hand. Fragmentary as they are, they offer us an invaluable opportunity to recover a female poetic voice — one that responds powerfully to those of her male counterparts.

We expect that readers will discover here material that is both surprising and moving; and we hope that these readings will provide a new sense of the vitality of the cultures of the ancient Mediterranean.

Historical Background

Mesopotamia

Mesopotamia, the "land between the rivers," encompassed an area roughly equivalent to present-day Iraq. The city-states that made up the civilizations of Mesopotamia clustered along the Tigris and Euphrates rivers, whose waters fed the irrigation systems that supported the vast husbandry needed to sustain urban life. But while an abundance of fertile land made Mesopotamia desirable, a lack of natural boundaries made it difficult to unite and vulnerable to invasion, and its political history is a stormy one.

Civilization first arose in Sumer, the southernmost portion of Mesopotamia, around 3500 B.C.E.; a dozen Sumerian city-states emerged as powers some seven hundred years later. With their invention of writing by 3300 B.C.E., the Sumerians became the first people to leave behind not just artifacts, but words. Sumerian script is known as cuneiform, meaning wedge-shaped (from the Latin *cuneus,* "wedge"). Its characteristic triangular marks were made by pressing a reed stylus into a damp clay tablet, which was subsequently left to bake to rock-like hardness in the sun. Cuneiform spread by trade, conquest, and diplomacy throughout Mesopotamia. Adapted by each people to the needs of their own language, it served as the regional writing system for over three millennia. The complexities of cuneiform took many years to master, and literacy was the special skill of an elite class of scribes trained to staff the vast religious/political bureaucracies typical of Mesopotamian societies.

Shortly after 2400 B.C.E. the Sumerians were conquered by a Semitic people from Akkad, the neighboring region to the north. The two cultures had long been in contact, and the Akkadians had already adopted many elements of Sumerian civilization, including writing. The Akkadians established the first known empire, which stretched from the Mediterranean to the Persian Gulf. The empire did not last long, however, and fell to invaders around 2250 B.C.E. Toward the end of the following century, the Sumerians regained control over Sumer and Akkad, but when their capital city, Ur, was sacked by invaders 108 years later, this empire, too, disintegrated into independent city-states.

A second Semitic people, the Amorites, who had established their capital in Akkad in Babylon, were the next to unify the region, extending their rule throughout Mesopotamia to create the Babylonian Empire in the mid-1700s B.C.E. As had the Akkadians before them, the Babylonians built their civilization on the foundations laid by the Sumerians. The language of business and government was Akkadian, but scribes were required to master Sumerian as well, and Sumerian culture was studied intensively. A city of unrivaled splendor, Babylon became the cultural center of Mesopotamia, a reputation it kept for some thousand years, long after its political power had faded.

The Sumerian and Babylonian literature in this section dates from this first cycle of Mesopotamian history. The subsequent history of the region should also be briefly told, for its names are linked to the fates of the other peoples of the ancient Mediterranean. Raided by the Hittites, an Indo-European speaking people who had settled in Asia Minor (present-day Turkey), and other invaders, the Babylonian Empire crumbled around 1600 B.C.E. Numerous small kingdoms rose and fell over the ensuing 500 years, but the next sizeable empire was built by the Assyrians from the north of Mesopotamia, who brutally subjugated not only all of Mesopotamia but also Syria, Palestine, and even Egypt. Assyrian rule was notoriously harsh, yet as custodians of the now many-layered civilization of Mesopotamia the Assyrians were scrupulous, and in their great library at Ninevah were preserved the writings of Babylon and Sumer. The Assyrian Empire fell in 612 B.C.E., and Babylon enjoyed a final cultural flowering with the Neo-Babylonian Empire, ruled by yet another Semitic people, the Chaldeans. Their empire lasted until 539 B.C.E., when the entire region was conquered from the east by the Persians.

Egypt

As in Mesopotamia, civilization in Egypt grew up along a river, the 750-mile length of the Nile. But while the Tigris and Euphrates were prone to disastrous and unpredictable floods (the floods of Mesopotamian myth are rooted in experience), the Nile was gentle and reliable. Each year, on schedule, it swelled, overflowed its banks, and then receded, depositing a nutrient-rich layer of silt over the farmland. Protected to the south by a series of cataracts and to the east and west by vast deserts, Egypt developed with relatively little interference from outsiders for much of its long history.

Civilization emerged in Egypt at roughly the same time it appeared in Sumer. The two regions were probably in contact, and the Egyptians may have even learned the idea of writing from the Sumerians. Unlike cuneiform, which began inauspiciously as a method for noting transactions and inventories, Egyptian hieroglyphs were from the start intended to record spoken language. As in Mesopotamia, the complexities of the writing system gave rise to a professionally trained scribal class. Throughout Egyptian history, literacy was the privilege of scribes and priests and a source of considerable power. Whether there is any direct connection between cuneiform and hieroglyphics is a matter of ongoing debate; what is certain is that Egypt had developed its own form of writing by about 3100 B.C.E., for that is when we find recorded the name of its first king, Narmer, who unified the regions of Lower (northern) Egypt and Upper (southern) Egypt into a single country. The subsequent history of Egypt unfolds against the successions of thirty ruling dynasties and is marked by three eras of great stability and achievement known as Old Kingdom, Middle Kingdom, and New Kingdom.

The Old Kingdom comprises the Third to Sixth Dynasties (c. 2700 – 2200 B.C.E.). This period saw the construction of the greatest of the pyramids – colossal tombs filled with treasure to accompany the king (or *pharaoh,* from the Egyptian word for *great house* or *palace*) on his journey to the afterlife. Having ruled on earth as a god incarnate, he would now rejoin the gods in immortality.

High taxes, a string of crop failures, and the crippling expense of lavish burials brought an end to the Sixth Dynasty; nobles rebelled, reclaiming their provinces, and civil war ensued. Order returned with the Middle Kingdom, presided over by the kings of the Eleventh and Twelfth Dynasties (c. 2050–1800 B.C.E.). Instead of grandiose tombs, these rulers focused on public works (today's "infrastructure") such as irrigation projects. They also extended the kingdom to the south with the conquest of gold-rich Nubia. Civil wars of succession followed the Twelfth Dynasty, and Egypt suffered a major invasion for the first time when a largely Semitic people known as the Hyksos entered from Palestine and conquered the Delta region.

Toward the middle of the sixteenth century the Egyptians finally mobilized to expel the invaders. They pursued the Hyksos all the way into Palestine, thereby ushering in the New Kingdom (c. 1570–1090 B.C.E.), Egypt's age of empire. The kings of the Eighteenth Dynasty reclaimed Nubia and extended Egyptian rule from Palestine north through Phoenicia (roughly present-day Lebanon) and east through Syria to the Euphrates. Their capital city, Thebes, surpassed even Babylon in magnificence, and tribute poured in from the conquered as well as from neighboring powers. During the mid-fourteenth century, most of Egypt's Middle Eastern possessions fell away from the empire. The kings of the Nineteenth Dynasty entered into extended warfare with the Hittites (who had expanded into the region) to recapture the territories, but they were eventually forced to settle for a peace treaty in 1269 B.C.E.

Egypt's long decline had begun. Priests and merchants gained power; kings lost it. Libyans invaded from the west in 940 B.C.E. and established a dynasty. Two centuries later, the Kushites of Nubia conquered Egypt from the south and founded the Twenty-fifth Dynasty. The Assyrians were next, invading from the east and subsuming Egypt into their empire in 671 B.C.E. They were quickly routed (with help from Greek mercenaries), but in 525 B.C.E. the country fell again, this time to the Persians. Two hundred years later, Alexander the Great conquered the country for Greece, and under the Greek dynasty that he installed, Egypt passed into the Hellenistic Age.

Hebrews

Our major source for the history of the Hebrews is their great work, the Bible. Historians must approach it warily, however, being careful to sift historical fact from religious and poetic truths. A seminomadic people, the Hebrews probably did, as the Bible narrates, come out of Sumer and migrate to the southeastern

Mediterranean sometime after 1900 B.C.E. Later, some of them moved on to Egypt, most likely during the period of Hyksos occupation. With the advent of the New Kingdom, the Hebrews would have been forced into service as laborers on the vast construction projects typical of Egyptian rulers. Eventually, many Hebrews left Egypt and sought to rejoin the rest of their people in Palestine. The Bible sets the story of their departure during the reign of Ramses II, which would place it shortly after 1300 B.C.E.

In a loose confederation of twelve tribes—an era known as the days of judges (temporary leaders in times of military danger)—the Hebrews successfully carved out a territory for themselves in Palestine by 1200 B.C.E. In an attempt to fend off invasions from a people who were eventually to be known as the Philistines, the Hebrews later regrouped as a monarchy and reached their greatest glory as a temporal power under Kings David and Solomon in the tenth century. After 922 B.C.E., the realm split into two kingdoms: northern Israel, with its capital at Samaria; and southern Judah, with its capital at Jerusalem. Israel fell to the Assyrian Empire in 722 B.C.E.; its people were deported (the famous "ten lost tribes" of Israel) and replaced with other settlers. Judah withstood the Assyrian assault but fell in 586 B.C.E. to the conquering forces of the Neo-Babylonian Empire, which exiled a great portion of the population to Babylon. Seventy years later, the Persian conquerors of the Neo-Babylonian Empire allowed the Jews to return to their homeland, and many did.

Although it retained a large measure of autonomy, the new state of Judah was under foreign domination for most of the rest of its existence, belonging first to the Hellenistic empire of Egypt, then to the Roman Empire. In response to uprisings in the early part of the common era, the Romans destroyed Jerusalem in 70 C.E. and again in 132 C.E., putting an end to the Hebrews' unity and independence as a people until the founding of the state of Israel in the twentieth century.

Greece

The Greek peninsula was the site of two Greek-speaking civilizations in the ancient world. The first was built by the Mycenaeans (so-called after their most important city, Mycenae), who took over the peninsula around 2000 B.C.E. Their chief teachers in the arts of civilization were the Minoans, whose vigorous culture on the island of Crete was already fully established. (The pupils repaid their teachers none too handsomely, conquering Crete in 1450 B.C.E.) The Mycenaeans were seafaring traders, but also pirates and raiders, and they probably did, as later Greek epics relate, destroy the city of Troy on the coast of Asia Minor, although we do not know under what circumstances.

Starting around 1200 B.C.E., a new wave of barbarian tribes, the Dorian Greeks, descended into the peninsula, overwhelming the Mycenaeans, who fled to the Aegean Islands and eventually settled the Aegean coast of Asia Minor. For the next several hundred years, our historical record is a blank. These "dark years" of Greek history are especially intriguing to scholars. It appears now that toward the end of their dominance the Mycenaeans knew writing, which they had either adapted from the Minoans or directed the Minoans to adapt for them. While we have no indications that their script, known as Linear B, was ever used for anything but palace inventories, its sudden and total eclipse is a mystery which at the very least underscores the fragility of literacy in the ancient world. When the Greeks begin to write again, in the eighth century B.C.E., their script bears no traces of Linear B, but instead employs a new concept, the alphabet. The first alphabet, known as Old Canaanite, was developed around 1500 B.C.E. in the eastern Mediterranean. From it all alphabets—such visually diverse systems as Hebrew, Arabic, and Latin—ultimately derive. Its immediate descendant was Linear Phoenician, the alphabet adapted by the Greeks, whose decisive contribution was the addition of letters to represent vowel sounds. Interestingly, the intellectual forefront of the new Hellenic culture (from *Hellas,* the ancient Greek name for *Greece*) was not the peninsula but the Asia Minor coast—a region called Ionia—where the first philosophers and poets arose among the descendants of the displaced Mycenaeans.

Greece developed as a confederation of fiercely independent, intensely competitive city-states. Their political development was diverse, and they variously experienced (and named) four major forms of government: monarchy, oligarchy, tyranny, and democracy. In a mountainous country with little arable land, overpopulation was a constant concern. Between 750 and 550 B.C.E. Greece established numerous colonies along the Black Sea coast and at key points around the Mediterranean, thus siphoning off potentially disruptive excesses of Greek citizens while at the same time creating new opportunities for trade. By the end of this period, Athens and Sparta had emerged as the two most important and powerful city-states.

The main foreign threat to Greece was Persia, which began to amass a huge empire in the mid-sixth century. (Remember that the Persians conquered the Neo-Babylonian Empire in 539 B.C.E. and Egypt in 525 B.C.E.) Extending their rule across Asia Minor, the Persians subjugated the cities of Ionia in 549 B.C.E. (The subsequent flight of many Ionian Greeks did much to spread Hellenic culture throughout the Greek world.) In 499 B.C.E. the Ionians rebelled and appealed to Athens for help; Greece entered into war with Persia, dramatically triumphing in 479 B.C.E. after coming perilously close to defeat.

Athens, whose fleet had been largely responsible for the last-minute victory, emerged from the conflict with a new sense of energy and self-confidence. It became the leading city-state of Greece and entered into an astonishing period of artistic and intellectual vigor known as the Golden Age. To combat the continuing Persian threat, Athens formed and led the Delian League, a naval alliance that succeeded in reclaiming Ionia in 468 B.C.E. At this point, the alliance could have disbanded, but Athens now repressed any attempts at secession. The Athenians claimed to be leading a union of democratic states, an example to the rest of Hellas. To some of its members, but especially to Sparta and its allies, the league had become the Athenian empire, and they accused Athens of tyranny. Mounting tensions led to the Peloponnesian War in 431 B.C.E. The war, which pitted Sparta against Athens, eventually involved—and exhausted—all of Greece. Athens surrendered in 404 B.C.E. and was stripped of its empire.

The politically unstable and economically depressed Greece of the fourth century left ample opportunity for a strong, decisive leader. Such a person emerged in Macedonia, a region just north of Greece, in Philip II, who conquered Greece and forced its city-states into a league to wage a campaign against Persia. After Philip's assassination in 336 B.C.E., his twenty-year-old son, Alexander, took command. With an army drawn from Macedonia and the Greek league, Alexander reclaimed Asia Minor, Syria, Palestine, and Egypt from the Persians. He defeated the Persian king decisively in Mesopotamia in 331 B.C.E., then marched on to conquer the rest of the Persian Empire, reaching as far as India. Alexander died suddenly at the age of thirty-two, and his vast empire was carved into three: the Ptolemaic Empire (Egypt and Palestine; Ptolemy was the name of the new dynasty Alexander had installed in Egypt); the Seleucid Empire (Alexander's Asian conquests, including most of the eastern provinces of the former Persian empire); and Macedonia and Greece.

In this configuration, the ancient Mediterranean passed into the Hellenistic (meaning Greek-like — that is, based in Greek culture) Age. The Seleucid Empire soon splintered into various kingdoms, and Greece regained independence from Macedonia. The light of Hellenism was to burn brightest and longest in Alexandria, Egypt, the capital of the Ptolemies, and it is with the fall of this city in 30 B.C.E. to a new power, Rome, that historians date the end of the Hellenistic Age.

Rome

Rome was probably no more than a collection of villages — the meeting place for a group of tribes called the Latins — when the Etruscans conquered it after 625 B.C.E. The Etruscans had established the first civilization in Italy, probably during the ninth century B.C.E. Under the Etruscan kings, Rome grew into an important city-state; its people worshipped the Etruscans' gods and observed their customs, and they mastered the Etruscan arts of building and writing. (The Etruscans had adopted the alphabet, along with other elements of their civilization, from the Greeks, who had colonized the southern portion of Italy. Etruscan writing has never been deciphered. Along with an undeciphered Minoan script known as Linear A, it remains one of the most tantalizing "locked doors" of the ancient Mediterranean world.)

In 509 B.C.E. the Romans overthrew their Etruscan king. Determined never again to suffer the absolute power of a monarch, they founded their independent state as a republic (from the Latin *res publicum*, which roughly translates as "something that concerns everyone"), governed by two chief executives (*consuls*), each elected to a one-year term, and an advisory body of nobles (*patricians*) called the senate. As the republic evolved, ordinary citizens (*plebeians*) gradually won the right to elect one of the consuls as well as their own body of representatives.

During the early phase of the republic, to 133 B.C.E., Rome expanded through warfare and alliances to become the dominant power of the Hellenistic Age. After first subduing all of Italy, Rome fought and destroyed the great naval power of Carthage (a wealthy city in Africa near present-day Tunis, originally founded as a Phoenician colony), in the process gaining control over Sicily, Sardinia, Corsica, Spain, and the portion of Africa around Carthage itself. To the east, Rome subdued a newly militant Macedonia, established power over Greece, forced the Seleucid Empire out of Asia Minor, and extended its protection to Egypt and Judea.

During the late phase of the republic, Rome suffered three civil wars as rival generals led their armies against each other for control of the state. The empire continued to grow, for each general consolidated his power base by conquest.

The last of these wars ended in 30 B.C.E., with the victory of Caesar Octavian over the combined forces of Mark Antony and Cleopatra, the queen of Egypt.

With the triumph of Octavian, the republic effectively came to an end, for he ruled as Augustus, Rome's first emperor. To ensure stability and legitimize his rule, Augustus preserved republican institutions such as the senate. For the rest of its history, Rome would be ruled in this way—a thinly disguised dictatorship we call the empire. During the first two centuries of the common era, Roman dominion reached its greatest extent, and the empire stretched from Britain to the Euphrates and around the entire perimeter of the Mediterranean.

Culturally, Rome came of age in the Hellenistic world, and its artistic thought was shaped by Greece. Roman literature flowered first in the late republic and reached its classical peak in the Augustan Age. The majority of the Roman selections here are drawn from this most creative period.

Further Readings

Alter, Robert, and Frank Kermode, eds. *The Literary Guide to the Bible*. Cambridge: Harvard University Press, 1987.

Boardman, John, Jasper Griffin, and Oswyn Murray, eds. *The Oxford History of the Classical World*. Oxford: Oxford University Press, 1986.

Burkert, Walter. *The Orientalizing Revolution: Near Eastern Influence on Greek Culture in the Early Archaic Age*. Cambridge: Harvard University Press, 1992.

Hallo, William, and W. K. Simpson. *The Ancient Near East: A History*. New Haven: Yale University Press, 1974.

Ogilvie, R. M. *Roman Literature and Society*. Harmondsworth, England: Penguin Books, 1988.

Saggs, H. W. F. *The Greatness That Was Babylon*. New York: New American Library, 1962.

Vernant, J. P. *The Origins of Greek Thought*. Ithaca, N.Y.: Cornell University Press, 1982.

ANONYMOUS (c. 1500–1200 B.C.E.)
Ancient Babylon

Enuma Elish, the Babylonian creation epic, recounts the origins of the gods and of the world, culminating in the birth of Marduk, patron god of Babylon. The forces of chaos, embodied in the goddess Tiamat and her children, threaten to take over the universe until Marduk leads the defense. After Tiamat's defeat, Marduk declares Babylon the ritual center of the world. He establishes cosmic order with the movements of the planets and the division of time, and he creates humanity to serve the gods.

The text is preserved on clay tablets written during the first millennium B.C.E., but the epic was probably composed earlier, perhaps sometime between 1500 and 1200 B.C.E. Presumably many of the elements of the story are much older still. The epic was used ritually, recited or performed during the annual festival for the new year in Babylon. The audience at this celebration included all of the royal governors, courtiers, and officers, and it was at this time that the king's mandate to rule as Marduk's earthly representative was renewed.

The epic's creation myths show many parallels to later accounts in the Bible and in Hesiod's *Theogony*. Its vivid dialogue and action invite comparisons with the epics of Homer, the *Epic of Gilgamesh*, and the *Erra Epic*.

from **Enuma Elish**

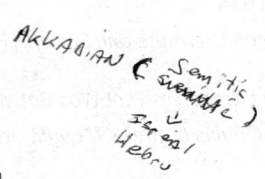

The Babylonian Creation Epic

Tablet 1

When skies above were not yet named,[1]
Nor earth below pronounced by name,
Apsu, the first one, their begetter
And maker Tiamat, who bore them all,[2]
Had mixed their waters together,   5
But had not formed pastures, nor discovered reed-beds;
When yet no gods were manifest,
Nor names pronounced, nor destinies decreed,
Then gods were born within them.
Lahmu (and) Lahamu emerged, their names pronounced.[3]   10
As soon as they matured, were fully formed,

*Translated by Stephanie Dalley.

---

1. The Babylonians called the epic by its opening words, *Enuma Elish*, "When skies above."
2. Apsu, father of the primeval gods, is the personification of the body of freshwater beneath the earth. Tiamat, "Ocean," is the primordial mother of the gods.
3. Primeval heroes, controllers of water and fishing.

Anshar (and) Kishar[4] were born, surpassing them.
They passed the days at length, they added to the years.
Anu[5] their first-born son rivalled his forefathers:
Anshar made his son Anu like himself,
And Anu begot Nudimmud[6] in his likeness.   15
He, Nudimmud, was superior to his forefathers:
Profound of understanding, he was wise, was very strong at arms.
Mightier by far than Anshar his father's begetter,
He had no rival among the gods his peers.
The gods of that generation would meet together   20
And disturb Tiamat, and their clamour reverberated.
They stirred up Tiamat's belly,
They were annoying her by playing inside Anduruna.[7]
Apsu could not quell their noise
And Tiamat became mute before them;   25
However grievous their behaviour to her,
However bad their ways, she would indulge them.
Finally Apsu, begetter of the great gods,
Called out and addressed his vizier Mummu,   30
    "O Mummu, vizier who pleases me!
    Come, let us go to Tiamat!"
They went and sat in front of Tiamat,
And discussed affairs concerning the gods their sons.
Apsu made his voice heard
And spoke to Tiamat in a loud voice,   35
    "Their ways have become very grievous to me,
    By day I cannot rest, by night I cannot sleep.
    I shall abolish their ways and disperse them!
    Let peace prevail, so that we can sleep."   40
When Tiamat heard this,
She was furious and shouted at her lover;
She shouted dreadfully and was beside herself with rage,
But then suppressed the evil in her belly.
    "How could we allow what we ourselves created to perish?   45
    Even though their ways are so grievous, we should bear it patiently."
Mummu replied and counselled Apsu;
The vizier did not agree with the council of his earth mother.
    "O father, put an end to their troublesome ways,
    So that she may be allowed to rest by day and sleep at night."   50
Apsu was pleased with him, his face lit up
At the evil he was planning for the gods his sons.

---

4. "Whole Sky" and "Whole Earth."
5. "Sky," patron god of Uruk, head of the older generation of gods.
6. A name for Ea or Enki, god of wisdom and

incantations, who sent the Seven Sages to teach the arts and skills of civilization to humanity.
7. Name of the gods' dwelling.

Mummu hugged him,
Sat on his lap and kissed him rapturously.
But everything they plotted between them   55
Was relayed to the gods their sons.
The gods listened and wandered about restlessly;
They fell silent, they sat mute.
Superior in understanding, wise and capable,
Ea[8] who knows everything found out their plot,   60
Made for himself a design of everything, and laid it out correctly,
Made it cleverly, his pure spell was superb.
He recited it and it stilled the waters.
He poured sleep upon him so that he was sleeping soundly,
Put Apsu to sleep, drenched with sleep.   65
Vizier Mummu the counsellor (was in) a sleepless daze.
Ea unfastened his belt, took off his crown,
Took away his mantle of radiance and put it on himself.
He held Apsu down and slew him;
Tied up Mummu and laid him across him.   70
He set up his dwelling on top of Apsu,
And grasped Mummu, held him by a nose-rope.
When he had overcome and slain his enemies,
Ea set up his triumphal cry over his foes,
Then he rested very quietly inside his private quarters   75
And named them Apsu and assigned chapels,
His own residence there.

[In the ensuing 350 lines, omitted here, Qingu and other gods urge Tiamat to avenge the
death of her husband. She assembles an army, which Ea and his allies hesitate to oppose,
until Ea's son Marduk agrees to lead the defending forces.]

Tablet IV

They founded a princely shrine for him,
And he took up residence as ruler before his fathers, (who proclaimed)
   "You are honoured among the great gods.
   Your destiny is unequalled, your word (has the power of) Anu!
   O Marduk, you are honoured among the great gods.   5
   Your destiny is unequalled, your word (has the power of) Anu!
   From this day onwards your command shall not be altered.
   Yours is the power to exalt and abase.
   May your utterance be law, your word never be falsified.
   None of the gods shall transgress your limits.   10
   May endowment, required for the gods' shrines
   Wherever they have temples, be established for your place.

---

8. God of Wisdom.

O Marduk, you are our champion!
We hereby give you sovereignty over all of the whole universe.
Sit in the assembly and your word shall be pre-eminent!   15
May your weapons never miss, may they smash your enemies!
O lord, spare the life of him who trusts in you,
But drain the life of the god who has espoused evil!"
They set up in their midst one constellation,
And then they addressed Marduk their son,   20
  "May your decree, O lord, impress the gods!
  Command to destroy and to recreate, and let it be so!
  Speak and let the constellation vanish!
  Speak to it again and let the constellation reappear."
He spoke, and at his word the constellation vanished.   25
He spoke to it again and the constellation was recreated.
When the gods his fathers saw how effective his utterance was,
They rejoiced, they proclaimed: "Marduk is King!"
They invested him with sceptre, throne, and staff-of-office.
They gave him an unfaceable weapon to crush the foe.   30
  "Go, and cut off the life of Tiamat! ➞ OCEAN
  Let the winds bear her blood to us as good news!"
The gods his fathers thus decreed the destiny of the lord
And set him on the path of peace and obedience.
He fashioned a bow, designated it as his weapon,   35
Feathered the arrow, set it in the string.
He lifted up a mace and carried it in his right hand,
Slung the bow and quiver at his side,
Put lightning in front of him,
His body was filled with an ever-blazing flame.   40
He made a net to encircle Tiamat within it,
Marshalled the four winds so that no part of her could escape.
South Wind, North Wind, East Wind, West Wind,
The gift of his father Anu, he kept them close to the net at his side.
He created the evil wind, the tempest, the whirlwind,   45
The Four Winds, the Seven Winds, the tornado, the unfaceable facing wind.
He released the winds which he had created, seven of them.
They advanced behind him to make turmoil inside Tiamat.
The lord raised the flood-weapon, his great weapon,
And mounted the frightful, unfaceable storm-chariot.   50
He had yoked to it a team of four and had harnessed to its side
"Slayer," "Pitiless," "Racer," and "Flyer;"
Their lips were drawn back, their teeth carried poison.
They know not exhaustion, they can only devastate.
He stationed on his right Fiercesome Fight and Conflict.   55
On the left Battle to knock down every contender.
Clothed in a cloak of awesome armour,
His head was crowned with a terrible radiance.

The Lord set out and took the road,
And set his face towards Tiamat who raged out of control.   60
In his lips he gripped a spell,
In his hand he grasped a herb to counter poison.
Then they thronged about him, the gods thronged about him;
The gods his fathers thronged about him, the gods thronged about him.
The Lord drew near and looked into the middle of Tiamat: 65
He was trying to find out the strategy of Qingu her lover.
As he looked, Qingu's mind became confused,
His will crumbled and his actions were muddled.
As for the gods his helpers, who marched at his side,
When they saw the warrior, the leader, their looks were strained.   70
Tiamat cast her spell. She did not even turn her neck.
In her lips she was holding falsehood, lies, wheedling,
    "[How powerful is] your attacking force, O lord of the gods!
    The whole assembly of them has gathered to your place!"
The Lord lifted up the flood-weapon, his great weapon   75
And sent a message to Tiamat who feigned goodwill, saying:
    "Why are you so friendly on the surface
    When your depths conspire to muster a battle force?
    Just because the sons were noisy (and) disrespectful to their fathers,
    Should you, who gave them birth, reject compassion?   80
    You named Qingu as your lover,
    You appointed him to rites of Anu-power, wrongfully his.
    You sought out evil for Anshar, king of the gods,
    So you have compounded your wickedness against the gods my fathers!
    Let your host prepare! Let them gird themselves with your weapons!   85
    Stand forth, and you and I shall do single combat!"
When Tiamat heard this,
She went wild, she lost her temper.
Tiamat screamed aloud in a passion,
Her lower parts shook together from the depths.   90
She recited the incantation and kept casting her spell.
Meanwhile the gods of battle were sharpening their weapons.
Face to face they came, Tiamat and Marduk, sage of the gods.
They engaged in combat, they closed for battle.
The Lord spread his net and made it encircle her,   95
To her face he dispatched the evil wind, which had been behind:
Tiamat opened her mouth to swallow it,
And he forced in the evil wind so that she could not close her lips.
Fierce winds distended her belly;
Her insides were constipated and she stretched her mouth wide.   100
He shot an arrow which pierced her belly,
Split her down the middle and slit her heart,
Vanquished her and extinguished her life.

He threw down her corpse and stood on top of her.
When he had slain Tiamat, the leader,   105
He broke up her regiments; her assembly was scattered.
Then the gods her helpers, who had marched at her side,
Began to tremble, panicked, and turned tail.
Although he allowed them to come out and spared their lives.
They were surrounded, they could not flee.   110
Then he tied them up and smashed their weapons.
They were thrown into the net and sat there ensnared.
They cowered back, filled with woe.
They had to bear his punishment, confined to prison.
And as for the dozens of creatures, covered in fearsome rays,   115
The gang of demons who all marched on her right,
He fixed them with nose-ropes and tied their arms.
He trampled their battle-filth beneath him.
As for Qingu, who had once been the greatest among them,
He defeated him and counted him among the dead gods,   120
Wrested from him the Tablet of Destinies,[9] wrongfully his,
Sealed it with (his own) seal and pressed it to his breast.
When he had defeated and killed his enemies
And had proclaimed the submissive foe his slave,
And had set up the triumphal cry of Anshar over all the enemy,   125
And had achieved the desire of Nudimmud, Marduk the warrior
Strengthened his hold over the captive gods,
And to Tiamat, whom he had ensnared, he turned back.
The Lord trampled the lower part of Tiamat,
With his unsparing mace smashed her skull,   130
Severed the arteries of her blood,
And made the North Wind carry it off as good news.
His fathers saw it and were jubilant: they rejoiced,
Arranged to greet him with presents, greetings gifts.
The Lord rested, and inspected her corpse.   135
He divided the monstrous shape and created marvels (from it).
He sliced her in half like a fish for drying:
Half of her he put up to roof the sky,
Drew a bolt across and made a guard hold it.
Her waters he arranged so that they could not escape.   140
He crossed the heavens and sought out a shrine;
He levelled Apsu, dwelling of Nudimmud.
The Lord measured the dimensions of Apsu
And the large temple which he built in its image, was Esharra:

---

9. A book recording everyone's fate.

In the great shrine Esharra, which he had created as the sky,   145
He founded cult centres for Anu, Ellil, and Ea.[10]

Tablet V

He fashioned stands for the great gods.
As for the stars, he set up constellations corresponding to them.
He designated the year and marked out its divisions,
Apportioned three stars each to the twelve months.
When he had made plans of the days of the year,   5
He founded the stand of Neberu[11] to mark out their courses,
So that none of them could go wrong or stray.
He fixed the stand of Ellil and Ea together with it,
Opened up gates in both ribs,
Made strong bolts to left and right.   10
With her liver he located the Zenith;
He made the crescent moon appear, entrusted night (to it)
And designated it the jewel of night to mark out the days.
  "Go forth every month without fail in a corona,
  At the beginning of the month, to glow over the land.   15
  You shine with horns to mark out six days;
  On the seventh day the crown is half.
  The fifteenth day shall always be the mid-point, the half of each month.[12]
  When Shamash looks at you from the horizon,
  Gradually shed your visibility and begin to wane.   20
  Always bring the day of disappearance close to the path of Shamash,[13]
  And on the thirtieth day, the year is always equalized, for Shamash is
    responsible for the year."
Marduk grouped the spittle of Tiamat and made clouds scud.
Raising winds, making rain,
Making fog billow, by collecting her poison,   25
He assigned for himself and let his own hand control it.
He placed her head, opened up springs: water gushed out.
He opened the Euphrates and the Tigris from her eyes.
He piled up clear-cut mountains from her udder,
Bored waterholes to drain off the catchwater.   30
He laid her tail across, tied it fast as the cosmic bond
And placed the Apsu beneath his feet.

---

10. The tablet ends with the following post-script: "146 lines. Fourth tablet 'When skies above.' Not complete. Written according to a tablet whose lines were canceled. Nabubelshu son of Naid-Marduk, son of a smith, wrote it for the life of himself and the life of his house, and deposited it in Ezida."

11. "Crossing Place," the name of the planet Jupiter.

12. The word for the fifteenth day of the month, *shabattu*, is related to the Hebrew term "sabbath."

13. The sun god.

He set her thigh to make fast the sky,
With half of her he made a roof; he fixed the earth.
When he had designed earth's cult, created its rites,
He threw down the reins and made Ea take them.   35
The Tablet of Destinies, which Qingu had appropriated, he fetched
And took it and presented it for a first reading to Anu.
[The gods of] battle whom he had ensnared were disentangled;
He led (them) as captives into the presence of his fathers.
And as for the eleven creatures that Tiamat had created,   40
Smashed their weapons, tied them at his feet,
Made images of them and had them set up at the door of Apsu.
  "Let this be a sign that will never in future be forgotten!"
The gods looked, and their hearts were full of joy at him.
Lahmu and Lahamu and all his fathers   45
Embraced him, and Anshar the king proclaimed that there should be a reception
    for him.
Anu, Enlil, and Ea each presented him with gifts.
Damkina his mother exclaimed with joy at him;
She made him beam [inside (?)] his fine (?) house.   50
Marduk appointed Usmu, who had brought his greetings present as good news,
To be vizier of the Apsu, to take care of shrines.
The Igigi[14] assembled, and all of them did obeisance to him.
The Anunnaki,[15] each and every one, kissed his feet.
The whole assembly collected together to prostrate themselves.
They stood, they bowed, "Yes, King indeed!"   55
His fathers took their fill of his manliness,
[They took off his clothes] which were enveloped in the dust of combat.
With cypress they sprinkled his body.
He put on a princely garment,
A royal aura, a splendid crown.   60
He took up a mace and grasped it in his right hand.
He set a dragon at his feet,
Slung the staff of peace and obedience at his side.
Lahmu and Lahamu made their voices heard and spoke to the Igigi,
  "Previously Marduk was our beloved son   65
  But now he is your king. Take heed of his command."
Next they spoke and proclaimed in unison,
  "LUGAL-DIMMER-ANKIA is his name.[16] Trust in him!"
When they gave kingship to Marduk,   70
They spoke an oration for him, for blessing and obedience.
  "Henceforth you shall be the provider of shrines for us.
  Whatever you command, we shall perform ourselves."

---

14. A group of younger gods.
15. A group of fifty gods, sons of Anu and
    judges of the underworld.

16. Sumerian for "King of the gods of heaven
    and earth."

Marduk made his voice heard and spoke,
Addressed his words to the gods his fathers,   75
  "Over the Apsu, the sea-green dwelling,
  In front of Esharra, which I created for you,
  Where I strengthened the ground beneath it for a shrine,
  I shall make a house to be a luxurious dwelling for myself
  And shall found his cult centre within it,   80
  And I shall establish my private quarters, and confirm my kingship.
  Whenever you come up from the Apsu for an assembly,
  Your night's resting place shall be in it, receiving you all.
  Whenever you come down from the sky for an assembly,
  Your night's resting place shall be in it, receiving you all.   85
  I hereby name it Babylon, home of the great gods.
  We shall make it the center of religion."
The gods his fathers listened to this command of his, and said,
  "Babylon, whose name you have just pronounced,
  Found there our night's resting place forever!"[17]   90

Tablet VI

When Marduk heard the speech of the gods,
He made up his mind to perform miracles.
He spoke his utterance to Ea,
And communicated to him the plan that he was considering.
  "Let me put blood together, and make bones too.   5
  Let me set up primeval man: Man shall be his name.
  Let me create a primeval man.
  The work of the gods shall be imposed (on him), and so they shall be at leisure.
  Let me change the ways of the gods miraculously,
  So they are gathered as one yet divided in two."   10
Ea answered him and spoke a word to him,
Told him his plan for the leisure of the gods.
  "Let one who is hostile to them be surrendered (up),
  Let him be destroyed, and let people be created (from him).
  Let the great gods assemble,   15
  Let the culprit be given up, and let them convict him."
Marduk assembled the great gods,
Gave (them) instructions pleasantly, gave orders.
The gods paid attention to what he said.
The king addressed his words to the Anunnaki,   20
  "Your election of me shall be firm and foremost.
  I shall declare the laws, the edicts within my power.

---

17. Twenty fragmentary lines follow, ending with a postscript identifying the tablet's ownership—rather pointedly—as "Palace of Assurbanipal, king of the world, king of Assyria."

Whosoever started the war,
And incited Tiamat, and gathered an army,
Let the one who started the war be given up to me,   25
And he shall bear the penalty for his crime, that you may dwell in peace."
The Igigi, the great gods, answered him,
Their lord Lugal-dimmer-ankia, counsellor of gods,
  "It was Qingu who started the war,
  He who incited Tiamat and gathered an army!"   30
They bound him and held him in front of Ea,
Imposed the penalty on him and cut off his blood.
He created mankind from his blood,
Imposed the toil of the gods (on man) and released the gods from it.
When Ea the wise had created mankind,   35
Had imposed the toil of the gods on them—
That deed is impossible to describe,
For Nudimmud performed it with the miracles of Marduk—
Then Marduk the king divided the gods,
The Anunnaki, all of them, above and below.   40
He assigned his decrees to Anu to guard,
Established three hundred as a guard in the sky;
Did the same again when he designed the conventions of earth,
And made the six hundred dwell in both heaven and earth.
When he had directed all the decrees,   45
Had divided lots for the Anunnaki, of heaven and of earth,
The Anunnaki made their voices heard
And addressed Marduk their lord,
  "Now, O Lord, that you have set us free,
  What are our favours from you?   50
  We would like to make a shrine with its own name.
  We would like our night's resting place to be in your private quarters, and to
    rest there.
  Let us found a shrine, a sanctuary there.
  Whenever we arrive, let us rest within it."
When Marduk heard this,   55
His face lit up greatly, like daylight.
  "Create Babylon, whose construction you requested!
  Let its mud bricks be moulded, and build high the shrine!"
The Anunnaki began shovelling.
For a whole year they made bricks for it.   60
When the second year arrived,
They had raised the top of Esagila in front of the Apsu;
They had built a high ziggurrat[18] for the Apsu.
They founded a dwelling for Anu, Ellil, and Ea likewise.

---

18. A terraced pyramid crowned with a temple.

In ascendancy he settled himself in front of them,   65
And his 'horns' look down at the base of Esharra.
When they had done the work on Esagila,
And the Anunnaki, all of them, had fashioned their individual shrines,
The three hundred Igigi of heaven and the Anunnaki of the Apsu all assembled.
The Lord invited the gods his fathers to attend a banquet   70
In the great sanctuary which he had created as his dwelling.
     "Indeed, Bab-ili is your home too![19]
     Sing for joy there, dwell in happiness!"
The great gods sat down there,
And set out the beer mugs; they attended the banquet.   75
When they had made merry within,
They themselves made an offering in splendid Esagila.
All the decrees and designs were fixed.
All the gods divided the stations of heaven and earth.
The fifty great gods were present, and   80
The gods fixed the seven destinies for the cult.
The Lord received the bow, and set his weapon down in front of them.
The gods his fathers looked at the net which he had made,
Looked at the bow, how miraculous her construction,
And his fathers praised the deeds that he had done.   85
Anu raised (the bow) and spoke in the assembly of gods,
He kissed the bow. "May she go far!"[20]
He gave to the bow her names, saying,
     "May Long and Far be the first, and Victorious the second;
     Her third name shall be Bowstar, for she shall shine in the sky."   90
He fixed her position among the gods her companions.
When Anu had decreed the destiny of the bow,
He set down her royal throne. "You are highest of the gods!"
And Anu made her sit in the assembly of gods.
The great gods assembled   95
And made Marduk's destiny highest; they themselves did obeisance.
They swore an oath for themselves,
And swore on water and oil, touched their throats.
Thus they granted that he should exercise the kingship of the gods
And confirmed for him mastery of the gods of heaven and earth.   100

Anshar gave him another name: ASARLUHI.[21]
     "At the mention of his name we shall bow down!
     The gods are to pay heed to what he says:

19. "Babylon" is written phonetically in this
    line as "Bab-ili," to emphasize its meaning
    of "Gate of God."
20. The bow is apparently treated as a mani-
    festation of Ishtar.

21. Originally a separate god, with powers of
    magic and healing, here assimilated with
    Marduk.

His command is to have priority above and below.
The son who avenged us shall be the highest!   105
His rule shall have priority; let him have no rival!
Let him act as shepherd over the dark-headed people, his creation.
Let his way be proclaimed in future days, never forgotten.
He shall establish great offerings for his fathers.
He shall take care of them, he shall look after their shrines.   110
He shall let them smell the offering, and make their chant joyful.
Let him breathe on earth as freely as he always does in heaven.
Let him designate the dark-headed people to revere him,
That mankind may be mindful of him, and name him as their god.
Let their interceding goddess pay attention when he opens his mouth.   115
Let offerings be brought [to] their god and their goddess.
Let them never be forgotten! Let them cleave to their god.
Let them keep their country pre-eminent, and always build shrines.
Though the dark-headed people share out the gods,
As for us, no matter by which name we call him, he shall be our god.   120
Come, let us call him by his fifty names!
His ways shall be proclaimed, and his deeds likewise!"[22]

        . . . . .

With fifty epithets the great gods
Called his fifty names, making his way supreme.
May they always be cherished, and may the older explain to the younger.   125
Let the wise and learned consult together,
Let the father repeat them and teach them to the son.
Let the ear of shepherd and herdsman be open,
Let him not be negligent to Marduk, the Ellil of the gods.
May his country be made fertile, and himself be safe and sound.   130
His word is firm, his command cannot alter;
No god can change his utterance.
When he is angry, he does not turn his neck aside;
In his rage and fury no god dare confront him.
His thoughts are deep, his emotions profound;   135
Criminals and wrongdoers pass before him.

The scribe wrote down the secret instruction which older men had recited in his
        presence,
And set it down for future men to read.
May the peoples of Marduk whom the Igigi gods created
Weave the tale and call upon his name   140
In remembrance of the song of Marduk
Who defeated Tiamat and took the kingship.

---

22. An extended listing follows, but is omitted
here. Some names are of formerly independent gods, now identified with Marduk; others describe various aspects of his
power.

ANONYMOUS (c. 2300 B.C.E.)

Egypt

Pyramid texts are among the oldest writings in the world. They were found carved on the interior walls of the pyramids of rulers from the Fifth and Sixth dynasties of Egypt (c. 2500–2180 B.C.E.). The texts consist of incantations and spells to ensure the king's resurrection and his success in earning immortality as a god in the afterlife. In order to achieve immortality, the soul had to purify itself and defeat a variety of hostile underworld forces. Priests recited the texts during the several stages of the burial itself and again during subsequent offerings of food and drink at the tomb. The texts of Unas are the best preserved of the examples that have come down to us. The last king of the Fifth Dynasty, Unas died around 2300 B.C.E.

Although the emphasis on cannibalism in the first selection soon disappeared from the tradition of pyramid texts, the practice is reflected in the many regional myths of generational succession among the gods. Hesiod's *Theogony*, for example, tells of how the god Zeus triumphed over his father, Cronos, who devoured his own children in order to forestall the succession to his throne. The brief second selection shows Unas in a far humbler relationship to the gods he hopes to rejoin.

from *The Pyramid Texts of Unas*

[Sky rains, stars darken]

Sky rains, stars darken,
The vaults quiver, earth's bones tremble,
The planets stand still
At seeing Unas rise as power,
A god who lives on his fathers,   5
Who feeds on his mothers!

Unas is master of cunning,
Whose mother knows not his name;
Unas's glory is in heaven,
His power is in the horizon;   10
Like Atum, his father, his begetter,
Though his son, he is stronger than he!

The forces of Unas are behind him,
His helpers are under his feet,
His gods on his head, his serpents on his brow,   15
Unas's lead-serpent is on his brow,

Translated by Miriam Lichtheim.

Soul-searcher whose flame consumes,
Unas's neck is in its place.

Unas is the bull of heaven
Who rages in his heart,
Who lives on the being of every god,
Who eats their entrails
When they come, their bodies full of magic
From the Isle of Flame.[1]

Unas is one equipped who has gathered his spirits,
Unas has risen as Great One, as master of servants,
He will sit with his back to Geb,[2]
Unas will judge with Him-whose-name-is-hidden
On the day of slaying the eldest.
Unas is lord of offerings who knots the cord,
Who himself prepares his meal.

Unas is he who eats men, feeds on gods,
Master of messengers who sends instructions:
It is Horn-grasper in Kehau who lassoes them for Unas,
It is Serpent Raised-head who guards, who holds them for him,
It is He-upon-the-willows who binds them for him.
It is Khons, slayer of lords, who cuts their throats for Unas,
Who tears their entrails out for him,
He the envoy who is sent to punish.
It is Shesmu[3] who carves them up for Unas,
Cooks meals of them for him in his dinner-pots.

Unas eats their magic, swallows their spirits:
Their big ones are for his morning meal,
Their middle ones for his evening meal,
Their little ones for his night meal,
And the oldest males and females for his fuel.
The Great Ones in the northern sky light him fire
For the kettles' contents with the old ones' thighs,
For the sky-dwellers serve Unas,
And the pots are scraped for him with their women's legs.

He has encompassed the two skies,
He has circled the two shores;
Unas is the great power that overpowers the powers,
Unas is the divine hawk, the great hawk of hawks,
Whom he finds on his way he devours whole.

20

25

30

35

40

45

50

55

---

1. A heavenly region.
2. The god of earth, known as the father of the
   gods.

3. The god of oil and wine.

Unas's place is before all the nobles in the horizon,
Unas is god, oldest of the old,
Thousands serve him, hundreds offer to him,
Great-Power rank was given him by Orion, father of gods.

Unas has risen again in heaven,   60
He is crowned as lord of the horizon.
He has smashed bones and marrow,
He has seized the hearts of gods,
He has eaten the Red, swallowed the Green.[4]
Unas feeds on the lungs of the wise,   65
Likes to live on hearts and their magic;
Unas abhors licking the coils of the Red
But delights to have their magic in his belly.

The dignities of Unas will not be taken from him,
For he has swallowed the knowledge of every god;   70
Unas's lifetime is forever, his limit is eternity
In his dignity of "If-he-likes-he-does if-he-hates-he-does-not,"
As he dwells in the horizon for all eternity.
Lo, their power is in Unas's belly,
Their spirits are before Unas as broth of the gods,   75
Cooked for Unas from their bones.
Lo, their power is with Unas,
Their shadows are taken from their owners,
For Unas is of those who risen is risen, lasting lasts.
Nor can evildoers harm Unas's chosen seat   80
Among the living in this land for all eternity!

[Unas is gods' steward, behind the mansion of Re]

Unas is gods' steward, behind the mansion of Re,
Born of Wish-of-the-gods, who is in the bow of Re's bark;[5]
Unas squats before him,
Unas opens his boxes,
Unas unseals his decrees,   5
Unas seals his dispatches,
Unas sends his messengers who tire not,
Unas does what Unas is told.

---

4. The "Red" is the crown of Lower Egypt (the
northern half of the country, "lower" because farther down the Nile); the "Green" is
Wadjet, the cobra goddess of Lower Egypt.

5. Probably a reference to the goddess Maat
("Truth"), daughter of Re.

HESIOD (EIGHTH CENTURY B.C.E.)
Greece

The *Theogony* names Hesiod as its author, but our only information about him comes from the purportedly autobiographical references within the poems ascribed to him, especially *Works and Days*, in which the narrator relates that his father fled poverty in Asia Minor and came to mainland Greece. Although the alphabet was introduced into Greece in the early eighth century B.C.E., we cannot say whether Hesiod was literate. The *Theogony,* however, clearly belongs in the tradition of oral composition and performance. Like the *Iliad* and the *Odyssey,* it is composed in dactylic hexameter (the meter characteristic of epic verse), uses a special amalgam of dialects adapted to the meter, and includes "formulas"— repeated phrases that facilitated oral composition.

The *Theogony*'s account of how the cosmos came into being and of the genealogy and social order of the gods is representative of a widespread type of literary composition describing the creation of the universe; the opening of Genesis (and its subsequent genealogies) may be said to be another example. The *Theogony* draws on traditional mythological material, and its account shows remarkable parallels with a second millennium B.C.E. Hittite text from Asia Minor as well as with the Babylonian *Enuma Elish* in this section. Hesiod traces hundreds of deities descended from three lineages: the Night, the Sea, and Heaven and Earth. Those descended from Heaven and Earth are given prominence because Heaven and Earth are also the progenitors of the current and (we are to understand) permanent divine regime under the leadership of Zeus, whose rule (after struggles detailed in the *Theogony*) is now beyond challenge.

from *Theogony*

[Now let us begin with the Olympian Muses]

Now let us begin with the Olympian Muses who sing for their father Zeus and delight his great soul, telling with harmonious voices of things past and present and to come. Sweet song pours from their mouths and never wearies; the house of their father Zeus the Thunderer laughs as the lily-like voice of the goddesses floats through it; the peaks of snowy Olympus and the homes of the gods echo with the sound. They lift their immortal voices to celebrate first the venerable primeval generation of the gods, born from Mother Earth and huge Father Sky, and then the gods who are descended from them and from whom all blessings flow. Secondly, they honor Zeus, the father of gods and men, both at the beginning and at the end of their song, since he is the greatest of the gods and the first in power. Next the Olympian Muses, the daughters of Zeus the lord of the aegis, delight the soul of Zeus on Mount Olympus by singing of mankind and of

Translated by Norman O. Brown.

the mighty Giants. These Muses were born in Pieria to Mnemosyne [Memory], the queen of the hills of Eleuther, after her union with Father Zeus the son of Cronus; their nature is forgetfulness of evil and rest from cares. On nine successive nights did Zeus the lord of wisdom unite with her, going to her sacred bed unknown to the rest of the gods; and when the year was up, as the seasons revolved and the months waned and many days had passed, she gave birth to nine daughters all of one mind, all with spirits dedicated to song, all carefree in their hearts. A little way from the topmost peak of snowy Olympus were they born, and that is where their smooth dancing floor and their beautiful home is; near them the Graces and Passion keep festive house. As soon as they were born, this immortal choir went in procession to Olympus, glorying in the beauty of their voice. The dark earth echoed all around as they sang, and under their feet a lovely sound leaped up as they went to their father—their father the king of heaven, the sole possessor of the thunder and the blasting lightning-bolt, who by his power conquered his father Cronus, who in his wisdom assigned to each of the gods their properties and settled their privileges.

Such was the song of the Muses whose home is Olympus—nine daughters of great Zeus: Clio and Euterpe and Thalia and Melpomene; Terpsichore and Erato and Polyhymnia and Urania; also Calliope; Calliope is the most exalted of them all, since it is she who attends on the majesty of kings. Whenever the daughters of great Zeus observe the birth of one of those appointed by Zeus to be kings and decide to honor him, they pour sweet dew upon his tongue, and the words flow like honey from his lips. All the people look up to him as he in judgment gives straight verdicts; with his sure eloquence he knows how to bring even large disputes to a quick end. Kings must have strength of mind for this—that they may secure redress for people who are wronged in the market place, their gentle words winning eager consent. Such a king, as he enters the assembly, receives worship like a god and gentle reverence: he is conspicuous in the assembled multitude. Such is the sacred gift of the Muses to mankind. It is the gift of the Muses and of the archer-god Apollo that makes men on earth singers and musicians; it is the gift of Zeus that makes men kings. Fortunate is the man whom the Muses love: sweet words flow from his lips. If someone has sorrow and is sick at heart and stunned with fresh trouble on his mind, and if a servant of the Muses sings of the glorious deeds of men in former times or of the blessed gods whose home is Olympus, he quickly forgets his bad thoughts and no longer remembers his troubles: the gifts of these goddesses instantly divert the mind.

Daughters of Zeus, I greet you; add passion to my song, and tell of the sacred race of gods who are forever, descended from Earth and starry Sky, from dark Night, and from salty Sea. Tell how in the beginning the gods and the earth came into being, as well as the rivers, the limitless sea with its raging surges, the shining stars, and the broad sky above—also how they divided the estate and distributed privileges among themselves, and how they first established themselves in the folds of Mount Olympus. Relate these things to me, Muses whose home is Olympus, from the beginning; tell me which of them first came into being.

[First of all, the Void came into being]

First of all, the Void came into being, next broad-bosomed Earth, the solid and eternal home of all, and Eros [Desire], the most beautiful of the immortal gods, who in every man and every god softens the sinews and overpowers the prudent purpose of the mind. Out of Void came Darkness and black Night, and out of Night came Light and Day, her children conceived after union in love with Darkness. Earth first produced starry Sky, equal in size with herself, to cover her on all sides. Next she produced the tall mountains, the pleasant haunts of the gods, and also gave birth to the barren waters, sea with its raging surges—all this without the passion of love. Thereafter she lay with Sky and gave birth to Ocean with its deep current, Coeus and Crius and Hyperion and Iapetus. Thea and Rhea and Themis [Law] and Mnemosyne [Memory]: also golden-crowned Phoebe and lovely Tethys.[1] After these came cunning Cronus, the youngest and boldest of her children; and he grew to hate the father who had begotten him.

Earth also gave birth to the violent Cyclopes—Thunderer, Lightner, and bold Flash—who made and gave to Zeus the thunder and the lightning-bolt. They were like the gods in all respects except that a single eye stood in the middle of their foreheads, and their strength and power and skill were in their hands.

There were also born to Earth and Sky three more children, big, strong, and horrible, Cottus and Briareus and Gyes. This unruly brood had a hundred monstrous hands sprouting from their shoulders, and fifty heads on top of their shoulders growing from their sturdy bodies. They had monstrous strength to match their huge size.

[Of all the children born of Earth and Sky]

Of all the children born of Earth and Sky these were the boldest, and their father hated them from the beginning. As each of them was about to be born, Sky would not let them reach the light of day; instead he hid them all away in the bowels of Mother Earth. Sky took pleasure in doing this evil thing. In spite of her enormous size, Earth felt the strain within her and groaned. Finally she thought of an evil and cunning stratagem. She instantly produced a new metal, gray steel, and made a huge sickle. Then she laid the matter before her children; the anguish in her heart made her speak boldly: "My children, you have a savage father; if you will listen to me, we may be able to take vengeance for his evil outrage: he was the one who started using violence."

This was what she said; but all the children were gripped by fear, and not one

---

1. These are some of the more benign members of the generally violent older generation of gods called Titans. Of Crius little is known; Hyperion and Thea are the parents of Helios, the sun; Iapetus is the father of Prometheus; Rhea is the mother of Zeus; Themis, the guardian of social order among the gods, bore Zeus a number of children, including the Seasons and the Fates; Mnemosyne is the mother of the Muses; Coeus and Phoebe are the parents of Leto, who bore Apollo and Artemis to Zeus; and Tethys is a goddess of the sea and the wife of Ocean.

of them spoke a word. Then great Cronus, the cunning trickster, took courage and answered his good mother with these words: "Mother, I am willing to undertake and carry through your plan. I have no respect for our infamous father, since he was the one who started using violence."

This was what he said, and enormous Earth was very pleased. She hid him in ambush and put in his hands the sickle with jagged teeth, and instructed him fully in her plot. Huge Sky came drawing night behind him and desiring to make love; he lay on top of Earth stretched all over her. Then from his ambush his son reached out with his left hand and with his right took the huge sickle with its long jagged teeth and quickly sheared the organs from his own father and threw them away, backward over his shoulder. But that was not the end of them. The drops of blood that spurted from them were all taken in by Mother Earth, and in the course of the revolving years she gave birth to the powerful Erinyes [Spirits of Vengeance] and the huge Giants with shining armor and long spears. As for the organs themselves, for a long time they drifted round the sea just as they were when Cronus cut them off with the steel edge and threw them from the land into the waves of the ocean; then white foam issued from the divine flesh, and in the foam a girl began to grow. First she came near to holy Cythera, then reached Cyprus, the land surrounded by sea. There she stepped out, a goddess, tender and beautiful, and round her slender feet the green grass shot up. She is called Aphrodite by gods and men, because she grew in the *froth*,[2] and also Cytherea, because she came near to Cythera, and the Cyprian, because she was born in watery Cyprus. Eros [Desire] and beautiful Passion were her attendants both at her birth and at her first going to join the family of the gods. The rights and privileges assigned to her from the beginning and recognized by men and gods are these: to preside over the whispers and smiles and tricks which girls employ, and the sweet delight and tenderness of love.

[More genealogies follow, culminating in the account of the birth of the children of Cronus and Rhea.]

[Rhea submitted to the embraces of Cronus]

Rhea submitted to the embraces of Cronus and bore him children with a glorious destiny: Hestia, Demeter, and Hera, who walks on golden sandals; Hades, the powerful god whose home is underground and whose heart is pitiless; Poseidon, the god whose great blows make the earth quake; and Zeus the lord of wisdom, the father of gods and men, whose thunder makes the broad earth tremble. As each of these children came out of their mother's holy womb onto her knees, great Cronus swallowed them. His purpose was to prevent the kingship of the gods from passing to another one of the august descendants of Sky; he had been told by Earth and starry Sky that he was destined to be overcome by his own son. For that reason he kept a sleepless watch and waited for his own children to be born and then

---

2. The word *aphros* in Greek means foam; the poet associates it here with the name of the goddess (although the words are not actually etymologically related).

swallowed them. Rhea had no rest from grief; so, when she was about to give birth to Zeus, the father of gods and men, she begged her own dear parents, Earth and starry Sky, to help her contrive a plan whereby she might bear her child without Cronus' knowing it, and make amends to the vengeful spirits of her father Sky. Earth and Sky listened to their daughter and granted her request; they told her what was destined to happen to King Cronus and to his bold son. When she was about to give birth to great Zeus, her youngest child, they sent her to the rich Cretan town of Lyctus. Huge Mother Earth undertook to nurse and raise the infant in the broad land of Crete. Dark night was rushing on as Earth arrived there carrying him, and Lyctus was the first place where she stopped. She took him and hid him in an inaccessible cave, deep in the bowels of holy earth, in the dense woods of Mount Aegeum. Then she wrapped a huge stone in baby blankets and handed it to the royal son of Sky, who then was king of the gods. He took the stone and swallowed it into his belly—the fool! He did not know that a stone had replaced his son, who survived, unconquered and untroubled, and who was going to overcome him by force and drive him from his office and reign over the gods in his place.

The young prince grew quickly in strength and stature. After years had passed Cronus the great trickster fell victim to the cunning suggestions of Mother Earth and threw up his own children again. The first thing he vomited was the stone, the last thing he had swallowed; Zeus set it up on the highways of the earth in holy Pytho under the slopes of Parnassus, to be a sign and a wonder to mankind thereafter.

Zeus also set free his father's brothers from the cruel chains in which their father Sky had in foolish frenzy bound them. They gratefully remembered his kindness and gave him the thunder and the lightning-bolt and flash, which huge Earth had kept hidden till then. In these weapons Zeus trusts; they make him master over gods and men.

[The *Theogony* goes on to recount the gift of fire to men by the Titan Prometheus, the creation of the first woman, and the Olympian gods' victorious struggle, under Zeus's leadership, against the Titans, whom they relegate permanently to the netherworld. The poem ends with an account of the children born to the Olympian gods.]

THE BIBLE

(EARLY FIRST MILLENNIUM B.C.E.)
Babylon

Genesis, meaning "beginning," is the first of the five books of Moses with which the Bible begins. These books are known collectively in Hebrew as the Torah, or "law." Chapters 1 through 11 form the opening section, a primeval history that serves as a prelude to the history of the Hebrew people and their relations with

God. The stories in these chapters are modeled after older Near Eastern accounts of creation, flood, and the subsequent ordering of the world such as those found in the *Enuma Elish* and the *Epic of Gilgamesh*.

Genesis is the product of several stages of composition, reflecting successive reworkings of these polytheistic stories to suit an increasingly monotheistic religion. The initial account, known as the Yahwistic version (from *Yahweh,* the name given to God by the Hebrews), probably dates to around the time of Solomon (the early tenth century B.C.E.). This version was revised by a later writer known as the Elohist (from *Elohim,* the name that he gave to God). Still later, a writer or group of writers known as the Priestly source made further revisions.

The process has left interesting differences between the two creation stories given here. Genesis 1 is a Priestly account of creation. It may have replaced an earlier, less strictly monotheistic account. (Several psalms preserve elements of stories in which Yahweh must defeat other primordial forces in order to establish the world.) The Yahwistic story of Eden that follows portrays a more mysterious and tentative relationship between God and his creation.

from The Bible

GENESIS 1–11

[The Creation Story]

1

In the beginning God created the heavens and the earth. Now the earth was formless and empty, darkness was over the surface of the deep,[1] and the Spirit of God was hovering over the waters.

And God said, "Let there be light," and there was light. God saw that the light was good, and he separated the light from the darkness. God called the light "day" and the darkness he called "night." And there was evening, and there was morning—the first day.

And God said, "Let there be an expanse between the waters to separate water from water."[2] So God made the expanse and separated the water under the expanse from the water above it. And it was so. God called the expanse "sky." And there was evening, and there was morning—the second day.

And God said, "Let the water under the sky be gathered to one place, and let dry ground appear." And it was so. God called the dry ground "land," and the gathered waters he called "seas." And God saw that it was good.

Then God said, "Let the land produce vegetation: seed-bearing plants and trees on the land that bear fruit with seed in it, according to their various kinds."

New International Version

---

1. "The deep," *tehom* in Hebrew, is related to Akkadian "Tiamat."
2. Whereas *Enuma Elish* shows the primeval gods being born from the mingling of Apsu and Tiamat, the Bible pointedly shows God beginning by *separating* the two—natural, not divine—bodies of water.

And it was so. The land produced vegetation: plants bearing seed according to their kinds and trees bearing fruit with seed in it according to their kinds. And God saw that it was good. And there was evening, and there was morning—the third day.

And God said, "Let there be lights in the expanse of the sky to separate the day from the night, and let them serve as signs to mark seasons and days and years, and let them be lights in the expanse of the sky to give light on the earth." And it was so. "God made two great lights—the greater light to govern the day and the lesser light to govern the night. He also made the stars. God set them in the expanse of the sky to give light on the earth, to govern the day and the night, and to separate light from darkness. And God saw that it was good. And there was evening, and there was morning—the fourth day.

And God said, "Let the water teem with living creatures, and let birds fly above the earth across the expanse of the sky." So God created the great creatures of the sea and every living and moving thing with which the water teems, according to their kinds, and every winged bird according to its kind. And God saw that it was good. God blessed them and said, "Be fruitful and increase in number and fill the water in the seas, and let the birds increase on the earth." And there was evening, and there was morning—the fifth day.

And God said, "Let the land produce living creatures according to their kinds: livestock, creatures that move along the ground, and wild animals, each according to its kind." And it was so. God made the wild animals according to their kinds, the livestock according to their kinds, and all the creatures that move along the ground according to their kinds. And God saw that it was good.

Then God said, "Let us make man in our image, in our likeness, and let them rule over the fish of the sea and the birds of the air, over the livestock, over all the earth, and over all the creatures that move along the ground."

So God created man in his own image,
in the image of God he created him;
male and female he created them.

God blessed them and said to them, "Be fruitful and increase in number; fill the earth and subdue it. Rule over the fish of the sea and the birds of the air and over every living creature that moves on the ground."

Then God said, "I give you every seed-bearing plant on the face of the whole earth and every tree that has fruit with seed in it. They will be yours for food. And to all the beasts of the earth and all the birds of the air and all the creatures that move on the ground—everything that has the breath of life in it—I give every green plant for food." And it was so.

God saw all that he had made, and it was very good. And there was evening and there was morning—the sixth day.

2

Thus the heavens and the earth were completed in all their vast array.

By the seventh day God had finished the work he had been doing; so on the seventh day he rested from all his work. And God blessed the seventh day and made it holy, because on it he rested from all the work of creating that he had done. This is the account of the heavens and the earth when they were created.[3]

When the LORD God made the earth and the heavens, no shrub of the field had yet appeared on the earth and no plant of the field had yet sprung up; the LORD God had not sent rain on the earth and there was no man to work the ground, but streams came up from the earth and watered the whole surface of the ground. And the LORD God formed man from the dust of the ground[4] and breathed into his nostrils the breath of life, and man became a living being.

Now the LORD God had planted a garden in the east, in Eden; and there he put the man he had formed. And the LORD God made all kinds of trees grow out of the ground—trees that were pleasing to the eye and good for food. In the middle of the garden were the tree of life and the tree of the knowledge of good and evil.

A river watering the garden flowed from Eden, and from there it divided; it had four headstreams. The name of the first is the Pishon; it winds through the entire land of Havilah, where there is gold. (The gold of that land is good; aromatic resin and onyx are also there.) The name of the second river is the Gihon; it winds through the entire land of Cush. The name of the third river is the Tigris; it runs along the east side of Asshur. And the fourth river is the Euphrates.[5]

The LORD God took the man and put him in the Garden of Eden to work it and take care of it. And the LORD God commanded the man, "You are free to eat from any tree in the garden; but you must not eat from the tree of the knowledge of good and evil, for when you eat of it you will surely die."

The LORD God said, "It is not good for the man to be alone. I will make a helper suitable for him."

Now the LORD God had formed out of the ground all the beasts of the field and all the birds of the air. He brought them to the man to see what he would name them; and whatever the man called each living creature, that was its name. So the man gave names to all the livestock, the birds of the air and all the beasts of the field.

But for man no suitable helper was found. So the LORD God caused the man to fall into a deep sleep; and while he was sleeping, he took one of the man's ribs and closed up the place with flesh. Then the LORD God made a woman from the rib he had taken out of the man, and he brought her to the man.

The man said,

"This is now bone of my bones
and flesh of my flesh;
she shall be called woman,
for she was taken out of man."[6]

---

3. This is the conclusion to the Priestly account of creation. Next comes a different ("Yahwistic") account of the creation of humanity.

4. "Man" in Hebrew, *adam*, is here derived from "ground," *adamah*.

5. Eden is thus located in southern Mesopotamia.

6. "Woman," *ishshah*, is seen as formed from "man," *ish*.

For this reason a man will leave his father and mother and be united to his wife, and they will become one flesh.

The man and his wife were both naked, and they felt no shame.

3

Now the serpent was more crafty than any of the wild animals the LORD God had made. He said to the woman. "Did God really say, 'You must not eat from any tree in the garden'?"

The woman said to the serpent, "We may eat fruit from the trees in the garden, but God did say, 'You must not eat fruit from the tree that is in the middle of the garden, and you must not touch it, or you will die.'"

"You will not surely die," the serpent said to the woman. "For God knows that when you eat of it your eyes will be opened, and you will be like God, knowing good and evil."

When the woman saw that the fruit of the tree was good for food and pleasing to the eye, and also desirable for gaining wisdom, she took some and ate it. She also gave some to her husband, who was with her, and he ate it. Then the eyes of both of them were opened, and they realized they were naked; so they sewed fig leaves together and made coverings for themselves.

Then the man and his wife heard the sound of the LORD God as he was walking in the garden in the cool of the day, and they hid from the LORD God among the trees of the garden. But the LORD God called to the man, "Where are you?"

He answered, "I heard you in the garden, and I was afraid because I was naked; so I hid."

And he said, "Who told you that you were naked? Have you eaten from the tree that I commanded you not to eat from?"

The man said, "The woman you put here with me—she gave me some fruit from the tree, and I ate it."

Then the LORD God said to the woman, "What is this you have done?"

The woman said, "The serpent deceived me, and I ate."

So the LORD God said to the serpent, "Because you have done this,

"Cursed are you above all the livestock
and all the wild animals!
You will crawl on your belly
and you will eat dust
all the days of your life.
And I will put enmity
between you and the woman,
and between your offspring and hers;
he will crush your head, and you will strike his heel."

To the woman he said,

"I will greatly increase your pains in childbearing;
with pain you will give birth to children.

Your desire will be for your husband,
and he will rule over you."

To Adam he said, "Because you listened to your wife and ate from the tree about which I commanded you, 'You must not eat of it.'

"Cursed is the ground because of you;
through painful toil you will eat of it
all the days of your life.
It will produce thorns and thistles for you,
and you will eat the plants of the field.
By the sweat of your brow you will eat your food
until you return to the ground,
   since from it you were taken;
   for dust you are
   and to dust you will return."

Adam named his wife Eve, because she would become the mother of all the living.[7]

The LORD God made garments of skin for Adam and his wife and clothed them. And the LORD God said, "The man has now become like one of us, knowing good and evil. He must not be allowed to reach out his hand and take also from the tree of life and eat, and live forever." So the LORD God banished him from the Garden of Eden to work the ground from which he had been taken. After he drove the man out, he placed on the east side of the Garden of Eden cherubim and a flaming sword flashing back and forth to guard the way to the tree of life.

4

Adam lay with his wife Eve, and she conceived and gave birth to Cain. She said, "With the help of the LORD I have brought forth a man."[8] Later she gave birth to his brother Abel.

Now Abel kept flocks, and Cain worked the soil. In the course of time Cain brought some of the fruits of the soil as an offering to the LORD. But Abel brought fat portions from some of the firstborn of his flock. The LORD looked with favor on Abel and his offering, but on Cain and his offering he did not look with favor. So Cain was very angry, and his face was downcast.

Then the LORD said to Cain, "Why are you angry? Why is your face downcast? If you do what is right, will you not be accepted? But if you do not do what is right, sin is crouching at your door; it desires to have you, but you must master it."

Now Cain said to his brother Abel, "Let's go out to the field." And while they were in the field, Cain attacked his brother Abel and killed him.

Then the LORD said to Cain, "Where is your brother Abel?"

"I don't know," he replied. "Am I my brother's keeper?"

---

7. "Eve" means "living."

8. "Cain" sounds like the Hebrew for "brought forth."

The LORD said, "What have you done? Listen! Your brother's blood cries out to me from the ground. Now you are under a curse and driven from the ground, which opened its mouth to receive your brother's blood from your hand. When you work the ground, it will no longer yield its crops for you. You will be a restless wanderer on the earth."

Cain said to the LORD, "My punishment is more than I can bear. Today you are driving me from the land, and I will be hidden from your presence; I will be a restless wanderer on the earth, and whoever finds me will kill me."

But the LORD said to him, "Very well: if anyone kills Cain, he will suffer vengeance seven times over." Then the LORD put a mark on Cain so that no one who found him would kill him. So Cain went out from the LORD's presence and lived in the land of Nod[9] east of Eden.

Cain lay with his wife, and she became pregnant and gave birth to Enoch. Cain was then building a city, and he named it after his son Enoch. To Enoch was born Irad, and Irad was the father of Mehujael, and Mehujael was the father of Methushael, and Methushael was the father of Lamech.

Lamech married two women, one named Adah and the other Zillah. Adah gave birth to Jabal; he was the father of those who live in tents and raise livestock. His brother's name was Jubal; he was the father of all who play the harp and flute. Zillah also had a son, Tubal-Cain, who forged all kinds of tools out of bronze and iron. Tubal-Cain's sister was Naamah.

Lamech said to his wives,

"Adah and Zillah, listen to me;
wives of Lamech, hear my words.
I have killed a man for wounding me,
a young man for injuring me.
If Cain is avenged seven times,
then Lamech seventy-seven times."

Adam lay with his wife again, and she gave birth to a son and named him Seth,[10] saying, "God has granted me another child in place of Abel, since Cain killed him." Seth also had a son, and he named him Enosh. At that time men began to call on the name of the LORD.

5

This is the written account of Adam's line.

When God created man, he made him in the likeness of God. He created them male and female; at the time they were created, he blessed them and called them "man."

When Adam had lived 130 years, he had a son in his own likeness, in his own image; and he named him Seth. After Seth was born, Adam lived 800 years and had other sons and daughters. Altogether, Adam lived 930 years, and then he died.

When Seth had lived 105 years, he became the father of Enosh. And after he

---

9. "Nod" means "wandering." 10. "Seth" probably means "granted."

became the father of Enosh, Seth lived 807 years and had other sons and daughters. Altogether, Seth lived 912 years, and then he died.

When Enosh had lived 90 years, he became the father of Kenan. And after he became the father of Kenan, Enosh lived 815 years and had other sons and daughters. Altogether, Enosh lived 905 years, and then he died.

When Kenan had lived 70 years, he became the father of Mahalalel. And after he became the father of Mahalalel, Kenan lived 840 years and had other sons and daughters. Altogether, Kenan lived 910 years, and then he died.

When Mahalalel had lived 65 years, he became the father of Jared. And after he became the father of Jared, Mahalalel lived 830 years and had other sons and daughters. Altogether, Mahalalel lived 895 years, and then he died.

When Jared had lived 162 years, he became the father of Enoch. And after he became the father of Enoch, Jared lived 800 years and had other sons and daughters. Altogether, Jared lived 962 years, and then he died.

When Enoch had lived 65 years, he became the father of Methuselah. And after he became the father of Methuselah, Enoch walked with God 300 years and had other sons and daughters. Altogether, Enoch lived 365 years. Enoch walked with God; then he was no more, because God took him away.

When Methuselah had lived 187 years, he became the father of Lamech. And after he became the father of Lamech, Methuselah lived 782 years and had other sons and daughters. Altogether, Methuselah lived 969 years, and then he died.

When Lamech had lived 182 years, he had a son. He named him Noah and said, "He will comfort us[11] in the labor and painful toil of our hands caused by the ground the LORD has cursed." After Noah was born, Lamech lived 595 years and had other sons and daughters. Altogether, Lamech lived 777 years, and then he died.

After Noah was 500 years old, he became the father of Shem, Ham and Japheth.

6

When men began to increase in number on the earth and daughters were born to them, the sons of God saw that the daughters of men were beautiful, and they married any of them they chose. Then the LORD said, "My Spirit will not remain in man forever, for he is mortal; his days will be a hundred and twenty years."

The Nephilim were on the earth in those days—and also afterward—when the sons of God went to the daughters of men and had children by them. They were the heroes of old, men of renown.

The LORD saw how great man's wickedness on the earth had become, and that every inclination of the thoughts of his heart was only evil all the time. The LORD was grieved that he had made man on the earth, and his heart was filled with pain. So the LORD said, "I will wipe mankind, whom I have created, from the face of the

---

11. "Noah" sounds like the Hebrew for "to comfort."

earth—men and animals, and creatures that move along the ground, and birds of the air—for I am grieved that I have made them." But Noah found favor in the eyes of the LORD.

This is the account of Noah. Noah was a righteous man, blameless among the people of his time, and he walked with God. Noah had three sons: Shem, Ham and Japheth.

Now the earth was corrupt in God's sight and was full of violence. God saw how corrupt the earth had become, for all the people on earth had corrupted their ways. So God said to Noah, "I am going to put an end to all people, for the earth is filled with violence because of them. I am surely going to destroy both them and the earth. So make yourself an ark of cypress' wood; make rooms in it and coat it with pitch inside and out. This is how you are to build it: The ark is to be 300 cubits long, 50 cubits wide and 30 cubits high.[12] Make a roof for it and finish the ark to within one cubit of the top. Put a door in the side of the ark and make lower, middle and upper decks. I am going to bring floodwaters on the earth to destroy all life under the heavens, every creature that has the breath of life in it. Everything on earth will perish. But I will establish my covenant with you, and you will enter the ark—you and your sons and your wife and your sons' wives with you. You are to bring into the ark two of all living creatures, male and female, to keep them alive with you. Two of every kind of bird, of every kind of animal and of every kind of creature that moves along the ground will come to you to be kept alive. You are to take every kind of food that is to be eaten and store it away as food for you and for them."

Noah did everything just as God commanded him.

7

The LORD then said to Noah, "Go into the ark, you and your whole family, because I have found you righteous in this generation. Take with you seven pairs of every kind of clean animal, a male and its mate, and two of every kind of unclean animal, a male and its mate, and also seven pairs of every kind of bird, male and female, to keep their various kinds alive throughout the earth. Seven days from now I will send rain on the earth for forty days and forty nights, and I will wipe from the face of the earth every living creature I have made."

And Noah did all that the LORD commanded him.

Noah was six hundred years old when the floodwaters came on the earth. And Noah and his sons and his wife and his sons' wives entered the ark to escape the waters of the flood. Pairs of clean and unclean animals, of birds and of all creatures that move along the ground, male and female, came to Noah and entered the ark, as God had commanded Noah. And after the seven days the floodwaters came on the earth.

In the six hundredth year of Noah's life, on the seventeenth day of the second month—on that day all the springs of the great deep burst forth, and the

---

12. A cubit was about eighteen inches.

floodgates of the heavens were opened. And rain fell on the earth forty days and forty nights.

On that very day Noah and his sons, Shem, Ham and Japheth, together with his wife and the wives of his three sons, entered the ark. They had with them every wild animal according to its kind, all livestock according to their kinds, every creature that moves along the ground according to its kind and every bird according to its kind, everything with wings. Pairs of all creatures that have the breath of life in them came to Noah and entered the ark. The animals going in were male and female of every living thing, as God had commanded Noah. Then the LORD shut him in.

For forty days the flood kept coming on the earth, and as the waters increased they lifted the ark high above the earth. The waters rose and increased greatly on the earth, and the ark floated on the surface of the water. They rose greatly on the earth, and all the high mountains under the entire heavens were covered. The waters rose and covered the mountains to a depth of more than twenty feet.[13] Every living thing that moved on the earth perished—birds, livestock, wild animals, all the creatures that swarm over the earth, and all mankind. Everything on dry land that had the breath of life in its nostrils died. Every living thing on the face of the earth was wiped out; men and animals and the creatures that move along the ground and the birds of the air were wiped from the earth. Only Noah was left, and those with him in the ark.

The waters flooded the earth for a hundred and fifty days.

8

But God remembered Noah and all the wild animals and the livestock that were with him in the ark, and he sent a wind over the earth and the waters receded. Now the springs of the deep and the floodgates of the heavens had been closed, and the rain had stopped falling from the sky. The water receded steadily from the earth. At the end of the hundred and fifty days the water had gone down, and on the seventeenth day of the seventh month the ark came to rest on the mountains of Ararat. The waters continued to recede until the tenth month, and on the first day of the tenth month the tops of the mountains became visible.

After forty days Noah opened the window he had made in the ark and sent out a raven, and it kept flying back and forth until the water had dried up from the earth. Then he sent out a dove to see if the water had receded from the surface of the ground. But the dove could find no place to set its feet because there was water over all the surface of the earth; so it returned to Noah in the ark. He reached out his hand and took the dove and brought it back to himself in the ark. He waited seven more days and again sent out the dove from the ark. When the dove returned to him in the evening, there in its beak was a freshly plucked olive leaf! Then Noah knew that the water had receded from the earth. He waited seven more days and sent the dove out again, but this time it did not return to him.

By the first day of the first month of Noah's six hundred and first year, the

---

13. In Hebrew, "fifteen cubits."

water had dried up from the earth. Noah then removed the covering from the ark and saw that the surface of the ground was dry. By the twenty-seventh day of the second month the earth was completely dry.

Then God said to Noah, "Come out of the ark, you and your wife and your sons and their wives. Bring out every kind of living creature that is with you—the birds, the animals, and all the creatures that move along the ground—so they can multiply on the earth and be fruitful and increase in number upon it."

So Noah came out, together with his sons and his wife and his sons' wives. All the animals and all the creatures that move along the ground and all the birds—everything that moves on the earth—came out of the ark, one kind after another.

Then Noah built an altar to the LORD and, taking some of all the clean animals and clean birds, he sacrificed burnt offerings on it. The LORD smelled the pleasing aroma and said in his heart: "Never again will I curse the ground because of man, even though every inclination of his heart is evil from childhood. And never again will I destroy all living creatures, as I have done.

> "As long as the earth endures,
> seedtime and harvest,
> cold and heat,
> summer and winter,
> day and night
> will never cease."

9

Then God blessed Noah and his sons, saying to them, "Be fruitful and increase in number and fill the earth. The fear and dread of you will fall upon all the beasts of the earth and all the birds of the air, upon every creature that moves along the ground, and upon all the fish of the sea; they are given into your hands. Everything that lives and moves will be food for you. Just as I gave you the green plants, I now give you everything.

"But you must not eat meat that has its lifeblood still in it. And for your lifeblood I will surely demand an accounting. I will demand an accounting from every animal. And from each man, too, I will demand an accounting for the life of his fellow man.

> "Whoever sheds the blood of man,
> by man shall his blood be shed;
> for in the image of God has God made man.

As for you, be fruitful and increase in number; multiply on the earth and increase upon it."

Then God said to Noah and to his sons with him: "I now establish my covenant with you and with your descendants after you and with every living creature that was with you—the birds, the livestock and all the wild animals, all those that came out of the ark with you—every living creature on earth. I establish my covenant with you: Never again will all life be cut off by the waters of a flood; never again will there be a flood to destroy the earth."

And God said, "This is the sign of the covenant I am making between me and you and every living creature with you, a covenant for all generations to come: I have set my rainbow in the clouds, and it will be the sign of the covenant between me and the earth.[14] Whenever I bring clouds over the earth and the rainbow appears in the clouds, I will remember my covenant between me and you and all living creatures of every kind. Never again will the waters become a flood to destroy all life. Whenever the rainbow appears in the clouds, I will see it and remember the everlasting covenant between God and all living creatures of every kind on the earth."

So God said to Noah, "This is the sign of the covenant I have established between me and all life on the earth."

The sons of Noah who came out of the ark were Shem, Ham and Japheth. (Ham was the father of Canaan.) These were the three sons of Noah, and from them came the people who were scattered over the earth.

Noah, a man of the soil, proceeded to plant a vineyard. When he drank some of its wine, he became drunk and lay uncovered inside his tent. Ham, the father of Canaan, saw his father's nakedness and told his two brothers outside. But Shem and Japheth took a garment and laid it across their shoulders; then they walked in backward and covered their father's nakedness. Their faces were turned the other way so that they would not see their father's nakedness.

When Noah awoke from his wine and found out what his youngest son had done to him, he said,

> "Cursed be Canaan!
> The lowest of slaves will he be to his brothers."
> He also said,
> "Blessed be the LORD, the God of Shem!
> May Canaan be the slave of Shem.
> May God extend the territory of Japheth;
> may Japheth live in the tents of Shem,
> and may Canaan be his slave."

After the flood Noah lived 350 years. Altogether, Noah lived 950 years, and then he died.

10

This is the account of Shem, Ham and Japheth, Noah's sons, who themselves had sons after the flood.

The sons of Japheth: Gomer, Magog, Madai, Javan, Tubal, Meshech and Tiras.

The sons of Gomer: Ashkenaz, Riphath and Togarmah.

The sons of Javan: Elishah, Tarshish, the Kittim and the Rodanim. (From

---

14. Compare God's literal rainbow to Marduk's bow personified as Ishtar in *Enuma Elish.*

these the maritime peoples spread out into their territories by their clans within their nations, each with its own language.)

The sons of Ham: Cush, Mizraim, Put and Canaan.

The sons of Cush: Seba, Havilah, Sabtah, Raamah and Sabtecah.

The sons of Raamah: Sheba and Dedan.

Cush was the father of Nimrod, who grew to be a mighty warrior on the earth. He was a mighty hunter before the LORD; that is why it is said, "Like Nimrod, a mighty hunter before the LORD." The first centers of his kingdom were Babylon, Erech, Akkad and Calneh, in Shinar. From that land he went to Assyria, where he built Nineveh, Rehoboth Ir, Calah and Resen, which is between Nineveh and Calah; that is the great city.

Mizraim was the father of the Ludites, Anamites, Lehabites, Naphtuhites, Pathrusites, Casluhites (from whom the Philistines came) and Caphtorites.

Canaan was the father of Sidon his firstborn, and of the Hittites, Jebusites, Amorites, Girgashites, Hivites, Arkites, Sinites, Arvadites, Zemarites and Hamathites.

Later the Canaanite clans scattered and the borders of Canaan reached from Sidon toward Gerar as far as Gaza, and then toward Sodom, Gomorrah, Admah and Zeboiim, as far as Lasha.

These are the descendants of Ham by their clans and languages, in their territories and nations.

Sons were also born to Shem, whose older brother was Japheth; Shem was the ancestor of all the sons of Eber.

The sons of Shem: Elam, Asshur, Arphaxad, Lud and Aram.

The sons of Aram: Uz, Hul, Gether and Meshech.

Arphaxad was the father of Shelah, and Shelah the father of Eber.

Two sons were born to Eber: One was named Peleg, because in his time the earth was divided; his brother was named Joktan.

Joktan was the father of Almodad, Sheleph, Hazarmaveth, Jerah, Hadoram, Uzal, Diklah, Obal, Abimael, Sheba, Ophir, Havilah and Jobab. All these were sons of Joktan. The region where they lived stretched from Mesha toward Sephar, in the eastern hill country.

These are the sons of Shem by their clans and languages, in their territories and nations. These are the clans of Noah's sons, according to their lines of descent, within their nations. From these the nations spread out over the earth after the flood.

11

Now the whole world had one language and a common speech. As men moved eastward, they found a plain in Shinar[15] and settled there.

They said to each other, "Come, let's make bricks and bake them thoroughly." They used brick instead of stone, and tar instead of mortar. Then they said, "Come, let us build ourselves a city, with a tower that reaches to the heavens,

---

15. Babylonia.

so that we may make a name for ourselves and not be scattered over the face of the whole earth."

But the LORD came down to see the city and the tower that the men were building. The LORD said, "If as one people speaking the same language they have begun to do this, then nothing they plan to do will be impossible for them. Come, let us go down and confuse their language so they will not understand each other."

So the LORD scattered them from there over all the earth, and they stopped building the city. That is why it was called Babel[16]—because there the LORD confused the language of the whole world. From there the LORD scattered them over the face of the whole earth.

THE BIBLE (SIXTH CENTURY B.C.E.)
Babylon

The Book of Job—one of the greatest wisdom texts of antiquity and a searching challenge to the very limits of human wisdom—explores the theological as well as the psychological implications of God's willingness to permit suffering on earth. The book thus explores on a personal level the same problems that were being raised in earlier works: the sacking of Babylon in the *Erra Epic,* Antigone's outcry against Creon's rule in Sophocles' play. As great as the problems of misrule might be when the responsible figure is a mortal king or the god of pestilence, the problem is even more severe in the context of monotheism, where God alone is ultimately to blame.

In developing his searching inquiry, the author of the poetic body of the Book of Job used an old second-millennium folktale, perhaps written down around 900 B.C.E. and appearing here as the prose frame at the beginning and end of the book. Probably writing during the period of exile in Babylon during the sixth century B.C.E., the poet structured his poem in the form of an initial outcry by Job, followed by a series of speeches by Job's friends Eliphaz, Bildad, and Zophar. Each friend makes three speeches attempting to mollify Job or to justify God's actions. In the course of their speeches, they begin increasingly to accept many of Job's premises, while his replies become increasingly ironic, often parodying commonplaces from wisdom literature and the Psalms. Following the friends' speeches and Job's final reply, God suddenly speaks from the whirlwind and silences Job, in the enigmatic inner conclusion that occurs before the return to the prose frame story.

Job's unrelenting quest for justice and his open accusations of God clearly disturbed the book's ancient editors, and the text as it appears in the Bible shows different attempts to soften Job's later speeches and to strengthen the friends' replies. The version presented here removes the major alterations: two long

---

16. I.e., Babylon; the writer intentionally ignores the name's actual meaning, "Gate of God," ironically suggesting instead that *babel* derives from *balal,* "to confuse."

speeches that must originally have been made by the friends but were later given to Job, and a repetitive set of speeches later added in and attributed to a new character named Elihu.

from **The Bible**

The Book of Job

1

There was a man in the land of Uz,[1] whose name was Job; and that man was perfect and upright, and one that feared God, and eschewed evil.

And there were born unto him seven sons and three daughters.

His substance also was seven thousand sheep, and three thousand camels, and five hundred yoke of oxen, and five hundred she asses, and a very great household; so that this man was the greatest of all the men of the east.

And his sons went and feasted in their houses, every one his day; and sent and called for their three sisters to eat and to drink with them.

And it was so, when the days of their feasting were gone about, that Job sent and sanctified them, and rose up early in the morning, and offered burnt offerings according to the number of them all: for Job said, It may be that my sons have sinned, and cursed God in their hearts. Thus did Job continually.

Now there was a day when the sons of God came to present themselves before the LORD, and Satan[2] came also among them.

And the LORD said unto Satan, Whence comest thou? Then Satan answered the LORD, and said, From going to and fro in the earth, and from walking up and down in it.

And the LORD said unto Satan, Hast thou considered my servant Job, that there is none like him in the earth, a perfect and an upright man, one that feareth God, and escheweth evil?

Then Satan answered the LORD, and said, Doth Job fear God for nought?

Hast not thou made an hedge about him, and about his house, and about all that he hath on every side? thou hast blessed the work of his hands, and his substance is increased in the land.

But put forth thine hand now, and touch all that he hath, and he will curse thee to thy face.

And the LORD said unto Satan, Behold, all that he hath is in thy power; only upon himself put not forth thine hand. So Satan went forth from the presence of the LORD.

And there was a day when his sons and his daughters were eating and drinking wine in their eldest brother's house:

King James Version.

---

1. Probably Edom in southern Palestine; interestingly, Job is not a Hebrew, though he calls upon the God of Israel.

2. Literally, "the Accuser."

And there came a messenger unto Job, and said, The oxen were plowing, and the asses feeding beside them:

And the Sabeans[3] fell upon them, and took them away; yea, they have slain the servants with the edge of the sword; and I only am escaped alone to tell thee.

While he was yet speaking, there came also another, and said, The fire of God is fallen from heaven, and hath burned up the sheep, and the servants, and consumed them; and I only am escaped alone to tell thee.

While he was yet speaking, there came also another, and said, The Chaldeans[4] made out three bands, and fell upon the camels, and have carried them away, yea, and slain the servants with the edge of the sword; and I only am escaped alone to tell thee.

While he was yet speaking, there came also another, and said, Thy sons and thy daughters were eating and drinking wine in their eldest brother's house:

And, behold, there came a great wind from the wilderness, and smote the four corners of the house, and it fell upon the young men, and they are dead; and I only am escaped alone to tell thee.

Then Job arose, and rent his mantle, and shaved his head, and fell down upon the ground, and worshipped,

And said, Naked came I out of my mother's womb, and naked shall I return thither: the LORD gave, and the LORD hath taken away; blessed be the name of the LORD.

In all this Job sinned not, nor charged God foolishly.

2

Again there was a day when the sons of God came to present themselves before the LORD, and Satan came also among them to present himself before the LORD.

And the LORD said unto Satan, From whence comest thou? And Satan answered the LORD, and said, From going to and fro in the earth, and from walking up and down in it.

And the LORD said unto Satan, Hast thou considered my servant Job, that there is none like him in the earth, a perfect and an upright man, one that feareth God, and escheweth evil? and still he holdeth fast his integrity, although thou movedst me against him, to destroy him without cause.

And Satan answered the LORD, and said, Skin for skin, yea, all that a man hath will he give for his life.

But put forth thine hand now, and touch his bone and his flesh, and he will curse thee to thy face.

And the LORD said unto Satan, Behold, he is in thine hand; but save his life.

So went Satan forth from the presence of the LORD, and smote Job with sore boils from the sole of his foot unto his crown.

And he took him a potshered to scrape himself withal; and he sat down among the ashes.

---

3. Nomads from Arabia.   4. A people from southern Mesopotamia.

Then said his wife unto him, Dost thou still retain thine integrity? curse God, and die.

But he said unto her, Thou speakest as one of the foolish women speaketh. What? shall we receive good at the hand of God, and shall we not receive evil? In all this did not Job sin with his lips.

Now when Job's three friends heard of all this evil that was come upon him, they came every one from his own place; Eliphaz and Temanite, and Bildad the Shuhite, and Zophar the Naamathite[5] for they had made an appointment together to come to mourn with him and to comfort him.

And when they lifted up their eyes afar off, and knew him not, they lifted up their voice, and wept; and they rent every one his mantle, and sprinkled dust upon their heads toward heaven.

So they sat down with him upon the ground seven days and seven nights, and none spake a word unto him: for they saw that his grief was very great.

3

After this opened Job his mouth, and cursed his day.

And Job spake, and said,

Let the day perish wherein I was born, and the night in which it was said, There is a man child conceived.

Let that day be darkness; let not God regard it from above, neither let the light shine upon it.

Let darkness and the shadow of death stain it; let a cloud dwell upon it; let the blackness of the day terrify it.

As for that night, let darkness seize upon it; let it not be joined unto the days of the year, let it not come into the number of the months.

Lo, let that night be solitary, let no joyful voice come therein.

Let them curse it that curse the day, who are ready to raise up their mourning.

Let the stars of the twilight thereof be dark; let it look for light, but have none; neither let it see the dawning of the day:

Because it shut not up the doors of my mother's womb, nor hid sorrow from mine eyes.

Why died I not from the womb? why did I not give up the ghost when I came out of the belly?

Why did the knees prevent me? or why the breasts that I should suck?

For now should I have lain still and been quiet, I should have slept: then had I been at rest,

With kings and counsellers of the earth, which built desolate places for themselves;

Or with princes that had gold, who filled their houses with silver:

Or as an hidden untimely birth I had not been; as infants which never saw light.

There the wicked cease from troubling; and there the weary be at rest.

---

5. Job's friends are from northwestern Arabia.

There the prisoners rest together; they hear not the voice of the oppressor.

The small and great are there; and the servant is free from his master.

Wherefore is light given to him that is in misery, and life unto the bitter in soul;

Which long for death, but it cometh not; and dig for it more than for hid treasures;

Which rejoice exceedingly, and are glad, when they can find the grave?

Why is light given to a man whose way is hid, and whom God hath hedged in?

For my sighing cometh before I eat, and my roarings are poured out like the waters.

For the thing which I greatly feared is come upon me, and that which I was afraid of is come unto me.

I was not in safety, neither had I rest, neither was I quiet; yet trouble came.

4

Then Eliphaz the Temanite answered and said,

If we assay to commune with thee, wilt thou be grieved? but who can withhold himself from speaking?

Behold, thou hast instructed many, and thou hast strengthened the weak hands.

Thy words have upholden him that was falling, and thou hast strengthened the feeble knees.

But now it is come upon thee, and thou faintest; it toucheth thee, and thou art troubled.

Is not this thy fear, thy confidence, thy hope, and the uprightness of thy ways?

Remember, I pray thee, who ever perished, being innocent? or where were the righteous cut off?

Even as I have seen, they that plow iniquity, and sow wickedness, reap the same.

By the blast of God they perish, and by the breath of his nostrils are they consumed.

The roaring of the lion, and the voice of the fierce lion, and the teeth of the young lions, are broken.

The old lion perisheth for lack of prey, and the stout lion's whelps are scattered abroad.

Now a thing was secretly brought to me, and mine ear received a little thereof.

In thoughts from the visions of the night, when deep sleep falleth on men,

Fear came upon me, and trembling, which made all my bones to shake.

Then a spirit passed before my face; the hair of my flesh stood up:

It stood still, but I could not discern the form thereof: an image was before mine eyes, there was a silence, and I heard a voice, saying,

Shall mortal man be more just than God? shall a man be more pure than his maker?

Behold, he put no trust in his servants; and his angels he charged with folly:

How much less in them that dwell in houses of clay, whose foundation is in the dust, which are crushed before the moth?

They are destroyed from morning to evening: they perish for ever without any regarding it.

Doth not their excellency which is in them go away? they die, even without wisdom.

5

Call now, if there be any that will answer thee; and to which of the saints wilt thou turn?

For wrath killeth the foolish man, and envy slayeth the silly one.

I have seen the foolish taking root: but suddenly I cursed his habitation.

His children are far from safety, and they are crushed in the gate, neither is there any to deliver them.

Whose harvest the hungry eateth up, and taketh it even out of the thorns, and the robber swalloweth up their substance.

Although affliction cometh not forth of the dust, neither doth trouble spring out of the ground;

Yet man is born unto trouble, as the sparks fly upward.

I would seek unto God, and unto God would I commit my cause:

Which doeth great things and unsearchable; marvellous things without number:

Who giveth rain upon the earth, and sendeth waters upon the fields:

To set up on high those that be low; that those which mourn may be exalted to safety.

He disappointeth the devices of the crafty, so that their hands cannot perform their enterprise.

He taketh the wise in their own craftiness: and the counsel of the froward is carried headlong.

They meet with darkness in the daytime, and grope in the noonday as in the night.

But he saveth the poor from the sword, from their mouth, and from the hand of the mighty.

So the poor hath hope, and iniquity stoppeth her mouth.

Behold, happy is the man whom God correcteth: therefore despise not thou the chastening of the Almighty:

For he maketh sore, and bindeth up: he woundeth, and his hands make whole.

He shall deliver thee in six troubles: yea, in seven there shall no evil touch thee.

In famine he shall redeem thee from death: and in war from the power of the sword.

Thou shalt be hid from the scourge of the tongue: neither shalt thou be afraid of destruction when it cometh.

At destruction and famine thou shalt laugh: neither shalt thou be afraid of the beasts of the earth.

For thou shalt be in league with the stones of the field: and the beasts of the field shall be at peace with thee.

And thou shalt know that thy tabernacle shall be in peace; and thou shalt visit they habitation, and shalt not sin.

Thou shalt know also that thy seed shall be great, and thine offspring as the grass of the earth.

Thou shalt come to thy grave in a full age, like as a shock of corn cometh in in his season.

Lo this, we have searched it, so it is; hear it, and know thou it for thy good.

6

But Job answered and said,

Oh that my grief were throughly weighed, and my calamity laid in the balances together!

For now it would be heavier than the sand of the sea: therefore my words are swallowed up.

For the arrows of the Almighty are within me, the poison whereof drinketh up my spirit: the terrors of God do set themselves in array against me.

Doth the wild ass bray when he hath grass? or loweth the ox over his fodder?

Can that which is unsavoury be eaten without salt? or is there any taste in the white of an egg?

The things that my soul refused to touch are as my sorrowful meat.

Oh that I might have my request; and that God would grant me the thing that I long for!

Even that it would please God to destroy me; that he would let loose his hand, and cut me off!

Then should I yet have comfort; yea, I would harden myself in sorrow: let him not spare; for I have not concealed the words of the Holy One.

What is my strength, that I should hope? and what is mine end, that I should prolong my life?

Is my strength the strength of stones? or is my flesh of brass?

Is not my help in me? and is wisdom driven quite from me?

To him that is afflicted pity should be shewed from his friend; but he forsaketh the fear of the Almighty.

My brethren have dealt deceitfully as a brook, and as the stream of brooks they pass away;

Which are blackish by reason of the ice, and wherein the snow is hid:

What time they wax warm, they vanish: when it is hot, they are consumed out of their place.

The paths of their way are turned aside; they go to nothing, and perish.

The troops of Tema looked, the companies of Sheba waited for them.

They were confounded because they had hoped; they came thither, and were ashamed.

For now ye are nothing; ye see my casting down, and are afraid.

Did I say, Bring unto me? or, Give a reward for me of your substance?

Or, Deliver me from the enemy's hand? or, Redeem me from the hand of the mighty?

Teach me, and I will hold my tongue: and cause me to understand wherein I have erred.

How forcible are right words! but what doth your arguing reprove?

Do ye imagine to reprove words, and the speeches of one that is desperate, which are as wind?

Yea, ye overwhelm the fatherless, and ye dig a pit for your friend.

Now therefore be content, look upon me; for it is evident unto you if I lie.

Return, I pray you, let it not be iniquity; yea, return again, my righteousness is in it.

Is there iniquity in my tongue? cannot my taste discern perverse things?

7

Is there not an appointed time to man upon earth? are not his days also like the days of an hireling?

As a servant earnestly desireth the shadow, and as an hireling looketh for the reward of his work:

So am I made to possess months of vanity, and wearisome nights are appointed to me.

When I lie down, I say, When shall I arise, and the night be gone? and I am full of tossings to and fro unto the dawning of the day.

My flesh is clothed with worms and clods of dust; my skin is broken, and become loathsome.

My days are swifter than a weaver's shuttle, and are spent without hope.

O remember that my life is wind: mine eye shall no more see good.

The eye of him that hath seen me shall see me no more: thine eyes are upon me, and I am not.

As the cloud is consumed and vanisheth away: so he that goeth down to the grave shall come up no more.

He shall return no more to his house, neither shall his place know him any more.

Therefore I will not refrain my mouth; I will speak in the anguish of my spirit; I will complain in the bitterness of my soul.

Am I a sea, or a whale, that thou settest a watch over me?[6]

When I say, My bed shall comfort me, my couch shall ease my complaint;

Then thou scarest me with dreams, and terrifiest me through visions:

So that my soul chooseth strangling, and death rather than my life.

I loathe it; I would not live alway: let me alone; for my days are vanity.

---

6. Job ironically compares himself to the conquered Tiamat in *Enuma Elish*.

What is man, that thou shouldest magnify him? and that thou shouldest set thine heart upon him?

And that thou shouldest visit him every morning, and try him every moment?

How long wilt thou not depart from me, nor let me alone till I swallow down my spittle?

I have sinned; what shall I do unto thee, O thou preserver of men? why hast thou set me as a mark against thee, so that I am a burden to myself?

And why dost thou not pardon my transgression, and take away mine iniquity? for now shall I sleep in the dust; and thou shalt seek me in the morning, but I shall not be.

8

Then answered Bildad the Shuhite, and said,

How long wilt thou speak these things? and how long shall the words of thy mouth be like a strong wind?

Doth God pervert judgment? or doth the Almighty pervert justice?

If thy children have sinned against him, and he have cast them away for their transgression;

If thou wouldest seek unto God betimes, and make thy supplication to the Almighty;

If thou wert pure and upright; surely now he would awake for thee, and make the habitation of thy righteousness prosperous.

Though thy beginning was small, yet thy latter end should greatly increase.

For inquire, I pray thee, of the former age, and prepare thyself to the search of their fathers:

(For we are but of yesterday, and know nothing, because our days upon earth are a shadow:)

Shall not they teach thee, and tell thee, and utter words out of their heart?

Can the rush grow up without mire? can the flag grow without water?[7]

Whilst it is yet in his greenness, and not cut down, it withereth before any other herb.

So are the paths of all that forget God; and the hypocrite's hope shall perish:

Whose hope shall be cut off, and whose trust shall be a spider's web.

He shall lean upon his house, but it shall not stand: he shall hold it fast, but it shall not endure.

He is green before the sun, and his branch shooteth forth in his garden.

His roots are wrapped about the heap, and seeth the place of stones.

If he destroy him from his place, then it shall deny him, saying, I have not seen thee.

Behold, this is the joy of his way, and out of the earth shall others grow.

Behold, God will not cast away a perfect man, neither will he help the evil doers:

---

7. Materials for making paper and pens.

Till he fill thy mouth with laughing, and thy lips with rejoicing.

They that hate thee shall be clothed with shame; and the dwelling place of the wicked shall come to nought.

9

Then Job answered and said,

I know it is so of a truth: but how should man be just with God?

If he will contend with him, he cannot answer him one of a thousand.

He is wise in heart, and mighty in strength: who hath hardened himself against him, and hath prospered?

Which removeth the mountains, and they know not: which overturneth them in his anger.

Which shaketh the earth out of her place, and the pillars thereof tremble.

Which commandeth the sun, and it riseth not; and sealeth up the stars.

Which alone spreadeth out the heavens, and treadeth upon the waves of the sea.

Which maketh Arcturus, Orion, and Pleiades, and the chambers of the south.

Which doeth great things past finding out; yea, and wonders without number.

Lo, he goeth by me, and I see him not: he passeth on also, but I perceive him not.

Behold, he taketh away, who can hinder him? who will say unto him, What doest thou?

If God will not withdraw his anger, the proud helpers do stoop under him.

How much less shall I answer him, and choose out my words to reason with him?

Whom, though I were righteous, yet would I not answer, but I would make supplication to my judge.

If I had called, and he had answered me; yet would I not believe that he had hearkened unto my voice.

For he breaketh me with a tempest, and multiplieth my wounds without cause.

He will not suffer me to take my breath, but filleth me with bitterness.

If I speak of strength, lo, he is strong: and if of judgment, who shall set me a time to plead?

If I justify myself, mine own mouth shall condemn me: if I say, I am perfect, it shall also prove me perverse.

Though I were perfect, yet would I not know my soul: I would despise my life.

This is one thing, therefore I said it, He destroyeth the perfect and the wicked.

If the scourge slay suddenly, he will laugh at the trial of the innocent.

The earth is given into the hand of the wicked: he covereth the faces of the judges thereof; if not, where, and who is he?

Now my days are swifter than a post: they flee away, they see no good.

They are passed away as the swift ships: as the eagle that hasteth to the prey.

If I say, I will forget my complaint, I will leave off my heaviness, and comfort myself:

I am afraid of all my sorrows, I know that thou wilt not hold me innocent.

If I be wicked, why then labour I in vain?

If I wash myself with snow water, and make my hands never so clean;

Yet shalt thou plunge me in the ditch, and mine own clothes shall abhor me.

For he is not a man, as I am, that I should answer him, and we should come together in judgment.

Neither is there any daysman betwixt us, that might lay his hand upon us both.

Let him take his rod away from me, and let not his fear terrify me:

Then would I speak, and not fear him; but it is not so with me.

10

My soul is weary of my life; I will leave my complaint upon myself; I will speak in the bitterness of my soul.

I will say unto God, Do not condemn me; shew me wherefore thou contendest with me.

Is it good unto thee that thou shouldest oppress, that thou shouldest despise the work of thine hands, and shine upon the counsel of the wicked?

Hast thou eyes of flesh? or seest thou as man seeth?

Are thy days as the days of man? are thy years as man's days,

That thou inquirest after mine iniquity, and searchest after my sin?

Thou knowest that I am not wicked; and there is none that can deliver out of thine hand.

Thine hands have made me and fashioned me together round about; yet thou dost destroy me.

Remember, I beseech thee, that thou hast made me as the clay; and wilt thou bring me into dust again?

Hast thou not poured me out as milk, and curdled me like cheese?

Thou hast clothed me with skin and flesh, and hast fenced me with bones and sinews.

Thou hast granted me life and favour, and thy visitation hath preserved my spirit.

And these things hast thou hid in thine heart: I know that this is with thee.

If I sin, then thou markest me, and thou wilt not acquit me from mine iniquity.

If I be wicked, woe unto me; and if I be righteous, yet will I not lift up my head. I am full of confusion; therefore see thou mine affliction;

For it increaseth. Thou huntest me as a fierce lion: and again thou shewest thyself marvellous upon me.

Thou renewest thy witnesses against me, and increasest thine indignation upon me; changes and war are against me.

Wherefore then hast thou brought me forth out of the womb? Oh that I had given up the ghost, and no eye had seen me!

I should have been as though I had not been; I should have been carried from the womb to the grave.

Are not my days few? cease then, and let me alone, that I may take comfort a little,

Before I go whence I shall not return, even to the land of darkness and the shadow of death;

A land of darkness, as darkness itself; and of the shadow of death, without any order, and where the light is as darkness.

11

Then answered Zophar the Naamathite, and said,

Should not the multitude of words be answered? and should a man full of talk be justified?

Should thy lies make men hold their peace? and when thou mockest, shall no man make thee ashamed?

For thou hast said, My doctrine is pure, and I am clean in thine eyes.

But oh that God would speak, and open his lips against thee;

And that he would shew thee the secrets of wisdom, that they are double to that which is! Know therefore that God exacteth of thee less than thine iniquity deserveth.

Canst thou by searching find out God? canst thou find out the Almighty unto perfection?

It is as high as heaven; what canst thou do? deeper than hell; what canst thou know?

The measure thereof is longer than the earth, and broader than the sea.

If he cut off, and shut up, or gather together, then who can hinder him?

For he knoweth vain men: he seeth wickedness also; will he not then consider it?

For vain man would be wise, though man be born like a wild ass's colt.

If thou prepare thine heart, and stretch out thine hands toward him;

If iniquity be in thine hand, put it far away, and let not wickedness dwell in thy tabernacles.

For then shalt thou lift up thy face without spot; yea, thou shalt be steadfast, and shalt not fear:

Because thou shalt forget thy misery, and remember it as waters that pass away:

And thine age shall be clearer than the noonday; thou shalt shine forth, thou shalt be as the morning.

And thou shalt be secure, because there is hope; yea, thou shalt dig about thee, and thou shalt take thy rest in safety.

Also thou shalt lie down, and none shall make thee afraid; yea, many shall make suit unto thee.

But the eyes of the wicked shall fail, and they shall not escape, and their hope shall be as the giving up of the ghost.

12

And Job answered and said,

No doubt but ye are the people, and wisdom shall die with you.

But I have understanding as well as you; I am not inferior to you: yea, who knoweth not such things as these?

I am as one mocked of his neighbour, who calleth upon God, and he answereth him: the just upright man is laughed to scorn.

He that is ready to slip with his feet is as a lamp despised in the thought of him that is at ease.

The tabernacles of robbers prosper, and they that provoke God are secure; into whose hand God bringeth abundantly.

But ask now the beasts, and they shall teach thee; and the fowls of the air, and they shall tell thee:

Or speak to the earth, and it shall teach thee: and the fishes of the sea shall declare unto thee.

Who knoweth not in all these that the hand of the LORD hath wrought this?

In whose hand is the soul of every living thing, and the breath of all mankind.

Doth not the ear try words? and the mouth taste his meat?

With the ancient is wisdom; and in length of days understanding.

With him is wisdom and strength, he hath counsel and understanding.

Behold, he breaketh down, and it cannot be built again: he shutteth up a man, and there can be no opening.

Behold, he withholdeth the waters, and they dry up: also he sendeth them out, and they overturn the earth.

With him is strength and wisdom: the deceived and the deceiver are his.

He leadeth counsellers away spoiled, and maketh the judges fools.

He looseth the bond of kings, and girdeth their loins with a girdle.

He leadeth princes away spoiled, and overthroweth the mighty.

He removeth away the speech of the trusty, and taketh away the understanding of the aged.

He poureth contempt upon princes, and weakeneth the strength of the mighty.

He discovereth deep things out of darkness, and bringeth out to light the shadow of death.

He increaseth the nations, and destroyeth them: he enlargeth the nations, and straiteneth them again.

He taketh away the heart of the chief of the people of the earth, and causeth them to wander in a wilderness where there is no way.

They grope in the dark without light, and he maketh them to stagger like a drunken man.

13

Lo, mine eye hath seen all this, mine ear hath heard and understood it.

What ye know, the same do I know also: I am not inferior unto you.

Surely I would speak to the Almighty, and I desire to reason with God.

But ye are forgers of lies, ye are all physicians of no value.

O that ye would altogether hold your peace! and it should be your wisdom.

Hear now my reasoning, and hearken to the pleadings of my lips.

Will ye speak wickedly for God? and talk deceitfully for him?

Will ye accept his person? will ye contend for God?

Is it good that he should search you out? or as one man mocketh another, do ye so mock him?

He will surely reprove you, if ye do secretly accept persons.

Shall not his excellency make you afraid? and his dread fall upon you?

Your remembrances are like unto ashes, your bodies to bodies of clay.

Hold your peace, let me alone, that I may speak, and let come on me what will.

Wherefore do I take my flesh in my teeth, and put my life in mine hand?

Though he slay me, yet will I trust in him: but I will maintain mine own ways before him.

He also shall be my salvation: for an hypocrite shall not come before him.

Hear diligently my speech, and my declaration with your ears.

Behold now, I have ordered my cause; I know that I shall be justified.

Who is he that will plead with me? for now, if I hold my tongue, I shall give up the ghost.

Only do not two things unto me: then will I not hide myself from thee.

Withdraw thine hand far from me: and let not thy dread make me afraid.

Then call thou, and I will answer: or let me speak, and answer thou me.

How many are mine iniquities and sins? make me to know my transgression and my sin.

Wherefore hidest thou thy face, and holdest me for thine enemy?

Wilt thou break a leaf driven to and fro? and wilt thou pursue the dry stubble?

For thou writest bitter things against me, and makest me to possess the iniquities of my youth.

Thou puttest my feet also in the stocks, and lookest narrowly unto all my paths; thou settest a print upon the heels of my feet.

And he, as a rotten thing, consumeth, as a garment that is moth eaten.

14

Man that is born of a woman is of few days, and full of trouble.

He cometh forth like a flower, and is cut down: he fleeth also as a shadow, and continueth not.

And dost thou open thine eyes upon such an one, and bringest me into judgment with thee?

Who can bring a clean thing out of an unclean? not one.

Seeing his days are determined, the number of his months are with thee, thou hast appointed his bounds that he cannot pass;

Turn from him, that he may rest, till he shall accomplish, as an hireling, his day.

For there is hope of a tree, if it be cut down, that it will sprout again, and that the tender branch thereof will not cease.

Though the root thereof wax old in the earth, and the stock thereof die in the ground;

Yet through the scent of water it will bud, and bring forth boughs like a plant.

But man dieth, and wasteth away: yea, man giveth up the ghost, and where is he?

As the waters fail from the sea, and the flood decayeth and drieth up:

So man lieth down, and riseth not: till the heavens be no more, they shall not awake, nor be raised out of their sleep.

O that thou wouldest hide me in the grave, that thou wouldest keep me secret, until thy wrath be past, that thou wouldest appoint me a set time, and remember me!

If a man die, shall he live again? all the days of my appointed time will I wait, till my change come.

Thou shalt call, and I will answer thee: thou wilt have a desire to the work of thine hands.

For now thou numberest my steps: dost thou not watch over my sin?

My transgression is sealed up in a bag, and thou sewest up mine iniquity.

And surely the mountain falling cometh to nought, and the rock is removed out of his place.

The waters wear the stones: thou washest away the things which grow out of the dust of the earth; and thou destroyest the hope of man.

Thou prevailest for ever against him, and he passeth: thou changest his countenance, and sendest him away.

His sons come to honour, and he knoweth it not; and they are brought low, but he perceiveth it not of them.

But his flesh upon him shall have pain, and his soul within him shall mourn.

15

Then answered Eliphaz the Temanite, and said,

Should a wise man utter vain knowledge, and fill his belly with the east wind?

Should he reason with unprofitable talk? or with speeches wherewith he can do no good?

Yea, thou castest off fear, and restrainest prayer before God.

For thy mouth uttereth thine iniquity, and thou choosest the tongue of the crafty.

Thine own mouth condemneth thee, and not I: yea, thine own lips testify against thee.

Art thou the first man that was born? or wast thou made before the hills?

Hast thou heard the secret of God? and dost thou restrain wisdom to thyself?

What knowest thou, that we know not? what understandest thou, which is not in us?

With us are both the grayheaded and very aged men, much elder than thy father.

Are the consolations of God small with thee? is there any secret thing with thee?

Why doth thine heart carry thee away? and what do thy eyes wink at,

That thou turnest thy spirit against God, and lettest such words go out of thy mouth?

What is man, that he should be clean? and he which is born of a woman, that he should be righteous?

Behold, he putteth no trust in his saints; yea, the heavens are not clean in his sight.

How much more abominable and filthy is man, which drinketh iniquity like water?

I will shew thee, hear me; and that which I have seen I will declare;

Which wise men have told from their fathers, and have not hid it:

Unto whom alone the earth was given, and no stranger passed among them.

The wicked man travaileth with pain all his days, and the number of years is hidden to the oppressor.

A dreadful sound is in his ears: in prosperity the destroyer shall come upon him.

He believeth not that he shall return out of darkness, and he is waited for of the sword.

He wandereth abroad for bread, saying, Where is it? he knoweth that the day of darkness is ready at his hand.

Trouble and anguish shall make him afraid; they shall prevail against him, as a king ready to the battle.

For he stretcheth out his hand against God, and strengtheneth himself against the Almighty.

He runneth upon him, even on his neck, upon the thick bosses of his bucklers:

Because he covereth his face with his fatness, and maketh collops of fat on his flanks.

And he dwelleth in desolate cities, and in houses which no man inhabiteth, which are ready to become heaps.

He shall not be rich, neither shall his substance continue, neither shall he prolong the perfection thereof upon the earth.

He shall not depart out of darkness; the flame shall dry up his branches, and by the breath of his mouth shall he go away.

Let not him that is deceived trust in vanity: for vanity shall be his recompence.

It shall be accomplished before his time, and his branch shall not be green.

He shall shake off his unripe grape as the vine, and shall cast off his flower as the olive.

For the congregation of hypocrites shall be desolate, and fire shall consume the tabernacles of bribery.

They conceive mischief, and bring forth vanity, and their belly prepareth deceit.

16

Then Job answered and said,

I have heard many such things: miserable comforters are ye all.

Shall vain words have an end? or what emboldeneth thee that thou answerest?

I also could speak as ye do: if your soul were in my soul's stead, I could heap up words against you, and shake mine head at you.

But I would strengthen you with my mouth, and the moving of my lips should assuage your grief.

Though I speak, my grief is not assuaged: and though I forbear, what am I eased?

But now he hath made me weary: thou hast made desolate all my company.

And thou hast filled me with wrinkles, which is a witness against me: and my leanness rising up in me beareth witness to my face.

He teareth me in his wrath, who hateth me: he gnasheth upon me with his teeth; mine enemy sharpeneth his eyes upon me.

They have gaped upon me with their mouth; they have smitten me upon the cheek reproachfully; they have gathered themselves together against me.

God hath delivered me to the ungodly, and turned me over into the hands of the wicked.

I was at ease, but he hath broken me asunder: he hath also taken me by my neck, and shaken me to pieces, and set me up for his mark.

His archers compass me round about, he cleaveth my reins asunder, and doth not spare; he poureth out my gall upon the ground.

He breaketh me with breach upon breach, he runneth upon me like a giant.

I have sewed sackcloth upon my skin, and defiled my horn in the dust.

My face is foul with weeping, and on my eyelids is the shadow of death;

Not for any injustice in mine hands: also my prayer is pure.

O earth, cover not thou my blood, and let my cry have no place.

Also now, behold, my witness is in heaven, and my record is on high.

My friends scorn me: but mine eye poureth out tears unto God.

O that one might plead for a man with God, as a man pleadeth for his neighbour!

When a few years are come, then I shall go the way whence I shall not return.

17

My breath is corrupt, my days are extinct, the graves are ready for me.

Are there not mockers with me? and doth not mine eye continue in their provocation?

Lay down now, put me in a surety with thee; who is he that will strike hands with me?

For thou hast hid their heart from understanding: therefore shalt thou not exalt them.

He that speaketh flattery to his friends, even the eyes of his children shall fail.

He hath made me also a byword of the people; and aforetime I was as a tabret.

Mine eye also is dim by reason of sorrow, and all my members are as a shadow.

Upright men shall be astonied at this, and the innocent shall stir up himself against the hypocrite.

The righteous also shall hold on his way, and he that hath clean hands shall be stronger and stronger.

But as for you all, do ye return, and come now: for I cannot find one wise man among you.

My days are past, my purposes are broken off, even the thoughts of my heart.

They change the night into day: the light is short because of darkness.

If I wait, the grave is mine house: I have made my bed in the darkness.

I have said to corruption, Thou art my father: to the worm, Thou art my mother, and my sister.

And where is now my hope? as for my hope, who shall see it?

They shall go down to the bars of the pit, when our rest together is in the dust.

18

Then answered Bildad the Shuhite, and said,

How long will it be ere ye make an end of words? mark, and afterwards we will speak.

Wherefore are we counted as beasts, and reputed vile in your sight?

He teareth himself in his anger: shall the earth be forsaken for thee? and shall the rock be removed out of his place?

Yea, the light of the wicked shall be put out, and the spark of his fire shall not shine.

The light shall be dark in his tabernacle, and his candle shall be put out with him.

The steps of his strength shall be straitened, and his own counsel shall cast him down.

For he is cast into a net by his own feet, and he walketh upon a snare.

The gin shall take him by the heel, and the robber shall prevail against him.

The snare is laid for him in the ground, and a trap for him in the way.

Terrors shall make him afraid on every side, and shall drive him to his feet.

His strength shall be hungerbitten, and destruction shall be ready at his side.

It shall devour the strength of his skin: even the firstborn of death shall devour his strength.

His confidence shall be rooted out of his tabernacle, and it shall bring him to the king of terrors.

It shall dwell in his tabernacle, because it is none of his: brimstone shall be scattered upon his habitation.

His roots shall be dried up beneath, and above shall his branch be cut off.

His remembrance shall perish from the earth, and he shall have no name in the street.

He shall be driven from light into darkness, and chased out of the world.

He shall neither have son nor nephew among his people, nor any remaining in his dwellings.

They that come after him shall be astonied at his day, as they that went before were affrighted.

Surely such are the dwellings of the wicked, and this is the place of him that knoweth not God.

19

Then Job answered and said,

How long will ye vex my soul, and break me in pieces with words?

These ten times have ye reproached me: ye are not ashamed that ye make yourselves strange to me.

And be it indeed that I have erred, mine error remaineth with myself.

If indeed ye will magnify yourselves against me, and plead against me my reproach:

Know now that God hath overthrown me, and hath compassed me with his net.

Behold, I cry out of wrong, but I am not heard: I cry aloud, but there is no judgment.

He hath fenced up my way that I cannot pass, and he hath set darkness in my paths.

He hath stripped me of my glory, and taken the crown from my head.

He hath destroyed me on every side, and I am gone: and mine hope hath he removed like a tree.

He hath also kindled his wrath against me, and he counteth me unto him as one of his enemies.

His troops come together, and raise up their way against me, and encamp round about my tabernacle.

He hath put my brethren far from me, and mine acquaintance are verily estranged from me.

My kinsfolk have failed, and my familiar friends have forgotten me.

They that dwell in mine house, and my maids, count me for a stranger: I am an alien in their sight.

I called my servant, and he gave me no answer; I intreated him with my mouth.

My breath is strange to my wife, though I intreated for the children's sake of mine own body.

Yea, young children despised me; I arose, and they spake against me.

All my inward friends abhorred me: and they whom I loved are turned against me.

My bone cleaveth to my skin and to my flesh, and I am escaped with the skin of my teeth.

Have pity upon me, have pity upon me, O ye my friends; for the hand of God hath touched me.

Why do ye persecute me as God, and are not satisfied with my flesh?

O that my words were now written! oh that they were printed in a book!

That they were graven with an iron pen and lead in the rock for ever!

For I know that my redeemer liveth, and that he shall stand at the latter day upon the earth:

And though after my skin worms destroy this body, yet in my flesh shall I see God:

Whom I shall see for myself, and mine eyes shall behold, and not another; though my reins be consumed within me.

But ye should say, Why persecute we him, seeing the root of the matter is found in me?

Be ye afraid of the sword: for wrath bringeth the punishments of the sword, that ye may know there is a judgment.

20

Then answered Zophar the Naamathite, and said,

Therefore do my thoughts cause me to answer, and for this I make haste.

I have heard the check of my reproach, and the spirit of my understanding causeth me to answer.

Knowest thou not this of old, since man was placed upon earth,

That the triumphing of the wicked is short, and the joy of the hypocrite but for a moment?

Though his excellency mount up to the heavens, and his head reach unto the clouds;

Yet he shall perish for ever like his own dung: they which have seen him shall say, Where is he?

He shall fly away as a dream, and shall not be found: yea, he shall be chased away as a vision of the night.

The eye also which saw him shall see him no more; neither shall his place any more behold him.

His children shall seek to please the poor, and his hands shall restore their goods.

His bones are full of the sin of his youth, which shall lie down with him in the dust.

Though wickedness be sweet in his mouth, though he hide it under his tongue;

Though he spare it, and forsake it not; but keep it still within his mouth:

Yet his meat in his bowels is turned, it is the gall of asps within him.

He hath swallowed down riches, and he shall vomit them up again: God shall cast them out of his belly.

He shall suck the poison of asps: the viper's tongue shall slay him.

He shall not see the rivers, the floods, the brooks of honey and butter.

That which he laboured for shall he restore, and shall not swallow it down: according to his substance shall the restitution be, and he shall not rejoice therein.

Because he hath oppressed and hath forsaken the poor; because he hath violently taken away an house which he builded not;

Surely he shall not feel quietness in his belly, he shall not save of that which he desired.

There shall none of his meat be left; therefore shall no man look for his goods.

In the fulness of his sufficiency he shall be in straits: every hand of the wicked shall come upon him.

When he is about to fill his belly, God shall cast the fury of his wrath upon him, and shall rain it upon him while he is eating.

He shall flee from the iron weapon, and the bow of steel shall strike him through.

It is drawn, and cometh out of the body; yea, the glittering sword cometh out of his gall: terrors are upon him.

All darkness shall be hid in his secret places: a fire not blown shall consume him; it shall go ill with him that is left in his tabernacle.

The heaven shall reveal his iniquity; and the earth shall rise up against him.

The increase of his house shall depart, and his goods shall flow away in the day of his wrath.

This is the portion of a wicked man from God, and the heritage appointed unto him by God.

21

But Job answered and said,

Hear diligently my speech, and let this be your consolations.

Suffer me that I may speak; and after that I have spoken, mock on.

As for me, is my complaint to man? and if it were so, why should not my spirit be troubled?

Mark me, and be astonished, and lay your hand upon your mouth.

Even when I remember I am afraid, and trembling taketh hold on my flesh.

Wherefore do the wicked live, become old, yea, are mighty in power?

Their seed is established in their sight with them, and their offspring before their eyes.

Their houses are safe from fear, neither is the rod of God upon them.

Their bull gendereth, and faileth not; their cow calveth, and casteth not her calf.

They send forth their little ones like a flock, and their children dance.

They take the timbrel and harp, and rejoice at the sound of the organ.

They spend their days in wealth, and in a moment go down to the grave.

Therefore they say unto God, Depart from us; for we desire not the knowledge of thy ways.

What is the Almighty, that we should serve him? and what profit should we have, if we pray unto him?

Lo, their good is not in their hand: the counsel of the wicked is far from me.

How oft is the candle of the wicked put out! and how oft cometh their destruction upon them! God distributeth sorrows in his anger.

They are as stubble before the wind, and as chaff that the storm carrieth away.

God layeth up his iniquity for his children: he rewardeth him, and he shall know it.

His eyes shall see his destruction, and he shall drink of the wrath of the Almighty.

For what pleasure hath he in his house after him, when the number of his months is cut off in the midst?

Shall any teach God knowledge? seeing he judgeth those that are high.

One dieth in his full strength, being wholly at ease and quiet.

His breasts are full of milk, and his bones are moistened with marrow.

And another dieth in the bitterness of his soul, and never eateth with pleasure.

They shall lie down alike in the dust, and the worms shall cover them.

Behold, I know your thoughts, and the devices which ye wrongfully imagine against me.

For ye say, Where is the house of the prince? and where are the dwelling places of the wicked?

Have ye not asked them that go by the way? and do ye not know their tokens,

That the wicked is reserved to the day of destruction? they shall be brought forth to the day of wrath.

Who shall declare his way to his face? and who shall repay him what he hath done?

Yet shall he be brought to the grave, and shall remain in the tomb.

The clods of the valley shall be sweet unto him, and every man shall draw after him, as there are innumerable before him.

How then comfort ye me in vain, seeing in your answers there remaineth falsehood?

22

Then Eliphaz the Temanite answered and said,

Can a man be profitable unto God, as he that is wise may be profitable unto himself?

Is it any pleasure to the Almighty, that thou art righteous? or is it gain to him, that thou makest thy ways perfect?

Will he reprove thee for fear of thee? will he enter with thee into judgment?

Is not thy wickedness great? and thine iniquities infinite?

For thou hast taken a pledge from thy brother for nought, and stripped the naked of their clothing.

Thou hast not given water to the weary to drink, and thou hast withholden bread from the hungry.

But as for the mighty man, he had the earth; and the honourable man dwelt in it.

Thou hast sent widows away empty, and the arms of the fatherless have been broken.

Therefore snares are round about thee, and sudden fear troubleth thee;

Or darkness, that thou canst not see; and abundance of waters cover thee.

Is not God in the height of heaven? and behold the height of the stars, how high they are!

And thou sayest, How doth God know? can he judge through the dark cloud?

Thick clouds are a covering to him, that he seeth not; and he walketh in the circuit of heaven.

Hast thou marked the old way which wicked men have trodden?

Which were cut down out of time, whose foundation was overflown with a flood:

Which said unto God, Depart from us: and what can the Almighty do for them?

Yet he filled their houses with good things: but the counsel of the wicked is far from me.

The righteous see it, and are glad: and the innocent laugh them to scorn.

Whereas our substance is not cut down, but the remnant of them the fire consumeth.

Acquaint now thyself with him, and be at peace: thereby good shall come unto thee.

Receive, I pray thee, the law from his mouth, and lay up his words in thine heart.

If thou return to the Almighty, thou shalt be built up, thou shalt put away iniquity far from thy tabernacles.

Then shalt thou lay up gold as dust, and the gold of Ophir as the stones of the brooks.

Yea, the Almighty shall be thy defence, and thou shalt have plenty of silver.

For then shalt thou have thy delight in the Almighty, and shalt lift up thy face unto God.

Thou shalt make thy prayer unto him, and he shall hear thee, and thou shalt pay thy vows.

Thou shalt also decree a thing, and it shall be established unto thee: and the light shall shine upon thy ways.

When men are cast down, then thou shalt say, There is lifting up; and he shall save the humble person.

He shall deliver the island of the innocent: and it is delivered by the pureness of thine hands.

23

Then Job answered and said,

Even to day is my complaint bitter: my stroke is heavier than my groaning.

Oh that I knew where I might find him! that I might come even to his seat!

I would order my cause before him, and fill my mouth with arguments.

I would know the words which he would answer me, and understand what he would say unto me.

Will he plead against me with his great power? No; but he would put strength in me.

There the righteous might dispute with him; so should I be delivered for ever from my judge.

Behold, I go forward, but he is not there; and backward, but I cannot perceive him:

On the left hand, where he doth work, but I cannot behold him: he hideth himself on the right hand, that I cannot see him:

But he knoweth the way that I take: when he hath tried me, I shall come forth as gold.

My foot hath held his steps, his way have I kept, and not declined.

Neither have I gone back from the commandment of his lips; I have esteemed the words of his mouth more than my necessary food.

But he is in one mind, and who can turn him? and what his soul desireth, even that he doeth.

For he performeth the thing that is appointed for me: and many such things are with him.

Therefore am I troubled at his presence: when I consider, I am afraid of him.

For God maketh my heart soft, and the Almighty troubleth me:

Because I was not cut off before the darkness, neither hath he covered the darkness from my face.

24

Why, seeing times are not hidden from the Almighty, do they that know him not see his days?

Some remove the landmarks; they violently take away flocks, and feed thereof.

They drive away the ass of the fatherless, they take the widow's ox for a pledge.

They turn the needy out of the way: the poor of the earth hide themselves together.

Behold, as wild asses in the desert, go they forth to their work; rising betimes for a prey: the wilderness yieldeth food for them and for their children.

They reap every one his corn in the field: and they gather the vintage of the wicked.

They cause the naked to lodge without clothing, that they have no covering in the cold.

They are wet with the showers of the mountains, and embrace the rock for want of a shelter.

They pluck the fatherless from the breast, and take a pledge of the poor.

They cause him to go naked without clothing, and they take away the sheaf from the hungry;

Which make oil within their walls, and tread their winepresses, and suffer thirst.

Men groan from out of the city, and the soul of the wounded crieth out: yet God layeth not folly to them.

They are of those that rebel against the light; they know not the ways thereof, nor abide in the paths thereof.

The murderer rising with the light killeth the poor and needy, and in the night is as a thief.

The eye also of the adulterer waiteth for the twilight, saying, No eye shall see me: and disguiseth his face.

In the dark they dig through houses, which they had marked for themselves in the daytime: they know not the light.

For the morning is to them even as the shadow of death: if one know them, they are in the terrors of the shadow of death.

"He is swift as the waters; their portion is cursed in the earth: he beholdeth not the way of the vineyards.

Drought and heat consume the snow waters: so doth the grave those which have sinned.

The womb shall forget him; the worm shall feed sweetly on him; he shall be no more remembered; and wickedness shall be broken as a tree."

He evil entreateth the barren that beareth not: and doeth not good to the widow.

He draweth also the mighty with his power: he riseth up, and no man is sure of life.

Though it be given him to be in safety, whereon he resteth; yet his eyes are upon their ways.

They are exalted for a little while, but are gone and brought low; they are taken out of the way as all other, and cut off as the tops of the ears of corn.

And if it be not so now, who will make me a liar, and make my speech nothing worth?

25

Then answered Bildad the Shuhite, and said,

Dominion and fear are with him, he maketh peace in his high places.

Is there any number of his armies? and upon whom doth not his light arise?

How then can man be justified with God? or how can he be clean that is born of a woman?

Behold even to the moon, and it shineth not; yea, the stars are not pure in his sight.

How much less man, that is a worm? and the son of man, which is a worm?[8]

26

But Job answered and said,

How hast thou helped him that is without power? how savest thou the arm that hath no strength?

How hast thou counselled him that hath no wisdom? and how hast thou plentifully declared the thing as it is?

To whom hast thou uttered words? and whose spirit came from thee?

Dead things are formed from under the waters, and the inhabitants thereof.

---

8. At this point, an ancient editor has inserted several lines from Job's reply (verses 1–4 of Chapter 26), thereby attributing the balance of Bildad's speech to Job.

Hell is naked before him, and destruction hath no covering.

He stretcheth out the north over the empty place, and hangeth the earth upon nothing.

He bindeth up the waters in his thick clouds; and the cloud is not rent under them.

He holdeth back the face of his throne, and spreadeth his cloud upon it.

He hath compassed the waters with bounds, until the day and night come to an end.

The pillars of heaven tremble and are astonished at his reproof.

He divideth the sea with his power, and by his understanding he smiteth through the proud.

By his spirit he hath garnished the heavens; his hand hath formed the crooked serpent.

Lo, these are parts of his ways: but how little a portion is heard of him? but the thunder of his power who can understand?

27

Moreover Job continued his parable, and said,

As God liveth, who hath taken away my judgment; and the Almighty, who hath vexed my soul;

All the while my breath is in me, and the spirit of God is in my nostrils;

My lips shall not speak wickedness, nor my tongue utter deceit.

God forbid that I should justify you: till I die I will not remove mine integrity from me.

My righteousness I hold fast, and will not let it go: my heart shall not reproach me so long as I live.

Let mine enemy be as the wicked, and he that riseth up against me as the unrighteous.

For what is the hope of the hypocrite, though he hath gained, when God taketh away his soul?

Will God hear his cry when trouble cometh upon him?

Will he delight himself in the Almighty? will he always call upon God?

I will teach you by the hand of God: that which is with the Almighty will I not conceal.

Behold, all ye yourselves have seen it; why then are ye thus altogether vain?

Zophar replied: This is the portion of a wicked man with God, and the heritage of oppressors, which they shall receive of the Almighty.

If his children be multiplied, it is for the sword: and his offspring shall not be satisfied with bread.

Those that remain of him shall be buried in death: and his widows shall not weep.

Though he heap up silver as the dust, and prepare raiment as the clay;

He may prepare it, but the just shall put it on, and the innocent shall divide the silver.

He buildeth his house as a moth, and as a booth that the keeper maketh.

The rich man shall lie down, but he shall not be gathered: he openeth his eyes, and he is not.

Terrors take hold on him as waters, a tempest stealeth him away in the night.

The east wind carrieth him away, and he departeth: and as a storm hurleth him out of his place.

For God shall cast upon him, and not spare: he would fain flee out of his hand.

Men shall clap their hands at him, and shall hiss him out of his place.

28

Surely there is a vein for the silver, and a place for gold where they fine it.

Iron is taken out of the earth, and brass is molten out of the stone.

He setteth an end to darkness, and searcheth out all perfection: the stones of darkness, and the shadow of death.

The flood breaketh out from the inhabitant; even the waters forgotten of the foot: they are dried up, they are gone away from men.

As for the earth, out of it cometh bread: and under it is turned up as it were fire.

The stones of it are the place of sapphires: and it hath dust of gold.

There is a path which no fowl knoweth, and which the vulture's eye hath not seen:

The lion's whelps have not trodden it, nor the fierce lion passed by it.

He putteth forth his hand upon the rock; he overturneth the mountains by the roots.

He cutteth out rivers among the rocks; and his eye seeth every precious thing.

He bindeth the floods from overflowing; and the thing that is hid bringeth he forth to light.

But where shall wisdom be found? and where is the place of understanding?

Man knoweth not the price thereof; neither is it found in the land of the living.

The depth saith, It is not in me: and the sea saith, It is not with me.

It cannot be gotten for gold, neither shall silver be weighed for the price thereof.

It cannot be valued with the gold of Ophir, with the precious onyx, or the sapphire.

The gold and the crystal cannot equal it: and the exchange of it shall not be for jewels of fine gold.

No mention shall be made of coral, or of pearls: for the price of wisdom is above rubies.

The topaz of Ethiopia shall not equal it, neither shall it be valued with pure gold.

Whence then cometh wisdom? and where is the place of understanding?

Seeing it is hid from the eyes of all living, and kept close from the fowls of the air.

Destruction and death say, We have heard the fame thereof with our ears.

God understandeth the way thereof, and he knoweth the place thereof.

For he looketh to the ends of the earth, and seeth under the whole heaven;

To make the weight for the winds; and he weigheth the waters by measure.

When he made a decree for the rain, and a way for the lightning of the thunder:

Then did he see it, and declare it; he prepared it, yea, and searched it out.

And unto man he said, Behold, the fear of the Lord, that is wisdom; and to depart from evil is understanding.

29

Moreover Job continued his parable, and said,

Oh that I were as in months past, as in the days when God preserved me;

When his candle shined upon my head, and when by his light I walked through darkness;

As I was in the days of my youth, when the secret of God was upon my tabernacle;

When the Almighty was yet with me, when my children were about me;

When I washed my steps with butter, and the rock poured me out rivers of oil;

When I went out to the gate through the city, when I prepared my seat in the street!

The young men saw me, and hid themselves: and the aged arose, and stood up.

The princes refrained talking, and laid their hand on their mouth.

The nobles held their peace, and their tongue cleaved to the roof of their mouth.

When the ear heard me, then it blessed me; and when the eye saw me, it gave witness to me:

Because I delivered the poor that cried, and the fatherless, and him that had none to help him.

The blessing of him that was ready to perish came upon me: and I caused the widow's heart to sing for joy.

I put on righteousness, and it clothed me: my judgment was as a robe and a diadem.

I was eyes to the blind, and feet was I to the lame.

I was a father to the poor: and the cause which I knew not I searched out.

And I brake the jaws of the wicked, and plucked the spoil out of his teeth.

Then I said, I shall die in my nest, and I shall multiply my days as the sand.

My root was spread out by the waters, and the dew lay all night upon my branch.

My glory was fresh in me, and my bow was renewed in my hand.

Unto me men gave ear, and waited, and kept silence at my counsel.

After my words they spake not again; and my speech dropped upon them.

And they waited for me as for the rain; and they opened their mouth wide as for the latter rain.

If I laughed on them, they believed it not; and the light of my countenance they cast not down.

I chose out their way, and sat chief, and dwelt as a king in the army, as one that comeforteth the mourners.

30

But now they that are younger than I have me in derision, whose fathers I would have disdained to have set with the dogs of my flock.

Yea, whereto might the strength of their hands profit me, in whom old age was perished?

For want and famine they were solitary; fleeing into the wilderness in former time desolate and waste.

Who cut up mallows by the bushes, and juniper roots for their meat.

They were driven forth from among men, (they cried after them as after a thief;)

To dwell in the clifts of the valleys, in caves of the earth, and in the rocks.

Among the bushes they brayed; under the nettles they were gathered together.

They were children of fools, yea, children of base men: they were viler than the earth.

And now am I their song, yea, I am their byword.

They abhor me, they flee far from me, and spare not to spit in my face.

Because he hath loosed my cord, and afflicted me, they have also let loose the bridle before me.

Upon my right hand rise the youth; they push away my feet, and they raise up against me the ways of their destruction.

They mar my path, they set forward my calamity, they have no helper.

They came upon me as a wide breaking in of waters: in the desolation they rolled themselves upon me.

Terrors are turned upon me: they pursue my soul as the wind: and my welfare passeth away as a cloud.

And now my soul is poured out upon me; the days of affliction have taken hold upon me.

My bones are pierced in me in the night season: and my sinews take no rest.

By the great force of my disease is my garment changed: it bindeth me about as the collar of my coat.

He hath cast me into the mire, and I am become like dust and ashes.

I cry unto thee, and thou dost not hear me: I stand up, and thou regardest me not.

Thou art become cruel to me: with thy strong hand thou opposest thyself against me.

Thou liftest me up to the wind; thou causest me to ride upon it, and dissolvest my substance.

For I know that thou wilt bring me to death, and to the house appointed for all living.

Howbeit he will not stretch out his hand to the grave, though they cry in his destruction.

Did not I weep for him that was in trouble? was not my soul grieved for the poor?

When I looked for good, then evil came unto me: and when I waited for light, there came darkness.

My bowels boiled, and rested not: the days of affliction prevented me.

I went mourning without the sun: I stood up, and I cried in the congregation.

I am a brother to dragons, and a companion to owls.

My skin is black upon me, and my bones are burned with heat.

My harp also is turned to mourning, and my organ into the voice of them that weep.

31

I made a covenant with mine eyes; why then should I think upon a maid?

For what portion of God is there from above? and what inheritance of the Almighty from on high?

Is not destruction to the wicked? and a strange punishment to the workers of iniquity?

Doth not he see my ways, and count all my steps?

If I have walked with vanity, or if my foot hath hasted to deceit;

Let me be weighed in an even balance, that God may know mine integrity.

If my step hath turned out of the way, and mine heart walked after mine eyes, and if any blot hath cleaved to mine hands;

Then let me sow, and let another eat; yea, let my offspring be rooted out.

If mine heart have been deceived by a woman, or if I have laid wait at my neighbour's door;

Then let my wife grind unto another, and let others bow down upon her.

For this is an heinous crime; yea, it is an iniquity to be punished by the judges.

For it is a fire that consumeth to destruction, and would root out all mine increase.

If I did despise the cause of my manservant or of my maidservant, when they contended with me;

What then shall I do when God riseth up? and when he visiteth, what shall I answer him?

Did not he that made me in the womb make him? and did not one fashion us in the womb?

If I have withheld the poor from their desire, or have caused the eyes of the widow to fail;

Or have eaten my morsel myself alone, and the fatherless hath not eaten thereof;

(For from my youth he was brought up with me, as with a father, and I have guided her from my mother's womb;)

If I have seen any perish for want of clothing, or any poor without covering;

If his loins have not blessed me, and if he were not warmed with the fleece of my sheep;

If I have lifted up my hand against the fatherless, when I saw my help in the gate:

Then let mine arm fall from my shoulder blade, and mine arm be broken from the bone.

For destruction from God was a terror to me, and by reason of his highness I could not endure.

If I have made gold my hope, or have said to the fine gold, Thou art my confidence;

If I rejoiced because my wealth was great, and because mine hand had gotten much;

If I beheld the sun when it shined, or the moon walking in brightness;

And my heart hath been secretly enticed, or my mouth hath kissed my hand:

This also were an iniquity to be punished by the judge: for I should have denied the God that is above.

If I rejoiced at the destruction of him that hated me, or lifted up myself when evil found him:

Neither have I suffered my mouth to sin by wishing a curse to his soul.

If the men of my tabernacle said not, Oh that we had of his flesh! we cannot be satisfied.

The stranger did not lodge in the street: but I opened my doors to the traveller.

If I covered my transgressions as Adam, by hiding mine iniquity in my bosom:

Did I fear a great multitude, or did the contempt of families terrify me, that I kept silence, and went not out of the door?

Oh that one would hear me! behold, my desire is, that the Almighty would answer me, and that mine adversary had written a book.

Surely I would take it upon my shoulder, and bind it as a crown to me.

I would declare unto him the number of my steps; as a prince would I go near unto him.

If my land cry against me, or that the furrows likewise thereof complain;

If I have eaten the fruits thereof without money, or have caused the owners thereof to lose their life:

Let thistles grow instead of wheat, and cockle instead of barley. The words of Job are ended.

[Chapters 32–37 in the received text, omitted here, are a latter addition in which a new character, Elihu, is abruptly introduced. Elihu's long speech reiterates the three friends' argument. The text then resumes.]

38

Then the LORD answered Job out of the whirlwind, and said,

Who is this that darkeneth counsel by words without knowledge?

Gird up now thy loins like a man; for I will demand of thee, and answer thou me.

Where wast thou when I laid the foundations of the earth? declare, if thou hast understanding.

Who hath laid the measures thereof, if thou knowest? or who hath stretched the line upon it?

Whereupon are the foundations thereof fastened? or who laid the corner stone thereof;

When the morning stars sang together, and all the sons of God shouted for joy?

Or who shut up the sea with doors, when it brake forth, as if it had issued out of the womb?

When I made the cloud the garment thereof, and thick darkness a swaddling-band for it,

And brake up for it my decreed place, and set bars and doors,

And said, Hitherto shalt thou come, but no further: and here shall thy proud waves be stayed?

Hast thou commanded the morning since thy days; and caused the dayspring to know his place;

That it might take hold of the ends of the earth, that the wicked might be shaken out of it?

It is turned as clay to the seal; and they stand as a garment.

And from the wicked their light is withholden, and the high arm shall be broken.

Hast thou entered into the springs of the sea? or hast thou walked in the search of the depth?

Have the gates of death been opened unto thee? or hast thou seen the doors of the shadow of death?

Hast thou perceived the breadth of the earth? declare if thou knowest it all.

Where is the way where light dwelleth? and as for darkness, where is the place thereof,

That thou shouldest take it to the bound thereof, and that thou shouldest know the paths to the house thereof?

Knowest thou it, because thou wast then born? or because the number of thy days is great?

Hast thou entered into the treasures of the snow? or hast thou seen the treasures of the hail,

Which I have reserved against the time of trouble, against the day of battle and war?

By what way is the light parted, which scattereth the east wind upon the earth?

Who hath divided a watercourse for the overflowing of waters, or a way for the lightning of thunder;

To cause it to rain on the earth, where no man is; on the wilderness, wherein there is no man;

To satisfy the desolate and waste ground; and to cause the bud of the tender herb to spring forth?

Hath the rain a father? or who hath begotten the drops of dew?

Out of whose womb came the ice? and the hoary frost of heaven, who hath gendered it?

The waters are hid as with a stone, and the face of the deep is frozen.

Canst thou bind the sweet influences of Pleiades, or loose the bands of Orion?

Canst thou bring forth Mazzaroth in his season? or canst thou guide Arcturus with his sons?

Knowest thou the ordinances of heaven? canst thou set the dominion thereof in the earth?

Canst thou lift up thy voice to the clouds, that abundance of waters may cover thee?

Canst thou send lightnings, that they may go, and say unto thee, Here we are?

Who hath put wisdom in the inward parts? or who hath given understanding to the heart?

Who can number the clouds in wisdom? or who can stay the bottles of heaven,

When the dust groweth into hardness, and the clods cleave fast together?

Wilt thou hunt the prey for the lion? or fill the appetite of the young lions,

When they couch in their dens, and abide in the covert to lie in wait?

Who provideth for the raven his food? when his young ones cry unto God, they wander for lack of meat.

39

Knowest thou the time when the wild goats of the rock bring forth? or canst thou mark when the hinds do calve?

Canst thou number the months that they fulfil? or knowest thou the time when they bring forth?

They bow themselves, they bring forth their young ones, they cast out their sorrows.

Their young ones are in good liking, they grow up with corn; they go forth, and return not unto them.

Who hath sent out the wild ass free? or who hath loosed the bands of the wild ass?

Whose house I have made the wilderness, and the barren land his dwellings.

He scorneth the multitude of the city, neither regardeth he the crying of the driver.

The range of the mountains is his pasture, and he searcheth after every green thing.

Will the unicorn be willing to serve thee, or abide by thy crib?

Canst thou bind the unicorn with his band in the furrow? or will he harrow the valleys after thee?

Wilt thou trust him, because his strength is great? or wilt thou leave thy labour to him?

Wilt thou believe him, that he will bring home thy seed, and gather it into thy barn?

Gavest thou the goodly wings unto the peacocks? or wings and feathers unto the ostrich?

Which leaveth her eggs in the earth, and warmeth them in dust,

And forgetteth that the foot may crush them, or that the wild beast may break them.

She is hardened against her young ones, as though they were not hers: her labour is in vain without fear;

Because God hath deprived her of wisdom, neither hath he imparted to her understanding.

What time she lifteth up herself on high, she scorneth the horse and his rider.

Hast thou given the horse strength? hast thou clothed his neck with thunder?

Canst thou make him afraid as a grasshopper? the glory of his nostrils is terrible.

He paweth in the valley, and rejoiceth in his strength: he goeth on to meet the armed men.

He mocketh at fear, and is not affrighted; neither turneth he back from the sword.

The quiver rattleth against him, the glittering spear and the shield.

He swalloweth the ground with fierceness and rage: neither believeth he that it is the sound of the trumpet.

He saith among the trumpets, Ha, ha; and he smelleth the battle afar off, the thunder of the captains, and the shouting.

Doth the hawk fly by thy wisdom, and stretch her wings toward the south?

Doth the eagle mount up at thy command, and make her nest on high?

She dwelleth and abideth on the rock, upon the crag of the rock, and the strong place.

From thence she seeketh the prey, and her eyes behold afar off.

Her young ones also suck up blood: and where the slain are, there is she.

40

Moreover the LORD answered Job, and said,

Shall he that contendeth with the Almighty instruct him? he that reproveth God, let him answer it.

Then Job answered the LORD, and said,

Behold, I am vile; what shall I answer thee? I will lay mine hand upon my mouth.

Once have I spoken; but I will not answer: yea, twice; but I will proceed no further.

Then answered the LORD unto Job out of the whirlwind, and said,

Gird up thy loins now like a man: I will demand of thee, and declare thou unto me.

Wilt thou also disannul my judgment? wilt thou condemn me, that thou mayest be righteous?

Hast thou an arm like God? or canst thou thunder with a voice like him?

Deck thyself now with majesty and excellency; and array thyself with glory and beauty.

Cast abroad the rage of thy wrath: and behold every one that is proud, and abase him.

Look on every one that is proud, and bring him low; and tread down the wicked in their place.

Hide them in the dust together; and bind their faces in secret.

Then will I also confess unto thee that thine own right hand can save thee.

Behold now behemoth, which I made with thee; he eateth grass as an ox.

Lo now, his strength is in his loins, and his force is in the navel of his belly.

He moveth his tail like a cedar: the sinews of his stones are wrapped together.

His bones are as strong pieces of brass; his bones are like bars of iron.

He is the chief of the ways of God: he that made him can make his sword to approach unto him.

Surely the mountains bring him forth food, where all the beasts of the field play.

He lieth under the shady trees, in the covert of the reed, and fens.

The shady trees cover him with their shadow; the willows of the brook compass him about.

Behold, he drinketh up a river, and hasteth not: he trusteth that he can draw up Jordan into his mouth.

He taketh it with his eyes: his nose pierceth through snares.

41

Canst thou draw out leviathan with an hook? or his tongue with a cord which thou lettest down?

Canst thou put an hook into his nose? or bore his jaw through with a thorn?

Will he make many supplications unto thee? will he speak soft words unto thee?

Will he make a covenant with thee? wilt thou take him for a servant for ever?

Wilt thou play with him as with a bird? or wilt thou bind him for thy maidens?

Shall the companions make a banquet of him? shall they part him among the merchants?

Canst thou fill his skin with barbed irons? or his head with fish spears?

Lay thine hand upon him, remember the battle, do no more.

Behold, the hope of him is in vain: shall not one be cast down even at the sight of him?

None is so fierce that dare stir him up: who then is able to stand before me?

Who hath prevented me, that I should repay him? whatsoever is under the whole heaven is mine.

I will not conceal his parts, nor his power, nor his comely proportion.

Who can discover the face of his garment? or who can come to him with his double bridle?

Who can open the doors of his face? his teeth are terrible round about.

His scales are his pride, shut up together as with a close seal.

One is so near to another, that no air can come between them.

They are joined one to another, they stick together, that they cannot be sundered.

By his neesings a light doth shine, and his eyes are like the eyelids of the morning.

Out of his mouth go burning lamps, and sparks of fire leap out.

Out of his nostrils goeth smoke, as out of a seething pot or caldron.

His breath kindleth coals, and a flame goeth out of his mouth.

In his neck remaineth strength, and sorrow is turned into joy before him.

The flakes of his flesh are joined together: they are firm in themselves; they cannot be moved.

His heart is as firm as a stone; yea, as hard as a piece of the nether millstone.

When he raiseth up himself, the mighty are afraid: by reason of breakings they purify themselves.

The sword of him that layeth at him cannot hold: the spear, the dart, nor the habergeon.

He esteemeth iron as straw, and brass as rotten wood.

The arrow cannot make him flee: slingstones are turned with him into stubble.

Darts are counted as stubble: he laugheth at the shaking of a spear.

Sharp stones are under him: he spreadeth sharp pointed things upon the mire.

He maketh the deep to boil like a pot: he maketh the sea like a pot of ointment.

He maketh a path to shine after him; one would think the deep to be hoary.

Upon earth there is not his like, who is made without fear.

He beholdeth all high things: he is a king over all the children of pride.

42

Then Job answered the LORD, and said,

I know that thou canst do every thing, and that no thought can be withholden from thee.

Who is he that hideth counsel without knowledge? therefore have I uttered that I understood not; things too wonderful for me, which I knew not.

Hear, I beseech thee, and I will speak: I will demand of thee, and declare thou unto me.

I have heard of thee by the hearing of the ear: but now mine eye seeth thee.

Wherefore I abhor myself, and repent in dust and ashes.

And it was so, that after the LORD had spoken these words unto Job, the LORD said to Eliphaz the Temanite, My wrath is kindled against thee, and against thy two friends: for ye have not spoken of me the thing that is right, as my servant Job hath.

Therefore take unto you now seven bullocks and seven rams, and go to my servant Job, and offer up for yourselves a burnt offering; and my servant Job shall pray for you: for him will I accept: lest I deal with you after your folly, in that ye have not spoken of me the thing which is right, like my servant Job.

So Eliphaz the Temanite and Bildad the Shuhite and Zophar the Naamathite went, and did according as the LORD commanded them: the LORD also accepted Job.

And the LORD turned the captivity of Job, when he prayed for his friends: also the LORD gave Job twice as much as he had before.

Then came there unto him all his brethren, and all his sisters, and all they that had been of his acquaintance before, and did eat bread with him in his house: and they bemoaned him, and comforted him over all the evil that the LORD had brought upon him: every man also gave him a piece of money, and every one an earring of gold.

So the LORD blessed the latter end of Job more than his beginning: for he had fourteen thousand sheep, and six thousand camels, and a thousand yoke of oxen, and a thousand she asses.

He had also seven sons and three daughters.

And he called the name of the first, Jemima; and the name of the second, Kezia; and the name of the third, Keren-happuch.[9]

And in all the land were no women found so fair as the daughters of Job: and their father gave them inheritance among their brethren.

After this lived Job an hundred and forty years, and saw his sons, and his sons' sons, even four generations.

So Job died, being old and full of days.

ANONYMOUS (SECOND MILLENNIUM B.C.E.)
Assyria/Babylonia

This haunting Akkadian poem describes the struggle for control of the underworld between Ishtar, the goddess of love, and her sister Ereshkigal, the queen of the underworld. Ereshkigal defeats Ishtar but spares her life on the condition that she surrender her husband, Dumuzi, as hostage.

The Descent of Ishtar dates from sometime during the second millennium B.C.E. The poem was performed in the Assyrian capital of Nineveh in connection with an annual ritual that featured the bathing and anointing of a statue of Dumuzi. It is based on an earlier Sumerian poem, *The Descent of Inanna,* in which Dumuzi is described as dying and rising again, thus causing seasonal fertility. (A

---

9. In this return to the folktale frame, Job's
new daughters have names meaning Dove,
Cinnamon, and Horn of eye-shadow.

similar mythical explanation of seasonal renewal can be found in the story of Persephone's abduction in the *Hymn to Demeter*.) *The Descent of Ishtar's* chilling description of the underworld House of Dust later found its way into the *Epic of Gilgamesh,* where it serves to motivate Gilgamesh's horror of death and leads to his subsequent search for immortality.

The Descent of Ishtar to the Underworld

To Kurnugi, land of no return,[1]
Ishtar daughter of Sin[2] was determined to go;
The daughter of Sin was determined to go
To the dark house, dwelling of Erkalla's god,[3]
To the house which those who enter cannot leave,   5
On the road where travelling is one-way only,
To the house where those who enter are deprived of light,
Where dust is their food, clay their bread.
They see no light, they dwell in darkness,
They are clothed like birds, with feathers.   10
Over the door and the bolt, dust has settled.
Ishtar, when she arrived at the gate of Kurnugi,
Addressed her words to the keeper of the gate,
   "Here gatekeeper, open your gate for me,
   Open your gate for me to come in!   15
   If you do not open the gate for me to come in,
   I shall smash the door and shatter the bolt,
   I shall smash the doorpost and overturn the doors,
   I shall raise up the dead and they shall eat the living:
   The dead shall outnumber the living!"   20
The gatekeeper made his voice heard and spoke,
He said to great Ishtar,
   "Stop, lady, do not break it down!
   Let me go and report your words to queen Ereshkigal."
The gatekeeper went in and spoke to Ereshkigal,   25
   "Here she is, your sister Ishtar,
   Who holds the great *keppū-*toy,[4]
   Stirs up the Apsu in Ea's presence."
When Ereshkigal heard this,
Her face grew livid as cut tamarisk,   30
Her lips grew dark as the rim of a pitch-coated vessel.

Translated by Stephanie Dalley.

1. *Kurnugi* is Sumerian for "Land of No Return."
2. The moon god (also spelled Su'en).
3. *Erkalla,* "The Great City," is another name for the underworld. It is ruled by Ereshkigal and her husband Nergal, who is often assimilated with Erra; he is called Herakles in Greek.
4. Perhaps a top, made to spin with a whip.

"What brings her to me? What has incited her against me?
Surely not because I drink water with the Anunnaki,
I eat clay for bread, I drink muddy water for beer?
Should I weep for young men forced to abandon their sweethearts?   35
Should I weep for girls wrenched from their lovers' laps?
Should I weep for the infant child, expelled before its time?
Go, gatekeeper, open your gate to her.
Treat her according to the ancient rites."
The gatekeeper went. He opened the gate to her.   40
    "Enter, my lady: may Kutha give you joy,[5]
May the palace of Kurnugi be glad to see you."
He let her in through the first door, but stripped away the great crown on her
    head.
    "Gatekeeper, why have you taken away the great crown on my head?"
    "Go in, my lady. Such are the rites of the Mistress of Earth."   45
He let her in through the second door, but stripped away the rings in her ears.
    "Gatekeeper, why have you taken away the rings in my ears?"
    "Go in, my lady. Such are the rites of the Mistress of Earth."
He let her in through the third door, but stripped away the beads around her neck.
    "Gatekeeper, why have you taken away the beads around my neck?"   50
    "Go in, my lady. Such are the rites of the Mistress of Earth."
He let her in through the fourth door, but stripped away the fasteners at her
    breast.
    "Gatekeeper, why have you taken away the fasteners at my breast?"
    "Go in, my lady. Such are the rites of the Mistress of Earth."
He let her in through the fifth door, but stripped away the girdle of birth-stones
    around her waist.   55
    "Gatekeeper, why have you taken away the girdle of birthstones around my
    waist?"
    "Go in, my lady. Such are the rites of the Mistress of Earth."
He let her in through the sixth door, but stripped away the bangles on her wrists
    and ankles.
    "Gatekeeper, why have you taken away the bangles from my wrists and ankles?"
    "Go in, my lady. Such are the rites of the Mistress of Earth."   60
He let her in through the seventh door, but stripped away the proud garment of
    her body.
    "Gatekeeper, why have you taken away the proud garment of my body?"
    "Go in, my lady. Such are the rites of the Mistress of Earth."
As soon as Ishtar went down to Kurnugi,
Ereshkigal looked at her and trembled before her.   65
Ishtar did not deliberate, but leant over her.
Ereshkigal made her voice heard and spoke,
Addressed her words to Namtar her vizier,

---

5. Kutha was a city sacred to Nergal; here the
name is used for the underworld itself.

'Go, Namtar, send out against her sixty diseases:
Disease of the eyes to her eyes,   70
Disease of the arms to her arms,
Disease of the feet to her feet,
Disease of the heart to her heart,
Disease of the head to her head,
To every part of her.'
After Ishtar the mistress of the land had gone down to Kurnugi,   75
No bull mounted a cow, no donkey impregnated a jenny,
No young man impregnated a girl in the street,
The young man slept in his private room,
The girl slept in the company of her friends.   80
Then Papsukkal, vizier of the great gods, hung his head, his face became gloomy;
He wore mourning clothes, his hair was unkempt.
Dejected, he went and wept before Sin his father,
His tears flowed freely before king Ea.
   "Ishtar has gone down to the Earth and has not come up again.   85
   As soon as Ishtar went down to Kurnugi
   No bull mounted a cow, no donkey impregnated a jenny,
   No young man impregnated a girl in the street,
   The young man slept in his private room,
   The girl slept in the company of her friends."   90
Ea, in the wisdom of his heart, created a person.
He created Good-looks the playboy.[6]
   "Come, Good-looks, set your face towards the gate of Kurnugi.
   The seven gates of Kurnugi shall be opened before you.
   Ereshkigal shall look at you and be glad to see you.   95
   When she is relaxed, her mood will lighten.
   Get her to swear the oath by the great gods.
   Raise your head, pay attention to the waterskin,
   Saying, 'Hey, my lady, let them give me the waterskin, that I may drink water
      from it.'"
                                     (*And so it happened. But*)   100
When Ereshkigal heard this,
She struck her thigh and bit her finger.
   "You have made a request of me that should not have been made!
   Come, Good-looks, I shall curse you with a great curse.
   I shall decree for you a fate that shall never be forgotten.   105
   Bread begged from the city's bakers shall be your food,
   The city drains shall be your only drinking place,
   The shade of a city wall your only standing place,
   Threshold steps your only sitting place,
   The drunkard and the thirsty shall slap your cheek."   110

---

6. Literally, "His appearance is bright."

Ereshkigal made her voice heard and spoke;
She addressed her words to Namtar her vizier,
   "Go, Namtar, knock at Egalgina,
   Decorate the threshold steps with coral,
   Bring the Anunnaki out and seat (them) on golden thrones,   115
   Sprinkle Ishtar with the waters of life and conduct her into my presence."
Namtar went, knocked at Egalgina,
Decorated the threshold steps with coral,
Brought out the Anunnaki, seated (them) on golden thrones,
Sprinkled Ishtar with the waters of life and brought her to her (sister).   120
He let her out through the first door, and gave back to her the proud garment of
   her body.
He let her out through the second door, and gave back to her the bangles for her
   wrists and ankles.
He let her out through the third door, and gave back to her the girdle of birth
   stones around her waist.
He let her out through the fourth door, and gave back to her the fasteners at her
   breast.
He let her out through the fifth door, and gave back to her the beads around her
   neck.   125
He let her out through the sixth door, and gave back to her the rings for her ears.
He let her out through the seventh door, and gave back to her the great crown for
   her head.
   "Swear that she has paid you her ransom, and give her back (in exchange) for
   him,
   For Dumuzi, the lover of her youth.
   Wash (him) with pure water, anoint him with sweet oil,   130
   Clothe him in a red robe, let the lapis lazuli pipe play.
   Let temple prostitutes raise a loud lament."
Then Belili[7] tore off her jewellery,
Her lap was filled with eyestones.
Belili heard the lament for her brother, she struck the jewellery from her body,   135
The eyestones with which the front of the wild cow was filled.
   "You shall not rob me (forever) of my only brother!
   On the day when Dumuzi comes back up, (and) the lapis lazuli pipe and the
   carnelian ring come up with him,
   (When) male and female mourners come up with him,
   The dead shall come up and smell the smoke offering."   140

---

7. Sister of Dumuzi; in the longer Sumerian
   version, she pleads for Dumuzi's periodic
   release. Compare this with Persephone's

seasonal return from the underworld in the
Greek myth.

ANONYMOUS (SEVENTH CENTURY B.C.E.)
Greece

The *Homeric Hymn to Aphrodite* and the *Homeric Hymn to Demeter* (from both of which we give substantial selections here) belong to a body of poems in epic meter that in antiquity were generally attributed to Homer. Linguistic and stylistic evidence has since disproved the attribution, although the poems clearly draw on traditional mythology and story patterns. As a genre, the hymn was highly popular in the archaic and classical periods of Greece (the seventh to the fifth centuries B.C.E.). The hymns ascribed to Homer are thought to have been composed for performance at public religious festivals as preludes to epic songs.

The *Homeric Hymn to Aphrodite* opens by acknowledging the irresistible power of Aphrodite, the goddess of erotic love. All beings mortal and divine (with only three exceptions) are helpless before her, and even Zeus, the supreme deity, has often been at her mercy. In the subsequent narrative, Zeus turns the tables on the goddess, causing her to fall in love with a young man—Anchises, a cousin of the Trojan king, Priam. Disguising herself as a girl from the countryside, Aphrodite seduces Anchises. His poignant expression of fear when he discovers her identity reflects the peril inherent in mortal-immortal liaisons—a recurrent motif in early Greek mythology and literature. From this union of Aphrodite with Anchises, however, the Trojan hero Aeneas will be born. Aphrodite predicts for him an endless line of descendants, which, centuries later, becomes an important thematic element in Vergil's *Aeneid*.

Homeric Hymn to Aphrodite

Muse, tell me the things done by golden Aphrodite,
the one from Cyprus,[1] who arouses sweet desire for gods
and who subdues the races of mortal humans,
and birds as well, who fly in the sky, as well as all beasts
—all those that grow on both dry land and the sea.   5
They all know the things done by the one with the beautiful garlands, the one
      from Kythera.[2]
But there are three whose minds she cannot win over or deceive.
The first is the daughter of aegis-bearing Zeus, bright-eyed Athena.
For she takes no pleasure in the things done by golden Aphrodite.
What does please her is wars and what is done by Ares,   10
battles and fighting, as well as the preparation of splendid pieces of craftsmanship.

Translated by Gregory Nagy.

1. Aphrodite is always associated with the island of Cyprus, thought to have been either the place of her birth or the island onto which she first stepped after her birth in the sea, as described in Hesiod's *Theogony*.
2. According to Hesiod, after Aphrodite's birth in the sea, she drifted near the island of Kythera before reaching Cyprus.

For she was the first to teach mortal humans to be craftsmen
in making war-chariots and other things on wheels, decorated with bronze.
And she it is who teaches maidens, tender of skin, inside the palaces,
the skill of making splendid pieces of craftsmanship, putting it firmly into each
    one's mind.   15
The second is the renowned Artemis,[3] she of the golden shafts: never
has she been subdued in lovemaking by Aphrodite, lover of smiles.
For she takes pleasure in the bow and arrows, and the killing of wild beasts in the
    mountains,
as well as lyres, groups of singing dancers, and high-pitched shouts of celebration.
Also shaded groves and the city of just men.   20
The third one not to take pleasure in the things done by Aphrodite is that young
    Maiden full of honorableness,
Hestia,[4] who was the first-born child of Kronos, the one with the crooked mind,
as well as the last and youngest, through the Will of Zeus, holder of the aegis.[5]
She was the Lady who was wooed by Poseidon and Apollo.
But she was quite unwilling, and she firmly refused.   25
She had sworn a great oath, and what she said became what really happened.
She swore, as she touched the head of her father Zeus, the aegis-bearer,
that she would be a virgin for all days to come, that illustrious goddess.
And to her Father Zeus gave a beautiful honor, as a compensating substitute for
    marriage.
She is seated in the middle of the house, getting the richest portion.   30
And in all the temples of the gods she has a share in the honor
Among all the mortals, she is the senior goddess.
These are the three that she could not persuade in their minds.
As for all the rest, there is nothing that has escaped Aphrodite:
none of the blessed gods nor any of mortal humans.   35
She even led astray the perception of Zeus, the one who delights in the thunder,
the one who is the very greatest and the one who has the very greatest honor as his
    share.
But even his well-formed mind is deceived by her, whenever she wants,
as she mates him with mortal women with the greatest of ease,
unbeknownst to Hera, his sister and wife,   40
who is the best among all the immortal goddesses in her great beauty.
She was the most glorious female to be born to Kronos, the one with the crooked
    mind,
and to her mother, Rhea. And Zeus, the one whose resources are inexhaustible,
made her his honorable wife, one who knows the ways of affection.
But even upon her Zeus put sweet desire in her heart   45
—desire to make love to a mortal man, so that

---

3. The chaste goddess of the hunt is Apollo's
   sister.
4. Hestia, whose name means "hearth" or
   "fireplace," was the first child swallowed by

her father Cronus and the last disgorged,
according to Hesiod.
5. The aegis is Zeus' shield.

not even she may go without mortal lovemaking
and get a chance to gloat at all the other gods,
with her sweet laughter, Aphrodite, lover of smiles,
boasting that she can make the gods sleep with mortal women,   50
who then bear mortal sons to immortal fathers,
and how she can make the goddesses sleep with mortal men.
And so he put sweet desire in her heart—desire for Anchises.
At that time, he was herding cattle at the steep peaks of Mount Ida, famous for its
      many springs.
To look at him and the way he was shaped was like looking at the immortals.   55
When Aphrodite, lover of smiles, saw him,
she fell in love with him. A terrible desire seized her in her mind.
She went to Cyprus, entering her temple fragrant with incense,
to Paphos.[6] That is where her sacred precinct is, and her altar, fragrant with
      incense.
She went in and closed the shining doors.   60
Then the Graces bathed her and anointed her with oil
—the kind that gives immortality, glistening on the complexion of the gods, who
      last for all time.
Immortal it was, giver of pleasures, and it had the fragrance of incense.
Then she wrapped all her beautiful clothes around her skin.
She was decked out in gold, Aphrodite, lover of smiles.   65
She rushed toward Troy, leaving behind fragrant Cyprus.
Making her way with the greatest of ease, high up among the clouds.
She arrived at Mount Ida, famous for its many springs, nurturing mother of beasts.
She went straight for the herdsmen's homestead, up over the mountain. Following
      her came
gray wolves and lions with fierce looks, fawning on her;   70
bears too, and nimble leopards, who cannot have their fill of devouring deer,
came along. Seeing them, she was delighted in her heart, in her thoughts,
and she put desire where their hearts were. So they all
went off in pairs and slept together in shaded nooks.
She in the meantime came to the well-built shelters   75
and found him left all alone at the herdsmen's homestead,
that hero Anchises, who had the beauty of the gods.
All the others went after the herds, along the grassy pastures,
while he was left all alone at the herdsmen's homestead,
pacing back and forth, playing tunes on his lyre that pierce the inside.   80
She stood before him, the daughter of Zeus, Aphrodite,
looking like an unwed maiden in size of length and appearance.
She did not want him to notice her with his eyes and be frightened of her.
When Anchises saw her he was filled with wonder as he took note
of her appearance and size of length and splendid clothes.   85
For she wore a robe that was more resplendent than the brightness of fire.

---

6. A city in Cyprus.

She had twisted brooches, and shiny earrings in the shape of flowers.
Around her tender throat were the most beautiful necklaces.
It was a thing of beauty, golden, decorated with every sort of design. Like the moon
it glowed all around her tender breasts, a marvel to behold.   90
Seized with love, Anchises said to her:
"Hail, my Lady, you who come here to this home, whichever of the blessed ones
    you are,
Artemis or Leto or golden Aphrodite
or Themis of noble birth or bright-eyed Athena.
Or perhaps you are one of the graces, you who have come here. They are the ones   95
who keep company with all the gods and are called immortal.
Or you are one of those Nymphs who range over beautiful groves,
or one of those Nymphs who inhabit this beautiful mountain,
and the fountainheads of rivers and grassy meadows.
For you, on some high peak, in a spot with a view going all round,   100
I will set up an altar, and I will perform for you beautiful sacrifices
every year as the season comes round. And I wish that you in turn may have a
    kindly-disposed heart towards me.
Grant that I become a man who is distinguished among the Trojans.
Make the genealogy that comes after me become a flourishing one. And make me
live a very long life and see the light of the sun,   105
blessed in the midst of the people. And let me arrive at the threshold of old age."
Then Aphrodite, daughter of Zeus, answered him:
"Anchises, most glorious of earth-born men!
I am no goddess. Why do you liken me to the female immortals?
No, I am a mortal. The mother that bore me was a woman.   110
My father is Otreus, famed for his name. Maybe you have heard of him.
He rules over all of Phrygia, with its strong-walled fortresses.
But I know your language as well as my own.
The nursemaid who brought me up in the palace was a Trojan. Ever since I was
    a small child,
she brought me up, having taken me from my dear mother.   115
That is why I know your language as well as my own.
But then, the one with the golden wand, the Argos-killer Hermes, abducted me,
taking me from a festival of song and dance in honor of Artemis, the one with the
    golden arrows.
There were many of us nymphs there, maidens worth many cattle as bride-price.
We were having a good time, and a crowd so large that you couldn't count them
    was standing around us in a circle.   120
Then it was that the one with the golden wand, the Argos-killer, abducted me.
He carried me over many fields of mortal humans
and over vast stretches of land unclaimed and unsettled, where wild beasts,
eaters of raw flesh, roam about, in and out of their shaded lairs.
I thought that my feet would never again touch the earth, grower of grain.   125
And he said that I, in your bed, the bed of Anchises, would be called your
lawfully-wedded wife, and that I would give you splendid children.

But once he pointed this out and made note of it, straightaway
he went back, that powerful Argos-killer, to that separate group, the immortals.
I in the meantime reached you here, and there is an overpowering compulsion
    that I have in me. 130
In the name of Zeus, in the name of your parents, I appeal to you as I touch your
    knees.
Your parents must be noble, for base ones could never have conceived such a one
    as you.
Take me, virgin that I am, inexperienced in making love,
and show me to your father and to your caring mother
and to your brothers, those born from the same parents. 135
I will not be an unseemly in-law for them, but a seemly one indeed.
And send a messenger quickly to the Phrygians, trainers of swift horses,
to tell my father and my mother, however much she grieves.
They will send you plenty of gold, and woven clothing as well.
Take these abundant and splendid things as dowry. 140
After you have done so, prepare a lovely wedding-feast
that gives honor to both humans and immortals."
After she said these things, she put sweet desire in his heart
and Anchises was seized with love. He said these words, calling out to her:
"If you are mortal, and if a woman was the mother who gave birth to you, 145
and if Otreus is your father, famed for his name, as you say he is,
and if you have come here because of the Immortal Conductor,[7]
Hermes, and if you are to be called my wife for all days to come,
then it is impossible for any god or any mortal human
to hold me back, right here, from joining with you in making love, 150
right now, on the spot—not even if the one who shoots from afar, Apollo himself,
takes aim from his silver bow and shoots his arrows that bring misery.
Then, O lady who looks like the gods, I would willingly,
once I have been in your bed, go down into the palace of Hades below."
So saying, he took her by the hand. And Aphrodite, lover of smiles, 155
went along, with her face turned away and her eyes downcast,
towards the bed, all nicely made, which had already been arranged for the lord,
all nicely made with soft covers. And on top lay skins of
bears and lions, who roar with their deep voices,
which he himself had killed on the lofty mountainsides. 160
And when they went up into the sturdy bed,
he first took off the jewelry shining on the surface of her body
—the twisted brooches and the shiny earrings in the shape of flowers.
Then he undid her girdle and her resplendent garments.
He stripped them off and put them on a silver-studded stool, 165
Anchises did. And then, by the will of the gods and by fate,

---

7. Hermes, the divine messenger, conducts
    travelers to their destinations and guides
    the souls of the dead to the underworld.

he lay next to the immortal female, mortal male that he was. He did not know
    what he was really doing.
But when the time comes for herdsmen to drive back to the fold
their cattle and sturdy sheep, back from the flowery pastures,
then it was that Aphrodite poured sweet sleep over Anchises,   170
sweet and pleasurable. She in the meantime put back on her beautiful clothes,
    which covered again the surface of her body.
Now that her skin was again beautifully covered over, the resplendent goddess
stood by the bed, and the well-built roof-beam
—her head reached that high up. And beauty shone forth from her cheeks
—an immortal beauty, the kind that marks the one with the beautiful garlands,
    the goddess from Kythera.   175
Then she woke him from his sleep and called out to him, saying:
"Rise up, son of Dardanos! Why do you sleep such a sleep without awakening?
See if I look like
what you noticed when you first saw me with your eyes."
So she spoke, and he, fresh out of his sleep, straightaway heeded her word.   180
As soon as he saw the neck and the beautiful eyes of Aphrodite,
he was filled with fright and he turned his eyes away, in another direction.
Then he hid his beautiful face with a cloak,
and, praying to her, addressed her with winged words:
"The first time I ever laid eyes on you, goddess,   185
I knew you were a god. But you did not speak to me accurately.
Now I appeal to you by touching your knees, in the name of Zeus the holder of the
    aegis,
don't let me become disabled, don't let me live on like that among humans!
Please, take pity! I know that no man is full of life, able,
if he sleeps with immortal goddesses."   190
He was answered by the daughter of Zeus, Aphrodite:
"Anchises, most glorious of mortal humans!
Take heart, and do not be too afraid in your thoughts.
You should have no fear of that I would do any kind of bad thing to you,
or that any of the other blessed ones would. For you are dear indeed to the gods. 195
And you will have a dear son, who will be king among the Trojans.
And following him will be generations after generations for all time to come.
His name will be Aineias, since it was an unspeakable[8] grief that took hold of
    me—grief that I had fallen into the bed of a mortal man."

[Aphrodite's speech continues, pointing out examples of other gods who fell in love with
mortals but acknowledging her extreme embarrassment at sharing their vulnerability. The
hymn ends with the goddess informing Anchises that his son will be raised by mountain
nymphs, and warning him to conceal the identity of his son's mother and his encounter with
her.]

---

8. Aphrodite connects the name of Aineias
   with the Greek adjective *ainos*, meaning
   "unspeakable, terrible"; the two words are
   not actually related etymologically, although they sound alike.

ANONYMOUS (SEVENTH CENTURY B.C.E.)
Greece

The *Homeric Hymn to Demeter* exhibits the hallmarks of oral composition in its meter, diction, and style (including the use of repeated phrases, or formulas). It can be dated, though only approximately, to the mid- or late seventh century B.C.E. As with the *Hymn to Aphrodite,* the ancient attribution of this hymn to the poet of the *Iliad* and *Odyssey* is certainly incorrect, but we have no positive evidence to determine its true authorship.

The *Hymn's* subject is the grief of Demeter, goddess of the fruits of the earth, over the rape of her daughter Persephone by Hades, god of the underworld. Significant above all are the consequences of Demeter's wrath, both at Hades— who has taken the girl to live with him in the underworld—and at Zeus, Persephone's father, who sanctioned the rape. Demeter withdraws from the company of gods and withholds her fertility functions, so that the earth is made barren; famine results, threatening human beings with extinction and depriving the gods of their due offerings. The motif of a god's withdrawal, with resulting universal infertility, occurs in ancient Egyptian, Babylonian, Ugaritic, and Hittite mythology, which add to their parallels with the *Hymn to Demeter* the distinctive feature that the gods themselves are threatened with starvation.

Despite pleas from the gods on Olympus, Demeter does not relent until she has seen her daughter and has secured her return from the underworld for at least part of every year—those seasons when the earth is fruitful. In its central section, the *Hymn* suggests that because Demeter—disguised as an old woman, in her chosen exile from Olympus—was hospitably received by the people of Eleusis (a town near Athens), she revealed to them in return the secrets of agriculture and the mysteries that promise happiness after death. Throughout antiquity, Demeter and Persephone were worshipped in an important cult at Eleusis, whose rituals were guarded by the initiates with utmost secrecy.

Homeric Hymn to Demeter

Demeter I being to sing, the fair-tressed awesome goddess,
herself and her slim-ankled daughter whom Aidoneus[1]
seized; Zeus gave her, heavy-thundering and mighty-voiced,
gave her, without the consent of Demeter, the bright fruit and golden sword,
as she played with the deep-breasted daughters of Ocean,   5
plucking flowers in the lush meadow—roses, crocuses,
and lovely violets, irises and hyacinth and the narcissus,
which Earth grew as a snare for the flower-faced maiden

Translated by Helene P. Foley.

1. Hades, god of the underworld.

in order to gratify by Zeus's design the Host-to-Many,[2]
a flower wondrous and bright, awesome for all to see,   10
for the immortals above and for mortals below.
From its root a hundred fold bloom sprang up and smelled
so sweet that the whole vast heaven above
and the whole earth laughed, and the salty swell of the sea.
The girl marvelled and stretched out both hands at once   15
to take the lovely toy. The earth with its wide ways yawned
over the Nysian plain; the lord host-to-many rose up on her
with his immortal horses, the celebrated son of Kronos;[3]
he snatched the unwilling maid into his golden chariot
and led her off lamenting. She screamed with a shrill voice,   20
calling on her father, the son of Kronos highest and best.
Not one of the immortals or of humankind
heard her voice, nor the olives bright with fruit,
except the daughter of Persaios; tender of heart,
she heard her from her cave. Hekate[4] of the delicate veil.   25
And lord Helios, brilliant son of Hyperion, heard
the maid calling her father the Son of Kronos. But he sat apart
from the gods, aloof in a temple ringing with prayers,
and received choice offerings from humankind.
Against her will Hades took her by the design of Zeus   30
with his immortal horses—her father's brother,
commander and host-to-many, the many-named son of Kronos.
So long as the goddess gazed on earth and starry heaven,
on the sea flowing strong and full of fish,
and on the beams of the sun, she still hoped   35
to see her dear mother and the race of immortal gods.
For so long hope charmed her strong mind despite her distress.
The mountain peaks and the depths of the sea echoed
in response to her divine voice, and her goddess mother heard.
Sharp grief seized her heart, and she tore the veil   40
on her ambrosial hair with her own hands.
She cast a dark cloak on her shoulders
and sped like a bird over dry land and sea,
searching. No one was willing to tell her the truth,
not one of the gods or mortals;   45
no bird of omen came to her as truthful messenger.
Then for nine days divine Deo[5] roamed over the earth,
holding torches ablaze in her hands;
in her grief she did not once taste ambrosia
or nectar sweet-to-drink, nor bathed her skin.   50

---

2. A euphemistic epithet of Hades.
3. Hades, like Zeus, was the son of the Titans
   Kronos and Rheia.

4. A divinity regularly associated with the
   goddess Artemis and with Persephone.
5. Demeter.

But when the tenth Dawn came shining on her,
Hekate met her, holding a torch in her hands,
to give her a message. She spoke as follows:
"Divine Demeter, giver of seasons and glorious gifts,
who of the immortals or mortal men   55
seized Persephone and grieved your heart?
For I heard a voice but did not see with my eyes
who he was. To you I say at once the whole truth."
Thus Hekate spoke. The daughter of fair-tressed Rheia[6]
said not a word, but rushed off at her side   60
holding torches ablaze in her hands.
They came to Helios, the observer of gods and mortals,
and stood before his horses. The most august goddess spoke:
"Helios, respect me as a god does a goddess, if ever
with word or deed I pleased your heart and spirit.   65
The daughter I bore, a sweet sprout noble in form—
I heard her voice throbbing through the barren air
as if she were suffering violence. But I did not see her with my eyes.
With your rays you look down through the bright air
on the whole of the earth and the sea.   70
Tell me the truth about my child. Have you somewhere
seen who of gods or mortal men took her
by force from me against her will and went away?"
Thus she spoke and the son of Hyperion replied:
"Daughter of fair-tressed Rheia, mighty Demeter,   75
you will know. For I greatly revere and pity you
grieving for your slim-ankled daughter. No other
of the gods was to blame but cloud-gathering Zeus,
who gave her to Hades his brother to be called
his fertile wife. With his horses Hades   80
snatched her screaming into the misty gloom.
But, Goddess, give up for good your great lamentation.
You must not nurse in vain insatiable anger.
Among the gods Aidoneus is not an unsuitable bridegroom,
commander-to-many and Zeus' own brother of the same stock.   85
As for honor, he got his third at the world's first division,
and dwells with those whose rule has fallen to his lot."
He spoke and called to his horses. At his rebuke
they bore the swift chariot lightly, like long-winged birds.
A more terrible and brutal grief seized the heart   90
of Demeter, angry now at the son of Kronos with his dark clouds.
Withdrawing from the assembly of the gods and high Olympus
she went among the cities and fertile fields of men,

---

6. The mother of Demeter as well as of Zeus
   and Hades.

disguising her beauty for a long time. No one of men
nor low-girt women recognized her when they looked,   95
until she came to the house of skillful Keleos,
the man then ruler of fragrant Eleusis.
There she sat near the road, grief in her heart,
where citizens drew water from the Maiden's Well
in the shade—an olive bush had grown overhead—   100
like a very old woman cut off from child-bearing
and the gifts of garland-loving Aphrodite.
Such are the nurses to children of law-giving kings
and the keepers of stores in their echoing halls.
The daughters of Keleos, son of Eleusis, saw her   105
as they came to fetch water easy-to-draw and bring it
in bronze vessels to their dear father's halls.
Like four goddesses they were in the flower of youth,
Kallidike, Kleisidike, Demo and fair Kallithoe,
who was the first born in birth of them all.   110
They did not know her—gods are hard for mortals to see.
Standing near her, they spoke winged words.
"Who are you, old woman, of those born long ago?
From where? Why have you gone from the city nor
draw near its homes? Women are there in the shadowy halls   115
of your age as well as others born younger,
who would care for you both in word and in deed."
They spoke, and the most august goddess replied:
"Dear children, whoever of womankind you are,
greetings. I will tell you my tale. For it is not wrong   120
to tell you the truth now you ask."

[Demeter proceeds to fabricate a tale about herself and concludes by appealing successfully
to Celeus' daughters to take her into their household. The old woman (as she appears)
becomes the nurse of their infant brother. Her plan to make him immortal is brought to an
abrupt end, however, when the child's horrified mother disturbs the goddess in the act of
putting the child (who flourishes under this divine ministration) into the fire. Demeter reveals
herself, commands the Eleusinians to build her a temple and promises to teach them her
sacred rites.]

The shrine grew as the goddess decreed.
But once they finished and ceased their toil,
each went off home. Then golden-haired Demeter
remained sitting apart from all the immortals,   125
wasting with desire for her deep-girt daughter.
For mortals she ordained a terrible and brutal year
on the deeply-fertile earth. The ground released
no seed, for bright-crowned Demeter kept it buried.
In vain the oxen dragged many curved plows down   130
the furrows. In vain much white barley fell on the earth.
She would have destroyed the whole mortal race

by cruel famine, and stolen the glorious honor of gifts
and sacrifices from those having homes on Olympus,
if Zeus had not seen and pondered their plight in his heart. 135
First he roused golden-winged Iris to summon
fair-tressed Demeter, so lovely in form.
Zeus spoke and Iris obeying the dark-clouded
son of Kronos, raced swiftly between heaven and earth.
She came to the citadel of fragrant Eleusis 140
and found in her temple dark-robed Demeter.
Addressing her, she spoke winged words:
"Demeter, Zeus the father with his unfailing knowledge
bids you rejoin the tribes of immortal gods.
Go and let Zeus's word not remain unfulfilled." 145
Thus she implored, but Demeter's heart was unmoved.
Then the father sent in turn all the blessed immortals;
one by one they kept coming and pleading
and offered her many glorious gifts and whatever
honors she might choose among the immortal gods. 150
Yet not one could bend the mind and thought
of the raging goddess, who harshly spurned their pleas.
Never, she said, would she mount up to fragrant
Olympus nor release the seed from the earth,
until she saw with her eyes her own fair-faced child. 155
When Zeus, heavy-thundering and mighty-voiced,
heard this, he sent down the Slayer of Argos[7] to Erebos[8]
with his golden staff to wheedle Hades with soft words
and lead back holy Persephone from the misty gloom
into the light to join the gods so that her mother 160
might see her with her eyes and desist from anger.
Hermes did not disobey. At once he left Olympus' height
and plunged swiftly into the depths of the earth.
He met lord Hades inside his dwelling,
reclining on a bed with his shy spouse, strongly reluctant 165
through desire for her mother. [still she, Demeter,
was brooding on revenge for the deeds of the blessed gods].
The strong Slayer of Argos stood near and spoke:
"Dark-haired Hades, ruler of the dead, Father Zeus
bids me lead noble Persephone up from Erebos 170
to join us, so that her mother might see her with her eyes
and cease from anger and dread wrath against the gods.
For she is devising a great scheme to destroy
the helpless race of mortals born on earth,
burying the seed beneath the ground and obliterating 175

---

7. The Slayer of Argos was Hermes, the divine　　8. The underworld.
messenger.

divine honors. Her anger is terrible, nor does she go
among the gods, but sits aloof in her fragrant temple,
keeping to the rocky citadel of Eleusis."
Thus he spoke and Aidoneus, lord of the dead, smiled
with his brows, nor disobeyed king Zeus's commands.   180
At once he urged thoughtful Persephone:
"Go, Persephone, to the side of your dark-robed mother,
keeping the spirit and temper in your breast benign.
Do not be so sad and angry beyond the rest;
in no way among immortals will I be an unsuitable spouse,   185
myself a brother of father Zeus. And when you are here
you will have power over all that lives and moves,
and you will possess the greatest honors among the gods.
There will be punishment forevermore for those wrongdoers
who fail to appease your power with sacrifices,   190
performing proper rites and making due offerings."
Thus he spoke and thoughtful Persephone rejoiced.
Eagerly she leapt up for joy. But he
gave her to eat a honey-sweet pomegranate seed,
stealthily passing it around her, lest she once more stay forever   195
by the side of revered Demeter of the dark robe.
Then Aidoneus commander-to-many yoked
his divine horses before the golden chariot.
She mounted the chariot and at her side the strong
Slayer of Argos took the reins and whip in his hands,   200
and dashed from the halls. The horses flew eagerly;
swiftly they completed the long journey; not sea nor
river waters, not grassy glens nor mountain peaks
slowed the speed of the immortal horses,
slicing the deep air as they flew above these places.   205
He brought them to a halt where rich-crowned Demeter
waited before the fragrant temple. With one look she darted
like a maenad down a mountain shaded with woods.
On her side Persephone, [seeing] her mother's [radiant face],
[left chariot and horses,] and leapt down to run   210
[and fall on her neck in passionate embrace].
[While holding her dear child in her arms], her [heart
suddenly sensed a trick. Fearful, she] drew back
from [her embrace and at once enquired:]
"My child, tell me, you [did not taste] food [while below?]   215
Speak out [and hide nothing, so we both may know.]
[For if not], ascending [from miserable Hades],
you will dwell with me and your father, the
dark-clouded [son of Kronos], honored by all the gods.
But if [you tasted food], returning beneath [the earth]   220
you will stay a third part of the seasons [each year],

but two parts with myself and the other immortals.
When the earth blooms in spring with all kinds
of sweet flowers, then from the misty dark you will
rise again, a great marvel to gods and mortal men.   225
By what guile did the mighty Host to Many deceive you?"
Then radiant Persephone replied to her in turn:
"I will tell you the whole truth exactly, Mother.
The Slayer of Argos came to bring fortunate news
from my father, the son of Kronos, and the other gods   230
and lead me from Erebos so that seeing me with your eyes
you would desist from your anger and dread wrath
at the gods. Then I leapt up for joy, but he stealthily
put in my mouth a food honey-sweet, a pomegranate seed,
and compelled me against my will and by force to taste it.   235
For the rest—how seizing me by the shrewd plan of my father,
Kronos' son, he carried me off into the earth's depths—
I shall tell and elaborate all that you ask.
We were all in the beautiful meadow—
Leukippe, Phrono, Elektra, and Ianthe,   240
Melite, Iache, Rhodies, and Kallirhoe,
Melibosis, Tuche, and flower-faced Okurhoe,
Khryseis, Ianeira, Akaste, Admete,
Rhodope, Plouto, and lovely Kalypso,
Styx, Ourania and fair Galaxaura, Pallas,   245
rouser of battles, and Artemis, sender of arrows—
playing and picking lovely flowers with our hands,
soft crocus mixed with irises and hyacinth,
rose buds and lilies, a marvel to see, and the
narcissus that wide earth bore like a crocus.   250
As I joyously plucked it, the ground gaped from beneath,
and the mighty lord, Host-to-Many, rose from it
and carried me off beneath the earth in his goden chariot
much against my will. And I cried out at the top of my voice.
I speak the whole truth, though I grieve to tell it."   255
Then all day long, their minds at one, they soothed
each other's heart and soul in many ways,
embracing fondly, and their spirits abandoned grief,
as they gave and received joy between them.
Hekate of the delicate veil drew near them   260
and often caressed the daughter of holy Demeter;
from that time this lady served her as chief attendant.
To them Zeus, heavy-thundering and mighty-voiced,
sent as mediator fair-tressed Rheia to summon
dark-robed Demeter to the tribes of gods; he promised   265
to give her what honors she might choose among the gods.
He agreed his daughter would spend one third

of the revolving year in the misty dark, and two thirds
with her mother and the other immortals.
So he spoke and the goddess did not disobey his commands.   270
She darted swiftly down the peaks of Olympus
and arrived where the Rharian plain, once life-giving
udder of earth, now giving no life at all, stretched idle
and utterly leafless. For the white barley was hidden
by the designs of lovely-ankled Demeter. Yet as spring came on   275
the fields would soon ripple with long ears of grain;
and the rich furrows would grow heavy on the ground
with grain to be tied with bands into sheaves.
There she first alighted from the barren air.
Mother and daughter were glad to see each other   280
and rejoiced at heart. Rheia of the delicate veil then said:
"Come, child, Zeus, heavy-thundering and mighty-voiced,
summons you to rejoin the tribes of the gods;
he has offered to give what honors you choose among them.
He agreed that his daughter would spend one third   285
of the revolving year in the misty dark, and two thirds
with her mother and the other immortals.
He guaranteed it would be so with a nod of his head.
So come, my child, obey me; do not rage overmuch
and forever at the dark-clouded son of Kronos.   290
Now make the grain grow fertile for humankind."
So Rheia spoke, and rich-crowned Demeter did not disobey.
At once she sent forth fruit from the fertile fields
and the whole wide earth burgeoned with leaves
and flowers. She went to the kings who administer law,   295
Triptolemos and Diokles, driver of horses, mighty
Eumolpos and Keleos, leader of the people, and revealed
the conduct of her rites and taught her mysteries to all,[9]
holy rites which are not to be transgressed, nor pried into,
nor divulged. For a great awe of the gods stops the voice.   300
Blessed is the mortal on earth who has seen these rites,
but the uninitiate who has no share in them, never
has the same lot once dead in the dreary darkness.
When the great goddess had founded all her rites,
they left for Olympos to join the assembly of the other gods.   305
There they dwell by Zeus delighting-in-thunder, inspiring
awe and reverence. Highly blessed is the mortal
on earth whom they graciously favor with love.

---

9. It is not known just what the Eleusinian
mysteries consisted of, but initiation into
them offered the promise of renewal of
agricultural fertility and the possibility for the
initiate of mitigating, in some form, the grim
finality of death.

For soon they will send to the hearth of his great house
Ploutos, the god giving abundance to mortal men.   310
But come, you goddesses, dwelling in the town of
fragrant Eleusis, and sea-girt Paros, and rocky Antron,
revered Deo, mighty giver of seasons and glorious gifts,
you and your very fair daughter Persephone,
For my song grant gladly a living that warms the heart.   315
And I shall remember you and a new song as well.

ANONYMOUS (c. 1200 B.C.E.)
Ancient Mesopotamia

The *Epic of Gilgamesh* is the longest and greatest literary composition of ancient
Mesopotamia. Gilgamesh was an early king of the Sumerian city-state of Uruk
(today in central Iraq); he lived sometime between 2800 and 2500 B.C.E. Stories
about his adventures began to circulate soon after his death. Sometime between
2000 and 1600 B.C.E., the stories were gathered and linked to form an epic
written in Akkadian, the language of the Babylonian Empire. The epic continued
to evolve, reaching its final form around 1200 B.C.E. An account of the flood that
had been circulating separately was added at this time, and Gilgamesh's search
for fame was re'fashioned into the moving story of his search for the secret of
immortality after the death of his friend Enkidu. To learn the secret, Gilgamesh
journeys to see a survivor of the flood named Utanapishtim. Their encounter,
now the climax of the epic, raises his individual story to a wider context of the life
and death of civilization itself.

The *Epic of Gilgamesh* is the first great reworking of a common pool of stories
of friendship, seduction, adventure, and death into a broad exploration of the
meaning and limits of culture as a whole. The epic assesses culture against the
world of the gods, the world of nature, and the limits of human knowledge and
mortality. Parallels in later literature reflect this common heritage. The snake's role
in the epic finds an echo in the story of Eden in the Bible; the friendship of
Gilgamesh and Enkidu survives in the friendship of Achilles and Patroklus in the
Iliad; the theme of journey and return links the *Epic of Gilgamesh* to such narratives
as the *Odyssey* and the tale of Sindbad from the *Thousand and One Nights*.

The Epic of Gilgamesh

Tablet I

He who has seen everything, I will make known to the lands.
I will teach about him who experienced all things.
Anu granted him the totality of knowledge of all.

Translated by Maureen Gallery Kovacs.

He saw the Secret, discovered the Hidden,
he brought information of the time before the Flood.   5
He went on a distant journey, pushing himself to exhaustion,
but then was brought to peace.
He carved on a stone stela all of his toils,
and built the wall of Uruk-Haven,[1]
the wall of the sacred Eanna Temple, the holy sanctuary.   10
Look at its wall which gleams like copper,
inspect its inner wall, the likes of which no one can equal!
Take hold of the threshold stone—it dates from ancient times!
Go close to the Eanna Temple, the residence of Ishtar,[2]
such as no later king or man ever equaled!   15
Go up on the wall of Uruk and walk around,
examine its foundation, inspect its brickwork thoroughly.
Is not even the core of the brick structure made of kiln-fired brick,
and did not the Seven Sages[3] themselves lay out its plans?
One league city, one league palm gardens, one league lowlands, the open area of   20
   the Ishtar Temple,
three leagues and the open area of Uruk the wall encloses.
Find the copper tablet box,
open the hasp of its lock of bronze,
undo the fastening of its secret opening.
Take and read out from the lapis lazuli tablet   25
how Gilgamesh went through every hardship.

Supreme over other kings, lordly in appearance,
he is the hero, born of Uruk, the goring wild bull.
He walks out in front, the leader,
and walks at the rear, trusted by his companions.   30
Mighty net, protector of his people,
raging flood-wave who destroys even walls of stone!
Offspring of Lugalbanda, Gilgamesh is strong to perfection,
son of the august cow, Rimat-Ninsun, Gilgamesh is awesome to perfection.[4]
It was he who opened the mountain passes,   35
who dug wells on the flank of the mountain.
It was he who crossed the ocean, the vast seas, to the rising sun,
who explored the world regions, seeking life.
It was he who reached by his own sheer strength Utanapishtim, the Faraway,[5]
who restored the sanctuaries that the Flood had destroyed!   40

. . .

---

1. Literally, "Uruk-the-Sheepfold."
2. Goddess of love; she shared the Eanna
   Temple in Uruk with her father Anu.
3. Sent to the Gods to teach the arts of civilization to humanity.
4. Gilgamesh's father Lugalbanda was an ear-

lier king of Uruk; his mother is the divine
Ninsun. The motif of the "good cow" who
gives birth to kings is well documented in
Sumerian literature.
5. Utanapishtim is the hero of the Akkadian
version of the Flood story.

Who can compare with him in kingliness?
Who can say like Gilgamesh: "I am King!"?
Whose name, from the day of his birth, was called "Gilgamesh"?
Two-thirds of him is god, one-third of him is human.
The Great Goddess[6] designed(?) the model for his body,   45
she prepared his form,

       . . .

beautiful, handsomest of men.
He walks around in the enclosure of Uruk,
like a wild bull he makes himself mighty, head raised over others.
There is no rival who can raise his weapon against him.
His fellows stand at the alert, attentive to his orders.   50
The men of Uruk become anxious:
Gilgamesh does not leave a son to his father;
Is Gilgamesh the shepherd of Uruk-Haven,

       . . .

bold, eminent, knowing, and wise?
Gilgamesh does not leave a girl to her betrothed(?)!   55
The daughter of the warrior, the bride of the young man,
the gods kept hearing their complaints, so
the gods of the heavens implored Anu, Lord of Uruk:
   "You have indeed brought into being a mighty wild bull, head raised!
   There is no rival who can raise a weapon against him.
   His fellows stand (at the alert), attentive to his (orders?),   60
   Gilgamesh does not leave a son to his father,

       . . .

Is he the shepherd of Uruk-Haven,

       . . .

   bold, eminent, knowing, and wise?
   Gilgamesh does not leave a girl to her betrothed(?)!"   65
The daughter of the warrior, the bride of the young man,
Anu listened to their complaints,
and (the gods) called out to Aruru:
   "It was you, Aruru, who created this man(?),
   now create a counterpart to him.   70
   Let him be equal to Gilgamesh's stormy heart,
   let them be a match for each other so that Uruk may find peace!"
When Aruru heard this she created within herself the counterpart of Anu.
Aruru washed her hands, she pinched off some clay, and threw it into the
   wilderness.

---

6. The Mother Goddess, creator of humanity,
  known also as Aruru and Beletili.

In the wilderness she created valiant Enkidu,   75
born of Silence, endowed with strength by Ninurta.[7]
His whole body was shaggy with hair,
he had a full head of hair like a woman,
his locks billowed in profusion like Ashnan.[8]
He knew neither people nor settled living,   80
but wore a garment like Sumukan.[9]
He ate grasses with the gazelles,
and jostled at the watering hole with the animals;
as with animals, his thirst was slaked with water.

A notorious trapper   85
came face-to-face with him opposite the watering hole.
A first, a second, and a third day
he came face-to-face with him opposite the watering hole.
On seeing him the trapper's face went stark with fear,
and he and his animals drew back home.   90
He was rigid with fear; though stock-still
his heart pounded and his face drained of color.
He was miserable to the core,
and his face looked like one who had made a long journey.
The trapper addressed his father saying: 95
    "Father, a certain fellow has come from the mountains.
    He is the mightiest in the land,
    his strength is as mighty as the meteorite(?) of Anu!
    He continually goes over the mountains,
    he continually jostles at the watering place with the animals,   100
    he continually plants his feet opposite the watering place.
    I was afraid, so I did not go up to him.
    He filled in the pits that I had dug,
    wrenched out my traps that I had spread,
    released from my grasp the wild animals.   105
    He does not let me make my rounds in the wilderness!"
The trapper's father spoke to him saying:
    "My son, there lives in Uruk a certain Gilgamesh.
    There is no one stronger than he,
    he is as strong as the meteorite(?) of Anu.   110
    Go, set off to Uruk,
    tell Gilgamesh of this Man of Might.
    He will give you the harlot Shamhat, take her with you.
    The woman will overcome the fellow as if she were strong.

---

7. God of war.
8. Goddess of grain.

9. God of wild animals.

When the animals are drinking at the watering place   115
have her take off her robe and expose her sex.
When he sees her he will draw near to her,
and his animals, who grew up in his wilderness, will be alien to him."
He heeded his father's advice.
The trapper went off to Uruk,   120
he made the journey, stood inside of Uruk,
and declared to Gilgamesh:
"There is a certain fellow who has come from the mountains—
he is the mightiest in the land,
his strength is as mighty as the meteorite(?) of Anu!   125
He continually goes over the mountains,
he continually jostles at the watering place with the animals,
he continually plants his feet opposite the watering place.
I was afraid, so I did not go up to him.
He filled in the pits that I had dug,   130
wrenched out my traps that I had spread,
released from my grasp the wild animals.
He does not let me make my rounds in the wilderness!"
Gilgamesh said to the trapper:
"Go, trapper, bring the harlot, Shamhat, with you.   135
When the animals are drinking at the watering place
have her take off her robe and expose her sex.
When he sees her he will draw near to her,
and his animals, who grew up in his wilderness, will be alien to him."

The trapper went, bringing the harlot, Shamhat, with him.   140
They set off on the journey, making direct way.
On the third day they arrived at the appointed place,
and the trapper and the harlot sat down at their posts(?).
A first day and a second they sat opposite the watering hole.
The animals arrived and drank at the watering hole,   145
the wild beasts arrived and slaked their thirst with water.
Then he, Enkidu, offspring of the mountains,
who eats grasses with the gazelles,
came to drink at the watering hole with the animals,
with the wild beasts he slaked his thirst with water.   150
Then Shamhat saw him—a primitive,
a savage fellow from the depths of the wilderness!
"That is he, Shamhat! Release your clenched arms,
expose your sex so he can take in your voluptuousness.
Do not be restrained—take his energy!   155
When he sees you he will draw near to you.
Spread out your robe so he can lie upon you,
and perform for this primitive the task of womankind!

His animals, who grew up in his wilderness, will become alien to him,
and his lust will groan over you."   160
Shamhat unclutched her bosom, exposed her sex, and he took in her
    voluptuousness.
She was not restrained, but took his energy.
She spread out her robe and he lay upon her,
she performed for the primitive the task of womankind.
His lust groaned over her;   165
for six days and seven nights Enkidu stayed aroused,
and had intercourse with the harlot
until he was sated with her charms.
But when he turned his attention to his animals,
the gazelles saw Enkidu and darted off,
the wild animals distanced themselves from his body.   170
Enkidu's body was utterly depleted,
his knees that wanted to go off with his animals went rigid;
Enkidu was diminished, his running was not as before.
But then he drew himself up, for his understanding had broadened.   175
Turning around, he sat down at the harlot's feet,
gazing into her face, his ears attentive as the harlot spoke.
The harlot said to Enkidu:
    "You are beautiful, Enkidu, you are become like a god.
    Why do you gallop around the wilderness with the wild beasts?   *crossed*   180
    Come, let me bring you into Uruk-Haven,   *threshold*
    to the Holy Temple, the residence of Anu and Ishtar,
    the place of Gilgamesh, who is wise to perfection,
    but who struts his power over the people like a wild bull."
What she kept saying found favor with him.   185
Becoming aware of himself, he sought a friend.
Enkidu spoke to the harlot:
    "Come, Shamhat, take me away with you
    to the sacred Holy Temple, the residence of Anu and Ishtar,
    the place of Gilgamesh, who is wise to perfection,
    but who struts his power over the people like a wild bull.   190
    I will challenge him.
    Let me shout out in Uruk: 'I am the mighty one!'
    Lead me in and I will change the order of things;
    he whose strength is mightiest is the one born in the wilderness!"   195
    "Come, let us go," (she replied) "so he may see your face.
    I will lead you to Gilgamesh—I know where he will be.
    Look about, Enkidu, inside Uruk-Haven,
    where the people show off in skirted finery,
    where every day is a day for some festival,   200
    where the lyre and drum play continually,
    where harlots stand about prettily,

exuding voluptuousness, full of laughter,
and on the couch of night the sheets are spread.
Enkidu, you who do not know how to live,   205
I will show you Gilgamesh, a man of joy and sorrow.
Look at him, gaze at his face—
he is a handsome youth, with freshness,
his entire body exudes voluptuousness.
He has mightier strength than you,   210
without sleeping day or night!
Enkidu, it is your wrong thoughts you must change!
It is Gilgamesh whom Shamash[10] loves,
and Anu, Enlil,[11] and Ea[12] have enlarged his mind.
Even before you came from the mountain
Gilgamesh in Uruk had dreams about you."   215

Gilgamesh got up and revealed the dream, saying to his mother:
"Mother, I had a dream last night.
Stars of the sky appeared,
and some kind of meteorite(?) of Anu fell next to me.
I tried to lift it but it was too mighty for me,   220
I tried to turn it over but I could not budge it.
The Land of Uruk was standing around it,
the whole land had assembled about it,
the populace was thronging around it,
the Men clustered about it,   225
and kissed its feet as if it were a little baby.
I loved it and embraced it as a wife.
I laid it down at your feet,
and you made it compete with me."

prophetic visions they foretell the future

The mother of Gilgamesh, the wise, all-knowing, said to her Lord;   230
Rimat-Ninsun, the wise, all-knowing, said to Gilgamesh:
"As for the stars of the sky that appeared
and the meteorite(?) of Anu which fell next to you,
which you tried to lift but it was too mighty for you,
which you tried to turn over but were unable to budge it,   235
which you laid down at my feet,
and I made it compete with you,
and you loved and embraced it as a wife:
There will come to you a mighty man, a comrade who saves his friend—
he is the mightiest in the land, he is strongest,   240
his strength is mighty as the meteorite(?) of Anu!
You loved him and embraced him as a wife;

---

10. The sun god, Gilgamesh's protector.
11. Chief god in the Sumerian pantheon.

12. God of Wisdom and of the underworld sea.

and it is he who will repeatedly save you.
Your dream is good and propitious!"
A second time Gilgamesh said to his mother: 245
    "Mother, I have had another dream:
    At the gate of my marital chamber there lay an axe,
    and people had collected about it.
    The Land of Uruk was standing around it,
    the whole land had assembled about it,   250
    the populace was thronging around it.
    I laid it down at your feet,
    I loved it and embraced it as a wife,
    and you made it compete with me."
The mother of Gilgamesh, the wise, all-knowing, said to her son;   255
Rimat-Ninsun, the wise, all-knowing, said to Gilgamesh:
    "The axe that you saw is a man,
    whom you love and embrace as a wife,
    but whom I have made compete with you.
    There will come to you a mighty man, a comrade who saves his friend—   260
    he is the mightiest in the land, he is strongest,
    he is as mighty as the meteorite(?) of Anu!"
Gilgamesh spoke to his mother saying:
    "By the command of Enlil, the Great Counselor, so may it come to pass!
    May I have a friend and adviser,   265
    a friend and adviser may I have!
    You have interpreted for me the dreams about him!"
After the harlot recounted the dreams of Gilgamesh to Enkidu
the two of them made love.

Tablet II

Enkidu sits in front of her.[13]
Enkidu knew nothing about eating bread for food,
and of drinking beer he had not been taught.
The harlot spoke to Enkidu, saying:
    "Eat the food, Enkidu, it is the way one lives.   5
    Drink the beer, as is the custom of the land."
Enkidu ate the food until he was sated,
he drank the beer—seven jugs!—and became expansive and sang with joy!
He was elated and his face glowed.
He splashed his shaggy body with water,   10
and rubbed himself with oil, and turned into a human.
Shamhat pulled off her clothing,
and clothed him with one piece

---

13. Thirty-three lines are missing here; the   from parallels in the earlier Old Babylonian
next fifteen lines are restored in their place   version, as are several later passages.

while she clothed herself with a second.
She took hold of him as gods do
and brought him to the hut of the shepherds.

The shepherds gathered all around about him,
they marveled to themselves:
    "How the youth resembles Gilgamesh—
    tall in stature, towering up to the battlements over the wall! 20
    Surely he was born in the mountains;
    his strength is as mighty as the meteorite of Anu!"
They placed food in front of him,
they placed beer in front of him;
Enkidu did not eat or drink, but squinted and stared. 25
Enkidu scattered the wolves, he chased away the lions.
The herders could lie down in peace,
for Enkidu was their watchman.

            . . .

Then he raised his eyes and saw a man.
He said to the harlot: 30
    "Shamhat, have that man go away!
    Why has he come? I will call out his name!"
The harlot called out to the man
and went over to him and spoke with him.
    "Young man, where are you hurrying? 35
    Why this arduous pace?"
The young man spoke, saying to Enkidu:
    "They have invited me to a wedding,
    as is the custom of the people,
    to make the selection of brides. 40
    I have heaped up tasty delights for the wedding on the ceremonial platter.
    For the King of Broad-Marted Uruk,
    open is the veil of the people for choosing a girl.
    For Gilgamesh, the King of Broad-Marted Uruk,
    open is the veil of the people for choosing. 45
    He will have intercourse with the 'destined wife,'
    he first, the husband afterward.
    This is ordered by the counsel of Anu,
    from the severing of his umbilical cord it has been destined for him."
At the young man's speech Enkidu's face flushed with anger. 50
Enkidu walked in front, and Shamhat after him.[14]
He walked down the street of Uruk-Haven, . . .
He blocked the way through Uruk the Sheepfold.

---

14. Several lines are missing; Enkidu presumably resolves to go and challenge Gilgamesh.

The land of Uruk stood around him,
the whole land assembled about him,
the populace was thronging around him,   55
and kissed his feet as if he were a little baby. . . .
For Ishara the bed of marriage is ready,
for Gilgamesh as for a god a counterpart is set up.   60
Enkidu blocked the entry to the marital chamber,
and would not allow Gilgamesh to be brought in.
They grappled with each other at the entry to the marital chamber,
in the street they attacked each other, the public square of the land.
The doorposts trembled and the wall shook.   65

[The next seven lines are from the earlier version.]

Gilgamesh bent his knees, with his other foot on the ground,
his anger abated and he turned his chest away.
After he turned his chest Enkidu said to Gilgamesh:
    "Your mother bore you ever unique,
    the Wild Cow of the Enclosure, Ninsun,   70
    your head is elevated over other men,
    Enlil has destined for you the kingship over the people."

                                        · · ·
They kissed each other and became friends.[15]

                                        · · ·
Enkidu made a declaration to Gilgamesh:

[Enkidu speaks to Gilgamesh:]

    "In order to protect the Cedar Forest   75
    Enlil assigned Humbaba[16] as a terror to human beings—
    Humbaba's roar is a Flood, his mouth is Fire, and his breath is Death!
    He can hear 100 leagues away any rustling in his forest!
    Who would go down into his forest?
    Enlil assigned him as a terror to human beings,   80
    and whoever goes down into his forest paralysis will strike!"
Gilgamesh spoke to Enkidu saying:

                                        · · ·
    "Who, my Friend, can ascend to the heavens?
    Only the gods can dwell forever with Shamash.
    As for human beings, their days are numbered,   85
    and whatever they keep trying to achieve is but wind!
    Now you are afraid of death—
    what has become of your bold strength?

---

15. A fragmentary passage describes Enkidu's
sorrow at the loss of his strength. Gilgamesh proposes journeying to the Cedar
Forest to kill its protector Humbaba and

cut down the cedars. Enkidu reacts with
fear.
16. A demon, grandson of the sacred Cedar
Forest.

I will go in front of you,
and your mouth can call out: 'Go on closer, do not be afraid!'   90
Should I fall, I will have established my fame.
They will say: 'It was Gilgamesh who locked in battle with Humbaba the
    Terrible!'
You were born and raised in the wilderness,
a lion leaped up on you, so you have experienced it all!'

I will undertake it and I will cut down the Cedar.   95
It is I who will establish fame for eternity!
Come, my friend, I will go over to the forge
and have them cast the weapons in our presence!"
Holding each other by the hand they went over to the forge.
The craftsmen sat and discussed with one another.   100

    "The hatchet should be one talent in weight,
    Their swords should be one talent,[17] and their armor as well. . . ."
Gilgamesh said to the men of Uruk:
    "Listen to me, . . . you men of Uruk, . . .
    I want to make myself more mighty, and will go on a distant journey!   105
    I will face fighting such as I have never known,
    I will set out on a road I have never traveled!
    Give me your blessings!
    I will enter the city gate of Uruk, . . .
    I will devote myself to the New Year's Festival.   110
    I will perform the New Year's ceremonies,
    The New Year's Festival will take place, . . .
    They will keep shouting 'Hurrah!'. . ."
Enkidu spoke to the Elders: 115

    "Say to him that he must not go to the Cedar Forest—
    the journey is not to be made!"
                    . . .
The Noble Counselors of Uruk arose and
delivered their advice to Gilgamesh:
    "You are young, Gilgamesh, your heart carries you off—   120
    you do not know what you are talking about!

    Humbaba's roar is a Flood,
    his mouth is Fire, his breath Death!
    He can hear any rustling in his forest 100 leagues away!
    Who would go down into his forest?   125
    Who among even the Igigi gods can confront him?

---

17. A unit of weight, perhaps 0.65 pound.

In order to keep the Cedar safe, Enlil[18] assigned him as a terror to human
   beings."
Gilgamesh listened to the statement of his Noble Counselors.

Tablet III

The Elders spoke to Gilgamesh, saying:
   "Gilgamesh, do not put your trust in your vast strength,
   but keep a sharp eye out, make each blow strike its mark!
      'The one who goes on ahead saves the comrade.'
      'The one who knows the route protects his friend.'   5
   Let Enkidu go ahead of you;
   he knows the road to the Cedar Forest,
   he has seen fighting, has experienced battle.
   Enkidu will protect the friend, will keep the comrade safe.
   Let his body urge him back to the wives."   10
[The Elders speak to Enkidu:]
   "In our Assembly we have entrusted the King to you,
   and on your return you must entrust the King back to us!"
Gilgamesh spoke to Enkidu, saying:
   "Come on, my friend, let us go to the Egalmah Temple,   15
   to Ninsun, the Great Queen;
   Ninsun is wise, all-knowing.
   She will put the advisable path at our feet."
Taking each other by the hand,
Gilgamesh and Enkidu walked to the Egalmah,   20
   to Ninsun, the Great Queen.
Gilgamesh arose and went to her.
   "Ninsun, even though I am extraordinarily strong,
   I must now travel a long way to where Humbaba is,
   I must face fighting such as I have not known,   25
   and I must travel on a road that I do not know!
   Until the time that I go and return,
   until I reach the Cedar Forest,
   until I kill Humbaba the Terrible,
   and eradicate from the land something baneful that Shamash hates,   30
   intercede with Shamash on my behalf!
   If I kill Humbaba and cut his Cedar
   let there be rejoicing all over the land,
   and I will erect a monument of the victory before you!"

The words of Gilgamesh, her son,   35
grieving Queen Ninsun heard over and over.
Ninsun went into her living quarters.

---

18. The chief Sumerian god, god of destinies.

She washed herself with the purity plant,
she donned a robe worthy of her body,
she donned jewels worthy of her chest,   40
she donned her sash, and put on her crown.
She sprinkled water from a bowl onto the ground.

          . . .

She went up to the roof and set incense in front of Shamash,
she offered fragrant cuttings, and raised her arms to Shamash.
  "Why have you imposed—nay, inflicted!—a restless heart on my son,
    Gilgamesh?   45
  Now you have touched him so that he wants to travel
  a long way to where Humbaba is!
  He will face fighting such as he has not known,
  and will travel on a road that he does not know!
  Until he goes away and returns,   50
  until he reaches the Cedar Forest,
  until he kills Humbaba the Terrible,
  and eradicates from the land something baneful that you hate,
  on the day that you see him on the road
  may Aja, the Bride,[19] without fear remind you,   55
  and command also the Watchmen of the Night,
  the stars, and at night your father, Sin."

[Long passage missing.]

She (Ninsun) banked up the incense and uttered the ritual words.
She called to Enkidu and would give him instructions:
  "Enkidu the Mighty, you are not of my womb,   60
  but now I speak to you along with the sacred votaries of Gilgamesh,
  the high priestesses, the holy women, the temple servers."
She laid a pendant on Enkidu's neck, . . . [saying]
  "I have taken Enkidu; Enkidu to Gilgamesh I have taken."[20]   65

          . . .

[The Elders said:]

  "Enkidu will protect the friend, will keep the comrade safe.
  Let his body urge him back to the wives.
  In our Assembly we have entrusted the King to you,
  and on your return you must entrust the King back to us!"[21]

Tablet IV

At twenty leagues they broke for some food,
at thirty leagues they stopped for the night,

---

19. Wife of the sun god, Shamash.
20. Five lines are missing; Gilgamesh appar-

ently stresses his ability to carry out his
wishes.
21. The rest of their speech is fragmentary.

walking fifty leagues in a whole day,
a walk of a month and a half.
On the third day they drew near to the Lebanon.   5
They dug a well facing Shamash, the setting sun. . . .
Gilgamesh climbed up a mountain peak,
made a libation of flour, and said:
    "Mountain, bring me a dream, a favorable message from Shamash."
Enkidu prepared a sleeping place for him for the night;   10
a violent wind passed through so he attached a covering.
He made him lie down. . . .
While Gilgamesh rested his chin on his knees,
sleep that pours over mankind overtook him.
In the middle of the night his sleep came to an end,   15
so he got up and said to his friend:
    "My friend, did you not call out to me? Why did I wake up?
    Did you not touch me? Why am I so disturbed?
    Did a god pass by? Why are my muscles trembling?
    Enkidu, my friend, I have had a dream—   20
    and the dream I had was deeply disturbing!
    In the mountain gorges, the mountain fell down on me!"

        . . .

He who was born in the wilderness,
Enkidu, interpreted the dream for his friend:
    "My friend, your dream is favorable,   25
    The dream is extremely important.
    My friend, the mountain which you saw in the dream is Humbaba.
    It means we will capture Humbaba, and kill him
    and throw his corpse into the wasteland.
    In the morning there will be a favorable message from Shamash."   30

At twenty leagues they broke for some food,
at thirty leagues they stopped for the night,
walking fifty leagues in a whole day,
a walk of a month and a half.
They dug a well facing Shamash; . . .   35
Gilgamesh climbed up a mountain peak,
made a libation of flour, and said:
    "Mountain, bring me a dream, a favorable message from Shamash."
Enkidu prepared a sleeping place for him for the night;
a violent wind passed through so he attached a covering.   40

        . . .

While Gilgamesh rested his chin on his knees,
sleep that pours over mankind overtook him.
In the middle of the night his sleep came to an end,
so he got up and said to his friend:

"My friend, did you not call out to me? Why did I wake up?   45
Did you not touch me? Why am I so disturbed?
Did a god pass by? Why are my muscles trembling?
Enkidu, my friend, I have had a dream,
besides my first dream I have had a second.
And the dream I had—so striking, so . . ., so disturbing!   50
I was grappling with a wild bull of the wilderness,
with his bellow he split the ground, a cloud of dust rose to the sky.
I sank to my knees in front of him. . . .
My tongue hung out, My temples throbbed;
he gave me water to drink from his waterskin."   55
"My friend," (Enkidu said) "the god to whom we go
is not the wild bull! He is totally different!
The wild bull that you saw is Shamash, the protector,
in difficulties he holds our hand.
The one who gave you water to drink from his waterskin   60
is your (personal) god, who brings honor to you, Lugalbanda.
We should join together and do one thing,
a deed such as has never before been done in the land."

At twenty leagues they broke for some food,
at thirty leagues they stopped for the night,   65
walking fifty leagues in a whole day,
a walk of a month and a half.
They dug a well facing Shamash; . . .
Gilgamesh climbed up a mountain peak,
made a libation of flour, and said: 70
    "Mountain, bring me a dream, a favorable message from Shamash."
Enkidu prepared a sleeping place for him for the night;
a violent wind passed through so he attached a covering.

                           . . .
While Gilgamesh rested his chin on his knees,
sleep that pours over mankind overtook him.   75
In the middle of the night his sleep came to an end,
so he got up and said to his friend:
    "My friend, did you not call out to me? Why did I wake up?
    Did you not touch me? Why am I so disturbed?
    Did a god pass by? Why are my muscles trembling?   80
    Enkidu, my friend, I have had a third dream,
    and the dream I had was deeply disturbing.
    The heavens roared and the earth rumbled;
    then it became deathly still, and darkness loomed.
    A bolt of lightning cracked and a fire broke out,   85
    and where it kept thickening, there rained death.
    The the white-hot flame dimmed, and the fire went out,

and everything that had been falling around turned to ash.
Let us go down into the plain so we can talk it over."
Enkidu heard the dream that he had presented and said to Gilgamesh:[22]   90

At twenty leagues they broke for some food,
at thirty leagues they stopped for the night,
walking fifty leagues in a whole day,
a walk of a month and a half.
They dug a well facing Shamash; . . .   95
Gilgamesh climbed up a mountain peak,
made a libation of flour, and said:
    "Mountain, bring me a dream, a favorable message from Shamash."
Enkidu prepared a sleeping place for him for the night;
a violent wind passed through so he attached a covering.   100

. . .

While Gilgamesh rested his chin on his knees,
sleep that pours over mankind overtook him.
In the middle of the night his sleep came to an end,
so he got up and said to his friend:
    "My friend, did you not call out to me? Why did I wake up?   105
    Did you not touch me? Why am I so disturbed?
    Did a god pass by? Why are my muscles trembling?
    Enkidu, my friend, I have had a fourth dream,
    and the dream I had was deeply disturbing.[23]

. . .

Enkidu listened to his dream, and said: 110
    "The dream that you had is favorable, it is extremely important!
    My friend, we will achieve victory over him,
    Humbaba, against whom we rage, and triumph over him.
    In the morning there will be a favorable message from Shamash."[24]   115

His tears were running in the presence of Shamash.
    "What you said in Uruk, be mindful of it, stand by me!"
Gilgamesh, the offspring of Uruk-Haven,
Shamash heard what issued from his mouth,   120
and suddenly there resounded a warning sound from the sky.
    "Hurry, stand by him so that Humbaba does not enter the forest,
    and does not go down into the thickets and hide!
    He has not put on his seven coats of armor,
    he is wearing only one, but has taken off six."[25]   125

---

22. Enkidu's reply is missing.
23. Gilgamesh's dream is missing.
24. A fifth dream follows, now fragmentary.

The text resumes with Gilgamesh appealing to the sun god Shamash.

25. In a fragmentary passage, Enkidu expresses fear.

Gilgamesh spoke to Enkidu, saying:
  "Why, my friend, . . . we have crossed over all the mountains together; . . .
  my friend, you who are so experienced in battle, . . .
  you need not fear death. . . .
  Let your voice bellow forth like the kettledrum,   130
  let the stiffness in your arms depart,
  let the paralysis in your legs go away.
  Take my hand, my friend, we will go on together.
  Your heart should burn to do battle
  —pay no heed to death, do not lose heart!   135
  The one who watches from the side is a careful man,
  but the one who walks in front protects himself and saves his comrade,
  and through their fighting they establish fame!"
As the two of them reached the evergreen forest
they cut off their talk, and stood still.   140

Tablet V[26]

They stood at the forest's edge,
gazing at the top of the Cedar Tree,
gazing at the entrance to the forest.
Where Humbaba would walk there was a trail,
the roads led straight on, the path was excellent.   5
Then they saw the Cedar Mountain, the Dwelling of the Gods, the throne dais of
    Irnini.[27]
Across the face of the mountain the Cedar brought forth luxurious foliage,
its shade was good, extremely pleasant.
The thornbushes were matted together, the woods were a thicket, . . .
the Forest was surrounded by a ravine two leagues long.[28]   10
      . . .

Humbaba spoke to Gilgamesh, saying:
  "An idiot and a moron should give advice to each other,
  but you, Gilgamesh, why have you come to me?
  Give advice, Enkidu, you 'son of a fish,' who does not even know his own
    father,
  to the large and small turtles which do not suck their mother's milk!   15
  When you were still young I saw you but did not go over to you; . . .
  Now, you have brought Gilgamesh into my presence,
  Here you stand, an enemy, a stranger. . . .
  I would feed your flesh to the screeching vulture, the eagle, and the vulture!"

---

26. This entire tablet is fragmentary; several
passages have been restored on the basis
of Babylonian and Assyrian versions.

27. A name for Ishtar, in her ferocious aspect.

28. Humbaba appears, frightening Enkidu anew. Gilgamesh consoles him,
but in the following lines Humbaba
mocks his words.

Gilgamesh spoke to Enkidu, saying: 20
  "My Friend, Humbaba's face keeps changing!"[29]
Enkidu spoke to Gilgamesh, saying:
  "Why, my friend, are you whining so pitiably,
  hiding behind your whimpering?
  Now there, my friend, . . . (it is time)   25
  to send the Flood, to crack the Whip.
  Do not snatch your feet away, do not turn your back;
  strike ever harder!"

              . . .

The ground split open with the heels of their feet,
as they whirled around in circles Mt. Hermon and Lebanon split.   30
The white clouds darkened,
death rained down on them like fog.
Shamash raised up against Humbaba mighty tempests—
Southwind, Northwind, Eastwind, Westwind, Whistling Wind,
Piercing Wind, Blizzard, Bad Wind, Wind of Simurru,   35
Demon Wind, Ice Wind, Storm, Sandstorm—
thirteen winds rose up against him and covered Humbaba's face.
He could not butt through the front, and could not scramble out the back,
so that Gilgamesh's weapons were in reach of Humbaba.
Humbaba begged for his life, saying to Gilgamesh: 40
  "You are young yet, Gilgamesh, your mother gave birth to you,
  and you are the offspring of Rimat-Ninsun
  It was at the instigation of Shamash, Lord of the Mountain,
  that you were roused to this expedition.
  O scion of the heart of Uruk, King Gilgamesh!   45

              . . .

  Gilgamesh, let me go,
  I will dwell with you as your servant.
  As many trees as you command me I will cut down for you,
  I will guard for you myrtle wood, wood fine enough for your palace!"
Enkidu addressed Gilgamesh, saying: 50
  "My friend, do not listen to Humbaba!"

              . . .

[Humbaba spoke to Enkidu:]

  "You understand the rules of my forest, . . .
  you are aware of all the things 'So ordered by Enlil.'
  I should have carried you up, and killed you at the very entrance to the
    branches of my forest.   55
  I should have fed your flesh to the screeching vulture, the eagle, and the
    vulture.

---

29. In two missing lines, it is now Gilgamesh
    who expresses fear.

An impression from a neo-Assyrian period seal, depicting the slaying of
Humbaba.

So now, Enkidu, clemency is up to you.
   Speak to Gilgamesh to spare my life!"
Enkidu addressed Gilgamesh, saying:
   "My friend, take Humbaba, Guardian of the Cedar Forest,
   grind up, kill, pulverize and . . . him!   60
   Humbaba, Guardian of the Forest, grind up, kill, pulverize and . . . him!"

[Long passage fragmentary or deleted.]

[Enkidu speaks again to Gilgamesh:]

   "Before the Preeminent God Enlil hears,
   and the gods are full of rage at us.
   Enlil is in Nippur, Shamash is in Sippar.   65
   Erect an eternal monument proclaiming how Gilgamesh killed Humbaba."
Humbaba heard (all this and said,) . . .
   "May he not live the longer of the two,
   may Enkidu not have any 'shore' more than his friend Gilgamesh!"
Enkidu spoke to Gilgamesh, saying: 70
   "My friend, I have been talking to you but you have not been listening to me,
   You have been listening to the curse of Humbaba."[30]

---

30. In forty fragmentary lines, Gilgamesh and
Enkidu slay Humbaba; in the only complete line, "they pulled out his insides
including his tongue."

They cut through the Cedar
While Gilgamesh cuts down the trees, Enkidu searches through the urmazallu.
Enkidu addressed Gilgamesh, saying: 75
  "My friend, we have cut down the towering Cedar whose top scrapes the sky.
  Make from it a door 72 cubits high, 24 cubits wide,
  one cubit thick, its fixture, its lower and upper pivots will be out of one piece.
  Let them carry it to Nippur, the Euphrates will carry it down, Nippur will
    rejoice.
They tied together a raft, . . . Enkidu steered it,   80
while Gilgamesh held the head of Humbaba.

Tablet VI

(Gilgamesh) washed out his matted hair and cleaned up his equipment,
shaking out his locks down over his back,
throwing off his dirty clothes and putting on clean ones.
He wrapped himself in regal garments and fastened the sash.
When Gilgamesh placed his crown on his head,   5
Princess Ishtar raised her eyes to the beauty of Gilgamesh.
  "Come along, Gilgamesh, be you my husband,
  to me grant your lusciousness.
  Be you my husband, and I will be your wife.
  I will have harnessed for you a chariot of lapis lazuli and gold,   10
  with wheels of gold and 'horns' of electrum.
  It will be harnessed with great storming mountain mules!
  Come into our house, with the fragrance of cedar.
  And when you come into our house the doorpost and throne dais will kiss your
    feet.
  Bowed down beneath you will be kings, lords, and princes.   15
  The Lullubu people will bring you the produce of the mountains and
    countryside as tribute.
  Your she-goats will bear triplets, your ewes twins,
  your donkey under burden will overtake the mule,   *Strength*
  your steed at the chariot will be bristling to gallop,
  your ox at the yoke will have no match."   20
Gilgamesh addressed Princess Ishtar saying:
  "What would I have to give you if I married you?
  Do you need oil or garments for your body?
  Do you lack anything for food or drink?
  I would gladly feed you food fit for a god,
  I would gladly give you wine fit for a king,   25

                              . . .

  You are an oven who . . . ice,
  a half-door that keeps out neither breeze nor blast,

a palace that crushes down valiant warriors,   30
an elephant who devours its own covering,
pitch that blackens the hands of its bearer,
a waterskin that soaks its bearer through,
limestone that buckles out the stone wall,
a battering ram that attracts the enemy land,   35
a shoe that bites its owner's feet!
Where are your bridegrooms that you keep forever?
Where is your 'Little Shepherd' bird that went up over you?
See here now, I will recite the list of your lovers. . . .
Tammuz, the lover of your earliest youth,   40
for him you have ordained lamentations year upon year!
You loved the colorful 'Little Shepherd' bird
and then hit him, breaking his wing, so
now he stands in the forest crying 'My Wing'!
You loved the supremely mighty lion,   45
yet you dug for him seven and again seven pits.
You loved the stallion, famed in battle,
yet you ordained for him the whip, the goad, and the lash,
ordained for him to gallop for seven and seven hours,
ordained for him drinking from muddied waters,   50
you ordained for his mother Silili to wail continually.
You loved the Shepherd, the Master Herder,
who continually presented you with bread baked in embers,
and who daily slaughtered for you a kid.
Yet you struck him, and turned him into a wolf,   55
so his own shepherds now chase him
and his own dogs snap at his shins.
You loved Ishullanu, your father's date gardener,
who continually brought you baskets of dates,
and brightened your table daily.   60
You raised your eyes to him, and you went to him:
    'Oh my Ishullanu, let us taste of your strength,
    stretch out your hand to me, and touch our "vulva." '**31**
Ishullanu said to you:
    'Me? What is it you want from me?   65
    Has my mother not baked, and have I not eaten
    that I should now eat food under contempt and curses
    and that alfalfa grass should be my only cover against the cold?'

---

31. A pun; "vulva" sounds like "date palm" in
    Akkadian.

As you listened to these his words
you struck him, turning him into a dwarf,   70
and made him live in the middle of his garden of labors.
And now me! It is me you love, and you will ordain for me as for them!"

When Ishtar heard this
in a fury she went up to the heavens,
going to Anu, her father, and crying,   75
going to Antum, her mother, and weeping:
    "Father, Gilgamesh has insulted me over and over,
    Gilgamesh has recounted despicable deeds about me,
    despicable deeds and curses!"
Anu addressed Princess Ishtar, saying: 80
    "What is the matter? Was it not you who provoked King Gilgamesh?
    So Gilgamesh recounted despicable deeds about you,
    despicable deeds and curses!"
Ishtar spoke to her father, Anu, saying:
    "Father, give me the Bull of Heaven,   85
    so he can kill Gilgamesh in his dwelling.
    If you do not give me the Bull of Heaven,
    I will knock down the Gates of the Netherworld,
    I will smash the door posts, and leave the doors flat down,
    and will let the dead go up to eat the living!   90
    And the dead will outnumber the living!"
Anu addressed Princess Ishtar, saying:
    "If you demand the Bull of Heaven from me,
    there will be seven years of empty husks for the land of Uruk.
    Have you collected grain for the people?   95
    Have you made grasses grow for the animals?"
Ishtar addressed Anu, her father, saying:
    "I have heaped grain in the granaries for the people,
    I made grasses grow for the animals,
    in order that they might eat in the seven years of empty husks.   100
    I have collected grain for the people,
    I have made grasses grow for the animals."

When Anu heard her words,
he placed the nose-rope of the Bull of Heaven in her hand.
Ishtar led the Bull of Heaven down to the earth.   105
When it reached Uruk, . . . it climbed down to the Euphrates.
At the snort of the Bull of Heaven a hug pit opened up,
and a hundred Young Men of Uruk fell in.
At his second snort a huge pit opened up,
and two hundred Young Men of Uruk fell in.   110
At his third snort a huge pit opened up,

and Enkidu fell in up to his waist.
Then Enkidu jumped out and seized the Bull of Heaven by its horns.
The Bull spewed his spittle in front of him,
with his thick tail he flung his dung behind him. . . .   115
Enkidu stalked and hunted down the Bull of Heaven.
He grasped it by the thick of its tail
and held onto it with both his hands,
while Gilgamesh, like an expert butcher,
boldly and surely approached the Bull of Heaven.   120
Between the nape, the horns, . . . he thrust his sword.
After they had killed the Bull of Heaven,
they ripped out its heart and presented it to Shamash.
They withdrew, bowing down humbly to Shamash.
Then the brothers sat down together.   125
Ishtar went up onto the top of the Wall of Uruk-Haven,
cast herself into the pose of mourning, and hurled her woeful curse:
    "Woe unto Gilgamesh who slandered me and killed the Bull of Heaven!"
When Enkidu heard this pronouncement of Ishtar,
he wrenched off the Bull's hindquarter and flung it in her face: 130
    "If I could only get at you I would do the same to you!
    I would drape his innards over your arms!"
Ishtar assembled the (cultic women) of lovely-locks, joy-girls, and harlots,
and set them to mourning over the hindquarter of the Bull.
Gilgamesh summoned all the artisans and craftsmen.   135
All the artisans admired the thickness of its horns,
each fashioned from 30 minas of lapis lazuli!
Two fingers thick is their casing.
Six vats of oil the contents of the two
he gave as ointment to his personal god Lugalbanda.   140
He brought the horns in and hung them in the bedroom of the family head.
They washed their hands in the Euphrates,
and proceeded hand in hand,
striding through the streets of Uruk.
The men of Uruk gathered together, staring at them.   145
Gilgamesh said to the palace retainers:
    "Who is the bravest of the men?
    Who is the boldest of the males?
    —Gilgamesh is the bravest of the men,
    the boldest of the males!   150
    She at whom we flung the hindquarter of the Bull of Heaven in anger,
    Ishtar has no one that pleases her in the street!"

                                        . . .

Gilgamesh held a celebration in his palace.
The Young Men dozed off, sleeping on the couches of the night.

Enkidu was sleeping, and had a dream.   155
He woke up and revealed his dream to his friend.[32]

Tablet VII

"My friend, why are the Great Gods in conference?
In my dream Anu, Enlil, and Shamash held a council,
and Anu spoke to Enlil:
  'Because they killed the Bull of Heaven and have also slain Humbaba,
  the one of them who pulled up the Cedar of the Mountain must die!'   5
Enlil said: 'Let Enkidu die, but Gilgamesh must not die!'
But the Sun God of Heaven replied to valiant Enlil:
  'Was it not at my command that they killed the Bull of Heaven and Humbaba?
  Should now innocent Enkidu die?'
Then Enlil became angry at Shamash, saying: 10
  'It is you who are responsible because you traveled daily with them as their
    friend!' "
Enkidu was lying sick in front of Gilgamesh.
His tears flowing like canals, Gilgamesh said:
  "O brother, dear brother, why are they absolving me instead of my brother?"
Then Enkidu said: "So now must I become a ghost,   15
  to sit with the ghosts of the dead, to see my dear brother nevermore?"

Enkidu raised his eyes, and spoke to the door as if it were human:
  "You stupid wooden door,
  with no ability to understand!
  Already at twenty leagues I selected the wood for you, . . .   20
  your wood was without compare in my eyes.
  Seventy-two cubits was your height, 24 cubits your width, one cubit your
    thickness; . . .
  I fashioned you, and I carried you to Nippur.
  Had I known, O door, that this would be your gratitude . . .
  I would have taken an axe and chopped you up,   25
  and lashed your planks into a raft!

  But yet, O door, I fashioned you, and I carried you to Nippur!
  May a king who comes after me reject you, . . .
  may he remove my name and set his own name there!" . . .
Gilgamesh kept listening to his words, and retorted quickly,   30
Gilgamesh listened to the words of Enkidu, his Friend, and his tears flowed.
Gilgamesh addressed Enkidu, saying:
  "Friend, the gods have given you a mind broad and . . . deep.
  Though it behooves you to be sensible, you keep uttering improper things!

---

32. This account of Enkidu's dream is taken
    from a Hittite fragment.

Why, my Friend, does your mind utter improper things? 35
The dream is important but very frightening,
your lips are buzzing like flies.
Though there is much fear, the dream is very important.
To the living the gods leave sorrow,
to the living the dream leaves pain. 40
I will pray, and beseech the Great Gods,
I will seek . . . and appeal to your god.

What Enlil says . . . cannot go back,
What he has laid down cannot go back. . . ."

Just as dawn began to glow,   humaness 45
Enkidu raised his head and cried out to Shamash,
at the first gleam of the sun his tears poured fourth.
"I appeal to you, O Shamash, on behalf of my precious life,
because of that notorious trapper
who did not let me attain the same as my friend. 50
May the trapper not get enough to feed himself.
May his profit be slashed, and his wages decrease! . . .

After he had cursed the trapper to his satisfaction,
his heart prompted him to curse the Harlot.
"Come now, Harlot, I am going to decree your fate, 55
a fate that will never come to an end for eternity!
I will curse you with a Great Curse,
may my curses overwhelm you suddenly, in an instant!
May you not be able to make a household,
and not be able to love a child of your own! . . . 60
May dregs of beer stain your beautiful lap,
may a drunk soil your festal robe with vomit,

May you never acquire anything of bright alabaster, ...
may shining silver, man's delight, not be cast into your house,
may a gateway be where you take your pleasure, 65
may a crossroad be your home,
may a wasteland be your sleeping place,
may the shadow of the city wall be your place to stand,
may the thorns and briars skin your feet,
may both the drunk and the dry slap you on the cheek, 70

may the builder not seal the roof of your house,
may owls nest in the cracks of your walls!"
                                    . . .

When Shamash heard what his mouth had uttered,
he suddenly called out to him from the sky:

"Enkidu, why are you cursing the harlot, Shamhat,   75
she who fed you bread fit for a god,
she who gave you wine fit for a king,
she who dressed you in grand garments,
and she who allowed you to make beautiful Gilgamesh your comrade?
Now Gilgamesh is your beloved brother-friend!   80
He will have you lie on a grand couch,
will have you lie on a couch of honor.
He will seat you in the seat of ease, the seat at his left,
so that the princes of the world kiss your feet.
He will have the people of Uruk go into mourning and moaning over you, 85
will fill the happy people with woe over you.
And after you he will let his body bear a filthy mat of hair,
will don the skin of a lion and roam the wilderness."
As soon as Enkidu heard the words of valiant Shamash,
his agitated heart grew calm, his anger abated.   90
Enkidu spoke to the harlot, saying:
"Come, Shamhat, I will decree your fate for you.
Let my mouth which has cursed you, now turn to bless you!
May governors and nobles love you,
May he who is one league away bite his lip in anticipation,   95
may he who is two leagues away shake out his locks in preparation!
May the soldier not refuse you, but undo his buckle for you,
may he give you rock crystal, lapis lazuli, and gold,
may his gift to you be earrings of filigree.
May his supplies be heaped up. . . .   100
May the wife, the mother of seven, be abandoned because of you!"

Enkidu's innards were churning,
lying there so alone.
He spoke everything he felt, saying to his friend:
"Listen, my friend, to the dream that I had last night.   105
The heavens cried out and the earth replied,
and I was standing between them.
There appeared a man of dark visage—
his face resembled the Anzu:
his hands were the paws of a lion,   110
his nails the talons of an eagle!—
he seized me by my hair and overpowered me.
I struck him a blow, but he skipped about like a jump rope,
and then he struck me and capsized me like a raft,
and trampled on me like a wild bull.   115
He encircled my whole body in a clamp.
    'Help me, my friend!' I cried,
but you did not rescue me, you were afraid and did not."

"Then he turned me into a dove,
so that my arms were feathered like a bird.
Seizing me, he led me down to the House of Darkness, the dwelling of Irkalla, 120
to the House where those who enter do not come out,
along the road of no return,
to the House where those who dwell do without light,
where dirt is their drink, their food is of clay, 125
where, like a bird, they wear garments of feathers,
and light cannot be seen, they dwell in the dark,
and upon the door and bolt lies dust.
On entering the House of Dust,
everywhere I looked there were royal crowns gathered in heaps, 130
everywhere I listened, it was the bearers of crowns who in the past had ruled the
    land,
but who now served Anu and Enlil cooked meats,
served confections, and poured cool water from waterskins.
In the House of Dust that I entered
there sat the high priest and acolyte, 135
there sat the purification priest and ecstatic,
there sat the anointed priests of the Great Gods.
There sat Etana, there sat Sumukan,
there sat Ereshkigal, the Queen of the Netherworld.
Beletseri, the Scribe of the Netherworld, knelt before her, 140
she was holding the tablet (of destinies,) and was reading it out to her.
She raised her head and when she saw me—
    'Who has taken this man?' "[33]
"I who went through every difficulty,
remember me and forget not all that I went through with you." 145
[Gilgamesh replied:]
"My friend has had a dream that bodes ill."

Enkidu lies down a first day, a second day, . . .
a third day and fourth day, that Enkidu remains in his bed;
a fifth, a sixth, and seventh, that Enkidu remains in his bed; 150
an eighth, a ninth, a tenth, that Enkidu remains in his bed.
Enkidu's illness grew ever worse.
The eleventh and twelfth day his illness grew ever worse.
Enkidu drew up from his bed,
and called out to Gilgamesh.[34] 155

---

33. Fifty lines are missing. The text resumes
with the conclusion of Enkidu's speech.

34. Thirty fragmentary lines recount Enkidu's last words and his death.

Tablet VIII

Just as day began to dawn
Gilgamesh addressed his friend, saying:
　　"Enkidu, your mother, the gazelle,
　　and your father, the wild donkey, engendered you,
　　four wild asses raised you on their milk,   5
　　and the herds taught you all the grazing lands.
　　May the Roads of Enkidu to the Cedar Forest mourn you
　　and not fall silent night or day.
　　May the Elders of the broad city of Uruk-Haven mourn you.
　　May the peoples who gave their blessing after us mourn you.   10
　　May the men of the mountains and hills mourn you. . . .
　　May the pasture lands shriek in mourning as if it were your mother.
　　May the . . . cypress, and the cedar which we destroyed in our anger mourn
　　　　you.
　　May the bear, hyena, panther, tiger, water buffalo, jackal, lion, wild bull, stag,
　　　　ibex, all the creatures of the plains mourn you.   15
　　May the holy River Ulaja, along whose banks we grandly used to stroll, mourn
　　　　you.
　　May the pure Euphrates, to which we would libate water from our waterskins,
　　　　mourn you.
　　May the men of Uruk-Haven, whom we saw in our battle when we killed the
　　　　Bull of Heaven, mourn you.
　　May the farmer, who extols your name in his sweet work song, mourn you.   20
　　May the people of the broad city, who exalted your name, mourn you.
　　May the herder, who prepared butter and light beer for your mouth, mourn
　　　　you.
　　May . . ., who put ointments on your back, mourn you.
　　May . . ., who prepared fine beer for your mouth, mourn you.
　　May the harlot, with whom you rubbed yourself with oil and felt good, mourn
　　　　you. . . .   25
　　May the brothers go into mourning over you like sisters;
　　as for the lamentation priests, may their hair be shorn off on your behalf.
　　Enkidu, your mother and your father are in the wastelands,
　　I mourn you.
　　Hear me, O Elders of Uruk, hear me, O men!   30
　　I mourn for Enkidu, my friend,
　　I shriek in anguish like a mourner.
　　You, axe at my side, so trusty at my hand—
　　you, sword at my waist, shield in front of me,
　　you, my festal garment, a sash over my loins—   35
　　an evil demon appeared and took him away from me!
　　My friend, the swift mule, fleet wild ass of the mountain, panther of the
　　　　wilderness,

Enkidu, my friend, the swift mule, fleet wild ass of the mountain, panther of the
    wilderness,
after we joined together and went up into the mountain,
fought the Bull of Heaven and killed it,   40
and overwhelmed Humbaba, who lived in the Cedar Forest,
now what is this sleep which has seized you?
You have turned dark and do not hear me!"
But Enkidu's eyes do not move,
he touched his heart, but it beat no longer.   45
He covered his friend's face like a bride,
swooping down over him like an eagle,
and like a lioness deprived of her cubs
he keeps pacing to and fro.
He shears off his curls and heaps them onto the ground,   50
ripping off his finery and casting it away as an abomination.

Just as day began to dawn, Gilgamesh arose
and issued a call to the land:
    "You, blacksmith! You, lapidary! You, coppersmith!
    You, goldsmith! You, jeweler!   55
    Create 'My Friend,' fashion a statue of him.
    . . . he fashioned a statue of his friend.
    I had you recline on the great couch,
    indeed, on the couch of honor I let you recline,
    I had you sit in the position of ease, the seat at the left, so the princes of the
        world kissed your feet.   60
    I had the people of Uruk mourn and moan for you,
    I filled happy people with woe over you,
    and after you died I let a filthy mat of hair grow over my body,
    and donned the skin of a lion and roamed the wilderness."

[Some 160 lines are missing or fragmentary.]

Tablet IX

Over his friend, Enkidu, Gilgamesh cried bitterly, roaming the wilderness.
    "I am going to die!—am I not like Enkidu?!
    Deep sadness penetrates my core,
    I fear death, and now roam the wilderness—
    I will set out to the region of Utanapishtim, son of Ubartutu, and will go with
        utmost dispatch!   5
    When I arrived at mountain passes at nightfall,
    I saw lions, and I was terrified!
    I raised my head in prayer to Sin,
    to the Great Lady of the gods my supplications poured forth, 'Save me from
        them!' "

He was sleeping in the night, but awoke with a start with a dream: 10
A warrior enjoyed his life—
he raised his axe in his hand,
drew the dagger from his sheath,
and fell into their midst like an arrow.
He struck and he scattered them.[35] 15
When he reached Mount Mashu,
which daily guards the rising and setting of the Sun,
above which only the dome of the heavens reaches,
and whose flank reaches as far as the Netherworld below,
there were Scorpion-beings watching over its gate. 20
Trembling terror they inspire, the sight of them is death,
their frightening aura sweeps over the mountains.
At the rising and setting they watch over the Sun.
When Gilgamesh saw them, trembling terror blanketed his face,
but he pulled himself together and drew near to them. 25
The scorpion-being called out to his female:
　　"He who comes to us, his body is the flesh of gods!"
The scorpion-being, his female, answered him:
　　"Only two-thirds of him is a god, one-third is human."
The male scorpion-being called out, saying to the offspring of the gods: 30
　　"Why have you traveled so distant a journey?
　　Why have you come here to me,
　　over rivers whose crossing is treacherous?"

[Twenty-nine lines are only partially legible.]

[Gilgamesh answered and said:]
　　"I have come on account of my ancestor Utanapishtim, 35
　　who joined the Assembly of the Gods, and was given eternal life.
　　About Death and Life I must ask him!"
The scorpion-being spoke to Gilgamesh, saying:
　　"Never has there been, Gilgamesh, a mortal man who could do that.
　　No one has crossed through the mountains, 40
　　for twelve leagues it is darkness throughout—
　　dense is the darkness, and light there is none."[36]
Gilgamesh answered and said:
　　"Though it be in deep sadness and pain,
　　in cold or heat gasping after breath, I will go on! 45
　　Now! Open the Gate!"
The scorpion-being spoke to Gilgamesh, saying:
　　"Go on, Gilgamesh, fear not!

---

35. Thirty fragmentary lines describe the beginning of Gilgamesh's journey to find Utanapishtim.

36. In seventy missing lines, Gilgamesh persuades the scorpion-man to allow him through.

The Mashu mountains I give to you freely,
the mountains, the ranges, you may traverse.   50
In safety may your feet carry you. . . .

As soon as Gilgamesh heard this
he heeded the utterances of the scorpion-being.
Along the Road of the Sun he journeyed—
one league he traveled . . . , dense was the darkness, light there was none.   55
Neither what lies ahead nor behind does it allow him to see.
Two leagues he traveled, dense was the darkness, light there was none,
neither what lies ahead nor behind does it allow him to see.
Three leagues he traveled, dense was the darkness, light there was none,
neither what lies ahead nor behind does it allow him to see. . . .   60
Four leagues he traveled . . . , dense was the darkness, light there was none,
neither what lies ahead nor behind does it allow him to see.
Five leagues he traveled . . . , dense was the darkness, light there was none,
neither what lies ahead nor behind does it allow him to see.
Six leagues he traveled . . . , dense was the darkness, light there was none,   65
neither what lies ahead nor behind does it allow him to see.
Seven leagues he traveled . . . , dense was the darkness, light there was none,
neither what lies ahead nor behind does it allow him to see.
Eight leagues he traveled and cried out (?),
dense was the darkness, light there was none,   70
neither what lies ahead nor behind does it allow him to see.
Nine leagues he traveled, the North Wind licked at his face,
dense was the darkness, light there was none,
neither what lies ahead nor behind does it allow him to see.
Ten leagues he traveled; the end of the road is near. . . .   75
Eleven leagues he traveled and came out before the sunrise.
Twelve leagues he traveled and it grew brilliant.

Before him there were trees of precious stones,
and he went straight to look at them.
The tree bears carnelian as its fruit,   80
laden with clusters of jewels, dazzling to behold,
—it bears lapis lazuli as foliage,
bearing fruit, a delight to look upon.

[A long description of the jewelled garden here is too illegible to be transcribed.]

Tablet X

The tavern-keeper Siduri who lives by the seashore, . . .
the pot-stand was made for her, the golden fermenting vat was made for her.
She is covered with a veil.

Gilgamesh was roving about, wearing a skin,
having the flesh of the gods in his body,   5
but sadness deep within him,
looking like one who has been traveling a long distance.
The tavern-keeper was gazing off into the distance,
puzzling to herself, she said,
wondering to herself: 10
   "That fellow is surely a murderer!
   Where is he heading?"
As soon as the tavern-keeper saw him, she bolted her door,
bolted her gate, bolted the lock.
But at her noise Gilgamesh pricked up his ears,   15
lifted his chin to look about and then laid his eyes on her.
Gilgamesh spoke to the tavern-keeper, saying:
   "Tavern-keeper, what have you seen that made you bolt your door,
   bolt your gate, bolt the lock?
   If you do not let me in I will break your door, and smash the lock!   20
Gilgamesh said to the tavern-keeper:
   "I am Gilgamesh, I killed the Guardian!
   I destroyed Humbaba who lived in the Cedar Forest,
   I slew lions in the mountain passes!
   I grappled with the Bull that came down from heaven, and killed him." 25
The tavern-keeper spoke to Gilgamesh, saying:
   "If you are Gilgamesh, who killed the Guardian,
   who destroyed Humbaba who lived in the Cedar Forest,
   who slew lions in the mountain passes,
   who grappled with the Bull that came down from heaven, and killed him, 30
   why are your cheeks emaciated, your expression desolate?
   Why is your heart so wretched, your features so haggard?
   Why is there such sadness deep within you?
   Why do you look like one who has been traveling a long distance
   so that ice and heat have seared your face?   35
   Why do you roam the wilderness?"
Gilgamesh spoke to her, to the tavern-keeper he said:
   "Tavern-keeper, should not my cheeks be emaciated?
   Should my heart not be wretched, my features not haggard?
   Should there not be sadness deep within me?   40
   Should I not look like one who has been traveling a long distance,
   and should ice and heat not have seared my face?
   Should I not roam the wilderness?
   My friend, the wild ass who chased the wild donkey, panther of the wilderness,
   Enkidu, the wild ass who chased the wild donkey, panther of the wilderness, 45
   we joined together, and went up into the mountain.

We grappled with and killed the Bull of Heaven,
we destroyed Humbaba who lived in the Cedar Forest,
we slew lions in the mountain passes!
My friend, whom I love deeply, who went through every hardship with me, 50
Enkidu, whom I love deeply, who went through every hardship with me,
the fate of mankind has overtaken him.
Six days and seven nights I mourned over him
and would not allow him to be buried
until a maggot fell out of his nose. 55
I was terrified by his appearance,
I began to fear death, and so roam the wilderness.
The issue of my friend oppresses me,
so I have been roaming long trails through the wilderness.
The issue of Enkidu, my friend, oppresses me, 60
so I have been roaming long roads through the wilderness.
How can I stay silent, how can I be still?
My friend whom I love has turned to clay.
Am I not like him? Will I lie down, never to get up again?"[37]
Gilgamesh spoke to the tavern-keeper, saying: 65
"So now, tavern-keeper, what is the way to Utanapishtim?
What are its markers? Give them to me! Give me the markers!
If possible, I will cross the sea;
if not, I will roam through the wilderness."
The tavern-keeper spoke to Gilgamesh, saying: 70
"There has never been, Gilgamesh, any passage whatever,
there has never been anyone since days of yore who crossed the sea.
The one who crosses the sea is valiant Shamash, except for him who can cross?
The crossing is difficult, its ways are treacherous—
and in between are the Waters of Death that bar its approaches! 75
And even if, Gilgamesh, you should cross the sea,
when you reach the Waters of Death what would you do?
Gilgamesh, over there is Urshanabi, the ferryman of Utanapishtim.
'The stone things'[38] are with him, he is in the woods picking mint.
Go on, let him see your face. 80
If possible, cross with him;
if not, you should turn back."

When Gilgamesh heard this
he raised the axe in his hand,
drew the dagger from his belt, 85

---

37. The text notably omits a reply by the tavern-keeper; in the earlier Old Babylonian version, she had urged Gilgamesh not to worry about death but to be content with the pleasures of life.

38. No one is sure what they are.

and slipped stealthily away after them.
Like an arrow he fell among the stone things.
From the middle of the woods their noise could be heard.
Urshanabi, the sharp-eyed, saw. . . .
When he heard the axe, he ran toward it.[39]   90

Gilgamesh spoke to Urshanabi, saying:
    "Now, Urshanabi! What is the way to Utanapishtim?
    What are its markers? Give them to me! Give me the markers!
    If possible, I will cross the sea;
    if not, I will roam through the wilderness!"   95

Urshanabi spoke to Gilgamesh, saying:
    "It is your hands, Gilgamesh, that prevent the crossing!
    You have smashed 'the stone things,' you have pulled out their retaining ropes.
    'The stone things' have been smashed, their retaining ropes pulled out!
    Gilgamesh, take the axe in your hand, go down into the woods,   100
    and cut down 300 punting poles each 60 cubits in length.
    Strip them, attach caps, and bring them to the boat!"
When Gilgamesh heard this
he took up the axe in his hand, drew the dagger from his belt,
and went down into the woods,   105
and cut 300 punting poles each 60 cubits in length.
He stripped them and attached caps, and brought them to the boat.
Gilgamesh and Urshanabi boarded the boat,
Gilgamesh launched the boat and they sailed away.
By the third day they had traveled a stretch of a month and a half, and   110
Urshanabi arrived at the Waters of Death.
Urshanabi said to Gilgamesh:
    "Hold back, Gilgamesh, take a punting pole,
    but your hand must not pass over the Waters of Death!
    Take a second, Gilgamesh, a third, and a fourth pole,   115
    take a fifth, Gilgamesh, a sixth, and a seventh pole,
    take an eighth, Gilgamesh, a ninth, and a tenth pole,
    take an eleventh, Gilgamesh, and a twelfth pole!"
In twice 60 rods Gilgamesh had used up the punting poles.
Then he loosened his waist-cloth for a sail;   120
Gilgamesh stripped off his garment
and held it up on the mast with his arms.

Utanapishtim was gazing off into the distance,
puzzling to himself he said, wondering to himself:
    "Why are 'the stone things' of the boat smashed to pieces?   125

---

39. In a fragmentary passage, Gilgamesh and
Urshanabi perhaps fight over the stone
things. Urshanabi then asks Gilgamesh
why he has come; he answers by repeating
his speech to the tavern-keeper.

And why is someone not its master sailing on it?
The one who is coming is not a man of mine."[40]

Utanapishtim said to Gilgamesh:
"Why are your cheeks emaciated, your expression desolate?
Why is your heart so wretched, your features so haggard?   130
Why is there such sadness deep within you?
Why do you look like one who has been traveling a long distance
so that ice and heat have seared your face?
Why do you roam the wilderness?"

Gilgamesh spoke to Utanapishtim saying: 135
"Should not my cheeks be emaciated, my expression desolate?
Should my heart not be wretched, my features not haggard?
Should there not be sadness deep within me?
Should I not look like one who has been traveling a long distance,
and should ice and heat not have seared my face?   140
Should I not roam the wilderness?
My friend who chased wild asses in the mountain, the panther of the
    wilderness,
Enkidu, my friend, who chased wild asses in the mountain, the panther of the
    wilderness,
we joined together, and went up into the mountain.
We grappled with and killed the Bull of Heaven,   145
we destroyed Humbaba who dwelled in the Cedar Forest,
we slew lions in the mountain passes!
My friend, whom I love deeply, who went through every hardship with me,
Enkidu, my friend, whom I love deeply, who went through every hardship with
    me,
the fate of mankind has overtaken him.   150
Six days and seven nights I mourned over him
and would not allow him to be buried
until a maggot fell out of his nose.
I was terrified by his appearance,
I began to fear death, and so roam the wilderness.   155
The issue of my friend oppresses me,
so I have been roaming long trails through the wilderness.
The issue of Enkidu, my friend, oppresses me,
so I have been roaming long roads through the wilderness.
How can I stay silent, how can I be still?   160
My friend whom I love has turned to clay;
Enkidu, my friend whom I love, has turned to clay!
Am I not like him? Will I lie down never to get up again?"
Gilgamesh spoke to Utanapishtim, saying:

---

40. Gilgamesh arrives and meets Utana-
    pishtim.

"That is why I must go on, to see Utanapishtim whom they call 'The Faraway.'   165
I went circling through all the mountains,
I traversed treacherous mountains, and crossed all the seas—
that is why sweet sleep has not mellowed my face,
through sleepless striving I am strained,
my muscles are filled with pain.   170
I had not yet reached the tavern-keeper's area before my clothing gave out.
I killed bear, hyena, lion, panther, tiger, stag, red-stag, and beasts of the
     wilderness;
I ate their meat and wrapped their skins around me.
The gate of grief must be bolted shut, sealed with pitch and bitumen!
Utanapishtim spoke to Gilgamesh, saying: 175
"Why, Gilgamesh, do you feel such sadness?
You who were created from the flesh of gods and mankind!

[Long but only partially legible passage follows.]

You have toiled without cease, and what have you got?
Through toil you wear yourself out,
you fill your body with grief,   180
your long lifetime you are bringing near (to a premature end)!
Mankind, whose offshoot is snapped off like a reed in a canebreak,

No one can see death,
no one can see the face of death,
no one can hear the voice of death,   185
yet there is savage death that snaps off mankind.
For how long do we build a household?
For how long do we seal a document?
For how long do brothers share the inheritance?
For how long is there to be jealousy in the land?   190
For how long has the river risen and brought the overflowing waters,
so that dragonflies drift down the river?
The face that could gaze upon the face of the Sun
has never existed ever.
How alike are the sleeping and the dead.   195
The image of Death cannot be depicted. . . .
After Enlil had pronounced the blessing,
the Anunnaki, the Great Gods, assembled.
Mammetum, she who fashions destiny, determined destiny with them.
They established Death and Life,   200
but they did not make known 'the days of death.'"

Tablet XI

Gilgamesh spoke to Utanapishtim, the Faraway:
"I have been looking at you,

but your appearance is not strange—you are like me!
You yourself are not different—you are like me!
My mind was resolved to fight with you,   5
but instead my arm lies useless over you.
Tell me, how is it that you stand in the Assembly of the Gods, and have found
   life?"
Utanapishtim spoke to Gilgamesh, saying:
  "I will reveal to you, Gilgamesh, a thing that is hidden,
  a secret of the gods I will tell you!   10
  Shuruppak, a city that you surely know,
  situated on the banks of the Euphrates,
  that city was very old, and there were gods inside it.
  The hearts of the Great Gods moved them to inflict the Flood.
  Their Father Anu uttered the oath of secrecy,   15
  Valiant Enlil was their Adviser,
  Ninurta was their Chamberlain,
  Ennugi was their Minister of Canals.
  Ea, the Clever Prince, was under oath with them
  so he repeated their talk to the reed house: 20
    'Reed house, reed house! Wall, wall!
    Hear, O reed house! Understand, O wall!
    O man of Shuruppak, son of Ubartutu:
    Tear down the house and build a boat!
    Abandon wealth and seek living beings!   25
    Spurn possessions and keep alive living beings!
    Make all living beings go up into the boat.
    The boat which you are to build,
    its dimensions must measure equal to each other:
    its length must correspond to its width.   30
    Roof it over like the Apsu.'[41]
I understood and spoke to my lord, Ea:
    'My lord, thus is the command which you have uttered
    I will heed and will do it.
    But what shall I answer the city, the populace, and the Elders?'   35
Ea spoke, commanding me, his servant:
    'You, well then, this is what you must say to them:
      "It appears that Enlil is rejecting me
      so I cannot reside in your city,
      nor set foot on Enlil's earth.   40
      I will go down to the Apsu to live with my lord, Ea,
      and upon you he will rain down abundance,
      a profusion of fowl, myriad fishes.
      He will bring to you a harvest of wealth,

---

41. The freshwater sea beneath the earth, the
    domain of the god Ea or Enki.

in the morning he will let loaves of bread shower down,   45
and in the evening a rain of wheat!"'
Just as dawn began to glow
the land assembled around me—
the carpenter carried his hatchet,
the reed worker carried his flattening stone,   50
The child carried the pitch,
the weak brought whatever else was needed.
On the fifth day I laid out her exterior.
It was a field in area,
its walls were each 10 times 12 cubits in height,   55
the sides of its top were of equal length, 10 times 12 cubits each.
I laid out its interior structure and drew a picture of it.
I provided it with six decks,
thus dividing it into seven levels.[42]
The inside of it I divided into nine compartments.   60
I drove plugs to keep out water in its middle part.
I saw to the punting poles and laid in what was necessary.
Three times 3,600 units of raw bitumen I poured into the bitumen kiln,
three times 3,600 units of pitch I put into it,
there were three times 3,600 porters of casks who carried (vegetable) oil,   65
apart from the 3,600 units of oil which they consumed
and two times 3,600 units of oil which the boatman stored away.
I butchered oxen for the meat,
and day upon day I slaughtered sheep.
I gave the workmen ale, beer, oil, and wine, as if it were river water,   70
so they could make a party like the New Year's Festival.

The boat was finished by sunset.
The launching was very difficult.
They had to keep carrying a runway of poles front to back,
until two-thirds of it had gone into the water.   75
Whatever I had I loaded on it:
whatever silver I had I loaded on it,
whatever gold I had I loaded on it.
All the living beings that I had I loaded on it,
I had all my kith and kin go up into the boat,   80
all the beasts and animals of the field and the craftsmen I had go up.
Shamash had set a stated time:
'In the morning I will let loaves of bread shower down,
and in the evening a rain of wheat!
Go inside the boat, seal the entry!'   85

---

42. The boat is described as a cube, rather than an ordinary boat, in a theological allusion to the dimensions of a ziggurat, the Mesopotamian stepped tower with four to seven levels on top of which stood a temple.

That stated time had arrived.
In the morning he let loaves of bread shower down,
and in the evening a rain of wheat.
I watched the appearance of the weather—
the weather was frightful to behold!   90
I went into the boat and sealed the entry.
For the caulking of the boat, to Puzuramurri, the boatman,
I gave the palace together with its contents.
Just as dawn began to glow
there arose from the horizon a black cloud.   95
Adad[43] rumbled inside of it,
before him went Shullat and Hanish,
heralds going over mountain and land.
Erragal pulled out the mooring poles,
forth went Ninurta and made the dikes overflow.   100
The Anunnaki lifted up the torches,
setting the land ablaze with their flare.
Stunned shock over Adad's deeds overtook the heavens,
and turned to blackness all that had been light.
The land shattered like a pot.   105
All day long the South Wind blew,
blowing fast, submerging the mountain in water,
overwhelming the people like an attack.
No one could see his fellow,
they could not recognize each other in the torrent.   110
The gods were frightened by the Flood,
and retreated, ascending to the heaven of Anu.
The gods were cowering like dogs, crouching by the outer wall.
Ishtar shrieked like a woman in childbirth,
the sweet-voiced Mistress of the Gods wailed: 115
    'The olden days have alas turned to clay,
    because I said evil things in the Assembly of the Gods!
    How could I say evil things in the Assembly of the Gods,
    ordering a catastrophe to destroy my people?!
    No sooner have I given birth to my dear people   120
    than they fill the sea like so many fish!'
The gods—those of the Anunnaki—were weeping with her,
the gods humbly sat weeping, sobbing with grief,
their lips burning, parched with thirst.
Six days and seven nights   125
came the wind and flood, the storm flattening the land.
When the seventh day arrived, the storm was pounding,
the flood was a war—struggling with itself like a woman writhing in labor.

---

43. The storm god. Erragal, below, is the god   Anunnaki are a group of fifty gods, sons of
    of death; Ninurta is the god of war. The   Anu.

The sea calmed, fell still, the whirlwind and flood stopped up.
I looked around all day long—quiet had set in   130
and all the human beings had turned to clay!
The terrain was as flat as a roof.
I opened a vent and fresh air fell upon the side of my nose.
I fell to my knees and sat weeping,
tears streaming down the side of my nose.   135
I looked around for coastlines in the expanse of the sea,
and at twelve leagues there emerged a region of land.
On Mt. Nimush the boat lodged firm,
Mt. Nimush held the boat, allowing no sway.**44**
One day and a second Mt. Nimush held the boat, allowing no sway.   140
A third day, a fourth, Mt. Nimush held the boat, allowing no sway.
A fifth day, a sixth, Mt. Nimush held the boat, allowing no sway.
When a seventh day arrived
I sent forth a dove and released it.
The dove went off, but came back to me;   145
no perch was visible so it circled back to me.
I sent forth a swallow and released it.
The swallow went off, but came back to me;
no perch was visible so it circled back to me.
I sent forth a raven and released it.   150
The raven went off, and saw the waters slither back.
It eats, it scratches, it bobs, but does not circle back to me.
Then I sent out everything in all directions and sacrificed a sheep.
I offered incense in front of the mountain-ziggurat.
Seven and seven cult vessels I put in place,   155
and into their bowls I poured reeds, cedar, and myrtle.
The gods smelled the savor,
the gods smelled the sweet savor,
and collected like flies over a sacrifice.
Just then Beletili arrived.   160
She lifted up the large flies (beads) which Anu had made for his enjoyment:**45**
  'You gods, as surely as I shall not forget this lapis lazuli around my neck,
  may I be mindful of these days, and never forget them!
  The gods may come to the incense offering,
  but Enlil may not come to the incense offering,   165
  because without considering he brought about the Flood
  and consigned my people to annihilation.'
Just then Enlil arrived.
He saw the boat and became furious,

---

44. This may be a 9,000-foot peak in eastern
    Iraq.
45. A necklace with beads in the form of flies,
representing the dead offspring of the
mother goddess Beletili/Aruru.

he was filled with rage at the Igigi gods:[46]   170
   'Where did a living being escape?
   No man was to survive the annihilation!'
Ninurta spoke to Valiant Enlil, saying:
   'Who else but Ea could devise such a thing?
   It is Ea who knows every machination!'   175
Ea spoke to Valiant Enlil, saying:
   'It is you, O Valiant One, who is the Sage of the Gods.
   How, how could *you* bring about a Flood without consideration?
   Charge the violation to the violator,
   charge the offense to the offender,   180
   but be compassionate lest (mankind) be cut off,
   be patient lest they be killed.
   Instead of your bringing on the Flood,
   would that a lion had appeared to diminish the people!
   Instead of your bringing on the Flood,   185
   would that a wolf had appeared to diminish the people!
   Instead of your bringing on the Flood,
   would that famine had occurred to slay the land!
   Instead of your bringing on the Flood,
   would that Pestilent Erra had appeared to ravage the land!   190
   It was not I who revealed the secret of the Great Gods,
   I only made a dream appear to Atrahasis[47] and (thus) he heard the secret of
     the gods.
   Now then! The deliberation should be about him!'
Enlil went up inside the boat
and, grasping my hand, made me go up.   195
He had my wife go up and kneel by my side.
He touched our forehead and, standing between us, he blessed us:
   'Previously Utanapishtim was a human being.
   But now let Utanapishtim and his wife become like us, the gods!
   Let Utanapishtim reside far away, at the Mouth of the Rivers.'   200
They took us far away and settled us at the Mouth of the Rivers.''

"Now then, (Gilgamesh,) who will convene the gods on your behalf,
that you may find the life that you are seeking?
Wait! You must not lie down for six days and seven nights."
As soon as he sat down with his head between his legs   205
sleep, like a fog, blew upon him.
Utanapishtim said to his wife:
"Look there! The man, the youth who wanted eternal life!
Sleep, lie a fog, blew over him."

---

46. A group of lesser gods who did manual
   labor for the Anunnaki.
47. Atrahasis, "Exceedingly Wise," is the hero

of an earlier Flood epic, from which this
account draws; here the name is applied
to Utanapishtim.

His wife said to Utanapishtim the Faraway: 210
   "Touch him, let the man awaken.
   Let him return safely by the way he came.
   Let him return to his land by the gate through which he left."
Utanapishtim said to his wife:
   "Mankind is deceptive, and will deceive you.   215
   Come, bake loaves for him and keep setting them by his head
   and draw on the wall each day that he lay down."
She baked his loaves and placed them by his head
and marked on the wall the day that he lay down.
The first loaf was dessicated,   220
the second stale, the third moist, the fourth turned white, . . .
the fifth sprouted gray (mold), the sixth is still fresh.
The seventh—suddenly he touched him and the man awoke.
Gilgamesh said to Utanapishtim:
   "The very moment sleep was pouring over me   225
   you touched me and alerted me!"
Utanapishtim spoke to Gilgamesh, saying:
   "Look over here, Gilgamesh, count your loaves!
   You should be aware of what is marked on the wall!
   Your first loaf is dessicated,   230
   the second stale, the third moist, your fourth turned white, . . .
   the fifth sprouted gray mold, the sixth is still fresh.
   The seventh—at that instant you awoke!"
Gilgamesh said to Utanapishtim the Faraway:
   "O woe! What shall I do, Utanapishtim, where shall I go?   235
   The Snatcher has taken hold of my flesh,
   in my bedroom Death dwells,
   and wherever I set foot there too is Death!"

Utanapishtim said to Urshanabi, the ferryman:
   "May the harbor reject you, may the ferry landing reject you!   240
   May you who used to walk its shores be denied its shores!
   The man in front of whom you walk, matted hair chains his body,
   animal skins have ruined his beautiful skin.
   Take him away, Urshanabi, bring him to the washing place.
   Let him wash his matted hair in water.   245
   Let him cast away his animal skin and have the sea carry it off,
   let his body be moistened with fine oil,
   let the wrap around his head be made new,
   let him wear royal robes worthy of him!
   Until he goes off to his city,   250
   until he sets off on his way,
   let his royal robe not become spotted, let it be perfectly new!"
Urshanabi took him away and brought him to the washing place.
He washed his matted hair with water. . . .

He cast off his animal skin and the sea carried it off. 255
He moistened his body with fine oil,
and made a new wrap for his head.
He put on a royal robe worthy of him.
Until he went away to his city,
until he set off on his way, 260
his royal robe remained unspotted, it was perfectly clean.
Gilgamesh and Urshanabi boarded the boat,
they cast off the boat, and sailed away.

The wife of Utanapishtim the Faraway said to him:
    "Gilgamesh came here exhausted and worn out. 265
    What can you give him so that he can return to his land with honor?"
Then Gilgamesh raised a punting pole
and drew the boat to shore.
Utanapishtim spoke to Gilgamesh, saying:
    "Gilgamesh, you came here exhausted and worn out. 270
    What can I give you so you can return to your land?
    I will disclose to you a thing that is hidden, Gilgamesh,
    a secret I will tell you.
    There is a plant like a boxthorn,
    whose thorns will prick your hand like a rose. 275
    If your hands reach that plant you will become a young man again."
Hearing this, Gilgamesh opened a conduit(?) to the Apsu
and attached heavy stones to his feet.
They dragged him down, to the Apsu they pulled him.
He took the plant, though it pricked his hand, 280
and cut the heavy stones from his feet,
letting the waves throw him onto its shores.
Gilgamesh spoke to Urshanabi, the ferryman, saying:
    "Urshanabi, this plant is a plant against decay
    by which a man can attain his survival. 285
    I will bring it to Uruk-Haven,
    and have an old man eat the plant to test it.
    The plant's name is 'The Old Man Becomes a Young Man.'[48]
    Then I will eat it and return to the condition of my youth."
At twenty leagues they broke for some food, 290
at thirty leagues they stopped for the night.
Seeing a spring and how cool its waters were,
Gilgamesh went down and was bathing in the water.
A snake smelled the fragrance of the plant,

---

48. This is probably the meaning of "Gilgamesh."

silently came up and carried off the plant.   295
While going back it sloughed off its casing.
At that point Gilgamesh sat down, weeping,
his tears streaming over the side of his nose.
    "Counsel me, O ferryman Urshanabi!
For whom have my arms labored, Urshanabi?   300
For whom has my heart's blood roiled?
I have not secured any good deed for myself,
but done a good deed for the 'lion of the ground'!
Now the high waters are coursing twenty leagues distant,
as I was opening the conduit(?) I turned my equipment over into it.   305
What can I find to serve as a marker for me?
I will turn back from the journey by sea and leave the boat by the shore!"

At twenty leagues they broke for some food,
at thirty leagues they stopped for the night.
They arrived in Uruk-Haven.   310
Gilgamesh said to Urshanabi, the ferryman:
    "Go up, Urshanabi, onto the wall of Uruk and walk around.
Examine its foundation, inspect its brickwork thoroughly—
is not even the core of the brick structure of kiln-fired brick,
and did not the Seven Sages themselves lay out its plan?   315
One league city, one league palm gardens, one league lowlands, the open area
    of the Ishtar Temple,
three leagues and the open area of Uruk the wall encloses."

HOMER (EIGHTH CENTURY B.C.E.)
Greece

The *Iliad*'s central themes—friendship and fame, human and divine relations,
and a hero's confrontation with his own mortality—will be familiar to readers of
the Babylonian *Epic of Gilgamesh,* which may have reached Greece through
trading contacts in Asia Minor during the period when the *Iliad* was being
shaped. The *Iliad,* whose title means "the story of Ilium" (Troy), was itself the
product of a centuries-old oral narrative tradition about the Trojan War, an
enduring subject around which a rich and elaborate mythology developed.
    The events of the *Iliad* are concentrated into a few crucial days in the final
year of the ten-year struggle. It begins with the strife between Achilles,
preeminent among the Greek heroes, and Agamemnon, king of Mycenae and
leader of the Greek forces. Their rift causes Achilles to withdraw from the war,
and he returns to it only after his friend Patroclus is killed by Hector, son of
Priam, the Trojan king. The final scene in our selection narrates the meeting of

Achilles and Priam in the poem's last book, when each expresses his compassion for the other.

The *Iliad* is thought to have taken the form in which we now have it in the early to mid-eighth century B.C.E., having been preceded by countless oral recreations of its story. Although numerous individuals must have left their mark on it as they sang different versions of the story, Homer is the name that has come down to us from antiquity as the creator of both the *Iliad* and the *Odyssey*. We know nothing whatever of Homer; but by his name we refer to the poet to whose artistic imprint these complex works owe their unmistakable coherence and unforgettable beauty. It is impossible to overstate their influence on later European literature.

from Iliad

Book 1 [The Rage of Achilles]

Rage—Goddess[1] sing the rage of Peleus' son Achilles,
murderous, doomed, that cost the Achaeans[2] countless losses,
hurling down to the House of Death so many sturdy souls,
great fighters' souls, but made their bodies carrion,
feasts for the dogs and birds,   5
and the will of Zeus was moving toward its end.
Begin, Muse, when the two first broke and clashed,
Agamemnon lord of men and brilliant Achilles.
    What god drove them to fight with such a fury?
Apollo the son of Zeus and Leto. Incensed at the king   10
he swept a fatal plague through the army—men were dying
and all because Agamemnon spurned Apollo's priest.
Yes, Chryses approached the Achaeans' fast ships
to win his daughter back, bringing a priceless ransom
and bearing high in hand, wound on a golden staff,   15
the wreaths of the god, the distant deadly Archer.
He begged the whole Achaean army but most of all[3]
the two supreme commanders, Atreus' two sons,
"Agamemnon, Menelaus—all Argives geared for war!
May the gods who hold the halls of Olympus give you   20
Priam's[4] city to plunder, then safe passage home.

Translated by Robert Fagles.

---

1. The goddess is the Muse, who is also invoked in the opening line of the *Odyssey*. In
early Greek poetry the Muse (sometimes in
the plural) is represented as the ultimate
source of the poet's skill; she is considered
to have witnessed the great deeds of the
past, which are the subject of epic poetry,
and can thus guarantee the authenticity of
the poet's song.

2. A Homeric name for the Greek forces, also
called Argives (from the city of Argos) and
Danaans (referring to their descent from a
mythical King Danaus who was said to have
been given refuge in Argos).
3. Apollo, the archer god, can inflict disease
but is also the god of healing.
4. Priam is king of Troy and father of Hector,
the city's chief defender.

Just set my daughter free, my dear one . . . here,
accept these gifts, this ransom. Honor the god
who strikes from worlds away—the son of Zeus, Apollo!"
    And all ranks of Achaeans cried out their assent: 25
"Respect the priest, accept the shining ransom!"
But it brought no joy to the heart of Agamemnon.
The king dismissed the priest with a brutal order
ringing in his ears: "Never again, old man,
let me catch sight of you by the hollow ships!   30
Not loitering now, not slinking back tomorrow.
The staff and the wreaths of god will never save you then.
The girl—I won't give up the girl. Long before that,
old age will overtake her in *my* house, in Argos,
far from her fatherland, slaving back and forth   35
at the loom, forced to share my bed!
                    Now go,
don't tempt my wrath—and you may depart alive."
    The old man was terrified. He obeyed the order,
turning, trailing away in silence down the shore
where the roaring battle lines of breakers crash and drag.   40
And moving off to a safe distance, over and over
the old priest prayed to the son of sleek-haired Leto,
lord Apollo, "Hear me, Apollo! God of the silver bow
who strides the walls of Chryse and Cilla[5] sacrosanct—
lord in power of Tenedos—Smintheus,[6] god of the plague!   45
If I ever roofed a shrine to please your heart,
ever burned the long rich bones of bulls and goats
on your holy altar, now, now bring my prayer to pass.
Pay the Danaans back—your arrows for my tears!"
    His prayer went up and Phoebus Apollo heard him.   50
Down he strode from Olympus' peaks, storming at heart
with his bow and hooded quiver slung across his shoulders.
The arrows clanged at his back as the god quaked with rage,
the god himself on the march and down he came like night.
Over against the ships he dropped to a knee, let fly a shaft   55
and a terrifying clash rang out from the great silver bow.
First he went for the mules and circling dogs but then,
launching a piercing shaft at the men themselves,
he cut them down in droves—
and the corpse-fires burned on, night and day, no end in sight.   60
    Nine days the arrows of god swept through the army.

---

5. Chryse and Cilla are towns to the south of Troy; the priest's name is taken from the town of Chryse. Tenedos is an island off the coast near Troy.

6. This epithet is thought to come from the Cretan word for "mouse" and to refer either to an early stage of worship of the god in animal form or to Apollo as a protector against mice, which destroy the crops.

On the tenth Achilles called all ranks to muster—
the impulse seized him, sent by white-armed Hera[7]
grieving to see Achaean fighters drop and die.
Once they'd gathered, crowding the meeting grounds,
the swift runner Achilles rose and spoke among them: 65
"Son of Atreus, now we are beaten back, I fear,
the long campaign is lost. So home we sail . . .
if we can escape our death—if war and plague
are joining forces now to crush the Argives.   70
But wait: let us question a holy man,
a prophet, even a man skilled with dreams—
dreams as well can come our way from Zeus—
come, someone to tell us why Apollo rages so,
whether he blames us for a vow we failed, or sacrifice.   75
If only the god would share the smoky savor of lambs
and full-grown goats, Apollo might be willing, still,
somehow, to save us from this plague."
                                      So he proposed
and down he sat again as Calchas rose among them,
Thestor's son, the clearest by far of all the seers   80
who scan the flight of birds. He knew all things that are,
all things that are past and all that are to come,
the seer who had led the Argive ships to Troy
with the second sight that god Apollo gave him.
For the armies' good the seer began to speak: 85
"Achilles, dear to Zeus . . .
you order me to explain Apollo's anger,
the distant deadly Archer? I will tell it all.
But strike a pact with me, swear you will defend me
with all your heart, with words and strength of hand.   90
For there is a man I will enrage—I see it now—
a powerful man who lords it over all the Argives,
one the Achaeans must obey . . . A mighty king,
raging against an inferior, is too strong.
Even if he can swallow down his wrath today,   95
still he will nurse the burning in his chest
until, sooner or later, he sends it bursting forth.
Consider it closely, Achilles. Will you save me?"
    And the matchless runner reassured him: "Courage!
Out with it now, Calchas. Reveal the will of god,   100
whatever you may know. And I swear by Apollo
dear to Zeus, the power you pray to, Calchas,
when you reveal god's will to the Argives—no one,
not while I am alive and see the light on earth, no one

---

7. The wife (and sister) of Zeus, patriarch of
the gods who live on Mt. Olympus.

will lay his heavy hands on you by the hollow ships.   105
None among all the armies. Not even if you mean
Agamemnon here who now claims to be, by far,
the best of the Achaeans."
                      The seer took heart
and this time he spoke out, bravely: "Beware—
he casts no blame for a vow we failed, a sacrifice.   110
The god's enraged because Agamemnon spurned his priest,
he refused to free his daughter, he refused the ransom.
That's why the Archer sends us pains and he will send us more
and never drive this shameful destruction from the Argives,
not till we give back the girl with sparkling eyes   115
to her loving father—no price, no ransom paid—
and carry a sacred hundred bulls to Chryse town.
Then we can calm the god, and only then appease him."
    So he declared and sat down. But among them rose
the fighting son of Atreus, lord of the far-flung kingdoms,   120
Agamemnon—furious, his dark heart filled to the brim,
blazing with anger now, his eyes like searing fire.
With a sudden, killing look he wheeled on Calchas first:
"Seer of misery! Never a word that works to my advantage!
Always misery warms your heart, your prophecies—   125
never a word of profit said or brought to pass.
Now, again, you divine god's will for the armies,
bruit it about, as fact, why the deadly Archer
multiplies our pains: because I, I refused
that glittering price for the young girl Chryseis.   130
Indeed, I prefer *her* by far, the girl herself,
I want her mine in my own house! I rank her higher
than Clytemnestra, my wedded wife—she's nothing less
in build or breeding, in mind or works of hand.
But I am willing to give her back, even so,   135
if that is best for all. What I really want
is to keep my people safe, not see them dying
But fetch me another prize, and straight off too
else I alone of the Argives go without my honor.
That would be a disgrace. You are all witness   140
look—*my* prize is snatched away!"
                         But the swift runner
Achilles answered him at once, "Just how, Agamemnon,
great field marshal . . . most grasping man alive,
how can the generous Argives give you prizes now?
I know of no troves of treasure, piled, lying idle,   145
anywhere. Whatever we dragged from towns we plundered,
all's been portioned out. But collect it, call it back
from the rank and file? *That* would be the disgrace.

So return the girl to the god, at least for now.
We Achaeans will pay you back, three, four times over,   150
if Zeus will grant us the gift, somehow, someday,
to raze Troy's massive ramparts to the ground."
    But King Agamemnon countered, "Not so quickly,
brave as you are, godlike Achilles—trying to cheat *me*.
Oh no, you won't get past me, take me in that way!   155
What do you want? To cling to your own prize
while I sit calmly by—empty-handed here?
Is that why you order me to give her back?
No—if our generous Argives *will* give me a prize,
a match for my desires, equal to what I've lost,   160
well and good. But if they give me nothing
I will take a prize myself—your own, or Ajax'
or Odysseus'[8] prize—I'll commandeer her myself
and let that man I go to visit choke with rage!
Enough. We'll deal with all this later, in due time.   165
Now come, we haul a black ship down to the bright sea,
gather a decent number of oarsmen along her locks
and put aboard a sacrifice, and Chryseis herself,
in all her beauty . . . we embark her too.
Let one of the leading captains take command.   170
Ajax, Idomeneus, trusty Odysseus or you, Achilles,
you—the most violent man alive—so you can perform
the rites for us and calm the god yourself."
                    A dark glance
and the headstrong runner answered him in kind: "Shameless—
armored in shamelessness—always shrewd with greed!   175
How could any Argive soldier obey your orders,
freely and gladly do your sailing for you
or fight your enemies, full force? Not I, no.
It wasn't Trojan spearmen who brought me here to fight.
The Trojans never did *me* damage, not in the least,   180
they never stole my cattle or my horses, never
in Phthia where the rich soil breeds strong men
did they lay waste my crops. How could they?
Look at the endless miles that lie between us . . .
shadowy mountain ranges, seas that surge and thunder.   185
No, you colossal, shameless—we all followed you,
to please you, to fight for you, to win your honor
back from the Trojans—Menelaus and you, you dog-face!
What do *you* care? Nothing. You don't look right or left.
And now you threaten to strip me of my prize in person—   190

---

8. Two of the preeminent Achaean warriors.

the one I fought for long and hard, and sons of Achaea
handed her to me.
          My honors never equal yours,
whenever we sack some wealthy Trojan stronghold—
my arms bear the brunt of the raw, savage fighting,
true, but when it comes to dividing up the plunder   195
the lion's share is yours, and back I go to my ships,
clutching some scrap, some pittance that I love,
when I have fought to exhaustion.
                No more now—
back I go to Phthia.[9] Better that way by far,
to journey home in the beaked ships of war.   200
I have no mind to linger here disgraced,
brimming your cup and piling up your plunder."
   But the lord of men Agamemnon shot back,
"*Desert,* by all means—if the spirit drives you home!
I will never beg you to stay, not on *my* account.   205
Never—others will take my side and do me honor,
Zeus above all, whose wisdom rules the world.
You—I hate you most of all the warlords
loved by the gods. Always dear to your heart,
strife, yes, and battles, the bloody grind of war.   210
What if you are a great soldier? That's just a gift of god.
Go home with your ships and comrades, lord it over your Myrmidons![10]
You *are* nothing to me—you and your overweening anger!
But let this be my warning on your way:
since Apollo insists on taking my Chryseis,[11]   215
I'll send her back in my own ships with *my* crew.
But I, I will be there in person at your tents
to take Briseis in all her beauty, your own prize—
so you can learn just how much greater I am than you
and the next man up may shrink from matching words with me,   220
from hoping to rival Agamemnon strength for strength!"
   He broke off and anguish gripped Achilles.
The heart in his rugged chest was pounding, torn . . .
Should he draw the long sharp sword slung at his hip,
thrust through the ranks and kill Agamemnon now?—   225
or check his rage and beat his fury down?
As his racing spirit veered back and forth,
just as he drew his huge blade from its sheath,

---

9. Achilles' home in Thessaly, in the north of
   mainland Greece.

10. Achilles' warrior companions who came
   with him from Phthia.

11. Her name means simply "daughter of
   Chryseis."

down from the vaulting heavens swept Athena,[12]
the white-armed goddess Hera sped her down: 230
Hera loved both men and cared for both alike.
Rearing behind him Pallas seized his fiery hair—
only Achilles saw her, none of the other fighters—
struck with wonder he spun around, he knew her at once,
Pallas Athena! the terrible blazing of those eyes,   235
and his winged words went flying: "Why, why now?
Child of Zeus with the shield of thunder, why come now?
To witness the outrage Agamemnon just committed?
I tell you this, and so help me it's the truth—
he'll soon pay for his arrogance with his life!"   240

    Her gray eyes clear, the goddess Athena answered,
"Down from the skies I come to check your rage
if only you will yield.
The white-armed goddess Hera sped me down:
she loves you both, she cares for you both alike.   245
Stop this fighting, now. Don't lay hand to sword.
Lash him with threats of the price that he will face.
And I tell you this—and I *know* it is the truth—
one day glittering gifts will lie before you,
three times over to pay for all his outrage.   250
Hold back now. Obey us both."

                So she urged
and the swift runner complied at once: "I must—
when the two of you hand down commands, Goddess,
a man submits though his heart breaks with fury.
Better for him by far. If a man obeys the gods   255
they're quick to hear his prayers."

                And with that
Achilles stayed his burly hand on the silver hilt
and slid the huge blade back in its sheath.
He would not fight the orders of Athena.
Soaring home to Olympus, she rejoined the gods   260
aloft in the halls of Zeus whose shield is thunder.

    But Achilles rounded on Agamemnon once again,
lashing out at him, not relaxing his anger for a moment:
"Staggering drunk, with your dog's eyes, your fawn's heart!
Never once did you arm with the troops and go to battle   265
or risk an ambush packed with Achaea's picked men—
you lack the courage, you can see death coming.

---

12. Pallas Athena, Zeus's daughter, and Hera,   Trojans. Athena is goddess of war as well
his wife, are partisans of the Greek side in   as of the civilizing arts.
the conflict and perpetually hostile to the

Safer by far, you find, to foray all through camp,
commandeering the prize of any man who speaks against you.
King who devours his people! Worthless husks, the men you rule—   270
if not, Atrides,[13] this outrage would have been your last.
I tell you this, and I swear a mighty oath upon it . . .
by this, this scepter, look,
that never again will put forth crown and branches,
now it's left its stump on the mountain ridge forever,   275
nor will it sprout new green again, now the brazen ax
has stripped its bark and leaves, and now the sons of Achaea
pass it back and forth as they hand their judgments down,
upholding the honored customs whenever Zeus commands—
This scepter will be the mighty force behind my oath: 280
someday, I swear, a yearning for Achilles will strike
Achaea's sons and all your armies! But then, Atrides,
harrowed as you will be, *nothing* you do can save you—
not when your hordes of fighters drop and die,
cut down by the hands of man-killing Hector![14] Then—   285
then you will tear your heart out, desperate, raging
that you disgraced the best of the Achaeans!"
                                             Down on the ground
he dashed the scepter studded bright with golden nails,
then took his seat again.

[After Achilles withdraws from the war, the fighting between Greeks and Trojans resumes.
Thanks to the prowess of the warrior Diomedes, the Greeks have considerable success on
the battlefield, prompting Hector to return to the city to instruct the Trojans to appeal to the
goddess Athena for aid. Before departing again for battle Hector visits his own house,
looking for his wife, Andromache, and their infant son.]

Book 6 [Hector Returns to Troy]

A flash of his helmet
and off he strode and quickly reached his sturdy,
well-built house. But white-armed Andromache—
Hector could not find her in the halls.
She and the boy and a servant finely gowned   5
were standing watch on the tower, sobbing, grieving.
When Hector saw no sign of his loyal wife inside
he went to the doorway, stopped and asked the servants,
"Come, please, tell me the truth now, women.
Where's Andromache gone? To my sister's house?   10

---

13. Achilles addresses Agamemnon as "son of
    Atreus." A warrior will often be referred
    to, as here, only by his patronymic, which
    designates him as "son of. . . ."

14. The leading Trojan warrior, son of King
    Priam.

To my brothers' wives with their long flowing robes?
Or Athena's shrine where the noble Trojan women
gather to win the great grim goddess over?"
    A busy, willing servant answered quickly,
"Hector, seeing you want to know the truth,   15
she hasn't gone to your sisters, brothers' wives
or Athena's shrine where the noble Trojan women
gather to win the great grim goddess over.
Up to the huge gate-tower of Troy she's gone
because she heard our men are so hard-pressed,   20
the Achaean fighters coming on in so much force.
She sped to the wall in panic, like a madwoman—
the nurse went with her, carrying your child."
    At that, Hector spun and rushed from his house,
back by the same way down the wide, well-paved streets   25
throughout the city until he reached the Scaean Gates,
the last point he would pass to gain the field of battle.
There his warm, generous wife came running up to meet him,
Andromache the daughter of gallant-hearted Eetion
who had lived below Mount Placos[15] rich with timber,   30
in Thebe below the peaks, and ruled Cilicia's people.
His daughter had married Hector helmed in bronze.
She joined him now, and following in her steps
a servant holding the boy against her breast,
in the first flush of life, only a baby,   35
Hector's son, the darling of his eyes
and radiant as a star . . .
Hector would always call the boy Scamandrius,[16]
townsmen called him Astyanax, Lord of the City,
since Hector was the lone defense of Troy.   40
The great man of war breaking into a broad smile,
his gaze fixed on his son, in silence. Andromache,
pressing close beside him and weeping freely now,
clung to his hand, urged him, called him: "Reckless one,
my Hector—your own fiery courage will destroy you!   45
Have you no pity for him, our helpless son? Or me,
and the destiny that weighs me down, your widow,
now so soon. Yes, soon they will kill you off,
all the Achaean forces massed for assault, and then,
bereft of you, better for me to sink beneath the earth.   50
What other warmth, what comfort's left for me,
once you have met your doom? Nothing but torment!

---

15. Andromache's father ruled an area to the
    south of Troy, near Mt. Ida.

16. Hector has named his son after the Trojan
    river Scamander. Astyanax literally means
    "lord of the city."

I have lost my father. Mother's gone as well.
Father . . . the brilliant Achilles laid him low
when he stormed Cilicia's city filled with people,   55
Thebe with her towering gates. He killed Eetion,
not that he stripped his gear—he'd some respect at least—
for he burned his corpse in all his blazoned bronze,
then heaped a grave-mound high above the ashes
and nymphs of the mountain planted elms around it,   60
daughters of Zeus whose shield is storm and thunder.
And the seven brothers I had within our halls . . .
all in the same day went down to the House of Death,
the great godlike runner Achilles butchered them all,
tending their shambling oxen, shining flocks.   65
                              And mother,
who ruled under the timberline of woody Placos once—
he no sooner haled her here with his other plunder
than he took a priceless ransom, set her free
and home she went to her father's royal halls
where Artemis,[17] showering arrows, shot her down.   70
You, Hector—you are my father now, my noble mother,
a brother too, and you are my husband, young and warm and strong!
Pity me, please! Take your stand on the rampart here,
before you orphan your son and make your wife a widow.
Draw your armies up where the wild fig tree stands,   75
there, where the city lies most open to assault,
the walls lower, easily overrun. Three times
they have tried that point, hoping to storm Troy,
their best fighters led by the Great and Little Ajax,
famous Idomeneus, Atreus' sons, valiant Diomedes.[18]   80
Perhaps a skilled prophet revealed the spot—
or their own fury whips them on to attack."
    And tall Hector nodded, his helmet flashing:
"All this weighs on my mind too, dear woman.
But I would die of shame to face the men of Troy   85
and the Trojan women trailing their long robes
if I would shrink from battle now, a coward.
Nor does the spirit urge me on that way.
I've learned it all too well. To stand up bravely,
always to fight in the front ranks of Trojan soldiers,   90
winning my father great glory, glory for myself.
For in my heart and soul I also know this well:

---

17. The goddess Artemis is Apollo's sister, the
    daughter of Zeus and Leto.
18. Andromache names some of the major
    Greek warriors; two were named Ajax, so

they were distinguished by the epithets
Great (for the Ajax who takes part in the
embassy to Achilles in Book 9) and Little.

the day will come when sacred Troy must die,
Priam must die and all his people with him,
Priam who hurls the strong ash spear. . .

[handwritten: Hector knows he will die eventually, but he wants to die having glory]

                                Even so,   95
it is less the pain of the Trojans still to come
that weighs me down, not even of Hecuba herself
or King Priam, or the thought that my own brothers
in all their numbers, all their gallant courage,
may tumble in the dust, crushed by enemies—   100
That is nothing, nothing beside your agony
when some brazen Argive hales you off in tears,
wrenching away your day of light and freedom!
Then far off in the land of Argos you must live,
laboring at a loom, at another woman's beck and call,   105
fetching water at some spring, Messeis or Hyperia,[19]
resisting it all the way—
the rough yoke of necessity at your neck.
And a man may say, who sees you streaming tears,
'There is the wife of Hector, the bravest fighter   110
they could field, those stallion-breaking Trojans,
long ago when the men fought for Troy.' So he will say
and the fresh grief will swell your heart once more,
widowed, robbed of the one man strong enough
to fight off your day of slavery.   115
                          No, no,
let the earth come piling over my dead body
before I hear your cries, I hear you dragged away!"
   In the same breath, shining Hector reached down
for his son—but the boy recoiled,
cringing against his nurse's full breast,   120
screaming out at the sight of his own father,
terrified by the flashing bronze, the horsehair crest,
the great ridge of the helmet nodding, bristling terror—
so it struck his eyes. And his loving father laughed,
his mother laughed as well, and glorious Hector,   125
quickly lifting the helmet from his head,
set it down on the ground, fiery in the sunlight,
and raising his son he kissed him, tossed him in his arms,
lifting a prayer to Zeus and the other deathless gods:
"Zeus, all you immortals! Grant this boy, my son,   130
may be like me, first in glory among the Trojans,
strong and brave like me, and rule all Troy in power
and one day let them say, 'He is a better man than his father!'—

---

19. Messeis was a spring in Sparta, Hyperia in
    northern Greece.

when he comes home from battle bearing the bloody gear
of the mortal enemy he has killed in war—   135
a joy to his mother's heart."
                    So Hector prayed
and placed his son in the arms of his loving wife.
Andromache pressed the child to her scented breast,
smiling through her tears. Her husband noticed,
and filled with pity now, Hector stroked her gently,   140
trying to reassure her, repeating her name: "Andromache,
dear one, why so desperate? Why so much grief for me?
No man will hurl me down to Death, against my fate.
And fate? No one alive has ever escaped it,
neither brave man nor coward, I tell you—   145
it's born with us the day that we are born.
So please go home and tend to your own tasks,
the distaff and the loom, and keep the women
working hard as well. As for the fighting,
men will see to that, all who were born in Troy   150
but I most of all."
                    Hector aflash in arms
took up his horsechair-crested helmet once again.
And his loving wife went home, turning, glancing
back again and again and weeping live warm tears.
She quickly reached the sturdy house of Hector,   155
man-killing Hector,
and found her women gathered there inside
and stirred them all to a high pitch of mourning.
So in his house they raised the dirges for the dead,
for Hector still alive, his people were so convinced   160
that never again would he come home from battle,
never escape the Argives' rage and bloody hands.

[As Zeus fulfills the promise he made to Thetis in Book 1. The battle turns against the
Greeks—so much so that the Trojans are able to drive them back to their ships and encamp
in the plain nearby waiting to attack on the following day. The Greek leaders send an
embassy of three warriors—Odysseus, Ajax, and Achilles's old tutor Phoenix—to persuade
Achilles to rejoin the fighting. Odysseus enumerates a long list of gifts Agamemnon has
offered to bestow on Achilles (including marriage to Agamemnon's daughter) if he will return
to battle.]

Book 9 [The Embassy to Achilles]

The famous runner Achilles rose to his challenge:
"Royal son of Laertes, Odysseus, great tactician . . .
I must say what I have to say straight out,
must tell you how I feel and how all this will end—
so you won't crowd around me, one after another,   5
coaxing like a murmuring clutch of doves.

I hate that man like the very Gates of Death
who says one thing but hides another in his heart.
I will say it outright. That seems best to me.
Will Agamemnon win me over? Not for all the world,
I swear it—nor will the rest of the Achaeans. 10
No, what lasting thanks in the long run
for warring with our enemies, on and on, no end?
One and the same lot for the man who hangs back
and the man who battles hard. The same honor waits
for the coward and the brave. They both go down to Death, 15
the fighter who shirks, the one who works to exhaustion.
And what's laid up for me, what pittance? Nothing—
and after suffering hardships, year in, year out,
staking my life on the mortal risks of war. 20
    Like a mother bird hurrying morsels back
to her wingless young ones—whatever she can catch—
but it's all starvation wages for herself.
                                        So for me.
Many a sleepless night I've bivouacked in harness,
day after bloody day I've hacked my passage through, 25
fighting other soldiers to win their wives as prizes.
Twelve cities of men I've stormed and sacked from shipboard,
eleven I claim by land, on the fertile earth of Troy.
And from all I dragged off piles of splendid plunder,
hauled it away and always gave the lot to Agamemnon, 30
that son of Atreus—always skulking behind the lines,
safe in his fast ships—and he would take it all,
he'd parcel out some scraps but keep the lion's share.
Some he'd hand to the lords and kings—prizes of honor—
and they, they hold them still. From me alone, Achilles 35
of all Achaeans, he seizes, he keeps the wife I love . . .
Well *let* him bed her now—
enjoy her to the hilt!
                Why must we battle Trojans,
men of Argos? Why did he muster an army, lead us here,
that son of Atreus? Why, why in the world if not 40
for Helen with her loose and lustrous hair?
Are *they* the only men alive who love their wives,
those sons of Atreus? Never! Any decent man,
a man with sense, loves his own, cares for his own
as deeply as I, I loved that woman with all my heart, 45
though I won her like a trophy with my spear . . .
But now that he's torn my honor from my hands,
robbed me, lied to me—don't let him try me now.
I know *him* too well—he'll never win me over!

                                No, Odysseus,

let him rack his brains with you and the other captains   50
how to fight the raging fire off the ships. Look—
what a mighty piece of work he's done without *me!*
Why, he's erected a rampart, driven a trench around it,
broad, enormous, and planted stakes to guard it. No use!
He still can't block the power of man-killing Hector!   55
No, though as long as *I* fought on Achaea's lines
Hector had little lust to charge beyond his walls,
never ventured beyond the Scaean Gates and oak tree.
There he stood up to me alone one day—
and barely escaped my onslaught.   60
                    Ah but now,
since I have no desire to battle glorious Hector,
tomorrow at daybreak, once I have sacrificed
to Zeus and all the gods and loaded up my holds
and launched out on the breakers—watch, my friend,
if you'll take the time and care to see me off,   65
and you will see my squadrons sail at dawn,
fanning out on the Hellespont that swarms with fish,
my crews manning the oarlocks, rowing out with a will,
and if the famed god of the earthquake grants us safe passage,
the third day out we raise the dark rich soil of Phthia.   70
There lies my wealth, hoards of it, all I left behind
when I sailed to Troy on this, this insane voyage—
and still more hoards from here: gold, ruddy bronze,
women sashed and lovely, and gleaming gray iron,
and I will haul it home, all I won as plunder.   75
All but my prize of honor . . .
he who gave that prize has snatched it back again—
what outrage! That high and mighty King Agamemnon,
that son of Atreus!
                Go back and tell him all,
all I say—out in the open too—so other Achaeans   80
can wheel on him in anger if he still hopes—
who knows?—to deceive some other comrade.
                            Shameless,
inveterate—armored in shamelessness! Dog that he is,
he'd never dare to look me straight in the eyes again.
No, I'll never set heads together with that man—   85
no planning in common, no taking common action.
He cheated me, did me damage, wrong! But never again,
he'll never rob me blind with his twisting words again!
Once is enough for him. Die and be damned for all I care!
Zeus who rules the world has ripped his wits away.   90
His gifts, I loathe his gifts . . .
I wouldn't give you a splinter for that man!

Not if he gave me ten times as much, twenty times over, all
he possesses now, and all that could pour in from the world's end—
not all the wealth that's freighted into Orchomenos,[20] even into Thebes,
Egyptian Thebes[21] where the houses overflow with the greatest troves of treasure.   95
Thebes with the hundred gates and through each gate battalions,
two hundred fighters surge to war with teams and chariots—
no, not if his gifts outnumbered all the grains of sand
and dust in the earth—no, not even then could Agamemnon
bring my fighting spirit round until he pays me back,   100
pays full measure for all his heartbreaking outrage!
  His daughter . . . I will marry no daughter of Agamemnon.
Not if she rivaled Aphrodite in all her golden glory,
not if she matched the crafts of clear-eyed Athena,
not even then would I make *her* my wife! No,   105
let her father pitch on some other Argive—
one who can please *him*, a greater king than I.
If the gods pull me through and I reach home alive,
Peleus needs no help to fetch a bride for me himself.   110
Plenty of Argive women wait in Hellas and in Phthia,
daughters of lords who rule their citadels in power.
Whomever I want I'll make my cherished wife—at home.
Time and again my fiery spirit drove me to win a wife,
a fine partner to please my heart, to enjoy with her   115
the treasures my old father Peleus piled high.
I say no wealth is worth my life! Not all they claim
was stored in the depths of Troy, that city built on riches,
in the old days of peace before the sons of Achaea came—
not all the gold held fast in the Archer's rocky vaults,   120
in Phoebus Apollo's house on Pytho's sheer cliffs!
Cattle and fat sheep can all be had for the raiding,
tripods all for the trading, and tawny-headed stallions.
But a man's life breath cannot come back again—
no raiders in force, no trading brings it back,   125
once it slips through a man's clenched teeth.
                                        Mother tells me,
the immortal goddess Thetis with her glistening feet,
that two fates bear me on to the day of death.
If I hold out here and I lay siege to Troy,
my journey home is gone, but my glory never dies.   130
If I voyage back to the fatherland I love,
my pride, my glory dies . . .

---

20. A city in Boeotia in central Greece, famous
    for its wealth in the Mycenaean period (c.
    1400–1200 B.C.E.), centuries before the
    Iliad was sung in its present form.

21. The *Iliad* preserves the ancient memory of
    this Egyptian city's prosperity and power,
    at their height not later than the 14th
    century B.C.E..

[handwritten margin note: Achilles has 2 choices — stay & fight in Troy — have glorious life or avoid fighting and live.]

true, but the life that's left me will be long,
the stroke of death will not come on me quickly.
    One thing more. To the rest I'd pass on this advice: 135
sail home now! You will never set your eyes
on the day of doom that topples looming Troy.
Thundering Zeus has spread his hands above her—
her armies have taken heart!
                                            So you go back
to the great men of Achaea. You report my message—   140
since this is the privilege of senior chiefs—
let *them* work out a better plan of action,
use their imaginations now to save the ships
and Achaea's armies pressed to their hollow hulls.
This maneuver will never work for them, this scheme   145
they hatched for the moment as I raged on and on.

[Agamemnon's lavish offer fails to persuade Achilles to reenter the battle, although the embassy's appeals to him on the basis of friendship have their effect; he will not leave Troy as he had threatened, but he refuses to fight until enemy fire comes to his own ships. The Greeks continue to suffer increasingly drastic reverses, until finally, with many of their major fighters wounded and with the Trojans menacing their ships, Patroclus tries to convince Achilles to rejoin the fighting.]

Book 16 [*Patroclus Fights and Dies*]

So they fought to the death around that benched beaked ship
as Patroclus reached Achilles, his great commander,
and wept warm tears like a dark spring running down
some desolate rock face, its shaded currents flowing.
And the brilliant runner Achilles saw him coming,   5
filled with pity and spoke out winging words:
"Why in tears, Patroclus?
Like a girl, a baby running after her mother,
begging to be picked up, and she tugs her skirts,
holding her back as she tries to hurry off—all tears,   10
fawning up at her, till she takes her in her arms . . .
That's how you look, Patroclus, streaming live tears.
But why? Some news for the Myrmidons, news for me?
Some message from Phthia that you alone have heard?
They tell me Menoetius,[22] Actor's son, is still alive,   15
and Peleus, Aeacus' son, lives on among his Myrmidons—
if both our fathers had died, we'd have some cause for grief.
Or weeping over the Argives, are you? Seeing them die
against the hollow ships, repaid for their offenses?

---

22. Patroclus's father.

Out with it now! Don't harbor it deep inside you.   20
We must share it all."
                              With a wrenching groan
you answered your friend, Patroclus O my rider:
"Achilles, son of Peleus, greatest of the Achaeans,
spare me your anger, please—
such heavy blows have overwhelmed the troops.   25
Our former champions, all laid up in the ships,
all are hit by arrows or run through by spears.
There's powerful Diomedes brought down by an archer,
Odysseus wounded, and Agamemnon too, the famous spearman,
and Eurypylus took an arrow-shot in the thigh . . .   30
Healers are working over them, using all their drugs,
trying to bind the wounds—
                              But *you* are intractable, Achilles!
Pray god such anger never seizes *me,* such rage you nurse.
Cursed in your own courage! What good will a man,
even one in the next generation, get from you   35
unless you defend the Argives from disaster?
You heart of iron! He was not your father,
the horseman Peleus—Thetis was not your mother.
Never. The salt gray sunless ocean gave you birth
and the towering blank rocks—your temper's so relentless.
But still, if down deep some prophecy makes you balk,   40
some doom your noble mother revealed to you from Zeus,
well and good: at least send *me* into battle, quickly.
Let the whole Myrmidon army follow my command—
I might bring some light of victory to our Argives!   45
And give me your own fine armor to buckle on my back,
so the Trojans might take *me* for you, Achilles, yes,
hold off from attack, and Achaea's fighting sons
get second wind, exhausted as they are . . .
Breathing room in war is all too brief.   50
We're fresh, unbroken. The enemy's battle-weary—
we could roll those broken Trojans back to Troy,
clear of the ships and shelters!"
                              So he pleaded,
lost in his own great innocence . . .
condemned to beg for his own death and brutal doom.   55
And moved now to his depths, the famous runner cried,
"No, no, my prince, Patroclus, what are you saying?
Prophecies? None that touch me. None I know of.
No doom my noble mother revealed to me from Zeus,
just this terrible pain that wounds me to the quick—   60
when one man attempts to plunder a man his equal,
to commandeer a prize, exulting so in his own power.

Achilles still won't go back —

That's the pain that wounds me, suffering such humiliation.
That girl—the sons of Achaea picked her as my prize,
and I'd sacked a walled city, won her with my spear   65
but right from my grasp he tears her, mighty Agamemnon,
that son of Atreus! Treating me like some vagabond,
some outcast stripped of all my rights . . .
                                        Enough.
Let bygones be bygones now. Done is done.
How on earth can a man rage on forever?   70
Still, by god, I said I would not relax my anger,
not till the cries and carnage reached my own ships.
So you, you strap my splendid armor on your back,
you lead our battle-hungry Myrmidons into action!—
if now, in fact, the black cloud of the Trojans   75
blasts down on the ships with full gale force,
our backs to the breaking surf but clinging still
to a cramped strip of land—the Argives, lost.
The whole city of Troy comes trampling down on us,
daring, wild—why? They cannot see the brow of my helmet   80
flash before their eyes—Oh they'd soon run for their lives
and choke the torrent-beds of the field with all their corpses
if only the mighty Agamemnon met me with respect:
now, as it is, they're fighting round our camp!
No spear rages now in the hand of Diomedes,   85
keen to save the Argives from disaster . . .
I can't even hear the battle cry of Agamemnon
break from his hated skull. But it's man-killing Hector
calling his Trojans on, his war cries crashing round me,
savage cries of his Trojans sweeping the whole plain,   90
victors bringing the Argive armies to their knees.
Even so, Patroclus, fight disaster off the ships,
fling yourself at the Trojans full force—
before they gut our hulls with leaping fire
and tear away the beloved day of our return.   95
But take this command to heart—obey it to the end.
So you can win great honor, great glory for me
in the eyes of all the Argive ranks, and they,
they'll send her back, my lithe and lovely girl,
and top it off with troves of glittering gifts.   100
Once you have whipped the enemy from the fleet
you must come back, Patroclus. Even if Zeus
the thundering lord of Hera lets you seize your glory,
you must not burn for war against these Trojans,
madmen lusting for battle—not without *me*—   105
you will only make *my* glory that much less . . .
You must not, lost in the flush and fire of triumph,

slaughtering Trojans outright, drive your troops to Troy—
what if one of the gods who never die comes down
from Olympus heights to intervene in battle?
The deadly Archer loves his Trojans dearly.   110
No, you must turn back—
soon as you bring the light of victory to the ships.
Let the rest of them cut themselves to pieces on the plain!
Oh would to god—Father Zeus, Athena and lord Apollo—   115
not one of all these Trojans could flee his death, not one,
no Argive either, but we could stride from the slaughter
so we could bring Troy's hallowed crown of towers
toppling down around us—you and I alone!"

          . . .

    But Achilles strode back to his shelter now   120
and opened the lid of the princely inlaid sea chest
that glistening-footed Thetis stowed in his ship to carry,
filled to the brim with war-shirts, windproof cloaks
and heavy fleecy rugs. And there it rested . . .
his handsome, well-wrought cup. No other man   125
would drink the shining wine from its glowing depths,
nor would Achilles pour the wine to any other god,
none but Father Zeus. Lifting it from the chest
he purified it with sulphur crystals first
then rinsed it out with water running clear,   130
washed his hands and filled it bright with wine.
And then, taking a stand before his lodge, he prayed,
pouring the wine to earth and scanning the high skies
and the god who loves the lightning never missed a word:
"King Zeus—Pelasgian Zeus,[23] lord of Dodona's holy shrine,   135
dwelling far away, brooding over Dodona's bitter winters!
Your prophets dwelling round you, Zeus, the Selli
sleeping along the ground with unwashed feet . . .
If you honored me last time and heard my prayer
and rained destruction down on all Achaea's ranks,   140
now, once more, I beg you, bring my prayer to pass!
I myself hold out on shore with the beached ships here
but I send my comrade forth to war with troops of Myrmidons—
Launch glory along with him, high lord of thunder, Zeus!
Fill his heart with courage—so even Hector learns   145
if Patroclus has the skill to fight his wars alone,
my friend-in-arms, or his hands can rage unvanquished
only when I go wading in and face the grind of battle.

---

23. Pelasgian is a name used elsewhere in the
    poem to denote the region of Achilles's
    home in northern Greece; in the west of
    that region, in Dodona, was an ancient
    oracle of Zeus. The Selloi seem to have
    been the priests of Zeus at Dodona.

But once he repels the roaring onslaught from the ships
let him come back to me and our fast fleet—unharmed—   150
with all my armor round him, all our comrades
fighting round my friend!"
                              So Achilles prayed
and Zeus in all his wisdom heard those prayers.
One prayer the Father granted, the other he denied:
Patroclus would drive the onslaught off the ships—   155
that much Zeus granted, true,
but denied him safe and sound return from battle.

[After Achilles agrees to let Patroclus enter the battle wearing Achilles's armor, Patroclus valiantly manages to turn the battle against the Trojans but is killed by Hector with assistance from Apollo. Hector strips Achilles's armor from Patroclus's body. Bitter fighting ensues over the body, and the news of Patroclus's death is brought to Achilles.]

Book 18 [The Shield of Achilles]

So the men fought on like a mass of whirling fire
as swift Antilochus[24] raced the message toward Achilles.
Sheltered under his curving, beaked ships he found him,
foreboding, deep down, all that had come to pass.
Agonizing now he probed his own great heart: 5
"Why, why? Our long-haired Achaeans routed again,
driven in terror off the plain to crowd the ships, but why?
Dear gods, don't bring to pass the grief that haunts my heart—
the prophecy that mother revealed to me one time . . .
she said the best of the Myrmidons—while I lived—   10
would fall at Trojan hands and leave the light of day.
And now he's dead, I know it. Menoetius' gallant son,
my headstrong friend! And I told Patroclus clearly,
'Once you have beaten off the lethal fire, quick,
come back to the ships—you must not battle Hector!' "   15
    As such fears went churning through his mind
the warlord Nestor's son drew near him now,
streaming warm tears, to give the dreaded message:
"Ah son of royal Peleus, what you must hear from me!
What painful news—would to god it had never happened!   20
Patroclus has fallen. They're fighting over his corpse.
He's stripped, naked—Hector with that flashing helmet,
Hector has your arms!"
                        So the captain reported.
A black cloud of grief came shrouding over Achilles.
Both hands clawing the ground for soot and filth,   25

---

24. A Greek warrior, son of Nestor and friend
    of Achilles.

he poured it over his head, fouled his handsome face
and black ashes settled onto his fresh clean war-shirt.
Overpowered in all his power, sprawled in the dust,
Achilles lay there, fallen . . .
tearing his hair, defiling it with his own hands.   30
And the women he and Patroclus carried off as captives
caught the grief in their hearts and keened and wailed,
out of the tents they ran to ring the great Achilles,
all of them beat their breasts with clenched fists,
sank to the ground, each woman's knees gave way.   35
Antilochus kneeling near, weeping uncontrollably,
clutched Achilles' hands as he wept his proud heart out—
for fear he would slash his throat with an iron blade.
Achilles suddenly loosed a terrible, wrenching cry
and his noble mother heard him, seated near her father,   40
the Old Man of the Sea in the salt green depths,
and she cried out in turn. And immortal sea-nymphs
gathered round their sister, all the Nereids[25] dwelling
down the sounding depths, they all came rushing now—
Glitter, blossoming Spray and the swells' Embrace,   45
Fair-Isle and shadowy Cavern, Mist and Spindrift,
ocean nymphs of the glances pooling deep and dark,
Race-with-the-Waves and Headlands' Hope and Safe Haven,
Glimmer of Honey, Suave-and-Soothing, Whirlpool, Brilliance,
Bounty and First Light and Speeder of Ships and buoyant Power,   50
Welcome Home and Bather of Meadows and Master's Lovely Consort,
Gift of the Sea, Eyes of the World and the famous milk-white Calm
and Truth and Never-Wrong and the queen who rules the tides in beauty
and in rushed Glory and Healer of Men and the one who rescues kings
and Sparkler, Down-from-the-Cliffs, sleek-haired Strands of Sand   55
and all the rest of the Nereids dwelling down the depths.
The silver cave was shimmering full of sea-nymphs,
all in one mounting chorus beating their breasts
as Thetis launched the dirge: "Hear me, sisters,
daughters of Nereus, so you all will know it well—   60
listen to all the sorrows welling in my heart!
I am agony—
                    mother of grief and greatness—O my child!
Yes, I gave birth to a flawless, mighty son . . .
the splendor of heroes, and he shot up like a young branch,
like a fine tree I reared him—the orchard's crowning glory—   65
but only to send him off in the beaked ships to Troy
to battle Trojans! Never again will I embrace him

---

25. Thetis's sisters, daughters of the sea-god   different aspects of the sea, as the literal
    Nereus. Many of their names are etymo-   translation of them here makes clear.
    logically related to, or descriptive of,

striding home through the doors of Peleus' house.
And long as I have him with me, still alive,
looking into the sunlight, he is racked with anguish.   70
And I, I go to his side—nothing I do can help him.
Nothing. But go I shall, to see my darling boy,
to hear what grief has come to break his heart
while he holds back from battle."
                                       So Thetis cried
as she left the cave and her sisters swam up with her,   75
all in a tide of tears, and billowing round them now
the ground swell heaved open. And once they reached
the fertile land of Troy they all streamed ashore,
row on row in a long cortege, the sea-nymphs
filing up where the Myrmidon ships lay hauled,   80
clustered closely round the great runner Achilles . . .
As he groaned from the depths his mother rose before him
and sobbing a sharp cry, cradled her son's head in her hands
and her words were all compassion, winging pity: "My child—
why in tears? What sorrow has touched your heart?   85
Tell me, please. Don't harbor it deep inside you.
Zeus has accomplished everything you wanted,
just as you raised your hands and prayed that day.
All the sons of Achaea are pinned against the ships
and all for want of you—they suffer shattering losses."   90
     And groaning deeply the matchless runner answered,
"O dear mother, true! All those burning desires
Olympian Zeus has brought to pass for me—
but what joy to me now? My dear comrade's dead—
Patroclus—the man I loved beyond all other comrades,   95
loved as my own life—I've lost him—Hector's killed him,
stripped the gigantic armor off his back, a marvel to behold—
my burnished gear! Radiant gifts the gods presented Peleus
that day they drove you into a mortal's marriage bed . . .
I wish you'd lingered deep with the deathless sea-nymphs,   100
lived at ease, and Peleus carried home a mortal bride.
But now, as it is, sorrows, unending sorrows must surge
within your heart as well—for your own son's death.
Never again will you embrace him striding home.
My spirit rebels—I've lost the will to live,   105
to take my stand in the world of men—unless,
before all else, Hector's battered down by my spear
and gasps away his life, the blood-price for Patroclus,
Menoetius' gallant son he's killed and stripped!"
     But Thetis answered, warning through her tears,   110
"You're doomed to a short life, my son, from all you say!
For hard on the heels of Hector's death your death

must come at once—"
                    "Then let me die at once"—
Achilles burst out, despairing—"since it was not my fate
to save my dearest comrade from his death! Look,   115
a world away from his fatherland he's perished,
lacking me, my fighting strength, to defend him.
But now, since I shall not return to my fatherland . . .
nor did I bring one ray of hope to my Patroclus,
nor to the rest of all my steadfast comrades,   120
countless ranks struck down by mighty Hector—
No, no, here I sit by the ships . . .
a useless, dead weight on the good green earth—
I, no man my equal among the bronze-armed Achaeans,
not in battle, only in wars of words that others win.   125
If only strife could die from the lives of gods and men
and anger that drives the sanest man to flare in outrage—
bitter gall, sweeter than dripping streams of honey,
that swarms in people's chests and blinds like smoke—
just like the anger Agamemnon king of men   130
has roused within me now . . .
                    Enough.
Let bygones be bygones. Done is done.
Despite my anguish I will beat it down,
the fury mounting inside me, down by force.
But now I'll go and meet that murderer head-on,   135
that Hector who destroyed the dearest life I know.
For my own death, I'll meet it freely—whenever Zeus
and the other deathless gods would like to bring it on!
Not even Heracles fled his death, for all his power,
favorite son as he was to Father Zeus the King.   140
Fate crushed him, and Hera's savage anger.[26]
And I too, if the same fate waits for me . . .
I'll lie in peace, once I've gone down to death.
But now, for the moment, let me seize great glory!—
and drive some woman of Troy or deep-breasted Dardan[27]   145
to claw with both hands at her tender cheeks and wipe away
her burning tears as the sobs come choking from her throat—
they'll learn that I refrained from war a good long time!
Don't try to hold me back from the fighting, mother,
love me as you do. You can't persuade me now."   150

[Thetis travels to Olympus to ask the divine craftsman Hephaestus to make armor for Achilles, to replace that worn by Patroclus and stripped from his body by Hector.]

[handwritten margin note: willing death for free Patroclus]

---

26. Hera hated Zeus's son Heracles because he was born to a mortal woman, Alcmene, whom Zeus had seduced.

27. The Dardanians were neighbors and allies of the Trojans, related to them through their ancestor Dardanus.

. . . Thetis burst into tears, her voice welling:
"Oh Hephaestus—who of all the goddesses on Olympus,
who has borne such withering sorrows in her heart?
Such pain as Zeus has given me, above all others!
Me out of all the daughters of the sea he chose   5
to yoke to a mortal man, Peleus, son of Aeacus,
and I endured his bed, a mortal's bed, resisting
with all my will. And now he lies in the halls,
broken with grisly age, but now my griefs are worse.
Remember? Zeus also gave me a son to bear and breed,   10
the splendor of heroes, and he shot up like a young branch,
like a fine tree I reared him—the orchard's crowning glory—
but only to send him off in the beaked ships to Troy
to battle Trojans! Never again will I embrace him
striding home through the doors of Peleus' house.   15
And long as I have him with me, still alive,
looking into the sunlight, he is racked with anguish.
I go to his side—nothing I do can help him. Nothing.
That girl the sons of Achaea picked out for his prize—
right from his grasp the mighty Agamemnon tore her,   20
and grief for her has been gnawing at his heart.
But then the Trojans pinned the Achaeans tight
against their sterns, they gave them no way out,
and the Argive warlords begged my son to help,
they named in full the troves of glittering gifts   25
they'd send his way. But at that point he refused
to beat disaster off—refused himself, that is—
but he buckled his own armor round Patroclus,
sent him into battle with an army at his back.
And all day long they fought at the Scaean Gates,   30
that very day they would have stormed the city too,
if Apollo had not killed Menoetius' gallant son
as he laid the Trojans low—Apollo cut him down
among the champions there and handed Hector glory.
So now I come, I throw myself at your knees,   35
please help me! Give my son—he won't live long—
a shield and helmet and tooled greaves with ankle-straps
and armor for his chest. All that he had was lost,
lost when the Trojans killed his steadfast friend.
Now he lies on the ground—his heart is breaking."   40

   And the famous crippled Smith[28] replied, "Courage!
Anguish for all that armor—sweep it from your mind.

---

28. Different myths give differing accounts of
the lameness of Hephaestus, god of the
forge; either he was lame from birth or as
a result of having been thrown from
Olympus by Zeus or Hera.

If only I could hide him away from pain and death,
that day his grim destiny comes to take Achilles,
as surely as glorious armor shall be his, armor   45
that any man in the world of men will marvel at
through all the years to come—whoever sees its splendor."

With that he left her there and made for his bellows,
turning them on the fire, commanding, "Work—to work!"
And the bellows, all twenty, blew on the crucibles,   50
breathing with all degrees of shooting, fiery heat
as the god hurried on—a blast for the heavy work,
a quick breath for the light, all precisely gauged
to the god of fire's wish and the pace of the work in hand.
Bronze he flung in the blaze, tough, durable bronze   55
and tin and priceless gold and silver, and then,
planting the huge anvil upon its block, he gripped
his mighty hammer in one hand, the other gripped his tongs.
And first Hephaestus makes a great and massive shield,
blazoning well-wrought emblems all across its surface,   60
raising a rim around it, glittering, triple-ply
with a silver shield-strap run from edge to edge
and five layers of metal to build the shield itself,
and across its vast expanse with all his craft and cunning
the god creates a world of gorgeous immortal work.   65
There he made the earth and there the sky and the sea
and the inexhaustible blazing sun and the moon rounding full
and there the constellations, all that crown the heavens,
the Pleiades and the Hyades, Orion in all his power too
and the Great Bear[29] that mankind also calls the Wagon: 70
she wheels on her axis always fixed, watching Orion,
and she alone is denied a plunge in the Ocean's baths.
And he forged on the shield two noble cities filled
with mortal men. With weddings and wedding feasts in one
and under glowing torches they brought forth the brides   75
from the women's chambers, marching through the streets
while choir on choir the wedding song rose high
and the young men came dancing, whirling round in rings
and among them the flutes and harps kept up their stirring call—
women rushed to the doors and each stood moved with wonder.   80
And the people massed, streaming into the marketplace
where a quarrel had broken out and two men struggled
over the blood-price for a kinsman just murdered.
One declaimed in public, vowing payment in full—
the other spurned him, he would not take a thing—   85
so both men pressed for a judge to cut the knot.

---

29. The "Big Dipper."

Description of
War & Peace.

The crowd cheered on both, they took both sides,
but heralds held them back as the city elders sat
on polished stone benches, forming the sacred circle,
grasping in hand the staffs of clear-voiced heralds,   90
and each leapt to his feet to plead the case in turn.
Two bars of solid gold shone on the ground before them;
a prize for the judge who'd speak the straightest verdict.
  But circling the other city camped a divided army
gleaming in battle-gear, and two plans split their ranks: 95
to plunder the city or share the riches with its people,
hoards the handsome citadel stored within its depths.
But the people were not surrendering, not at all.
They armed for a raid, hoping to break the siege—
loving wives and innocent children standing guard   100
on the ramparts, flanked by elders bent with age
as men marched out to war. Ares[30] and Pallas led them,
both burnished gold, gold the attire they donned, and great,
magnificent in their armor—gods for all the world,
looming up in their brillance, towering over troops.   105
And once they reached the perfect spot for attack,
a watering place where all the herds collected,
there they crouched, wrapped in glowing bronze.
Detached from the ranks, two scouts took up their posts,
the eyes of the army waiting to spot a convoy,   110
the enemy's flocks and crook-horned cattle coming . . .
Come they did, quickly, two shepherds behind them,
playing their hearts out on their pipes—treachery
never crossed their minds. But the soldiers saw them,
rushed them, cut off at a stroke the herds of oxen   115
and sleek sheep-flocks glistening silver-gray
and killed the herdsmen too. Now the besiegers,
soon as they heard the uproar burst from the cattle
as they debated, huddled in council, mounted at once
behind their racing teams, rode hard to the rescue,   120
arrived at once, and lining up for assault
both armies battled it out along he river banks—
they raked each other with hurtling bronze-tipped spears.
And Strife and Havoc plunged in the fight, and violent Death—
now seizing a man alive with fresh wounds, now one unhurt,   125
now hauling a dead man through the slaughter by the heels,
the cloak on her back stained red with human blood.
So they clashed and fought like living, breathing men
grappling each other's corpses, dragging off the dead.
  And he forged a fallow field, broad rich plowland   130

---

30. The god of war.

tilled for the third time, and across it crews of plowmen
wheeled their teams, driving them up and back and soon
as they'd reach the end-strip, moving into the turn,
a man would run up quickly
and hand them a cup of honeyed, mellow wine   135
as the crews would turn back down along the furrows,
pressing again to reach the end of the deep fallow field
and the earth churned black behind them, like earth churning,
solid gold as it was—that was the wonder of Hephaestus' work.

    And he forged a king's estate where harvesters labored,   140
reaping the ripe grain, swinging their whetted scythes.
Some stalks fell in line with the reapers, row on row,
and others the sheaf-binders girded round with ropes,
three binders standing over the sheaves, behind them
boys gathering up the cut swaths, filling their arms,   145
supplying grain to the binders, endless bundles.
And there in the midst the king,
scepter in hand at the head of the reaping-rows,
stood tall in silence, rejoicing in his heart.
And off to the side, beneath a spreading oak,   150
the heralds were setting out the harvest feast,
they were dressing a great ox they had slaughtered,
while attendant women poured out barley, generous,
glistening handfuls strewn for the reapers' midday meal.

    And he forged a thriving vineyard loaded with clusters,   155
bunches of lustrous grapes in gold, ripening deep purple
and climbing vines shot up on silver vine-poles.
And round it he cut a ditch in dark blue enamel
and round the ditch he staked a fence in tin.
And one lone footpath led toward the vineyard   160
and down it the pickers ran
whenever they went to strip the grapes at vintage—
girls and boys, their hearts leaping in innocence,
bearing away the sweet ripe fruit in wicker baskets.
And there among them a young boy plucked his lyre,   165
so clear it could break the heart with longing,
and what he sang was a dirge for the dying year,
lovely . . . his fine voice rising and falling low
as the rest followed, all together, frisking, singing,
shouting, their dancing footsteps beating out the time.   170

    And he forged on the shield a herd of longhorn cattle,
working the bulls in beaten gold and tin, lowing loud
and rumbling out of the farmyard dung to pasture
along a rippling stream, along the swaying reeds.
And the golden drovers kept the herd in line,   175
four in all, with nine dogs at their heels,

their paws flickering quickly—a savage roar!—
a crashing attack—and a pair of ramping lions
had seized a bull from the cattle's front ranks—
he bellowed out as they dragged him off in agony.   180
Packs of dogs and the young herdsmen rushed to help
but the lions ripping open the hide of the huge bull
were gulping down the guts and the black pooling blood
while the herdsmen yelled the fast pack on—no use.
The hounds shrank from sinking teeth in the lions,   185
they balked, hunching close, barking, cringing away.
     And the famous crippled Smith forged a meadow
deep in a shaded glen for shimmering flocks to graze,
with shepherds' steadings, well-roofed huts and sheepfolds.
     And the crippled Smith brought all his art to bear   190
on a dancing circle, broad as the circle Daedalus[31]
once laid out on Cnossos spacious fields
for Ariadne the girl with lustrous hair.
Here young boys and girls, beauties courted
with costly gifts of oxen, danced and danced,   195
linking their arms, gripping each other's wrists.
And the girls wore robes of linen light and flowing,
the boys wore finespun tunics rubbed with a gloss of oil,
the girls were crowned with a bloom of fresh garlands,
the boys swung golden daggers hung on silver belts.   200
And now they would run in rings on their skilled feet,
nimbly, quick as a crouching potter spins his wheel,
palming it smoothly, giving it practice twirls
to see it run, and now they would run in rows,
in rows crisscrossing rows—rapturous dancing.   205
A breathless crowd stood round them struck with joy
and through them a pair of tumblers dashed and sprang,
whirling in leaping handsprings, leading out the dance.
     And he forged the Ocean River's mighty power girdling
round the outmost rim of the welded indestructible shield.   210
     And once the god had made that great and massive shield
he made Achilles a breastplate brighter than gleaming fire,
he made him a sturdy helmet to fit the fighter's temples,
beautiful, burnished work, and raised its golden crest
and made him greaves of flexing, pliant tin.   215
                                             Now,
when the famous crippled Smith had finished off
that grand array of armor, lifting it in his arms
he laid it all at the feet of Achilles' mother Thetis—

---

31. Master craftsman, famous in myth for his
    elaborate constructions designed for the
    family of King Minos of Crete, Ariadne's
    father, in the chief Cretan city, Cnossos.

and down she flashed like a hawk from snowy Mount Olympus
bearing the brilliant gear, the god of fire's gift.   220

[Armed with the weapons forged for him by Hephaestus, Achilles returns to battle,
slaughtering numerous Trojans in revenge for the killing of Patroclus. Apollo, always a Trojan
partisan, diverts Achilles's relentless pursuit by taking the form of a Trojan warrior in order
to draw Achilles away from the rest of the retreating Trojans, all of whom flee into the
city—except Hector, who remains outside the walls.]

Book 22 [The Death of Hector]

So all through Troy the men who had fled like panicked fawns
were wiping off their sweat, drinking away their thirst,
leaning along the city's massive ramparts now
while Achaean troops, sloping shields to shoulders,
closed against the walls. But there stood Hector,   5
shackled fast by his deadly fate, holding his ground,
exposed in front of Troy and the Scaean Gates.
And now Apollo turned to taunt Achilles:
"Why are you chasing *me?* Why waste your speed?—
son of Peleus, you a mortal and I a deathless god.   10
You still don't know that I am immortal, do you?—
straining to catch me in your fury! Have you forgotten?
There's a war to fight with the Trojans you stampeded,
look, they're packed inside their city walls, but you,
you've slipped away out here. You can't kill *me*—   15
I can never die—it's not my fate!"
                        Enraged at that,
Achilles shouted in mid-stride, "You've blocked my way,
you distant, deadly Archer, deadliest god of all—
you made me swerve away from the rampart there.
Else what a mighty Trojan army had gnawed the dust   20
before they could ever straggle through their gates!
Now you've robbed me of great glory, saved their lives
with all your deathless ease. Nothing for you to fear,
no punishment to come. Oh I'd pay you back
if I only had the power at my command!"   25

   No more words—he dashed toward the city,
heart racing for some great exploit, rushing on
like a champion stallion drawing a chariot full tilt,
sweeping across the plain in easy, tearing strides—
so Achilles hurtled on, driving legs and knees.   30
   And old King Priam was first to see him coming,
surging over the plain, blazing like the star
that rears at harvest, flaming up in its brilliance,—
far outshining the countless stars in the night sky,

that star they call Orion's Dog[32]—brightest of all   35
but a fatal sign emblazoned on the heavens,
it brings such killing fever down on wretched men.
So the bronze flared on his chest as on he raced—
and the old man moaned, flinging both hands high,
beating his head and groaning deep he called,   40
begging his dear son who stood before the gates,
unshakable, furious to fight Achilles to the death.
The old man cried, pitifully, hands reaching out to him,
"Oh Hector! Don't just stand there, don't, dear child,
waiting that man's attack—alone, cut off from friends!   45
You'll meet your doom at once, beaten down by Achilles,
so much stronger than you—that hard, headlong man.
Oh if only the gods loved him as much as I do . . .
dogs and vultures would eat his fallen corpse at once!—
with what a load of misery lifted from my spirit.   50
That man who robbed me of many sons, brave boys,
cutting them down or selling them off as slaves,
shipped to islands half the world away . . .
Even now there are two, Lycaon and Polydorus[33]—
I cannot find them among the soldiers crowding Troy,   55
those sons Laothoë bore me, Laothoë queen of women.
But if they are still alive in the enemy's camp,
then we'll ransom them back with bronze and gold.
We have hoards inside the walls, the rich dowry
old and famous Altes presented with his daughter.   60
But if they're dead already, gone to the House of Death,
what grief to their mother's heart and mine—we gave them life.
For the rest of Troy, though, just a moment's grief
unless you too are battered down by Achilles.
Back, come back! Inside the walls, my boy!   65
Rescue the men of Troy and the Trojan women—
don't hand the great glory to Peleus' son,
bereft of your own sweet life yourself.
                                                     Pity me too!—
still in my senses, true, but a harrowed, broken man
marked out by doom—past the threshold of old age . . .   70
and Father Zeus will waste me with a hideous fate,
and after I've lived to look on so much horror!
My sons laid low, my daughters dragged away
and the treasure-chambers looted, helpless babies
hurled to the earth in the red barbarity of war . . .   75

---

32. Also called Sirius, the brightest star in the   Achilles, Polydorus in Book 20 and Ly-
late summer sky.   caon in Book 21.
33. These sons of Priam were killed by

my sons' wives hauled off by the Argives' bloody hands!
And I, I last of all—the dog before my doors
will eat me raw, once some enemy brings me down
with his sharp bronze sword or spits me with a spear,
wrenching the life out of my body, yes, the very dogs   80
I bred in my own halls to share my table, guard my gates—
mad, rabid at heart they'll lap their master's blood
and loll before my doors.
                            Ah for a young man
all looks fine and noble if he goes down in war,
hacked to pieces under a slashing bronze blade—   85
he lies there dead . . . but whatever death lays bare,
all wounds are marks of glory. When an old man's killed
and the dogs go at the gray head and the gray beard
and mutilate the genitals—that is the cruelest sight
in all our wretched lives!"   90
                            So the old man groaned
and seizing his gray hair tore it out by the roots
but he could not shake the fixed resolve of Hector.
And his mother wailed now, standing beside Priam,
weeping freely, loosing her robes with one hand
and holding out her bare breast with the other,   95
her words pouring forth in a flight of grief and tears:
"Hector, my child! Look—have some respect for *this*!
Pity your mother too, if I ever gave you the breast
to soothe your troubles, remember it now, dear boy—
beat back that savage man from safe inside the walls!   100
Don't go forth, a champion pitted against him—
merciless, brutal man. If he kills you now,
how can I ever mourn you on your deathbed?—
dear branch in bloom, dear child I brought to birth!—
Neither I nor your wife, that warm, generous woman . . .   105
Now far beyond our reach, now by the Argive ships
the rushing dogs will tear you, bolt your flesh!"

     So they wept, the two of them crying out
to their dear son, both pleading time and again
but they could not shake the fixed resolve of Hector.   110
No, he waited Achilles, coming on, gigantic in power.
As a snake in the hills, guarding his hole, awaits a man—
bloated with poison, deadly hatred seething inside him,
glances flashing fire as he coils round his lair . . .
so Hector, nursing his quenchless fury, gave no ground,   115
leaning his burnished shield against a jutting wall,
but harried still, he probed his own brave heart:
"No way out. If I slip inside the gates and walls,

Polydamas will be first to heap disgrace on me—
he was the one who urged me to lead our Trojans   120
back to Ilium just last night, the disastrous night
Achilles rose in arms like a god. But did I give way?
Not at all. And how much better it would have been!
Now my army's ruined, thanks to my own reckless pride,
I would die of shame to face the men of Troy   125
and the Trojan women trailing their long robes . . .
Someone less of a man than I will say, 'Our Hector—
staking all on his own strength, he destroyed his army!'
So they will mutter. So now, better by far for me
to stand up to Achilles, kill him, come home alive   130
or die at his hands in glory out before the walls.
But wait—what if I put down my studded shield
and heavy helmet, prop my spear on the rampart
and go forth, just as I am, to meet Achilles,
noble Prince Achilles . . .   135
why, I could promise to give back Helen, yes,
and all her treasures with her, all those riches
Paris once hauled home to Troy in the hollow ships—
and they were the cause of all our endless fighting—
Yes, yes, return it all to the sons of Atreus now   140
to haul away, and then, at the same time, divide
the rest with all the Argives, all the city holds,
and then I'd take an oath for the Trojan royal council
that we will hide nothing! Share and share alike the hoards
our handsome citadel stores within its depths and—   145
Why debate, my friend? Why thrash things out?
I must not go and implore him. He'll show no mercy,
no respect for me, my rights—he'll cut me down
straight off—stripped of defenses like a woman
once I have loosed the armor off my body.   150
No way to parley with that man—not now—
not from behind some oak or rock to whisper,
like a boy and a young girl, lovers' secrets
a boy and girl might whisper to each other . . .
Better to clash in battle, now, at once—   155
see which fighter Zeus awards the glory!"
                                        So he wavered,
waiting there, but Achilles was closing on him now
like the god of war, the fighter's helmet flashing,
over his right shoulder shaking the Pelian[34] ash spear,

[handwritten margin note: This is realistic interpretation of how a man would feel. Hector doesn't want to lose his honor.]

---

34. Achilles's spear, made of wood from Mt.
    Pelion, had been given to him by his
    father.

that terror, and the bronze around his body flared 160
like a raging fire or the rising, blazing sun.
Hector looked up, saw him, started to tremble,
nerve gone, he could hold his ground no longer,
he left the gates behind and away he fled in fear—
and Achilles went for him, fast, sure of his speed 165
as the wild mountain hawk, the quickest thing on wings,
launching smoothly, swooping down on a cringing dove
and the dove flits out from under, the hawk screaming
over the quarry, plunging over and over, his fury
driving him down to beak and tear his kill— 170
so Achilles flew at him, breakneck on in fury
with Hector fleeing along the walls of Troy,
fast as his legs would go. On and on they raced,
passing the lookout point, passing the wild fig tree
tossed by the wind, always out from under the ramparts 175
down the wagon trail they careered until they reached
the clear running springs where whirling Scamander[35]
rises up from its double wellsprings bubbling strong—
and one runs hot and the steam goes up around it,
drifting thick as if fire burned at its core 180
but the other even in summer gushes cold
as hail or freezing snow or water chilled to ice . . .
And here, close to the springs, lie washing-pools
scooped out in the hollow rocks and broad and smooth
where the wives of Troy and all their lovely daughters 185
would wash their glistening robes in the old days,
the days of peace before the sons of Achaea came . . .
Past these they raced, one escaping, one in pursuit
and the one who fled was great but the one pursuing
greater, even greater—their pace mounting in speed 190
since both men strove, not for a sacrificial beast
or oxhide trophy, prizes runners fight for, no,
they raced for the life of Hector breaker of horses.
Like powerful stallions sweeping round the post for trophies,
galloping full stretch with some fine prize at stake, 195
a tripod, say, or woman offered up at funeral games
for some brave hero fallen—so the two of them
whirled three times around the city of Priam,
sprinting at top speed while all the gods gazed down,
and the father of men and gods broke forth among them now: 200
"Unbearable—a man I love, hunted round his own city walls

---

35. The Trojan river, after which Hector's son
 is named.

and right before my eyes. My heart grieves for Hector.
Hector who burned so many oxen in my honor, rich cuts,
now on the rugged crests of Ida, now on Ilium's heights.
But now, look, brilliant Achilles courses him round   205
the city of Priam in all his savage, lethal speed.
Come, you immortals, think this through. Decide.
Either we pluck the man from death and save his life
or strike him down at last, here at Achilles' hands—
for all his fighting heart."
                    But immortal Athena,   210
her gray eyes wide, protested strongly: "Father!
Lord of the lightning, king of the black cloud,
what are you saying? A man, a mere mortal,
his doom sealed long ago? You'd set him free
from all the pains of death?
                    Do as you please—   215
but none of the deathless gods will ever praise you."
    And Zeus who marshals the thunderheads replied,
"Courage, Athena, third-born of the gods, dear child.
Nothing I said was meant in earnest, trust me,
I mean you all the good will in the world. Go.   220
Do as your own impulse bids you. Hold back no more."
    So he launched Athena already poised for action—
down the goddess swept from Olympus' craggy peaks.
    And swift Achilles kept on coursing Hector, nonstop
as a hound in the mountains starts a fawn from its lair,   225
hunting him down the gorges, down the narrow glens
and the fawn goes to ground, hiding deep in brush
but the hound comes racing fast, nosing him out
until he lands his kill. So Hector could never throw
Achilles off his trail, the swift racer Achilles—   230
time and again he'd make a dash for the Dardan Gates,
trying to rush beneath the rock-built ramparts, hoping
men on the heights might save him, somehow, raining spears
but time and again Achilles would intercept him quickly,
heading him off, forcing him out across the plain   235
and always sprinting along the city side himself—
endless as in a dream . . .
when a man can't catch another fleeing on ahead
and he can never escape nor his rival overtake him—
so the one could never run the other down in his speed   240
nor the other spring away. And how could Hector have fled
the fates of death so long? How unless one last time,
one final time Apollo had swept in close beside him,
driving strength in his legs and knees to race the wind?
And brilliant Achilles shook his head at the armies,   245

[handwritten margin note: Zeus feeling sympathy for Hector.]

never letting them hurl their sharp spears at Hector—
someone might snatch the glory, Achilles come in second.
But once they reached the springs for the fourth time,
then Father Zeus held out his sacred golden scales:
in them he placed two fates of death that lays men low—   250
one for Achilles, one for Hector breaker of horses—
and gripping the beam mid-haft the Father raised it high
and down went Hector's day of doom, dragging him down
to the strong House of Death—and god Apollo left him.
Athena rushed to Achilles, her bright eyes gleaming,   255
standing shoulder-to-shoulder, winging orders now:
"At last our hopes run high, my brilliant Achilles—
Father Zeus must love you—
we'll sweep great glory back to Achaea's fleet,
we'll kill this Hector, mad as he is for battle!   260
No way for him to escape us now, no longer—
not even if Phoebus the distant deadly Archer
goes through torments, pleading for Hector's life,
groveling over and over before our storming Father Zeus.
But you, you hold your ground and catch your breath   265
while I run Hector down and persuade the man
to fight you face-to-face."
                So Athena commanded
and he obeyed, rejoicing at heart—Achilles stopped,
leaning against his ashen spearshaft barbed in bronze.
And Athena left him there, caught up with Hector at once.   270
and taking the build and vibrant voice of Deiphobus
stood shoulder-to-shoulder with him, winging orders:
"Dear brother, how brutally swift Achilles hunts you—
coursing you round the city of Priam in all his lethal speed!
Come, let us stand our ground together—beat him back."   275
    "Deiphobus!"—Hector, his helmet flashing, called out to her—
"dearest of all my brothers, all these warring years,
of all the sons that Priam and Hecuba produced!
Now I'm determined to praise you all the more,
you who dared—seeing me in these straits—   280
to venture out from the walls, all for *my* sake,
while the others stay inside and cling to safety."
    The goddess answered quickly, her eyes blazing,
"True, dear brother—how your father and mother both
implored me, time and again, clutching my knees,   285
and the comrades round me begging me to stay!
Such was the fear that broke them, man for man,
but the heart within me broke with grief for you.
Now headlong on and fight! No letup, no lance spared!
So now, now we'll *see* if Achilles kills us both   290

and hauls our bloody armor back to the beaked ships
or he goes down in pain beneath your spear."
   Athena luring him on with all her immortal cunning—
and now, at last, as the two came closing for the kill
it was tall Hector, helmet flashing, who led off: 295
"No more running from you in fear, Achilles!
Not as before. Three times I fled around
the great city of Priam—I lacked courage then
to stand your onslaught. Now my spirit stirs me
to meet you face-to-face. Now kill or be killed!   300
Come, we'll swear to the gods, the highest witnesses—
the gods will oversee our binding pacts. I swear
I will never mutilate you—merciless as you are—
if Zeus allows me to last it out and tear your life away.
But once I've stripped your glorious armor, Achilles,   305
I will give your body back to your loyal comrades.
Swear you'll do the same."
                    A swift dark glance
and the headstrong runner answered, "Hector, stop!
You unforgivable, you . . . don't talk to me of pacts.
There are no binding oaths between men and lions—   310
wolves and lambs can enjoy no meeting of the minds—
they are all bent on hating each other to the death.
So with you and me. No love between us. No truce
till one or the other falls and gluts with blood
Ares who hacks at men behind his rawhide shield.   315
Come, call up whatever courage you can muster.
Life or death—now prove yourself a spearman,
a daring man of war! No more escape for you—
Athena will kill you with my spear in just a moment.
Now you'll pay at a stroke for all my comrades' grief,   320
all you killed in the fury of your spear!"
                    With that,
shaft poised, he hurled and his spear's long shadow flew
but seeing it coming glorious Hector ducked away,
crouching down, watching the bronze tip fly past
and stab the earth—but Athena snatched it up   325
and passed it back to Achilles
and Hector the gallant captain never saw her.
He sounded out a challenge to Peleus' princely son:
"You missed, look—the great godlike Achilles!
So you knew nothing at all from Zeus about my death—   330
and yet how sure you were! All bluff, cunning with words,
that's all you are—trying to make me fear you,
lose my nerve, forget my fighting strength.
Well, you'll never plant your lance in my back

Handwritten margin notes:

Athena made Hector believe she was a friend.

Athena gives Achilles back his spear. She favors Achilles

as I flee *you* in fear—plunge it through my chest   335
as I come charging in, if a god gives you the chance!
But now it's for you to dodge *my* brazen spear—
I wish you'd bury it in your body to the hilt.
How much lighter the war would be for Trojans then
if you, their greatest scourge, were dead and gone!"   340
  Shaft poised, he hurled and his spear's long shadow flew
and it struck Achilles' shield—a dead-center hit—
but off and away it glanced and Hector seethed,
his hurtling spear, his whole arm's power poured
in a wasted shot. He stood there, cast down . . .   345
he had no spear in reserve. So Hector shouted out
to Deiphobus bearing his white shield—with a ringing shout
he called for a heavy lance—
                                but the man was nowhere near him,
vanished—
                yes and Hector knew the truth in his heart
and the fighter cried aloud, "My time has come!   350
At last the gods have called me down to death.
I thought he was at my side, the hero Deiphobus—
he's safe inside the walls, Athena's tricked me blind.
And now death, grim death is looming up beside me,
no longer far away. No way to escape it now. This,   355
this was their pleasure after all, sealed long ago—
Zeus and the son of Zeus, the distant deadly Archer—
though often before now they rushed to my defense.
So now I meet my doom. Well let me die—
but not without struggle, not without glory, no,   360
in some great clash of arms that even men to come
will hear of down the years!"
                            And on that resolve
he drew the whetted sword that hung at his side,
tempered, massive, and gathering all his force
he swooped like a soaring eagle   365
launching down from the dark clouds to earth
to snatch some helpless lamb or trembling hare.
So Hector swooped now, swinging his whetted sword
and Achilles charged too, bursting with rage, barbaric,
guarding his chest with the well-wrought blazoned shield,   370
head tossing his gleaming helmet, four horns strong
and the golden plumes shook that the god of fire
drove in bristling thick along its ridge.
Bright as that star amid the stars in the night sky,
star of the evening, brightest star that rides the heavens,   375
so fire flared from the sharp point of the spear Achilles
brandished high in his right hand, bent on Hector's death,

scanning his splendid body—where to pierce it best?
The rest of his flesh seemed all encased in armor,
burnished, brazen—*Achilles'* armor that Hector stripped   380
from strong Patroclus when he killed him—true,
but one spot lay exposed,
where collarbones lift the neckbone off the shoulders,
the open throat, where the end of life comes quickest—*there*
as Hector charged in fury brilliant Achilles drove his spear   385
and the point went stabbing clean through the tender neck
but the heavy bronze weapon failed to slash the windpipe—
Hector could still gasp out some words, some last reply . . .
he crashed in the dust—
                         godlike Achilles gloried over him:
"Hector—surely you thought when you stripped Patroclus' armor   390
that you, you would be safe! Never a fear of me—
far from the fighting as I was—you fool!
Left behind there, down by the beaked ships
his great avenger waited, a greater man by far—
that man was I, and I smashed your strength! And you—   395
the dogs and birds will maul you, shame your corpse
while Achaeans bury my dear friend in glory!"
    Struggling for breath, Hector, his helmet flashing,
said, "I beg you, beg you by your life, your parents—
don't let the dogs devour me by the Argive ships!   400
Wait, take the princely ransom of bronze and gold,
the gifts my father and noble mother will give you—
but give my body to friends to carry home again,
so Trojan men and Trojan women can do me honor
with fitting rites of fire once I am dead."   405
    Staring grimly, the proud runner Achilles answered,
"Beg no more, you fawning dog—begging me by my parents!
Would to god my rage, my fury would drive me now
to hack your flesh away and eat you raw—
such agonies you have caused me! Ransom?   410
No man alive could keep the dog-packs off you,
not if they haul in ten, twenty times that ransom
and pile it here before me and promise fortunes more—
no, not given if Dardan Priam should offer to weigh out
your bulk in gold! Not even then will your noble mother   415
lay you on your deathbed, mourn the son she bore . . .
The dogs and birds will rend you—blood and bone!"
    At the point of death, Hector, his helmet flashing,
said, "I know you well—I see my fate before me.
Never a chance that I could win you over . . .   420
Iron inside your chest, that heart of yours.
But now beware, or my curse will draw god's wrath

[handwritten marginal note: Hector prophesize in his dying that Apollo & [Paris] will kill Achi]

upon your head, that day when Paris[36] and lord Apollo—
for all your fighting heart—destroy you at the Scaean Gates!"
    Death cut him short. The end closed in around him.
Flying free of his limbs   425
his soul went winging down to the House of Death,
wailing his fate, leaving his manhood far behind,
his young and supple strength. But brilliant Achilles
taunted Hector's body, dead as he was, "Die, die!   430
For my own death, I'll meet it freely—whenever Zeus
and the other deathless gods would like to bring it on!"
    With that he wrenched his bronze spear from the corpse,
laid it aside and ripped the bloody armor off the back.
And the other sons of Achaea, running up around him,   435
crowded closer, all of them gazing wonder-struck
at the build and marvelous, lithe beauty of Hector.
And not a man came forward who did not stab his body,
glancing toward a comrade, laughing: "Ah, look here—
how much softer he is to handle now, this Hector,   440
than when he gutted our ships with roaring fire!"
    Standing over him, so they'd gloat and stab his body.
But once he had stripped the corpse the proud runner Achilles
took his stand in the midst of all the Argive troops
and urged them on with a flight of winging orders: 445
"Friends—lords of the Argives, O my captains!
Now that the gods have let me kill this man
who caused us agonies, loss on crushing loss—
more than the rest of all their men combined—
come, let us ring their walls in armor, test them,   450
see what recourse the Trojans still may have in mind.
Will they abandon the city heights with this man fallen?
Or brace for a last, dying stand though Hector's gone?
But wait—what am I saying? Why this deep debate?
Down by the ships a body lies unwept, unburied—   455
Patroclus . . . I will never forget him,
not as long as I'm still among the living
and my springing knees will lift and drive me on.
Though the dead forget their dead in the House of Death,
I will remember, even there, my dear companion.   460
                                                    Now,
come, you sons of Achaea, raise a song of triumph!
Down to the ships we march and bear this corpse on high—
we have won ourselves great glory. We have brought

---

36. Hector's brother, whose seduction of
    Menelaos' wife Helen was the cause of the
    war.

magnificent Hector down, that man the Trojans
glorified in their city like a god!"
                                    So he triumphed   465
and now he was bent on outrage, on shaming noble Hector.
Piercing the tendons, ankle to heel behind both feet,
he knotted straps of rawhide through them both,
lashed them to his chariot, left the head to drag
and mounting the car, hoisting the famous arms aboard,   470
he whipped his team to a run and breakneck on they flew,
holding nothing back. And a thick cloud of dust rose up
from the man they dragged, his dark hair swirling round
that head so handsome once, all tumbled low in the dust—
since Zeus had given him over to his enemies now   475
to be defiled in the land of his own fathers.
    So his whole head was dragged down in the dust.
And now his mother began to tear her hair . . .
she flung her shining veil to the ground and raised
a high, shattering scream, looking down at her son.   480
Pitifully his loving father groaned and round the king
his people cried with grief and wailing seized the city—
for all the world as if all Troy were torched and smoldering
down from the looming brows of the citadel to her roots.
Priam's people could hardly hold the old man back,   485
frantic, mad to go rushing out the Dardan Gates.
He begged them all, groveling in the filth,
crying out to them, calling each man by name,
"Let go, my friends! Much as you care for me,
let me hurry out of the city, make my way,   490
all on my own, to Achaea's waiting ships!
I must implore that terrible, violent man . . .
Perhaps—who knows?—he may respect my age,
may pity an old man. He has a father too,
as old as I am—Peleus sired him once,   495
Peleus reared him to be the scourge of Troy
but most of all to me—he made my life a hell.
So many sons he slaughtered, just coming into bloom . . .
but grieving for all the rest, one breaks my heart the most
and stabbing grief for him will take me down to Death—   500
my Hector—would to god he had perished in my arms!
Then his mother who bore him—oh so doomed,
she and I could glut ourselves with grief."
    So the voice of the king rang out in tears,
the citizens wailed in answer, and noble Hecuba[37]   505
led the wives of Troy in a throbbing chant of sorrow:

---

37. Hector's mother.

"O my child—my desolation! How can I go on living?
What agonies must I suffer now, now *you* are dead and gone?
You were my pride throughout the city night and day—
a blessing to us all, the men and women of Troy: 510
throughout the city they saluted you like a god.
You, you were their greatest glory while you lived—
now death and fate have seized you, dragged you down!"

    Her voice rang out in tears, but the wife of Hector
had not heard a thing. No messenger brought the truth   515
of how her husband made his stand outside the gates.
She was weaving at her loom, deep in the high halls,
working flowered braiding into a dark red folding robe.
And she called her well-kempt women through the house
to set a large three-legged cauldron over the fire   520
so Hector could have his steaming hot bath
when he came home from battle—poor woman,
she never dreamed how far he was from bathing,
struck down at Achilles' hands by blazing-eyed Athena.
But she heard the groans and wails of grief from the rampart now   525
and her body shook, her shuttle dropped to the ground,
she called out to her lovely waiting women, "Quickly—
two of you follow me—I must see what's happened.
That cry—that was Hector's honored mother I heard!
My heart's pounding, leaping up in my throat,   530
the knees beneath me paralyzed—Oh I know it . . .
something terrible's coming down on Priam's children.
Pray god the news will never reach my ears!
Yes but I dread it so—what if great Achilles
has cut my Hector off from the city, daring Hector,   535
and driven him out across the plain, and all alone?—
He may have put an end to that fatal headstrong pride
that always seized my Hector—never hanging back
with the main force of men, always charging ahead,
giving ground to no man in his fury!"

                          So she cried,   540
dashing out of the royal halls like a madwoman,
her heart racing hard, her women close behind her.
But once she reached the tower where soldiers massed
she stopped on the rampart, looked down and saw it all—
saw him dragged before the city, stallions galloping,   545
dragging Hector back to Achaea's beaked warships—
ruthless work. The world went black as night
before her eyes, she fainted, falling backward.
gasping away her life breath . . . .
She flung to the winds her glittering headdress,   550
the cap and the coronet, braided band and veil,

all the regalia golden Aphrodite gave her once,
the day that Hector, helmet aflash in sunlight,
led her home to Troy from her father's house
with countless wedding gifts to win her heart.   560

[After Hector is killed, Achilles holds Patroclus's funeral, followed by the customary athletic
games in celebration and commemoration of the dead hero. Meanwhile, Hector's body
remains unburied. Priam, at Zeus's prompting and despite Hecuba's efforts to dissuade him,
makes his way across the battlefield at night to Achilles's tent to offer him ransom for the
body of Hector.]

Book 24 [Achilles and Priam]

The majestic king of Troy slipped past the rest
and kneeling down beside Achilles, clasped his knees
and kissed his hands, those terrible, man-killing hands
that had slaughtered Priam's many sons in battle.
Awesome—as when the grip of madness seizes one   5
who murders a man in his own fatherland and flees
abroad to foreign shores, to a wealthy, noble host,
and a sense of marvel runs through all who see him—
so Achilles marveled, beholding majestic Priam.
His men marveled too, trading startled glances.   10
But Priam prayed his heart out to Achilles:
"Remember your own father, great godlike Achilles—
as old as I am, past the threshold of deadly old age!
No doubt the countrymen round about him plague him now,
with no one there to defend him, beat away disaster.   15
No one—but at least he hears you're still alive
and his old heart rejoices, hopes rising, day by day,
to see his beloved son come sailing home from Troy.
But I—dear god, my life so cursed by fate . . .
I fathered hero sons in the wide realm of Troy   20
and now not a single one is left, I tell you.
Fifty sons I had when the sons of Achaea came,
nineteen born to me from a single mother's womb
and the rest by other women in the palace. Many,
most of them violent Ares cut the knees from under.   25
But one, one was left me, to guard my walls, my people—
the one you killed the other day, defending his fatherland,
my Hector! It's all for him I've come to the ships now,
to win him back from you—I bring a priceless ransom.
Revere the gods, Achilles! Pity me in my own right,   30
remember your own father! I deserve more pity . . .
I have endured what no one on earth has ever done before—
I put to my lips the hands of the man who killed my son."

Those words stirred within Achilles a deep desire
to grieve for his own father. Taking the old man's hand   35
he gently moved him back. And overpowered by memory
both men gave way to grief. Priam wept freely
for man-killing Hector, throbbing, crouching
before Achilles' feet as Achilles wept himself,
now for his father, now for Patroclus once again,   40
and their sobbing rose and fell throughout the house.
Then, when brilliant Achilles had had his fill of tears
and the longing for it had left his mind and body,
he rose from his seat, raised the old man by the hand
and filled with pity now for his gray head and gray beard,   45
he spoke out winging words, flying straight to the heart:
"Poor man, how much you've borne—pain to break the spirit!
What daring brought you down to the ships, all alone,
to face the glance of the man who killed your sons,
so many fine brave boys? You have a heart of iron.   50
Come, please, sit down on this chair here . . .
Let us put our griefs to rest in our own hearts,
rake them up no more, raw as we are with mourning.
What good's to be won from tears that chill the spirit?
So the immortals spun our lives that we, we wretched men   55
live on to bear such torments—the gods live free of sorrows.
There are two great jars that stand on the floor of Zeus's halls
and hold his gifts, our miseries one, the other blessings.
When Zeus who loves the lightning mixes gifts for a man,
now he meets with misfortune, now good times in turn.   60
When Zeus dispenses gifts from the jar of sorrows only,
he makes a man an outcast—brutal, ravenous hunger
drives him down the face of the shining earth,
stalking far and wide, cursed by gods and men.
So with my father, Peleus: What glittering gifts   65
the gods rained down from the day that he was born!
He excelled all men in wealth and pride of place,
he lorded the Myrmidons, and mortal that he was,
they gave the man an immortal goddess for a wife.
Yes, but even on him the Father piled hardships,   70
no powerful race of princes born in his royal halls,
only a single son he fathered, doomed at birth,
cut off in the spring of life—
and I, I give the man no care as he grows old
since here I sit in Troy, far from my fatherland,   75
a grief to you, a grief to all your children . . .
And you too, old man, we hear you prospered once:
as far as Lesbos, Macar's kingdom, bounds to seaward,

Phrygia east and upland, the Hellespont vast and north—
that entire realm, they say, you lorded over once,   80
you excelled all men, old king, in sons and wealth.
But then the gods of heaven brought this agony on you—
ceaseless battles round your walls, your armies slaughtered.
You must bear up now. Enough of endless tears,
the pain that breaks the spirit.   85
Grief for your son will do no good at all.
You will never bring him back to life—
sooner you must suffer something worse.''

[Achilles returns Hector's body to Priam and offers to delay the fighting until the Trojans have performed Hector's funeral rites. Priam brings his son's body back to Troy and the poem ends with with grief-stricken Trojans mourning their fallen defender.]

HOMER (EIGHTH CENTURY B.C.E.)
Greece

The subject of the *Odyssey* is the ten-year-long return of the Greek hero Odysseus, after the fall of Troy, to his home on the island of Ithaca. In four of the poem's twenty-four books, Odysseus is the first-person narrator of his voyage through uncharted territories. He relates his travels (beginning with our Book 9 selection) to the Phaeacians on the island of Scheria, where he has taken refuge after being shipwrecked in a storm brought on by Poseidon, ruling divinity of the sea.

Odysseus' encounters with unfamiliar beings and their customs serve to delineate the contrast between civilized and noncivilized existence, bringing to the fore the idea of culture itself. In Book Nine, Polyphemos, one of the Cyclopes—a group of giants living without agriculture or social organization, so that each family is literally a "law unto itself"—makes a mockery of the fundamental norms of social relations in early Greece in a grisly perversion of the inviolable code of hospitality. The episode establishes Odysseus as a master strategist who through sheer intelligence and perspicacity outwits his vastly more powerful adversary—an aspect of heroism less evident in the *Iliad*. In this poem's second half, Odysseus' wife, Penelope, is depicted as sharing these same qualities. Together, they bring about the defeat of Penelope's corrupt suitors, who in Odysseus' absence have overrun and exploited his entire household.

The *Odyssey* is generally thought (on linguistic grounds) to have reached its present form at a slightly later date than the *Iliad*. In its description (in Book 8) of a bard accompanying himself on the lyre and responding to the requests of an attentive audience, it gives us our earliest picture of how an epic may originally have been composed and sung.

from Odyssey

Book 1 [Invocation]

Tell me, Muse, of the man of many ways, who was driven
far journeys, after he had sacked Troy's sacred citadel.
Many were they whose cities he saw, whose minds he learned of,
many the pains he suffered in his spirit on the wide sea,
struggling for his own life and the homecoming of his companions.   5
Even so he could not save his companions, hard though
he strove to; they were destroyed by their own wild recklessness,
fools, who devoured the oxen of Helios, the Sun God,
and he took away the day of their homecoming. From some point
here, goddess, daughter of Zeus, speak, and begin our story.   10
    Then all the others, as many as fled sheer destruction,
were at home now, having escaped the sea and the fighting.
This one alone, longing for his wife and his homecoming,
was detained by the queenly nymph Kalypso, bright among goddesses,
in her hollowed caverns, desiring that he should be her husband.   15
But when in the circling of the years that very year came
in which the gods had spun for him his time of homecoming
to Ithaka, not even then was he free of his trials
nor among his own people. But all the gods pitied him
except Poseidon; he remained relentlessly angry   20
with godlike Odysseus, until his return to his own country.

[Odysseus, after being shipwrecked on his voyage homeward in a storm brought on by the sea-god Poseidon, manages to swim to shore on the island of Scheria, where, although his identity is unknown, he is given shelter by the king and queen of the Phaeacians. They entertain him at a feast in which a singer sings about the Trojan War, including Odysseus's own exploits. Observing his guest weeping at the songs, King Alkinoos asks Odysseus to reveal his name and to explain the cause of his grief.]

Book 9 [The Wanderings of Odysseus]

Then resourceful Odysseus spoke in turn and answered him:
'O great Alkinoos, pre-eminent among all people,
surely indeed it is a good thing to listen to a singer
such as this one before us, who is like the gods in his singing;
for I think there is no occasion accomplished that is more pleasant   5
than when festivity holds sway among all the populace,
and the feasters up and down the houses are sitting in order
and listening to the singer, and beside them the tables are loaded

Translated by Richmond Lattimore.

with bread and meats, and from the mixing bowl the wine steward
draws the wine and carries it about and fills the cups. This   10
seems to my own mind to be the best of occasions.
But now your wish was inclined to ask me about my mournful
sufferings, so that I must mourn and grieve even more. What then
shall I recite to you first of all, what leave till later?
Many are the sorrows the gods of the sky have given me.   15
Now first I will tell you my name, so that all of you
may know me, and I hereafter, escaping the day without pity,
be your friend and guest, though the home where I live is far away from you.
I am Odysseus son of Laertes, known before all men
for the study of crafty designs, and my fame goes up to the heavens.   20
I am at home in sunny Ithaka. There is a mountain
there that stands tall, leaf-trembling Neritos, and there are islands
settled around it, lying one very close to another.
There is Doulichion and Same, wooded Zakynthos,
but my island lies low and away, last of all on the water   25
toward the dark, with the rest below facing east and sunshine,
a rugged place, but a good nurse of men; for my part
I cannot think of any place sweeter on earth to look at.
For in truth Kalypso,[1] shining among divinities, kept me
with her in her hollow caverns desiring me for her husband,   30
and so likewise Aiaian Circe[2] the guileful detained me
beside her in her halls, desiring me for her husband,
but never could she persuade the heart within me. So it is
that nothing is more sweet in the end than country and parents
ever, even when far away one lives in a fertile   35
place, when it is in alien country, far from his parents.
But come, I will tell you of my voyage home with its many
troubles, which Zeus inflicted on me as I came from Troy land.
'From Ilion the wind took me and drove me ashore at Ismaros
by the Kikonians. I sacked their city and killed their people,   40
and out of their city taking their wives and many possessions
we shared them out, so none might go cheated of his proper
portion. There I was for the light foot and escaping,
and urged it, but they were greatly foolish and would not listen,
and then and there much wine was being drunk, and they slaughtered   45
many sheep on the beach, and lumbering horn-curved cattle.
But meanwhile the Kikonians went and summoned the other

---

1. The nymph Kalypso (whose name means
   "the one who conceals"), on whose island
   Odysseus took refuge after an earlier shipwreck in which all his companions were
   lost, kept him with her for seven years, until
   Zeus obliged her to let Odysseus continue
   his journey home.

2. On his return from Troy, before reaching
   Kalypso's island, Odysseus and his companions on the one remaining ship reach
   Circe's island of Aiaia, where they stay for a
   year before setting out for Ithaca again.

Kikonians, who were their neighbors living in the inland country,
more numerous and better men, well skilled in fighting
men with horses, but knowing too at need the battle 50
on foot. They came at early morning, like flowers in season
or leaves, and the luck that came our way from Zeus was evil,
to make us unfortunate, so we must have hard pains to suffer.
Both sides stood and fought their battle there by the running
ships, and with bronze-headed spears they cast at each other, 55
and as long as it was early and the sacred daylight increasing,
so long we stood fast and fought them off, though there were more of them;
but when the sun had gone to the time for unyoking of cattle,
then at last the Kikonians turned the Achaians back and beat them,
and out of each ship six of my strong-greaved companions 60
were killed, but the rest of us fled away from death and destruction.
　'From there we sailed on further along, glad to have escaped death,
but grieving still at heart for the loss of our dear companions.
Even then I would not suffer the flight of my oarswept vessels
until a cry had been made three times for each of my wretched 65
companions, who died there in the plain, killed by the Kikonians.
Cloud-gathering Zeus drove the North Wind against our vessels
in a supernatural storm, and huddled under the cloud scuds
land alike and the great water. Night sprang from heaven.
The ships were swept along yawing down the current; the violence 70
of the wind ripped our sails into three and four pieces. These then,
in fear of destruction, we took down and stowed in the ships' hulls,
and rowed them on ourselves until we had made the mainland.
There for two nights and two days together we lay up,
for pain and weariness together eating our hearts out. 75
But when the fair-haired Dawn in her rounds brought on the third day,
we, setting the masts upright, and hoisting the white sails on them,
sat still, and let the wind and the steersmen hold them steady.
And now I would have come home unscathed to the land of my fathers,
but as I turned the hook of Maleia,[3] the sea and current 80
and the North Wind beat me off course, and drove me on past Kythera.
　'Nine days then I was swept along by the force of the hostile
winds on the fishy sea, but on the tenth day we landed
in the country of the Lotus-Eaters, who live on a flowering
food, and there we set foot on the mainland, and fetched water, 85
and my companions soon took their supper there by the fast ships.
But after we had tasted of food and drink, then I sent
some of my companions ahead, telling them to find out
what men, eaters of bread, might live here in this country.
I chose two men, and sent a third with them, as a herald. 90
My men went on and presently met the Lotus-Eaters,

---

3. The southernmost tip of the Peloponnesus.

nor did these Lotus-Eaters have any thoughts of destroying
our companions, but they only gave them lotus to taste of.
But any of them who ate the honey-sweet fruit of lotus
was unwilling to take any message back, or to go   95
away, but they wanted to stay there with the lotus-eating
people, feeding on lotus, and forget the way home. I myself
took these men back weeping, by force, to where the ships were,
and put them aboard under the rowing benches and tied them
fast, then gave the order to the rest of my eager   100
companions to embark on the ships in haste, for fear
someone else might taste of the lotus and forget the way home,
and the men quickly went aboard and sat to the oarlocks,
and sitting well in order dashed the oars in the gray sea.
  'From there, grieving still at heart, we sailed on further   105
along, and reached the country of the lawless outrageous
Cyclopes who, putting all their trust in the immortal
gods, neither plow with their hands nor plant anything,
but all grows for them without seed planting, without cultivation,
wheat and barley and also the grapevines, which yield for them   110
wine of strength, and it is Zeus' rain that waters it for them.
These people have no institutions, no meetings for counsels;
rather they make their habitations in caverns hollowed
among the peaks of the high mountains, and each one is the law
for his own wives and children, and cares nothing about the others.   115
  'There is a wooded island that spreads, away from the harbor,
neither close in to the land of the Cyclopes nor far out
from it; forested; wild goats beyond number breed there,
for there is no coming and going of human kind to disturb them,
nor are they visited by hunters, who in the forest   120
suffer hardships as they haunt the peaks of the mountains,
neither again is it held by herded flocks, nor farmers,
but all its days, never plowed up and never planted,
it goes without people and supports the bleating wild goats.
For the Cyclopes have no ships with cheeks of vermilion,   125
nor have they builders of ships among them, who could have made the
strong-benched vessels, and these if made could have run them sailing
to all the various cities of men, in the way that people
cross the sea by means of ships and visit each other,
and they could have made this island a strong settlement for them.   130
For it is not a bad place at all, it could bear all crops
in season, and there are meadow lands near the shores of the gray sea,
well watered and soft; there could be grapes grown there endlessly,
and there is smooth land for plowing, men could reap a full harvest
always in season, since there is very rich subsoil. Also   135
there is an easy harbor, with no need for a hawser
nor anchor stones to be thrown ashore nor cables to make fast;

one could just run ashore and wait for the time when the sailors'
desire stirred them to go and the right winds were blowing.
Also at the head of the harbor there runs bright water,   140
spring beneath rock, and there are black poplars growing around it.
There we sailed ashore, and there was some god guiding
us in through the gloom of the night, nothing showed to look at,
for there was a deep mist around the ships, nor was there any moon
showing in the sky, but she was under the clouds and hidden.   145
There was none of us there whose eyes had spied out the island,
and we never saw any long waves rolling in and breaking
on the shore, but the first thing was when we beached the well-benched vessels.
Then after we had beached the ships we took all the sails down,
and we ourselves stepped out onto the break of the sea beach,   150
and there we fell asleep and waited for the divine Dawn.
   'But when the young Dawn showed again with her rosy fingers,
we made a tour about the island, admiring everything
there, and the nymphs, daughters of Zeus of the aegis,[4] started
the hill-roving goats our way for my companions to feast on.   155
At once we went and took from the ships curved bows and javelins
with long sockets, and arranging ourselves in three divisions
cast about, and the god granted us the game we longed for.
Now there were twelve ships that went with me, and for each one nine goats
were portioned out, but I alone had ten for my portion.   160
So for the whole length of the day until the sun's setting,
we sat there feasting on unlimited meat and sweet wine;
for the red wine had not yet given out in the ships, there was
some still left, for we all had taken away a great deal
in storing jars when we stormed the Kikonians' sacred citadel.   165
We looked across at the land of the Cyclopes, and they were
near by, and we saw their smoke and heard sheep and goats bleating.
But when the sun went down and the sacred darkness came over,
then we lay down to sleep along the break of the seashore;
but when the young Dawn showed again with her rosy fingers,   170
then I held an assembly and spoke forth before all:
"The rest of you, who are my eager companions, wait here,
while I, with my own ship and companions that are in it,
go and find out about these people, and learn what they are,
whether they are savage and violent, and without justice,   175
or hospitable to strangers and with minds that are godly."
   'So speaking I went aboard the ship and told my companions
also to go aboard, and to cast off the stern cables,
and quickly they went aboard the ship and sat to the oarlocks,
and sitting well in order dashed the oars in the gray sea.   180
But when we had arrived at the place, which was nearby, there

---

4. The aegis is Zeus's shield.

at the edge of the land we saw the cave, close to the water,
high, and overgrown with laurels, and in it were stabled
great flocks, sheep and goats alike, and there was a fenced yard
built around it with a high wall of grubbed-out boulders   185
and tall pines and oaks with lofty foliage. Inside
there lodged a monster of a man, who now was herding
the flocks at a distance away, alone, for he did not range with
others, but stayed away by himself; his mind was lawless,
and in truth he was a monstrous wonder made to behold, not   190
like a man, an eater of bread, but more like a wooded
peak of the high mountains seen standing away from the others.
  'At that time I told the rest of my eager companions
to stay where they were beside the ship and guard it. Meanwhile
I, choosing out the twelve best men among my companions,   195
went on, but I had with me a goatskin bottle of black wine,
sweet wine, given me by Maron, son of Euanthes
and priest of Apollo, who bestrides Ismaros; he gave it
because, respecting him with his wife and child, we saved them
from harm. He made his dwelling among the trees of the sacred   200
grove of Phoibos Apollo, and he gave me glorious presents.
He gave me seven talents of well-wrought gold, and he gave me
a mixing bowl made all of silver, and gave along with it
wine, drawing it off in storing jars, twelve in all. This was
a sweet wine, unmixed, a divine drink. No one of his servants   205
or thralls that were in his household knew anything about it,
but only himself and his dear wife and a single housekeeper.
Whenever he drank this honey-sweet red wine, he would pour out
enough to fill one cup, then twenty measures of water
were added, and the mixing bowl gave off a sweet smell;   210
magical; then would be no pleasure in holding off. Of this
wine I filled a great wineskin full, and took too provisions
in a bag, for my proud heart had an idea that presently
I would encounter a man who was endowed with great strength,
and wild, with no true knowledge of laws or any good customs.   215
  'Lightly we made our way to the cave, but we did not find him
there, he was off herding on the range with his fat flocks.
We went inside the cave and admired everything inside it.
Baskets were there, heavy with cheeses, and the pens crowded
with lambs and kids. They had all been divided into separate   220
groups, the firstlings in one place, and then the middle ones,
the babies again by themselves. And all his vessels, milk pails
and pans that he used for milking into, were running over
with whey. From the start my companions spoke to me and begged me
to take some of the cheeses, come back again, and the next time 225
to drive the lambs and kids from their pens, and get back quickly
to the ship again, and go sailing off across the salt water;

but I would not listen to them, it would have been better their way,
not until I could see him, see if he would give me presents.
My friends were to find the sight of him in no way lovely.   230
    'There we built a fire and made sacrifice, and helping
ourselves to the cheeses we ate and sat waiting for him
inside, until he came home from his herding. He carried a heavy
load of dried-out wood, to make a fire for his dinner,
and threw it down inside the cave, making a terrible   235
crash, so in fear we scuttled away into the cave's corners.
Next he drove into the wide cavern all from the fat flocks
that he would milk, but he left all the male animals, billygoats
and rams, outside in his yard with the deep fences. Next thing,
he heaved up and set into position the huge door stop,   240
a massive thing; no twenty-two of the best four-wheeled
wagons could have taken that weight off the ground and carried it,
such a piece of sky-towering cliff that was he set over
his gateway. Next he sat down and milked his sheep and his bleating
goats, each of them in order, and put lamb or kid under each one   245
to suck, and then drew off half of the white milk and put it
by in baskets made of wickerwork, stored for cheeses,
but let the other half stand in the milk pails so as to have it
to help himself to and drink from, and it would serve for his supper.
But after he had briskly done all his chores and finished,   250
at last he lit the fire, and saw us, and asked us a question:
"Strangers, who are you? From where do you come sailing over the watery
ways? Is it on some business, or are you recklessly roving
as pirates do, when they sail on the salt sea and venture
their lives as they wander, bringing evil to alien people?"[5]   255
    'So he spoke, and the inward heart in us was broken
in terror of the deep voice and for seeing him so monstrous;
but even so I had words for an answer, and I said to him:
"We are Achaians coming from Troy, beaten off our true course
by winds from every direction across the great gulf of the open   260
sea, making for home, by the wrong way, on the wrong courses.
So we have come. So it has pleased Zeus to arrange it.
We claim we are of the following of the son of Atreus,
Agamemnon, whose fame now is the greatest thing under heaven,
such a city was that he sacked and destroyed so many   265
people; but now in turn we come to you and are suppliants
at your knees, if you might give us a guest present or otherwise
some gift of grace, for such is the right of strangers. Therefore
respect the gods, O best of men. We are your suppliants,

---

5. The code of hospitality required a host to
offer a visitor food, shelter, and gifts for his
journey before asking him to identify himself; the Cyclops's ominous greeting itself thus
violates established practice, even before he
takes any further action.

and Zeus the guest god, who stands behind all strangers with honor   270
due them, avenges any wrong toward strangers and suppliants."
  'So I spoke, but he answered me in pitiless spirit:
"Stranger, you are a simple fool, or come from far off,
when you tell me to avoid the wrath of the gods or fear them.
The Cyclopes do not concern themselves over Zeus of the aegis,   275
nor any of the rest of the blessed gods, since we are far better
than they, and for fear of the hate of Zeus I would not spare
you or your companions either, if the fancy took me
otherwise. But tell me, so I may know: where did you
put your well-made ship when you came? Nearby or far off?"   280
  'So he spoke, trying me out, but I knew too much and was not
deceived, but answered him in turn, and my words were crafty:
"Poseidon, Shaker of the Earth, has shattered my vessel.
He drove it against the rocks on the outer coast of your country,
cracked on a cliff, it is gone, the wind on the sea took it;   285
but I, with these you see, got away from sudden destruction."
  'So I spoke, but he in pitiless spirit answered
nothing, but sprang up and reached for my companions,
caught up two together and slapped them, like killing puppies,
against the ground, and the brains ran all over the floor, soaking   290
the ground. Then he cut them up limb by limb and got supper ready,
and like a lion reared in the hills, without leaving anything,
ate them, entrails, flesh and the marrowy bones alike. We
cried out aloud and held our hands up to Zeus, seeing
the cruelty of what he did, but our hearts were helpless.   295
But when the Cyclops had filled his enormous stomach, feeding
on human flesh and drinking down milk unmixed with water,
he lay down to sleep in the cave sprawled out through his sheep. Then I
took counsel with myself in my great-hearted spirit
to go up close, drawing from beside my thigh the sharp sword,   300
and stab him in the chest, where the midriff joins on the liver,
feeling for the place with my hand; but the second thought stayed me;
for there we too would have perished away in sheer destruction,
seeing that our hands could never have pushed from the lofty
gate of the cave the ponderous boulder he had propped there.   305
So mourning we waited, just as we were, for the divine Dawn.
  'But when the young Dawn showed again with her rosy fingers,
he lit his fire, and then set about milking his glorious
flocks, each of them in order, and put lamb or kid under each one.
But after he had briskly done all his chores and finished,   310
again he snatched up two men, and prepared them for dinner,
and when he had dined, drove his fat flocks out of the cavern,
easily lifting off the great doorstone, but then he put it
back again, like a man closing the lid on a quiver.
And so the Cyclops, whistling loudly, guided his fat flocks   315

to the hills, leaving me there in the cave mumbling my black thoughts
of how I might punish him, how Athene might give me that glory.
And as I thought, this was the plan that seemed best to me.
The Cyclops had lying there beside the pen a great bludgeon
of olive wood, still green. He had cut it so that when it dried out   320
he could carry it about, and we looking at it considered
it to be about the size for the mast of a cargo-carrying
broad black ship of twenty oars which crosses the open
sea; such was the length of it, such the thickness, to judge by
looking. I went up and chopped a length of about a fathom,   325
and handed it over to my companions and told them to shave it
down, and they made it smooth, while I standing by them sharpened
the point, then put it over the blaze of the fire to harden.
Then I put it well away and hid it under the ordure
which was all over the floor of the cave, much stuff lying   330
about. Next I told the rest of the men to cast lots, to find out
which of them must endure with me to take up the great beam
and spin it in Cyclops' eye when sweet sleep had come over him.
The ones drew it whom I myself would have wanted chosen,
four men, and I myself was the fifth, and allotted with them.   335
With the evening he came back again, herding his fleecy
flocks, but drove all his fat flocks inside the wide cave
at once, and did not leave any outside in the yard with the deep fence,
whether he had some idea, or whether a god so urged him.
When he had heaved up and set in position the huge door stop,   340
next he sat down and started milking his sheep and his bleating
goats, each of them in order, and put lamb or kid under each one.
But after he had briskly done all his chores and finished,
again he snatched up two men and prepared them for dinner.
Then at last I, holding in my hands an ivy bowl   345
full of the black wine, stood close up to the Cyclops and spoke out:
"Here, Cyclops, have a drink of wine, now you have fed on
human flesh, and see what kind of drink our ship carried
inside her. I brought it for you, and it would have been your libation
had you taken pity and sent me home, but I cannot suffer   350
your rages. Cruel, how can any man come and visit
you ever again, now you have done what has no sanction?"
    'So I spoke, and he took it and drank it off, and was terribly
pleased with the wine he drank and questioned me again, saying:
"Give me still more, freely, and tell me your name straightway   355
now, so I can give you a guest present to make you happy.
For the grain-giving land of the Cyclopes also yields them
wine of strength, and it is Zeus' rain that waters it for them;
but this comes from where ambrosia and nectar flow in abundance."
    'So he spoke, and I gave him the gleaming wine again. Three times   360
I brought it to him and gave it to him, three times he recklessly

drained it, but when the wine had got into the brains of the Cyclops,
then I spoke to him, and my words were full of beguilement:
"Cyclops, you ask me for my famous name. I will tell you
then, but you must give me a guest gift as you have promised.   365
Nobody is my name. My father and mother call me
Nobody, as do all the others who are my companions."
    'So I spoke, and he answered me in pitiless spirit:
"Then I will eat Nobody after his friends, and the others
I will eat first, and that shall be my guest present to you."   370
    'He spoke and slumped away and fell on his back, and lay there
with his thick neck crooked over on one side, and sleep who subdues all
came on and captured him, and the wine gurgled up from his gullet
with gobs of human meat. This was his drunken vomiting.
Then I shoved the beam underneath a deep bed of cinders,   375
waiting for it to heat, and I spoke to all my companions
in words of courage, so none should be in a panic, and back out;
but when the beam of olive, green as it was, was nearly
at the point of catching fire and glowed, terribly incandescent,
then I brought it close up from the fire and my friends about me   380
stood fast. Some great divinity breathed courage into us.
They seized the beam of olive, sharp at the end, and leaned on it
into the eye, while I from above leaning my weight on it
twirled it, like a man with a brace-and-bit who bores into
a ship timber, and his men from underneath, grasping   385
the strap on either side whirl it, and it bites resolutely deeper.
So seizing the fire-point-hardened timber we twirled it
in his eye, and the blood boiled around the hot point, so that
the blast and scorch of the burning ball singed all his eyebrows
and eyelids, and the fire made the roots of his eye crackle.   390
As when a man who works as a blacksmith plunges a screaming
great ax blade or plane into cold water, treating it
for temper, since this is the way steel is made strong, even
so Cyclops' eye sizzled about the beam of the olive.
He gave a giant horrible cry and the rocks rattled   395
to the sound, and we scuttled away in fear. He pulled the timber
out of his eye, and it blubbered with plenty of blood, then
when he had frantically taken it in his hands and thrown it
away, he cried aloud to the other Cyclopes, who live
around him in their own caves along the windy pinnacles.   400
They hearing him came swarming up from their various places,
and stood around the cave and asked him what was his trouble:
"Why, Polyphemos, what do you want with all this outcry
through the immortal night and have made us all thus sleepless?
Surely no mortal against your will can be driving your sheep off?   405
Surely none can be killing you by force or treachery?"

'Then from inside the cave strong Polyphemos answered:
"Good friends, Nobody is killing me by force or treachery."**6**
'So then the others speaking in winged words gave him an answer:
"If alone as you are none uses violence on you, 410
why, there is no avoiding the sickness sent by great Zeus;
so you had better pray to your father, the lord Poseidon."
'So they spoke as they went away, and the heart within me
laughed over how my name and my perfect planning had fooled him.
But the Cyclops, groaning aloud and in the pain of his agony, 415
felt with his hands, and took the boulder out of the doorway,
and sat down in the entrance himself, spreading his arms wide,
to catch anyone who tried to get out with the sheep, hoping
that I would be so guileless in my heart as to try this;
but I was planning so that things would come out the best way, 420
and trying to find some release from death, for my companions
and myself too, combining all my resource and treacheries,
as with life at stake, for the great evil was very close to us.
And as I thought, this was the plan that seemed best to me.
There were some male sheep, rams, well nourished, thick and fleecy, 425
handsome and large, with a dark depth of wool. Silently
I caught these and lashed them together with pliant willow
withes, where the monstrous Cyclops lawless of mind had used to
sleep. I had them in threes, and the one in the middle carried
a man, while the other two went on each side, so guarding 430
my friends. Three rams carried each man, but as for myself,
there was one ram, far the finest of all the flock. This one
I clasped around the back, snuggled under the wool of the belly,
and stayed there still, and with a firm twist of the hands and enduring
spirit clung fast to the glory of this fleece, unrelenting. 435
So we grieved for the time and waited for the divine Dawn.
'But when the young Dawn showed again with her rosy fingers,
then the male sheep hastened out of the cave, toward pasture,
but the ewes were bleating all through the pens unmilked, their udders
ready to burst. Meanwhile their master, suffering and in 440
bitter pain, felt over the backs of all his sheep, standing
up as they were, but in his guilelessness did not notice
how my men were fastened under the breasts of his fleecy
sheep. Last of all the flock the ram went out of the doorway,
loaded with his own fleece, and with me, and my close counsels. 445
Then, feeling him, powerful Polyphemos spoke a word to him:
"My dear old ram, why are you thus leaving the cave last of
the sheep? Never in the old days were you left behind by

---

6. There is an aural pun in the Greek here. The word for "Nobody" in Polyphemos's answer about his adversary sounds virtually exactly like the word for "intelligence."

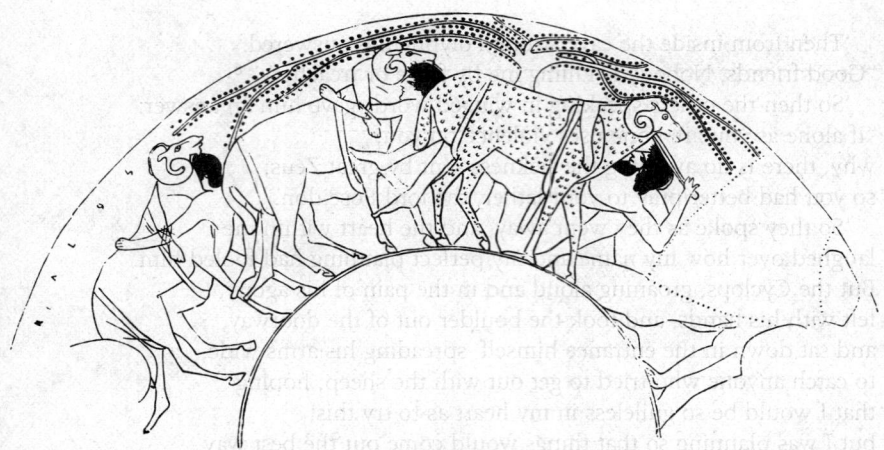

A vase painting showing Odysseus and his followers escaping the cave of
Polyphemos. 480–460 B.C.E.

the flock, but long-striding, far ahead of the rest would pasture
on the tender bloom of the grass, be first at running rivers,   450
and be eager always to lead the way first back to the sheepfold
at evening. Now you are last of all. Perhaps you are grieving
for your master's eye, which a bad man with his wicked companions
put out, after he had made my brain helpless with wine, this
Nobody, who I think has not yet got clear of destruction.   455
If only you could think like us and only be given
a voice, to tell me where he is skulking away from my anger,
then surely he would be smashed against the floor and his brains go
spattering all over the cave to make my heart lighter
from the burden of all the evils this niddering Nobody gave me."   460
    'So he spoke, and sent the ram along from him, outdoors,
and when we had got a little way from the yard and the cavern,
first I got myself loose from my ram, then set my companions
free, and rapidly then, and with many a backward glance, we
drove the long-striding sheep, rich with fat, until we reached   465
our ship, and the sight of us who had escaped death was welcome
to our companions, but they began to mourn for the others;
only I would not let them cry out, but with my brows nodded
to each man, and told them to be quick and to load the fleecy
sheep on board our vessel and sail out on the salt water.   470
Quickly they went aboard the ship and sat to the oarlocks,
and sitting well in order dashed the oars in the gray sea.
But when I was as far from the land as a voice shouting
carries, I called out aloud to the Cyclops, taunting him:
"Cyclops, in the end it was no weak man's companions   475

you were to eat by violence and force in your hollow
cave, and your evil deeds were to catch up with you, and be
too strong for you, hard one, who dared to eat your own guests
in your own house, so Zeus and the rest of the gods have punished you."

'So I spoke, and still more the heart in him was angered. 480
He broke away the peak of a great mountain and let it
fly, and threw it in front of the dark-prowed ship by only
a little, it just failed to graze the steering oar's edge,
but the sea washed up in the splash as the stone went under, the tidal
wave it made swept us suddenly back from the open 485
sea to the mainland again, and forced us on shore. Then I
caught up in my hands the very long pole and pushed her
clear again, and urged my companions with words, and nodding
with my head, to throw their weight on the oars and bring us
out of the threatening evil, and they leaned on and rowed hard. 490
But when we had cut through the sea to twice the previous distance
again I started to call to Cyclops, but my friends about me
checked me, first one then another speaking, trying to soothe me:
"Hard one, why are you trying once more to stir up this savage
man, who just now threw his missile in the sea, forcing 495
our ship to the land again, and we thought once more we were finished
and if he had heard a voice or any one of us speaking,
he would have broken all our heads and our ship's timbers
with a cast of a great jagged stone, so strong is his throwing."

'So they spoke, but could not persuade the great heart in me, 500
but once again in the anger of my heart I cried to him:
"Cyclops, if any mortal man ever asks you who it was
that inflicted upon your eye this shameful blinding,
tell him that you were blinded by Odysseus, sacker of cities.
Laertes is his father, and he makes his home in Ithaka." 505

'So I spoke, and he groaned aloud and answered me, saying:
"Ah now, a prophecy spoken of old is come to completion.
There used to be a man here, great and strong, and a prophet,
Telemos, Eurymos' son, who for prophecy was pre-eminent
and grew old as a prophet among the Cyclopes. This man told me 510
how all this that has happened now must someday be accomplished,
and how I must lose the sight of my eye at the hands of Odysseus.
But always I was on the lookout for a man handsome
and tall, with great endowment of strength on him, to come here;
but now the end of it is that a little man, niddering, feeble, 515
has taken away the sight of my eye, first making me helpless
with wine. So come here, Odysseus, let me give you a guest gift
and urge the glorious Shaker of the Earth to grant you conveyance
home. For I am his son, he announces himself as my father.
He himself will heal me, if he will, but not any other 520
one of the blessed gods, nor any man who is mortal."

'So he spoke, but I answered him again and said to him:
"I only wish it were certain I could make you reft of spirit
and life, and send you to the house of Hades, as it is certain
that not even the Shaker of the Earth will ever heal your eye for you."   525
'So I spoke, but he then called to the lord Poseidon
in prayer, reaching both arms up toward the starry heaven:
"Hear me, Poseidon who circle the earth, dark-haired. If truly
I am your son, and you acknowledge yourself as my father,
grant that Odysseus, sacker of cities, son of Laertes,   530
who makes his home in Ithaka, may never reach that home;
but if it is decided that he shall see his own people,
and come home to his strong-founded house and to his own country,
let him come late, in bad case, with the loss of all his companions,
in someone else's ship, and find troubles in his household."   535
'So he spoke in prayer, and the dark-haired god heard him.
Then for the second time lifting a stone far greater
he whirled it and threw, leaning into the cast his strength beyond measure,
and the stone fell behind the dark-prowed ship by only
a little, it just failed to graze the steering oar's edge,   540
and the sea washed up in the splash as the stone went under; the tidal
wave drove us along forward and forced us onto the island.
But after we had so made the island, where all the rest of
our strong-benched ships were waiting together, and our companions
were sitting about them grieving, having waited so long for us,   545
making this point we ran our ship on the sand and beached her,
and we ourselves stepped out onto the break of the sea beach,
and from the hollow ships bringing out the flocks of the Cyclops
we shared them out so none might go cheated of his proper
portion; but for me alone my strong-greaved companions   550
excepted the ram when the sheep were shared, and I sacrificed him
on the sands to Zeus, dark-clouded son of Kronos, lord over
all, and burned him the thighs; but he was not moved by my offerings,
but still was pondering on a way how all my strong-benched
ships should be destroyed and all my eager companions.   555
So for the whole length of the day until the sun's setting,
we sat there feasting on unlimited meat and sweet wine.
But when the sun went down and the sacred darkness came over,
then we lay down to sleep along the break of the seashore;
but when the young Dawn showed again with her rosy fingers,   560
then I urged on the rest of my companions and told them
to go aboard their ships and to cast off the stern cables,
and quickly they went aboard the ships and sat to the oarlocks,
and sitting well in order dashed their oars in the gray sea.
From there we sailed on further along, glad to have escaped death,   565
but grieving still at heart for the loss of our dear companions.

KABTI-ILANI-MARDUK

(EARLY EIGHTH CENTURY B.C.E.)

Babylon

This extraordinary poem was written, as its closing lines inform us, by Kabti-ilani-Marduk, a priest of Marduk, the patron god of Babylon. The poem depicts a time of troubles, characterized both by civil unrest and by incursions of nomadic invaders, during which Marduk's temple was sacked. Kabti-ilani-Marduk, who probably lived in the first half of the eighth century B.C.E. seeks to explore the roots of the disorder, and especially to explain how Marduk could have allowed his own temple to be overrun. The poet wants to show that Marduk himself was not defeated by hostile forces and that he did not simply desert his own people; in particular, the poem exonerates the priesthood of Marduk from accusations of neglect of their duties.

More generally, the poet outlines the nature of responsible and irresponsible government, implicitly admonishing the rulers of Babylon through his story of the consequences of power politics among the gods. Erra, the god of pestilence, persuades Marduk to journey away from Babylon and then usurps his place. He is moved to hatch this plot not from some pure, mythic love of violence but at the behest of his seven disease demons. Normally mere henchmen, here they are shown as a kind of military-pestilential complex, fomenting a war so as to keep their own weapons and tactics in good order; they argue that a spectacular first strike against a weaker opponent will improve Erra's standing at home. Erra, for his part, approves their plan because he realizes that he can use the ensuing disorder to dominate his fellow gods. His depredations end only when his counselor Ishum manages to calm him down. The poem is a striking instance of mythic material used for acute social and political analysis, all presented with vivid dialogue and moving descriptions of the war and its effects.

The Erra Epic

Tablet I

I sing of the son of the lord of the inhabited lands, creator of the universe,
of Hendursanga, Enlil's first-born son,[1] governor of the world,
bearer of the august scepter, guardian of the dark-headed ones, shepherd of
      humanity:
Ishum, glorious warrior whose hands are made to brandish his furious weapons,

Translated by David Damrosch.

Note on translation: This translation is based on the edition and Italian translation by Luigi Cagni; the translator also adopted a number of readings from translations by René Labat and by Stephanie Dalley.

---

1. Enlil is the chief Sumerian deity; Hendur-sanga is a name for his son Ishum, war leader of the gods, herald and adviser to Erra.

at the flash of whose impetuous spear Erra himself, most valiant of the gods,
    trembles on his throne!   5
When Erra's heart urges him on to battle,
he says to his weapons, "Spread on yourselves the poison of death!"
and to the Seven,[2] heroes unequalled, "Strap your weapons on!"
To you, Ishum, he says, "I am ready to march;
you are the torch, we see by your light;   10
you are the herald, the gods follow your lead;
you are the blade, it is you who will slay."

"Then let us go, Erra!" Ishum replies. "To lay waste the lands,
how it refreshes your spirit, how it gladdens your heart!"
Yet Erra's arms are heavy, as of one who needs sleep.   15
He says to himself, "Should I arise? Should I lie down some more?"
He says to his weapons: "Remain in the corner!"
He says to the Seven, heroes unequalled, "Go back to your homes!"
Until you wake him, Ishum, he stays in his bed,
given over to pleasure with Mami, his wife.   20
O Engidudu,[3] lord who prowls at night, the prince's vigilant guardian,
he watches over the youths and the maidens and makes them shine like day.

But as for the Seven, heroes unequalled, their nature is different indeed.
Their origin is strange, they are replete with terrors,
whoever sees them is horror-struck; their breath is fatal.   25
Mortals tremble, they dare not approach them;
Ishum is their bulwark, a door closed before them.
When Anu, king of the gods, impregnated the Earth,
she bore him seven gods, and he called them the Seven.
They stood before him, and he fixed their destinies.   30
He called the first to give him this order:
"Wherever you spread terror, may you have no rival!"
He said to the second, "Burn like fire, and scorch like flame!"
He said to the third, "Take the features of a lion: those who see you will return to
    nothingness!"
He said to the fourth, "When you raise your furious weapons, the mountains will
    crumble!"   35
He said to the fifth, "Howl like the wind, and search across the sphere of the
    universe!"
He ordered the sixth, "Go from the heights to the depths, and let no one be
    spared!"
He charged the seventh with viper's venom, saying, "Destroy the living!"
After Anu had fixed the destinies of all of the Seven,
he gave them to Erra, champion of the gods, saying, "These will march at your
    side.   40

---

2. The seven disease demons, Erra's lieuten-   3. A name for Erra.
   ants.

If the tumult of the inhabited lands becomes distressing to you,
and your heart is moved to wreak destruction,
to kill the dark-headed ones and slaughter the cattle of Shakkan,[4]
then let these be your furious weapons, may they march by your side!"

And now they brandish their arms in rage,   45
saying to Erra: "Get up! Go to it!
Why do you stay in the city, like a feeble old man,
why do you stay at home, like a weak little child?
Like those who do not take the field, should we eat women's bread?
As though we did not know battle, should we tremble, full of fear?   50
For young men, going to war is like going to a feast!
Even a prince who stays in town cannot eat his bread in peace;
he is mocked by his people, and his person is despised.
How can he measure up against those who take the field?
The one who stays in town, however great his strength,   55
in what can he prevail over one who takes the field?
City bread in plenty cannot compare to flat loaves baked in embers,
the sweetest beer cannot compare to water from a goatskin,
nor can a terraced palace be compared to a hut in the field.
Valiant Erra, go into the field, and let your arms resound!   60
Launch your battle-cry so strongly that all who hear will tremble;
that the Igigi,[5] hearing it, may magnify your name;
that the Anunnaki,[6] hearing it, may tremble at your name;
that all the gods, hearing it, may bow beneath your yoke;
that kings, hearing it, may fall down at your feet;   65
that the nations, hearing it, may bring their tribute to you;
that the demons, hearing it, may hide themselves away;
that the powerful, hearing it, may bite their lips in fear;
that the high mountains, hearing it, may shudder and bow their heads;
that the oceans, hearing it, may surge and drown all they produce;   70
that in the ancient forest, the tree-trunks may be shattered;
that in the densest cane-field, the reeds may all be broken;
that the humans may be filled with fear, and quiet their tumult down;
that the beasts be filled with panic, and all return to clay;
seeing all this, may the gods your fathers glorify your valor!   75
Valiant Erra, why have you shunned the field, to rest within the city?
Even the cattle of Shakkan and the other animals scorn us.
O valiant Erra, to you we speak, may our words not displease you!
Before the entire human land becomes too strong for us,
may you take our words to heart!   80
For the Anunnaki, who love silence, you should do a good deed—
the Anunnaki, troubled by the humans' noise, no longer can sleep.

---

4. God of cattle and herdsmen.   6. A group of fifty gods, sons of Anu, judges of
5. A group of gods.   the underworld.

The cattle are trampling down the pastures, the life of the land,
the laborer in his fields is weeping bitterly;
the lion and the wolf are carrying off the cattle of Shakkan,   85
and the shepherd, concerned for his flock, has no rest day or night: it is you he
    implores!
And we, who knew the mountain passes, have completely forgotten the way.
Across our weapons of war the spider has stretched her webs;
our trusty bow, rebelling, has become too strong for us,
the sharp edge of our arrow has been blunted,   90
and our sword is covered with rust instead of blood!"

The valiant Erra heard them;
the words of the Seven pleased him like fine oil.
He opened his mouth and said to Ishum,
"Why, having heard this, do you sit silent and still?   95
Open the way, I would take the path of war!
The Seven, heroes unequalled, are to accompany me;
let my valiant weapons march at my sides,
and as for you, march before me and behind me!"

When Ishum heard these words,   100
he opened his mouth and replied to valiant Erra,
"Lord Erra, why do you plan evil against the gods?
Why do you plan evil, to lay waste the lands and exterminate their people?"

Erra opened his mouth and spoke; to Ishum, his herald, he replied:
"Attend, Ishum, and hear what I have to say!   105
As for the inhabitants of the lands, whom you ask me to spare,
O herald of the gods, wise Ishum, whose counsel is good,
in heaven I am a wild bull, on earth I am a lion!
Among the nations I am the king, among the gods the ferocious one.
Among the Igigi I am the most valiant, among the Anunnaki the most powerful.   110
Among the cattle I am the butcher, among the mountains the wild ram.
In the cane-field, I am the fire; in the forest, the battle-axe.
On the path of war, I am the standard.
I howl like the wind, I thunder like Adad,[7]
like Shamash[8] I survey the entire sphere of the universe.   115
When I go into the field, I am at home like a wild sheep,
when I go up to heaven, I make my home there too.
All of the gods dread battle with me,
but the humans, the dark-headed ones, hold me in contempt!
And so I—since they fear my name no longer,   120
and since they follow their own inclination, rejecting the word of Marduk[9]—
I will stir lord Marduk to anger: I will cause him to leave his throne;
I will destroy the human race!"

---

7. God of storms.
8. God of the sun.

9. Patron god of Babylon, hero of *Enuma Elish*.

Then valiant Erra turned his face toward Shuanna,[10] city of the king of the gods;
he entered Esagil,[11] palace of heaven and earth, and came before Marduk's
    presence.   125
He opened his mouth and spoke to the king of the gods:
"How could it be that your regalia, insignia of your sovereignty, are blemished,
though they should be full of splendor like the stars of heaven?
How could it be that the appearance of your royal crown is dimmed,
though it should illuminate the temple Ehalanki like your tower Etemenanki?"[12]   130

The king of the gods opened his mouth and spoke;
to Erra, champion of the gods, he returned these words:
"Valiant Erra, as for this task you urge me to undertake,
long ago I stirred myself to anger; I left my throne, and I brought about the Flood;
I left my throne, and the bonds of heaven and earth were untied,   135
And then the heavens trembled; the stars were shaken, and did not return to their
    place;
the underworld was stirred up, and the fruit of the furrows grew scarce: a tribute
    imposed forever.
When I had untied the bonds of heaven and earth, the deep waters dried up, and
    the floods ebbed away.
I returned and saw this: it was hard to bring the waters back!
The fertility of living things had diminished, and I could not return them to their
    former state,   140
until, like a farm laborer, I had taken their seed in my own hands,
and until I had built a house and installed myself within.
The appearance of my regalia, tarnished by the deluge, was darkened.
I assigned to Girru[13] the task of renewing the splendor of my features, and
    purifying my vestments.
After he had restored the splendor of my regalia, and had completed this work for
    me,   145
and I had put back on the crown of my sovereignty and had resumed my place,
my features expressed haughtiness, and my look was awesome.
As for the humans who survived the flood and witnessed this work,
should I now wield my arms and destroy the rest?
As for the wise craftsmen, I had sent them into the Abyss, and I did not ordain
    their return.   150
And as for the materials, the rosewood and rock crystal, I had changed their
    location and revealed it to no one.
And so, for the work you propose, O valiant Erra,
where can be found the rosewood, flesh of the gods, insignia of the king of the
    universe?
It is the pure wood, the august youth, fitted for sovereignty,

---

10. A name for Babylon.
11. Marduk's temple.
12. Ehelanki is a shrine in Babylon; Eteme-

nanki is the great ziggurat tower of Marduk.
13. God of fire.

whose root, reaching a hundred leagues into the waters of the great ocean, attains
    the foundations of the nether world;   155
whose root stretches up to the height of the heaven of Anu.
Where is the translucent sapphire, which I had set aside?
Where is Ninildu, great carpenter of my divinity,
who carries the golden adze, and who knows all timbers,
who makes his work shine like day, and who bows before me?   160
Where is Gushkinbanda, creator of god and of man, whose hands are pure?
Where is Ninagal, bearer of the hammer and anvil,
who cuts hard copper as if it were leather, and who makes the needed tools?
Where are the precious stones to be found, product of the vast ocean, ornaments
    of my crown?
Where are now the Seven Sages of the Abyss, the holy carp,   165
filled like their father Ea with sublime understanding, adept at purifying my
    body?"[14]

Hearing him, valiant Erra stepped forward; he opened his mouth and spoke to
    lord Marduk.
"I, Marduk, I will retrieve the rock crystal that you desire,
I will bring back the pure rosewood that you desire."
Hearing this, Marduk opened his mouth and spoke to valiant Erra: 170
"If I should leave my throne again, the bonds of heaven and earth would be
    untied,
the waters would rise up and flood the land.
Bright day would change to darkness,
the tempest would arise and cover the stars;
the evil wind would blow and block the sight of mankind, the progeny of the
    living;   175
demons would ascend from the nether world, and death would seize the living;
until I had resumed my arms, who would repel them?"

Hearing this, Erra opened his mouth and spoke to lord Marduk:
"O prince Marduk, until you have returned to your home, vestments purified by
    Girru,
until you have returned to your place, until that very moment,   180
I myself will take your place, and I will make fast the bonds of heaven and earth!
I will go up to heaven and give the Igigi their orders,
I will descend to the Abyss and assign the Anunnaki's tasks.
I will chase the savage demons to the Land of No Return;
I will unleash my furious weapons against them.   185
As for the evil wind, I will tie up its wings like a bird,
and at that house which you enter, O prince Marduk,
to the right and the left of your door, like guardian bulls,

---

14. Ea, god of freshwater and wisdom, sent
the Seven Sages in the form of fish to teach
humanity the arts of civilization.

I will cause the divine Anu and Enlil to lie!"
Lord Marduk heard him out; he was pleased by the words Erra said.
He arose from his inaccessible throne, and turned his face toward the Anunnaki's
    dwelling.

Tablet II [15]

Erra entered Emeslam and occupied the throne.
He consulted with himself about what he should do,
but his heart was raging and gave him no reply.
To Ishum he repeated his commands:
"Make the way open: I wish to take the path of war!
The day is over, the term is at an end.
I say: Let the splendor of the rays of Shamash be dimmed!
I will cover the face of the Moon at night!
To Adad I will say: 'Hold back your well-springs,
withdraw your clouds, and stop the snow and the rain!'
To Marduk and to Ea I will carry this news:
The one who has flourished in times of abundance will be buried in times of
    distress;
the one who has travelled on well-watered roads will return on a pathway of dust!
To the king of the gods I will say: 'Reside in Esagil;
the words you have spoken will be carried out, your orders will be fulfilled;
but if the dark-headed ones cry out to you, do not grant their prayers!'
I will destroy the nations and reduce them to heaps of debris.
I will lay the cities low and reduce them all to desert.
I will shatter the mountains and slaughter the cattle on them;
I will stir up the oceans and destroy the things they produce;
I will devastate cane-field and forest, burning them up like fire;
I will slaughter the people, leaving no soul alive.
I will not spare a single one, that they could multiply;
I will not let the cattle of Shakkan or any animal escape.
I will take charge over one city after another:
The son will no longer think of the health of his father, nor the father care for the
    son.
The mother will plot her daughter's misfortune in the midst of the joys of love.
Into the dwelling of the gods, forbidden to the wicked, I will cause the wicked to
    enter;
into the dwelling of princes I will introduce the scoundrel.
I will cause beasts to enter the city,
and I will empty it of people.
I will cause them to strike at the hearts of the mountains;

line numbers in margin: 190, 5, 10, 15, 20, 25, 30

---

15. The first seventy-five lines of this tablet are
fragmentary; the predicted natural disasters occur after Marduk departs. When the
text resumes, Erra is taking advantage of
the chaos to seize power.

wherever they set their foot, I will devastate that place;
I will cause wild beasts of the steppe to roam about the city.
I will render omens evil; I will devastate the holy precincts.   35
Into the dwellings of the gods I will bring the demon Saghulhaga;
the palace of kings I will bring to ruin.
I will silence the cry of humanity, and deprive them of every joy!"

Tablet III

Erra, in his rage, listens to no one;
he ignores the counsel he is given,
a lion in appearance and in voice.
Then to Ishum, who marches before him, he says these words:
"I will change the sunlight into darkness!   5
I will take the wise man in his house, and I will cut short his days!
As for the just man, the good intercessor, I will cut off his life,
and in his place I will put the wicked man, the cut-throat.
I will alter the human heart: the father will not heed his son,
and the daughter will speak hatefully to her mother.   10
I will render their speech evil: they will forget their god,
and against their goddess they will speak vile insults.
I will raise up brigands to block the roads,
and within the cities, neighbors will steal each other's goods,
while the lion and the wolf attack the cattle of Shakkan.   15
I will enrage the goddess of creation and she will put an end to childbirth;
I will deprive the wet-nurse of the crying of infants and of children.
I will disrupt the song of the workers in the fields;
shepherd and herdsman will forget the shelter of their hut.
I will strip the clothing from the human body: 20
the young will creep naked through their cities,
and I will make them, naked, descend to the nether world.
They will lack the sacrificial sheep to save their life;
even for the prince the lamb needed for the oracles of Shamash will be rare,
and one who is ill will long in vain for the roasted meat for his offering!"[16]   25

Ishum was filled with pity, and said to himself,
"Alas for my people, against whom Erra is enraged!
They have aroused the vengeance of valiant Nergal; now, as in days of combat,
when he killed the conquered Asakku, his arms do not tire;
as if to bind the wicked Anzu, he stretches out his net!"[17]   30
Then Ishum opened his mouth and spoke; to valiant Erra he said these words:
"Why have you had evil thoughts against god and humankind?
Why these endless evil thoughts against the humans, the dark-headed ones?"

---

16. Several dozen fragmentary lines detail
Erra's depredations and the gods' distress.
When the text resumes, Ishum responds.

17. The Asakku were a group of demons;
Anzu was a lion-headed eagle.

Erra opened his mouth and spoke; to Ishum, his herald, he said these words:
"You know the decrees of the Igigi, and the Anunnakis' counsel;   35
you give orders to humanity, the dark-headed ones, and open their
    understanding:
why then do you speak as one who knows nothing?
Why do you counsel me as though you did not know what Marduk has said?
The king of the gods has abandoned his throne—
how could the nations remain stable?   40
He has put aside the crown of his sovereignty:
kings and princes, like slaves, forget their duties.
He has loosened the buckle of his belt,
and the chain linking god and mortals is unfastened: it is hard to retie!
The terrible Girru has made Marduk's precious regalia shine like day, has raised
    up again his divine splendor.   45
His right hand has seized the mace, his great weapon,
and the glance of lord Marduk is fearsome.
O herald of the gods, wise Ishum, whose counsel is benevolent,
why do the words of Marduk displease you?"   50

Ishum opened his mouth and spoke to valiant Erra:
"Warrior Erra, you grasp the reins of heaven,
you are lord of all the earth, you are master of the nations;
you stir up the oceans, you lay the mountains low;
you govern humanity, you give the cattle pasture;   55
Esharra is at your disposal, Engurra is in your hands;
you control Shuanna, you give orders for Esagil;
you gather together all the sacred ordinances: the gods fear you,
the Igigi revere you, the Anunnaki tremble before you.
If you render a decision, even Anu heeds you,   60
even Enlil obeys you. Without you, would there be hostilities,
and without you, would there be battle?
A breastplate of battle is your robe!
And yet you say in your heart: 'They have despised me!'

Tablet IV

"Valiant Erra, you have not feared the name of Marduk;
of the city of the king of the gods, Dimkurkurra, "Bond of the Nations," you have
    broken the bond.
You have altered your divine nature and taken the form of a man;
you have put on your weapons and entered inside the city;
in Babylon, you have spoken as a master, like one who has conquered a city.   5
The people of Babylon, used to growing freely like the reeds of the canals, are all
    clustered around you.
The one who knew no weapons, has his sword unsheathed;
the one who knew no arrow, now his bow is bent;
he who knew no combat, his battle is engaged;

he who knew no haste, flies like a bird;   10
the slow one passes the swift, the feeble surpasses the strong.
Against the governor, provider of their holy city, great insults are spoken;
the gate of Babylon, canal of their abundance, the people themselves have blocked
    up;
they have put the sanctuary of Babylon to fire, as if they were their own
    conquerors!
And you, you marched before them as their herald!   15
You struck with an arrow the great wall Imgur-Enlil—'Ah, my heart!' it exclaimed.
The throne of Muhra, custodian of the entry, you drowned in the blood of
    children.
The inhabitants of Babylon are birds, and you the decoy—
you led them into the net, to be captured and destroyed, O valiant Erra!
Then you left the city, and you went yet further: 20
You assumed the features of a lion and entered into the palace.
Seeing you, the troops put on their arms,
and the heart of the governor, Babylon's protector, became enraged.
He ordered his army to pillage like enemy looters,
and the captain of the guard he incited to evil: 25
'When I send you into the city, my brave one,
fear no god and dread no mortal;
young and old together, put them all to death,
do not spare a single babe or suckling!
Strip off Babylon's riches as your plunder!'   30
The king's army assembled and entered the city;
the arrow blazes, the sword is thrust!
The free man, protected by the holiness of Anu and of Dagan, you have called to
    arms;
you have spilled their blood like water down the city's drains,
you have opened their veins, and made the river flow in blood!   35

"The great lord Marduk has seen this and exclaimed 'Alas!'
His heart was seized, an inexpiable curse was on his lips.
He swore that he would never again drink the river's water;
he shunned their blood and refused to enter Esagil.
'Alas, Babylon,' he cried, 'whose head I ripened like a palm tree, now withered by
    the wind!   40
Alas, Babylon, which I filled with seeds like a pine-cone, whose fullness I cannot
    enjoy!
Alas, Babylon, which I planted like a lush garden, whose fruits I cannot taste!
Alas, Babylon, which like a crystal seal I set at the throat of Anu!
Alas, Babylon, which I held in my hands like the tablet of destiny, and entrusted
    to no one else!'
Thus spoke lord Marduk: 45
'Let the river routes dry up, till they are passable on foot!
May the wells lose thirty fathoms of water, that no one may survive!

May they need to haul the sailor's boat a hundred leagues to reach the waters of the sea!'

"As for Sippar, primeval city, which the Lord of the Lands did not let the Deluge drown, for it was dear in his sight,
against the will of Shamash you have destroyed its wall, you have felled its rampart.
And in Uruk, seat of Anu and of Ishtar—city of courtesans, of temple slaves and prostitutes, 50
all those whom Ishtar has deprived of husbands, devoting them to her service—
there the cries of Sutean men and women now ring out![18]
They rouse within Esagil eunuchs and transvestites,
whose masculinity Ishtar, to inspire the people with awe, had changed to femininity, 55
bearers of rapiers, of knives, of pruning knives and knives of flint,
those who, to rejoice the heart of Ishtar, give themselves over to abominations;
over these you have placed a cruel and pitiless governor,
who oppresses the people and transgresses their rites.
Ishtar herself, seized with rage, is angered at Uruk as well: 60
she raises an enemy who sweeps away the people like grain before onrushing water.
The citizens of Daksa lament without respite the loss of E'ugal,[19] committed to ruins.
The enemy you have raised up does not know when to stop!

"Ishtaran, god of Der, says these words:
'You have made a desert of my city; 65
you have broken those inside it like reeds,
and swept their cry away like foam upon the water!
Even me you have not left free: you have delivered me to the Suteans.
And so, on account of Der, my city,
no longer will I render judgments, I will not hand down decisions for the land, 70
I will give no more orders, nor make my wishes known!' "

(Erra answered thus:)[20] "Since the people have forsaken equity, embracing violence instead,
since they have abandoned what is just and have turned to plotting evil,
therefore I have unleashed the seven winds against this single country!
Whoever does not die in battle will perish from the plague; 75
whoever does not die of plague, the enemy will plunder;
whoever the enemy does not plunder will be robbed by the thief;
whoever the thief does not rob will be raked by the weapons of the king;

18. The Suteans were semitic nomads, traditional enemies of the settled Akkadians.
19. A major temple of Enlil.
20. The speaker of the following lines is not identified and may still be Ishtaran, though Erra seems more likely. Similarly, the next speech is unattributed but appears to be Ishum's reply to Erra.

whoever is not raked by the weapons of the king will be struck down by the prince;
whoever the prince does not strike down, will be drowned by the storms of Adad;   80
whoever is not drowned by Adad, will be carried off by Shamash;
whoever escapes into the open will be smitten by the wind;
whoever goes into his own house will be struck down by a demon;
whoever climbs to a high place will perish of thirst;
whoever descends into a valley, will perish from the waters;   85
heights and valleys alike will all be fatal!
The governor of the city will speak to his mother thus:
'If only, on the day you bore me, I had been blocked within your womb!
If only you had died in childbirth, and our lives had ended then!
You delivered me into a city whose wall has collapsed;   90
its people become like cattle, and the butcher is their god!'
The net is tightly woven, there is none who can escape.
Whoever sires a son and exclaims: 'Behold my son,
whom I have raised: he will avenge me!'—
that son I will give over to death, and his father must inter him;   95
and then I will give the father to death, and there will be none to dig his grave.
Whoever has built a house, and exclaims: 'This is my dwelling,
this is what I have made, and within it I shall take my rest:
on the day my destiny claims my life, here I will find my resting-place'—
him will I give over to death, and I will have his dwelling plundered;   100
and once it has been sacked, I will give the house to another."

"O valiant Erra," (Ishum responded), "you have slain the just,
and you have slain the unjust alike!
You have slain the one who offended you,
and you have slain the one who has not offended you.   105
You have slain the priest zealous in bringing offerings to his god,
and you have slain the palace attendant, servant of his king.
You have slain the elders in their rooms,
and you have slain the young maiden in her bed.
Yet none of this has calmed you in the least!   110
You say within your heart: 'They have held me in contempt!'
As you say within your heart, O valiant Erra:
'I wish to fell the strong and terrify the weak;
I wish to kill the commander, and scatter his troops in flight;
I wish to shatter the chamber of the sanctuary and the parapet of the wall,
    destroying the city's vital strength;   115
I wish to tear apart the mooring-post, that the boat be pulled away by the current;
I wish to shatter the rudder, that the ship not be able to land;
I wish to shiver the mainmast, and tear its rigging off!
I wish to dry up the mother's breast, that her infant not survive;
I wish to dam the springs, that the rivers lose their water;   120
I wish to send earthquakes through the nether world, that even the heavens may
    shake;

I wish to extinguish the splendor of Shulpae's rays,[21] and cast aside the stars;
I wish to sever the roots of trees, that their buds may not unfold;
I wish to undermine the walls, that their pinnacles may totter,
and I will go to the throne of the king of the gods, that his counsel no longer
    hold!' "   125

When valiant Erra heard Ishum's words, they pleased him like fine oil.
Then valiant Erra spoke thus:
"The sea-folk, the sea-folk; the Subartean, the Subartean; the Assyrian, the
    Assyrian;
the Elamite, the Elamite; the Kassite, the Kassite;
the Sutean, the Sutean; the Gutean, the Gutean; the Lullubean, the Lullubean;[22]   130
one country, another country; one city, another city; one house, another house;
one man, another man; one brother, his brother, without mercy:
May they all kill each other!
Only then may Akkad arise again, destroy them all and rule over them!"

Then valiant Erra said these words to his herald Ishum: 135
"Go, Ishum! Satisfy the longing of your heart to do all that you've said!"
Ishum turned his face toward mount Hihi,[23]
the Seven, heroes unequalled, pressing on behind him.
The hero reached mount Hihi:
he raised his hand and destroyed the mountain,   140
razing mount Hihi to the ground,
and he uprooted the trunks of the forest of cypress.
Once the royal road was cleared, Erra followed after Ishum.
He annihilated the cities and reduced them to desert,
he destroyed the mountains and slaughtered their cattle,   145
he stirred the oceans up and did not spare their produce,
he devastated cane and reed fields, and burned them up like fire,
he cursed the cattle and reduced them all to clay.

Tablet V

When Erra had calmed himself and returned to his throne,
all the gods looked toward his face.
Igigi and Anunnaki alike were full of fear.
Erra opened his mouth, and spoke to all the gods:
"Listen well, all of you! Pay attention to my words!   5
Truly, in this time of fault now past, I plotted wickedness;
my heart burned with rage, and I wished to slaughter the human race.
Like a mercenary shepherd, I stole the leader of the flock;
like one who knows no husbandry, I cut the orchard down;

---

21. A major Sumerian god, identified with the
    planet Jupiter.
22. Erra names various groups both within

southern Mesopotamia and to the north,
east, and west.
23. A mythical mountain, birthplace of Anzu.

like one who lays a country waste, I treated good and evil alike: I killed them all!   10
Yet one cannot pull a corpse from the mouth of a raging lion,
and where one is in a rage, another cannot give counsel!
Without Ishum, my herald, what more might have happened?
Where would your temple supplies be, where would your high priest be?
Where would your food offerings be? No longer would you smell incense!"   15

Ishum opened his mouth and spoke; to valiant Erra he addressed these words:
"Valiant one, listen well! Pay attention to my words!
Very well then, may you now be calm! We wish to be at your service;
in the day of your wrath, who can affront you?"

Erra heard this, and his visage cleared;   20
His radiant features shone like a sunlit day.
He entered Emeslam and occupied his throne,
while Ishum gave orders concerning the ruined people of Akkad:
"Let the remnant of the people begin to multiply again!
May little ones walk the roads with their elders once again.   25
May the weakened Akkadian overcome the mighty Sutean,
may each of you lead seven in tow, as though they were sheep!
May you reduce their cities to ruin, and their grazing lands to desert,
and bring their massive booty into Shuanna!
You will return the gods of your land, no longer angry, to their thrones in safety;   30
you will cause Shakkan and Nisaba[24] to descend to their land again.
The steppe will again produce its riches, and the sea will provide its tribute;
you will make the fields, laid waste, productive once again.
The governors of all the cities will bear their massive tribute into Shuanna.
May the temples now in ruins raise their heads like the rising sun,   35
may the Tigris and Euphrates flow with water in abundance;
let all governors bring supplies to the providers for Esagil and for Babylon.
For years without number, may you praise the great lord Nergal[25] and valiant
   Ishum:
be it said that Erra, consumed with anger, planned to destroy the lands and their
   people,
but Ishum, his counselor, calmed him down and saved a remnant!   40
To Kabti-ilani-Marduk, son of Dabibi, composer of these tablets,
I revealed these verses at night; when he recited them in the morning,
he did not omit a single line, nor did he add a line."

Erra heard this and expressed his approbation;
he was pleased with Ishum, his herald, and the gods all joined in his praise.   45
And then spoke valiant Erra thus:
"As for the god who esteems this song, may his sanctuary grow in wealth,
but the god who rejects it, may he never more smell incense!

---

24. Goddess of grain.

25. The god of death, here identified with
   Erra.

The king who magnifies my name will have lordship over the world,
the prince who proclaims the praise of my valor, he will have no rival!   50
The singer who chants this song will not perish from the plague,
but his words will please both king and prince alike!
The scribe who commits it to memory will escape the land of the enemy, and will
    be honored in his own land;
In the sanctuary of the wise, where they will continually proclaim my name, I will
    give wisdom to them.
In the house where these tablets are placed, should Erra become enraged, should
    the Seven turn murderous again,   55
the sword of destruction will not approach them, but safety will lie upon them.
May this song endure forever, may it last throughout all time!
May all the lands hear it and celebrate my valor,
may all people come to know it, and magnify my name!"

[Postscript to the copy from Assur.]

I, Assurbanipal, great king, mighty king, king of the world, king of Assyria, son of   60
Esarhaddon king of Assyria, son of Sennacherib king of Assyria, wrote,
checked, and collated this tablet in the company of scholars in accordance
with clay tablets and wooden writing boards, exemplars from Assyria, Sumer
and Akkad, and put it in my palace for royal reading. Whoever erases my
written name and writes his own name, may Nabu,[26] the scribe of all, erase
his name.   65

HESIOD (EIGHTH CENTURY B.C.E.)
Greece

Hesiod's *Theogony* chronicles the struggles on Olympus that establish Zeus's indisputable supremacy. In *Works and Days,* it is justice, given to human beings by Zeus, that (the poem tells us) distinguishes humankind from wild beasts. The occasion for *Works and Days*—and for the poet's invoking the justice of Zeus—purports to be a quarrel between Hesiod and his brother Perses, whom he accuses of unjustly trying to claim a larger portion of the land that the two have inherited from their father.

    The dispute gives rise to Hesiod's complaints against corrupt authority (especially, we can presume, those judges who let Perses get away with his grab) and to his reflections on the rigors and sorrows of human existence in

Translated by Dorothea Wender.

26. God of writing and wisdom.

his contemporary world. The myth about the creation of woman (in the form of Pandora) accounts in part for the suffering intrinsic to the human condition, while the myth of the five generations describes the collective decline of the human race from its earliest stage of equality with the gods, to its present state, characterized by endless labor and pain. Hesiod's exhortations to overcome idleness and restrain greed by means of honest toil (now that work is unavoidably the human lot) are combined in the last half of the poem with practical instructions on how the industrious peasant should spend his day, according to the season, interspersed with ethical precepts designed to ensure him stable prosperity. Literary works of instruction and exhortation known as "wisdom texts" existed in the Near East as early as the middle of the third millenium B.C.E.; Hesiod's poem shows their influence in form as well as content.

from Works and Days

[O Perses, store this in your heart]

O Perses, store this in your heart; do not
Let Wicked Strife persuade you, skipping work,
To gape at politicians and give ear
To all the quarrels of the market place.
He has n time for courts and public life   5
Who has not stored up one full year's supply
Of corn, Demeter's gift,[1] got from the earth.
When you have grain piled high, you may dispute
And fight about the goods of other men.
But *you* will never get this chance again: 10
Come, let us settle our dispute at once,
And let our judge be Zeus, whose laws are just.
We split our property in half, but you
Grabbed at the larger part and praised to heaven
The lords who love to try a case like that,   15
Eaters of bribes. The fools! They do not know
That half may be worth more by far than whole,
Nor how much profit lies in poor man's bread.

The gods desire to keep the stuff of life
Hidden from us. If they did not, you could   20
Work for a day and earn a year's supplies;
You'd pack away your rudder, and retire
The oxen and the labouring mules. But Zeus
Concealed the secret, angry in his heart
At being hoodwinked by Prometheus,[2]   25

---

1. Demeter is goddess of agricultural crops and presides over the harvest.

2. The story of how the Titan Prometheus tricked Zeus is told in the *Theogony*.

And so he thought of painful cares for men.
First he hid fire. But the son of Iapetos
Stole it from Zeus the Wise, concealed the flame
In a fennel stalk, and fooled the Thunderer.

Then, raging, spoke the Gatherer of Clouds:[3]   30
'Prometheus, most crafty god of all,
You stole the fire and tricked me, happily,
You, plague on all mankind and on yourself.
They'll pay for fire: I'll give another gift
To men, an evil thing for their delight,   35
And all will love this ruin in their hearts.
So spoke the father of men and gods, and laughed.

He told Hephaistos[4] quickly to mix earth
And water, and to put in it a voice
And human power to move, to make a face   40
Like an immortal goddess, and to shape
The lovely figure of a virgin girl.
Athene was to teach the girl to weave,
And golden Aphrodite[5] to pour charm
Upon her head, and painful, strong desire,   45
And body-shattering cares. Zeus ordered, then,
The killer of Argos, Hermes,[6] put in
Sly manners, and the morals of a bitch.
The son of Kronos spoke, and was obeyed.
The Lame God moulded earth as Zeus decreed   50
Into the image of a modest girl,
Grey-eyed Athene made her robes and belt,
Divine Seduction and the Graces gave
Her golden necklaces, and for her head
The Seasons wove spring flowers into a crown.   55
Hermes the Messenger put in her breast
Lies and persuasive words and cunning ways;
The herald of the gods then named the girl
Pandora[7] for the gifts which all the gods
Had given her, this ruin of mankind.   60

The deep and total trap was now complete;
The Father sent the gods' fast messenger

---

3. An epithet of Zeus, whose dominion is the sky.
4. The divine craftsman.
5. Goddess of love and sexuality.
6. Hermes, the divine messenger, is also a renowned thief and the patron deity of thieves.
7. The name means "all gifts." Woman in this account is viewed as a construction, fabricated by joining together disconnected elements, rather than as an integrated being.

To bring the gift to Epimetheus.[8]
And Epimetheus forgot the words
His brother said, to take no gift from Zeus,   65
But send it back, lest it should injure men.
He took the gift, and understood, too late.

Before this time men lived upon the earth
Apart from sorrow and from painful work,
Free from disease, which brings the Death-gods in.   70
But now the woman opened up the cask,
And scattered pains and evils among men.
Inside the cask's hard walls remained one thing,
Hope, only, which did not fly through the door.
The lid stopped her, but all the others flew,   75
Thousands of troubles, wandering the earth.
The earth is full of evils, and the sea.
Diseases come to visit men by day
And, uninvited, come again at night
Bringing their pains in silence, for they were   80
Deprived of speech by Zeus the Wise. And so
There is no way to flee the mind of Zeus.

And now with art and skill I'll summarize
Another tale, which you should take to heart,
Of how both gods and men began the same.   85
The gods, who live on Mount Olympus, first
Fashioned a golden race of mortal men;
These lived in the reign of Kronos, king of heaven,[9]
And like the gods they lived with happy hearts
Untouched by work or sorrow. Vile old age   90
Never appeared, but always lively-limbed,
Far from all ills, they feasted happily.
Death came to them as sleep, and all good things
Were theirs; ungrudgingly, the fertile land
Gave up her fruits unasked. Happy to be   95
At peace, they lived with every want supplied,
[Rich in their flocks, dear to the blessed gods.]

And then this race was hidden in the ground.
But still they live as spirits of the earth,
Holy and good, guardians who keep off harm,   100

---

8. Brother of Prometheus.
9. Father of Zeus and the other Olympian
   gods. His reign was thought of as a golden
   age of simplicity and plenty, subsequent to
   which men's lives underwent progressive
   hardships and physical and moral degeneration. The myth of the deteriorating ages of
   man represented by successively inferior
   metals has parallels in Babylonian and Persian mythology, as well as in the Book of
   Daniel.

Givers of wealth: this kingly right is theirs.
The gods, who live on Mount Olympus, next
Fashioned a lesser, silver race of men:
Unlike the gold in stature or in mind.
A child was raised at home a hundred years   105
And played, huge baby, by his mother's side.
When they were grown and reached their prime, they lived
Brief, anguished lives, from foolishness, for they
Could not control themselves, but recklessly
Injured each other and forsook the gods;   110
They did not sacrifice, as all tribes must, but left
The holy altars bare. And, angry, Zeus
The son of Kronos, hid this race away,
For they dishonoured the Olympian gods.

The earth then hid this second race, and they   115
Are called the spirits of the underworld,
Inferior to the gold, but honoured, too.
And Zeus the father made a race of bronze,
Sprung from the ash tree, worse than the silver race,
But strange and full of power. And they loved   120
The groans and violence of war; they ate
No bread; their hearts were flinty-hard; they were
Terrible men; their strength was great, their arms
And shoulders and their limbs invincible.
Their weapons were of bronze, their houses bronze;   125
Their tools were bronze: black iron was not known.
They died by their own hands, and nameless, went
To Hades' chilly house. Although they were
Great soldiers, they were captured by black Death,
And left the shining brightness of the sun.   130

But when this race was covered by the earth,
The son of Kronos made another, fourth,
Upon the fruitful land, more just and good,
A godlike race of heroes, who are called
The demi-gods—the race before our own.   135
Foul wars and dreadful battles ruined some;
Some sought the flocks of Oedipus,[10] and died
In Cadmus' land, at seven-gated Thebes;
And some, who crossed the open sea in ships,
For fair-haired Helen's sake, were killed at Troy.   140
These men were covered up in death, but Zeus

---

10. A reference to the struggle between the
    sons of Oedipus for power in the city of
    Thebes. (See Sophocles's *Antigone*.)

The son of Kronos gave the others life
And homes apart from mortals, at Earth's edge.
And there they live a carefree life, beside
The whirling Ocean, on the Blessed Isles.   145
Three times a year the blooming, fertile earth
Bears honeyed fruits for them, the happy ones.
And Kronos is their king, far from the gods,
For Zeus released him from his bonds, and these,
The race of heroes, will deserve their fame.   150

Far-seeing Zeus then made another race,
The fifth, who live now on the fertile earth.
I wish I were not of this race, that I
had died before, or had not yet been born.
This is the race of iron. Now, by day,   155
Men work and grieve unceasingly; by night,
They waste away and die. The gods will give
Harsh burdens, but will mingle in some good;
Zeus will destroy this race of mortal men,
When babies shall be born with greying hair.   160
Father will have no common bond with son,
Neither will guest with host, nor friend with friend;
The brother-love of past days will be gone.
Men will dishonour parents, who grow old
Too quickly, and will blame and criticize   165
With cruel words. Wretched and godless, they
Refusing to repay their bringing up,
Will cheat their aged parents of their due.
Men will destroy the towns of other men.
The just, the good, the man who keeps his word   170
Will be despised, but men will praise the bad
And insolent. Might will be Right, and shame
Will cease to be. Men will do injury
To better men by speaking crooked words
And adding lying oaths;   175

                    · · ·

O Perses, follow right; control your pride.
For pride is evil in a common man.
Even a noble finds it hard to bear;
It weighs him down and leads him to disgrace.
The road to justice is the better way,   180
For Justice in the end will win the race
And Pride will lose: the simpleton must learn
This fact through suffering. The god of Oaths
Runs faster than a crooked verdict; when
Justice is dragged out of the way by men   185

Who judge dishonestly and swallow bribes,
A struggling sound is heard; then she returns
Back to the city and the homes of men,
Wrapped in a mist and weeping, and she brings
Harm to the crooked men who drove her out. 190
But when the judges of a town are fair
To foreigner and citizen alike,
Their city prospers and her people bloom;
Since Peace is in the land, her children thrive;
Zeus never marks them out for cruel war. 195
Famine and blight do not beset the just,
Who till their well-worked fields and feast. The earth
Supports them lavishly; and on the hills
The oak bears acorns for them at the top
And honey-bees below; their woolly sheep 200
Bear heavy fleeces, and their wives bear sons
Just like their fathers. Since they always thrive,
They have no need to go on ships, because
The plenty-bringing land gives them her fruit.

But there are some who till the fields of pride 205
And work at evil deeds; Zeus marks them out,
And often, all the city suffers for
Their wicked schemes, and on these men, from heaven
The son of Kronos sends great punishments,
Both plague and famine, and the people die. 210
Their wives are barren, and their villages
Dwindle, according to the plan of Zeus.
At other times the son of Kronos will
Destroy their army, or will snatch away
Their city wall, or all their ships at sea. 215
You lords, take notice of his punishment.
The deathless gods are never far away;
They mark the crooked judges who grind down
Their fellow-men and do not fear the gods.
Three times ten thousand watchers-over-men, 220
Immortal, roam the fertile earth for Zeus.
Clothed in a mist, they visit every land
And keep a watch on law-suits and on crimes.
One of them is the virgin, born of Zeus,
Justice, revered by all the Olympian gods. 225
Whenever she is hurt by perjurers,
Straightway she sits beside her father Zeus,
And tells him of the unjust hearts of men,
Until the city suffers for its lords
Who recklessly, with mischief in their minds, 230

Pervert their judgments crookedly. Beware,
You lords who swallow bribes, and try to judge
Uprightly, clear your minds of crookedness.
He hurts himself who hurts another man,
And evil planning harms the planner most.   235

The eye of Zeus sees all, and understands,
And when he wishes, marks and does not miss
How just a city is, inside. And I
Would not myself be just, nor have my son
Be just among bad men: for it is bad   240
To be an honest man where felons rule;
I trust wise Zeus to save me from this pass.
But you, O Perses, think about these things;
Follow the just, avoiding violence.
The son of Kronos made this law for men: 245
That animals and fish and winged birds
Should eat each other, for they have no law.
But mankind has the law of Right from him,
Which is the better way. And if one knows
The law of Justice and proclaims it, Zeus   250
Far-seeing gives one great prosperity.
But if a man, with knowledge, swears an oath
Committing perjury and harming right
Beyond repair, his family will be cursed
In after times, and come to nothing. He   255
Who keeps his oath will benefit his house.

I say important things for you to hear,
O foolish Perses: Badness can be caught
In great abundance, easily; the road
To her is level, and she lives near by.   260
But Good is harder, for the gods have placed
In front of her much sweat; the road is steep
And long and rocky at the first, but when
You reach the top, she is not hard to find.

That man is best who reasons for himself,   265
Considering the future. Also good
Is he who takes another's good advice.
But he who neither thinks himself nor learns
From others, is a failure as a man.

O noble Perses, keep my words in mind,   270
And work till Hunger is your enemy
And till Demeter, awesome, garlanded,
Becomes your friend and fills your granary.
For Hunger always loves a lazy man;

Both gods and men despise him, for he is   275
Much like the stingless drone, who does not work
But eats, and wastes the effort of the bees.
But you must learn to organize your work
So you may have full barns at harvest time.
From working, men grow rich in flocks and gold   280
And dearer to the deathless gods. In work
There is no shame; shame is in idleness.
And if you work, the lazy man will soon
Envy your wealth: a rich man can become
Famous and good. No matter what your luck,   285
To work is better; turn your foolish mind
From other men's possessions to your own,
And earn your living, as I tell you to.
A cringing humbleness accompanies
The needy man, a humbleness which may   290
Destroy or profit him. The humble are
The poor men, while the rich are self-assured.
Money should not be seized; that gold which is
God's gift is better. If a man gets wealth
By force of hands or through his lying tongue,   295
As often happens, when greed clouds his mind
And shame is pushed aside by shamelessness,
Then the gods blot him out and blast his house
And soon his wealth deserts him. Also, he
Who harms a guest or suppliant, or acts   300
Unseemly, sleeping with his brother's wife,
Or in his folly, hurts an orphan child,
Or he who picks rough quarrels, and attacks
His father at the threshold of old age,
He angers Zeus himself, and in the end   305
He pays harsh penalties for all his sins.

Now, shut your foolish heart against these things
And sacrifice to the immortal gods
With reverence and ritual cleanliness,
And burn the glorious thigh-bones; please the gods   310
With incense and libations, when you go
To bed, and when the holy light returns,
That they may favour you, with gracious hearts
And spirits, so that you may buy the lands
Of other men, and they may not buy yours.   315

Invite your friend, but not your enemy,
To dine; especially, be cordial to
Your neighbour, for if trouble comes at home,
A neighbour's there, at hand; while kinsmen take

Some time to arm themselves. It is a curse   320
To have a worthless neighbour; equally,
A good one is a blessing; he who is
So blest possesses something of great worth.
No cow of yours will stray away if you
Have watchful neighbours. Measure carefully   325
When you must borrow from your neighbour, then,
pay back the same, or more, if possible,
And you will have a friend in time of need.

Shun evil profit, for dishonest gain
Is just the same as failure. Love your friends.   330

ARCHILOCHUS
(SEVENTH CENTURY B.C.E.)
TYRTAEUS (SEVENTH CENTURY B.C.E.)
SOLON (c. 640–558 B.C.E.)
Greece

As increasingly complex forms of political and social organization developed throughout Greece in the seventh century B.C.E., the experience of belonging to a community, with all the entailed responsibilities and benefits, became a subject for reflection. A number of poetic forms lent themselves to the expression of community-centered concerns at this period (literary prose came only much later); among them was the elegy. Ancient critics made a formal distinction between elegiac and lyric poetry, the elegy being accompanied by the flute, the lyric being sung to a stringed instrument called the lyre. In addition, the elegy's distinctive meter, consisting of two-line sequences, set it apart from the stanzaic structure of lyric verse. In later periods the term elegy came exclusively to denote poetry of mourning, but in early Greece elegiac meter was used for poetry on a wide variety of subjects, notably that of political address as well as private reflection. All of the poems in this selection, with the exception of Archilochus's "Heart, my heart" and "I don't like a tall general, swaggering" are elegies.

Archilochus, who lived in the mid-seventh century B.C.E. and came from the island of Paros, is the first practitioner of elegy whose work survives to us (although he wrote in other verse forms as well). In a striking departure from the way in which Homer and even Hesiod present themselves in their poetry, Archilochus represents himself as a citizen, a member of a political entity, deeply affected by the loss of his fellow citizens.

Tyrtaeus, Archilochus's younger contemporary from Sparta, returns us to an image of battle reminiscent of the *Iliad* (and clearly influenced by it). Here, however, the call to valor is a call to patriotism; the context for Tyrtaeus was his city's war with a neighboring territory, and he exhorts his fellow Spartans to brave action on the battlefield by reminding them of each individual's dependence on the city for which he fights.

Solon was both a poet and a crucial figure in Athenian political history who was responsible for far-reaching constitutional reforms. The broad civic (rather than simply military) obligation of citizens to the community that sustains them is a major theme of Solon's poetry. His emphasis on justice and individual righteous behavior recalls Hesiod's *Works and Days,* while his unshakable commitment to the city—Athens—as the environment that best allows the individual to flourish, has much in common with Thucydides in his *Funeral Oration.*

ARCHILOCHUS

[I am a servant of the War Lord]

I am a servant of the War Lord
and of the Muses, knowing their desirable gift.

[I don't like a tall general, swaggering]

I don't like a tall general, swaggering,
proud of his curls, with a fancy shave.
I'd rather have a short man, who looks
bow-legged, with a firm stride, full of heart.

[Some Thracian exults in an excellent shield]

Some Thracian exults in an excellent shield,
which I left—not willingly—by a bush.
I saved myself. What do I care for that shield?
To hell with it. I'll buy one again, no worse.

[Heart, my heart churning with fathomless cares]

Heart, my heart churning with fathomless cares,
get up! Fight! Heave your chest against the foe,
standing firm near the enemy's shafts.
And don't exult openly in victory,

Poems by Archilochus are translated by Diane J. Rayor.

nor in defeat collapse at home and weep.   5
But rejoice in joys and chafe at evils—
not too much. Recognize what rhythm holds men.

[No townsman, Perikles, will blame us]

No townsman, Perikles,[1] will blame us for groaning
with cares, nor will the city celebrate feasts:
Such men the waves of the thundering sea
washed under, that our lungs are swollen
with sorrow. But for incurable ills, my friend,   5
the gods created powerful endurance
as a drug. Pain strikes one, then another.
Now it turns to us and we groan over a bloody
wound; next it'll turn to someone else. So now
endure, driving back womanly grief.   10

TYRTAEUS

[I would not say anything for a man nor take account of him]

I would not say anything for a man nor take account of him
    for any speed of his feet or wrestling skill he might have,
not if he had the size of a Cyclops and strength to go with it,
    not if he could outrun Bóreas, the North Wind of Thrace,
not if he were more handsome and gracefully formed than Tithónos,[1]   5
    or had more riches than Midas[2] had, or Kínyras[3] too,
not if he were more of a king than Tantalid Pelops,[4]
    or had the power of speech and persuasion Adrastos[5] had,
not if he had all splendors except for a fighting spirit.
    For no man ever proves himself a good man in war   10
unless he can endure to face the blood and the slaughter,
    go close against the enemy and fight with his hands.
Here is courage, mankind's finest possession, here is
    the noblest prize that a young man can endeavor to win,

Poems by Tyrtaeus and Solon are translated by Richmond Lattimore.

Archilochus
1. One of Archilochus's friends, otherwise un-
    known.
Tyrtaeus
1. The lover of the Dawn goddess; legendary
    as a young man, for his beauty.
2. A mythical Phrygian king whose touch
    turned things to gold.

3. A legendary king of Cyprus, famous for his
    wealth.
4. A mythical king for whom the Peloponnese,
    where he ruled, was named; the grandfa-
    ther of Agamemnon and Menelaus (see
    Selection 8).
5. A king of Argos, in the Peloponnese.

and it is a good thing his city and all the people share with him   15
   when a man plants his feet and stands in the foremost spears
relentlessly, all thought of foul flight completely forgotten,
   and has well trained his heart to be steadfast and to endure,
and with words encourages the man who is stationed beside him.
   Here is man who proves himself to be valiant in war.   20
With a sudden rush he turns to flight the rugged battalions
   of the enemy, and sustains the beating waves of assault.
And he who so falls among the champions and loses his sweet life,
   so blessing with honor his city, his father, and all his people,
with wounds in his chest, where the spear that he was facing has transfixed   25
   that massive guard of his shield, and gone through his breastplate as well,
why, such a man is lamented alike by the young and the elders,
   and all his city goes into mourning and grieves for his loss.
His tomb is pointed to with pride, and so are his children,
   and his children's children, and afterward all the race that is his.   30
His shining glory is never forgotten, his name is remembered,
   and he becomes an immortal, though he lies under the ground,
when one who was a brave man has been killed by the furious War God
   standing his ground and fighting hard for his children and land.
But if he escapes the doom of death, the destroyer of bodies,   35
   and wins his battle, and bright renown for the work of his spear,
all men give place to him alike, the youth and the elders,
   and much joy comes his way before he goes down to the dead.
Aging, he has reputation among his citizens. No one
   tries to interfere with his honors or all he deserves;   40
all men withdraw before his presence, and yield their seats to him,
   the youth, and the men his age, and even those older than he.
Thus a man should endeavor to reach this high place of courage
   with all his heart, and, so trying, never be backward in war.

SOLON

[This city of ours will never be destroyed]

This city of ours[1] will never be destroyed by the planning
   of Zeus, nor according to the wish of the immortal gods;
such is she who, great hearted, mightily fathered, protects us,
   Pallas Athene, whose hands are stretched out over our heads.

Solon
1. Athens.

But the citizens themselves in their wildness are bent on destruction   5
   of their great city, and money is the compulsive cause.
The leaders of the people are evil-minded. The next stage
   will be great suffering, recompense for their violent acts,
for they do not know enough to restrain their greed and apportion
   orderly shares for all as if at a decorous feast.   10

   they are tempted into unrighteous acts and grow rich.

   sparing the property neither of the public nor of the gods,
they go on stealing, by force or deception, each from the other,
   nor do the solemn commitments of Justice keep them in check;
but she knows well, though silent, what happens and what has been happening,
   and in her time she returns to extract a full revenge;   15
for it comes upon the entire city as a wound beyond healing,
   and quickly it happens that foul slavery is the result,
and slavery wakens internal strife, and sleeping warfare,
   and this again destroys many in the pride of their youth,
for from enemies' devising our much-adored city is afflicted   20
   before long by conspiracies so dear to wicked men.
Such evils are churning in the home country, but, of the impoverished,
   many have made their way abroad on to alien soil,
sold away, and shamefully going in chains of slavery.

Thus the public Ruin invades the house of each citizen,   25
   and the courtyard doors no longer have strength to keep it away,
but it overleaps the lofty wall, and though a man runs in
   and tries to hide in chamber or closet, it ferrets him out.
So my spirit dictates to me: I must tell the Athenians
   how many evils a city suffers from Bad Government,   30
and how Good Government displays all neatness and order,
   and many times she must put shackles on the breakers of laws.
She levels rough places, stops Glut and Greed, takes the force from Violence;
   she dries up the growing flowers of Despair as they grow;
she straightens out crooked judgments given, gentles the swollen   35
   ambitions, and puts an end to acts of divisional strife;
she stills the gall of wearisome Hate, and under her influence
   all life among mankind is harmonious and does well.

[I gave the people as much privilege as they have a right to]

I gave the people as much privilege as they have a right to:
   I neither degraded them from rank nor gave them free hand;
and for those who already held the power and were envied for money,

I worked it out that they also should have no cause for complaint.
I stood there holding my sturdy shield over both the parties;
    I would not let either side win a victory that was wrong.

                              . . .

Thus would the people be best off, with the leaders they follow:
    neither given excessive freedom nor put to restraint;
for Glut gives birth to Greed, when great prosperity suddenly
    befalls those people who do not have an orderly mind.

                              . . .

    Acting where issues are great, it is hard to please all.

[My purpose was to bring my scattered people back]

My purpose was to bring my scattered people back
together. Where did I fall short of my design?
I call to witness at the judgment seat of time
one who is noblest, mother of Olympian
divinities, and greatest of them all, Black Earth.
I took away the mortgage stones[1] stuck in her breast,
and she, who went a slave before, is now set free.
Into this sacred land, our Athens, I brought back
a throng of those who had been sold, some by due law,
though others wrongly; some by hardship pressed to escape
the debts they owed; and some of these no longer spoke
Attic, since they had drifted wide around the world,
while those in the country had the shame of slavery
upon them, and they served their masters' moods in fear.
These I set free; and I did this by strength of hand,
welding right law with violence to a single whole.
So have I done, and carried through all that I pledged.
I have made laws, for the good man and the bad alike,
and shaped a rule to suit each case, and set it down.
Had someone else not like myself taken the reins,
some ill-advised or greedy person, he would not
have held the people in. Had I agreed to do
what pleased their adversaries at that time, or what
they themselves planned to do against their enemies,
our city would have been widowed of her men. Therefore,
I put myself on guard at every side, and turned
among them like a wolf inside a pack of dogs.

[My purpose was to bring]
1. Among Solon's democratic reforms was his
abolition of serfdom, including the cancel-
lation of all existing debts and mortgages.

SOPHOCLES (496–406 B.C.E.)
Greece

Tragic drama in Greece was closely associated with the city of Athens. It was regarded in antiquity as originating there, and it was certainly in the hands of Athenian playwrights that it flourished with the support and participation of Athenian citizens. In the sixth century B.C.E., Athens established a competition in tragedy, held at an annual civic and religious festival honoring the god Dionysus. An individual was chosen by lot from the community at large to be in charge of the festival. It was that person's responsibility to select the major participants: three competing playwrights, each of whom would produce four plays for the occasion; the financial sponsors, who as a service to the city provided money for the staging of the plays; the chorus members; and the judges, who awarded the prizes. Audiences were huge, by modern standards: the Theater of Dionysus where the tragedies were performed, located just below the Acropolis in Athens, held 14,000 people.

The fifth century B.C.E. was especially rich in tragic drama, including the plays of Aeschylus, Sophocles, and Euripides, among others. Over a lifetime that practically spanned the century, Sophocles wrote 123 plays, many of which took first prize in the competition; he also held, at different times, important military, political, and religious offices in Athens.

The myth of Oedipus provided the subject for tragedies by Aeschylus and Euripides as well as for three of Sophocles' seven surviving plays. Although one

Sophocles. Roman copy of bronze original erected in the Theater of Dionysus, Athens.

play (by Aeschylus) on a historical subject is extant, and we know of others, most tragedies were based on episodes from mythology familiar to their audience; through them the poets explored issues fundamental to the political, moral, and intellectual concerns of their city, as *Antigone* powerfully demonstrates.

Antigone

Characters

ANTIGONE	HAEMON
ISMENE	TEIRESIAS
CHORUS OF THEBAN ELDERS	A MESSENGER
CREON	EURYDICE
A GUARD	

[When Oedipus, the father of Antigone and Ismene, was exiled from Thebes, after the discovery that he had unknowingly murdered his father and married his mother, his sons Eteocles and Polyneices became rivals for their father's throne. Despite his equal claim, Polyneices was expelled from Thebes by his brother. Polyneices thereupon raised an army captained by himself and six leading Argive warriors, and marched against Thebes. The attacking army was defeated and the two brothers died at each other's hands, leaving Creon, the brother of Oedipus's wife (and mother) Jocasta, as the city's new ruler.]

Scene

Thebes, before the royal palace. Antigone and Ismene emerge from its great central door.

ANTIGONE: My sister, my Ismene, do you know
    of any suffering from our father sprung
    that Zeus does not achieve for us survivors?
    There's nothing grievous, nothing free from doom,
    not shameful, not dishonored, I've not seen.   5
    Your sufferings and mine.
    And now, what of this edict which they say
    the commander has proclaimed to the whole people?
    Have you heard anything? Or don't you know
    that the foes' trouble comes upon our friends?   10
ISMENE: I've heard no word, Antigone, of our friends.
    Not sweet nor bitter, since that single moment
    when we two lost two brothers
    who died on one day by a double blow.
    And since the Argive army went away   15
    this very night, I have no further news
    of fortune or disaster for myself.
ANTIGONE: I knew it well, and brought you from the house
    for just this reason, that you alone may hear.
ISMENE: What is it? Clearly some news has clouded you.   20

Translated by Elizabeth Wyckoff.

ANTIGONE: It has indeed. Creon will give the one
of our two brothers honor in the tomb;
the other none.
Eteocles, with just entreatment treated,
as law provides he has hidden under earth   25
to have full honor with the dead below.
But Polyneices' corpse who died in pain,
they say he has proclaimed to the whole town
that none may bury him and none bewail,
but leave him unwept, untombed, a rich sweet sight   30
for the hungry birds' beholding.
Such orders they say the worthy Creon gives
to you and me—yes, yes I say to *me*—
and that he's coming to proclaim it clear
to those who know it not.   35
Further: he has the matter so at heart
that anyone who dares attempt the act
will die by public stoning in the town.
So there you have it and you soon will show
if you are noble, or fallen from your descent.
ISMENE: If things have reached this stage, what can I do,
poor sister, that will help to make or mend?   40
ANTIGONE: Think will you share my labor and my act.
ISMENE: What will you risk? And where is your intent?
ANTIGONE: Will you take up that corpse along with me?
ISMENE: To bury him you mean, when it's forbidden?
ANTIGONE: My brother, and yours, though you may wish he were not.   45
I never shall be found to be his traitor.
ISMENE: O hard of mind! When Creon spoke against it!
ANTIGONE: It's not for him to keep me from my own.
ISMENE: Alas, Remember, sister, how our father
perished abhorred, ill famed.   50
Himself with his own hand, through his own curse
destroyed both eyes.
Remember next his mother and his wife
finishing life in the shame of the twisted strings.
And third two brothers on a single day,   55
poor creatures, murdering, a common doom
each with his arm accomplished on the other.
And now look at the two of us alone.
We'll perish terribly if we force law
and try to cross the royal vote and power.   60
We must remember that we two are women
so not to fight with men.
And that since we are subject to strong power
we must hear these orders, or any that may be worse.

So I shall ask of them beneath the earth   65
forgiveness, for in these things I am forced,
and shall obey the men in power. I know
that wild and futile action makes no sense.

ANTIGONE: I wouldn't urge it. And if now you wished
to act, you wouldn't please me as a partner.   70
Be what you want to; but that man shall I
bury. For me, the doer, death is best.
Friend shall I lie with him, yes friend with friend,
when I have dared the crime of piety.
Longer the time in which to please the dead   75
than that for those up here.
There shall I lie forever. You may see fit
to keep from honor what the gods have honored.

ISMENE: I shall do no dishonor. But to act
against the citizens. I cannot.

ANTIGONE: That's your protection. Now I go, to pile   80
the burial-mound for him, my dearest brother.

ISMENE: Oh my poor sister. How I fear for you!

ANTIGONE: For me, don't borrow trouble. Clear your fate.

ISMENE: At least give no one warning of this act;
you keep it hidden, and I'll do the same.   85

ANTIGONE: Dear God! Denounce me. I shall hate you more
if silent, not proclaiming this to all.

ISMENE: You have a hot mind over chilly things.

ANTIGONE: I know I please those whom I most should please.

ISMENE: If but you can. You crave what can't be done.   90

ANTIGONE: And so, when strength runs out, I shall give over.

ISMENE: Wrong from the start, to chase what cannot be.

ANTIGONE: If that's your saying, I shall hate you first,
and next the dead will hate you in all justice.
But let me and my own ill-counselling   95
suffer this terror. I shall suffer nothing
as great as dying with a lack of grace.

ISMENE: Go, since you want to. But know this: you go
senseless indeed, but loved by those who love you.

*[Ismene returns to the palace; Antigone leaves by one of the side entrances.
The Chorus now enters from the other side.]*

CHORUS: Sun's own radiance, fairest light ever shone on the gates of Thebes,   100
then did you shine, O golden day's
eye, coming over Dirce's[1] stream,

---

1. A river on the western side of Thebes.

on the Man who had come from Argos[2] with all his armor
running now in headlong fear as you shook his bridle free.

He was stirred by the dubious quarrel of Polyneices.   105
So, screaming shrill,
like an eagle over the land he flew,
covered with white-snow wing,
with many weapons,
with horse-hair crested helms.   110

He who had stood above our halls, gaping about our seven gates,
with that circle of thirsting spears.
Gone, without our blood in his jaws,   115
before the torch took hold on our tower-crown.
Rattle of war at his back; hard the fight for the dragon's foe.

The boasts of a proud tongue are for Zeus to hate.
So seeing them streaming on
in insolent clangor of gold,   120
he struck with hurling fire him who rushed
for the high wall's top,
to cry conquest abroad.

Swinging, striking the earth he fell
fire in hand, who in mad attack,   125
had raged against us with blasts of hate.
He failed. He failed of his aim.
For the rest great Ares[3] dealt his blows about,
first in the war-team.   130

The captains stationed at seven gates
fought with seven and left behind
their brazen arms as an offering
to Zeus who is turner of battle.
All but those wretches, sons of one man,   135
one mother's sons, who sent their spears
each against each and found the share
of a common death together.

Great-named Victory comes to us
answering Thebe's warrior-joy.   140
Let us forget the wars just done
and visit the shrines of the gods.
All, with night-long dance which Bacchus[4] will lead,
who shakes Thebe's acres.

---

2. This refers collectively to the invading army
raised by Polyneices in Argos.
3. The god of war.

4. The god Dionysus, closely associated with
the city of Thebes. [See Euripides' *Bacchae*]

[Creon enters from the palace.]

Now here he comes, the king of the land,   145
Creon, Menoeceus' son,
newly named by the gods' new fate.
What plan that beats about his mind
has made him call this council-session,
sending his summons to all?   150

CREON: My friends, the very gods who shook the state
with mighty surge have set it straight again.
So now I sent for you, chosen from all,
first that I knew you constant in respect
to Laius' royal power; and again   155
when Oedipus had set the state to rights,
and when he perished, you were faithful still
in mind to the descendants of the dead.
When they two perished by a doubt fate,
on one day struck and striking and defiled   160
each by his own hand, now it comes that I
hold all the power and the royal throne
through close connection with the perished men.
You cannot learn of any man the soul,
the mind, and the intent until he shows   165
his practice of the government and law.
For I believe that who controls the state
and does not hold to the best plans of all,
but locks his tongue up through some kind of fear,
that he is worst of all who are or were.   170
And he who counts another greater friend
than his own fatherland, I put him nowhere.
So I—may Zeus all-seeing always know it—
could not keep silent as disaster crept
upon the town, destroying hope of safety.   175
Nor could I count the enemy of the land
friend to myself, not I who know so well
that she it is who saves us, sailing straight,
and only so can we have friends at all.
With such good rules shall I enlarge our state.   180
And now I have proclaimed their brother-edict.
In the matter of the sons of Oedipus,
citizens, know: Eteocles who died,
defending this our town with champion spear,
is to be covered in the grave and granted   185
all holy rites we give the noble dead.
But his brother Polyneices whom I name
the exile who came back and sought to burn

his fatherland, the gods who were his kin,
who tried to gorge on blood he shared, and lead   190
the rest of us as slaves—
it is announced that no one in this town
may give him burial or mourn for him.
Leave him unburied, leave his corpse disgraced,
a dinner for the birds and for the dogs.   195
Such is my mind. Never shall I, myself,
honor the wicked and reject the just.
The man who is well-minded to the state
from me in death and life shall have his honor.

CHORUS: This resolution, Creon, is your own,
in the matter of the traitor and the true.   200
For you can make such rulings as you will
about the living and about the dead.

CREON: Now you be sentinels of the decree.

CHORUS: Order some younger man to take this on.

CREON: Already there are watchers of the corpse.   205

CHORUS: What other order would you give us, then?

CREON: Not to take sides with any who disobey.

CHORUS: No fool is fool as far as loving death.

CREON: Death is the price. But often we have known
men to be ruined by the hope of profit.   210

[Enter, from the side, a guard.]

GUARD: Lord, I can't claim that I am out of breath
from rushing here with light and hasty step,
for I had many haltings in my thought
making me double back upon my road.
My mind kept saying many things to me: 215
"Why go where you will surely pay the price?"
"Fool, are you halting? And if Creon learns
from someone else, how shall you not be hurt?"
Turning this over, on I dilly-dallied.
And so a short trip turns itself to long.   220
Finally, though, my coming here won out.
If what I say is nothing, still I'll say it.
For I come clutching to one single hope
that I can't suffer what is not my fate.

CREON: What is it that brings on this gloom of yours?   225

GUARD: I want to tell you first about myself.
I didn't do it, didn't see who did it.
It isn't right for me to get in trouble.

CREON: Your aim is good. You fence the fact around.
It's clear you have some shocking news to tell.   230

GUARD: Terrible tidings make for long delays.

CREON: Speak out the story, and then get away.
GUARD: I'll tell you. Someone left the corpse just now,
    burial all accomplished, thirsty dust
    strewn on the flesh, the ritual complete.   235
CREON: What are you saying? What man has dared to do it?
GUARD: I wouldn't know. There were no marks of picks,
    no grubbed-out earth. The ground was dry and hard,
    no trace of wheels. The door left no sign.
    When the first fellow on the day-shift showed us,   240
    we all were sick with wonder.
    For he was hidden, not inside a tomb,
    light dust upon him, enough to turn the curse,
    no wild beast's track, nor track of any hound
    having been near, nor was the body torn.   245
    We roared bad words about, guard against guard,
    and came to blows. No one was there to stop us.
    Each man had done it, nobody had done it
    so as to prove it on him—we couldn't tell.
    We were prepared to hold to red-hot iron,   250
    to walk through fire, to swear before the gods
    we hadn't done it, hadn't shared the plan,
    when it was plotted or when it was done.
    And last, when all our sleuthing came out nowhere,
    one fellow spoke, who made our heads to droop   255
    low toward the ground. We couldn't disagree.
    We couldn't see a chance of getting off.
    He said we had to tell you all about it.
    We couldn't hide the fact.
    So he won out. The lot chose poor old me   260
    to win the prize. So here I am unwilling,
    quite sure you people hardly want to see me.
    Nobody likes the bringer of bad news.
CHORUS: Lord, while he spoke, my mind kept on debating.
    Isn't this action possibly a god's?   265
CREON: Stop now, before you fill me up with rage,
    or you'll prove yourself insane as well as old.
    Unbearable, your saying that the gods
    take any kindly forethought for this corpse.
    Would it be they had hidden him away,   270
    honoring his good service, his who came
    to burn their pillared temples and their wealth,
    even their land, and break apart their laws?
    Or have you seen them honor wicked men?
    It isn't so.   275
    No, from the first there were some men in town
    who took the edict hard, and growled against me,

who hid the fact that they were rearing back,
not rightly in the yoke, no way my friends.
These are the people—oh it's clear to me— 280
who have bribed these men and brought about the deed.
No current custom among men as bad
as silver currency. This destroys the state;
this drives men from their homes; this wicked teacher
drives solid citizens to acts of shame. 285
It shows men how to practise infamy
and know the deeds of all unholiness.
Every least hireling who helped in this
brought about then the sentence he shall have.
But further, as I still revere great Zeus, 290
understand this, I tell you under oath,
if you don't find the very man whose hands
buried the corpse, bring him for me to see,
not death alone shall be enough for you
till living, hanging, you make clear the crime. 295
For any future grabbings you'll have learned
where to get pay, and that it doesn't pay
to squeeze a profit out of every source.
For you'll have felt that more men come to doom
through dirty profits than are kept by them. 300

GUARD: May I say something? Or just turn and go?
CREON: Aren't you aware your speech is most unwelcome?
GUARD: Does it annoy your hearing or your mind?
CREON: Why are you out to allocate my pain?
GUARD: The doer hurts your mind. I hurt your ears. 305
CREON: You are a quibbling rascal through and through.
GUARD: But anyhow I never did the deed.
CREON: And you the man who sold your mind for money!
GUARD: Oh!
How terrible to guess, and guess at lies!
CREON: Go pretty up your guesswork. If you don't 310
show me the doers you will have to say
that wicked payments work their own revenge.
GUARD: Indeed, I pray he's found, but yes or no,
taken or not as luck may settle it,
you won't see me returning to this place. 315
Saved when I neither hoped nor thought to be,
I owe the gods a mighty debt of thanks.

[*Creon enters the palace. The Guard leaves by the way he came.*]

CHORUS: Many the wonders but nothing walks stranger than man.
This thing[5] crosses the sea in the winter's storm,

---

5. This remarkable creature, man.

making his path through the roaring waves.   320
And she, the greatest of gods, the earth—
ageless she is, and unwearied—he wears her away
as the ploughs go up and down from year to year
and his mules turn up the soil.

Gay nations of birds he snares and leads,   325
wild beast tribes and the salty brood of the sea,
with the twisted mesh of his nets, this clever man.
He controls with craft the beasts of the open air,
walkers on hills. The horse with his shaggy mane
he holds and harnesses, yoked about the neck,   330
and the strong bull of the mountain.

Language, and thought like the wind
and the feelings that make the town,
he has taught himself, and shelter against the cold,
refuge from rain. He can always help himself.   335
He faces no future helpless. There's only death
that he cannot find an escape from. He has contrived
refuge from illnesses once beyond all cure.

Clever beyond all dreams
the inventive craft that he has   340
which may drive him one time or another to well or ill.
When he honors the laws of the land and the gods' sworn right
high indeed is his city; but stateless the man
who dares to dwell with dishonor. Not by my fire,
never to share my thoughts, who does these things.   345

[The Guard enters with Antigone.]

My mind is split at this awful sight.
I know her. I cannot deny
Antigone is here.
Alas, the unhappy girl,
her unhappy father's child.   350
Oh what is the meaning of this?
It cannot be you that they bring
for breaking the royal law,
caught in open shame.

GUARD: This is the woman who has done the deed.   355
We caught her at the burying. Where's the king?

[Creon enters.]

CHORUS: Back from the house again just when he's needed.
CREON: What must I measure up to? What has happened?
GUARD: Lord, one should never swear off anything.

Afterthought makes the first resolve a liar.   360
I could have vowed I wouldn't come back here
after your threats, after the storm I faced.
But joy that comes beyond the wildest hope
is bigger than all other pleasure known.
I'm here, though I swore not to be, and bring   365
this girl. We caught her burying the dead.
This time we didn't need to shake the lots;
mine was the luck, all mine.
So now, lord, take her, you, and question her
and prove her as you will. But I am free.   370
And I deserve full clearance on this charge.

CREON: Explain the circumstance of the arrest.

GUARD: She was burying the man. You have it all.

CREON: Is this the truth? And do you grasp its meaning?

GUARD: I saw her burying the very corpse   375
you had forbidden. Is this adequate?

CREON: How was she caught and taken in the act?

GUARD: It was like this: when we got back again
struck with those dreadful threatenings of yours,
we swept away the dust that hid the corpse.   380
We stripped it back to slimy nakedness.
And then we sat to windward on the hill
so as to dodge the smell.
We poked each other up with growling threats
if anyone was careless of his work.   385
For some time this went on, till it was noon.
The sun was high and hot. Then from the earth
up rose a dusty whirlwind to the sky,
filling the plain, smearing the forest-leaves,
clogging the upper air. We shut our eyes,   390
sat and endured the plague the gods had sent.
So the storm left us after a long time.
We saw the girl. She cried the sharp and shrill
cry of a bitter bird which sees the nest
bare where the young birds lay.   395
So this same girl, seeing the body stripped,
cried with great groanings, cried a dreadful curse
upon the people who had done the deed.
Soon in her hands she brought the thirsty dust,
and holding high a pitcher of wrought bronze   400
she poured the three libations for the dead.
We saw this and surged down. We trapped her fast;
and she was calm. We taxed her with the deeds
both past and present. Nothing was denied.
And I was glad, and yet I took it hard.   405

One's own escape from trouble makes one glad;
but bringing friends to trouble is hard grief.
Still, I care less for all these second thoughts
than for the fact that I myself am safe.

CREON: You there, whose head is drooping to the ground,   410
do you admit this, or deny you did it?

ANTIGONE: I say I did it and I don't deny it.

CREON (TO THE GUARD): Take yourself off wherever you wish to go
free of a heavy charge.

CREON (TO ANTIGONE): You—tell me not at length but in a word.   415
You knew the order not to do this thing?

ANTIGONE: I knew, of course I knew. The word was plain.

CREON: And still you dared to overstep these laws?

ANTIGONE: For me it was not Zeus who made that order.
Nor did that Justice who lives with the gods below   420
mark out such laws to hold among mankind.
Nor did I think your orders were so strong
that you, a mortal man, could over-run
the gods' unwritten and unfailing laws.
Not now, nor yesterday's, they always live,   425
and no one knows their origin in time.
So not through fear of any man's proud spirit
would I be likely to neglect these laws,
draw on myself the gods' sure punishment.
I knew that I must die; how could I not?   430
even without your warning. If I die
before my time, I say it is a gain.
Who lives in sorrows many as are mine
how shall he not be glad to gain his death?
And so, for me to meet this fate, no grief.   435
But if I left that corpse, my mother's son,
dead and unburied I'd have cause to grieve
as now I grieve not.
And if you think my acts are foolishness
the foolishness may be in a fool's eye.   440

CHORUS: The girl is bitter. She's her father's child.
She cannot yield to trouble; nor could he.

CREON: These rigid spirits are the first to fall.
The strongest iron, hardened in the fire,
most often ends in scraps and shatterings.   445
Small curbs bring raging horses back to terms.
Slave to his neighbor, who can think of pride?
This girl was expert in her insolence
when she broke bounds beyond established law.
Once she had done it, insolence the second,   450
to boast her doing, and to laugh in it.

I am no man and she the man instead
if she can have this conquest without pain.
She is my sister's child, but were she child
of closer kin than any at my hearth,   455
she and her sister should not so escape
their death and doom. I charge Ismene too.
She shared the planning of this burial.
Call her outside. I saw her in the house,
maddened, no longer mistress of herself.   460
The sly intent betrays itself sometimes
before the secret plotters work their wrong.
I hate it too when someone caught in crime
then wants to make it seem a lovely thing.

ANTIGONE: Do you want more than my arrest and death?   465
CREON: No more than that. For that is all I need.
ANTIGONE: Why are you waiting? Nothing that you say
    fits with my thought. I pray it never will.
    Nor will you ever like to hear my words.
    And yet what greater glory could I find   470
    than giving my own brother funeral?
    All these would say that they approved my act
    did fear not mute them.
    (A king is fortunate in many ways,
    and most, that he can act and speak at will.)   475
CREON: None of these others see the case this way.
ANTIGONE: They see, and do not say. You have them cowed.
CREON: And you are not ashamed to think alone?
ANTIGONE: No, I am not ashamed. When was it shame
    to serve the children of my mother's womb?
CREON: It was not your brother who died against him, then?
ANTIGONE: Full brother, on both sides, my parents' child.
CREON: Your act of grace, in his regard, is crime.
ANTIGONE: The corpse below would never say it was.
CREON: When you honor him and the criminal just alike?   485
ANTIGONE: It was a brother, not a slave, who died.
CREON: Died to destroy this land the other guarded.
ANTIGONE: Death yearns for equal law for all the dead.
CREON: Not that the good and bad draw equal shares.
ANTIGONE: Who knows that this is holiness below?   490
CREON: Never the enemy, even in death, a friend.
ANTIGONE: I cannot share in hatred, but in love.
CREON: Then go down there, if you must love, and love
    the dead. No woman rules me while I live.

[Ismene is brought from the palace under guard.]

CHORUS: Look there! Ismene is coming out.   495
   She loves her sister and mourns,
   with clouded brow and bloodied cheeks,
   tears on her lovely face.
CREON: You, lurking like a viper in the house,
   who sucked me dry. I looked the other way 500
   while twin destruction planned against the throne.
   Now tell me, do you say you shared this deed?
   Or will you swear you didn't even know?
ISMENE: I did the deed, if she agrees I did.
   I am accessory and share the blame.   505
ANTIGONE: Justice will not allow this. You did not
   wish for a part, nor did I give you one.
ISMENE: You are in trouble, and I'm not ashamed
   to sail beside you into suffering.
ANTIGONE: Death and the dead, they know whose act it was. 510
   I cannot love a friend whose love is words.
ISMENE: Sister, I pray, don't fence me out from honor,
   from death with you, and honor done the dead.
ANTIGONE: Don't die along with me, nor make your own
   that which you did not do. My death's enough. 515
ISMENE: When you are gone what life can be my friend?
ANTIGONE: Love Creon. He's your kinsman and your care.
ISMENE: Why hurt me, when it does yourself no good?
ANTIGONE: I also suffer, when I laugh at you.
ISMENE: What further service can I do you now?   520
ANTIGONE: To save yourself. I shall not envy you.
ISMENE: Alas for me. Am I outside your fate?
ANTIGONE: Yes. For you chose to live when I chose death.
ISMENE: At least I was not silent. You were warned.
ANTIGONE: Some will have thought you wiser. Some will not. 525
ISMENE: And yet the blame is equal for us both.
ANTIGONE: Take heart. You live. My life died long ago.
   And that has made me fit to help the dead.
CREON: One of these girls has shown her lack of sense
   just now. The other had it from her birth.   530
ISMENE: Yes, lord. When people fall in deep distress
   their native sense departs, and will not stay.
CREON: You chose your mind's distraction when you chose
   to work out wickedness with this wicked girl.
ISMENE: What life is there for me to live without her? 535
CREON: Don't speak of her. For she is here no more.
ISMENE: But will you kill your own son's promised bride?[6]

---

6. Antigone is to marry Creon's son Haemon.

CREON: Oh, there are other furrows for his plough.

ISMENE: But where the closeness that has bound these two?

CREON: Not for my sons will I choose wicked wives.

ISMENE: Dear Haemon, your father robs you of your rights.

CREON: You and your marriage trouble me too much.

ISMENE: You will take away his bride from your own son?

CREON: Yes. Death will help me break this marriage off.

CHORUS: It seems determined that the girl must die.   545

CREON: You helped determine it. Now, no delay!
    Slaves, take them in. They must be women now.
    No more free running.
    Even the bold will fly when they see Death
    drawing in close enough to end their life.   550

[Antigone and Ismene are taken inside.]

CHORUS: Fortunate they whose lives have no taste of pain.
    For those whose house is shaken by the gods
    escape no kind of doom. It extends to all the kin
    like the wave that comes when the winds of Thrace[7]
    run over the dark of the sea.   555
    The black sand of the bottom is brought from the depth;
    the beaten capes sound back with a hollow cry.

    Ancient the sorrow of Labdacus'[8] house, I know.
    Dead men's grief comes back, and falls on grief.
    No generation can free the next.   560
    One of the gods will strike. There is no escape.
    So now the light goes out
    for the house of Oedipus, while the bloody knife
    cuts the remaining root. Folly and Fury have done this.

    What madness of man, O Zeus, can bind your power?   565
    Not sleep can destroy it who ages all,
    nor the weariless months the gods have set. Unaged in time
    monarch you rule of Olympus' gleaming light.
    Near time, far future, and the past,
    one law controls them all: 570
    any greatness in human life brings doom.

    Wandering hope brings help to many men.
    But others she tricks from their giddy loves,
    and her quarry knows nothing until he has walked into flame.
    Word of wisdom it was when someone said,   575
    "The bad becomes the good

---

7. A region in northern Greece, believed to be the home of the north wind, Boreas.

8. The grandfather of Oedipus and great-grandfather of Antigone.

to him a god would doom."
Only briefly is that one from under doom.

[Haemon enters from the side.]

Here is your one surviving son.
Does he come in grief at the fate of his bride,   580
in pain that he's tricked of his wedding?
CREON: Soon we shall know more than a seer could tell us.
Son, have you heard the vote condemned your bride?
And are you here, maddened against your father,
or are we friends, whatever I may do?   585
HAEMON: My father, I am yours. You keep me straight
with your good judgment, which I shall ever follow.
Nor shall a marriage count for more with me
than your kind leading.
CREON: There's my good boy. So should you hold at heart   590
and stand behind your father all the way.
It is for this men pray they may beget
households of dutiful obedient sons,
who share alike in punishing enemies,
and give due honor to their father's friends.   595
Whoever breeds a child that will not help
what has he sown but trouble for himself,
and for his enemies laughter full and free?
Son, do not let your lust mislead your mind,
all for a woman's sake, for well you know   600
how cold the thing he takes into his arms
who has a wicked woman for his wife.
What deeper wounding than a friend no friend?
Oh spit her forth forever, as your foe.
Let the girl marry somebody in Hades.   605
Since I have caught her in the open act,
the only one in town who disobeyed,
I shall not now proclaim myself a liar,
but kill her. Let her sing her song of Zeus
who guards the kindred.   610
If I allow disorder in my house
I'd surely have to licence it abroad.
A man who deals in fairness with his own,
he can make manifest justice in the state.
But he who crosses law, or forces it,   615
or hopes to bring the rulers under him,
shall never have a word of praise from me.
The man the state has put in place must have
obedient hearing to his least command
when it is right, and even when it's not.   620

He who accepts this teaching I can trust,
ruler, or ruled, to function in his place,
to stand his ground even in the storm of spears,
a mate to trust in battle at one's side.
There is no greater wrong than disobedience.   625
This ruins cities, this tears down our homes,
this breaks the battle-front in panic-rout.
If men live decently it is because
discipline saves their very lives for them.
So I must guard the men who yield to order,   630
not let myself be beaten by a woman.
Better, if it must happen, that a man
should overset me.
I won't be called weaker than womankind.
CHORUS: We think—unless our age is cheating us—   635
that what you say is sensible and right.
HAEMON: Father, the gods have given men good sense,
the only sure possession that we have.
I couldn't find the words in which to claim
that there was error in your late remarks.   640
Yet someone else might bring some further light.
Because I am your son I must keep watch
on all men's doing where it touches you.
their speech, and most of all, their discontents.
Your presence frightens any common man   645
from saying things you would not care to hear.
But in dark corners I have heard them say
how the whole town is grieving for this girl,
unjustly doomed, if ever woman was,
to die in shame for glorious action done.   650
She would not leave her fallen, slaughtered brother
there, as he lay, unburied, for the birds
and hungry dogs to make an end of him.
Isn't her real desert a golden prize?
This is the undercover speech in town.   655
Father, your welfare is my greatest good.
What loveliness in life for any child
outweighs a father's fortune and good fame?
And so a father feels his children's faring.
Then, do not have one mind, and one alone   660
that only your opinion can be right.
Whoever thinks that he alone is wise,
his eloquence, his mind, above the rest,
come the unfolding, shows his emptiness.
A man, though wise, should never be ashamed   670
of learning more, and must unbend his mind.

Have you not seen the trees beside the torrent,
the ones that bend them saving every leaf,
while the resistant perish root and branch?
And so the ship that will not slacken sail,   675
the sheet drawn tight, unyielding, overturns.
She ends the voyage with her keel on top.
No, yield your wrath, allow a change of stand.
Young as I am, if I may give advice,
I'd say it would be best if men were born   680
perfect in wisdom, but that failing this
(which often fails) it can be no dishonor
to learn from others when they speak good sense.

CHORUS: Lord, if your son has spoken to the point
you should take his lesson. He should do the same.   685
Both sides have spoken well.

CREON: At my age I'm to school my mind by his?
This boy instructor is my master, then?

HAEMON: I urge no wrong. I'm young, but you should watch
my actions, not my years, to judge of me.   690

CREON: A loyal action, to respect disorder?

HAEMON: I wouldn't urge respect for wickedness.

CREON: You don't think she is sick with that disease?

HAEMON: Your fellow-citizens maintain she's not.

CREON: Is the town to tell me how I ought to rule?   695

HAEMON: Now there you speak just like a boy yourself.

CREON: Am I to rule by other mind than mine?

HAEMON: No city is property of a single man.

CREON: But custom gives possession to the ruler.

HAEMON: You'd rule a desert beautifully alone.   700

CREON (TO THE CHORUS): It seems he's firmly on the woman's side.

HAEMON: If you're a woman. It is you I care for.

CREON: Wicked, to try conclusions with your father.

HAEMON: When you conclude unjustly, so I must.

CREON: An I unjust, when I respect my office?   705

HAEMON: You tread down the gods' due. Respect is gone.

CREON: Your mind is poisoned. Weaker than a woman!

HAEMON: At least you'll never see me yield to shame.

CREON: Your whole long argument is but for her.

HAEMON: And you, and me, and for the gods below.   710

CREON: You shall not marry her while she's alive.

HAEMON: Then she shall die. Her death will bring another.

CREON: Your boldness has made progress. Threats, indeed!

HAEMON: No threat, to speak against your empty plan.

CREON: Past due, sharp lessons for your empty brain.   715

HAEMON: If you weren't father, I should call you mad.

CREON: Don't flatter me with "father," you woman's slave.

HAEMON: You wish to speak but never wish to hear.
CREON: You think so? By Olympus, you shall not
    revile me with these tauntings and go free.   720
    Bring out the hateful creature; she shall die
    full in his sight, close at her bridegroom's side.
HAEMON: Not at my side her death, and you will not
    ever lay eyes upon my face again.
    Find other friends to rave with after this.   725

[Haemon leaves, by one of the side entrances.]

CHORUS: Lord, he has gone with all the speed of rage.
    When such a man is grieved his mind is hard.
CREON: Oh, let him go, plan superhuman action.
    In any case the girls shall not escape.
CHORUS: You plan for both the punishment of death?   730
CREON: Not her who did not do it. You are right.
CHORUS: And what death have you chosen for the other?
CREON: To take her where the foot of man comes not.
    There shall I hide her in a hollowed cave
    living, and leave her just so much to eat   735
    as clears the city from the guilt of death.
    There, if she prays to Death, the only god
    of her respect, she may manage not to die.
    Or she may learn at last and even then
    how much too much her labor for the dead.   740

[Creon returns to the palace.]

CHORUS: Love unconquered in fight, love who falls on our havings.
    You rest in the bloom of a girl's unwithered face.
    You cross the sea, you are known in the wildest lairs.
    Not the immortal gods can fly,
    nor men of a day. Who has you within him is mad.   745
    You twist the minds of the just. Wrong they pursue and are ruined.
    You made this quarrel of kindred before us now.
    Desire looks clear from the eyes of a lovely bride:
    power as strong as the founded world.
    For there is the goddess at play with whom no man can fight.   750

[Antigone is brought from the palace under guard.]

Now I am carried beyond all bounds.
My tears will not be checked.
I see Antigone depart
to the chamber where all men sleep.
ANTIGONE: Men of my fathers' land, you see me go   755
    my last journey. My last sight of the sun,
    then never again. Death who brings all to sleep

       takes me alive to the shore
       of the river underground.
       Not for me was the marriage-hymn, nor will anyone start the song   760
       at a wedding of mine. Acheron[9] is my mate.

CHORUS: With praise as your portion you go
       in fame to the vault of the dead.
       Untouched by wasting disease,
       not paying the price of the sword,   765
       of your own motion you go.
       Alone among mortals will you descend
       in life to the house of Death.

ANTIGONE: Pitiful was the death that stranger died,
       our queen once, Tantalus' daughter[10]. The rock   770
       it covered her over, like stubborn ivy it grew.
       Still, as she wastes, the rain
       and snow companion her.
       Pouring down from her mourning eyes comes the water that soaks the
          stone.   775.
       My own putting to sleep a god has planned like hers.

CHORUS: God's child and god she was.
       We are born to death.
       Yet even in death you will have your fame,
       to have gone like a god to your fate,   780
       in living and dying alike.

ANTIGONE: Laughter against me now. In the name of our fathers' gods,
       could you not wait till I went? Must affront be thrown in my face?
       O city of wealthy men.
       I call upon Dirce's spring.   785
       I call upon Thebe's grove in the armored plain,
       to be my witnesses, how with no friend's mourning,
       by what decree I go to the fresh-made prison-tomb.
       Alive to the place of corpses, an alien still,
       never at home with the living nor with the dead.   790

CHORUS: You went to the furthest verge
       of daring, but there you found
       the high foundation of justice, and fell.
       Perhaps you are paying your father's pain.

---

9. A river believed to be at the boundary between the upper world and Hades. The name Acheron was sometimes used to refer generally to the Underworld as a whole. Young women who died before marriage were said to be the brides of Hades.

10. Tantalus's daughter is Niobe, who was supposed to have compared herself favorably to the goddess Leto, because she had numerous children while Leto had only two. Leto's children, however, were the gods Apollo and Artemis, who avenged the slight to their mother's reputation by killing the children of Niobe. Niobe herself was said to have been turned into a figure of stone on Mt. Sipylus in Lydia, the water that ran perpetually down the face of the rock being her ceaseless tears.

ANTIGONE: You speak of my darkest thought, my pitiful father's fame,   795
   spread through all the world, and the doom that haunts our house,
   the royal house of Thebes.
   My mother's marriage-bed.
   Destruction where she lay with her husband-son,
   my father. These are my parents and I their child.   800
   I go to stay with them. My curse is to die unwed.
   My brother, you found your fate when you found your bride,
   found it for me as well. Dead, you destroy my life.

CHORUS: You showed respect for the dead.
   So we for you: but power   805
   is not to be thwarted so.
   Your self-sufficiency has brought you down.

ANTIGONE: Unwept, no wedding-song, unfriended, now I go
   the road laid down for me.
   No longer shall I see this holy light of the sun.   810
   No friend to bewail my fate.

[Creon enters from the palace.]

CREON: When people sing the dirge for their own deaths
   ahead of time, nothing will break them off
   if they can hope that this will buy delay.
   Take her away at once, and open up   815
   the tomb I spoke of. Leave her there alone.
   There let her choose: death, or a buried life.
   No stain of guilt upon us in this case,
   but she is exiled from our life on earth.

ANTIGONE: O tomb, O marriage-chamber, hollowed out   820
   house that will watch forever, where I go.
   To my own people, who are mostly there;
   Persephone has taken them to her.
   Last of them all, ill-fated past the rest,
   shall I descend, before my course is run.   825
   Still when I get there I may hope to find
   I come as a dear friend to my dear father,
   to you, my mother, and my brother too.
   All three of you have known my hand in death.
   I washed your bodies, dressed them for the grave,   830
   poured out the last libation at the tomb.
   Last, Polyneices knows the price I pay
   for doing final service to his corpse.
   And yet the wise will know my choice was right.
   Had I had children or their father dead,   835
   I'd let them moulder. I should not have chosen
   in such a case to cross the state's decree.
   What is the law that lies behind these words?

One husband gone, I might have found another,
or a child from a new man in first child's place,
but with my parents hid away in death,
no brother, ever, could spring up for me.
Such was the law by which I honored you.
But Creon thought the doing was a crime,
a dreadful daring, brother of my heart.
So now he takes and leads me out by force.
No marriage-bed, no marriage-song for me,
and since no wedding, so no child to rear.
I go, without a friend, struck down by fate,
live to the hollow chambers of the dead.
What divine justice have I disobeyed?
Why, in my misery, look to the gods for help?
Can I call any of them my ally?
I stand convicted of impiety,
the evidence my pious duty done.
Should the gods think that this is righteousness,
in suffering I'll see my error clear.
But if it is the others who are wrong
I wish them no greater punishment than mine.

CHORUS: The same tempest of mind
    as ever, controls the girl.

CREON: Therefore her guards shall regret
    the slowness with which they move.

ANTIGONE: That word comes close to death.

CREON: You are perfectly right in that.

ANTIGONE: O town of my fathers in Thebe's land,
    O gods of our house.
    I am led away at last.
    Look, leaders of Thebes,
    I am last of your royal line.
    Look what I suffer, at whose command,
    because I respected the right.

[Antigone is led away. The slow procession should begin during the preceding passage.]

CHORUS: Danaë[11] suffered too.
    She went from the light to the brass-built room,
    chamber and tomb together. Like you, poor child,
    she was of great descent, and more, she held and kept

840

845

850

855

860

865

870

875

---

11. Danaë was a virgin imprisoned by her father, who feared a prediction that he would be killed at the hands of a child that would someday be born to her; Zeus entered the prison room in the form of a shower of golden rain and impregnated Danae.

the seed of the golden rain which was Zeus.
Fate was terrible power.
You cannot escape it by wealth or war.
No fort will keep it out, no ships outrun it.   880

Remember the angry king,
son of Dryas,[12] who raged at the god and paid,
pent in a rock-walled prison. His bursting wrath
slowly went down. As the terror of madness went,
he learned of his frenzied attack on the god.   885
Fool, he had tried to stop
the dancing women possessed of god,
the fire of Dionysus, the songs and flutes.

Where the dark rocks divide
sea from sea in Thrace   890
is Salmydessus whose savage god
beheld the terrible blinding wounds
dealt to Phineus' sons by their father's wife.[13]
Dark the eyes that looked to avenge their mother.
Sharp with her shuttle she struck, and blooded her hands.   895

Wasting they wept their fate,
settled when they were born
to Cleopatra, unhappy queen.
She was a princess too, of an ancient house,
reared in the cave of the wild north wind, her father.   900
Half a goddess but, child, she suffered like you.

[Enter, from the side Teiresias, the blind prophet, led by a boy attendant.]

TEIRESIAS: Elders of Thebes, we two have come one road,
two of us looking through one pair of eyes.
This is the way of walking for the blind.
CREON: Teiresias, what news has brought you here?   905
TEIRESIAS: I'll tell you. You in turn must trust the prophet.
CREON: I've always been attentive to your counsel.
TEIRESIAS: And therefore you have steered this city straight.
CREON: So I can say how helpful you have been.
TEIRESIAS: But now you are balanced on a razor's edge.   910
CREON: What is it? How I shudder at your words!
TEIRESIAS: You'll know, when you hear the signs that I have marked

---

12. Lycurgus, a king of Thrace who was said
to have attacked Dionysus and his followers. Dionysus drove him mad, so that he
was eventually imprisoned by his own
people.
13. Cleopatra, in mythology the daughter of

the north wind, Boreas. She married
Phineus, king of the Thracian city of Salmydessus, to whom she bore two sons.
Phineus later imprisoned her and remarried; his second wife persecuted both Cleopatra and her sons, blinding the two boys.

I sat where every bird of heaven comes
in my old place of augury, and heard
bird-cries I'd never known. They screeched about   915
goaded by madness, inarticulate.
I marked that they were tearing one another
with claws of murder. I could hear the wing-beats.
I was afraid, so straight away I tried
burnt sacrifice upon the flaming altar.   920
No fire caught my offerings. Slimy ooze
dripped on the ashes, smoked and sputtered there.
Gall burst its bladder, vanished into vapor;
the fat dripped from the bones and would not burn.
These are the omens of the rites that failed,   925
as my boy here has told me. He's my guide
as I am guide to others.
Why has this sickness struck against the state?
Through your decision.
All of the altars of the town are choked   930
with leavings of the dogs and birds; their feast
was on that fated, fallen Polyneices.
So the gods will have no offering from us,
not prayer, nor flame of sacrifice. The birds
will not cry out a sound I can distinguish,   935
gorged with the greasy blood of that dead man.
Think of these things, my son. All men may err
but error once committed, he's no fool
nor yet unfortunate, who gives up his stiffness
and cures the trouble he has fallen in.   940
Stubbornness and stupidity are twins.
Yield to the dead. Why goad him where he lies?
What use to kill the dead a second time?
I speak for your own good. And I am right.
Learning from a wise counsellor is not pain   945
if what he speaks are profitable words.

CREON: Old man, you all, like bowmen at a mark,
have bent your bows at me. I've had my share
of seers. I've been an item in your accounts.
Make profit, trade in Lydian silver-gold,   950
pure gold of India; that's your chief desire.
But you will never cover up that corpse.
Not if the very eagles tear their food
from him, and leave it at the throne of Zeus.
I wouldn't give him up for burial   955
in fear of that pollution. For I know
no mortal being can pollute the gods.
O old Teiresias, human beings fall;

the clever ones the furthest, when they plead
a shameful case so well in hope of profit.   960
TEIRESIAS: Alas!
    What man can tell me, has he thought at all . . .
CREON: What hackneyed saw is coming from your lips?
TEIRESIAS: How better than all wealth is sound good counsel.
CREON: And so is folly worse than anything.   965
TEIRESIAS: And you're infected with that same disease.
CREON: I'm reluctant to be uncivil to a seer . . .
TEIRESIAS: You're that already. You have said I lie.
CREON: Well, the whole crew of seers are money-mad.
TEIRESIAS: And the whole tribe of tyrants grab at gain.   970
CREON: Do you realize you are talking to a king?
TEIRESIAS: I know. Who helped you save this town you hold?
CREON: You're a wise seer, but you love wickedness.
TEIRESIAS: You'll bring me to speak the unspeakable, very soon.
CREON: Well, speak it out. But do not speak for profit.   975
TEIRESIAS: No, there's no profit in my words for you.
CREON: You'd better realise that you can't deliver
    my mind, if you should sell it, to the buyer.
TEIRESIAS: Know well, the sun will not have rolled its course
    many more days, before you come to give   980
    corpse for these corpses, child of your own loins.
    For you've confused the upper and lower worlds.
    You sent a life to settle in a tomb;
    you keep up here that which belongs below
    the corpse unburied, robbed of its release.   985
    Not you, nor any god that rules on high
    can claim him now.
    You rob the nether gods of what is theirs.
    So the pursuing horrors lie in wait
    to track you down. The Furies sent by Hades   990
    and by all gods will even you with your victims.
    Now say that I am bribed! At no far time
    shall men and women wail within your house.
    And all the cities that you fought in war
    whose sons had burial from wild beasts, or dogs,   995
    or birds that brought the stench of your great wrong
    back to each hearth, they move against you now.
    A bowman, as you said, I send my shafts,
    now you have moved me, straight. You'll feel the wound.
    Boy, take me home now. Let him spend his rage   1000
    on younger men, and learn to calm his tongue,
    and keep a better mind than now he does.

[Exit.]

CHORUS: Lord, he has gone. Terrible prophecies!
              And since the time when I first grew grey hair
              his sayings to the city have been true.   1005
CREON: I also know this. And my mind is torn.
              To yield is dreadful. But to stand against him.
              Dreadful to strike my spirit to destruction.
CHORUS: Now you must come to counsel, and take advice.
CREON: What must I do? Speak, and I shall obey.   1010
CHORUS: Go free the maiden from that rocky house.
              Bury the dead who lies in readiness.
CREON: This is your counsel? You would have me yield?
CHORUS: Quick as you can. The gods move very fast
              when they bring ruin on misguided men.   1015
CREON: How hard, abandonment of my desire.
              But I can fight necessity no more.
CHORUS: Do it yourself. Leave it to no one else.
CREON: I'll go at once. Come, followers, to your work.
              You that are here round up the other fellows.   1020
              Take axes with you, hurry to that place
              that overlooks us.
              Now my decision has been overturned
              shall I, who bound her, set her free myself.
              I've come to fear it's best to hold the laws   1025
              of old tradition to the end of life.

              [Exit.]

CHORUS: God of the many names, Semele's golden child,
              child of Olympian thunder, Italy's lord.[14]
              Lord of Eleusis, where all men come
              to mother Demeter's plain.   1030
              Bacchus, who dwell in Thebes,
              by Ismenus' running water,
              where wild Bacchic women are at home,
              on the soil of the dragon seed.

              Seen in the glaring flame, high on the double mount,   1035
              with the nymphs of Parnassus[15] at play on the hill,
              seen by Kastalia's flowing stream.
              You come from the ivied heights,
              from green Euboea's shore.
              In immortal words we cry   1040
              your name, lord, who watch the ways,
              the many ways of Thebes.

---

14. Dionysus.   **15.** The mountain below which is the site
                                                                               of Apollo's oracle at Delphi.

This is your city, honored beyond the rest,
the town of your mother's miracle-death.
Now, as we wrestle our grim disease,   1045
come with healing step from Parnassus' slope
or over the moaning sea.

Leader in dance of the fire-pulsing stars,
overseer of the voices of night,
child of Zeus, be manifest,   1050
with due companionship of Maenad maids[16]
whose cry is but your name.

[Enter one of those who left with Creon, as messenger.]

MESSENGER: Neighbors of Cadmus, and Amphion's[17] house,
there is no kind of state in human life
which I now dare to envy or to blame.   1055
Luck sets it straight, and luck she overturns
the happy or unhappy day by day.
No prophecy can deal with men's affairs.
Creon was envied once, as I believe,
for having saved this city from its foes   1060
and having got full power in this land.
He steered it well. And he had noble sons.
Now everything is gone.
Yes, when a man has lost all happiness,
he's not alive. Call him a breathing corpse.   1065
Be very rich at home. Live as a king.
But once your joy has gone, though these are left
they are smoke's shadow to lost happiness.
CHORUS: What is the grief of princes that you bring?
MESSENGER: They're dead. The living are responsible.   1070
CHORUS: Who died? Who did the murder? Tell us now.
MESSENGER: Haemon is gone. One of his kin drew blood.
CHORUS: But whose arm struck? His father's or his own?
MESSENGER: He killed himself. His blood is on his father.
CHORUS: Seer, all too true the prophecy you told!   1075
MESSENGER: This is the state of things. Now make your plans.

[Enter, from the palace, Eurydice.]

CHORUS: Eurydice is with us now, I see.
Creon's poor wife. She may have come by chance.
She may have heard something about her son.
EURYDICE: I heard your talk as I was coming out   1080

---

16. Dionysus's followers.

17. A mythical king of Thebes, husband
of Niobe.

to greet the goddess Pallas with my prayer.
And as I moved the bolts that held the door
I heard of my own sorrow.
I fell back fainting in my women's arms.
But say again just what the news you bring.   1085
I, whom you speak to, have known grief before.

MESSENGER: Dear lady, I was there, and I shall tell,
leaving out nothing of the true account.
Why should I make it soft for you with tales
to prove myself a liar? Truth is right.   1090
I followed your husband to the plain's far edge,
where Polyneices' corpse was lying still
unpitied. The dogs had torn him all apart.
We prayed the goddess of all journeyings,
and Pluto, that they turn their wrath to kindness,   1095
we gave the final purifying bath,
then burned the poor remains on new-cut boughs,
and heaped a high mound of his native earth.
Then turned we to the maiden's rocky bed,
death's hollow marriage-chamber.   1100
But, still far off, one of us heard a voice
in keen lament by that unblest abode.
He ran and told the master. As Creon came
he heard confusion crying. He groaned and spoke:
"Am I a prophet now, and do I tread   1105
the saddest of all roads I ever trod?
My son's voice crying! Servants, run up close,
stand by the tomb and look, push through the crevice
where we built the pile of rock, right to the entry.
Find out if that is Haemon's voice I hear   1110
or if the gods are tricking me indeed."
We obeyed the order of our mournful master.
In the far corner of the tomb we saw
her, hanging by the neck, caught in a noose
of her own linen veiling.   1115
Haemon embraced her as she hung, and mourned
his bride's destruction, dead and gone below,
his father's actions, the unfated marriage.
When Creon saw him, he groaned terribly,
and went toward him, and called him with lament: 1120
"What have you done, what plan have you caught up,
what sort of suffering is killing you?
Come out, my child, I do beseech you, come!"
The boy looked at him with his angry eyes,
spat in his face and spoke no further word.   1125
He drew his sword, but as his father ran,

he missed his aim. Then the unhappy boy,
in anger at himself, leant on the blade.
It entered, half its length, into his side.
While he was conscious he embraced the maiden,   1130
holding her gently. Last, he gasped out blood,
red blood on her white cheek.
Corpse on a corpse he lies. He found his marriage.
Its celebration in the halls of Hades.
So he has made it very clear to men   1135
that to reject good counsel is a crime.

[Eurydice returns to the house.]

CHORUS: What do you make of this? The queen has gone
    in silence. We know nothing of her mind.
MESSENGER: I wonder at her, too. But we can hope
    that she has gone to mourn her son within   1140
    with her own women, not before the town.
    She knows discretion. She will do no wrong.
CHORUS: I am not sure. This muteness may portend
    as great disaster as a loud lament.
MESSENGER: I will go in and see if some deep plan   1145
    hides in her heart's wild pain. You may be right.
    There can be heavy danger in mute grief.

*[The messenger goes into the house. Creon enters with his followers. They are
carrying Haemon's body on a bier.]*

CHORUS: But look, the king draws near.
    His own hand brings
    the witness of his crime,   1150
    the doom he brought on himself.
CREON: O crimes of my wicked heart,
    harshness bringing death.
    You see the killer, you see the kin he killed.
    My planning was all unblest.   1155
    Son, you have died too soon.
    Oh, you have gone away
    through my fault, not your own.
CHORUS: You have learned justice, though it comes too late.
CREON: Yes, I have learned in sorrow. It was a god who struck,   1160
    who has weighted my head with disaster; he drove me to wild strange
        ways,
    his heavy heel on my joy.
    Oh sorrows, sorrows of men.

[Re-enter the messenger, from a side door of the palace.]

MESSENGER: Master you hold one sorrow in your hands
        but you have more, stored up inside the house.   1165.
CREON: What further suffering can come on me?
MESSENGER: Your wife has died. The dead man's mother in deed,
        poor soul, her wounds are fresh.
CREON: Hades, harbor of all,
        you have destroyed me now.   1170
        Terrible news to hear, horror the tale you tell.
        I was dead, and you kill me again.
        Boy, did I hear you right?
        Did you say the queen was dead,
        slaughter on slaughter heaped?   1175

[The central doors of the palace begin to open.]

CHORUS: Now you can see. Concealment is all over.

[The doors are open, and the corpse of Eurydice is revealed.]

CREON: My second sorrow is here. Surely no fate remains
        which can strike me again. Just now, I held my son in my arms.
        And now I see her dead.   1180
        Woe for the mother and son.
MESSENGER: There, by the altar, dying on the sword,
        her eyes fell shut. She wept her older son
        who died before, and this one. Last of all
        she cursed you as the killer of her children.
CREON: I am mad with fear. Will no one strike   1185
        and kill me with cutting sword?
        Sorrowful, soaked in sorrow to the bone!
MESSENGER: Yes, for she held you guilty in the death
        of him before you, and the elder dead.
CREON: How did she die?   1190
MESSENGER: Struck home at her own heart
        when she had heard of Haemon's suffering.
CREON: This is my guilt, all mine. I killed you, I say it clear.
        Servants, take me away, out of the sight of men.
        I who am nothing more than nothing now.   1195
CHORUS: Your plan is good—if any good is left.
        Best to cut short our sorrow.
CREON: Let me go, let me go. May death come quick,
        bringing my final day.
        O let me never see tomorrow's dawn.   1200
CHORUS: That is the future's. We must look to now.
        What will be is in other hands than ours.
CREON: All my desire was in that prayer of mine.
CHORUS: Pray not again. No mortal can escape
        the doom prepared for him.   1205

CREON: Take me away at once, the frantic man who killed
        my son, against my meaning. I cannot rest.
        My life is warped past cure. My fate has struck me down.

[Creon and his attendants enter the house.]

CHORUS: Our happiness depends
        on wisdom all the way.   1210
        The gods must have their due.
        Great words by men of pride
        bring greater blows upon them.
        So wisdom comes to the old.

THUCYDIDES (c. 460–400 B.C.E.)
Greece

Thucydides, an Athenian, was not simply an observer of the Peloponnesian War
but a participant in it; he was for a time a general in that protracted conflict
between Athens and Sparta, which convulsed the entire Greek world, as almost
every city-state was drawn in—willingly or not—in support of one side or the
other. He described the war, accurately enough, as being unprecedented in the
Greek world in its magnitude and severity; it lasted from 431 to 404 B.C.E., was
fought all across the map of Greece, and involved enormous numbers of people
and resources.

    Thucydides' account of this struggle, written in eight books, set a standard
of accuracy and objectivity for later historical writing. His purpose, he stated in
the opening chapters, was to identify not the superficial pretexts but the
underlying causes of the conflict, the fundamental social forces that were
responsible for it, so that future generations could recognize them when they
recurred, as he believed was inevitable—"human nature," as he wrote "being
always the same."

    Among the striking features of Thucydides' history are the numerous
speeches he reports; some he heard himself, others he reconstructed. Pericles, by
far the most important and influential Athenian statesman during the middle
decades of the fifth century B.C.E., delivered the *Funeral Oration* (at which
Thucydides may well have been present) as a memorial to the men who fell in
battle in the first year of the war. His representation of the humane, participatory
Athenian democracy of this period—attentive to "unwritten" moral laws reminiscent of those invoked by Antigone in Sophocles' play—contrasts dramatically
with the imperialist doctrine of power and expediency later endorsed by the
Athenians in the "Melian Dialogue."

from *The History of the Peloponnesian War*

Pericles' Funeral Oration

In the same winter[1] the Athenians, following their annual custom, gave a public funeral for those who had been the first to die in the war. These funerals are held in the following way: two days before the ceremony the bones of the fallen are brought and put in a tent which has been erected, and people make whatever offerings they wish to their own dead. Then there is a funeral procession in which coffins of cypress wood are carried on wagons. There is one coffin for each tribe, which contains the bones of members of that tribe. One empty bier is decorated and carried in the procession: this is for the missing, whose bodies could not be recovered. Everyone who wishes to, both citizens and foreigners, can join in the procession, and the women who are related to the dead are there to make their laments at the tomb. The bones are laid in the public burial-place, which is in the most beautiful quarter outside the city walls. Here the Athenians always bury those who have fallen in war. The only exception is those who died at Marathon,[2] who, because their achievement was considered absolutely outstanding, were buried on the battlefield itself.

When the bones have been laid in the earth, a man chosen by the city for his intellectual gifts and for his general reputation makes an appropriate speech in praise of the dead, and after the speech all depart. This is the procedure at these burials, and all through the war, when the time came to do so, the Athenians followed this ancient custom. Now, at the burial of those who were the first to fall in the war Pericles, the son of Xanthippus, was chosen to make the speech. When the moment arrived, he came forward from the tomb and, standing on a high platform, so that he might be heard by as many people as possible in the crowd, he spoke as follows:

'Many of those who have spoken here in the past have praised the institution of this speech at the close of our ceremony. It seemed to them a mark of honour to our soldiers who have fallen in war that a speech should be made over them. I do not agree. These men have shown themselves valiant in action, and it would be enough, I think, for their glories to be proclaimed in action, as you have just seen it done at this funeral organized by the state. Our belief in the courage and manliness of so many should not be hazarded on the goodness or badness of one man's speech. Then it is not easy to speak with a proper sense of balance, when a man's listeners find it difficult to believe in the truth of what one is saying. The man who knows the facts and loves the dead may well think that an oration tells less than what he knows and what he would like to hear: others who do not know so much may feel envy for the dead, and think the orator over-praises them, when he speaks of exploits that are

Translated by Rex Warner.

beyond their own capacities. Praise of other people is tolerable only up to a certain point, the point where one still believes that one could do oneself some of the things one is hearing about. Once you get beyond this point, you will find people becoming jealous and incredulous. However, the fact is that this institution was set up and approved by our forefathers, and it is my duty to follow the tradition and do my best to meet the wishes and the expectations of every one of you.

'I shall begin by speaking about our ancestors, since it is only right and proper on such an occasion to pay them the honour of recalling what they did. In this land of ours there have always been the same people living from generation to generation up till now, and they, by their courage and their virtues, have handed it on to us, a free country. They certainly deserve our praise. Even more so do our fathers deserve it. For to the inheritance they had received they added all the empire we have now, and it was not without blood and toil that they handed it down to us of the present generation. And then we ourselves, assembled here today, who are mostly in the prime of life, have, in most directions, added to the power of our empire and have organized our State in such a way that it is perfectly well able to look after itself both in peace and in war.

'I have no wish to make a long speech on subjects familiar to you all: so I shall say nothing about the warlike deeds by which we acquired our power or the battles in which we or our fathers gallantly resisted our enemies, Greek or foreign. What I want to do is, in the first place, to discuss the spirit in which we faced our trials and also our constitution and the way of life which has made us great. After that I shall speak in praise of the dead, believing that this kind of speech is not inappropriate to the present occasion, and that this whole assembly, of citizens and foreigners, may listen to it with advantage.

'Let me say that our system of government does not copy the institutions of our neighbours. It is more the case of our being a model to others, than of our imitating anyone else. Our constitution is called a democracy because power is in the hands not of a minority but of the whole people. When it is a question of settling private disputes, everyone is equal before the law; when it is a question of putting one person before another in positions of public responsibility, what counts is not membership of a particular class, but the actual ability which the man possesses. No one, so long as he has it in him to be of service to the state, is kept in political obscurity because of poverty. And, just as our political life is free and open, so is our day-to-day life in our relations with each other. We do not get into a state with our next-door neighbour if he enjoys himself in his own way, nor do we give him the kind of black looks which, though they do no real harm, still do hurt people's feelings. We are free and tolerant in our private lives; but in public affairs we keep to the law. This is because it commands our deep respect.

'We give our obedience to those whom we put in positions of authority, and we obey the laws themselves, especially those which are for the protection of the oppressed, and those unwritten laws which it is an acknowledged shame to break.

'And here is another point. When our work is over, we are in a position to enjoy all kinds of recreation for our spirits. There are various kinds of contests and sacrifices regularly throughout the year; in our own homes we find a beauty and a good taste which delight us every day and which drive away our cares. Then the greatness of our city brings it about that all the good things from all over the world flow in to us, so that to us it seems just as natural to enjoy foreign goods as our own local products.

'Then there is a great difference between us and our opponents, in our attitude towards military security. Here are some examples: Our city is open to the world, and we have no periodical deportations in order to prevent people observing or finding out secrets which might be of military advantage to the enemy. This is because we rely, not on secret weapons, but on our own real courage and loyalty. There is a difference, too, in our educational systems. The Spartans, from their earliest boyhood, are submitted to the most laborious training in courage; we pass our lives without all these restrictions, and yet are just as ready to face the same dangers as they are. Here is a proof of this: When the Spartans invade our land, they do not come by themselves, but bring all their allies with them; whereas we, when we launch an attack abroad, do the job by ourselves, and, though fighting on foreign soil, do not often fail to defeat opponents who are fighting for their own hearths and homes. As a matter of fact none of our enemies has ever yet been confronted with our total strength, because we have to divide our attention between our navy and the many missions on which our troops are sent on land. Yet, if our enemies engage a detachment of our forces and defeat it, they give themselves credit for having thrown back our entire army; or, if they lose, they claim that they were beaten by us in full strength. There are certain advantages, I think, in our way of meeting danger voluntarily, with an easy mind, instead of with a laborious training, with natural rather than with state-induced courage. We do not have to spend our time practising to meet sufferings which are still in the future; and when they are actually upon us we show ourselves just as brave as these others who are always in strict training. This is one point in which, I think, our city deserves to be admired. There are also others:

'Our love of what is beautiful does not lead to extravagance; our love of the things of the mind does not make us soft. We regard wealth as something to be properly used, rather than as something to boast about. As for poverty, no one need be ashamed to admit it: the real shame is in not taking practical measures to escape from it. Here each individual is interested not only in his own affairs but in the affairs of the state as well: even those who are mostly occupied with their own business are extremely well-informed on general politics—this is a peculiarity of ours: we do not say that a man who takes no interest in politics is a man who minds his own business; we say that he has no business here at all. We Athenians, in our own persons, take our decisions on policy or submit them to proper discussions: for we do not think that there is an incompatibility between words and deeds; the worst thing is to rush into action before the consequences have been properly debated. And this is another point where we differ from other people. We are capable at the same time of taking risks and of estimating them beforehand. Others are brave out of ignorance; and, when they stop to think, they begin to fear. But the man who can most truly be accounted brave is he who best knows the meaning of what is sweet in life and of what is terrible, and then goes out undeterred to meet what is to come.

'Again, in questions of general good feeling there is a great contrast between us and most other people. We make friends by doing good to others, not by receiving good from them. This makes our friendship all the more reliable, since we want to keep alive the gratitude of those who are in our debt by showing continued goodwill to them: whereas the feelings of one who owes us something lack the same enthusiasm, since he knows that, when he repays our kindness, it will be more like paying back a debt than giving something spontaneously. We are unique in this. When we do kindnesses to others, we do not do them out of any calculations of profit or loss: we do them without afterthought, relying on our free liberality. Taking everything together then, I declare that our city is an education to Greece, and I declare that in my opinion each single one of our citizens, in all the manifold aspects of life, is able to show himself the rightful lord and owner of his own person, and do this, moreover, with exceptional grace and exceptional versatility. And to show that this is no empty boasting for the present occasion, but real tangible fact, you have only to consider the power which our city possesses and which has been won by those very qualities which I have mentioned. Athens, alone of the states we know, comes to her testing time in a greatness that surpasses what was imaged of her. In her case, and in her case alone, no invading enemy is ashamed at being defeated, and no subject can complain of being governed by people unfit for their responsibilities. Mighty indeed are the marks and monuments of our empire which we have left. Future ages will wonder at us, as the present age wonders at us now. We do not need the praises of a Homer, or of anyone else whose words may delight us for the moment, but whose estimation of facts will fall short of what is really true. For our adventurous spirit has forced an entry into every sea and into every land; and everywhere we have left behind us everlasting memorials of good done to our friends or suffering inflicted on our enemies.

'This, then, is the kind of city for which these men, who could not bear the thought of losing her, nobly fought and nobly died. It is only natural that every one of us who survive them should be willing to undergo hardships in her service. And it was for this reason that I have spoken at such length about out city, because I wanted to make it clear that for us there is more at stake than there is for others who lack our advantages; also I wanted my words of praise for the dead to be set in the bright light of evidence. And now the most important of these words has been spoken. I have sung the praises of our city; but it was the courage and gallantry of these men, and of people like them, which made her splendid. Nor would you find it true in the case of many of the Greeks, as it is true of them, that no words can do more than justice to their deeds.

'To me it seems that the consummation which has overtaken these men shows us the meaning of manliness in its first revelation and in its final proof. Some of them, no doubt, had their faults; but what we ought to remember first is their gallant conduct against the enemy in defence of their native land. They have blotted out evil with good, and done more service to the commonwealth than they ever did harm in their private lives. No one of these men weakened because he wanted to go on enjoying his wealth: no one put off the awful day in the hope that he might live to escape his poverty and grow rich. More to be desired than such things, they chose to check the enemy's pride. This, to them, was a risk most glorious, and they accepted it, willing to strike down the enemy and relinquish everything else. As for success or failure, they left that in the doubtful hands of Hope, and when the reality of battle was before their faces, they put their trust in their own selves. In the fighting, they thought it more honourable to stand their ground and suffer death than to give in and save their lives. So they fled from the reproaches of men, abiding with life and limb the brunt of battle; and, in a small moment of time, the climax of their lives, a culmination of glory, not of fear, were swept away from us.

'So and such they were, these men—worthy of their city. We who remain behind may hope to be spared their fate, but must resolve to keep the same daring spirit against the foe. It is not simply a question of estimating the advantages in theory. I could tell you a long story (and you know it as well as I do) about what is to be gained by beating the enemy back. What I would prefer is that you should fix your eyes every day on the greatness of Athens as she really is, and should fall in love with her. When you realize her greatness, then reflect that what made her great was men with a spirit of adventure, men who knew their duty, men who were ashamed to fall below a certain standard. If they ever failed in an enterprise, they made up their minds that at any rate the city should not find their courage lacking to her, and they gave to her the best contribution that they could. They gave her their lives, to her and to all of us, and for their own selves they won praises that never grow old, the most splendid of sepulchres—not the sepulchre in which their bodies are laid, but where their glory remains eternal in men's minds, always there on the right occasion to stir others to speech or to action. For famous men have the whole earth as their memorial: it is not only the inscriptions on their graves in their own country that mark them out; no, in foreign lands also, not in any visible form but in people's hearts, their memory abides and grows. It is for you to try to be like them. Make up your minds that happiness depends on being free, and freedom depends on being courageous. Let there be no relaxation in face of the perils of the war. The people who have most excuse for despising death are not the wretched and unfortunate, who have no hope of doing well for themselves, but those who run the risk of a complete reversal in their lives, and who would feel the difference most intensely, if things went wrong for them. Any intelligent man would find a humiliation caused by his own slackness more painful to bear than death, when death comes to him unperceived, in battle, and in the confidence of his patriotism.

'For these reasons I shall not commiserate with those parents of the dead, who are present here. Instead I shall try to comfort them. They are well aware that they have grown up in a world where there are many changes and chances. But this is good fortune—for men to end their lives with honour, as these have done, and for you honourably to lament them: their life was set to a measure where death and happiness went hand in hand. I know that it is difficult to convince you of this. When you see other people happy you will often be reminded of what used to make you happy too. One does not feel sad at not having some good thing which is outside one's experience: real grief is felt at the loss of something which one is used to. All the same, those of you who are of the right age must bear up and take comfort in the thought of having more children. In your own homes these new children will prevent you from brooding over those who are no more, and they will be a help to the city, too, both in filling the empty places, and in assuring her security. For it is impossible for a man to put forward fair and honest views about our affairs if he has not, like everyone else, children whose lives may be at stake. As for those of you who are now too old to have children, I would ask you to count as gain the greater part of your life, in which you have been happy, and remember that what remains is not long, and let your hearts be lifted up at the thought of the fair fame of the dead. One's sense of honour is the only thing that does not grow old, and the last pleasure, when one is worn out with age, is not, as the poet said, making money, but having the respect of one's fellow men.

'As for those of you here who are sons or brothers of the dead, I can see a hard struggle in front of you. Everyone always speaks well of the dead, and, even if you rise to the greatest heights of heroism, it will be a hard thing for you to get the reputation of having come near, let alone equalled, their standard. When one is alive, one is always liable to the jealousy of one's competitors, but when one is out of the way, the honour one receives is sincere and unchallenged.

'Perhaps I should say a word or two on the duties of women to those among you who are now widowed. I can say all I have to say in a short word of advice. Your great glory is not to be inferior to what God has made you, and the greatest glory of a woman is to be least talked about by men, whether they are praising you or criticizing you. I have now, as the law demanded, said what I had to say. For the time being our offerings to the dead have been made, and for the future their children will be supported at the public expense by the city, until they come of age. This is the crown and prize which she offers, both to the dead and to their children, for the ordeals which they have faced. Where the rewards of valour are the greatest, there you will find also the best and bravest spirits among the people. And now, when you have mourned for your dear ones, you must depart.'

PLATO (427–348 B.C.E.)
Greece

Plato's *Apology* purports to be the speech Socrates delivered in his own defense at his trial in 399 B.C.E., when he was seventy years old. (The word *apologia* in the Greek title of this work simply means "defense;" it has none of the connotations of regret or retraction associated with the English word *apology*.) Our knowledge of Socrates' life and thought comes from the writings of a few of his younger contemporaries, most notably, Plato. Socrates himself left no written record of his ideas or activities; his chosen vehicle for philosophical inquiry was oral discourse with his fellow Athenians. It was Plato who gave these conversations their literary form: in a set of works structured as dialogues, he reproduces Socrates' manner of questioning and eliciting responses, of turning each discussion into a process of intellectual discovery in the course of which the rational basis of belief is tested and the overriding value of moral goodness is affirmed. In the *Apology* (which for the most part describes, rather than reproduces, Socrates' approach as an interlocutor), Socrates says that he considers it a moral obligation and a service to Athens to be the conscience of the city—exposing ignorance, shallowness, and hypocrisy where he finds it—although he is aware that in doing so he incurs the animosity of many Athenians. Perhaps because his youthful followers learned from him to question conventional attitudes and to reject the pretensions of many of those in authority, Socrates was brought to trial on charges of impiety and of corrupting the youth. Such was the resentment against him that, despite the inability of his prosecutors to substantiate their accusations, he was convicted and condemned to death.

from *The Apology*

[The Trial of Socrates]

I do not know, gentlemen of the jury, how my accusers affected you; as for me, I was almost carried away in spite of myself, so persuasively did they speak. And yet, hardly anything of what they said is true. Of the many lies they told, one in particular surprised me, namely that you should be careful not to be deceived by an accomplished speaker like me. That they are not ashamed to be immediately proved wrong by the facts, when I show myself not to be an accomplished speaker at all, that I think is most shameless on their part—unless indeed they call an accomplished speaker the man who speaks the truth. If they mean that, I would agree that I am an orator, but not after their manner, for indeed, as I say, practically nothing they said was true. From me you will hear the whole truth, though not, by Zeus, gentlemen, expressed in embroidered and stylized phrases like theirs, but things spoken at random and expressed in the first words that come to mind, for I put my trust in the justice of what I say, and let none of you expect anything else. It would not be fitting at my age, as it might be for a young man, to toy with words when I appear before you.

One thing I do ask and beg of you, gentlemen: if you hear me making my defence in the same kind of language as I am accustomed to use in the market place by the bankers' tables, where many of you have heard me, and elsewhere, do not be surprised or create a disturbance on that account. The position is this: this is my first appearance in a lawcourt, at the age of seventy; I am therefore simply a stranger to the manner of speaking here. Just as if I were really a stranger, you would certainly excuse me if I spoke in that dialect and manner in which I had been brought up, so too my present request seems a just one, for you to pay no attention to my manner of speech—be it better or worse—but to concentrate your attention on whether what I say is just or not, for the excellence of a judge lies in this, as that of a speaker, in telling the truth.

It is right for me, gentlemen, to defend myself first against the first lying

Translated by G. M. A. Grube.

accusations made against me and my first accusers, and then against the later accusations and the later accusers. There have been many who have accused me to you for many years now, and none of their accusations are true. These I fear much more than I fear Anytus and his friends, though they too are formidable. These earlier ones, however, are more so, gentlemen; they got hold of most of you from childhood, persuaded you and accused me quite falsely, saying that there is a man called Socrates, a wise man, a student of all things in the sky and below the earth, who makes the worse argument the stronger. Those who spread that rumour, gentlemen, are my dangerous accusers, for their hearers believe that those who study these things do not even believe in the gods. Moreover, these accusers were numerous, they have been at it a long time; also, they spoke to you at an age when you would most readily believe them, some of you being children and adolescents, and they won their case by default, as there was no defence.

What is most absurd in all this is that one cannot even know or mention their names unless one of them is a writer of comedies.[1] Those who maliciously and slanderously persuaded you, those too, who, when persuaded themselves then persuaded others, all those are most difficult to deal with: one cannot bring one of them into court or refute him; one is simply fighting with shadows in making one's defence, and cross-examining when no one answers. I want you to realize too that my accusers are of two kinds: those who have accused me recently, and the old ones I mention; and to think that I must first defend myself against the latter, for you have also heard their accusations first, and to a much greater extent than the more recent.

Very well then. I must surely defend myself and attempt to uproot from your minds in so short a time the slander that has resided there so long. I wish this may happen, if it is in any way better for you and me, and that my defence may be successful, but I think this is very difficult and I am fully aware of how difficult it is. Even so, let the matter proceed as the gods may wish, but I must obey the law and make by defence.

Let us then take up the case from its beginning. What is the accusation from which arose the slander in which Meletus trusted when he wrote out the charge against me? What did they say when they slandered me? I must, as if they were my actual prosecutors, read the affidavit they would have sworn. It goes something like this: Socrates is guilty of wrongdoing in that he busies himself studying things in the sky and below the earth; he makes the worse into the stronger argument, and he teaches these same things to others.[2] You have seen this yourselves in the comedy of Aristophanes, a Socrates swinging about there, saying he was walking on air and talking a lot of other nonsense about things of which I know nothing at all. I do not speak in contempt of such knowledge, if someone is wise in these

---

1. Aristophanes had parodied (and misrepresented) Socrates in his comedy the *Clouds*, produced in 423 B.C.E.
2. "Making the worse argument into the stronger" was the practice of the Sophists, professional teachers of rhetoric, who—for a substantial fee—taught their students to ar-

gue effectively without regard to the moral implications of their arguments. Socrates's accusers conveniently confused Socrates with the Sophists, although his attempt to guide people to reason and to live ethically on the basis of rationality had nothing in common with Sophistic teaching.

things—lest Meletus bring more cases against me—but, gentlemen, I have no part in it, and on this point I call upon the majority of you as witnesses. I think it right that all those of you who have heard me conversing, and many of you have, should tell each other if anyone of you has ever heard me discussing such subjects to any extent at all. From this you will learn that the other things said about me by the majority are of the same kind. Not one of them is true.

One of you might perhaps interrupt me and say: "But Socrates, what is your occupation? From where have these slanders come? For surely if you did not busy yourself with something out of the common, all these rumours and talk would not have arisen unless you did something other than most people. Tell us what it is, that we may not speak inadvisedly about you." Anyone who says that seems to be right, and I will try to show you what has caused this reputation and slander. Listen then. Perhaps some of you will think I am jesting, but be sure that all that I shall say is true. What has caused my reputation is none other than a certain kind of wisdom. What kind of wisdom? Human wisdom, perhaps. It may be that I really possess this, while those whom I mentioned just now are wise with a wisdom more than human: else I cannot explain it, for I certainly do not possess it, and whoever says I do is lying and speaks to slander me. Do not create a disturbance, gentlemen, even if you think I am boasting, for the story I shall tell does not originate with me, but I will refer you to a trustworthy source. I shall call upon the god at Delphi[3] as witness to the existence and nature of my wisdom, if it be such. You know Chairephon. He was my friend from youth, and the friend of most of you, as he shared your exile and your return.[4] You surely know the kind of man he was, how impulsive in any course of action. He went to Delphi at one time and ventured to ask the oracle—as I say, gentlemen, do not create a disturbance—he asked if any man was wiser than I, and the Pythian replied that no one was wiser. Chairephon is dead, but his brother will testify to you about this.

Consider that I tell you this because I would inform you about the origin of the slander. When I heard of this reply I asked myself: "Whatever does the god mean? What is his riddle? I am very conscious that I am not wise at all: what then does he mean by saying that I am the wisest? For surely he does not lie: it is not legitimate for him to do so." For a long time I was at a loss: then I very reluctantly turned to some such investigation as this: I went to one of those reputed wise, thinking that there, if anywhere, I could refute the oracle and say to it: "This man is wiser than I, but you said I was." Then, when I examined this man—there is no need for me to tell you his name, he was one of our public men—my experience was something like this: I thought that he appeared wise to many people and especially to himself, but he was not. I then tried to show him that he thought himself wise, but that he was not. As a result he came to dislike me, and so did

---

3. Apollo, whose oracle was located at Delphi.
4. In 404 B.C.E., an oligarchic coup (supported by the Spartan leadership) overthrew the democratic government in Athens. The oligarchs, who came to be known as the Thirty Tyrants, terrorized Athens with their brutality and corruption for the better part of a year; many prominent democrats fled into exile until the restoration of the democracy in 403.

many of the bystanders. So I withdrew and thought to myself: "I am wiser than this man; it is likely that neither of us knows anything worthwhile, but he thinks he knows something when he does not, whereas when I do not know, neither do I think I know; so I am likely to be wiser to this small extent, that I do not think I know what I do not know." After this I approached another man, one of those thought to be wiser than he, and I thought the same thing, and so I came to be disliked both by him and by many others.

After that I proceeded systematically. I realized, to my sorrow and alarm, that I was getting unpopular, but I thought that I must attach the greatest importance to the god's oracle, so I must go to all those who had any reputation for knowledge to examine its meaning. And by the dog,[5] gentlemen of the jury—for I must tell you the truth—I experienced something like this: in my investigation in the service of the god I found that those who had the highest reputation were nearly the most deficient, while those who were thought to be inferior were more knowledgeable. I must give you an account of my journeyings as if they were labours I had undertaken to prove the oracle irrefutable. After the politicians, I went to the poets, the writers of tragedies and dithyrambs[6] and the others, intending in their case to catch myself being more ignorant then they. So I took up those poems with which they seemed to have taken most trouble and asked them what they meant, in order that I might at the same time learn something from them. I am ashamed to tell you the truth, gentlemen, but I must. Almost all the bystanders explained the poems better than their authors could. I soon realized that poets do not compose their poems with knowledge, but by some inborn talent and by inspiration, like seers and prophets who also say many fine things without any understanding of what they say. The poets seemed to me to have had a similar experience. At the same time I saw that, because of their poetry, they thought themselves very wise men in other respects, which they were not. So there again I withdrew, thinking that I had the same advantage over them as I had over the politicians.

Finally I went to the craftsmen, for I was conscious of knowing practically nothing, and I knew that I would find that they had knowledge of many fine things. In this I was not mistaken; they knew things I did not know, and to that extent they were wiser than I. But, gentlemen of the jury, the good craftsmen seemed to me to have the same fault as the poets: each of them, because of his success at his craft, thought himself very wise in other most important pursuits, and this error of theirs overshadowed the wisdom they had, so that I asked myself, on behalf of the oracle, whether I should prefer to be as I am, with neither their wisdom nor their ignorance, or to have both. The answer I gave myself and the oracle was that it was to my advantage to be as I am.

As a result of this investigation, gentlemen of the jury, I acquired much unpopularity, of a kind that is hard to deal with and is a heavy burden; many slanders came from these people and a reputation for wisdom, for in each case the bystanders thought that I myself possessed the wisdom that I proved that my

---

5. An oath occasionally used by Socrates, unknown elsewhere.

6. A form of choral poetry, written for public
performance.

interlocutor did not have. What is probable, gentlemen, is that in fact that god is wise and that his oracular response meant that human wisdom is worth little or nothing, and that when he says this man, Socrates, he is using my name as an example, as if he said: "This man among you, mortals, is wisest who, like Socrates, understands that this wisdom is worthless." So even now I continue this investigation as the gods bade me—and I go around seeking out anyone, citizen or stranger, whom I think wise. Then if I do not think he is, I come to the assistance of the god and show him that he is not wise. Because of this occupation, I do not have the leisure to engage in public affairs to any extent, nor indeed to look after my own, but I live in great poverty because of my service to the god.

Furthermore, the young men who follow me around of their own free will, those who have most leisure, the sons of the very rich, take pleasure in hearing people questioned; they themselves often imitate me and try to question others. I think they find an abundance of men who believe they have some knowledge but know little or nothing. The result is that those whom they question are angry, not with themselves but with me. They say: "That man Socrates is a pestilential fellow who corrupts the young." If one asks them what he does and what he teaches to corrupt them, they are silent, as they do not know, but, so as not to appear at a loss, they mention those accusations that are available against all philosophers, about "things in the sky and things below the earth," about "not believing in the gods" and "making the worse the stronger argument;" they would not want to tell the truth, that they have been proved to lay claim to knowledge when they know nothing. These people are ambitious, violent and numerous; they are continually and convincingly talking about me; they have been filling your ears for a long time with vehement slanders against me. From them Meletus[7] attacked me, and Anytus and Lycon, Meletus being vexed on behalf of the poets, Anytus on behalf of the craftsmen and the politicians, Lycon on behalf of the orators, so that, as I started out by saying, I should be surprised if I could rid you of so much slander in so short a time. That, gentlemen of the jury, is the truth for you. I have hidden or omitted nothing. I know well enough that this very conduct makes me unpopular, and this is proof that what I say is true, that such is the slander against me, and that such are its causes. If you look into this either now or later, this is what you will find.

Let this suffice as a defence against the charges of my earlier accusers. After this I shall try to defend myself against Meletus, that good and patriotic man, as he says he is, and my later accusers. As these are a different lot of accusers, let us again take up their sworn deposition. It goes something like this: Socrates is guilty of corrupting the young and of not believing in the gods in whom the city believes, but in other new divinities. Such is their charge. Let us examine it point by point.

He says that I am guilty of corrupting the young, but I say that Meletus is guilty of dealing frivolously with serious matters, of irresponsibly bringing people into court, and of professing to be seriously concerned with things about none of

---

7. Meletus was Socrates' chief accuser, although Anytus, the wealthiest, was probably the most influential.

which he has ever cared, and I shall try to prove that this is so. Come here and tell me, Meletus. Surely you consider it of the greatest importance that our young men be as good as possible?—Indeed I do.

Come then, tell the jury who improves them. You obviously know, in view of your concern. You say you have discovered the one who corrupts them, namely me, and you bring me here and accuse me to the jury. Come, inform the jury and tell them who it is. You see, Meletus, that you are silent and know not what to say. Does this not seem shameful to you and a sufficient proof of what I say, that you have not been concerned with any of this. Tell me, my good sir, who improves our young men?—The laws.

That is not what I am asking, but what person, who has previously acquired knowledge of the laws?—These jurymen,[8] Socrates.

How do you mean, Meletus? Are these able to educate the young and improve them?—Certainly.

All of them, or some but not others?—All of them.

Very good, by Hera. You mention a great abundance of benefactors. But what about the audience? Do they improve the young or not?—They do, too.

What about the members of Council?[9] The Councillors, also.

But, Meletus, what about the assembly? Do members of the assembly corrupt the young, or do they all improve them?—They improve them.

All the Athenians, it seems, make the young into fine good men, except me, and I alone corrupt them. Is that what you mean?—That is most definitely what I mean.

You condemn me to a great misfortune. Does this also apply to horses do you think? That all men improve them and one individual corrupts them. Or is quite the contrary true, one individual is able to improve them, or very few, namely the horse breeders, whereas the majority, if they have horses and use them, corrupt them. Is that not the case, Meletus, both with horses and all other animals? Of course it is, whether you and Anytus say so or not. It would be a very happy state of affairs if only one person corrupted our youth, while the others improved them.

You have made it sufficiently obvious, Meletus, that you have never had any concern for our youth; you show your indifference clearly; that you have given no thought to the subjects about which you bring me to trial.

And by Zeus, Meletus, tell us also whether it is better for a man to live among good or wicked fellow-citizens. Answer, my good man, for I am not asking a difficult question. Do not the wicked always do some harm to their nearest neighbours, whereas good people benefit them?—Certainly.

And does the man exist who would rather be harmed than benefited by his associates? Answer, my good sir, for the law orders you to answer. Is there any man who wants to be harmed?—Of course not.

Come now, do you accuse me here of corrupting the young and making them

---

8. Athenian juries were huge, consisting of as many as 500 men for this trial; there was no judge.

9. The deliberative body of 500 men who prepared the agenda for the assembly, which was the chief decision-making body in Athens and open to the participation of all adult males—perhaps some 40,000 people.

worse deliberately or unwillingly?—Deliberately.

What follows, Meletus? Are you so much wiser at your age than I am at mine that you understand that wicked people always do some harm to their closest neighbours while good people do them good, but I have reached such a pitch of ignorance that I do not realize this, namely that if I make one of my associates wicked I run the risk of being harmed by him so that I do such a great evil deliberately, as you say. I do not believe you, Meletus, and I do not think anyone else will. Either I do not corrupt the young or, if I do, it is unwillingly, and you are lying in either case. Now if I corrupt them unwillingly, the law does not require you to bring people to court for such unwilling wrongdoings, but to get hold of them privately, to instruct them and exhort them; for clearly, if I learn better, I shall cease to do what I am doing unwillingly. You, however, have avoided my company and were unwilling to instruct me, but you bring me here, where the law requires one to bring those who are in need of punishment, not of instruction.

[Socrates, by questioning Meletus and exposing the logical fallacies in his argument about Socrates' irreligiosity, quickly disposes of that charge.]

I do not think, gentlemen of the jury, that it requires a prolonged defence to prove that I am not guilty of the charges in Meletus' deposition, but this is sufficient. On the other hand, you know that what I said earlier is true, that I am very unpopular with many people. This will be my undoing, if I am undone, not Meletus or Anytus but the slanders and envy of many people. This has destroyed many and will, I think, continue to do so. There is no danger that it will stop at me.

Someone might say: "Are you not ashamed, Socrates, to have followed the kind of occupation that has led to your being now in danger of death?" However, I should be right to reply to him: "You are wrong, sir, if you think that a man who is any good at all should take into account the risk of life or death; he should look to this only in his actions, whether what he does is right or wrong, whether he is acting like a good or a bad man." According to your view, all the heroes who died at Troy were inferior people, especially the son of Thetis who was so contemptuous of danger compared with disgrace.[10] When he was eager to kill Hector, his goddess mother warned him, as I believe, in some such words as these: "My child, if you avenge the death of your comrade, Patroclus, and you kill Hector, you will die yourself, for your death is to follow immediately after Hector's." Hearing this, he despised death and danger and was much more afraid to live a coward who did not avenge his friends. "Let me die at once," he said, after attacking his killer, "rather than remain here, a laughingstock by the curved ships, a burden upon the earth." Do you think he gave thought to death and danger?

This is the truth of the matter, gentlemen of the jury: wherever a man has taken a position that he believes to be best, or has been placed by his commander, there he must I think remain and face danger, without a thought for death or

10. Achilles, in Book 18 of the *Iliad,* risks his
life to avenge the death of Patroclus. (See
the *Iliad,* Book 18.)

anything else, rather than disgrace. It would have been a dreadful way to behave, gentlemen of the jury, if, at Potidaea[11] Amphipolis and Delium, I had, at the risk of death, like anyone else, remained at my post where those you had elected to command had ordered me, and then, when the god ordered me, as I thought and believed, to live the life of a philosopher, to examine myself and others, I had abandoned my post for fear of death or anything else. That would have been a dreadful thing, and then I might truly have justly been brought here for not believing in the gods, disobeying the oracle, fearing death, and thinking I was wise when I was not. To fear death, gentlemen, is no other than to think oneself wise when one is not, to think one knows what one does not know. No one knows whether death may not be the greatest of all blessings for a man, yet men fear it as if they knew that it is the greatest of evils. And surely it is the most blameworthy ignorance to believe that one knows what one does not know. It is perhaps on this point and in this respect, gentlemen, that I differ from the majority of men, and if I were to claim that I am wiser than anyone in anything, it would be in this, that, as I have no adequate knowledge of things in the underworld, so I do not think I have. I do know, however, that it is wicked and shameful to do wrong, to disobey one's superior, be he god or man. I shall never fear or avoid things of which I do not know, whether they may not be good rather than things that I know to be bad. Even if you acquitted me now and did not believe Anytus, who said to you that either I should not have been brought here in the first place, or that now I am here, you cannot avoid executing me, for if I should be acquitted, your sons would practice the teachings of Socrates and all be thoroughly corrupted. If you said to me in this regard: "Socrates, we do not believe Anytus now; we acquit you, but only on condition that you spend no more time on this investigation and do not practise philosophy, and if you are caught doing so you will die;" if, as I say, you were to acquit me on those terms, I would say to you: "Gentlemen of the jury, I am grateful and I am your friend, but I will obey the god rather than you, and as long as I draw breath and am able, I shall not cease to practise philosophy, to exhort you and to point out to anyone of you whom I happen to meet: Good Sir, you are an Athenian, a citizen of the greatest city with the greatest reputation for both wisdom and power; are you not ashamed of your eagerness to possess as much wealth, reputation and honours as possible, while you do not care for nor give thought to wisdom or truth, or the best possible state of your soul?" Then, if one of you disputes this and says he does care, I shall not let him go at once or leave him, but I shall question him, examine him and test him, and if I do not think he has attained the goodness that he says he has, I shall reproach him because he attaches little importance to the most important things and greater importance to inferior things. I shall treat in this way anyone I happen to meet, young and old, citizen and stranger, and more so the citizens because you are more kindred to me. Be sure that this is what the god orders me to do, and I think there is no greater blessing for the city than my service to the god. For I go around

---

11. Potidaea, Amphipolis, and Delium were the locations of battles in the Peloponnesian war, where Socrates had fought.

doing nothing but persuading both young and old among you not to care for your body or your wealth in preference to or as strongly as for the best possible state of your soul, as I say to you: "Wealth does not bring about excellence, but excellence brings about wealth and all other public and private blessings for men."

Now if by saying this I corrupt the young, this advice must be harmful, but if anyone says that I give different advice, he is talking nonsense. On this point I would say to you, gentlemen of the jury: "Whether you believe Anytus or not, whether you acquit me or not, do so on the understanding that this is my course of action, even if I am to face death many times. Do not create a disturbance, gentlemen, but abide by my request not to cry out at what I say but to listen, for I think it will be to your advantage to listen, and I am about to say other things at which you will perhaps cry out. By no means do this. Be sure that if you kill the sort of man I say I am, you will not harm me more than yourselves. Neither Meletus nor Anytus can harm me in any way, he could not harm me, for I do not think it is permitted that a better man be harmed by a worse; certainly he might kill me, or perhaps banish or disfranchise me, which he and maybe others think to be great harm, but I do not think so. I think he is doing himself much greater harm doing what he is doing now, attempting to have a man executed unjustly. Indeed, gentlemen of the jury, I am far from making a defence now on my own behalf, as might be thought, but on yours, to prevent you from wrongdoing by mistreating the god's gift to you by condemning me; for if you kill me you will not easily find another like me. I was attached to this city by the god—though it seems a ridiculous thing to say—as upon a great and noble horse which was somewhat sluggish because of its size and needed to be stirred up by a kind of gadfly. It is to fulfill some such function that the god has placed me in the city. I never cease to rouse everyone of you, to persuade and reproach you all day long and everywhere I find myself in your company.

Another such man will not easily come to be among you, gentlemen, and if you believe me you will spare me. You might easily strike out at me as people do when they are aroused from a doze; if convinced by Anytus you could easily kill me, and then you could sleep on for the rest of your days, unless the god, in his care for you, sent you someone else. That I am the kind of person to be a gift of the god to the city you might realize from the fact that it does not seem like human nature for me to have neglected all my own affairs and to have tolerated this neglect now for so many years while I was always concerned with you, approaching each one of you like a father or an elder brother to persuade you to care for virtue. Now if I profited from this by charging a fee for my advice, there would be some sense to it, but you can see for yourselves that, for all their shameless accusations, my accusers have not been able in their impudence to bring forward a witness to say that I have ever received a fee or ever asked for one. I, on the other hand, have a convincing witness that I speak the truth, my poverty.

It may seem strange that while I go around and give this advice privately and interfere in private affairs, I do not venture to go to the assembly and there advise the city. You have heard me give the reason for this in many places. I have a divine sign from the god which Meletus has ridiculed in his deposition. This began when I was a child. It is a voice, and whenever it speaks it turns me away from something I am about to do, but it never encourages me to do anything. This is what has prevented me from taking part in public affairs, and I think it was quite right to prevent me. Be sure, gentlemen of the jury, that if I had long ago attempted to take part in politics, I should have died long ago, and benefitted neither you nor myself. Do not be angry with me for speaking the truth; no man will survive who genuinely opposes you or any other crowd and prevents the occurrence of many unjust and illegal happenings in the city. A man who really fights for justice must lead a private, not a public, life if he is to survive for even a short time.

[Socrates describes two incidents of civil disobedience on his part, in which he disobeyed official directives—one under the democratic government and one under the oligarchy—that he believed to be illegal.]

Very well, gentlemen of the jury. This, and maybe other similar things, is what I have to say in my defence. Perhaps one of you might be angry as he recalls that when he himself stood trial on a less dangerous charge, he begged and implored the jury with many tears, that he brought his children and many of his friends and family into court to arouse as much pity as he could, but that I do none of these things, even though I may seem to be running the ultimate risk. Thinking of this, he might feel resentful and angry and cast his vote in anger. If there is such a one among you—I do not deem there is, but if there is—I think it would be right to say in reply: "My good sir, I too have a household and, in Homer's phrase, I am not born from oak or rock but from men, so that I have a family, indeed three sons, gentlemen of the jury, of whom one is an adolescent while two are children. Nevertheless, I will not beg you to acquit me by bringing them here. Why do I do none of these things? Not through arrogance, gentlemen, nor through lack of respect for you. Whether I am brave in the face of death is another matter, but with regard to my reputation and yours and that of the whole city, it does not seem right to me to do these things, especially at my age and with my reputation. For it is generally believed, whether it be true or false, that in certain respects Socrates is superior to the majority of men. Now if those of you who are considered superior, be it in wisdom or courage or whatever other virtue makes them so, are seen behaving like that, it would be a disgrace. Yet I have often seen them do this sort of thing when standing trial, men who are thought to be somebody, doing amazing things as if they thought it a terrible thing to die, and as if they were to be immortal if you did not execute them. I think these men bring shame upon the city so that a stranger, too, would assume that those who are outstanding in virtue among the Athenians, whom they themselves select from themselves to fill offices of state and receive other honours, are in no way better than women. You should not act like that, gentlemen of the jury, those of you who have any reputation at all, and if we do, you should not allow it. You should make it very clear that you will more readily convict a man who performs these pitiful dramatics in court and so makes the city a laughingstock, than a man who keeps quiet.

Quite apart from the question of reputation, gentlemen, I do not think it right to supplicate the jury and to be acquitted because of this. It is not the purpose of a juryman's office to give justice as a favour to whomever seems good to him, but to judge according to law, and this he has sworn to do. We should not accustom you to perjure yourselves, nor should you make a habit of it. This is irreverent conduct for either of us.

Do not deem it right for me, gentlemen of the jury, that I should act towards you in a way that I do not consider to be good or just or pious, especially, by Zeus, as I am being prosecuted by Meletus here for impiety; clearly, if I convinced you by my supplication to do violence to your oath of office, I would be teaching you not to believe in the gods, and my defence would convict me of not believing in them, as my accusers do now, gentlemen of the jury. This is far from being the case, gentlemen, for I do believe in them as none of my accusers do. I leave it to you and the god to judge me in the way that will be best for me and for you.

[The jury now gives its verdict of guilty, and Meletus asks for the penalty of death.]

There are many other reasons for my not being angry with you for convicting me, gentlemen of the jury, and what happened was not unexpected. I am much more surprised at the number of votes cast on each side, for I did not think the decision would be by so few votes but by a great many. As it is, a switch of only thirty votes would have acquitted me.[12] I think myself that I have been cleared on Meletus' charges, and it is clear to all that, if Anytus and Lycon had not joined him in accusing me, he would have been fined a thousand drachmas for not receiving a fifth of the votes.

He assesses the penalty at death. What counter-assessment should I propose to you, gentlemen of the jury?[13] Clearly it should be a penalty I deserve, and what do I deserve to suffer or to pay because I have deliberately not led a quiet life but have neglected what occupies most people: wealth, household affairs, the position of general or public orator or the other offices, the political clubs and factions that exist in the city? I thought myself too honest to survive if I occupied myself with those things. I did not follow that path that would have made me of no use either to you or to myself, but I went to each of you privately and conferred upon him what I say is the greatest benefit, by persuading him not to care for any of his belongings before caring that he himself should be as good and as wise as possible, not to care for the city's possessions more than for the city itself, and to care for other things in the same way. What do I deserve for being such a man? Some good, gentlemen of the jury, if I must truly make an assessment according to my deserts, and something suitable. What is suitable for a benefactor who needs leisure to exhort you? Nothing is more suitable, gentlemen, than for such a man to be fed in the Prytaneum,[14] much more suitable for him than for anyone of you who has won a victory at Olympia with a pair or a team of horses. The Olympian victor makes you think yourself happy, I make you be happy. Besides, he does not

---

12. The vote seems to have been 280 to 220. A tie vote would have been equivalent to acquittal. In order to discourage frivolous lawsuits, prosecutors who did not obtain a fifth of the votes were subject to a fine; Socrates humorously suggests that had he had only one accuser instead of three, that accuser would have fallen short of the requisite fifth of the total votes.

13. The defendant was legally entitled to propose a counterpenalty, such as exile.

14. A kind of town hall, where visiting dignitaries and Olympic victors were entertained.

need food, but I do. So if I must make a just assessment of what I deserve, I assess it at this: free meals in the Prytaneum.

When I say this you may think, as when I spoke of appeals to pity and entreaties, that I speak arrogantly, but that is not the case, gentlemen of the jury, rather it is like this: I am convinced that no man willingly does wrong, but I am not convincing you of this, for we have talked together but a short time. If it were the law with us, as it is elsewhere, that a trial for life should not last one but many days, you would be convinced, but now it is not easy to dispel great slanders in a short time. Since I am convinced that I wrong no one, I am not likely to wrong myself, to say that I deserve some evil and to make some such assessment against myself. What should I fear? That I should suffer the penalty Meletus has assessed against me, of which I say I do not know whether it is good or bad? Am I then to choose in preference to this something that I know very well to be an evil and assess the penalty at that? Imprisonment? Why should I live in prison, always subjected to the ruling magistrates? A fine, and imprisonment until I pay it? That would be the same thing for me, as I have no money. Exile? for perhaps you might accept that assessment.

I should have to be inordinately fond of life, gentlemen of the jury, to be so unreasonable as to suppose that other men will easily tolerate my company and conversation when you, my fellow citizens, have been unable to endure them, but found them a burden and resented them so that you are now seeking to get rid of them. Far from it, gentlemen. It would be a fine life at my age to be driven out of one city after another, for I know very well that wherever I go the young men will listen to my talk as they do here. If I drive them away, they will themselves persuade their elders to drive me out; if I do not drive them away, their fathers and relations will drive me out on their behalf.

Perhaps someone might say: But Socrates, if you leave us will you not be able to live quietly, without talking? Now this is the most difficult point on which to convince some of you. If I say that it is impossible for me to keep quiet because that means disobeying the god, you will not believe me and will think I am being ironical. On the other hand, if I say that it is the greatest good for a man to discuss virtue every day and those other things about which you hear me conversing and testing myself and others, for the unexamined life is not worth living for man, you will believe me even less.

[Socrates says that his friends (including Plato) have urged him to propose a fine; he proposes an absurdly small one. The jury now votes again and sentences Socrates to death.]

It is for the sake of a short time, gentlemen of the jury, that you will acquire the reputation and the guilt, in the eyes of those who want to denigrate the city, of having killed Socrates, a wise man, for they will say that I am wise even if I am not. If you had waited but a little while, this would have happened of its own accord. You see my age, that I am already advanced in years and close to death. I am saying this not to all of you but to those who condemned me to death, and to these same jurors I say: Perhaps you think that I was convicted for lack of such words as might have convinced you, if I thought I should say or do all I could to avoid my sentence. Far from it. I was convicted because I lacked not words but boldness and shamelessness and the willingness to say to you what you would most gladly have heard from me, lamentations and tears and my saying and doing many things that I say are unworthy of me but that you are accustomed to hear from others. I did not think then that the danger I ran should make me do anything mean, nor do I now regret the nature of my defence. I would much rather die after this kind of defence than live after making the other kind. Neither I nor any other man should, on trial or in war, contrive to avoid death at any cost. Indeed it is often obvious in battle that one could escape death by throwing away one's weapons and by turning to supplicate one's pursuers, and there are many ways to avoid death in every kind of danger if one will venture to do or say anything to avoid it. It is not difficult to avoid death, gentlemen of the jury, it is much more difficult to avoid wickedness, for it runs faster than death. Slow and elderly as I am, I have been caught by the slower pursuer, whereas my accusers, being clever and sharp, have been caught by the quicker, wickedness. I leave you now, condemned to death by you, but they are condemned by truth to wickedness and injustice. So I maintain my assessment, and they maintain theirs. This perhaps had to happen, and I think it is as it should be.

Now I want to prophesy to those who convicted me, for I am at the point when men prophesy most, when they are about to die. I say gentlemen, to those who voted to kill me, that vengeance will come upon you immediately after my death, a vengeance much harder to bear than that which you took in killing me. You did this in the belief that you would avoid giving an account of your life, but I maintain that quite the opposite will happen to you. There will be more people to test you, whom I now held back, but you did not notice it. They will be more difficult to deal with as they will be younger and you will resent them more. You are wrong if you believe that by killing people you will prevent anyone from reproaching you for not living in the right way. To escape such tests is neither possible nor good, but it is best and easiest not to discredit others but to prepare oneself to be as good as possible. With this prophecy to you who convicted me, I part from you.

I should be glad to discuss what has happened with those who voted for my acquittal during the time that the officers of the court are busy and I do not yet have to depart to my death. So, gentlemen, stay with me awhile, for nothing prevents us from talking to each other while it is allowed. To you, as being my friends, I want to show the meaning of what has occurred. A surprising thing has happened to me, judges—you I would rightly call judges. At all previous times my usual mantic sign frequently opposed me, even in small matters, when I was about to do something wrong, but now that, as you can see for yourselves, I was faced with what one might think, and what is generally thought to be, the worst of evils, my divine sign has not opposed me, either when I left home at dawn, or when I came into court, or at any time that I was about to say something during my speech. Yet in other talks if often held me back in the middle of my speaking, but now it has opposed no word or deed of mine. What do I think is the reason for this? I will tell you. What has happened to me may well be a good thing, and those of us who believe death to be an evil are certainly mistaken. I have convincing proof of this, for it is impossible that my customary sign did not oppose me if I was not about to do what was right.

Let us reflect that there is good hope that death is a blessing, for it is one of two things: either the dead are nothing and have no perception of anything, or it is, as we are told, a change for the soul from here to another place. If it is complete lack of perception, like a dreamless sleep, then death would be a great advantage. For I think that if one had to pick out that night during which a man slept soundly and did not dream, put beside it the other nights and days of his life, and then see how many days and nights had been better and more pleasant than that night, not only a private person but the great king would find them easy to count compared with the other days and nights. If death is like this I say it is an advantage, for all eternity would then seem to be no more than a single night. If, on the other hand, death is a change from here to another place, and what we are told is true and all who have died are there, what greater blessing could there be, gentlemen of the jury? If anyone arriving in Hades will have escaped from those who call themselves judges here, and will find those true judges who are said to sit in judgement there, Minos[15] and Radamanthus and Aeacus and Triptolemus and the other demi-gods who have been upright in their own life, would that be a poor kind of change? Again, what would one of you give to keep company with Orpheus[16] and Musaeus, Hesiod and Homer? I am willing to die many times if that is true. It would be a wonderful way for me to spend my time whenever I met Palamedes and Ajax, the son of Telamon, and any other of the men of old who died through an unjust conviction, to compare my experience with theirs. I think it would be pleasant. Most important, I could spend my time testing and examining people there, as I do here, as to who among them is wise, and who thinks he is, but is not.

You too must be of good hope as regards death, gentlemen of the jury, and keep this one truth in mind, that a good man cannot be harmed either in life or in death, and that his affairs are not neglected by the gods. What has happened to me now has not happened of itself, but it is clear to me that it was better for me to die now and to escape from trouble. That is why my divine sign did not oppose me at any point. So I am certainly not angry with those who convicted me, or with my accusers. Of course that was not their purpose when they accused and convicted me, but they thought they were hurting me, and for this they deserve blame. This much I ask from them: when my sons grow up, avenge yourselves by causing them the same kind of grief that I caused you, if you think they care for money or anything else more than they care for virtue, or if they think they are somebody when they are nobody. Reproach them as I reproach you, that they do not care for the right things and think they are worthy when they are not worthy of anything. If you do this, I shall have been justly treated by you, and my sons also.

Now the hour to part has come. I go to die, you go to live. Which of us goes to the better lot is known to no one, except the god.

---

15. Minos, Radamanthus, and Aeacus were famous in myth as just men who became judges of the dead in the underworld. Triptolemus, an Eleusinian to whom Demeter taught both agriculture and the rites of her worship, is not elsewhere associated with the underworld.

16. Orpheus and Musaeus are legendary poets.

LUCRETIUS (98?–55 B.C.E.)
Rome

Lucretius's poem *On the Nature of Things* has its antecedents in such didactic poems as Hesiod's *Works and Days,* with its emphatic moral lessons (and its connections to Near Eastern wisdom literature). The stated purpose of Lucretius's poem is to challenge and dispel the superstitions of his contemporaries, including those about divine intervention in human life and, most especially, those about the terrors of death. To counter these fears, Lucretius expounded the teachings of Epicurus, a Greek philosopher of the early third century B.C.E., whose theory of the material nature of the universe, through its combination of physics and ethical precepts, proposed ways to achieve peace of mind and freedom from irrational anxiety. Epicurus depicted the entire universe as a combination of perpetually moving atoms: human beings are formed of them, as everything else in the world must also be, including the gods. When a person dies, the soul's atoms cease to coalesce, so that death is final; fears of punishment in the underworld are groundless and therefore foolish. Nominally addressing his friend Memmius, Lucretius set forth the philosophical doctrine of Epicurus in clear and forceful language that a wide audience might understand and learn from.

from *On the Nature of Things [De Rerum Natura]*

[Mother of all the Romans]

Mother of all the Romans, delight of men and gods,
life-giving Venus,[1] who under the gliding constellations
fill with teeming life the sea that bears our ships
and land that bears our crops—through you each living creature
is conceived and issues forth to look upon the sunlight;   5
at your coming, O goddess, the winds and clouds of heaven
are put to flight; for you the skillful earth brings forth
her sweetest flowers; for you the ocean levels smile;
and heaven, now grown calm, pours forth its gentle light.
For when the day puts on her lovely dress of spring   10
and the life-bringing West Wind blows with all his force,
then first the birds of heaven herald your approach,
for it is your power, goddess, that strikes them to the heart.
And cattle all run wild and prance through the rich pastures
and swim the rapid rivers: they are enthralled by your charm   15
and follow wherever you lead them with a keen desire.

Translated by James H. Mantinband.

---

1. The Roman goddess of love and fertility,
   identified with the Greek goddess

Aphrodite; mother of Aeneas [see the
Aeneid in this section].

And through the seas and mountains and the rushing rivers,
the leafy dwellings of the birds, and the verdant meadows,
their hearts are all inspired by you with gentle passion,
so that they long to reproduce their several species.   20
Since you alone, O goddess, are the Queen of Nature,
and since without you, nothing comes into the daylight,
nothing happy, nothing beautiful is created,
I crave your help in writing these verses, which I am trying
to fashion on the Nature of the Universe   25
for Memmius, my good friend, the man whom you have wished
always to excel, endowed with every gift.
Therefore, goddess, grant a lasting grace to my words,
and meanwhile cause the brutal works of war to cease,
to sleep and to be still, on every land and sea.   30
For you alone can bless mankind with tranquil peace,
since it is mighty Mars who is the Lord of War
and all its brutal works, and he often lies in your lap,
entirely conquered by the eternal wound of love,
and looking upward with his shapely neck bent back,   35
he feasts his avid eyes upon you, hungry for love;
his breath is hanging upon your lips as he reclines.
And you, O goddess, bend over him as he lies there
upon your holy body, and shed your honeyed words,
and for your Romans, glorious goddess, seek placid peace.   40
For in such troubled times, I cannot do my work
with quiet mind, nor can the noble Memmius
at such a time be wanting to the common safety.

   It now remains for you to devote receptive ears
and a keen mind, removed from cares, to the True Reason,   45
lest my gifts, set forth for you with faithful zeal,
be scornfully cast aside before they are understood.
For I am about to disclose to you the laws of heaven
and of the gods; I shall unfold the beginnings of things
whence Nature creates all things, increases and fosters them,   50
and whither this same Nature dissolves and reduces them,
—which we shall designate by some such names as Matter,
and Generative Bodies, and the Seeds of Things
and likewise call them by the name of First Bodies,
because from these First Elements all things are made.   55

[Therefore death is nothing to us]

Therefore death is nothing to us, for it matters not,
since the nature of the mind is known to be mortal;

and just as, in the days of old, we felt no distress
when Carthaginians[2] were pouring in to do battle,
and when the entire world, shaken by war's dread tumult,   5
reeled and trembled under the lofty vault of heaven,
and all men were in doubt, not knowing to which empire
all humanity on land and sea would be subject:—
so, when we shall be no more, when body and spirit,
by whose union we exist, have been separated,   10
nothing more will be able to touch us, who shall not be,
nothing at all will be able to affect our senses,
not though earth were fused with sea or sea with sky.
And even granted that the nature of mind and spirit
still had the power to feel, when torn away from the body,   15
that is nothing to us, who are brought into existence
by the wedlock of body and spirit, joined and made one.
And even if the atoms that compose our body
were reassembled by time and brought to their present arrangement,
and to this arrangement the light of life were given—   20
even that would not be any concern of ours,
once the chain of memory had been snapped and broken.
We, who are now, are not concerned with ourselves that were
in any previous time, nor touched by former sufferings.
For when you look back at all the tremendous expanse   25
of unmeasured time, and think how many and varied
are the atoms' movements, then you might believe with ease
that these same atoms that now compose us, have been arranged
many times before in the same combinations.
But our mind cannot recall or remember this: 30
for a break in life has intervened, and the atoms' motions
all have wandered far astray from any sensation.
For if the future holds misery and woe for a man,
then he himself will have to exist in that future time
in order to suffer. But death removes us from this fate,   35
denying existence to the self that would suffer thus;
so we may be sure we have nothing to fear in death:
one who no longer is, cannot be miserable,
or differ at all from one who never has been born,
when immortal death has taken mortal life away.   40

    And therefore when you see a man resenting his lot,
that after death his corpse will molder in the tomb,
or be destroyed by fire or the jaws of beasts,
you may be certain that his words do not ring true,

---

2. Rome and Carthage, in north Africa, were
embroiled in a series of wars fought at long
intervals, beginning in the mid-third century B.C.E. and ending with Roman victory
and domination more than a century later.

that deep in his heart there lurks some secret pang, although   45
he may deny the belief in sensation after death.
I think he does not admit what he professes, and why;
and he does not completely remove himself from life,
but unconsciously makes something of himself survive.
For when a living man anticipates the thought   50
that after death the birds and beasts will rend his body,
he pities himself: he does not distinguish between himself
and the outcast corpse; but imagines himself to be that object,
and, standing there, he projects his own feelings into it.
And so he resents having been born mortal: he does not see   55
that in real death there will not be another self
to mourn his own departure or to stand by and suffer
with the agony of being mangled or cremated.
For if it is a bad thing after death to be mauled
by wild beasts' jaws, why should it not be just as painful   60
to be roasted in the blazing flames on a funeral pyre,
or to lie embalmed in honey, suffocated
and stiff with cold upon a slab of chilly marble,
or to be crushed beneath a heavy load of earth?

   "No longer now your happy home and your good wife   65
shall welcome you, nor your sweet children come a-running
to win the first kiss, touching your heart with silent joy!
No more prosperity, no protection for your family.
Alas, unhappy wretch!" men say, "one fatal day
has cheated you of all the blessings of this life!"   70
But they do not go on to add: "And now no yearning
for all these lost delights can touch you any more."
If they could clearly see, and spoke accordingly,
they would rid their hearts of weighty fears and torments!
"Yes, you are now at peace in the quiet sleep of death   75
and will remain so forever, free of pain and grief;
but we, beside you as you burn on the dreadful pyre,
we have wept insatiably for you, and no day
shall ever come to lift the load of grief from our hearts."
Of such a man we should ask, why all this bitterness,   80
if a body returns to sleep and peaceful repose,
what reason to pine and weep with everlasting sorrow?

   Thus, again, men speak, when they recline at the banquet
with goblets in their hands and garlands on their brows—
they say in their hearts: "How short the enjoyment for us poor mortals!   85
Soon it will be gone and it can never return!"
As if in death the chief calamity for them
will be that they are parched and shrivelled by burning thirst,
or tormented by the longing for anything.
For no one misses himself, nor does he long for life,   90

when mind and body alike are peacefully asleep.
And even if that sleep should be made everlasting,
no longing for ourselves would torment us at all.
And yet the vital atoms dispersed throughout the body
are not wandering far away from the sensory motions,   95
when a man wakes up from sleep and collects his wits.
Death, then, must be thought to be even less than sleep,
if anything can be less than what we see to be nothing:
for there is a greater dispersion of the disturbed matter
once we are dead, nor can anyone awake and arise   100
whom once the chilly end of life has overtaken.
     Suppose that Nature herself should suddenly find a voice
and reprimand some one of us in such words as these:
"What grieves you, mortal, making you indulge yourself
in all these lamentations? Why weep and wail at death?   105
For if your life until this moment has been pleasant,
if all your blessings have not flowed away like water
in a leaky vase, and been wasted and unenjoyed,
why not, O foolish man, retire, as a dinner guest
who has had his fill, and take your rest in peace and quiet?   110
But if all your blessings have been spilt and lost,
if life is odious to you, why seek to prolong it,
when you will only be a prey to future misfortunes?
Why not rather make an end of life and affliction?
For I have no new invention or contrivance   115
that can please you: everything remains the same.
If your body is not already worn out with years
and your limbs decrepit, still nothing new can happen,
even though you should outlive all generations,
even though you never were to die at all."   120
What could we answer Nature, except that she is right,
and the argument she sets forth is a valid one?
But suppose some aged person should complain
—some miserable man bewailing imminent doom—
would she not be right to scold him all the more: 125
"Away with tears, you villain! Cease your lamentations!
Before you withered, you tasted all the joys of life;
but since you always want what you haven't and scorn what you have,
your life has slipped away unblessed and unfulfilled.
And death is standing by your head, without your knowledge,   130
before you can retire, sated, from the banquet.
But come now, and dismiss what is not meet for your years.
Depart: make room for your children, since you have no choice."
She would be right, in my opinion, thus to reproach.
For the old is always thrust aside to make a place   135
for the new; one thing is built from the wreckage of another.

But there is no black pit of Hell awaiting us:
atoms are needed for future generations' growth,
and when they have lived their lives they will follow you.
Earlier generations have gone, and future ones   140
will do the same: one thing will always grow from another.
No man has life in freehold: we all are merely tenants.
Look back at all the ages that passed before our birth
and see how utterly they count to us as nothing.
This is the mirror Nature is holding up for us   145
to see the time that is to come when we are dead.
Is this so terrible? Is it so very depressing?
Is it not more tranquil than the deepest sleep?

And as for all the tortures that are said to exist
in Hell, they all exist for us here in this life.   150
There is no fabled Tantalus,[3] trembling with vain fears,
at the mighty rock poised in the air above him;
but rather, in this life, it is groundless superstition
oppressing mortals, who fear any fate that may befall.
No Tityos[4] lies in Hell, torn by ravening birds—   155
indeed, how could they ever find enough sustenance
in that mighty chest for all eternity?
It would not matter how huge his Titanic body is,
covering not only nine acres with outstretched limbs,
but the entire globe of the earth—yet even so   160
he will not be able to suffer everlasting pain,
nor furnish everlasting food from his own body.
But our Tityos is here, prostrated by passion;
the ravening birds that tear him apart are his own emotions—
anxieties and lusts and gnawing jealousies.   165
Sisyphus[5] too is here in this life, before our eyes,
thirsting for official insignia, lictor's rods,
and cruel axes, a bitter and frustrated man.
For to strive for empty, unattainable power,
and to endure toils and labors because of this,   170
is just like pushing a boulder up the steepest hill,
laboriously, and when it reaches the very top,
it rolls down again, headlong, to the level of the plain.
Again, to be always feeding an ungrateful mind,

---

3. In the myth of Tantalus, which Lucretius
discredits, he was punished for a hideous
crime against his own son by being consigned to a perpetual punishment in Hades,
whereby (among other things) a stone was
suspended over his head, threatening at
every moment to crush him.
4. The subject of another myth about punish-

ment after death, Tityos was stretched on
the ground in the underworld while vultures ate his liver.
5. A further example of the purported miseries
of the underworld. Sisyphus was obliged
forever to push a boulder uphill, which,
when it approached the top of the hill,
always rolled back down to the bottom.

never able to satisfy it with life's blessings,   175
just as the seasons of the year do with mankind
when they come circling round with fruits and varied delights,
yet we are never surfeited with the fruits of life—
this, I think, is what is meant by the tale of maidens
young and lovely, carrying water in leaky vessels,[6]   180
which, no matter how they try, can never be filled.
Cerberus and the Furies and the pitch-black darkness

the jaws of Tartarus belching forth their hideous fires,
all these do not and cannot exist anywhere,
but in this life we fear retribution for our sins,   185
and the fear is in proportion to the crime,
punishments, prison, being cast from the terrible Rock,
the lash, the hangman, pitch and torches and branding-irons—
and even if these are absent, still the guilty conscience
in frightened anticipation, torments itself with whips,   190
and does not see what end there can be to its misery,
or what is the final limit of the punishments,
fearing that these will be even greater after death.
So foolish men make for themselves a Hell on earth.

This is something you can tell yourself at times: 195
"Even good King Ancus[7] looked his last at the light,
and he was a far, far better man than you, you scoundrel!
And many other kings and potentates have died,
men who were mighty monarchs and ruled over great kingdoms.
Even the Great King[8] who built a road across the sea   200
and gave his soldiers a road to take them over the water,
teaching them to march on foot across the brine,
and scorning the ocean's roar with charging cavalry—
even he was robbed of the light and poured out his spirit.
Scipio,[9] thunderbolt of war and terror of Carthage,   205
gave his bones to the earth the same as the meanest slave.
Add to these the discoverers of knowledge and beauty,
add the companions of the Muses, Homer among them,
their only king—yes, even he was laid to rest.
Democritus,[10] when ripe old age reminded him   210
that his mind and intellect were beginning to fail,

---

6. The daughters of the mythical king Danaus
were punished for a crime they had committed by being made to draw water perpetually in leaky jars.
7. One of the early kings of Rome.
8. The fifth-century Persian king Xerxes I,
against whom the Greeks fought the Persian wars; his army and fleet of ships were

so vast that he bridged the Hellespont
with them.
9. Roman statesman and general who conquered and destroyed Carthage in 146
B.C.E.
10. A Greek philosopher of the mid-fifth century B.C.E.

of his own free will offered his head to death.
Epicurus himself, when his life had run its course,
died: he whose genius surpassed the entire race of men,
who outshone other men as the sun outshines the stars.   215
Will *you*, then flinch and hesitate to meet your death?
You whose life is all but dead, though you live and see,
you who squander the greater part of your time in sleep,
and even when awake are snoring still and dreaming!
You whose mind is terrified by groundless fears,   220
who cannot even discover what it is that ails you,
when you are hounded by your troubles, you drunken wretch,
drifting on the wandering waves of fantasy!"

   Men clearly feel that there is a burden on their minds
whose weight oppresses them; but if they could recognize   225
what are the reasons for this oppression, if they could see
whence comes this burden of misery into their hearts,
they would not live their lives as we now see they do,
with no one knowing what he wants, but always seeking
to escape, as if by moving he could throw off the burden.   230
The owner of a stately mansion will venture forth,
utterly bored at home, then suddenly return
because he feels no better off when out of doors.
So off he drives to his country house at breakneck speed,
as if he were in a hurry to save a house on fire.   235
But when he reaches the threshold he begins to yawn,
or falls into the deepest sleep of oblivion,
or else he rushes all the way back to the city again.
So each man flees himself, but, as you can plainly see,
the self he cannot escape clings to him against his will.   240
He hates himself because he is sick, not knowing the cause;
if only he knew this, he would throw everything aside
and he would devote himself to studying Nature,
since what is at stake is not the passing hour,
but all the time to come—the lot for all mankind   245
through the eternal lapse of time after our death.

   What is this evil lust for life that holds us in fear
and makes us slaves to such anxiety and danger?
There is a definite end of life for mortal men.
Death cannot be avoided: everyone must die.   250
Besides, we live our lives the same from day to day;
nor can we create new pleasures by living longer;
as long as we lack what we desire, it seems more precious
than anything else; but when we have it, we want something different.
One long unchanging thirst for life keeps us always gasping. 255
We never know what fortune the years to come will bring,
what lies in store for us, or what the end will be.

By prolonging life we do not take away one bit
from the duration of our death; we cannot diminish
the time we shall be dead after we leave the earth.   260
However many generations you may live,
the same eternal death will still be waiting for you.
The time of Non-existence will be no less for him
who made an end of life at sunset yesterday,
than for him who perished many months and years before.   265

ANONYMOUS (THIRD MILLENNIUM B.C.E.)
Sumer

These Sumerian compositions of the third millennium B.C.E. reveal how stories of
the gods were used as the basis for the continuance of society. In the first poem,
Inanna, the goddess of love, celebrates her seduction by Dumuzi. Because it was
believed that their periodic union gave rise to seasonal fertility, this poem was
performed at annual agricultural festivals. For all its mythic resonance, the poem
is notable for the very human concern that Inanna (Ishtar) shows: What will she
tell her mother that she has been doing?

The second poem formed part of a sacred marriage ceremony in which the
king would renew his intimate connection to the gods by having intercourse with

Alabaster vase from Uruk,
possibly representing the sacred
marriage of Inanna (Ishtar). Early
Sumerian period, third quarter of
the fourth millennium B.C.E..

a priestess playing the role of Inanna. This ceremony, too, would have been carried out annually. Political and agricultural stability were both expected to follow from this earthly translation of the union of Inanna and Dumuzi.

from *Sacred Marriage Texts of Sumer*

The Ecstasy of Love

Last night, as I, the queen, was shining bright,
Last night, as I, the queen of heaven, was shining bright,
As I was shining bright, as I was dancing about,
As I was uttering a song at the brightening of the oncoming night,
He met me, he met me,   5
The Lord Kuli-Anna[1] met me,
The lord put his hand into my hand,
Ushumgalanna embraced me.

"Come now, wild bull, set me free, I must go home,
Kuli-Enlil, set me free, I must go home,   10
What shall I say to deceive my mother!
What shall I say to deceive my mother Ningal!"

"Let me inform you, let me inform you.
Inanna, most deceitful of women, let me inform you:
'My girl friend took me with her to the public square,   15
She entertained me there with music and dancing,
Her chant, the sweet, she sang for me.
In sweet rejoicing I whiled away the time there—
Thus deceitfully stand up to your mother,
While we by the moonlight indulge our passion,   20
I will prepare for you a bed pure, sweet, and noble,
Will while away the sweet time with you in joyful fulfillment.'"

I have come to our mother's gate,   25
I, in joy I walk,
I have come to Ningal's gate,
I, in joy I walk.
To my mother he will say the word,
He will sprinkle cypress oil on the ground,   30
To my mother Ningal he will say the word,
He will sprinkle cypress oil on the ground,

Translated by S. N. Kramer.

---

1. Kuli-Anna is a name for Dumuzi, as are
   Ushumgalanna, Kuli-Enlil, and
   Amaushumgalanna.

He whose dwelling is fragrant,
Whose word brings deep joy.

My lord is seemly for the holy lap,   35
Amaushumgalanna, the son-in-law of Sin,[2]
The lord Dumuzi is seemly for the holy lap,
Amaushumgalanna, the son-in-law of Sin.
My lord, sweet is your increase,
Tasty your plants and herbs in the plain,   40
Amaushumgalanna, sweet is your increase,
Tasty your plants and herbs in the plain.

Blessing on the Wedding Night

"Guidance of the house of Eridu,[3]
radiance of the house of Sin,
habitation of the Eanna[4]:
this house has been presented to you.
In my enduring house which floats like a cloud,   5
Whose name in truth, is a goodly vision,
Where a fruitful bed, lapis-bedecked,
Gibil[5] had purified for you in the great shrine,
He who is well-suited for 'queenship,'
The lord has erected his altar,   10
In his reed-filled house which he has purified for you, he performs your rites.

The sun has gone to sleep, the day has passed,
As in bed you gaze lovingly upon him,
As you caress the lord,
Give life unto the lord,   15
Give the staff and crook unto the lord."
She craves it, she craves it, she craves the bed,
She craves the bed of the rejoicing heart, she craves the bed,
She craves the bed of the sweet lap, she craves the bed,
She craves the bed of kingship, she craves the bed,   20
She craves the bed of queenship, she craves the bed.
By his sweet, by his sweet, by his sweet bed,
By his sweet bed of the rejoicing heart, by his sweet bed,
By his sweet bed of the sweet lap, by his sweet bed,
By his sweet bed of kingship, by his sweet bed,   25

---

2. God of the moon.
3. Eridu was a founder of the royal line of
   Sumer. As the poem begins, the poet, or a
   god, is addressing Inanna.

4. The name of the temple where the ritual is
   taking place.
5. Gibil is a divine craftsman.

By his sweet bed of queenship, by his sweet bed,
He covers the bed for her, covers the bed for her,
He covers the bed for her, covers the bed for her.

The beloved speaks to the king on his sweet bed,
Speaks to him words of life, words of long days.   30

Ninshubur, the trustworthy vizier of the Eanna,
Took him by his right forearm,
Brought him blissfully to the lap of Inanna:
"May the lord whom you have called to your heart,
The king, your beloved husband, enjoy long days at your holy lap, the sweet,   35
Give him a reign favorable and glorious,
Give him the throne of kingship on its enduring foundation,
Give him the people-directing scepter, the staff and the crook,
Give him an enduring crown, a diadem which ennobles the head,
From where the sun rises, to where the sun sets,   40
From south to north,
From the Upper Sea to the Lower Sea,
From where the halub tree grows to where the cedar grows,
Over all Sumer and Akkad give him the staff and the crook,
May he exercise the shepherdship of the dark-headed people wherever they
    dwell,
    45
May he like the farmer make productive the fields.
May he multiply the sheepfolds like a trustworthy shepherd.

Under his reign may there be plants, may there be grain,
At the river, may there be overflow,
In the field may there be late-grain,   50
In the marshland may the fish and birds make much chatter,
In the canebrake may the old reeds, the young reeds grow high,
In the steppe may the trees grow high,
In the forests may the deer and the wild goats multiply,
May the watered garden produce honey and wine,   55
In the trenches may the lettuce and cress grow high,
In the palace may there be long life,
Into the Tigris and Euphrates may flood water be brought,
On their banks may the grass grow high, may the meadows be covered,
May the holy queen of vegetation pile high the grain heaps and mounds,   60
Oh my queen, queen of the universe, the queen who encompasses the universe,
May he enjoy long days at your holy lap."

The king goes with lifted head to the holy lap,
He goes with lifted head to the holy lap of Inanna,
The king going with lifted head,   65
Going to my queen with lifted head,
Embraces the priestess.

ANONYMOUS

(MID-SECOND MILLENNIUM B.C.E.)

Egypt

These delightful, anonymous poems survive on scraps of pottery and on several scrolls—compilations with names like "Songs of Excellent Enjoyment"—placed in tombs for the pleasure of the deceased. During the course of the New Kingdom (1570–1090 B.C.E.), and probably before that as well, the living performed them at parties and sang them in the fields. More than fifty such poems survive, forming the most extensive body of ancient Near Eastern love poetry known to us. Motifs from the poems recur in The Song of Songs and in the poetry of Greece, Rome, and India.

from *Love Poems from Egypt*

[*If I am not with you, where will you set your heart?*]

If I am not with you, where will you set your heart?
If you do not embrace me, where will you go?
If good fortune comes your way, you still cannot find happiness.
But if you try to touch my thighs and breasts,
Then you'll be satisfied.   5

Because you remember you are hungry
    would you then leave?
Are you a man thinking only of his stomach?
Would you walk off from me
    concerned with your stylish clothes
and leave me the sheet?

Because of hunger
    would you then leave me?
Take then my breast: 10
    for you its gift overflows.
Better indeed is one day in your arms
    than a hundred thousand anywhere on earth.

[*Distracting is the foliage of my pasture*]

Distracting is the foliage of my pasture:
the mouth of my girl is a lotus bud,
her breasts are mandrake apples,

All poems in this selection are translated by William Kelly Simpson.

her arms are vines,
her eyes are fixed like berries,
her brow a snare of willow,
and I the wild goose!
My beak snips her hair for bait,
as worms for bait in the trap.

[My heart is not yet happy with your love]

My heart is not yet happy with your love,
my wolf cub, so be lascivious unto drunkenness.

Yet I will not leave it unless sticks beat me off
to dally in the Delta marshes
or driven to the land of Khor with cudgels and maces
to the land of Kush[1] with palm switches
to the highground with staves
to the lowland with rushes.

So I'll not heed their arguments
to leave off needing you.

[The voice of the turtledove speaks out]

The voice of the turtledove speaks out. It says:
day breaks, which way are you going?
Lay off, little bird,
must you so scold me?

I found my lover on his bed,
and my heart was sweet to excess.

We said:

I shall never be far away from you
while my hand is in your hand,
and I shall stroll with you
in every favorite place.

He set me as first of the girls
and he does not break my heart.

[My heart remembers well your love]

My heart remembers well your love.
One half of my temple was combed,

My heart is not yet

1. Khor is the region of Syria and Palestine;
   Kush is Nubia, in the far south.

I came rushing to see you,
and I forgot my hair.

[I embrace her]

I embrace her,
and her arms open wide,
I am like a man in Punt,[1]
like someone overwhelmed with drugs.

I kiss her,
her lips open,
and I am drunk   5
without a beer.

[How well the lady knows to cast the noose]

How well the lady knows to cast the noose
yet still escape the cattle tax.

With her hair she throws lassoes at me,
with her eyes she catches me,
with her necklace entangles me
and with her seal ring brands me.

[Why need you hold converse with your heart?]

Why need you hold converse with your heart?
To embrace her is all my desire.
As Amun[1] lives, I come to you,
my loin cloth on my shoulder.

[I found the lover at the ford]

I found the lover at the ford,
His feet set in the water;
he builds a table there for feasts
and sets it out with beer.

He brings a blush to my skin,   5
for he is tall and lean.

I embrace her
1. Source of exotic spices and produce.

Why need you
1. God of the sun, also called Amun-Re or Re.

[I passed by her house in the dark]

I passed by her house in the dark,
I knocked and no one opened.
What a beautiful night for our doorkeeper!

Open, door bolts!
Door leaves you are my fate, you are my genie.   5
Our ox will be slaughtered for you inside.
Door leaves do not use your strength.

A long-horned bull will be slaughtered to the bolt.
a short-horned bull to the door pin,
a wild fowl to the threshold,   10
and its fat to the key.

But all the best parts of our ox
shall go to the carpenter's boy,
so he'll make us a door of grass
and a door bolt of reeds,   15

And any time when the lover comes
he'll find her house open,
he'll find beds made with linen sheets
and in them a lovely girl.

And the girl will say to me: 20
this place belongs to the captain's boy!

THE BIBLE

(MID- TO LATE FIRST MILLENNIUM B.C.E.)

Israel

A loosely ordered collection of lyrics, the Song of Songs is presented in the Bible as a cycle of wedding songs from the time of King Solomon. The poems undoubtedly circulated in various forms for several centuries before the final compilation was made, probably in the third century B.C.E. Although there is no consistent formal structure to the poems, the speakers throughout are a bride, her groom, and a chorus of attendants or friends.

The Song has no overt religious content, and justification for its inclusion in the Bible was a matter of early rabbinical debate. The decision in favor (c. 100 B.C.E.) was partly based on precedent: Hebrew prophets such as Hosea and Isaiah had used imagery from love poetry to describe the relations between God and Israel. It was thus possible to interpret the Song allegorically along similar lines.

Modern scholarship tends to stress instead the Song's thematic links to older fertility myths. However, we can also think of the poems as infusing theology back into daily life, for they endow their lovers with elements of mystery not found in the earlier Egyptian love poems.

from **The Bible**

THE SONG OF SONGS

[Let him kiss me with the kisses of his mouth]

The Song of Songs, which is Solomon's.

Let him kiss me with the kisses of his mouth.
Your love is more delightful than wine;
delicate is the fragrance of your perfume,
your name is an oil poured out,
and that is why the maidens love you.   5
Draw me in your footsteps, let us run.
The King has brought me into his rooms;
you will be our joy and our gladness.
We shall praise your love above wine;   10
how right it is to love you.

[I am black but lovely, daughters of Jerusalem]

I am black but lovely, daughters of Jerusalem,
like the tents of Kedar,
like the pavilions of Salmah.[1]
Take no notice of my swarthiness,
it is the sun that has burnt me.   5
My mother's sons turned their anger on me,
they made me look after the vineyards.
Had I only looked after my own!

—How beautiful you are, my love,
how beautiful you are!   10
Your eyes are doves.
—How beautiful you are, my Beloved,
and how delightful!
All green is our bed.
—The beams of our house are of cedar,   15
the panelling of cypress.

Jerusalem Bible translation.

1. Or Solomon.

—I am the rose of Sharon,[2]
the lily of the valleys.
—As a lily among the thistles,
so is my love among the maidens.   20
—As an apple tree among the trees of the orchard,
so is my Beloved among the young men.
In his longed-for shade I am seated
and his fruit is sweet to my taste.
He has taken me to his banquet hall,   25
and the banner he raises over me is love.
Feed me with raisin cakes,
restore me with apples,
for I am sick with love.
His left arm is under my head,   30
his right embraces me.
—I charge you,
daughters of Jerusalem,
by the gazelles, by the hinds of the field,
not to stir my love, nor rouse it,   35
until it please to awake.

[See where he stands]

See where he stands
behind our wall.
He looks in at the window,
he peers through the lattice.
My Beloved lifts up his voice,   5
he says to me,
'Come then, my love,
my lovely one, come.
For see, winter is past,
the rains are over and gone.   10
The flowers appear on the earth.
The season of glad songs has come,
the cooing of the turtledove is heard in our land.
The fig tree is forming its first figs
and the blossoming vines give out their fragrance.   15
Come then, my love,
my lovely one, come.
My dove, hiding in the clefts of the rock,
in the coverts of the cliff,
show me your face,   20

---

2. A rich plain along the Mediterranean coast.

let me hear your voice;
for your voice is sweet
and your face is beautiful.

On my bed, at night, I sought him
whom my heart loves.   25
I sought but did not find him.
So I will rise and go through the City;
in the streets and the squares
I will seek him whom my heart loves.
The watchmen came upon me   30
on their rounds in the City:
'Have you seen him whom my heart loves?'
Scarcely had I passed them
than I found him whom my heart loves.
I held him fast, nor would I let him go   35
till I had brought him
into my mother's house,
into the room of her who conceived me.

[How beautiful you are, my love]

How beautiful you are, my love,[3]
how beautiful you are!
Your eyes, behind your veil,
are doves;
your hair is like a flock of goats   5
frisking down the slopes of Gilead.
Your teeth are like a flock of shorn ewes
as they come up from the washing.
Each one has its twin,
not one unpaired with another.   10
Your lips are a scarlet thread
and your words enchanting.
Your cheeks, behind your veil,
are halves of pomegranate.
Your neck is the tower of David   15
built as a fortress,
hung round with a thousand bucklers,
and each the shield of a hero.
Your two breasts are two fawns,
twins of a gazelle,   20
that feed among the lilies.

---

3. This poem is spoken by the groom.

Before the dawn-wind rises,
before the shadows flee,
I will go to the mountain of myrrh,
to the hill of frankincense. 25
You are wholly beautiful, my love,
and without a blemish.
Come from Lebanon, my promised bride,
come from Lebanon, come on your way.
Lower your gaze, from the heights of Amana, 30
from the crests of Senir and Hermon,[4]
the haunt of lions,
the mountains of leopards.
You ravish my heart,
my sister, my promised bride, 35
you ravish my heart
with a single one of your glances,
with one single pearl of your necklace.
What spells lie in your love,
my sister, my promised bride! 40

[I sleep, but my heart is awake]

I sleep, but my heart is awake.
I hear my Beloved knocking.
'Open to me, my sister, my love,
my dove, my perfect one,
for my head is covered with dew, 5
my locks with the drops of night.'
—'I have taken off my tunic,
am I to put it on again?
I have washed my feet,
am I to dirty them again?' 10
My Beloved thrust his hand
through the hole in the door;
I trembled to the core of my being.
Then I rose to open to my Beloved,
myrrh ran off my hands, 15
pure myrrh off my fingers,
on to the handle of the bolt.
I opened to my Beloved,
but he had turned his back and gone!
My soul failed at his flight. 20
I sought him but I did not find him,

---

4. The mountain home of the Syrian goddess
   of fertility.

I called to him but he did not answer.
The watchmen came upon me
as they made their rounds in the City.
They beat me, they wounded me,   25
they took away my cloak,
they who guard the ramparts.
I charge you, daughters of Jerusalem,
if you should find my Beloved,
what must you tell him?   30
That I am sick with love.
What makes your Beloved better than other lovers,
O loveliest of women?
What makes your Beloved better than other lovers,
to give us a charge like this?   35
My Beloved is fresh and ruddy,
to be known among ten thousand.
His head is golden, purest gold,
his locks are palm fronds
and black as the raven.   40
His eyes are doves
at a pool of water,
bathed in milk,
at rest on a pool.
His cheeks are beds of spices,   45
banks sweetly scented.
His lips are lilies,
distilling pure myrrh.
His hands are golden, rounded,
set with jewels of Tarshish.   50
His belly a block of ivory
covered with sapphires.
His legs are alabaster columns
set in sockets of pure gold.
His appearance is that of Lebanon,   55
unrivalled as the cedars.
His conversation is sweetness itself,
he is altogether lovable.
Such is my Beloved, such is my friend,
O daughters of Jerusalem.   60

[You are beautiful as Tirzah, my love]

You are beautiful as Tirzah,[5] my love,
fair as Jerusalem.

---

5. Former capital of Israel.

Turn your eyes away,
for they hold me captive.

The maidens saw her, and proclaimed her blessed,
queens and concubines sang her praises:
'Who is this arising like the dawn,
fair as the moon,
resplendent as the sun,
terrible as an army with banners?'

How beautiful are your feet in their sandals,
O prince's daughter!
The curve of your thighs is like the curve of a necklace,
work of a master hand.
Your navel is a bowl well rounded
with no lack of wine,
your belly a heap of wheat
surrounded with lilies.
Your two breasts are two fawns,
twins of a gazelle.
Your neck is an ivory tower.
Your eyes, the pools of Heshbon,
by the gate of Bath-rabbim.
Your nose, the Tower of Lebanon,
sentinel facing Damascus.
Your head is held high like Carmel,[6]
and its plaits are as dark as purple;
a king is held captive in your tresses.
How beautiful you are, how charming,
my love, my delight!
In stature like the palm tree,
its fruit-clusters your breasts.
'I will climb the palm tree,' I resolved,
'I will seize its clusters of dates.'
May your breasts be clusters of grapes,
your breath sweet-scented as apples,
your speaking, superlative wine.

Wine flowing straight to my Beloved,
as it runs on the lips of those who sleep.
I am my Beloved's, and his desire is for me.

---

6. A prominent mountain on the Mediterranean coast.

Come, my Beloved, let us go to the fields.
We will spend the night in the villages,
and in the morning we will go to the vineyards.
We will see if the vines are budding,
if their blossoms are opening,   45
if the pomegranate trees are in flower.
Then I shall give you the gift of my love.
The mandrakes yield their fragrance,
the rarest fruits are at our doors;
the new as well as the old,   50
I have stored them for you, my Beloved.
Ah, why are you not my brother,
nursed at my mother's breast!
Then if I met you out of doors, I could kiss you
without people thinking ill of me.   55
I should lead you, I should take you
into my mother's house, and you would teach me!
I should give you spiced wine to drink,
juice of my pomegranates.
His left arm is under my head   60
and his right embraces me.
I charge you,
daughters of Jerusalem,
not to stir my love, nor rouse it,
until it please to awake.   65

[Who is this coming up from the desert/leaning on her Beloved?]

Who is this coming up from the desert
leaning on her Beloved?
I awakened you under the apple tree,
there where your mother conceived you,
there where she who gave birth to you conceived you.   5
Set me like a seal on your heart,
like a seal on your arm.
For love is strong as Death,
jealousy relentless as Sheol.[7]
The flash of it is a flash of fire,   10
a flame of Yahweh himself.
Love no flood can quench,
no torrents drown.

---

7. The underworld.

ALCAEUS (MID-SEVENTH TO EARLY SIXTH CENTURY B.C.E.)

SAPPHO (MID-SEVENTH TO EARLY SIXTH CENTURY B.C.E.)

Greece

Lyric poetry in Greece—composed in stanzas, sung by performers accompanying themselves on the lyre—flourished vigorously in the Aegean islands in the seventh and sixth centuries B.C.E. Like elegiac poetry (from which it differed musically and metrically), and unlike the epic, the lyric poetry of this period lent itself especially to the expression of intense personal emotion and to statements of the individual's values; most often lyric themes were those of private rather than public experience, and presupposed an audience closely associated with the poet.

Sappho and Alcaeus were contemporaries (born c. 630 B.C.E.) from the island of Lesbos at a time when it was torn by civil conflict. Of all the lyricists, Alcaeus is the one whose poetry most explicitly reflects the political conditions of the day. He was equally influential, however, for his poems celebrating the pleasures of camaraderie in a convivial setting, in which wine is a prominent feature; there is evidence that most of Alcaeus's verse may have been composed to be sung at symposia (drinking parties) among friends and political allies.

As with Alcaeus, what remains to us of Sappho's poetry is largely fragmentary: only the first poem we give has been preserved in its entirety. Sappho is the earliest of the very few female poets of antiquity whose work has survived in any form, providing us with an irreplaceable alternative to the male perspective that prevails throughout this entire section. Her audience, too, seems to have been a circle of intimate friends; their companionship—valued for its own sake rather than as an expression of political solidarity, as is often the case in Alcaeus's writings—is the focus of much of her surviving verse. In poems like "Some say . . . ," she asserts the primacy of private affections, claiming for them a heroic stature to rival epic subject matter.

ALCAEUS

[Zeus rains upon us]

Zeus rains upon us, and from the sky comes down
enormous winter. Rivers have turned to ice.

. . .

Dash down the winter. Throw a log on the fire
and mix the flattering wine (do not water it too much) and bind on round our
    foreheads soft ceremonial wreaths of spun fleece.

5

Poems by Alcaeus are translated by Richmond Lattimore.

We must not let our spirits give way to grief.
By being sorry we get no further on, my Bukchis.[1] Best of all defenses is to mix
    plenty of wine, and drink it.

[Wet your whistle with wine now]

Wet your whistle with wine now, for the dog star, wheeling up the sky,
brings back summer, the time all things are parched under the searing heat.
Now the cicada's cry, sweet in the leaves, shrills from beneath his wings.
Now the artichoke flowers, women are lush, ask too much of their men,
who grow lank, for the star burning above withers their brains and knees.   5

SAPPHO

[On the throne of many hues, Immortal Aphrodite]

On the throne of many hues, Immortal Aphrodite,
child of Zeus, weaving wiles—I beg you
not to subdue my spirit, Queen,
with pain or sorrow

but come—if ever before   5
having heard my voice from far away
you listened, and leaving your father's
golden home you came

in your chariot yoked with swift, lovely
sparrows bringing you over the dark earth   10
thick-feathered wings swirling down
from the sky through mid-air

arriving quickly—you, Blessed One,
with a smile on your unaging face
asking again what have I suffered   15
and why am I calling again

and in my wild heart what did I most wish
to happen to me: "Again whom must I persuade
back into the harness of your love?
Sappho, who wrongs you?   20

For if she flees, soon she'll pursue,
she doesn't accept gifts, but she'll give,

Poems by Sappho are translated by Diane J. Rayor.

Zeus rains

1. The name of one of Alcaeus's friends.

if not now loving, soon she'll love
even against her will."

Come to me now again, release me from
this pain, everything my spirit longs
to have fulfilled, fulfill, and you
be my ally.   25

[Some say an army of horsemen]

Some say an army of horsemen, others
say foot-soldiers, still others, a fleet,
is the fairest thing on the dark earth:
I say it is whatever one loves.

Everyone can understand this—   5
consider that Helen,[1] far surpassing
the beauty of mortals, leaving behind
the best man of all,

sailed away to Troy. She had no
memory of her child or dear parents,   10
since she was led astray
[by Kypris][2]

                                        . . . lightly

. . . reminding me now of Anaktoria[3]
being gone,   15

I would rather see her lovely step
and the radiant sparkle of her face
than all the war-chariots in Lydia[4]
and soldiers battling in shining bronze.

[To me it seems]

To me it seems
that man has the fortune of gods,
whoever sits beside you, and close,

Some say

1. Helen left her husband Menelaos to follow
   the Trojan prince Paris to Troy.
2. Aphrodite, the goddess of love. There is a
   gap in the text at this point.

3. One of Sappho's friends.
4. A country in western Asia Minor that
   was prosperous and powerful in this
   period.

who listens to you sweetly speaking
and laughing temptingly;   5
my heart flutters in my breast,
whenever I look quickly, for a moment—
I say nothing, my tongue broken,
a delicate fire runs under my skin,
my eyes see nothing, my ears roar,   10
cold sweat rushes down me,
trembling seizes me,
I am greener than grass,
to myself I seem
needing but little to die.   15

But all must be endured, since . . .

[Evening Star who gathers everything]

Evening Star who gathers everything
shining dawn scattered—
you bring the sheep and the goats,
you bring the child back to its mother.

[The sweet apple reddens on a high branch]

The sweet apple reddens on a high branch
high upon highest, missed by the applepickers:
no, they didn't miss, so much as couldn't touch.

IBYCUS (MID-SIXTH CENTURY B.C.E.)
ANACREON (c. 582–c. 485 B.C.E.)
Greece

Ibycus and Anacreon were mid-sixth century B.C.E. contemporaries born at
opposite ends of the Greek map (Ibycus in the west and Anacreon on the Ionian
coast). Both poets came to live and write at the court of the island of Samos under
the patronage of its ruler. Ibycus composed primarily for choral performance,
while Anacreon's love songs, like Alcaeus's, suited individual performance in the
setting of the symposium; both enlarged the lyric repertory of erotic imagery.

IBYCUS

[In Spring, quince trees]

In Spring, quince trees
irrigated with streams
from rivers, in the Virgins'
inviolate garden, and vinebuds
growing beneath shady shoots   5
of vinetwigs bloom. But for me
Love rests for no season:
blazing with lightning
Thracian Boreas,
darting from Kypris, dark   10
with parching madness, shameless,
violently shakes
my senses from the depth.

[Again Love]

Again Love, glancing meltingly
beneath royal blue eyelids,
with myriad enchantments throws me
into the infinite nets of Kypris.
Yes, I tremble at his approach,   5
as a yoke-bearing horse,
    a prizewinner near old age,
goes to the contest unwillingly
    with the swift chariots.

ANACREON

[Lad, glancing like a virgin]

Lad, glancing like a virgin,
I seek you, but you don't hear,
not knowing that you
are my soul's charioteer.

[The dice of Love]

The dice of Love are
madness and turmoil.

All poems in this selection are translated by Diane J. Rayor.

[Again Love struck me]

Again Love struck me like a smith with a giant
hammer, and washed me in a wintry torrent.

[Thracian filly]

Thracian filly, why do you
look with eyes askance
and stubbornly flee me, and why
do you think I've no skill?
Understand this: I could well   5
throw a bridle on you,
and holding the reins I could turn
you round the goal of the track.
But now you graze the meadows
and, frisking nimbly, play,   10
since you've no dextrous horseman,
no easy rider.

CATULLUS (84?–54? B.C.E.)
Rome

The Rome to which Gaius Valerius Catullus moved from his native Verona was
the political as well as the intellectual center of Italy under the republic in the first
century B.C.E. In the more than one hundred highly varied poems by Catullus that
survive, however, politics is never his subject (although he pokes fun at a number
of public figures). His poems are primarily concerned with love—for men as well
as women—with friendship, and with poetry itself. They are frequently colloquial in tone and for the most part clearly set in Rome, allowing us valuable
glimpses of contemporary social behavior in that city; their intended initial
audience was probably the poet's close circle of literary friends.

Together with Horace, Catullus is the heir to the poetic forms and themes
of the Greek lyric poets, although unlike their poetry, his works and Horace's
were written to be recited rather than sung. He shows special affinity for
Sappho, directly imitating her poetry on occasion. A number of poems addressed to a woman he calls Lesbia (in an allusion to his literary forebears,
Sappho and Alcaeus, who were from the Aegean island of Lesbos) chart the
course of an ardent love affair that ultimately ends in anguished disillusionment. We do not know whether the passionate narrative presented in these
poems was real or fictive, but our uncertainty does nothing to diminish their
power.

[My Lesbia, let us live and love]*

My Lesbia, let us live and love
And not care tuppence for old men
Who sermonise and disapprove.
Suns when they sink can rise again,
But we, when our brief light has shone,   5
Must sleep the long night on and on.
Kiss me: a thousand kisses, then
A hundred more, and now a second
Thousand and hundred, and now still
Hundreds and thousands more, until   10
The thousand thousands can't be reckoned
And we've lost track of the amount
And nobody can work us ill
With the evil eye by keeping count.

[How many kisses satisfy]*

How many kisses satisfy,
How many are enough and more,
You ask me, Lesbia. I reply,
As many as the Libyan sands
Sprinkling the Cyrenaic[1] shore   5
Where silphium grows, between the places
Where old King Battus's tomb stands
And Jupiter Ammon has his shrine
In Siwa's sweltering oasis;
As many as the stars above   10
That in the dead of midnight shine
Upon men's secrecies of love.
When he has all those kisses, mad-
Hungry Catullus will have had
Enough to slake his appetite—   15
So many that sharp eyes can't tell
The number, and the tongues of spite
Are too confused to form a spell.

[Enough, Catullus, of this silly whining]*

Enough, Catullus, of this silly whining;
What you can see is lost, write off as lost.

*Translated by James Michie.

How many kisses satisfy
1. Cyrene was a city in Libya, thought to have

been founded by a Greek named Battus in
the seventh century B.C.E.

Not long ago the sun was always shining,
And, loved as no girl ever will be loved,
She led the way and you went dancing after.
Those were the days of lovers' games and laughter   5
When anything you wanted she approved;
That was a time when the sun really shone.
But now she's cold, you too must learn to cool;
Weak though you are, stop groping for what's gone,   10
Stop whimpering, and be stoically resigned.
Goodbye, my girl. Catullus from now on
Is adamant: he has made up his mind:
He won't beg for your favour like a bone.
You'll feel the cold, though, you damned bitch, when men   15
Leave *you* alone. What life will you have then?
Who'll visit you? Who'll think you beautiful? Who'll
Be loved by you? Parade you as his own?
Whom will you kiss and nibble then?
                              Oh fool,
Catullus, stop this, stand firm, become stone.   20

[Furius and Aurelius, loyal comrades]*

Furius and Aurelius, loyal comrades,
Who'd travel with me to remotest India,
Where the beaches pounded by the Eastern Ocean
    Boom to the rollers' thud,

Into Hyrcania,[1] languorous Arabia,   5
Among the Scythians or the archer Parthians,
Or to the plains which Nile, the seven-tongued river,
    Darkens with churned-up mud,

Who'd march on foot across the Alpine passes
To view the trophy-sites of mighty Caesar,[2]   10
The Rhine in Gaul, or the outlandish Britons
    Fenced by their sullen strait—

Staunch friends, ready to share all hazards with me,
Anything that the will of heaven proposes,
Please take this message to my girl, a few short   15
    Words to express my hate:

Good luck to her, let her enjoy her lovers,
The whole three hundred that she hugs together,

Furius and Aurelius, loyal comrades
1. A territory on the Caspian Sea.

2. Julius Caesar; the first invasion of Britain took place in 55 B.C.E.

Loving none truly, by grim repetition
    Wringing them all sperm-dry.   20

Let her not look to find my love unaltered;
Through her own fault it lies in ruins, fallen
Like a wildflower at a field's edge that the ploughshare
    Touches and passes by.

[She swears she'd rather marry me]*

She swears she'd rather marry me
Than anyone—even Jupiter,[1]
Supposing he were courting her.
She swears; but what a girl will swear
To the man who loves her ought to be   5
Scribbled on water, scrawled on air.

[I can remember, Lesbia, when you swore]*

I can remember, Lesbia, when you swore
You were mine and mine only, called me more
Desirable than Jove.[1] I loved you then,
And not just in the way that other men
Love mistresses, but as a father cares   5
For his own sons and daughters, for his heirs.
Now that I know you, you're much cheaper, lighter,
And yet desire in me flares even brighter.
'How can that be?' you say. In love deceit
Freezes affection, though it stokes up heat.   10

[If in recalling former kindnesses]†

If in recalling former kindnesses there's pleasure
    When a man reflects that he has been true
Nor broken solemn promise nor in any pact
    Abused the Gods' goodwill to fool his fellow men,
Then many joys remain in store for you, Catullus,   5
    Through a long lifetime from this ungrateful love.
For whatever kind things men can say or
    do
    To anyone, these you have said and done,

---

†*Translated by Guy Lee.*

She swears

1. The supreme deity of the Romans, identified with the Greek god Zeus.

I can remember

1. Another name for Jupiter.

But credited to ingratitude they have all been wasted.
    So now why torture yourself any more?   10
Why not harden your heart and tear yourself away
    And stop being wretched against the Gods' will?
It's difficult to break with long love suddenly.
    It's difficult, but this you must somehow do.
This is your only chance. You must win through to this.   15
    Possible or not, this you must achieve.
O Gods, if you can pity or have ever brought
    Help at last to any on the point of death,
Look on my wretchedness and if I have led a decent life
    Take away from me this deadly disease,   20
Which like a paralysis creeping into my inmost being
    Has driven from my heart every happiness.
I do not ask now that she love me in return
    Or, what's impossible, that she be chaste.
I pray for my own health, to be rid of this foul sickness.   25
    O Gods, grant me this for my true dealing.

[Travelling through many nations][†]

Travelling through many nations and through many seas[1]
    I have come, brother, for these poor funeral rites,
That I might render you the last dues of the dead
    And vainly comfort your dumb ashes,
Because Fortune has robbed me of your self, alas,   5
    Poor brother, unfairly taken from me.
But now, meanwhile, accept these gifts which by old custom
    Of the ancestors are offered in sad duty
At funeral rites, gifts drenched in a brother's tears,
    And forever, brother, greetings and farewell.   10

HORACE (65–8 B.C.E.)
Rome

A writer of great versatility, Horace (whose Latin name was Quintus Horatius
Flaccus) produced a substantial and varied body of poetry. In addition to a
collection of lyric poems organized into four books—the Odes, from which our

---

Travelling through many nations
1. Catullus's brother died in the region of Asia

Minor called the Troad, after its principal
city, Troy.

selection is drawn—his writings include literary criticism and philosophical meditations (often combined) in the form of satires and epistles in verse. From these latter groups of poems we learn a considerable number of biographical details. Horace's father was a slave who had been freed; he saw to Horace's education, sending him to Athens to study philosophy. There Horace grew to know the poetic traditions of Greece and was profoundly influenced by Archilochus, Sappho, and Alcaeus, as many of his odes attest. (Compare his Ode "You see how deep . . ." with Alcaeus's "Zeus rains upon us," presented earlier in this section.) Although not an innovator of formal poetic features, Horace brilliantly synthesized traditional elements from earlier Greek and Roman writers and deservedly claimed for himself the remarkable achievement of having successfully adapted to the Latin language the extraordinarily complex rhythms of Greek lyric poetry.

Through the poet Vergil, Horace met Maecenas, the preeminent literary patron of the time and a powerful friend of the emperor Augustus. From within the elite circle around Maecenas, Horace wrote a number of poems on Roman civic themes. Most frequently, however, his lyrics, like those of his Greek predecessors, represent private emotions and sensibilities, within which an appreciation of the transience of all things mortal is often central. In many of his poems Horace's perspective is framed by images of the natural world, and in others by those of the impersonal life of the city.

[Winter's fists unclench at the touch of spring] *

Winter's fists unclench at the touch of spring and western breezes,
　　dried-out keels are drawn down to the waves,
flocks are no longer at ease in stables, farmers at firesides,
　　meadows are no longer white with frost.

Under a hovering moon come dancers led by white Aphrodite,　　　　　　5
　　the slender Graces join hands with the nymphs
lightly to waltz on the grass, as Cyclops[1] under sweltering Vulcan
　　forge bolts of lightning for the storms to come.

Now is the time to garland glistening hair with green myrtle
　　or flowers, as the freed earth rejoices in birth;　　　　　　　　　　10
now a gift to Faunus[2] is proper, in shadowy groves a victim,
　　whatever is to his taste, ewe lamb or kid.

Death with his drained-out face will drum at destitute cottage
　　and royal castle. You have been lucky, Sestius:[3]

*Translated by Joseph P. Clancy.

Winter's fists

1. According to some mythological traditions, the Cyclopes were assistants to the god Hephaestus [see *Iliad*, Book 18], with whom Vulcan, the Roman god of fire and of the forge, was identified.

2. A deity who protects flocks, herds, and agriculture in general.

3. Sestius, Horace's friend, was a prominent figure in Roman political life in the middle of the 1st century B.C.E.

all of life is only a little, no long-term plans are allowed.
  Soon night and half-remembered shapes and drab   15

Pluto's[4] walls will be closing in; enter his halls and you're done with
  tosses of dice that crown you toastmaster,
marveling glances at slim young Lycidas, for whom all the boys are
  now burning, and the girls will soon catch fire.   20

[What slim youth, Pyrrha][†]

What slim youth, Pyrrha, drenched in perfumed oils,
Lying in an easy grotto among roses, roses,
  Now woos, and watches you
  Gathering back your golden hair,

With artless elegance? How many a time   5
Will he cry out, seeing all changed, the gods, your promise,
  And stare in wondering shock
  At winds gone wild on blackening seas!

Now fondling you, his hope, his perfect gold,
He leans on love's inviolable constancy, not dreaming   10
  How false the breeze can blow.
  Ah, pity all those who have not found

Your glossy sweetness out! My shipwreck's tale
Hangs, told in colors, on Neptune's temple wall,[1] a votive
  Plaque, with salvaged clothes   15
  Still damp, vowed to the sea's rough lord.

[You see how deep Soracte stands in snow][†]

You see how deep Soracte[1] stands in snow,
A hoary blaze, the laboring forests cringing
  Under the load, the rivers standing
  Pinned in their course by piercing ice.

Heap logs in plenty on the grate, melt off   5
The cold, and tilt the crock up by both handles,

---

†Translated by Cedric Whitman.

---

4. Pluto is one of the names of the god of the
  underworld.

What slim youth

1. The Roman god of the sea, identified with
  the Greek Poseidon. Sailors who had survived shipwreck would often dedicate to

Neptune a tablet or picture to commemorate the event, along with the clothes they
had worn at sea.

You see how deep

1. A mountain north of Rome, which was
  visible from the city.

Good revel master, pour the four year
Vintage out with freer hand.

Leave all the rest to the gods; once they have laid
Asleep these winds that now go brawling over   10
    The boiling sea, no more will cypress
    Shiver and flail, nor aged ash.

Let be what comes tomorrow, reckoning
Pure gain whatever gift of days your fortune
    Yields, and in youth be not disdainful   15
    Of love in all its sweetness; dance,

While yet no sorry white head nods upon
Your springtime shoulders; look to the piazza,
    The pleasure walks, the hushed whisper
    By nightfall at the trysting hour;   20

When a girl's laughter happily betrays
Her hiding place, lurked in a secret corner;
    Then plunder a trinket from her finger,
    Or languidly protesting arm.

[Don't ask, Leuconoë, the forbidden question] *

Don't ask, Leuconoë, the forbidden question, how long
the gods have given to you and to me: don't imagine
fortunetellers know. Better to take what is coming,
whether Jove allows us more winters, or this that now
wearies the Etruscan sea as it beats on the cliffs   5
is the last. Be sensible: strain the wine: in a little life,
take no long looks ahead. As we talk, time spites us
and runs: reap today: save no hopes for tomorrow.

[Those wars, Venus, are long over] *

Those wars, Venus, are long over,
    and now you provoke them again. Please, please, spare me.
I am not what I was when dear
    Cinara ruled me. Put an end to your efforts,

cruel mother of sweet Cupids,   5
    to soften the stiffness of a man now fifty
by your gentle orders: go where
    the young men invite you with flattering prayers.

This is a better time for you
    to bring, drawn by your swans' glowing wings, your joy to   10
the home of Paulus Maximus,[1]
    if you're looking for the kind of heart to catch fire.

For he is noble and handsome,
    and speaks well in defending his troubled clients,
a young man of many talents   15
    who will carry the banner of your service far;

and whenever he is happy
    to have conquered the gifts of a spendthrift rival,
he will set your marble statue
    under a cedar roof, beside the Alban lakes.   20

There you will breathe in plentiful
    incense, and you will find delight in the music
of the Berecyntian[2] flute
    mingled with the strings, with the pipe not forgotten;

there, twice every day, the boys   25
    and delicate virgins will chant the praises of
your divinity, their white feet
    beating the ground in tripletime Salian[3] dance.

As for me, not woman nor boy
    nor the hope that believes its feelings are returned   30
pleases me now, nor drinking bouts,
    nor having fresh flowers wound about my forehead.

But why, ah Ligurinus,[4] why
    does a tear now and then run trickling down my cheek?
Why does my tongue, once eloquent,   35
    fall, as I'm talking, into ungracious silence?

At night I see you in my dreams,
    now caught, and I hold you, now I follow as you
run away, over the grassy
    Field of Mars,[5] over flowing streams, with your hard heart.   40

Those wars

1. A prominent member of Roman society
   who was a friend of the emperor Augustus.
2. An instrument used in the worship of several Roman deities, notably the
   god Bacchus.

3. The Salians were legendary dancers.
4. The addressee of this poem is unknown;
   the name may be imaginary.
5. A public area near the Tiber, popular with
   the Romans as a place for exercise and
   entertainment.

Akhnaten and Nefertiti offering libations to the Aten. Fragment from a balustrade from the Great Palace, Amarna. Egyptian, Eighteenth Dynasty (fourteenth century B.C.E.).

ANONYMOUS (c. 1300 B.C.E.)
Egypt

For most of its history, ancient Egypt was a thoroughly polytheistic society. But King Akhnaten, who ruled from 1350 to 1334 B.C.E., espoused the worship of a single god, the sun disk, or Aten. Akhnaten emphasized the international supremacy of the Aten by pointing out that the sun shines on all peoples equally. He presented himself as the Aten's son, the chief intermediary between the Aten and humanity. The worship of the Aten may not have been true monotheism, especially given the king's own quasi-divine role. Nevertheless, the cults of the old gods were systematically repressed, and even their names were removed from public inscriptions. Artistic reforms were undertaken as well, with a new realism emerging in portaiture.

This hymn was found inscribed on a wall of the tomb of Ay, a high official in Akhnaten's court. It gives an almost anthropological view of the different races and emphasizes the Aten's tender care for his whole creation. The worship of the Aten was a remarkable episode in Egyptian history. It is almost as though the Egyptians were trying to see the world whole for the first time, uniting the many peoples of their cosmopolitan empire under the Aten while accepting their great diversity. The moment did not last long, however. After Akhnaten's death, the older gods were reestablished and his own name was supressed in turn.

The Great Hymn to the Aten

Adoration of Re-Harakhti-who-rejoices-in-the horizon In-his-name-Shu-who-is-Aten, living forever; the great living Aten who is in jubilee, the lord of all that the Disk encircles, lord of sky, lord of earth, lord of the house-of-Aten in Akhet-Aten; and of the King of Upper and Lower Egypt, who lives by Maat,[1] the Lord of the Two Lands,[2] Neferkheprure, Sole-one-of-Re; the Son of Re who lives by Maat, the Lord of Crowns, Akhenaten, great in his lifetime; and his beloved great Queen, the Lady of the Two Lands, Nefer-nefru-Aten Nefertiti, who lives in health and youth forever. The Vizier, the Fanbearer on the right of the King, Ay; he says:

Splendid you rise in heaven's horizon,
O living Aten, creator of life!
When you have dawned in the eastern horizon,
You fill every land with your beauty.
You are beauteous, great, radiant,   5
High over every land;
Your rays embrace the lands,
To the limit of all that you made.
Being Re, you reach their limits,
You bend them for the son whom you love;   10
Though you are far, your rays are on earth,
Though one sees you, your strides are unseen.

When you set in the western horizon,
Earth is in darkness as if in death;
One sleeps in chambers, heads covered,   15
One eye does not see another.
Were they robbed of their goods,
That are under their heads,
People would not remark it.
Every lion comes from its den,   20
All the serpents bite;
Darkness hovers, earth is silent,
As their maker rests in the horizon.

Earth brightens when you dawn in the horizon,
When you shine as Aten of daytime;   25
As you dispel the dark,
As you cast your rays,
The Two Lands are in festivity.
Awake they stand on their feet,
You have roused them;   30

Translated by Miriam Lichtheim.

1. *Maat* means "truth."

2. Upper and Lower Egypt, united by the first pharaoh.

Bodies cleansed, clothed,
Their arms adore your appearance.
The entire land sets out to work,
All beasts browse on their herbs;
Trees, herbs are sprouting,   35
Birds fly from their nests,
Their wings greeting your spirit.
All flocks frisk on their feet,
All that fly up and alight,
They live when you dawn for them.   40
Ships fare north, fare south as well,
Roads lie open when you rise;
The fish in the river dart before you,
Your rays are in the midst of the sea.

Who makes seed grow in women,   45
Who creates people from sperm;
Who feeds the son in his mother's womb,
Who soothes him to still his tears.
Nurse in the womb,
Giver of breath,   50
To nourish all that he made.
When he comes from the womb to breathe,
On the day of his birth,
You open wide his mouth,
You supply his needs.   55
When the chick in the egg speaks in the shell,
You give him breath within to sustain him;
When you have made him complete,
To break out from the egg,
He comes out from the egg,   60
To announce his completion,
Walking on his legs he comes from it.

How many are your deeds,
Though hidden from sight,
O Sole God beside whom there is none!   65
You made the earth as you wished, you alone,
All peoples, herds, and flocks;
All upon earth that walk on legs,
All on high that fly on wings,
The lands of Khor and Kush,
The land of Egypt.   70
You set every man in his place,
You supply their needs;
Everyone has his food,

His lifetime is counted.
Their tongues differ in speech,
Their characters likewise;
Their skins are distinct,
For you distinguished the peoples.

You made Hapy[3] in the underworld;
You bring him when you will,
To nourish the people,
For you made them for yourself.
Lord of all who toils for them,
Lord of all lands who shines for them,
Aten of daytime, great in glory!
All distant lands, you make them live,
You made a heavenly Hapy descend for them;
He makes waves on the mountains like the sea,
To drench their fields and their towns.
How excellent are your ways, O Lord of eternity!
A Hapy from heaven for foreign peoples,
And all lands' creatures that walk on legs,
For Egypt the Hapy who comes from the underworld.

Your rays nurse all fields,
When you shine they live, they grow for you;
You made the seasons to foster all that you made,
Winter to cool them, heat that they taste you.
You made the far sky to shine therein,
To behold all that you made;
You alone, shining in your form of living Aten,
Risen, radiant, distant, near.
You made millions of forms from yourself alone,
Towns, villages, fields, the river's course;
All eyes observe you upon them,
For you are the Aten of daytime on high.

You are in my heart,
There is no other who knows you,
Only your son, Neferkheprure, Sole-one-of-Re,
Whom you have taught your ways and your might.
Those on earth come from your hand as you made them,
When you have dawned they live,
When you set they die;
You yourself are lifetime, one lives by you.

75

80

85

90

95

100

105

110

---

3. Hapy is the god who controls the Nile's
annual inundation.

All eyes are on your beauty until you set,   115
All labor ceases when you rest in the west;
When you rise you stir everyone for the King,
Every leg is on the move since you founded the earth.
You rouse them for your son who came from your body,
The King who lives by Maat, the Lord of the Two Lands,   120
Neferkheprure, Sole-one-of-Re,
The Son of Re who lives by Maat, the Lord of crowns,
Akhenaten, great in his lifetime;
And the great Queen whom he loves, the Lady of the Two Lands,
Nefer-nefru-Aten Nefertiti, living forever.   125

ANONYMOUS (c. 1900 B.C.E.)
Egypt

This remarkable autobiography begins with the death of the first king of the Twelfth Dynasty, Amenemhet I, in 1961 B.C.E. Upon hearing the news, the courtier Sinuhe flees Egypt, apparently fearing that the new dynasty will not survive its founder's death. The ensuing story describes Sinuhe's survival and eventual prosperity in Syria and Palestine. He returns in old age to the court of Amenemhet's successor, Sesostris I, where he is received with honor and, most importantly, granted a traditional burial and funerary rites.

The story survives in various manuscripts from the Twelfth Dynasty onward. It is usually supposed that it was copied from an inscription in Sinuhe's tomb, although neither a tomb nor any other record of Sinuhe has ever been discovered. Almost four thousand years old, the "Story of Sinuhe" is a masterpiece of realistic narration.

The Story of Sinuhe

The Prince, Count, Governor of the domains of the sovereign in the lands of the Asiatics, true and beloved Friend of the King, the Attendant Sinuhe, says:

I was an attendant who attended his lord, a servant of the royal harem, waiting on the Princess, the highly praised Royal Wife of King Sesostris in Khenemsut, the daughter of King Amenemhet in Kanefru, Nefru, the revered.[1]

Year 30, third month of the inundation, day 7: the god ascended to his horizon. The King of Upper and Lower Egypt, Sehetepibre, flew to heaven and

Translated by Miriam Lichtheim.

---

1. Sinuhe is an official of Princess Nefru,
daughter of Amenemhet and wife of her
brother Sesostris I. Khenemsut and Kanefru
are the pyramid towns of Sesostris and his
father.

united with the sun-disk, the divine body merging with its maker. Then the residence was hushed; hearts grieved; the great portals were shut; the courtiers were head-on-knee; the people moaned.

His majesty, however, had despatched an army to the land of the Tjemeh, with his eldest son as its commander, the good god Sesostris. He had been sent to smite the foreign lands and to punish those of Tjehenu.[2] Now he was returning, bringing captives of the Tjehenu and cattle of all kinds beyond number. The officials of the palace sent to the western border to let the king's son know the event that had occurred at the court. The messengers met him on the road, reaching him at night. Not a moment did he delay. The falcon flew with his attendants, without letting his army know it.

But the royal sons who had been with him on this expedition had also been sent for. One of them was summoned while I was standing there. I heard his voice, as he spoke, while I was in the near distance. My heart fluttered, my arms spread out, a trembling befell all my limbs. I removed myself in leaps, to seek a hiding place. I put myself between two bushes, so as to leave the road to its traveler.

I set out southward. I did not plan to go to the residence. I believed there would be turmoil and did not expect to survive it. I crossed Maaty near Sycamore; I reached Isle-of-Snefru. I spent the day there at the edge of the cultivation. Departing at dawn I encountered a man who stood on the road. He saluted me while I was afraid of him. At dinner time I reached "Cattle-Quay." I crossed in a barge without a rudder, by the force of the westwind. I passed to the east of the quarry, at the height of "Mistress of the Red Mountain." Then I made my way northward.[3] I reached the "Walls of the Ruler," which were made to repel the Asiatics and to crush the Sand-farers. I crouched in a bush for fear of being seen by the guard on duty upon the wall.

I set out at night. At dawn I reached Peten. I halted at "Isle-of-Kem-Wer." An attack of thirst overtook me; I was parched, my throat burned. I said, "This is the taste of death." I raised my heart and collected myself when I heard the lowing sound of cattle and saw Asiatics. One of their leaders, who had been in Egypt, recognized me. He gave me water and boiled milk for me. I went with him to his tribe. What they did for me was good.

Land gave me to land. I traveled to Byblos; I returned to Qedem. I spent a year and a half there. Then Ammunenshi, the ruler of Upper Retenu,[4] took me to him, saying to me: "You will be happy with me; you will hear the language of Egypt." He said this because he knew my character and had heard of my skill, Egyptians who were with him having borne witness for me. He said to me: "Why have you come here? Has something happened at the residence?" I said to him: "King Sehetepibre departed to the horizon, and one did not know the circumstances." But I spoke in half-truths: "When I returned from the expedition to the land of the Tjemeh, it was reported to me and my heart grew faint. It carried me away on the

---

2. Tjemeh and Tjehenu are names of two Libyan peoples.
3. Sinuhe began by traveling south. He turns northward upon crossing the Nile, perhaps

inspired by the downstream (northward) drift of his rudderless boat.
4. A region in parts of Palestine and Syria.

path of flight, though I had not been talked about: no one had spat in my face; I had not heard a reproach; my name had not been heard in the mouth of the herald. I do not know what brought me to this country; it is as if planned by god. As if a Delta-man saw himself in Yebu, a marsh-man in Nubia."[5]

Then he said to me: "How then is that land without that excellent god, fear of whom was throughout the lands like Sakhmet[6] in a year of plague?" I said to him in reply: "Of course his son has entered into the palace, having taken his father's heritage.

> He is a god without peer,
> No other comes before him;
> He is lord of knowledge, wise planner, skilled leader,
> One goes and comes by his will.

> He was the smiter of foreign lands,
> While his father stayed in the palace,
> He reported to him on commands carried out.

> He is a champion who acts with his arm,
> A fighter who has no equal,
> When seen engaged in archery,
> When joining the melee.

> Horn-curber who makes hands turn weak,
> His foes can not close ranks;
> Keen-sighted he smashes foreheads,
> None can withstand his presence.

> Wide-striding he smites the fleeing,
> No retreat for him who turns him his back;
> Steadfast in time of attack,
> He makes turn back and turns not his back.

> Stouthearted when he sees the mass,
> He lets not slackness fill his heart;
> Eager at the sight of combat,
> Joyful when he works his bow.

> Clasping his shield he treads under foot,
> No second blow needed to kill;
> None can escape his arrow,
> None turn aside his bow.

> The Bowmen flee before him,
> As before the might of the goddess;
> As he fights he plans the goal,
> Unconcerned about all else.

> Lord of grace, rich in kindness,
> He has conquered through affection;

---

5. I.e., at the opposite end of the country.   6. Goddess of war.

His city loves him more than itself,
Acclaims him more than its own god.

Men outdo women in hailing him,
Now that he is king;
Victor while yet in the egg,
Set to be ruler since his birth.

Augmenter of those born with him,
He is unique, god-given;
Happy the land that he rules!

Enlarger of frontiers,
He will conquer southern lands,
While ignoring northern lands,
Though made to smite Asiatics and tread on Sand-farers!

"Send to him! Let him know your name as one who inquires while being far from his majesty. He will not fail to do good to a land that will be loyal to him."

He said to me: "Well then, Egypt is happy knowing that he is strong. But you are here. You shall stay with me. What I shall do for you is good."

He set me at the head of his children. He married me to his eldest daughter. He let me choose for myself of his land, of the best that was his, on his border with another land. It was a good land called Yaa. Figs were in it and grapes. It had more wine than water. Abundant was its honey, plentiful its oil. All kinds of fruit were on its trees. Barley was there and emmer, and no end of cattle of all kinds. Much also came to me because of the love of me; for he had made me chief of a tribe in the best part of his land. Loaves were made for me daily, and wine as daily fare, cooked meat, roast fowl, as well as desert game. For they snared for me and laid it before me, in addition to the catch of my hounds. Many sweets were made for me, and milk dishes of all kinds.

I passed many years, my children becoming strong men, each a master of his tribe. The envoy who came north or went south to the residence stayed with me. I let everyone stay with me. I gave water to the thirsty; I showed the way to him who had strayed; I rescued him who had been robbed. When Asiatics conspired to attack the Rulers of Hill-Countries, I opposed their movements. For this ruler of Retenu made me carry out numerous missions as commander of his troops. Every hill tribe against which I marched I vanquished, so that it was driven from the pasture of its wells. I plundered its cattle, carried off its families, seized their food, and killed people by my strong arm, by my bow, by my movements and my skillful plans. I won his heart and he loved me, for he recognized my valor. He set me at the head of his children, for he saw the strength of my arms.

There came a hero of Retenu,
To challenge me in my tent.
A champion was he without peer,
He had subdued it all.
He said he would fight with me,
He planned to plunder me,

He meant to seize my cattle
At the behest of his tribe.

The ruler conferred with me and I said: "I do not know him; I am not his ally,
that I could walk about in his camp. Have I ever opened his back rooms or
climbed over his fence? It is envy, because he sees me doing your commissions. I
am indeed like a stray bull in a strange herd, whom the bull of the herd charges,
whom the longhorn attacks. Is an inferior beloved when he becomes a superior?
No Asiatic makes friends with a Delta-man. And what would make papyrus cleave
to the mountain?[7] If a bull loves combat, should a champion bull retreat for fear
of being equaled? If he wishes to fight, let him declare his wish. Is there a god who
does not know what he has ordained, and a man who knows how it will be?"

At night I strung my bow, sorted my arrows, practiced with my dagger,
polished my weapons. When it dawned Retenu came. It had assembled its tribes;
it had gathered its neighboring peoples; it was intent on this combat.

He came toward me while I waited, having placed myself near him. Every
heart burned for me; the women jabbered. All hearts ached for me thinking: "Is
there another champion who could fight him?" He raised his battle-axe and shield,
while his armful of missiles fell toward me. When I had made his weapons attack
me, I let his arrows pass me by without effect, one following the other. Then,
when he charged me, I shot him, my arrow sticking in his neck. He screamed; he
fell on his nose; I slew him with his axe. I raised my war cry over his back, while
every Asiatic shouted. I gave praise to Mont,[8] while his people mourned him. The
ruler Ammunenshi took me in his arms.

Then I carried off his goods; I plundered his cattle. What he had meant to do
to me I did to him. I took what was in his tent; I stripped his camp. Thus I became
great, wealthy in goods, rich in herds. It was the god who acted, so as to show
mercy to one with whom he had been angry, whom he had made stray abroad.
For today his heart is appeased.

A fugitive fled his surroundings
    I am famed at home.
A laggard lagged from hunger—
    I give bread to my neighbor.
A man left his land in nakedness—
    I have bright clothes, fine linen.
A man ran for lack of one to send—
    I am rich in servants.
My house is fine, my dwelling spacious—
    My thoughts are at the palace!

Whichever god decreed this flight have mercy, bring me home! Surely you
will let me see the place in which my heart dwells! What is more important than
that my corpse be buried in the land in which I was born! Come to my aid! What

---

7. Papyrus grows in fertile lowland like
   Sinuhe's native Nile Delta; the mountains

are dry and implicitly less cultivated (in
both senses).

8. Patron god of warriors.

if the happy event should occur![9] May god pity me! May he act so as to make happy the end of one whom he punished! May his heart ache for one whom he forced to live abroad! If he is truly appeased today, may he hearken to the prayer of one far away! May he return one whom he made roam the earth to the place from which he carried him off!

May Egypt's king have mercy on me, that I may live by his mercy! May I greet the mistress of the land who is in the palace! May I hear the commands of her children! Would that my body were young again! For old age has come; feebleness has overtaken me. My eyes are heavy, my arms weak; my legs fail to follow. The heart is weary; death is near. May I be conducted to the city of eternity! May I serve the Mistress of All![10] May she speak well of me to her children; may she spend eternity above me!

Now when the majesty of King Kheperkare was told of the condition in which I was, his majesty sent word to me with royal gifts, in order to gladden the heart of this servant like that of a foreign ruler. And the royal children who were in his palace sent me their messages. Copy of the decree brought to this servant concerning his return to Egypt:

Horus: Living in Births; the Two Ladies: Living in Births; the King of Upper and Lower Egypt: Kheperkare; the Son of Re: Sesostris, who lives forever. Royal decree to the Attendant Sinuhe:

This decree of the King is brought to you to let you know: That you circled the foreign countries, going from Qedem to Retenu, land giving you to land, was the counsel of your own heart. What had you done that one should act against you? You had not cursed, so that your speech would be reproved. You had not spoken against the counsel of the nobles, that your words should have been rejected. This matter—it carried away your heart. It was not in my heart against you. This your heaven in the palace lives and prospers to this day.[11] Her head is adorned with the kingship of the land; her children are in the palace. You will store riches which they give you; you will live on their bounty. Come back to Egypt! See the residence in which you lived! Kiss the ground at the great portals, mingle with the courtiers! For today you have begun to age. You have lost a man's strength. Think of the day of burial, the passing into reveredness.

A night is made for you with ointments and wrappings from the hand of Tait.[12] A funeral procession is made for you on the day of burial; the mummy case is of gold, its head of lapis lazuli. The sky is above you as you lie in the hearse, oxen drawing you, musicians going before you. The dance of the funerary dancers is done at the door of your tomb; the offering-list is read to you; sacrifice is made before your offering-stone. Your tomb-pillars, made of white stone, are among those of the royal children. You shall not die abroad! Nor shall Asiatics inter you. You shall not be wrapped in the skin of a ram to serve as your coffin. Too long a roaming of the earth! Think of your corpse, come back!

---

9. I.e., death.
10. Sinuhe identifies the queen with the sky goddess, who shields souls in the underworld.

11. I.e., Princess Nefru is secure as the new queen.
12. Goddess of weaving, including mummy-wrappings.

This decree reached me while I was standing in the midst of my tribe. When it had been read to me, I threw myself on my belly. Having touched the soil, I spread it on my chest. I strode around my camp shouting: "What compares with this which is done to a servant whom his heart led astray to alien lands? Truly good is the kindness that saves me from death! Your spirit will grant me to reach my end, my body being at home!"

Copy of the reply to this decree:

The servant of the Palace, Sinuhe, says: In very good peace! Regarding the matter of this flight which this servant did in his ignorance. It is your spirit, O good god, lord of the Two Lands, which Re loves and which Mont lord of Thebes favors; and Amun lord of Thrones-of-the-Two-Lands, and Sobk-Re lord of Sumenu, and Horus, Hathor, Atum with his Ennead, and Sopdu-Neferbau-Semseru the Eastern Horus, and the Lady of Yemet—many she enfold your head—and the conclave upon the flood, and Min-Horus of the hill-countries, and Wereret lady of Punt, Nut, Haroeris-Re, and all the gods of Egypt and the isles of the sea—may they give life and joy to your nostrils, may they endue you with their bounty, may they give you eternity without limit, infinity without bounds! May the fear of you resound in lowlands and highlands, for you have subdued all that the sun encircles! This is the prayer of this servant for his lord who saves from the West.

The lord of knowledge who knows people knew in the majesty of the palace that this servant was afraid to say it. It is like a thing too great to repeat. The great god, the peer of Re, knows the heart of one who has served him willingly. This servant is in the hand of one who thinks about him. He is placed under his care. Your Majesty is the conquering Horus; your arms vanquish all lands. May then your Majesty command to have brought to you the prince of Meki from Qedem, the mountain chiefs from Keshu, and the prince of Menus from the lands of the Fenkhu. They are rulers of renown who have grown up in the love of you. I do not mention Retenu—it belongs to you like your hounds.

Lo, this flight which the servant made—I did not plan it. It was not in my heart; I did not devise it. I do not know what removed me from my place. It was like a dream. As if a Delta-man saw himself in Yebu, a marsh-man in Nubia. I was not afraid; no one ran after me. I had not heard a reproach; my name was not heard in the mouth of the herald. Yet my flesh crept, my feet hurried, my heart drove me; the god who had willed this flight dragged me away. Nor am I a haughty man. He who knows his land respects men. Re has set the fear of you throughout the land, the dread of you in every foreign country. Whether I am at the residence, whether I am in this place, it is you who covers this horizon. The sun rises at your pleasure. The water in the river is drunk when you wish. The air of heaven is breathed at your bidding. This servant will hand over his possessions to the brood which this servant begot in this place. This servant has been sent for! Your Majesty will do as he wishes! One lives by the breath which you give. As Re, Horus, and Hathor love your august nose,[13] may Mont lord of Thebes wish it to live forever!

---

13. The nose, associated with the breath of life, was seen as a center of sensation and emotion.

I was allowed to spend one more day in Yaa, handing over my possessions to my children, my eldest son taking charge of my tribe; all my possessions became his—my serfs, my herds, my fruit, my fruit trees. This servant departed southward. I halted at Horusways. The commander in charge of the garrison sent a message to the residence to let it be known. Then his majesty sent a trusted overseer of the royal domains with whom were loaded ships, bearing royal gifts for the Asiatics who had come with me to escort me to Horusways. I called each one by his name, while every butler was at his task. When I had started and set sail, there was kneading and straining beside me, until I reached the city of Itj-tawy.

When it dawned, very early, they came to summon me. Ten men came and ten men went to usher me into the palace. My forehead touched the ground between the sphinxes, and the royal children stood in the gateway to meet me. The courtiers who usher through the forecourt set me on the way to the audience-hall. I found his majesty on the great throne in a kiosk of gold. Stretched out on my belly, I did not know myself before him, while this god greeted me pleasantly. I was like a man seized by darkness. My soul was gone, my limbs trembled; my heart was not in my body, I did not know life from death.

His majesty said to one of the courtiers: "Lift him up, let him speak to me." Then his majesty said: "Now you have come, after having roamed foreign lands. Flight has taken its toll of you. You have aged, have reached old age. It is no small matter that your corpse will be interred without being escorted by Bowmen.[14] But don't act thus, don't act thus, speechless though your name was called!" Fearful of punishment I answered with the answer of a frightened man: "What has my lord said to me, that I might answer it? It is not disrespect to the god! It is the terror which is in my body, like that which caused the fateful flight! Here I am before you. Life is yours. May your Majesty do as he wishes!"

Then the royal daughters were brought in, and his majesty said to the queen: "Here is Sinuhe, come as an Asiatic, a product of nomads!" She uttered a very great cry, and the royal daughters shrieked all together. They said to his majesty: "Is it really he, O king, our lord?" Said his majesty: "It is really he!" Now having brought with them their necklaces, rattles, and sistra, they held them out to his majesty:

> Your hands upon the radiance, eternal king,
> Jewels of heaven's mistress!
> The Golden One gives life to your nostrils,
> The Lady of Stars enfolds you!
>
> Southcrown fared north, northcrown south,
> Joined, united by your majesty's word.
> While the Cobra decks your brow,
> You deliver the poor from harm.
> Peace to you from Re, Lord of Lands!
> Hail to you and the Mistress of All!
>
> Slacken your bow, lay down your arrow,
> Give breath to him who gasps for breath!

---

14. I.e., by the rough nomads.

Give us our good gift on this good day,
Grant us the son of northwind, Bowman born in Egypt!

He made the flight in fear of you,
He left the land in dread of you!
A face that sees you shall not pale,
Eyes that see you shall not fear!

His majesty said: "He shall not fear, he shall not dread!" He shall be a
Companion among the nobles. He shall be among the courtiers. Proceed to the
robing-room to wait on him!"

I left the audience-hall, the royal daughters giving me their hands. We went
through the great portals, and I was put in the house of a prince. In it were
luxuries: a bathroom and mirrors. In it were riches from the treasury; clothes of
royal linen, myrrh, and the choice perfume of the king and of his favorite courtiers
were in every room. Every servant was at his task. Years were removed from my
body. I was shaved; my hair was combed. Thus was my squalor returned to the
foreign land, my dress to the Sand-farers. I was clothed in fine linen; I was
anointed with fine oil. I slept on a bed. I had returned the sand to those who dwell
in it, the tree-oil to those who grease themselves with it.

I was given a house and garden that had belonged to a courtier. Many
craftsmen rebuilt it, and all its woodwork was made anew. Meals were brought to
me from the palace three times, four times a day, apart from what the royal
children gave without a moment's pause.

A stone pyramid was built for me in the midst of the pyramids. The masons
who build tombs constructed it. A master draughtsman designed in it. A master
sculptor carved in it. The overseers of construction in the necropolis busied
themselves with it. All the equipment that is placed in a tomb-shaft was supplied.
Mortuary priests were given me. A funerary domain was made for me. It had fields
and a garden in the right place, as is done for a Companion of the first rank. My
statue was overlaid with gold, its skirt with electrum. It was his majesty who
ordered it made. There is no commoner for whom the like has been done. I was
in the favor of the king, until the day of landing[15] came.

Colophon   It is done from beginning to end as it was found in writing.

ANONYMOUS (c. 1200 B.C.E.)
Egypt

This mysterious story was found on a papyrus copied—or written—by an
Egyptian scribe named Ennana, who lived around 1200 B.C.E. Its protagonists

------

15. I.e., death.

bear the names of two gods: Anubis was god of the dead and embalming; Bata was a pastoral god, often pictured as a ram or as a bull. Whether or not they are divine in this story is unclear. They may be gods, or they may be essentially human characters who share some traits with divine namesakes. In either case, the story mixes magical and earthly realism with a full presentation of familial and psychological conflict.

The Two Brothers

It is said, there were two brothers, of the same mother and the same father. Anubis was the name of the elder, and Bata the name of the younger. As for Anubis, he had a house and a wife; and his young brother was with him as if he were a son. He was the one who made clothes for him, and he went behind his cattle to the fields. He was the one who did the plowing, and he harvested for him. He was the one who did for him all kinds of labor in the fields. Indeed, his young brother was an excellent man. There was none like him in the whole land, for a god's strength was in him.

Now when many days had passed, his young brother was tending his cattle according to his daily custom. And he returned to his house in the evening, laden with all kinds of field plants, and with milk, with wood, and with every good thing of the field. He placed them before his elder brother, as he was sitting with his wife. Then he drank and ate and [went to sleep in] his stable among his cattle.

Now when it had dawned and another day had come, he took foods that were cooked and placed them before his elder brother. Then he took bread for himself for the fields, and he drove his cattle to let them eat in the fields. He walked behind his cattle, and they would say to him: "The grass is good in such-and-such a place." And he heard all they said and took them to the place of good grass that they desired. Thus the cattle he tended became exceedingly fine, and they increased their offspring very much.

Now at plowing time his elder brother said to him: "Have a team of oxen made ready for us for plowing, for the soil has emerged and is right for plowing. Also, come to the field with seed, for we shall start plowing tomorrow." So he said to him. Then the young brother made all the preparations that his elder brother had told him to make.

Now when it had dawned and another day had come, they went to the field with their seed and began to plow. And their hearts were very pleased with this work they had undertaken. And many days later, when they were in the field, they had need of seed. Then he sent his young brother, saying: "Hurry, fetch us seed from the village." His young brother found the wife of his elder brother seated braiding her hair. He said to her: "Get up, give me seed, so that I may hurry to the field, for my elder brother is waiting for me. Don't delay." She said to him: "Go, open the storeroom and fetch what you want. Don't make me leave my hairdo unfinished."

Then the youth entered his stable and fetched a large vessel, for he wished to take a great quantity of seed. He loaded himself with barley and emmer and came out with it. Thereupon she said to him: "How much is what you have on your

Translated by Miriam Lichtheim.

shoulder?" He said to her: "Three sacks of emmer and two sacks of barley, five in all, are on my shoulder." So he said to her. Then she spoke to him saying: "There is great strength in you. I see your vigor daily." And she desired to know him as a man. She got up, took hold of him, and said to him: "Come, let us spend an hour lying together. It will be good for you. And I will make fine clothes for you."

Then the youth became like a leopard in his anger over the wicked speech she had made to him; and she became very frightened. He rebuked her, saying: "Look, you are like a mother to me; and your husband is like a father to me. He who is older than I has raised me. What is this great wrong you said to me? Do not say it to me again! But I will not tell it to anyone. I will not let it come from my mouth to any man." He picked up his load; he went off to the field. He reached his elder brother, and they began to work at their task. When evening had come, his elder brother returned to his house. And his young brother tended his cattle, loaded himself with all things of the field, and drove his cattle before him to let them sleep in their stable in the village.

Now the wife of his elder brother was afraid on account of the speech she had made. So she took fat and grease and made herself appear as if she had been beaten, in order to tell her husband, "It was your young brother who beat me." Her husband returned in the evening according to his daily custom. He reached his house and found his wife lying down and seeming ill. She did not pour water over his hands in the usual manner; nor had she lit a fire for him. His house was in darkness, and she lay vomiting.

Her husband said to her: "Who has had words with you?" She said to him: "No one has had words with me except your young brother. When he came to take seed to you, he found me sitting alone. He said to me: 'Come, let us spend an hour lying together; loosen your braids.' So he said to me. But I would not listen to him. 'Am I not your mother? Is your elder brother not like a father to you?' So I said to him. He became frightened and he beat me, so as to prevent me from telling you. Now if you let him live, I shall die! Look, when he returns, do not let him live! For I am ill from this evil design which he was about to carry out in the morning."

Then his elder brother became like a leopard. He sharpened his spear and took it in his hand. Then his elder brother stood behind the door of his stable, in order to kill his younger brother when he came in the evening to let his cattle enter the stable. Now when the sun had set he loaded himself with all the plants of the field according to his daily custom. He returned, and as the lead cow was about to enter the stable she said to her herdsman: "Here is your elder brother waiting for you with his spear in order to kill you. Run away from him." He heard what his lead cow said, and when another went in she said the same. He looked under the door of his stable and saw the feet of his elder brother as he stood behind the door with his spear in his hand. He set his load on the ground and took off at a run so as to flee. And his elder brother went after him with his spear.

Then his young brother prayed to Pre-Harakhti,[1] saying: "My good lord! It is you who judge between the wicked and the just!" And Pre heard all his plea; and Pre made a great body of water appear between him and his elder brother, and it

---

1. A name for the sun god Re or Ra.

was full of crocodiles. Thus one came to be on the one side, and the other on the other side. And his elder brother struck his own hand twice, because he had failed to kill him. Then his young brother called to him on this side, saying: "Wait here until dawn! When the Aten[2] has risen, I shall contend with you before him; and he will hand over the wicked to the just! For I shall not be with you any more. I shall not be in the place in which you are. I shall go to the Valley of the Pine."

Now when it dawned and another day had come, and Pre-Harakhti had risen, one gazed at the other. Then the youth rebuked his elder brother, saying: "What is your coming after me to kill me wrongfully, without having listened to my words? For I am yet your young brother, and you are like a father to me, and your wife is like a mother to me. Is it not so that when I was sent to fetch seed for us your wife said to me: 'Come, let us spend an hour lying together'? But look, it has been turned about for you into another thing." Then he let him know all that had happened between him and his wife. And he swore by Pre-Harakhti, saying: "As to your coming to kill me wrongfully, you carried your spear on the testimony of a filthy whore!" Then he took a reed knife, cut off his phallus, and threw it into the water; and the catfish swallowed it. And he grew weak and became feeble. And his elder brother became very sick at heart and stood weeping for him loudly. He could not cross over to where his young brother was on account of the crocodiles.

Then his young brother called to him, saying: "If you recall something evil, will you not also recall something good, or something that I have done for you? Go back to your home and tend your cattle, for I shall not stay in the place where you are. I shall go to the Valley of the Pine. But what you shall do for me is to come and look after me, when you learn that something has happened to me. I shall take out my heart and place it on top of the blossom of the pine. If the pine is cut down and falls to the ground, you shall come to search for it. If you spend seven years searching for it, let your heart not be disgusted. And when you find it and place it in a bowl of cool water, I shall live to take revenge on him who wronged me. You will know that something has happened to me when one puts a jug of beer in your hand and it ferments. Do not delay at all when this happens to you."

Then he went away to the Valley of the Pine; and his elder brother went to his home, his hand on his head and smeared with dirt.[3] When he reached his house, he killed his wife, cast her to the dogs, and sat mourning for his young brother.

Now many days after this, his young brother was in the Valley of the Pine. There was no one with him, and he spent the days hunting desert game. In the evening he returned to sleep under the pine on top of whose blossom his heart was. And after many days he built a mansion for himself with his own hand in the Valley of the Pine, filled with all good things, for he wanted to set up a household.

Coming out of his mansion, he encountered the Ennead[4] as they walked about administering the entire land. Then the Ennead addressed him in unison, saying: "O Bata, Bull of the Ennead, are you alone here, having left your town on account of the wife of Anubis, your elder brother? He has killed his wife and you are avenged of all the wrong done to you." And as they felt very sorry for him,

---

2. The disk of the sun.
3. Signs of mourning.

4. The council of nine major gods.

Pre-Harakhti said to Khnum[5]: "Fashion a wife for Bata, that he not live alone!" Then Khnum made a companion for him who was more beautiful in body than any woman in the whole land, for the fluid of every god was in her. Then the seven Hathors[6] came to see her, and they said with one voice: "She will die by the knife."

He desired her very much. She sat in his house while he spent the day hunting desert game, bringing it and putting it before her. He said to her: "Do not go outdoors, lest the sea snatch you. I cannot rescue you from it, because I am a woman like you. And my heart lies on top of the blossom of the pine. But if another finds it, I shall fight with him." Then he revealed to her all his thoughts.

Now many days after this, when Bata had gone hunting according to his daily custom, the young girl went out to stroll under the pine which was next to her house. Then she saw the sea surging behind her, and she started to run before it and entered her house. Thereupon the sea called to the pine, saying: "Catch her for me!" And the pine took away a lock of her hair. Then the sea brought it to Egypt and laid it in the place of the washermen of Pharaoh. Thereafter the scent of the lock of hair got into the clothes of Pharaoh. And the king quarreled with the royal washermen, saying: "A scent of ointment is in the clothes of Pharaoh!" He quarreled with them every day, and they did not know what to do.

The chief of the royal washermen went to the shore, his heart very sore on account of the daily quarrel with him. Then he realized that he was standing on the shore opposite the lock of hair which was in the water. He had someone go down, and it was brought to him. Its scent was found to be very sweet, and he took it to Pharaoh.

Then the learned scribes of Pharaoh were summoned, and they said to Pharaoh: "As for this lock of hair, it belongs to a daughter of Pre-Harakhti in whom there is the fluid of every god. It is a greeting to you from another country. Let envoys go to every foreign land to search for her. As for the envoy who goes to the Valley of the Pine, let many men go with him to fetch her." His majesty said: "What you have said is very good." And they were sent.

Now many days after this, the men who had gone abroad returned to report to his majesty. But those who had gone to the Valley of the Pine did not return, for Bata had killed them, leaving only one of them to report to his majesty. Then his majesty sent many soldiers and charioteers to bring her back, and with them was a woman into whose hand one had given all kinds of beautiful ladies' jewelry. The woman returned to Egypt with her, and there was jubilation for her in the entire land. His majesty loved her very very much, and he gave her the rank of Great Lady. He spoke with her in order to make her tell about her husband, and she said to his majesty: "Have the pine felled and cut up." The king sent soldiers with their tools to fell the pine. They reached the pine, they felled the blossom on which was Bata's heart, and he fell dead at that moment.

When it had dawned and the next day had come, and the pine had been felled, Anubis, the elder brother of Bata, entered his house. He sat down to wash his hands. He was given a jug of beer, and it fermented. He was given another of

---

5. The potter god who shapes bodies.

6. Manifestations of the sky goddess Hathor, who foretell a child's fate at birth.

wine, and it turned bad. Then he took his staff and his sandals, as well as his clothes and his weapons, and he started to journey to the Valley of the Pine. He entered the mansion of his young brother and found his young brother lying dead on his bed. He wept when he saw his young brother lying dead. He went to search for the heart of his young brother beneath the pine under which his young brother had slept in the evening. He spent three years searching for it without finding it.

When he began the fourth year, his heart longed to return to Egypt, and he said: "I shall depart tomorrow." So he said in his heart. When it had dawned and another day had come, he went to walk under the pine and spent the day searching for it. When he turned back in the evening, he looked once again in search of it and he found a fruit. He came back with it, and it was the heart of his young brother! He fetched a bowl of cool water, placed it in it, and sat down according to his daily custom.

When night had come, his heart swallowed the water, and Bata twitched in all his body. He began to look at his elder brother while his heart was in the bowl. Then Anubis, his elder brother, took the bowl of cool water in which was the heart of his young brother and let him drink it. Then his heart stood in its place, and he became as he had been. Thereupon they embraced each other, and they talked to one another.

Then Bata said to his elder brother: "Look, I shall change myself into a great bull of beautiful color, of a kind unknown to man, and you shall sit on my back. By the time the sun has risen, we shall be where my wife is, that I may avenge myself. You shall take me to where the king is, for he will do for you everything good. You shall be rewarded with silver and gold for taking me to Pharaoh. For I shall be a great marvel, and they will jubilate over me in the whole land. Then you shall depart to your village."

When it had dawned and the next day had come, Bata assumed the form which he had told his elder brother. Then Anubis, his elder brother, sat on his back. At dawn he reached the place where the king was. His majesty was informed about him; he saw him and rejoiced over him very much. He made a great offering for him, saying: "It is a great marvel." And there was jubilation over him in the entire land. Then the king rewarded his elder brother with silver and gold, and he dwelled in his village. The king gave him many people and many things, for Pharaoh loved him very much, more than anyone else in the whole land.

Now when many days had passed, Bata entered the kitchen, stood where the Lady was, and began to speak to her, saying: "Look, I am yet alive!" She said to him: "Who are you?" He said to her: "I am Bata. I know that when you had the pine felled for Pharaoh, it was on account of me, so that I should not live. Look, I am yet alive! I am a bull." The Lady became very frightened because of the speech her husband had made to her. Then he left the kitchen.

His majesty sat down to a day of feasting with her. She poured drink for his majesty, and he was very happy with her. Then she said to his majesty: "Swear to me by God, saying: 'Whatever she will say, I will listen to it!' " He listened to all that she said: "Let me eat of the liver of this bull; for he is good for nothing." So she said to him. He became very vexed over what she had said, and the heart of Pharaoh was very sore.

When it had dawned and another day had come, the king proclaimed a great offering, namely, the sacrifice of the bull. He sent one of the chief royal slaughterers to sacrifice the bull. And when he had been sacrificed and was carried on the shoulders of the men, he shook his neck and let fall two drops of blood beside the two doorposts of his majesty, one on the one side of the great portal of Pharaoh, and the other on the other side. They grew into two big Persea trees, each of them outstanding. Then one went to tell his majesty: "Two big Persea trees have grown this night—a great marvel for his majesty—beside the great portal of his majesty." There was jubilation over them in the whole land, and the king made an offering to them.

Many days after this, his majesty appeared at the audience window of lapis lazuli with a wreath of all kinds of flowers on his neck. Then he mounted a golden chariot and came out of the palace to view the Persea trees. Then the Lady came out on a team behind Pharaoh. His majesty sat down under one Persea tree and the Lady under the other. Then Bata spoke to his wife: "Ha, you false one! I am Bata! I am alive in spite of you. I know that when you had the pine felled for Pharaoh, it was on account of me. And when I became a bull, you had me killed."

Many days after this, the Lady stood pouring drink for his majesty, and he was happy with her. Then she said to his majesty: "Swear to me by God, saying: 'Whatever she will say, I will listen to it!' So you shall say." He listened to all that she said. She said: "Have the two Persea trees felled and made into fine furniture." The king listened to all that she said. After a short while his majesty sent skilled craftsmen. They felled the Persea trees of Pharaoh, and the Queen, the Lady, stood watching it. Then a splinter flew and entered the mouth of the Lady. She swallowed it, and in a moment she became pregnant. The king ordered made of the trees whatever she desired.

Many days after this, she gave birth to a son. One went to tell his majesty: "A son has been born to you." He was fetched, and a nurse and maids were assigned to him. And there was jubilation over him in the whole land. The king sat down to a feastday and held him on his lap. From that hour his majesty loved him very much, and he designated him as Viceroy of Kush. And many days after this, his majesty made him crown prince of the whole land.

Now many days after this, when he had spent many years as crown prince of the whole land, his majesty flew up to heaven.[7] Then the king[8] said: "Let my great royal officials be brought to me, that I may let them know all that has happened to me." Then his wife was brought to him. He judged her in their presence, and they gave their assent. His elder brother was brought to him, and he made him crown prince of the whole land. He spent thirty years as king of Egypt. He departed from life; and his elder brother stood in his place on the day of death.

Colophon   It has come to a good end under the scribe of the treasury, Kagab, and the scribes of the treasury, Hori and Meremope. Written by the scribe Ennana, the owner of this book. Whoever maligns this book, Thoth[9] will contend with him.

---

7. I.e., died.
8. Now Bata.

9. The gods' messenger, patron of wisdom and writing.

THE BIBLE (c. 900 B.C.E.)
Israel

One of the masterpieces of biblical narrative, the story of Joseph forms the final third of the Book of Genesis. It serves as a bridge between the history of the patriarchs and matriarchs of Israel (Genesis 12–36) and the story of Moses and the flight from Egypt in the ensuing Book of Exodus. The story may have been written in the cosmopolitan court of Solomon in the late tenth century B.C.E., or it may be of later date.

The narrative shows great psychological depth in its portrayal of the tensions in Joseph's family and their gradual resolution. It also provides an extended look at how the clan-based Hebrews viewed imperial Egyptian society. As the tale of a person from Palestine making good in Egypt, "The Joseph Story" is especially fascinating to read in juxtaposition with the "Story of Sinuhe," in which the narrator flees Egypt and establishes himself in Palestine. The story also invites comparisons with parallel motifs in earlier literature—the use of dream in Gilgamesh, the adulterous wife in "The Two Brothers." Centuries later, the same material was reworked for inclusion in the Qur'an, the holy book of Islam.

from **The Bible**

Genesis 37–50

The Joseph Story

37

This is the story of Joseph.

Joseph was seventeen years old. As he was still young, he was shepherding the flock with his brothers, with the sons of Bilhah and Zilpah his father's wives. Joseph informed their father of the evil spoken about them.

Israel[1] loved Joseph more than all his other sons, for he was the son of his old age, and he had a coat with long sleeves made for him. But his brothers, seeing how his father loved him more than all his other sons, came to hate him so much that they could not say a civil word to him.

Now Joseph had a dream, and he repeated it to his brothers. "Listen," he said, "to this dream I have had. We were binding sheaves in the countryside; and my sheaf, it seemed, rose up and stood upright; then I saw your sheaves gather round and bow to my sheaf." "So you want to be king over us," his brothers retorted, "or

---

New International Version translation.

---

1. Jacob received the name Israel ("He who wrestles with God") after struggling all night with an angel who tried to kill him (Genesis 32).

to lord it over us?" And they hated him still more, on account of his dreams and of what he said. He had another dream which he told to his brothers.

"Look, I have had another dream," he said. "I thought I saw the sun, the moon and eleven stars, bowing to me." He told his father and brothers, and his father scolded him. "A fine dream to have!" he said to him. "Are all of us then, myself, your mother and your brothers, to come and bow to the ground before you?" His brothers were jealous of him, but his father kept the thing in mind.

His brothers went to pasture their father's flock at Shechem. Then Israel said to Joseph, "Are not your brothers with the flock at Shechem? Come, I am going to send you to them." "I am ready," he replied. He said to him, "Go and see how your brothers and the flock are doing, and bring me word." He sent him from the valley of Hebron, and Joseph arrived at Shechem.

A man found him wandering in the countryside and the man asked him, "What are you looking for?" "I am looking for my brothers," he replied. "Please tell me where they are pasturing their flock." The man answered, "They have moved on from here; indeed I heard them say, 'Let us go to Dothan.'" So Joseph went after his brothers and found them at Dothan.

They saw him in the distance, and before he reached them they made a plot among themselves to put him to death. "Here comes the man of dreams," they said to one another. "Come on, let us kill him and throw him into some well; we can say that a wild beast devoured him. Then we shall see what becomes of his dreams."

But Reuben[2] heard, and he saved him from their violence. "We must not take his life," he said. "Shed no blood," said Reuben to them, "throw him into this well in the wilderness, but do not lay violent hands on him"—intending to save him from them and to restore him to his father. So, when Joseph reached his brothers, they pulled off his coat, the coat with long sleeves that he was wearing, and catching hold of him they threw him into the well, an empty well with no water in it. They then sat down to eat.

Looking up they saw a group of Ishmaelites who were coming from Gilead, their camels laden with gum, tragacanth, balsam and resin, which they were taking down into Egypt. Then Judah said to his brothers, "What do we gain by killing our brother and covering up his blood? Come, let us sell him to the Ishmaelites, but let us not do any harm to him. After all, he is our brother, and our own flesh." His brothers agreed.

Now some Midianite merchants were passing, and they drew Joseph up out of the well. They sold Joseph to the Ishmaelites for twenty silver pieces, and these men took Joseph to Egypt.[3] When Reuben went back to the well there was no sign of Joseph. Tearing his clothes, he went back to his brothers. "The boy has disappeared," he said. "What am I going to do?"

They took Joseph's coat and, slaughtering a goat, they dipped the coat in the blood. Then they sent back the coat with long sleeves and had it taken to their

---

2. Joseph's oldest brother.
3. Two traditions appear to have been combined here; in one version, the brothers sell Joseph to Ishmaelite traders; in the other, Reuben discovers that Joseph has been kidnapped from the pit by Midianites.

father, with the message, "This is what we have found. Examine it and see whether or not it is your son's coat." He examined it and exclaimed, "It is my son's coat! A wild beast has devoured him. Joseph has been the prey of some animal and has been torn to pieces." Jacob, tearing his clothes and putting on a loin-cloth of sackcloth, mourned his son for a long time. All his sons and daughters came to comfort him, but he refused to be comforted. "No," he said, "I will go down in mourning to Sheol, beside my son." And his father wept for him.

Meanwhile the Midianites had sold him in Egypt to Potiphar, one of Pharaoh's officials and commander of the guard.

38

It happened at that time that Judah left his brothers, to go down and stay with an Adullamite called Hirah. There Judah saw the daughter of a Canaanite called Shua.[4] He made her his wife and slept with her. She conceived and gave birth to a son whom she named Er. She conceived again and gave birth to a son whom she named Onan. Yet again she gave birth to a son whom she named Shelah. She was at Chezib when she gave birth to him.

Judah took a wife for his first-born Er, and her name was Tamar. But Er, Judah's first-born, offended Yahweh greatly, so Yahweh brought about his death. Then Judah said to Onan, "Take your brother's wife, and do your duty as her brother-in-law, to produce a child for your brother." But Onan, knowing the child would not be his, spilt his seed on the ground every time he slept with his brother's wife, to avoid providing a child for his brother. What he did was offensive to Yahweh, so he brought about his death also. Then Judah said to his daughter-in-law Tamar, "Return home as a widow to your father, and wait for my son Shelah to grow up," for he was thinking, "He must not die like his brothers." So Tamar went back home to her father.

A long time passed, and then Shua's daughter, the wife of Judah, died. After Judah had been comforted[5] he went up to Timnah to the men who sheared his sheep, himself and Hirah, his Adullamite friend. This was reported to Tamar, "Listen, your father-in-law is going up to Timnah for the shearing of his sheep." She therefore changed her widow's clothes, wrapped a veil around her, and sat down, heavily swathed, where the road to Enaim branches off the road to Timnah. Shelah had now grown up, as she saw, and yet she had not been given to him as his wife.

Judah, seeing her, took her for a prostitute, since her face was veiled. Going up to her on the road, he said, "Come, let me sleep with you." He did not know that she was his daughter-in-law. "What will you give me to sleep with me?" she asked. "I will send you a kid from the flock," he answered. "Agreed, if you give me a pledge until you send it," she answered. "What pledge shall I give you?" he asked. "Your seal, your cord and the stick you are holding," she answered. He gave them to her and slept with her, and she conceived by him. Then she rose and left him, and taking off her veil she put on her widow's weeds.

---

4. Judah is marrying a non-Hebrew wife, always a problem in Genesis.

5. I.e., when the period of mourning had ended.

Judah sent the kid by his Adullamite friend to recover the pledge from the woman. But he did not find her. He inquired from the men of the place, "Where is the prostitute who was by the roadside at Enaim?" "There has been no prostitute there," they answered. So returning to Judah he said, "I did not find her. What is more, the men of the place told me there had been no prostitute there." "Let her keep what she has," Judah replied, "or we shall become a laughing-stock. At least I sent her this kid, even though you did not find her."

About three months later it was reported to Judah, "Your daughter-in-law has played the harlot; furthermore, she is pregnant, as a result of her misconduct." "Take her outside and burn her," said Judah. But as she was being led off she sent this message to her father-in-law, "It was the man to whom these things belong who made me pregnant. Look at them," she said, "and see whose seal and cord and stick these are." Judah examined them and then said, "She is in the right, rather than I. This comes of my not giving her to my son Shelah to be his wife." He had no further intercourse with her.

When the time for her confinement came she was found to have twins in her womb. During the delivery one of them put out a hand, and the midwife caught it and tied a scarlet thread to it, saying, "This is the first to arrive." But he drew his hand back, and it was his brother who came out first. Then she said, "What a breach you have opened for yourself!" So he was named Perez.[6] The his brother came out with the scarlet thread on his hand, so he was named Zerah.[7]

39

Now Joseph had been taken down into Egypt. Potiphar the Egyptian, one of Pharaoh's officials and commander of the guard, bought him from the Ishmaelites who had brought him down there. Yahweh was with Joseph, and everything went well with him. He lodged in the house of his Egyptian master, and when his master saw how Yahweh was with him and how Yahweh made everything succeed that he turned his hand to, he was pleased with Joseph and made him his personal attendant; and his master put him in charge of his household, entrusting everything to him. And from the time he put him in charge of his household and all his possessions, Yahweh blessed the Egyptian's household out of consideration for Joseph; Yahweh's blessing extended to all his possessions, both household and estate. So he left Joseph to handle all his possessions, and with him at hand, concerned himself with nothing beyond the food he ate.

Now Joseph was well built and handsome, and it happened some time later that his master's wife looked desirously at him and said, "Sleep with me." But he refused, and answered his master's wife, "Because of me, my master does not concern himself with what happens in the house; he has handed over all his possessions to me. He is no more master in this house than I am. He has withheld nothing from me except yourself, because you are his wife. How could I do anything so wicked, and sin against God?" Although she spoke to Joseph day after day he would not agree to sleep with her and surrender to her.

---

6. Perez means "breaking out."

7. Zerah can mean "scarlet" or "brightness."

But one day Joseph in the course of his duties came to the house, and there was not a servant there indoors. The woman caught hold of him by his tunic and said, "Sleep with me." But he left the tunic in her hand and ran out of the house. Seeing he had left the tunic in her hand and left the house, she called her servants and said to them, "Look at this! He has brought us a Hebrew to insult us. He came to me to sleep with me, but I screamed, and when he heard me scream and shout he left his tunic beside me and ran out of the house."

She put the tunic down by her side until the master came home. Then she told him the same tale, "The Hebrew slave you bought us came to insult me. But when I screamed and called out he left his garment by my side and made his escape." When the master heard his wife say, "This is how your slave treated me," he was furious. Joseph's master had him arrested and committed to the jail where the king's prisoners were kept.

And there in jail he stayed. But Yahweh was with Joseph. He was kind to him and made him popular with the chief jailer. The chief jailer put Joseph in charge of all the prisoners in the jail, making him responsible for everything done there. The chief jailer did not need to interfere with Joseph's administration, for Yahweh was with him, and Yahweh made everything he undertook successful.

40

It happened some time later that the king of Egypt's cupbearer and his baker offended their master the king of Egypt. Pharaoh was angry with his two officials, the chief cupbearer and the chief baker, and put them under arrest in the house of the commander of the guard, in the jail where Joseph was a prisoner. The commander of the guard assigned Joseph to them to attend to their wants, and they remained under arrest for some time.

Now both of them had dreams on the same night, each with its own meaning for the cupbearer and the baker of the king of Egypt, who were prisoners in the jail. When Joseph came to them in the morning, he saw that they looked gloomy, and he asked the two officials who were with him under arrest in his master's house, "Why these black looks today?" They answered him, "We have had a dream, but there is no one to interpret it." "Are not interpretations God's business?" Joseph asked them. "Come, tell me."

So the chief cupbearer described his dream to Joseph, telling him, "In my dream I saw a vine in front of me. On the vine were three branches; no sooner had it budded than it blossomed, and its clusters became ripe grapes. I had Pharaoh's cup in my hand; I picked the grapes and squeezed them into Pharaoh's cup, and put the cup into Pharaoh's hand." "Here is the interpretation of it," Joseph told him. "The three branches are three days. In another three days Pharaoh will release you and restore you to your place. Then you will hand Pharaoh his cup, as you did before, when you were his cupbearer. But be sure to remember me when things go well with you, and do me the kindness of reminding Pharaoh about me, to get me out of this house. I was kidnaped from the land of the Hebrews in the first place, and even here I have done nothing to warrant imprisonment."

The chief baker, seeing that the interpretation had been favorable, said to

Joseph, "I too had a dream; there were three trays of cakes on my head. In the top tray there were all kinds of Pharaoh's favorite cakes, but the birds ate them off the tray on my head." Joseph gave him this answer. "Here is the interpretation of it: the three trays are three days. In another three days Pharaoh will release you and hang you on a gallows, and the birds will eat the flesh off your bones."

And so it happened; the third day was Pharaoh's birthday and he gave a banquet for all his officials, and he released the chief cupbearer and the chief baker in the presence of his officials. The chief cupbearer he restored to his position as cupbearer, to hand Pharaoh his cup; the chief baker he hanged. It was as Joseph had said in his interpretation. But the chief cupbearer did not remember Joseph: he forgot him.

41

Two years later it happened that Pharaoh had a dream: he was standing by the Nile, and there, coming up from the Nile, were seven cows, sleek and fat, and they began to feed among the rushes. And seven other cows, ugly and lean, came up from the Nile after them; and these went over and stood beside the other cows on the bank of the Nile. The ugly and lean cows ate the seven sleek and fat cows. Then Pharaoh awoke.

He fell asleep and dreamed a second time: there, growing on one stalk, were seven ears of corn full and ripe. And sprouting up after them came seven ears of corn, meager and scorched by the east wind. The scanty ears of corn swallowed the seven full and ripe ears of corn. Then Pharaoh awoke; it was a dream.

In the morning Pharaoh, feeling disturbed, had all the magicians and wise men of Egypt summoned to him. Pharaoh told them his dream, but no one could interpret it for Pharaoh. Then the chief cupbearer addressed Pharaoh, "Today I must recall my offenses. Pharaoh was angry with his servants and put myself and the chief baker under arrest in the house of the commander of the guard. We had a dream on the same night, he and I, and each man's dream had a meaning for himself. There was a young Hebrew with us, one of the slaves belonging to the commander of the guard. We told our dreams to him and he interpreted them, giving each of us the interpretation of his dream. It turned out just as he interpreted for us: I was restored to my place, but the other man was hanged."

Then Pharaoh had Joseph summoned, and they hurried him from prison. He shaved and changed his clothes, and came into Pharaoh's presence. Pharaoh said to Joseph, "I have had a dream which no one can interpret. But I have heard it said of you that when you hear a dream you can interpret it." Joseph answered Pharaoh, "I do not count. It is God who will give Pharaoh a favorable answer."

So Pharaoh told Joseph, "In my dream I was standing on the bank of the Nile. And there were seven cows, fat and sleek, coming up out of the Nile, and they began to feed among the rushes. And seven other cows came up after them, starved, ugly and lean; I have never seen such poor cows in all the land of Egypt. The lean and ugly cows ate up the seven fat cows. But when they had eaten them up, it was impossible to tell they had eaten them, for they remained as lean as before. Then I woke up. And then again in my dream, there, growing on one stalk, were seven ears of corn, beautifully ripe; but sprouting up after them came seven ears of corn, withered, meager and scorched by the east wind. The shriveled ears of corn swallowed the seven ripe ears of corn. I told the magicians this, but no one could tell me the meaning."

Joseph told Pharaoh, "Pharaoh's dreams are one and the same: God has revealed to Pharaoh what he is going to do. The seven fine cows are seven years and the seven ripe ears of corn are seven years; it is one and the same dream. The seven gaunt and lean cows coming up after them are seven years, as are the seven shriveled ears of corn scorched by the east wind: there will be seven years of famine. It is as I have told Pharaoh: God has revealed to Pharaoh what he is going to do. Seven years are coming, bringing great plenty to the whole land of Egypt, but seven years of famine will follow them, when all the plenty in the land of Egypt will be forgotten, and famine will exhaust the land. The famine that is to follow will be so very severe that no one will remember what plenty the country enjoyed. The reason why the dream came to Pharaoh twice is because the event is already determined by God, and God is impatient to bring it about.

"Pharaoh should now choose a man who is intelligent and wise to govern the land of Egypt. Pharaoh should take action and appoint supervisors over the land, and impose a tax of one fifth on the land of Egypt during the seven years of plenty. They will collect all food produced during these good years that are coming. They will store the corn in Pharaoh's name, and place the food in the towns and hold it there. This food will serve as a reserve for the land during the seven years of famine that will afflict the land of Egypt. And so the land will not be destroyed by the famine."

Pharaoh and all his ministers approved of what he had said. Then Pharaoh asked his ministers, "Can we find any other man like this, possessing the spirit of God?" So Pharaoh said to Joseph, "Seeing that God has given you knowledge of all this, there can be no one as intelligent and wise as you. You shall be my chancellor, and all my people shall respect your orders; only this throne shall set me above you." Pharaoh said to Joseph, "I hereby make you governor of the whole land of Egypt." Pharaoh took the ring from his hand and put it on Joseph's. He clothed him in fine linen and put a gold chain around his neck. He made him ride in the best chariot he had after his own, and they cried before him "Make way!" This is the way he was made governor of the whole land of Egypt.

Pharaoh said to Joseph, "I am Pharaoh: without your permission no one is to move hand or foot throughout the whole land of Egypt." Pharaoh named Joseph Zaphenath-paneah, and gave him Asenath the daughter of Potiphera, priest of On, for his wife.[8] Joseph traveled through the land of Egypt.

Joseph was thirty years old when he appeared before Pharaoh king of Egypt. After leaving Pharaoh's presence Joseph went through the whole land of Egypt. During the seven years of plenty, the soil yielded generously. He collected all the food of the seven years when there was an abundance in the land of Egypt, and

---

8. Joseph's assimilation into Egyptian society is to be sealed with the bestowal of an Egyptian name and a wife from a prominent priestly family.

allotted food to the towns, placing in each the food from the surrounding countryside. Joseph stored the corn like the sand of the sea, so much that they stopped reckoning, since it was beyond all estimating.

Before the year of famine came, two sons were born to Joseph: Asenath, the daughter of Potiphera priest of On, bore him these. Joseph named the first-born Manasseh, "Because," he said, "God has made me forget all my suffering and all my father's household."[9] He named the second Ephraim, "Because," he said, "God has made me fruitful in the country of my misfortune."[10]

Then the seven years of plenty that there had been in the land of Egypt came to an end. The seven years of famine began to come as Joseph had said. There was famine in every country, but there was bread to be had throughout the land of Egypt. When the whole country began to feel the famine, the people cried out to Pharaoh for bread. But Pharaoh told all the Egyptians, "Go to Joseph and do what he tells you."—There was famine all over the world.—Then Joseph opened all the granaries and sold grain to the Egyptians. The famine grew worse in the land of Egypt. People came to Egypt from all over the world to buy grain from Joseph, for the famine had grown severe throughout the world.

42

Jacob, seeing that there was grain for sale in Egypt, said to his sons, "Why do you stand looking at one another? I hear," he said, "that there is grain for sale in Egypt. Go down and buy grain for us there, that we may survive and not die." So ten of Joseph's brothers went down to buy grain in Egypt. But Jacob did not send Joseph's brother Benjamin with his brothers. "Nothing must happen to him," he said.[11]

Israel's sons with others making the same journey went to buy grain, for there was famine in the land of Canaan. It was Joseph, as the man in authority over the country, who sold the grain to all comers. So Joseph's brothers went and bowed down before him, their faces touching the ground. When Joseph saw his brothers he recognized them. But he did not make himself known to them, and he spoke harshly to them. "Where have you come from?" he asked. "From the land of Canaan to buy food," they replied.

So Joseph recognized his brothers, but they did not recognize him. Joseph, remembering the dreams he had had about them, said to them, "You are spies. You have come to discover the country's weak points." "No, my lord," they told him, "your servants have come to buy food. We are all sons of the same man. We are honest men, your servants are not spies." "Not so!" he replied. "It is the country's weak points you have come to discover." "Your servants are twelve brothers," they said, "sons of the same man, from the land of Canaan. The youngest, we should explain, is at present with our father, and the other one is no more." Joseph answered them, "It is as I said, you are spies. This is the test you are to undergo: as sure as Pharaoh lives you shall not leave unless your youngest

---

9. Manasseh sounds like the Hebrew for "forget."

10. Ephraim sounds like the Hebrew for "twice fruitful."

11. Benjamin, Jacob's youngest son, is Joseph's only full brother.

brother comes here. Send one of your number to fetch your brother; you others will remain under arrest, so that your statements can be tested to see whether or not you are honest. If not, then as sure as Pharaoh lives you are spies." Then he kept them all in custody for three days.

On the third day Joseph said to them, "Do this and you shall keep your lives, for I am a man who fears God. If you are honest men let one of your brothers be kept in the place of your detention; as for you, go and take grain to relieve the famine of your families. You shall bring me your youngest brother; this way your words will be proved true, and you will not have to die!" This they did. They said to one another, "Truly we are being called to account for our brother. We saw his misery of soul when he begged our mercy, but we did not listen to him and now this misery has come home to us." Reuben answered them, "Did I not tell you not to wrong the boy? But you did not listen, and now we are brought to account for his blood." They did not know that Joseph understood, because there was an interpreter between them. He left them and wept. Then he went back to them and spoke to them. Of their number he took Simeon and had him bound while they looked on.

Joseph gave the order to fill their panniers with corn, to put back each man's money in his sack, and to give them provisions for the journey. This was done for them. They loaded the grain on their donkeys and went away. But when they camped for the night one of them opened his corn sack to give fodder to his donkey and saw his money in the mouth of his sack. He said to his brothers, "My money has been put back; here it is in my corn sack." Their hearts sank, and they looked at one another in panic, saying, "What is this that God has done to us?"

Returning to their father Jacob in the land of Canaan, they gave him a full report of what had happened to them. "The man who is lord of the land spoke harshly to us, taking us for men spying on the country. We told him, 'We are honest men, we are not spies. We are twelve brothers, sons of the same father. One of us is no more, and the youngest is at present with our father in the land of Canaan.' But the man who is lord of the land said to us, 'This is how I shall know if you are honest: leave one of your brothers with me. Take the grain your families stand in need of, and go. But bring me back your youngest brother and then I shall know that you are not spies but honest men. Then I will hand over your brother to you, and you can trade in the country.'"

As they emptied their sacks, each discovered his bag of money in his sack. On seeing their bags of money they were afraid, and so was their father. Then their father Jacob said to them, "You are robbing me of my children; Joseph is no more; Simeon is no more; and now you want to take Benjamin. All this I must bear."

Then Reuben said to his father, "You may put my two sons to death if I do not bring him back to you. Put him in my care and I will bring him back to you." But he replied, "My son is not going down with you, for now his brother is dead he is the only one left. If any harm came to him on the journey you are to undertake, you would send me down to Sheol with my white head bowed in grief."

43

But the country was hard pressed by famine, and when they had finished eating the grain they had brought from Egypt their father said to them, "Go back and buy us a little food." "But the man expressly warned us," Judah told him. "He said, 'You will not be admitted to my presence unless your brother is with you.' If you are ready to send our brother with us, we are willing to go down and buy food for you. But if you are not ready to send him we will not go down, for the man told us, 'You will not be admitted to my presence unless your brother is with you.' " Then Israel said, "Why did you bring this misery on me by telling the man you had another brother?" They replied, "He kept questioning us about ourselves and our kinsfolk, 'Is your father still alive?' and, 'Have you a brother?' That is why we told him. How could we know he was going to say, 'Bring your brother down here?' " Judah said to his father Israel, "Send the boy with me. Let us start off and go, so that we may save our lives and not die, we, you, and our dependents. I will go surety for him, and you can hold me responsible for him. If I do not bring him back to you and set him before you, let me bear the blame all my life. Indeed, if we had not wasted so much time we should have been back again by now!"

Then their father Israel said to them, "If it must be so, then do this: take some of the land's finest products in your panniers, and carry them down to the man as a gift, a little balsam, a little honey, gum, tragacanth, resin, pistachio nuts and almonds. Take double the amount of money with you and return the money put back in the mouths of your sacks; it may have been a mistake. Take your brother, and go back to the man. May El Shaddai move the man to be kind to you, and allow you to bring back your other brother and Benjamin. As for me, if I must be bereaved, bereaved I must be."

The men took this gift; they took double the amount of money with them, and Benjamin. They started off and went down to Egypt. They presented themselves to Joseph. When Joseph saw Benjamin with them he said to his chamberlain, "Take these men to the house. Slaughter a beast and prepare it, for these men are to eat with me at midday." The man did as Joseph had ordered, and took the men to Joseph's house.

The men were afraid at being taken to Joseph's house, thinking, "We are being taken there because of the money replaced in our corn sacks the first time. They will set on us; they will fall on us and make slaves of us, and take our donkeys too." So they went up to Joseph's chamberlain and spoke to him at the entrance to the house. "By your leave, sir," they said, "we came down once before to buy food, and when we reached camp and opened our corn sacks, there was each man's money in the mouth of his sack, to its full amount. But we have brought it back with us, and we have brought more money with us to buy food. We do not know who put the money in our corn sacks." "Peace to you," he replied, "do not be afraid. Your God and your father's God has put a treasure in your corn sacks. Your money reached me safely." And he brought Simeon out to them.

The man took the men into Joseph's house. He offered them water to wash their feet, and gave their donkeys fodder. They arranged their gift while they waited for Joseph to come at midday, for they had heard they were to dine there.

When Joseph arrived at the house they offered him the gift they had with them, and bowed before him to the ground. But he greeted them kindly, asking, "Is your father well, the old man you told me of? Is he still alive?" "Your servant our father is well," they replied, "he is still alive," and they bowed low in homage.

Looking up he saw his brother Benjamin, his mother's son. "Is this your youngest brother," he asked, "of whom you told me?" Then he said to him, "God be good to you, my son." Joseph hurried out, for his heart was moved at the sight of his brother and he was near to weeping. He went into his room, and there he wept. After bathing his face he returned and, controlling himself, gave the order: "Serve the meal." He was served separately; so were they, and so were the Egyptians who ate in his household, for Egyptians cannot take food with Hebrews: they have a horror of it. They were placed opposite him each according to his rank, from the eldest to the youngest, and the men looked at one another in amazement. He had portions carried to them from his own dish, the portion for Benjamin being five times larger than any of the others. They drank with him and were happy.

44

Joseph gave this order to his chamberlain: "Fill these men's sacks with as much food as they can carry, and put each man's money in the mouth of his sack. And put my cup, the silver one, in the mouth of the youngest one's sack as well as the money for his grain." He carried out the instructions Joseph had given.

When morning came and it was light, the men were sent off with their donkeys. They had scarcely left the city, and had not gone far before Joseph said to his chamberlain, "Away now and follow those men. When you catch up with them say to them, 'Why did you reward good with evil? Is this not the one my lord uses for drinking and also for reading omens? What you have done is wrong.' "

So when he caught up with them he repeated these words. They asked him, "What does my lord mean? Your servants would never think of doing such a thing. Look, the money we found in the mouths of our corn sacks we brought back to you from the land of Canaan. Are we likely to have stolen the silver or gold from your master's house? Whichever of your servants is found to have it shall die, and we ourselves shall be slaves of my lord." "Very well, then," he replied, "it shall be as you say. The one on whom it is found shall become my slave, but the rest of you can go free." Each of them quickly lifted his corn sack to the ground, and each opened his own. He searched them, beginning with the eldest and ending with the youngest, and found the cup in Benjamin's sack. Then they tore their clothes, and when each man had reloaded his ass they returned to the city.

When Judah and his brothers arrived at Joseph's house he was still there, so they fell on the ground in front of him. "What is this deed you have done?" Joseph asked them. "Did you not know that a man such as I am is a reader of omens?" "What can we answer my lord?" Judah replied. "What can we say? How can we clear ourselves? God himself has uncovered your servants' guilt. Here we are then, my lord's slaves, we no less than the one in whose possession the cup was found." "I could not think of doing such a thing," he replied. "The man in whose possession the cup was found shall be my slave, but you can go back safe and sound to your father."

Then Judah went up to him and said, "May it please my lord, let your servant have a word privately with my lord. Do not be angry with your servant, for you are like Pharaoh himself. My lord questioned his servants, 'Have you father or brother?' And we said to my lord, 'We have an old father, and a younger brother born of his old age. His brother is dead, so he is the only one left of his mother, and his father loves him.' Then you said to your servants, 'Bring him down to me that my eyes may look on him.' We replied to my lord, 'The boy cannot leave his father. If he leaves him, his father will die.' But you said to your servants, 'If your youngest brother does not come down with you, you will not be admitted to my presence again.' When we went back to your servant my father, we repeated to him what my lord had said. So when our father said, 'Go back and buy us a little food,' we said, 'We cannot go down. If our youngest brother is with us, we will go down, for we cannot be admitted to the man's presence unless our youngest brother is with us.' So your servant our father said to us, 'You know that my wife bore me two children. When one left me, I said that he must have been torn to pieces. And I have not seen him to this day. If you take this one from me too and any harm comes to him, you will send me down to Sheol with my white head bowed in misery.' If I go to your servant my father now, and we have not the boy with us, he will die as soon as he sees the boy is not with us, for his heart is bound up with him. Then your servants will have sent your servant our father down to Sheol with his white head bowed in grief. Now your servant went surety to my father for the boy. I said: If I do not bring him back to you, let me bear the blame before my father all my life. Let your servant stay, then, as my lord's slave in place of the boy, I implore you, let the boy go back with his brothers. How indeed could I go back to my father and not have the boy with me? I could not bear to see the misery that would overwhelm my father."

45

Then Joseph could not control his feelings in front of all his retainers, and he exclaimed, "Let everyone leave me." No one therefore was present with him while Joseph made himself known to his brothers, but he wept so loudly that all the Egyptians heard, and the news reached Pharaoh's palace.

Joseph said to his brothers, "I am Joseph. Is my father really still alive?" His brothers could not answer him, they were so dismayed at the sight of him. Then Joseph said to his brothers, "Come closer to me." When they had come closer to him he said, "I am your brother Joseph whom you sold into Egypt. But now, do not grieve, do not reproach yourselves for having sold me here, since God sent me before you to preserve your lives. For this is the second year there has been famine in the country, and there are still five years to come of no plowing or reaping. God sent me before you to make sure that your race would have survivors in the land and to save your lives, many lives at that. So it was not you who sent me here but God, and he has made me father to Pharaoh, lord of all his household and administrator of the whole land of Egypt.

"Return quickly to your father and tell him, 'Your son Joseph says this: God has made me lord of all Egypt. Come down to me at once. You shall live in the country of Goshen[12] where you will be near me, you, your children and your

---

12. An area of grazing land in the Nile delta.

grandchildren, your flocks, your cattle and all your possessions. I will provide for you there, for there are still five years of famine, and I do not want you to be in need, you and your household and all you have.' You can see with your own eyes, and my brother Benjamin can see too that it is my own mouth speaking to you. Give my father a full report of all the honor I enjoy in Egypt, and of all you have seen. Then hurry and bring my father down here."

Then throwing his arms around the neck of his brother Benjamin he wept; and Benjamin wept on his shoulder. He kissed all his brothers, weeping over them. After which his brothers talked with him.

News reached Pharaoh's palace that Joseph's brothers had come, and Pharaoh was pleased to hear it, as were his servants. Pharaoh told Joseph, "Say to your brothers, 'Do this: load your beasts and go off to the land of Canaan. Fetch your father and families, and come back to me. I will give you the best the land of Egypt offers, and you shall feed on the fat of the land.' And you, for your part, give them this command: 'Do this: take wagons from the land of Egypt, for your little ones and your wives. Get your father and come. Never mind about your property, for the best that the land of Egypt offers is yours.' "

Israel's sons did as they were told. Joseph gave them wagons as Pharaoh had ordered, and he gave them provisions for the journey. To each and every one he gave a festal garment, and to Benjamin three hundred shekels of silver and five festal garments. And he sent his father ten donkeys laden with the best that Egypt offered, and ten she-donkeys laden with grain, bread and food for his father's journey. Then he sent his brothers on their way. His final words to them were, "Do not be upset on the journey."

And so they left Egypt. When they reached the land of Canaan and their father Jacob, they gave him this report, "Joseph is still alive. Indeed it is he who is administrator of the whole land of Egypt." But he was as one stunned, for he did not believe them. However, when they told him all Joseph had said to them, and when he saw the wagons that Joseph had sent to fetch him, the spirit of their father Jacob revived, and Israel said, "That is enough! My son Joseph is still alive. I must go and see him before I die."

46

Israel left with his possessions, and reached Beersheba. There he offered sacrifices to the God of his father Isaac. God spoke to Israel in a vision at night, "Jacob, Jacob," he said. "I am here," he replied. "I am God, the God of your father," he continued. "Do not be afraid of going down to Egypt, for I will make you a great nation there. I myself will go down to Egypt with you. I myself will bring you back again, and Joseph's hand shall close your eyes." Then Jacob left Beersheba. Israel's sons conveyed their father Jacob, their little children and their wives in the wagons Pharaoh had sent to fetch him.

Taking their livestock and all that they had acquired in the land of Canaan, they went to Egypt, Jacob and all his family with him: his sons and his grandsons, his daughters and his granddaughters, in a word, all his children he took with him to Egypt.

These are the names of Israel's sons who came to Egypt,[13] Reuben, Jacob's first-born, and the sons of Reuben: Hanoch, Pallu, Hezron, Carmi. The sons of Simeon: Jemuel, Jamin, Ohad, Jachin, Zohar, and Shaul the son of the Canaanite woman. The sons of Levi: Gershon, Kohath, Merari. The sons of Judah: Er, Onan, Shelah, Perez, and Zerah (though Er and Onan died in the land of Canaan), and Hezron and Hamul, sons of Perez. The sons of Issachar: Tola, Puvah, Jashub and Shimron. The sons of Zebulun: Sered, Elon, Jahleel. These are the sons that Leah had born to Jacob in Paddan-aram, besides his daughter Dinah; in all, his sons and daughters numbered thirty-three.

The sons of Gad: Ziphion, Haggi, Shuni, Ezbon, Eri, Arodi, and Areli. The sons of Asher: Imnah, Ishvah, Ishvi, Beriah, with their sister Serah; the sons of Beriah: Heber and Malchiel. These are the sons of Zilpah whom Laban gave to his daughter Leah; she bore these to Jacob—sixteen persons.

The sons of Rachel, wife of Jacob: Joseph and Benjamin. Born to Joseph in Egypt were: Manasseh and Ephraim, children of Asenath, the daughter of Potiphera priest of On. The sons of Benjamin: Bela, Becher, Ashbel, Gera, Naaman, Ehi, Rosh, Muppim, Huppim and Ard. These are the sons that Rachel bore to Jacob—fourteen persons in all.

The sons of Dan: Hushim. The sons of Naphtali: Jahzeel, Guni, Jezer and Shillem. These are the sons of Bilhah whom Laban gave to his daughter Rachel; she bore these to Jacob—seven persons in all.

The people who went to Egypt with Jacob, of his own blood and not counting the wives of Jacob's sons, numbered sixty-six all told. Joseph's sons born to him in Egypt were two in number. The members of the family of Jacob who went to Egypt totaled seventy.

Israel sent Judah ahead to Joseph, so that the latter might present himself to him in Goshen. When they arrived in the land of Goshen, Joseph had his chariot made ready and went up to meet his father Israel in Goshen. As soon as he appeared he threw his arms around his neck and for a long time wept on his shoulder. Israel said to Joseph, "Now I can die, now that I have seen you again, and seen you still alive."

Then Joseph said to his brothers and his father's family, "I will go up and break the news to Pharaoh. I will tell him, 'My brothers and my father's family who were in the land of Canaan have come to me. The men are shepherds and look after livestock, and they have brought their flocks and cattle and all their possessions.' Thus, when Pharaoh summons you and asks, 'What is your occupation?', you are to say, 'Ever since our boyhood your servants have looked after livestock, we and our fathers before us.' And so you will be able to stay in the land of Goshen." For the Egyptians have a horror of all shepherds.

---

13. The text lists all the children of Joseph and his brothers—the founders of the twelve tribes of Israel.

47

So Joseph went and told Pharaoh, "My father and brothers, along with their flocks and cattle and all their possessions, have come from the land of Canaan and are now in the land of Goshen." He had taken five of his brothers, and he now presented them to Pharaoh. Pharaoh asked his brothers, "What is your occupation?" and they gave Pharaoh the answer, "Your servants are shepherds, like our fathers before us." They went on to tell Pharaoh, "We have come to stay for the present in this land, for there is no pasture for your servants' flocks, the land of Canaan is hard pressed by famine. Now give your servants leave to stay in the land of Goshen." Then Pharaoh said to Joseph, "They may stay in the land of Goshen, and if you know of any capable men among them, put them in charge of my own livestock."

Jacob and his sons went to Egypt where Joseph was. Pharaoh, king of Egypt, heard of this and said to Joseph, "Your father and brothers have come to you. The country of Egypt is open to you: settle your father and brothers in the best region." Joseph brought his father and presented him to Pharaoh. Jacob blessed Pharaoh. Pharaoh asked Jacob, "How many years of life can you reckon?" "My life of wandering has lasted one hundred and thirty years," Jacob told Pharaoh, "few years and unhappy, falling short of the years of my fathers in their life of wandering." Jacob blessed Pharaoh and left Pharaoh's presence. Joseph settled his father and brothers, giving them a holding in the land of Egypt, and in the best region of the land, namely the land of Rameses, according to Pharaoh's command.

Joseph provided his father, brothers and all his father's family with food according to the number of their dependents.

There was no bread in the whole land, for the famine had grown so severe that the land of Egypt and the land of Canaan were weakened with hunger. Joseph accumulated all the money there was to be found in the land of Egypt and in the land of Canaan, in return for the grain which men were buying, and he brought the money to Pharaoh's palace.

When all the money in the land of Egypt and in the land of Canaan had run out, the Egyptians all came to Joseph: "Give us bread," they said. "Have we to perish before your eyes? For our money has come to an end." Joseph answered, "Hand over your livestock; I am willing to give you bread in exchange for your livestock, if your money has come to an end." So they brought their livestock to Joseph, and Joseph gave them bread, in exchange for horses and livestock, whether sheep or cattle, and for donkeys. Thus he fed them that year with bread, in exchange for all their livestock.

When that year was over, they came to him the next year, and said to him, "We cannot hide it from my lord: the truth is, our money has run out and the livestock is in my lord's possession. There is nothing left for my lord except our bodies and our land. Have we to perish before your eyes, we and our land? Buy us and our land in exchange for bread; we with our land will be Pharaoh's serfs. But give us something to sow, that we may keep our lives and not die and the land may not become desolate."

Thus Joseph acquired all the land in Egypt for Pharaoh, since one by one the Egyptians sold their estates, so hard pressed were they by the famine, and the whole country passed into Pharaoh's possession.[14] As for the people, he reduced them to serfdom from one end of Egypt to the other. The only land he did not acquire belonged to the priests, for the priests received an allowance from Pharaoh and lived on the allowance that Pharaoh gave them. Therefore they did not have to sell their land.

Then Joseph said to the people, "This is how we stand: I have bought you out, with your land, on Pharaoh's behalf. Here is seed for you so that you can sow the land. But when harvest comes you must give a fifth to Pharaoh. The other four fifths you can have for sowing your fields, to provide food for yourselves and your households, and food for your dependents." "You have saved our lives," they replied. "If we may enjoy my lord's favor, we will be Pharaoh's serfs." So Joseph made a statute, still in force today, concerning the soil of Egypt: a fifth goes to Pharaoh. The land of the priests alone did not go to Pharaoh.

The Israelites stayed in the land of Egypt, in the country of Goshen. They acquired property there; they were fruitful and increased in numbers greatly. Jacob lived seventeen years in the land of Egypt, and the length of his life was a hundred and forty-seven years. When Israel's time to die drew near he called his son Joseph and said to him, "If I enjoy your favor, place your hand under my thigh and promise to be kind and good to me, do not bury me in Egypt. When I sleep with my fathers, carry me out of Egypt and bury me in their tomb." "I will do as you say," he replied. "Swear to me," he insisted. So he swore to him, and Israel sank back on the pillow.

48

Some time later it was reported to Joseph, "Your father has been taken ill." So he took with him his two sons Manasseh and Ephraim. When Jacob was told, "Look, your son Joseph has come to you," Israel, summoning his strength, sat up in bed. "El Shaddai appeared to me at Luz in the country of Canaan," Jacob told Joseph, "and he blessed me, saying to me, 'I will make you fruitful and increase you in numbers. I will make you a group of peoples and give this country to your descendants after you, to own in perpetuity.' Now your two sons, born to you in the land of Egypt before I came to you in Egypt, shall be mine; Ephraim and Manasseh shall be as much mine as Reuben and Simeon. But with regard to the children you have had since them, they shall be yours, and they shall be known by their brothers' names for the purpose of their inheritance.

"When I was on my way from Paddan,[15] to my sorrow death took your mother Rachel[16] from me, in the land of Canaan, on the journey while we were

---

14. The writer uses the story of the famine to account for the fact that, in the feudal Egyptian system, all land except for religious property was considered to be owned by the king.

15. Northwest Mesopotamia.

16. Mother of Joseph and Benjamin.

still some distance from Ephrath. I buried her there on the road to Ephrath at Bethlehem."

When Israel saw Joseph's two sons, he asked, "Who are these?" "They are my sons, whom God has given me here," Joseph told his father. "Then bring them to me," he said, "that I may bless them." Israel's sight was failing because of his great age, and so he could not see. Joseph therefore made them come closer to him and he kissed and embraced them. Then Israel said Joseph, "I did not think that I should see you again, but God has let me see your family as well." Joseph took them from his lap and bowed to the ground.

Joseph took hold of the two of them, Ephraim with his right hand so that he should be on Israel's left, and Manasseh with his left hand, so that he should be on Israel's right, and brought them close to him. But Israel held out his right hand and laid it on the head of Ephraim, the younger, and his left on the head of Manasseh, crossing his hands—Manasseh was, in fact, the elder.[17] Then he blessed Joseph saying:

> "May God in whose presence my fathers Abraham and Isaac walked,
> may God who has been my shepherd from my birth until this day,
> may the angel who has been my savior from all harm, bless these boys,
> may my name live on in them, and the names of my fathers Abraham and Isaac.
> May they grow and increase on the earth."

Joseph saw that his father was laying his right hand on the head of Ephraim, and this upset him. He took his father's hand and tried to shift it from the head of Ephraim to the head of Manasseh. Joseph protested to his father, "Not like that, father! This one is the elder; put your right hand on his head." But his father refused. "I know, my son, I know," he said. "He too shall become a people; he too shall be great. Yet his younger brother shall be greater than he, and his descendants shall become a multitude of nations."

So he blessed them that day saying:

> "May you be a blessing in Israel; may they say,
> 'God make you like Ephraim and Manasseh!' "

In this way he put Ephraim before Manasseh.

Then Israel said to Joseph, "Now I am about to die. But God will be with you and take you back to the country of your fathers. As for me, I give you a Shechem more than your brothers, the one I took from the Amorites with my sword and my bow."

49

Jacob called his sons and said, "Gather together that I may declare to you what lies before you in time to come.

---

17. This scene recalls an earlier episode in which Jacob himself tricked his blind father Isaac into giving him the blessing meant for his brother Esau (Genesis 27).

[The body of Chapter 49, omitted here, is an independent account of Jacob's final words to his sons, characterizing the natures of the different tribes of Israel.]

He blessed them, giving to each one an appropriate blessing.

Then he gave them these instructions, "I am about to be gathered to my people. Bury me near my fathers, in the cave that is in the field of Ephron the Hittite, in the cave in the field at Machpelah, opposite Mamre, in the land of Canaan, which Abraham bought from Ephron the Hittite as a burial plot. There Abraham was buried and his wife Sarah. There Isaac was buried and his wife Rebekah. There I buried Leah.[18] I mean the field and the cave in it that were bought from the sons of Heth."

When Jacob had finished giving his instructions to his sons, he drew his feet up into the bed, and breathing his last was gathered to his people.

50

At this, Joseph threw himself on his father, covering his face with tears and kissing him. Then Joseph ordered the doctors in his service to embalm his father. The doctors embalmed Israel, and it took them forty days, for embalming takes forty days to complete.

The Egyptians mourned him for seventy days. When the period of mourning for him was over, Joseph said to Pharaoh's household, "If I may presume to enjoy your favor, please see that this message reaches Pharaoh's ears, 'My father made me swear an oath: I am about to die, he said, I have a tomb which I dug for myself in the land of Canaan, and there you must bury me. So now I seek leave to go up and bury my father, and then I shall come back.' " Pharaoh replied, "Go up and bury your father, in accordance with the oath he made you swear."

Joseph went up to bury his father, all Pharaoh's servants and the palace dignitaries going up with him, joined by all the dignitaries of the land of Egypt, as well as all Joseph's family and his brothers, along with his father's family. They left no one in the land of Goshen but their dependents, with their flocks and their cattle. Chariots also and horsemen went up with them; it was a very large retinue. On arriving at Goren-ha-atad, which is across the Jordan, they performed there a long and solemn lamentation, and Joseph observed three days' mourning for his father. When the Canaanites, the inhabitants of the land, witnessed the mourning at Goren-ha-atad they exclaimed, "This is a solemn act of mourning for the Egyptians." For this reason they call this place Abel-mizraim[19]—it is across the Jordan.

His sons did what he had ordered them to do for him. His sons carried him to the land of Canaan and buried him in the cave in the field at Machpelah opposite Mamre, which Abraham had bought from Ephron the Hittite as a burial plot.

Then Joseph returned to Egypt, he and his brothers, along with all those who had come up with him for his father's burial.

Seeing that their father was dead, Joseph's brothers said, "What if Joseph

---

18. Jacob's first wife, Rachel's older sister.   19. "Mourning for the Egyptians."

intends to treat us as enemies and repay us in full for all the wrong we did him?" So they sent this message to Joseph: "Before your father died he gave us this order: 'You must say to Joseph: Oh forgive your brothers their crime and their sin and all the wrong they did you.' Now therefore, we beg you, forgive the crime of the servants of your father's God." Joseph wept at the message they sent to him.

His brothers came themselves and fell down before him. "We present ourselves before you," they said, "as your slaves." But Joseph answered them, "Do not be afraid; is it for me to put myself in God's place? The evil you planned to do me has by God's design been turned to good, that he might bring about, as indeed he has, the deliverance of a numerous people. So you need not be afraid; I myself will provide for you and your dependents." In this way he reassured them with words that touched their hearts.

So Joseph stayed in Egypt with his father's family; and Joseph lived a hundred and ten years. Joseph saw the third generation of Ephraim's children, as also the children of Machir, Manasseh's son, who were born on Joseph's lap. At length Joseph said to his brothers, "I am about to die; but God will be sure to remember you kindly and take you back from this country to the land that he promised on oath to Abraham, Isaac and Jacob." And Joseph made Israel's sons swear an oath, "When God remembers you with kindness be sure to take my bones from here."

Joseph died at the age of a hundred and ten; they embalmed him and laid him in his coffin in Egypt.

HERODOTUS (c. 485–c. 425 B.C.E.)
Greece

Ancient historiography originates with Herodotus's account of the wars between Persia and Greece. In his introduction, Herodotus describes the history he has written as the "exposition of his researches" in order to emphasize that, in gathering information, he has relied above all on empirical observation and that his historical method, unlike that of the mythologizing chronicles of his predecessors, is based on the critical evaluation of evidence. In the course of his investigations into the causes of Persian imperialism, Herodotus traveled widely to (among other places) Egypt, Phoenicia, Mesopotamia, and Scythia, including in his work detailed ethnographic reports on many nations with whom the Persians had contact,—from Lydia and Babylon to Egypt, India and others. His account serves to document at the same time the pervasive and profound influences of the Eastern world on Greek life and thought.

Fundamental to Herodotus's narrative is his belief in a continuous cycle in human affairs, in which prosperity and decline alternate perpetually through every nation's history. This cycle, as Herodotus sees it, is an expression of divine justice, which exacts retribution for the unjust acquisition of power. As in the case of Croesus—whose eventual downfall was traced back five generations to an ancestor who usurped the Lydian throne by killing the king—retribution may come late, but it comes inevitably. Herodotus recounts that, years after the meeting described in this selection, Croesus was disastrously defeated and captured by the Persian king Cyrus; as he was about to be put to death, Croesus called out the name of Solon, remembering his wise words about the transience of happiness.

from *The Histories*

The Story of Solon and Croesus

When all these nations had been added to the Lydian empire,[1] and Sardis[2] was at the height of her wealth and prosperity, all the great Greek teachers of that epoch, one after another, paid visits to the capital. Much the most distinguished of them was Solon the Athenian,[3] the man who at the request if his countrymen had made a code of laws for Athens. He was on his travels at the time, intending to be away ten years, in order to avoid the necessity of repealing any of the laws he had made. That, at any rate, was the real reason of his absence, though he gave it out that what he wanted was just to see the world. The Athenians could not alter any of Solon's laws without him, because they had solemnly sworn to give them a ten years' trial.

For this reason, then—and also no doubt for the pleasure of foreign travel—Solon left home and, after a visit to the court of Amasis[4] in Egypt, went to Sardis to see Croesus.

Croesus entertained him hospitably in the palace, and three or four days after his arrival instructed some servants to take him on a tour of the royal treasuries and point out the richness and magnificence of everything. When Solon had made as thorough an inspection as opportunity allowed, Croesus said: " 'Well, my Athenian friend, I have heard a great deal about your wisdom, and how widely you have travelled in the pursuit of knowledge. I cannot resist my desire to ask you a question: who is the happiest man you have ever seen?' "

The point of the question was that Croesus supposed himself to be the happiest of men. Solon, however, refused to flatter, and answered in strict accordance with his view of the truth. "An Athenian," he said, "called Tellus."[5]

Croesus was taken aback. "And what," he asked sharply, "is your reason for this choice?"

"There are two good reasons," said Solon, "first, his city was prosperous, and he had fine sons, and lived to see children born to each of them, and all these

Translated by Aubrey de Selincourt.

1. Lydia, under the rule of Croesus in the mid-sixth century B.C.E., was the most powerful kingdom in Asia Minor until its defeat by Persia in 546 B.C.E.
2. Sardis was the capital city of Lydia.
3. The Athenian lawgiver (born c. 640 B.C.E.), whose poetry is presented earlier in this section. It is unlikely, for reasons of chro-

nology, that Solon and Croesus ever actually met, but both were so renowned that Herodotus could use the contrast between them to illustrate an ethical point.
4. King of Egypt.
5. Solon uses the name of a typical Athenian citizen.

children surviving; and, secondly, after a life which by our standards was a good one, he had a glorious death. In a battle with the neighbouring town of Eleusis, he fought for his countrymen, routed the enemy, and died like a soldier; and the Athenians paid him the high honour of a public funeral on the spot where he fell."

All these details about the happiness of Tellus, Solon doubtless intended as a moral lesson for the king; Croesus, however, thinking he would at least be awarded second prize, asked who was the next happiest person whom Solon had seen.

"Two young men of Argos," was the reply; "Cleobis and Biton. They had enough to live on comfortably; and their physical strength is proved not merely by their success in athletics, but much more by the following incident. The Argives were celebrating the festival of Hera, and it was most important that the mother of the two young men should drive to the temple in her ox-cart; but it so happened that the oxen were late in coming back from the fields. Her two sons therefore, as there was no time to lose, harnessed themselves to the cart and dragged it along, with their mother inside, for a distance of nearly six miles, until they reached the temple. After this exploit, which was witnessed by the assembled crowd, they had a most enviable death—a heaven-sent proof of how much better it is to be dead than alive. Men kept crowding round them and congratulating them on their strength, and women kept telling the mother how lucky she was to have such sons, when, in sheer pleasure at this public recognition of her sons' act, she prayed the goddess Hera, before whose shrine she stood, to grant Cleobis and Biton, who had brought her such honour, the greatest blessing that can fall to mortal man.

"After her prayer came the ceremonies of sacrifice and feasting; and the two lads, when all was over, fell asleep in the temple—and that was the end of them, for they never woke again.

"The Argives had statues made of them, which they sent to Delphi[6] as a mark of their particular respect."

Croesus was vexed with Solon for giving the second prize for happiness to the two young Argives, and snapped out: "That's all very well, my Athenian friend; but what of my own happiness? Is it so utterly contemptible that you won't even compare me with mere common folk like those you have mentioned?"

"My lord," replied Solon, "I know God is envious of human prosperity and likes to trouble us; and you question me about the lot of man. Listen then: as the years lengthen out, there is much both to see and to suffer which one would wish otherwise. Take seventy years as the span of a man's life: those seventy years contain 25,200 days, without counting intercalary months. Add a month every other year, to make the seasons come round with proper regularity, and you will have thirty-five additional months, which will make 1,050 additional days. Thus the total of days for your seventy years is 26,250, and not a single one of them is like the next in what it brings. You can see from that, Croesus, what a chancy thing

---

6. Delphi was the most important religious
site in Greece, located on the mainland
above the Gulf of Corinth.

life is. You are very rich, and you rule a numerous people; but the question you asked me I will not answer, until I know that you have died happily. Great wealth can make a man no happier than moderate means, unless he has the luck to continue in prosperity to the end. Many very rich men have been unfortunate, and many with a modest competence have had good luck. The former are better off than the latter in two respects only, whereas the poor but lucky man has the advantage in many ways; for though the rich have the means to satisfy their appetites and to bear calamities, and the poor have not, the poor, if they are lucky, are more likely to keep clear of trouble, and will have besides the blessings of a sound body, health, freedom from trouble, fine children, and good looks.

"Now if a man thus favoured dies as he has lived, he will be just the one you are looking for: the only sort of person who deserves to be called happy. But mark this: until he is dead, keep the word 'happy' in reserve. Till then, he is not happy, but only lucky.

"Nobody of course can have all these advantages, any more than a country can produce everything it needs: whatever it has, it is bound to lack something. The best country is the one which has most. It is the same with people: no man is ever self-sufficient—there is sure to be something missing. But whoever has the greatest number of the good things I have mentioned, and keeps them to the end, and dies a peaceful death, that man, my lord Croesus, deserves in my opinion to be called happy.

"Look to the end, no matter what it is you are considering. Often enough God gives a man a glimpse of happiness, and then utterly ruins him."

These sentiments were not of the sort to give Croesus any pleasure; he let Solon go with cold indifference, firmly convinced that he was a fool. For what could be more stupid than to keep telling him to look at the "end" of everything, without any regard to present prosperity?

After Solon's departure Croesus was dreadfully punished, presumably because God was angry with him for supposing himself the happiest of men.

[Croesus lived to witness his country's defeat and the capture of Sardis by the Persians under their king, Cyrus, in 546 B.C.E. As he was on the point of being put to death, he invoked the name of Solon. Upon explaining to Cyrus the lesson that Solon had tried to teach him, Croesus was pardoned by Cyrus and his life spared.]

THE BIBLE (AFTER 538 B.C.E.)
Palestine

The biblical Book of Ruth is set in the days of Judges, an era that preceded the establishment of the Hebrew monarchy in the late eleventh century B.C.E. It was probably composed much later, however, most likely after the Israelites returned from exile in Babylon around 538 B.C.E.

On the death of her husband, Ruth chooses to return to Bethlehem in Judah with her Hebrew mother-in-law, Naomi; she will share the fortunes of her new family rather than stay with her own people in the land of Moab. The relationship between Ruth and Naomi is one of the most beautiful in biblical literature. The sympathetic portrayal of the Moabite Ruth suggests that the story may have been meant to combat fifth- and fourth-century decrees requiring Hebrew men to divorce their foreign wives and marry only within the covenant community.

from *The Bible*

The Book of Ruth

In the days when the judges ruled, there was a famine in the land, and a man from Bethlehem in Judah, together with his wife and two sons, went to live for a while in the country of Moab.[1] The man's name was Elimelech, his wife's name Naomi, and the names of his two sons were Mahlon and Kilion. They were Ephrathites from Bethlehem in Judah. And they went to Moab and lived there.

Now Elimelech, Naomi's husband, died, and she was left with her two sons. They married Moabite women, one named Orpah and the other Ruth. After they had lived there about ten years, both Mahlon and Kilion also died, and Naomi was left without her two sons and her husband.

When she heard in Moab that the LORD had come to the aid of his people by providing food for them, Naomi and her daughters-in-law prepared to return home from there. With her two daughters-in-law she left the place where she had been living and set out on the road that would take them back to the land of Judah.

Then Naomi said to her two daughters-in-law, "Go back, each of you, to your mother's home. May the LORD show kindness to you, as you have shown to your dead and to me. May the LORD grant that each of you will find rest in the home of another husband."

Then she kissed them and they wept aloud and said to her, "We will go back with you to your people."

But Naomi said, "Return home, my daughters. Why would you come with me? Am I going to have any more sons, who could become your husbands? Return home, my daughters; I am too old to have another husband. Even if I thought there was still hope for me—even if I had a husband tonight and then gave birth to sons—would you wait until they grew up? Would you remain unmarried for them? No, my daughters. It is more bitter for me than for you, because the LORD's hand has gone out against me!"

At this they wept again. Then Orpah kissed her mother-in-law good-by, but Ruth clung to her.

New International Version translation.

---

1. The Moabites, east of the Dead Sea, were often enemies of the Israelites.

"Look," said Naomi, "your sister-in-law is going back to her people and her gods. Go back with her."

But Ruth replied, "Don't urge me to leave you or to turn back from you. Where you go I will go, and where you stay I will stay. Your people will be my people and your God my God. Where you die I will die, and there I will be buried. May the LORD deal with me, be it ever so severely, if anything but death separates you and me." When Naomi realized that Ruth was determined to go with her, she stopped urging her.

So the two of them went on until they came to Bethlehem. When they arrived in Bethlehem, the whole town was stirred because of them, and the women exclaimed, "Can this be Naomi?"

"Don't call me Naomi," she told them. "Call me Mara,[2] because the Almighty has made my life very bitter. I went away full, but the LORD has brought me back empty. Why call me Naomi? The LORD has afflicted me; the Almighty has brought misfortune upon me."

So Naomi returned from Moab accompanied by Ruth the Moabitess, her daughter-in-law, arriving in Bethlehem as the barley harvest was beginning.

Now Naomi had a relative on her husband's side, from the clan of Elimelech, a man of standing, whose name was Boaz.

And Ruth the Moabitess said to Naomi, "Let me go to the fields and pick up the leftover grain behind anyone in whose eyes I find favor."

Naomi said to her, "Go ahead, my daughter." So she went out and began to glean in the fields behind the harvesters. As it turned out, she found herself working in a field belonging to Boaz, who was from the clan of Elimelech.

Just then Boaz arrived from Bethlehem and greeted the harvesters, "The LORD be with you!"

"The LORD bless you!" they called back.

Boaz asked the foreman of his harvesters, "Whose young woman is that?"

The foreman replied, "She is the Moabitess who came back from Moab with Naomi. She said, 'Please let me glean and gather among the sheaves behind the harvesters.' She went into the field and has worked steadily from morning till now, except for a short rest in the shelter."

So Boaz said to Ruth, "My daughter, listen to me. Don't go and glean in another field and don't go away from here. Stay here with my servant girls. Watch the field where the men are harvesting, and follow along after the girls. I have told the men not to touch you. And whenever you are thirsty, go and get a drink from the water jars the men have filled."

At this, she bowed down with her face to the ground. She exclaimed, "Why have I found such favor in your eyes that you notice me—a foreigner?"

Boaz replied, "I've been told all about what you have done for your mother-in-law since the death of your husband—how you left your father and mother and your homeland and came to live with a people you did not know

---

2. "Bitter."

before. May the LORD repay you for what you have done. May you be richly rewarded by the LORD, the God of Israel, under whose wings you have come to take refuge."

"May I continue to find favor in your eyes, my lord," she said. "You have given me comfort and have spoken kindly to your servant—though I do not have the standing of one of your servant girls."

At mealtime Boaz said to her, "Come over here. Have some bread and dip it in the wine vinegar."

When she sat down with the harvesters, he offered her some roasted grain. She ate all she wanted and had some left over. As she got up to glean, Boaz gave orders to his men, "Even if she gathers among the sheaves, don't embarrass her. Rather, pull out some stalks for her from the bundles and leave them for her to pick up, and don't rebuke her."

So Ruth gleaned in the field until evening. Then she threshed the barley she had gathered, and it amounted to about half a bushel. She carried it back to town, and her mother-in-law saw how much she had gathered. Ruth also brought out and gave her what she had left over after she had eaten enough.

Her mother-in-law asked her, "Where did you glean today? Where did you work? Blessed be the man who took notice of you!"

Then Ruth told her mother-in-law about the one at whose place she had been working. "The name of the man I worked with today is Boaz," she said.

"The LORD bless him," Naomi said to her daughter-in-law. "The LORD has not stopped showing his kindness to the living and the dead." She added, "That man is our close relative; he is one of our next of kin."

Then Ruth the Moabitess said, "He even said to me, 'Stay with my workers until they finish harvesting all my grain.'"

Naomi said to Ruth her daughter-in-law, "It will be good for you, my daughter, to go with his girls, because in someone else's field you might be harmed."

So Ruth stayed close to the servant girls of Boaz to glean until the barley and wheat harvests were finished. And she lived with her mother-in-law.

One day Naomi her mother-in-law said to her, "My daughter, should I not try to find a home for you, where you will be well provided for? Is not Boaz, with whose servant girls you have been, a kinsman of ours? Tonight he will be winnowing barley on the threshing floor. Wash and perfume yourself, and put on your best clothes. Then go down to the threshing floor, but don't let him know you are there until he has finished eating and drinking. When he lies down, note the place where he is lying. Then go and uncover his feet and lie down. He will tell you what to do."

"I will do whatever you say," Ruth answered. So she went down to the threshing floor and did everything her mother-in-law told her to do.

When Boaz had finished eating and drinking and was in good spirits, he went over to lie down at the far end of the grain pile. Ruth approached quietly, uncovered his feet and lay down. In the middle of the night something startled the man, and he turned and discovered a woman lying at his feet.

"Who are you?" he asked.

"I am your servant Ruth," she said. "Spread the corner of your garment over me, since you are my next of kin."[3]

"The LORD bless you, my daughter," he replied. "This kindness is greater than that which you showed earlier. You have not run after the younger men, whether rich or poor. And now, my daughter, don't be afraid. I will do for you all you ask. All my fellow townsmen know that you are a woman of noble character. Although it is true that I am near of kin, there is a kinsman nearer than I. Stay here for the night, and in the morning if he wants to redeem, good; let him redeem. But if he is not willing, I vow that, as surely as the LORD lives, I will do it. Lie here until morning."

So she lay at his feet until morning, but got up before anyone could be recognized; and he said, "Don't let it be known that a woman came to the threshing floor."

He also said, "Bring me the shawl you are wearing and hold it out." When she did so, he poured into it six measures of barley and put it on her. Then he went back to town.

When Ruth came to her mother-in-law, Naomi asked, "How did it go, my daughter?"

Then she told her everything Boaz had done for her and added, "He gave me these six measures of barley, saying, 'Don't go back to your mother-in-law empty-handed.'"

Then Naomi said, "Wait, my daughter, until you find out what happens. For the man will not rest until the matter is settled today."

Meanwhile Boaz went up to the town gate and sat there. When the kinsman he had mentioned came along, Boaz said, "Come over here, my friend, and sit down." So he went over and sat down.

Boaz took ten of the elders of the town and said, "Sit here," and they did so. Then he said to the kinsman, "Naomi, who has come back from Moab, is selling the piece of land that belonged to our brother Elimelech. I thought I should bring the matter to your attention and suggest that you buy it in the presence of these seated here and in the presence of the elders of my people. If you will redeem it, do so. But if you will not, tell me, so I will know. For no one has the right to do it except you, and I am next in line."

"I will redeem it," he said.

Then Boaz said, "On the day you buy the land from Naomi and from Ruth the Moabitess, you acquire the dead man's widow, in order to maintain the name of the dead with his property."

At this, the kinsman said, "Then I cannot redeem it because I might endanger my own estate. You redeem it yourself. I cannot do it."

(Now in earlier times in Israel, for the redemption and transfer of property to

---

3. To spread his garment over her would mean to take her as his wife; as her next of kin, it would be Boaz's responsibility to protect the widow and maintain her deceased husband's family line (an exception to the ordinary prohibition of marriage of brother and sister-in-law).

become final, one party took off his sandal and gave it to the other. This was the method of legalizing transactions in Israel.)

So the kinsman said to Boaz, "Buy it yourself." And he removed his sandal.

Then Boaz announced to the elders and all the people. "Today you are witnesses that I have bought from Naomi all the property of Elimelech, Kilion and Mahlon. I have also acquired Ruth the Moabitess, Mahlon's widow, as my wife, in order to maintain the name of the dead with his property, so that his name will not disappear from among his family or from the town records. Today you are witnesses!"

Then the elders and all those at the gate said, "We are witnesses. May the LORD make the woman who is coming into your home like Rachel and Leah[4] who together built up the house of Israel. May you have standing in Ephrathah and be famous in Bethlehem. Through the offspring the LORD gives you by this young woman, may your family be like that of Perez, whom Tamar bore to Judah."[5]

So Boaz took Ruth and she became his wife. And the LORD enabled her to conceive, and she gave birth to a son. The women said to Naomi: "Praise be to the LORD, who this day has not left you without a kinsman. May he become famous throughout Israel! He will renew your life and sustain you in your old age. For your daughter-in-law, who loves you and who is better to you than seven sons, has given him birth."

Then Naomi took the child, laid him in her lap and cared for him. The women living there said, "Naomi has a son." And they named him Obed. He was the father of Jesse, the father of David.[6]

This, then, is the family line of Perez:

Perez was the father of Hezron, Hezron the father of Ram, Ram the father of Amminadab, Amminadab the father of Nahshon, Nahshon the father of Salmon, Salmon the father of Boaz, Boaz the father of Obed, Obed the father of Jesse, and Jesse the father of David.

THUCYDIDES (c. 460–c. 400 B.C.E.)
Greece

Early in the fifth century B.C.E., Persia, under King Darius and his son Xerxes, was largely successful in gaining political control of the nearby Greek cities in Asia Minor and finally invaded Greece itself in 490 B.C.E. and again in 480. Athens played a decisive role in the defense of Greece at the battle of Marathon in 490 and in the Persian defeat at Salamis in 480. As a result, it was under Athenian

---

4. The sisters who were the wives of the patriarch Isaac.
5. See Genesis 38.

6. Thus Naomi, Ruth, and Boaz become progenitors of Israel's greatest king.

hegemony that the Greek cities were subsequently organized into a defensive league to protect themselves against further potential aggression by Persia; the cities contributed money to Athens, which maintained a fleet for the general protection. Athenian domination over the league grew increasingly inflexible in the middle decades of the century, as Athens made tribute payments compulsory and refused to allow member cities to withdraw from the league, forcibly punishing efforts to do so. Thucydides' history of the Peloponnesian War [See the introductory headnote to Pericles' Funeral Oration] is thus a history of the growth—and ultimate dissolution—of the Athenian empire, and of the reactions of the rest of Greece. "What made war inevitable," Thucydides writes, "was the growth of Athenian power and the fear which this caused in Sparta."

The small Aegean island of Melos was one of the few to have remained independent of both the Athenian league and the Spartan alliance. In 416 B.C.E., with a view to increasing its resources, Athens sent a naval expedition to coerce the unwilling Melians into the empire as tribute-paying league members. Thucydides reports a dialogue between the Athenian generals and the Melian leaders in which the brutality and amoral cynicism of imperial power in action is fully revealed.

from *The History of the Peloponnesian War*

[The Melian Dialogue]

The Athenians also made an expedition against the island of Melos. They had thirty of their own ships, six from Chios[1] and two from Lesbos; 1,200 hoplites,[2] 300 archers, and twenty mounted archers, all from Athens; and about 1,500 hoplites from the allies and the islanders.

The Melians are a colony from Sparta. They had refused to join the Athenian empire like the other islanders, and at first had remained neutral without helping either side; but afterwards, when the Athenians had brought force to bear on them by laying waste their land, they had become open enemies of Athens.

Now the generals Cleomedes, the son of Lycomedes, and Tisias, the son of Tisimachus, encamped with the above force in Melian territory and, before doing any harm to the land, first of all sent representatives to negotiate. The Melians did not invite these representatives to speak before the people, but asked them to make the statement for which they had come in front of the governing body and the few.[3] The Athenian representatives then spoke as follows:

'So we are not to speak before the people, no doubt in case the mass of the people should hear once and for all and without interruption an argument from us which is both persuasive and incontrovertible, and should so be led astray. This, we realize, is your motive in bringing us here to speak before the few. Now suppose that you who sit here should make assurance doubly sure. Suppose that

Translated by Rex Warner.

---

1. Chios and Lesbos, islands in the eastern Aegean off the coast of Asia Minor, were under Athenian domination at this time.

2. Heavily armed infantrymen.
3. Leaders of the Melian oligarchy governing the island.

you, too, should refrain from dealing with every point in detail in a set speech, and should instead interrupt us whenever we say something controversial and deal with that before going on to the next point? Tell us first whether you approve of this suggestion of ours.'

The Council of the Melians replied as follows:

'No one can object to each of us putting forward our own views in a calm atmosphere. That is perfectly reasonable. What is scarcely consistent with such a proposal is the present threat, indeed the certainty, of your making war on us. We see that you have come prepared to judge the argument yourselves, and that the likely end of it all will be either war, if we prove that we are in the right, and so refuse to surrender, or else slavery.'

ATHENIANS: If you are going to spend the time in enumerating your suspicions about the future, or if you have met here for any other reason except to look the facts in the face and on the basis of these facts to consider how you can save your city from destruction, there is no point in our going on with this discussion. If, however, you will do as we suggest, then we will speak on.

MELIANS: It is natural and understandable that people who are placed as we are should have recourse to all kinds of arguments and different points of view. However, you are right in saying that we are met together here to discuss the safety of our country and, if you will have it so, the discussion shall proceed on the lines that you have laid down.

ATHENIANS: Then we on our side will use no fine phrases saying, for example, that we have a right to our empire because we defeated the Persians, or that we have come against you now because of the injuries you have done us—a great mass of words that nobody would believe. And we ask you on your side not to imagine that you will influence us by saying that you, though a colony of Sparta, have not joined Sparta in the war, or that you have never done us any harm. Instead we recommend that you should try to get what it is possible for you to get, taking into consideration what we both really do think; since you know as well as we do that, when these matters are discussed by practical people, the standard of justice depends on the equality of power to compel and that in fact the strong do what they have the power to do and the weak accept what they have to accept.

MELIANS: Then in our view (since you force us to leave justice out of account and to confine ourselves to self-interest)—in our view it is at any rate useful that you should not destroy a principle that is to the general good of all men—namely, that in the case of all who fall into danger there should be such a thing as fair play and just dealing, and that such people should be allowed to use and to profit by arguments that fall short of a mathematical accuracy. And this is a principle which affects you as much as anybody, since your own fall would be visited by the most terrible vengeance and would be an example to the world.

ATHENIANS: As for us, even assuming that our empire does come to an end, we are not despondent about what would happen next. One is not so much frightened of being conquered by a power which rules over others, as Sparta does (not that we are concerned with Sparta now), as of what would happen if a ruling power is attacked and defeated by its own subjects. So far as this point is concerned, you can leave it to us to face the risks involved. What we shall do now is to show you that it is for the good of our own empire that we are here and that it is for the preservation of your city that we shall say what we are going to say. We do not want any trouble in bringing you into our empire, and we want you to be spared for the good both of yourselves and of ourselves.

MELIANS: And how could it be just as good for us to be the slaves as for you to be the masters?

ATHENIANS: You, by giving in, would save yourselves from disaster; we, by not destroying you, would be able to profit from you.

MELIANS: So you would not agree to our being neutral, friends instead of enemies, but allies of neither side?

ATHENIANS: No, because it is not so much your hostility that injures us; it is rather the case that, if we were on friendly terms with you, our subjects would regard that as a sign of weakness in us, whereas your hatred is evidence of our power.

MELIANS: Is that your subjects' idea of fair play—that no distinction should be made between people who are quite unconnected with you and people who are mostly your own colonists or else rebels whom you have conquered?

ATHENIANS: So far as right and wrong are concerned they think that there is no difference between the two, that those who still preserve their independence do so because they are strong, and that if we fail to attack them it is because we are afraid. So that by conquering you we shall increase not only the size but the security of our empire. We rule the sea and you are islanders, and weaker islanders too than the others; it is therefore particularly important that you should not escape.

MELIANS: But do you think there is no security for you in what we suggest? For here again, since you will not let us mention justice, but tell us to give in to your interests, we, too, must tell you what our interests are and, if yours and ours happen to coincide, we must try to persuade you of the fact. Is it not certain that you will make enemies of all states who are at present neutral, when they see what is happening here and naturally conclude that in course of time you will attack them too? Does not this mean that you are strengthening the enemies you have already and are forcing others to become your enemies even against their intentions and their inclinations?

ATHENIANS: As a matter of fact we are not so much frightened of states on the continent. They have their liberty, and this means that it will be a long time before they begin to take precautions against us. We are more concerned about islanders like yourselves, who are still unsubdued, or subjects who have already become embittered by the constraint which our empire imposes on them. These are the people who are most likely to act in a reckless manner and to bring themselves and us, too, into the most obvious danger.

MELIANS: Then surely, if such hazards are taken by you to keep your empire and by your subjects to escape from it, we who are still free would show ourselves great cowards and weaklings if we failed to face everything that comes rather than submit to slavery.

ATHENIANS: No, not if you are sensible. This is no fair fight, with honour on one side and shame on the other. It is rather a question of saving your lives and not resisting those who are far too strong for you.

MELIANS: Yet we know that in war fortune sometimes makes the odds more level than could be expected from the difference in numbers of the two sides. And if we surrender, then all our hope is lost at once, whereas, so long as we remain in action, there is still a hope that we may yet stand upright.

ATHENIANS: Hope, that comforter in danger! If one already has solid advantages to fall back upon, one can indulge in hope. It may do harm, but will not destroy one.

But hope is by nature an expensive commodity, and those who are risking their all on one cast find out what it means only when they are already ruined; it never fails them in the period when such a knowledge would enable them to take precautions. Do not let this happen to you, you who are weak and whose fate depends on a single movement of the scale. And do not be like those people who, as so commonly happens, miss the chance of saving themselves in a human and practical way, and, when every clear and distinct hope has left them in their adversity, turn to what is blind and vague, to prophecies and oracles and such things which by encouraging hope lead men to ruin.

MELIANS: It is difficult, and you may be sure that we know it, for us to oppose your power and fortune, unless the terms be equal. Nevertheless we trust that the gods will give us fortune as good as yours, because we are standing for what is right against what is wrong; and as for what we lack in power, we trust that it will be made up for by our alliance with the Spartans, who are bound, if for no other reason, then for honour's sake, and because we are their kinsmen, to come to our help. Our confidence, therefore, is not so entirely irrational as you think.

ATHENIANS: So far as the favour of the gods is concerned, we think we have as much right to that as you have. Our aims and our actions are perfectly consistent with the beliefs men hold about the gods and with the principles which govern their own conduct. Our opinion of the gods and our knowledge of men lead us to conclude that it is a general and necessary law of nature to rule whatever one can. This is not a law that we made ourselves, nor were we the first to act upon it when it was made. We found it already in existence, and we shall leave it to exist for ever among those who come after us. We are merely acting in accordance with it, and we know that you or anybody else with the same power as ours would be acting in precisely the same way. And therefore, so far as the gods are concerned, we see no good reason why we should fear to be at a disadvantage. But with regard to your views about Sparta and your confidence that she, out of a sense of honour, will come to your aid, we must say that we congratulate you on your simplicity but do not envy you your folly. In matters that concern themselves or their own constitution the Spartans are quite remarkably good; as for their relations with others, that is a long story, but it can be expressed shortly and clearly by saying that of all people we know the Spartans are most conspicuous for believing that what they like doing is honourable and what suits their interests is just. And this kind of attitude is not going to be of much help to you in your absurd quest for safety at the moment.

MELIANS: But this is the very point where we can feel most sure. Their own self-interest will make them refuse to betray their own colonists, the Melians, for that would mean losing the confidence of their friends among the Hellenes[4] and doing good to their enemies.

ATHENIANS: You seem to forget that if one follows one's self-interest one wants to be safe, whereas the path of justice and honour involves one in danger. And, where danger is concerned, the Spartans are not, as a rule, very venturesome.

MELIANS: But we think that they would even endanger themselves for our sake and count the risk more worth taking than in the case of others, because we are so close to the Peloponnese that they could operate more easily, and because they

---

4. Greeks.

can depend on us more than on others, since we are of the same race and share the same feelings.

ATHENIANS: Goodwill shown by the party that is asking for help does not mean security for the prospective ally. What is looked for is a positive preponderance of power in action. And the Spartans pay attention to this point even more than others do. Certainly they distrust their own native resources so much that when they attack a neighbour they bring a great army of allies with them. It is hardly likely therefore that, while we are in control of the sea, they will cross over to an island.

MELIANS: But they still might send others. The Cretan sea[5] is a wide one, and it is harder for those who control it to intercept others than for those who want to slip through to do so safely. And even if they were to fail in this, they would turn against your own land and against those of your allies left unvisited by Brasidas.[6] So, instead of troubling about a country which has nothing to do with you, you will find trouble nearer home, among your allies, and in your own country.

ATHENIANS: It is a possibility, something that has in fact happened before. It may happen in your case, but you are well aware that the Athenians have never yet relinquished a single siege operation through fear of others. But we are somewhat shocked to find that, though you announced your intention of discussing how you could preserve yourselves, in all this talk you have said absolutely nothing which could justify a man in thinking that he could be preserved. Your chief points are concerned with what you hope may happen in the future, while your actual resources are too scanty to give you a chance of survival against the forces that are opposed to you at this moment. You will therefore be showing an extraordinary lack of common sense if, after you have asked us to retire from this meeting, you still fail to reach a conclusion wiser than anything you have mentioned so far. Do not be led astray by a false sense of honour—a thing which often brings men to ruin when they are faced with an obvious danger that somehow affects their pride. For in many cases men have still been able to see the dangers ahead of them, but this thing called dishonour, this word, by its own force of seduction, has drawn them into a state where they have surrendered to an idea, while in fact they have fallen voluntarily into irrevocable disaster, in dishonour that is all the more dishonourable because it has come to them from their own folly rather than their misfortune. You, if you take the right view, will be careful to avoid this. You will see that there is nothing disgraceful in giving way to the greatest city in Hellas when she is offering you such reasonable terms—alliance on a tribute-paying basis and liberty to enjoy your own property. And, when you are allowed to choose between war and safety, you will not be so insensitively arrogant as to make the wrong choice. This is the safe rule—to stand up to one's equals, to behave with deference towards one's superiors, and to treat one's inferiors with moderation. Think it over again, then, when we have withdrawn from the meeting, and let this be a point that constantly recurs to your minds—that you are discussing the fate of your country, that you have only one country, and that its future for good or ill depends on this one single decision which you are going to make.

---

5. The part of the Aegean around the island of Crete, south of Melos.

6. A Spartan general.

The Athenians then withdrew from the discussion. The Melians, left to themselves, reached a conclusion which was much the same as they had indicated in their previous replies. Their answer was as follows:

'Our decision, Athenians, is just the same as it was at first. We are not prepared to give up in a short moment the liberty which our city has enjoyed from its foundation for 700 years. We put our trust in the fortune that the gods will send and which has saved us up to now, and in the help of men—that is, of the Spartans; and so we shall try to save ourselves. But we invite you to allow us to be friends of yours and enemies to neither side, to make a treaty which shall be agreeable to both you and us, and so to leave our country.'

The Melians made this reply, and the Athenians, just as they were breaking off the discussion, said:

'Well, at any rate, judging from this decision of yours, you seem to us quite unique in your ability to consider the future as something more certain than what is before your eyes, and to see uncertainties as realities, simply because you would like them to be so. As you have staked most on and trusted most in Spartans, luck, and hopes, so in all these you will find yourselves most completely deluded.'

The Athenian representatives then went back to the army, and the Athenian generals, finding that the Melians would not submit, immediately commenced hostilities and built a wall completely round the city of Melos, dividing the work out among the various states. Later they left behind a garrison of some of their own and some allied troops to blockade the place by land and sea, and with the greater part of their army returned home. The force left behind stayed on and continued with the siege.

Meanwhile the Melians made a night attack and captured the part of the Athenian lines opposite the market-place. They killed some of the troops, and then, after bringing in corn and everything else useful that they could lay their hands on, retired again and made no further move, while the Athenians took measures to make their blockade more efficient in future. So the summer came to an end.

In the following winter the Spartans planned to invade the territory of Argos, but when the sacrifices for crossing the frontier turned out unfavourably, they gave up the expedition. The fact that they had intended to invade made the Argives suspect certain people in their city, some of whom they arrested, though others succeeded in escaping.

About this same time the Melians again captured another part of the Athenian lines where there were only a few of the garrison on guard. As a result of this, another force came out afterwards from Athens under the command of Philocrates, the son of Demeas. Siege operations were now carried on vigorously and, as there was also some treachery from inside, the Melians surrendered unconditionally to the Athenians, who put to death all the men of military age whom they took, and sold the women and children as slaves. Melos itself they took over for themselves, sending out later a colony of 500 men.

EURIPIDES (480? B.C.E.–406 B.C.E.)
Greece

Together with Aeschylus and Sophocles, the two other major Athenian tragedians of the fifth century B.C.E., Euripides shaped the future of tragic drama as a genre. His innovative writings were controversial, and largely unpopular, in his lifetime—he won first prize only four times out of twenty-two entries in the annual competition at the festival known as the City Dionysia, and he was often the subject of parody in contemporary comedies. His works were greatly prized, however, in the century after his death and thereafter, especially for the psychological depth of their characters. Aristotle called him the "most tragic" of the playwrights.

The *Bacchae* is concerned with the baffling, enigmatic nature of the god Dionysus, the very god at whose festival (and, according to the Athenians, in whose presence) the drama was performed. Dionysus seems to be both an exotic visitor from the East and a native Theban son; at once the liberating source of pleasure and release for human beings and the overpowering manipulator of their actions and responses; the benign promoter of fertility as well as a violent force of calamitous destruction. All these aspects are evident in the *Bacchae*, which in its representation of the god's female worshippers reflects several historically documented cult practices. Euripides, remarkably, makes the god himself the protagonist of the tragedy. Within the play, Dionysus, the patron deity of drama, both directs the action and is himself an actor, taking the part of a stranger devoted to the worship of Dionysus. Even Euripides' contemporaries recognized the extraordinary qualities of the *Bacchae*, his last play: Performed posthumously in 406, it won one of his rare first prizes.

Bacchae

Characters

DIONYSUS, *the son of the god Zeus and the mortal Semele*

PENTHEUS (*pronounced as two syllables,* PEN-*theus), the king of Thebes, whose crown has been bestowed on him by his grandfather Cadmus*

CADMUS, *the grandfather of Pentheus, and of Dionysus*

TIRESIAS, *the blind seer*

AGAVE, *Pentheus' mother, the daughter of Cadmus*

THE CHORUS, *the adepts of Dionysus, who have followed him from Asia, and who are thus strangers in Thebes. They are the Bacchae, also known as Bacchants, or Maenads, who are entirely dedicated to the ecstatic worship of the god*

There are two messengers—one a cowherd and one who goes with Pentheus on his journey to Cithaeron—and a guard.

Translated by C.K. Williams.

The royal palace of Thebes. To one side, a tomb covered with vines, and the rubble of a house, with smoke rising from it.

[*Enter Dionysus.*]

DIONYSUS: I am Dionysus.[1] I am Bacchus.
Bromius[2] and Iacchus.
Dithyrambus and Evius.
I am a god, the son of Zeus,
but I have assumed the semblance of a mortal,   5
and come to Thebes, where my mother, Semele,
the daughter of King Cadmus, gave birth to me.
Her midwife was the lightning bolt that killed her.
There is the river Dirce,[3] and there the stream
Ismenus. Over there, near the palace,   10
is my mother's tomb, and her ruined house,
still smoldering with the living flame of Zeus,
Hera's unrelenting hatred towards her.
I praise Cadmus. He made the ruins hallowed ground,
dedicated to his daughter. I myself   15
caused these vines to grow so thickly on them.

I was in Phrygia[4] before I came here,
and Lydia, where the earth flows gold. I passed
the broiling plains of Persia, and Bactria's[5]
walled towns. The Medes[6] then, their freezing winters,   20
then opulent Arabia and down
along the bitter, salt-sea coast of Asia
where Hellenes[7] and barbarians mingle
in teeming, beautifully towered cities.
When I had taught my dances there, established   25
the rituals of my mystery, making
my divinity manifest to mortals,

1. Son of Zeus and a mortal woman, Semele—
the daughter of King Cadmus of Thebes, a
city in central Greece—Dionysus (also
called Bacchus) is the god of burgeoning
vegetation, especially of the grapevine, and
of wine. Zeus visited Semele in disguise,
whereupon his jealous wife Hera persuaded
Semele to extract from him a promise Hera
knew would result in Semele's death: that
Zeus should appear before her in his true
form. Zeus was obliged to fulfill the promise and Semele, pregnant with Dionysus,
was killed by fire from his thunderbolt.
Zeus rescued his unborn child, whom he
put in his thigh and removed after a full
term of gestation.
2. Bromius, Iacchus, Dithyrambus, and Evius

are all titles of Dionysus. Bromius, used
frequently throughout the play, means the
"roarer" or "thunderer"; it may refer to the
bellowing of a bull—a form in which Dionysus sometimes manifested himself.
3. Dirce, a spring on Mount Cithaeron, near
Thebes, is named for a mythical Theban
queen who had been a follower of Dionysus.
4. Phrygia, a country in western Asia Minor,
was bordered on the west by the kingdom
of Lydia.
5. Bactria was a province of Persia.
6. The Medes were inhabitants of a territory to
the southwest of the Caspian Sea.
7. The Greek name for Greek-speaking peoples.

I came to Greece, to Thebes, the first Greek city
I've caused to shriek in ecstasy for me,
the first whose women I've clothed in fawnskin and in   30
whose hands I've placed my ivy spear, the thyrsus.[8]
Why did I choose Thebes? Because my mother's sisters,
who should have been the last to even *think*
of saying such a thing, started rumors:
that Dionysus was *not* the son of Zeus,   35
that Semele's lover had been a mortal
and she'd imputed the disgrace to Zeus, a fraud
Cadmus had contrived. They kept whispering
that Zeus destroyed her because she'd lied and said
he was her lover. Therefore I've stung them   40
with madness, and goaded them raving from their houses.
They're living on the mountain now, delirious,
dressed, as I've compelled them to be dressed,
in the garments of my rituals.
And all the rest, the whole female seed of Thebes,   45
I've driven frenzied out of house and home.
They're with the daughters of King Cadmus now,
huddled on bare rocks beneath the pines.
This city must learn, and know, against its will or not,
that it is uninitiated in my mysteries.   50
As for Semele, her memory
will be vindicated when I appear
to mortal eyes as the power she bore Zeus.
Cadmus has abdicated now to Pentheus,
the son of Agave, another of his daughters,   55
and Pentheus is warring with divinity
by excluding me from rituals
and not invoking my name in prayers.

Because of this, I'm going to demonstrate to him
and to all Thebes the god I really am.   60
When order is established, I'll go on,
revealing my identity in other lands.
But if, by rage and force of arms, the citizens
of Thebes drive the Bacchae from the mountain,
then I lead the army of my Maenads[9] into war.   65
This is why I have assumed a mortal shape,
shedding my divine form for a human's.

[Dionysus calls to the Chorus.]

---

8. The thyrsus was a wand that was wound
   around with ivy and carried by the followers of Dionysus.

9. Maenads were female worshippers of Dionysus who followed him as he journeyed
   through different lands.

Now, women, come: all you who left the ramparts
of Tmolus,[10] who left Lydia, left barbarian lands
to follow me and worship me, my women: come.   70
Bring the drum we brought from Phrygia,
the drum that pulses with the beat of Mother Earth.
Surround the royal walls of Pentheus with thunder:
let the city of King Cadmus see!

I am going to the gorges of Cithaeron now;   75
I am going to the Bacchae, to their dances.

[Enter Chorus. Exit Dionysus.]

CHORUS: Down
  from Asia, down
   from sacred Tmolus
 I have soared and
  soar, still, for   80
   Bromius, in
 the labor, difficult,
  difficult
   and sweet, the
 sweet, exacting labor
  of exalting   85
   him, of crying
 out
  for him, *Bacchus,*
   holy Bacchus!   90

 Who is in
  the road,
   who
 is in
  the   95
   streets and who
 is in
  the palace, in
   its chambers?
 Be here,   100
  now, be
   here, anyone,
 anywhere, be
  here, lips
   dedicated,   105
 pious, purified, be

---

10. A mountain in Lydia.

here, now, as
   I, as all, all
sing the
   ancient
     blessings, the   110
ancient, hallowed
   blessings
     of Dionysus!   115

Blessed, blessed
   and happy,
     blessed and
blessed again
   are they who,   120
     in the holy
rituals,
   consecrate themselves,
     who
know the   125
   mysteries.
     Blessed
in spirit, blessed
   spirit fused,
     fused
with and consecrated   130
   to the holy
     bands upon
the mountains,
   the bands   135
     of Bacchus praying
in the mountains,
   blessing, praising
     Bacchus, holy
Bacchus,   140
   blessed
     with purity and
blessed
   with prayer. And
     the rituals   145
of our great mother
   Cybele,[11] and
     the rituals

---

11. A fertility goddess in Lydia and Phrygia whose cult was introduced into Greece in the fifth century, and who in turn was closely connected with Dionysus and his worship.

of the ivy-covered
 thyrsus and the ritual
  of its rattling,   150
of the rattling of
 the ivy of
  the holy wand,
holy
 thyrsus, and   155
  the ritual
of the holy, ivy-
 covered crown of
  Bacchus.   160

Plummet
 down, now,
  Bacchants, plummet
down,
 hover,   165
  Bacchants, down,
down from
 Phrygia, down
  its mountains,
down   170
 to here, the
  broad
ways here, lead
 Bromius down,
  Bromius,   175
Dionysus, god, son
 of god and
  god, lead
him down!
 Bromius! Roarer!   180
 Roarer!
Once, she,
 his
  mother, of
whom, in
 agony, and in   185
  a blast
of fire from
 Zeus, he
  was born;
once,   190
 his mother, from
  whom he

was torn out
   by Zeus's lightning . . .
      And   195
she died with
   it, and he,
      then,
by his father,   200
   Zeus, son
      of Cronos,
was caught,
   uplifted, and,
      that   205
instant, pinned,
   with golden
      clips,
into his holy
   thigh, and
      he kept   210
him there, a
   secret
      from his wife,
a gold-
   bound secret
      from Hera,   215
wife of
   Zeus . . .
      And it was
Zeus who,   220
   when the
      time
the fates deemed
   proper
      came,   225
it was
   Zeus who
      brought him
forth again, to   230
   his birth
      again,
a god,
   though, now,
      horned,   235
horns rising
   like
      a bull's
now, horns

flourished, garlanded
  with
  beast-nourished
    serpents, and
    his Maenads,
too, in their
  tresses, too,
    weave
serpents, all
  his holy
    Maenads.
Thebes, O
  Thebes, who nurtured
    her, Semele,
garland now
  yourself, Thebes, with
    ivy garlands
now and
  with myrtle, luscious
    myrtle, crown
yourself and
  with oak and
    fir-twigs; be the
Bacchant now,
  yourself, and
    dappled fawnskins
wrap
  upon yourself,
    and
white curls of
  braided wool,
    take unto
yourself the wild
  thyrsus now,
    behold, now,
yourself, behold,
  holy now,
    all the land,
yourself and all
  the land, shall
    dance now,
dance
  again, when
    Bromius leads
the dance
  onto the

240

245

250

255

260

265

270

275

280

285

holy
mountain!
  Bromius
    calls
his band and
  leads them
    where, already,
one band
  waits, the band
    of women
waits, driven
  from their
    looms, driven
from
  their shuttles,
    stung,
stung by
  Dionysus, from
    themselves!

Oh, and
  you, the
    holy
caves of
    Crete, the
      dens
of the Curetes,[12]
  the
    caves where
Zeus was
  born and where
    the drum,
too, was
  born, was given
    by you, you
who wear
  three helmets,
    you,
Corybants, you
  who made my
    leather drum for
me and
  danced for

290

295

300

305

310

315

320

325

12. In myth, the Curetes were votaries of Rhea, the Cretan mother goddess. They were often identified with Cybele's attendants, the Corybantes.

me, and who,
dancing out
the Bacchic rites,
mixed
the drumbeat
into the wild,
ecstatic dances   330
with the sharp,
sweet calling
crying
of the flute, and
handed
it, my   335
drum, to her, Mother
Rhea, so
that she
could hand it
to the Satyrs, who   340
were wild with
dancing, too,
and
brought
it to the dances
now   345
in which
Dionysus, in
his gigantic
year,[13] in
his festival
exults—   350
Holy Dionysus!

Delectable he
is, delectable,
upon   355
the mountain and he
falls out of
the holy bands, onto
the ground; delectable   360
he is, in the
holy   365

---

13. One of the rites practiced by women and
sacred to Dionysus took place in alternate
years; the ritual included dancing on a
mountainside and, in at least some Di-
onysiac cults, it was documented as involving the practice of tearing an animal to
pieces and eating it raw.

fawnskin, and he
  joyfully
    devours the living
flesh of new-
  ly slaughtered goats and
    on the mountain
now, again,
  in Phrygia,
    in Lydia, and
always, rushing
  everywhere
    before
us, sweetly calling,
  is
    Bromius!
And the earth
  flows, flows
    beneath us, then
milk
  flows, and wine
    flows,
and nectar
  flows, like
    flame,
like the fire
  from Syria, from
    the frankincense,
delectable, the
  flame that
    flows, now,
from
  his torch, and rushes,
    flowing now,
from his thyrsus
  as he whirls
    it, runs
with it, rushes,
  driving on his
    dancers with
it, roaring
  on
    with it, and
his locks
  flow thickly and
    his locks dance
and *Onwards,*

370

375

380

385

390

395

400

405

410

Bacchae, he
   is roaring, Onwards,
Bacchae,
  blazing with
   the gold of
golden Tmolus,
  Evohe! he
   roars, Evohe! he
calls, Sing
  to Dionysus,
   Sing!
And make
  the drums, make
   the
drums
  roar, let the drums
   honor
Bacchus, let
  the flute shriek, and
   the holy
shriekings
  and delectable and
   holy and now
shriek again, it
  is woven
   now, together,
the holy flute,
  the way up
   to the
mountain,
  holiness and
   mountain!
And the
  Bacchant
   then, as
joyful
  as a foal
   near
its mother,
  grazing, leaps
   cavorts,
prances, so
  she dances
   now,
the Bacchant,
  and she

415

420

425

430

435

440

445

450

455

soars
  now, being, 460
   now,
    joy-
fully, playfully,
  the 465
   Bacchant.

[Enter Tiresias.]

TIRESIAS: Who is at the gates? Call Cadmus from the house:
the son of Agenor, who came from Sidon
to build the walls and towers of Thebes.
Tell him Tiresias is here. He'll know why. 470
He and I, ancient and more ancient, have made vows:
to adorn ourselves with fawnskins, with Bacchic wands,
and to wreathe shoots of ivy in our hair.

[Enter Cadmus.]

CADMUS: I knew it was you, old friend. I was in the palace,
but I recognized that wise old voice of yours. 475
You always know a voice like that, the wisdom in it.
Here I am, in the god's equipment, all prepared.
He's my daughter's son. We have to lift him high,
as high as possible—Dionysus,
who's revealed himself to mortals as a god. 480
Now, where will the dancing be? Show me
where my feet should go: they'll dance; we'll toss
these old white manes of ours. Explain where,
Tiresias, old man to old man: you're wise.
I'll dance all day and night and not get tired, 485
beating my thyrsus on the ground. In our joy,
we've even forgotten how we've gotten on.
TIRESIAS: That's it, that's how I feel, young, too.
I'll dance, I'll take my chances.
CADMUS: Shall we ride in a chariot to the mountain? 490
TIRESIAS: No, we'll walk, it will show more reverence.
CADMUS: We're both old, but shall I lead you?
TIRESIAS: The god will lead us without our trying.
CADMUS: Are we the only men who'll dance for Dionysus?
TIRESIAS: Only we can see. The rest of them are mad. 495
CADMUS: Let's not waste time. Let me lead you there.
TIRESIAS: Here, take my hand in yours.
CADMUS: I'm only human: I won't despise the gods.
TIRESIAS: Compared with their wisdom, ours is nothing.
What comes down to us, from our fathers, 500
out of ancient time, no argument's more powerful

than that: the wisest mind can't theorize past that.
When I put on my ivy now, and go to dance,
they'll say, "Old fool, shameless fool,"
but the god makes no distinction, old or young: 505
he wants us all to honor him, he wants
us united in his exaltation.

CADMUS: Since you can't see this sight, Tiresias,
let me tell you what's about to happen.
Pentheus, the son of Echion,   510
to whom I've resigned my powers as king,
is rushing towards the palace. He seems agitated.

[Enter Pentheus.]

PENTHEUS: I happened to be gone from Thebes, now I hear
awful evils have erupted in the city.
Our women have deserted home to perpetrate   515
false Bacchic mysteries in the dark woods
on the mountain, dancing to celebrate their upstart
deity, Dionysus . . . whoever Dionysus is.
They fill great bowls of wine, then they creep
into the bushes and lie down for lusting men.   520
Priestesses, they say they are, Maenads,
sworn to Bacchus. I say if it's anyone
they're dedicated to, it's Aphrodite.
Some of them I've had trapped: they're in prison,
chained. The rest are in the hills.   525
I'll track them down, all of them, even Agave,
my mother, and her sisters, Ino,[14]
and Autonoe, the mother of Actaeon.
I'll have them all in cages.
I'll stamp out these obscene orgies.   530
There's an intruder, too, I hear, a foreigner,
a sorcerer, a charlatan, from Lydia.
Long, scented yellow hair, they say, cheeks like wine,
with Aphrodite's[15] love charms in his eyes.
Day and night he mixes with young girls,   535
holding his mysteries up for them to admire.
Once I get him here, though, inside the walls,
he won't be tossing his locks or beating the ground
with his famous thyrsus. Not when I have his head.
He's the one who claims Dionysus is a god,   540
that he was stitched into the thigh of Zeus,

---

14. Agave, Ino, and Autonoe were the sisters
of Semele. Actaeon, Autonoe's son, was
turned into a stag for an offense against

the goddess Artemis and was devoured by
his own hunting dogs.

15. Aphrodite was the goddess of erotic love.

when really the child and the mother were both
consumed by lightning, because she'd lied
and said that Zeus had been her lover.
I don't know who this stranger is,   545
but doesn't such insulting outrage deserve hanging?

[He sees Cadmus and Tiresias.]

Not another miracle! Look: the seer,
rigged up in dappled fawnskin—Tiresias himself.
And my mother's father, you, too, decked out
like a Bacchant with your thyrsus. Ridiculous!   550
Are you both senile? I'm ashamed, Grandfather.
Shake that ivy off, right away;
let go of that thyrsus. Tiresias,
you instigated this! One more imported deity,
more flocks of birds for you to read,   555
more burnt offerings to get fees for!
You're fortunate you're old, that's why
you're not shackled with the Bacchae
for having brought these wretched rites to Thebes.
Whenever wine gleams at a women's feast,   560
I say nothing's healthy in those mysteries.

CHORUS LEADER: This is impiety! Stranger, do you offer reverence
neither to the gods, nor to Cadmus,
who sowed the crop of those born of the earth?[16]
You, the son of Echion, will you deny your race?   565

TIRESIAS: If a wise man finds an honest case to argue,
being eloquent is hardly difficult.
As for you, though your glibness gives you the air
of being sane, there's nothing rational about you.
A man who influences others with overbearing   570
is dangerous for his city: he lacks reason.
This new god you're subjecting to ridicule,
I can't tell you how great he'll be
throughout Greece.
                    There are, young man,
two principles for humankind: first, the goddess   575
Demeter—you can call her that, or Earth—
who nourishes us with solid food. Then comes
the son of Semele, equal in power, who invented
and introduced to mortals the liquid of the grape,

---

16. One of the myths about Thebes was that
Cadmus had populated the city by sowing
in plowed furrows the teeth of a sacred
snake he had killed; from the sown teeth
armed men sprang up.

which gives weak humans surcease from pain,   580
when they're glutted with the liquor of the vine,
and gives us sleep, to forget the evils of our days.
There is no other remedy for our affliction.
He, a god himself, is poured as a libation to the gods,
it's thanks to him men have these blessings.   585

You sneer at him being sewn into the thigh
of Zeus? I'll teach you what that really means.
When Zeus snatched the newborn from the lightning
and carried him up onto Olympus as a god,
Hera wanted to throw the child from heaven,   590
but Zeus, in his godly wisdom, countered her.
Breaking off a fragment of the ether
the world floats in, he made a doll, a Dionysus-
doll, that he showed Hera. But men confused
the words: they garbled "showed" to "sewed" and made   595
the story up about his having "sewed"
the god in his thigh to hide him from Hera.

And this god is a prophet, too: the Bacchic
frenzy gives the power of foresight; when
Bacchus fully infiltrates the body   600
of whoever is possessed, they foretell the future.
Dionysus even has a share
of the god of war: an army will be ranged
with arms for battle—before a lance is lifted,
a panic suddenly takes them and they flee.   605
This dementia also comes from Dionysus.
Someday you'll see him soaring on the rocks
at Delphi, leaping with pine torches
on the double cliffs, his Bacchic thyrsus
whirling, lashing, great in all Greece.   610
Pentheus, listen: don't believe that power
dominates in human life, and though
your sick imagination makes you think it,
don't believe you're sane. Welcome the god,
offer him libations, be a Bacchant, wear garlands.   615
It's not Dionysus who'll compel
a woman to be virtuous: chastity
is a part of one's nature or it's not;
even plunged in the deliriums of ritual,
a woman who is truly chaste won't be corrupted.   620

You know you're proud when your name is glorified,
when the multitude cries "Pentheus!" from the towers.
I believe the god is pleased by homage, too.

Therefore both Cadmus and I, the butt of your jokes,
will wreathe our heads with ivy and we'll dance: 625
gray-haired or not, both of us will dance
You won't persuade me to fight the god.
You're mad, and there are no drugs to heal you,
because you must be drugged to be this painfully mad.

CHORUS LEADER: Old man, Apollo would approve your words. 630
Honoring the great god Bromius proves your wisdom.

CADMUS: My boy, the advice Tiresias is offering is good.
Believe him. Live with us. Don't break tradition.
For the moment, you're distracted, deluded.
But besides, even if the god isn't a god, 635
say he is: it's a pious lie. Semele,
the mother of a god: consider the honor
it brings our family and remember Actaeon:
his death, how horrible it was; the hounds
he'd raised with meat from his own hands, 640
tearing him to pieces on the mountain,
because he bragged he could outhunt Artemis.
Don't let that be you. Here, I'll crown you
with ivy: stay with us, offer homage to the god.

PENTHEUS: Don't touch me! Go play with your Bacchus, 645
but don't wipe your madness off on me.
And Tiresias, the instructor of your foolishness,
will pay for this.

[Enter guards.]

                    Someone, quickly, go,
now, to the place where he observes his birds.
Take a lever, turn the whole thing over, demolish it, 650
throw his sacred garlands to the storming winds.
There's no way I can hurt him more than that.
The rest of you, patrol the city.
That girlish stranger who's introduced this new plague
and fouled our beds—I want him. Track him down 655
and when you find him, tie him up, bring him here,
so he can get what he deserves, death by stoning.
He'll rue the Bacchic orgies he'll find in Thebes.

[Exit guards.]

TIRESIAS: You poor fool. You don't know the meaning
of your own words. Before, you were insane, 660
now you're raving. Come, Cadmus, we'll pray for him.
May the god have pity on the wild man and may
he not inflict reprisals on the city.
Come, we'll support one another.

Hold your thyrsus. Two old men,   665
we mustn't fall, we would be disgraced.
We must serve Bacchus, son of Zeus, and so we will.
Cadmus, beware that Pentheus doesn't make your house
repent. This isn't prophecy, but fact:
the fool speaks foolishness.   670

[*Exit Pentheus to the palace. Exit Cadmus and Tiresias to Cithaeron.*]

CHORUS: Holiness, queen
  of all the
   gods, Holiness,
 who to
  the earth
   hovers
 down, on   675
  gold
   wings, down
 to us: do   680
  you hear
   him? Do you
 hear this
  Pentheus, his
   unholy,   685
 raging insolence
  against the
   god? Against
 Bromius, son of
  Semele, most
   blessed, most   690
 holy, of the
  divine, who,
   at the god's
 lovely garlanded
  celebration, has   695
   this gift, to
 dance, to bring men,
  to bring men
   together in   700
 the dance, and
  this,
   when the
 flute shrieks, to
  laugh, and   705
   this, to
 stop cares, to
  stop

woe, and
when the glistening
   wine   710
     into the holy,
ivy-bearing
   god-feast comes,
     to banish   715
everything, to wrap
   us all
     in sleep.

Tongues
   without bits;
     defiance   720
without law:
   together
     they create
disaster.   725
   But this, the
     life
of calm, the
   life of rational
     tranquillity, this   730
sustains us, this
   holds our house
     together.

The gods
   are far from
     us: how far   735
in their azure
   are they, how
     far they
are, in their   740
   eons: but still
     they
watch us,
   see us, see
     our actions,   745
watch
   our
     goings on.

Knowledge
   is not wisdom:
     cleverness   750

is not, not
  without
    awareness
of our
  death,   755
  not
without recalling
  just how
    brief   760
our flare
  is. He
    who overreaches
will, in his
  overreaching, lose   765
    what
he possesses,
  betray
    what
he has   770
  now. That
    which is
beyond us,
  which is
    greater   775
than
  the human, the
    unattainably
great, is
  for   780
    the mad, or
for those
  who listen
    to
the mad, and then   785
  believe
    them.

Oh, let me, let
  me go, let
    me go   790
to Cyprus,
  Aphrodite's
    island, where
the heart's
  beguilers,   795
    tempters

of men's
  hearts
    live.

Oh, there at   800
  Paphos,[17]
    where, with
no rain,
  the river
    with a hundred   805
mouths
  brings forth gigantic
    harvests.
There, or
  Pieria, lovely
    Pieria, where   810
Olympus
  is, where
    the muses
have their holy   815
  place; take me
    there,
Master, O
  Bromius, there
    the Graces   820
are, there
  Desire, and there
    the Bacchants
can lawfully
  enact their holy   825
    rites.
The god, the
  son of
    Zeus, finds
rituals
  joyful! He   830
    cherishes
peace, and peace
  cherishes
    the   835
young. He
  brings goodness to

---

17. A city on the southwest coast of Cyprus; a
    center of the worship of Aphrodite.

both
rich and
  lesser mortals,
    offering
all, all
  happiness, all
    wine,   840
all
  painlessness
    and pleasure.
They, though,
  who
    will not take   845
these
  gifts, who
    refuse
the happiness of
  those
    who choose to   855
live a life
  rich by
    day and
blessed at night, those
  he detests! He   860
    detests excess,
detests
  insatiable, excessive
    men!   865
And so, what
  the common man
    thinks, what
the simple
  man believes, the   870
    most
humble, that
  I, too,
    will
take   875
  as my
    example.

[Enter guards, leading Dionysus, bound. Enter Pentheus.]

GUARD: Pentheus, here we are: we've hunted down
  the prey you wanted. Except . . .
  the animal was tame: he didn't try to run,   880
  he never lost the flushed wine color in his cheeks.

He just smiled, gave us his hands, told us
we'd better tie him. I felt ashamed. "Stranger,"
I said, "I'm doing this against my will:
it's Pentheus who gave the order."   885
And those women you had chained, locked
in the dungeon? Well, they're gone now.
They're off in the meadows, dancing,
calling on their god Bromius. The chains around
their legs just snapped, the barred doors   890
came open by themselves: no mortal did all that.
This person who's come to Thebes is full of miracles.
But all this is your responsibility.
PENTHEUS: Untie his hands, he's in my net,
he won't be dancing out of this.   895
Well, you're not impossible to look at, are you?
Women wouldn't think so, anyway. Not in Thebes,
they wouldn't, which is why you're here, of course.
What a mane of hair you have: very seductive.
Look at it falling down your cheeks.   900
Good hand holds for a wrestler.
And how white your skin is: you must be careful
about staying out of the sun.
Oh, yes, handsome you, in the shade,
hunting with Aphrodite. All right, who are you?   905
DIONYSUS: I'll tell you, I have no secrets.
You've heard of Tmolus of the thousand flowers?
PENTHEUS: I know it, it flanks the town of Sardis.
DIONYSUS: I come from there, my country is Lydia.
PENTHEUS: Why have you brought these rituals to Greece?   910
DIONYSUS: By command of Dionysus, son of Zeus.
PENTHEUS: Is there a Zeus in Lydia spawning new gods?
DIONYSUS: No, it's your Zeus, who married Semele.
PENTHEUS: He commanded you . . . Face to face, or in a dream?
DIONYSUS: He revealed his mysteries face to face.   915
PENTHEUS: And these mysteries: what are they?
DIONYSUS: They are forbidden, unutterable to unbelievers.
PENTHEUS: What do they confer on those who sacrifice?
DIONYSUS: It would be sacrilege to tell, but there's great good.
PENTHEUS: You're clever. You want to make me curious.   920
DIONYSUS: The mysteries detest an impious man.
PENTHEUS: You say you saw the god: what form did he take?
DIONYSUS: Any form he wanted to—it wasn't my doing.
PENTHEUS: Another evasion. You make no sense.
DIONYSUS: Sense *is* nonsense, for a fool.   925
PENTHEUS: Is Thebes the first stop on your god's itinerary?
DIONYSUS: No, foreigners everywhere dance to him.

PENTHEUS: Foreigners are less intelligent than Greeks.
DIONYSUS: In this, more intelligent: customs vary.
PENTHEUS: Do you perform your mysteries by day, or at night?   930
DIONYSUS: Usually at night: there's more awe in darkness.
PENTHEUS: And for women, more treachery and corruption.
DIONYSUS: There's corruption in broad daylight, too.
PENTHEUS: Cheap sophistries! You'll pay for them.
DIONYSUS: *You'll* pay, for your impiety and stubbornness.   935
PENTHEUS: Well, Bacchic backtalk. You wrestle well, with words.
DIONYSUS: Tell me, how do you propose to punish me?
PENTHEUS: First I'll shear those lovely locks of yours.
DIONYSUS: My hair is holy: I've grown it for the god.
PENTHEUS: Now your thyrsus, you'll hand that over.   940
DIONYSUS: You'll have to take it: it belongs to Dionysus.
PENTHEUS: Now I'll put you in chains, in prison.
DIONYSUS: The god will free me, when I want him to.
PENTHEUS: Call him all you like, you and your Bacchae.
DIONYSUS: He's here now, seeing what I'm suffering.   945
PENTHEUS: Where is he? I don't see anything.
DIONYSUS: He's with me. You're unholy. You can't see.
PENTHEUS: Tie him up! He's scorning Thebes and me!
DIONYSUS: I am sane. I won't be bound by the insane.
PENTHEUS: I say bind him! I'm the power here, not you!   950
DIONYSUS: Your power is mortal, you don't know what
                you're doing: you don't even know who you are.
PENTHEUS: I am Pentheus. Son of Echion. Son of Agave.
DIONYSUS: Pentheus, Pentheus, you'll repent that name.[18]
PENTHEUS: Take him. Lock him up. Put him in the stable.   955
            If it's dark he wants, give him darkness.
            Go dance there. And your women,
            your accomplices, I'll sell them as slaves,
            or keep them in my house, laboring at looms,
            instead of beating on their maddening drums.   960
DIONYSUS: Take me. What isn't to be suffered won't be.
            But you: Dionysus, whom you've offered outrage to,
            whose very being you deny, will punish you.
            Wrong us, it's him you bind in chains.

[The guards lead Dionysus off. Pentheus follows.]

CHORUS: Queen   965
            Dirce, you are
                the daughter

---

18. The name "Pentheus" sounds like the
    Greek word for "grief," *penthos.*

of Achelous;[19]
  holy
    Dirce, more
than holy, for   970
  to you Zeus
    once
touched his
  child, touched him   975
    to your waters
as he tore
  him from the unrelenting
    fire
and placed him   980
  in his thigh and
    roared:
You
  are Dithyrambus!
    Into my male   985
womb, come!
  You
    are Bacchus!
Come, I will
  reveal you to   990
    Thebes!
You
  are Bacchus!
    They
shall call   995
  you
    Bacchus!
But you, Dirce,
  blessed
    river, you   1000
thrust me from
  you, you thrust the
    garlanded
bands who dance
  near you. Why   1005
    thrust me from
you this way? Why
  shun me
    so? Soon,
though, by   1010

---

19. A river in the southwest part of mainland
    Greece.

the luscious grapes
of Dionysus'
vines, I swear
soon the name
Bromius
will have
a meaning for
you, too.

Rage, and
rage and rage
is what
he, this
earth-child,
this
Pentheus,
dragon's
seed, this
monstrous
son
of Echion,[20]
reveals, an earth-
child, just
as the monstrous
giants are,
children of
the earth, as
they, gory, wild-
faced, rage, so
he, daring,
daring to dare
gods, rages, and
will
dare, soon,
too, to
threaten
me, with
chains, and who
already, in
his house, in
the darkness of
his prison,
has

1020

1025

1030

1035

1040

1045

1050

---

20. One of the armed men who sprang up
from the earth when Cadmus sowed the
dragon's teeth. He married Cadmus's
daughter Agave; Pentheus was his son.

my dancing
comrade.

Do
you see us?
Do you
see these
things, son
of Zeus?
Dionysus,
do you see
our battle,
our suffering
in
oppression?
Come, be
with us, come
down from
Olympus,
come whirl
your thyrsus with
its golden
face
quell
this vile person's
insolence
and violence!

Are you on
Nysa[21] now, which
nurtures
beasts, or are
you now,
Dionysus,
guiding with your
wand bands
of dancers in
the mountains of
Corycia?
Or on

21. According to some versions of the myth, the child Dionysus was raised by nymphs on a mountain called Nysa. The chorus refers here to several mountainous areas frequented by Dionysus: Corycia is part of Mount Parnassus, while Pieria is on the northern side of Mount Olympus in Thessaly, in the northern part of mainland Greece.

Olympus, in
the forest
where
Orpheus played
his lyre and brought, 1095
with his
muse, the
trees
to him and
the ferocious 1100
beasts to
him, are
you there? Oh,
Pieria,
blessed, 1105
honors you and with
your own cries,
Evius, honors
you, and he
will come 1110
dance
in Bacchic
celebrations, and
over the
roaring river 1115
Axios[22] will
spin
his Maenads, and
over the
rich 1120
waters of
Lydias
spin them,
Lydias,
bliss-giver, 1125
father, whose lovely
waters make that
land of horses
gleam.

[Dionysus' voice is heard from offstage.]

DIONYSUS: Listen! 1130
Listen to me, Bacchae!

---

22. Axios and Lydias are Macedonian rivers.

I am calling! Listen, Bacchae, listen to me!

CHORUS: Who? To
    whom
      listen? 1135
Whose
    call? Whose
      call, O
Evius, where
    are you to listen 1140
      to, Evius?

DIONYSUS: Again! Listen! I call again!
The son of Zeus, the son of Semele, calls again!

CHORUS: *Bromius!*
    Roarer! 1145
      You!
Lord! You
    come to us, oh,
      be here, lord!

DIONYSUS: *Earthquake! Be here! Shake the world!* 1150
Come, shudder the foundations of the world!

CHORUS: Look, the
    palace, Pentheus,
      his palace, look,
it shudders, the 1155
    whole palace trembles, now
      it falls!
Dionysus!
    Look! Dionysus!
      Loved one! 1160
Dionysus now is in
    the palace! Love him,
      oh, we adore
him! Look, the lintels
    craze, and 1165
      look, the stones
craze! Over
    the pillars, crazing,
      the stone shatters!
Listen, now: Bromius! 1170
    Bromius roars! He roars
      now, Bromius!

DIONYSUS: *Roar, lightning! Roar, bolt! Fire!*
Let the fire consume! Consume and roar!

CHORUS: Look! 1175
    The fire, look,
      it roars

upon
   the tomb
      of Semele! Look!   1180
The fire-
   bolt, Zeus's
      fire,
it falls upon
   the fire of
      Semele!   1185
Fall,
   Maenads!
      Fall!
There, the   1190
   ground, fall
      to it!
Tremble! Look!
   Our lord, the
      son   1195
of Zeus, has
   brought these
      high
halls
   down to
      ruin.   1200

[*Enter Dionysus.*]

DIONYSUS: Ah, my Oriental women: did you fall?
      Why? Was it fear that made you fall?
      You saw the house of Pentheus, when Dionysus
      made it shake, and you were shaken, too, by fear.   1205
      Come, no fear now, no fall: rise.
CHORUS LEADER: O Light, without you there was no dance,
      I was lost without you, Light.
DIONYSUS: Were you lost when I was locked in there?
      In the dark there, in the net of Pentheus?   1210
      Did you think that I was lost?
CHORUS LEADER: I was lost. What else, without you, but lost?
      The man who has no god had you. How are you free?
DIONYSUS: I saved myself. It took no effort.
CHORUS LEADER: But he'd bound your hands in knots!   1215
DIONYSUS: That was how I took my vengeance on him,
      how I humiliated him: he tried to bind me,
      his hands, though, never touched me;
      he fed on his desires. A bull was in there,
      by its stall—my jail, he thought. He took his ropes   1220
      and bent to wind them on its knees and hooves.

He was panting: *rage!* He was sweating, dripping,
biting at his lips. I was right there next to him.
I watched him. I was quiet. Then Bromius
revealed himself. The house shook! The grave   1225
of Semele shot flames! Pentheus cried out.
He thought the palace was in flames.
Where are all my slaves? he cried. He ran.
The slaves ran. *Water!* he shouted, *from the river,*
from Achelous, but all their work was futile.   1230
Then he stopped. He thought of me: I might escape.
He drew a pitch-black sword and ran into the palace.
But it seems Bromius must have made a shape,
in the courtyard: Pentheus stabbed at it,
at the gleaming air, as though it were me.   1235
Bacchus wasn't finished, though, humiliating him.
The palace crashes down, everything is shattered.
Now Pentheus can see the bitterness my chains
have brought him. His sword falls. He's exhausted.
A man, a mortal, dares to struggle with a god!   1240
I left him there. I walked out quietly to you.
Pentheus! What is he to me? I imagine he'll be coming.
Listen to him tramping through the courtyard.
I'll be patient: let him rage. Wise men
know how to practice self-control.   1245

[Enter Pentheus and guards.]

PENTHEUS: Terrible: that stranger, that man I had in chains . . .
        he's escaped . . . *You!*
        What are you doing here, at the gate?
        How did you get out?
DIONYSUS: Step calmly with your anger.   1250
PENTHEUS: How did you escape your bonds?
DIONYSUS: Weren't you listening when I told you
        someone would be here to free me?
PENTHEUS: Someone? You keep making riddles.
DIONYSUS: Someone who makes grapevines grow for human beings.   1255
PENTHEUS: The gift of wine! You reproach this god yourself!
        I want the tower gates all closed.
DIONYSUS: Can't gods leap over walls?
PENTHEUS: You're very wise. Except when you should be wise.
DIONYSUS: Wisest of all when I have to be.   1260
        Wait, though, someone's running towards us.
        He's coming from the mountain with a message.
        We'll wait, we won't try to run away.

[Enter Messenger.]

MESSENGER: Pentheus. King of Thebes.
  I come from Cithaeron,   1265
  where the white snow gleams
  and falls and never falters . . .
PENTHEUS: Is this news urgent?
MESSENGER: I've seen the holy Bacchae, the women from Thebes,
  who shot bare-legged out of the city like arrows.   1270
  I want to tell it to you, lord,
  to the entire city. It's astonishing,
  a miracle . . . May I speak freely, though?
  You have a temper, lord. I'm afraid
  of you, of your royal rage.   1275
PENTHEUS: Speak, I won't hurt you. Tell me everything.
  Being angry with an honest man is wrong.
  The more scandalous the things you tell about
  the Bacchae, though, the more the man who gave
  the women those ideas is going to suffer.   1280
MESSENGER: Our cattle were just coming up
  the last ridge to the high meadow.
  The sun was barely in the sky,
  just starting to warm the ground,
  when I saw them, the dancers, all three   1285
  troops of them, with their leaders.
  Autonoe first, then Agave, your mother,
  and finally, Ino.
  All of them were sound asleep, some
  stretched out on pine boughs,   1290
  others lying modestly here and there
  among the oak leaves, their heads on the ground.
  They were drunk with wine, but not
  the way you say, intoxicated with shrieking
  flutes and driven into ecstasies   1295
  tracking Aphrodite in the bushes.
  But then your mother, hearing
  the lowing of our stock, was on her feet,
  letting out a ritual scream, and then
  the rest of the Bacchae, in one bound,   1300
  as though with a single mind, woke,
  too, rubbing their eyes like children.
  There were old women and young,
  and unmarried girls: all wonderfully
  well disciplined. They shook their long hair   1305
  out over their shoulders. The ones whose
  fawnskin robes had slipped refastened them
  with living snakes, whose tongues
  flickered over the women's cheeks.

I saw mothers who'd abandoned babies;   1310
their breasts gorged with milk, they held
wolf cubs in their arms, or young
gazelles, and were suckling them.
Now they all put garlands on their heads,
flowering myrtle and oak leaves.   1315
Now one, with her thyrsus, strikes
a rock: living water fountains up.
Another drives her wand into the ground:
the god jets up a spring of wine.
If they wanted milk to drink,   1320
they scratched at the earth with their nails
and milk streamed for them, and pure honey
spurted from the tips of their wands.
If you had been there, sire,
if you had seen these miracles,   1325
believe me, the god whom you abuse now
you'd supplicate with prayers.

We, the shepherds and cow-tenders,
all of us there watching, were all
talking at once by then, trying   1330
to explain to one another the wonderful
and awful things they were doing.
Then someone, a wanderer, who'd spent
time in town and had a way
with words, said to us: "Listen,   1335
all of you who live up here
on the holy highlands
of the mountains, don't you want
to curry favor with the king?
Let's hunt down Agave for him   1340
and drag her from those dances."
We let him talk us into it.
We set up ambush in the brush,
camouflaged with leaves. The women,
when the time came, started dancing.   1345
Suddenly their wands were whirling,
then the women, whirling, spinning,
were crying out, "O Iacchus,
O Bromius, O son of Zeus,
O Lord of Cries,"   1350
then everything, all of them,
the whole mountain, all the wild
animals, went Bacchic, too,

nothing was unmoved; the women ran,
and it all ran with them.   1355

Agave came leaping past my hiding
place and I leaped out
to try to capture her,
but she was howling now: "Bitches,
dogs who hunt with me, it's *us*   1360
these men are hunting! Look! Follow
me! Arm yourself with thyrsi!"
Then it was we who had to run,
to keep from being torn apart.
They swooped down on our grazing   1365
cattle: bare-handed, they attacked.
Watch: a bellowing heifer, udders
gorged—a woman picks it bodily up,
and tears it limb from limb.
Watch now: full-grown cows,   1370
dismembered. Ribs,
hooves, flying this way, that way,
catching on the pine boughs,
hanging there, dribbling gore.
Even bulls, all power and arrogance,   1375
rage rising in their horns:
soft, young hands wrestle them
to the earth and flay them, faster
than your royal eyes could blink.
Then the women, like a flock of birds,   1380
soared out across the lowlands,
along the river Asopus, where the rich
cornfields of the Thebans are.
Now, at the foot of Cithaeron,
the two hamlets, Hysiae   1385
and Eurythrae, are invaded,
the women are attacking,
plundering. They tear children
from their houses, and whatever they put
on their backs stays there,   1390
without straps, even bronze and iron.
They carried fire on their hair
and weren't scorched. Now the men
had had enough: in rage, they rose,
took up their weapons. What we see   1395
next is dreadful, lord.
The men throw their spears, and draw

no blood; the women, though, let loose
their *wands,* and *wound* the men and
the men run! . . . Women defeating men!   1400
Certainly a god was in it.
The women went back then
to the springs the god had gushed
out of the earth, and washed away
the blood, the snakes licked the drops   1405
from their cheeks.
                  Master,
this god, whoever he may be,
I don't know, but welcome him to Thebes.
He's great in other ways as well,   1410
but beyond all that, they say
it's he who gave mortals wine,
which eases our suffering.
If we didn't have our wine, there
wouldn't be sexual love: what pleasure   1415
would there be for humans then?

[*Exit Messenger.*]

CHORUS LEADER: I don't know how to speak freely
    to a king: I'm afraid, but I will say it,
    I will cry it out: Dionysus is divine!
    Dionysus cedes nothing to the other gods!   1420
PENTHEUS: Everything is roaring closer, like a fire.
    This outrage of the Bacchae:
    humiliation for all Greece!
    To the gates. No time to lose.
    I want all the horses, all the shields;   1425
    every soldier who can snap a bowstring,
    every trooper who can lift a lance.
    We march on the Bacchae!
    This is beyond endurance.
    To have to suffer this from women!   1430
DIONYSUS: You pretend to listen, Pentheus,
    but you don't pay attention.
    You wronged me, but still, I'll tell you again:
    don't war against a god. Stay at peace.
    Bromius won't allow his Bacchae to be driven   1435
    from where the mountain cries in ecstasy.
PENTHEUS: Don't preach at me. You were chained, you escaped.
    Keep your freedom. Shall I punish you again?
DIONYSUS: In your place, I'd offer sacrifice to him,
    instead of sacrilege and fighting the bit.   1440
    You're mortal, he's a god.

PENTHEUS: I'll make sacrifice. Women's blood,
       pouring down the flanks of Cithaeron. As they deserve.
DIONYSUS: You'll be routed, shamed, disgraced.
       They'll lift their ivied wands,   1445
       your bronze shields will wilt.
PENTHEUS: There's no way to pin this stranger, is there?
       Chain him or unchain him, he still won't be quiet.
DIONYSUS: Listen, friend! We still can make this turn out well.
PENTHEUS: By doing what, obeying my own slaves?   1450
DIONYSUS: I'll bring the women here, with no recourse to arms.
PENTHEUS: Another of your traps.
DIONYSUS: I'll use my powers to save you: is that a trap?
PENTHEUS: You and these powers conspire to save your rituals.
DIONYSUS: I have conspired, but with the god.   1455
PENTHEUS: Bring my weapons. You: not another word.
DIONYSUS: Wait! Wouldn't you like to see them on the mountain?
PENTHEUS: See? Yes, I'd give gold to see that.
DIONYSUS: That? Why such a wild craving to see that?
PENTHEUS: I'd hate to see them drunk, if they were drunk.   1460
DIONYSUS: Even if you hate it, though, you'd like to see?
PENTHEUS: I could hide. Under the pines, and watch quietly.
DIONYSUS: Hide or not, they might sniff you out.
PENTHEUS: Yes. Let them behold me openly.
DIONYSUS: Are you ready now? Shall I take you there?   1465
PENTHEUS: Take me there. Let's not waste time.
DIONYSUS: First, put on a dress, a long, linen dress.
PENTHEUS: A dress? Do I have to be demoted to a woman?
DIONYSUS: If they see you as a man, they'll kill you.
PENTHEUS: You're right. Again. You always seem to know.   1470
DIONYSUS: Dionysus taught me what to know.
PENTHEUS: What is it you know next?
DIONYSUS: We'll go inside. I'll put you in your dress.
PENTHEUS: The dress? Still? A woman's dress? Shame.
DIONYSUS: Don't you want to see the Maenads?   1475
PENTHEUS: What sort of costume will you dress me in?
DIONYSUS: I'll put you in a wig. You'll have long curls.
PENTHEUS: Put me in a wig? . . . with long curls?
DIONYSUS: The long dress, and a net for the long curls.
PENTHEUS: Long dress . . . a net for the long curls.   1480
DIONYSUS: Then a thyrsus for your hand; and a fawnskin.
PENTHEUS: A woman's costume? No, I won't; I can't.
DIONYSUS: Blood will flow if you battle the Bacchae.
PENTHEUS: Yes, first we have to scout them out.
DIONYSUS: Better than hunting one evil with another.   1485
PENTHEUS: How get through the city, though, and not be seen?
DIONYSUS: We'll take the alleys and back ways: I'll lead you.

PENTHEUS: Just so the Bacchae can't mock me.
             Come inside now. I'll make up my mind.
DIONYSUS: As you please, you make up your mind.   1490
PENTHEUS: I'll go in, then either I'll come out in arms
             or go with you, and follow your advice.

[Exit Pentheus into the palace.]

DIONYSUS: He's in the net now, women. He'll get to see
             his Bacchae. He'll get what he deserves . . to die.
             Dionysus, you are near now; your task,   1495
             too, is near: your revenge, our vengeance.
             Make him insane. Give him ecstasy, and madness.
             In his right mind, he'd never wear that woman's dress,
             but driven from his sense, he'll slide right into it.
             I want him to be the laughingstock of Thebes,   1500
             led through the streets, costumed as a woman,
             after all the bragging that made him seem so fearsome.
             I'll go in now, I'll put him in his dress:
             he'll take it to Hades with him
             when his mother slaughters him.   1505
                                      Then, at last,
             he'll know; Dionysus is a god.
             Dionysus is the son of Zeus.
             Dionysus is, for humans, fiercest and most sweet.

[Exit Dionysus into the palace.]

CHORUS: Oh, will I, some-
           time, in the all-
             night dances, dance   1510
         again, bare-
           foot, rapt,
             again, in
         Bacchus, all
           in Bacchus,   1515
             again?

         Will I
           throw my bared
             throat
         back, to the cool   1520
           night back, the
             way,
         oh, in the green joys
           of the meadow, the
             way   1525
         a fawn

frisks, leaps,
   throws itself
as it finds itself
  safely past
    the frightening
hunters, past the
  nets, the
    houndsmen
urging on
  their straining
    hounds, free
now, leaping, tasting
  free wind now,
    being wind
now as it leaps
  the plain, the
    stream
and river, out
  at last, out from
    the human,
free, back
  into the
    green,
rich, dapple-
  shadowed tresses of the
    forest.

What is
  wisdom?
    What
the fairest
  gift the gods
    can offer
us
  below?
    What
is nobler
  than
    to hold
a dominating
  hand
    above
the bent
  head of
    the enemy?
The fair, the

1530

1535

1540

1545

1550

1555

1560

1565

1570

noble, how
  we
cherish, how
  we welcome
    them.   1575

Hardly
  stirring, hardly
    seeming   1580
to happen, it
  happens sometimes
    so
slowly, the power
  of the gods, but   1585
    it does, then,
stir, does
  come
    to pass, and,
inexorably, comes   1590
  to punish
    humans,
who honor first
  self-pride, and
    turn,   1595
their judgment
  torn, their reason
    torn,
demented, from
  the   1600
    holy.

The first step
  of the gods, it
    hardly, in
its great   1605
  time, seems
    to stir, the
first step
  of the godly hunt
    of   1610
the unholy, first
  step
    of the revenge
on those who
  put themselves   1615

    beyond
and
  over
    law.

So little
  does
    it cost
to understand
  that *this*
    has power, whatever
is divine; so
  little
    cost
to comprehend
  that what has
    long
been lawful,
  over
    centuries,
comes forever
  out
    of Nature.

What is
  wisdom?
    What
the fairest
  gift the gods
    can offer
us
  below?
    What
is nobler
  than
    to hold
a dominating
  hand
    above
the bent
  head of
    the enemy?
The fair, the
  noble, how
    we

1620

1625

1630

1635

1640

1645

1650

1655

cherish, how
  we welcome
    them.   1660

He
  is happy who,
    from the
storm, from
  the   1665
    ocean,
reaches
  harbor, and he,
    he   1670
is happy who,
  out of
    labor, out
of toil,
  has   1675
    risen. And
the one
  with wealth, and
    the one with
power surpassing   1680
  others: he
    is happy.

And hope: there
  are
    countless hopes.   1685
Hopes
  come one
    by one, some
end well and
  others   1690
    merely end.
But he who
  lives,
    day by
single day,   1695
  in
    happiness, he,
and only he,
  will I name
    blessed.   1700

[Enter Dionysus from the palace. He turns and calls back to Pentheus.]

DIONYSUS: If you still want to see what you shouldn't see,
      if you desire what shouldn't be desired, come out.
      Pentheus, come out here, let me see you.
      Maenad, Bacchant, woman: show us your long dress,
      show us how you'll scout your mother and her troop.   1705

[Enter Pentheus, dressed as a Bacchant.]

      Why, you look like one of the daughters of Cadmus.
PENTHEUS: Look! What I see! I think I see two suns
      and Thebes, too, twice: the seven-gated fortress, twice.
      And you, you seem to be a bull, out there before me,
      the double horns sprouting on your forehead: 1710
      were you an animal before, the way now you're a bull?
DIONYSUS: The god is with us now. He's not angry now.
      He's made peace. You see now what you ought to see.
PENTHEUS: What do I look like now?
      Do I stand like Ino or my mother?   1715
DIONYSUS: When I see you, I might be seeing them.
      Wait, a curl has come loose.
      I'll tuck it in its net; it must have fallen.
PENTHEUS: It must have fallen, I was in there dancing
      Bacchic dances, shaking my head backwards and forwards . . .   1720
DIONYSUS: Hold your head still now. I'll be your maid.
      I'll put the curl back, like this.
PENTHEUS: You'll put it back. Yes, I'm in your hands.
DIONYSUS: But wait, your sash has slipped. The pleats
      are disarrayed; the hem is too low.   1725
PENTHEUS: Not on the right too low; on the left, though . . .
      Watch, when I lift my left leg, this way . . .
DIONYSUS: You're going to think that I'm your closest friend,
      when you see how surprisingly chaste the Bacchae are.
PENTHEUS: Would a good Bacchant hold her thyrsus this way,   1730
      in her right hand, or like this, in her left?
DIONYSUS: The right hand, yes. Now the right leg, lift that.
      I commend your change of mind.
PENTHEUS: Tell me, could I lift Cithaeron now—
      Bacchae, cliffs, all of it: could I?   1735
DIONYSUS: You could, if you wanted to. Your mind before
      wasn't healthy, now you have the mind you should.
PENTHEUS: Will I need levers, or shall I tear the cliffs up
      with my hands and put them on my shoulders?
DIONYSUS: Now wait: don't destroy the Nymphs' groves,   1740
      the sacred places where Pan plays his flute.
PENTHEUS: You're right. One shouldn't need brute force
      to conquer women. I'll stay out of sight in the pines.

DIONYSUS: You'll have the proper hiding place to hide;
  then, when you're hidden, you'll spy on the Maenads. 1745
PENTHEUS: Yes, I can see them now, in the bushes,
  little birds, trapped in the toils of love.
DIONYSUS: That's your mission, isn't it? To keep an eye on them?
  You might catch them at it, unless they catch you . . .
PENTHEUS: Take me through Thebes now. Let all Thebes see 1750
  the single person man enough to dare all this.
DIONYSUS: You and only you will suffer for this city.
  Ordeals await you, they are fated for you.
  Come, I'll lead you there safely.
  You'll return with someone else. 1755
PENTHEUS: My mother . . .
DIONYSUS: . . . a model for all men . . .
PENTHEUS: That's my purpose.
DIONYSUS: You'll be carried home . . .
PENTHEUS: You're spoiling me! 1760
DIONYSUS: . . . in your mother's arms.
PENTHEUS: . . . No, you're *spoiling* me
DIONYSUS: Yes, I *want* to spoil you, in my way.
PENTHEUS: I'll have what I deserve.
DIONYSUS: You'll have the outcome you deserve. 1765
  You are awe-inspiring.
  Your outcome will inspire awe.
  Your fame will reach the heavens.

[Exit Pentheus towards Cithaeron.]

Agave! Listen to me! Listen to me, daughters
of Cadmus! I am calling! Hold out your hands! 1770
I lead this young man to his ordeal.
The victory will be for me, and for Bromius.
The rest will be revealed.

[Exit Dionysus.]

CHORUS: Now, hounds,
  now, 1775
   quickly, hounds
 of madness, quickly
  to the mountain,
   quickly
 to the bands 1780
  of Cadmus' daughters—
   sting
 them, goad
  them on,
   lead 1785

them to the man
    costumed
        as a woman, to
the frenzied
    spy, goad
        them. First his   1790
mother will
    see him, on
        the smooth
stone cliff, or   1795
    on his tree, will
        see him
watching, and
    will call
        the others
to her, the other   1800
    Maenads to
        be with her.
"Who is
    this?" she'll
        call. "Who   1805
is this who
    searches for
        the
daughters of   1810
    Cadmus in the
        mountain,
on our
    mountain?
        Bacchae,"   1815
she'll
    call, "*Bacchae,*
        was he
from woman
    born? *Who*
        dared   1820
spill blood to
    bear him? Surely
        not a
woman, surely   1825
    a
        lioness, yes,
not a
    woman but some
        monstrous   1830
Gorgon, from

     Lydia, a
       monster."

Justice
   now! Let justice   1835
      go
forth clearly
   now! Justice
      goes
forth with   1840
   her sword
     now!
Justice thrusts
   through
      the throat   1845
now of the
   godless, lawless
     unjust son
of Echion, earth-
   born offspring   1850
     of the snake.

No justice and no
   judgment and
     no
law has he, to   1855
   rise against
     you, Bacchic
one, against your
   secret worship
     and your   1860
mother's; with
   force, insanity,
     frenzy,
did he
   rise as   1865
     though
to conquer the
   unconquerable
     with his frenzy and
his force.   1870
   Death,
     though,
death will
   temper him and
     tame him; implacable   1875

death chastises
  minds which
    do
not understand the
  things
    of gods.   1880

To understand
  that we
    are mortal
is to live
  without insufferable
    pain.   1885

I hardly envy
  wisdom; my
    joy,   1890
instead, is
  hunting down
    those other
values, great
  and clear, that
    lead   1895
life towards
  the
    good:
to be, day-
  long, night-
    long,   1900
reverent,
  pure, and
    to
give my
  honor to
    the gods   1905
by casting
  out
    those customs
which
  are outside
    justice.   1910

Justice
  now! Justice
    goes
forth clearly   1915

now! Justice
   goes
forth with
   her sword
     now!
Justice thrusts
   through
     the throat
now of the
   godless, lawless,
     unjust son
of Echion, earth-
   born offspring
     of the snake.

A bull be,
   Bacchus, or a
     serpent, many-
headed, be,
   or a lion,
     like a flame
be. Hunt
   the hunter,
     Bacchus, hunt
him, be the
   fighter, Bacchus, now,
     throw the net
now, laughing, lethal,
   pull him
     down now, let
him fall,
   beneath
     the herd
of Maenads, let
   him fall
     now.

[Enter Messenger.]

MESSENGER: O house, O famous house:
   all Greece once thought you fortunate.
   Cadmus came from Sidon, sowing the earth-
   born dragon's harvests in the serpent's land.
   Now I, a slave, mourn for you.
CHORUS: What? What news from the Bacchae?
MESSENGER: The son of Echion, Pentheus, is dead.

1920

1925

1930

1935

1940

1945

1950

1955

1960

CHORUS: King Bromius! You
    reveal your
       greatness!
MESSENGER: What are you saying? What do these words mean?
    Does my master's anguish give you joy?   1965
CHORUS: Ecstasy, for
    us, the Asian
      strangers: no
  chains, no
    terror
      now!
MESSENGER: Do you think no men are left in Thebes?   1970
CHORUS: Dionysus now! Not
    Thebes!
      Dionysus
  has power   1975
    over
      me!
MESSENGER: I can pardon what you feel—still, women:
    rejoicing in misfortune isn't right.   1980
CHORUS: What doom, tell
    me, did he
      die,
  the tyrant, the
    man of unjust   1985
      accomplishments?
MESSENGER: When we'd marched out of Thebes, past
    the last farms, then the river Asopus, we headed
    into the hills of Cithaeron, Pentheus and I—
    I was accompanying my master—and the stranger   1990
    who was the escort for our spying mission.
    After a while we stopped: grass, a valley.
    Stay down, be quiet, watch your step—
    we want to see, not be seen. Ahead of us,
    the hills move in: cliffs, a cut,   1995
    water wandering through, pines and shade,
    and there they are, sitting quietly, the Maenads,
    peacefully working with their hands.
    A few were wreathing tendrils of ivy on a tattered
    thyrsus, some were chanting Bacchic songs   2000
    to one another, like fillies when their harnesses
    are taken off at night. Pentheus,
    though, poor Pentheus, couldn't see the women.
    "Stranger," he said, "from where we are—
    I can't make them out, the imposter Maenads.   2005

If I could climb a high pine on the cliff,
I could see their shameless orgies."

Suddenly, the stranger now: a miracle.
He reaches into the sky, and, seizing the topmost
branch of a pine tree, he drags it down,   2010
down and down, until it touches the black earth,
until it's bent, curved, the way a bow is curved,
the way a wooden rim is curved on pegs to form a wheel.

With his two hands the stranger bent it, tough
mountain pine: this wasn't mortal's work.   2015
Now, taking Pentheus, he puts him on the branches
of the pine and, sliding the trunk through his hands,
he lets it rise . . . gently, though, so it wouldn't
throw its rider. Pentheus wasn't thrown,
he rode it up until it towered   2020
into the towering air, and the Maenads
saw him . . . He didn't see them, though.

Now, suddenly, as Pentheus appeared in the sky,
the stranger vanished and a voice was in the sky—
it had to have been Dionysus—crying: 2025
"Women! I've brought the man who mocks us:
you, me, my mysteries—take revenge!"

As he cried, a light of sacred fire formed,
linking earth and heaven: the high air
suddenly went still, and everything, sky, forest,   2030
leaf and creature, everything was still.

The women, too, not sure what they had heard,
stood still, looking around them. Then the voice
again, his command, clearer now, and they heard it
now, the daughters of Cadmus; Agave, the mother   2035
of Pentheus, her sisters, all the Bacchae
heard him now, and understood, and ran,
flew, like darting doves, through the glade,
over the boiling stream, over the jagged stones.
They were soaring now, the god's breath maddening them.   2040
Finally they saw him, Pentheus, in his tree.
Scaling a cliff that towered across from him,
they pitched stones at their pitiful target,
and branches, and some even threw their thyrsi.
He was out of reach of their passion,   2045
but he was helpless, wretched, treed.
They sheared limbs from oaks then, and there they were,
with wooden levers, prying at the roots.

Again they failed. Then Agave shouted: 2050
"Maenads, here! Circle the tree! Hold on to it!
We have to catch the animal who's mounted there.
He'll reveal the secrets of the dances of the god!"
How many hands were on that tree!
They wrenched it from the ground. And he,
he fell . . . So high he was, and he was falling, 2055
moaning: he'd begun to understand his doom.

The first one at him was the priestess of the slaughter,
his own mother. She fell upon him, and he,
that she, poor Agave, might recognize him, tore
his headband off and, touching her cheek, shrieked 2060
at her: "*Me!* It's me! It's Pentheus, Mother.
Your son! You are my *mother!* Look at me!
I've made mistakes, but I'm your son: don't kill me!"

Agave was foaming at the mouth, though.
Her eyes were rolling, wild; she was mad, 2065
utterly possessed by Bacchus: what Pentheus said
was nothing to her. She took him by the arm,
the left arm, under the elbow, then she planted
a foot against his ribs and tore his arm off.
Not by herself: it was the power of the god 2070
that put so much force into her hands.

Ino was working at his other side,
clawing at the flesh. And Autonoe
and the rest of them, the whole horde of them,
were swarming over him and everything 2075
by then was one horrifying scream:
he, groaning with the little breath left in him,
they, howling in triumph. One had a forearm,
one had one of his feet, still warm in its sandal.
His ribs were stripped of flesh, and all the women, 2080
all those bloody hands, were throwing pieces of him
back and forth between them as though it were a game.

Now the body is scattered. Parts at the base
of the cliff, parts hidden in the undergrowth.
His pitiful head his mother happened on; 2085
she took it in her hands, impaled it,
like a mountain lion's, on her thyrsus,
and now she's carrying it home across Cithaeron,
leaving her sisters in the dances of the Maenads.
She's here now, in Thebes, carrying her hideous 2090
trophy, exulting, calling on her Bacchus,
her partner in the hunt, comrade in the capture—

but all her crown of victory will really be
is tears. I want away from this calamity.
I'm leaving now, before Agave reaches the palace.   2095
To know your human limits, to revere the gods,
is the noblest and I think the wisest course
that mortal men can follow.

[*Exit Messenger.*]

CHORUS: Dance
    now! Exult   2100
      and dance
now, Bacchae!
    Exult and dance the
      misery of
Pentheus, offspring   2105
    of
      the Snake, who
took a woman's
    dress, took
      the
holy   2110
    thyrsus and
      took with it the
road marked out
    by the Bull, to   2115
      Hades.

O Theban
    Bacchae! What
      a song of
victory have you   2120
    wailed, what
      triumph wailed,
a victory of tears
    and
      mourning. How   2125
lovely is
    the conflict, how
      lovely,
with one's bloody
    hand   2130
      embracing,
lovely, one's
    own
      child!
But here is Agave, here is the mother of Pentheus.   2135

Her eyes are wild. Welcome now the joyous
dancers of the God of Evohe!

[Enter Agave. She carries the head of Pentheus.]

AGAVE: Bacchae! Asians!
CHORUS: What do you
   want of
    us?   2140
AGAVE: Look what we
   have! What we
    bring home!
CHORUS: We can
   see it. I welcome you,   2145
    fellow dancer.
AGAVE: I caught it by
   myself,
    this offspring   2150
  of a savage
   lion, and with no
    net: look!
CHORUS: In what
   wilderness?   2155
AGAVE: Cithaeron . . .
CHORUS: Cithaeron? . . .
AGAVE: . . . butchered him.
CHORUS: Who
   struck him
    first?   2160
AGAVE: I
  had the honor first.
CHORUS: Blessed
   Agave!
AGAVE: So I'm called
   among my   2165
    pack!
CHORUS: No
   one else? . . .   2170
AGAVE: Cadmus . . .
CHORUS: Cadmus?
AGAVE: His daughters,
   after me,
  after I   2175
   had touched,
    touched,
  too, the
   beast. Blessed

              hunting!   2180
Now take part
in
    the feast!
CHORUS: Take
         part? Pitiful   2185
         woman!
AGAVE: Look, though,
        the bull
        is
        young, look,   2190
        his mane
        is soft, his
cheeks
    are barely
        downed.   2195
CHORUS: At least he
seems, yes,
    with
his mane, to be
    a savage   2200
    animal.
AGAVE: Our god, Bacchus,
        hunter,
        whipped,
        cunningly, his pack   2205
        of women on
        the beast!
CHORUS: Our lord god,
         yes, is a
         hunter.   2210
AGAVE: Do you praise
        me?
CHORUS: I
         praise
         you.   2215
AGAVE: And
        the Cadmeans,
        soon? . . .
CHORUS: . . . and
         your son, Pentheus . . .   2220
AGAVE: . . . will praise his
        mother for . . .
CHORUS: . . . her savage . . .
AGAVE: . . . catch, lion . . .

CHORUS: . . . born, prod-   2225
            igious . . .

AGAVE: . . . catch . . .

CHORUS: . . . caught
            prodigiously.

AGAVE: Prodigious   2230
            catch.

CHORUS: Do you
            exult?

AGAVE: I
            exult!   2235
                Greatness have
                    I
            accomplished, great
                the deeds, great
                and shining!   2240

CHORUS LEADER: Show it now, poor woman. Show your blessed trophy
        to the people. Let them behold your victory.

AGAVE: Thebans! Citizens!
            Everyone who lives beneath these high towers,
            look! Come see the beast the daughters of Cadmus   2245
            hunted down, not with nets, not with spears,
            but with the white nails of our hands.
            Who is the hunter, armed with useless spears,
            who'll dare boast now, when all needed
            were our hands to bring the creature down   2250
            and tear it completely to pieces?

            Where's my father?
            Old, good Cadmus, he should be here.
            And my child, Pentheus, find him for me, too.
            Have him bring a ladder; have him stand it   2255
            here to nail the lion's head to the cornice.
            I captured it myself, and brought it here.

*[Enter Cadmus, with attendants carrying a litter with the remains of
Pentheus.]*

CADMUS: Come this way, please . . . . Put the dreadful burden
            which was Pentheus here, before the palace.
            I've brought the body back: I searched forever.   2260
            It was in the folds of Cithaeron, torn to shreds,
            scattered through the impenetrable forest,
            no two parts of him in any single spot.
            When they described the atrocity my daughters
            had committed, I'd returned to the walls of the town   2265
            with old Tiresias: we'd been with the Bacchae.

I turned back again, up to the mountain,
where I gathered the body of this boy,
murdered by the Maenads. I saw Autonoe there,
Aristaeus' wife, the mother of poor Actaeon,   2270
and I saw Ino, both of them, still in the thickets,
pitiful women, still stung with frenzy, still insane.
Now someone has told me that Agave,
still possessed by the god, has come to Thebes . . .
And they were right, I see her,   2275
a dismal sight to have to behold.

AGAVE: Father, you can boast now; the daughters you sired
are more noble than any other mortal's.
I speak of all of us, but especially me,
who have left the loom and shuttle and risen   2280
to greatness: hunting wild creatures with my hands.

Look what I have here in my arms:
a trophy for the palace. Here, Father,
take it in your hands, glory in my kill.
Invite your friends to feast, for you   2285
are blessed, blessed by our accomplishments.

CADMUS: I cannot watch this. This is grief that has no measure.
What your poor hands accomplished was butchery.
A lovely victim you have murdered for the gods,
whom you call for Thebes and me to celebrate.   2290
Anguish for you, anguish, too, for me.
With justice, but with too much severity,
Lord Bromius, our own blood, has ruined us.

AGAVE: Complaining, scowling: old age makes men sour!
Would my son at least could be a happy hunter,   2295
like his mother, when he goes out on the chase
with his young friends from Thebes.
But all he does is struggle with the god.
Father, he needs talking to, by you.
Someone call him, let me see him.   2300
Let him see his mother, Agave the blessed.

CADMUS: Child, if consciousness should come to you
of what you've done, how grievously you'll suffer.
If you could pass your life in your present mind,
we'd never call you happy but at least   2305
you wouldn't know how miserable you are.

AGAVE: But this is wonderful! What could cause pain here?

CADMUS: First, turn your eyes upwards, towards the sky.

AGAVE: There. Why should I look into the sky, though?

CADMUS: Does the sky look the same? Might it be changing?   2310

AGAVE: Yes, it is; it's more transparent, clearer.

CADMUS: And do you still feel flurries of excitement in you?
AGAVE: I don't know what you mean . . . No . . . Yes . . .
　　　　Yes, something is changing, my mind is calmer.
CADMUS: Can you hear me? Can you answer clearly?　　　　　　2315
AGAVE: What were we saying, Father? I've forgotten.
CADMUS: In whose household did you marry?
AGAVE: You gave me to Echion, the sown-man they called him.
CADMUS: And what child did you bear your husband there?
AGAVE: Pentheus was the outcome of our marriage.　　　　　　2320
CADMUS: Now, whose head are you holding in your arms?
AGAVE: A lion's . . . The huntresses . . . They told me . . .
CADMUS: Look right at it. One look will be enough.
AGAVE: What? What am I seeing? What is in my hands?
CADMUS: Look carefully. Study it more closely.　　　　　　　2325
AGAVE: I see horror. I see suffering. I see grief.
CADMUS: Does it still look like a lion?
AGAVE: No, Pentheus: I am holding his head.
CADMUS: Yes, now you know, I mourn Pentheus.
AGAVE: Who killed him? Why is he in *my* hands?　　　　　　2330
CADMUS: Savage truth, how long you took to come to light.
AGAVE: Tell me, my heart is trembling with it.
CADMUS: You killed him. With your sisters.
AGAVE: Where did it happen? At home? Where?
CADMUS: Where Actaeon was dismembered by his hounds.　　　　2335
AGAVE: On Cithaeron? Why was my poor Pentheus there?
CADMUS: He went to mock the gods, and your rituals.
AGAVE: But we, why were we there?
CADMUS: You were mad. The city was possessed by Dionysus.
AGAVE: I see now. Dionysus has destroyed us.　　　　　　　2340
CADMUS: You enraged him. You denied he was god.
AGAVE: My son's beloved body, where is it, Father?
CADMUS: There he is, what I could find of him.
AGAVE: Is he decently put back together?
　　　　Why did Pentheus have to suffer for my madness?　　　2345
CADMUS: He, too, refused the god, and the god,
　　　　for this, has ruined us all—
　　　　you, this boy: our whole house is ruined.
　　　　And I, with no male heirs, have to see him now,
　　　　this branching of your womb, the new light　　　　　2350
　　　　of our house, shamefully destroyed.

　　　　O child, you held our house together, you,
　　　　my daughter's son, how the city was in awe of you.
　　　　No one looking at your face would dare affront my age—
　　　　you'd have punished them as they deserved.　　　　　2355
　　　　Now I'll be exiled, my honors stripped from me.

I, the great Cadmus, sower of the race of Thebes,
who harvested the most lovely of harvests.
O dearest of men, you are no longer living
but you are still, child, among those I love   2360
beyond all else. Who will stroke my beard now?
Who embrace me, call me Grandfather, ask me,
"Has anyone offended you, old man, not shown you
adequate respect? Disturbed, dishonored you?
Tell me who it was, Grandfather, I'll punish him."   2365
Now I am nothing. You, a ruin. Your mother
only to be pitied, and her unhappy sisters, too.
Is there anyone who scorns the gods? Look now
at this murdered boy: now, believe!

CHORUS LEADER: I grieve with you, Cadmus: your daughter's son   2370
    has justice now, but so much grief for you.

AGAVE: Father, look at me, how my destiny has turned.

[She kneels to the body of Pentheus.]

Who is this person? Who is this corpse?
Who am I? How can I, in all reverence,
knowing that my hands dismembered him   2375
and are polluted with his blood,
dare to touch him, dare take him
to my breast, dare sing his dirge to him?
But how can I not? What other hands
can care for you, my child?   2380

O old man, come help me, help me
touch this wretched boy. Show me
where to lay his head, show me how
to put his body back together.

Look, his arms are so well muscled,   2385
his legs so strong, but his face, oh,
dearest face, its cheek is barely feathered.
This flesh I nurtured once, I kiss.
The fragments of this body I loved
once, I lay in place.   2390

How am I doing this? How can I touch
my crime with my polluted hands?
With what robes shall I veil you, child?
Here: I'll give you mine. I'll hide your head.
Here, hide your shattered, bloodstained body.   2395

[She covers the body with her veil. Dionysus appears, as himself, above.]

DIONYSUS: I am Dionysus. I am Bacchus.
　　　　　　Bromius and Iacchus.
　　　　　　Dithyrambus and Evius.
　　　　　　I am the son of Zeus.
　　　　　　I have come to the country of the Thebans,   2400
　　　　　　where Semele, the daughter of King Cadmus,
　　　　　　bore me in a blaze of lightning.
　　　　　　When I arrived in Thebes, there was blasphemy.
　　　　　　"He was born of mortals," they were saying.
　　　　　　Slander. Irreverence. Impiety.   2405
　　　　　　I offered these people everything.
　　　　　　How did they repay my generosity?
　　　　　　With malice, ingratitude, and lies.

　　　　　　Now I shall recite your future for you.
　　　　　　First, your future will be suffering.   2410
　　　　　　Then your future will be suffering again.
　　　　　　Banishment and slavery and pain.
　　　　　　You will be driven from this city.
　　　　　　You will be hounded into other lands.
　　　　　　Captives in a war.   2415
　　　　　　Chains. Slavery. Toil.
　　　　　　Your lives will wear away like sand.

　　　　　　Behold our Pentheus. He found the death
　　　　　　he deserved: torn to pieces.

　　　　　　You beheld him. You beheld his lies.   2420
　　　　　　His impudence. You beheld him
　　　　　　when he tried to chain me and abused me
　　　　　　and tried—and *dared* to try—
　　　　　　to punish me.
　　　　　　I am Dionysus! Behold me!   2425

　　　　　　The hands that should have been the last
　　　　　　to do this to him were the very hands
　　　　　　that did it. Why? Because he did
　　　　　　what he should not have done.

　　　　　　And now your doom, Agave, is this: 2430
　　　　　　for you and for your sisters—exile.
　　　　　　You must expiate your crime.
　　　　　　You are polluted, you cannot stay
　　　　　　in the precincts of these graves.

　　　　　　And Cadmus: there are ordeals for you.   2435
　　　　　　You will be transfigured into a snake.
　　　　　　And Harmonia, the daughter of Ares, whom you won

as wife despite your being mortal,
she, too, will be a beast, a snake.
Then both of you, drawn by oxen in a cart,   2440
will, according to the oracle of Zeus,
lead an innumerable barbarian horde
to lay waste cities, to ravage and destroy.
And when the shrine of Apollo is sacked,
the hordes will turn, and the turning   2445
and the coming back, will be tragic.

Ares, in the end, will save you and save
Harmonia and bring your lives
into the country of the blessed.

This is the decree of Dionysus,   2450
the son not of a human but of Zeus.
If you had understood your mortal natures
when you refused to understand them,
the son of Zeus would have been your ally.
You would now be in blessedness.   2455

CADMUS: Dionysus, we implore you, we have offended.
DIONYSUS: You learned too late to know me.
When you had time, you did not know me.
CADMUS: We confess that, but your punishment is harsh.
DIONYSUS: I am a god! You outraged my divinity.   2460
CADMUS: Gods should not resemble mortals in anger.
DIONYSUS: Long ago, my father, Zeus, ordained all this.
AGAVE: Father, the sentence is decreed: banishment.
DIONYSUS: Why do you delay your doom?
CADMUS: Oh, my child, to what a terrible fate   2465
have we been reduced.
You, your pitiful sisters, and myself, all wretched.
An old man, to have to live a stranger among strangers.
There is an oracle as well that I will lead
a ragged barbarian army against Hellas. My wife,   2470
Harmonia, the daughter of Ares, will be a savage snake,
and I, too, will be a snake, and against the altars
and the graves of Greece will lead those spears.
And no respite. I will cross the river Acheron,[23]
as it plunges down, and have, still, no peace.   2475
AGAVE: And me, O Father, banishment!
To be torn from you!

---

23. The Acheron River was said to form one of
    the boundaries of the underworld.

CADMUS: My poor child, why put your arms around me?
  A white swan sheltering its hoary, helpless father.
AGAVE: Tell me, where shall I go, outcast from my country?   2480
CADMUS: I don't know, child. Your father is no help.
AGAVE: Farewell, my house; farewell,
  my country. Banished from my home,
  exiled from everything I love.
  What is left for me?   2485
CADMUS: Poor daughter: go to Aristaeus, Actaeon's father.
AGAVE: I am mourning for you, Father.
CADMUS: And I, daughter, these tears are for you,
  and for your sisters.
AGAVE: How terrible the blows Dionysus   2490
  struck against your house.
DIONYSUS: I suffered terribly,
  my name, in Thebes, deprived of honor.
AGAVE: Goodbye, Father.
CADMUS: Child, poor child, farewell.   2495
  Faring well, though, will be hard for you.
AGAVE: Take me away from here, to my sisters,
  the sisters of my endless exile.
  Let awful Cithaeron never see me again.
  Let me never set my eyes on Cithaeron again,   2500
  and let me never see another thyrsus,
  to bring this back to me again.

  All of that I leave, all
  of it, to other Bacchae.

  [Exit Agave.]

CHORUS: Many forms are   2505
  there of the
   divine.
  Many things the
   gods accomplish
   unexpectedly.   2510
  What we waited
   for does not
   come to pass, while
  for what remained
   undreamed the god   2515
   finds ways.
  Just such
   doing was this
   doing.

  [Exit all.]

VERGIL (70–19 B.C.E.)
Rome

Vergil (Latin name Publius Vergilius Maro) channeled his genius and ambition exclusively through traditional Greek genres, but his poems reinvent the themes and forms they inherit in the service of Roman politics, culture, and ideology. The *Aeneid*, Vergil's last monumental work and the labor of a decade, is inspired simultaneously by the *Iliad* and the *Odyssey* and composed in dactylic hexameter. In twelve books, Vergil follows his eponymous hero from the smoking ruins of Troy to the shores of Italy, where Aeneas becomes the living link between the legendary Homeric age and the Rome in which Vergil lived and wrote, then at the crucial moment of its transition to empire.

Like Odysseus, (and Gilgamesh before him), Aeneas must voyage and endure; like Achilles, his half-human, half-divine nature meets its greatest challenges in combat and the clash of arms. But while the self-awareness of the Homeric heroes exalts them, Aeneas displays a far more modern consciousness. Both a maker and an agent of history, Aeneas is burdened by the fate that selects him as Rome's glorious progenitor. Caught between obligations to the past and to the future, Aeneas puts collective values before personal goals, accepting responsibility for ends that he can neither control nor wholly envision. Nowhere is this more evident than in Book 4, where Aeneas must choose between his love for Dido, queen of Carthage, and his destiny. Vergil's orchestration of Trojan past, Roman future, and vivid psychological present created an imperial mythology for Augustus Caesar, Vergil's patron and the first Roman emperor. Yet Vergil's celebration of Roman triumph is also suffused with a sense of its price: above all, of the pity of war. The profundity and virtuosity of Vergil's epic, combined with the longevity of Roman influence and the Latin language in European civilization, make the *Aeneid* the most influential single poem in Western literature.

from *Aeneid*

Book 4 [The Passion of the Queen[1]]

The queen, for her part, all that evening ached[1]
With longing that her heart's blood fed, a wound
Or inward fire eating her away.

Translated by Robert Fitzgerald.

---

1. Aeneas, son of Aphrodite and the Trojan Anchises (see the *Homeric Hymn to Aphrodite*), escapes the sack of Troy and, at the gods' urging, sails for Italy with a group of comrades in order to build a new settlement of Trojan descendants there. Driven by stormwinds to the coast of North Africa, the fleet lands at Carthage, a city recently founded by Queen Dido, a daughter of the ruling family of Tyre in Phoenicia. Dido has recently fled her native city after her brother's treacherous murder of her husband. and, sympathetic to the distress of the homeless Trojans, receives them hospitably. Aeneas recounts to her the destruction of Troy and the subsequent wanderings of his band of survivors until their arrival in Carthage.

The manhood of the man, his pride of birth,
Came home to her time and again; his looks,   5
His words remained with her to haunt her mind,
And desire for him gave her no rest.
                                        When Dawn
Swept earth with Phoebus' torch and burned away
Night-gloom and damp, this queen, far gone and ill,
Confided to the sister of her heart: 10
"My sister Anna, quandaries and dreams
Have come to frighten me—such dreams!
                                        Think what a stranger
Yesterday found lodging in our house:
How princely, how courageous, what a soldier.
I can believe him in the line of gods,   15
And this is no delusion. Tell-tale fear
Betrays inferior souls. What scenes of war
Fought to the bitter end he pictured for us!
What buffetings awaited him at sea!
Had I not set my face against remarriage   20
After my first love died and failed me, left me
Barren and bereaved—and sick to death
At the mere thought of torch and bridal bed—
I could perhaps give way in this one case
To frailty. I shall say it: since that time   25
Sychaeus, my poor husband, met his fate,
And blood my brother shed stained our hearth gods,
This man alone has wrought upon me so
And moved my soul to yield. I recognize
The signs of the old flame, of old desire.   30
But O chaste life, before I break your laws,
I pray that Earth may open, gape for me
Down to its depth, or the omnipotent
With one stroke blast me to the shades, pale shades
Of Erebus[2] and the deep world of night!   35
That man who took me to himself in youth
Has taken all my love; may that man keep it,
Hold it forever with him in the tomb."
At this she wept and wet her breast with tears.
But Anna answered:
                        "Dearer to your sister   40
Than daylight is, will you wear out your life,
Young as you are, in solitary mourning,
Never to know sweet children, or the crown
Of joy that Venus brings? Do you believe

---

2. The underworld.

This matters to the dust, to ghosts in tombs?
Granted no suitors up to now have moved you,
Neither in Libya nor before, in Tyre—
Iarbas[3] you rejected, and the others,
Chieftains bred by the land of Africa
Their triumphs have enriched—will you contend
Even against a welcome love? Have you
Considered in whose lands you settled here?
On one frontier the Gaetulans,[4] their cities,
People invincible in war—with wild
Numidian horsemen, and the offshore banks,
The Syrtës; on the other, desert sands,
Bone-dry, where fierce Barcaean nomads range.
Or need I speak of future wars brought on
From Tyre, and the menace of your brother?
Surely by dispensation of the gods
And backed by Juno's will, the ships from Ilium[5]
Held their course this way on the wind.

                    Sister,
What a great city you'll see rising here,
And what a kingdom, from this royal match!
With Trojan soldiers as companions in arms
By what exploits will Punic[6] glory grow!
Only ask the indulgence of the gods,
Win them with offerings, give your guests ease,
And contrive reasons for delay, while winter
Gales rage, drenched Orion storms at sea,
And their ships, damaged still, face iron skies."
This counsel fanned the flame, already kindled,
Giving her hesitant sister hope, and set her
Free of scruple. Visiting the shrines
They begged for grace at every altar first,
Then put choice rams and ewes to ritual death
For Ceres Giver of Laws,[7] Father Lyaeus,
Phoebus, and for Juno most of all
Who has the bonds of marriage in her keeping.
Dido herself, splendidly beautiful,
Holding a shallow cup, tips out the wine

45

50

55

60

65

70

75

80

---

3. Iarbas was a North African king and an
   unsuccessful suitor of the widowed Queen
   Dido.
4. The people of Iarbas's kingdom.
5. Troy.
6. Phoenician.
7. Ceres was the Roman goddess of agricultural fertility. She was called "lawgiver"
presumably because of her regulation of the
processes of agriculture. Lyaeus is an epithet of Dionysus, or Bacchus, also a deity
associated with fertility (see Euripides' *Bacchae* in this section). Juno, daughter of
Saturn and wife of the supreme deity, Jupiter, is especially associated with marriage
and domesticity.

On a white shining heifer, between the horns,
Or gravely in the shadow of the gods
Approaches opulent altars. Through the day
She brings new gifts, and when the breasts are opened   85
Pores over organs, living still, for signs.
Alas, what darkened minds have soothsayers!
What good are shrines and vows to maddened lovers?
The inward fire eats the soft marrow away,
And the internal wound bleeds on in silence.   90
Unlucky Dido, burning, in her madness
Roamed through all the city, like a doe
Hit by an arrow shot from far away
By a shepherd hunting in the Cretan woods—
Hit by surprise, nor could the hunter see   95
His flying steel had fixed itself in her;
But though she runs for life through copse and glade
The fatal shaft clings to her side.
                        Now Dido
Took Aeneas with her among her buildings,
Showed her Sidonian wealth, her walls prepared,   100
And tried to speak, but in mid-speech grew still.
When the day waned she wanted to repeat
The banquet as before, to hear once more
In her wild need the throes of Ilium,
And once more hung on the narrator's words.   105
Afterward, when all the guests were gone,
And the dim moon in turn had quenched her light,
And setting stars weighed weariness to sleep,
Alone she mourned in the great empty hall
And pressed her body on the couch he left: 110
She heard him still, though absent—heard and saw him.
Or she would hold Ascanius[8] in her lap,
Enthralled by him, the image of his father,
As though by this ruse to appease a love
Beyond all telling.
                        Towers, half-built, rose   115
No farther; men no longer trained in arms
Or toiled to make harbors and battlements
Impregnable. Projects were broken off,
Laid over, and the menacing huge walls
With cranes unmoving stood against the sky.   120
As soon as Jove's[9] dear consort saw the lady
Prey to such illness, and her reputation

---

8. Aeneas' son, also called Iulus; his mother
Creusa died in the sack of Troy.

9. Jupiter, supreme deity of the Roman pantheon.

Standing no longer in the way of passion,
Saturn's daughter said to Venus:
                              "Wondrous!
Covered yourself with glory, have you not,   125
You and your boy, and won such prizes, too.
Divine power is something to remember
If by collusion of two gods one mortal
Woman is brought low.
                    I am not blind.
Your fear of our new walls has not escaped me,   130
Fear and mistrust of Carthage at her height,
But how far will it go? What do you hope for,
Being so contentious? Why do we not
Arrange eternal peace and formal marriage?
You have your heart's desire: Dido in love,   135
Dido consumed with passion to her core.
Why not, then, rule this people side by side
With equal authority? And let the queen
Wait on her Phrygian[10] lord, let her consign
Into your hand her Tyrians as a dowry."   140
Now Venus knew this talk was all pretence,
All to divert the future power from Italy
To Libya; and she answered:
                        "Who would be
So mad, so foolish as to shun that prospect
Or prefer war with you? That is, provided   145
Fortune is on the side of your proposal.
The fates here are perplexing: would one city
Satisfy Jupiter's will for Tyrians
And Trojan exiles? Does he approve
A union and a mingling of these races?   150
You are his consort: you have every right
To sound him out. Go on, and I'll come, too."
But regal Juno pointedly replied:
"That task will rest with me. Just now, as to
The need of the moment and the way to meet it,   155
Listen, and I'll explain in a few words.
Aeneas and Dido in her misery
Plan hunting in the forest, when the Titan
Sun comes up with rays to light the world.
While beaters in excitement ring the glens   160
My gift will be a black raincloud, and hail,

[handwritten margin note: Venus knows what Juno's plans.]

---

10. Troy was situated in Phrygia, a large terri-
    tory in Anatolia, in northwestern Asia
    Minor.

A downpour, and I'll shake heaven with thunder.
The company will scatter, lost in gloom,
As Dido and the Trojan captain come
To one same cavern. I shall be on hand,
And if I can be certain you are willing,
There I shall marry them and call her his.
A wedding, this will be."

Juno – the Goddess of Marriage

                Then Cytherea,[11]
Not disinclined, nodded to Juno's plea,
And smiled at the stratagem now given away.   170
Dawn came up meanwhile from the Ocean stream,
And in the early sunshine from the gates
Picked huntsmen issued: wide-meshed nets and snares,
Broad spearheads for big game, Massylian horsemen
Trooping with hounds in packs keen on the scent.   175
But Dido lingered in her hall, as Punic
Nobles waited, and her mettlesome hunter
Stood nearby, cavorting in gold and scarlet,
Champing his foam-flecked bridle. At long last
The queen appeared with courtiers in a crowd,   180
A short Sidonian cloak edged in embroidery
Caught about her, at her back a quiver
Sheathed in gold, her hair tied up in gold,
And a brooch of gold pinning her scarlet dress.
Phrygians came in her company as well,   185
And Iulus, joyous at the scene. Resplendent
Above the rest, Aeneas walked to meet her,
To join his retinue with hers. He seemed—
Think of the lord Apollo in the spring
When he leaves wintering in Lycia   190
By Xanthus'[12] torrent, for his mother's isle
Of Delos, to renew the festival;
Around his altars Cretans, Dryopës,
And painted Agathyrsans raise a shout,
But the god walks the Cynthian ridge alone   195
And smooths his hair, binds it in fronded laurel,
Braids it in gold; and shafts ring on his shoulders.
So elated and swift, Aeneas walked
With sunlit grace upon him.
                Soon the hunters,
Riding in company to high pathless hills,   200
Saw mountain goats shoot down from a rocky peak

---

11. An epithet of Venus, who was especially
associated with the island of Cythera (see
the *Homeric Hymn to Aphrodite*).

12. A river in the Trojan plain.

And scamper on the ridges; toward the plain
Deer left the slopes, herding in clouds of dust
In flight across the open lands. Alone,
The boy Ascanius, delightedly riding   205
His eager horse amid the lowland vales,
Outran both goats and deer. Could he only meet
Amid the harmless game some foaming boar,
Or a tawny lion down from the mountainside!
Meanwhile in heaven began a rolling thunder,   210
And soon the storm broke, pouring rain and hail.
Then Tyrians and Trojans in alarm—
With Venus' Dardan grandson[13]—ran for cover
Here and there in the wilderness, as freshets
Coursed from the high hills.
                    Now to the self-same cave   215
Came Dido and the captain of the Trojans.
Primal Earth herself and Nuptial Juno
Opened the ritual, torches of lightning blazed,
High Heaven became witness to the marriage,
And nymphs cried out wild hymns from a mountain top.   220
That day was the first cause of death, and first
Of sorrow. Dido had no further qualms
As to impressions given and set abroad;
She thought no longer of a secret love
But called it marriage. Thus, under that name,   225
She hid her fault.
                 Now in no time at all
Through all the African cities Rumor goes—
Nimble as quicksilver among evils.

                                    . . .

In those days Rumor took an evil joy
At filling countrysides with whispers, whispers,   230
Gossip of what was done, and never done:
How this Aeneas landed, Trojan born,
How Dido in her beauty graced his company,
Then how they reveled all the winter long
Unmindful of the realm, prisoners of lust.   235
These tales the scabrous goddess put about
On men's lips everywhere. Her twisting course
Took her to King Iarbas, whom she set
Ablaze with anger piled on top of anger.

Handwritten margin notes: Dido is having an affair. Juno arranged this marriage. This is not a real marriage; Virgil thinks marriage is. Dido feels. Dido & Aeneas are having a love affair.

---

13. Ascanius, whose grandfather Anchises was
a Dardanian prince.

. . . Before his altars 240
King Iarbas, crazed by the raw story,
Stood, they say, amid the Presences,
With supplicating hands, pouring out prayer:
"All powerful Jove, to whom the feasting Moors
At ease on colored couches tip their wine, 245
Do you see this? Are we then fools to fear you
Throwing down your bolts? Those dazzling fires
Of lightning, are they aimless in the clouds
And rumbling thunder meaningless? This woman
Who turned up in our country and laid down 250
A tiny city at a price, to whom
I gave a beach to plow—and on my terms—
After refusing to marry me has taken
Aeneas to be master in her realm.
And now Sir Paris[14] with his men, half-men, 255
His chin and perfumed hair tied up
In a Maeonian[15] bonnet, takes possession.
As for ourselves, here we are bringing gifts
Into these shrines—supposedly your shrines—
Hugging that empty fable."
                 Pleas like this 260
From the man clinging to his altars reached
The ears of the Almighty. Now he turned
His eyes upon the queen's town and the lovers
Careless of their good name; then spoke to Mercury,[16]
Assigning him a mission:
                 "Son, bestir yourself, 265
Call up the Zephyrs, take to your wings and glide.
Approach the Dardan captain where he tarries
Rapt in Tyrian Carthage, losing sight
Of future towns the fates ordain. Correct him,
Carry my speech to him on the running winds: 270
No son like this did his enchanting mother
Promise to us, nor such did she deliver
Twice from peril at the hands of Greeks.
He was to be the ruler of Italy,
Potential empire, armorer of war; 275
To father men from Teucer's noble blood[17]
And bring the whole world under law's dominion.
If glories to be won by deeds like these

---

14. Iarbas identifies Aeneas with his Trojan relative Paris, whose seduction of his host Menelaos's wife Helen started the Trojan War.

15. Phrygian.

16. Mercury was known as the divine messenger.

17. Teucer was the first Trojan king.

[handwritten note: The God Jove is very different from Zeus. He is very strict, wants duty + loyalty. Achilles allows passion to rule him.]

Cannot arouse him, if he will not strive
For his own honor, does he begrudge his son,
Ascanius, the high strongholds of Rome?
What has he in mind? What hope, to make him stay   280
Amid a hostile race and lose from view
Ausonian progeny,[18] Lavinian lands?
The man should sail: that is the whole point.   285
Let this be what you tell him, as from me."
He finished and fell silent. Mercury
Made ready to obey the great command
Of his great father, and he first tied on
The golden sandals, winged, that high in air   290
Transport him over seas or over land
Abreast of gale winds; then he took the wand
With which he summons pale souls out of Orcus[19]
And ushers others to the undergloom,
Lulls men to slumber or awakens them,   295
And open dead men's eyes.

Alighting tiptoe
On the first hutments, there he found Aeneas
Laying foundations for new towers and homes.
He noted well the swordhilt the man wore,
Adorned with yellow jasper; and the cloak   300
Aglow with Tyrian dye upon his shoulders—
Gifts of the wealthy queen, who had inwoven
Gold thread in the fabric. Mercury
Took him to task at once:

                              "Is it for you
To lay the stones for Carthage's high walls,   305
Tame husband that you are, and build their city?
Oblivious of your own world, your own kingdom!
From bright Olympus he that rules the gods
And turns the earth and heaven by his power—
He and no other sent me to you, told me   310
To bring this message on the running winds:
What have you in mind? What hope, wasting your days
In Libya? If future history's glories
Do not affect you, if you will not strive
For your own honor, think of Ascanius,   315
Think of the expectations of your heir,
Iulus, to whom the Italian realm, the land

---

18. The Ausonians were early inhabitants of
    southern Italy; Ausonia refers to Italy in
    general.

19. Like Erebus, Orcus was one of the names
    for the underworld.

Of Rome, are due."
                          And Mercury, as he spoke,
Departed from the visual field of mortals
To a great distance, ebbed in subtle air.   320
Amazed, and shocked to the bottom of his soul
By what his eyes had seen, Aeneas felt
His hackles rise, his voice choke in his throat.
As the sharp admonition and command
From heaven had shaken him awake, he now   325
Burned only to be gone, to leave that land
Of the sweet life behind. What can he do? How tell
The impassioned queen and hope to win her over?
What opening shall he choose? This way and that
He let his mind dart, testing alternatives,   330
Running through every one. And as he pondered
This seemed the better tactic: he called in
Mnestheus, Sergestus and stalwart Serestus,
Telling them:
                  "Get the fleet ready for sea,
But quietly, and collect the men on shore.   335
Lay in ship stores and gear."
        As to the cause
For a change of plan, they were to keep it secret,
Seeing the excellent Dido had no notion,
No warning that such love could be cut short;
He would himself look for the right occasion,   340
The easiest time to speak, the way to do it.
The Trojans to a man gladly obeyed.
The queen, for her part, felt some plot afoot
Quite soon—for who deceives a woman in love?
She caught wind of a change, being in fear   345
Of what had seemed her safety. Evil Rumor,
Shameless as before, brought word to her
In her distracted state of ships being rigged
In trim for sailing. Furious, at her wits' end,
She traversed the whole city, all aflame   350
With rage, like a Bacchantë driven wild[20]
By emblems shaken, when the mountain revels
Of the odd year possess her, when the cry
Of Bacchus rises and Cithaeron calls
All through the shouting night. Thus it turned out   355
She was the first to speak and charge Aeneas:

---

20. Bacchantes were worshippers of the god
    Bacchus.

"You even hoped to keep me in the dark
As to this outrage, did you, two-faced man,
And slip away in silence? Can our love
Not hold you, can the pledge we gave not hold you,   360
Can Dido not, now sure to die in pain?
Even in winter weather must you toil
With ships, and fret to launch against high winds
For the open sea? Oh, heartless!
                              Tell me now,
If you were not in search of alien lands   365
And new strange homes, if ancient Troy remained,
Would ships put out for Troy on these big seas?
Do you go to get away from me? I beg you,
By these tears, by your own right hand, since I
Have left my wretched self nothing but that—   370
Yes, by the marriage that we entered on,
If ever I did well and you were grateful
Or found some sweetness in a gift from me,
Have pity now on a declining house!
Put this plan by, I beg you, if a prayer   375
Is not yet out of place.
Because of you, Libyans and nomad kings
Detest me, my own Tyrians are hostile;
Because of you, I lost my integrity
And that admired name by which alone   380
I made my way once toward the stars.
                         To whom
Do you abandon me, a dying woman,
Guest that you are—the only name now left
From that of husband? Why do I live on?
Shall I, until my brother Pygmalion comes   385
To pull my walls down? Or the Gaetulan
Iarbas leads me captive? If at least
There were a child by you for me to care for,
A little one to play in my courtyard
And give me back Aeneas, in spite of all,   390
I should not feel so utterly defeated,
Utterly bereft."
                 She ended there.
The man by Jove's command held fast his eyes
And fought down the emotion in his heart.
At length he answered:
                    "As for myself, be sure   395
I never shall deny all you can say,
Your majesty, of what you meant to me.

[handwritten margin note: Dido's people are mad at her b/c of Aeneas]

Never will the memory of Elissa[21]
Stale for me, while I can still remember
My own life, and the spirit rules my body.
As to the event, a few words. Do not think
I meant to be deceitful and slip away.
I never held the torches of a bridegroom,
Never entered upon the pact of marriage.
If Fate permitted me to spend my days
By my own lights, and make the best of things
According to my wishes, first of all
I should look after Troy and the loved relics
Left me of my people. Priam's great hall
Should stand again; I should have restored the tower
Of Pergamum[22] for Trojans in defeat.
But now it is the rich Italian land
Apollo tells me I must make for: Italy,
Named by his oracles. There is my love;
There is my country. If, as a Phoenician,
You are so given to the charms of Carthage,
Libyan city that it is, then tell me,
Why begrudge the Teucrians new lands
For homesteads in Ausonia? Are we not
Entitled, too, to look for realms abroad?
Night never veils the earth in damp and darkness,
Fiery stars never ascend the east,
But in my dreams my father's troubled ghost[23]
Admonishes and frightens me. Then, too,
Each night thoughts come of young Ascanius,
My dear boy wronged, defrauded of his kingdom,
Hesperian lands of destiny. And now
The gods' interpreter, sent by Jove himself—
I swear it by your head and mine—has brought
Commands down through the racing winds! I say
With my own eyes in full daylight I saw him
Entering the building! With my very ears
I drank his message in! So please, no more
Of these appeals that set us both afire.
I sail for Italy not of my own free will."
During all this she had been watching him
With face averted, looking him up and down

400

405

415

420

425

430

435

---

21. Another name for Dido.
22. An important citadel in northwest Asia
Minor near Troy and, in myth, allied with
the Trojan cause.

23. Aeneas's father Anchises died during
their early wanderings, after they escaped the sack of Troy.

In silence, and she burst out raging now:
"No goddess was your mother. Dardanus
Was not the founder of your family.
Liar and cheat! Some rough Caucasian cliff
Begot you on flint. Hyrcanian tigresses
Tendered their teats to you. Why should I palter?
Why still hold back for more indignity?
Sigh, did he, while I wept? Or look at me?
Or yield a tear, or pity her who loved him?
What shall I say first, with so much to say?
The time is past when either supreme Juno
Or the Saturnian father[24] viewed these things
With justice. Faith can never be secure.
I took the man in, thrown up on this coast
In dire need, and in my madness then
Contrived a place for him in my domain,
Rescued his lost fleet, saved his shipmates' lives.
Oh, I am swept away burning by furies!
Now the prophet Apollo, now his oracles,
Now the gods' interpreter, if you please,
Sent down by Jove himself, brings through the air
His formidable commands! What fit employment
For heaven's high powers! What anxieties
To plague serene immortals! I shall not
Detain you or dispute your story. Go,
Go after Italy on the sailing winds,
Look for your kingdom, cross the deepsea swell!
If divine justice counts for anything,
I hope and pray that on some grinding reef
Midway at sea you'll drink your punishment
And call and call on Dido's name!
From far away I shall come after you
With my black fires, and when cold death has parted
Body from soul I shall be everywhere
A shade to haunt you! You will pay for this,
Unconscionable! I shall hear! The news will reach me
Even among the lowest of the dead!"
At this abruptly she broke off and ran
In sickness from his sight and the light of day,
Leaving him at a loss, alarmed, and mute
With all he meant to say. The maids in waiting

440

445

450

455

460

465

470

475

---

24. Jupiter, son of Saturn.

Caught her as she swooned and carried her   480
To bed in her marble chamber.

                    Duty-bound,
Aeneas, though he struggled with desire
To calm and comfort her in all her pain,
To speak to her and turn her mind from grief,   485
And though he sighed his heart out, shaken still
With love of her, yet took the course heaven gave him
And went back to the fleet. Then with a will
The Teucrians fell to work and launched the ships
Along the whole shore: slick with tar each hull   490
Took to the water. Eager to get away,
The sailors brought oar-boughs out of the woods
With leaves still on, and oaken logs unhewn.
Now you could see them issuing from the town
To the water's edge in streams, as when, aware   495
Of winter, ants will pillage a mound of spelt
To store it in their granary; over fields
The black battalion moves, and through the grass
On a narrow trail they carry off the spoil;
Some put their shoulders to the enormous weight   500
Of a trundled grain, while some pull stragglers in
And castigate delay; their to-and-fro
Of labor makes the whole track come alive.
At that sight, what were your emotions, Dido?
Sighing how deeply, looking out and down   505
From your high tower on the seething shore
Where all the harbor filled before your eyes
With bustle and shouts! Unconscionable Love,
To what extremes will you not drive our hearts!
She now felt driven to weep again, again   510
To move him, if she could, by supplication,
Humbling her pride before her love—to leave
Nothing untried, not to die needlessly.
"Anna, you see the arc of waterfront
All in commotion: they come crowding in   515
From everywhere. Spread canvas calls for wind,
The happy crews have garlanded the sterns.
If I could brace myself for this great sorrow,
Sister, I can endure it, too. One favor,
Even so, you may perform for me.   520
Since that deserter chose you for his friend
And trusted you, even with private thoughts,
Since you alone know when he may be reached,
Go, intercede with our proud enemy.

Remind him that I took no oath at Aulis[25]   525
With Danaans to destroy the Trojan race;
I sent no ship to Pergamum. Never did I
Profane his father Anchisës' dust and shade.
Why will he not allow my prayers to fall
On his unpitying ears? Where is he racing?   530
Let him bestow one last gift on his mistress:
This, to await fair winds and easier flight.
Now I no longer plead the bond he broke
Of our old marriage, nor do I ask that he
Should live without his dear love, Latium,[26]   535
Or yield his kingdom. Time is all I beg,
Mere time, a respite and a breathing space
For madness to subside in, while my fortune
Teaches me how to take defeat and grieve.
Pity your sister. This is the end, this favor—   540
To be repaid with interest when I die."
She pleaded in such terms, and such, in tears,
Her sorrowing sister brought him, time and again.
But no tears moved him, no one's voice would he
Attend to tractably. The fates opposed it;   545
God's will blocked the man's once kindly ears.
And just as when the north winds from the Alps
This way and that contend among themselves
To tear away an oaktree hale with age,
The wind and tree cry, and the buffeted trunk   550
Showers high foliage to earth, but holds
On bedrock, for the roots go down as far
Into the underworld as cresting boughs
Go up in heaven's air: just so this captain,
Buffeted by a gale of pleas   555
This way and that way, dinned all the day long,
Felt their moving power in his great heart,
And yet his will stood fast; tears fell in vain.
On Dido in her desolation now
Terror grew at her fate. She prayed for death,   560
Being heartsick at the mere sight of heaven.
That she more surely would perform the act
And leave the daylight, now she saw before her
A thing one shudders to recall: on altars
Fuming with incense where she placed her gifts,   565

25. At aulis, where Agamemnon marshalled   effort to avenge the abduction of Helen by
    the Greek expedition against Troy, the   sacking Troy.
    chieftains swore an oath of loyalty to his   26. The region of Italy around and to the
                                                       south of Rome.

The holy water blackened, the spilt wine
Turned into blood and mire. Of this she spoke
To no one, not to her sister even. Then, too,
Within the palace was a marble shrine
Devoted to her onetime lord, a place   570
She held in wondrous honor, all festooned
With snowy fleeces and green festive boughs.
From this she now thought voices could be heard
And words could be made out, her husband's words,
Calling her, when midnight hushed the earth;   575
And lonely on the rooftops the night owl
Seemed to lament, in melancholy notes,
Prolonged to a doleful cry. And then, besides,
The riddling words of seers in ancient days,
Foreboding sayings, made her thrill with fear.   580
In nightmare, fevered, she was hunted down
By pitiless Aeneas, and she seemed
Deserted always, uncompanioned always,
On a long journey, looking for her Tyrians
In desolate landscapes—   585
                              as Pentheus[27] gone mad
Sees the oncoming Eumenidës and sees
A double sun and double Thebes appear,
Or as when, hounded on the stage, Orestës
Runs from a mother armed with burning brands,   590
With serpents hellish black,
And in the doorway squat the Avenging Ones.
So broken in mind by suffering, Dido caught
Her fatal madness and resolved to die.
She pondered time and means, then visiting   595
Her mournful sister, covered up her plan
With a calm look, a clear and hopeful brow.
"Sister, be glad for me! I've found a way
To bring him back or free me of desire.
Near to the Ocean boundary, near sundown,   600
The Aethiops' farthest territory lies,
Where giant Atlas turns the sphere of heaven
Studded with burning stars. From there
A priestess of Massylian stock has come;
She had been pointed out to me: custodian   605
Of that shrine named for daughters of the west,
Hesperidës; and it is she who fed

---

27. The Theban king whose hostility to the
    god Dionysus resulted in his destruction,
    as dramatized by Euripides in the *Bacchae*.

The dragon, guarding well the holy boughs
With honey dripping slow and drowsy poppy.
Chanting her spells she undertakes to free   610
What hearts she wills, but to inflict on others
Duress of sad desires; to arrest
The flow of rivers, make the stars move backward,
Call up the spirits of deep Night. You'll see
Earth shift and rumble underfoot and ash trees   615
Walk down mountainsides. Dearest, I swear
Before the gods and by your own sweet self,
It is against my will that I resort
For weaponry to magic powers. In secret
Build up a pyre in the inner court   620
Under the open sky, and place upon it
The arms that faithless man left in my chamber,
All his clothing, and the marriage bed
On which I came to grief—solace for me
To annihilate all vestige of the man,   625
Vile as he is: my priestess shows me this."
While she was speaking, cheek and brow grew pale.
But Anna could not think her sister cloaked
A suicide in these unheard-of rites;
She failed to see how great her madness was   630
And feared no consequence more grave
Than at Sychaeus' death. So, as commanded,
She made the preparations. For her part,
The queen, seeing the pyre in her inmost court
Erected huge with pitch-pine and sawn ilex,   635
Hung all the place under the sky with wreaths
And crowned it with funereal cypress boughs.
On the pyre's top she put a sword he left
With clothing, and an effigy on a couch,
Her mind fixed now ahead on what would come.   640
Around the pyre stood altars, and the priestess,
Hair unbound, called in a voice of thunder
Upon three hundred gods, on Erebus,
On Chaos, and on triple Hecatë,[28]
Three-faced Diana. Then she sprinkled drops   645
Purportedly from the fountain of Avernus.[29]
Rare herbs were brought out, reaped at the new moon
By scythes of bronze, and juicy with a milk

---

28. Hecate was a divinity associated with Persephone, queen of the underworld, as well
as with the goddess Diana; she is often
represented as a woman with three bodies.

29. A lake near Naples, thought to be an entrance
to the underworld.

Of dusky venom; then the rare love-charm
Or caul torn from the brow of a birthing foal   650
And snatched away before the mother found it.
Dido herself with consecrated grain
In her pure hands, as she went near the altars,
Freed one foot from sandal straps, let fall
Her dress ungirdled, and, now sworn to death,   655
Called on the gods and stars that knew her fate.
She prayed then to whatever power may care
In comprehending justice for the grief
Of lovers bound unequally by love.
The night had come, and weary in every land   660
Men's bodies took the boon of peaceful sleep.
The woods and the wild seas had quieted
At that hour when the stars are in mid-course
And every field is still; cattle and birds
With vivid wings that haunt the limpid lakes   665
Or nest in thickets in the country places
All were asleep under the silent night.
Not, though, the agonized Phoenician queen:
She never slackened into sleep and never
Allowed the tranquil night to rest   670
Upon her eyelids or within her heart.
Her pain redoubled; love came on again,
Devouring her, and on her bed she tossed
In a great surge of anger.
      So awake,   675
She pressed these questions, musing to herself:
"Look now, what can I do? Turn once again
To the old suitors, only to be laughed at—
Begging a marriage with Numidians
Whom I disdained so often? Then what? Trail   680
The Ilian ships and follow like a slave
Commands of Trojans? Seeing them so agreeable,
In view of past assistance and relief,
So thoughtful their unshaken gratitude?
Suppose I wished it, who permits or takes   685
Aboard their proud ships one they so dislike?
Poor lost soul, do you not yet grasp or feel
The treachery of the line of Laömedon?[30]
What then? Am I to go alone, companion
Of the exultant sailors in their flight?   690
Or shall I set out in their wake, with Tyrians,
With all my crew close at my side, and send

---

30. A king of Troy.

The men I barely tore away from Tyre
To sea again, making them hoist their sails
To more sea-winds? No: die as you deserve,   695
Give pain quietus with a steel blade.
                                    Sister,
You are the one who gave way to my tears
In the beginning, burdened a mad queen
With sufferings, and thrust me on my enemy.   700
It was not given me to lead my life
Without new passion, innocently, the way
Wild creatures live, and not to touch these depths.
The vow I took to the ashes of Sychaeus
Was not kept."   705
                    So she broke out afresh
In bitter mourning. On his high stern deck
Aeneas, now quite certain of departure,
Everything ready, took the boon of sleep.
In dream the figure of the god returned   710
With looks reproachful as before: he seemed
Again to warn him, being like Mercury
In every way, in voice, in golden hair,
And in the bloom of youth.
                        "Son of the goddess,   715
Sleep away this crisis, can you still?
Do you not see the dangers growing round you,
Madman, from now on? Can you not hear
The offshore westwind blow? The woman hatches
Plots and drastic actions in her heart,   720
Resolved on death now, whipping herself on
To heights of anger. Will you not be gone
In flight, while flight is still within your power?
Soon you will see the offing boil with ships
And glare with torches; soon again   725
The waterfront will be alive with fires,
If Dawn comes while you linger in this country.
Ha! Come, break the spell! Woman's a thing
Forever fitful and forever changing."
At this he merged into the darkness. Then   730
As the abrupt phantom filled him with fear,
Aeneas broke from sleep and roused his crewmen:
"Up, turn out now! Oarsmen, take your thwarts!
Shake out sail! Look here, for the second time
A god from heaven's high air is goading me   735
To hasten our break away, to cut the cables.
Holy one, whatever god you are,
We go with you, we act on your command

Most happily! Be near, graciously help us,
Make the stars in heaven propitious ones!"   740
He pulled his sword aflash out of its sheath
And struck at the stern hawser. All the men
Were gripped by his excitement to be gone,
And hauled and hustled. Ships cast off their moorings,
And an array of hulls hid inshore water   745
As oarsmen churned up foam and swept to sea.
Soon early Dawn, quitting the saffron bed
Of old Tithonus, cast new light on earth,
And as air grew transparent, from her tower
The queen caught sight of ships on the seaward reach   750
With sails full and the wind astern. She knew
The waterfront now empty, bare of oarsmen.
Beating her lovely breast three times, four times,
And tearing her golden hair,
      "O Jupiter,"   755
She said, "will this man go, will he have mocked
My kingdom, stranger that he was and is?
Will they not snatch up arms and follow him
From every quarter of the town? and dockhands
Tear our ships from moorings? On! Be quick   760
With torches! Give out arms! Unship the oars!
What am I saying? Where am I? What madness
Takes me out of myself? Dido, poor soul,
Your evil doing has come home to you.
Then was the right time, when you offered him   765
A royal scepter. See the good faith and honor
But rise up from my bones, avenging spirit!
Harry with fire and sword the Dardan countrymen
Now, or hereafter, at whatever time
The strength will be afforded. Coast with coast   770
In conflict, I implore, and sea with sea,
And arms with arms: may they contend in war,
Themselves and all the children of their children!"
Now she took thought of one way or another,
At the first chance, to end her hated life,   775
And briefly spoke to Barcë, who had been
Sychaeus' nurse; her own an urn of ash
Long held in her ancient fatherland.
       "Dear nurse,
Tell Sister Anna to come here, and have her   780
Quickly bedew herself with running water
Before she brings our victims for atonement.
Let her come that way. And you, too, put on
Pure wool around your brows. I have a mind

To carry out that rite to Stygian Jove[31]   785
That I have readied here, and put an end
To my distress, committing to the flames
The pyre of that miserable Dardan."
At this with an old woman's eagerness
Barcë hurried away. And Dido's heart   790
Beat wildly at the enormous thing afoot.
She rolled her bloodshot eyes, her quivering cheeks
Were flecked with red as her sick pallor grew
Before her coming death. Into the court
She burst her way, then at her passion's height   795
She climbed the pyre and bared the Dardan sword—
A gift desired once, for no such need.
Her eyes now on the Trojan clothing there
And the familiar bed, she paused a little,
Weeping a little, mindful, then lay down   800
And spoke her last words:

               "Remnants dear to me
While god and fate allowed it, take this breath
And give me respite from these agonies.
I lived my life out to the very end   805
And passed the stages Fortune had appointed.
Now my tall shade goes to the under world.
I built a famous town, saw my great walls,
Avenged my husband, made my hostile brother
Pay for his crime. Happy, alas, too happy,   810
If only the Dardanian keels had never
Beached on our coast." And here she kissed the bed.
"I die unavenged," she said, "but let me die.
This way, this way, a blessed relief to go
Into the undergloom. Let the cold Trojan,   815
Far at sea, drink in this conflagration
And take with him the omen of my death!"
Amid these words her household people saw her
Crumpled over the steel blade, and the blade
Aflush with red blood, drenched her hands. A scream   820
Pierced the high chambers. Now through the shocked city
Rumor went rioting, as wails and sobs
With women's outcry echoed in the palace
And heaven's high air gave back the beating din,
As though all Carthage or old Tyre fell   825
To storming enemies, and, out of hand,
Flames billowed on the roofs of men and gods.

---

31. The mythical Styx was the principal river
of the underworld.

Her sister heard and trembling, faint with terror,
Lacerating her face, beating her breast,
Ran through the crowd to call the dying queen: 830
"It came to this, then, sister? You deceived me?
The pyre meant this, altars and fires meant this?
What shall I mourn first, being abandoned? Did you
Scorn your sister's company in death?
You should have called me out to the same fate!   835
The same blade's edge and hurt, at the same hour,
Should have taken us off. With my own hands
Had I to build this pyre, and had I to call
Upon our country's gods, that in the end
With you placed on it there, O heartless one,   840
I should be absent? You have put to death
Yourself and me, the people and the fathers
Bred in Sidon, and your own new city.
Give me fresh water, let me bathe her wound
And catch upon my lips any last breath   845
Hovering over hers."
              Now she had climbed
The topmost steps and took her dying sister
Into her arms to cherish, with a sob,
Using her dress to stanch the dark blood flow.   850
But Dido trying to lift her heavy eyes
Fainted again. Her chest-wound whistled air.
Three times she struggled up on one elbow
And each time fell back on the bed. Her gaze
Went wavering as she looked for heaven's light   855
And groaned at finding it. Almighty Juno,
Filled with pity for this long ordeal
And difficult passage, now sent Iris down
Out of Olympus to set free
The wrestling spirit from the body's hold.   860
For since she died, not at her fated span
Nor as she merited, but before her time
Enflamed and driven mad, Proserpina[32]
Had not yet plucked from her the golden hair,
Delivering her to Orcus of the Styx.   865
So humid Iris through bright heaven flew
On saffron-yellow wings, and in her train
A thousand hues shimmered before the sun.
At Dido's head she came to rest.
                  "This token   870

---

32. Persephone, wife of Hades, lord of the
    underworld.

Sacred to Dis[33] I bear away as bidden
And free you from your body."

Saying this,

She cut a lock of hair. Along with it
Her body's warmth fell into dissolution,
And out into the winds her life withdrew.

875

THE BIBLE (LATE FIRST CENTURY C.E.)
Palestine or Greece (?)

The Gospel According to Luke and the Acts of the Apostles, together comprise a two-volume work describing the life and teachings of Jesus and the early history of the church. Their authorship is unknown, but they were traditionally attributed to Luke the Physician, a Gentile convert and friend of the apostle Paul. Written in Greek, his works date from the late first century C.E. Much of Luke's gospel is based on the earlier gospel of Mark, with substantial information added from oral tradition and from other written sources now lost. The selections presented here are the opening five gospel chapters—describing the birth of Jesus, his childhood, and his early ministry; the final three gospel chapters, describing Jesus' betrayal, trial, crucifixion, death, and resurrection—and the opening two chapters of Acts, recounting the beginnings of the church up through Pentecost.

Throughout his account, Luke interweaves events and teachings, setting the Hebrew tradition in counterpoint against the wider world of the Roman empire, of which Palestine was then a part. Although the imperial culture posed a threat to the preservation of local ethnic identity, it also provided the means to spread the universalist message of the gospels. This is vividly dramatized in the miraculous ability of the apostles to be understood by all peoples at Pentecost.

The Gospel According to Luke 1–5, 22–24

1

Inasmuch as many have undertaken to compile a narrative of the things which have been accomplished among us, just as they were delivered to us by those who from the beginning were eyewitnesses and ministers of the word, it seemed good to me also, having followed all things closely for some time past, to write an

---

Revised Standard Version translation.

---

33. One of the names of Hades.

orderly account for you, most excellent Theophilus, that you may know the truth concerning the things of which you have been informed.

In the days of Herod,[1] king of Judea, there was a priest named Zechariah, of the division of Abijah; and he had a wife of the daughters of Aaron, and her name was Elizabeth. And they were both righteous before God, walking in all the commandments and ordinances of the Lord blameless.

But they had no child, because Elizabeth was barren, and both were advanced in years.

Now while he was serving as priest before God when his division was on duty, according to the custom of the priesthood, it fell to him by lot to enter the temple of the Lord and burn incense. And the whole multitude of the people were praying outside at the hour of incense. And there appeared to him an angel of the Lord standing on the right side of the altar of incense. And Zechariah was troubled when he saw him, and fear fell upon him. But the angel said to him, "Do not be afraid, Zechariah, for your prayer is heard, and your wife Elizabeth will bear you a son, and you shall call his name John.

> And you will have joy and gladness,
> and many will rejoice at his birth;
> for he will be great before the Lord,
> and he shall drink no wine nor strong drink,
> and he will be filled with the Holy Spirit,
> even from his mother's womb.
> And he will turn many of the sons of Israel to the Lord their God,
> And he will go before him in the spirit and power of Elijah,[2]
> to turn the hearts of the fathers to the children,
> and the disobedient to the wisdom of the just,
> to make ready for the Lord a people prepared."

And Zechariah said to the angel, "How shall I know this? For I am an old man, and my wife is advanced in years." And the angel answered him, "I am Gabriel, who stand in the presence of God; and I was sent to speak to you, and to bring you this good news. And behold, you will be silent and unable to speak until the day that these things come to pass, because you did not believe my words, which will be fulfilled in their time." And the people were waiting for Zechariah, and they wondered at his delay in the temple. And when he came out, he could not speak to them, and they perceived that he had seen a vision in the temple; and he made signs to them and remained dumb. And when his time of service was ended, he went to his home.

After these days his wife Elizabeth conceived, and for five months she hid herself, saying, "Thus the Lord has done to me in the days when he looked on me, to take away my reproach among men."

In the sixth month the angel Gabriel was sent from God to a city of Galilee

---

1. Herod the Great ruled Palestine under Roman control from 37 to 4 B.C.E.
2. In the biblical book of Malachi, the great prophet Elijah is described as returning as God's messenger before the final days of the world.

named Nazareth, to a virgin betrothed to a man whose name was Joseph, of the house of David; and the virgin's name was Mary. And he came to her and said, "Hail, O favored one, the Lord is with you!" But she was greatly troubled at the saying, and considered in her mind what sort of greeting this might be. And the angel said to her, "Do not be afraid, Mary, for you have found favor with God. And behold, you will conceive in your womb and bear a son, and you shall call his name Jesus.

> He will be great, and will be called the Son of the Most High;
> and the Lord God will give to him the throne of his father David,[3]
> and he will reign over the house of Jacob[4] for ever;
> and of his kingdom there will be no end."

And Mary said to the angel, "How can this be, since I have no husband?"

> And the angel said to her,
> "The Holy Spirit will come upon you,
> and the power of the Most High will overshadow you;
> therefore the child to be born will be called holy,
> the Son of God.

And behold, your kinswoman Elizabeth in her old age has also conceived a son; and this is the sixth month with her who was called barren. For with God nothing will be impossible." And Mary said, "Behold, I am the handmaid of the Lord; let it be to me according to your word." And the angel departed from her.

In those days Mary arose and went with haste into the hill country, to a city of Judah, and she entered the house of Zechariah and greeted Elizabeth. And when Elizabeth heard the greeting of Mary, the babe leaped in her womb; and Elizabeth was filled with the Holy Spirit and she exclaimed with a loud cry, "Blessed are you among women, and blessed is the fruit of your womb! And why is this granted me, that the mother of my Lord should come to me? For behold, when the voice of your greeting came to my ears, the babe in my womb leaped for joy. And blessed is she who believed that there would be fulfillment of what was spoken to her from the Lord."

> And Mary said,
> "My soul magnifies the Lord,
> and my spirit rejoices in God my Savior,
> for he has regarded the low estate of his handmaiden.
> For behold, henceforth all generations will call me blessed;
> for he who is mighty has done great things for me,
> and holy is his name.
> And his mercy is on those who fear him
> from generation to generation.
> He has shown strength with his arm,

---

3. David (reigned c. 1000 to 965 B.C.E.), second king of Israel.

4. Jacob was the legendary patriarch whose twelve sons founded the twelve tribes of Israel.

> he has scattered the proud in the imagination of their hearts,
> he has put down the mighty from their thrones,
> and exalted those of low degree;
> he has filled the hungry with good things,
> and the rich he has sent empty away.
> He has helped his servant Israel,
> in remembrance of his mercy,
> as he spoke to our fathers,
> to Abraham and to his posterity for ever."

And Mary remained with her about three months, and returned to her home.

Now the time came for Elizabeth to be delivered, and she gave birth to a son. And her neighbors and kinsfolk heard that the Lord had shown great mercy to her, and they rejoiced with her. And on the eighth day they came to circumcise the child; and they would have named him Zechariah after his father, but his mother said, "Not so; he shall be called John." And they said to her, "None of your kindred is called by this name." And they made signs to his father, inquiring what he would have him called. And he asked for a writing tablet, and wrote, "His name is John." And they all marveled. And immediately his mouth was opened and his tongue loosed, and he spoke, blessing God. And fear came on all their neighbors. And all these things were talked about through all the hill country of Judea; and all who heard them laid them up in their hearts, saying, "What then will this child be?" For the hand of the Lord was with him.

And his father Zechariah was filled with the Holy Spirit, and prophesied, saying,

> "Blessed be the Lord God of Israel,
> for he was visited and redeemed his people,
> and has raised up a horn of salvation for us
> in the house of his servant David,
> as he spoke by the mouth of his holy prophets from of old,
> that we should be saved from our enemies,
> and from the hand of all who hate us;
> to perform the mercy promised to our fathers,
> and to remember his holy covenant,
> the oath which he swore to our father Abraham, to grant us
> that we, being delivered from the hand of our enemies,
> might serve him without fear,
> in holiness and righteousness before him all the days of our life.
> And you, child, will be called the prophet of the Most High;
> for you will go before the Lord to prepare his ways,
> to give knowledge of salvation to his people
> in the forgiveness of their sins,
> through the tender mercy of our God,
> when the day shall dawn upon us from on high
> to give light to those who sit in darkness and in the shadow of death,
> to guide our feet into the way of peace."

And the child grew and became strong in spirit, and he was in the wilderness till the day of his manifestation to Israel.

2

In those days a decree went out from Caesar Augustus[5] that all the world should be enrolled. This was the first enrollment, when Quirinius was governor of Syria. And all went to be enrolled, each to his own city. And Joseph also went up from Galilee, from the city of Nazareth, to Judea, to the city of David, which is called Bethlehem, because he was of the house and lineage of David, to be enrolled with Mary his betrothed, who was with child. And while they were there, the time came for her to be delivered. And she gave birth to her first-born son and wrapped him in swaddling cloths, and laid him in a manger, because there was no place for them in the inn.

And in that region there were shepherds out in the field, keeping watch over their flock by night. And an angel of the Lord appeared to them, and the glory of the Lord shone around them, and they were filled with fear. And the angel said to them, "Be not afraid; for behold, I bring you good news of a great joy which will come to all the people; for to you is born this day in the city of David a Savior, who is Christ the Lord. And this will be a sign for you: you will find a babe wrapped in swaddling cloths and lying in a manger." And suddenly there was with the angel a multitude of the heavenly host praising God and saying,

"Glory to God in the highest,
and on earth peace among men with whom he is pleased!"

When the angels went away from them into heaven, the shepherds said to one another, "Let us go over to Bethlehem and see this thing that has happened, which the Lord has made known to us." And they went with haste, and found Mary and Joseph, and the babe lying in a manger. And when they saw it they made known the saying which had been told them concerning this child; and all who heard it wondered at what the shepherds told them. But Mary kept all these things, pondering them in her heart. And the shepherds returned, glorifying and praising God for all they had heard and seen, as it had been told them.

And at the end of eight days, when he was circumcised, he was called Jesus, the name given by the angel before he was conceived in the womb.

And when the time came for their purification according to the law of Moses, they brought him up to Jerusalem to present him to the Lord (as it is written in the law of the Lord, "Every male that opens the womb shall be called holy to the Lord") and to offer a sacrifice according to what is said in the law of the Lord, "a pair of turtledoves, or two young pigeons." Now there was a man in Jerusalem, whose name was Simeon, and this man was righteous and devout, looking for the consolation of Israel, and the Holy Spirit was upon him. And it had been revealed to him by the Holy Spirit that he should not see death before he had seen the Lord's Christ.[6] And inspired by the Spirit he came into the temple; and when the parents brought in the child Jesus, to do for him according to the custom of the law, he took him up in his arms and blessed God and said,

---

5. Augustus was Roman emperor from 27 B.C.E. to 14 C.E.; the census was taken in 7 to 6 B.C.E.

6. "Christ" is a translation of the Hebrew "Messiah," "the anointed one."

"Lord, now lettest thou thy servant depart in peace,
according to thy word;
for mine eyes have seen thy salvation
which thou hast prepared in the presence of all peoples,
a light for revelation to the Gentiles,
and for glory to thy people Israel."
And his father and his mother marveled at what was said about him; and Simeon
    blessed them and said to Mary his mother,
"Behold, this child is set for the fall and rising of many in Israel,
and for a sign that is spoken against
(and a sword will pierce through your own soul also),
that thoughts out of many hearts may be revealed."

And there was a prophetess, Anna, the daughter of Phanuel, of the tribe of Asher; she was of a great age, having lived with her husband seven years from her virginity, and as a widow till she was eighty-four. She did not depart from the temple, worshiping with fasting and prayer night and day. And coming up at that very hour she gave thanks to God, and spoke of him to all who were looking for the redemption of Jerusalem.

And when they had performed everything according to the law of the Lord, they returned into Galilee, to their own city, Nazareth. And the child grew and became strong, filled with wisdom; and the favor of God was upon him.

Now his parents went to Jerusalem every year at the feast of the Passover. And when he was twelve years old, they went up according to custom; and when the feast was ended, as they were returning, the boy Jesus stayed behind in Jerusalem. His parents did not know it, but supposing him to be in the company they went a day's journey, and they sought him among their kinsfolk and acquaintances; and when they did not find him, they returned to Jerusalem, seeking him. After three days they found him in the temple, sitting among the teachers, listening to them and asking them questions; and all who heard him were amazed at his understanding and his answers. And when they saw him they were astonished; and his mother said to him, "Son, why have you treated us so? Behold, your father and I have been looking for you anxiously." And he said to them, "How is it that you sought me? Did you not know that I must be in my Father's house?" And they did not understand the saying which he spoke to them. And he went down with them and came to Nazareth, and was obedient to them; and his mother kept all these things in her heart.

And Jesus increased in wisdom and in stature, and in favor with God and man.

3

In the fifteenth year of the reign of Tiberius Caesar,[7] Pontius Pilate being governor of Judea, and Herod being tetrarch of Galilee, and his brother Philip tetrarch of the region of Ituraea and Trachonitis,[8] and Lysanias tetrarch of Abilene, in the

---

7. 26 or 27 C.E.
8. The Roman governor Pilate now ruled Judea directly; the remainder of the kingdom of Herod the Great was divided between his sons Herod Antipas and Philip, as tetrarchs (rulers of a subordinate territory).

high-priesthood of Annas and Caiaphas, the word of God came to John the son of Zechariah in the wilderness; and he went into all the region about the Jordan, preaching a baptism of repentance for the forgiveness of sins. As it is written in the book of the words of Isaiah the prophet,

"The voice of one crying in the wilderness:
Prepare the way of the Lord,
make his paths straight.
Every valley shall be filled,
and every mountain and hill shall be brought low,
and the crooked shall be made straight,
and the rough ways shall be made smooth;
and all flesh shall see the salvation of God."

He said therefore to the multitudes that came out to be baptized by him, "You brood of vipers! Who warned you to flee from the wrath to come? Bear fruits that befit repentance, and do not begin to say to yourselves, 'We have Abraham as our father'; for I tell you, God is able from these stones to raise up children to Abraham. Even now the axe is laid to the root of the trees; every tree therefore that does not bear good fruit is cut down and thrown into the fire."

And the multitudes asked him, "What then shall we do?" And he answered them, "He who has two coats, let him share with him who has none; and he who has food, let him do likewise." Tax collectors also came to be baptized, and said to him, "Teacher, what shall we do?" And he said to them, "Collect no more than is appointed you." Soldiers also asked him, "And we, what shall we do?" And he said to them, "Rob no one by violence or by false accusation, and be content with your wages."

As the people were in expectation, and all men questioned in their hearts concerning John, whether perhaps he were the Christ, John answered them all, "I baptize you with water; but he who is mightier than I is coming, the thong of whose sandals I am not worthy to untie; he will baptize you with the Holy Spirit and with fire. His winnowing fork is in his hand, to clear his threshing floor, and to gather the wheat into his granary, but the chaff he will burn with unquenchable fire."

So, with many other exhortations, he preached good news to the people. But Herod the tetrarch, who had been reproved by him for Herodias, his brother's wife,[9] and for all the evil things that Herod had done, added this to them all, that he shut up John in prison.

Now when all the people were baptized, and when Jesus also had been baptized and was praying, the heaven was opened, and the Holy Spirit descended upon him in bodily form, as a dove, and a voice came from heaven, "Thou art my beloved Son; with thee I am well pleased."

Jesus, when he began his ministry, was about thirty years of age, being the son (as was supposed) of Joseph, the son of Heli, the son of Matthat, the son of Levi,

---

9. Herod had married his brother's wife, in
   violation of Jewish law.

the son of Melchi, the son of Jannai, the son of Joseph, the son of Mattathias, the son of Amos, the son of Nahum, the son of Esli, the son of Naggai, the son of Maath, the son of Mattathias, the son of Semein, the son of Josech, the son of Joda, the son of Joanan, the son of Rhesa, the son of Zerubbabel, the son of Shealtiel, the son of Neri, the son of Melchi, the son of Addi, the son of Cosam, the son of Elmadam, the son of Er, the son of Joshua, the son of Eliezer, the son of Jorim, the son of Matthat, the son of Levi, the son of Simeon, the son of Judah, the son of Joseph, the son of Jonam, the son of Eliakim, the son of Melea, the son of Menna, the son of Mattatha, the son of Nathan, the son of David, the son of Jesse, the son of Obed, the son of Boaz, the son of Sala, the son of Nahshon, the son of Amminadab, the son of Admin, the son of Arni, the son of Hezron, the son of Perez, the son of Judah, the son of Jacob, the son of Isaac, the son of Abraham, the son of Terah, the son of Nahor, the son of Serug, the son of Reu, the son of Peleg, the son of Eber, the son of Shelah, the son of Cainan, the son of Arphaxad, the son of Shem, the son of Noah, the son of Lamech, the son of Methuselah, the son of Enoch, the son of Jared, the son of Mahalaleel, the son of Cainan, the son of Enos, the son of Seth, the son of Adam, the son of God.[10]

4

And Jesus, full of the Holy Spirit, returned from the Jordan, and was led by the Spirit for forty days in the wilderness, tempted by the devil. And he ate nothing in those days; and when they were ended, he was hungry. The devil said to him, "If you are the Son of God, command this stone to become bread." And Jesus answered him, "It is written, 'Man shall not live by bread alone.'" And the devil took him up, and showed him all the kingdoms of the world in a moment of time, and said to him, "To you I will give all this authority and their glory; for it has been delivered to me, and I give it to whom I will. If you, then, will worship me, it shall all be yours." And Jesus answered him, "It is written,

> 'You shall worship the Lord your God,
>   and him only shall you serve.'"

And he took him to Jerusalem, and set him on the pinnacle of the temple, and said to him, "If you are the Son of God, throw yourself down from here; for it is written,

> 'He will give his angels charge of you, to guard you,'

and

> 'On their hands they will bear you up,
>   lest you strike your foot against a stone,'"

And Jesus answered him, "It is said, 'You shall not tempt the Lord your God.'" And when the devil had ended every temptation, he departed from him until an opportune time.

---

10. Whereas Matthew's gospel traces Jesus's lineage back to Abraham, Luke makes a point of extending his ancestry to the founder of the entire human race.

And Jesus returned in the power of the Spirit into Galilee, and a report concerning him went out through all the surrounding country. And he taught in their synagogues, being glorified by all.

And he came to Nazareth, where he had been brought up; and he went to the synagogue, as his custom was, on the sabbath day And he stood up to read; and there was given to him the book of the prophet Isaiah. He opened the book and found the place where it was written.

> "The Spirit of the Lord is upon me,
> because he has anointed me to preach good news to the poor.
> He has sent me to proclaim release to the captives
> and recovering of sight to the blind,
> to set at liberty those who are oppressed,
> to proclaim the acceptable year of the Lord."

And he closed the book, and gave it back to the attendant, and sat down; and the eyes of all in the synagogue were fixed on him. And he began to say to them, "Today this scripture has been fulfilled in your hearing." And all spoke well of him, and wondered at the gracious words which proceeded out of his mouth; and they said, "Is not this Joseph's son?" And he said to them, "Doubtless you will quote to me this proverb, 'Physician, heal yourself; what we have heard you did at Capernaum, do here also in your own country.' " And he said, "Truly, I say to you, no prophet is acceptable in his own country. But in truth, I tell you, there were many widows in Israel in the days of Elijah, when the heaven was shut up three years and six months, when there came a great famine over all the land; and Elijah was sent to none of them but only to Zarephath, in the land of Sidon, to a woman who was a widow. And there were many lepers in Israel in the time of the prophet Elisha; and none of them was cleansed, but only Naaman the Syrian." When they heard this, all in the synagogue were filled with wrath. And they rose up and put him out of the city, and led him to the brow of the hill on which their city was built, that they might throw him down headlong. But passing through the midst of them he went away.

And he went down to Capernaum, a city of Galilee. And he was teaching them on the sabbath; and they were astonished at his teaching, for his word was with authority.[11] And in the synagogue there was a man who had the spirit of an unclean demon; and he cried out with a loud voice, "Ah! What have you to do with us, Jesus of Nazareth? Have you come to destroy us? I know who you are, the Holy One of God." But Jesus rebuked him, saying, "Be silent, and come out of him!" And when the demon had thrown him down in the midst, he came out of him, having done him no harm. And they were all amazed and said to one another, "What is this word? For with authority and power he commands the unclean spirits, and they come out." And reports of him went out into every place in the surrounding region.

And he arose and left the synagogue, and entered Simon's house. Now

---

11. Rabbis usually taught in the name of their
    teachers rather than on their own authority.

Simon's mother-in-law was ill with a high fever, and they besought him for her. And he stood over her and rebuked the fever, and it left her; and immediately she rose and served them.

Now when the sun was setting, all those who had any that were sick with various diseases brought them to him; and he laid his hands on every one of them and healed them. And demons also came out of many, crying, "You are the Son of God!" But he rebuked them, and would not allow them to speak, because they knew that he was the Christ.

And when it was day he departed and went into a lonely place. And the people sought him and came to him, and would have kept him from leaving them; but he said to them, "I must preach the good news of the kingdom of God to the other cities also; for I was sent for this purpose." And he was preaching in the synagogues of Judea.

5

While the people pressed upon him to hear the word of God, he was standing by the lake of Gennesaret. And he saw two boats by the lake; but the fishermen had gone out of them and were washing their nets. Getting into one of the boats, which was Simon's, he asked him to put out a little from the land. And he sat down and taught the people from the boat. And when he had ceased speaking, he said to Simon, "Put out into the deep and let down your nets for a catch." And Simon answered, "Master, we toiled all night and took nothing! But at your word I will let down the nets." And when they had done this, they enclosed a great shoal of fish; and as their nets were breaking, they beckoned to their partners in the other boat to come and help them. And they came and filled both the boats, so that they began to sink. But when Simon Peter saw it, he fell down at Jesus' knees, saying, "Depart from me, for I am a sinful man, O Lord." For he was astonished, and all that were with him, at the catch of fish which they had taken; and so also were James and John, sons of Zebedee, who were partners with Simon. And Jesus said to Simon, "Do not be afraid; henceforth you will be catching men." And when they had brought their boats to land, they left everything and followed him.

While he was in one of the cities, there came a man full of leprosy; and when he saw Jesus, he fell on his face and besought him, "Lord, if you will, you can make me clean." And he stretched out his hand, and touched him, saying, "I will; be clean." And immediately the leprosy left him. And he charged him to tell no one; but "go and show yourself to the priest, and make an offering for your cleansing, as Moses commanded, for a proof to the people" But so much the more the report went abroad concerning him; and great multitudes gathered to hear and to be healed of their infirmities. But he withdrew to the wilderness and prayed.

On one of those days, as he was teaching, there were Pharisees[12] and teachers of the law sitting by, who had come from every village of Galilee and Judea and from Jerusalem; and the power of the Lord was with him to heal. And behold, men were bringing on a bed a man who was paralyzed, and they sought to bring him

---

12. A group of strict observers of Jewish law.

in and lay him before Jesus; but finding no way to bring him in, because of the crowd, they went up on the roof and let him down with his bed through the tiles into the midst before Jesus. And when he saw their faith he said, "Man, your sins are forgiven you." And the scribes and the Pharisees began to question, saying, "Who is this that speaks blasphemies? Who can forgive sins but God only?" When Jesus perceived their questionings, he answered them, "Why do you question in your hearts? Which is easier, to say, 'Your sins are forgiven you,' or to say, 'Rise and walk'? But that you may know that the Son of man has authority on earth to forgive sins"—he said to the man who was paralyzed—"I say to you, rise, take up your bed and go home." And immediately he rose before them, and took up that on which he lay, and went home, glorifying God. And amazement seized them all, and they glorified God and were filled with awe, saying, "We have seen strange things today."

After this he went out, and saw a tax collector, named Levi, sitting at the tax office; and he said to him, "Follow me." And he left everything, and rose and followed him.

And Levi made him a great feast in his house; and there was a large company of tax collectors and others sitting at table with them. And the Pharisees and their scribes murmured against his disciples, saying, "Why do you eat and drink with tax collectors and sinners?"[13] And Jesus answered them, "Those who are well have no need of a physician, but those who are sick; I have not come to call the righteous, but sinners to repentance.

And they said to him, "The disciples of John fast often and offer prayers, so do the disciples of the Pharisees, but yours eat and drink." And Jesus said to them, "Can you make wedding guests fast while the bridegroom is with them? The days will come, when the bridegroom is taken away from them, and then they will fast in those days." He told them a parable also: "No one tears a piece from a new garment and puts it upon an old garment; if he does, he will tear the new, and the piece from the new will not match the old. And no one puts new wine into old wineskins; if he does, the new wine will burst the skins and it will be spilled and the skins will be destroyed. But new wine must be put into fresh wineskins. And no one after drinking old wine desires new; for he says, 'The old is good.' "[14]

22

Now the feast of Unleavened Bread drew near, which is called the Passover. And the chief priests and the scribes were seeking how to put him to death; for they feared the people.

Then Satan entered into Judas called Iscariot, who was of the number of the twelve; he went away and conferred with the chief priests and captains how he

---

13. Tax collectors were despised both because they typically extorted all they could and because they were agents of the Roman occupation.

14. In Chapters 6–21, Jesus chooses the rest of his twelve disciples and continues to teach and perform miracles, arousing increasing hostility from the religious authorities.

might betray him to them. And they were glad, and engaged to give him money. So he agreed, and sought an opportunity to betray him to them in the absence of the multitude.

Then came the day of Unleavened Bread, on which the passover lamb had to be sacrificed.[15] So Jesus sent Peter and John, saying, "Go and prepare the passover for us, that we may eat it." They said to him, "Where will you have us prepare it?" He said to them, "Behold, when you have entered the city, a man carrying a jar of water will meet you: follow him into the house which he enters, and tell the householder, 'The Teacher says to you, Where is the guest room, where I am to eat the passover with my disciples?' And he will show you a large upper room furnished; there make ready." And they went, and found it as he had told them; and they prepared the passover.

And when the hour came, he sat at table, and the apostles with him. And he said to them, "I have earnestly desired to eat this passover with you before I suffer; for I tell you I shall not eat it until it is fulfilled in the kingdom of God." And he took a cup, and when he had given thanks he said, "Take this, and divide it among yourselves; for I tell you that from now on I shall not drink of the fruit of the vine until the kingdom of God comes." And he took bread, and when he had given thanks he broke it and gave it to them, saying, "This is my body which is given for you. Do this in remembrance of me." And likewise the cup after supper, saying, "This cup which is poured out for you is the new covenant in my blood. But behold the hand of him who betrays me is with me on the table. For the Son of man goes as it has been determined; but woe to that man by whom he is betrayed!" And they began to question one another, which of them it was that would do this.

A dispute also arose among them, which of them was to be regarded as the greatest. And he said to them, "The kings of the Gentiles exercise lordship over them; and those in authority over them are called benefactors. But not so with you; rather let the greatest among you become as the youngest, and the leader as one who serves. For which is the greater, one who sits at table, or one who serves? Is it not the one who sits at table? But I am among you as one who serves.

"You are those who have continued with me in my trials; and I assign to you, as my Father assigned to me, a kingdom, that you may eat and drink at my table in my kingdom, and sit on thrones judging the twelve tribes of Israel.

"Simon, Simon, behold, Satan demanded to have you, that he might sift you like wheat, but I have prayed for you that your faith may not fail; and when you have turned again, strengthen your brethren." And he said to him, "Lord, I am ready to go with you to prison and to death." He said, "I tell you, Peter, the cock will not crow this day, until you three times deny that you know me."

And he said to them, "When I sent you out with no purse or bag or sandals, did you lack anything?" They said, "Nothing." He said to them, "But now, let him who has a purse take it, and likewise a bag. And let him who has no sword sell his mantle and buy one. For I tell you that this scripture must be fulfilled in me, 'And

---

15. Passover commemorates God's deliverance of the Israelites from slavery in Egypt; as they fled, the Hebrews had to eat unleavened bread, lacking time for baking.

he was reckoned with transgressors'; for what is written about me has its fulfillment." And they said, "Look, Lord, here are two swords." And he said to them, "It is enough."

And he came out, and went, as was his custom, to the Mount of Olives; and the disciples followed him. And when he came to the place he said to them, "Pray that you may not enter into temptation." And he withdrew from them about a stone's throw, and knelt down and prayed, "Father, if thou art willing, remove this cup from me; nevertheless not my will, but thine, be done." And when he rose from prayer, he came to the disciples and found them sleeping for sorrow, and he said to them, "Why do you sleep? Rise and pray that you may not enter into temptation."

While he was still speaking, there came a crowd, and the man called Judas, one of the twelve, was leading them. He drew near to Jesus to kiss him; but Jesus said to him, "Judas, would you betray the Son of man with a kiss?" And when those who were about him saw what would follow, they said, "Lord, shall we strike with the sword?" And one of them struck the slave of the high priest and cut off his right ear. But Jesus said, "No more of this!" And he touched his ear and healed him. Then Jesus said to the chief priests and officers of the temple and elders, who had come out against him, "Have you come out as against a robber, with swords and clubs? When I was with you day after day in the temple, you did not lay hands on me. But this is your hour, and the power of darkness."

Then they seized him and led him away, bringing him into the high priest's house. Peter followed at a distance; and when they had kindled a fire in the middle of the courtyard and sat down together, Peter sat among them. Then a maid, seeing him as he sat in the light and gazing at him, said, "This man also was with him." But he denied it, saying, "Woman, I do not know him." And a little later some one else saw him and said, "You also are one of them." But Peter said, "Man, I am not." And after an interval of about an hour still another insisted, saying, "Certainly this man also was with him; for he is a Galilean." But Peter said, "Man, I do not know what you are saying." And immediately, while he was still speaking, the cock crowed. And the Lord turned and looked at Peter. And Peter remembered the word of the Lord, how he had said to him, "Before the cock crows today, you will deny me three times." And he went out and wept bitterly.

Now the men who were holding Jesus mocked him and beat him; they also blindfolded him and asked him, "Prophesy! Who is that struck you?" And they spoke many other words against him, reviling him.

When day came, the assembly of the elders of the people gathered together, both chief priests and scribes; and they led him away to their council, and they said, "If you are the Christ, tell us." But he said to them, "If I tell you, you will not believe; and if I ask you, you will not answer. But from now on the Son of man shall be seated at the right hand of the power of God." And they all said, "Are you the Son of God, then?" And he said to them, "You say that I am." And they said, "What further testimony do we need? We have heard it ourselves from his own lips."

23

Then the whole company of them arose, and brought him before Pilate. And they began to accuse him, saying, "We found this man perverting our nation, and forbidding us to give tribute to Caesar, and saying that he himself is Christ a king." And Pilate asked him, "Are you the King of the Jews?" And he answered him, "You have said so." And Pilate said to the chief priests and the multitudes, "I find no crime in this man." But they were urgent, saying, "He stirs up the people, teaching throughout all Judea, from Galilee even to this place."

When Pilate heard this, he asked whether the man was a Galilean. And when he learned that he belonged to Herod's jurisdiction, he sent him over to Herod, who was himself in Jerusalem at that time. When Herod saw Jesus, he was very glad, for had long desired to see him, because he had heard about him, and he was hoping to see some sign done by him. So he questioned him at some length; but he made no answer. The chief priests and the scribes stood by, vehemently accusing him. And Herod with his soldiers treated him with contempt and mocked him; then, arraying him in gorgeous apparel, he sent him back to Pilate. And Herod and Pilate became friends with each other that very day, for before this they had been at enmity with each other.

Pilate then called together the chief priests and the rulers and the people, and said to them, "You brought me this man as one who was perverting the people; and after examining him before you, behold, I did not find this man guilty of any of your charges against him; neither did Herod, for he sent him back to us. Behold, nothing deserving death has been done by him; I will therefore chastise him and release him."

But they all cried out together, "Away with this man, and release to us Barabbas"—a man who had been thrown into prison for an insurrection started in the city, and for murder. Pilate addressed them once more, desiring to release Jesus; but they shouted out, "Crucify, crucify him!" A third time he said to them, "Why, what evil has he done? I have found in him no crime deserving death; I will therefore chastise him and release him." But they were urgent, demanding with loud cries that he should be crucified. And their voices prevailed. So Pilate gave sentence that their demand should be granted. He released the man who had been thrown into prison for insurrection and murder, whom they asked for; but Jesus he delivered up to their will.

And as they led him away, the seized one Simon of Cyrene, who was coming in from the country, and laid on him the cross, to carry it behind Jesus. And there followed him a great multitude of the people, and of women who bewailed and lamented him. But Jesus turning to them said, "Daughters of Jerusalem, do not weep for me, but weep for yourselves and for your children. For behold, the days are coming when they will say, 'Blessed are the barren, and the wombs that never bore, and the breasts that never gave suck!' Then they will begin to say to the mountains, 'Fall on us'; and to the hills, 'Cover us.' For if they do this when the wood is green, what will happen when it is dry?"[16]

Two others also, who were criminals, were led away to be put to death with him. And when they came to the place which is called The Skull, there they

---

16. I.e., if the innocent Jesus meets such a fate, what will become of guilty Jerusalem as a whole?

crucified him, and the criminals, one on the right and one on the left. And Jesus said, "Father, forgive them; for they know not what they do." And they cast lots to divide his garments. And the people stood by, watching; but the rulers scoffed at him, saying, "He saved others; let him save himself, if he is the Christ of God, his Chosen One!" The soldiers also mocked him, coming up and offering him vinegar, and saying, "If you are the King of the Jews, save yourself!" There was also an inscription over him, "This is the King of the Jews."

One of the criminals who were hanged railed at him, saying, "Are you not the Christ? Save yourself and us!" But the other rebuked him, saying, "Do you not fear God, since you are under the same sentence of condemnation? And we indeed justly; for we are receiving the due reward of our deeds; but this man has done nothing wrong." And he said, "Jesus, remember me when you come in your kingly power." And he said to him, "Truly, I say to you, today you will be with me in Paradise."

It was now about the sixth hour, and there was darkness over the whole land until the ninth hour,[17] while the sun's light failed; and the curtain of the temple was torn in two. Then Jesus, crying with a loud voice, said, "Father, into thy hands I commit my spirit!" And having said this he breathed his last. Now when the centurion saw what had taken place, he praised God, and said, "Certainly this man was innocent!" And all the multitudes who assembled to see the sight, when they saw what had taken place, returned home beating their breasts. And all his acquaintances and the women who had followed him from Galilee stood at a distance and saw these things.

Now there was a man named Joseph from the Jewish town of Arimathea. He was a member of the council, a good and righteous man, who had not consented to their purpose and deed, and he was looking for the kingdom of God. This man went to Pilate and asked for the body of Jesus. Then he took it down and wrapped it in a linen shroud, and laid him in a rock-hewn tomb, where no one had ever yet been laid. It was the day of Preparation, and the sabbath was beginning. The women who had come with him from Galilee followed, and saw the tomb, and how his body was laid; then they returned, and prepared spices and ointments. On the sabbath they rested according to the commandment.

24

But on the first day of the week, at early dawn, they went to the tomb, taking the spices which they had prepared. And they found the stone rolled away from the tomb, but when they went in they did not find the body. While they were perplexed about this, behold, two men stood by them in dazzling apparel; and as they were frightened and bowed their faces to the ground, the men said to them, "Why do you seek the living among the dead? Remember how he told you, while he was still in Galilee, that the Son of man must be delivered into the hands of sinful men, and be crucified, and on the third day rise." And they remembered his words, and returning from the tomb they told all this to the eleven and to all the

---

17. From noon to 3 P.M.

rest. Now it was Mary Magdalene and Joanna and Mary the mother of James and the other women with them who told this to the apostles; but these words seemed to them an idle tale, and they did not believe them.

That very day two of them were going to a village named Emmaus, about seven miles from Jerusalem, and talking with each other about all these things that had happened. While they were talking and discussing together, Jesus himself drew near and went with them. But their eyes were kept from recognizing him. And he said to them, "What is this conversation which you are holding with each other as you walk?" And they stood still, looking sad. Then one of them, named Cleopas, answered him, "Are you the only visitor to Jerusalem who does not know the things that have happened there in these days?" And he said to them, "What things?" And they said to him, "Concerning Jesus of Nazareth, who was a prophet mighty in deed and word before God and all the people, and how our chief priests and rulers delivered him up to be condemned to death, and crucified him. But we had hoped that he was the one to redeem Israel. Yes, and besides all this, it is now the third day since this happened. Moreover, some women of our company amazed us. They were at the tomb early in the morning and did not find his body; and they came back saying that they had even seen a vision of angels, who said that he was alive. Some of those who were with us went to the tomb, and found it just as the women had said; but him they did not see." And he said to them, "O foolish men, and slow of heart to believe all that the prophets have spoken! Was it not necessary that the Christ should suffer these things and enter into his glory?" And beginning with Moses and all the prophets, he interpreted to them in all the scriptures the things concerning himself.

So they drew near to the village to which they were going. He appeared to be going further, but they constrained him, saying, "Stay with us, for it is toward evening and the day is now far spent." So he went in to stay with them. When he was at table with them, he took the bread and blessed, and broke it, and gave it to them. And their eyes were opened and they recognized him: and he vanished out of their sight. They said to each other, "Did not our hearts burn within us while he talked to us on the road, while he opened to us the scriptures?" And they rose that same hour and returned to Jerusalem; and they found the eleven gathered together and those who were with them, who said, "The Lord has risen indeed, and has appeared to Simon!" Then they told what had happened on the road, and how he was known to them in the breaking of the bread.

As they were saying this, Jesus himself stood among them. But they were startled and frightened, and supposed that they saw a spirit. And he said to them, "Why are you troubled, and why do questionings rise in your hearts? See my hands and my feet, that it is I myself; handle me, and see; for a spirit has not flesh and bones as you see that I have." And while they still disbelieved for joy, and wondered, he said to them, "Have you anything here to eat?" They gave him a piece of broiled fish, and he took it and ate before them.

Then he said to them, "These are my words which I spoke to you, while I was still with you, that everything written about me in the law of Moses and the prophets and the psalms must be fulfilled." Then he opened their minds to understand the scriptures, and said to them, "Thus it is written, that the Christ should suffer and on the third day rise from the dead, and that repentance and forgiveness of sins should be preached in his name to all nations, beginning from Jerusalem. You are witnesses of these things. And behold, I send the promise of my Father upon you; but stay in the city, until you are clothed with power from on high."

Then he led them out as far as Bethany, and lifting up his hands he blessed them. While he blessed them, he parted from them. And they returned to Jerusalem with great joy, and were continually in the temple blessing God.

Acts of the Apostles 1, 2

1

In the first book, O Theophilus, I have dealt with all that Jesus began to do and teach, until the day when he was taken up, after he had given commandment through the Holy Spirit to the apostles whom he had chosen. To them he presented himself alive after his passion by many proofs, appearing to them during forty days, and speaking of the kingdom of God. And while staying with them he charged them not to depart from Jerusalem, but to wait for the promise of the Father, which, he said, "you heard from me, for John baptized with water, but before many days you shall be baptized with the Holy Spirit."

So when they had come together, they asked him, "Lord, will you at this time restore the kingdom to Israel?" He said to them, "It is not for you to know times or seasons which the Father has fixed by his own authority. But you shall receive power when the Holy Spirit has come upon you; and you shall be my witnesses in Jerusalem and in all Judea and Samaria and to the end of the earth." And when he had said this, as they were looking on, he was lifted up, and a cloud took him out of their sight. And while they were gazing into heaven as he went, behold, two men stood by them in white robes, and said, "Men of Galilee, why do you stand looking into heaven? This Jesus, who was taken up from you into heaven, will come in the same way as you saw him go into heaven."

Then they returned to Jerusalem from the mount called Olivet, which is near Jerusalem, a sabbath day's journey away; and when they had entered, they went up to the upper room, where they were staying, Peter and John and James and Andrew, Philip and Thomas, Bartholomew and Matthew, James the son of Alphaeus and Simon the Zealot and Judas the son of James. All these with one accord devoted themselves to prayer, together with the women and Mary the mother of Jesus, and with his brothers.

In those days Peter stood up among the brethren (the company of persons was in all about a hundred and twenty), and said, "Brethren, the scripture had to be fulfilled, which the Holy Spirit spoke beforehand by the mouth of David, concerning Judas who was guide to those who arrested Jesus. For he was numbered among us, and was allotted his share in this ministry. (Now this man bought a field with the reward of his wickedness; and falling headlong he burst

Revised Standard Version translation.

open in the middle and all his bowels gushed out. And it became known to all the inhabitants of Jerusalem, so that the field was called in their language Akeldama, that is, Field of Blood.) For it is written in the book of Psalms.

> 'Let his habitation become desolate, and let there be no one to live in it';
> and
> > 'His office let another take.'

So one of the men who have accompanied us during all the time that the Lord Jesus went in and out among us, beginning from the baptism of John until the day when he was taken up from us—one of these men must become with us a witness to his resurrection." And they put forward two, Joseph called Barsabbas, who was surnamed Justus, and Matthias. And they prayed and said, "Lord, who knowest the hearts of all men, show which one of these two thou hast chosen to take the place in this ministry and apostleship from which Judas turned aside, to go to his own place." And they cast lots for them, and the lot fell on Matthias; and he was enrolled with the eleven apostles.

2

When the day of Pentecost had come, they were all together in one place. And suddenly a sound came from heaven like the rush of a mighty wind, and it filled all the house where they were sitting. And there appeared to them tongues as of fire, distributed and resting on each one of them. And they were all filled with the Holy Spirit and began to speak in other tongues, as the Spirit gave them utterance.

Now there were dwelling in Jerusalem Jews, devout men from every nation under heaven. And at this sound the multitude came together, and they were bewildered, because each one heard them speaking in his own language.[1] And they were amazed and wondered, saying, "Are not all these who are speaking Galileans? And how is it that we hear, each of us in his own native language? Parthians and Medes and Elamites and residents of Mesopotamia, Judea and Cappadocia, Pontus and Asia, Phrygia and Pamphylia, Egypt and the parts of Libya belonging to Cyrene, and visitors from Rome, both Jews and proselytes, Cretans and Arabians, we hear them telling in our own tongues the mighty works of God." And all were amazed and perplexed, saying to one another, "What does this mean?" But others mocking said, "They are filled with new wine."

But Peter, standing with the eleven, lifted up his voice and addressed them, "Men of Judea and all who dwell in Jerusalem, let this be known to you, and give ear to my words. For these men are not drunk, as you suppose, since it is only the third hour of the day;[2] but this is what was spoken by the prophet Joel:

> 'And in the last days it shall be, God declares,
> that I will pour out my Spirit upon all flesh,
> and your sons and your daughters shall prophesy,
> and your young men shall see visions,

---

1. An inversion of the splintering of languages   **2.** 9 A.M.
   at the Tower of Babel (Genesis 11).

and your old men shall dream dreams;
yea, and on my menservants and my maidservants in those days
I will pour out my Spirit; and they shall prophesy.
And I will show wonders in the heaven above
and signs on the earth beneath,
blood, and fire, and vapor of smoke;
the sun shall be turned into darkness
and the moon into blood,
before the day of the Lord comes,
the great and manifest day.
And it shall be that whoever calls on the name of the Lord shall be saved.'

"Men of Israel, hear these words: Jesus of Nazareth, a man attested to you by God with mighty works and wonders and signs which God did through him in your midst, as you yourselves know—this Jesus, delivered up according to the definite plan and foreknowledge of God, you crucified and killed by the hands of lawless men. But God raised him up, having loosed the pangs of death, because it was not possible for him to be held by it. For David says concerning him,

'I saw the Lord always before me,
for he is at my right hand that I may not be shaken;
therefore my heart was glad, and my tongue rejoiced;
moreover my flesh will dwell in hope.
For thou wilt not abandon my soul to Hades,
nor let thy Holy One see corruption.
Thou hast made known to me the ways of life;
thou wilt make me full of gladness with thy presence.'

"Brethren, I may say to you confidently of the patriarch David that he both died and was buried, and his tomb is with us to this day. Being therefore a prophet, and knowing that God had sworn with an oath to him that he would set one of his descendants upon his throne, he foresaw and spoke of the resurrection of the Christ, that he was not abandoned to Hades, nor did his flesh see corruption. This Jesus God raised up, and of that we all are witnesses. Being therefore exalted at the right hand of God, and having received from the Father the promise of the Holy Spirit, he has poured out this which you see and hear. For David did not ascend into the heavens; but he himself says,

'The Lord said to my Lord, Sit at my right hand,
till I make thy enemies a stool for thy feet.'

Let all the house of Israel therefore know assuredly that God has made him both Lord and Christ, this Jesus whom you crucified."

Now when they heard this they were cut to the heart, and said to Peter and the rest of the apostles, "Brethren, what shall we do?" And Peter said to them, "Repent, and be baptized every one of you in the name of Jesus Christ for the forgiveness of your sins; and you shall receive the gift of the Holy Spirit. For the promise is to you and to your children and to all that are far off, every one whom the Lord our God calls to him." And he testified with many other words and exhorted them, saying, "Save yourselves from this crooked generation." So those who received his word were baptized, and there were added that day about three thousand souls. And they devoted themselves to the apostles' teaching and fellowship, to the breaking of bread and the prayers.

And fear came upon every soul; and many wonders and signs were done through the apostles. And all who believed were together and had all things in common; and they sold their possessions and goods and distributed them to all, as any had need. And day by day, attending the temple together and breaking bread in their homes, they partook of food with glad and generous hearts, praising God and having favor with all the people. And the Lord added to their number day by day those who were being saved.

OVID (43 B.C.E.–17 C.E.)
Rome

Ovid's earliest work—the three volumes of *Amores*—represents the transformation elegiac poetry underwent in the hands of the Roman poets of the first century B.C.E. In contrast to the wide range of subject matter that characterizes Greek elegy, in the writings of the Roman elegists—of whom Ovid (Publius Ovidius Naso) was the last—erotic themes predominate, developing into what amounts to a new and distinctive genre. Although in Ovid's work (as in that of Tibullus and Propertius, contemporary writers of amatory elegy) love does not have the tragic dimensions with which Vergil endows it in his *Aeneid* (See *Aeneid* Book 4, in this section)—and although Ovid explicitly draws a contrast between the grandeur of epic themes and the more modest aims of his chronicle of the everyday vicissitudes of his love affair with a woman (probably fictive) he calls Corinna—the poet often humorously compares the arduous course of love with the rigors and perils of war. Despite his ironic self-deprecation, Ovid expended great care on his elegies, revising them into an edition of three books from an original five, as the epigram to the whole collection indicates.

Some years later Ovid did attempt an epic poem, the *Metamorphoses,* which takes as its subject the phenomenon of *change:* beginning with the transition from chaos to order that created the world, it narrates and gives coherence to numerous Greek and Roman legends about how gods and mortals altered their physical forms—often to pursue or evade each other, sometimes as a truer reflection of their natures.

A virtual archive of mythology, the *Metamorphoses* was an endlessly valuable resource for artists, both literary and visual, of later centuries; in the early modern period, the poem's depictions of the amorous adventures of the gods were often drawn upon to allegorize the activities of a contemporary aristocracy. Ovid never completed his epic. For reasons not clearly known (but sometimes thought to be connected with his publication of a long erotic elegy, the *Ars Amatoria,* or *Art of Love*), Ovid was abruptly banished by the emperor Augustus to a frontier outpost on the Black Sea, where he died after ten years in exile.

from *Amores*

Epigram by the Poet

We are our author's book. Before, we comprised five sections,
  Now we're cut down to three. The decision was his.
You still may derive no pleasure from reading us—but remember,
  With two of us gone, your labour is that much less.

[Every lover's on active service]

Every lover's on active service, my friend, active service, believe me,
  And Cupid has his headquarters in the field.
Fighting and love-making belong to the same age-group—
  In bed as in war, old men are out of place.
A commander looks to his troops for gallant conduct,   5
  A mistress expects no less.
Soldier and lover both keep night-long vigil,
  Lying rough outside their captain's (or lady's) door.
The military life brings long route-marches—but just let his mistress
  Be somewhere ahead, and the lover too   10
Will trudge on for ever, scale mountains, ford swollen rivers,
  Thrust his way through deep snow.
Come embarkation-time *he* won't talk of 'strong north-easters',
  Or say it's 'too late in the season' to put to sea.
Who but a soldier or lover would put up with freezing   15
  Nights—rain, snow, sleet? The first
Goes out on patrol to observe the enemy's movements,
  The other watches his rival, an equal foe.
A soldier lays siege to cities, a lover to girls' houses,
  The one assaults city gates, the other front doors.   20
Night attacks are a great thing. Catch your opponents sleeping
  And unarmed. Just slaughter them where they lie.
That's how the Greeks dealt with Rhesus[1] and his wild Thracians
  While rustling those famous mares.
Lovers, too, will take advantage of slumber (her husband's),   25
  Strike home while the enemy sleeps: getting past
Night patrols and eluding sentries are games both soldiers
  And lovers need to learn.
Love, like war, is a toss-up. The defeated can recover,
  While some you might think invincible collapse;   30
So if you've got love written off as an easy option

Translated by Peter Green.

---

1. In a grisly episode of the Trojan War narrated in Book 10 of the *Iliad*, the Greek warriors Odysseus and Diomedes killed the Trojan ally Rhesus and his fellow Thracians at night as they slept, and drove the slain Rhesus's prized horses back to the Greek camp.

You'd better think twice. Love calls
For guts and initiative. Great Achilles sulks for Briseis[2]—
Quick, Trojans, smash through the Argive wall!
Hector went into battle from Andromache's embraces   35
    Helmeted by his wife.
Agamemnon[3] himself, the Supremo, was struck into raptures
    At the sight of Cassandra's tumbled hair;
Even Mars[4] was caught on the job, felt the blacksmith's meshes—
    Heaven's best scandal in years. Then take   40
My own case. I was idle, born to leisure *en déshabillé,*
    Mind softened by lazy scribbling in the shade.
But love for a pretty girl soon drove the sluggard
    To action, made him join up.
And just look at me now—fighting fit, dead keen on night exercises: 45
    If you want a cure for slackness, fall in love!

[A second batch of verses by that naughty provincial poet]

A second batch of verses[5] by that naughty provincial poet,
    Naso, the chronicler of his own
Wanton frivolities; another of Love's commissions (warning
    To puritans: *This volume is not for you*).
I want my works to be read by the far-from-frigid virgin   5
    On fire for her sweetheart, by the boy
In love for the very first time. May some fellow-sufferer,
    Perusing my anatomy of desire,
See his own passion reflected there, cry in amazement:
    'Who told this scribbler about my private affairs?'   10
One time, I recall, I got started on an inflated epic
    About War in Heaven,[6] with all
Those hundred-handed monsters, and Earth's fell vengeance, and towering
    Ossa piled on Olympus (plus Pelion too).

Every lover's on active service

2. The personages (and themes) of Greek mythology, exalted in epic poetry, are frequently subjected to a humorously ironic—
and deflating—treatment by the Roman
elegists. Here Achilles' devastating wrath
over the loss of Briseis and his withdrawal
from the Trojan War, which propel the plot
of the *Iliad,* are pictured as a case of mere ill
humor.
3. The commander of the Greek army brought
the Trojan princess and seer Cassandra,
King Priam's daughter, home to Argos as a
prize of war.
4. Book 8 of the *Odyssey* recounts the adulterous love affair of Ares (identified with Mars,

in Roman mythology) and Aphrodite (Venus). Aphrodite's husband Hephaestus, the
divine blacksmith, trapped the lovers by
constructing a mesh of delicate golden filaments that pinned them, unaware, to the
bed as they made love.

A second batch of verses

5. This is the opening poem of the second
book of the *Amores.*
6. Invoking a traditional epic subject—the
struggle for supremacy in heaven, such as
the version narrated by Hesiod in his
Theogony—Ovid alludes to an episode in
which a pair of giants tried to pile two
mountains on top of a third, so as to scale
them and lay siege to heaven.

But while I was setting up Jove[7]—stormclouds and thunderbolts gathered   15
   Ready to hand, a superb defensive barrage—
My mistress staged a lock-out. I dropped Jupiter and his lightnings
   That instant, didn't give him another thought.
Forgive me, good Lord, if I found your armoury useless—
   Her shut door ran to larger bolts   20
Than any *you* wielded. I went back to verses and compliments,
   My natural weapons. Soft words
Remove harsh door-chains. There's magic in poetry, its power
   Can pull down the bloody moon,
Turn back the sun, make serpents burst asunder   25
   Or rivers flow upstream.
Doors are no match for such spellbinding, the toughest
   Locks can be open-sesamed by its charms.
But epic's a dead loss for me. I'll get nowhere with swift-footed
   Achilles, or with either of Atreus' sons.[8]   30
Old what's-his-name[9] wasting twenty years on war and travel,
   Poor Hector dragged in the dust—
No good. But lavish fine words on some young girl's profile
   And sooner or later she'll tender herself as the fee,
An ample reward for your labours. So farewell, heroic   35
   Figures of legend—the *quid*
Pro quo you offer won't tempt me. A bevy of beauties
   All swooning over my love-songs—that's what *I* want.

[A hot afternoon: siesta-time]

A hot afternoon: siesta-time. Exhausted,
   I lay sprawled across my bed.
One window-shutter was closed, the other stood half-open,
   And the light came sifting through
As it does in a wood. It recalled that crepuscular glow at sunset   5
   Or the trembling moment between darkness and dawn,
Just right for a modest girl whose delicate bashfulness
   Needs some camouflage. And then—
In stole Corinna, long hair tumbled about her
   Soft white throat, a rustle of summer skirts,   10
Like some fabulous Eastern queen *en route* to her bridal-chamber—
   Or a top-line city call-girl, out on the job.
I tore the dress off her—not that it really hid much,
   But all the same she struggled to keep it on:
Yet her efforts were unconvincing, she seemed half-hearted—   15
   Inner self-betrayal made her give up.

   A second batch of verses

7. Another name for Jupiter, the supreme deity of the Roman pantheon.

8. Agamemnon and Menelaus.
9. Odysseus.

When at last she stood naked before me, not a stitch of clothing,
   I couldn't fault her body at any point.
Smooth shoulders, delectable arms (I saw, I touched them),
   Nipples inviting caresses, the flat   20
Belly outlined beneath that flawless bosom,
   Exquisite curve of a hip, firm youthful thighs.
But why catalogue details? Nothing came short of perfection,
   And I clasped her naked body close to mine.
Fill in the rest for yourselves! Tired at last, we lay sleeping.   25
   May my siestas often turn out that way!

LUCIUS APULEIUS (SECOND CENTURY C.E.)
Roman North Africa

Lucius Apuleius was born in the Roman province of Africa around 125 C.E. He
studied in Carthage (a city in North Africa near today's Tunis) and Athens, visited
Rome, then probably settled back in Carthage. Apuleius produced poems, orations,
and philosophical works, but he is best known for his satiric masterpiece, originally
titled *Metamorphoses* but later known as *Asinus Aureus—The Golden Ass*.

    Consumed with insatiable curiosity (among other appetites), Lucius, the
story's hero, dabbles in magic and finds himself accidentally transformed into the
shape of a donkey. He wanders in search of release, a sort of comic Odysseus,
providing the author with an opportunity to paint a vivid and darkly comic
portrait of life in the cosmopolitan Roman Empire, mixing the magical and the
marvelous with the debased and the depraved. Lucius's bodily transformation is
paralleled by confusions of languages and cultures, and the adventure culminates
with conversion to the worship of Isis, the Egyptian goddess of the moon and
ruler of change itself.

from *The Golden Ass*

Prologue

But[1] I would like to tie together different sorts of tales for you in that Milesian style
of yours,[2] and to caress your ears into approval with a pretty whisper, if only you
will not begrudge looking at Egyptian papyrus inscribed with the sharpness of a
reed from the Nile, so that you may be amazed at men's forms and fortunes

---

Translated by J. Arthur Hanson.

1. The narrator begins as if in mid-conversa-
   tion.

2. Stories in the style of the florid erotic tales
   of a Greek writer, Aristides of Miletus.

transformed into other shapes and then restored again in an interwoven knot. I begin my prologue. Who am I? I will tell you briefly. Attic Hymettos and Ephyrean Isthmos and Spartan Taenaros, fruitful lands preserved for ever in even more fruitful books, form my ancient stock.[3] There I served my stint with the Attic tongue in the first campaigns of childhood. Soon afterwards, in the city of the Latins, as a newcomer to Roman studies I attacked and cultivated their native speech with laborious difficulty and no teacher to guide me. So, please, I beg your pardon in advance if as a raw speaker of this foreign tongue of the Forum I commit any blunders. Now in fact this very changing of language corresponds to the type of writing we have undertaken, which is like the skill of a rider jumping from one horse to another. We are about to begin a Greekish story. Pay attention, reader, and you will find delight.

[Lucius, our hero, is travelling on business through Thessaly in northern Greece. After hearing various marvelous stories from fellow travellers, he finds lodging in a strange city. His hosts are Milo, a miser; Pamphile, his wife; and Fotis, their seductive servant. Lucius goes looking for excitement in town.]

[Seduction in the Enchanted Land of Thessaly]

As soon as night had been scattered and a new sun brought day, I emerged from sleep and bed alike. With my anxiety and my excessive passion to learn the rare and the marvellous, considering that I was staying in the middle of Thessaly, the native land of those spells of the magic art which are unanimously praised throughout the entire world, and recalling that the story told by my excellent comrade Aristomenes had originated at the site of this very city, I was on tenterhooks of desire and impatience alike, and I began to examine each and every object with curiosity. Nothing I looked at in that city seemed to me to be what it was; but I believed that absolutely everything had been transformed into another shape by some deadly mumbo-jumbo: the rocks I hit upon were petrified human beings, the birds I heard were feathered humans, the trees that surrounded the city wall were humans with leaves, and the liquid in the fountains had flowed from human bodies. Soon the statues and pictures would begin to walk, the walls to speak, the oxen and other animals of that sort to prophesy; and from the sky itself and the sun's orb there would suddenly come an oracle.

I was in such a state of shock, or rather so dumbfounded by my torturous longing, that, although I found no trace or vestige whatever of what I longed to see, I continued to circulate anyway.

[Lucius meets a relation, who warns him to beware of his hostess, who is a sorceress. He returns home determined to see her in action. He decides to enlist the aid of Fotis, whom he finds in the kitchen.]

---

3. The narrator claims descent from several
   different regions in Greece: Athens,
   Corinth, and Sparta.

She herself was neatly dressed in a linen tunic and had a dainty, bright red band tied up under her breasts. She was turning the cooking pot round and round with her flower-like hands, and she kept shaking it with a circular motion, at the same time smoothly sliding her own body, gently wiggling her hips, softly shaking her supple spine, beautifully rippling. I was transfixed by the sight, utterly stunned. I stood in amazement, as did a part of me which had been lying limp before. Finally I spoke. "How gorgeously, my Photis," I said, "and how delightfully you twist your little pot with your buttocks! What a delicious stew you are cooking! A man would be lucky—surely even blessed—if you would let him dip his finger in there."

Then she, with her wit and her ready tongue, retorted: "Get away, poor boy; get as far away as you can from my oven, because if my little flame should blow against you even slightly, you will burn deep inside and no one will be able to extinguish your fire except me. I can season things deliciously, and I know how to shake a pot and a bed to your equal delight."

As she spoke she looked around at me and laughed. But I did not move away until I had carefully scrutinised every aspect of her appearance. Yet why should I mention anything else, since my exclusive concern has always been with a person's head and hair, to examine it intently first in public and enjoy it later at home? The reasoning behind this preference of mine is deliberate and well-considered: namely, as the dominant part of the body openly located for clear visibility, it is the first thing to meet our eyes. Secondly, what the cheerful colour of flowery clothing does for the rest of the body, its own natural lustre does for the head. Finally, when most women want to prove their own real loveliness, they take off all their garments, remove their clothes: they wish to show their beauty naked, knowing that they will be better liked for the rosy blush of their skin than for the golden colour of their dress. However—though it is forbidden to mention this and I hope that such a horrible illustration of this point will never occur—if you were to strip the hair from the head of the most extraordinary and beautiful woman and rob her face of its natural decoration, even if she were descended from heaven, born out of the sea, and raised by the waves, even, I say, if she were Venus herself, surrounded by the whole chorus of Graces and accompanied by the entire throng of Cupids, wearing her famous girdle, breathing cinnamon, and sprinkling balsam—if she came forth bald she could not attract even her husband Vulcan.

But think what it is like when hair shines with its own lovely colour and brilliant light, and when it flashes lively against the sunbeams or gently reflects them; or when it shifts its appearance to produce opposite charms, now glistening gold compressed into the smooth shadows of honey, now with raven-blackness imitating the dark blue flowerets on pigeons' necks; or when it is anointed with Arabian oils and parted with a sharp comb's fine tooth and gathered at the back so as to meet the lover's eyes and, like a mirror, reflect an image more pleasing than reality; or when, compact with all its tresses, it crowns the top of her head or, let out in a long train, it flows down over her back. In short, the significance of a woman's coiffure is so great that, no matter how finely attired she may be when she steps out in her gold, robes, jewels, and all her other finery, unless she has embellished her hair she cannot be called well-dressed.

In my Photis' case, her coiffure was not elaborate, but its casualness gave her added charm. Her luxuriant tresses were softly loosened to hang down over her neck, then they spread over her shoulders and momentarily rested upon the slightly curved border of her tunic; they were then gathered in a mass at the end and fastened in a knot to the crown of her head.

I could no longer endure the excruciating torture of such intense pleasure, but rushed toward her and planted that most delicious of kisses on the spot where her hair rose toward the top of her head. Then she twisted her neck and turned toward me with a sidelong glance of those biting eyes. "Well, well, my schoolboy," she said, "that is a bittersweet appetiser you are sampling. Be careful not to catch a chronic case of bitter indigestion from eating too sweet honey."

"How so, my merry one?" I replied. "I am prepared, if you will revive me now with one little kiss, to be stretched out over your fire and barbecued." And with that I held her tight and began to kiss her. Her ardour now began to rival my own, and she grew with me to an equal intensity of passion. Her mouth was open now, her breath like cinnamon and her tongue darting against mine with a touch like nectar, her passion unrestrained in her desire for me.

"I am dying," I said. "No, I am already dead unless you have mercy."

After another long kiss she answered, "Cheer up! Because I want what you want, I have become your slave, and our pleasure will not be postponed much longer. When the first lights are lit I will come to your bedroom. So go away now and prepare your forces, because all night long I will make war on you bravely and with all my heart."

After this bantering conversation we separated.

[Fotis becomes Lucius's lover, and enables him to spy on Pamphile as she changes herself into an owl. Lucius persuades Fotis to steal the sorceress's magic ointment for him, but she brings Lucius the wrong box: instead of an owl, he becomes a donkey, a form he will be trapped in until he manages to find some rose blossoms to eat. The bulk of the book describes Lucius's adventures among scoundrels, swindlers and thieves. All the while, he hears strange stories, and sharply observes the world around him, even when he is set to hard labor at a baker's millstone.]

[The Degradation of Lucius and His Fellow Slaves] Ch. 13

After most of the day was past and I was worn out, they took off my rope-collar, disconnected me from the machine, and fastened me to the manger. Although I was exceedingly exhausted, desperately in need of repairing my strength, and really dead from hunger, yet my habitual curiosity held me spellbound and made me quite anxious. So I postponed the plentiful dinner at hand and took a certain pleasure in carefully observing the routine of this undesirable workshop.

Good gods, what stunted little men they were! The whole surface of their skin was painted with livid welts. Their striped backs were merely shaded, not covered, by the tattered patchwork they wore: some had thrown on a tiny cloth that just covered their loins, but all were clad in such a way that you could discern them clearly through their rags. Their foreheads were branded, their heads half-shaved, and their feet chained. They were hideously sallow too, and their eyelids were eaten away by the smoky darkness of scorching murk until they were quite weak-sighted; like boxers who fight sprinkled with dust, they were dirtily white-washed with a floury ash.

As for my comrades, the animals, what can I say? How can I describe their condition? What a sight! Those old mules and feeble geldings stood round the manger with their heads sunk down, munching through piles of chaff; their necks sagged from the rotting decay of sores; their flabby nostrils were distended from constant coughing; their chests were ulcerated from the continual rubbing of the rope harnesses; their flanks were bare to the bone from everlasting whipping, their hoofs stretched out to abnormal dimensions from their multiple circling, and their entire hide rough with decay and mangy starvation.

The funereal example of my fellow-slaves made me fear for myself. Recalling the happy Lucius I once was, now driven to the utmost degradation, I lowered my head and grieved. Nowhere was there any consolation for my tortured existence, except one: I was revived by my innate curiosity, since everyone now took little account of my presence and freely did and said whatever they wished. That divine inventor of ancient poetry among the Greeks, desiring to portray a hero of the highest intelligence, was quite right to sing of a man who acquired the highest excellence by visiting many cities and learning to know various peoples.[4] In fact, I now remember the ass that I was with thankful gratitude because, while I was concealed under his cover and schooled in a variety of fortunes, he made me better-informed, if less intelligent. And so here is a story, better than all the others and delightfully elegant, which I have decided to bring to your ears. So here goes.

The baker who bought me was a good man in general and extremely temperate, but he had drawn as mate the worst and by far the most depraved woman in the world, who brought such dishonour to his bed and hearth that even I, by Hercules, often groaned silently for his sake. That vile woman lacked not a single fault. Her soul was like some muddy latrine into which absolutely every vice had flowed. She was cruel and perverse, crazy for men and wine, headstrong and obstinate, grasping in her mean thefts and a spendthrift in her loathsome extravagances, an enemy of fidelity and a foe to chastity. Furthermore she scorned and spurned all the gods in heaven, and, instead of holding a definite faith, she used the false sacrilegious presumption of a god, whom she would call "one and only",[5] to invent meaningless rites to cheat everyone and deceive her wretched husband, having sold her body to drink from dawn and to debauchery the whole day.

Such being the kind of woman she was, she persecuted me with extraordinary hatred. Even before dawn, while she was still in bed, she would shout out for the apprentice-ass to be yoked to the mill-wheel. Then the very moment she came out of her room she would insistently order me to be whipped over and over again while she watched. And although all the other animals were released for dinner on time, she had me put to the manger much later. This cruelty very greatly increased my natural curiosity about her behaviour. You see, I had heard a young man regularly visiting her bedroom, and I longed with all my heart to see his face, if

---

4. A reference to Homer's opening words about Odysseus.

5. Apparently an allusion to Christianity.

only the covering over my head had allowed my eyes any freedom. My ingenuity would not have failed, one way or another, to expose that terrible woman's scandalous affairs.

[In due course, the wife is entertaining her lover, a handsome young priest, when the baker returns home unexpectedly. She hides her lover under a wooden bin, but Lucius exposes him by treading on his hand.]

The baker, however, was not particularly moved at this damage to his honour. His face was calm and his expression kind as he began to speak caressingly to the bloodlessly pale and trembling boy.

"You have nothing harsh to fear from me, son," he said. "I am not barbarous, and I do not share the boorishness of rustic morality. I will not model myself on the fuller's savagery and kill you with lethal sulphur fumes, and I will not even invoke the strictness of the law to try you on capital charges under the statutes against adultery. You are such a charming and pretty boy: I will treat you as the joint property of my wife and me. Instead of a probate to split an estate, I will institute a suit to share common assets, contending that without controversy or dissension we three should enter into contract in the matter of one bed. You see, I have always lived in such harmony with my spouse that, in accordance with the teachings of the wise, we both have the same tastes. But the principle of equity does not permit a wife to have greater right of ownership than her husband."

When he had finished mocking the boy with the gentleness of this speech, he led him off to bed. Reluctantly the boy followed; and the miller, locking up his virtuous wife in another room, lay alone with the boy and enjoyed the most gratifying revenge for his ruined marriage. But when first the Sun's bright wheel gave birth to day, he summoned the two strongest slaves in the house, ordered them to lift the boy up as high as they could, and then flogged his buttocks with a rod.

[Lucius's misadventures culminate when he is exhibited as a tourist attraction and comes to the attention of a wealthy woman with unusual tastes.]

Among the crowds was a certain influential and wealthy lady, who, after paying for a look at me just like everyone else and enjoying my various tricks, out of her constant wonder at me gradually conceived a wondrous desire for me. She took no remedy for her insane passion but, like some asinine Pasiphae,[6] ardently yearned for my embraces. She therefore bargained with my keeper, offering him a large price to lie with me for one night; and he agreed, not the least concerned whether anything pleasant could result for me, but content only with his own gain.

We had just finished supper and left my owner's dining room when we met the lady, who had already been waiting for a long time in my room. Good gods, what luxurious and splendid fittings! Four eunuchs were hastily making a bed for

---

6. The wife of king Minos of Crete, who mated with a bull and gave birth to the Minotaur, half man and half bull.

us on the ground out of a large number of pillows airily puffed out with soft feathers. Over these they carefully laid covers coloured with gold cloth and Tyrian purple, and on top they scattered some other pillows, small but quite numerous, the kind that refined women use to support their chins and necks. They did not delay their mistress's pleasure by their continued presence, but closed the bedroom door and went away. Inside wax candles sparkled with brilliant light and whitened the night's darkness for us.

Then she stripped herself of all her clothes, including the band with which she had bound her lovely breasts. Standing next to the light, she anointed herself all over with oil of balsam from a pewter jar, and lavishly rubbed me down with the same, but with much greater eagerness. She even moistened my nostrils with frankincense. Then she kissed me intimately—not the sort of kisses tossed about in a whorehouse, the money-begging kisses of prostitutes or the money-refusing kisses of customers, but pure and uncorrupted. And she spoke to me with tender affection, saying "I desire you," "I want you," "It is you alone I love," "I can not live without you," and all the other expressions women use to stimulate their lovers and to declare their own feelings. Next she took me by my halter and made me lie down, as I had learned to do. I obeyed readily, because I did not think my task would be anything new or difficult, and especially since for the first time in a long while I was about to enjoy the passionate embraces of a very beautiful woman. Furthermore I had saturated myself with a generous quantity of the finest wine and aroused my desire for sex with the heady fragrance of the ointment.

I was distressed, however, and not a little frightened as I wondered how I, with so many and such large legs, could mount such a delicate lady; or how I could embrace such a soft, translucent body, all compact of milk and honey, with my hard hoofs; or how I could kiss those fine lips reddened by ambrosial dew with my great monstrous misshapen mouth with its stone-sized teeth. Finally, even though she was itching for it to the tips of her toes, how could the woman contain my huge organ? Woe unto me if I should rupture the noble lady and get thrown to the beasts to provide part of my owner's gladiatorial show. Meantime she kept repeating tender words and constant kisses and sweet moans with eyes that bit into me. Finally she said, "I am holding you, I am holding you, my little dove, my sparrow." And as she spoke she demonstrated that my calculations had been vain and my fear pointless, because she clasped me very tightly and took in absolutely all of me—yes, all of me. In fact every time I tried to spare her and pull back my buttocks, she would push closer with a mad thrust, grab my spine, and cling in an even closer embrace, until, by Hercules, I believed that I did not even have enough to fulfil her desire, and that the Minotaur's mother might have had reason to take her pleasure with her mooing paramour. After we had passed a busy and sleepless night the woman departed, avoiding the complicity of daylight, after agreeing to the same price for another night.

My trainer was not unhappy to dispense these joys at her command, because he was not only taking in a very large profit but also rehearsing a new show for his master, to whom he unhesitatingly disclosed our entire sexual performance. The master rewarded his freedman generously, and decided that I should take part in his public spectacle. Since that excellent wife of mine could not be considered because of her social position, and absolutely no one else could be found even for a high price, a depraved woman was procured, one already sentenced by the governor's order to be thrown to the beasts, to appear with me in a packed theatre and exhibit the loss of her virtue.[7]

I awaited the day of the show in a state of terrible suspense and great torment, frequently wishing to kill myself rather than be polluted by the infection of that depraved woman or shamed by the disgrace of a public spectacle. But, lacking a human hand and fingers, I had no way to unsheath a sword with my round, misshapen hoof. In this uttermost catastrophe I consoled myself with just one slender hope: spring in her moment of birth was now painting everything with her flowery jewels and clothing the meadows with crimson brilliance; and recently the roses had burst their thorny covers and sparkled forth, exhaling their spicy fragrance—roses that could restore me to the Lucius I used to be.[8]

And now the day appointed for the show had come. I was led to the outside wall of the theatre, escorted by crowds in an enthusiastic parade. The opening of the show was given over to actors' mimic dances; meanwhile I enjoyed myself standing in front of the gate, browsing on the lush, rich grass which grew right in the entrance-way, and occasionally refreshing my inquisitive eyes with a delightful glimpse of the show through the open gate.

There were boys and girls in the bloom of verdant youth, outstanding in beauty, resplendent in costume, and graceful in movement, all ready to dance the Greek Pyrrhic. They went through beautiful dance-cycles with carefully arranged patterns, now turning into a rounded circle, now linked into a slanting chain, then wedged into a hollow square, then split into separate sections. But when the horn's concluding note had unravelled the knotted complexities of their alternating movements, the curtain was raised, the screens folded back, and the stage was set.

There stood a wooden mountain, constructed with lofty craftsmanship to resemble the famous mountain of which the bard Homer sang, Mount Ida. It was planted with bushes and live trees, and at its very peak, from a flowing fountain made by the designer's hand, it poured river-water. A few goats were browsing among the low grasses, and a young man, beautifully attired like the Phrygian shepherd Paris, with exotic robes flowing over his shoulders and a golden tiara covering his head, was feigning mastery of the flock. Then a radiantly beautiful boy appeared, naked except for an ephebic cape covering his left shoulder. He attracted all eyes with his blond curls, and from his hair projected little golden wings symmetrically attached; a caduceus and wand identified him as Mercury.[9] He danced forward, carrying in his right hand an apple gilded with gold leaf, which he held out to the person who was acting Paris. Then, after indicating Jupiter's instructions with a nod, he quickly and elegantly retraced his steps and disappeared.

---

7. Lucius now recounts the woman's criminal history, omitted here.

8. Lucius can only return to human form by eating roses.

9. Messenger of the gods.

[Indecent Proposal and Judgment of Paris] Ch. 17

[Paris is commanded to judge who is the most beautiful goddess: Juno, queen of the gods; Minerva, goddess of wisdom; or Venus, goddess of love. He awards the prize to Venus after she promises him her human daughter Helen — over whom the Trojan War will subsequently be fought. Lucius comments on his verdict.]

Why are you so surprised, you cheap ciphers—or should I say sheep of the courts, or better still vultures in togas—if nowadays all jurors hawk their verdicts for a price, since at the world's beginning an adjudication between gods and men was corrupted by beauty's influence, and a country shepherd, chosen judge on the advice of great Jupiter, sold the first verdict for a profit of pleasure, resulting in the destruction of himself and his entire race? And it was the same, by Hercules, with a second and yet another celebrated case among the far-famed princes of the Achaeans, when Palamedes, a man of superior learning and wisdom, was condemned for treason because of false accusations, or mediocre Ulysses was preferred to great Ajax, who was supreme in martial valour.[10] And what kind of a trial was that one held by the Athenians, those skilful legislators and teachers of all knowledge? Is it not true that that divinely wise old man,[11] whom the Delphic god pronounced superior to all other mortals in intelligence, was attacked by the lies and malice of an utterly worthless faction, accused of being a corruptor of the young—whom he was in fact keeping in rein—and murdered with the poisonous juice of a baleful herb? He bequeathed to his fellow-citizens the stain of eternal disgrace, because even to this day the best philosophers choose his holy school and in their jealous pursuit of happiness swear by his very name.

But I am afraid one of you may reproach me for this attack of indignation and think to himself, "So, now are we going to have to stand an ass lecturing us on philosophy?" So I shall return to the story at the point where I left it.

After the judgement of Paris was completed, Juno and Minerva went off stage, gloomy and acting angry, proclaiming with gestures their wrath at being defeated. Venus, on the other hand, joyfully and gaily proclaimed her happiness by dancing with her entire chorus. Then, from a hidden pipe at the very peak of the mountain, saffron dissolved in wine came spurting up into the air and rained down in a fragrant shower, sprinkling the goats that were grazing all round, until, dyed to a greater beauty, they exchanged their natural whiteness for a yellow hue. Finally, when the theatre was filled with the delightful fragrance, a chasm in the earth opened and swallowed up the wooden mountain.

And now a soldier came hurrying across the theatre floor in answer to the audience's demands, to fetch the woman from the public prison, the one who I told you had been condemned to the beasts for her manifold crimes and engaged to make an illustrious match with me. And now a bed, evidently meant to serve as our honeymoon couch, was being elaborately made up, shining with Indian tortoise-shell, piled high with a feathered mattress, and spread with a flowery silk coverlet.

---

10. Two famous mythical examples of unjust verdicts.

11. Socrates, condemned to death by drinking hemlock.

But as for me, besides my shame at indulging in sexual intercourse in public, besides the contagion of this damnable polluted woman, I was greatly tormented by the fear of death; for I thought to myself that, when we were in fact fastened together in Venus' embrace, any wild animal that might be let in to slaughter the woman could not possibly turn out to be so intelligently clever or so skilfully educated or so temperately moderate as to mangle the woman lying attached to my loins while sparing me on the grounds that I was unconvicted and innocent. So now I was afraid not for my honour, but for my very life. While my trainer gave his full attention to the proper fitting of our couch, and all the slaves were busy, some occupied with preparations for the hunting-spectacle, the others spellbound by the sensual pleasure of the show, I was allowed free rein for my own devices. Besides, no one thought that such a tame ass needed to be watched very carefully. So I slowly moved forward without being observed until I reached the nearest gate, and then hurled myself forward with the utmost rapidity. I covered six whole miles at full speed and arrived at the town of Cenchreae, which is well-known as part of the illustrious territory of the Corinthians, and is washed by the Aegean Sea and the Saronic Gulf. The port there is a safe harbour for ships and has a large population. I avoided the crowds, therefore, and chose a hidden stretch of shore. There, right next to the spray from the breakers, I stretched out in a soft hollow of sand to refresh my weary body, for the Sun's chariot had raced round the last turning-post of the day. As I surrendered myself to the evening's quiet, sweet sleep overwhelmed me.

About the first watch of the night I awoke in sudden fright and saw, just emerging from the waves of the sea, the full circle of the moon glistening with extraordinary brilliance. Surrounded by the silent mysteries of dark night, I realised that the supreme goddess now exercised the fullness of her power; that human affairs were wholly governed by her providence; that not only flocks and wild beasts but even lifeless things were quickened by the divine favour of her light and might; and that individual bodies on land, in the sky, and in the sea grew at one period in consequence of her waxing and diminished at another in obedience to her waning. Since fate, it seemed, was now satiated with the number and intensity of my sufferings, and was offering me the hope, albeit late, of deliverance, I decided to pray to the august image of the goddess present before me. Quickly I shook off my sluggish sleep and arose happily and eagerly. Desiring to purify myself I went at once to bathe in the sea, plunging my head under the waves seven times, because the divine Pythagoras[12] had declared that number to be especially appropriate to religious rituals. Then, my face covered with tears, I prayed to the mighty goddess.

"O queen of heaven—whether you are bountiful Ceres, the primal mother of crops, who in joy at the recovery of your daughter took away from men their primeval animal fodder of acorns and showed them gentler nourishment, and now dwell in the land of Eleusis; or heavenly Venus, who at the first foundation

---

12. Greek mathematician and philosopher, sixth century B.C.E., who taught of the transmigration of souls.

of the universe united the diversity of the sexes by creating Love and propagated the human race through ever-recurring progeny, and now are worshipped in the island sanctuary of Paphos; or Phoebus' sister,[13] who brought forth populous multitudes by relieving the delivery of offspring with your soothing remedies, and now are venerated at the illustrious shrine of Ephesus; or dreaded Proserpina[14] of the nocturnal howls, who in triple form repress the attacks of ghosts and keep the gates to earth closed fast, roam through widely scattered groves and are propitiated by diverse rites—you who illumine every city with your womanly light, nourish the joyous seeds with your moist fires, and dispense beams of fluctuating radiance according to the convolutions of the Sun—by whatever name, with whatever rite, in whatever image it is meet to invoke you: defend me now in the uttermost extremes of tribulation, strengthen my fallen fortune, grant me rest and peace from the cruel mischances I have endured. Let this be enough toil, enough danger. Rid me of this dreadful four-footed form, restore me to the sight of my own people, restore me to the Lucius I was. But if some divine power that I have offended is harassing me with inexorable savagery, at least let me die, if I may not live."

[Venus appears to Lucius.]

all of the people of all the world worship her as all the goddess

"Behold, Lucius, moved by your prayers I have come, I the mother of the universe, mistress of all the elements, and first offspring of the ages, mightiest of deities, queen of the dead, and foremost of heavenly beings; my one person manifests the aspect of all gods and goddesses. With my nod I rule the starry heights of heaven, the health-giving breezes of the sea, and the plaintive silences of the underworld. My divinity is one, worshipped by all the world under different forms, with various rites, and by manifold names. In one place the Phrygians, first-born of men, call me Pessinuntine Mother of the Gods, in another the autochthonous people of Attica call me Cecropian Minerva, in another the sea-washed Cyprians call me Paphian Venus; to the arrow-bearing Cretans I am Dictynna Diana, to the trilingual Sicilians Ortygian Proserpina, to the ancient people of Eleusis Attic Ceres; some call me Juno, some Bellona, others Hecate, and still others Rhamnusia; the people of the two Ethiopias, who are lighted by the first rays of the Sun-God as he rises every day, and the Egyptians, who are strong in ancient lore, worship me with the rites that are truly mine and call me by my real name, which is Queen Isis. I have come in pity at your misfortunes; I have come in sympathy and good will. Now stop your tears and cease your lamentation; banish your grief. Now by my providence your day of salvation is dawning. So, therefore, pay careful attention to these commands of mine. The day which will be the day born from this night has been proclaimed mine by everlasting religious observance: on that day, when the winter's tempests are lulled and the ocean's storm-blown waves are calmed, my priests dedicate an untried keel to the now navigable sea and consecrate it as the first fruits of voyaging. You must await this

---

13. Diana, patroness of childbirth, was worshipped at Ephesus as an Asiatic fertility goddess.

14. Queen of the underworld.

rite with an attitude both calm and reverent. At my command, my priest, as part of his equipment for the procession, will carry in his right hand a garland of roses attached to the sistrum.[15] So do not hesitate, but eagerly push through the crowd and join the procession, relying on my good will; go right up to the priest and gently, as if you were going to kiss his hand, pluck the roses and cast off at once the hide of that wretched beast which I have long detested. And do not shrink from any of my instructions because it seems difficult: for at this very moment when I come to you I am present there too and am instructing my priest in his sleep about what he must do next. At my command the tight-packed crowd of people will give way before you, and no one in the midst of the joyous rites and festive revelries will shrink from the unsightly aspect that you present. Nor will anyone misinterpret your sudden transformation and prefer charges against you out of spite.

You will clearly remember and keep forever sealed deep in your heart the fact that the rest of your life's course is pledged to me until the very limit of your last breath. Nor is it unjust that you should owe all the time you have to live to her by whose benefit you return to the world of men. Moreover you will live in happiness, you will live in glory, under my guardianship. And when you have completed your life's span and travel down to the dead, there too, even in the hemisphere under the earth, you will find me, whom you see now, shining among the shades of Acheron and holding court in the deep recesses of the Styx, and while you dwell in the Elysian fields I will favour you and you will constantly worship me.[16] But if by assiduous obedience, worshipful service, and determined celibacy you win the favour of my godhead, you will know that I—and I alone—can even prolong your life beyond the limits determined by your fate."

This was the end of the holy revelation, and the invincible divinity now withdrew into herself. At once I was quickly released from sleep, and I rose in a confusion of fear and joy, and covered with sweat.

[Lucius Recovers His Human Form]

[Lucius recovers his human form, then undergoes a series of initiations into the worship of Isis and her divine husband Osiris. He moves to Rome and becomes a devotee at the temple of Isis, shaving his head and selling his clothes to do so; he earns his living as a lawyer. The book ends with a final vision.]

Finally, after just a few days, he that is mightiest of the great gods, the highest of the mightiest, the loftiest of the highest, and the sovereign of the loftiest, Osiris, appeared to me in a dream. He had not transformed himself into a semblance other than his own, but deigned to welcome me face to face with his own venerable utterance, bidding me unhesitatingly to continue as now to win fame in the courts as an advocate and not fear the slanders of detractors which my

---

15. A musical instrument, used in rituals of Isis.

16. Acheron and Styx are underworld rivers; the Elysian fields are the dwelling place of blessed souls.

industrious pursuit of legal studies had aroused in Rome. Furthermore, to avoid my serving his mysteries as an undistinguished member of the faithful, he elected me to the college of his *pastophori*,[17] and even made me a member of the quinquennial board of directors. Then, once more shaving my head completely, neither covering up nor hiding my baldness, but displaying it wherever I went, I joyfully carried out the duties of that ancient priesthood, founded in the days of Sulla.[18]

> The man who went through praising hair ended up w/ a shaved head as a priest.

---

17. "Shrine-bearers."   18. Some 250 years earlier.

Lady writing a love letter. Temple sculpture of the eleventh century C.E. from Khajuraho in central India.

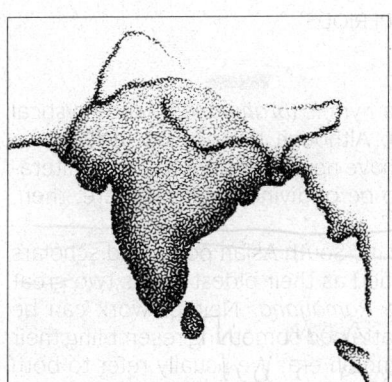

SECTION II

South Asia:
Early and
Middle Periods

As a physical landscape South Asia, comprising present-day Pakistan, India, Nepal, Bangladesh, and Sri
Lanka, is vast and varied. As a literary landscape, it
comprises dozens of languages with a complex and
fascinating record of literary activity stretching back
more than three thousand years. In the "early period" (to the end of the first millennium C.E.) literature in South Asia finds expression above all in
Sanskrit and Tamil, languages radically different not
only in respect to their linguistic identity but also in
respect to their ethnic and regional identities; the
next half-millennium or so, the "middle period," is
marked by the emergence of new literary languages
and new forms of subjectivity and of political, social,
and religious consciousness.

Sanskrit belongs to the Indo-European family of
languages; its presence in the northwest of the subcontinent is attested to as early as the first millennium B.C.E. During the next thousand years Sanskrit
spread throughout South Asia to become the first of
several pan-Indian literary languages (the others being Persian in the later middle period and English in
the modern period).

The name Sanskrit means, among other things,
"refined" or "ritually purified." (It is one of the very
few language names that does not commemorate an
ethnic identity.) Initially, Sanskrit seems to have been
employed principally for religious purposes. Writings
related to this religion include the hymns of the Veda
("[sacred] knowledge," from the same Indo-
European root, *weid*, that gave us our English words

wit and *wisdom*), prose commentaries on the hymns (*brahmanas*), and mystical and philosophical speculations (*upanishads*). Although these texts include the most ancient Sanskrit writings, South Asians have never considered them "literature" in as much as they were considered to be of divine origins. Where, then, does the Sanskrit literary tradition begin?

Since at least the fifth or sixth centuries C.E., South Asian poets and scholars reflecting on their literary history have identified as their oldest works two great Sanskrit "epics": the *Mahabharata* and the *Ramayana*. Neither work can be dated with any specificity, but both probably attained something resembling their current form around the beginning of the common era. We usually refer to both works as epics (they share features in common with Homeric poems), but for South Asians they are often thought to represent different genres. The *Ramayana* is regarded as a poem (*kavya*), indeed it is thought to be the first poem, while the *Mahabharata* is classified as history (*itihasa*). Despite this distinction, the two works are similar in form as well as in content.

The concerns of these texts are above all social, political, and male in perspective: What does it mean to live in a world of power, to live with our "own," to deal with "others"? What is a king? What is the nature of war? What is the "right thing to do" (*dharma*)? What is the proper relationship between men and women? The responses the two epics provide to these questions are markedly different. Between them they provide a kind of spectrum of responses to the most pressing questions of the human condition.

The influence that the *Mahabharata* and the *Ramayana* have exerted on the literary history of South Asia has been fundamental. Even Sanskrit literature of a much later period is devoted to rethinking and rewriting their stories. This is especially true of Sanskrit drama (whose relationship to these epics is strikingly close to the relationship that existed between Greek drama and the Homeric epics). The history of virtually every regional literature, too, is marked—in some cases even initiated—by adaptations of the epics. Today their influence continues to be strong, as witnessed by large-scale television versions of both epics in India in the 1980s. The religious associations of Sanskrit were such that apart from the two "epics" we have no "literature" in Sanskrit before the common era.

The literary imagination was to find expression in other languages, probably in the Prakrits—regional dialects related to Sanskrit that are the ancestors of modern languages of northern India. Little of this literature has survived, however, and with few exceptions later Prakrit works are derivative of Sanskrit literature.

Religious movements such as Buddhism and Jainism arose in opposition to Vedic practice during the fifth century B.C.E. and explicitly rejected Sanskrit, at least initially, for their own doctrinal writings. In part, this rejection was a practical decision: The new sects hoped to attract converts by using a common language. However, the decision was also ideological, for the sects defined themselves in opposition to vedic culture and its Sanskrit idiom. Languages espoused by these new sects provided literary opportunities; thus some of the oldest texts that exhibit features of what the later Indian tradition thinks of as literature are in Pali, an early Buddhist language. These texts also include some of the first works ascribed to women, for the Buddhist monastic community included women as members.

Within three or four hundred years of the founding of these religious movements, however, many of their adherents in the north had switched to Sanskrit for their writings. The reasons were undoubtedly as complex as the process is unclear, yet the effect was to "liberate" Sanskrit and make it available for general intellectual use. Among the great innovators in this cultural convergence were Buddhist poets of the first centuries of the common era, who worked in a new environment created by—if not actually at the courts of—central Asians newly immigrant into the subcontinent. The most celebrated of these poets is Ashvaghosha, who turned vernacular tales about the Buddha into a form of Sanskrit poetry that quickly came to be regarded as a "classical" standard.

Freed by the examples of the epics and the efforts of the Buddhists from its exclusively Vedic domain, Sanskrit became the chosen instrument for expressing a vast range of intellectual and artistic concerns. The Sanskrit literature that evolved over the next 1500 years (100–1600 or so) includes every conceivable genre of imaginative and expository writing and constitutes perhaps the largest and richest single body of literature in all premodernity. A truly representative sampling—that would include something from the large number of Sanskrit dramas or from the immensely influential story literature—is impossible within the confines of this book. But the flavor of Sanskrit literature can be suggested by the selections of lyric poetry included here. A decidedly nonreligious species of writing in what is often and quite erroneously represented as a uniquely religion-obsessed culture, lyric poetry is one of the great achievements of Sanskrit art. The lyric was also the single genre to offer women a literary voice in early India, though unfortunately even this was rather rare. (It is only toward the end of the middle period, in the fifteenth to seventeenth centuries, that we find in southern India a few larger-scale compositions in Sanskrit by women.)

Despite the everyday concerns of Sanskrit literature, there is evidence that the language was never widely used for everyday purposes. Instead, Sanskrit was studied as a "father" tongue, and it existed in a state of some tension with the "mother" tongues—the various regional languages. (The situation can be compared with the relationship of Latin to the emerging regional languages of medieval Europe.) Only one regional language, Tamil, the language of the southernmost region of India, succeeded in creating its own distinct literary tradition during the early period (up to about 1000 C.E.)

Tamil belongs to the Dravidian family of languages—a family exclusive to South Asia—and its literary history stretches back to at least a century or two before the common era. The earliest Tamil poetry—called *sangam,* or "literary academic" poetry—shares a highly systematized and detailed repertoire of literary conventions, indicating how acutely aware its poets were that they inhabited a linguistically and culturally distinct region. Central to Tamil poetry is the genre distinction between the "interior" and "exterior" worlds—the inner world of the emotional life of lovers, the outer world of the public lives of warriors and kings. More than just a literary convention, these worlds provided a way of envisioning the human condition in terms of two complementary spheres of experience.

The influence of Tamil poetry spread early into the world of Sanskrit poetry. But the lines of influence were also reversed, as Sanskrit literature exercised a powerful influence on later Tamil poetry. This was far from a passive reception of dominant cultural forms, however, as the adaptation of the *Ramayana* by Kampan, Tamil's greatest poet (twelfth century), makes clear: Kampan did not merely translate the earlier Sanskrit work; he rethought it and reworked some of its key scenes and themes.

A powerful component in the development of South Asian writing, however, is indeed a growing self-conscious differentiation between Sanskrit and the mother tongues. The "Middle Period" of South Asian literary history (roughly 1000–1800) may in fact be taken as constituted by the emergence of new literary languages to express new forms of subjectivity, new worlds of political experience, new kinds of religious consciousness. For example, Kannada, the language of the southern region of India called Karnataka, had been a vehicle for literary work from at least the ninth century C.E. Its earliest writers, however, had largely emulated Sanskrit models. A truly distinctive form of Kannadan literature came into existence in the tenth century, with the rise of new religious movements broadly known as "devotionalism," which expressed a more direct, less socially constrained relationship with the divine. Similarly in the north, regional languages such as Avadhi and Braj (ancestors of modern Hindi) became the vehicles for expressing an altogether new kind of subjectivity, as in the strikingly innovative autobiography from the beginning of the seventeenth century, the *Ardhakatha-naka* of Banarasi, and a new kind of religious politics, as in the songs of the low-caste weaver poet Kabir, which contest and seek to transcend the divisions in the social and religious communities of the fifteenth century.

Historical and Cultural Background

An early form of Sanskrit and the Vedic religious practices were brought to South Asia by peoples who are thought to have entered the region from the northwest probably a little before 1000 B.C.E. In successive waves of migration they gradually fanned out over the northern plains and along the Ganges River. Before their arrival the northwest had been home to what is known as the Harappan civilization, in the Indus River valley (largely in present-day Pakistan), which flourished for perhaps five hundred years (about 1500 B.C.E.). Archaeological evidence makes it clear that Harappan civilization was extremely advanced; writing was known, though it has yet to be deciphered. It is probable, though as yet unproven, that something of its culture also survived in the new civilizations that would take shape over the next millennium.

These civilizations began to take on distinctive traits after 1000 B.C.E. with the growth of cities and settled kingdoms, especially in the northeast. The Sanskrit texts often refer to four social orders: Vedic priests (*brahmans*), warriors (*kshatriyas*), merchants (*vaishyas*), and servants (*shudras*). Eventually, numerous "subcastes" would appear. It was especially in the religious world of the Brahman priests and the fire cult they maintained and the sacred texts associated with this cult (the *vedas*) that these social orders were represented as an ideological model. Whatever the everyday reality of this hierarchy, it and the religious worldview in which it was embedded were the objects of frequent contention from about the middle of the first millennium B.C.E. onward. New social-religious communities, such as the Buddhists and the Jains, came into existence then which presented themselves as alternatives to Vedic society. Brahmanic developments in the wake of these movements and interaction with local religious practices initiated the gradual metamorphosis of Vedic practice into the diverse collection of local religions we group together under the umbrella term *Hinduism*.

Political regional autonomy was the rule in South Asia, with numerous dynastic kingdoms fostering great cultural diversity. Regional kingdoms were occasionally, however, brought into loose imperial formations. Among the most important of these were the Maurya Empire (third to fourth centuries B.C.E.), the last of whose kings, Ashoka, patronized the Buddhists; the central Asian Kushan Empire in the north and northwest (first century C.E.), which also adopted Buddhism; and the Gupta Empire (fourth to sixth centuries C.E.), which made its presence felt throughout much of the northern half of the subcontinent. Crippled by repeated invasions of Hun tribes (part of the same wave of invasions that brought down the Roman Empire in the west), the Gupta Empire gradually disintegrated, and autonomous regional kingdoms reasserted themselves. New incursions from central Asia had lasting effects.

Starting in the eleventh century, Turkic peoples from central Asia and Afghanistan began a series of invasions that eventually led to the establishment of the Delhi Sultanate in 1206. The Sultanate lasted for almost two centuries, bringing much of the subcontinent under Turkic rule. A second major period of Islamic influence occurred from the sixteenth to the eighteenth centuries with the Mughal Empire.

Too often painted in stark terms of conquest and mutual animosity, the interactions of the Islamic immigrants with the very heterogeneous peoples of the subcontinent were actually quite complex, creating particularly Indian types of Islamic culture. Sometimes the results were the creation of altogether new forms of religious and cultural identity. From a cultural standpoint, a major consequence was the introduction of Persian, yet another trans-regional language in the South Asian cultural landscape.

NB Alternate spellings (Siva, Shiva, etc.) have been allowed to stand.

Further Readings

Biardeau, Madeleine. *Hinduism: The Anthropology of a Civilization*. Delhi: Oxford University Press, 1989.

Chatterji, Suniti Kumar, ed. "Part III: Major Languages and Literature of Modern India." *The Cultural Heritage of India*. Vol. 5. Calcutta: Ramakrishna Mission Institute of Culture, 1978.

Das, Sisir Kumar. *A History of Indian Literature*. Vol. 8. New Delhi: Sahitya Akademi, 1991.

Davies, C. Collin. *An Historical Atlas of the Indian Peninsula*. Oxford: Oxford University Press, 1959.

Dimock, Edward C. et al. *The Literatures of India: An Introduction*. Chicago: University of Chicago Press, 1974.

Gonda, Jan, ed. *A History of Indian Literature*. 10 vols. Wiesbaden, Germany: Otto Harrossowitz, 1973.

Hardy, Peter. "Islam in South Asia." *Encyclopedia of Religions*. Vol. 7. Ed. Mircea Eliade. New York: Macmillan. 390–404.

Kosambi, D. D. *The Culture and Civilisation of Ancient India in Historical Outline* London: Routledge & Kegan Paul, 1965.

Kulke, Hermann, and Dieter Rothermund. *A History of India*. Totowa, N.J.: Barnes and Noble, 1986.

O'Flaherty, Wendy Doniger. *Hindu Myths: A Sourcebook*. Harmondsworth, England: Penguin, 1975.

Robinson, Richard. *Buddhism: A Historical Introduction*. 3rd ed. Belmont, CA: Dickenson, 1982.

Winternitz, Maurice. *History of Indian Literature*. 3 vols. Delhi: Motilal Banarsidass. 1959–67.

KRISHNA DVAIPAIYANA VYASA

(FOURTH CENTURY B.C.E.)

India

The *Mahabharata*, or the Great Tale of the Bharata War, started as an oral epic. It was composed (that is, recited, modified, and transmitted) over the course of many centuries, beginning in the middle of the first millennium B.C.E. The written text of some 100,000 verses probably dates from early in the common era. It is traditionally attributed to Krishna Dvaipaiyana Vyasa, about whom we know nothing except what emerges from the poem itself.

The story concerns the dispute between two sets of claimants to the throne of Hastinapura, a city the text locates near modern Delhi. Though often referred to in the poem as brothers, they are actually first cousins—the sons of the brothers Pandu and Dhritarashtra. After years of struggle, the kingdom is provisionally partitioned between them. But Duryodhana, the eldest son of Dhritarashtra, decides to seize the share of the Pandavas (the sons of Pandu). He settles on the ruse of a dice game with Yudhishthira, the eldest son of Pandu.

The first selection presents this dramatic gambling match. Yudhishthira, a weak and confused person, is nevertheless an embodiment of "law" (*dharma*) itself as a duly consecrated King. The tricky Duryodhana is playing through a proxy, his uncle Shakuni. The focal point of the selection is the humiliation of Draupadi, the wife of the Pandavas. (They have married her conjointly.) Her humiliation is the key moment of the epic, releasing energies on both sides that cannot be contained. Inexorably, the story builds to the terrible slaughter that will destroy the sons of Dhritarastra, leaving the sons of Pandu victors who, as they realize near the end of the poem, are really dead in life, for they have destroyed everything they fought for.

Just before the great battle begins in the epic from the *Mahabharata* is the celebrated *Bhagavad Gita,* or "Song of the Blessed One." In our second selection, the action begins with a description of "the field of Kuru," "the field of sacred duty (*dharma*)," where the question posed is what actually is "duty" in the context of this war. Krishna, a close companion of Arjuna, one of the Pandavas, discourses on the nature of the war and convinces Arjuna that it is right for him to do battle.

from *The Mahabharata*

The Friendly Dice Game

2.52

VAISHAMPAYANA

Then Vidura[1] set forth with noble steeds
swift and strong, well broken to the car.

Translated by Daniel H. H. Ingalls.

---

1. The half-caste son of Vyasa, and therefore
   half-brother to King Dhritarashtra.

Compelled by order of King Dhritarashtra
he journeyed to the five wise Pandavas.

He flew along the road; he reached the royal city.   5
The wise counselor entered and was honored by the priests.

He came to the king's citadel as bright as Kubera's palace,[2]
and approached the son of Law, the Law itself, Yudhishthira.

Yudhishthira the king, invincible,
ever firm in truth and great of soul,   10
then greeted Vidura with all respect
and asked of Dhritarashtra and his sons.

YUDHISHTHIRA
I see your heart, O half-caste, is unhappy.
And yet, the news you bring is good, I trust?
His sons, I trust, obey the ancient king;   15
the Kuru tribesmen follow his command?

VIDURA
The ancient king is well, as are his children:
He sits among his godlike family
happy with virtuous and obedient sons,
knowing no sorrow, self-reliant, strong.   20

But this is the message given me by the king,
bidding me first ask your health and welfare:
"Your cousins have built a court as fair as yours
that I would gladly have you see, my son.

"Come to it, Pandava, with your four brothers   25
and enjoy yourself at a friendly game of dice.
We will rejoice to see you, as will also
the Kuru lords whom we have brought together."

You will see the stocks of dice provided there
by Dhritarashtra the magnificent,   30
and all the players that he has assembled.
Such was I bid to ask you. Pray accept.

YUDHISHTHIRA
If we should gamble, I fear there will be quarrels.
What man, aware of what it leads to, gambles?
But I ask you what you think the proper course,   35
for all of us take counsel by your word.

---

2. Kubera was the god of riches and treasure
   and presiding deity of the northern quarter
   of space.

VIDURA

I know that gambling is the source of evil
and I made great efforts to prevent it;
in spite of which the king has sent me.
Hear and choose with wisdom what is best.   40

YUDHISHTHIRA

What other gamblers will attend the game
in addition to the sons of Dhritarashtra?
I ask you, Vidura; tell me who they are,
those others brought together by the king.

VIDURA

The king of Gandhara, Shakuni, O king,   45
that gambler swift of hand who knows his dice;
Prince Vivimshati and Citrasena,
Purumitra, true to his word, and Jaya.

YUDHISHTHIRA

Fearful gamblers have been brought together,
experts in the art, who use deceit.   50
But the world, they say, is in the power of fate;
I will not fail to gamble with the experts.

For how can I not wish to come
when Dhritarashtra sends his bidding?
—a son must wish what his father bids—   55
So I accept the invitation.

But with Shakuni I have no wish to gamble
and will not do so unless he challenges.
Only if challenged I will not refuse,
for so I have sworn as my eternal vow.   60

VAISHAMPAYANA

So spoke the King of Law to Vidura
and bid with haste make ready for the journey.
Next morning he departed with his men,
and with his ladies led by Draupadi.

"Fate takes along our wits as a bright light takes our vision,   65
and we are in the power of fate as if bound to it by cords."

So spoke Yudhishthira in setting forth with the half-caste;
the invitation did not please the enemy-taming king.

The slayer of foes mounted the car that Bahlika had given;
surrounded by his brothers the son of Law drove forth,   70

drove shining with royal glory and accompanied by brahmans,[3]
summoned by Dhritarashtra and by the hour of fate.

He drove to Hastinapura to Dhritarashtra's palace
and there the lawful Pandava met the ancient king.

He met the teacher Drona, and Bhishma, Karna, Kripa,   75
greeting each in his degree and greeting Drona's son.

And there the great-armed king met also Somadatta
together with Duryodhana, Shakuni, and Shalya.

He met Jayadratha and Kuru lords by hundreds,
and all the other kings that had assembled there.   80

Then the great-armed king accompanied by his brothers
entered the inner chamber of learned Dhritarashtra.

He saw Queen Gandhari with daughters-in-law beside her,
bright as the star Rohini among its lesser stars.

He greeted Queen Gandhari and in return was greeted.   85
He saw the king his uncle blind except in wit.

The old king kissed his head and the heads of the kneeling princes,
the younger sons of Pandu, Bhima and the rest.

There was joy among the Kurus at the coming of their cousins
to see these handsome Pandavas, these tigers among men.   90

They took their leave and were shown to chambers decked with jewels,
where all their ladies met them, led by Draupadi.

But not so glad of heart were the Dhartarashtra ladies
when they saw how Draupadi fairly blazed with gems.   95

The heroes left their wives with promise to meet later;
they engaged in manly exercise and had their bodies oiled
and rubbed with sandal paste; and so in peaceful spirit
they heard the priestly blessing and said their evening prayers.

After a rich repast they returned to the jeweled chambers,   100
and as their ladies sang to them, the Pandavas lay down.

They passed the happy night in amorous engagement
and awoke refreshed next morning to praises of their bards.

The happy night had passed. They said their morning prayers
and entered the fair court where the gamblers stood in wait.   105

---

3. Priests and scholars.

2.53

SHAKUNI

The carpet is laid, Yudhishthira; all wait upon your coming.
The dice are put in place; let us set the rules of play.

YUDHISHTHIRA

Dicing is deception. It needs no warrior's courage;
it needs no ruler's judgment. Why praise dicing, king?

For men accord no honor to the deceptions of a gambler.   5
Do not beat us, Shakuni, by such dishonest means.

SHAKUNI

He alone can long endure at gambling
who can reckon numbers and recognize deceit,
who never tires in moving of the dice,
who has the wit to understand the play.   10

It is the way you draw the dice that wins
and only that, when you will call it fate.
Let us gamble, king, and no more hesitate;
set stakes and make no more delay.

YUDHISHTHIRA

I would rather heed the words of Devala the holy,   15
who ever visits our battles, those gates to heaven's world.

"That sort of play is evil where gamblers use deception.
To win by rightful war is the proper sort of play.

"Nobles do not act like slaves; they do not use deception.
An honest and straightforward fight is the way of real men."   20

We seek to use our wealth in aid of worthy brahmans;
whether one win or lose, it is wrong to gamble with such wealth.

I like not wealth or pleasure when purchased by deception;
even when the gambler is honest, I do not praise the game.

SHAKUNI

The learned fights the ignorant: by deceit, Yudhishthira?   25
the wise against the foolish: who calls out deceit?

Just so you fight me here. But if you find deception,
or if you are afraid, of course you may withdraw.

YUDHISHTHIRA

Challenged, I will not refuse, for I have made that promise;
and fate is strong, O Shakuni; I stand at its command.   30

So say in this assembly with whom am I to gamble?
Who can set stakes against me? Let the play begin

DURYODHANA
O lord of tribes, it is I will stake my gold and jewels;
but for my sake my uncle, Shakuni, will dice.

YUDHISHTHIRA
It is wrong that one should gamble on another's wager;   35
you know as well as I. But take him if you wish.

VAISHAMPAYANA
As the game was about to begin, many kings and nobles
followed Dhritarashtra into the fair court.

Bhisma, Drona, Kripa, and wise Vidura
came with the others, but they were not so glad of heart.   40

Singly and in couples the lion-necked heroes
seated themselves about on the many brilliant thrones.

The court was then resplendent with these assembled nobles,
as heaven is resplendent with its assembled gods,

for all of them were brilliant, Veda—knowing[4] heroes.   45
Then straightaway began the friendly game of dice.

YUDHISHTHIRA
I have a pearl necklace born of the deep ocean,
costly and fair, Duryodhana, and the pearls are set in gold.

This is my wager, king. What have you that is equal?
If not, I have won first turn to draw from the stock of dice.   50

DURYODHANA
Indeed I too have pearls and many kinds of treasure.
I am no miser with my wealth. See, I have won the draw.

VAISHAMPAYANA
Then Shakuni drew the dice, who knew the art of dicing.
"I have won," said Shakuni to King Yudhishthira.

SHAKUNI
You have lost much wealth: horses, elephants, and brothers.   55
Tell me, son of Kunti, does any wealth remain?

YUDHISHTHIRA
I am the chief of all and well loved of my brothers;
If beaten I will work for you myself in servitude.

VAISHAMPAYANA
The gambler heard the words; etc. . . .

---

4. Sacred text.

SHAKUNI
This was most ill done to lose yourself at wager;   60
when wealth remains, O king, it is ill to lose oneself.

VAISHAMPAYANA
He spoke and with proud glance herded his captives singly,
drawing to him the heroes that had stood at stake.

SHAKUNI
There still is left your dear queen, a single unwon wager.
Set Draupadi at stake; by her win back yourself.   65

YUDHISHTHIRA
The mean of tall and short; the mean of black and gold,
whose eyes are lit by passion: with her I wager you.

Whose eyes are autumn lotuses, whose breath is the autumn lotus,
whose beauty is that of Sri[5] who lives in the autumn lotus;

a woman of such kindliness and of such perfect beauty,   70
of such consummate virtue, as ever man could wish;

whose careful management extends to my meanest shepherd,
ever the first to wake, ever the last to sleep;

the sweat upon whose face smells of jasmine flowers;
long-haired, narrow-waisted, smooth-skinned, loving-eyed: 75

with this fair-waisted queen, the daughter of Pancala,
with dear-limbed Draupadi: come, I wager you.

VAISHAMPAYANA
So spoke the King of Law and at his words there mounted
a cry of horror from the elders of the court.

All began to speak; the court was in an uproar.   80
Bhisma, Drona, Kripa, were overwhelmed with grief.

Vidura held his head as if fainting from a blow;
he sat with lowered face, breath hissing like a snake.

But Dhritarashtra was glad. He asked over and over
"Has he won, Has my son won?" unable to hide his joy.   85

Karna was passing glad and Duhshasana exulted;
but others at the court could not hold back their tears.

Shakuni was sure of himself. As though without reflection
he approached the dice once more, and said simply "I have won."

---

5. The goddess of royalty and wealth.

2.59

DURYODHANA

Come, half-caste! Bring Draupadi to court:
the dear consort of the Pandavas.
We'll put her straight to work. It will be a pleasure
to watch her clean the floor with servant girls.

VIDURA

Fool! you put a noose around your neck   5
and yet are unaware of what you do:
a simpleton that teeters on a cliff,
a boy that would show off by teasing tigers.

The snakes are on your head, their fangs filled with poison;
stir them not up, you fool, or you will soon be dead.   10

Queen Draupadi I think has not become your servant;
the king was not her master when he made the bet.

This young king is like the bamboo tree
that comes in fruit only in time to perish.
For gambling brings on deadly enmity: 15
he knows it not but he is ripe for death.

Be not spiteful. Turn not the knife in the wound,
nor summon payment from a helpless man.
Speak not that word by which, although
another trembles, you go yourself to hell.   20

We call it "overspeaking" when a word
so falls upon another's tenderness
that day and night he suffers from the pain.
A wise man guards himself from overspeech.

You know of the goat—the thieves had lost the knife   25
until the goat by digging with his hoof
revealed the means of cutting his own throat.
So you: don't dig at hatred that may kill you.

Some men are silent, saying not a word
of village dweller or of forester;   30
but when a holy man appears in town,
perfect in wisdom, they bark at him like dogs.

You do not realize, Duryodhana,
that at this dice game you have opened up
a gateway sloping down to hell, through which   35
how many Kuru lords must follow you!

Gourds may sink and stones may float,
ships may lose themselves on water,
but this stupid son of Dhritarashtra
will never heed my good advice.   40

The end is near. Destruction of the Kurus,
cruel and all-devouring, will ensue
from this one prince who spurns the words of Kavya,[6]
the advice of friends, and only grows in greed.

2.60

VAISHAMPAYANA
Duryodhana cried out, "I spurn your words,"
and turned away from the half-caste with contempt.
His eyes sought out the usher of the court,
to whom among those noble lords he spoke.

"You, usher, bring us Draupadi.   5
You are not frightened of the Pandavas.
The half-caste here opposes me from fear
and from his never having wished me well."

He spoke. The bard who served the court as usher
left quickly in obedience to the king.   10
As a dog might steal into a pride of lions
he made his way to the Pandavas' chief queen.

THE USHER
Yudhishthira, mad with dicing,
has lost you to Duryodhana.
So come to Dhritarashtra's chamber;   15
I am to lead you to your work.

DRAUPADI
O usher, how can such a thing be true?
What son of kings would put his wife at wager?
Was the king out of his mind with dicing,
or was it that no other wealth remained?   20

THE USHER
It was when no other wealth remained
that King Yudhishthira put up the wager;
for first the king had wagered his four brothers
and next himself; last of all were you.

---

6. Also called Shukra, a mythological authority on politics.

DRAUPADI

Go now, bard's son, to the court and ask my lord this question: 25
whether he first lost himself or whether first lost me.
Find out the answer and come back; then lead me as you say.

VAISHAMPAYANA

He went straight to the court and told Yudhishthira her question:
"Draupadi asks of whom you were master when you lost,
'whether you first lost yourself, or whether first lost me.'"   30

As though he were in a swoon Yudhishthira sat silent.
He said no word to the bard's son, whether of good or ill.

DURYODHANA

Let Krsna Draupadi come here and ask her question,
here in the court where all may hear both her words and his.

VAISHAMPAYANA

Again at the king's command he went to the royal harem   35
and said to Draupadi, trembling as he spoke:

THE USHER

The courtiers, lady, order you to come
and I fear destruction for the Kauravas.
The worthless king will not keep fortune long
if my lady Draupadi goes down to court.   40

DRAUPADI

The ordainer surely has ordained it thus,
for both the wise and foolish feel his hand.
But he has given us one highest law
and he will give me peace if I obey it.

      . . .

VAISHAMPAYANA

In single garment, with knot turned down, weeping and in her courses,[7]   45
the daughter of Panchala kings knelt before her uncle.

From where he stood Duryodhana observed
the expression of their faces. To the bard's son
he spoke exultant: "Bring her here, right here,
where the lords may speak to her directly.   50

The bard was subject to Duryodhana
but feared the anger of the highborn queen.
He faltered in obedience and asked,
"What shall I say to the lady Draupadi?"

---

7. Traditionally Indian women are secluded
   during their menstrual periods and dress in
   a single garment.

DURYODHANA
Duhshasana! My foolish usher
trembles with fear of Wolfbelly Bhima.
Go bring us Draupadi yourself.
What can her helpless husbands do?

VAISHAMPAYANA
The younger prince heard his brother's words
and rose with anger-reddened eyes.
He strode up to the audience chamber
and thus addressed Queen Draupadi.

"Come, Pancali, come! You have been won.
Look without shame on King Duryodhana.
Your love belongs to the Kurus; the lovely prize
is fairly won. Come down with me to the court."

Mindless what to do, the queen arose
and passed a hand across her bloodless face,
then ran in desperation toward the chambers
of the royal ladies of the Kauravas.

With speed Duhshasana ran after,
cursing at her in his wrath.
By her hair he seized the fleeing queen,
by her long and wavy, jet-black hair.

That hair that had been bathed in holy water
at ending of a royal consecration
the sons of Pandu now could not protect
from insult at a Dhartarastra's hand.

Duhshasana seized and pulled her toward the court
as the wind pulls at the thrashing plantain tree,
Pancala's daughter of the jet black hair,
a married queen, like a woman without a man.

With slender body bending at his force
she whispered, "No! I wear a single garment;
I am unclean! You cannot be so vile
as to bring me in this state before the court."

To which he answered, seizing with rough hand
the soft black tresses of the trembling queen,
"Call on what gods you wish: not Krishna, Jisnu,
Hari, Nara, shall stop my taking you.

"Be you unclean, it makes no difference;
or in a single garment or stark naked.
You have been won at dice and are our slave
and masters do with slave girls as they wish."

Her hair fell dissheveled, her garment slipped 95
as she was shaken by Duhshasana.
In deep shame and burning indignation
the beautiful queen spoke with lowered voice.

DRAUPADI
Here present in the court are learned men,
men like Indra,[8] who perform the rites, 100
my elders and lords the equals of my elders;
they must not see me in my present state.

This is an outrage! You are being shameful!
Stop stripping me¡ Stop pulling me about!
These sons of kings will not permit such wrong 105
even if all the gods should give you aid.

The royal son of Law[9] stands in the law,
and law is subtle: only the wise can grasp it.
But even at my lord's command I will not
give up honor and commit a sin. 110

This is a villainy to drag me so
among the Kurus when I am unclean.
But does no one cry out shame upon you?
Surely it cannot be that they approve?

Shame! Shame! The law of Bharatas, 115
the warrior code of honor is destroyed
when all the Kurus gathered here at court
see how the law of Kurus is transgressed.

Drona and Bhisma must have lost their strength
together with the great-souled Vidura. 120
Do not the elders of the Kauravas
perceive the unlawful conduct of their king?

VAISHAMPAYANA
The queen spoke these pitiable words
and cast a glance upon her hero husbands,
raising the anger of the Pandava hearts 125
to blazing fire by her sidelong glance.

Not their lost kingdom, not the wealth,
not all the lost gems of highest price,
gave Pandu's sons such pain as Draupadi
gave by that one anguished sidelong glance. 130

---

8. King of the gods.

9. Yudhishthira, who is viewed as the
embodiment of Dharma.

Duhshasana, observing how the queen
had looked upon her helpless hero lords,
shook her roughly until she almost swooned,
with cruel laughter calling her his slave.

Karna was passing glad to her that word;   135
he gave honor to the prince and laughed aloud.
The King of Gandhara, son of Subala,
also gave Duhshasana applause.

But others who were present at the court,
except those two and King Duryodhana,   140
felt bitter anguish as they saw the queen,
dark Draupadi, so pulled about the court.

BHISMA
My good lady, the law is a subtle thing;
I cannot answer rightly what you ask.
A gambler cannot bet what is not his: 145
true; but a wife lies in her husband's power.

Again, I know that King Yudhishthira
would forsake the world before forsaking truth,
and Yudhishthira admits that he has lost;
I cannot answer rightly what you ask.   150

There is no equal to Shakuni in dicing,
but he gave to King Yudhishthira his choice;
the king does not accuse him of deceit;
I cannot answer rightly what you ask.

DRAUPADI
No. The king was challenged by these gamblers,   155
villainous, wicked men who use deceit;
of his own free will he never sought to gamble.
How can you tell me that he had his choice?

An honest man, the noblest of you all,
he never recognized the treachery.   160
As he was beaten out of all his wealth
and only then agreed upon the wager—

answer me, Kurus who attend this court,
you nobles who have daughters of your own
and daughters-in-law to spur your rightful judgment,   165
answer me the question I have put!

VAISHAMPAYANA
She spoke these pitiable words and wept,
casting her eyes once more upon her husbands,

the while Duhshasana kept up his cry
of bitter words and cruel epithets.   170

Then Bhima, seeing the defenseless queen
in such condition in a single garment
so treated, looked at King Yudhishthira
and in ungovernable fury spoke.

2.61

BHIMA

A gambler often keeps a wench but never bets her;
even to such a creature he shows some decency.

What stirs my wrath is not that the tribute of Benares
and other tribute given at your assumption of the realm,

not that the chariots and gold, the armor and the weapons,   5
the kingdom, and ourselves, and you, have all been lost:

these things stir not my wrath—for were you not sole master?
but this I say was wrongly done to wager Draupadi;

for she who came to us a blameless maid is by your doing
now tortured by these Kurus, these double-dealing brutes.   10

On her account my wrath is stirred and I bring it down on you.
I will brand your arms. Sahadeva, bring me fire!

ARJUNA

Never have you spoken words like this, Bhima.
Our enemies have broken your respect for law.

Give them no such satisfaction. Hold to what is lawful.   15
The rightful and the eldest brother must not be defied.

Challenged by his foe, he minds the code of warriors
and gambles at the other's wish. Hereby he wins us fame.

BHIMA

If I knew him to have acted so like an egoist
I would hold his two arms in the fire until they burned to ash.   20

VAISHAMPAYANA

Then seeing the sons of Pandu pained and Draupadi mistreated,
a younger son of the Kuru king, Vikarna, rose and spoke.

VIKARNA

Answer the question, nobles, that Draupadi has set us.
If we decide unjustly, we shall pay for it in hell.

Bhisma and Dhritarashtra, the oldest of the Kurus,   25
withhold their word of judgment, as does Vidura the wise.

Kripa too, and Drona, the teacher of us all,
our two foremost brahmans, have answered not a word.

So let the other nobles who are here assembled
put by their love and hatred and answer as they think.   30

Consider well the question that Draupadi has set us
and speak up, every nobleman, what side of it you choose.

VAISHAMPAYANA
He spoke. He spoke to them again, to all those there assembled,
but the nobles answered not a word, either of good or ill.

Then after asking many times those noblemen, Vikarna,   35
wringing his hands in anguish and breathing deeply, spoke.

VIKARNA
So be it, noblemen; speak or speak not your judgment;
I think it proper here in either case to give my own.

Four vices, as they say, are often found in princes:
hunting, drinking, dice, and the vice of fornication.   40

A man attached to one of these lets go his hold on virtue,
and what he does unbridled the world does not approve.

It is true we find here Pandu's son too much attached to dicing,
for on a gambler's challenge he wagered Draupadi.

But not only does the queen belong to all the Pandavas;   45
she was wagered by one Pandava when he had lost himself.

Furthermore, Shakuni sought the wager, naming the queen outright.
Considering these facts, I find she is not won.

VAISHAMPAYANA
When the lords had heard him out, a mighty roar resounded
of nobles favoring Vikarna and blaming Shakuni.   50

At length the sound subsided and Karna, filled with anger,
stretched forth his jeweled arm in challenge and replied.

KARNA
I see in this Vikarna a fatal twist of temper,
a rod to kindle fire that burns the rod itself.

The others have said nothing though urged to give their judgment;   55
I infer their judgment to be that Draupadi is won.

But you, young son of Dhritarashtra, will perish by your nonsense,
a child who rises as an elder to give judgment in the hall.

You do not know the law, young brother of Duryodhana,
if you would call the queen unwon when she is surely won.   60

How think you Draupadi can be unwon, Vikarna,
when the eldest of the Pandavas pledged everything he owned

and Draupadi, as lying within that everything, most surely
and lawfully is won. The conclusion is not to be denied.

Yes, Draupadi was named; but the Pandava consented.   65
What reason can you give by which she becomes unwon?

Perhaps you think it wrong that in a single garment
she was brought to the hall. On that too hear my word.

To one wife, O Kuru prince, the gods allot one husband;
this woman with her many husbands stands ajudged a whore.   70

Bringing her to the hall was nothing strange I think
whether in single garment or in her naked skin.

Whatever property existed in Pandava possession,
their woman and they themselves, all has been rightly won.

This boy Vikarna is a fool who tries to speak with wisdom.   75
Duhshasana! Strip off the clothes of the servants we have won!

VAISHAMPAYANA
The sons of Pandu heard his words. Without delay the brothers
took off their upper robes and sat bare-breasted in the court.

Then Prince Duhshasana in the midst of that assembly
began to strip the single garment by force from Draupadi.   80

But ever as he drew away her robe, another garment
identical in form assumed its very place.

At this there rose a murmur, swelling to an uproar,
from all the courtiers as they saw this wonder of the age;

above which Bhima's voice was heard from lips that shook with anger.   85
Pressing one hand on the other, he shouted out this oath.

BHIMA
Hear my words, O nobles who have come from all countries,
words that no man has spoken and none will speak again;

words that having said, if I should fail to do them,
may I never join my ancestors in the world of joy to come: 90

I will take one day in battle this wicked, lowborn outcaste
and I swear that day I will rip out his breast and drink his living blood.

VAISHAMPAYANA

The nobles heard his oath and shivered as they heard it;
they gave him their applause and blamed Duhshasana.

Only when the garments grew to a heap upon the carpet   95
did the prince, ashamed and weary, give over his attempt.

But a chilling cry of shame arose from every witness,
whether men or gods. Then, seeing there the Pandavas

and that the Kauravas answered not the question,
the common folk cried out, reviling the old king.   100

The Song of the Blessed One [Bhagavad Gita]

THE FIRST TEACHING: ARJUNA'S DEJECTION

DHRITARASHTRA

Sanjaya, tell me what my sons
and the sons of Pandu did when they met,
wanting to battle on the field of Kuru,
on the field of sacred duty?

SANJAYA[1]

Your son Duryodhana, the king,   5
seeing the Pandava forces arrayed,
approached his teacher Drona
and spoke in command.

"My teacher, see
the great Pandava army arrayed   10
by Drupada's son,
your pupil, intent on revenge.

Here are heroes, mighty archers
equal to Bhima[2] and Arjuna[3] in warfare,
Yuyudhana, Virata, and Drupada,   15
your sworn foe on his great chariot.

Here too are Dhrishtaketu, Cekitana,
and the brave king of Benares;

Translated by Barbara Stoler Miller.

---

1. The charioteer and messenger of King Dhritarashtra.

2. The second son of Pandu.

3. The third son of Pandu.

Purujit, Kuntibhoja,
and the manly king of the Shibis.

Yudhamanyu is bold,
and Uttamaujas is brave;
the sons of Subhadra and Draupadi
all command great chariots.

Now, honored priest, mark
the superb men on our side
as I tell you the names
of my army's leaders.

They are you and Bhishma,[4]
Karna and Kripa, a victor in battles,
your own son Ashvatthama,
Vikarna, and the son of Somadatta.

Many other heroes also risk
their lives for my sake,
bearing varied weapons
and skilled in the ways of war.

Guarded by Bhishma, the strength
of our army is without limit;
but the strength of their army,
guarded by Bhima, is limited.

In all the movements of battle,
you and your men,
stationed according to plan,
must guard Bhishma well!"

Bhishma, fiery elder of the Kurus,
roared his lion's roar
and blew his conch horn,
exciting Duryodhana's delight.

Conches and kettledrums,
cymbals, tabors, and trumpets
were sounded at once
and the din of tumult arose.

Standing on their great chariot
yoked with white stallions,
Krishna and Arjuna, Pandu's son,
sounded their divine conches.

20

25

30

35

40

45

50

55

---

4. The grand-uncle of the Pandavas.

Krishna blew Pancajanya,[5] won from a demon;
Arjuna blew Devadatta,[6] a gift of the gods;
fierce wolf-bellied Bhima blew Paundra,[7]
his great conch of the east.   60

Yudhishthira, Kunti's son, the king,
blew Anantavijaya,[8] conch of boundless victory;
his twin brothers Nakula and Sahadeva
blew conches resonant and jewel toned.

The king of Benares, a superb archer,   65
and Shikhandin on his great chariot,
Drishtadyumna, Virata, and indomitable Satyaki,
all blew their conches.

Drupada, with his five grandsons,
and Subhadra's strong-armed son,
each in his turn blew   70
their conches, O King.

The noise tore the hearts
of Dhritarashtra's sons,
and tumult echoed   75
through heaven and earth.

Arjuna, his war flag a rampant monkey,
saw Dhritarashtra's sons assembled
as weapons were ready to clash,
and he lifted his bow.   80

He told his charioteer:
  "Krishna,
  halt my chariot
  between the armies!
  Far enough for me to see   85
  these men who lust for war,
  ready to fight with me
  in the strain of battle.

  I see men gathered here,
  eager to fight,   90
  bent on serving the folly
  of Dhritarashtra's son."

When Arjuna had spoken,
Krishna halted
their splendid chariot   95
between the armies.

---

5. The name of Krishna's conch shell.   7. The name of Bhisma's conch shell.
6. The name of Arjuna's conch shell.   8. The name of Yudhishthira's conch shell.

Facing Bhishma and Drona
and all the great kings,
he said, "Arjuna, see
the Kuru men assembled here!"   100

Arjuna saw them standing there:
fathers, grandfathers, teachers,
uncles, brothers, sons,
grandsons, and friends.

He surveyed his elders   105
and companions in both armies,
all his kinsmen
assembled together.

Dejected, filled with strange pity,
he said this: 110
    "Krishna, I see my kinsmen
    gathered here, wanting war.

My limbs sink,
my mouth is parched,
my body trembles,   115
the hair bristles on my flesh.

The magic bow slips
from my hand, my skin burns,
I cannot stand still,
my mind reels.   120

I see omens of chaos,
Krishna; I see no good
in killing my kinsmen
in battle.

Krishna, I seek no victory,   125
or kingship or pleasures.
What use to us are kingship,
delights, or life itself?

We sought kingship, delights,
and pleasures for the sake of those   130
assembled to abandon their lives
and fortunes in battle.

They are teachers, fathers, sons,
and grandfathers, uncles, grandsons,
fathers and brothers of wives,   135
and other men of our family.

I do not want to kill them
even if I am killed, Krishna;

not for kingship of all three worlds,
much less for the earth!

What joy is there for us, Krishna,
in killing Dhritarashtra's sons?
Evil will haunt us if we kill them,
though their bows are drawn to kill.

Honor forbids us to kill
our cousins, Dhritarashtra's sons;
how can we know happiness
if we kill our own kinsmen?

The greed that distorts their reason
blinds them to the sin they commit
in ruining the family, blinds them
to the crime of betraying friends.

How can we ignore the wisdom
of turning from this evil
when we see the sin
of family destruction, Krishna?

When the family is ruined,
the timeless laws of family duty
perish; and when duty is lost,
chaos overwhelms the family.

In overwhelming chaos, Krishna,
women of the family are corrupted;
and when women are corrupted,
disorder is born in society.

This discord drags the violators
and the family itself to hell;
for ancestors fall when rites
of offering rice and water lapse.

The sins of men who violate
the family create disorder in society
that undermines the constant laws
of caste and family duty.

Krishna, we have heard
that a place in hell
is reserved for men
who undermine family duties.

I lament the great sin
we commit when our greed

140

145

150

155

160

165

170

175

for kingship and pleasures
drives us to kill our kinsmen.

If Dhritarashtra's armed sons
kill me in battle when I am unarmed
and offer no resistance,
it will be my reward."

Saying this in the time of war,
Arjuna slumped into the chariot
and laid down his bow and arrows,
his mind tormented by grief.

THE SECOND TEACHING:
PHILOSOPHY AND SPIRITUAL DISCIPLINE

SANJAYA
Arjuna sat dejected,
filled with pity,
his sad eyes blurred by tears.
Krishna gave him counsel.

LORD KRISHNA
Why this cowardice
in time of crisis, Arjuna?
The coward is ignoble, shameful,
foreign to the ways of heaven.

Don't yield to impotence!
It is unnatural in you!
Banish this petty weakness from your heart.
Rise to the fight, Arjuna!

ARJUNA
Krishna, how can I fight
against Bhishma and Drona[9]
with arrows
when they deserve my worship?

It is better in this world
to beg for scraps of food
than to eat meals
smeared with the blood
of elders I killed

180

185

5

10

15

20

---

9. The former is the grand-uncle of the Pandavas; the latter is their teacher. Both are
allied, albeit reluctantly, with Duryodhana.

at the height of their power
while their goals
were still desires.

We don't know which weight
is worse to bear—
our conquering them
or their conquering us.
We will not want to live
if we kill
the sons of Dhritarashtra
assembled before us.

The flaw of pity
blights my very being;
conflicting sacred duties
confound my reason.
I ask you to tell me
decisively—Which is better?
I am your pupil.
Teach me what I seek!

I see nothing
that could drive away
the grief
that withers my senses;
even if I won kingdoms
of unrivaled wealth
on earth
and sovereignty over gods.

SANJAYA
Arjuna told this
to Krishna—then saying,
"I shall not fight,"
he fell silent.
Mocking him gently,
Krishna gave this counsel
as Arjuna sat dejected,
between the two armies.

LORD KRISHNA
You grieve for those beyond grief,
and you speak words of insight;
but learned men do not grieve
for the dead or the living.

25

30

35

40

45

50

55

60

Never have I not existed,
nor you, nor these kings;
and never in the future
shall we cease to exist.

Just as the embodied self
enters childhood, youth, and old age,
so does it enter another body;
this does not confound a steadfast man.

Contacts with matter make us feel
heat and cold, pleasure and pain.
Arjuna, you must learn to endure
fleeting things—they come and go!

When these cannot torment a man,
when suffering and joy are equal
for him and he has courage,
he is fit for immortality.

Nothing of nonbeing comes to be,
nor does being cease to exist;
the boundary between these two
is seen by men who see reality.

Indestructible is the presence
that pervades all this;
no one can destroy
this unchanging reality.

Our bodies are known to end,
but the embodied self is enduring,
indestructible, and immeasurable;
therefore, Arjuna, fight the battle!

He who thinks this self a killer
and he who thinks it killed,
both fail to understand;
it does not kill, nor is it killed.

It is not born,
it does not die;
having been,
it will never not be;
unborn, enduring,
constant, and primordial,
it is not killed
when the body is killed.

Arjuna, when a man knows the self
to be indestructible, enduring, unborn,
unchanging, how does he kill
or cause anyone to kill?

As a man discards
worn-out clothes
to put on new
and different ones,
so the embodied self
discards
its worn-out bodies
to take on other new ones.

Weapons do not cut it,
fire does not burn it,
waters do not wet it,
wind does not wither it.

It cannot be cut or burned;
it cannot be wet or withered;
it is enduring, all-pervasive,
fixed, immovable, and timeless.

It is called unmanifest,
inconceivable, and immutable;
since you know that to be so,
you should not grieve!

If you think of its birth
and death as ever-recurring,
then too, Great Warrior,
you have no cause to grieve!

Death is certain for anyone born,
and birth is certain for the dead;
since the cycle is inevitable,
you have no cause to grieve!

Creatures are unmanifest in origin,
manifest in the midst of life,
and unmanifest again in the end.
Since this is so, why do you lament?

Rarely someone
sees it,
rarely another
speaks it,
rarely anyone

hears it—
even hearing it,
no one really knows it.

The self embodied in the body
of every being is indestructible;
you have no cause to grieve
for all these creatures, Arjuna!

Look to your own duty;
do not tremble before it;
nothing is better for a warrior
than a battle of sacred duty.

The doors of heaven open
for warriors who rejoice
to have a battle like this
thrust on them by chance.

If you fail to wage this war
of sacred duty,
you will abandon your own duty
and fame only to gain evil.

People will tell
of your undying shame,
and for a man of honor
shame is worse than death.

The great chariot warriors will think
you deserted in fear of battle;
you will be despised
by those who held you in esteem.

Your enemies will slander you,
scorning your skill
in so many unspeakable ways—
could any suffering be worse?

If you are killed, you win heaven;
if you triumph, you enjoy the earth;
therefore, Arjuna, stand up
and resolve to fight the battle!

Impartial to joy and suffering,
gain and loss, victory and defeat,
arm yourself for the battle,
lest you fall into evil.

145

150

155

160

165

170

175

180

VALMIKI (SECOND CENTURY B.C.E.)
North India

The *Ramayana* ("adventures of Rama") is not only considerably shorter than the *Mahabharata* (about a quarter of its length), it is also more recent. It began its life as an oral epic well after the *Mahabharata,* although it reached its present form somewhat earlier—perhaps a little before the first century of the common era. The traditional attribution of the poem is to Valmiki. As with Vyasa, the creator of the older epic, we know little about Valmiki other than what the poem itself tells us.

The *Ramayana* looks back to the *Mahabharata* as it attempts to offer different solutions to the problems raised there. Again, the action centers initially around a dispute over the succession to the throne of a major state—this time Ayodhya, capital of the eastern province of Kosala (in the present-day state of Bihar). The aged king, Dasharatha, wishes to appoint his eldest son, Rama, as his successor. However, one of the king's younger wives, Kaikeyi, demands the appointment of her own son, Bharata. The king once made certain promises to Kaikeyi, and the first selection, from Book 2, focuses on the critical moment when he is forced to keep them by denying the kingship to Rama and instead sending him into exile. Again, the moral fulcrum of the narrative lies in the problem of *dharma,* "what is right." Rama believes that any promise his father made must be kept, no matter what the cost. He adheres to a higher, almost spiritualized vision of kingship by accepting exile rather than launching a struggle for the throne.

The main action of the epic begins in Book 3, our second selection, which takes place during Rama's banishment in the wilderness. The demon king Ravana abducts the hero's wife, in part as revenge for Rama's attack on Shurpanakha, Ravana's sister. As in the *Mahabharata,* the narrative focuses on violence perpetrated against a woman, and again war ensues. This time the antagonists are not brothers, however, but a demon race dwelling far from the world of Ayodhya.

from THE RAMAYANA

Book 2

SARGA 7 [*Now, Kaikeyi's family servant*]

1. Now, Kaikeyi's family servant, who had lived with her from the time of her birth, had happened to ascend to the rooftop terrace that shone like the moon.

2–3. From the terrace Manthara could see all Ayodhya—the king's way—newly sprinkled, the lotuses and waterlilies strewn about, the costly ornamental

Translated by Sheldon I. Pollock.

pennants and banners, the sprinkling of sandalwood water, and the crowds of freshly bathed people.

4–5. Seeing a nursemaid standing nearby, Manthara asked, "Why is Rama's mother so delighted and giving away money to people, when she has always been so miserly? Tell me, why are the people displaying such boundless delight? Has something happened to delight the lord of earth? What is he planning to do?"

6. Bursting with delight and out of sheer gladness the nursemaid told the hunchback Manthara about the greater majesty in store for Raghava:

7. "Tomorrow on Pusya day[1] King Dasharatha is going to consecrate Rama Raghava as prince regent, the blameless prince who has mastered his anger."

8. When she heard what the nursemaid said, the hunchback was furious and descended straightway from the terrace that was like the peak of Mount Kailasa.[2]

9. Consumed with rage, the malevolent Manthara approached Kaikeyi as she lay upon her couch, and she said:

10. "Get up, you foolish woman! How can you lie there when danger is threatening you? Don't you realize that a flood of misery is about to overwhelm you?

11. "Your beautiful face has lost its charm. You boast of the power of your beauty, but it has proved to be as fleeting as a river's current in the hot season."

12. So she spoke, and Kaikeyi was deeply distraught at the bitter words of the angry, malevolent hunchback.

13. "Manthara," she replied, "is something wrong? I can tell by the distress in your face how sorely troubled you are."

14. Hearing Kaikeyi's gentle words the wrathful Manthara spoke—and a very clever speaker she was.

15. The hunchback grew even more distraught, and with Kaikeyi's best interests at heart, spoke out, trying to sharpen her distress and turn her against Raghava:

16. "Something is very seriously wrong, my lady, something that threatens to ruin you. For King Dasharatha is going to consecrate Rama as prince regent.

17. "I felt myself sinking down into unfathomable danger, stricken with grief and sorrow, burning as if on fire. And so I have come here, with your best interests at heart.

---

1. An auspicious day in the lunar calendar.

2. Holy mountain in the far north of India; dwelling place of the god Shiva

18. "When you are sorrowful, Kaikeyi, I am too, and even more, and, when you prosper, so do I. There is not the slightest doubt of this.

19. "You were born into a family of kings, you are a queen of the lord of earth. My lady, how can you fail to know that the ways of kings are ruthless?

20. "Your husband talks of righteousness, but he is deceiving you; his words are gentle but he is cruel. You are too innocent to understand, and so he has utterly defrauded you like this.

21. "When expedient, your husband reassures you, but it is all worthless. Now that there is something of real worth he is ready to bestow it upon Kausalya.

22. "Having got Bharata out of the way by sending him off to your family, the wicked man shall tomorrow establish Rama in unchallenged kingship.

23. "He is an enemy pretending to be your husband. He is like a viper, child, whom you have taken to your bosom and lovingly mothered.

24. For what an enemy or a snake would do if one ignored them, King Dasharatha is now doing to you and your son.

25. "The man is evil, his assurances false, and, by establishing Rama in the kingship, dear child who has always known comfort, he will bring ruin upon you and your family.

26. "Kaikeyi, the time has come to act, and you must act swiftly, for your own good. You must save your son, yourself, and me, my enchanting beauty."

27. After listening to Manthara's speech, the lovely woman rose from the couch and presented the hunchback with a lovely piece of jewelry.

28. And, when she had given the hunchback the jewelry, Kaikeyi, most beautiful of women, said in delight to Manthara,

29. "What you have reported to me is the most wonderful news. How else may I reward you, Manthara, for reporting such good news to me?

30. "I draw no distinction between Rama and Bharata, and so I am perfectly content that the king should consecrate Rama as king.

31. "You could not possibly tell me better news than this, or speak more welcome words, my well-deserving woman. For what you have told me I will give you yet another boon, something you might like more—just choose it!"

The end of the seventh *sarga* of the *Ayodhyakanda* of the *Sri Ramayana*.

SARGA 8 [But Manthara was beside herself with rage and sorrow]

1. But Manthara was beside herself with rage and sorrow. She threw the jewelry away and said spitefully:

2. "You foolish woman, how can you be delighted at such a moment? Are you not aware that you stand in the midst of a sea of grief?

3. "It is Kausalya who is fortunate; it is her son the eminent brahmans will consecrate as the powerful prince regent tomorrow, on Pusya day.

4. "Once Kausalya secures this great object of joy, she will cheerfully eliminate her enemies. And you will have to wait on her with hands cupped in reverence, like a serving woman.

5. "Delight is truly in store for Rama's exalted women, and all that is in store for your daughters-in-law is misery, at Bharata's downfall."

6. Seeing how deeply distressed Manthara was as she spoke, Queen Kaikeyi began to extol Rama's virtues:

7. "Rama knows what is right, his gurus have taught him self-restraint. He is grateful, truthful, and honest, and as the king's eldest son, he deserves to be prince regent.

8. "He will protect his brothers and his dependents like a father; and long may he live! How can you be upset, hunchback, at learning of Rama's consecration?

9. "Surely Bharata as well, the bull among men, will obtain the kingship of his fathers and forefathers after Rama's one hundred years.

10. "Why should you be upset, Manthara, when we have prospered in the past, and prosper now, and shall have good fortune in the future? For he obeys me even more scrupulously than he does Kausalya."

11. When she heard what Kaikeyi said, Manthara was still more sorely troubled. She heaved a long and hot sigh and then replied:

12. "You are too simple-minded to see what is good for you and what is not. You are not aware that you are sinking in an ocean of sorrow fraught with disaster and grief.

13. "Raghava will be king, Kaikeyi, and then the son of Raghava, while Bharata will be debarred from the royal succession altogether.

14. "For not all the sons of a king stand in line for the kingship, my lovely. Were all of them to be so placed, grave misfortune would ensue.

15. "That is why kings place the powers of kingship in the hands of the eldest, faultless Kaikeyi, however worthy the others.

16. "Like a helpless boy that son of yours, the object of all your motherly love, will be totally excluded from the royal succession and from its pleasures as well.

17. "Here I am, come on your behalf, but you pay me no heed. Instead, you want to reward me in token of your rival's good luck!

18. "Surely once Rama secures unchallenged kingship he will have Bharata sent off to some other country—if not to the other world!

19. And you had to send Bharata, a mere boy, off to your brother's, though knowing full well that proximity breeds affection, even in insentient things.

20. "Now, Raghava will protect Lakshmana, just as Saumitri will protect Rama, for their brotherly love is as celebrated as that of the Asvins.[3]

21. "And so Rama will do no harm to Lakshmana, but he will to Bharata without question.

22. "So let your son go straight from Rajagriha[4] to the forest. That is the course I favor, and it is very much in your own best interests.

23. "For in this way good fortune may still befall your side of the family—if, that is, Bharata secures, as by rights he should, the kingship of his forefathers.

24. "Your child has known only comfort, and, at the same time, he is Rama's natural enemy. How could the one, with his fortunes lost, live under the sway of the other, whose fortunes are thriving?

25. "Like the leader of an elephant herd attacked by a lion in the forest, your son is about to be set upon by Rama, and you must save him.

26. "Then, too, because of your beauty's power you used to spurn your co-wife, Rama's mother, so proudly. How could she fail to repay that enmity?

27. "When Rama secures control of the land, Bharata will be lost for certain. You must therefore devise some way of making your son the king and banishing his enemy this very day."

The end of the eighth *sarga* of the *Ayodhyakanda* of the *Sri Ramayana*.

SARGA 9 [So Manthara spoke]

1. So Manthara spoke, and Kaikeyi, her face glowing with rage, heaved a long and burning sigh and said to her:

2. "Today, at once, I will have Rama banished to the forest, and at once have Bharata consecrated as prince regent.

3. "But now, Manthara, think: In what way can Bharata, and not Rama, secure the kingship?"

4. So Queen Kaikeyi spoke, and the malevolent Manthara answered her, to the ruin of Rama's fortunes:

5. "Well then, I shall tell you, Kaikeyi—and pay close attention—how your son Bharata may secure sovereign kingship."

---

3. Twin deities, typically represented as beings of great beauty.

4. Bharata is currently visiting his mother's family in the northwest city of Rajagriha.

[Handwritten notes in top margin: "Diff. between Greek Gods & Hindu Gods. Demon King Ravona had gotten an oath from the Gods that he could not be destroyed by Vishnu is born in human form, but posses the spirit of a Go—"]

6. Hearing Manthara's words, Kaikeyi half rose from her sumptuous couch and exclaimed:

7. "Tell me the way, Manthara! How can Bharata, and not Rama, secure the kingship?"

8. So the queen spoke, and the malevolent hunchback answered her, to the ruin of Rama's fortunes:

9–11. "When the gods and *asuras*[5] were at war, your husband went with the royal seers to lend assistance to the king of the gods, and he took you along. He set off toward the south, Kaikeyi, to the Dandakas and the city called Vaijayanta. It was there that Timidhvaja ruled, the same who is called Shambara, a great *asura* of a hundred magic powers. He had given battle to Shakra, and the host of gods could not conquer him.

12–13. "In the great battle that followed, King Dasharatha was struck unconscious, and you, my lady, conveyed him out of battle. But there, too, your husband was wounded by weapons, and once again you saved him, my lovely. And so in his gratitude he granted you two boons.

14. "Then, my lady, you said to your husband, 'I shall choose my two boons when I want them,' and the great king consented. I myself was unaware of this, my lady, until you yourself told me, long ago.

15. "You must now demand these two boons of your husband: the consecration of Bharata and the banishment of Rama for fourteen years.

16. "Now go into your private chamber, daughter of Asvapati, as if in a fit of rage. Put on a dirty garment, lie down on the bare ground, and don't speak to him, don't even look at him.

17. "Your husband has always adored you, I haven't any doubt of it. For your sake the great king would even go through fire.

18. "The king could not bring himself to anger you, nor even bear to look at you when you are angry. He would give up his own life to please you.

19. "The lord of the land is powerless to refuse your demand. Dull-witted girl, recognize the power of your beauty.

20. "King Dasharatha will offer gems, pearls, gold, a whole array of precious gifts—but pay no mind to them.

21. "Just keep reminding Dasharatha of those two boons he granted at the battle of the gods and *asuras*. Illustrious lady, you must not let this opportunity pass you by.

22–23. "When the great king Raghava helps you up himself and offers you a boon, then you must ask him for this one, first making sure he swears to it: 'Banish

---

5. Antigods.

Rama to the forest for nine years and five, and make Bharata king of the land, the bull among kings.'

24. "In this way Rama will be banished and cease to be 'the pleasing prince,' and your Bharata, his rival eliminated, will be king.

25. "And by the time Rama returns from the forest, your steadfast son and his supporters will have struck deep roots and won over the populace.

26. "I think it high time you overcame your timidity. You must forcibly prevent the king from carrying out Rama's consecration."

27. And so Manthara induced her to accept such evil by disguising it as good, and Kaikeyi, now cheered and delighted, replied:

28. "Hunchback, I never recognized your excellence, nor how excellent your advice. Of all the hunchbacks in the land there is none better at devising plans.

29. "You are the only one who has always sought my advantage and had my interests at heart. I might never have known, hunchback, what the king intended to do.

30. "There are hunchbacks who are misshapen, crooked and hideously ugly—but not you, you are lovely, you are bent no more than a lotus in the breeze.

31. "Your chest is arched, raised as high as your shoulders, and down below your waist, with its lovely navel, seems as if it had grown thin in envy of it.

32. "Your girdle-belt beautifies your hips and sets them jingling. Your legs are set strong under you, while your feet are long.

33. "With your wide buttocks, Manthara, and your garment of white linen, you are as resplendent as a wild goose when you go before me.

34. "And this huge hump of yours, wide as the hub of a chariot wheel—your clever ideas must be stored in it, your political wisdom and magic powers.

35. "And there, hunchback, is where I will drape you with a garland made of gold, once Bharata is consecrated and Raghava has gone to the forest.

36. "When I have accomplished my purpose, my lovely, when I am satisfied, I will anoint your hump with precious liquid gold.

37. "And for your face I will have them fashion an elaborate and beautiful forehead mark of gold and exquisite jewelry for you, hunchback.

38. "Dressed in a pair of lovely garments you shall go about like a goddess; with that face of yours that challenges the moon, peerless in visage; and you shall strut holding your head high before the people who hate me.

39. "You too shall have hunchbacks, adorned with every sort of ornament, to humbly serve you, hunchback, just as you always serve me."

40. Being flattered in this fashion, she replied to Kaikeyi, who still lay on her luxurious couch like a flame of fire on an altar:

41. "One does not build a dike, my precious, after the water is gone. Get up, apprise the king, and see to your own welfare!"

42. Thus incited, the large-eyed queen went with Manthara to her private chamber, puffed up with the intoxicating power of her beauty.

43. There the lovely lady removed her pearl necklace, worth many hundred thousands, and her other costly and beautiful jewelry.

44. And then, under the spell of the hunchback Manthara's words, the golden Kaikeyi got down upon the floor and said to her:

45. "Hunchback, go inform the king that I will surely die right here unless Bharata receives as his portion the land and Raghava, as his, the forest."

46. And uttering these ruthless words, the lady put all her jewelry aside and lay down upon the ground bare of any spread, like a fallen *kimnara* woman.[6]

47. Her face enveloped in the darkness of her swollen rage, her fine garlands and ornaments stripped off, the wife of the lord of men grew distraught and took on the appearance of a darkened sky, when all the stars have set.

The end of the ninth *sarga* of the *Ayodhyakanda* of the *Sri Ramayana*.

SARGA 10 [Now, when the great king had given orders]

1. Now, when the great king had given orders for Raghava's consecration, he gladly entered the inner chamber to tell his beloved wife the good news.

2. But when the lord of the world saw her fallen on the ground and lying there in a posture so ill-befitting her, he was consumed with sorrow.

3. The guileless old man saw her on the floor, that guileful young wife of his, who meant more to him than life itself.

4. He began to caress her affectionately, as a great bull elephant in the wilderness might caress his cow wounded by the poisoned arrow of a hunter lurking in the forest.

5. And, as he caressed his lotus-eyed wife with his hands, sick with worry and desire, he said to her:

6-7. "I do not understand, my lady, why you should be angry. Has someone offended you, or shown you disrespect, that you should lie here in the dust, my precious, and cause me such sorrow? What reason have you to lie upon

---

6. A semidivine creature of great beauty.

the floor as if possessed by a spirit, driving me to distraction, when you are so precious to me?

8. "I have skilled physicians, who have been gratified in every way. They will make you well again. Tell me what hurts you, my lovely.

9. "Is there someone to whom you would have favor shown, or has someone aroused your disfavor? The one shall find favor at once, the other incur my lasting disfavor.

10. "Is there some guilty man who should be freed, or some innocent man I should execute? What poor man should I enrich, what rich man impoverish?

11–12. "I and my people, we all bow to your will. I could not bring myself to thwart any wish of yours, not if it cost me my life. Tell me what your heart desires, for all the earth belongs to me, as far as the wheel of my power reaches."

13. So he spoke, and now encouraged, she resolved to tell her hateful plan. She then commenced to cause her husband still greater pain.

14. "No one has mistreated me, my lord, or shown me disrespect. But there is one wish I have that I should like you to fulfill.

15. "You must first give me your promise that you are willing to do it. Then I shall reveal what it is I desire."

16. So his beloved Kaikeyi spoke, and the mighty king, hopelessly under the woman's power, said to her with some surprise:

17. "Do you not yet know, proud lady, that except for Rama, tiger among men, there is not a single person I love as much as you?

18. "Take hold of my heart, rip it out, and examine it closely, my lovely Kaikeyi; then tell me if you do not find it true.

19. "Seeing that I have the power, you ought not to doubt me. I will do what will make you happy, I swear to you by all my acquired merit."

20. His words filled her with delight, and she made ready to reveal her dreadful wish, which was like a visitation of death:

21. "Let the three and thirty gods, with Indra at their head, hear how you in due order swear an oath and grant me a boon.

22–23. "Let the sun and moon, the sky, the planets, night and day, the quarters of space, heaven and earth, let all the *gandharvas*[7] and *raksasas*,[8] the spirits that stalk the night, the household gods in every house, and all the other spirits take heed of what you have said.

24. "This mighty king, who is true to his word and knows the ways of

---

7. Heavenly musicians.   **8.** Demons.

righteousness, in full awareness grants me a boon—let the deities give ear to this for me."

25. Thus the queen ensnared the great archer and called upon witnesses. She then addressed the king, who in his mad passion had granted her a boon.

26. "I will now claim the two boons you once granted me, my lord. Hear my words, your Majesty.

27. "Let my son Bharata be consecrated with the very rite of consecration you have prepared for Raghava.

28. "Let Rama withdraw to Dandaka wilderness and for nine years and five live the life of an ascetic, wearing hides and barkcloth garments and matted hair.

29. "Let Bharata today become the uncontested prince regent, and let me see Raghava depart this very day for the forest."

30. When the great king heard Kaikeyi's ruthless demands, he was shaken and unnerved, like a stag at the sight of a tigress.

31. The lord of men gasped as he sank down upon the bare floor. "Oh damn you!" he cried in uncontrollable fury before he fell into a stupor, his heart crushed by grief.

32. Gradually the king regained his senses and then, in bitter sorrow and anger, he spoke to Kaikeyi, with fire in his eyes:

33. "Malicious, wicked woman, bent on destroying this House! Evil woman, what evil did Rama or I ever do to you?

34. "Raghava has always treated you just like his own mother. What reason can you have for trying to wreck his fortunes, of all people?

35. "It was sheer suicide to bring you into my home. I did it unwittingly, thinking you a princess—and not a deadly poisonous viper.

36. "When praise for Rama's virtues is on the lips of every living soul, what crime could I adduce as pretext for renouncing my favorite son?

37. "I would sooner renounce Kausalya, or Sumitra, or sovereignty, or life itself, than Rama, who so cherishes his father.

38. "The greatest joy I know is seeing my first-born son. If I cannot see Rama, I shall lose my mind.

39. "The world might endure without the sun, or crops without water, but without Rama life could not endure within my body.

40. "Enough then, give up this scheme, you evil-scheming woman. I beg you! Must I get down and bow my head to your feet?"

41. His heart in the grip of a woman who knew no bounds, the guardian of the

earth began helplessly to cry, and as the queen extended her feet he tried in vain to touch them, and collapsed like a man on the point of death.

The end of the tenth *sarga* of the *Ayodhyakanda* of the *Sri Ramayana*.

SARGA 11 [*The king lay there, in so unaccustomed a posture*]

1–2. The king lay there, in so unaccustomed a posture, so ill-befitting his dignity, like Yayati[9] himself, his merit exhausted, fallen from the world of the gods. But the woman was unafraid, for all the fear she awoke. She was misfortune incarnate and had yet to secure her fortunes. Once more she tried to force him to fulfill the boon.

3. "You are vaunted, great king, as a man true to his word and firm in his vows. How then can you be prepared to withhold my boon?"

4. So Kaikeyi spoke, and King Dasharatha, faltering for a moment, angrily replied:

5. "Vile woman, mortal enemy! Will you not be happy, will you not be satisfied until you see me dead, and Rama, the bull among men, gone to the forest?

6. "To satisfy Kaikeyi Rama must be banished to the forest, but if I keep my word in this, then I must be guilty of another lie. My infamy will be unequaled in the eyes of the people and my disgrace inevitable."

7. While he was lamenting like this, his mind in a whirl, the sun set and evening came on.

8. To the anguished king lost in lamentation, the night, adorned with the circlet of the moon, no longer seemed to last a mere three watches.

9. Heaving burning sighs, aged King Dasharatha sorrowfully lamented in his anguish, his eyes fixed upon the sky.

10. "I do not want you to bring the dawn—here, I cup my hands in supplication. But no, pass as quickly as you can, so that I no longer have to see this heartless, malicious Kaikeyi, the cause of this great calamity."

11. But with this, the king cupped his hands before Kaikeyi and once more, begging her mercy, he spoke:

12. "Please, I am an old man, my life is nearly over. I am desolate, I place myself in your hands. Dear lady, have mercy on me for, after all, I am king.

13. "Truly it was thoughtless of me, my fair-hipped lady, to have said those things just now. Have mercy on me, please, my child. I know you have a heart."

14. So the pure-hearted king lamented, frantically and piteously, his eyes

---

9. A legendary king, who went to heaven for
   his good deeds, but there committed a sin,
   and so was exiled.

reddened and dimmed by tears, but the malicious, black-hearted woman only listened and made no reply.

15. And as the king stared at the woman he loved but could not appease, whose demand was so perverse—for the exile of his own son—he once again was taken faint, overcome with grief, and dropped unconscious to the floor.

The end of the eleventh *sarga* of the *Ayodhyakanda* of the *Sri Ramayana*.

SARGA 16 [Rama saw his father, with a wretched look and his mouth all parched]

1. Rama saw his father, with a wretched look and his mouth all parched, slumped upon his lovely couch, Kaikeyi at his side.

2. First he made an obeisance with all deference at his father's feet and then did homage most scrupulously at the feet of Kaikeyi.

3. "Rama!" cried the wretched king, his eyes brimming with tears, but he was unable to say anything more or to look at him.

4. As if his foot had grazed a snake, Rama was seized with terror to see the expression on the king's face, one more terrifying than he had ever seen before.

5. For the great king lay heaving sighs, racked with grief and remorse, all his senses numb with anguish, his mind stunned and confused.

6. It was as if the imperturbable, wave-wreathed ocean had suddenly been shaken with perturbation, as if the sun had been eclipsed, or a seer had told a lie.

7. His father's grief was incomprehensible to him, and the more he pondered it, the more his agitation grew, like that of the ocean under a full moon.

8. With his father's welfare at heart, Rama struggled to comprehend, "Why does the king not greet me, today of all days?

9. "On other occasions, when Father might be angry, the sight of me would calm him. Why then, when he looked at me just now, did he instead become so troubled?

10. "He seems desolate and grief-stricken, and his face has lost its glow." Doing obeisance to Kaikeyi, Rama spoke these words:

11. "I have not unknowingly committed some offense, have I, to anger my father? Tell me, and make him forgive me.

12. "His face is drained of color, he is desolate and does not speak to me. It cannot be, can it, that some physical illness or mental distress afflicts him? But it is true, well-being is not something one can always keep.

13. "Some misfortune has not befallen the handsome prince Bharata, has it, or courageous Satrughna,[10] or one of my mothers?

14. "I should not wish to live an instant if his Majesty, the great king, my father, were angered by my failure to satisfy him or do his bidding.

15. "How could a man not treat him as a deity incarnate, in whom he must recognize the very source of his existence in this world?

16. "Can it be that in anger you presumed to use harsh words with my father, and so threw his mind into such turmoil?

17. "Answer my questions truthfully, my lady: What has happened to cause this unprecedented change in the lord of men?

18. "At the bidding of the king, if enjoined by him, my guru, father, king, and benefactor, I would hurl myself into fire, drink deadly poison, or drown myself in the sea.

19. "Tell me then, my lady, what the king would have me do. I will do it, I promise. Rama need not say so twice."

20. The ignoble Kaikeyi then addressed these ruthless words to Rama, the upright and truthful prince:

21. "Long ago, Raghava, in the war of the gods and *asuras,* your father bestowed two boons on me, for protecting him when he was wounded in a great battle.

22. "By means of these I have demanded of the king that Bharata be consecrated and that you, Raghava, be sent at once to Dandaka wilderness.

23. "If you wish to ensure that your father be true to his word, and you to your own, best of men, then listen to what I have to say.

24. "Abide by your father's guarantee, exactly as he promised it, and enter the forest for nine years and five.

25. "Forgo the consecration and withdraw to Dandaka wilderness, live there seven years and seven, wearing matted hair and barkcloth garments.

26. "Let Bharata rule this land from the city of the Kosalans, with all the treasures it contains, all its horses, chariots, elephants."

27. When Rama, slayer of enemies, heard Kaikeyi's hateful words, like death itself, he was not the least disconcerted, but only replied,

28. "So be it. I shall go away to live in the forest, wearing matted hair and barkcloth garments, to safeguard the promise of the king.

---

10. The fourth son of Dasharatha and close companion of Bharata.

29. "But I want to know why the lord of earth, the invincible tamer of foes, does not greet me as he used to?

30. "You need not worry, my lady. I say it to your face: I shall go to the forest—rest assured—wearing barkcloth and matted hair.

31. "Enjoined by my father, my benefactor, guru, and king, a man who knows what is right to do, what would I hesitate to do in order to please him?

32. "But there is still one thing troubling my mind and eating away at my heart: that the king does not tell me himself that Bharata is to be consecrated.

33. "For my wealth, the kingship, Sita, and my own dear life I would gladly give up to my brother Bharata on my own, without any urging.

34. "How much more readily if urged by my father himself, the lord of men, in order to fulfill your fond desire and safeguard his promise?

35. "So you must reassure him. Why should the lord of earth keep his eyes fixed upon the ground and fitfully shed these tears?

36. "This very day let messengers depart on swift horses by order of the king to fetch Bharata from his uncle's house.

37. "As for me, I shall leave here in all haste for Dandaka wilderness, without questioning my father's word, to live there fourteen years."

38. Kaikeyi was delighted to hear these words of Rama's, and trusting them implicitly, she pressed Raghava to set out at once.

39. "So be it. Men shall go as messengers on swift horses to bring home Bharata from his uncle's house.

40. "But since you are now so eager, Rama, I do not think it wise to linger. You should therefore proceed directly from here to the forest.

41. "That the king is ashamed and does not address you himself, that is nothing, best of men, you needn't worry about that.

42. "But so long as you have not hastened from the city and gone to the forest, Rama, your father shall neither bathe nor eat."

43. "Oh curse you!" the king gasped, overwhelmed with grief, and upon the gilt couch he fell back in a faint.

44. Rama raised up the king, pressed though he was by Kaikeyi—like a horse whipped with a crop—to make haste and depart for the forest.

45. Listening to the ignoble Kaikeyi's hateful words, so dreadful in their consequences, Rama remained unperturbed and only said to her,

46. "My lady, it is not in the hopes of gain that I suffer living in this world. You should know that, like the seers, I have but one concern and that is righteousness.

47. "Whatever I can do to please this honored man I will do at any cost, even if it means giving up my life.

48. "For there is no greater act of righteousness than this: obedience to one's father and doing as he bids.

49. "Even unbidden by this honored man, at your bidding alone I shall live for fourteen years in the desolate forest.

50. "Indeed, Kaikeyi, you must ascribe no virtue to me at all if you had to appeal to the king, when you yourself are so venerable in my eyes.

51. "Let me only take leave of my mother, and settle matters with Sita. Then I shall go, this very day, to the vast forest of the Dandakas.

52. "You must see to it that Bharata obeys Father and guards the kingdom, for that is the eternal way of righteousness."

53. When his father heard Rama's words, he was stricken with such deep sorrow that he could not hold back his sobs in his grief and broke out in loud weeping.

54. Splendid Rama did homage at the feet of his unconscious father and at the feet of that ignoble woman, Kaikeyi, then he turned to leave.

55. Reverently, Rama circled his father and Kaikeyi, and withdrawing from the inner chamber, he saw his group of friends.

56. Laksmana, the delight of Sumitra, fell in behind him, his eyes brimming with tears, in a towering rage.

57. Reverently circling the equipment for the consecration, but careful not to gaze at it, Rama slowly went away.

58. The loss of the kingship diminished his great majesty as little as night diminishes the loveliness of the cool-rayed moon, beloved of the world.

59. Though he was on the point of leaving his native land and going to the forest, he was no more discomposed than one who has passed beyond all things of this world.

60. Holding back his sorrow within his mind, keeping his every sense in check, and fully self-possessed he made his way to his mother's residence to tell her the sad news.

61. As Rama entered her residence, where joy still reigned supreme, as he reflected on the sudden wreck of all his fortunes, even then he showed no sign of discomposure, for fear it might endanger the lives of those he loved.

The end of the sixteenth *sarga* of the *Ayodhyakanda* of the *Sri Ramayana*.

Book 3

SARGA 16 [After their bath, Rama, Sita, and Laksmana left the bank of the Godavari for their ashram]

1. After their bath Rama, Sita, and Laksmana left the bank of the Godavari for their ashram.[11]

2. Returning to the ashram, Raghava and Laksmana performed the morning rites and then returned to the leaf hut.

3. Great-armed Rama sat with Sita before the leaf hut, shining like the moon beside the sparkling star Citra, and began to converse with his brother Laksmana about one thing and another.

4. As Rama was sitting there engrossed in conversation, a certain *rakshasa*[12] woman chanced to come that way.

5. She was the sister of Ravana, the ten-necked *rakshasa*, and her name was Shurpanakha. Coming upon Rama, she stared at him as if he were one of the thirty gods.

6–7. Rama had long arms, the chest of a lion, eyes like lotus petals. Though delicate, he was very strong and bore all the signs of royalty. He was swarthy as the blue lotus, radiant as the love-god Kandarpa, the very image of Indra—and when the *rakshasa* woman saw him, she grew wild with desire.

8–10. Rama was handsome, the *rakshasa* woman was ugly, he was shapely and slim of waist, she misshapen and potbellied; his eyes were large, hers were beady, his hair was jet black, and hers the color of copper; he always said just the right thing and in a sweet voice, her words were sinister and her voice struck terror; he was young, attractive, and well mannered, she ill mannered, repellent, an old hag. And yet, the god of love, who comes to life in our bodies, had taken possession of her, and so she addressed Rama:

11. "Your hair is matted in the manner of ascetics, yet you have a wife with you and bear bow and arrows. How is it you have come into this region, the haunt of *rakshasas*?"

12. Questioned in this fashion by the *rakshasa* woman Shurpanakha, the slayer of enemies in his open manner proceeded to tell her everything.

13. "There was a king named Dasharatha, courageous as one of the thirty gods. I am his eldest son, named Rama, known to people far and wide.

14. "This is Laksmana, my devoted younger brother, and this my wife, the princess of Videha, known as Sita.

---

11. Dwelling place of ascetics.   12. A sort of antihuman; demon.

15. "I was compelled to come to live in the forest by command of my mother and my father, the lord of men, and I wanted to do what is right, for doing right has always been my chief concern.

16. "But I should like to know about you. Tell me, who are you? To whom do you belong? For what purpose have you come here? Tell me truthfully."

17. Hearing his words and consumed with passion, the *rakshasa* woman replied, "Listen, then, Rama, I shall tell you, and my words will be truthful.

18. "My name is Shurpanakha. I am a *rakshasa* woman, who can take on any form at will, and I roam this wilderness all alone, striking terror into every living thing.

19. "The *rakshasa* named Ravana, the lord of all *rakshasas*, is my brother, so too the powerful Kumbhakarna, who lies ever fast asleep.

20. "So is Vibhisana, but he is righteous and does not behave like a *rakshasa*. My other brothers are Khara and Dusana, famed for their might in battle.

21. "But I am prepared to defy them all, Rama, for I have never seen anyone like you. I approach you as I would a husband, with true love, best of men. Be my husband forevermore; what do you want with Sita?

22. "She is ugly and misshapen and unworthy of you. I alone am suited to you; look upon me as your wife.

23. "I will devour this misshapen slut, this hideous human female with her pinched waist, along with this brother of yours.

24. "And then, my beloved, you shall roam Dandaka with me, viewing all the different mountain peaks and forests."

25. Thus addressed by the wild-eyed creature, Kakutstha[13] burst out laughing but then went on to reply with customary eloquence.

The end of the sixteenth *sarga* of the *Aranyakanda* of the *Sri Ramayana*.

SARGA 17

1. As Shurpanakha stood there bound tight in the bonds of desire, Rama smiled and, humoring her, replied in jest:

2. "I am already married, my lady, and I love my wife. And for women such as you, to have a rival wife is a source of bitter sorrow.

3. "But my younger brother here is of good character, handsome, powerful, majestic, and still unmarried. His name is Laksmana.

---

13. Another name for Rama.

4. "He has never had a woman before and is in need of a wife. He is young and handsome and will make a good husband, one suited to such beauty as yours.

5. "Accept my brother as your husband, large-eyed, shapely lady. With no rival wife the two of you will be inseparable as sunlight and Mount Meru."

6. When the *rakshasa* woman, wild with desire, heard Rama address her in this way, she promptly forsook him and said to Laksmana:

7. "I shall make you a lovely wife, one befitting your beauty. And together we shall roam so pleasantly all through Dandaka."

8. Lakshman smiled at the words of the *rakshasa* woman Shurpanakha and with customary eloquence made this fitting reply:

9. "Why would you want to be my wife, lotuslike beauty? I am completely subject to the will of my noble brother; I am a slave, and she who is my wife must be a slave as well.

10. "Become instead the junior wife of my noble brother, large-eyed lady of unblemished beauty. He is prosperous, and with him your fortunes, too, will prosper and you will be happy.

11. "Soon enough he will turn away from this misshapen slut, this hideous old wife with her pinched waist, and give his love to you alone.

12. "What man with any sense would reject this singular beauty of yours, my fair and shapely lady, and bestow his affections on a human female?"

13. So Laksmana spoke, and the potbellied, hideous creature, unused to teasing, thought he was in earnest.

14. Then as Rama, the invincible slayer of enemies, sat with Sita before the leaf hut, the *rakshasa* woman addressed him once more, wild with desire.

15. "It is on account of this misshapen slut, this hideous old wife with her pinched waist, that you care so little for me.

16. "I am going to devour this human female at once, before your very eyes; then, free of any rival, I shall live happily with you."

17. And with this, she flew into a rage, and with eyes flashing like firebrands she shot toward the fawn-eyed princess, like a giant meteor toward the star Rohini.

18. But as she was about to fall upon Sita, like the very noose of Death, mighty Rama angrily restrained her and said to Laksmana:

19. "Never tease savage, ignoble creatures, Saumitri. Look at Vaidehi, dear brother; she is frightened half to death.

20. "Now, tiger among men, mutilate this misshapen slut, this potbellied, lustful *rakshasa* woman."

21. So Rama spoke, and powerful Lakshmana, in full view of his brother, drew his sword and in a rage cut off the creature's ears and nose.

22. The dreadful Shurpanakha, her ears and nose hacked off, gave out an earsplitting roar as she fled back into the forest the way she had come.

23. Mutilated, spattered with blood, and all the more dreadful now, the *rakshasa* woman roared incessantly, like a storm cloud when the rains come.

24. Gushing blood all over, a terror to behold, she disappeared into the deep forest, howling, her arms outstretched.

25. She made her way then to her brother, the awesome Khara, who was in Janasthana together with a troop of *rakshasas*. Mutilated, she fell before him to the ground, like a bolt of lightning from the sky.

26. Spattered with blood, wild with fear and confusion, Khara's sister told him the whole story—how Rama had come into the forest with his wife and Lakshmana, and how she herself had been mutilated.

The end of the seventeenth *sarga* of the *Aranyakanda* of the *Sri Ramayana*.

KAMPAN (TWELFTH CENTURY C.E.)

India

Kampan was a Tamil poet who most likely lived in the twelfth century C.E. His *Ramayana* is regarded as one of the literary masterpieces of the Tamil language. The story Kampan narrates is essentially the same as that presented by Valmiki, but the manner in which the story is presented is very different. In the present selection, for instance, the Tamil poet focuses on the woman in a different way, exploring her emotional response in far greater depth. Among the sources Kampan drew on for his narrative are motifs and conventions associated with *sangam* (literary academic) poetry and the folklore of southern India. Perhaps the most distinctive feature of Kampan's text is that it explicitly presents Rama as an incarnation of the god Vishnu, one of the three supreme gods of classical Hinduism (the divinity of Rama in Valmiki's poem is a more complicated matter). In this it follows the tradition established by the poetry of the Tamil saints of the sixth to ninth centuries C.E.

from **The Ramayana**

[Patalam Five: Shurpunakha]

1. 2829

And the heroes saw the river Godavari
    which was like the poems of the great poets,
a sublime ornament for the earth
    with fields of profound wealth
and its episodes that are watering places
    for rescue from the heat, with its flow
through the five landscapes of poetry,[1]
    clear and lovely and sweetly running.

2. 2830

With her bright face glittering, gracious
    as a lotus where the bees gather
and the glowing eyes of her water lilies
    that absorb and hold sweet fragrance
while her hands, the clear waves,
    one after another, were picking up and scattering
beautiful flowers, the holy river shone
    as if bowing at the noble sight of them.

3. 2831

And O the river seemed to cry out,
    cry out and grieve and grieve
with risen love, as if the moving water
    were shedding cool drops of tears
spreading from her lovely eyes
    of newly open water lilies that had to see
this sadness, those young men[2] who were honest
    and faultless living in the forest.

4. 2832

The bowman of the long bow saw
    the cakravaka birds[3] peacefully

Translated by George L. Hart and Hank Heifitz.

---

1. The five different types of Tamil love poetry, associated with five stages of love.
2. Rama and Laksmana.

3. Love birds condemned to spend their
   nights apart.

closing their eyes on their beds
    of lotuses and looked at the breasts
of his woman, while she whose ornaments
    were lovely looked at the hills
glittering with their jewels and her mind
    turned to her great lord's arms.

5. 2833

And that highest being when he saw
    the swaying walk of a wild goose
smiled a little and looked
    at Sita walking near him
and she saw how a male elephant
    coming back from drinking at the water
moved and a sudden smile
    showed across her face.

20. 2848

"Has the sun who is lord of light not seen this radiance,
this glow of a being whose smile is like glistening moonlight,
that he goes on his way without shame in his heart, spreading
his lesser light on high through all the distances?

21. 2849

"This man with his huge shoulders like towering mountains
has a lower lip for which no comparison possible
on this earth is adequate. What could I ever find
to say that marks a redness even greater than coral?

22. 2850

"For the happiness of encircling this lovely waist that dispels
the darkness, I think that not even a golden robe
could have done the tapas of that bark garment[4]
for this noble being who shines as brightly as the moon.

23. 2851

"Ah! if instead of matted hair, he was wearing
the black tuft[5] of a young man with its curls

---

4. Religious penance consisting of wearing
   rough garments.

5. The signs, respectively, of an ascetic and
   a warrior.

all through it like long clouds hanging down,
surely he would put an end to every woman's life.

24. 2852

"If the best of ornaments, radiating light, were to embrace
this body, could they make its loveliness grow any more?
Does the beauty of the faultless ruby, king of gems,
shine any brighter by the presence of some other jewel?

25. 2853

"When Brahma[6] created this body, collecting and displaying
every virtue possible, keeping nothing back, then blame
came to him since Indra, ruler of all the worlds, though he beg
for more, in beauty is not worth the dust on those feet!"

. . .

80. 2908

Whenever a dark cloud appeared or she happened to look at a column
of blue sapphires, she would join her palms in praise, with her body
so on fire that even a giant moonstone that is moistened
by the moon's touch would catch fire from her and burn.

81. 2909

So that the huge lovely moon would never find her
nor the cool north wind nor the God of Love, she almost went
to the safety of a deep mountain cave where there lives
an angry snake, with sharp, terrifying fangs.

82. 2910

Then, as the flame grew higher and higher, not knowing
what to do next, with her breasts burning and pouring out
three times more fire than before, she began to roll
around on a bed of long, fresh, golden shoots.

83. 2911

The form of the hero took shape before her burning eyes
and thinking she was seeing him, huge and dark as a monsoon cloud,[7]
she was pained and ashamed and stunned as that body
vanished away and she fell to the ground, in great suffering.

---

6. The creator god.

7. Rama is represented as dark in complexion.

84. 2912

As a black cloud passed, she tried to press it to her breasts,
imagining it was her lord and when she saw those clouds
warming up and dissolving, she would weep! Was there
any end at all to that unholy woman's delusion?

85. 2913

Though it seemed as if she were caught in the blazing fire that consumes
a universe, that mindless woman did not lose her life
saved by the drug of her desire to have that man
with his body the color of the dark ocean and then to live!

99. 2927

She tried to press her nose back on.
    She breathed like fire in a forge.
She hammered her hands on the ground and grasping
    her two large breasts,
she looked at them and her body broke out
    sweating. She went running
on her great strong legs everywhere
    and she weakened as the blood flowed.

100. 2928

She wandered in a flooding swamp of her own blood
    that came streaming down like a waterfall
swollen full by many springs and, through calling out
    all those names of her family
that can frighten even Death, made
    the gods run away in terror.
Unable to bear the pain, she stood there and summoned them,
    speaking in a torrent of words.

101. 2929

"You! with your power on this wide earth, are you not offended by these
holy men wandering carrying bows who have made me not able
any more to raise my head before the gods! O incomparable mountain
who lifted Siva's[8] own mountain! Won't you come look at these things?

---

8. The destroyer god, who dwells on Mt.
   Kailasa.

102. 2930

"The world encircled by the roaring ocean believes that no one
takes a tiger's cub even when the mother is gone. Is this
a lie? O you who are stronger than Asuras and gods and the three[9]
who are highest! Won't you come to see the pain I feel?

103. 2931

"You saw the back of Indra when you fought him as he was riding
the king of elephants who trumpeted in battle and, fighting for him,
there was a dense army of gods! You defeated him in war. He broke out sweating
and barely escaped with his life! Won't you come to see the shame I feel?

104. 2932

"You who are served by wind, fire, and water and Death
who is cruel time, and the sky and the planets! Have you lost
your strength? Do you retreat before two men, you who seized
the sword you carry out of the mighty hand of great Siva!

105. 2933

"Though in form they resemble the God of Love, why do you not show
your anger at these men not worth the dust under the soles of your sandals,
O strength! who, lifting your arms, broke Kailasa and the tusks of the Elephants
of Space[10] who flow with musth, whose feet make the dust sparkle!

106. 2934

"Has his strength abandoned Ravana who has the power even to destroy
the gods who wear fragrant garlands that are filled with nectar?
Has strength left his younger brothers? Has it gone to stay
with men, the meat of whose bodies is meant to be food for our race?

107. 2935

"Did this happen because of the power of two holy men who are hiding
in the great forest thick with trees or because Raksasas good at killing
have given up? You! whose hands are so strong your enemies can only
be Siva or Brahma or Visnu! Will you look at the pain I feel?

---

9. Brahma, Visnu, Siva.

10. Mythic beasts said to guard the cardinal points of space.

108. 2936

"Where Indra and Brahma on his flower and the other gods ask for your orders
and the women of heaven sing to wish you long life and the seven worlds
praise you, sitting in the midst of your court under your umbrella unrivaled
like the moon, can I who am your servant, with no shame, show you my face?

109. 2937

"Am I to remain here crying out my pain while that man admires
his arms after he kicked and rolled me across the ground so that my strength
broke and faded and then he cut off my nose? Should I have to endure this
in Khara's forest? O brother who moved Siva's mountain! O my brother!

110. 2938

"Isn't your good name sullied by this stain, because I acted
without a sense of shame and due to my lust, I have lost my nose?
You whose arms have the great fame of having fought and tired
out the Elephants of Space! You broke their tusks! Ravana! Ravana!

111. 2939

"And you my nephew![11] My nephew! You who made the gods serve you,
who put Indra himself in chains and wiped out clans of Asuras!
Am I to die here, because of this disgrace, I who sinned and had
my nose and my ears cut off by those two in the middle of the forest!

112. 2940

"Once the seven worlds grew angry and came against you and you,
strong in your rage, broke them with a single bow and scattered them
in all the directions. Then, chaining Indra's legs, you put him
in a great prison! My nephew! Won't you come face the strength of men?

113. 2941

"You whose murderous force can split rocks with the weapons in your giant
hands! Khara! Dusana![12] You others born as Rakshasas and ornamented
with jewels that flash apart the darkness! Do you sleep on the earth
like Kumbhakarna[13] with his sharply honed weapons? Can't you hear me calling?"

---

11. Indrajit, son of Ravana and "conqueror of
Indra."

12. Brother of Shurpanakha and Khara's
general, respectively.
13. Brother of Ravana.

114. 2942

As the Raksasi, she who was the enemy, went on shouting out these things,
wailing and lamenting as she rolled on the beautiful earth, he came,
who by that river had finished the full morning rites of his tapas, a mountain
of emerald, whose long arms with their strong sturdy hands held a bow.

115. 2943

Looking at his face as he came, she beat her belly and her raining
tears and the torrents of her blood turned the rich soil to mud.
"By the sin of love risen in me for the beauty of your body, ah
my lord! See what I have suffered!" and she fell on the ground before him.

116. 2944

Within the beauty of his heart that has no equal, he knew something evil
had been done by this woman whose hair was spreading loose and he realized
it must have been his younger brother that same day who had cut off
her long ears and her nose. He said to her, "Woman! Who are you?"

117. 2945

Hearing these words, the strong Raksasi said, "Don't you know me?
My brother is Ravana whose rage silenced even a single word
raised against him in any of the worlds, he who holds heaven
and all other worlds by his cruel spear with its leaflike blade."

118. 2946

"Why have you left those Raksasas with all their power and come here
so far away, to where we live and carry on our tapas?" he said,
and she answered him, "O best cure for the cruel sickness of desire
burning me like hot charcoal! Don't you remember my coming yesterday?"

119. 2947

"Was it you walking here yesterday, like the goddess Sri on her lotus
full of honey, with your long dark eyes like lovely fishes?"
"When a woman has lost her nipples, her ears with their earrings, her nose
like a vine, O king with handsome eyes! isn't her beauty destroyed?"

120. 2948

The king, looking into the face of his strong younger brother and smiling
just a little said to him, "Hero! What evil thing did she intend
to do that you at once cut off her long ears and her nose like a vine?"
and the great hero, bowing to his brother's feet, gave him this answer.

121. 2949

"Whether she meant to use her sharp teeth and consume what she had tracked
or whether a crowd of malevolent Raksasas somewhere behind her
was urging her on, she came running, evil, with her eyes spitting fire
at your noble woman. She was in a towering rage beyond belief."

122. 2950

Before Laksmana with his curving, well-strung bow had finished, the Raksasi,
their enemy, said, "You are from a rich land bright with rivers where by a stream
a pregnant frog, furious at the sight of her husband hovering near a conch,
troubles the water! Doesn't a woman's heart burn when she sees her rival?"

123. 2951

That being who is past the reach of words said to her, "We came here
searching for the great clan of Raksasas to destroy them all who fight
in their strength against the weak. Run now far from this forest where truth
is sought, or else you will be killed as you give us these vicious answers."

124. 2952

"Since Brahma whose hair never turns white nor does his skin wrinkle
and all the other gods are subjects and pay tribute to Ravana,
it would be wrong of you to hurry me away. I have something else,
something different to tell you, if you have any sense of what's best for you!

125. 2953

"Ravana will tear out the tongue of the man who tells him his sister
has had her nose cut off, lost to her forever. He is not
a cultured gentleman. By cutting off my nose, you ended your clan
without escape! You have poured all your beauty out on barren ground.

126. 2954

"The gods in heaven and the kings on the earth and those who rule
where the great Nagas live will stay where they are now protecting
their own heads! Who is there to protect you? Care for me and I
will protect you, but if you will not, then be aware that Ravana exists!

127. 2955

"Though women who are firmly modest should not boast of their own might,
yet I speak out to you because of my love, great with desire.
Won't you tell your younger brother that I am stronger than anyone
in this world, and the honored sister of him who is stronger than the gods?

128. 2956

"In your mighty battles, I will stand by you and protect you. I can
pick you up and carry you away on the air! I can give you endless fruit
as delicious as meat! Why reject your protector? I will give you anything
you wish for! Tell me what you gain from this one who is delicate as a flower!

129. 2957

"Among women who wear their lovely ornaments here on the earth
or in the sky, who are young and beautiful and accomplished, the finest
in their clans, who can summon for themselves whatever they may want,
will you tell me if there is a single one fit to be compared with me?

130. 2958

"So what if you made me lose my nose, now that it's gone, if you can't bear it,
instantly I will create it again! I will be beautiful again! Am I
any less a woman if in this way I gain the fortune of your grace?
Isn't a long nose rising on a woman's face only a frill?

131. 2959

"If I want someone and he doesn't want me, mustn't he be impotent?
Isn't my life yours, because of the love that has risen in me?
Beauty that others may look at and desire, isn't that a poison?
Shouldn't you welcome a body that only a husband will caress?

132. 2960

"You! as if Siva and Brahma who on his flower faces the directions[14]
and Visnu and Indra with his devastating thunderbolt had joined in one
to stand here! Is Kama whose flower arrows take life away from the worlds
your younger brother too? He is as merciless as this one has been.

133. 2961

"Is there any reason for you to have cut off my nose and made a hole
    show, you with your war anklets
beautifully fashioned of gold! unless you had the thought in your mind,
    'She will stay here with us, she will
not go, she who has this form that is delight.' So that no stranger
    might ever look at me, you cut it,
didn't you? Did you harm me? Because I understood your wish, don't I know
    that my love is twice as strong?

---

14. Brahma has four faces, one looking in each
    direction.

134. 2962

"If the Raksasas with their spears and their great anger like unquenchable fire
  should come to know what has happened
and see it in their rage, all the worlds would be destroyed because of you
  who have wronged me. Born in a lineage
so high, with Righteousness always in your minds, you would not cause the
  worlds
  to be destroyed! Consider carefully
and stay here with me, in happiness, clear of blame, saving all life,"
  she said and, standing up, bowed down to him.

135. 2963

"I still have the arrow that ended the life of Tadaka, the mother
  of your mother who was a Raksasi guilty
of causing pain such as living beings here had never known
  and now I have taken on as my tapas
to live in the forest where I exist to destroy the enemy race
  of Raksasas who around their shoulders
wear garlands of thick, lovely flowers. Strong Raksasi!" said the Lord,
  "Stop behaving in a way so low!

136. 2964

"We are the sons of Dasaratha, the wheel of whose law ruled the world
  unrivaled! Obeying our mother's command,
we entered the forest where fragrance is everywhere. Brahmins and great sadhus
  have asked us to destroy the race
of Raksasas whose army is an ocean with no shore to be seen.
  Only then will we reenter our city
where the mansions of the families rise like ancient mountains. Take these things
  to heart. Understand them clearly,

137. 2965

"You should not be thinking that these are just any two men,
  even though the great gods themselves
were defeated, unable to stand against the Raksasas who do not
  travel the path of virtues.
Bring, if you can, everyone you think is powerful, all of them,
  the Raksasas with their sharp spears
smelling of flesh and all the Yaksas[15] who always win their victories!
  Then right in front of you we will kill them."

---

15. Semidivine beings, whose king is Kubera,
    brother of Shurpanakha.

138. 2966

"Yes, you can kill them," she said, "you can be told what strategies
 they will try, you can win
and end their string of victories, you can overcome every one
 of their tricks if only you see me
not as a woman with a gaping mouth, with all of my teeth showing
 because my upper lip has been cut away!
Listen to me! You who come from a land where water nourishes
 all grains and offers them to the people!

139. 2967

"Even if you don't give her up, she whose arms are as graceful as bamboo,
 would I be nothing at all to you?
If you are determined to go into battle against the Raksasas who are outlaws,
 who are ignorant and murderous, then
since I understand the various magic powers of their intricate weapons,
 won't I be able to repel them?
Don't you know what the proverb says, that a snake is the one
 to search out the lair of a snake?

140. 2968

"If you feel that you must keep this woman in your heart, still you should
 realize that if you intend to fight
and prevail on the battlefield against the Raksasas, we three here together
 could make that field a pool
of blood! Should that give you pain? And if then you will marry me
 to this young prince who does not realize
what there is to gain, I would never weaken even before him
 who has imprisoned[16] the sun and the moon.

141. 2969

"On the day you return to your city, when it will be filled with great joy,
 I will skillfully take on whatever form
you wish for, and if your younger brother should say, 'How can I live
 with a woman who has had her nose
cut off completely?' even though it was he who became enraged and cut at me
 in his anger that could not be satisfied,
won't you tell him he has been living for a very long time
 with a woman who has no waist at all?"

---

16. Ravana.

142. 2970

The younger brother glanced at his spear with its bright blade like a leaf,
  thinking to pierce her as she spoke
and he said, "If we don't free ourselves by killing her right now,
  she will trouble us for a long time.
O king, what is your will?" The Lord said, "That would be the right thing
  to do, if she doesn't leave us alone!"
and the Raksasi thought, "These men will show me no compassion.
  I will lose my life if I stay."

143. 2971

She said to them, "Could I ever bear to live with you after I have
  lost my nose as lovely
as a long vine and my two ears and the nipples of both my breasts?
  What I said was meant to find out
all about you. Now I will bring him who is swifter than the wind,
  him who is crueler than fire,
Khara, who will be your Death!" and she set out, feeling herself
  full of hatred that had no calming.

ASHVAGHOSHA (c. 100 C.E.)
India

The *Life of the Buddha* [*Buddhacarita*] is one of two long poems, three plays, and
assorted hymns and discourses written by Ashvaghosha, the first of the great
Buddhist poets in Sanskrit. Tradition associates Ashvaghosha with the court of
King Kanishka I, who ruled sometime between the middle and the end of the first
century C.E. in the northern part of present-day India.

The passage presented here is known as the episode of the "four signs." It
relates a crucial moment in the life of Shakyamuni, a young prince, when a series
of events convinces him to undertake the quest for spiritual awakening that will
result in his transformation into Buddha (which means "awakened" in Sanskrit).
It had been foretold at Shakyamuni's birth that he was destined to become either
a great king or a master of *dharma* (here the word takes on a special Buddhist
meaning of spiritual teaching). Hoping for a king rather than a holy man, his
father, King Shuddhodana, raises Shakyamuni in perfect comfort, shielding him
from anything that might provoke a distaste for worldly pleasures. One day,
however, the prince accidentally encounters four men: an old man, a sick man,
a dead man, and a man who has renounced the world. He thereby realizes the
nature of mortality and the possible responses to its inevitable course, and he
decides to seek his spiritual enlightenment.

The Enlightenment of the Buddha. Sandstone sculpture of the first century C.E. from Sanchi in central India.

from The Life of Buddha [Buddhacarita]

The Four Signs

LIFE IN THE PALACE

The prince passed through infancy and in course of time duly underwent the ceremony of initiation. And it took him but a few days to learn the sciences suitable to his race, the mastery of which ordinarily requires many years.

But, as the king of the Sakyas had heard from the great seer, Asita, that the prince's future goal would be the supreme beatitude, he feared lest he should go to the forests and therefore he turned him to sensual pleasures.

Then from a family possessed of long-standing good conduct he summoned for him the goddess of Fortune in the shape of a maiden, Yasodhara by name, of widespread renown, virtuous and endowed with beauty, modesty and gentle bearing.

The prince, radiant with wondrous beauty like Sanatkumara,[1] took his delight with the Sakya king's daughter-in-law, as the Thousand-eyed with Saci.[2]

The monarch, reflecting that the prince must see nothing untoward that might agitate his mind, assigned him a dwelling in the upper storeys of the palace and did not allow him access to the ground.

Translated by E. H. Johnston.

---

1. "Eternal Youth," one of the four sons of the god Brahmā.

2. The god Indra (who is said to have one thousand eyes) with his wife.

Then in the pavilions, white as the clouds of autumn, with apartments suited to each season and resembling heavenly mansions come down to earth, he passed the time with the noble music of singing-women.

For the palace was glorious as Kailasa,[3] with tambourines whose frames were bound with gold and which sounded softly beneath the strokes of women's fingers, and with dances that rivalled those of the beautiful Apsarases.[4]

There the women delighted him with their soft voices, charming blandishments, playful intoxications, sweet laughter, curvings of eyebrows and sidelong glances.

Then, a captive to the women, who were skilled in the accessories of love and indefatigable in sexual pleasure, he did not descend from the palace to the ground, just as one who has won Paradise by his merit does not descend to earth from the heavenly mansion.

THE PRINCE'S PERTURBATION

Then upon a time he listened to songs celebrating the forests, with their soft grass, with their trees resounding with koïls' calls, and with their adornment of lotusponds.

Then hearing of the entrancing character of the city groves, beloved of the womenfolk, he set his heart on an expedition outside, like an elephant confined inside a house.

Then the king learnt of the state of mind of that heart's desire, styled his son, and directed a pleasure excursion to be prepared worthy of his love and majesty and of his son's youth.

And, reflecting that the prince's tender mind might be perturbed thereby, he forbade the appearance of afflicted common folk on the royal road.

Then with the greatest gentleness they cleared away on all sides those whose limbs were maimed or senses defective, the aged, sick and the like, and the wretched, and made the royal highway supremely magnificent.

Then, when the road had been made beautiful, the prince, after receiving permission, descended at the proper time in full splendour with well-trained attendants from the top of the palace, and approached the king.

Thereon the ruler of men, with tears in his eyes, gazed long at his son and kissed him on the head; and with his voice he bade him set forth, but out of affection he did not let him go in his mind.

Then the prince mounted a golden chariot, to which were harnessed four well-broken horses with golden gear, and with a driver who was manly, skilful and reliable.

Then, like the moon with the constellations mounting to the sky, he proceeded with a suitable retinue towards the road which was bestrewn with

---

3. Mountain in the Himalayas, where the god Siva resides.

4. Divine females, often represented as the dancing girls of the gods.

heaps of brilliant flowers and made gay with hanging wreaths and fluttering banners.

And very slowly he entered the royal highway, which was carpeted with the halves of blue lotuses in the shape of eyes open to their widest in excitement, as all around the citizens gazed at him.

Some praised him for his gracious bearing, others worshipped him for his glorious appearance, but for his benignity others wished him sovereignty and length of days.

From the great houses humpbacks and swarms of dwarfs and Kiratas[5] poured forth, and from the meaner houses women; and all bowed down as to the flag in the procession of the god.

Hearing the news from their servants, "the prince, they say, is going out," the women obtained leave from their elders and went out on to the balconies in their desire to see him.

They gathered together in uncontrollable excitement, obstructed by the slipping of their girdle-strings, as they put their ornaments on at the report, and with their eyes still dazed by sudden awakening from sleep.

They frightened the flocks of birds on the houses with the jingling of belts, the tinkling of anklets and the clatter of their steps on the stairs, and reproached each other for jostling.

But some of these magnificent women, though longing made them try to rush, were delayed in their movements by the weight of their hips and full breasts.

But another, though well able to move with speed, checked her steps and went slowly, modestly shrinking as she covered up the ornaments worn in intimacy.

Unquiet reigned in the windows then, as the women were crowded together in the mutual press, with their earrings ever agitated by collisions and their ornaments jingling.

But the lotus-faces of the women, emerging from the windows and mutually setting their earrings in perpetual commotion, seemed like lotuses stuck on to the pavilions.

Then with its palaces full to bursting with young women, who threw the lattices open in their excitement, the city appeared as magnificent on all sides as Paradise with its heavenly mansions full of Apsarases.

From the narrowness of the windows the faces of these glorious women, with their earrings resting on each other's cheeks, seemed like bunches of lotus-flowers tied to the windows.

The women, looking down at the prince in the street, seemed as if wishing to descend to earth, while the men, gazing up at him with upraised faces, seemed as if wishing to rise to heaven.

Beholding the king's son in the full glory of his beauty and majesty, the

---

5. Usually forest-dwelling hunters: here presumably harem guards.

women murmured low, "Blessed is his wife," with pure minds and from no baser motive;

For they held him in reverent awe, reflecting that he with the long stout arms, in form like the visible presence of the god whose symbols are flowers,[6] would, it was said, resign his royal pomp and follow the religious law.

Thus the first time that the prince saw the royal highway, it was thronged with respectful citizens, clad in cleanly sober guise; and he rejoiced and felt in some degree as if he were being re-created.

But when the Suddhadhivasa gods[7] saw that city as joyful as Paradise itself, they created the illusion of an old man in order to incite the king's son to leave his home.

Then the prince saw him overcome with senility and different in form to other men. His interest was excited and, with gaze steadily directed on the man, he asked the charioteer:—

"Good charioteer, who is this man with white hair, supporting himself on the staff in his hand, with his eyes veiled by the brows, and limbs relaxed and bent? Is this some transformation in him, or his original state, or mere chance?"

When the chariot-driver was thus spoken to, those very same gods confounded his understanding, so that, without seeing his error, he told the prince the matter he should have withheld:—

"Old age it is called, that which has broken him down,—the murderer of beauty, the ruin of vigour, the birthplace of sorrow, the grave of pleasure, the destroyer of memory, the enemy of the senses.

For he too sucked milk in his infancy, and later in course of time he crawled on the ground; in the natural order he became a handsome youth and in the same natural order he has now reached old age."

At these words the king's son started a little and addressed the charioteer thus, "Will this evil come upon me also?" Then the charioteer said to him:—

"Inevitably by force of time my long-lived lord will know this length of his days. Men are aware that old age thus destroys beauty and yet they seek it."

Then, since his mind was purified by his intentions in the past and his good merit had been accumulated through countless epochs, he was perturbed in his lofty soul at hearing of old age, like a bull on hearing the crash of a thunderbolt near by.

Fixing his eyes on the old man, he sighed deeply and shook his head; and looking on the festive multitude he uttered these words in his perturbation:—

"Thus old age strikes down indiscriminately memory and beauty and valour, and yet with such a sight before its eyes the world is not perturbed.

This being so, turn back the horses, charioteer; go quickly home again. For how can I take my pleasure in the garden, when the fear of old age rules in my mind?"

So at the bidding of his master's son the driver turned back the chariot. Then the prince returned to the same palace, but so lost in anxiety that it seemed to him empty.

---

6. The god of love, who (like Cupid) has a bow, made of flowers with a black bowstring of bees.

7. "Dwelling in a pure abode," one of numerous categories of gods in the Buddhist cosmology, who typically announce the birth of the Buddha.

But even there he found no relief, as he ever dwelt on the subject of old age; therefore once more with the permission of the king he went out, all being ordered as before.

Thereupon the same gods created a man with body afflicted by disease, and the son of Śuddhodana saw him, and, keeping his gaze fixed on him, he said to the charioteer:—

"Who is this man with swollen belly and body that heaves with his panting? His shoulders and arms are fallen in, his limbs emaciated and pale. He calls out piteously, "mother," as he leans on another for support."

Then the charioteer replied to him, "Good Sir, it is the mighty misfortune called disease, developed in full force from the disorder of the humours, that has made this man, once so competent, no longer master of himself."

Thereupon the king's son looked at the man compassionately and spoke, "Is this evil peculiar to him, or is the danger of disease common to all men?"

Then the chariot-driver said, "Prince, this evil is shared by all. For men feast and yet they are thus oppressed by disease and racked by pain".

Hearing this truth, he was perturbed in mind and trembled like the reflection of the moon on rippling water; and in his pity he uttered these words in a somewhat low tone:—

"This is the calamity of disease for mankind and yet the world sees it and feels no alarm. Vast, alas, is the ignorance of men, who sport under the very shadow of disease.

Turn back the chariot, charioteer, from going outside; let it go straight to the palace of the chief of men. And on hearing of the danger of disease, my mind is repelled from pleasures and shrinks, as it were, into itself."

Then he turned back with all feeling of joy gone and entered the palace, given over to brooding; and seeing him thus returned a second time, the lord of the earth made enquiry.

But when he learnt the reason for his return, he felt himself already abandoned by him. And he merely reprimanded the officer in charge of clearing the road, and angry though he was, imposed no severe punishment on him.

And he further arranged for his son the application of sensual attractions in the highest degree, hoping, "Perhaps he will be held by the restlessness of the senses and not desert us".

But when in the women's apartments his son took no pleasure in the objects of sense, sounds and the rest, then he directed another excursion outside with the thought that it might cause a change of mood.

And as out of his affection he understood his son's state of mind and took no account of the dangers of passion, he ordered suitable courtesans to be present there, as skilled in the arts.

Then the royal highway was decorated and guarded with especial care; and the king changed the charioteer and chariot and sent the prince off outside.

Then as the king's son was going along, those same gods fashioned a lifeless man, so that only the charioteer and the prince, and none other, saw the corpse being borne along.

Thereon the king's son asked the charioteer, "Who is being carried along yonder by four men and followed by a dejected company? He is dressed out gorgeously and yet they bewail him".

Then the driver's mind was overcome by the pure-natured Suddhadhivasa gods and, though it should not have been told, he explained this matter to the lord of mankind:—

"This is someone or other, lying bereft of intellect, senses, breath and qualities, unconscious and become like a mere log or bundle of grass. He was brought up and cherished most lovingly with every care and now he is being abandoned."

Hearing the driver's reply, he was slightly startled and said, "Is this law of being peculiar to this man, or is such the end of all creatures?"

Then the driver said to him, "This is the last act for all creatures. Destruction is inevitable for all in the world, be he of low or middle or high degree".

Then, steadfast-minded though he was, the king's son suddenly became faint on hearing of death, and, leaning with his shoulder against the top of the chariot rail, he said in a melodious voice:—

"This is the end appointed for all creatures, and yet the world throws off fear and takes no heed. Hardened, I ween, are men's hearts; for they are in good cheer, as they fare along the road.

Therefore, charioteer, let our chariot be turned back; for it is not the time or place for pleasure-resorts. For how could a man of intelligence be heedless here in the hour of calamity, when once he knows of destruction?"

Though the king's son spoke to him thus, he not merely did not turn back but in accordance with the king's command went on to the Padmasanda grove,[8] which had been provided with special attractions.

There the prince saw that lovely grove like the grove of Nandana,[9] with young trees in full bloom, with intoxicated koïls[10] flitting joyously about, and with pavilions and tanks beautiful with lotuses.

THE WOMEN REJECTED

Then the women went forth from the city garden, their eyes dancing with excitement, to meet the king's son, as if he were a bridegroom arriving.

And, as they approached him, their eyes opened wide in wonder and they welcomed him respectfully with hands folded like lotus-buds.

And they stood around him, their minds absorbed in love, and seemed to drink him in with eyes that were moveless and blossomed wide in ecstasy.

For the glory of the brilliant signs on his person,[11] as of ornaments born on him, made the women deem him to be the god of love in bodily form.

---

8. A place where day-lotuses grow.
9. The heavenly garden of Indra.
10. Indian cuckoos.

11. Physical marks—often very specific signs such as the "wheel" on the foot in the case of an emperor—indicate a person's character and destiny.

Some opined from his benignity and gravity that the moon had come down to earth in person with his rays veiled.

Enthralled by his beauty, they writhed suppressedly, and, smiting each other with their glances, softly sighed.

But despite such allurements the prince firmly guarded his senses, and in his perturbation over the inevitability of death, was neither rejoiced nor distressed.

He, the supreme man, saw that they had no firm footing in the real truth, and with mind that was at the same time both perturbed and steadfast he thus meditated:—

"Do these women then not understand the transitoriness of youth, that they are so inebriated with their own beauty, which old age will destroy?

Surely they do not perceive anyone overwhelmed by illness, that they are so full of mirth, so void of fear in a world in which disease is a law of nature.

And quite clearly they sport and laugh so much at ease and unperturbed, because they are ignorant of death who carries all away.

For what rational being would stand or sit or lie at ease, still less laugh, when he knows of old age, disease and death?

But he is just like a being without reason, who, on seeing another aged or ill or even dead, remains indifferent and unmoved.

For when one tree is shorn both of its flowers and its fruit and falls or is cut down, another tree is not distressed thereby."

Then their garlands and ornaments worn in vain, their excellent arts and endearments all fruitless, the women suppressed the god of love in his birthplace, their hearts, and returned to the city with their hopes frustrated.

Then the son of earth's guardian saw the glory of the women in the city garden withdrawn again in the evening and, meditating on the transitoriness of everything, he entered his dwelling.

But when the king heard that his son was averse from the objects of sense, then like an elephant with a dart in its heart, he did not lie down that night. Thereon wearing himself out with all kinds of counsels with his ministers, he found no means, other than the passions, for restraining his son's purpose.

FLIGHT

Though the son of the Sakya king was thus tempted by priceless objects of sense, he felt no contentment, he obtained no relief, like a lion pierced deeply in the heart by a poisoned arrow.

Then longing for spiritual peace, he set forth outside with the king's permission in order to see the forest, and for companions he had a retinue of ministers' sons, chosen for their reliability and skill in converse.

He went out, mounted on the good horse Kanthaka, the bells of whose bit were of fresh gold and whose golden trappings were beautified with waving chowries, and so he resembled a *karṇikara*[12] emblem mounted on a flag-pole.

Desire for the forest as well as the excellence of the land led him on to the more distant jungle-land, and he saw the soil being ploughed, with its surface broken with the tracks of the furrows like waves of water.

When he saw the ground in this state, with the young grass torn up and scattered by the ploughs and littered with dead worms, insects and other creatures, he mourned deeply as at the slaughter of his own kindred.

And as he observed the ploughmen with their bodies discoloured by wind, dust and the sun's rays, and the oxen in distress with the labour of drawing, the most noble one felt extreme compassion.

Then alighting from his horse, he walked slowly over the ground, overcome with grief. And as he considered the coming into being and the passing away of creation, he cried in his affliction, "How wretched this is."

And desiring to reach perfect clearness with his mind, he stopped his friends who were following him, and proceeded himself to a solitary spot at the root of a *jambu*-tree,[13] whose beautiful leaves were waving in all directions.

And there he sat down on the clean ground, with grass bright like beryl; and reflecting on the origin and destruction of creation he took the path of mental stillness.

And his mind at once came to a stand and at the same time he was freed from mental troubles such as desire for the objects of sense. And he entered into the first trance of calmness which is accompanied by gross and subtle cogitation and which is supermundane in quality.

Then he obtained possession of concentration of mind, which springs from discernment and yields extreme ecstasy and bliss, and thereafter, rightly perceiving in his mind the course of the world, he meditated on this same matter.

"A wretched thing it is indeed that man, who is himself helpless and subject to the law of old age, disease and destruction, should in his ignorance and the blindness of his conceit, pay no heed to another who is the victim of old age, disease or death.

For if I, who am myself such, should pay no heed to another whose nature is equally such, it would not be right or fitting in me, who have knowledge of this, the ultimate law."

As he thus gained correct insight into the evils of disease, old age and death, the mental intoxication relating to the self, which arises from belief in one's strength, youth and life, left him in a moment.

He did not rejoice nor yet was he downcast; doubt came not over him, nor sloth, nor drowsiness. And he felt no longing for sensual pleasures, no hatred or contempt for others.

---

12. A type of tree.   13. Rose-apple tree.

The Offering of the Four Bowls. Gandharan, 2nd to 5th century
A.D. Stone (schist); Baltimore Museum of Art

While this pure passionless state of mind grew within his lofty soul, there came up to him a man in mendicant's clothes, unseen of other men.

The king's son asked him, "Tell me, who are you?" On this he explained to him, "O bull among men, I am a *sramana*,[14] who in fear of birth and death have left the home life for the sake of salvation.

Since the world is subject to destruction, I desire salvation and seek the blessed incorruptible stage. I look with equal mind on kinsman and stranger, and longing for and hatred of the objects of sense have passed from me.

I dwell wherever I happen to be, at the root of a tree or in a deserted temple, on a hill or in the forest, and I wander without ties or expectations in search of the highest good, accepting any alms I may receive."

After saying this, he flew up to the sky before the prince's very eyes; for he was a heavenly being who in that form had seen other Buddhas and had encountered him to rouse his attention.

When that being went like a bird to heaven, the best of men was thrilled and amazed. And then he gained awareness of *dharma*[15] and set his mind on the way to leave his home.

---

14. Wandering mendicant, especially Buddhist or Jain.

15. Doctrine of the Buddha.

ANONYMOUS (500–1500 C.E.)
India

Sanskrit epic poetry was written in quatrains—syntactically self-contained four-line stanzas expressing a complete thought and able to stand alone. The quatrain became the basic building block of classical Sanskrit poetry. Poets also explored the possibilities of using the quatrain as a complete poem in its own right (the translations that follow often abandon this rigid form). These four-line works, called *muktaka*, or "separated" poems, were apparently gathered into collections by the poets themselves. From about 1000 C.E., anthologies containing *muktakas* from many poets replaced these earlier collections, and the names of the poets were often lost in the process. It is from these later anthologies that the anonymous poems in this selection derive.

The thousands of *muktaka* thus preserved for us are as manifold and complex as life itself. A typical anthology will begin with invocations of the gods, proceed through all the various stages and domains of human existence, and end with poems dealing with renunciation of the world.

The lyrics illustrate not only the emotional universe of Sanskrit, however, but also its aesthetic project, the ways in which Indian poets sought to produce a complete literary experience in four lines of verse, and to do so by generating as pure a representation of emotion as they could. The anonymity of this poetry, the fact that it is never anchored in a given time or place or historical personality—you will find almost nothing comparable to "Easter 1916," "Westminster Bridge," "miser Catulle"—is a *decision* on the part of the poets rather than a lack. The thousands of poems found in inscriptions, typically praise-poems to kings, show that sensitivity to time and place could be profound when it was felt to be appropriate. But in this genre there operates a literary sensibility that believed the highest forms of poetry were able to express human emotion in a way permitting a sensitive reader to relive that emotion as a pure distillate of aesthetic pleasure; any local specificity would only diminish this potential for universalization.

from *Love Poems from the Sanskrit*

[Deep in night]

Deep in night
a lonely wanderer listens to heavy
moving clouds crashing
all over sullen heaven
the longing overcomes him
tears fill his eyes

5

Translated by W. S. Merwin and J. Moussaieff Masson.

he sings
the agony of his loneliness
then the villagers know that travelling
away from someone we love   10
is like dying
they will not speak of it
suddenly even their pride
is far behind them

[How have you come to be/ so thin]

How have you come to be
so thin
why are you trembling
why are you so
pale oh   5
simple girl
and she answered the lord of her life
all these things
just happen for no reason
sighing as she said it   10
and turning away to let
tears fall

[She let him in]

She let him in
she did not turn away from him
there was no anger in her words
she simply looked straight at him
as though there had never been   5
anything between them

[Lush clouds]

Lush clouds in
dark sky of tears she saw *my love*
if you leave me now she
said and could not say more
twisting my shirt   5
toe gripping dust
after that what she
did all words

are helpless to repeat and
they know it and give up   10

[Middle of night]

Middle of night
season of rains season
for love
heavy clouds rolling
thunder   5
small village asleep in soft rain
lonely traveller sings in tears
girl whose lover is far away
hears the singing
shuts her eyes over what she sees   10
longing longing
still weeping
later and later in the dark

[Conquering the whole earth]

Conquering the whole earth
as I have done
the essence of it is one
city
in that city one house   5
in that house only one
room
and even there one bed
in that bed the woman above all others
the essence of the kingdom's happiness   10
shining like a jewel

[I know]

I know
I shook like a vine
he kissed me
touched my two breasts as he pleased
pushed the necklace aside   5
I remember that much
but what next
the letting go

the body turning to water
but after that
I keep trying to remember
and I cannot

[To go if you have really decided]

To go
if you have really decided
then you will go
why hurry
two or three oh little while stay
while I look at
your face
living we are water running from
a bucket
who knows
whether I will see you
and you will see
me again

[Daughter of the mountain]

Daughter of
the mountain
look at the full moon
you can see a man
who loves a dark woman
night
she is that black shape
lying on top of him
wrapped around him
he exhausted after loving
she dripping nectar onto him[1]

[Lakshman little brother]

Lakshman
little brother
the mouth of the murderous sun

---

1. The black spot of the moon is imagined to
   be a black woman on top of her white lover.

Convention has it that the moon oozes
nectar.

opens on the horizon
let us hide in the shade here
of the green tree

   Rama
   beloved brother
   it is night now
   we are in the dark
   there is no sun
   what you see is the moon

Gentle Lakshman
how do you know

   I see the face
   of a deer
   on the moon

oh god
oh my love where are you
my Sita my wife
with the moon your face
and the face of the deer on it[2]

[Some in this world insist]

Some in this world insist
that a certain whatever-it-is
that has no taste of
joy or sorrow
no qualities
is Release
they are fools

to my mind her
body unfurling

---

2. The situation is this: Rama is wandering in the forest with his younger brother Lakshman. Lakshman is no doubt attempting to distract him from brooding over the loss of Sita. He is, the verse suggests, on the verge of madness for he can no longer distinguish night from day. The poetic convention is that for a man burning with the fever of love, even moonbeams, generally regarded as soothing, burn him. But this conventional figure is completely forgotten in the next lines. The words "deer" (where we see a face, Indians see a deer or a hare in the moon) and "moon," common epithets for a beautiful woman (referring to her eyes and face respectively) remind Rama of Sita and the depth of his loss. The imaginative experience involves the pathos of lovers separated by forces beyond their control.

with joy of being young
flowering out of love
her eyes floating as with wine and
words wandering with love
then the undoing of the knot
of her sari
that
is Release

[I like sleeping with somebody different]

I like sleeping with somebody
   different

   often

It's nicest when my husband is
   in a foreign country

   and there's rain in the streets at night
   and wind

   and nobody

[He who stole my virginity]

He who stole my virginity
is the same man
I am married to
and these are the same
spring nights and
this is the same moment of
the jasmine's opening
with winds just coming of age carrying
the scent of its flowers mingled.
with pollen from Kadamba trees
to wake desire
in its nakedness
I am no different yet I
long with my heart
for the delicate
love-making back there under
the dense cane-trees
by the bank of the river
Narmada in
the Vindhya mountains

[Hiding in the cucumber garden]

Hiding in the
cucumber garden
simple country girl shivers
with desire
her lover on a low cot   5
lies tired with love
she melts into his body
with joy
his neck tight in her arms
one of her feet   10
flicking a necklace of
sea shells hanging
on a vine
on the fence
rattles them to scare off   15
foxes there in the dark

[Sky dark]

Sky dark
black smudge-fire clouds
earth dark
thick blanket of young grass yes
now is the time for making love   5
those whose lovers are not with them
call softly to death

VARIOUS AUTHORS (100 B.C.E.–250 C.E.)
India

Among the finest literary creations in the Tamil language is a corpus of
approximately 2400 poems collected in eight *sangam* (literary academic poetry)
anthologies. The poems selected here are drawn from the five anthologies
classified as *akam* poems, poems of the interior world. Each *akam* poem depicts
a moment in the story of two lovers. The moment is described by one of the
lovers or by someone who knows of them, such as the girl's close friend or her
mother, or another lover of the man's. An especially striking feature of many
akam poems is the way in which the poet uses landscape as a mirror of the
emotional lives of the characters. The author and the anthology in which it is
found are listed at the end of each selection.

from **Love Poems from the Tamil**

On Mothers

Mothers

That dignified old woman,

with white hair
that has given up
all fragrant things,

and withered breasts   5
with nipples like eyes
crinkled as the ironwood seed,

she has a much-loved son who, all alone,

    like a drop of curd
    flicked by a childish milkmaid's   10
    fingernail
    curdling a whole pitcher of milk,

brought grief
to an army of enemies.

Maturaipputan Ilanakanar
Purananuru 276

Mothers

The old woman's hair
was white, feather
of the fisher heron.

Her delight

    when she heard
    that her son fell in battle   5
    felling an elephant,

was greater
than at his birth,

and her tears
were more than the scatter of drops   10
hanging from all the great swaying bamboos

All poems in this selection are translated by A. K. Ramanujan.

after the rains
on the Bamboo Mountains.

Punkanuttiraiyar
Purananuru 277

Mothers

There, in the very middle
of battle-camps
   that heaved like the seas,

pointing at the enemy
   the tongues of lances,
new-forged and whetted,   5

urging soldiers forward
   with himself at the head
in a skirmish of arrow and spear,

cleaving through
   an oncoming wave of foes,   10
forcing a clearing,

he had fallen
in that space
   between armies,   15
his body hacked to pieces:

   when she saw him there
   in all his greatness,
   mother's milk flowed again
   in the withered breasts   20
   of this mother
   for her warrior son
   who had no thought of retreat.

Auvaiyar
Purananuru 295

A Leaf in Love and War

The chaste trees,[1] dark-clustered,
blend with the land
that knows no dryness;

---

1. "Its dark leaves were used by women in love as leaf-skirts, and as emblematic wreaths by warriors during a siege. The poem points to the irony of this double-edged image" (Ramanujan).

the colors on the leaves
mob the eyes.

> We've seen those leaves
> on jeweled women,
> on their mounds
> of love.

Now the chaste wreath lies slashed
on the ground, so changed, so mixed
with blood, the vulture snatches it
with its beak,
thinking it raw meat.

> We see this too
> just because a young man
> in love with war
> wore it for glory.

Veripatiya Kamakkanniyar
Purananuru 271

Peace Poem

Waist thin as the purslane creeper,
gait heavy as with grief,

the young Brahman came at night
and entered the fortress quickly.

The words he spoke
were few,

and the ladders, the wooden bolts,
came down,

and the war bells
were loosened

from the flanks
of the veteran elephants.

Maturai Velacan
Purananuru 305

What She Said

"O your hair," he said,
"it's like rainclouds
moving between
branches of lightning.

It parts five ways
between gold ornaments,
braided with a length of flowers
and the fragrant screwpine.

"O your smiles, your glistening teeth,
words sheer honey,
mouth red as coral,
O fair brow,
I want to tell you
something,
listen, stop and listen,"

he said, and stopped me.

Came close,
to look closer
at my brow, my hands, my eyes,
my walk, my speech,
and said, searching
for metaphors:

 "Amazed, it grows small, but it isn't the crescent.
 Unspotted, it isn't the moon.
 Like bamboo, yet it isn't on a hill.
 Lotuses, yet there's no pool.
 Walk mincing, yet no peacock.
 The words languish, yet you're not a parrot,"

and so on.[2]

On and on he praised my parts
with words gentle and sly,
looked for my weakening
like a man with a net
stalking an animal,

watched me
as my heart melted,
stared at me
like a butcher at his prey,

O he saluted me, saluted me,
touched me O he touched me,
a senseless lusting elephant
no goad could hold back.

---

2. The flattery used by the suitor is rife with
 clichés.

Salute and touch,
and touch again he did,

but believe me, friend,
I still think he is not really

a fool by nature.

Kapilar
Kalittokai 55

What She Said: to Her Girl Friend

O you, you wear flowers of gold,
their colors made in fire,
complete with pollen,
while the flowers on creeper and branch
are parched, waterless.
Your lovely forearm stacked
with jeweled bracelets,
shoulders soft as a bed of down,

is it right not to let me
live at your feet?
                    he said.

And didn't let go at that,
but stayed on to grab
all my hair
scented with lemon grass,
my hair-knot held together
by the gold shark's-mouth,
and with a finger
he twisted tight
the garland in my hair
and smelled it too.

Not only that, he took
my fingers
    (unfolding now
    like crocus buds,
    I suppose)

to cover his bloodshot eyes
and fetched a huge sigh,
blowing hot like a blacksmith
into his bellows.

And,   30

   like a deluded bull-elephant
   fondling with his trunk
   his beloved female,

he fondled my young painted breasts
till the paint rubbed off   35
on his rough hands.
Then he stroked me all over,
just about everywhere.

Yet friend,
with that act of his   40
I was rid
of all my troubles.

And I tell you this
only so that you can go
and persuade Mother: 45

May the sweet smells
of my marriage in our house
cling to no man
but him,
and that will be good.   50

It will guarantee a lasting place for us
in this world that doesn't last.

Kapilar
Kalittokai 54

What She Said: to Her Girl Friend, and What Her Girl Friend Said in Reply

"Friend,
like someone who gets drunk secretly
on hard liquor
till his body begins to ooze with it,
and goes on to brag shamelessly   5
till listeners shiver,
and then gets caught
with the stolen liquor in his hand,

I too got caught
with my secret in my hands: 10

my goatherd lover's
string of jasmine
that I'd twined in my hair

fell before my foster-mother[3]
as she loosened my hair   15
to smear it with butter,[4]

and embarrassed her
before Father, Mother,
and others in the house.

And she   20
didn't ask a thing about it,
or get angry,
but like someone
shaking off a live coal
she shook it off   25
and moved into the backyard.

Then I
dried my hair perfumed with sandal,
knotted it,
and picking up the end   30
of my blue flower-border dress
    that comes down to the floor
I tiptoed in fear
and hid
in the thick of the forest."   35

"O you got scared because of that?
No fears. Even as you wore
your young man's garlands,
they too have conspired
to give you to him.   40

They'll pour soft sand
in the wide yard,
put curtains all around,
and make a wedding there
very soon.   45
            Not only all day today,
but all night yesterday,
we've been scheming
to do just that."

Uruttiran
Kalittokai 115

---

3. Either her personal maid or her father's
   second wife.

4. Hair is typically oiled in South Asia.

The Girl Friend Describes the Bull Fight

With the first rains

white clusters of the wild jasmine
backed by fresh thorn
are budding
on nodes once dry   5
in the cool rain lands.

The bud of the glory lily
looks like a ladle first,
then becomes a fire
when the red petals open   10
gathering the embers,
and it sways like a drunk.

The bilberry, flowering,
gives nothing but blue gems.

Weaving such blossom   15
in their wreaths,
cowherds vie with all they have,
enter the stalls
to let loose the bulls,
horns whittled sharp   20
as the Lord's own pickaxes.

There, in the middle ground,
where the brides wait,
men gather
again and again   25
ready to master the bulls,
sounding like rumbling and thunder,
raising dust clouds, and smoke,
offer the right things
to the gods   30
in watering places,
under the banyan tree
and the ancient mango.

There, they leap into the field.

Look, the bull,   35
raised horns and skin tawny
as certain silkmoths,
he skewers to death
the cowherd who sprang
heedless of the look in the animal's eyes,   40

carries the carcass high and shakes it
on his horns,

> like the warrior Bhima[5]
> making good his oath
> sworn among enemies,
> cleaving the heart
> of the man
> who dared put a hand
> to the tresses
> of his lovely wife.

Look at that black bull,
a moon-mark on his brow,[6]
carry and shake the cowherd,
skewered and gutted
(the wreaths on his head
were flowers once on the caverned hills):

> like the raging androgynous god,
> whose one half is His woman,
> who dances at the end of time
>   when lives wear all their sorrows,
> cleaves the heart of the Death-god,
> that rider of buffaloes,
> and feeds Death's own guts
> to His famished barbaric minions.

Look at that other bull
with spotted ears,
smooth reds
on his white body.
Teased by the fighters,
he throws that daredevil, that herdsman,
with the points of his horns,

> like Ashvatthama[7] in grief and rage
> not mindful of the darkness
> whirling
> on his shoulders

---

5. Second son of Paṇḍu and a hero of the
   Mahābhārata. Bhima ripped open the chest
   of Duhśāsana, and drank his blood, to fulfil
   the vow he took when Duhśāsana assaulted
   Draupadi during "The Friendly Dice
   Game."

6. The bull is being compared to Siva, who
   wears a crescent moon in his headdress.
7. Another Mahabharata figure, son of Drona.
   He sought to avenge his father's death by a
   nighttime raid on the camp of the
   Pandavas.

that eunuch
who slew his father.

But now the herdsmen
play flutes,
good omens
for you and your man
wearing blue-gem bilberry flowers.   80

[Saying this, the girl friend went to the man and said:]

That bull is wilder
than an elephant
gone wild:
do not loosen   85
your hand's grip
on him,
and the shoulders of our girl
will bring you victory flags.   90

Only to that man
who takes on that murderous bull,
carries a staff on his shoulder,
plays melancholy notes on his flute,
we will give our girl   95
with dark flowing hair.

Among men who take on a bull,
no one is equal to me, says he,
standing among the cows,
bragging of his power.   100

Surely, one day, not too far,
he will take us too:
for, looking at him,
my left eye throbs,
which is a good omen.   105

There, the bulls are faint,
and the men have wounds all over.
The cowherd girls
with dark fragrant hair,
taking hints   110
from their herdsman-lovers,
move into the cool groves
of jasmine.

Uruttirann
Kalittokai 101

What She Said: to Her Girl Friend, After a Tryst at Night (which Turned Out to Be a Fiasco)

My well-dressed friend,
listen to what happened.
It has set the whole village laughing.

It's the dead of night, very dark,
no sign of life,   5
and I'm waiting
all dressed up, lovely shawl,
best jewels,
for our soft broad-chested man,

when that old cripple, that Brahman[8]   10
turns up,
the one you're always asking me to respect,
bald head, rough blanket,
hands and legs shortened by leprosy,
the fellow who never leaves our street.   15

He bends low
to take a good look at me
and says,
          "Standing here
at this unearthly hour?
Who are you?"   20

He won't leave my side
like an old bull
who has sighted hay;
he opens his satchel, saying,
"Lady, come, have some betel,[9] won't you?"   25

I stand there, say nothing.
"Listen, girl," he says,
    stepping back a little.

"I've caught you.
I'm a demon too, but not your kind.   30
Be good to me. If you trouble me,
I'll grab all the offerings of this village,
and you'll get nothing."

And he jabbers on.
I can see by now the old fellow is a bit scared,   35
maybe thinking I'm some demon woman,

---

8. Priest, highest of the four social orders.
9. Chewing the tender leaf of betel, containing areca nut, spices, and often tobacco, is a common custom.

so I pick up a fistful of sand and throw it
in his face, and he howls and howls.

It was as if a trap laid by hunters
for a tiger, a fearless, striped, cruel-eyed tiger,   40
had caught instead a puny jackal.

What a sight for someone
waiting to see a lover!
The whole village is laughing
at this old Brahman whose life   45
is a daily farce.

Kapilar
Kalittokai 65

The Hunchback and the Dwarf: A Dialogue

Hunchback woman,
the way you move is gentle
and crooked as a reflection
in the water,
              what good deeds
did you do that I should want you so?   5

  O mother! (she swore to herself) Some
  auspicious moment made you dwarf,
  so tiny you're almost invisible,
  you whelp born to a man-faced owl,
  how dare you stop us to say   10
  you want us? Would such midgets
  ever get to touch such as us!

Lovely one,
            curvaceous,
                      convex
as the blade of a plough,
you strike me with a love   15
I cannot bear.
              I can live
only by your grace.

  (Look at this creature!)
  You dwarf, standing piece of timber,
  you've yet to learn the right approach
  to girls. At high noon   20
  you come to hold
  our hand and ask us to your place.
  Have you had any women?

Good woman,
        your waist is higher   25
than your head, your face a stork,
plucked and skinned,
with a dagger for a beak,
            listen to me.
If I take you in the front, your hump
juts into my chest; if from the back   30
it'll tickle me in odd places.
           So I'll not
even try it. But come close anyway and let's touch
side to side.

    Chi,[10] you're wicked. Get lost! You half-man!
    As creepers hang on only to the crook of a tree   35
    there are men who'd love to hold this hunch
    of a body close, though nothing fits. Yet, you lecher,
    you ask for us sideways. What's so wrong
    with us, you ball, you bush of a man.
    Is a gentle hunchback type far worse than a cake   40
    of black beans?

But I've fallen for you
(he said, and went after her).
O look, my heart,
at the dallying of this hunchback!   45

    Man, you stand
    like a creepy turtle stood up by somebody,
    hands flailing in your armpits.
    We've told you we're not for you. Yet you hang around.
    Look, he walks now like Kama.[11]   50

Yes, the love-god with arrows, brother to Cama.
Look at this love-god!
           Come now, let's find joy.
you in me, me in you; come, let's ask and tell
which parts we touch.

I swear by the feet of my king.   55
All right, O gentle-breasted one. I too will give up
mockery.
        But I don't want this crowd in the palace
laughing at us, screaming when we do it,

---

10. An exclamation.   **11.** God of love.

"Hey, hey! Look at them mounting,
leaping like demon on demon!"
                              O shape   60
of unbeaten gold, let's get away from the palace
to the wild jasmine bush. Come,
let's touch close, hug hard,
and finish the unfinished:
then we'll be   65
like a gob of wax on a parchment
made out in a court full of wise men,
and stamped
to a seal.
        Let's go.

                                        Marutanilanakanar
                                        Kalittokai 94

BASAVANNA (C. 900–1100 C.E.)
DEVARA DASIMAYYA (C. 900–1100 C.E.)
MAHADEVIYAKKA (C. 900–1100 C.E.)
India

The poems selected here—written in Kannada, after Tamil the oldest literary
language of southern India—belong to a genre termed *vachanas* (sayings,
utterances). They were composed between the tenth and twelfth centuries in the
religious community of the Lingayats or Virashaivas. This community arose in
part as a devotionalist movement opposed to the caste system of Hinduism. Thus
many of the *vachana* poets were members of the lowest caste and illiterate. The
poems typically end with a direct address to a local embodiment of the god Shiva,
one of the three major deities of Hinduism. The third poet represented here,
Mahadeviyakka, is one of a number of women who composed *vachanas*.

from **The Kannada**

BASAVANNA

[Like a monkey on a tree]

Like a monkey on a tree
it leaps from branch to branch:

Translated by A. K. Ramanujan.

how can I believe or trust
this burning thing, this heart?[1]
It will not let me go
to my Father,
my lord of the meeting rivers.

[Shiva, you have no mercy]

Shiva, you have no mercy.
Shiva, you have no heart.

Why why did you bring me to birth,
    wretch in this world,
    exile from the other?

Tell me, lord,
don't you have one more
little tree or plant
made just for me?

[You can make them talk]

You can make them talk
if the serpent
has stung
them.

You can make them talk
if they're struck
by an evil planet.[2]

But you can't make them talk
if they're struck dumb
by riches.

    Yet when Poverty the magician
    enters, they'll speak
    at once,

        O lord of the meeting rivers.

---

1. The heart as a monkey is a traditional image for the restless distracted heart (*manas*). In Kannada, the word *mana* or *manas* could mean either heart and mind. In this poem, the Lord is the Father: a favorite stance of bhakti or personal devotion. Other stances are Lover/Beloved and Master/Servant.

2. Struck by misfortune, the action of malefic planets. The rich unregenerate worldling is a familiar target in the vacanas. The Virashaiva movement was a movement of the poor, the underdog.

[The crookedness of the serpent]

The crookedness of the serpent
is straight enough for the snake-hole.

The crookedness of the river
is straight enough for the sea.

And the crookedness of our Lord's men
is straight enough for our Lord!

[Before/ the grey reaches the cheek]

Before
    the grey reaches the cheek,
    the wrinkle the rounded chin
    and the body becomes a cage of bones:

before
    with fallen teeth
    and bent back
    you are someone else's ward:

before
    you drop your hand to the knee
    and clutch a staff:

before
    age corrodes
    your form:

before
    death touches you:

        worship
        our lord
        of the meeting rivers!

[Feet will dance]

Feet will dance,
eyes will see,
tongue will sing,
and not find content.
What else, what else
shall I do?

I worship with my hands,
the heart is not content.
What else shall I do?

Shiva as Lord of the Dance. Bronze sculpture from c. 1000 C.E. Tiruppulam, south India.

Listen, my lord,
it isn't enough.
I have it in me
to cleave thy belly
and enter thee

O lord of the meeting rivers!   15

[I don't know anything like time-beats and metre]

I don't know anything like time-beats and metre
nor the arithmetic of strings and drums;
I don't know the count of iamb and dactyl.[3]

My lord of the meeting rivers,
as nothing will hurt you
I'll sing as I love.

[In the mother's womb]

In the mother's womb
the child does not know
his mother's face

---

3. The familiar vacana opposition of *measure* v. *spontaneity*. Iamb and dactyl are here used as loose English equivalents for two metric units in Kannada.

nor can *she* ever know
his face.   5

The man in the world's illusion
does not know the Lord

nor the Lord him,

Ramanatha.

DEVARA DASIMAYYA

[A fire in every act and look and word]

A fire
in every act and look and word.
Between man and wife
a fire.
In the plate of food   5
eaten after much waiting
a fire.
In the loss of gain
a fire.
And in the infatuation   10
of coupling
a fire.

You have given us
five fires
and poured dirt in our mouths   15

O Ramanatha.[4]

[For what shall I handle a dagger]

For what
shall I handle a dagger
O lord?

What can I pull it out of,
or stab it in,   5

when You are all the world,

O Ramanatha?

---

4. Name of the devotee's god.

[The earth is your gift]

The earth is your gift,
the growing grain your gift,
the blowing wind your gift.

What shall I call these curs
who eat out of your hand
and praise everyone else?   5

[I'm the one who has the body]

I'm the one who has the body,
you're the one who holds the breath.

You know the secret of my body,
I know the secret of your breath.

That's why your body   5
is in mine.

You know
and I know, Ramanatha,

the miracle

of your breath   10
in my body.

[Fire can burn]

Fire can burn
but cannot move.

Wind can move
but cannot burn.

Till fire joins wind   5
it cannot take a step.

Do men know
it's like that
with knowing and doing?

[Monkey on a monkeyman's stick]

Monkey on a monkeyman's stick
puppet at the end of a string

I've played as you've played
I've spoken as you've told me
I've been as you've let me be

O engineer of the world
lord white as jasmine

I've run
till you cried halt.

MAHADEVIYAKKA

[O mother I burned]

O mother[5] I burned
in a flameless fire

O mother I suffered
a bloodless would

mother I tossed
without a pleasure:

loving my lord white as jasmine
I wandered through unlikely worlds.

[Would a circling surface vulture]

Would a circling surface vulture
    know such depths of sky
    as the moon would know?

would a weed on the riverbank
    know such depths of water
    as the lotus would know?

would a fly darting nearby
    know the smell of flowers
    as the bee would know?

O lord white as jasmine
    only you would know
    the way of your devotees:
    how would these,

these
    mosquitoes
    on the buffalo's hide?

---

5. Exclamation of intense feeling.

[Other men are thorn under the smooth leaf]

Other men are thorn
under the smooth leaf.
I cannot touch them,
go near them, nor trust them,
nor speak to them confidences.   5

Mother,
because they all have thorns
in their chests,
                    I cannot take
any man in my arms but my lord

        white as jasmine.   10

[Who cares]

Who cares
    who strips a tree of leaf
    once the fruit is plucked?

Who cares
    who lies with the woman
    you have left?   5

Who cares
    who ploughs the land
    you have abandoned?

After this body has known my lord
    who cares if it feeds
    a dog
    or soaks up water?   10

[Like an elephant lost from his herd]

Like an elephant
lost from his herd
suddenly captured,

remembering his mountains,
    his Vindhyas,[6]   5
        I remember.

---

6. Mountain range in central India.

A parrot
came into a cage
remembering his mate,
    I remember.   10

O lord white as jasmine
show me
your ways.
    Call me: Child, come here,
      come this way.

[Better than meeting and mating all the time]

Better than meeting
and mating all the time
is the pleasure of mating once
after being far apart.

When he's away   5
I cannot wait
to get a glimpse of him.

Friend, when will I have it
both ways,
be with Him   10
yet not with Him,
my lord white as jasmine?

KABIR (C. 1450 C.E.)
North India

These songs were composed by Kabir, a fifteenth-century weaver from northern
India, in the vernacular of his region. They express with great poignancy the
social and religious vision of a man striving to transcend the conflicts facing him
in his world—the choice between high caste and low caste, between Hinduism
and Islam. The unmistakable candor, sincerity, and power of these songs have
kept them an integral part of popular culture in northern India, where to this day
one often hears the phrase "As Kabir says . . . ."

from *The Bijak*

[Saints, I see the world is mad]

Saints, I see the world is mad.
If I tell the truth they rush to beat me,
if I lie they trust me.
I've seen the pious Hindus, rule-followers,
early morning bath-takers—   5
killing souls, they worship rocks.
They know nothing.
I've seen plenty of Muslim teachers, holy men
reading their holy books
and teaching their pupils techniques.   10
They know just as much.
And posturing yogis, hypocrites,
hearts crammed with pride,
praying to brass, to stones, reeling
with pride in their pilgrimage,   15
fixing their caps and their prayer-beads,
painting their brow-marks and arm-marks,
braying their hymns and their couplets,
reeling. They never heard of soul.
The Hindu says Ram is the Beloved,   20
the Turk says Rahim.
Then they kill each other.
No one knows the secret.
They buzz their mantras from house to house,
puffed with pride.   25
The pupils drown along with their gurus.
In the end they're sorry.
Kabir says, listen saints:
they're all deluded!
Whatever I say, nobody gets it.   30
It's too simple.

[Brother, where did your two gods come from]

Brother, where did your two gods come from?
Tell me, who made you mad?
Ram, Allah, Keshav, Karim, Hari, Hazrat—

   so many names.
   So many ornaments, all one gold,   5

All poems in this section are translated by Linda Hess and Shukdev Singh.

it has no double nature.
For conversation we make two—
this *namaz,* that *puja,*
this Mahadev, that Muhammed,
this Brahma, that Adam,
this a Hindu, that a Turk,
but all belong to earth.
Vedas, Korans, all those books,
those Mullas and those Brahmins—
so many names, so many names,
but the pots are all one clay.
Kabir says, nobody can find Ram,
both sides are lost in schisms.
One slaughters goats, one slaughters cows,
they squander their birth in isms.

[Pandit, look in your heart for knowledge]

Pandit, look in your heart for knowledge.
Tell me where untouchability
came from, since you believe in it.
Mix red juice, white juice and air—
a body bakes in a body.[1]
As soon as the eight lotuses
are ready, it comes
into the world. Then what's
untouchable?
Eighty-four hundred thousand vessels
decay into dust, while the potter
keeps slapping clay
on the wheel, and with a touch
cuts each one off.
We eat by touching, we wash
by touching, from a touch
the world was born.
So who's untouched? asks Kabir.
Only he
who has no taint of Maya.

---

1. *Ghat,* with the conventional double meaning of body and clay pot, initiates the metaphor of pot and potter which is worked out in this poem in detail. The potter is considered untouchable in North India, and clay vessels are unclean, the cheap unbaked ones being thrown away after a single use. The body is commonly referred to as a pot—one whose clay, as the poet points out here, surrounds the eight lotuses or chakras, channels of spiritual energy. The vessels of line 10 (*basan*) have the obvious secondary meaning of passions (*basana*); one finds the word printed both ways. The potter's wheel has been inferred from *pat,* defined as a washerman's stone slab or a millstone, but basically meaning any level surface. The pots are cut off the wheel with a string or wire.

[When you die, what do you do with your body]

When you die, what do you do with your body?
Once the breath stops
you have to put it away.
There are several ways to deal
with spoiled flesh.   5
Some burn it, some bury it
in the ground.
Hindus prefer cremation,
Turks burial.
But in the end, one way or another,   10
both have to leave home.
Death spreads the karmic net
like a fisherman snaring fish.
What is a man without Ram?
A dung beetle in the road.   15
Kabir says, you'll be sorry later
when you go from this house
to that one.

[It's a heavy confusion]

It's a heavy confusion.
Veda, Koran, holiness, hell, woman, man,
a clay pot shot with air and sperm . . .
When the pot falls apart, what do you call it?
Numskull! You've missed the point.   5
It's all one skin and bone, one piss and shit,
one blood, one meat.
From one drop, a universe.
Who's Brahman? Who's Shudra?
Brahma *rajas,* Shiva *tamas,* Vishnu *sattva* . . .   10
Kabir says, plunge into Ram!
There: No Hindu. No Turk.

[So much pain, a mine of pain]

So much pain, a mine of pain.
You'll save yourself when you know Ram.
The Ram-knowing trick is the only trick
that doesn't land you in a trap.
The world sticks to its own tricks,   5
it certainly doesn't listen to me.
Gold, silk, horses, women,
a lot of wealth
last a little time.

From a little money
a man goes crazy.
He doesn't hear news
of the King of Death.
When the terror comes,
his face shrivels.
Cheated, he learns
his nectar was poison.
I make, I kill, I burn,
I eat, I fill
the land and water.
Spotless is my name.[2]

[No one knows the secret of the weaver]

No one knows the secret of the weaver
who spread his warp through the universe.
He dug two ditches, sky and earth,[3]
made two spools, sun and moon,[4]
filled his shuttle with a thousand threads,
and weaves till today: a difficult length!
Kabir says, they're joined by actions.
Good threads and bad,
that fellow weaves both.

[The road the pandits took]

The road the pandits took,
crowds took.

Ram's pass is a high one.
Kabir keeps climbing.

[Man in his stupid acts]

Man in his stupid acts—
iron mail from head to toe.
Why bother to raise your bow?
No arrow can pierce that.

---

2. Originally a name for God, Niranjan (without spot/stain) through sectarian mythology came to be associated with *kal* or Death.
3. Indian looms are set in dug-out places in the ground. In tantric symbolism the earth is the lowest chakra (*muladhara*) and sky the highest (*sahasrara*).

4. The *nari* (nali/nari, "tube") is a small spool that is inserted in the shuttle; it has a hollow center through which the thread is drawn out. The two *nadi* (channels) on either side of the spine in tantric physiology are often called sun and moon.

BANARASI (SEVENTEENTH CENTURY C.E.)
India

Written in 1641, the heyday of Mughal rule, *Half a Tale* [*Ardhakathanaka*] is the most striking example of autobiography in premodern India; in fact, it is virtually unique. *Ardhakathanaka* tells the story of a self-aware and articulate merchant-scholar, a member of the Jain community. (The Jains had both monastic and lay orders; members of the latter were typically merchants.) It concerns in part a search for religious meaning, although the tone is far removed from the fervent devotionalism of the preceding selections. Written in the vernacular, in this case a mixed dialect of Braj and eastern Hindi, *Ardhakathanaka* is a rare example of literary expression outside the patronage of any court. Long ignored, it is increasingly held to be an important document for our understanding of the cultural, intellectual, and social history of Mughal India, especially in revealing the new sense of self-awareness that emerged during that period.

Half a Tale [Ardhakathanaka]

My name is Banarasi, a name which carries the stamp of the city that gave birth to two Tirthankaras.[1] I will now relate to you the story of my life because it occurred to me that I should make my history public.

I will speak of my life from my early childhood to the present, describing what I saw and experienced; and to this narrative I will also sometimes add things I have heard from others. In this manner, I will relate the events of my past in broad outlines, but the future I do not know; only the All-knowing can know that.

I will narrate my story in the common language of middle India (madhyadesa), freely revealing all that lies concealed. And though I will speak to you of my virtues, I will also disclose my sins and follies.

Listen attentively friends as I unveil my past.

I am a Jain[2] belonging to the clan of Srimals, who were once princely Rajputs[3] living in Biholi, a village near the town of Rohtak in the region known as Madhyadesa of our good land of Bharat. These Rajputs were converted to Jainism under the influence of a great teacher, and, giving up their earlier life of violence, they took to the practice of wearing a mala, a garland, inscribed with the true mantra; hence they came to be called Srimals. My ancestors bore the gotra-name[4] Biholia, for they had once been defenders of Biholi.

I was now fourteen and began to develop a keen desire to pursue further studies, and so I went to Pandit Devadutt, who was a knowledgeable scholar. I studied with him a number of standard works on a wide variety of subjects. My

Translated by Mukund Lath.

1. Jain deities.
2. Religious sect.
3. Members of a high caste in North India.
4. Lineage name.

studies included two lexical texts, the *Namamala* and the *Anekarthakosa*.[5] I also took lessons in jyotisa (astronomy cum astrology), alankara (poetics), and erotics, in which latter subject I read a work called *Laghukoka*[6] by Pandit Koka. In addition, I also studied the *Khandasphuta*[7] which is a work in four hundred verses. I spent the whole of Vikram[8] 1657 intent upon studying and reflecting deeply on whatever I had learnt.

But I had also another, equally strong, passion. For I was in love and I gave myself up to this consuming passion with the whole-hearted yearning and devotion of a sufi fakir.[9] Single-mindedly I meditated upon the object of my desire. My beloved occupied my entire vision. Forever I thought of her, paying no heed to propriety or family honour. I even stooped to stealing money and jewels from my father so that I could buy her costly presents and offer her the choicest sweets. Following the right etiquette in such matters, I called myself the 'slave' of my beloved, always referring to myself as the 'poor one'.

After four months of summer had passed, the weather turned cool. During this pleasant season, two Jain sadhus[10] named Bhanchand and Ramchand came to sojourn in Jaunpur. Both were disciples of a great teacher called Abhaydharma, who was a Svetambara monk of the Kharataragaccha sect[11] of Jainism, a religion which reveals the path of fearlessness. Bhanchand was the more intelligent and knowledgeable of the two. Ramchand was yet a young boy; he still wore the attire of householders, such as novice sadhus do. Devotees of the sect to which they belonged often came piously to visit these two. I, too, followed the custom of my community and went to see them at the upasraya, a religious building where Jain sadhus stay. I became friendly with Bhanchand and my attachment to him grew so much that I spent all my days in his company, often returning home quite late at night. With him I began earnestly to study the sacred texts of Jainism. I studied a large number of works including hymns to various Tirthankaras,[12] hundreds of well-known verses on different religious topics and a treatise on the proper ritual for bathing a Jina image. I also studied texts dealing with samayika meditation and penances for sin. Besides Jain texts I also studied lexicons and works on prosody. An important work I studied was the famous *Srutabodha*. Another was the *Chandakosa*.[13] I was a diligent student and spent much time memorising texts and reciting them with the right enunciation. I had become quite religious and did my best to acquire the eight merits of a good Jain.

I also began to write and commenced work on a book called *Pancasandhi* dealing with an important aspect of Sanskrit grammar. But I was still leading a dual life. Though I was fully devoted to the task of acquiring knowledge, yet I did not give up my amorous pursuits. I composed a book of poems containing a thousand verses with love as the central theme, though, ostensibly, the book was

---

5. Dictionaries.
6. A treatise on erotics.
7. An unidentified text; its name suggests a work on astronomy.
8. Calendrical reckoning (approx. C.E. minus 57 years).
9. Muslim ascetic.

10. Ascetics.
11. A monk who goes "clothed in white" (as opposed to the naked Jain monks) and belongs to a sect especially devoted to scholarship.
12. Jain saints.
13. Treatises on metrics.

about all the major human sentiments, which have been classified as the nine rasas.[14] Reflecting back, I realize that I had become a false poet, an author of words and sentiments expressing falsehood.

Devoted thus entirely to my two consuming passions, I was doing nothing to earn money. I was so lost in the labours of love and learning that often I even forgot to eat my meals. Where then was the time for thinking of paltry things like money?

I spent two whole years in this state of abandon, despite severe admonitions from my parents. By Vikram 1659, however, I was satiated with books and amour. I now set out to fetch my bride from her father's home. I put on all my finery, and attended by a livery of servants, travelled happily in a palanquin to Khairabad, the home of my father-in-law.

I was now fifteen years and ten months old. After a month in Khairabad, I suddenly fell sick with a disgusting disease caused by a morbid condition of the windy humour (vata). The skin all over my body became like that of a leper. My very bones ached and my hair began to fall. Innumerable eruptions appeared all over my arms and legs and soon I was so unsightly that people shunned my company. My father-in-law and my brother-in-law refused to sit with me at meals. I was so repellant that none wanted even to come near me. My sins were bearing fruit once again.

In Vikram 1662 (A.D. 1605), during the month of Kartik, after the monsoon was over, the great emperor Akbar breathed his last in Agra. The alarming news of his death spread fast and soon reached Jaunpur. People felt suddenly orphaned and insecure without their sire. Terror raged everywhere; the hearts of men trembled with dire apprehension; their faces became drained of colour.

I was sitting upon a flight of stairs in my house when I heard the dreadful news, which came as a sharp and sudden blow. It made me shake with violent, uncontrollable agitation. I reeled, and losing my balance, fell down the stairs in a faint. My head hit the stone floor and began to bleed profusely, turning the courtyard red. Everyone present rushed to my help. My dear parents were in utter agony. My mother put my head in her lap and applied a piece of burnt cloth to my wound in order to stop the flow of blood. I was then quickly put to bed with my sobbing mother at my side.

The whole town was in a tremor. Everyone closed the doors of his house in panic; shop-keepers shut down their shops. Feverishly, the rich hid their jewels and costly attire underground; many of them quickly dumped their wealth and their ready capital on carriages and rushed to safe, secluded places. Every householder began stocking his home with weapons and arms. Rich men took to wearing thick, rough clothes such as are worn by the poor, in order to conceal their status, and walked the streets covered in harsh woolen blankets or coarse cotton wrappers. Women shunned finery, dressing in shabby, lustreless clothes. None could tell the status of a man from his dress and it became impossible to distinguish the rich from the poor. There were manifest signs of panic everywhere

---

14. Aesthetic moods.

although there was no reason for it since there were really no thieves or robbers about.

The commotion subsided after ten days, when a letter arrived from Agra bearing news that all was well in the capital. The situation returned to normal. Let me give you the gist of the news the letter carried. Akbar had died in the month of Kartik, in the year 1662 Vikram, after a reign of fifty-two years; now Akbar's eldest son, Prince Salim, had been enthroned as king to rule from Agra, like his father. Salim had assumed the title of Sultan Nuruddin Jahangir; his power reigned supreme and unchallenged throughout the land.

This news came as a great relief and people heartily hailed the new king.

To the joy of my parents, I, too, soon regained my health. We celebrated the end of the days of gloom with much festivity, distributing alms to the poor and gifts to friends and relations.

Soon after these events I went alone one day to my room at the roof-top and sat down to think and reflect. I began seriously to question the state of my faith and belief.

"I have been an ardent devotee of Siva," I said to myself, "but when I fell down the stairs and was severely hurt, Siva did not come to my aid." This thought nagged me constantly and made me neglect my daily ritual to Siva. My heart was no longer in it, and one day I simply put the Siva-conch[15] away.

Indeed, a strange mood had come over me. For that conch was not the only thing I put away. One day, in the company of a few close friends, I strolled down to the bridge over the Gomti, taking with me the manuscript of my book of poems on love, and began reciting verses from it to my friends. But as I read, a sudden thought violently perturbed me: "A man who utters a single lie," I reflected, "suffers in hell; yet here I am with a whole book full of nothing but falsehood—how can I ever be redeemed?" I looked down at the flowing waters, and on the spur of the moment, flung away the manuscript into the river, as though it was so much waste paper. My friends rushed to stop me from this impulsive act, but the deed was done. The folios of my poems were lying scattered over waters running deep and fearful. The book was now beyond retrieval. My friends were greatly distressed, but all they could do was to lament over the quirks of destiny.

My father was glad to hear the news. "Perhaps this is a sign that my son is undergoing a real change for the better," he happily remarked, "there is yet hope for the future of my family."

I had made two good friends, both very close and dear to me. One was Narottamdas, the grandson of Benidas of the Khobra gotra. The other was Thanmal Badaliya. The three of us were greatly attached to each other. We made a merry trio, spending all our time in each other's company.

One day, taking a carriage we went together to offer worship at a Jain shrine. After performing the usual rites of propitiation, the three of us approached the deity with folded palms and, in unison, made the following supplication: "O Lord,

---

15. Refers to an earlier episode of Banarasi's
    religious development.

grant us wealth, for then we shall have occasion to come and offer worship at your shrine again."

After that day the three of us became still more attached to each other, one in body and soul. We began to spend every hour of the day together in sweet conversation.

Then, during that year, in the spring month of Phalgun, a rich friend of ours named Tarachand Mothiya, who was a son of Nema, invited me to join him in a marriage party which was soon to proceed out of town. Balchand was the groom. Narottamdas was travelling with it and I, too, was prevailed upon to go. I began to look for some money to take with me, and sold a few pearls which I had put aside for bad times. They fetched me thirty-two rupees, which sum I took with me on my journey.

When I returned I had no money left. I hastened to sell my stock of cloth for whatever I could get and had to be satisfied with four rupees less than my cost price. I used this money to pay off some interest that had fallen due. I was free of debt but a pauper once again.

I went to see Narottam at his house. He welcomed me warmly and forced me to share his meal. I told him I was bankrupt, with nothing left and nowhere to go. He implored me to come and live with him. He assured me that I was like a brother to him and that whatever was his was also mine. His house, he added, was always open to those whom he loved. I was hesitant and protested that others in his family, especially his wife, may not like my being there. But he silenced me with these words: "Can you think of anyone in my family who will say anything to hurt you?"

He insisted that I could not refuse. He now made it a habit to address me as 'brother'; he also treated me like one, and we were always inseparable.

One day, when Narottamdas was with Tarachand Mothiya, Tarachand offered him some work. He asked Narottam to travel as his agent to Patna, taking me with him. He gave us money and we began making preparations for our departure. Then, on an auspicious day, we performed the propitiatory rites customary for people setting out on a long journey and crossed the Yamuna with tilak-marks[16] on our foreheads.

We were three of us, Narottam, I, and his father-in-law: all young, able Srimal men. We hired a carriage for our journey but took no serving men.

We had hired our carriage at Firozabad and we were to travel on it up to Shahzadpur, about half way on the road to Patna. When we reached Shahzadpur we paid our fare and decided to cover the rest of the journey on foot, hiring a porter to carry our luggage.

We decided to leave Shahzadpur as early in the morning as possible. That night, about five hours after sunset, the moonlight suddenly became very bright and we were deceived into thinking that day was about to dawn. So we immediately set out on our way. But as the light was yet dim, we could not properly make out our path. We strayed towards the south and soon entered a

---

16. Dots or stripes drawn on the forehead,
    here for good luck.

thick forest. It was not long before we realized that we were completely lost in the middle of a desolate jungle. Our porter suddenly lost his wits and began to scream and howl in panic. He threw down the luggage he was carrying and ran away into the wilderness. We had no choice but to carry the load ourselves. We divided it into three bundles, one for each of us. But the journey now became an ordeal. We tried to ease our burden by constantly shifting the weight from head to shoulders, but this was hardly of any help. Soon it was midnight and yet we were still far away from anywhere. We were miserable and almost demented with fatigue, singing and crying in the same breath like men who have suddenly gone mad.

After a little while, we entered a part of the forest where robbers lived in little hamlets of their own. A man espied us and shouted: "Who goes there?" We were seized with terror. Our lips were parched and suddenly glued together. We could not bring ourselves to utter a single word and began fervently to pray to God.

The man we had encountered was the chief of the robbers himself. Seeing him, I had a timely inspiration. I pronounced a benediction upon the man, chanting a sacred verse in Sanskrit in the manner of a pious Brahman. My trick worked. The robber chief took us for learned Brahmans, and approaching us, humbly bowed at our feet with deep respect. He also offered to give us shelter for the night.

"Consider me your humble servant, O venerable ones," he said. "Come with me and I will take you to my village where you can spend the night in the chaupal.[17] Do not be afraid of me, for as God is my witness, I mean you no harm."

We quietly followed the robber chief to his village, and, true to his word, he gave us a place for the night.

But we were still trembling violently with fear, our hearts pounding and our faces drained of all colour. As soon as we were alone, we hurriedly hunted for some loose yarn and quickly spun it into four sacred threads (*janeu*) such as every Brahman must wear. We then hung three of the sacred threads across our shoulders, and kept the fourth conspicuously out for all to see. Then, fetching some mud and a little water from a nearby pond, we smeared our foreheads with holy tilak-marks[18] befitting pious Brahmans. Our disguise now complete, we waited quietly for the morning to come. But we were still seized with fear and remained huddled together in a crouching position till about six hours later when light dawned and the rising sun turned the clouds red.

The robber chief approached us on a horse with a retinue of twenty men. When he came near us, he folded his palms and deeply bowed his head in veneration. I blessed him, again loudly intoning a sacred benedictory verse.

"Come venerable Brahmans, let me lead you out of the forest and show you the road," the chief said.

Obediently, we followed him with our bundles on our head. The man meant well and took us along a path that led out of the forest. After we had walked for about three kos,[19] we reached the road to Fatehpur.

---

17. Assembly hall in a village used also for shelter for travelers.
18. Here the "tilak-marks" are caste signs.

19. Literally "cry," a measure of distance (how far one can hear a human cry; calculated at a little over two miles).

"This road will take you to your destination," the robber chief assured us. Pointing to a clump of trees in the distance, he added: "There, across those trees, lies Fatehpur."

He then begged leave of us and we blessed him heartily, chanting "May you live long," and began to walk towards Fatehpur.

In Vikram 1699, my third son, the only surviving child I had, also died. His death rent my heart with agony. I was wretched and miserable with sorrow. Worldly attachments are powerful bonds, for they bind both the ignorant and the knowing. Two years have now passed since my son's death, and I still feel desolate. I find myself unable to overcome my sorrow and my attachment to his memory remains an unbearable pain.

My story is now complete. I am fifty-five years of age, and I live in Agra with my wife in reasonably comfortable circumstances. I married thrice, and had two daughters and seven sons. But all my children died. And now my wife and I are alone like winter trees that have shed all their greenery, standing bare and denuded. Looking at it in the light of the absolute vision, you may declare that as a man takes unto himself, so he sheds. But can any man rooted in this world ever see things in such a light? A man feels enriched when he takes something unto himself and utterly lost when he is deprived of even a trifle.

I will now end. But before I do so, I would like to speak to you of my present good and bad attributes.

First, then, my good points. As a poet I am matchless in composing verses on spiritual themes, which I recite with great art and impact. I know Prakrit and Sanskrit and can intone these languages with faultless pronunciation. I also know many vernacular languages. In my use of language I am ever alive to nuances of words and meanings.

My temper is naturally forgiving. I am easily content, and not readily moved by worldly cares. I am sweet of tongue and good at mixing with people for I have great forbearance and shun harsh language. My intentions are unsullied; so the counsel I give usually proves helpful to others. I have no foul or vicious habits, and I do not run after other men's wives. I have a true, unwavering faith in Jainism, and a steadfast mind which remains unshaken in its determination. I am pure in heart and always strive for equanimity.

These are my various virtues, both small and big. None of them really touch supreme heights and none are quite without shortcomings.

Now for my bad points. I said I have little of anger, pride or cunning, yet my greed for money is great. A little gain makes me inordinately happy and a little loss plunges me into the depths of despair. I am indolent by nature and slow in my work, hardly ever wanting to stir out of my house.

I do not perform sacred religious rituals; I never utter the holy mantras, never sit for meditations (tapa) and never exercise self-restraint. Neither do I perform puja[20] nor practise charity.

I am overfond of laughter, and love to poke fun at everything. I delight in

---

20. Worship.

playing the clown and acting the buffoon, indulging in these capers with great relish and gusto. I often utter things that should not be said without any sense of shame, revelling in narrating unutterable stories and escapades with much glee. I love to relate fictitious stories, often quite scandalous, and try to pass them off as true especially when I am in the midst of a large gathering. When I am in the mood for fun, nothing can restrain me from telling fanciful lies or untruths.

I sometimes break into a dance when I am alone. Yet I am also prone to sudden, irrational feelings of sheer dread.

Such is my temper. The good in my character alternates with the bad.

I have now done with all that I had to say about myself. Yet what I have said pertains mostly to my visible conduct and actions: things that could be seen or discovered by all. But in a man's life there is much that is too subtle to be so palpable. Of this, however, only God can know.

Also, I must confess that I spoke mostly of things I could best recollect. I have also deliberately remained silent about certain of my deeds which were perversities of such gross proportions that I cannot speak of them to anyone. Yet you must grant that I have not entirely shied away from speaking of my faults and follies. This at least is something quite unusual since people are careful to conceal even their smallest misdoings although they be petty things of common occurrence. A man who confesses to his faults is a Kevalin,[21] a realized soul.

But none can report all that happens, not even the all-knowing Kevalin. Even in the tiny span of a day, a man passes through myriad states of consciousness. The all-knowing Kevalin can perceive them, but even he cannot describe them in their fulness. And who can know more than the Kevalin? The wisest, most occult of sages can know only a part of what the Kevalin knows. Compared to them I am nothing but a primitive earthworm with no more than the haziest of awareness. How could I have revealed all? A man's life has much that is subtly secret and profoundly beyond grasp. What I have reported is certainly the grossest of the gross part of my life. For as I said, I have spoken mainly of my outward conduct and behaviour.

I have narrated to you the story of fifty-five years of my life. The full span of a man's life is a hundred and ten years. I have lived only half of this span. I do not know what is to come in the future. God alone can know that.

All men at all times can be divided into three categories; the truly praiseworthy, the utterly despicable, and those who fall between these two.

The truly praiseworthy men are those who, in speaking of others, speak only of their merits, deliberately drawing a veil over their faults. When such men speak of themselves, they speak only of faults and never of their merits.

The utterly despicable have just the contrary traits. They only speak of faults in others while boasting of their own merits. Never do they utter a word about their own blemishes.

I am one who falls in between. I speak unreservedly of both faults and merits in others as well as myself.

---

21. In Jain theology, one liberated from the
    cycle of rebirth.

Today, as I complete my tale, it is Monday, the fifth of the bright half of the month Agrahayana, Vikram 1698 (A.D. 1641). I now live in Agra and I am, let me repeat, a Jain of the Srimal clan, Banarasi Biholia by name and an Adhyatmi by conviction. It occurred to me that I should make the story of my life public, and so I have narrated the events that have happened during these last fifty-five years. The future I do not know; I shall face it as it comes.

The story of the last fifty-five years of my life covers half the number of days allotted to man. I have, therefore, named my story 'Half a Tale'.

Wicked men will mock at my tale. But friends will surely give it a glad and attentive ear and recite it to each other.

Before I finish I would like to extend my good wishes to all who may read my story or listen to it or recite it to others.

"SAGE IN MEDITATION." KANG HUI-AN,
1419–65. Early Yi dynasty. National
Museum of Korea.

SECTION III
East Asia: Early and Middle Periods

China
Japan
Korea

CHINA

The German philosopher Friedrich Nietzsche once suggested that the value of a nation resided in its ability to give to ordinary, daily experience the "stamp of the eternal." One can imagine the writers in this section agreeing with his criterion, for not only does it perfectly capture the effect of so much of Chinese literature, it also touches on the deepest assumptions underlying Chinese culture itself. In China, what one marvels at is the commonplace, what one celebrates is the mundane. Even as they occasionally note the strange and extraordinary, China's writers never tire of the everyday. If one had to settle on a single characteristic that most clearly distinguishes the literature of China from that of the West, it would be this resolute emphasis on the actual moment, this clear-eyed focus on the here and now.

Readers new to Chinese literature are often struck by its immense time span and essential unity of thought. China is, in fact, the oldest continuous civilization in the world, the keeper of an unbroken literary tradition stretching back some 2500 years. The earliest works of this tradition, a collection of texts known as the Confucian classics, were enshrined at the center of the educational system during the Han Dynasty (206 B.C.E. to 220 C.E.) and remained there until the early years of our own century. Studied and memorized by each succeeding generation of scholars, the histories, anecdotes, poetry, and philosophy of the classics provide an intellectual bond, a common currency of allusion and reference that links China's present effortlessly to its past for 2000 years.

On a deeper level, continuity and unity flow from the Chinese writing system itself, a system unlike those of the West in concept and implication. Unlike Indo-European languages, Chinese is not written phonetically by means of an alphabet. Rather, each word has its own unique sign—a visual emblem of the entire word-idea called a *character* or *calligraph*. Many basic characters originated as *pictographs,* drawings that visually represent what they signify. For example, the character for "sun" (日) originated as a simple line drawing of the sun (⊙). Yet even in the earliest examples of Chinese script that have been discovered—inscriptions on bone from the second millennium B.C.E.,—pictographs were being combined to form *ideographs,* representations of abstract ideas. Thus sun and moon next to each other signify "brightness" (明); the sun showing through a tree (木) signifies "east" (東).

Because they embody the meaning of a word instead of merely recording its sound, Chinese characters overcome the difficulties that arise with phonetic scripts as spoken language changes over the centuries and from region to region. Today, Mandarin and Cantonese, to name only the two most widely spoken Chinese dialects, are farther apart in sound than French and Italian. In Mandarin, the word for "shoe," for example, is pronounced *xie*; the Cantonese word is *hai*. Clearly, if they relied on a phonetic script, the two dialects could no longer communicate. As it is, the gulf between them disappears in writing, for *xie* and *hai* are written with the same character (鞋).

Writing not only links colloquial dialects to each other, it also connects them to a third entity known as classical Chinese (*wen-yen,* or "literary language"). Arising in the late fourth century B.C.E. and formalized during the Han Dynasty, classical Chinese presumably reflected the spoken language of the time. However, it survived as a purely written language, the preferred vehicle for literary expression, until the early twentieth century, even as the spoken language continued to change. Classical Chinese differs from colloquial Chinese (*pai-hua,* or "plain speech") mainly in syntax; the two overlap in vocabulary and use the same characters. Although many characters have shifted in meaning as the spoken language diverged from the classical, many key words have survived the centuries completely intact. Certain words at the heart of the culture—for example, 仁, meaning a sense of human relatedness; or 恕, meaning sympathy, forgiveness; or 孝, meaning devotion to family and respect for one's elders—are a part of today's vernacular but also occurred with virtually the same senses in ancient texts.

These fundamental facts about the Chinese language are certainly important in understanding the "conservative," seemingly immutable nature of Chinese culture. Traditional Chinese literature is still, at least partially, accessible to contemporary readers in a way that ancient literatures of other cultures are not. A student of modern English could not read the works of Chaucer without special training, whereas a student of modern Chinese could make some sense of *The Analects* (*Lun-yü),* purportedly an account of a series of discourses between Confucius and his disciples. Less than 600 years separate us from Chaucer; almost twenty-five centuries separate us from Confucius.

For Western readers approaching Chinese literature in translation, the first challenge is not so much what is said, but what is *not* said. One of the finest Western interpreters of Chinese was misled into believing that, because the word "love" does not often occur in the literature of China, there is no tradition of love poems in Chinese. If he was thinking of effusions of passion, he was right; but if he was thinking of expressions of devotion between two human beings, he could not be more wrong. Chinese writers considered emotions too intense for words. Chinese love poems are indirect—passion is conveyed subtly and with understatement. A neutral and modest reference to "feeling" will touch a Chinese reader deeply, eliciting emotions far more intense than the most lavish verbal display.

Another adjustment that Western readers must make is in their expectations of originality, which does not have the exalted place on the scale of values in China that it does in the modern West. Many images, thoughts, and attitudes encountered in Chinese writing will undoubtedly seem novel and even exotic to Western readers. But more often than not such effects are due to the disparity between Western and Chinese cultures. To Chinese readers, the same passages would probably seem reassuringly familiar, neither exceptional nor exceptionable.

What, then, do the Chinese value in their literature? One clue is a quotation from Confucius's *Analects*: "I merely transmit, I do not create; I love and revere the ancients." Chinese writers took their cue from Confucius even when they had something original to say. The virtue of their writing lay in its affirmation of age-old truths, not in the discovery of new ones. Except for a brief period called the Six Dynasties (roughly from the third century C.E. to the end of the sixth century C.E.), Chinese writers strove toward an elegance that was spare rather than contrived. Modesty of character, a major tenet of Chinese philosophy, was reflected in modesty of means, and readers admired the seeming artlessness and inevitability of the compositions. This seeming effortlessness is, of course, the product of much effort, for there is art of a very high order in Chinese writing. Chinese poets, for example, strove for their limpid style while at the same time fulfilling the demands of intricate poetic forms.

The literature of China is vast, and the selections here can give only a sample of its great variety. In addition to the obvious proportion of poetry, readers will find many snippets and extracts that are more difficult to classify—selections of philosophical discourse and aphorisms; literary anecdotes and criticism; official and legendary history. Chinese forms and genres do not find exact Western counterparts, nor, in fact, does the Chinese concept of literature. The closest Chinese term, *wenxue* (pinyin) includes both our "literature" and "literary studies." Writing commentary on the classics was a scholarly tradition from the Han Dynasty onward. In the West, we would classify such commentary as "secondary" works—derivatives rather than the genuine article. In China, however, commentary on the past is part of the ongoing literary enterprise.

Wen means not only "script" or "text," but refers to any kind of marks that reveal inner essence. The most famous instances of *wen* in this sense are the stripes of the tiger manifesting tigerness and the spots of a leopard manifesting leopardness. (Just so are Chinese characters marks that indicate essence.) *Wen* also refers to culture: the outward manifestation of an inner sense of civility that reflects virtue. *Hsüeh* means "learning," but it can also designate a "school," as in *xuexcao*. "Written learning" is an inadequate translation for *wenxue*, but it conveys something of a sense of what literature is to the Chinese. Official documents, transcribed folksongs, memorial inscriptions, philosophy, history, commentary, poetry, anecdote, fact approached through fiction, fiction grounded in fact—all are *wenxue*.

The problem with many Western presentations of Chinese literature — which includes not only popular translations but scholarly exegeses — is that too often the texts are considered as codes to be broken rather than as worlds to be inhabited. Western students have been misled to look for counterparts to their own genres and literary forms, just as Western linguists have vainly searched in Chinese for exact counterparts to their own grammar. The result has been a distortion of the value of Chinese literature on the basis of its likeness or unlikeness to Western literature. What has fascinated students of early Chinese literature in the West is not always what the Chinese value in their own tradition. To put it perhaps oversimplistically, Chinese literature does not so much embody a constant search for truth as it exemplifies a continuing reaffirmation of traditional verities.

The best of Chinese literature is astonishing by any aesthetic standards, whether Western or Eastern. The Japanese admired the Chinese canon when their own culture was being shaped. Indeed, there is a large body of original poems written in classical Chinese by Japanese scholars. The intellectuals of eighteenth-century France took a special interest in the fugitive translations of Chinese literature that were beginning to appear. Chinese literature influenced the early founders of modernism, especially Ezra Pound and the poets of the imagist group. Just as, in the 1960s, this literature became the favorite reading of many young hippie Americans, it will doubtless continue to enlighten and charm readers for centuries to come.

Historical and Cultural Background

The civilization of China arose in the fertile basin of the Yellow River not long after the first civilizations began in Mesopotamia, Egypt, and the Indus Valley; there is some evidence that Chinese civilization is even older — dating from the fifth millennium B.C.E. Ancient Chinese historical annals date the founding of China to 2852 B.C.E. and describe the eras of the Three Sovereigns, the Five Kings, and the Hsia and Shang dynasties. Modern historians long regarded all of these eras as legendary. However, archaeological finds of the early twentieth century not only validated the existence of the Shang but found that the succession of Shang kings coincided almost exactly with the list given in Chinese literary sources, leading some scholars to speculate that accounts of the Hsia Dynasty may be accurate as well. Excavations of Shang sites also yielded the earliest examples of Chinese writing.

The subsequent history of China has traditionally been told within the framework supplied by the rise and fall of dynasties, which serve as reference points for discussions of culture. We speak, for example, of a Sung Dynasty painting or a T'ang Dynasty porcelain.

In 1027 B.C.E., the Shang were overthrown by the Chou, a Chinese people to the northwest who adopted the more advanced Shang culture and established feudal rule over the Chinese city-states. In 771 B.C.E., the Chou capital fell to invaders from the west. Chou kings reestablished an eastern capital, but they never fully recovered their authority, and the Eastern Chou period was a troubled one. During the first portion, a time known as the Spring and Autumn period (770–476 B.C.E.), subordinate states grew in power and independence. The situation worsened during the treacherous political maneuvering and increasingly ruthless warfare of the Warring States period (403–221 B.C.E.). It was during these chaotic times that China's greatest philosophers were to emerge. Historians speak of ''100 schools of philosophy,'' each offering solutions to the problems of how to govern, social organization, and individual conduct. While none of the philosophers seems to have had an effect on the rulers of his day, the three whose works are included in this section—Confucius, Lao-tzu, and Chuang-tzu— ultimately exerted a profound and lasting influence on Chinese culture.

In 256 B.C.E. the state of Ch'in overthrew the Chou Dynasty and within twenty-five years subjugated the remaining states, unifying China for the first time. As a sign of superiority over the Chou kings, the first Ch'in ruler gave himself the exalted title we translate as emperor. The Ch'in established the mechanism of central bureaucracy that would serve later dynasties well, dividing the empire into administrative units and standardizing weights and measures, currency, the width of cart axles, and the characters of the writing system. China's borders were extended in all directions, and various battlements on the northern frontier were joined to form the Great Wall. Ch'in laws, however, were cruel and severe, the products of a philosophy called Legalism. In 213 B.C.E., all books except for practical manuals on such subjects as agriculture were ordered burned, and scholars were persecuted. Classical texts survived only by being carefully hidden or committed to memory.

A rebellion brought the downfall of the Ch'in in 206 B.C.E. The leader of the victorious forces, a commoner, founded the Han Dynasty and ruled as its first emperor. The Han, divided by historians into Former or Western Han (206 B.C.E.–9 C.E.) and Later or Eastern Han (23–220 C.E.), gave Chinese culture its definitive form and served as a model for subsequent dynasties. Han emperors relaxed the stringent laws of the Ch'in, instituted Confucianism as the state philosophy, recruited scholars to staff the bureaucracy, and set up an imperial academy to train civil servants by teaching the Confucian classics. The empire expanded still farther, and Chinese control over great stretches of the Central Asian steppe resulted in the fabled Silk Road, a trade route that linked China by land to the Kushan Empire and ultimately to the Hellenistic world of Greece and Rome. Over this road, Chinese emissaries traveled to India and Persia. It was also over this road that Buddhism first began to filter back into China, where its influence would ultimately prove more lasting than in its native India.

After the first century C.E., the Han entered into a long decline, and civil unrest, palace intrigues, and rebellious generals finally brought the dynasty to a close. China now began the long era of political disunity called by historians the Six Dynasties (220–589). The history of the period is complex, but a brief summary provides the reference points needed for the literature here. China split first into three kingdoms for more than a generation. The Chin Dynasty united the two northern kingdoms in 265, and in 280 succeeded in briefly reuniting all of China. Constant invasions from the north and west, however, forced the Chin to move their capital south to Nanking, after which the dynasty is known as Eastern Chin (318–420), the first of the six dynasties centered in Nanking, for which the period is named. The north, meanwhile, experienced the rise and fall of successive kingdoms—sixteen in all—established by various invaders from the steppe. Over the course of two centuries, these peoples were gradually assimilated, and the resulting multiethnic society added great vibrancy to Chinese culture.

The Sui Dynasty, the last of the six southern dynasties, succeeded in reuniting all of China in 589, but overextended itself and was quickly succeeded by the T'ang Dynasty (618–907). Under the T'ang emperors, China once again reached out to the world. At its height, T'ang China was a vast, prosperous, cosmopolitan empire with close cultural ties to Persia, Japan, Korea (then known as Silla), and India. Caravan trade along the Silk Road was reestablished. The arts flourished, especially poetry. To search out the most brilliant minds for its bureaucracy, the T'ang emperors introduced a more highly structured version of the civil service examinations of the Han. The most prestigious degree was the *chin-shih*, a literature degree that demanded not only complete mastery of the Confucian classics but also the ability to compose poetry. The examinations established a gentry class of literati in China that served as the backbone of its government until the early twentieth century. From the T'ang on, most men of letters served for a time as government officials, and most high officials were also accomplished in the arts of poetry, calligraphy, and painting.

We use the locution "men of letters" intentionally, for Confucian philosophy relegated women to distinctly second-class citizenship. The imperial examinations were closed to them, and it was generally only in a family setting—and this rarely—that women were encouraged in scholarly or literary pursuits. Thus it was, for example, that one of China's finest historians was a woman, Pan Chao; her brother, Pan Ku, who had learned the family "trade" of writing, died, and she took over. Nevertheless, there were women writers in every dynasty. During the T'ang Dynasty, the *Ch'uan T'ang Shih*, a collection of poetry in the *shih* form included 190 women among its 2200 anthologized poets. Literacy was officially restricted to Buddhist nuns, Taoist priestesses, concubines, and courtesans, though these women were often very well educated indeed. (The situation was to eventually change somewhat: during the Ch'ing Dynasty in the eighteenth and nineteenth centuries, a period outside our present survey, a woman's ability to write poetry was considered part of her dowry.) Possibly the only class of women to keep up a steady stream of literary production were courtesans, who wrote copiously in the folk song genre and who stood by definition outside the realm of Confucian codes.

In the middle of the eighth century, T'ang power began to wane. The armies guarding the distant frontiers gathered power, weakening central bureaucratic control. The event that signaled the beginning of the end was the rebellion led by An Lu-shan, a general from the northeastern frontier who swept across China with his armies, capturing the capital and forcing the emperor to flee to the mountains. The rebellion is particularly notable because it touched the lives of the two greatest T'ang poets, Tu Fu and Li Po, and because the story of the dynasty's fleeing emperor and his concubine forms the subject of Po Chü-yi's masterpiece, "A Song of Unending Sorrow," which is included here.

After the T'ang Dynasty, China experienced fifty years of civil war, during which time the north and south again developed separately. The country was reunited in 960 under the Sung Dynasty. The Sung was another era of great cultural brilliance, especially in painting. Some of the most familiar modern technologies were invented or developed during the Sung—including gunpowder, paper currency, printing (centuries before Gutenberg), and the compass used in navigation. Wealth, luxury, and taste prevailed; trade and commerce flourished, resulting in the growth of great cities. The capital, Kaifeng, held over 260,000 households—a population estimated at more than one million people. By comparison, London at the time had a population of only 18,000.

Invading Chin Tartars forced the Sung to abandon their capital in 1126 and flee south, and for the rest of the period under consideration here China was again divided. The Southern Sung Dynasty (1127–1279) held the south; the powerful Chin Dynasty (1126–1234) ruled the north.

A Note on Transliteration

There are two systems generally used for romanizing or transliterating Chinese words in the English-speaking world. The older of the two, the Wade-Giles system, has today been largely supplanted by the *pinyin* system introduced by the People's Republic of China in the 1950s. However, because so many important scholarly works on China predate *pinyin,* a sensible practice has been established, which we follow here: Wade-Giles is used for discussions of pre-1950 or prerevolutionary China and *pinyin* is used for topics in contemporary China. At the start of each headnote, however, we include the *pinyin* version of the author's name in brackets next to the Wade-Giles version. For example, Chuang-tzu [Zhuangzi]. In some instances, such as "Shanghai" and "Wang Wei," there are no differences in the two systems.

Further Readings

Birch, Cyril, ed. *Anthology of Chinese Literature.* 2 vols. New York: Grove Press, 1972.

Chan, Wing-tsit. *A Source Book in Chinese Philosophy.* Princeton: Princeton University Press, 1963.

Liu, James J.Y. *The Art of Chinese Poetry.* Chicago: University of Chicago Press, 1962.

Liu, Wu-chi, and Irving Lo, eds. *Sunflower Splendor: Three Thousand Years of Chinese Poetry.* Bloomington: Indiana University Press, 1990.

Nienhauser, William. *Indiana Companion to Traditional Chinese Literature.* Bloomington: Indiana University Press, 1986.

CONFUCIUS (551–479 B.C.E.)
China

The man whose honorific name K'ung-fu-tzu (Master K'ung) has been Latinized since the sixteenth century as Confucius was known in his own day as K'ung Ch'iu; the name he chose for himself or his "style"-name was Chung-ni.* Born into a declining aristocratic family in the state of Lu (roughly, present-day Shantung province), Confucius was reduced to relative poverty when young and had to make a living in a number of menial occupations. He served briefly as an official during his middle years but soon returned to private life, lecturing and traveling with his disciples.

Confucius lived during an era of drastic social upheavals known as the Spring and Autumn period, when the disastrous consequences of warfare among China's numerous feudal states bred uncertainties about the meaning of life in the minds of the rulers and ruled alike. During this troubled time, Confucius emerged as a great educator, discussing many issues and addressing numerous problems in life, society, and politics. His doctrines have come to be known as Confucianism.

Lun-yü, familiar in English as the Analects, was not written by Confucius himself but was compiled by his disciples or their followers. Its twenty books or chapters contain brief, concise notes of conversations between Confucius and his disciples. (The English title is actually somewhat misleading. Lun-yü can be literally translated as "discussion talk," but it properly means "conversation" or "discourse.") The notes can be bewilderingly fragmentary, and since much of their original context has undoubtedly been lost, the meaning of certain passages is irretrievable.

During the Han Dynasty, the Analects, along with the rest of the Confucian texts, became the official "core curriculum" for scholars, a position they held until the early years of the twentieth century. As such, they helped shape Chinese thinking for more than two millennia. Probably the only work in Western civilization that can be placed on a par with the Analects, both in terms of generic form and subsequent influence, would be Plato's Republic.

Selected Analects [Lun-yü]

Someone asked Confucius how to elevate virtue, purge evil, and clarify confusion. Confucius said, "Good question! Put service first and gain after; is this not elevating virtue? Attack your own evils, not those of others; is this not purging evil? And suppose you forget yourself and affect your relatives because of a temporary fit of anger; is that not confusion?" (12:21)

Translated by Thomas Cleary.

*A Chinese author is identified not only by his given name (ming), but also by his style or courtesy name (tzu), as well as by his pen name or literary name (hao). Woman authors, however, do not always enjoy the full panoply of nominals.

A pupil asked about friendship. Confucius said, "Speak truthfully and guide them in good ways. If they do not agree, then stop and do not disgrace yourself for them." (12:23)

Confucius said to a student, "Be an exemplary man of learning, not a trivial pedant." (6:13)

Confucius said, "Not cultivating virtue, not learning, not being able to take to justice on hearing it, and not being able to change what is not good: these are my worries." (7:3)

Confucius said, "Be dutiful at home, brotherly in public; be discreet and trustworthy, love all people, and draw near to humanity. If you have extra energy as you do that, then study literature." (1:7)

Confucius said, "At the age of fifteen I set my heart on learning. At thirty I was established. At forty I was unwavering. At fifty I knew the order of Heaven. At sixty I listened receptively. At seventy I followed my heart's desire without going too far." (2:4)

One of the disciples was studying for employment.
Confucius said, "Learn a lot, eliminate the doubtful, and speak discreetly about the rest; then there will be little blame. See a lot, eliminate the perilous, act prudently on the rest; then there will be little regret. When your words are seldom blamed and your actions seldom regretted, employment will be there." (2:18)

Confucius said, "It is after the coldest weather that you know the pine and the cedar outlast the withering." (9:29)

Confucius said of his foremost disciple, "He is wise indeed! He subsists on bare essentials and lives in a poor neighborhood; for other people this would mean intolerable anxiety, but he is consistently happy. Wise indeed is he!" (6:11)

Confucius said, "Don't worry about the recognition of others; worry about your own lack of ability." (14:32)

Confucius said, "Don't worry that other people don't know you; worry that you don't know other people." (1:16)

Confucius said to a disciple, "Shall I teach you how to know something? Realize you know it when you know it, and realize you don't know it when you don't." (2:17)

Confucius said, "Uncle Tai can be said to have been perfect in virtue. He conceded kingship three times, yet the people never found out or appreciated it." (8:1)

Confucius said, "A person can spread the Way, but the Way is not to aggrandize a person." (15:29)

Confucius said, "If you associate with those who are not centered in their actions, you will become either too uninhibited or too inhibited. Those who are too uninhibited are too aggressive, while those who are too inhibited are too passive." (13:21)

Confucius said, "Cultivated people are easy to work for but hard to please. If you try to please them in the wrong way, they are not pleased. When they employ people, they consider their capacities.

"Petty people are hard to work for but easy to please. Even if you please them by something that is wrong, they are still pleased. When they employ people, they expect everything." (13:25)

Confucius said, "Cultivated people are serene but not haughty. Petty people are haughty but not serene." (13:26)

Confucius said, "Clever talkers who put imperious expressions on their faces have little humaneness indeed." (1:3)

Confucius said, "I will have nothing to do with those who are free but not honest, childlike but not sincere, straightforward but not trustworthy." (8:16)

A disciple asked Confucius, "How is it when everyone in your hometown likes you?"

Confucius said, "Not good enough."

The disciple asked, "How about if everyone in your hometown dislikes you?"

Confucius said, "Not good enough. It is better when the good among the people like you and the bad dislike you." (13:24)

Confucius said, "A knight who is concerned about a dwelling place is not worthy of being considered a knight." (14:3)

Confucius said, "When I am with a group of people all day and the conversation never touches on matters of justice but inclines to the exercise of petty wit, I have a hard time." (15:17)

Confucius said of his foremost disciple, "I can talk to him all day, and he doesn't contradict me, as if he were ignorant. From what I observe of his private life after he has gone home, however, I find he has the ability to apply what he's learned. He is no ignoramus." (2:9)

Confucius said, "See what they do, observe the how and why, and examine their basic premises. How can people hide? How can people hide?" (2:10)

Confucius said, "I do not teach the uninspired or enlighten the complacent. When I bring out one corner to show people, if they do not come back with the other three, I do not repeat." (7:8)

Confucius said, "It is all right to talk of higher things to those who are at least middling, but not to those who are less than middling." (6:21)

Confucius said, "Enliven the ancient and also know what is new; then you can be a teacher." (2:11)

Confucius said, "If you don't talk with those worth talking to, you lose people. If you talk with those not worth talking to, you lose words. Knowers do not lose people, and they do not lose words either." (15:8)

Confucius said to a pupil, "Do you think I have come to know many things by studying them?"
The pupil said, "Yes. Isn't it so?"
Confucius said, "No. I penetrate them by their underlying unity." (15:3)

Confucius said, "Study without thinking, and you are blind; think without studying, and you are in danger." (2:16)

A pupil asked Confucius, "If one is poor but does not curry favor, or is rich but not haughty, how would that be?"
Confucius said, "Fine, but not as good as one who is poor but takes pleasure in the Way, or one who is rich but still courteous." (1:15)

Confucius said, "Exemplary people understand matters of justice; small people understand matters of profit." (1:16)

Confucius said, "The knowing enjoy water, the humane enjoy mountains. The knowing are diligent; the humane are quiet. The knowing are happy, the humane are long-lived." (6:23)

When at ease, Confucius was relaxed and genial. (7:4)

Confucius said, "Even if my fare is plain and my lifestyle austere, I still find pleasure in them. Riches and status unjustly attained are to me like floating clouds." (7:15)

An official of the state of Chu asked one of Confucius' disciples about the teacher, but the disciple didn't answer. Confucius remarked, "Why didn't you say, 'His character is such that he gets so enthusiastic that he forgets to eat, and is so happy that he forgets worries; he is not conscious of impending death'?" (7:18)

A certain student was sleeping in the daytime.

Confucius said, "Rotten wood cannot be sculpted, a manure wall cannot be plastered. What admonition is there for me to give?" (5:10)

Confucius also said, "At first the way I dealt with people was to listen to their words and trust they would act on them. Now I listen to their words and observe whether they act on them. It was within my power to change this." (5:10)

Confucius said, "Good people should be slow to speak but quick to act." (4:24)

One of the disciples always used to say, "Neither harming nor importuning—how can this not be good?"

Confucius said, "How can this way be enough to be considered good?" (9:28)

Someone asked Confucius how to serve ghosts and spirits.

Confucius said, "As long as you are unable to serve people, how can you serve ghosts?"

The inquirer also asked about death.

Confucius said, "As long as you do not know life, how can you know death?" (11:12)

Confucius said, "To eat your fill but not apply your mind to anything all day is a problem. Are there no games to play? Even that would be smarter than doing nothing." (17:22)

A disciple asked Confucius, "Do cultivated people value courage?"

Confucius said, "Cultivated people consider justice foremost. When cultivated people have courage without justice, they become rebellious. When petty people have courage without justice, they become brigands." (17:23)

LAO-TZU [LAOZI] (SIXTH CENTURY B.C.E.)
China

Little can be said definitively about the life of the sage who is honorifically called Lao-tzu. According to Ssu-ma Ch'ien, a historian who lived four centuries later, Lao-tzu was named Li Erh and was from the south, possibly the state of Ch'u (roughly the region covering the present-day provinces of Hunan and Hupei). The scarcity of biographical data has fostered a supernaturalized Lao-tzu in popular literature and has led some modern scholars to question whether he actually existed at all.

Like his contemporary Confucius, Lao-tzu (assuming that he existed) rose as a profound philosopher at a time when philosophy was most needed as a remedy for social chaos. The two masters, however, stood for different, if not diametrically opposite, ideals and precepts. While Confucius considered himself a transmitter of ancient tradition, Lao-tzu questioned established values and the status quo. One of his key notions is that of Tao, or the Way things in the universe come into existence as they do. Both individuals and governments must conform to the Tao by practicing *wu wei,* or nondoing. Difficult to translate succinctly, *wu wei* does not imply passivity or inaction, but rather it serves as an injunction against "being or acting as that which you are not." Perhaps the closest we can come in current Western terms would be to say that to practice *wu wei* is to live in a state of constant epiphany before the ordinary, and to let that state guide our relations with all things in the world.

Tao Te Ching, the only work attributed to Lao-tzu, was actually not written by the sage himself. Like the *Analects* of Confucius, it is a compilation by disciples of what they had noted down or remembered of their master's sayings. Apart from its philosophical wisdom, it is marked by its artless simplicity, vivid imagery, and piquant wit.

from *Tao-Te Ching*

[Existence is beyond the power of words]

Existence is beyond the power of words
To define:
Terms may be used
But are none of them absolute.
In the beginning of heaven and earth there were no words,   5
Words came out of the womb of matter;
And whether a man dispassionately
Sees to the core of life
Or passionately
Sees the surface,   10
The core and the surface
Are essentially the same,
Words making them seem different
Only to express appearance.
If name be needed, wonder names them both: 15
From wonder into wonder
Existence opens.

[Thirty spokes are made one]

Thirty spokes are made one by holes in a hub
By vacancies joining them for a wheel's use

Translated by Witter Bynner.

The use of clay in moulding pitchers
Comes from the hollow of its absence;
Doors, windows, in a house,
Are used for their emptiness: 5
Thus we are helped by what is not
To use what is.

[Rid of formalized wisdom and learning]

19

Rid of formalized wisdom and learning
People would be a hundredfold happier,
Rid of conventionalized duty and honor
People would find their families dear.
Rid of legalized profiteering   5
People would have no thieves to fear.
These methods of life have failed, all three,
Here is the way, it seems to me:
Set people free,
As deep in their hearts they would like to be,   10
From private greeds
And wanton needs.

[Existence is infinite, not to be defined]

32

Existence is infinite, not to be defined;
And, though it seem but a bit of wood in your hand, to carve as you please,
It is not to be lightly played with and laid down.
When rulers adhered to the way of life,
They were upheld by natural loyalty: 5
Heaven and earth were joined and made fertile,
Life was a freshness of rain,
Subject to none,
Free to all.
But men of culture came, with their grades and their distinctions;   10
And as soon as such differences had been devised
No one knew where to end them,
Though the one who does know the end of all such differences
Is the sound man:
Existence   15
Might be likened to the course
Of many rivers reaching the one sea.

[There is no need to run outside]

47

There is no need to run outside
For better seeing,
Nor to peer from a window. Rather abide
At the center of your being;
For the more you leave it, the less you learn.   5
Search your heart and see
If he is wise who takes each turn:
The way to do is to be.

[Real words are not vain]

81

Real words are not vain,
Vain words not real;
And since those who argue prove nothing
A sensible man does not argue.
A sensible man is wiser than he knows,   5
While a fool knows more than is wise.
Therefore a sensible man does not devise resources:
The greater his use to others
The greater their use to him,
The more he yields to others   10
The more they yield to him.
The way of life cleaves without cutting:
Which, without need to say,
Should be man's way.

ANONYMOUS (NINTH–FIFTH CENTURY B.C.E.)

The fountainhead of Chinese poetry is the *Book of Songs* [*Shih-ching*], a compilation of 305 songs representing a variety of musical forms. Few of the songs can be accurately dated, but the bulk of them came into being approximately between 1000 and 700 B.C.E., during the Chou Dynasty. More than half are folk songs (*feng*) from various regions; the rest are categorized as courtly songs (*ya*) or ritual songs (*sung*). The bulk of the songs had been passed down orally, constantly modified in form and language, until they were transcribed and gathered into the *Book of Songs* during Confucius's time.

Credit for compiling the songs was in fact traditionally given to Confucius. When Confucianism established its position as orthodoxy during the Han Dynasty, the *Book of Songs* was enshrined as one of the Confucian classics—the central texts of a scholarly education. The diction and imagery of its songs thus influenced generations of scholars and writers.

Two of the four songs included here, "In the south is a tree with drooping boughs" and "Where the scrub elm skirts the wood" are *feng*. The first is a song of benediction; the second describes a hunter's seduction of a lovesick girl. The other two songs are *ya*. "Pick a fern, pick a fern, ferns are high" is a soldier's lament and may have been sung by soldiers in unison to keep time as they marched. "Don't escort the big chariot" is a homily on the travails of life.

from **Book of Songs [Shih-ching]**

[In the south is a tree with drooping boughs]*

4

In the south is a tree with drooping boughs;
The cloth-creeper binds it.
Oh, happy is our lord;
Blessings and boons secure him!

In the south is a tree with drooping boughs;   5
The cloth-creeper covers it.
Oh, happy is our lord;
Blessings and boons protect him!

In the south is a tree with drooping boughs;
The cloth-creeper encircles it.   10
Oh, happy is our lord;
Blessings and boons surround him!

[Where the scrub elm skirts the wood]†

23

Lies a dead deer on yonder plain
whom white grass covers,
A melancholy maid in spring
                    is luck
                         for   5
                            lovers.

*Translated by Arthur Waley.
†Translated by Ezra Pound.

Where the scrub elm skirts the wood,
be it not in white mat bound,
as a jewel flawless found,
   dead as doe is maidenhood.

Hark!
Unhand my girdle-knot,
   stay, stay, stay
   or the dog
   may
   bark.

[Pick a fern, pick a fern, ferns are high]†

167

Pick a fern, pick a fern, ferns are high,
"Home," I'll say: home, the year's gone by,
no house, no roof, these huns on the hoof.
Work, work, work, that's how it runs,
We are here because of these huns.

Pick a fern, pick a fern, soft as they come,
I'll say "Home."
Hungry all of us, thirsty here,
no home news for nearly a year.

Pick a fern, pick a fern, if they scratch,
I'll say "Home," what's the catch?
I'll say, "Go home," now October's come.
King wants us to give it all,
no rest, spring, summer, winter, fall,
Sorrow to us, sorrow to you.
We won't get out of here till we're through.

When it's cherry-time with you,
we'll see the captain's car go thru,
four big horses to pull that load.
That's what comes along our road,
What do you call three fights a month,
and won 'em all?

Four car-horses strong and tall
and the boss who can drive 'em all
as we slog along beside his car,
ivory bow-tips and shagreen case

†Translated by Ezra Pound.

to say nothing of what we face
sloggin' along in the Hien-yün war.

Willows were green when we set out,
it's blowin' an' snowin' as we go   30
down this road, muddy and slow,
hungry and thirsty and blue as doubt
(no one feels half of what we know).

[Don't escort the big chariot]*

206

Don't escort the big chariot;
You will only make yourself dusty.
Don't think about the sorrows of the world;
You will only make yourself wretched.

Don't escort the big chariot;   5
You won't be able to see for dust.
Don't think about the sorrows of the world;
Or you will never escape from your despair.

Don't escort the big chariot;
You'll be stifled with dust.   10
Don't think about the sorrows of the world;
You will only load yourself with care.

CHUANG-TZU [ZHUANGZI]

(369–286 B.C.E.)

China

Chuang Chou, known by his honorific name of Chuang-tzu, was a native of the
state of Sung, today's Honan province. Born into an aristocratic family, Chuang-
tzu grew up in a rich tradition of learning and refinement. Nevertheless, except
for a short stint as a clerk in the local government, he declined all offers of official
positions. Chuang-tzu's noninvolvement in public affairs was in keeping with his
adherence to the Taoist principle of nondoing, which he learned from his master
Lao-tzu. As a philosopher, Chuang-tzu's major contribution was his exploration
of relativism—the idea that there are no absolute qualities, only individual

*Translated by Arthur Waley.

viewpoints. His concerns are a natural extension of the Taoist insistence on reverence for the uniqueness of all creation.

Chuang-tzu lived during the Warring States period, a time that saw the numerous small states of China consolidated into seven major kingdoms. It was in the wake of this step toward unification of the nation that the formation of the writing style known today as Classical Chinese began. The sophistication of the new style enabled Chuang-tzu to include descriptive amplifications in his narrative, in contrast to the sketchiness of the *Analects* and the *Tao-te Ching*.

In his writings, Chuang-tzu characteristically uses fictions—stories and parables—to illustrate truths. "Wandering About at Large" focuses on the theme that the world of each of us is necessarily provincial, because each person's perspective is limited. We are tempted—both as individuals and as a species—to see our world as the "real" one, but our experience determines what we know and what we can imagine. "The Identity of Things" attacks hierarchical notions of reality (that one thing is more important than another, for example, or that one being is superior to another). It also explores the flaws in our tendency to bipolar logic—the world of either/or choices: this/that, right/wrong, light/dark. All interpretation is an imposition, according to Chuang-tzu, and it has the pitfall of reducing phenomena to abstract meaning—seeing "treeness," for example, rather than the tree itself. Taoism suggests that such abstractions can cause us to lose contact with reality.

"In the World of Men" teaches us that utility is a subjective concept, not an inherent quality in things or ideas. The proper question is not, Is *x* useful? but rather, For whom is *x* useful, and when? To be useless to others, it turns out, may be quite useful to one's self, and wisdom may even reside in being useless to as many others as possible. In "Autumn Waters," the final selection, Chuang-tzu ridicules a famous ancient logician who thought he understood everything because he could reduce everything to analytical abstractions. Chuang-tzu attacks this form of knowledge as narrow and provincial. Persuasive as analytical understanding appears to be, its mode of investigation is to "take apart," whereas true knowledge, Taoists maintain, is direct and unanalytical. True understanding transcends analysis: as Lao-tzu would say, "The truth cannot be told."

Wandering About at Large

In the vast reaches of the north there is a fish named K'un: its size cannot be gauged but it is at least several thousand leagues (*li*). When transformed into a bird, its name is P'eng. P'eng's span is beyond measuring: at least several thousand leagues. When it rages, its wings are like a cloud hung from heaven. This bird, when the sea moves, migrates toward the southern reaches, called the Pool of Heaven. In the Book of Wonders many strange things are recorded: it says there that when the P'eng migrates to the southern reaches, the waters are stirred for three thousand leagues; when it beats its wings, a typhoon results, and when it rises ninety thousand leagues, it leaves behind a gale that lasts for six months. Horses in the wild, bits of dust, living things are all blown about. The blue-azure of the sky, its true color, is distorted; its remoteness and limitless horizon is distorted; from its vantage point from above, it would be as it was.

Translated by Eugene Eoyang.

Moreover, if the depths of the water are not great, then there is not buoyancy enough to float a large boat. Pour out a cup of water into a hollow in the ground, and a mustard seed will float on it; put the *cup* in the water, and it will become stuck: the water is shallow and the vessel large. If a wind lacks force, it will lack the strength to keep great wings airborne. To rise ninety thousand leagues therefore requires this kind of wind from below: only then can it be mounted. With the blue sky at its back, and nothing to stop him and nothing in his way, he heads south.

The cicada and the dove laughed and said: "We take off and dart from elm to elm: there are times when we don't make it and fall to the ground. How can anything travel south flying at ninety thousand leagues? Three meals on an outing to the country and one returns, with the belly still full; for a trip of a hundred miles, grain must be pounded the night before; and for a trip of a thousand miles, three months' provisions must be stored." What do these worms know? A little knowledge does not amount to great wisdom; a few years of life is not the same as many years of experience. How does one know? The morning-glory [literally "the morning mushroom"] knows nothing of moonrise and moonset: one season's cicada knows nothing of spring and autumn. They live only a short term. South of Ch'u, there is a tree called Ming-ling, which counts five hundred years as one spring and five hundred years as one autumn. In very ancient times, there was a great tree for which eight thousand years was one spring, and eight thousand years one autumn. Even down to the present, Peng-tsu is well-known for his longevity. If everyone were to compare themselves to him, wouldn't they feel sorry for themselves?

The questions T'ang asked of Chi say the same thing: "In the sparse wastes of the north there is a vast ocean, the Pool of Heaven, with a fish several thousand leagues wide and who knows how long, named K'un. There is also a bird named P'eng, with a back like T'ai Mountain, wings like clouds hanging down from the sky. Flapping up a whirlwind winding around like goat-horns, it rises ninety thousand leagues, breaking through the clouds, and with only the blue sky at its back, it heads toward the south, and the southern deep. The marsh quail laughed at this and said: "So what? I take off and go up for some distance before I glide down amidst weeds and brambles. This is also the ultimate in flying. So what?" Which shows the difference between the little and the great. So it is that those who know how to govern a district, to administer a region, and who have the virtues of a ruler that qualify them for leading a nation, they all regard themselves in this way. Yet, Sung Jung-tzu would have laughed at them, for though the entire world censures him, he would not have been crushed. He firmly distinguished between what he thought of himself and what the world thought of him and he clearly marked off the limits of honor and of shame. But this is as far as he went. Toward the world, he was in no way unsettled. He had not yet grounded himself firmly.

Lieh-tzu rode on the wind, and took to its airy ways, but he returned in a fortnight. In matters of his own welfare, he had no worries. Still, while this enabled him to avoid moving about on his own, he had, nevertheless, to depend on something else. Whether one depends on the processes of heaven and earth or seizes upon the shifts in the six elements, one will wander ceaselessly, and this is the evil of being dependent. Therefore, it is said that the supreme man is without self; the holy man is without merit; *the exalted man is anonymous.*

Yao wished to yield his throne to Hsü-yu and said: "When the sun and moon come out in the midst of torch fires that burn steadily, wouldn't it be difficult to see them in the glare? When seasonal rains fall, wouldn't irrigating the marshland be too much effort? Then you should take over the reins of government, for if I continue to administer the country, all I would see would be my own shortcomings. Please take over." Hsü-yu answered: "With you in charge, the country is under control; if I were to stand in your place, it would only be for vanity. But vanity is only the shadow of reality, and I would be but a shadow. The wren may build its nest in a thick forest but he uses only one branch; the tapir may drink from the stream, but only to quench his thirst. Go back, my lord, I would be of no use in government. Even if a cook is not attending to the kitchen, the master of ceremonies does not skip over the sacrificial vessels to take his place."

Chien-wu said to Lien-shu: "I have heard Chieh-yü talk. His words are big but not to the point; they wander all over the place but never hit home. I am overwhelmed by his words: they are like the stars of the Milky Way, and as numberless. But they are beside the point and have nothing to do with the world of men."

"What kind of talk?" Lien-shu asked.

"He said: 'Far away in the mountain of Ku-she, there lived a holy man. His flesh was like ice and snow, and he was as tender as a young maiden. He didn't eat five grains but inhaled the wind and imbibed the dew. He rode the cloud-drifts and mounted a flying dragon, and wandered beyond even the four seas. His intense powers spared creatures from disease and caused the crops to flourish every year.' To my mind, these words were mad, so I didn't believe them."

Lien-shu said: "Of course. A blind man cannot appreciate the sight of an elegant figure, nor a deaf man the sound of a bell and drum. Yet who's to say only the body may be afflicted with blindness and deafness? It can happen to the mind as well—as your words demonstrate! This man has the virtues of responsiveness: to comprehend a thousand things as one. Though the world calls out of its chaos, who would manage its affairs? This man cannot be harmed by things: though the floodwaters reach heaven, he would not drown. In a great drought, when metal and stone melt and the hills and mountains are scorched, he will not be hot. From his earthly remains one could fashion a Yao or a Shun, so why would he be willing to manage such things? A man of Sung, who sold ceremonial caps, went to Yüeh, but the people of Yüeh cut their hair short, and decorated their bodies, so had no use for them. Yao ruled over the people in the world, and controlled the governments within the seas, yet after, when he went to see the Four Masters in far-away Ku-she Mountain, south of the Fen River, he mourned deeply for his kingdom.

Hui-tzu said to Chuang-tzu: "The King of Wei left me a melon seed. I planted it and it grew to a size that could contain fully five gallons. With liquid in it, it was too heavy to lift. Cut in two for ladles, there was nothing that it wasn't too big for. Therefore, because it was useless, I broke it up."

Chuang-tzu said: "You are obtuse in matters concerning the importance of usefulness. There was a man of Sung who excelled at concocting an ointment for chapped hands. For generations, his family was in the business of treating silk. A stranger heard of this, and offered to buy the method for a hundred pieces of gold. Whereupon the family was convened, and they all agreed: 'For generations we have treated silk and never earned more than a few pieces of gold. Now one morning we can sell it for a hundred pieces. Give it to him.' The stranger took it and went to advise the King of Wu, who was having difficulties with Yüeh. The King of Wu sent him to command his forces. It was winter. There was a naval battle with Yüeh, and Yüeh suffered a great defeat. The conquered territories were parceled out, and he received a fiefdom. Now, the properties of the ointment were the same—whether to prevent chapped hands (which may be used to gain a fiefdom), or to treat silk. The difference lies in how you use it. Now, you have a gourd that holds five gallons: why not make a large vessel out of it, to float down the river with? Instead, you worry that it is too big. It appears you still have cobwebs in your head."

Hui-tzu said to Chuang-tzu: "I have a big tree which people call 'the tree of heaven.' Its large roots are so dense and swollen as to be beyond measuring; its small branches are so twisted that they can't be lined up with a straightedge. If it were standing in the road, a carpenter wouldn't even take notice. Now your words are equally large and useless. Which is why the multitudes pay no attention."

Chuang-tzu said: "You alone do not notice the wildcat, how it crouches low to lie in ambush for the unwary. It leaps everywhere, nothing is too high or too low until it falls into a trap and perishes in the net. Then, there is the yak—as big as a cloud dropped from heaven, really huge! But it cannot catch mice. Now, your big tree bothers you because it is useless. Why not plant it in Never-never land, in the great barren wastes, where you can stroll to and fro beside it and can lie down free and easy beneath it? It will not be axed, and it will be free from harm. What possible distress could uselessness cause?"

The Oneness of Things

Tzu-ch'i of the Southern Suburb sat at his place, leaning against a table, looking up at the sky, and sighed. Distracted, he looked as if he had lost touch. Yen-ch'eng tzu-yu was standing by, in front of him, and said, "What's this? Your body could be a withered tree, and your mind is like dead ashes. Surely the person leaning at this table today is not the same person who was leaning at this table before?"

Tzu-ch'i said, "Yen, don't you start asking. Just now, I was outside myself. Do you understand? You hear the sounds of humans, but know nothing of the sounds of the earth. Or if you have heard the sounds of the earth, you haven't heard the sounds of heaven."

Tzu-yu said: "Would you please explain that?"

Tzu-ch'i replied: "The Great Earth exhales, and it is called 'wind.' There are times when it doesn't blow. But when it does, a thousand caves will bellow. Are you the only one who has never heard the rushing of the wind? The awesome

Translated by Eugene Eoyang.

heights of the mountain forests, the hollows of huge trees—a hundred span around—are like noses, mouths, ears, goblets, bowls, puddles, pools. And the wind whistles, exclaims, sighs, howls, wails, moans, first high notes, then low notes. A light wind produces minor chords, a gale brings forth major chords. When the fierce wind blows over, all the stops are empty. Have you not noticed this in the swaying and bending of trees in the wind?"

Tzu-yu said: "The music of the earth is made through countless hollows; the music of humans is made on the pipes; may I ask about the music of the spheres?"

Tzu-ch'i said: "These melodies are all different, but every one of them is self-generated, all of them self-realized. Who is there that would initiate these sounds? Great understanding opens up; small knowledge closes in. Great discourse is limpid and clear; small discourse is petty and wordy. Asleep, the soul wanders; awake, the body is set free. Associations mean involvement, and every day one mind contends with another. There are hesitations, inhibitions, and qualms. Small fears are annoying; large fears disturbing. Some set out like a mechanical contrivance with the function of making out what is from what is not; others maintain themselves with alliance pacts, taking charge to keep up their superiority. Some decay and die as in autumn and winter, while their words daily diminish; others sink so far that they cannot come back again. Some are repressed, as if all bound up; their words outdated, like a dried-up moat, their hearts edging toward death, incapable of regeneration.

Joy and outrage, sorrow and happiness, anxiety and relief, flexibility and firmness, sedateness and agitation—these express our moods. Music derives from the void, and moisture produces mushrooms. Day and night alternate with each other and no one knows from whence they sprout. Oh, my! Dawn and dusk bear this out: if we ask their origin. Without them, there is no *I*; and without an *I*, there is nothing to experience them. This is very near to the truth, but we do not know what makes it so. If this is the reality of things, it would be difficult to solve their mysteries. I believe this reality to be possible, but I cannot see its manifestations. It exists, but without form. The hundred joints, the nine apertures (eyes, ears, nose, mouth, nostrils, etc.), the six organs (heart, liver, spleen, lungs, kidneys, etc.) all coexist together. Which one am I most attached to? Which would you say? Their existence is an internal matter: as if all were functionaries. These functionaries are not up to governing themselves, and take turns as governor and governed, and thus retain true governance. Whether you find the reality or do not find it, it does not matter, for reality itself is unaffected. Once the parts are in place, they operate without interruption to the very end. Whether on edge with each other, or working smoothly together, the process exhausts itself like a runaway horse that cannot be stopped. Isn't this a shame? To sweat and strain all one's life, with no sign of accomplishment; blithely working oneself to death and not know to what end one is working toward, is this not pitiful? One may say: 'there is no death' but to what purpose? When the body wears out, the spirit goes with it. How can this not be called sad? Is the life of man so thoughtless? Or am I alone so blithe when everyone else is not?

Men are influenced by what they think: Who alone is not so influenced? And not only those who know the ups and downs and who think for themselves: fools also have such thoughts and influences. To not have such thoughts about what is and what is not, is like going to Yüeh today and arriving there yesterday. It would be like making something that isn't, is. To make something that isn't—though one had the powers of the sage Yü—would be impossible to know. How could I know it, then?

Words are not mere wind: words have something to say; what they say, however, is not absolute. So, do words exist? Or don't they? There are those who distinguish words from the chirping of birds. Some see a difference there and some see no difference at all.

How can the Tao be both obscure to the perceptions and distinguishable as true and false? How can words be obscure and real or unreal? How can the Tao be past and yet not present? How can words be present and not possible? The Tao is obscured by small-mindedness. Words are obscured by vain-gloriousness. Thus, the "right" and "wrong" of the Confucians and the Mohists.[1] What one calls "right" the other considers "wrong": and what one calls "wrong," the other considers "right." If one wishes to make "right" the other's "wrong," and to make "wrong" the other's "right," there is nothing better than insight.

There is nothing that is not object (a "that"), and nothing that is not subject (a "this"). The self does not see itself as the "other"; the self, however, knows the "other." Which is why it is said: " 'That' derives from 'this'; and 'this' also proceeds from 'that.' " Which is saying that "this" and "that" arise from each other. Where there is life there is death; where there is death, there is life. Where there is possibility, there is also impossibility, and where there is impossibility, there is possibility. Because reality exists, so too unreality; and if unreality exists, so does reality. Existence in the eyes of the sage is not seen this way, but in the light of eternity, the truth is determined. For "this" is also "that," and "that" is also "this." According to "that" there is a true and false; according to "this" there is a true and false. Thus, there is a "that" and a "this": or is there no "that" and no "this"? To resist opposing "that" and "this" is the very point of the Tao. This point is the center of a sphere of innumerable mutual influences. The "trues" are as numberless as the "untrues." Which is why it is better to use insight. To point to something that is to illustrate something that is not is not as good as to point to something which is not to illustrate what is not. To use a horse to illustrate what isn't a horse, isn't as good as using what isn't a horse to illustrate that a horse is not something else. All creation is an index; everything is a horse.

The possible is possible; the impossible impossible. The Tao follows this course to achieve its purpose. Things are merely labeled to be so. But do they exist? That which exists, exists. Or do they not exist? That which is nonexistent does not exist. Things which are, therefore, exist; things which are, therefore, are possible. Nonexistent things do not exist; nonexistent things are not possible. Which is why a rafter and a pillar, ugliness and the beauty Hsi Shih, greatness,

---

1. The Mohists formed a school that followed the precepts of Mo-tzu, a contemporary of Confucius who preached a doctrine of universal love, and who based his teachings on the concept of righteousness (i)—whereas Confucius based his ethics on the concept of relatedness (jen). From the fifth century to the third century B.C.E., the Mohists constituted the bitterest rivals of the Confucian school.

cunning, craftiness, strangeness, in the scheme of the Tao, are all one. Individualities comprise the whole; but the whole diminishes them. All things—incomplete or diminished—can yet be regarded as one. Only those with transcendent wisdom can see through to things as one. Reality is not used but seen from the multiplicity of things. This multiplicity has its "uses"; these "uses" are effective; this "effectiveness" is successful. When success is achieved, the ultimate is reached. When the ultimate is reached, and one doesn't know what it is, we call it the Tao.

To work the spirit and the mind as one, and not know they are identical, is like "three in the morning." What is "three in the morning"? A keeper of monkeys, distributing acorns, said: "Only three acorns and four at night." The monkeys were incensed. "Well, then," he said, "You'll have four in the morning and three at night." At this, the monkeys were well pleased. What one calls reality has no consequences on the reality, but does affect the response, whether of anger or satisfaction. The cause for this is subjectivity.

The sage accommodates himself to reality and nonreality, abides by the scales of Heaven. This is called the two-fold path.

The knowledge of the ancients was ultimate. How? They were not yet aware that things existed. That was ultimate and exhaustive, and could not be improved upon. Then they recognized the existence of things, but had yet to make distinctions between them. Finally, they began to make distinctions, but had yet to distinguish between reality and unreality. When reality and nonreality appear, the Tao is undermined. As the Tao fails, so the affections succeed. Now, is this success and this failure real? Or are they unreal? If this success and failure are real, then Chao-wen plays the lute; and if they aren't, he doesn't play. Chao-wen's lute, Shih-kuang's baton, Hui-tzu's rhetoric: their knowledge—all three—was incomparable, and each excelled in an art which he practiced to the end of his life. Because they loved their art, they were different from others. And because they loved their art, they wanted to make it clear to others. But they were not enlightened as a result of their efforts. Which is why one ends up with obscure abstractions as hardness (in a stone) and whiteness (in a horse). His son played with Chao-wen's instruments all his life, and all his life never realized anything. If this can be called realization, than I am also realized; but if this cannot be called realization, then everything, including me, remains unrealized. Therefore the glimmerings out of chaos are valued by the Sage. He doesn't use reality but derives what is called insight from within the multitude of things.

Now, there are words, like these. I don't know if they are of the same order as that which is real. Perhaps they are not of the same order. Of, and not of, the same order. They may be of the same order, but they may be different from the other nonentities. Never mind. Let's try these words: There was a beginning; there was a time before the beginning began; there was a time before the beginning of a beginning of a time before the beginning. There is existence; there is nonexistence. There is a time before existence and nonexistence; there was a time before the time before there was nonexistence. When, all of a sudden, nonexistence came into being, no one knew whether the roots of nonexistence lay in existence or nonexistence. Now, though I have just said something, I do not know whether what I have said really said something, or whether it said nothing. In all the world, nothing is as big as the tip of a wisp in autumn, and Mount T'ai is small. There's no one older than a child who is short-lived and Peng-tsu is young. The universe and I were both created at the same time, and the multitude of things and I are one. But, if they are one, what about words? If you consider those things as one, they are not words. The one with words would make two. Two and one would make three. And so it goes. If skilled mathematicians are not up to this, how about ordinary people? Thus, from nonexistence proceeding to existence, one reaches three, what would happen if one proceeded from existence to existence? Let's not proceed. Let's stop here.

The Tao existed before there were distinctions, and words existed before posterity. To cope with reality, demarcations were set up. And words indicated those demarcations. There is a "left" and there is a "right"; there are "discussions" and there are "deliberations"; there are "distinctions" and there are "discriminations"; there are "contentions" and there are "rivalries." These are the so-called "eight propositions." Things outside the universe, the sage allows but does not discuss. Things within the universe, the sage discusses but does not decide. In the *Ch'un Ch'iu,* which documents history and the annals of ancient kings, the sages discussed but did not dispute. True, there are distinguishable things, but there are also things not distinguishable, as there are things that can't be discriminated.

"How is that?"

"The sage comprehends the thing itself, while the common man contrasts things with each other. Which is why it is said that the one who makes distinctions does not see. Thus, the great Tao is inexpressible; the great distinctions are beyond words; great virtue is in not being virtuous. Great modesty is not humble; great courage is not bold. The Tao on display is not the Tao; words that split hairs do not see to the heart of the matter. Constant benevolence fails. Flagrant modesty will not be believed. Presumptuous courage will not succeed. These five attributes seem to be round, but tend toward being square. Therefore, wisdom that stops at what it does not know is the highest wisdom."

Who knows the distinction that cannot be expressed, the Way that cannot be expressed, the Way that cannot be followed? If there is such a one who possesses this knowledge, then he holds what is called the "storehouse of the heavens"— which may be replenished but is never full, drained but never empty, the source for which is unknown. This is called "the light within."

Long ago, Yao asked Shun: "I wish to attack Tsung, Kuei, and Hsü-ao in the south, but I can't figure out why? Can you tell me?"

Shun said: "Those are three backwater countries. It's no wonder you can't explain it. Long ago, ten suns emerged among the multitude of things, and shone on everything. By how much does the radiance of virtue exceed these suns?"

Yeh-Chüeh asked Wang I: "Do you know in what way things are identical?"

"How should I know?"

"Do you know those things which you don't know?"

"How should I know?"

"Then, how about the ignorance of things?"

"How should I know?" came the reply once again, "but let me try this: How do I know that what I think I know isn't something I don't know? How do I know that what I think I don't know isn't really something I really do know? Now, let me ask you this: people who sleep in the damp end up half-dead, with an ache in their back—but what about the mudfish? To live in the trees is perilous and precarious,—but what about a monkey? Now, of these three, who has the right idea of a place to live? Men feed on the flesh of herbivores; deer feed on autumn grass; centipedes find locusts tasty; owls relish mice. Of the four, who knows how to eat? Monkeys cohabit with monkeys; buck with doe; mudfish sport with other fish. Men find Mao Ch'iang, or "the beautiful concubine," attractive: but fish would dive for the deep at the sight of her, birds would head for the skies, and deer would dart away for dear life. Of these four, who knows what beauty is? The way I see it, the principles of righteousness and benevolence, the path of right and wrong, is a morass of confusion—how can I possibly know the difference?"

Yeh-Chüeh said: "If you do not know what is good or bad, then must it be that the perfect man also does not know?"

Wang I said: "The Perfect Man is superhuman: when the great marshes are scorched, he is not burned; when the great waterways freeze over, he feels no cold; when the mountains are split asunder by bolts of lightning, and the seas tremble in the typhoon, he is not frightened. Such a man rides the clouds, mounts the sun and the moon, and wanders beyond the four seas. Death and life have no effect on him, so how can notions of good and bad?"

Chü-chüeh-tzu asked Ch'ang-wu-tzu: "I have heard the Masters say, 'The exalted man does not concern himself with the affairs of the world, he does not achieve rewards, nor avoid penalties; he is not curious to find out; nor does he explain the ineffable. He has no utterance for what can be expressed, but he can communicate the inexpressible.' Thus, he roams beyond the reach of the dirt and dust of this world. The Master considered this idle talk, but I consider it the workings of the mysterious Tao. I ask you, what do you think?"

Ch'ang-wu-tzu said: "The Yellow Emperor himself would hear these words with skepticism, so how could you expect Confucius to understand them? Besides, you jump to conclusions: you see an egg and look for a cock to crow; you see a cross-bow and envision a duck roasting on a spit. Let me try out a few conjectures on you, which I want you to consider as conjecture. How does one stand by the sun and moon and hold the universe in one's hands? The one who does, relates one thing to another, puts aside chaos and confusion, and treats menials on a par. The ordinary man shifts about, while the sage is ingenuous. Ten thousand years are as one, pure and simple; ten thousand things pursue their course, and exist together. How do I know that love of life is not an illusion? How do I know that fearing death isn't like the lost soul weeping because he cannot find the way home? "Beautiful concubine" was the daughter of Ai, the border guard. When she was captured by Chin, tears flowed onto her dress but when she arrived at the palace, and shared the royal couch, and ate the most sumptuous food, she then wondered why she had wept at all. How do I know that the dead do not regret their first quest for life? Those who dream of getting drunk may end up by morning in tears; those who dream of crying and sobbing may find themselves hunting in the fields when day breaks. In a dream, one is not aware one is dreaming; indeed, one can even interpret a dream in the midst of the dream. Only when awake does one know one has been dreaming. Maybe there will be one day a great awakening at which we will realize that this life has been one great dream. Fools think they are awake, and know it with insistence, whether prince or pauper. Confucius and you are both part of a dream; when I say you are part of a dream, I am also dreaming. These assertions are paradoxical: thousands of generations from now, a great sage will appear and explain them in a day.

Suppose you and I argue; you win out instead of me; is your argument right, mine wrong? Or, suppose I win out instead of you, is my argument right and yours wrong? Must one be right and the other wrong? Or can both be right, or both wrong? You and I cannot reach any agreement, so meanwhile people are left in the dark. Who should I get to set things right? If I choose someone who agrees with you as the arbiter, then he will agree with you in his judgment, so how can he be fair? And if I choose one who agrees with me as arbiter, then he will agree with me, so how can he be fair? And, if I choose someone who disagrees with both you and me, then he will differ from both of us, so how can he be fair in judging between us? And, if I choose someone who agrees with both you and me, then he will agree with both of us, so how can he judge between us in all fairness? As a result, you, I, everyone cannot come to understand each other, and wait for someone else. What is the so-called "harmony with the workings of heaven"? Let us consider: "We have 'is' and 'is not,' 'right' and 'not right'; but if 'is' exists, then the opposite of 'is' must be 'is not' and there is no distinction. If there is a 'right' then the opposite of 'right' must be 'not right,' and there would be no distinction. The mutual dependency of changing sounds, if they do not depend on each other, is said to "harmonize with the workings of heaven." Because of this, one can live out the years in boundless fulfillment. Forget the years, forget notions of right and wrong, and you will establish yourself in the realm of the infinite."

Shade asked shadow: "Before, you moved about, now you stay still; before, you sat down, now you get up. Why are you so shiftless and lacking in purpose?"

Shadow replied: "My existence depends on the existence of something else; that on which my existence depends itself depends on something else. My dependence is like the skin shed by a snake, or the wings of a cicada. How do I know what will happen? How do I know when something will not happen?"

Once Chuang Chou dreamed he was a butterfly, fluttering happily about like a butterfly. It did not know it was Chuang Chou. Suddenly it awoke and realized it was Chou. Now, we don't know whether it was Chou dreaming he was a butterfly in his dream, or a butterfly now dreaming it was Chou. There must be a difference between Chou and the butterfly: this is the so-called "transformation of things."

from *In the World of Men*

[The Usefulness of Trees]

A carpenter named Shih went to the kingdom of Chi: when he reached Ch'ü-yüan he saw an oak tree used as an altar: its girth was wide enough to hide oxen; it

Translated by Eugene Eoyang.

spanned a hundred cubits, its height approached the mountains; at eighty feet, the branches spread out, a score or more, each the size of a small boat. Crowds milled around it, but the master carpenter didn't give it any notice, and went on without stopping. His apprentice stared his fill and, catching up to Carpenter Shih, said: "Since I picked up the axe and followed in your service, I have never seen a piece of wood to match this tree. Why does the Master walk right by without glancing at it even for a moment?"

"That's enough. Don't waste your breath. That's a worthless piece of wood. If you made a boat out of it, it would sink; if you made a coffin, it would rot in no time; if you made furniture out of it, it would collapse on the spot; if you made a door, the sap would seep through; if you made a pillar, it would be worm-eaten. It's a completely worthless piece of wood, and because it is so useless, it has lived so long."

Later, when Carpenter Shih had returned home, the oak tree appeared to him in a dream: "Why do you make comparisons with me? Are you comparing me with 'usable' trees? Like the pear, the orange, the grapefruit, and all species of fruit-bearing plants? When the fruit ripens, they are stripped and treated ignominiously: first, the big branches are cut, and the little branches are pulled off. Thus the value of the trees embitters their life, they are not allowed to live out their heaven-ordained years, are cut off midway in their life span. They bring upon themselves the mutilation and abuse of the mob. There is nothing that this does not apply to. So I cultivated uselessness for a long time. Near death now, I have reached this state, and that is of great use to me. Let us suppose I were useful, do you think I would have attained such a size as this? Besides, you and I are both things. By what right does one thing judge another? And what does a worthless mortal fellow like you know about a worthless tree like me?"

When Carpenter Shih woke up, he tried to interpret the dream. His disciple said: "If the tree were so set on being useless, then why is it a sacred tree?"

"If secrets have no words, that also must have just happened, since the tree did not know itself as being free from harm and injury. If it were not an altar, would it not have been cut down? Thus its manner of survival was different from that of others, and to compare its disposition with those would be wide of the mark."

Tzu-ch'i of Nan-po was travelling in the mountains of Shang, when he saw a big tree of extraordinary size. A thousand chariot teams could be sheltered in its shade. Tzu-ch'i said: "What kind of tree is this? It must yield an extraordinary amount of wood. Then he looked up and saw the smaller branches all gnarled and twisted, totally unfit for rafters or beams. Looking down, he saw the great roots of the tree, too pliant and supple to make good wood for coffins. He licked the leaves, and his mouth burned and hurt. He sniffed at it, and it made one drunk for fully three days. Tzu-ch'i said: "This tree is not so useful, after all. And because of this, it has attained to such size. Ah! the wise man is useless in the same way."

In the state of Sung, there is a region called Ching-shih, where the catalpa, the cedar, and the mulberry flourish. But those that grow above a few spans are used for monkey posts; they are cut; those of three or four yards are cut down to make roofbeams; those of seven or eight yards, are cut down to make sideboards for the coffins of the aristocrats. As a result they never live out their alloted life-span, and are axed in their prime. This is the calamity of being useful. Thus in the book of Chieh, cows with white faces, pigs with upturned snouts, men with piles were all taboo, and could not be used as offerings to the river. This was known to the shamans, so they considered these things ill-fated. But to the sage, on the other hand, these things were blessed.

There was a deformed man without limbs named Shu, whose chin hung over his navel, whose shoulders were higher than his head, whose top-knot pointed skyward; his viscera were in the upper half of his body, and his thigh-bones were his ribs. By sharpening needles, and by washing clothes, he eked out a living. By winnowing grains of rice, he was able to support ten or more people. When soldiers were conscripted, this misshapen man bared his arms along with the others; when there was great effort required, because he was subject to so many maladies, the burden of the work was never placed on him. But when provisions were distributed, he would receive three bushels of grain and ten bundles of firewood. With his deformity, Shu was still able to take care of his body, and live out his years: how much more than if he were crippled in mind!

Confucius went to Ch'u. There was a madman named Chieh-yü who passed by his door, saying: "Oh phoenix, oh phoenix, that virtue has fallen on such hard times! The world of tomorrow is beyond waiting for, and the world of yesterday cannot be dismissed. When the Tao prevails, the sage achieves his purpose; when the Tao fails, the sage merely survives. Nowadays, he barely escapes punishment. The joys of life are as light as a feather, but no one knows how to keep them going; the calamities of life are as heavy as earth, yet no one knows how to avert them. Enough of this! Approaching men with notions of virtue, watch out, watch out! to mark out the way and rush on ahead. False light, false light, do not mislead me in my journey. My path is erratic; do not injure my steps. Mountain trees undermine themselves; grease-fires consume themselves; the cassia is edible, and for that is cut down; the lacquer tree is useful, so it is scarred with a knife. Everybody knows the use of the useful, but no one knows the use of the useless."

from *Autumn Waters*

[The Boundaries of Knowing and Not Knowing]

Kung-sun Lung asked Wei-mou: "When I was young I learned the wisdom of former kings; when I was older, I could understand the workings of selflessness and right-mindedness, relate similarity to dissimilarity, distinguish between "hardness" and "whiteness," what is and what is not, possibility and impossibility; I struggled through the teachings of the hundred schools, and exhausted the subtleties of innumerable points of view. I thought I had reached the ultimate. Now, I hear Chuang-tzu's words and I am lost and bewildered. I don't know if my arguments are inadequate, or my understanding is awry, but it seems I have nothing to say. Would you explain this?"

Translated by Eugene Eoyang.

Prince Mou leaned on his bench, heaved a sigh, looked up toward heaven, and laughed. He said: "Have you never heard of the frog who lived in a shallow well. Talking to the turtle of the Eastern Sea, he said: "How happy I am! I hop out onto the railing of the well, then go in for a rest whenever I want into the crevices where a brick is missing; when I go in the water, it comes up to my haunches and holds up my chin; when I slip into the mud, my feet are covered and my ankles disappear. When I look at small crabs and tadpoles, they can't do what I can, for I have the waters of this ditch all to myself, and can enjoy the pleasures of the well. This is the greatest! Why don't you come and look for yourself?"

The turtle of the Eastern Sea had hardly put his left foot in when his right knee got caught. Whereupon, he drew back and began telling about the sea: "A thousand leagues wouldn't be enough to measure its vastness; a thousand yards wouldn't be enough to plumb its depths. In the days of Yü, when it flooded nine years out of ten, its water level did not rise; in the days of T'ang, when there was drought seven years out of eight, its shoreline did not recede. No pushing or shifting, for a moment or for long, no matter how much the tide advances and recedes—this is the great joy of the Eastern Sea. When the frog heard this, he was suddenly stupefied, and found himself at a loss. How you are at the boundaries of knowing and not-knowing, right and wrong, and still you look askance at Chuang-tzu's words. This is like making a gnat shoulder a mountain, or a millipede race the river. That won't do!"

"The detailed and subtle discussions on knowing and not-knowing will provide an advantage for a time—but isn't it like the frog in the broken-down well? Whereas the other [Chuang-tzu] is just now walking about in the Yellow Springs [the underworld] or ascending into heaven. For him, there is no south, no north, he is free in every direction: he is awash in the bottomless depths; with no east, no west, he starts out with dark mysteries, and ends up with great insight. You come blithely along and analyze him for petty points! Isn't this like looking at the sky through a straw or pointing to the earth with an awl? Those things are too small! Off with you! Or, haven't you heard of the youngest children of Shou-ling, who were learning to walk in Han-tan: but before they went home, they had lost the knack, so they had to crawl back on their hands and knees. Now, if you don't go, you may forget what you knew before, and lose your means of livelihood."

Kung-sun Lung's mouth was wide open and would not close, his tongue was stuck and would not come loose. There and then, he withdrew and walked away.

ANONYMOUS (THIRD CENTURY B.C.E.)
China

Consisting of thirty-three books, each on an individual state, *Intrigues of the Warring States [Chan-kuo Ts'e]* records, or rather recreates, the major events during the Warring States period (403–221 B.C.E.). The stories were first recorded during the third century B.C.E., although the text that has come down to us is the product of later editing during the Western Han and Northern Sung periods.

With several states waging deadly wars and treacherous diplomacy against each other, the Warring States period saw the decline of feudal patriotism—the system of loyalties that had provided political stability during the preceding Chou Dynasty. Scholars no longer dutifully served their own state, wandering instead from one state to the next, offering their expertise in statecraft to the highest bidder. The eloquent Su Ch'in, in the selection from the *Book of Yen,* was such a figure. With other scholars, however, feudal patriotism died hard. Among these was Ching K'o, whose abortive attempt to assassinate the King of Ch'in, the archenemy of his native state, has remained for centuries the model for heroic self-sacrifice.

A hallmark of this historic work is its extensive use of dialogues, such as the one between Su-Ch'in and the King of Yen. Also characteristic is a penchant for parables, many of which, frequently alluded to by later writers, have furnished expressions and aphorisms still current in everyday Chinese conversation. In a literary tradition where the demarcation between history and fiction was never clear-cut, *Intrigues of the Warring States* exerted a strong influence on later narratives.

from Intrigues of the Warring States [Chan-kuo Ts'e]

THE BOOK OF CH'I

[Lord Meng-ch'ang Is Persuaded to Keep His Retainer]

Lord Meng-ch'ang had a retainer he was not too happy with and he wanted to get rid of him. But Lu (Chung-)lien said to Lord Meng-ch'ang: "If apes and monkeys left the woods and took to the water, they would not be the equals of fish and turtles; for passing through rugged terrain and for climbing cliffs, thousand-league horses are not as good as the fox. When Ts'ao Mei flashed his three-foot sword, an army couldn't subdue him; but take the three-foot sword away, put a hoe in his hands, let him live with farmers in the field, and he wouldn't be even as good as a farmer. If strengths are abandoned in favor of shortcomings, then Yao himself would be found inadequate. Now if we force someone to do something he can't and call him incompetent; if we teach someone who cannot understand and call him dense; and because of their stupidity get rid of them, and because of their incompetence, abandon them, we will have removed any means of communicating with the rejected and the abandoned, and they will come back seeking revenge. This, surely, wouldn't be the example you would want to set for the world, would it?"

Lord Meng-ch'ang said: "All right, then," and he did not send the man away.

Translated by Eugene Eoyang.

[Feng Hsuan Provides Loyalty for Lord Meng-ch'ang]

There was a man of Ch'i named Feng Hsuan who was so poor he couldn't support himself, so he sent word to Lord Meng-ch'ang that he wished to serve as his attendant. Lord Meng-ch'ang said: "What ambitions does he have?"

"No ambitions," came the reply.

"What abilities?"

"No abilities," he was told. Lord Meng-ch'ang then laughed, and received him, saying: "Alright."

The staff assumed that their lord did not think much of the newcomer, so they fed him the humblest fare. He stayed for a while, then, leaning on a post, stroking his longsword, he sang a song with these words: "Longsword! Let's go home! Not even a fish in our meals." The staff reported this to Lord Meng-ch'ang, who said: "Feed him as a guest of the court." He stayed for a while, and then once again he stroked his sword, and sang this song: "Longsword! Let's go home! We don't even have a chariot to ride out in!" The retainers all laughed and reported this to Lord Meng-ch'ang, who said: "Give him a chariot, like those of the others!" Thereupon, he mounted his chariot, raised his sword, and passing among his friends, he would say: "Lord Meng-ch'ang treats me like a guest!" But, after a while, once again he stroked his sword and sang: "Longsword! Let's go home! I'm not treated as one of them!" The staff began to hate him, for they thought him grasping and insatiable. Lord Meng-ch'ang asked: "Does he have a family?"

"A mother," came the reply.

Lord Meng-ch'ang sent someone to her with provisions, so that she would never go hungry. And after that, Feng Hsuan never sang his song again.

Some time later, Lord Meng-ch'ang issued a proclamation, asking if there were any among his retainers with experience handling accounts who could collect revenues in the region of Hsieh. Feng Hsuan replied that he could. Lord Meng-ch'ang marveled at this: "Who is this?" he asked.

"He is the one who sang to his sword that they should go home," said the retainers.

Lord Meng-ch'ang laughed: "So he can do something after all! I have been remiss and haven't taken much notice of him." He then asked Feng Hsuan to step forward and addressed him, apologetically: "I have been much occupied, vexed by worries, and have become abstracted and inattentive: I am swamped by affairs of state, and therefore have treated you most reprehensibly. Yet, you are not offended, and are even willing to collect revenues for me in the region of Hsieh?"

Feng Hsuan replied: "Yes, I am."

So he prepared his cart and arranged his baggage, taking along the tax records. As he left, he said: "When I have finished collecting the tax revenue, is there anything you would like me to bring back for you?"

Lord Meng-ch'ang said: "Take a look around, and see if I need anything."

Feng Hsuan hurried to Hsieh, sent out messengers calling everyone to straighten out their accounts. When the accounts had all been settled, he announced a mythical edict which returned all the revenue back to the people, and burned the records. At this, the people all cheered.

Feng hurried back to Ch'i, and asked for an audience early in the morning. Lord Meng-ch'ang wondered at his quickness, put on his ceremonial robes, and gave him an audience:

"Did you collect the revenues? How comes it that you've returned so quickly?"

"The revenues have been collected," came the reply.

"And what have you brought back for me?"

Feng Hsuan said: "You asked me to bring back whatever I thought you seem to need. I concluded that in your palace, since there was an abundance of wealth, stables teeming with horses and dogs, beautiful women of every rank, that what you lacked was loyalty. I therefore took it upon myself to secure loyalty for you."

Lord Meng-ch'ang said: "And where is this loyalty?"

"Now, you have the territory of Hsieh, but you do not much care for its people, which is why you exploit them. I proclaimed a mythical edict from you, which released the people from their tax obligation, and burned the records. The populace all cheered. This is how I secured loyalty for you."

Lord Meng-ch'ang was not happy about this, but he said: "Alright. You may go."

A full year later, the King of Ch'i called Lord Meng-ch'ang and told him: "I cannot afford to continue in my service a minister of my predecessor." So Lord Meng-ch'ang left the country for Hsieh: he had not gone one hundred leagues before the people, holding their old folk up, and with their children in tow, all turned out to welcome him as he came down the road. At the end of the day, Lord Meng-ch'ang looked up Feng Hsuan: "Sir, the loyalty which you secured for me I saw for myself today."

Feng Hsuan said: "The crafty hare has three burrows, to avoid being killed. Now, we have but one burrow. It isn't time yet to sit down and relax. Let me dig out a second burrow."

Lord Meng-ch'ang conferred upon him fifty chariots, five hundred catties[1] of gold, and with it, he journeyed west to Liang. There, he said to King Hui: "The kingdom of Ch'i has just released its great minister Lord Meng-ch'ang, and he is now free to serve someone else. Whoever secures his services will be prosperous and mighty in arms."

Immediately, the King of Liang vacated a high post by making his minister a general, and sent an envoy with a thousand vessels of gold and a hundred carts to offer to Lord Meng-ch'ang. But Feng Hsuan rushed there first to forewarn Lord Meng-ch'ang. "A thousand vessels of gold is quite a treasure; a hundred carts is no small caravan. Ch'i should hear of this."

The Liang emissary approached Lord Meng-ch'ang three times, but each time Lord Meng-ch'ang adamantly refused their offer to go back with them. The King of Ch'i heard of it, and both he and his ministers were nervous and apprehensive. They sent the Assistant Grand Tutor with an offer of a thousand catties of gold, two beautifully tooled chariots, a formal ceremonial sword, and a letter, in which he apologized to Lord Meng-ch'ang in these words: "I am terribly unfortunate, bedeviled by evil spirits haunting my ancestral temples and surrounded by toadies

---

1. A Chinese pound.

for ministers. We have committed offenses against you, which I cannot allow. Would you consider looking after the ancestral temples of the former kings? Would you come back now and govern the people?"

Feng Hsuan advised Lord Meng-ch'ang: "Ask him to place the sacred vessels of the former kings in ancestral temples set up in Hsieh."

When the temples were completed, Feng Hsuan reported to Lord Meng-ch'ang: "The three burrows are now finished, sir. You may now relax and enjoy yourself."

That Lord Meng-ch'ang was able to serve as minister for several decades without the slightest mishap befalling him was due largely to the foresight of Feng Hsuan.

[King Hsuan Learns About Fear]

King Hsuan of Ching (Ch'u) asked his assembled ministers: "I hear that the people in the North fear Chao Hsi-hsu. Is that true?" The assembled ministers kept silent, all except Chiang Yi, who said: "The tiger hunts all the animals for food, but when he caught a fox, the fox said: 'You dare not eat me. The almighty has made me leader of all the animals. If you eat me now, you will be violating the will of Heaven. Now if you don't believe, come with me and we'll see, with me in front and you behind. You will see that when all the animals see us, no one will dare to face us; they will run away.' "

The tiger wondered about this, so he followed him. When the animals saw them, indeed, they all ran away. The tiger did not know that the animals feared him: he thought it was the fox. Now, your majesty's territory spans some five thousand leagues, and you have a million soldiers who bear arms for you, which you have delegated to Chao Hsi-hsu. This is why the northern regions fear Hsi-hsu. What they really fear is your majesty's army, in the same way that the animals were all actually afraid of the tiger."

THE BOOK OF CH'U

[A Rogue Becomes a Lord]

Chuang Hsin said to King Hsiang of Ch'u: "Your majesty has Marquis Chou on his left, and Marquis Hsia on his right; in your entourage are Lord Yen-ling and Lord Shou-ling. Since all they do is to indulge in wanton pleasures, and no one looks after how well the country is governed, Ying (the capital of Ch'u) is in peril."

King Hsiang said: "You are a contrary old rogue! Do you want to wish misfortune on Ch'u?"

Chuang Hsin said: "I merely report honestly the way things really are: I wouldn't dare wish ill-fortune on this country. But if your majesty indulges these four men without let-up, then the state of Ch'u is doomed. I request permission to repair to Chao, where I can wait and watch."

He stayed there five months. In that time, Ch'in moved against the territories of Yen, the city of Ying (the capital of Ch'u), the regions of Wu, Shang Tsai, and

Ch'en. King Hsiang took cover in Ch'eng-yang, whereupon he sent messengers to seek out Chuang Hsin in Chao. Chuang Hsin agreed to come. When he arrived, King Hsiang said: "I was not able to follow your advice, so that now, things have come to this. What shall I do?"

Chuang Hsin replied: "I have heard folk say, 'When the hare is spotted, it's still not too late to send the hound; when sheep have strayed off, it's not too late to repair the pen.' I have heard that in times past, T'ang and Wu flourished with a hundred leagues, while Chieh and Chou came to nought even with everything under the sun. Now, although Ch'u is small, if you take the long and short of it, it still extends several thousand leagues. And what's wrong with even a hundred?

Haven't you seen the dragonfly, with his six legs, four wings, darting and hovering between heaven and earth, diving down to peck on mosquitoes for food, soaring upward for sweet dew to drink? He thinks himself free from calamity, and has no conflict with man. He does not know that a boy, scarce four feet tall, is dabbing honey on some sticky string, and will bring him down from twenty feet and above to become food for ants. But, after all, what's a small thing like a dragonfly?

The yellow sparrow, for example, dips down to peck at grain, perches upon a branch of a luxuriant tree, flaps his wings and flies off. He thinks himself free from calamity, and has no conflict with man. He does not know that a young prince, with bird-shot in his left hand and pellets in his right, will bring him down from a height of nearly sixty feet, and does not know that decoys will lure him to his death. Flying among the trees in the morning, in no time he will end up a tasty dish at night, when he falls into the hands of a young prince. But, after all, what's a small thing like a sparrow?

Consider the yellow crane, who roams the rivers and oceans, and dwells in a great swamp, diving down for eel and carp, and reaching up for chestnuts and tasty shoots. He flaps his six pinions and glides on thin air, banking here and there, soaring high on the wind. He thinks himself free from calamity, and has no conflict with man. He doesn't know that an archer is sharpening his shaft, arranging his black bow, and adjusting his retrieving line, all designed to bring him down from more than five hundred feet, where, struck by the arrow, and pulled by the line, he is brought down from thin air. Roaming the rivers and streams in the morning, he falls into a boiling pot by night. But, after all, what's a small thing like a yellow crane?

So let us take the case of the Marquis Tsai-ling: he traveled in the south around the high range, climbed Mount Wu in the north, drank from the streams of Ju-ch'i, and tasted the fish of the Hsiang river. Here he embraces young girls, there he sports with old favorites, gallivanting about in the middle of Kao-ts'ai, with no concern for affairs of state. Little does he know that Tzu-fa has received orders from King Hsuan to bring him to court, bound with the vermilion cord. But, after all, what's a small thing like the troubles of Marquis Ling?

Your majesty's affair, for example, involves Marquis Chou on the one side and Marquis Hsia on the other, and Prince Yen-ling and Prince Shou-ling in attendance: they feed off the grain collected from the fiefs, carry away gold tribute from all directions, and go off gallivanting in Yun-meng [a district in Hupei province]. They do not attend to affairs of state. Little do they know that Marquis Jang has already received an order from the King of Ch'in to cut off the Min pass, to strand the King of Ch'u outside."

King Hsiang, when he heard this, turned pale and trembled with fear. Whereupon he then and there grasped his sceptre and enfeoffed Chuang Hsin with the title, Lord of Yang-ling, and gave him the region of Huai-pei.

[Loyalty Is Sometimes Punished]

There was a man who hated Su Ch'in and said to the King of Yen: "Lord Wu-an (i.e., Su Ch'in), is the most faithless man in the empire. Your majesty has equipped him with ten thousand chariots, honored him at court, as if to proclaim to all the world that you prefer the company of small people."

When Lord Wu-an came back from Ch'i, the King of Yen would not give him hospitality. He addressed the King of Yen: "I was a mere rustic from Eastern Chou (Tung Chou) when I first met you, without a thing to commend me, yet you welcomed me from the outside, and singled me out within your palace. Now that I have served you, Sir, as minister, annexed ten cities, shored up a faltering state, you won't even listen to me. It must be because someone has spoken to you against me behind my back, claiming that I am disloyal. If what I do is disloyal, it is unfortunate for you, for ministers as loyal as Wei-sheng, as upright as Po Yi, as devoted as Tseng Shen, three of the noblest models, could hardly serve you, could they?"

"And why not?"

"If I were that kind of minister, I'd hardly serve you," Su Ch'in said, "for as devoted as Tseng Shen was, he would never leave his parents for even one night abroad, so how could I have gone to Ch'i? If I were as upright as Po Yi, I couldn't accept the fruits of indolence, and would consider even fealty to King Wu demeaning: I would not serve him but leave the lord of Ku-chu and starve to death alone in the mountains of Shou-yang. Would anyone so upright have been willing, as I was, to travel a thousand leagues to serve a weak ruler of Yen in trouble? Or say I were as faithful as Wei-sheng, who waited for his loved one even when she did not come, holding onto the pilings of the pier until he drowned to death. Were I that faithful would I have been willing to further the interest of Yen and Ch'in in Ch'i and still receive great distinction doing it? For those who are faithful are faithful for themselves, and not for others. Pretenses at self-abnegation, do not achieve results. The Three Kings stayed in power, the Five Rulers maintained their preeminence, not by abnegating themselves, so why should your majesty? Otherwise, Ch'i would not have exploited Ying-ch'iu, and you, Sir, would not have crossed the borders of Ch'u or be eyeing the regions outside your territories. When I left my aged mother in Chou to serve you, I had to abandon the arts of self-denial, and plot out ways of advancing and making progress. My bent evidently does not coincide with yours: you want a self-denying minister, whereas

I am ambitious and eager to move ahead. This is why I say that loyalty and piety would be punished by your majesty."

The King of Yen said: "How can loyalty and faithfulness be punished?"

"Your majesty does not know about a neighbor of mine who was sent far from home on a mission. His wife had a lover and when the husband came back, the lover became apprehensive, but the wife reassured him: 'My lord, don't worry, I have already poisoned the wine that my husband will be served when he returns.' When the husband arrived after two days, the wife sent the concubine to bring in the jug of wine. The concubine knew the wine was poisoned, and that if she brought it in, her master would die, and that if she betrayed her mistress, then she would be dispatched, so she fell flat out, and spilled the wine. The husband was furious and gave her a sound thrashing. But, because the concubine fell down and spilled the wine, the husband was saved and the wife spared. Loyalty as devoted as this, however, didn't spare her a thrashing. This is the kind of loyalty that is punished."

"Now my conduct of affairs is ill-fated, and I am like the concubine who spilled the wine. For though I serve you, Sir, in honor and for the benefit of the state, I am being punished today. I fear that those who will serve you in the future will not dare to act on their own. Where I have won the confidence of Ch'i for you, and have never misled her, those who will be sent to negotiate with Ch'i will not have my say, and though they have the intelligence of a Yao or Shun, they will not dare to exercise their own initiative."

THE BOOK OF YEN

[Sword Play in Ch'in's Territories]

Prince Tan of Yen, the heir to the throne, after being hostage at Ch'in, returned to see Ch'in destroy the Six States, and poise its armies on the Yi River. Fearing the worst, the Prince addressed his tutor Chu Wu with apprehension: "Yen and Ch'in cannot both stand. Would the Grand Tutor devise a well-conceived scheme?" Wu replied: "Ch'in's territories are all over the place. If they can intimidate Han, Wei, and Chao, then the region north of the Yi River will not be secure. Of what use is your grievance if it will only goad the dragon?" The Prince said: "Alright, then, what do I do?" The Grand Tutor said: "Let me think of something."

Meanwhile, a certain General Fan ran away from Ch'in and arrived in Yen: the Prince offered him sanctuary. The Grand Tutor Chu Wu remonstrated with him: "You can't do that! The savagery of Ch'in and his growing hostilities toward Yen are enough to make the heart shudder; what will happen when he hears that General Fan is here? It would be like leaving meat in the path of a hungry tiger. Nothing can save us from catastrophe now! Even if you had the wise Kuan-tzu or the clever Yen-tzu, they couldn't come up with a way out. You must quickly abandon him to the Hsiung-nu to dispose of, then negotiate treaties in the west with the three Tsin [Han, Chao, and Wei], conclude an alliance in the south with Ch'i and Ch'u, and make a parley in the north with the Ch'an-yu [the chieftain of the Huns]. Only then can you figure out what to do next!"

Prince Tan said: "The Grand Tutor's plan wastes time and would take forever.

It's completely confused and couldn't be done in a little while. And that's not the only consideration. General Fan has gone through many obstacles in order to get here, and we will not, in the end, be pressured by the might of Ch'in to abandon all principles of mercy by leaving him to the Hsiung-nu. My mind is made up, and my fate is sealed. Think of something else!"

Chu Wu said: "In Yen, there is a Master T'ien Kuang, who is profoundly wise and deeply courageous. Perhaps he can help."

The Prince said: "You have to but command!" He went to see T'ien Kuang and told him that the Prince wanted to discuss affairs of state with him. T'ien Kuang said, "I shall obey, with all due respect," and went with him. The Prince welcomed him on his knees, led him to his place, and asked him to sit down. When he was seated, and they were alone, the Prince left his seat and said: "Yen and Ch'in cannot both stand. Would you, Sir, give this matter your attention?"

T'ien Kuang said: "I have heard when the fabulous Ch'i-ch'i horse was hale and hearty, it could cover a thousand leagues in one day, but when it was in its last days, even an old nag could outrun it. Now, the Prince has heard of me as I was in my prime, and you are not aware that my powers have long ago deserted me. Although I cannot presume to settle momentous affairs of state myself, I can recommend Ching K'o as someone who might help."

The Prince said: "Would you, Sir, be good enough to introduce us to Ching K'o?"

"Most assuredly!" T'ien Kuang said, and got up to go.

The Prince saw him to the gate, and said: "I am indebted to you for your good counsel, but as these are important affairs of state, I would wish that you wouldn't let word of this get out."

T'ien Kuang bowed with a smile: "Of course." And with this he took his leave and went to see Ching K'o.

"You and I have been good friends," he said to Ching K'o, "as everyone in Yen knows. Now, the Prince has heard of me in my prime, and not knowing that I am not what I used to be, he said to me, 'Yen and Ch'in cannot both stand, please give this matter your attention.' I could not overlook you, so I spoke of you to the Prince, and now he wants you to go see him in the palace."

Ching K'o said: "You have but to command."

T'ien Kuang said: "I have heard that honorable men conduct themselves in such a way as to leave no cause for anyone to doubt them. But just now the Prince said to me, 'The things we've just discussed are important matters of state, please don't let any word of this get out.' Which means that the Prince has doubts about me. And anyone whose conduct is not above suspicion is not a true man of integrity." And since he wanted his suicide to be a spur to Ching K'o, he said: "Please hurry on to the Prince, and tell him that I am already dead, and am silenced forever." With that, he cut his own throat and died.

When K'o saw the Prince, he told him that T'ien Kuang had died, silenced by his own hand forever. The Prince bowed again and again, knelt down and wept, and said, after a while: "When I asked Master T'ien to keep close counsel, I was thinking only of the success of any plans we may make. Now, Master T'ien has died to protect our confidence. How could I imagine that he would do such a thing?"

Ching K'o sat down. The Prince got up, bowed toward him, and said: "Master T'ien did not know that I was not worthy of him. Yet he sent you to me, and you seem willing to give me counsel, so Heaven has taken pity on Yen, and has not abandoned us. At the moment, Ch'in has a voracious appetite, and her wants cannot be satisfied. Not until she has all the territories under the sun, or the fealty of all the kings within the oceans, will she have enough. As of now, Ch'in has already seized the King of Han, and absorbed her territories, also has raised an army south against Ch'u, north toward Chao, and Wang Chien with troops in the tens of thousands, is heading for Chang Yeh, and Li Hsin is coming out right into Tai-yuan and Yun-chung. Chao cannot hold out against Ch'in, and will be subjugated, and when that happens, it will be a catastrophe for Yen, for Yen is too small and weak to survive several military engagements. Now we figure the country is not up to facing Ch'in, even if the whole population were mobilized. All the various clans now swear fealty to Ch'in: they would not dare support any attempt to oppose her. But I have a secret plan. I'm foolish enough to think that if we found the bravest man there is, sent him to Ch'in to look around and gave him lots of wealth, the king would be so greedy for his goods that he would be able to have his way. Truly to steal back and return to everyone the territories invaded by the King of Ch'in—just like Ts'ao Mei with the Duke Huan of Ch'i—would be a marvelous thing. But if that isn't possible, he will be assassinated. Then, the generals would seize control of the army on the outside, and there would be great confusion within; lord and minister would suspect each other, and the various clans would band together and force restitutions that would break Ch'in's hold. This is my fondest wish, but I do not know who to send, if my minister Ching won't consider it."

After some time, Ching K'o said: "This is a very important affair of state: I doubt whether I am up to the task." The Prince implored him, kept insisting and wouldn't take no for an answer, until finally he agreed. Thereupon he was promoted to the highest rank, lodged in the best apartments, consulted daily by the Prince, and was given the best of everything—chariots, women, whatever he wanted was duly granted Ching K'o.

A considerable period of time passed, and Ching K'o still had not shown any signs of proceeding with the plan. Meantime, Ch'in, through General Wang Chien, invaded Chao, capturing the King of Chao, taking all her lands, advancing the army to the northern reaches, all the way to the southern border of Yen. Prince Tan was fearful, and asked Ching K'o: "The Ch'in army is about to cross the Yi River any day or night now, and though I would like to indulge you indefinitely, I can't afford to any longer."

Ching K'o said: "If my prince hadn't mentioned it, I would have broached the subject myself. But to proceed now would be pointless: I have nothing yet with which to gain Ch'in's confidence. But now there's General Fan, for whom the King of Ch'in has offered a reward of a thousand catties of gold and a fiefdom of ten thousand families. If only one could get one's hands on General Fan's head, that along with the map of the Tu-k'ang region of Yen would surely secure an audience with the Ch'in king, and then I would be able to avenge my prince."

The Prince said: "General Fan has undergone many hardships to seek refuge here. I will not tolerate any breach of propriety while he is in my custody. Please, Sir, consider another alternative!"

Ching K'o knew that the Prince would not permit it, so he went to see Fan Yu-ch'i in secret: "Ch'in's offense against you is grave. Your father and mother and the rest of your family have all been massacred. And now I hear there is a price on the General's head of a thousand catties of gold and a fiefdom of ten thousand families! What do you make of this?"

General Fan raised his head toward heaven, sighed aloud, and with tears in his eyes, he said: "My every thought pierces me to the marrow. But I don't know what I should do!"

K'o replied: "What would you say if I had an idea that could save the state of Yen from calamity, and also repay the General's enemy?"

Fan Yu-ch'i leaned forward and asked: "What is it?"

Ching K'o: "Let me deliver your head to Ch'in, and the Ch'in king will be delighted to grant me an audience. Then, with my left hand holding his sleeve, my right will strike at his heart. Thus the General will be avenged on his enemy, and the state of Yen will be rid of the shame of grave insult. What does the General say to this?"

Fan Yu-ch'i bared his throat, grasped his wrist, and said: "Day and night, I have gnashed my teeth and afflicted my heart, but now I have heard what I want!" With this he cut his throat and died.

When the Prince heard this, he hurried to the prostrate corpse in tears, moaning in lamentation: but since there was nothing that could be done about it, he took Fan Yu-ch'i's head, and put it in a sealed box. Then he looked high and low for the best dagger in all the land, and found the dagger of a certain Hsu of Chao, which he bought for a hundred gold pieces, and had workman temper in poison. He also tested it on people: when so much as a trickle of blood was drawn, not one survived. It was wrapped up and sent along to Ching K'o. Now, in the state of Yen, there was someone named Ch'in Wu-yang, who had killed a man when he was in his thirteenth year, whom no one dared cross, and he was assigned to accompany Ching K'o on his mission. Ching K'o was waiting for someone else whom he wanted along with him, but lived very far away and had not yet arrived. Still, Ching K'o waited for him and did not set out. The Prince bore with him, but he was anxious lest Ching K'o change his mind, so he asked again: "Time is running out. Why isn't the minister Ching carrying out our plan? Perhaps I had better send Ch'in Wu-yang on ahead."

Ching K'o was indignant, and he yelled at the Prince: "Since I am the poor fool who is going and will not return, and since I am the one to go straight into the invulnerable and invincible Ch'in army with only a dagger, I naturally delayed a bit, waiting for my friend whom I wanted along as a companion. But since the Prince is so impatient, I'll be on my way right now!" And with that, he set out at last.

The Prince and those who knew of the mission all donned their white robes and caps to see him off. When they reached the waters of the Yi, they invoked the gods and asked for a blessing on the mission. Kao Chien-li struck up a mournful melody on his lute, and Ching K'o sang along, harmonizing in a minor key. The men all had tears running down their cheeks, as Ching K'o stepped forward and sang:

> The wind blows and blows,
> The Yi waters are cold!
> Stout fellows once gone,
> Oh, will never come back!

Then he sang of The Magnanimous Knight, and the other officers glared at him, their hair bristling under their caps. Ching K'o mounted his chariot and went, without so much as a glance back. When he arrived in Ch'in, he made gifts of a thousand pieces of gold to the Tutor Meng Chia, who was a key member of the King's privy council. Chia spoke on his behalf to the King of Ch'in: "The King of Yen is truly awed by the might of your majesty, and does not dare to organize troops to raise a hand against you; he wishes to offer his fealty to you, to serve you as one of your vassals, and to make tributes as a protectorate if he is allowed to retain his ancestral temples. And since he was fearful and did not want to come in person, he sent the decapitated head of Fan Yu-ch'i, along with the maps of the Tu-k'ang region of Yen, all under seal. The King of Yen has sent an envoy to pay his respects, and to attend to your majesty's wishes!"

When the King of Ch'in heard this, he was very pleased. He instructed the entire court to turn out to receive the envoy from Yen in the Hsien-yang palace. Ching K'o offered up the box with Fan Yu-ch'i's head, and Ch'in Wu-yang presented the portfolio with the map. When they approached the throne, however, Ch'in Wu-yang grew pale with fear, and the assembly wondered at this. Ching K'o noticed this and laughed. Stepping forward, he apologized to the throne: "He's a rube who comes from among the northern barbarians, and since he has never seen real royalty, naturally, he is a bit terrified. If your majesty would make allowances for him and let him stay out here until the audience is over."

Ching K'o took the map and presented it, unrolling the map until the dagger wrapped up in it was exposed, whereupon he seized the sleeve of the King with his left hand and with his right, he struck out at him. But, before he could get to him, the King of Ch'in jumped, drew back, got up, tearing his sleeve, and reached for his sword. As the sword was long, it wouldn't come out of its scabbard, for in his panic, the King left the scabbard upright, which is why it was hard to draw out. Ching K'o chased the King, who circled around a pillar and darted away. The assembled court was aghast, and all collapsed into chaos, without any notion of what to do. According to the rules of the Ch'in court, courtiers who approached the throne were not allowed to carry arms, so the assembled guards were all some distance from the royal dais, and could not approach. Further, at this critical point, there was no time to call the guards, which is why Ching K'o could— unchecked—pursue the King of Ch'in. The King, in his disarray, had nothing with which to strike back at K'o, so he resorted to using his fists. Just then, the physician Hsia Wu-ch'ieh threw his medicine pouch at K'o, which enabled the Ch'in king to go behind a pillar, but being still confused, he was at a loss as to what to do next. Everyone around then yelled: "Your majesty, pull out your sword!" And the King managed to draw it, and with it struck out at K'o, cutting his left thigh. Ching K'o withdrew, and threw his dagger at the Ch'in king, but he missed, hitting the pillar. The King of Ch'in then struck K'o repeatedly, inflicting eight wounds. K'o realized at this point that he had failed, and spreading his legs against a pillar, he laughed derisively and cursed out: "The mission has failed! And all because I tried to strip him alive, and force him to return the lands that he had invaded, thus avenging my Prince." At this the attendants all surrounded him and stabbed him to death, while the King fell into a dead faint. When it came time later to mete out rewards for meritorious action, everyone at court was found undeserving, except for Hsia Wu-ch'ieh who was awarded two thousand taels of gold with these words: "Wu-ch'ieh is devoted to me, for he threw his medicine pouch at K'o." From then on, Ch'in was furious at Yen: she sent additional troops to besiege Chao and called upon General Wang Chien to attack Yen. In ten months, the town of Chi in Yen fell. King Hsi, and Prince Tan, together with the remnants of their army, fled east to Liao-tung for safety. But the Ch'in general Li Hsin tracked them down and attacked the Yen king, who in his panic, took the suggestion of King Chia of Tai, and had Prince Tan executed, and with his head sued for peace. But Ch'in pressed on, and after five years, destroyed Yen completely, capturing Hsi, the King. Ch'in then proceeded to consolidate all her territories. Afterward, Ching K'o's old companion Kao Chien-li, playing on his lute, caught sight of the Ch'in emperor, and tried to beat him over the head with his lute to avenge the state of Yen, but he too failed and was killed.

CH'Ü YÜAN [QU YUAN] (378?–340 B.C.E.)
China

Ch'ü Yüan, China's first known poet, was born into an aristocratic family in the southern state of Ch'u, one of the seven major powers during the Warring States period. After finishing his schooling, he was appointed to a prominent official position. Political rivals succeeded in turning the King of Ch'u against him, however, and he was dismissed from court in disgrace. Ch'ü Yüan was bitterly sorrowful over the future of the state and of its people, as well as his own personal fate. According to legend, he eventually drowned himself in the Milo River.

Paradoxically, what was unfortunate for Ch'ü Yüan turned out to be most fortunate for literature, for he gave form to his profound sorrow in one of China's greatest lyric poems, "On Encountering Sorrow" ["Li-sao"]. The first part of the poem presents a biographical account of the poet's ancestry, his efforts at self-cultivation, and his ideal of an enlightened government. The second part is devoted to the poet's imaginary travels to a heavenly world, travels that represent his frustrated quest for his ideals. In the last part, the poet continues his travels in search of an understanding goddess but ends up in despair. Finally, he decides to join P'eng Hsien, a legendary courtier who drowned himself after his counsel was ignored by his king.

The style of the poetry of the state of Ch'ü, represented by the exuberant imagery and magnificent diction of "On Encountering Sorrow," greatly influenced later poets, especially those of the Han Dynasty.

On Encountering Sorrow [Li Sao]

UNLIKE the other Chu-tzu poems, for whose authorship the second-century commentator Wang I is often our only authority, this poem was from a fairly early date associated with the name of Ch'ü Yüan, and there seems little reason for quarrelling with the traditional attribution. It may, however, be of interest to consider to what extent the personality which confronts us in Li Sao corresponds to the Ch'ü Yüan of Ssŭ-ma Ch'ien's biography.

Like him, the author of Li Sao is a Ch'u nobleman. (All noblemen in ancient China were descended from the gods, and Li Sao opens with a declaration of the poet's divine ancestry from Kao Yang.) Like him, he is a victim of slanderous misrepresentation and royal folly. Like him, his conception of honor and purity sets him at odds with a society fallen into evil ways.

Beyond that the resemblances end. The Li Sao poet is a magician who journeys in an airborne chariot to the fairyland of the West, compelling gods and spirits to wait upon him. Somehow the magic is not quite strong enough, however, and the dispirited poet ends in complete despair, disillusioned alike with the world of men and with the supernatural world through which he has been travelling.

The way in which we interpret Li Sao rests ultimately on whether or not we believe the last two lines of the poem to be authentic. If they are, it looks as though the poet's celestial journey in quest of fair women is an allegory of the rejected courtier's unsuccessful search for a wise prince. The 'place where P'eng Hsien dwells' used to be taken as a reference to the waters of the river, and the poet's final resolution to go there as an announcement of his intention to drown himself. This is by no means certain, and I am inclined to believe that 'following P'eng Hsien' meant devoting oneself to occult training.

In a sense the interpretation makes little difference to our picture of the poet. Allegory or no allegory, the fact remains that Ch'ü Yüan took a rather specialized kind of magic-making as the central theme of his poem, thereby demonstrating that he was familiar with such matters and perhaps expert in them.

The escape from human miseries by means of a journey into the supernatural world, in which the poet, like a lord of the universe, seizes the stars in his grasp and commands the gods as his lackeys, later became a stock-in-trade of the Chinese poet. But it was Ch'ü Yüan who first used this theme and who wrote the earliest long narrative poem to survive. It seems not unreasonable to suppose that he may have got the idea for his theme and also for the form of his poem from hearing recitals by Ch'u shamans in which they gave an account of their journeys through the spirit-lands. Recitals of this kind are extremely common among shamans in other parts of the world and references to 'spirit-journeys' are by no means uncommon in early Chinese literature.

—DAVID HAWKES

Scion of the High Lord Kao Yang,[1]
Po Yung was my father's name.
When She T'i[2] pointed to the first month of the year,
On the day keng yin,[3] I passed from the womb.
My father, seeing the aspect of my nativity,   5

Translated by David Hawkes.

---

1. Divine ancestor of both the Ch'u and Ch'in royal houses.
2. A constellation.

3. Name of the twenty-seventh day in the sexagenary cycle.

Took omens to give me an auspicious name.
The name he gave me was True Exemplar;
The title he gave me was Divine Balance[4]

Having from birth this inward beauty,
I added to it fair outward adornment;
I dressed in selinea and shady angelica,
And twined autumn orchids to make a garland.
Swiftly I sped, as in fearful pursuit,
Afraid Time would race on and leave me behind.
In the morning I gathered the angelica on the mountains;   15
In the evening I plucked the sedges of the islets.

The days and months hurried on, never delaying;
Springs and autumns sped by in endless alternation:
And I thought how the trees and flowers were fading and falling,
And feared that my Fairest's beauty would fade too.   20
'Gather the flower of youth and cast out the impure!
'Why will you not change the error of your ways?
'I have harnessed brave coursers for you to gallop forth with:
'Come, let me go before and show you the way!

'The three kings[5] of old were most pure and perfect: 25
'Then indeed fragrant flowers had their proper place.
'They brought together pepper and cinnamon;
'All the most-prized blossoms were woven in their garlands.
'Glorious and great were those two, Yao and Shun,[6]
'Because they had kept their feet on the right path.   30
'And how great was the folly of Chieh and Chou,[7]
'Who hastened by crooked paths, and so came to grief.

'The fools enjoy their careless pleasure,
'But their way is dark and leads to danger.
'I have no fear for the peril of my own person,   35
'But only lest the chariot of my lord should be dashed.
'I hurried about your chariot in attendance,
'Leading you in the tracks of the kings of old.'
But the Fragrant One refused to examine my true feelings:
He lent ear, instead, to slander, and raged against me.   40

How well I know that loyalty brings disaster;
Yet I will endure: I cannot give it up.
I called on the ninefold heaven to be my witness,

---

4. "True Exemplar" and "Divine Balance" are
   pseudonyms. They could be word-plays on
   "P'ing" and "Yüan".
5. Yü, T'ang, and Wu, founders of the Hsia,
   Shang, and Chou dynasties.

6. Legendary Sage-kings.
7. Last kings of the Hsia and Shang dynasties,
   traditionally described as monsters of iniquity.

And all for the sake of the Fair One, and no other.
[Interpolation]

There once was a time when he spoke with me in frankness;   45
But then he repented and was of another mind.
I do not care, on my own count, about this divorcement,
But it grieves me to find the Fair One so inconstant.

I had tended many an acre of orchids,   50
And planted a hundred rods of melilotus;
I had raised sweet lichens and the cart-halting flower,
And asarums mingled with fragrant angelica,
And hoped that when leaf and stem were in fullest bloom,
When the time had come, I could reap a fine harvest.   55
Though famine should pinch me, it is small matter;
But I grieve that all my blossoms should waste in rank weeds.

All others press forward in greed and gluttony,
No surfeit satiating their demands:
Forgiving themselves, but harshly judging others;   60
Each fretting his heart away in envy and malice.
Madly they rush in the covetous chase,
But not after that which *my* heart sets store by.
For old age comes creeping and soon will be upon me,
And I fear I shall not leave behind an enduring name.   65

In the mornings I drank the dew that fell from the magnolia;
At evening ate the petals that dropped from chrysanthemums.
If only my mind can be truly beautiful,
It matters nothing that I often faint for famine.
I pulled up roots to bind the valerian   70
And thread the castor plant's fallen clusters with;
I trimmed sprays of cassia for plaiting melilotus,
And knotted the lithe, light trails of ivy.

I take my fashion from the good men of old:
A garb unlike that which the rude world cares for: 75
Though it may not accord with present-day manners,
I will follow the pattern that P'eng Hsien[8] has left.
Heaving a long sigh, I brush away my tears,
Grieving for man's life, so beset with hardships.
I have always loved pretty things to bind myself about with,   80
And so mornings I plaited and evenings I twined.

When I had finished twining my girdle of orchids,
I plucked some angelicas to add to its beauty.

---

8. A shaman ancestor, i.e. a long-dead shaman   late tradition says that he lived in the Shang
who has become a guide to the initiate. A   Dynasty and that he drowned himself.

It is this that my heart takes most delight in,
And though I died nine times, I should not regret it.   85
What I do resent is the Fair One's waywardness:
Because he will never look to see what is in men's hearts.
All your ladies were jealous of my delicate beauty;
They chattered spitefully, saying I loved wantonness.

Truly, this generation are cunning artificers!   90
From square and compass they turn their eyes and change the true measurement,
They disregard the ruled line to follow their crooked fancies:
To emulate in flattery is their only rule.
But I am sick and sad at heart and stand irresolute:
I alone am at a loss in this generation.   95
But I would rather quickly die and meet dissolution
Before I ever would consent to ape *their* behaviour.

Eagles do not flock like birds of lesser species;
So it has ever been since the olden time.
How can the round and square ever fit together?   100
How can different ways of life ever be reconciled?
Yet humbling one's spirit and curbing one's pride,
Bearing blame humbly and enduring insults,
But keeping pure and spotless and dying in righteousness:
Such conduct was greatly prized by the wise men of old.   105

Repenting, therefore, that I had not conned the way more closely,
I halted, intending to turn back again—
To turn about my chariot and retrace my road
Before I had advanced too far along the path of folly.
I walked my horses through the marsh's orchid-covered margin;   110
I galloped to the hill of pepper-trees and rested there.
I could not go in to him for fear of meeting trouble,
And so, retired, I would once more fashion my former raiment.

I made a coat of lotus and water-chestnut leaves,
And gathered lotus petals to make myself a skirt.   115
I will no longer care that no one understands me,
As long as I can keep the sweet fragrance of my mind.
High towered the lofty hat on my head;
The longest of girdles dangled from my waist.
Fragrance and richness mingled in sweet confusion.   120
The brightness of their lustre has remained undimmed.

. . .

Pepper is all wagging tongue and lives only for slander;
And even stinking Dogwood seeks to fill a perfume bag.
Since they only seek advancement and labour for position,
What fragrance have they deserving our respect?   125

Since, then, the world's way is to drift the way the tide runs,
Who can stay the same and not change with all the rest?
Seeing the behaviour of Orchid and Pepper flower,
What can be expected from cart-halt and selinea?
They have cast off their beauty and come to this: 130
Only my garland is left to treasure.
Its penetrating perfume does not easily desert it,
And even to this day its fragrance has not faded.

I will follow my natural bent and please myself;
I will go off wandering to look for a lady.   135
While my adornment is in its pristine beauty
I will travel all around looking both high and low.
Since Ling Fen had given me a favourable oracle,
I reckoned a lucky day to start my journey on.
I broke a branch of jasper to take for my meat,   140
And ground fine jasper meal for my journey's provisions.

'Harness winged dragons to be my coursers;
'Let my chariot be of fine work of jade and ivory!
'How can I live with men whose hearts are strangers to me?
'I am going a far journey to be away from them.'   145
I took the way that led towards the K'un-lun mountain:
A long, long road with many a turning in it.
The cloud-embroidered banner flapped its great shade above us;
And the jingling jade yoke-bells tinkled merrily.

I set off at morning from the Ford of Heaven;   150
At evening I came to the world's western end.
Phoenixes followed me, bearing up my pennants,
Soaring high aloft with majestic wing-beats.
'See, I have come to the desert of Moving Sands!'
Warily I drove along the banks of the Red Water;[9]   155
Then, beckoning the water-dragons to make a bridge for me,
I summoned the God of the West to take me over.

Long was the road that lay ahead and full of difficulties;
I sent word to my other chariots to take a short route and wait.
The road wound leftwards round the Pu Chou Mountain:[10]   160
I marked out the Western Sea as our meeting-place.
There I marshalled my thousand chariots,
And jade hub to jade hub we galloped on abreast.

---

9. The Moving Sands of mythological geography no doubt derive from travelers' tales of the Gobi Desert. The Red Water is one of the colored rivers that flow from K'un-lun.

10. The northwest pillar of heaven against which Kung Kung butted his head in the theomachia which tilted the earth downward in the southeast. It is also the gate of the underworld.

My eight dragon-steeds flew on with writhing undulations;
My cloud-embroidered banners flapped on the wind.   165

I tried to curb my mounting will and slacken the swift pace;
But the spirits soared high up, far into the distance.
We played the Nine Songs and danced the Nine Shao dances:[11]
I wanted to snatch some time for pleasure and amusement.
But when I had ascended the splendour of the heavens,   170
I suddenly caught a glimpse below of my old home.
The groom's heart was heavy and the horses for longing
Arched their heads back and refused to go on.

ENVOI

Enough! There are no true men in the state: no one to understand me.
Why should I cleave to the city of my birth?   175
Since none is worthy to work with in making good government,
I will go and join P'eng Hsien in the place where he abides.

FU HSÜAN [FU XUAN]

(THIRD CENTURY C.E.)

China

Fu Hsüan was a poet of the early Chin Dynasty. During his time, the period of the
Three Kingdoms (220 C.E.–262 or 280 C.E.), which had seen the tripartition of
China, was ended, and the nation was once again unified. Peace and relative
social stability brought about a period in which both literature and art prospered.

From the time of the Han Dynasty, when a taste for elaborate court poetry
was established, Chinese poetry had primarily moved in an elitist direction,
cultivating intricate forms, ornate rhetorical devices, and inbred allusions.
Alongside this learned tradition, however, existed a breath of fresh air: a genre
called *yüeh-fu*, which had its roots in folk song. *Yüeh-fu* refers literally to a
division of the bureaucracy, the Bureau of Music. Scholars employed in this
bureau were charged with collecting folk songs as a means of gauging the
national mood: "Find out what the people are singing about and report back to
me," was the essence of their edicts. The poetic virtues of the songs did not go
unnoticed, and a tradition began of writing in their simple, down-to-earth style.

Fu Hsüan wrote in the *yüeh-fu* tradition. In plain language, his poems depict

---

11. Not the Nine Songs of *Ch'u Tz'ü*, but those
of Ch'i. The Nine Shao were danced to
these songs.

with sympathy the poor and the unfortunate, especially women who were downtrodden and suppressed by male-dictated ethical codes.

Woman*

How sad it is to be a woman!
Nothing on earth is held so cheap.
Boys standing leaning at the door
Like Gods fallen out of Heaven.
Their hearts brave the Four Oceans,   5
The wind and dust of a thousand miles.
No one is glad when a girl is born;
By her the family sets no store.
When she grows up, she hides in her room
Afraid to look a man in the face.   10
No one cries when she leaves her home—
Sudden as clouds when the rain stops.
She bows her head and composes her face,
Her teeth are pressed on her red lips:
She bows and kneels countless times.   15
She must humble herself even to the servants.
His love is distant as the stars in Heaven,
Yet the sunflower bends toward the sun.
Their hearts more sundered than water and fire—
A hundred evils are heaped upon her.   20
Her face will follow the years' changes;
Her lord will find new pleasures.
They that were once like substances and shadow
Are now as far as Hu from Ch'in.[1]
Yet Hu and Ch'in shall sooner meet   25
Than they whose parting is like Ts'an and Ch'en.[2]

T'AO CH'IEN [TAO QIAN] (365–427 C.E.)
China

A native of Hsinyang in present-day Kiangsi province, T'ao Ch'ien (also known as T'ao Yüan-ming), was the literary giant of the late Chin period and arguably

*Translated by Arthur Waley.

---

1. Two lands.   2. Two stars.

China's greatest pastoral poet. Despite the fact that he was the scion of a bureaucratic family, T'ao Ch'ien was reduced to poverty because he did not want a job in the bureaucracy, and had occasionally even to resort to begging in order to support his aging mother and himself. At thirty-two, he was made a magistrate, but he resigned this post after only one year, and after ten years in public service, returned to his rustic life.

The late Chin period was marked by turbulent disorder. In the face of repeated barbarian invasions from the north, the imperial court had moved southward to Nanjing in 318 C.E. Subsequently, the Chin house (today referred to as Eastern or Later Chin by historians) was plagued by the factional strife and political corruption that would eventually cause its downfall. T'ao Ch'ien's withdrawal into a rural life was his way of distancing himself from corrupt bureaucratic politics.

However, T'ao Ch'ien was not merely an escapist. During his time, the influence of Confucianism had significantly waned, yielding ground to Taoism and to a newcomer, Buddhism. T'ao Ch'ien's philosophy has often been said to be a harmonious combination of elements from these three sources, but in his love of nature and adherence to a natural way of living, involving no extraneous efforts, he was clearly closer to Taoism than anything else.

The Seasons Come and Go, Four Poems*

The seasons come and go: late spring is upon us. The spring garments are ready and, as the scenery is inviting, I stroll out by myself, with feelings of joy mixed with sadness.

1

By and by, the seasons come and go,
My, my! What a fine morning!
I put on my spring cloak
And set out east for the outskirts.
Mountains are cleansed by lingering clouds;   5
Sky is veiled by fine mist.
A wind comes up from the south,
Winging over the new sprouts.

2

Bank to bank, the stream is wide;
I rinse, then douse myself.
Scene by scene, the distant landscape;
I am happy as I look out.
People have a saying: 5
"A heart at peace is easy to please."
So I brandish this cup,
Happy to be by myself.

*Translated by Eugene Eoyang.

3

Peering into the depths of the stream,[1]
I remember the pure waters of the Yi,
There students and scholars worked together,
And, carefree, went home singing.
I love their inner peace,   5
Awake or asleep, I'd change places,
But, alas, those times are gone—
We can no longer bring them back.

4

In the morning and at night
I rest in my house.
Flowers and herbs are all in place;
Trees and bamboos cast their shadows.
A clear-sounding lute lies on my bed,   5
And there's half a jug of coarse wine.
Huang and T'ang[2] are gone forever:
Sad and alone, here I am.

On Returning to My Garden and Field, Two Selections[†]

1

When I was young, I did not fit into the common mold,
By instinct, I love mountains and hills.
By error, I fell into this dusty net
And was gone from home for thirteen years.
A caged bird yearns for its native woods;   5
The fish in a pond recalls old mountain pool.
Now I shall clear the land at the edge of the southern wild,
And, clinging to simplicity, return to garden and field.
My house and land on a two-acre lot,
My thatched hut of eight or nine rooms—   10
Elms and willows shade the eaves back of the house,
Peach and plum trees stand in a row before the hall.
Lost in a haze is the distant village,
Where smoke hovers above the homes.
Dogs bark somewhere in deep lanes,   15
Cocks crow atop the mulberry trees.
My home is free from dust and care,

[†]*Translated by Wu-chi Liu.*

---

1. Alluding to the ancient lustration rites held   2. The legendary emperors Huang-ti and Yao.
   in the spring, on the bank of the Yi River.

In a bare room there is leisure to spare.
Long a prisoner in a cage,
I am now able to come back to nature.   20

2

I plant beans at the foot of the southern hill;
The grass is thick and bean sprouts are sparse.
At dawn, I rise and go out to weed the field;
Shouldering the hoe, I walk home with the moon.
The path is narrow, grass and shrubs are tall,   5
And evening dew dampens my clothes.
Wet clothes are no cause for regret
So long as nothing goes contrary to my desire.

Miscellaneous Poems, Six Selections*

1

A man has no roots.
Blown about—like dust on the road,
In all directions, he tumbles with the wind:
Our lives are brief enough.
We come into this world as brothers and sisters: 5
But why must we be tied to flesh and blood?
Let's enjoy our happiness:
Here's a jug of wine, call in the neighbors.
The best times don't come often:
Each day dawns only once.   10
The seasons urge us on—
Time waits for no man.

2

Bright sun lights out over the western bank,
Pale moon comes out from behind the eastern ridge.
Far-reaching, this million-mile brilliance;
Transcendent, this scene in space.
A breeze comes through the window in my room.   5
At night the mat and pillow are cold.
The weather shifts: I sense the seasons change;
Unable to sleep, I know how long the night is.
I'd like to say something, but no one's around,
So I raise my cup, and toast my own shadow.   10
Days and months pass by—

*Translated by Eugene Eoyang

One cannot keep pace with ambition.
Thinking these thoughts, I am depressed;
Right through till dawn, I find rest impossible.

3

Bright blossoms seldom last long;
Life's ups-and-downs can't be charted.
What was a lotus flower in spring,
Is now the seed-husk of autumn.
Severe frost freezes the wild grass: 5
Decay has yet to finish it off.
Sun and moon come back once more,
But where I go, no sun will shine.
I look back longingly on times gone by—
Remembering the past wounds my soul.   10

4

A noble ambition spans the four seas;
Mine is simpler: not to grow old.
I'd like my family all in one place,
My sons and grandsons all caring for each other.
I want a goblet and a lute to greet each day,   5
And my wine casks never to run dry.
Belt loosened, I drink pleasure to the dregs:
I rise late, and retire early.
How can today be compared to yesterday?
My heart harbored both ice and coal.   10
In time, ashes return to ashes, dust to dust—
And vain is the way of fame and glory.

5

When I was young and in my prime,
If times were sad, I was happy on my own.
With brave plans that went beyond the sea,
I spread my wings, and dreamt of great flights.
But the course of time has run me down,   5
And my zest for life has begun to wane.
Enjoyment no longer makes me happy,
Each and every thing means more worry.
My strength is beginning to peter out,
I sense the change: one day's not like the last.   10
The hurrying barge can't wait for a moment:
It pulls me along and gives no rest.
The road ahead: how much farther?

Ch'en Hung-shou (1598–
1652). Handscroll illustrating
an ode of T'ao Ch'ien.

I don't know where I will come to rest.
The ancients begrudged a shadow's inch-of-time: 15
When I think of this, it makes me shudder.

6

Years ago, when I heard the words of my elders,
I'd cover my ears, not liking what they said.
Now that I am fifty years old,
These things suddenly matter.
To recapture the joys of my youth—   5
Does not appeal to me in the slightest.
Going, going, it's very quickly gone.
Who ever lives this life twice?
Let's use the household money for entertainment,
Before the years catch up with us.   10
I have children, but no money left:
No use leaving post-mortem trusts.

In Praise of Poor Scholars*

All creatures, each has a home:
The solitary cloud alone has none.
Here and there, into thin air, it vanishes:

*Translated by Eugene Eoyang

When do you ever see its traces?
Morning glow breaks through night's mist;   5
Flocks of birds fly off together—
One by one, winging out of the woods,
Not to return again until nightfall.
Know your strengths, keep to trodden ways.
Who hasn't known cold and hunger?   10
Those who know me: if they are no longer here—
That's it then. Why complain?

LIU I-CH'ING [LIU YIQING]

(403–444 C.E.)
China

Liu I-ch'ing was a prince of the royal family of the Sung Dynasty. Although
known as a generous patron of literary talent, he was reportedly not a particularly
gifted writer himself, and his *New Talk of the Town,* [Shih-shuo hsin-yu] therefore,
may actually have been compiled by many hands.

Although fictional elements are by no means rare in China's early historical
narratives, prose fiction as a genre arose relatively late. During the fifth century,
Buddhism, with its emphasis on the other world, inspired a number of prose
works telling stories of the supernatural and the miraculous. During this same
period, Taoism (which considers other-worldly speculation pointless) inspired a
vogue among the intelligentsia for *ch'ing-t'an,* or pure discourse unsullied by
worldly (i.e., everyday, practical) concerns. Both genres had a significant impact
on the evolution of Chinese fictional narrative.

New Talk of the Town, a collection of anecdotes and sayings of literati past
and present, is an example of *ch'ing-t'an.* Written in a pithy style approaching oral
presentation, these short pieces aim at entertainment rather than edification, but
they do reflect the spirit of the age.

from **New Talk of the Town [Shih-shuo hsin-yu]**

Repartee [The Presence of the Two Sons of an Official Is Requested by the Twelve-Year-Old Emperor, to the Official's Trepidation]

[The ceremonial respect for authority in Chinese history was not mere ritual, for rulers were
often terrifying in their absolute power. A minister was admired not only for loyalty,
bordering on servility, but for his wit and tact. The following exchange involves the two sons

Translated by Eugene Eoyang.

of Chūng Yú (died 230 C.E.), both of whom were successful officials; it records a disarming instance of the awe in which the two held the Emperor.]*

Chūng Yú and Chūng Húi were much praised when they were small. At around the age of twelve, the Emperor of Wèn of Wéi heard about them, and said to their father Chūng Yú: "You may bring your two sons to court." They were thus commanded to appear. At the audience, Chung Yu's face broke out in beads of sweat. The Emperor asked: "Why are you perspiring?" To this, Chūng Yú replied:

> "Overcome with fear and trepidation,
> I cannot control my perspiration."

Then, turning to Chung Hui, the Emperor asked:
"And why do you *not* sweat?" To which, Hui replied:

> "Here I'm trembling and shivering yet,
> How could I possibly dare to sweat!"

[Learning: Pettiness and Envy Among Brilliant Minds]

[The following story concerns pettiness and envy among brilliant minds. Ma Jung (79–166 C.E.) was perhaps the most famous scholar of his generation, whose commentaries on the classics won him a great reputation and attracted a considerable following. Cheng Hsüan (127–200 C.E.) one of his most brilliant students, eventually surpassed his master, as this anecdote indicates.]

Cheng Hsüan was a disciple of Ma Jung, and had not been able to meet with the master for three years. Ma Jung's chief assistant would relay what the master said, and that was it. One day, the calculations on the astrolabe did not come out correctly and no one among the students could work it out. Someone said that Cheng Hsüan might be able to figure it out, so Ma Jung sent for him. With one turn, Cheng Hsüan was able to solve the problem, to the astonishment of all.

Later, Cheng Hsüan, upon completing his studies, took his leave and went home (east to Shantung). At that point, Ma Jung was sorry that his secrets on the Classic of Music and the Classic of Rites would go east with Hsüan. Afraid that Hsüan would now make a name for himself, Ma Jung became jealous. Hsüan, for his part, was on the alert, for he suspected an ambush. So he sat under a bridge, on top of the water, in wooden overshoes. Jung consequently turned his divining wheel to locate him, and then announced to those around him, "Hsüan is under the ground, above the water, and resting on wood. This must mean he is dead." And with that, he called off the search. Hsüan was thus able to escape in the end.

[Noble Ladies: The Story of Wang Chao-chün]

[The story of Wang Chao-chün is one of the most celebrated in all of Chinese literature: recounted in the official histories as well as in other chronicles; memorialized in verse (Li Po, for one, has two poems on the theme); recorded on a scroll found at Tun-huang; alluded to

---

*Through an accident of transliteration, Chung Yü and Chung Yu look very similar; in the Chinese, the names and the way they are pronounced are, of course, very different.

in many *tz'u* during the Sung period; the subject of dramas during the Yuan period; the variants differ in technique and in their details, but the essential story is the same. In the Han palace there were so many concubines that the emperor gave away his most beautiful woman by mistake to a Hsiung-nu chieftain. The ill-starred concubine, going out of loyalty to her country into what was considered an unspeakable exile among barbarians, became the central figure in a drama of pathos and self-sacrifice.]

In the palace of the Han emperor Yüan (who reigned 48 B.C.E. to 32 B.C.E.), there were so many ladies that he had portraits painted of each of them for reference. Instead of calling for them in person, they were summoned right away by means of the portraits. Now, among the ladies, there was a long-standing practice of offering bribes to the court painter.

Wang Chao-chün was exceptionally beautiful, but her disposition was such that she would not stoop to a bribe. The painter, as a result, spitefully distorted her portrait.

Later, when the Hsiung-nu came to the Han court to conclude an alliance, he sought a beautiful lady from the Han emperor. The emperor thought Wang Chao-chün dispensable and decided to give her up, but when he summoned her and saw her in person, he regretted his decision. But, since he had affixed his seal to the pact, there was no turning back on his word, and so he had to let her go.

[Outlandish Figures: The Drunkard]

[The total abandon of the drunkard has about it something of the aura of innocence. Vulnerable, totally without inhibitions, the drunkard seems to undercut the hypocrisy of social conventions, as the following episode shows.]

Liu Ling was constantly under the influence and totally abandoned in his behavior. Once he took off all his clothes and stood stark naked in the room. The people all made fun of him, but Ling said: "Heaven and earth are my abode; these rooms, this house are my trousers. What are you doing in my trousers?"

ANONYMOUS (FIRST CENTURY? C.E.)
China

Circulated in the second century C.E., this *yüeh-ju* is attributed to Lady Pan, a concubine of the Han emperor Ch'ung, who reigned from 32 to 37 C.E.

Song of Regret

To begin I cut fine silk of Ch'i,
white and pure as frost or snow,

Translated by Burton Watson.

shape it to make a paired-joy fan,
round, round as the luminous moon,
to go in and out of my lord's breast;   5
when lifted, to stir him a gentle breeze.
But always I dread the coming of autumn,
cold winds that scatter the burning heat,
when it will be laid away in the hamper,
love and favor cut off midway.   10

WANG WEI (701–761 C.E.)
China

Wang Wei was born in Hotung (present-day Jungchi in Shanhsi province). From early childhood, he was recognized as a prodigy and began to compose poems at the age of nine. After earning the *chin-shih* degree at twenty-one, he was appointed to various official positions. In addition to his fame as one of the leading poets of the T'ang Dynasty, a period regarded by the Chinese as their golden age of poetry, Wang Wei was also a great innovator in calligraphy and landscape painting.

A spiritual heir to T'ao Ch'ien, Wang Wei was a great admirer of natural beauty and idyllic country life. His poems, like his paintings, never delineate the details of nature, but rely instead on a few suggestive strokes to convey an effect of pure elegance. In his later years, Wang Wei became increasingly absorbed in the beauty of nature and thus detached himself from society: "I love only the stillness, / The world's affairs no longer trouble my heart."

Seeing Someone Off*

Dismounting, I offer you wine
And ask, "Where are you bound?"
You say, "I've found no fame or favors;
"I must return to rest in the South Mountain."
You leave, and I ask no more—   5
White clouds drift on and on.

To Subprefect Chang*

In late years, I love only the stillness,
The world's affairs no longer trouble my heart.

Translated by Irving Y. Lo.

Looking at myself: no far-reaching plans;
All I know: to return to familiar woods—
The pine winds blow and loosen my sash;   5
The mountain moon shines upon me playing the lute.
You ask for reasons for failure or success—
Fisherman's song enters the riverbanks deep.

Birdsong Brook*

Mind at peace, cassia flowers fall,
Night still, spring mountain empty.
Moon rising startles mountain birds
Now and again sing from spring brook.

Suffering from Heat†

The red sun fills the sky and the earth,
And fiery clouds are packed into hills and mountains.
Grasses and trees are all parched and shriveled;
Rivers and swamps, all utterly dried.
In light white silks I feel that my clothes are heavy;   5
Under dense trees I grieve that the shade is thin.
My mat of rushes cannot be approached;
My clothes of linen are washed again and again.

I long to escape beyond space and time;
In vast emptiness, dwell alone and apart.   10
Then long winds from a myriad miles would come.
Rivers and seas would cleanse me of trouble and dirt.
Then would I find that my body causes suffering;
Then would I know that my mind is still unawake.
I would suddenly enter the Gate of Pleasant Dew   15
And be at ease in the clear, cool joy.

†*Translated by Hugh M. Stimson.*

LI PO [LI BAI] (701?–762? C.E.)
China

Li Po's ancestral home was probably in Ch'engchi (near present-day T'ienshi, in Kansu province). Early in the seventh century, however, his ancestors were banished to Central Asia, where they lived for almost a century before Li Po's father brought the family back to China proper, settling in Ssuchuan [Sichuan] when Li Po was about six years old.

Li Po spent most of his life joining various reclusive groups or traveling around the country visiting friends and scenic spots. When he was forty- two, he was introduced by a friend to the imperial court, where his poetic talent so impressed the emperor that he was immediately appointed to an official position. But Li Po was too unconventional to confine himself to the rigors of court life, and three years later he found himself roaming again. Toward the end of his life, Li Po was exiled for his involvement in the famous An Lu-shan rebellion; he died shortly after the punishment was lifted.

More than any other T'ang poet, Li Po is "romantic" in the full sense of the word. In his poems we hear him deriding various forms of social vanity that suppress spontaneous individuality ("Bringing in the Wine"); we feel the pulse of

Su Han-ch'en (active 1124– 1162 C.E.), *A Lady on a Garden Terrace.*

human psyche and emotions ("The River-Merchant's Wife: A Letter" and "Written in Behalf of My Wife"). Above all we see the poet's true self—forthright, unconstrained, and somewhat hedonistic.

    Fully exploring the possibilities of folk songs, Li Po was versatile stylistically. His poems are known for their grandeur and forcefulness, but they do not lack subtlety. Deservedly, Li Po keeps a supreme place in the history of Chinese poetry, where he is known as "The Transcendent Exile from Heaven."

The River-Merchant's Wife: A Letter*

While my hair was still cut straight across my forehead
I played about the front gate, pulling flowers.
You came by on bamboo stilts, playing horse,
You walked about my seat, playing with blue plums.
And we went on living in the village of Chokan: 5
Two small people, without dislike or suspicion.

At fourteen I married My Lord you.
I never laughed, being bashful.
Lowering my head, I looked at the wall.
Called to, a thousand times, I never looked back.   10

At fifteen I stopped scowling,
I desired my dust to be mingled with yours
For ever and for ever and for ever.
Why should I climb the look out?

At sixteen you departed,   15
You went into far Ku-to-yen, by the river of swirling eddies,
And you have been gone five months.
The monkeys make sorrowful noise overhead.

You dragged your feet when you went out.
By the gate now, the moss is grown, the different mosses,   20
Too deep to clear them away!
The leaves fall early this autumn, in wind.
The paired butterflies are already yellow with August
Over the grass in the West garden:
They hurt me. I grow older.   25

If you are coming down through the narrows of the river Kiang
Please let me know beforehand.
And I will come out to meet you
         As far as Cho-fu-Sa.

Translated by Ezra Pound.

Written in Behalf of My Wife†

To cleave a running stream with a sword,
The water will never be severed.
My thoughts that follow you in your wanderings
Are as interminable as the stream.
Since we parted, the grass before our gate   5
In the autumn lane has turned green in spring.
I sweep it away but it grows back,
Densely it covers your footprints.
The singing phoenixes were happy together;
Startled, the male and the female each flies away.   10
On which mountaintop have the drifting clouds stayed?
Once gone, they never are seen to return.
From a merchant traveling to Ta-lou,
I learn you are there at Autumn Cove.
In the Liang Garden[1] I sleep in an empty embroidered bed;   15
On the Yang Terrace you dream of the drifting rain.[2]
Three times my family has produced a prime minister;
Then moved to west Ch'in since our decline.
We still have our old flutes and songs,
Their sad notes heard everywhere by neighbors.   20
When the music rises to the purple clouds,
I cry for the absence of my beloved.
I am like a peach tree at the bottom of a well,
For whom will the blossoms smile?
You are like the moon high in the sky,   25
Unwilling to cast your light on me.
I cannot recognize myself when I look in the mirror,
I must have grown thin since you left home.
If only I could own the fabled parrot
To tell you of the feelings in my heart!   30

Bringing in the Wine†

[written to music]

See how the Yellow River's waters move out of heaven.
Entering the ocean, never to return.
See how lovely locks in bright mirrors in high chambers,

†Translated by Joseph J. Lee.
†Translated by Witter Bynner.

---

1. A region in southeastern Honan.
2. Yang Terrace refers to the general area on the Yangtze. The line alludes not only to Li Po's whereabouts, but also to Sung Yü's "Shen-nü Fu."

Though silken-black at morning, have changed by night to snow.
. . . Oh, let a man of spirit venture where he pleases   5
And never tip his golden cup empty toward the moon!
Since heaven gave the talent, let it be employed!
Spin a thousand pieces of silver, all of them come back!
Cook a sheep, kill a cow, whet the appetite,
And make me, of three hundred bowls, one long drink!   10
. . . To the old master, Ts'ên,
And the young scholar, Tan-ch'iu,

Bring in the wine!
Let your cups never rest!
Let me sing you a song!   15
Let your ears attend!
What are bell and drum, rare dishes and treasure?
Let me be forever drunk and never come to reason!
Sober men of olden days and sages are forgotten,
And only the great drinkers are famous for all time   20
. . . Prince Ch'ên paid at a banquet in the Palace of Perfection
Ten thousand coins for a cask of wine, with many a laugh and quip.
Why say, my host, that your money is gone?
Go and buy wine and we'll drink it together!
My flower-dappled horse,   25
My furs worth a thousand,
Hand them to the boy to exchange for good wine,
And we'll drown away the woes of ten thousand generations!

Farewell to Meng Hao-jan§

I took leave of you, old friend, at the
Yellow Crane Pavilion;
In the mist and bloom of March, you went
down to Yang-chou:
A lonely sail, distant shades, extinguished   5
by blue—
There, at the horizon, where river meets sky.

Drinking Alone in the Moonlight‡

From a pot of wine among the flowers
I drank alone. There was no one with me—
Till, raising the cup, I asked the bright moon
To bring me my shadow and make us three.

§Translated by Eugene Eoyang.
‡Translated by Witter Bynner

Alas, the moon was unable to drink   5
And my shadow tagged me vacantly;
But still for a while I had these friends
To cheer me through the end of spring. . .
I sang, the moon encouraged me.
I danced. My shadow tumbled after.   10

As long as I knew, we were boon companions.
And then I was drunk, and we lost one another.
. . . Shall goodwill ever be secure?
I watch the long road of the River of Stars.

TU FU [DU FU] (712–772 C.E.)
China

Tu Fu was a native of Hsiangyang, located in present-day Honan province. When
he was twenty, he began traveling around the country, meeting scholars and
poets, including Li Po. The two poets became lifelong friends, and their
friendship found sincere expression in poems such as "Dreaming of Li Po." Tu Fu
sat for the civil service examination several times but never passed it, and he was
in his forties before he was finally appointed to a minor official position. In his
later years Tu Fu lived mostly in Ch'engtu. In 772, he died on his way to visit
friends.

Tu Fu's life was marked by poverty, instability, anxiety, and frustration. He
was especially affected by the devastation and human suffering he witnessed in
the aftermath of the An Lu-shan rebellion, and in his poems he voiced his
concern for his family, for the people of China, and for the state. In the history of
Chinese literature, Tu Fu's name is most often mentioned in the same breath with
that of Li Po, the two forming twin peaks in the land of poetry. Although Li Po's
poetry largely transcends social realities, Tu Fu was in fact a realist—"a
poet-historian," as he is often called—and he used his gifts to call attention to the
urgent social conditions of his time.

Meandering River, Two Poems*

1

A single petal swirling diminishes the spring.
Ten thousand dots adrift in the wind, they sadden me.
Shouldn't I then gaze at flowers about to fall before my eyes?

Translated by Irving Y. Lo.

Never disdain the hurtful wine that passes through my lips.
In a small pavilion by the river nest the kingfisher birds;   5
Close by a high tomb in the royal park lie stone unicorns.
This, a simple law of nature: seek pleasure while there's time.
Who needs drifting fame to entangle this body?

2

Returning from court day after day, I pawn my spring clothes;
Every time I come home drunk from the riverbank.
A debt of wine is a paltry, everyday affair;
To live till seventy is rare since Time began.
Deep among the flowers, butterflies press their way;   5
The slow-winged dragonflies dot the water.
I'd whisper to the wind and light: "Together let's tarry;
We shall enjoy the moment, and never contrary be."

Dreaming of Li Po, Two Poems[†]

1

Parted by death, we swallow remorse;
Apart in life, we always suffer.
South of the river, miasmal place,
From the banished exile, not a word!
Old friend, you appeared in a dream,   5
It shows you have long been in my thoughts.
Perhaps it wasn't your living soul[1]
The way's too far, it couldn't be done.
Your spirit came: and the maples were green;
Your spirit left: the mountain pass darkened.   10
Friend, now that you're ensnared down there,[2]
How did you manage to wing away?
Moonlight shines full on the rafters,
Yet I wonder if it isn't your reflection.
The waters are deep, the waves expansive: 15
They won't let the water-dragon prevail!

[†]*Translated by Eugene Eoyang.*

"Dreaming of Li Po, Two Poems"

1. The popular conception distinguished between the soul of a living being and the soul of a dead being. The soul of a living being was more circumscribed in its movements, but the soul of the deceased could roam at will across great distances.
2. The image of the net plays an important role in both this and the next poem. Here reference is made to the net of the law. The injustice of this net moves Tu Fu to write in "Twenty Rhymes to Li Po": "When they applied the old laws to your case,/Was there no one to point this out?" It is against this net of the law, which has kept Li Po in exile away from the capital, that Tu Fu rails.

2

Drifting clouds pass by all day long;
The wanderer is long in getting here.
Three nights now you've entered my dreams—
Which shows how good a friend you are.
But your leave-takings are hurried,   5
Bitterly you say, it's not easy to come;
The river's waters are wind-blown and choppy,
And you're afraid to lose your oars.
Outside the door, you scratch your white head,
As if a lifetime's ambition were forfeit.   10
Officials teem in the capital city,[3]
Yet you alone are wretched.
Who says the net is wide,[4]
When it tangles such a man in his old age?
An imperishable fame of a thousand years   15
Is but a paltry, after-life affair.

Random Pleasures: Nine Quatrains*

1

See a traveler in sorrow: deeper is his grief
As wanton spring steals into the river pavilion—
True, the flowers will rush to open,
Yet how the orioles will keep up their songs.

2

Those peach and plum trees planted by hand are not without a master:
The rude wall is low; still it's my home.
But 'tis just like the spring wind, that master bully:
Last night it blew so many blossomed branches down.

Translated by Irving Y. Lo

---

3. Cf. "For Li Po," "Two years I've been in the Eastern Capital,/And had my fill of cunning and conniving."
4. Here, the net is the net of Heaven (cf. Ch. 78 of the *Tao Te Ching:* "Heaven's net is wide; Coarse are the meshes, yet nothing slips through"—Waley translation). Hawkes (*A Little Primer of Tu Fu*, Oxford University Press, 1967, p. 97) contrasts the net here with that in the first poem: "The net here is not the net of the law . . . but the net with which the Emperor, as a fisher of men, gathers up men of talent to put in positions of responsibility. Li Po, one of the biggest fish of all, has managed to elude the imperial fisherman." This contrast, between the "net of the law" and "the net of Heaven," is critical to an understanding of both poems.

3

How well they know my study's low and small—
The swallows from the riverside find reason to visit me often:
Carrying mud to spot and spoil my lute and books,
And trailing a flight of gnats that strike my face.

4

March is gone, and April's come:
Old fellow, how many more chances to welcome the spring?
Don't think of the endless affairs beyond the hereafter;
Just drain your lifetime's few allotted cups.

5

Heartbroken—there springtime river trickles to its end:
Cane in hand, I slowly pace and stand on fragrant bank.
How impertinent the willow catkins to run off with the wind;
So fickle, the peach blossoms to drift with the stream!

6

I've grown so indolent I never leave the village;
At dusk I shout to the boy to shut the rustic gate.
Green moss, raw wine, calm in the grove;
Blue water, spring breeze, dusk on the land.

7

Path-strewn catkins spread out a white carpet;
Stream-dotting lotus leaves mound up green coins.
By the bamboo roots, a young pheasant unseen;
On the sandbank, ducklings by their mother, asleep.

8

West of my house, young mulberry leaves are ready for picking;
Along the river, new wheat, so tender and soft.
How much more is left of life when spring has turned to summer?
Don't pass up good wine, sweeter than honey.

9

The willows by the gate are slender and graceful
Like the waist of a girl at fifteen.
Morning came, and who could fail to see
Mad wind had snapped the longest branch.

Two Quatrains†

1

I lounge on the jetty in the fragrance of catalpa
The fresh young buds all seem too young to fly
I'll stay drunk until the wind's through blowing
Could I bear, if I were sober, the rains come smash, and scatter?

2

Beyond the gate the cormorant had gone and not returned
Now on the sandbank, suddenly, he greets my waiting eye
From this moment he must know my mind
And every day return a hundred times.

Night§

Over sheer banks a menacing wind moves,
In a cold room the candle shadow dims,
The mountain ape sleeps out in the frost,
And the river bird flies deep into night.
Sitting alone I befriend a manly sword,
With a mournful song, sigh at my short gown.
Smoke and dust encircle the palace gate;
White head pays no heed to a stout heart.

5

Jade Flower Palace**

The stream swirls. The wind moans in
The pines. Grey rats scurry over
Broken tiles. What prince, long ago,
Built this palace, standing in

†*Translated by Jerome P. Seaton.*
§*Translated by Jan W. Walls.*
****Translated by Kenneth Rexroth.*

Ruins beside the cliffs? There are 5
Green ghost fires in the black rooms.
The shattered pavements are all
Washed away. Ten thousand organ
Pipes whistle and roar. The storm
Scatters the red autumn leaves. 10
His dancing girls are yellow dust.
Their painted cheeks have crumbled
Away. His gold chariots
And courtiers are gone. Only
A stone horse is left of his 15
Glory. I sit on the grass and
Start a poem, but the pathos of
It overcomes me. The future
Slips imperceptibly away.
Who can say what the years will bring? 20

Restless Night[††]

The cool of bamboo invades my room;
moonlight from the fields fills the corners of the court;
dew gathers till it falls in drops;
a scattering of stars, now there, now gone.
A firefly threading the darkness makes his own light; 5
birds at rest on the water call to each other;
all these lie within the shadow of the sword—
Powerless I grieve as the clear night passes.

PO CHÜ-YI [BAI JUYI] (772–846 C.E.)
China

Po Chü-yi is generally regarded as the third greatest poet of the T'ang period,
surpassed only by Li Po and Tu Fu. A native of the province of Shensi, Po Chü-yi
was born into a scholar official's family. After earning the *chin-shih* degree at
twenty-nine, Po Chü-yi was appointed to a succession of official posts in various
parts of the empire. His long life and broad experience enabled him to be the most
prolific poet of the T'ang period, leaving us a corpus of over three thousand poems.

Despite his successful official career, Po Chü-yi was an advocate of the
impoverished and underprivileged. With Yüan Chen, another poet, Po Chü-yi
formed a literary comradeship, one purpose of which was to promote the socially

[††]*Translated by Burton Watson.*

utilitarian functions of poetry. In many of his poems, such as "Bitter Cold, Living in the Village," "The Old Man of Hsin-feng with the Broken Arm" and "An Old Charcoal Seller," Po Chü-yi expresses his boundless sympathy for unfortunate people and protests social inequities. In the famous "A Song of Unending Sorrow," however, Po Chü-yi was more ambivalent; he castigates the rulers for their sumptuous way of living, but he obviously savors the love between the emperor and his beautiful consort.

Stylistically, Po Chü-yi endeavored to revitalize the *yüeh-fu,* a poetic genre that came into being during the Han period and was rooted in folk song. Indeed, many of Po Chü-yi's poems were written in such a colloquial diction that some critics have called them "pseudo–folk songs."

Bitter Cold, Living in the Village*

In the twelfth month of the Eighth Year,
On the fifth day, a heavy snow fell.
Bamboos and cypress all perished from the freeze.
How much worse for people without warm clothes!

As I looked around the village,   5
Of ten families, eight or nine were in need.
The north wind was sharper than the sword,
And homespun cloth could hardly cover one's body.
Only brambles were burnt for firewood,
And sadly people sat at night to wait for dawn.   10

From this I know that when winter is harsh,
The farmers suffer most.
Looking at myself, during these days—
How I'd shut tight the gate of my thatched hall,
Cover myself with fur, wool, and silk,   15
Sitting or lying down, I had ample warmth.
I was lucky to be spared cold or hunger,
Neither did I have to labor in the field.

Thinking of that, how can I not feel ashamed?
I ask myself what kind of man am I.   20

The Old Man of Hsin-feng with the Broken Arm†1

An old man from Hsin-feng, eighty-eight years old,
Hair on his temples and his eyebrows white as snow.

*Translated by Irving Y. Lo.
†Translated by Eugene Eoyang.

1. Author's subtitle "To Warn Against Militarism: New Music Bureau Ballads" (*Hsin
Yüeh-fu*), No. 9. Each poem in Po Chü-yi's

"New Music Bureau Ballads" carries a similar subtitle, which states the moral implied.

Leaning on his great-great-grandson, he walks to the front of the inn,
His left arm on the boy's shoulder, his right arm broken.
I ask the old man how long has his arm been broken,   5
And how it came about, how it happened.
The old man said he grew up in the Hsin-feng district.
He was born during blessed times, without war or strife.
And he used to listen to the singing and dancing in the Pear Garden,
Knew nothing of banner and spear, or bow and arrow.   10
Then, during the T'ien-pao period, a big army was recruited:
From each family, one was taken out of every three,
And of those chosen, where were they sent?
Five months, ten thousand miles away, to Yunnan,
Where, it is said, the Lu River runs,   15
Where, when flowers fall from pepper trees, noxious fumes rise;
Where, when a great army fords the river, with its seething eddies,
Two or three out of ten never reach the other side.

The village, north and south, was full of the sound of wailing,
Sons leaving father and mother, husbands leaving wives.   20
They all said, of those who went out to fight the barbarians,
Not one out of a thousand lived to come back.
At the time, this old man was twenty-four,
And the army had his name on their roster.

"Then, late one night, not daring to let anyone know,   25
By stealth, I broke my arm, smashed it with a big stone.
Now I was unfit to draw the bow or carry the flag,
And I would be spared the fighting in Yunnan.
Bone shattered, muscles ached, it wasn't unpainful,
But I could count on being rejected and sent home.   30

"This arm has been broken now for over sixty years:
I've lost one limb, but the body's intact.
Even now, in cold nights, when the wind and rain blow,
Right up to daybreak, I hurt so much I cannot sleep,
But I have never had any regrets.   35
At least, now I alone have survived.
Or else, years ago at the River Lu,
I would have died, my spirit fled, and my bones left to rot:
I would have wandered, a ghost in Yunnan looking for home,
Mourning over the graves of ten thousands."   40

So the old man spoke: I ask you to listen.
Have you not heard of the Prime Minister of the K'ai-yüan period,
     Sung K'ai-fu?
How he wouldn't reward frontier campaigns, not wanting to glorify war?
And, have you not heard of Yang Kuo-chung, the Prime Minister of the T'ien-pao
     period?

Wishing to seek favor, he achieved military deeds at the frontier,   45
But, before he could pacify the frontier, the people became disgruntled:
Ask the old man of Hsin-feng with the broken arm!

An Old Charcoal Seller†

An old charcoal seller
Cuts firewood, burns coal by the southern mountain.
His face, all covered with dust and ash, the color of smoke,
The hair at his temples is gray, his ten fingers black.
The money he makes selling coal, what is it for?   5
To put clothes on his back and food in his mouth.
The rags on his poor body are thin and threadbare;
Distressed at the low price of coal, he hopes for colder weather.
Night comes, an inch of snow has fallen on the city,
In the morning, he rides his cart along the icy ruts,   10
His ox weary, he hungry, and the sun already high.
In the mud by the south gate, outside the market, he stops to rest.
All of a sudden, two dashing riders appear;
An imperial envoy, garbed in yellow (his attendant in white),
Holding an official dispatch, he reads a proclamation.   15
Then turns the cart around, curses the ox, and leads it north.
One cartload of coal—a thousand or more vessels!
No use appealing to the official spiriting the cart away:
Half a length of red lace, a slip of damask
Dropped on the ox—is payment in full!   20

To My Brothers and Sisters Adrift in Troubled Times
This Poem of the Moon‡

[Since the disorders in Ho-nan and the famine in Kuan-nêi, my brothers and sisters have
been scattered. Looking at the moon, I express my thoughts in this poem, which I send to my
eldest brother at Fou-liang, my seventh brother at Yü-ch'ien, my fifteenth brother at
Wu-chiang and my younger brothers and sisters at Fu-li and Hsia-kuêi.]

My heritage lost through disorder and famine,
My brothers and sisters flung eastward and westward,
My fields and gardens wrecked by the war,
My own flesh and blood become scum of the street,
I moan to my shadow like a lone-wandering wildgoose,   5
I am torn from my root like a water-plant in autumn:
I gaze at the moon, and my tears run down
For hearts, in five places, all sick with one wish.

†*Translated by Eugene Eoyang.*
‡*Translated by Witter Bynner.*

A Song of Unending Sorrow†

China's Emperor, craving beauty that might shake an empire,
Was on the throne for many years, searching, never finding,
Till a little child of the Yang clan, hardly even grown,
Bred in an inner chamber, with no one knowing her,
But with graces granted by heaven and not to be concealed,   5
At last one day was chosen for the imperial household.
If she but turned her head and smiled, there were cast a hundred spells,
And the powder and paint of the Six Palaces faded into nothing.
. . . It was early spring. They bathed her in the Flower-Pure Pool,
Which warmed and smoothed the creamy-tinted crystal of her skin,   10
And, because of her languor, a maid was lifting her
When first the Emperor noticed her and chose her for his bride.
The cloud of her hair, petal of her cheek, gold ripples of her crown when she
      moved,
Were sheltered on spring evenings by warm hibiscus-curtains;
But nights of spring were short and the sun arose too soon,   15
And the Emperor, from that time forth, forsook his early hearings
And lavished all his time on her with feasts and revelry,
His mistress of the spring, his despot of the night.
There were other ladies in his court, three thousand of rare beauty,
But his favours to three thousand were concentered in one body.   20
By the time she was dressed in her Golden Chamber, it would be almost evening;
And when tables were cleared in the Tower of Jade, she would loiter, slow with
      wine.
Her sisters and her brothers all were given titles;
And, because she so illumined and glorified her clan,
She brought to every father, every mother through the empire,   25
Happiness when a girl was born rather than a boy.
. . . High rose Li Palace, entering blue clouds,
And far and wide the breezes carried magical notes
Of soft song and slow dance, of string and bamboo music.
The Emperor's eyes could never gaze on her enough—   30
Till war-drums, booming from Yü-yang, shocked the whole earth
And broke the tunes of *The Rainbow Skirt and the Feathered Coat*.
The Forbidden City, the nine-tiered palace, loomed in the dust
From thousands of horses and chariots headed southwest.
The imperial flag opened the way, now moving and now pausing—   35
But thirty miles from the capital, beyond the western gate,
The men of the army stopped, not one of them would stir
Till under their horses' hoofs they might trample those moth-eyebrows . . . .
Flowery hairpins fell to the ground, no one picked them up,
And a green and white jade hair-tassel and a yellow-gold hairbird.   40
The Emperor could not save her, he could only cover his face.
And later when he turned to look, the place of blood and tears

Was hidden in a yellow dust blown by a cold wind.
. . . At the cleft of the Dagger-Tower Trail they criss-crossed through a cloud-line
Under O-mêi Mountain. The last few came. 45
Flags and banners lost their colour in the fading sunlight . . .
But as waters of Shu are always green and its mountains always blue,
So changeless was His Majesty's love and deeper than the days.
He stared at the desolate moon from his temporary palace.
He heard bell-notes in the evening rain, cutting at his breast. 50
And when heaven and earth resumed their round and the dragon-car faced home,
The Emperor clung to the spot and would not turn away
From the soil along the Ma-wêi Slope, under which was buried
That memory, that anguish. Where was her jade-white face?
Ruler and lords, when eyes would meet, wept upon their coats 55
As they rode, with loose rein, slowly eastward, back to the capital.
. . . The pools, the gardens, the palace, all were just as before,
The Lake T'ai-yi hibiscus, the Wêi-yang Palace willows;
But a petal was like her face and a willow-leaf her eyebrow—
And what could he do but cry whenever he looked at them? 60
. . . Peach-trees and plum-trees blossomed, in the winds of spring;
Lakka-foliage fell to the ground, after autumn rains;
The Western and Southern Palaces were littered with late grasses,
And the steps were mounded with red leaves that no one swept away.
Her Pear-Garden Players became white-haired 65
And the eunuchs thin-eyebrowed in her Court of Pepper-Trees;
Over the throne flew fire-flies, while he brooded in the twilight.
He would lengthen the lamp-wick to its end and still could never sleep.
Bell and drum would slowly toll the dragging night-hours
And the River of Stars grow sharp in the sky, just before dawn, 70
And the porcelain mandarin-ducks on the roof grow thick with morning frost
And his covers of kingfisher-blue feel lonelier and colder
With the distance between life and death year after year;
And yet no beloved spirit ever visited his dreams.
. . . At Lin-ch'iung lived a Taoist priest who was a guest of heaven, 75
Able to summon spirits by his concentrated mind.
And people were so moved by the Emperor's constant brooding
That they besought the Taoist priest to see if he could find her.
He opened his way in space and clove the ether like lightning,
Up to heaven, under the earth, looking everywhere. 80
Above, he searched the Green Void, below, the Yellow Spring;
But he failed, in either place, to find the one he looked for.
And then he heard accounts of an enchanted isle at sea,
A part of the intangible and incorporeal world,
With pavilions and fine towers in the five-coloured air, 85
And of exquisite immortals moving to and fro,
And of one among them—whom they called The Ever True—
With a face of snow and flowers resembling hers he sought.

So he went to the West Hall's gate of gold and knocked at the jasper door
And asked a girl, called Morsel-of-Jade, to tell The Doubly-Perfect.   90
And the lady, at news of an envoy from the Emperor of China,
Was startled out of dreams in her nine-flowered canopy.
She pushed aside her pillow, dressed, shook away sleep,
And opened the pearly shade and then the silver screen.
Her cloudy hair-dress hung on one side because of her great haste,   95
And her flower-cap was loose when she came along the terrace,
While a light wind filled her cloak and fluttered with her motion
As though she danced *The Rainbow Skirt and the Feathered Coat.*
And the tear-drops drifting down her sad white face
Were like a rain in spring on the blossom of the pear.   100
But love glowed deep within her eyes when she bade him thank her liege,
Whose form and voice had been strange to her ever since their parting—
Since happiness had ended at the Court of the Bright Sun,
And moons and dawns had become long in Fairy-Mountain Palace.
But when she turned her face and looked down toward the earth   105
And tried to see the capital, there were only fog and dust.
So she took out, with emotion, the pledges he had given
And, through his envoy, sent him back a shell box and gold hairpin,
But kept one branch of the hairpin and one side of the box,
Breaking the gold of the hairpin, breaking the shell of the box;   110
"Our souls belong together," she said, "like this gold and this shell—
Somewhere, sometime, on earth or in heaven, we shall surely meet."
And she sent him, by his messenger, a sentence reminding him
Of vows which had been known only to their two hearts:
"On the seventh day of the Seventh-month, in the Palace of Long Life,   115
We told each other secretly in the quiet midnight world
That we wished to fly in heaven, two birds with the wings of one,
And to grow together on the earth, two branches of one tree."
. . . Earth endures, heaven endures; some time both shall end,
While this unending sorrow goes on and on for ever.   120

LI CH'ING-CHAO [LI QINGZHAO]

(1084?–c. 1151 C.E.)

China

Indisputably China's most noted woman poet, Li Ch'ing-chao lived during a
period straddling the Northern and the Southern Sung dynasties. The daughter
of a distinguished man of letters from Tsi-nan, Shantung, she married a scholar

named Chao Ming-ch'eng. At the time of the invasion of the Chin Tartars (the event that caused the Sung to move their capital south, ushering in the Southern Sung period), the couple hastily made their escape southward, but the husband died after they reached Chienk'ang (present-day Nanjing). Lonely and wretched, the poet spent the rest of her life in Hangchou and Chinhua.

In addition to inheriting an extremely rich tradition of poetry from the T'ang, the Sung Dynasty saw the flourishing of a newly popular form called *tz'u*. Originating in popular song, *tz'u* were written to fit certain specified tunes. Like many other Sung poets, Li Ch'ing-chao wrote mostly in the *tz'u* tradition.

In Li Ch'ing-chao's poems, of which only some fifty are extant, we hear the many voices of the poet, the facets of a distinctly feminine sensibility. To her, the blissful matrimonial life was only to be recaptured in poetry ("Tune: 'Magnolia Blossoms, Abbreviated' " and "Tune: 'Song of Picking Mulberry' "). Except for a few bright moments of delight ("Tune: 'Manifold Little Hills' "), most of her poems convey the sorrow and melancholy of widowhood. She was incomparable in depicting personal feelings with vigor and honesty and in transcending the subjective and the merely anecdotal.

Tune: *Spring at Wu-ling*

The wind subsides—a fragrance
   of petals freshly fallen;
it's late in the day—I'm too tired
   to comb my hair.
Things remain but he is gone
   and with him everything.
On the verge of words: tears flow.

I hear at Twin Creek spring it's still lovely;   5
how I long to float there on a small boat—
But I fear at Twin Creek my frail "grasshopper" boat
could not carry this load of grief.

Tune: *A Southern Song*

In the sky the Milky Way turns;
here on earth a curtain drops.
A chill collects on the pillow-mat, wet with tears.
I get up to untie my silk gown,
   wondering what hour of night it is.   5

The blue-tinted lotus pod is small
the gold-spotted lotus leaves are sparse.
Old-time weather, old-time clothes

Translated by Eugene Eoyang.

only bring back memories
  but nothing like real old times.   10

Tune: Tipsy in the Flower's Shade

Thin mists—thick clouds—sad all day long.
The gold animal spurts incense from its head.
Once more it's the Festival of Double Nine[1]:
On the jade pillow—through mesh bed curtains—
the chill of midnight starts seeping through.   5

At the eastern hedge[2] I drink a cup after dusk;
furtive fragrances fill my sleeve.
Don't say one can't be overwhelmed:
when the west wind furls up the curtain,
I'm more fragile than the yellow chrysanthemum.   10

Tune: Manifold Little Hills

Spring has come to the gate—spring's grasses green;
some red blossoms on the plum tree burst open,
others have yet to bloom.
Azure clouds gather, grind out jade into dust.
Let's keep this morning's dream: 5
break open a jug of spring!

Flower's shadows press at the gate;
translucent curtains thin out pale moonlight.
It's a lovely evening!
Over two years—three times—you've missed the spring.   10
Come back!
Let's enjoy this one to the full!

Tune: Magnolia Blossoms, Abbreviated

From the pole of the flower vendor
I bought a sprig of spring about to bloom,

---

1. The Double Nine refers to the ninth day of
   the ninth month by the lunar calendar
   (which corresponds to early October),
   which the Chinese call *Ch'ung Yang*. On this
   day, the custom is to climb to high ground,
   take some wine in which chrysanthemum
   petals have been dropped, and compose
   poetry. The festival was especially important to Li Ch'ing-chao, because it was associated with T'ao Ch'ien, the poet whom she
   and her husband preferred to all others and
   who was known for his poems on the
   chrysanthemum.
2. Referring to T'ao Ch'ien's famous lines:
   "Picking chrysanthemums by the eastern
   hedge / I catch sight of the distant southern
   hills."

tear-speckled, lightly sprinkled,
still touched by a rose mist and dawn's early dew.

Should my beloved chance to ask,
if my face weren't fair as a flower's,
I'd put one aslant in my hair,
then ask him to look and compare.

Tune: The Charm of Nien-nu

　　Lonely courtyard,
once more slanting wind, misty rain,
the double-hinged door must be shut.
Graceful willow, delicate blossoms,
　　Cold Food Day approaches,
and with it every kind of unsettling weather.
　　I work out a few ingenious rhymes,
　　clear my head of weak wine,
　　exceptional, the taste of idleness.
Migrating wild geese wing out of sight
but they cannot convey my teeming thoughts.

In my pavilion, cold for days with spring chill,
　　the curtains are drawn on all sides.
I am too weary to lean over the balustrade.
The incense sputters, the quilt feels cold,
　　I am just awake from a dream.
No dallying in bed for one who grieves,
　　when clear dew descends with the dawn,
　　and the *wu-t'ung* tree is about to bud.
There are so many diversions in spring.
The sun is rising: the fog withdraws;
see: it will be a fine day after all.

Tune: As in a Dream: A Song (Two Lyrics)

1

How many evenings in the arbor by the river,
when flushed with wine we'd lose our way back.
The mood passed away, returning late by boat
we'd stray off into a spot thick with lotus,
　　and thrashing through
　　　　　　　　and thrashing through
startle a shoreful of herons by the lake.

2

Last night, a bit of rain, gusty wind,
a deep sleep did not dispel the last of the wine.
I ask the maid rolling up the blinds—
but she replies: "The crab apple is just as it was."
    Doesn't she know?
                doesn't she know?
The leaves should be lush and the petals frail.

Tune: Sand of Silk-washing Stream (Two Lyrics)

1

Mild and peaceful spring glow, Cold Food Day.
From a jade censer, incense curls out in wisps of smoke.
My dream returns me to the hills of my pillow, hiding my hairpins.
The sea swallows have not yet come,
    idly we duel with blades of grass.
By the river the plum trees have bloomed,
    catkins sprout from the willow,
and at dusk scattered showers
    sprinkle the garden swing.

2

In the little courtyard, by the side window,
    spring's colors deepen,
with the double blinds unfurled
    the gloom thickens.
Upstairs, wordless,
    the strumming of a jasper lute.

Far-off hills, jutting peaks,
    hasten the thinning of dusk,
Gentle wind blowing rain
    plays with light shade.
Pear blossoms are about to fall
    but there's no helping that.

Tune: Song of Picking Mulberry[1]

In the evening gusts of wind and rain
    washed away embers of daylight.

---

1. This lyric has also been attributed to anonymous authorship and appeared under the
   tune-title Ch'ou nu-erh.

I stop playing on the pipe
and touch up my face in front of my mirror.

Through the thin red silk my cool flesh glistens   5
  lustrous as snow fresh with fragrance.
  With a smile I say to my beloved:
"Tonight, inside the mesh curtains, the pillow and mat are cool."

Tune: Telling of Innermost Feelings

Night found me so flushed with wine;
  I was slow to undo my hair.
The plum petals still stuck onto a dying branch.
Waking up, the scent of wine stirred me from spring sleep;
  my dream once broken, there was no going back.   5

  Now it's quiet,
  the moon hovers above,
  the kingfisher blinds are drawn.
Still: I feel the fallen petals;
still: I touch their lingering scent;   10
still: I hold onto a moment of time.

JAPAN

Premodern or classical Japanese literature extends from earliest times to the Meiji
Restoration of 1868, a change in government that ended a long period of
isolationism and opened Japan to the West. The date is a convenience, of course,
for literary practice did not change overnight. Nevertheless, the Japanese themselves find it a useful reference point for separating the world of "then" from the
world of "now." In its classical period, Japanese literature defined itself largely
against the influence and example of China; in the modern period, it has
responded in various ways to the literature of the West. This section treats
Japanese literature up to 1600, the beginning of the Edo period (a change in
government that moved the capital to Edo, present-day Tokyo).

Like almost all literatures except those of the West, Japanese literature was
founded on the lyric. That is, it holds the lyric poem to be the highest form of
artistic expression, and the lyric sensibility infuses its other literary genres, such
as drama and prose narrative. So close is the Japanese identification with the lyric
that its most characteristic poetic form, the *tanka,* or "short poem," is alternatively called *waka,* which means simply "Japanese poem." Exceedingly brief by

Western norms, the *tanka* consists of 31 syllables divided into five lines. (The pattern is 5-7-5-7-7.) For centuries, Japanese poets cultivated this small plot, and from it entire worlds of human experience blossomed.

The poetics (a treatise on poetic theory) for a lyric-based literature was supplied early on, though not, interestingly, at the very dawn of the tradition. The earliest extant Japanese works are three compilations of the eighth century C.E., *Kojiki* ("Records of Ancient Matters"), *Nihon Shoki* ("Records of Japan"), and *Man'yōshū* ("Collection for Ten Thousand Generations" or "of Ten Thousand Leaves"). *Kojiki* and *Nihon Shoki* were considered historical accounts of the Age of the Gods through the early sovereigns of Japan. Today, we would say they combine myth, legend, anecdote, and history. Both are prose narratives, though they also include poems and songs, and both anthologize traditional, orally transmitted material as well as earlier written sources, now lost. As such, they served as valuable sourcebooks for later writers, and they remain essential for understanding early Japan.

The *Man'yōshū* is the first extant collection of poetry and the glory of early Japanese literature. It would be impossible to overstate the esteem in which the collection is held in Japan. Compiled in the latter portion of the eighth century, in part from no longer extant earlier collections, it contains well over four thousand poems, ranging from anonymous works transmitted orally from early times through contemporary poems by the anthology's compilers. In view of later developments, the variety of its forms is most remarkable. *Tanka* are certainly well represented, but there are also many long poems, *chōka*, and these often contain narrative elements and a decidedly public voice, addressing issues of concern to society such as war, historical events, and affairs of state.

The earliest writings of Japan, then, offered many possible directions for development. Yet, for whatever reason, no critical ntelligence of sufficient power or influence arose in response to these works to formulate a literary theory based on prose, on narrative, or on poetry of the public realm. After the *Man'yōshū*, Japan's poets grew more subjective, and it is this intimate, personal, yet social lyricism that came to distinguish most Japanese poetry.

In the early part of the tenth century, the poet Ki no Tsurayuki and others compiled the *Kokinshū*, the first of twenty-one royally comissioned *waka* collections. The collection came to be considered a standard, so much so that to refer to something as the *Kokinshū* of its kind was a formula of high praise. Tsurayuki's preface to the collection is the first major work of Japanese literary criticism in Japan, and it formulated the poetics that set the essential project of Japanese literature for centuries. In the opening of the preface, often referred to by later writers, Tsurayuki set out to differentiate Japanese poetry:

> The poetry of Japan has its roots in the human heart [or, mind] and flourishes in the countless leaves of words. Because human beings possess interests of so many kinds, it is in poetry that they give expression [to what they think and experience]. Hearing the warbler sing among the blossoms and the frog that lives in the waters—is there any living being not given to song? It is poetry which, without exertion, moves heaven and earth, stirs the feelings of gods and spirits invisible to the eye, softens relations between men and women, calms the hearts of fierce warriors.

The human heart (or, mind), Tsurayuki says, is the seed or cause of words. Japanese poetry is thus *expressionist,* that is, it concerns itself with giving form to an inner, emotional response to the outer world of experience. (In lieu of a title, collections like the *Kokinshū* precede each poem with a brief statement of the circumstances or subject the poem responds to.) Japanese poetry is also *affective,* that is, its goal is to produce in the reader the response that moved the poet. The expressive-affective ideal of poetry is that of a "transfer" from heart to heart of what is most moving.

The third sentence is also important. Tsurayuki asks rhetorically whether poetry is not the natural expression of *all* living things. That emphasis shows how we Western readers ought not to suppose that Japanese poetry — for all its valuing of cultivated lyricism — is inherently elitist. It is true that the majority of poems that have come down to us were written by a small elite largely centered around the court, and that in this rarified milieu the crafting of verse became a subtle and exquisite affair. But the assumption underlying the Japanese view of poetry is something quite different: Poetry is a natural form of expression, something everyone is presumed capable of creating. An experience of sufficient emotional intensity was as likely to prompt a *tanka* from a peasant as from a courtier. The royal anthologies, the most famous repositories of classical poetry, underscored this point by including poetry by illiterates, by a beggar or a prostitute, for example. Even *renga* linked verse, a particularly intricate and demanding form, was mastered by illiterate peasants, who composed orally and recited their efforts.

Orality in general retained a strong presence in Japanese literature. Correspondence commonly included poetry, and the recipient of a letter was expected to read any poems it contained aloud in a sort of heightened speech-song called cantillation. Even lengthy prose works were written to be recited rather than read. Versions of this practice still survive. Tsurayuki's invocation of warbler- and frog-song thus strikes deeper than the casual reader first realizes: literature in Japan was human song and to be voiced.

In another work, Tsurayuki has his narrator write in her diary, "Surely both in China and Japan art is that which is created when we are unable to suppress our feeling." Japanese ideas about literature were founded to no little extent by knowledge of the "classical" model of China, whose civilization was already highly advanced when Japan's was newly forming. There is a consistent lag of about 350 years between Chinese practice and Japanese adaptation. The insular nation guarded itself from its huge continental neighbor by the time lag to adapt to native tastes, by periodic rejection of the foreign, as well as by an almost religious veneration of the unique properties, real and supposed, of Japanese language and society.

As is often pointed out, classical Chinese served much the same purpose in East and Southeast Asia as Latin did in medieval Europe. It was the language of scholarship, of education and cultivation. (There is a sizeable body of poetry by both Korean and Japanese poets in classical Chinese.) The Japanese initially borrowed Chinese characters to write their own language. While the gift of writing was, of course, a great step for Japan, the system was extremely cumbersome, for the Japanese language is much different from Chinese. During the ninth century, the Japanese developed two syllabaries based on simplified Chinese characters. (A syllabary is a writing system in which each symbol stands for a syllable.) However, links with Chinese, both spoken and written, remained in the language to varying degrees. (Today, Japanese is written with a mixture of Chinese characters and Japanese syllabic symbols.)

Classical Chinese remained the preferred medium for most philosophical and legal texts, histories, essays and religious writings in Japan until the nineteenth century. But classical Japanese poetry, the foundation of Japanese literature, shunned Sinified pronunciations (words pronounced in the Chinese manner) and Chinese loanwords, emphasizing instead pure Japanese, which could be written entirely with the syllabaries, avoiding Chinese characters altogether. A syllabary, like an alphabet, is inherently democratic: Anyone can learn to write "by ear," connecting the limited repertoire of signs with sounds. Perhaps the happiest consequence was the opening of the literary enterprise to women. Women did not normally receive a formal education in classical Chinese, but because literature emphasized pure Japanese, women could write — and not as marginal voices but straight to the heart of the tradition. Women were authors in Japan from earliest mythic times, and Japanese is the sole literature for which it is agreed that the greatest writer is a woman: Murasaki Shikibu, author of *The Tale of Genji*.

Japanese poetics is distinguished from other lyric-based aesthetics in its early acceptance of fictionality. To simplify complex matters, we can say that literature is assumed to be factual in the absence of evidence to the contrary. That is, we assume that the poet actually had the experience that prompted the poem. Fictionality is accommodated to factuality when a poet responds to an imagined experience as though it were real. A poem attributed to an animal, for example, is clearly fictional. (Poems were attributed to animals in the spirit of the *Kokinshū* preface.) A more pervasive practice was the poetry match, in which poets composed on set topics. By the eleventh century most poetry was created in response to the topics set for competitions. Fictional poetry is now judged by how intensely it affects a reader, not how faithfully it reports an actual experience.

A second distinguishing mark of Japanese literature is the early acceptance of prose narrative and drama as critically esteemed genres. By 1010, less than a century after the *Kokinshū* preface, Murasaki Shikibu had, in her *Tale of Genji*, produced in prose the greatest work in the whole literature, justifying it (in the "Fireflies" chapter) by analogy both to histories and to Buddhist practice: Fiction gives what is lacking, most moving, and religiously suggestive to cold fact.

The Tale of Genji is studded with lyrics — the characters often communicate in verse. In this we discover another distinctive feature of Japanese literature, the compatibility of narrative and lyric: poems are typically embedded like gemstones in longer prose works, where they serve to embody moments of particular emotional intensity. The selections from the *Tales of Ise* included here show this trait in its ideal form.

This tendency to use brief poetic units as building blocks of larger artistic wholes is evident in its purest form in the royal *waka* anthologies themselves. These did not order their contents chronologically or by author, but by subject matter (the seasons, love, and so on). Organization grew increasingly subtle, reaching perfection with the eighth anthology, the *Shinkokinshū* of the early thirteenth century, which can actually be read as a single, extended work of nearly 2,000 poems (10,000 lines).

With *nō* plays and their comic interludes, *kyōgen,* drama obtained admired status. *Nō* developed gradually from a variety of popular entertainment forms. Its sudden flowering and achievement of literary prestige was largely the work of two men, the actor and playwright Kan'ami (1333–1384) and his even greater son, the actor, playwright, and critic Zeami (?1364–?1443). Zeami's critical writings in particular were instrumental in positioning *nō* within the framework of Japan's lyric poetics (as amplified to include narratives). In the manner of narrative works, *nō* texts combine prose and poetry. But the essence of *nō* theatre is, of course, performance, and the text must be understood as only one element of what in contemporary terms we might call total theatre. *Nō* performance includes masks, music, mime, dance, chant, and a stylized form of acting. In its method of performance and its central use of narrative and lyric, it is unique in the theatres of the world.

The selections here illustrate the progression of the lyric-based literature in pure Japanese that has been the subject of this introduction. Thus, the usual "narrow" definition of Japanese literature has been used, excluding Japanese writings in Chinese, as well as writings in Ainu (the language of an earlier people in the Japanese islands), or in the Ryukyuan dialect-language. By modern western convention, we ignore many histories included in the broader Japanese concept of literature. Space constraints account for omission of many kinds of poetry and song, of performance, and of narrative.

Historical Background

The early Stone Age culture of Japan seems to have given way around 300 B.C.E. to communities based on agriculture and metal-working—developments that paved the way there as elsewhere for the beginning of civilization. The technologies had probably been brought by a new wave of arrivals from the nearby Korean peninsula. After a period of warfare (a Chinese chronicle of the Han Dynasty speaks of Japan as comprising "more than one hundred countries" at war), a more or less stable configuration of regional states seems to have emerged—tribal confederations, more accurately—ruled by a dominant aristocratic warrior class headed by royalty.

By around 300 C.E., a warrior clan on the Yamato plain, near present day Osaka, had accrued enough power to style themselves as "great kings" over the regional aristocracy. From here on, the political history of Japan is customarily divided into periods according to the seat of the government, and literary history follows suit. (It also uses designations such as medieval, modern, etc.)

During the Yamato era, which lasted roughly four centuries, close relations with Korea continued, and Chinese culture, which the Korean ruling class had adopted, passed increasingly into Japan. During the sixth century, Buddhism, Confucianism, administrative systems, and writing all entered Japan mostly through Korea. Beginning in the seventh century, Japan began to send students and ambassadors directly to China, a practice that continued for some 200 years.

Though it persisted, the philosophy of Confucius did not find especially fertile ground in Japan. Buddhism, however, proved a lasting and powerful influence. The Japanese took especially to the religious aspects of Buddhism (the Chinese, in contrast, had focused on the philosophical side). Buddhism had the advantage of meshing easily with the ancient state religion, Shintō. Shintō is a shamanistic religion, shamans being mediums between humankind and divinities. When not protective deities or spirits of the dead, the divinities of Shintō are largely natural divinities—mountains, rivers, thunder, and so on. The chief divinity is female, the sun goddess. Shamans, too, are almost all female (the chief exception being the monarch, who ruled as the leading shaman). Shintō is a religion of communion with, invocation of, and appeasement of spirits, including the recent dead. Its strong feminine component is another cultural factor supporting the uncontested acceptance of women as writers and the relatively high position of women in society generally: women monarchs were common in early times.

Toward the end of the seventh century centralized power increased, and administrative systems adapted from Chinese models were instituted. While Western histories have generally referred to the rulers of Japan as emperors from this point on, the concept of empire had no place in classical Japan. "Sovereign" or "monarch" remain more accurate titles.

In 710, the capital was moved to Nara. With the Nara period, we enter true historical time, though our knowledge is far from complete. This was the period of Japanese literature's three founding works, *Kojiki, Nihon Shoki*, and *Man'yōshū*. In 794, the capital moved again, this time to Heian (present-day Kyoto), where it remained for over one thousand years. The Heian era was one of courtly refinement and great artistic brilliance. Literary development was rapid, as was development in other social and cultural spheres. The capital grew to perhaps the most populous city in the world, and decade upon decade passed in peace.

The Heian also witnessed the rise of the *samurai* — regional warriors nominally in the service of the government but capable of stirring up trouble. Regional military forces emerged, increasing in strength and sapping the power of the nobility of the ruling Fujiwara houses. That vast family grew to preeminence in the ninth century and retained its grip on power for 200 years. They monopolized all key government posts and, by marrying their daughters to the sovereign, controlled the court as well: after the birth of an heir, the Fujiwara would force the sovereign into retirement and rule as regents for the child. Things began to change when a series of "retired" sovereigns reasserted control from 1072 to 1156. But struggles over royal succession brought in rival military forces with their taste for conflict. At first the Taira family (who had supplanted the Fujiwara in power) triumphed over the armies of the Minamoto family. Their control was brief—they were overthrown by the Minamoto in 1185. The long rivalry and bloody warfare between the Taira and Minamoto clans furnished a rich subject for later literature.

The ensuing period, dated from either 1156 or 1186 and extending to 1603, is often referred to as medieval or feudal Japan, though it is more specifically divided into four periods, Kamakura, Nambokuchō, Muromachi, and Azuchi-Momoyama. The victorious Minamoto generals moved the administrative center east to Kamakura, away from the distractions of the Heian court. Their control lasted until 1339, when the country was plunged into disastrous civil war over two rival lines of sovereigns (the Nambokuchō period). Peace was forged in 1399 with the formation of a military and increasingly "feudal" society. Powerful regional lords ruled under the central control (now waxing, now waning) of a *bakufu* (government by military aristocracy) run by the *shogun*, the commander-in-chief to the figurehead sovereign. Regional warfare was common. In this newly militaristic society, the status of women declined. Buddhism offered a consolation to many in these chaotic times, especially the Pure Lands and Zen sects, which ascended over the Tendai and Shingon sects that had dominated the Heian period. In literature, this was the time of the flowering *nō* drama and *renga* linked verse.

A Note on Japanese Names and Pronunciation

Names are given here in contemporary style and according to representations of contemporary Japanese pronunciation. Surnames precede given names, as in

Ariwara (surname) Narihira (given name). Beyond this point, the matter of names in Japan is more complicated. Modern abbreviations simplify more ancient practice and have been used here: thus, Kakinomoto Hitomaro instead of Kakinomoto no Asomi no Hitomaro. By convention, some writers are known by their pen name versions of given names, while others are known by their (sometimes pseudo-) surnames. There is no single rule or style to be followed. One simply adopts some version of current Japanese practice.

A rough approximation of modern Japanese pronunciation is possible with vowels sounded as in Spanish (or Italian, Latin) and consonants as in English except for *r*, which is pronounced with the slightest touch of *the tip* of the tongue behind the area touched for English *l*, so giving it features of English *l*, *r*, and *d*. The stress accent on Japanese syllables is lighter than in English. There is also a light accent. Following the usual practice, Old Japanese has here been standardized into modern. Two diacritical marks are used: an apostrophe to indicate the end of a syllable and a macron to indicate lengthening of *o* or *u*. Thus, *Man'yōshū* is pronounced divided as *man-yō-shū* rather than *ma-nyō-shū*, and with the second and third vowels longer in duration than the first. Long *a*, *e*, and *i* are represented doubled as *aa*, *ee*, and *ii*.

Further Reading

Keene, Donald. *World Within Walls*. New York: Holt Rinehart Winston, 1976. (premodern, ca. 1600–1868)

———. *Dawn to the West*. 2 vols. New York: Holt Rinehart Winston, 1984.

Konishi, Jin'ichi. *A History of Japanese Literature*. 5 vols., Princeton: Princeton University Press. Volume 1: *The Archaic and Ancient Ages*, 1984; Volume 2: *The Early Middle Ages*, 1986; Volume 3: *The High Middle Ages*, 1991.

Miner, Earl, Hiroko Odagiri, and Robert E. Morrell. *The Princeton Companion to Classical Japanese Literature*. Princeton: Princeton University Press, 1985.

Note: At present the most authoritative version in English consists of Konishi's three volumes followed by Keene's two in the 1984 work, but both authors assume certain kinds of knowledge. In Miner et al. there is a concise literary history (Part 1); there are also chronologies (Part 2) and other information. But all is premodern.

KAKINOMOTO HITOMARO
(fl. 680–700; d. 708–715 C.E.)

YAMANO(U)E OKURA (660–c. 733 C.E.)

Japan

Kakinomoto Hitomaro and Yamano(u)e Okura are generally regarded as the foremost poets of the *Man'yōshū* (c. 760), the first great anthology of Japanese poetry, containing about 4,500 poems.

Kakinomoto Hitomaro has long been revered as a virtual deity within the world of poetry. For centuries after his death, the supposed date of his birth was a closely guarded secret, known only to a few. He perfected the chōka (long poem), which dealt with both official and personal subjects.

In Hitomaro's poetry, the simple and the complex are impossible to distinguish. The first poem selected here, ("at Cape Kara . . .") which concerns a man who is parting from his wife, reflects enormously complicated Japanese marriage customs. Family property was passed down matrilineally—that is, from mother to daughter. Thus a husband moved in with (or visited) his wife. If he was then assigned duty to another part of the county, as is assumed to be the case in this poem, separation or divorce was the result. Over a lifetime, both sexes might have a series of spouses, official or unofficial.

In the second poem, ("The Quick Gallop"), a man mourns the death of his wife. In the Shinto religion, efforts were made to remember the newly dead, both to comfort mourners and to pacify the possibly angry spirit of the deceased. In the third poem ("The land of Sanuki . . .") the poet describes his shipwreck during a typhoon. He encounters a lifeless body and addresses it—or its spirit—in order to pacify it. Hitomaro seeks to pacify and console himself as well. He speaks in gentle ironies: We meet disaster, yet the world is divine; if your wife were here . . . ; what a rough place to sleep. In Japanese the poem can be read so that the complete text is an incomplete sentence stressing its last word, wife; the same word begins the first envoy—or short concluding stanza—which finally brings the sentence to a close.

Yamano(u)e Okura studied for a while in China, and in the dialogue presented here he writes Chinese-style social criticism. The criticism is implicit; no names are provided. But the poet makes the point that the country is not well ruled—hence the apologetic prose at the end to soften the criticism. The poem consists of a double *chōka,* something very rare. In the first *chōka* (lines 1–29), a poor man speaks, emphasizing the cold as an image of his bad fortune. In the second *chōka* (lines 30–70), a man wholly destitute replies. Traces of new (Chinese) learning appear in references to Buddhist and Confucian tenets. Thus to be born human (line 38) is a blessing, since it is a requisite for Buddhist enlightenment. The greater care of parents than of wife and children (lines 50–53) is Confucian. (We could not guess from this poem that property in Japan was inherited matrilineally.)

The translator follows the usual interpretation wherein the poet himself speaks the envoy. The original, however, has no noun or pronoun as a subject.

It is conceivable that the destitute man continues talking, or that a voice speaks on behalf of the human race.

The morality based on rational grounds, the striking imagery appealing to all our senses, and the uneven, jerky, hard-hitting style are typical of Okura's poetry. By the end, we feel Okura's concern: we know that poverty and hunger continue in "this world."

from **Man'Yōshū**

KAKINOMOTO HITOMARO

On Parting from His Wife as He Set Out from Iwami for the Capital

At Cape Kara
on the Sea of Iwami,
where the vines
   crawl on the rocks,
rockweed of the deep   5
grows on the reefs
and sleek seaweed
grows on the desolate shore.
As deeply do I
think of my wife   10
who swayed toward me in sleep
   like the lithe seaweed.
Yet few were the nights
we had slept together
before we were parted   15
like crawling vines uncurled.
And so I look back,
still thinking of her
with painful heart,
this clench of inner flesh,   20
but in the storm
of fallen scarlet leaves
on Mount Watari,
crossed as on
   a great ship,   25
I cannot make out the sleeves
she waves in farewell.
For she, alas,
is slowly hidden
like the moon   30
   in its crossing

Translated by Ian Hideo Levy.

between the clouds
over Yagami Mountain
just as the evening sun
coursing through the heavens
has begun to glow,
            and even I
who thought I was a brave man
find the sleeves
of my well-woven robe
drenched with tears.

Envoys

The quick gallop
of my dapple-blue steed
races me to the clouds,
passing far away
from where my wife dwells.

O scarlet leaves
falling on the autumn mountainside:
stop, for a while, the storm
your strewing makes, that I might glimpse
the place where my wife dwells.

On the Death of His Wife

She was my wife,
to whom my thoughts gathered
thick as the spring leaves,
like the myriad branches budding
on the zelkova tree
on the embankment (a short step
from her gate),
that we would bring
and look at together
while she was of this world.
She was my wife,
on whom I depended,
but now, unable to break
the course of this world,
she shrouds herself from me
in heavenly white raiments
on a withered, sun-simmered plain,
and rises away in the morning
like a bird,

and conceals herself
like the setting sun.
Each time our infant,
the memento she left,
cries out in hunger,
I, though a man,
having nothing to give it,
hug it to my breast.
Inside the wedding house
where the pillows we slept on
lie pushed together,
I live through the days
desolate and lonely
and sigh through the nights.
Lament as I may,
I know nothing I can do.
Long for her as I may,
I have no way to meet her.
And so when someone said,
"The wife you long for
dwells on Hagai Mountain,
    of the great bird,"
I struggled up here,
kicking the rocks apart,
but it did no good:
my wife, whom I thought
was of this world,
is ash.[1]

Envoys

The autumn moon crosses the heavens
as it did when I watched last year,
but my wife, who watched with me—
the drift of the year has taken her.

Leaving my wife on Hikide Mountain
by the Fusuma Road,
I think of the path she has taken,
and I am hardly alive.

I come home
and gaze inside:
facing outward

20
25
30
35
40
45
50
55

---

1. "Is ash": the line alludes to the Buddhist practice of cremation, then new to Japan. Since there is so little Buddhism elsewhere in Hitomaro, it may be an addition.

on the haunted floor,
my wife's boxwood pillow.   60

[Upon seeing a dead man lying among the rocks on the island of Samine in Sanuki]

The land of Sanuki,
    fine in sleek seaweed:
is it for the beauty of the land
that we do not tire
    to gaze upon it?   5
Is it for its divinity
that we deem it most noble?
Eternally flourishing,
    with the heavens
        and the earth,
    with the sun   10
        and the moon,
the very face of a god—
so it has come down
    through the ages.   15

Casting off
from Naka harbor,
we came rowing.
Then tide winds
blew through the clouds;
on the offing   20
we saw the rustled waves,
on the strand
we saw the roaring crests.
Fearing the whale-hunted seas,
our ship plunged through—   25
we bent those oars!
Many were the islands
near and far,
but we beached on Samine—
    beautiful its name—   30
and built a shelter
    on the rugged shore.
Looking around,
        we saw you
lying there   35
on a jagged bed of stones,
the beach
    for your finely woven pillow,

by the breakers' roar.
    If I knew your home,
I would go and tell them.
If your wife knew,
she would come and seek you out.
But she does not even know the road,
    straight as a jade spear.
Does she not wait for you,
    worrying and longing,
your beloved wife?

Envoys

If your wife were here,
she would gather and feed you
the starwort that grows
on the Sami hillsides,
but is its season not past?

Making a finely woven pillow
of the rocky shore
    where waves from the offing
        draw near,
you, who sleep there!

YAMANO(U)E OKURA

A Dialogue of the Poor with the Destitute

"On nights when rain falls,
    mixed with wind,
on nights when snow falls,
    mixed with rain,
I am cold.
And the cold
    leaves me helpless:
I lick black lumps of salt
and suck up melted dregs of *sake*.
Coughing and sniffling,
I smooth my uncertain wisps
    of beard.
I am proud—
    I know no man
        is better than me.
But I am cold.
I pull up my hempen nightclothes

and throw on every scrap
of cloth shirt that I own.
But the night is cold.   20
And I wonder how a man like you,
 even poorer than myself,
with his father and mother
starving and freezing,
with his wife and children   25
begging and begging
  through their tears,
can get through the world alive
  at times like this."
"Wide, they say,   30
  are heaven and earth—
but have they shrunk for me?
Bright, they say,
  are the sun and moon—
but do they refuse to shine for me?   35
Is it thus for all men,
  or for me alone?
Above all, I was born human,
I too toil for my keep—
as much as the next man—   40
yet on my shoulders hangs
a cloth shirt
not even lined with cotton,
these tattered rags
thin as strips of seaweed.   45
In my groveling hut,
 my tilting hut,
sleeping on straw
cut and spread right on the ground,
with my father and mother   50
 huddled at my pillow
and my wife and children
 huddled at my feet,
I grieve and lament.
Not a spark rises in the stove,   55
and in the pot
a spider has drawn its web.
I have forgotten
what it is to cook rice!
As I lie here,   60
a thin cry tearing from my throat—
  a tiger thrush's moan—
then, as they say,

to slice the ends
of a thing already too short,
to our rough bed
comes the scream of the village headman
    with his tax collecting whip.
Is it so helpless and desperate,
the way of life in this world?"

Envoy

I find this world
a hard and shameful place.
But I cannot fly away—
I am not a bird.

ONO NO KOMACHI (fl. 835–857 C.E.)
ARIWARA NARIHIRA (825–880 C.E.)
KI NO TSURAYUKI (c. 872?–945? C.E.)
IZUMI SHIKIBU (b. 976? C.E.)
Japan

The four poets presented here are among the most admired of the *Kokinshū* (910 C.E.), the first and most prestigious of twenty-one royal anthologies. The *Kokinshū* is ordered topically (poems about the seasons, poems about love, and so on) rather than by author. The result is less an anthology than a complete artistic whole in which each individual poem takes its place. Ono no Komachi and Ariwara Narihira are numbered among the Six Poetic Sages, a title that comes from their having been singled out in the *Kokinshū* preface. Komachi focused attention on the poetic figure of the passionate woman. Indeed, the legends that have evolved about Komachi's life as a woman of passion have been so enduring that her historical reality remains veiled for us today. Narihira was also famous as a lover, though he was less intense, and more reflective and difficult in his style. Ki no Tsurayuki was the complete poet and critic, and his was presumably the genius behind the *Kokinshū*. Izumi Shikibu, the greatest poet of her time, was, with Murasaki Shikibu, one of the many brilliant writers at the salon of Joto Mon'in, a royal consort. Quickwitted, amorous, religious, maternal and a prolific poet, she is often difficult to interpret.

    These poets mark the dawn of a continuous poetic tradition in Japan. They are confident even in their questions, certain even of their bewilderment. Their world is one in which things can be named, collected, and confidently arranged.

It is no accident that this was the age that articulated a systematic poetics (in Ki no Tsurayuki's preface to the *Kokinshū*) that has outlasted the centuries. There were great works before, but the unbroken tradition of Japanese literature in all its guises begins here.

from **The Early Royal Anthologies [Kokinshū]**

ONO NO KOMACHI

[The cherry blossoms]

The cherry blossoms
Have passed with loss of color,
   While to no avail
Age takes my beauty as it falls
In the long rain of my regret.

[For waking daylight]

For waking daylight,
Then it can be understood!
   But even in dreams!
To avoid me there in fear of gossip—
That is too much misery to be borne.

[Although my feet / never rest in running to you]

Although my feet
Never rest in running to you
   On the path of dreams,
Such nights of spectral love
Match no moment face-to-face.

[No hue of passion / marks that thing which fades away]

No hue of passion
Marks that thing which fades away:
   In the world of love
Find that in the male heart
Pretending to be abloom with love!

All poems in this selection translated by Earl Miner.

[Longing for your loving]

Longing for your loving,
Without a moon to light my way,
   Waking in passion's fire
My breast swift conflagration,
My yearning heart reduced to char.

ARIWARA NARIHIRA

[Though the blackness]

Through the blackness
Of the darkness of desiring heart
   Wandering bewildered—
Is this called reality or dream?
You who know the world of love, decide!

[Full sleep does not come]

Full sleep does not come.
Full waking still eludes me,
   And night breaks with dawn:
So far am I a listless spring thing
Imbued with reverie's long rain.

[This is not that moon]

This is not that moon.
It cannot be this is the spring
   Known as spring before.
I myself am that alone
Remaining as it ever was . . .

[At last we find ourselves / upon the road that all must travel]

"At last we find ourselves
Upon the road that all must travel"—
   So had I heard, too,
But never had it occurred to me
The time is then and now.

KI NO TSURAYUKI

[Composed when I visited a mountain temple]

"Composed when I visited a mountain temple."
  I found my dwelling;
It was on hillslopes of spring
  That I slept the night,
And even throughout my dreams
The cherry blossoms kept up their fall.

[On hearing the hototogisu sing]

"On hearing the hototogisu sing."[1]
  During June's long rains
The sky itself fills with music,
  And, hototogisu,
What anguish is that you feel
To give the whole night to song?

[Composed at royal command]

"Composed at royal command."
  Is it Kasuga,
The fields where they go for greens,
  Those young women
With sleeves of whitened linen
Beckoning the one who sees?

[As urged by desire]

  As urged by desire
I go in hunt of my beloved,
  On the winter night
The river wind blows up so cold
That I hear the plovers cry.

[On the death of his cousin, Ki no Tomonori]

On the death of his cousin, Ki no Tomonori.
  Tomorrow is unknown,
So much of myself have I been sure,

---

1. A sort of cuckoo, rather like a nightingale.

But all has turned to dark:
Today it is him I think of
That casts me into all this grief!

[A mother returning to the capital from Tosa]

A mother returning to the capital from Tosa thinks
of her daughter who died in that province.

   Thinking her alive,
I keep forgetting she is not,
   Asking of one now dead,
"Where has that girl slipped off to?"
And the shock renews the grief.

IZUMI SHIKIBU

Love

   Whether my long dark hair
Be tangled is more than I can care:
   As I lie beside you,
You, darling, are so loving
As to start by stroking it aside.

The same

The same
   My darling will believe
He dwells in lapis lazuli,
   Because our bedding
Sparkles with string after string
Of drops of our bejewelled tears.

[Composed after my lover had abandoned me]

Composed after my lover had abandoned me. On a
pilgrimage to Kibune Shrine I saw fireflies by
the sacred river.

   Heavy at heart,
I take the fireflies from the marsh
   To be my very soul
Departed somehow from my body
And flickering in the gloom.

[Written to someone when I was ill]

Written to someone when I was ill.
  Soon to be no more!
As a keepsake of this world
  Taken to the next,
I long to have you come for loving
If just once more but make it now.

[Sent to her lover]

Sent to her lover "on seeing the extraordinary
whiteness of the frost."
  Marking everything
The frost also lies on the sleeve
  Of the pillowing arm,
And in morning light it looks
Like "whitened hemp" of olden times.
             (Izumi Shikibu Diary)

[Sent to His Eminence Shōku]

Sent to His Eminence Shōku.
  Out of darkness
To travel yet a darker path
  I must set forth:
Illuminate the great distance,
Blest moon arising on the hills!

ANONYMOUS (c. 950 C.E.)
Japan

An evocative, romantic mystery, the *Tales of Ise* consists of some 125 brief episodes centering on 209 poems. No satisfactory explanation exists for its title (though episode 69, included here, does indeed take place in Ise). The date is also uncertain: the earliest estimate is c. 875; the latest and more likely is c. 950 C.E. The episodes usually begin with a recurring phrase: "Once there was a certain man . . ." This man is generally presumed to be modeled on Ariwara Narihira, one of the foremost poets of the *Kokinshū*, the first royal anthology (910 C.E.). Episodes often seem to be taken verbatim, or with slight modifications, from *Kokinshū*, although some scholars believe the influence flowed the other way. In the first episode, the man appears newly dressed in adult clothing; he will be an "old man" before the tales are over. Quick-witted and amorous, he is the model for numerous courtly males in later literature. A certain air of doom also hangs over him: the Ariwaras were losers in the political struggles at court.

Together with *The Tale of Genji,* the *Tales of Ise* came to define the essence of court romance for later centuries. Both works, but especially the *Tales,* illustrate the compatibility of prose and verse in Japanese literature. The *Tales* also shows the distinctive Japanese tendency to consolidate ever briefer artistic units into new, larger wholes. Few things looking so simple are so complex. A first reading reveals little of the Shinto and esoteric Buddhist depths of these brief accounts. And few works, when fully understood, are so revealing about the possibilities of literature.

from The Tales of Ise *[Ise Monogatari]*

[Glimpsing Two Sisters]

Once a man who had lately come of age went hunting on his estate at Kasuga village, near the Nara capital. In the village there lived two beautiful young sisters. The man caught a glimpse of the sisters through a gap in their hedge. It was startling and incongruous indeed that such ladies should dwell at the ruined capital, and he wished to meet them. He tore a strip from the skirt of his hunting costume, dashed off a poem, and sent it in. The fabric of the robe was imprinted with a moss-fern design.

> Like the random pattern of this robe,
> Dyed with the young purple
> From Kasuga Plain—
> Even thus is the wild disorder
> Of my yearning heart.

No doubt it had occurred to him that this was an interesting opportunity for an adaptation of the poem that runs,

> My thoughts have grown disordered
> As random patterns dyed on cloth
> Reminiscent of Shinobu in Michinoku—
> And who is to blame?
> Surely not I.

People were remarkably elegant in those days.

[Plum Blossoms and the Past][1]

Once when the ex-empress was living in the eastern Fifth Ward, a certain lady occupied the western wing of her house. Quite without intending it, a man fell

Translated by Helen Craig McCullough; the translation of the first poem "Like the random pattern" and the preceding three sentences ("It was startling . . . moss-fern design") by Earl Miner.

1. This episode features Narihira's greatest and, for the translator, most difficult poem.

deeply in love with the lady and began to visit her; but around the Tenth of the First Month she moved away without a word, and though he learned where she had gone, it was not a place where ordinary people could come and go. He could do nothing but brood over the wretchedness of life. When the plum blossoms were at their height in the next First Month, poignant memories of the year before drew him back to her old apartments. He stared at the flowers from every conceivable standing and sitting position, but it was quite hopeless to try to recapture the past. Bursting into tears, he flung himself onto the floor of the bare room and lay there until the moon sank low in the sky. As he thought of the year before, he composed this poem:

> Is not the moon the same?
> The spring
> The spring of old?
> Only this body of mine
> Is the same body . . .

He went home at dawn, still weeping.

[Weeping Over Poems]

Once a certain man decided that it was useless for him to remain in the capital. With one or two old friends, he set out toward the east in search of a province in which to settle. Since none of the party knew the way, they blundered ahead as best they could, until in time they arrived at a place called Yatsuhashi in Mikawa Province. (It was a spot where the waters of a river branched into eight channels, each with a bridge, and thus it had come to be called Yatsuhashi—"Eight Bridges.") Dismounting to sit under a tree near this marshy area, they ate a meal of parched rice. Someone glanced at the clumps of sweet flags blooming luxuriantly in the marsh. "Compose a poem on the topic, 'A Traveler's Emotions,' beginning each line with a letter from 'flags,'" he said. The man recited,

> From far Cathay,
> Long has the robe been a comfort
> As is the wife I miss,
> Gone from sight into the distance,
> Sorrows being what travel brings.

They all wept onto their dried rice until it swelled with the moisture.

On they journeyed to the province of Suruga. At Mount Utsu the road they were to follow was dark, narrow, and overgrown with ivy vines and maples. As they contemplated it with dismal forebodings, a wandering ascetic appeared and asked, "What are you doing on a road like this?" The man, recognizing him as someone he had once known by sight, gave him a message for a lady in the capital:

> Beside Mount Utsu
> In Suruga
> I can see you
> Neither waking
> Nor, alas, even in my dreams.

At Mount Fuji a pure white snow had fallen, even though it was the end of the Fifth Month.

> Fuji is a mountain
> That knows no seasons.
> What time does it take this for,
> That it should be dappled
> With fallen snow?

To speak in terms of the mountains hereabout, Mount Fuji is as tall as twenty Mount Hiei's piled on top of one another. In shape it resembles a salt-cone.

Continuing on their way, they came to a mighty river flowing between the provinces of Musashi and Shimōsa. It was called the Sumidagawa. The travelers drew together on the bank, thinking involuntarily of home. "How very far we have come!" The ferryman interrupted their laments: "Come aboard quickly; it's getting late." They got into the boat and prepared to cross, all in wretched spirits, for there was not one among them who had not left someone dear to him in the capital.

A bird about the size of a snipe—white, with a red bill and red legs—happened to be frolicking on the water as it ate a fish. Since it was of a species unknown in the capital, none of them could identify it. They consulted the ferryman, who replied with an air of surprise, "It is a capital-bird, of course." Then one of the travelers recited this poem:

> If you are what your name implies,
> Let me ask you,
> Capital-bird,
> Does all go well
> With my beloved?

Everyone in the boat burst into tears.

[A Poem Gets Completed] [2]

Once a man went to the province of Ise as an Imperial Huntsman. The Ise [Shrine Priestess's] mother had sent word that he was to be treated better than the ordinary run of imperial representatives, and the [Priestess] accordingly looked after his needs with great solicitude, seeing him off to hunt in the morning and allowing him to come to her own residence when he returned in the evening.

On the night of the second day of this hospitable treatment, the man suggested that they might become better acquainted. The [Priestess] was not unwilling, but with so many people about it was impossible to arrange a meeting in private. However, since the man was in charge of the hunting party, he had not

---

2. This episode is thought by some to explain the title. The Shrine Priestess seems so dazzled that she cannot wait for the man to send his *aubade* (next-morning poem, or poem of dawn, when the lovers separate, from *alba,* literally "white").

been relegated to some distant quarter, but had been lodged rather close to the [Priestess's] own sleeping chamber, and so the [Priestess] went to his room around eleven o'clock that night, after the household had quieted down. He was lying on his bed wide awake, staring out into the night. When he saw her by the faint light of the moon, standing with a little girl in front of her, he led her joyfully into the bedchamber; but though she stayed from eleven o'clock until two-thirty, she took her leave without exchanging vows with him.

The man, bitterly disappointed, spent a sleepless night. The next morning, despite his impatience, he could not very well send a message, and was obliged to wait anxiously for word from the [Priestess]. Soon after dawn she sent this poem without an accompanying letter:

> Did you, I wonder, come here,
> Or might I have gone there?
> I scarcely know . . .
> Was it dream or reality—
> Did I sleep or wake?

Shedding tears of distress, he sent her this:

> I too have groped
> In utter darkness.
> Can you not determine tonight
> Which it might have been—
> Whether dream or reality?

Then he went off on a hunting excursion. As he galloped over the plain his thoughts strayed to the coming night. Might he not hope to meet [her] as soon as the others had gone to bed? But word of his presence had reached the governor of the province, who was also in charge of the [Priestess's] affairs, and that official proceeded to entertain him at a drinking party that lasted all night. It was impossible to see [her], and since he was to leave at dawn for Owari Province there could be no further opportunity, even though he was quite frantic with longing, as indeed was [she].

As dawn approached, [she] sent him a farewell cup of wine with a poem inscribed on the saucer. He picked up the vessel and examined it.

> Since ours was a relationship no deeper
> Than a creek too shallow
> To wet a foot-traveler's garb . . .

The last two lines were missing. He took a bit of charcoal from a pine torch and supplied them:

> I shall surely again cross
> Osaka Barrier.

At daybreak he set out toward the province of Owari.

The [Priestess] was the one who served during the reign of Emperor Seiwa; she was a daughter of Emperor Montoku and a sister of Prince Koretaka.

SEI SHŌNAGON (c. 966?–1017? C.E.)
Japan

Sei (shorthand for "Kiyowara family") Shōnagon was a star in the literary circle of the royal consort Teishi. Her masterpiece, *The Pillow Book* (*Makura no Soshi*), consists of numerous prose sections—jottings, we are to presume, made in a bedside notebook—and sixteen poems. The sections are conventionally viewed as falling into two broad categories: diary-like entries and the now-famous lists of things or enumerations of such modern appeal ("Things That Make One's Heart Beat Faster," "Rare Things"). Yet the very first section, given here, shows this distinction to be inadequate. Two features in particular deserve special attention. One is the almost total and unparalleled absence of verse with the courtly prose. The other is the author's exquisite sense of her own subjectivity: it will be five centuries before a European author, the French essayist Montaigne, writes with such an awareness.

Sei Shōnagon knew her way around a royal court and all its intrigues. Her chief demand was that the court—and the world, for that matter—be observable. She knew how to make it memorable. Her education included Chinese, and while she may not have known as much of that language as she liked to pretend, the point is that she knew it at all. Had the occasion arisen, she could easily have invented a list called "Things Concealed from Others in Order to Understand Ourselves."

from *The Pillow Book [Makura no Soshi]*

In Spring It Is the Dawn[1]

In spring it is the dawn that is most beautiful. As the light creeps over the hills, their outlines are dyed a faint red and wisps of purplish cloud trail over them.

In summer the nights. Not only when the moon shines, but on dark nights too, as the fireflies flit to and fro, and even when it rains, how beautiful it is!

In autumn the evenings, when the glittering sun sinks close to the edge of the hills and the crows fly back to their nests in threes and fours and twos; more charming still is a file of wild geese, like specks in the distant sky. When the sun has set, one's heart is moved by the sound of the wind and the hum of the insects.

In winter the early mornings. It is beautiful indeed when snow has fallen during the night, but splendid too when the ground is white with frost; or even when there is no snow or frost, but it is simply very cold and the attendants hurry from room to room stirring up the fires and bringing charcoal, how well this fits

Translated by Ivan Morris.

1. These associations between hours and seasons become essential to understanding Japanese literature.

the season's mood! But as noon approaches and the cold wears off, no one bothers to keep the braziers alight, and soon nothing remains but piles of white ashes.

Things That Make One's Heart Beat Faster

Sparrows feeding their young. To pass a place where babies are playing. To sleep in a room where some fine incense has been burnt. To notice that one's elegant Chinese mirror has become a little cloudy. To see a gentleman stop his carriage before one's gate and instruct his attendants to announce his arrival. To wash one's hair, make one's toilet, and put on scented robes; even if not a soul sees one, these preparations still produce an inner pleasure.

It is night and one is expecting a visitor. Suddenly one is startled by the sound of rain-drops, which the wind blows against the shutters.

Once I Saw Yukinari[2]

Once I saw Yukinari, the Controller First Secretary, engaged in a long conversation with a lady near the garden fence by the western side of the Empress's Office. When at last they had finished, I came out and asked, "Who was she?" "Ben no Naishi," he replied. "And what on earth did you find to discuss with her for such a long time? If the Major Controller had seen you, she would have left you quickly enough." "And who can have told you about that business?" asked Yukinari, laughing. "As a matter of fact, that is precisely what I was discussing with her. I was trying to persuade her not to leave me even if the Major Controller did see us."

Yukinari is a most delightful man. To be sure, he does not make any particular effort to display his good points and simply lets people take him as he appears, so that in general he is less appreciated than he might be. But I, who have seen the deeper side of his nature, know what an unusual person he really is. I said this one day to the Empress, who was well aware of it herself. In the course of our conversations he often says, "A woman yields to one who has taken pleasure in her; a knight dies for one who has shown him friendship." We used to say that our feelings for each other were like the willows on Tōtōmi Beach.

Yet the young women at Court heartily detest Yukinari and openly repeat the most disagreeable things about him. "What an ugly man he is!" they say. "Why can't he recite sutras and poems like other people? He really is most unpleasant." Yukinari, for his part, never speaks to any of them.

"I could love a woman," he said one day, "even if her eyes were turned up, her eyebrows spread all over her forehead, and her nose crooked. But she must have a prettily shaped mouth and a good chin and neck, and I couldn't stand an unattractive voice. Of course I would prefer her not to have any bad feature. There's really something sad about a woman with an ugly face." As a result, all the Court ladies with pointed chins or other unattractive features have become Yukinari's bitter enemies, and some of them have even spoken badly of him to the Empress.

---

2. This study of Yukinari is really a self-study.

I was the first person he employed to take messages to the Empress, and he always called on me when he wanted to communicate with her. If I was in my room, he would send for me to the main part of the Palace, or else he would come directly into the women's quarters to give me his message. Even if I was at home, he would write to me or come himself, saying, "In case you are not returning to Court at once, would you please send someone to Her Majesty informing her that I have such-and-such a message." "Surely you could tell a messenger yourself directly," I said; but he would have none of it.

On one such occasion I suggested to Yukinari that one should "take things as they are" and not always stick to the same habits. "But such is my nature," he replied, "and that is something one cannot change."

"Well then," I said in a surprised tone, "what is the meaning of 'Do not be afraid'?"

Yukinari laughed and said, "There has no doubt been a lot of talk lately about our being so friendly. But what of it? Even if we were as intimate as people think, that would be nothing to be ashamed of. Really you could let me see your face."

"O no," I replied, "I cannot possibly do that. I am extremely ugly, and you said you could never love an ugly woman."

"Are you really?" he said. "In that case you had better not let me see you."

Often thereafter, when it would have been easy for Yukinari to look at me in the normal course of things, he covered his face with a fan or turned aside. In fact he never once saw me. To think that he took what I said about my ugliness quite seriously!

Towards the end of the Third Month it becomes too warm for winter cloaks, and often Chamberlains who are on night watch in the Senior Courtiers' Chamber wear only the over-robes of their Court costumes, leaving off their trouser-skirts and trains. Early one morning in that month, when Lady Shikibu and I had been sleeping in the outer part of a room in the Empress's Office, the sliding-door was pushed open and the Emperor and Empress entered. We were thrown into utter confusion and did not know what to do with ourselves, which greatly amused Their Majesties. Hastily we threw on our Chinese jackets, tucking our hair inside, and then we heaped the bed-clothes and everything else in a great pile. Their Majesties walked across the room and, standing behind this pile, watched the men going between the Palace and the guard house. Several courtiers approached our room and spoke to us, without suspecting who was inside the room. "Do not let them see we are here," His Majesty said with a chuckle.

Before long Their Majesties left. "Come along, both of you," said the Empress. I replied that we would come as soon as we had made up our faces, and we stayed where we were.

Lady Shikibu and I were still discussing how splendid Their Majesties had looked when, through a small opening in the blinds (where the frame of our curtain of state was pressed against the sliding-door in the back of the room), we noticed the dark silhouette of a man. At first we thought that it must be Noritaka and continued to talk without paying any particular attention. Presently a beaming face appeared through the opening in the blinds. We still took it to be Noritaka, but after a quick look we were amused to find that we were mistaken.

Laughing heartily, we rearranged our curtain of state so that we were properly hidden. Too late, though. The man turned out to be none other than Yukinari; and he had seen me full-face. After all my past efforts this was extremely vexing. Lady Shikibu, on the other hand, had been looking safely in the other direction.

"Well," said Yukinari, stepping forward, "now I have really managed to see you completely."

"We thought it was Noritaka," I explained, "and so we didn't bother to hide properly. But why, may I ask, did you examine me so carefully when in the past you said that you would never look at me?"

"I have been told," said he, "that a woman's face is particularly attractive when she rises in the morning. So I came here hoping for a chance to peep into one of the ladies' rooms and see something interesting. I was already watching you when Their Majesties were here, but you suspected nothing."

Then, as I recall, he walked straight into the room.

Unsettling Things

The feeling of a mother whose son is a priest and has gone into the mountains for a twelve-year retreat.

One arrives after nightfall in an unfamiliar place. For fear of being too conspicuous, one refrains from lighting a lamp; but one prefers to sit near the other people in the room, even though they are hidden by the dark.

A servant is newly employed and his character unfamiliar; yet one has entrusted a valuable object to him. He is supposed to deliver it to someone's house and now he is late in returning.

A baby who is still unable to talk falls over backwards. Someone picks him up, but he starts crying.

Eating strawberries in the dark.

A festival where one does not recognize any of the participants.

Rare Things

A son-in-law who is praised by his adoptive father; a young bride who is loved by her mother-in-law.

A silver tweezer that is good at plucking out the hair.

A servant who does not speak badly about his master.

A person who is in no way eccentric or imperfect, who is superior in both mind and body, and who remains flawless all his life.

People who live together and still manage to behave with reserve towards each other. However much these people may try to hide their weaknesses, they usually fail.

To avoid getting ink stains on the notebook into which one is copying stories, poems, or the like. If it is a very fine notebook, one takes the greatest care not to make a blot; yet somehow one never seems to succeed.

When people, whether they be men or women or priests, have promised each other eternal friendship, it is rare for them to stay on good terms until the end.

A servant who is pleasant to his master.

One has given some silk to the fuller and, when he sends it back, it is so beautiful that one cries out in admiration.

Adorable Things

The face of a child drawn on a melon.

A baby sparrow that comes hopping up when one imitates the squeak of a mouse; or again, when one has tied it with a thread round its leg and its parents bring insects or worms and pop them in its mouth—delightful!

A baby of two or so is crawling rapidly along the ground. With his sharp eyes he catches sight of a tiny object and, picking it up with his pretty little fingers, takes it to show to a grown-up person.

A child, whose hair has been cut like a nun's, is examining something; the hair falls over his eyes, but instead of brushing it away he holds his head to the side. The pretty white cords of his trouser-skirt are tied round his shoulders, and this too is most adorable.

A young Palace page, who is still quite small, walks by in ceremonial costume.

One picks up a pretty baby and holds him for a while in one's arms; while one is fondling him, he clings to one's neck and then falls asleep.

The objects used during the Display of Dolls.[3]

One picks up a tiny lotus leaf that is floating on a pond and examines it. Not only lotus leaves, but little hollyhock flowers, and indeed all small things, are most adorable.

An extremely plump baby, who is about a year old and has a lovely white skin, comes crawling towards one, dressed in a long gauze robe of violet with the sleeves tucked up.

A little boy of about eight who reads aloud from a book in his childish voice.

Pretty, white chicks who are still not fully fledged and look as if their clothes are too short for them; cheeping loudly, they follow one on their long legs, or walk close to the mother hen.

Duck eggs.

An urn containing the relics of some holy person.

Wild pinks.

One Day, When Her Majesty Was Surrounded by Several Ladies[4]

One day, when Her Majesty was surrounded by several ladies, I remarked in connexion with something that she had said, "There are times when the world so

---

3. The Display of Dolls fell on the third day of the third Month.

4. This describes the way in which *The Pillow Book* was begun. For all its bows to royalty, this shows the author's self-analysis.

exasperates me that I feel I cannot go on living in it for another moment and I want to disappear for good. But then, if I happen to obtain some nice white paper, Michinoku paper, or white decorated paper, I decide that I can put up with things as they are a little longer. Or, if I can spread out a finely woven, green straw mat and examine the white bordering with its vivid black patterns, I somehow feel that I cannot turn my back on this world, and life actually seems precious to me."

"It really doesn't take much to console you," said the Empress, laughing. "I wonder what sort of a person it was who gazed at the moon on Mount Obasute."

The ladies who were in attendance also teased me. "You've certainly found a cheap prayer for warding off evil," they said.

Some time later, when I was staying at home and absorbed in various petty worries, a messenger brought me twenty rolls of magnificent paper from Her Majesty. "Come back quickly," she wrote, adding, "I am sending you this because of what you told me the other day. It seems to be of poor quality, however, and I am afraid you will not be able to use it for copying the Sutra of Longevity." It delighted me that Her Majesty should have remembered something that I myself had completely forgotten. Even if an ordinary person had sent me the present, I should have been overjoyed. How much more pleasing when it came from the Empress herself! I was so excited that I could not frame a proper reply, but simply sent Her Majesty this poem:

> Thanks to the paper that the Goddess gave,
> My years will now be plenteous as the crane's.

"Make sure that the Empress is asked the following," I told the messenger. "Am I expecting too many years?" My reward for the messenger, a general maid from the Table Room, was an unlined green costume.

Then I immediately used the paper I had received to write my collection of notes. I felt a glow of delight and all my worries began to disappear.

A couple of days later a messenger dressed in red arrived with a straw mat. "Here you are," he said. "And who may you be?" said my maid severely. "Such impudence!" However, the man simply put down the mat and left. I told the maid to ask him where he came from, but he had already disappeared. She brought me the mat, which was an unusually beautiful one with a splendid white border, of the type used by high dignitaries. I felt it must be the Empress who had sent it, but as I was not quite sure I told someone to look for the messenger. Everyone was greatly puzzled, but I did not think the matter was worth discussing since the messenger was nowhere to be found. It occurred to me that, if he had delivered the mat to the wrong place, he would be sure to come back and say so. I should have liked to send someone to Her Majesty's palace to discover the truth of the affair. Then I decided that the mystery must be deliberate and that the mat could only have come from the Empress. This thought filled me with joy. Having heard nothing further after two days, I knew there could be no doubt about the matter, and I sent a message to Lady Sakyō telling her what had happened. "Has any of this come to your ears?" I asked. "Please inform me secretly of what you have heard. In any case do not let anyone know that I have asked you."

"Her Majesty did it all in great secret," was Lady Sakyō's reply. "On no account tell anyone now or later that I informed you."

Delighted that everything I had suspected was now clear, I wrote a letter, telling the messenger to lay it on the balustrade in Her Majesty's palace when no one was looking. In his nervousness, however, he placed it in such a way that it fell off the side and landed under the stairs.

MURASAKI SHIKIBU (978?–1014? C.E.)
Japan

"Evening Faces" ("Yūgao") is the fourth chapter of *The Tale of Genji,* the greatest work of Japanese literature. Genji, the hero of the book, was born fifteen years before we meet him here. He is the son of a low-ranking but favorite royal concubine and the emperor. To spare him from palace intrigues, his father made him a commoner, assigning him to the Marimoto clan, or Genji. Hence his name, which gave no hint of his royal lineage. Because of his magical aura or charisma, he was given the name Radiant Genji [Hikaru Genji]. (No character in the book has a name in the standard sense of an inherited family name and a given name.)

The book begins by focusing on Genji's relations with women throughout the first three chapters. The rainy-night discussion of women in the second chapter is one of the most self-contained of the work's fifty-four chapters, but a few connections and conventions need to be explained. Rokujō, who is mentioned in the opening paragraph, is identified later: it is the place where Genji has an affair with a high-born, somewhat older woman. It is perhaps her jealous spirit that kills Yūgao, the chapter's heroine. The ties that children formed with a wetnurse were considered close ones; Genji's visit to his is aided by her son, Koremitsu. He is Genji's faithful attendant, as Yūgao's is Ukon.

4   Yūgao ("Evening Faces") takes her name, as do so many characters in the story, from a poem mentioning a flower having the same name. When she hands the flower to Genji, she is permitting him to woo her. (Today the eroticism may be missed, but in the time of *Genji* the gesture was highly charged.) Yūgao's poem is more important than her appearance; as is clear from Chapter 51 of the *Pillow Book,* women even preferred not to be seen. Genji also hides his appearance from Yūgao. The courtly romance here involves youth, glimpses of the couple making love, essential communications by means of poems, the shock of a malevolent spirit bringing darkness and death, and the revelation that the precious beauty and anguish of life are mutually dependent.

Other characters appear late in the chapter. Tō no Chūjō is Genji's closest friend and an often comic foil. He preceded Genji as Yūgao's lover. (In fact, he has unknowingly had a daughter by her, as Ukon will discover many chapters later.) The "lady of the locust shell," Utsusemi, had been pursued in vain earlier by Genji; their attachment remains unconsummated.

The chapter concludes with the longest example of the author's intervention in the story. The Japanese suppose a number of court ladies as the narrators of

Frontispiece to a sutra scroll. Japanese, Heian period, 12th century C.E. Itsukushima Jinja Homotsukan, Hiroshima

Genji's story, but imagine that the author herself may intrude at moments such as this.

The clear and appealing translation obscures the complex style of the original, which usually omits mention of persons and flows on unceasingly as if each chapter were a single sentence. Older manuscripts include no punctuation at all and use indentation solely to set off poems. A more beautiful, more complex, and yet more natural style cannot be imagined. Seven or eight centuries before the English novel was born, a Japanese lady serving in the salon of a royal consort created one of the greatest literary works in the world.

from *The Tale of Genji*

Evening Faces

On his way from court to pay one of his calls at Rokujō, Genji stopped to inquire after his old nurse, Koremitsu's mother, at her house in Gojō. Gravely ill, she had become a nun. The carriage entrance was closed. He sent for Koremitsu and while he was waiting looked up and down the dirty, cluttered street. Beside the nurse's house was a new fence of plaited cypress. The four or five narrow shutters above had been raised, and new blinds, white and clean, hung in the apertures. He caught outlines of pretty foreheads beyond. He would have judged, as they moved about, that they belonged to rather tall women. What sort of women might they

Translated by Edward G. Seidensticker.

be? His carriage was simple and unadorned and he had no outrunners. Quite certain that he would not be recognized, he leaned out for a closer look. The hanging gate, of something like trelliswork, was propped on a pole, and he could see that the house was tiny and flimsy. He felt a little sorry for the occupants of such a place—and then asked himself who in this world had more than a temporary shelter.[1] A hut, a jeweled pavilion, they were the same. A pleasantly green vine was climbing a board wall. The white flowers, he thought, had a rather self-satisfied look about them.

" 'I needs must ask the lady far off yonder,' "[2] he said, as if to himself.

An attendant came up, bowing deeply. "The white flowers far off yonder are known as 'evening faces,' "[3] he said. "A very human sort of name—and what a shabby place they have picked to bloom in."

It was as the man said. The neighborhood was a poor one, chiefly of small houses. Some were leaning precariously, and there were "evening faces" at the sagging eaves.

"A hapless sort of flower. Pick one off for me, would you?"

The man went inside the raised gate and broke off a flower. A pretty little girl in long, unlined yellow trousers of raw silk came out through a sliding door that seemed too good for the surroundings. Beckoning to the man, she handed him a heavily scented white fan.

"Put it on this. It isn't much of a fan, but then it isn't much of a flower either."

Koremitsu, coming out of the gate, passed it on to Genji.

"They lost the key, and I have had to keep you waiting. You aren't likely to be recognized in such a neighborhood, but it's not a very nice neighborhood to keep you waiting in."

Genji's carriage was pulled in and he dismounted. Besides Koremitsu, a son and a daughter, the former an eminent cleric, and the daughter's husband, the governor of Mikawa, were in attendance upon the old woman. They thanked him profusely for his visit.

The old woman got up to receive him. "I did not at all mind leaving the world, except for the thought that I would no longer be able to see you as I am seeing you now. My vows seem to have given me a new lease on life, and this visit makes me certain that I shall receive the radiance of Lord Amitābha with a serene and tranquil heart." And she collapsed in tears.

Genji was near tears himself. "It has worried me enormously that you should be taking so long to recover, and I was very sad to learn that you have withdrawn from the world. You must live a long life and see the career I make for myself. I am sure that if you do you will be reborn upon the highest summits of the Pure Land. I am told that it is important to rid oneself of the smallest regret for this world."

Fond of the child she has reared, a nurse tends to look upon him as a paragon even if he is a half-wit. How much prouder was the old woman, who somehow

---

1. Compare Anonymous, *Kokinshū* 987:
   Where in all this world shall I call home?
   A temporary shelter is my home.
2. Compare: Anonymous, *Kokinshū* 1007:
   I needs must ask the lady far off yonder

What flower it is off there that blooms so white.

3. The *Yūgao, Lagenaria siceraria,* is a kind of gourd.

gained stature, who thought of herself as eminent in her own right for having been permitted to serve him. The tears flowed on.

Her children were ashamed for her. They exchanged glances. It would not do to have these contortions taken as signs of a lingering affection for the world.

Genji was deeply touched. "The people who were fond of me left me when I was very young. Others have come along, it is true, to take care of me, but you are the only one I am really attached to. In recent years there have been restrictions upon my movements, and I have not been able to look in upon you morning and evening as I would have wished, or indeed to have a good visit with you. Yet I become very depressed when the days go by and I do not see you. 'Would that there were on this earth no final partings.' "[4] He spoke with great solemnity, and the scent of his sleeve, as he brushed away a tear, quite flooded the room.

Yes, thought the children, who had been silently reproaching their mother for her want of control, the fates had been kind to her. They too were now in tears.

Genji left orders that prayers and services be resumed. As he went out he asked for a torch, and in its light examined the fan on which the "evening face" had rested. It was permeated with a lady's perfume, elegant and alluring. On it was a poem in a disguised cursive hand that suggested breeding and taste. He was interested.

"I think I need not ask whose face it is,
So bright, this evening face, in the shining dew."

"Who is living in the house to the west?" he asked Koremitsu. "Have you perhaps had occasion to inquire?"

At it again, thought Koremitsu. He spoke somewhat tartly. "I must confess that these last few days I have been too busy with my mother to think about her neighbors."

"You are annoyed with me. But this fan has the appearance of something it might be interesting to look into. Make inquiries, if you will, please, of someone who knows the neighborhood."

Koremitsu went in to ask his mother's steward, and emerged with the information that the house belonged to a certain honorary vice-governor.[5] "The husband is away in the country, and the wife seems to be a young woman of taste. Her sisters are out in service here and there. They often come visiting. I suspect the fellow is too poorly placed to know the details."

His poetess would be one of the sisters, thought Genji. A rather practiced and forward young person, and, were he to meet her, perhaps vulgar as well—but the easy familiarity of the poem had not been at all unpleasant, not something to be pushed away in disdain. His amative propensities, it will be seen, were having their way once more.

---

4. Compare Ariwara Narihira, *Kokinshū* 901 and *Tales of Ise* 84:
   Would that my mother might live a thousand years.
   Would there were on this earth no final partings.

5. The word in original text is *Yōmei no suke.* Once thought among the undecipherables in the *Genji*, it is now thought to refer to someone who has the title but not the perquisites of vice-governor.

Carefully disguising his hand, he jotted down a reply on a piece of notepaper and sent it in by the attendant who had earlier been of service.

"Come a bit nearer, please. Then might you know
Whose was the evening face so dim in the twilight."

Thinking it a familiar profile, the lady had not lost the opportunity to surprise him with a letter, and when time passed and there was no answer she was left feeling somewhat embarrassed and disconsolate. Now came a poem by special messenger. Her women became quite giddy as they turned their minds to the problem of replying. Rather bored with it all, the messenger returned empty-handed. Genji made a quiet departure, lighted by very few torches. The shutters next door had been lowered. There was something sad about the light, dimmer than fireflies, that came through the cracks.

At the Rokujō house, the trees and the plantings had a quiet dignity. The lady herself was strangely cold and withdrawn. Thoughts of the "evening faces" quite left him. He overslept, and the sun was rising when he took his leave. He presented such a fine figure in the morning light that the women of the place understood well enough why he should be so universally admired. On his way he again passed those shutters, as he had no doubt done many times before. Because of that small incident he now looked at the house carefully, wondering who might be within.

"My mother is not doing at all well, and I have been with her," said Koremitsu some days later. And, coming nearer: "Because you seemed so interested, I called someone who knows about the house next door and had him questioned. His story was not completely clear. He said that in the Fifth Month or so someone came very quietly to live in the house, but that not even the domestics had been told who she might be. I have looked through the fence from time to time myself and had glimpses through blinds of several young women. Something about their dress suggests that they are in the service of someone of higher rank.[6] Yesterday, when the evening light was coming directly through, I saw the lady herself writing a letter. She is very beautiful. She seemed lost in thought, and the women around her were weeping."

Genji had suspected something of the sort. He must find out more.

Koremitsu's view was that while Genji was undeniably someone the whole world took seriously, his youth and the fact that women found him attractive meant that to refrain from these little affairs would be less than human. It was not realistic to hold that certain people were beyond temptation.

"Looking for a chance to do a bit of exploring, I found a small pretext for writing to her. She answered immediately, in a good, practiced hand. Some of her women do not seem at all beneath contempt."

"Explore very thoroughly, if you will. I will not be satisfied until you do."

The house was what the guardsman would have described as the lowest of the low, but Genji was interested. What hidden charms might he not come upon!

---

6. They wear *shibira*, apparently a sort of apron or jacket indicating a small degree of formality.

Suzumushi ("The Bell Cricket") painting from The Tale of Genji Scroll. Attributed to Takayoshi. Japanese, Heian period, 12th century C.E. In the Gotoh Museum, Tokyo

He had thought the coldness of the governor's wife, the lady of "the locust shell," quite unique. Yet if she had proved amenable to his persuasions the affair would no doubt have been dropped as a sad mistake after that one encounter. As matters were, the resentment and the distinct possibility of final defeat never left his mind. The discussion that rainy night would seem to have made him curious about the several ranks. There had been a time when such a lady would not have been worth his notice. Yes, it had been broadening, that discussion! He had not found the willing and available one, the governor of Iyo's daughter, entirely uninteresting, but the thought that the stepmother must have been listening coolly to the interview was excruciating. He must await some sign of her real intentions.

The governor of Iyo returned to the city. He came immediately to Genji's mansion. Somewhat sunburned, his travel robes rumpled from the sea voyage, he was a rather heavy and displeasing sort of person. He was of good lineage, however, and, though aging, he still had good manners. As they spoke of his province, Genji wanted to ask the full count of those hot springs, but he was somewhat confused to find memories chasing one another through his head. How foolish that he should be so uncomfortable before the honest old man! He remembered the guardsman's warning that such affairs are unwise,[7] and he felt sorry for the governor. Though he resented the wife's coldness, he could see that from the husband's point of view it was admirable. He was upset to learn that the governor meant to find a suitable husband for his daughter and take his wife to the provinces. He consulted the lady's young brother upon the possibility of another meeting. It would have been difficult even with the lady's cooperation, however, and she was of the view that to receive a gentleman so far above her would be extremely unwise.

---

7. This is curious, since the guardsman's warning was not against women of the lower classes but against fickle women. There have been theories that some part of his discourse has been lost.

Yet she did not want him to forget her entirely. Her answers to his notes on this and that occasion were pleasant enough, and contained casual little touches that made him pause in admiration. He resented her chilliness, but she interested him. As for the stepdaughter, he was certain that she would receive him hospitably enough however formidable a husband she might acquire. Reports upon her arrangements disturbed him not at all.

Autumn came. He was kept busy and unhappy by affairs of his own making, and he visited Sanjō infrequently. There was resentment.

As for the affair at Rokujō, he had overcome the lady's resistance and had his way, and, alas, he had cooled toward her. People thought it worthy of comment that his passions should seem so much more governable than before he had made her his. She was subject to fits of despondency, more intense on sleepless nights when she awaited him in vain. She feared that if rumors were to spread the gossips would make much of the difference in their ages.

On a morning of heavy mists, insistently roused by the lady, who was determined that he be on his way, Genji emerged yawning and sighing and looking very sleepy. Chūjō, one of her women, raised a shutter and pulled a curtain aside as if urging her lady to come forward and see him off. The lady lifted her head from her pillow. He was an incomparably handsome figure as he paused to admire the profusion of flowers below the veranda. Chūjō followed him down a gallery. In an aster robe that matched the season pleasantly and a gossamer train worn with clean elegance, she was a pretty, graceful woman. Glancing back, he asked her to sit with him for a time at the corner railing. The ceremonious precision of the seated figure and the hair flowing over her robes were very fine.

He took her hand.

"Though loath to be taxed with seeking fresher blooms,
I feel impelled to pluck this morning glory.

"Why should it be?"

She answered with practiced alacrity, making it seem that she was speaking not for herself but for her lady:

"In haste to plunge into the morning mists,
You seem to have no heart for the blossoms here."

A pretty little page boy, especially decked out for the occasion, it would seem, walked out among the flowers. His trousers wet with dew, he broke off a morning glory for Genji. He made a picture that called out to be painted.

Even persons to whom Genji was nothing were drawn to him. No doubt even rough mountain men wanted to pause for a time in the shade of the flowering tree,[8] and those who had basked even briefly in his radiance had thoughts, each in accordance with his rank, of a daughter who might be taken into his service, a

---

8. In the preface to the *Kokinshū* one of the "poetic immortals" is likened to a woodcutter resting under a cherry tree in full bloom.

not ill-formed sister who might perform some humble service for him. One need not be surprised, then, that people with a measure of sensibility among those who had on some occasion received a little poem from him or been treated to some little kindness found him much on their minds. No doubt it distressed them not to be always with him.

I had forgotten: Koremitsu gave a good account of the fence peeping to which he had been assigned. "I am unable to identify her. She seems determined to hide herself from the world. In their boredom her women and girls go out to the long gallery at the street, the one with the shutters, and watch for carriages. Sometimes the lady who seems to be their mistress comes quietly out to join them. I've not had a good look at her, but she seems very pretty indeed. One day a carriage with outrunners went by. The little girls shouted to a person named Ukon that she must come in a hurry. The captain[9] was going by, they said. An older woman came out and motioned to them to be quiet. How did they know? she asked, coming out toward the gallery. The passage from the main house is by a sort of makeshift bridge. She was hurrying and her skirt caught on something, and she stumbled and almost fell off. 'The sort of thing the god of Katsuragi might do,'[10] she said, and seems to have lost interest in sightseeing. They told her that the man in the carriage was wearing casual court dress and that he had a retinue. They mentioned several names, and all of them were undeniably Lord Tō no Chūjō's guards and pages."

"I wish you had made positive identification." Might she be the lady of whom Tō no Chūjō had spoken so regretfully that rainy night?

Koremitsu went on, smiling at this open curiosity. "I have as a matter of fact made the proper overtures and learned all about the place. I come and go as if I did not know that they are not all equals. They think they are hiding the truth and try to insist that there is no one there but themselves when one of the little girls makes a slip."

"Let me have a peep for myself when I call on your mother."

Even if she was only in temporary lodgings, the woman would seem to be of the lower class for which his friend had indicated such contempt that rainy evening. Yet something might come of it all. Determined not to go against his master's wishes in the smallest detail and himself driven by very considerable excitement, Koremitsu searched diligently for a chance to let Genji into the house. But the details are tiresome, and I shall not go into them.

Genji did not know who the lady was and he did not want her to know who he was. In very shabby disguise, he set out to visit her on foot. He must be taking her very seriously, thought Koremitsu, who offered his horse and himself went on foot.

"Though I do not think that our gentleman will look very good with tramps for servants."

To make quite certain that the expedition remained secret, Genji took with him only the man who had been his intermediary in the matter of the "evening

---

9. Tō no Chūjō.
10. Tradition held that the god of Katsuragi, south of Nara, was very ugly and built a bridge which he used only at night.

faces" and a page whom no one was likely to recognize. Lest he be found out even so, he did not stop to see his nurse.

The lady had his messengers followed to see how he made his way home and tried by every means to learn where he lived; but her efforts came to nothing. For all his secretiveness, Genji had grown fond of her and felt that he must go on seeing her. They were of such different ranks, he tried to tell himself, and it was altogether too frivolous. Yet his visits were frequent. In affairs of this sort, which can muddle the senses of the most serious and honest of men, he had always kept himself under tight control and avoided any occasion for censure. Now, to a most astonishing degree, he would be asking himself as he returned in the morning from a visit how he could wait through the day for the next. And then he would rebuke himself. It was madness, it was not an affair he should let disturb him. She was of an extraordinarily gentle and quiet nature. Though there was a certain vagueness about her, and indeed an almost childlike quality, it was clear that she knew something about men. She did not appear to be of very good family. What was there about her, he asked himself over and over again, that so drew him to her?

He took great pains to hide his rank and always wore travel dress, and he did not allow her to see his face. He came late at night when everyone was asleep. She was frightened, as if he were an apparition from an old story. She did not need to see his face to know that he was a fine gentleman. But who might he be? Her suspicions turned to Koremitsu. It was that young gallant, surely, who had brought the strange visitor. But Koremitsu pursued his own little affairs unremittingly, careful to feign indifference to and ignorance of this other affair. What could it all mean? The lady was lost in unfamiliar speculations.

Genji had his own worries. If, having lowered his guard with an appearance of complete unreserve, she were to slip away and hide, where would he seek her? This seemed to be but a temporary residence, and he could not be sure when she would choose to change it, and for what other. He hoped that he might reconcile himself to what must be and forget the affair as just another dalliance; but he was not confident.

On days when, to avoid attracting notice, he refrained from visiting her, his fretfulness came near anguish. Suppose he were to move her in secret to Nijō. If troublesome rumors were to arise, well, he could say that they had been fated from the start. He wondered what bond in a former life might have produced an infatuation such as he had not known before.

"Let's have a good talk," he said to her, "where we can be quite at our ease."

"It's all so strange. What you say is reasonable enough, but what you do is so strange. And rather frightening."

Yes, she might well be frightened. Something childlike in her fright brought a smile to his lips. "Which of us is the mischievous fox spirit? I wonder. Just be quiet and give yourself up to its persuasions."

Won over by his gentle warmth, she was indeed inclined to let him have his way. She seemed such a pliant little creature, likely to submit absolutely to the most outrageous demands. He thought again of Tō no Chūjō's "wild carnation," of the equable nature his friend had described that rainy night. Fearing that it would be useless, he did not try very hard to question her. She did not seem likely to indulge in dramatics and suddenly run off and hide herself, and so the fault must have been Tō no Chūjō's. Genji himself would not be guilty of such negligence—though it did occur to him that a bit of infidelity[11] might make her more interesting.

The bright full moon of the Eighth Month came flooding in through chinks in the roof. It was not the sort of dwelling he was used to, and he was fascinated. Toward dawn he was awakened by plebeian voices in the shabby houses down the street.

"Freezing, that's what it is, freezing. There's not much business this year, and when you can't get out into the country you feel like giving up. Do you hear me, neighbor?"

He could make out every word. It embarrassed the woman that, so near at hand, there should be this clamor of preparation as people set forth on their sad little enterprises. Had she been one of the stylish ladies of the world, she would have wanted to shrivel up and disappear. She was a placid sort, however, and she seemed to take nothing, painful or embarrassing or unpleasant, too seriously. Her manner elegant and yet girlish, she did not seem to know what the rather awful clamor up and down the street might mean. He much preferred this easygoing bewilderment to a show of consternation, a face scarlet with embarrassment. As if at his very pillow, there came the booming of a foot pestle,[12] more fearsome than the stamping of the thunder god, genuinely earsplitting. He did not know what device the sound came from, but he did know that it was enough to awaken the dead. From this direction and that there came the faint thump of fulling hammers against coarse cloth; and mingled with it—these were sounds to call forth the deepest emotions—were the calls of geese flying overhead. He slid a door open and they looked out. They had been lying near the veranda. There were tasteful clumps of black bamboo just outside and the dew shone as in more familiar places. Autumn insects sang busily, as if only inches from an ear used to wall crickets at considerable distances. It was all very clamorous, and also rather wonderful. Countless details could be overlooked in the singleness of his affection for the girl. She was pretty and fragile in a soft, modest cloak of lavender and a lined white robe. She had no single feature that struck him as especially beautiful, and yet, slender and fragile, she seemed so delicately beautiful that he was almost afraid to hear her voice. He might have wished her to be a little more assertive, but he wanted only to be near her, and yet nearer.

"Let's go off somewhere and enjoy the rest of the night. This is too much."

"But how is that possible?" She spoke very quietly. "You keep taking me by surprise."

There was a newly confiding response to his offer of his services as guardian in this world and the next. She was a strange little thing. He found it hard to believe that she had had much experience of men. He no longer cared what people might think. He asked Ukon to summon his man, who got the carriage ready. The

---

11. On whose part, his or the girl's? The passage is obscure.

12. *Karausu*. The mortar was sunk in the floor and the pestle was raised by foot and allowed to fall.

women of the house, though uneasy, sensed the depth of his feelings and were inclined to put their trust in him.

Dawn approached. No cocks were crowing. There was only the voice of an old man making deep obeisance to a Buddha, in preparation, it would seem, for a pilgrimage to Mitake.[13] He seemed to be prostrating himself repeatedly and with much difficulty. All very sad. In a life itself like the morning dew, what could he desire so earnestly?

"Praise to the Messiah to come," intoned the voice.

"Listen," said Genji, "He is thinking of another world.

"This pious one shall lead us on our way
As we plight our troth for all the lives to come."

The vow exchanged by the Chinese emperor and Yang Kuei-fei seemed to bode ill, and so he preferred to invoke Lord Maitreya, the Buddha of the Future; but such promises are rash.

"So heavy the burden I bring with me from the past,
I doubt that I should make these vows for the future."

It was a reply that suggested doubts about his "lives to come."

The moon was low over the western hills. She was reluctant to go with him. As he sought to persuade her, the moon suddenly disappeared behind clouds in a lovely dawn sky. Always in a hurry to be off before daylight exposed him, he lifted her easily into his carriage and took her to a nearby villa. Ukon was with them. Waiting for the caretaker to be summoned, Genji looked up at the rotting gate and the ferns that trailed thickly down over it. The groves beyond were still dark, and the mist and the dews were heavy. Genji's sleeve was soaking, for he had raised the blinds of the carriage.

"This is a novel adventure, and I must say that it seems like a lot of trouble.

"And did it confuse them too, the men of old,
This road through the dawn, for me so new and strange?

"How does it seem to you?"
She turned shyly away.

"And is the moon, unsure of the hills it approaches,
Foredoomed to lose its way in the empty skies?

"I am afraid."
She did seem frightened, and bewildered. She was so used to all those swarms of people, he thought with a smile.

The carriage was brought in and its traces propped against the veranda while a room was made ready in the west wing. Much excited, Ukon was thinking about earlier adventures. The furious energy with which the caretaker saw to preparations made her suspect who Genji was. It was almost daylight when they alighted

---

13. In the Yoshino Mountains, south of Nara.

from the carriage. The room was clean and pleasant, for all the haste with which it had been readied.

"There are unfortunately no women here to wait upon His Lordship." The man, who addressed him through Ukon, was a lesser steward who had served in the Sanjō mansion of Genji's father-in-law. "Shall I send for someone?"

"The last thing I want. I came here because I wanted to be in complete solitude, away from all possible visitors. You are not to tell a soul."

The man put together a hurried breakfast, but he was, as he had said, without serving women to help him.

Genji told the girl that he meant to show her a love as dependable as "the patient river of the loons."[14] He could do little else in these strange lodgings.

The sun was high when he arose. He opened the shutters. All through the badly neglected grounds not a person was to be seen. The groves were rank and overgrown. The flowers and grasses in the foreground were a drab monotone, an autumn moor. The pond was choked with weeds, and all in all it was a forbidding place. An outbuilding seemed to be fitted with rooms for the caretaker, but it was some distance away.

"It is a forbidding place,"[15] said Genji. "But I am sure that whatever devils emerge will pass me by."

He was still in disguise. She thought it unkind of him to be so secretive, and he had to agree that their relationship had gone beyond such furtiveness.

"Because of one chance meeting by the wayside
The flower now opens in the evening dew.

"And how does it look to you?"

"The face seemed quite to shine in the evening dew.
But I was dazzled by the evening light."

Her eyes turned away. She spoke in a whisper.

To him it may have seemed an interesting poem.

As a matter of fact, she found him handsomer than her poem suggested, indeed frighteningly handsome, given the setting.

"I hid my name from you because I thought it altogether too unkind of you to be keeping your name from me. Do please tell me now. This silence makes me feel that something awful might be coming."

"Call me the fisherman's daughter."[16] Still hiding her name, she was like a little child.

"I see. I brought it all on myself? A case of *warekara*?"[17]

---

14. Compare: Umanofuhito Kunihito, *Man-yōshū* 4458:
    The patient river of the patient loons
    Will not run dry. My love will still
    outlast it.
15. The repetition in almost identical language suggests a miscopying.
16. Compare: Anonymous, *Shinkokinshū* 1701, and "Courtesan's Song," *Wakan Rōeishū* 722:

A fisherman's daughter, I spend my
    life by the waves,
The waves that tell us nothing. I
    have no home.
17. Compare: Fujiwara Naoiko, *Kokinshū* 807:
    The grass the fishermen take, the *warekara*:
    "I did it myself." I shall weep but I shall
    not hate you.

And so, sometimes affectionately, sometimes reproachfully, they talked the hours away.

Koremitsu had found them out and brought provisions. Feeling a little guilty about the way he had treated Ukon, he did not come near. He thought it amusing that Genji should thus be wandering the streets, and concluded that the girl must provide sufficient cause. And he could have had her himself, had he not been so generous.

Genji and the girl looked out at an evening sky of the utmost calm. Because she found the darkness in the recesses of the house frightening, he raised the blinds at the veranda and they lay side by side. As they gazed at each other in the gathering dusk, it all seemed very strange to her, unbelievably strange. Memories of past wrongs quite left her. She was more at ease with him now, and he thought her charming. Beside him all through the day, starting up in fright at each little noise, she seemed delightfully childlike. He lowered the shutters early and had lights brought.

"You seem comfortable enough with me, and yet you raise difficulties."

At court everyone would be frantic. Where would the search be directed? He thought what a strange love it was, and he thought of the turmoil the Rokujō lady was certain to be in.[18] She had every right to be resentful, and yet her jealous ways were not pleasant. It was that sad lady to whom his thoughts first turned. Here was the girl beside him, so simple and undemanding; and the other was so impossibly forceful in her demands. How he wished he might in some measure have his freedom.

It was past midnight. He had been asleep for a time when an exceedingly beautiful woman appeared by his pillow.

"You do not even think of visiting me, when you are so much on my mind. Instead you go running off with someone who has nothing to recommend her, and raise a great stir over her. It is cruel, intolerable." She seemed about to shake the girl from her sleep. He awoke, feeling as if he were in the power of some malign being. The light had gone out. In great alarm, he pulled his sword to his pillow and awakened Ukon. She too seemed frightened.

"Go out to the gallery and wake the guard. Have him bring a light."

"It's much too dark."

He forced a smile. "You're behaving like a child."

He clapped his hands and a hollow echo answered. No one seemed to hear. The girl was trembling violently. She was bathed in sweat and as if in a trance, quite bereft of her senses.

"She is such a timid little thing," said Ukon, "frightened when there is nothing at all to be frightened of. This must be dreadful for her."

Yes, poor thing, thought Genji. She did seem so fragile, and she had spent the whole day gazing up at the sky.

"I'll go get someone. What a frightful echo. You stay here with her." He pulled Ukon to the girl's side.

---

18. We do not learn much about "the Rokujō lady" until Chapter 9. There is a theory that "Evening Faces" was written consid-erably later than the present succession of chapters has it.

The lights in the west gallery had gone out. There was a gentle wind. He had few people with him, and they were asleep. They were three in number: a young man who was one of his intimates and who was the son of the steward here, a court page, and the man who had been his intermediary in the matter of the "evening faces." He called out. Someone answered and came up to him.

"Bring a light. Wake the other, and shout and twang your bowstrings. What do you mean, going to sleep in a deserted house? I believe Lord Koremitsu was here."

"He was. But he said he had no orders and would come again at dawn."

An elite guardsman, the man was very adept at bow twanging. He went off with a shouting as of a fire watch. At court, thought Genji, the courtiers on night duty would have announced themselves, and the guard would be changing. It was not so very late.

He felt his way back inside. The girl was as before, and Ukon lay face down at her side.

"What is this? You're a fool to let yourself be so frightened. Are you worried about the fox spirits that come out and play tricks in deserted houses? But you needn't worry. They won't come near me." He pulled her to her knees.

"I'm not feeling at all well. That's why I was lying down. My poor lady must be terrified."

"She is indeed. And I can't think why."

He reached for the girl. She was not breathing. He lifted her and she was limp in his arms. There was no sign of life. She had seemed as defenseless as a child, and no doubt some evil power had taken possession of her. He could think of nothing to do. A man came with a torch. Ukon was not prepared to move, and Genji himself pulled up curtain frames to hide the girl.

"Bring the light closer."

It was a most unusual order. Not ordinarily permitted at Genji's side, the man hesitated to cross the threshold.

"Come, come, bring it here! There is a time and place for ceremony."

In the torchlight he had a fleeting glimpse of a figure by the girl's pillow. It was the woman in his dream. It faded away like an apparition in an old romance. In all the fright and horror, his confused thoughts centered upon the girl. There was no room for thoughts of himself.

He knelt over her and called out to her, but she was cold and had stopped breathing. It was too horrible. He had no confidant to whom he could turn for advice. It was the clergy one thought of first on such occasions. He had been so brave and confident, but he was young, and this was too much for him. He clung to the lifeless body.

"Come back, my dear, my dear. Don't do this awful thing to me." But she was cold and no longer seemed human.

The first paralyzing terror had left Ukon. Now she was writhing and wailing. Genji remembered a devil a certain minister had encountered in the Grand Hall.[19]

---

19. The *Okagami* tells how Fujiwara Tadahira met a devil in the Shishinden. It withdrew when informed that he was on the emperor's business.

"She can't possibly be dead." He found the strength to speak sharply. "All this noise in the middle of the night—you must try to be a little quieter." But it had been too sudden.

He turned again to the torchbearer. "There is someone here who seems to have had a very strange seizure. Tell your friend to find out where Lord Koremitsu is spending the night and have him come immediately. If the holy man is still at his mother's house, give him word, very quietly, that he is to come too. His mother and the people with her are not to hear. She does not approve of this sort of adventure."

He spoke calmly enough, but his mind was in a turmoil. Added to grief at the loss of the girl was horror, quite beyond describing, at this desolate place. It would be past midnight. The wind was higher and whistled more dolefully in the pines. There came a strange, hollow call of a bird. Might it be an owl? All was silence, terrifying solitude. He should not have chosen such a place—but it was too late now. Trembling violently, Ukon clung to him. He held her in his arms, wondering if she might be about to follow her lady. He was the only rational one present, and he could think of nothing to do. The flickering light wandered here and there. The upper parts of the screens behind them were in darkness, the lower parts fitfully in the light. There was a persistent creaking, as of someone coming up behind them. If only Koremitsu would come. But Koremitsu was a nocturnal wanderer without a fixed abode, and the man had to search for him in numerous places. The wait for dawn was like the passage of a thousand nights. Finally he heard a distant crowing. What legacy from a former life could have brought him to this mortal peril? He was being punished for a guilty love, his fault and no one else's, and his story would be remembered in infamy through all the ages to come. There were no secrets, strive though one might to have them. Soon everyone would know, from his royal father down, and the lowest court pages would be talking; and he would gain immortality as the model of the complete fool.

Finally Lord Koremitsu came. He was the perfect servant who did not go against his master's wishes in anything at any time; and Genji was angry that on this night of all nights he should have been away, and slow in answering the summons. Calling him inside even so, he could not immediately find the strength to say what must be said. Ukon burst into tears, the full horror of it all coming back to her at the sight of Koremitsu. Genji too lost control of himself. The only sane and rational one present, he had held Ukon in his arms, but now he gave himself up to his grief.

"Something very strange has happened," he said after a time. "Strange—'unbelievable' would not be too strong a word. I wanted a priest—one does when these things happen—and asked your reverend brother to come."

"He went back up the mountain yesterday. Yes, it is very strange indeed. Had there been anything wrong with her?"

"Nothing."

He was so handsome in his grief that Koremitsu wanted to weep. An older man who has had everything happen to him and knows what to expect can be depended upon in a crisis; but they were both young, and neither had anything to suggest.

Koremitsu finally spoke. "We must not let the caretaker know. He may be dependable enough himself, but he is sure to have relatives who will talk. We must get away from this place."

"You aren't suggesting that we could find a place where we would be less likely to be seen?"

"No, I suppose not. And the women at her house will scream and wail when they hear about it, and they live in a crowded neighborhood, and all the mob around will hear, and that will be that. But mountain temples are used to this sort of thing. There would not be much danger of attracting attention." He reflected on the problem for a time. "There is a woman I used to know. She has gone into a nunnery up in the eastern hills. She is very old, my father's nurse, as a matter of fact. The district seems to be rather heavily populated, but the nunnery is off by itself."

It was not yet full daylight. Koremitsu had the carriage brought up. Since Genji seemed incapable of the task, he wrapped the body in a covering and lifted it into the carriage. It was very tiny and very pretty, and not at all repellent. The wrapping was loose and the hair streamed forth, as if to darken the world before Genji's eyes.

He wanted to see the last rites through to the end, but Koremitsu would not hear of it. "Take my horse and go back to Nijō, now while the streets are still quiet."

He helped Ukon into the carriage and himself proceeded on foot, the skirts of his robe hitched up. It was a strange bedraggled sort of funeral procession, he thought, but in the face of such anguish he was prepared to risk his life. Barely conscious, Genji made his way back to Nijō.

"Where have you been?" asked the women. "You are not looking at all well."

He did not answer. Alone in his room, he pressed a hand to his heart. Why had he not gone with the others? What would she think if she were to come back to life? She would think that he had abandoned her. Self-reproach filled his heart to breaking. He had a headache and feared he had a fever. Might he too be dying? The sun was high and still he did not emerge. Thinking it all very strange, the women pressed breakfast upon him. He could not eat. A messenger reported that the emperor had been troubled by his failure to appear the day before.

His brothers-in-law came calling.

"Come in, please, just for a moment." He received only Tō no Chūjō and kept a blind between them. "My old nurse fell seriously ill and took her vows in the Fifth Month or so. Perhaps because of them, she seemed to recover. But recently she had a relapse. Someone came to ask if I would not call on her at least once more. I thought I really must go and see an old and dear servant who was on her deathbed, and so I went. One of her servants was ailing, and quite suddenly, before he had time to leave, he died. Out of deference to me they waited until night to take the body away. All this I learned later. It would be very improper of me to go to court with all these festivities coming up,[20] I thought, and so I stayed

---

20. There were many Shinto rites during the Ninth Month.

away. I have had a headache since early this morning—perhaps I have caught cold. I must apologize."

"I see. I shall so inform your father. He sent out a search party during the concert last night, and really seemed very upset." Tō no Chūjō turned to go, and abruptly turned back. "Come now. What sort of brush did you really have? I don't believe a word of it."

Genji was startled, but managed a show of nonchalance. "You needn't go into the details. Just say that I suffered an unexpected defilement. Very unexpected, really."

Despite his cool manner, he was not up to facing people. He asked a younger brother-in-law to explain in detail his reasons for not going to court. He got off a note to Sanjō with a similar explanation.

Koremitsu came in the evening. Having announced that he had suffered a defilement, Genji had callers remain outside, and there were few people in the house. He received Koremitsu immediately.

"Are you sure she is dead.?" He pressed a sleeve to his eyes.

Koremitsu too was in tears. "Yes, I fear she is most certainly dead. I could not stay shut up in a temple indefinitely, and so I have made arrangements with a venerable priest whom I happen to know rather well. Tomorrow is a good day for funerals."

"And the other woman?"

"She has seemed on the point of death herself. She does not want to be left behind by her lady. I was afraid this morning that she might throw herself over a cliff. She wanted to tell the people at Gojō, but I persuaded her to let us have a little more time."

"I am feeling rather awful myself and almost fear the worst."

"Come, now. There is nothing to be done and no point in torturing yourself. You must tell yourself that what must be must be. I shall let absolutely no one know, and I am personally taking care of everything."

"Yes, to be sure. Everything is fated. So I tell myself. But it is terrible to think that I have sent a lady to her death. You are not to tell your sister, and you must be very sure that your mother does not hear. I would not survive the scolding I would get from her."

"And the priests too: I have told them a plausible story." Koremitsu exuded confidence.

The women had caught a hint of what was going on and were more puzzled than ever. He had said that he had suffered a defilement, and he was staying away from court; but why these muffled lamentations?

Genji gave instructions for the funeral. "You must make sure that nothing goes wrong."

"Of course. No great ceremony seems called for."

Koremitsu turned to leave.

"I know you won't approve, said Genji, a fresh wave of grief sweeping over him, "but I will regret it forever if I don't see her again. I'll go on horseback."

"Very well, if you must." In fact Koremitsu thought the proposal very ill advised. "Go immediately and be back while it is still early."

Genji set out in the travel robes he had kept ready for his recent amorous excursions. He was in the bleakest despair. He was on a strange mission and the terrors of the night before made him consider turning back. Grief urged him on. If he did not see her once more, when, in another world, might he hope to see her as she had been? He had with him only Koremitsu and the attendant of that first encounter. The road seemed a long one.

The moon came out, two nights past full. They reached the river. In the dim torchlight, the darkness off towards Mount Toribe was ominous and forbidding; but Genji was too dazed with grief to be frightened. And so they reached the temple.

It was a harsh, unfriendly region at best. The board hut and chapel where the nun pursued her austerities were lonely beyond description. The light at the altar came dimly through cracks. Inside the hut a woman was weeping. In the outer chamber two or three priests were conversing and invoking the holy name in low voices. Vespers seemed to have ended in several temples nearby. Everything was quiet. There were lights and there seemed to be clusters of people in the direction of Kiyomizu. The grand tones in which the worthy monk, the son of the nun, was reading a sutra brought on what Genji thought must be the full flood tide of his tears.

He went inside. The light was turned away from the corpse. Ukon lay behind a screen. It must be very terrible for her, thought Genji. The girl's face was unchanged and very pretty.

"Won't you let me hear your voice again?" He took her hand. "What was it that made me give you all my love, for so short a time, and then made you leave me to this misery?" He was weeping uncontrollably.

The priests did not know who he was. They sensed something remarkable, however, and felt their eyes mist over.

"Come with me to Nijō," he said to Ukon.

"We have been together since I was very young. I never left her side, not for a single moment. Where am I to go now? I will have to tell the others what has happened. As if this weren't enough, I will have to put up with their accusations." She was sobbing. "I want to go with her."

"That is only natural. But it is the way of the world. Parting is always sad. Our lives must end, early or late. Try to put your trust in me." He comforted her with the usual homilies, but presently his real feelings came out. "Put your trust in me—when I fear I have not long to live myself." He did not after all seem likely to be much help.

"It will soon be light," said Koremitsu. "We must be on our way."

Looking back and looking back again, his heart near breaking, Genji went out. The way was heavy with dew and the morning mists were thick. He scarcely knew where he was. The girl was exactly as she had been that night. They had exchanged robes and she had on a red singlet of his. What might it have been in other lives that had brought them together? He managed only with great difficulty to stay in his saddle. Koremitsu was at the reins. As they came to the river Genji fell from his horse and was unable to remount.

"So I am to die by the wayside? I doubt that I can go on."

Koremitsu was in a panic. He should not have permitted this expedition, however strong Genji's wishes. Dipping his hands in the river, he turned and made supplication to Kiyomizu. Genji somehow pulled himself together. Silently invoking the holy name, he was seen back to Nijō.

The women were much upset by these untimely wanderings. "Very bad, very bad. He has been so restless lately. And why should he have gone out again when he was not feeling well?"

Now genuinely ill, he took to his bed. Two or three days passed and he was visibly thinner. The emperor heard of the illness and was much alarmed. Continuous prayers were ordered in this shrine and that temple. The varied rites, Shinto and Confucian and Buddhist, were beyond counting. Genji's good looks had been such as to arouse forebodings. All through the court it was feared that he would not live much longer. Despite his illness, he summoned Ukon to Nijō and assigned her rooms near his own. Koremitsu composed himself sufficiently to be of service to her, for he could see that she had no one else to turn to. Choosing times when he was feeling better, Genji would summon her for a talk, and she soon was accustomed to life at Nijō. Dressed in deep mourning, she was a somewhat stern and forbidding young woman, but not without her good points.

"It lasted such a very little while. I fear that I will be taken too. It must be dreadful for you, losing your only support. I had thought that as long as I lived I would see to all your needs, and it seems sad and ironical that I should be on the point of following her." He spoke softly and there were tears in his eyes. For Ukon the old grief had been hard enough to bear, and now she feared that a new grief might be added to it.

All through the Nijō mansion there was a sense of helplessness. Emissaries from court were thicker than raindrops. Not wanting to worry his father, Genji fought to control himself. His father-in-law was extremely solicitous and came to Nijō every day. Perhaps because of all the prayers and rites the crisis passed—it had lasted some twenty days—and left no ill effects. Genji's full recovery coincided with the final cleansing of the defilement. With the unhappiness he had caused his father much on his mind, he set off for his apartments at court. For a time he felt out of things, as if he had come back to a strange new world.

By the end of the Ninth Month he was his old self once more. He had lost weight, but emaciation only made him handsomer. He spent a great deal of time gazing into space, and sometimes he would weep aloud. He must be in the clutches of some malign spirit, thought the women. It was all most peculiar.

He would summon Ukon on quiet evenings. "I don't understand it at all. Why did she so insist on keeping her name from me? Even if she *was* a fisherman's daughter it was cruel of her to be so uncommunicative. It was as if she did not know how much I loved her."

"There was no reason for keeping it secret. But why should she tell you about her insignificant self? Your attitude seemed so strange from the beginning. She used to say that she hardly knew whether she was waking or dreaming. Your refusal to identify yourself, you know, helped her guess who you were. It hurt her that you should belittle her by keeping your name from her."

"An unfortunate contest of wills. I did not want anything to stand between us; but I must always be worrying about what people will say. I must refrain from things my father and all the rest of them might take me to task for. I am not permitted the smallest indiscretion. Everything is exaggerated so. The little incident of the 'evening faces' affected me strangely and I went to very great trouble to see her. There must have been a bond between us. A love doomed from the start to be fleeting—why should it have taken such complete possession of me and made me find her so precious? You must tell me everything. What point is there in keeping secrets now? I mean to make offerings every week, and I want to know in whose name I am making them."

"Yes, of course—why have secrets now? It is only that I do not want to slight what she made so much of. Her parents are dead. Her father was a guards captain. She was his special pet, but his career did not go well and his life came to an early and disappointing end. She somehow got to know Lord Tō no Chūjō—it was when he was still a lieutenant. He was very attentive for three years or so, and then about last autumn there was a rather awful threat from his father-in-law's house. She was ridiculously timid and it frightened her beyond all reason. She ran off and hid herself at her nurse's in the western part of the city. It was a wretched little hovel of a place. She wanted to go off into the hills, but the direction she had in mind has been taboo since New Year's. So she moved to the odd place where she was so upset to have you find her. She was more reserved and withdrawn than most people, and I fear that her unwillingness to show her emotions may have seemed cold."

So it was true. Affection and pity welled up yet more strongly.

"He once told me of a lost child. Was there such a one?"

"Yes, a very pretty little girl, born two years ago last spring."

"Where is she? Bring her to me without letting anyone know. It would be such a comfort. I should tell my friend Tō no Chūjō, I suppose, but why invite criticism? I doubt that anyone could reprove me for taking in the child. You must think up a way to get around the nurse."

"It would make me very happy if you were to take the child. I would hate to have her left where she is. She is there because we had no competent nurses in the house where you found us."

The evening sky was serenely beautiful. The flowers below the veranda were withered, the songs of the insects were dying too, and autumn tints were coming over the maples. Looking out upon the scene, which might have been a painting, Ukon thought what a lovely asylum she had found herself. She wanted to avert her eyes at the thought of the house of the "evening faces." A pigeon called, somewhat discordantly, from a bamboo thicket. Remembering how the same call had frightened the girl in that deserted villa, Genji could see the little figure as if an apparition were there before him.

"How old was she? She seemed so delicate, because she was not long for this world, I suppose."

"Nineteen, perhaps? My mother, who was her nurse, died and left me behind. Her father took a fancy to me, and so we grew up together, and I never once left her side. I wonder how I can go on without her. I am almost sorry that we were so close.[21] She seemed so weak, but I can see now that she was a source of strength."

"The weak ones do have a power over us. The clear, forceful ones I can do without. I am weak and indecisive by nature myself, and a woman who is quiet and withdrawn and follows the wishes of a man even to the point of letting herself be used has much the greater appeal. A man can shape and mold her as he wishes, and becomes fonder of her all the while."

"She was exactly what you would have wished, sir." Ukon was in tears. "That thought makes the loss seem greater."

The sky had clouded over and a chilly wind had come up. Gazing off into the distance, Genji said softly:

"One sees the clouds as smoke that rose from the pyre,
And suddenly the evening sky seems nearer."

Ukon was unable to answer. If only her lady were here! For Genji even the memory of those fulling blocks was sweet.

"In the Eighth Month, the Ninth Month, the nights are long,"[22] he whispered, and lay down.

The young page, brother of the lady of the locust shell, came to Nijō from time to time, but Genji no longer sent messages for his sister. She was sorry that he seemed angry with her and sorry to hear of his illness. The prospect of accompanying her husband to his distant province was a dreary one. She sent off a note to see whether Genji had forgotten her.

"They tell me you have not been well.

"Time goes by, you ask not why I ask not.
Think if you will how lonely a life is mine.

"I might make reference to Masuda Pond."[23]

This was a surprise; and indeed he had not forgotten her. The uncertain hand in which he set down his reply had its own beauty.

"Who, I wonder, lives the more aimless life.

"Hollow though it was, the shell of the locust
Gave me strength to face a gloomy world.

"But only precariously."

So he still remembered "the shell of the locust." She was sad and at the same time amused. It was good that they could correspond without rancor. She wished no further intimacy, and she did not want him to despise her.

As for the other, her stepdaughter, Genji heard that she had married a guards lieutenant. He thought it a strange marriage and he felt a certain pity for the

---

21. This would seem to be a poetic allusion, but none has been satisfactorily identified.
22. Po Chü-i, Collected Works, XIX, "The Fulling Blocks at Night."

23. Compare: Anonymous, *Shūishū* 804:
Long the roots of the Masuda water shield,
Longer still the aimless, sleepless nights.

lieutenant. Curious to know something of her feelings, he sent a note by his young messenger.

"Did you know that thoughts of you had brought me to the point of expiring?

"I bound them loosely, the reeds beneath the eaves,[24]
And reprove them now for having come undone."

He attached it to a long reed.

The boy was to deliver it in secret, he said. But he thought that the lieutenant would be forgiving if he were to see it, for he would guess who the sender was. One may detect here a note of self-satisfaction.

Her husband was away. She was confused, but delighted that he should have remembered her. She sent off in reply a poem the only excuse for which was the alacrity with which it was composed:

"The wind brings words, all softly, to the reed,
And the under leaves are nipped again by the frost."

It might have been cleverer and in better taste not to have disguised the clumsy handwriting. He thought of the face he had seen by lamplight. He could forget neither of them, the governor's wife, seated so primly before him, or the younger woman, chattering on so contentedly, without the smallest suggestion of reserve. The stirrings of a susceptible heart suggested that he still had important lessons to learn.

Quietly, forty-ninth-day services were held for the dead lady in the Lotus Hall on Mount Hiei. There was careful attention to all the details, the priestly robes and the scrolls and the altar decorations. Koremitsu's older brother was a priest of considerable renown, and his conduct of the services was beyond reproach. Genji summoned a doctor of letters with whom he was friendly and who was his tutor in Chinese poetry and asked him to prepare a final version of the memorial petition. Genji had prepared a draft. In moving language he committed the one he had loved and lost, though he did not mention her name, to the mercy of Amitābha.

"It is perfect, just as it is. Not a word needs to be changed." Noting the tears that refused to be held back, the doctor wondered who might be the subject of these prayers. That Genji should not reveal the name, and that he should be in such open grief—someone, no doubt, who had brought a very large bounty of grace from earlier lives.

Genji attached a poem to a pair of lady's trousers which were among his secret offerings:

"I weep and weep as today I tie this cord.
It will be untied in an unknown world to come."

He invoked the holy name with great feeling. Her spirit had wandered

---

24. The girl is traditionally called Nokiba-no-
ogi, "the reeds beneath the eaves."

uncertainly these last weeks. Today it would set off down one of the ways of the future.

His heart raced each time he saw Tō no Chūjō. He longed to tell his friend that "the wild carnation" was alive and well; but there was no point in calling forth reproaches.

In the house of the "evening faces," the women were at a loss to know what had happened to their lady. They had no way of inquiring. And Ukon too had disappeared. They whispered among themselves that they had been right about that gentleman, and they hinted at their suspicions to Koremitsu. He feigned complete ignorance, however, and continued to pursue his little affairs. For the poor women it was all like a nightmare. Perhaps the wanton son of some governor, fearing Tō no Chūjō, had spirited her off to the country? The owner of the house was her nurse's daughter. She was one of three children and related to Ukon. She could only long for her lady and lament that Ukon had not chosen to enlighten them. Ukon for her part was loath to raise a stir, and Genji did not want gossip at this late date. Ukon could not even inquire after the child. And so the days went by bringing no light on the terrible mystery.

Genji longed for a glimpse of the dead girl, if only in a dream. On the day after the services he did have a fleeting dream of the woman who had appeared that fatal night. He concluded, and the thought filled him with horror, that he had attracted the attention of an evil spirit haunting the neglected villa.

Early in the Tenth Month the governor of Iyo left for his post, taking the lady of the locust shell with him. Genji chose his farewell presents with great care. For the lady there were numerous fans,[25] and combs of beautiful workmanship, and pieces of cloth (she could see that he had had them dyed specially) for the wayside gods. He also returned her robe, "the shell of the locust."

"A keepsake till we meet again, I had hoped,
And see, my tears have rotted the sleeves away."

There were other things too, but it would be tedious to describe them. His messenger returned empty-handed. It was through her brother that she answered his poem.

"Autumn comes, the wings of the locust are shed.
A summer robe returns, and I weep aloud."

She had remarkable singleness of purpose, whatever else she might have. It was the first day of winter. There were chilly showers, as if to mark the occasion, and the skies were dark. He spent the day lost in thought.

"The one has gone, to the other I say farewell.
They go their unknown ways. The end of autumn."

He knew how painful a secret love can be.

---

25. Because the sound of the word ōgi, "fan,"
bodes well for a reunion, fans were often
given as farewell presents.

I had hoped, out of deference to him, to conceal these difficult matters; but I have been accused of romancing, of pretending that because he was the son of an emperor he had no faults. Now, perhaps, I shall be accused of having revealed too much.

MONK SAIGYŌ (1118–1190 C.E.)
FUJIWARA SHUNZEI (c. 1175?–?1250 C.E.)
FUJIWARA TEIKA (1162–1241 C.E.)
PRINCESS SHOKUSHI (d. 1201 C.E.)
FUJIWARA SHUNZEI'S DAUGHTER
(c. 1175?–?1250 C.E.)
Japan

These poets are five of the brightest lights of the *Shinkokinshū* ("New Kokinshū"), the eighth and, by general consent, finest of the twenty-one royal poetry anthologies. The Japanese regard the poets of the *Shinkokinshū* period (1183–1235) as their most profound, admiring in particular their subtle allusions to earlier poetry, their meditations on Tendai Buddhism, their descriptions of nature, and the depth they bring to the conventional poetic figure of the passionate woman.

Poetry by now had become largely fictional—imagined responses to artificially posed situations. Such poetry required intense depth and a supremely magical quality in order to appeal to readers—or even to poets, who looked on poetry as both a contest for fame and a religious vocation. The compilers of the *Shinkokinshū* brought to perfection the practice, which had begun with the *Kinkoshū*, of creating a new artistic continuum from sequences of brief poems. The collection is organized in sequences of 100 poems each and can actually be read as a single, extended work of almost 10,000 lines.

As for the poets, the monk Saigyō is counted as one of the three most beloved poets in Japan. Fujiwara Shunzei defined the poetic ideals of the age in terms of affecting deprivation (*sabi*, the beauty and desolation of loneliness or solitude), ethereal beauty (*yōen*) and, especially, mystery and depth (*yūgen*). His son, Fujiwara Teika, is increasingly being considered one of the three or four greatest Japanese poets. Too difficult a person to sentimentalize, he was his own harshest critic. To him we also owe a number of the best manuscript transcriptions of earlier great works, including *The Tale of Genji*. He also distinguished himself in a rare way: his gifted imitators were also to achieve greatness. Among them was the poet known simply as Fujiwara Shunzei's Daughter. Her talent was so great that Fujiwara Teika, who was her uncle, adopted her. Another gifted woman writer, Princess Shokushi, shows that the beauty sought was truly refined and proud.

from *The Eighth Royal Anthology [Shinkokinshū]*

MONK SAIGYŌ

[While denying his heart]

While denying his heart,
Even a monk cannot but know
   The bleak beauty.
From the marsh a single snipe
Flies off into autumn dusk.

[I hope no longer]

I hope no longer
That any friend will come to visit
   This village in the hills,
Where if not for loneliness
Living would be a wretched thing.

[The crickets cry]

The crickets cry—
With the quelling cold of night
   Autumn takes its way,
As they gradually seem to falter,
Those cries that fade afar.

[In Tsu province]

In Tsu province
Naniwa knew spring glories
   Now no more than dream!
Over the frost-withered reed leaves
The cold winds cross to farther ends.

[We realized our love]

We realized our love.
And from those nights of vanished dreams

All poems in this selection translated by Earl Miner.

Would I never wake,
In spite of everlasting sleep
In the darkness of vain desire.[1]

FUJIWARA SHUNZEI

[As evening falls]

As evening falls,
Along the fields the autumn wind
   Pierces to the bone,
And quails raise their anguished cries
Among Fukakusa's deep grass.[2]

[Longing for the past]

Longing for the past,
The hermit's grass-thatched hut
   In a shower at night:
Do not call a freshening of tears,
Hototogisu singing here at last.[3]

[Will some other poet]

Will some other poet,
When once again the orange trees bloom
   Recall with longing
Something of me when I as well
Will have become a person of the past?

[Upon Fushimi Hill]

Upon Fushimi Hill,
From this dark shelter of the pines
   I gaze off beyond,
Where with daybreak on the fields
The ripples of the breeze pass by.

---

1. The dream of love is held in balance with the reality of religion.
2. Recalling Ariwara Narihira's exchange of poems with a woman in Fukakusa, a place that had disappeared.
3. The hototogisu is a variety of cuckoo, similar to the western nightingale.

[Shining with raindrops]

Shining with raindrops
Across the blooms of orange trees
    The breeze makes way,
And at last the hototogisu
Sings from somewhere in low clouds.

[Worldly attachments]

Worldly attachments
Join together numerous desires,
    And while I ponder this,
In the emptiness of the sky[4]
A white cloud melts away from view.

[The imagined image]

The imagined image
Of the form of cherry blossoms
    I hold as ideal view,
And how many ridges have I crossed
For what were white clouds on those peaks?[5]

FUJIWARA TEIKA

[Looking far beyond]

Looking far beyond
Neither blossoms nor colored leaves[6]
    Need be wished for:
Wretched thatched huts along the cove
In the thickening autumn dusk.

[A woman on love at dawn parting]

My image of you—
It too alters with your departure
    At dawn's temple bell

---

4. The character for "sky" designates literal "emptiness" and also the Buddhist doctrine of lack of real existence.

5. The clouds imagined as flowers are more attractive than actual flowers.

6. A dispute exists as to whether or not these are autumnal leaves.

When it is always sad to find
The sky streaked with first light.[7]

[Across the heavens]

Across the heavens
In the fragrance of plum blossoms[8]
   The haze increases;
The smoke-like pallor does not exempt
The moon on the brief spring night.

[On the brief spring night]

On the brief spring night
The floating bridge of dreams
   Breaks all apart,
And from the peak a bank of clouds
Takes leave into the empty sky.[9]

[Blossoms of the plum]

Blossoms of the plum
Transfer from the tree their fragrance
   To rest upon the sleeve,
Where moonbeams vie in glistening
As they filter through the eaves.

[Crimson it is]

Crimson it is,
The dew catching and reflecting
   The morning sunlight
And the whole region all aglow
With wild carnation flowers.

[A single traveler]

A single traveler,
His sleeves blow back and forth

---

7. A woman on her lover's rare and too brief visit.
8. Plum and haze are spring emblems in section 1 of *The Pillow Book*.

9. The imagery of lines 1–3 conveys waking up; the personification of lines 4–5 describes the scene. Line 2 is the title of the last chapter of *The Tale of Genji*. "Sky" is discussed in note 4.

In the autumn wind
When the evening sun turns desolate[10]
The hanging bridge between the peaks.

[One of three love poems presented at the palace in the Third Month of 1213]

Our reflections—
Where the two Streams of Longing met,
  Let them at least join!
What matter if, like drifting foam,
We soon vanish in the current.

[I leave the capital]

I leave the capital
As morning rises on the mountain,
  Where upon the crest
The tearful dew of parting
Scatters with gusts of autumn wind.

[For straw-mat bedding / in the waiting night]

For straw-mat bedding—
In the waiting night the autumn
  Wind grows very late,
And she spreads out the moonlight—
The Lady of the Uji Bridge.[11]

["Like whitened hemp"]

The sleeves that mark our parting
  Accumulate the dew,
And with its flesh-piercing color
The chill wind of autumn blows.[12]

---

10. "Desolate" modifies both "sun" and
   "bridge."
11. This poem echoes a questioning earlier
   poem. "The Bridge Lady" is the title of one
   of the Uji chapters of *The Tale of Genji;* it
   may also indicate a goddess.

12. Parting in tears and in the dew, (with
   additional erotic suggestions) the lovers
   don garments used as bedclothes. The
   man leaves the woman's house in a white
   wind, contrary to an earlier poem, which
   depicts wind without any color.

PRINCESS SHOKUSHI

[The dawn arrives]

The dawn arrives
Announced by the crowing cocks
    That call some hope
To a pillow fraught with longing
In the long dream of vain desire.

[Hidden Love]

O cord of life,
If you must break, then break now!
    If I must live on,
The fearful strain of holding out
Will be too much for me to bear.

[Guide me on my way]

Guide me on my way—
Across waves that leave no trace
    My boat rows on
And its destination uncertain—
O salt wind gusting from all sides!

[The cherry petals gone]

The cherry petals gone,
No special color makes its claim;
    Gazing in reverie,
From somewhere in the vacant sky[13]
The spring rain gently falls.

FUJIWARA SHUNZEI'S DAUGHTER

[On the topic "Love and Clouds"]

"On the topic 'Love and Clouds' "
    Its flames suppressed,
Desire's great fire will consume me.
    Its very smoke

---

13. Sky and emptiness are discussed in note 4.

Vanishing without trace in clouds
Whose only end is desolation.[14]

[On the topic "Love in Spring"]

An image of you
Forms in the hazed over moon
    That has found lodging:
In a spring not that of old
On sleeves glistening with tears.[15]

[The orange flowers]

The orange flowers
Glow all about the region
    Of some brief sleep,
And in a dream of times bygone
His scented sleeves return to mind.[16]

[Haze by the river]

The Lady of the Bridge—[17]
The morning frost upon her sleeves
    Chills them further,
And the spring haze drifts along
In the Uji River's wind.

[To my house]

To my house his path
Has along its wayside grasses
    Withered, withered,
And rarer still his footprints
In the frost that makes all pale.

[A gentle breeze]

A gentle breeze
Comes to a sleeve that dozes

---

14. The imagery suggests cremation.
15. See Narihira's poem, Tales of Ise, episode 4.
16. Alluding to an anonymous Kokinshū

poem in which the blossoms recall a lover who used them to scent sleeves.
17. See note 11.

Scenting with blossoms
A pillow rich in the fragrance
Of dream on a brief spring night.

A SEQUENCE OF SEVEN POEMS BY VARIOUS POETS FROM THE SHINKOKINSHŪ

These poems are taken from Book 6 of the twenty divisions of the *Shinkokinshū*. Among the winter poems, the seven presented here belong to a group of twenty-eight poems having snow as their central image, as well as to a briefer subsequence of thirteen poems emphasizing human concerns. The first four poems are by older and, on the whole, lesser poets; the more recent poems are by more impressive poets. (This controlled fluctuation in poetic quality was part of the aesthetic strategy of the anthology's compilers. Lesser poems provided a mental respite, in preparation for the more challenging greater poems.)

In the poems presented below, the customary headnote (a statement describing the occasion the poem is responding to) has been omitted. Following each translation is the poet's name and a review of motifs. By paying close attention to the motifs, we see how the techniques used by these poets were able to integrate poems written on widely varied subjects into a kind of continuous narrative or sequence. Beyond their intrinsic interest, sequences of this kind foretell the genius of *renga* or linked poetry (like the selections from *One Hundred Stanzas by Three Poets at Ginase* included later in this section), which was at this period only a pastime from the rigors of composing serious poems such as the ones presented here.

[As they sound]

As they sound—
The bamboo wattlings of the fence
Crack beneath the piling snow.

[Fujiwara Norikane. Indoors, bamboo fence, snow. Sleeper awaking. Predawn. Surprise.]

[The crowing cock]

The crowing cock
Announces arrival of the dawn—
But it is the snow
That radiates the peak of Otowa,
"Mountain of Feathered Sound."

[Fujiwara Takakura. Bird(s), light, mountains, snow. Observer of daybreak sounds and sights. Dawn. Pleasure in beauty. Hearing from, and looking at, the outside of the house.]

All poems in this selection translated by Earl Miner and Robert H. Brower.

[In the mountains]

In the mountains
Even the single path must lie
    Buried from the sight,
For in the capital snow has fallen
Together with the colored leaves.

[Fujiwara Ietsune. Distant mountains, trees, snow. Capital dweller thinking of life in the mountains (and someone dear?). Day. Pensive tone. Only outdoors conceived; speaker's position unclear.]

[Was it not enough / to know loneliness]

Was it not enough
To know loneliness without this?
    Along the hillslopes
The oaks drop their withered leaves
And silently the snow still falls.

[Fujiwara Kunifusa. Hills, trees, snow. Observer out of doors (hills). Daytime. Loneliness.]

[There is no shelter]

There is no shelter
Where I can rest my weary horse
    And brush my laden sleeves:
Sano ford and adjoining fields
Spread with a twilight in the snow.

[Fujiwara Teika. Horse, river and neighborhood, snow. Rider during heavy snowfall. Out of doors. Bleak scene as light is failing.]

[The path of him I long for]

The path of him I long for
Across foothills to where I wait
    Must be all hidden:
The snow weighs unbearably
In the cedars beyond my eaves.

[Teika. Hills (and mountains), narrow road, trees, snow. Evening (when a lover visits). Lonely scene imagined by a waiting woman.]

[Beneath the piling snow]

Beneath the piling snow
The bamboos at Fushimi village

Crack loudly in the dark:
Even the path to love in dreams
Snaps to waking underneath the snow.

[Fujiwara Ariie. Village south of the capital, bamboos, snow. Night. Dream of visiting her lover broken by sound of bamboos cracking under heavy snowfall. Pathos of romance.]

ANONYMOUS (1300–1330 C.E.)
Japan

The Tale of the Heike describes the defeat of the Heike (or Taira) family by the Genji (or Minamoto) family. The story is as familiar in Japan as is the Bible or the Arthurian legend in the West. Covering the bloody period between c. 1131 and 1191, the *Tale* existed in numerous versions, the best known of which were those of the *biwa hōshi* or "lute priests"—itinerant blind minstrels who recited to their own lute accompaniment. The extracts here are taken from the most respected of these oral versions, the one associated with the reciter Kakuichi (c. 1300–1371). It consists of twelve parts subdivided into numbered, titled episodes, and a sequel.

In its imaginative role, majesty, and sweep, this is the Japanese epic, a miscellaneous grouping in the manner of the Western romance epic (there is no agreement on the "structure" of its parts); in many ways, it is epic-by-collection. The *Tale* also differs from most Western epics in the prominence given to women and children. The collective viewpoint is that of the people of Kyoto. They had trembled before the mighty Heike family, who are now reported dead or humiliatingly led captive through the streets of the capital. Yet the Heike receive admiration and sympathy in defeat, for they had taken up the refined ways of the court. Among the iron-willed, militaristic Genji, on the other hand, only the doomed Yoshitsune seems to receive full approval.

The selections here begin with the famous opening words and thereafter come from later books: the death of the impetuous Yoshinaka (9:4); the death of the young Atsumori (9:16); and the separation of Yokubue from her beloved (10:8). The first of these episodes displays the ethos of the warrior, including women warriors. The second is a favorite that has inspired dramatic versions in both nō and kabuki. The third, one of the most popular, shows both how Japanese concepts of love involve yearning for the unattainable and how Buddhism offered consolation for human misery. The elegiac emphasis heard here increases as the work progresses, a quality which brings the *Tale* closer to epics outside the Graeco-Roman tradition.

The *Tale* is a typically Japanese work in three respects. First, it combines prose narrative with verse lyrics. Second, the assembly of diverse matter is more important than the plot. Third, the boundaries of fact and fiction are the harder to draw because they so often cross. The *Tale* is a fitting counterpart, in a later age, to *The Tale of Genji*, showing the heartrending beauty of human suffering in war.

Buddhism, with its stress on evanescence, underlies the opening passage, in which the first sentence alludes to the death of Shakamuni (depicted by his entry into Nirvana as a Buddha) at the Jetavana Temple (Gion Shoja in Japanese, providing the title for the opening chapter). Shakamuni's passing causes the great teak trees to shed their leaves and animals to weep tears. As this rich tapestry unfolds, Buddhism is only one of the many designs included.

from The Tale of the Heike [Heike Monogatari]

[Opening]*

At the Jetavana Temple / the bell sounds out / the impermanence of all things / as it tolls its knell. / That the color of the flowers / on the great teak trees / foretells the fall of the proud / is wholly suitable. / Those who utter large claims / will not long continue— / their times like a spring night / when dreams quickly break. / Those who display bravery / fall down in the end: / as victims of the tempest / are blown off like the dust.

[The Death of Kiso]†

Kiso no Yoshinaka had brought with him from Shinano two female attendants, Tomoe and Yamabuki. Yamabuki had fallen ill and stayed in the capital. Of the two, Tomoe was especially beautiful, with white skin, long hair, and charming features. She was also a remarkably strong archer, and as a swordswoman she was a warrior worth a thousand, ready to confront a demon or god, mounted or on foot. She handled unbroken horses with superb skill; she rode unscathed down perilous descents. Whenever a battle was imminent, Yoshinaka sent her out as his first captain, equipped with strong armor, an oversized sword, and a mighty bow; and she performed more deeds of valor than any of his other warriors. Thus she was now one of the seven who remained after all the others had fled or perished.

There were rumors that Yoshinaka was making for the Tanba Road by way of Nagasaka, and also that he was heading north through the Ryūge Pass. In actuality, he was fleeing toward Seta in the hope of finding Imai no Shirō Kanehira. Kanehira himself had started back toward the capital with furled banner, worried about his master, after having lost all but fifty of his eight hundred defenders at Seta. The two arrived simultaneously at Uchide-no-hama in the vicinity of Ōtsu, recognized one another from about three hundred and fifty feet away, and galloped together.

Lord Kiso took Kanehira by the hand, "I meant to die at the Rokujō riverbed, but I broke through a swarm of enemies and came away here because I wanted to find you."

"Your words do me great honor," Kanehira said. "I meant to die at Seta, but I have come this far because I was worried about you."

*Translated by Earl Miner.
†Translated by Helen McCullough.

"I see that our karma tie is still intact. My warriors scattered into the mountains and woods after the enemy broke our formations; some of them must still be nearby. Have that furled banner of yours raised!"

More than three hundred riders responded to the unfurling of Imai's banner—men who had fled from the capital or Seta, or who had come from some other place. Yoshinaka was overjoyed. "Why can't we fight one last battle, now that we have a force of this size? Whose is the band I see massed over there?"

"They say the commander is Ichijō no Jirō Tadayori from Kai."

"What is his strength?"

"He is supposed to have six thousand riders."

"Then we are well matched! If we must meet death, let it be by galloping against a worthy foe and falling outnumbered." Yoshinaka rode forward in the lead.

That day, Lord Kiso was attired in a red brocade *hitatare,* a suit of armor laced with thick Chinese damask, and a horned helmet. At his side, he wore a magnificent oversized sword; high on his back, there rode a quiver containing the few arrows left from his earlier encounters, all fledged with eagle tail feathers. He grasped a rattan-wrapped bow and sat in a gold-edged saddle astride his famous horse Oniashige [Roan Demon], a very stout and brawny animal. Standing in his stirrups, he announced his name in a mighty voice "You must have heard of Kiso no Kanja in the past; now you see him! I am the Morning Sun Commander Minamoto no Yoshinaka, Director of the Imperial Stables of the Left and Governor of Iyo Province. They tell me you are Ichijō no Jirō from Kai. We are well matched! Cut off my head and show it to Yoritomo!" He galloped forward, shouting.

"The warrior who has just announced his name is their Commander-in-Chief," Ichijō no Jirō said. "Wipe out the whole force, men! Get them all, young retainers! Kill them!"

The easterners moved to surround Yoshinaka with their superior numbers, each hoping to be the one to take his head. Yoshinaka's three hundred riders galloped lengthwise, sidewise, zigzag, and crosswise in the midst of the six thousand foes and finally burst through to the rear, only fifty strong.

As the fifty went on their way after having broken free, they came to a defensive position manned by two thousand riders under the command of Toi no Jirō Sanehira. Again, they broke through and went on. Again, they galloped through enemy bands—here four or five hundred. there two or three hundred, or a hundred and forty or fifty, or a hundred—until only five of them were left. Even then, Tomoe remained alive.

"Quickly, now," Lord Kiso said to Tomoe. "You are a woman, so be off with you; go wherever you please. I intend to die in battle, or to kill myself if I am wounded. It would be unseemly to let people say, 'Lord Kiso kept a woman with him during his last battle.' "

Reluctant to flee, Tomoe rode with the others until she could resist no longer. Then she pulled up. "Ah! If only I could find a worthy foe! I would fight a last battle for His Lordship to watch," she thought.

As she sat there, thirty riders came into view, led by Onda no Hachirō Moroshige, a man renowned in Musashi Province for his great strength. Tomoe galloped into their midst, rode up alongside Moroshige, seized him in a powerful grip, pulled him down against the pommel of her saddle, held him motionless, twisted off his head, and threw it away. Afterward, she discarded armor and helmet and fled toward the eastern provinces.

Tezuka no Tarō Mitsumori died in battle; Tezuka no Bettō fled. Only two horsemen remained, Imai no Shirō Kanehira and Lord Kiso.

"I have never noticed it before, but my armor seems heavy today," Lord Kiso said.

"You are not tired yet, and your horse is still strong. Why should you find a suit of armor heavy? You are discouraged because there is nobody left to fight on our side. But you should think of me as a man worth a thousand ordinary warriors. I will hold off the enemy awhile with my last seven or eight arrows. That place over there is the Awazu Pine Woods: kill yourself among the trees."

As the two rode, whipping their horses, a new band of fifty warriors appeared. "Get into the pine woods. I will hold these enemies at bay," Kanehira said.

"I ought to have perished in the capital. My only reason for fleeing here was that I wanted to die with you. Let's not be killed in different places; let's go down together." Lord Kiso brought his mount alongside Kanehira's, ready to gallop forward.

Kanehira leaped down and took his master's horse by the mouth. "No matter how glorious a warrior's earlier reputation may have been, an ignoble death means eternal disgrace. You are tired; there are no forces following you. If you are isolated by the enemy and dragged down to your death by some fellow's insignificant retainer, people will say, 'So-and-So's retainer killed the famous Lord Kiso, the man known throughout Japan.' I would hate to see that happen. Please, please, go into the pine woods."

"Well, then . . ." Lord Kiso galloped toward the Awazu Pine Woods.

Kanehira dashed into the fifty riders alone, stood in his stirrups, and announced his name in a mighty voice. "You must have heard of me long ago; see me now with your own eyes! I am Imai no Shirō Kanehira, aged thirty-three, foster brother to Lord Kiso. The Kamakura Lord Yoritomo himself must know that such a person exists. Kill me and show him my head!" He fired off his remaining eight arrows in a fast and furious barrage that felled eight men on the spot. (It is impossible to say whether or not they were killed.) Then he drew his sword and galloped slashing from place to place, without meeting a man willing to face him. Many were the trophies he amassed! The easterners surrounded him and let fly a hail of arrows, hoping to shoot him down, but none of their shafts found a chink in his armor or penetrated its stout plates, and he remained uninjured.

Lord Kiso galloped toward the Awazu Pine Woods, a lone rider. The shadows were gathering on the Twenty-First of the First Month, and a thin film of ice had formed. Unaware that a deep paddy field lay in front of him, he sent his horse plunging into the mire. The animal sank below its head and stayed there, motionless, despite furious flogging with stirrups and whip. Lord Kiso glanced backward, worried about Kanehira, and Ishida no Jirō Tamehisa, who was hard on his heels, drew his bow to the full and sent an arrow thudding into his face. Mortally wounded, he sagged forward with the bowl of his helmet against the horse's neck.

Two of Tamehisa's retainers went up and took Lord Kiso's head. Tamehisa impaled it on the tip of his sword, raised it aloft, and announced in a mighty voice,

"Miura no Ishida no Jirō Tamehisa has killed Lord Kiso, the man known throughout Japan!"

Kanehira heard the shout as he battled. "I don't need to fight to protect anyone now. Take a look, easterners! This is how the bravest man in Japan commits suicide!" He put the tip of his sword in his mouth, jumped headlong from his horse, and perished, run through. Thus, it turned out that there was no combat worthy of the name at Awazu.

[The Death of Atsumori]

Kumagae no Jirō Naozane walked his horse toward the beach after the defeat of the Heike. "The Taira nobles will be fleeing to the water's edge in the hope of boarding rescue vessels," he thought. "Ah, how I would like to grapple with a high-ranking Commander-in-Chief!" Just then, he saw a lone rider splash into the sea, headed toward a vessel in the offing. The other was attired in a crane-embroidered *nerinuki* silk *hitatare,* a suit of armor with shaded green lacing, and a horned helmet. At his waist, he wore a sword with gilt bronze fittings; on his back, there rode a quiver containing arrows fledged with black-banded white eagle feathers. He grasped a rattan-wrapped bow and bestrode a white-dappled reddish horse with a gold-edged saddle. When his mount had swum out about a hundred and fifty or two hundred feet, Naozane beckoned him with his fan.

"I see that you are a Commander-in-Chief. It is dishonorable to show your back to an enemy. Return!"

The warrior came back. As he was leaving the water, Naozane rode up alongside him, gripped him with all his strength, crashed with him to the ground, held him motionless, and pushed aside his helmet to cut off his head. He was sixteen or seventeen years old, with a lightly powdered face and blackened teeth—a boy just the age of Naozane's own son Kojirō Naoie, and so handsome that Naozane could not find a place to strike.

"Who are you? Announce your name. I will spare you," Naozane said.

"Who are you?" the youth asked.

"Nobody of any importance: Kumagae no Jirō Naozane, a resident of Musashi Province."

"Then it is unnecessary to give you my name. I am a desirable opponent for you. Ask about me after you take my head. Someone will recognize me, even if I don't tell you."

"Indeed, he must be a Commander-in-Chief," Naozane thought. "Killing this one person will not change defeat into victory, nor will sparing him change victory into defeat. When I think of how I grieved when Kojirō suffered a minor wound, it is easy to imagine the sorrow of this young lord's father if he were to hear that the boy had been slain. Ah, I would like to spare him!" Casting a swift glance to the rear, he discovered Sanehira and Kagetoki coming along behind him with fifty riders.

"I would like to spare you," he said, restraining his tears, "but there are Genji warriors everywhere. You cannot possibly escape. It will be better if I kill you than if someone else does it, because I will offer prayers on your behalf."

"Just take my head and be quick about it."

Overwhelmed by compassion, Naozane could not find a place to strike. His senses reeled, his wits forsook him, and he was scarcely conscious of his surroundings. But matters could not go on like that forever: in tears, he took the head.

"Alas! No lot is as hard as a warrior's. I would never have suffered such a dreadful experience if I had not been born into a military house. How cruel I was to kill him!" He pressed his sleeve to his face and shed floods of tears.

Presently, since matters could not go on like that forever, he started to remove the youth's armor *hitatare* so that he might wrap it around the head. A brocade bag containing a flute was tucked in at the waist. "Ah, how pitiful! He must have been one of the people I heard making music inside the stronghold just before dawn. There are tens of thousands of riders in our eastern armies, but I am sure none of them has brought a flute to the battlefield. Those court nobles are refined men!"

When Naozane's trophies were presented for Yoshitsune's inspection, they drew tears from the eyes of all the beholders. It was learned later that the slain youth was Tayū Atsumori, aged seventeen, a son of Tsunemori, the Master of the Palace Repairs Office.

After that, Naozane thought increasingly of becoming a monk.

The flute in question is said to have been given by Retired Emperor Toba to Atsumori's grandfather Tadamori, who was a skilled musician. I believe I have heard that Tsunemori, who inherited it, turned it over to Atsumori because of his son's proficiency as a flautist. Saeda [Little Branch] was its name. It is deeply moving that music, a profane entertainment, should have led a warrior to the religious life.

Yokobue

Although the corporeal being of the Komatsu Middle Captain Koremori remained at Yashima, his spirit strayed ceaselessly to the capital. The figures of his wife and children at home were always by his side, never forgotten for an instant. It was meaningless to live on with matters thus, he told himself. Shortly before dawn on the Fifteenth of the Third Month in the first year of Genryaku, he stole away from his Yashima quarters with three attendants—Yosōbyōe Shigekage, a page called Ishidōmaru, and a groom known as Takesato, whom he took because he was said to understand boats. Setting out from Yūki-no-ura in Awa Province aboard a small craft, he rowed across the Naruto Straits toward Kii Province, passed Waka, Fukiage, the Tamatsushima Shrine (where Sotoorihime had once appeared as a divinity), and the shrines at Nichizen and Kokuken, and so arrived at Kii Harbor.

"I would like to follow the mountains from here to the city, to see and be seen by my beloved family one last time," he thought. "But it is bad enough that Shigehira has already been captured, paraded through the avenues, and humiliated in the capital and Kamakura. What a terrible disgrace for my dead father if I should be taken too!" Time after time, he was seized by the urge to go, but he always fought it down, and in the end he went to Mount Kōya instead.

On Mount Kōya, there dwelt a holy man who was an old acquaintance of Koremori's, Saitō Takiguchi Tokiyori (a son of Saitō Saemondaifu Mochiyori of Sanjō), who had been one of Shigemori's samurai. As a thirteen-year-old boy, Tokiyori had taken up a post in the Palace Guards, where he had proceeded to fall in love with one of Kenreimon'in's lesser attendants, a girl called Yokobue. His father gave him a severe scolding when he heard about it. "I had intended to marry you into an influential family so you could rise in the world. Now I find you have got yourself involved with a nobody."

"There was once a Queen Mother of the West," the youth said to himself, "but she no longer exists; we hear of Dongfang Shuo, but we cannot see him. In a world where the young may die before the old, human existence is like a spark from a flint. Even what we call a long life does not last more than seventy or eighty years, and the prime of that span is a mere two decades or thereabouts. What is to be gained by spending even a brief time with an uncongenial wife in this dreamlike, evanescent existence? Yet I will seem disobedient to my father if I marry the one I love. The situation is a friend to me: it shows that I ought to renounce the harsh world for the path of truth." He cut off his hair and went to perform pious exercises at the Ōjōin in Saga, aged nineteen.

"I could have accepted it if he had broken with me," Yokobue thought when she heard the news, "but it was unkind to go to such lengths. Why couldn't he have told me if he was planning to become a monk? Even though he may not want to see me, I will find him and tell him how I feel." One day toward dusk, she left the capital and wandered off in the direction of Saga. As was to have been expected of the season, which was past the Tenth of the Second Month, the spring breeze from Umezu carried the nostalgic scent of plum blossoms, and haze veiled the moonlight on the Ōi River. She must have considered it entirely Tokiyori's fault that she was suffering such unhappiness.

Yokobue had been told that the Takiguchi Novice was at the Ōjōin, but she did not know which cloister was his, and she began a pathetic search, pausing here and stopping there. At length, she heard a voice intoning sacred words inside a ruined monks' dwelling. Thinking that it sounded like his, she sent in a message by the maid who had accompanied her. "I have come all this way looking for you. Please let me see you just once as a monk."

The Takiguchi Novice peeped through a crack in the sliding partition, his heart racing. Even the most resolute pursuer of enlightenment would have wavered at such a moment, moved to pity by her exhausted appearance. But he turned her away without a meeting. "The person you want is not here," he sent someone out to say. "You must have come to the wrong place." Although Yokobue's heart swelled with indignation at his coldness, she had to restrain her tears and go home.

"This is a quiet place where a man can recite the sacred name without interference," the Takiguchi Novice said to a cloister mate. "But I parted from a girl I still loved, and now she has found me here. Even though I hardened my heart the first time, I don't think I can do it if she comes again. I must bid you farewell." He left Saga for Mount Kōya and took up residence at the Shōjōshin'in.

Word reached the Takiguchi Novice that Yokobue had also entered the religious life. He sent her a poem:

> Although you harbored
> such feelings of resentment
>   that you shaved your head,
> what happiness to know
> you have entered the true Way!

Yokobue answered with this:

> That I shaved my head
> was not because I harbored
>   resentment toward you.
> Yours is a heart praiseworthy
> for steadfast devotion.

Perhaps because Yokobue was borne down by the heavy burden of her sorrows, she soon breathed her last at the Hokkeji in Nara, where she had gone to live. Upon hearing the news, the Takiguchi Novice redoubled his pious exertions, displaying a zeal so intense that his father recognized him as his son again. Everyone close to him revered him and called him "the holy man at Mount Kōya."

Middle Captain Koremori went to visit the Novice. In the old days at the capital, this samurai had been an elegant gentleman in an unfigured hunting robe and high cap, his garments stylishly draped and his side hair smoothed. Now, when the Middle Captain saw him for the first time since his renunciation of the world, it must have cost him a pang of envy to recognize a true seeker after enlightenment—a man who resembled an emaciated old monk (though he was not yet thirty), dressed in a deep black robe and a black surplice. It seemed that the Seven Sages of the Bamboo Groves in Jin or the Four Graybeards of Mount Shang in Han could have been no more impressive to behold.

ZEAMI (KANZE MOTOKIYO)

(1364–1443 C.E.)

Japan

Nō plays are traditionally divided into five categories by the kind of character represented by the principal or *shite* role: plays of gods, of warriors, of women, of mad ones, and of devils. *Kagekiyo,* a play of anonymous authorship, belongs to the fourth and most numerous category—plays in which the *shite* is a mad person (male or female) or a person from "modern" times. The plays are also placed in two additional categories, depending on whether the *shite* represents a spirit or a living person. A play featuring a spirit is a dream play (*mugen*); one whose chief character is alive is called a "present" play (*genzaimono*). Finally, some *nō* plays consist of a single act (*tanshiki*) and some of two acts (*fukushiki*). The form the Japanese consider the most beautiful—that is, the most fully expressive of the essence of nō—is the two-act dream play (*fukushiki mugen nō*) with the spirit of a woman in the *shite* role. In such plays, the secondary or *waki* role is commonly that of a visiting monk. There are various accompanying characters (*tsure*) and other refinements as well.

Kagekiyo is a one-act "present" play. Its four characters include the title character (the *shite* role), his daughter Hitomaru (*tsure* or *shitezure*), an attendant (*tomo, shitezure no tomo*), and a village headman (the *waki* role). Having supported the Heike cause (see headnote to *The Tale of the Heike*), Kagekiyo is banished by the victorious Genji to what is now southeastern Kyushu. Although near death, he remains hot-tempered. The drama turns on deep motives that are sometimes contradictory and not always resolved. Kagekiyo is self-centered and proud of his military feats, but he is also shamed by his present status as a beggar. He speaks contemptuously about his daughter, but when he meets her after a long separation their bond is fully established. Hitomaru has searched for him out of filial devotion and shares his strong spirit. The other characters handle the events of the plot.

The seeming simplicity of the plot is belied by various formal features, the most typical of which is the ending in two phases. The first phase involves Kagekiyo's deeds at the crucial Battle of Yashima, which begins with high bravery and concludes in comedy. The second phase contains the final speech, in which the chorus speaks for Kagekiyo for nine lines, for Hitomaru for one line, and finally for a narrator who speaks the last three lines, which may be more literally rendered: "Their final words mingle as one voice, / this the sole relic of parent and child, / this the sole relic of parent and child." The comedy at the end of the first phase and the abrupt conclusion of the second phase with its switches from mind to mind are very Japanese and typical of nō drama.

Kagekiyo, A Nō Drama

Persons

HITOMARU, *Daughter of Kagekiyo*	*Tsure*
ATTENDANT	*Tomo*
AKUSHICHIBYŌE KAGEKIYO,	
(Kagekiyo the Hot-tempered)	*Shite*
VILLAGE HEADMAN	*Waki*

Place

Miyazaki, Hyūga Province (in southeastern Kyushu)

Season

Indefinite

Stage-attendants bring in a framework straw-thatched hut hung all round with a curtain and place it before the Orchestra.

Translated by Gakujutsu Shinkōkai

1

  HITOMARU, *wearing a* tsure *mask, wig, brocade outer-kimono, and painted gold-patterned under-kimono and her* ATTENDANT, *wearing a* suō *robe, trailing divided skirt, plain kimono and carrying a short sword at his side, appear, cross the Bridgeway and enter the stage.*

HITOMARU and ATTENDANT: A zephyr whispered he was living still,
shidai A zephyr whispered he was living still,
   But what has become of his life of dew?
CHORUS: A zephyr whispered he was living still,
jidori But what has become of his life of dew?   5
HITOMARU: I am Hitomaru, a girl living
sashi At Kamegae-ga-yatsu in Kamakura.
   My father, Kagekiyo the Hot-tempered,
   sided with the Heike clan,
   And incurred the hatred of the Genji.   10
   They banished him to Miyazaki,
   A village, in Hyūga Province,
   And there in exile he has lived for many years.
   Though unused to journeying far,
   I am armed against all perils,   15
   Encouraged by the thought
   Of seeing my dear father.
HITOMARU and ATTENDANT: Yearning after him, on the pillow
sage-uta I lay my head and weep
   And wet my sleeves already moist   20
   With the evening dew of the wayside grass.
age-uta Sagami lies behind us,
   Sagami lies behind us,
   Whom shall we ask for guidance
   On our distant journey?   25
   Through Tōtōmi Province we pass,
   Crossing the lake[1] by ferry-boat,
   And on to Mikawa with the Eight Bridges.
   Inured to wind and road,
   Oh! how long before we see Miyako!
   Oh! how long before we see Miyako!   30
ATTENDANT: Travelling in haste, we have already reached Miyazaki in Hyūga.
   Here it would be well to ask where your father lives.

   *[*HITOMARU *stands by the Waki seat, and the* ATTENDANT *stands beside her.]*

2

  KAGEKIYO *is sitting in the hut, wearing a "Kagekiyo" mask, pointed hood, broad-sleeved robe and plain kimono.*

---

1. I.e. Lake Hamana.

KAGEKIYO: *[Speaks from within the hut.]* Behind the gate the pine-trees shadow
          I live alone year in, year out.
          Blind to the serene light of sun and moon,
          I hardly feel the passing of the hours.
          In the deep, unending darkness of my hut   5
          I only wake and sleep.
          Owning not a change of robe
          To shield me from the sun and snow,
          My bones are bent, my flesh decayed.
CHORUS: If to leave the world it be one's fate,
age-uta If to leave the world it be one's fate,
          Better far to wear the holy robes of black.
          A different way I chose, and now I find
          My plight repulsive even to myself.
          None pities me nor comes to solace me,
          None pities me nor comes to solace me.

          [The curtain is removed from the hut.]

    3

          [HITOMARU and the ATTENDANT *turn toward the hut.]*

HITOMARU: How strange that from within this hut of thatch,
          Desolate beyond a habitation,
          A human voice is heard.
          Is it a beggar dwelling there?
          Better that we stand beyond
          The shadow of its eaves.
KAGEKIYO: Our eyes know not when autumn first comes in, yet we know it from
          the murmur of the wind; so do I feel a visitor from some unknown place.
HITOMARU: Alas! Not knowing where to seek my father,
          There is no house in which to rest.
KAGEKIYO: In truth, the Three Worlds do not exist in space, and can to
          nothingness diminish.
          Whom then should you ask for in this void?
            How could we reply
            Where the sought one lives?
ATTENDANT: O master of the hut! I have something to ask you.
KAGEKIYO: Who are you?
ATTENDANT: Do you know where lives the exile?
KAGEKIYO: The exile? Whom do you mean? What is his name?
ATTENDANT: It is Kagekiyo the Hot-tempered, a Heike warrior.
KAGEKIYO: I have heard of him, indeed, but being blind never have I seen him.
          A wretched life, they say, he lives
          And my pity stirs for him.
          Go elsewhere
          And others ask for information.

ATTENDANT: He is not to be found here. We must go farther and enquire again.

[HITOMARU *and the* ATTENDANT *retire to the stage-attendants' seat.*]

4

KAGEKIYO: How strange! For who should be the visitor but the daughter of this blind man? Long ago I fell in love with a courtesan of Atsuta in Owari Province, and in course of time a child was born to me. She was a girl, and therefore being not important, I left her in the charge of the mistress of a pleasure-house at Kamegae-ga-yatsu in Kamakura.

Desolate at the years of parting,
From afar she comes to speak to me.

CHORUS: Her speech I heard,
age-uta Her face I could not see.
Oh! the pity of my sightless eyes!
I let her pass without my name revealing,
Out of my dear love for her,
Out of my dear love for her.

[KAGEKIYO *lowers his face.*]

5

[HITOMARU *and the* ATTENDANT *go along the bridgeway as far as the first pine and the* ATTENDANT *turns toward the curtain.*]

ATTENDANT: Is there anyone about?

The VILLAGE HEADMAN, *wearing a striped kimono and* suō *robe and trailing skirt and carrying a short sword at his side, appears on the bridgeway.*

HEADMAN: You ask for some one. What do you want?

ATTENDANT: Do you know the house of the exile?

HEADMAN: There are several, which one are you seeking?

ATTENDANT: We are seeking a Heike warrior by the name of Kagekiyo the Hot-tempered.

HEADMAN: [*Turns toward the* Metsuke Pillar.] On your way you must have passed a thatched hut beneath the hill. Was there no one inside?

ATTENDANT: Yes, there was a blind beggar.

HEADMAN: That blind beggar is the man you seek. How strange! [HITOMARU *starts weeping.*] When I spoke about Kagekiyo, the lady wept bitter tears of sorrow. What, I wonder, ails her?

ATTENDANT: You have reason to wonder. I shall tell you. This lady is the daughter of Kagekiyo, and longing to see her father once again before he dies, has travelled from afar to find him. If I presume not too much on your kindness, please persuade him to receive his daughter.

HEADMAN: How strange! Is this lady Kagekiyo's daughter? Pray calm yourself and hear me speak. Your father has become blind. In distress he has shaved his head and taken the name of Kōtō of Hyūga to live on the charity of travellers and villagers like myself. Perhaps, he was too ashamed to reveal himself to you. I will accompany you once more to his hut, and call him by his real name. If he answers, then you may present yourself and together you can talk of all things past and present. Please come this way.

[HITOMARU *and the* ATTENDANT *enter the stage and go to the* Waki *seat. The* HEADMAN *stands near the* shite *pillar, facing the hut.*]

6

HEADMAN: Kagekiyo! Are you in? [*Approaches the hut and taps the pillar twice. Then he steps away and stands near the* Metsuke *pillar. Stops his ears with his hands. Lowers his hands.*]

KAGEKIYO: Quiet, Fellow! Quiet! My mind is troubled enough without your noisy shouting. Only a little while ago some one came from my distant home, but ashamed of my poverty and my state, I could not reveal my name and turned her from my door.
A thousand streams of tears drench my sleeves![2]

I have now awakened to the thought that all is a dream and I myself but a dream shadow. If you call a beggar dead to the world 'Kagekiyo the Hot-tempered,' how will he answer?

CHORUS: In Hyūga, the sun-facing land,
In Hyūga, the sun-facing land,
I find a name becoming me.
Call me by the old name
I myself cast off
When my bow was laid aside
And I, whose passion now lies dead,
Will burn with bitter wrath.

KAGEKIYO: [KAGEKIYO *strikes his knee with his right hand.*] Here must I live,

CHORUS: Here must I live;
A blind man losing his staff
Could I be likened to,
If I the hatred bring upon my head
Of those, whose charity I seek.

[KAGEKIYO *fumbles for the staff.*]

Deformity brings ill reason
As with me now.
Forgive my bitter tongue.

---

[2]Line from a Chinese poem by Sugawara-no-Michizane:
More than three years have passed since I left home;
Tears fall in a thousand lines.
All, all is like a dream;
From time to time I look up at the sky.
The poem was composed when he was in exile in Dazaifu.

KAGEKIYO: [KAGEKIYO *turns toward the* HEADMAN *and joins his hands.*] My eyes are
        darkened,
CHORUS: My eyes are darkened,
        Yet I can tell the thoughts of man
        By a single uttered word.

        [KAGEKIYO *looks upward to the left.*]

        If there is a breeze in the hill-top pines,
        I know what it will scatter blooms like snow.
        From dreams like these to wake,
        Wherein alone a blind man sees
        The cherries blooming,
        Oh! how bitter, how bitter!

        [KAGEKIYO *lowers his face.*]

        And on the rocky beach
        I hear the noise of falling waves,
        And know the evening tide is flowing.

        [KAGEKIYO *makes a gesture of listening.*]

        I am a former warrior of the Heike;
        And I will entertain you with the tales of battle.

        [KAGEKIYO *comes out of the hut, taking the staff in his hand, and sits down in
        the center.*]

   7

KAGEKIYO: I said harsh things to you just now. My mind was over-wrought. Pray
        forgive me.
HEADMAN: Never mind. We understand and do not take it seriously. Were there
        not some people here before me?
KAGEKIYO: No, no one came to see me save yourself.
HEADMAN: You are not telling the truth. You know a young lady came here,
        who called herself Kagekiyo's daughter. Why do you conceal it? Hearing
        her tale, so deeply was my heart moved that I have brought her back
        again.
             Come here at once, and speak with your father.

        [*Speaks to* HITOMARU.]

HITOMARU: Father! It is I, Hitomaru, who have come.

        [Sits down by KAGEKIYO's *side and takes hold of his sleeve with her hand.*]

        Where lies your pity
        To receive me thus, after my long journey,
        Through rain and wind, dew and frost?

[*Weeps.*]

Is your father's love the less
Because his child's a girl?
O cruel, cruel!

[*Weeps again.*]

KAGEKIYO: I thought to have disguised myself,
But all in vain; I know not what to do
With my shameful, wretched self.

[*Lowers his face.*]

If you in all your youthful grace
Should own this wretch your father,
All the world would talk.
Oh! Think me not heartless
For deceiving you.

[*Puts his hand on her shoulder.*]

CHORUS: I, whose house was ever warm
sage-uta To greet the passing stranger,
Was angry if he did not call,
Now close my door to hide myself
From my own child.
Oh! how wretched I am!

[KAGEKIYO *lets go of* HITOMARU *and weeps.*]

age-uta On the warships of the Heike,
On the warships of the Heike,
Warriors were crowded,
Shoulder to shoulder, knee to knee,
Leaving no space between.
Among them all,
Kagekiyo shone like the moon.
My advice was sought
By war commanders
Of the Imperial ship.
The clan of Heike boasted many
Brave in battle and in counsel wise,
But none to equal Kagekiyo.
I, envied by all
When called to live
With my princely masters,
An now a broken horse
Outstripped by every jade.

[KAGEKIYO *sinks to the floor, lowering his face.*]

8

HEADMAN: O pathetic speech! Dear child, be seated here. Kagekiyo, your daughter
has a favour to ask of you.

[Speaks to HITOMARU. *She resumes her seat, while the* HEADMAN *sits down
next the* ATTENDANT.*]*

KAGEKIYO: What is it?

HEADMAN: She says that she would like to hear your exploits at the battle of
Yashima. Please tell her the tale.

KAGEKIYO: Such a desire is not quite becoming in a girl, but out of compassion for
her filial love in coming here from such a distance, I will comply with her
request. When the tale is finished, you must persuade her to return home
at once.

HEADMAN: Yes, I will persuade her, as soon as your tale is over.

KAGEKIYO: It was towards the end of the third month of the third year of Juei. We
katari   of the Heike in ships and the Genji on land were arrayed along the coast
for the impending decisive battle.

Then said Noritsune, Lord of Noto,
"All last year,
Neither at Muroyama of Harima,
Nor Mizushima of Bitchū,
Nor again at Hiyodorigoe,
Did our warriors a single victory gain,
Because of Yoshitsune's battle strategy.
O for some strategic plan
To destroy this Yoshitsune!"
I thought to myself, "After all the Hōgan is not above an ordinary
mortal; it would be easy to destroy him, if I am prepared to give my life
for it." Telling Noritsune what was in my heart I bade him a long farewell.
The moment I set foot on land,
The Genji troops rush towards me,
Crying "Death to the enemy."

[KAGEKIYO dances while the following lines are being chanted.]

CHORUS: At sight of this, I, Kagekiyo,
age-uta   At sight of this, I, Kagekiyo,
Say to myself, "What noise!"
And brandishing my halberd in the setting sun,
I cut and slash to right and left;
The flinching foemen take to flight
In disarray in all directions.
Pressing hard upon them,

KAGEKIYO: "Fie on you, you cowards!

CHORUS: "Fie on you, you cowards!" I shout;
"Be ashamed before the watching eyes
Of both the Genji and the Heike!"

Confident in victory in single combat,
I cry and cry again, with my halberd by my side,
"I am Kagekiyo of the Heike clan!"
And pursue them fiercely,
Trying to stop and capture one.
I grasp the neck-piece
Of Mionoya's helmet,
But alas! I fail to hold it.
Two, three times he flees from me;
I pursue him still;
He is a foe too worthy to let slip.
At last I leap upon him, seize his helmet,
And pull and tug at it with violent shouts.
Suddenly it breaks, leaving the neck-piece in my hand,
Giving its owner another chance to flee.
Some distance off he stops to turn and say,
"You have, indeed, a devilish strength of arm."
In reply I say to him,
"You have a neck-bone more powerful still!"
And we parted from each other
With shouts of laughter.

9

CHORUS: Such tales of ancient times I still remember,
But I am old and weak, and to my shame confess
My mind confused is growing.
My life with all its ills is coming to a close.
Go home now, and pray for my departed soul.
Your prayers for me will be
A light in darkest night,
A bridge across the desolate plain.
"Farewell, daughter!" I say.

[KAGEKIYO *takes hold of his staff and stands up.* HITOMARU, *the* ATTENDANT *and the* HEADMAN *all stand up with him.* KAGEKIYO *goes toward the* shite *pillar, and as* HITOMARU *passes him on her way to the bridgeway, he turns around and places his hand on her shoulder.*]

"Farewell, father! I go."

[HITOMARU *goes along the Bridgeway, followed by the* ATTENDANT *and the* HEADMAN, *and all disappear behind the curtain.*]

In the sorrowing minds of child and father
This simple parting forever dwells,
This simple parting forever dwells.

[KAGEKIYO *looks after* HITOMARU *and then, turning to the front, weeps.*]

IIO SŌGI (1421–1502 C.E.)
BOTANKA SHŌHAKU (1443–1527 C.E.)
SAIOKUEN SŌCHŌ (1448–1532 C.E.)

The three poets included here are not represented by their individual works but by extracts from a joint effort, a long poem called *One Hundred Stanzas by Three Poets at Minase* (*Minase Sangin Hyakuin*). The poem is probably the most famous example of *renga*, one of two forms of linked poetry—a fascinating and distinctively Japanese genre. *Renga* began as a diversion, a sort of game for facile poets. It was later accepted as serious literature by modeling its language on that of court poetry (*waka*), establishing elaborate canons and gaining court approval.

The typical *renga* sequence of 100 stanzas was composed by three or four poets writing stanzas in rapid alternation. Decades of poetic practice had made the writers so adept that a stanza might be composed, checked, written down, and repeated aloud in less than three minutes. The most fundamental principle of composition was that each stanza had to form a semantic unit with, and only with, its immediate predecessor. Thus the hundred stanzas emerged linked in an ongoing chain.

Linked poetry was written on the fronts and backs of four folded sheets (eight sides in all). The front of the first sheet was devoted to a dignified introduction of eight stanzas. The first stanza, or *hokku,* was a factual description of the scene at the poets' meeting; subsequent stanzas were predominantly fictional. The back of the last sheet contained an eight-stanza conclusion. In between, with fourteen stanzas per side, was the development, the most varied and agitated part of the sequence. The remaining conventions of *renga* were so elaborate that they defy simple description. The code covered topics and subtopics, imagery, motifs, and even variations in quality and degrees of connectedness between stanzas.

The greatest *renga* sequences are characterized by controlled variation. They honor the *renga* code, manipulate it, and transform it with originality. In successful practice, a single strong poet exercised a role like that of a conductor. Sogi, for example, ensured that the beauty of the total sequence always took precedence over the brilliance of any one part, and other able *renga* poets never composed as well as with him.

For its spirit and principles, linked poetry is indebted to collections of court poetry such as the *Shinkokinshū*, which first explored ways of gathering independent poetic units into a larger artistic whole. Linked poetry bequeathed its three-part structure to the *nō* drama. It is quintessentially Japanese in its asymmetry and poetic associations (see the opening section to Sei Shōnagon's *Pillow Book*). Some critics have been tempted to trace the principles of linked poetry throughout later and even contemporary literature. This goes perhaps too far. Yet its uniqueness and influence is undisputed. Linked poetry is a truly Japanese phenomenon, both in its aesthetic spirit and its lack of counterparts in other literatures.

One Hundred Stanzas by Three Poets at Minase
[Minase Sangin Hyakuin]

SŌGI

[Despite some snow]

Despite some snow
the base of hills spreads with haze
the twilight scene

Design. No relation. Spring. Rising Things. Peaks.
In this most famous of renga *hokku*, haze designates spring, a season long thought best for
dawn, as autumn was for evening. Gotoba had a royal palace at Minase, where he wrote a
tanka Sōgi echoes.

SHŌHAKU

[Despite some snow]

Despite some snow
the base of hills spreads with haze
the twilight scene
where the waters flow afar
the village glows with sweet plum flowers

Design. Close. Spring. Waters. Trees. Residences.
The movement suggests temporal progress with the melting of snow in 1. "Yuku mizu"
seems to recall a poem in the *Kokinshū* (15: 793) on Minase River. This *waki* (or second
stanza) is not a flower stanza, because it uses a named flower, the plum.

SŌCHŌ

[Where the waters flow afar]

Where the waters flow afar
the village glows with sweet plum flowers
in the river wind
a single stand of willow trees
shows spring color

Design-Ground. Close. Spring. Waters. Trees.
This *daisan* (third stanza) advances spring a bit more, suggesting that willows are in full leaf
but still fresh. When stirred by wind they were thought loveliest.

Translated by Earl Miner.

SŌGI

[In the river wind]

In the river wind
a single stand of willow trees
shows spring color
the break of day shows distinct
sounds of the punting of a boat

Ground-Design. Distant-Close. Miscellaneous. Waters. Night.
Daybreak is considered nightbreak: hence, Night. So also does Sōgi emphasize what is
heard. The connection is that between the boat and the river of 3. "Distinct" governs both
"day shows" and "sounds," as "spreads with haze" does "hills" and "scene" in the
opening stanza: a form of zeugma or yoking common in linked poetry.

SHŌHAKU

[The break of day]

The break of day shows distinct
sounds of the punting of a boat
does not the moon
of a fog-enveloped night
stay yet in the sky

Ground-Design. Close-Distant. Autumn. Radiance. Night. Rising Things.
The language is somewhat prosaic (although it would be poetic in haikai), but the image of
the moon ensures that this is not a ground stanza. Shōhaku emphasizes the stillness implied
by 5 with night fog. In it a faint glow suggests that the moon has not yet set. The first moon
stanza, expected as stanza 8.

SŌCHŌ

[Does not the moon]

Does not the moon
of a fog-enveloped night
stay yet in the sky
as wide fields settle with the frost
autumn has approached its end

Ground. Close-Distant. Autumn. Falling Things.
The stanza has commonplace imagery and is syntactically fragmented, but it fits well in the
sequence, opposing a falling to a rising thing and suggesting that the end of autumn made
the moon more appreciated in 5.

SŌGI

[As wide fields settle with the frost]

As wide fields settle with the frost
autumn has approached its end
　the insects cry out
but without regard for such desires
　the grasses wither

Design. Close-Distant. Autumn. Insects. Plants.
This is fresh in conception and yet central to Japanese thinking about autumn and insects.
Given the essential character (hon'i) of renga imagery, unnamed insects were thought more
comprehensive and moving. This is, therefore, the sole use allowed in a hundred stanzas.

SHŌHAKU

[The insects cry out]

　The insects cry out
but without regard for such desires
　the grasses wither
as I come to the fence in visit
the once covered path is clear

Design-Ground. Close-Distant. Miscellaneous. Residences.
"The once-covered path" is new in renga diction, and it suggests that the person visited is
as much gone as the path is changed. This concludes the front of the first sheet: three poems
on spring and three on autumn, the two most esteemed seasons.

KOREA

In considering Korean literature, we must first make it clear that we mean
literature written in the Korean language, not all literature written by Koreans. The
distinction is important, for the fundamental fact that confronts students of
Korean literature is this: until well into the nineteenth century, literate Koreans
wrote almost exclusively in classical Chinese, which in East Asia enjoyed the same
authority and prestige as did Latin in the medieval West. Of the writings that have
come down to us from before 1850, less than one percent are in Korean. Nor did
a script for Korean exist until the fifteenth century, when scholars devised an

alphabet under the patronage of King Sejong. Prior to this, writers interested in recording Korean borrowed Chinese graphs to transcribe the sound and sense of Korean words.

Linguistic and literary evidence indicates that Koreans learned to use the Chinese script at the earliest stage of their history, from at least the fourth century C.E. on. In the mid-seventh century, a royal academy was established, modeled on the Chinese system of the T'ang Dynasty. As in China, the curriculum was grounded in the Confucian classics, and the goal was to train scholars for civil service examinations. Again as in China, the system produced a privileged social class of *literati,* or lettered men. (Women were excluded from both the academy and the examinations.) It was this class that controlled the canon of classical literature and critical discourse in Korea. The literati adopted as official the Chinese genres and their hierarchy, with their clear distinction between most esteemed genres (poetry and certain prose genres) and lesser genres (literary miscellany, fictional narratives, and drama), and they intended their writings as contributions to Chinese culture.

And how they wrote! Poems were produced on every conceivable occasion; the courtiers must have thought in verse. If a soldier, merchant, female entertainer, or slave is mentioned in history, it is because of his or her unexpected ability to write poetry in Chinese. It was even common practice to write poems on house walls or in public places for passersby to enjoy; this poetry was not considered graffiti. Some literati, and some enterprising women, wrote in Korean, although vernacular poetry and prose enjoyed little esteem. Still, within the native Korean tradition, poetry held pride of place, as it did in China. Other genres in Korean remained low in status and have not been fully appreciated until modern times.

Generalizations about early Korean poetry are difficult to frame, for very little has come down to us. From the unified Silla period (beginning in the mid-seventh century) through the Koryŏ period (935–1392), we know of only forty-one extant poems. Twenty-five of these, dating from the Silla and early Koryŏ, are known as *hyangga,* "native songs" (as opposed to poetry in classical Chinese). Eleven *hyangga* are devotional poems written by the Buddhist monk Kyunyŏ; the remaining fourteen were written by members of the elite corps of knights or by Buddhist monks. The other sixteen poems, known simply as Koryŏ songs, are folk songs and poems by commoners.

After the creation of the Korean alphabet, writing in Korean grew more common. The two most enduring poetic forms to develop were the *sijo* and *kasa.* Both were written initially by the literati, then from the eighteenth century on largely by commoners. The selections in this section—a sampling of *hyangga, sijo,* and *kasa,* as well as prose works by women writers—thus represent a spectrum of native sensibility and experience.

Aside from basic similarities in topics, imagery, tropes, allusions, and other devices, Korean poetry is characterized by its musicality, the consistency with which it celebrates cultural values, and its close relationship to the audience. In Korea, all poetry was meant to be sung, and its forms and styles reflect melodic origins. The basis of its prosody is a line of alternating metric segments of three or four syllables, the rhythm that is probably most natural to the Korean language. Extant musical notations indicate that the musical divisions of, for example, a popular song of medieval Korea are different from its poetic (stanzaic) division; a musical division is signaled by an interjection followed by a refrain. Nonsense jingles or onomatopoetic representations of the sound of musical instruments attest to the refrain's musical origin and function.

Considered as a living performance art, poetry becomes a collective enterprise involving the poet, the singer, and the audience. The singer of a poem takes on the role of lyric persona—the disembodied voice of poetry itself. (If the singer is also the poet, he or she has multiple roles of composer and singer, poet and lyric persona.) The audience, for its part, validates the song through its understanding and appreciation, which derive from a shared knowledge of traditional poetic norms and conventions. We can even say that the audience helps shape the song through its expectations. Thus, poet and audience together reaffirm their common culture.

We can see this reaffirmation in the recurrence of certain themes—such as nature, love, friendship, time, and praise—as well as certain topics and images. Taken up again and again, by generation after generation, such themes become cultural touchstones, and the poetry of the past—the poet's own tradition—takes on the character of a resource to be freely drawn on rather than a burden to be thrown off. Like their Chinese and Japanese counterparts, Korean poets knew that a literary text that draws nothing from its predecessors is inconceivable, and that originality does not mean repudiating all that has gone before. Indeed, links to the past were valued, for they endow poems with rich overtones and multiple meanings unavailable through any other means. Far from being overwhelmed by tradition, successful poets found their own unique voice through a skillful use of the poetic techniques at their disposal.

Historical Background

From the time of the emergence of the Three Kingdoms in the early centuries of our era, Korea maintained its independence and cultural identity throughout history. The three kingdoms—Koguryŏ in the north, and Paekche and Silla in the south—consolidated earlier tribal federations and states, which in turn had evolved from the earliest Stone Age cultures of the peninsula. Relations with the more advanced neighboring culture of China were complex. Elements of Chinese culture such as writing, Confucianism, and Buddhism were quickly absorbed, yet China's recurring territorial ambitions were a source of tension. During the first century B.C.E., the Chinese had overthrown an earlier state in northern Korea and colonized the area. During the early- and mid-seventh century C.E., Koguryŏ, which extended north into southern Manchuria, successfully fought off invasions by the Chinese as well as by northeastern nomadic peoples.

Supported by T'ang Dynasty China, Silla conquered the other two kingdoms during the latter part of the seventh century, unifying the peninsula. The northern territories of Koguryŏ (into Manchuria) reformed as the state of Parhae—as seen by many Korean historians—and soon came into direct confrontation with Silla. But Parhae eventually collapsed and was overtaken by nomadic peoples, and the development of Korean society and culture henceforth takes place on the peninsula proper.

During the Silla period, Buddhism flourished and a royal academy was established on the Chinese model. The eighth century saw a gradual weakening of the Silla government and the corresponding growth of numerous regional powers. After the final disintegration of Silla in the ninth century, the ruler of one of these regional powers again unified the peninsula, founding the Koryŏ dynasty, from which we derive our word "Korea." The Koryŏ lasted almost five hundred years surviving even the Mongol invasions and overlordship of the thirteenth and fourteenth centuries.

Following the collapse of the Mongol empire in the fourteenth century, a Korean general named Yi Sŏnggye declared himself king, founding the Chosŏn Dynasty. Chosŏn ruled in a succession of twenty-six monarchs until Japan annexed Korea in 1910. The early Chosŏn was a time of great cultural flowering, with development of movable type for printing, the creation of the Korean alphabet, and the establishment of many centers of learning, including a prestigious royal academy. Buddhism, hitherto the official state religion, was replaced with the ethical system of neo-Confucianism.

A Japanese invasion of 1592 inaugurated a period of disturbances. The Japanese withdrew in defeat in 1598, but trouble came soon after from the north with invasions by the Manchu, who also threatened, and eventually toppled, the Ming dynasty in China.

Beginning in the mid-seventeenth century, significant changes occurred in Korean society. Agricultural advances raised the standard of living for common people. Many scholars set aside the abstract theorizing dear to Confucianists to found the Sirhak, or Practical Learning School, which held that theory should have practical applications for society and the nation. The Sirhak turned their attention to such matters as administrative reform, education, commerce, technology, history, and the Korean language. This language was increasingly used for the lengthy prose works called *sosŏl,* or narrative fiction. The *sosŏl* is not a literary form equivalent to the novel, as many Western scholars mistakenly think. Originally, it was a derogatory term meaning "small talk," and the term was eventually used by writers when they translated the English term "novel," hence the confusion. By the twentieth century, but not before, *sosŏl* came to correspond to the Western novel. But even in our day, the East Asian *sosŏl* is different from the Western novel, as some critics are beginning to point out (e.g., Fujii, *Complicit Fictions,* Berkeley, 1993).

Further Reading

Eckert, Carter J. et al. *Korea Old and New: A History.* Seoul: Ilchokak, 1990.

Lee, Peter H. *Celebration of Continuity: Themes in Classic East Asian Poetry.* Cambridge: Harvard University Press, 1979.

————. *Anthology of Korean Literature from Early Times to the Nineteenth Century.* 2nd ed. Honolulu: University of Hawaii Press, 1990.

Rutt, Richard. *The Bamboo Grove: An Introduction to Sijo.* Berkeley: University of California Press, 1971.

Fujii, *Complicit Fictions.* Berkeley: University of California Press, 1993.

Pronounciation Guide

Chŏng Ch'ŏl (jung chul)
Chosŏn (cho-sun)
Ch'ungdam (choong-dahm)
Hŏ Nansŏrhŏn (huh nan-sol-hun)
Hwang Chini (hwang jin-ee)
hyangga (hyang-gah)
Kwangdŏk (kwang-duhk)

Kyunyŏ (kyun-yuh)
sasŏl sijo (sah-sol si-jo)
Sejong (se-jong)
sijo (si-jo)
Silla (shilla)
Yŏngjae (young-jay)
Yun Sŏndo (yoon son-do)

KWANGDŎK (fl. 661–681 C.E.)
MASTER WŎLMYŎNG (fl. 742–765 C.E.)
MASTER CH'UNGDAM (fl. 742–765 C.E.)
HŬIMYŎNG (fl. 742–765 C.E.)
MONK YŎNGJAE (fl. 785–798 C.E.)
CH'ŎYONG (fl. 875–886 C.E.)
GREAT MASTER KYUNYŎ (923–973 C.E.)
Korea

Vernacular poetry dating from the seventh through the tenth centuries is called
hyangga [hyang-gah], meaning "native songs" or "Korean songs" as opposed to
poetry written in classical Chinese. As in most vernacular poetry in Korea,
hyangga are songs, emphasizing orality, the vibrant relation between poet and
audience, and between poetry and music. On the basis of the surviving examples,
we may say that there are three forms: a stanza of four lines; two stanzas of four
lines; and two stanzas of four lines plus a stanza of two lines. In the ten-line
version, the ninth line usually begins with an interjection, analogous to the
English "Ah," which indicates heightened emotions an a change in tempo and
pitch and also presages the poem's conclusion. Buddhist poems occupy two-
thirds of extant *hyangga*—a reflection of the fact that Buddhism was the dominant
religion for almost nine hundred years (527–1392) during the earlier kingdoms
of Silla and Koryŏ.[1]

---

1. Silla [shilla] (57 B.C.–A.D. 935), an ancient
Korean kingdom, had its capital in Kyŏngju
in southeastern Korea. Koryŏ (918–1392),

a medieval Korean kingdom, had its capital
in Kaesŏng in west-central Korea.

KWANGDŎK

[In the first stanza the speaker asks the moon to undertake a journey to the West where Amitāyus (Infinite Life) resides. The second amplifies the praise of the virtues of Amitāyus. The last stanza presents a rhetorical question in which the speaker affirms that flesh, that stands between the promised land and this world, must be annihilated.]

Prayer to Amitāyus

O Moon,
Go to the West, and
Pray to Amitāyus
And say

That there is one who
Adores the judicial throne, and
Longs for the Pure Land,
Praying before Him with folded hands.

Can the forty-eight vows be met
If this flesh remains unannihilated?

MASTER WŎLMYŎNG

[Written by Master Wŏlmyŏng (Moon Brightness) in memory of his sister, the poem is built on a single theme of separation through death, in the first stanza on the image of a crossroad and in the second on the image of the tree. The branches come from the same source, the trunk: but leaves which grow on the branches, when fallen, are permanently separated from one another. In the final line, the assurance of a meeting after death consoles the speaker, dispelling the uncertainty expressed in the second stanza, and the image echoes that of Homer, who, underscoring the brevity of human life, compared the generation of men to leaves (*Iliad* 6:146–150).]

Requiem

On the hard road of life and death
That is near our land.
You went, afraid,
Without words.

All poems in this selection translated by Peter H. Lee.

We know not where we go,
Leaves blown, scattered,
Though fallen from the same tree,
By the first winds of autumn.

Abide, Sister, perfect your ways,
Until we meet in the Pure Land.

MASTER CH'UNGDAM

[This is a eulogy by Master Ch'ungdam written to praise Knight Kip'a, a member of the *hwarang*, a group of leading knights in the ancient kingdom of Silla. By introducing a correspondence between the knight and the pine, the poet asserts that his moral beauties endure. The knight, through his integrity, not only scorns mutability but imposes a sense of order on the landscape.]

Ode to Knight Kip'a

The moon that pushes her way
Through the thickets of clouds,
Is she not pursuing
The white clouds?

Knight Kip'a once stood by the water,
Reflecting his face in the blue.
Henceforth I shall seek and gather
Among pebbles the depth of his mind.

Knight, you are the towering pine
That scorns frost, ignores snow.

HŬIMYŎNG

[On behalf of her son who has lost his eyesight, Hŭimyŏng implores the Thousand-Armed and Thousand-Eyed "Sound Observer" (Bodhisattva Who Observes the Sounds of the World), painted on the north wall of Punhwang Monastery.]

Hymn to the Thousand-Eyed Sound Observer

Falling on my knees,
Pressing my hands together,
Thousand-Eyed Merciful Goddess,
I implore thee.

Yield me,
Who lacks,
One among your thousand eyes,
By your mystery restore me whole.

If you grant me one of your many eyes,
O the bounty, then, of your charity.

MONK YŎNGJAE

[Intending to spend his last days on South Peak in retirement, the monk Yŏngjae was crossing Taehyŏn Ridge when he met sixty thieves. The bandits drew their swords and threatened him; but he showed no fear and revealed his identity. Since the bandits had heard of his reputation as a poet, they asked him to compose an impromptu poem. The poem is a revelation of the process of attaining enlightenment: the swords that "glitter in the bushes" aid the poet to comprehend the relations between illusion and enlightenment. It is the enlightened poet who in turn enlightens the bandits.]

Meeting with Bandits

My mind that knew not its true self,
The mind that wandered in the dark and deep,
Now is started out for bodhi,
Now is awakened to light.

But on my way to the city of light,
I meet with a band of thieves.
Their swords glitter in the bushes—
Things-as-they-are and things-as-they are not.

Well, bandits and I both meditate on the Truth;
But is that sufficient for tomorrow?

CH'ŎYONG

Ch'ŏyong, one of the seven sons of the Dragon King of the Eastern Sea, married a beautiful woman. Seeing that she was extremely beautiful, a demon of plague transformed himself into a man and attacked her in her room while Ch'ŏyong was away. But Ch'ŏyong returned, and witnessing the scene, he calmly sang the following song, which so moved the demon that he went away. The Ch'ŏyong mask was later used to exorcise evil spirits, usually on New Year's Eve, and his image was pasted on the gates.]

Song of Ch'ŏyong

Having caroused far into the night
In the moonlit capital,
I return home and in my bed,
Behold, four legs.

Two were mine,
Whose are the other two?
Two were mine.
No, no, they are taken.

GREAT MASTER KYUNYŎ

[This is the sixth of eleven poems inspired by "Vows on the Practices of the Bodhisattva." The mind is the ignorant soil which suffers from "the blight of affliction." If
"sweet dharma rain" falls over the dried and barren soil of the mind, the blight will
be dispelled, the grass will grow, and the soil will bear the "golden fruit of knowledge."
The autumn field must be illuminated by the moon, a recurring symbol for enlightenment.]

from *Eleven Devotional Poems*

To the Majestic Assembly of Buddhas

To the majestic assembly of Buddhas
In the dharma realm.
I fervently pray
For the sweet rain of truth.

Dispel the blight of affliction
Rooted deep in the soil of ignorance,
And wet the mind's field of the living,
Where good grasses struggle to grow.

Ah, the mind is a moonlit autumn field
Ripe with the golden fruit of knowledge.

HWANG HŬI (1363–1452 C.E.)
KING SŎNGJONG (1457–1494 C.E.)
SONG SUN (1493–1583 C.E.)
YI HWANG (1501–1571 C.E.)
YU HŬI-CH'UN (1513–1577 C.E.)
HWANG CHINI (c. 1506–1544 C.E.)
KWŎN HOMUN (1532–1587 C.E.)
SŎNG HON (1535–1598 C.E.)
CHŎNG CH'ŎL (1537–1594 C.E.)
YI TŎKHYŎNG (1561–1613 C.E.)
YUN SŎNDO (1587–1671 C.E.)
YI MYŎNGHAN (1595–1645 C.E.)

Korea

SIJO

Each line of the *sijo,* the most popular, elastic, and mnemonic of Korean poetic forms, consists of four metric segments, with a minor pause occurring at the
end of the second segment and a major one at the end of the fourth. An emphatic syntactic division is usually introduced in the third line in the form of a
countertheme, paradox, resolution, judgment, command, or exclamation. The
introduction of a deliberate twist in phrasing or meaning is often a test of a
poet's originality. The following scheme shows the syllable-count pattern of the
sijo:

$$
\begin{array}{cccc}
\tfrac{3}{4} & 4 & \tfrac{3}{4} & 4 \\
\tfrac{3}{4} & 4 & \tfrac{3}{4} & 4 \\
3 & 5 & 4 & \tfrac{3}{4}
\end{array}
$$

The *sijo* was transmitted orally, as a song. It was not until the beginning of the
eighteenth century that such poems were written down.

The great number of variants of a given poem reflects the oral nature of the
sijo. We are not sure which *sijo* are composed spontaneously during performances. In any event, the singer was free to alter phrases or lines whenever his
memory failed him or his creativity inspired him. Always, the spoken word was
the basis of his artistic creation. The *sijo* has proved to be a form well-suited to
express the poet's sense of the world and response to a given situation. Simplicity
and sensitive rendering of the poet's own microcosm in relation to the world at
large characterize the form.

The last song included in this selection is an example of the *sasŏl sijo*, in which more than two metric segments in each line, except for the first in the third line, are added. Most *sasŏl sijo* are written anonymously, usually not at court. What hastened the rise of this poetic form was the eighteenth-century rupture of a system of beliefs that served to perpetuate existing social formations and power structures. Innovations introduced by the *sasŏl sijo* writers include the introduction of new topics regarding love and other matters as well as a change of scale, voice, diction, and rhetorical patterns. A marked feature is enumeration, or listing of details.

HWANG HŬI

[Spring has come to a country village]*

Spring has come to a country village;
How much there is to be done!
I knit a net and
A servant tills the fields and sows:
But who will pluck the sweet herbs
That grow on the back-hill?

KING SŎNGJONG

[Stay]*

Stay:
Will you go? Must you go?
Is it in weariness you go? From disgust?
Who advised you, who persuaded you?
Say why you are leaving,
You, who are breaking my heart.[1]

SONG SUN

[I have spent ten years]*

I have spent ten years
Building a grass hut;
Now winds occupy half,
The moon fills the rest.

*Translated by Peter H. Lee.

---

1. Addressed to Yu Hoin (1445–1494), assistant section chief of the Ministry of Works and the king's favorite courtier.

Alas, I cannot let you come in.
But I shall receive you outside.[1]

[I discuss with my heart]*

I discuss with my heart
Whether to retire from court.
My heart scorns the intent:
"How could you leave the king?"
"Heart, stay here and serve him,
My old body must go."

[Do not grieve, little birds]*

Do not grieve, little birds,
Over the falling blossoms:
They're not to blame, it's the wind
Who loosens and scatters the petals.
Spring is leaving us.
Don't hold it against her.

YI HWANG

[The green hills—how can it be]*

The green hills—how can it be
            that they are green eternally?
Flowing streams—how can it be;
            night and day do they never stand still?
We also, we can never stop,
            we shall grow green eternally.

YU HǓICH'UN

[A little bunch of parsley]†

A little bunch of parsley,
            which I dug and rinsed myself.
I did it for no one else,
            but simply to give it to you.

†Translated by Richard Rutt.

1. Also attributed to Kim Changsaeng (1548–
   1631).

The flavor is not so very pungent;
        taste it, once more taste it, and see.

HWANG CHINI

[I will break the back]†

I will break the back
        of this long, midwinter night,
folding it double,
        cold beneath my spring quilt,
that I may draw out
        the night, should my love return.

KWŎN HOMUN

[Nature makes clear the windy air]*

Nature makes clear the windy air,
And bright the round moon.
In the bamboo garden, on the
Pine fence, not a speck of dust.
How fresh and fervent my life
With a long lute and piled scrolls!

SŎNG HON

[The mountain is silent]*

The mountain is silent,
The water without form.
A clear breeze has no price,
The bright moon no lover.
Here, after their fashion,
I will grow old in peace.

CHŎNG CH'ŎL

[Snow has fallen on the pine-woods]*

Snow has fallen on the pine-woods,
        and every bough has blossomed.
I should like to pluck a branch
        and send it to where my lord is.

---

†Translated by David R. McCann.

After he has looked at it,
              what matter if the snow-flowers melt?

[Could my heart but be removed][†]

Could my heart but be removed
              and assume the moon's bright shape
To be hung there bright and shining
              in the vast expanse of heaven.
I could go where my dear lord is,
              and pour my light upon him.

YI TŎKHYŎNG

[The moon hangs in the sky, bright, full]*

The moon hangs in the sky, bright, full.
Since the dawn,
It has met wind and frost.
Alas, soon it will sink.
But no, wait, I say,
And shine on the gold cup of my drunken guest.

YUN SŎNDO

Songs of Five Friends*

How many friends have I? Count them:
Water and stone, pine and bamboo—
The rising moon on the east mountain,
Welcome, it too is my friend.
What need is there, I say,
To have more friends than five?

They say clouds are fine: I mean the color.
But, alas, they often darken.
They say winds are clear; I mean the sound.
But, alas, they often cease to blow.
It is only the *water,* then,
That is perpetual and good.

Why do flowers fade so soon
Once they are in their glory?
Why do grasses yellow so soon
Once they have grown tall?
Perhaps it is the *stone,* then,
That is constant and good.

Flowers bloom when it is warm;
Leaves fall when days are cool.
But, O *pine,* how is it
That you scorn frost, ignore snow?
I know now even your roots are,
Straight among the Nine Springs.

You are not a tree, no,
Nor a plant, not even that.
Who let you shoot so straight;
What makes you empty within?
You are green in all seasons,
Welcome, *bamboo,* my friend.

YI MYŎNGHAN

[Do not draw back your sleeves and go]*

Do not draw back your sleeves and go,
My own,
With tears I beg you.
Over the long dike green with grass
Look, the sun goes down.
You will regret it, lighting the lamp
By the tavern window,
Sleepless and alone.

[If my dreams]*

If my dreams
Left their footprints on the road,
The path beneath my love's window
Would be worn down, though it is stone.
Alas, in the country of dream
No roads endure, no traces remain.

ANONYMOUS

from *Sasŏl Sijo*

[Cricket, cricket]*

Cricket, cricket,
O sad cricket,

you keep vigil till the moon sinks,
with your long and short notes;
each sad note
of your lonely cry
wakes me from a fitful sleep.
Chirp on, tiny insect,
you alone know my misery
in this empty room.

HŎ NANSŎRHON (1563–1589 C.E.)
KIM INGYŎM (1707–?)
Korea

Kasa

The *kasa* originated as song lyrics written to prevailing *kasa* tunes. It is characterized by a lack of stanzaic division, varying length, a tendency toward description and exposition, as well as, at times, lyricism, and by its verbally and syntactically balanced parallel phrases. Emerging as a new genre toward the middle of the fifteenth century, the form was perfected by such masters as Chŏng Ch'ŏl (1537–1594) and Hŏ Nansŏrhon, who was an accomplished poet in Chinese and Korean. Hŏ Nansŏrhon's is a dramatic narrative written by a woman on unrequited love.

As third secretary, Kim Ingyŏm accompanied the Korean diplomatic mission to Japan. The party, consisting of some five hundred members, left Seoul on September 9, 1763 and arrived in Edo (Tokyo) in 1764. They returned to Seoul on August 5, 1764. The work runs to some four thousand lines, and the present selection shows what was expected of a writer in a foreign country such as Japan. The scenes depicted occurred on two days in February 1764.

HŎ NANSŎRHON

A Woman's Sorrow

Yesterday I fancied I was young;
But today, I am aging.
What use is there in recalling
The joyful days of my youth?

Translated by Peter H. Lee.

Now I am old, to recount
My sad story chokes me.
When Father begot me, Mother reared me,
When they took pains to bring me up,
They dreamed, not of a duchess or marchioness,
But at least of a bride fit for a gentleman.
Through the retribution of karma
And the ties chanced by a matchmaker,
I met as if in a dream
A valiant man known as frivolous,
And I served him with care, as if trodding on ice.
When I reached fifteen, counted sixteen,
The inborn beauty in me blossomed,
And with this face and this body
I vowed a union of a hundred years.
The flow of time was sudden;
The gods too were jealous of my beauty,
Spring breezes and autumn water,
They flew like a shuttle.
And my face once young and fair
Has become ugly to look at.
I know my image in the mirror;
So who will love me now?
Blush not, my self, and reproach no one.
Do you say a new customer showed up
At a tavern where men cluster?
When flowers smiled in the setting sun,
He left home for no fixed place
On a white horse with a gold whip.
Where does he stop to enjoy himself?
How far he went I don't know;
I'll hear no word from him.
Our ties are broken,
But I still think of him.
I don't see him at all, but I still yearn for him.
Long is a day, cruel is a month.
The plum trees by my window,
How many times have they fallen?
The winter night is bitter cold,
And snow, or some mixture, descends.
Long, long is a summer's day,
And a dreary rain comes too.
And spring with flowers and willows
Have no feeling for me.
When the autumn moon enters my room

And crickets chirp on the couch,
A long sigh and salty tears
In vain make me recall the past.
It is hard to bring this cruel life to an end.
But when I examine myself, I shouldn't despair so.
Turning the blue lamp around,
I play "A Song of Blue Lotus,"
Holding the green zither aslant,
As my sorrow commands me.
As though the rain on the Hsiao and Hsiang
Beat over the rustling bamboo leaves,
As though the crane returned whooping
After a span of a thousand years,
Fingers may stylishly pluck
The old familiar tune;
But who will listen in the room
Except for the lotus-brocade curtains?
I feel that my entrails are torn to pieces.
I would rather fall asleep
To see him at least in a dream.
But for what enmity
Do the leaves falling in the wind
And the insects piping among the grasses
Wake me from sleep?
The Weaver and Herdboy in the sky[1]
Meet once on the seventh day of the seventh moon—
However hard it is to cross the Milky Way—
And never miss this yearly encounter.
But since he left me alone,
What magic water separates him from me,
And what makes him silent about his comings and goings?
Leaning on the balustrade, I gaze at the path he took—
Dewdrops glitter on the grass,
Evening clouds pass by, birds sing sadly
In the green bamboo grove.
Numberless are the sorrowful;
But can there by anyone as wretched as I?
Love, you caused me this grief;
I don't know whether I shall live or die.

---

1. The Herdboy and Weaver were constellations in Chinese astronomy, on both sides
of the Milky Way. Condemned to a year-
long separation, they meet once on the
night of the seventh day of the seventh
lunar month, when magpies form a bridge
across the river of stars. The motif is as old
as the *Book of Songs*.

KIM INGYŎM

Grand Trip to Japan

On the twenty-third I fell ill,
lying in the official hostel.
Our hosts bring me their poems,
they are heaped like a hill.
Sickness aside, I answer them;
how taxing this chore is!
Regulated verse, broken-off lines,
old style verse, regulated couplets—
some one hundred thirty pieces.
Because I dashed them off on draft paper,
upon revision I've discarded a half.
If I have to work like this every day,
it will be too much to bear. . . .
The rich and noble in the city
bring presents, many in kind and amount.
But I return them all as before.
One scholar, his hand on the brow,
begs me a hundred times to accept,
rubbing hands together sincerely.
Touched with pity,
I accept a piece of ink stick.
When I offer him Korean paper,
brushes and ink sticks,
he too takes only one ink stick. . . .
Before dawn on the twenty-fourth,
they arrive in streams.
How hard to talk by means of writing,
how annoying to cap their verses.
Braving my illness,
and mindful of our mission
to awe them and enhance our prestige,
I exert myself for dear life,
wield my brush like wind and rain,
and harmonize with them.
When they revise their verses,
they put their heads together—
their writings bid fair to inundate me.
I compose for another round;
they respond with another pile.
I am old and infirm,
and the task saps my vigor.

Translated by Peter H. Lee.

I wouldn't mind it if I were young,
but they traveled thousands of miles
with packed food and waited for months
just to get our opinions.
If we deny them our writing,
how disappointed they would be!
We write on and on
for the old and young, the high and low.
We work as a matter of duty
night and day, without rest.

ANONYMOUS (NINETEENTH CENTURY)
Korea

Prose by Women

Women have not been silent in Korean literature. Some secretly taught themselves classical Chinese, much as Lady Wortley Montague taught herself Latin, and some were gifted poets in Chinese forms. Because the Korean alphabet, which was invented between 1443 and 1444, was easier to learn than Chinese, it was thought to be a script for women who used it as the medium for refined literature.

"Lament for a Needle" is a delightful prose piece gracefully written by an anonymous woman. The author of "The Dispute of a Woman's Seven Companions," also anonymous, rebukes those members of her own sex concerned with self-recognition. Her engaging story is told with great simplicity to her friends gathered around a brazier on a winter night. It is interesting to note that she praises the humility of the thimble, portrayed as the loyal servant of the house who has mastered the secret of life.

Lament for a Needle

On a certain day of a certain month in a certain year, a certain widow addresses a needle with a few words. To a woman the needle is an indispensable tool, though commonly people do not cherish it. You are only a small thing, but I mourn you greatly, because so many memories are connected with you. Alas, what a loss, what a pity! It has been twenty-seven years since I first held you in my hand. How could a sensitive human being feel otherwise? How sad! Holding back my tears and calming my heart, I bid my last farewell to you by hastily writing down this account of your deeds and my memories.

Translated by Peter H. Lee.

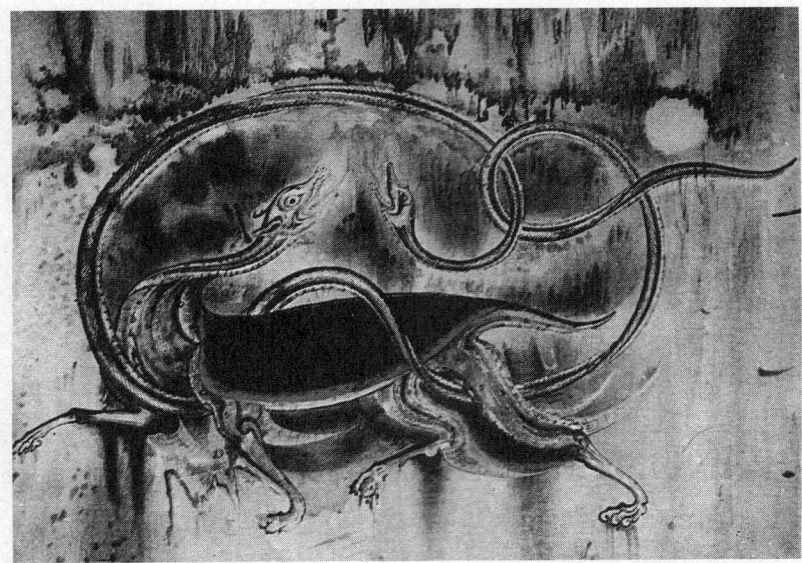

Tortoise-Serpent in the mural painting in a Koguryo tomb (500–650 AD). From *Korea: Tradition and Transformation* by Andrew C. Nahm. Courtesy, Andrew C. Nahm.

Years ago, my uncle-in-law was chosen as the head of the Winter Solstice Felicitation mission to China, and upon his return from Peking he gave me dozens of needles. I sent some to my parents' home, some to my relatives, and divided the rest among my servants. I then chose you, and got to know you, and we have been together ever since. How sad! The ties between us are of an extraordinary nature. Although I have lost or broken many other needles, I have kept you for years. You may be unfeeling, but how could I not love you and be charmed by you! What a loss, what a disappointment!

I was unlucky, I had no children, but I went on living. Moreover, our fortunes began to fail, so I devoted myself to sewing, and you helped me forget my sorrow and manage my household. Today I bid you farewell. Alas, this must have come about through the jealousy of the spirits and the enmity of Heaven.

How regrettable, my needle, how pitiful! You were a special gift of fine quality, a thing out of the ordinary, prominent among ironware. Deft and swift like some knight-errant, straight and true like royal subject, your sharp point seemed to talk, your round eye seemed to see. When I embroidered phoenixes and peacocks on thick or thin silk, your wondrously agile movements seemed the workings of a spirit. No human effort could have matched yours.

Alas! Children may be precious, but they leave when the time comes. Servants may be obedient, but they grumble at times. When I consider your subtle talents, so responsive to my needs, you are far better than children or servants. I made you a silver case enameled in five colors and carried you on the tie-string of my blouse, a lady's trinket. I used to feel you there whenever I ate or slept, and we became friends. Before beaded screens in summer or by lamplight in winter, I used to quilt, broad-stitch, hem, sew, or make finishing stitches with double thread, and your movement was like a phoenix brandishing its tail. When I sewed stitch by stitch, your two ends went together harmoniously to attach seam to seam. Indeed, your creative energy was endless.

I intended to live with you for a hundred years, but, alas, my needle! On the tenth day of the tenth month of this year, at the hour of the Dog (7–9 P.M.), while I was attaching a collar to a court robe in dim lamplight, you broke. You caught me unawares, and I was stunned. Alas, you had broken in two. My spirit was numbed and my soul flew away, as if my heart had been pulverized and my brain smashed. When I recovered from my long faint, I touched you and tried to put you back together, but it was no use. Not even the mystic arts of a renowned physician could prolong your life nor a village artisan patch you up. I felt as if I had lost an arm or a leg. How pitiful, my needle! I felt at my collar, but no trace of you remained.

Alas, it was my fault. I ended your innocent life, so whom else could I loathe or reproach? How can I ever hope to see an adept nature or ingenious talent like yours again? Your exquisite shape haunts my eyes, and your special endowments fill me with yearning. If you have any feeling, we will meet again in the underworld to continue our companionship. I hope we may share happiness and sorrow, and live and die together. Alas, my needle!

The Dispute of a Woman's Seven Companions

The lifelong companions of a woman are seven: a yardstick, a pair of scissors, a needle, blue and pink threads, a thimble, a long-handled iron, and a regular iron. The lady of a household is in charge of them all, and none of them can keep a secret from the others.

A certain lady who often used to work with the help of her seven indispensable companions one day felt sleepy and dozed off.

Brandishing her slender body, the yardstick said, "Friends, listen. I am so perceptive I can measure the long, the short, the narrow and the wide. It's because of me that my lady does not fail in her work. Don't you think my merits far exceed yours?"

Thereupon, the scissors grew angry. Shaking her long mouth, she replied, "Don't praise yourself so. Without my mouth nothing could be shaped or formed. It is only through my services that your measurements become reality. Hence my merits excel yours."

The needle reddened. "Don't argue, my two friends. However well you measure or cut, nothing is accomplished without me. So I am the first in merit," she retorted.

The blue and pink threads roared with laughter. "Don't talk nonsense. The

Translated by Peter H. Lee.

proverb says, 'Three bushels of pearls have to be strung to become a treasure.' What could you accomplish without us?"

Then the old thimble laughed. "Don't quarrel, threads. Let me cut in. I cover tactfully the sore spot in the fingers of the old and young, so that they can finish their work easily. So how can you say I'm without merit? Like a shield on the battlefield, I help to get the work done, no matter how difficult it is."

The long-handled iron, fuming with rage, moved forward in a single stride. "You all want to show off your talents, but listen to me if you don't want to be called fools. My foot can smooth out wrinkles and correct what is crooked and bent. It's my work you're taking the credit for. Without me, you'd be ashamed to face our mistress no matter how hard you tried."

Choking with laughter the iron said, "How true the word of the long-handled iron. Were it not for our services, who could talk about rewards?"

Their wordy warfare woke up the lady, who suddenly rose up in anger. "What merits are you talking about? It is my eyes and hands that make you do what you do. How can you wrangle impudently behind my back and indulge in self-praise?"

The yardstick sighed and mumbled, "How unkind and unfeeling is human-kind. How could she measure anything without me? As if this is not enough, she uses me to thrash the maidservants. I've held out this long only because I happen to be strong, and it saddens me that our mistress takes no notice of this."

The scissors joined in tearfully, "How unkind my mistress is. Day after day she forces open my mouth and cuts thick and hard fabrics just as she pleases. But if I am not to her liking, she strikes my two cheeks with an iron hammer, accuses me of having thick lips or blunt edges and whets me. For her to talk like that after all she's done to me."

The needle heaved a long sigh, "I was made from an iron stick belonging to the fairy Ma-ku of Mount Ti'en-t'ai and polished for ten years on a rock: She inserts thick and thin threads through my eye and makes a hole with my leg through all kinds of dress goods. What an odious chore! Overcome with fatigue, sometimes I pierce her under the fingernail and draw blood, but there's no relief."

The blue and pink threads chimed in, "How can we tell all our sorrow? Clothes of men and women, fine quilts, children's colorful dresses—how could one sew a single seam of these without us? When lazy ladies and girls pull us through the needle's eye too hard, or when we cannot pass through it easily, they curse us in unspeakable language. What is our crime, and how can we bear this grief?"

"My resentment is immeasurable," the long-handled iron complained. "For what retribution am I stuck in a brazier day and night throughout the seasons? After children have used me sloppily to iron the clothes for their dolls, they stick me in any old way until some woman picks me up and scolds me for not being warm enough, or for being too light or too heavy. They make me feel there is no place for me in the world."

"Your sorrow is like mine," the iron said, "so there is no point rehearsing it. They put burning charcoal in my mouth; it's like the tyrant Chou's cruel punishments of roasting and branding. Only because my face is tough and hardened can I bear it. And that's not all. Lazy women will put off their work for ten or even fifteen days. Then they blame me for the wrinkles that will not come out."

The old thimble leaped forward and waved her hand, saying, "Listen, girls. I'm half dead from overwork too; stop chattering on and on. If our mistress hears, all your sins will be visited on me."

"What if she does?" all replied. "She cannot manage without us."

The lady finally scolded, "You dared to criticize my behavior while I was asleep," and dismissed them all. They were withdrawing in despair when the old thimble fell prostrate. "The young ones acted thoughtlessly. Please calm your anger and forgive them," she begged the lady.

Thereupon the lady called all of them together. "I forgive you for the sake of the old thimble," she said. She promised the thimble never to be parted from her, and to this day she cherishes her as her most intimate friend.

"The Birth of Tristram." Woodcut from Wynkyn de Worde's *Morte D'Arthur*, 1498. Rylands Library, Manchester, England.

SECTION IV
Medieval Europe

The term *Middle Ages,* (or *medieval*) coined during the Renaissance in Italy, was not intended as a compliment. It looks backward to ancient Rome and forward to a beginning Renaissance, dismissing what happened in between. The most striking aspect of medieval literature in western Europe is variety. Despite the predominance of Christianity, there is influence from ancient Roman and Germanic pagan cultures, and to a lesser extent from Islamic and Jewish cultures as well. Despite the prevalence of Latin as the language of literacy, there are literary traditions of some sophistication in both Germanic vernaculars (German, Anglo-Saxon, Old Norse) and Romance vernaculars (Provençal, French, Italian, Gallego-Portuguese, Spanish). The literature of this period takes many forms—from learned treatises in prose and learned allegories in poetry, religious sermons and saints' lives, to love lyrics, courtly romances, heroic epics, and animal fables. But with all the different influences, languages, and genres, common sources and common themes provide continuity across the many centuries and peoples of medieval Europe. The classics of ancient Rome from the Mediterranean, the Judeo-Christian bible from the Near East, the myths of King Arthur and his knights from the Celtic northwest, and the concept of courtly love from southern France make their way into virtually all medieval literatures.

Medieval literature begins in the last years of the ancient Roman Empire, as that civilization was being attacked spiritually by Christianity and physically by various tribes. The early fathers of the church (e.g., Augustine), like the philosopher Boethius, were Roman-educated and wrote in Latin for Roman audiences, but their works were formative influences on Christian thought and literature throughout the Middle Ages.

Augustine, the major theologian of the early Catholic faith in the West, traces in his *Confessions* his own conversion from pagan to Christian, from self-centered, lustful, and ambitious man of the world to devoted servant of God, in part through episodes that most of his readers can identify with. Boethius, whose writings transmitted classical philosophy, Platonic and Aristotelian, to the early Middle Ages, presents himself in *The Consolation of Philosophy* as an intellectual caught up in self-pity, who must be led by the figure of Philosophy (classical learning and logical thinking) to understand and accept his fate within the larger scheme of good and evil in the world. Most of the issues that concern these early writers and the philosophical and allegorical modes they use to deal with them recur frequently in succeeding centuries, and their works offer powerful models to later writers and messages that have relevance for later readers.

The historical struggle between Christianity and pagan religions is reflected in the stories of early martyrs.[1] Some of the twelfth-century French epics (*chansons de geste* like the *Song of Roland*) also draw on historic conflicts between pagans and Christians, particularly Saracens and Franks in Spain, but these are treated as military rather than intellectual encounters. For the most part, it is the personal struggle that dominates the texts presented in this medieval section, whether in moral terms—individuals struggling against their baser instincts—or in social terms—individual needs in opposition to the claims of society. The settings of these conflicts are vastly different from those we face today, but the human problems, social and moral, are quite similar at times.

Hildegard of Bingen, a renowned abbess of the same period, preached and wrote against the corruption of her world; her contemporaries, even religious and secular leaders, widely sought her advice because of her visions in which the voice of God spoke to her. She does not reveal her motives as openly as the monk Abelard,[2] but her struggles both with herself and with authority are nonetheless revealed in her letters, while her extraordinary powers of imagination are evident in her visions and poems.

Jean de Meun, a learned man of the thirteenth century, continued in a more polemical and didactic vein the open-ended *Romance of the Rose,* a poem that Guillaume de Lorris had written as an allegory of young, self-centered love. Dante (1265–1321), a lyric poet and author of prose treatises in philosophy, language, and political theory, brings together the moral, philosophical, religious, and cultural issues of earlier writers with political concerns of his own time and experience in an all-encompassing narrative poem, *The Divine Comedy.* The

---

1. The dramas of the tenth-century nun, Hrotsvit, offer an interesting example, with a touch of early feminism and sometimes with humor. Her Christian martyrs are mainly women who expose the emptiness of the faith of pagan men by their courageous acceptance of torture and death and also by their learning and eloquence.

2. Abelard, one of the most important philosophers in the early twelfth century, recounts in "The Story of His Misfortunes" the history of his problems with what he sees as a hostile world, though he provokes much of the hostility by his intellectual arrogance and his self-indulgence, particularly the showing up of his teachers and the seduction of his brilliant student Heloise.

Comedy sets the conversion of the individual from sin to grace within the vast context of contrasting worlds, the corrupt world of Hell and the ideal world of Paradise, which together house an impressive array of characters from contemporary life, history, and literature. They tell their own stories of political, moral, or emotional struggles, some in victory, some in defeat, driven by the same kinds of lust and ambition that moved Augustine and that move us still today.

Much later in the fourteenth century, Christine de Pizan (c. 1364–c. 1429) wrote an allegory that also deals with religion, history, philosophy, and the arts, but in a world entirely inhabited and fashioned by women. *The City of Ladies* is her answer to the vast literature of misogyny she had been exposed to. Christine's interest in learning had been encouraged by her father, a physician and astrologer at the court of Charles V of France, and by various powerful friends, including the king and the chancellor of the University of Paris. But it was only when her husband died, leaving her as the sole support for herself, her children, and her mother, that she used that learning to write on a variety of subjects — from warfare and political theory to biography, love, and women. She went on to become a highly successful author, with an international reputation and invitations from English and Italian courts.

The focus of writers mentioned so far is on the morality and behavior of the individual, though some are also concerned with the effects of individual actions on society. Their mode of presentation is mainly prose or allegorical poetry, often entertaining and moving but primarily didactic, unlike the lyrics, heroic epics, and romances, secular genres composed primarily for entertainment; these lighter works, however, can also carry serious messages about personal conduct and social responsibility. The lyrics offer a brief but intense expression of the human condition, the emotions of grief, desire, joy, anger, unsatisfied yearning or frustrated desire for a love that either is never satisfied or can no longer be satisfied, fear of death and decay, or religious devotion. The Provençal lyrics of the twelfth century, such as those of Bernart de Ventadorn, introduce the concept of "courtly love," a love befitting a member of a court, which involves devoted service and striving to be worthy of the person loved, and which contributes to the quality of life at the court. This concept, with its idealization of the beloved, makes its way into other vernacular lyric and romance traditions, and continues to influence their treatment of love, even when they move beyond the original courtly and aristocratic audiences. Indeed, with considerable modification, the influence of such lyrics has persisted to the present.

The narrative genres of heroic epic and romance fulfill a different purpose. Though the plot may hinge on the hero's conflicting motivations or desires, the resolution of such conflict must be in harmony with the needs and values of his society. In the epics the hero's story is part of the history of his people, and his death may well mean their destruction as in *Beowulf*. To serve society, the hero must perform heroic actions, fighting monsters or defeating hostile armies, and these actions can provoke envy and betrayal, even death. Violent deaths in a heroic society demand revenge; the endless cycle of fighting and death ultimately means the end of a people or of a dynasty. The mood of epic is therefore tragic, while courtly romance is comic (in the sense of ending happily). In Arthurian romance the setting is not historic, but ideal; in this world, conflicts can be resolved, and death, when it occurs, is not allowed to determine the action. The values of Arthur's court are ideal social values: justice, defense of the weak and oppressed, condemnation of evil or violence for its own sake. Individuals learn to harmonize their personal needs and desires with the demands of their societies, so they can satisfy the one while serving the other. Love is an inspiration to social service rather than an obstacle to it.

At least, that is true of the genre of medieval romance in its early stages, in most of the works of twelfth and early thirteenth-century French and German poets, whom Chrétien de Troyes and Wolfram von Eschenbach represent here. It is not true of the many versions of the Tristan story, where the adulterous nature of the love puts it into insoluble conflict with society. It is not always true in the *Lais* of Marie de France (late twelfth century), where the social setting, court, family, or marriage can be oppressive and sterile, and the trapped individual can only be rescued by a love that is freely given. Nor is it true of the later Arthurian romances—the thirteenth-century prose romances, particularly the Grail romances, or their last medieval expression in Thomas Malory's *Morte D'Arthur* (c. 1471) where the problems can no longer be resolved because they have struck at the center of the court, the king and queen, and because the Grail quest is now perceived as an individual quest for salvation that takes the best knights away from the secular world, instead of inspiring them in its service.

To some extent, the seeds of trouble were always present in the Arthurian court, even in the earliest romances of Chrétien, where court customs threatened to provoke hostilities, but they were contained there. The problems of envy and jealousy, of lust for undeserved honor and power, are inherent in the human condition. They are treated satirically in the animal stories collected around Renard the Fox beginning in the late twelfth century and in the fables of Marie de France. These and other aspects are satirized by Chaucer (c. 1340–c. 1400), on all levels of society and in a variety of literary genres, in *Canterbury Tales*.

There is satire and much else in the Spanish texts of the late Middle Ages included here. Juan Ruiz's *Book of Good Love* has been described variously as an erotic pseudo-autobiography and an "art of love," and as a sober example of proper Christian behavior and an "art of poetry"; its multicultural perspective reflects the coexistence in medieval Spain of Christians, Jews, and Moors. Equally rich and ambiguous is Fernando de Rojas's *Celestina*, which has been called a tragicomedy, the first European novel, and a "novel in disguise." Janus-like, it looks both backward toward medieval literary and philosophical concerns and forward toward new interrogations of these traditions and the ensuing development of new forms, while presenting individual human lives in a society that it views as chaotically meaningless and godless.

Historical Background

Two momentous decisions of the Roman emperor Constantine (ruled 310–337) helped set the stage for the Middle Ages. In 313, Constantine extended official recognition to Christianity, whose adherents had been growing in both numbers and wealth. In 330, he moved the capital east to the ancient Greek city of Byzantium, renamed Constantinople (which is present-day Istanbul).

By 400, Christianity had become the state religion, and the empire was partitioned for administrative purposes. The Eastern, or Byzantine, empire survived into the fifteenth century. The Western empire, long decaying internally, collapsed over the course of the fifth century, overwhelmed by a massive influx of

Germanic tribes. The last Roman emperor was deposed by a Germanic chieftain named Odoacer in 476.

The ensuing thousand years – to roughly 1500 – are conventionally called the Middle Ages. The early Middle Ages (to 1000) was a time of invasion and instability. Determined to reassert its authority over the West, Constantinople sent the Ostrogoths, a neighboring Germanic tribe, to retake Italy. Their leader, Theodoric, reinstituted Roman law and ruled until 526. Elsewhere, Germanic kingdoms rose and fell – Visigoths in Spain, Franks in France – whose rulers acknowledged the sovereignty of Constantinople and were given Roman titles in return. All in all, the period saw a gradual interpenetration of cultures rather than the total eclipse of one by the other.

After Theodoric's death, Byzantine armies conquered North Africa and Italy. The Eastern empire's presence in Italy was reduced to a mere foothold, however, when the peninsula was overrun from the north by yet another Germanic tribe, the Lombards. North Africa in turn fell to an entirely new regional power, Islam: during the seventh and eighth centuries, Arab armies consolidated an empire that reached from the borders of Byzantium across Africa and up into Spain. Islam retained a strong presence in Spain throughout the Middle Ages, and Arab ships dominated the Mediterranean for several centuries. Ultimately, it was not Constantinople but the Latin Church that reestablished the frontiers of Europe. Having grown up within the empire, the Church had adopted imperial organization, with an administrative hierarchy of clergy in provincial cities and a central authority, the pope, in Rome.

The Church was central to the medieval world: when the kingdoms of the Middle Ages thought of themselves as part of a whole, it was not Europe they called it, but Christendom. From the clergy, schooled in Latin, came most of the literate members of society. Education remained in the hands of the Church. Monasteries were important scholarly as well as spiritual centers, and it was in their libraries that the classical texts known to the early Middle Ages survived. Convents offered education and some realm of authority to women, but only to daughters of the nobility. Male monasteries, too, were largely the province of the well-born and/or well-off, closed to all but the most gifted poor men. In general, the lines of literacy in the early Middle Ages were less male/female then religious/secular. Later, as universities became centers of learning, dominated by the clergy, women were denied entry even to the profession of medicine, which had long been open to them. Certainly women were excluded from the priesthood and therefore from the church hierarchy. But outside the Church women had more access to power than misogynist doctrines would seem to suggest. When there was no male heir, women might inherit land and, in some cases, rule it. In the absence of a husband or the minority of a son, women frequently exercised authority as regents.

The Church also had a hand in secular government. Bishops, abbots, and abbesses (into the twelfth century) were drawn from the nobility and some ruled as lords over extensive estates. These swore fealty as vassals to secular lords and fulfilled a vassal's military obligations: a bishop might even lead troops in battle. Later government bureaucracy relied on the services of clerics because of their training and literacy, and some higher clergy held administrative or advisory positions. The relationship between church and state, however, was rarely untroubled, and the history of the Middle Ages traces an ongoing struggle between popes and kings to define respective spheres of authority.

In the secular sphere, different forces dominated in different periods. The early Middle Ages witnessed the ascendancy of the Franks. Under their leader Clovis, who was converted with the help of his Christian wife Clotilda—not an unusual circumstance—the Franks were the first important conquest of the Church in the sixth century. During the next two centuries, they extended their rule over much of France and into Germany. In 732 Frankish troops turned back Arab armies at Tours, an important battle that ended Islamic attempts to push beyond the Pyrenees.

Under Charlemagne (who ruled from 768 to 814), Frankish dominion reached its height. Charlemagne conquered the Lombards in Italy, extended German holdings, and pushed Frankish power over the Pyrenees into Moorish Spain. In 800, Pope Leo III crowned Charlemagne "Emperor and Augustus," recognizing a new Western empire and sending a signal of independence to Constantinople. Charlemagne ruled from Aachen in present-day Germany, where his court was the center of a brief intellectual and artistic renaissance, but his empire was short-lived. His grandsons divided it into three kingdoms, which were later consolidated into two; these developed separately as France and Germany. Legends of Charlemagne's achievements persisted, however, furnishing a rich subject for later medieval literature.

The ninth and tenth centuries brought new waves of invasions: Norsemen (northmen, also known as Vikings), who raided coastal towns and moved inland up rivers; Magyar horsemen (Hungarians), who swept in from the east; Arab ships that attacked from the Mediterranean. The Vikings in particular had a lasting influence on the new civilization of Europe, especially through their assimilation in Germany and their presence in France, where as the Normans they controlled a large territory. The Norman Conquest in 1066 placed the French-speaking ex-Vikings legitimately on the English throne, affecting the subsequent history not only of England but also of the English language: hitherto purely Germanic, English entered into a new cycle of development that integrated French (Latin) elements.

The Magyar invasions were turned back by Otto I, the German king who emerged as the most powerful ruler since Charlemagne. His kingdom united an expanded Germany with northern Italy, and he was crowned emperor by the pope in 961. For the rest of the Middle Ages and beyond, Germany formed the core of the Holy Roman Empire, the nominal protector of the papacy. German kings had the strongest claim to the imperial throne, though they could only secure it through coronation in Rome. Disagreements between emperors and popes over whose authority was supreme provoked the most explosive of the many medieval confrontations between spiritual and secular authority.

The early Middle Ages also saw the development of feudalism, a hierarchy of loyalties and obligations that structured medieval society. Based on the holding of land by one lord from another, the central relationship of feudalism was the bond between lord and vassal. A vassal pledged fealty (loyalty) to a lord in return for a fief—an estate from the lord's holdings. Peasants worked the land either as serfs, essentially owned by the local lord, or as his tenants. The vassal might in turn have vassals of his own; the lord might be vassal to another lord. The obligations between lord and vassal were many, but the fundamental exchange was that of the lord to protect his vassal and the vassal to serve his lord, especially militarily. In theory, feudalism produced a hierarchy of vassalage that extended from the lowliest knight to the king—a gigantic cavalry in perpetual readiness for mobilization. In reality, feudalism suffered fragmentation and fostered a powerful regional nobility, technically vassals to the king, yet largely autonomous.

Knights, originally mounted soldiers quartered in a lord's household as a private army, came to constitute a lesser nobility, often holding fiefs and earning a large degree of independence. With the increasingly elaborate and ritualized character of knightly warfare and the influence of courtly literature, knighthood became central to the nobility's self-image, and there grew around it a system of ethical ideals known as chivalry (from *chevalier,* the French word for knight). A fusion of Christian and military values, chivalry emphasized honor, bravery, courtesy, piety, and loyalty. During the Crusades—the military expeditions undertaken by the European Christians in the eleventh, twelfth, and thirteenth centuries to recover the Holy Land from the Moslems—chivalry found its ultimate expression in the creation of knightly orders and monastic communities of knights such as the Knights Templar.

The clergy formed its own privileged class, although some were also feudal lords. The upper ranks usually came from the nobility, while the lower clergy—especially parish priests—tended to come from the peasantry and were often little better educated than their flock.

The high Middle Ages (1100–1300) began with a sense of confidence, with the borders of Europe largely secured. The economy, in decline since the late Roman empire, started to revive. A newly rich merchant class evolved and spread throughout Europe. As the economy revived, so did the cities and towns, home not only to merchants but also to artisans and tradespeople. To the three classes of feudal society—the nobles, the church, and the peasants—the towns added a new and disturbing "middle class" virtually outside the feudal system.

The Church's power and prestige reached its apex. In 1095 the pope declared the First Crusade, calling on the sovereigns of Europe to retake the Holy Land from Islam. Although faith certainly played a role in the Crusades, the expeditions—eight in all—increasingly became acts of plunder and conquest, deepening the mutual antagonism between the Latin West and East whether Byzantium or Islam. Viewed from a political or religious standpoint, the Crusades were a failure. In the long run, their contribution lay in stimulating trade.

Intellectually, the high Middle Ages were marked by the dissemination of Roman learning and the recovery of Greek learning from the Moors in Spain. Islamic scholars had preserved the works of Greek thinkers and had themselves made important advances in mathematics and other fields. Latin texts and basic works of Roman law were also newly available. Universities began to form in Bologna in the twelfth century and in Paris in the thirteenth century. A major project of medieval scholars was the reconciliation of Church doctrine with the newly recovered works of Aristotle, a synthesis of faith and reason.

Politically, England and France began a gradual movement toward national monarchies. Lawyers staffed government bureaucracies replacing feudal custom with centralized Roman law. Nobility, clergy, and townspeople organized councils to represent their concerns in the shifting power structure, laying the foundations for parliamentary systems of government. The Holy Roman Empire, in contrast, began a long process of fragmentation that saw Germany splinter into ever smaller, increasingly autonomous principalities. In Italy independent cities made rich by trade annexed surrounding lands to form city-states. Neither Germany nor Italy would unify as a centralized nation-state until the nineteenth century.

The late Middle Ages (1300–1500) were a troubled period of transition.

Crop failures led to recurrent famine; trade routes that had brought wealth now brought disease, and pestilence swept Europe. The most famous plague, the Black Death, struck around 1348 and wiped out as much as two-fifths of the population. The futile Hundred Years' War between France and England (1337–1453), fought entirely on French soil, wreaked terrible suffering on the population. New military technology — gunpowder, artillery, and professional armies — made knights increasingly obsolete and finally destroyed the power base of the feudal structure. Gangs of disbanded mercenary troops roamed the countryside, causing as much terror as the war itself. The disastrous conditions of the time ignited social unrest in three great peasant revolts and many lesser urban riots. France emerged from the war as a centralized state with a strong monarchy, but not before the duchy of Burgundy almost carved out its own empire. England gave up its claims to French soil and turned its attention to becoming a naval power, but not before suffering a lengthy civil war of succession.

Emerging national sentiments lessened the hold of the Church, and the papacy, in disarray and disrepute for most of the late Middle Ages, lost much of its political influence. Intellectually, the Church was increasingly challenged by an emphasis on rational inquiry, and the synthetic systems of the high Middle Ages crumbled. Classical humanism flourished in Italy; independently of the Church-sponsored universities, humanist scholars pursued knowledge for its own sake, reestablishing a tradition of secular education whose greatest weapon would be the newly invented printed book. Even spiritually, the Church was losing ground, and internal dissent and calls for reform would soon culminate in the Protestant Reformation.

Spain, whose small Christian principalities had been slowly pushing back the Moorish frontier, suddenly arrived as a major power when the kingdoms of Castile and Aragon merged through marriage. In 1492 the Spanish recaptured the last Moorish stronghold at Granada, exiling the Jews and attempting to convert the Muslims by force. In the same year Spain sponsored a voyage by an explorer named Christopher Columbus, who failed in his mission to find a sea route to India but accidentally stumbled onto something of even greater potential.

Further Reading

Erich Auerbach, *Mimesis*. Princeton: Princeton University Press, 1953.

Marc Bloch, *The Feudal Society*. Chicago: University of Chicago Press, 1961.

Caroline Walker Bynum, *Jesus as Mother: Studies in the Spirituality of the High Middle Ages*. Berkeley: University of California Press, 1982.

Norman F. Cantor, *The Meaning of the Middle Ages*. Boston: Allyn and Bacon, 1973.

Ernst Curtius, *European Literature and the Decline of the High Middle Ages*. Princeton: Princeton University Press, Bollingen, 1953.

Joan Ferrante, *Woman as Image in Medieval Literature*. New York: Columbia University Press, 1975. (Labyrinth Paperback.)

Penelope Schine Gold, *The Lady and the Virgin*. Chicago: Chicago University Press, 1985.

Frederick Goldin, *The Mirror of Narcissus in the Courtly Love Lyric*. Ithaca: Cornell University Press, 1967.

Robert Hanning, *The Individual in Twelfth Century Romance*. New Haven: Yale University Press, 1977.

Friedrich Heer, *The Medieval World*. New York: Mentor, 1961.

J. Huizinga, *The Waning of the Middle Ages*. New York: Doubleday Anchor, 1973.

W. T. H. Jackson, *The Literature of the Middle Ages*. New York: Columbia University Press, 1960.

SAINT AUGUSTINE [AURELIUS AUGUSTINUS] (354–430)
Roman North Africa

In the *Confessions,* the first autobiography in Western Christendom, Augustine tells the story of his early life in what is today Algeria and of his conversion to Christianity. After 376, he went to Rome where he taught rhetoric and then to Milan. He was converted in 387, joined a monastic community, and in 395, became the bishop of Hippo, where he died during the siege of the Vandals. Beginning with his childhood, and writing in Latin, he describes his experiences as the son of an educated pagan father and a Christian mother, St. Monica, whose devotion was ultimately an important influence on him, and he dwells on the defects in his character: his impatience with his studies and his delight in bouts of delinquency like the theft of the pears, the incident described in the first selection here; his pursuit of sex and the distractions of the stage when he is sent to school in the city; and his early career, teaching young men to practice law for profit, preferring honesty but clearly not rejecting manipulation of the truth ("the tricks of pleading"), while living with a woman to whom he was not married. In many details Augustine led the life typical of a middle-class suburban youth, with all the advantages of devoted parents, good education, and easy access to a profitable career, aided by native intelligence and abetted by a desire for comfort and pleasure. It is not the way we might expect the life of a major saint and theologian of the Catholic faith to begin, nor is it the way the lives of most saints begin. Augustine's writing holds us with the honesty of its introspection and the liveliness of its description.

from *Confessions*

Book 2 [Stealing the Pears]

It is certain, O Lord, that theft is punished by your law, the law that is written in men's hearts and cannot be erased however sinful they are. For no thief can bear that another thief should steal from him, even if he is rich and the other is driven to it by want. Yet I was willing to steal, and steal I did, although I was not compelled by any lack, unless it were the lack of a sense of justice or a distaste for what was right and a greedy love of doing wrong. For of what I stole I already had plenty, and much better at that, and I had no wish to enjoy the things I coveted by stealing, but only to enjoy the theft itself and the sin. There was a pear-tree near our vineyard, loaded with fruit that was attractive neither to look at nor to taste. Late one night a band of ruffians, myself included, went off to shake down the fruit and carry it away, for we had continued our games out of doors until well after dark, as was our pernicious habit. We took away an enormous quantity of

Translated by R. S. Pine-Coffin.

pears, not to eat them ourselves, but simply to throw them to the pigs. Perhaps we ate some of them, but our real pleasure consisted in doing something that was forbidden.

Look into my heart, O God, the same heart on which you took pity when it was in the depths of the abyss. Let my heart now tell you what prompted me to do wrong for no purpose, and why it was only my own love of mischief that made me do it. The evil in me was foul, but I loved it. I loved my own perdition and my own faults, not the things for which I committed wrong, but the wrong itself. My soul was vicious and broke away from your safe keeping to seek its own destruction, looking for no profit in disgrace but only for disgrace itself.

Book 3 [Love and Lust]

I went to Carthage, where I found myself in the midst of a hissing cauldron of lust. I had not yet fallen in love, but I was in love with the idea of it, and this feeling that something was missing made me despise myself for not being more anxious to satisfy the need. I began to look around for some object for my love, since I badly wanted to love something. I had no liking for the safe path without pitfalls, for although my real need was for you, my God, who are the food of the soul, I was not aware of this hunger. I felt no need for the food that does not perish, not because I had had my fill of it, but because the more I was starved of it the less palatable it seemed. Because of this my soul fell sick. It broke out in ulcers and looked about desperately for some material, worldly means of relieving the itch which they caused. But material things, which have no soul, could not be true objects for my love. To love and to have my love returned was my heart's desire, and it would be all the sweeter if I could also enjoy the body of the one who loved me.

So I muddied the stream of friendship with the filth of lewdness and clouded its clear waters with hell's black river of lust. And yet, in spite of this rank depravity, I was vain enough to have ambitions of cutting a fine figure in the world. I also fell in love, which was a snare of my own choosing. My God, my God of mercy, how good you were to me, for you mixed much bitterness in that cup of pleasure! My love was returned and finally shackled me in the bonds of its consummation. In the midst of my joy I was caught up in the coils of trouble, for I was lashed with the cruel, fiery rods of jealousy and suspicion, fear, anger, and quarrels.

Book 3 [The Attractions of the Theatre]

I was much attracted by the theatre, because the plays reflected my own unhappy plight and were tinder to my fire. Why is it that men enjoy feeling sad at the sight of tragedy and suffering on the stage, although they would be most unhappy if they had to endure the same fate themselves? Yet they watch the plays because they hope to be made to feel sad, and the feeling of sorrow is what they enjoy. What miserable delirium this is! The more a man is subject to such suffering himself, the more easily he is moved by it in the theatre. Yet when he suffers himself, we call it misery: when he suffers out of sympathy with others, we call it pity. But what sort of pity can we really feel for an imaginary scene on the stage? The audience is not called upon to offer help but only to feel sorrow, and the more they are pained the more they applaud the author. Whether this human agony is based on fact or is simply imaginary, if it is acted so badly that the audience is not moved to sorrow, they leave the theatre in a disgruntled and critical mood; whereas, if they are made to feel pain, they stay to the end watching happily.

This shows that sorrow and tears can be enjoyable. Of course, everyone wants to be happy; but even if no one likes being sad, is there just the one exception that, because we enjoy pitying others, we welcome their misfortunes, without which we could not pity them? If so, it is because friendly feelings well up in us like the waters of a spring. But what course do these waters follow? Where do they flow? Why do they trickle away to join that stream of boiling pitch, the hideous flood of lust? For by their own choice they lose themselves and become absorbed in it. They are diverted from their true course and deprived of their original heavenly calm.

Book 4 [Playing Shepherd to the Wind]

During those years I was a teacher of the art of public speaking.[1] Love of money had gained the better of me and for it I sold to others the means of coming off the better in debate. But you know, Lord, that I preferred to have honest pupils, in so far as honesty has any meaning nowadays, and I had no evil intent when I taught the tricks of pleading, for I never meant them to be used to get the innocent condemned but, if the occasion arose, to save the lives of the guilty. From a distance, my God, you saw me losing my foothold on this treacherous ground, but through clouds of smoke you also saw a spark of good faith in me; for though, as I schooled my pupils, I was merely abetting their futile designs and their schemes of duplicity, nevertheless I did my best to teach them honestly.

In those days I lived with a woman, not my lawful wedded wife but a mistress whom I had chosen for no special reason but that my restless passions had alighted on her. But she was the only one and I was faithful to her. Living with her I found out by my own experience the difference between the restraint of the marriage alliance, contracted for the purpose of having children, and a bargain struck for lust, in which the birth of children is begrudged, though, if they come, we cannot help but love them.

I remember too that once, when I had decided to enter a competition for reciting dramatic verse, a sorcerer sent to ask me how much I would pay him to make certain that I won. I loathed and detested these foul rites and told him that even if the prize were a crown of gold that would last for ever, I would not let even a fly be killed to win it. For he would have slaughtered living animals in his ritual, and by means of these offerings he would have pretended to invoke the aid of his demons in my favour. But, O God of my heart, it was not from a pure love of you that I rejected this wickedness. I had not learnt how to love you, for when I

---

1. The art of public speaking is rhetoric—the art of using language to persuade an audience, here in a court of law.

thought of you I imagined you as some splendid being, but entirely physical. Does not the soul which pines for such fantasies *break its troth with you?* Does it not trust in false hopes and *play shepherd to the wind?* But while I would not let this man offer sacrifice for me to his devils, all the time I was offering myself as a sacrifice to them because of my false beliefs. For if we play shepherd to the wind, we find pasture for the devils, because by straying from the truth we give them food for laughter and fill their cup of pleasure.

BOETHIUS [ANICIUS MANLIUS SEVERINUS] (c. 480–524)
Roman Empire

The Roman philosopher Boethius wrote Latin commentaries and translations of Greek philosophers and treatises on logic and music that were major sources of medieval learning. Accused of treason, he was imprisoned by Theodoric, king of the Ostrogoths. While awaiting execution, he wrote *The Consolation of Philosophy,* which influenced medieval poets as well as philosophers. His personification of Philosophy is a model for Jean de Meun's Reason (in *The Roman de la Rose*) and Dante's Philosophy (in his *Convivio* or *The Banquet)* and his Virgil and Beatrice (in the *Divine Comedy*), to name only the most obvious. A personification of learning and logical thought, she comes to the imprisoned philosopher when he is consumed by self-pity and giving vent to his grief in poetry. She appears as a separate character, though in fact she represents the learning and logic that is already present in his mind but is not functioning. By the end of the work, which is written mainly in prose, with poems interspersed, she has brought him around to see himself not as the victim of an unjust fate but as someone who is finally happier than those fortune seems to favor; in their evil and ignorance, they are unable to achieve the good that is really desired by all, while he, for all his apparent misfortune, has achieved it, and with it a power and a reality they can never attain.

from *The Consolation of Philosophy*

BOOK 1

[Philosophy and the Muses]

While I was quietly thinking these thoughts over to myself and giving vent to my sorrow with the help of my pen, I became aware of a woman standing over me.

Translated by V. E. Watts.

She was of awe-inspiring appearance, her eyes burning and keen beyond the usual power of men. She was so full of years that I could hardly think of her as of my own generation, and yet she possessed a vivid colour and undiminished vigour. It was difficult to be sure of her height, for sometimes she was of average human size, while at other times she seemed to touch the very sky with the top of her head, and when she lifted herself even higher, she pierced it and was lost to human sight. Her clothes were made of imperishable material, of the finest thread woven with the most delicate skill. (Later she told me that she had made them with her own hands.) Their colour, however, was obscured by a kind of film as of long neglect, like statues covered in dust. On the bottom hem could be read the embroidered Greek letter Pi, and on the top hem the Greek letter Theta.[1] Between the two a ladder of steps rose from the lower to the higher letter. Her dress had been torn by the hands of marauders who had each carried off such pieces as he could get. There were some books in her right hand, and in her left hand she held a sceptre.

At the sight of the Muses of Poetry at my bedside dictating words to accompany my tears, she became angry.

"Who," she demanded, her piercing eyes alight with fire, "has allowed these hysterical sluts to approach this sick man's bedside? They have no medicine to ease his pains, only sweetened poisons to make them worse. These are the very women who kill the rich and fruitful harvest of Reason with the barren thorns of Passion. They habituate men to their sickness of mind instead of curing them. If as usual it was only some ordinary man you were carrying off a victim of your blandishments, it would matter little to me—there would be no harm done to my work. But this man has been nourished on the philosophies of Zeno and Plato.[2] Sirens is a better name for you and your deadly enticements: be gone, and leave him for my own Muses to heal and cure."

These rebukes brought blushes of shame into the Muses' cheeks, and with downcast eyes they departed in a dismal company. Tears had partly blinded me, and I could not make out who this woman of such imperious authority was. I could only fix my eyes on the ground overcome with surprise and wait in silence for what she would do next. She came closer and sat down on the edge of my bed. I felt her eyes resting on my face, downcast and lined with grief. Then sadly she began to recite . . .

[The Good and Strong, the Bad, the Weak]

Then I cried out in wonder at the magnitude of her promises. "Not that I don't think you can do it," I said. "Only do not keep me waiting, now that you have whetted my appetite."

"First then," she said, "that the good are always strong and that the wicked always bereft of all power, these are facts you will be able to see, the one being

---

1. In another work, Boethius speaks of two kinds of philosophy, practical (moral philosophy and ethics) and theoretical or speculative (theology, metaphysics and phys-

ics), represented here by the first letters of their names in Greek, Pi and Theta.
2. The Greek philosopher Zeno is credited with the invention of logic.

proved by the other. For since good and evil are opposites, the weakness of evil is shown by establishing the strength of good, and vice versa. So to strengthen your confidence in my teaching, I will proceed along both ways and prove my assertions doubly.

"Now, there are two things on which all the performance of human activity depends, will and power. If either of them is lacking, there is no activity that can be performed. In the absence of the will, a man is unwilling to do something and therefore does not undertake it; and in the absence of the power to do it, the will is useless. So that if you see someone who wants to get something which he cannot get, you can be sure that what he has been lacking is the power to get what he wanted."

"It is obvious," I said, "and cannot be denied."

"And if you see a man who has done what he wanted, you will hardly doubt that he had the power to do it, will you?"

"No."

"Therefore, men's power or ability is to be judged by what they can do, and their weakness by what they can't do."

"I agree."

"Do you, then, remember how earlier in the argument we reached the conclusion that the instinctive direction of the human will, manifested through a variety of pursuits, was entirely towards happiness?"

"I remember that this was proved as well."

"And you recall that happiness is the good itself and similarly that since they seek happiness, all men desire the good?"

"Not so much recall it, as hold it fixed in my mind."

"So that without any difference of instinct all men, good and bad alike, strive to reach the good."

"Yes, that follows."

"But surely men become good by acquiring goodness?"

"Yes."

"So that good men obtain what they are looking for?"

"It seems so."

"But if the wicked obtained what they want—that is goodness—they could not be wicked?"

"No."

"Since, then, both groups want goodness, and one obtains it and the other doesn't, surely there can be no doubt of the power of the good and the weakness of the bad?"

"Anyone who does doubt it is no judge either of reality or the logic of argument."

"Again," she said, "suppose there were two men who are set the same natural task, and one of them performs and completes it by natural action, while the other cannot manage the natural action, but uses another method contrary to nature, and does not actually complete the task but approximates to someone completing it; which would you say had the more power?"

"I can guess what you mean," I said, "but I would like to have it more clearly put."

"You will not deny that the action of walking is natural and human, will you?"

"No."

"And presumably you have no doubt that it is the natural function of the feet?"

"No, indeed."

"If, then, one man is able to proceed on foot and goes walking, and another lacks the natural function of the feet and tries to walk on his hands, which may properly be considered the more able or powerful?"

"Ask me another! No one could doubt that the man who can do the natural action is more able than the one who can't."

"Well, the supreme good is the goal of good men and bad alike, and the good seek it by means of a natural activity—the exercise of their virtues—while the bad strive to acquire the very same thing by means of their various desires, which isn't a natural method of obtaining the good. Or don't you agree?"

"Yes, for what follows is also obvious; from what I have already admitted it follows that the good are powerful and the bad weak."

"You anticipate correctly. As the doctors like to think, it is a sign of a constitution strong and fighting back. But seeing you are so quick of understanding, I will pile the arguments on. Just think how great the weakness is that we see in wicked men; they can't even reach the goal to which almost by compulsion their natural inclination leads them. What if they were deserted by this great and almost invincible help, and nature ceased to show them the way?

"Think of the extent of the weakness impeding the wicked. It is not as if the prizes they failed to win were mere sports trophies. The quest in which they fail is the quest for the highest and most important of all things, and success is denied these wretched men in the very pursuit they toil at night and day to the exclusion of all else, the same pursuit in which the strength of the good stands out.

"If a man by walking could reach a point beyond which there was nowhere for him to go, you would consider him the champion at walking. In the same way you must judge the man who achieves the goal of all endeavour, beyond which there is nothing, to be supreme in power. The opposite of this is also true; those who do not gain it are obviously lacking in all power.

"For I ask you, what is the cause of this flight from virtue to vice? If you say it is because they do not know what is good, I shall ask what greater weakness is there than the blindness of ignorance. And if you say that they know what they ought to seek for, but pleasure sends them chasing off the wrong way, this way too, they are weak through lack of self control because they cannot resist vice. And if you say they abandon goodness and turn to vice knowingly and willingly, this way they not only cease to be powerful, but cease to be at all. Men who give up the common goal of all things that exist, thereby cease to exist themselves. Some may perhaps think it strange that we say that wicked men, who form the majority of men, do not exist; but that is how it is. I am not trying to deny the wickedness of the wicked; what I do deny is that their existence is absolute and complete existence. Just as you might call a corpse a dead man, but couldn't simply call it a man, so I would agree that the wicked are wicked, but could not agree that they have unqualified existence. A thing exists when it keeps its proper place and preserves its own nature. Anything which departs from this ceases to exist, because its existence depends on the preservation of its nature.

"To the objection that evil men do have power, I would say that this power of theirs comes from weakness rather than strength. For they would not have the power to do the evil they can if they could have retained the power of doing good. This power only makes it more clear that they can do nothing, for if, as we concluded a short time ago, evil is nothing, it is clear that since they can only do evil, the wicked can do nothing."

"Obviously."

"But I want you to understand the exact nature of the power we are talking about. A moment ago we decided that there is nothing with greater power than the supreme good."

"That is so."

"But supreme goodness cannot do evil."

"No."

"Now, no one thinks of human beings as omnipotent, do they?"

"Not unless they are mad."

"But men can do evil?"

"I only wish they couldn't."

"It is obvious, therefore, that since a power that can only do good is omnipotent, while human beings who can also do evil are not, these same human beings who can do evil are less powerful. In addition to this we have shown that all forms of power are to be included among those things worth pursuing, and that all these worthwhile objects of pursuit are related to the good as to a kind of aggregate of their nature. Now, the ability to commit a crime cannot be a form of goodness, and is therefore not worth pursuing. But all forms of power are worth seeking after, so that it is obvious that the ability to do evil is not a form of power.

"From all this the power of good men is obvious and, beyond all doubt, so is the weakness of bad men. And it is clear that what Plato said in the *Gorgias* is true, namely that only the wise can achieve their desire, while the wicked busy themselves with what gives pleasure without being able to achieve their real objective. Their actions depend on the belief that they are going to obtain the good they desire through the things that give them pleasure. But they do not obtain it, because evil things cannot reach happiness."

ANONYMOUS (EIGHTH CENTURY)
England

Dating from the eighth century, "The Seafarer," an Old English elegy of 124 lines in all, is composed in alliterative verse. The first section, given here, deals with the wonders and miseries of life at sea, whereas the second contains moral reflections on the brevity of human existence and the glories of the heavens. It is generally supposed that there are at least two authors of this text, which may be a secular poem with a Christian appendage, or an allegory for human exile upon life's waters. Ezra Pound's rendering of the first part, free and remarkably evocative, conveys, as few texts have, a feeling of and for the sea.

The Seafarer

May I for my own self song's truth reckon,
Journey's jargon, how I in harsh days
Hardship endured oft.
Better breast-cares have I abided,
Known on my keel many a care's hold,   5
And dire sea-surge, and there I oft spent
Narrow nightwatch nigh the ship's head
While she tossed close to cliffs. Coldly afflicted,
My feet were by frost benumbed.
Chill its chains are; chafing sighs   10
Hew my heart round and hunger begot
Mere-weary[1] mood. Lest man know not
That he on dry land loveliest liveth,
List how I, care-wretched, on ice-cold sea,
Weathered the winter, wretched outcast   15
Deprived of my kinsmen;
Hung with hard ice-flakes, where hail-scur[2] flew,
There I heard naught save the harsh sea
And ice-cold wave, at whiles the swan cries,
Did for my games the gannet's clamor,   20
Sea-fowls' loudness was for me laughter,
The mews' singing all my mead-drink.
Storms, on the stone-cliffs beaten, fell on the stern
In icy feathers; full oft the eagle screamed
With spray on his pinion.
                              Not any protector   25
May make merry man faring needy.
This he little believes, who aye in winsome life
Abides 'mid burghers some heavy business,
Wealthy and wine-flushed, how I weary oft
Must bide above brine.   30
Neareth nightshade, snoweth from north,
Frost froze the land, hail fell on earth then,
Corn of the coldest. Nathless[3] there knocketh now

Translated by Ezra Pound.

---

1. Sea-weary.
2. Hail-storms.

3. Notwithstanding.

The heart's thought that I on high streams
The salt-wavy tumult traverse alone.   35
Moaneth always my mind's lust
That I fare forth, that I afar hence
Seek out a foreign fastness.
For this there's no moody-lofty man over earth's midst,
Not though he be given his good, but will have in his youth greed;   40
Nor his deed to the daring, nor his king to the faithful
But shall have his sorrow for sea-fare
Whatever his lord will.
He hath not heart for harping, nor in ring-having
Nor winsomeness to wife, nor world's delight   45
Nor any whit else save the wave's slash,
Yet longing comes upon him to fare forth on the water.
Bosque⁴ taketh blossom, cometh beauty of berries,
Fields to fairness, land fares brisker,
All this admonisheth man eager of mood,   50
The heart turns to travel so that he then thinks
On flood-ways to be far departing.
Cuckoo calleth with gloomy crying,
He singeth summerward, bodeth sorrow,
The bitter heart's blood. Burgher knows not—   55
He the prosperous man—what some perform
Where wandering them widest draweth.
So that but now my heart burst from my breastlock,
My mood 'mid the mere-flood,
Over the whale's acre, would wander wide.   60
On earth's shelter cometh oft to me,
Eager and ready, the crying lone-flyer,
Whets for the whale-path the heart irresistibly,
O'er tracks of ocean; seeing that anyhow
My lord deems to me this dead life   65
On loan and on land, I believe not
That any earth-weal eternal standeth
Save there be somewhat calamitous
That, ere a man's tide go, turn it to twain.
Disease or oldness or sword-hate   70
Beats out the breath from doom-gripped body.
And for this, every earl whatever, for those speaking after—
Laud of the living, boasteth some last word,
That he will work ere he pass onward,
Frame on the fair earth 'gainst foes his malice,   75

---

4. Grove.

Daring ado,[5] . . .
So that all men shall honor him after
And his laud beyond them remain 'mid the English,
Aye, for ever, a lasting life's-blast,
Delight 'mid the doughty.
       Days little durable,   80
And all arrogance of earthen riches,
There come now no kings nor Caesars
Nor gold-giving lords like those gone.
Howe'er in mirth most magnified,
Whoe'er lived in life most lordliest,   85
Drear all this excellence, delights undurable!
Waneth the watch, but the world holdeth.
Tomb hideth trouble. The blade is layed low.
Earthly glory ageth and seareth.
No man at all going the earth's gait,   90
But age fares against him, his face paleth,
Gray-haired he groaneth, knows gone companions,
Lordly men, are to earth o'ergiven,
Nor may he then the flesh-cover, whose life ceaseth,
Nor eat the sweet nor feel the sorry,   95
Nor stir hand nor think in mid heart,
And though he strew the grave with gold,
His born brothers, their buried bodies
Be an unlikely treasure hoard.

ANONYMOUS (EIGHTH CENTURY)
England

Anonymously composed, like virtually all the heroic epics of the Middle Ages, *Beowulf* is a poem about a mythic hero of a historic sixth-century tribe, the Geats. It is interspersed with references to historic people and events, and realistic descriptions of the tragic effects of heroic values. Beowulf wins honor in his youth by saving the Danes from the ravages of the monster Grendel (the first excerpt included here) and the monster's mother. Half a century later, when he is king of the Geats, Beowulf defeats but is killed by a dragon who has ravaged his own land. After Beowulf's death, his people do not survive long. There is a self-destructive aspect to the heroic ethos, in which honor can be won only by defeating an enemy, and it can be maintained only if the deaths of relatives are

---

5. Brave deeds.

avenged. The second excerpt describes the hopelessness of attempts to control the destruction with peace-making marriages.

from *Beowulf*

[Beowulf Defeats the Archbeast Grendel]

The fiend wasted no time, but for a start snatched up a sleeping man. He tore him apart in an instant, crunched the body, drank blood from its veins, and gulped it down in great bites until he had wholly swallowed the dead man, even the hands and feet. Then he advanced nearer. Reaching out with his open hand, the fiend was about to take hold of the hero on his bed. But Beowulf at once saw the hostile move and propped himself up on his elbow. The archbeast soon realized that nowhere in the world had he ever met a man with such might in the grip of his hand. Although terror-struck, he could get away none the faster. He had never met anything like this in his life before; his one idea was to slink off to his hiding-place to rejoin the fellowship of devils. But at this point Beowulf remembered the promise which he had made earlier in the evening. He stood upright and gripped Grendel so tightly that the talons cracked to bursting. The monster fought to escape, but Beowulf closed with him. The fiend was trying to break loose and make a bolt for his fen-refuge; yet, as he knew only too well, his talons were fast in an enemy clutch. That was a fatal expedition which the demon made to Heorot.[1] The hall thundered with the hubbub. Every one of the Danes who lived in the stronghold, soldiers and chieftains alike, was seized with extreme panic. The furious contestants for the mastery of the hall raged till the building rang. It was a miracle that the beautiful banqueting hall withstood such combatants without falling flat to the ground; but it was firmly braced inside and out with iron clamps forged by skilled craftsmen. They say that where the two antagonists fought, bench after bench inlaid with gold was uprooted from the floor. Till then the most farsighted among the Danes had never imagined that anybody might wreck their splendid ivory-inlaid hall by ordinary means, or destroy it by dint of cunning (barring fire, which would envelop it in flame). A stupendous din went up. Pure terror laid hold of the Danes, and of everyone outside the hall who heard the howling; the dreadful scream of God's adversary wailing his defeat; the prisoner of hell bellowing over his wound. He was fast in the clutch of the strongest man alive.

[The Uselessness of a Treaty]

Sometimes Hrothgar's[2] daughter carried goblets of ale to the senior chieftains in succession—as she handed the flagon round I heard people call her Freawaru. Young and adorned with gold, she was promised in marriage to Froda's

Translated by David Wright.

---

1. Heorot is the great hall of the Danes, which Grendel invades.

2. Hrothgar is king of the Danes.

good-looking son, Prince Ingeld of the Heathobards.[3] King Hrothgar arranged it, and thinks it a good plan to end the many bitter feuds between the Danes and the Heathobards through this girl. But after the death of a prince it seldom happens that the spear lies idle for long, however beautiful the bride may be.

"For it may gall Prince Ingeld, and every man of his race, when he enters the banqueting hall with his bride, that the treasures of the Heathobards, the arms and armour that their ancestors once wielded, should glitter upon the backs of her Danish retainers now being banqueted.

"But in the battle the Heathobards had led their comrades, as well as their own lives, to destruction. Sooner or later, when drinking has begun, some fierce old spearman who remembers everything, including the massacre of his comrades, will recognize one of the swords. In bitterness of heart he will begin to sound some young fellow and stir up trouble with talk like this: 'My friend, can you recognize that weapon which your own father last carried into battle, when these brave Danes killed him and held the field after the death of Withergyld and the destruction of our men? Now the son of one of his killers is swaggering in his armour in our banqueting hall, bragging of that slaughter and flaunting a sword which by rights should be yours.' In this manner he will egg him on at every turn, and lash him with blistering words, until the day shall come when one of Freawaru's Danish retainers, drenched in blood from a sword-thrust, forfeits his life for what his father did; while the man who killed him escapes because he knows the neighbourhood. Then on both sides the oaths of the chieftains will quickly be broken. Bitter hatred must swell in Ingeld's breast, while, owing to his anguish of mind, his love for his wife must cool. That is why I do not think much of this friendship of the Heathobards, or consider the peace treaty with the Danes to be either real or lasting."

ALCUIN (c. 735–804)
England/France

Alcuin was a distinguished scholar and teacher, born in England and active there for most of his life. In 782 he accepted Charlemagne's invitation to the imperial court in Aachen, where he was a principal force in the revival of classical learning and the establishment of an enduring educational system. This lyric, written like nearly all his verse in classical Latin meter, begins as a personal lament for a lost nightingale; but the grief is forgotten as soon as it is expressed, and the poem concentrates on the message embodied in the sweetly singing bird. Hearing this creature, guided by instinct, singing to its Creator, the listener may sense something of

---

3. The Heathobards are an unidentified tribe. They were apparently seafaring and lived for a while along the Baltic Sea.

the rapture of the angels in their eternal song of praise; for the nightingale was given by God and Nature to man to wake him to his own true life of praise and devotion.

The Nightingale

Nightingale in the broom, the hand which stole you
from me was envious of my joy.
You filled my heart with sweet-sounding poetry
and my unhappy mind with honeyed song.
May throngs of birds come at once from all sides   5
to lament with me for you in Pierian song. Spurned though you were
for your colour, for your singing you were not spurned;
your swelling voice sounded in your narrow throat,
repeating its sweet tunes in different melodies,
always singing odes to the Creator.   10
On gloomy nights your adorable voice never ceased
your sacred songs, my pride and beauty.
What wonder is it that the cherubim and seraphim praise
the Almighty in eternal song, if your voice has such power?
How happy is he who both day and night   15
with such zeal always has songs for the Lord on his lips!
Neither food and drink were sweeter to you than song,
nor were the bonds of companionship with other birds.
This was the gift of Nature and of Nature's kindly creator
whom you praised with unceasing voice,   20
in order to urge us when sodden with wine and slumber
to shake off the idleness of our minds, clogged with sleep.
What you did, ignorant of reason or understanding,
with natural instinct as your much nobler guide,
everyone with active understanding and powerful reason   25
ought to have done for some time with their speech.
The greatest rewards shall await eternally in the heights of heaven
the man who forever praises the eternal king.

ANONYMOUS (c. 1000)
Germany

The lyric presented here is preserved in a manuscript of the eleventh century that contains forty-eight other poems of various types—some on religious and historical

Translated by Peter Godman.

subjects, some of themes of secular love—known collectively as the *Cambridge Songs*. This song is written in quatrains of rhymed iambic couplets, which was the most common meter of liturgical hymns. (Secular and religious lyrics adopted each other's meters and expressions throughout the Middle Ages). The strategy of beginning a lyric with a description of the season and then comparing the mood of nature with that of the speaker is a widespread feature of the medieval lyric, in both Latin and the vernacular languages. The contrast between the joyful reawakening of life in spring and the sadness of the speaker became one of the most common themes of the medieval lyric in the centuries that followed.

The Sighs of a Woman in Spring

Softly the west wind blows;
Gaily the warm sun goes;
The earth her bosom sheweth,
And with all sweetness floweth.

Goes forth the scarlet spring,   5
Clad with all blossoming,
Sprinkles the fields with flowers,
Leaves on the forest.

Dens for four-footed things,
Sweet nests for all with wings.   10
On every blossomed bough
Joy ringeth now.

I see it with my eyes,
I hear it with my ears,
But in my heart are sighs,   15
And I am full of tears.

Alone with thought I sit,
And blench, remembering it;
Sometimes I lift my head,
I neither hear nor see.   20

Do thou, O Spring most fair,
Squander thy care
On flower and leaf and grain.
—Leave me alone with pain![1]

Translated by Helen Waddell.

---

1. The translation of this last line trivializes the
   original: *Nam mea lanquet anima*, ("For my
   soul languishes.")

Hildegard of Bingen, a Vision from *Scivias*. Otto Müller Verlag, Salzburg, 1954.

HILDEGARD OF BINGEN (1098–1179)
Germany

This German Benedictine nun had many talents: her opinions on theology, prophecies, attacks on corruption, and advice on professional, personal, and medical problems were widely valued. She was an able administrator of a convent, who could hold her own with the bishops of her district. She was a gifted poet and composer of music, a student of female physiology, and a prolific correspondent (hundreds of letters to and from her survive—she corresponded with four popes, two emperors, and St. Bernard of Clairvaux). She had had, from her childhood, divine visions in which the voice of God interpreted the extraordinary things she saw or decried the corruption of the world and the Church, or gave her answers to questions that people put to her, in her extensive travels around Germany, about the conduct of their lives. She described these visions in three books, written in Latin, of which one, the *Scivias,* has survived in a manuscript with illustrations done probably under her guidance. The passages cited here give only a limited sense of the scope of her imagination and the power of her expression.

from **Scivias**

Book 1: Vision Three, The Universe and Its Symbolism

After this I saw a vast instrument, round and shadowed, in the shape of an egg, small at the top, large in the middle and narrowed at the bottom; outside it, surrounding its circumference, there was bright fire with, as it were, a shadowy zone under it. And in that fire there was a globe of sparkling flame so great that the whole instrument was illuminated by it, over which three little torches were arranged in such a way that by their fire they held up the globe lest it fall. And that globe at times raised itself up, so that much fire flew to it and thereby its flames lasted longer; and sometimes sank downward and great cold came to it, so that its flames were more quickly subdued. But from the fire that surrounded the instrument issued a blast with whirlwinds, and from the zone beneath it rushed forth another blast with its own whirlwinds, which diffused themselves hither and thither throughout the instrument. In that zone, too, there was a dark fire of such great horror that I could not look at it, whose force shook the whole zone, full of thunder, tempest and exceedingly sharp stones both large and small. And while it made its thunders heard, the bright fire and the winds and the air were in commotion, so that lightning preceded those thunders; for the fire felt within itself the turbulence of the thunder.

But beneath that zone was purest ether, with no zone beneath it, and in it I saw a globe of white fire and great magnitude over which two little torches were placed, holding that globe so that it would not exceed the measure of its course. And in that ether were scattered many bright spheres, into which the white globe from time to time poured itself out and emitted its brightness, and then moved back under the globe of red fire and renewed its flames from it, and then again sent them out into those spheres. And from that ether too a blast came forth with its whirlwinds, which spread itself everywhere throughout the instrument.

And beneath that ether I saw watery air with a white zone beneath it, which diffused itself here and there and imparted moisture to the whole instrument. And when it suddenly contracted it sent forth sudden rain with great noise, and when it gently spread out it gave a pleasant and softly falling rain. But from it too came a blast with its whirlwinds, which spread itself throughout the aforementioned instrument.

And in the midst of these elements was a sandy globe of great magnitude, which these elements had so surrounded that it could not waver in any direction. But as these elements and these blasts contended with each other, by their strength they made it move a little.

And I saw between the North and the East a great mountain, which to the North had great darkness and to the East had great light, but in such a way that the light could not reach the darkness, nor the darkness the light.

And again I heard the voice from Heaven, saying to me:

1.   The visible and temporal is a manifestation of the invisible and eternal   God, Who made all things by His will, created them so that His Name would be known and glorified, showing in them not just the things that are visible and temporal, but also the things that are invisible and eternal. Which is demonstrated by this vision you are perceiving.

2.   The firmament in the likeness of an egg and what it signifies   For this *vast instrument, round and shadowy, in the shape of an egg, small at the top, large in the middle and narrowed at the bottom*, faithfully shows Omnipotent God,

Translated by Mother Columba Hart and Jane Bishop.

incomprehensible in His Majesty and inestimable in His mysteries and the hope of all the faithful; for humanity at first was rude and rough and simple in its actions, but later was enlarged through the Old and New Testaments, and finally at the end of the world is destined to be beset with many tribulations.

3.   On the bright fire and the shadowy zone   *Outside it, surrounding its circumference, there is bright fire with, as it were, a shadowy zone under it.* This shows that God consumes by the fire of His vengeance all those who are outside the true faith, and those who remain within the Catholic faith He purifies by the fire of His consolation; thus He throws down the darkness of devilish perversity, as He did also when the Devil wanted to oppose himself to God though God had created him, and so fell defeated into perdition.

4.   On the placement of the sun and the three stars   *And in that fire there is a globe of sparkling flame, so great that the whole instrument is illuminated by it,* which in the splendour of its brightness shows that within God the Father is His ineffable Only-Begotten, the sun of justice with the brilliance of burning charity, of such great glory that every creature is illumined by the brightness of His light; *over which three little torches are arranged in such a way that by their fire they hold up the globe lest it fall;* that is, [the Trinity] shows how by its arrangement the Son of God, leaving the angels in the heavenly places, descended to earth and showed humans, who exist in soul and body, heavenly things, so that, glorifying Him by serving Him, they reject all harmful error, and magnify Him as the true Son of God incarnate through the true Virgin, when the angel foretold Him and when humans, living in soul and body, with faithful joy received Him.

6.   On the descent of the sun and what it signifies   So, indeed, *sometimes it sinks downwards and great cold comes to it, so that its flames are more quickly subdued.* This shows that the Only-Begotten of God, born of a virgin and hence inclined to be merciful to human poverty, incurred many miseries and sustained great physical anguish; but after He had shown Himself to the world in a bodily shape, He passed from the world and returned to the Father, while His disciples stood by, as it is written:

. . .

9.   On the second wind and its whirlwinds   *But from the zone beneath it rushes forth another blast with its own whirlwinds* because the rage of the Devil, knowing God and fearing Him, sends out the worst dishonor and the most evil utterances, *which diffuse themselves hither and thither throughout the instrument,* since in the world useful and useless rumors spread themselves abroad in many ways among the peoples.

10.   On the dark fire and the thunder and the sharp stones   *In this zone also there is a dark fire of such horror that you cannot look at it.* This means that the ancient betrayer's most evil and most vile snares vomit forth blackest murder with such great passion that the human intellect cannot fathom its insanity; *whose force shakes the whole zone,* because murder includes in its horror all diabolical malignities. In the first man born hatred boiled up out of anger and led to fratricide, *full of thunder, tempest and exceedingly sharp stones large and small,* for murder is full of avarice, and drunkenness and extreme hardness of heart, which run riot relentlessly both in great murders and in minor vices. *While it makes its thunders heard, the bright fire and the winds and the air are all in commotion,* because when murder cries out in its eagerness to shed blood, it arouses the justice of Heaven and an outburst of flying rumors and an increased disposition to vengeance on the part of right judgment; *so that lightning precedes those thunders, for the fire feels in itself the turbulence of the thunder,* for the manifestation of divine scrutiny exceeds and suppresses evil, since the Divine Majesty, before the sound of that insanity manifests itself in public, forsees it with that watchful eye to which all things are naked.

ANONYMOUS (c. 1100?)
France

The term "chanson de geste" can mean song of great deeds or song of the race or family. It denotes medieval epic French poems whose plots arise from an historical setting, very often the court of Charlemagne or his son; the first and greatest of these is *La Chanson de Roland*. There are historic elements in *The Song of Roland*—the French invasion of Spain under Charlemagne in 778 and the destruction of their rearguard—but it was Christian Basques, not Saracens, who ambushed them, and it was a disaster, not a glorious victory. Among the slain was Hruodlandus, Prefect of Brittany. *The Chanson de Roland* transforms this kernel into a combat between Christians and pagans or good and evil. The embarrassing defeat was slowly transformed in oral tradition into the victory described in the second part of this *chanson de geste,* where Charlemagne takes revenge for the deaths of his nephew Roland and the other heroes of the rearguard. Roland contributes to the tragedy by publicly offending his stepfather, Ganelon, who is already envious of Roland's glory. Ganelon plots with the Saracen enemy to ambush and kill Roland and coincidentally the entire rearguard, the flower of Charlemagne's army. In the first excerpt, Roland and his friend Oliver have just realized that the Saracens are approaching in overwhelming numbers. Oliver wants Roland to sound his horn and alert Charlemagne to their danger so he will return with the rest of the army, but Roland considers it shameful to ask for help and refuses, preferring to die rather than to lose his honor. Once they have been defeated and know they are dying, Roland is ready to sound the horn, so Charlemagne can come back and take revenge, but Oliver objects, throwing Roland's words back at him. The dying Oliver strikes Roland, whom he does not recognize, asks his forgiveness, and dies reconciled with him. Roland's consistent opposition to the pagans and his absolute acceptance of what he regarded as his duty are ultimately rewarded when he alone is escorted to heaven by angels. The gap in the lines of this translation is intended to suggest the rhythm of the original; it does not occur in the text.

from **Song of Roland**

[Roland Refuses to Blow His Horn]

84

"Roland, my friend,   let the Oliphant[1] sound!
King Charles will hear it,   his host will all turn back,
His valiant barons   will help us in this fight."
Roland replies,   "Almighty God forbid
That I bring shame   upon my family,   5
And cause sweet France   to fall into disgrace!
I'll strike that horde   with my good Durendal;[2]
My sword is ready,   girded here at my side,
And soon you'll see   its keen blade dripping blood.
The Saracens   will curse the evil day   10
They challenged us,   for we will make them pay."

85

"Roland, my friend,   I pray you, sound your horn!
King Charlemagne,   crossing the mountain pass,
Won't fail, I swear it,   to bring back all his Franks.
"May God forbid!"   Count Roland answers then.   15
"No man on earth   shall have the right to say
That I for pagans   sounded the Oliphant!
I will not bring   my family to shame.
I'll fight this battle;   my Durendal shall strike
A thousand blows   and seven hundred more;   20
You'll see bright blood   flow from the blade's keen steel.
We have good men;   their prowess will prevail,
And not one Spaniard   shall live to tell the tale."

86

Oliver says,   "Never would you be blamed;
I've seen the pagans,   the Saracens of Spain.   25
They fill the valleys,   cover the mountain peaks;
On every hill,   and every wide-spread plain,
Vast hosts assemble   from that alien race;
Our company   numbers but very few."
Roland replies,   "The better, then, we'll fight!   30
The saints and angels,   almighty God forbid
That I betray   the glory of sweet France!"

Translated by Patricia Terry.

---

1. The oliphant is Roland's ivory horn.   2. Durendal is Roland's sword.

Better to die   than learn to live with shame—
Charles loves us more   as our keen swords win fame."

87

Roland's a hero,   and Oliver is wise;   35
Both are so brave   men marvel at their deeds.
When they mount chargers,   take up their swords and shields,
Not death itself   could drive them from the field.
They are good men;   their words are fierce and proud.
With wrathful speed   the pagans ride to war.   40
Oliver says,   "Roland, you see them now.
They're very close,   the King too far away.
You were too proud   to sound the Oliphant:
If Charles were with us,   we would not come to grief.
Just look up there!   Close to the Aspre Pass,   45
The rearguard stands,   grieving for what must come.
To fight this battle   means not to fight again."
Roland replies,   "Don't speak so foolishly!"
Cursed be the heart   that cowers in the breast!
We'll hold our ground;   if they will meet us here,   50
Our foes will find us   ready with sword and spear."

88

When Roland sees   the fight will soon begin,
Lions and leopards   are not so fierce as he.
Calling the Franks,   he says to Oliver:
"Noble companion,   my friend, don't talk that way!
The Emperor Charles,   who left us in command   55
Of twenty thousand   he chose to guard the pass,
Made very sure   no coward's in their ranks.
In his lord's service   a man must suffer pain,
Bitterest cold   and burning heat endure;   60
He must be willing   to lose his flesh and blood.
Strike with your lance,   and I'll wield Durendal—
The king himself   presented it to me—
And if I die,   whoever takes my sword
Can say its master   has nobly served his lord."   65

[Oliver and Roland Before the Battle]
91

At Roncevaux   Count Roland passes by,
Riding his charger,   swift-running Veillantif.
He's armed for battle,   splendid in shining mail.

As he parades,   he brandishes his lance,
Turning the point   straight up against the sky,   5
And from the spearhead   a banner flies, pure white,
With long gold fringes   that beat against his hands.
Radiant, fair to see,   he laughs for joy.
Now close behind him   comes Oliver, his friend,
With all the Frenchmen   cheering their mighty lord.   10
Fiercely his eyes   confront the Saracens;
Respectfully, fondly   he gazes at the Franks,
Speaking these gallant words   to cheer their hearts:
"Barons, my lords,   softly now, keep the pace!
Here come the pagans   looking for martyrdom.   15
We'll have such plunder   before the day is out,
As no French king   has ever won before!"
And at this moment   the armies join in war.

92

Oliver says,   "I have no heart for words.
You were too proud   to sound the Oliphant: 20
No help at all   you'll have from Charlemagne.
It's not his fault—   he doesn't know our plight,
Nor will the men   here with us be to blame.
But now, ride on,   to fight as you know how.
Barons, my lords,   in battle hold your ground!   25
And in God's name,   I charge you, be resolved
To strike great blows   for those you have to take.
Let's not forget   the war-cry of King Charles!"
He says these words,   and all the Franks cry out;
No one who heard   that mighty shout, "Montjoie!"   30
Would soon forget   the valor of these men.
And then, how fiercely,   God! they begin to ride,
Spurring their horses   to give their utmost speed,
They race to strike—   what else is there to do?
The Saracens stand firm;   they won't retreat.   35
Pagans and Christians,   behold! in battle meet.

[Angels Take Roland's Soul to Paradise]

128

Count Roland sees   the slaughter of the Franks.
He says these words   to Oliver his friend:
"Noble companion,   how does it look to you?
So many Franks   lie dead upon the field—
Well could we weep   for that fair land, sweet France,   5
Which will not see   these valiant lords again.

Oh! Charles, my friend,   if only you were here!
Oliver, brother,   how can we call him back?
Is there no way   for us to send him word?"
Oliver answers,   "No, I do not know how.   10
Better to die   than lose our honor now."

129

Then Roland says,   "I'll sound the Oliphant.
King Charles will hear it   on the high mountain pass;
I promise you,   the Franks will all turn back."
Oliver answers,   "Then you would bring disgrace   15
And such dishonor   on your whole family
The shame of it   would last them all their lives.
Three times I asked,   and you would not agree;
You still can do it,   but not with my consent.
To sound the horn   denies your valor now.   20
And both your arms   are red with blood of foes!"
The Count replies,   "I've struck some pretty blows."

[Roland and Oliver in Battle]

147

Oliver knows   he has a fatal wound.
He longs for vengeance—   he'll never have enough.
In the melee   he fights on valiantly,
He cuts through spears,   the pagans' studded shields,
And feet and fists   and saddle-trees and spines.   5
Whoever watched him   cut pagans limb from limb,
Bodies piled up   around him on the ground,
Would know that once   he'd seen a noble lord.
The Count remembers   the war-cry of King Charles,
And loud and clear   his voice rings out, "Montjoie!"   10
He calls to Roland,   summons his friend and peer,
"My lord, companion,   come fight beside me now!
We'll part in sorrow   before the sun goes down."

148

Roland is there;   he sees Oliver's face,
The skin is ashen,   so pallid it looks grey,   15
And from his wounds   bright blood is spurting out;
Its heavy drops   flow down him to the ground.
"O God!" says Roland,   "I don't know what to do

Was such great valor   destined to be cut down!
My noble friend,   you'll have no peer on earth.   20
Alas, sweet France!   Now you have fallen low,
Bereft of vassals,   so many valiant men;
The Emperor Charles   will sorely feel the lack."
With these words Roland   faints on his horse's back.

149

Here is Count Roland   unconscious on his horse;   25
Oliver, wounded   and very close to death,
Has bled so much   that both his eyes are dimmed:
Now far or near   he can't see well enough
To give a name   to any man alive.
When he encounters   Count Roland in the field,   30
Oliver strikes him,   cleaving his golden helm
Brilliant with jewels—   the nose-piece cracks in two—
And yet the blade   does not touch face or head.
Roland's eyes open,   and looking at his friend,
Softly and gently   he asks him only this: 35
"My lord, companion,   it's Roland—did you know?
I've always loved you;   did you intend that blow?
You gave no challenge   before you charged at me."
Oliver says,   "I recognize your voice,
But I can't see you—   God keep you in His sight!   40
I struck at you!   I pray you, pardon me."
Roland replies,   "I am not hurt at all;
I do forgive you,   here and in front of God."
When he had spoken,   each leaned down toward his friend.
So, with great love,   they parted in the end.   45

[Death of Count Roland]

169

High are the hills   and very high the trees,
The four great blocks   of polished marble shine;
On the green grass   the Count is lying still.
A Saracen   watches with steady eyes:
This man feigned death,   hiding among the slain;   5
His face and body   he had besmeared with blood.
Now he stands up   and dashes forward fast—
He's handsome, strong   and very valiant too,
But he won't live   to profit from his pride;
He falls on Roland,   seizing him and his arms,   10

And says these words: "Charles' nephew lost the fight!
When I go home,   his sword shall be my prize."
But as he pulls it,   Roland comes back to life.

170

Count Roland feels   the pagan take his sword,
And opening his eyes,   he says just this: 15
"You look to me   like no one on our side!"
Raising the horn   he'd wanted to keep safe,
He strikes the helmet   shining with gold and jewels,
Shatters the steel,   smashes the skull and bones;
He puts both eyes   out of the pagan's head,   20
And sends his body   crashing against the ground.
And then he asks him,   "How did you get so brave,
Dog, to attack me   with or without just cause?
Whoever heard this   would say you were insane!
But I have cracked   the Oliphant's broad bell;   25
Its gold and crystals   were shattered as it fell."

171

Now Roland feels   that he is going blind.
The Count stands upright,   using what strength remains;
All of the color   has vanished from his face.
In front of him   there is a dark grey stone.   30
He strikes ten blows   in bitterness and grief;
The steel blade grates   but will not break or dent.
Then Roland cries: "O Holy Mary, help!
O Durendal,   alas for your fair fame!
My life is over,   you won't be in my care.   35
We've won such battles   together in the field,
So many lands   we've conquered, you and I,
For Charles to rule   whose beard is silver-grey.
No man must have you   who fights and runs away!
You have been long   in a good vassal's hands;   40
You'll have no equal   in all of holy France."

172

Count Roland strikes   the hard sardonyx stone;
The steel blade grates   but will not chip or break.
When Roland sees   he can't destroy his sword,
Then, to himself,   grieving, he speaks its praise: 45
"O Durendal,   how fair you are, and bright!
Against the sunlight   your keen steel gleams and flames!

Charles was that time   in Moriane's Vales
When by God's will   an angel from the sky
Said to bestow you   upon a chieftain Count: 50
The noble King   girded you at my side.
With you I won him   Anjou and Brittany,
Conquered Poitou   and after that all Maine,
With you I won him   that free land, Normandy,
Conquered Provence,   and then all Aquitaine,   55
And Lombardy,   Romagna after that.
With you I won him   Bavaria, Flanders,
Bulgaria,   and all of Poland too.
Constantinople   paid homage to King Charles,
In Saxony   he does as he desires.   60
With you I conquered   the Irish and the Scots,
And England too   the King holds as his own.
So many countries   we've won him, many lands
Ruled by King Charles   whose flowing beard is white.
For your sake now   I suffer grief and pain—   65
Better to die   than leave you here in Spain.
Almighty Father,   keep sweet France from that shame!"

173

Count Roland strikes   against a dark grey stone;
More of it falls   than I can make you see.
The steel blade grates   but will not crack or break;   70
Against the sky   it springs back up again.
Count Roland knows   he can't destroy his sword.
Then, to himself,   he quietly laments:
"O Durendal,   holy you are, and fair!
You have great relics   within your hilt of gold: 75
Saint Peter's tooth,   drops of Saint Basil's blood,
Hairs from the head   of my lord Saint Denis,
Part of a garment   that Holy Mary wore—
For any pagan   to hold you would be wrong;
Only by Christians   can you be rightly served.   80
May you not fall   into a coward's hands!
Many wide lands   we've conquered, you and I,
For Charles to rule   whose flowing beard is white;
They have increased   his majesty and might."

174

Count Roland feels   the very grip of death   85
Which from his head   is reaching for his heart.
He hurries then   to go beneath a pine;

In the green grass   he lies down on his face,
Placing beneath him   the sword and Oliphant;
He turns his head   to look toward pagan Spain.   90
He does these things   in order to be sure
King Charles will say,   and with him all the Franks,
The noble Count   conquered until he died.
He makes confession,   for all his sins laments,
Offers his glove   in God in penitence.   95

175

Now Roland feels   his time has all run out.
He looks toward Spain   from high on a steep hill.
And with one hand   beating his breast, he says:
"God, I have sinned   against Thy holy name.
Forgive the sins,   the great ones and the less,   100
That I committed   from my first hour of life
To this last day   when I have been struck down."
And now toward God   he raises his right glove;
A flight of angels   comes from the skies above.

176

And now Count Roland,   lying beneath a pine,   105
Has turned his face   to look toward pagan Spain;
And he begins   remembering these things:
The many lands   his valor won the King,
Sweet France, his home,   the men of his own line,
And Charlemagne   who raised him in his house—   110
The memories   make him shed tears and sigh.
But not forgetting   how close he is to death,
He prays that God   forgive him all his sins:
"O my true Father,   O Thou who never lied,
Thou who delivered   Lazarus from the grave,   115
Who rescued Daniel   out of the lions' den,
Keep now my soul   from every peril safe,
Forgive the sins   that I have done in life."
Roland's right glove   he offers now to God.
Saint Gabriel comes   and takes it from his hand.   120
His head sinks down   to rest upon his arm;
Hands clasped in prayer,   Roland has met his end.
God sends from heaven   the angel Cherubin,
Holy Saint Michael   who saves us from the sea,
And with these two   the angel Gabriel flies.   125
Count Roland's soul   they bring to Paradise.

MARCABRU (fl. 1129–1150)
France

Marcabru was one of the earliest troubadours, the poet-musicians of Provence in the eleventh, twelfth, and thirteenth centuries, and one of the most inventive in language, form, and imagery. He wrote in Provençal, the language of medieval southern France. Though he did not compose love songs, he attacked the circumstances that fostered the deterioration of the ideals represented in such songs. He denounces the immorality of the courtly class, the lost sense of its mission, the false, seductive, language of its entertainments. In his prophetic stance he used rough words and striking images whose vernacular immediacy and rich allusiveness often make them hard to understand today. But there is considerable variety in his work, and other songs of his assume the voice of a degenerate high-born character—the kind he elsewhere excoriates—who unwittingly condemns himself. In still other songs, such as "By the Fountain in the Orchard," Marcabru sets a dialogue going that draws its significance from the situation of the two speakers: both characters are outside the walls of the court; the woman is alone in the open, the man sees a sexual conquest, both are free of the policing presence of society. This situation tests the class quality and the ethical integrity of the two characters, and, as is usual in Marcabru, the woman emerges with the dignity appropriate to her station, while the man is exposed and defeated. This song dramatizes the conception of passionate love fostered by the troubadours and adopted in lyrics and romances in succeeding generations in European literature: human love is true and sanctionable when it accords with social order and Providential design; otherwise it is false, bitter, lustful, and destructive. This is a dialogue between the voices of true and false love. The differences in the language of the two speakers, their misunderstandings, their mutually incomprehensible desires reveal the ethical status of each one. Observing how they talk past each other, we can make out the courtly ideals promoted by the early vernacular lyric. We can sense, too, in the young woman's situation and in her lament and longing, the spirit of the time during the Crusades.

By the Fountain in the Orchard

I

By the fountain in the orchard,
where the grass is green along the sandy banks,
under the shade of a planted tree,
beset among white flowers
and the ancient song of the new season,   5
I found her alone, without companion,
this girl who wants no pleasure with me.

Translated by Frederick Goldin.

II

She was a young girl, the body on her beautiful,
the daughter of a castle lord.
And just as I ventured the thought that the birds   10
must be filling her with joy, and all the green,
and this sweet new season, this spring,
and she would gladly hear my patter—
just then the look and manner of her changed.

III

Her eyes welled up with tears beside the fountain,   15
she sighed from the depths of her heart.
"Jesus," she said, "King of the world,
because of You my great grief increases,
the shame done unto You now brings me down,
for the best of all this world   20
are going off to serve You, such is Your pleasure.

IV

"Away with You goes my beloved,
my handsome, gentle, valiant, noble friend;
no part of him stays here with me but the great distress,
the constant desire, and the tears.   25
Ai! cursed be King Louis,[1]
who gave the orders and preached the sermons
that brought on grief invading my heart."

V

When I heard how the spirit in her was gone,
I came up to her along the clear stream.   30
"O beautiful," I said, "with too much weeping
the face grows pale, the color fades.
You have no reason to despair, now,
for He Who makes the woods burst into leaf
can give you all the joy you need."   35

VI

"Lord," she said, "I do believe
that God may pity me

---

1. Louis VII, king of France, was a leader of
   the Second Crusade in 1147.

in the world to come, time without end,
like many another sinner.
But in this world He wrests from me the only one   40
who made my joy grow great; who cares but little for me,
for he has gone so far away."

BERNART DE VENTADORN

(fl. 1150–1180)
France

This is one of the most famous and most widely praised lyrics of the troubadours, the poet-musicians of southern France, in part because of the entrancing image in the first strophe. All we know of its author is that he was a commoner. This song is a *canso,* a song of several strophes (usually five to seven), often concluding (as here) with an envoi or *tornada.* The *canso* was devoted exclusively to the theme of *fin' amors,* or "courtly love." Such love was befitting a person of the court, and it distinguished that individual from those lacking the refinement and self-discipline of the courtly class. The object of this love never appears in the *canso;* she is present only in the lover's praise and complaints. In his praise he depicts her as ideally beautiful, a radiant figure in whom the distinguishing virtues of courtliness are fully realized; in his complaints he curses the obstacles that keep him at a distance, and reproaches her for her imperiousness and lack of concern. For at the heart of courtly love is a strange erotic paradox: this long-enduring love reveals and perfects the lover's courtly quality *as long as distance separates him from the beloved;* she may respond to his courtship and his song but always across an ineradicable distance and always leaving his longing and uncertainty intact. Though courtly love was strictly a literary theme, a fiction in which the noble audience could behold its high-minded image and justify its privileged position, the troubadours depicted the lover's joy and suffering as actual experiences. They analyzed the consequences of the courtly love relation—the enhanced refinement, the tested loyalty, the celebration of courtly worth, the perpetual tension, the moral uncertainty, the dangers of disillusionment—through a series of subsidiary themes, many of which are powerfully realized in this song.

When I See the Lark Moving

I

When I see the lark moving
its wings in joy against the light,

Translated by Frederick Goldin.

rising up into forgetfulness, letting go, and falling
for the sweetness that comes to its heart,
ai! such envy then comes over me
of everyone I see rejoicing,
it makes me wonder that my heart
at once does not melt with desire.

II

I, weary, how much I thought I knew
about love, and how little I know,
because I cannot keep myself from loving
her from whom I shall get no favor.
She has it all: she bore off my heart, and me,
and herself, and the whole world.
And when she took herself away from me, she left me nothing
but desire and a heart still wanting.

III

I have no longer had the power of myself,
I have not been my own man, from that moment
when she let me look into her eyes,
into a mirror that gives me pleasure, even now.
Mirror, since I beheld myself in you,
the sighs from my depths have slain me,
and I am lost to myself, as he was lost—
the fair Narcissus in the fountain.

IV

I give up all hope in fair ladies,
I shall not put my faith in them again.
As much as I used to exalt them,
now I shall abandon them.
For I do not see a single one who stands by me
against her who destroys me and brings me down.
I shall fear and distrust them all,
for they are all alike, I know it well.

V

This is how she shows herself a woman indeed,
my lady, and I reproach her for it:
she does not want what one ought to want,
and that which one forbids her to do, she does.

I have fallen in evil grace,
I have acted like the madman on the bridge,
and why this happens to me I do not know,
except that I climbed too high on the mountain.   40

VI

Kindness, in truth, is lost,
and I never knew it till now;
for she who ought to have it most
has none, and where shall I seek it?
Ah, to look at her it does not seem   45
that she would let this man, miserable with desire,
who can know no health without her,
die, and never come to his aid.

VII

Since these things do not avail me with my lady:
prayer, pity, the rights I have;   50
and since it brings her no pleasure
that I love her, I shall not tell her again.
Thus I part from her, I renounce my service and song.
She has given me death, and I will answer her with death,
and I go away, since she does not retain me,   55
a broken man, in exile, I know not where.

VIII

Tristan, you shall have nothing more from me,
for I go away, a broken man, I know not where.
I forsake all song, I renounce it,
and far from joy and love shall hide myself away.   60

MARIE DE FRANCE (fl. 1160–1190)
France

We do not know the exact identity of the French medieval poet, Marie de France, although some have suggested she was a half-sister of Henry II of England. She probably wrote for the French-speaking English court. Besides her *Lais,* she wrote a collection of beast fables, based on Aesop (*Isopet* or *Little Aesop.*)

The *lai* is a short verse narrative poem related to the romance in setting and theme and composed for the same sort of audience. In the prologue to the *Lais,* Marie de France begins with a standard remark about the duty to share the knowledge one has, but then she suggests a deeper meaning in her work. She might have translated some of her material from Latin to French, as many of her contemporaries did, thereby establishing her scholarly credentials; but, she chose to put these tales into verse. In her twelve *lais,* Marie deals with love in a variety of forms and human relations: love between husband and wife, between adulterous lovers, between young lovers, between a possessive father and his daughter; self-indulgent love and self-sacrificing love; sterile love and fertile love; enduring devotion and brief flirtation.

In "Yonec" she describes a love that is willed by the imagination of a young woman trapped in marriage with an old and jealous husband who imprisons her in a tower. A knight comes to her as a bird and visits her whenever she wants him, until the husband, alerted by the joy she cannot conceal, sets a trap that fatally wounds the lover. The woman is empowered by this treachery to leap from the tower and follow her lover to his land, where he gives her a ring to make her husband forget what has happened and a sword for the son she will have, who will eventually avenge his father when he visits his tomb with his mother and his stepfather.

In the *Fables* Marie tells old and new stories and derives morals from them, frequently using them to make a point about social responsibility, which seems to take direct aim at members of her audience, as we see in "The Wolf and the Lamb."

from Lais

Prologue

Whoever has received knowledge
and eloquence in speech from God
should not be silent or secretive
but demonstrate it willingly.
When a great good is widely heard of,   5
then, and only then, does it bloom,
and when that good is praised by many,
it has spread its blossoms.
The custom among the ancients—
as Priscian testifies—   10
was to speak quite obscurely
in the books they wrote,
so that those who were to come after
and study them
might gloss the letter   15
and supply its significance from their own wisdom.
Philosophers knew this,
they understood among themselves

Translated by Robert Hanning and Joan Ferrante.

that the more time they spent,
the more subtle their minds would become   20
and the better they would know how to keep themselves
from whatever was to be avoided.
He who would guard himself from vice
should study and understand
and begin a weighty work   25
by which he might keep vice at a distance,
and free himself from great sorrow.
That's why I began to think
about composing some good stories
and translating from Latin to Romance;   30
but that was not to bring me fame:
too many others have done it.
Then I thought of the *lais* I'd heard.
I did not doubt, indeed I knew well,
that those who first began them   35
and sent them forth
composed them in order to preserve
adventures they had heard.
I have heard many told;
and I don't want to neglect or forget them.   40
To put them into word and rhyme
I've often stayed awake.

Yonec

The lady lived in great sorrow,
with tears and sighs and weeping;
she lost her beauty,
as one does who cares nothing for it.
She would have preferred   5
death to take her quickly.

It was the beginning of April
when the birds begin their songs.
The lord arose in the morning
and made ready to go to the woods.   10
He had the old woman get up
and close the door behind him—
she followed his command.
The lord went off with his men.
The old woman carried a psalter   15
from which she intended to read the psalms.
The lady, awake and in tears,
saw the light of the sun.

She noticed that the old woman
had left the chamber.
She grieved and sighed
and wept and raged:
"I should never have been born!
My fate is very harsh.
I'm imprisoned in this tower
and I'll never leave it unless I die.
What is this jealous old man afraid of
that he keeps me so imprisoned?
He's mad, out of his senses;
always afraid of being deceived.
I can't even go to church
or hear God's service.
If I could speak to people
and enjoy myself with them
I'd be very gracious to my lord
even if I didn't want to be.
A curse on my family,
and on all the others
who gave me to this jealous man,
who married me to his body.
It's a rough rope that I pull and draw.
He'll never die—
when he should have been baptized
he was plunged instead in the river of hell;
his sinews are hard, his veins are hard,
filled with living blood.
I've often heard
that one could once find
adventures in this land
that brought relief to the unhappy.
Knights might find young girls
to their desire, noble and lovely;
and ladies find lovers
so handsome, courtly, brave, and valiant
that they could not be blamed,
and no one else would see them.
If that might be or ever was,
if that has ever happened to anyone,
God, who has power over everything,
grant me my wish in this."
When she'd finished her lament,
she saw, through a narrow window,
the shadow of a great bird.
She didn't know what it was.

It flew into the chamber;
its feet were banded; it looked like a hawk
of five or six moultings.
It alighted before the lady.
When it had been there awhile
and she'd stared hard at it,
it became a handsome and noble knight.
The lady was astonished;
her blood went cold, she trembled,
she was frightened—she covered her head.
The knight was very courteous,
he spoke first:
"Lady," he said, "don't be afraid.
The hawk is a noble bird,
although its secrets are unknown to you.
Be reassured
and accept me as your love.
That," he said, "is why I came here.
I have loved you for a long time,
I've desired you in my heart.
Never have I loved any woman but you
nor shall I ever love another,
yet I couldn't have come to you
or left my own land
had you not asked for me.
But now I can be your love."
The lady was reassured;
she uncovered her head and spoke.
She answered the knight,
saying she would take him as her lover
if he believed in God,
and if their love was really possible.
For he was of great beauty.
Never in her life
had she seen so handsome a knight—
nor would she ever.
"My lady," he said, "you are right.
I wouldn't want you to feel
guilt because of me,
or doubt or suspicion.
I do believe in the creator
who freed us from the grief
that Adam, our father, led us into
when he bit into the bitter apple.
He is, will be, and always was
the life and light of sinners.

65

70

75

80

85

90

95

100

105

110

[handwritten margin note:] She wants him to be a true believer

With that the knight departed,
leaving his love in great joy.
In the morning she rose restored;
she was happy all week.
Her body had now become precious to her,   115
she completely recovered her beauty.
Now she would rather remain here
than look for pleasure elsewhere.
She wanted to see her love all the time
and enjoy herself with him.   120
As soon as her lord departed,
night or day, early or late,
she had him all to her pleasure.
God, let their joy endure!
Because of the great joy she felt,   125
because she could see her love so often,
her whole appearance changed.
But her lord was clever.
In his heart he sensed
that she was not what she had been.   130
He suspected his sister.
He questioned her one day,
saying he was astonished
that the lady now dressed with care.
He asked her what it meant.   135
The old woman said she didn't know—
no one could have spoken to her,
she had no lover or friend—
it was only that she was now more willing
to be alone than before.   140
His sister, too, had noticed the change.
Her lord answered:
"By my faith," he said, "I think that's so.
But you must do something for me.
In the morning, when I've gotten up   145
and you have shut the doors,
pretend you are going out
and leave her lying there alone.
Then hide yourself in a safe place,
watch her and find out   150
what it is, and where it comes from,
that gives her such great joy."
With that plan they separated.
Alas, how hard it is to protect yourself

from someone who wants to trap you,
to betray and deceive you!

He left in great sorrow.
She followed him with loud cries.
She leapt out a window—
it's a wonder that she wasn't killed,
for it was at least twenty feet high
where she made her leap,
naked beneath her gown.
She followed the traces of blood
that flowed from the knight
onto the road.
She followed that road and kept to it
until she came to a hill.
In the hill there was an opening,
red with his blood.
She couldn't see anything beyond it
but she was sure
that her love had gone in there.
She entered quickly.
She found no light
but she kept to the right road
until it emerged from the hill
into a beautiful meadow.
When she found the grass there wet with blood,
she was frightened.
She followed the traces through the meadow
and saw a city not far away.
The city was completely surrounded by walls.
There was no house, no hall or tower,
that didn't seem entirely of silver.
The buildings were very rich.
Going toward the town there were marshes,
forests, and enclosed fields.
On the other side, toward the castle,
a steam flowed all around,
where ships arrived—
there were more than three hundred sails.
The lower gate was open;
the lady entered the city,
still following the fresh blood
through the town to the castle.
No one spoke to her,
she met neither man nor woman.

When she came to the palace courtyard,
she found it covered with blood.   200
She entered a lovely chamber
where she found a knight sleeping.
She did not know him, so she went on
into another larger chamber.
There she found nothing but a bed   205
with a knight sleeping on it;
she kept going.
She entered the third chamber
and on that bed she found her love.

. . .

On their way, they passed the chapter house,   210
where they found a huge tomb
covered with a cloth of embroidered silk,
a band of precious gold running from one side to the other.
At the head, the feet, and at the sides
burned twenty candles.   215
The chandeliers were pure gold,
the censers amethyst,
which through the day perfumed
that tomb, to its great honor.
They asked and inquired   220
of people from that land
whose tomb it was,
what man lay there.
The people began to weep
and, weeping, to recount   225
that it was the best knight
the strongest, the most fierce,
the most handsome and the best loved,
that had ever lived.
"He was king of this land;   230
no one was ever so courtly.
At Caerwent he was discovered
and killed for the love of a lady.
Since then we have had no lord,
but have waited many days,   235
just as he told and commanded us,
for the son the lady bore him."
When the lady heard that news,
she called aloud to her son.
"Fair son," she said, "you hear   240
how God has led us to this spot.
Your father, whom this old man murdered,
lies here in this tomb.

Now I give and commend his sword to you.
I have kept it a long time for you."
Then she revealed, for all to hear,
that the man in the tomb was the father and this was his son,   245
and how he used to come to her,
how her lord had betrayed him—
she told the truth.
Then she fainted over the tomb   250
and, in her faint, she died.
She never spoke again.
When her son saw that she had died,
he cut off his stepfather's head.   255
Thus with his father's sword
he avenged his mother's sorrow.
When all this had happened,
when it became known through the city,
they took the lady with great honor   260
and placed her in the coffin.
Before they departed
they made Yonec their lord.

Long after, those who heard this adventure
composed a lay about it,   265
about the pain and the grief
that they suffered for love.

from *The Fables*

The Wolf and the Lamb

This tells of wolf and lamb who drank
Together once along a bank.
The wolf right at the spring was staying
While lambkin down the stream was straying.
The wolf then spoke up nastily,   5
For argumentative was he,
Saying to lamb, with great disdain,
"You give me such a royal pain!"
The lamb made this reply to him,
"Pray sir, what's wrong?"—"Are your eyes dim!   10
You've so stirred up the water here,
I cannot drink my fill, I fear,
I do believe I should be first,
Because I've come here dying of thirst."

Translated by Harriet Spiegel.

The little lamb then said to him,   15
"But sir, 'twas you who drank upstream.
My water comes from you, you see."
"What!" snapped the wolf. "You dare curse me?"
"Sir, I had no intention to!"
The wolf replied, "I know what's true.   20
Your father treated me just so
Here at this spring some time ago—
It's now six months since we were here."
"So why blame me for that affair?
I wasn't even born, I guess."   25
"So what?" the wolf responded next;
"You really are perverse today—
You're not supposed to act this way."
The wolf then grabbed the lamb so small,
Chomped through his neck, extinguished all.   30
    And this is what our great lords do,
The viscounts and the judges too,
With all the people whom they rule:
False charge they make from greed so cruel.
To cause confusion they consort   35
And often summon folk to court.
They strip them clean of flesh and skin,
As the wolf did to the lambkin.

CHRÉTIEN DE TROYES (fl. 1170–1190)
France

Chrétien de Troyes, a French poet who spent some time at the court of Marie de Champagne and Phillip of Flanders, was the author of some of the earliest Arthurian romances. Although fighting is still a main element of the plot in his romances, new values of public service have replaced the old ones of honor and revenge. Knights are expected to fight for justice and to defend the weak and oppressed, not simply to increase their own glory. The most successful knights in this world are inspired by their love for a woman, but that love is supposed to inspire them to serve society, not to interfere with their service. In *The Knight with the Lion,* however, the hero, Yvain, is so obsessed with winning honor by fighting that he leaves his wife and his responsibilities to defend her land and goes off on unspecified adventures with Gawain. When he does not return within the allotted time, she sends a messenger to denounce and reject him. He goes mad and must work his way back to sanity and to his wife by a series of battles in defense of women who are endangered or exploited or abused. The most striking is presented in "The Weaving Maidens," which describes women working in a silk factory, a medieval sweatshop, with conditions that may have parallels with those of the cloth manufacturers of northern France. Certainly Chrétien seems to be making a comment on the indifference of his audience to the women's plight, when he shows the noble family who live in the same castle. They presumably benefit from the work done there but seem oblivious to the workers' suffering as they sit in a garden listening to their daughter read a romance.

Yvain's companion in his adventures is not a fellow knight—indeed, Gawain is not available even for those adventures that should have been his responsibility—but a lion, whom the knight had rescued. In "The Devotion of a Lion," the animal shows extraordinary gratitude and devotion, to the point of attempting suicide when he thinks Yvain is dead.

from *The Knight with the Lion*

[The Devotion of a Lion]

When he reached a clearing, he saw a lion and a serpent, which was holding the lion by the tail and scorching his haunches with burning fire. Sir Yvain spent little time looking at this strange sight. When he considered which of the two he would help, he decided to go to aid the lion, because a serpent with its venom and treachery deserved nothing but harm. The serpent was venomous, and fire was darting from its mouth, so full of evil was the creature.

Intending first to kill the serpent, Sir Yvain drew his sword and advanced. He held his shield before his face as a protection against the flames gushing from the serpent's throat, which was more gaping than a pot. If the lion attacked him later, there would be a fight; yet whatever happened after, he still wished to aid the lion. Pity urged him and pleaded that he help and support the noble and honorable beast.

With his keen-cutting sword he attacked the evil serpent, pinning it to the ground and slicing it in two. He then struck it again and again until he had cut and hacked it to pieces. But he had to sever a piece of the lion's tail because the head of the wretched serpent still gripped the tail. He cut off as little as necessary; in fact, he could not have removed less. When he had freed the lion, he expected that the lion would spring at him and he would have to fight, but to the lion such an idea never occurred. Hear what the lion did. In a manner befitting the worthy and nobly born, he began to show that he was surrendering. He stood on his hind legs, stretched out his forepaws together to the knight, and bowed his head to the ground. Then he knelt down, his whole face wet with tears of humility. For certain Sir Yvain realized that the lion was thanking him and humbling himself before him, since he had delivered him from death by killing the serpent. This adventure delighted Yvain. He cleaned the serpent's venomous filth from his sword, which he then placed back in its scabbard. Then he resumed his journey. The lion

Translated by David Staines.

walked close beside him, never to leave him, but to accompany him always to serve and to protect him.

The lion went ahead on the road. Because he was in front, he caught in the wind the scent of wild beasts grazing. Hunger and his natural instinct urged him to go hunting prey for his own food. This was the way Nature intended him to act. He set out on the trail a little until he had shown his master that he had sniffed out and taken up the scent of a wild animal. He then stopped and looked at him, for he sought to please him and had no intention of acting against his will. By such behavior, Yvain realized that the lion was showing him that he awaited his direction. He understood and knew that if he held back, the lion would hold back, and if he followed him, the lion would catch the game he had scented.

. . .

Alas, Sir Yvain almost lost sense when this time he neared the spring and the stone and the chapel.[1] A thousand times he called himself wretched and miserable. He was so distraught that he fell in a faint; his sharp sword dropped from its scabbard and the point pierced through the meshes of his hauberk close to the neck below the cheek. There is no mail that does not break open, and the sword cut the skin of the neck beneath the gleaming mail and made his blood spill. The sight convinced the lion that his master and companion was dead. Greater than ever before was the anger he experienced, as the display of his grief commenced. Never have I heard told or described such grief. He threw himself about, clawing himself and screaming. He wanted to kill himself with the sword he thought had killed his good master. With his teeth he grabbed the sword from him, laid it on a fallen tree, and steadied it on a trunk behind, fearing it might slip when he hurled his breast against it. He had almost accomplished his desire when Yvain recovered from his swoon. The lion had been rushing at death like a wild boar, careless of where he impaled himself. Now, however, he took restraint.

[The Weaving Maidens]

Pressured and provoked into coming up by the porter's rude insolence, Sir Yvain went straight past him without saying a word and came upon a great high hall that was recently built. In front of it was a courtyard enclosed by large, round, pointed stakes, between which he saw as many as three hundred maidens inside, engaged in different kinds of embroidery, sewing threads of gold and silk as best they could. They were so poor that many had nothing on their heads and no belts around their waists. Their jackets were torn at the breasts and elbows; the shifts on their backs were soiled. From hunger and pain their faces were

---

1. The spring, the stone, and the chapel are the setting of Yvain's first adventure, in which he fatally wounded the knight defending the spring. Pursuing the knight to his castle, Yvain was trapped there, fell in love with his widow, and married her, thereby accepting responsibility to defend the spring. When he sees it again, he is reminded of his wife, his neglect of her, and her rejection of him.

pale, their necks thin. They all noticed him looking at them, and bowed their heads and wept. For a long time they remained there without the will to do anything. Wretched as they were, they were unable to raise their eyes from the ground.

When Sir Yvain had watched them a while, he turned and rode back to the gate. The porter barred the way. "It is no use, dear master, you will not go away now," he yelled at him. "You will want to be outside now, but wanting that, I swear, avails you not. Before you leave, you will have suffered so much shame that you will be unable to bear more. It was unwise of you to enter here, for there is no escape."

"Dear brother, I have no wish to escape," he replied. "But tell me, on your father's soul, the young ladies I have seen in this castle weaving cloths of silk and gold embroidery, whence have they come? I am delighted by their work. But I am disturbed by their thin bodies and the sad expressions on their pale faces. I believe they would be beautiful and charming if they had what pleased them."

"I shall say nothing to you," he replied. "Find someone else to tell you."

"So I will, since there's nothing more to do."

Yvain searched until he found the entrance to the courtyard where the young ladies were working. He stood before them all and greeted them together. He saw the teardrops running from their eyes and falling as they wept. "May it be God's pleasure to take this sorrow from your hearts and turn it to joy," he said to them. "I do not know the cause of your sorrow."

"God hear your call!" one answered. "You shall know who we are and from what land. I suppose that is what you wish to ask."

"Yes, that is why I came here," he said.

"Sir, a long time ago it happened that the King of the Isle of Maidens was traveling through many courts and countries in search of news. He continued traveling, like a born fool, until he fell into this peril. It was an evil hour when he arrived here. We prisoners undeservedly suffer the misery and disgrace of it. You can be certain such awful shame will be yours too unless they agree to accept ransom for you.

"In any case, it happened that our lord came to this castle, which is the home of two sons of the devil. Do not think this an idle tale, for they are the offspring of a woman and a demon. They were to fight the king, who was exceedingly alarmed. He was not yet eighteen years old, and they would have cut him in half as though he were a gentle lamb. The king was terrified, and escaped as best he could, swearing to send here every year, as long as he lived, thirty maidens from his kingdom. This tribute brought about his release. And it was settled by oath that the tribute should last as long as the two demons were alive. On the day they were overcome and defeated in combat, he would be released from this duty, and we, who are subjected to painful lives of misery and disgrace, would be set free. We shall never have anything to please us. Now I chatter like a child in referring to being set free. We shall never leave here.

"Always we shall weave cloths of silk. Never shall we be better dressed. Always we shall be poor and naked, and always suffer hunger and thirst. Never shall we be able to earn enough to have better food. We have hardly any bread, a little in the morning and less in the evening. Never, for her handiwork, will any maiden earn more than four deniers[2] from the pound to live on, and that cannot give us enough clothing and food. Those who earn twenty sous[3] a week are still not without burden. The truth, be certain, is that every one of us does at least twenty sous' worth of work or more. That amount would make a duke wealthy. We are destitute, and our employer becomes rich from our earnings. We lie awake most of the night, and work all day to earn our living, for he threatens us with bodily harm when we rest. So we dare not rest. But why talk more? We have so much misery and disgrace that I cannot tell you the fifth of it. Still we are often furious and enraged at the sight of young and worthy knights dying in combat against the two demons; they pay much for their accommodation, as you will tomorrow. Whether you wish to or not, tomorrow you will have to fight entirely on your own and lose your reputation against two devils incarnate."

"May God, the true King of Heaven, protect me and give you honor and joy, if it be His will," Sir Yvain answered, "Now I must go and see the people inside and learn how they will receive me."

"Go now, sir. The Giver of All Goodness save you."

He then went away and entered the hall, where he found no one, good or evil, who would speak to them of anything.

Sir Yvain, the maiden, and the lion passed through the house and went out into a garden. They did not discuss or even mention stabling their horses, but it did not matter; those who expected to have the horses had done the stabling. I do not know if they were wise in their expectations, for in the end the knight will have a horse that is all rested. The horses had oats and hay and straw up to their bellies.

Sir Yvain entered the garden with his party following him. He saw a noble man reclining on his side on a silk rug. In front of him a maiden was reading from a romance—I do not know about whom. A lady had come to recline there and hear the romance. She was the maiden's mother, and the lord was her father. They enjoyed watching and listening to her very much, for they had no other children. Not more than sixteen, she was so beautiful and charming that the god of Love, had he seen her, would have become her servant and caused her never to love anyone but him. To be her servant, he would have set aside his divinity and taken on human form. He would have struck his own body with the arrow whose wound never heals unless an untrue physician tends it. It is wrong for anyone to recover unless treachery is discovered there, and anyone healed another way is not a true lover. If the story pleased you, I could go on telling you of these wounds until I reached some ending. But soon there would be someone who would say I was telling you of a dream. People today do not fall in love or love as they used to. They do not even have the desire to hear talk of love.

---

2. The *denier* is a penny, a twelfth of a *sou*.
3. The *sou* is the equivalent of an English shilling,

a twentieth of a pound, a little more than a dime.

WALTHER VON DER VOGELWEIDE

(c. 1170–1230)

Germany

Walther von der Vogelweide created a greater variety of lyrical forms, and treated a greater range of poetic themes, than any other *Minnesinger*. During the Civil War in Germany, he supported first one side, then the other, and finally turned to Frederick II, the grandson of Barbarossa, who gave him a house with the fireside he had always longed for. His love songs differ from others in their emphasis on reciprocity: he depicts *Minne*—courtly love—as a bond between equals and in some lyrics challenges traditional representations of love by imagining a simpler, more direct relation. He composed the first sustained and specifically pointed political songs of the German Middle Ages. He represents the singer—that is, himself—as the creator and guarantor of the renown of those he serves: of his lady in the (fictional) love songs, of his noble patron in the political and didactic songs. The inventiveness and boldness of his thought, the continual assertion of his performer's pride, the brilliant structure of his strophes, the immediacy of his needy presence (he continually proclaims both his unsurpassed merit and his undeserved indigence), the beauty and directness of his language—the combination of all these traits is unique, and he is generally considered the greatest German lyric poet of the Middle Ages.

The lyric presented here has come to be known as Walther's "elegy," largely because of the painful awakening depicted in the first two strophes. But these bitter complaints, which sound so personal, are meant to exemplify the inability of human beings to save themselves, and of any society to endure on its own strength without corruption. The song then brings forth its triumphant theme, the Crusade. The horrified awakening can be the beginning of a new life, of redemption in service of God; the knight's profession can be the way to his salvation, sanctified forever in the voyage across the sea.

Alas, Where Have They Vanished

I

Alas, where have they vanished, all my years!
Have I dreamed my life, or is it real?
That which I thought was something, *was* it something?
Then I have long been sleeping and do not know it.
Now I have awakened, and everything seems strange   5
that used to be familiar as this hand of mine.
The people and the land where from a child I was raised—

Translated by Frederick Goldin.

have all turned strange to me, as though it were all lies.
The children that I played with now are old and slow.
The field is cultivated, all the woods cut down.   10
If the water did not flow still as it used to flow,
in truth I would consider my misfortune great.
Many are slow to greet me who knew me once quite well.
The world is everywhere full of the loss of grace.
When I think back on many and many a glorious day   15
all fallen from me like a blow struck on the water, then
evermore, alas.

II

Alas, how poorly these young people present themselves today,
whose spirits soared rejoicing, once, in times gone by.
They know only worries, ach, how can they live that way?   20
Wherever in this world I turn, no one is content,
dancing, laughing, singing pass on into care.
No Christian man has ever seen a year so wretched.
Look at the ladies, how they dress their hair,
and our knights, so splendid, clothed in peasant dress.   25
Now here are these cruel letters come to us from Rome:[1]
we are authorized to suffer, we are despoiled of joy.
It offends me deeply—we used to live well in this land—
that I must trade away my laughter, that I must choose to weep.
The birds in the wild forests are cast down by our lament: 30
then what wonder is it if I come to despair?
Ach, fool, what am I saying in my worthless rage?
Who chases after pleasures *here* has lost them *there,*
evermore, alas.

III

Alas, how we are poisoned with things that taste so sweet.   35
I see amidst the honey the bitter gall afloat.
Outside the world is fair—white, green, and red,
and inside black, black the darkness of death.
Let him whom the world has misled now look upon his hope:
he is, with such soft penance, set free from mighty sin.   40
You who are knights, reflect on this, it is for you.

---

1. The excommunication of Frederick II, the
   Holy Roman Emperor, by Pope Gregory IX,
   in 1227.

You bear the brilliant helms, the meshes of hard rings,
the strong shields, the consecrated swords.
Would God that I were worthy of that victory!
Then I, a needy man, would win great wages,   45
but I do not mean vast acres or the gold of kings.
Salvation's crown of ages I myself would wear,
that a soldier fighting for pay could win with his spear.[2]
Could I make that beloved voyage across the sea,
then I would sing rejoicing, and nevermore "alas,"   50
nevermore "alas."

GACE BRULÉ (fl. 1180–1212)
France

The *trouvères* of northern France also took up the themes and ideas of the
troubadours. Among the most celebrated of the singers of France was Gace Brulé,
a knight of Champagne, who knew the songs of the troubadours well and was
especially influenced by Bernart de Ventadorn, to whose lyrics he alludes
explicitly. The lyric presented here is a skillfully wrought fabric of courtly
themes. The songs of the birds heard in Brittany remind him of his native land,
Champagne, where he first heard them; the mood of remembrance and
contemplation evokes the image of his beloved. The succeeding strophes
continue this intricate and unending alternation of distant memory and live
experience: the central event of the past, the kiss, continues to take place in the
lonely present: his lips still feel it; the lingering feeling of the kiss is the cause of
his torment, which recalls the joy of its first occurrence. The inaccessibility of the
beloved, the crazed look of the lover, the competition of the false lovers who win
the favor denied to the true one—these too are traditional themes; here their
expressive power is renewed through the pattern of the song.

The Little Birds of My Homeland

I

The little birds of my homeland
I have heard here in Brittany.
By their song I realize

Translated by Frederick Goldin.

---

2. A possible reference to Longinus, a Roman
soldier who, according to legend, was converted at the foot of the Cross at the Crucifixion.

I heard them, once,
in sweet Champagne,
if I am not mistaken.   5
They've put me into such a pleasant study,
I have started out on this new song,
so that I may attain
what Love has now for so long promised me.   10

II

By long waiting I am discomfited,
and speak not one word of complaint.
That takes away my joy in song, my laughter,
for no one whom Love rules and torments
can think of anything else.   15
My body and my face
I find so many times beset,
that I have taken on a madman's look:
whatever others may transgress in love,
I never did her any other wrong.   20

III

On a kiss my sweet gentle lady
stole away my heart.
How mad of my heart to quit me
for her who torments me.
Alas! I never felt it   25
when it went from me.
She ravished it away so gently,
drew it to her on a sigh.
She fills my mad heart with desire,
but will never feel pity for me.   30

IV

That kiss I remember well,
so well that in my mind
not an hour passes but on my lips
I feel what has betrayed me.
When she allowed,   35
Lord God! what I am telling of,
why did she not warn me of my death!
She is aware that I am dying

of the pain of this long waiting,
wherefor my face loses color, has grown pale.   40

V

Thus she bears away my laughter and play
and causes me to die of longing.
Love makes me pay dearly again
and again for her company.
Alas, I dare not go to her: 45
the false lovers get me condemned there
for the madman's look on me.
Seeing them ply their words with her, I am undone,
for not one of them can find
the smallest treachery in her.   50

GOTTFRIED VON STRASSBURG

(fl. 1210)

Germany

This great German Romantic poet was probably well read in Latin and in French.
He had a gift for language and an affinity for classical poetry, mythology, and
music. Basing his German version of the popular story of the doomed lovers
Tristan and Isolde on the Anglo-Norman text by the poet Thomas, with its echoes
of Abelard and Heloise (the gifted pair of intellectuals who fell in love over their
studies) Gottfried raises the love to an almost mystic level. He uses religious
language to describe it in the prologue, calling their story a kind of eucharist
("bread") to all noble hearts, treating the love potion as a symbol of the bond
between them that makes one being of the two, and describing the cave in which
they spend their exile as an allegorical shrine of ideal love, where they need no
food or company but subsist on love, on mutual desire and on the literature and
music they share. Unfortunately, they also have to exist in the real world, in
which Isolde is married to Tristan's uncle, King Mark. Eventually Mark's jealousy
of Isolde, despite his love for Tristan, forces Tristan to leave court.

In other versions the lovers meet again before they die, but we do not know
if Gottfried would have included those episodes, had he finished the poem, or
whether he deliberately left their fate suspended because he was uncomfortable
with Thomas's ending. Either way, his audience would have known that the
lovers could not be truly united except in death.

from *Tristan*

from the *Prologue [The Sorrow and Joy of Love]*

He that never had sorrow of love never had joy of it either! In love, joy and sorrow ever went hand in hand! With them we must win praise and honour or come to nothing without them! If the two of whom this love-story tells had not endured sorrow for the sake of joy, love's pain for its ecstasy within one heart, their name and history would never have brought such rapture to so many noble spirits! Today we still love to hear of their tender devotion, sweet and ever fresh, their joy, their sorrow, their anguish, and their ecstasy. And although they are long dead, their sweet name lives on and their death will endure for ever to the profit of well-bred people, giving loyalty to those who seek loyalty, honour to those who seek honour. For us who are alive their death must live on and be for ever new. For wherever still today one hears the recital of their devotion, their perfect loyalty, their hearts' joy, their hearts' sorrow—

This is bread to all noble hearts. With this their death lives on. We read their life, we read their death, and to us it is sweet as bread.

Their life, their death are our bread. Thus lives their life, thus lives their death. Thus they live still and yet are dead, and their death is the bread of the living.

And whoever now desires to be told of their life, their death, their joy, their sorrow, let him lend me his heart and ears—he shall find all that he desires!

[Enduring Sorrow for the Sake of Joy]

Now when the maid and the man, Isolde and Tristan, had drunk the draught, in an instant that arch-disturber of tranquility was there, Love, waylayer of all hearts, and she had stolen in! Before they were aware of it she had planted her victorious standard there and bowed them beneath her yoke. They who were two and divided now became one and united. No longer were they at variance. Isolde's hatred was gone. Love, the reconciler, had purged their hearts of enmity, and so joined them in affection that each was to the other as limpid as a mirror. They shared a single heart. Her anguish was his pain: his pain her anguish. The two were one both in joy and in sorrow, yet they hid their feelings from each other. This was from doubt and shame. She was ashamed, as he was. She went in doubt of him, as he of her. However blindly the craving in their hearts was centered on one desire, their anxiety was how to begin. This masked their desire from each other.

When Tristan felt the stirrings of love he at once remembered loyalty and honour, and strove to turn away. 'No, leave it, Tristan,' he was continually thinking to himself, 'pull yourself together, do not take any notice of it.' But his heart was impelled towards her. He was striving against his own wishes, desiring against his desire. He was drawn now in one direction, now in another. Captive that he was, he tried all that he knew in the snare, over and over again, and long maintained his efforts.

Translated by A. T. Hatto.

[The Blind Sweetness of Love]

The loyal man was afflicted by a double pain: when he looked at her face and sweet Love began to wound his heart and soul with her, he bethought himself of Honour, and it retrieved him. But this in turn was the sign for Love, his liege lady, whom his father had served before him, to assail him anew, and once more he had to submit. Honour and Loyalty harassed him powerfully, but Love harassed him more. Love tormented him to an extreme, she made him suffer more than did Honour and Loyalty combined. His heart smiled upon Isolde, but he turned his eyes away: yet his greatest grief was when he failed to see her. As is the way of captives, he fixed his mind on escape and how he might elude her, and returned many times to this thought: 'Turn one way, or another! Change this desire! Love and like elsewhere!' But the noose was always there. He took his heart and soul and searched them for some change: but there was nothing there but Love—and Isolde.

And so it fared with her. Finding this life unbearable, she, too, made ceaseless efforts. When she recognized the lime that bewitching Love had spread and saw that she was deep in it, she endeavoured to reach dry ground, she strove to be out and away. But the lime kept clinging to her and drew her back and down. The lovely woman fought back with might and main, but stuck fast at every step. She was succumbing against her will. She made desperate attempts on many sides, she twisted and turned with hands and feet and immersed them ever deeper in the blind sweetness of Love, and of the man. Her limed senses failed to discover any path, bridge, or track that would advance them half a step, half a foot, without Love being there too. Whatever Isolde thought, whatever came uppermost in her mind, there was nothing there, of one sort or another, but Love, and Tristan.

This was all below the surface, for her heart and her eyes were at variance— Modesty chased her eyes away, Love drew her heart towards him. That warring company, a Maid and a Man, Love and Modesty, brought her into great confusion; for the Maid wanted the Man, yet she turned her eyes away: Modesty wanted Love, but told no one of her wishes. But what was the good of that? A Maid and her Modesty are by common consent so fleeting a thing, so short-lived a blossoming, they do not long resist. Thus Isolde gave up her struggle and accepted her situation. Without further delay the vanquished girl resigned herself body and soul to Love and to the man.

Isolde glanced at him now and again and watched him covertly, her bright eyes and her heart were now in full accord. Secretly and lovingly her heart and eyes darted at the man rapaciously, while the man gave back her looks with tender passion. Since Love would not release him, he too began to give ground. Whenever there was a suitable occasion the man and the maid came together to feast each other's eyes. These lovers seemed to each other fairer than before—such is Love's law, such is the way with affection. It is so this year, it was so last year and it will remain so among all lovers as long as Love endures, that while their affection is growing and bringing forth blossom and increase of all loveable things, they please each other more than ever they did when it first began to burgeon. Love that bears increase makes lovers fairer than at first. This is the seed of Love, from which it never dies.

Love seems fairer than before and so Love's rule endures. Were Love to seem the same as before, Love's rule would soon wither away.

[The Nourishment of Love]

Some people are smitten with curiosity and astonishment, and plague themselves with the question how these companions, Tristan and Isolde, nourished themselves in this wasteland? I will tell them and assuage their curiosity. They looked at one another and nourished themselves with that! Their sustenance was the eye's increase. They fed in their grotto on nothing but love and desire. The two lovers who formed its court had small concern for their provender. Hidden away in their hearts they carried the best nutriment to be had anywhere in the world, which offered itself unasked ever fresh and new. I mean pure devotion, love made sweet as balm that consoles body and sense so tenderly, and sustains the heart and spirit—this was their best nourishment. Truly, they never considered any food but that from which the heart drew desire, the eyes delight, and which the body, too, found agreeable. With this they had enough. Love drove her ancient plough for them, keeping pace all the time, and gave them an abundant store of all those things that go to make heaven on earth.

Nor were they greatly troubled that they should be alone in the wilds without company. Tell me, whom did they need in there with them, and why should anyone join them? They made an even number: there were simply one and one. Had they included a third in the even pair which they made, there would have been an uneven number, and they would have been much encumbered and embarrassed by the odd one. Their company of two was so ample a crowd for this pair that good King Arthur never held a feast in any of his palaces that gave keener pleasure or delight. In no land could you have found enjoyment for which these two would have given a brass farthing to have with them in their grotto. Whatever one could imagine or conceive elsewhere in other countries to make a paradise, they had with them there. They would not have given a button for a better life, save only in respect of their honour. What more should they need? They had their court, they were amply supplied with all that goes to make for happiness. Their loyal sevitors were the green lime, the sunshine and the shade, the brook and its banks. flowers, grass, blossoms, and leaves, so soothing to the eye. The service they received was the song of the birds, of the lovely, slender nightingale, the thrush and blackbird, and other birds of the forest. Siskin and calander-lark vied in eager rivalry to see who could give the best service. These followers served their ears and sense unendingly. Their high feast was Love, who gilded all their joys; she brought them King Arthur's Round Table as homage and all its company a thousand times a day! What better food could they have for body or soul? Man was there with Woman, Woman there with Man. What else should they be needing? They had what they were meant to have, they had reached the goal of their desire.

Now some people are so tactless as to declare (though I do not accept it myself) that other food is needed for this pastime. I am not so sure that it is. There is enough here in my opinion. But if anyone has discovered better nourishment in this world let him speak in the light of his experience. There was a time when I, too, led such a life, and I thought it quite sufficient.

. . .

Those faithful denizens, Tristan and his mistress, had arranged their leisure and exertions very pleasantly in the woods and glades of their wilderness. They were always at each other's side. In the mornings they would stroll to the meadow through the dew, where it had cooled the grass and the flowers. The cool field was their recreation. They talked as they walked to and fro, and they listened as they went to the sweet singing of the birds. Then they would turn aside to where the cool spring murmured, and would hearken to its music as it slid down on its path. Where it entered the glade they used to sit and rest and listen to its purling and watch the water flow, a joy they never tired of.

But when the bright sun began to climb and the heat to descend, they withdrew to their lime-tree in quest of its gentle breezes. This afforded them pleasure within and without their breasts—the tree rejoiced both their hearts and their eyes. With its leaves the fragrant lime refreshed both air and shade for them; from its shade the breezes were gentle, fragrant, cool. The bench beneath the lime was flowers and grass, the best-painted lawn that ever lime-tree had. Our constant lovers sat there together and told love-tales of those whom love had ruined in days gone by.

When they tired of stories they slipped into their refuge and resumed their well-tried pleasure of sounding their harp, and singing sadly and sweetly. They busied their hands and their tongues in turn. They performed amorous lays and their accompaniments, varying their delight as it suited them: for if one took the harp it was for the other to sing the tune with wistful tenderness. And indeed the strains of both harp and tongue, merging their sound in each other, echoed in that cave so sweetly that it was dedicated to sweet Love for her retreat most fittingly as 'La fossiure a la gent amant'.[1]

[Tristan and Isolde Shall Forever Remain One]

If Isolde was ever united with Tristan in one heart and bond, it will always remain fresh, it will endure for ever! But I will ask one thing: to whichever corners of the earth you go, take care of yourself, my life! For when I am orphaned of you, then I, your life, will have perished. I will guard myself, your life, with jealous care, not for my sake but yours, knowing that our two lives are one. We are one life and flesh. Keep your thoughts on me, your very life, your Isolde. Let me see my life again, in you, as soon as ever possible; and may you see yours in me! The life we share is in your keeping. Now come here and kiss me. You and I, Tristan and Isolde, shall for ever remain one and undivided! Let this kiss be a seal upon it that I am yours, that you are mine, steadfast till death, but one Tristan and Isolde!

---

1. "The cave of lovers," which gives its title to the chapter.

WOLFRAM VON ESCHENBACH

(fl. 1200–1210)
Germany

Little is known about the author, except that he must have begun *Parzival* around 1197 or 1198. We assume, from the text, that he must have been a knight, proud though poor. He spent some time at the court of Landgrave Hermann, and may have competed in the singing contest there, the subject of the second act of Wagner's*Tannhauser*. Also working with a French source, Chrétien's *Perceval* or *The Story of the Grail,* though he denies it, Wolfram resolves the problems of loyalty and love, and their occasional clash, which had troubled Chrétien in the Arthurian world, by moving his hero into a higher world, the realm of the Grail, where he can serve God and man and his lady all at the same time. And by not making the Grail world very different from the Arthurian, except in the religious symbolism of its central ritual, seen in the last selection presented here, Wolfram manages to keep chivalric adventure as the main plot device. Chrétien had condemned fighting and violence in the beginning of his story, and then had no action for his hero to engage in, but Wolfram, who was a knight himself and approved of fighting, allows his hero to fight, because his Grail knights are a military order, like the Knights Templar.

Parzival is brought up in the woods, ignorant of the chivalry that killed his father because his mother wants to protect him from his father's fate. She has taught him little about religion except that God is brilliant, so when he first sees knights in bright armor, he mistakes them for gods, as is described in the first selection presented here. Subsequently, he learns what Knights are, and he decides he wants to be one and goes to Arthur's court to be made a knight without any sense of what it involves. He learns quickly and is able to rescue the woman whom he will marry from a devastating siege, whose effects on the population are described with realistic touches (that contrast with the splendor of the Grail procession).

from *Parzival*

[Parzival Mistakes the Knights for Gods]

One day he went out hunting along a mountain slope. He broke off a branch from a tree for the whistle the leaf would make. Right near him ran a path, and there he heard the sound of horses' hooves. He began to brandish his javelot and said, "What is this I hear? O, if only the Devil would just come along now in his furious rage! I would stand up to him for sure. My mother says he is a terror, but I think her bravery is a little daunted." And thus he stood eager for battle, when look!

Translated by Helen M. Mustard and Charles E. Passage.

there came three knights galloping along, as fair as anyone could wish and armed from the feet upward. The lad thought for sure that each one was a god, and so he stood there no longer but fell to his knees on the path. Loud cried the lad then, "Help, God! You surely have help to give!"

The rider in front flew into a rage to see the lad laying there in the path: "This stupid Waleis[1] is holding up our swift journey."—A thing we Bavarians get praise for I have to say about Waleis people too: they are stupider than Bavarian folks, and yet, like them, of manly stout-heartedness. Anyone born in these two countries grows up a marvel of cleverness.

Just then there came along at a gallop a splendidly adorned knight who was in a great hurry. He was riding in pursuit of those who had got a head start on him, two knights, namely, who had abducted a lady in his land. He considered this a disgrace and grieved at the plight of the maiden, who had ridden on before him in a deplorable state. These three knights here were his own vassals. He was riding a fine Castilian horse; there was very little of his shield that was whole; and his name was Karnahkarnanz, *le comte* Ulterlec. "Who is blocking our way?" said he, and rode over to the lad, to whom he seemed to have the form of a god, for never had he seen anything so bright. His surcoat swept the dew, his stirrups, adjusted to either foot to just the right length, rang with little golden bells, and his right arm chimed with bells whenever he raised it in greeting or to strike. It was meant to ring loud at his sword strokes, for this hero was eager for renown. Thus rode the rich prince, woundrously adorned.

Then of him who was a garland of all the flowers of manly beauty Karnahkarnanz asked, "Young Sir, have you seen two knights ride past who could not keep the knightly code? They are perpetrating rape and are lacking in honor. They are abducting a maiden."

But say what he might, the lad still thought he was God, just as Lady Herzeloyde[2] the Queen had told him when she explained His bright shining. And so he cried out in all seriousness, "Help me now, God of help!" And *le fils du roi* Gahmuret fell down in an attitude of prayer.

The prince said, "I am not God, though I gladly do His commandment. What you see here are four knights, if you would only look aright."

The lad asked further, "You speak of *knights*: what is that? If you do not have God's kind of power, then tell me: who bestows knighthood?"

"That King Arthur does. Young Sir, if you come to his house, he will give you the name of knight so that you will never need to be ashamed of it. You may well be of knightly race."—And by the warriors he was scrutinized, and God's handiwork was manifest in him.—I have this from the adventure, which with truth was told me so. Never had man's beauty been more nobly realized since Adam's time, and hence his praise was wide among women.

---

1. A Welshman.

2. Parzival's mother, whose name means "heart's grief" in German.

But then the lad spoke again, and laughter arose at it, "Ay, Knight God, what may you be? You have so many rings tied around your body, up there, and down here."[3] And therewith the lad's hand laid hold of iron wherever he could find it on the prince, and he began to inspect the armor. "My mother's ladies wear their rings on strands and they don't fit so close together as these." The lad spoke further to the prince, just as the thoughts came to him, "What is this good for, that fits you so well? I can't pick it off."

Then the prince showed him his sword. "You see, anyone seeking battle with me I ward off with blows, and to protect myself against his, I have to put this on, and both for shot and for stab I have to wear armor like this."

But the lad quickly replied, "If stags wore pelts like that, my javelot would not wound a single one. And a good many fall dead before me."

The knights were chafing at his delay with the lad who was so simple. "God shield you," said the prince. "Would that your beauty were mine! God would have conferred upon you the uttermost that could be wished for, if only you had intelligence. May God's power keep you from harm."

[Parzival Is About to Be a Knight]

The lad said, "God keep you! as my mother told me to say before I left her house. I see many Arthurs here: which one will make me a knight?"

Iwanet[4] burst out laughing and said, "The right one you do not see, but it won't be long before you do." He led him inside the great hall where the worthy company was.

In spite of the din he was able to say, "God keep you gentlemen all, and especially the King and his wife. My mother charged me on my life to greet *them* in particular. And those that have a place at the Round Table because of their deserved renown, she bade me greet them too. But one piece of knowledge I lack: I don't know which one of you is the host. To *him* a knight has sent a message—I saw him and he was red all over[5] . . . and he says he will wait for him outside there. I think he wants to fight. Also, he is sorry that he spilled wine on the Queen. O, if only I had received those clothes of his from the King's hand! I would be very pleased: they look so knightly!"

The free-spoken lad was much elbowed about, hustled this way and that. They noticed his beauty. Their own eyes saw that never was more lovely form lorded or ladied, for God was in a good humor when He created Parzival. And thus he who feared terror but little was brought before Arthur. No one could be hostile to him in whom God invented perfection. The Queen too gazed at him before she left the great hall where she had had the wine spilled on her.

---

3. Parzival has never seen armor or chain mail.
4. Iwanet is a squire in Arthur's court.
5. The knight in red armor is Ither, who came to Arthur's court to claim land, and seized the goblet as a symbolic gesture, but spilled the wine on the queen.

Then Arthur looked at the lad, and to the simple youth he said, "Young Sir, may God repay your greeting. I will gladly serve you with my life and my possessions. I am indeed of a mind to do so."

"God grant that that is really so! The time seems to me a year since I was supposed to become a knight, and that is more bad than good. Now do not make me wait any longer, grant me the honor of knighthood!"

"That I will and gladly," said his host, "if my dignity suffices. You are so pleasing that my gift to you shall be of precious worth. Indeed I will not fail to do it, but you must wait until tomorrow morning and I will fit you out properly."

The high-born lad halted there awkward as a crane, and said "I will not beg for anything here. A knight came riding toward me. If I can't get his armor I don't care who talks about kingly gifts. Those my mother can give me, for after all she is a queen."

Then Arthur said to the lad, "That armor is worn by such a man that I would not dare give to you. I have had to live with worry as it is, and through no fault of mine, ever since I lost his homage. He is Ither of Gaheviez, who rammed sorrow through my joy."

"A generous king *you* would be, if a gift like that were too great for you!" said Keie[6] then. "Let him have it, and let him go out there and face him on the meadow! As long as someone has to bring us the goblet, here is the string and there is the top: let the boy do the spinning. He will be praised for it among the women. He will often have to risk quarrels and take such chances, and I don't care about either of their lives. You have to lose a dog or two to get a boar's head."

"I hate to deny him," said Arthur in good faith, "only I fear he may be killed just when I am about to help him to knighthood."

. . .

On both sides of the street stood a great crowd of people. Slingers and foot soldiers, a long line of them, came bearing arms, and a large number of dart throwers. At the same time he saw many brave foot soldiers, the best in the country, with long stout lances, sharp and whole. Also, as I heard the story, many merchants stood there too with axes and javelots, as their guild masters had ordered. They all had skins slack from hunger. The queen's marshal led him with difficulty through their midst as far as the courtyard. There defenses had been prepared. There were towers over the living quarters, mural towers, tower keeps, and half turrets, certainly more of them than he had ever seen before. From all sides knights came forth to greet him, some on horseback, some on foot, and this sorry crowd was also the color of ashes or sickly clay.—My master, the Count of Wertheim,[7] would not have liked to be a soldier there: he couldn't have survived on their allowance.—Want had reduced them to starvation. They had neither cheese, nor meat, nor bread; they had no use for toothpicks, and no grease from

---

6. Keie (or Kay) is Arthur's seneschal, who is normally insulting or mocking, as he is here.

7. Wolfram was apparently a vassal of the Count of Wertheim, and a poor one at that.

their lips soiled the wine they drank. Their bellies had caved in, their hips were protruding and lean, and their skin was shriveled right to their ribs like Hungarian leather. Hunger had driven their flesh away, and from privation they could do nothing but endure it. There was mighty little to drip into their fires.

But if I were to twit them about it, I would show very poor sense, for where I have often dismounted and where I am addressed as Sir, at home in my own house, it is uncommon for a mouse to find delight. Mice have to steal their food, but I, from whom nobody has to hide it, can't even find it openly. And it happens all too often to me, Wolfram of Eschenbach, that I put up with such comfort!

[The Procession of the Grail]

There where sat many a valorous knight, Sorrow itself was borne into their presence. In through the door dashed a squire, bearing a lance in his hand. This rite sharpened their sorrow. Blood gushed from the point and ran down the shaft to the hand that bore it and on into the sleeve. And now there was weeping and wailing throughout the whole wide hall. The people of thirty lands could not have wept so many tears. The squire bore the lance in his hands all around the four walls until he reached the door again and ran out. Stilled then was the people's mourning, called forth by the sorrow of which they had been reminded by this lance borne in the hand of the squire.

If it will not weary you, I shall tell you now with what courtesy service was offered here. At the end of the great hall a door of steel was opened and in came two maidens of noble birth—now note how they are attired—so fair that they could have given love's reward if any knight there had earned it with his service. Each wore a wreath of flowers on her loose-flowing hair and bore in her hand a golden candlestick in which was a burning candle. Their hair was wavy, long, and fair—but we must not forget to tell how they were dressed. The Countess of Tenabroc and her companion wore gowns of brown wool, each drawn tight with a girdle about the waist. Following them came a duchess and her companion, their lips aglow like the red of the fire, carrying two little ivory stools. They bowed, all four, and the two set the stools in front of the host. This service was performed to perfection. Then they stood in a group together, all four dressed alike and fair to see.

But look how quickly they have been joined by more ladies, four times two, who had a duty to perform. Four carried tall candles, the other four were not displeased to be the bearers of a precious stone so clear that in the day the sun shone through. It was a garnet hyacinth, long and wide, and he who measured it for a table top had cut it thin that it might be light to carry. At this sumptuous table the host ate. All eight maidens went straight to the host and bowed their heads before him. Four laid the table top on the snow-white ivory of the stools placed there before, and stepped back decorously to stand with the first four.

Two princesses were seen approaching now, most beautifully dressed. They carried two knives as sharp as fishbones, displaying them, since they were so rare, on two cloths, each one separately. They were of silver hard and white and wrought with cunning skill, so keenly sharpened they could very likely have cut even steel. Preceding the silver knives came other ladies needed for service here, four maids of a purity free from reproach, carrying candles that cast a gleam upon the silver.

After them came the queen.[8] So radiant was her countenance that everyone thought the dawn was breaking. She was clothed in a dress of Arabian silk. Upon a deep green achmardi she bore the perfection of Paradise, both root and branch. That was a thing called the Grail,[9] which surpasses all earthly perfection. Repanse de Schoye was the name of her whom the Grail permitted to be its bearer. Such was the nature of the Grail that she who watched over it had to preserve her purity and renounce all falsity.

Before the Grail came lights of no small worth, six vessels of clear glass, tall and beautifully formed, in which balsam was burning sweetly. When they had advanced a proper distance from the door, the queen and all the maidens bearing the balsam bowed courteously. Then the queen free of falsity placed the Grail before the host. The story relates that Parzival looked often at her who bore the Grail, yet thought only that it was her cloak he was wearing. The seven now withdrew, as was fitting, to join the first eighteen. Their noblest member they placed in the center, with twelve on either side, I was told, and the maiden with the crown stood there in all her beauty.

For the knights assembled in the great hall stewards were assigned, one for each group of four, all bearing heavy gold basins and followed by comely pages carrying white towels. Splendor enough was there to be seen. A hundred tables—there must have been that many—were now brought into the hall, each was placed before four of the noble knights, and white cloths were spread carefully upon them. The host then took water for washing his hands—he had long since lost his joyful spirits—and Parzival too washed in the same water and, like his host, dried his hands on a bright-colored silk towel which a count's son on bended knee was quick to offer them. In the spaces between, where . . . no tables were, four squires were stationed to serve those who sat at each table. Two of them knelt and carved; the other two brought food and drink and attended them zealously.

---

8. The "queen," Repanse de Schoye, is the sister of the Grail king. Her name, apparently French, may mean "thought of joy," though it could also be "refuge" or "regret of joy." Wolfram frequently played with French names.

9. The Grail is a vessel—supposedly containing the blood of Christ—with power from God to sustain those who serve it, and the Grail quest adds a religious motivation to the secular culture of chivalry. In Wolfram it draws the finest knight away from Arthur's service—Parzival becomes the Grail king—without disrupting Arthur's court, but in the *Morte D'Arthur* by Malory, the quest contributes to the disintegration of the Arthurian world.

Listen now as I tell you more of this splendor. Four carts brought costly vessels of gold to every knight who was there. Around the four walls they were drawn, and four knights with their own hands placed the vessels on the tables, each one followed by a clerk whose duty it was to collect and count them later after the meal was over.

Now listen and you shall hear more. A hundred squires, so ordered, reverently took bread in white napkins from before the Grail, stepped back in a group and, separating, passed the bread to all the tables. I was told, and I tell you too, but on *your* oath, not mine—hence if I deceive you, we are liars all of us— that whatsoever one reached out his hand for, he found it ready, in front of the Grail, food warm or food cold, dishes new or old, meat tame or game. "There never was anything like that," many will say. But they will be wrong in their angry protest, for the Grail was the fruit of blessedness, such abundance of the sweetness of the world that its delights were very like what we are told of the kingdom of heaven.

ANONYMOUS
(TWELFTH–THIRTEENTH CENTURY)
France

Renard the Fox is the greatest of the beast epics—a sociopolitical satire in which predatory animals and their natural prey represent the various inhabitants of a monarchy. The authors of these tales attack with gusto and an implied idealism the government of their country, its legal system and Church, the formalities of feudalism, the hollow protection offered the underprivileged, and the unre- deemed brutality of peasants.

When Renard the Fox, a great lord in the court of King Noble the Lion, is tried and condemned for murdering a chicken, the effect is richly comic, but the underlying message is that the predations of a human *seigneur* would similarly be part of his nature. The Renard stories spread throughout European vernacular literatures, leaving their mark on Chaucer's "Nun's Priest's Tale" and Goethe's famous adaptation, *Reineke Fuchs*.

In the passage that follows, the badger, Grinbert, kinsman to Renard, goes to visit the fox at Maupertuis, described as a fortress but also clearly a den. Grinbert has been preceded as ambassador by Tibert the cat and Bruin the bear, both of whom were grievously mistreated by Renard. Grinbert persuades Renard to confess his sins, which gives the fox a chance to rejoice in past successes. Then they must leave for the court of King Noble, where Renard is to be tried for committing adultery with the wolf's wife, Hersent. Renard bids farewell to his family and says a moving prayer, but he is soon shown to be unreformed.

King Noble the Lion furious with Renard the Fox - manuscript illumination.
Bibliothèque Nationale, Paris.

from *Renard the Fox*

[Renard's Confession]

Then Grinbert,[1] with the king's permission,
Started out to perform his mission.
Through meadow and wood he went; no lack
Of sweat was pouring off his back,
And still he had far to go before   5
He would be close to Renard's front door.
At vespers he came upon a lane,
And at nightfall found Renard's domain.
The walls rose high above his head;
There were narrow passageways that led   10
To where he found a low-vaulted door
Into a courtyard. Then, still more*
Afraid of what Renard would do
If he should hear him coming through,
He hugged the walls and waited to see—   15
That was Grinbert at Maupertuis.[2]
As soon as his visitor had stepped
Onto the turning bridge* and crept

Translated by Patricia Terry.
*The translation conforms to the octosyllabic couplets of the original.

---

1. Grinbert (Gran BER): the king's ambassador, a badger.

2. Maupertuis (Mow pair TWEE): Renard's
   home.

Along the passageways—even then,
Before Grinbert came into his den,
Hindquarters first and head to the rear,
Renard knew who was coming near.
He welcomed Grinbert with warm delight,
Wrapped both arms around him tight,
And two soft pillows behind him pressed,
Because his cousin was his guest.
I think Grinbert was very wise
To keep his message for a surprise
Until he'd had enough to eat,
But after dinner, feeling replete,
"My lord," he said, "everyone knows
The way you lie and cheat—it shows.
I'm here to tell you the king demands,
No, not demands—the king commands
That at his palace you submit
To whatever sentence he deems fit.
Why wage a war you cannot win?
What did you want of Ysengrin?[3]
Why harm Tibert? Why hurt Bruin?
You have betrayed them to your ruin.
I'd like to offer you some cheer,
But I think your time to die is near,
And all your children will share your fate.
Break this seal and you'll get it straight.
Just read the words that are written here."
Renard listens, and shakes with fear.
He trembles, as he breaks the seal,
For what that gesture may reveal.
He reads the first few words and sighs,
Well understanding what meets his eyes.
    "Noble the lion, whose majesty
Prevails throughout these lands where he
Over all the beasts is king and lord,
Promises Renard he cannot afford
To ignore this summons: he'll pay dear
If tomorrow he does not appear
To make amends for his misdeeds.
Not silver and not gold he needs,
And let no champion give him hope;
He'll pay his debt with a hangman's rope."
    A terrible message for Renard!
Inside his chest his heart beat hard,

20

25

30

35

40

45

50

55

60

---

3. Ysengrin the wolf.

His face took on a somber hue.
"For God's sake, Grinbert, what shall I do?
Pity a poor defenseless captive!   65
Alas that I have this hour to live,
If I must hang until I'm dead
Tomorrow. I wish I'd been instead
A monk at Cluny or Citeaux!
But many of them are false, and so   70
I'd soon have wanted to depart;
In that case better not to start."
"You've other things to worry about!"
Said Grinbert. "And while you're here without
People around you, I suggest   75
That it would be well if you confessed.
Confess your sins to me at least—
Since I don't see any closer priest."
"My lord Grinbert," Renard replies,
I think your counsel very wise;   80
I'm close to death for my transgression,
And if you hear my true confession
I've nothing at all to lose thereby,
And I am saved if I have to die.
   Listen! I heartily repent   85
For what I did with Dame Hersent[4]
Who is the wife of Ysengrin.
She tried to cover up that sin
But no one believed her—that was shrewd
For she was well and truly screwed.   90
May God preserve my soul from Hell,
So many time I rang her bell—
Mea culpa!—if I have to face
Ysengrin, I'll lose the case.
How to deny that he's been cheated,   95
Three times imprisoned and defeated!
Now I will tell you all about it.
I made him fall into the pit
Just as he carried off a sheep.
Lucky for him he got to keep   100
Any skin at all, for it was shed
In a hundred blows before he fled.
When I had trapped him as I planned,
There were three shepherds close at hand
Who beat him like a balky ass."   105
Another time I helped him pass

---

4. Hersent the wolf's wife.

Through an entrance to a rich man's larder,
But getting out was a great deal harder,
For his belly swelled still more with each
Of three hams he found within his reach.   110
I set him to fishing through the ice;
His tail was caught as in a vise.
I made him fish in a pool one night
When the full moon was very bright,
And its reflection, white and round,   115
Looked like a lovely cheese he'd found.
So once again I had my wish—
He ended up on a load of fish.
A hundred times I took him in
With the guileful schemes my wits can spin.   120
Thanks to me he had a tonsured head.
Then he saw how well the canons fed
And thought their life wouldn't be so hard;
Those fools gave him their sheep to guard!
I could talk all day and not be done   125
Telling you how I had my fun.
There's not one beast in Noble's court
Who wouldn't give me a bad report.
When I led Tibert into the net
He thought that it was rats he'd get.   130
In all Pinte's[5] family there lives
One aunt; her other relatives,
Cocks and hens alike, were able
To fill a place at my dinner table.
When a cow and ox and the mighty boar   135
With other beasts stood at my door
Well armed, Ysengrin, in the lead,
Was sure that he had all he'd need
To win. There were on his side as well,
With the watchdog, Loudmouth Roenel,   140
Seven times twenty dogs and bitches
All of whom soon needed stitches,
Having most foully been betrayed—
I'd gotten to everyone they paid.
I certainly have no cause to boast   145
Of how I routed that great host—
Only by guile were they defeated.
I watched as long as they retreated

---

5. Pinte the hen who came to King Noble's
   court to accuse Renard of murdering her
   relatives.

And in salute stuck out my tongue.
God! What I did when I was young!
But now, *mea culpa!* true remorse
Turns my life from its sinful course."   150
"Renard, Renard," Grinbert begins,
"I've heard the confession of your sins
And all the evil you have done.
Your trial, By God's will, may yet be won.   155
Take care from now on to do no wrong."
"May God not let me live so long,"
Renard replied, "that all my ways
Are not deserving of His praise."   160
He shows a pious resolution,
Kneels, and Grinbert gives absolution
In French and in the tongue of Rome.
Next morning, before Renard left home,
He kissed his children and his wife,   165
All of them fearing for his life.
When the time of separation came,
"My sons," he said, "defend our name!
However this misadventure goes,
Protect my castles against our foes.   170
Against a count, against a king,
For months you won't need to fear a thing—
No count or baron, no lord would dare
Rob your head of a single hair.
You'll never be so much as grazed,   175
If you keep every drawbridge raised
And are well provisioned—for seven years
You'll stand them off and have no fears.
What more is there for me to say?
I commend you now to God, and pray   180
That He will bring me back once more."
With that he knelt down on the floor;
Because he would have to leave his lair,
Renard began to say a prayer.
   "God, King, in your omnipotence,   185
Let my craft and my common sense
Not be lost to me out of fear
When before the king I must appear
To answer Ysengrin in court.
Whatever he chooses to report   190
Let me make it harmless to admit,
Or find some way of denying it;
And let me come back to Maupertuis
Alive and well, so that I may be

Avenged on those who seek my disgrace." 195
Renard fell down upon his face,
Then, beating his breast for what he'd done,
Made the sign against the evil one.
    And now the noble lords will go
To court; on their way swift rivers flow; 200
There are narrow trails to follow past
High mountain ridges until at last
They ride across a level plain.
Renard is really feeling the strain;
That's why, in the woods, they go astray 205
And find no footpath, road or way
Until, where farmland had been cleared,
A barn that belonged to nuns appeared.
Surely one would find inside
The best of what the world can provide: 210
Cheese and milk and lambs they keep,
Geese and oxen, cows and sheep,
And young ones they fatten up to eat.
"Come on!" said Renard. "Don't drag your feet!
Now I can see where we went wrong. 215
There's underbrush to follow along
To the henyard, then it's straight ahead."
"Renard, Renard," the badger said,
"Does God not know what you say that for?
Foul unbelieving son of a whore, 220
Stinking glutton—I thought you craved,
Pleading for mercy, to be saved!
I heard your confession, did I not?"
Replied Renard, "I quite forgot.
I'm ready now. Let's go on like friends." 225
"Renard, Renard, it never ends!
God himself you will try to trick!
On you repentance can never stick.
How you came to be so mad, God knows!
Your life may be coming to a close, 230
And scarcely have you confessed before
You turn around and sin once more.
Evil has marked you out as prey.
Let's go now. A curse upon the day
When you were severed from your mother!" 235
"You do very well to say so, brother!
But now let's go our way in peace."
To make his cousin's scolding cease
Renard was keeping very quiet
As to the farm—he dared not try it, 240

But he craned his neck a little when
He caught a sight of a lovely hen,
Sadly thinking he'd rather have fed
And paid the price, though it were his head!

NA CASTELLOZA

(EARLY THIRTEENTH CENTURY)

France

Castelloza is an unusual name, perhaps a pseudonym. It appears attached to three Provençal poems in the found texts, but we know nothing about her. In the scant information that is provided in the prose poems, the poet speaks of a husband and a lover, and she also addresses another woman poet, but none of this has helped to identify her. In the text presented here she asserts her love and the pleasure she takes in pleading her case, even though it is not considered proper for a lady to do so. Elsewhere she explains her unusual forthrightness: "I shall have set a very bad example for other women in love, because it's the man who usually sends a message . . . yet . . . this was right for me." And: "the more a lady happens to love, [the more] she should court a knight, if she sees prowess and heroism in him."

Friend, If I Found You Charming

I. Friend, if I found you charming, humble, open, and compassionate, I would love you indeed—since now I realize that I find you wicked, despicable, and haughty toward me, yet I make songs to make your good name heard; which is why I cannot keep from making everyone praise you when most you cause me harm and anger.

II. Never shall I consider you worthy, nor shall I love you from the heart or with trust; in truth I'll see if ever it would do me any good to show you a cruel and hateful heart.—I will never do it, for I don't want you to be able to say that I ever had the heart to be negligent toward you; you would have some defense, if I had committed negligence toward you.

III. I know well that it pleases me, even though everyone says that it's very improper for a lady to plead her own cause with a knight, and make him so long a sermon all the time. But whoever says that doesn't know how to discern well at

Translated by William Paden.

all. I want to pray before I let myself die, since in prayer I find much sweet healing when I pray to the one from whom I get great care.

IV. He is quite a fool who reproaches me for loving you, since it is so very pleasing to me; and he who says it doesn't know how it is with me, nor has he seen you with the eyes I saw you with when you told me not to worry, for at any time it could happen that I would again have joy. From your mere word I have a rejoicing heart.

V. All other love I consider nothing—so know well that joy no longer sustains me, but for yours which delights me and heals me when most pain and distress come to me. By my lamentation and lays I always hope to enjoy you, friend, because I cannot convert; I have no joy, nor do I expect help, except only as much as I'll get while sleeping.

VI. From now on I don't know why I present myself to you, for I've tested with evil and with good your hard heart—which my own doesn't renounce. And I don't send you this, for I say it to you myself: I shall die if you don't want to make me rejoice with whatever joy; and if you let me die you will commit a sin, and you'll be in torment for it, and I'll be more sought after at Judgment.

HEINRICH VON MORUNGEN

(fl. 1200; d. 1222)

Germany

The form and the defining themes of the troubadour *canso* were adopted in other areas and languages. In German-speaking lands the influence of the troubadours of southern France and the *trouvères* of northern France combined with a native lyric tradition to produce a distinctive body of lyrics, known collectively as the *Minnesang,* that is, songs about *Minne* or courtly love. (The word *Minne* is etymologically related to English "mind" and designates that elevated passion— sexual desire complicated and enhanced by thought, and channeled into courtly forms of behavior—which the troubadours called *fin' amors.*)

The songs of Heinrich von Morungen—a nobleman, who died in a cloister—are characterized by the variety of their forms, their immediacy to the audience, and their arresting imagery. The lyric presented here is one of the most famous and most variously interpreted of the entire *Minnesang.* It depicts the deepest traits of the courtly love relation: the tense and unending—and unendable—oscillation of the lover between adoration and disillusionment, soaring joy and painful doubt; the tantalizing unreadability of the beloved (reflected in the instability of her image), and the intensification of self-consciousness in the "I." From another point of view one can detect the awareness of the performer before his audience—notice the dramatic strategy in the second strophe ("Behold!"), and the allusions to elements of their common culture, to Narcissus in the third strophe, for example, and to the Virgin in the fourth: ("The very heaven . . . she is the good one").

It Fared with Me as with a Child

I

It fared with me as with a child
that caught sight of its glowing image in a mirror
and reached in toward its own reflection
so long, till it broke the mirror to pieces;
then all its pleasure turned to pain and discontent.   5
So I, once, thought I'd live in joy forever
when I beheld my lady, beautiful, dearly loved,
through whom, beside the pleasure, it has fared painfully with me.

II

Minne, who increases the joy of the world,
behold! she brought me my lady in the way of a dream   10
where my body was turned toward sleep,
lost in the vision of its great delight.
Then I beheld her excellence, her noble radiance,
beautiful, exalted among women,
only there was some little wound upon   15
her small red mouth, the source of every joy.

III

I felt great dread therefore,
that her sweet mouth should pale, that was so red.
And so I now raised up new laments,
since my heart offered itself to such tribulation,   20
that my eyes made me look on such distress—
like a certain child, unthinking, inexperienced,
who caught sight of his shadow in a spring
and now must love it till he dies.

IV

Women more exalted in character and spirit   25
the very heaven can nowhere embrace—
she is the good one.[1] To my loss, and fearing loss,

Translated by Frederick Goldin.

---

1. The virtue of the beloved, compared to that
   of the Virgin.

I must keep my distance and cleave to her forever.
Ach, the pain of it! I imagined I had reached the goal:
her noble and rejoicing love.   30
Now here I stand, barely at the beginning.
Therefore my joy is gone, and my soaring dream.

GIACOMO DA LENTINO (fl. 1200–1250)
Italy

Giacomo da Lentino was a notary in the imperial court of Frederick II in Sicily, a
setting that favored the continuation of the themes and poetic practices of the
troubadours. He was among the first to write lyrics in Italian in this courtly manner,
even adopting many of the key terms of his poetic ancestors. He is generally
regarded as the inventor of the sonnet. In the example that follows, he uses the
sonnet form in exemplary fashion. The second quatrain, celebrating the physical
beauty of his lady and the joy that she gives, seems to undo the impression of piety
conveyed by the first, which speaks only of devotion to God and the joys of
Paradise; the last six lines, or sestet, resolve this conflict, revealing that the two
devotions coincide, that the beloved, as the magnet of his gaze, draws him to his
salvation. The role played by the lady in this sonnet is a development of one of the
fundamental themes of the courtly love lyric, that of the ameliorating effect of the
beloved image. The extension of this effect to the gates of Paradise is an innovation
that continues through all the "schools" of Italian lyric poetry in the Middle Ages.
Until Dante, it is used simply as an elaborate literary compliment. In Dante this
figurative theme illustrates a literal belief with narrative details.

I Have Set My Heart to Serving God

I have set my heart to serving God
so that I may go to Paradise,
the holy place, where, as I have heard,
there is no end of converse, laughter, joys.

Without my lady I would not want to go there—   5
she of the blonde hair and radiant face—
for lacking her I can rejoice nowhere,
parted from my lady in that place.

But I do not mean by this pronouncement
that I would want to sin in Heaven—I forswear;   10
but only to behold her beautiful deportment,

Translated by Frederick Goldin.

that gentle, loving look, that face so fair;
for I would dwell forever in contentment
to see my lady standing in glory there.

ANONYMOUS (THIRTEENTH CENTURY)
Norway/Iceland

"The Grief of Gudrun" comes from the pre-Christian oral tradition of Norway
and Iceland. Its written form, dating from the tenth century, was preserved in a
thirteenth-century collection called *The Elder Edda,* a collection of poems
primarily lyric rather than narrative. It comes from the legends of the Volsungs,
King Sigmond and his descendants, familiar in modern times from Wagner's
operas. The tradition reflects ancient conflicts between the Burgundians and the
Huns. Brynhild, originally one of Odin's valkyries—the shield-maidens who
guide the dead to Valhalla—is portrayed here as the sister of Atli (Attila the Hun).

In all versions of the Gudrun/Sigurd/Brynhild triangle, Gudrun is the
innocent victim of her brother's (Gunnar's) treachery. Gunnar, desiring the gold
that Sigurd acquired when he killed the dragon Fafnir, deceived Sigurd with a
magical drink that caused him to forget his commitment to Brynhild and marry
Gudrun instead. Brynhild then conspired in Sigurd's murder and killed herself.

The gap in the lines exists in the original text.

from **The Elder Edda**

The Grief of Gudrun

Close to death   in her despair,
Gudrun sat grieving   over Sigurd.
She did not wail   or wring her hands,
nor did she weep   like other women.

Noblemen came   to give her comfort,   5
spoke wise words   to soothe her heart.
Yet Gudrun could not   give way to tears;
burdened by grief,   her heart would break.

Great ladies   decked in gold
sat with Gudrun;   each one spoke.   10
telling the sorrows   she had suffered,
the bitterest   each one had borne.

Translated by Patricia Terry.

Gjuki's sister,   Gjaflaug said:
"I think no woman   in the world
hapless as I am—   five husbands,
three daughters,   three sisters,
eight brothers lost;   and I live on."

Yet Gudrun could not   give way to tears;
hating those   who had killed her husband,
she sat with Sigurd,   her heart like stone.

Then said Herborg,   queen of the Huns:
"I have greater   griefs to tell.
At war in the south,   my seven sons,
and then my husband—   all have been slain;
my father and mother,   my four brothers,
all, when the wind   whipped the waves,
were struck down   in their ship at sea.

"I alone laid them out,   I alone buried them,
I alone gave them   an honored grave.
All this I suffered   in just one season,
and no one came   to comfort me.

"Then I was caught   and held a captive
in that same season;   I was a slave.
Every day   I had to dress
my lord's lady,   and lace her shoes.

"Her jealous spite   spared me no threats,
and she would beat me   hard blows.
No house could boast   a better master,
not have I met   a mistress worse."

Yet Gudrun could not   give way to tears;
hating those   who had killed her husband,
she sat with Sigurd,   her heart like stone.

Gjuki's daughter,   Gullrond, spoke:
"Foster-mother,   your wisdom fails you—
how shall a young wife   listen to words?"
She told them not to keep   the dead prince concealed.

She swept off the sheet   that covered Sigurd,
and placed a pillow   at Gudrun's knees:
"Look at your beloved!   Lay your lips on his,
the way you kissed   when the king was alive."

Gudrun looked   once at her lord;
she saw his hair   streaming with blood,

15

20

25

30

35

40

45

50

the keen eyes dead   in the king's face,
the great sword wound   in Sigurd's breast.

She sank to the ground   against the pillow,   55
her hair fell loose,   her cheeks flushed red;
drops as of rain   ran down to her knees.

Then Gjuki's daughter,   Gudrun, wept
so that the tears   streamed through her hair;
geese in the yard   began to shriek,   60
the famous birds   that belonged to Gudrun.

Gjuki's daughter,   Gullrond, said:
"No man and woman   in all the world
were ever given   so great a love.
Sister, I know   you never felt at peace   65
anywhere   away from Sigurd."

Gudrun said:
"My Sigurd was   to Gjuki's sons
as garlic stands   taller than grass,
or like a bright stone   on a string of beads,   70
a priceless jewel   among the princes.

"My lord's warriors   honored me once
more than any   of Odin's maids:
now I am so little,   like a winter leaf
clinging to a willow,   since the king is dead.   75

"I miss in the hall,   I miss in bed,
my companion   killed by Gjuki's sons,
Gjuki's sons   who gave me to grief,
who made their sister's   bitter sorrow.

"May all who live here   leave your lands   80
as you cast aside   the oaths you swore!
Gunnar, you'll get   no joy from the gold—
the rings will drive you   to your death,
because you swore   an oath with Sigurd.

"There was greater happiness   in this house   85
before my Sigurd   saddled Grani,
and they left   on a luckless day
to woo Brynhild,   the worst of women,"

Then said Brynhild,   Budli's daughter:
"May she mourn   her man and children,   90
who taught you, Gudrun,   to shed tears,
and gave you this day   the gift of speech."

Gjuki's daughter,   Gullrond, said:
"Accursed woman,   don't speak such words!
Ever have you proved   the bane of princes,   95
all the world   wishes you ill;
seven kings   you've brought to sorrow,
widows you've made   of many wives."

Then said Brynhild,   Budli's daughter:
"Atli bears the guilt   of all this grief,   100
Atli, my brother,   Budli's son.

"Around a hero   in the Hunnish hall
flickered the light   of Fafnir's lair,
and I paid   for the prince's journey,
for that sight   I still can see."   105

She stood by a pillar,   summoning her strength;
fire burned   in Brynhild's eyes,
baneful venom   flew from her lips,
when she saw the wounds,   how Sigurd died.

GUILLAUME DE LORRIS (fl. 1230–1235)
JEAN DE MEUN [JEAN CHOPINEL]
(c. 1240–1305)
France

Guillaume de Lorris began *The Romance of the Rose,* a poem written in French
about a young lover who in a dream enters an idyllic garden of Love in the spring,
joins in the dance of Love's companions (Idleness, Diversion, Courtesy, Joy, and
others), sees himself in the mirror of Narcissus, is shot by the arrows of Love, and
falls in love with a rosebud. The rosebud seems to represent a woman, the Rose
for whom Guillaume claims to write the poem, though the Narcissism of this
kind of love is also obvious. The poet describes the pursuit of the rosebud and her
reactions up to the kiss and the imprisonment of the rosebud in a tower, with a
sympathetic if ironic view of the lover's folly. Whether Guillaume died before he
could finish, as Jean de Meun says, or intentionally left the story suspended, as
some have argued, we do not know.

    In any case, Jean de Meun went on with it in a rather different tone, putting
extensive polemical or didactic discourses in the mouths of various personifications
and human characters, who speak on a variety of subjects from justice to optics,
with emphasis on clerical corruption and misogyny, though Jean also developed

Translated by Charles Dahlberg.

the struggle between the forces or attributes of the lover and those of the lady into a full-scale psychoneurosis. Though there is a good deal of antifeminism in the text, and the poem ends with what can only be called a rape of the rosebud, there is also the curiously affecting speech of an old woman who laments the loss of her beauty and the gifts and attention it brought her, and who wants the young woman to profit from her mistakes, not by avoiding a life of pleasure, but by making it work for her. Though the old woman is morally offensive in her deceptiveness and greed and in her desire for revenge, she also makes a case for the mistreatment of women by men and the natural desire of women to be free—a subject that influenced Chaucer in his treatment of the wife of Bath in the *Canterbury Tales* and that has understandably attracted the attention of modern feminists.

from *The Romance of the Rose*

[The Dream of Narcissus and the Fountain]

Many men say that there is nothing in dreams but fables and lies, but one may have dreams which are not deceitful, whose import becomes quite clear afterward. We may take as witness an author named Macrobius, who did not take dreams as trifles, for he wrote of the vision which came to King Scipio.[1] Whoever thinks or says that to believe in a dream's coming true is folly and stupidity may, if he wishes, think me a fool; but, for my part, I am convinced that a dream signifies the good and evil that come to men, for most men at night dream many things in a hidden way which may afterward be seen openly.

In the twentieth year of my life, at the time when Love exacts his tribute from young people, I lay down one night, as usual, and slept very soundly. During my sleep I saw a very beautiful and pleasing dream; but in this dream was nothing which did not happen almost as the dream told it. Now I wish to tell this dream in rhyme, the more to make your hearts rejoice, since Love both begs and commands me to do so. And if anyone asks what I wish the romance to be called, which I begin here, it is the Romance of the Rose, in which the whole art of love is contained. Its matter is good and new; and God grant that she for whom I have undertaken it may receive it with grace. It is she who is so precious and so worthy to be loved that she should be called Rose.

I became aware that it was May, five years or more ago; I dreamed that I was filled with joy in May, the amorous month, when everything rejoices, when one sees no bush or hedge that does not wish to adorn itself with new leaves.

. . .

When I heard the birds singing, I began to go out of my mind wondering by what art or what device I could enter the garden. But I could never discover any place where I could get in; you see, I didn't know whether there were opening, path, or place by which one might enter. There was not even any one there who might show me one, for I was alone. I was very distressed and anguished until at

---

1. The commentary of the Latin writer and philosopher Macrobius (fl. 400) on the dream of Scipio in Cicero's *Republic,* discusses the various kinds of dreams, their divine, demonic, or physiological causes, and their prophetic meanings.

last I remembered that it had never in any way happened that such a beautiful garden had no door or ladder or opening of some sort. Then I set out rapidly, tracing the outline of the enclosure and extent of the square walled area until I found a little door that was very narrow and tight. No man entered there by any other place. Since I didn't know how to look for any other entrance, I began to knock on the door. I knocked and rapped a great deal and listened many times to see whether I might hear anyone coming. Finally a very sweet and lovely girl opened the wicket, which was made of hornbeam. She had hair as blond as a copper basin, flesh more tender than that of a baby chick, a gleaming forehead, and arched eyebrows. The space between her eyes was not small but very wide in measure. She had a straight, well-made nose, and her eyes, which were gray-blue like those of a falcon, caused envy in the harebrained. Her breath was sweet and savory, her face white and colored, her mouth small and a little full; she had a dimple in her chin. Her neck was of good proportion, thick enough and reasonably long, without pimples or sores. From here to Jerusalem no woman has a more beautiful neck; it was smooth and soft to the touch. She had a bosom as white as the snow upon a branch, when it has just fallen. Her body was well made and svelte; you would not have had to seek anywhere on earth to find a woman with a more beautiful body. She had a pretty chaplet of gold embroidery. There was never a girl more elegant or better arrayed; nor would I have described her right. Above the chaplet of gold embroidery was one of fresh roses, and in her hand she held a mirror. Her hair was arranged very richly with a fine lace. Both sleeves were well sewn into a beautifully snug fit, and she had white gloves to keep her white hands from turning brown. She wore a coat of rich green from Ghent, cord-stiched all around. It certainly seemed from her array that she was hardly busy. By the time that she had combed her hair carefully and prepared and adorned herself well, she had finished her day's work. She led a good and happy life, for she had no care nor trouble except only to turn herself out nobly.

When the girl with gracious heart had opened the door to me, I thanked her nicely and asked her name and who she was. She was not haughty toward me, nor did she disdain to reply.

"I am called Idleness,"[2] she said, "by people who know me. I am a rich and powerful lady, and I have a very good time, for I have no other purpose than to enjoy myself and make myself comfortable, to comb and braid my hair. I am the intimate acquaintance of Diversion, the elegant charmer who owns this garden and who had the trees imported from Saracen land and planted throughout the garden.

. . .

When the inscription had made clear to me that this was indeed the true fountain of the fair Narcissus,[3] I drew back a little, since I dared not look within. When I remembered Narcissus and his evil misfortune, I began to be afraid. But

---

2. Idleness is the gatekeeper of the garden of Love because courtly love is a game that can be played only by the rich and the leisured.
3. Narcissus scorned the love of a young woman, Echo, who cursed him to a similar fate of unrequited love. When he saw his own reflection in water, he fell in love with its beauty, and when he finally recognized that his love could never be satisfied, he died.

then I thought that I might be able to venture safely to the fountain, without fear of misfortune, and that I was foolish to be frightened of it. I approached the fountain, and when I was near I lowered myself to the ground to see the running water and the gravel at the bottom, clearer than fine silver. It is the fountain of fountains; there is none so beautiful in all the world. The water is always fresh and new; night and day it issues in great waves from two deep, cavernous conduits. All around, the short grass springs up thick and close because of the water. In winter it cannot die, nor can the water stop flowing.

At the bottom of the fountain were two crystal stones upon which I gazed with great attention. There is one thing I want to tell you which, I think, you will consider a marvel when you hear it: when the sun, that sees all, throws its rays into the fountain and when its light descends to the bottom, then more than a hundred colors appear in the crystals which, on account of the sun, become yellow, blue, and red. The crystals are so wonderful and have such power that the entire place—trees, flowers, and whatever adorns the garden—appears there all in order. To help you understand, I will give you an example. Just as the mirror shows things that are in front of it, without cover, in their true colors and shapes, just so, I tell you truly, do the crystals reveal the whole condition of the garden, without deception, to those who gaze into the water, for always, wherever they are, they see one half of the garden, and if they turn, then they may see the rest. There is nothing so small, however hidden or shut up, that is not shown there in the crystal as if it were painted in detail.

It is the perilous mirror in which proud Narcissus gazed at his face and his gray eyes; on account of this mirror he afterward lay dead, flat on his back. Whoever admires himself in this mirror can have no protection, no physician, since anything that he sees with his eyes puts him on the road of love. This mirror has put many a valiant man to death, for the wisest, most intelligent and carefully instructed are all surprised and captured here. Out of this mirror a new madness comes upon men. Here hearts are changed; intelligence and moderation have no business here, where there is only the simple will to love, where no one can be counseled. For it is here that Cupid, son of Venus, sowed the seed of love that has dyed the whole fountain, here that he stretched his nets and placed his snares to trap young men and women; for Love wants no other birds. Because of the seed that was sown this fountain has been rightly called the Fountain of Love, about which several have spoken in many places in books and in romances; but, when I have revealed the mystery, you will never hear the truth of the matter better described.

I wanted to remain there forever, gazing at the fountain and the crystals, which showed me the hundred thousand things that appeared there; but it was a painful hour when I admired myself there. Alas! How I have sighed since then because of that deceiving mirror. If I had known its powers and qualities, I would never have approached it, for now I have fallen into the snare that has captured and betrayed many a man.

Among a thousand things in the mirror, I saw rosebushes loaded with roses; they were off to one side, surrounded closely by a hedge. I was seized by so great a desire for them that not for Pavia or Paris would I have left off going there where I saw this splendid thicket. When this madness, by which many other men have been seized, had captured me, I straightway drew near to the rosebushes. Mark well: when I was near, the delicious odor of the roses penetrated right into my entrails. Indeed, if I had been embalmed, the perfume would have been nothing in comparison with that of the roses. Had I not feared to be attacked or roughly treated, I would have cut at least one that I might hold it in my hand to smell the perfume; but I was afraid that I might repent such an action which might easily provoke the wrath of the lord of the garden. There were great heaps of roses; none under heaven were as beautiful. There were small, tight buds, some a little larger, and some of another size that were approaching their season and were ready to open. The little ones are not to be despised; the broad, open ones are gone in a day, but the buds remain quite fresh at least two or three days. These buds pleased me greatly. I did not believe that there were such beautiful ones anywhere. Whoever might grasp one should hold it a precious thing. If I could have a chaplet of them, I would love no possession as much.

Among these buds I singled out one that was so very beautiful that, after I had examined it carefully, I thought that none of the others was worth anything beside it; it glowed with a color as red and as pure as the best that Nature can produce, and she had placed around it four pairs of leaves, with great skill, one after the other. The stem was straight as a sapling, and the bud sat on the top, neither bent nor inclined. Its odor spread all around; the sweet perfume that rose from it filled the entire area. And when I smelled its exhalation, I had no power to withdraw, but would have approached to take it if I had dared stretch out my hand to it. But the sharp and piercing thorns that grew from it kept me at a distance. Cutting, sharp spikes, nettles, and barbed thorns allowed me no way to advance, for I was afraid of hurting myself.

[Women Maintain Their Freedom as Best They Can]

"Certainly, dear son, my tender young one, if my youth were present, as yours is now, the vengeance that I would take on them could not rightly be written. Everywhere I came I would work such wonders with those scoundrels, who valued me so lightly and who vilified and despised me when they so basely passed by near me, that one would never have heard the like. They and others would pay for their pride and spite; I would have no pity on them. For with the intelligence that God has given me—just as I have preached to you—do you know what condition I would put them in? I would so pluck them and seize their possessions, even wrongly and perversely, that I would make them dine on worms and lie naked on dunghills, especially and first of all those who loved me with more loyal heart and who more willingly took trouble to serve and honor me. If I could, I wouldn't leave them anything worth one bud of garlic until I had everything in my purse and had put them all into poverty; I would make them stamp their feet in living rage behind me. But to regret it is worth nothing; what has gone cannot come. I would never be able to hold any man, for my face is so wrinkled that they don't even protect themselves against my threat. A long time ago the scoundrels who despised me told me so, and from that time on I took to weeping. O God. But it still pleases me when I think back on it. I rejoice in my thought and my limbs become lively again. Remembering all that happened gives me all the blessings of the world, so that however they may have deceived me, at least I have had my fun.

A young lady is not idle when she leads a gay life, especially she who thinks about acquiring enough to take care of her expenses.

. . .

"Moreover, women are born free. The law, which takes away the freedom in which Nature placed them, has put them under conditions. Nature is not so stupid that she has Marotte born only for Robichon, if we put our wits to work, nor Robichon only for Marietta or Agnes or Perette. Instead, fair son, never doubt that she has made all us women for all men and all men for all women, each woman common to every man and every man common to each woman. Thus, when they are engaged, captured by law, and married, in order to prevent quarreling, contention, and murder and to help in the rearing of children, who are their joint responsibility, they still exert themselves in every way, these ladies and girls, ugly or beautiful, to return to their freedoms. They maintain their freedom as best they can; as a result, many evils will come, do come, and have come many times in the past. In fact, I would count over ten of them straightway, but I pass on, since I would be worn out and you overburdened with listening before I had numbered them.

"But pay good attention to Nature, for in order that you may see more clearly what wondrous power she has I can give you many examples which will show this power in detail. When the bird from the green wood is captured and put in a cage, very attentively and delicately cared for there within, you think that he sings with a gay heart as long as he lives; but he longs for the branching woods that he loved naturally, and he would want to be on the trees, no matter how well one could feed him. He always plans and studies how to regain his free life. He tramples his food under his feet with the ardor that his heart fills him with, and he goes trailing around his cage, searching in great anguish for a way to find a window or hole through which he might fly away to the woods. In the same way, you know, all women of every condition, whether girls or ladies, have a natural inclination to seek out voluntarily the roads and paths by which they might come to freedom, for they always want to gain it.

"It is the same, I tell you, with the man who goes into a religious order and comes to repent of it afterward. He needs only a little more grief to hang himself. He complains and goes frantic until he is completely tormented by the great desires that come to him. He wants to find out how he can regain the freedom that he has lost. The will is not moved on account of any habit that one may take, no matter what place one goes to give oneself up to religion.

DANTE ALIGHIERI (1265–1321)
Italy

Born in Florence, Dante was a lyric poet and political figure exiled because of his politics in 1302. He spent the rest of his life in exile, living in different cities and courts of Northern Italy. During this time, he wrote his *Divine Comedy*, perhaps as a political message to his countrymen.

from **The Divine Comedy**

HELL

Canto 5 [From that initial circle I went down]

The first active sinners Dante meets in Hell are the lustful, those who indulged their sexual desires with no thought to their social responsibilities. It is the obsessive aspect of their passion and their willful self-deception that Dante condemns, not sexual love, witness the former lovers Dante puts in Paradise in Canto 9. Most of the souls Dante sees here are reigning queens, who satisfied their personal appetites at great cost to their lands. The bestial aspect of such obsession is shown in King Minos, the infernal guardian at the beginning of the section who now communicates his judgments by coiling his tail; the surrender to uncontrolled passion is represented by the "hurricane," and the self-deceptive aspect of the sin is seen in the story Francesca tells about her affair, casting it in the romantic frame of the tale of Lancelot and Guinevere, blaming the legendary lovers for inspiring her affair. But she rewrites their story, making Lancelot the active partner in the first kiss instead of Guinevere, as she presumably revises her own story, to whitewash her role, and to disguise the physical aspect under the clichés of courtly love ("Love, that can quickly seize the gentle heart," "Love, that releases no beloved from loving").

From that initial circle I went down
descending to the second, which contains,
enclosing as it does a lesser space,
a harsher pain to sting them till they shriek.
There horrifying Minos[1] stands and snarls   5
upon the threshold, scrutinising sins:
he judges and despatches with his coils,
by which I mean that when the hapless soul
appears before him, it confesses all,
and this great connoisseur of sinfulness   10
decides on its allotted place in hell;
the times he twines his tail determining
how many levels down the soul must fall.
Before him always stands a crowd, and each
comes forward for the verdict in his turn.   15
They speak, they hear and then are hurled below.
'Oh you who come to pain's own residence,'
said Minos when he saw me, and left off
performance of his high official rites,
'be careful how you enter; whom you trust;   20

Translated by Tom Phillips.

Hell, Canto 5

1. According to Greek myth, Minos, king of Crete, was the son of Europa and Zeus in the guise of a bull. He is judge of the underworld in Vergil's *Aeneid*. Dante adds the tail.

and don't be fooled by this wide entranceway.'
And then my guide to him, 'Why shout like that?
Do not obstruct his destined way ahead,
for this is willed where will and power are one;
all further questions are superfluous.'   25
From now I start to hear the tones of grief,
and come where frequent wailing strikes my ears.
I came into a place where light was dumb,
which bellowed like the tempest-beaten sea
when warring winds assault it from all sides.   30
The hellish hurricane unresting sweeps
the swirling souls in its rapacious wake
and thrashes and torments them as they whirl.
With devastation now they're face to face,
a scene of weeping, howling and lament   35
where they revile divine omnipotence.
It dawned on me that those who undergo
such torture must be <u>carnal sinners</u>, who
submit all reason to their appetite.
And just as starlings when cold weather comes   40
are lofted by their wings in huge dense flocks,
so back and forth and up and down are swept
the wicked spirits in that blast of wind;
nor are they comforted at all by hope
of any rest, much less relief from pain.   45
And just as cranes strung out in stretching lines
chant dirges as they travel through the air,
I watched the moaning shades go passing by
suspended in the maelstrom I described;
which made me ask, 'Oh master, who are they,   50
the beings whom the black air scourges so?'
And straight away he said, 'The first of them
whose history you'd want me to relate
was Empress over many different tongues
and so abandoned to luxurious vice   55
she legalised her own licentiousness
and thus forestalled the censure she deserved.
She is <u>Semiramis</u>,[2] who as we read
was wife to <u>Ninos</u> and succeeded him:
she held the land where now the Sultan rules.   60
Next, faithless to Sichaeus' ashes,[3] comes

---

2. <u>Semiramis</u> was supposed to have succeeded her husband as ruler of Assyria, to have founded the city of Babylon, and to have had an affair with her son, which she justified by making incest legal.

3. The widow of Sychaeus was Dido, who had an affair with Aeneas, which kept him temporarily from pursuing his destiny to found Trojan civilization in Italy, ultimately in Rome.

the one who killed herself possessed by love.
Luxurious Cleopatra follows her:
see Helen now, round whom revolved an age
of tragedy: see great Achilles too   65
who fought his final battle against love.
See Paris, Tristan[4] . . . and a thousand shades
or more he singled out to show and name
whom love had severed from this life of ours.
Then, having heard my mentor name these Knights   70
and Ladies of times past, my pity grew,
and I was lost in my bewilderment.
'Oh poet,' I began, 'I'd like to speak
with those that fly together as a pair
and seem to be so weightless on the wind.'   75
And he, 'You'll see, when they draw nearer us,
if you request them by that love of theirs,
the force that drives them on, that they will come.'
The wind steered them towards us, and at once
I raised my voice. 'Oh wearied souls, unless   80
Another One forbids it, come and speak.'
Like doves with wings held high and motionless
that drift on air supported by their will
when drawn by longing for their pleasant nest,
these separated now from Dido's flock   85
and came towards us through the sickly air,
such was the tender force of my appeal.
'Oh living creatures, gracious and benign
that brave the purple darkness of the air
to visit us who stained the world blood red;   90
were He our friend, the Universal King,
we'd pray to Him to grant you peace, since you
have pity on our sad calamity.
Whatever you would like to speak about
or hear, we'll hear and speak about with you   95
within the present respite of the wind.
My birthplace hugs that shore, where, making peace
with its attendant streams, the Po descends.
Love that so quickly fires the gentle heart
ensnared this man through that fair body's form   100
I now am stripped of (it still grieves me how).
Love that releases none, if loved, from love
ensnared me with such strong delight in him
it still won't let me go, as you can see.

---

4. Achilles, Paris, and Tristan shared, in medieval legend, the role of royal princes who became involved in illicit affairs to their own and their countries' harm.

Love led us on towards a single death.   105
Caïna's depth greets him who quenched our lives.'
Such were the words that floated down from them.
And when I'd listened to these injured souls
I bowed my head and held it low so long
the Poet asked at last, 'What's on your mind?'   110
And then I answered him and said, 'Alas
how many sweet reflections and desires
have led them on to this distressing state.'
Then turning back to speak to them, I said,
'Francesca,[5] how your torment makes me weep   115
for sadness and for sympathy; but say,
by what, in your delightful time of sighs,
and how, did love announce itself, and bring
the stirrings of those dubious desires?'
And she to me, 'There is no greater grief   120
than when in wretchedness one calls to mind
one's happy times: your mentor knows this too.
But if you've such a keen desire to know
the story of our love, how it took root,
I'll talk of it as one who speaks and weeps.   125
One day for our amusement we began
to read the tale of Lancelot,[6] how love
had made him prisoner. We were alone,
without the least suspicion in our minds:
but more and more our eyes were forced to meet,   130
our faces to turn pale by what we read.
One passage in particular became
the source of our defeat: when we read how
the infatuated lover saw the smile
he'd longed to see and kissed it, this man here   135
who never shall be parted from my side,
all trembling as he did it, kissed my mouth.
The book was Gallehault, a go-between
and he who wrote it played that role for us.
That day we read no further word of it.'   140
As this first spirit spoke the other wept.

---

5. Francesca da Rimini, according to early
   accounts, had an affair with her husband's
   younger brother, Paolo, who was himself
   married but had served as proxy at their
   betrothal. As she tells it, the husband surprised them in the first flush of love and
   killed them both, but in reality the deaths
   took place at least a decade after the marriage, and long after the birth of children to
   both. Dante's Francesca expects her husband to go to the section reserved for
   fratricides (Caina) in the lowest circle of
   Hell (for traitors).
6. The story of Lancelot and Guinevere is told
   in a thirteenth-century French prose romance; Gallehault is the friend who arranged for the lovers to meet.

For pity like a dying man, I swooned
and fell as bodies fall that fall down dead.

Canto 10 [*Onwards through a hidden alleyway*]

Just inside the inner city of Hell, Dante finds a vast cemetery of open tombs. This is the circle of heretics, specifically of those who did not believe in an afterlife, so they are condemned to tombs representing the death they expected, but the lids are open, revealing the life they did not expect. They are grouped with their followers because leading others into error is part of their sin, and the souls will involve Dante temporarily in error. Dante has strong ties to the two souls he meets here— political in one case, personal in the other—but he distresses both of them; the souls are also connected with each other, by the marriage of their children, but they ignore each others' feelings throughout.

The first soul, Farinata, recognizes Dante as a fellow Tuscan and Florentine. Farinata had been the leader of the Ghibelline faction, the party that supported the emperor, while Dante's family is Guelph, the party that supported the pope and the republic; in fact, Dante is actually a White Guelph, a member of the pro-empire faction, which had evolved after Farinata's time, so their political positions are not opposed. But Farinata does not know that and does not wait to find out. He attacks Dante as an enemy, and Dante responds in kind; they exchange taunts of exile, Dante announcing that Farinata's party was never allowed to return to the city, and Farinata that Dante would soon know what exile was like. (Dante was in exile by the time he wrote the poem, but the poem is set in the year 1300, two years before his exile began, so the Dante in the poem is disturbed by the news.) They attack each other even though they are on the same side, a good example of the way political factionalism works mindlessly against peace.

Their argument is interrupted by the other soul, Cavalcanti, the father of one of Dante's closest friends and fellow poets, Guido Cavalcanti, who asks why his son is not there. He and Dante confuse each other because, like heretics, both are working from limited knowledge. Dante does not know that Cavalcanti is unaware of the present (a particular punishment of these heretics who were concerned only with the present), and Cavalcanti does not know that Dante does not know. All three are left worse off for the encounter, Farinata because of the fate of his people, Cavalcanti because he thinks his son is dead, and Dante because he learns he will be exiled.

Now onwards through a hidden alleyway
between these tortures and the city walls
my master went and I came close behind.
'Oh paragon of moral strength,' I said,
'who lead me down according to your will   5
along the spirals of iniquity,
speak, satisfy my anxious need to know;
these people, lying in the sepulchres,
is one allowed to see them? All the lids
are open wide and nobody stands guard.'   10
And he to me, 'They'll all be well locked up

Translated by Tom Phillips.

when they come back here from Jehosophat[1]
and bring their bodies which they left above.
This cemetery is the ground reserved
for Epicurus[2] and his followers   15
who state that soul and body die one death.
And as for that you questioned me about
it shall be answered soon, and in this place,
as shall that other wish you've kept from me.'
'Kind guide, it's not that I conceal my heart,'   20
I said, 'but only keep my speeches short
as often you've encouraged me to do.'
'Tuscan! who make your way, a living man
across the fiery city, and who speak
with such refinement, please stay here awhile.   25
Your dialect reveals that you were born
a native of that noble fatherland
of which my treatment was perhaps too harsh.'
This sound it was that suddenly burst out
of one such grave and made me in my fear   30
draw even closer to my master's side,
who said to me, 'Turn round! Why act like that?
Look now, at Farinata, risen there;
waist upwards he's entirely visible.'
But I was staring at his face by then.   35
He'd now stretched upright, chest and brow thrown back
as though he had a high contempt for hell.
At once my guide with prompt decisive hands
urged me towards him through the sepulchres,
and as he did so told me, 'Watch your words.'   40
When I had reached the limits of his tomb
he eyed me half-contemptuously awhile
then asked me, 'You, who were your ancestors?'
And I who was most willing to comply
left nothing out but openly told all.   45
He raised his eyebrows somewhat as I spoke,
and said, 'Their bitter animosity towards
myself, my forbears, and my party too
obliged me twice to scatter them abroad.'
I answered him, 'Though they were driven out,   50
they still came back, both times, from every point,

Handwritten margin notes: Virgil being almost respectable to Farinata

Handwritten margin notes: Farinata holds all hell in contempt

---

Hell, Canto 10.

1. Jehosophat is the valley in which the Last
   Judgment is supposed to have taken place
   (Joel 3:2, 3:12).

2. Epicurus was an ancient Greek philosopher
   whose followers taught that pleasure or the
   lack of pain is the highest good; they were
   thought also to deny an afterlife of the soul.

an art your faction hasn't mastered yet.'
Alongside him another shade reared up,
with face and chin emerging into view;
he must have heaved himself on to his knees. 55
He looked each side of me, as though impelled
to check if someone else was with me there
but when this expectation had proved vain
he said, through tears, 'If your high genius
allows you passage through this purblind gaol 60
then where's my son? Why isn't he with you?'
'I do not come here on my own,' I said,
'for he that waits there guides me through, to her[3]
your Guido held perhaps in low esteem.'
The words he spoke, his mode of punishment 65
had by this time spelled out his name for me;
that's why I'd given such a full reply.
Then all at once he sprang up straight and cried,
'What? You said, "held". Is he not still alive?
Is gentle light not visiting his eyes?' 70
When he became aware that I had made
some kind of pause before I answered him
he just fell backwards and was seen no more.
That first imposing soul at whose request
I'd halted did not move meanwhile 75
a muscle on his face, nor turn his neck
nor shift his body's attitude at all
but carried on from where he had left off,
'To think they're not yet masters of that art;
why, that torments me more than does this bed. 80
The face of her that rules this lower realm
shall not become rekindled fifty times
before you'll know what price that art exacts.
So tell me, by your wish to reach again
the lovely world, why with their every law 85
these people treat my clan so brutally?'
'The havoc and the heavy massacre,'
I said, 'that dyed the Arbia[4] red, make this
the issue upon which our temple dwells.'
He sighed and shook his head and then replied, 90

---

3. The translator takes the Italian pronoun *cui*
   to refer to Beatrice, who will be mentioned
   at the end of the canto as the one who will
   tell Dante about his destiny. It might also
   refer to Vergil, Dante's guide.
4. The Arbia is a river at the site of the battle of
   Monataperti at which Ghibelline forces

killed many Florentine Guelphs in 1260.
The Guelphs never forgave them for that
slaughter, but they seem to have forgotten
that Farinata was the one who alone kept
his party from destroying the city after the
defeat, as he reminds Dante.

'I was not on my own when that was done
nor surely would have joined in without cause:
yet I was on my own when all the rest
resolved to stamp out Florence. It was I
that spoke out openly in her defense.'   95
'And now,' I begged him, 'to ensure your seed
eventually might come to find repose
untie this knot that's tangled up my wits.
It seems, if I hear right, that you can see
events which time has yet to bring about   100
while no such process makes the present clear.'
'Like those who have defective sight,' he said,
'we see what lies a long way off, for such
is what the high Lord's light still shines upon.
When things approach or actually take place   105
our intellects are wholly at a loss;
and so, unless some other brings us word
we have no knowledge of your human state.
From this you'll understand, that instantly
the doors of future time have been shut fast   110
our own awareness will die utterly.'
Whereat, regretting my offence, I said,
'Would you inform the one who just fell back
his son is still in living company,
and let him know that if I earlier   115
was silent in response to what he said
it's just that my ideas were still confused
by that misapprehension you've resolved.'
But now my master called for my return
and so I pressed the soul more urgently   120
to speak of those who shared that place with him.
'A thousand shades or more,' he said, 'lie here;
the second Frederick[5] and the cardinal
are both within, but I'll not mention more.'
With that he disappeared, and I walked back   125
towards the poet of antiquity
turning that message over in my mind
which seemed to carry threats against myself.
He started off, and as we went along
enquired, 'What's this that's made you so perplexed?'   130
I answered him as fully as I could.

---

5. Frederick II was emperor from 1215 to
1250; Dante respected him as a political
leader but places him in this circle because
of his reputed refusal to believe in the life of
the soul. The cardinal is Ottaviano degli

Ubaldini (born sometime after 1273), who
was reported to have said, "If there is a soul,
I have lost it a thousand times for the
Ghibellines."

'Keep fresh within your mind the things you've heard
against yourself,' the sage advised, 'and note,'
and here his finger pointed up above
'when you shall face the gentle radiance   135
of her whose lovely eyes see everything,
you'll understand from her your quest in life.'
This said he turned his feet towards the left
and, veering from the wall, we made our way
towards the centre following a path   140
that struck across a valley whose foul stench
was nauseating high up as we were.

PURGATORY

Canto 4 [When any of our faculties retains/ a strong impression]

*Along the lower edge of the mountain of Purgatory, outside the gate where purgation really begins,
Dante meets a series of souls who are literally "doing time," waiting for a period that corresponds
to the time they neglected their religious duties, before they can begin to climb the mountain and
purify themselves in order to enter paradise. Among these souls Dante meets an old friend, Belacqua, who is still as lazy and cynical as he was on earth. He makes fun of Vergil's lecture on
astronomy and of Dante's desire to climb. In comparison to Belacqua, who sits like a rock, scarcely
moving his head and speaking in very short sentences, Dante seems all energy and action, even
though he has been exhausted by his earlier climb. In contrast to other mountains, the mountain
of Purgatory is steepest at the bottom: the climb to purge oneself of sinful impulses is hard to begin,
but increasingly easier to finish.*

When any of our faculties retains
a strong impression of delight or pain,
the soul will wholly concentrate on that,
    neglecting any other power it has[1]
(and this refutes the error that maintains   5
that—one above the other—several souls
    can flame in us); and thus, when something seen
or heard secures the soul in stringent grip,
time moves and yet we do not notice it.
    The power that perceives the course of time   10
is not the power that captures all the mind;
the former has no force—the latter binds.
    And I confirmed this by experience,

Translated by Allen Mandelbaum.

Purgatory, Canto 4

1. The soul has different powers, including
the senses and reason, but it is one soul, not
several, as some believe.

hearing that spirit in my wonderment;
for though the sun had fully climbed fifty   15
 degrees, I had not noticed it, when he
came to the point at which in unison
those souls cried out to us: "Here's what you want."
 The farmer, when the grape is darkening,
will often stuff a wider opening   20
with just a little forkful of his thorns,
 than was the gap through which my guide and I,
who followed after, climbed, we two alone,
after that company of souls had gone.
 San Leo can be climbed, one can descend   25
to Noli and ascend Cacume and
Bismantova[2] with feet alone, but here
 I had to fly: I mean with rapid wings
and pinions of immense desire, behind
the guide who gave me hope and was my light.   30
 We made our upward way through rifted rock;
along each side the edges pressed on us;
the ground beneath required feet and hands.
 When we had reached the upper rim of that
steep bank, emerging on the open slope,   35
I said: "My master, what way shall we take?"
 And he to me: "Don't squander any steps;
keep climbing up the mountain after me
until we find some expert company."
 The summit was so high, my sight fell short;   40
the slope was far more steep than the line drawn
from middle-quadrant to the center point.
 I was exhausted when I made this plea:
"O gentle father, turn around and see—
I will be left alone unless you halt."   45
 "My son," he said, "draw yourself up to there,"
while pointing to a somewhat higher terrace,
which circles all the slope along that side.
 His words incited me; my body tried;
on hands and knees I scrambled after him   50
until the terrace lay beneath my feet.
 There we sat down together, facing east,
in the direction from which we had come:
what joy—to look back at a path we've climbed!
 My eyes were first set on the shores below,   55

---

2. San Leo in Urbino and Bismantova in
 Emilia refer to very steep ascents, and Noli
 in Liguria, to a steep descent.

and then I raised them toward the sun; I was
amazed to find it fall upon our left.
    And when the poet saw that I was struck
with wonder as I watched the chariot
of light passing between the north and us,[3]
    he said to me: "Suppose Castor and Pollux
were in conjunction with that mirror there,
which takes the light and guides it north and south,
    then you would see the reddish zodiac
still closer to the Bears as it revolves—
unless it has abandoned its old track.
    If you would realize how that should be,
then concentrate, imagining this mountain
so placed upon this earth that both Mount Zion
    and it, although in different hemispheres,
share one horizon; therefore, you can see,
putting your mind to it attentively,
    how that same path which Phaethon drove so poorly
must pass this mountain on the north, whereas
it skirts Mount Zion on the southern side."
    I said: "My master, surely I have never—
since my intelligence seemed lacking—seen
as clearly as I now can comprehend,
    that the mid-circle of the heavens' motion
(one of the sciences calls it Equator),
which always lies between the sun and winter,
    as you explained, lies as far north of here
as it lies southward of the site from which
the Hebrews, looking toward the tropics, saw it.
    But if it please you, I should willingly
learn just how far it is we still must journey:
the slope climbs higher than my eyes can follow."
    And he to me: "This mountain's of such sort
that climbing it is hardest at the start;
but as we rise, the slope grows less unkind.
    Therefore, when this slope seems to you so gentle
that climbing farther up will be as restful
as traveling downstream by boat, you will
    be where this pathway ends, and there you can

60

65

70

75

80

85

90

---

3. Dante is amazed to see the sun in the
northeast rather than the southeast, and
Vergil has to explain why with a combination of astronomic and mythological terms.
The main point is that Purgatory is at the
center of the southern hemisphere on the
opposite side of the earth from Jerusalem,
the center of the northern hemisphere.

expect to put your weariness to rest.   95
I say no more, and this I know as truth."
   And when his words were done, another voice
nearby was heard to say: "Perhaps you will
have need to sit before you reach that point!"
   Hearing that voice, both of us turned around,   100
and to the left we saw a massive boulder,
which neither he nor I—before—had noticed.
   We made our way toward it and toward the people
who lounged behind that boulder in the shade,
as men beset by listlessness will rest.   105
   And one of them, who seemed to me exhausted,
was sitting with his arms around his knees;
between his knees, he kept his head bent down.
   "O my sweet lord," I said, "look carefully
at one who shows himself more languid than   110
he would have been were laziness his sister!"
   Then that shade turned toward us attentively,
lifting his face, but just along his thigh,
and said: "Climb, then, if you're so vigorous!"
   Then I knew who he was, and the distress   115
that still was quickening my breath somewhat
did not prevent my going to him; and
   when I had reached him, scarcely lifting up
his head, he said: "And have you fathomed how
the sun can drive his chariot on your left?"   120
   The slowness of his movements, his brief words
had stirred my lips a little toward a smile;
then I began: "From this time on, Belacqua,
   I need not grieve for you; but tell me, why
do you sit here? Do you expect a guide?   125
Or have you fallen into your old ways?"
   And he: "O brother, what's the use of climbing?
God's angel, he who guards the gate, would not
let me pass through to meet my punishment.
   Outside that gate the skies must circle round   130
as many times as they did when I lived—
since I delayed good sighs until the end—
   unless, before then, I am helped by prayer
that rises from a heart that lives in grace;
what use are other prayers—ignored by Heaven?"   135
   And now the poet climbed ahead, before me,
and said: "It's time; see the meridian
touched by the sun; elsewhere, along the Ocean,
   night now has set its food upon Morocco."

PARADISE

Canto 9 [Fair Clemence, after I had been enlightened]

The souls Dante meets in the heaven of Venus, those who succumbed to the influence of passionate love in their lives, are very different from the self-centered souls of the two previous selections, the hostile souls of the heretics or the lazy Belacqua. These souls are moved by the love of God to share their joy with others and to share the joy of others with Dante. They do not need to hear Dante's desire to satisfy it, reading his thoughts reflected in God as in a mirror, and they are eager to pass him on to other souls in the same section who can satisfy his desire further. The first to speak to him in Canto 9 is Cunizza, a woman famous for her love affairs and many marriages, who is now able to say "this planet's radiance conquered me." She shows no trace of sinful lust, though she is still passionate about the corruption in her land. She introduces Dante to the love-poet Folco, who later became a monk and bishop. Folco compares himself without shame to the most passionate classical lovers, and then introduces Dante to the most surprising soul of all, Rahab, the prostitute in the book of Joshua, the first in this group of souls, Folco tells us, to be led out of Hell by Christ, when he rescued the souls of the Jews in the Old Testament. Rahab the prostitute, who was interpreted by medieval Christians as a figure for the Church because she had helped Joshua, a Christ figure, to enter Jericho, is contrasted with the pope and cardinals of the contemporary Church, who are committing adultery with Christ's bride (the Church) and who neglect Christ's teachings in their concern with worldly matters.

Fair Clemence,[1] after I had been enlightened
by your dear Charles, he told me how his seed
would be defrauded, but he said: "Be silent
    and let the years revolve." All I can say
is this: lament for vengeance well-deserved   5
will follow on the wrongs you are to suffer.
    And now the life-soul of that holy light
turned to the Sun that fills it even as
the Goodness that suffices for all things.
    Ah, souls seduced and creatures without reverence,   10
who twist your hearts away from such a Good,
who let your brows be bent on emptiness!
    And here another of those splendors moved
toward me; and by its brightening without,
it showed its wish to please me. Beatrice,   15
    whose eyes were fixed on me, as they had been
before, gave me the precious certainty
that she consented to my need to speak.
    "Pray, blessed spirit, may you remedy—
quickly—my wish to know," I said. "Give me   20
proof that you can reflect the thoughts I think."

Translated by Allen Mandelbaum.

Paradise, Canto 9

1. Clemence is either the wife or the daughter of Charles Martel (1271–1295), the King of Hungary, whom Dante met in the previous canto.

Botticelli, illustration to Dante's *Paradiso*, Canto XX. Kupferstichka-binett, Staatliche Museen, Berlin.

At which that light, one still unknown to me,
out of the depth from which it sang before,
continued as if it rejoiced in kindness:
"In that part of indecent Italy   25
that lies between Rialto and the springs
from which the Brenta and the Piave stream,
    rises a hill—of no great height—from which
a firebrand[2] descended, and it brought
much injury to all the land about.   30
    Both he and I were born of one same root:
Cunizza was my name, and I shine here
because this planet's radiance conquered me.
    But in myself I pardon happily
the reason for my fate; I do not grieve—   35
and vulgar minds may find this hard to see.
    Of the resplendent, precious jewel that stands
most close to me within our heaven, much
fame still remains and will not die away
    before this hundredth year returns five times: 40
see then if man should not seek excellence—
that his first life bequeath another life.

---

2. The firebrand is Cunizza's brother, Ezzelino
   III da Romano, a tyrant whom Dante saw in
   Canto 12 of Hell.

Feltre[3] shall yet lament the treachery
of her indecent shepherd—act so filthy
that for the like none ever entered prison.   45
   The vat to hold the blood of the Ferrarese
would be too large indeed, and weary he
who weighs it ounce by ounce—the vat that he,
   generous priest, will offer up to show
fidelity to his Guelph party; and   50
such gifts will suit the customs of that land.
   Above are mirrors—Thrones[4] is what you call them—
and from them God in judgment shines on us;
and thus we think it right to say such things."
   Here she was silent and appeared to me   55
to turn toward other things, reentering
the wheeling dance where she had been before.
   The other joy, already known to me
as precious, then appeared before my eyes
like a pure ruby struck by the sun's rays.   60
   On high, joy is made manifest by brightness.
as, here on earth, by smiles; but down below,
the shade grows darker when the mind feels sorrow.
   "God can see all," I said, "and, blessed spirit,
your vision is contained in Him, so that   65
no wish can ever hide itself from you.
   Your voice has always made the heavens glad.
as has the singing of the pious fires
that make themselves a cowl of their six wings:
   why then do you not satisfy my longings?   70
I would not have to wait for your request
if I could enter you as you do me."[5]
   "The widest valley into which the waters
spread from the sea that girds the world," his words
began, "between discrepant shores, extends   75
   eastward so far against the sun, that when
those waters end at the meridian,
that point—when they began—was the horizon.
   I lived along the shoreline of that valley
between the Ebro and the Magra, whose   80

---

3. The bishop of Feltre surrendered political
   refugees who had put themselves under his
   protection to their enemies and they were
   all killed.
4. Thrones are one of the orders of angels,
   called "mirrors" because they reflect God's
   will to the souls. The Seraphim, referred to

in ll 68–69 as the "fires" with six wings, are
a higher order of angels.
5. The line reads literally, "if I could *inyou*
   myself as you *inme* yourself." The verbs
   created out of pronouns emphasize the
   intense union of the souls.

brief course divides the Genoese and Tuscans.[6]

    Beneath the same sunset, the same sunrise,
lie both Bougie and my own city, which
once warmed its harbor with its very blood.

    Those men to whom my name was known, called me 85
Folco; and even as this sphere receives
my imprint, so was I impressed with its;

    for even Belus' daughter, wronging both
Sychaeus and Creusa, did not burn
more than I did, as long as I was young;[7] 90

    nor did the Rhodopean woman whom
Demophoön deceived, nor did Alcides
when he enclosed Iole in his heart.

    Yet one does not repent here; here one smiles—
not for the fault, which we do not recall, 95
but for the Power that fashioned and foresaw.

    For here we contemplate the art adorned
by such great love, and we discern the good
through which the world above forms that below.

    But so that all your longings born within 100
this sphere may be completely satisfied
when you bear them away, I must continue.

    You wish to know what spirit is within
the light that here beside me sparkles so,
as would a ray of sun in limpid water. 105

    Know then that Rahab lives serenely in
that light, and since her presence joins our order.
she seals that order in the highest rank.

    This heaven, where the shadow cast by earth
comes to a point, had Rahab as the first 110
soul to be taken up when Christ triumphed.

    And it was right to leave her in this heaven
as trophy of the lofty victory
that Christ won, palm on palm, upon the cross,

    for she had favored the initial glory 115
of Joshua within the Holy Land—
which seldom touches the Pope's memory.

    Your city, which was planted by that one
who was the first to turn against his Maker,[8]

---

6. Folco identifies his city Marseilles by its
position along the Mediterranean coast between Italy and Spain, and directly across
from the North African city of Bougie.
7. Belus's daughter is Dido, who wronged
both her dead husband Sychaeus and
Aeneas's wife Creusa by her affair with

Aeneas and then killed herself when he
deserted her. The Rhodopean woman is
Phyllis, who hanged herself when she
thought her lover, Demophoön, had left
her. Alcides is Hercules, who was killed
because of his wife's jealousy of his new
love, Iole.

the one whose envy cost us many tears—   120
   produces and distributes the damned flower
that turns both sheep and lambs from the true course,
for of the shepherd it has made a wolf.
   For this the Gospel and the great Church Fathers
are set aside and only the Decretals[9]   125
are studied—as their margins clearly show.
   On these the Pope and cardinals are intent.
Their thoughts are never bent on Nazareth,
where Gabriel's open wings were reverent.
   And yet the hill of Vatican as well   130
as other noble parts of Rome that were
the cemetery for Peter's soldiery
   will soon be freed from priests' adultery."

GUIDO CAVALCANTI (c. 1259–1300)
Italy

Guido Cavalcanti was the most important of a group of Florentine poets who
produced a body of lyrics that has come to be known as the Dolce Stil
Nuovo—the "sweet new style," a phrase drawn from a critical passage in Dante's
Purgatorio (XXIV, 52ff). Both the physical setting of the court and the social
tenets of courtly love have disappeared in the lyrics of the stilnovists. Love
remains the chief subject, however, and they speculate about its origin, its nature,
and its effect. The phenomenon of love takes place now in a more complex
setting, which includes the mental and physical organization of the lover, the
urban space across which the beloved lady's inspiring image is borne to him, and
the cosmic order, which is connected to the love relation through influence and
analogy. The primary agents of this communication are the "spirits"—highly
refined and specialized material substances produced in the body, which
maintain the network of human faculties and make human beings sentient in the
world. Visual spirits, for example, bear the image of the thing seen to the eyes and
then to the brain, which abstracts the essence of the thing from its "accidents" or
inessential properties; spirits then carry the commands of the mind back to the

---

8. Florence is Dante's city, planted by the
devil, "the first to turn against his maker"; it
distributes the florin, "the damned flower,"
one of the strongest currencies in contemporary Europe, and turns the shepherd, the

pope, and other clerics, into a wolf, a
symbol of greed in the *Comedy*.
9. Decretals are papal decrees, usually comments on or modifications in ecclesiastical
law.

senses and sinews. Sighs, too, are spirits that go out into the world—and even to the border of this world and the next—bearing and receiving images. The stilnovisti drew their imagery and many of their ideas from the fields of medicine, natural philosophy, and theology; in so doing, they were able to work out in detail the universal context of inner experience, setting humans in a world that extended from the streets of the city to the highest heaven. By excluding everything in the poetic tradition that was no longer expressive, and by broadening the sources of poetry, they gave new life and new possibilities to the lyric. Through their innovations, the lyric was able to express the concerns and experiences of a world far removed from that of the court—a city world under the stress of dynamic forces, rather than a court world ordered by stable, endlessly circling patterns.

In the following lyric, one can observe many of the distinctive traits of the stilnovist lyric. The action of the spirits, the processes of desire and intellection, the longing to decode the metaphysical message of beauty, and the ambition of the stilnovisti to compose lyrics that only a spiritually privileged elite could understand—these are all brilliantly conveyed in the proliferating image of the lady and the star.

[I see in the eyes of my lady]

I see in the eyes of my lady
a light full of spirits of love,
bearing to my heart a sweetness never known,
so that a joyous life awakens there.

Something happens to me in her presence,   5
which I cannot describe to the intellect:
it seems to me as I gaze that a lady issues forth
from her lips—one so beautiful that the mind
cannot grasp it, because at once
another is born of her, of a beauty never seen,   10
from whom it seems a star arises
and proclaims: "Your blessedness is come forth."

There, where this beautiful lady appears,
a voice is heard preceding her; and seems,
moved by goodness and humility, to sing her name   15
so sweetly, that if I try to recount it,
I feel that her greatness makes me tremble;
and sighs in my soul bestir themselves,
which say: "Behold, if you gaze upon this one,
you will see her goodness and power ascended into heaven." 20

Translated by Frederick Goldin.

JUAN RUIZ (1283–1350)
Spain

All that we know about the creator of this intriguing text (composed in 1330 and revised by him in 1343) is his identity, summed up in a single laconic phrase: "I, Juan Ruiz, archpriest of Hita." Not only is this a small amount of information, but the name "Juan Ruiz" is most probably a pseudonym, akin to the English "John Doe." The author may have chosen to disguise his true identity because the irreverent nature of this book may have jeopardized his position as archpriest. Despite the lack of specific biographical data, however, the author offers us a very well developed profile of himself and his ethical and literary values by means of his self-presentation as the protagonist and author of his text.

While acknowledging—indeed celebrating—racial and religious diversity in his text, Juan Ruiz is most concerned with the perennial problem of human interpretation on its broadest level. This interest is illustrated by his presentation of many perspectives on the same issue or event. "Debate between the Greeks and Romans" offers us a prime example of the archpriest's exploration of interpretation per se, offering, in essence, a parable of interpretation (and its inevitable ambiguities) whereby each of the two disputants is convinced by the definitive truth of his own view. Both nonetheless are mistaken.

So that we do not miss the point of the archpriest's treatment of interpretation (simultaneously comical but very serious) and its challenges for the reader or listener, he follows the sign-language debate between the Greek scholar and the Roman ruffian with an episode detailing five mutually contradictory astrological predictions regarding the untimely death of King Alcáraz's son. Much to our astonishment, they all prove to be true.

This profound interrogation of interpretation is thematized by the archpriest in his text, where the term "Good Love" has various meanings: it serves as the book's title and it also refers to the go-between who helps him to meet women as well as (very daringly) both to the carnal love between the sexes and to the spiritual love of God.

from *The Book of Good Love*

Debate Between the Greeks and Romans

Here it tells how every man in the midst of his cares should be merry; and of the debate that the Greeks and the Romans had with one another.

It is the saying of a wise man, and Cato said it, that among the cares man has in his heart he should intersperse pleasures and merry words, for much sadness brings much sin.

Translated by Raymond S. Willis.

And since a person cannot laugh at sensible things, I will insert a few jokes here; whenever you hear them pay attention only to the way they are put into song and verse.

Understand my words correctly and ponder their meaning; don't let it happen to you as it happened to the wise man from Greece with the Roman hoodlum of very little knowledge, when Rome petitioned Greece for learning.

Once upon a time the Romans had no laws, and they went to ask for them from the Greeks who did have them; the Greeks answered that the Romans did not deserve them, nor would they be able to understand them because they had so little knowledge;

although, if the Romans did want laws in order to conduct themselves by them, it was first of all necessary for them to hold a debate with the wise men of Greece in order to determine whether the Romans could understand laws and deserved to have them: this was the gracious answer they gave in order to get out of it.

The Romans answered that this suited them [and they would do it] gladly; they drew up a signed agreement for the debate; but since they would not be able to understand the language which they themselves did not speak, they asked to debate by means of gestures and the sign-language used by learned men.

Both parties agreed on a specified day for the contest; the Romans were in distress; they did not know what to do because they were not educated and would not be able to understand the Greek doctors nor their great wisdom.

While they were in this difficulty, a certain citizen told them to select a hoodlum, a Roman roughneck, and [tell him that] whatever gestures God might inspire him to make with his hand, these he should make; and it was good advice for them.

They approached a hoodlum, who was very big and pugnacious; they told him: "We have an appointment with the Greeks to debate by gestures; ask for anything you want and we will give it to you: only spare us from this contest."

They put on him rich robes of great price, as though he were a doctor of philosophy; he climbed up onto the lecture seat and said boastfully: "Now let those Greeks come, challenge and all."

A Greek stepped forth, a very polished doctor, selected from among the Greeks and highly renowned among all; he mounted the other high seat, with all the people assembled; they began their gestures, as had been agreed upon.

The Greek rose, calmly, slowly, and held out one finger, the one next to the thumb; then he sat down in his place. The hoodlum rose, savage and in a bad temper;

he held out three fingers towards the Greek, the thumb and the two fingers next to it, like a trident, with the last two fingers folded in; quickly he sat down, gazing at his robes.

The Greek stood up and held out his open palm, and then he sat down, he with his fine mind; the hoodlum got up, he with his vacuous fancies, and stuck out his clenched fist: he wanted to get into a brawl.

The Greek sage said to all the Greeks: "The Romans deserve laws, I will not deny them to them." All the people arose in peace and with calm; Rome gained great honor through a worthless tramp.

They asked the Greek what he had said to the Roman by his gestures, and what he had answered him. He said: "I said that there is one God; the Roman said He was One in Three Persons, and made a sign to that effect.

Next I said that all was by the will of God; he answered that God held everything in his power, and he spoke truly. When I saw that they understood and believed in the Trinity, I understood that they deserved assurance of [receiving] laws."

They asked the hoodlum what his notion was; he replied: "He said that with his finger he would smash my eye; I was mighty unhappy about this and I got mighty angry, and I answered him with rage, with anger, and with fury,

that, right in front of everybody, I would smash his eyes with my two fingers and his teeth with my thumb; right after that he told me to watch him because he would give me a big slap on my ears [that would leave them] ringing.

I answered him that I would give him such a punch that in all his life he would never get even for it. As soon as he saw that he had the quarrel in bad shape, he quit making threats in a spot where they thought nothing of him."

This is why the proverb of the shrewd old woman says: "No word is bad if you don't take it badly." You will see that my word is well said if it is well understood: understand my book well and you will have a lovely lady.

Whatever joke you may hear, don't despise it; the nature of the book must be understood by you as subtle, an art [knowledge] of praising and vilifying, cryptic and graceful; you won't find here just one of a thousand troubadours.

You will find many herons, you won't find a single egg; not every new tailor can do a good job of mending; don't imagine that I am impelled to compose poems as a fool does: what good love says, I will prove to you with good reasoning.

The text speaks to everyone in general; people of good sense will discern its wisdom; as for frivolous young people, let them refrain from folly: let him who is fortunate select the better side.

The utterances of good love are veiled: strive to find their true meanings; if you understand the meaning of what is said or hit upon the sense, you will not speak ill of the book which you now censure.

Where you think it is telling lies, it is speaking the greatest truth; in the bright-colored stanzas is where great ugliness lies; judge a statement to be complimentary or derogatory, point by point [with hairsplitting reasoning]; praise or condemn the stanzas for their points [musical notes].

I, this book, am akin to all instruments of music: according as you point [play music] well or badly, so, most assuredly, will I speak; in whatever way you choose to speak, make a point [stop] there and hold fast; if you know how to point me [pluck my strings], you will always hold me in mind.

Here it says how by nature men and the other beasts desire to couple with females.

As Aristotle says, and a true thing it is, the whole world exerts itself for two things: the first is to find sustenance, the other thing is to couple with a pleasant female.

GIOVANNI BOCCACCIO (1313–1375)
Italy

After spending part of his youth at Naples (1327–1341), Boccaccio lived mostly in Florence. He is considered, with Petrarch, one of the first writers of the Italian Renaissance; his scholarly works in Latin were written toward the end of his life, when a spiritual crisis caused him to reject vernacular writing as sinful. Framed within a story of ten young Florentines fleeing the plague in the city and amusing themselves in the country, partly by storytelling, Boccaccio presents 100 short stories, ten each day—which explains the word "decameron," ten days in Greek. The stories come in a variety of moods—comic, tragic, romantic—and in a variety of settings—ancient and contemporary, exotic and familiar. Boccaccio values love (of body and of soul), justice, generosity, and cleverness, (learning from one's experiences, coping with life and other people, often by a clever use of words). A storyteller who uses his ongoing or "frame" characters, to tell the stories of other characters themselves using stories or witty remarks to get what they want or to get out of trouble. Boccaccio is fascinated by the power of words and the power of laughter. The tale of Chichibio is a good example.

from *Decameron*

Sixth Day, Fourth Tale

Chichibio, cook to Currado Gianfigliazzi, changes Currado's anger to laughter, and so escapes the punishment with which Currado had threatened him.

Lauretta was silent, and they all praised Nonna; whereupon the queen ordered Neifile to follow next. And she said:

Amorous ladies, although quick wits often provide speakers with useful and witty words, yet Fortune, which sometimes aids the timid, often puts words into their mouths which they would never have thought of in a calm moment. This I intend to show you by my tale.

As everyone of you must have heard and seen, Currado Gianfigliazzi was always a noble citizen of our city, liberal and magnificent, leading a gentleman's life, continually delighting in dogs and hawks, and allowing his more serious affairs to slide. One day near Peretola his falcon brought down a crane, and finding it to be plump and young he sent it to his excellent cook, a Venetian named Chichibio, telling him to roast it for supper and see that it was well done.

Chichibio, who was a bit of a fool, prepared the crane, set it before the fire, and began to cook it carefully. When it was nearly done and giving off a most savoury odour, there came into the kitchen a young peasant woman, named Brunetta, with

Translated by Richard Aldington.

whom Chichibio was very much in love. Smelling the odour of the bird and seeing it, she begged Chichibio to give her a leg of it. But he replied with a snatch of song:

"You won't get it from me, Donna Brunetta, you won't get it from me."

This made Donna Brunetta angry, and she said:

"God's faith, if you don't give it me, you'll never get anything you want from me."

In short, they had high words together. In the end Chichibio, not wanting to anger his lady-love, took off one of the crane's legs, and gave it to her. A little later the one-legged crane was served before Currado and his guests. Currado was astonished at the sight, sent for Chichibio, and asked him what had happened to the other leg of the crane. The lying Venetian replied:

"Sir, cranes only have one leg and one foot."

"What the devil d'you mean," said Currado angrily, "by saying they have only one leg and foot? Did I never see a crane before?"

"It's as I say, Sir," Chichibio persisted, "and I'll show it you in living birds whenever you wish."

Currado would not bandy further words from respect to his guests, but said:

"Since you promise to show me in living birds something I never saw or heard of, I shall be glad to see it tomorrow morning. But, by the body of Christ, if it turns out otherwise I'll have you tanned in such a way that you'll remember my name as long as you live."

When day appeared next morning, Currado, who had not been able to sleep for rage all night, got up still furious, and ordered his horses to be brought. He made Chichibio mount a pad, and took him in the direction of a river where cranes could always be seen at that time of day, saying:

"We'll soon see whether you were lying or not last night."

Chichibio, seeing that Currado was still angry and that he must try to prove his lie, which he had not the least idea how to do, rode alongside Currado in a state of consternation, and would willingly have fled if he had known how. But as he couldn't do that, he kept gazing round him and thought everything he saw was a crane with two legs. But when they came to the river, he happened to be the first to see a dozen cranes on the bank, all standing on one leg as they do when they are asleep. He quickly pointed them out to Currado, saying:

"Messer, you can see that what I said last evening is true, that cranes have only one leg and one foot; you have only to look at them over there."

"Wait," said Currado, "I'll show you they have two."

And going up closer to them, he shouted: "Ho! Ho!" And at this the cranes put down their other legs and, after running a few steps, took to flight. Currado then turned to Chichibio, saying:

"Now, you glutton, what of it? D'you think they have two?"

In his dismay Chichibio, not knowing how the words came to him, replied:

"Yes, messer, but you didn't shout 'ho! ho!' to the bird last night. If you had shouted, it would have put out the other leg and foot, as those did."

Currado was so pleased with this answer that all his anger was converted into merriment and laughter, and he said:

"Chichibio, you're right; I ought to have done so."

So with this quick and amusing answer Chichibio escaped punishment, and made his peace with his master.

GEOFFREY CHAUCER (1340–1400)
England

The most important writer of Middle English, the poet Geoffrey Chaucer, joined the English army's invasion of France in 1359, was captured, and was ransomed by King Edward III in 1360; after 1367, when he was given a life pension by the King, he remained in the royal service. After periods of French and Italian influence, he began *The Canterbury Tales* in 1387. Chaucer created a vivid social satire in his *Canterbury Tales*. In the prologue he describes a group of people of different ranks and professions setting off together on a pilgrimage. He focuses on each of them, detailing their physical characteristics, their clothes, and something of their lives and habits. He rarely criticizes his characters directly, but uses clothes or actions that are not appropriate to their position to satirize them. The characters also reveal themselves, for good or bad, in their conversations, in the prologues to the individual tales, and in the tales themselves, which range from courtly to coarse, from saint's life to dirty tricks, from tragic to farcical. The prologue for the Wife of Bath describes her various marriages, the domination of some of her husbands, and her rebellion against the misogyny of others. The tale she tells, set in the world of Arthurian knights, questions stereotypical notions of sexual hierarchy, of class, even of age. Beginning with a snide attack on friars who abuse their positions of trust to seduce women, it focuses on a knight who commits a rape but is saved from execution by the queen (Guinevere) if he can discover what it is that all women want. The trick, however, is that to discover the answer he has to act it out—that is, he has to give himself and his body into the power of his wife, who thereby avenges the rape. And, it is implied, if he wants to continue to have a beautiful and faithful wife, he must leave the relationship in her control.

from *The Canterbury Tales*

The Wife of Bath's Tale

In the old days when King Arthur ruled the nation,
Whom Welshmen speak of with such veneration,
This realm we live in was a fairy land.
The fairy queen danced with her jolly band
On the green meadows where they held dominion. 5

Translated by Theodore Morrison.

This was, as I have read, the old opinion;
I speak of many hundred years ago.
But no one sees an elf now, as you know,
For in our time the charity and prayers
And all the begging of these holy friars   10
Who swarm through every nook and every stream
Thicker than motes of dust in a sunbeam,
Blessing our chambers, kitchens, halls, and bowers,
Our cities, towns, and castles, our high towers,
Our villages, our stables, barns, and dairies,   15
They keep us all from seeing any fairies,
For where you might have come upon an elf
There now you find the holy friar himself
Working his district on industrious legs
And saying his devotions while he begs.   20
Women are safe now under every tree.
No incubus is there unless it's he,
And all they have to fear from him is shame.
     It chanced that Arthur had a knight who came
Lustily riding home one day from hawking,   25
And in his path he saw a maiden walking
Before him, stark alone, right in his course.
This young knight took her maidenhead by force,
A crime at which the outcry was so keen
It would have cost his neck, but that the queen,   30
With other ladies, begged the king so long
That Arthur spared his life, for right or wrong,
And gave him to the queen, at her own will,
According to her choice, to save or kill.
     She thanked the king, and later told this knight,   35
Choosing her time, "You are still in such a plight
Your very life has no security.
I grant your life, if you can answer me
This question: what is the thing that most of all
Women desire? Think, or your neck will fall   40
Under the ax! If you cannot let me know
Immediately, I give you leave to go
A twelvemonth and a day, no more, in quest
Of such an answer as will meet the test.
But you must pledge your honor to return   45
And yield your body, whatever you may learn."
     The knight sighed; he was rueful beyond measure.
But what! He could not follow his own pleasure.
He chose at last upon his way to ride
And with such answer as God might provide   50
To come back when the year was at the close.

Geoffrey Chaucer, from an illuminated manuscript, now in the National Portrait Gallery, London.

He seeks out every house and every place
Where he has any hope, by luck or grace,
Of learning what thing women covet most.   55
But he could never light on any coast
Where on this point two people would agree,
For some said wealth and some said jollity,
Some said position, some said sport in bed
And often to be widowed, often wed.   60
Some said that to a woman's heart what mattered
Above all else was to be pleased and flattered.
That shaft, to tell the truth, was a close hit.
Men win us best by flattery, I admit,
And by attention. Some say our greatest ease   65
Is to be free and do just as we please,
And not to have our faults thrown in our eyes,
But always to be praised for being wise.
And true enough, there's not one of us all
Who will not kick if you rub us on a gall.   70
Whatever vices we may have within,
We won't be taxed with any fault or sin.
        Some say that women are delighted well
If it is thought that they will never tell
A secret they are trusted with, or scandal.   75
But that tale isn't worth an old rake handle!

We women, for a fact, can never hold
A secret. Will you hear a story told?
Then witness Midas! For it can be read
In Ovid that he had upon his head   80
Two ass's ears that he kept out of sight
Beneath his long hair with such skill and sleight
That no one else besides his wife could guess.
He loved her well, and trusted her no less.
He begged her not to make his blemish known,   85
But keep her knowledge to herself alone.
She swore that never, though to save her skin,
Would she be guilty of so mean a sin,
And yet it seemed to her she nearly died
Keeping a secret locked so long inside.   90
It swelled about her heart so hard and deep
She was afraid some word was bound to leap
Out of her mouth, and since there was no man
She dared to tell, down to a swamp she ran—
Her heart, until she got there, all agog—   95
And like a bittern booming in the bog
She put her mouth close to the watery ground:
"Water, do not betray me with your sound!
I speak to you, and you alone," she said.
"Two ass's ears grow on my husband's head!   100
And now my heart is whole, now it is out.
I'd burst if I held it longer, past all doubt."
Safely, you see, awhile you may confide
In us, but it will out; we cannot hide
A secret. Look in Ovid if you care   105
To learn what followed; the whole tale is there.

    This knight, when he perceived he could not find
What women covet most, was low in mind;
But the day came when homeward he must ride,
And as he crossed a wooded countryside   110
Some four and twenty ladies there by chance
He saw, all circling in a woodland dance,
And toward this dance he eagerly drew near
In hope of any counsel he might hear.
But the truth was, he had not reached the place   115
When dance and all, they vanished into space.
No living soul remained there to be seen
Save an old woman sitting on the green,
As ugly a witch as fancy could devise.
As he approached her she began to rise   120
And said, "Sir knight, here runs no thoroughfare.
What are you seeking with such anxious air?

Tell me! The better may your fortune be.
We old folk know a lot of things," said she.
    "Good mother," said the knight, "my life's to pay,   125
That's all too certain, if I cannot say
What women covet most. If you could tell
That secret to me, I'd requite you well."
    "Give me your hand," she answered. "Swear me true
That whatsoever I next ask of you,   130
You'll do it if it lies within your might
And I'll enlighten you before the night."
    "Granted, upon my honor," he replied.
    "Then I dare boast, and with no empty pride,
Your life is safe," she told him. "Let me die   135
If she, the queen, won't say the same as I.
Let's learn if the haughtiest of all who wear
A net or coverchief upon their hair
Will be so forward as to answer 'no'
To what I'll teach you. No more; let us go."   140
With that she whispered something in his ear,
And told him to be glad and have no fear.
    When they had reached the court, the knight declared
That he had kept his day, and was prepared
To give his answer, standing for his life.   145
Many the wise widow, many the wife,
Many the maid who rallied to the scene,
And at the head as justice sat the queen.
Then silence was enjoined; the knight was told
In open court to say what women hold   150
Precious above all else. He did not stand
Dumb like a beast, but spoke up at command
And plainly offered them his answering word
In manly voice, so that the whole court heard.
    "My liege and lady, most of all," said he,   155
"Women desire to have the sovereignty
And sit in rule and government above
Their husbands, and to have their way in love.
This is what most you want. Spare me or kill
As you may like; I stand here by your will."   160
    No widow, wife, or maid gave any token
Of contradicting what the knight had spoken.
He should not die; he should be spared instead;
He well deserved his life, the whole court said.
    The old woman whom the knight met on the green   165
Sprang up at this. "My sovereign lady queen,
Before your court has risen, do me right!
I taught, myself, this answer to the knight,

For which he pledged his honor in my hand,
Solemnly, that the first thing I demand,   170
He'd do it, if it lay within his might.
Before the court I ask you, then, sir knight,
To take me," said the woman, "as your wife,
For well you know that I have saved your life.
Deny me, on your honor, if you can."   175
    "Alas," replied this miserable man,
"That was my promise, it must be confessed.
For the love of God, though, choose a new request!
Take all my wealth, and let my body be."
    "If that's your tune, then curse both you and me,"   180
She said. "Though I am ugly, old, and poor,
I'll have, for all the metal and the ore
That under earth is hidden or lies above,
Nothing, except to be your wife and love."
    "My love? No, my damnation, if you can!   185
Alas," he said, "that any of my clan
Should be so miserably misallied!"
    All to no good; force overruled his pride,
And in the end he is constrained to wed,
And marries his old wife and goes to bed.   190
    Now some will charge me with an oversight
In failing to describe the day's delight,
The merriment, the food, the dress at least.
But I reply, there was no joy nor feast;
Nothing but sorrow and sharp misery.   195
He married her in private, secretly,
And all day after, such was his distress,
Hid like an owl from his wife's ugliness.
    Great was the woe this knight had in his head
When in due time they both were brought to bed.   200
He shuddered, tossed, and turned, and all the while
His old wife lay and waited with a smile.
"Is every knight so backward with a spouse?
Is it," she said, "a law in Arthur's house?
I am your love, your own, your wedded wife.   205
I am the woman who has saved your life.
I've never done you anything but right.
Why do you treat me this way the first night?
You must be mad, the way that you behave!
Tell me my fault, and as God's love can save,   210
I will amend it, truly, if I can."
    "Amend it?" answered this unhappy man.
"It never can be amended, truth to tell.
You are so loathsome and so old as well,

And your low birth besides is such a cross 215
It is no wonder that I turn and toss.
God take my woeful spirit from my breast!"
   "Is this," she said, "the cause of your unrest?"
"No wonder!" said the knight. "It truly is."
   "Now sir, she said, "I could amend all this 220
Within three days, if it should please me to,
And if you deal with me as you should do.
   "But since you speak of that nobility
That comes from ancient wealth and pedigree,
As if *that* constituted gentlemen, 225
I hold such arrogance not worth a hen!
The man whose virtue is pre-eminent,
In public and alone, always intent
On doing every generous act he can,
Take him—he is the greatest gentleman! 230
Christ wills that we should claim nobility
From him, not from old wealth or family.
Our elders left us all that they were worth
And through their wealth and blood we claim high birth,
But never, since it was beyond their giving, 235
Could they bequeath to us their virtuous living;
Although it first conferred on them the name
Of gentlemen, they could not leave that claim!
   "Dante the Florentine on this was wise:
'Frail is the branch on which man's virtues rise'— 240
Thus runs his rhyme—'God's goodness wills that we
Should claim from him alone nobility.'
Thus from our elders we can only claim
Such temporal things as men may hurt and maim.
   "It's plain enough that true nobility 245
Is not bequeathed along with property,
For many a lord's son does a deed of shame
And yet, God knows, enjoys his noble name.
But he, though scion of a noble house
And elders who were wise and virtuous, 250
Who will not follow his elders, who are dead,
But leads, himself, a shameful life instead,
He is not noble, be he duke or earl.
It is the churlish deed that makes the churl.
And therefore, my dear husband, I conclude 255
That though my ancestors were rough and rude,
Yet may Almighty God confer on me
The grace to live, as I hope, virtuously.
Call me of noble blood when I begin
To live in virtue and to cast out sin. 260

"As for my poverty, at which you grieve,
Almighty God in whom we all believe
In willful poverty chose to lead his life,
And surely every man and maid and wife
Can understand that Jesus, heaven's king,   265
Would never choose a low or vicious thing.
A poor and cheerful life is nobly led;
So Seneca and others have well said.
The man so poor he doesn't have a stitch
Who thinks himself repaid, I count as rich.   270
He that is covetous, he is the poor man,
Pining to have the things he never can.
It is of cheerful mind, true poverty.
Juvenal says about it happily:
'The poor man as he goes along his way   275
And passes thieves is free to sing and play.'
Poverty is a good we loathe, a great
Reliever of our busy worldly state,
A great amender also of our minds
As he that patiently will bear it finds.   280
And poverty, for all it seems distressed,
Is a possession no one will contest.
Poverty, too, by bringing a man low,
Helps him the better God and self to know.
Poverty is a glass where we can see   285
Which are our true friends, as it seems to me.
So, sir, I do not wrong you on this score;
Reproach me with my poverty no more.
    "Now, sir, you tax me with my age; but, sir,
You gentlemen of breeding all aver   290
That men should not despise old age, but rather
Grant an old man respect, and call him 'father.'
    "If I am old and ugly, as you have said,
You have less fear of being cuckolded,
For ugliness and age, as all agree,   295
Are notable guardians of chastity.
But since I know in what you take delight,
I'll gratify your worldly appetite.
    "Choose now, which of two courses you will try:
To have me old and ugly till I die   300
But evermore your true and humble wife,
Never displeasing you in all my life,
Or will you have me rather young and fair
And take your chances on who may repair
Either to your house on account of me   305
Or to some other place, it well may be.

Now make your choice, whichever you prefer."
  The knight took thought, and sighed, and said to her
At last, "My love and lady, my dear wife,
In your wise government I put my life.   310
Choose for yourself which course will best agree
With pleasure and honor, both for you and me.
I do not care, choose either of the two;
I am content, whatever pleases you."
  "Then have I won from you the sovereignty,   315
Since I may choose and rule at will?" said she.
  He answered, "That is best, I think, dear wife."
  "Kiss me," she said. "Now we are done with strife,
For on my word, I will be both to you,
That is to say, fair, yes, and faithful too.   320
May I die mad unless I am as true
As ever wife was since the world was new.
Unless I am as lovely to be seen
By morning as an empress or a queen
Or any lady between east and west,   325
Do with my life or death as you think best.
Lift up the curtain, see what you may see."
  And when the knight saw what had come to be
And knew her as she was, so young, so fair,
His joy was such that it was past compare.   330
He took her in his arms and gave her kisses
A thousand times on end; he bathed in blisses.
And she obeyed him also in full measure
In everything that tended to his pleasure.
  And so they lived in full joy to the end.   335
And now to all us women may Christ send
Submissive husbands, full of youth in bed,
And grace to outlive all the men we wed.
And I pray Jesus to cut short the lives
Of those who won't be governed by their wives;   340
And old, ill-tempered niggards who hate expense,
God promptly bring them down with pestilence!

CHRISTINE DE PIZAN (c. 1364–1429)
France

In the *Mutation of Fortune*, a narrative poem written in 1403, the French author
Christine de Pizan describes how Fortune appears to her when she is in deep

depression over the death of her husband—Etienne de Castel—whom she married in 1379, and who was to become secretary to Charles VI—and turns her into a man so she can face the demands of her new life, support her three children, fight with the government bureaucracy over her husband's claims, and succeed as a professional writer. She is not comfortable with her new role, but she accepts it as a necessity for herself and her family.

Christine's interest in learning had been encouraged by her father, a physician and astrologer at the court of Charles V of France, and by various powerful friends, including the king and the chancellor of the University of Paris. In the beginning of the *The Book of the City of Ladies,* a French prose work of 1405, she is again in a moment of depression, this time brought on by reading the latest in a series of misogynous texts that make women out to be hopelessly sinful creatures. Though the descriptions of women in these books contrast with Christine's own experience of women of every class, she is unsettled by them and begins to feel that God has mistreated her by making her a woman, until three personifications appear to her (reflecting the influence of Boethius's *The Consolation of Philosophy*) and console her. They are Reason, Rectitude, and Justice, and they tell her of all the contributions women have made to civilization. It is from this knowledge that she builds her city of ladies.

from The Mutation of Fortune

[*Fortune Changes Christine into a Man*]

I was in this state [of grief for her husband] for a long time, refusing all pleasures, without hope of joy or solace. Our troubled ship was carried now here, now there, all winds harmful to it, for there was no one who knew enough to pilot it. I thought that I could never guide it back, but would remain on that sea that divides grief from joy all my life, on the wrong side of happiness which had fled from me, and that alarmed me. But it did not continue; I was later to take many steps on land. To be brief, my sorrow and my weeping were such that even Fortune had pity on my distress and wanted to befriend and help me, as a good mistress. But her help was wondrous—perhaps it was even more dangerous.

Exhausted by long weeping, I remained as if dead. Then I fell asleep and my mistress, who has offered joy to many, came towards me and touched me all over my body. Each part, I remember well, she held in her hands and massaged. Then she left and I remained. When our ship, carried by the waves of the sea, broke against a rock with a great crash, I awoke and immediately, without any doubt, felt myself completely transformed. I felt my body to be much stronger, the weeping I had been engaged in abated. Then I touched myself and was amazed. Fortune did not hate me if she so transformed me, for quite suddenly she changed the fear and doubt in which I had been floundering. I felt myself much relieved, my flesh changed and strengthened, my voice deepened, and my body harder and swifter. But the ring that Hymen [marriage] had given me, fell from my finger which troubled me, with good reason, for I loved it dearly.

Translated by Joan M. Ferrante.

I got up easily. I did not remain in the indolence of weeping which had increased my distress. I found a strong and bold heart in me, which astonished me, but then I recognized that I had become a true man. I was amazed by the adventure. I raised my eyes, by chance, saw the sail and mast all broken, for the bad weather had torn the ropes. Our ship was badly shattered and cracked and the water was pouring in. It was already so filled that if the rocks on which we struck had not interfered, it would have sunk to the bottom. When I saw it thus in danger, I began to fix it myself. With nails and mortar, I rejoined and hammered the planks and gathered moss on the rocks and fixed it in the cracks in great bunches to make it watertight. I had the water bailed. In short, I knew what to do to handle the ship. What I did not know myself about guiding it, I learned, so I became a good pilot, as I had to be to help myself and my people, if I didn't want us to die there.

Now I was a true man—this is no fable—capable of piloting a ship. Fortune taught me that craft, and so took hold of me. As you hear this, I am still a man, and have been so already for more than thirteen years, though it would please me three times as much to be a woman still, as I was when I spoke with Hymen. But since Fortune has estranged me from that life, so that I shall never be lodged there again, I shall remain a man and keep myself with my lady [Fortune] however much I find a harshness in her service that destroys me. But I have to live there until I die—God deliver me to salvation. So I drew myself away from those rocks, I steered my ship and brought it to the place from which I had departed.

from *The Book of the City of Ladies*

[*Here Begins the Book of the City of Ladies*]

1. Here begins The Book of the City of Ladies, *whose first chapter tells why and for what purpose this book was written.*

One day as I was sitting alone in my study surrounded by books on all kinds of subjects, devoting myself to literary studies, my usual habit, my mind dwelt at length on the weighty opinions of various authors whom I had studied for a long time. I looked up from my book, having decided to leave such subtle questions in peace and to relax by reading some light poetry. With this in mind, I searched for some small book. By chance a strange volume came into my hands, not one of my own, but one which had been given to me along with some others. When I held it open and saw from its title page that it was by Mathéolus,[1] I smiled, for though I had never seen it before, I had often heard that like other books it discussed respect for women. I thought I would browse through it to amuse myself. I had not been reading for very long when my good mother called me to refresh myself with some supper, for it was

Translated by Earl Jeffrey Richards.

---

1. Mathéolus wrote a *Book of Lamentations* in Latin in about 1300, expressing misogyny in Ovidian verse. It was translated into French in the late fourteenth century.

evening. Intending to look at it the next day, I put it down. The next morning, again seated in my study as was my habit, I remembered wanting to examine this book by Mathéolus. I started to read it and went on for a little while. Because the subject seemed to me not very pleasant for people who do not enjoy lies, and of no use in developing virtue or manners, given its lack of integrity in diction and theme, and after browsing here and there and reading the end, I put it down in order to turn my attention to more elevated and useful study. But just the sight of this book, even though it was of no authority, made me wonder how it happened that so many different men—and learned men among them—have been and are so inclined to express both in speaking and in their treatises and writings so many wicked insults about women and their behavior. Not only one or two and not even just this Mathéolus (for this book had a bad name anyway and was intended as a satire) but, more generally, judging from the treatises of all philosophers and poets and all the orators—it would take too long to mention their names—it seems that they all speak from one and the same mouth. They all concur in one conclusion: that the behavior of women is inclined to and full of every vice. Thinking deeply about these matters, I began to examine my character and conduct as a natural woman and, similarly, I considered other women whose company I frequently kept, princesses, great ladies, women of the middle and lower classes, who had graciously told me of their most private and intimate thoughts, hoping that I could judge impartially and in good conscience whether the testimony of so many notable men could be true. To the best of my knowledge, no matter how long I confronted or dissected the problem, I could not see or realize how their claims could be true when compared to the natural behavior and character of women. Yet I still argued vehemently against women, saying that it would be impossible that so many famous men—such solemn scholars, possessed of such deep and great understanding, so clear-sighted in all things, as it seemed—could have spoken falsely on so many occasions that I could hardly find a book on morals where, even before I had read it in its entirety, I did not find several chapters or certain sections attacking women, no matter who the author was. This reason alone, in short, made me conclude that, although my intellect did not perceive my own great faults and, likewise, those of other women because of its simpleness and ignorance, it was however truly fitting that such was the case. And so I relied more on the judgment of others than on what I myself felt and knew. I was so transfixed in this line of thinking for such a long time that it seemed as if I were in a stupor. Like a gushing fountain, a series of authorities, whom I recalled one after another, came to mind, along with their opinions on this topic. And I finally decided that God formed a vile creature when He made woman, and I wondered how such a worthy artisan could have deigned to make such an abominable work which, from what they say, is the vessel as well as the refuge and abode of every evil and vice. As I was thinking this, a great unhappiness and sadness welled up in my heart, for I detested myself and the entire feminine sex, as though we were monstrosities in nature. And in my lament I spoke these words:

"Oh, God, how can this be? For unless I stray from my faith, I must never doubt that Your infinite wisdom and most perfect goodness ever created anything which was not good. Did You yourself not create woman in a very special way and since that time did You not give her all those inclinations which it pleased You for her to have? And how could it be that You could go wrong in anything? Yet look at all these accusations which have been judged, decided, and concluded against women. I do not know how to understand this repugnance. If it is so, fair Lord God, that in fact so many abominations abound in the female sex, for You Yourself say that the testimony of two or three witnesses lends credence, why shall I not doubt that this is true? Alas, God, why did You not let me be born in the world as a man, so that all my inclinations would be to serve You better, and so that I would not stray in anything and would be as perfect as a man is said to be? But since Your kindness has not been extended to me, then forgive my negligence in Your service, most fair Lord God, and may it not displease You, for the servant who receives fewer gifts from his lord is less obliged in his service." I spoke these words to God in my lament and a great deal more for a very long time in sad reflection, and in my folly I considered myself most unfortunate because God had made me inhabit a female body in this world.

[Here Christine Describes How Three Ladies Appeared to Her]

2. Here Christine describes how three ladies appeared to her and how the one who was in front spoke first and comforted her in her pain.

So occupied with these painful thoughts, my head bowed in shame, my eyes filled with tears, leaning on the pommel of my chair's armrest, I suddenly saw a ray of light fall on my lap, as though it were the sun. I shuddered then, as if wakened from sleep, for I was sitting in a shadow where the sun could not have shone at that hour. And as I lifted my head to see where this light was coming from, I saw three crowned ladies standing before me, and the splendor of their bright faces shone on me and throughout the entire room. Now no one would ask whether I was surprised, for my doors were shut and they had still entered. Fearing that some phantom had come to tempt me and filled with great fright, I made the Sign of the Cross on my forehead.

Then she who was the first of the three smiled and began to speak, "Dear daughter, do not be afraid, for we have not come here to harm or trouble you but to console you, for we have taken pity on your distress, and we have come to bring you out of the ignorance which so blinds your own intellect that you shun what you know for a certainty and believe what you do not know or see or recognize except by virtue of many strange opinions. You resemble the fool in the prank who was dressed in women's clothes while he slept; because those who were making fun of him repeatedly told him he was a woman, he believed their false testimony more readily than the certainty of his own identity. Fair daughter, have you lost all sense? Have you forgotten that when fine gold is tested in the furnace, it does not change or vary in strength but becomes purer the more it is hammered and handled in different ways? Do you not know that the best things are the most debated and the most discussed? If you wish to consider the question of the highest form of reality, which consists in ideas or celestial substances, consider whether the greatest philosophers who have lived and whom you support against your own sex have ever resolved whether ideas are false and contrary to the truth. Notice how these same philosophers contradict and criticize one another, just as you have seen in the *Metaphysics* where Aristotle takes their opinions to task and speaks similarly of Plato and other philosophers. And note, moreover, how even Saint Augustine and the Doctors of the Church have criticized Aristotle in certain passages, although he is known as the prince of philosophers in whom both natural and moral philosophy attained their highest level. It also seems that you think that all the words of the philosophers are articles of faith, that they could never be wrong. As far as the poets of whom you speak are concerned, do you not know that they spoke on many subjects in a fictional way and that often they mean the contrary of what their words openly say? One can interpret them according to the grammatical figure of *antiphrasis*, which means, as you know, that if you call something bad, in fact, it is good, and also vice versa. Thus I advise you to profit from their works and to interpret them in the manner in which they are intended in those passages where they attack women. Perhaps this man, who called himself Mathéolus in his own book, intended it in such a way, for there are many things which, if taken literally, would be pure heresy. As for the attack against the estate of marriage—which is a holy estate, worthy and ordained by God—made not only by Mathéolus but also by others and even by the *Romance of the Rose* where greater credibility is averred because of the authority of its author, it is evident and proven by experience that the contrary of the evil which they posit and claim to be found in this estate through the obligation and fault of women is true. For where has the husband ever been found who would allow his wife to have authority to abuse and insult him as a matter of course, as these authorities maintain? I believe that, regardless of what you might have read, you will never see such a husband with your own eyes, so badly colored are these lies. Thus, in conclusion, I tell you, dear friend, that simplemindedness has prompted you to hold such an opinion. Come back to yourself, recover your senses, and do not trouble yourself anymore over such absurdities. For you know that any evil spoken of women so generally only hurts those who say it, not women themselves."

FRANÇOIS VILLON [FRANÇOIS DE MONTCORBIER, OR FRANÇOIS DE LOGES] (1431–1463?)

France

François de Montcorbier adopted the last name of his patron, the chaplain of a university church who adopted him in about 1438. Villon received a Master of Arts degree from the Sorbonne before he was twenty-one, and spent his life repeatedly under arrest, or wandering to escape it, for brawls, robberies, and other escapades. His *Petit Testament* parodies the style of a legal testament; his *Grand Testament,* of

2000 lines, is more melancholy, without losing its humor. In 1462, he was sentenced to be hanged, after a street fight, but the sentence was commuted in 1463 to ten years of banishment. He then disappeared, and remains popular as a colorful outlaw. Villon's lyrics are deeply rooted in tradition and in the facts of life of their time; drawing on these two sources, he gives a vivid and permanent form to the ephemeral moment. As a university student, a criminal, a jailbird, and a wanderer, Villon had a broad schooling in the varieties of human life and language. He was no less broadly acquainted with the poetic movements of his time. He organized most of his lyrics into two cycles, in each of which the speaker—an outlaw and a fugitive, possessing nothing—bequeaths a "legacy" to various persons who shared his times. There are many figures represented and voices heard—those of pimps and prostitutes as well as those of prominent personages—and many kinds of language—from street slang and obscenities to learned and refined speech. The speaker's body is given a voice as well, for it is the object of his continual awareness and concern, a principal source of his moods and of his self-recognition as a mortal, as a participant in the mortality of all God's creatures. For human beings, however much they differ in fortune and circumstance, are all human through their bodies, and all bodies come to the same end.

Most of these elements in Villon's poetry—the arrangement of lyrics into cycles that follow the movements of the speaker's inner life; the immediate presence of historical and personal reality, as well as gloom and the awareness of disaster and decay; the inclusion of different voices and points of view, and of various metrical forms in which to express them—are characteristic of lyric poetry in France in the fourteenth and fifteenth centuries. It is partly through the immense increase in the subjects of poetic representation, and the inclusion of many kinds of popular language not previously recognized as poetic, that Villon surpasses other poets of his time and tradition. With his outlaw's point of view, his mortal and physical consciousness, and his urban attitude—he is the poet of the city, of Paris. Villon was to enlarge the domain of poetry so that there remained no subject unworthy of poetic language, and no language unworthy of poetic form.

Hanged Men

Brother humans who live on after us
Don't let your hearts harden against us
For if you have pity on wretches like us
More likely God will show mercy to you
You see us five, six, hanging here   5
As for the flesh we loved too well
A while ago it was eaten and has rotted away
And we the bones turn to ashes and dust
Let no one make us the butt of jokes
But pray God that he absolve us all.   10

Don't be insulted that we call you
Brothers, even if it was by Justice
We were put to death, for you understand

Translated by Galway Kinnell.

Not every person has the same good sense
Speak up for us, since we can't ourselves   15
Before the son of the virgin Mary
That his mercy toward us shall keep flowing
Which is what keeps us from hellfire
We are dead, may no one taunt us
But pray God that he absolve us all.   20

The rain has rinsed and washed us
The sun dried us and turned us black
Magpies and ravens have pecked out our eyes
And plucked our beards and eyebrows
Never ever can we stand still   25
Now here, now there, as the wind shifts
At its whim it keeps swinging us
Pocked by birds worse than a sewing thimble

Therefore don't join in our brotherhood
But pray God that he absolve us all.   30

Prince Jesus, master over all
Don't let us fall into hell's dominion
We've nothing to do or settle down there
Men, there's nothing here to laugh at
But pray God that he absolve us all.   35

Our Lady[1]

Lady of heaven, regent of earth
Empress over the swamps of hell
Receive me your humble Christian
Let me be counted among your elect
Even though I'm without any worth   5
My lady and mistress your merits
Are greater by far than my sinfulness
And without them no soul could deserve
Or enter heaven, I'm not acting
In this faith I want to live and die.   10

Tell your son I belong to him
May he wash away my sins
And forgive me as he did the Egyptian woman[2]

---

1. In his poetic *Testament* or Will, Villon be-
queathes this ballade to his "poor mother,"
to help her pray to the Virgin.
2. Saint Mary the Egyptian was a prostitute in
Alexandria who joined a pilgrimage out of
mere curiosity, paying for her passage, according to legend, by plying her trade—a
Villonesque touch; she was converted in
Jerusalem through the influence of the Virgin's image and thereafter lived a reclusive
life of penance in the wilderness.

Or Theophilus[3] the priest
Who with your help was acquitted and absolved   15
Though he'd made a pact with the devil
Keep me from ever doing that
Virgin who bore with unbroken hymen
The sacrament we celebrate at Mass
In this faith I want to live and die.   20

I'm just a poor old woman
Who knows nothing and can't read
On the walls of my parish church I see
A paradise painted with harps and lutes
And a hell where they boil the damned   25
One gives me a fright, one great bliss and joy
Let me have the good place, mother of God
To whom sinners all must turn
Filled with faith, sincere and eager
In this faith I want to live and die.   30

Virgin so worthy, princess, you bore
Iesus who reigns without end or limit
Lord Almighty who took on our weakness
Left heaven and came down to save us
Offering his precious youth to death   35
Now such is our Lord, such I acknowledge him
In this faith I want to live and die.[4]

THOMAS MALORY (c. 1471)
England

Sir Thomas Malory, who belonged to an old Warwickshire family, was, at various
times, a soldier—a loyalist, then a rebel—a member of Parliament, and five or six
years later, a fugitive from justice. Imprisoned eight times, he made two dramatic
escapes; it was during his last imprisonment that he wrote his Arthurian
romance: Le Morte D'Arthur, testifying to England's heroic past. Drawing on the
vast compendia of Arthurian, Tristan, and Grail stories in the French vulgate
cycles of the thirteenth century, Malory set the Tristan-Isolde affair at the center
of Le Morte D'Arthur, his long prose romance.

---

3. The story of Theophilus, saved from his
pact with the Devil through the intervention of the Virgin, was popular all through
the Middle Ages.

4. In this concluding stanza, or envoi, the first
letters of the first six lines, read downward,
form an acrostic of the poet's name.

The Launcelot-Guinevere affair, with certain important similarities, is told on either side of the Tristan story. It brings the problem of adultery with the king's wife to the heart of the Arthurian court, which it will help to destroy. Malory makes Launcelot an exemplum of the courtly paradox—the knight who has achieved the highest level of chivalry through his service to his lady, Guinevere, but who fails in the highest quest of all, for the Grail, precisely because of that love. Though he remains the finest knight within the Arthurian circle, Launcelot is unable to give up chivalric values, like helping the weaker side in a tournament even if it is the sinners' side (the black knights in the second selection). He is therefore unable to achieve the Grail quest, while the knights who do, Galahad and Perceval, do not continue to serve in the world but die shortly after their quests are accomplished.

from *Le Morte D'Arthur*

[How Sir Launcelot Found the Old Chapel and Saw the Altar]

Then Sir Launcelot looked by him, and saw an old chapel, and there he weened to have found people; and Sir Launcelot tied his horse till a tree, and there he did off his shield and hung it upon a tree. And then he went to the chapel door, and found it waste and broken. And within he found a fair altar, full richly arrayed with cloth of clean silk, and there stood a fair clean candlestick, which bare six great candles, and the candlestick was of silver. And when Sir Launcelot saw this light he had great will for to enter into the chapel, but he could find no place where he might enter; then was he passing heavy and dismayed. Then he returned and came to his horse and did off his saddle and bridle, and let him pasture, and unlaced his helm, and ungirt his sword, and laid him down to sleep upon his shield tofore the cross.

How Sir Launcelot, half sleeping and half waking, saw a sick man borne in a litter, and how he was healed by the Sangrail

And so he fell asleep; and half waking and sleeping he saw come by him two palfreys all fair and white, the which bare a litter, therein lying a sick knight. And when he was nigh the cross he there abode still. All this Sir Launcelot saw and beheld, for he slept not verily; and he heard him say,

"O sweet Lord, when shall this sorrow leave me? And when shall the holy vessel come by me, wherethrough I shall be blessed? For I have endured thus long, for little trespass."

A full great while complained the knight thus, and always Sir Launcelot heard it.

With that Sir Launcelot saw the candlestick with the six tapers come before the cross, and he saw nobody that brought it. Also there came a table of silver, and

Edited by Janet Cowen.

the holy vessel of the Sangrail,[1] which Launcelot had seen aforetime in King Petchere's house.[2]

And therewith the sick knight sat up, and held up both his hands, and said, "Fair sweet Lord, which is here within this holy vessel, take heed unto me that I may be whole of this malady."

And therewith on his hands and on his knees he went so nigh that he touched the holy vessel and kissed it, and anon he was whole; and then he said, "Lord God, I thank Thee, for I am healed of this sickness."

So when the holy vessel had been there a great while it went unto the chapel with the chandelier and the light, so that Launcelot wist not where it was become; for he was overtaken with sin that he had no power to rise against[3] the holy vessel; wherefore after that many men said of him shame, but he took repentance after that.

Then the sick knight dressed him up and kissed the cross; anon his squire brought him his arms, and asked his lord how he did.

"Certes," said he, "I thank God right well, through the holy vessel I am healed. But I have marvel of this sleeping knight that had no power to awake when this holy vessel was brought hither."

"I dare right well say," said the squire, "that he dwelleth in some deadly sin whereof he was never confessed."

"By my faith," said the knight, "whatsomever he be he is unhappy, for as I deem he is of the fellowship of the Round Table, the which is entered into the quest of the Sangrail."

"Sir," said the squire, "here I have brought you all your arms save your helm and your sword, and therefore by mine assent now may ye take this knight's helm and his sword;" and so he did.

And when he was clean armed he took Sir Launcelot's horse, for he was better than his; and so departed they from the cross.

[How Sir Launcelot Heard a Voice and Called Himself Wretched, Unhappy, and Ashamed]

Then anon Sir Launcelot waked, and sat him up, and bethought him what he had seen there, and whether it were dreams or not.

Right so heard he a voice that said, "Sir Launcelot, more harder than is the stone, and more bitter than is the wood, and more naked and barer than is the leaf of the fig tree;[4] therefore go thou from hence, and withdraw thee from this holy place."

And when Sir Launcelot heard this he was passing heavy and wist not what

---

1. The Sangrail is the Holy Grail. In Malory, God's blood is in the vessel, giving it the power to cure the sick knight when he kisses it.
2. King Petchere or Pescheors is the Fisher King, the Grail king who appears in Chrétien and in Wolfram. It is a play on the French word *pescheor,* "sinner," which in

Middle French also means "fisherman." Since Saint Peter was a "fisher of men," and a fish is an ancient symbol of Christians, the pun is particularly suitable.

3. In the presence of the holy vessel.
4. A fig tree becomes barren in the gospel when Christ curses it (Matthew 21:19).

to do, and so departed sore weeping, and cursed the time that he was born. For then he deemed never to have had worship more. For those words went to his heart, till that he knew wherefore he was called so.

Then Sir Launcelot went to the cross and found his helm, his sword, and his horse taken away. And then he called himself a very wretch, and most unhappy of all knights; and there he said,

"My sin and my wickedness have brought me unto great dishonour. For when I sought worldly adventures for worldly desires, I ever achieved them and had the better in every place, and never was I discomfit in no quarrel, were it right or wrong. And now I take upon me the adventures of holy things, and now I see and understand that mine old sin hindereth me and shameth me, so that I had no power to stir nor speak when the holy blood appeared afore me."

[Sir Launcelot and the Black Knights]

How Sir Launcelot jousted with many knights, and he was taken

And then mounted upon his horse, and rode into a forest, and held no highway. And as he looked afore him he saw a fair plain, and beside that a fair castle, and afore the castle were many pavilions of silk and of diverse hue. And him seemed that he saw there five hundred knights riding on horseback; and there were two parties; they that were of the castle were all on black horses and their trappers black, and they that were without were all on white horses and trappers, and every each hurtled to other that it marvelled Sir Launcelot. And at the last him thought they of the castle were put to the worse.

Then thought Sir Launcelot for to help there the weaker party in increasing of his chivalry. And so Sir Launcelot thrust in among the party of the castle, and smote down a knight, horse and man, to the earth. And then he rushed here and there, and did marvellous deeds of arms and then he drew out his sword, and struck many knights to the earth, so that all those that saw him marvelled that ever one knight might do so great deeds of arms.

But always the white knights held them nigh about Sir Launcelot, for to tire him and wind him. But at the last, as a man may not ever endure, Sir Launcelot waxed so faint of fighting and travailing, and was so weary of his great deeds, but he might not lift up his arms for to give one stroke, so that he weened never to have borne arms; and then they all took and led him away into a forest, and there made him to alight and to rest him.

And then all the fellowship of the castle were overcome for the default of him.

Then they said all unto Sir Launcelot, "Blessed be God that ye be now of our fellowship, for we shall hold you in our prison;" and so they left him with few words.

And then Sir Launcelot made great sorrow, "For never or now was I never at tournament nor jousts but I had the best, and now I am shamed." And then he said, "Now I am sure that I am more sinfuller than ever I was."

Thus he rode sorrowing, and half a day he was out of despair, till that he came into a deep valley. And when Sir Launcelot saw he might not ride up into the mountain, he there alit under an apple tree, and there he left his helm and his shield, and put his horse unto pasture. And then he laid him down to sleep.

And then him thought there came an old man afore him, the which said, "Ah, Launcelot of evil faith and poor belief, wherefore is thy will turned so lightly toward thy deadly sin?" And when he had said thus he vanished away, and Launcelot wist not where he was become.

Then he took his horse, and armed him; and as he rode by the way he saw a chapel where was a recluse, which had a window that she might see up to the altar. And all aloud she called Launcelot, for that he seemed a knight errant. And then he came, and she asked him what he was, and of what place, and where about he went to seek.

[How Sir Launcelot Recounted His Vision, and Had It Interpreted for Him]

And then he told her all together by word, and the truth how it befell him at the tournament. And after told her his advision that he had had that night in his sleep, and prayed her to tell him what it might mean, for he was not well content with it.

"Ah, Launcelot," said she, "as long as ye were knight of earthly knighthood ye were the most marvellous man of the world, and most adventurous. Now," said the lady, "sithen ye be set among the knights of heavenly adventures, if adventure fell thee contrary at that tournament have thou no marvel, for that tournament yesterday was but a tokening of Our Lord. And notforthan there was none enchantment, for they at the tournament were earthly knights.

. . .

"The day of Pentecost, when King Arthur held his court, it befell that earthly kings and knights took a tournament together, that is to say the quest of the Sangrail. The earthly knights were they the which were clothed all in black, and the covering betokeneth the sins whereof they be not confessed. And they with the covering of white betokeneth virginity, and they that chose chastity. And thus was the quest begun in them. Then thou beheld the sinners and the good men, and when thou sawest the sinners overcome, thou inclinest to that party for bobaunce and pride of the world, and all that must be left in that quest, for in this quest thou shalt have many fellows and thy betters. For thou are so feeble of evil trust and good belief, this made it when thou were there where they took thee and led thee into the forest.

"And anon there appeared the Sangrail unto the white knights, but thou was so feeble of good belief and faith that thou mightest not abide it for all the teaching of the good man, but anon thou turnest to the sinners, and that caused thy misadventure that thou shouldst know good from evil and vain glory of the world, the which is not worth a pear. And for great pride thou madest great sorrow that thou haddest not overcome all the white knights with the covering of white by whom was betokened virginity and chastity; and therefore God was wroth with you, for God loveth no such deeds in this quest. And this advision signifieth that thou were of evil faith and of poor belief, the which will make thee to fall into the deep pit of hell if thou keep thee not.

"Now have I warned thee of thy vain glory and of thy pride, that thou hast many times erred against thy Maker. Beware of everlasting pain, for of all earthly knights I have most pity of thee, for I know well thou hast not thy peer of any earthly sinful man."

FERNANDO DE ROJAS (c. 1465–1541)
Spain

Fernando de Rojas was a *converso*—a Jew who converted to Christianity in order to avoid permanent expulsion from his homeland as a result of a royal decree of 1492. Few other biographical facts are known about him and the circumstances under which he wrote *La Celestina*. However, he does offer some information in an acrostic poem that precedes the text proper. If we combine the first letters of each stanza, we learn the following: "The Bachelor [i.e., lawyer] Fernando de Rojas finished the comedy of Calisto and Melibea and was born in Puebla de Montalbán." Some further indirectly communicated information is supplied by a letter from "the author to a friend," which also precedes the narrative. In the letter he explains that he found the first act he reproduces in his text in Salamanca with no indication as to its author. Rojas goes on to say that during a two-week vacation he added the subsequent acts (offering a total of sixteen acts in the 1499 version and twenty-one acts in the expanded 1502 edition). Also new in the later edition is a prologue that officially changed the title of the work from the *Comedy of Calixto and Melibea* to the *Tragicomedy of Calixto and Melibea*.

In spite of this significant renaming of his text (intended to emphasize its more somber aspects), it has since the sixteenth century been referred to as *La Celestina* because of the powerful portrayal of the bawd who effects the liaison between the two young lovers, Melibea and Calixto. Celestina is characterized very vividly in her various vocations as pedcler, procuress, and witch, and Rojas defies literary norms by combining a story about upper-class lovers with a striking fascination for the world of the underclass in all its seaminess. The clash of values extends to the upper class as well, however, for we see that even Calixto and Melibea are driven by a very uncourtly lust and a craving for domination.

The passages included here are among the most famous speeches in all of Spanish literature, for they testify with great eloquence to the power of human subjectivity and its defiance of social strictures. Melibea confesses her illicit affair to her father, killing herself thereafter, since life without Calixto would be meaningless. Even more surprisingly, her father, Pleberio, who has functioned not only as an exemplary and loving father but as a spokesman for Stoic *ataraxia* (restraint), is utterly devastated by Melibea's untimely death. It is important to note that Pleberio does not condemn his daughter's behavior as a revengeful father of Spanish Golden Age *comedia* (or traditional drama) would do—as a horrible stain on the family's honor. He is too deeply destroyed on a personal level to care about social sanctions. In these passages, as throughout this text, Rojas brilliantly explodes the convention of character decorum, whereby individuals are made to function as expressions of class, gender, or other sociocultural typecasting.

from *The Celestina*

[Melibea Confesses Her Affair and Kills Herself]

MELIBEA: Everyone has left me, and I've now contrived a way of dying. It gives me some consolation to know that soon we shall be together, I and my dear lover Calisto. I will shut the door, so that no one may come up to prevent my death. They shan't prevent my going. No one shall stop the way by which very soon I shall be able to visit him today who visited me last night. Everything has conformed to my plan, and I shall have time to tell my lord Pleberio the cause of my premature end. I am greatly wronging his grey hairs, bringing much grief to his old age. Many sorrows will fall on him because of my sin. I leave him in great desolation. But even if my death should shorten my parents' days, others have certainly been crueller to theirs. Prusias, king of Bithynia killed his father, for no reason, having no grievance against him; Ptolemy king of Egypt killed his father, his mother, his brothers, and his wife in order to enjoy a mistress; and Orestes murdered his mother Clytemnestra; the cruel Emperor Nero had his mother Agrippina killed just for the joy he took in murder. They are wicked, they are the true parricides, but I am not. If I give pain by my death, at least I am expiating the crime of causing them grief. Others have been far more cruel, and killed sons and brothers. Beside their crimes mine will appear slight. Philip, king of Macedon; Herod, king of Judah; Constantine, emperor of Rome; Laodice, queen of Cappadocia, and the witch Medea: all of them killed their dear children and lovers for no reason and preserved their own lives. Finally I remember the great cruelty of Phrates, king of the Parthians, who killed his old father Orodos, his only son, and thirty brothers and sisters in order to leave no heir. These crimes were wicked indeed, for they killed their elders, descendants, and brothers, while remaining safe themselves. It is true that even so we should not imitate their evil-doing. But it is now out of my hands. You, Lord, who have been witness to what I've said, you see how little is my strength, how my liberty is lost, how my feelings have been captured by love for that gentleman who is dead, a love so powerful that it destroys the love I have for my living parents.

PLEBERIO: What are you doing up there, Melibea? Why are you alone? What do you want to say to me? Would you like me to come up?

MELIBEA: Don't attempt to come up here, Father, or you'll interrupt what I want to say to you. Soon you'll be weeping for the death of your only daughter. I have come to my end. I am drawing near to my rest and you to your sorrow, I to my comfort and you to your grief. Now is the time when I shall have company and you will be alone. There'll be no need of instruments to soothe my sorrow, only of bells for the burial of my body. If you can listen without weeping you'll hear the desperate cause of my forced but happy

Translated by J. M. Cohen.

departure. Do not interrupt me with words or tears, or you'll suffer more by not knowing why I have died than by seeing me dead. Ask me no questions, and do not demand to know more than I wish to tell you. For when the heart is heavy with grief, the ears are closed to counsel, and at such times good advice rather inflames than allays the passions. Listen, dear Father, to my last words, and if you receive them as I hope, you will not blame my fault. You can see and hear the mourning that afflicts the whole city. You can hear the tolling of bells, the shouting of the people, the barking of dogs and the clash of arms. I was the cause of all this. I have today clothed in sackcloth and mourning the majority of the city's gentlemen, I have left many servants masterless, I have robbed many poor and destitute people of alms and relief, I have been the occasion for sending the most accomplished man ever endowed with graces to keep company with the dead. I have sent out of the land of the living the pattern of nobility and gallantry, of charm and adornment, of speech, carriage, courtesy, and virtue. Thanks to me earth enjoys before her time the noblest body and freshest youth ever born into the world in our days. Though it will astonish you to hear of my strange sin, I will tell you more fully what happened.

Many days ago, Father, a knight named Calisto, whom you knew well, was grieving for love of me. You knew his parents also, and his noble descent; he was famous for his virtues and his courtesy to everyone. He was so tortured by his love and had so little opportunity of speaking to me that he disclosed his passion to a wise and cunning old woman called Celestina, whom he sent to visit me and who dragged the secret of my love from my heart. I told her what I had concealed from my beloved mother. She found a way of winning me to her will, and brought his desires and mine to fruition. He loved me greatly and he was not disappointed. She contrived the sweet and ill-fated consummation of his desires. Subdued by love for him I let him into your house. He scaled the walls of your garden with a ladder, and overcame my resistance. I lost my virginity, and we enjoyed the sinful pleasures of our love for almost a month. Last night he came in the usual way, and just as he was about to return home, Fortune, in her mutability, disposing of all things in her disorderly way, put an end to our joy. The walls were high, the night was dark, the ladder was weak, and the servants he brought with him unused to this kind of service. He was descending in a hurry, having heard a noise in the road where his servants were waiting, and in his confusion failed to see the rungs, put a foot out into the void and fell. Alas, he fell on his head and scattered his brains over the stones and the wall. The Fates cut short his life. They cut him off unconfessed and with him all my hopes, my joy and delight in his company. How cruel it would be, Father, after his death from that fall, that I should live on in grief! His death calls for mine. It invites me, it compels me to be swift and allows no delay. It summons me to fall also. so that I may follow him in everything. It shall not be said of me that dead and gone is soon forgotten. I shall content him in my death, since I had not time to do so in my life. O my loved lord Calisto! Wait for me, I am coming. Wait if you expect me, and don't blame me for staying to give this last account to my father, for I owe him this and much more. Beloved father, I beg you if you loved me in my painful life that is now over, that we may be buried together and our funerals be celebrated together also. Before my welcome release I would say some words of consolation to you that I have chosen and gathered from those ancient books that you made me read for the improvement of my mind. But alas, my memory is confused by the tumult of my grief, and by the sight of your ill-restrained tears trickling down your wrinkled cheeks, and so I have forgotten them. Carry my farewell to my dear mother, and tell her carefully the sad reasons for my death. I am glad not to see her here. Accept, dear father, the penalties of old age; for in a long life sorrows must be endured. Receive this tribute to your years, and receive your beloved daughter in your arms. I grieve for myself, I grieve for you, and much more for my old mother. God be with you and her. To him I offer my soul, and to you for burial my body, that is now coming down to you.

[Pleberio Bewails His Misery and Curses Celestina]

Pleberio returns to his room weeping bitterly, and Alisa asks him the cause of his sudden grief. He tells her of their daughter's death, and shows her Melibea's shattered body. The work concludes with his lamentation.

ALISA: What's the matter, Pleberio? Why are you weeping and crying? I have been lying here senseless since I fainted on hearing that our daughter was in pain. But now your shouts and groans have roused me. Your tears and grief and unaccustomed lamentations have struck me to the heart, revived my numbed senses, and dispelled my previous sorrow. One grief, one passion has driven out the other. Tell me what you are bewailing. Why are you cursing your honourable old age? Why are you tearing your white hair? Why do you call on death? Why are you scratching your venerable face? Has something terrible happened to Melibea? In God's name tell me, for if she is suffering I no longer want to live.

PLEBERIO: Oh, oh, noble wife! Our joy is drowned, and all our happiness gone. Our life is worth nothing now. There is no pain like that of sudden grief, one unexpected blow following on another. It will drive you quickly to the tomb. But I cannot weep alone for the sad loss that has struck us both. Here is the daughter you bore and I engendered. Gaze on her shattered body. She told me the cause, but I learnt it more fully from her sorrowful maid. Join me in weeping our latter years that have now come upon us, all of you who come to share my grief. Help me, my friends, to bewail my misery. My daughter who was my sole treasure! It would be cruelty in me to outlive you. My seventy years were riper for the grave than your twenty. The due order of death was reversed by the grief that overwhelmed you. My hair has grown white only from sorrow, and earth should receive it more gladly than the fair locks that lie here. The rest of my days will be too many. I will complain against death for being so slow and leaving me here alone, now that you have gone. What have I left in life now that I have lost your delightful company? Get up from where she lies, Alisa, and if any life is left in you join me in bewailing her, pour it out in groans and sighs and lamentations. But if your spirit has joined hers, if you have already left this life of grief, why have you wished me to suffer everything alone? You women have the advantage over us that a great grief can painlessly remove you from the world, or at least make you swoon and thus give you some ease. What a hard heart has a father, that it does not break with grief at the loss of its one beloved child! For whom did I build towers? For whom did I acquire honours? For whom did I plant trees? For whom construct ships? O hard earth, how can you still support my steps? Where will my disconsolate old age find shelter? O Fortune, you are indeed minister and steward of temporal wealth, how mutable you are! Why did you not turn your cruel wrath on me? Why did you not overwhelm with your changing tides me who am truly your subject? Why did you not destroy my wealth? Why did you not burn my house? Why did you not reduce my great inheritance to dust? You might have left me that flourishing plant, over which you should have had no power. O fickle Fortune, if you had given me an unhappy youth and a glad old age, you would not have perverted nature. I could have borne the cruelty of your deceptions better in my strong and vigorous youth than in my weak and declining age.

O life full of griefs and miseries! O world, world! Many men have said many things of you, many have inveighed against you for your deceits. they have said many things of you by hearsay, but I will speak from the sad experience of one whose sales and purchases at your deceptive fair have not gone well, of one who has long concealed your double-dealing for fear of arousing your wrath by my hatred, and so that you should not prematurely wither this flower that has today fallen into your grasp. But now I am not afraid, for I have nothing more to lose. Now I am weary of your company. I am like a poor traveller who sings loudly on his way since he has nothing to fear from the cruel highwaymen. I believed in my youth that you and your deeds were governed by some order. But now that I have seen the pro and contra of your dealings, I find in you only a maze of error, a frightful desert, a den of wild beasts, a game in which men go round in circles, a lake full of mud, a country choked with thorns, a high mountain, a stony meadow, a field swarming with snakes, an orchard all blossom and no fruit, a fountain of cares, a river of tears, a sea of miseries, labour without profit, sweet poison, vain hope, false joy, and real sorrow. Feed us, false world, with the food of your delights, and in the tastiest morsel we find the hook. We cannot escape it for it has ensnared our wills. You promise much but perform nothing. You throw us from you so that we shall not beg you to keep your empty promises. Carelessly and thoughtlessly we run in the meadows of your rank vices, and you show us the trap when we have no chance of turning back. Many have forsaken you for fear you might suddenly forsake them, and they will count themselves lucky when they see the reward you have given this poor old man in payment for his long services. You put out our eyes and then anoint our brows to comfort us. So that no sad man shall find himself alone in adversity, you hurt everyone. You tell us that it consoles miserable men like myself to have companions in sorrow. But I am alone in my grief, disconsolate and old.

No man's misfortune is like mine. Though I search my weary memory of the present and the past I can find no one who has suffered a similar grief. If I recall the stoical patience of Paulus Emilius, whose two sons were killed within a week yet who bore his loss with such courage that the Roman people took more comfort from him than he from them, I am not consoled, for he had two sons left to him, whom he had adopted. What sort of companion in my grief should I find in the Athenian captain Pericles, or in the valiant Xenophon, since their sons died in foreign lands? It could not have cost Pericles much not to change countenance but to keep a calm expression, or for Xenophon to tell the messenger who brought him the sad news of his son's death that he would receive no penalty because he himself felt no sorrow. There is no resemblance here to my misfortune.

Even less could you say, O world full of evils, that Anaxagoras and I were alike in our grief and loss, and that I could repeat of my beloved daughter what he said of his only son: 'Being mortal, I knew that whatever I engendered must die.' For my Melibea killed herself before my eyes, of her own free will, driven to it by the cruel love that tortured her, whereas his son was killed in righteous battle. There is no loss like mine. A stricken old man, I seek comfort but find nothing to comfort me. The royal prophet David, who wept when his son was sick, refused to weep for him dead since he said it was almost madness to weep for what could not be remedied, and he had many children left to comfort him in his loss. But I am not weeping for her sad death, but for the terrible manner of it. O my unhappy daughter, with you I lose the fears and apprehensions that alarmed me every day. Your death alone has had the power to free me from anxieties.

What shall I do when I go to your room and find it empty? What shall I do when you do not answer my knock? Who could fill the void that you leave in me? No one has lost what I have lost today, not the valiant Lambas of Auria, Duke of Athens, who with his own hands threw his wounded son overboard into the sea. All these were deaths suffered in the cause of honour. But what forced my daughter to slay herself was the mighty power of love. False world, what comfort can you give me in my tired old age? How can you expect me to remain alive, now that I know the tricks and snares, the chains and nets, in which you capture our weak wills? Where have you taken my daughter? Who will be my companion in my companionless home? Who will look after me in my failing years? O love, love, I did not think you had the strength and power to kill your victims. You wounded me in my youth, but I survived your fires. Why did you let me go, only to pay me out for my escape in my old age? I thought myself free from your snares when I came to the age of forty and was happy in my wife's company and in the fruit of our union that you have plucked today. I did not think you would visit your spite against the fathers upon the children, or know that you could wound with the sword and burn with fire. You leave the clothes untouched but wound the heart. You make men love the ugly and think it beautiful. Who gave you such power? Who gave you so unsuitable a name? If you were love indeed, you would love your servants. If they lived happily they would not kill themselves, as my beloved daughter has done.

What is the fate of your servants and ministers? The false pander Celestina died at the hands of the most faithful servants she had ever recruited in your poisonous cause. They were beheaded, Calisto fell from the wall, and my beloved daughter chose to die the same death in order to follow him. You were the cause of all this. They have given you a sweet name, but you perform bitter deeds, and you do not give equal rewards. The law is wicked that is not fair to all. We rejoice at the sound of your name, but our dealings with you make us sad. Happy are those whom you have never known or never noticed. Some, induced by an error of the senses, have called you a god. But it is a strange god that kills its own children, as you kill your followers. In defiance of all reason, you give the richest gifts to those who serve you least, so that in the end you may draw them into your painful dance. You are an enemy to your friends, a friend to your enemies. Why do you act without rhyme or reason? They paint you as a poor blind boy, and put a bow in your hand with which you shoot at random; but it is your ministers that are blind, for they never feel or see how harsh is the reward you give to those who serve you. Your fire is a burning flash that leaves no mark where it strikes. Its flames are fed with the souls and lives of human beings, so numberless that if I tried to count them I do not know where I should begin. Not only of Christians, but of pagans and Jews; and all in requital for their worship of you. What would you say of Macias, who in our day died of love, and of whose sad end you were the cause? What did Paris do for you? And Helen? And Hypermnestra? And Aegisthus? Everyone knows the answer. What payment did you give to Sappho, Ariadne, and Leander? You would not leave even David and Solomon unharmed. And did not Samson pay the penalty for trusting her in whom you forced him to put his faith? There are many more whom I leave unmentioned, for my own evils are a sufficient theme.

I complain of the world because it created me in its bosom; because if it had not given me life I should not have fathered Melibea. If she had not been born I should not have loved her; if I had not loved I would cease to complain and my old age would not be desolate. O my daughter, my dear companion, dashed to pieces on the ground, why would you not let me prevent your death? Why did you not take pity on your darling mother, whom you loved? Why did you behave so cruelly to your old father? Why did you leave me in torment? Why did you leave me sad and alone in this vale of tears?

ANONYMOUS (FIFTEENTH CENTURY)
England

In this poem we see some of the defining features of the Middle English lyric at its best. The meaning and effect are conveyed by vivid images that are both simple and rich in allusiveness (the dew, for example, is a symbol of multiple significance, including the Holy Spirit and divine grace in its range of meaning; its initiating text is the story of Gideon's fleece, Judges 6:37–40). The language is simple and close to popular usage, but it can convey complex ideas and feelings. The word *makeles,* for example, in the second line, means "matchless," signifying not only the Virgin's uniqueness as the mother of God, but also her exemption from the ordinary "match," since the Middle English word *make* also means "mate"; consider also the different meanings of *stille.* The message is simple and directly stated, but its enterprise is tremendous: it seeks to translate mystery into experience—the greatest mystery of all, the miracle of the Virgin Birth, the beginning of human redemption, and also the most interior experience, that of the sentient imagination. The tone of wonder and admiration is strengthened by a powerful irony: the maiden, a simple girl, chooses as her son the King of Kings.

I Sing of a Maiden

I sing of a maiden
that is makeles,[1]
Kings of alle kinges
to[2] here sone she ches.[3]

He cam also[4] stille   5
ther[5] his moder was
as dew in Aprille
that falleth on the gras.

He cam also stille
to his moderes bowr   10
as dew is Aprille
that falleth on the flowr.

He cam also stille
ther his moder lay
as dew in Aprille   15
that falleth on the spray.[6]

Moder and maiden
was never none but she:
well may swich[7] a lady
Godes moder be.   20

---

1. Matchless/mateless.
2. For, as.
3. Chose.
4. As.

5. Where.
6. Small branches and foliage.
7. Such.

Dervishes dancing to music, from a
Persian manuscript, c. 1485 C.E. Dublin,
Chester Beatty Library (mms. 163).

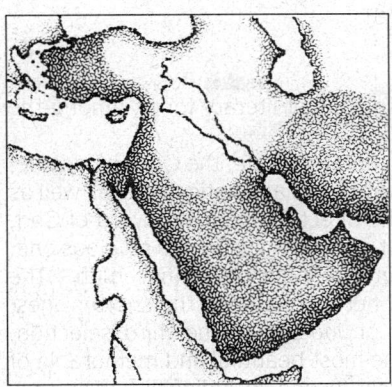

SECTION V
Early and Classical Middle East

The development of Arabic, Persian, and Turkish literatures was closely bound up with the emergence of the Islamic religion in seventh-century Arabia, the Arab conquests that followed, and the classical Islamic civilization that resulted in most of what we today call the Middle East.

When the Qur'an (Arabic *qur'ān,* recitation; also familiar as the Koran) the holy book of Islam, was revealed to the Arabian Prophet Muhammad during the seventh century C.E., it heralded the advent not only of a new religious civilization but of a sophisticated literary culture as well. The first literature of the Islamic world was in Arabic, the language of the Arabs and of the Qur'an. For a few centuries, Arabic remained the sole literary language. But later, literatures developed in Persian, Turkish, and other languages. These literary cultures drew from their progenitor; their writers were usually schooled in Arabic letters as well as their own.

Arabic literature began before Islam in a period called the Jāhiliyya. This literature of a partly Bedouin society was dominated by poetry, the poet often acting as the oracle of his tribe. Poems such as "Arabian Ode in 'L,' " written by the sixth-century poet Shanfarā, are still considered by modern Arabs to be among the finest examples of their art. Alongside the dominant male poetic voice was a female one, generally specialized in elegiac verse, like that of al-Khansā', whose elegies for her brother have ensured her literary immortality. Indeed, poetry has remained to the present time the most prestigious of literary forms among the Arabs.

With its powerful imagery and its often incantatory style, the Qur'an became, along with the pre-Islamic poetic corpus, a literary and aesthetic model as well as a religious one. For Muslims, the Qur'an is the direct, unmediated word of God, and as such it is as perfect from a literary point of view as it is from a religious one. The Qur'an is divided into 114 chapters or *suras* in Arabic of varying length. "The Forenoon" and "The Darkening," presented here, are among the shorter ones, dealing with the call to Islam and the Day of Judgment. The third selection, "Joseph," is generally agreed to be one of the most beautiful and memorable of the longer *suras,* relating the story of the biblical Joseph, including his adventures with his brothers and his period in Egypt. Joseph is represented as the paragon of beauty in Islam; this confrontation with the Egyptian ruler's wife becomes one of the most haunting incidents recurring in later literary and mystical texts, where the wife is known as Zulaykhā.

The Arab-Islamic conquests of the seventh and eighth centuries created a multinational empire from Spain to Afghanistan. This cosmopolitan society drew virtually without prejudice from the cultures of the region, spawning a sophisticated literature far greater in richness and quantity than the literatures of either the classical Mediterranean world or medieval Europe. Paper had recently been invented in China and its dissemination throughout the Islamic world had much to do with this literary florescence, but so too did the opening of cultural channels and the circulation of ideas across an unprecedented geographical expanse. Scholars and writers could begin their careers in what is today Portugal and end them on the banks of the Red Sea or on the borders of the Hindu Kush.

The works that have come down to us from the classical period of this highly sophisticated culture are numerous.[1] One of the literary genres dominating the prose corpus is *adab,* an anecdotal genre designed at once to be edifying and entertaining. To characterize it strictly as prose can be, however, misleading. In its various forms, *adab* can include Qur'anic verses, poetry, and traditions of the Prophet. These traditions, called *hadīth,* are collections of sayings and descriptions of the actions of the Prophet, designed to serve as guides for the daily life of the Muslim. The ninth-century Arab writer, al-Jāhiz is generally recognized as the greatest master of Arabic *adab.*

The heterogeneous nature of the Islamic empire led eventually to linguistic diversity, and even al-Jāhiz used some Persian in his Arabic works. Given the diversity of the culture, it should come as no surprise that literary genres once conceived as typically Arabic should surface in other languages of the Islamic empire, such as Persian. It is here that a connection can be seen with the works of the thirteenth-century writer, Saʿdī and the fourteenth-century writer ʿUbayd-i Zākānī. That they are, in fact, literary cousins of the Arabic *adab* can be seen from their similar discourse, with its mixture of prose, verse, and interwoven religious text.

The characters who populated medieval Arabic anecdotal works ranged from rulers and judges to misers and party crashers. This anecdotal literature was a generic cousin to an indigenous Arabic form invented by the tenth-century writer

---

1. The classical period of Islamic civilization coincided with the European Middle Ages. "Classical" and "medieval" are thus loosely interchangeable in general discussions of Islamic culture.

Badī^c al-Zamān al-Hamadhānī. His *Maqāmāt* (loosely translated as "seances") were a literary tour de force executed in rhymed prose *saj*^c and featuring a sort of picaresque hero whose existence centered around his eloquence on the one hand and his ability to outwit his listeners and gain from them on the other.

Literature flourished in the Islamic West as it did in the Islamic East. The eleventh-century Andalusian author Ibn Hazm, shows us another dimension of anecdotal prose literature in *The Dove's Neckring,* his treatise on the psychology of love. The emergence of courtly love themes in Hispano-Arabic literature has often been linked to the popularity of the troubadours in neighboring Provence.

From quite early on in the development of Islamic orthodoxy, rumblings of asceticism and mysticism could be heard. Islamic mysticism spawned its own literature in Arabic, and especially, in Persian. Farīd al-Dīn ^cAttār, Rūmī, and Jāmī are but a few of the names. One of the most beloved of stories in Islam, that of Joseph and the Egyptian ruler's wife was redefined and recast in a mystical setting. Generally, asceticism and mysticism attracted individuals dissatisfied with what they perceived to be the loss of the personal dimension in the religious experience, buried under legalistic discussions and ritualized practice. These competing trends, the mystical and the legal, were harmonized by the great thinker al-Ghazālī, whose autobiography focuses on this dilemma.

Al-Ghazālī's autobiography, like that of Saint Augustine, recounts a religious quest. The autobiographical writing of the great twelfth-century Syrian warrior-writer, Usāma ibn Munqidh is different. His saga takes place during the Crusades and some of his observations of the Western combatants are by now classic, their insights into cultural differences as illuminating today as they were seven centuries ago.

The Islamization of regions such as Iran and Turkey did not mean a homogenization of culture. Distinctive genres flourished; distinctive discourses developed. The Persian epic, for example, finds no parallel in Arabic letters. The Persian poet Firdawsī's famous epic, *Shāh Nāma,* dramatically recounts the adventures of the heroes of pre-Islamic Iran. As such, it has remained a monument to Iranian (as opposed to Islamic) cultural identification. Its influence in the twentieth century is still felt: one of the first cultural acts of the Khomeini regime was to ban this work.

Fortunately, literature seems to be able to transcend politics and political borders. Names may change, but genres, like the *ghazal*—a lyric form cultivated by Arab, Persian, and Turkish poets alike—remind us that the Islamic world, despite its linguistic diversity, had a unified and rich culture.

Historical Background

Muhammad (570?–632 C.E.), the Prophet of Islam, was born in Mecca, a thriving commercial center in Arabia. When he was about forty, he felt himself selected to be the prophet of God, the same unique God that had spoken through such prophets as Abraham, Moses, and Jesus. Against the idolatry, materialism, and social injustice he perceived around him, Muhammad preached an uncompromising monotheism. *Islām,* "submission" or "surrender," to God's will was the paramount principle of faith; by acknowledging God's transcendence, one became *muslim,* "submissive."

In 622 Muhammad left an increasingly hostile Mecca for Yathrib, an agricultural town to the north. His voyage subsequently became known as the Hegira (*hijra*, "emigration"), the town as Medina (*al-Madina*, "the City [of the Prophet]"), and the year as the first of the new Islamic calendar. (The era before 622 is known simply as the Jāhiliyya, or "pagan" era.) In Medina, Muhammad consolidated his political and spiritual authority, and the basic practices of the Islamic community, or *umma*, evolved. By 630 the entire Arabian peninsula had been brought under Muhammad's leadership, and traditionally divisive tribal and blood loyalities were subsumed—at least theoretically—in the unifying idea of *umma*.

After Muhammad's death, leadership passed to a series of four caliphs (from *khalīfa*, successor) distinguished by their close ties to the Prophet. Arab armies began to expand Islamic domination, winning Syria, Egypt, and northern Libya from the Byzantine empire, and conquering the Sassanian Persian empire to the east. From these territories, the heritage of eastern Hellenism—especially its philosophic and scientific writings—passed into Islamic culture, laying the foundation for a brilliant scholarly tradition that produced important advances in astronomy, medicine, natural sciences, and mathematics. From Iran, long open to Indian as well as Mediterranean influence, materials of Hindu civilization passed into the Islamic intellectual storehouse.

A civil war of succession followed, and power passed to the founder of the Umayyad Dynasty (661–750), the first dynastic caliphate. Expansion continued: in the West newly converted Berber tribes helped extend Muslim rule across North Africa and into the Iberian Peninsula; in the east the frontier was pushed to the Indus River. Everywhere, Arabic followed as the language of religion and administration. The importance of preserving the meaning of the Qur'an encouraged the crystalization of a "classical" Arabic language, which remained the literary standard even as spoken dialects continued to evolve.

A rebellion in 750 brought the Abbasid Dynasty (750–1258) to power. Within a few years, however, a new Umayyad Dynasty (756–1031) established itself in Spain, ending forever the political unity of Islam. Henceforth, the empire comprised a shifting mosaic of major powers, these often further fragmented into semiautonomous kingdoms and principalities.

The Abbasid Dynasty, with its capital in Baghdad, witnessed the rise of a strong Persian presence in Islam as the Arabic warrior elite that had prevailed during the Umayyad Dynasty gave way to a bureaucracy staffed largely by Persian gentry.

By the time of the Islamic conquest, the Persian civilization was already an ancient one. The first Persian empire, founded in the sixth century B.C.E., fell to Alexander the Great in 331 B.C.E., ushering in a period of Hellenistic influence under the Seleucids. Parthian rule followed, succeeded in turn by the Sassanian empire (224–642). These changes had been accompanied by a linguistic evolution from Old Iranian to Pahlavi, or Middle Iranian. Little literature survives from these early eras, although an important epic tradition had clearly been established.

For the first 200 years of Abbasid rule, Arabic remained the sole literary language, and, fueled in no small part by Arabic-speaking Persians, the period marks a high point in Arabic letters and scholarship. Jews and Christians, protected as always under Islamic law, added still more facets to the intellectual community. At the same time, the Persian language was undergoing a further metamorphosis, absorbing Arabic vocabulary and borrowing the Arabic script.

This newly formulated "classical" Persian began an independent literary life in the tenth century, inspired both by the vigorous Arabic-Islamic literary culture and Persia's own heroic past.

Turkish tribes, meanwhile, had become an important new ethnic presence. Initially brought from the central Asian steppe to serve as slave troops, Turks gradually assumed virtually all political power, with the rule of the Seljuk Turks in Iran beginning in the eleventh century serving as a decisive moment. The most lasting Turkish formation, however, was the Ottoman empire, which began to consolidate its power in Anatolia (Asia Minor) during the fourteenth century, lasting another six centuries until World War I. During the course of the fifteenth century, the Ottoman Turks finished off the Byzantine empire, and made inroads into Eastern Europe. During the following century, they extended their rule over virtually the entire Arabic-speaking world.

Writings in various Turkic dialects exist from the onset of the Turkish presence in the Islamic world. As the Ottomans came to prominence, however, so did their dialect. Culturally oriented toward Persia, Ottoman Turkish absorbed Persian and Arabic elements and adopted the Arabic script. During the latter part of the fifteenth century, the language of the Ottoman capital at Istanbul (formerly Constantinople) became the literary standard, and the stability and wealth of the new empire contributed to the flowering of the third major Islamic literature.

A Note on Transliteration

There is no single, universally accepted system for transliterating from the Arabic alphabet. The differences between systems, however, are minimal, and generations of readers have learned to take minor variations in spellings and diacritical marks (symbols added to a letter to modify its pronounciation) in stride. Here, readers will notice occasional discrepancies between our text and the translations.

One fact that accounts for many spelling variations is that written Arabic does not usually indicate short vowels, and thus vowel sounds are open to some interpretation. The Persian poet here spelled Firdawsī, for example, may be found in other works listed as Ferdousī or Firdausī. Long vowels may be marked with an accent (á), a circumflex (â), or a macron (ā). The macron is currently the most widely accepted symbol; some of the translations, however, use the accent or the circumflex. Full scholarly transliteration also demands the use of subscript dots to distinguish "emphatic" consonants (ḥ, ṣ, ṭ, and so on), for which the Arabic alphabet has separate letters. Again, a few of the translations here employ them, others do not. Necessary for specialists, they can safely be ignored by the general reader.

Finally, readers will notice two diacritical marks that are especially prevalent in Arabic, the hamza (ɔ) and the ᶜayn (ᶜ). The hamza indicates a glottal stop, the ᶜayn a sort of gargling sound deep in the throat. While special characters are sometimes used for these, common substitutes are a turned comma for the hamza (') and an apostrophe for ᶜayn (').

N. B. In this section, headings to the notes offer the language of the original text instead of the writer's country or region.

Further Readings

Grunebaum, G. E. von. *Medieval Islam: A Study in Cultural Orientation.* 2d ed. Chicago: University of Chicago Press, 1971.

Nicholson, R. A. *A Literary History of the Arabs.* 1907. Reprint. Cambridge: Cambridge University Press, 1969.

Rahman, Fazlur. *Islam.* Anchor Books Edition. Garden City, N.Y.: Doubleday, 1968.

Rypka, Jan. *History of Iranian Literature.* Translated from the German by P. van Popta-Hope, and edited and revised by the authors. Dordrecht: D. Reidel Publishing Co., 1968.

Schimmel, Annemarie. *Mystical Dimensions of Islam.* Chapel Hill: University of North Carolina Press, 1975.

Yarshater, Ehsan, ed. *Persian Literature.* Albany, N.Y.: Bibliotheca Persica, 1988.

SHANFARĀ (SIXTH CENTURY)
Arabic

"Arabian Ode in 'L' " [*Lāmīyat al-'Arab*], attributed to the poet Shanfarā, is one of the most famous pre-Islamic odes. The ode (*qasīda*) was a favored classical Arabic poetic form. Technically, it challenged a poet to sustain not only the same meter but also the same rhyme throughout. The title of this example comes from the fact that the rhyme that repeats at the end of each line of the original Arabic employs the letter "L." As in the case for other pre-Islamic poets, Shanfara's name and works lived for generations in the mouths of professional reciters (*rāwīs*) before being transcribed and collected by early Islamic scholars. Tradition classifies him as one of the brigand or outlaw poets. Proud exiles from the tribal communities, their poetry often celebrates the fierce independence of their existence.

Arabian Ode in "L"

Get up the chests of your camels
    and leave, sons
of my mother, I lean to a tribe
    other than you.

    What must be is at hand.
The moon is full,
    mounts and saddle frames secured
for distant crossings.   5

In this land is a refuge for a man
    from wrongs,
for one fearing scalding hatred,
    a place to withdraw.   10

    By your life! It crowds on no man
who travels by night,
    in fear or in desire,
and keeps his wits about him.   15

I have in place of you other kin:
    the wolf, unwearying runner,
the darting sand leopard,
    the bristle-necked hyena.   20

    These are my clan. They don't reveal
a secret given in trust,

Translated by Michael A. Sells.

and they don't abandon a man
for his crimes.

They are the scornful ones,
   the fierce, though I
at first sight of the prey
   am fiercer.   25

   As recompense for losing those
who don't repay a favor,
   in whose nearness
I cannot feel ease,   30

I have three friends: a brave
   heart, a bare
blade, and a long
   bow of yellow wood,   35

   Smooth and taut,
sonorous,
   bedecked with jeweled tokens,
secured with a crossbelt.   40

And when it lets the arrow slip
   it twangs,
like a child-bereft mother,
   grief-struck, who moans and wails.

   I'm no quick-to-thirst,
herd ill-pastured at dusk,
   calves ill-fed   45
though their mother's udders are untied,

No foul-breathed cringer,
   wife-clinging,
asking her in every affair   50
   what to do,

   No ostrich,
gangly, stupefied,
   as if a sparrow were beating up and down
in his heart,   55

No malingerer, stay-at-home,
   woman-chaser,
evening and morning coated with kohl
   and perfume,   60

   No tick,
worthless, indolent,

leaping up, when startled,
unarmed,

Nor bewildered by the dark
   when the towering emptiness
turns astray the traveler, lagging,
   frantic, losing his way.

   When my sole pads
meet the gravel flint
   it flies up sparking,
shattered.

I push hunger on
   until it dies,
drive attention from it,
   forget.

   I'd sooner slurp the dust,
a dry mouthful,
   than take some man's
condescending favors.

Where I not shunning blame
   I would lack
no food, no drink,
   no ease of life,

   But this hard soul
gives me no rest
   when wronged
until I move on,

Wrapping my insides
   around an empty stomach pit,
like a weaver's threads
   spun and twisted.

———————

   I part at dawn on meager fare
like a wolf
   led on, desert into desert,
scrawny, grey.

He sets out at dawn, hungry,
   quick into the wind,
slicing down where the ravine ends
   and veering.

   He moves on in pursuit of food.
It eludes him.

65

70

75

80

85

90

95

100

He howls. His mates respond,
hunger-worn,

Thin as the new moon,
   ashen-faced, like arrow shafts
rattling around
   in the hand of a gambler,   105

   Like a queen bee,
swarm roused   110
   by the two poles of a cliff-dangling
honey-gatherer,

Wide-jawed, gape-mouthed,
   as if their jaws
were the sides of a split stick,   115
   grinning, grim.

   He howls in the empty spaces,
they howl,
   as if they and he were bereaved women
on the high ridge, wailing.   120

His eyelids sag. He grows silent.
   They follow his lead.
They, he, forlorn,
   take heart from one another.

   He turns back. They turn back,   125
surging, hard pressed,
   keeping composure
over what they hide.

The sand grouse drink what I leave behind.
   They approach the water hole   130
after a night journey,
   their sides rumbling.

   I resolved. They did.
We raced. Their wings fell limp
   while I stood in front at ease   135
with my robe tucked up.

I turned away.
   They tumbled to the rim,
crops and gullets
   squeezing and pulsing,   140

   As if their clatter
on both sides of the water hole

were groups of men from caravans,
letting themselves down,

Congregating from all sides
   and taken in
like droves of camels
   at a wayside pool.   145

   They gulped swiftly and passed on
at dawn
   like panic-stricken riders
from Uháza.   150

———————

I know the earth's face well.
   There I stretch out,
restless,
   dried out vertebrae and a crooked back,   155

   An arm for a pillow,
worn to the bone,
   joints standing up like bone cubes
strewn by a gambler.   160

And if the mother of dust
   grieves for Shánfara now,
long did she find satisfaction in him
   before!

   His crimes track him down,   165
They cast lots
   for the choicest piece
of his hamstrung flesh.

When he sleeps
   they spend the night,   170
eyes open, quick to his ruin,
   working their way in.

   Shánfara, friend of cares!
Time after time they return
   like quartan fever   175
or worse.

When they come down
   I drive them out.
They turn back from all sides
   upon me.   180

   Though you might see me
sun-beaten as a sand daughter,

ragged, shoeless,
with worn feet,

Still am I the master of patience,
   wearing its armor
over the heart of a sand cat,
   shod with resolution.

   Sometimes I have nothing,
sometimes all I need.
   Only one who gives himself,
far-seeing, will prosper.

I don't lose nerve in adversity,
   exposing weakness,
nor do I prance, self-satisfied,
   in my riches.

   The hot-neck fool will not provoke
my self-command, and I am not seen
   begging at the heels of conversations
and slandering.

On how many a night of ill luck
   when the hunter burns his bow
for fuel.
   and his arrow wood.

   Have I trodden through darkness and drizzle.
on fire with hunger,
   grinding inside, shivering,
filled with dread.

Then have I widowed women
   and orphaned children,
returning as I began,
   the night a blacker black.

   When next morning in Ghumaysá[1]
two groups met,
   one asking about me,
the other being asked:

"Last night our dogs were whining."
   "A wolf prowling, or a hyena?"
"Just a faint sound, then silence."
   "Perhaps a startled grouse, or a hawk?"

185

190

195

200

205

210

215

220

---

1. An obscure place name.

"If a jinni,[2]
   what an ill-boding night visitor!
and a man, no,
   men don't act like that."

   To how many a day of the dog star,   225
when the sun drools heat
   and snakes writhe
on the burning ground,
Have I turned my face,
   no veil to protect it   230
but the tattered shreds
   of an Athami cloak.[3]

   With hair down my back,
flying up
   when the wind takes it   235
in uncombed clumps,

Unoiled, unloused,
   encrusted,
a full turn of seasons
   without a rinse of mallow.   240

   How many a desert plain, wind-swept,
like the surface of a shield,
   empty, impenetrable,
have I cut through on foot,

Joining the near end to the far,   245
   then looking out from a summit,
crouching sometimes,
   then standing,

   While mountain goats, flint-yellow,
graze around me,   250
   meandering like maidens
draped in flowing shawls.

They become still in the setting sun,
   around me, as if I were a white-foot,
bound for the high mountain meadow,   255
   tall-horned.

---

2. A spirit capable of assuming human or
   animal form to exercise supernatural powers over people. *Jinn* were part of pre-
   Islamic beliefs.

3. A cloak from Atham, an obscure place
   name.

AL-KHANSĀ' (SEVENTH CENTURY)
Arabic

Al-Khansā' was a pre-Islamic poet famous for her elegies mourning the death of her brother, Sakhr, who was killed in battle (c. 615 C.E.). The genre in which she wrote, the *rithā*, or poetic elegy, became associated more with the female voice than with the male voice. Most often, the *rithā*, was written to mourn the death of a father or a brother.

[Oh, would that my mother]

Oh, would that my mother had never borne me sound and straight,
    and that I had been dust in the hands of the midwives,
And that heaven had fallen on the earth and covered it over,
    and that everyone, barefoot and shod, had died.
On the morning that the announcer of Sakhr's death came   5
    and frightened me, and bequeathed to me grief full of anxieties.
I said to him, "What are you saying?" And he replied, "Ibn
    ᶜAmr is dead." May his mother be bereft of him!
After you I will never enjoy any favor, and I will never weep
    at the request of a woman bereft.   10
Let death work its will with my relatives after him; let them
    get a second draught of it after the first.

[It is as if Ṣakhr]

It is as if Ṣakhr had never made a morning raid with
    his horsemen, and had never urged on the thin noble she-camels,
And had never requited his true friends, nor clad himself in the
    gray dust of battle raised by the horses' hooves,
Had never made in the noonday heat for his men a canopy of his   5
    beautiful cloak.
So weep for Sakhr ibn ᶜAmr, for he was an easy man to deal with
    whenever fate was harsh to the people,
Generous and sweet when his aid was requested, but bitter and
    sour when he wished to be.   10
And Khansā' weeps sadly in the dark and calls to her brother,
    but he, dust-covered, makes no reply.

Translated by James Bellamy.

THE QUR'AN (THE KORAN)
(SEVENTH CENTURY)
Arabic

As the sacred book of Islam, the Qur'an (Arabic *qur'ān,* meaning "recitation" or "text to be recited") is considered by Muslim believers to be the direct word of God revealed to the Prophet Muhammad through the intervention of the angel Gabriel. Preserved both orally and in written form during the Prophet's lifetime, the revelations were collected under the caliph 'Uthmān some twenty years after the Prophet's death and an authorized text was prepared. The Qur'an is organized by chapters (*sūras*), not in chronological order of revelation but according to the length of the *sūra.* After the brief opening *sūra* known as *al-fātiha,* the chapters are arranged from the longest to the shortest. The *sūras* are also classified by their locus of revelation, the Meccan having been revealed in Mecca, the Medinan in Medina. The Meccan chapters, shorter and more dynamic, are often exhortations and calls to religion with appropriate interjections about events such as the Day of Judgment. The typical Medinan chapters (which occur later than the Meccan chapters) tend to be more legally oriented, directed to the organization of the Muslim community (*umma*). The *sūra* of Joseph (*sūra* 12) is universally considered by Muslims and non-Muslims alike to be a narrative masterpiece. Because of the Qur'an's religious nature as the revealed word of the deity, Muslim scholars speak of its inimitability (*i'jāz al-Qur'ān*). This doctrine signifies both literary and aesthetic as well as doctrinal and moral perfection on the part of the Holy Book.

from The Qur'an [Koran]

SÛRA 81

The Darkening

In the Name of God, the Merciful, the Compassionate

When the sun shall be darkened,
when the stars shall be thrown down,
when the mountains shall be set moving,
when the pregnant camels shall be neglected,
when the savage beasts shall be mustered,　　5
when the seas shall be set boiling,
when the souls shall be coupled,

Translated by Arthur J. Arberry.

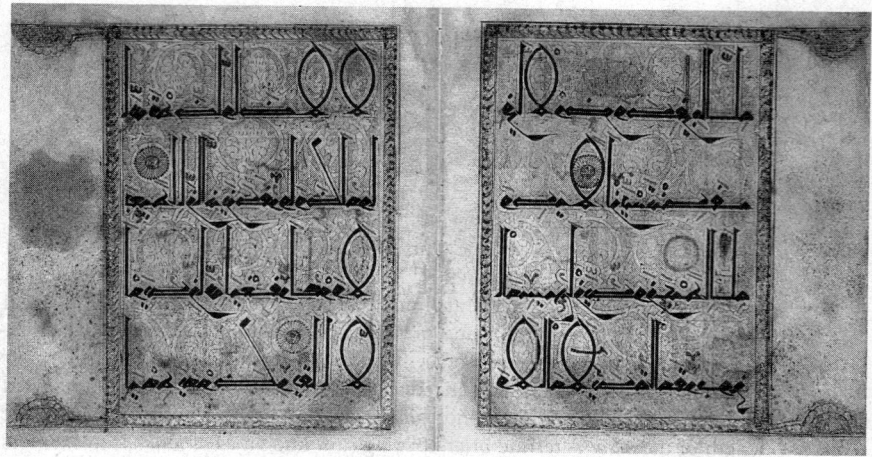

A page from the Qur'an, from a manuscript produced in Iraq or Iran, eleventh
century C.E.

when the buried infant shall be asked for what sin she was slain,
when the scrolls shall be unrolled,
when heaven shall be stripped off,
when Hell shall be set blazing,   10
when Paradise shall be brought nigh,
then shall be a soul know what it has produced.

No! I swear by the slinkers,
the runners, the sinkers,
by the night swarming,   15
by the dawn sighing,
truly this is the word of a noble Messenger
having power, with the Lord of the Throne secure,
obeyed, moreover trusty.   20

Your companion is not possessed;
he truly saw him on the clear horizon;
he is not niggardly of the Unseen.

And it is not the word of an accursed Satan;
where then are you going?   25

It is naught but a Reminder
unto all beings,
for whosoever of you who would go straight;
but will you shall not, unless God wills,
the Lord of all Being.   30

SÛRA 93

The Forenoon

In the Name of God, the Merciful, the Compassionate

By the white forenoon
and the brooding night!
Thy Lord has neither forsaken thee nor hates thee
and the Last shall be better for thee than the First.
Thy Lord shall give thee, and thou shalt be satisfied.   5

Did He not find thee an orphan, and shelter thee?
Did He not find thee erring, and guide thee?
Did He not find thee needy, and suffice thee?

As for the orphan, do not oppress him,
and as for the beggar, scold him not;   10
and as for thy Lord's blessing, declare it.

SÛRA 12

Joseph

In the Name of God, the Merciful, the Compassionate

Alif Lam Ra[1]
Those are the signs of the Manifest Book.
We have sent it down as an Arabic Koran;
    haply you will understand.

We will relate to thee the fairest of stories
in that We have revealed to thee this Koran,   5
though before it thou wast one of the heedless.

When Joseph said to his father, "Father, I saw
eleven stars, and the sun and the moon; I saw them
    bowing down before me."
He said, "O my son, relate not thy vision   10
to thy brothers, lest they devise against thee
some guile. Surely Satan is to man
    a manifest enemy.
So will thy Lord choose thee, and teach thee
the interpretation of tales, and perfect His   15

---

1. Three Arabic letters. Groups of two to five
letters appear at the beginning of 29 *suras*.
Known as the "isolated letters" (*al-harûf
al-muqatta^cāt*), their meaning, while the
subject of much speculation, remains a
mystery. A certain mystical significance has
become attached to them.

blessing upon thee and upon the House of Jacob,
as He perfected it formerly on thy fathers
Abraham and Isaac; surely thy Lord is
    All-knowing, All-wise."
(In Joseph and his brethren were signs for those   20
    who ask questions.)
When they said, "Surely Joseph and his brother
are dearer to our father than we, though
we are a band. Surely our father is
    in manifest error.   25
Kill you Joseph, or cast him forth into
some land, that your father's face may be
free for you, and therefore you may be
    a righteous people."
One of them said, "No, kill not Joseph,   30
but cast him into the bottom of the pit
and some traveller will pick him out,
    if you do aught."
They said, "Father, what ails thee, that thou
trustest us not with Joseph? Surely we are his   35
    sincere well-wishers.
Send him forth with us tomorrow, to
frolic and play; surely we shall be
    watching over him."
He said, "It grieves me that you should go with him, 40
and I fear the wolf may eat him, while you
    are heedless of him."
They said, "If the wolf eats him, and we a band,
    then are we losers!"
So when they went with him, and agreed to put him 45
in the bottom of the well, and We revealed to him,
"Thou shalt tell them of this their doing
    when they are unaware,"
And they came to their father in the evening,
    and they were weeping.   50
They said, "Father, we went running races, and
left Joseph behind with our things; so the wolf
ate him. But thou wouldst never believe us,
    though we spoke truly."
And they brought his shirt with false blood on it. 55
He said, "No; but your spirits tempted you
to do somewhat. But come, sweet patience!
And God's succour is ever there to seek against
    that you describe."
Then came travellers, and they sent one of them,   60
a water-drawer, who let down his bucket.

[handwritten annotation:] they deliberately lured Joseph out to hurt him.

"Good news!" he said. "Here is a young man."
So they hid him as merchandise; but God knew
   what they were doing.
Then they sold him for a paltry price, a   65
handful of counted dirhams; for they set
   small store by him.
He that bought him, being of Egypt,
said to his wife, "Give him goodly lodging,
and it may be that he will profit us,   70
or we may take him for our own son."
So We established Joseph in the land, and
that We might teach him the interpretation
of tales. God prevails in His purpose, but
   most men know not.   75
And when he was fully grown, We gave him
judgment and knowledge. Even so We recompense
   the good-doers.

Now the woman in whose house he was
solicited him, and closed the doors on them.   80
"Come," she said, "take me!" "God be my refuge,"
he said, "Surely my lord has given me
a goodly lodging. Surely the evildoers
   do not prosper."
For she desired him; and he would have taken her,   85
but that he saw the proof of his Lord.
So was it, that We might turn away from him
evil and abomination; he was one of
   Our devoted servants.
They raced to the door; and she tore his shirt   90
from behind. They encountered her master
by the door. She said, "What is the recompense
of him who purposes evil against thy folk,
but that he should be imprisoned, or
   a painful chastisement?"   95
Said he, "It was she that solicited me";
and a witness of her folk bore witness,
"If his shirt has been torn from before
then she has spoken truly, and he is
   one of the liars;   100
but if it be that his shirt has been torn
from behind, then she has lied, and he is
   one of the truthful."
When he saw his shirt was torn from behind
he said, "This is of your women's guile; surely   105
   your guile is great.

Joseph, turn away from this; and thou, woman,
ask forgiveness of thy crime; surely thou art
   one of the sinners."
Certain women that were in the city said,
"The Governor's wife has been soliciting her
page; he smote her heart with love; we see her
   in manifest error."
When she heard their sly whispers, she sent
to them, and made ready for them a repast,
then she gave to each one of them a knife.   115
"Come forth, attend to them," she said.
And when they saw him, they so admired him
that they cut their hands, saying, "God save us!
This is no mortal; he is no other   120
   but a noble angel."
"So now you see," she said. "This is he you
blamed me for. Yes, I solicited him, but
he abstained. Yet if he will not do what I
command him, he shall be imprisoned, and be   125
   one of the humbled."
He said, "My Lord, prison is dearer to me
than that they call me to; yet if Thou
turnest not from me their guile, then I
shall yearn towards them, and so become   130
   one of the ignorant."
So his Lord answered him, and He turned
away from him their guile; surely He is
   the All-hearing, the All-knowing.
Then it seemed good to them, after they had   135
seen the signs, that they should imprison
   him for a while.
And there entered the prison with him
two youths. Said one of them. "I dreamed
that I was pressing grapes." Said the other,   140
"I dreamed that I was carrying on my head
bread, that birds were eating of. Tell us
its interpretation; we see that thou art
   of the good-doers."
He said, "No food shall come to you   145
for your sustenance, but ere it comes to you
I shall tell you its interpretation.
That I shall tell you is of what God
has taught me. I have forsaken the creed
of a people who believe not in God   150
and who moreover are unbelievers in
   the world to come.

And I have followed the creed of my fathers,
Abraham, Isaac and Jacob. Not ours is it
to associate aught with God. That is of God's   155
bounty to us, and to men; but most men
    are not thankful.
Say, which is better, my fellow-prisoners—
many gods at variance, or God the One,
    the Omnipotent?   160
That which you serve, apart from Him, is
nothing but names yourselves have named,
you and your fathers; God has sent down
no authority touching them. Judgment
belongs only to God; He has commanded   165
that you shall not serve any but Him.
That is the right religion; but
    most men know not.
Fellow-prisoners, as for one of you, he shall
pour wine for his lord; as for the other,   170
he shall be crucified, and birds will eat
of his head. The matter is decided
    whereon you enquire."
Then he said to the one he deemed
should be saved of the two, "Mention me   175
in thy lord's presence." But Satan caused him
to forget to mention him to his master,
so that he continued in the prison
    for certain years.

And the king said, "I saw in a dream   180
seven fat kine,[2] and seven lean ones
devouring them; likewise seven green ears
of corn, and seven withered. My counsellors,
pronounce to me upon my dream, if you are
    expounders of dreams."   185
"A hotchpotch of nightmares!" they said.
"We know nothing of the interpretation
    of nightmares."
Then said the one who had been delivered,
remembering after a time, "I will   190
myself tell you its interpretation;
    so send me forth."

"Joseph, thou true man, pronounce to us
regarding seven fat kine, that seven lean ones

---

2. Cattle.

[handwritten marginal note:] He is preaching the doctrine of one God not many Gods, and the doctrine of the world to come.

were devouring, seven green ears of corn, and   195
seven withered; haply I shall return to the men,
   haply they will know."
He said, "You shall sow seven years
after your wont; what you have harvested   200
leave in the ear, excepting a little
   whereof you eat.
Then thereafter there shall come upon you
seven hard years, that shall devour what
you have laid up for them, all but a little   205
   you keep in store.
Then thereafter there shall come a year
wherein the people will be succoured
   and press in season."

The king said, "Bring him to me!" And
when the messenger came to him, he   210
said, "Return unto thy lord, and ask
of him, 'What of the women who cut
their hands?' Surely my Lord has knowledge
   of their guile."
"What was your business, women," he said,   215
"when you solicited Joseph?" "God save us!"
they said, "We know no evil against him."
The Governor's wife said, "Now the truth
is at last discovered; I solicited him; he
   is a truthful man."   220
"That, so that he may know I betrayed him not
secretly, and that God guides not the guile
   of the treacherous.
Yet I claim not that my soul was innocent—
surely the soul of man incites to evil—   225
except inasmuch as my Lord had mercy;
truly my Lord is All-forgiving,
   All-compassionate."
The king said, "Bring him to me! I would
attach him to my person." Then, when he   230
had spoken with him, he said, "Today
thou art established firmly in our favour
   and in our trust."
He said, "Set me over the land's storehouses; I
   am a knowing guardian."   235
So We established Joseph in the land, to
make his dwelling there wherever he would.
We visit with Our mercy whomsoever We
will, and We leave not to waste the wage

[handwritten marginal note:] the Name of Benjamin is never mentioned. He's known as the brother of Joseph

of the good-doers.
Yet is the wage of the world to come better
for those who believe, and are godfearing.

And the brethren of Joseph came, and
entered unto him, and he knew them, but
   they knew him not.
When he had equipped them with their equipment
he said, "Bring me a certain brother of yours
from your father. Do you not see
that I fill up the measure, and am
   the best of hosts?
But if you bring him not to me, there shall
be no measure for you with me, neither shall
   you come nigh me."
They said, "We will solicit him of our father;
   that we will do."
He said to his pages, "Put their merchandise
in their saddlebags; haply they will recognize it
when they have turned to their people; haply
   they will return."
So, when they had returned to their father,
they said, "Father, the measure was denied
to us; so send with us our brother, that we
may obtain the measure; surely we shall be
   watching over him."
He said, "And shall I entrust him to you
otherwise than as I entrusted before
his brother to you? Why, God is the best
guardian, and He is the most merciful
   of the merciful."
And when they opened their things, they found
their merchandise, restored to them. "Father,"
they said, "what more should we desire?
See, our merchandise here is restored to us.
We shall get provision for our family,
and we shall be watching over our brother;
we shall obtain an extra camel's load—that
   is an easy measure."
He said, "Never will I send him with you
until you bring me a solemn pledge by God
that you will surely bring him back to me
unless it be that you are encompassed."
When they had brought him their solemn pledge
he said, "God shall be Guardian
   over what we say."

He also said, "O my sons, enter not   285
by one door; enter by separate doors.
Yet I cannot avail you anything
against God; judgment belongs not to any
but God. In Him I have put my trust;   290
and in Him let all put their trust
  who put their trust."

And when they entered after the manner
their father commanded them, it availed them
nothing against God; but it was a need
in Jacob's soul that he so satisfied.   295
Verily he was possessed of a knowledge
for that We had taught him; but
  most men know not.
And when they entered unto Joseph, he said,
taking his brother into his arms,   300
"I am thy brother; so do not despair of
  that they have done."
Then, when he had equipped them with
their equipment, he put his drinking-cup
into the saddlebag of his brother.   305
Then a herald proclaimed, "Ho, cameleers,
  you are robbers!"
They said, turning to them, "What is it that
  you are missing?"
They said, "We are missing the king's goblet.   310
Whoever brings it shall receive a camel's load;
  that I guarantee."
"By God," they said, "you know well that we
came not to work corruption in the land.
  We are not robbers."   315
They said, "And what shall be its recompense
  if you are liars?"
They said, "This shall be its recompense—
in whoever's saddlebag the goblet is found,
he shall be its recompense. So we recompense   320
  the evildoers."
So he made beginning with their sacks, before
his brother's sack, then he pulled it out
of his brother's sack. So We contrived
for Joseph's sake; he could not have taken his   325
brother, according to the king's doom, except
that God willed. Whomsoever We will, We
raise in rank; over every man of knowledge
  is One who knows.

[Handwritten margin note:] Joseph's planning to trap the brothers into repentous. Benjamin is let in on his secret. He only revealed himself to Benjamin.

[Handwritten margin note:] If he is a thief, a brother of his was a thief before. They were talking about Joseph.

They said, "If he is a thief, a brother of his
was a thief before." But Joseph secreted it
in his soul and disclosed it not to them, saying,
"You are in a worse case; God knows very well
    what you are describing."   330
They said, "Mighty prince, he has a father,
aged and great with years; so take one of us
in his place; we see that thou art one
    of the good-doers."   335
He said, "God forbid that we should take
any other but him in whose possession
we found the goods; for if we did so, we
    would be evildoers."   340
When they despaired of moving him, they
conferred privily apart. Said the eldest of
them, "Do you not know how your father has taken
a solemn pledge from you by God, and aforetime   345
you failed regarding Joseph? Never will I
quit this land, until my father gives me
leave, or God judges in my favour; He is
    the best of judges.   350
Return you all to your father, and say,
'Father, thy son stole; we do not testify
except that we know; we were no guardians
    of the Unseen.
Enquire of the city wherein we were, and the   355
caravan in which we approached; surely
    we are truthful men.' "

"No!" he said. "But your spirits tempted you
to do somewhat. But come, sweet patience!
Haply God will bring them all to me; He is   360
    the All-knowing, the All-wise."
And he turned away from them, and said,
"Ah, woe is me for Joseph!" And his eyes
turned white because of the sorrow that
    he choked within him.   365
"By God," they said, "thou wilt never cease
mentioning Joseph till thou art consumed, or
    among the perishing."
He said, "I make complaint of my anguish
and my sorrow unto God; I know from God   370
    that you know not.
Depart, my sons, and search out tidings
of Joseph and his brother. Do not despair
of God's comfort; of God's comfort

no man's despairs, excepting the people   375
  of the unbelievers."

So, when they entered unto him, they said,
"O mighty prince, affliction has visited us
and our people. We come with merchandise
of scant worth. Fill up to us the measure,   380
and be charitable to us; surely God recompenses
  the charitable."
He said, "Are you aware of what you did
with Joseph and his brother, when you
  were ignorant?"   385
They said, "Why, art thou indeed Joseph?"
"I am Joseph," he said. "This is my brother.
God has indeed been gracious unto us.
Whosoever fears God, and is patient—
surely God leaves not to waste the wage   390
  of the good-doers."
"By God," they said, "God has indeed
preferred thee above us, and certainly
  we have been sinful."
He said, "No reproach this day shall be on you;   395
God will forgive you; He is the most merciful
  of the merciful.
Go, take this shirt, and do you cast it
on my father's face, and he shall recover
his sight; then bring me your family   400
  all together."
So, when the caravan set forth, their father
said, "Surely I perceive Joseph's scent, unless
  you think me doting."
The said, "By God, thou art certainly in   405
  thy ancient error."
But when the bearer of good tidings came
to him, and laid it on his face, forthwith
  he saw once again.
He said, "Did I not tell you I know from God   410
  that you know not?"
They said, "Our father, ask forgiveness
of our crimes for us; for certainly
  we have been sinful."
He said, "Assuredly I will ask my Lord   415
to forgive you; He is the All-forgiving,
  the All-compassionate."

So, when they entered unto Joseph,
he took his father and mother into his arms

saying, "Enter you into Egypt, if God will,   420
   in security."
And he lifted his father and mother
upon the throne; and the others fell down
prostrate before him: "See, father," he said,
"this is the interpretation of my vision   425
of long ago; my Lord has made it true.
He was good to me when He brought me forth
from the prison, and again when He
brought you out of the desert, after that
Satan set at variance me and my brethren.   430
My Lord is gentle to what He will; He is
   the All-knowing, the All-wise.
O my Lord, Thou has given me to rule,
and Thou hast taught me the interpretation
of tales. O Thou, the Originator of the   435
heavens and earth, Thou art my Protector
in this world and the next. O receive me
to Thee in true submission, and join me
   with the righteous."

That is of the tidings of the Unseen that   440
We reveal to thee; thou wast not with them
when they agreed upon their plan, devising.
Yet, be thou ever so eager, the most part of
   men believe not.
Thou askest of them no wage for it;   445
it is nothing but a reminder
   unto all beings.
How many a sign there is in the heavens
and in the earth that they pass by, turning
   away from it!   450
And the most part of them believe not in God,
   but they associate
other gods with Him. Do they feel secure
that there shall come upon them no enveloping
of the chastisement of God, or that the   455
Hour shall not come upon them suddenly
   when they are unaware?

   Say: "This is my way.
I call to God with sure knowledge,
I and whoever follows after me.
To God be glory! And I am not   460
   among the idolaters."

We sent not forth any before thee, but
men We revealed to of the people living
in the cities. Have they not journeyed
in the land? Have they not beheld   465
how was the end of those before them? Surely
the abode of the world to come is better
for those that are godfearing. What,
   do you not understand?   470
Till, when the Messengers despaired, deeming
they were counted liars, Our help came to them
and whosoever We willed was delivered. Our
might will never be turned back from the people
   of the sinners.   475
In their stories is surely a lesson to
men possessed of minds; it is not a tale
forged, but a confirmation of what is before
it, and a distinguishing of every thing,
and a guidance, and a mercy to a people   480
   who believe.

DHŪ AL-RUMMA (696?–735?)
Arabic

Dhū al-Rumma was the nickname of Ghaylān ibn ʿUkba, a famous Arab poet of the
early Islamic period. He hailed from a family of poets and was himself an authority
on poetry. His extensive use of rare terms earned him great visibility among the
later lexicographers, who quoted profusely from his verses. He earned the title of
"seal (i.e., the last) of the classical poets," because of the close links of his poetry to
the Bedouin ode, or *qasīda*—a form widely cultivated by the pre-Islamic Arab
poets. *Qasīdas* would continue to be written for some time—the form, in fact,
would later be taken up by Persian poets—but the distinctive voice of the early
desert poets sounds for the last time in the work of Dhū al-Rumma.

To the Encampments of Máyya

To the encampments of Máyya,[1]
   both of you,

Translated by Michael A. Sells.

---

1. A woman's name. Al-Rumma's love for
   Máyya was constant; he is said to have
   courted her for twenty years.

a well-meant word
   and distant greeting:

   May the rain-star Arcturus
be over you still . . .
   and the rains of the Pleiades,
pouring down and spreading,

Though it was you
   who stirred a lover's
disheartened desire,
   until the eye shed

   Tears, yes, that nearly,
on knowing a campsite as Máyya's,
   if not released,
would have killed,

Though I was already nearing thirty
   and my friends had learned better
and good sense had begun
   to weigh down folly.

   When distance turns other lovers,
the first premonition
   of loving Máyya
will still be with me.

Nearness of her
   cannot impoverish desire,
nor distance, wherever she might be,
   run it dry.

   The inner whisper
of memory,
   reminiscence of Máyya,
is enough to bruise your heart.

Desires have their way,
   circulate freely,
but I can't see your share of my heart
   given away.

   Though in parting some love
is effaced and disappears,
   yours in me is made over
and compounded.

You came to mind
   when a doe ariel passed us,

5

10

15

20

25

30

35

40

right flank turned to the camel mounts,
  neck lowered,

A doe of the sands, earth-hued,
with a white blaze on the forehead
  and the forenoon sun
clear upon her back.

She leaves her fawn
  on a dune, a grassy dune
in Múshrif, the glance of her eye
  gleaming around him,

Gazing at us as if we intended harm
where we would meet him,
  approaching us,
then backing away.

She is her like, in shoulder,
  neck and eye,
but Máyya is more radiant than she, still—
  more beautiful.

After sleep she is languor.
The house exudes her fragrance.
  She adorns it
when she appears in the morning,

As if her anklets and ivory
  were entwined around a calotrope
stopping the water's flow
  in the bed of a wadi,

With buttocks like a soft dune
over which a rain shower falls
  matting the sand
as it sprinkles down,

Her hair-fall
  over the lower curve of her back,
soft as the moringa's gossamer flowers,
  curled with pins and combed,

With long cheek hollows
where tears flow,
  and a lengthened curve at the breast sash
where it crosses and falls.

You see her ear pendant
  along the exposed ridge of her neck,

45

50

55

60

65

70

75

80

swaying out,
    dangling over the abyss.

With a red thornberry tooth-twig,   85
fragrant as musk and Indian ambergris
    brought in in the morning,
she reveals

Petals of a camomile
    cooled by the night   90
to which the dew has risen at evening
    from Ráma oasis,

    Wafting in on all sides
with the earth scent of the garden,
    redolent as a musk pod   95
falling open.

The white gleam of her teeth,
    her immoderate laugh,
almost, to the unhearing
    speak secrets.   100

    She is the cure, she the disease,
memory of her, misgiving,
    desire dead
were it not for the affliction of distance.

Far-flung!   105
    her tribe cut off
behind biting winds
    that scour the hard ground.

    How many a crow,
cawing separation,   110
    like a highborn Nubian woman
wailing the dead.

Has confirmed my foreboding,
    Máyya changing direction,
striking fire   115
    with the staff of parting.

    Let the spouse of Máyya weep
that purebred camels kneel
    worn out at the end of night
before the house of Mai.   120

Die miserably
    husband of Mai!

Hearts belonging to Máyya
　　are free to blemish, pure.

　　Had they left her a choice,
she would have chosen well.   125
　　One like Máyya does not belong
with the likes of you.

As if I sleep on a bed of awls
　　while her spouse sleeps,
stretched out,   130
　　on a sandy hillock.

　　When I say Máyya is near
the desert stretches out,
　　dust-hued,   135
as far as the eye can see.

Mai has packed up and gone.
　　Right there is her abode!
Left to the limping crow
　　and ring-necked dove.   140

　　When I complained to Máyya of love
that she might reward me
　　for my affections, she said:
You're not being serious!

Keeping me off,   145
　　leading me on,
when she saw that the spector of love
　　had almost made off with my body.

　　　────────

　　How many a noonday heat,
far from Mai,   150
　　the pace of my thick-humped mare unbroken,
the black-white locusts twitching

In pathless wastelands
　　whose stillness
in the mirage of forenoon and midday   155
　　almost blots out the gaze,

　　As if the flat hill summits
were entwined in pure silk
　　parting at times to reveal them,
then sewed back,   160

When the chameleon
　　struck by the heat

begins to twist his head
  and reel—

How many a rider
drunk on sleeplessness
    as if swaying from the two ropes
on a concave well   165

Have I shaken from his stupor
    as he nodded his head
like a staggering drinker   170
    after his last drop of wine.

    When he expires in the saddle
I bring him back to life
    with your memory. The fleet roans   175
lean to their gallop.

When the end of the whip frays
    and the bodies of the camels
are worn to sickles
    then Sáydah besets them.   180

———————

    She has stubby ears
and a long upper nape,
    a cheek polished
like the mirror of a foreign lady,

The eyes of a black-horn,   185
    solitary,
lips like Yemeni leather
    that flap loosely when she paces,

    A leg like the shadow of a wolf,
stride met   190
    by the lower foreleg
twisted out wide by the shinbone,

At full gallop
    when the black of night
is parted from the riders   195
    by the pale horizon of dawn.

    When I call out "aaj!"
or intone the camel driver's song
    she lifts a tail like under-wing feathers
as if pregnant or false-pregnant.   200

You see her
    when I have imposed upon her

every hardship, before the trail camels,
   their forelegs pulling in air,

   Her legs surging,   210
body lunging,
   wary of threats,
head raised,

Tawny, towering,
   as if a bite-scarred rough-flank   215
bore me in the saddle
   through the empty regions.

   ————————

   He turns the herd,
driving and urging, their flanks
   like boulder-strewn ground   220
in a field of brush grass.

They grazed dry pastures
   until they became as thin
as well-straightened spear shafts
   from Khatt.   225

   Until there came a day
when in their sand hollows
   ostrich eggs
nearly split in the blaze.

He continued to beguile them,   230
   as they stood, thirst-parched,
as if on the crowns of their heads
   were a flock of birds,

   One a promontory
at the dust hour   235
   when locusts expire
from the force of heat.

   ————————

You see the wind play
   where she travels at nightfall
between her and what she will find   240
   where she arrives at dawn.

   As if the camels
through the far-flung, trackless barrens
   were boats floating
in the desert of the Tigris.   245

My heart refused everything
  but memory of Máyya.
She-with-many-guises, playful and serious,
  troubled it.

AL-JĀHIZ (776?–868?)
Arabic

Al-Jāhiz, the master stylist of classical Arabic prose, is most notably associated
with *adab,* a medieval Arabic genre that combined anecdotal prose, poetry,
sacred text, proverb, and story. Al-Jāhiz (whose name means "the goggle-eyed")
was born and died in Basra (in present-day Iraq), one of the major centers of
medieval Islamic scholarship. He had an astounding literary and scholarly range,
extending from philosophy and religion to works oriented to the general reader.
His works on rhetoric and poetic composition are as renowned as his works on
varied character types, such as misers. Al-Jāhiz was a master at observing his
fellow human beings, and all his works demonstrate a lively wit. His *Book of
Misers* [*Kitāb al-Bukhalā'*] is a classic; some of its anecdotes appear even today in
children's magazines all over the Arab world.

from *Book of Misers*

The Glass Lamp

One day Abū ʿAbd Allāh al-Marwazī paid a visit to a *shaikh** from Khurāsān, and
the latter had just lit one of those green pottery lamps. "Upon my soul," exclaimed
Abū ʿAbd Allāh, "you do nothing right. I grumbled at you for using stone lamps,
and you think to please me [by replacing them] with pottery. Do you not know
that stone and earthenware literally drink oil?" "Excuse me," replied the *shaikh,* "I
gave this lamp to a friend of mine who is an oil merchant, and he put it in his filter
for a month, so that it is super-saturated and will never absorb any more." "That
is not my point. That may be a good way you have discovered of dealing with that
problem. But do you not know that the flame continually burning at the end of the
wick dries out the part of the lamp it is in contact with? When this place is
saturated the flame soaks up the oil from it and burns it. If you were to compare
the amount of oil absorbed from this place with the amount drawn up into the
wick, you would find that the former is greater."

"Moreover the part of the lamp that is in contact with the wick is always
running with oil. I am told that if a lighted lamp is placed inside a empty one, after

Translated by Charles Pellat.
**A religious official or leader of an Arab village.*

one night or two at the outside the underneath one is full of oil. You can observe it also if you look at the salt and bran placed underneath a lamp to level it: they are absolutely soaked in oil. All this represents loss and waste such as can be condoned only by spendthrifts. Such people are continually providing others with food and drink, but at least they occasionally reap some benefit from it, trifling though it may be; whereas all you are doing is giving food and drink to the flame. And on the Day of Resurrection God will feed the flames with those that have fed them during their lifetime!"

"Then what should one do, pray?" asked the *shaikh*.

"Get a glass lamp. Glass is better than any other material: it is non-porous and non-absorbent, and does not collect dust. As a rule the only way to remove dust is either to rub the lamp hard or else to set light to it, and either way the effect is to dry the lamp out still further. Glass, on the other hand, withstands water and wine better than pure gold; and moreover it is manufactured, whereas gold is in its natural state. If gold is to be preferred for its hardness, glass is superior by virtue of its cleanness. Finally, glass is transparent, while gold is opaque. Furthermore, since the wick in a glass lamp is situated at the centre, the edges do not get heated by the flame as they do in an ordinary lamp. When a ray of light strikes the glass, the flame and the lamp together become a single source of light, reflecting each other's rays. This effect can be observed when a ray of light strikes a mirror, the surface of water or a piece of glass: its brightness is doubled, and if it shines in someone's eye it dazzles and may even blind him. It is said in the Koran: 'God is the light of the heavens and of the earth. This light is like a niche in which is a torch set in a glass like a glittering star; the torch is lit with oil from a sacred tree, an olive neither of the East nor of the West, whose oil glows even when no fire touches it. It is light upon light. God guides to His light whom He pleases.' Oil in a glass lamp is 'light upon light,' brightness upon twofold brightness. In addition to this advantage there is the point that a glass lamp is handsomer than a stone or pottery one."

A Tale About Tammām b. Ja'far

Tammām b. Ja'far was mean about food with an excessive meanness. He would heap reproaches on people who had eaten his bread and pursue them with his spite, sometimes even going as far as to claim that it was lawful for him to put them to death.

If a guest of his should say: "There is no one on earth better than me at walking and running," he would reply: "What else do you expect, seeing that you eat enough for ten? It is not the belly that gives strength to the legs? May God not reward him that praises you."

But if the same guest said: "No, by God, I cannot walk, for I am too weak, and get out of breath after thirty paces," he would reply: "And how do you expect to be able to walk, seeing that you have put twenty porters' loads into your belly? Do you not know that to be spry one must eat lightly? How can anyone move freely when sated? A man who is overburdened with food cannot kneel down and prostrate himself, let alone go for a long walk."

Suppose the guest complained of a bad tooth, explaining that he did not sleep a wink the previous night because of the shooting pain. He would retort: "I am surprised that you complain of one tooth and not of all of them, and that you still have one left in your head! What molar could stand up to such crushing and grinding? By God, the mills of Syria would soon grow weary and the stoutest pestle be worn out by such a task! Indeed, your toothache seems to me to have come very late. Spare yourself, for moderation is a blessing; and do not maltreat yourself, for abuse is a calamity!"

But if he said: "I have never suffered from toothache; not one tooth of mine has ever shifted in my life," Tammām would reply: "Idiot! Chewing hardens the gum tissue, strengthens the teeth, tans the skin and consolidates the roots, whereas disuse weakens the teeth. The mouth is a part of the human body, and the same is true of the jaw as of the whole organism: work and exercise strengthen it, whereas prolonged inactivity makes it weak and soft. But go gently: overwork will weaken the strongest, for there is a limit and a compass to everything. [And have a care:] if you have not got toothache, have you not got a bellyache?"

If the same guest said: "By God, I drink a lot of water: I doubt whether there is anyone in the world who drinks more than I," he would reply: "Earth and clay need water to moisten and soak them: is not the amount needed proportional to the amount of soil to be moistened? It would not surprise me if you drank all the water of the Euphrates, seeing the quantity of food you eat and the size of your mouthfuls! Do you know what you do? You take your pleasure and do not see yourself. Ask someone who will speak straightforwardly to you, and you will see that all the water of the Tigris would not suffice [to wet] the contents of your stomach!"

But if he said: "I have not drunk a drop of water all day, and yesterday I did not take so much as half a pint: no one on earth drinks less than I do," Tammām would reply: "Obviously you leave no room for water: you put away such a hoard in your belly that there would be no space for it. Indeed, it is surprising that you have not got indigestion. For the man who does not drink with meals does not realize how much he is eating, and if he overdoes it he runs the risk of getting indigestion."

If he said: "I cannot sleep a wink all night, and insomnia is killing me," Tammām would reply: "How on earth do you expect to sleep, with your stomach swollen and rumbling? Thirst alone would prevent you sleeping and keep you awake all night! If a man drinks a lot it makes him piss, and how can he get to sleep if he spends all night drinking and pissing?"

But if he said: "I go off to sleep the moment I lay my head [on the pillow], and sleep like a log till morning," he would reply: "Good heavens! Food intoxicates, numbs and clouds the mind; it saturates the brain and arteries, and makes the whole body sodden. I would expect you to sleep day and night!"

If he said: "I do not feel like anything to eat this morning," Tammām would reply: "Beware of eating very lightly, for to eat little when you are not hungry is worse for you than eating a lot when you are. Indeed, the very table says, 'Alas for the man who never feels like anything to eat!' Besides, how could you possibly have an appetite today, seeing that yesterday you ate enough for ten?"

A Fine Line of Patter

An old vagrant met a young one new to the profession, and asked him how he was. "God's curses on vagrancy," he cried, "and on them that follow such a miserable, unprofitable calling! It lines the face all unbeknownst, and drags a man down. Have you ever come across a successful vagrant?" The old vagrant turned angrily to his young colleague and said: "Just you talk a little less, for you exaggerate. A man such as you cannot succeed because you are not predestined to, and anyway you are not grown-up yet. Vagrancy demands men. Why do you say such things?" Then he turned [to the crowd] and said: "Pray listen to me. Do you not know that vagrancy is a noble, enjoyable, pleasing calling? Vagrants enjoy boundless happiness; their task it is to rove the world by stages, and to pace out the earth; they are the successors of Alexander the Great, who reached the East and the West. No matter where they stop, they need fear no harm. They go wherever they wish, getting the best there is to be had in every town . . . They are serene and content with their lot, and have no worries about families, possessions, houses or property: wherever they stop they find their pittance. I myself once went just as I am to a town in Media and stopped in the great mosque, with a towel round [my body], a palmetto cord round my head and an oleander stick in my hand. Quite a crowd collected around me, as though I were al-Hajjāj b. Yūsuf[1] in his pulpit. I said to them: 'Good people, I come from Syria, to be precise from a town called al-Maṣṣīṣa,[2] and I am descended from conquerors and monks [who walked] in the way of God, from the gallopers and the protectors of Islam. I have taken part with my father in fourteen expeditions, seven by sea and seven on land; I have fought with the Armenian (say "God's blessing on Abū al-Ḥasan"), with 'Amr b. 'Ubaid Allāh[3] (say "God's blessing on Abū Ḥafs"), with al-Baṭṭāl b. al-Husain[4] and many more. I have been to Constantinople and prayed in the mosque of Maslama b. 'Abd al-Malik.[5] If you have heard my name, so much the better; if not, let me introduce myself: I am Ibn al-Ghuzayyil b. al-Rakkān al-Maṣṣīṣī, known and celebrated on all the borders, he who smites with sword and lance. I am one of the bulwarks of Islam, and I challenged the king of Byzantium under the walls of Tarsus . . . I fled with a party of merchants, but we were cut off by brigands. I call on God and on you for protection. If you see fit to restore one of the pillars of Islam to his home and country, [I rely on you].' By God, before I had finished my speech the *dirhams*[6] were raining on me from all sides: I went away with more than a hundred pieces of silver."

Then the young man fell on him and kissed his head, crying: "You are the master of goodness. May God reward you on behalf of your brothers!"

---

1. A famous governor, known for his cruelty, who died in 714 C.E.
2. A town in Asia Minor.
3. Emir of Melitene, who died in 863 C.E.
4. A warrior from the Umayyad period who becomes a legendary hero.
5. Son of the caliph ᶜAbd al-Malik, who fought the Byzantines.
6. Silver coin.

A Late Supper

Maḥfūz an-Naqqāsh accompanied me one night from the Friday Mosque.[7] When I got near his house, and his house was closer to the Friday Mosque than mine, he asked me to spend the night at his home saying: "Where will you go in this rain and cold, given that my house is your house, and you are in darkness and you have no lantern? I have some colostrum[8] the like of which no one has seen and some excellent dates which can only be eaten with the colostrum." So I went along with him. He delayed a while, then brought me a cup of colostrum and a platter of dates. But when I stretched out [my arm], he said: "Abū 'Uthmān, this is colostrum with its thickness, and it is nighttime with its sluggishness. Besides, it is a rainy and damp night and you are a man already advanced in age and you still complain of hemiplegia. You get extremely thirsty and, in principle, you do not eat dinner. If you eat the colostrum and do not overdo it, you will be neither an eater nor an abstainer, you will irritate your nature and then will stop eating, no matter how appetizing it might be for you. If, however, you overdo it, we will spend a bad night worrying about your state, and we will not prepare any wine or honey for you. I have only said this to you lest you say tomorrow: it was such and such. By God, I am on the horns of a dilemma: because if I did not bring it to you after having mentioned it to you, you would say: he has been miserly with it and has changed his mind about it. But if I brought it to you and did not warn you nor mention all that would happen to you with it, you would say: he had no pity on me and did not advise me. However, I am cleared from both sides: if you wish, it is eating and dying and if you wish, then some suffering but sleeping in health."

I have never laughed the way I laughed that night. I ate it all and it was only the laughter, liveliness, and delight which digested it, as far as I know. If there had been someone with me who understood the flavor of what he said, the laughter would have destroyed me or killed me. But the laughter of he who is alone is not the same as that shared with friends.

AL-KHATĪB AL-BAGHDĀDĪ (d. 1071)
Arabic

Al-Khatīb al-Baghdādī, whose name means the Baghdadi preacher, was, like al-Jāhiz, an author with an immense literary range. Al-Khatīb's broader fame is linked to his abilities as a *muhaddith*, a specialist in the transmission of *hadīth*, the traditions of the Prophet Muhammad. But as an author, al-Khatīb has to his name works of history, such as *The History of Baghdad* [*Ta'rīkh Baghdād*], a text that is

---

7. The mosque where obligatory Friday prayers are held.

8. Milk secreted shortly before and after parturition.

still widely used as a source for that city's history, as well as works more theological and literary in orientation. His *Book of Misers* [*Kitāb al-Bukhalā'*] is less concrete but no less sophisticated than that of his predecessor al-Jāhiz.

from *Book of Misers*

A Delicate Sensibility

A certain important man wished to have people come to his table and eat his food, except that he could not bear to see a mouth chewing anything. So he complained about that to a friend of his with whom he was on intimate terms. His friend said to him: "What if you were to take some food which they would eat without chewing?" He said: "Is that possible?" "Yes," he said, "prepare for them a *siritrāta*, and it is a *fālūdhaja* [sweetmeat composed of starch, water, and honey], which would not be well cooked over fire and would therefore not thicken. They will swallow it and will not need to chew it." So the man said to his friend: "You have comforted me. This is the easiest thing for me, nothing is difficult for me except the noise of the chewing only." So he ordered the stew, and it was made and placed in a large bowl and he brought those whom he wished to invite. People then sat in the courtyard of the house while the man sat in a room overlooking them so that he could watch how they ate. After a while, his friend with whom he was on intimate terms went up to see him and found him unconscious. So he waited until he regained his consciousness and then said to him: "How are you, Sir, and what hit you?" He said, "My friend, swallowing, by God, is harder on me than chewing!"

FIRDAWSĪ (941?–1020?)

Persian

The *Shāh Nāma* is the Iranian national epic. Replete with adventure and romance, it chronicles the majestic history of pre-Islamic Iran from the first mythological ruler to the last Sassanian king, defeated in the seventh century by the Muslim Arab forces. About its author, Firdawsī, we know little other than that he was born near Tus, in eastern Iran, into a landed though not particularly wealthy family. As befits the man regarded as the immortal national poet of Iran, however, his life is surrounded with legends. Relying on at least one written source that we know of, and most likely on other sources both written and oral as well, he worked on his epic for about thirty years, finally completing it around 1000 C.E. Structurally, the *Shāh Nāma* consists of some fifty thousand lines divided into an introduction and fifty chapters, each of which chronicles the reign of a king.

Translated by Fedwa-Malti Douglas.

Integrated into the first half of this historical framework is a traditional cycle of Iranian stories known as the Seistan cycle, which relate the adventures of the great hero Rostam and his descendents. As with other heroes of world literature, Rostam is of extraordinary descent (from a long line of Seistan kings—hence the name of the cycle) and birth (by caesarean section). His strength and endurance are superhuman, yet he is human in his feelings and failings. His long life—he lives for three hundred years—uncoils relentlessly according to a pre-ordained fate, and after heroic deeds in the service of king after king, he dies a ignoble and unheroic death. Rostam spends only one night with a woman, but from that night issues a son, Sohrāb. Here, the two meet in deadly battle, each unaware of the other's identity. The story of Sohrāb and Rostam has had great appeal for English readers, and translations appeared as early as the mid-nineteenth century.

from *The Shâh Nâma*

The Tragedy of Sohráb and Rostám

The Death of Sohráb

Again they firmly hitched their steeds, as ill—
Intentioned fate revolved above their heads.
Once more they grappled hand to hand. Each seized
The other's belt and sought to throw him down.
Whenever evil fortune shows its wrath,   5
It makes a block of granite soft as wax.
Sohráb had mighty arms, and yet it seemed
The skies above had bound them fast. He paused
In fear; Rostám stretched out his hands and seized
That warlike leopard by his chest and arms.   10
He bent that strong and youthful back, and with
A lion's speed, he threw him to the ground.
Sohráb had not the strength; his time had come.
Rostám knew well he'd not stay down for long.
He swiftly drew a dagger from his belt   15
And tore the breast of that stout-hearted youth.
He writhed upon the ground; groaned once aloud,
Then thought no more of good and ill. He told
Rostám, "This was the fate allotted me.
The heavens gave my key into your hand.   20
It's not your fault. It was this hunchback fate,
Who raised me up then quickly cast me down.
While boys my age still spent their time in games,
My neck and shoulders stretched up to the clouds.
My mother told me who my father was.   25
My love for him has ended in my death.

Translated by Jerome W. Clinton.

Whenever you should thirst for someone's blood,
And stain your silver dagger with his gore,
Then Fate may thirst for yours as well, and make
Each hair upon your trunk a sharpened blade.   30
Now should you, fishlike, plunge into the sea,
Or cloak yourself in darkness like the night,
Or like a star take refuge in the sky,
And sever from the earth your shining light,
Still when he learns that earth's my pillow now,   35
My father will avenge my death on you.
A hero from among this noble band
Will take this seal and show it to Rostám.
'Sohráb's been slain, and humbled to the earth,'
He'll say, 'This happened while he searched for you.' "   40
    When he heard this, Rostám was near to faint.
The world around grew dark before his eyes.
And when Rostám regained his wits once more,
He asked Sohráb with sighs of grief and pain,
"What sign have you from him—Rostám? Oh, may   45
His name be lost to proud and noble men!"
"If you're Rostám," he said, "you slew me while
Some evil humor had confused your mind.
I tried in every way to draw you forth,
But not an atom of your love was stirred.   50
When first they beat the war drums at my door,
My mother came to me with bloody cheeks.
Her soul was racked by grief to see me go.
She bound a seal upon my arm, and said,
'This is your father's gift, preserve it well.   55
A day will come when it will be of use.'
Alas, its day has come when mine has passed.
The son's abased before his father's eyes.
My mother with great wisdom thought to send
With me a worthy pahlaván[1] as guide.   60
The noble warrior's name was Zhende Razm,
A man both wise in action and in speech.
He was to point my father out to me,
And ask for him among all groups of men.
But Zhende Razm, that worthy man, was slain.   65
And at his death my star declined as well.
Now loose the binding of my coat of mail,
And look upon my naked, shining flesh."

---

1. A hero; becomes *paladin* in English.

When he unloosed his armor's ties and saw
That seal, he tore his clothes and wept.   70
"Oh, brave and noble youth, and praised among
All men, whom I have slain with my own hand!"
He wept a bloody stream and tore his hair;
His brow was dark with dust, tears filled his eyes.
Sohráb then said, "But this is even worse.   75
You must not fill your eyes with tears. For now
It does no good to slay yourself with grief.
What's happened here is what was meant to be."
    When the radiant sun had left the sky,
And Tahamtán had not returned to camp,   80
Some twenty cavaliers rode off to see
How matters stood upon the field of war.
They saw two horses standing on the plain,
Both caked with dirt. Rostám was somewhere else.
Because they did not see his massive form   85
Upon the battlefield and mounted on
His steed, the heroes thought that he'd been slain.
The nobles all grew fearful and perplexed.
They sent a message swiftly to the shah,[2]
"The throne of majesty has lost Rostám."   90
From end to end the army cried aloud,
And suddenly confusion filled the air.
Kavús commanded that the horns and drums
Be sounded, and his marshal, Tus, approached.
Then Kavús spoke, "Be quick, and send a scout   95
From here to view the battlefield
And see how matters stand with bold Sohráb.
Must we lament the passing of Irán?
If by his hand the brave Rostám's been slain,
Who from Irán will dare approach this foe?   100
We now must strike a wide and general blow;
We dare not tarry long upon this field."
    And while a tumult rose within their camp,
Sohráb was speaking thus with Tahamtán,
"The situation of the Turks has changed   105
In every way, now that my days are done.
Be kind to them, and do not let the shah
Pursue this war or urge his army on.
It was for me the Turkish troops rose up,
And mounted this campaign against Irán.   110

---

2. Iranian ruler.

I it was who promised victory, and I
Who strove in every way to give them hope.
They should not suffer now as they retreat.
Be generous with them, and let them go."
  Rostám then mounted Rakhsh, as swift as dust.   115
His eyes bled tears, his lips were chilled with sighs.
He wept as he approached the army's camp,
His heart was filled with pain at what he'd done.
When they first spied his face, the army of Irán
Fell prostrate to the earth in gratitude,   120
And loudly praised the Maker of the World,
That he'd returned alive and well from war.
But when they saw him thus, his chest and clothes
All torn, his body heavy and his face
Begrimed by dust, they asked him all at once,   125
"What does this mean? Why are you sad at heart?"
He told them of his strange and baffling deed,
Of how he'd slain the one he held most dear.
They all began to weep and mourn with him,
And filled the earth and sky with loud lament.   130
At last he told the nobles gathered there,
"It seems my heart is gone, my body too.
Do not pursue this battle with the Turks.
The evil I have done is quite enough."
And when he left that place, the pahlaván   135
Returned with weary heart to where he lay.
The noble lords accompanied their chief,
Men like Gudárz and Tus and Gostahám.
The army all together loosed their tongues,
And gave advice and counsel to Rostám,   140
"Yazdán alone can remedy this wound;
He yet may ease this burden's weight for you."
He grasped a dagger in his hand, and made
To cut his worthless head from his own trunk.
The nobles hung upon his arm and hand, and tears   145
Of blood poured from the lashes of their eyes.
Gudárz said to Rostám, "What gain is there
If by your death you set the world in flames?
Were you to give yourself a hundred wounds,
How would that ease the pain of brave Sohráb?   150
If some time yet remains for him on earth,
He'll live, and you'll remain with him, at peace.
But if this youth is destined to depart,
Look on the world, who's there that does not die?
The head that wears a helmet and the head   155
That wears a crown, to death we all are prey."

Rostám Asks Kay Kavús for the Nushdarú

Rostám called wise Gudárz and said to him,
"Depart from here upon your swiftest steed,
And take a message to Kavús the shah.
Tell him what has befallen me. With my   160
Own dagger I have torn the breast of my
Brave son—oh, may Rostám not live for long!
If you've some recollection of my deeds,
Then share with me a portion of my grief,
And from your store send me the *nushdarú*,   165
That medicine which heals whatever wound.
It would be well if you sent it to me
With no delay, and in a cup of wine.
By your good grace, my son may yet be cured,
And like his father stand before your throne."   170
The *sepahbód*[3] Gudárz rode like the wind,
And gave Kavús the message from Rostám.

   Kavús replied, "If such an elephant
Should stay alive and join our royal court,
He'll make his father yet more powerful.   175
Rostám will slay me then, I have no doubt.
When I may suffer evil at his hands,
What gift but evil should I make him now?
You heard him, how he said, 'Who is Kavús?
If he's the shah, then who is Tus?' And with   180
That chest and neck, that mighty arm and fist,
In this wide world, who's there to equal him?
Will he stand humbly by my royal seat,
Or march beneath my banner's eagle wings?"

   Gudárz heard his reply, then turned and rode   185
Back to Rostám as swift as wind-borne smoke.
"The evil nature of the shah is like
The tree of war, perpetually in fruit.
You must depart at once and go to him.
Perhaps you can enlighten his dark soul."   190

Rostám Mourns Sohráb

Rostám commanded that a servant bring
A robe and spread it by the river's bank.
He gently laid Sohráb upon the robe,
Then mounted Rakhsh and rode toward the shah.

---

3. A title that means general; can be used for
   shahs and heroes as well.

But as he rode, his face toward the court,   195
They overtook him swiftly with the news,
"Sohráb has passed from this wide world; he'll need
A coffin from you now, and not a crown.
'Father!' he cried, then sighed an icy wind,
Then wept aloud and closed his eyes at last."   200
   Rostám dismounted from his steed at once.
Dark dust replaced the helmet on his head.
He wept and cried aloud, "Oh, noble youth,
And proud, courageous seed of pahlaváns!
The sun and moon won't see your like again,   205
No more will shield or mail, nor throne or crown.
Who else has been afflicted as I've been?
That I should slay a youth in my old age
Who is the grandson of world-conquering Sam,
Whose mother's seed's from famous men as well.   210
It would be right to sever these two hands.
No seat be mine henceforth save darkest earth.
What father's ever done a deed like this?
I now deserve abuse and icy scorn.
Who else in all this world has slain his son,   215
His wise, courageous, youthful son?
How Zal the golden will rebuke me now,
He and the virtuous Rudabé as well.
What can I offer them as my excuse?
What plea of mine will satisfy their hearts?   220
What will the heroes and the warriors say
When word of this is carried to their ears?
And when his mother learns, what shall I say?
How can I send a messenger to her?
What can I say? Why did I slay him when   225
He'd done no crime? Why blacken all his days?
How will her sire, that worthy pahlaván,
Report this to his pure and youthful child?
He'll call this seed of Sam[4] a godless wretch,
And heap his curses on my ancient head.   230
Alas, who could have known this precious child
Would quickly grow to cypress height, or that
He'd raise this host and think of arms and war,
Or that he'd turn my shining day to night."
   Rostám commanded that the body of   235
His son be covered with a royal robe.

---

4. Rostám's grandfather.

He'd longed to sit upon the throne and rule;
His portion was a coffin's narrow walls.
The coffin of Sohráb was carried from
The field. Rostám returned to his own tent.   240
They set aflame Sohráb's pavilion while
His army cast dark dust upon their heads.
They threw his tents of many colored silk,
His precious throne and leopard saddle cloth
Into the flames, and tumult filled the air.   245
   He cried aloud, "Oh, youthful conqueror!
Alas, that stature and that noble face!
Alas, that wisdom and that manliness!
Alas, what sorrow and heart-rending loss—
No mother near, heart pierced by father's blade!"   250
His eyes wept bloody tears, he tore the earth,
And rent the kingly garments on his back.
   Then all the pahlaváns and Shah Kavús
Sat with him in the dust beside the road.
They spoke to him with counsel and advice—   255
In grief Rostám was like one driven mad—
"This is the way of fortune's wheel. It holds
A lasso in this hand, a crown in that.
As one sits happily upon his throne,
A loop of rope will snatch him from his place.   260
Why is it we should hold the world so dear?
We and our fellows must depart this road.
The longer we have thought about our wealth,
The sooner we must face that earthy door.
If heaven's wheel knows anything of this,   265
Or if its mind is empty of our fate,
The turning of the wheel it cannot know,
Nor can it understand the reason why.
One must lament that he should leave this world,
Yet what this means at last, I do not know."   270
   Then Kay Kavús spoke to Rostám at length,
"From Mount Alborz to the frailest reed,
The turning heavens carry all away.
You must not fix your heart upon this world.
One sets off quickly on the road, and one   275
Will take more time, but all pass on to death.
Content your heart with his departure and
Give careful heed to what I tell you now.
If you should bring the heavens down to earth,
Or set the world aflame from end to end,   280
You won't recall from death the one who's gone.

His soul's grown ancient in that other manse.
Once from afar I saw his arms and neck,
His lofty stature and his massive chest.
The times impelled him and his martial host   285
To come here now and perish by your hand.
What can you do? What remedy is there
For death? How long can you bewail his loss?"
   Rostám replied, "Though he himself is gone,
Humán still sits upon this ample plain,   290
His Turkish and his Chinese chiefs as well.
Retain no hint of enmity toward them,
But strengthened by Yazdán and your command,
Let Zavaré guide all their army home."
   "Oh, famous pahlaván," said Shah Kavús,   295
"This war has caused you suffering and loss.
Though they have done me many grievous wrongs,
And though Turán has set Irán aflame,
Because my heart can feel your heavy pain,
I'll think no more of them and let them go,"   300

BADĪ^C AL-ZAMĀN AL-HAMADHĀNĪ

(969?–1008)

Arabic

The *maqāma* (plural, *maqāmāt*) is an indigenous Arabic literary form, a tale
crafted in rhymed prose (*saj^c*) with occasional portions in verse. Usually
translated as "seance" or "assembly," it is closely related to the anecdotal *adab*.
Al-Hamadhānī is credited by most literary historians with having invented the
maqāma. Born, as his name reveals, in Hamadān, he seems to have spent his life
traveling from one court to another. He died in Herāt, in present-day Afghanistan. According to a delighted account by a contemporary, al-Hamadhānī's
verbal virtuosity was dazzling; his nickname, Badī^c al-Zaman, means "wonder of
the age." The hero of the *maqāma* is likewise a verbal virtuoso—a clever rogue
whose exploits are related by a narrator whose path continually crosses the
hero's. The two even share adventures. Eloquence and a ready wit are among the
chief tools of the rogue hero's trade. This and other literary qualities have led
some scholars to link the classical Arabic *maqāma* to the Spanish picaresque
novel, a genre named for *its* rogue hero, or *picaro*. Certain is that al-Hamadhānī's
invention, including its stock hero and narrator, spread throughout the Islamic
world, and the ensuing centuries saw *Maqāmāt* written in Persian, Turkish, and
even Hebrew.

from *The Maqāmāt*

Portrait of a Parvenu

THE MAḌĪRA[1] (LATE TENTH CENTURY)

'Isā ibn Hishām told us the following: I was in Basra with Abu'l-Fatḥ al-Iskandarī, a master of language—when he summoned elegance, it responded; when he commanded eloquence, it obeyed. I was present with him at a reception given by some merchant, and we were served a *maḍīra,* one that commended the civilization of cities. It quivered in the dish and gave promise of bliss and testified that Muʿāwiya,[2] God have mercy on him, was Imam.[3] It was in a bowl such that looks glided off it and brilliance rippled in it. When it took its place on the table and its home in our hearts, Abu'l-Fatḥ al-Iskandarī started to curse it and him who offered it, to abuse it and him who ate it, to revile it and him who cooked it. We thought that he was jesting, but the fact was the reverse, for his jest was earnest, indeed. He withdrew from the table and left the company of brothers. We had the *maḍīra* removed, and our hearts were removed with it, our eyes followed behind it, our mouths watered after it, our lips smacked, and our livers were kindled. Nevertheless, we joined with him in parting with it and inquired of him concerning it, and he said, "My story about the *maḍīra* is longer than the pain of my being deprived of it, and if I tell you about it, I am in danger of arousing aversion and wasting time."

We said, "Come on!" and he continued.

"When I was in Baghdad a certain merchant invited me to a *maḍīra* and stuck to me like a creditor and like the dog to the companions of al-Raqīm.[4] So I accepted his invitation, and we set out for his house. All the way he praised his wife, for whom, he said, he would give his life's blood. He described her skill in preparing the *maḍīra* and her refinement in cooking it, and he said, 'O my master, if you could see her, with the apron round her middle, moving about the house, from the oven to the pots and from the pots to the oven, blowing on the fire with her mouth and pounding the spices with her hand; if you could see the smoke blacken that beautiful face and leave its marks on that smooth cheek, then you would see a sight which would dazzle the eyes! I love her because she loves me. It is bliss for a man to be vouchsafed the help of his wife and to be aided by his helpmate, especially if she is of his kin. She is my cousin on my father's side, her

Translated by Bernard Lewis.

1. A stew of spiced meat.
2. Caliph, founder of the Umayyad Dynasty.
3. leader of the community, a reference to the disputed legitimacy of this ruler.
4. A reference to the story of the People of the Cave which appears in Sûra 18 of the Qur'an. The People of the Cave are often associated with the Seven Sleepers of Eph-

esus, in the Christian tradition a group of young men who escaped persecution under the Emperor Decius by hiding in a cave and sleeping there for many years. Al-Raqīm may be the dog or the village closest to the cave. Others understand this reference to allude to a separate incident altogether.

flesh is my flesh, her town is my town, her uncles are my uncles, her root is my root. She is however better natured and better looking that I.'

"So he wearied me with his wife's qualities until we reached the quarter where he lived, and then he said, 'O my master, look at this quarter! It is the noblest quarter of Baghdad. The worthy vie to settle here, and the great compete to dwell here. None but merchants live here, for a man can be judged by his neighbor. My house is the jewel in the middle of a necklace of houses, the center of their circle. How much, O my master, would you say was spent on each house? Make a rough guess, if you don't know exactly.'

"I answered, 'A lot.'

"He said, 'Glory be to God, how great is your error! You just say "a lot." ' Then he sighed deeply and said, 'Glory to Him who knows all things.'

"Then we came to the door of his house, and he said, 'This is my house. How much, O my master, would you say I spent on this doorway? By God, I spent more than I could afford and enough to reduce me to poverty. What do you think of its workmanship and shape? By God, have you seen its like? Look at the fine points of craftsmanship in it, and observe the beauty of its lattice-work; it is as if it had been drawn with a compass. Look at the skill of the carpenter in making this door. From how many pieces did he make it? You may well say, "How should I know?" It is made of a single piece of teak, free from worm or rot. If it is moved, it moans, and if it is struck, it hums. Who made it, sir? Abū Ishāq ibn Muhammad al-Basrī made it, and he is, by God, of good repute, skillful in the craft of doors, dextrous with his hands in his work. God, what a capable man he is! By my life, I would never call on anyone but him for such a task.'

" 'And this door ring which you see, I bought it in the curio market from 'Imrān the curio dealer, for three Mu'izzī dinars. And how much yellow copper does it contain, sir? It contains six *ratls*! It turns on a screw in the door. Turn it, by God! Then strike it and watch. By my life, one should not buy a door ring from anyone but " 'Imrān, who sells nothing but treasures.' "

"Then he rapped on the door, and we entered the hall, and he said, 'May God preserve you, O house! May God not destroy you, O walls! How strong are your buttresses, how sound your construction, how firm your foundation! By God, observe the steps and scrutinize the inside and the outside of the house, and ask me, "How did you obtain it, and by what devices did you acquire and gain possession of it?" I had a neighbor called Abū Sulaymān, who lived in this quarter. He had more wealth than he could store and more valuables than he could weigh. He died, may God have mercy on him, leaving an heir who squandered his inheritance on wine and song and dissipated it between backgammon and gambling. I feared lest the guide of necessity lead him to sell the house and he sell it in a moment of desperation or leave it exposed to ruination. Then I would see my chance of buying it slip away, and my grief would continue to the day of my death.'

" 'So I got some clothes of a kind difficult to sell and brought them and offered them to him and chaffered with him until he agreed to buy them on credit. The luckless regard credit as a gift, and the unsuccessful reckon it as a present. I asked him for a document for the amount, and he drew one up in my favor. Then

I neglected to claim what was due until he was in the direst straits. And then I came and demanded what he owed. He asked for a delay, to which I agreed; he asked me for more clothes, which I brought him; and I asked him to give me his house as security and as a pledge in my hand. He did so, and then I induced him in successive negotiation to sell it to me so that it became mine by rising fortune, lucky chance, and a strong arm. Many a man works unwittingly for others, but I, praise be to God, am lucky and successful in matters such as these. Just think, O my master, that a few nights ago when I was sleeping in the house together with my household, there was a knock at the door. I asked, "Who is this untimely caller?" and there was a woman with a necklace of pearls, as clear as water and as delicate as a mirage, offering it for sale. I took it from her as if by theft, so low was the price for which I bought it. It will be of obvious value and abundant profit, with the help and favor of God. I have only told you this story so that you may know how lucky I am in business, for good luck can make water flow from stones. God is great! Nobody will inform you more truthfully than you yourself, and no day is nearer than yesterday. I bought this mat at an auction. It was brought out of the houses of the Ibn al-Furāt family when their assets were confiscated and seized. I had been looking for something like this for a long time and had not found it. "Fate is a pregnant woman;" no one knows what it will bear. It chanced that I was at Bāb al-Ṭāq, and this mat was displayed in the market. I weighed out so many dinars[5] for it. By God, look at its fineness, its softness, its workmanship, its color, for it is of immense value. Its like occurs only rarely. If you have heard of Abū 'Imrān the mat maker, it is he who made it. He has a son who has now succeeded him in his shop, and only with him can the finest mats be found. By my life, never buy mats from any shop but his, for a true believer gives good advice to his brothers, especially those admitted to the sanctity of his table. But let us return to the *madīra,* for the hour of noon has come. Slave! Basin and water!'

"God is great, I thought, release draws nearer and escape becomes easier.

"The slave stepped forward, and the merchant said, 'Do you see this slave? He is of Greek origin and brought up in Iraq. Come here, slave! Uncover your head! Raise your leg! Bare your arm! Show your teeth! Walk up and down!'

"The slave did as he said, and the merchant said, 'By God, who bought him? By God, Abu'l-Abbās bought him from the slave-dealer. Put down the basin and bring the jug!'

"The slave put it down and the merchant picked it up, turned it around, and looked it over; then he struck it and said, 'Look at this yellow copper—like a glowing coal or a piece of gold! It is Syrian copper, worked in Iraq. This is not one of those wornout valuables, though it has known the houses of kings and has circulated in them. Look at its beauty and ask me, "When did you buy it?" By God, I bought it in the year of the famine, and I put it aside for this moment. Slave! The jug!'

"He brought it, and the merchant took it and turned it around and said, 'Its spout is part of it, all one piece. This jug goes only with this basin, this basin goes

---

5. Gold coins.

only with this seat of honor, this seat of honor fits only in this house, and this house is beautiful only with this guest! Pour the water, slave, for it is time to eat! By God, do you see this water? How pure it is, as blue as a cat's eye, as clear as a crystal rod! It was drawn from the Euphrates and served after being kept overnight so that it comes as bright as the tongue of flame from a candle and clear as a tear. What counts is not the liquid, but the receptacle. Nothing will show you the cleanliness of the receptacles more clearly than the cleanliness of what you drink. And this kerchief! Ask me about its story! It was woven in Jurjān and worked in Arrajān. I came across it and I bought it. My wife made part of it into a pair of drawers and part of it into a kerchief. Twenty ells went into her drawers, and I snatched this amount away from her hand. I gave it to an embroiderer who worked it and embroidered it as you see. Then I brought it home from the market and stored it in a casket and reserved it for the most refined of my guests. No Arab of the common people defiled it with his hands, nor any woman with the corners of her eyes. Every precious thing has its proper time, and every tool its proper user. Slave! Set the table, for it is growing late! Bring the dish, for the argument has been long! Serve the food, for the talk has been much!'

"The slave brought the table, and the merchant turned it in its place and struck it with his fingertips and tested it with his teeth and said, 'May God give prosperity to Baghdad! How excellent are its products, how refined its craftsmen! By God, observe this table, and look at the breadth of its surface, the slightness of its weight, the hardness of its wood, and the beauty of its shape.'

"I said, 'This is all fine, but when do we eat?'

" 'Now,' he said. 'Slave! Bring the food quickly. But please observe that the legs and the table are all of one piece.' "

Abu'l-Fath said, "I was fuming, and I said to myself, 'There is still the baking and its utensils, the bread and its qualities, and where the wheat was originally bought, and how an animal was hired to transport it, in what mill it was ground, in what tub it was kneaded, in what oven it was baked, and what baker was hired to bake it. Then there is still the firewood, when it was cut, when it was brought, and how it was set out to dry; and then the baker and his description, the apprentice and his character, the flour and its praises, the yeast and its commentary, the salt and its saltiness. And then there are the plates, who got them, how he acquired them, who used them, and who made them; and the vinegar, how its grapes were selected or its fresh dates were bought, how the press was limed, how the juice was extracted, how the jars were tarred, and how much each cask was worth. And then there were the vegetables, by what devices they were picked, in what grocery they were packed, with what care they were cleaned. And then there is the *madīra,* how the meat was bought, the fat was paid for, the pot set up, the fire kindled, the spices pounded so that the cooking might excell and the gravy be thick. This is an affair that overflows and a business that has no end.'

"So I rose, and he asked, 'What do you want?'

"I said, 'A need that I must satisfy.'

"He said, 'O my master! You are going to a privy which shames the spring residence of the amir and the autumn residence of the vizier! Its upper part is plastered and its lower part is whitewashed; its roof is terraced and its floor is paved with marble. Ants slip off its walls and cannot grip; flies walk on its floor and slither along. It has a door with panels of teak and ivory combined in the most perfect way. A guest could wish to eat there.'

" 'Eat there yourself,' I said. 'The privy is not part of the bargain.'

"Then I made for the door and hurried as I went. I began to run, and he followed me, shouting, 'O Abu'l-Fath, the *madīra!* The youngsters thought that *al-madīra* was my byname, and they began to shout it. I threw a stone at one of them, so angry was I, but the stone hit a man on his turban and pierced his head. I was seized and beaten with shoes, both old and new, and showered with blows, both worthy and vicious, and thrown into prison. I remained for two years in this misfortune, and I swore that I would never eat a *madīra* as long as I lived. Have I done wrong in this, O people of Hamadān?"

'Isā ibn Hishām said, "We accepted his excuse and joined in his vow, saying 'The *madīra* has brought misfortune on the noble and has exalted the unworthy over the worthy.' "

IBN HAZM (d. 1064)
Arabic

The Dove's Neckring (*Twaq al-Hamāma*), written by the Andalusian scholar and legist Ibn Hazm, is a work of great universal appeal. It was supposedly written in answer to a request by a friend who wished Ibn Hazm to describe love and its various manifestations. Part of the appeal of the work lies in its autobiographical elements. It also provides readers with a personal view of Andalusian society during the eleventh century.

from *The Dove's Neckring*

[Of Various Loves]

Because betrayal is so common a characteristic of the beloved, fidelity on her part has come to be regarded as extraordinary; therefore its rare occurrence in persons loved is thought to counterbalance its frequency among lovers. I have a little poem on this subject.

> Small faithfulness in the beloved
> Is most exceedingly approved,
> While lovers' great fidelity
> Is taken unremarkably.

Translated by A. J. Arberry.

> So cowards, rarely brave in war,
> Are more applauded when they are
> Than heroes, who sustain all day
> The heat and fury of the fray.

A particularly base type of betrayal is when the lover sends an emissary to the beloved, entrusting all his secrets to his keeping, and then the messenger strives and contrives to convert the beloved's interest to himself, and captures her affection to the exclusion of his principal. I put this situation in rhyme as follows.

> I sent an envoy unto thee,
>   Intending so my hopes to gain;
> I trusted him too foolishly;
>   Now he has come between us twain.
>
> He loosed the cords of my true love,
>   Then neatly tied his own instead;
> He drove me out of all whereof
>   I might have well been tenanted.
>
> I, who had called him to the stand,
>   Am now a witness to his case:
> I fed him at my table, and
>   Now hang myself upon his grace.

Finally there is the separation which is caused by death, that final parting from which there is no hope of a return. This is indeed a shattering and back-breaking blow, a fateful catastrophe; it is a lamentable woe, overshadowing the blackness of night itself; it cuts off every hope, erases all ambition, and causes the most sanguine to despair of further meeting. Here all tongues are baffled; the cord of every remedy is severed; no other course remains open but patient fortitude, willing or perforce. It is the greatest affliction that can assail true lovers; and he who is struck down by it has nothing left but to lament and weep, until either he perishes himself or wearies of his lamentations. It is the wound which cannot heal, the anguish which never passes, the sorrow which is constantly renewed, as ever his poor body crumbles that thou hast committed to the dust. On this matter I have the following to say.

> What things soe'er
> May come to pass,
> Cry not alas
> While hope is there.
>
> Haste not thy heart
> To gloom to yield:
> All is not sealed
> Till life depart.
>
> But when the veil
> Of death descends
> Then all hope ends,
> All comforts fail.

I have seen this happen to many people, and can relate to you a personal experience of the same order; for I am also one who has been afflicted by this calamity and surprised by this misfortune. I was deeply in love with, and passionately enamoured of, a certain slave-girl once in my possession, whose name was Nu'm. She was a dream of desire, a paragon of physical and moral beauty, and we were in perfect harmony. She had known no other man before me, and our love for each other was mutual and perfectly satisfying. Then the fates ravished her from me, and the nights and passing days carried her away; she became one with the dust and stones. At the time of her death I was not yet twenty, and she younger than I. For seven months thereafter I never once put off my garments; my tears ceased not to flow, though I am a man not given to weeping, nor discovering relief in lamentation. And by Allah, I have not found consolation for her loss even to this day. If ransoms could have been of avail, I would have ransomed her with everything of which I stand possessed, my inheritance and all my earnings, aye, and with the most precious limb of my body, swiftly and willingly. Since her death life has never seemed sweet to me; I have never forgotten her memory, nor been intimate with any other woman. My love for her blotted out all that went before, and made anathema to me all that came after it.

I can tell you with regard to myself, that in my youth I enjoyed the loving friendship of a certain slave-girl who grew up in our house, and who at the time of my story was sixteen years old. She had an extremely pretty face, and was moreover intelligent, chaste, pure, shy, and of the sweetest disposition. She was not given to jesting, and was most sparing of her favours; she had a wonderful complexion, which she always kept closely veiled. Innocent of every vice, and of very few words, she kept her eyes modestly cast down. Moreover she was extremely cautious, and guiltless of all faults, ever maintaining a serious mien; charming in her withdrawal, she was naturally reserved, and most graceful in repelling unwelcome advances. She seated herself with becoming dignity, and was most sedate in her behaviour; the way she fled from masculine attentions like a startled bird was delightful to behold. No hopes of easy conquest were to be entertained so far as she was concerned; none could look to succeed in his ambitions if these were aimed in her direction; eager expectation found no resting-place in her. Her lovely face attracted all hearts, but her manner kept at arm's length all who came seeking her; she was far more glamorous in her refusals and rejections than those other girls, who rely upon easy compliance and the ready lavishing of their favours to make them interesting to men. In short, she was dedicated to earnestness in all matters, and had no desire for amusement of any kind; for all that she played the lute most beautifully. I found myself irresistibly drawn towards her, and loved her with all the violent passion of my youthful heart. For two years or thereabouts I laboured to the utmost of my powers to win one syllable of response from her, to hear from her lips a single word, other than the usual kind of banalities that may be heard by everyone; but all my efforts proved in vain.

Now I remember a party that was held in our residence, on one of those occasions that are commonly made the excuse for such festivities in the houses of persons of rank. The ladies of our household and of my brother's also, God have mercy on his soul, were assembled together, as well as the womenfolk of our retainers and faithful servants, all thoroughly nice and jolly folk. The ladies remained in the house for the earlier part of the day, and then betook themselves to a belvedere that was attached to our mansion, overlooking the garden and giving a magnificent view of the whole of Cordova; the bays were constructed with large open windows. They passed their time enjoying the panorama through the lattice openings, myself being among them.

I recall that I was endeavouring to reach the bay where she was standing, to enjoy her proximity and to sidle up close to her. But no sooner did she observe me in the offing than she left that bay and sought another, moving with consummate grace. I endeavoured to come to the bay to which she had departed, and she repeated her performance and passed on to another. She was well aware of my infatuation, while the other ladies were entirely unconscious of what was passing between us; for there was a large company of them, and they were all the time moving from one alcove to another to enjoy the variety of prospects, each bay affording a different view from the rest.

You must realize, my friend, that women have keener eyes to detect admiration in a man's heart, than any benighted traveller has to discover a track in the desert. Well, at last the ladies went down into the garden; and the dowagers and duchesses among them entreated the mistress of the girl to let them hear her sing. She commanded her to do so; and she thereupon took up her lute and tuned it with a pretty shyness and modesty, the like of which I had never seen; though it is true of course that things are doubly beautiful in the eyes of their admirers. Then she began to sing those famous verses of al-ʿAbbās ibn al-Aḥnaf.

> My heart leapt up, when I espied
> A sun sink slowly in the west,
> Its beauty in that bower to hide
> Where lovely ladies lie at rest:
>
> A sun embodied in the guise
> Of a sweet maiden of delight,
> The ripple of her rounded thighs
> A scroll of parchment, soft and white.
>
> No creature she of human kind,
> Though human fair and beautiful,
> And neither sprite, although designed
> In faery grace ineffable.
>
> Her body was a jasmine rare,
> Her perfume sweet as amber scent,
> Her face a pearl beyond compare,
> Her all, pure light's embodiment.
>
> All shrouded in her pettigown
> I watched her delicately pass,

> Stepping as light as thistledown
> That dances on a crystal glass.

And by my life, it was as though her plectrum was plucking at the strings of my heart. I have never forgotten that day, nor shall forget it until the time comes for me to leave this transient world. That was the most I was ever given to see her, or to hear her voice.

Then my father, the vizier, God rest his soul, moved from our new mansion in Rabad al-Zāhira on the eastern side of Cordova to our old residence on the western side, in the quarter of Balat Mughith; this was on the third day of the accession of Muhammad al-Mahdī, to the Caliphate.[1] I followed him in February 1009; but the girl did not come with us, for reasons that obliged her to remain behind. Thereafter, when Hishām al-Mu'aiyad[2] succeeded to the throne, we were sufficiently preoccupied with the misfortunes which came upon us, thanks to the hostility of his ministers; we were sorely tried by imprisonment, surveillance and crushing fines, and were finally obliged to go into hiding. Civil war raged far and wide; all classes suffered from its dire effects, and ourselves in particular. At last my father the vizier died, God have mercy on his soul, our situation being still as I have described, on the afternoon of Saturday, June 22, 1012.

Things remained unchanged with us thereafter, until presently the day came when we again had a funeral in the house, one of our relatives having deceased. I saw her standing there amid the clamour of mourning, all among the weeping and wailing women. She revived that passion long buried in my heart, and stirred my now still ardour, reminding me of an ancient troth, an old love, an epoch gone by, a vanished time, departed months, faded memories, periods perished, days forever past, obliterated traces. She renewed my griefs and reawakened my sorrows; and though upon that day I was afflicted and cast down for many reasons, yet I had indeed not forgotten her; only my anguish was intensified, the fire smouldering in my heart blazed into flame, my unhappiness was exacerbated, my despair was multiplied. Passion drew forth from my breast all that lay hidden within it; my soul answered the call, and I broke out into plaintive rhyme.

> They weep for one now dead,
> High honoured in his tomb;
> Those tears were better shed
> For him who lives in gloom.
>
> O wonder, that they sigh
> For him who is at rest
> Yet mourn not me, who die
> Most cruelly oppressed.

Then destiny struck its heaviest blows, and we were banished from our loved abodes; the armies of the Berbers triumphed over us. I set forth from Cordova[3] on July 13, 1013, and after that one glimpse of her she vanished from my sight for six

---

1. Muhammad al-Mahdī reigned from 1009 to 1010.

2. Hisham al-Mu'aiyad reigned from 976 to 1009 and from 1010 to 1013.

3. A city in Spain.

long years and more. Then I came again into Cordova in February 1019, and lodged with one of our womenfolk; and there I saw her. I could scarcely recognize her, until someone said to me, 'This is So-and-so'; her charms were so greatly changed. Gone was her radiant beauty, vanished her wondrous loveliness; faded now was that lustrous complexion which once gleamed like a polished sword or an Indian mirror; withered was the bloom on which the eye once gazed transfixed seeking avidly to feast upon its dazzling splendour only to turn away bewildered. Only a fragment of the whole remained, to tell the tale and testify to what the complete picture had been. All this had come to pass because she took too little care of herself, and had lacked the guardian hand which had nourished her during the days of our prosperity, when our shadow was long in the land; as also because she had been obliged to besmirch herself in those inevitable excursions to which her circumstances had driven her, and from which she had formerly been sheltered and exempted.

For women are as aromatic herbs, which if not well tended soon lose their fragrance; they are as edifices which, if not constantly cared for, quickly fall into ruin. Therefore it has been said that manly beauty is the truer, the more solidly established, and of higher excellence, since it can endure, and that without shelter, onslaughts the merest fraction of which would transform the loveliness of a woman's face beyond recognition: such enemies as the burning heat of the noonday, the scorching wind of the desert, every air of heaven, and all the changing moods of the seasons.

If I had enjoyed the least degree of intimacy with her, if she had been only a little kind to me, I would have been beside myself with happiness; I verily believe that I would have died for joy. But it was her unremitting aloofness which schooled me in patience, and taught me to find consolation. This then was one of those cases in which both parties may excusably forget, and not be blamed for doing so: there has been no firm engagement that should require their loyalty, no covenant has been entered into obliging them to keep faith, no ancient compact exists, no solemn plighting of troths, the breaking and forgetting of which should expose them to justified reproach.

Here is a story which I have often heard told concerning a certain Berber king. An Andalusian gentleman, finding himself in financial difficulties, had sold a female slave whom he loved passionately; she was bought by a man of the Berber country. The poor fellow who sold her never imagined that his heart would follow her in the way it did. When she reached her purchaser's home, her former owner almost expired. So he searched out the man to whom he had sold her and offered him all his possessions, and himself to boot, if he would restore her to him; but the Berber refused.

The Andalusian then besought the inhabitants of the town to prevail upon him; but not one of them came to his assistance. Almost out of his mind, he bethought himself of appealing to the king; he therefore stood without the palace, and uttered a loud cry. The king, who was seated in a lofty chamber overlooking the courtyard, heard his shout and ordered him to be admitted. The Andalusian entered the royal presence, and standing before his Berber majesty he told his story, and implored and supplicated him to have compassion.

The king, much touched by his plight, commanded that the man who had bought the girl should be summoned to court. He duly came; and the king said, "This poor fellow is a stranger; you can see what a state he is in. I intercede with you personally on his behalf." But the purchaser refused, saying, "I am more deeply in love with her than he is, and I fear that if you return her to him I myself shall be standing here tomorrow imploring your aid, and in an even worse case." The king and all his courtiers offered him of their own riches to let her go; but he persisted in his refusal, pleading as his excuse the affection he bore her.

The audience having by now dragged on a long time, and there being no sign whatsoever that the purchaser would give way and consent, the king said to the Andalusian, "My good sir, I can do nothing more for you than this. I have striven to the utmost of my powers on your behalf; and you see how he excuses himself on the grounds that he loves her more than you do, and fears he may come to even greater evil than yourself. You had best endure patiently what Allah has decreed for you."

The Andalusian thereupon exclaimed, "Have you no means at all then of helping me?"

"Can I do anything more for you than entreat him, and offer him money?" the king answered.

The Andalusian, being in despair, bent himself double, and with his hands clutching his feet he threw himself down from the topmost height of the audience-chamber to the earth. The king cried out in alarm, and his slaves below ran to where the man was lying. It was his fate not to be greatly injured by the fall, and he was brought up to the king again.

"What did you intend by doing that?" the king said to him.

"O king," the man replied, "I cannot live any longer, now that I have lost her."

Then he would have thrown himself down a second time, but he was prevented.

"Allah is great!" the king thereupon exclaimed. "I have hit upon the just arbitrament of this problem." Turning to the purchaser he said, "Good sir, do you claim that your love for the girl is greater than his, and do you state that you fear to come to the same pass as he is in?"

"Yes," replied the Berber.

"Very well," went on the king. "Your friend here has given us a clear indication of his love; he hurled himself down, and would have died, but that Almighty God preserved him. Now do you stand up and prove your love is true; cast yourself down from the topmost point of this pavilion, as your friend did. If you die, it will mean that your appointed time has come; if you live, you will have the better right to the girl, seeing that she is at present your property; and your companion in distress shall then go away. But if you refuse to jump, I will take the girl from you, whether you like it or not, and will hand her over to him."

At first the Berber held back, but then he said, "I will cast myself down." But when he came near the opening, and looked into the yawning void below him, he drew himself back again.

"By Allah," cried the king, "it shall be as I have said."

The man tried again, but shrunk away once more.

When he would not take the plunge, the king shouted to him, "Do not make sport of us! Ho, slaves, seize his hands and pitch him to the ground!"

The Berber, seeing the king thus resolved, exclaimed, "O king, I am content: let him have the girl."

The king replied, "Allah give thee a good recompense!"

So saying, he bought the girl from him and gave her over to her former owner; and the two departed.

AL-GHAZALI (1058?–1111)
Arabic

A brilliant legist, philosopher-theologian, and professor, al-Ghazali has entered the annals of world literature through his spiritual autobiography. Al-Ghazali began his career as a professor of religious sciences in Baghdad, where he produced important works on philosophy and Islamic orthodoxy. Dissatisfied with the intellectual life he was leading, however, he left his teaching post, abandoned his family, and for ten years explored the mystical side of Islam. *The Rescuer from Error [al-Munqidh min al-Dala]* is his autobiographical account of this intellectual and spiritual saga. Al-Ghazali was more than simply someone who solved his own personal crisis, however. In a later work, *Revitalization of Religious Sciences [Ihya' ʿ-Ulum ad-Din]*, he turned his personal experience to use in unifying two divergent strands in medieval Islamic society: religious orthodoxy and mysticism.

from *The Rescuer from Error*

The Ways of Mysticism

When I had finished with these sciences, I next turned with set purpose to the method of mysticism (or Sufism). I knew that the complete mystic "way" includes both intellectual belief and practical activity; the latter consists in getting rid of the obstacles in the self and in stripping off its base characteristics and vicious morals, so that the heart may attain to freedom from what is not God and to constant recollection of Him.

The intellectual belief was easier to me than the practical activity. I began to acquaint myself with their belief by reading their book, such as *The Food of the Hearts* by Abu Talib al-Makki (God have mercy upon him), the works of al-Harith al-Muhasibi, the various anecdotes about al-Junayd, ash-Shibli and Abu Yazid al-Bistami (may God sanctify their spirits),[1] and other discourses of their leading

Translated by W. Montgomery Watt.

men. I thus comprehended their fundamental teachings on the intellectual side, and progressed, as far as is possible by study and oral instruction, in the knowledge of mysticism. It became clear to me, however, that what is most distinctive of mysticism is something which cannot be apprehended by study, but only by immediate experience (ahawq—literally "tasting"), by ecstasy and by a moral change. What a difference there is between *knowing* the definition of health and satiety, together with their causes and presuppositions, and *being,* healthy and satisfied! What a difference between being acquainted with the definition of drunkenness—namely, that it designates a state arising from the domination of the seat of the intellect by vapours arising from the stomach—and being drunk! Indeed, the drunken man while in that condition does not know the definition of drunkenness nor the scientific account of it; he has not the very least scientific knowledge of it. The sober man, on the other hand, knows the definition of drunkenness and its basis, yet he is not drunk in the very least. Again the doctor, when he is himself ill, knows the definition and causes of health and the remedies which restore it, and yet is lacking in health. Similarly there is a difference between knowing the true nature and causes and conditions of the ascetic life and actually leading such a life and forsaking the world.

I apprehended clearly that the mystics were men who had real experiences, not men of words, and that I had already progressed as far as was possible by way of intellectual apprehension. What remained for me was not to be attained by oral instruction and study but only by immediate experience and by walking in the mystic way.

Now from the sciences I had laboured at and the paths I had traversed in my investigation of the revelational and rational sciences (that is, presumably, theology and philosophy), there had come to me a sure faith in God most high, in prophethood (or revelation), and in the Last Day. These three credal principles were firmly rooted in my being, not through any carefully argued proof, but by reason of various causes, coincidences and experiences which are not capable of being stated in detail.

It had already become clear to me that I had no hope of the bliss of the world to come save through a God-fearing life and the withdrawal of myself from vain desire. It was clear to me too that the key to all this was to sever the attachment of the heart to worldly things by leaving the mansion of deception and returning to that of eternity, and to advance towards God most high with all earnestness. It was also clear that this was only to be achieved by turning away from wealth and position and fleeing from all time-consuming entanglements.

Next I considered the circumstances of my life, and realized that I was caught in a veritable thicket of attachments. I also considered my activities, of which the best was my teaching and lecturing, and realized that in them I was dealing with sciences that were unimportant and contributed nothing to the attainment of eternal life.

After that I examined my motive in my work of teaching, and realized that it

---

1. Al-Makkī, al-Muhāsibī, al-Junayd, ash-
Shiblī, and al-Bistāmī are all well-known
mystics.

was not a pure desire for the things of God, but that the impulse moving me was the desire for an influential position and public recognition. I saw for certain that I was on the brink of a crumbling bank of sand in imminent danger of hell-fire unless I set about to mend my ways.

I reflected on this continuously for a time, while the choice still remained open to me. One day I would form the resolution to quit Baghdad and get rid of these adverse circumstances; the next day I would abandon my resolution. I put one foot forward and drew the other back. If in the morning I had a genuine longing to seek eternal life, by the evening the attack of a whole host of desires had reduced it to impotence. Worldly desires were striving to keep me by their chains just where I was, while the voice of faith was calling, "To the road! to the road! What is left of life is but little and the journey before you is long. All that keeps you busy, both intellectually and practically, is but hypocrisy and delusion. If you do not prepare *now* for eternal life, when will you prepare? If you do not now sever these attachments, when will you sever them?" On hearing that the impulse would be stirred and the resolution made to take to flight.

Soon, however, Satan would return. "This is a passing mood," he would say; "do not yield to it, for it will quickly disappear; if you comply with it and leave this influential position, these comfortable and dignified circumstances where you are free from troubles and disturbances, this state of safety and security where you are untouched by the contentions of your adversaries, then you will probably come to yourself again and will not find it easy to return to all this."

For nearly six months beginning with Rajab 488 A.H.[2] I was continuously tossed about between the attractions of worldly desires and the impulses towards eternal life. In that month the matter ceased to be one of choice and become one of compulsion. God caused my tongue to dry up so that I was prevented from lecturing. One particular day I would make an effort to lecture in order to gratify the hearts of my following, but my tongue would not utter a single word nor could I accomplish anything at all.

This impediment in my speech produced grief in my heart, and at the same time my power to digest and assimilate food and drink was impaired; I could hardly swallow or digest a single mouthful of food. My powers became so weakened that the doctors gave up all hope of successful treatment. "This trouble arises from the heart; they said, "and from there it has spread through the constitution; the only method of treatment is that the anxiety which has come over the heart should be allayed."

Thereupon, perceiving my impotence and having altogether lost my power of choice, I sought refuge with God most high as one who is driven to Him, because he is without further resources of his own. He answered me, He who 'answers him who is driven (to Him by affliction) when he calls upon Him'.[3] He made it easy for my heart to turn away from position and wealth, from children and friends. I openly professed that I had resolved to set out for Mecca, while privately I made arrangements to travel to Syria. I took this precaution in case the Caliph and all my friends should oppose my resolve to make my residence in Syria. This stratagem

---

2. July 1095 C.E.   **3.** Qur'an 27, 63.

for my departure from Baghdad I gracefully executed, and had it in my mind never to return there. There was much talk about me among all the religious leaders of 'Iraq, since none of them would allow that withdrawal from such a state of life as I was in could have a religious cause, for they looked upon that as the culmination of a religious career; that was the sum of their knowledge.

Much confusion now came into people's minds as they tried to account for my conduct. Those at a distance from 'Iraq supposed that it was due to some apprehension I had of action by the government. On the other hand those who were close to the governing circles and had witnessed how eagerly and assiduously they sought me and how I withdrew from them and showed no great regard for what they said, would say, "This is a supernatural affair; it must be an evil influence which has befallen the people of Islam and especially the circle of the learned."

I left Baghdad, then, I distributed what wealth I had, retaining only as much as would suffice myself and provide sustenance for my children. This I could easily manage, as the wealth of 'Iraq was available for good works, since it constitutes a trust fund for the benefit of the Muslims. Nowhere in the world have I seen better financial arrangements to assist a scholar to provide for his children.

In due course I entered Damascus, and there I remained for nearly two years with no other occupation then the cultivation of retirement and solitude, together with religious and ascetic exercises, as I busied myself purifying my soul, improving my character and cleansing my heart for the constant recollection of God most high, as I had learnt from my study of mysticism. I used to go into retreat for a period in the mosque of Damascus, going up the minaret of the mosque for the whole day and shutting myself in so as to be alone.

At length I made my way from Damascus to the Holy House (that is, Jerusalem). There I used to enter into the precinct of the Rock every day and shut myself in.

Next there arose in me a prompting to fulfill the duty of the Pilgrimage, gain the blessings of Mecca and Medina, and perform the visitation of the Messenger of God most high (peace be upon him), after first performing the visitation of al-Khalīl, the Friend of God (God bless him).[4] I therefore made the journey to the Hijaz.[5] Before long, however, various concerns, together with the entreaties of my children, drew me back to my home (country); and so I came to it again, though one time no one had seemed less likely than myself to return to it. Here, too, I sought retirement, still longing for solitude and the purification of the heart for the recollection (of God). The events of the interval, the anxieties about my family, and the necessities of my livelihood altered the aspect of my purpose and impaired the quality of my solitude, for I experienced pure ecstasy only occasionally, although I did not cease to hope for that; obstacles would hold me back, yet I always returned to it.

I continued at this stage for the space of ten years, and during these periods of solitude there were revealed to me things innumerable and unfathomable. This much I shall say about that in order that others may be helped: I learnt with certainty

---

4. That is, Abraham, who is buried in the cave of Machpelah under the mosque at Hebron, which is called 'al-Khalīl' in Arabic; similarly the visitation of the Messenger is the formal visit to his tomb at Medina.

5. A district of western Arabia that includes the holy cities of Mecca and Medina.

that it is above all the mystics who walk on the road of God; their life is the best life, their method the soundest method, their character the purest character; indeed, were the intellect of the intellectuals and the learning of the learned and the scholarship of the scholars, who are versed in the profundities of revealed truth, brought together in the attempt to improve the life and character of the mystics, they would find no way of doing so; for to the mystics all movement and all rest, whether external or internal, brings illumination from the light of the lamp of prophetic revelation; and behind the light of prophetic revelation there is no other light on the face of the earth from which illumination may be received.

In general, then, how is a mystic "way" (*tarīqah*) described? The purity which is the first condition of it (as bodily purity is the prior condition of formal Worship for Muslims) is the purification of the heart completely from what is other than God most high; the key to it, which corresponds to the opening act of at adoration in prayer,[6] is the sinking of the heart completely in the recollection of God; and the end of it is complete absorption (*fanā*) in God. At least this is its end relatively to those first steps which almost come within the sphere of choice and personal responsibility; but in reality in the actual mystic "way" it is the first step, what comes before it being, as it were, the antechamber for those who are journeying towards it.

With this first stage of the "way" there begin the revelations and visions. The mystics in their waking state now behold angels and the spirits of the prophets; they hear their speaking to them and are instructed by them. Later, a higher state is reached; instead of beholding forms and figures, they come to stages in the "way" which it is hard to describe in language; if a man attempts to express these, his words inevitably contain what is clearly erroneous.

In general what they manage to achieve is nearness to God; some, however, would conceive of this as "inherence" (*hulūl*) some as "union" (*ittihād*), and some as "connection" (*wusūl*) All that is erroneous. In my book, *The Noblest Aim,* I have explained the nature of the error here. Yet he who has attained the mystic "state" need do no more than say:

> Of the things I do not remember, what was, was;
> Think it good; do not ask an account of it.
>   (Ibn al-Mu'tazz).

In general the man to whom He has granted no immediate experience at all, apprehends no more of what prophetic revelation really is than the name. The miraculous graces given to the saints are in truth the beginnings of the prophets; and that was the first "state" of the Messenger of God (peace be upon him) when he went out to Mount Hirā,[7] and was given up entirely to his Lord, and worshipped, so that the bedouin said, "Muhammad loves his Lord passionately."

Now this is a mystical "state" which is realized in immediate experience by

---

6. Literally, the "prohibition," *tahrīm;* the opening words of the rites of the Muslim Worship, "God is great," are known as *takbīrat at-tahrīm,* the prohibitory adora-tion, "because it forbids to the worshipper what was previously allowable."

7. The place where the Prophet Muhammad received the first revelations.

those who walk in the way leading to it. Those to whom it is not granted to have immediate experience can become assured of it by trial (contact with mystics or observation of them) and by hearsay, if they have sufficiently numerous opportunities of associating with mystics to understand that (ecstasy) with certainty means of what accompanies the "states." Whoever sits in their company derives from them this faith; and none who sits in their company is pained.

Those to whom it is not even granted to have contacts with mystics may know with certainty the possibility of ecstasy by the evidence of demonstration, as I have remarked in the section entitled *The Wonders of the Heart* of my *Revival of the Religious Sciences.*

Certainly reached by demonstration is *knowledge* ('ilm); actual acquaintance with that "state" is *immediate experience* (dhawq); the acceptance of it as probable from hearsay and trial (or observation) is *faith* (īmān). These are three degrees. "God will raise those of you who have faith and those who have been given knowledge in degrees (of honour)."[8]

Behind the mystics, however, there is a crowd of ignorant people. They deny this fundamentally, they are astonished at this line of thought, they listen and mock. "Amazing," they say, "What nonsense they talk!" About such people God most high has said: "Some of them listen to you, until, upon going out from you, they say to those to whom knowledge has been given, 'What did he say just now?' These are the people on whose hearts God sets a seal and they follow their passions."[9] He makes them deaf, and blinds their sight.

Among the things that necessarily became clear to me from my practice of the mystic "way" was the true nature and special characteristics of prophetic revelation. The basis of that must undoubtedly be indicated in view of the urgent need for it.

YEHUDA HALEVY (1085?–1141?)
Hebrew

Although classified in this section with Arabic writers and poets, Yehuda Halevy was one of the most brilliant of the Hebrew poets who modeled themselves after Arabic literature in medieval Spain, Provençe, and the Near East. He was born in Muslim Toledo on the borders of Christian Spain, and then traveled to various centers of Jewish scholarship. In Andalusia, he formed a lasting friendship with the famous poet and philosopher Moses Ibn Ezra. He later settled in Toledo, where he practiced medicine; after concerted attacks there on Jews by Christians, he returned to the Muslim area of Cordoba.

Halevy was also known as a philosopher. In his *Book of the Kuzari* he

---

8. Qur'an 58, 12.
9. Qur'an 47, 18.

developed a philosophy of history, as a dialogue between intuitive religious truths and speculative logical or rational truths, giving preference to the former. He left on a pilgrimage to Palestine around 1140, staying in Alexandria on the way. The place of his death has never been determined.

[Soaring Wind]*

Soaring wind, when the day's
heat begins to wane, bear

greetings to my companion:
All I ask is remembrance

of that parting day,
love's first pact

under the leaves
of an apple tree.

[Life's Source]*

Toward life's true source I run,
fleeing senseless barren days, to
see my King's visage my sole intent:
only before Him do I tremble, I
exalt no other—if I but beheld
Him in a dream I would sleep an
endless sleep and never rise—
having gazed at His face within
my heart's core, my eyes would
no longer seek vision without.

USĀMA IBN MUNQIDH (1095–1188)
Arabic

The Crusades began in 1095, the same year that Usāma ibn Munqidh was born in Syria. Usāma was a nobleman and a warrior, and his family's castle can still be visited in the mountains of western Syria. In his classic work, *The Book of Reflections* (*Kitāb al-Iᶜtibār*), East meets West, but also, autobiography meets anecdote. Usāma is an interesting narrator: he describes life with his family and

*Translated by Ammiel Alcalay.

life with the Crusaders. These delightful and candid evaluations are unparalleled in medieval Arabic literature. At the same time, they show what Arabs of the period felt about the Western invaders.

from The Book of Reflections

USAMAH: A Muslim View of the Crusaders

Mysterious are the works of the Creator, the author of all things! When one comes to recount cases regarding the Franks, he cannot but glorify Allah (exalted is he!) and sanctify him, for he sees them as animals possessing the virtues of courage and fighting, but nothing else, just as animals have only the virtues of strength and carrying loads. I shall now give some instances of their doings and their curious mentality.

In the army of King Fulk, son of Fulk, was a Frankish reverend knight who had just arrived from their land in order to make the holy pilgrimage and then return home. He was of my intimate fellowship and kept such constant company with me that he began to call me "my brother." Between us were mutual bonds of amity and friendship. When he resolved to return by sea to his homeland, he said to me:

"My brother, I am leaving for my country and I want thee to send with me thy son (my son, who was then fourteen years old, was at that time in my company) to our country, where he can see the knights and learn wisdom and chivalry. When he returns, he will be like a wise man."

Thus there fell upon my ears words which would never come out of the head of a sensible man; for even if my son were to be taken captive, his captivity could not bring him a worse misfortune than carrying him into the lands of the Franks. However, I said to the man:

"By thy life, this has been exactly my idea. But the only thing that prevented me from carrying it out was the fact that his grandmother, my mother, is so fond of him that she did not this time let him come out with me until she exacted an oath from me to the effect that I would return him to her."

Thereupon he asked, "Is thy mother still alive?" "Yes," I replied. "Well," said he, "disobey her not."

A case illustrating their curious medicine is the following:

The lord of al-Munaytirah[1] wrote to my uncle asking him to dispatch a physician to treat certain sick persons among his people. My uncle sent him a Christian physician named Thābit. Thābit was absent but ten days when he returned. So we said to him, "How quickly hast thou healed thy patients!" He said:

Translated by Philip K. Hitt.

---

1. In Lebanon near Afqah, the source of Nahr-Ibrāhīm, i.e., ancient Adonis.

They brought before me a knight in whose leg an abscess had grown, and a woman afflicted with imbecility.[2] To the knight I applied a small poultice until the abscess opened and became well; and the woman I put on diet and made her humor wet. Then a Frankish physician came to them and said, "This man knows nothing about treating them." He then said to the knight, "Which wouldst thou prefer, living with one leg or dying with two?" The latter replied, "Living with one leg." The physician said, "Bring me a strong knight and a sharp ax." A knight came with the ax. And I was standing by. Then the physician laid the leg of the patient on a block of wood and bade the knight strike his leg with the ax and chop it off at one blow. Accordingly he struck it—while I was looking on—one blow, but the leg was not severed. He dealt another blow, upon which the marrow of the leg flowed out and the patient died on the spot. He then examined the woman and said, "This is a woman in whose head there is a devil which has possessed her. Shave off her hair." Accordingly they shaved it off and the woman began once more to eat their ordinary diet—garlic and mustard. Her imbecility took a turn for the worse. The physician then said, "The devil has penetrated through her head." He therefore took a razor, made a deep cruciform incision on it, peeled off the skin at the middle of the incision until the bone of the skull was exposed, and rubbed it with salt. The woman also expired instantly. Thereupon I asked them whether my services were needed any longer, and when they replied in the negative I returned home, having learned of their medicine what I knew not before.

I have, however, witnessed a case of their medicine which was quite different from that.

The king of the Franks[3] had for treasurer a knight named Bernard, who (may Allah's curse be upon him!) was one of the most accursed and wicked among the Franks. A horse kicked him in the leg, which was subsequently infected and which opened in fourteen different places. Every time one of these cuts would close in one place, another would open in another place. All this happened while I was praying for his perdition. Then came to him a Frankish physician and removed from the leg all the ointments which were on it and began to wash it with very strong vinegar. By this treatment all the cuts were healed and the man became well again. He was up again like a devil.

Another case illustrating their curious medicine is the following:

In Shayzar we had an artisan named abu-al-Fath, who had a boy whose neck was afflicted with scrofula. Every time a part of it would close, another part would open. This man happened to go to Antioch on business of his, accompanied by his son. A Frank noticed the boy and asked his father about him. Abu-al-Fath replied, "This is my son." The Frank said to him, "Wilt thou swear by thy religion that if I prescribe to thee a medicine which will cure thy boy, thou wilt charge nobody fees for prescribing it thyself? In that case, I shall prescribe to thee a medicine which will cure the boy." The man took the oath and the Frank said:

---

2. Arabic *nashāf*, "dryness," is not used as a name of a disease. I take the word therefore to be Persian *nishāf*—"imbecility."

3. Fulk of Anjou, king of Jerusalem (1131–1142).

"Take uncrushed leaves of glasswort, burn them, then soak the ashes in olive oil and sharp vinegar. Treat the scrofula[4] with them until the spot on which it is growing is eaten up. Then take burnt lead, soak it in ghee butter[5] and treat him with it. That will cure him."

The father treated the boy accordingly, and the boy was cured. The sores closed, and the boy returned to his normal condition of health.

I have myself treated with this medicine many who were afflicted with such disease, and the treatment was successful in removing the cause of the complaint.

Everyone who is a fresh emigrant from the Frankish lands is ruder in character than those who have become acclimatized and have held long association with the Moslems. Here is an illustration of their rude character.

Whenever I visited Jerusalem I always entered the Aqsa Mosque,[6] beside which stood a small mosque which the Franks had converted into a church. When I used to enter the Aqsa Mosque, which was occupied by the Templars[7] who were my friends, the Templars would evacuate the little adjoining mosque so that I might pray in it. One day[8] I entered this mosque, repeated the first formula, "Allah is great," and stood up in the act of praying, upon which one of the Franks rushed on me, got hold of me and turned my face eastward, saying, "This is the way thou shouldst pray!" A group of Templars hastened to him, seized him and repelled him from me. I resumed my prayer. The same man, while the others were otherwise busy, rushed once more on me and turned my face eastward, saying, "This is the way thou shouldst pray!" The Templars again came in to him and expelled him. They apologized to me, saying, "This is a stranger who has only recently arrived from the land of the Franks and he has never before seen anyone praying except eastward." Thereupon I said to myself, "I have had enough prayer." So I went out, and have ever been surprised at the conduct of this devil of a man, at the change in the color of his face, his trembling, and his sentiment at the sight of one praying towards the *qiblah*.[9]

I saw one of the Franks come to al-Amīr Muᶜīn-al-Dīn (may Allah's mercy rest upon his soul!) when he was in the Dome of the Rock,[10] and say to him, "Dost thou want to see God as a child?" Muᶜīn-al-Dīn said, "Yes." The Frank walked ahead of us until he showed us the picture of Mary with Christ (may peace be upon him!) as an infant in her lap. He then said, "This is God as a child." But Allah is exalted far above what the infidels say about him!

The Franks are void of all zeal and jealousy. One of them may be walking along with his wife. He meets another man who takes the wife by the hand and steps aside to converse with her while the husband is standing on one side waiting

---

4. A skin disease.
5. Clarified butter.
6. A holy mosque in Jerusalem.
7. Knights of the Temple, a crusading order.
8. About 1140.

9. The direction of the Kaᶜbah in the holy city, Mecca.
10. *al-sakhrah*, the mosque, standing near al-Aqsa in Jerusalem.

for his wife to conclude the conversation. If she lingers too long for him, he leaves her alone with the conversant and goes away.

Here is an illustration which I myself witnessed:

When I used to visit Nāblus,[11] I always took lodging with a man named Muᶜizz, whose home was a lodging house for the Moslems. The house had windows which opened to the road, and there stood opposite to it on the other side of the road a house belonging to a Frank who sold wine for the merchants. He would take some wine in a bottle and go around announcing it by shouting, "So and so, the merchant, has just opened a cask full of this wine. He who wants to buy some of it will find it in such and such a place." The Frank's pay for the announcement made would be the wine in that bottle. One day this Frank went home and found a man with his wife in the same bed. He asked him, "What could have made thee enter into my wife's room?" The man replied, "I was tired, so I went in to rest." "But how," asked he, "didst thou get into my bed?" The other replied, "I found a bed that was spread, so I slept in it." "But," said he, "my wife was sleeping together with thee!" The other replied, "Well, the bed is hers. How could I therefore have prevented her from using her own bed?" "By the truth of my religion," said the husband, "if thou shouldst do it again, thou and I would have a quarrel." Such was for the Frank the entire expression of his disapproval and the limit of his jealousy.

Another illustration:

We had with us a bath-keeper named Sālim, originally an inhabitant of al-Maᶜarrah,[12] who had charge of the bath of my father (may Allah's mercy rest upon his soul!). This man related the following story:

"I once opened a bath in al-Maᶜarrah in order to earn my living. To this bath there came a Frankish knight. The Franks disapprove of girding a cover around one's waist while in the bath. So this Frank stretched out his arm and pulled off my cover from my waist and threw it away. He looked and saw that I had recently shaved off my pubes. So he shouted, "Sālim!" As I drew near him he stretched his hand over my pubes and said, "Sālim, good! By the truth of my religion, do the same for me." Saying this, he lay on his back and I found that in that place the hair was like his beard. So I shaved it off. Then he passed his hand over the place and, finding it smooth, he said, "Sālim, by the truth of my religion, do the same to madame [al-dāma]" (al-dāma in their language means the lady), referring to his wife. He then said to a servant of his, "Tell madame to come here." Accordingly the servant went and brought her and made her enter the bath. She also lay on her back. The knight repeated, "Do what thou hast done to me." So I shaved all that hair while her husband was sitting looking at me. At last he thanked me and handed me the pay for my service."

Consider now this great contradiction! They have neither jealousy nor zeal, but they have great courage, although courage is nothing but the product of zeal and of ambition to be above ill repute.

Here is a story analogous to the one related above:

---

11. Neapolis, ancient Shechem.

12. Maᶜarrat-al-Nuᶜmān, between Hamāh and Aleppo.

I entered the public bath in Ṣūr [Tyre] and took my place in a secluded part. One of my servants thereupon said to me, "There is with us in the bath a woman." When I went out, I sat on one of the stone benches and behold! the woman who was in the bath had come out all dressed and was standing with her father just opposite me. But I could not be sure that she was a woman. So I said to one of my companions, "By Allah, see if this is a woman," by which I meant that he should ask about her. But he went, as I was looking at him, lifted the end of her robe and looked carefully at her. Thereupon her father turned toward me and said, "This is my daughter. Her mother is dead and she has nobody to wash her hair. So I took her in with me to the bath and washed her head." I replied, "Thou hast well done! This is something for which thou shalt be rewarded [by Allah]!"

A curious case relating to their medicine is the following, which was related to me by William of Bures, the lord of Ṭabarayyah [Tiberias], who was one of the principal chiefs among the Franks. It happened that William had accompanied al-Amīr Muʿīn-al-Dīn (may Allah's mercy rest upon his soul!) from ʿAkka to Ṭabarayyah when I was in his company too. On the way William related to us the following story in these words:

"We had in our country a highly esteemed knight who was taken ill and was on the point of death. We thereupon came to one of our great priests and said to him, 'Come with us and examine so and so, the knight.' 'I will,' he replied, and walked along with us, while were were assured in ourselves that if he would only lay his hand on him the patient would recover. When the priest saw the patient, he said, 'Bring me some wax.' We fetched him a little wax, which he softened and shaped like the knuckles of fingers, and he stuck one in each nostril. The knight died on the spot. We said to him, 'He is dead.' 'Yes,' he replied, 'he was suffering great pain, so I closed up his nose that he might die and get relief.'

Let this go and let us resume the discussion regarding Harim.[13]

We shall now leave the discussion of their treatment of the orifices of the body to something else.

I found myself in Ṭabarayyah at the time the Franks were celebrating one of their feasts. The cavaliers went out to exercise with lances. With them went out two decrepit, aged women whom they stationed at one end of the race course. At the other end of the field they left a pig which they had scalded and laid on a rock. They then made the two aged women run a race while each one of them was accompanied by a detachment of horsemen urging her on. At every step they took, the women would fall down and rise again, while the spectators would laugh. Finally one of them got ahead of the other and won that pig for a prize.

I attended one day a duel in Nāblus between two Franks. The reason for this was that certain Moslem thieves took by surprise one of the villages of Nāblus. One of the peasants of that village was charged with having acted as guide for the

---

13. A hemistich quoted from the pre-Islamic
poet Zuhayr ibn-abi-Sulma al-Muzani.

thieves when they fell upon the village. So he fled away. The king[14] sent and arrested his children. The peasant thereupon came back to the king and said, "Let justice be done in my case. I challenge to a duel the man who claimed that I guided the thieves to the village." The king then said to the tenant who held the village in fief, "Bring forth someone to fight the duel with him." The tenant went to his village, where a blacksmith lived, took hold of him and ordered him to fight the duel. The tenant became thus sure of the safety of his own peasants, none of whom would be killed and his estate ruined.

I saw this blacksmith. He was a physically strong young man, but his heart failed him. He would walk a few steps and then sit down and ask for a drink. The one who had made the challenge was an old man, but he was strong in spirit and he would rub the nail of his thumb against that of the forefinger in defiance, as if he was not worrying over the duel. Then came the viscount, the seignior of the town, and gave each one of the two contestants a cudgel and a shield and arranged the people in a circle around them.

The two met. The old man would press the blacksmith backward until he would get him as far as the circle, then he would come back to the middle of the arena. They went on exchanging blows until they looked like pillars smeared with blood. The contest was prolonged and the viscount began to urge them to hurry, saying, "Hurry on." The fact that the smith was given to the use of the hammer proved now of great advantage to him. The old man was worn out and the smith gave him a blow which made him fall. His cudgel fell under his back. The smith knelt down over him and tried to stick his fingers into the eyes of his adversary, but could not do it because of the great quantity of blood flowing out. Then he rose up and hit his head with the cudgel until he killed him. They then fastened a rope around the neck of the dead person, dragged him away and hanged him. The lord who brought the smith now came, gave the smith his own mantle, made him mount the horse behind him, and rode off with him. This case illustrates the kind of jurisprudence and legal decisions the Franks have—may Allah's curse be upon them!

I once went in the company of al-Amīr Muⁱīn-al-Dīn (may Allah's mercy rest upon his soul!) to Jerusalem. We stopped at Nāblus. There a blind man, a Moslem, who was still young and was well dressed, presented himself before al-Amīr carrying fruits for him and asked permission to be admitted into his service in Damascus. The Amīr consented. I inquired about this man and was informed that his mother had been married to a Frank whom she had killed. Her son used to practice ruses against the Frankish pilgrims and co-operate with his mother in assassinating them. They finally brought charges against him and tried his case according to the Frankish way of procedure.

They installed a huge cask and filled it with water. Across it they set a board of wood. They then bound the arms of the man charged with the act, tied a rope around his shoulders, and dropped him into the cask, their idea being that in case he was innocent, he would sink in the water and they would then lift him up with

---

14. Fulk of Anjou, king of Jerusalem again.

the rope so that he might not die in the water; and in case he was guilty, he would not sink in the water. This man did his best to sink when they dropped him into the water, but he could not do it. So he had to submit to their sentence against him—may Allah's curse be upon them! They pierced his eyeballs with red-hot awls.

Later this same man arrived in Damascus. Al-Amīr Muʿīn-al-Dīn (may Allah's mercy rest upon his soul!) assigned him a stipend large enough to meet all his needs and said to a slave of his, "Conduct him to Burhān-al-Dīn al-Balkhi (may Allah's mercy rest upon his soul!) and ask him on my behalf to order somebody to teach this man the Koran and something of Moslem jurisprudence." Hearing that, the blind man remarked, "May triumph and victory be thine! But this was never my thought." "What didst thou think I was going to do for thee?" asked Muʿīn-al-Dīn. The blind man replied, "I thought thou wouldst give me a horse, a mule and a suit of armor and make me a knight." Muʿīn-al-Dīn then said, "I never thought that a blind man could become a knight."

Among the Franks are those who have become acclimatized and have associated long with the Moslems. These are much better than the recent comers from the Frankish lands. But they constitute the exception and cannot be treated as a rule.

Here is an illustration. I dispatched one of my men to Antioch on business. There was in Antioch at that time al-Ra'īs Theodoros Sophianos, to whom I was bound by mutual ties of amity. His influence in Antioch was supreme. One day he said to my man, "I am invited by a friend of mine who is a Frank. Thou shouldst come with me so that thou mayest see their fashions." My man related the story in the following words:

"I went along with him and we came to the home of a knight who belonged to the old category of knights who came with the early expeditions of the Franks. He had been by that time stricken off the register and exempted from service, and possessed in Antioch an estate on the income of which he lived. The knight presented an excellent table, with food extraordinarily clean and delicious. Seeing me abstaining from food, he said, "Eat, be of good cheer! I never eat Frankish dishes, but I have Egyptian women cooks and never eat except their cooking. Besides, pork never enters my home." I ate, but guardedly, and after that we departed.

As I was passing in the market place, a Frankish woman all of a sudden hung to my clothes and began to mutter words in their language, and I could not understand what she was saying. This made me immediately the center of a big crowd of Franks. I was convinced that death was at hand. But all of a sudden that same knight approached. On seeing me, he came and said to that woman, "What is the matter between thee and this Moslem?" She replied, "This is he who has killed my brother Hurso." This Hurso was a knight in Afāmiyah who was killed by someone of the army of Hamāh. The Christian knight shouted at her, saying, "This is a bourgeois (i.e., a merchant) who neither fights nor attends a fight." He also yelled at the people who had assembled, and they all dispersed. Then he took me by the hand and went away. Thus the effect of that meal was my deliverance from certain death."

FARĪD AL-DĪN ᶜATTĀR (1142?–1230?)
Persian

A poet and mystic, Farīd al-Dīn ᶜAttār lived in Nishapur, an important center of mysticism, where he practiced as a pharmacist (hence "attar"). He produced mystical literature in poetry and prose, as well as an influential collection of biographies of mystic saints. His epic poem *The Conference of the Birds* [*Mantiq al-Tayr*], given here in a prose translation, is his most enduringly popular work. This poetic adventure tells of the search on the part of all the birds for the mythical bird known as the Sīmurgh, whom they regard as their king. Of the thousands of birds that gather, only thirty birds (*sī murgh* in Persian) finally embark on the journey. A mystical allegory of the pilgrim soul's search for union with God, the poem ends when the thirty, *sī murgh,* understand that they themselves are the being they so ardently seek.

from *The Conference of the Birds*

The Bird Parliament

All of the birds of the world, known and unknown, were assembled together. They said: "No country in the world is without a king. How comes it, then, that the kingdom of the birds is without a ruler? This state of things cannot last. We must make effort together and search for one; for no country can have a good administration and a good organization without a king."

So they began to consider how to set out on their quest. The Hoopoe,[1] excited and full of hope, came forward and placed herself in the middle of the assembled birds. On her breast was the ornament which symbolized that she had entered the way of spiritual knowledge; the crest on her head was as the crown of truth, and she had knowledge of both good and evil.

"Dear Birds," she began, "I am one who is engaged in divine warfare, and I am a messenger of the world invisible. I have knowledge of God and of the secrets of creation. When one carries on his beak, as I do, the name of God, Bismillah, it follows that one must have knowledge of many hidden things. Yet my days pass restlessly and I am concerned with no person, for I am wholly occupied by love for the King. I can find water by instinct, and I know many other secrets. I talk with Solomon and am the foremost of his followers. It is astonishing that he neither asked nor sought for those who were absent from his kingdom, yet when I was away from him for a day he sent his messengers everywhere, and, since he could not be without me for a moment, my worth is established forever. I carried his letters, and I was his confidential companion. The bird who is sought after by

Translated by S. C. Nott.

---

1. A bird.

the prophet Solomon merits a crown for his head. The bird who is well spoken of by God, how can he trail his feathers in the dust? For years I have travelled by sea and land, over mountains and valleys. I covered an immense space in the time of the deluge; I accompanied Solomon on his journeys, and I have measured the bounds of the world.

"I know well my King, but alone I cannot set out to find him. Abandon your timidity, your self-conceit and your unbelief, for he who makes light of his own life is delivered from himself; he is delivered from good and evil in the way of his beloved. Be generous with your life. Set your feet upon the earth and step out joyfully for the court of the King. We have a true King, he lives behind the mountains called Kāf. His name is Simurgh and he is the King of birds. He is close to us, but we are far from him. The place where he dwells is inaccessible, and no tongue is able to utter his name. Before him hang a hundred thousand veils of light and darkness, and in the two worlds no one has power to dispute his kingdom. He is the sovereign lord and is bathed in the perfection of his majesty. He does not manifest himself completely even in the place of his dwelling, and to this no knowledge or intelligence can attain. The way is unknown, and no one has the steadfastness to seek it, though thousands of creatures spend their lives in longing. Even the purest soul cannot describe him, neither can the reason comprehend: these two eyes are blind. The wise cannot discover his perfection nor can the man of understanding perceive his beauty. All creatures have wished to attain to this perfection and beauty by imagination. But how can you tread that path with thought? How measure the moon from the fish? So thousands of heads go here and there, like the ball in polo, and only lamentations and sighs of longing are heard. Many lands and seas are on the way. Do not imagine that the journey is short; and one must have the heart of a lion to follow this unusual road, for it is very long and the sea is deep. One plods along in a state of amazement, sometimes smiling, sometimes weeping. As for me, I shall be happy to discover even a trace of him. That would indeed be something, but to live without him would be a reproach. A man must not keep his soul from the beloved, but must be in a fitting state to lead his soul to the court of the King. Wash your hands of this life if you would be called a man of action. For your beloved, renounce this dear life of yours, as worthy men. If you submit with grace, the beloved will give his life for you.

"An astonishing thing! The first manifestation of the Simurgh took place in China in the middle of the night. One of his feathers fell on China and his reputation filled the world. Everyone made a picture of this feather, and from it formed his own system of ideas, and so fell into a turmoil. This feather is still in the picture-gallery of that country; hence the saying, 'Seek knowledge, even in China!'

"But for his manifestation there would not have been so much noise in the world concerning this mysterious Being. This sign of his existence is a token of his glory. All souls carry an impression of the image of his feather. Since the description of it has neither head nor tail, beginning nor end, it is not necessary to say more about it. Now, any of you who are for this road, prepare yourselves, and put your feet on the Way."

When the Hoopoe had finished, the birds began excitedly to discuss the glory of this King, and seized with longing to have him for their own sovereign, they were all impatient to be off. They resolved to go together; each became a friend to the other and an enemy to himself. But when they began to realize how long and painful their journey was to be, they hesitated, and in spite of their apparent good will began to excuse themselves, each according to his type.

One bird said to the Hoopoe: "O you who know the road of which you have told us and on which you wish us to accompany you, to me the way is dark, and in the gloom it appears to be very difficult, and many parasangs in length."

The Hoopoe replied: "We have seven valleys to cross, and only after we have crossed them shall we discover the Simurgh. No one has ever come back into the world who has made this journey, and it is impossible to say how many parasangs there are in front of us. Be patient, O fearful one, since all those who went by this road were in your state.

"The first valley is the Valley of the Quest, the second the Valley of Love, the third is the Valley of Understanding, the fourth is the Valley of Independence and Detachment, the fifth of Pure Unity, the sixth is the Valley of Astonishment, and the seventh is the Valley of Poverty and Nothingness, beyond which one can go no farther."

When the birds had listened to this discourse of the Hoopoe their heads dropped down, and sorrow pierced their hearts. Now they understood how difficult it would be for a handful of dust like themselves to bend such a bow. So great was their agitation that numbers of them died then and there. But others, in spite of their distress, decided to set out on the long road. For years they travelled over mountains and valleys, and a great part of their life flowed past on this journey. But how is it possible to relate all that happened to them? It would be necessary to go with them and see their difficulties for oneself, and to follow the wanderings of this long road. Only then could one realize what the birds suffered.

In the end, only a small number of all this great company arrived at that sublime place to which the Hoopoe had led them. Of the thousands of birds, almost all had disappeared. Many had been lost in the ocean; others had perished on the summits of the high mountains, tortured by thirst; others had had their wings burnt and their hearts dried up by the fire of the sun; others were devoured by tigers and panthers; others died of fatigue in the deserts and in the wilderness, their lips parched and their bodies overcome by the heat. Some went mad and killed each other for a grain of barley; others, enfeebled by suffering and weariness, dropped on the road, unable to go farther; others, bewildered by the things they saw, stopped where they were, stupefied; and many who had started out from curiosity or pleasure, perished without an idea of what they had set out to find.

So then out of all those thousands of birds, only thirty reached the end of the journey. And even these were bewildered, weary and dejected, with neither feathers nor wings. But now they were at the door of this Majesty that cannot be described, whose essence is incomprehensible—that Being who is beyond human reason and knowledge. Then flashed the lightning of fulfilment, and a hundred worlds were consumed in a moment. They saw thousands of suns, each more resplendent than the other, thousands of moons and stars all equally beautiful, and seeing all this they were amazed and agitated like a dancing atom of dust, and they cried out: "O Thou who art more radiant than the sun! Thou who hast reduced the sun to an atom, how can we appear before Thee? Ah, why have we so uselessly endured all this suffering on the Way? Having renounced ourselves and all things, we now cannot obtain that for which we have striven. Here it little matters whether we exist or not."

Then the birds, who were so disheartened that they resembled a cock half-killed, sank into despair. A long time passed. When, at a propitious moment, the door suddenly opened, there stepped out a noble Chamberlain, one of the courtiers of the Supreme Majesty. He looked them over and saw that out of thousands, only these thirty birds were left.

He said: "Now then, O Birds, where have you come from, and what are you doing here? What is your name? O you who are destitute of everything, where is your home? What do they call you in the world? What can be done with a feeble handful of dust like you?"

"We have come," they said, "to acknowledge the Simurgh as our King. Through love and desire for him we have lost our reason and our peace of mind. Very long ago, when we started on this journey, we were thousands, and now only thirty of us have arrived at this sublime court. We cannot believe that the King will scorn us after all the sufferings we have gone through. Ah, no! He cannot but look on us with the eye of benevolence!"

The Chamberlain replied: "O you whose minds and hearts are troubled, whether you exist or do not exist in the universe, the King has his being always and eternally. Thousands of worlds of creatures are no more than an ant at his gate. You bring nothing but moans and lamentations. Return then to whence you came, O vile handful of earth!"

At this the birds were petrified with astonishment. Nevertheless, when they came to themselves a little, they said: "Will this great King reject us so ignominiously? And if he really has this attitude to us, may he not change it to one of honour? Remember Majnūn, who said: 'If all the people who dwell on earth wished to sing my praises, I would not accept them; I would rather have the insults of Laila.[2] One of her insults is more to me than a hundred compliments from another woman!' "

"The lightning of his glory manifests itself," said the Chamberlain, "and it lifts up the reason of all souls. What benefit is there if the soul be consumed by a hundred sorrows? What benefit is there at this moment in either greatness or littleness?"

The birds, on fire with love, said: "How can the moth save itself from the flame when it wishes to be one with the flame? The friend we seek will content us by allowing us to be united to him. If now we are refused, what is there left for us

---

2. The classic Arabic star-crossed lovers.

to do? We are like the moth who wished for union with the flame of the candle. They begged him not to sacrifice himself so foolishly and for such an impossible aim, but he thanked them for their advice and told them that since his heart was given to the flame forever, nothing else mattered."

Then the Chamberlain, having tested them, opened the door; and as he drew aside a hundred curtains, one after the other, a new world beyond the veil was revealed. Now was the light of lights manifested, and all of them sat down on the masnad, the seat of the Majesty and Glory. They were given a writing which they were told to read through; and reading this, and pondering, they were able to understand their state. When they were completely at peace and detached from all things, they became aware that the Simurgh was there with them, and a new life began for them in the Simurgh. All that they had done previously was washed away. The sun of Majesty sent forth his rays, and in the reflection of each other's faces these thirty birds (si-murgh) of the outer world contemplated the face of the Simurgh of the inner world. This so astonished them that they did not know if they were still themselves or if they had become the Simurgh. At last, in a state of contemplation, they realized that they were the Simurgh and that the Simurgh was the thirty birds. When they gazed at the Simurgh they saw that it was truly the Simurgh who was there, and when they turned their eyes toward themselves they saw that they themselves were the Simurgh. And perceiving both at once, themselves and Him, they realized that they and the Simurgh were one and the same being. No one in the world has ever heard of anything to equal it.

Then they gave themselves up to meditation, and after a little they asked the Simurgh, without the use of tongues, to reveal to them the secret of the mystery of the unity and plurality of beings. The Simurgh, also without speaking, made this reply: "The sun of my majesty is a mirror. He who sees himself therein sees his soul and his body, and sees them completely. Since you have come as thirty birds, si-murgh, you will see thirty birds in this mirror. If forty or fifty were to come, it would be the same. Although you are now completely changed, you see yourselves as you were before.

"Can the sight of an ant reach to the far-off Pleiades? And can this insect lift an anvil? Have you ever seen a gnat seize an elephant in its teeth? All that you have known, all that you have seen, all that you have said or heard—all this is no longer that. When you crossed the valleys of the Spiritual Way and when you performed good tasks, you did all this by my action; and you were able to see the valleys of my essence and my perfections. You, who are only thirty birds, did well to be astonished, impatient and wondering. But I am more than thirty birds. I am the very essence of the true Simurgh. Annihilate then yourselves gloriously and joyfully in me, and in me you shall find yourselves."

Thereupon the birds at last lost themselves forever in the Simurgh—the shadow was lost in the sun, and that is all.

All that you have heard or seen or known is not even the beginning of what you must know, and since the ruined habitation of this world is not your place you must renounce it. Seek the trunk of the tree, and do not worry about whether the branches do or do not exist.

When a hundred thousand generations had passed, the mortal birds surrendered themselves spontaneously to total annihilation. No man, neither young nor old, can speak fittingly of death or immortality. Even as these things are far from us, so the description of them is beyond all explanation or definition. If my readers wish for an allegorical explanation of the immortality that follows annihilation, it will be necessary for me to write another book. So long as you are identified with the things of the world you will not set out on the Path, but when the world no longer binds you, you enter as in a dream, and knowing the end, you see the benefit. A germ is nourished among a hundred cares and loves so that it may become an intelligent and acting being. It is instructed and given the necessary knowledge. Then death comes and everything is effaced, its dignity is thrown down. This that was a being has become the dust of the street. It has several times been annihilated; but in the meanwhile it has been able to learn a hundred secrets of which previously it had not been aware, and in the end it receives immortality, and is given honour in place of dishonour. Do you know what you possess? Enter into yourself and reflect on this. So long as you do not realize your nothingness and so long as you do not renounce your self-pride, your vanity and your self-love, you will never reach the heights of immortality. On the Way you are cast down in dishonour and raised in honour.

And now my story is finished; I have nothing more to say.

IBN AL-ʿARABĪ (d. 1240)
Arabic

Known as al-Shaykh al-Akbar (The Greatest Shaykh), Ibn al-ʿArabī is possibly one of the greatest mystics of Islam. He was born in Andalusia, and lived in Spain and North Africa. An inveterate traveler, he journeyed East to perform the pilgrimage to Mecca and expand his intellectual and geographical horizons to include the Eastern lands of the Islamic world. Ibn al-ʿArabī was the most prolific of the mystic writers, with *The Meccan Revelations [al-Futūhāt al-Makkiyya]* being his most famous work. His influence extended beyond his own century and continues today. The poem here, "Gentle Now, Doves of the Thornberry and Moringa Thicket" (*alā yā hammāmāti l-arākati wa l-bāni*) typically mingles the thought and vocabulary of sacred and profane love.

Gentle Now, Doves of the Thornberry and Moringa Thicket

Gentle now,
doves of the thornberry and moringa thicket,
don't add to my heart-ache
your sighs.

Translated by Michael A. Sells.

Gentle now,
or your sad cooing
will reveal the love I hide
the sorrow I hide away.

I echo back, in the evening,
in the morning, echo,
the longing of a love-sick lover,
the moaning of the lost.

In a grove of tamarisks
spirits wrestled,
bending the limbs down over me,
passing me away.

They brought yearning,
breaking of the heart,
and other new twists of pain,
putting me through it.

Who is there for me in Jámᶜ,
and the Stoning-Place at Mína,
who for me at Tamarisk Grove,
or at the way-station of Naᶜmān?

Hour by hour
they circle my heart
in rapture, in love-ache,
and touch my pillars with a kiss.

As the best of creation
circled the Kaᶜba,
which reason with its proofs
called unworthy,

And kissed the stones there—
and he was the Natiq!
And what is the house of stone
compared to a man or a woman?

They swore, and how often!
they'd never change—piling up vows.
She who dyes herself red with henna
is faithless.

A white-blazed gazelle
is an amazing sight,
red-dye signalling,
eyelids hinting,

Pasture between breastbones   45
and innards.
Marvel,
a garden among the flames!

My heart can take on
any form: 50
a meadow for gazelles,
a cloister for monks,

For the idols, sacred ground,
Ka^cba for the circling pilgrim,
the tables of the Torah,   55
the scrolls of the Qur^án.

I profess the religion of love;
wherever its caravan turns long the way,
that is the belief,
the faith I keep.   60

Like Bishr,
Hind and her sister,
love-mad Qays and his lost Láyla,
Máyya and her lover Ghaylán.

JALĀL AL-DĪN RŪMĪ (1207?–1273)
Persian

A theologian and a mystic, Jalāl al-Dīn Rūmī was born in Balkh. As a child, he fled with his family from his native city and after years of traveling through the central Islamic lands, the group finally made Konya, the Seljug capital, their home. There, Rūmī's infatuation with another mystic, Shams al-Dīn, known as Shams-i Tabrīzī (*shams* means sun), altered his life: the poem here speaks of their reunion in the language of mystical love. Generally considered the most brilliant of the Persian mystic poets, Rūmī founded the Mawlawi order, one of the fraternal mystical orders that began to form during the thirteenth century.

[Blessed Moment]

Blessed moment. Here we sit in this palace of love, you and I.
We have two shapes, two bodies, but a single soul, you and I.

Translated by Talat Sait Halman.

The colors of the gardens and the songs of the birds
Among the flower-beds will make us immortal, you and I.

The stars of heaven will come out to gaze at us—   5
We shall show the stars the moon herself, you and I.

United in ecstasy, we shall no longer be you or I.
Rescued from foolish babble, we shall rejoice, you and I.

All the bright-plumed birds of paradise will plunge into grief
When they hear us laughing merrily, you and I.   10

SAᶜDÎ (1200?–1292)
Persian

Born in Shiraz, Saᶜdî studied in Baghdad, made more than one pilgrimage to
Mecca, and travelled widely. He is best known for *The Rose Garden* [*Gulistan*], a
marvelous example of Persian *adab* literature. Like its Arabic cousin, the Persian
adab runs the gamut from prose to poetry. *The Rose Garden* covers topics ranging
from rulers to mystics to erotic exploits. (On the cover of an English translation,
for example, it is billed as "the Persian counterpart to the Kama Sutra.") This is
certainly quite a claim, but it does testify to the appeal of the work, which was one
of the first oriental texts translated into a European language, and this as early as
the seventeenth century. As a compendium of worldly wisdom, it is unsurpassed.

from *The Rose Garden* [*Gulistan*]

[*The Thorn Without the Rose*]

The beautiful wife of a man died but her mother, a decrepit old hag, remained in
the house on account of the dowry. The man saw no means of escaping from
contact with her until a company of friends paid him a visit of condolence and one
of them asked him how he bore the loss of his beloved. He replied: "It is not as
painful not to see my wife as to see the mother of my wife."

> The rose has been destroyed and the thorn remained.
> The treasure has been taken and the serpent left[1]
> It is better that one's eye be fixed on a spear-head
> Than that it should behold the face of an enemy.

Translated by Edward Rehatsek

---

1. Generally in Eastern legend, the serpent   treasure is removed; here, the opposite
   guarding a treasure is killed before the   takes place.

It is incumbent to sever connection with a thousand friends
Rather than to behold a single foe.

[A Beauty Brings a Beverage]

I remember having in the days of my youth passed through a street, intending to
see a moon-faced beauty. It was in Temuz[2] whose heat dried up the saliva in the
mouth and whose simum[3] boiled the marrow in my bones. My weak human
nature being unable to endure the scorching sun, I took refuge in the shadow of
a wall, wishing someone might relieve me from the summer heat and quench my
fire with some water; and lo, all of a sudden, from the darkness of the porch of a
house a light shone forth, namely a beauty, the grace of which the tongue of
eloquence is unable to describe. She came out like the rising dawn after an obscure
night or the water of immortality gushing from a dark cavern, carrying in her hand
a bowl of snow-water, into which sugar had been poured and essence of roses
mixed. I knew not whether she had perfumed it with rose-water or whether a few
drops from her rosy face had fallen into it. In short, I took the beverage from her
beautiful hands, drank it and began to live again.

> The thirst of my heart cannot be quenched
> By sipping limpid water even if I drink oceans of it.

Blessed is the man of happy destiny whose eye
Alights every morning on such a countenance.
One drunk of wine awakens at midnight,
One drunk of the cupbearer on the morn of resurrection.

[A Leave-Taking]

In the year when Muhammad Khovarezm Shah concluded peace with the king of
Khata to suit his own purpose, I entered the cathedral mosque of Kashgar and saw
an extremely handsome, graceful boy as described in the simile:

> Thy master has taught thee to coquet and to ravish hearts,
> Instructed thee to oppose, to dally, to blame and to be severe.
> A person of such figure, temper, stature and gait
> I have not seen; perhaps he learnt these tricks from a fairy.

He was holding in his hand the introduction of Zamak-sharni's Arabic syn-
tax and reciting: *Zaid struck Amru and was the injurer of Amru*. I said: "Boy!
Khovarezm and Khata have concluded peace, and the quarrel between Zaid and
Amru still subsists!" He smiled and asked for my birthplace. I replied: "The soil of
Shiraz." He continued: "What rememberest thou of the compositions of Sa'di?" I
recited:

---

2. The month of July.

3. The name of a fearfully hot wind blowing in
the African deserts.

"I am tired by a nahvi[4] who makes a furious attack
Upon me, like Zaid in his opposition to Amru.
When Zaid submits he does not raise his head
And how can elevation subsist when submission is the regent."[5]

He considered awhile and then said: "Most of his poetry current in this country is in the Persian language. If thou wilt recite some, it will be more easily understood." Then I said:

"When thy nature has enticed thee with syntax
It blotted out the form of intellect from our heart.
Alas, the hearts of lovers are captive in thy snare.
We are occupied with thee but thou with Amru and Zaid."

The next morning, when I was about to depart, some people told him that I was Sa'di, whereon he came running to me and politely expressed his regret that I had not revealed my identity before so that he might have girded his loins to serve me in token of the gratitude due to the presence of a great man.

In spite of thy presence no voice came to say: I am he.

He also said: "What would it be if thou wert to spend in this country some days in repose that we might derive advantage by serving thee?" I replied: "I cannot on account of the following adventure which occurred to me:

I beheld an illustrious man in a mountain region
Who had contentedly retired from the world into a cave.
Why, said I, comest thou not into the city
For once to relax the bonds of thy heart?
He replied: "Fairy-faced maidens are there.
When clay is plentiful, elephants will stumble."

This I said. Then we kissed each other's heads and faces and took leave of each other.

What profits it to kiss a friend's face
And at the same time to take leave of him?
Thou wouldst say that he who parts from friends is an apple.
One half of his face is red and the other yellow.

If I die not of grief on the day of separation
Reckon me not faithful in friendship.

[A Dervish Utters Wise Words]

A man in patched garments[6] accompanied us in a caravan to the Hejaz and one of the Arab amirs presented him with a hundred dinars to spend upon his family but

---

4. A student of syntax.
5. The play on words is on two grammatical terms, the nominative *refa'*, which also

means raising, elevating, and the genitive *jarr*, which also means pulling, submitting.
6. A dervish.

robbers of the Kufatcha tribe suddenly fell upon the caravan and robbed it clean of everything. The merchants began to wail and to cry, uttering vain shouts and lamentations.

> Whether thou implorest or complainest
> The robber will not return the gold again.

The dervish[7] alone had not lost his equanimity and showed no change. I asked: "Perhaps they have not taken thy money?" He replied: "Yes, they have but I was not so much accustomed to that money that separation therefrom could grieve my heart":

> The heart must not be tied to any thing or person
> Because to take off the heart is a difficult affair.

I replied: "What thou hast said resembles my case because, when I was young, my intimacy with a young man and my friendship for him were such that his beauty was the Qiblah[8] of my eye and the chief joy of my life union with him":

> Perhaps an angel in heaven but no mortal
> Can be on earth equal in beauty of form to him.
> I swear by the amity, after which companionship is illicit,
> No human sperm will ever become a man like him.

All of a sudden the foot of his life sank into the mire of non-existence. The smoke[9] of separation arose from his family. I kept him company on his grave for many days and one of my compositions on his loss is as follows:

> Would that on the day when the thorn of fate entered thy foot
> The hand of heaven had struck a sword on my head;
> So that this day my eye could not see the world without thee.
> Here I am on thy grave, would that it were over my head.

> He who could take neither rest nor sleep
> Before he had first scattered roses and narcissi.
> The turns of heaven have strewn the roses of his face.[10]
> Thorns and brambles are growing on his tomb.

After separation from him I resolved and firmly determined to fold up the carpet of pleasure during the rest of my life and to retire from mixing in society:

> Last night I strutted about like a peacock in the garden of union
> But today, through separation from my friend, I twist my head like a snake.
> The profit of the sea would be good if there were no fear of waves.
> The company of the rose would be sweet if there were no pain from thorns.

---

7. A Muslim mystic.
8. The direction toward Mecca in which all Moslems are bound to turn when they say their orisons; in Bombay they turn to the west and do not err much in doing so.

9. Grief.
10. More freely translated this would be "have blanched the roses of his cheeks."

[Looking from a Lover's Eye]

A king of the Arabs, having been informed of the relations subsisting between Laila and Mejnun, with an account of the latter's insanity, to the effect that he had in spite of his great accomplishments and eloquence, chosen to roam about in the desert and to let go the reins of self-control from his hands; he ordered him to be brought to his presence, and this having been done, he began to reprove him and to ask him what defect he had discovered in the nobility of the human soul that he adopted the habits of beasts and abandoned the society of mankind. Mejnun replied:

> *"Many friends have blamed me for loving her.*
> *Will they not see her one day and understand my excuse?"*

> Would that those who are reproving me
> Could see thy face, O ravisher of hearts,
> That instead of a lemon in thy presence
> They might heedlessly cut their hands.[11]

That the truth may bear witness to the assertion: *This is he for whose sake ye blamed me.*[12]

The king expressed a wish to see the beauty of Laila in order to ascertain the cause of so much distress. Accordingly he ordered her to be searched for. The encampments of various Arab families having been visited, she was found, conveyed to the king and led into the courtyard of the palace. The king looked at her outward form for some time and she appeared despicable in his sight because the meanest handmaids of his harem excelled her in beauty and attractions. Mejnun, who shrewdly understood the thoughts of the king, said: "It would have been necessary to look from the window of Mejnun's eye at the beauty of Laila when the mystery of her aspect would have been revealed to thee."

> *If the record of the glade which entered my ears*
> *Had been heard by the leaves of the glade they would have lamented with me.*
> *O company of friends, say to him who is unconcerned*
> *"Would that thou knewest what is in a pining heart!"*

> Who are healthy have no pain from wounds.
> I shall tell my grief to no one but a sympathizer.
> It is useless to speak of bees to one
> Who never in his life felt their sting.
> As long as thy state is not like mine
> My state will be but an idle tale to thee.

---

11. Zuleikha, the wife of Potiphar, knowing that her female friends would be extremely surprised at the wonderful beauty of Joseph, of whom they previously thought ill, used a stratagem to change their mind, as appears from the Qur'an, Ch. XII. v. 31, which gave rise to the allusion in the above verses; 'and when she had heard of their subtle behaviour, she sent unto them and prepared a banquet for them and she gave to each of them a knife; and then said to Joseph come forth to them. And when they saw him they praised him greatly and they cut their own hands and said: "O Allah, this is not a mortal, he is no other than an angel, deserving the highest respect." '

12. Qur'an, Ch. XII, part of v. 32.

[A Qazi Is Saved by His Wit]

It is related that the qazi[13] of Hamdan, having conceived affection towards a farrier-boy and the horseshoe of his heart being on fire, he sought for some time to meet him, roaming about and seeking for opportunities, according to the saying of chroniclers:

> That straight tall cypress my eyes beheld
> It robbed me of my heart and threw me down.
> Those wanton eyes have taken my heart with a lasso.
> If thou desirest to preserve thy heart shut thy eyes.

I was informed that the boy, who had heard something of the qazi's passion, happening to meet him in a thoroughfare, manifested immense wrath, assailed the qazi with disrespectful and insulting words, snatched up a stone and left no injury untried. The qazi said to an ullemma[14] of repute who happened to be of the same opinion with him:

> "Look at that sweetheart and his getting angry,
> And that bitter knot of his sweet eyebrow."

The Arab says: "*A slap from a lover is a raisin.*"[15]

> A blow from the hand on the mouth
> Is sweeter than eating bread with one's own hand.

In the same way the boy's impudence might be indicating kindness as padshahs utter hard words whilst they secretly wish for peace:

> Grapes yet unripe are sour.
> Wait two or three days, they will become sweet.

After saying these words he returned to his court of justice, where some respectable men connected with him kissed the ground of service and said: "With thy permission we shall, doing obeisance, speak some words to thee although they may be contrary to politeness because illustrious men have said:

> It is not permissible to argue on every topic.
> To find fault with great men is wrong.

"But as in consequence of favours conferred by thy lordship in former times upon thy servants it would be a kind of treachery to withhold the opinion they entertain, they inform thee that the proper way is not to yield to thy inclinations concerning this boy but to fold up the carpet of lascivious desires because thy dignity as qazi is high and must not be polluted by a base crime. The companion thou hast seen is this, and our words thou hast heard are these:

> One who has done many disreputable things
> Cares nothing for the reputation of anyone.

---

13. Or qadi, a Muslim judge.
14. In Arabic, ʿulamâ', plural of ʿâlim, meaning a class of learned men in Islam.

15. 'Sweet like a raisin.'

> Many a good name of fifty years
> Was trodden under foot by one bad name."[16]

The qazi approved of the unanimous advice of his friends and appreciated their good opinion as well as their steadfast fidelity, saying that the view taken by his beloved friends on the arrangement of his case was perfectly right and their arguments admitting of no contradiction. Nevertheless:

> *Although love ceases in consequence of reproval*
> *I heard that just men sometimes concoct falsehoods.*

> Blame me as much as thou listest
> Because blackness cannot be washed off from a negro.

> Nothing can blot out my remembrance of thee.
> I am a snake with broken head and cannot turn.

These words he said and sent some persons to make inquiries about him,[17] spending boundless money because it is said that whoever has gold in his hand possesses strength of arm and he who has no worldly goods has no friends in the whole world:

> Whoever has seen gold droops his head,
> Although he may be hard to bend like iron-backed scales.[18]

In short, one night he obtained privacy but during that night the police obtained information that the qazi is spending the whole of it with wine in his hand and a sweetheart on him bosom, enjoying himself, not sleeping, and singing:

> Has this cock perhaps not crowed at the proper time this night
> And have the lovers not had their fill of embrace, and kiss
> Whilst alas for only a moment the eye of confusion is asleep?
> Remain awake that life may not elapse in vain
> Till thou hearest the morning call from the Friday-mosque
> Or the noise of kettle-drums on Atabek's palace-gate.
> Lips against lips like the cock's eye[19]
> Are not to part at the crowing of a silly cock.

Whilst the qazi was in this state one of his dependants entered and said: "Arise and run as far as thy feet will carry thee because the envious have not only obtained a handle for vexation but have spoken the truth. We may, whilst the fire of confusion is yet burning low, perchance extinguish it with the water of stratagem but when it blazes up high it may destroy a world." The qazi, however, replied:

> "When the lion has his claws on the game
> What boots it if a jackal makes his appearance?

---

16. Or "by one imprudent act deserving a bad name."
17. That is to say, about the above-mentioned farrier boy.
18. Because when the scales are very heavily filled, even the iron rod from which they are suspended must bend.
19. The cock's eye designates a certain brilliant red flower to which beautiful lips are also sometimes compared.

> Keep thy face on the face of the friend and leave
> The foe to chew the back of his own hand in rage."

The same night information was also brought to the king that in his realm such a wickedness had been perpetrated and he was asked what he thought of it. He replied: "I know that he is one of the most learned men, and I account him to be the paragon of our age. As it is possible that enemies have devised a plot against him, I give no credit to this accusation unless I obtain ocular evidence because philosophers have said:

> He who grasps the sword in haste
> Will repenting carry the back of his hand to his teeth and bite it."

I heard that at dawn the king with some of his courtiers arrived at the pillow of the qazi, saw a lamp standing, the sweetheart sitting, the wine spilled, the goblet broken and the qazi plunged in the sleep of drunkenness, unaware of the realm of existence. The king awakened him gently and said: "Get up for the sun has risen." The qazi, who perceived the state of affairs, asked: "From what direction?" The sultan was astonished and replied: "From the east as usual." The qazi exclaimed: "Praise be to Allah! The door of repentance is yet open because according to tradition *the gate of repentance will not be locked against worshippers till the sun rises in its setting place.*"[20]

> These two things impelled me to sin:
> My ill-luck and my imperfect understanding.
> If thou givest me punishment I deserve it
> And if thou forgivest pardon is better than revenge.

The king replied: "As thou knowest that thou must suffer capital punishment, it is of no use to repent. *But their faith availed them not after they had beholden our vengeance.*[21]

> "What is the use to promise to forego thieving
> When a lasso cannot be thrown up to the palace?
> Say to the tall man: 'Do not pluck the fruit,'
> For he who is short cannot reach the branch.

"For thee, who hast committed such wickedness, there is no way of escape." After the king had uttered these words, the men appointed for the execution took hold of him, whereon he said: "I have one word more to speak in the service of the sultan." The king, who heard him, asked: "What is it?" And he recited:

> "Thou who shakest the sleeve of displeasure upon me
> Expect not that I shall withdraw my hand from thy skirt.
> If escape be impossible from this crime which I committed
> I trust to the clemency which thou possessest."

---

20. It is well known that the rising of the sun in the west instead of the east will be one of the signs of the resurrection and Day of Judgment.

21. Qur'an, Ch. XL, last verse, i.e., 85.

The king replied: "Thou hast adduced this wonderful sally and hast enounced a strange maxim but it is impossible according to reason and contrary to usage that thy accomplishments and eloquence should this day save thee from the punishment which I have decreed; and I consider it proper to throw thee headlong from the castle that others may take an example." He continued: "O lord of the world, I have been nourished by the bounty of this dynasty, and this crime was not committed only by me in the world. Throw another man headlong that I may take the example." The king burst out laughing, pardoned his crime and said to his dependents who desired the qazi to be slain:

> "Everyone of you who are bearers of your own faults
> Ought not to blame others for their defects."

[Falling into the Sea]

A virtuous and beauteous youth
Was pledged to a chaste maiden.
I read that in the great sea
They fell into a vortex together.
When a sailor came to take his hand,
Lest he might die in that condition,
He said in anguish from the waves:
"Leave me. Take the hand of my love."
Whilst saying this, he despaired of life.
In his agony he was heard to exclaim:
"Learn not the tale of love from the wretch
Who forgets his beloved in distress."
Thus the lives of the lovers terminated.
Learn from what has occurred that thou mayest know
Because Sa'di is of the ways and means of love affairs
Well aware in the Arabian city of Baghdad.
Tie thy heart to the heart-charmer thou possessest
And shut thy eye to all the rest of the world.
If Mejnun and Laila were to come to life again
They might indite a tale of love on this occurrence.

ᶜUBAYD-I ZĀKĀNĪ (d. 1371)

Persian

Zākānī can justifiably be considered the master satirist of medieval Persian literature. Born in Qazvīn, he studied in Baghdad before settling in Shiraz, where he was a contemporary of the poet Hāfiz. Much of the wit in his satirical works derives from a juxtaposition of the sacred and profane, sometimes tending to the obscene. Zākānī's satire is not for everyone: his works, as one Western critic puts it, "were, and continue to be, condemned as self-serving vulgarity."

[A Sequence of Satiric Anecdotes]

Sultan Maḥmūd[1] was attending a sermon in the Mosque. Talhak went there after him. When he arrived, the preacher stood up and said that if anyone had committed pederasty, then on the Day of Judgment the youth whom he had abused would be placed on his neck, and he would have to carry him over the Bridge of Doom. Sultan Maḥmūd wept. Talhak said, "O Sultan, do not weep but be of good cheer. On that day you won't have to go on foot either."

The Caliph al-Mahdī once got separated from his party during a hunt. In the night he came to a Bedouin's house. The Bedouin was sitting at a meal and had a jug of wine in front of him. When they had drunk a glass, al-Mahdī said, "I am one of al-Mahdī's courtiers." They drank another glass, and al-Mahdī said, "I am one of al-Mahdī's amirs." When they had drunk a third glass, he said, "I am al-Mahdī." The Bedouin took the jug away and said, "You drank the first glass and claimed to be a courtier. With the second glass you claimed to be an amir, and with the third, to be Caliph. If you drink another glass, you will surely claim to be God Almighty." The next day when the Caliph's party arrived, the Bedouin fled in fear. Al-Mahdī commanded that he should be found and brought before him, whereupon he gave him some gold pieces. The Bedouin said, "I bear witness that you speak truth, even if you make the fourth claim."

A man announced that he was God. He was brought before the Caliph who said to him. "Last year there was someone here who claimed to be a prophet. He was executed." "That was well done," said the man, "for I had not sent him."

A Qazvīnī[2] went to war against the heretics with a huge shield. From the fortress they threw a stone which hit him on the head and wounded him. The Qazvīnī was furious and said, "Are you blind, man? Can't you see a shield as big as this that you have to throw a stone straight on to my head?"

A number of Qazvīnīs went to war against the heretics. When they came back from the battle, each of them was carrying the head of a heretic on a pole. One of them had a foot on his pole. They asked him, "Who killed this one?" He answered, "I did." They asked him, "Why didn't you bring his head?" He answered, "They took his head away before I got there."

Translated by Bernard Lewis.

1. Sultan Maḥmūd of Ghazna, who reigned from 998 to 1030.
2. Qazvin, where ʿUbayd-i Zākānī was born, was the main base for campaigns against the Ismāʿīlī stronghold at Alamūt.

Someone asked Mawlānā 'Aḍud al-Dīn, "How is it that in the time of the Caliphs many men claimed to be God or Prophet, and now they do not?" He replied, "The men of our time are so beset by oppression and hunger that they reck nothing of God or Prophet."

A Rāzī, Gīlānī, and a Qazvīnī went together on pilgrimage. The Qazvīnī was bankrupt, the Rāzī and the Gīlānī were rich. When the Rāzī put his hand on the curtain ring of the Ka'ba, he said, "O God, in thanksgiving to Thee for bringing me here safely I set free my slaves Balban and Banafsha." When the Gīlānī grasped the curtain ring, he said, "In thanksgiving for this I set free my slaves Mubārak and Sunqur." When the Qazvīnī grasped the curtain ring he said, "O God, Thou knowest I have neither Balban nor Sunqur, neither Banafsha nor Mubārak. In thanksgiving for this, therefore, I set free my old Fāṭima with a triple divorce."

In the time of the Caliph Wāthiq a woman laid claim to prophethood. The Caliph asked her, "Was Muḥammad a Prophet?" "Certainly," she replied. "Then," said the Caliph, "since Muḥammad said, 'There will be no Prophet after me,' your claim is false." The woman replied, "He said, 'There will be no Prophet after me,' He did not say, 'There will be no Prophetess after me.' "

One day when Sultan Maḥmūd was hungry, they brought him a dish of eggplant. He liked it very much and said, "Eggplant is an excellent food." A courtier began to praise the eggplant with great eloquence. When the sultan grew tired of the dish he said, "Eggplant is a very harmful thing," whereupon the courtier began to speak in hyperbole of the harmful qualities of the eggplant. "Man alive," said the sultan, "have you not just now uttered the praises of the eggplant?" "Yes," said the courtier, "but I am your courtier and not the eggplant's courtier. I have to say what pleases you, not what pleases the eggplant."

A tumbler scolded his son and said, "You do no work and you waste your life in idleness. How often must I tell you to practice somersaults and to learn how to dance on a rope and to make a dog jump through a hoop so that you can achieve something with your life. If you don't listen to me, I swear by God I shall abandon you to the *madrasa* to learn their dead and useless science and to become a scholar so as to live in contempt and misery and adversity and never be able to earn a penny wherever you go."

Shaykh Sharaf al-Dīn Darguzīnī asked Mawlānā 'Aḍud al-Dīn, "Where in the Qur'ān has God spoken of shaykhs?" He answered, "At the side of the learned in this verse, 'Shall the learned and the ignorant be treated in the same manner?' "

Mawlānā Sharaf al-Dīn Dāmghānī was passing by the door of a mosque just as the mosque servant got hold of a dog and beat him inside the mosque. The dog howled. Mawlānā opened the mosque door, and the dog fled. The mosque servant abused Mawlānā. "My friend," said Mawlānā, "excuse the dog. He has no understanding; that is why he went into the mosque. We others, who have understanding, you will never see us in the mosque."

A Khurāsānī went to a physician and said, "My wife is ill. What should I do?" The physician said, "Bring me a specimen in a bottle tomorrow. Then I will look and tell you." By chance the Khurāsānī himself felt ill later that day. Next day he came to the physician with a bottle with a piece of string tied round the middle. The physician asked, "Why did you tie on this string?" The man said, "I also felt sick. The upper half is my water and the lower half is my wife's." Next day the physician repeated this story to everybody. A Qazvīnī was present and said, "Master, please excuse him, for the Khurāsānī has no sense. Was the string tied inside or outside the bottle?"

They asked a wise man, "Why do the nomads never need a physician?" He answered, "As the wild ass needs no vet."

Shams-i Muẓaffar said one day to his disciples, "One should learn when one is young. What one learns in youth one never forgets in age. It is now fifty years since I learned the first verse of the Qur'ān and I can still remember it, though I never read it since."

A man said, "I have pain in my eyes and as a cure I use Qur'ān verses and prayers." Talhak said to him, "But you should use a little eye-salve too."

The devil was asked, "Which group of people do you love best?" He replied, "The market brokers [dallāl]." They asked him why. He answered, "Not only do they speak falsehood, which in itself delights me, but they swear to it as well."

A king had three wives, one Persian, one Arab, and one Coptic. One night he lay beside the Persian woman and asked her, "What time is it?" She answered, "It is the hour of dawn." He asked her, "How do you know?" She answered, "Because the scent of the roses and basil is rising and the birds are beginning to sing." The next night he lay with the Arab woman and asked her the same question. She answered, "It is the hour of dawn. I know it because the pearls of my necklace feel cold against my breast." On the third night he lay with the Coptic woman and he asked her the same question and she answered, "It is the hour of dawn. I know because I have to go to stool."[3]

In the month of Ramaḍān someone said to a dealer, "In this month there is no business." He answered "God give long life to the Jews and the Christians."

A man met another man who was riding on a wretched donkey. "Where are you going?" he asked. "I am going to the Friday prayer," answered the other. "Woe

---

3. The first two answers contain well-known
   literary themes used in dawn poetry.

betide you, it's only Tuesday," said the first. "Yes," said the rider, "but I shall be lucky if this donkey can bring me to the mosque by Saturday."

Abū Dulaf became a Shiʿite and used to say that whoever did not declare himself a Shiʿite was a child of fornication. His son said to him, "I am not of your sect." Abū Dulaf answered, "Yes, indeed, by God. I bedded your mother before I bought her."

A man said to a woman, "I would like to taste you, to know which has a better flavor, you or my wife." She answered, "Ask my husband, he has tasted us both."

Abū Nuwās saw a drunken man and looked at him in wonderment. He was asked, "Why do you find this funny? You yourself are in the same state every day." Abū Nuwās replied, "I have never seen a drunken man before." "How is that?" they asked him. "Because," he replied, "I am always the first to get drunk and the last to recover so I don't know what happens to those who get drunk after I do."

One day Abū Nuwās was seen with a glass of wine in his hand, a bunch of grapes on his right, and a dish of raisins on his left, and every time he drank from the glass he took a grape and a raisin. "What does this mean?" they asked him, and he replied, "This is the Father, the Son, and the Holy Ghost."

A Bedouin was eating with all five fingers. He was asked, "Why do you behave like this?" "If I were to eat with only three," he replied, "the other fingers would be angry." They said to another Bedouin, "You are eating with five fingers." "Yes," he said, "what can I do? I have no more."

Abu'l-Hārith was asked, "Can a man of eighty have a child?" He answered them, "Yes, if he has a neighbor of twenty."

A man with bad breath came to a physician and complained of a toothache. When the physician opened his mouth, a terrible smell came out. The physician said, "This is not my job. Go to the sweepers."

A bore visited a sick man and stayed with him too long. The sick man said, "I am plagued with too many visitors." The bore said, "I will go and shut the door." "Yes," said the sick man, "but from the outside."

A man who claimed to be a prophet was brought before the Caliph al-Muʿtasim. Al-Muʿtasim said, "I bear witness that you are a stupid prophet." The man replied, "I have only come to people like you."

A man said to Ḥajjāj, "I saw you yesterday in a dream, and it seemed that you were in Paradise!" Ḥajjāj replied, "If your dream is true, then the injustice in the hereafter is even greater than in this world."

They said to a Ṣūfī, "Sell your cloak." He replied, "If a fisherman sells his net, with what shall he fish?"

A Bedouin went on pilgrimage and reached Mecca ahead of the others. He grasped the curtains of the Ka'ba and said, "O God, forgive me before the crowd gets to You."

A man married a woman, and on the fifth day after the wedding she bore a child. The man went to the market and bought tablets and ink. They asked him, "What is this?" He answered, "A child that can come into the world after five days can go to school after another three."

The mark of the fool is that he comes at the wrong time and stays too long.

HĀFIZ (1300?–1388?)
Persian

Hāfiz is the master of the *ghazal*, a short lyrical poem. His name means "he who has memorized the *Qur'an*." Little is certain of his life other than that he lived in Shiraz and was apparently attached to a mystical order. It is perhaps not coincidental, then, that much of his lyrical and often apparently erotic poetry can be understood in mystical terms.

I Cease Not from Desire*

I cease not from desire till my desire
Is satisfied; or let my mouth attain
My love's red mouth, or let my soul expire,
Sighed from those lips that sought her lips in vain.
Others may find another love as fair;   5
Upon her threshold I have laid my head,
The dust shall cover me, still lying there,
When from my body life and love have fled.

My soul is on my lips ready to fly,
But grief beats in my heart and will not cease,   10
Because not once, not once before I die,
Will her sweet lips give all my longing peace.
My breath is narrowed down to one long sigh

*Translated by Gertrude Bell.

For a red mouth that burns my thoughts like fire;
When will that mouth draw near and make reply   15
To one whose life is straitened with desire?
When I am dead, open my grave and see
The cloud of smoke that rises round thy feet:
In my dead heart the fire still burns for thee;
Yea, the smoke rises from my winding-sheet!   20
Ah, come, Beloved! for the meadows wait
Thy coming, and the thorn bears flowers instead
Of thorns, the cypress fruit, and desolate
Bare winter from before thy steps has fled.
Hoping within some garden ground to find   25
A red rose soft and sweet as thy soft cheek,
Through every meadow blows the western wind,
Through every garden he is fain to seek.
Reveal thy face! that the whole world may be
Bewildered by thy radiant loveliness;   30
The cry of man and woman comes to thee,
Open thy lips and comfort their distress!
Each curling lock of thy luxuriant hair
Breaks into barbèd hooks to catch my heart,
My broken heart is wounded everywhere   35
With countless wounds from which the red drops start.
Yet when sad lovers meet and tell their sighs,
Not without praise shall Hafiz' name be said,
Not without tears, in those pale companies
Where joy has been forgot and hope has fled.   40

Light in Darkness†

High-nesting in the stately fir,
The enduring nightingale again
Unto the rose in passionate strain
Singeth: "All ill be far from her!"

"In gratitude for this, O rose,   5
That thou the Queen of Beauty art,
Pity nightingales' mad heart,
Be not contemptuous of those."

I do not rail against my fate
When thou dost hide thy face from me;   10
Joy wells not of propinquity
Save in the heart once desolate.

†*Translated by Arthur S. Arberry.*

If other men are gay and glad
That life is joy and festival,
I do exult and glory all   15
Because her beauty makes me sad.

And if for maids of Paradise
And heavenly halls the monk aspires,
The Friend fulfils my heart's desires,
The Tavern will for heaven suffice.   20

Drink wine, and let the lute vibrate;
Grieve not; if any tell to thee,
"Wine is a great iniquity",
Say, "Allah is compassionate!"

Why, Hafiz, art thou sorrowing,   25
Why is thy heart in absence rent?
Union may come of banishment,
And in the darkness light doth spring.

O Ask Not†

O love, how have I felt thy pain!
    Ask me not how—
O absence, how I drank thy bane!
    Ask me not how—

In quest, throughout the world I err'd,   5
And whom, at last, have I preferr'd?
    O ask not whom—

In hope her threshold's dust to spy,
How streamed down my longing eye!
    O ask not how—   10

Why bite my friends their lips, displeas'd?
Know they what ruby lip I seiz'd?
    O ask not when—

But yester-night, this very ear
Such language from her mouth did hear—
    O ask not what—   15

Like Hafiz, in love's mazy round,
My feet, at length, their goal have found,
    O ask not where.

†*Translated by H. H.*

[If I follow in her tracks she stirs up trouble]

If I follow in her tracks she stirs up trouble,
and if I rest from the search she rises up in anger.

And if on the road for a moment, out of loyalty,
I fall on her tracks like dust, like the wind she flees.

And if I seek half a kiss, a hundred taunts, like sugar,   5
spill down from the jewel-box of her mouth.

That deceit which I see in your eyes
mixes many a good name with the dust of the road.

The rise and fall of Love's desert is the snare of affliction.
Where is the lionhearted who is unafraid of affliction?   10

Seek life and patience, for the great wheel, with its sleight-of-hand,
plays a thousand tricks more strange than these.

Hafiz, place your head on the threshold of submission,
for if you argue, time will argue back.

[Don't ask how many complaints I have about her black curls]

Don't ask how many complaints I have about her black curls.
I am so undone because of her that it's beyond telling.

Let no one abandon heart and faith in hope of fidelity.
I did. Do not ask me how sorry I am.

With one gulp of wine which troubles no one
I drew such fire from the ignorant that it's beyond telling.

Ascetic, leave us in peace. And this ruby wine,
do not ask how it steals my heart and faith.

Seclusion and peace were my desire but
the glance I caught from that narcissus is beyond telling.

On this road there are conversations which melt the soul.
Each man has such a quarrel that it's beyond telling.

I asked the great sphere of Heaven about his condition.
He said, "Don't ask how much pain I feel from the mallet's blow."

Translated by H. H.

I said to her, "With whose blood did you color your hair?"
She said, "Hafiz, by the Koran, this story is so long it's beyond telling."

JÂMÎ (1414–1492)
Persian

Regarded as one of the greatest authors of the medieval Persian romance, Jāmī
was a member of a mystical order and spent most of his life at the Timurid court
at Herāt. Prolific and versatile, he excelled in all literary genres and also produced
works on such subjects as theory, poetics, rhetoric and grammar. Among his
finest creations are seven epic poems, known collectively as *The Seven Thrones*
(*Haft Ourang*, the Persian name for the constellation Ursa Major). Three of these
poems are romances. For his topics, Jāmī drew from both Islamic and Greco-
Islamic materials, ranging from the beloved Joseph and Zulaykhā story to the
legend of the star-crossed lovers, Laylā and Majnūn. His frequent use of allegory
links his romantic plots with the world of mysticism.

The Women of Memphis
[from Yūsuf u Zulaikhā, *Joseph and Zulaikha*]

Love is ill suited with peace and rest:
Scorn and reproaches become him best.
Rebuke gives strength to his tongue, and blame
Wakes the dull spark to a brighter flame.
Blame is the censor of Love's bazaar: 5
It suffers no rust the pure splendour to mar.
Blame is the whip whose impending blow
Speeds the willing lover and wakes the slow;
And the weary steed who can hardly crawl
Is swift of foot when reproaches fall.   10
When the rose of the secret had opened and blown,
The voice of reproach was a bulbul in tone.[1]

The women of Memphis, who heard the tale first,
The whispered slander received and nursed.

Translated by Ralph T. H. Griffith.

---

1. An allusion to the bulbul's love of the rose,
   whose beauty, according to Persian legend,
   he sings.

Then, attacking Zulaikha for right and wrong,   15
Their uttered reproaches were loud and long:
"Heedless of honour and name she gave
The love of her heart to the Hebrew slave,
Who lies so deep in her soul enshrined
That to sense and religion her eyes are blind.   20
She loves her servant. 'Tis strange to think
That erring folly so low can sink;
But stranger still that the slave she woos
Should scorn her suit and her love refuse.
His cold eye to hers he never will raise;   25
He never will walk in the path where she strays.
He stops if before him her form he sees;
If she lingers a moment he turns and flees.
When her lifted veil leaves her cheek exposed,
With the stud of his eyelash his eye is closed.   30
If she weeps in her sorrow he laughs at her pain,
And closes each door that she opens in vain.
It may be that her form is not fair in his eyes,
And his cold heart refuses the proffered prize.
If once her beloved one sat with us   35
He would sit with us ever, not treat us thus.
Our sweet society ne'er would he leave,
But joy unending would give and receive.
But not all have this gift in their hands: to enthral
The heart they would win is not given to all.   40
There is many a woman, fair, good, and kind,
To whom never the heart of a man inclined;
And many a Laila with soft black eye.
The tears of whose heart-blood are never dry."

    Zulaikha heard, and resentment woke   45
To punish the dames for the words they spoke.
She summoned them all from the city to share
A sumptuous feast which she bade prepare.
A delicate banquet meet for kings
Was spread with the choicest of dainty things.   50
Cups filled with sherbet of every hue
Shone as rifts in a cloud when the sun gleams through.
There were goblets of purest crystal filled
With wine and sweet odours with art distilled.
The golden cloth blazed like the sunlight; a whole   55
Cluster of stars was each silver bowl.
From goblet and charger rare odours came;
There was strength for the spirit and food for the frame.

All daintiest fare that your lip would taste,
From fish to fowl, on the cloth was placed.   60
It seemed that the fairest their teeth had lent
For almonds, their lips for the sugar sent.
A mimic palace rose fair to view
Of a thousand sweets of each varied hue,
Where instead of a carpet the floor was made   65
With bricks of candy and marmalade.
Fruit in profusion, of sorts most rare,
Piled in baskets, bloomed fresh and fair.
Those who looked on their soft transparency felt
That the delicate pulp would dissolve and melt.   70
Bands of boys and young maidens, fine
As mincing peacocks, were ranged in line;
And the fair dames of Memphis, like Peris eyed,
In a ring on their couches sat side by side.
They tasted of all that they fancied, and each   75
Was courteous in manner and gentle in speech.

　　The feast was ended; the cloth was raised,
And Zulaikha sweetly each lady praised.
Then she set, as she planned in her wily breast,
A knife and an orange beside each guest: 80
An orange, to purge the dark thoughts within
Each jaundiced heart with its golden skin.
One hand, as she bade them, the orange clasped,
The knife in the other was firmly grasped.
Thus she addressed them: "Dames fair and sweet,   85
Most lovely of all when the fairest meet,
Why should my pleasure your hearts annoy?
Why blame me for loving my Hebrew boy?
If your eyes with the light of his eyes were filled,
Each tongue that blames me were hushed and stilled.   90
I will bid him forth, if you all agree,
And bring him near for your eyes to see."
"This, even this," cried each eager dame,
"Is the dearest wish that our hearts can frame.
Bid him come; let us look on the lovely face   95
That shall stir our hearts with its youthful grace.
Already charmed, though our eyes never fell
On the youth we long for, we love him well.
These oranges still in our hands we hold,
To sweeten the spleen with their skins of gold.   100
But they please us not, for he is not here:
Let not one be cut till the boy appear."

She sent the nurse to address him thus:
"Come, free-waving cypress, come forth to us.
Let us worship the ground which thy dear feet press,   105
And bow down at the sight of thy loveliness.
Let our love-stricken hearts be thy chosen retreat,
And our eyes a soft carpet beneath thy feet."

But he came not forth, like a lingering rose
Which the spell of the charmer has failed to unclose.   110
Then Zulaikha flew to the house where he dwelt,
And in fond entreaty before him knelt:
"My darling, the light of these longing eyes,
Hope of my heart," thus she spoke with sighs,
"I fed on the hope which thy words had given;   115
But that hope from my breast by despair is driven.
For thee have I forfeited all: my name
Through thee has been made a reproach and shame.
I have found no favour: thou wouldst not fling
One pitying look on so mean a thing.   120
Yet let not the women of Memphis see
That I am so hated and scorned by thee.
Come, sprinkle the salt of thy lip to cure
The wounds of my heart and the pain I endure.
Let the salt be sacred: repay the debt   125
Of the faithful love thou shouldst never forget."

The heart of Yusuf grew soft at the spell
Of her gentle words, for she charmed so well.
Swift as the wind from her knees she rose,
And decked him gay with the garb she chose.   130
Over his shoulders she drew with care,
The scented locks of his curling hair,
Like serpents of jet-black lustre seen
With their twisted coils where the grass is green.
A girdle gleaming with gold, round the waist   135
That itself was fine as a hair, she braced.
I marvel so dainty a waist could bear
The weight of the jewels that glittered there.
She girt his brow with bright gems; each stone
Of wondrous beauty enhanced his own.   140
On his shoes were rubies and many a gem,
And pearls on the latchets that fastened them.
A scarf, on whose every thread was strung
A loving heart, on his arm was hung.
A golden ewer she gave him to hold,   145
And a maid brow-bound with a fillet of gold
In her hand a basin of silver bore,

And shadow-like moved as he walked before.
If a damsel had looked, she at once had resigned
All joy of her life, all the peace of her mind.   150
Too weak were my tongue if it tried to express
The charm of his wonderful loveliness.

　　Like a bed of roses in perfect bloom
The secret treasure appeared in the room.
The women of Memphis beheld him, and took   155
From that garden of glory the rose of a look.
One glance at his beauty o'erpowered each soul
And drew from their fingers the reins of control.
Each lady would cut through the orange she held,
As she gazed on that beauty unparalleled.   160
But she wounded her finger, so moved in her heart,
That she knew not her hand and the orange apart.
One made a pen of her finger, to write
On her soul his name who had ravished her sight—
A reed which, struck with the point of the knife,   165
Poured out a red flood from each joint in the strife.
One scored a calendar's lines in red
On the silver sheet of her palm outspread,
And each column, marked with the blood-drops, showed
Like a brook when the stream o'er the bank has flowed.   170

　　When they saw that youth in his beauty's pride:
"No mortal is he," in amaze they cried.
"No clay and water composed his frame,
But, a holy angel, from heaven he came."
" 'Tis my peerless boy," cried Zulaikha, "long   175
For him have I suffered reproach and wrong.
I told him my love for him, called him the whole
Aim and desire of my heart and soul.
He looked on me coldly; I bent not his will
To give me his love and my hope fulfill.   180
He still rebelled: I was forced to send
To prison the boy whom I could not bend.
In trouble and toil, under lock and chain,
He passed long days in affliction and pain.
But his spirit was tamed by the woe he felt,   185
And the heart that was hardened began to melt.
Keep your wild bird in a cage and see
How soon he forgets that he once was free."

　　Of those who wounded their hands, a part
Lost reason and patience, and mind and heart.   190
To weak the sharp sword of his love to stay,

They gave up their souls ere they moved away.
The reason of others grew dark and dim,
And madness possessed them for love of him.
Bare-headed, bare-footed, they fled amain,   195
And the light that had vanished ne'er kindled again.
To some their senses at length returned,
But their hearts were wounded, their bosoms burned.
They were drunk with the cup which was full to the brim.
And the birds of their hearts were ensnared by him.   200
Nay, Yusuf's love was a mighty bowl
With varied power to move the soul.
One drank the wine till her senses reeled;
To another, life had no joy to yield;
One offered her soul his least wish to fulfil;   205
One dreamed of him ever, but mute and still.
But only the woman to whom no share
Of the wine was vouchsafed could be pitied there.

ANONYMOUS
Arabic

An established classic in both Eastern and Western literature, *The Thousand and
One Nights* (*Alf Layla wa-Layla,* also known in English as *The Arabian Nights*)
enjoyed little success among the medieval Arab intelligentsia, who favored the
stylistically more ambitious *adab* works. But the *Nights* did have strong links to
adab literature, in much the same way that the *maqâma* did. Narratively, the
Nights is composed of enframed stories. The frame story itself is the tale of
Shahrasād (long familiar in English as Sheherazade), the new bride of King
Shahryār. Once betrayed, the king has come to fear infidelity so much that he
kills each wife after but one night with her. To forestall her own death, Shahrasād
tells the king each night a story, stopping always at its climax: to learn the ending,
he must let her live for one more day. After one thousand and one nights, his
heart is finally melted. Into this frame are set stories gathered from various parts
of the Islamic world and India. *The Nights* was not composed all at once, but
evolved over many centuries. The frame story has been traced to India, and it was
possibly as a collection of Hindu and Buddhist tales that *The Nights* first made its
way into Persian. During the ninth century, a Persian version was translated into
Arabic. *The Nights* continued to evolve in Arabic, with new stories in all
probability replacing old ones. The collection was especially popular in Egypt
during the period of Mamlūk rule (1250–1517), and it was then that the *Nights*
probably took its final form, though the word "final" is somewhat misleading:

there is no single canonical text, and some versions include stories not found in other versions.

from **The Thousand and One Nights**

[The Tale of King Yunan and the Sage Duban]

There was once a king call Yunan, who reigned in one of the cities of Persia, in the province of Zuman.[1] This king was afflicted with leprosy, which had defied the physicians and the sages, who, for all the medicines they gave him to drink and all the ointments they applied, were unable to cure him. One day there came to the city of King Yunan a sage called Duban. This sage had read all sorts of books, Greek, Persian, Turkish, Arabic, Byzantine, Syriac, and Hebrew, had studied the sciences, and had learned their groundwork, as well as their principles and basic benefits. Thus he was versed in all the sciences, from philosophy to the lore of plants and herbs, the harmful as well as the beneficial. A few days after he arrived in the city of King Yunan, the sage heard about the king and his leprosy and the fact that the physicians and the sages were unable to cure him. On the following day, when God's morning dawned and His sun rose, the sage Duban put on his best clothes, went to King Yunan and, introducing himself, said, "Your Majesty, I have heard of that which has afflicted your body and heard that many physicians have treated you without finding a way to cure you. Your Majesty, I can treat you without giving you any medicine to drink or ointment to apply." When the king heard this, he said, "If you succeed, I will bestow on you riches that would be enough for you and your grandchildren. I will bestow favors on you, and I will make you my companion and friend." The king bestowed robes of honor on the sage, treated him kindly, and then asked him, "Can you really cure me from my leprosy without any medicine to drink or ointment to apply?" The sage replied, "Yes, I will cure you externally." The king was astonished, and he began to feel respect as well as great affection for the sage. He said, "Now, sage, do what you have promised." The sage replied, "I hear and obey. I will do it tomorrow morning, the Almighty God willing." Then the sage went to the city, rented a house, and there he distilled and extracted medicines and drugs. Then with his great knowledge and skill, he fashioned a mallet with a curved end, hollowed the mallet, as well as the handle, and filled the handle with his medicines and drugs. He likewise made a ball. When he had perfected and prepared everything, he went on the following day to King Yunan and kissed the ground before him.

But morning overtook Shahrazad, and she lapsed into silence. Then her sister Dinarzad said, "What a lovely story!" Shahrazad replied, "You have heard nothing yet.

Translated by Husain Haddawy.

---

1. Modern Armenia.

Tomorrow night I shall tell you something stranger and more amazing if the king spares me and lets me live!"

THE TWELFTH NIGHT

The following night Dinarzad said to her sister Shahrazad, "Please, sister, finish the rest of the story of the fisherman and the demon." Shahrazad replied, "With the greatest pleasure":

I heard, O King, that the fisherman said to the demon:

The sage Duban came to King Yunan and asked him to ride to the playground to play with the ball and mallet. The king rode out, attended by his chamberlains, princes, viziers,[2] and lords and eminent men of the realm. When the king was seated, the sage Duban entered, offered him the mallet, and said, "O happy King, take this mallet, hold it in your hand, and as you race on the playground, hold the grip tightly in your fist, and hit the ball. Race until your perspire, and the medicine will ooze from the grip into your perspiring hand, spread to your wrist, and circulate through your entire body. After you perspire and the medicine spreads in your body, return to your royal palace, take a bath, and go to sleep. You will wake up cured, and that is all there is to it." King Yunan took the mallet from the sage Duban and mounted his horse. The attendants threw the ball before the king, who, holding the grip tightly in his fist, followed it and struggled excitedly to catch up with it and hit it. He kept galloping after the ball and hitting it until his palm and the rest of his body began to perspire, and the medicine began to ooze from the handle and flow through his entire body. When the sage Duban was certain that the medicine had oozed and spread through the king's body, he advised him to return to his palace and go immediately to the bath. The king went to the bath and washed himself thoroughly. Then he put on his clothes, left the bath, and returned to his palace.

As for the sage Duban, he spent the night at home, and early in the morning, he went to the palace and asked for permission to see the king. When he was allowed in, he entered and kissed the ground before the king; then, pointing toward him with his hand, he began to recite the following verses:

The virtues you fostered are great;
For who but you could sire them?
Yours is the face whose radiant light
Effaces the night dark and grim.
Forever beams your radiant face;
That of the world is still in gloom.

---

2. Ministers.

You rained on us with ample grace,
As the clouds rain on thirsty hills,
Expending your munificence,
Attaining your magnificence.

When the sage Duban finished reciting these verses, the king stood up and embraced him. Then he seated the sage beside him, and with attentiveness and smiles, engaged him in conversation. Then the king bestowed on the sage robes of honor, gave him gifts and endowments, and granted his wishes. For when the king had looked at himself the morning after the bath, he found that his body was clear of leprosy, as clear and pure as silver. He therefore felt exceedingly happy and in a very generous mood. Thus when he went in the morning to the reception hall and sat on his throne, attended by the Mamluks[3] and chamberlains, in the company of the viziers and the lords of the realm, and the sage Duban presented himself, as we have mentioned, the king stood up, embraced him, and seated him beside him. He treated him attentively and drank and ate with him.

But morning overtook Shahrazad, and she lapsed into silence. Then her sister Dinarzad said, "Sister, what a lovely story!" Shahrazad replied, "The rest of the story is stranger and more amazing. If the king spares me and I am alive tomorrow night, I shall tell you something even more entertaining."

THE THIRTEENTH NIGHT

The following night Dinarzad said to her sister Shahrazad, "Sister, if you are not sleepy, tell us one of your lovely little tales to while away the night." Shahrazad replied, "With the greatest pleasure":

I heard, O happy King who is praiseworthy by the Grace of God, that King Yunan bestowed favors on the sage, gave him robes of honor, and granted his wishes. At the end of the day he gave the sage a thousand dinars and sent him home. The king, who was amazed at the skill of the sage Duban, said to himself, "This man has treated me externally, without giving me any draught to drink or ointment to apply. His is indeed a great wisdom for which he deserves to be honored and rewarded. He shall become my companion, confidant, and close friend." Then the king spent the night, happy at his recovery from his illness, at his good health, and at the soundness of his body. When morning came and it was light, the king went to the royal reception hall and sat on the throne, attended by his chief officers, while the princes, viziers, and lords of the realm sat to his right and left. Then the king called for the sage, and when the sage entered and kissed

---

3. Literally "slaves," members of a military force, originally of Caucasian slaves, who made themselves masters of Egypt in 1254 C.E. until their massacre in 1811.

the ground before him, the king stood up to salute him, seated him beside him, and invited him to eat with him. The king treated him intimately, showed him favors, and bestowed on him robes of honor and many other gifts. Then he spent the whole day conversing with him, and at the end of the day he ordered that he be given a thousand dinars. The sage went home and spent the night with his wife, feeling happy and thankful to God the Arbiter.

In the morning, the king went to the royal reception hall, and the princes and viziers came to stand in attendance. It happened that King Yunan had a vizier who was sinister, greedy, envious, and fretful, and when he saw that the sage had found favor with the king, who bestowed on him much money and many robes of honor, he feared that the king would dismiss him and appoint the sage in his place; therefore, he envied the sage and harbored ill will against him, for 'nobody is free from envy.' The envious vizier approached the king and, kissing the ground before him, said, "O excellent King and glorious Lord, it was by your kindness and with your blessing that I rose to prominence; therefore, if I fail to advise you on a grave matter, I am not my father's son. If the great King and noble Lord commands, I shall disclose the matter to him." The king was upset and asked, "Damn you, what advice have you got?" The vizier replied, "Your Majesty, 'He who considers not the end, fortune is not his friend.' I have seen your Majesty make a mistake, for you have bestowed favors on your enemy who has come to destroy your power and steal your wealth. Indeed, you have pampered him and shown him many favors, but I fear that he will do you harm." The king asked, "Whom do you accuse, whom do you have in mind, and at whom do you point the finger?" The vizier replied, "If you are asleep, wake up, for I point the finger at the sage Duban, who has come from Byzantium." The king replied, "Damn you, is he my enemy? To me he is the most faithful, the dearest, and the most favored of people, for this sage has treated me simply by making me hold something in my hand and has cured me from the disease that had defied the physicians and the sages and rendered them helpless. In all the world, east and west, near and far, there is no one like him, yet you accuse him of such a thing. From this day onward, I will give him every month a thousand dinars, in addition to his rations and regular salary. Even if I were to share my wealth and my kingdom with him, it would be less than he deserves. I think that you have said what you said because you envy him. This is very much like the situation in the story told by the vizier of King Sindbad[4] when the king wanted to kill his own son.

But morning overtook Shahrazad, and she lapsed into silence. Then her sister Dinarzad said, "Sister, what a lovely story!" Shahrazad replied, "What is this compared with what I shall tell you tomorrow night! It will be stranger and more amazing."

---

4. Not to be confused with Sindbad the Sailor.

THE FOURTEENTH NIGHT

The following night, when the king got into bed and Shahrazad got in with him, her sister Dinarzad said, "Please, sister, if you are not sleepy, tell us one of your lovely little tales to while away the night." Shahrazad replied, "Very well":

I heard, O happy King, that King Yunan's vizier asked, "King of the age, I beg your pardon, but what did King Sindbad's vizier tell the king when he wished to kill his own son?" King Yunan said to the vizier, "When King Sindbad, provoked by an envious man, wanted to kill his own son, his vizier said to him, 'Don't do what you will regret afterward.' "

[The Tale of the Husband and the Parrot]

I have heard it told that there was once a very jealous man who had a wife so splendidly beautiful that she was perfection itself. The wife always refused to let her husband travel and leave her behind, until one day when he found it absolutely necessary to go on a journey. He went to the bird market, bought a parrot, and brought it home. The parrot was intelligent, knowledgeable, smart, and retentive. Then he went away on his journey, and when he finished his business and came back, he brought the parrot and inquired about his wife during his absence. The parrot gave him a day-by-day account of what his wife had done with her lover and how the two carried on in his absence. When the husband heard the account, he felt very angry, went to his wife, and gave her a sound beating. Thinking that one of her maids had informed her husband about what she did with her lover in her husband's absence, the wife interrogated her maids one by one, and they all swore that they had heard the parrot inform the husband.

When the wife heard that it was the parrot who had informed the husband, she ordered one of her maids to take the grinding stone and grind under the cage, ordered a second maid to sprinkle water over the cage, and ordered a third to carry a steel mirror and walk back and forth all night long. That night her husband stayed out, and when he came home in the morning, he brought the parrot, spoke with it, and asked about what had transpired in his absence that night. The parrot replied, "Master, forgive me, for last night, all night long, I was unable to hear or see very well because of the intense darkness, the rain, and the thunder and lightning." Seeing that it was summertime, during the month of July, the husband replied, "Woe unto you, this is no season for rain." The parrot said, "Yes, by God, all night long, I saw what I told you." The husband, concluding that the parrot had lied about his wife and had accused her falsely, got angry, and he grabbed the parrot and, taking it out of the cage, smote it on the ground and killed it. But after the parrot's death, the husband heard from his neighbors that the parrot had told the truth about his wife, and he was full of regret that he had been tricked by his wife to kill the parrot.

King Yunan concluded, "Vizier, the same will happen to me."

But morning overtook Shahrazad, and she lapsed into silence. Then her sister Dinarzad said, "What a strange and lovely story!" Shahrazad replied, "What is this compared with what I shall tell you tomorrow night! If the king spares me and lets me live, I shall tell you something more amazing." The king thought to himself, "By God, this is indeed an amazing story."

THE FIFTEENTH NIGHT

The following night Dinarzad said to her sister Shahrazad, "Please, sister, if you are not sleepy, tell us one of your lovely little tales, for they entertain and help everyone to forget his cares and banish sorrow from the heart." Shahrazad replied, "With the greatest pleasure." King Shahrayar added, "Let it be the remainder of the story of King Yunan, his vizier, and the sage Duban, and of the fisherman, the demon, and the jar." Shahrazad replied, "With the greatest pleasure":

I heard, O happy King, that King Yunan said to his envious vizier, "After the husband killed the parrot and heard from his neighbors that the parrot had told him the truth, he was filled with remorse. You too, my vizier, being envious of this wise man, would like me to kill him and regret it afterward, as did the husband after he killed the parrot." When the vizier heard what King Yunan said, he replied, "O great king, what harm has this sage done to me? Why, he has not harmed me in any way. I am telling you all this out of love and fear for you. If you don't discover my veracity, let me perish like the vizier who deceived the son of the king." King Yunan asked his vizier, "How so?" The vizier replied:

[The Tale of the King's Son and the She-Ghoul]

It is said, O happy King, that there was once a king who had a son who was fond of hunting and trapping. The prince had with him a vizier appointed by his father the king to follow him wherever he went. One day the prince went with his men into the wilderness, and when he chanced to see a wild beast, the vizier urged him to go after it. The prince pursued the beast and continued to press in pursuit until he lost its track and found himself alone in the wilderness, not knowing which way to turn or where to go, when he came upon a girl, standing on the road, in tears. When the young prince asked her, "Where do you come from?" she replied, "I am the daughter of an Indian king. I was riding in the wilderness when I dozed off and in my sleep fell of my horse and found myself alone and helpless." When the young prince heard what she said, he felt sorry for her, and he placed her behind him on his horse and rode on. As they passed by some ruins, she said, "O my lord, I wish to relieve myself here." He let her down and she went into the ruins. Then he went in after her, ignorant of what she was, and discovered that she was a she-ghoul, who was saying to her children, "I brought you a good, fat boy."

They replied, "Mother, bring him to us, so that we may feed on his innards." When the young prince heard what they said, he shook with terror, and fearing for his life, ran outside. The she-ghoul followed him and asked, "Why are you afraid?" and he told her about his situation and his predicament, concluding, "I have been unfairly treated." She replied, "If you have been unfairly treated, ask the Almighty God for help, and he will protect you from harm." The young prince raised his eyes to Heaven . . .

But morning overtook Shahrazad, and she lapsed into silence. Then her sister Dinarzad said, "What a strange and lovely story!" Shahrazad replied, "What is this compared with what I shall tell you tomorrow night! It will be even stranger and more amazing."

THE SIXTEENTH NIGHT

The following night Dinarzad said, "Please, sister if you are not sleepy, tell us one of your lovely little tales." Shahrazad replied, "I shall with pleasure":

I heard, O King, that the vizier said to King Yunan:

When the young prince said to the she-ghoul, "I have been unfairly treated," she replied, "Ask God for help, and He will protect you from harm." The young prince raised his eyes to Heaven and said, "O Lord, help me to prevail upon my enemy, for 'everything is within your power,'" When the she-ghoul heard his invocation, she gave up and departed, and he returned safely to his father and told him about the vizier and how it was he who had urged him to pursue the beast and drove him to his encounter with the she-ghoul. The king summoned the vizier and had him put to death.

The vizier added, "You too, your Majesty, if you trust, befriend, and bestow favors on this sage, he will plot to destroy you and cause your death. Your Majesty should realize that I know for certain that he is a foreign agent who has come to destroy you. Haven't you seen that he cured you externally, simply with something you held in your hand?" King Yunan, who was beginning to feel angry, replied, "You are right, vizier. The sage may well be what you say and may have come to destroy me. He who has cured me with something to hold can kill me with something to smell." Then the king asked the vizier, "My vizier and good counselor, how should I deal with him?" The vizier replied, "Send for him now and have him brought before you, and when he arrives, strike off his head. In this way, you will attain your aim and fulfill your wish." The king said, "This is good and sound advice." Then he sent for the sage Duban, who came immediately, still feeling happy at the favors, the money, and the robes the king had bestowed on him. When he entered, he pointed with his hand toward the king and began to recite the following verses:

> If I have been remiss in thanking you,
> For whom then have I made my verse and prose?
> You granted me your gifts before I asked,
> Without deferment and without excuse.
> How can I fail to praise your noble deeds,
> Inspired in private and in public by my muse?
> I thank you for your deeds and for your gifts,
> Which, though they bend my back, my care reduce.

The king asked, "Sage, do you know why I have had you brought before me?" The sage replied, "No, your Majesty." The king said "I brought you here to have you killed and to destroy the breath of life within you." In astonishment Duban asked, "Why does your Majesty wish to have me put to death, and for what crime?" The king replied, "I have been told that you are a spy and that you have come to kill me. Today I will have you killed before you kill me. I will have you for lunch before you have me for dinner." Then the king called for the executioner and ordered him, saying, "Strike off the head of this sage and rid me of him! Strike!"

When the sage heard what the king said, he knew that because he had been favored by the king, someone had envied him, plotted against him, and lied to the king, in order to have him killed and get rid of him. The sage realized then that the king had little wisdom, judgment, or good sense, and he was filled with regret, when it was useless to regret. He said to himself, "There is no power and no strength, save in God the Almighty, the Magnificent. I did a good deed but was rewarded with an evil one." In the meantime, the king was shouting at the executioner, "Strike off his head." The sage implored, "Spare me, your Majesty, and God will spare you; destroy me, and God will destroy you." He repeated the statement, just as I did, O demon, but you too refused, insisting on killing me. King Yunan said to the sage, "Sage, you must die, for you have cured me with a mere handle, and I fear that you can kill me with anything." The sage replied, "This is my reward from your Majesty. You reward good with evil." The king said, "Don't stall; you must die today without delay." When the sage Duban became convinced that he was going to die, he was filled with grief and sorrow, and his eyes overflowed with tears. He blamed himself for doing a favor for one who does not deserve it and for sowing seeds in a barren soil and recited the following verses:

> Maimuna was a foolish girl,
> Though from a sage descended,
> And many with pretense to skill
> Are e'en on dry land upended.

The executioner approached the sage, bandaged his eyes, bound his hands, and raised the sword, while the sage cried, expressed regret, and implored, "For God's sake, your Majesty, spare me, and God will spare you; destroy me, and God will destroy you." Then he tearfully began to recite the following verses:

They who deceive enjoy success,
While I with my true counsel fail
And am rewarded with disgrace.
If I live, I'll nothing unveil;
If I die, then curse all the men,
The men who counsel and prevail.

Then the sage added, "Is this my reward from your Majesty? It is like the reward of the crocodile." The king asked, "What is the story of the crocodile?" The sage replied, "I am in no condition to tell you a story. For God's sake, spare me, and God will spare you. Destroy me, and God will destroy you," and he wept bitterly.

Then several noblemen approached the king and said, "We beg your Majesty to forgive him for our sake, for in our view, he has done nothing to deserve this." The king replied, "You do not know the reason why I wish to have him killed. I tell you that if I spare him, I will surely perish, for I fear that he who has cured me externally from my affliction, which had defied the Greek sages, simply by having me hold a handle, can kill me with anything I touch. I must kill him, in order to protect myself from him." The sage Duban implored again, "For God's sake, your Majesty, spare me, and God will spare you. Destroy me, and God will destroy you." The king insisted, "I must kill you."

Demon, when the sage realized that he was surely going to die, he said, "I beg your Majesty to postpone my execution until I return home, leave instructions for my burial, discharge my obligations, distribute alms, and donate my scientific and medical books to one who deserves them. I have in particular a book entitled *The Secret of Secrets,* which I should like to give you for safekeeping in your library." The king asked, "What is the secret of this book?" The sage replied, "It contains countless secrets, but the chief one is that if your Majesty has my head struck off, opens the book on the sixth leaf, reads three lines from the left page, and speaks to me, my head will speak and answer whatever you ask."

The king was greatly amazed and said, "Is it possible that if I cut off your head and, as you say, open the book, read the third line, and speak to your head, it will speak to me? This is the wonder of wonders." Then the king allowed the sage to go and sent him home under guard. The sage settled his affairs and on the following day returned to the royal palace and found assembled there the princes, viziers, chamberlains, lords of the realm, and military officers, as well as the king's retinue, servants, and many of his citizens. The sage Duban entered, carrying an old book and a kohl[5] jar containing powder. He sat down, ordered a platter, and poured out the powder and smoothed it on the platter. Then he said to the king, "Take this book, your Majesty, and don't open it until after my execution. When my head is cut off, let it be placed on the platter and order that it be pressed on

---

5. Cosmetic, used by Eastern, especially Muslim, women to darken the eyelids.

the powder. Then open the book and begin to ask my head a question, for it will then answer you. There is no power and no strength save in God, the Almighty, the Magnificent. For God's sake, spare me, and God will spare you; destroy me, and God will destroy you." The king replied, "I must kill you, especially to see how your head will speak to me." Then the king took the book and ordered the executioner to strike off the sage's head. The executioner drew his sword and, with one stroke, dropped the head in the middle of the platter, and when he pressed the head on the powder, the bleeding stopped. Then the sage Duban opened his eyes and said, "Now, your Majesty, open the book." When the king opened the book, he found the pages stuck. So he put his finger in his mouth, wetted it with his saliva, and opened the first page, and he kept opening the pages with difficulty until he turned seven leaves. But when he looked in the book, he found nothing written inside, and he exclaimed, "Sage, I see nothing written in this book." The sage replied, "Open more pages." The king opened some more pages but still found nothing, and while he was doing this, the drug spread through his body—for the book had been poisoned—and he began to heave, sway, and twitch.

But morning overtook Shahrazad, and she lapsed into silence. Then her sister Dinarzad said, "Sister, what an amazing and entertaining story!" Shahrazad replied, "What is this compared with what I shall tell you tomorrow night if the king spares me and lets me live!"

THE SEVENTEENTH NIGHT

The following night Dinarzad said to her sister Shahrazad, "Please, sister, if you are not sleepy, tell us one of your lovely little tales to while away the night." The king added, "Let it be the rest of the story of the sage and the king and of the fisherman and the demon." Shahrazad replied, "Very well, with the greatest pleasure":

I heard, O King, that when the sage Duban saw that the drug had spread through the king's body and that the king was heaving and swaying, he began to recite the following verses:

For long they ruled us arbitrarily,
But suddenly vanished their powerful rule.
Had they been just, they would have happily
Lived, but they oppressed, and punishing fate
Afflicted them with ruin deservedly,
And on the morrow the world taunted them,
" 'Tis tit for tat; blame not just destiny."

As the sage's head finished reciting the verses, the king fell dead, and at that very moment the head too succumbed to death. Demon, consider this story.

But morning overtook Shahrazad, and she lapsed into silence. Then her sister Dinarzad said, "Sister, what an entertaining story!" Shahrazad replied, "What is this compared with what I shall tell you tomorrow night if I live!"

FUZŪLĪ (1480?–1556?)
Turkish

Muhammad ibn Sulaymān, whose pen name was Fuzūlī, is considered one of the most illustrious figures in classical Turkish literature. Fuzūlī came from an educated family and was an accomplished author in all three classical Islamic languages: Arabic, Persian, and Turkish. It is, however, his literary output in Turkish, in the Azerbaijan dialect, that has placed Fuzūlī's name in the limelight. His popularity has not waned over the centuries among Turkish speakers. The poem here, a *ghazal,* is from his collection of lyrics in Turkish.

[My love has tired me of my life]

My love has tired me of my life—will she not tire of cruelty?
My sigh has set the spheres on fire—will not the candle of my passion burn?

On those who faint and fail for her, my love bestows a healing drug
Why does she give none to me; does she not think that I am sick?

I hid my pain from her. They said tell it to your love.
And if I tell that faithless one—I do not know, will she believe, or will she not?

In the night of separation, my soul burns, my eye weeps blood
My cries awaken; does my black fate never wake?

Against the rose of your cheek red tears stream from my eye
Dear love, this is the time of roses, will not these flowing waters cloud?

It was not I who turned to you but you who drove my sense away
When the fool who blames me sees you, will he not be put to shame?

Fuzuli is a crazy lover and a byword among folk
Ask then what kind of love is this—of such a love does he not tire?

Translated by Bernard Lewis.

Bronze Benin head (sixteenth century).
The Metropolitan Museum of Art.

SECTION VI
Africa: The Epic Tradition

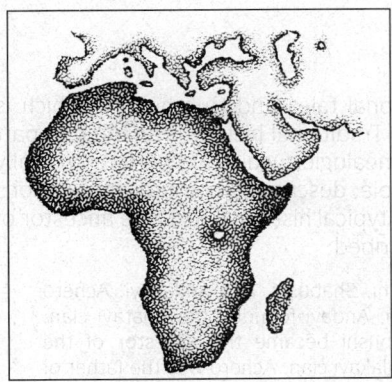

The epic in Africa is born again and again; it combines several oral genres: songs, incantations, proverbs, praise poetry, narrative, and sometimes genealogy. Oral praise poetry, which is equivalent to a panegyric, is produced throughout Africa to celebrate a hero or heroine, or a respected animal, or sometimes both at the same time as in S. K. Lekgothoane's "Praises of Animals in Northern Section":

It is the yellow leopard with the spots
The yellow leopard of the cliffs
It is the leopard of the broad cheeks
Yellow leopard of the broad face, I-do-not-fear

The real subjects in this excerpt are the chiefs of the Tlokwa of Lesotho. An equally well-known genre in Africa is the traditional narrative of an important historical figure such as Chaka the Zulu, Liongo Fumo of East Africa, Muhammed Toure of Songhay, or Idris Alooma of Kanem-Bornu. Dedan Kimathi, the Kenyan freedom fighter, is made legendary through the eyes of a Gikuyu schoolboy in *Weep Not Child,* a novel by Ngugi wa Thiong'o:

Dedan can change himself into anything—a white man, a bird, or a tree. He can also turn himself into an aeroplane. He learnt all this in the Big War.

The accounts of such figures, presented as fact, often contain elements difficult for the outsider to believe, but it is this legendary quality that enforces belief and a sense of affiliation. An essential distinction is always maintained between invented, fictional tales and true history, which is often the province only of elders or priests. Traditional history is an integral part of the life of many African peoples, as are genealogies, which are performed orally and function as a charter for a group of people, describing their present relations in terms of their lineages from the past. In a typical historical text, the ancestor of the Abasamia clan in western Kenya is described:

[He] had five sons: Achero, Andaayi, Aswani, Shabushi, and Andakayi. Achero became the ancestor of the Abachero clan; Andayi founded the Abatayi clan; Aswani founded the Abayonga clan; Shabushi became the ancestor of the Abakambuli; and Andakayi founded the Abalakayi clan. Achero was the father of Luyo, father of Mwamba, father of Miya.

The recitation is in fact a poetic exercise in name-dropping, since every name alludes to some person or group the hearer is expected to recognize.

When we combine praise with narrative, we get epic. Today researchers keep uncovering so much new epic and heroic poetry that the form cannot be thought of as confined to any one of Africa's four language groups: Click (macro-khoisan), Afro-Asiatic, Savanna-Sahara, and Niger-Congo. Heroic epics are as common in Africa as anywhere else, for the same reasons. Just as the Greek Oedipus and Theseus, the Hebrew Moses, the German Siegfried, and the Irish Cu Chulainn—heroes of the ancient Mediterranean and Europe—are historically related because the peoples are contiguous, so the lives of African heroes often include similar incidents: unusual birth, precocious growth, enormous physical strength and bravery in slaying monsters or enemies, and eventual leadership or fathering of a people. Anthropologist Clyde Kluckhohn found the theme of slaying monsters in thirty-seven of the fifty world-wide cultures he studied for their myth themes. He interpreted it psychologically in his *Myth and Mythmaking*:

Not infrequently, the elaboration of the theme has a faintly Oedipal flavor. Thus in Bantu Africa (and beyond) a hero is born to a woman who survives after a monster has eaten her spouse (and everyone else). The son immediately turns into a man, slays a monster or monsters, restores his people—but not his father—and becomes chief.

In African forms of this hero legend, the Oedipal theme is often disguised by making it seem that the son is avenging his father. The components of this epic also include a favorite African motif, the all-devouring monster who swallows whole towns of people and buildings. The final incident will then be the rescuing of the victims from the monster's belly.

The epic selections presented here refer to events that happened as early as the eighth or tenth century. All were recorded in modern times. Face-to-face oral transmission was for many centuries, and still is, a perfectly adequate channel for the production and enjoyment of this kind of art. Although writing, recording, broadcasting, or printing an epic alters its status as living entertainment, it does not diminish it. In an age of increased African literacy, print affords recognition to an ancient art, especially when the many nights required for a full performance do not seem to be available any more. Printed texts and translations can manage sometimes to reflect the active intervention of audiences, commenting on the action, applauding the narrator, and even helping out the person running the tape recorder. Historical reconstruction enables us to imagine where and when an epic would have been performed, and what audience would have especially appreciated it. All these texts, then, should be read as libretti for performance, like Sophocles' *Antigone* or Racine's *Phaedra*.

Historical Background

The epics in this section are drawn from West Africa, Egypt, and the island of Madagascar. The borders of the region known as West Africa are the Sahara to the north, the Atlantic Ocean to the west and south, and the basin of Lake Chad to the east. Its northern portion forms the greater part of the Sudan, a broad belt of sahel (semidesert) modulating to savanna (flat grasslands) that stretches across Africa south of the Sahara. Below the Sudan is a forested coastal region called Guinea.

The West African epics included in this section come from three Sudanese empires: Ghana, Mali, and Songhay. They flourished successively from the eighth through the sixteenth centuries, and each in its time controlled lucrative trade between West Africa and the Mediterranean. The trans-Sahara trade routes were ancient — probably as old as the desert itself (which emerged by around 2000 B.C.E.). Mediterranean civilizations offered horses, luxury goods, and — above all — salt. West Africa offered ivory, slaves, and gold from the valleys of the Senegal and Niger rivers. During the sixth century B.C.E., the Phoenician colony of Carthage (near present-day Tunis) tried to establish direct contact with West Africa by sea. But the attempt failed, and the desert routes remained the monopoly of mediating Saharan peoples.

The first written mention of Ghana appears in an Arab chronicle of the late eighth century. Arabs united under Islam had by this time amassed an empire that stretched from Spain across North Africa and east as far as Afghanistan. In the process they came into possession of the northern ends of the trans-Sahara trade routes. Over the ensuing centuries, Islam spread gradually into West Africa, largely through trading contacts, and Muslim geographers and chroniclers left descriptions of the kingdoms they encountered.

Ghana arose in the Sahel between the Senegal and Niger rivers (far north of the present-day coastal nation of Ghana, to which it is unrelated). By the time the Arabs encountered it, the kingdom—if not the empire—was probably several centuries old. Excavations have confirmed Arabic records that tell of stone cities and surrounding farmlands. The court was wealthy and powerful, and the king commanded the allegiance of numerous lesser rulers. Muslims found welcome not only as traders but also as administrators and legal advisers to the king.

In the mid-eleventh century, Ghana was attacked and occupied for a time by the Almoravids, a group of North African nomadic peoples united under a militant version of Islam. The occupation—possibly combined with a series of droughts—undermined the empire, and its satellite kingdoms grew increasingly independent.

During the early thirteenth century, the Keita kings of Mali, a gold-rich region of the uppermost Niger valley, emerged as the new regional power. Under King Son-Jara (or Sundiata, r. 1230–1255), Mali extended its dominion along the length of the upper Niger, around the Niger Bend, and west to the Atlantic coast, subsuming the former empire of Ghana in a much larger formation. Mali controlled the Sahara trade far more effectively than Ghana had. The West African commercial centers of Gao, Walata, and Jenne were firmly under Malian control, and the capital, Niani, grew into a major city.

The Keita kings were Muslim. Several even made the pilgrimage to Mecca, among them Mansa Musa, who ruled in the early fourteenth century. Musa's pilgrimage earned him lasting fame when, during his stay in Egypt, so much gold flowed from his purse that a decade-long inflation ensued. He returned to Mali with a retinue of scholars, scientists, artists, and architects, transforming Timbuktu into the most important intellectual center of Islam south of the Sahara.

Mali went into a decline in the fifteenth century, and, as with Ghana, its subject kingdoms began to splinter away. The next power to arise were the Songhay, whose kings ruled from the city of Gao on the Niger Bend. The Songhay were brought into the Mali empire by Mansa Musa but succeeded in throwing off Malian control in 1375. In the fifteenth century, they reached out to form their own empire, which extended in a broad arc along the Niger River and north to the Sahara. Songhay dominance lasted until 1591, when the empire was conquered by the Sa^cdi Dynasty of Morocco.

Madagascar lies off the southeastern coast of Africa. Its people, the Malagasy, are of Indonesian and Afro-Arab ancestry; the Malagasy language is Malayo-Polynesian with some Bantu and Arabic vocabulary. This multicultural mixture is typical of the East African coastal territories, which from ancient times were visited by ships trading along the coast of South Asia. In all likelihood, Indonesian migrations to Africa and Madagascar began before the birth of Christ or what we now call the common era. Muslim traders arrived from East Africa between the ninth and fourteenth centuries. Europeans discovered Madagascar in 1500, and in the seventeenth century the French established settlements.

The Malagasy epic excerpted here is from the Merina people, who inhabit the central plateau of the island. Their kingdom, Imerina, was founded by a forceful visionary ruler Andrianampoinimerina (r. 1782–1810), known as the "Prince in the Heart of Imerina." His son, Radama I, who ruled from 1810 to 1828, opened the island to British influence; Christian missionaries put the Malagasy language into writing and started schools. After his death, his xenophobic widow Ranavalona I (r. 1828–1861) expelled all Europeans and reinstated traditional beliefs and customs. Then in another reversal, Ranavalona's successors again welcomed Europeans. Despite much resistance, Madagascar eventually succumbed to the French and underwent sixty-two years of colonial rule. Independence was won in 1958.

Further Readings

Davidson, Basil. *African Civilization Revisited from Antiquity to Modern Times.* Trenton N.J.: Africa World Press, 1991.

Finnegan, Ruth. *Oral Literature in Africa.* Oxford: Clarendon Press, 1970.

Okpewho, Isidore. *African Oral Tradition.* Bloomington: Indiana University Press, 1992.

Scheub, Harold. *African Oral Narratives, Proverbs, Riddles, Poetry and Song.* Boston: G. K. Hall, 1977.

———. "A Review of African Oral Traditions and Literature." *African Studies Review* June–September 1985: 1–72.

Zell, Hans M., et al. *A New Reader's Guide to African Literature.* New York: Africana, 1983.

MERINA PEOPLE
Madagascar

The Merina (pronounced *Mairn'*, the "Elevated People") are the largest and most influential (1,200,000) of Madagascar's eighteen dialect groups. From the seventeenth century until 1896, when France invaded and colonized the island, the Merina state ("Imerina") expanded through military conquest and forced labor. The colossus of Merina history is Andrianampoinimerina ("Prince in the heart of Imerina"), whose imposing presence was the incarnation of kingly authority. Ibonia's heroic deeds in the epic seem to allude to this divine king. The Merina have produced eloquent oratory, innumerable proverbs, and a remarkable kind of oral poetry, *hainteny* (pron. *hine-tenny*), in which men and women court each other. Famous for blending this poetry with European literary forms is the poet Jean-Joseph Rabearivelo (1901–1937).

The epic from which this episode comes narrates the typical biography of a legendary hero of royal parentage: unusual birth, precocious strength, a quest for his betrothed, tests and combats, supernatural aid, a struggle with the abductor of the beloved, final victory, and marriage. The epic was probably recited in and for the royal court of nineteenth-century Imerina, a rigidly stratified society having a female sovereign. This early episode depicts the testing of Beautiful-Rich, the hero's mother, who proves to be nearly as heroic as her son will be. By featuring the mother early in this recitation, the Merina bard combines praise poetry, flattering his audience, with narration.

At the beginning of this excerpt, Skyfather expresses dismay that his favorite son, Prince of the Center, has no heir. The prince sends Beautiful-Rich, his barren wife, to the diviner, Great-Echo, who in turn sends her to a certain rock to capture a locust that will enable her to conceive. Beautiful-Rich displays perfect determination in seeking out the diviner and "masculine" courage in her quest for a magical object that will fulfill her destiny. She returns home pregnant with the hero.

from *Ibonia*

[Beautiful-Rich Goes to Seek the Locust]

Skyfather then went out and mounted his golden throne.
He made a speech:
"Now I have completed the welcome meal for the four men,
    but not the one for Prince of the Center.
We will arrange two groups facing each other.   5
    That means a hundred bulls, a hundred oxen and the rest.
I have had the guns and cannons fired with a single charge,

Collected by L. Dahle, a Norwegian missionary; translated by Lee Haring from the published version.

and the discharge was lost in the earth,
        because there is no child to cry.[1]
Beautiful-Rich is barren.   10
The Prince of the Center has fathered no child.
What I have to say to you then,
    Beautiful-Rich and Prince of the Center, is this:
      All now is well,
          your greatness up to now is all very well—   15
      but there is no child to cry."

Now when Beautiful-Rich heard that,
    she was perturbed. She wept, she cried out,
      she covered her husband with tears up to the neck,
    Prince of the Center. Then she said,   20
"Prince, men are assembled here;
    much wealth is here.
    Only a single calabash[2] is denied to us,
      and swine and curs must inherit this kingdom and land."
"I will not take another wife," said Prince of the Center.   25
"Go you to get help from Great-Echo [the diviner].
    Get a childbearing charm from him."

So Beautiful-Rich set out to get help from Great-Echo.
    With her she took ten women
      and a hundred men carrying guns, spears, and muskets.   30

When they reached Great-Echo's place, Great-Echo said,
"The 'line for two' is not made by my foot,
    The 'line for four' is not made by my hand.[3]
What will happen next year I see this year,
    what will happen tomorrow I see today.   35
So I know even before you open your mouth
    what brings you here grieving. It is your need for a child.
How many men accompany you, how many women accompany you?"

Beautiful-Rich said, "A hundred men,
carrying a hundred guns, a hundred spears, and a hundred muskets,   40
    and ten women carrying ten round stones."

"Eehh, woman!" said Great-Echo.
    "He will be a hard man on earth.
      A thousand years in your womb,
      a hundred men inside you,   45

---

1. Crying means that the child is alive but also
    that there will be no child to weep for
    Skyfather himself when he dies.
2. A bowl-shaped container made from a large
    gourd.

3. Refers to arrangements of stones used in
    sikidy, or divination. The divine says he is
    the channel, not the creator, of the divina-
    tion signs.

and ten years will you carry him, O Beautiful-Rich.
　　If you consent, then that is what I will give you.
　　But if you do not consent, you will have no other child.
Then go home—
　　for he is a trouble child. Trouble, that one,   50
　　　and a calamity child.
He is a thunderbolt, he is lightning.
　　On earth he will kill his father,
　　　　　　　in the womb he will kill his mother."

Then Beautiful-rich said, "Oh yes, sir,   55
　　for it is bad to have nothing, even trouble,
　　　and the child is the heir to the father."

　　　　　　　Great-Echo said, "So be it.
If you agree, then go you to Male-Rock-of-Thousand-Corners.
　　Lightning will also be there.   60
　　　Animals will be there.
　　　　Deadly things will be there too.
But when you go there,
　　have each of your women carry two cannonballs
　　　and you carry three.   65
A locust you will get there, as your childbearing charm.
A thousand strong men will meet you there,
　　　　　but those thousand strong men will flee,
　　for the male locust will madden the ox
　　　and will pass over the Male-Rock-of-Thousand-Corners."   70

　　　　　Then she set out.
When she arrived near the stone,
　　waterspouts, winds, thunderbolts, hail fell upon her.
　　　So did all deadly things.
Seven times did the ten women fall,   75
　　but Beautiful-Rich was the only one who did not fall.
As she approached Male-Rock-of-Thousand-Corners,
　　there were more deadly things.
When she came to the north of the rock,
　　　　　　　there was the locust, on top of it.   80
Male-Rock-of-Thousand-Corners sank down
　　level with the ground.
Then again her ten servant women fell, crushing their hands,
　　but Beautiful-Rich was the only one who did not fall.
The locust was bombarded with bullets   85
　　so that Beautiful-Rich could catch him,
but that locust did not die.
　　He seemed ever more alive, to look at him.
Then Beautiful-Rich bound up her loins like a man

to catch the locust 90
   and she caught the locust.
It carried them up, flying.
  Beautiful-Rich almost reached the sky—
   but she would not fall:
    she was sitting atop the stone. 95
Then it came down to earth,
  but did not enlarge its hole;
  it fell into the same place as before.
Beautiful-Rich slid into the stone[4]
   and took the locust to make a childbearing charm. 100

Then each of the oldest trees in the world began to speak:
  "I am the childbearing charm."
  "I am the childbearing charm."
When Beautiful-Rich had arrived
  among the childbearing charms— 105
  among Does-Not-Wither-When-Transplanted,
   and Does-Not-Dry-When-Planted,
    Thousand-Goat-Horns,
    Hundred-in-the-Womb—
she went into the forest to get Single-Trunk.[5] 110
But when she reached the top of Single-Trunk,
    it was the locust who seized the charm.
Then came back Beautiful-Rich, traversing on spiderwebs,
  not touching the sky,
   not touching the blossoms on the trees as she passed, 115
   not walking on the ground.

SONINKÉ PEOPLE
West Africa

These excerpts come from two versions of poetic narratives about the Ghana empire and were recounted by Soninké *griots*—a regional term of uncertain origin for professional wordsmiths found throughout the Sahel. Known in Soninké as *geseré, griots* serve as historians, genealogists, praise-singers, compos-

---

4. Victory over the stone and the locust establish her supremacy over the mineral and animal realms. By the time she enters the male rock, she is carrying the seed.

5. A second charm will give force to the first one.

ers, musicians, spokesmen, arbiters, tutors, and ambassadors. Their female counterparts, *griottes,* perform many of the same functions.

Ghana, once called Wagadu, was described by eighth-century Arab writers as the "land of gold." With its capital at Kumbi Saleh in southeastern Mauritania, Ghana controlled trade in gold, ivory, salt, and slaves between North Africa and the forest region to the south. After reaching its peak in the eleventh century, Ghana declined and many of its Soninké-speaking peoples scattered across West Africa, carrying with them the story of the Bida snake and its role in the empire's fall.

The first text was recorded from a Soninké *griot* named Diara Sylla, transcribed and translated by Mamadou Soumare, and annotated by Germaine Dieterlen and Youssouf Cissé for publication in French in 1977. The second text was recorded from Jiri Silla in 1965 at Yerere, Mali, by Malamine Cissé and translated by Abdoulaye Bathily for publication in French in 1977.

from *The Oral Epic of the Ghana Empire*

[A Message Left for a Vulture to Convey]

[Diara Sylla first tells his listeners about Dinga Khoré, ancestor of the descendants of the Ghana empire. In this version, they came from India via Yemen and Israel to an unidentified place in Africa approximately a thousand miles east of present-day Mauritania. Toward the end of his life, Dinga left a message for a vulture to convey to his descendants.]

. . . I have a message I would like to entrust to you.

The vulture replied, "We are at your service."

Dinga spoke again: "After my death, when all the sacrifices have been made, you
    will tell my descendants to go toward the West.

There is a place there called Kumbi, there is a well at that place, and there is
    something in the well. People talk with that creature, for it is not an ordinary
    creature. My descendants will only settle down there after they have reached
    an understanding with the creature in question."

[The vulture transmitted the message to one of Dinga's sons, Djabé Cissé.]

Djabé Cissé asked, "How can one find this place?"

The vulture replied, "You will kill forty fillies for us, one a day."

The lungs and the liver are for me, the vulture, and the remainder of the meat you
    will give to the hyena."

[After the sacrifices were made, the vulture explained what the descendants of Dinga would find at Kumbi.]

. . . . after their arrival at Kumbi, they will find there a well and inside the well a
    monster.

They will be called upon to make a contract with this creature.

[Djabé Cissé and his people set off with the hyena and the vulture for Kumbi.]

Told by Diara Sylla and Jiri Silla; translated and summarized by Thomas A. Hale.

They walked for forty days before reaching Kumbi. At their arrival the hyena
stopped at the edge of a well and the vulture perched at the top of a tree near
the well.

The vulture said then to the children of Dinga, "Here is Kumbi, here is the well."
Then a loud noise arose from the well.

The voice asked who was there, and the vulture replied that they were the children
of Dinga, and that they had come to settle there.

At these words, an enormous snake rose out of the well. He was very black, he had
a crest on his head like that of a rooster, and the crest was very red.

He said, "No one will settle here."

Djabé replied, "We will settle here, for our father at the end of his life ordered us
to come to Kumbi. And this is certainly Kumbi: here is the well! We shall
settle here."

"Agreed!" said the snake called Bida. "But there are conditions for that."

Djabé declared then, "We are ready to listen to these conditions."

"Fine!" replied Bida.

"Each year," he said, "in the seventh month, on the seventh day of the seventh
month, you will offer me 100 heifers, 100 fillies, and 100 girls."

"Agreed," said Djabé, "but each year, the loss of 100 heifers, 100 fillies, and 100
girls will amount to the ruin of the country."

They bargained and finally agreed on one filly and one girl—but the filly will be the
best in the entire country and the girl the most beautiful in the entire country.

[Djabé won the title of King of Wagadu as the result of a competition to lift four heavy drums.
The snake then gave him conditional power to rule.]

When Djabé was installed as ruler, Bida declared to him that he will be supplied
with people and goods as long as he honors the contract that links them
together.

[A Time for Sacrifice]

[When the time for the sacrifice came next year, the people prepared themselves.]

At the end of the rainy season, in the seventh month and on the seventh day, all
the people gathered and the sacrifice was carried out.

The morning of the sacrifice, the morning of the solemn day, everyone turned up
before the door of the ruler, drummers as well as citizens, all gathered in this
spot.

As for the girl, she was already dressed, dressed in such an extraordinary way that
you had to see it to appreciate it.

The filly was so fat that it was beyond commentary.

When they arrived near the well, the cortege divided in two.

The *griots* were always in front of the ruler, competing with each other in turn
until they arrived at the edge of the well.

Before the *griots* could return to the ruler with their songs, Bida the snake
suddenly surged out of the well and made a terrifying loud noise.

[After coming out and going back into the well twice, the snake appeared again for a final time.]

He wrapped himself around the girl and the filly. He carried them in his lair.
The ruler and his people returned to the town.

[The snake kept his promise. Gold rained down on the country and the people prospered. But during the annual sacrifice to Bida another year, after the third appearance of the snake from the well, a man attacked it.]

Mahamadu the Taciturn cut off his head with his sabre.
At the very moment his head fell away, the serpent cried out: "Seven stars, seven luminous stars,"
"Seven famines, seven great famines,"
"Seven rainy seasons, seven entire rainy seasons."
"No rain will fall in the country of Wagadu."
"And even less gold."
"People will say that Mahamadu the Taciturn ruined Wagadu!"

[The Flight of Wagadu]

[After the flight of the Wagadu people from the land, some people went home to see what was left.]

They found that everyone was dead.
Wagadu emigrated.
It divided into three groups.
One went along the banks of the river.
One group headed toward the Sahel.
And the third left by the middle way.
The one that left by the middle maintained the use of the Soninké language.

[Today, all that remains at Kumbi are some ruins. But the Soninké people live on in many parts of the Sahel from Senegal to Niger. An archaic form of their language has become the occult tongue of Songhay sorcerors and *griots*.]

SONGHAY PEOPLE
West Africa

Mali began to lose control of its territory by the mid-fifteenth century. The Songhay empire, based in Gao on the Niger River in southeastern Mali, expanded to absorb a large part of Mali and other areas. From 1463 to 1492, Sonni Ali Ber laid the foundation for Askia Mohammed, a ruler of Soninké origin who built a vast empire from 1493 to 1528.

Tomb of
the Askia
Dynasty
near Gao,
Mali.

Our knowledge of Songhay history comes both from the Timbuktu chronicles, written in Arabic by Moslem scribes close to the ruling elite, and from *griots*, known in Songhay as *jeseré*, derived from the Soninké *geseré*. Songhay oral narratives were originally chanted in Soninké.

Askia Mohammed spread Islam to new areas of West Africa, and for this reason the religion has a much higher profile here than in the other epics in this section. But traditional Songhay beliefs and magic play equally significant roles. Like Son-Jara and other epic heroes, Askia Mohammed was born under extraordinary circumstances and had to overcome great obstacles. Called Mamar Kassaye (Mohammed, son of Kassaye), he appears as the killer of Sonni Ali Ber, referred to here as his uncle Si.

from The Oral Epic of Askia Mohammed

[By Subterfuge, Kassaye Saves Her Son]

Kassaye is the woman.
It is Si who is the man, it is he who is on the throne, it is he who is the chief.
Kassaye is his sister, she is in his compound.
Any husband who marries Kassaye, and if she gives birth,
The seers have said "Listen"—they told Si it is Kassaye who   5
    will give birth to a child who will kill him and take over the
    throne of Gao.
It is Kassaye who will give birth to a child.
That child will kill Si and will take the position of ruler.

Excerpted from a 1602-line version chanted in Songhay by Nouhou Malio in Saga, Niger, on December 30, 1980, and January 26, 1981. Recorded, translated, annotated, and published by Thomas A. Hale; this is the first English version of the epic.

Si also heard about this.
All the children that Kassaye gave birth to,   10
As soon as Kassaye delivered it, Si killed it.
Every child that Kassaye delivered, as soon as it was born, Si killed it.
Until she had given birth to seven children,
Which her brother Si killed.
Kassaye had enough, she said she would no longer take a husband.   15
She stayed like that.
Si is on his throne,
While Kassaye remained like that.
Until, until, until, until one day, much later, in the middle of the night,
A man came who was wearing beautiful clothes.   20
He was a real man, he was tall, someone who looked good in
white clothes, his clothes were really beautiful.
One could smell perfume everywhere.
He came in to sit down next to Kassaye.
They chatted with each other, they chatted, they chatted.   25
He said to her, "It is really true.
"Kassaye, I would like to make love with you.
"Once we make love together,
"You will give birth to a boy,
"Whom Si will not be able to kill,   30
"It is he who will kill Si and will become the ruler."
Kassaye said to him, "What?"
He said, "By Allah."
She said, "Good, in the name of Allah."
Each night the man came.   35
It is during the late hours that he came.
Each time during the coolness of the late evening.
Until Kassaye became pregnant by him.
Kassaye carried her pregnancy.
Kassaye had a Bargantché captive.   40
It is the Bargantché woman who is her captive, she lives in her house, and she too
    is pregnant.
They remained like that.
Kassaye kneeled down to give birth.
The captive kneeled down to give birth.
So Kassaye, Kassaye gave birth to a boy.   45
The captive gave birth to a girl.
Then Kassaye took the daughter of the captive, she took her home with her.
She took her son and gave it to the captive.
So the people left for the palace.
They said to Si: 50
"The Bargantché captive has given birth."
He said, "What did she get?"
They said, "A boy."

He said, "May Allah be praised, may our Lord give him a long life and may he be
  useful."
Then they were thoughtful for a moment.   55
They got up and informed him that Kassaye had given birth.
They asked, "What did she get?"
They answered, "A girl."
He said, "Have them bring it to me."
They brought it to him, he killed it.   60
It is the boy who remained with the captive and Kassaye.

[By this subterfuge, Kassaye saves her son, who becomes a servant working for his uncle. Of
noble origin, he must nevertheless pass as a slave.]

[Mamar Kassaye Sees His Father]

He became a young man tall and very strong, a tall young man.
The children in the compound,
They are the ones who insult him by saying that they don't know his father.
Also, they call him the little slave of Si.
"The little slave of Si, the little slave of Si."   5
They called him "little slave of Si," and said, "We don't know your father, you
  don't have a father.
"Who is your father?"
Then he came home to his mother's house and told her that the children in the
  compound were really bothering him.
They say to him, "Who is your father?"
She told him, "Go sit down, you'll see your father."   10
She said to him, "Look, take this ring in your hand.
"But don't put it on your finger,
"Until you get to the river.
"Then you put it on your finger.
"At that moment, you will see your father."   15
Mamar took the ring to the river.
Then he put the ring on his middle finger.
The water opened up.
Under the water there are so many cities, so many cities, so many cities, so many
  villages, and so many people.
It is his father too who is the chief.   20
They too get themselves ready, they go out to go to the prayer ground.
He said, "That's the way it is."
His father greets him with an embrace.
There is his son, there is his son.
Yes, the prince whom he fathered while away,   25
The chief's son whom he fathered while away has come.
He said to him, "Now go return to your home, you do not stay here.

"Go return home."

His father gave him a white stallion, really white, really, really, really, really, really, really, really white like, like percale.[1]

He gave him all the things necessary.

He gave him two lances.

He gave him a saber, which he wore.

He gave him a shield.

He bid him good-bye.

[Armed by his real father from the underwater spirit world, Mamar Kassaye sets out to take power from his evil uncle. He chooses to do so on a Moslem holy day. Pretending to demonstrate his loyalty to Si, he races his horse up to the ruler three times in succession, stopping each time just before the ruler.]

[Mamar Kassaye Kills His Uncle]

He and his people go out, they went to the prayer ground.

They are at the prayer ground.

Then Mamar went around them and headed directly for them.

They were about to start the prayer.

They said, "Stop, just stop, a prince from another place is coming to pray with us.   5

"A prince from another place is coming to pray with us."

The horse gallops swiftly, swiftly, swiftly, swiftly, swiftly, swiftly he is
    approaching.

He comes into view suddenly, leaning forward on his mount.

Until, until, until, until, until, until, until he touches the prayer skin of his uncle,
    then he reins his horse there.

Those who know him say that he is like the little captive of Si.   10

Actually, he does resemble the little captive of Si, he has the same look as the little
    captive of Si.

Did you see him! When I saw him I thought that it was the little captive of Si.

He retraced his path only to return again.

Until be brought the horse to the same place, where he reined it again.

Now he made it gallop again.   15

As he approaches the prayer skin of his uncle,

He reins his horse.

He unslung his lance, and pierced his uncle with it until the lance touched the
    prayer skin.

Until the spear went all the way to the prayer skin.

[Mamar Kassaye decides to atone for the killing of his uncle by making a pilgrimage to Mecca, an event that actually took place between 1497 and 1498. On his way, he forces Islam on many peoples.]

---

1. A type of finely woven cotton cloth.

[Mamar Kassaye Imposes Islam on Many Villages]

In each village where he stopped during the day, for example, this place,
If he arrives in mid-afternoon, he stops there and spends the night.
Early in the morning, they pillage and they go on to the next village, for example,
  Liboré.
The cavalier who goes there,
He traces on the ground for the people the plan for the mosque.   5
Once the plan for the foundation is traced,
The people build the mosque.
It is at that time,
Mamar Kassaye comes to dismount from his horse.

· · ·

They teach them prayers from the Koran.   10
Any villages that refuse, he destroys the village, burns it, and moves on.

[After his return from Mecca, Mamar Kassaye continues to impose Islam on the territories he conquers. But he does not always succeed. He cannot escape the fact that, when
he was an infant, he was nursed during the day by a woman from another ethnic group,
the Bargantché of northern Benin. This milk tie is as strong as the tie of blood that
links people together in families and clans. For this reason, when Mamar Kassaye sets
out to conquer the Bargantché, he encounters difficulty and must call upon his mother for
help.]

[Mamar Kassaye Asks His Mother For Help and Escapes]

His mother, Kassaye, had told him, "Long ago,
"I told him not to fight against the Bargantché.
"He cannot beat them, for he has in his stomach the milk of a Bargantché."

Now, she took some cotton seeds in her hand and said, "Take."
She took an egg, a chicken egg, and she said to him, "Take."   5
She took a stone, a river stone, she told him, "Take."
"If you go," if he goes to the Bargantché,
If the Bargantché chase him,
He should put all his horses before him and he should be the only one behind.
He should scatter the cotton seeds behind him.   10
They will become a dense bushy barrier between him and them.
If they chop it down,
This dense bush will not prevent anything.
They will clear the bush in order to find him.
If the bush does not help at all,   15
This time, if they are still hunting him,
He should put all his cavalry in front of him.
He should throw the stone behind him.
It will become a big mountain that will be a barrier between them.

If the big mountain does not help them,   20
And when they chase him again,
He should put all his cavalry in front of him again,
Leaving himself in the rear.
He should throw the egg behind him.
The egg will become a river to separate them.   25

He escaped from the Bargantché, the Bargantché who live along the river.
He never again fought against them.
Now, he just passed through their country, to go and start again his reign.

[Nouhou Malio does not tell us what happened to Mamar Kassaye. But we know from the chronicles that he was overthrown by one of his sons, Askia Moussa, in 1528, and exiled to an island in the Niger River. He died ten years later. The empire then experienced a series of rulers descended from Askia Mohammed—some good, some bad—for the remainder of the century. On April 12, 1591, an army sent by the Sultan of Morocco across the Sahara defeated the Songhay, an event that not only destroyed their empire, but marked the final chapter in the rise of a great Sahelian civilization whose stories still echo across the region in the tales of modern *griots*.]

BEDOUIN PEOPLE
Egypt

The action of *Sirat Bani Hilal,* an epic that recounts the migration of the Hilali, a group of Bedouin Arabs, from Arabia to Tunis, takes place in the eighth or ninth century. The excerpt presented here was recorded on March 10, 1983, by one of the many Egyptian poet-reciters who keep this ancient tradition alive. "The Story of Amir Khafaji" recounts the rescue of Dawaba, daughter of King Amir Khafaji of Iraq, by the hero Abu Zayd (who, however, does not marry her, as he would in a European folktale). Enjoying the king's hospitality as they travel westward, Abu Zayd and his three nephews are assumed to be slaves because they say they are wandering poets and praise-singers. Abu Zayd entertains the court. Dawaba, Amir's daughter, violates custom to descend among the Arabs because she hopes that Abu Zayd's nephew, the handsome Yunis, will perform. To save the situation, Abu Zayd, who really is a poet, recites until dawn. Then when a black slave arrives bearing a letter, Abu Zayd asks to see it; the slave, incredulous at his literacy, accompanies him into Amir's *diwan,* or men's council. The king weeps on discovering that the rival king al-Tash al-Khorasani is extorting tribute, including Dawaba, from him and that he threatens the destruction of Iraq if it is not delivered. During the recitation, the audience comments upon the behavior of the characters.

from *Sirat Bani Hilal*

The Story of Amir Khafaji

Dawaba descended in full regalia [*adalha*[1]]
(Audience: Really.)

from atop the lofty fortress,
kohl[2]-darkened eyes beautifying her form, as was her custom
at her father's, and she went to the dwelling.
The maiden entered the *diwans*,   5
she is eloquent with wisdom for all,
she meets the Arabs in session,
Arabs honored with chairs.[3]
"Dawaba," he said, "O handsome of stature,
O maiden, perform now your duties,   10
I hope you know the proper art.
Why do you come among the Arabs?
Why do you come inside the *diwans*?
O woman wearing earrings, coquettish,
a scandal, a lack of conduct: 15
you are a dishonor among the tribes.
Is this a council for women?
I swear by the path of trust,
a scandal, a lack of conduct,
O maiden, be wary of censure!"   20
Dawaba says to him, "O my father,
yield me the sanctuary of your trust."
"Dawaba, your words speak to me,
may you be welcome among the Arabs."
"O my father, if the slave's like this,   25
then how are his masters in poetry?
Then how are his masters in poetry?
O dark one, why not be silent,
let the handsome one bring forth an ode."
(Audience: Really she wants to get Yunis[4] to speak any way she can)
Yunis said, said the Emir Yunis: 30
"What's to be done about unjust times?
We are neither poets nor praise-singers,
have not even a verse inside a poem,
we shut fast a window on those troubles

Told by Awadallah Abd aj-Jalil Ali; translated by Susan Slyomovic.

---

1. Makeup, earrings.
2. Black eye makeup used by women.

3. Chairs are a sign of government and authority according to the bard.
4. Nephew of the hero, Abu Zayd.

and Abu Zayd flings wide paths and doors." 35
Abu Zayd said to him, "O my nephew,"
in the language of Najd, a strange language,
"O my son, cease your words,
O Yunis, your words are childish words.
I am your uncle the hero Abu Zayd, 40
the lion does not eat my portion,
neither in our *wadis*[5] nor our homeland.
I myself am the warrior Abu Zayd,
I have sworn not to pass by the wretched.
O son, cease your speaking, 45
when am I ever confused how to reject a request?"
Abu Zayd said to him, "O Amir,
hear my words, O Sultan:
the day we set forth from our country
we spread forth our hands praying for the inhabitants, 50
each made poetry for thirty,
every last one, thirty days.
They were standing in rows,
by God, this night we spend with you, O Sultan,
if you bid me to stop I shall stop, 55
as my gift, I refuse no fee."
He said to him, "O poet, divert us,
your night will be the happiest of times."
He said, "O night," to invoke the Beautiful One,[6]
an invocation to the Prophet, sheltered by clouds. 60
He drew on the bowstring, sang of the Beloved
until dawn's rays widened into light.

Abu Zayd stared with his eyes,
yet performed the obligatory prayer to the Merciful One.
He observes the slave coming forward, 65
with a firman[7] stuck in his head,
with a letter stuck in his head.
See the slave, purchased with money!
Abu Zayd went towards him,
he said to him, "Good morning, O lad of Mirgan, 70
good morning, O my cousin.
(Audience: Really)
My mother and your mother were sisters,
as for you, your mother is Masuda
and I, my mother was named Zayd al-Mal,
but where are you going and from where do you come? 75

---

5. Oases.   7. Royal order in writing.
6. The Prophet.

The news of yourself, give me a sign."
The slave said to him, "I come from al-Khorasani,
from al-Tash al-Khorasani."
Abu Zayd said to him, "Good, show me the letter,
I would see the writing of the title."   80
He said to Abu Zayd, "Enough, O vile black slave
ill-mannered, you show no respect.
How can Mameluke[8] writing
be read by slaves from Sunnar?"
Abu Zayd nagged at him   85
until he caused him to enter the diwan,
(*Audience: he is politicking*)
when he caused him to enter the diwans
he found the assembly abustle.
(*Audience: he fell into the trap*)

The slave said to Amir, "Behold, O father of Dawaba,
a letter from al-Tash al-Khorasani."
When Amir saw the letter,   90
his tears fell first, wetting his caftan
(*Audience: his color changed*)
Amir wept, tears of his eyes,
his tears upon the cheek, descending,
fate and parting tormented him,   95
all present were astonished by him.
Amir wept, tears of his eyes,
when no one fulfills one's needs
when no one asks after one's sadness, why?"
His tears fell first, wetting his cheeks,   100
he wept, drenching his clothes.
Salama the hero had said to him:
"Why tears descending, what happened to you?
O stalwart camel, you spit in rage,
O Amir, why weep, what happened to you?   105
You weep, O Shaykh, and what to do?
I swear by the path of trust!"
Amir said to Abu Zayd, "Then forbear your words,
an evil day brought you among us,
(*Audience: O Protector*)
so you O little slave are ill-omened,   110
they turn you loose in the wadis,[9]
The night you passed in my home
you brought it, like the close walls, down upon me."
Abu Zayd said to him, "Show me the letter,

---

8. The Mamelukes were the dominant class in   **9.** River valleys.
Egypt.

I shall explain what the address contains."
Amir said to him, "Then you know how to read?"
Abu Zayd said to him, "I am schooled in the Koran.
(*Audience: ya salam*)[10]
First, this old man[11] is a healer,
I heal all the sick,
secondly, this old man is a preacher,
I read the a's and d's,
thirdly, this old man is a poet,
I make art and bring forth poems,
fourthly, this old man is a horseman,
my spirit is young in my spear thrust."
Then Amir gave him the letter,
Abu Zayd set forth the firman:
"The letter begins, the Jew says:
O Amir,[12] I want tribute.
Beware refusing the tithe of goods!
I want ninety she-camels,
fruitful, long-necked ones,
I want ninety he-camels
of the spitting kind, roaring ones,
I want ninety kohl-black horses,
their tail hairs sweeping the sands,
I want ninety portions of flour,
the choice grains that sleep on the sieve
(*Audience: that's the way it is*)
and ninety portions of henna
for the hair of the foreigner's daughters.
We want ninety lances,
their spearpoints, two thirds of a gintar.
I want ninety spears,
whose teeth wound men
and besides all these,
hear my words, O son of Durgham,
from you, I want Dawaba
in the temple, she will bring forth poems.
I want, I want ninety fair maidens,
the choicest of the daughters of Islam.
If you bring all these
we shall meet as friends meet,
and if you do not bring all these
I proclaim destruction for your homeland!"

115

120

125

130

135

140

145

150

---

10. An exclamation.
11. Conversing with Amir, Abu Zayd refers to

himself as "your uncle" in the sense of
"this old man in front of you."
12. Prince.

MANINKA PEOPLE
Mali

"Son-Jara" is an epic of the Mandé, whose languages include Mandinka, Maninka, Khasonke, Bamana, Jula, and Wangara. The indigenous term for the old empire of Mali, which flourished in the thirteenth and fourteenth centuries, is *Manden,* sometimes spelled *Mandin* or *Manding.* A person from the Manden heartland is a *Maninka,* sometimes spelled Malinké.

In the wake of the regional instability left by the decline of Ghana, Mali rose in the thirteenth century because of the efforts of Son-Jara (or Sundiata) Keita. Mali reached a peak in the mid-fourteenth century, when Mansa Musa made an extraordinary pilgrimage to Mecca. Today the cultural heritage of the Mali empire is preserved by *griots* who are called *jeli* or *jali* in the many Mandé languages of Mali, eastern Senegal, The Gambia, Guinea-Bissau, upper Guinea, northern Liberia, and northwestern Côte d'Ivoire*. The peoples of the ancient Manden region—the Maninka, the Bambana, the Jula, and the Mandinka, among others—recognize Son-Jara and his accomplishments every seven years by sending representatives to reroof a sacred house in Kangaba, a town in southwestern Mali that is the center of the Manden. From Ghana to Mali we see an evolution in the form of the West African epic. The 3083-line source of these excerpts is more detailed and more focused on the rise and exploits of a single hero, and it contains references to the new religion in the region, Islam.

from *The Oral Epic of Son-Jara*

[A Family Rivalry]

[Fa-Digi Sisòkò explains how two hunters managed to kill a buffalo that had been devastating the farmers of Du. They received as a reward a woman named Sugulun Kòndè, who rejected them. They then traded her to the King of the Manden,[1] Fata Magan, in exchange for his sister, Nakana Tiliba, and a token that the King had received from his ancestor Bilal, a man of African origin who was the first *muezzin* or prayer-caller for Muhammad, founder of Islam.]

"You must give me your ugly maid.   (Mmm)
"My forefather Bilal,   (Indeed)
"When he departed from the Messenger of God,   (True)
"He designed a certain token,   (Mmm)
"Saying that his ninth descendant,   (Indeed) 5

Told by Fa-Digi Sisòkò in the Maninka language on March 9, 1968, in Kita, Mali; recorded by Charles S. Bird and translated, annotated, and published by John W. Johnson in 1986. This is the first linear, or verse, version in English from the Mandé heartland of what has become the most widely read epic from West Africa.

*Previously known in English as the Ivory Coast.

---

1. The homeland of the Mandé-speaking peoples.

"Having taken his first wife,   (True)
"When he takes his second wife,   (Indeed)
"Must add that token to that marriage.   (Mmm)
"I am adding that token
"Together with Nakana Tiliba,   (Mmm)   10
"And giving them to you,
"You must give me your ugly little maid."
That token was added to Nakana Tiliba,
Exchanging her for Sugulun Kòndè.   (Indeed)
It is said that Fata Magan, the Handsome   15
Took the Kòndè maiden to bed.   (Mmm)
His Berete wife became pregnant.   (Indeed)
His Kòndè wife became pregnant.   (Indeed)

[Birth of Son-Jara]

[The birth of children both to the new wife and the King's first wife set the stage for family rivalry known in the Manden as *fadenya,* or father-centeredness. It is marked by competition between sons of the same father but different mothers. In the short run the outcome of the rivalry between Son-Jara and his half-brother determined who would rule the Manden. In the excerpts that follow, Wizard, Biribiriba, and Magan Konate are praise names for Son-Jara based on his talents, actions, and paternal lineage. Couscous is a dish of North African origin composed of a meat-and-vegetables stew on a bed of steamed semolina.]

One day as dawn was breaking,   (Indeed)
The Berete woman gave birth to a son.   (Indeed)
She cried out, "Ha! Old Women!   (Indeed)
"That which causes co-wife conflict
"Is nothing but the co-wife's child.   (True)   5
"Go forth and tell my husband   (Indeed)
"His first wife has borne him a son."   (Indeed)
    . . .
The Berete woman,
She summoned to her a holy-man,
Charging him to pray to God,   (Indeed)   10
So Son-Jara would not walk.   (Indeed)
And summoned to her an Omen Master,   (Indeed)
For him to read the signs in sand,   (Indeed)
So Son-Jara would not walk.   (Indeed)
For nine years, Son-Jara crawled upon the ground.   (Indeed)   15
Magan Kònatè could not rise.   (Indeed)
    . . .
On the tenth day of Dòmba,   (Indeed)
The Wizard's mother cooked some couscous,   (Indeed)
Sacrificial couscous for Son-Jara.
Whatever woman's door she went to,   (Indeed)   20
The Wizard's mother would cry: (Indeed)

"Give me some sauce of baobab[2] leaf."   (Indeed)
The woman would retort,
"I have some sauce of baobab leaf,
"But it is not to give to you.
"Go tell that cripple child of yours   25

"That he should harvest some for you.   (Mmm)
"Twas my son harvested these for me."   (True)

[Baobab Tree]

[The scene of the baobab tree marks the beginning of Son-Jara's rise to power. *Griots,* realizing the significance of what is happening, begin to compose praises to celebrate him. He shows his hunting prowess early and gives other signs of his future greatness. The audience constantly replies to and reinforces the bard. His mother is the first to praise him.]

  "*O Kapok Tree and Flame Tree!*"   (Fa-Digi, that's true)
"My mother,   (Mmm)
"That baobab there in Manden country,
"That baobab from which the best sauce comes,   (Indeed)
"Where is that baobab, my mother?"   (Indeed)   5
"Ah, my lame one,   (Indeed)
"You have yet to walk,"   (Indeed)

The Wizard took his right foot,
And put it before his left.   (Indeed)
His mother followed behind him,   10
And sang these songs for him:
  "*Tunyu Tanya!*   (Indeed)
  "*Brave men fit well among warriors!*   (Indeed)
  "*Tunyu tanya!*   (Indeed)
  "*Brave men fit well among warriors!*   (Indeed)   15
  "*Ma'an Kònatè, you have risen!*"   (Indeed)

  "*Muddy water,*   (Indeed)
  "*Do not compare yourself to water among the stones.*   (Indeed)
  "*That among the stones is pure, wasili!*   (Indeed)
  "   (Indeed)   20
  "   (Indeed)
  "*And a good reputation.*   (Indeed)
  "*Khalif Magan Kònatè has risen.*   (True)

  "*Great snake, O great snake,*   (Indeed)
  "*I will tolerate you.*   (Indeed)   25
  "*Should you confront me, toleration.*   (Indeed)

---

2. A very large and distinctive tree that serves
   as a rich source of sustenance for both
   humans and animals throughout the Sahel.

"O great snake upon the path,   (Indeed)
"Whatever confronts me, I will tolerate."   (Indeed)

"Arrow-shaft of happiness.   (Indeed)
"It is in one hundred.   (Indeed)   30
"The one hundred dead,
"All but Son-Jara.   (True)
"The higher stones get crushed!   (Indeed)
"Who can mistake the Destroyer-of-Origins!
"And this by the hand of Nare Magan Kònatè!"   35

Hey! Biribiriba came forward.   (Indeed)
He shook the baobab tree.   (Indeed)
A young boy fell out.
His leg was broken.
The bards thus sing, "Leg-Crushing-Ruler!   40
"Magan Kònatè has risen!"   (Indeed)
He shook the baobab again.   (Indeed)
Another young boy fell out.
His arm was broken   (Indeed)
The bards thus sing, "Arm-Breaking-Ruler!   45
"Magan Kònatè has risen!"   (Indeed)
He shook the baobab again.   (Indeed)
Another young boy fell out.   (Indeed)
His neck was broken.   (Indeed)
And thus the bards sing, "Neck-Breaking-Ruler!   50
"Magan Kònatè has risen!"   (Indeed)
The Wizard uprooted the baobab tree,
And laid it across his shoulder.   (Mmm)
Nare Magan Kònatè rose up.   (Indeed)

A crowd of women surged out: yrrrrrrr.   (Indeed)   55
    "Why have you come today?   (Indeed)
    "What a spectacle!   (Indeed)
    "Have they no reason to be here?   (Indeed)
    "What a spectacle!   (Indeed)

    "O witch-wives!   (Indeed)   60
    "O witch-wives of the Manden!
    "You go find the answer.   (Indeed)
    "Today's cannot be found by searching."   (Indeed)

    "The Master of men, O power, power, power.   (Indeed)
    "One without people, the wind, the wind.   65
    "The woman put the child in a web,
    "A web of sorcery!"   (Mmm)

They fixed their eyes on Magan Son-Jara standing there:
"Come, let us go!

"Nare Magan Kònatè has risen!   70

"Living alone, I know it.   (Indeed)
"After coming to understand that,   (Indeed)
"Bearer of good children, have no shame.   (Indeed)
"Whenever there's a crowd, have no shame."

"Having power,   (Indeed)   75
"If you prepare yourself for the powerful,
"They will respect you."   (Indeed)

"The pocket sees only today,
"Its eye is not on tomorrow.   (Indeed)
"The pocket sees only today,   (Indeed)   80
"Its eye is not on tomorrow.
"A fortunate man's happiness occurs while he lives.   (Indeed)
"The unfortunate man's happiness occurs after he dies.
"O misery!   (Indeed)
"But one should not kill himself for misery.   85
"No one knows where misery leads.   (True)
"Khalif Magan Kònatè!

"The one for those behind is Kapok.
"Tunyu tanya!   (Indeed)
"Ours is the Flame Tree,   90
"The golden Flame Tree!   (Mmm)
"Khalif Magan Kònatè has risen!"

Biribiriba came forward.   (Mmm)
He planted the baobab behind his mother's house:
"In and about the Manden,   (Mmm)   95
"From my mother they must seek these leaves!"   (Mmm)
To which his mother said, "I do not think I heard."   (Mmm)
"Ah, my mother,   (Indeed)
"Now all the Manden baobabs are yours."
"I do not think I heard."   100
"Ah, my mother,   (Indeed)
"All those women who refused you leaves,
"They all must seek those leaves from you."   (Indeed)
His mother fell upon her knees, gejebu![3]
On both her knees,   105
And laid her head aside the baobab.   (Indeed)

"For years and years,
"My ear was deaf.   (Indeed)

---

3. An ideophone—a descriptive word that creates an emotion—for the sound of Son-Jara's mother kneeling on the ground; later ideophones are found on lines 184, 187, and 235: "fèsè," "dèndèlen," and "bilika." (See footnote 6.)

"Only this year
"Has my ear heard news. 110
"Khalif Magan Kònatè has risen!" (That's true)
Biribiriba! (Indeed)
Since he began to walk, (Indeed)
Whenever he went into the bush, (Mmm)
Were he to kill some game, (Indeed) 115
He would give his elder the tail,
And think no more of it.

    . . .

    Took up the bow! (Indeed)
    Simbon, Master-of-the-Bush!
    Took up the bow! 120
    Took up the bow!
    Ruler of bards and smiths (Indeed)
    Took up the bow!
    Took up the bow!
    The Kòndè woman's child, 125
    Answerer-of-Needs,
    He took up the bow.
    Sugulun's Ma'an took up the bow!

    The Wizard has risen!
    King of Nyani, Nare Magan Kònatè! 130
    The Wizard has risen! (Indeed)
Ah! Bèmba! (Indeed)
Whenever he went to the bush, (Indeed)
Were he to kill some game, (Indeed)
He would give to his elder the tail, 135
And think no more of it.

    . . .

As Biribiriba walked forth one day, (That's true)
A jinn[4] came upon him,
And laid his hand on Son-Jara's shoulder:
"O Son-Jara! (Mmm) 140
"In the Manden, there's a plot against you. (Mmm)
"That spotted dog you see before you, (Indeed)
"Is an offering made against you, (Indeed) 145
"So that you not rule the bards, (Indeed)
"So that you not rule the smiths,
"So, the three and thirty warrior clans,
"That you rule over none of them. (Mmm)
"When you go forth today, (Mmm) 150
"Make an offering of a safo-dog, (Indeed)

---

4. A spirit.

"Should God will it,
"The Manden will be yours!"   (Indeed)

Ah! Bèmba!
On that, Biribiriba went forth, my father,   155
And made an offering of a safo-dog,[5]
And hung a weight around its neck,
And fastened an iron chain about it.   (Indeed)
Even tomorrow morning,
The Europeans will imitate him.   160
Whenever the Europeans leave a dog,   (Mmm)
Its neck weight,
They fasten that dog with an iron chain, Manden!   (Indeed)

O! Bèmba!
He hung a weight around the dog's neck,   165
And fastened it with a chain.   (Mmm)
That done, whatever home he passed before,   (Indeed)
The people stood gaping at him:
"Causer-of-Loss!   (Indeed)
"A cow with its neckweight,   170
"But a dog with a neckweight?"   (Indeed)
To which the Wizard did retort:
"Leave me be!   (True)
"Cast your eyes on the dog of the prince.
"There's not a tooth in that dog's mouth!   175
"But there are teeth in my dog's mouth,
"My commoner's dog. Leave me be!
"My dog's name is Tomorrow's Affair."   (Indeed)

Son-Jara's sacrificial dog,
That dog was called Tomorrow's Affair.   180

From his neckweight he broke loose,
And also from his chain,   (Indeed)
And charged the dog of Dankaran Tuman,   (Indeed)
And ripped him into shreds, fèsè fèsè fèsè!   (Indeed)
And stacked one piece atop the other.   (Indeed)   185
The mother of Dankaran Tuman, she wrung her hands atop her head,
And gave a piercing cry: "dèndèlen!   (Indeed)
"That a dog would bite a dog,   (Indeed)
"A natural thing in the Manden.   (Indeed)
"That a dog would kill a dog,   190

---

5. A favorite sacrifice, but its exact nature is
   obscure. The dog is considered an animal
   possessed of extraordinary occult power.

"A natural thing in the Manden.
"That a dog shred another like an old cloth,
"My mother, there must be something with his master!"
Dankaran Tuman replied, "Ah! my mother,   (Mmm)
"I called my dog Younger-Leave-Me-Be.   (Mmm)   195
"Ah! My mother, do not sever the bonds of family.   (True)
"My mother!   (Indeed)
"That is the dog that stalked the bush
"To go and kill some game,
"Bringing it back to me, my mother.   (True)   200
"Do not sever the bonds of family, my mother!"   (True)

The mother of Dankaran Tuman had no answer: (Indeed)
"One afternoon, the time will come for Son-Jara to depart.   (Mmm)
"Indeed what the wise men have said,   (Mmm)
"His time is for the morrow.   (Mmm)   205
"The one that I have borne,   (Mmm)
"He is being left behind without explanation.   (Mmm)
"Son-Jara,   (Mmm)
"The Kònde woman's offspring,   (Mmm)
"He will take the Manden tribute,   (Mmm)   210
"And he will rule the bards,   (Mmm)
"And he will rule the smiths,   (Indeed)
"And rule the funès and the cordwainers.   (Indeed)
"The Manden will be his.
"That time will yet arrive,   (Indeed)   215
"And that by the hand of Nare Magan Kònate.
"Nothing leaves its time behind."
    O Biribiriba!
    Kirikisa, Spear-of-Access, Spear-of-Service!
    People of Kaya, Son-Jara entered Kaya.   220
    All this by the hand of Nare Magan Kònate.
    Gaining power is not easy!   (Indeed)
Ah! Bèmba!   (Indeed)
The mother of King Dankaran Tuman,   (Indeed)
When the Wizard had left the bush,   (Indeed)   225
And offered his flesh-and-blood-brother the tail,   (Indeed)
And when he said, "Here take the tail,"
She retorted: "Your mother, Sugulun Kònde, will take the tail!   (Indeed)
"And your younger sister, Sugulun Kulukan,   (Indeed)
"And your younger brother, Manden Bukari.   (Indeed)   230
"Go and seek a place to die,   (Indeed)
"If not, I will chop through your necks,
"Cutting a handspan down into the ground.
"Be it so; you'll never return to the Manden again."   (Indeed)

Son-Jara bitterly wept, bilika[6] bilika!	(Indeed) 235
And went to tell his mother.	(Indeed)
His mother said,	(Indeed)
"Ah! My child,	(Indeed)
"Be calm. Salute your brother.	(Indeed) 240
"Had he banished you as a cripple,	
"Where would you have gone?	
"Let us at least agree on that.	
"Let us depart.	
"What sitting will not solve,	245
"Travel will resolve."	(That's true)

[Son-Jara's Sister Is of Help]

[Son-Jara grows up, becomes a great hunter, and relinquishes his claim to the throne after the death of his father. His half-brother, Dankaran Tuman, forces Son-Jara into exile at the insistence of his mother, the powerful and jealous first wife. Son-Jara returns later to a homeland conquered by the sorcerer king Sumamuru. Unable to defeat the enemy at first because of Sumamuru's far greater occult power, Son-Jara retreats. But his sister offers to help.]

Son-Jara's flesh-and-blood-sister, Sugulun Kulunkan,	(Indeed)
She said, "O Magan Son-Jara,	(Indeed)
"One person cannot fight this war.	(Indeed)
"Let me go seek Sumamuru.	(Indeed)
"Were I then to reach him,	5
"To you I will deliver him,	(Indeed)
"So that the folk of the Manden be yours,	(Indeed)
"And all the Mandenland your shield."	(Indeed)
Sugulun Kulunkan arose,	(Indeed)
And went up to the gates of Sumamuru's fortress:	(Indeed) 10

"Brave child of the Warrior,	
"And Deliverer-of-the-Benign.	
"Sumamuru came amongst us	(Indeed)
"With pants of human skin.	
"Sumamuru came amongst us	(Indeed)
"With shirt of human skin.	15
"Sumamuru came amongst us	
"With helm of human skin.	(Indeed)
"Come open the gates, Susu Mountain Sumamuru!	(Indeed) 20
"Come make me your bed companion!"	(Indeed)
Sumamuru came to the gates:	(Indeed)

---

6. An ideophone for the sound of falling tears. An *ideophone* is a descriptive word that creates an emotion. "It creates a picture; it is sensual, enabling the listener to identify a feeling, a sound, color, texture, expression, movement, or silence through his own senses. The ideophone is poetic; it is in the purest sense imagery" (Philip A. Noss, "Description in Gbaya Literary Art," in *African Folklore*, ed. Richard M. Dorson. Garden City: Doubleday, 1972, p. 75).

"What manner of person are you?"   (Indeed)
"It is I Sugulun Kulunkan!"   (Indeed)
"Well, now, Sugulun Kulunkan,   (Indeed) 25
"If you have come to trap me,   (Indeed)
"To turn me over to some person,   (Indeed)
"Know that none can ever vanquish me.   (Indeed)
"I have found the Manden secret,   (Indeed)

He lay Sugulun Kulunkan down on the bed.   (Indeed) 30
After one week had gone by,
Sugulun Kulunkan spoke up: (Indeed)
"Ah, my husband,   (Indeed)
"Will you not let me go to the Manden,   (Indeed)
"That I may get my bowls and spoons,   35
"For me to build my household here?"   (Indeed)

Sugulun returned to reveal those secrets
To her flesh-and-blood-brother, Son-Jara.   (Indeed)
The sacrifices did Son-Jara thus discover.   (Indeed)

[Son-Jara Defeats Sumamuru]

[Armed with the information needed to defeat Sumamuru, Son-Jara sets off with his army to attack the enemy. After a series of battles, he and his lieutenants close in on Sumamuru. Their victory sets the stage for the rise of the Mali empire. In the final lines, Sumamuru disappears into a mountain at the village of Kulu-Kòrò, thirty miles northeast of Bamako, capital of present-day Mali.]

Fa-Koli with his darts charged up:
  "O Colossus,   (Indeed)
  "We have taken you!   (That's the truth)
  "We have taken you, Colossus!
  "We have taken you, Colossus!   5
  "We have taken you!"   (Indeed)
Tura Magan held him at bladepoint.   (Indeed)
Sura, the Jawara patriarch held him at bladepoint.   (Indeed)
Fa-Koli came up and held him at bladepoint.
Son-Jara held him at bladepoint: (Indeed) 10
  "We have taken you, Colossus!   (That's the truth)
  "We have taken you!"   (Indeed)
Sumamuru dried up on the spot: nyònyòwu!   (Indeed)
He has become the sacred fetish of Kulu-Kòrò   (Indeed)
The Bambara[7] worship that now, my father.   15
Susu Mountain Sumamuru,
He became that sacred fetish. (That's the truth, indeed, father, yes, yes, yes, yes)

---

7. A Mandè people living in Mali. They have remained most strongly attached to their own belief system and most resistant to Islam.

Gianlorenzo Bernini, *The Ecstasy of St. Teresa*, 1645–52. Marble, lifesize. Cornaro Chapel, S. Maria della Vittoria, Rome.

SECTION VII
Early Modern Europe

The early modern period in European literature extends from the late fourteenth century to about 1750, from the Renaissance to the Baroque period, and finally to neoclassicism. The Renaissance is most clearly distinguished from the medieval period by a distinctly different attitude toward the culture of ancient Greece and Rome. Although there was an awareness during the Middle Ages of the many remains, physical and literary, of ancient culture, such things were not at the center of medieval concerns. The Renaissance had begun in Italy in the fourteenth century and from there spread to the other parts of Europe. Ancient culture was viewed as a kind of model, a way to understand human experience. It was a time of cultural rebirth, "rebirth" being the meaning of the French word "renaissance," which was later applied to the period. Renaissance scholars eagerly cultivated the artifacts of ancient culture. In literature this meant locating, editing, and publishing ancient manuscripts, often hidden away and preserved in monastery libraries. Understanding these texts involved mastering the intricacies of the classical languages, especially Latin. This led to the birth of the science of philology, the technical study of the language found in these texts.

Complicating this enterprise was the fact that ancient Greek and Roman culture had been pagan while European culture was now Christian. The Catholic Church was the only organized religious body—aside from small Jewish communities—at the beginning of the Early Modern period. The new methods of studying and editing ancient literary texts could be applied to Christian texts as well, to the Bible and to the early Christian writings of the fathers of the Church. These techniques, combined with nationalist stirrings in many countries and what were perceived as abuses within the Catholic Church, resulted in a period of religious upheaval that swept through the sixteenth century. The result was that the sixteenth century was racked by religious wars, which finally ended in a permanent division of Europe: the Protestant North and the Catholic South.

A basic preoccupation of Renaissance scholars was the search for self-knowledge. It was here that the classical models seemed especially useful: if you could understand your own experience in terms of the experiences described in classical literature, your own experience became more meaningful. This secular movement was known as humanism, for its concentration on human values and possibilities. Renaissance literature thus often had an introspective quality that was lacking during the Middle Ages. It was a period that developed a new interest in autobiographical writing, as we will see in Montaigne's "Of Cannibals," presented in this section.

Technological developments also generated a reshaping of European society at the beginning of the late medieval period. Contemporary observers were ambivalent. The invention of the printing press was a benefit while the newly discovered gunpowder was an evil. The fact that a common soldier could lay low a nobleman with a simple firearm, or that artillery made armor increasingly useless except for show, transformed military chivalry into mere display, although display itself was significant for this culture. Nevertheless, the development of the printed book was to be the distinctive hallmark of the period. Texts, ancient and modern, could be disseminated in a standardized form more quickly and more inexpensively than handwritten manuscripts, thus making the knowledge of the period accessible to a far greater number of readers.

A single event was to decisively reshape the view of the world in this period: the discovery of the New World by Columbus in 1492. It was an era of exploration, of colonization and economic expansion, which rarely was for the good of native populations but inspired the European imagination. Such discoveries had few precedents in classical literature and previous European experience. The chief European contact with an alien civilization had been a long and complex interaction with the Muslim countries around the Mediterranean. The discovery of America encouraged other voyages that led to a bewildering variety of cultural otherness and brought Europe into more intimate contact with the cultures of Asia and Africa. This confrontation with non-European otherness resulted in two conflicting tendencies. On the one hand, there was the kind of self-questioning we see in Montaigne's essay on the cannibals. On the other, there was the conviction that the Christian culture of Europe was superior to other cultures, an attempted denial of the other that was to result in the seventeenth century in the rise of racism and colonialism. But the disquieting presence of the other remained impossible to ignore.

Renaissance culture, like the periods that immediately followed it, was obsessed by form. A renewed interest in the rules of art and writing of the ancient classics focused attention on the careful creation of form, on what we would call technique. Form itself became a kind of meaning, and some literary forms became very closely associated with certain kinds of subject matter. In poetry, the sonnet is a clear example of this, perfected according to Renaissance standards, by

Petrarch in the fourteenth century. The sonnet was associated with frustrated love, both physical and spiritual. Merely glancing at a poem and seeing that it was a sonnet raised expectations in a reader that skillful poets could shape through the way they made use of the sonnet form. In prose, the concern for form resulted in a renewed interest in the principles of classical rhetoric, the art of arranging language so as to make it more persuasive. The Roman orator Cicero was a model in this area, a model that writers could imitate or—as often in the seventeenth century—react against.

The baroque period responded to Renaissance form by distorting it, by twisting its shapes to express a vision of a world of extremes, such as that of God and man, very difficult to reconcile. Neoclassicism was to emerge in the seventeenth century as a reaction to this. Obsessed with symmetry and balance, it dominated Europe through the eighteenth century. The neoclassicists sought to express attitudes and ideas that were seen as having universal value, and Renaissance practice was codified into neoclassical law, which allowed no exceptions. The center of neoclassical culture in Europe by the middle of the seventeenth century was in France, where it had become the official artistic policy of the French court, and from there it spread to the rest of Europe where it was eagerly, and more or less effectively, imitated.

The works in this section exemplify these movements and impulses. The central figure in the early northern Renaissance was Erasmus, who dominated the European intellectual culture of his time. His editions of the New Testament and of the church fathers, his voluminous writings on social and religious questions, his many letters, and his varied humorous works offered a stature few have had since. But in the sixteenth century Europe was splitting into Protestant and Catholic camps and his attempts to mediate between the two had little lasting effect, and his vision of a harmonious society organized around a Christianity that was understood primarily as perfect charity was not a forecast of what would follow.

At the same time in Italy Machiavelli was working out ideas about the control of political power, a view that he believed much more realistic. Italy was still the center of European culture in the early sixteenth century. A key figure, because of the brilliance of his work as a sculptor, painter, and architect, and because of his long life, was Michelangelo, who has since also come to be recognized as one of the most accomplished poets of his time. His exchange of sonnets with Vittoria Colonna emphasized spiritual love and demonstrated one set of possibilities for the form. The contrast between Michelangelo's muscular energy and agitation and Colonna's serenity is a striking one for two people who were so close. A different kind of longing is expressed in the sonnets of Gaspara Stampa, in which physical desire is central and overpowering. But in all these poems, the energy is controlled by the tight and precise form that focuses the energy all the more sharply.

In Spain religious and mystical impulses were given striking expression in the prose writings of Saint Teresa of Avila, whose accounts of her own religious experience bear classical and definitive witness to human consciousness overwhelmed by a sense of God's presence.

The literary culture of France in the mid-sixteenth century was especially brilliant, as Italian and classical forms and impulses were being adopted by an already vigorous native tradition. Here too the contribution of women writers is significant. The sonnet was effectively transposed into French and Lyons became an important poetic center. Among the several women active there, Louise Labé was especially successful in using this cultivated form for the elegant expression of her own longings. Marguerite d' Angoulême, sister of Francis I and later to become Queen of Navarre, made herself the center of a literary circle in which her own writing stands out most sharply. Her chief work is the *Heptameron,* which follows the tradition of story collections begun by Boccaccio in his *Decameron* but relies heavily on experiences she herself was familiar with.

Two prose writers, supreme and idiosyncratic, dominate French Renaissance literature: Rabelais and Montaigne. François Rabelais created a unique synthesis of many branches of learning and of popular culture in the five volumes of his *Gargantua and Pantagruel.* This enormous text, outsized as are its giant heroes, satirizes Renaissance ideas about balance and order at the same time that it expresses and embodies Renaissance ideas about education and about social and political concerns. At the end of the sixteenth century, the measured, reflective voice of Michel de Montaigne expresses, in his *Essays,* an equally individual reaction to the ideas and events of his time. He questions, without quite rejecting, the accepted values of style and education, using his own experience as a constant test of the value of what his culture has passed on to him.

England became another vibrant center for later Renaissance literature toward the end of the sixteenth century, with Shakespeare as its undisputed master. His plays have become central to world theater, and his sonnets reveal his supreme skills of formal control, combining passion and precision in their expression. Equally accomplished in his own way was John Donne. With restless virtuosity he shifted from the erotic to the spiritual. The culmination of English Renaissance literature, with neoclassicism now the dominant form is found in the works of John Milton. In *Paradise Lost,* the last great Renaissance epic, Milton carefully worked out a powerful synthesis of classical and Christian themes.

In Spain, Miguel Cervantes partakes of both the Renaissance and the baroque; *Don Quixote,* a comic masterpiece, is a complex novel that has provided the world with an archetype of the man engaged in a mad attempt to enact his fantasies in a world finding no use for them.

The center of European neoclassical culture was France. Especially important are the writers encouraged by Louis XIV, the Sun King, as he liked to be called, and some of the most brilliant of these writers were dramatists. The supreme achievement of neoclassical tragedy is found in the work of Racine, whose dark and stately dramas achieve a synthesis of elegance and intensity that was the ideal of neoclassical culture.

We can thus see that the early modern period was a time both like and unlike our own. Although obsession with religious matters and the belief in the supreme importance of form may seem somewhat strange to us, the questions raised about the status of the individual, about the exercise of political power, and about the presence of cultural otherness are questions we are still wrestling with. The vitality of the literature of this period comes from just these questions.

Historical Background

What we now think of as modern Europe actually had its beginnings in the sixteenth century when the feudalism of the Middle Ages began to yield to a more dynamic structure of society. The decisive turning point was the Renaissance, which by 1600 had reached its final flourishing. During this latter period there arose a number of features we recognize as distinctively modern, including the revival of both urban life and a fertile urban culture, growth of business enterprises stoked by private capital, dedication to classical scholarship and observation of the world, rising literacy, a surge of works written not in Latin but in the vernacular, an expanding bureaucracy, and establishment of increasingly independent, powerful and often warring city-states. As towns expanded into the surrounding countryside and consolidated themselves into corporate and more highly organized states, conflict between—and within—city states proliferated. In *The Prince,* Machiavelli pragmatically counseled would-be rulers how to acquire power, found a state, and keep it—in a very real and unidealized world marked by human weakness and desire.

When Machiavelli proclaimed that he loved his country (Florence) more than his soul, he aligned himself with civil rather than Christian virtues. In this, he signals a crucial shift away from Christian ethics and toward humanist and republican values. Besides Martin Luther, no other figure exerted a greater impact on western culture in the first half of the sixteenth century. In the north, the humanist movement brought the study of the classics within the compass of a larger Christian framework, and a Christian humanist such as Erasmus was able to make sophisticated fun of human foibles even as he championed down-to-earth Christian values. Similarly, Rabelais lampooned the Church's excesses, even as he argued the essential goodness of human nature. Linked with humanism was an increase in literacy and rise of national feeling expressed in vernacular works.

All of these wide-ranging social and political developments were linked to dramatic changes in the economic structure of early modern Europe, a period marked by an ever more rapid revolution. During that time, Europe saw tremendous economic expansion, the explosion of sea and land trade, the replacement of serfdom with a system of capitalist rent, and the general advance and maturation of western capitalism. After two centuries of stagnation, famine, and plagues throughout Europe, populations began to increase after 1500. This, along with technological advances, fueled Europe's transformation into a world economic system. New commodities were transported from new lands, particularly spices and luxury goods from the East. During the sixteenth century, Venice reached prominence as a commercial and shipping center. A century later, the Atlantic coast had begun to replace the Mediterranean as the center of commerce. The Dutch, with the help of a new and cheaper cargo ship, dominated much Baltic trade. Merchants, traders, entrepreneurs, and bankers amassed capital in unprecedented quantities. Not surprisingly, the sixteenth century is known as "the bourgeois century."

In the first half of the sixteenth century, the most important political development was the emergence of the modern sovereign state. In the era of the Tudor sovereigns in England, the monarchial system grew stronger, more centralized, and more organized. In addition to larger bureaucracies and mounting national debts, states now marshalled large and professional armies, sent out diplomats, and supported a princely court—where music, painting, and poetry were pursued in a refined and exclusionary manner. The Renaissance paragon was the perfect gentleman, reinforcing the point that education and statecraft were directed at young men. The efforts to regulate the economy in order to reinforce state power—what is known as mercantilism—had its beginnings but did not fully emerge until after 1650, when more systematic economic plans were drawn up. From roughly 1494 to 1564, Europe's internationally regulated political arena was dominated by France and Spain under the Valois kings and Charles I, respectively. Both countries regularly sent armies into weaker states while England remained aloof from continental matters. By the last forty years of the century, most wishes for a united Europe and Christendom were erased by increasing national consciousness as well as by Charles V's abdication in 1555 of the largest empire the world has ever known: the Holy Roman Empire.

Yet it was not only nation-states, monarchies, and trade patterns that changed. Social patterns altered as well. What demographers label the modern marriage pattern emerged. Unlike the Middle Ages when wives were usually younger than their husbands, brides in late sixteenth century were generally mature and usually the same age as their grooms. The consolidation of state power brought a number of problems having to do with race and ethnicity. As the state power increased, so, too, did an ideal of unquestioning allegiance to the state, conformity to the prevailing culture, and intolerance for those different. Witches were fervidly hunted. The status of Jews progressively worsened, not only in England and France but also in Spain, where in 1492 they were offered the choice of expulsion or conversion. Elsewhere, however, in Holland as well as Italian states, exiled Jews were admitted, though often forced to live in segregated communities or ghettos (the word originates in Venice).

At about the same time that Italy had its High Renaissance, Germany became the center of the Protestant Reformation, a spiritual watershed that thwarted forever any hopes for the religious unity of the West. The crusade began in 1517 with Martin Luther's *Ninety-five Theses*, a protest against the profligacy and materialism of the Church, in particular the generation of papal revenue by selling indulgences or pardons for sins. Luther's act led to excommunication in 1520 but he retained protection from German princes. Within four years, Luther had a sizable following for his theology, known as Lutheranism; he advocated a return to an earlier and simpler Christianity, grounded not in the popes, bishops, or councils, not in rituals and relics, but in the Bible. Such religious reforms succeeded in fragmenting Western Christianity into a number of camps, including Lutheranism, a more militant Protestantism known as Calvinism, and Anabaptism, as well as Anglicanism, which took form under Henry VIII as the Church of England. To this general movement may be added the reforms staged by the Catholic Church upon itself—particularly at the Council of Trent in Italy (1545–1563)—a movement known as the Counter-Reformation that by 1600 had begun to win back adherents. Nonetheless, the religious problem was ultimately settled in Germany, France, and the Netherlands by the Religious Wars, a series of conflicts that did not end until 1609.

With the seventeenth century came the dawning of the baroque era, a name that itself suggests the age's opulence, grandeur, nonclassical dynamism, and sweeping gestures as well as a search for supreme order and stability. The idea of Europe was fully in place, though it was no longer centered in Rome, stretching instead across the entire continent. The period from 1648 to 1789, the Age of Monarchy, was characterized by a new breed of ruler who aspired to absolute power in both name and deed. Among the new rulers was Louis XIV, the self-proclaimed Sun King who immortalized his name with a palace at Versailles, and a court life that established France as an artistic and literary center. Similarly in England, under Elizabeth I as well as the first two Stuarts, James I and Charles I, a system of court patronage and court literature flourished. Yet the Stuart Accession that begins with James I in 1603 also charts a gradual course away from monarchy and court life to a republic in 1649, and finally in 1660, after twenty years of civil war and revolution, to a restored but limited monarchy wherein the crown had to acknowledge a citizen's rights as well as Parliament's power in financial matters. After 1688, private businesses as well as Parliament offered a formidable rival to the power and prestige of court, and this too exerted a profound pressure on the period's literature and art. Despite the Thirty Years' War, the last continent-wide conflict between the Protestants and the Roman Catholics, the idea of Europe continued to be fortified; by 1715, a tenuous but workable balance of power existed between five principal military states— England, Austria, France, Prussia, and Russia.

It has been argued that the Scientific Revolution did more to prepare the world for modernity than the Renaissance and Reformation combined. The crisis of conscience that Europe underwent from 1685 to 1715 was largely prompted by the Scientific Revolution, when age-old beliefs about the universe—as well as the place of humanity in it—were displaced by discoveries in physics and astronomy. The telescope and the microscope, both invented around 1600, enabled scientists to see what had never before been seen. In such a climate, the ground was prepared for reason to replace faith, skepticism to meet dogma, and natural law to contest Scripture; human nature was seen as potentially good and people were thought to be capable of self-government. Such beliefs would find their fullest flowering in the later period known alternatively as the Enlightenment and the Age of Reason.

Further Reading

Burckhardt, Jakob. *The Civilization of the Renaissance in Italy*. New York: Mentor Classic, New American Library, (1960).

Bush, Douglas. *The Renaissance and English Humanism*. Toronto: University of Toronto Press (1968).

Ferguson, Wallace K. *The Renaissance*. New York: Holt, Rinehart and Winston (1940).

Ferguson, Wallace K., Robert S. Lopez, George Sarton, Roland H. Bainton, Leicester Bradner, and Erwin Panofsky. *The Renaissance: Six Essays*. New York: Harper Paperback Editions (1962).

Kristeller, Paul Oskar. *Renaissance Thought and Its Sources*. New York: Columbia University Press (1979).

Rabil, Albert, Jr., ed. *Renaissance Humanism: Foundations, Forms and Legacy*. Philadelphia: University of Pennsylvania Press, (1988).

FRANCESCO PETRARCH (1304–1374)
Italy

Francesco Petrarca, known in English as Petrarch, was born in Arezzo, Italy, but spent much of the first part of his life in Avignon in southern France. Here he met the woman he called Laura: his feelings for her are the subject of his love poems. She died of the plague in 1348, and her death is a crucial event in the *Rime sparse* (*Scattered Rhymes or Lyrics*), as they are called, including sonnets, songs, sestinas, ballads, and madrigals.

Petrarch was famous in his lifetime for his extensive writings in Latin, but his love poetry in Italian started a tradition that spread throughout Europe and was the basic model for European love poetry for centuries to come. Though Petrarch is a contemporary of Chaucer, he is a figure who dissociates himself from the Middle Ages. Even in his return to the classical, he is seen to mark an opening to the modern.

[O Heavenly Father: after wasted days]*

O Heavenly Father: after wasted days,
And all these hungry nights when my desire
Ran in my veins with new replenished fire
At recollection of her lovely ways;
O Heavenly Father, lend the hand to raise   5
Me to the good life whereto I aspire,
Rescue my feet from the encompassing mire
And from the traps my adversary lays.
Father, today the eleventh year is turning
Since that unhappy day of desolation   10
When the yoke first upon my shoulders lay.
Have mercy, Lord, on my long shameful yearning,
Lead thou my thoughts to a better destination,
Remind them, thou wast crucified today.

[She used to let her golden hair fly free]*

She used to let her golden hair fly free
For the wind to toy and tangle and molest;
Her eyes were brighter than the radiant west.
(Seldom they shine so now.) I used to see

*Translated by Morris Bishop.

Pity look out of those deep eyes on me. 5
('It was false pity,' you would now protest.)
I had love's tinder heaped within my breast;
What wonder that the flame burned furiously?
She did not walk in any mortal way,
But with angelic progress; when she spoke, 10
Unearthly voices sang in unison.
She seemed divine among the dreary folk
Of earth. You say she is not so today?
Well, though the bow's unbent, the wound bleeds on.

[Charged with oblivion my ship careers / through stormy combers]†

Charged with oblivion my ship careers
Through stormy combers in the depth of night;
Left lies Charybdis, Scylla[1] to the right;
My master—nay, my foe sits aft and steers.
Wild fancies ply the oars, mad mutineers, 5
Reckless of journey's end or tempest's might;
The canvas splits 'gainst the relentless spite
Of blasts of hopes and sighs and anxious fears.
A rain of tears, a blinding mist of wrath
Drench and undo the cordage, long since worn 10
And fouled in knots of ignorance and error;
The two sweet lights[2] are lost that showed my path,
Reason and art lie 'neath the waves forlorn: *love is coldly irrational*
What hope of harbor now? I cry in terror.

[Life hurries on, a frantic refugee]*

Life hurries on, a frantic refugee,
And Death, with great forced marches, follows fast;
And all the present leagues with all the past *present links up to past and*
And all the future to make war on me. *haunts you when you are afra*
Anticipation joins to memory *of future.* 5
To search my soul with daggers; and at last,
Did not damnation set me so aghast, *suicide, he goes to hell so he doesn't*
I'd put an end to thinking, and be free. *want to*

---

†*Translated by Thomas G. Bergin.*

1. Charybdis and Scylla were legendary monsters who threatened sailors in the strait between Italy and Sicily.

2. The two lights in this and the following sonnet are Laura's eyes.

The few glad moments that my heart has known
Return to me; then I foresee in dread
The winds upgathering against my ways,
Storm in the harbor, and the pilot prone,
The mast and rigging down; and dark and dead
The lovely lights whereon I used to gaze.

[handwritten margin note: he would like things to be better but the way it is going he sees shipwreck. Some relationship is not going well]

[handwritten: 10]

[The ardour and the odour and dark wonder]‡

The ardour and the odour and dark wonder
Of my sweet laurel and her golden glamour
That offered quiet from the dusty clamour,
Death the Despoiler tramples down in thunder.
As when the moon presses the proud sun under,
So now my lights go out, my voices stammer;
On Death I cry to halt Death's heavy hammer—
With such black thoughts Love tears my heart asunder.
O lovely lady, brief the sleep you slumbered:
An instant only, then amid the numbered
You woke to gaze with them on God's deep glory:
And if my verse its cunning still recovers,
Among the noble minds, the noble lovers
It shall record your name, your deathless story.

[handwritten margin note: he sees his lover in the afterlife. "elevating theme" writers promise of immortality through the lover being celebrated in a work lit. you will die old but you will be remembered as young and beautiful]

[handwritten: 5]

DESIDERIUS ERASMUS (1466–1536)
Netherlands / Switzerland

Desiderius Erasmus was born in Rotterdam in the Netherlands around 1466.
Trained in schools that emphasized religious practice as opposed to theological
dogma, he was himself ordained a priest in 1492. Through his writings, all of
which were in Latin, he became the central European intellectual figure of his
time. He died in Basel, Switzerland, in 1536. *The Praise of Folly,* his best known
work, was published in 1511. It is a satiric work in which the female figure of
Folly, the goddess of foolishness, speaks in the first person.

‡*Translated by Joseph Auslander.*

Fool sees himself in mirror from Erasmus, *The Praise of Folly.*

from The Praise of Folly

[Sweetening the Sourness of the Masculine Mind with Female Folly]

But because it was necessary to add just a pinch more of reason to the male, who is naturally destined for the administration of affairs, Jupiter took me into his counsel on this occasion (as on others) so that he might provide for this extra bit of reason as well as he could; and I very quickly gave him advice worthy of myself, namely, that he join woman to man (for women are foolish and silly creatures, but nevertheless amusing and pleasant) so that by living with him she can season and sweeten the sourness of the masculine mind with her folly. For where Plato is uncertain whether to place women among rational or irrational creatures, he intended no more than to point out the extraordinary folly of that sex. And if by chance a woman should wish to be considered wise, she simply shows that she is twice foolish, since she is attempting something 'completely against the grain,' as they say, like someone bringing 'a bull to a chinashop.' For a fault is redoubled if someone tries to gloss it over with unnatural disguises and to work against the

Translated by Clarence Miller.

inborn bias of the mind. The Greek proverb says "An ape is still an ape, even if it is dressed up in royal purple"; just so, a woman is still a woman—that is, a fool—no matter what role she may try to play.

Still, I don't think women are so foolish as to be angry at me because I, who am both a woman and Folly herself, attribute folly to them. For if they see the matter in the right light, they will recognize that they owe it to folly that they are better off than men in so many ways. First, because of their beauty, which they quite rightly value above everything else and which protects them so well that they can tyrannize even over tyrants. Where do men get their rough features, coarse skin, bushy beards—all of them clearly signs of old age? Where but from the vice of prudence? Women, on the other hand, have soft cheeks, a high voice, a delicate and smooth complexion, so that they seem to preserve forever unchanged the marks of adolescence. Then again, what do women want more than anything else in the world? Isn't it to be most attractive to men? Isn't that the reason for so many toiletries, cosmetics, baths, coiffures, lotions, perfumes, so many clever ways of highlighting, painting, disguising their faces, eyes, and skin? Now, is there anything which makes them more attractive to men than folly? What is there that men will not grant to women? But what recompense do men expect but pleasure? Now, women have no way of giving pleasure except through folly. No one will deny this if he takes the trouble to consider how childishly men talk, how frivolously they act when they have decided to indulge in the pleasure to be found in women. There you have it: the source from which springs the first and foremost pleasure in life.

But there are some people—especially old men—who are boozers rather than woman-chasers and who find the greatest pleasure in drinking bouts. Whether there can be a really fine party with no women present is a question I leave to others. But this much is certain: without the spice of folly there is no such thing as an enjoyable party. So much so that if there is no one who can make people laugh, either by genuine or simulated folly, they get some *comedian*—and pay him a good fee too—or find some ridiculous hanger-on to dispel the silence and boredom of the party with his laughable (that is, foolish) quips. What good would it do to stuff the belly with so many hors d'oeuvres, so many tidbits and delicacies, unless the eyes and ears too, indeed, unless the whole mind be replenished with laughter, jokes, and witticisms? But I am the one and only deviser of such delicacies. Of course, those customary amusements at parties—such as choosing a master of the revels, playing dice, drinking each other's health, *passing the bottle around the table,* having everybody (one after the other) sing a song, dancing around and cutting up—all these pastimes were hardly invented by the seven sages of Greece but rather were thought up by us for the well-being of the human race. But the nature of all such amusements is that the more foolish they are, the more they contribute to the life of mortals. Indeed, a sad life can hardly be called life at all. But sad it must be unless you employ such entertainments to dispel the inherent tedium of living.

But perhaps there will be some who do not care for this kind of pleasure either, who find their satisfaction in the mutual affection and companionship of friends. Friendship, they keep insisting, takes precedence over everything else. It is just as essential as air or fire or water, so pleasurable that we can no more do without it than we can do without the sun, and (finally) so honorable (as if that had anything to do with it) that philosophers have not hesitated to place it among the chief goods of life. But what if I can show that I constitute this great blessing 'from stem to stern'? I will not demonstrate it through the crocodile's dilemma, or the argument of the growing heap, or the argument of the horns,[1] or any other dialectical subtlety of that sort. Rather I will use simple evidence to make it 'as plain as the nose on your face,' as they say. Tell me now, to wink at a friend's faults, to be deceived, to be blind to his vices, to imagine them away, even to love and admire certain notorious vices as if they were virtues—surely this is not far from folly? What about the man who kisses the mole on his mistress or the one who is delighted with his sweetheart's polyp, or the doting father who insists his cross-eyed boy merely has a slight squint—what is all this, I say, but sheer folly? They can call it as foolish as they like—they can say it over and over again—but it is this very same foolishness that brings friends together and keeps them together. I am talking about mortal men, none of whom is born without faults (indeed, he is best who is afflicted with the fewest); as for these gods of wisdom, either they never strike up any friendship at all, or they occasionally fall into a gloomy and unpleasant sort of friendship, and even that with very few men (I hesitate to say with none at all) because most men are foolish—indeed, there is no one who does not have many foolish delusions—and, of course, friendship cannot spring up except between those who are alike. But if it should happen that some of these severe wisemen should become friendly with each other, their friendship is hardly stable or long-lasting, because they are so sour and sharp-sighted that they detect their friends' faults with an eagle eye and 'a bloodhound's nostril,' so to speak. Nevertheless, they are completely blind to their own faults and utterly ignore the wallet hanging on their own backs.[2] Therefore, since man's nature is such that no personality can be discovered which is not subject to many faults, and when you add to this the great variety of temperaments and interests, the many mistakes and errors and accidents to which the lives of mortals are subject, how could the joy of friendship possibly last even for a single hour among these 'critics who ferret out every fault' if it were not for that quality which the Greeks designate by the remarkable word υη, which may be translated either "folly" or "an easy-going temperament"? And what about this: isn't Cupid, the author and father of all friendship, completely blind? Just as *things not beautiful seem beautiful to him,* so too he is responsible for a similar phenomenon among you: to each his own seems fair, 'Punch dotes on Judy, Jack must have his Jill.' Such things happen everywhere and are laughed at everywhere, but still it is just such laughable absurdities that fit and join together the whole frame-work of society and make the wheels of life run smoothly.

Now, what has been said about friendship is even more applicable to marriage, which is, after all, no more than an inseparable joining of two lives into one. Good lord! how many divorces (or things worse than divorces) would be

---

1. The names of certain technical kinds of dialectical argumentation.

2. A wallet in Erasmus's time was a large sack.

happening everywhere if it were not that the everyday life of married couples is supported and sustained by flattery, laughing things off, taking it easy, being deceived, pretending things are not as they are—all of which belong to my retinue. Good grief! how few marriages would take place if the bridegroom prudently investigated the pranks played long before the wedding by that refined and (to all appearances) modest maiden. And then, of the marriages actually entered into, how very few would last if many of the wife's carryings on did not remain secret from her husband, either through his negligence or his stupidity. Such blindness is quite rightly attributed to folly, but it is this same folly which makes it possible for the wife to remain in her husband's good graces and he in hers, for the home to remain peaceful and their relatives to remain on good terms. The deceived husband is a standing joke. People call him cuckold. They make fun of his horns and whatnot when he kisses away the tears of his whorish wife. But how much happier it is to be thus deceived than to eat out your own heart with jealous suspicion and to turn everything into a tragic uproar!

In short, without me no companionship among friends, no blending of lives in marriage can be either pleasant or stable. The people would no longer tolerate their prince, nor the master his servant, nor the maidservant her mistress, nor the teacher his pupil, nor one friend another, nor the wife her husband, nor the landlord his tenant, nor a soldier his barracks-buddy, nor one messmate another, if in their relations with one another they did not sometimes err, sometimes flatter, sometimes wisely overlook things, sometimes soothe themselves with the sweet salve of folly.

* * *

Even so, I can imagine the philosophers' objections: "But to be caught in the toils of such folly, to err, to be deceived, to be ignorant—such an existence is itself miserable." One thing is sure: such it is to be a man. But I don't see why they should call him miserable, since this is the way you are born, this is the way you are formed and fashioned, this is the common lot of everyone. But nothing is miserable merely because it follows its own nature, unless perhaps someone thinks man's lot is deplorable because he cannot fly like the birds, or run on all fours like other animals, and is not armed with horns like a bull. But by the same token, he should argue that even a fine, thoroughbred horse is unhappy because he has never learned grammar and doesn't eat pancakes, or that a bull is miserable because he cannot work out in the gym. Therefore, just as a horse who is ignorant of grammar is not miserable, so too, a man who is a fool is not unhappy, because these things are inherent in their natures.

But these word-jugglers are back at it again: "The knowledge of various branches of learning," they say, "was especially added to human nature so that with their help he could use his mental skill to compensate for what Nature left out." As if it were the least bit likely that Nature, who was so alert in providing for gnats (and even for tiny flowers and blades of grass), should have nodded only in equipping mankind, so that there should be a need for the different branches of learning—which were actually thought up by Theutus, a spirit quite hostile to mankind, as instruments of man's utter ruination. So little do they contribute to man's happiness, that they defeat the very purpose for which they were supposedly invented—as that most wise king in Plato cleverly argues concerning the invention of writing. Thus, the branches of learning crept in along with the other plagues of man's life, and from the very same source from which all shameful crimes arise, namely, the demons—who also derive their name from this fact, since "demon" comes from δαημονες ("scientes," knowing ones). Now the simple people of the golden age, who were not armed with any formal learning, lived their lives completely under the guidance of natural impulses. What need was there for grammar when everyone spoke the same language and when speech served no other purpose than to let one person understand another? What use was there for dialectic, when there was no disagreement among conflicting opinions? What room was there for rhetoric when there were no litigious troublemakers? What demand was there for legal learning when there was no such thing as bad morals—for good laws undoubtedly sprang from bad conduct. Then too, they had more reverence than to pry into the secrets of Nature with irreligious curiosity—to measure the stars, their motions and effects, to seek the causes of mysterious phenomena—for they considered it unlawful for mortals to seek knowledge beyond the limits of their lot. As for what is beyond the range of the furthest stars, the madness of exploring such things never even entered their minds. But when the purity of the golden age had gradually declined, then evil spirits, as I said, first began to invent the learned disciplines, but only a few at first and even those taken up only by a few. Afterwards, the superstition of the Chaldeans and the idle frivolity of the Greeks added hundreds more, all of them nothing but forms of mental torture, so painful that the grammar of even one language is more than enough to make life a perpetual agony.

Still, even among these disciplines, the ones held in highest esteem are those which come closest to the ordinary understanding—that is, the folly—of mankind. Theologians starve, physicists freeze, astronomers are ridiculed, logicians are ignored. *"One physician alone is worth whole hosts of other men."* And even among physicians, the more ignorant, bold, and thoughtless one of them is, the more he is valued by these high and mighty princes. Besides, medicine ((certainly as it is now practiced by most doctors)) is nothing but a subdivision of flattery, just like rhetoric. The next rank beneath the doctors belongs to pettifogging lawyers; in fact, I wonder if they don't hold the highest rank of all, since their profession—not to speak of it myself—is universally ridiculed as asinine by the philosophers. Still, all business transactions, from the smallest to the greatest, are absolutely controlled by these asses. They acquire large estates, while a theologian who has carefully read through whole bookcases of divinity nibbles on dried peas, waging continual warfare with bedbugs and lice.

Moreover, just as those disciplines which are most closely related to Folly contribute most to happiness, so too, those men who have nothing whatever to do with any branch of learning and follow Nature as their only guide are by far the happiest of all. For she is completely adequate in every way, unless perhaps someone wants to leap over the bounds of human destiny. Nature hates disguises, and whatever has not been spoiled by artifice always produces the happiest results.

* * *

Do not all these witnesses cry out with one voice that all mortals are fools, even the pious? And that even Christ, though he was the wisdom of the Father, became somehow foolish in order to relieve the folly of mortals when he took on human nature and appeared in the form of a man? Just as he became sin in order to heal sins. Nor did he choose any other way to heal them but through the folly of the cross, through ignorant and doltish apostles. For them, too, he carefully prescribed folly, warning them against wisdom, when he set before them the example of children, lilies, mustard seed, and sparrows—stupid creatures lacking all intelligence, leading their lives according to the dictates of nature, artless and carefree—and also when he forbad them to be concerned about how they should speak before magistrates, and when he enjoined them not to examine dates and times, so as to keep them from relying on their own wisdom and make them depend on him heart and soul. To the same effect is the prohibition of God, the architect of the world, that they should not eat any fruit from the tree of knowledge, as if knowledge would poison their happiness. For that matter, Paul openly condemns knowledge as dangerous because it puffs men up. St. Bernard, I imagine, was following Paul when he interpreted the mountain on which Lucifer established his throne as the mountain of knowledge.

* * *

And now, to stop running through endless examples and to put it in a nutshell, it seems to me that the Christian religion taken all together has a certain affinity with some sort of folly and has little or nothing to do with wisdom. If you want some proof of this, notice first of all that children, old people, women, and retarded persons are more delighted than others with holy and religious matters and hence are always nearest to the altar, simply out of a natural inclination. Moreover, you see how those first founders of religion were remarkably devoted to simplicity and bitterly hostile to literature. Finally, no fools seem more senseless than those people who have been completely taken up, once and for all, with a burning devotion to Christian piety: they throw away their possessions, ignore injuries, allow themselves to be deceived, make no distinction between friend and foe, shudder at the thought of pleasure, find satisfaction in fasts, vigils, tears, and labors, shrink from life, desire death above all else—in short, they seem completely devoid of normal human responses, just as if their minds were living somewhere else, not in their bodies. Can such a condition be called anything but insanity? In this light, it is not at all surprising that the apostles seemed to be intoxicated with new wine and that Paul seemed mad to the judge Festus.

NICCOLÒ MACHIAVELLI (1469–1527)
Italy

Niccolò Machiavelli was born in Florence in 1469. He became actively involved in the administration of the Florentine republic, as an envoy, and was closely acquainted with figures like Caesar Borgia, but when the government was overthrown in 1512, when the Medicis returned, he was forced to retreat from the city. It was during this semiexile that he wrote the twenty-six chapters of *The Prince* in 1513, a work that has been a source of controversy since its publication in 1532. Since *The Prince* seems to advise the ruler to adopt a course that is expedient rather than moral, Machiavelli's name, rightly or wrongly, has become associated with political practices whose goal is success by any means. His other best-known works are the *Discorsi* (*Discourses*, (1513-17) and the comedy *La Mondragola* (*The Mandrake*, c. 1518).

from The Prince

[On Things for Which Men, and Particularly Princes, Are Praised or Blamed]

We now have left to consider what should be the manners and attitudes of a prince toward his subjects and his friends. As I know that many have written on this subject I feel that I may be held presumptuous in what I have to say, if in my comments I do not follow the lines laid down by others. Since, however, it has been my intention to write something which may be of use to the understanding reader, it has seemed wiser to me to follow the real truth of the matter rather than what we imagine it to be. For imagination has created many principalities and republics that have never been seen or known to have any real existence, for how we live is so different from how we ought to live that he who studies what ought to be done rather than what is done will learn the way to his downfall rather than to his preservation. A man striving in every way to be good will meet his ruin among the great number who are not good. Hence it is necessary for a prince, if he wishes to remain in power, to learn how not to be good and to use his knowledge or refrain from using it as he may need.

Putting aside then the things imagined as pertaining to a prince and considering those that really do, I will say that all men, and particularly princes because of their prominence, when comment is made of them, are noted as having some characteristics deserving either praise or blame. One is accounted liberal, another stingy, to use a Tuscan term—for in our speech avaricious (*avaro*) is

Translated by Thomas G. Bergin.

applied to such as are desirous of acquiring by rapine whereas stingy (*misero*) is the term used for those who are reluctant to part with their own—one is considered bountiful, another rapacious; one cruel, another tender-hearted; one false to his word, another trustworthy; one effeminate and pusillanimous, another wild and spirited; one humane, another haughty; one lascivious, another chaste; one a man of integrity and another sly; one tough and another pliant; one serious and another frivolous; one religious and another skeptical, and so on. Everyone will agree, I know, that it would be a most praiseworthy thing if all the qualities accounted as good in the above enumeration were found in a Prince. But since they cannot be so possessed nor observed because of human conditions which do not allow of it, what is necessary for the prince is to be prudent enough to escape the infamy of such vices as would result in the loss of his state; as for the others which would not have that effect, he must guard himself from them as far as possible but if he cannot, he may overlook them as being of less importance. Further, he should have no concern about incurring the infamy of such vices without which the preservation of his state would be difficult. For, if the matter be well considered, it will be seen that some habits which appear virtuous, if adopted would signify ruin, and others that seem vices lead to security and the well-being of the prince.

[Cruelty and Clemency and Whether It Is Better to Be Loved or Feared]

Now to continue with the list of characteristics. It should be the desire of every prince to be considered merciful and not cruel, yet he should take care not to make poor use of his clemency. Cesare Borgia[1] was regarded as cruel, yet his cruelty reorganized Romagna and united it in peace and loyalty. Indeed, if we reflect, we shall see that this man was more merciful than the Florentines who, to avoid the charge of cruelty, allowed Pistoia to be destroyed. A prince should care nothing for the accusation of cruelty so long as he keeps his subjects united and loyal; by making a very few examples he can be more truly merciful than those who through too much tender-heartedness allow disorders to arise whence come killings and rapine. For these offend an entire community, while the few executions ordered by the prince affect only a few individuals. For a new prince above all it is impossible not to earn a reputation for cruelty since new states are full of dangers. Virgil indeed has Dido[2] apologize for the inhumanity of her rule because it is new, in the words:

> Res dura et regni novitas me talia cogunt
> Moliri et late fines custode tueri.[3]

---

1. Cesare Borgia, the illegitimate son of Pope Alexander VI, had conquered the Northern Italian region of Romagna on behalf of his father, who made him Duke of Romagna. Famous for his violence and treachery, he became a noted example of the unscrupulous Renaissance warlord.

2. In Virgil's *Aeneid*, Dido is the queen of the newly established settlement of Carthage on the hostile North African coast.
3. Harsh conditions and the newness of my kingdom force me to undertake such things and to watch my boundaries far and wide with guards.

Machiavelli, oil painting by Santi di Tito (1536–1603). In the Palazzo Vecchio, Florence.

Nevertheless a prince should not be too ready to listen to talebearers nor to act on suspicion, nor should he allow himself to be easily frightened. He should proceed with a mixture of prudence and humanity in such a way as not to be made incautious by overconfidence nor yet intolerable by excessive mistrust.

Here the question arises; whether it is better to be loved than feared or feared than loved. The answer is that it would be desirable to be both but, since that is difficult, it is much safer to be feared than to be loved, if one must choose. For of men in general this observation may be made: they are ungrateful, fickle, and deceitful, eager to avoid dangers, and avid for gain, and while you are useful to them they are all with you, offering you their blood, their property, their lives, and their sons so long as danger is remote, as we noted above, but when it approaches they turn on you. Any prince, trusting only in their words and having no other preparations made, will fall to his ruin, for friendships that are bought at a price and not by greatness and nobility of soul are paid for indeed, but they are not owned and cannot be called upon in time of need. Men have less hesitation in offending a man who is loved than one who is feared, for love is held by a bond of obligation which, as men are wicked, is broken whenever personal advantage suggests it, but fear is accompanied by the dread of punishment which never relaxes.

Yet a prince should make himself feared in such a way that, if he does not thereby merit love, at least he may escape odium, for being feared and not hated may well go together. And indeed the prince may attain this end if he but respect the property and the women of his subjects and citizens. And if it should become necessary to seek the death of someone, he should find a proper justification and a public cause, and above all he should keep his hands off another's property, for men forget more readily the death of their father than the loss of their patrimony. Besides, pretexts for seizing property are never lacking, and when a prince begins to live by means of rapine he will always find some excuse for plundering others, and conversely pretexts for execution are rarer and are more quickly exhausted.

A prince at the head of his armies and with a vast number of soldiers under his command should give not the slightest heed if he is esteemed cruel, for without such a reputation he will not be able to keep his army united and ready for action. Among the marvelous things told of Hannibal is that, having a vast army under his command made up of all kinds and races of men and waging war far from his own country, he never allowed any dissension to arise either as between the troops and their leaders or among the troops themselves, and this both in times of good fortune and bad. This could only have come about through his most inhuman cruelty which, taken in conjunction with his great valor, kept him always an object of respect and terror in the eyes of his soldiers. And without the cruelty his other characteristics would not have achieved this effect. Thoughtless writers have admired his actions and at the same time deplored the cruelty which was the basis of them. As evidence of the truth of our statement that his other virtues would have been insufficient let us examine the case of Scipio,[4] an extraordinary leader not only in his own day but for all recorded history. His army in Spain revolted and for no other reason than because of his kind-heartedness, which had allowed more license to his soldiery than military discipline properly permits. His policy was attacked in the Senate by Fabius Maximus, who called him a corrupter of the Roman arms. When the Locrians had been mishandled by one of his lieutenants, his easy-going nature prevented him from avenging them or disciplining his officer, and it was à propos of this incident that one of the senators remarked, wishing to find an excuse for him, that there were many men who knew better how to avoid error themselves than to correct it in others. This characteristic of Scipio would have clouded his fame and glory had he continued in authority, but as he lived under the government of the Senate, its harmful aspect was hidden and it reflected credit on him.

Hence, on the subject of being loved or feared I will conclude that since love depends on the subjects, but the prince has it in his own hands to create fear, a wise prince will rely on what is his own, remembering at the same time that he must avoid arousing hatred, as we have said.

[In What Manner Princes Should Keep Their Word]

How laudable it is for a prince to keep his word and govern his actions by integrity rather than trickery will be understood by all. Nonetheless we have in our times seen great things accomplished by many princes who have thought little of keeping their promises and have known the art of mystifying the minds of men. Such princes have won out over those whose actions were based on fidelity to their word.

---

4. Publius Cornelius Scipio, called "Africanus," was a Roman general who conquered Spain and defeated Carthage in the Second Punic War.

It must be understood that there are two ways of fighting, one with laws and the other with arms. The first is the way of men, the second is the style of beasts, but since very often the first does not suffice it is necessary to turn to the second. Therefore a prince must know how to play the beast as well as the man. This lesson was taught allegorically by the ancient writers who related that Achilles and many other princes were brought up by Chiron the Centaur, who took them under his discipline. The clear significance of this half-man and half-beast preceptorship is that a prince must know how to use either of these two natures and that one without the other has no enduring strength. Now since the prince must make use of the characteristics of beasts he should choose those of the fox and the lion, though the lion cannot defend himself against snares and the fox is helpless against wolves. One must be a fox in avoiding traps and a lion in frightening wolves. Such as choose simply the rôle of a lion do not rightly understand the matter. Hence a wise leader cannot and should not keep his word when keeping it is not to his advantage or when the reasons that made him give it are no longer valid. If men were good, this would not be a good precept, but since they are wicked and will not keep faith with you, you are not bound to keep faith with them.

A prince has never lacked legitimate reasons to justify his breach of faith. We could give countless recent examples and show how any number of peace treaties or promises have been broken and rendered meaningless by the faithlessness of princes, and how success has fallen to the one who best knows how to counterfeit the fox. But it is necessary to know how to disguise this nature well and how to pretend and dissemble. Men are so simple and so ready to follow the needs of the moment that the deceiver will always find some one to deceive. Of recent examples I shall mention one. Alexander VI[5] did nothing but deceive and never thought of anything else and always found some occasion for it. Never was there a man more convincing in his asseverations nor more willing to offer the most solemn oaths nor less likely to observe them. Yet his deceptions were always successful for he was an expert in this field.

So a prince need not have all the aforementioned good qualities, but it is most essential that he appear to have them. Indeed, I should go so far as to say that having them and always practising them is harmful, while seeming to have them is useful. It is good to appear clement, trustworthy, humane, religious, and honest, and also to be so, but always with the mind so disposed that, when the occasion arises not to be so, you can become the opposite. It must be understood that a prince and particularly a new prince cannot practise all the virtues for which men are accounted good, for the necessity of preserving the state often compels him to take actions which are opposed to loyalty, charity, humanity, and religion. Hence he must have a spirit ready to adapt itself as the varying winds of fortune command him. As I have said, so far as he is able, a prince should stick to the path of good but, if the necessity arises, he should know how to follow evil.

---

5. Pope Alexander VI, Rodrigo Borgia, who
   ruled from 1492 to 1503, was notorious for
   his corruption and his worldliness.

A prince must take great care that no word ever passes his lips that is not full of the above mentioned five good qualities, and he must seem to all who see and hear him a model of piety, loyalty, integrity, humanity, and religion. Nothing is more necessary than to seem to possess this last quality, for men in general judge more by the eye than the hand, as all can see but few can feel. Everyone sees what you seem to be, few experience what you really are and these few do not dare to set themselves up against the opinion of the majority supported by the majesty of the state. In the actions of all men and especially princes, where there is no court of appeal, the end is all that counts. Let a prince then concern himself with the acquisition or the maintenance of a state; the means employed will always be considered honorable and praised by all, for the mass of mankind is always swayed by appearances and by the outcome of an enterprise. And in the world there is only the mass, for the few find their place only when the majority has no base of support. A certain prince of our own times, whom it would not be well to name, preaches nothing but peace and faith and yet is the enemy of both, and if he had observed either he would already on numerous occasions have lost both his state and his renown.

[The Influence of Fortune on Human Affairs and How It May Be Countered]

I am not ignorant of the fact that many have held and hold the opinion that the things of this world are so ordered by fortune and God that the prudence of mankind may effect little change in them, indeed is of no avail at all. On this basis it could be argued that there is no point in making any effort, but we should rather abandon ourselves to destiny. This opinion has been the more widely held in our day on account of the great variations in things that we have seen and are still witnessing and which are entirely beyond human conjecture. Sometimes indeed, thinking on such matters, I am minded to share that opinion myself. Nevertheless I believe, if we are to keep our free will, that it may be true that fortune controls half of our actions indeed but allows us the direction of the other half, or almost half. I would compare fortune to a river in flood, which when it breaks its bonds, deluges the surrounding plains, tears up trees and dwellings, here washing away the land and there building up new deposits. All flee before it, everyone must bow before the fury of the flood, for there is no checking it. Yet though this be so it does not signify that in quiet times men cannot make some provision against it, building levees and dikes so that when the river rises it may follow a channel prepared for it or at least have its first onrush rendered less impetuous and harmful. In like fashion fortune displays her greatest effect where there is no organized ability to resist and hence she directs her bolts where there have been no defenses or bulwarks prepared against her. And if you will consider Italy, the scene of the variations we have mentioned above and the motivating center thereof, you will find it an open field without dikes and without any kind of protection. Had it been protected by proper valor and ability, as were Germany, France, and Spain, it would not have suffered such great changes from the flood, which indeed might never have come. This I think should suffice as an argument against fortune in general.

Coming now to particular cases, I will note how we see such a prince reign happily today and meet his downfall tomorrow without any visible change in his nature and character. This is a result of causes we have already discussed, and a prince who depends entirely on fortune will not prosper when fortune changes. I further believe that a prince is fortunate when his conduct is in accord with the times and unsuccessful if his behavior is not so in tune. For we observe of men as they follow out the course of action necessary to the ends they seek, whether glory or riches, that one works cautiously, another impetuously, or one uses violence and another astuteness, or one is patient and another the contrary, yet success may attend any of these methods. And we may see that of two of the cautious type one attains his ends where the other fails, and similarly we may see two succeed though using different methods, one deliberate and the other impetuous, and this all depends on the temper of the times and whether or not it be in accord with the method of procedure. Hence it comes about, as I have said, that two using different methods may come to the same end, and of two following the same method one may succeed and the other fail. Herein lies the variation in prosperity, for if one prince conducts himself with patience and caution and the times are right for such conduct he will prosper, but if times and circumstances change and he does not alter his behavior he will fall. Nor is there any man so wise as to be able to adapt himself to such changes, both because we cannot be other than as nature inclines us and because one who has prospered by following one kind of policy will not be persuaded to abandon it. Hence the cautious man, when the time comes for bold action, is incapable of it and so falls, for if nature could be changed with the variation of times and circumstances fortune would not change.

My conclusion is, then, that, as fortune is variable and men fixed in their ways, men will prosper so long as they are in tune with the times and will fail when they are not. However, I will say that in my opinion it is better to be bold than cautious, for fortune is a woman and whoever wishes to win her must importune and beat her, and we may observe that she is more frequently won by this sort than by those who proceed more deliberately. Like a woman, too, she is well disposed to young men, for they are less circumspect and more violent and more bold to command her.

BALDESSARE CASTIGLIONE
(1478–1529)
Italy

Baldesar Castiglione was born in Mantua; he served in various official capacities at the courts of northern Italy, especially at the court of the Duke of Urbino. It was there that he set his chief work, *The Book of the Courtier,* in which a group of

Portrait of Baldassare
Castiglione by Raphael, 1516.
In the Louvre, Paris.

nobles hold a series of conversations in which they attempt to describe the ideal courtier. Published in 1528, this work defined the standards of the ideal courtier for the rest of Renaissance Europe. Castiglione, himself regarded as a model courtier, died in 1529 in Spain where he had been sent as papal envoy.

from **The Book of the Courtier**

[Should the Courtier Be Deprived of Love]

Then signor Gasparo[1] said: "I remember that last evening, in discussing the accomplishments of the Courtier, these gentlemen wished him to be in love; and since, in summarizing what has been said so far, we might conclude that a Courtier who has to lead his prince to virtue by his worth and authority will almost have to be old (because knowledge very rarely comes before a certain age, and especially knowledge in those things that are learned through experience)—I do not know how it can be fitting for him, if he is advanced in age, to be in love. For, as has been said this evening, love is not a good thing in old men, and those things which in young men are the delights, courtesies, and elegances so pleasing to women, in old men amount to madness and ridiculous ineptitude, and whoever indulges in them will cause some women to despise him and others to deride him. So if this Aristotle of yours, as an old Courtier, were in love and did the things that young lovers do

Translated by Charles Singleton.

1. Gasparo Pallavicino, a friend of Castiglione's.

(like some whom we have seen in our time), I fear he would forget to instruct his prince, and children would perhaps mock him behind his back, and women would scarcely have any pleasure from him except to poke fun at him."

Then signor Ottaviano[2] said: "As all the other accomplishments assigned to the Courtier suit him, even though he be old, I do not think that we ought at all to deprive him of this happiness of loving."

"Nay," said signor Gasparo, "to deprive him of love is to give him a further perfection and to make him live happily, free of misery and calamity."

* * *

Then the Duchess[3] said: "I am glad, messer Pietro,[4] that you have had little to do in our discussion this evening, for now we shall the more confidently give you the burden of speaking, and of teaching the Courtier a love so happy that it brings with it neither blame nor displeasure; for it could well be one of the most important and useful conditions that have yet been attributed to him. Therefore, by your faith, tell us all that you know about it."

* * *

Whereupon messer Pietro, having first remained silent for a while, made ready as if to speak of something important, then said: "Gentlemen, in order to show that old men can love not only without blame but sometimes more happily than young men, I am obliged to enter upon a little discourse to explain what love is, and wherein lies the happiness that lovers can have. So I beg you to follow me attentively, for I hope to bring you to see that there is no man here to whom it is unbecoming to be in love. . . .

"I say, then, that, according to the definition of ancient sages, love is nothing but a certain desire to enjoy beauty; and, as our desire is only for things that are known, knowledge must always precede desire, which by its nature turns to the good but in itself is blind and does not know the good. Therefore nature has ordained that to every cognitive power there shall be joined an appetitive power; and as in our soul there are three modes of cognition, namely, by sense, by reason, and by intellect: so, from sense comes appetite, which we have in common with animals; from reason comes choice, which is proper to man; from intellect, whereby man can communicate with the angels, comes will. Thus, even as sense knows only those things which the senses perceive, appetite desires these and no other; and even as intellect is turned solely to the contemplation of intelligible things, the will feeds only upon spiritual good. Being by nature rational and placed as in the middle between these two extremes, man can choose (by descending to sense or rising to intellect) to turn his desires now in one direction and now in the other. In these two ways, therefore, men can desire beauty, which name is universally applied to all things, whether natural or artificial, that are made in the good proportion and due measure that befit their nature.

"But to speak of the beauty we have in mind, namely, that only which is seen in the human person and especially in the face, and which prompts the ardent

---

2. Ottaviano Fregoso, a nobleman of Genoa.
3. Elisabetta Gonzaga, the Duchess of Urbino, who presides over the gathering.

4. Pietro Bembo, a Venetian nobleman, famous as a poet and as an authority on the Neoplatonic theory of love.

desire we call love, we will say that it is an effluence of the divine goodness, which (although it is shed, like the sun's light, upon all created things), when it finds a face well proportioned and composed of a certain radiant harmony of various colors set off by light and shadow and by measured distance and limited outline, infuses itself therein and shines forth most beautifully and adorns and illumines with grace and a wondrous splendor the object wherein it shines, like a sunbeam striking upon a beautiful vase of polished gold set with precious gems. Thus, it agreeably attracts the eyes of men to itself, and, entering through them, impresses itself upon the soul, and moves and delights it throughout with a new sweetness; and, by kindling it, inspires it with a desire of itself."

MICHELANGELO BUONARROTI

(1475–1564)

Italy

Michelangelo Buonarroti, the greatest sculptor of the Renaissance, wrote poetry on and off throughout his long life. He was born in 1475 in a rural area near Florence, where he was trained as an artist. He eventually settled in Rome, working for Pope Julius II and gaining great fame as a sculptor and also as the painter (although a reluctant one) of the frescoes of the Sistine Chapel in the Vatican. He died in Rome in 1564. A tormented man, Michelangelo expressed many of the tensions in his life in his vigorous poetry, which was not published until 1623.

To Giovanni, the One from Pistoia, on Painting the Vault of the Sistine Chapel (1508–1512)[1]

I've already grown a goiter from this toil
as water swells the cats in Lombardy
or any other country they might be,
forcing my belly to hang under my chin,
　My beard to heaven, and my memory
I feel above its coffer. My chest a harp.
And ever above my face, the brush dripping,
making a rich pavement out of me.
　My loins have been shoved into my guts,

5

Translated by Sidney Alexander.

1. This poem, addressed to the humanist Giovanni di Benedetto da Pistoia, is the artist's description of himself painting the ceiling of the Sistine Chapel.

My arse serves to counterweigh my rump,   10
Eyelessly I walk in the void.
   Ahead of me my skin lies outstretched,
and to bend, I must knot my shoulders taut,
holding myself like a Syrian bow.
   Therefore, fallacious, strange   15
the judgment carried in the mind must fly,
for from a twisted gun one shoots awry.
   My dead picture defend
now, Giovanni, and also my honor,
for I'm in no good place, nor I a painter.   20

For Vittoria Colonna

High-born soul whose limbs and features fair
Mirror within your chaste and mollient members dear
How nature and heaven can draw near
And shape for us beauty beyond compare.

Resplendent spirit in whom one hopes and believes that there   5
Inwardly, as on your outward face appear,
Love, pity, mercy are—states so rare
Never so intimately bound with beauty were.

Love seizes me, locks me in beauty's prison
Pity and mercy with gentle glances beckoning   10
Seem to ring my heart with hopes to the horizon.

What usage, what governance, what reckoning
Denies this world? What cruelty? What ultimate negation
That soon or late death spares not so lovely a creation?[2]

[What marvel is it, if close to the fire]

What marvel is it, if close to the fire
I melted and burned; and now that it is spent
from without, from within I am afflicted and rent
and bit by bit reduced to ashes of a perished pyre?

Burning I used to see the source of my desire,   5
the lucent place whence depended my torment.
That sight alone lent me content
And death and dole to me were festivals and gyre.

---

2. The sonnet was written on the death of
  Michelangelo's friend, the poet Vittoria Colonna.

But when the splendor of that incendiary food
that burnt me and nurtured me flew off to heaven   10
One coal though covered, yet remained glowing.

And if love heap not up other wood
to see me aflame, not a single spark even
will remain of me, all to cinders and ashes going.

VITTORIA COLONNA (1490–1547)
Italy

Vittoria Colonna, born in 1490 into a noble family in Rome, was married to the
Marquis of Pescara. Although he was absent on military campaigns during most
of the marriage, his death in 1525 had a decisive effect on her. For the rest of her
life she lived in convents and became intensely interested in religion. In 1534 she
met Michelangelo, who became a close friend. In 1538 she published a collection
of sonnets, very spiritual in tone, on the death of her husband. Michelangelo was
present when she died in 1547, and he wrote several of his most notable sonnets
on her death.

[I live on this depraved and lonely cliff]*

I live on this depraved and lonely cliff
like a sad bird abhorring a green tree
or plashing water; I move forcefully
away from those I love, and I am stiff
even before myself, so that my thoughts   5
may rise and fly to him: sun I adore
and worship. Though their wings could hurry more,
they race only to him; the forest rots
until the instant when they reach that place.
Then deep in ecstasy, though brief, they feel   10
a joy beyond all earthly joy. I reel,
and yet if they could recreate his face
as my mind, craving and consuming, would,
then here perhaps I'd own the perfect good.

*Translated by Willis Barnstone.

[As when some hungry fledgling hears and sees]*

As when some hungry fledgling hears and sees
  His mother's wings beating around him, when
  She brings him nourishment, from which loving
  Both meal and her, he cheers up and rejoices,
  And deep within the nest, chafes and worries   5
    With desire to follow her, even flying,
    And offers thanks with such a caroling
    His tongue seems loosed beyond its usual power;
  So I, at times, when warm and living rays
    Come from the heavenly sun by which my heart   10
    Is fed, shine forth with such a lightening,
  And I find my pen moves, urged on always
    By an inner love, as if it had no part
    In what I say: it is his praise I sing.

MARGUERITE DE NAVARRE (MARGUERITE DE VALOIS) (1492–1549)

France

Marguerite was born in Angoulême in 1492. Her younger brother would become King Francis I of France. She had a literary education and was married in 1527 to the king of Navarre (of whose court she made a refuge for humanists). Often at the French court, she was much involved in the political events of her time and was associated with attempts to reform the Catholic Church from within. The *Heptameron* was apparently left incomplete at her death in 1549. In this first collection of French tales, which continues the tradition of Boccaccio's *Decameron,* a group of ten men and women, caught in the mountains by flooded streams, amuse themselves by telling each other stories.

from *Heptameron*

[Passion and Vengeance in the Naples Court]†

In the town of Amboise there was a certain mule-driver in the service of the Queen of Navarre, the sister of King Francis I, and it all happened while the Queen was

---

Translated by Barbara Howes.
†*Translated by P. A. Chilton; revised by Marcel Tetel.*

staying at Blois, around the time when she gave birth to a son.[1] The mule-driver had gone over to collect his quarterly pay, while his wife stayed behind in their house on the other side of the bridges in Amboise. Now the husband had a servant, and this man had been desperately in love with the wife for quite a while. One day, unable to stand it any longer, he had come out with his declaration. But being a very virtuous woman, she had given him a very sharp reply, and threatened to get her husband to give him a beating and throw him out of the house. After that the man had never dared open his mouth to her in this fashion again, or in any other way indicate his feelings. However, the flames of passion smoldered secretly away, until the fateful day when the husband went off to Blois. The lady of the house had gone to vespers in the church of Saint-Florentin, in the castle, and a long way from the house. Left to himself in the house, the servant got it into his head that he would take by force what he had failed to obtain by supplication and service. He broke an opening in the partition that separated the room where he slept from that of his mistress. The hole could not be seen, because it was covered by the curtain of his master's bed on one side, and by the curtain round the servant's bed on the other. So his foul intentions were not suspected, until the good lady had actually got into bed, accompanied by a little lass of eleven or twelve years of age. The poor woman had just fallen asleep, when the servant jumped through the hole and into bed with her, wearing nothing but his shirt, and clutching his bare sword in his hand. The moment she felt him by her side, she jumped up, and told him what she thought of him, like the virtuous woman she was. His love was no more than animal lust, and he would have understood the language his mules spoke better than he understood the virtuous appeals to reason that she now made. Indeed, what he did next proved him even more bestial than the animals with whom he had spent so much of his life. She ran too fast round the table for him to catch her, and was in any case so strong that she had already twice managed to struggle free from his clutches. He despaired of taking her alive, and stabbed her violently in the small of the back, thinking no doubt that the pain would make her surrender, where terror and manhandling had failed. However, the very opposite happened. Just as a good soldier will fight back all the more fiercely if he sees his own blood flowing, so the chaste heart of this lady was only strengthened in its resolve to run, and escape falling into the hands of this desperate man. As she struggled to get away, she reasoned with him as well as she was able, thinking she might somehow bring him to recognize the wrongness of his acts. But by now he was worked up into a frenzy, and was in no state to be moved by words of wisdom. He went on lunging at her with his sword, while she ran as fast as she could to get away. When at last she had lost so much blood that she felt death approaching, she raised her eyes to heaven and, joining her hands in prayer, gave thanks to her God.

"Thou art my strength, my virtue, my suffering and my chastity," she prayed, humbly beseeching that He would receive the blood, which, according to His commandment, was shed in veneration of the blood of His son. For she truly

---

1. The Queen is Marguerite herself. The teller of this story is Cisille, who is usually identi- fied with Louise of Savoy, the mother of Marguerite and King Francis.

believed that through Him were all her sins cleansed and washed from the memory of His wrath. And as she sank with her face to the floor, she sighed, "Into thy hands I commend my spirit, my spirit that was redeemed by thy great goodness."

Then the vicious brute stabbed her several times again, and, once she could no longer speak, and all her physical resistance was gone, he took the poor defenseless creature by force. When he had satisfied his lusts he made a speedy getaway, and in spite of all subsequent attempts to track him down, it had proved impossible to find him. The young girl who had been sleeping with the poor woman had been terrified, and had hidden under the bed. Once the man had disappeared she came out and went to her mistress. Finding that she was unable to speak and just lay there motionless, she ran to the window and called out for help from the neighbors. There were plenty of people in the town who were fond of her and thought highly of her, and they now rallied round immediately and fetched doctors to tend her. When they examined her they found twenty-five fatal wounds. They did what they could to help her, but to no avail. She lingered on for another hour, unable to speak, but indicating by movements of her eyes, and gestures of the hands, that her mind was still clear. A man of the church came and questioned her about the faith in which she died, and about her hope for salvation through Christ alone. Although she could only reply by signs, no words could have conveyed her meaning more clearly. And so, with joy on her face, and her eyes turned heavenward, her soul left this chaste body to return to its Creator. No sooner had the corpse been lifted from where it lay, prepared for burial and placed before the door of the house to await the burial party, than the poor husband arrived. There, completely unforewarned, he was confronted with the spectacle of his wife lying dead in front of his own house. When he heard how she had died, his grief was doubled. Indeed, so deep was his sorrow that he too came near to death. His wife, this martyr of chastity, was then laid to rest in the church of Saint-Florentin. All the virtuous women of the town were present, as was their duty, to do all possible honor to her name. For them it was a great blessing to have lived in the same town as one so virtuous. For women of more wanton ways the sight of such respect being paid to her body made them resolve to amend their lives.

FRANÇOIS RABELAIS (c. 1494–1553)

France

François Rabelais was born around 1494 in the French province of Touraine. Although ordained a priest and having entered first the Franciscan and then the Benedictine order, Rabelais left the monastery to work as a doctor. In 1532 he published his *Pantagruel,* and two years later, *Gargantua*. These works made him famous, but because they were frequently condemned by the authorities, he often moved from one place to another, while revising and expanding them, until his death in Paris in 1553. The story of the adventures of the giant Gargantua and his son Pantagruel is an exuberant mixture of popular culture and great learning that has always fascinated and perplexed readers.

from Gargantua

Chapter 7: How a Monk of Seuilly Saved the Abbey-Close from Being Sacked by the Enemy

So they went on, wasting, pillaging, and stealing till they arrived at Seuilly, where they robbed men and women alike and took everything they could; nothing was too hot or too heavy for them.[1] Although there was plague in almost every house, they broke into all of them and plundered everything inside; and none of them caught any infection, which is a most wonderful thing. For the priests, curates, preachers, physicians, surgeons, and apothecaries who went to visit, dress, heal, preach to, and admonish the sick had all died of the infection. Yet these robbing and murdering devils never took any harm. What is the reason for that, gentlemen? Consider the problem, I beg of you.

When the town was thus pillaged they went to the abbey in a horrible tumult, but they found it well bolted and barred. So the main body of their army marched on towards the ford of Vède, except for seven companies of foot and two hundred knights with their retainers, who remained there and broke down the walls of the close in order to ravage the vineyard. The poor devils of monks did not know which of their saints to turn to. Whatever the risk, they had the bell tolled for a meeting of the chapter, at which it was decided to march in a stately procession, rendered more effective by grand chants and litanies *contra hostium insidias*, and fine responses *pro pace*.[2]

There was in the abbey at that time a cloister monk, named Friar John of the Hashes, a young, gallant, sprightly, jovial, resourceful, bold, adventurous, resolute, tall, and thin fellow with a great gaping mouth and a fine outstanding nose. He was grand mumbler of matins, dispatcher of masses, and polisher off of vigils, and, to put it briefly, a true monk if ever there has been one since the monking world monked its first monkery; and moreover in the matter of his breviary he was a clerk to his very teeth.

Now when this monk heard the noise that the enemy were making in the close of their vineyard, he came out to see what they were doing; and finding them to be picking the grapes of their close, on which their provision for the whole year depended, he returned to the choir of the church, where the rest of the monks,

---

Translated by J. M. Cohen.

---

1. Gargantua's kingdom has been attacked by the disorganized army of King Picrochole.

2. "Against the treachery of the enemy"; "for peace."

Pantagruel tests his wits against the Parisian scholars (II.10). Illustration by Gustave Doré from *OEuvres de Rabelais* published by Garnier Freres, Paris, n. d. (1873 or shortly thereafter).

gaping like so many stuffed pigs, were singing: *Ini nim, pe, ne, ne, ne, ne, ne, ne, mum, num, ini, i, mi, i, mi, co, o, ne, no, ne, no no, no, rum, ne, num, num.*[3]

"That's shitten well sung!" he cried when he saw them. "But, for God's sake, why don't you sing: 'Baskets farewell; the harvest's done'? The devil take me if they aren't in our close, and so thoroughly cutting both vines and grapes that, God's body, there'll be nothing but gleanings there for the next four years. Tell me, by

---

3. The trembling monks garble the Latin words *impetum inimicorum*, "the attack of our enemies," which they are praying to be delivered from.

St James's belly, what shall we drink in all that time? What'll there be for us poor devils? Lord God, *da mihi potum.*"[4]

Then said the Prior of the convent: "What does this drunkard want here? Let him be taken to the punishment cell for disturbing the divine service!"

"But," said the monk, "what about the wine service? Let's see that isn't disturbed. For you yourself, my lord Prior, like to drink of the best, and so does every decent fellow. Indeed, no man of honour hates a good wine; which is a monkish saying. But these responses you're singing here are very much out of season, by God. Now tell me, why are our services short at the harvest-tide and the vintage, and during Advent too, and all the winter? The late Friar Mace Pelosse, of blessed memory, a true zealot for our faith—devil take me if he wasn't—told me the reason, as I remember. It was that we might press and make the wine properly at the vintage, and in winter drink it down. So listen to me, all you who love wine; and follow me too, in God's name. For I tell you boldly, may St Anthony's fire burn me if anyone tastes the grape who hasn't fought for the vine. Church property it is, by God, and hands off it! Devil take it, St Thomas of Canterbury was willing to die for the Church's goods, and if I were to die for them, shouldn't I be a Saint as well? But I shan't die, for all that. It's I that will be the death of others."

As he said this he threw off his heavy monk's cloak and seized the staff of his cross, which was made of the heart of a sorb-apple tree. It was as long as a lance, a full hand's grip round, and decorated in places with lily flowers, which were almost all rubbed away. Thus he went out in a fine cassock, with his frock slung over his shoulder, and rushed so lustily on the enemy, who were gathering grapes in the vineyard without order or ensign, trumpet or drum. For the standard-bearers and ensigns had put down their standards and ensigns beside the walls, the drummers had knocked in one side of their drums to fill them with grapes, the trumpeters were loaded with the fruit, and everyone was in disorder. He rushed, as I said, so fiercely on them, without a word of warning, that he bowled them over like hogs, striking right and left in the old fencing fashion.

He beat out the brains of some, broke the arms and legs of others, disjointed the neck-bones, demolished the kidneys, slit the noses, blackened the eyes, smashed the jaws, knocked the teeth down the throats, shattered the shoulder-blades, crushed the shins, dislocated the thigh-bones, and cracked the fore-arms of yet others. If one of them tried to hide among the thickest vines, he bruised the whole ridge of his back and broke the base of his spine like a dog's. If one of them tried to save himself by flight, he knocked his head into pieces along the lambdoidal suture. If one of them climbed into a tree, thinking he would be safe there, Friar John impaled him up the arse with his staff. If any one of his old acquaintance cried out: "Ha, Friar John, my friend, Friar John, I surrender!" he replied: "You can't help it. But you'll surrender your soul to all the devils as well." And he gave the fellow a sudden thumping.

---

4. "Give me a drink."

If any man was seized with such a spirit of rashness as to try to face up to him, then he showed his muscular strength by running him through the chest by way of the mediastine to the heart. In the case of others, thrusting under the hollow of their short ribs, he turned their stomachs over, so that they died immediately. Others he smote so fiercely through the navel that he made their bowels gush out. Others he struck on the ballocks and pierced their bum-gut. It was, believe me, the most hideous spectacle that ever was seen.

Some invoked St Barbara, others St George, other St Hands-off, others Our Lady of Cunault, of Loretto, of Good Tidings, of Lenou, of Rivière. Some called on St James, others on the Holy Shroud of Chambéry—but it was burnt three months later so completely that they could not save a single thread—others on the Shroud of Cadouin, others on St John of Angély, others on St Eutropius of Saintes, St Maximus of Chinon, St Martin of Candes, St Cloud of Cinais, the relics of Javarzay, and a thousand other pleasant little saints.

Some died without a word, others spoke without dying; some died as they spoke, others spoke as they died, and others cried aloud: "Confession! Confession! *Confiteor! Miserere! In manus!*"[5]

Such was the shouting of the wounded that the Prior of the abbey came out with all his monks; and when they saw these poor creatures tumbled there among the vines and mortally wounded, they confessed some of them. But whilst the priests amused themselves by taking confessions, the little monklings ran to the place where Friar John stood, and asked him how they could help him.

His reply was that they should slit the throats of those lying on the ground. So, leaving their great cloaks on the nearest fence, they began to cut the throats of those whom he had already battered, and to dispatch them. Can you guess with what instruments? With fine *whittles,* which are the little jack-knives with which the small children of our country shell walnuts.

Meanwhile, still wielding the staff of his cross, Friar John reached the breach which the enemy had made, while some of the little monks carried off the ensigns and standards to their cells, to cut them into garters. But when those who had made their confession tried to get out through this breach, the monk rained blows upon them, crying: "These men are shriven and repentant, and have earned their pardons. They'll go right to paradise, as straight as a sickle or the road to Faye."

Thus, by his prowess, all that part of the army that had got into the close was discomfited, to the number of thirteen thousand, six hundred and twenty-two, not counting the women and small children—as is always understood. For never did Maugis the Hermit—of whom it is written in the Deeds of the Four Sons of Aymon—wield his pilgrim's staff so valiantly against the Saracens as this monk swung the staff of his cross in his encounter with the enemy.

---

5. "I confess! Have mercy! Into your hands (I commit myself)!"

from *Pantagruel*

Chapter 2: Of the Nativity of the Most Redoubted Pantagruel

Gargantua at the age of four hundred, four score, and forty-four years begat his son Pantagruel upon his wife Badebec, daughter of the king of the Amaurots in Utopia, who died in childbirth; for he was so amazingly large and so heavy that he could not come into the world without suffocating his mother.

But in order fully to understand the cause and reason of the name which was given to him at baptism, you will note that in that year there was so great a drought throughout all the land of Africa, that thirty-six months, three weeks, four days, thirteen hours, and somewhat more passed without rain, and with the sun's heat so torrid that the whole earth was parched by it. Indeed the heat was no more violent in the days of Elijah than it was then. For there was not a tree in the land that had either leaf or flower. The grass lost its green; the rivers drained away; the springs ran dry; the poor fish, abandoned by their own element, strayed and cried on the ground most horribly; the birds fell from the air through lack of dew; the wolves, foxes, stags, boars, deer, hares, rabbits, weasels, martens, badgers, and other animals were to be found dead in the fields, with their throats gaping. As for men, their case was most piteous. You would have seen them lolling out their tongues like greyhounds that have run for six hours; many threw themselves into wells; others crept into a cow's belly, to be in the shade, and these Homer calls *Alibantes*. The whole country was at a standstill. It was pitiable to see the pains that mortals took to save themselves from this dreadful plight. It was hard work to keep the holy water in the churches from being exhausted. But they so organized it, by the advice of My Lords the Cardinals and the Holy Father, that no one dared to take more than one dip. Yet when anyone entered the church you might have seen scores of poor thirsty souls coming up behind him, and him distributing it to anyone who had his mouth wide open to catch a drop of it, like the wicked rich man, in order that nothing should be lost. Oh, how fortunate in that year was the man who had a cool and well furnished cellar!

The Philosopher relates, in debating the question why the waters of the sea are salt, that at the time when Phoebus handed over the driving of his light-giving chariot to his son Phaeton, the said Phaeton, unskilled in the art and not knowing how to follow the ecliptic line between the two tropics of the sun's orbit, strayed from his track and approached so near to the earth that he dried up all the lands beneath him, scorching a large portion of the sky which the philosophers call *Via lactea*[6] and simpletons call St James's Path, although the more highfalutin' poets say that it is the region where Juno's milk fell when she suckled Hercules. That was the time when the earth was so heated that it burst into a great sweat, which caused it to sweat out the whole sea, which for that reason is salt, for all sweat is salt; which you will admit to be true if you taste your own, or that of pox-patients when they make them sweat. It is all one to me.

An almost similar case occurred in that year. For one Friday, when everyone

---

6. The Milky Way.

was at devotions, and they were making a fine procession with all manner of litanies and grand sermons, calling on God Almighty to deign with his eye of mercy to look down on them in their great distress, great drops of water were plainly seen to break out of the earth, as when someone bursts into a copious sweat. And the poor people began to rejoice, as if this had been something to their profit. For some said that there was not a drop of moisture in the air from which they could expect rain, and that the earth was making up for this lack. Other learned people said that it was rain from the Antipodes, about which Seneca tells in the fourth book of his *Questiones naturales,* in speaking of the origin and source of the River Nile. But they were mistaken. For after the procession, when each one wanted to gather up some of this dew and drink it by the bowlful, they found that it was only brine, saltier and far nastier than sea-water.

And because Pantagruel was born on that very day, his father gave him the name he did: for *Panta* in Greek is equivalent to *all,* and *Gruel,* in the Hagarene language, is as much as to say *thirsty;* by this meaning to infer that at the hour of the child's nativity the world was all thirsty, and also seeing, in a spirit of prophecy, that one day his son would be ruler over the thirsty, as was demonstrated to him at that very hour by another sign even more convincing. For when the child's mother Badebec was being delivered of him and the midwives were waiting to receive him, there came first out of her womb sixty-eight muleteers, each pulling by the collar a mule heavily laden with salt; after which came out nine dromedaries loaded with hams and smoked ox-tongues, seven camels loaded with salted eels; and then twenty-four cartloads of leeks, garlics, and onions: all of which greatly alarmed the said midwives.

But some of them said: "Here is fine fare. We were only drinking slackly, not like Saxons. This is bound to be a good sign. These are spurs to wine." And whilst they were gossiping amongst themselves about such little matters, out came Pantagruel, as shaggy as a bear. Whereupon one of them said in a spirit of prophecy: "He is born with all his hair. He will perform wonders; and if he lives he'll reach a ripe age."

Chapter 8: How Pantagruel, When at Paris, Received a Letter from his Father Gargantua, Together with a Copy of the Same

As you may well suppose, Pantagruel studied very hard. For he had a double-sized intelligence and a memory equal in capacity to the measure of twelve skins and twelve casks of oil. But while he was staying in Paris, he one day received a letter from his father which read as follows:

Most dear Son,

Among the gifts, graces, and prerogatives with which the Sovereign Creator, God Almighty, endowed and embellished human nature in the beginning, one seems to me to stand alone, and to excel all others; that is the one by which we can, in this mortal state, acquire a kind of immortality and, in the course of this transitory life, perpetuate our name and seed; which we do by lineage sprung from us in lawful marriage. By this means there is in some sort restored to us what was taken from us by the sin of our first parents, who were told that, because they had not been obedient to the commandment of God the Creator, they would die, and that by death would be brought to nothing that magnificent form in which man has been created.

But by this method of seminal propagation, there remains in the children what has perished in the parents, and in the grandchildren what has perished in the children, and so on in succession till the hour of the Last Judgement, when Jesus Christ shall peacefully have rendered up to God His Kingdom, released from all danger and contamination of sin. Then all generations and corruptions shall cease, and the elements shall be free from their continuous transformations, since peace, so long desired, will then be perfect and complete, and all things will be brought to their end and period.

Not without just and equitable cause, therefore, do I offer thanks to God, my Preserver, for permitting me to see my grey-haired age blossom afresh in your youth. When, at the will of Him who rules and governs all things, my soul shall leave this mortal habitation, I shall not now account myself to be absolutely dying, but to be passing from one place to another, since in you, and by you, I shall remain in visible form here in this world, visiting and conversing with men of honour and my friends as I used to do. Which conversation of mine has been, thanks to God's aid and grace, although not free from sin, I confess—for we all sin, and continually pray to God to wipe out our sins—at least without evil intention.

If the qualities of my soul did not abide in you as does my visible form, men would not consider you the guardian and treasure-house of the immortality of our name; in which case my pleasure would be small, considering that the lesser part of me, which is my body, would persist, and the better part, which is the soul, and by which our name continues to be blessed among men, would be bastardized and degenerate. This I say not out of any distrust of your virtue, which I have already tried and approved, but in order to encourage you more strongly to proceed from good to better. For what I write to you at present is not so much in order that you may live in this virtuous manner as that you may rejoice in so living and in so having lived, and may strengthen yourself in the like resolution for the future, for the furtherance and perfection of these ends I have, as you will easily remember, spared no expense. Indeed, I have helped you towards them as if I treasured nothing else in this world but to see you, in my lifetime, a perfect model of virtue, honour, and valour, and a paragon of liberal and high-minded learning. I might seem to have desired nothing but to leave you, after my death, as a mirror representing the person of me your father, and if not as excellent and in every way as I wish you, at least desirous of being so.

But although my late father Grandgousier, of blessed memory, devoted all his endeavours to my advancement in all perfection and political knowledge, and although my labour and study were proportionate to—no, even surpassed—his desire; still, as you may well understand, the times were not as fit and favorable for learning as they are to-day, and I had no supply of tutors such as you have. Indeed the times were still dark, and mankind was perpetually reminded of the miseries and disasters wrought by those Goths who had destroyed all sound scholarship. But, thanks be to God, learning has been restored in my age to its former dignity and enlightenment. Indeed I see such improvements that nowadays I should have difficulty in getting a place among little schoolboys, in the lowest class, I who in my youth was reputed, with some justification, to be the most learned man of the century. Which I do not say out of vain boastfulness, although I might commendably do so in writing to you,—for which you have the authority of Marcus Tullius in his work on Old Age, and Plutarch's statement in his book entitled: *How a Man may praise himself without Reproach*—but in order to inspire you to aim still higher.

Now every method of teaching has been restored, and the study of languages has been revived: of Greek, without which it is disgraceful for a man to call himself a scholar, and of Hebrew, Chaldean, and Latin. The elegant and accurate art of printing, which is now in use, was invented in my time, by divine inspiration; as, by contrast, artillery was inspired by diabolical suggestion. The whole world is full of learned men, of very erudite tutors, and of most extensive libraries, and it is my opinion that neither in the time of Plato, of Cicero, nor of Papinian were there such facilities for study as one finds today. No one, in future, will risk appearing in public or in any company, who is not well polished in Minerva's workshop. I find robbers, hangmen, free-booters, and grooms nowadays more learned than the doctors and preachers were in my time.

Why, the very women and girls aspire to the glory and reach out for the celestial manna of sound learning. So much so that at my present age I have been compelled to learn Greek, which I had not despised like Cato, but which I had not the leisure to learn in my youth. Indeed I find great delight in reading the *Morals* of Plutarch, Plato's magnificent *Dialogues*, the *Monuments* of Pausanias, and the *Antiquities* of Athenaeus, while I wait for the hour when it will please God, my Creator, to call me and bid me leave this earth.

Therefore, my son, I beg you to devote your youth to the firm pursuit of your studies and to the attainment of virtue. You are in Paris. There you will find many praiseworthy examples to follow. You have Epistemon for your tutor, and he can give you living instruction by word of mouth. It is my earnest wish that you shall become a perfect master of languages. First of Greek, as Quintilian advises; secondly, of Latin; and then of Hebrew, on account of the Holy Scriptures; also of Chaldean and Arabic, for the same reason; and I would have you model your Greek style on Plato's and your Latin on that of Cicero. Keep your memory well stocked with every tale from history, and here you will find help in the Cosmographes of the historians. Of the liberal arts, geometry, arithmetic, and music, I gave you some smattering when you were still small, at the age of five or six. Go on and learn the rest, also the rules of astronomy. But leave divinatory astrology and Lully's art alone, I beg of you, for they are frauds and vanities. Of Civil Law I would have you learn the best texts by heart, and relate them to the art of philosophy. And as for the knowledge of Nature's works, I should like you to give careful attention to that too; so that there may be no sea, river, or spring of which you do not know the fish. All the birds of the air, all the trees, shrubs, and bushes of the forest, all the herbs of the field, all the metals deep in the bowels of the earth, the precious stones of the whole East and the South—let none of them be unknown to you.

Then scrupulously peruse, the books of the Greek, Arabian, and Latin doctors once more, not omitting the Talmudists and Cabalists, and by frequent dissertations gain a perfect knowledge of that other world which is man. At some hours of the day also, begin to examine the Holy Scriptures. First the New Testament and the Epistles of the Apostles in Greek; and then the Old Testament, in Hebrew. In short, let me find you a veritable abyss of knowledge. For, later, when you have grown into a man, you will have to leave this quiet and repose of study, to learn chivalry and warfare, to defend my house, and to help our friends in every emergency against the attacks of evil-doers.

Furthermore, I wish you shortly to show how much you have profited by your studies, which you cannot do better than by publicly defending a thesis in every art against all persons whatsoever, and by keeping the company of learned men, who are as common in Paris as elsewhere.

But because, according to the wise Solomon, Wisdom enters not into the malicious heart, and knowledge without conscience is but the ruin of the soul, it befits you to serve, love, and fear God, to put all your thoughts and hopes in Him, and by faith grounded in charity to be so conjoined with Him that you may never be severed from Him by sin. Be suspicious of the world's deceits and set not your heart on vanity; for this life is transitory, but the word of God remains eternal. Be helpful to all your neighbours, and love them as yourself. Respect your tutors, avoid the company of those whom you would not care to resemble, and do not omit to make use of those graces which God has bestowed on you. Then, when you see that you have acquired all the knowledge to be gained in those parts, return to me, so that I may see you and give you my blessing before I die.

My son, the peace and grace of Our Lord be with you. Amen.

From Utopia, this seventeenth day of the month of March,

Your father, Gargantua

After receiving and reading this letter, Pantagruel took fresh courage and was inspired to make greater advances than ever. Indeed, if you had seen him studying and measured the progress he made, you would have said that his spirit among the books was like fire among the heather, so indefatigable and ardent was it.

SAINT TERESA OF AVILA (1515–1582)
Spain

Teresa de Cepeda y Ahumada, generally known as Saint Teresa of Avila, was born there to a noble family in 1515. After a devout childhood—she ran away at the age of seven to seek martyrdom among the Moors—she became a Carmelite nun and mystic, as Teresa de Jesus, leading a life of intense personal religious experience, and she also led a movement to reform the Carmelite community, (the Discalced or Barefoot Carmelites). With St. John of the Cross, she founded seventeen new convents of friars and traveled widely. Her mystical writings focus on prayer as the essential expression of the love of God and are based on her own experience, which she describes vividly and effectively: the piercing of her heart (described in her *Vida* [Life, 1552–1565]), is thought to have taken place in 1559. She died in 1582 and was canonized in 1622. In 1970 she was the first woman to be proclaimed doctor of the Catholic Church.

from *The Life of Saint Teresa*

[The Pain and Bliss of Saint Teresa]

The infant soul should be soothed by the caresses of love, which shall draw forth its love in a gentle way, and not, as they say, by force of blows. This love should be inwardly under control, and not as a cauldron, fiercely boiling because too much fuel has been applied to it, and out of which everything is lost. The source of the fire must be kept under control, and the flame must be quenched in sweet tears, and not with those painful tears which come out of these emotions, and which do so much harm.

In the beginning, I had tears of this kind. They left me with a disordered head and a wearied spirit, and for a day or two afterwards unable to resume my prayer. Great discretion, therefore, is necessary at first, in order that everything may proceed gently, and that the operations of the spirit may be within; all outward manifestations should be carefully avoided.

These other impetuosities are very different. It is not we who apply the fuel; the fire is already kindled, and we are thrown into it in a moment to be consumed. It is

Translated by David Lewis.

by no efforts of the soul that it sorrows over the wound which the absence of our Lord has inflicted on it; it is far otherwise; for an arrow is driven into the entrails to the very quick, and into the heart at times, so that the soul knows not what is the matter with it, nor what it wishes for. It understands clearly enough that it wishes for God, and that the arrow seems tempered with some herb which makes the soul hate itself for the love of our Lord, and willingly lose its life for Him. It is impossible to describe or explain the way in which God wounds the soul, nor the very grievous pain inflicted, which deprives it of all self-consciousness; yet this pain is so sweet, that there is no joy in the world which gives greater delight. As I have just said, the soul would wish to be always dying of this wound.

This pain and bliss together carried me out of myself, and I never could understand how it was. Oh, what a sight a wounded soul is!—a soul, I mean, so conscious of it, as to be able to say of itself that it is wounded for so good a cause; and seeing distinctly that it never did anything whereby this love should come to it, and that it does come from that exceeding love which our Lord bears it. A spark seems to have fallen suddenly upon it, that has set it all on fire. Oh, how often do I remember, when in this state, those words of David: "Quemadmodum desiderat cervus ad fontes aquarum"![1] They seem to me to be literally true of myself.

When these impetuosities are not very violent, they seem to admit of a little mitigation—at least, the soul seeks some relief, because it knows not what to do—through certain penances; the painfulness of which, and even the shedding of its blood, are no more felt than if the body were dead. The soul seeks for ways and means to do something that may be felt, for the love of God; but the first pain is so great, that no bodily torture I know of can take it away. As relief is not to be had here, these medicines are too mean for so high a disease. Some slight mitigation may be had, and the pain may pass away a little, by praying God to relieve its sufferings: but the soul sees no relief except in death, by which it thinks to attain completely to the fruition of its good. At other times, these impetuosities are so violent, that the soul can do neither this nor anything else; the whole body is contracted, and neither hand nor foot can be moved: if the body be upright at the time, it falls down, as a thing that has no control over itself. It cannot even breathe; all it does is to moan—not loudly, because it cannot: its moaning, however, comes from a keen sense of pain.

Our Lord was pleased that I should have at times a vision of this kind: I saw an angel close by me, on my left side, in bodily form. This I am not accustomed to see, unless very rarely. Though I have visions of angels frequently, yet I see them only by an intellectual vision, such as I have spoken of before. It was our Lord's will that in this vision I should see the angel in this wise. He was not large, but small of stature, and most beautiful—his face burning, as if he were one of the highest angels, who seem to be all of fire: they must be those whom we call cherubim. Their names they never tell me; but I see very well that there is in heaven so great a difference between one angel and another, and between these and the others, that I cannot explain it.

---

1. Psalm 51: "As the longing of the hart for the fountains of waters, so is the longing of my soul for Thee, O my God."

I saw in his hand a long spear of gold, and at the iron's point there seemed to be a little fire. He appeared to me to be thrusting it at times into my heart, and to pierce my very entrails; when he drew it out, he seemed to draw them out also, and to leave me all on fire with a great love of God. The pain was so great, that it made me moan; and yet so surpassing was the sweetness of this excessive pain, that I could not wish to be rid of it. The soul is satisfied now with nothing less than God. The pain is not bodily, but spiritual; though the body has its share in it, even a large one. It is a caressing of love so sweet which now takes place between the soul and God, that I pray God of His goodness to make him experience it who may think that I am lying.

During the days that this lasted, I went about as if beside myself. I wished to see, or speak with, no one, but only to cherish my pain, which was to me a greater bliss than all created things could give me.

I was in this state from time to time, whenever it was our Lord's pleasure to throw me into those deep trances, which I could not prevent even when I was in the company of others, and which, to my deep vexation, came to be publicly known. Since then, I do not feel that pain so much, but only that which I spoke of before—I do not remember the chapter—which is in many ways very different from it, and of greater worth. On the other hand, when this pain, of which I am now speaking, begins, our Lord seems to lay hold of the soul, and to throw it into a trance so that there is no time for me to have any sense of pain or suffering, because fruition ensues at once. May He be blessed for ever, who hath bestowed such great graces on one who has responded so ill to blessings so great!

LOUISE LABÉ (c. 1520–1565)

France

Little is known about the details of Louise Labé's life, although there has been much speculation. She was born in Lyons, France, about 1520 and was married to a prosperous ropemaker: thus her nickname, "La Belle Cordière" or the beautiful ropemaker. She was a prominent figure in the literary life of Lyons at a time when it was an important cultural center. In 1555 her *Works* were published, including twenty-three sonnets admired for their striking combination of high literary polish, expression of classical learning, and intense emotion. The poems describe the feelings of a woman involved in an absorbing love affair, and they are forthright and carefully crafted.

[I'm living and dying]*

I'm living and dying, as I burn and drown.
I scorch even as I freeze:

*Translated by Patricia Terry and Mary Ann Caws.

My life is too sweet and yet too harsh.
Together mingle there great pain and joy:
   I laugh and tears come sudden to my eyes,
Grief torments me even in my pleasure:
I am verdant even as I wither.
My happiness departs; it will not stay.
   So does love inconstant lead me on:
And when I think I cannot bear the pain,
I am surprised to find that it has gone.
   Then when I believe my joy is sure,
That I am close to what I most desire,
Love restores me to my grief again.

[O handsome chestnut eyes]†

O handsome chestnut eyes, evasive gaze,
O fiery sighs and falling tears, O night
obscurely black through which I wait for light
for nothing, O clear dawn of futile days!
O lamentations, O obstinate desires,
O wasted time, O grief scattered about,
O thousand deaths, O thousand nets throughout
my life among the worst insidious fires,
O laughing lips, brow, hair, arms, hands, and fingers,
O funereal lute, viol, bow, and voice!
A woman's heart always has a burned mark.
I sob because of you. Your fire lingers
in every place my seared heart would rejoice,
except in you who keep no single spark.

[Although I cry]†

Although I cry and though my eyes still shed
tears for the seasons I once spent with you,
and while my voice—suppressing sobs, subduing sighs—still rings out vaguely spirited,
while my hand can still pluck the supple string
of the exquisite Lute to sing your grace
and while my arms care only to embrace
your lovely body and to share your being,
while this is true I have no wish to die.
But when I feel my eyes begin to spin,
my voice is broken and my fingers lack
all power, then waiting in my mortal skin

†*Translated by Willis Barnstone.*

my spirit has no lover's glow, and I
pray death to make my brightest day turn black.

[Don't blame me, ladies, if I've loved]†

Don't blame me, ladies, if I've loved. No sneers
if I have felt a thousand torches burn,
a thousand wounds, a thousand daggers turn
in me, if I have burnt my life with tears.
Especially, leave my good name alone.
If I have failed, my hurt is very plain.
Don't sharpen razors to increase my pain,
but know that love, whom none of you have known,
needing no Vulcan to excuse your flame,
nor beautiful Adonis for your shame,
can make you fall in love and anywhere.
You will have fewer chances for relief,
your passion will be stronger and more rare,
and so beware of a more shattering grief.

ANONYMOUS CATALAN BALLAD

(SIXTEENTH CENTURY)

Spain

This sixteenth-century ballad is written in Catalan, the language of Barcelona and the surrounding province, which resembles Provençal. The sentiment of this "romance" is expressed with a typical directness and an autobiographical feeling. As with many anonymous writings, this one is ascribed to a woman. "Anon" is a woman, said Virginia Woolf.

Two Gifts

When I was a girl
I had many lovers.
Now that I'm big,
I only have two:
one a fancy tailor,
the other a weaver.
What can I do?
Both want my love.

†*Translated by Willis Barnstone.*

Spring is coming
with many flowers,
carnations, roses,
violets of all colors.
I'll go to my father's
garden, pick a few,
give the tailor flowers
and the weaver my love.
If they don't want them,
God rid me of both.

GASPARA STAMPA (c. 1523–1554)

Italy

Gaspara Stampa was born in Padua around 1523 but lived most of her life in
Venice. There her literary and musical talent made her the object of considerable
attention in the society of the cultured nobility in which she moved. Her poetry
was published shortly after her death in 1554 as *Rhymes*. The most intense of her
sonnets are the result of her passionate affair with Count Collaltino di Collalto. It
is his name, derived from the Italian word *colle* (hill), that she often plays on in
her poetry. She is much admired for the force and directness of the feelings
expressed in her work.

from *Rhymes*

Night of Love

O night to me more splendid and more blessèd
Than the most blessèd and most splendid days;
Night worthy of the most exalted praise,
Not just of mine, unworthy and distressèd;

You alone have been the faithful giver
Of all my joys; you've made the bitter taste
Of this life sweet and dear, for you've replaced
Within my arms the one who's bound me ever.

I just regret that I did not become
Lucky Alemena[1] then, for whom the dawn

Translated by Frank Warnke.

---

1. Alemena was the mother of Hercules by the
   god Zeus. Engendering the hero was a
   project that lasted three nights.

Postponed, against all custom, its returning;
But I can never say such good has come
From you, clear night, for even now my song
Cannot subdue the matter of its yearning.

Send Back My Heart to Me, Relentless One

Send back my heart to me, relentless one,
Who, tyrant-like, do hold and tear it so,
And do to it, and me, just what is done
By tigers and lions to the hapless doe.

Eight days have passed, at least a year to me;
No messages, no letters, do I get,
Despite the vows with which you were so free:
Fountain of valor, Count, and of deceit!

Am I Hercules or Samson, do you suppose,
To bear such sorrow now that we're apart?
I'm young, a woman, half out of my mind,
And, most of all, I'm here without my heart,
You being gone, in whom I used to find
Defense, who were for me strength and repose.

Love, Having Elevated Her to Him, Inspires Her Verses

If, being a woman so abject and vile,
I nonetheless can bear so high a flame,
Why should I not give to the world the same,
At least in part, in proper wealth and style?

If Love, with a new, unprecedented spark,
Could raise me to a place I could not reach,
Why cannot pain and pen combine to teach
Such arts as, never known, shall find their mark?

And if this does not lie in Nature's art,
Then let it be by miracle, whose power

Can conquer, transcend, and every limit break.
How this may be I cannot say for sure,
But well I know the fortune I partake,
And through it a new style engraves my heart.

By Now This Waiting So Has Wearied Me

By now this waiting so has wearied me,
So vanquished am I by desire and grief
For him who, absent, grants me no relief,
So faithless, so forgetful, still is he,

That I turn and beg that she will give me ease,
Who with her sickle makes the world turn white
And gives to all the final blow; my plight
Such sorrow wrings from me, such anguished pleas.

But she is deaf to this my wretched crying,
And scorns my scattered thoughts disturbed and vain,
Like him who, deaf to me, grants no replying.
Thus with lament that from my eyes distills
I wake the pity of these waves, this main,
While he, lighthearted, lives among his hills.

MICHEL DE MONTAIGNE (1533–1592)
France

Michel de Montaigne was born in 1533 on his family's estate in southwestern France. After an excellent humanist education, he studied law but then withdrew from public life and retired into a tower on his estate to devote himself to his reading. There in 1572 he began to write his essays, a form that he is credited with inventing and naming. His *Essays,* first published in 1580, would occupy him until his death in 1592. With their reflective and skeptical tone, they earned him long-lasting fame as an author within his own lifetime and beyond.

from *Essays*

Of Cannibals

When King Pyrrhus passed over into Italy, after he had reconnoitered the formation of the army that the Romans were sending to meet him, he said: "I do not know what barbarians these are" (for so the Greeks called all foreign nations), "but the formation of this army that I see is not at all barbarous." The Greeks said as much of the army that Flamininus brought into their country, and so did Philip, seeing from a knoll the order and distribution of the Roman camp, in his kingdom, under Publius Sulpicius Galba. Thus we should beware of clinging to vulgar opinions, and judge things by reason's way, not by popular say.

I had with me for a long time a man who had lived for ten or twelve years in that other world which has been discovered in our century, in the place where Villegaignon landed, and which he called Antarctic France.[1] This discovery of a boundless country seems worthy of consideration. I don't know if I can guarantee

Translated by Donald M. Frame.

1. The region that is now Brazil.

Piglike Sea Monster near Iceland north of Faroe Islands. From Olaus
Magnus, *Carta Marina*. Bayerische Staatsbib iothek, Munich.

that some other such discovery will not be made in the future, so many personages
greater than ourselves having been mistaken about this one. I am afraid we have
eyes bigger than our stomachs, and more curiosity than capacity. We embrace
everything, but we clasp only wind.

Plato brings in Solon, telling how he had learned from the priests of the city
of Saïs in Egypt that in days of old, before the Flood, there was a great island
named Atlantis, right at the mouth of the Strait of Gibraltar, which contained more
land than Africa and Asia put together, and that the kings of that country, who not
only possessed that island but had stretched out so far on the mainland that they
held the breadth of Africa as far as Egypt, and the length of Europe as far as
Tuscany, undertook to step over into Asia and subjugate all the nations that
border on the Mediterranean, as far as the Black Sea; and for this purpose crossed
the Spains, Gaul, Italy, as far as Greece, where the Athenians checked them; but
that some time after, both the Athenians and themselves and their island were
swallowed up by the Flood.

It is quite likely that that extreme devastation of waters made amazing
changes in the habitations of the earth, as people maintain that the sea cut off
Sicily from Italy—

'Tis said an earthquake once asunder tore
These lands with dreadful havoc, which before
Formed but one land, one coast

—VIRGIL

Cyprus from Syria, the island of Euboea from the mainland of Boeotia; and elsewhere joined lands that were divided, filling the channels between them with sand and mud:

> A sterile marsh, long fit for rowing, now
> Feeds neighbor towns, and feels the heavy plow.
> —HORACE

But there is no great likelihood that that island was the new world which we have just discovered; for it almost touched Spain, and it would be an incredible result of a flood to have forced it away as far as it is, more than twelve hundred leagues; besides, the travels of the moderns have already almost revealed that it is not an island, but a mainland connected with the East Indies on one side, and elsewhere with the lands under the two poles; or, if it is separated from them, it is by so narrow a strait and interval that it does not deserve to be called an island on that account.

It seems that there are movements, some natural, others feverish, in these great bodies, just as in our own. When I consider the inroads that my river, the Dordogne, is making in my lifetime into the right bank in its descent, and that in twenty years it has gained so much ground and stolen away the foundations of several buildings, I clearly see that this is an extraordinary disturbance; for if it had always gone at this rate, or was to do so in the future, the face of the world would be turned topsy-turvy. But rivers are subject to changes: now they overflow in one direction, now in another, now they keep to their course. I am not speaking of the sudden inundations whose causes are manifest. In Médoc, along the seashore, my brother, the sieur d'Arsac, can see an estate of his buried under the sands that the sea spews forth; the tops of some buildings are still visible; his farms and domains have changed into very thin pasturage. The inhabitants say that for some time the sea has been pushing toward them so hard that they have lost four leagues of land. These sands are its harbingers; and we see great dunes of moving sand that march half a league ahead of it and keep conquering land.

The other testimony of antiquity with which some would connect this discovery is in Aristotle, at least if that little book *Of Unheard-of Wonders* is by him. He there relates that certain Carthaginians, after setting out upon the Atlantic Ocean from the Strait of Gibraltar and sailing a long time, at last discovered a great fertile island, all clothed in woods and watered by great deep rivers, far remote from any mainland; and that they, and others since, attracted by the goodness and fertility of the soil, went there with their wives and children, and began to settle there. The lords of Carthage, seeing that their country was gradually becoming depopulated, expressly forbade anyone to go there any more, on pain of death, and drove out these new inhabitants, fearing, it is said, that in course of time they might come to multiply so greatly as to supplant their former masters and ruin their state. This story of Aristotle does not fit our new lands any better than the other.

This man I had was a simple, crude fellow—a character fit to bear true witness; for clever people observe more things and more curiously, but they interpret them; and to lend weight and conviction to their interpretation, they cannot help altering history a little. They never show you things as they are, but bend and disguise them according to the way they have seen them; and to give credence to their judgment and attract you to it, they are prone to add something to their matter, to stretch it out and amplify it. We need a man either very honest, or so simple that he has not the stuff to build up false inventions and give them plausibility; and wedded to no theory. Such was my man; and besides this, he at various times brought sailors and merchants, whom he had known on that trip, to see me. So I content myself with his information, without inquiring what the cosmographers say about it.

We ought to have topographers who would give us an exact account of the places where they have been. But because they have over us the advantage of having seen Palestine, they want to enjoy the privilege of telling us news about all the rest of the world. I would like everyone to write what he knows, and as much as he knows, not only in this, but in all other subjects; for a man may have some special knowledge and experience of the nature of a river or a fountain, who in other matters knows only what everybody knows. However, to circulate this little scrap of knowledge, he will undertake to write the whole of physics. From this vice spring many great abuses.

Now, to return to my subject, I think there is nothing barbarous and savage in that nation, from what I have been told, except that each man calls barbarism whatever is not his own practice; for indeed it seems we have no other test of truth and reason than the example and pattern of the opinions and customs of the country we live in. *There* is always the perfect religion, the perfect government, the perfect and accomplished manners in all things. Those people are wild, just as we call wild the fruits that Nature has produced by herself and in her normal course; whereas really it is those that we have changed artificially and led astray from the common order, that we should rather call wild. The former retain alive and vigorous their genuine, their most useful and natural, virtues and properties, which we have debased in the latter in adapting them to gratify our corrupted taste. And yet for all that, the savor and delicacy of some uncultivated fruits of those countries is quite as excellent, even to our taste, as that of our own. It is not reasonable that art should win the place of honor over our great and powerful mother Nature. We have so overloaded the beauty and richness of her works by our inventions that we have quite smothered her. Yet wherever her purity shines forth, she wonderfully puts to shame our vain and frivolous attempts:

> Ivy comes readier without our care;
> In lonely caves the arbutus grows more fair;
> No art with artless bird song can compare.
> —PROPERTIUS

All our efforts cannot even succeed in reproducing the nest of the tiniest little bird, its contexture, its beauty and convenience; or even the web of the puny spider. All things, says Plato, are produced by nature, by fortune, or by art; the greatest and most beautiful by one or the other of the first two, the least and most imperfect by the last.

These nations, then, seem to me barbarous in this sense, that they have been fashioned very little by the human mind, and are still very close to their original naturalness. The laws of nature still rule them, very little corrupted by ours; and they are in such a state of purity that I am sometimes vexed that they were unknown earlier, in the days when there were men able to judge them better than we. I am sorry that Lycurgus and Plato did not know of them; for it seems to me that what we actually see in these nations surpasses not only all the pictures in which poets have idealized the golden age and all their inventions in imagining a happy state of man, but also the conceptions and the very desire of philosophy. They could not imagine a naturalness so pure and simple as we see by experience; nor could they believe that our society could be maintained with so little artifice and human solder. This is a nation, I should say to Plato, in which there is no sort of traffic, no knowledge of letters, no science of numbers, no name for a magistrate or for political superiority, no custom of servitude, no riches or poverty, no contracts, no successions, no partitions, no occupations but leisure ones, no care for any but common kinship, no clothes, no agriculture, no metal, no use of wine or wheat. The very words that signify lying, treachery, dissimulation, avarice, envy, belittling, pardon—are unheard of. How far from this perfection would he find the republic that he imagined: *Men fresh sprung from the gods* [Seneca].

> These manners nature first ordained.
> —VIRGIL

For the rest, they live in a country with a very pleasant and temperate climate, so that according to my witnesses it is rare to see a sick man there; and they have assured me that they never saw one palsied, bleary-eyed, toothless, or bent with age. They are settled along the sea and shut in on the land side by great high mountains, with a stretch about a hundred leagues wide in between. They have a great abundance of fish and flesh which bear no resemblance to ours, and they eat them with no other artifice than cooking. The first man who rode a horse there, though he had had dealings with them on several other trips, so horrified them in this posture that they shot him dead with arrows before they could recognize him.

Their buildings are very long, with a capacity of two or three hundred souls; they are covered with the bark of great trees, the strips reaching to the ground at one end and supporting and leaning on one another at the top, in the manner of some of our barns, whose covering hangs down to the ground and acts as a side. They have wood so hard that they cut with it and make of it their swords and grills to cook their food. Their beds are of a cotton weave, hung from the roof like those in our ships, each man having his own; for the wives sleep apart from their husbands.

They get up with the sun, and eat immediately upon rising, to last them through the day; for they take no other meal than that one. Like some other Eastern peoples, of whom Suidas tells us, who drank apart from meals, they do not drink then; but they drink several times a day, and to capacity. Their drink is made of some root, and is of the color of our claret wines. They drink it only lukewarm. This beverage keeps only two or three days; it has a slightly sharp taste, is not at all heady, is good for the stomach, and has a laxative effect upon those who are not used to it; it is a very pleasant drink for anyone who is accustomed to it. In place of bread they use a certain white substance like preserved coriander. I have tried it; it tastes sweet and a little flat.

The whole day is spent in dancing. The younger men go to hunt animals with bows. Some of the women busy themselves meanwhile with warming their drink, which is their chief duty. Some one of the old men, in the morning before they begin to eat, preaches to the whole barnful in common, walking from one end to the other, and repeating one single sentence several times until he has completed the circuit (for the buildings are fully a hundred paces long). He recommends to them only two things: valor against the enemy and love for their wives. And they never fail to point out this obligation, as their refrain, that it is their wives who keep their drink warm and seasoned.

There may be seen in several places, including my own house, specimens of their beds, of their ropes, of their wooden swords and the bracelets with which they cover their wrists in combats, and of the big canes, open at one end, by whose sound they keep time in their dances. They are close shaven all over, and shave themselves much more cleanly than we, with nothing but a wooden or stone razor. They believe that souls are immortal, and that those who have deserved well of the gods are lodged in that part of heaven where the sun rises, and the damned in the west.

They have some sort of priests and prophets, but they rarely appear before the people, having their home in the mountains. On their arrival there is a great feast and solemn assembly of several villages—each barn, as I have described it, makes up a village, and they are about one French league from each other. The prophet speaks to them in public, exhorting them to virtue and their duty; but their whole ethical science contains only these two articles: resoluteness in war and affection for their wives. He prophesies to them things to come and the results they are to expect from their undertakings, and urges them to war or holds them back from it; but this is on the condition that when he fails to prophesy correctly, and if things turn out otherwise than he has predicted, he is cut into a thousand pieces if they catch him, and condemned as a false prophet. For this reason, the prophet who has once been mistaken is never seen again.

Divination is a gift of God; that is why its abuse should be punished as imposture. Among the Scythians, when the soothsayers failed to hit the mark, they were laid, chained hand and foot, on carts full of heather and drawn by oxen, on which they were burned. Those who handle matters subject to the control of human capacity are excusable if they do the best they can. But these others, who come and trick us with assurances of an extraordinary faculty that is beyond our ken, should they not be punished for not making good their promise, and for the temerity of their imposture?

They have their wars with the nations beyond the mountains, further inland, to which they go quite naked, with no other arms than bows or wooden swords ending in a sharp point, in the manner of the tongues of our boar spears. It is astonishing what firmness they show in their combats, which never end but in slaughter and bloodshed; for as to routs and terror, they know nothing of either.

Each man brings back as his trophy the head of the enemy he has killed, and sets it up at the entrance to his dwelling. After they have treated their prisoners well for a long time with all the hospitality they can think of, each man who has a prisoner calls a great assembly of his acquaintances. He ties a rope to one of the prisoner's arms, by the end of which he holds him, a few steps away, for fear of being hurt, and gives his dearest friend the other arm to hold in the same way; and these two, in the presence of the whole assembly, kill him with their swords. This done, they roast him and eat him in common and send some pieces to their absent friends. This is not, as people think, for nourishment, as of old the Scythians used to do; it is to betoken an extreme revenge. And the proof of this came when they saw the Portuguese, who had joined forces with their adversaries, inflict a different kind of death on them when they took them prisoner, which was to bury them up to the waist, shoot the rest of their body full of arrows, and afterward hang them. They thought that these people from the other world, being men who had sown the knowledge of many vices among their neighbors and were much greater masters than themselves in every sort of wickedness, did not adopt this sort of vengeance without some reason, and that it must be more painful than their own; so they began to give up their old method and to follow this one.

I am not sorry that we notice the barbarous horror of such acts, but I am heartily sorry that, judging their faults rightly, we should be so blind to our own. I think there is more barbarity in eating a man alive than in eating him dead; and in tearing by tortures and the rack a body still full of feeling, in roasting a man bit by bit, in having him bitten and mangled by dogs and swine (as we have not only read but seen within fresh memory, not among ancient enemies, but among neighbors and fellow citizens, and what is worse, on the pretext of piety and religion), than in roasting and eating him after he is dead.

Indeed, Chrysippus and Zeno, heads of the Stoic sect, thought there was nothing wrong in using our carcasses for any purpose in case of need, and getting nourishment from them; just as our ancestors, when besieged by Caesar in the city of Alésia, resolved to relieve their famine by eating old men, women, and other people useless for fighting.

> The Gascons once, 'tis said, their life renewed
> By eating of such food.
> —JUVENAL

And physicians do not fear to use human flesh in all sorts of ways for our health, applying it either inwardly or outwardly. But there never was any opinion so disordered as to excuse treachery, disloyalty, tyranny, and cruelty, which are our ordinary vices.

So we may well call these people barbarians, in respect to the rules of reason, but not in respect to ourselves, who surpass them in every kind of barbarity.

Their warfare is wholly noble and generous, and as excusable and beautiful as this human disease can be; its only basis among them is their rivalry in valor. They are not fighting for the conquest of new lands, for they still enjoy that natural abundance that provides them without toil and trouble with all necessary things in such profusion that they have no wish to enlarge their boundaries. They are still in that happy state of desiring only as much as their natural needs demand; anything beyond that is superfluous to them.

They generally call those of the same age, brothers; those who are younger, children; and the old men are fathers to all the others. These leave to their heirs in common the full possession of their property, without division or any other title at all than just the one that Nature gives to her creatures in bringing them into the world.

If their neighbors cross the mountains to attack them and win a victory, the gain of the victor is glory, and the advantage of having proved the master in valor and virtue; for apart from this they have no use for the goods of the vanquished, and they return to their own country, where they lack neither anything necessary nor that great thing, the knowledge of how to enjoy their condition happily and be content with it. These men of ours do the same in their turn. They demand of their prisoners no other ransom than that they confess and acknowledge their defeat. But there is not one in a whole century who does not choose to die rather than to relax a single bit, by word or look, from the grandeur of an invincible courage; not one who would not rather be killed and eaten than so much as ask not to be. They treat them very freely, so that life may be all the dearer to them, and usually entertain them with threats of their coming death, of the torments they will have to suffer, the preparations that are being made for that purpose, the cutting up of their limbs, and the feast that will be made at their expense. All this is done for the sole purpose of extorting from their lips some weak or base word, or making them want to flee, so as to gain the advantage of having terrified them and broken down their firmness. For indeed, if you take it the right way, it is in this point alone that true victory lies:

> It is no victory
> Unless the vanquished foe admits your mastery.
> —CLAUDIAN

The Hungarians, very bellicose fighters, did not in olden times pursue their advantage beyond putting the enemy at their mercy. For having wrung a confession from him to this effect, they let him go unharmed and unransomed, except, at most, for exacting his promise never again to take up arms against them.

We win enough advantages over our enemies that are borrowed advantages, not really our own. It is the quality of a porter, not of valor, to have sturdier arms and legs; agility is a dead and corporeal quality; it is a stroke of luck to make our enemy stumble, or dazzle his eyes by the sunlight; it is a trick of art and technique, which may be found in a worthless coward, to be an able fencer. The worth and value of a man is in his heart and his will; there lies his real honor. Valor is the strength, not of legs and arms, but of heart and soul; it consists not in the worth of our horse or our weapons, but in our own. He who falls obstinate in his courage, *if he has fallen, he fights on his knees* [Seneca]. He who relaxes none of his assurance, no matter how great the danger of imminent death; who, giving up his soul, still looks firmly and scornfully at his enemy—he is beaten not by us, but by fortune; he is killed, not conquered.

The most valiant are sometimes the most unfortunate. Thus there are triumphant defeats that rival victories. Nor did those four sister victories, the fairest that the sun ever set eyes on—Salamis, Plataea, Mycale, and Sicily—ever dare match all their combined glory against the glory of the annihilation of King Leonidas[2] and his men at the pass of Thermopylae.

Who ever hastened with more glorious and ambitious desire to win a battle

---

2. During the invasion of Greece by the Persians in 480 B.C., King Leonidas of Sparta and a small army held off a vastly superior Persian force for two days at Thermopylae before being wiped out.

than Captain Ischolas to lose one? Who ever secured his safety more ingeniously and painstakingly than he did his destruction? He was charged to defend a certain pass in the Peloponnesus against the Arcadians. Finding himself wholly incapable of doing this, in view of the nature of the place and the inequality of the forces, he made up his mind that all who confronted the enemy would necessarily have to remain on the field. On the other hand, deeming it unworthy both of his own virtue and magnanimity and of the Lacedaemonian name to fail in his charge, he took a middle course between these two extremes, in this way. The youngest and fittest of his band he preserved for the defense and service of their country, and sent them home; and with those whose loss was less important, he determined to hold this pass, and by their death to make the enemy buy their entry as dearly as he could. And so it turned out. For he was presently surrounded on all sides by the Arcadians, and after slaughtering a large number of them, he and his men were all put to the sword. Is there a trophy dedicated to victors that would not be more due to these vanquished? The role of true victory is in fighting, not in coming off safely; and the honor of valor consists in combating, not in beating.

To return to our story. These prisoners are so far from giving in, in spite of all that is done to them, that on the contrary, during the two or three months that they are kept, they wear a gay expression; they urge their captors to hurry and put them to the test; they defy them, insult them, reproach them with their cowardice and the number of battles they have lost to the prisoners' own people.

I have a song composed by a prisoner which contains this challenge, that they should all come boldly and gather to dine off him, for they will be eating at the same time their own fathers and grandfathers, who have served to feed and nourish his body. "These muscles," he says, "this flesh and these veins are your own, poor fools that you are. You do not recognize that the substance of your ancestors' limbs is still contained in them. Savor them well; you will find in them the taste of your own flesh." An idea that certainly does not smack of barbarity. Those that paint these people dying, and who show the execution, portray the prisoner spitting in the face of his slayers and scowling at them. Indeed, to the last gasp they never stop braving and defying their enemies by word and look. Truly here are real savages by our standards; for either they must be thoroughly so, or we must be; there is an amazing distance between their character and ours.

The men there have several wives, and the higher their reputation for valor the more wives they have. It is a remarkably beautiful thing about their marriages that the same jealousy our wives have to keep us from the affection and kindness of other women, theirs have to win this for them. Being more concerned for their husbands' honor than for anything else, they strive and scheme to have as many companions as they can, since that is a sign of their husbands' valor.

Our wives will cry "Miracle!" but it is no miracle. It is a properly matrimonial virtue, but one of the highest order. In the Bible, Leah, Rachel, Sarah, and Jacob's wives gave their beautiful handmaids to their husbands; and Livia seconded the appetites of Augustus, to her own disadvantage; and Stratonice, the wife of King Deiotarus, not only lent her husband for his use a very beautiful young chambermaid in her service, but carefully brought up her children, and backed them up to succeed to their father's estates.

And lest it be thought that all this is done through a simple and servile bondage to usage and through the pressure of the authority of their ancient customs, without reasoning or judgment, and because their minds are so stupid that they cannot take any other course, I must cite some examples of their capacity. Besides the warlike song I have just quoted, I have another, a love song, which begins in this vein: "Adder, stay; stay, adder, that from the pattern of your coloring my sister may draw the fashion and the workmanship of a rich girdle that I may give to my love; so may your beauty and your pattern be forever preferred to all other serpents." This first couplet is the refrain of the song. Now I am familiar enough with poetry to be a judge of this: not only is there nothing barbarous in this fancy, but it is altogether Anacreontic. Their language, moreover, is a soft language, with an agreeable sound, somewhat like Greek in its endings.

Three of these men, ignorant of the price they will pay some day, in loss of repose and happiness, for gaining knowledge of the corruptions of this side of the ocean; ignorant also of the fact that of this intercourse will come their ruin (which I suppose is already well advanced: poor wretches, to let themselves be tricked by the desire for new things and to have left the serenity of their own sky to come and see ours!)—three of these men were at Rouen, at the time the late King Charles IX was there.[3] The king talked to them for a long time; they were shown our ways, our splendor, the aspect of a fine city. After that, someone asked their opinion, and wanted to know what they had found most amazing. They mentioned three things, of which I have forgotten the third, and I am very sorry for it; but I still remember two of them. They said that in the first place they thought it very strange that so many grown men, bearded, strong, and armed, who were around the king (it is likely that they were talking about the Swiss of his guard) should submit to obey a child, and that one of them was not chosen to command instead. Second (they have a way in their language of speaking of men as halves of one another), they had noticed that there were among us men full and gorged with all sorts of good things, and that their other halves were beggars at their doors, emaciated with hunger and poverty; and they thought it strange that these needy halves could endure such an injustice, and did not take the others by the throat, or set fire to their houses.

I had a very long talk with one of them; but I had an interpreter who followed my meaning so badly, and who was so hindered by his stupidity in taking in my ideas, that I could get hardly any satisfaction from the man. When I asked him what profit he gained from his superior position among his people (for he was a captain, and our sailors called him king), he told me that it was to march foremost in war. How many men followed him? He pointed to a piece of ground, to signify as many as such a space could hold; it might have been four or five thousand men. Did all his authority expire with the war? He said that this much remained, that when he visited the villages dependent on him, they made paths for him through the underbrush by which he might pass quite comfortably.

All this is not too bad—but what's the use? They don't wear breeches.

---

3. Charles IX became king of France in 1560 at the age of ten; he died in 1574.

MIGUEL DE CERVANTES SAAVEDRA

(1547–1616)

Spain

Miguel de Cervantes Saavedra, the greatest figure in Spanish literature, was born in Alcalá de Henares in 1547. He had an eventful military career, in Italy, fighting in the battle of *Lepanto* (1571), in which he lost his left hand; returning to Spain with his brother, he was captured by Barbary pirates. Both brothers were taken to Algiers as slaves. When his ransom was paid by the Trinitarian friars, he returned to Spain. He wrote in a variety of forms including the twelve short stories of the *Novelas ejemplares* (*Exemplary Stories*), the pastoral romance *La Galatea* (1585), many plays after 1585, as well as verse and verse romance. His masterpiece is *Don Quixote*: the first part was published in 1605 and the second in 1615, a year before the author's death. A satire on the romances of chivalry, this tale of the adventures of a mad and impoverished nobleman who becomes a wandering knight, a role which in his own time existed only in literature, is one of the world's most influential novels and—as is now recognized—one of the most complex.

from *Don Quixote*

[The Quality and Way of Life of the Famous Knight Don Quixote]

In a certain village in La Mancha, which I do not wish to name, there lived not long ago a gentleman—one of those who have always a lance in the rack, an ancient shield, a lean hack and a greyhound for coursing. His habitual diet consisted of a stew, more beef than mutton, of hash most nights, boiled bones on Saturdays, lentils on Friday, and a young pigeon as a Sunday treat; and on this he spent three-quarters of his income. The rest of it went on a fine cloth doublet, velvet breeches and slippers for holidays, and a homespun suit of the best in which he decked himself on weekdays. His household consisted of a housekeeper of rather more than forty, a niece not yet twenty, and a lad for the field and market, who saddled his horse and wielded the pruning-hook.

Our gentleman was verging on fifty, of tough constitution, lean-bodied, thin-faced, a great early riser and a lover of hunting. They say that his surname was Quixada or Quesada—for there is some difference of opinion amongst authors on this point. However, by very reasonable conjecture we may take it that he was called Quexana. But this does not much concern our story; enough that we do not depart by so much as an inch from the truth in the telling of it.

The reader must know, then, that this gentleman, in the times when he had nothing to do—as was the case for most of the year—gave himself up to the reading of books of knight errantry; which he loved and enjoyed so much that he almost entirely forgot his hunting, and even the care of his estate. So odd and foolish, indeed, did he grow on this subject that he sold many acres of cornland to buy these books of chivalry to read, and in this way brought home every one he could get. And of them all he considered none so good as the works of the famous Feliciano de Silva. For his brilliant style and those complicated sentences seemed to him very pearls, especially when he came upon those love-passages and challenges frequently written in the manner of: 'The reason for the unreason with which you treat my reason, so weakens my reason that with reason I complain of your beauty'; and also when he read: 'The high heavens that with their stars divinely fortify you in your divinity and make you deserving of the desert that your greatness deserves.'

These writings drove the poor knight out of his wits; and he passed sleepless nights trying to understand them and disentangle their meaning, though Aristotle himself would never have unravelled or understood them, even if he had been resurrected for that sole purpose. He did not much like the wounds that Sir Belianis gave and received, for he imagined that his face and his whole body must have been covered with scars and marks, however skillful the surgeons who tended him. But, for all that, he admired the author for ending his book with the promise to continue with that interminable adventure, and often the desire seized him to take up the pen himself, and write the promised sequel for him. No doubt he would have done so, and perhaps successfully, if other greater and more persistent preoccupations had not prevented him.

Often he had arguments with the priest of his village, who was a scholar and a graduate of Siguenza, as to which was the better knight—Palmerin of England or Amadis of Gaul.[1] But Master Nicholas, the barber of that village, said that no one could compare with the Knight of the Sun. Though if anyone could, it was Sir Galaor, brother of Amadis of Gaul. For he had a very accommodating nature, and was not so affected nor such a sniveller as his brother, though he was not a bit behind him in the matter of bravery.

In short, he so buried himself in his books that he spent the nights reading from twilight till daybreak and the days from dawn till dark; and so from little sleep and much reading, his brain dried up and he lost his wits. He filled his mind with all that he read in them, with enchantments, quarrels, battles, challenges, wounds, wooings, loves, torments and other impossible nonsense; and so deeply did he steep his imagination in the belief that all the fanciful stuff he read was true, that to his mind no history in the world was more authentic. He used to say that the Cid Ruy Diaz must have been a very good knight, but that he could not be compared to the Knight of the Burning Sword, who with a single backstroke had cleft a pair of fierce and monstrous giants in two. And he had an even better opinion of Bernardo del Carpio for slaying the enchanted Roland at Roncesvalles,[2] by making use of Hercules' trick when he throttled the Titan Antaeus in his arms.

---

1. Heroes of narrative works about knights-errant. The many volumes of the adventures of Amadis, written in several western European languages, were especially popular.

2. There are many stories about Roland, the heroic nephew of Charlemagne, who supposedly died in battle against the Moors at Roncesvalles in the Pyrenees.

He spoke very well of the giant Morgante; for, though one of that giant brood who are all proud and insolent, he alone was affable and well-mannered. But he admired most of all Reynald of Montalban, particularly when he saw him sally forth from his castle and rob everyone he met, and when in heathen lands overseas he stole that idol of Mahomet, which history says was of pure gold. But he would have given his housekeeper and his niece into the bargain, to deal the traitor Galaon a good kicking.

In fact, now that he had utterly wrecked his reason he fell into the strangest fancy that ever a madman had in the whole world. He though it fit and proper, both in order to increase his renown and to serve the state, to turn knight errant and travel through the world with horse and armour in search of adventures, following in every way the practice of the knights errant he had read of, redressing all manner of wrongs, and exposing himself to chances and dangers, by the overcoming of which he might win eternal honour and renown. Already the poor man fancied himself crowned by the valour of his arm, at least with the empire of Trebizond; and so, carried away by the strange pleasure he derived from these agreeable thoughts, he hastened to translate his desires into action.

The first thing that he did was to clean some armour which had belonged to his ancestors, and had lain for ages forgotten in a corner, eaten with rust and covered with mould. But when he had cleaned and repaired it as best he could, he found that there was one great defect: the helmet was a simple head-piece without a visor. So he ingeniously made good this deficiency by fashioning out of pieces of pasteboard a kind of half-visor which, fitted to the helmet, gave the appearance of a complete head-piece. However, to see if it was strong enough to stand up to the risk of a sword-cut, he took out his sword and gave it two strokes, the first of which demolished in a moment what had taken him a week to make. He was not too pleased at the ease with which he had destroyed it, and to safeguard himself against this danger, reconstructed the visor, putting some strips of iron inside, in such a way as to satisfy himself of his protection; and, not caring to make another trial of it, he accepted it as a fine jointed headpiece and put it into commission.

Next he went to inspect his hack, but though, through leanness, he had more quarters than there are pence in a groat, and more blemishes than Gonella's horse,[3] which was nothing but skin and bone, he appeared to our knight more than the equal of Alexander's Bucephalus[4] and the Cid's Babieca.[5] He spent four days pondering what name to give him; for, he reflected, it would be wrong for the horse of so famous a knight, a horse so good in himself, to be without a famous name. Therefore he tried to fit him with one that would signify what he had been before his master turned knight errant, and what he now was; for it was only right that as his master changed his profession, the horse should change his name for a sublime and high-sounding one, befitting the new order and the new calling he

---

3. Gonella was the court jester of the Duke of Ferrara and became a legendary personality in his own right. There were jokes about his incredibly skinny horse.

4. Alexander the Great, ruler of Macedon and conqueror of much of the known world, had a famous horse named Bucephalus.

5. The horse of Rodrigo Díaz de Bivar, called "The Cid" and hero of the twelfth-century Spanish poem of the same name.

professed. So, after many names invented, struck out and rejected, amended, cancelled and remade in his fanciful mind, he finally decided to call him Rocinante, a name which seemed to him grand and sonorous, and to express the common horse he had been before arriving at his present state: the first and foremost of all hacks in the world.

Having found so pleasing a name for his horse, he next decided to do the same for himself, and spent another eight days thinking about it. Finally he resolved to call himself Don Quixote. And that is no doubt why the authors of this true history, as we have said, assumed that his name must have been Quixada and not Quesada, as other authorities would have it. Yet he remembered that the valorous Amadis had not been content with his bare name, but had added the name of his kingdom and native country in order to make it famous, and styled himself Amadis of Gaul. So, like a good knight, he decided to add the name of his country to his own and call himself Don Quixote de la Mancha. Thus, he thought, he very clearly proclaimed his parentage and native land and honoured it by taking his surname from it.

Now that his armour was clean, his helmet made into a complete head-piece, a name found for his horse, and he confirmed in his new title, it struck him that there was only one more thing to do: to find a lady to be enamoured of. For a knight errant without a lady is like a tree without leaves or fruit and a body without a soul. He said to himself again and again: 'If I for my sins or by good luck were to meet with some giant hereabouts, as generally happens to knights errant, and if I were to overthrow him in the encounter, or cut him down the middle or, in short, conquer him and make him surrender, would it not be well to have someone to whom I could send him as a present, so that he could enter and kneel down before my sweet lady and say in tones of humble submission: "Lady, I am the giant Caraculiambro, lord of the island of Malindrania, whom the never-sufficiently-to-be-praised knight, Don Quixote de la Mancha, conquered in single combat and ordered to appear before your Grace, so that your Highness might dispose of me according to your will"?' Oh, how pleased our knight was when he had made up this speech, and even gladder when he found someone whom he could call his lady. It happened, it is believed, in this way: in a village near his there was a very good-looking farm girl, whom he had been taken with at one time, although she is supposed not to have known it or had proof of it. Her name was Aldonza Lorenzo, and she it was he thought fit to call the lady of his fancies; and, casting around for a name which should not be too far away from her own, yet suggest and imply a princess and great lady, he resolved to call her Dulcinea del Toboso—for she was a native of El Toboso—,a name which seemed to him as musical, strange and significant as those others that he had devised for himself and his possessions.

[Don Quixote's Success in the Dreadful and Never Before Imagined Adventure of the Windmills]

At that moment they caught sight of some thirty or forty windmills, which stand on that plain, and as soon as Don Quixote saw them he said to his squire: "Fortune is guiding our affairs better than we could have wished. Look over there, friend Sancho Panza, where more than thirty monstrous giants appear. I intend to do battle with them and take all their lives. With their spoils we will begin to get rich, for this is a fair war, and it is a great service to God to wipe out such a wicked brood from the face of the earth."

"What giants?" asked Sancho Panza.

"Those you see there," replied his master, "with their long arms. Some giants have them about six miles long."

"Take care, your worship," said Sancho; "those things over there are not giants but windmills, and what seem to be their arms are the sails, which are whirled round in the wind and make the millstone turn."

"It is quite clear," replied Don Quixote, "that you are not experienced in this matter of adventures. They are giants, and if you are afraid, go away and say your prayers, whilst I advance and engage them in fierce and unequal battle."

As he spoke, he dug his spurs into his steed Rocinante, paying no attention to his squire's shouted warning that beyond all doubt they were windmills and no giants he was advancing to attack. But he went on, so positive that they were giants that he neither listened to Sancho's cries nor noticed what they were, even when he got near them. Instead he went on shouting in a loud voice: "Do not fly, cowards, vile creatures, for it is one knight alone who assails you."

At that moment a slight wind arose, and the great sails began to move. At the sight of which Don Quixote shouted: "Though you wield more arms than the giant Briareus, you shall pay for it!" Saying this, he commended himself with all his soul to his Lady Dulcinea, beseeching her aid in his great peril. Then, covering himself with his shield and putting his lance in the rest, he urged Rocinante forward at a full gallop and attacked the nearest windmill, thrusting his lance into the sail. But the wind turned it with such violence that it shivered his weapon to pieces, dragging the horse and his rider with it, and sent the knight rolling badly injured across the plain. Sancho Panza rushed to his assistance as fast as his ass could trot, but when he came up he found that the knight could not stir. Such a shock had Rocinante given him in their fall.

"Oh my goodness!" cried Sancho. "Didn't I tell your worship to look what you were doing, for they were only windmills? Nobody could mistake them, unless he had windmills on the brain."

"Silence, friend Sancho," replied Don Quixote. "Matters of war are more subject than most to continual change. What is more, I think—and that is the truth—that the same sage Friston who robbed me of my room and my books has turned those giants into windmills, to cheat me of the glory of conquering them. Such is the enmity he bears me; but in the very end his black arts shall avail him little against the goodness of my sword."

"God send it as He will," replied Sancho Panza, helping the knight to get up and remount Rocinante, whose shoulders were half dislocated.

WILLIAM SHAKESPEARE (1564–1616)
England

William Shakespeare was born in Stratford-upon-Avon in 1564, and worked as an actor and as a playwright in London. His history plays, tragedies, comedies, and romances have made him the world's most famous and most frequently performed playwright. He later retired from the stage and withdrew to Stratford, dying there in 1616. His 154 sonnets, written in the mid 1590s, were published in 1609. They are concerned with a tangle of relationships between the first person speaker and a handsome young man, a dark complexioned older woman, and a rival poet. They have generated an enormous amount of criticism and commentary of every conceivable kind. The late romance, *The Tempest* (1611), one of Shakespeare's last plays, is often seen as the culmination of his dramatic art.

Shall I Compare Thee to a Summer's Day

Shall I compare thee to a summer's day?
Thou art more lovely and more temperate.
Rough winds do shake the darling buds of May,
And summer's lease hath all too short a date.
Sometimes too hot the eye of heaven shines,   5
And often is his gold complexion dimmed;
And every fair from fair sometime declines,
By chance, or nature's changing course, untrimmed;
But thy eternal summer shall not fade,
Nor lose possession of that fair thou ow'st,   10
Nor shall Death brag thou wand'rest in his shade,
When in eternal lines to time thou grow'st.
   So long as men can breathe or eyes can see,
   So long lives this, and this gives life to thee.

When, in Disgrace with Fortune and Men's Eyes

When, in disgrace with Fortune and men's eyes,
I all alone beweep my outcast state,
And trouble deaf heaven with my bootless cries,
And look upon myself and curse my fate,
Wishing me like to one more rich in hope,
Featured like him, like him with friends possessed,
Desiring this man's art, and that man's scope,
With what I most enjoy contented least;
Yet in these thoughts myself almost despising,

Haply I think on thee, and then my state,
Like to the lark at break of day arising
From sullen earth, sings hymns at heaven's gate;
   For thy sweet love rememb'red such wealth brings,
   That then I scorn to change my state with kings.

My Mistress' Eyes Are Nothing Like the Sun

My mistress' eyes are nothing like the sun;
Coral is far more red than her lips' red;
If snow be white, why then her breasts are dun;
If hairs be wires, black wires grow on her head.
I have seen roses damasked, red and white,
But no such roses see I in her cheeks,
And in some perfumes is there more delight
Than in the breath that from my mistress reeks.
I love to hear her speak, yet well I know
That music hath a far more pleasing sound.
I grant I never saw a goddess go;
My mistress when she walks treads on the ground.
   And yet, by heaven, I think my love as rare
   As any she belied with false compare.

The Tempest

Names of the Actors

ALONSO, *King of Naples*

SEBASTIAN, *his brother*

PROSPERO, *the right Duke of Milan*

ANTONIO, *his brother, the usurping Duke of Milan*

FERDINAND, *son to the King of Naples*

GONZALO, *an honest old councillor*

ADRIAN *and*
FRANCISCO, } *lords*

CALIBAN, *a savage and deformed slave*

TRINCULO, *a jester*

STEPHANO, *a drunken butler*

MASTER *of a ship*

BOATSWAIN

MARINERS

MIRANDA, *daughter to Prospero*

ARIEL, *an airy spirit*

IRIS
CERES,
JUNO, } *[presented by] spirits*
NYMPHS
REAPERS,

[Other Spirits attending on Prospero]

Scene

An uninhabited island

Sketch of the Swan made in 1596 by
Aernout van Buchell. Drawing by
Johannes de Witt. Bibliotheek der
Rijksuniversiteit Utrecht.

Act I

Scene 1[1]

> [*A tempestuous noise of thunder and lighting heard. Enter a Shipmaster and a Boatswain.*]

MASTER: Boatswain!

BOATSWAIN: Here, Master. What cheer?

MASTER: Good,[2] speak to the mariners. Fall to 't yarely,[3] or we run ourselves aground. Bestir, bestir! [*Exit.*]

> [*Enter Mariners.*]

BOATSWAIN: Heigh, my hearts! Cheerly, cheerly, my hearts! Yare, yare! Take in the topsail. Tend[4] to the Master's whistle.—Blow[5] till thou burst thy wind, if room enough![6]   5

> [*Enter Alonso, Sebastian, Antonio, Ferdinand, Gonzalo, and others.*]

Act I, Scene 1

1. Location: on board ship, off the island's coast.
2. I.e., it's good you've come, or, my good fellow.
3. Nimbly.
4. Attend.
5. Addressed to the wind.
6. As long as we have sea room enough.

ALONSO: Good Boatswain, have care. Where's the Master? Play the men.[7]

BOATSWAIN: I pray now, keep below.

ANTONIO: Where is the Master, Boatswain?

BOATSWAIN: Do you not hear him? You mar our labor. Keep[8] your cabins! You do assist the storm.

GONZALO: Nay, good,[9] be patient.

BOATSWAIN: When the sea is. Hence! What cares these roarers[10] for the name of king? To cabin! Silence! Trouble us not.

GONZALO: Good, yet remember whom thou hast aboard.

BOATSWAIN: None that I more love than myself. You are a councillor; if you can command these elements to silence and work the peace of the present,[11] we will not hand[12] a rope more. Use your authority. If you cannot, give thanks you have lived so long and make yourself ready in your cabin for the mischance of the hour, if it so hap.[13]—Cheerly, good hearts!—Out of our way, I say. *[Exit.]*

GONZALO: I have great comfort from this fellow. Methinks he hath no drowning mark upon him; his complexion is perfect gallows.[14] Stand fast, good Fate, to his hanging! Make the rope of his destiny our cable, for our own doth little advantage.[15] If he be not born to be hanged, our case is miserable.[16] *[Exeunt (courtiers).]*

[Enter Boatswain.]

BOATSWAIN: Down with the topmast! Yare! Lower, lower! Bring her try wi' the main course.[17] *(A cry within.)* A plague upon this howling! They are louder than the weather or our office.[18]

[Enter Sebastian, Antonio, and Gonzalo.]

Yet again? What do you here? Shall we give o'er[19] and drown? Have you a mind to sink?

SEBASTIAN: A pox o' your throat, you bawling, blasphemous, incharitable dog!

BOATSWAIN: Work you, then.

ANTONIO: Hang, cur! Hang, you whoreson, insolent noisemaker! We are less afraid to be drowned than thou art.

---

7. Act like men (?) ply, urge the men to exert themselves (?).
8. Remain in.
9. Good fellow.
10. Waves or winds, or both: spoken to as though they were "bullies" or blusterers.
11. Bring calm to our present circumstances.
12. Handle.
13. Happen.

14. Appearance shows he was born to be hanged (and therefore, according to the proverb, in no danger of drowning).
15. Our own cable is of little benefit.
16. Circumstances are desperate.
17. Sail her close to the wind by means of the mainsail.
18. I.e., the noise we make at our work.
19. Give up.

GONZALO: I'll warrant him for drowning,[20] though the ship were no stronger than a nutshell and as leaky as an unstanched[21] wench.

BOATSWAIN: Lay her ahold, ahold![22] Set her two courses.[23] Off to sea again! Lay her off!

[Enter Mariners, wet.]

MARINERS: All lost! To prayers, to prayers! All lost! 40

[The Mariners run about in confusion, exiting at random.]

BOATSWAIN: What, must our mouths be cold?[24]

GONZALO:
The King and Prince at prayers! Let's assist them,
For our case is as theirs.

SEBASTIAN: I am out of patience.

ANTONIO:
We are merely[25] cheated of our lives by drunkards. 45
This wide-chapped[26] rascal! Would thou mightst lie drowning
The washing of ten tides![27]

GONZALO: He'll be hanged yet,
Though every drop of water swear against it
And gape at wid'st[28] to glut[29] him. 50

[A confused noise within.] "Mercy on us!"—
"We split,[30] we split!"—"Farewell my wife and children!"—
"Farewell, brother!"—We split, we split, we split!"

[Exit Boatswain.]

ANTONIO: Let's all sink wi' the King.

SEBASTIAN: Let's take leave of him.

[Exit (with Antonio).]

GONZALO: Now would I give a thousand furlongs of sea for an acre of barren 55
ground: long heath,[31] brown furze,[32] anything. The wills above be done!
But I would fain[33] die a dry death.

[Exit.]

---

20. Guarantee that he will never be drowned.
21. Insatiable, loose, unrestrained (suggesting also "incontinent" and "menstrual").
22. Ahull, close to the wind.
23. Sails, i.e., foresail as well as mainsail, set in an attempt to get the ship back out into open water.
24. I.e., must we drown in the cold sea, or, let us heat up our mouths with liquor.
25. Utterly.
26. With mouth wide open.
27. Pirates were hanged on the shore and left until three tides had come in.
28. Wide open.
29. Swallow.
30. Break apart.
31. Heather.
32. Furze gorse, a weed growing on wasteland
33. Rather.

Scene 2[1]

[Enter Prospero (in his magic cloak) and Miranda.]

MIRANDA:
    If by your art,[2] my dearest father, you have
    Put the wild waters in this roar, allay[3] them.
    The sky, it seems, would pour down stinking pitch,
    But that the sea, mounting to th' welkin's cheek,[4]
    Dashes the fire out. O, I have suffered   5
    With those that I saw suffer! A brave[5] vessel,
    Who had, no doubt, some noble creature in her,
    Dashed all to pieces. O, the cry did knock
    Against my very heart! Poor souls, they perished.   10
    Had I been any god of power, I would
    Have sunk the sea within the earth or ere[6]
    It should the good ship so have swallowed and
    The freighting[7] souls within her.
PROSPERO: Be collected.[8]
    No more amazement.[9] Tell your piteous[10] heart
    There's no harm done.   15
MIRANDA: O, woe the day!
PROSPERO: No harm.
    I have done nothing but[11] in care of thee,
    Of thee, my dear one, thee, my daughter, who
    Art ignorant of what thou art, naught knowing
    Of whence I am, nor that I am more better[12]
    Than Prospero, master of a full[13] poor cell,   20
    And thy no greater father.
MIRANDA: More to know
    Did never meddle[14] with my thoughts.
PROSPERO: 'Tis time
    I should inform thee farther. Lend thy hand
    And pluck my magic garment from me. So,

[Laying down his magic cloak and staff.]

Act I, Scene 2

1. Location: the island, near Prospero's cell.
On the Elizabethan stage, this cell is implicitly at hand throughout the play, although
in some scenes the convention of flexible
distance allows us to imagine characters in
other parts of the island.
2. Magic.
3. Pacify.
4. Sky's face.
5. Gallant, splendid.

6. Before.
7. Forming the cargo.
8. Calm, composed.
9. Consternation.
10. Pitying.
11. Except.
12. Of higher rank.
13. Very.
14. Mingle.

Lie there, my art.—Wipe thou thine eyes. Have comfort.   25
The direful spectacle of the wreck,[15] which touched
The very virtue[16] of compassion in thee,
I have with such provision[17] in mine art
So safely ordered that there is no soul—
No, not so much perdition[18] as an hair   30
Betid[19] to any creature in the vessel
Which[20] thou heard'st cry, which thou saw'st sink. Sit down,
For thou must now know farther.
MIRANDA [*sitting*]:   You have often
Begun to tell me what I am, but stopped
And left me to a bootless inquisition,[21]   35
Concluding, "Stay, not yet."
PROSPERO: . The hour's now come;
The very minute bids thee ope thine ear.
Obey, and be attentive. Canst thou remember
A time before we came unto this cell?
I do not think thou canst, for then thou wast not   40
Out[22] three years old.
MIRANDA: Certainly, sir, I can.
PROSPERO:
By what? By any other house or person?
Of anything the image, tell me, that
Hath kept with thy remembrance.
MIRANDA: 'Tis far off,
And rather like a dream than an assurance   45
That my remembrance warrants.[23] Had I not
Four or five women once that tended me?
PROSPERO:
Thou hadst, and more, Miranda. But how is it
That this lives in thy mind? What seest thou else
In the dark backward and abysm of time?[24]   50
If thou rememberest aught[25] ere thou cam'st here,
How thou cam'st here thou mayst.
MIRANDA: But that I do not.
PROSPERO:
Twelve year since, Miranda, twelve year since,
Thy father was the Duke of Milan and
A prince of power.   55
MIRANDA: Sir, are not you my father?

---

15. Shipwreck.
16. Essence.
17. Foresight.
18. Loss.
19. Happened.
20. Whom.

21. Profitless inquiry.
22. Fully.
23. Certainty that my memory guarantees.
24. Abyss of the past.
25. Anything.

PROSPERO:

    Thy mother was a piece[26] of virtue, and
    She said thou wast my daughter; and thy father
    Was Duke of Milan, and his only heir
    And princess no worse issued.[27]

MIRANDA: O the heavens!

    What foul play had we, that we came from thence?   60
    Or blessed was 't we did?

PROSPERO: Both, both, my girl.

    By foul play, as thou sayst, were we heaved thence,
    But blessedly holp[28] hither.

MIRANDA: O, my heart bleeds

    To think o' the teen[29] that I have turned you to,
    Which is from[30] my remembrance! Please you, farther.   65

PROSPERO:

    My brother and thy uncle, called Antonio—
    I pray thee mark me—that a brother should
    Be so perfidious!—he whom next[31] thyself
    Of all the world I loved, and to him put
    The manage[32] of my state, as at that time   70
    Through all the seigniories[33] it was the first,
    And Prospero the prime[34] duke, being so reputed
    In dignity, and for the liberal arts
    Without a parallel; those being all my study,
    The government I cast upon my brother   75
    And to my state grew stranger,[35] being transported[36]
    And rapt in secret studies. Thy false uncle—
    Dost thou attend me?

MIRANDA: Sir, most heedfully.

PROSPERO:

    Being once perfected[37] how to grant suits,
    How to deny them, who t' advance and who   80
    To trash[38] for overtopping,[39] new created
    The creatures[40] that were mine, I say, or changed 'em,
    Or else new formed 'em;[41] having both the key[42]

---

26. Masterpiece, exemplar.
27. No less nobly born, descended.
28. Helped.
29. To trouble I've caused you to remember or put you to.
30. Out of.
31. Next to.
32. Management, administration.
33. I.e., city-states of northern Italy.
34. First in rank and importance.
35. I.e., withdrew from my responsibilities as duke.

36. Carried away.
37. Grown skillful.
38. Check a hound by tying a cord or weight to its neck.
39. Running too far ahead of the pack; surmounting, exceeding one's authority.
40. Dependents.
41. I.e., either changed their loyalties and duties or else created new ones.
42. (1) key for unlocking (2) tool for tuning stringed instruments.

Of officer and office, set all hearts i' the state
To what tune pleased his ear, that[43] now he was   85
The ivy which had hid my princely trunk
And sucked my verdure out on 't.[44] Thou attend'st not.

MIRANDA:
      O, good sir, I do.

PROSPERO: I pray thee, mark me.
I, thus neglecting worldly ends, all dedicated
To closeness[45] and the bettering of my mind   90
With that which, but by being so retired,
O'erprized all popular rate,[46] in my false brother
Awaked an evil nature; and my trust,
Like a good parent,[47] did beget of[48] him
A falsehood in its contrary as great   95
As my trust was, which had indeed no limit,
A confidence sans[49] bound. He being thus lorded[50]
Not only with what my revenue yielded
But what my power might else[51] exact, like one
Who,[52] having into[53] truth by telling of it,   100
Made such a sinner of his memory
To[54] credit his own lie, he did believe
He was indeed the Duke, out o'[55] the substitution
And executing th' outward face of royalty[56]
With all prerogative. Hence his ambition growing—   105
Dost thou hear?

MIRANDA: Your tale, sir, would cure deafness.

PROSPERO:
To have no screen between this part he played
And him he played it for,[57] he needs will be[58]
Absolute Milan.[59] Me, poor man, my library
Was dukedom large enough. Of temporal[60] royalties   110

---

43. So that.
44. Vitality. Out of it.
45. Retirement, seclusion.
46. I.e., were it not that its private nature caused me to neglect my public responsibilities, had a value far beyond what public opinion could appreciate, or, simply because it was done in such seclusion, had a value not appreciated by popular opinion.
47. (Alludes to the proverb that good parents often bear bad children.)
48. In.
49. Without.
50. Raised to lordship, with power and wealth.
51. Otherwise, additionally.

52. I.e., who, by repeatedly telling the lie (that he was indeed Duke of Milan,) made his memory such a confirmed sinner against truth that he began to believe his own lie.
53. Unto, against.
54. So as to.
55. As a result of.
56. And (as a result of) his carrying out all the visible functions of royalty.
57. To have no separation or barrier between his role and himself. (Antonio wanted to act in his own person, not as substitute.)
58. Insisted on becoming.
59. Unconditional Duke of Milan.
60. Practical prerogatives and responsibilities of a sovereign.

He thinks me now incapable; confederates[61]—
So dry[62] he was for sway[63]— wi' the King of Naples
To give him[64] annual tribute, do him homage,
Subject his[65] coronet to his[66] crown, and bend[67]
The dukedom yet[68] unbowed—alas, poor Milan!—   115
To most ignoble stooping.

MIRANDA: O the heavens!

PROSPERO:
Mark his condition[69] and th' event,[70] then tell me
If this might be a brother.

MIRANDA: I should sin
To think but[71] nobly of my grandmother.   120
Good wombs have borne bad sons.   120

PROSPERO: Now the condition.
This King of Naples, being an enemy
To me inveterate, hearkens[72] my brother's suit,
Which was that he,[73] in lieu o' the premises[74]
Of homage and I know not how much tribute,
Should presently extirpate[75] me and mine   125
Out of the dukedom and confer fair Milan,
With all the honors, on my brother. Whereon,
A treacherous army levied, one midnight
Fated to th' purpose did Antonio open
The gates of Milan, and, i' the dead of darkness,   130
The ministers for the purpose[76] hurried thence[77]
Me and thy crying self.

MIRANDA: Alack, for pity!
I, not remembering how I cried out then,
Will cry it o'er again. It is a hint[78]   135
That wrings[79] mine eyes to 't.

PROSPERO: Hear a little further,
And then I'll bring thee to the present business
Which now's upon 's, without the which this story
Were most impertinent.[80]

MIRANDA: Wherefore[81] did they not
That hour destroy us?

---

61. Conspires, allies himself.
62. Thirsty.
63. Power.
64. I.e., the King of Naples.
65. Antonio's.
66. The King of Naples.
67. Make bow down.
68. Hitherto.
69. Pact.
70. Outcome.
71. Other than.

72. Listens to.
73. The King of Naples.
74. In return for the stipulation.
75. At once remove.
76. Agents employed to do this.
77. From there.
78. Occasion.
79. (1) constrains (2)wrings fears from.
80. Irrelevant.
81. Why.

PROSPERO: Well demanded,[82] wench.[83]   140
            My tale provokes that question. Dear, they durst not,
            So dear the love my people bore me, nor set
            A mark so bloody[84] on the business, but
            With colors fairer[85] painted their foul ends.
            In few,[86] they hurried us aboard a bark,[87]
            Bore us some leagues to sea, where they prepared   145
            A rotten carcass of a butt,[88] not rigged,
            Nor tackle,[89] sail, nor mast; the very rats
            Instinctively have quit[90] it. There they hoist us,
            To cry to th' sea that roared to us, to sigh
            To th' winds whose pity, sighing back again,   150
            Did us but loving wrong.[91]
MIRANDA: Alack, what trouble
            Was I then to you!
PROSPERO: O, a cherubin
            Thou wast that did preserve me. Thou didst smile,
            Infused with a fortitude from heaven,   155
            When I have decked[92] the sea with drops full salt,
            Under my burden groaned, which[93] raised in me
            An undergoing stomach,[94] to bear up
            Against what should ensue.
MIRANDA: How came we ashore?
PROSPERO: By Providence divine.   160
            Some food we had, and some fresh water, that
            A noble Neapolitan, Gonzalo,
            Out of his charity, who being then appointed
            Master of this design, did give us, with
            Rich garments, linens, stuffs,[95] and necessaries,   165
            Which since have steaded much.[96] So, of[97] his gentleness,
            Knowing I loved my books, he furnished me
            From mine own library with volumes that
            I prize above my dukedom.
MIRANDA: Would[98] I might
            But ever[99] see that man!   170

---

82. Asked.
83. (Here a term of endearment.)
84. I.e., make obvious their murderous intent.
    (From the practice of marking with the
    blood of the prey those who have partici-
    pated in a successful hunt.)
85. Apparently more attractive.
86. Few words.
87. Ship.
88. Cask, tub.
89. Neither rigging.
90. Abandoned.

91. I.e., the winds pitied Prospero and Mi-
    randa, though of necessity they blew them
    from shore.)
92. Covered (with salt tears); adorned.
93. I.e., the smile.
94. Courage to go on.
95. Supplies.
96. Been of much use.
97. Similarly, out of.
98. I wish.
99. I.e., someday.

PROSPERO: Now I arise.

[He puts on his magic cloak.]

Sit still, and hear the last of our sea sorrow.[100]
Here in this island we arrived; and here
Have I, thy schoolmaster, made thee more profit[101]
Than other princess'[102] can, that have more time
For vainer[103] hours and tutors not so careful.   175
MIRANDA:
Heavens thank you for 't! And now, I pray you, sir—
For still 'tis beating in my mind—your reason
For raising this sea storm?
PROSPERO: Know thus far forth:
By accident most strange, bountiful Fortune,
Now my dear lady,[104] hath mine enemies   180
Brought to this shore; and by my prescience
I find my zenith[105] doth depend upon
A most auspicious star, whose influence[106]
If now I court not, but omit,[107] my fortunes
Will ever after droop. Here cease more questions.   185
Thou art inclined to sleep. 'Tis a good dullness,[108]
And give it way.[109] I know thou canst not choose.

[Miranda sleeps.]

Come away,[110] servant, come! I am ready now.
Approach, my Ariel, come.

[Enter Ariel.]

ARIEL: 190
All hail, great master, grave sir, hail! I come
To answer thy best pleasure; be 't to fly,
To swim, to dive into the fire, to ride
On the curled clouds, to thy strong bidding task[111]
Ariel and all his quality.[112]
PROSPERO: Hast thou, spirit,
Performed to point[113] the tempest that I bade thee?   195

---

100. Sorrowful adventure at sea.
101. Profit more.
102. Princesses. (Or the word may be *princes*,
     referring to royal children both male and
     female.)
103. More foolishly spent.
104. Refers to Fortune, not Miranda.
105. Height of fortune. (Astrological term.)

106. Astrological power.
107. Ignore.
108. Drowsiness.
109. Let it happen (i.e., don't fight it).
110. Come away.
111. Make demands upon.
112. (1) Fellow spirits; (2) abilities.
113. To the smallest detail.

ARIEL: To every article.
            I boarded the King's ship. Now on the beak,[114]
            Now in the waist,[115] the deck,[116] in every cabin,
            I flamed amazement.[117] Sometimes I'd divide
            And burn in many places; on the topmast,   200
            The yards, and bowsprit would I flame distinctly,[118]
            Then meet and join. Jove's lightning, the precursors
            O' the dreadful thunderclaps, more momentary
            And sight-outrunning[119] were not.[120] The fire and cracks
            Of sulfurous roaring the most mighty Neptune[121]   205
            Seem to besiege and make his bold waves tremble,
            Yea, his dread trident shake.
PROSPERO: My brave spirit!
            Who was so firm, so constant, that this coil[122]
            Would not infect his reason?
ARIEL: Not a soul
            But felt a fever of the mad[123] and played   210
            Some tricks of desperation. All but mariners
            Plunged in the foaming brine and quit the vessel,
            Then all afire with me. The King's son, Ferdinand,
            With hair up-staring[124]—then like reeds, not hair—
            Was the first man that leapt; cried, "Hell is empty,   215
            And all the devils are here!"
PROSPERO: Why, that's my spirit!
            But was not this nigh shore?
ARIEL: Close by, my master.
PROSPERO:
            But are they, Ariel, safe?
ARIEL: Not a hair perished.
            On their sustaining garments[125] not a blemish,
            But fresher than before; and, as thou bad'st[126] me,   220
            In troops[127] I have dispersed them 'bout the isle.
            The King's son have I landed by himself,
            Whom I left cooling[128] of the air with sighs
            In an odd angle[129] of the isle, and sitting,
            His arms in this sad knot.[130]   *[He folds his arms.]*   225

---

114. Prow.
115. Midships.
116. Poop deck at the stern.
117. Struck terror in the guise of fire, i.e, Saint
     Elmo's fire.
118. In different places.
119. Swifter than sight.
120. Could not have been.
121. Roman god of the sea.
122. Tumult.

123. I.e., such as madmen feel.
124. Standing on end.
125. Garments that buoyed them up in the
     sea.
126. Ordered.
127. Groups.
128. Cooling.
129. Corner.
130. (Folded arms are indicative of mel-
     ancholy.)

PROSPERO: Of the King's ship,
      The mariners, say how thou hast disposed,
      And all the rest o' the fleet.
ARIEL: Safely in harbor
      Is the King's ship; in the deep nook,[131] where once
      Thou called'st me up at midnight to fetch dew[132]
      From the still-vexed Bermudas,[133] there she's hid;   230
      The mariners all under hatches stowed,
      Who, with a charm joined to their suffered labor,[134]
      I have left asleep. And for the rest o' the fleet,
      Which I dispersed, they all have met again
      And are upon the Mediterranean float[135]   235
      Bound sadly home for Naples,
      Supposing that they saw the King's ship wrecked
      And his great person perish.
PROSPERO: Ariel, thy charge
      Exactly is performed. But there's more work.
      What is the time o' the day?   240
ARIEL: Past the mid season.[136]
PROSPERO:
      At least two glasses.[137] The time twixt six and now
      Must by us both be spent most preciously.
ARIEL:
      Is there more toil? Since thou dost give me pains,[138]
      Let me remember[139] thee what thou hast promised,
      Which is not yet performed me.   245
PROSPERO: How now? Moody?
      What is't thou canst demand?
ARIEL: My liberty.
PROSPERO:
      Before the time be out? No more!
ARIEL: I prithee,
      Remember I have done thee worthy service,
      Told thee no lies, made thee no mistakings, served
      Without or grudge or grumblings. Thou did promise   250
      To bate[140] me a full year.
PROSPERO: Dost thou forget
      From what a torment I did free thee?

---

131. Bay.
132. (Collected at midnight for magical purposes; compare with line 324.)
133. Ever stormy Bermudas. (Perhaps refers to the then recent Bermuda shipwreck; see play Introduction. The Folio text reads "Bermoothes.")
134. By means of a spell added to all the labor they have undergone.
135. Sea.
136. Noon.
137. Hourglasses.
138. Labors.
139. Remind.
140. Remit, deduct.

ARIEL: No.

PROSPERO:

    Thou dost, and think'st it much to tread the ooze

    Of the salt deep,

    To run upon the sharp wind of the north,   255

    To do me[141] business in the veins[142] o' the earth

    When it is baked[143] with frost.

ARIEL: I do not, sir.

PROSPERO:

    Thou liest, malignant thing! Hast thou forgot

    The foul witch Sycorax, who with age and envy[144]

    Was grown into a hoop?[145] Hast thou forgot her?   260

ARIEL: No, sir.

PROSPERO:

    Thou hast. Where was she born? Speak. Tell me.

ARIEL:

    Sir, in Argier.[146]

PROSPERO: O, was she so? I must

    Once in a month recount what thou hast been

    Which thou forgett'st. This damned witch Sycorax,   265

    For mischiefs manifold and sorceries terrible

    To enter human hearing, from Argier,

    Thou know'st, was banished. For one thing she did[147]

    They would not take her life. Is not this true?

ARIEL: Ay, sir.   270

PROSPERO:

    This blue-eyed[148] hag was hither brought with child[149]

    And here was left by the sailors. Thou, my slave,

    As thou report'st thyself, was then her servant;

    And, for[150] thou wast a spirit too delicate

    To act her earthy and abhorred commands,   275

    Refusing her grand hests,[151] she did confine thee,

    By help of her more potent ministers

    And in her most unmitigable rage,

    Into a cloven pine, within which rift

    Imprisoned thou didst painfully remain   280

    A dozen years; within which space she died

---

141. Do for me.
142. Veins of minerals, or, underground streams, thought to be analogous to the veins of the human body.
143. Hardened.
144. Malice.
145. I.e., so bent over with age as to resemble a hoop.

146. Algiers.
147. (Perhaps a reference to her pregnancy, for which her life would be spared.)
148. With dark circles under the eyes or with blue eyelids, implying pregnancy.
149. Pregnant.
150. Because.
151. Commands.

And left thee there, where thou didst vent thy groans
As fast as mill wheels strike.[152] Then was this island—
Save[153] for the son that she did litter[154] here,
A freckled whelp,[155] hag-born[156]—not honored with   285
A human shape.

ARIEL: Yes, Caliban her son.[157]

PROSPERO:
Dull thing, I say so:[158] he, that Caliban
Whom now I keep in service. Thou best know'st
What torment I did find thee in. Thy groans
Did make wolves howl, and penetrate the breasts   290
Of ever-angry bears. It was a torment
To lay upon the damned, which Sycorax
Could not again undo. It was mine art,
When I arrived and heard thee, that made gape[159]   295
The pine and let thee out.

ARIEL: I thank thee, master.

PROSPERO:
If thou more murmur'st, I will rend an oak
And peg thee in his[160] knotty entrails till
Thou hast howled away twelve winters.

ARIEL: Pardon, master.
I will be correspondent[161] to command
And do my spiriting[162] gently.[163]   300

PROSPERO: Do so, and after two days
I will discharge thee.

ARIEL: That's my noble master!
What shall I do? Say what? What shall I do?

PROSPERO:
Go make thyself like a nymph o' the sea. Be subject
To no sight but thine and mine, invisible   305
To every eyeball else. Go take this shape
And hither come in 't. Go, hence with diligence!

[Exit (Ariel).]

Awake, dear heart, awake! Thou hast slept well.
Awake!

---

152. As the blades of a mill wheel strike the
water.
153. Except.
154. Give birth to.
155. Offspring. (Used of animals.)
156. Born of a female demon.
157. (Ariel is probably concurring with Prospero's comment about a "freckled

whelp," not contradicting the point
about "A human shape.")
158. I.e., exactly, that's what I said, you dull-
ard.
159. Open wide.
160. Its.
161. Responsive, submissive.
162. Duties as a spirit.
163. Willingly, ungrudgingly.

MIRANDA: The strangeness of your story put
　　　　Heaviness[164] in me.   310
PROSPERO:　　　Shake it off. Come on,
　　　　We'll visit Caliban, my slave, who never
　　　　Yields us kind answer.
MIRANDA:　　　　　　　'Tis a villain, sir,
　　　　I do not love to look on.
PROSPERO:　　　　　　　But, as 'tis,
　　　　We cannot miss[165] him. He does make our fire,
　　　　Fetch in our wood, and serves in offices[166]   315
　　　　That profit us.—What ho! Slave! Caliban!
　　　　Thou earth, thou! Speak.
CALIBAN(*within*): There's wood enough within.
PROSPERO:
　　　　Come forth, I say! There's other business for thee.
　　　　Come, thou tortoise! When?[167]

　　　　[Enter Ariel like a water nymph.]

　　　　Fine apparition! My quaint[168] Ariel,   320
　　　　Hark in thine ear.　　　　　　　　　　　*[He whispers.]*
ARIEL:　　　　My lord, it shall be done.　　　　　　　*[Exit.]*
PROSPERO:
　　　　Thou poisonous slave, got[169] by the devil himself
　　　　Upon thy wicked dam,[170] come forth!

　　　　[Enter Caliban.]

CALIBAN:
　　　　As wicked[171] dew as e'er my mother brushed
　　　　With raven's feather from unwholesome fen[172]
　　　　Drop on you both! A southwest[173] blow on ye   325
　　　　And blister you all o'er!
PROSPERO:
　　　　For this, be sure, tonight thou shalt have cramps,
　　　　Side-stitches that shall pen thy breath up. Urchins[174]
　　　　Shall forth at vast[175] of night that they may work   330
　　　　All exercise on thee. Thou shalt be pinched

---

164. Drowsiness.
165. Do without.
166. Functions, duties.
167. (An exclamation of impatience.)
168. Ingenious.
169. Begotten, sired.
170. Mother. (Used of animals.)
171. Mischievous, harmful.

172. Marsh, bog.
173. I.e., wind thought to bring disease.
174. Hedgehogs; here, suggesting goblins in the guise of hedgehogs.
175. Lengthy, desolate time. (Malignant spirits were thought to be restricted to the hours of darkness.)

As thick as honeycomb,[176] each pinch more stinging
Than bees that made 'em.[177]

CALIBAN: I must eat my dinner.
This island's mine, by Sycorax my mother,
Which thou tak'st from me. When thou cam'st first,   335
Thou strok'st me and made much of me, wouldst give me
Water with berries in 't, and teach me how
To name the bigger light, and how the less,[178]
That burn by day and night. And then I loved thee   340
And showed thee all the qualities o' th' isle,
The fresh springs, brine pits, barren place and fertile.
Cursed be I that did so! All the charms[179]
Of Sycorax, toads, beetles, bats, light on you!
For I am all the subjects that you have,
Which first was mine own king; and here you sty[180] me   345
In this hard rock, whiles you do keep from me
The rest o' th' island.

PROSPERO: Thou most lying slave,
Whom stripes[181] may move, not kindness! I have used thee,
Filth as thou art, with humane[182] care, and lodged thee
In mine own cell, till thou didst seek to violate   350
The honor of my child.

CALIBAN:
Oho, Oho! Would 't had been done!
Thou didst prevent me; I had peopled else[183]
This isle with Calibans.

MIRANDA: Abhorred slave,[184]
Which any print[185] of goodness wilt not take,   355
Being capable of all ill! I pitied thee,
Took pains to make thee speak, taught thee each hour
One thing or other. When thou didst not, savage,
Know thine own meaning, but wouldst gabble like
A thing most brutish, I endowed thy purposes[186]   360
With words that made them known. But thy vile race,[187]
Though thou didst learn, had that in 't which good natures
Could not abide to be with; therefore wast thou

---

176. I.e., all over, with as many pinches as a
     honeycomb has cells.
177. I.e., the honeycomb.
178. I.e., the sun and the moon. (See Genesis
     1:16: "God then made two great lights:
     the greater light to rule the day, and the
     less light to rule the night.")
179. Spells.
180. Confine as in a sty.

181. Lashes.
182. (Not distinguished as a word from *hu-man.*)
183. Otherwise populated.
184. "Abhorred slave . . . prison (Sometimes
     assigned by editors to Prospero.)
185. Imprint, impression.
186. Meanings, desires.
187. Natural disposition: species, nature.

Deservedly confined into this rock,
Who hadst deserved more than a prison   365

CALIBAN:
You taught me language, and my profit on 't
Is I know how to curse. The red plague[188] rid[189] you
For learning[190] me your language!

PROSPERO: Hagseed,[191] hence!
Fetch us in fuel, and be quick, thou'rt best,[192]
To answer other business.[193] Shrugg'st thou, malice?   370
If thou neglect'st or dost unwillingly
What I command, I'll rack thee with old[194] cramps,
Fill all thy bones with aches,[195] make thee roar
That beasts shall tremble at thy din.

CALIBAN: No, pray thee.
[Aside.] I must obey. His art is of such power   375
It would control my dam's god, Setebos,[196]
And make a vassal of him.

PROSPERO: So, slave, hence!

[Exit Caliban.]

[Enter Ferdinand; and Ariel, invisible,[197] playing and singing. (Ferdinand
does not see Prospero and Miranda)]

[Ariel's Song.]

ARIEL:
Come unto these yellow sands,
    And then take hands;
Curtsied when you have,[198] and kissed   380
    The wild waves whist;[199]
Foot it featly[200] here and there,
    And, sweet sprites,[201] bear
The burden.[202] Hark, hark!

                    [Burden, dispersedly[203] (within).] Bow-wow.   385
The watchdogs bark.

                    [Burden, dispersedly within.] Bow-wow.

---

188. Plague characterized by red sores and evacuation of blood.
189. Destroy.
190. Teaching.
191. Offspring of a female demon.
192. You'd be well advised.
193. Perform other tasks.
194. Such as old people suffer, or, plenty of.
195. (Pronounced "aitches.")
196. (A god of the Patagonians, named in Robert Eden's *History of Travel*, 1577.)

197. (Ariel wears a garment that by convention indicates he is invisible to the other characters.)
198. When you have curtsied.
199. Kissed the waves into silence, or, kissed while the waves are being hushed.
200. Dance nimbly.
201. Spirits.
202. Refrain, undersong.
203. I.e., from all directions, not in unison.

Hark, hark! I hear
The strain of strutting chanticleer
   Cry Cock-a-diddle-dow. 390

FERDINAND:
   Where should this music be? I' th' air or th' earth?
   It sounds no more; and sure it waits upon[204]
   Some god o' th' island. Sitting on a bank,[205]
   Weeping again the King my father's wreck,
   This music crept by me upon the waters, 395
   Allaying both their fury and my passion[206]
   With its sweet air. Thence[207] I have followed it,
   Or it hath drawn me rather. But 'tis gone.
   No, it begins again.

   [Ariel's Song.]

ARIEL:
   Full fathom five thy father lies. 400
      Of his bones are coral made.
   Those are pearls that were his eyes.
      Nothing of him that doth fade
   But doth suffer a sea change
   Into something rich and strange. 405
   Sea nymphs hourly ring his knell.[208]

                    [Burden (within).] Ding dong.
   Hark, now I hear them, ding dong bell.

FERDINAND:
   The ditty does remember[209] my drowned father.
   This is no mortal business, nor no sound 410
   That the earth owes.[210] I hear it now above me.

PROSPERO *[to Miranda]:*
   The fringed curtains of thine eye advance[211]
   And say what thou seest yond.

MIRANDA: What is 't? A spirit?
   Lord, how it looks about! Believe me, sir,
   It carries a brave[212] form. But 'tis a spirit. 415

PROSPERO:
   No, wench, it eats and sleeps and hath such senses
   As we have, such. This gallant which thou seest

---

204. Serves, attends.
205. Sandbank.
206. Grief.
207. I.e, from the bank on which I sat.
208. Announcement of a death by the tolling of a bell.

209. Commemorate.
210. Owns.
211. Raise.
212. Excellent.

Was in the wreck; and, but[213] he's something stained
With grief, that's beauty's canker,[214] thou mightst call him
A goodly person. He hath lost his fellows   420
And strays about to find 'em.

MIRANDA: I might call him
A thing divine, for nothing natural
I ever saw so noble.

PROSPERO [aside]:   It goes on,[215] I see,
As my soul prompts it.—Spirit, fine spirit, I'll free thee
Within two days for this.   425

FERDINAND [seeing Miranda]: Most sure, the goddess
On whom these airs[216] attend!—Vouchsafe[217] my prayer
May[218] know if you remain[219] upon this island,
And that you will some good instruction give
How I may bear me[220] here. My prime[221] request,
Which I do last pronounce, is—O you wonder![222]—   430
If you be maid or no?[223]

MIRANDA: No wonder, sir,
But certainly a maid.

FERDINAND: My language? Heavens!
I am the best[224] of them that speak this speech,
Were I but where 'tis spoken.

PROSPERO [coming forward]   How? The best?
What wert thou if the King of Naples heard thee?   435

FERDINAND:
A single[225] thing, as I am now, that wonders
To hear thee speak of Naples.[226] He does hear me,[227]
And that he does I weep.[228] Myself am Naples,
Who with mine eyes, never since at ebb,[229] beheld
The King my father wrecked.   440

MIRANDA: Alack, for mercy!

FERDINAND:
Yes, faith, and all his lords, the Duke of Milan
And his brave son[230] being twain.

---

213. Except that.
214. Somewhat disfigured; cankerworm (feeding on buds and leaves).
215. I.e., My plan works.
216. Songs.
217. Grant.
218. I.e., that I may know.
219. Dwell.
220. Conduct myself.
221. Chief.
222. (Miranda's name means "to be wondered at.")

223. I e, a human maiden as opposed to a goddess or married woman.
224. I.e., in birth.
225. Solitary, being at once King of Naples and myself; (2) feeble.
226. The King of Naples.
227. I.e., the King of Naples does hear my words, for I am King of Naples.
228. I.e., and I weep at this reminder that my father is seemingly dead, leaving me heir.
229. I.e., dry, not weeping.
230. (The only reference in the play to a son of Antonio.)

PROSPERO [aside]: The Duke of Milan
And his more braver[231] daughter could control[232] thee,
If now 'twere fit to do 't. At the first sight
They have changed eyes.[233]—Delicate Ariel, 445
I'll set thee free for this. [To Ferdinand.] A word, good sir.
I fear you have done yourself some wrong.[234] A word!

MIRANDA [aside]:
Why speaks my father so ungently? This
Is the third man that e'er I saw, the first 450
That e'er I sighed for. Pity move my father
To be inclined my way!

FERDINAND: O, if a virgin,
And your affection not gone forth, I'll make you
The Queen of Naples.

PROSPERO: Soft, sir! One word more.
[Aside.] They are both in either's power's; but this[235] swift business
I must uneasy[236] make, lest too light[237] winning 455
Make the prize light.[238] [to Ferdinand.] One word more: I charge thee
That thou attend[239] me. Thou dost here usurp
The name thou ow'st[240] not, and hast put thyself
Upon this island as a spy, to win it
From me, the lord on 't.[241] 460

FERDINAND: No, as I am a man.

MIRANDA:
There's nothing ill can dwell in such a temple.
If the ill spirit have so fair a house,
Good things will strive to dwell with 't.[242]

PROSPERO: Follow me.—
Speak not you for him; he's a traitor.—Come,
I'll manacle thy neck and feet together. 465
Seawater shalt thou drink; thy food shall be
The fresh-brook mussels, withered roots, and husks
Wherein the acorn cradled. Follow.

FERDINAND: No!
I will resist such entertainment[243] till
Mine enemy has more power. 470

[He draws, and is charmed[244] from moving.]

---

231. More splendid.	**239.** Follow, obey.
232. Refute.	**240.** Ownest.
233. Exchanged amorous glances.	**241.** Of it.
234. I.e., spoken falsely.	**242.** I.e., expel the evil and occupy the *temple*,
235. Each in the other's.	the body.
236. Difficult.	**243.** Treatment.
237. Easy.	**244.** Magically prevented.
238. Cheap.	

MIRANDA: O dear father,
Make not too rash[245] a trial of him, for
He's gentle,[246] and not fearful.[247]

PROSPERO: What, I say,
My foot[248] my tutor?—Put thy sword up, traitor,
Who mak'st a show but dar'st not strike, thy conscience
Is so possessed with guilt. Come, from thy ward,[249]   475
For I can here disarm thee with this stick
And make thy weapon drop. *[He brandishes his staff.]*

MIRANDA *[trying to hinder him]:* Beseech you, father!

PROSPERO:
Hence! Hang not on my garments.

MIRANDA: Sir, have pity!
I'll be his surety.[250]

PROSPERO: Silence! One word more
Shall make me chide thee, if not hate thee. What,   480
An advocate for an impostor? Hush!
Thou think'st there is no more such shapes as he,
Having seen but him and Caliban. Foolish wench,
To the most of men this is a Caliban,
And they to[251] him are angels.   485

MIRANDA: My affections
Are then most humble; I have no ambition
To see a goodlier man.

PROSPERO *[to Ferdinand]:* Come on, obey.
Thy nerves[252] are in their infancy again
And have no vigor in them.

FERDINAND: So they are.
My spirits,[253] as in a dream, are all bound up.   490
My father's loss, the weakness which I feel,
The wreck of all my friends, nor this man's threats
To whom I am subdued, are but light[254] to me,
Might I but through my prison once a day
Behold this maid. All corners else[255] o' th' earth   495
Let liberty make use of; space enough
Have I in such a prison.

PROSPERO *[aside]:* It works. *[To Ferdinand.]* Come on.—
Thou hast done well, fine Ariel! *[To Ferdinand.]* Follow me.
[To Ariel.] Hark what thou else shalt do me.[256]

---

245. Harsh.
246. Wellborn.
247. Frightening, dangerous, or perhaps, cowardly.
248. Subordinate, (Miranda, the foot, presumes to instruct Prospero, the head.)
249. Defensive posture (in fencing).

250. Guarantee.
251. Compared to.
252. Sinews.
253. Vital powers.
254. Unimportant.
255. Other corners, regions.
256. For me.

MIRANDA [*to Ferdinand*]:   Be of comfort.
    My father's of a better nature, sir,   500
    Than he appears by speech. This is unwonted[257]
    Which now came from him. —
PROSPERO [*to Ariel*]:   Thou shalt be as free
    As mountain winds; but then[258] exactly do
    All points of my command.
ARIEL: To th' syllable.
PROSPERO [*to Ferdinand*]:
    Come, follow. [*To Miranda.*] Speak not for him.   505

    [*Exeunt.*]

Act II

Scene 1[1]

[*Enter Alonso, Sebastian, Antonia, Gonzalo, Adrian, Francisco, and others.*]

GONZALO [*to Alonso*]:
    Beseech you, sir, be merry. You have cause,
    So have we all, of joy, for our escape
    Is much beyond our loss. Our hint[2] of woe
    Is common; every day some sailor's wife,
    The masters of some merchant, and the merchant,[3]   5
    Have just our theme of woe. But for the miracle,
    I mean our preservation, few in millions
    Can speak like us. Then wisely, good sir, weigh
    Our sorrow with[4] our comfort.
ALONSO: Prithee, peace.
SEBASTIAN [*aside to Antonio*]: He receives comfort like cold porridge.[5]   10
ANTONIO [*aside to Sebastian*]: The visitor[6] will not give him o'er[7] so
SEBASTIAN: Look, he's winding up the watch of his wit; by and by it will strike.
GONZALO [*to Alonso*]: Sir—
SEBASTIAN [*aside to Antonio*]: One. Tell.[8]
GONZALO: When every grief is entertained[9]   15
    That's offered, comes to th' entertainer—

---

257. Unusual.
258. Until then, or, if that is to be so.

    Act II, Scene 1

  1. Location: another part of the island.
  2. Occasion.
  3. Officers of some merchant vessel and the merchant himself, the owner.
  4. Against.
  5. (Punningly suggested by *peace*, i.e., "peas" or "pease," a common ingredient of porridge.)

  6. One taking nourishment and comfort to the sick, as Gonzalo is doing.
  7. Abandon him.
  8. Keep count.
  9. When every sorrow that presents itself is accepted without resistance, there comes to the recipient.

SEBASTIAN: A dollar.[10]

GONZALO: Dolor comes to him, indeed. You have spoken truer than you purposed.

SEBASTIAN: You have taken it wiselier than I meant you should.

GONZALO: *[to Alonso]*: Therefore, my lord—   20

ANTONIO: Fie, what a spendthrift is he of his tongue!

ALONSO *[to Gonzalo]*: I prithee, spare.[11]

GONZALO: Well, I have done. But yet—

SEBASTIAN *[aside to Antonio]*: He will be talking.

ANTONIO *[aside to Sebastian]*: Which, of he or Adrian, for a good wager, first begins   25
     to crow?[12]

SEBASTIAN: The old cock.[13]

ANTONIO: The cockerel.[14]

SEBASTIAN: Done, The wager?

ANTONIO: A laughter.[15]   30

SEBASTIAN: A match![16]

ADRIAN: Though this island seem to be desert[17]—

ANTONIO: Ha, ha, ha!

SEBASTIAN: So, you're paid.[18]   35

ADRIAN: Uninhabitable and almost inaccessible—

SEBASTIAN: Yet—

ADRIAN: Yet—

ANTONIO: He could not miss 't.[19]

ADRIAN: It must needs be[20] of subtle, tender, and delicate temperance.[21]   40

ANTONIO: Temperance[22] was a delicate[23] wench.

SEBASTIAN: Ay, and a subtle,[24] as he most learnedly delivered.[25]

ADRIAN: The air breathes upon us here most sweetly.

SEBASTIAN: As if it had lungs, and rotten ones.

ANTONIO: Or as 'twere perfumed by a fen.   45

---

10. Widely circulated coin, the German thaler and the Spanish piece of eight. (Sebastian puns on *entertainer* in the sense of innkeeper; to Gonzalo, *dollar* suggests "dolor," grief.)
11. Forbear, cease.
12. Which of the two, Gonzalo or Adrian, do you bet will speak (crow) first?
13. I.e., Gonzalo.
14. I.e., Adrian.
15. (1) Burst of laughter; (2) sitting of eggs. (When Adrian, the *cockerel*, begins to speak two lines later, Sebastian loses the bet. The Folio speech prefixed in lines 38–39 are here reversed so that Antonio enjoys his laugh as the prize for winning, as in the proverb "He who laughs last laughs best" or "He laughs that wins." The Folio assignment can work in the theater, however, if Sebastian pays for losing with a sardonic laugh of concession.)

16. A bargain; agreed.
17. Uninhabited.
18. I.e., you've had your laugh.
19. (1) Avoid saying "Yet"; (2) miss the island.
20. Has to be.
21. Mildness of climate.
22. A girl's name.
23. (Here it means "given to pleasure, voluptuous"; in line 44, "pleasant." Antonio is evidently suggesting that *tender, and delicate temperance* sounds like a Puritan phrase, which Antonio then mocks by applying the words to a woman rather than an island. He began this bawdy comparison with a double entendre on *inaccessible*, (line 40.)
24. (Here it means "tricky, sexually crafty"; in line 44 "delicate.")
25. Uttered. (Sebastian joins Antonio in baiting the Puritans with his use of the pious cant phrase *learnedly delivered.*)

GONZALO: Here is everything advantageous to life.   50

ANTONIO: True, save[26] means to live.

SEBASTIAN: Of that there's none, or little.

GONZALO: How lush and lusty[27] the grass looks! How green!

ANTONIO: The ground indeed is tawny.[28]

SEBASTIAN: With an eye[29] of green in 't.   55

ANTONIO: He misses not much.

SEBASTIAN: No. He doth but[30] mistake the truth totally.

GONZALO: But the rarity of it is—which is indeed almost beyond credit—

SEBASTIAN: As many vouched[31] rarities are.

GONZALO: That our garments, being, as they were, drenched in the sea, hold   60
notwithstanding their freshness and glosses, being rather new-dyed than
stained with salt water.

ANTONIO: If but one of his pockets[32] could speak, would it not say he lies?

SEBASTIAN: Ay, or very falsely pocket[33] up his report.[34]

GONZALO: Methinks our garments are now as fresh as when we put them on first   65
in Afric, at the marriage of the King's fair daughter Claribel to the King
of Tunis.

SEBASTIAN: 'Twas a sweet marriage, and we prosper well in our return.

ADRIAN: Tunis was never graced before with such a paragon to[35] their queen.

GONZALO: Not since widow Dido's[36] time.   70

ANTONIO [aside to Sebastian]: Widow? A pox o' that! How came that "widow" in?
Widow Dido!

SEBASTIAN: What if he had said, "widower Aeneas" too? Good Lord, how you
take[37] it!

ADRIAN [to Gonzalo]: "Widow Dido" said you? You make me study of[38] that. She   75
was of Carthage, not of Tunis.

GONZALO: This Tunis, sir, was Carthage.

ADRIAN: Carthage?

GONZALO: I assure you, Carthage.

ANTONIO: His word is more than the miraculous harp.[39]   80

---

26. Except.
27. Healthy.
28. Dull brown, yellowish.
29. Tinge, or spot (perhaps with reference to Gonzalo's eye or judgment).
30. Merely.
31. Allegedly real though strange sights.
32. I.e., because they are muddy.
33. I.e., conceal, suppress; often used in the sense of "receive unprotestingly, fail to respond to a challenge."
34. (Sebastian's jest is that the evidence of Gonzalo's soggy and sea-stained pockets would confute Gonzalo's speech and his reputation for truth telling.)
35. For.

36. Queen of Carthage, deserted by Aeneas. (She was, in fact, a widow when Aeneas, a widower, met her, but Antonio may be amused at Gonzalo's prudish use of the term "widow" to describe a woman deserted by her lover.)
37. Understand, respond to, interpret.
38. Think about.
39. (Alludes to Amphion's harp, with which he raised the walls of Thebes: Gonzalo has exceeded that deed by recreating ancient Carthage—wall and houses—mistakenly on the site of modern-day Tunis. Some Renaissance commentators believed, like Gonzalo, that the two sites were near each other.)

SEBASTIAN: He hath raised the wall, and houses too.

ANTONIO: What impossible matter will he make easy next?

SEBASTIAN: I think he will carry this island home in his pocket and give it his son for an apple.

ANTONIO: And, sowing the kernels[40] of it in the sea, bring forth more islands.   85

GONZALO: Ay.[41]

ANTONIO: Why, in good time.[42]

GONZALO [to Alonso]: Sir, we were talking[43] that our garments seem now as fresh as when we were at Tunis at the marriage of your daughter, who is now queen.   90

ANTONIO: And the rarest[44] that e'er came there.

SEBASTIAN: Bate,[45] I beseech you, widow Dido.

ANTONIO: O, widow Dido? Ay, widow Dido.

GONZALO: Is not, sir, my doubtlet[46] as fresh as the first day I wore it? I mean, in a sort.[47]   95

ANTONIO: That "sort"[48] was well fished for.

GONZALO: When I wore it at your daughter's marriage.

ALONSO:
    You cram these words into mine ears against
    The stomach of my sense.[49] Would I had never
    Married[50] my daughter there! For, coming thence,   100
    My son is lost and, in my rate,[51] she too,
    Who is so far from Italy removed
    I ne'er again shall see her. O thou mine heir
    Of Naples and of Milan, what strange fish
    Hath made his meal on thee?   105

FRANCISCO: Sir, he may live.
    I saw him beat the surges[52] under him
    And ride upon their backs. He trod the water,
    Whose enmity he flung aside, and breasted
    The surge most swoll'n that met him. His bold head   110
    'Bove the contentious waves he kept, and oared
    Himself with his good arms in lusty[53] stroke.
    To th' shore, that o'er his[54] wave-worn basis bowed,[55]

---

40. Seeds.
41. (Gonzalo may be reasserting his point about Carthage, or he may be responding ironically in Antonio, who, in turn, answers sarcastically.)
42. (An expression of ironical acquiescence or amazement, i.e., "sure, right away.")
43. Saying.
44. Most remarkable, beautiful.
45. Abate, except, leave out. (Sebastian says sardonically, surely you should allow widow Dido to be an exception.)
46. Close-fitting jacket.

47. In a way.
48. (Antonio plays on the idea of drawing lots and on "fishing" for something to say.)
49. My appetite for hearing them.
50. Given in marriage.
51. Estimation, opinion.
52. Waves.
53. Vigorous.
54. Its.
55. I.e., that projected out over the base of the cliff that had been eroded by the surf, thus seeming to bend down toward the sea.

As[56] stooping to relieve him. I not doubt   115
He came alive to land.
ALONSO: No, no, he's gone.
SEBASTIAN [to Alonso]:
          Sir, you may thank yourself for this great loss,
          That[57] would not bless our Europe with your daughter,
          But rather[58] loose[59] her to an African,   120
          Where she at least is banished from your eye,[60]
          Who hath cause to wet the grief on 't.[61]
ALONSO: Prithee, peace.
SEBASTIAN:
          You were kneeled to and importuned[62] otherwise
          By all of us, and the fair soul herself   125
          Weighed between loathness and obedience at
          Which end o' the beam should bow.[63] We have lost your son,
          I fear, forever. Milan and Naples have
          More widows in them of this business' making[64]
          Than we bring men to comfort them.   130
          The fault's your own.
ALONSO: So is the dear'st[65] o' the loss.
GONZALO: My lord Sebastian.
          The truth you speak doth lack some gentleness
          And time[66] to speak it in. You rub the sore   135
          When you should bring the plaster.[67]
SEBASTIAN: Very well.
ANTONIO: And most chirurgeonly.[68]
GONZALO [to Alonso]:
          It is foul weather in us all, good sir,   140
          When you are cloudy.
SEBASTIAN [to Antonio]: Fowl[69] weather?
ANTONIO [to Sebastian]:   Very foul.
GONZALO:
          Had I plantation[70] of this isle, my lord—

---

56. As if.
57. You who.
58. Would rather.
59. (1) Release, let loose; (2) lose.
60. Is not constantly before your eye to serve
    as a reproachful reminder of what you
    have done.
61. I.e., your eye, which has good reason to
    weep because of this, or, Claribel, who has
    good reason to weep for it.
62. Urged, implored.
63. Claribel herself was poised uncertainly
    between unwillingness to marry and obe-
    dience to her father as to which end of the
    scales should sink, which should prevail.

64. On account of this marriage and sub-
    sequent shipwreck.
65. Heaviest, most costly.
66. Appropriate time.
67. (A medical application.)
68. Like a skilled surgeon. (Antonio mocks
    Gonzalo's medical analogy of a *plaster*
    applied curatively to a wound.)
69. With a pun on *foul*, returning to the
    imagery of lines 30–35.
70. Colonization (with subsequent wordplay
    on the literal meaning, "planting.")

ANTONIO [to Sebastian]:
> He'd sow 't with nettle seed.   145

SEBASTIAN: Or docks, or mallows.[71]

GONZALO:
> And were the king on 't, what would I do?

SEBASTIAN: Scape[72] being drunk for want[73] of wine.

GONZALO:
> I' the commonwealth I would by contraries[74]
> Execute all things; for no kind of traffic[75]   150
> Would I admit; no name of magistrate;
> Letters[76] should not be known; riches, poverty,
> And use of service,[77] none; contract, succession,[78]
> Bourn, bound of land, tilth,[79] vineyard, none;
> No use of metal, corn,[80] or wine, or oil;   155
> No occupation; all men idle, all,
> And women too, but innocent and pure;
> No sovereignty—

SEBASTIAN: Yet he would be king on 't.   160

ANTONIO: The latter end of his commonwealth forgets the beginning.

GONZALO:
> All things in common nature should produce
> Without sweat or endeavor. Treason, felony,
> Sword, pike,[81] knife, gun, or need of any engine[82]
> Would I not have; but nature should bring forth,   165
> Of its own kind, all foison,[83] all abundance,
> To feed my innocent people.

SEBASTIAN: No marrying 'mong his subjects?

ANTONIO: None, man, all idle—whores and knaves.

GONZALO:
> I would with such perfection govern, sir,   170
> T' excel the Golden Age.[84]

SEBASTIAN: 'Save[85] His Majesty!

ANTONIO:
> Long live Gonzalo!

GONZALO: And—do you mark me, sir?

---

71. (Weeds used as antidotes for nettle stings.)
72. Escape.
73. Lack. (Sebastian jokes sarcastically that this hypothetical ruler would be saved from dissipation only by the barrenness of the island.)
74. By what is directly opposite to usual custom.
75. Trade.
76. Learning.
77. Custom of employing servants.
78. Holding of property by right or inheritance.
79. Boundaries, property limits, tillage of soil.
80. Grain.
81. Lance.
82. Instrument of warfare.
83. Plenty.
84. The age, according to Hesiod, when Cronus, or Saturn, ruled the world; an age of innocence and abundance.
85. God save.

ALONSO:
 Prithee, no more. Thou dost talk nothing to me.

GONZALO: I do well believe Your Highness, and did it to minister occasion[86] to 175
 these gentlemen, who are of such sensible[87] and nimble lungs that they
 always use[88] to laugh at nothing.

ANTONIO: 'Twas you we laughed at.

GONZALO: Who in this kind of merry fooling am nothing to you; so you may
 continue, and laugh at nothing still. 180

ANTONIO: What a blow was there given!

SEBASTIAN: An[89] it had not fallen flat-long.[90]

GONZALO: You are gentlemen of brave mettle;[91] you would lift the moon out of
 her sphere[92] if she would continue in it five weeks without changing.

[Enter Ariel (invisible) playing solemn music.]

SEBASTIAN: We would so, and then go a-batfowling.[93] 185

ANTONIO: Nay, good my lord, be not angry.

GONZALO: No, I warrant you, I will not adventure my discretion so weakly.[94] Will
 you laugh me asleep? For I am very heavy.[95]

ANTONIO: Go sleep, and hear us.[96]

[All sleep except Alonso, Sebastian, and Antonio.]

ALONSO:
 What, all so soon asleep? I wish mine eyes 190
 Would, with themselves, shut up my thoughts.[97] I find
 They are inclined to do so.

SEBASTIAN: Please you, sir,
 Do not omit[98] the heavy[99] offer of it.
 It seldom visits sorrow; when it doth, 195
 It is a comforter.

ANTONIO: We two, my lord,
 Will guard your person while you take your rest,
 And watch your safety.

ALONSO: Thank you. Wondrous heavy. 200

---

86. Furnish opportunity.
87. Sensitive.
88. Are accustomed.
89. If.
90. With the flat of the sword, i.e., ineffectu-
 ally. (Compare with "fallen flat.")
91. Temperament, courage. (The sense of
 metal, indistinguishable as a form from
 mettle, continues the metaphor of the
 sword.)
92. Orbit. (Literally, one of the concentric
 zones occupied by planets in Ptolemaic
 astronomy.)
93. Hunting birds at night with lantern and

bat, or "stick"; also, gulling a
simpleton. (Gonzalo is the simpleton, or
fowl, and Sebastian will use the moon as
his lantern.)
94. Risk my reputation for discretion for so
 trivial a cause (by getting angry at these
 sarcastic fellows).
95. Sleepy.
96. I.e., get ready for sleep, and we'll do our
 part by laughing.
97. Would shut off my melancholy brooding
 when they close themselves in sleep.
98. Neglect.
99. Drowsy.

[Alonso sleeps. Exit Ariel.]

SEBASTIAN:
What a strange drowsiness possesses them!

ANTONIO:
It is the quality o' the climate.

SEBASTIAN: Why
Doth it not then our eyelids sink? I find not
Myself disposed to sleep.   205

ALONSO: Nor I. My spirits are nimble.
They[100] fell together all, as by consent;[101]
They dropped, as by a thunderstroke. What might,
Worthy Sebastian. O, what might—? No more.
And yet methinks I see it in thy face,   210
What thou shouldst be. Th' occasion speaks thee,[102] and
My strong imagination sees a crown
Dropping upon thy head.

SEBASTIAN: What, art thou waking?

ANTONIO:
Do you not hear me speak?   215

SEBASTIAN: I do, and surely
It is a sleepy[103] language, and thou speak'st
Out of thy sleep. What is it thou didst say?
This is a strange repose, to be asleep
With eyes wide open—standing, speaking, moving—   220
And yet so fast asleep.

ANTONIO: Noble Sebastian,
Thou lett'st thy fortune sleep—die, rather; wink'st[104]
Whiles thou art waking.

SEBASTIAN: Thou dost snore distinctly;[105]   225
There's meaning in thy snores.

ANTONIO:
I am more serious than my custom. You
Must be so too if heed[106] me, which to do
Trebles thee o'er.[107]

SEBASTIAN: Well, I am standing water.[108]   230

ANTONIO:
I'll teach you how to flow.

---

100. The sleepers.
101. Common agreement.
102. Opportunity of the moment calls upon
     you, i.e., proclaims you usurper of
     Alonso's crown.
103. Dreamlike, fantastic.

104. (You) shut your eyes.
105. Articulately.
106. If you heed.
107. Makes you three times as great and rich.
108. Water that neither ebbs nor flows, at a
     standstill.

SEBASTIAN: Do so. To ebb[109]
          Hereditary sloth[110] instructs me.
ANTONIO: O,
          If you but knew how you the purpose cherish   235
          Whiles thus you mock it![111] How, in stripping it,[112]
          You more invest[113] it! Ebbing men, indeed,
          Most often do so near the bottom[114] run
          By their own fear or sloth.
SEBASTIAN: Prithee, say on.
          The setting[115] of thine eye and cheek proclaim   240
          A matter[116] from thee, and a birth indeed
          Which throes[117] thee much to yield.[118]
ANTONIO: Thus, sir:
          Although this lord[119] of weak remembrance,[120] this   245
          Who shall be of as little memory
          When he is earthed,[121] hath here almost persuaded—
          For he's a spirit of persuasion, only
          Professes to persuade[122]—the King his son's alive,
          'Tis as impossible that he's undrowned   250
          As he that sleeps here swims.
SEBASTIAN: I have no hope
          That he's undrowned.
ANTONIO: O, out of that "no hope"
          What great hope have you! No hope that way[123] is   255
          Another way so high a hope that even
          Ambition[124] cannot pierce a wink[125] beyond,
          But doubt discovery there. Will you grant with me
          That Ferdinand is drowned?
SEBASTIAN: He's gone.   260
ANTONIO: Then tell me,
          Who's the next heir of Naples?

---

109. Decline.
110. Natural laziness and the position of
     younger brother, one who cannot in-
     herit.
111. If you only knew how much you really
     enhance the value of ambition even
     while your words mock your purpose.
112. I.e., how the more you speak flippantly
     of ambition, the more you, in effect,
     affirm it.
113. Clothe. (Antonio's paradox is that, by
     skeptically stripping away illusions, Se-
     bastian can see the essence of a situation
     and the opportunity it presents or that, by
     disclaiming and deriding his purpose, Se-
     bastian shows how valuable it really is.)
114. I.e., on which unadventurous men may go
     aground and miss the tide of fortune.

115. Set expression (of earnestness).
116. Matter of importance.
117. Causes pain, as in giving birth.
118. Give forth, speak about.
119. I.e., Gonzalo.
120. (1) Power of remembering; (2) being re-
     membered after his death.
121. Buried.
122. Whose whole function (as a privy coun-
     cillor) is to persuade.
123. I.e., in regard to Ferdinand's being saved.
124. Ambition itself cannot see any further than
     that hope (of the crown), is unsure of
     finding anything to achieve beyond it or
     even there.
125. Glimpse.

SEBASTIAN: Claribel.

ANTONIO:

        She that is Queen of Tunis; she that dwells

        Ten leagues beyond man's life;[126] she that from Naples   265

        Can have no note,[127] unless the sun were post[128]—

        The Man i' the Moon's too slow—till newborn chins

        Be rough and razorable;[129] she that from[130] whom

        We all were sea-swallowed, though some cast[131] again,

        And by that destiny to perform an act   270

        Whereof what's past is prologue, what to come

        In yours and my discharge.[132]

SEBASTIAN: What stuff is this? How say you?

        'Tis true my brother's daughter's Queen of Tunis,

        So is she heir of Naples, twixt which regions   275

        There is some space.

ANTONIO: A space whose every cubit[133]

        Seems to cry out, "How shall that Claribel

        Measure us[134] back to Naples? Keep[135] in Tunis,

        And let Sebastian wake."[136] Say this were death   280

        That now hath seized them, why, they were no worse

        Than now they are. There be[137] that can rule Naples

        As well as he that sleeps, lords that can prate[138]

        As amply and unnecessarily

        As this Gonzalo. I myself could make   285

        A chough of as deep chat.[139] O, that you bore

        The mind that I do! What a sleep were this

        For your advancement! Do you understand me?

SEBASTIAN:

        Methinks I do.

ANTONIO: And how does your content[140]   290

        Tender[141] your own good fortune?

SEBASTIAN: I remember

        You did supplant your brother Prospero.

ANTONIO: True.

        And look how well my garments sit upon me,   295

---

126. I.e., further than the journey of a life-
     time.
127. News, intimation.
128. Messenger.
129. Ready for shaving.
130. On our voyage from.
131. Were disgorged (with a pun on *casting* of
     parts for a play).
132. Performance.
133. Ancient measure of length of about
     twenty inches.

134. I.e., traverse the cubits, find her way.
135. Stay. (Addressed to Claribel.)
136. I.e., to his good fortune.
137. There are those.
138. Speak foolishly.
139. I could teach a jackdaw to talk as wisely,
     or, be such a garrulous talker myself.
140. Desire, inclination.
141. Regard, look after.

Much feater[142] than before. My brother's servants
Were then my fellows. Now they are my men.
SEBASTIAN: But, for your conscience?
ANTONIO:
    Ay, sir, where lies that? If 'twere a kibe,[143]
    'Twould put me to[144] my slipper; but I feel not   300
    This deity in my bosom. Twenty consciences
    That stand twixt me and Milan,[145] candied[146] be they[147]
    And melt ere they molest![148] Here lies your brother,
    No better than the earth he lies upon,
    If he were that which now he's like—that's dead,   305
    Whom, I, with this obedient steel, three inches of it,
    Can lay to bed forever; whiles you, doing thus,[149]
    To the perpetual wink[150] for aye[151] might put
    This ancient morsel, this Sir Prudence, who
    Should not[152] upbraid our course. For all the rest,   310
    They'll take suggestion[153] as a cat laps milk;
    They'll tell the clock[154] to any business that
    We say befits the hour.
SEBASTIAN: Thy case, dear friend,
    Shall be my precedent. As thou gott'st Milan,
    I'll come by Naples. Draw thy sword. One stroke   315
    Shall free thee from the tribute[155] which thou payest,
    And I the king shall love thee.
ANTONIO: Draw together;
    And when I rear my hand, do you the like   320
    To fall it[156] on Gonzalo.   *[They draw.]*
SEBASTIAN: O, but one word.

    [They talk apart.]

    [Enter Ariel (invisible), with music and song.]

ARIEL: *[to Gonzalo]*
    My master through his art foresees the danger
    That you, his friend, are in, and sends me forth—
    For else his project dies—to keep them living.   325

                             [Sings in Gonzalo's ear.]

---

142. More becomingly, fittingly.
143. Chilblain, here a sore on the heel.
144. Oblige me to wear.
145. The dukedom of Milan.
146. Frozen, congealed in crystalline form.
147. May they be.
148. Interfere.
149. Similarly. (The actor makes a stabbing gesture.)

150. Sleep, closing of eyes.
151. Ever.
152. Would not then be able to.
153. Respond to prompting.
154. I.e., agree, answer appropriately, chime.
155. (See 1.2.z 113–124.)
156. Let it fall.

                    While you here do snoring lie,
                    Open-eyed conspiracy
                         His time[157] doth take.
                    If of life you keep a care,
                    Shake off slumber, and beware.   330
                         Awake, awake!

ANTONIO: Then let us both be sudden.[158]

GONZALO: *[waking]* Now, good angels preserve the King!

        [The others wake.]

ALONSO:
                Why, how now, ho, awake? Why are you drawn?
                Wherefore this ghastly looking?   335

GONZALO: What's the matter?

SEBASTIAN:
                Whiles we stood here securing[159] your repose,
                Even now, we heard a hollow burst of bellowing
                Like bulls, or rather lions. Did 't not wake you?
                It struck mine ear most terribly.   340

ALONSO: I heard nothing.

ANTONIO:
                O, 'twas a din to fright a monster's ear,
                To make an earthquake! Sure it was the roar
                Of a whole herd of lions.

ALONSO: Heard you this, Gonzalo?   345

GONZALO:
                Upon mine honor, sir, I heard a humming,
                And that a strange one too, which did awake me.
                I shaked you, sir, and cried.[160] As mine eyes opened,
                I saw their weapons drawn. There was a noise,
                That's verily.[161] 'Tis best we stand upon our guard,   350
                Or that we quit this place. Let's draw our weapons.

ALONSO:
                Lead off this ground, and let's make further search
                For my poor son.

GONZALO: Heavens keep him from these beasts!
                For he is, sure, i' th' island.   355

ALONSO: Lead away.

ARIEL *[aside]*:
                Prospero my lord shall know what I have done.
                So, King, go safely on to seek thy son.

        [Exeunt (separately).]

---

157. Opportunity.   160. Called out.
158. Quick.   161. True.
159. Standing guard over.

Scene 2[1]

[Enter Caliban with a burden of wood. A noise of thunder heard.]

CALIBAN:
    All the infections that the sun sucks up
    From bogs, fens, flats,[2] on Prosper fall, and make him
    By inchmeal[3] a disease! His spirits hear me,
    And yet I needs must[4] curse. But they'll nor[5] pinch,
    Fright me with urchin shows,[6] pitch me i' the mire,   5
    Nor lead me, like a firebrand,[7] in the dark
    Out of my way, unless he bid 'em. But
    For every trifle are they set upon me,
    Sometimes like apes, that mow[8] and chatter at me
    And after bite me; then like hedgehogs, which   10
    Lie tumbling in my barefoot way and mount
    Their pricks at my footfall. Sometimes am I
    All wound with[9] adders, who with cloven tongues
    Do hiss me into madness.

[Enter Trinculo.]

                Lo, now, lo!
    Here comes a spirit of his, and to torment me   15
    For bringing wood in slowly. I'll fall flat.
    Perchance he will not mind[10] me.   *[He lies down.]*

TRINCULO: Here's neither bush nor shrub to bear off[11] any weather at all. And another storm brewing; I hear it sing i' the wind. Yond same black cloud, yond huge one, looks like a foul bombard[12] that would shed his[13] liquor.   20 If it should thunder as it did before, I know not where to hide my head. Yond same cloud cannot choose but fall by pailfuls. *[Seeing Caliban.]* What have we here, a man or a fish? Dead or alive? A fish, he smells like a fish; a very ancient and fishlike smell; a kind of not-of-the-newest Poor John.[14] A strange fish! Were I in England now, as once I was, and had but   25 this fish painted,[15] not a holiday fool there but would give a piece of silver. There would this monster make a man.[16] Any strange beast there makes a man. When they will not give a doit[17] to relieve a lame beggar,

---

    Act II, Scene 2

1. Location: another part of the island.
2. Swamps.
3. Inch by inch.
4. Have to.
5. Neither.
6. Elvish apparitions shaped like hedgehogs.
7. They in the guise of a will-o'-the-wisp.
8. Make faces.
9. Entwined by.
10. Notice.

11. Keep off.
12. Dirty leather jug.
13. Its.
14. Salted fish, type of poor fare.
15. I.e., painted on a sign set up outside a booth or tent at a fair.
16. (1) Make one's fortune; (2) be indistinguishable from an Englishman.
17. Small coin.

they will lay out ten to see a dead Indian. Legged like a man, and his fins
like arms! Warm, o' my troth![18] I do now let loose my opinion, hold it[19]   30
no longer: this is no fish, but an islander, that hath lately suffered[20] by a
thunderbolt. [*Thunder.*] Alas, the storm is come again! My best way is to
creep under his gaberdine.[21] There is no other shelter hereabout. Misery
acquaints a man with strange bedfellows. I will here shroud[22] till the
dregs[23] of the storm be past.   35

[*He creeps under Caliban's garment.*]

[*Enter Stephano, singing, (a bottle in his hand).*]

STEPHANO:
"I shall no more to sea, to sea,
Here shall I die ashore—"
This is a very scurvy tune to sing at a man's funeral.
Well, here's my comfort.   [*Drinks.*]

[*Sings.*]

"The master, the swabber,[24] the boatswain, and I,   40
The gunner and his mate,
Loved Mall, Meg, and Marian, and Margery,
But none of us cared for Kate.
For she had a tongue with a tang,[25]
Would cry to a sailor, 'Go hang!'   45
She loved not the savor of tar nor of pitch,
Yet a tailor might scratch her where'er she did itch.[26]
Then to sea, boys, and let her go hang!"
This is a scurvy tune too. But here's my comfort.

[*Drinks.*]

CALIBAN: Do not torment me![27] O!   50
STEPHANO: What's the matter?[28] Have we devils here? Do you put tricks upon 's[29]
with savages and men of Ind,[30] ha? I have not scaped drowning to be
afeard now of your four legs. For it has been said, "As proper[31] a man as
ever went on four legs[32] cannot make him give ground"; and it shall be
said so again while Stephano breathes at[33] nostrils.   55

---

18. By my faith.
19. Hold it in.
20. I.e., died.
21. Cloak, loose upper garment.
22. Take shelter.
23. I.e., last remains (as in a *bombard* or jug, line 20)
24. Crew member whose job is to wash the decks.
25. Sting.
26. (A dig at tailors for their supposed effeminacy and a bawdy suggestion of satisfying a sexual craving.)

27. (Caliban assumes that one of Prospero's spirits has come to punish him.)
28. What's going on here?
29. Trick us with conjuring shows.
30. India.
31. Handsome.
32. (The conventional phrase would supply *two legs,* but the creature Stephano thinks he sees has four).
33. At the.

CALIBAN: This spirit torments me! O!

STEPHANO: This is some monster of the isle with four legs, who hath got, as I take it, an ague.[34] Where the devil should he learn[35] our language? I will give him some relief, if it be but for that.[36] If I can recover[37] him and keep him tame and get to Naples with him, he's a present for any emperor that ever trod on neat's leather.[38] 60

CALIBAN: Do not torment me, prithee. I'll bring my wood home faster.

STEPHANO: He's in his fit now and does not talk after the wisest.[39] He shall taste of my bottle. If he have never drunk wine afore,[40] it will go near to[41] remove his fit. If I can recover[42] him and keep him tame, I will not take too much[43] for him. He shall pay for him that hath[44] him,[45] and that soundly. 65

CALIBAN: Thou dost me yet but little hurt; thou wilt anon,[46] I know it by thy trembling. Now Prosper works upon thee.

STEPHANO: Come on your ways. Open your mouth. Here is that which will give language to you, cat. Open your mouth.[47] This will shake your shaking. I can tell you, and that soundly. *[Giving Caliban a drink.]* You cannot tell who's your friend. Open your chaps[48] again. 70

TRINCULO: I should know that voice. It should be—but he is drowned, and these are devils. O, defend me! 75

STEPHANO: Four legs and two voices—a most delicate[49] monster! His forward voice now is to speak well of his friend; his backward voice[50] is to utter foul speeches and to detract. If all the wine in my bottle will recover him,[51] I will help[52] his ague. Come. *[Giving a drink.]* Amen! I will pour some in thy other mouth. 80

TRINCULO: Stephano!

STEPHANO: Doth thy other mouth call me?[53] Mercy, mercy! This is a devil, and no monster. I will leave him. I have no long spoon.[54]

TRINCULO: Stephano! If thou beest Stephano, touch me and speak to me, for I am Trinculo—be not afeard—thy good friend Trinculo. 85

STEPHANO: If thou beest Trinculo, come forth. I'll pull thee by the lesser legs. If

---

34. Fever. (Probably both Caliban and Trinculo are quaking; see lines 56 and 81.)
35. Could he have learned.
36. I.e., for knowing our language.
37. Restore.
38. Cowhide.
39. In the wisest fashion.
40. Before.
41. Be in a fair way to.
42. Restore.
43. I.e., no sum can be too much.
44. Possesses, receives.
45. I.e., anyone who wants him will have to pay dearly for him.
46. Presently.
47. (Allusion to the proverb "Good liquor will make a cat speak.")

48. Jaws.
49. Ingenious.
50. (Trinculo and Caliban are facing in opposite directions. Stephano supposes the monster to have a rear end that can emit *foul speeches* or foul-smelling wind at the monster's *other mouth,* line 95.)
51. Even if it takes all the wine in my bottle to cure him.
52. Cure.
53. I.e., call me by name, know supernaturally who I am.
54. (Allusion to the proverb "He that sups with the devil has need of a long spoon.")

any be Trinculo's legs, these are they. *[Pulling him out.]* Thou art very
Trinculo indeed! How cam'st thou to be the siege[55] of this mooncalf?[56]
Can he vent[57] Trinculos?

TRINCULO: I took him to be killed with a thunderstroke. But art thou not   90
    drowned, Stephano? I hope now thou art not drowned. Is the storm
    overblown?[58] I hid me under the dead mooncalf's gaberdine for fear of
    the storm. And art thou living, Stephano? O Stephano, two Neapolitans
    scaped! *[He capers with Stephano.]*

STEPHANO: Prithee, do not turn me about. My stomach is not constant.[59]   95

CALIBAN:
    These be fine things, an if[60] they be not spirits.
    That's a brave[61] god, and bears[62] celestial liquor.
    I will kneel to him.

STEPHANO: How didst thou scape? How cam'st thou hither? Swear by this bottle
    how thou cam'st hither. I escaped upon a butt of sack[63] which the sailors   100
    heaved o'erboard—by this bottle,[64] which I made of the bark of a tree
    with mine own hands since[65] I was cast ashore.

CALIBAN *[kneeling]:* I'll swear upon that bottle to be thy true subject, for the liquor
    is not earthly.

STEPHANO: Here. Swear then how thou escapedst.   105

TRINCULO: Swum ashore, man, like a duck. I can swim like a duck, I'll be sworn.

STEPHANO: Here, kiss the book.[66] Though thou canst swim like a duck, thou art
    made like a goose.

[Giving him a drink.]

TRINCULO: O Stephano, hast any more of this?

STEPHANO: The whole butt, man. My cellar is in a rock by the seaside, where my   110
    wine is hid.—How now, mooncalf? How does thine ague?

CALIBAN: Hast thou not dropped from heaven?

STEPHANO: Out o' the moon, I do assure thee. I was the Man i' the Moon when
    time was.[67]

CALIBAN:
    I have seen thee in her, and I do adore thee.
    My mistress showed me thee, and thy dog, and thy bush.[68]   115

STEPHANO: Come, swear to that. Kiss the book. I will furnish it anon with new
    contents. Swear.

---

55. Excrement.
56. Monstrous or misshapen creature (whose
    deformity is caused by the malignant in-
    fluence of the moon).
57. Excrete, defecate.
58. Blown over.
59. Unsteady.
60. If.
61. Fine, magnificent.
62. He carries.

63. Barrel of Canary wine.
64. I.e., I swear by this bottle.
65. After.
66. I.e., bottle (but with ironic reference to the
    practice of kissing the Bible in swearing an
    oath; see *I'll be sworn* in line 128)
67. Once upon a time.
68. (The Man in the Moon was popularly
    imagined to have with him a dog and a
    bush of thorn.)

[Giving him a drink.]

TRINCULO: By this good light,[69] this is a very shallow monster! I afeard of him? A
very weak monster! The Man i' the Moon? A most poor credulous
monster! Well drawn,[70] monster, in good sooth![71]   120
CALIBAN *[to Stephano]*:
I'll show thee every fertile inch o' th' island,
And I will kiss thy foot. I prithee, be my god.
TRINCULO: By this light, a most perfidious and drunken monster! When 's god's
asleep, he'll rob his bottle.[72]
CALIBAN:
I'll kiss thy foot. I'll swear myself thy subject.   125
STEPHANO: Come on then. Down, and swear.

[Caliban kneels.]

TRINCULO: I shall laugh myself to death at this puppy-headed monster. A most
scurvy monster! I could find in my heart to beat him—
STEPHANO: Come, kiss.
TRINCULO: But that the poor monster's in drink.[73] An abominable monster!   130
CALIBAN:
I'll show thee the best springs. I'll pluck thee berries.
I'll fish for thee and get thee wood enough.
A plague upon the tyrant that I serve!
I'll bear him no more sticks, but follow thee,
Thou wondrous man.   135
TRINCULO: A most ridiculous monster, to make a wonder of a poor drunkard!
CALIBAN:
I prithee, let me bring thee where crabs[74] grow,
And I with my long nails will dig thee pignuts,[75]
Show thee a jay's nest, and instruct thee how
To snare the nimble marmoset.[76] I'll bring thee   140
To clustering filberts, and sometimes I'll get thee
Young scamels[77] from the rock. Wilt thou go with me?
STEPHANO: I prithee now, lead the way without any more talking.—Trinculo, the
King and all our company else[78] being drowned, we will inherit[79]

---

69. By God's light, by this good light from
    heaven.
70. Well pulled (on the bottle).
71. Truly, indeed.
72. I.e., Caliban wouldn't even stop at robbing
    his god of his bottle if he could catch him
    asleep.
73. Drunk.
74. Crab apples, or perhaps crabs.
75. Earthnuts, edible tuberous roots.

76. Small monkey.
77. (Possibly *seamews*, mentioned in Stra-
    chey's letter, or shellfish, or perhaps from
    squamelle "furnished with little scales."
    Contemporary French and Italian travel
    accounts report that the natives of Patago-
    nia in South America ate small fish de-
    scribed as *tort scameux* and *squame*.)
78. In addition, besides ourselves.
79. Take possession.

here.—Here, bear my bottle.—Fellow Trinculo, we'll fill him by and by   145
   again.

CALIBAN (*sings drunkenly*):
   Farewell, master, farewell, farewell!

TRINCULO: A howling monster; a drunken monster!

CALIBAN:
   No more dams I'll make for fish,
      Nor fetch in firing[80]   150
         At requiring,
      Nor scrape trenchering,[81] nor wash dish.
         'Ban, 'Ban, Ca–Caliban
         Has a new master. Get a new man![82]
   Freedom, high-day! High-day, freedom! Freedom, high-day,[83]   155
   freedom!

STEPHANO: O brave monster! Lead the way.   *[Exeunt.]*

Act III

Scene 1[1]

[Enter Ferdinand, bearing a log.]

FERDINAND:
   There be some sports are painful, and their labor
   Delight in them sets off.[2] Some kinds of baseness[3]
   Are nobly undergone,[4] and most poor[5] matters
   Point to rich ends. This my mean[6] task
   Would be as heavy to me as odious, but[7]   5
   This mistress which I serve quickens[8] what's dead
   And makes my labors pleasures. O, she is
   Ten times more gentle than her father's crabbed,
   And he's composed of harshness, I must remove
   Some thousands of these logs and pile them up,   10
   Upon a sore injunction.[9] My sweet mistress
   Weeps when she sees me work and says such baseness

---

80. Firewood.
81. Trenchers, wooden plates.
82. (Addressed to Prospero.)
83. Holiday.

   Act III, Scene 1
1. Location: Before Prospero's cell.
2. Some pastimes are laborious, but the pleasure we get from them compensates for
   the effort. (Pleasure is *set off* by labor as a
   jewel is set off by its foil.)
3. Menial activity.

4. Undertaken.
5. Poorest.
6. Lowly.
7. Were it not that.
8. Gives life to.
9. Severe command.

Had never like executor.[10] I forget;[11]
But these sweet thoughts do even refresh my labors,
Most busy lest when I do it.[12]   15

[Enter Miranda; and Prospero (at a distance, unseen).]

MIRANDA: Alas now, pray you,
Work not so hard, I would the lightning had
Burnt up those logs that you are enjoined[13] to pile!
Pray, set it down and rest you. When this[14] burns,
'Twill weep[15] for having wearied you. My father
Is hard at study. Pray now, rest yourself.   20
He's safe for these[16] three hours.
FERDINAND: O most dear mistress,
The sun will set before I shall discharge[17]
What I must strive to do.
MIRANDA: If you'll sit down,
I'll bear your logs the while. Pray, give me that.   25
I'll carry it to the pile.
FERDINAND: No, precious creature,
I had rather crack my sinews, break my back,
Than you should such dishonor undergo
While I sit lazy by.
MIRANDA: It would become me
As well as it does you; and I should do it
With much more ease, for my good will is to it,   30
And yours it is against.
PROSPERO *[aside]:*   Poor worm, thou art infected!
This visitation[18] shows it.
MIRANDA: You look wearily.
FERDINAND:
No, noble mistress, 'tis fresh morning with me
When you are by[19] at night. I do beseech you—
Chiefly that I might set it in my prayers—   35
What is your name?
MIRANDA: Miranda.—O my father,
I have broke your hest[20] to say so.

---

10. I.e., was never before undertaken by so
    noble a being.
11. I.e., I forget that I'm supposed to be
    working, or, I forget my happiness, op-
    pressed by my labor.
12. I.e., busy at my labor but with my mind on
    other things (?) (The line may be in need
    of emendation.)
13. Commanded.

14. I.e., the log.
15. I.e., exude resin.
16. The next.
17. Complete.
18. (1) Miranda's visit to Ferdinand; (2) visita-
    tion of the plague, i.e., infection of love.
19. Nearby.
20. Command.

FERDINAND: Admired Miranda![21]
          Indeed the top of admiration, worth
          What's dearest[22] to the world! Full many a lady
          I have eyed with best regard,[23] and many a time   40
          The harmony of their tongues hath into bondage
          Brought my too diligent[24] ear. For several[25] virtues
          Have I liked several women, never any
          With so full soul but some defect in her
          Did quarrel with the noblest grace she owed[26]   45
          And put it to the foil.[27] But you, O you,
          So perfect and so peerless, are created
          Of[28] every creature's best!
MIRANDA: I do not know
          One of my sex; no woman's face remember,
          Save, from my glass, mine own. Nor have I seen   50
          More that I may call men than you, good friend,
          And my dear father. How features are abroad[29]
          I am skilless[30] of; but, my modesty,[31]
          The jewel in my dower, I would not wish
          Any companion in the world but you;   55
          Nor can imagination form a shape,
          Besides yourself, to like of.[32] But I prattle
          Something[33] too wildly, and my father's precepts
          I therein do forget.
FERDINAND: I am in my condition[34]
          A prince, Miranda; I do think, a king—   60
          I would,[35] not so!—and would no more endure
          This wooden slavery[36] than to suffer
          The flesh-fly[37] blow[38] my mouth. Hear my soul speak:
          The very instant that I saw you did
          My heart fly to your service, there resides   65
          To make me slave to it, and for your sake
          Am I this patient log-man.
MIRANDA: Do you love me?

---

21. (Her name means "to be admired or won-
    dered at.")
22. Most treasured.
23. Thoughtful and approving attention.
24. Attentive.
25. Various (also in line 43).
26. Owned.
27. (1) overthrew it (as in wrestling) (2)
    served as a *foil*, or "contrast," to set it off.
28. Out of.

29. What people look like in other places.
30. Ignorant.
31. Virginity.
32. Be pleased with, be fond of.
33. Somewhat.
34. Rank.
35. Wish (it were).
36. Being compelled to carry wood.
37. Insect that deposits its eggs in dead flesh.
38. Befoul with fly eggs.

FERDINAND:
> O heaven, O earth, bear witness to this sound,
> And crown what I profess with kind event[39]
> If I speak true! If hollowly,[40] invert[41]   70
> What best is boded[42] me to mischief?[43] I
> Beyond all limit of what[44] else i' the world
> Do love, prize, honor you.

MIRANDA *[weeping]:*   I am a fool
> To weep at what I am glad of.

PROSPERO *[aside]:*   Fair encounter
> Of two most rare affections! Heavens rain grace   75
> On that which breeds between 'em!

FERDINAND: Wherefore weep you?

MIRANDA:
> At mine unworthiness, that dare not offer
> What I desire to give, and much less take
> What I shall die[45] to want.[46] But this is trifling,
> And all the more it seeks to hide itself   80
> The bigger bulk it shows. Hence, bashful cunning,[47]
> And prompt me, plain and holy innocence!
> I am your wife, if you will marry me;
> If not, I'll die your maid.[48] To be your fellow[49]
> You may deny me, but I'll be your servant   85
> Whether you will[50] or no.

FERDINAND: My mistress,[51] dearest,
> And I thus humble ever.

MIRANDA: My husband, then?

FERDINAND: Ay, with a heart as willing[52]
> As bondage e'er of freedom. Here's my hand   90

MIRANDA *[clasping his hand]:*
> And mine, with my heart in 't. And now farewell
> Till half an hour hence.

FERDINAND: A thousand thousand![53]

> *[Exeunt (Ferdinand and Miranda, separately).]*

---

39. Favorable outcome.
40. Insincerely, falsely.
41. Turn.
42. In store for.
43. Harm.
44. Whatever.
45. (Probably with an unconscious sexual meaning that underlies all of lines 77–81.)
46. Through lacking.

47. Coyness.
48. Handmaiden, servant.
49. Mate, equal.
50. Desire it.
51. I.e., the woman I adore and serve (not an illicit sexual partner).
52. Desirous.
53. I.e., a thousand thousand farewells.

PROSPERO:

> So glad of this as they I cannot be,
> Who are surprised with all;[54] but my rejoicing
> At nothing can be more. I'll to my book,   95
> For yet ere suppertime must I perform
> Much business appertaining.[55]   *[Exit.]*

Scene 2[1]

[Enter Caliban, Stephano, and Trinculo.]

STEPHANO: Tell not me. When the butt is out,[2] we will drink water, not a drop
before. Therefore bear up and board 'em.[3] Servant monster, drink to me.

TRINCULO: Servant monster? The folly[4] of this island!

> They say there's but five upon this isle. We are three of them; if th' other
> two be brained[5] like us, the state totters.   5

STEPHANO: Drink, servant monster, when I bid thee.

> Thy eyes are almost set[6] in thy head. *[Giving a drink.]*

TRINCULO: Where should they be set[7] else? He were a brave[8] monster indeed if
they were set in his tail.

STEPHANO: My man-monster hath drowned his tongue in sack. For my part, the   10
sea cannot drown me. I swam, ere I could recover[9] the shore, five and
thirty leagues[10] off and on.[11] By this light,[12] thou shalt be my lieutenant,
monster, or my standard.[13]

TRINCULO: Your lieutenant, if you list;[14] he's no standard.[15]

STEPHANO: We'll not run,[16] Monsieur Monster.   15

TRINCULO: Nor go[17] neither, but you'll lie[18] like dogs and yet say nothing neither.

STEPHANO: Mooncalf, speak once in thy life, if thou beest a good mooncalf.

CALIBAN:

> How does thy honor? Let me lick thy shoe.
> I'll not serve him. He is not valiant.

---

54. By everything that has happened, or,
withal, "with it."
55. Related to this.

Act III, Scene 2

1. Location: another part of the island.
2. Empty.
3. (Stephano uses the terminology of maneuvering at sea and boarding a vessel under
attack as a way of urging an assault on the
liquor supply.)
4. I.e., stupidity found on.
5. Are endowed with intelligence.
6. Fixed in a drunken stare, or, sunk, like the
sun.
7. Placed.

8. Fine, splendid.
9. Gain, reach.
10. Units of distance, each equaling about
three miles.
11. Intermittently.
12. (An oath: by the light of the sun.)
13. Standard-bearer, ensign (as distinguished
from *lieutenant,* lines 16–17).
14. Prefer.
15. I.e., not able to stand up.
16. (1) retreat; (2) urinate (taking Trinculo's
standard, line 17, in the old sense of
"conduit.")
17. Walk.
18. (1) Tell lies; (2) lie prostrate (3) excrete.

TRINCULO: Thou liest, most ignorant monster, I am in case to jostle a constable.[19]   20
Why, thou debauched[20] fish thou, was there ever man a coward that
hath drunk so much sack[21] as I today? Wilt thou tell a monstrous lie
being but half a fish and half a monster?

CALIBAN:
Lo, how he mocks me! Wilt thou let him, my lord?

TRINCULO: "Lord," quoth he? That a monster should be such a natural![22]   25

CALIBAN:
Lo, lo, again! Bit him to death, I prithee.

STEPHANO: Trinculo, keep a good tongue in your head.
If you prove a mutineer—the next tree![23] The poor monster's my subject,
and he shall not suffer indignity.

CALIBAN:
I thank my noble lord. Wilt thou be pleased   30
To hearken once again to the suit I made to thee?

STEPHANO: Marry,[24] will I. Kneel and repeat it. I will stand, and so shall Trinculo.

[Caliban kneels.]

[Enter Ariel, invisible.][25]

CALIBAN:
As I told thee before, I am subject to a tyrant,
A sorcerer, that by his cunning hath
Cheated me of the island.   35

ARIEL *[mimicking Trinculo]*:
Thou liest.

CALIBAN: Thou liest, thou jesting monkey, thou!
I would my valiant master would destroy thee.
I do not lie.

STEPHANO: Trinculo, if you trouble him any more in's tale, by this hand, I will   40
supplant[26] some of your teeth.

TRINCULO: Why, I said nothing.

STEPHANO: Mum, then, and no more.—Proceed.

CALIBAN:
I say by sorcery he got this isle;
From me he got it. If thy greatness will   45
Revenge it on him—for I know thou dar'st,
But this thing[27] dare not—

STEPHANO: That's most certain.

---

19. I.e., in fit condition, made valiant by
drink, to taunt or challenge the police.
20. (1) Seduced away from proper service and
allegiance; (2) depraved.
21. Spanish white wine.
22. (1) idiot; (2) natural as opposed to unnatural, monsterlike.

23. I.e., you'll hang.
24. I.e., indeed. (Originally an oath, "by the
Virgin Mary.")
25. I.e., wearing a garment to connote invisibility.
26. Uproot, displace.
27. I.e., Trinculo.

CALIBAN:
> Thou shalt be lord of it, and I'll serve thee.

STEPHANO: How now shall this be compassed?[28] Canst thou bring me to the   50
> party?

CALIBAN:
> Yea, yea, my lord. I'll yield him thee asleep,
> Where thou mayst knock a nail into his head.

ARIEL: Thou liest; thou canst not.

CALIBAN:
> What a pied ninny's[29] this! Thou scurvy patch![30]—   55
> I do beseech thy greatness, give him blows
> And take his bottle from him. When that's gone
> He shall drink naught but brine, for I'll not show him
> Where the quick freshes[31] are.

STEPHANO: Trinculo, run into no further danger. Interrupt the monster one word   60
> further[32] and, by this hand, I'll turn my mercy out o' doors[33] and make
> a stockfish[34] of thee.

TRINCULO: Why, what did I? I did nothing. I'll go farther off.[35]

STEPHANO: Didst thou not say he lied?

ARIEL: Thou liest.   65

STEPHANO: Do I so? Take thou that. *[He beats Trinculo.]*
> As you like this, give me the lie[36] another time.

TRINCULO: I did not give the lie. Out o' your wits and hearing too? A pox o' your
> bottle! This can sack and drinking do. A murrain[37] on your monster, and
> the devil take your fingers!   70

CALIBAN: Ha, ha, ha!

STEPHANO: Now, forward with your tale. *[To Trinculo.]*
> Prithee, stand further off.

CALIBAN:
> Beat him enough. After a little time
> I'll beat him too.   75

STEPHANO: Stand farther.—Come, proceed.

CALIBAN:
> Why, as I told thee, 'tis a custom with him
> I' th' afternoon to sleep. There thou mayst brain him,
> Having first seized his books; or with a log
> Batter his skull, or paunch[38] him with a stake,   80
> Or cut his weasand[39] with thy knife. Remember
> First to possess his books, for without them

---

28. Achieved.
29. Fool in motley.
30. Fool.
31. Running springs.
32. I.e., one more time.
33. I.e., forget about being merciful.

34. Dried cod beaten before cooking.
35. Away.
36. Call me a liar to my face.
37. Plague. (Literally, a cattle disease.)
38. Stab in the belly.
39. Windpipe.

He's but a sot,[40] as I am, nor hath not
One spirit to command. They all do hate him
As rootedly as I. Burn but his books. 85
He has brave utensils[41]—for so he calls them—
Which, when he has a house, he'll deck withal.[42]
And that most deeply to consider is
The beauty of his daughter. He himself
Calls her a nonpareil. I never saw a woman 90
But only Sycorax my dam and she;
But she as far surpasseth Sycorax
As great'st does least.

STEPHANO: Is it so brave[43] a lass?

CALIBAN:
Ay, lord. She will become[44] thy bed, I warrant, 95
And bring thee forth brave brood.

STEPHANO: Monster, I will kill this man. His daughter and I will be king and
queen—save Our Graces!—and Trinculo and thyself shall be viceroys.
Dost thou like the plot, Trinculo?

TRINCULO: Excellent. 100

STEPHANO: Give me thy hand. I am sorry I beat thee; but, while thou liv'st, keep
a good tongue in thy head.

CALIBAN:
Within this half hour will he be asleep.
Wilt thou destroy him then?

STEPHANO: Ay, on mine honor. 105

ARIEL [aside]: This will I tell my master.

CALIBAN:
Thou mak'st me merry; I am full of pleasure.
Let us be jocund.[45] Will you troll the catch[46]
You taught me but whilere?[47]

STEPHANO: At thy request, monster, I will do reason, 110
any reason.[48]—Come on, Trinculo, let us sing. [Sings.]
"Flout[49] 'em and scout[50] 'em
And scout 'em and flout 'em!
Thought is free."

CALIBAN: That's not the tune. 115

[Ariel plays the tune on a tabor[51] and pipe.]

STEPHANO: What is this same?

---

40. Fool.
41. Fine furnishings.
42. Furnish it with.
43. Splendid, attractive.
44. Suit (sexually).
45. Jovial, merry.

46. Sing the round.
47. Only a short time ago.
48. Anything reasonable.
49. Scoff at.
50. Deride.
51. Small drum.

TRINCULO: This is the tune of our catch, played by the picture of Nobody.[52]

STEPHANO: If thou beest a man, show thyself in thy likeness. If thou beest a devil,
　　　　take 't as thou list.[53]

TRINCULO: O, forgive me my sins!   120

STEPHANO: He that dies pays all debts.[54] I defy thee.
　　　　Mercy upon us!

CALIBAN: Art thou afeard?

STEPHANO: No, monster, not I.

CALIBAN:
　　　　Be not afeard. The isle is full of noises,   125
　　　　Sounds, and sweet airs, that give delight and hurt not.
　　　　Sometimes a thousand twangling instruments
　　　　Will hum about mine ears, and sometimes voices
　　　　That, if I then had waked after long sleep,
　　　　Will make me sleep again; and then, in dreaming,   130
　　　　The clouds methought would open and show riches
　　　　Ready to drop upon me, that when I waked
　　　　I cried to dream[55] again.

STEPHANO: This will prove a brave kingdom to me, where I shall have my music
　　　　for nothing.   135

CALIBAN: When Prospero is destroyed.

STEPHANO: That shall be by and by.[56] I remember the story.

TRINCULO: The sound is going away. Let's follow it, and after do our work.

STEPHANO: Lead, monster; we'll follow. I would I could see this taborer! He lays
　　　　it on.[57]   140

TRINCULO: Wilt come? I'll follow, Stephano.

　　　　[Exeunt (following Ariel's music).]

Scene 3[1]

[Enter Alonso, Sebastian, Antonio, Gonzalo, Adrian, Francisco, etc.]

GONZALO:
　　　　By r' lakin,[2] I can go no further, sir.
　　　　My old bones aches. Here's a maze trod indeed
　　　　Through forthrights and meanders![3] By your patience,
　　　　I needs must[4] rest me.

---

52. (Refers to a familiar figure with head,
arms, and legs but no trunk.)

53. I.e., take my defiance as you please, as best
you can.

54. I.e., if I have to die, at least that will be the
end of all my woes and obligations.

55. Desirous of dreaming.

56. Very soon.

57. I.e., plays the drum vigorously.

　　Act III, Scene 3.

1. Location: another part of the island.

2. By our Ladykin, by our Lady.

3. Paths straight and crooked.

4. Have to.

ALONSO: Old lord, I cannot blame thee,
   Who am myself attached[5] with weariness,   5
   To th' dulling of my spirits.[6] Sit down and rest.
   Even here I will put off my hope, and keep it
   No longer for[7] my flatterer. He is drowned
   Whom thus we stray to find, and the sea mocks
   Our frustrate[8] search on land. Well, let him go.   10

   [Alonso and Gonzalo sit.]

ANTONIO *[aside to Sebastian]:*
   I am right[9] glad that he's so out of hope.
   Do not, for[10] one repulse, forgo the purpose
   That you resolved t' effect.
SEBASTIAN *[to Antonio]:* The next advantage
   Will we take throughly.[11]
ANTONIO *[to Sebastian]:* Let it be tonight,
   For, now[12] they are oppressed with travel,[13] they   15
   Will not, nor cannot, use[14] such vigilance
   As when they are fresh.
SEBASTIAN *[to Antonio]:* I say tonight. No more.

   [Solemn and strange music; and Prospero on the top,[15] invisible.]

ALONSO:
   What harmony is this? My good friends, hark!
GONZALO: Marvelous sweet music!

   *[Enter several strange shapes, bringing in a banquet, and dance about it with
   gentle actions of salutations; and, inviting the King, etc., to eat, they depart.]*

ALONSO:
   Give us kind keepers,[16] heavens! What were these?   20
SEBASTIAN
   A living[17] drollery.[18] Now I will believe
   That there are unicorns; that in Arabia
   There is one tree, the phoenix'[19] throne, one phoenix
   At this hour reigning there.

---

5. Seized.
6. To the point of being dull-spirited.
7. As.
8. Frustrated.
9. Very.
10. Because of.
11. Thoroughly.
12. Now that.
13. (Spelled *trauaile* in the Folio and carrying
  the sense of labor as well as traveling.)
14. Apply.

15. At some high point of the tiring-house or
  the theatre, on a third level above the
  gallery.
16. Guardian angels.
17. With live actors.
18. Comic entertainment, caricature, puppet
  show.
19. Mythical bird consumed to ashes every
  five hundred to six hundred years, only to
  be renewed into another cycle.

ANTONIO: I'll believe both;
    And what does else want credit,[20] come to me   25
    And I'll be sworn 'tis true. Travelers ne'er did lie,
    Though fools at home condemn 'em.
GONZALO: If in Naples
    I should report this now, would they believe me
    If I should say I saw such islanders?
    For, certes,[21] these are people of the island,   30
    Who, though they are of monstrous[22] shape, yet note,
    Their manners are more gentle, kind, than of
    Our human generation you shall find
    Many, nay, almost any.
PROSPERO [aside]:   Honest lord,
    Thou hast said well, for some of you there present   35
    Are worse than devils.
ALONSO: I cannot too much muse[23]
    Such shapes, such gesture, and such sound, expressing—
    Although they want[24] the use of tongue—a kind
    Of excellent dumb discourse.
PROSPERO [aside]:   Praise in departing.[25]
FRANCISCO:
    They vanished strangely.
SEBASTIAN: No matter, since   40
    They have left their viands[26] behind, for we have stomachs.[27]
    Will 't please you taste of what is here?
ALONSO: Not I.
GONZALO:
    Faith, sir, you need not fear. When we were boys,
    Who would believe that there were mountaineers[28]
    Dewlapped[29] like bulls, whose throats had hanging at 'em   45
    Wallets[30] of flesh? Or that there were such men
    Whose heads stood in their breasts?[31] Which now we find
    Each putter-out of five for one[32] will bring us
    Good warrant[33] of.

---

20. Lack credence.
21. Certainly.
22. Unnatural.
23. Wonder at.
24. Lack.
25. I.e., save your praise until the end of the performance. (Proverbial.)
26. Provisions.
27. Appetites.
28. Mountain dwellers.
29. Having a dewlap, or fold of skin hanging from the neck, like cattle.
30. Pendent folds of skin, wattles.
31. (I.e., like the Anthropophagi described in *Othello*, 1.3.146)
32. One who invests money or gambles on the risks of travel on the condition that the traveler who returns safely is to receive five times the amount deposited; hence, any traveler
33. Assurance.

ALONSO: I will stand to[34] and feed,
           Although my last[35]—no matter, since I feel   50
           The best[36] is past. Brother, my lord the Duke,
           Stand to, and do as we.   *[They approach the table.]*

           [Thunder and lightning. Enter Ariel, like a harpy,[37] claps his wings upon the
           table, and with a quaint device[38] the banquet vanishes.[39]]

ARIEL:

           You are three men of sin, whom Destiny—
           That hath to instrument this lower world
           And what is in 't—the never-surfeited sea
           Hath caused to belch up you,[40] and on this island   55
           Where man doth not inhabit, you 'mongst men
           Being most unfit to live. I have made you mad;
           And even with suchlike valor[41] men hang and drown
           Their proper[42] selves. *[Alonso, Sebastian, and Antonio draw their swords.]*
               You fools! I and my fellows
           Are ministers of Fate. The elements
           Of whom[43] your swords are tempered[44] may as well
           Wound the loud winds, or with bemocked-at[45] stabs
           Kill the still-closing waters, as diminish
           One dowl[46] that's in my plume. My fellow ministers   65
           Are like[47] invulnerable. If[48] you could hurt,
           Your swords are now too massy[49] for your strengths
           And will not be uplifted. But remember—
           For that's my business to you—that you three
           From Milan did supplant good Prospero;   70
           Exposed unto the sea, which hath requit[50] it,
           Him and his innocent child; for which foul deed
           The powers, delaying, not forgetting, have
           Incensed the seas and shores, yea, all the creatures,
           Against your peace. Thee of thy son, Alonso,   75
           They have bereft; and do pronounce by me
           Ling'ring perdition,[51] worse than any death

---

34. Fall to; take the risk.
35. Even if this were to be my last meal.
36. Best part of life.
37. A fabulous monster with a woman's face and breasts and a vulture's body, supposed to be a minister of divine vengeance.
38. Ingenious stage contrivance.
39. I.e., the food vanishes; the table remains until line 82.
40. You whom Destiny, controller of the sublunary world as its instrument, has caused the ever hungry sea to belch up.

41. I.e., the reckless valor derived from madness.
42. Own.
43. Which.
44. Composed and hardened.
45. Scorned.
46. Soft, fine feather.
47. Likewise, similarly.
48. Even if.
49. Heavy.
50. Requited, avenged.
51. Ruin, destruction.

Can be at once, shall step by step attend
You and your ways; whose[52] wraths to guard you from—
Which here, in this most desolate isle, else[53] falls   80
Upon your heads—is nothing[54] but heart's sorrow
And a clear[55] life ensuing.

[He vanishes in thunder; then, to soft music, enter the shapes again, and dance, with mocks and mows,[56] and carrying out the table.]

PROSPERO:

Bravely[57] the figure of this harpy hast thou
Performed, my Ariel; a grace it had devouring.[58]
Of my instruction hast thou nothing bated[59]   85
In what thou hadst to say. So,[60] with good life[61]
And observation strange,[62] my meaner[63] ministers
Their several kinds[64] have done. My high charms work,
And these mine enemies are all knit up
In their distractions.[65] They now are in my power;
And in these fits I leave them, while I visit   90
Young Ferdinand, whom they suppose is drowned,
And his and mine loved darling.   *[Exit above.]*

GONZALO:

I' the name of something holy, sir, why[66] stand you
In this strange stare?   95

ALONSO: O, it[67] is monstrous, monstrous!
Methought the billows[68] spoke and told me of it;
The winds did sing it to me, and the thunder,
That deep and dreadful organ pipe, pronounced
The name of Prosper; it did bass my trespass.[69]
Therefor[70] my son i' th' ooze is bedded; and   100
I'll seek him deeper than e'er plummet[71] sounded.[72]
And with him there lie mudded.   *[Exit.]*

---

52. (Refers to the heavenly powers.)
53. Otherwise.
54. There is no way.
55. Unspotted, innocent.
56. Mocking gestures and grimaces.
57. Finely, dashingly.
58. I.e., you gracefully caused the banquet to disappear as if you had consumed it (with puns on *grace,* meaning "gracefulness" and "a blessing on the meal," and on *devouring,* meaning "a literal eating" and "an all-consuming or ravishing grace").
59. Abated, omitted.
60. In the same fashion.
61. Faithful reproduction.
62. Exceptional attention to detail.
63. I.e., subordinate to Ariel.
64. Individual parts.
65. Trancelike state.
66. (Gonzalo was not addressed in Ariel's speech to the *three men of sin,* line 53, and is not, as they are, in a maddened state; see lines 105–107.)
67. I.e., my sin (also in line 96)
68. Waves.
69. Proclaim my trespass like a bass note in music.
70. In consequence of that.
71. A lead weight attached to a line for testing depth.
72. Probed, tested the depth of.

SEBASTIAN: But one fiend at a time,
  I'll fight their legions o'er.[73]
ANTONIO: I'll be thy second.

        [Exeunt (Sebastian and Antonio).]

GONZALO:
  All three of them are desperate.[74] Their great guilt, 105
  Like poison given to work a great time after,
  Now 'gins to bite the spirits.[75] I do beseech you,
  That are of suppler joints, follow them swiftly
  And hinder them from what this ecstasy[76]
  May now provoke them to. 110
ADRIAN   Follow, I pray you.

        [Exeunt omnes.]

Act IV

Scene 1[1]

[Enter Prospero, Ferdinand, and Miranda.]

PROSPERO:
  If I have too austerely punished you,
  Your compensation makes amends, for I
  Have given you here a third[2] of mine own life,
  Or that for which I live; who once again
  I tender[3] to thy hand. All thy vexations 5
  Were but my trials of thy love, and thou
  Hast strangely[4] stood the test. Here, afore heaven,
  I ratify this my rich gift. O Ferdinand,
  Do not smile at me that I boast her off,[5]
  For thou shalt find she will outstrip all praise 10
  And make it halt[6] behind her.
FERDINAND: I do believe it
  Against an oracle.[7]

---

73. One after another.
74. Despairing and reckless.
75. Sap their vital powers through anguish.
76. Mad frenzy.

 Act IV, Scene 1

1. Location: before Prospero's cell.
2. I.e., Miranda, into whose education Prospero has put a third of his life (?) or who represents a large part of what he cares about, along with his dukedom and his learned study (?)
3. Offer.

4. Extraordinarily.
5. I.e., praise her so, or, perhaps an error for "boast of her"; the Folio reads "boast her of."
6. Limp.
7. Even if an oracle should declare otherwise.

PROSPERO:

 Then, as my gift and thine own acquisition
 Worthily purchased, take my daughter. But
 If thou dost break her virgin-knot before   15
 All sanctimonious[8] ceremonies may
 With full and holy rite be ministered,
 No sweet aspersion[9] shall the heavens let fall
 To make this contract grow; but barren hate,
 Sour-eyed disdain, and discord shall bestrew   20
 The union of your bed with weeds[10] so loathly
 That you shall hate it both. Therefore take heed,
 As Hymen's lamps shall light you.[11]

FERDINAND: As I hope

 For quiet days, fair issue,[12] and long life,
 With such love as 'tis now, the murkiest den,   25
 The most opportune place, the strong'st suggestion[13]
 Our worser genius[14] can,[15] shall never melt
 Mine honor into lust, to[16] take away
 The edge[17] of that day's celebration
 When I shall think or[18] Phoebus' steeds are foundered[19]   30
 Or Night kept chained below.

PROSPERO: Fairly spoke.

 Sit then and talk with her. She is thine own.

 [Ferdinand and Miranda sit and talk together.]

 What,[20] Ariel! My industrious servant, Ariel!

 [Enter Ariel.]

ARIEL:

 What would my potent master? Here I am.

PROSPERO:

 Thou and thy meaner fellows[21] your last service   35
 Did worthily perform, and I must use you
 In such another trick.[22] Go bring the rabble,[23]

---

8. Sacred.
9. Dew, shower.
10. (In place of the flowers customarily strewn on the marriage bed.)
11. I.e., as you long for happiness and concord in your marriage. (Hymen was the Greek and Roman god of marriage; his symbolic torches, the wedding torches, were supposed to burn brightly for a happy marriage and smokily for a troubled one.)
12. Offspring.

13. Temptation.
14. Evil genius, or, evil attendant spirit.
15. Is capable of.
16. So as to.
17. Keen enjoyment, sexual ardor.
18. Either.
19. Broken down, made lame. (Ferdinand will wait impatiently for the bridal night.)
20. Now then.
21. Subordinates.
22. Device.
23. Band, i.e., the *meaner fellows* of line 35.

O'er whom I give thee power, here to this place.
Incite them to quick motion, for I must
Bestow upon the eyes of this young couple   40
Some vanity[24] of mine art. It is my promise,
And they expect it from me.

ARIEL: Presently?[25]

PROSPERO: Ay, with a twink.[26]

ARIEL:

Before you can say "Come" and "Go,"
And breathe twice, and cry "So, so,"   45
Each one, tripping on his toe,
Will be here with mop and mow.[27]
Do you love me, master? No?

PROSPERO:

Dearly, my delicate Ariel. Do not approach
Till thou dost hear me call.   50

ARIEL: Well; I conceive.[28]   [*Exit.*]

PROSPERO:

Look thou be true;[29] do not give dalliance
Too much the rein. The strongest oaths are straw
To the fire i' the blood. Be more abstemious,
Or else good night[30] your vow!

FERDINAND: I warrant[31] you, sir,
The white cold virgin snow upon my heart[32]   55
Abates the ardor of my liver.[33]

PROSPERO: Well.
Now come, my Ariel! Bring a corollary,[34]
Rather than want[35] a spirit. Appear, and pertly![36]—
No tongue![37] All eyes! Be silent.   [*Soft music.*]

[*Enter Iris.*][38]

IRIS:

Ceres,[39] most bounteous lady, thy rich leas[40]   60
Of wheat, rye, barley, vetches,[41] oats, and peas;

---

24. (1) illusion; (2) trifle; (3) desire for admiration, conceit.
25. Immediately.
26. In the twinkling of an eye.
27. Gestures and grimaces.
28. Understand.
29. True to your promise.
30. I.e., say good-bye to.
31. Guarantee.
32. I.e., the ideal of chastity and consciousness of Miranda's chaste innocence enshrined in my heart.

33. (As the presumed seat of the passions.)
34. Surplus, extra supply.
35. Lack.
36. Briskly.
37. All the beholders are to be silent (lest the spirits vanish).
38. Goddess of the rainbow and Juno's messenger.
39. Goddess of the generative power of nature.
40. Meadows.
41. Plants for forage, fodder.

Thy turfy mountains, where live nibbling sheep,
And flat meads[42] thatched with stover,[43] them to keep;
Thy banks with pionèd and twillèd[44] brims,
Which spongy[45] April at thy hest[46] betrims   65
To make cold nymphs chaste crowns; and thy broom groves,[47]
Whose shadow the dismissed bachelor[48] loves,
Being lass-lorn; thy poll-clipped[49] vineyard;
And thy sea marge,[50] sterile and rocky hard,
Where thou thyself dost air:[51] the queen o' the sky,[52]   70
Whose watery arch[53] and messenger am I,
Bids thee leave these, and with her sovereign grace,

[Juno descends[54] (slowly in her car).]

Here on this grass plot, in this very place,
To come and sport. Her peacocks[55] fly amain.[56]
Approach, rich Ceres, her to entertain.[57]   75

[Enter Ceres.]

CERES:

Hail, many-colored messenger, that n'er
Dost disobey the wife of Jupiter,
Who with thy saffron[58] wings upon my flowers
Diffusest honeydrops, refreshing showers,
And with each end of thy blue bow[59] dost crown   80
My bosky[60] acres and my unshrubbed down,[61]
Rich scarf[62] to my proud earth. Why hath thy queen
Summoned me hither to this short-grassed green?

IRIS:

A contract of true love to celebrate,
And some donation freely to estate[63]   85
On the blest lovers.

CERES: Tell me, heavenly bow,

---

42. Meadows.
43. Winter fodder for cattle.
44. Undercut by the swift current and protected by roots and branches that tangle to form a barricade.
45. Wet.
46. Command.
47. Clumps of broom, gorse, yellow-flowered shrub.
48. Rejected male lover.
49. Pruned, lopped at the top, or *pole-clipped*, "hedged in with poles"
50. Shore.
51. You take the air, go for walks.
52. I.e., Juno.

53. Rainbow.
54. I.e., starts her descent from the "heavens" above the stage (?)
55. Birds sacred to Juno and used to pull her chariot.
56. With full speed.
57. Receive.
58. Yellow.
59. I.e., rainbow.
60. Wooded.
61. Open upland.
62. (The rainbow is like a colored silk band adorning the earth.)
63. Bestow.

	If Venus or her son,[64] as[65] thou dost know,	
	Do now attend the Queen? Since they did plot	
	The means that[66] dusky[67] Dis my daughter got,[68]	
	Her and her[69] blind boy's scandaled[70] company	90
	I have forsworn.	
IRIS:	Of her society[71]	
	Be not afraid: I met her deity[72]	
	Cutting the clouds towards Paphos,[73] and her son	
	Dove-drawn[74] with her. Here thought they to have done[75]	
	Some wanton[76] charm upon this man and maid,	95
	Whose vows are that no bed-right shall be paid	
	Till Hymen's torch be lighted; but in vain.	
	Mars's hot minion[77] is returned[78] again;	
	Her waspish-headed[79] son has broke his arrows,	
	Swears he will shoot no more, but play with sparrows[80]	100
	And be a boy right out.[81]	

[Juno alights.]

CERES:	Highest Queen of state,[82]	
	Great Juno, comes; I know her by her gait.[83]	
JUNO		
	How does my bounteous sister?[84] Go with me	
	To bless this twain, that they may prosperous be,	
	And honored in their issue.[85] *[They sing.]*	105
JUNO:		
	Honor, riches, marriage blessing,	
	Long continuance, and increasing,	
	Hourly joys be still[86] upon you!	
	Juno sings her blessings on you.	
CERES:		
	Earth's increase, foison plenty,[87]	110
	Barns and garners[88] never empty,	

---

64. I.e., Cupid.
65. As far as.
66. Whereby.
67. Dark.
68. (Pluto, or *Dis,* god of the infernal regions, carried off Proserpina, daughter of Ceres, to be his bride in Hades.)
69. I.e., Venus'.
70. Scandalous.
71. Company.
72. I.e., Her Highness.
73. Place on the island of Cyprus, sacred to Venus.
74. (Venus' chariot was drawn by doves.)

75. Placed.
76. Lustful spell.
77. I.e., Venus, the beloved of Mars.
78. I.e., returned to Paphos.
79. Hotheaded, peevish.
80. (Supposedly lustful, and sacred to Venus.)
81. Outright.
82. Most majestic Queen.
83. I.e., majestic bearing.
84. I.e., fellow goddess (?)
85. Offspring.
86. Always.
87. Plentiful harvest.
88. Granaries.

Vines with clustering bunches growing,
Plants with goodly burden bowing;

Spring come to you at the farthest
In the very end of harvest![89]   115
Scarcity and want shall shun you;
Ceres' blessing so is on you.

FERDINAND:
This is a most majestic vision, and
Harmonious charmingly.[90] May I be bold
To think these spirits?   120

PROSPERO: Spirits, which by mine art
I have from their confines called to enact
My present fancies.

FERDINAND: Let me live here ever!
So rare a wondered[91] father and a wife
Makes this place Paradise.

[Juno and Ceres whisper, and send Iris on employment.]

PROSPERO: Sweet now, silence!
Juno and Ceres whisper seriously;   125
There's something else to do. Hush and be mute,
Or else our spell is marred.

IRIS *[calling offstage]*:
You nymphs, called naiads,[92] of the windring[93] brooks,
With your sedged[94] crowns and ever-harmless[95] looks,
Leave your crisp[96] channels, and on this green land   130
Answer your summons; Juno does command.
Come, temperate[97] nymphs, and help to celebrate
A contract of true love. Be not too late.

[Enter certain nymphs.]

You sunburned sicklemen,[98] of August weary,[99]
Come hither from the furrow[100] and be merry.   135
Make holiday; your rye-straw hats put on,
And these fresh nymphs encounter[101] every one
In country footing.[102]

---

89. I.e., with no winter in between.
90. Enchantingly.
91. Wonder-performing, wondrous.
92. Nymphs of springs, rivers, or lakes.
93. Wandering, winding (?).
94. Made of reeds.
95. Ever innocent.
96. Curled, rippled.

97. Chaste.
98. Harvesters, field workers who cut down grain and grass.
99. I.e., weary of the hard work of the harvest.
100. I.e., plowed fields.
101. Join.
102. Country dancing.

[Enter certain reapers, properly[103] habited. They join with the nymphs in a graceful dance, towards the end whereof Prospero starts suddenly, and speaks; after which, to a strange, hollow, and confused noise, they heavily[104] vanish.]

PROSPERO *[aside]*:
 I had forgot that foul conspiracy
 Of the beast Caliban and his confederates   140
 Against my life. The minute of their plot
 Is almost come. *[To the Spirits.]* Well done! Avoid;[105] no more!

FERDINAND *[to Miranda]*:
 This is strange. Your father's in some passion
 That works[106] him strongly.

MIRANDA: Never till this day
 Saw I him touched with anger so distempered.   145

PROSPERO:
 You do look, my son, in a moved sort,[107]
 As if you were dismayed. Be cheerful, sir.
 Our revels[108] now are ended. These our actors,
 As I foretold you, were all spirits and
 Are melted into air; into thin air;   150
 And, like the baseless fabric[109] of this vision,
 The cloud-capped towers, the gorgeous palaces,
 The solemn temples, the great globe[110] itself,
 Yea, all which it inherit,[111] shall dissolve,
 And, like this insubstantial pageant faded,   155
 Leave not a rack[112] behind. We are such stuff
 As dreams are made on,[113] and our little life
 Is rounded[114] with a sleep. Sir, I am vexed.
 Bear with my weakness. My old brain is troubled.
 Be not disturbed with[115] my infirmity.   160
 If you be pleased, retire[116] into my cell
 And there repose. A turn or two I'll walk
 To still my beating[117] mind.

FERDINAND, MIRANDA: We wish your peace.

[Exeunt (Ferdinand and Miranda).]

---

103. Suitably.
104. Slowly, dejectedly.
105. Withdraw.
106. Affects, agitates.
107. Troubled state, condition.
108. Entertainment, pageant.
109. Unsubstantial theatrical edifice or contrivance.
110. (With a glance at the Globe Theatre.)
111. Who subsequently occupy it.
112. Wisp of cloud.
113. Of.
114. Surrounded (before birth and after death), or crowned, rounded off.
115. By.
116. Withdraw, go
117. Agitated.

PROSPERO:
　　Come with a thought![118] I thank thee, Ariel, Come.

　　[Enter Ariel.]

ARIEL:
　　Thy thoughts I cleave[119] to. What's thy pleasure?   165
PROSPERO: Spirit,
　　We must prepare to meet with Caliban.
ARIEL:
　　Ay, my commander. When I presented[120] Ceres,
　　I thought to have told thee of it, but I feared
　　Lest I might anger thee.
PROSPERO:
　　Say again, where didst thou leave these varlets?   170
ARIEL:
　　I told you, sir, they were red-hot with drinking;
　　So full of valor that they smote the air
　　For breathing in their faces, beat the ground
　　For kissing of their feet; yet always bending[121]
　　Towards their project. Then I beat my tabor,   175
　　At which, like unbacked[122] colts, they pricked their ears,
　　Advanced[123] their eyelids, lifted up their noses
　　As[124] they smelt music. So I charmed their ears
　　That calflike they my lowing[125] followed through
　　Toothed briers, sharp furzes, pricking gorse,[126] and thorns,   180
　　Which entered their frail shins. At last I left them
　　I' the filthy-mantled[127] pool beyond your cell,
　　There dancing up to the chins, that the foul lake
　　O'erstunk[128] their feet.
PROSPERO: This was well done, my bird.
　　Thy shape invisible retain thou still.   185
　　The trumpery[129] in my house, go bring it hither,
　　For stale[130] to catch these thieves.
ARIEL: I go, I go.   *[Exit.]*

---

118. I.e., on the instant, or, summoned by my thought, no sooner thought of than here.
119. Cling, adhere.
120. Acted the part of, or, introduced.
121. Aiming.
122. Unbroken, unridden.
123. Lifted up.
124. As if.
125. Mooing.
126. Prickly shrubs.

127. Covered with a slimy coating.
128. Smelled worse than, or, caused to stink terribly.
129. Goods, the *glistering apparel* mentioned in the following stage direction.
130. (1) Decoy; (2) out-of-fashion garments (with possible further suggestions of "horse piss," as in line 198, and "steal," pronounced like *stale*). For *stale* could also mean "fit for a prostitute."

PROSPERO:
 A devil, a born devil, on whose nature
 Nurture can never stick; on whom my pains,
 Humanely taken, all, all lost, quite lost!   190
 And as with age his body uglier grows,
 So his mind cankers.[131] I will plague them all,
 Even to roaring.

[Enter Ariel, loaden with glistering apparel, etc.]

         Come, hang them on this line.[132]

*[(Ariel hangs up the showy finery; Prospero and Ariel remain,[133] invisible.)
Enter Caliban, Stephano, and Trinculo, all wet.]*

CALIBAN:
 Pray you, tread softly, that the blind mole may
 Not hear a foot fall. We now are near his cell.   195
STEPHANO: Monster, your fairy, which you say is a harmless fairy, has done little
 better than played the jack[134] with us.
TRINCULO: Monster, I do smell all horse piss, at which my nose is in great
 indignation.   200
STEPHANO: So is mine. Do you hear, monster? If I should take a displeasure
 against you, look you—
TRINCULO: Thou wert but a lost monster.
CALIBAN:
 Good my lord, give me thy favor still.
 Be patient, for the prize I'll bring thee to
 Shall hoodwink this mischance.[135] Therefore speak softly.
 All's hushed as midnight yet.
TRINCULO: Ay, but to lose our bottles in the pool—
STEPHANO: There is not only disgrace and dishonor in that monster, but an
 infinite loss.   210
TRINCULO: That's more to me than my wetting. Yet this is your harmless fairy,
 monster!
STEPHANO: I will fetch off my bottle, though I be o'er ears[136] for my labor.
CALIBAN:
 Prithee, my king, be quiet. Seest thou here,   215
 This is the mouth o' the cell. No noise, and enter.
 Do that good mischief which may make this island
 Thine own forever, and I thy Caliban
 For aye thy footlicker.

---

131. Festers, grows malignant.
132. Lime tree or linden.
133. (The staging is uncertain. They may instead exit here and return with the spirits
 at line 256.)
134. (1) Knave; (2) will-o'-the-wisp.

135. (Misfortune is to be prevented from doing further harm by being hooded like a
 hawk and also put out of remembrance.)
136. I.e., totally submerged and perhaps
 drowned.

STEPHANO: Give me thy hand. I do begin to have bloody thoughts.   220
TRINCULO *[seeing the finery]:* O King Stephano! O peer![137]
    O worthy Stephano! Look what a wardrobe here is for thee!
CALIBAN:
    Let it alone, thou fool, it is but trash.
TRINCULO Oho, monster! We know what belongs to a frippery.[138] O King
    Stephano!   *[He puts on a gown.]*   225
STEPHANO: Put off[139] that gown, Trinculo. By this hand,
    I'll have that gown.
TRINCULO Thy Grace shall have it.
CALIBAN:
    The dropsy[140] drown this fool! What do you mean
    To dote thus on such luggage?[141] Let 't alone   230
    And do the murder first. If he awake,
    From toe to crown[142] he'll fill our skins with pinches,
    Make us strange stuff.
STEPHANO: Be you quiet, monster.—Mistress line,[143] is not this my jerkin?[144] *[He*
    takes it down.] Now is the jerkin under the line.[145] Now, jerkin, you are   235
    like[146] to lose your hair and prove a bald[147] jerkin.
TRINCULO Do, do![148] We steal by line and level,[149] an 't like[150] Your Grace.
STEPHANO: I thank thee for that jest. Here's a garment for 't. *[He gives a garment.]*
    Wit shall not go unrewarded while I am king of this country. "Steal by
    line and level" is an excellent pass of pate.[151] There's another garment   240
    for 't.
TRINCULO Monster, come, put some lime[152] upon your fingers, and away with the
    rest.
CALIBAN:
    I will have none on 't. We shall lose our time,

---

137. (Alludes to the old ballad beginning, "King Stephen was a worthy peer.")
138. Place where cast-off clothes are sold.
139. Put down, or, take off.
140. Disease characterized by the accumulation of fluid in the connective tissue of the body.
141. Cumbersome trash.
142. Head.
143. (Addressed to the linden or lime tree upon which, at line 193, Ariel hung the *glistering apparel.)*
144. Jacket made of leather.
145. Under the lime tree (with punning sense of being south of the equinoctial line or equator; sailors on long voyages to the southern regions were popularly supposed to lose their hair from scurvy or

other diseases. Stephano also quibbles bawdily on losing hair through syphilis, and in *Mistress* and *jerkin.)*
146. Likely
147. (1) Hairless, napless; (2) meager.
148. I.e., bravo. (Said in response to the jesting or to the taking of the jerkin, or both.)
149. I.e., by means of plumb lime and carpenter's level, methodically (with pun on *line,* "lime tree," line 238, and *steal,* pronounced like *stale,* i.e, prostitute, continuing Stephano's bawdy quibble).
150. If it please.
151. Sally of wit. (The metaphor is from fencing.)
152. Birdlime, sticky substance (to give Caliban sticky fingers).

And all be turned to barnacles,[153] or to apes   245
With foreheads villainous[154] low.
STEPHANO: Monster, lay to[155] your fingers. Help to bear this[156] away where my
    hogshead[157] of wine is, or I'll turn you out of my kingdom. Go to,[158]
    carry this.
TRINCULO And this.   250
STEPHANO: Ay, and this.

[They load Caliban with more and more garments.]

*[A noise of hunters heard. Enter divers spirits, in shape of dogs and hounds,
hunting them about, Prospero and Ariel setting them on.]*

PROSPERO: Hey, Mountain, hey!
ARIEL: Silver! There it goes, Silver!   255
PROSPERO: Fury, Fury!, There, Tyrant, there! Hark! Hark!

[Caliban, Stephano, and Trinculo are driven out.]

Go, charge my goblins that they grind their joints
With dry[159] convulsions,[160] shorten up their sinews
With aged[161] cramps, and more pinch-spotted make them
Than pard[162] or cat o' mountain.[163]
ARIEL: Hark, they roar!   260
PROSPERO:
Let them be hunted soundly.[164] At this hour
Lies at my mercy all mine enemies.
Shortly shall all my labors end, and thou
Shalt have the air at freedom. For a little[165]
Follow, and do me service.   *[Exeunt.]*   265

Act V

Scene 1[1]

[Enter Prospero in his magic robes, (with his staff) and Ariel.]

PROSPERO:
    Now does my project gather to a head.

---

153. Barnacle geese, formerly supposed to be
    hatched from barnacles attached to trees
    or to rotting timber; here, evidently used,
    like *apes*, as types of simpletons.
154. Miserably.
155. Start using.
156. I.e., the *glistering apparel.*
157. Large cask.
158. (An expression of exhortation or remon-
    strance.)
159. Associated with age, arthritic (?).

160. Cramps.
161. Characteristic of old age.
162. Panther or leopard.
163. Wildcat.
164. Thoroughly (and suggesting the sounds
    of the hunt).
165. Little while longer.

Act V, Scene 1
1. Location: before Prospero's cell.

My charms crack[2] not, my spirits obey, and Time
Goes upright with his carriage.[3] How's the day?

ARIEL:
On[4] the sixth hour, at which time, my lord,
You said our work should cease.   5

PROSPERO: I did say so,
When first I raised the tempest. Say, my spirit,
How fares the King and 's followers?

ARIEL: Confined together
In the same fashion as you gave in charge,
Just as you left them; all prisoners, sir,
In the line grove[5] which weather-fends[6] your cell.   10
They cannot budge till your release.[7] The King,
His brother, and yours abide all three distracted,[8]
And the remainder mourning over them.
Brim full of sorrow and dismay; but chiefly
Him that you termed, sir, the good old lord, Gonzalo.   15
His tears runs down his beard like winter's drops
From eaves of reeds.[9] Your charm so strongly works 'em
That if you now beheld them your affections[10]
Would become tender.

PROSPERO: Dost thou think so, spirit?

ARIEL:
Mine would, sir, were I human.[11]   20

PROSPERO: And mine shall.
Hast thou, which art but air, a touch,[12] a feeling
Of their afflictions, and shall not myself,
One of their kind, that relish all as sharply
Passion as they,[13] be kindlier[14] moved than thou art?
Though with their high wrongs I am struck to the quick,   25
Yet with my nobler reason 'gainst my fury
Do I take part. The rarer[15] action is
In virtue than in vengeance. They being penitent,
The sole drift of my purpose doth extend
Not a frown further. Go release them. Ariel.   30

---

2. Collapse, fail. (The metaphor is probably
   alchemical, as in *project* and *gather to a head*,
   line 1.)
3. Its burden. (Time is no longer heavily burdened and so can go *upright*, "standing
   straight and unimpeded.")
4. Approaching.
5. Grove of lime trees.
6. Protects from the weather.
7. You release them.
8. Out of their wits.

9. Thatched roofs.
10. Disposition, feelings.
11. (Spelled *humane* in the Folio and encom-
    passing both senses.)
12. Sense, apprehension.
13. Who experience human passions as
    acutely as they.
14. (1) More sympathetically; (2) more natu-
    rally, humanly
15. Nobler.

My charms I'll break, their senses I'll restore,
And they shall be themselves.

ARIEL: I'll fetch them, sir.

[Exit.]

[Prospero traces a charmed circle with his staff.]

PROSPERO:
Ye elves of hills, brooks, standing lakes, and groves,[16]
And ye that on the sands with printless foot
Do chase the ebbing Neptune, and do fly him   35
When he comes back; you demi-puppets[17] that
By moonshine do the green sour ringlets[18] make,
Whereof the ewe not bites; and you whose pastime
Is to make midnight mushrooms,[19] that rejoice
To hear the solemn curfew;[20] by whose aid,   40
Weak masters[21] though ye be, I have bedimmed
The noontide sun, called forth the mutinous winds,
And twixt the green sea and the azured vault[22]
Set roaring war; to the dread rattling thunder
Have I given fire,[23] and rifted[24] Jove's stout oak[25]   45
With his own bolt;[26] the strong-based promontory
Have I made shake, and by the spurs[27] plucked up
The pine and cedar; graves at my command
Have waked their sleepers, oped, and let 'em forth
By my so potent art. But this rough[28] magic   50
I here abjure, and when I have required[29]
Some heavenly music—which even now I do—
To work mine end upon their senses that[30]
This airy charm[31] is for, I'll break my staff,
Bury it certain fathoms in the earth,   55
And deeper than did ever plummet sound
I'll drown my book.   *[Solemn music.]*

[Here enters Ariel before; then Alonso, with a frantic gesture, attended by
Gonzalo; Sebastian and Antonio in like manner, attended by Adrian and

---

16. (This famous passage is an embellished
    paraphrase of Goldring's translation of
    Ovid's *Metamorphoses*, 7.197–219.)
17. Puppets of half size, i.e., elves and fairies.
18. Fairy rings, circles in grass (actually pro-
    duced by mushrooms).
19. Mushrooms appearing overnight.
20. Evening bell, usually rung at nine o'clock
    ushering in the time when spirits are
    abroad.
21. I.e., subordinate spirits, as in 4.1.35 (?)
22. I.e., the sky.
23. I have discharged the dread rattling thun-
    derbolt.
24. Riven, split.
25. A tree that was sacred to Jove.
26. Lightning bolt.
27. Roots.
28. Violent.
29. Requested.
30. The senses of those whom.
31. I.e., music.

*Francisco. They all enter the circle which Prospero had made, and there stand
charmed; which Prospero observing, speaks:]*

[*To Alonso.*] A solemn air,[32] and[33] the best comforter
To an unsettled fancy,[34] cure thy brains,
Now useless, boiled[35] within thy skull! [*To Sebastian and Antonio.*] There
   stand,   60
For you are spell-stopped.—
Holy Gonzalo, honorable man,
Mine eyes, e'en sociable[36] to the show[37] of thine,
Fall[38] fellowly drops. [*Aside.*] The charm dissolves apace,   65
And as the morning steals upon the night,
Melting the darkness, so their rising senses
Begin to chase the ignorant fumes[39] that mantle[40]
Their clearer[41] reason.—O good Gonzalo,
My true preserver, and a loyal sir   70
To him thou follow'st! I will pay thy graces[42]
Home[43] both in word and deed.—Most cruelly
Didst thou, Alonso, use me and my daughter.
Thy brother was a furtherer[44] in the act.—
Thou art pinched[45] for 't now, Sebastian. [*To Antonio.*] Flesh and blood,   75
You, brother mine, that entertained ambition,
Expelled remorse[46] and nature,[47] whom,[48] with Sebastian,
Whose inward pinches therefore are most strong,
Would here have killed your king, I do forgive thee,
Unnatural though thou art.—Their understanding   80
Begins to swell, and the approaching tide
Will shortly fill the reasonable shore[49]
That now lies foul and muddy. Not one of them
That yet looks on me, or would know me.—Ariel,
Fetch me the hat and rapier in my cell.

[*Ariel goes to the cell and returns immediately.*]

---

32. Song.
33. I.e., which is
34. imagination
35. I.e., extremely agitated.
36. Sympathetic.
37. Appearance.
38. Let fall
39. Fumes that render them incapable of comprehension.
40. Envelop.

41. Growing clearer.
42. Requite your favors and virtues.
43. Fully.
44. Accomplice.
45. Punished, afflicted.
46. Pity.
47. Natural feeling.
48. I.e., who.
49. Shores of reason, i.e., minds. (Their reason returns, like the incoming tide.)

I will discase[50] me and myself present   85
As I was sometime Milan.[51] Quickly, spirit!
Thou shalt ere long be free.

[Ariel sings and helps to attire him.]

ARIEL:
    Where the bee sucks, there suck I.
    In a cowslip's bell I lie;
    There I couch[52] when owls do cry.   90
    On the bat's back I do fly
    After[53] summer merrily.
  Merrily, merrily shall I live now
  Under the blossom that hangs on the bough.

PROSPERO:
  Why, that's my dainty Ariel! I shall miss thee,   95
  But yet thou shalt have freedom. So, so, so.[54]
  To the King's ship, invisible as thou art!
  There shalt thou find the mariners asleep
  Under the hatches. The Master and the Boatswain
  Being awake, enforce them to this place,   100
  And presently,[55] I prithee.

ARIEL:
  I drink the air before me and return
  Or ere[56] your pulse twice beat.   *[Exit.]*

GONZALO:
  All torment, trouble, wonder, and amazement
  Inhabits here. Some heavenly power guide us   105
  Out of this fearful[57] country!

PROSPERO: Behold, sir King,
  The wronged Duke of Milan, Prospero.
  For more assurance that a living prince
  Does now speak to thee, I embrace thy body;
  And to thee and thy company I bid   110
  A hearty welcome.   *[Embracing him.]*

ALONSO: Whe'er thou be'st he or no,
  Or some enchanted trifle[58] to abuse[59] me,
  As late[60] I have been, I not know. Thy pulse

---

50. Disrobe.
51. In my former appearance as Duke of Mi-
    lan.
52. Lie.
53. I.e., pursuing.
54. (Expresses approval of Ariel's help as
    valet.)

55. Immediately.
56. Before.
57. Frightening.
58. Trick of magic.
59. Deceive.
60. Lately.

Beats as of flesh and blood; and, since I saw thee,
Th' affliction of my mind amends, with which   115
I fear a madness held me. This must crave[61]—
An if this be at all[62]—a most strange story.[63]
Thy dukedom I resign,[64] and do entreat
Thou pardon me my wrongs.[65] But how should Prospero
Be living, and be here?
PROSPERO [to Gonzalo]: First, noble friend,
Let me embrace thine age,[66] whose honor cannot
Be measured or continued.   [Embracing him.]
GONZALO: Whether this be
Or be not, I'll not swear.
PROSPERO: You do yet taste
Some subtleties[67] o' th' isle, that will not let you
Believe things certain. Welcome, my friends all!   125
[Aside to Sebastian and Antonio.] But you, my brace[68] of lords, were I so
    minded,
I here could pluck His Highness' frown upon you
And justify you[69] traitors. At this time
I will tell no tales.
SEBASTIAN: The devil speaks in him.
PROSPERO: No.
[To Antonio.] For you, most wicked sir, whom to call brother   130
Would even infect my mouth, I do forgive
Thy rankest fault—all of them; and require
My dukedom of thee, which perforce[70] I know
Thou must restore.
ALONSO: If thou be'st Prospero,
Give us particulars of thy preservation,   135
How thou hast met us here, whom[71] three hours since
Were wrecked upon this shore; where I have lost—
How sharp the point of this remembrance is!—
My dear son Ferdinand.
PROSPERO: I am woe[72] for 't, sir.
ALONSO:
Irreparable is the loss, and Patience   140
Says it is past her cure.

---

61. Require.
62. If this is actually happening.
63. I.e., explanation.
64. (Alonso made arrangement with Antonio
    at the time of Prospero's banishment for
    Milan to pay tribute to Naples; see
    1.2.113–127.)
65. Wrongdoings.

66. Your venerable self.
67. Illusions, magical powers (playing on the
    idea of "pastries, concoctions").
68. Pair.
69. Prove you to be
70. Necessarily.
71. I.e., who.
72. Sorry.

PROSPERO: I rather think
    You have not sought her help, of whose soft grace[73]
    For the like loss I have her sovereign[74] aid
    And rest myself content.

ALONSO: You the like loss?

PROSPERO:
    As great to me as late,[75] and supportable   145
    To make the dear loss, have I[76] means much weaker
    Than you may call to comfort you; for I
    Have lost my daughter.

ALONSO: A daughter?
    O heavens, that they were living both in Naples,   150
    The king and queen there! That[77] they were, I wish
    Myself were mudded[78] in that oozy bed
    Where my son lies. When did you lose your daughter?

PROSPERO:
    In this last tempest. I perceive these lords
    At this encounter do so much admire[79]   155
    That they devour their reason[80] and scarce think
    Their eyes do offices of truth, their words
    Are natural breath.[81] But, howsoever you have
    Been jostled from your senses, know for certain
    That I am Prospero and that very duke   160
    Which was thrust forth of[82] Milan, who most strangely
    Upon this shore, where you were wrecked, was landed
    To be the lord on 't. No more yet of this,
    For 'tis a chronicle of day by day.[83]
    Not a relation for a breakfast nor   165
    Befitting this first meeting. Welcome, sir.
    This cell's my court. Here have I few attendants,
    And subjects none abroad.[84] Pray you, look in.
    My dukedom since you have given me again,
    I will requite[85] you with as good a thing,   170
    At least bring forth a wonder to content ye
    As much as me my dukedom.

[Here Prospero discovers[86] Ferdinand and Miranda, playing at chess.]

---

73. By whose mercy
74. Efficacious.
75. Recent.
76. To make the deeply felt loss bearable, I have.
77. So that.
78. Buried in the mud.
79. Wonder
80. I.e., are openmouthed, dumbfounded.

81. Scarcely believe that their eyes inform them accurately as to what they see or that their words are naturally spoken.
82. From.
83. Requiring days to tell.
84. Away from here, anywhere else.
85. Repay.
86. I.e., by opening a curtain, presumably rearstage.

MIRANDA: Sweet lord, you play me false.[87]

FERDINAND: No, my dearest love,
I would not for the world.   175

MIRANDA:
Yes, for a score of kingdoms you should wrangle,
And I would call it fair play.[88]

ALONSO: If this prove
A vision[89] of the island, one dear son
Shall I twice lose.

SEBASTIAN: A most high miracle!

FERDINAND [approaching his father]:
Though the seas threaten, they are merciful;   180
I have cursed them without cause.   [He kneels.]

ALONSO: Now all the blessings
Of a glad father compass[90] thee about!
Arise, and say how thou cam'st here.

[Ferdinand rises.]

MIRANDA: O, wonder!
How many goodly creatures are there here!
How beauteous mankind is! O brave[91] new world   185
That has such people in 't!

PROSPERO: 'Tis new to thee.

ALONSO:
What is this maid with whom thou wast at play?
Your eld'st[92] acquaintance cannot be three hours.
Is she goddess that hath severed us,
And brought us thus together?   190

FERDINAND: Sir, she is mortal;
But by immortal Providence she's mine.
I chose her when I could not ask my father
For his advice, nor thought I had one. She
Is daughter to this famous Duke of Milan,
Of whom so often I have heard renown,   195
But never saw before; of whom I have
Received a second life; and second father
This lady makes him to me.

---

87. I.e., press your advantage
88. I.e., yes, even if we were playing for twenty kingdoms, something less than the whole world, you would still press your advantage against me, and I would lovingly let you do it as though it were fair play, or, if you were to play not just for stakes but literally for kingdoms, my com-plaint would be out of order in that your "wrangling" would be proper

89. Illusion.
90. Encompass, embrace.
91. Splendid, gorgeously appareled, handsome.
92. Longest.

ALONSO: I am hers.

But O, how oddly will it sound that I

Must ask my child forgiveness! 200

PROSPERO: There, sir, stop.

Let us not burden our remembrances with

A heaviness[93] that's gone.

GONZALO: I have inly[94] wept,

Or should have spoke ere this. Look down, you gods,

And on this couple drop a blessed crown!

For it is you that have chalked forth the way[95] 205

Which brought us hither.

ALONSO: I say amen, Gonzalo!

GONZALO:

Was Milan thrust from Milan,[96] that his issue

Should become kings of Naples? O, rejoice

Beyond a common joy, and set it down

With gold on lasting pillars: In one voyage 210

Did Claribel her husband find at Tunis,

And Ferdinand, her brother, found a wife

Where he himself was lost; Prospero his dukedom

In a poor isle; and all of us ourselves

When no man was his own.[97] 215

ALONSO: *[to Ferdinand and Miranda]*: Give me your hands.

Let grief and sorrow still[98] embrace his[99] heart

That[100] doth not wish you joy!

GONZALO: Be it so! Amen!

[Enter Ariel, with the Master and Boatswain amazedly following.]

O, look, sir, look, sir! Here is more of us.

I prophesied, if a gallows were on land,

This fellow could not drown.—Now, blasphemy,[101] 220

That swear'st grace o'erboard,[102] not an oath[103] on shore?

Hast thou no mouth by land? What is the news?

BOATSWAIN:

The best news is that we have safely found

Our King and company; the next, our ship—

Which, but three glasses[104] since, we gave out[105] split— 225

---

93. Sadness.
94. Inwardly.
95. Marked as with a piece of chalk the pathway.
96. Was the Duke of Milan.
97. All of us have found ourselves and our sanity when we all had lost our senses.
98. Always.

99. That person's.
100. Who.
101. I.e., blasphemer.
102. I.e., you who banish heavenly grace from the ship by your blasphemies.
103. Aren't you going to swear an oath
104. I.e., hours.
105. Reported, professed to be.

Is tight and yare[106] and bravely[107] rigged as when
We first put out to sea.

ARIEL: *[aside to Prospero]:* Sir, all this service
Have I done since I went.

PROSPERO: *[aside to Ariel]:*   My tricksy[108] spirit!

ALONSO:
These are not natural events; they strengthen[109]
From strange to stranger. Say, how came you hither?   230

BOATSWAIN:
If I did think, sir, I were well awake,
I'd strive to tell you. We were dead of sleep,[110]
And—how we know not—all clapped under hatches,
Where but even now, with strange and several[111] noises
Of roaring, shrieking, howling, jingling chains,   235
And more diversity of sounds, all horrible,
We were awaked; straightway at liberty;
Where we, in all her trim, freshly beheld
Our royal, good, and gallant ship, our Master
Cap'ring to eye her.[112] On a trice,[113] so please you,   240
Even in a dream, were we divided from them[114]
And were brought moping[115] hither.

ARIEL: *[aside to Prospero]:*   Was 't well done?

PROSPERO: *[aside to Ariel]:*
Bravely, my diligence. Thou shalt be free.

ALONSO:
This is as strange a maze as e'er men trod,
And there is in this business more than nature   245
Was ever conduct[116] of. Some oracle
Must rectify our knowledge.

PROSPERO: Sir, my liege,
Do not infest[117] your mind with beating on[118]
The strangeness of this business. At picked[119] leisure,
Which shall be shortly, single[120] I'll resolve[121] you,   250
Which to you shall seem probable,[122] of every
These[123] happened accidents;[124] till when, be cheerful
And think of each thing well.[125] *[Aside to Ariel.]* Come hither, spirit.

---

106. Ready.
107. Splendidly.
108. Ingenious, sportive.
109. Increase.
110. Deep in sleep.
111. Diverse.
112. Dancing for joy to see.
113. In an instant.
114. I.e., the other crew members.
115. In a daze.

116. Guide
117. Harass, disturb.
118. Worrying about.
119. Chosen, convenient.
120. Privately, by my own human powers.
121. Satisfy, explain to.
122. Plausible.
123. About every one of these.
124. Occurrences.
125. Favorably.

Set Caliban and his companions free.
Untie the spell. *[Exit Ariel.]* How fares my gracious sir?   255
There are yet missing of your company
Some few odd[126] lads that you remember not.

[Enter Ariel, driving in Caliban, Stephano, and Trinculo, in their stolen apparel]

STEPHANO: Every man shift[127] for all the rest,[128] and let no man take care for
himself; for all is but fortune. Coragio,[129] bully monster,[130] coragio!   260

TRINCULO: If these be true spies[131] which I wear in my head, here's a goodly sight.

CALIBAN:
O Setebos, these be brave[132] spirits indeed!
How fine[133] my master is! I am afraid
He will chastise me.   265

SEBASTIAN: Ha, ha!
What things are these, my lord Antonio?
Will money buy 'em?

ANTONIO: Very like. One of them
Is a plain fish, and no doubt marketable.

PROSPERO:
Mark but the badges[134] of these men, my lords,   270
Then say if they be true.[135] This misshapen knave,
His mother was a witch, and one so strong
That could control the moon, make flows and ebbs,
And deal in her command without her power.[136]
These three have robbed me, and this demidevil—   275
For he's a bastard[137] one—had plotted with them
To take my life. Two of these fellows you
Must know and own.[138] This thing of darkness I
Acknowledge mine.

CALIBAN: I shall be pinched to death.

ALONSO:
Is not this Stephano, my drunken butler?   280

SEBASTIAN: He is drunk now. Where had he wine?

---

126. Unaccounted for.
127. Provide.
128. (Stephano drunkenly gets wrong the saying "Every man for himself.")
129. Courage.
130. Gallant monster. (Ironical.)
131. Accurate observers (i.e., sharp eyes)
132. Handsome.
133. Splendidly attired
134. Emblems of cloth or silver worn by re-

tainers to indicate whom they serve. (Prospero refers here to the stolen clothes as emblems of their villainy.)
135. Honest.
136. Wield the moon's power, either without her authority or beyond her influence, or, even though to do so was beyond Sycorax's own power
137. Counterfeit.
138. Recognize, admit as belonging to you.

ALONSO:
>And Trinculo is reeling ripe.[139] Where should they
>Find this grand liquor that hath gilded[140] 'em?
>*[To Trinculo.]* How cam'st thou in this pickle?[141]

TRINCULO: I have been in such a pickle since I saw you last that, I fear me, will   285
>never out of my bones. I shall not fear flyblowing.[142]

SEBASTIAN: Why, how now, Stephano?

STEPHANO: O, touch me not! I am not Stephano, but a cramp.

PROSPERO: You'd be king o' the isle, sirrah?[143]   290

STEPHANO: I should have been a sore[144] one, then.

ALONSO: *[pointing to Caliban]:*
>This is a strange thing as e'er I looked on.

PROSPERO:
>He is as disproportioned in his manners
>As in his shape.—Go, sirrah, to my cell.
>Take with you your companions. As you look   295
>To have my pardon, trim[145] it handsomely.

CALIBAN:
>Ay, that I will; and I'll be wise hereafter
>And seek for grace.[146] What a thrice-double ass
>Was I to take this drunkard for a god
>And worship this dull fool!   300

PROSPERO: Go to. Away!

ALONSO:
>Hence, and bestow your luggage where you found it.

SEBASTIAN: Or stole it, rather.

>*[Exeunt Caliban, Stephano, and Trinculo.]*

PROSPERO:
>Sir, I invite Your Highness and your train
>To my poor cell, where you shall take your rest
>For this one night; which, part of it, I'll waste[147]   305
>With such discourse as, I not doubt, shall make it
>Go quick away: the story of my life,
>And the particular accidents[148] gone by
>Since I came to this isle. And in the morn

---

139. Stumblingly drunk.
140. (1) Flushed, made drunk; (2) covered with gilt (suggesting the horse urine)
141. (1) Fix, predicament (2) pickling brine (in this case, horse urine).
142. I.e., being fouled by fly eggs (from which he is saved by being pickled).
143. (Standard form of address to an inferior, here expressing reprimand.)

144. (1) Tyrannical; (2) sorry, inept; (3) wracked by pain.
145. Prepare, decorate.
146. Pardon, favor.
147. Spend.
148. Occurrences.

I'll bring you to your ship, and so to Naples, 310
Where I have hope to see the nuptial
Of these our dear-beloved solemnized;
And thence retire me[149] to my Milan, where
Every third thought shall be my grave.

ALONSO: I long
To hear the story of your life, which must 315
Take[150] the ear strangely.

PROSPERO: I'll deliver[151] all;
And promise you calm seas, auspicious gales,
And sail so expeditious that shall catch
Your royal fleet far off.[152] *[Aside to Ariel.]* My Ariel, chick,
That is thy charge. Then to the elements 320
Be free, and fare thou well!—Please you, draw near.[153]

[Exeunt omnes (except Prospero).]

Epilogue

[Spoken by PROSPERO.]

Now my charms are all o'erthrown,
And what strength I have 's mine own,
Which is most faint. Now, 'tis true,
I must be here confined by you
Or set to Naples. Let me not, 5
Since I have my dukedom got
And pardoned the deceiver, dwell
In this bare island by your spell,
But release me from my bands[1]
With the help of your good hands.[2] 10
Gentle breath[3] of yours my sails
Must fill, or else my project fails,
Which was to please. Now I want[4]
Spirits to enforce,[5] art to enchant,
And my ending is despair, 15
Unless I be relieved by prayer,[6]

---

149. Return.
150. Take effect upon, enchant.
151. Declare, relate.
152. Enable you to catch up with the main part of your royal fleet, now afar off enroute to Naples (see 1.2.235–236)
153. I.e., enter my cell.

Epilogue

1. Bonds.
2. I.e., applause (the noise of which would break the spell of silence).
3. Favorable breeze (produced by hands clapping or favorable comment).
4. Lack.
5. Control.
6. I.e., Prospero's petition to the audience.

Which pierces so that it assaults[7]
Mercy itself, and frees[8] all faults.
As you from crimes[9] would pardoned be,
Let your indulgence[10] set me free.   *[Exit.]*   20

JOHN DONNE (1572–1631)
England

John Donne was born in London in 1572 to a good family; he was reared as a
Roman Catholic, attended Oxford, Cambridge, and Lincoln's Inn, where he was
well educated in theology and law. Overcoming his own religious scruples, he
was ordained an Anglican priest in 1615. He became dean of Saint Paul's
Cathedral in London in 1621, and was famous for the sermons he preached
there. Throughout his lifetime, Donne composed poetry, concerned with both
love (in the various senses of the word including the erotic) and religion, which
was only published after his death in 1631. The main figure of the group known
as the metaphysical poets, Donne is now recognized as the greatest lyric poet in
English of his time.

Holy Sonnet [Death be not proud]

Death be not proud, though some have called thee
Mighty and dreadfull, for, thou are not soe,
For, those, whom thou think'st, thou dost overthrow,
Die not, poore death, nor yet canst thou kill mee;
From rest and sleepe, which but thy pictures bee,   5
Much pleasure, then from thee, much more must flow,
And soonest our best men with thee doe goe,
Rest of their bones, and soules deliverie.
Thou'art slave to Fate, chance, kings, and desperate men,
And dost with poyson, warre, and sickness dwell,   10
And poppie, 'or charmes can make us sleepe as well,
And better then thy stroke; why swell'st thou then?
One short sleepe past, wee wake eternally,
And death shall be no more, Death thou shalt die.

---

7. Rightfully gains the attention of.
8. Obtains forgiveness for.
9. Sins.

10. (1) humoring, lenient approval; (2) remission of punishment for sin.

Holy Sonnet [Batter my heart, three person'd God]

Batter my heart, three person'd God; for, you
As yet but knocke, breathe, shine, and seeke to mend;
That I may rise, and stand, o'erthrow mee, 'and bend
Your force, to breake, blowe, burn and make me new.
I, like an usurpt towne, to'another due,   5
Labour to'admit you, but Oh, to no end,
Reason your viceroy in mee, mee should defend,
But is captiv'd, and proves weake or untrue,
Yet dearely'I love you, and would be lov'd faine,
But am betroth'd unto your enemie,   10
Divorce mee,'untie, or breake that knot againe,
Take mee to you, imprison mee, for I
Except you'enthrall mee, never shall be free,
Nor ever chast, except you ravish mee.

Goodfriday, 1613. Riding Westward.

Let man's Soule be a Spheare, and then, in this,
The'intelligence that moves, devotion is,
And as the other Spheares, by being growne
Subject to forraigne motions, lose their owne,
And being by others hurried every day,   5
Scarce in a yeare their naturall forme obey:
Pleasure or businesse, so, our Soules admit
For their first mover, and are whirld by it.
Hence is't, that I am carryed towards the West
This day, when my Soules forme bends toward the East.   10
There I should see a Sunne, by rising set,
And by that setting endlesse day beget;
But that Christ on this Crosse, did rise and fall,
Sinne had eternally benighted all.
Yet dare I'almost be glad, I do not see   15
That spectacle of too much weight for mee.
Who sees Gods face, that is selfe life, must dye;
What a death were it then to see God dye?
It made his owne Lieutenant Nature shrinke,
It made his footstoole crack, and the Sunne winke.   20
Could I behold those hands which span the Poles,
And turne all spheares at once peirc'd with those holes?
Could I behold that endlesse height which is
Zenith to us, and to'our Antipodes,
Humbled below us? or that blood which is   25
The seat of all our Soules, if not of his,
Make durt of dust, or that flesh which was worne

By God, for his apparell, rag'd, and torne?
If on these things I durst not looke, durst I
Upon his miserable mother cast mine eye,   30
Who was Gods partner here, and furnish'd thus
Halfe of that Sacrifice, which ransom'd us?
Though these things, as I ride, be from mine eye,
They'are present yet unto my memory,
For that looks towards them; and thou look'st towards mee,   35
O Saviour, as thou hang'st upon the tree;
I turne my backe to thee, but to receive
Corrections, till thy mercies bid thee leave.
O thinke mee worth thine anger, punish mee,
Burne off my rusts, and my deformity,   40
Restore thine Image, so much, by thy grace,
That thou may'st know mee, and I'll turne my face.

The Anniversary

   All kings, and all their favorites,
    All glory' of honors, beauties, wits,
The sun itself, which makes times, as they pass,
Is elder by a year, now, than it was
When thou and I first one another saw;   5
All other things to their destruction draw,
   Only our love hath no decay;
This, no tomorrow hath, nor yesterday;
Running it never runs from us away,
But truly keeps his first, last, everlasting day,   10

   Two graves must hide thine and my corse;
If one might, death were no divorce:
Alas, as well as other princes, we
(Who prince enough in one another be)
Must leave at last in death, these eyes, and ears,   15
Oft fed with true oaths, and with sweet salt tears;
   But souls where nothing dwells but love
(All other thoughts being inmates) then shall prove
This, or a love increaséd there above,
When bodies to their graves, souls from their graves remove.   20

   And then we shall be throughly blest,
    But we no more than all the rest;
Here upon earth, we're kings, and none but we
Can be such kings, nor of such subjects be;

Who is so safe as we, where none can do 25
Treason to us, except one of us two?
  True and false fears let us refrain,
Let us love nobly, 'and live, and add again
Years and years unto years, till we attain
To write threescore, this is the second of our reign. 30

JOHN MILTON (1608–1674)
England

John Milton was born in London in 1608 and was educated at St. Paul's School
and Cambridge University, afterward making a long trip to Italy, on a two-year
European tour, to perfect his learning. He devoted himself to the Puritan cause
and primary school,—then becoming Latin secretary to Cromwell. By 1652, at
the age of 44, he had lost his eyesight from too much intense work; hampered
by political disappointments in later life, he consecreted himself exclusively to
his poetry until his death in 1674. His greatest work is *Paradise Lost,* first
published in 1667. It is an epic poem dealing with God's creation of the universe,
Satan's revolt against God, and especially the fall of Adam and Eve through their
original sin, which has tainted all humankind. The poem, controversial from
Milton's own time on, is regarded as one of the great monuments of English
literature.

from *Paradise Lost*

From Book 1 [*Of Man's First Disobedience*]

Of Man's First Disobedience, and the Fruit
Of that Forbidden Tree, whose mortal taste
Brought Death into the World, and all our woe,
With loss of *Eden,* till one greater Man
Restore us, and regain the blissful Seat, 5
Sing Heav'nly Muse, that on the secret top
Of *Oreb,* or of *Sinai,* didst inspire
That Shepherd, who first taught the chosen Seed,
In the Beginning how the Heav'ns and Earth
Rose out of *Chaos:* Or if *Sion* Hill 10
Delight thee more, and *Siloa's* Brook that flow'd
Fast by the Oracle of God; I thence

Invoke thy aid to my advent'rous Song,
That with no middle flight intends to soar
Above th' *Aonian* Mount,[1] while it pursues   15
Things unattempted yet in Prose or Rhyme.
And chiefly Thou O Spirit, that dost prefer
Before all Temples th' upright heart and pure,
Instruct me, for Thou know'st; Thou from the first
Wast present, and with mighty wings outspread   20
Dove-like satst brooding on the vast Abyss
And mad'st it pregnant: What in me is dark
Illumine, what is low raise and support;
That to the highth of this great Argument
I may assert Eternal Providence,   25
And justify the ways of God to men.
    Say first, the Heav'n hides nothing from thy view
Nor the deep Tract of Hell, say first what cause
Mov'd our Grand Parents in that happy State,
Favor'd of Heav'n so highly, to fall off   30
From thir Creator, and transgress his Will
For one restraint, Lords of the World besides?
Who first seduc'd them to that foul revolt?
Th' infernal Serpent;[2] hee it was, whose guile
Stirr'd up with Envy and Revenge, deceiv'd   35
The Mother of Mankind; what time his Pride
Had cast him out from Heav'n, with all his Host
Of Rebel Angels, by whose aid aspiring
To set himself in Glory above his Peers,
He trusted to have equall'd the most High,   40
If he oppos'd; and with ambitious aim
Against the Throne and Monarchy of God
Rais'd impious War in Heav'n and Battle proud
With vain attempt. Him the Almighty Power
Hurl'd headlong flaming from th' Ethereal Sky   45
With hideous ruin and combustion down
To bottomless perdition, there to dwell
In Adamantine Chains and penal Fire,
Who durst defy th' Omnipotent to Arms.
Nine times the Space that measures Day and Night   50
To mortal men, hee with his horrid crew
Lay vanquisht, rolling in the fiery Gulf
Confounded though immortal: But his doom
Reserv'd him to more wrath; for now the thought

---

1. Mount Helicon, sacred to the Muses, the
   goddesses of classical poetic inspiration.

2. Satan, the archangel whose revolt against
   God has just been defeated.

Both of lost happiness and lasting pain 55
Torments him, round he throws his baleful eyes
That witness'd huge affliction and dismay
Mixt with obdúrate pride and steadfast hate:
At once as far as Angels' ken he views
The dismal Situation waste and wild, 60
A Dungeon horrible, on all sides round
As one great Furnace flam'd, yet from those flames
No light, but rather darkness visible
Serv'd only to discover sights of woe,
Regions of sorrow, doleful shades, where peace 65
And rest can never dwell, hope never comes
That comes to all; but torture without end
Still urges, and a fiery Deluge, fed
With ever-burning Sulphur unconsum'd:
Such place Eternal Justice had prepar'd 70
For those rebellious, here thir Prison ordained
In utter darkness, and thir portion set
As far remov'd from God and light of Heav'n
As from the Center thrice to th' utmost Pole.
O how unlike the place from whence they fell! 75
There the companions of his fall, o'erwhelm'd
With Floods and Whirlwinds of tempestuous fire,
He soon discerns, and welt'ring by his side
One next himself in power, and next in crime,
Long after known in *Palestine,* and nam'd 80
Beëlzebub. To whom th' Arch-Enemy,
And thence in Heav'n call'd Satan, with bold words
Breaking the horrid silence thus began.
    If thou beest hee; But O how fall'n! how chang'd
From him, who in the happy Realms of Light 85
Cloth'd with transcendent brightness didst outshine
Myriads though bright: If he whom mutual league,
United thoughts and counsels, equal hope,
And hazard in the Glorious Enterprise,
Join'd with me once, now misery hath join'd 90
In equal ruin: into what Pit thou seest
From what highth fall'n, so much the stronger prov'd
He with his Thunder: and till then who knew
The force of those dire Arms? yet not for those,
Nor what the Potent Victor in his rage 95
Can else inflict, do I repent or change,
Though chang'd in outward luster; that fixt mind
And high disdain, from sense of injur'd merit,
That with the mightiest rais'd me to contend,

And to the fierce contention brought along   100
Innumerable force of Spirits arm'd
That durst dislike his reign, and mee preferring,
His utmost power with adverse power oppos'd
In dubious Battle on the Plains of Heav'n.
And shook his throne. What though the field be lost?   105
All is not lost; the unconquerable Will,
And study of revenge, immortal hate,
And courage never to submit or yield:
And what is else not to be overcome?
That Glory never shall his wrath or might   110
Extort from me. To bow and sue for grace
With suppliant knee, and deify his power
Who from the terror of this Arm so late
Doubted his Empire, that were low indeed,
That were an ignominy and shame beneath   115
This downfall; since by Fate the strength of Gods
And this Empyreal substance cannot fail,
Since through experience of this great event
In Arms not worse, in foresight much advanc't,
We may with more successful hope resolve   120
To wage by force or guile eternal War
Irreconcilable to our grand Foe,
Who now triúmphs, and in th' excess of joy
Sole reigning holds thy Tyranny of Heav'n.

From Book 4 [Two of far nobler shape erect and tall]

Two of far nobler shape erect and tall,
Godlike erect, with native Honor clad
In naked Majesty seem'd Lords of all,
And worthy seem'd, for in thir looks Divine
The image of thir glorious Maker shone,   5
Truth, Wisdom, Sanctitude severe and pure,
Severe, but in true filial freedom plac't;
Whence true authority in men; though both
Not equal, as thir sex not equal seem'd;
For contemplation hee and valor form'd,   10
For softness shee and sweet attractive Grace,
Hee for God only, shee for God in him:
His fair large Front and Eye sublime declar'd
Absolute rule; and Hyacinthine Locks
Round from his parted forelock manly hung   15
Clust'ring, but not beneath his shoulders broad:

Shee as a veil down to the slender waist
Her unadorned golden tresses wore
Dishevell'd, but in wanton ringlets wav'd
As the Vine curls her tendrils, which impli'd   20
Subjection, but requir'd with gentle sway,
And by her yielded, by him best receiv'd,
Yielded with coy submission, modest pride,
And sweet reluctant amorous delay.
Nor those mysterious parts were then conceal'd,   25
Then was not guilty shame: dishonest shame
Of Nature's works, honor dishonorable,
Sin-bred, how have ye troubl'd all mankind
With shows instead, mere shows of seeming pure,
And banisht from man's life his happiest life,   30
Simplicity and spotless innocence.
So pass'd they naked on, nor shunn'd the sight
Of God or Angel, for they thought no ill:
So hand in hand they pass'd, the loveliest pair
That ever since in love's imbraces met,   35
Adam the goodliest man of men since born
His Sons, the fairest of her Daughters *Eve.*
Under a tuft of shade that on a green
Stood whispering soft, by a fresh Fountain side
They sat them down, and after no more toil   40
To thir sweet Gard'ning labor than suffic'd
To recommend cool *Zephyr,* and made ease
More easy, wholesome thirst and appetite
More grateful, to thir Supper Fruits they fell,
Nectarine Fruits which the compliant boughs   45
Yielded them, side-long as they sat recline
On the soft downy Bank damaskt with flow'rs:
The savory pulp they chew, and in the rind
Still as they thirsted scoop the brimming stream;
Nor gentle purpose, nor endearing smiles   50
Wanted, nor youthful dalliance as beseems
Fair couple, linkt in happy nuptial League,
Alone as they. About them frisking play'd
All Beasts of th' Earth, since wild, and of all chase
In Wood or Wilderness, Forest or Den;   55
Sporting the Lion ramp'd, and in his paw
Dandl'd the Kid; Bears, Tigers, Ounces, Pards
Gamboll'd before them, th' unwieldy Elephant
To make them mirth us'd all his might, and wreath'd
His Lithe Proboscis; close the Serpent sly   60
Insinuating, wove with Gordian twine

His braided train, and of his fatal guile
Gave proof unheeded; others on the grass
Couch, and now fill'd with pasture gazing sat,
Or Bedward ruminating; for the Sun   65
Declin'd was hasting now with prone career
To th' Ocean Isles, and in th' ascending Scale
Of Heav'n the Stars that usher Evening rose:
When *Satan* still in *gaze,* as first he stood,
Scarce thus at length fail'd speech recover'd sad.   70
    O Hell! what do mine eyes with grief behold,
Into our room of bliss thus high advanc't
Creatures of other mould, earth-born perhaps,
Not Spirits, yet to heav'nly Spirits bright
Little inferior; whom my thoughts pursue   75
With wonder, and could love, so lively shines
In them Divine resemblance, and such grace
The hand that form'd them on thir shape hath pour'd.
Ah gentle pair, yee little think how nigh
Your change approaches, when all these delights   80
Will vanish and deliver ye to woe,
More woe, the more your taste is now of joy;
Happy, but for so happy ill secur'd
Long to continue, and this high seat your Heav'n
Ill fenc't for Heav'n to keep out such a foe   85
As now is enter'd; yet no purpos'd foe
To you whom I could pity thus forlorn
Though I unpitied: League with you I seek,
And mutual amity so strait, so close,
That I with you must dwell, or you with me   90
Henceforth; my dwelling haply may not please
Like this fair Paradise, your sense, yet such
Accept your Maker's work; he gave it me,
Which I as freely give; Hell shall unfold,
To entertain you two, her widest Gates,   95
And send forth all her Kings; there will be room,
Not like these narrow limits, to receive
Your numerous offspring; if no better place,
Thank him who puts me loath to this revenge
On you who wrong me not for him who wrong'd.   100
And should I at your harmless innocence
Melt, as I do, yet public reason just,
Honor and Empire with revenge enlarg'd,
By conquering this new World, compels me now
To do what else though damn'd I should abhor.   105

From Book 9 [Confounded long they sat, as struck'n mute]

Confounded long they sat, as struck'n mute,[3]
Till *Adam,* though not less than *Eve* abasht,
At length gave utterance to these words constrain'd.
   O *Eve,* in evil hour thou didst give ear
To that false Worm, of whomsoever taught   5
To counterfeit Man's voice, true in our Fall,
False in our promis'd Rising; since our Eyes
Op'n'd we find indeed, and find we know
Both Good and Evil, Good lost, and Evil got,
Bad Fruit of Knowledge, if this be to know,   10
Which leaves us naked thus, of Honor void,
Of Innocence, of Faith, of Purity,
Our wonted Ornaments now soil'd and stain'd,
And in our Faces evident the signs
Of foul concupiscence; whence evil store;   15
Even shame, the last of evils; of the first
Be sure then. How shall I behold the face
Henceforth of God or Angel, erst with joy
And rapture so oft beheld? those heav'nly shapes
Will dazzle now this earthly, with thir blaze   20
Insufferably bright. O might I here
In solitude live savage, in some glade
Obscur'd, where highest Woods impenetrable
To Star or Sun-light, spread thir umbrage broad,
And brown as Evening: Cover me ye Pines,   25
Ye Cedars, with innumerable boughs
Hide me, where I may never see them more.
But let us now, as in bad plight, devise
What best may for the present serve to hide
The Parts of each from other, that seem most   30
To shame obnoxious, and unseemliest seen,
Some Tree whose broad smooth Leaves together sew'd,
And girded on our loins, may cover round
Those middle parts, that this new comer, Shame,
There sit not, and reproach us as unclean.   35
   So counsell'd hee, and both together went
Into the thickest Wood, there soon they chose
The Figtree, not that kind for Fruit renown'd,

---

3. At this point Satan in the form of a serpent has persuaded Eve to eat the fruit of the Tree of Knowledge, and she has persuaded Adam to eat it as well.

But such as at this day to *Indians* known
In *Malabar* or *Decan* spreads her Arms
Branching so broad and long, that in the ground
The bended Twigs take root, and Daughters grow
About the Mother Tree, a Pillar'd shade
High overarch't, and echoing Walks between;
There oft the *Indian* Herdsman shunning heat
Shelters in cool, and tends his pasturing Herds
At Loopholes cut through thickest shade: Those Leaves
They gather'd, broad as *Amazonian* Targe,
And with what skill they had, together sew'd,
To gird thir waist, vain Covering if to hide
Thir guilt and dreaded shame; O how unlike
To that first naked Glory. Such of late
Columbus found th' *American* so girt
With feather'd Cincture, naked else and wild
Among the Trees on Isles and woody Shores.
Thus fenc't, and as they thought, thir shame in part
Cover'd, but not at rest or ease of Mind,
They sat them down to weep, nor only Tears
Rain'd at thir Eyes, but high Winds worse within
Began to rise, high Passions, Anger, Hate,
Mistrust, Suspicion, Discord, and shook sore
Thir inward State of Mind, calm Region once
And full of Peace, now toss't and turbulent:
For Understanding rul'd not, and the Will
Heard not her lore, both in subjection now
To sensual Appetite, who from beneath
Usurping over sovran Reason claim'd
Superior sway: From thus distemper'd breast,
Adam, estrang'd in look and alter'd style,
Speech intermitted thus to *Eve* renew'd.
   Would thou hadst heark'n'd to my words, and stay'd
With me, as I besought thee, when that strange
Desire of wand'ring this unhappy Morn,
I know not whence possess'd thee; we had then
Remain'd still happy, not as now, despoil'd
Of all our good, sham'd, naked, miserable.
Let none henceforth seek needless cause to approve
The Faith they owe; when earnestly they seek
Such proof, conclude, they then begin to fail.
   To whom soon mov'd with touch of blame thus *Eve.*
What words have past thy Lips, *Adam* severe,
Imput'st thou that to my default, or will

40

45

50

55

60

65

70

75

80

Of wand'ring, as thou call'st it, which who knows
But might as ill have happ'n'd thou being by,
Or to thyself perhaps: hadst thou been there,   85
Or here th' attempt, thou couldst not have discern'd
Fraud in the Serpent, speaking as he spake;
No ground of enmity between us known,
Why hee should mean me ill, or seek to harm.
Was I to have never parted from thy side?   90
As good have grown there still a lifeless Rib.
Being as I am, why didst not thou the Head
Command me absolutely not to go,
Going into such danger as thou said'st?
Too facile then thou didst not much gainsay,   95
Nay, didst permit, approve, and fair dismiss.
Hadst thou been firm and fixt in thy dissent,
Neither had I transgress'd, nor thou with mee.
    To whom then first incenst *Adam* repli'd.
Is this the Love, is this the recompense   100
Of mine to thee, ingrateful *Eve,* express't
Immutable when thou wert lost, not I,
Who might have liv'd and joy'd immortal bliss,
Yet willingly chose rather Death with thee:
And am I now upbraided, as the cause   105
Of thy transgressing? not enough severe,
It seems, in thy restraint: what could I more?
I warn'd thee, I admonish'd thee, foretold
The danger, and the lurking Enemy
That lay in wait; beyond this had been force,   110
And force upon free Will hath here no place.
But confidence then bore thee on, secure
Either to meet no danger, or to find
Matter of glorious trial; and perhaps
I also err'd in overmuch admiring   115
What seem'd in thee so perfet, that I thought
No evil durst attempt thee, but I rue
That error now, which is become my crime,
And thou th' accuser. Thus it shall befall
Him who to worth in Woman overtrusting   120
Lets her Will rule; restraint she will not brook,
And left to herself, if evil thence ensue,
Shee first his weak indulgence will accuse.
    Thus they in mutual accusation spent
The fruitless hours, but neither self-condemning,   125
And of thir vain contést appear'd no end.

From Book 12 [*To whom thus also th'Angel last repli'd*]

To whom thus also th' Angel last repli'd:[4]
This having learnt, thou hast attain'd the sum
Of wisdom; hope no higher, though all the Stars
Thou knew'st by name, and all th' ethereal Powers,
All secrets of the deep, all Nature's works,   5
Or works of God in Heav'n, Air, Earth, or Sea,
And all the riches of this World enjoy'dst,
And all the rule, one Empire; only add
Deeds to thy knowledge answerable, add Faith,
Add Virtue, Patience, Temperance, add Love,   10
By name to come call'd Charity, the soul
Of all the rest: then wilt thou not be loath
To leave this Paradise, but shalt possess
A paradise within thee, happier far.
Let us descend now therefore from this top   15
Of Speculation; for the hour precise
Exacts our parting hence; and see the Guards,
By mee encampt on yonder Hill, expect
Thir motion, at whose Front a flaming Sword,
In signal of remove, waves fiercely round;   20
We may no longer stay: go, waken *Eve;*
Her also I with gentle Dreams have calm'd
Portending good, and all her spirits compos'd
To meek submission: thou at season fit
Let her with thee partake what thou hast heard,   25
Chiefly what may concern her Faith to know,
The great deliverance by her Seed to come
(For by the Woman's Seed) on all Mankind,
That ye may live, which will be many days,
Both in one Faith unanimous though sad,   30
With cause for evils past, yet much more cheer'd
With meditation on the happy end.
   He ended, and they both descend the Hill;
Descended, *Adam* to the Bow'r where *Eve*
Lay sleeping ran before, but found her wak't;   35
And thus with words not sad she him receiv'd.
   Whence thou return'st, and whither went'st, I know;

---

4. The Archangel Michael has explained to
Adam God's plan for the redemption of
humankind.

For God is also in sleep, and Dreams advise,
Which he hath sent propitious, some great good
Presaging, since with sorrow and heart's distress   40
Wearied I fell asleep: but now lead on;
In mee is no delay; with thee to go,
Is to stay here; without thee here to stay,
Is to go hence unwilling; thou to mee
Art all things under Heav'n, all places thou,   45
Who for my wilful crime art banisht hence.
This further consolation yet secure
I carry hence; though all by mee is lost,
Such favor I unworthy am voutsaf't,
By mee the Promis'd Seed shall all restore.   50
   So spake our Mother *Eve,* and *Adam* heard
Well pleas'd, but answer'd not; for now too nigh
Th' Arch-Angel stood, and from the other Hill
To thir fixt Station, all in bright array
The Cherubim descended; on the ground   55
Gliding meteorous, as Ev'ning Mist
Ris'n from a River o'er the marish glides,
And gathers ground fast at the Laborer's heel
Homeward returning. High in Front advanc't,
The brandisht Sword of God before them blaz'd   60
Fierce as a Comet; which with torrid heat,
And vapor as the *Libyan* Air adust,[5]
Began to parch that temperate Clime; whereat
In either hand the hast'ning Angel caught
Our ling'ring Parents, and to th' Eastern Gate   65
Led them direct, and down the Cliff as fast
To the subjected Plain; then disappear'd.
They looking back, all th' Eastern side beheld
Of Paradise, so late thir happy seat,
Wav'd over by that flaming Brand, the Gate   70
With dreadful Faces throng'd and fiery Arms:
Some natural tears they dropp'd, but wip'd them soon;
The World was all before them, where to choose
Thir place of rest, and Providence thir guide:
They hand in hand with wand'ring steps and slow,   75
Through *Eden* took thir solitary way.

---

5. Burned like the air in the desert of Libya.

ANDREAS GRYPHIUS [ANDREAS GREIF] (1616–1664)
Germany

Andreas Gryphius, poet and playwright, was born and died in Glogau in Silesia, a part of Germany devastated by the Thirty Years' War. After studying in Holland, he returned to his native city to occupy a position as a municipal official. After early work in Latin, he began to publish poetry in German in 1637. In his lifetime he came to be recognized as the foremost German poet of his age and the first great master of the sonnet in the language. The violent contrasts in his poetry and its preoccupation with mortality are characteristic of the German baroque.

Human Misery*

What are we men indeed? Grim torment's habitation,
A toy of fickle luck, wisp in time's wilderness,
A scene of bitter fear and filled with keen distress,
And tapers burned to stubs, snow's quick evaporation.

This life does flee away like jest or conversation;
Those who before us laid aside the body's dress
And in the domesday-book of monster mortalness
Old entry found, have left our mind's and heart's sensation.

Just as an empty dream from notice lightly flees,
And as a stream is lost whose course no might may cease,
So must our honor, fame, our praise and name be ended.

What presently draws breath, must perish with the air,
What after us will come, someday our grave will share.
What do I say? We pass as smoke on strong winds wended.

SOR VIOLANTE DO CÉU (VIOLANTE MONTESINO) (1602?–1693)
Portugal

In 1630 Sor Violante entered the order of Our Lady of the Rosary. She was a playwright (*Saint Eufemia*) as well as a baroque poet, under the influence of the

*Translated by George C. Schoolfield.

baroque Spanish poet Góngora and given to meditating on life's passing and on divine love. She practices the conceit or *concetto* (the keystone of the movement called *conceptismo*), the idea with a twist toward which the writing leads necessarily, through turnings and deviations.

Voice of a Dissipated Woman Inside a Tomb, Talking to Another Woman Who Presumed to Enter a Church with the Purpose of Being Seen and Praised by Everyone, Who Sat Down Near a Sepulcher Containing This Epitaph, Which Curiously Reads:*

You fool yourself and live a crazy day
or year, dizzy with adventures, and bent
solely on pleasures! Know the argument
of rigid doom and find a wiser way.
Consider that here, buried in the earth,
a dazzling and commended beauty lies,
and all live things are nothing, dust, and worth
less than the nothing of your life and lies.
Consider that when rigid death is come,
it laughs at beauty and discernment, and
what seems entirely certain fades in doubt.
Learn from this tomb what you will soon become,
and live more prudently till that command
is heard: the end which ends with no way out.

CATHERINA REGINA VON GREIFFENBERG (1633–1694)
Germany

Catherina Regina von Greiffenberg was born into a noble Austrian family; because her family was Protestant, she was forced to flee from Catholic Austria and she spent the later years of her life in Nuremberg, Germany, where she died in 1694. Her collected poems, including 250 sonnets, were published in 1662. Her intensely religious poetry, based on her own inner experiences rather than on dogmatic teaching, made a deep impression on her contemporaries. Long

---

*Translated by Willis Barnstone.

neglected, she has in recent years come to be seen as one of the most forceful poets in German of her time.

On the Ineffable Inspiration of the Holy Ghost*

Lightning invisible, you dark bright light
Heart-filling strength, being yet ungrasped!
A godlike thing has come upon the spirit
That moves and rules me; I sense a spare light.

Of itself the soul is not so very light.
It is a wonder-wind, a spirit, a being weaving,
The eternal power of breath become arch-enemy,
Kindling energy in me, this heaven flaming.

You mirror-color-sight, you wonder-tinted shining!
You shimmer in and out, ungraspable, oh clear;
The spirit's dove-flights gleam in the sun of truth.

The pool moved by God is, even troubled, clear!
First the sun of spirit will set the moon
Alight; then turning, the earth will come clear too.

JEAN RACINE (1639–1699)
France

Jean Racine, the greatest French tragic playwright, was born at La Ferté-Milon in 1639. He received a strict and thorough education under religious auspices and became the most prominent playwright of his time, receiving extensive patronage from Louis XIV. *Phaedra* was first performed and published in 1677. Immediately thereafter Racine left the commercial theater and was named official historian to the king, a post he held until his death in 1699. *Phaedra* focuses on a subject drawn from ancient Greek drama: the story of Phaedra's desperate love for her stepson Hippolytus. It is widely admired as one of Racine's greatest tragedies.

Racine's Preface to Phaedra[†]

HERE is another tragedy of which I have borrowed the subject from Euripides. Although I have followed a slightly different route from that author as regards the plot, I have not failed

---

*Translated by Mary Ann Caws and Fred J. Nichols.
[†]Translated by John Cairncross.

to enrich my play with everything which seemed to me to be most striking in his. Even if I owed him only the idea of Phaedra's character, I should be justified in saying that I owe him what is probably the clearest and most closely-knit play I have written. I am not surprised that this character should have met with such a favourable reception in Euripides' day and that it should still be so successful in our time, since it possesses all the qualities required by Aristotle in a tragic hero, that is, the ability to arouse pity and terror. For Phaedra is neither entirely guilty nor altogether innocent. She is involved by her destiny, and by the anger of the gods, in an unlawful passion at which she is the very first to be horrified. She makes every effort to overcome it. She prefers to let herself die rather than declare it to anyone. And, when she is forced to disclose it, she speaks with such embarrassment that it is clear that her crime is a punishment of the gods rather than an urge flowing from her own will.

I have even been at pains to make her slightly less odious than in the tragedies of the ancients, where she resolves of her own accord to accuse Hippolytus. I felt that calumny was somewhat too low and foul to be put in the mouth of a princess whose sentiments were otherwise so noble and virtuous. This baseness seemed to me to be more appropriate to a nurse, who could well have more slave-like inclinations, and who nevertheless launches this false accusation only in order to save the life and honour of her mistress. Phaedra consents to it only because she is in such a state of excitement as to be out of her mind, and she appears a moment later in order to exculpate her innocent victim and declare the truth.

In Euripides and Seneca, Hippolytus is accused of having violated his stepmother: Vim corpus tulit. But here he is only accused of having intended to do so. I wished to spare Theseus a degree of agitation which could have detracted from the sympathy aroused by him among the spectators.

As regards the role of Hippolytus, I had noticed that the ancients reproached Euripides with having portrayed him as a sage free from any imperfection. As a result, the young prince's death caused much more indignation than pity. I felt obliged to leave him one weakness which would make him slightly guilty towards his father, without however depriving him in any way of the nobility with which he spares Phaedra's honour and allows himself to be mistreated without accusing her. I regard as a weakness the passion he feels in spite of himself for Aricia, who is the daughter and sister of his father's mortal enemies.

This character—Aricia—was not invented by me. Virgil says that Hippolytus married her, and had a son by her, after Aesculapius had brought him back to life. And I have also read in certain authors that Hippolytus married and took to Italy a young Athenian lady of high birth who was called Aricia and who gave her name to a small Italian town.

I cite these authorities, because I have been very scrupulous in trying to follow the classical account. I have even been faithful to the story of Theseus as recounted by Plutarch.

It was in this historian that I found that what gave rise to the belief that Theseus went down to the underworld to abduct Prosperpine was a journey by this prince in Epirus towards the source of the Acheron to a king whose wife Pirithous wished to carry off and who kept Theseus prisoner after having put Pirithous to death. In this way, I have endeavoured to retain the credibility of the story without losing anything of the ornaments of the legend which constitutes a rich source of poetry. And the rumor of Theseus' death, based on this legendary journey, gives rise to Phaedra's profession of love which becomes one of the main causes of her downfall, since she would never have dared to speak had she believed that her husband was alive.

For the rest, I do not as yet dare to affirm that this play is my best tragedy. I leave it to the readers and to time to decide as to its real value. What I can affirm is that in no other play of mine is virtue given greater prominence. The slightest transgressions are severely punished. The very thought of crime is regarded with as much horror as crime itself. Weaknesses caused by love are treated as real weaknesses. The passions are portrayed merely in order to show the aberrations to which they give rise; and vice is painted throughout in colours which bring out its hideousness and hatefulness. That is really the objective which everyone working for the public should have in mind. And it is what the tragedians of early times aimed at above all else. Their theatre was a school in which virtue was taught not less well than in the schools of the philosophers. Hence it was that Aristotle *did not disdain to lend a hand to the composition of Euripides' tragedies. It would be greatly to be desired that modern writings were as sound and full of useful precepts as the works of these poets. This might perhaps provide a means of reconciling to tragedy a host of people famous for their piety and their doctrine who have recently condemned it and who would no doubt pass a more favourable judgement on it if writers were as keen to edify their spectators as to amuse them, thereby complying with the real purpose of tragedy.*

Phaedra

Characters

THESEUS, *son of Aegeus, King of Athens*

HIPPOLYTUS, *son of Theseus and Antiope, Queen of the Amazons*

THERAMENES, *Hippolytus' mentor*

ISMENE, *Aricia's confidante*

PHAEDRA, *wife of Theseus, daughter of Minos and Pasiphae*

ARICIA, *princess of the blood royal of Athens*

OENONE, *Phaedra's nurse and confidante*

PANOPE, *a woman of Phaedra's retinue*

The scene is in Troezen, a town in the Peloponnese

Act I

Scene I

HIPPOLYTUS: It is resolved, Theramenes. I go.
    I will depart from Troezen's pleasant land.
    Torn by uncertainty about the King,
    I am ashamed of standing idly by.
    For over half a year I have not heard   5
    Of my dear father Theseus' destiny
    Nor even by what far sky he is concealed.

THERAMENES: And, where, my lord, would you make search for him?
    Already, to allay your rightful fears,
    I have scoured both the seas that Corinth joins;[1]   10
    I have sought news of Theseus on the shores
    Of Acheron, the river of the dead;
    Elis I searched, then sailed past Tenaros

Translated by John Cairncross.

---

1. The isthmus of Corinth links the main part of Greece with the peninsula of the Peloponnese. The two seas are the Ionian and the Aegean. The River Acheron has its source in the mountains of Epirus in northwest Greece. Theramenes' wanderings took him from there southward to Elis, a province on the western shore of the Peloponnese, then to Tenaros on its southern tip, and finally to the Aegean Sea on the east side of Greece.

On to the sea where Icarus came down.
What makes you hope that you may find his trace   15
In some more favoured region of the world?
Who knows indeed if it is his desire
To have the secret of his absence known?
And whether, as we tremble for his life,
He is not tasting all the joys of love,   20
And soon the outraged victim of his wiles. . . .

HIPPOLYTUS: No more of this, Theramenes. The King
Has seen the errors of his amorous youth.
He is above unworthy dalliance,
And, stronger than his old inconstancy,   25
Phaedra has in his heart long reigned alone.
But, to be brief, I must make search for him
Far from this city where I dare not stay.

THERAMENES: Since when do you, my lord, fear to frequent
These peaceful haunts you cherished as a boy,   30
Which I have seen you many a time prefer
To the loud pomp of Athens and the court?
What peril, or what trouble, drives you hence?

HIPPOLYTUS: Those happy days are gone, and all is changed,
Since to these shores the mighty gods have sent   35
The child of Minos and Pasiphae.[2]

THERAMENES: I understand. The cause of your distress
Is known to me. Phaedra distresses you.
Theseus' new wife had scarcely seen you than
Your exile gave the measure of her power.   40
But now her hate that never let you be
Has vanished or is greatly on the wane.
Besides what perils threaten you from her—
A woman dying or who seeks to die?
Racked by a malady she will not name,   45
Tired of herself and of the light of day,
Phaedra has not the strength to do you ill.

HIPPOLYTUS: I do not fear her vain hostility.
If I go hence, I flee, let me confess,
Another enemy . . . Aricia,   50
Last of a line that plotted Theseus' death.

THERAMENES: What! Would you stoop to persecute her too?
Though she is sprung of Pallas' cruel race,[3]

---

2. Minos was King of Crete, and later judge in Hades. Pasiphae was the daughter of the Sun. She had two daughters by Minos— Ariadne and Phaedra (the latter being the one that Hippolytus has in mind). Aphrodite, the goddess of love, inspired Pasiphae with a monstrous passion for a bull, and from this union there was born the Minotaur, half man, half bull. Theseus brought back Phaedra from Greece after killing the monster in its labyrinth.

    She never joined in her false brothers' schemes.

    Why hate her then if she is innocent?   55

HIPPOLYTUS: I would not flee her if I hated her.

THERAMENES: My lord, may I explain your sudden flight?

    Are you no more the man that once you were,

    Relentless foe of all the laws of love

    And of a yoke Theseus himself has borne?   60

    Will Venus whom you haughtily disdained

    Vindicate Theseus after all these years

    By forcing you to worship with the throng

    Of ordinary mortals at her shrine?

    Are you in love?   65

HIPPOLYTUS: My friend, what have you said?

    You who have known me since I first drew breath,

    You ask me shamefully to disavow

    The feelings of a proud disdainful heart?

    The Amazon, my mother, with her milk[4]

    Suckled me on that pride you wonder at.   70

    And I myself, on reaching man's estate,

    Approved my nature when I knew myself.

    Serving me with unfeignéd loyalty,

    You would relate my father's history.

    You know how, as I hung upon your words,   75

    My heart would glow at tales of his exploits

    When you portrayed Theseus, that demi-god,

    Consoling mortals for Alcides' loss.[5]

    Monsters suppressed and brigands brought to book—

    Procrustes, Sciron, Sinis, Cercyon;   80

    The giants' bones in Epidaurus strewn

    And Crete red with the slaughtered Minotaur.

    But, when you told me of less glorious deeds,

    His word pledged and believed in countless lands:

    Helen in Sparta ravished from her home,   85

    Salamis, scene of Periboea's tears;

    Others whose very names he has forgot,

    Too trusting spirits all deceived by him;

    Wronged Ariadne crying to the winds;[6]

---

3. Pallas was descended from Erechtheus, the original King of Athens and son of the earth god. Aegeus, Theseus's father, had obtained the throne by adoption. Aricia's brothers plotted Theseus's downfall, but were discovered and put to death.

4. Antiope (Hippolyta).

5. Hercules.

6. Minos' daughter, Phaedra's sister, who led Theseus through the labyrinth and thus enabled him to kill the Minotaur; she eloped with Theseus, and was abandoned by him on the island of Naxos.

Phaedra abducted, though for lawful ends; 90
You know how, loath to hear this sorry tale,
I often urged you quickly to conclude,
Happy could I have kept the shameful half
Of these adventures from posterity.
And am I to be vanquished in my turn? 95
And can the gods have humbled me so far?
In base defeat the more despicable
Since countless exploits plead on his behalf,
Whereas no monsters overcome by me
Have given me the right to err like him. 100
And, even if I were fated to succumb,
Should I have chosen to love Aricia?
Should not my wayward feelings have recalled
That she is barred from me eternally?
King Theseus frowns upon her and decrees 105
That she shall not prolong her brothers' line:
He fears this guilty stock will blossom forth,
And has, so that her name shall end with her,
Condemned her to be single till she dies—
No marriage torch shall ever blaze for her. 110
Should I espouse her cause and brave his wrath?
Set an example to foolhardiness?
And, on a foolish passion launched, my youth . . .
THERAMENES: Ah! when your hour has once but struck, my lord,
Heaven of our reasons takes but little heed. 115
Theseus opens your eyes despite yourself.
His hatred of Aricia has fanned
Your passion and has lent her added grace.
Besides, my lord, why fear a virtuous love?
If it is sweet, will you not dare to taste? 120
And will you always shyly flee from it?
Can you go wrong where Hercules has trod?
What hearts has Venus' power not subdued?
Where would you be yourself, who fight her now,
If, combating her love, Antiope 125
Had never been consumed for Theseus?
However, what avails this haughty tone?
Confess it, all is changed; for some days past
You are less often seen, aloof and proud,
Speeding your chariot along the shore, 130
Or, skilful in the seagod Neptune's art,
Bending an untamed courser to the curb.
The woods less often to your cries resound;
Your eyes grow heavier with secret fire.
There is no doubt, you are consumed with love. 135

You perish from a malady you hide.
Has fair Aricia enraptured you?
HIPPOLYTUS: Theramenes, I go to seek the King.
THERAMENES: And will you see Phaedra before you leave,
  My lord?   140
HIPPOLYTUS: I mean to. You may tell her so.
  See her I must, since duty so commands.
  But what new burden weighs Oenone down?

Scene 2

OENONE: Alas, my lord what cares can equal mine?
  The Queen is almost at her destined end.
  In vain I watch over her night and day.
  She's dying from a hidden malady;
  Eternal discord reigns within her mind.   5
  Her restless anguish tears her from her bed.
  She longs to see the light, and yet, distraught
  With pain, she bids me banish everyone . . .
  But here she comes.
HIPPOLYTUS: Enough. I'll take my leave   10
  And will not show her my detested face.

Scene 3

PHAEDRA: No further. Here, Oenone, let us stay.
  I faint, I fall; my strength abandons me.
  My eyes are dazzled by the daylight's glare,
  And my knees, trembling, give beneath my weight.
  Alas!   5
OENONE: May our tears move you, mighty gods!
PHAEDRA: How these vain jewels, these veils weigh on me!
  What meddling hand has sought to re-arrange
  My hair, by braiding it across my brow?
  All things contrive to grieve and thwart me, all.
OENONE: How all her wishes war among themselves! 10
  Yourself, condemning your unlawful plans,
  A moment past, bade us adorn your brow;
  Yourself, summoning up your former strength,
  Wished to come forth and see the light again.
  Scarce have you seen it than you long to hide; 15
  You hate the daylight you come forth to see.
PHAEDRA: O shining founder of an ill-starred line,
  You, whom my mother dared to boast her sire,[7]

---

7. The Sun was Pasiphae's father and hence
 Phaedra's grandfather.

Who blush perhaps to see me thus distraught,
Sungod, for the last time, I look on you.   20
OENONE: What? you will not give up this fell desire?
And will you, always saying no to life,
Make mournful preparation for your death?
PHAEDRA: Would I were seated in the forest's shade!
When can I follow through the swirling dust   25
The lordly chariot's flight along the course?
OENONE: What?
PHAEDRA: Madness! Where am I, what have I said?
Whither have my desires, my reason strayed?
Lost, lost, the gods have carried it away.
Oenone, blushes sweep across my face;   30
My grievous shame stands all too clear revealed,
And tears despite me fill my aching eyes.
OENONE: If you must blush, blush for your silence, for
It but inflames the fury of your ills.
Deaf to our wild entreaties, pitiless,   35
Will you allow yourself to perish thus?
What madness cuts you off in mid career?
What spell, what poison, has dried up the source?
Thrice have the shades of night darkened the skies
Since sleep last made its entry in your eyes,   40
And thrice the day has driven forth dim night
Since last your fainting lips took nourishment.
What dark temptation lures you to your doom?
What right have you to plot to end your life?
In this you wrong the gods from whom you spring,   45
You are unfaithful to your wedded lord;
Unfaithful also to your hapless sons,
Whom you would thrust beneath a heavy yoke.
Remember, that same day their mother dies,
Hope for the alien woman's son revives,   50
For that fierce enemy of you and yours,
That youth whose mother was an Amazon,
Hippolytus . . .
PHAEDRA: God!
OENONE: *That* reproach struck home.
PHAEDRA: Ah! wretched woman, what name crossed your lips?
OENONE: Your anger now bursts forth, and rightly so.   55
I love to see you shudder at the name.
Live then. Let love and duty spur you on.
Live. Do not give a Scythian's son a chance
To lord it with his harsh and odious rule
Over the pride of Greece and of the gods.   60
Do not delay! for every moment kills.

                Haste to replenish your enfeebled strength
                While yet the fires of life, though all but spent,
                Are burning and can still flame bright again.
PHAEDRA: I have prolonged my guilty days too far.   65
OENONE: What, are you harried by some keen remorse?
                What crime could ever bring you to this pass?
                Your hands were never stained with guiltless blood.
PHAEDRA: Thanks be to Heaven, my hands have done no wrong.
                Would God my heart were innocent as they!   70
OENONE: What fearful project then have you conceived
                Which strikes such terror deep into my heart?
PHAEDRA: I have revealed enough. Spare me the rest.
                I die, and my grim secret dies with me.
OENONE: Keep silence then, inhuman one, and die;   75
                But seek some other hand to close your eyes.
                Although the candle of your life burns low,
                I will go down before you to the dead.
                Thither a thousand different roads converge,
                My misery will choose the shortest one.   80
                When have I ever failed you, cruel one?
                Remember, you were born into my arms.
                For you I have lost country, children, all.[8]
                Is this how you reward fidelity?
PHAEDRA: What do you hope to gain by violence?   85
                If I should speak, you would be thunderstruck.
OENONE: And what, ye gods, could be more terrible
                Than seeing you expire before my eyes?
PHAEDRA: Even when you know my crime and cruel fate,
                I yet will die, and die the guiltier.   90
OENONE: By all the tears that I have shed for you,
                And by your faltering knees I hold entwined,
                Deliver me from dire uncertainty.
PHAEDRA: You wish it. Rise.
OENONE: Speak. I await your words.
PHAEDRA: What shall I say to her and where begin?   95
OENONE: Wound me no longer by such vain affrights!
PHAEDRA: O hate of Venus! Anger-laden doom!
                Into what dark abyss love hurled my mother![9]
OENONE: Ah, Queen, forget; and for all time to come
                Eternal silence seal this memory.   100
PHAEDRA: O sister Ariadne, of what love
                You died deserted on a barren shore!

---

8. The nurse had accompanied Phaedra from her native Crete to Athens.

9. An allusion to Pasiphae's monstrous passion for the bull.

OENONE: What ails you, and what mortal agony
     Drives you to fury against all your race?
PHAEDRA: Since Venus wills it, of this unblest line   105
     I perish, I, the last and wretchedest.
OENONE: You are in love?
PHAEDRA: Love's furies rage in me.
OENONE: For whom?
PHAEDRA: Prepare to hear the crowning woe.
     I love . . . I tremble, shudder at the name;
     I love . . .   110

[Oenone leans forward]

PHAEDRA: You know that prince whom I myself
     So long oppressed, son of the Amazon?
OENONE: Hippolytus?
PHAEDRA: *You* have pronounced his name.
OENONE: Merciful heavens! My blood chills in my veins.
     O grief! O crime! O lamentable race!
     Ill-fated journey and thrice ill-starred coast!   115
     Would we had never neared your dangerous shores!
PHAEDRA: My malady goes further back. I scarce
     Was bound by marriage to Aegeus' son;[10]
     My peace of mind, my happiness seemed sure.
     Athens revealed to me my haughty foe.   120
     As I beheld, I reddened, I turned pale.
     A tempest raged in my distracted mind.
     My eyes no longer saw. I could not speak.
     I felt my body freezing, burning; knew
     Venus was on me with her dreaded flames,   125
     The fatal torments of a race she loathes.
     By sleepless vows, I thought to ward her off.
     I built a temple to her, rich and fair.
     No hour went by but I made sacrifice,
     Seeking my reason in the victims' flanks.   130
     Weak remedies for love incurable!
     In vain my hand burned incense on the shrine.
     Even when my lips invoked the goddess' name,
     I worshipped *him*. His image followed me.
     Even on the altar's steps, my offerings   135
     Were only to the god I dared not name.
     I shunned him everywhere. O crowning woe!
     I found him mirrored in his father's face!
     Against myself at last I dared revolt.
     I spurred my feelings on to harass him.   140

---

10. Theseus.

To banish my adoréd enemy,
I feigned a spite against this stepson, kept
Urging his exile, and my ceaseless cries
Wrested him from a father's loving arms.
I breathed more freely since I knew him gone.   145
The days flowed by, untroubled, innocent.
Faithful to Theseus, hiding my distress,
I nursed the issue of our ill-starred bed.
Ah vain precautions! Cruel destiny!
Brought by my lord himself to Troezen's shores,   150
I saw once more the foe I had expelled.
My open wound at once poured blood again.
The fire no longer slumbers in the veins.
Venus in all her might is on her prey.
I have a fitting horror for my crime;   155
I hate this passion and I loathe my life.
Dying, I could have kept my name unstained,
And my dark passion from the light of day;
Your tears, your pleas have forced me to confess,
And I shall not regret what I have done,   160
If you, respecting the approach of death,
Will cease to vex me with reproaches, and
Your vain assistance will not try to fan
The last faint flicker still alight in me.

Scene 4

PANOPE: Would I could hide from you the grievous news,
My lady, but I cannot hold it back.
Death has abducted your unconquered lord
And this mischance is known to all but you.
OENONE: What, Panope?   5
PANOPE: The Queen in vain, alas!
Importunes heaven for Theseus' safe return,
For, from the vessels just arrived in port,
Hippolytus, his son, has learned his death.
PHAEDRA: God!
PANOPE: Athens is divided in its choice
Of master. Some favour the prince, your son,   10
Others, forgetful of the State's decrees,[11]
Dare to support the foreign woman's son.
Rumour even has it that a bold intrigue
Wishes to give Aricia the throne.
I deemed it right to warn you of this threat.   15

---

11. Which ruled out the succession of anyone
    even partly of non-Greek blood.

      Hippolytus is ready to set sail,
      And in this turmoil it is to be feared
      He may win fickle Athens to his cause.
OENONE: Panope, cease! You may be sure the Queen
      Will give due heed to this important news.   20

Scene 5

OENONE: Ah Queen, I had relinquished you to death
      And thought to follow you down to the tomb.
      I had no longer words to turn you back;
      But this news bids you steer another course.
      Now all is changed, and fortune smiles on you.   5
      The King is dead, and you must take his place.
      He leaves a son with whom your duty lies—
      A slave without you; if you live, a king.
      On whom in his misfortune can he lean?
      If you are dead, no hand will dry his tears;   10
      And his fond cries, borne upwards to the gods,
      Will bring his forbears' anger down on you.
      Live then, no longer tortured by reproach.
      Your love becomes like any other love.
      Theseus, in dying, has dissolved the bonds   15
      Which made your love a crime to be abhorred.
      You need no longer dread Hippolytus,
      And you may see him and be guiltless still.
      Perhaps, convinced of your hostility,
      He is prepared to captain the revolt.
      Quick, undeceive him; bend him to your will.
      King of these fertile shores, Troezen is his.
      But well he knows the laws assign your son   20
      The soaring ramparts that Minerva built,[12]
      Both of you have a common enemy.
      Join forces then against Aricia.
PHAEDRA: Then be it so. Your counsels have prevailed.
      I'll live, if I can be recalled to life,   25
      And if the love I bear my son can still
      In this grim hour revive my failing strength.

Act II

Scene 1

ARICIA: Hippolytus has asked to see me here?
      Hippolytus wishes to say farewell?
      Ismene, are you not mistaken?

---

12. Athens.

ISMENE: No.
    This is the first result of Theseus' death.
    Make ready to receive from every side   5
    Allegiances that Theseus filched from you.
    Aricia is mistress of her fate,
    And soon all Greece will bow the knee to her.
ARICIA: This was no rumour then, Ismene. Now
    My enemy, my tyrant is no more.   10
ISMENE: Indeed. The gods no longer frown on you,
    And Theseus wanders with your brother's shades.
ARICIA: By what adventure did he meet his end?
ISMENE: The tales told of his death are past belief.
    They say that in some amorous escapade   15
    The waters closed over his faithless head.
    The thousand tongues of rumour even assert
    That with Pirithous he went down to Hell,
    Beheld Cocytus[13] and the sombre shores.
    Showed himself living to the shades below,   20
    But that he could not, from the house of death,
    Recross the river whence is no return.
ARICIA: Can mortal man, before he breathes his last,
    Descend into the kingdom of the dead?   25
    What magic lured him to that dreaded shore?
ISMENE: You alone doubt it. Theseus is no more.
    Athens is stricken; Troezen knows the news,
    And now pays tribute to Hippolytus.
    Here in this palace, trembling for her son,   30
    Phaedra takes counsel with her anxious friends.
ARICIA: But will Hippolytus be kinder than
    His father was to me, loosen my chains,
    And pity my mishaps?
ISMENE: I think he will.
ARICIA: Do you not know severe Hippolytus?   35
    How can you hope that he will pity me,
    Honouring in me alone a sex he spurns?
    How constantly he has avoided us,
    Haunting those places which he knows we shun!
ISMENE: I know the tales of his unfeelingness;   40
    But I have seen him in your presence, and
    The legend of Hippolytus' reserve
    Doubled my curiosity in him.
    His aspect did not tally with his fame;
    At the first glance from you he grew confused.   45

---

13. The river of the underworld.

His eyes, seeking in vain to shun your gaze,
Brimming with languor, took their fill of you.
Although the name of lover wounds his pride,
He has a lover's eye, if not his tongue.

ARICIA: How avidly, Ismene, does my heart,   60
Drink in these sweet, perhaps unfounded words!
O you who know me, can it be believed
That the sad plaything of a ruthless fate,
A heart that always fed on bitterness,
Should ever know the frenzied pangs of love?   65
Last of the issue of Earth's royal son,[14]
I only have escaped the scourge of war.
I lost, all in their springtime's flowering,
Six brothers, pride of an illustrious line.
The sword swept all away and drenched the earth,   70
Which drank, unwillingly, Erechtheus' blood.
You know that, since their death, a cruel law
Forbids all Greeks to seek me as their wife,
Since it was feared my marriage might some day
Kindle my brothers' ashes into life.   75
But you recall with what disdain I viewed
These moves of a suspicious conqueror,
For, as a lifelong enemy of love,
I rendered thanks to Theseus' tyranny,
Which merely helped to keep me fancy free.   80
My eyes had not yet lighted on his son.
Not that my eyes alone yield to the charm
Of his much vaunted grace, his handsomeness,
Bestowed by nature, but which he disdains,
And seems not even to realize he owns.   85
I love and prize in him far nobler gifts—
His father's virtues, not his weaknesses.
I love, let me confess, that manly pride,
Which never yet has bowed beneath love's yoke.
Phaedra in vain gloried in Theseus' sighs.   90
I am more proud, and spurn the easy prize
Of homage to a thousand others paid
And of a heart accessible to all.
But to bring an unbending spirit down,
To cause an aching where no feeling was,   95
To stun a conqueror with his defeat,
In vain revolt against a yoke he loves,
That rouses my ambition, my desire.

---

14. Erechtheus.

Even Hercules was easier to disarm.
Vanquished more often than Hippolytus,   100
He yielded a less glorious victory.
But, dear Ismene, what rash hopes are these?
For his resistance will be all too strong.
You yet may hear me, humble in my grief,
Bewail the very pride I now admire.   105
Hippolytus in love? By what excess
Of fortune could I . . .
ISMENE: You yourself will hear.
Hither he comes.

Scene 2

HIPPOLYTUS: Princess, before I go
I deemed it right to let you know your fate.
My father is no more. My fears divined
The secret of his lengthy absence. Death,
Death only, ending his illustrious deeds,
Could hide him from the universe so long.   5
The gods at last deliver to the Fates
Alcides' friend, companion, and his heir.
I feel that, silencing your hate, even you
Hear in good part the honours due to him.
One hope alone tempers my mortal grief.   10
I can release you from a stern control,
Revoking laws whose harshness I deplore.
Yourself, your heart, do with them what you will;
And in this Troezen, now assigned to me
As my sage grandsire Pittheus' heritage,   15
Which with a single voice proclaimed me king,
I leave you free as I am; nay, more free.
ARICIA: Limit your boundless generosity.
By honouring me, despite adversity,
My lord, you place me, more than you believe,   20
Beneath those laws from which you set me free.
HIPPOLYTUS: Athens, uncertain whom to choose as heir,
Talks of yourself, of me, and the Queen's son.
ARICIA: Me?
HIPPOLYTUS: I would not wish to deceive myself.
My claim appears to be annulled by law   25
Because my mother was an Amazon.
But, if my only rival for the throne
Were Phaedra's son, my stepbrother, I could
Protect my rights against the law's caprice.
If I do not assert my claim, it is   30

To hand, or rather to return, to you
A sceptre given to your ancestors
By that great mortal whom the earth begot.
Adoption placed it in Aegeus' hands.
Theseus, his son, defended and enlarged   35
The bounds of Athens, which proclaimed him king
And left your brothers in oblivion.
Athens recalls you now within her walls.
Too long has she deplored this endless feud;
Too long your noble kinsmen's blood has flown,   40
Drenching the very fields from which it sprang.
If Troezen falls to me, the lands of Crete
Offer a rich domain to Phaedra's son.
But Attica is yours. And I go hence
To unify our votes on your behalf.   45

ARICIA: At all I hear, astounded and amazed,
I almost fear a dream deceives my ears.
Am I awake? Is it to be believed?
What god, my lord, inspired you with the thought?
How rightly is your glory spread abroad!   50
And how the truth surpasses your renown!
You in my favour will renounce your claim?
Surely it was enough to keep your heart
So long free from that hatred of my line,   55
That enmity . . .

HIPPOLYTUS: I hate you, Princess? No.
However my aloofness be decried,
Do you believe a monster gave me birth?
What churlish breeding, what unbending hate
Would not have melted at the sight of you?
Could I resist the soft beguiling spell . . .   60

ARICIA: What! My lord . . .

HIPPOLYTUS: No, I cannot now draw back!
Reason, I see, gives way to violence.
And, since I have begun to speak my mind,
Princess, I must go on: I must reveal
A secret that my heart can not conceal.   65
Before you stands a pitiable prince,
Signal example of rash arrogance.
I who, in proud rebellion against love,
Have long mocked other captives' sufferings,
Who, pitying the shipwrecks of the weak,   70
Had thought to watch them always from the shore,
Am now, in bondage to the common law,
Cut from my moorings by a surging swell.

A single blow has quelled my recklessness:
My haughty spirit is at last in thrall.   75
For six long months ashamed and in despair,
Pierced by the shaft implanted in my side,
I battle with myself, with you, in vain.
Present I flee you; absent, you are near.
Deep in the woods, your image follows me.   80
The light of day, the shadows of the night,
Everything conjures up the charms I flee;
Each single thing delivers up my heart.
And, sole reward for all my fruitless care,
I seek but cannot find myself again.   85
Bow, chariot, javelins, all importune me;
The lessons Neptune taught me are forgot.[15]
My idle steeds no longer know my voice,
And only to my cries the woods resound.
Perhaps the tale of so uncouth a love   90
Brings, as you listen, blushes to your face.
What words with which to offer you a heart!
How strange a conquest for so fair a maid!
But you should prize the offering the more.
Remember that I speak an unknown tongue,
And do not scorn my clumsy gallantry,   95
Which, but for you, I never would have known.

Scene 3

THERAMENES: The Queen is coming, Prince. She looks for you.
HIPPOLYTUS: For me?
THERAMENES: I do not know what she intends.
        You have been sent for by her messenger.
        Before you leave, Phaedra would speak with you.
HIPPOLYTUS: What can I say? And what can she expect . . .   5
ARICIA: Consent at least, my lord, to hear her speak.
        Although she was your bitter enemy,
        You owe some shade of pity to her tears.
HIPPOLYTUS: Meanwhile you go. I leave, and am in doubt
        Whether I have offended my beloved,   10
        Or if my heart that I commit to you . . .
ARICIA: Go, Prince. Pursue your generous designs.
        Make Athens' state pay homage to me. All
        The gifts you offer to me I accept.
        But Athens' empire, glorious though it be,   15
        Is not your most endearing offering.

---

15. The seagod was also the god of horses.

Scene 4

HIPPOLYTUS: Are you all ready? But I see the Queen.
　　　　Let everyone prepare with all despatch
　　　　To sail. Go, give the signal; hasten back,
　　　　And free me from a tedious interview.

Scene 5

PHAEDRA:

[To Oenone at the back of the stage.]

　　　　He comes . . . My blood sweeps back into my heart.
　　　　Forgotten are the words I had prepared.
OENONE: Think of your son, who hopes in you alone.
PHAEDRA: They say that you are leaving us at once.
　　　　My lord. I come to join my tears to yours.　　　　　　　5
　　　　I come to tell you of a mother's fears.
　　　　My son is fatherless, and soon, too soon,
　　　　He must behold my death as well. Even now,
　　　　Numberless enemies beset his youth.
　　　　You, only you, can see to his defence.　　　　　　　10
　　　　But I am harried by remorse within.
　　　　I fear lest you refuse to hear his cries.
　　　　I tremble lest you visit on a son
　　　　Your righteous anger at a mother's crimes.
HIPPOLYTUS: How could I ever be so infamous?　　　　　　　15
PHAEDRA: If you should hate me, I would not complain,
　　　　For I appeared resolved to do you ill.
　　　　Deep in my inmost heart you could not read.
　　　　I drew upon myself your enmity,
　　　　And where I dwelt, I would not suffer you.　　　　　　　20
　　　　With unrelenting hate, I sought to be
　　　　Divided from you by a waste of seas.
　　　　I even ordained by an express decree
　　　　That in my presence none should speak your name.
　　　　But, if the punishment should fit the crime,　　　　　　　25
　　　　If hate alone could bring your hate on me,
　　　　Never did woman merit pity more
　　　　And less, my lord, deserve your enmity.
HIPPOLYTUS: A mother jealous of her children's rights
　　　　Rarely forgives another woman's son,　　　　　　　30
　　　　I realize; and from a second bed
　　　　Awkward suspicion all too often springs.
　　　　Another would have taken like offence,
　　　　And at her hands I might have suffered more.

PHAEDRA: Ah! My lord, heaven, I dare here attest,   35
        Has quite dispensed me from the common rule.
        Far other is the care that weighs on me.
HIPPOLYTUS: Lady, it is too early yet to grieve.
        Who knows, your husband may be still alive.
        Heaven may vouchsafe him to your tears again.   40
        Protected by the seagod, not in vain
        Will Theseus call on mighty Neptune's aid.
PHAEDRA: No mortal visits twice the house of death.
        Since Theseus has beheld the sombre shores,
        In vain you hope a god will send him back,   45
        And hungry Acheron holds fast his prey.
        But no, he is not dead; he lives, in you.
        Always I think I see my husband's face.
        I see him, speak to him, and my fond heart . . .
        My frenzied love bursts forth in spite of me.   50
HIPPOLYTUS: In this I see the wonder of your love.
        Dead as he is, Theseus still lives for you.
        Still does his memory inflame your heart.
PHAEDRA: Yes, Prince, I pine, I am on fire for him.
        I love King Theseus, not as once he was,   55
        The fickle worshipper at countless shrines,
        Dishonouring the couch of Hades' god;[16]
        But constant, proud, and even a little shy;
        Enchanting, young, the darling of all hearts,
        Fair as the gods; or fair as you are now.   60
        He had your eyes, your bearing, and your speech.
        His face flushed with your noble modesty.
        When towards my native Crete he cleft the waves,[17]
        Well might the hearts of Minos' daughters burn!
        What were you doing then? Why without you   65
        Did he assemble all the flower of Greece?
        Why could you not, too young, alas, have fared
        Forth with the ship that brought him to our shores?
        You would have slain the monstrous Cretan bull
        Despite the windings of his endless lair.   70
        My sister[18] would have armed you with the thread,
        To lead you through the dark entangled maze—
        No. *I* would have forestalled her. For my love
        Would instantly have fired me with the thought.
        I, only I, would have revealed to you   75

---

16. Pluto, King of the underworld.   18. Ariadne.
17. On the expedition to Crete against the
    Minotaur.

The subtle windings of the labyrinth.
What care I would have lavished on your head!
A thread would not have reassured my fears.
Affronting danger side by side with you,
I would myself have wished to lead the way,   80
And Phaedra, with you in the labyrinth,
Would have returned with you or met her doom.

HIPPOLYTUS: What do I hear? Have you forgotten that
King Theseus is my father, you his wife?

PHAEDRA: What makes you think, my lord, I have forgot,   85
Or am no longer mindful of my name?

HIPPOLYTUS: Forgive me. Blushing, I confess your words
Were innocent, and I misunderstood.
For very shame I cannot bear your gaze.
I go . . .   90

PHAEDRA: Ah, cruel, you have understood
Only too well. I have revealed enough.
Know Phaedra then, and all her wild desires.
I burn with love. Yet, even as I speak,
Do not imagine I feel innocent,
Nor think that my complacency has fed   95
The poison of the love that clouds my mind.
The hapless victim of heaven's vengeances,
I loathe myself more than you ever will.
The gods are witness, they who in my breast
Have lit the fire fatal to all my line.   100
Those gods whose cruel glory it has been
To lead astray a feeble mortal's heart.
Yourself recall to mind the past, and how
I shunned you, cruel one, nay, drove you forth.
I strove to seem to you inhuman, vile;   105
The better to resist, I sought your hate.
But what availed my needless sufferings?
You hated me the more, I loved not less.
Even your misfortunes lent you added charms.
I pined, I drooped, in torments and in tears.   110
Your eyes alone could see that it is so,
If for a moment they could look at me.
Nay, this confession to you, ah! the shame,
Think you I made it of my own free will?
I meant to beg you, trembling, not to hate   115
My helpless children, whom I dared not fail.
My foolish heart, alas, too full of you,
Could talk to you of nothing but yourself.
Take vengeance. Punish me for loving you.
Come, prove yourself your father's worthy son,   120

And of a vicious monster rid the world.
I, Theseus' widow, dare to love his son!
This frightful monster must not now escape.
Here is my heart. Here must your blow strike home.
Impatient to atone for its offence,   125
I feel it strain to meet your mighty arm.
Strike. Or if it's unworthy of your blows,
Or such a death too mild for my deserts,
Of if you deem my blood too vile to stain
Your hand, lend me, if not your arm, your sword.   130
Give me it!

OENONE: Ah! What are you doing? God!
Someone is coming. You must not be seen.
Come, let's go in, quick, to avoid disgrace.

Scene 6

THERAMENES: Can that be Phaedra who was dragged away?
Why, my lord, why this sudden, sharp dismay?
I find you without sword, aghast and pale.

HIPPOLYTUS: Flee, flee, Theramenes. I cannot speak,
Nor without horror look upon myself.   5
Phaedra. . . . No, mighty gods, let us consign
This shameful secret to oblivion.

THERAMENES: If you will leave, the sails are all unfurled.
But Athens has already made her choice.
Her chieftains have consulted all the tribes.
Your brother rules; and Phaedra wins the day.[19]   10

HIPPOLYTUS: Phaedra?

THERAMENES: A herald speaking Athens' will
Into her hands conveyed the reins of state.
Her son is king, my lord.

HIPPOLYTUS: Oh God, who knows
Her heart, is it her virtue you reward?   15

THERAMENES: Meanwhile, vague rumours say the King still lives,
And even that in Epirus he was seen.
But I, who sought him there, my lord, I know . . . .

HIPPOLYTUS: No matter. Let us study every clue.
Have this new rumour traced back to its source.   20
But, if it does not then prove credible,
Let us depart and, at whatever cost,[20]
Replace the sceptre in more worthy hands.

---

19. I.e. half-brother, son of Theseus and   **20.** That is, even at the cost of a rebellion.
Phaedra, whereas Hippolytus' mother was
Antiope (Hippolyta).

ACT III

Scene 1

PHAEDRA: Ah, take away those royal honours. How
    Can you importune me to show myself?
    And why seek to beguile my grieving heart?
    Rather conceal me. I have said too much.
    My frantic passion has revealed itself.   5
    I have said what should never have been heard.
    God! how he listened to me. By what shifts
    He long pretended not to understand.
    How his whole being hankered to be gone.
    And how his blushes added to my shame.   10
    Why did you ever thwart my baneful plan?
    Ah! when his sword was pointed at my breast,
    Did he turn pale for me, or did he wrench
    It from me? I had but to touch it once
    To make it horrible for him, and for   15
    The wretched sword to soil his cruel hands.

OENONE: Thus your misfortunes breed self-pity, and
    Only inflame a fire you ought to quench.
    Daughter of Minos, should you not aspire
    To seek your peace of mind in nobler cares?   20
    Resort to flight from an ungrateful youth,
    Reign, and assume the guidance of the State?

PHAEDRA: I reign? I bring a State beneath my rule,
    When reason reigns no longer over me;
    When I have lost my self-dominion; when   25
    Beneath a shameful sway I scarcely breathe;
    When I am dying?

OENONE: Flee.

PHAEDRA: I cannot go.

OENONE: You sent him into exile. Shun him now.

PHAEDRA: Too late, too late. He knows my mad desires.
    I have transgressed the bounds of modesty.   30
    I to Hippolytus have bared my shame,
    And hope, despite me, has seduced my heart,
    You yourself, rallying my failing strength
    When on my lips my soul was hovering,
    By guileful counsels brought me back to life.   35
    You gave me glimpses of a sinless love.

OENONE: Alas! guilty or no of your mishaps,
    What would I not have done to save your life?
    But, if by insults you were ever stung,
    Can you forget a haughty youth's disdain?   40
    God! with what cruel, stern, unfeeling heart

He left you well-nigh prostrate at his feet!
How odious his uncompromising pride!
Why did not Phaedra see him with my eyes?

PHAEDRA: He may discard this pride that angers you.   45
Bred in the forests, he is wild like them.
Hardened by rude upbringing, he perhaps
For the first time listens to words of love.
Perhaps his silence mirrors his surprise,
And our reproaches are too violent.   50

OENONE: An Amazon, forget not, gave him birth.

PHAEDRA: Though a barbarian, yet did she love.

OENONE: He hates all women with a deadly hate.

PHAEDRA: No rival, then, will triumph over me.
In short, the time for good advice is past.   55
Serve my wild heart, Oenone, not my head.
If he is inaccessible to love,
Let us attack him at some weaker point.
He seemed attracted by an empire's rule.
He could not hide it; Athens beckoned him.   60
Thither his vessels' prows were headed, and
The white sails fluttered, streaming in the wind.
Oenone, play on his ambition. Go,
Dazzle him with the glitter of the crown.
Let him assume the sacred diadem.   65
Myself to bind it on is all I ask,
Yielding to him the power I cannot hold.
He will instruct my son how to command;
Perhaps he will be father to the boy.
Mother and son I will commit to him.   70
In short, try every means to win him round.
Your words will find a readier ear than mine.
Urge! Weep! Paint Phaedra at death's door.
You may assume a supplicating tone.
I will endorse it, whatsoe'er you do.   75
Go. Upon your success depends my fate.

Scene 2

PHAEDRA: O you who see the depths of this my shame,
Relentless Venus, is my fall complete?
Your cruelty could go no further. Now
You triumph. All your arrows have struck home.
O cruel goddess! if you seek new fame,   5
Attack a more rebellious enemy.
Frigid Hippolytus, flouting your wrath,
Has at your altars never bowed the knee.

Your name seems to offend his haughty ear.
Goddess, avenge yourself. Our cause is one.   10
Make him love . . . but Oenone, you are back.
Did he not listen? Does he loathe me still?

Scene 3

OENONE: Your love is vain and you must stifle it,
O Queen, and summon up your former strength.
The King we thought was dead will soon be here;
Theseus is come; Theseus is on his way.
Headlong, the crowd rushes to welcome him.   5
I had gone out to seek Hippolytus
When, swelling to the heavens a thousand cries . . .
PHAEDRA: My husband lives. Oenone, say no more.
I have confessed a love that soils his name.
He is alive, and more I will not know.
OENONE: What?   10
PHAEDRA: I foretold it but you would not hear.
Your tears prevailed over my keen remorse.
I died this morning worthy to be mourned;
I took your counsel and dishonoured die.
OENONE: You mean to die?   15
PHAEDRA: Great God, what have I done?
My husband and his son are on their way.
I will behold the witness of my guilt
Observe me as I dare approach the King,
My heart heavy with sighs he heard unmoved,
My eyes wet with the tears the wretch disdained. 20
Mindful of Theseus' honour, as he is,
Will he conceal from him my fierce desires?
Will he be false to father and to king,
Restrain the horror that he feels for me?
His silence would be vain, Oenone, for   25
I know my baseness, and do not belong
To those bold wretches who with brazen front
Can revel in their crimes unblushingly.
I know my transports and recall them all.
Even now I feel these very walls, these vaults,   30
Will soon give tongue and, with accusing voice,
Await my husband to reveal the truth.
Then, death, come free me from so many woes.
Is it so terrible to cease to live?
Death holds no terrors for the wretched. No.   35
I fear only the name I leave behind,
For my poor children what a heritage.

The blood of Jove should make their spirit swell;[21]
But, whatsoever pride that blood inspires,
A mother's crime lies heavy on her sons.   40
I tremble lest reports, alas, too true,
One day upbraid them with a mother's guilt.
I tremble lest, crushed by this odious weight,
Neither will ever dare hold up his head.

OENONE: Ah! do not doubt it. Pity both of them.
Never was fear more justified than yours.   45
But why expose them to such base affronts?
And why bear witness now against yourself?
That way lies ruin. Phaedra, they will say,
Fled from the dreaded aspect of her lord.
Hippolytus is fortunate indeed.   50
By laying down your life, you prove him right.
How can I answer your accuser's charge?
I shall be all too easy to confound.
I shall behold his hideous triumph as
He tells your shame to all who care to hear.   55
Ah! sooner let the flames of heaven descend.
But tell me frankly do you love him still?
How do you view this overweening prince?

PHAEDRA: He is a fearful monster in my eyes.   60

OENONE: Then why concede him such a victory?
You fear him. Dare then to accuse him first
Of the offence he soon may charge you with.
Nothing is in his favour; all is yours—
His sword, left by good fortune in your hands,   65
Your present agitation, your past grief,
His father, turned against him by your cries,
And, last, his exile you yourself obtained.

PHAEDRA: Should I oppress and blacken innocence?

OENONE: All I need is your silence to succeed.
Like you I tremble and I feel remorse.   70
Sooner would I affront a thousand deaths,
But, since without this remedy you die,
For me your life must come before all else.
Therefore I'll speak. Despite his wrath, the King   75
Will do naught to his son but banish him.
A father when he punishes is still
A father, and his judgement will be mild.
But, even if guiltless blood must still be shed,
What does your threatened honour not demand?   80

---

21. Jove (Zeus) was father to Minos and
    grandfather to Phaedra.

It is too precious to be compromised.
Its dictates, all of them, must be obeyed.
And, to safeguard your honour, everything,
Yes, even virtue, must be sacrified.
But who comes here? Theseus!   85
PHAEDRA: Hippolytus!
In his bold gaze my ruin is writ large.
Do as you will. My fate is in your hands.
My whirling mind has left me powerless.

Scene 4

THESEUS: Fortune at last ceases to frown on me,
O Queen, and in your arms again . . .
PHAEDRA: No more.
Do not profane your transports of delight.
No more do I deserve this tenderness.
You have been outraged. Jealous fortune's blows   5
During your absence have not spared your wife.
I am unworthy to approach you, and
Henceforth my only thought must be to hide.

Scene 5

THESEUS: Why this cold welcome to your father?
HIPPOLYTUS: Sire,
Phaedra alone can solve this mystery.
But, if my ardent wish can move you still,
Allow me never to set eyes on her.
Suffer your trembling son to disappear   5
For ever from the place where Phaedra dwells.
THESEUS: You, my son, leave me?
HIPPOLYTUS: Yes. It was not I
Who sought her. You, my lord, you brought her here.
For you, on leaving, brought Aricia
And your Queen, Phaedra, here to Troezen's shore.   10
You even committed them into my care.
But, since your safe return, why should I stay?
Long have I squandered in the woods of Greece
My manhood's skill on paltry enemies.
Should not I, fleeing shameful idleness,   15
Redden my javelins in more glorious blood?
Before you had attained my present years,
More than one tyrant, monsters more than one,
Had felt the might of your unconquered arm;
Even then, you were the scourge of insolence.   20
You had cleared all the shores of both the seas.
The traveller now fares freely through the land.

> Hercules, resting on his laurels' fame,
> Already for his labours looked to you.
> And I, a glorious father's unknown son,   25
> Lag far behind even my mother's deeds.
> Let me at least show you my mettle and,
> If some fell monster has escaped your sword,
> Place at your feet its honourable spoils.
> Or let the memory of a glorious death,   30
> Engraving in eternity my life,
> Prove to the universe I was your son.

THESEUS: What do I see? What horror spread around
> Drives back from me, distraught, my family?
> If I return, so feared, so undesired,   35
> O heaven! why did you free me from my gaol?
> I had one friend alone.[22] He rashly tried
> To seize the consort of Epirus' King.
> I served his amorous plan reluctantly;
> But fate in anger blinded both of us.   40
> The tyrant took me by surprise unarmed.
> Pirithous I beheld, a woeful sight,
> Thrown to fierce monsters by the barbarous king,
> Who fed them on the blood of helpless men.
> Me he confined in sombre caves profound   45
> Nearby the shadowy kingdom of the dead.
> The gods at last relented towards me and
> Allowed me to outwit my guardian.
> I purged the world of a perfidious knave.
> And his own monsters battened on his flesh.   50
> But when I joyfully prepare to meet
> My dearest ones, all that the gods have spared,
> Nay, when my soul, that is its own again,
> Would feast itself upon so dear a sight,
> Only with shudders am I welcomed home;   55
> Everyone flees, rejecting my embrace.
> Myself, filled with the horror I inspire,
> Would I were prisoner in Epirus still.
> Speak! Phaedra tells of outrage done to me.
> Who played me false? Why am I unavenged?   60
> Has Greece, so often guarded by my arm,
> Afforded shelter to the criminal?
> You do not answer. Is my son, my own
> Dear son, in league, then, with my enemies?
> Let us go in and end this grim suspense.   65

---

22. Pirithous.

Let us discover criminal and crime,
And Phaedra tell us why she is distraught.

Scene 6

HIPPOLYTUS: What meant these words that made my blood run cold?
Will Phaedra, still in her delirium,
Denounce herself, bring ruin on her head?
O God! What will the King say then? How love
Has spread its baleful poison through the house!   5
Myself, full of a passion he condemns,
As once he knew me, so he finds me still.
Gloomy forebodings terrify my soul.
But innocence has surely naught to fear.
Come, let me with some new and happier   10
Approach revive my father's tenderness,
And tell him of a love he may oppose
But which it is not in his power to change.

Act IV

Scene 1

THESEUS: What do I hear? A reckless libertine
Conceived this outrage on his father's name?
How harshly you pursue me, destiny.
I know not where I am, whither I go.
O son! O ill-rewarded tenderness!   5
Daring the scheme, detestable the thought.
To gain his lustful and nefarious ends,
The shameless villain had resort to force.
I recognized the sword he drew on her,
That sword I gave him for a nobler use.   10
Could all the ties of blood not hold him back?
Phaedra was slow in bringing him to book?
In keeping silent, Phaedra spared the knave?
OENONE: Rather did Phaedra spare a father's tears.
Ashamed of a distracted lover's suit,   15
And of the vicious passion she had caused,
Phaedra, my lord, was dying and her hand
Was on the point of cutting short her days.
I saw her raise her arm, I ran to her.
I, only I, preserved her for your love,   20
And, pitying her distress and your alarm,
Reluctantly I lent her tears a voice.
THESEUS: The criminal! He blenched despite himself.
As I drew near, I saw him start with fear.

I was astonished by his joyless mien;   25
His cold embraces froze my tenderness
But had this guilty love that eats him up
Already, even in Athens, shown itself?
OENONE: My lord, recall how oft the Queen complained.
Infamous love gave rise to all her hate.   30
THESEUS: And here in Troezen this flamed up again?
OENONE: My lord, I have related all I know.
The grieving Queen too long remains alone;
Allow me to withdraw and go to her.

Scene 2

THESEUS: Ah, it is he. Great gods! what eye would not
Be duped like mine by such nobility?
Must needs the brow of an adulterer
Be bright with virtue's sacred character?
And ought we not by fixed and certain signs   5
To see into perfidious mortals' hearts?
HIPPOLYTUS: May I inquire of you what baleful cloud
Has overcast, my lord, your regal brow?
Will you not venture to confide in me?
THESEUS: Villain! How dare you come before me now?   10
Monster, the thunderbolt too long has spared!
Last of the brigands whom I swept away!
After the frenzy of your wicked lust
Has driven you to assault your father's bed,
You dare to show your hateful face to me,   15
Here in this place full of your infamy,
And seek not out, under an unknown sky,
Countries to which your fame has never spread.
Flee, villain, flee. Brave not my hatred here
Not tempt my anger that I scarce restrain.   20
I have my portion of eternal shame
To have begot so criminal a son,
Without his death, disgrace to my renown,
Soiling the glory of my labours past.
Flee, and if you desire not to be joined   25
To all the villains fallen by my hand,
Take care that never does the shining sun
Behold you in these palaces again.
Flee then, and never more return;
And of your hideous presence purge my realm.   30
And, Neptune, in time past if my strong hand
Of infamous assassins cleared your shores,
Remember that, to recompense my deeds,

You swore to grant the first of my desires.
In the long hardships of a cruel gaol   35
I did not call on your immortal power;
With miser's care I put aside your aid,
Holding it in reserve for greater needs.
I call upon you now. Revenge my wrong.
I give this villain over to your wrath;   40
Drown in his blood his shameless foul desires.
Your favours will be measured by your rage.

HIPPOLYTUS: Phaedra accuses me of sinful love?
So infinite a horror numbs my soul.
So many unforeseen and heavy blows   45
Rain down upon me that I cannot speak.

THESEUS: Villain, you thought that Phaedra would conceal
In craven silence your vile insolence.
You should not, as you fled, have dropped the sword
That, in her hands, established your guilt.   50
Rather should you have crowned your perfidy
And at one stroke robbed her of speech and life.

HIPPOLYTUS: Rightly indignant at so black a lie,
I ought, my lord, to let the truth speak out,
But I shall not resolve this mystery   55
Out of the deep respect that seals my lips.
And, if you will not deepen your distress,
Look at my life; remember who I am.
Like virtue, crime advances by degrees,
Whoever goes beyond the bounds of law   60
Can in the end flout the most sacred rules.
No less than virtue, crime has its degrees,
And innocence has never yet been known
To swing at once to licence's extreme.
A single day cannot change virtuous men   65
To craven and incestuous murderers.
Reared by a virtuous Amazon from birth,
I never had belied my mother's blood.
Pittheus, esteemed the wisest far of men,
Instructed me after I left her hands.   70
I do not seek to paint myself too fair;
But, if one virtue is my birthright, that
Is above all, my lord, as I have shown,
Hate of the crime that they accuse me of.
That is what I am famous for in Greece,   75
I carried virtue to the sternest lengths,
My obdurate austerity is known;
The daylight is not purer than my heart.
Yet I, they say, fired by unholy love . . .

THESEUS: Yes, by that very pride you stand condemned.   80
         The reason why you were so cold is clear;
         Phaedra alone entranced your lustful eyes.
         And, by all other charms unmoved, your heart
         Disdained to glow with innocent desire.

HIPPOLYTUS: No, father, for this may not be concealed,   85
         I have not scorned to glow with virtuous love,
         And at your feet confess my real offence.
         I am in love; in love despite your ban.
         Aricia is mistress of my heart
         And Pallas' daughter has subdued your son.   90
         I worship her and, flouting your command,
         For her alone I pine, I am consumed.

THESEUS: You love her? God! The ruse is gross indeed!
         You feign to err to justify yourself.

HIPPOLYTUS: For half a year I have been deep in love.   95
         Trembling, I came to tell you so myself.
         What! Can no word of mine unseal your eyes?
         What fearful oath, to move you, must I swear?
         May heaven and earth and everything that is . . .

THESEUS: Foulness goes hand in hand with perjury.   100
         Cease! Spare me an importunate harangue,
         If your false virtue has no other stay.

HIPPOLYTUS: To you I may seem false and full of guile.
         Phaedra does justice to me in her heart.

THESEUS: Ah! how my wrath grows at your shamelessness.   105

HIPPOLYTUS: What time and what the place of banishment?

THESEUS: Were you beyond Alcides' pillars, still[23]
         Would I believe your villainy too near.

HIPPOLYTUS: Crushed by the crime that you suspect me of,
         If you desert me who will pity me?   110

THESEUS: Go seek out friends who in their viciousness
         Applaud adultery and incest. These
         Villains and ingrates, lawless, honourless,
         Will shelter evildoers such as you.

HIPPOLYTUS: You harp on incest and adultery.   115
         I will say nought; but Phaedra, as you know,
         My lord, is of a mother, of a line,
         Richer in all these horrors than my own.

THESEUS: What! are there no bounds to your frantic rage?
         For the last time, begone from out my sight.   120

---

23. The Pillars of Hercules, at the western end
    of the Mediterranean; hence any ex-
    tremely remote locality.

Go, libertine, before a father's wrath
Has you with ignominy torn from hence.

Scene 3

THESEUS: Unhappy youth! Haste to your certain doom.
By the stream dreaded even of the gods
Neptune has given and will fulfil his word.
A god of vengeance follows hard on you.
I loved you and, in spite of your offence,   5
My heart is stirred for you forebodingly.
But you have forced me to pronounce your doom.
Was ever wretched father outraged so?
O God who see my overwhelming grief,
How could I have begot so foul a child?   10

Scene 4

PHAEDRA: My Lord, I come stricken with terror, for
Your dreaded voice has reached me and I fear
Your menace may be given prompt effect.
If it is not too late, then spare your son.
Respect your flesh and blood, I beg of you,   5
And save me from the horror of his cries.
Do not lay up for me the endless grief
Of causing bloodshed by a father's hand.
THESEUS: No, Queen, my hand has not bathed in his blood,
But still the villain will not now escape.   10
Immortal hands are with his downfall charged.
This Neptune owes me. You will be avenged.
PHAEDRA: This Neptune owes you. What? Your anger calls . . .
THESEUS: How! You already fear I may be heard?
Rather unite your wishes with my own.   15
In all their heinousness depict his crimes;
Stir up my sluggish cold resentment, for
You do not know the measure of his crimes.
His fury showers affronts upon your name.
Your mouth, he says, speaks nothing but deceit;   20
He swears Aricia has won his heart,
And that he loves her.
PHAEDRA: What!
THESEUS: Those were his words.
But I am not the dupe of vain pretence.
Let us expect swift justice from the god.   25
I shall myself to Neptune's altars, there
To urge fulfilment of immortal oaths.

Scene 5

PHAEDRA: He's gone. What tidings have assailed my ears!
    What smouldering fire awakens in my heart!
    God! What a thunderbolt! What baleful news!
    Flying with but one thought to aid his son,
    I tore myself from pale Oenone's arms,   5
    Yielding to the remorse that tortured me.
    Who knows how far repentance would have gone?
    Perhaps I might even have accused myself?
    Perhaps, had not my voice died in my throat,
    The frightful truth would have escaped my lips.   10
    Hippolytus can love but loves not me.
    Aricia has won his heart, his troth.
    Ah! when, inexorable to my pleas,
    Hippolytus put on a front of steel,
    I thought his heart for ever closed to love,   15
    And against women all alike was armed.
    Another none the less has conquered him.
    She has found favour in his cruel eyes.
    Perhaps he has a heart easy to move.
    Alone of women me he cannot bear.   20
    And I was hastening to his defence!

Scene 6

PHAEDRA: Oenone, do you know what I have heard?
OENONE: No, but I still am trembling, to be frank.
    As you rushed forth, I blenched at your intent.
    I was afraid you would destroy yourself.
PHAEDRA: Who would have thought it? There was someone else.   5
OENONE: What!
PHAEDRA: Yes. Hippolytus is deep in love.
    This shy, unconquerable enemy,
    Whom my respect displeased, my tears annoyed,
    Whom I could never speak to unafraid,
    Submissive, tamed, proclaims his own defeat.   10
    Aricia is mistress of his heart.
OENONE: Aricia?
PHAEDRA: Ah! unplumbed depths of woe!
    For what new torments have I spared myself?
    All I have suffered, jealous torments, fears,
    Raging desire, the horror of remorse,   15
    A cruel, harsh, intolerable slight,
    Were a mere foretaste of my torments now.
    They love each other. By what spell did they
    Deceive me? How, where did they meet, since when?
    You knew. Why did you let me be misled?   20

Why did you keep from me their stealthy love?
Were they seen oft exchanging looks and words?
Deep in the forests were they wont to hide?
Alas! They had the utmost liberty.
Heaven smiled upon their innocent desires.   25
They followed where love led them, conscience free.
For them the dawn rose shining and serene.
And I, rejected by all living things,
I hid myself from day, I shunned the light;
Death was the only god I dared invoke.   30
I waited for the moment of my end,
Feeding on gall and drinking deep of tears.
Too closely watched, I did not even dare
Give myself up in freedom to my grief.
Trembling, this baleful pleasure I enjoyed   35
And, cloaking with a feignéd calm my woes,
Was often driven to forego my tears.

OENONE: What good will their love do them? Never will
They meet again.

PHAEDRA: Their love will always live.
Even as I speak, ah cruel, deadly thought!   40
They flout the fury of my insane rage.
Despite this exile which will sever them
They swear a thousand oaths never to part.
No. No. Their happiness is gall to me.
Oenone, pity my wild jealousy.   45
Aricia must perish, and the King
Be stirred to wrath against her odious race.
No trifling retribution will suffice.
The sister has outdone her brothers' crime.
I will implore him in my jealous rage.   50
What am I doing? I have lost my mind!
I, jealous? and 'tis Theseus I implore!
My husband is alive and yet I pine.
For whom? Whose heart have I been coveting?
At every word my hair stands up on end.   55
Henceforth the measure of my crimes is full.
I reek with foulest incest and deceit.
My hands, that strain for murder and revenge,
Burn with desire to plunge in guiltless blood.
Wretch! and I live and can endure the gaze   60
Of the most sacred sun from which I spring.
My grandsire is the lord of all the gods;
My forebears fill the sky, the universe.
Where can I hide? In dark infernal night?
No, there my father holds the urn of doom.   65

Destiny placed it in his ruthless hands.
Minos judges in hell the trembling dead.
Ah! how his horror-stricken shade will start
To see before him his own daughter stand,
Forced to admit to such a host of sins   70
And some, perhaps, unknown even in hell!
What, father, will you say to that dread sight?
I see your hand slip from the fateful urn;
I see you searching for new punishments,
Yourself your own kin's executioner.   75
Forgive me. Venus' wrath has doomed your race.
Your daughter's frenzy shows that vengeance forth.
Alas, my sad heart never has enjoyed
The fruits of crimes whose dark shame follows me.
Dogged by misfortune to my dying breath,   80
I end upon the rack a life of pain.

OENONE: Ah, Queen! dismiss these unbecoming fears,
And of your error take a different view.
You are in love. We cannot change our fate.
By destined magic you were swept along.   85
Is that so strange or so miraculous?
Has love then triumphed only over you?
Frailty is human and but natural.
Mortal, you must a mortal's lot endure.
This thraldom was imposed long, long ago.   90
The gods themselves that in Olympus dwell,
Who smite the evildoer with their bolt,
Have sometimes felt unlawful passions' fire.

PHAEDRA: Great gods! What counsels dare you offer me?
Even to the last you seek to poison me.   95
Wretch! Thus it is that you have caused my doom.
You, when I fled from life, you called me back;
At your entreaties duty was forgot;
It was _you_ made me see Hippolytus.
You meddling fool. Why did your impious lips,   100
Falsely accusing him, besmirch his life?
You may have killed him, if the gods have heard
A maddened father's sacrilegious wish.
I'll hear no more. Hence, loathsome monster, hence.
Go, leave me to my pitiable fate.   105
May the just heavens reward you fittingly,
And may your punishment forever fright
All who, as you have done, by base deceit
Pander to ill-starred princes' weaknesses,
Urging them on to yield to their desires,   110

And dare to smooth the path of crime for them,
Vile flatterers, the most ill-fated boon
The anger of the gods can make to kings!
OENONE: Ah God! to save her what have I not done;
But this is the reward I have deserved.   115

Act V

Scene 1

ARICIA: What, in this peril you refuse to speak?
You leave a loving father undeceived?
Cruel one, can you, by my tears unmoved,
Consent without a sigh to part from me?
Go hence and leave to my grieving heart.   5
But, if you go, at least preserve your life.
Defend your honour from a foul reproach
And force your father to revoke your doom.
There still is time. Wherefore, from what caprice,
Will you let Phaedra's slander hold the field?   10
Tell Theseus all.
HIPPOLYTUS: Ah, what have I not said?
Should I make known the outrage to his bed
And by an all too frank confession bring
Over my father's brow a blush of shame?
This odious secret you alone have pierced.   15
My sole confidants are the gods and you.
Judge of my love, I have not hid from you
All I desired to hide even from myself.
But, since you have been sworn to secrecy,
Forget, if it be possible, my words.   20
And never may your pure unsullied lips
Recount the details of this horrid scene.
Let's trust the justice of the gods above.
Their interest lies in vindicating me.
Sooner or later Phaedra will be brought   25
To book and meet an ignominious doom.
That is the only boon I ask of you.
My anger takes all other liberties.
Reject the bondage under which you pine;
Dare to accompany me in my flight.   30
Tear yourself free from an unhallowed spot
Where virtue breathes a foul, polluted air.
Let us to cover our escape exploit
The wild confusion that my downfall spreads.

I can provide you with the means for flight.   35
The only guards controlling you are mine.
Mighty defenders will take up our cause.
Argos awaits us; Sparta summons us.
Let's bear our grievance to our new allies.
Phaedra must never profit from our fall[24]   40
And drive us both from off my father's throne,
Making her son the heir to our estates.
Now is our chance. We must lay hands on it.
What holds you back? You seem to hesitate.
Only your interest thus emboldens me.   45
When I am ardent, why are you so cold?
Are you afraid to share an exile's lot?

ARICIA: Alas! How pleasant to be banished thus!
With what delight, linking my fate with yours,
By all the world forgotten I would live!   50
But, since we are not joined by that sweet bond,
Could I in honour flee from here with you?
I know that, even by the strictest code,
I may throw off your father's tutelage.
No bond of home or parents holds me back,   55
And flight from tyrants is permissible.
You love me, though, my lord, and my good name

HIPPOLYTUS: No. No. Your honour is too dear to me.
I come before you with a nobler plan.
Flee from my foes. Flee as my wedded wife.   60
Alone in exile, since heaven wills it so,
We need no man's consent to pledge our faith.
Not always torches blaze for Hymen's rites.
Not far from Troezen's gates, among these tombs,
My princely forebears' ancient burial place,   65
There stands a shrine dreaded of perjurers.
There mortals never swear an oath in vain.
Who breaks his word is punished instantly,
And men forsworn, afraid of certain death,
Are held in check by this most dreaded threat.   70
There, if you trust me, we will ratify
By solemn oath our everlasting love,
Taking to witness this old temple's god.
We'll pray him to be father to us both.
I'll call to witness the most sacred gods,   75
And chaste Diana, Juno the august,

---

24. I.e. profit by obtaining the kingdom which
    normally would have gone to Hippolytus
    and Aricia.

And all the gods, witnesses of my love,
Will lend their blessing to my holy vows.
ARICIA: The King is coming. Flee, make haste. To cloak
My own departure, I will stay awhile. 80
Go now, but leave me someone I can trust
To lead my steps to the appointed place.

Scene 2

THESEUS: O God! lighten the darkness of my mind.
Show me the truth that I am searching for.
ARICIA: Make ready, dear Ismene, for our flight.

Scene 3

THESEUS: Your colour changes and you seem aghast,
Lady. What was the young prince doing here?
ARICIA: My lord, he took eternal leave of me.
THESEUS: You have subdued that proud rebellious heart,
And his first raptures were inspired by you. 5
ARICIA: My lord, I cannot well deny the truth.
Your unjust hatred is not shared by him.
He did not treat me like a criminal.
THESEUS: I know. He swore eternal love to you.
Do not rely on that inconstant heart,
For he to others swore the self same oaths. 10
ARICIA: He, Sire?
THESEUS: You ought to have restrained him. How
Could you endure to share his fickle heart?
ARICIA: And how could you allow such calumny
To tarnish the bright glory of his life? 15
Have you so little knowledge of his heart?
Can you not tell baseness from innocence?
Must from your eyes alone an odious cloud
Conceal his virtues which shine bright to all?
I cannot let him further be maligned. 20
Stop and repent of your assassin's prayer.
Fear, my lord, fear lest the unbending heavens
Hate you enough to grant you your desire.
Oft in their wrath they take our sacrifice.
Often their gifts are sent to scourge our sins. 25
THESEUS: In vain you seek to cover his offence.
Your passion blinds you to his faults. But I
Have faith in sure, trustworthy witnesses.
I have seen tears which surely were not feigned.
ARICIA: Take care, my lord. Invincible, your hands 30
Have freed the world from monsters numberless;
But all are not destroyed. You still let live

One . . . But your son forbids me to proceed.
Knowing his wishes, I respect you still.
I would not grieve him if I dared to speak.   35
Following his restraint, I shall withdraw
Rather than let the truth escape my lips.

Scene 4

THESEUS (*alone*)   What does she mean, and what do these words hide,
Begun and broken off, begun again?
Is it their aim to trick me by a feint?
Are they in league to put me on the rack?
But I myself, despite my stern resolve,   5
What plaintive voice cries in my inmost heart?
A lurking flash of pity harrows me.
I'll have Oenone questioned once again:
I must have more light thrown upon the crime.
Guards, bring Oenone out to me alone.   10

Scene 5

PANOPE: I do not know what the Queen purposes,
But her distraction is a fearful sight.
Mortal despair cries from her haggard face,
And death has laid its paleness on her cheeks.
Oenone, driven out with shame, has plunged   5
Already into the unsounded sea.
We do not know what led her to this death;
The waves have closed for ever over her.
THESEUS: What?
PANOPE: This dark action did not calm the Queen.
Distraction seems to swell her wavering heart.   10
Sometimes, to soothe her secret sufferings,
She takes her children, bathes them in her tears;
Then, suddenly, renouncing mother's love,
Shuddering with horror, will have none of them.
This way and that, she wanders aimlessly;   15
Wildly she looks at us, but knows us not.
She thrice has written, then has changed her mind,
And thrice torn up the letter she began.
See her, we beg you. We implore your help.
THESEUS: Oenone's dead, and Phaedra seeks to die.   20
Call back my son, let him defend himself
And speak to me! I'll lend a willing ear.

[Alone.]

Do not be overhasty with your gifts,
Neptune! I wish my prayer may not be heard.
Perhaps I have believed false witnesses,   25
Lifting too soon my cruel hand to you.
Ah! if you act, how endless my despair!

  Scene 6

THESEUS: What have you done with him, Theramenes?
        I put him as a boy into your hands.
        But why the tears that trickle down your cheeks?
        What of my son?
THERAMENES: O tardy vain concern!
        O unavailing love! Your son's no more.   5
THESEUS: God!
THERAMENES: I have seen the best of mortals die,
        And the most innocent, I dare to add.
THESEUS: Dead? When I open wide my arms to him,
        The gods, impatient, hasten on his death?
        What blow, what thunderbolt snatched him away?   10
THERAMENES: Scarce were we issuing from Troezen's gates;
        He drove his chariot; round about him ranged,
        Copying his silence, were his cheerless guards.
        Pensive, he followed the Mycenae road,
        And let the reins hang loose upon his steeds.   15
        These haughty steeds, that once upon a time,
        Noble, high-spirited, obeyed his voice,
        Now dull of eye and with dejected air
        Seemed to conform to his despondent thoughts.
        A ghastly cry from out the water's depths   20
        That moment rent the quiet of the air.
        From the earth's entrails then a fearful voice
        Made answer with a groan to that dread cry.
        Deep in our hearts our blood with horror froze.
        The coursers' manes, on hearing, stood erect.   25
        And now, there rose upon the liquid plain
        A watery mountain seething furiously.
        The surge drew near, dissolved and vomited
        A raging monster from among the foam.
        His forehead huge was armed with fearsome horns   30
        And his whole body sheathed in yellow scales,
        Half bull, half dragon, wild, impetuous.
        His crupper curved in many a winding fold.
        The shore quaked with his long-drawn bellowings.
        The heavens beheld the monster, horror-struck;   35

It poisoned all the air; it rocked the earth.
The wave that brought it in recoiled aghast.
Everyone, throwing courage to the winds,
Took refuge in the temple near at hand.
Hippolytus alone, undaunted, stayed,   40
Reined in his steeds and seized his javelins,
Had at the monster and, with sure-flung dart,
Dealt him a gaping wound deep in his flank.
With rage and pain the monster, starting up,
Collapsed and, falling at the horses' feet,   45
Rolled over, opening wide his flaming jaws,
And covered them with smoke and blood and fire.
Carried away by terror, deaf, the steeds
No more responded to his curb or voice.
Their master spent his efforts all in vain.   50
They stained the bridle with their bloody foam.
In this wild tumult, it is even said,
A god appeared, goading their dusty flanks.
Over the rocks fear drove them headlong on;
The axle groaned and broke. Hippolytus   55
Saw his whole chariot shattered into bits.
He fell at last, entangled in the reins.
Forgive my grief. For me this picture spells
Eternal sorrow and perpetual tears.
I have beheld, my lord, your ill-starred son   60
Dragged by the horses that his hand had fed.
His voice that called them merely frightened them.
Onward they flew—his body one whole wound.
The plain resounded with our cries of woe.
At last they slackened their impetuous course.   65
They halted near the old ancestral tombs
Where all his royal forebears lie in state.
I and his guards hastened to him in tears.
The traces of his blood showed us the way.
The rocks were stained with it, the cruel thorns   70
Dripped with the bleeding remnants of his hair.
I saw him, called him; giving me his hand,
He opened and then straightway closed his eyes.
'Heaven takes my life, though innocent,' he cried.
'When I am dead, protect Aricia.   75
Friend, if my father ever learns the truth,
And pities the misfortunes of his son,
And would appease me in the life to come,
Tell him to show that princess clemency,

To give her back . . .'. And then he passed away,   80
And in my arms lay a disfigured corpse,
A tribute to the anger of the gods
That even his father would not recognize.

THESEUS: My son, fond hope I have myself destroyed!
Inexorable, all too helpful gods!   85
What keen remorse will haunt me all my life!

THERAMENES: Aricia then came upon the scene.
She came, my lord, fleeing your royal wrath,
Before the gods to pledge her faith to him.
As she drew near, she saw the reeking grass.   90
She saw, a grim sight for a lover's eyes,
Hippolytus, disfigured, deadly pale.
A while she tried to doubt her evil fate.
She sees the body of Hippolytus,
Yet still pursues the quest for her beloved.   95
But, in the end, only too sure 'tis he,
With one sad look, accusing heaven's spite,
Cold, moaning, and well nigh inanimate,
She falls, unconscious, at her sweetheart's feet.
Ismene, bending over her, in tears,   100
Summons her back to life, a life of pain.
And I have come, my lord, hating the world,
To tell you of Hippolytus' last wish
And to discharge the bitter embassy
Which he entrusted to me as he died.   105
But hither comes his deadly enemy.

Scene 7

THESEUS: Well, then, you triumph and my son's no more.
What grounds I have for fear! What cruel doubt
Gnaws at my heart, pleading his innocence!
But he is dead. Accept your victim. Joy
In his undoing, justified or no,   5
For I am willing to deceive myself.
Since you accuse him, I accept his guilt.
His death will make my tears flow fast enough
Without my seeking for enlightenment
Which could not ever bring him back to me   10
And might perhaps but sharpen my distress.
Let me flee, far from you and from these shores,
The bloody vision of my mangled son.
Stunned and pursued by this grim memory,
Would I were in another universe!   15

        Everything seems to brand my wicked wrath.
        My very name increases my despair.
        Less known of mortals, I could hide myself.
        I hate even the favours of the gods.
        And now I must bewail their murderous gifts,   20
        No longer tiring them with fruitless prayers.
        Whatever they have done for me, their aid
        Cannot give back what they have robbed me of.
PHAEDRA: No, Theseus. No, I must at last speak out.
        I must redress the wrong I did your son,   25
        For he was innocent.
THESEUS: Wretch that I am!
        If I condemned him, it was on your word.
        Cruel one, do you hope to be forgiven . . . .
PHAEDRA: Each moment's precious. Listen. It was I,
        Theseus, who on your virtuous, filial son   30
        Made bold to cast a lewd, incestuous eye.
        Heaven in my heart lit an ill-omened fire.
        Detestable Oenone did the rest.
        She feared your son, knowing my frenzy, might
        Reveal a guilty passion he abhorred.   35
        The wretch, exploiting my enfeebled state,
        Rushed to denounce Hippolytus to you.
        She has exacted justice on herself
        And found beneath the waves too mild a death.
        By now I would have perished by the sword,   40
        But first I wished to clear my victim's name.
        I wished, revealing my remorse to you,
        To choose a slower road down to the dead.
        I have instilled into my burning veins
        A poison that Medea brought to Greece.   45
        Already it has reached my heart and spread
        A strange chill through my body. Even now
        Only as through a cloud I see the bright
        Heaven and the husband whom I still defile.
        But death, robbing my eyes of light, will give   50
        Back to the sun its tarnished purity.
PANOPE: Ah! she is dying.
THESEUS: Would the memory
        Of her appalling misdeeds die with her!
        Let us, now that my error's all too clear,
        Go out and mourn over my ill-starred son.   55
        Let us embrace my cherished son's remains
        And expiate my mad atrocious wish,

Rendering him the honours he deserves,
And, to appease the anger of his shade,
Let his beloved, despite her brothers' crime,
Be as a daughter to me from this day.   60

San Agustin National Archeological Park.
Monolith of a warrior (left) and a god of
war, on mound dedicated to gods of war.

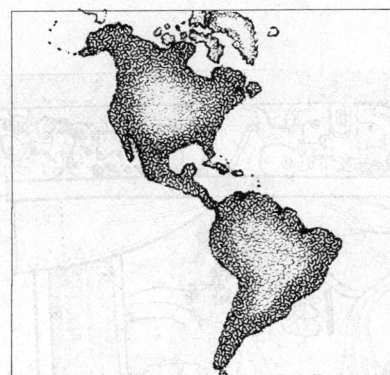

SECTION VIII
The Early Americas

The first inhabitants of the Americas—the peoples we know collectively as Indians—migrated across the Bering Strait from Asia between 25,000 and 40,000 years ago. Over the ensuing millennia, they migrated gradually over the North and South American continents, developing cultures suited to diverse geographic and climatic conditions. Our earliest evidence for the emergence of regional cultures dates from about 10,000 B.C.E.

Mexico, and Central and South America

Although advanced civilizations existed in the Americas from as early as 800 C.E., the most sophisticated Indian cultures—the Mayas (first century B.C.E.), the Aztecs (thirteenth century C.E.), and the Incas (thirteenth century C.E.) respectively—occupied central Mexico, Central America, and the high valleys of the Andes. When the Spanish conquistadors landed in the "new" world, the indigenous population may have been as large as forty-five million. We are including here selections from the cultural traditions of the three best-known societies: the Aztecs of Mexico, the Mayas of the Yucatan and Central America, and the Incas of what is now called Peru. These three groups represent, however, a tiny fraction of the 350 major tribal groups, fifteen cultural centers or advanced civilizations, and more than 160 linguis-

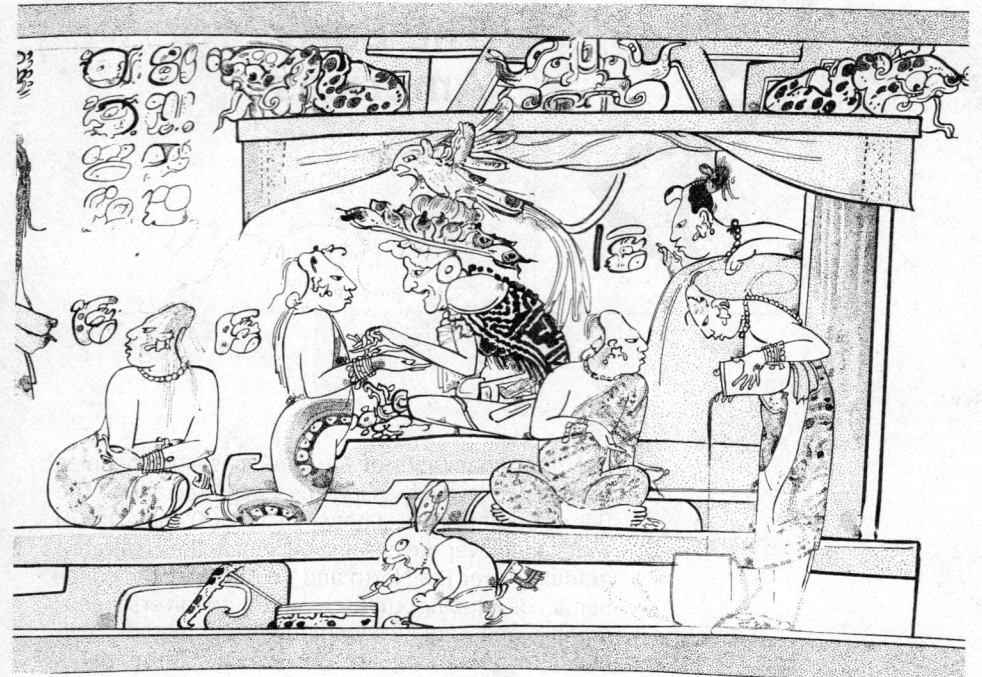

AND THEN THEY TOOK HOLD OF A HUMAN SACRIFICE: A classic Maya funerary vase painting from northern Guatemala, showing head lord of Xibalba, One Death, seated on his throne at right; (*The vase is in the Princeton University Art Museum.*)

tic groups that occupied Latin America. Building on the legacies of the societies that came before them, these civilizations were to develop advanced agricultural technology, sophisticated astronomical knowledge, stratified societies, and imperial political systems.

When speaking of the Aztecs it is usually the Mexicas, a Nahuatl-speaking warrior tribe, that is being referred to. The Mexicas, an uncultivated people, formed an alliance around 1246 C.E. with the aristocracy of the surviving Toltecs who preceded them as leaders of the Aztec state. The Mexicas built their capital city of Tenochtitlan in what is now central Mexico around 1325 and by 1376 they had made the transition from a clan (*calpulli*) society to a monarchy. In 1428, allied with the peoples of Texcoco and Tlacopan, they conquered the seat of the state in Atzcapotzalco. From then on the Mexicas reigned supreme, subjugating many other peoples who in retaliation were to later provide material and military help to Cortés, who conquered them in 1521.

Under the Mexicas, the Aztec empire became a warrior state. Although human sacrifice was practiced to an extent by other peoples in the empire, the Mexicas undertook such rituals to an unprecedented degree. Such fanaticism can be partly explained by the prominence that the deity Huitzilopochtli gained over the other deities of the Aztec pantheon. Huitzilopochtli, the Mexicas believed, required the daily sacrifice of human hearts in order for the sun to rise. This belief legitimized the casualties of their military expansion. By the mid-fifteenth century, when military expansion slowed down, the Mexicas resorted to the infamous "flower wars" or tournaments in which they battled other peoples, particularly the Tlaxcalans, in order to exchange captives, who were then sacrificed to the deities.

It is in this context that Aztec "literary" production should be understood. The "flower songs" included here are not "poetry" as we traditionally understand it. Rather they are the words forming a part of a ritual in which "ghost warriors" were called down from heaven to help in battle.

Our knowledge of the Mayan peoples can be traced back to around 2000 B.C.E., when they began to settle in the areas known today as Guatemala, Honduras, and El Salvador, and the Mexican states of Yucatan, Campeche, Tabasco, and Chiapas. Like the Mexicas, the Mayans had their roots in a civilization (the Olmecs) which flourished before them. Two of the most sophisticated achievements of the Mayas, hieroglyphic writing and the calendar, were developed as early as 500 C.E. but were not inscribed on stone until the first century B.C.E. There were two Mayan empires. The first was the Classic Period, which flourished between 317 and 889 C.E. in Petén, in what is today northern Guatemala. The richly inscribed architectural and sculptural wonders of Palenque, Tikal, and Copán date from this period. As the first empire declined because of overpopulation, environmental blight, and malnutrition, the center of Mayan civilization shifted northward to the Yucatan around 900 C.E. This second or New Empire was shaped by the Toltecs, a Nahuatl-speaking people of Mayan descent. They were militaristic and worshipped the god-king Quetzalcoatl or "Plumed Serpent," who figures prominently in the *Popol Vuh* or "Council Book" of the Maya-Quiché kingdom founded by their descendants.

The Mayas of both periods had a highly developed culture that was expressed in musical, dramatic, philosophical, and historical forms. Among the thousands of hieroglyphic works that they produced, only four survived the destruction wreaked by the conquistadors. The first, *Xahoh-Tun* [The Dance of Tun], is also known as *Rabinal Achí* in reference to the place — Rabinal — in which the transcribed Mayan oral text was found in the mid-nineteenth century. The events, which are thought to have taken place in the mid-fifteenth century C.E., revolve around the young warrior Cavek Quiché Vinak's challenge to an enemy lord, who in the end has him sacrificed. The other three — the *Popol Vuh, The Annals of the Cakchikels,* and *The Books of Chilam Balam* — all reproduce the cosmogonies of various Mayan peoples. Discovered on different dates in the seventeenth, eighteenth, and nineteenth centuries, these works are thought to have been created in the fifteenth century. Some, like the *Popol Vuh,* were written down in Mayan, just after the Spanish conquest in the sixteenth century. Like the *Popol Vuh,* which is a sacred book of counsel and prophesy, the various books of *Chilam Balam* (Chilam signifies *priest* and Balam, which denotes *jaguar,* refers to the last and greatest prophet before the conquest), were meant to be interpreted in ritual ceremonies. The *Annals of the Cakchiquels* describes in historical detail the bloody fight between the Cakchiquels and the Quichés in the middle of the fifteenth century. All of these reveal some Christian influence, a result of Indian scribes having been trained by the Spaniards. The scribes were used to aid the Spaniards in their evangelizing mission by translating Christian prayers, sermons, and catechisms into the Mayan languages.

The third civilization discussed here, the Incas, were the most sophisticated. They built their empire by skillful political organization, efficient administration of resources, and the invention and use of advanced military technology. Their religion tended toward monotheism, with the sun being their principal deity, whom they worshipped in sumptuous temples. Around 1100 C.E., the Incas began to populate the valley which was to become Cuzco, their capital city. By the time the Spaniards arrived, the Incas had extended their dominion over a territory that included today's Peru and Ecuador, and large portions of Bolivia, Chile, and Argentina. The Inca, which means "child of the sun," was a kind of emperor believed to be descended from the sun deity. He was the highest authority in the hereditary monarchy and had both military and priestly functions. Incan society was highly stratified, but its economy was predominantly collectivist. The success of the Incas was primarily due to their organizational abilities, which were perfected in a highly developed mathematical system. Like the Romans in Europe, the Incas were able to build an excellent highway system, stretching over 25,000 kilometers. They also constructed aqueducts, bridges, and large-scale buildings, such as those at Machu Picchu, and organized an efficient communication network of messenger-runners. Like the Romans, too, they imposed their language, Quechua, throughout their empire.

The Incas had an extensive and varied culture. Although they did not have writing, they did have a system of memorization based on knotted strings or *kipus* of different sizes, colors, and shapes. They had ritual dramatic forms that included dance, song, and pantomime. Their "lyric" forms were metaphysical, ritual, or epic in character. When the Spaniards conquered the Incan empire in the 1530s, it was at the height of its splendor under the rule of Atahualpa. As in the defeat of Moctezuma, the Spaniards took advantage of the rivalries among different groups, particularly that of Atahualpa's brother Huascar.

When we look back today at the legacies of the Aztecs, the Mayas, and the Incas, we find that the native texts recorded during the period of the Spanish conquests register a note of profound despondency, not only at the destruction of life and the great works of civilization, but more importantly at the loss of a guiding vision, whether epistemological or cosmological. The world as they had known it was no more. The Mayan books of *Chilam Balam*—for there are Chilam books from various Mayan sites—characterize this loss as the destruction of understanding and wisdom: "There was no longer any great teacher, any great orator, any supreme priest, when the change of rulers occurred upon [the] arrival [of the Spaniards]."* Similarly, in one of the surviving Aztec accounts of the defeat of Moctezuma, we can read: "Broken spears lie in the roads;/we have torn our hair in grief./The houses are roofless now, and their walls/are red with blood."† Worse still, there was no longer communication with the gods, as Durán's *History of the Indies* notes: "[The Aztecs] had no further answer from their oracles; then they regarded the gods as mute or dead."‡

The problems of transliteration and transcription that we encounter in dealing with Hispanic texts attest to a certain duality in Latin American cultures that continues even today—for example, in the literature of magical or marvelous realism (a noncontradictory combination of the rational and the supernatural) and in Cuban *santería* or Brazilian *candomblé*, African-based popular religions that combine Catholic saints and Yoruban *orixas* or deities in syncretic figures, each with its own style of dress, food and rhythm. Initially, this duality was related to

---

The Book of Chilam Balam of Chumayel (Norman: University of Oklahoma Press, 1967) p. 5.

†"The Story of the Conquest as Told by the Anonymous Authors of Tlatelolco," *The Broken Spears. The Aztec Account of the Conquest of Mexico,* trans. from Nahuatl into Spanish by Angel Maria Garibay K., trans. into English by Lysander Kemp, ed. Miguel León-Portilla (Boston: Beacon Press, 1962), p. 137.

‡D. Durán, *The Aztecs, The History of the Indies of New Spain* (New York: Orion, 1964) 77.

the reconciling of two entirely different visions of the world. This is most evident in the conquerors' accounts—letters to the kings, journals, chronicles, histories, etc.—of the nature of the places and peoples they encountered. For example, in the attempts made by Christopher Columbus to explain what he saw, there are constant references to his own repository of knowledge: from Christian scripture, Pliny's *Natural History*—the Latin text regarded as a scientific source book during the Middle Ages—and Marco Polo's *Travels* to chivalry romances and Renaissance epic poems. In many cases, this knowledge took precedence over what Columbus saw or heard. For example, when he heard the word "Cariba," supposedly an appellative for a neighboring tribe of warlike Indians, he assimilated it to "Caniba," which were the subjects of the Grand Khan of which Marco Polo writes.§ Likewise, certain beliefs that he had—that the lands he encountered bordered on Paradise, or that he expected to meet up with Cyclopes and mermaids—demonstrate that his epistemological framework overrode what he actually witnessed. However, despite such assimilations he was also careful to note the exoticism of many things: "I saw many trees very unlike ours, and many of them had branches of different kinds, and all coming from one root; one branch is of one kind and one of another, and they are so unlike each other that it is the greatest wonder in the world."**

The literature of conquest, colonization, and evangelization tells us much about native societies and their destruction. The oscillation between assimilation and differentiation, as noted by Columbus in his journal, however, was to remain a problem in most accounts of such "encounters" between civilizations and, more generally, for most interpretations of the nature of Latin American culture right up to the present.

The Dominican priest Bartolomé de Las Casas, who himself came with the conquistadors as an evangelist and was granted an *encomienda* or tract of land, underwent so strong a conversion to abolitionism that he eventually came to value the Indians more than his fellow Christians. His characterization of the natives as innocents—"poor lambs" in the excerpts from *The History of the Indies* presented here—and his energetic protest against the brutality of the conquistadors were put forth in many arguments and writings, but most notably in the *Very Brief Account of the Destruction of the Indies* (1522), which was immediately translated into six European languages. This work constituted the immediate pretext for the so-called Black Legend, according to which Spain was considered to have wreaked a destruction of indigenous peoples far more brutal than the violence of conquest by other European nations. The Black Legend was elaborated as a means to legitimize the challenges by England, the Low Countries, and France to Spain's possession of the Indies by papal and other international law.

The selections included here from Felipe Guamán Poma de Ayala, a Christianized Indian of noble, Incan lineage, and Garcilaso de la Vega (El Inca), a *mestizo* (part Native American and part European) of double royal lineage, offer two interesting variations on the interaction of identity, recognition, and knowledge. Both, as Indians, claim to have privileged knowledge that has enabled them to write a truer history of their native Peru. This knowledge is also used as a pretext for criticizing their respective targets—the colonial administration in Guamán Poma's case, European historiography as it relates to Peru in Garcilaso's—and for making a case for their own worth.

---

§*The Journal of Christopher Columbus* (London: Anthony Blond, 1968), 11/23/92, 11/26/92, 12/11/92.
***The Journal of Christopher Columbus*, 10/16/92.

Colonial literature was not, of course, institutionalized as such in its own time; it is, rather, the construct of literary scholarship dating from the nineteenth century and is currently in the process of reconstruction. t is this scholarship, intimately linked to intellectual projects to legitimize particula countries and Latin America in general by grounding cultural identity in a historical foundation, which led us to include all kinds of genres as literature, be they chronicles, ethnographies written by missionaries, the epic poetry of the elites, *autos sccramentales* or religious drama, the satirical writing of disgruntled *letrados* (administrative functionaries and others who disseminated information and knowledge) and those who were at odds with colonial rule, which was the exclusive domain of Spaniards. There was, of course, strictly literary writing, but it was the exception and it was very much under the influence of the Baroque ethos that the Cathol c Church and the Spanish and Portuguese crowns propagated throughout Latin America.

The Baroque influence—showy, intricate artifices interwoven with a mood of disillusionment and the signs of Iberian decadence and the Counter-Reformation—was taken to extremes in Latin America. There the formal acquires an almost independent existence, for the source of power is always distant and the mixture of races leads to a heterogeneous society in which strategies of simulation and dissimulation are required to "pass" from one stratum to another. The complication and proliferation of forms, intensified by recourse not only to this social and linguistic heterogeneity but also to the panoply of natural elements different from the European ones, mark Latin American literature. An excess of style, which was initially a means to approximate and even better models of European culture, became a way of life and art among many writers, enduring to this day in such expressive modes as magical or marvelous realism and the neobaroque (a twentieth-century reworking, in strictly literary terms, of this stylization).

North America

At the time of the first European contacts, the area currently occupied by the lower United States was home to some 240 tribes (or nations) distributed across six broad cultural regions: Northwest Coast, Plateau, Plains, Southwest, Eastern Woodlands, and Southeast.

There is no doubt that a rich and varied literary culture—from songs, stories, and dramatic oratory to chants and charms and curing spells—existed for thousands of years before the arrival of the Europeans. But the indigenous cultures of the present-day United States were oral cultures; they did not use alphabetic writing to record their thought or "literature." For an anthology such as this—indeed, for any anthology—the problem is apparent: how to represent the literature of a period when literature was not represented in textual form? Strictly speaking, of course, there is no way to do so; we cannot *read* Ind an literature from a time before the incursion of the Europeans because a written literature simply did not exist.

But because oral cultures are oriented toward continuity rather than change, it is at least possible to suggest that some later texts that we do have may serve as approximate representations of what we do not have. Any such assumptions, of course, must amount to at best an informed guess. We have decided that it is a guess worth chancing—at least in a limited way. Thus we have included a lengthy excerpt from a Navajo creation story, which, although it was first recorded in a written form in the nineteenth century, is probably not very different from versions of the story told hundreds of years earlier. (But that is something we can only guess, not know.) We have also included in this section a few examples classified as songs, charms, prophecies—genres that are entirely Western categories, that we can only speculate are consistent with the actual Native American oral versions that existed long before Columbus. The North American peoples whose works are included in this section are the Navajo, Kwakiutl, Crow, Iroquois, and Cherokee.

The Navajo migrated from southern Canada to the southwestern United States between the years 1000 and 1300 C.E., settling among the sedentary Pueblo peoples who had preceded them to the region far earlier. Although the Navajo raided their Pueblo neighbors, they also learned from them, adapting Pueblo techniques in agriculture, in the arts of pottery and weaving, and in ritual practices such as sand painting. The Navajo were also influenced by the Mexicans, from whom they later learned the silver-working techniques for which they are well-known today. In the seventeenth century, sheep—introduced to the New World by the Spanish—became important to the Navajo economy. Today, even after the disastrous "sheep reduction" program instituted by the federal government in the 1930s and 1940s, sheepherding remains important to the Navajo people. In 1864 the Navajo, caught up in the fighting between the Union and the Confederacy in the Civil War, were violently subdued in Santa Fe by Kit Carson, a colonel in the Union army and onetime "friend" of the Indian. They were then sent upon the "Long Walk" some 300 miles to imprisonment at Fort Sumner, southeast of Santa Fe. This was a traumatic event for the Navajo as the "Trail of Tears" was for the Cherokee (see below). In 1868 the Navajo were permitted to return to their homelands and to settle on a reservation that had been surveyed so that most of the best pastureland was left to the more numerous white settlers. The Navajo today are the most populous tribe in the United States.

The Kwakiutl are a Northwest Coast people. Their traditional homelands included the northern portion of Vancouver Island and the facing mainland. In common with several other peoples of the Northwest, Kwakiutl subsistence was heavily dependent upon salmon fishing, and important ritual activities were focused on the life cycle of the salmon. As Navajo silverwork and weaving are well-known throughout the world, so, too, are the woodworking skills of the Kwakiutl—their elaborately carved and painted memorial poles, house posts, and ceremonial utensils are among the best known of Indian arts.

Kwakiutl society was elaborately stratified, with each person holding an inherited position. The potlatch, a ceremonial distribution of gifts undertaken for a variety of reasons—to celebrate an important event or to affirm or establish status—is perhaps the Kwakiutl ritual activity most intensely studied by anthropologists. Dancing societies were another important institution; each society had a hierarchical repertoire of dances that told of ancestral encounters with supernatural beings in which gifts, social rankings, crests, and privileges were originally bestowed in a sort of potlatch of the gods.

The Crow are a Plains people who occupied the Yellowstone River country in what are today the states of Oregon and Montana. After obtaining horses from the Spanish (the horse had become extinct in the New World), Plains Indians developed a distinctive culture based on hunting the extensive buffalo herds that provided food, clothing, and housing. (For example, buffalo skins were used to construct the familiar conical *tipi*, or what we call the tepee, of the Plains.) They also conducted ritualized raiding activities designed to increase the supply of horses or to bring prestige to those who carried them out successfully (e.g., to warriors who killed or counted *coup* upon—touched—an enemy in battle).

The spiritual life of young Crow males, typical of Plains tribes generally, was rooted in individual mystical experience. A vision induced in an adolescent male by fasting and self-torture would reveal the supernatural guardian, usually an animal, who would confer upon him certain powers. The Lakota and the Cheyenne were traditional enemies of the Crow, and, as the whites advanced upon the Plains, the Crow made common cause with them against these enemy tribes. Thus, in 1868, when the Crow agreed to settle upon a reservation carved from some of their former territories in Montana, their history of cooperation with the whites helped them to obtain a better deal, relatively speaking, than the resisting Plains tribes. The Sun Dance of the Crow, once outlawed as a "heathenish practice," has, in somewhat modified form, had a great revival today, and serves as the center of the ritual life of many contemporary, traditional Crow people.

The Cherokee originally dwelt around the Great Lakes, but after defeat by the Delaware and Iroquois, they migrated south, and, around the year 1700, were settled around the northern Allegheny Mountains of eastern Tennessee and the western Carolinas. The southernmost group of Iroquoian speakers, the Cherokee, developed an economy based upon advanced agricultural techniques; social organization emphasized a division between red (war) villages, whose chiefs were under the rule of the supreme war chief, and white (peace) villages, whose chiefs answered to the supreme peace chief. Each village consisted of some thirty to sixty log cabins and a council house.

The response of the Cherokee to the increasing numbers of white invaders intruding upon Cherokee lands after the turn of the nineteenth century involved a complex and subtle combination of resistance and accommodation. In 1821 the mixed-blood Cherokee, George Guess, or Sequoyah, performed the extraordinary task of singlehandedly inventing a writing system — strictly speaking, a syllabary rather than an alphabet — for the Cherokee language. As result, many Cherokee persons also became literate in English.

Nonetheless, in 1830, under pressure from President Andrew Jackson, Congress passed the Indian Removal Act, which gave the president the authority to remove Indians east of the Mississippi from their traditional homelands to Indian Territory (present-day Oklahoma) west of the Mississippi. This was done in 1838, when approximately twelve thousand eastern Cherokee were forced by federal troops to set out, in the dead of winter, on the "Trail of Tears." Fully one third—four thousand people—died on that march. Today, the majority of Cherokee people live in the state of Oklahoma. Next to the Navajo, the Cherokee are the most populous tribe in the United States today.

The people called the Iroquois are not a single tribe but rather a loose confederation of five (the Mohawk, Oneida, Orondaga, Cayuga, and Seneca), and later (with the addition of the Tuscarora) six peoples speaking similar languages (the "Iroquoian" language group). The Iroquois lived in an area around the southern Great Lakes, and, in the seventeenth and eighteenth centuries, controlled a wide expanse of territory from the Great Lakes as far south and east as Albany.

The Iroquoian peoples relied on both agriculture and hunting for sustenance. The basic economic and social unit was the village, a grouping of "longhouses," each of which lodged many families. Indeed, the longhouse served as a central metaphor of society for the Iroquois. For example, the nations of the Iroquois League spoke of themselves as "people of the longhouse," meaning that the tribes together were as families in a dwelling. Society was matrilineal, with property owned by the women. The women also played a major role in the frequent and lengthy council meetings through which decisions involving the people were made. Renowned as fierce warriors, the Iroquois were able to organize effective resistance against French expansion south from Canada, and westward expansion by those English who would become Americans. The Iroquois supported the British in the Revolutionary War because, among other reasons, they were obviously in agreement with the British wish to contain the line of colonial settlement east of the Allegheny Mountains. American victory led to harsh consequences for the Iroquois. Today Iroquoian culture flourishes in a variety of complex ways, on both sides of the border between the United States and Canada.

Further Readings

Adorno, Rolona. *Guamán Poma de Ayala: Writing and Resistance in Colonial Peru*. Austin: University of Texas Press, 1986.

Allen, Paula Gunn, ed. *Studies in American Indian Literature*. New York: Modern Language Association, 1983.

Astrov, Margot, ed. *American Indian Prose and Poetry*. New York: Fawcett, 1973 [1946].

Bierhorst, John, ed. *Four Masterworks of American Indian Literature: Quetzalcoatl, The Ritual of Condolence, Cuceb, The Night Chant*. New York: Farrar, Straus & Giroux, 1974.

———. *In the Trail of the Wind: American Indian Poems and Ritual Orations*. New York: Farrar, Straus & Giroux, 1987 [1971].

———. *The Red Swan: Myths and Tales of the American Indians*. New York: Farrar, Straus & Giroux, 1976.

Burns, Allan F. *An Epoch of Miracles: Oral Literature of the Yucatec Maya*. Austin: University of Texas Press, 1983.

Jara, René and Spadaccini, Nicholas, eds. *1492–1992: Re/Discovering Colonial Writing*. Hispanic Issues No. 4. Minneapolis: The Prisma Institute, 1989.

Klor de Alva, Jorge. "Language, Politics, and Translation: Colonial Discourse and Classic Nahuatl in New Spain." In *The Art of Translation: Voices from the Field*. Ed. Rosanna Warren. Boston: Northeastern University Press, 1989.

Kroeber, Karl, ed. *Traditional American Indian Literatures: Texts and Interpretations*. Lincoln: University of Nebraska Press, 1981.

León-Portilla, Miguel. *Aztec Thought and Culture: A Study of the Ancient Nahuatl Mind*. Norman: University of Oklahoma Press, 1963.

———. *Pre-Columbian Literatures of Mexico*. Norman: University of Oklahoma Press, 1969.

MacCormak, Sabine. *Children of the Sun and Reason of State: Myths, Ceremonies, and Conflicts in Incan Peru*. 1992 Lecture Series, Working Papers No. 6, Department of Spanish and Portuguese, University of Maryland, College Park (1990).

Murray, David. *Forked Tongues: Speech, Writing and Representation in North American Indian Texts*. Bloomington: Indiana University Press, 1991.

O'Gorman, Edmundo. *The Invention of America*. Bloomington: Indiana University Press, 1961.

Ruoff, A. LaVonne Brown. *American Indian Literatures: An Introduction, Bibliographic Review, and Selected Bibliography*. New York: Modern Language Association, 1990.

Swann, Brian, and Arnold Krupat, eds. *Recovering the Word: Essays on Native American Literature*. Berkeley: University of California Press, 1987.

Wachtel, Nathan. *The Vision of the Vanquished. The Spanish Conquest of Peru Through Indian Eyes: 1530–1570*. Trans. Ben and Siân Reynolds. New York: Harper and Row, 1977.

Wiget, Andrew. *Native American Literature*. Boston: Twayne Publishers, 1985.

ANONYMOUS (MID-SIXTEENTH CENTURY)
Guatemala

The *Popol Vuh*—which can be translated as "Council Book" or "Council Paper"—of the Maya-Quiché Indians was written down in the Latin alphabet in the middle of the sixteenth century. The manuscript was found at a church in Chiche-castenango, Guatemala. At the beginning of the eighteenth century, it was translated into Spanish by a Dominican priest named Francisco Jimenez. The *Popol Vuh* is the most complete creation myth to survive the devastation wreaked by the Spanish conquistadors.

The *Popol Vuh* consists of four major sections. The first, excerpted here, contains the creation account and is analogous to the first chapter of Genesis, although contradicting it since the mud beings created by the Makers, apparent Adams, are destroyed because they have no understanding. The first part also tells of the deeds of Hunahpu and Xbalanque, twin gods who control the morning-star aspect of Venus or One Hunahpu, their father, and respectively become the sun and the moon ("little jaguar sun"). They were sent to earth to curb the pride of Zipacna, a self-aggrandizing figure who, like his father Seven Macaw, claimed to be the Maker. The second part includes other mythic accounts, such as that of the Ahup people who played ball with the lords of the Xibalba, the region of the dead, and the story, excerpted here, of Ixquic, the maiden who became pregnant from the saliva that dripped from the skull of one of the Ahub lords defeated in the ball game. The third and fourth parts tell the history of the Quichés under their first four leaders.

The *Popol Vuh* was originally a hieroglyphic "council book," which the Lords of Quiché consulted to determine the future. that is, to see as the first four humans had seen, "everything under the sky perfectly."* The most recent translator of the *Popol Vuh* into English, Dennis Tedlock, explains that the original hieroglyphic book probably contained astronomical tables that permitted diviners to set appropriate dates for ceremonies and political events. The book was not just read but performed in the interpretation and conduct of Quiché life.

Prayer Suggested by the Maya Andrés Xiloj to Help the Reading of the Popol Vuh

Make my guilt vanish,
Heart of Sky, Heart of Earth;
do me a favor,
give me strength, give me courage
in my heart, in my head,
since you are my mountain and my plain;
may there be no falsehood and no stain,

Translated by Dennis Tedlock, Popol Vuh: The Definitive Edition of the Mayan Book of the Dawn of Life and the Glories of Gods and Kings.

and may this reading of the Popol Vuh
come out clear as dawn,
and may the shifting of ancient times
be complete in my heart, in my head;
and make my guilt vanish,
my grandmothers, grandfathers,
and however many souls of the dead there may be,
you who speak with the Heart of Sky and Earth,
may all of you together give strength
to the reading I have undertaken.

from *Popol Vuh*

[And now for the messengers of One and Seven Death]

And now for the messengers of One and Seven Death: "You're going, you Military Keepers of the Mat, to summon One and Seven Hunahpu. You'll tell them, when you arrive:

" 'They must come,' the lords say to you. 'Would that they might come to play ball with us here. Then we could have some excitement with them. We are truly amazed at them. Therefore they should come,' say the lords, 'and they should bring their playthings, their yokes and arm guards should come, along with their rubber ball,' say the lords, you will say when you arrive," the messengers were told.

And these messengers of theirs are owls: Shooting Owl, One-legged Owl, Macaw Owl, Skull Owl, as the messengers of Xibalba are called.

There is Shooting Owl, like a point, just piercing.

And there is One-legged Owl, with just one leg; he has wings.

And there is Macaw Owl, with a red back; he has wings.

And there is also Skull Owl, with only a head alone; he has no legs, but he does have wings.

There are four messengers, Military Keepers of the Mat in rank.

And when they came out of Xibalba they arrived quickly, alighting above the ball court where One and Seven Hunahpu were playing, at the ball court called Great Abyss at Carchah. The owls, arriving in a flurry over the ball court, now repeated their words, reciting the exact words of One Death, Seven Death, Pus Master, Jaundice Master, Bone Scepter, Skull Scepter, House Corner, Blood Gatherer, Trash Master, Stab Master, Wing, Packstrap, as all the lords are named. Their words were repeated by the owls.

"Don't the lords One and Seven Death speak truly?"[1]

"Truly indeed," the owls replied. "We'll accompany you."

Translated by Dennis Tedlock.

---

1. That this line is part of the dialogue rather
than part of the narrative is made obvious
by the next line, which is clearly a reply.

"They're to bring along all their gaming equipment," say the lords.

"Very well, but wait for us while we notify our mother," they replied.

And when they went to their house, they spoke to their mother; their father had died:

"We're going, our dear mother, even though we've just arrived.[2] The messengers of the lord have come to get us:

" 'They should come,' he says," they say, giving us orders. "We'll leave our rubber ball behind here," they said, then they went to tie it up under the roof of the house. "Until we return—then we'll put it in play again."

They told One Monkey and One Artisan:

"As for you, just play and just sing,[3] write and carve to warm our house and to warm the heart of your grandmother." When they had been given their instructions, their grandmother Xmucane sobbed, she had to weep.

"We're going, we're not dying. Don't be sad," said One and Seven Hunahpu, then they left.

[After that One and Seven Hunahpu Left, guided down the road by the messengers]

After that One and Seven Hunahpu left, guided down the road by the messengers.

And then they descended the road to Xibalba, going down a steep cliff, and they descended until they came out where the rapids cut through, the roaring canyon narrows named Neck Canyon. They passed through there, then they passed on into the River of Churning Spikes. They passed through countless spikes but they were not stabbed.

And then they came to water again, to blood: Blood River. They crossed but did not drink. They came to a river, but a river filled with pus. Still they were not defeated, but passed through again.

And then they came to the Crossroads, but here they were defeated, at the Crossroads.

Red Road was one and Black Road another.

White road was one and Yellow Road another.

There were four roads, and Black Road spoke:

"I am the one you are taking. I am the lord's road," said the road. And they were defeated there: this was the Road of Xibalba.

And then they came to the council place of the lords of Xibalba, and they were defeated again there. The ones seated first there are just manikins, just woodcarvings dressed up by Xibalba. And they greeted the first ones:

"Morning,[4] One Death," they said to the manikin. "Morning, Seven Death," they said to the woodcarving in turn.

---

2. "Even though" is my translation of *xaet*. Antitheses are rather frequent in the speech of Hunahpu and Xbalanque.

3. The playing here (*tzuan-*) is specifically on the flute.

4. This is *calah [zalah]*, literally "clear, bright, plainly visible," used as a morning greeting in classical Quiché. Today the preferred greeting for the morning is *zakiric*, "it is getting light (or dawning)."

So they did not win out, and the lords of Xibalba shouted out with laughter over this. All the lords just shouted with laughter because they had triumphed; in their hearts they had beaten One and Seven Hunahpu. They laughed on until One and Seven Death spoke:

"It's good that you've come. Tomorrow you must put your yokes and arm guards into action," they were told.

"Sit here on our bench," they were told, but the only bench they were offered was a burning-hot rock.

So now they were burned on the bench; they really jumped around on the bench now, but they got no relief. They really got up fast, having burned their butts. At this the Xibalbans laughed again, they began to shriek with laughter, the laughter rose up like a serpent in their very cores,[5] all the lords of Xibalba laughed themselves down to their blood and bones.

"Just go in the house. Your torch and cigars will be brought to your sleeping quarters," the boys were told.

After that they came to the Dark House, a house with darkness alone inside. Meanwhile the Xibalbans shared their thoughts:

"Let's just sacrifice them tomorrow. It can only turn out to be quick; they'll die quickly because of our playing equipment, our gaming things," the Xibalbans are saying among themselves.

This ball of theirs is just a spherical knife. White Dagger is the name of the ball, the ball of Xibalba. Their ball is just ground down to make it smooth; the ball of Xibalba is just surfaced with crushed bone to make it firm.

[And One and Seven Hunahpu went inside Dark House]

And One and Seven Hunahpu went inside Dark House.

And then their torch was brought,[6] only one torch, already lit, sent by One and Seven Death, along with a cigar for each of them, also already lit, sent by the lords. When these were brought to One and Seven Hunahpu they were cowering,[7] here in the dark. When the bearer of their torch and cigars arrived, the torch was bright as it entered; their torch and both their cigars were burning. The bearer spoke:

" 'They must be sure to return them in the morning—not finished, but just as they look now. They must return them intact,' the lords say to you," they were told, and they were defeated. They finished the torch and they finished the cigars that had been brought to them.

And Xibalba is packed with tests, heaps and piles of tests.

This is the first one: the Dark House, with darkness alone inside.

---

5. *Cumatz* or "serpent" is a term for various kinds of disabling cramps.
6. The torch is *chah*, literally "pine"; in the present context it is the Quiché term for what is more widely known in Mesoamer-ica as *ocote* (a Nahua-derived term), a split-off stick of extremely resinous pine wood, still widely used for torches and kindling.
7. The verb here is *chocochoh*, which means to crouch "in a cowering manner."

Ceremonial ax - represents the
Olmec Rain God, which the Olmec
conceived of as part jaguar, part
"crying baby."

And the second is named Rattling House, heaving with cold inside, whistling with drafts, clattering with hail. A deep chill comes inside here.

And the third is named Jaguar House, with jaguars alone inside, jostling one another, crowding together, with gnashing teeth. They're scratching around; these jaguars are shut inside the house.

Bat House is the name of the fourth test, with bats alone inside the house, squeaking, shrieking, darting through the house. The bats are shut inside; they can't get out.

And the fifth is named Razor House, with blades alone inside. The blades are moving back and forth, ripping, slashing through the house.

These are the first tests of Xibalba, but One and Seven Hunahpu never entered into them, except for the one named earlier, the specified test house.

And when One and Seven Hunahpu went back before One and Seven Death, they were asked:

"Where are my cigars? What of my torch? They were brought to you last night!"

"We finished them, your lordship."

"Very well. This very day, your day is finished, you will die, you will disappear, and we shall break you off. Here you will hide your faces: you are to be sacrificed!" said One and Seven Death.

And then they were sacrificed and buried. They were buried at the Place of Ball Game Sacrifice, as it is called. The head of One Hunahpu was cut off; only his body was buried with his younger brother.

"Put his head in the fork of the tree that stands by the road," said One and Seven Death.

And when his head was put in the fork of the tree, the tree bore fruit. It would not have had any fruit, had not the head of One Hunahpu been put in the fork of the tree.

This is the calabash tree, as we call it today, or "the head of One Hunahpu," as it is said.

And then One and Seven Death were amazed at the fruit of the tree. The fruit grows out everywhere, and it isn't clear where the head of One Hunahpu is; now it looks just the way the calabashes look. All the Xibalbans see this, when they come to look.

The state of the tree loomed large in their thoughts, because it came about at the same time the head of One Hunahpu was put in the fork. The Xibalbans said among themselves:

"No one is to pick the fruit, nor is anyone to go beneath the tree," they said. They restricted themselves; all of Xibalba held back.

It isn't clear which is the head of One Hunahpu; now it's exactly the same as the fruit of the tree. Calabash tree came to be its name, and much was said about it. A maiden heard about it, and here we shall tell of her arrival.

[And here is the account of a maiden, the daughter of a lord named Blood Gatherer]

And here is the account of a maiden, the daughter of a lord named Blood Gatherer.

And this is when a maiden heard of it, the daughter of a lord. Blood Gatherer is the name of her father, and Blood Woman is the name of the maiden.

And when he heard the account of the fruit of the tree, her father retold it. And she was amazed at the account:

"I'm not acquainted with that tree they talk about. ' "Its fruit is truly sweet!" they say,' I hear," she said.

Next, she went all alone and arrived where the tree stood. It stood at the Place of Ball Game Sacrifice:

"What? Well! What's the fruit of this tree? Shouldn't this tree bear something sweet? They shouldn't die, they shouldn't be wasted. Should I pick one?" said the maiden.

And then the bone spoke; it was here in the fork of the tree:

"Why do you want a mere bone, a round thing in the branches of a tree?" said the head of One Hunahpu when it spoke to the maiden. "You don't want it," she was told.

"I do want it," said the maiden.

"Very well. Stretch out your right hand here, so I can see it," said the bone.

"Yes," said the maiden. She stretched out her right hand, up there in front of the bone.

And then the bone spit out its saliva, which landed squarely in the hand of the maiden.

And then she looked in her hand, she inspected it right away, but the bone's saliva wasn't in her hand.

"It is just a sign I have given you, my saliva, my spittle. This, my head, has nothing on it—just the bone, nothing of meat. It's just the same with the head of a great lord: it's just the flesh that makes his face look good. And when he dies, people get frightened by his bones. After that, his son is like his saliva, his spittle, in his being, whether it be the son of a lord or the son of a craftsman, an orator. The father does not disappear, but goes on being fulfilled. Neither dimmed nor destroyed is the face of a lord, a warrior, craftsman, orator. Rather, he will leave his daughters and sons. So it is that I have done likewise through you. Now go up there on the face of the earth; you will not die. Keep the word. So be it," said the head of One and Seven Hunahpu—they were of one mind when they did it.

This was the word Hurricane, Newborn Thunderbolt, Raw Thunderbolt had given them. In the same way, by the time the maiden returned to her home, she had been given many instructions. Right away something was generated in her belly, from the saliva alone, and this was the generation of Hunahpu and Xbalanque.

And when the maiden got home and six months had passed, she was found out by her father. Blood Gatherer is the name of her father.

[And after the maiden was noticed by her father, when he saw that she was now with child, all the lords then shared their thoughts]

And after the maiden was noticed by her father, when he saw that she was now with child, all the lords then shared their thoughts—One and Seven Death, along with Blood Gatherer:

"This daughter of mine is with child, lords. It's just a bastard," Blood Gatherer said when he joined the lords.

"Very well. Get her to open her mouth.[8] If she doesn't tell, then sacrifice her. Go far away and sacrifice her."

"Very well, your lordships," he replied. After that, he questioned his daughter:

"Who is responsible for the child in your belly, my daughter?" he said.

"There is no child, my father, sir; there is no man whose face I've known,"[9] she replied.

---

8. This is *chacoto uchi [uchii]*, literally "Dig it
   out of her mouth," an idiom for close
   questioning. In terms of the somatic mapping of actual or potential speech, as conceived by Quichés, this implies that she
   knows perfectly well what her father wants
   her to say; if her word were "in her belly,"
   on the other hand, it would mean that she

could not readily articulate a response even
if she wanted to.

9. This statement is not only true in its figurative reference to Blood Woman's sexual
   innocence, but in its literal sense: she has
   never known the (fleshly) face of the man
   responsible for her miraculous pregnancy.

"Very well. It really is a bastard you carry! Take her away for sacrifice, you Military Keepers of the Mat. Bring back her heart in a bowl, so the lords can take it in their hands this very day," the owls were told, the four of them.

Then they left, carrying the bowl. When they left they took the maiden by the hand, bringing along the White Dagger, the instrument of sacrifice.

"It would not turn out well if you sacrificed me, messengers, because it is not a bastard that's in my belly. What's in my belly generated all by itself when I went to marvel at the head of One Hunahpu, which is there at the Place of Ball Game Sacrifice. So please stop: don't do your sacrifice, messengers," said the maiden. Then they talked:

"What are we going to use in place of her heart? We were told by her father: 'Bring back her heart. The lords will take it in their hands, they will satisfy themselves, they will make themselves familiar with its composition. Hurry, bring it back in a bowl, put her heart in the bowl.' Isn't that what we've been told? What shall we deliver in the bowl? What we want above all is that you should not die," said the messengers.

"Very well. My heart must not be theirs, nor will your homes be here.[10] Nor will you simply force people to die, but hereafter, what will be truly yours will be the true bearers of bastards. And hereafter, as for One and Seven Death, only blood,[11] only nodules of sap, will be theirs. So be it that these things are presented before them, and not that hearts are burned before them. So be it: use the fruit of a tree,"[12] said the maiden. And it was red tree sap she went out to gather in the bowl.

After it congealed, the substitute for her heart became round. When the sap of the croton tree was tapped, tree sap like blood, it became the substitute for her blood. When she rolled the blood around inside there, the sap of the croton tree, it formed a surface like blood, glistening red now, round inside the bowl. When the tree was cut open by the maiden, the so-called cochineal croton, the sap is what she called blood, and so there is talk of "nodules of blood."

"So you have been blessed with the face of the earth. It shall be yours," she told the owls.

"Very well, maiden. We'll show you the way up there. You just walk on ahead; we have yet to deliver this apparent duplicate of your heart before the lords," said the messengers.

And when they came before the lords, they were all watching closely:

"Hasn't it turned out well?" said One Death.

"It has turned out well, your lordships, and this is her heart. It's in the bowl."

---

10. In the biological sense, this means that future owls will be free to move around the surface of the earth. If I am right in suspecting that the messenger owls of Xibalba correspond to the planet Mercury, the astronomical sense of this same statement would be that Mercury appears above the horizon on more days than it remains below.

11. "Blood" is a literal translation of *quic* [*qui4*], which also refers to gums and resins from trees (including latex), in this case the blood-red resin of the cochineal croton or "red tree."

12. This is a figurative reference to nodules of sap from the cochineal croton.

"Very well. So I'll look," said One Death, and when he lifted it up with his fingers, its surface was soaked with gore, its surface glistened red with blood.

"Good. Stir up the fire, put it over the fire," said One Death.

After that they dried it over the fire, and the Xibalbans savored the aroma. They all ended up standing here, they leaned over it intently. They found the smoke of the blood to be truly sweet!

And while they stayed at their cooking, the owls went to show the maiden the way out. They sent her up through a hole onto the earth, and then the guides returned below.

In this way the lords of Xibalba were defeated by a maiden; all of them were blinded.

And here, where the mother of One Monkey and One Artisan lived, was where the woman named Blood Woman arrived.

[And when the Blood Woman came to the mother of One Monkey and One Artisan]

And when the Blood Woman came to the mother of One Monkey and One Artisan,[13] her children were still in her belly, but it wasn't very long before the birth of Hunahpu and Xbalanque, as they are called.

And when the woman came to the grandmother, the woman said to the grandmother:

"I've come, mother, madam. I'm your daughter-in-law and I'm your child,[14] mother, madam," she said when she came here to the grandmother.

"Where do you come from? As for my lastborn children,[15] didn't they die in Xibalba? And these two remain as their sign and their word: One Monkey and One Artisan are their names. So if you've come to see my children, get out of here!" the maiden was told by the grandmother.

"Even so, I really am your daughter-in-law. I am already his, I belong to One Hunahpu. What I carry is his. One Hunahpu and Seven Hunahpu are alive, they are not dead. They have merely made a way for the light to show itself, madam mother-in-law, as you will see when you look at the faces of what I carry," the grandmother was told.

And One Monkey and One Artisan have been keeping their grandmother

---

13. In fact the mother (in the literal sense) of One Monkey and One Artisan has already died by this time; in the present passage the term "mother" is being used in its role-designating sense rather than in its genealogical sense. One Monkey and One Artisan are living alone with Xmucane, their father's mother, at this point; she is the only person they have who could fill the role of "mother."

14. The use of "child" here is metaphorical. A Quiché daughter-in-law takes up resi-

dence with her husband's family; in offering herself not only as a daughter-in-law but as a "child," Blood Woman both seeks the kind of acceptance a daughter would have and makes an offer of loyalty.

15. Given that Xmucane is never mentioned as having had any children other than One and Seven Hunahpu, she may be using *chipa [4hipa]* or "lastborn (youngest)" endearingly, in effect calling her sons, who were adults when they left home, "my little babies."

entertained: all they do is play and sing, all they work at is writing and carving, every day, and this cheers the heart of their grandmother.

And then the grandmother said:

"I don't want you, no thanks, my daughter-in-law. It's just a bastard in your belly, you trickster! These children of mine who are named by you are dead," said the grandmother.

"Truly, what I say to you is so!"[16]

"Very well, my daughter-in-law, I hear you. So get going, get their food so they can eat. Go pick a big netful of corn, then come back—since you are already my daughter-in-law,[17] as I understand it," the maiden was told.

"Very well," she replied.

After that, she went to the garden; One Monkey and One Artisan had a garden. The maiden followed the path they had cleared and arrived there in the garden, but there was only one clump,[18] there was no other plant, no second or third. That one clump had borne its ears. So then the maiden's heart stopped:

"It looks like I'm a sinner, a debtor! Where will I get the netful of food she asked for?" she said. And then the guardians of food were called upon by her:

"Come thou, rise up, come thou, stand up:
Generous Woman, Harvest Woman,
Cacao Woman, Cornmeal Woman,
thou guardian of the food of One Monkey, One Artisan,"

said the maiden.

And then she took hold of the silk, the bunch of silk at the top of the ear. She pulled it straight out, she didn't pick the ear, and the ear reproduced itself to make food for the net. It filled the big net.

And then the maiden came back, but animals carried her net. When she got back she went to put the pack frame in the corner of the house, so it would look to the grandmother as if she had arrived with a load.

And then, when the grandmother saw the food, a big netful:

"Where did that food of yours come from? You've leveled the place! I'm going to see if you've brought back our whole garden!" said the grandmother.

And then she went off, she went to look at the garden, but the one clump was still there, and the place where the net had been put at the foot of it was still obvious.

And the grandmother came back in a hurry, and she got back home, and she said to the maiden:

"The sign is still there. You really are my daughter-in-law! I'll have to keep

---

16. I take it that this sentence belongs to Blood Woman rather than Xmucane, given that it is followed with *utz bala,* "Very well," which signals the beginning of a reply and definitely belongs to Xmucane.

17. The grandmother isn't so much accepting Blood Woman's claim to kinship here as she is saying (with sarcasm) something

like, "If you *say* you're my daughter-in-law, then *act* like one." Quiché daughters-in-law, who live with the families of their husbands, are subject to the commands of their mothers-in-law, who give them heavy household tasks to do.

18. In Mesoamerica corn is properly grown in thick clumps, not stalk by stalk in single file; clumps survive high winds better.

watching what you do. These grandchildren of mine are already showing genius," the maiden was told.

Now this is where we shall speak of the birth of Hunahpu and Xbalanque.

[And this is their birth; we shall tell of it here]

And this is their birth; we shall tell of it here.

Then it came to the day of their birth, and the maiden named Blood Woman gave birth. The grandmother was not present when they were born; they were born suddenly. Two of them were born, named Hunahpu and Xbalanque. They were born in the mountains, and then they came into the house. Since they weren't sleeping:

"Throw them out of here! They're really loudmouths!" said the grandmother.

After that, when they put them on an anthill, they slept soundly there. And when they removed from there, they put them in brambles next.

And this is what One Monkey and One Artisan wanted: that they should die on the anthill and die in the brambles. One Monkey and One Artisan wanted this because they were rowdyish and flushed with jealousy. They didn't allow their younger brothers in the house at first, as if they didn't even know them, but even so they flourished in the mountains.

And One Monkey and One Artisan were great flautists and singers, and as they grew up they went through great suffering and pain. It had cost them suffering to become great knowers. Through it all they became flautists, singers, and writers, carvers. They did everything well. They simply knew it when they were born, they simply had genius. And they were the successors of their fathers who had gone to Xibalba, their dead fathers.

Since One Monkey and One Artisan were great knowers, in their hearts they already realized everything when their younger brothers came into being, but they didn't reveal their insight because of their jealousy. The anger in their hearts came down on their own heads;[19] no great harm was done. They were decoyed[20] by Hunahpu and Xbalanque, who merely went out shooting every day. These two got no love from the grandmother, or from One Monkey and One Artisan. They weren't given their meals; the meals had been prepared and One Monkey and One Artisan had already eaten them before they got there.

But Hunahpu and Xbalanque aren't turning red with anger; rather, they just let it go, even though they know their proper place, which they see as clear as day. So they bring birds when they arrive each day, and One Monkey and One Artisan

---

19. Andrés Xiloj remarked, "We see a person; we speak behind his back and he doesn't hear what we are murmuring. Then this murmur doesn't fall upon that person, but we are the ones who pay for it." A daykeeper, taking on the task of defending a person who has been the victim of witchcraft, asks in prayer that "the one who did this work should be the one to receive it."

20. The verb here is *poizaxic [poyizaxic]*; if English "doll" were a verb, this could be translated literally as "to be dolled"—that is, to be misled by a doll. Today *poyizaxic* is most commonly employed with reference to the use of scarecrows in fields.

eat them. Nothing whatsoever is given to Hunahpu and Xbalanque, either one of them. All One Monkey and One Artisan do is play and sing.

And then Hunahpu and Xbalanque arrived again, but now they came in here without bringing their birds, so the grandmother turned red:

"What's your reason for not bringing birds?" Hunahpu and Xbalanque were asked.

"There are some, our dear grandmother, but our birds just got hung up in a tree,"[21] they said, "and there's no way to get up the tree after them, our dear grandmother, and so we'd like our elder brothers to please go with us, to please go get the birds down," they said.

"Very well. We'll go with you at dawn," the elder brothers replied.

Now they had won, and they gathered their thoughts, the two of them, about the fall of One Monkey and One Artisan:

"We'll just turn their very being around with our words. So be it, since they have caused us great suffering. They wished that we might die and disappear—we, their younger brothers. Just as they wished us to be slaves here, so we shall defeat them there. We shall simply make a sign of it," they said to one another.

And then they went there beneath a tree, the kind named yellowwood, together with the elder brothers. When they got there they started shooting. There were countless birds up in the tree, chittering, and the elder brothers were amazed when they saw the birds. And not one of these birds fell down beneath the tree:

"Those birds of ours don't fall down; just go throw them down," they told their elder brothers.

"Very well," they replied.

And then they climbed up the tree, and the tree began to grow, its trunk got thicker.

After that, they wanted to get down, but now One Monkey and One Artisan couldn't make it down from the tree. So they said, from up in the tree:

"How can we grab hold?[22] You, our younger brothers, take pity on us! Now this tree looks frightening to us, dear younger brothers," they said from up in the tree. Then Hunahpu and Xbalanque told them:

"Undo your pants, tie them around your hips, with the long end trailing like a tail behind you, and then you'll be better able to move," they were told by their younger brothers.

"All right," they said.

And then they left the ends of their loinclothes trailing, and all at once these became tails. Now they looked like mere monkeys.

After that they went along in the trees of the mountains, small and great. They went through the forests, now howling, now keeping quiet in the branches of trees.

Such was the defeat of One Monkey and One Artisan by Hunahpu and Xbalanque. They did it by means of their genius alone.

---

21. When birds are shot they sometimes close their feet around the branch where they were sitting and then hang there, dead.
22. The verb stem here is *chanic,* translated on the basis of *chanih,* "keep in the fist." The tree is too thick for One Monkey and One Artisan to use their hands in coming down.

And when they got home they said, when they came to their grandmother and mother:

"Our dear grandmother, something has happened to our elder brothers. They've become simply shameless, they're like animals now," they said.

"If you've done something to your elder brothers, you've knocked me down and stood me on my head. Please don't do anything to your elder brothers, my dear grandchildren," the grandmother said to Hunahpu and Xbalanque. And they told their grandmother:

"Don't be sad, our dear grandmother. You will see the faces of our elder brothers again. They'll come, but this will be a test for you, our dear grandmother. Will you please not laugh[23] while we test their destiny?" they said.

And then they began playing. They played "Hunahpu Monkey."

[And then they sang, they played, they drummed]

And then they sang, they played, they drummed. When they took up their flutes and drums, their grandmother sat down with them, then they played, they sounded out the tune, the song that got its name then. "Hunahpu Monkey" is the name of the tune.

And then One Monkey and One Artisan came back, dancing when they arrived.

And then, when the grandmother looked, it was their ugly faces the grandmother saw. Then she laughed, the grandmother could not hold back her laughter, so they just left right away, out of her sight again, they went up and away in the forest.

"Why are you doing that, our dear grandmother? We'll only try four times; only three times are left. We'll call them with the flute, with song. Please hold back your laughter. We'll try again," said Hunahpu and Xbalanque.

Next they played again, then they came back, dancing again, they arrived again, in the middle of the patio of the house. As before, what they did was delightful; as before, they tempted their grandmother to laugh. Their grandmother laughed at them soon enough. The monkeys looked truly ridiculous, with the skinny little things below their bellies[24] and their tails wiggling in front of their breasts.[25] When they came back the grandmother had to laugh at them, and they went back into the mountains.

---

23. Among the contemporary Jacaltec Maya there are myths in which the hero tricks his elder brother or his mother's brothers into going up a tree that grows taller and maroons them, after which they turn into monkeys. The hero's mother than tries to reverse this transformation but fails.

24. This is *chi xiriric xe quipam*; Andrés Xiloj read it as "round little thing," chuckling as he did so. This refers not to the "bellies" of the monkeys (*quipam*) but to what is "be-

low" or "at the bottom of" (*xe*) their bellies.

25. This is *chi chilita he pu chuchi quiꝗux*, "that wag tails and at-edge-of-their-breasts." Andrés Xiloj read *chuchi* as "up against" in this context. Spider monkeys and howler monkeys both have very long prehensile tails; howlers are seldom observed, but spider monkeys are given to winding their tails around to the front of their bodies and all the way up to their chins.

"Please, why are you doing that, our dear grandmother? Even so, we'll try it a third time now," said Hunahpu and Xbalanque.

Again they played, again they came dancing, but their grandmother held back her laughter. Then they climbed up here, cutting right across the building, with thin red lips, with faces blank, puckering their lips, wiping their mouths and faces, suddenly scratching themselves. And when the grandmother saw them again, the grandmother burst out laughing again, and again they went out of sight because of the grandmother's laughter.

"Even so, our dear grandmother, we'll get their attention."

So for the fourth time they called on the flute, but they didn't come back again. The fourth time they went straight into the forest. So they told their grandmother:

"Well, we've tried, our dear grandmother. They came at first, and we've tried calling them again. So don't be sad. We're here—we, your grandchildren. Just love our mother, dear grandmother. Our elder brothers will be remembered. So be it: they have lived here and they have been named; they are to be called One Monkey and One Artisan," said Hunahpu and Xbalanque.

So they were prayed to by the flautists and singers among the ancient people, and the writers and carvers prayed to them. In ancient times they turned into animals, they became monkeys, because they just magnified themselves, they abused their younger brothers. Just as they wished them to be slaves, so they themselves were brought low. One Monkey and One Artisan were lost then, they became animals, and this is now their place forever.

Even so, they were flautists and singers; they did great things while they lived with their grandmother and mother.

ANONYMOUS (LATE SIXTEENTH CENTURY)
Tenochtitlán (Mexico City)

The flower song presented here was originally part of a bound manuscript dating from the end of the sixteenth century that contains ninety-one songs in Nahuatl, the Aztec language, transliterated into the Latin alphabet. A friar named Francisco Ximénez found the manuscript in his parish (Chichicastenango, Guatemala) sometime between 1701 and 1703, copied it, and added a Spanish translation. The manuscript remained with the Dominican order until 1830, when it was purchased by the library of the University of San Carlos in Guatemala City. Several scholars consulted it there, copied it, published Ximénez's translation or translated it into other languages. In 1861 Etienne Brasseur de Bourbourg, a Jesuit priest interested in indigenous texts, stole the manuscript and translated it into French. In 1911 the manuscript was acquired by the Newberry Library in Chicago. Exactly what term should be used to characterize the genre of these compositions is, as in the case of other pre-Hispanic Native American expressive

Sculpture of the god Xochipilli seated on a throne decorated with flowers and jewels; his body is tattooed with flowers and he has a mask over his face. He was the god of music, dancing, and love. Mexica (Aztec) culture. From Mexico City. Postclassic: 1300–1521 A.D. Museo Nacional de Antropologia. *Mexico City.*

forms, a matter of interpretation that must consider the cultural environment of the Aztecs rather than European literary forms. To call them lyric poetry, for example, would be to overlook their ritual nature, which included the accompaniment of drumming, dancing, and often a peculiar form of "flying" or "whirling" to earth from a platform placed on top of a pole. John Bierhorst, the translator of this excerpt, departs from the traditional translation of *xochitl/cuicatl* (flower song) as "poetry."* He believes that the two Nahuatl words are versions of each other, a kind of fixed metaphor that refers to persons, particularly "ghost warriors" whom the singer summoned back from the afterworld to earth. This return, enacted in the "flying" or "whirling" down from the platform, is also understood to be the source of music. Bierhorst cites the following examples: "From heaven, ah, come good flowers, good songs"; "As a song you're born, O Montezuma: as a flower you come to bloom on earth," and "God has formed you, has given you birth as a flower. He paints you as a song"; and "My songs are marching forth." The return of these ghost warriors permits, again according to Bierhorst, the reenactment of historical battles in such a way that the singer and his comrades emerge victorious, thus adding to the prestige of the Mexicas. This Flower Song is summarized as follows in Bierhorst's "Commentary," which is a gloss on each song: Revenant muses from the enemy city-states of Huexotzinco and Tlaxcala (that had joined Cortés against the Aztecs) summon ghost warriors from the afterworld to join the battle. An unnamed singer, most likely Aztec, declares having summoned the victim revenants. He then proceeds to call Aztec warriors to battle. In a fantasized battle the Huexotzincans and Tlaxcalans are defeated and sent to paradise as payment for the newly arrived ghosts, who now establish the Aztec kingdom or Mexico as paradise on earth.†

from Cantares Mexicanos: Songs of the Aztecs

Aztec Flower song

Where are you, singer? Here, let the flower drums appear. They're twirling down
    as plumes. They're littered as golden flowers.
You'd pleasure princes, lords, eagles, jaguars.
Ah, he's descended. The singer's at the drum. He's setting them free as plumes.
    He's dispersing the songs of Life Giver. Bellbird gives him the echo, singing
    along, spreading flowers. Let's have these flowers!
And how do I hear his songs? Ah! It's Life Giver who gives him the echo. Bellbird
    gives him the echo, singing along, spreading flowers. Let's have *these flowers!*
These jades are falling as a mist of plumes. Ah! They're your songs. And this is how
    Ayocuan, *yes,* Cuetzpal, utters them. It would seem indeed that this one has
    acquaintance with Life Giver.

Translated by John Bierhorst.

*John Bierhorst, trans. and introd., Cantares Mexicanos: Songs of the Aztecs (*Stanford: Stanford University Press*, 1985) 3–122.

†This account is based on Bierhorst, p. 438.

So this is how that lord, that vaunted one, comes creating them. Yes, with plumelike bracelet beads he pleasures the Only Spirit. How *else* would Life Giver acquiesce? How *else* could there be anything good on earth?

"Let me borrow for a moment, for a while, these jades and bracelets, these princes. I flower-spin these nobles. Here! As songs of mine I whirl them, ah! beside the drum.

"For a moment I have companions here in Huexotzinco, I, King Tecayehuatzin. I'm assembling jades, emeralds, princes. I flower-spin these nobles, ah!"

From heaven, ah, come good flowers, good songs. They put away our cares, they put away our pain. Ah, it's the Chichimec lord, Tecayehuatzin! Be pleasured.

Comrades are scattering down as plumelike popcorn flowers, spinning down as white morning glories, lords, princes, moving along these branches, inhaling this plumelike cornsilk flower *tree*.

A golden bellbird! A beautiful song! You're singing a beauty. And you that are warbling are there, it would seem, on the flower-*tree* branches, where flowers are swelling.

It would seem that you're a swan for Life Giver, a singer for God, you, the first of these singers to watch for the dawn.

"Though my heart desires shield flowers, Life Giver's flowers, what might happen to this heart of mine? Alas, it's for nothing that we've come to be born here on earth.

"I'm to pass away like a ruined flower. My fame will be nothing, my renown here on earth will be nothing. There may be flowers, there may be songs, but what might happen to this heart of mine? Alas, it's for nothing that we've come to be born here on earth.

"Friends, be pleasured! Let us put our arms around each other's shoulders here. We're living in a world of flowers here. No one when he's gone can enjoy the flowers, the songs, that lie outspread in this home of Life Giver.

"Earth is but a moment. Is the Place Unknown the same? Is there happiness and friendship? Is it not just here on earth that acquaintances are made?"

I've heard a song. I hear the fluting of the garland, Lord Ayocuan.

He's answered you. From within the house of flowers Aquiahuatzin has answered you. And Commander Ayapancatl.

"Life Giver, Spirit, where are you! I seek you time and again. For you I grieve, I, the singer. I give you pleasure.

"Popcorn flowers, plumelike popcorn flowers are drizzling into this house of green places, this house of paintings. I give you much pleasure."

It seems that there in Tlaxcala they're singing as jade gongs beside the drum. And there's a narcotic that's flower-narcotic. And Lord Xicotencatl, and Tizatlacatzin, and Camaxochitzin are entertained with this music, awaited with these flowers—they that are songs of the Only Spirit.

O Life Giver, it seems your home is everywhere. The Flower Mat is here! And princes, whirled as flowers there, are making prayers to you.

That multitude of flower trees is standing up beside the drum. As baby maize ears, yes, as plumes, they're spun. They're scattered. They're holy flowers.

Bellbird is singing in the plume arbor. He echoes the lords, he delights those eagle jaguars.

Flowers are sprinkling down. Let there be dancing beside the drum, O friends. Whom do we await? Our hearts are grieving.

He's the one. It's God! Hear him! He descends from heaven, singing. Angels echo him. They come fluting.

"I grieve, I, Cuauhtencoztli. Our flower drums stand wrapped in sadness. Is it true? Let it not be so. Our songs are good no more."

But let them arise! Let them appear! We live beyond, exist beyond. You're poor, my friend. Let me take you away. Arise beyond!

"I'm singing, alas." O friends, whatever you utter sings here!

"From where the Flower Court lies comes one of the nobles. Ah, it's Coyolchiuhqui. He comes singing through tears from the house of green places. Unhappy are the flowers, unhappy the songs. Everything created here is misery."

"The pain is hard. We move along in anguish. Motenchuatzin am I, and in grieving songs I plume-spin princes, lords, rulers, and Telpoloatl, Lord Tepoloatl. We're all alive in this house of green places. Unhappy the flowers, unhappy the songs. Everything created *here* is misery."

I've heard a song. I see him in Green Places, walking in Dawn's House along the flower shore, calling to turquoise swans and green-corn birds. It's the roseate swan Lord Monencauhtzin.

O friends, who are they that dwell within God's house of green-swan cacao flowers? Keep on tilling this plume garden. Let me, let me see them laughing like jade flutes, conversing like flower log drums. And might these lords and princes strike and resonate the turquoise-brilliant drums within this house of flowers?

Hear it! He's shrilling, warbling on the branches of the flower tree. He's shaking! It's the golden flower-bell, the rattle hummingbird, the swan, Lord Monencauhtzin. Like a gorgeous troupial fan he spreads his wings and soars beside the flower drum.

They've reached the top. Flowers have reached the top. The flowers are blooming in the presence of Life Giver. And He's given you the echo. Oh, heart!

You've brought down precious birds of God. Your songs, your riches, are plentiful. You're giving pleasure. Flowers are stirring.

"A singer am I, and everywhere I walk, everywhere I speak, the plume-like popcorn flowers sprinkle down on this flower court, this house of butter-flies.

"From Flower Place come all the whirling flowers that make hearts spin. They themselves come scattering, come strewing flowers, whirled ones, narcotic flowers."

They're entered upon the Flower Mat. And he who wings abundantly, who warbles in this home of yours, this picture house, is Xayacamach. Cacao flowers intoxicate his heart.

There's a beautiful song. And the one who shrills, who lifts his song, is Tlapalteuccitzin. Great is his pleasure. His flowers are sifting down. And the flowers are cacao flowers.

O friends, I seek you, running through all these gardens. And here you are. Pass away in gladness, pass away producing *songs*. I've arrived, I, your comrade, your comrade.

Among these flowers am I introducing tzitzi-weed flowers, mozo-weed flowers? Is that the way it is? Am I simple? Am I poor? O friends!

Who am I that soar? I compose. I flower-sing, I, a butterfly of song. Let my cares be put aside. Let my heart enjoy it.

I come from Home. I've descended, I, a swan of Green Places, arriving on earth. I spread my wings beside the flower drum. My songs are lifted. They're born on earth.

It seems that I myself am cultivating songs, keeping company with those who work the soil. I, your humble comrade, am snaring my plumelike ancestors as golden garlands.

I'm on guard in the flower fields, I, your poor little friend. With gorgeous flower fronds I thatch my troopers' flower tents, rejoicing in these fields of God. Be pleasured!

Pass away rejoicing greatly, you flower jewels, for He is Lord. Will you live again? Ah, your heart knows that you live forever.

I've arrived in the branches of the flower tree, I, Flower Hummingbird, delighting in the aroma, rejoicing. Sweet, fragrant, are my words.

With flowers you are prayed to, O God, O Life Giver. We bow down, we pleasure you beside the flower drum, O Water-Palace Lord.

The drums are kept: they're kept beyond in the house of green places. Your comrades War Declarer, Arrow Snake, and Rattle Eagle are awaiting You. These lords are sighing in flowers.

"This city of Huexotzinco has been coveted: it's hated: it lies encased with spines, bristling with javelins, this Huexotzinco."

Gongs, rattles, are ringing at your home in Huexotzinco. Tecayehuatzin, Lord Quecehuatl, stands guard there, fluting, singing in his home, in Huexotzinco.

Listen! God the father is descending. Jaguar eagle drums are ringing in his home. Gong music is ringing.

It would seem to be so. Ah, these flowers are plumes—yes, a trailing cape *of plumes*. It's in a house of pictures that the realm is held *in safety*, that the Only Spirit is held *in veneration*.

Your city in the Jade Land is ascending on an arrow fire of flowers. My city of the golden pictures is your home, O Only Spirit.

Friends, hear the words of a dream: the golden milk corn sustains us in summer, the roseate-swan green corn gives us life, and it bejewels us to know that friends' hearts have been converted to the faith.

CHRISTOPHER COLUMBUS [CRISTOFORO COLOMBO]
(1451–1506)
Italy

The long-standing controversy regarding Columbus and his "discovery" of a "new" world in 1492 received renewed attention in 1992, 500 years after his historic voyage. The undeniable events are that Columbus did land, due to a navigational error, on an island in what is now the Caribbean Sea. The landing was to become a symbol of the emergence of European modernity, of unprecedented developments in knowledge, politics, economics, and society. Columbus had set out on an expedition, financed by Ferdinand and Isabella, the king and queen of Spain, to find a westward sea route for the spice trade in the Far East. Much as he tried to persuade his royal sponsors of his success, he found no spices and was to return with only a few nuggets of gold. His journal compensates for such missing riches with a treasure trove of fantastic and marvelous descriptions. Many critics have remarked that he did not actually see what he recorded, but rather recorded what he had gleaned from his extensive readings: Amazons, mermaids, men with dogs' heads and tails. It is precisely because of the awe with which Columbus and other conquistadors viewed the New World that their accounts have been considered traditionally as founding texts of Latin American literature. This is especially evident in those works that can be characterized as exponents of "marvelous realism"—that is, a world view whose rationality includes supernatural events and explanations, at least from the perspective of an archetypically modern mentality.

The excerpts presented here register Columbus's ambivalence toward the people he encounters. He expresses wonder and admiration at their appearance and dwellings, but he considers them quite gullible and incapable of defending themselves, thus making them likely candidates for servitude and enslavement. Indeed, these latter attitudes manifested themselves markedly in Columbus's efforts to wrest gold and other riches from the native peoples.

The diary of Columbus's first voyage is available only in Father Bartolomé de Las Casas's edition of extracted passages, linked together by the priest's own summaries and enunciative indicators, such as "The admiral says" or "he says." Consequently, the priest's voice sometimes seems to intervene in Columbus's own account.

from *The Journal of Christopher Columbus*

THURSDAY/FRIDAY, OCTOBER 11/12, 1492

[Columbus describes the people of the new world]

"I,"[1] he says, " in order that they might feel great amity towards us, because I knew that they were a people to be delivered and converted to our holy faith rather by love than by force, gave to some among them some red caps and some glass beads, which they hung round their necks, and many other things of little value. At this they were greatly pleased and became so entirely our friends that it was a wonder to see. Afterwards they came swimming to the ships' boats, where we were, and brought us parrots and cotton thread in balls, and spears and many other things, and we exchanged for them other things, such as small glass beads and hawks' bells, which we gave to them. In fact, they took all and gave all, such as they had, with good will, but it seemed to me that they were a people very deficient in everything. They all go naked as their mothers bore them, and the women also, although I saw only one very young girl. And all those whom I did see were youths, so that I did not see one who was over thirty years of age; they were very well built, with very handsome bodies and very good faces. Their hair is coarse almost like the hairs of a horse's tail and short; they wear their hair down over their eyebrows, except for a few strands behind, which they wear long and never cut. Some of them are painted black, and they are the colour of the people of the Canaries, neither black nor white, and some of them are painted white and some red and some in any colour that they find. Some of them paint their faces, some their whole bodies, some only the eyes, and some only the nose. They do not bear arms or know them, for I showed to them swords and they took them by the blade and cut themselves through ignorance. They have no iron. Their spears are certain reeds, without iron, and some of these have a fish tooth at the end, while others are pointed in various ways. They are all generally fairly tall, good looking and well proportioned. I saw some who bore marks of wounds on their bodies, and I made signs to them to ask how this came about, and they indicated to me that people came from other islands, which are near, and wished to capture them, and they defended themselves. And I believe and still believe that they come here from the mainland to take them for slaves. They should be good servants and of quick intelligence, since I see that they very soon say all that is said to them, and I believe that they would easily be made Christians, for it appeared to me that they had no creed. Our Lord willing, at the time of my departure I will bring back six of them to Your Highnesses, that they may learn to talk. I saw no beast of any kind in this island, except parrots."

Translated by Cecil Jane.

---

1. When the speech is inside quotation marks, Columbus is speaking. Otherwise, it is Bartolomé de Las Casas, who is linking together Columbus's words.

SATURDAY, OCTOBER 13, 1492

[Exchanges]

The men were all of a good height, very handsome people. Their hair is not curly, but loose and coarse as the hair of a horse; all have very broad foreheads and heads, more so than has any people that I have seen up to now. Their eyes are very lovely and not small. They are not at all black, but the colour of Canarians, and nothing else could be expected, since this is in one line from east to west with the island of Hierro in the Canaries. Their legs are very straight, all alike; they have no bellies but very good figures.

This island is fairly large and very flat; the trees are very green and there is much water. In the centre of it, there is a very large lake; there is no mountain, and all is so green that it is a pleasure to gaze upon it. The people also are very gentle and, since they long to possess something of ours and fear that nothing will be given to them unless they give something, when they have nothing, they take what they can and immediately throw themselves into the water and swim. But all that they do possess, they give for anything which is given to them, so that they exchange things even for pieces of broken dishes and bits of broken glass cups.

SUNDAY, OCTOBER 14, 1492

[The people of the new world greet Columbus]

And I soon saw two or three villages, and the people all came to shore, calling us and giving thanks to God. Some brought us water, others various eatables: others, when they saw that I was not inclined to land, threw themselves into the sea and came, swimming, and we understood that they asked us if we had come from heaven. One old man got into the boat, and all the rest, men and women, cried in loud voices: "Come and see the men who have come from heaven; bring them food and drink." Many came and many women, each with something, giving thanks to God, throwing themselves on the ground and raising their hands to the sky, and then shouting to us that we should land.

. . .

These people are very unskilled in arms, as Your Highnesses will see from the seven whom I caused to be taken in order to carry them off that they may learn our language and return. However, when Your Highnesses so command, they can all be carried off to Castile or held captive in the island itself, since with fifty men they would be all kept in subjection and forced to whatever may be wished.

. . .

MONDAY, OCTOBER 15, 1492

[At daybreak, I hoisted sail]

To this island I gave the name *Santa Maria de la Concepción*," and about sunset, I anchored off the said point to learn if there were gold there, because those whom I had caused to be taken in the island of San Salvador told me that there they wore very large golden bracelets on the legs and arms. I can well believe that all that they said was a ruse in order to get away. It was nevertheless my wish not to pass any island without taking possession of it, although when one had been annexed, all might be said to have been. And I anchored and was there until to-day, Tuesday, when at dawn I went ashore in the armed boats and landed. The people, who were many, were naked and of the same type as those of the other island of San Salvador; they allowed us to go through the island and gave us what we asked of them.

. . .

This island is very green and flat and very fertile, and I have no doubt that all the year they sow and reap Indian corn, and equally other things. I saw many trees very unlike ours, and many of them had many branches of different kinds, and all coming from one root; one branch is of one kind and one of another, and they are so unlike each other that it is the greatest wonder in the world. How great is the difference between one and another! For example: one branch has leaves like those of a cane and another leaves like those of a mastic tree, and thus, on a single tree, there are five or six different kinds all so diverse from each other. They are not grafted, for it might be said that it is the result of grafting; on the contrary, they are wild and these people do not cultivate them. No creed is known to them and I believe that they would be speedily converted to Christianity, for they have a very good understanding. There are here fish, so unlike ours that it is a marvel; there are some shaped like dories, of the finest colours in the world, blue, yellow, red and of all colours, and others painted in a thousand ways, and the colours are so fine that no man would not wonder at them or be anything but delighted to see them.

FRIDAY, NOVEMBER 23, 1492

[Columbus is told of cannibals]

Beyond this cape there stretched out another land or cape, which also trended to the east, which those Indians whom he had with him called "Bohio." They said that this land was very extensive and that in it were people who had one eye in the forehead, and others whom they called "Canibals." Of these last, they showed great fear, and when they saw that this course was being taken, they were speechless, he says, because those people ate them and because they are very warlike.

TUESDAY, DECEMBER 11, 1492

[Understanding and misunderstanding]

"The Caniba are nothing else than the people of the Grand Khan, who must be very near here and possess ships, and they must come to take them captive, and as the prisoners do not return, they believe that they have been eaten. Every day we understand these Indians better and they us, although many times there has been misunderstanding."

BARTOLOMÉ DE LAS CASAS

(1474–1566)

Spain

Born in Seville, Bartolomé de Las Casas was the son of a military officer that accompanied Columbus on his first voyage to the "Indies." He was educated in the humanist tradition of the period at the University of Salamanca, graduating as a *licenciado* (equivalent to a master's degree) and eventually going on to complete his studies for the priesthood. In 1502 he accompanied the conquistador Nicolás de Ovando (1460–1518) who sailed to Santo Domingo (Hispaniola) to take over the governorship (1502–1509). After taking his vows as a Dominican priest in 1510, he moved to Cuba, where he gave a sermon critical of Spanish colonizers and in defense of the Indians. At age seventy he was named Bishop of Chiapas; he died in his nineties while on a trip to Spain.

Las Casas is a major historian, although a polemical and activist one. Since he was engaged in day-to-day administrative, legal, and Church matters—as a high Church official he was a major arbiter in the conduct of Church and State law, writing legal tracts and engaging in legal arguments—he did not have the time to write history as a scholar. Consequently, his major historical work, *The History of the Indies* took many years to complete, from 1527 to 1564. Las Casas made several trips to the Spanish court of the Emperor Charles V. There he debated with noted scholars such as Juan Ginés de Sepúlveda, a philosopher and translator of Aristotle's *Politics* into Latin, who in "The Just Causes of War Against the Indians" (1548) invoked the authority of classical antiquity, especially Aristotle and Aquinas, "on behalf of his concept of natural slavery."

Las Casas argued that the Indians were as rational as Christians and certainly more faithful to their religion, for they were willing to sacrifice life, the most precious gift to humankind, to serve their gods. "The nations who offered human sacrifices to their gods thereby showed, as deluded idolators, the high idea they had of the excellence of divinity, of the value of their gods, and how noble and high was their veneration of divinity. They consequently demonstrated that they possessed, better than other nations, natural reflection, rectitude of speech, and the judgment of reason; they employed their understanding better than the others. And in religious feeling they exceeded all the other nations, for the latter are the most religious nations in the world who, for the good of their peoples, offer their own children as sacrifices."* Las Casas was victorious against Sepúlveda, and laws protecting the Indians from enslavement were enacted. These laws, of course, were worth about as much as the paper they were printed on, as abuses against the Indians continued throughout the colonial period.

What makes Las Casas so remarkable to the modern reader is the extent to which he fought for the rights of the oppressed. Las Casas was the only defender of the Indians who tried to see things from their side. Others, like Francisco de Vitoria, theologian, jurist and professor at the University of Salamanca, although arguing against contemporary justifications of the wars waged in America against the Indians, nevertheless conceived of circumstances in which "just wars" are possible, such as when innocents seek protection against tyranny, thus leaving a loophole for those who argued that the Indians' cannibalism required action to protect the sacrificed victims. If at first he condoned the enslavement of Africans in order to save the "weaker" indigenous Native American peoples from painful toil, he eventually came to reject all forms of imposed labor. If at first he argued on behalf of Indian freedom together with a peaceful evangelization, he ultimately came to reject all forms of religious imposition.

from The History of the Indies

[The Horrors of the Conquest: The Conquest of Cuba]

At this time, when it was known in the island of Jamaica that Diego Velázquez had gone to settle and pacify . . . the island of Cuba, Juan de Esquivel, the deputy in Jamaica, agreed to send one Pánfilo de Narváez, a native of Valladolid . . . with thirty Spaniards, to aid Diego Velázquez—or else they bestirred themselves and asked permission to go there. All were archers, with their bows and arrows, in the use of which they were more practiced than the Indians.

This Pánfilo de Narváez was a man with an air of authority, tall of stature, and rather fair-haired, tending toward red. He was honorable and wise, but not very prudent; good company, with good habits, valiant in fighting against the Indians and would perhaps have been valiant against other peoples—but above all he had this defect, that he was very careless. . . .

With his band of bowmen he was well received by Diego Velázquez. . . . Velázquez promptly gave them shares of Indians, as if these were heads of cattle, so that the Indians would serve them, although they had brought some Jamaican Indians to do that wherever they went. Diego Velázquez made this Narváez his chief captain and always honored him in such a way that, after Velázquez, Narváez held first place in that island.

A few days later I went there, the said Diego Velázquez having sent for me because of our past friendship in this island of Hispaniola. We went together,

Translated by George Sanderlin.

*Bartolomé de Las Casas Apológtica Historia Summaria, vol. 2 (Mexico City: Universidad Nacional Autónoma de México, 1967) 183.

Narváez and I, for about two years, and secured the rest of that island, to the detriment of all of it, as will be seen.

[Las Casas tells how Velázquez terrorized the natives of eastern Cuba, near Cape Maisi, executed the chieftain Hatuey, and went on to Baracoa. Narváez landed at the Gulf of Guacayanabo, on the south coast near Maisi, and, on orders from Velázquez, invaded the province of Camagüey, in central Cuba.]

The Spaniards entered the province of Camagüey, which is large and densely populated . . . and when they reached the villages, the inhabitants had prepared as well as they could cassava bread from their food; what they called *guaminiqui-najes* from their hunting; and also fish, if they had caught any.

Immediately upon arriving at a village, the cleric Casas would have all the little children band together; taking two or three Spaniards to help him, along with some sagacious Indians of this island of Hispaniola, whom he had brought with him, and a certain servant of his, he would baptize the children he found in the village. He did this throughout the island . . . and there were many for whom God provided holy baptism because He had predestined them to glory. God provided it at a fitting time, for none or almost none of those children remained alive after a few months. . . .

When the Spaniards arrived at a village and found the Indians at peace in their houses, they did not fail to injure and scandalize them. Not content with what the Indians freely gave, they took their wretched subsistence from them, and some, going further, chased after their wives and daughters, for this is and always has been the Spaniards' common custom in these Indies. Because of this and at the urging of the said father, Captain Narváez ordered that after the father had separated all the inhabitants of the village in half the houses, leaving the other half empty for the Spaniards' lodging, no one should dare go to the Indians' section. For this purpose, the father would go ahead with three or four men and reach a village early; by the time the Spaniards came, he had already gathered the Indians in one part and cleared the other.

Thus, because the Indians saw that the father did things for them, defending and comforting them, and also baptizing their children, in which affairs he seemed to have more command and authority than others, he received much respect and credit throughout the island among the Indians. Further, they honored him as they did their priests, magicians, prophets, or physicians, who were all one and the same.

Because of this . . . it became unnecessary to go ahead of the Spaniards. He had only to send an Indian with an old piece of paper on a stick, informing them through the messenger that those letters said thus and so. That is, that they should all be calm, that no one should absent himself because he would do them no harm, that they should have food prepared for the Christians and their children ready for baptism, or that they should gather in one part of the village, and anything else that it seemed good to counsel them—and that if they did not carry these things out, the father would be angry, which was the greatest threat that could be sent them.

They performed everything with a very good will, to the best of their ability.

And great was the reverence and fear which they had for the letters, for they saw that through these what was being done in other, distant regions was known. It seemed more than a miracle to them. . . .

The Spaniards thus passed through certain villages of that province on the road they were taking. And because the folk of the villages . . . were eager to see such a new people and especially to see the three or four mares being taken there, at which the whole land was frightened—news of them flew through the island—many came to look at them in a large town called Caonao, the penultimate syllable long. And the Spaniards, on the morning of the day they arrived at the town, stopped to breakfast in a riverbed that was dry but for a few small pools. This riverbed was full of whetstones, and all longed to sharpen their swords on them and did. When they had finished their breakfast, they continued on the road to Caonao.

Along the road for two or three leagues there was an arid plain, where one found oneself thirsty after any work; and there certain Indians from the villages brought them some gourds of water and some things to eat.

They arrived at the town of Caonao in the evening. Here they found many people, who had prepared a great deal of food consisting of cassava bread and fish, because they had a large river close by and also were near the sea. In a little square were 2,000 Indians, all squatting because they have this custom, all staring, frightened, at the mares. Nearby was a large *bohio,* or large house, in which were more than 500 other Indians, close-packed and fearful, who did not dare come out.

When some of the domestic Indians the Spaniards were taking with them as servants (who were more than 1,000 souls . . .) wished to enter the large house, the Cuban Indians had chickens ready and said to them: "Take these—do not enter here." For they already knew that the Indians who served the Spaniards were not apt to perform any other deeds than those of their masters.

There was a custom among the Spaniards that one person, appointed by the captain, should be in charge of distributing to each Spaniard the food and other things the Indians gave. And while the captain was thus on his mare and the others mounted on theirs, and the father himself was observing how the bread and fish were distributed, a Spaniard, in whom the devil is thought to have clothed himself, suddenly drew his sword. Then the whole hundred drew theirs and began to rip open the bellies, to cut and kill those lambs—men, women, children, and old folk, all of whom were seated, off guard and frightened, watching the mares and the Spaniards. And within two credos, not a man of all of them there remains alive.

The Spaniards enter the large house nearby, for this was happening at its door, and in the same way, with cuts and stabs, began to kill as many as they found there, so that a stream of blood was running, as if a great number of cows had perished. Some of the Indians who could make haste climbed up the poles and woodwork of the house to the top, and thus escaped.

The cleric had withdrawn shortly before this massacre to where another small square of the town was formed, near where they had lodged him. This was in a large house where all the Spaniards also had to stay, and here about forty of the Indians who had carried the Spaniards' baggage from the provinces farther back were stretched out on the ground, resting. And five Spaniards chanced to be with the cleric. When these heard the blows of the swords and knew that the Spaniards were killing the Indians—without seeing anything, because there were certain houses between—they put hands to their swords and are about to kill the forty Indians . . . to pay them their commission.

The cleric, moved to wrath, opposes and rebukes them harshly to prevent them, and having some respect for him, they stopped what they were going to do, so the forty were left alive. The five go to kill where the others were killing. And as the cleric had been detained in hindering the slaying of the forty carriers, when he went he found a heap of dead, which the Spaniards had made among the Indians, which was certainly a horrible sight.

When Narváez, the captain, saw him he said: "How does Your Honor like what these our Spaniards have done?"

Seeing so many cut to pieces before him, and very upset at such a cruel event, the cleric replied: "That I commend you and them to the devil!"

The heedless Narváez remained, still watching the slaughter as it took place, without speaking, acting, or moving any more than if he had been marble. For if he had wished, being on the horseback and with a lance in his hands, he could have prevented the Spaniards from killing even ten persons.

Then the cleric leaves him, and goes elsewhere through some groves seeking Spaniards to stop them from killing. For they were passing through the groves looking for someone to kill, sparing neither boy, child, woman, nor old person. And they did more, in that certain Spaniards went to the road to the river, which was nearby. Then all the Indians who had escaped with wounds, stabs, and cuts—all who could flee to throw themselves into the river to save themselves—met with Spaniards who finished them.

Another outrage occurred which should not be left untold, so that the deeds of our Christians in these regions may be observed. When the cleric entered the large house where I said there were about 500 souls—or whatever the number, which was great—and saw with horror the dead there and those who had escaped above by the poles or woodwork, he said to them:

"No more, no more. Do not be afraid. There will be no more, there will be no more."

With this assurance, believing that it would be thus, an Indian descended, a well-disposed young man of twenty-five or thirty years, weeping. And as the cleric did not rest but went everywhere to stop the killing, the cleric then left the house. And just as the young man came down, a Spaniard who was there drew a cutlass or half sword and gives him a cut through the loins, so that his intestines fall out. . . .

The Indian, moaning, takes his intestines in his hands and comes fleeing out of the house. He encounters the cleric . . . and the cleric tells him some things about the faith, as much as the time and anguish permitted, explaining to him that if he wished to be baptized he would go to heaven to live with God. The sad one, weeping and showing pain as if he were burning in flames, said yes, and with this the cleric baptized him. He then fell dead on the ground. . . .

Of all that has been said, I am a witness. I was present and saw it, and I omit many other particulars in order to shorten the account.

FELIPE GUAMÁN POMA DE AYALA (1526–1613)
Peru

Felipe Guamán Poma de Ayala was a Christianized Indian of noble, Incan lineage. His *New Chronicle and Good Government,* addressed to the Spanish king in order to redress certain colonialist inequities, and thus also known as *Letter to a King,* offers an interesting perspective on the interaction of identity, valuation, and knowledge. In the first place, as an Indian, he claims to have privileged knowledge that enables him to write a truer history of his native Peru than that contained in previous chronicles. This knowledge is also used as a pretext for criticizing the colonial administration and for making a case for his own worth. Guamán, semieducated in the cultural forms of the Spaniards, opted for the chronicle, a genre of medieval origin analogous to "mythistory," whose starting point is always the beginning of the world, making its way through dynasties and generations, and finally reaching the present. The underlying purpose of his *Nueva Crónica* (New Chronicle) was the denunciation of Spanish injustices and the proposal of a *Buen Gobierno* or Good Government: "[I]t is not the Spanish administrators and employers who are the rightful owners of Peru. According to the laws of both God and man, we Indians are the proprietors." Guamán also subverts the apparent conformity to colonial rule by a deft masking of Andean ideas in European expressive forms. Most important in his critique of the Spaniards is his use of pictures, which unlike European illustrations do not follow the meaning of the text but, rather, precede it and guide it. Like all syncretic expression, these pictures accommodate a double reading. On one level of interpretation narrative events are represented; on another level this narrative representation is subverted by a subliminal message. The mapping of values in Andean space follows a different hierarchy than that of European space. While the center is the position of preferred value, as in European topology, the left always, signifies greater importance than the right. By placing Indian figures on the left and Spaniards on the right, Guamán thus inverts their status and by implication the hierarchy of colonialism.

from *Letter to a King*

The First Part of this Chronicle: The Indians of Peru

AUTHOR'S FAMILY

My history begins with the exemplary life which was led by my father Huaman Mallqui and my mother Curi Ocllo Coya, daughter of Tupec Inca Yupanqui, the Peruvian ruler.

My father interested himself in the education of his adopted son Martín de Ayala, a half-caste of mixed Spanish and Indian blood. He caused this boy to enter the service of God and take the habit of a Christian friar when only 12 years old. This was a happy chance for myself. For my half-brother Martín, once he had grown into a man, gave instruction to his brothers including myself. Thus I came to be able to write my "First New Chronicle," having been taught my letters at an early age.

As one of the principal Indians of Peru, my father had duly presented himself to the envoy of the Emperor Charles V, Don Francisco Pizarro, and other Spaniards in order to kiss their hands and offer peace and friendship to the Emperor. He was received by them at the port of Tumbes before their march to Caxamarca. My father was on the side of Inca Huascar, the legitimate ruler, whom he served as Viceroy. After his reception by the Christians he returned to his province.

My father served in an important capacity during all the wars, battles and revolts against the Spanish Crown. In one of these wars he was in the service of a loyal Captain named Luis de Avalos de Ayala, the father of the half-caste Martín about whom I have written, and they both took part in the bloody battle of Huarina. The Captain was umhorsed by a lance-thrust while fighting against the partisans of Gonzalo Pizarro. He was defended and saved from certain death by my father, who knocked down and killed Martín de Olmos, one of the rebel side. The Captain, on rising from the ground, acknowledged his debt and declared that my father, even though an Indian, deserved a grant of land from the Crown. Thus my father, having gained some honour from this service, thenceforward took the name of Ayala and adopted the style of Don Martín de Ayala.[1]

Translated by Christopher Dilke.

---

1. This story, in the precise form in which it is told, appears improbable or indeed impossible. Ayala arrived in Spain a year after the battle of Huarina in 1547. In other battles he fought on the same side as Martín de Olmos, who survived to be mayor of Cuzco in 1573.

The Second Part of this Chronicle: The Conquest

The first inhabitant of the Old World to discover our country was St. Bartholo-mew, who arrived from Jerusalem during the reign of the Inca Sinchi Roca.

It was much later that the way across the sea was opened up. Alexander VI, a Spaniard, was Pope and Maximilian I was the Holy Roman Emperor. Queen Joan was on the throne of Spain.[2] Already it was known that another ocean existed to the west of the Indies.

Our countries were properly discovered by two men: one of Columbus' companions and Pedro de Candia. When the former died he left his papers to his friend. Candia returned to Castile and reported that he had been ashore at Santa.

The way it happened was that the Inca Huayna Capac, who was in Cuzco, was told that some men with long beards and the appearance of corpses had landed in his Empire. He immediately gave the order that one of them—who turned out to be Candia—was to be brought by his messengers as freight to Cuzco, so that he could see him with his own eyes. In this way the two of them, the Inca and the Spaniard, got to know one another.

They communicated by signs. When Candia was asked what he ate, he replied that he lived on silver and gold. The Inca thereupon gave him some silver and gold-dust and a quantity of gold plate and had him returned by the messengers to Santa, where he found his companion lying dead. Candia trav-elled back to Spain alone, taking with him the precious gifts which he had obtained.[3]

He spread the news of the wealth to be found in Peru and reported that our people were dressed and shod in gold and silver, wore ornaments of these metals on their heads and hands and even walked on gold and silver floors. This was true to the extent that our Indians decorated themselves for their feasts and entertain-ments with bracelets, diadems and brooches made of the precious metals. And Candia added that a small kind of camel was to be found in our country, meaning the llama.

The greed for gold which was awakened by Candia's story caused a number of Spaniards to enlist themselves for the Conquest of our country. They were assisted by a Peruvian Indian who had been brought back to Spain as a captive and who was given the name of Felipe or Felipillo. This Indian learnt the Castilian tongue in order to be able to act as interpreter. The Spaniards could hardly wait for their arrival in Peru, so anxious were they to lay their hands on our treasures.

. . .

In 1532, when Charles V was King of Spain and also Holy Roman Emperor, Pizarro and Almagro, acting in their capacity as his ambassadors, received an envoy from the legitimate ruler Capac Apo Inca Tupac Cucihualpa Huascar, who came with a message of peace to greet them at the port of Tumbes. This envoy was my father Huaman Mallqui, who carried credentials from the capital city of Cuzco.

. . .

---

2. Ferdinand and Isabella were the Sovereigns in 1492.

3. Candia met, not the Inca, but an Incan nobleman at Tumbes.

The second ambassador to be received by the Spaniards was Rumiñavi, the commanding general of Atahuallpa. He presented himself with great ceremony before Pizarro and Almagro and requested them to remove their troops from the country. In exchange for their departure he offered them a large amount of gold and silver. The Spaniards refused the request, saying that they wished to meet and kiss hands with the Inca in their capacity as ambassadors of their King-Emperor and that they could not leave the country until they had done so.

The presents which Atahuallpa sent to Pizarro and Almagro and the factor Illán consisted of male servants and sacred virgins. Some of the virgins were also offered to the Spaniards' horses because, seeing them eating maize, the Peruvians took them for a kind of human being. Until that time, horses were unknown to our people and it seemed advisable to treat them with respect.

· · ·

To our Indian eyes, the Spaniards looked as if they were shrouded like corpses. Their faces were covered with wool, leaving only the eyes visible, and the caps which they wore resembled little red pots on top of their heads. Sometimes they also decorated their heads with plumes. Their swords appeared very long, since they had to be carried with the points turned in a backward direction. They were all dressed alike and talked together like brothers and ate at the same table. Only one of them seemed to have powers of command and he had a dark face, white teeth and flashing eyes. He often shouted at the others and they obeyed his orders.

· · ·

Franciso Pizarro, speaking for himself and Almagro, explained through the Indian interpreter Felipe that he was the messenger and ambassador of a great ruler who desired friendship with the Inca and that this was the only object of his mission to Peru. Atahuallpa listened with close attention to the words spoken by Pizarro and then by the interpreter. He answered with great dignity that he had no reason to doubt the fact of the Spaniards' long journey or their mission from an important ruler. However, he had no need to make any pact of friendship with them because he too was a great ruler in his own country.

After this reply Friar Vicente joined in the conversation. He came forward holding a crucifix in his right hand and a breviary in his left and introduced himself as another envoy of the Spanish ruler, who according to his account was a friend of God, and who often worshipped before the cross and believed in the Gospel. Friar Vicente called upon the Inca to renounce all other gods as being a mockery of the truth.

Atahuallpa's reply was that he could not change his belief in the Sun, who was immortal, and in the other Inca divinities. He asked Friar Vicente what authority he had for his own belief and the friar told him it was all written in the book which he held. The Inca then said: "Give me the book so that it can speak to me." The book was handed up to him and he began to eye it carefully and listen to it page by page. At last he asked: "Why doesn't the book say anything to me?" Still sitting on his throne, he threw it on to the ground with a haughty and petulant gesture.

Friar Vicente found his voice and called out that the Indians were against the Christian faith. Thereupon Pizarro and Almagro began to shout orders to their men, telling them to attack these Indians who rejected God and the Emperor. The

Spaniards began to fire their muskets and charged upon the Indians, killing them like ants.

It was 32 years since the outbreak of civil war between the two Inca brothers Huascar and Atahuallpa. During that period of time Franciso Pizarro, Diego de Almagro the elder and the younger, Gonzalo Pizarro, Carbajal and Hernández Girón had committed treason to the Crown and instigated disorder and unrest. They had all of them been driven by the ambition of poor men to make a fortune and become great lords in our country.

GARCILASO DE LA VEGA (EL INCA) (1539–1616)
Peru

Garcilaso de la Vega was part Native American, part European, of royal lineage on both sides. His father, Captain Sebastián de la Vega Vargas, opted to marry not Garcilaso's mother, the Incan princess Ñusta Champu Ocllo, whom he met in Peru, but a Spanish noble woman of his own status, Doña Luisa de los Ríos, who eventually became his sole heir when he died in 1560. Garcilaso continued to live with his father, the *Corregidor*, serving as his amanuensis. When Don Sebastián died, he left a sum of money for Garcilaso, now twenty-one, to go to Spain and continue his education. The young Garcilaso went to seek redress in the Spanish courts, but it was to no avail. He never returned to Peru, and remained in Spain, settling with relatives in Montilla, Andalusia. His brief absences, included taking part in the War of the Alpujarras (1570), in which he received the title of captain. Garcilaso eventually joined a religious order in Cordova after his relative, the marquis of Priego, died. Garcilaso had received an annuity from the marquis but when a cousin inherited the title, he was left without means. Losing all hope of inheritance, he turned to literature, particularly the Greeks and Italians: Plutarch, Boccaccio, and Ariosto. He seemed to be modeling himself after his illustrious forebear and namesake, Garcilaso de la Vega, the poet, who had ushered the Renaissance into Spain half a century earlier. In 1590 he published a translation of Leon Hebreo's *Dialoghi di amore (Dialogues on Love)*, a very influential neoplatonic treatise of the time. In Cordova he wrote *La Florida* (1605), an account of Hernando de Soto's explorations of Florida and his masterpiece, *The Royal Commentaries*, a two-volume work published between 1609 and 1617.* Unlike Guamán, Garcilaso chose to work the lofty genre of history, which, however, he mixed with autobiographical passages and the oral lore of native informants. Motivated by the desire to exalt the history of the Incas and to cast them as the first and greatest civilization of Peru, he disturbed the Spanish readers of his time and was subsequently criticized by professional historians for injecting heavy doses of myth. However, Garcilaso shrewdly justified his approach by pointing out that Greek and Roman histories also made use of legendary material. He also criticized the lapses and errors of Spanish historians like

"El Castillo," Chichén Itzá.

Francisco López de Gómara, Hernán Cortés's chaplain and biographer and author of an early and highly influential *General History of the Indies* (1552). Either for lack of direct information or ignorance of Quechua, the Incan language, Spanish historians misconstrued and mistranslated the history of the Incas.

from *Royal Commentaries of the Incas and General History of Peru*

Preface to the Reader

Though there have been learned Spaniards who have written accounts of the states of the New World, such as those of Mexico and Peru and the other kingdoms of the heathens, they have not described these realms so fully as they might have done. This I have remarked particularly in what I have seen written about Peru, concerning which, as a native of the city of Cuzco, which was formerly the Rome of that empire, I have fuller and more accurate information than that provided by

Translated by Harold V. Livermore.

*The title that Garcilaso gave his book is *Royal Commentaries,* which was published in 1609; *Of the Incas* has been added in English editions. *General History of Peru* is the title given by the Royal Council to Part Two, which appeared seven months after Garcilaso's death, as a way of disavowing connections with its implicit critiques of the Spaniards.

previous writers. It is true that these have dealt with many of the very remarkable achievements of that empire, but they have set them down so briefly that, owing to the manner in which they are told, I am scarcely able to understand even such matters as are well known to me. For this reason, impelled by my natural love for my native country, I have undertaken the task of writing these *Commentaries,* in which everything in the Peruvian empire before the arrival of the Spaniards is clearly and distinctly set down, from the rites of their vain religion to the government of their kings in time of peace and war, and all else that can be told of these Indians, from the highest affairs of the royal crown to the humblest duties of its vassals. I write only of the empire of the Incas, and do not deal with other monarchies, about which I can claim no similar knowledge. In the course of my history I shall affirm its truthfulness and shall set down no important circumstances without quoting the authority of Spanish historians who may have touched upon it in part or as a whole. For my purpose is not to gainsay them, but to furnish a commentary and gloss, and to interpret many Indian expressions which they, as strangers to that tongue, have rendered inappropriately. This will be fully seen in the course of my history, which I commend to the piety of those who may peruse it, with no other interest than to be of service to Christendom.

The Idolatry of the Indians and the Gods They Worshipped Before the Incas

For the better understanding of the idolatry, way of life, and customs of the Indians of Peru, it will be necessary for us to divide those times into two periods. First we shall say how they lived before the Incas, and then how the Inca kings governed, so as not to confuse the one thing with the other, and so that the customs and gods of one period are not attributed to the other. It must therefore be realized that in the first age of primitive heathendom there were Indians who were little better than tame beasts and others much worse than wild beasts. To begin with their gods, we may say that they were of a piece with the simplicity and stupidity of the times, as regards the multiplicity of gods and the vileness and crudity of the things the people worshipped. Each province, each tribe, each village, each quarter, each clan, each house had gods different from the rest, for they considered that other people's gods, being busy with other people's affairs, could not help them, but they must have their own. Thus they came to have so great a variety of gods, which were too numerous to count. They did not understand, as the gentile Romans did, how to create abstract gods such as Hope, Victory, Peace, and so on, for their thoughts did not rise to invisible things, and they worshipped what they saw, some in one way and others in another. They did not consider whether the things they worshipped were worthy of their worship and they had no self-respect, in the sense of refraining from worshipping things inferior to themselves. They only thought of distinguishing themselves from one another, and each from all the rest. Thus they worshipped grasses, plants, flowers, trees of all kinds, high hills, great rocks and nooks in them, deep caves, pebbles, and little pieces of stone of various colors found in rivers and streams, such as jasper. They worshipped the emerald, especially in the province now called Puerto

Viejo. They did not worship diamonds or rubies because these stones did not exist there. Instead they worshipped various animals, some for their ferocity, such as the tiger, lion, and bear: and consequently, regarding them as gods, if they chanced to meet them, they did not flee but fell down and worshipped them and let themselves be killed and eaten without escaping or making any defence at all. They also worshipped other animals for their cunning, such as the fox and monkeys. They worshipped the dog for its faithfulness and nobility, the wild cat for its quickness, and the bird they call *cuntur* for its size; and some natives worshipped eagles, because they boast of descending from them and also from the *cuntur*. Other peoples adored hawks for their quickness and ability in winning their food. They adored the owl for the beauty of its eyes and head; the bat for the keenness of its sight—it caused them much wonder that it could see at night. They also adored many other birds according to their whims. They adored great snakes for their monstrous size and fierceness (some of those in the Antis are about twenty-five or thirty feet long and as thick round as a man's thigh). They also considered other smaller snakes—where there were none so big as in the Antis—to be gods, and they adored lizards, toads, and frogs. In a word, there was no beast too vile and filthy for them to worship as a god, merely in order to differ from one another in their choice of gods, without adoring any real god or being able to expect any benefit from them. They were very simple in everything, like sheep without a shepherd. But we need not be surprised that such unlettered and untaught people should have fallen into these follies, for it is well known that the Greeks and Romans, who prided themselves so greatly on their learning, had thirty thousand gods when their empire was at its height.

The Great Variety of Other Gods They Had

There were many other Indians of various nations in this first period who chose their gods with rather more discrimination than these. They worshipped certain objects that were beneficial, such as streaming fountains and great rivers, which they argued gave them water to irrigate their crops.

Others adored the earth and called it "mother," because it gave them its fruits. Others the air they breathed, saying that men lived by it; others fire, because it warmed them and they cooked their food with it. Others worshipped a ram, because of the great flocks reared in their region; others the great chain of the Sierra Nevada, because of its height and wonderful grandeur and because many rivers used for irrigation flow from it; others maize or *sara*, as they call it, because it was their usual bread; others other cereals or legumes, according to what grew most abundantly in their provinces.

The coastal Indians, in addition to an infinity of other gods they had, even including those already mentioned, generally worshipped the sea, which they called *Mamacocha*, or "Mother Sea," implying that it was like a mother to them in sustaining them with its fish. They also worshipped the whale on account of its monstrous greatness. Besides these cults, which were common to the whole coast, various provinces and regions worshipped the fish most commonly caught there, holding that the first fish that was in the upper world (their word for heaven) was the origin of all other fish of the kind they ate and that it took care to send them plenty of its children to sustain their tribe. Thus in some provinces they worshipped the sardine, which they killed in greater quantity than any other fish, in others the skate, in others the dogfish, in others the goldfish for its beauty, in others the crab and other shellfish for lack of anything better in their waters or because they could not catch or kill anything else. In short, they worshipped and considered gods any fish that was more beneficial to them than the rest. So they had for gods not only the four elements, each separately, but also the compounds and forms of them, however vile and squalid. Other tribes, such as the Chirihuanas and the people of Cape Passau (that is, the southernmost and northernmost provinces of Peru) felt no inclination to worship anything, high or low, either from interest or fear, but lived and still live exactly like beasts, because the doctrine and teaching of the Inca kings did not reach them.

The Origin of the Inca Kings of Peru

While these peoples were living or dying in the manner we have seen, it pleased our Lord God that from their midst there should appear a morning star to give them in the dense darkness in which they dwelt some glimmerings of natural law, of civilization, and of the respect men owe to one another. The descendants of this leader should thus tame those savages and convert them into men, made capable of reason and of receiving good doctrine, so that when God, who is the sun of justice, saw fit to send forth the light of His divine rays upon those idolaters, it might find them no longer in their first savagery, but rendered more docile to receive the Catholic faith and the teaching and doctrine of our Holy Mother the Roman Church, as indeed they have received it—all of which will be seen in the course of this history. It has been observed by clear experience how much prompter and quicker to receive the Gospel were the Indians subdued, governed, and taught by the Inca kings than the other neighboring peoples unreached by the Incas' teachings, many of which are still today as savage and brutish as before, despite the fact that the Spaniards have been in Peru seventy years. And since we stand on the threshold of this great maze, we had better enter and say what lay within.

After having prepared many schemes and taken many ways to begin to give an account of the origin and establishment of the native Inca kings of Peru, it seemed to me that the best scheme and simplest and easiest way was to recount what I often heard as a child from the lips of my mother and her brothers and uncles and other elders about these beginnings. For everything said about them from other sources comes down to the same story as we shall relate, and it will be better to have it as told in the very words of the Incas than in those of foreign authors. My mother dwelt in Cuzco, her native place, and was visited there every week by the few relatives, both male and female, who escaped the cruelty and tyranny of Atahuallpa (which we shall describe in our account of his life). On these visits the ordinary subject of conversation was always the origin of the Inca kings, their greatness, the grandeur of their empire, their deeds and conquests, their government in peace and war, and the laws they ordained so greatly to the advantage of their vassals. In short, there was nothing concerning the most flourishing period of their history that they did not bring up in their conversations.

From the greatness and prosperity of the past they turned to the present, mourning their dead kings, their lost empire, and their fallen state, etc. These and similar topics were broached by the Incas and Pallas on their visits, and on recalling their departed happiness, they always ended these conversations with tears and mourning, saying: "Our rule is turned to bondage" etc. During these talks, I, as a boy, often came in and went out of the place where they were, and I loved to hear them, as boys always do like to hear stories. Days, months, and years went by, until I was sixteen or seventeen. Then it happened that one day when my family was talking in this fashion about their kings and the olden times, I remarked to the senior of them, who usually related these things: "Inca, my uncle, though you have no writings to preserve the memory of past events, what information have you of the origin and beginnings of our kings? For the Spaniards and the other peoples who live on their borders have divine and human histories from which they know when their own kings and their neighbors' kings began to reign and when one empire gave way to another. They even know how many thousand years it is since God created heaven and earth. All this and much more they know through their books. But you, who have no books, what memory have you preserved of your antiquity? Who was the first of our Incas? What was he called? What was the origin of his line? How did he begin to reign? With what men and arms did he conquer this great empire? How did our heroic deeds begin?"

The Inca was delighted to hear these questions, since it gave him great pleasure to reply to them, and turned to me (who had already often heard him tell the tale, but had never paid as much attention as then) saying:

"Nephew, I will tell you these things with pleasure: indeed it is right that you should hear them and keep them in your heart (this is their phrase for 'in the memory'). You should know that in olden times the whole of this region before you was covered with brush and heath, and people lived in those times like wild beasts, with no religion or government and no towns or houses, and without tilling or sowing the soil, or clothing or covering their flesh, for they did not know how to weave cotton or wool to make clothes. They lived in twos and threes as chance brought them together in caves and crannies in rocks and underground caverns. Like wild beasts they ate the herbs of the field and roots of trees and fruits growing wild and also human flesh. They covered their bodies with leaves and the bark of trees and animals' skins. Others went naked. In short, they lived like deer or other game, and even in their intercourse with women they behaved like beasts, for they knew nothing of having separate wives."

I must remark, in order to avoid many repetitions of the words "our father the Sun," that the phrase was used by the Incas to express respect whenever they mentioned the sun, for they boasted of descending from it, and none but Incas were allowed to utter the words: it would have been blasphemy and the speaker would have been stoned. The Inca said:

"Our father the Sun, seeing men in the state I have mentioned, took pity and was sorry for them, and sent from heaven to earth a son and a daughter of his to indoctrinate them in the knowledge of our father the Sun that they might worship him and adopt him as their god, and to give them precepts and laws by which they would live as reasonable and civilized men, and dwell in houses and settled towns, and learn to till the soil, and grow plants and crops, and breed flocks, and use the fruits of the earth like rational beings and not like beasts. With this order and mandate our father the Sun set these two children of his in Lake Titicaca, eighty leagues from here, and bade them go where they would, and wherever they stopped to eat or sleep to try to thrust into the ground a golden wand half a yard long and two fingers in thickness which he gave them as a sign and token: when this wand should sink into the ground at a single thrust, there our father the Sun wished them to stop and set up their court.

"Finally he told them: 'When you have reduced these people to our service, you shall maintain them in reason and justice, showing mercy, clemency, and mildness, and always treating them as a merciful father treats his beloved and tender children. Imitate my example in this. I do good to all the world. I give them my light and brightness that they may see and go about their business; I warm them when they are cold; and I grow their pastures and crops, and bring fruit to their trees, and multiply their flocks. I bring rain and calm weather in turn, and I take care to go round the world once a day to observe the wants that exist in the world and to fill and supply them as the sustainer and benefactor of men. I wish you as children of mine to follow this example sent down to earth to teach and benefit those men who live like beasts. And henceforward I establish and nominate you as kings and lords over all the people you may thus instruct with your reason, government, and good works.'

"When our father the Sun had thus made manifest his will to his two children he bade them farewell. They left Titicaca and travelled northwards, and wherever they stopped on the way they thrust the golden wand into the earth, but it never sank in. Thus they reached a small inn or resthouse seven or eight leagues south of this city. Today it is called Pacárec Tampu, 'inn or resthouse of the dawn.' The Inca gave it this name because he set out from it about daybreak. It is one of the towns the prince later ordered to be founded, and its inhabitants to this day boast greatly of its name because our first Inca bestowed it. From this place he and his wife, our queen, reached the valley of Cuzco which was then a wilderness."

THE NAVAJO PEOPLE
Southwestern United States

People the world over have stories of how the world began, and these stories serve—as Genesis does for the Judeo-Christian tradition—to provide a general world view for the culture in question. The Navajo creation story is not, as Genesis is not, made up of a single story, told or written by a named individual. Rather, any single *text* of the creation story is inevitably a composite made up of what various Navajo people have narrated or explained to one or another Euro-American at various times.

Although the Navajo came into contact with Europeans as early as the sixteenth century, it was not until the nineteenth century that informed and careful efforts to record their extensive ceremonial and, as we might say, "literary" expression were undertaken. Foremost among these efforts were those of Washington Matthews whose publications date from the early 1880s until the time of his death in 1905. In Matthews's *Navaho Legends* (1897) is found what author Paul Zolbrod calls "one of the earliest renditions of the Navajo account of the creation and the most comprehensive English text" available. Zolbrod's own text of the Navajo creation story, from which our selection is taken, began, as Zolbrod writes, as "an experiment in text retrieval," since his "original intention was to present an English version of the Navajo creation story as evidence of an ongoing pre-Columbian literary tradition in North America."* In the end, he may have done something like that—although as Zolbrod himself notes, his work mostly led him to "an expanded view of poetry and poetics, or an uncertain one," inasmuch as it is not and cannot be clear to what extent any "text retrieval" process, however careful and sophisticated, can actually retrieve what was never textualized.

An Athabascan people whose language is related to that of Canadian and Alaskan tribes, the Navajo arrived in the southwestern United States from a much more northerly point at a relatively recent date—between 1000 and 1300 C.E. They learned farming and weaving techniques from long-settled Pueblo people, acquired livestock from the Spanish in the seventeenth century, and developed silver-working skills from contact with Mexicans in the nineteenth century.

The creation story describes how the *Diné*—the name the Navajo use for themselves, meaning, roughly, "earth surface people"—ascended to the surface from the many worlds below the earth. Together with the Holy People, who lived in the twelfth and lowest level beneath the earth, the ancestors of the present-day Navajo, after a series of adventures, came to their homes and established their traditional ways of life. The most important figure in Navajo mythology is Changing Woman, daughter of First Man and First Woman (themselves created from two ears of corn). Her mating with the Sun and with Water produced two twins sons who were able to slay the monsters that disrupted the life of the *Diné* on this earth. As the anthropologist James F. Downs puts it, "The record of their victories is written in the landscape of the Navajo country. Prominent mountains, lava flows, and other natural features are identified with the carcasses of slain monsters."

from *The Navajo Creation Story [Diné Bahane]*

One

Of a time long, long ago these things are said.

It is said[1] that at *Tó bił dahisk'id* white arose in the east and was considered day. We now call that spot Place Where the Waters Crossed.

Translated by Paul Zolbrod.

Our selections come from pages 35–51 of Paul Zolbrod's Diné Bahanè: The Navajo Creation Story (Albuquerque: University of New Mexico Press, 1984). The quotation is from p. 5.

Blue arose in the south. It too was considered day. So the *Nílch'i dine'é*, who already lived there, moved around. We would call them Air-Spirit People in the language spoken today by those who are given the name *Bilagáana*, which means White Man.

In the west yellow arose and showed that evening had come. Then in the north black arose. So the Air-Spirit People lay down and slept.

. . .

At *Tó bił dahisk'id* where the streams came together water flowed in all directions. One stream flowed to the east. One stream flowed to the south. One stream flowed to the west. One stream flowed to the north.

Along three of those streams there were dwelling places. There were dwelling places along the stream that flowed east. There were dwelling places along the stream that flowed south. There were dwelling places along the stream that flowed west. But along the stream that flowed north there were no dwellings.

. . .

To the east there was a place called *Dą́ą́*. In the language of *Bilagáana*, the White Man that name means food. To the south there was a place called *Nahodoolá*. It is unknown what that name means. And to the west there was a place called *Lók'aatsoh sikaad*. In the White Man's language that name means Standing Reed. Nothing is said about a place to the north.

Also to the east there was a place called *Ásaa'łáá'ii*, which means One Dish. And also to the south there was a place called *Tó hadziłtił*, which means A Big Amount of Water Coming Out in the language of *Bilagáana*. And also to the west there was a place called *Dził łichíí' bee hooghan*. That name means House of Red Mountain. To the north there are no places that have been given names.

Then there was a place called *Leeyaa hooghan* to the east. In his language the White Man would give it the name Underground House. And there was another place called *Chiiłchintah* to the south. In the language he speaks *Bilagáana* would give it the name Among Aromatic Sumac. And there was another place called *Tsé łichíí' bee hooghan* to the west. In the language of his people the White Man would give it the name House of Red Rock. We hear of no places with names to the north.

. . .

In those early times dark ants dwelled there. Red ants dwelled there. Dragonflies dwelled there. Yellow beetles dwelled there.

Hard beetles lived there. Stone-carrier beetles lived there. Black beetles lived there. Coyote-dung beetles lived there.

Bats made their homes there. Whitefaced beetles made their homes there. Locusts made their homes there. White locusts made their homes there.

Those are the twelve groups who started life there. We call them *Nílch'idine'é*. In the language of *Bilagáana* the White Man that name means Air-Spirit People. For they are people unlike the five-fingered earth-surface people who come into the world today, live on the ground for a while, die at a ripe old age, and then leave the world. They are people who travel in the air and fly swiftly like the wind and dwell nowhere else but here.

Far to the east there was an ocean. Far to the south there was an ocean. Far to the west there was an ocean. And far to the north there was an ocean.

In the ocean to the east dwelled *Tééhooltsódii,* who was chief of the people there. In the White Man's language he can be called The One That Grabs Things In the Water. In the ocean to the south lived *Táłtł'ááh alééh.* His name means Blue Heron. In the ocean to the west *Ch'ał* made his home and was chief of those people. In the language of the White Man he would be called Frog. And in the ocean to the north dwelled *Ii'ni'jiłgaii.* In the White Man's language that name means Winter Thunder. He was chief among whoever those people were who lived there, it is said.

Two

It is also said that the Air-Spirit People fought among themselves. And this is how it happened. They committed adultery, one with another. Many of the men were to blame, but so were many of the women.

They tried to stop, but they could not help themselves.

Tééhooltsódii The One That Grabs Things In the Water, who was chief in the east, complained, saying this:

"They must not like it here," he said.

And *Táłtł'ááh álééh* the Blue Heron, who was chief in the south, also complained:

"What they do is wrong," he complained.

Ch'ał the Frog, who was chief in the west, also complained. But he took his complaint directly to the Air-Spirit people, having this to say to them:

"You shall no longer be welcome here where I am chief," is what he said.

"That is what I think of you."

And from his home in the north where he was chief, *Ii'ni'jiłgaii* the Winter Thunder spoke to them also.

"Nor are you welcome here!" he, too, said to them.

"Go away from this land."

"Leave at once!"

But the people still could not help it: one with another they continued to commit adultery. And when they did it yet another time and then argued with each other again, *Tééhooltsódii* The One That Grabs Things In the Water would no longer speak to them. *Táłtł'ááh álééh* the Blue Heron would no longer speak to them. Likewise *Ch'ał* the Frog would say nothing to them. And *Ii'ni'jiłgaii* the Winter Thunder refused to say anything.

Four days and four nights passed.

Then the same thing happened. Those who lived in the south repeated their sins: the men with the women and the women with the men. They committed adultery. And again they quarreled afterward.

One woman and one man sought *Tééhooltsódii* The One That Grabs Things In the Water in the east to try to straighten things out. But they were driven away. Then they went to *Táłtł'ááh álééh* the Blue Heron in the south. But they were again driven away. And they looked for *Ch'at* the Frog in the west. But they were driven away again. Finally they went to the north to speak with *Ii'ni'jitgaii* the Winter Thunder. He, too, drove them away, breaking his silence to say this to them:

"None of you shall enter here," he said to them.

"I do not wish to listen to you.

"Go away, and keep on going!"

That night the people held a council at *Nahodoolá* in the south. But they could not agree on anything. On and on they quarreled, until white arose in the east and it was again day. *Tééhooltsódii* The One That Grabs Things In the Water then spoke to them:

"Everywhere in this world you bring disorder," he said to them.

"So we do not want you here.

"Find some other place to live."

But the people did not leave right away. For four nights the women talked and squabbled, each blaming the other for what had happened. And for four nights the men squabbled and talked. They, too, blamed one another.

At the end of the fourth night as they were at last about to end their meeting, they all noticed something white in the east. They also saw it in the south. It appeared in the west, too. And in the north it also appeared.

It looked like an endless chain of white mountains. They saw it on all sides. It surrounded them, and they noticed that it was closing in on them rapidly. It was a high, insurmountable wall of water! And it was flowing in on them from all directions, so that they could escape neither to the east nor to the west; neither to the south nor to the north could they escape.

So, having nowhere else to go, they took flight. Into the air they went. Higher and higher they soared, it is said.

Three

It is also said that they circled upward until they reached the smooth, hard shell of the sky overhead. When they could go no higher they looked down and saw that water now covered everything. They had nowhere to land either above or below.

Suddenly someone with a blue head appeared and called to them:

"Here," he called to them.

"Come this way.

"Here to the east there is a hole!"

They found that hole and entered. One by one they filed through to the other side of the sky. And that is how they reached the surface of the second world.

. . .

The blue-headed creature was a member of the Swallow People. It was they who lived up there.

While the first world had been red, this world was blue. The swallows lived in blue houses, which lay scattered across a broad, blue plain. Each blue house was cone-shaped; each tapered toward the top where there was a blue entry hole.

At first the Swallow People gathered around the newcomers and watched them silently. Nobody from either group said anything to any member of the other. Finally, when darkness came and the exiled Air-Spirit People made camp for the night, the blue swallow left.

In the morning the insect people from the world below decided that someone should explore this new world. So they sent a plain locust and a white locust to the east, instructing them to look for people like themselves.

Two days came and went before the locusts returned. They said that they had traveled for a full day. And as darkness fell they reached what must have been the end of the world. For they came upon the rim of a great cliff that rose out of an abyss whose bottom could not be seen. Both coming and going, they said, they found no people, no plants, no rivers, no mountains. They found nothing but bare, blue, level ground.

Next the two messengers were sent south to explore. Again, two days came and went while they were gone. And they again reported that after traveling for a full day they reached the end of the world. And they reported again that neither in going nor in coming back could they find people or plants, mountains or rivers.

They were then sent to the west. And after that they were sent to the north. Both times they were gone for two days, and they reported each time that they reached the end of the world after traveling for a full day. They also reported that again they could find neither people nor plants and neither mountains nor rivers.

To the others they had only this to say:

"It seems that we are in the center of a vast, blue plain," was all that they could say.

"Wherever we went in this world we could find neither company nor food; neither rivers nor mountains could we find."

After the scouts had returned from their fourth trip, the Swallow People visited the camp of the newcomers. And they asked why they had sent someone to the east to explore.

This is what the insect people from the lower world replied:

"We sent them out to see what was in the land," they replied.

"We sent them out to see if there were people here like ourselves."

Then the swallows asked this:

"What did your scouts tell you?" they asked.

To which the newcomers replied this way:

"They told us that they reached the end of the world after traveling for a full day," they replied.

"They told us that wherever they went in this world they could find neither people nor plants. Neither rivers nor mountains could they find."

The swallows then asked why the insect people had sent their scouts to the south. And they were told that the locusts were sent south to see what was in the land. And when the swallows asked why scouts were sent to the west, they were told again that the locusts were to see what they could find in this blue world. Which is what they were told when they asked why scouts were sent to the north.

To all of which the Swallow People then had this to say:

"Your couriers spoke the truth," they then said.

"But their trips were not necessary.

"Had you asked us what the land contained, we would have told you.

"Had you asked us where this world ended, we would have told you.

"We could have saved you all that time and all that trouble.

"Until you arrived here, no one besides us has ever lived in this world. We are the only ones living here."

The newcomers then had this suggestion to make to the swallows:

"You are like us in many ways," they suggested.

"You understand our language.

"Like us you have legs; like us you have bodies; like us you have wings; like us you have heads.

"Why can't we become friends?"

To which the swallows replied:

"Let it be as you say," they replied.

"You are welcome here among us."

So it was that both sets of people began to treat each other as members of one tribe. They mingled one among the other and called each other by the familiar names. They called each other grandparent and grandchild, brother and sister; they called each other father and son, mother and daughter.

For twenty-three days they all lived together in harmony. But on the night of the twenty-fourth day, one of the strangers became too free with the wife of the swallow chief.

Next morning, when he found out what had happened the night before, the chief had this to say to the strangers:

"We welcomed you here among us," was what he had to say to them.

"We treated you as friends and as kin.

"And this is how you return our kindness!

"No doubt you were driven from the world below for just such disorderly acts.

"Well, you must leave this world, too; we will have you here no longer.

"Anyhow, this is a bad land. There is not enough food for all of us.

"People are dying here every day from hunger. Even if we allowed you to stay, you could not live here very long."

When they heard the swallow chief's words, the locusts took flight. And all the others followed. Having nowhere else to go, they flew skyward.

Into the air they went. Higher and higher they soared. They circled upward until they reached the smooth, hard shell of the sky overhead, it is said.

Four

It is also said that like the sky of the world below, this sky had a smooth, hard shell. And like the sky of the world below this one seemed to have no opening. When the insect people reached it they flew around and around, having nowhere to land either above or below.

But as they circled, they noticed a white face peering at them. This was the face of *Nítch'i*. In the language of *Bilagáana* the White Man he would be called Wind. And they heard him cry to them:

"Here!" he cried.

"Here to the south you will find an opening."

"Come this way."

So off they flew to the south, and soon they found a slit in the sky slanting upward in a southerly direction. One by one they flew through it to the other side. And that is how they reached the surface of the third world.

. . .

While the second world had been blue, this world was yellow. Here the exiles found no one but Yellow Grasshopper People, who lived in yellow holes in the ground along the banks of a river which flowed east through their yellow land.

At first the Yellow Grasshopper People said nothing. They gathered silently around the newcomers and stared at them. Nobody from either group spoke to anyone from the other. And when darkness finally came and the people from the world below made their camp, the grasshoppers left.

In the morning the wanderers sent out the same two locusts who had explored the second world.

First they flew to the east where they were gone for two days altogether. Then they flew to the south where they were gone for two more days. Then they flew to the west, where they were gone for another two days. And they flew to the north where for two additional days they were gone. Each time they returned with the same report.

For a full day they had journeyed, until by nightfall they arrived at the rim of a cliff that rose from some unseen place far, far below. And neither in going forth nor in coming back could they find people or plants, mountains or waters. The river along whose banks the Grasshopper People lived soon tapered off toward the east until it was a dry, narrow gully. Otherwise there was nothing to see in this world except flat, yellow countryside and the yellow grasshoppers who lived on it.

When the messengers returned from their fourth journey the two great chiefs of the Grasshopper People came to visit. And they asked the newcomers why they had someone fly to the east and to the west, to the south and to the north.

To which the insect people from the world below replied:

"We sent them to see what was in the land," they replied.

"We sent them to see if they could find people like ourselves."

Then the grasshopper chiefs asked:

"And what did they find?" they asked.

Answered the newcomers:

"They found nothing but the bare land," they answered.

"They found nothing but the cliffs that marked the edge of this world.

"They found no plants and no people. They found no mountains and no rivers.

"Even the river along whose banks your people live here in the center of this world tapers off until it is only a dry, narrow gully."

Replied the grasshopper chiefs then:

"You might have first asked us what the land contains," they replied.

"We could have saved your messengers all that trouble.

"We could have told you that there in nothing in this land but what you see right here.

"We have lived here for a long time, but we have seen nothing that you have not seen. And we have seen no other people until you came."

The insect people from the world below then spoke to the grasshopper chiefs as they had spoken to the Swallow People in the second world, saying these things to them:

"Come to think of it, you are somewhat like us," they said to them.

"Like us you have heads. Like us you have wings. Like us you have bodies. Like us you have legs.

"You even speak the way we speak.

"Perhaps we can join you here."

The grasshoppers consented, and the two groups quickly began to mingle. They embraced each other, and soon they were using the names of family and kin together. They called each other mother and daughter, father and son, brother and sister, grandparent and grandchild. It was as if they were all of the same tribe.

As before, all went well for twenty-three days. But as before, on the night of the twenty-fourth, one of the newcomers treated the chief of the grasshoppers exactly as the swallow chief had been treated in the second world.

When he discovered how he had been wronged, the grasshopper chief spoke this way to the insect people:

"No doubt you were sent away from the world below for such transgressions!" is how he spoke.

"No doubt you bring disorder wherever you go. No doubt you lack intelligence.

"Well, here too you shall drink no more of our water. Here too you shall eat no more of our food. Here too you shall breathe no more of our air.

"Get out of here!"

So the insect people took flight again. And again they circled round and round into the sky until they arrived at the smooth, hard shell of its outer crust, it is said.

Five

It is also said that they again had to circle around for quite some time, looking in vain for some way to get through the sky overhead. Finally they heard a voice bidding them fly to the west and look there. And they noticed a red head peering at them. The voice they heard and the head they saw belonged to *Níłch'i łichíí*. In the language of *Bilagáana* the White Man he would bear the name Red Wind.

Doing as they were told they found a passage which twisted around through the sky's other surface like the tendril of a vine. It had been made this way by the wind. They flew into it and wound their way to the other side. And that is how they reached the surface of the fourth world.

Four of the grasshoppers had come with them. One was white. One was blue.

One was yellow. And one was black. To this very day, in fact, we have grasshoppers of those four colors among us.

. . .

The surface of the fourth world was unlike the surface of any of the lower worlds. For it was a mixture of black and white. The sky above was alternately white, blue, yellow, and black, just as it had been in the worlds below. But here the colors were of a different duration.

In the first world each color lasted for about the same length of time each day. In the second world the blue and the black lasted just a little longer than the white and the yellow. But here in the fourth world there was white and yellow for scarcely any time, so long did the blue and black remain in the sky. As yet there was no sun and no moon; as yet there were no stars.

When they arrived on the surface of the fourth world, the exiles from the lower worlds saw no living thing. But they did observe four great snow-covered peaks along the horizon around them. One peak lay to the east. One peak lay to the south. One peak lay likewise to the west. And to the north there was one peak.

The insect people sent two scouts to the east, who returned at the end of the two days. Those two said that they had not been able to reach the eastern mountain after an entire day's flight. And although they had traveled far indeed they could see no living creature. Neither track nor trail could they see; not one sign of life were they able to detect.

Two scouts were then sent to the south. And when these two returned at the end of two full days they reported that after an entire day's flight they managed to reach a low range of mountains on this side of the great peak which lay in that direction.

They too had traveled very far. They too could see no living creature. But they did observe two different kinds of tracks the likes of which they had never seen before. They described them carefully, and from that description the tracks seemed to resemble those made these days in our own world by deer and turkey.

Two scouts were sent next to the west. And after two full days they returned, reporting that they could by no means reach the great peak which lay in that direction, no matter how fast they could fly in a single day and no matter how far. Neither in going forth nor in returning could they see any living creature. Not one sign of life were they able to see.

Finally, two scouts were sent to explore the land that lay to the north. And when they returned they had a different story to tell. For they reported that they had found a strange race unlike any other. These were people who cut their hair square in front. They were people who lived in houses in the ground. They were people who cultivated the soil so that things grew therein. They were now harvesting what they had planted, and they gave the couriers food to eat.

It was now evident to the newcomers that the fourth world was larger than any of the worlds below.

. . .

On the very next day, two members of the newly found race came to the camp of the exiles. They were called *Kiis'áanii,* they said, which in the language of

Bilagáana the White Man means People Who Live in Upright Houses. And they wished to invite the exiles to visit their village.

On the way they came to a stream which was red. The *Kiis'áanii* warned their guests not to wade through it. Otherwise the water would injure the feet of the newcomers. Instead they showed the insect people a square raft made of four logs. One log was of white pine. One log was of blue spruce. One log was of yellow pine. And one log was of black spruce. On this raft they all crossed to the opposite bank, where the people who had arrived from the third world visited the homes of the people who dwelled here in the fourth world.

The exiles were given corn and pumpkins to eat. And they were asked by their new friends to stay. For quite some time, in fact, they stayed in the village of the upright houses. There they lived well on the food that the *Kiis'áanii* gave them. Eventually they all lived together like the people of one tribe. Soon the two groups were using the names of family and kin between themselves. They called each other father and son, mother and daughter, grandparent and grandchild, brother and sister.

The land of the *Kiis'áanii* was a dry land. It had neither rain nor snow and there was little water to be found. But the people who had been dwelling there knew how to irrigate the soil to make things grow, and they taught the newcomers to do so.

Twenty-three days came and went, and twenty-three nights passed and all was well. And on the twenty-fourth night the exiles held a council meeting. They talked quietly among themselves, and they resolved to mend their ways and to do nothing unintelligent that would create disorder. This was a good world, and the wandering insect people meant to stay here, it is said.

Six

It is also said that late in the autumn of that year the newcomers heard a distant voice calling to them from far in the east.

They listened and waited, listened and waited. Until soon they heard the voice again, nearer and louder than before. They continued to listen and wait, listen and wait, until they heard the voice a third time, all the nearer and all the louder.

Continuing to listen, they heard the voice again, even louder than the last time, and so close now that it seemed directly upon them.

A moment later they found themselves standing among four mysterious beings. They had never seen such creatures anywhere before. For they were looking at those who would eventually become known as *Haashch'ééh dine'é*.

In the language of *Bilagáana* the White Man, that name means Holy People. For they are people unlike the earth-surfaced people who come into the world today, live on the ground for a while, die at a ripe old age, and then move on. These are intelligent people who can perform magic. They do not know the pain of being mortal. They are people who can travel far by following the path of the rainbow. And they can travel swiftly by following the path of the sunray. They can make the winds and the thunderbolts work for them so that the earth is theirs to control when they so wish.

The people who were then living on the surface of the fourth world were looking upon *Bits'íís łigaii*, which name means White Body. He is the one that the Navajo people who live in our own world would eventually call *Haashch'ééłti'í*, which in today's language means Talking God.

And they were looking upon *Bits'íís dootł'izh*. That name means Blue Body. He is the one that the Navajo people in our own world would eventually come to know as *Tó neinilí*, which means Water Sprinkler.

And they were looking upon *Bits'íís łitsoii*, or Yellow Body. He is the one that the Navajo people today call *Hashch'éoghan*. Nobody can be sure what that name means in today's language. Some say it means Calling God; some say that it means House God; and some say that it means Growling God.

And they were looking upon *Bits'íís łizhin*. In the White Man's language that name means Black Body. He is the one that the Navajo people living in this world would eventually come to know as *Haashch'ééshzhiní*, which means Black God. Sometimes he is also called the God of Fire.

Without speaking the Holy People made signs to those who were gathered there, as if to give them instructions. But the exiles could not understand their gestures. So they stood by helplessly and watched.

And after the gods had left, the people talked about that mysterious visit for the rest of that day and all night long, trying to determine what it meant.

. . .

As for the gods, they repeated their visit four days in a row. But on the fourth day, *Bits'íís łizhin* the Black Body remained after the other three departed. And when he was alone with the onlookers, he spoke to them in their own language. This is what he said:

"You do not seem to understand the Holy People," he said.

"So I will explain what they want you to know.

"They want more people to be created in this world. But they want intelligent people, created in their likeness, not in yours.

"You have bodies like theirs, true enough.

"But you have the teeth of beasts! You have the mouths of beasts! You have the feet of beasts! You have the claws of beasts!

"The new creatures are to have hands like ours. They are to have feet like ours. They are to have mouths like ours and teeth like ours. They must learn to think ahead, as we do.

"What is more, you are unclean!

"You smell bad.

"So you are instructed to cleanse yourselves before we return twelve days from now."

That is what *Bits'íís łizhin* the Black Body said to the insect people who had emerged from the first world to the second, from the second world to the third, and from the third world to the fourth world where they now lived.

. . .

Accordingly, on the morning of the twelfth day the people bathed carefully.

The women dried themselves with yellow corn meal. The men dried themselves with white corn meal.

Soon after they had bathed, they again heard the distant voice coming from far in the east.

They listened and waited as before, listened and waited. Until soon they heard the voice as before, nearer and louder this time. They continued to listen and wait, listen and wait, until they heard the voice a third time as before, all the nearer and all the louder.

Continuing to listen as before, they heard the voice again, even louder than the last time, and so close now that it seemed directly upon them, exactly as it had seemed before. And as before they found themselves standing among the same four *Haashch'ééh dine'é,* or Holy People as *Bilagáana* the White Man might wish to call them.

Bits'íís dootł'izh the Blue Body and *Bits'íís łizhin* the Black Body each carried a sacred buckskin. *Bits'íís łigaii* the White Body carried two ears of corn.

One ear of corn was yellow. The other ear was white. Each ear was completely covered at the end with grains, just as sacred ears of corn are covered in our own world now.

Proceeding silently, the gods laid one buckskin on the ground, careful that its head faced the west. Upon this skin they placed the two ears of corn, being just as careful that the tips of each pointed east. Over the corn they spread the other buckskin, making sure that its head faced east.

Under the white ear they put the feather of a white eagle.

And under the yellow ear they put the feather of a yellow eagle.

Then they told the onlooking people to stand at a distance.

So that the wind could enter.

Then from the east *Nítch'i łigai* the White Wind blew between the buckskins. And while the wind thus blew, each of the Holy People came and walked four times around the objects they had placed so carefully on the ground.

As they walked, the eagle feathers, whose tips protruded slightly from between the two buckskins, moved slightly.

Just slightly.

So that only those who watched carefully were able to notice.

And when the Holy People had finished walking, they lifted the topmost buckskin.

And lo! the ears of corn had disappeared.

In their place there lay a man and there lay a woman.

. . .

The white ear of corn had been transformed into our most ancient male ancestor. And the yellow ear of corn had been transformed into our most ancient female ancestor.

It was the wind that had given them life: the very wind that gives us our breath as we go about our daily affairs here in the world we ourselves live in!

When this wind ceases to blow inside of us, we become speechless. Then we die.

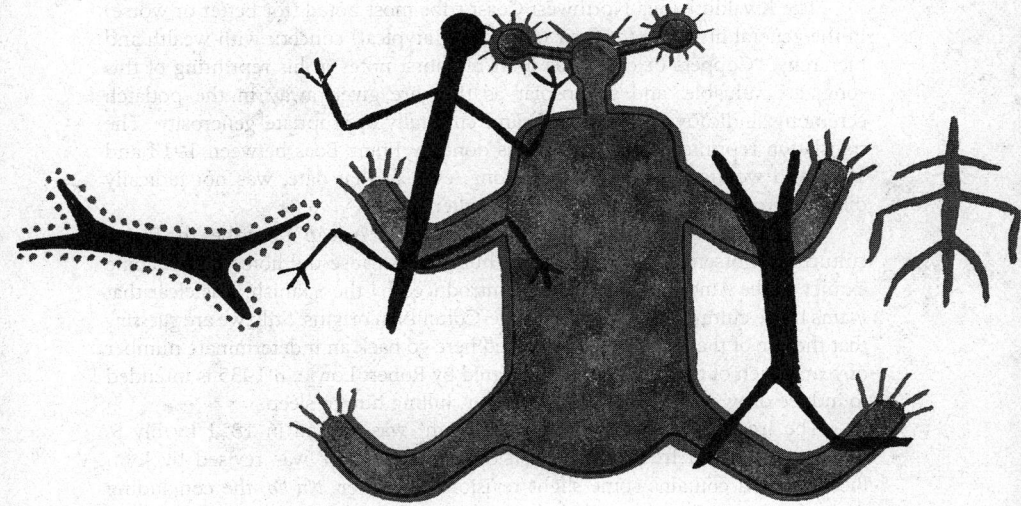

Cuyama. Curious bearlike being, showing superimposition. On a rock lying in a cave.

In the skin at the tips of our fingers we can see the trail of that life-giving wind.

Look carefully at your own fingertips.

There you will see where the wind blew when it created your most ancient ancestors out of two ears of corn, it is said.

THE KWAKIUTL PEOPLE
THE CROW PEOPLE
THE IROQUOIS PEOPLE
THE CHEROKEE PEOPLE

In contrast to *The Navajo Creation Story,* a lengthy and elaborated narrative, that tells Navajo people of their origins, the material presented next—a Kwakiutl song, a series of Crow "charms," an Iroquois oration, and a "magic formula" from the Iroquois and the Cherokee—is neither extensive nor story-like. Classifying these works by "genre," as noted earlier, is a Western practice; native people could have said *when* they were to be spoken, sung, or chanted, and *why* they would have been spoken, sung, or chanted, but they would not have offered the classifications (charm, oration, etc.) that we find useful.

The Kwakiutl are a Northwest Coast tribe most noted (for better or worse) in the general literature for their (apparently atypical) concern with wealth and hierarchy. "Coppers or coins," as John Bierhorst notes in his reprinting of this song, are valuable, and so, insofar as they are given away in the potlatch ceremony, indicative of high rank and culturally appropriate generosity. The translation reprinted by Bierhorst was done by Franz Boas between 1913 and 1914 and we are guessing that the song, even at that date, was not radically different from similar songs of a much earlier date.

"Five Charms to Make the Evening Warrior Fall Asleep" describes the Plains cultures of horsemanship and buffalo hunting. Because the horse had become extinct in the Americas, only being reintroduced by the Spanish, it is clear that Plains horse culture cannot have any pre-Columbian origins. Still, we are *guessing* that the use of the war charms discussed here go back an indeterminate number of years. Each of the five charms translated by Robert Lowie in 1935 is intended to induce drowsiness in an enemy warrior, lulling him to sleep.

The Iroquois "Oration on a Son's Death" was revised in 1851 by Ely S. Parker, himself an Iroquois; the version presented here was revised by John Bierhorst and contains some slight revisions of Parker. *Na-ho,* the concluding term of the oration means, in Bierhorst's note. I have finished; or, So be it. The Iroquois "magic formula" was translated by Arthur C. Parker in 1928.

We conclude with a charm in the form of a "medical prescription," as James Mooney called it sometime after 1888, from the Cherokee. Obviously this is not strictly "literature," for all that it has certain "poetic" properties. I have given the "free translation," for us, the "poetic" translation, but also included Mooney's interlinear "literal" translation to the original Cherokee.

THE KWAKIUTL PEOPLE

Song of a Chief's Daughter

Be ready, O chiefs' sons of the tribes! to be my husbands; for I come to make my husband a great chief through my father, for I am mistress, ha ha aya ha ha aya!

I, mistress, come to be your wife, O princes of the chiefs of the tribes! I am seated on coppers, and have many names and privileges that will be given by my father to my future husband, ha ha aya ha ha aya!

For my belt has been woven by my mother, which I use when I look after the dishes that will be given as a marriage present by my father to him who shall be my husband, when many kinds of food shall be given in the marriage feast by my father to him who shall be my husband, ha ha aya ha ha aya!

Translated by Franz Boas.

THE CROW PEOPLE

Five Charms to Make the Enemy Warrior Fall Asleep*

1

In the spring when we lie down under the young cherry-trees, with the grass green and the sun getting a bit warm, we feel like sleeping, don't we?

2

In the fall when there is a little breeze and we lie in some shelter, hearing the dry weeds rubbing against one another, we generally get drowsy, don't we?

3

In the daytime as the drizzle strikes the lodge pattering and we lie warming the soles of our feet, we fall asleep, don't we?

4

At night when we lie down, listening to the wind rustling through the bleached trees, we know not how we get to sleep but we fall asleep, don't we?

5

Having looked for a hollow among the thickest pines, we make a fresh camp there. The wind blows on us, and we, rather tired, lie down and keep listening to the rustling pines until we fall asleep.

THE IROQUOIS PEOPLE

Oration on a Son's Death†

My son, listen once more to the words of your mother. You were brought into life with her pains. You were nourished with her life. She has attempted to be faithful in raising you up. When you were young she loved you as her life. Your presence has been a source of great joy to her. Upon you she depended for support and comfort in her declining days. She had always expected to gain the end of the path of life before you. But you have outstripped her, and gone before her. Our great and wise creator has ordered it thus. By his will I am left to taste more of the miseries of this world. Your friends and relatives have gathered about your body, to look upon you for the last time. They mourn, as with one mind, your departure from among us. We, too, have but a few days more, and our journey shall be

---

*Translated by Robert Lowie.

†Translated by Ely S. Parker; revised by John Bierhorst.

ended. We part now, and you are conveyed from our sight. But we shall soon meet again, and shall again look upon each other. Then we shall part no more. Our maker has called you to his home. Thither will we follow. *Na-ho!*

Magic Formula*

You have no right to trouble me,
Depart, I am becoming stronger;
You are now departing from me,
You who would devour me;
I am becoming stronger, stronger.
Mighty medicine is now within me,
You cannot now subdue me—
I am becoming stronger,
I am stronger, stronger, stronger.

THE CHEROKEE PEOPLE

Charm (as a medical prescription)†

'ι'α' ɔⁿ'	Dι·'niskɔ ·li̇	Dv`nitlǪηǪꞮ'		
this-and	their heads	whenever they are ill		
αnìsGü'ya	αni'lɔ,'i'	vtsι"nαwa‛	anɔ̈"nvGa'	α'niDɑ́·ᵘwḗ
they men	they just passed by	beyond-it-stretched	they have come and said it	they (are) wizards
αni'lɔ ,'i'	vtsι"nαwa‛	αnɔ̈ "nι.Ga'	vts "nαwa'	Gɔ̈ 'tɫtα ͵ɑⁿ
they just passed by	beyond it stretched	they have come and said it	beyond it stretched	It (has been) rubbed
vtsι"nαwa‛	αnɔ "nι.Ga'	yă'		
beyond it stretched	they have come and said it	Sharp!		
'ι"α-N',ɔⁿ	na.'sGw ɔ̈ⁿ	ηι'niskɔ ·li'	Dv'nitlφησ·'.i‛	'ι'a' nι-vsti'
this-and	also	their heads	whenever they are ill	this so far like
ɔ·'Dali-Gù'Dli	anǪ·'skɔ̈ tlɔ̈'.i	DιDzɔ ‛·t'ιstɔ .ti'		
mountain-he climbs	it used to be held in the mouth	they to be blown with it		

Translated by Arthur C. Parker.
†*Translated by James Mooney.*

And This Is (for) When Their Heads Are Ill[†]

The men have just passed by, they have caused relief,
The wizards have just passed by, they have caused relief,
Relief has been rubbed, they have caused relief. Sharp!

R. Tagore, *Abstract Figure*. Lithograph.

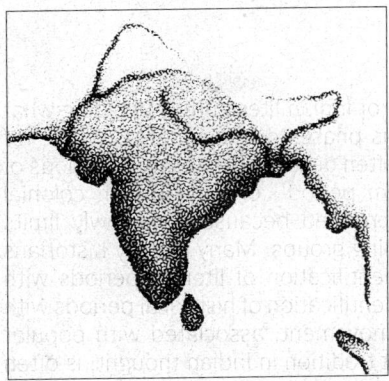

SECTION IX
Modern South Asia

At the outset it is necessary to indicate the enormous difficulties in presenting the literature of Modern South Asia as "Indian literature"—a designation that is more of a conceptual convenience than a reality. It would indeed be more accurate to refer to "Indian *literatures*," and even more specifically to refer to literature in the different regional languages, such as Gujarati, Marathi, Tamil, Kannada, Hindi, or Telegu. But while each of these languages has enjoyed a rich and lively literary tradition, the problem in the writing of literary history has always been one of relating them collectively to a "national" literature. What makes a novel in Marathi or Telegu or Bengali an example of Indian literature may have very little to do with the presence (or absence) of certain religious and cultural values, linguistic expressions, or traditions. Alternatively, to establish the place of origin of a literary work—here the Indian subcontinent—as the defining attribute of Indian literature is no less problematic, as a large number of works termed Indian are produced in diasporic settings.

What then defines a work as part of Indian literature? Perhaps we may have to remain content with the definition given by Sisir Kumar Das: "Indian literature is a record of memorable utterances of the Indian people, an entity which is not determined by political exigencies but defined by a feeling of communality that runs through centuries."[1]

[1] Sisir Kumar Das, *A History of Indian Literature 1800–1910*, vol. 7 (Delhi: Sahitva Akademi, 1991), 4.

Another problem in presenting a survey of Indian literature is deciding what historical categories best describe its various phases or movements. While, for the sake of convenience, Indian literature is often described in terms of periods of influence (the "Hindu period," the "Muslim period" or "the British colonial period"), that tendency is increasingly discredited because it narrowly limits literary production to works by dominant ruling groups. Many literary historians have tried to circumvent the problem of identification of literary periods with dominant powers by advocating instead an identification of historical periods with dominant genres. For instance, the *bhakti* movement, associated with popular devotional literature as well as with a protest tradition in Indian thought, is often described as inaugurating a "medieval" period in Indian literature; however, the word "medieval" does not have the same chronological connotations as it might in the Western tradition and is more suggestive, in the Indian context, of a period of historical transition between literary genres. Where the "ancient" period ends and the medieval begins, or where in turn the medieval period gives way to the modern, are questions complicated by the give-and-take of literary forms and styles between these various periods.

The selections included here do not attempt to cover every period of Indian literature, which they clearly cannot. The choices have been determined by considerations of readability, representativeness of genres (if not representativeness of historical period), and quality of translations. The selections show, first, that Indian literary forms have been in a state of constant experimentation, adapting and often recreating genres borrowed from both other world traditions and regional language traditions; and second, that Indian literature is an ethnically, racially, and religiously diverse literature that cannot be said to bear the stamp of a distinct national identity or recount a single national history. For example, two of the authors included here, Faiz Ahmed Faiz and Sara Suleri, come from Pakistan, but the historical experience of partition, political struggle, and pain of exile they describe blurs the boundaries between national histories and raises questions, through literary expression, about the very meaning of "national" literatures.

Most anthologies of Indian literature have tended to stress selections embodying a "spiritual tradition" (often equated, erroneously, with Hinduism). However, such selections are at best only a partial evocation of India's multireligious and multiethnic heritage. During the period of British colonial rule translations of certain types of works, such as the *Bhagavad Gita* or the *Ramayana,* were undertaken to prove the common origin of an Indo-European past. Representing the heyday of Orientalist enthusiasm for works of the Indian spiritual tradition, British colonial administrators regularly authorized English translations of works that pointed in the direction of a common Aryan past and a patriarchal tradition. Alternatively, Hindu legal and moral treatises like *The Laws of Manu* or the *Dharmasastra* were translated because of their importance in administering Hindu civil law in the British Indian courts. As a result, Hindu religious texts were made more widely available than any other kind of works; folktales and literature by social groups (including women) in particular fell outside the established Hindu caste hierarchy.[2] The Orientalist predilection for sacred Hindu texts, with which

---

[2]Susie Tharu and K. Lalita, eds., *Women Writing in India* (New York: Feminist Press, 1991).

India has been monolithically identified, continues even in modern anthologies of Indian literature, which tend to focus on the Hindu spiritual tradition. The selections included here are an attempt to address this imbalance by seeking out works outside the Vedic or Brahminical tradition that more accurately capture the fusion of secular and sacred strands in Indian literature.

Before English officially became the medium of instruction in Indian schools and colleges in 1835, Sanskrit, Persian, and Arabic were the dominant languages of use. Arabic, the language of the Koran, and Persian, the court language of the Mughals who ruled India from about the eleventh to seventeenth centuries, were languages acquired not only by Muslims but also by Hindus seeking positions in the Muslim administration. Of the two languages, Persian enjoyed greater popularity and was both a literary language and a language of administrators and the judiciary. Even as late as 1803 a prominent Bengali intellectual, Rammohun Roy, chose to write some of his most important pamphlets in the Persian language, which continued to be associated with an elite intellectual and cultural class. The poets Mirza Ghalib and Muhammed Iqbal celebrated the Persian lyric (or *ghazal*) in their own literary writings.

The introduction of English language and literature in 1835 infused Indian writing with not only new styles and inflections but also a new set of themes and concerns. The transmission of texts through printing rather than the manuscript tradition had a profound effect on the increased circulation of works, the translations of works from one regional language to another, and the emergence of a wider reading public; furthermore, printing contributed to the decline of traditional patronage, which had hitherto determined literary production. But while the introduction of English may have seemed to suggest the advent of modernization in India, the concerns of literary figures writing in both English and the vernacular languages indicate that modernization—including the rise of technology, the concentration of social life around urban centers rather than rural areas, the eradication of superstition and outmoded styles of thought and their replacement by ideas of the European enlightenment—always remained a contested issue. This is not to say that the reaction against Westernization and modernization invariably took the form of a nostalgic return to past traditions. Rather, as the literary career of Premchand (1880–1936), India's first modern writer, suggests, the challenge of modernization created productive conflicts within Indian intellectual life, which were often resolved by acts of cultural synthesis.

Historical Background

The history of modern India is underwritten by a number of mutually conflicting and reinforcing crosscurrents, stretching from the early period of British imperial rule in the mid-nineteenth century to the vigorous nationalist revolt against it in the late nineteenth and early twentieth century to the founding of India as a free state in 1947. To these various histories could be added the growth of a Muslim religious and political state in the form of Pakistan. Such a tumultuous history or series of histories takes, as backdrop, the intertwining of political conflict with religious belief, intense economic expansion, and industrial modernization, as well as natural disaster in the form of disease and famine.

Yet it would not be entirely incorrect to locate the beginnings of such a complex socio-demographic history in the Mutiny and Great Revolt of 1857–1859, which began as a military insurrection by Indian soldiers but soon became a populist revolt. The nature of that revolt has been much debated by historians, but it is fair to see it both as the first Indian war of independence as well as the final efforts of a tradition-bound India. Soon after the revolt was suppressed by British troops, the British Parliament successfully transferred power (via the 1858 Government of India Act) from the East India Company to the crown, whose power came to rest in what was undoubtedly the largest and most thoroughly entrenched imperial bureaucracy of the modern era. On one end, it was headed by a secretary of state and the fifteen-member Council of India; on the other, by British viceroys in Simla and Calcutta who in turn controlled nearly 1,500 Indian Civil Service (ICS) officials all through India. During the period, the British implemented policies of nonintervention with regard to religious belief and the autonomy of Indian princes, along with promises of racial "impartiality" as to the hiring of ICS officers. Such laissez-faire policies were often motivated as much by fear of further revolts as by a concern for human rights.

Racial equality proved elusive during Queen Victoria's reign, and the racial tension engendered by the 1857 mutiny saw a steady increase throughout the colonial period. The period was marked by British domination in the form of an escalating bureaucracy, racial arrogance and violent abuse of "natives," and an exclusionary social life centered on the British Club. Together, these images have proved one of the most enduring clichés as well as one of the clearest indictments of British imperial rule, a time when, as Rudyard Kipling put it, British officials "took up the White man's burden" by assuming lucrative positions in India. Throughout the period, relations between British officials — who often had little experience with Indian life — and native Indians remained aloof at best, marked on the British side by fear, suspicion, and concern with "native contamination." Although the ICS was officially open to Indians and Britons, by 1869 only one Indian candidate had managed to gain admittance. Nonetheless, the period of British colonialism saw intense economic expansion, fueled by a lucrative land tax, a governmental monopoly on the opium trade, and the maturation of textile, tea, and coal industries. But there was a considerable price to be paid; the growth of British imports led to a decline of Indian handcrafts. Together with such military actions as the conquest of Burma and suppression of native tribes in the northwest, the economic expansion often had a deleterious effect on native cultures and economies.

Against this backdrop, there was both rebellion and active campaigning for social reforms, particularly on issues of women's emancipation, child and even infant marriage, and female education. Somewhat paradoxically, the official British policy of nonintervention spawned innumerable local reform movements. Mahadev Ranade founded the Indian National Social Conference in 1897, which would become the principal organization promoting the reformation of Hinduism. After 1920, under the leadership of Mahatma Gandhi, it merged with the Indian National Congress to become a powerful mainstream political force. Although official support was lacking, there was unofficial and private backing, as well as official, though failed, attempts to reform India for the benefit of native Indians. Chief among such liberal British reformers was Lord Ripon, a viceroy venerated by the Indian populace for urging the abolition of racism and a system of representative government at both local precinct and municipal levels.

In December 1885, the Indian National Congress convened for the first time.

The meeting was a turning point in Indian history, for it contained not only the seeds of contemporary India but also a Muslim countercurrent that would lead to the creation of Pakistan. Furthermore, it marked a new India, one guided by an elite middle class group of intellectuals — lawyers, businessmen, journalists, and professors — who were devoted to peaceful political reform. Galvanized by the unpopular 1905 partition of Bengal, they launched boycotts, circulated petitions, and brought to the public's attention a wide range of economic and political reforms geared to providing education for all, opening up the ICS, and ending the exploitation of natural resources for British gain.

The Indian response to World War I was largely supportive, with Indian princes freely supplying money, arms, large amounts of goods, and men to the Allied cause. By Armistice Day over a million Indian troops were serving overseas. At the war's end, more than 100,000 Indian casualties had been sustained, over a third of them fatal. Such loyalty to Britain was, however, rewarded after the war with the enactment of a series of repressive measures known as the Rowlatt Acts, and in 1919, with the Jallianwalla Bagh massacre, which involved the killing of 400 unarmed civilians who had gathered to protest the duplicitous actions of Britain, whose promises of political reform were quickly abandoned in favor of policies reinstating prewar inequality and exploitation. Coming so shortly after years of loyal service to the Allied cause, the Rowlatt Acts and the Jallianwalla Bagh massacre transformed much of the Indian public from moderate and loyal supporters of the British *raj* into ardent nationalists. With the exception of the Mutiny of 1857, no single event would affect the future of India as did the events surrounding World War I.

Chief among those to call for a repeal of the Rowlatt or black acts was a young Indian named Mohandas Gandhi, considered one of the most promising young members of Congress. Gandhi's remarkable power lay in his ability to fuse politics with religion, and his unique political gift is inseparable from a sense of spiritual leadership that he communicated to the Indian people, who saw him as a *sadhu* ("saint") and worshipped him as a *mahatma* ("great-souled one"). Gandhi above all recognized what was a nearly unsurmountable problem: breaking down the mechanism of British colonial rule with an unarmed India. As cornerstones of his political movement, Gandhi chose the Vedic conception of *satya* ("truth") and *ahimsa* ("nonviolence"). With these two tools, Gandhi argued that the Indian people could bring British rule peacefully and inexorably to an end. In 1920, one year after the Jallianwalla Bagh massacre, Gandhi led the first of his national *satyagraha* ("devotion to truth") marches, calling for the boycott of all things British — from schools and courts of law, to elections and even land tax collectors. Charged with "promoting disaffection" toward the British *raj*, Gandhi was arrested and sentenced to six years in prison.

The period saw increasing tension between Britain and the Indian National Congress, the latter mirroring such divisions and ambivalence. Some members endorsed Gandhian noncooperation, other more conservative members urged partial cooperation and legislative reforms, and still others supported military insurrection against the crown. In particular, one emerging party, the Swaraj, was led by Motila Nehru, and took a more pragmatic and less orthodox Hindu position. Between Muslims and Hindus tensions similarly increased, fanned by doctrinal differences, in particular such practices as Muslim cow slaughter. By 1924, religious rioting had struck nearly every city in Northern India and by 1930, a Muslim separatist movement was gathering steam, not only in Northwest India, but also in eastern Bengal, Kashmir, and sections of the United Provinces. In Punjab, the great Urdu poet Muhammed Iqbal made the first call, in 1930, for a "final destiny" of Indian Muslims — in the form of a self-governing state. Throughout the 1930s, Muslims came to see the emerging Hindu *raj*, like the Hindu-led Congress, as a source of injustice and tyranny.

World War II witnessed the intensification of conflict between Britain and the Indian National Congress, as well as between Hindus and Muslims. In 1939 Britain declared India to be at war with Germany, and this act, arrived at without consultation on India's part, led to a number of antiwar protests staged by both Gandhi and Nehru. The Muslim League, on the other hand, generally supported the British war effort. In 1940, in what is known as the Lahore Resolution, the League proposed that all Muslim-majority areas be organized as "autonomous and sovereign" states. By 1940 Gandhi had organized his Quit India movement, an action that landed Gandhi and as many as 60,000 others in British jails and that prompted a British military crackdown on the Indian underground. By 1943, martial law was imposed to quell civil disobedience and violence — and would not be lifted until the war's end. With the breaking off of the talks of 1945, official negotiations between Hindus and Muslims had largely collapsed.

By 1945, Britain had resolved to transfer power to India, but the problem of finding an administration that could fairly represent the competing interests remained unresolvable. Differences between Muslims, Hindus, and Sikhs were not satisfactorily settled by Britain's initial division of India into three sections. By mid-1947, a period of bloody civil war began, prompted in part by a call for "Direct Action" on the part of Muslims. In 1947 Parliament quickly passed the Indian Independence Act, bringing about the demarcation of India from Pakistan. In the ensuing period of border rearrangement, as Muslims, Hindus, and Sikhs sought to seek shelter in the newly demarcated territories, nearly a million people were slaughtered, with Sikhs suffering particularly heavy casualties.

Post-partition India and Pakistan saw a number of tragedies stemming from economic instability, refugee resettlement, separation of Pakistani raw materials from Indian factories, political assassinations, and a continuing conflict between Pakistan and India. After independence, Nehru became India's first prime minister and Muhammed Ali Jinnah assumed leadership in Pakistan. Gandhi, who chose not to hold office, walked great distances, preaching nonviolence. When he was assassinated in 1948, Nehru remarked that "the light has gone out of our lives, and there is darkness everywhere." Yet Nehru in many ways continued Gandhi's policy of enlightened though secularized leadership, and his condemnation of a "caste-ridden" society proved crucial to India's modernization and its gradual escape from the religious violence and hatred that had plagued it in earlier years. Nonetheless, religious and political disputes would characterize Indian and Pakistani life for years afterward, with the first undeclared war between India and Pakistan beginning only two months after independence, and a second major conflict occurring in 1965, after Nehru's death. In 1970, under the rule of Indira Gandhi, India would defeat Pakistan in the Bangladesh war, leading to the establishment of the Peoples' Republic of Bangladesh in 1972. Well into the 1980s problems of poverty, gross social and economic inequality, and local communal religious violence would still plague both India and Pakistan, with the most notable examples being the Sikh uprisings and separatist movement throughout the 1980s, and the assassinations of Indira Gandhi in 1984 and Rajiv Gandhi, her son and successor, in 1991.

Further Readings

Chatterji, Suniti Kumar, ed. *The Cultural Heritage of India*. Vol. 5. Calcutta: Ramakrishna Mission Institute of Culture, 1978.

Das, Sisir Kumar. *A History of Indian Literature*. Vol. 7. New Delhi: Sahitya Akademi, 1991.

George, K. M., ed. *Comparative Indian Literature*. 2 vols. New Delhi: Macmillan, 1984.

Gonda, Jan, ed. *A History of Indian Literature*. 10 vols. Wiesbaden, Germany: Otto Harrossowitz, 1975.

Mukherjee, Meenakshi. *Realism and Reality: The Novel and Society in India*. Delhi: Oxford University Press, 1985.

Spear, Percival. *India: A Modern History*. Ann Arbor: University of Michigan Press, 1961.

Tharu, Susie, and K. Lalita, eds. *Women Writing in India*. 2 vols. New York: Feminist Press, 1991.

Viswanathan, Gauri. *Masks of Conquest: Literary Study and British Rule in India*. New York: Columbia University Press, 1989.

RABINDRANATH TAGORE (1861–1941)
India

After studying law in England, Rabindranath Tagore returned to India, managed his father's large estate, and became active in the Indian nationalist movement. He is widely recognized as one of India's greatest modern writers, achieving acclaim in a variety of modes, from poetry and drama to the novel and the essay. His major philosophical work, *Sadhana: The Realization of Life* (1913), expresses the basic ideas of sacred Hindu writings. He was awarded the Nobel Prize in literature in 1913. He wrote principally in Bengali, in both the traditional literary and everyday spoken forms of the language. One of his principal themes— illustrated in "The Editor"—concerns the supremacy of personal over public values. Such beliefs brought Tagore into sharp conflict with Mahatma Gandhi and others on the question of how independence from British rule was to be achieved.

The Editor

As long as my wife was alive, I did not pay much attention to Probha. As a matter of fact, I thought a great deal more about Probha's mother than I did of the child herself.

At that time my dealing with her was superficial, limited to a little petting, listening to her lisping chatter, and occasionally watching her laugh and play. As long as it was agreeable to me I used to fondle her, but as soon as it threatened to become tiresome I would surrender her to her mother with the greatest readiness.

At last, on the untimely death of my wife, the child dropped from her mother's arms into mine, and I took her to my heart.

But it is difficult to say whether it was I who considered it my duty to bring up the motherless child with twofold care, or my daughter who thought it her duty to take care of her wifeless father with a superfluity of attention. At any rate, it is a fact that from the age of six she began to assume the role of housekeeper. It was quite clear that this little girl constituted herself the sole guardian of her father.

I smiled inwardly but surrendered myself completely to her hands. I soon saw that the more inefficient and helpless I was the better pleased she became. I found that even if I took down my own clothes from the peg, or went to get my own umbrella, she put on such an air of offended dignity that it was clear that she thought I had usurped her right. Never before had she possessed such a perfect doll as she now had in her father, and so she took the keenest pleasure in feeding him, dressing him, and even putting him to bed. Only when I was teaching her the elements of arithmetic or the First Reader had I the opportunity of summoning up my parental authority.

Translated by William Radice.

Every now and then the thought troubled me as to where I should be able to get enough money to provide her with a dowry for a suitable bride-groom. I was giving her a good education, but what would happen if she fell into the hands of an ignorant fool?

I made up my mind to earn money. I was too old to get employment in a Government office, and I had not the influence to get work in a private one. After a good deal of thought I decided that I would write books.

If you make holes in a bamboo tube, it will no longer hold either oil or water, in fact its power of receptivity is lost; but if you blow through it, then, without any expenditure it may produce music. I felt quite sure that the man who is not useful can be ornamental, and he who is not productive in other fields can at least produce literature. Encouraged by this thought, I wrote a farce. People said it was good, and it was even acted on the stage.

Once having tasted of fame, I found myself unable to stop pursuing it farther. Days and days together I went on writing farces with an agony of determination.

Probha would come with her smile, and remind me gently: "Father, it is time for you to take your bath."

And I would growl out at her: "Go away, go away; can't you see that I am busy now? Don't vex me."

The poor child would leave me, unnoticed, with a face dark like a lamp whose light has been suddenly blown out.

I drove the maid-servants away, and beat the men-servants, and when beggars came and sang at my door I would get up and run after them with a stick. My room being by the side of the street, passers-by would stop and ask me to tell them the way, but I would request them to go to Jericho. Alas, no one took it into serious consideration that I was engaged in writing a screaming farce.

Yet I never got money in the measure that I got fun and fame. But that did not trouble me, although in the meantime all the potential bride-grooms were growing up for other brides whose parents did not write farces.

But just then an excellent opportunity came my way. The landlord of a certain village, Jahirgram, started a newspaper, and sent a request that I would become its editor. I agreed to take the post.

For the first few days I wrote with such fire and zest that people used to point at me when I went out into the street, and I began to feel a brilliant halo about my forehead.

Next to Jahirgram was the village of Ahirgram. Between the landlords of these two villages there was a constant rivalry and feud. There had been a time when they came to blows not infrequently. But now, since the magistrate had bound them both over to keep the peace, I took the place of the hired ruffians who used to act for one of the rivals. Every one said that I lived up to the dignity of my position.

My writings were so strong and fiery that Ahirgram could no longer hold up its head. I blackened with my ink the whole of their ancient clan and family.

All this time I had the comfortable feeling of being pleased with myself. I even became fat. My face beamed with the exhilaration of a successful man of genius. I admired my own delightful ingenuity of insinuation, when at some excruciating satire of mine, directed against the ancestry of Ahirgram, the whole of Jahirgram would burst its sides with laughter like an over-ripe melon. I enjoyed myself thoroughly.

But at last Ahirgram started a newspaper. What it published was starkly naked, without a shred of literary urbanity. The language it used was of such undiluted colloquialism that every letter seemed to scream in one's face. The consequence was that the inhabitants of both villages clearly understood its meaning.

But as I was hampered in my style by my sense of decency, my subtlety of sarcasm very often made but a feeble impression upon the power of understanding of both my friends and my enemies.

The result was that even when I won decidedly in this war of infamy my readers were not aware of my victory. At last in desperation I wrote a sermon on the necessity of good taste in literature, but found that I had made a fatal mistake. For things that are solemn offer more surface for ridicule than things that are truly ridiculous. And therefore my effort at the moral betterment of my fellow-beings had the opposite effect to that which I had intended.

My employer ceased to show me such attention as he had done. The honour to which I had grown accustomed dwindled in its quantity, and its quality became poor. When I walked in the street people did not go out of their way to carry off the memory of a word with me. They even went so far as to be frivolously familiar in their behavior towards me—such as slapping my shoulders with a laugh and giving me nicknames.

In the meantime my admirers had quite forgotten the farces which had made me famous. I felt as if I was a burnt-out match, charred to its very end.

My mind became so depressed that, no matter how I racked my brains, I was unable to write one line. I seemed to have lost all zest for life.

Probha had now grown afraid of me. She would not venture to approach me unless summoned. She had come to understand that a commonplace doll is a far better companion than a genius of a father who writes comic pieces.

One day I saw that the Ahirgram newspaper, leaving my employer alone for once, had directed its attack on me. Some very ugly imputations had been made against myself. One by one all my friends and acquaintances came and read to me the spiciest bits, laughing heartily. Some of them said that however one might disagree with the subject-matter, it could not be denied that it was cleverly written. In the course of the day at least twenty people came and said the same thing, with slight variations to break its monotony.

In front of my house there is a small garden. I was walking there in the evening with a mind distracted with pain. When the birds had returned to their nests, and surrendered themselves to the peace of the evening, I understood quite clearly that amongst the birds at any rate there were no writers of journalism, nor did they hold discussions on good taste.

I was thinking only of one thing, namely, what answer I could make. The disadvantage of politeness is that it is not intelligible to all classes of people. So I had decided that my answer must be given in the same strain as the attack. I was not going to allow myself to acknowledge defeat.

Just as I had come to this conclusion, a well-known voice came softly through the darkness of the evening, and immediately afterwards I felt a soft warm touch in the palm of my hand. I was so distracted and absent-minded that even though that voice and touch were familiar to me, I did not realise that I knew them.

But the next moment, when they had left me, the voice sounded in my ear, and the memory of the touch became living. My child had slowly come near to me once more, and had whispered in my ear, 'Father,' but not getting any answer she had lifted my right hand, and with it had gently stroked her forehead, and then silently gone back into the house.

For a long time Probha had not called me like that, nor caressed me with such freedom. Therefore it was that to-day at the touch of her love my heart suddenly began to yearn for her.

Going back to the house a little later, I saw that Probha was lying on her bed. Her eyes were half closed, and she seemed to be in pain. She lay like a flower which has dropped on the dust at the end of the day.

Putting my hand on her forehead, I found that she was feverish. Her breath was hot, and her pulse was throbbing.

I realised that the poor child, feeling the first symptoms of fever, had come with her thirsty heart to get her father's love and caresses, while he was trying to think of some stinging reply to send to the newspaper.

I sat beside her. The child, without speaking a word, took my hand between her two fever-heated palms, and laid it upon her forehead, lying quite still.

All the numbers of the Jahirgram and Ahirgram papers which I had in the house I burnt to ashes. I wrote no answer to the attack. Never had I felt such joy as I did, when I thus acknowledged defeat.

I had taken the child to my arms when her mother had died, and now, having cremated this rival of her mother, again I took her to my heart.

MAHATMA [MOHANDAS KARAMCHAND] GANDHI (1869–1948)
India/Gujarat

Mahatma Gandhi is widely seen as the foremost political and spiritual leader of modern India, notably in the struggle against British imperial rule. Educated in India and London and admitted to the bar in 1889, he gave up law practice to fight legislation against Indians. He was also a prolific writer, mainly in his native tongue, Gujarati. His writings are for the most part exercises in social philosophy and moral teaching. The extract presented here is from a memoir about Tolstoy Farm, named after the great Russian writer, Leo Tolstoy (with whom Gandhi corresponded). Gandhi helped set up the farm in 1910 while he was living in South Africa to promote ideals such as cooperative manual labor and nonviolence set forth by Tolstoy. It was in South Africa that he organized his first *Satyagraha* or campaign of civil disobedience. Although he repudiated the title "Mahatma," or "great-soul," it indicates his stature among those who knew him and his teaching.

from *Autobiography: The Story of my Experiments with Truth*

Tolstoy Farm

In this chapter I propose to string together a number of Tolstoy Farm reminiscences which are rather disjointed and for which therefore I must crave the reader's indulgence.

A teacher hardly ever had to teach the kind of heterogeneous class that fell to my lot, containing as it did pupils of all ages and both sexes, from boys and girls of about 7 years of age to young men of twenty and young girls of 12 or 13 years old. Some of the boys were wild and mischievous.

What was I to teach this ill-assorted group? How was I to be all things to all pupils? Again in what language should I talk to all of them? The Tamil and Telegu[1] children knew their own mother-tongue or English and a little Dutch. I could speak to them only in English. I divided the class into two sections—the Gujarati[2] section talked to in Gujarati and the rest in English. As the principal part of the teaching, I arranged to tell or read to them some interesting stories. I also proposed to bring them into close mutual contact and to lead them to cultivate a spirit of friendship and service. Then there was to be imparted some general knowledge of history and geography and in some cases of arithmetic. Writing was also taught, and so were some which formed part of our prayers, and to which therefore I tried to attract the Tamil children as well.

The boys and girls met freely. My experiment of co-education and Tolstoy Farm was the most fearless of its type. I dare not today allow, or train children to enjoy, the liberty which I had granted the Tolstoy Farm class. I have often felt that my mind then used to be more innocent than it is now, and that was due perhaps to my ignorance. Since then I have had bitter experiences, and have sometimes burnt my fingers badly. Persons whom I took to be thoroughly innocent have turned out corrupt. I have observed the roots of evil deep down in my own nature; and timidity has claimed me for its own.

I do not repent having made the experiment. My conscience bears witness that it did not do any harm. But as a child who has burnt himself with hot milk blows even into whey, my present attitude is one of extra caution.

A man cannot borrow faith or courage from others. The doubter is marked out for destruction, as the *Gita*[3] puts it. My faith and courage were at their highest at Tolstoy Farm. I have been praying to God to permit me to re-attain that height

Translated by Mahadev Desai.

---

1. Languages spoken in southern India.
2. Language spoken in the western state of Gujarat.

3. The *Bhagavad Gita*, a section of the *Mahabharata*, the renowned epic of ancient India (200 B.C.E.–200 C.E.).

but the prayer has not yet been heard, for the number of such suppliants before the Great White Throne is legion. The only consolation is that God has as many years as there are suppliants. I therefore repose full faith in Him and know that my prayer will be accepted when I have fitted myself for such grace.

This was my experiment. I sent the boys reputed to be mischievous and the innocent young girls to bathe in the same spot at the same time. I had fully explained the duty of self-restraint to the children, who were all familiar with my Satyagraha doctrine. I knew, and so did the children, that I loved them with a mother's love. The reader will remember the spring at some distance from the kitchen. Was it a folly to let the children meet there for bath and yet to expect them to be innocent? My eye always followed the girls as a mother's eye would follow a daughter. The time was fixed when all the boys and girls went together for a bath. There was an element of safety in the fact that they went in a body. Solitude was always avoided. Generally I also would be at the spring at the same time.

All of us slept on an open verandah. The boys and the girls would spread themselves around me. There was hardly a distance of three feet between any two beds. Some care was exercised in arranging the order of the beds, but any amount of such care would have been futile in the case of a wicked mind. I now see that God alone safeguarded the honour of those boys and girls. I made the experiment from a belief that boys and girls could thus live together without harm, and the parents with their boundless faith in me allowed me to make it.

One day one of the young men made fun of two girls, and the girls themselves or some child brought me the information. The news made me tremble. I made inquiries and found that the report was true. I remonstrated with the young men, but that was not enough. I wished the two girls to have some sign on their person as a warning to every young man that no evil eye might be cast upon them, and as a lesson to every girl that no one dare assail their purity. The passionate Ravana could not so much as touch Sita[4] with evil intent while Rama was thousands of miles away. What mark should the girls bear so as to give them a sense of security and at the same time to sterilise the sinner's eye? This question kept me awake for the night. In the morning I gently suggested to the girls that they might let me cut off their fine long hair. On the farm we shaved and cut the hair of one another and we therefore kept scissors and clipping machines. At first the girls would not listen to me. I had already explained the situation to the elderly women who could not bear to think of my suggestion but yet quite understood my motive, and they had finally accorded their support to me. They were both of them noble girls. One of them is alas! now no more. She was very bright and intelligent. The other is living and the mistress of a household of her own. They came round after all, and at once the very hand that is narrating this incident set to cut off their hair. And afterwards I analysed and explained my procedure before my class, with excellent results. I never heard of a joke again. The girls in question did not lose in any case;

---

4. Ravana and Sita were characters in the classic sixth-century B.C.E. epic the *Ramay-* *ana*, Ravana is the demon god of Lanka who abducts Sita from her husband Rama.

goodness knows how much they gained. I hope the young men still remember this incident and keep their eye from sin.

Experiments such as I have placed on record are not meant for imitation. Any teacher who imitates them would be incurring grave risk. I have here taken note of them only to show how far a man can go in certain circumstances and to stress the purity of the Satyagraha struggle. This very purity was a guarantee of its victory. Before launching on such experiment, a teacher has to be both father and mother to his pupils and to be prepared for all eventualities whatever, and only the hardest penance can fit him to conduct them.

This act of mine was not without its effect on the entire life of the settlers on the farm. As we had intended to cut down expenses to the barest minimum, we changed our dress also. In the cities the Indian men including Satyagrahis[5] put on European dress. Such elaborate clothing was not needed on the farm. We had all become labourers and therefore put on labourers' dress but in the European style, viz. workmen's trousers and shirts, which were imitated from prisoners' uniforms. We all used cheap trousers and shirts which could be had ready-made out of coarse blue cloth. Most of the ladies were good hands at sewing and took charge of the tailoring department.

As for food we generally had rice, dal, vegetable and *rotti* with porridge occasionally superadded. All this was served in a single dish which was not really a dish but a kind of bowl such as is supplied to prisoners in jail. We had made wooden spoons on the farm ourselves. There were three meals in the day. We had bread and homemade wheaten coffee at six o'clock in the morning, rice, *dal* and vegetable at eleven, and wheat pap and milk, or bread and coffee at half past five in the evening. After the evening meal we had prayers at seven or half past seven. At prayers we sang *bhajans*[6] and sometimes had readings from the *Ramayana*[7] or books on Islam. The *bhajans* were in English, Hindi and Gujarati. Sometimes we had one *bhajan* from each of the three languages, and sometimes only one. Everyone retired at 9 o'clock.

Many observed the *Ekadashi*[8] fast on the Farm. We were joined there by Sr. P. K. Kotwal who had much experience of fasting, and some of us followed him to keep the *Chaturmas*.[9] Ramzan[10] also arrived in the meanwhile. There were Mussalman youngsters among us, and we felt we must encourage them to keep the fasts. We arranged for them to have meals in the evening as well as in the early morning. Porridge, etc., were prepared for them in the evening. There was no meat, of course, nor did any one ask for it. To keep the Mussalman friends' company, the rest of us had only one meal a day in the evening. As a rule we finished our evening meal before sunset; so the only difference was that the others finished their supper about when the Mussalman boys commenced theirs. These

---

5. Those who observe the principle of *Satyagraha*, or "truth-force," passive resistance to injustice.
6. Devotional Hindu music.
7. A classic epic poem written around the sixth century B.C.E. See note 4.

8. The first day of the moon during which fasting is observed.
9. The fourth day of the moon, during which fasting is observed.
10. The obligatory Islamic practice of fasting from dawn to sunset for purification of the soul.

boys were so courteous that they did not put any one to extra trouble although they were observing fasts, and the fact that the non-Muslim children supported them in the matter of fasting left a good impression on all. I do not remember that there ever was a quarrel, much less a split, between the Hindu and the Mussalman boys on the score of religion. On the other hand I know that although staunch in their own beliefs, they all treated one another with respect and assisted one another in their respective religious observances.

Although we were living far from the amenities of city life, we did not keep even the commonest appliances against the possible attacks of illness. I had in those days as much faith in the nature cure of disease as I had in the innocence of children. I felt that there should not be disease as we lived a simple life, but if there was, I was confident of dealing with it. My booklet on health is a note book of my experiments and of my living faith in those days. I was proud enough to believe that illness for me was out of the question. I held that all kinds of diseases could be cured by earth and water treatment, fasting or changes in diet. There was not a single case of illness on the farm in which we used drugs or called in a doctor. There was an old man from North India, 70 years of age, who suffered from asthma cough, but whom I cured simply by changes in diet and water treatment. But I have now lost the courage and, in view of my two serious illnesses, I feel that I have forfeited even the right to make such experiments.

Tolstoy Farm proved to be a centre of spiritual purification and penance for the final campaign. I have serious doubts as to whether the struggle could have been prosecuted for eight years, whether we could have secured larger funds, and whether the thousands of men who participated in the last phase of the struggle would have borne their share in it, if there had been no Tolstoy Farm. Tolstoy Farm was never placed in the limelight, yet an Institution, which deserved it, attracted public sympathy to itself. The Indians saw that the Tolstoy Farmers were doing what they themselves were not prepared to do and what they looked upon in the light of hardship. This public confidence was a great asset to the movement when it was organised afresh on a large scale in 1913. One can never tell whether such assets give an account of themselves, and if yes, when. But I do not entertain and would ask the reader not to entertain a shadow of a doubt that such latent assets do in God's good time become patent.

PREMCHAND [DHANPAT RAI SRIVASTAV] (1880–1936)
India/Urda

Prolific in both Hindi and Urdu, Premchand is often described as India's first modern writer; he originally wrote in Urdu, but changed to Hindi to reach a wider audience. Using a short story form that fuses the allegory of traditional Indian narratives with the social realism of nineteenth-century European writers, Premchand explores the impact of urbanization, modernization, and commercialism on Indian village life. An impassioned social critic, he is also considered an idealist. "The Kafan" or "The Shroud" was first published in 1936.

The Shroud

Father and son sat in silence at the door of their hut before a burnt-out fire and inside Budhiya, the son's young wife, lay fainting in the throes of child-birth. From time to time such an agonizing cry came out of her that their hearts skipped a beat. It was a winter night, all was silent, and the whole village was obliterated in the darkness.

Ghisu said, "It looks as though she won't make it. You spent the whole day running around—just go in and have a look."

Annoyed, Madhav said, "If she's going to die why doesn't she get it over with? What can I do by looking?"

"You're pretty hard-hearted, aren't you? You live at your ease with somebody a whole year and then you don't give a damn about her."

"But I couldn't stand looking at her writhing and thrashing."

They were a family of untouchable leather-workers and had a bad name throughout the whole village. If Ghisu worked one day he'd take three off. Madhav was such a loafer that whenever he worked for a half hour he'd stop and smoke his pipe for an hour. So they couldn't get work anywhere. If there was even a handful of grain in the house then the two of them swore off work. After a couple of days fasting Ghisu would climb up a tree and break off branches for firewood and Madhav would bring it to the market to sell. And so long as they had any of the money they got for it they'd both wander around in idleness. There was no shortage of heavy work in the village. It was a village of farmers and there was any number of chores for a hard-working man. But whenever you called these two you had to be satisfied with paying them both for doing one man's work between them. If the two of them had been wandering ascetics there would have been absolutely no need for them to practice greater restraint or austerity to attain a saint's serenity and patience. This was their nature. A strange life theirs was! They owned nothing except for some clay pots; a few torn rags was all that covered their nakedness. They were free of worldly cares! They were loaded with debts, people abused them, beat them, but they didn't suffer. People would loan them a little something even though they were so poor there was no hope of getting it back. At the time of the potato and pea harvest they would go into other people's fields and dig up potatoes and gather peas and roast them or they'd pick sugarcane to suck at night. Ghisu had reached the age of sixty living this hand-to-mouth existence, and like a good son Madhav was following in his father's foot-steps in every way, and if anything he was adding luster to his father's fame. The two of them were sitting before the fire now roasting potatoes they'd dug up in some field. Ghisu's

Translated by David Rubin.

wife had died a long time ago. Madhav had been married last year. Since his wife had come she'd established order in the family and kept those two good-for-nothings' bellies filled. And since her arrival they'd become more sluggish than ever. In fact, they'd begun to let it go to their heads. If someone sent for them to do a job, they'd bare-facedly ask for twice the wages. This same woman was dying today in child-birth and it was as though they were only waiting for her to die so they could go to sleep in peace and quiet.

Ghisu took a potato and while he peeled it said, "Go and look, see how she is. She must be possessed by some ghost, what else? But the village conjurer wants a rupee for a visit."

Madhav was afraid that if he went into the hut Ghisu would do away with most of the potatoes. He said, "I'm scared to go in there."

"What are you afraid of? I'll be right here."

"Then why don't you go and look?"

"When my woman died I didn't stir from her side for three days. And then she'd be ashamed if I saw her bare like that when I've never even seen her face before. Won't she be worried about her modesty? If she sees me she won't feel free to thrash around."

"I've been thinking, if there's a baby what's going to happen? There's nothing we're supposed to have in the house—ginger, sugar, oil."

"Everything's going to be all right, God will provide. The very people who wouldn't even give us a pice[1] before will send for us tomorrow and give us rupees. I had nine kids and there was never a thing in the house but somehow or other the Lord got us through."

In a society where the condition of people who toiled day and night was not much better than theirs and where, on the other hand, those who knew how to profit from the weaknesses of the peasants were infinitely richer, it's no wonder they felt like this. We could even say that Ghisu was much smarter than the peasants and instead of being one of the horde of empty-headed toilers he'd found a place for himself in the disreputable society of idle gossipers. Only he didn't have the ability to stick to the rules and code of such idlers. So while others of his crowd had made themselves chiefs and bosses of the village, the whole community pointed at him in contempt. Nevertheless, there was the consolation that although he was miserably poor at least he didn't have to do the back-breaking labour the farmers did, and other people weren't able to take unfair advantage of his simplicity and lack of ambition.

They ate the potatoes piping hot. Since yesterday they'd eaten nothing and they didn't have the patience to let them cool. Several times they burned their tongues. When they were peeled the outside of the potatoes didn't seem very hot but as soon as they bit into them the inside burned their palates, tongues and throats. Rather than keep these burning coals in their mouths it was a lot safer to drop them down into their bellies, where there was plenty of equipment to cool them. So they swallowed them quickly, even though the attempt brought tears to their eyes.

---

1. A *paisa*, an Indian coin.

At this moment Ghisu recalled the Thakur's[2] wedding, which he'd attended twenty years before. The way the feast had gratified him was something to remember all his life, and the memory was still vivid today. He said, "I won't forget that feast. Since then I've never seen food like it or filled my belly so well. The bride's people crammed everybody with puris,[3] everybody! Bigshots and nobodies all ate puris fried in real ghee.[4] Relishes and curds with spices, three kinds of dried vegetables, a tasty curry, sweets—how can I describe how delicious that food was? There was nothing to hold you back, you just asked for anything you wanted and as much as you wanted. We ate so much that nobody had any room left for water. The people serving just kept on handing out hot, round, mouth-watering pastries on leaves. And we'd say 'Stop, you mustn't,' and put our hands over the plates to stop them but they kept right on handing it out. And when everybody'd rinsed his mouth we got *pan* and cardamom too.[5] But how could I take any *pan*? I couldn't even stand up. I just went and lay down in my blanket right away. That's how generous that Thakur was!"

Relishing the banquet in his imagination Madhav said, "Nobody feeds us like that now."

"Who'd feed us like that today? That was another age. Now everybody thinks about saving his money. Don't spend for weddings, don't spend for funerals! I ask you, if they keep on hoarding the wealth they've squeezed out of the poor, where are they going to put it? But they keep on hoarding. When it comes to spending any money they say they have to economize."

"You must have eaten a good twenty puris?"

"I ate more than twenty."

"I would have eaten fifty!"

"I couldn't have eaten any less than fifty. I was a husky lad in those days. You're not half so big."

After finishing the potatoes they drank some water and right there in front of the fire they wrapped themselves up in their dhotis and pulling up their knees they fell asleep—just like two enormous coiled pythons.

And Budhiya was still moaning.

2

In the morning Madhav went inside the hut and saw that his wife had turned cold. Flies were buzzing around her mouth. Her stony eyes stared upwards. Her whole body was covered with dust. The child had died in her womb.

Madhav ran to get Ghisu. Then they both began to moan wildly and beat their chests. When they heard the wailing the neighbours came running and according to the old tradition began to console the bereaved.

---

2. The title of Rajputs or landowners.
3. Deep-fried whole wheat puffed cake.
4. Clarified butter.

5. Pan is a digestive composed of betel nut, areca nuts, and other condiments; cardamom is a spice used in desserts.

But there was not much time for moaning and chest-beating. There was the worry about a shroud and wood for the pyre. The money in the house had disappeared like carrion in a kite's nest.

Father and son went weeping to the village zamindar.[6] He hated the sight of the two of them and several times he'd thrashed them with his own hands for stealing or for not coming to do the work they'd promised to do. He asked, "What is it, little Ghisu, what are you crying about? You don't show yourself much these days. It seems as though you don't want to live in this village."

Ghisu bowed his head all the way to the ground, his eyes full of tears, and said, "Excellency, an awful thing's happened to me. Madhav's woman passed away last night. She was in agony the whole time. The two of us never once left her side. We did whatever we could, gave her medicine—but to make a long story short, she gave us the slip. And now there's nobody left even to give us a piece of bread, master. We're ruined! My house has been destroyed! I'm your slave—except for you now who is there to see that she's given a decent funeral? Whatever we had we spent on medicine. If your excellency is merciful, then she'll have a good funeral. Whose door can we go to except yours?"

The zamindar was soft-hearted. But to be kind to Ghisu was like trying to dye a black blanket. He was tempted to say, "Get out and don't come back! When we send for you you don't show up but today when you're in a jam you come and flatter me. You're a sponging bastard!" But this was not the occasion for anger or scolding. Exasperated, he took out a couple of rupees and threw them on the ground. But he didn't utter a word of consolation. He didn't even look at Ghisu. It was as though he'd shoved a load off his head.

When the zamindar had given two rupees how could the shop-keepers and moneylenders of the village refuse? Ghisu knew how to trumpet the zamindar's name around. Somebody gave him a couple of annas, somebody else four. Within an hour Ghisu had harvested a tidy sum of five rupees. He got grain at one place, wood from somewhere else. And at noon Ghisu and Madhav went to the market to get a shroud. There were people already cutting the bamboo to make a litter for the corpse.

The tender-hearted women of the village came and looked at the dead woman, shed a few tears over her forlorn state and went away.

3

When they reached the market Ghisu said, "We have enough wood to burn her up completely, haven't we, Madhav?"

"Yes, there's plenty of wood, now we need the shroud."

"That's right, come along and we'll pick up a cheap one."

"Of course, what else? By the time we move the corpse it will be night—who can see a shroud at night?"

---

6. A landowner.

"What a rotten custom it is that somebody who didn't even have rags to cover herself while she was alive has to have a new shroud when she dies!"

"The shroud just burns right up with the body."

"And what's left? If we'd had these five rupees before then we could have got some medicine."

Each of them guessed what was in the other's mind. They went on wandering through the market, stopping at one cloth-merchant's shop after another. They looked at different kinds of cloth, silk and cotton, but nothing met with their approval. This went on until evening. Then the two of them, by some divine inspiration or other, found themselves in front of a liquor shop, and as though according to a previous agreement they went inside. For a little while they stood there, hesitant. Then Ghisu went up to where the tavern-keeper sat and said, "Sahuji, give us a bottle too."

Then some snacks arrived, fried fish was brought and they sat on the veranda and tranquilly began to drink.

After drinking several cups in a row they began to feel tipsy. Ghisu said, "What's the point of throwing a shroud over her? In the end it just burns up. She can't take anything with her."

Madhav looked toward heaven and said, as though calling on the gods to witness his innocence, "It's the way things are done in the world, otherwise why would people throw thousands of rupees away on Brahmans![7] Who can tell if anybody gets it in the next world or not?"

"The bigshots have lots of money to squander so let them squander it, but what have we got to squander?"

"But how will you explain it to people? Won't they ask, 'Where's the shroud?' "

Ghisu laughed. "So what? We'll say the money fell out of the knot in our dhotis and we looked and looked but couldn't find it. They won't believe it but they'll give the money again."

Madhav laughed too over this unexpected stroke of luck. He said, "She was good to us, that poor girl—even dying she got us fine things to eat and drink."

They'd gone through more than half a bottle. Ghisu ordered four pounds of puris. Then relish, pickle, livers. There was a shop right across from the tavern. Madhav brought everything back in a trice on a couple of leaf-platters. He'd spent one and a half rupees; only a few pice were left.

The two of them sat eating their puris in the lordly manner of tigers enjoying their kill in the jungle. They felt neither fear of being called to account nor concern for a bad reputation. They had overcome those sensibilities long before.

Ghisu said philosophically, "If our souls are content won't it be credited to her in heaven as a good deed?"

Respectfully Madhav bowed his head and confirmed, "Absolutely will! Lord, you know all secrets. Bring her to paradise—we bless her from our hearts . . . the way we've eaten today we've never eaten before in our whole lives."

---

7. Priestly caste of Hindus.

A moment later a doubt rose in his mind. He said, "What about us, are we going to get there some day too?"

Ghisu gave no answer to this artless question. He didn't want to dampen his pleasure by thinking about the other world.

"But if she asks us there, 'Why didn't you people give me a shroud?' what will you say?"

"That's a stupid question!"

"But surely she'll ask!"

"How do you know she won't get a shroud? Do you think I'm such a jackass? Have I been wasting my time in this world for sixty years? She'll have a shroud and a good one too."

Madhav was not convinced. He said, "Who'll give it? You've eaten up all the money. But she'll ask *me*. I was the one who put the cinnabar[8] in her hair at the wedding."

Getting angry, Ghisu said, "I tell you she'll have a shroud, aren't you listening?"

"But why don't you tell me who's going to give it?"

"The same people who gave before will give the money again—well, not the money this time but the stuff we need."

As the darkness spread and the stars began to glitter the gaiety of the tavern also increased steadily. People sang, bragged, embraced their companions, lifted the jug to the lips of friends. All was jollity, there was intoxication in the air. Anybody who came in got drunk in an instant from just a few drops, the very air of the place turned their heads more than the liquor. The sufferings of their lives drew them all there and after a little while they were no longer aware if they were alive or dead, not alive or not dead.

And father and son went on slopping it up with zest. Everyone was staring at them. How lucky the two of them were, they had a whole bottle between themselves.

When he was crammed full Madhav handed the left-over puris on a leaf to a beggar who was standing watching them with famished eyes. And for the first time in his life he experienced the pride, the happiness and the pleasure of giving.

Ghisu said, "Take it, eat it and say a blessing—the one who earned it is—well, she's dead. But surely your blessing will reach her. Bless her from your heart, that food's the wages for very hard labour."

Madhav looked heavenward again and said, "She'll go to heaven, Dada, she'll be a queen in heaven."

Ghisu stood up and as though bathing in waves of bliss he said, "Yes, son, she'll go to heaven. She didn't torment anybody, she didn't oppress anybody. At the moment she died she fulfilled the deepest wish of all our lives. If she doesn't go to heaven then will those big fat people go who rob the poor with both hands and swim in the Ganges and offer holy water in the temples to wash away their sins?"

---

8. A reddish pigment.

Their mood of credulity suddenly changed. Volatility is the special character-istic of drunkenness. Now was the turn for grief and despair.

"But Dada," Madhav said, "the poor girl suffered so much in this life! How much pain she had when she died."

He put his hands over his eyes and began to cry, he burst into sobs.

Ghisu consoled him. "Why weep, son? Be glad she's slipped out of this maze of illusion and left the whole mess behind her. She was very lucky to escape the bonds of the world's illusion so quickly."

And the two of them stood up and began to sing.

"Deceitful world, why do you dazzle us with your eyes? Deceitful world!"

The eyes of all the drunkards were glued on them and the two of them became intoxicated right to their hearts. Then they started to dance, they jumped and sprang, fell back, twisted, they gesticuclated, they mimed their feelings, and finally they collapsed dead drunk.

FAIZ AHMED FAIZ (1910–1984)
Pakistan/Lebanon

Faiz Ahmed Faiz, a Pakistani exile who spent his last years in Beirut, is one of the most celebrated modern writers of Urdu poetry. Although he uses traditional Indian literary forms and techniques, such as the imagery of romantic pain and pleasure of the Urdu *ghazal* or lyric poem, he does so in order to express the political criticisms of an exile in the symbolic form of a tragic lover.

Black Out

[Written during the India-Pakistan war of 1965]

Ever since the lights failed,
I have been searching to see how I could see.
Where have my eyes strayed in the dust?

You who know, give me proof.
Describe me to myself.
A bitter river rages in my veins.
And my heart, still longing for you,
flows on its poisonous waves.

5

Translated by Agha Shahid Ali.

Wait a little: perhaps from some other world
the hand of a prophet, carved in lightning,
is bringing me pearls for my lost eyes.

Wait till the river is stilled
and my submerged heart, annulled like a Sufi's,
is washed up, cleansed, on a welcoming shore.

I will then begin a new translation of hope.
I will complete the texts of love.

In Search of Vanished Blood

There's no sign of blood, not anywhere.
I've searched everywhere.
The executioner's hands are clean, his nails transparent.
The sleeves of each assassin are spotless.
No sign of blood: no trace of red,
not on the edge of the knife, none on the point of the sword.
The ground is without stains, the ceiling white.

This blood which has disappeared without leaving a trace
isn't part of written history: who will guide me to it?
It wasn't spilled in service of emperors—
    it earned no honor, had no wish granted.
It wasn't offered in rituals of sacrifice—
    no cup of absolution holds it in a temple.
It wasn't shed in any battle—
    no one calligraphed it on banners of victory.

But, unheard, it still kept crying out to be heard.
No one had the time to listen, no one the desire.
It kept crying out, this orphan blood,
but there was no witness. No case was filed.
From the beginning this blood was nourished only by dust.
Then it turned to ashes, left no trace, became food for dust.

Be Near Me

You who demolish me, you whom I love,
be near me. Remain near me when evening,
drunk on the blood of the skies,
becomes night, in its one hand
a perfumed balm, in the other
a sword sheathed in the diamond of stars.

Be near me when night laments or sings,
or when it begins to dance,
its steel-blue anklets ringing with grief.

Be here when longings, long submerged
in the heart's waters, resurface
and everyone begins to look:
Where is the assassin? In whose sleeve
is hidden the redeeming knife?

And when wine, as it is poured, is the sobbing
of children whom nothing will console—
when nothing holds,
when nothing is:
at that dark hour when night mourns,
be near me, my destroyer, my lover,
be near me.

Before You Came

Before you came,
things were as they should be:
the sky was the dead-end of sight,
the road was just a road, wine merely wine.

Now everything is like my heart,
a color at the edge of blood:
the grey of your absence, the color of poison, of thorns,
the gold when we meet, the season ablaze,
the yellow of autumn, the red of flowers, of flames,
and the black when you cover the earth
with the coal of dead fires.

And the sky, the road, the glass of wine?
The sky is a shirt wet with tears,
the road a vein about to break,
and the glass of wine a mirror in which
the sky, the road, the world keep changing.

Don't leave now that you're here—
Stay. So the world may become like itself again:
so the sky may be the sky,
the road a road,
and the glass of wine not a mirror, just a glass of wine.

The Rain of Stones Is Finished

[For Hassan Nasir, tortured to death in the Lahore Fort, 1959]

Today as I stared, suddenly a string snapped,
and the moon and sun were smashed in the sky.
No darkness is left in any corner, and no light—
behind me the road of fidelity lies broken,
   its lights extinguished, like my heart;   5
and nothing remains ahead. Friends, what will happen now?

Convoys of pain bearing cargoes of love must keep moving,
but someone else must now wave them forward.
And others must tend the garden where ardor blooms—
I can't: the dew of my eyes has dried: I won't weep again.   10
All rapture, the pure madness of passion, has ceased,
   and no one's left to bear the rain of stones.

That road behind me: it was always the Beloved's street.
It is now the color of her lips;
my blood, like a flag, has been unfurled there.   15
I have nothing left to give.

And a glass is being filled again.
Friends, let one of you now come forward,
for the cry has begun: "Who'll dare to drink this wine of love
   that is blood and poison? Who?"   20
This is the cry in the tavern after I'm gone.

Appointments

The walls, each inch of them, have turned black.
Darkness has climbed up to the noose of the ceiling.
All roads have been stamped out, their lights gone out.
Everyone has taken leave. I am alone,
and it's night, nothing but night.   5
It seems desolation will be my only companion,
for whatever may or may not be,
once again she has come to me for the night,
her one hand dyed red like a bride's,
the other wet with the blood of her victims,   10
her one eye poison, the other wine.

Years have passed since my heart's been anyone's destination,
and its wounds, in this desolation,
have lost their sheen—
Whom can I possibly ask to pour color into them?   15

But suddenly she is here, come
once again, without my asking,
that familiar one, Beloved death,
my enemy who erases sorrows like a friend,   20
my murderer who's also my lover.

Solitary Confinement

Wave of light on the horizon:
the city of grief awakes
and the eye too is restless—
but truly the city sleeps, the eye too sleeps.

Here in this dark where separation is endless,   5
I see dawn: I take it through the bars
and pour it into the heart, the cup
where I mix yesterday's poison with today's exile.
I drink.

A little light on the far, far horizon: 10
it brings news of another dawn, farther out, behind the horizon:
a song, the ghost of musk, the ravishing face of love
pass through here where there is no hope;
they pass and I'm again alone, restless with terrible hope.

I drink the poison and I drink the faint light.   15
I say, "To life,"
and long for my friends at home
and in countries I'll never see.
With them I used to raise a glass
to this planet   20
and to the beauty of woman.

Evening

The trees are dark ruins of temples,
seeking excuses to crumble
since who knows when—
their roofs are cracked,
their doors lost to ancient winds.   5
And the sky is a priest,
saffron marks on his forehead,
ashes smeared on his body.
He sits by the temples, worn to a shadow, not looking up.

Some terrible magician, hidden behind curtains,   10
has hypnotized Time

so this evening is a net
in which the twilight is caught.
Now darkness will never come—
and there will never be morning.   15

The sky waits for this spell to be broken,
for History to tear itself from this net,
for Silence to break its chains
so that a symphony of conch shells
may wake up the statues   20
and a beautiful, dark goddess,
her anklets echoing, may unveil herself.

Why complain? Holding up our sorrows as banners,
new lovers will emerge
from the lanes where we were killed   25
and embark, in caravans, on those highways of desire.
It's because of them that we shortened the distances of sorrow,
it's because of them that we went out to make the world our own,
we who were murdered in the darkest lanes.

We Who Were Executed

[After reading the letters of Julius and Ethel Rosenberg]

I longed for your lips, dreamed of their roses:
I was hanged from the dry branch of the scaffold.
I wanted to touch your hands, their silver light:
I was murdered in the half-light of dim lanes.

And there where you were crucified,   5
so far away from my words,
you still were beautiful:
color kept clinging to your lips—
rapture was still vivid in your hair—
light remained silvering in your hands.   10

When the night of cruelty merged with the roads you had taken,
I came as far as my feet could bring me,
on my lips the phrase of a song,
my heart lit up only by sorrow.
This sorrow was my testimony to your beauty—   15
Look! I remained a witness till the end,
I who was killed in the darkest lanes.

It's true—that not to reach you was fate—
but who'll deny that to love you
was entirely in my hands?   20

So why complain if these matters of desire
brought me inevitably to the execution grounds?

ISMAT CHUGTAI (1915–1992)
India

Ismat Chugtai, widely regarded as one of India's finest writers, can be credited
with giving to Urdu fiction a biting realism that used the language of everyday
speech and a widened scope that included hitherto unexplored areas of human
sensibility. Best known as a short story writer, Chugtai exposes in her fiction a
variety of social ills, including illiteracy and the abuse of women. In "Housewife"
she reveals the hollowness, irrelevance, and hypocrisy of the institution of
marriage.

Housewife

The day Mirza's new maid ambled into his house, there was a sensation in the
neighbourhood. The sweeper, who normally avoided work, stayed on and
scrubbed the floor with great vigour. The milkman, notorious for adulterating his
ware, brought milk clogged with cream.

Who could have named her Lajo—the coy one? Bashfulness was unknown to
Lajo. No one knew who begot her and abandoned her on the streets to a lonely
weeping childhood. Begging and starving, she reached an age when she could
snatch a living for herself. Youth etched her body into bewitching curves and this
became her only asset. The street initiated her into the mysteries of life.

She never haggled. If it was not a cash-down proposition, it would be sex on
credit. If the lover had no means, she would even give of herself free.

"Aren't you ashamed of yourself?" people asked.

"I am!" Lajo would blush brazenly.

"You'll regret it some day."

"I couldn't care less!"

How could she? With a face that was innocence itself, dark eyes, evenly set
teeth, a mellow complexion and a gait so swinging, so provocative?

Mirza was a bachelor. Flattening and baking chapatis daily had flattened out
his existence. He owned a small grocery shop which he pompously called
"General Store." The shop did not give any leisure to Mirza even to go to his home
town and get married.

Mirza's friend Bakhshi had picked up Lajo at a bus stop. Bakhshi's wife was
nine months pregnant and they needed a maid. Later, when Lajo was not

Translated by Fatima Ahmed.

required, Bakhshi deposited her at Mirza's. Instead of squandering away at brothels, he thought, why not let Mirza enjoy a free dish?

"God forbid. I won't have a tart in the house!" said Mirza warily. "Take her back!"

But Lajo had already made herself at home. With her skirt hiked up like a diaper, broom in hand, she was sweeping Mirza's house in dead earnest. When Bakhshi informed her of Mirza's refusal, it fell on deaf ears. She ordered him to arrange the pans on the kitchen shelf and went out to fetch water. "If you wish, I'll take you back home," Bakhshi said.

"Out with you! Are you my husband to leave me back at my mother's? Go! I'll tackle the Mian[1] myself!"

Bakhshi's departure left Mirza helpless. He ran out and took refuge in the mosque. He was not prepared to incur this extra expenditure. Moreover, she was bound to pilfer and cheat. What a mess Bakhshi had got him into!

But on returning home he held his breath. As though his late mother, Bi Amma, was back! The house was sparkling.

"Shall I serve dinner, Mian?" Lajo asked and disappeared into the kitchen.

Spinach and potato curry, *moong ki dal*[2] fried with onion and garlic—just the way Ammajii used to cook!

"How did you manage all this?" Mirza asked, baffled.

"Borrowed from the bania."

"Look, I'll pay your return fare. I just cannot afford a servant."

"Who wants to be paid?"

"But . . ."

"Is the food hot?" Lajo asked, slipping a fresh chapati into his plate.

"Not the food but I am certainly hot from top to toe!" Mirza wanted to shout as he went into his room to sleep.

"No, Mian, I am here for good!" Lajo threatened when he brought up the question again the next morning.

"But . . ."

"Didn't you like the food?"

"It's not that. . . ."

"Don't I scrub and clean well?"

"It's not that . . ."

"Then what is it?" Lajo flared up.

She had fallen in love, not with Mirza, but with the house. Bakhshi, the bastard had once rented a room for her. Its previous occupant had been Nandi—a buffalo. The buffalo was dead and gone to hell but had left behind his stench. And Bakhshi did not treat her well either. Now here she was, the unrivalled mistress of Mirza's house! Mirza was uncomplicated. He would sneak in, softly and quietly, and eat whatever was served.

Mirza, for his part checked the accounts a few times and was satisfied that Lajo did not cheat.

---

1. A term of endearment for one's spouse.   2. Cooked lentils.

At times she went across to Ramu's grandmother for a tete-a-tete. Ramu was Mirza's dissipated teenaged help in the store. He fell for Lajo the minute he saw her. It was he who told her of Mirza's frequent visits to the singing girls.

This hurt Lajo. After all, what was she for? Wherever employed, she had served well in every capacity. And here a full chaste week had passed! She had never felt so unwanted before. Several offers came her way but she was Mirza's maid. She rejected one and all, lest Mirza should become a laughing-stock. And here was Mirza an iceberg, or so he appeared. Lajo could not see the volcanoes erupting within him. He kept away from home deliberately.

Lajo's name was on every lip—today she slapped the milkman, yesterday she had aimed a dung-cake full in the face of the bania[3] and so on. The schoolmaster insisted on educating her. The Mullaji of the mosque burst into prayers in Arabic, beseeching God to ward off impending danger!

Mirza came home annoyed. Lajo had just had her bath. Strands of wet hair clung to her shoulders. Blowing into the kitchen fire had flushed her cheeks and filled her eyes with water. She ground her teeth at Mian's untimely entry.

Mirza almost toppled over! After a silent, uneasy meal, he picked up his walking-stick, went out and sat in the mosque. But he could not relax. Ceaseless thoughts of home made him restless. Unable to hold out any longer, he got back and found Lajo on the threshold, quarrelling with a man. The man slinked away the moment he saw Mirza.

"Who was that?" Mirza's tone was that of a suspicious husband.

"Raghava!"

"Raghava?" Mirza had been buying milk from him for years and yet did not know his name.

"Shall I prepare the hookah, Mian?" Lajo changed the subject.

"No! What was that man up to?"

"Was asking me how much milk he should bring from now on."

"What did you say?"

"I said: May God hasten your funeral! Bring the usual measure."

"Then?" Mirza was furious.

"Then I said: Bastard, go, feed the extra milk to your mother and sister!"

"The scoundrel! Don't let him set foot here again! I'll myself fetch milk on the way home from the store."

That night, after dinner, Mirza put on a starched freshly laundered kurta, stuck a scented piece of cottonwool in an ear, picked up his walking-stick and walked out.

Jealousy wrung Lajo's heart. She cursed the singing-girl and sat dumbfounded. Was Mirza really indifferent to her? 'How could that be?' she wondered.

The singing-girl was haggling with a customer. This upset Mirza. He turned away and made for the Lala's shop. There, he vented his anger on inflation, rising

---

3. A moneylender.

prices, national politics . . . and returned home at midnight, spent and irritated. He drank a lot of cold water but the fire in him continued to blaze.

A part of Lajo's smooth golden leg was visible from the open door. A careless turn in sleep tinkled her anklets. Mirza drained another glass of water and bundled up on his cot, cursing everything under the moon.

Ceaseless tossing in bed reduced his body to a blister. Litres of cold water bloated his stomach. The roundness of the leg behind the door was irresistible. Unknown fears strangled him. But the devil egged him on. From his bed to the kitchen, he had walked so many miles but now he couldn't move a step.

Then a very innocent idea crossed his mind. Were Lajo's leg not so exposed he wouldn't be so uncomfortable . . . Gradually, this idea took strength and so did Mirza. What if she woke up? Yet he had to take the risk—for the sake of his own safety.

He left his slippers under the cot, held his breath and tiptoed across, gingerly lifted the hem of the skirt and pulled it down slowly. He stood awhile, indecisively and turned away.

With one quick move, Lajo grabbed him. Mirza was speechless. He was never so wrong in life before. He struggled, pleaded but Lajo wouldn't let him go!

When he encountered Lajo the next morning, she blushed like a bride! Lajo, the victor, went about her chores boldly, humming a kajri.[4] Not a shadow of the night's happening flickered in her eyes. When Mirza sat down to breakfast, she sat on the doorstep, as usual, fanning the flies away.

That afternoon, when she brought his lunch to the shop he noticed a new lilt in her gait. Whenever Lajo came to the shop, people would stop by and enquire about the prices of groceries. She sold in a short while what Mirza couldn't during the entire day!

Mirza began to improve in his looks. People knew the reason and sizzled with envy. Mirza, in turn, grew nervous and ill at ease. The more Lajo looked after him, the more he was enamoured of her and the more afraid he was of the neighbours. She was utterly brazen. When she fetched his lunch, the entire bazaar throbbed with her presence.

"Don't bring lunch any more!" he told her one day.

"Why not?" Lajo's face fell. Staying home all by herself bored her. The bazaar was an interesting break.

Having stopped her from coming, many doubts assailed Mirza. He dropped in at odd hours to spy on her and she would insist on rewarding him fully for his attentions!

The day he caught her at a game of kabaddi[5] with street urchins, his anger knew no bounds. Her skirt was billowing in the wind. The boys were engrossed in the skirt. Mirza passed by, holding his head high with affected indifference. His discomfiture amused the onlookers.

Mirza had grown fond of Lajo. The very idea of separation drove him crazy.

---

4. A folk song of northern India.   5. A buyer of junk and old newspapers.

He was unable to concentrate on his shop. He feared that some day she might desert him.

"Mian, why not marry her?" Miran Mian suggested.

"God forbid!" he shouted. How could he form so sacred a relationship with a slut?

But that very evening, when he didn't find her at home, Mirza felt lost. The confounded Lala had been long on the wait. He had offered her a bungalow! Miran Mian, a friend from all accounts, had himself made a proposition to Lajo on the sly.

Mirza was losing hope when suddenly Lajo appeared. She had just gone across to Ramu's grandmother!

That day Mirza made up his mind to take Lajo for a wife even at the cost of his family's pride and prestige.

"But why, Mian?" Lajo asked, surprised at his proposal.

"Why not? Want to have a fling elsewhere?" he asked crossly.

"Why should I have a fling?"

"That Raoji is offering you a bungalow."

"I wouldn't spit on his bungalow!"

But the need for marriage completely escaped her. She was and would be his for life. A master like him was not easy to come by. Lajo knew what a gem Mirza was. All her previous masters inevitably ended up as her lovers. They would first have their fill then beat her up and kick her out. Mirza had always been tender and loving. He had bought her a few clothes and a pair of gold bangles. No one in seven generations of Lajo's family had even worn ornaments of pure gold.

When Mirza spoke of his plan to Ramu's grandmother, she too was surprised.

"Mian, why tie a bell around your neck?" she asked. "Is the slut making a fuss? A sound thrashing will set her right. Where beating up can do, why think of marriage."

But Mirza was obsessed with the idea.

"You there, are you hesitating on account of the difference in religion?" Ramu's grandmother asked Lajo.

"No, I've always regarded him as my husband."

Lajo looked upon even a passing lover as a passing husband and served him well. Riches were never showered upon her, yet she gave of herself fully—body and soul. Mirza was an exception, of course. Only Lajo knew the pleasure of the give-and-take game with him. Compared to him the others were pigs.

Also, marriage was for virgins. How did she qualify to be a bride? She begged and pleaded, but Mirza was bent upon entering into a legal contract of the *nikah*.[6]

That day, after the evening prayer, *nikah* was solemnised. Young girls of the neighbourhood sang wedding songs. Mirza entertained his friends. Lajo renamed Kaneez Fatima, became wife of Mirza Irfan Ali Beg.

Mirza imposed a ban on *lehngas*[7] and prescribed *churidar*[8] pyjamas. Lajo, however, was used to open space between her legs. This new imposition was a big

---

6. A Muslim wedding ceremony.
7. A long skirt.

8. Trousers worn under a loose shirt.

irritant. She could never get used to it. One day, at the first opportunity, she took off the pyjamas and was about to get into the *lehnga,* when Mirza turned up. In her confusion, she forgot to hold the skirt around her waist and dropped it to the floor.

"The devil take you!" Mirza thundered a Quranic curse. He hurriedly threw a bedsheet over her.

Lajo could not understand his annoyance and the grandiloquent oration that followed. Where had she erred? This very act had taken Mirza's breath away so many times in the past. Now he was so upset. He picked up the *lehnga* and actually fed it to the fire.

Mirza left, leaving Lajo shocked and uncomprehending. Discarding the sheet, she examined her body. Maybe some repulsive skin disease had erupted overnight.

When bathing under the tap in the open, she kept wiping her tears. Mithwa, son of the mason, climbed the terrace daily on the pretext of flying kites and watched her. She was so sad today she neither stuck out her thumb nor hurled a slipper at him. She wrapped the sheet around and went indoors.

With a heavy heart she got into the long trousers—as long as the devil's intestines. To add to her misery the cummerbund got lost inside the waistband. She shouted for help. Jullu, the neighbour's daughter, appeared and the tape was located. 'Which sadist could have adapted this rifle case for a feminine dress?' Lajo wondered.

Later, when Mirza returned home, the tape played truant once again. Lajo tried desparately to catch it with her fingers. Mirza found her nervousness endearing. After a combined concentrated chase, the tape was found.

But a ticklish problem popped up for Mirza. What used to be intoxicating coquetry in Lajo now turned to brazeness in his wife. The indecent ways of a flirt are unbecoming to respectable women. Lajo failed to be the bride of his dream—one who would blush at his amorous advances, be annoyed at his persistence and feign indifference to his attention. Lajo was a mere pavement slab.

Checking her at every step, Mirza curbed her excesses and tamed the wild in her—or so he thought. Also, he was no longer impatient to get back home in the evenings. Like all husbands, he spent more time with friends to avoid being labelled henpecked.

To make up for his frequent absences, he suggested engaging a maid. Lajo was furious. She knew of Mian's renewed visits to the singing-girls. She also knew that every man of the neighbourhood went there. But, in her own home, she would not tolerate another woman! Let anybody step into her kitchen and tinker with her glistening vessels, Lajo would tear her to bits! She would share Mirza with another woman but certainly would not share the home.

Mirza seemed to have installed Lajo in his house and forgotten all about her. For weeks he spoke only in monosyllables. When she was his mistress, all men had had eyes on her. Now that she had gained respectability, she became "mother, sister and daughter." No one cast even stray glance at the jute curtain—except the faithful Mithwa. He still flew kites on the roof, although only when Mirza was away and Lajo was bathing in the courtyard.

One night Mirza stayed away, celebrating Dassera with friends. He came home the next morning, had a quick wash and went off to the shop. Lajo was annoyed. It was then, while bathing, that her glance climbed up the terrace. Or may be that day Mithwa's stares pierced her wet body like so many spears.

Suddenly his kite snapped. The broken cord brushed sharply against Lajo's body. Lajo was startled. She got up quickly and ran into a room, absent-minded or deliberately forgetting to wrap the towel around her.

From then on, Mithwa was always found hanging around Mirza's house. Whenever Lajo wanted something from the market, she would draw the jute curtain aside and shout "Mithwa, don't stay put like a dunghill! Get us a few kachoris."[9]

If Mithwa did not appear on the terrace during her bath, she rattled the bucket loud enough to wake a corpse in its grave. The love, of which she had given so lavishly all her life, was now Mithwa's for the asking. If Mirza did not turn up for a meal, she would never waste the food but feed someone poor and needy. Who was needier than Mithwa?

Mirza was convinced that, chained down to wedlock, Lajo had become a genuine housewife. Had he not seen for himself, he would never have believed it. Seeing him on the doorstep so unexpectedly, she gave out a peal of laughter. She could not, even in her wildest dreams, imagine that Mirza would be so offended!

But Mithwa knew. Clutching his dhoti firmly with one hand, he bolted and stopped for breath only after he had crossed three villages! Mirza flogged Lajo so much that, had she been made of softer stuff, she would have breathed her last.

The news that Mirza had caught his wife with Mithwa spread throughout the village. People came in large numbers to watch the fun and were sorely disappointed to know that Mithwa, the hero, had fled and that the wife lay dismantled. Ramu's grandmother arrived and gathered her away.

One would think a flogging like that would turn Lajo against the very idea of Mirza. Far from it! Beating helped achieve what marriage could not. The bond was stronger. The minute she came to, Lajo enquired after Mirza. All her masters inevitably ended up as lovers. After giving her a sound thrashing, the question of pay was set aside. She slogged free and was beaten from time to time. But Mirza had always been good. Other masters had even "loaned" her to friends but Mirza regarded her as his own. Everyone advised her to run away and save her skin but she did not budge.

How was Mirza to face the world? He saw no way but to kill her in order to save his honour. Mirza Mian held him back. "Why must you stick your head in the noose for a bitch? Divorce the whore and forget her!"

Mirza divorced Lajo then and there and sent 32 rupees of dower, *mahr*, her clothes and other belongings over to Ramu's grandmother.

When Lajo heard of the divorce, she heaved a sigh of relief. *Nikah* had proved unlucky. All mishaps had been due to that.

"Is Mian still angry?" she asked Ramu's grandmother.

---

9. Deep-fried savory.

"Shan't set eyes on you. Wants you to get lost! Drop dead!"

The news of Mirza's divorce rocked the village. Lala sent out a feeler: "The bungalow is ready!"

"Dump your mother in it!" Lajo retorted.

After a fortnight in bed, Lajo was up on her feet again. The beating seemed to have spring-cleaned her and left her more glowing than ever. When buying pan or kachori, she took the whole bazaar by storm.

Mirza died a thousand deaths. Once he spotted her at the bania's arguing over something. The bania drooled. Mirza slinked away, avoiding notice.

"You are crazy, Mian! Why care for what she does? You have divorced her, haven't you?" Miran Mian asked.

"She has been my wife."

"If you want the truth, she was never your wife!"

"What about the *nikah?*"

"Thoroughly illegal!"

"How?"

"It was never valid. No one knows who begot her. And, I suppose, *nikah* with a bastard is not valid." Miran Mian passed the verdict.

"So the *nikah* never came into effect?" Mirza asked.

"Never!" confirmed Miran Mian.

"And I never lost face either? My family's reputation is intact!"

Mirza felt immensely relieved. "But what about the divorce?" he asked, worried.

"My dear Mian, no *nikah,* no divorce!"

"So the thirty-two rupees were wasted!" Mirza said sorrowfully.

In no time, news went bouncing all over the neighbourhood that Mirza was never married to his 'wife', that the *nikah* and divorce had both been unlawful.

When Lajo heard the news she danced with joy. The nightmare that was her marriage and divorce was over. What made her happiest was the fact that Mian had not lost face, after all. She had been genuinely grieved that he had lost his honour because of her. "What a boon it is to be a bastard," she thought. God forbid, were she a legitimate child . . . Even the idea of such a possibility made her shudder.

Lajo was feeling suffocated at Ramu's grandmother's. Thoughts of the house kept her worried. Mian could not have had it swept and dusted for fear of theft. The place must be in a mess.

One day Mirza was on his way to the shop when Lajo waylaid him.

"Mian, shall I resume duty from tomorrow?"

"Damn," said Mirza and walked away briskly. 'But I'll need a maid sooner or later,' he thought, 'May be this wretch if none other.'

Lajo did not wait for Mirza to make up his mind. She jumped into the house from the roof, tied up her *lehnga* and set to work.

That evening, on his return, Mirza held his breath. It was like the late Bi Amma come back! The house was sparkling clean. A faint smell of incense filled the air. The pitcher was filled with water and over that was placed a well-scrubbed bowl.

Mirza's heart went heavy with nostalgia. He ate the roast mutton and *parathas*[10] in hushed silence. As usual Lajo sat on the doorstep, fanning the flies away.

At night, when she spread jute[11] curtains on the kitchen floor and went to sleep, Mirza once again had a severe bout of thirst. He tossed and turned, listening to the provocative tinkle of her anklets. Fear clutched at his heart, as also a feeling of guilt. He felt he had been very unfair to her and had grossly underestimated the poor creature. A deep sense of regret overtook him. He lay cursing himself.

Then with a sudden "Damn it all," he got up, ran across and collected the housewife from the mat.

K. A. ABBAS (b. 1930)
India

In his many novels, short stories, and screenplays, K. A. Abbas, who writes in English, Hindi, and Urdu, has addressed the challenges of building a postcolonial Indian nation. "Maharaja's Elephant," written in Urdu and translated into English by Abbas, is a parable of India's transition from a feudal colony to a democratic nation. The genre of this work is the fable, a form with deep roots in Indian literary tradition and one which is itself linked to a kind of social order, in that it would normally be narrated collectively in a community setting.

Maharaja's Elephant

Once upon a time—and it seems it was very, very long ago—when Maharajas were Maharajas and not amusing mascots for airlines, the importance of a ruler was reckoned by the number of guns to which he was entitled as a royal salute, the population of his harem, and by the number of elephants in his *feelkhana*.[1]

Judged from his standards, Raja Suryakumar Chandrakumar Vijaysingh Shumsherjung of Chhamchhampur (only two crackers,[2] seven wives and one elephant) was not among the top ten or even top two hundred of the rulers of princely states. Indeed, his state (Area: 1704 square miles, population: 274589), nestling insignificantly somewhere in the barren plateaus of Central India, was no

Translated by K. A. Abbas.

---

10. A whole wheat griddled cake.
11. Flaxen material.

Maharaja's Elephant
1. *Feelkhana* can be translated as *feel* (elephant) *khana* (house).
2. Firecrackers.

bigger than a big Zamindari[3] estate, but nevertheless, its relations with the *Angrezi Sarkar*[4] were governed by the terms of a treaty that the great grandfather of the present ruler, the redoubtable Raja Narsingharao Bhimsingh Arjunsingh, had personally signed with Lord Canning.

As a matter of historical record, let it be stated that Chhamchhampur was not always so small and insignificant a state. There was a time when the writ of the Maharaja of Chhamchhampur ran over a great part of Rajputana and what is now known as Madhya Pradesh. But the successive Maharajas' overfondness for wine (extracted from the *mahoba* flowers that grew wild all over the state) and women (especially dancing girls the *chham-chham* sound of whose anklet bells was reputed to be the genesis of the state's name—chhamchhampur) had worked havoc with the martial qualities of the ruling family. One after another, various parts of the state had been swallowed up by the more energetic and avaricious rulers of neighbouring states, not to mention the big slice that had been conceded to the *firangees*[5] in return for the protection afforded by their troops against Chhamchhampur's marauding neighbours.

And thus it had come to pass that by the year 1945 the Maharaja of Chhamchhampur was left only with seven wives and one elephant, and when, under pressure of public opinion, the Viceroy ordered a further cut in the privy purse, the Maharaja found himself financially incapable of maintaining even such a depleted harem and *feelkhana*.

A man of ample girth, nevertheless he decieved to tighten his belt both literally and figuratively. He put all his wives (except the junior most who was naturally his favourite) on short rations, ordered a cut in their allowances and, on the pretext that robbers were rampant in the state capital, he divested them of their jewels which were duly deposited in the royal treasury for safekeeping, or so it was given out, while the fact was that the precious stones were taken out and sent to a firm of jewellers in Bombay, and the gold was melted and secretly sold to a bullion merchant in Delhi. Looking about for further economies, the Maharaja spotted Lakshmi, the solitary old cow elephant in the huge *feelkhana* that was originally designed to house a dozen elephants. According to the Comptroller of the Royal Household, the maintenance of the *feelkhana,* including the rations for the elephant and salary for the *mahout,*[6] came no less than Rs. 350/- per month—i.e. over four thousand per year! To the Maharaja's newly awakened sense of economy, this seemed a waste of good money, for after all he never rode on the elephant even for state procession, and the very idea of sitting cross-legged in an uncomfortable *howdah* struck him as ridiculous when he had a fleet of Daimlers and Packards for luxurious driving. So he decided to get rid of old Lakshmi. But he could not afford to lose face by making it public that he was closing down his *feelkhana* because he could no longer afford it. It had to be done with diplomatic circumspection and royal finesse. He was debating the issue in his mind when the Resident, Sir John Rollingstone (pronounced Rawlington) was announced.

---

3. The title to the land, or the system of
   revenue settlement.
4. English government.

5. Englishmen.
6. A man who trains and manages elephants.

Sir John was an officer of the Political Department who had risen from the ranks as it were. The son of a Manchester tailor, he had worked his way through college with the help of scholarships, crammed Latin and Ancient History to get into I.C.S., and had served for 20 years in various malarious moffusil[7] towns, first as Joint Magistrate and then as Collector, before he was drafted for the Political Department. A secret romanticist who spent all the leisure hours of his bachelor life reading Kipling and Churchill and Yeats-Brown, his original inferiority complex had been transformed into a fascination for what he regarded as the chivalry and old world charm of India's princely courts. As such he was more interested in preserving the traditional pomp, pageantry and ceremonial of the princely courts to which he was accredited than in such prosaic matters as the administration of justice and the improvement of the irrigation system for the benefit of the improverished *ryot*. No wonder Sir John Rollingstone was held in such affection and esteem by the princes he had served, but particularly by the Maharaja of Chhamchhampur.

And so it was natural that in recognition of his services, the Resident should receive a present from the Maharaja—and what present could be more appropriate for the romantic soul of Sir John Rollingstone than a royal elephant, the symbol and epitome of all that pomp and pageantry, chivalry and gallantry that the Manchester tailor's son had always associated with his mission in the princely states of India. And so he was duly grateful for the royal present, and felt greatly moved when the elephant and *mahout* arrived to take their new quarters in the compound of his bungalow. It seemed to him the crowning moment of his career in India.

But he had not yet reckoned with the economic problem of maintaining an elephant. The few thousands he had been able to put by in his bank account were soon gone into the building of an over-sized stable for the elephant. The royal beast had a royal appetite and soon a good bit of the Resident's far-from-ample salary was going into the purchase of sugarcane and other costly rations. The Political Department flatly refused to finance this elephantine adventure and made it clear that the Resident should regard himself lucky if he was not hauled up for so openly accepting a present from the Maharaja—which could easily be construed as illegal gratification. All this was mortifying to the sensitive soul of one who regarded himself as the heir to the Kipling tradition. But with characteristic British tenacity Sir John Rollingstone stuck loyally to the elephant, even if it meant his resignation from the club (as he could no longer pay for his whisky-soda bills), giving up of the summer vacation in the hills, and other such self-imposed economies. But as every evening he strolled over to the stable which he liked to call his *feelkhana,* he derived immense consolation from the thought that soon, when he retired, he would take the elephant with him to England where it would lend unparalleled distinction to his semi-detached cottage in Sunningdale or some such place. "That," he would be able to tell his envious neighbours, "is old Lakshmi, the royal elephant, that my friend the Maharaja of Chhamchhampur gave me as a present"—and it was a pleasant thrill to anticipate the look of envious

---

7 A provincial town.

wonderment it would produce on the faces of those who had never ventured to the fabulous and exotic lands "east of Suez."

But when the time came for his retirement and impending departure for England, Sir John was dismayed to learn of the immense cost of transporting his royal elephant to England—the train to Bombay and the ship's freight to London amounting to more than the total gratuity to which the retiring civilian was entitled after 25 years in the service of the Empire. He could expect little help or understanding from the Political Department in New Delhi, for meanwhile, a bunch of Gandhi-capped ex-Seditionists had persuaded Whitehall to transfer the Government of India to them, the Maharaja of Chhamchhampur along with many other rulers had agreed to the merger and integration of the state, and it seemed to Sir John Rollingstone (no longer pronounced Rawlington but even rudely spelt as Rolling Stone by the raw young Indian officials who had taken over the Secretariat) that the end of the world had come simultaneously with the loss of the brightest jewel in the British crown.

And so, with a heavy heart, he bid goodbye to Lakshmi and, by a regular deed—the last document he would sign in India—gifted the elephant to Ganga Ram, the old hereditary *mahout,* who was no less bewildered by the new developments than "Raalingam Saab" as he called the Resident.

With seven salams and many low bows of gratitude Ganga Ram accepted the gift but hardly had his old master's train steamed out of Chhamchhampur station than the poor *mahout* was obliged to revise his estimate of this good fortune that he thought had befallen him served with a notice to quit the stable, along with his *hathi,*[8] as the Resident's bungalow and all its out-houses were being converted by the new administration into a school. With a petition drafted for him by a professional scribe for a fee of two rupees, he went the round of all the offices but found no sympathy from the new officials. So poor Ganga Ram, suddenly rendered not only homeless but friendless and unwanted in the strange and incomprehensible new world which had risen round him, sat on the neck of old Lakshmi and led her by gentle proddings of his *ankush*[9] to his village where their arrival was heralded by much merriment by the village children.

It was his practical-minded wife, however, whose sharp tongue rudely made him aware of the economic crisis he had brought upon himself by accepting such a gift. Not only they had no place to accommodate the gigantic beast in their mud hut, the produce from their little piece of land (which an earlier Maharaja had given to Ganga Ram's father) was quite inadequate to feed their family, not to speak of the elephant which would eat more than a dozen human beings.

"Give it away to the temple on the hill—a gift to the gods," advised the Old Man of the village, and Ganga Ram, having exhausted his life's savings in feeding the animal just for three days, readily agreed.

With great ceremony, beating of drums and blowing of conches, players and intoning of holy *mantras,* the elephant was accepted by the *pujaris* and *pandits*[10]

---

8. Elephant.
9. A pointed prodding hook used by elephant-drivers.

10. *Pujaris* and *pandits* are Hindu priests.

of the temple who felt greatly exhilarated by the gift which proved—or so they thought—that faith was still very much alive, if a poor man like Ganga Ram could bring such a royal gift to the goddess.

To celebrate the occasion, the image of the goddess was placed on the back of the elephant and taken in procession round the surrounding villages, followed by a crowd mostly of children drawn less by devotion or faith and more by impish curiosity about an elephant.

But soon the *pujaris* of the temple also learnt the disturbing facts and figures of the royal appetite of the Maharaja's elephant. Since the people in the villages began migrating to the city to work in mills, and schools began to lure the simple-minded peasants away from the path of faith (or so the *pujaris* thought), the income of the temple from offerings and donations had been steadily dwindling, with the result that now if the elephant had to be fed the *pujaris* had to starve.

"Then let the beast starve," cried a young hot-head among the *pujaris*. "If we keep her a little longer we will all die of hunger."

The Head Priest advised caution. "Don't forget the elephant is a gift to the goddess—so we cannot allow her to starve. Moreover, the elephant, too, is a god—the incarnation of our Lord Ganapati of the elephant's head. We will be earning the displeasure of the gods if we illtreat this noble beast."

"Then you do want us to starve in order to feed this precious elephant?"

"No," the Head Priest calmly went on, "I only wish that this noble animal, this gift of the goddess, this incarnation of our Lord Ganapati, be gifted to the nation, to serve the people and to be served by them. Of course, that will also save us all from starvation but that is only incidental."

And so it came to be that on the auspicious day of August 15, old Lakshmi was decorated with sandalwood paste and vermillion and taken in procession to the office of the local Community Project and offered as a gift in the service of the people. Now it can be seen in a certain obscure corner of the country, busy with such humble chores as carrying loads of stone or cement or dragging a gigantic stone roller to level the road.

Which may appear to some like our old friend Sir John Rollingstone (pronounced Rawlington) as a sad come-down for a Maharaja's elephant but there are others, and Mahout Ganga Ram (who has been engaged again to look after Lakshmi) is one of them, who say that the old Lakshmi has never looked happier in her whole life.

SARA SULERI (b. 1953)
Pakistan

Sara Suleri, who now teaches English at Yale University, left her familial home in Pakistan to become a professional academic in the United States. Her autobiographical memoir, *Meatless Days,* is an elegy of that leave-taking, as well as a drama of individual survival as she adapts to her newfound diasporic home. "The Immoderation of Ifat," excerpted here, is an intensely personal account of her relationship with her sister in Pakistan, who dies tragically under questionable circumstances.

from **Meatless Days**

The Immoderation of Ifat

At first I thought she was the air I breathed, but Ifat was prior, prior. Before my mechanical bellows hit the air to take up their fanning habit, Ifat had preceded me, leaving her haunting aura in all my mother's secret crevices: in the most constructive period of my life she lay around me like an umbilical fluid, yellow and persistent. I was asleep inside her influence when I did not yet know how to sleep. In later years such envelopment would lend a curiosity to my regard, which was uncertain whether an inward musing would not suffice—since there was so much of her inside me—in place of what it meant to look at her. But how could I abstain from looking? For if Shahid was the apple of my eye when I was six, Ifat belonged to a more burnished complexion and was the golden apples of my soul.

Was she twin, or is that merely my imagination? Could it be possible that one egg in its efficient subdivisions became forgetful for a while—my company of cells went wandering off bemused and was not missed—until four years later they remembered to be born, the sleepy side of Ifat? It cannot be, for she was twinned before my time, her face already raising to the power of some other number, which danced about her shoulder like a spirit minuscule. And she needed no lessons from me about how to conduct her always instantaneous sleep! Sleep would come and hold her like a membrane does, until her voice at night was the only one I've heard to tell me quite so clearly, "There are two chords of voice inside my throat." Once it was day again, how I could listen to those humming things, which cajoled each other, danced and ran, in the manner that her face ran, too, weaving in and out of the eddies of her voice. They worked in unison at a display brilliant and precise as water, when water wishes to perform both in and out of light. So of course I was not needed to make Ifat two: before I had even dreamed of number, she had enacted out a multitude. There always were, for instance, several voices in her single throat.

I thought of it, the trick of Ifat's speech and the colloquy that it conducted with her face, when my friend Jonathan was kindly driving me through New Haven's unloveliness. He was driving me home—a kind thing to do—and it set him brooding on all the other ways he could be kind to me. "It's all very well, you know," he murmured, "to be obsessional." We were driving down a one-way street. "But why do it so thoroughly, arrest yourself in a prosopopoeic posture that retards you from your real work?" I looked out the window at people shoveling hateful snow. "Maybe this is my work," I suggested finally. Jonathan's hands left the wheel in a moment of abbreviated exasperation, but then he softened, liberal toward me. "Alright. So now you have to write about your sister's death."

"Nonsense!" I replied indignantly, and then the subject changed, as we reached home. But later on I wondered at that conversation, and the scandal in my voice when I cried out, "Nonsense!" What did it mean, I wondered. Then I realized what I must have known all along: of course, Ifat's story has nothing to do with dying; it has to do with the price a mind must pay when it lives in a beautiful body.

Of all her haunting aspects that return to me, I often am most pleased when I recollect her wrist. Ifat imposed an order on her bones that gave her gestures of an unsuspected strength: her wrists were such a vessel. There was no jar, no bottle in the house which could resist that flick of wrist, and in arm wrestling once she dropped Shahid down, to cries of everyone's amazement. We liked to watch her wield her slender tools with such efficient hygiene, so "Let Ifat open the olives," we'd agree, and when of course she did in one clean twist, our admiration exceeded olives. She was the nutty bone our teeth would hit when we wished to take upon our tongue that collusion of taste and texture. Ifat was always two. In moments when her affection felt most fierce to her, she would send out two fingers to bracelet tightly the wrist of whoever was beside her and gave her joy: when that wrist was mine, I had no way of uttering the honor to my radius and ulna. In later years, particularly, Ifat would suddenly and wordlessly grasp my wrist, making my hand, like a dying moth or a creature not knowing what to do with suffocation, flutter out, "Don't let go; don't let go."

"Don't let go, Ifat!" I screamed out in alarm when she veered me back and forth on the world's most perfect swing. There is a chinar tree[1] in Nathia Gali growing upon a silent verge: some large-spirited person has hung a swing from its most massive limb so that the seat swings out to hurtle a body over that chasmic valley, whose terraced rice fields gleam, green and tiny, thousands of feet below. That swing was one of Ifat's passions as a child, and once she had had her manic fill of movement, she would test my mettle by pushing me back and forth over that heart's leap of a fall. I did not know which I liked better: the ecstasy of space such motion gave me or the approval in Ifat's eye when—after I had collapsed trembling on the hill—she'd say, "That was brave of you, Sara, since you are so small!" She was always fair about making concessions to my size: even when I annoyed her, she would glance at me gloomily and say, "I suppose you can't help it, since you are so small." Of course I fought against such diminution, forcing my mind into a trot to keep up with her and the swiftness of her thought. "Shahid is also smaller than you," I reminded her once when she seemed to be slipping beyond my grasp. "That's different, he's a boy." But when I sought to question her on why my girlhood mattered to my size, she had passed away from listening: "Sara," she said firmly, "I can't explain what you're too young to see."

What I could see, however—even then, when she was eight—was the lasting glamour of a face that both did and did not know the nature of its impact. For her beauty's commonplace was not aware of what transpired on her face when feature fell in with spirit. It was my first experience of aesthetic joy to watch her expression spilling over with laughter, or amazement, or whatever else was

---

1. A flowering tree of northern India.

prompting her to feel alive at a given moment of the day. To such a sight my father responded with a bright delight, looking at her only with open admiration, but I sometimes noticed that my mother would seem saddened to be a witness of that gay excess. It was as though Ifat's grace was frightening to her, as she watched her child and had to contemplate what the world could exact from grace. How I must concentrate, she thought, in order to protect this girl from what could be the portion of such extravagance of face. It made her soul subdued and move in measure when she saw the sudden theater of Ifat's eyes: a theater unable to envisage a curtain or the quick falling of a duskless night. So Mamma gravely curtained Ifat then, adopting a twilight tone that seemed to say, bright daylight of my daughter, look at me and learn. But Ifat was too interested in adoration to consider what else my mother's manner could suggest: "Oh softness of my mother!" she'd exclaim. Thus lesson only gave occasion to what it sought to hide. "What gave you such green eyes, what gave you such softness?" Ifat adored.

Could that be it, an unwitting absorption of my mother's fear, that causes all those sharp angles to accrue around my earliest images of Ifat? I am crying along a roadside in Karachi that is a stony and resistant surface on which to run and cry, but she has left me far behind, so I know that I will never catch up with her and that I no longer want to be the only audience to my tears. Then, shortly after I am three years old, sitting on the deep veranda of a Karachi house, watching in admiration as Ifat twirls her weight upon a heavy rope that holds thick bamboo screens in place, now rolled stiffly up to let in the tepid evening breeze. Ifat dances, twirls and whirls—her white muslin frock is a further admiration round her limbs—until her forehead meets with sickening crack an evil abutment of plaster. How efficiently the fabric of her dress absorbs the abundance of her blood! I hear Ifat screaming "Papa, Papa!" shaking off her entanglement in rope and the sharpness of her fall and the little wounded sounds that Shahid and I keep darting round her. As Papa runs out from his study, Ifat is able to command, almost with impatience, "Now hold me while I die."

She didn't, of course, and her seven-year-old cranium was knitting before the three of us had really satisfied our taste for the glory of her wound. But Ifat still lay in her blue bed and behaved as though nothing could be averted now. It was as though her mastery over us had been extended beyond the weight of years—three over Shahid, four over me—to address us henceforth with the infinite knowledge of the grave. So it did not matter that two days later not even that cumbersome gauze bandage, an ill-tied turban on her head, could keep Ifat in her bed. Even when she was soon up again and playing, she still had that bloodletting over us, making her absolute and awesome to our eyes.

Some two decades later Ifat described her fall to me as though I had not been there, and it was entrancing to witness that event again from, as it were, the opposite angle of the room. She did not pay particular attention to the hurt itself nor to the imperious evocations of death that it unleashed in her. Instead, she told me about what it was like at night to wait for the moistness of that wound to heal and then to run a finger through her hair, feeling the increasingly stiff joy of that dry extraneous growth, with which she could tamper, if she chose. For Ifat, the event clinched her perception of bodily secrecy and the illicit texture of what happens when something is added onto or subtracted from flesh. For me, however, it was and still remains my sharpest consciousness of the publicity of blood.

Keen red blood, coursing down her leopard's skull! The image made me shudder many years afterward when we were merely playing and something in her imperiousness reminded of how she could hurt. For games were Ifat's provenance: she made us play and play until the very intensity of her invention made us feel as though we collaborated with her in the most significant work of our lives. When I woke in the morning, I would slowly think, I wonder what we will play today, and before I was properly awake, Ifat would be upon me, shaking me to action: "You're Belinda and Shahid's Pepito and I'm Diana"; "You're Gray Rabbit and Shahid is Mole and I'm the Crab"; "Today we're going to play at Holmes." Holmes was an elaborate invention through which Ifat made our toys familial to us: each one had its proper station of relationship, and new toys in the fold had to undergo a stringent initiation before they were admitted to that private world. A woollen animal knitted expressly for Shahid (What was Goodboy's sweet face meant to signify? A dog? Perhaps a bear?) was the bad-boy stranger in our games for months until Ifat declared, "He's home—he can be a good boy now." And so we solemnly welcomed him into our midst and named him Goodboy: Goodboy soon became so much a part of us that he even married the Princess of Loveliness—Ifat's favorite doll—after we had determined that he was her long-lost brother, most deserving to have her as his wife. They were intricately brothered and sistered, all our toys, as we made them wed and interwed.

" 'Who Killed Cock Robin?'—what a strange song it is, Ifat," I said to her one day. " 'I, said the sparrow, with my bow and arrow'—how odd that he should confess it straight-away!" "You know what he's confessing, don't you?" replied Ifat with a meaningful look that always made me feel most ignorant. "It's all about sex!" And then, rising to the horror on my face, she added, "Of course you know that's what nursery rhymes are all about!" Ifat looked pleased at this. "You know, don't you, that all those rhymes are just a way of telling children about the horrid parts of sex?" I at eight did not want to know, feeling squeamish at the relentlessness of her claim. "Don't tell me, Ifat, don't," I begged, until her satisfaction was nearly brimming over. "What!" she exclaimed cheerfully, " 'Put on the pan, says greedy Nan, / Let's sup before we go'? 'She cut off their tails with a carving knife / Did you ever see such a sight in your life'?—Come on, Sara, see what you must see!" I crumpled, seeing it, for Ifat's devastating knowledge seemed designed to rob me of the pale of innocence, insisting that innocence was a lie, a most pallid place to be! "Don't you think that there are some things you shouldn't tell me?" I asked her once, gloomily, after she had filled my evening with hair-raising representations of bodily functions. "Don't you think it may be bad for me?" "If you let it fester, that's your fault," Ifat answered in reproof. "Tomorrow I'll tell you why Jack Sprat could eat no fat and his wife could eat no lean!" And then, leaving me to contemplate her dreadful promise, she turned round and went to sleep.

What else could she be coupled with when she had her discourse by her? She presented herself to the world as a pair in the whitest days of her girlhood, so that looking and listening leaked their knowledge into one another in a magic of multiplication. Her talk was like a creature next to her, a golden retriever of Ifat's singular expression or, better still, a lion padding in startling fashion about the house. Years later, when Richard X. swept into my home with his dog Lulu by his side, something of his buoyancy made me tell him cautiously, "You can remind me slightly of my sister." I intended it to be the highest compliment that I could pay, not realizing at the time that to a man so conscious of the peculiarities of manhood such an analogy could only perplex. "Did you like her?" asked Richard in the wistful way he had of always saying in secret, "Please like me." "Like her?—Oh yes," I said quietly, "yes, I did like Ifat." But naming her put the unpronounceability of my life between us in a way that gave him unease: he did not wish to see me framed by family just then but to picture me alone instead and isolate me in his gaze.

"If anyone hurts you, Sara," Ifat said to me on the day I turned nineteen, "make sure you tell me who it is, so that I can kill them, slowly." For a moment she looked mournful with protection but then, at the execution of revenge, quite pleased. "I'll do a Dadi, chop up their livers into little bits and feed them to the crows," she added, echoing my Dadi's favorite curse. We had just driven to Gulberg Market in Lahore, and as she sat waiting for me in the car, she saw two vagabonds drive up to graze me slightly when I crossed the road. I think they only wished to startle me, wanting for some reason to see a woman look afraid, but swiftly came their punishment. Ifat drove fiercely after them, forced their car off the road, and then used her car as a battering ram, causing considerable damage to both vehicles. "Are you mad?" said the vagabonds, aghast. "How dare you touch my sister?" Ifat hissed. By then quite a crowd had gathered, in the habit of Lahore's instant assembly of spectatorship, so Ifat was surrounded with supporters cheering on her bravery. "Don't you have any sisters yourselves, you louts?" they told the astounded vagabonds. "Don't you understand what it is to protect the honor of your sister?" The vagabonds drove off without a word, dented and dumbfounded. "You've lost a headlight," I told Ifat as I got back into the car, noticing her knuckles white with rage. "If anyone hurts a hair of your head, Sara," Ifat told me as we drove home, "I will not let them live." Her voice seemed overburdened with knowledge at that moment: it made me stare down at the birthday cake sitting on my lap and think, "Dear god, don't let her hurt."

I had already watched her accrue the tragedy of adolescence, days she endured only in the deepest mourning. Even then there was an energy to her manner that belied her tone: "Oh, I am Wednesday's child!" she would exclaim. "Wednesday's, full of woe!" In that era she hated her body, which had become beautiful in a way that was too womanly for her tastes, hungry for childhood's swifter grace. So Ifat would hold her face fastidiously, a walking crown above such bodily disdain, as though she would concede to walking beside her body but would not inhabit it, not yet. "Look at the hair on my arms!" she said to me with horror. "It's too horrible—I'd need a forest fire to get rid of all this growth on my limbs!" She was by no means ready to accept the modifications in her own aesthetic that existence was imposing on her and disavowed its strictures, even when they gave her great increments of grace. Thus Ifat left her body sitting by the fire and sauntered off to stare out the window in the opposite direction, for there were always several Ifats with us in a room. Hinged to her like a hotel door, what could I do but keep ushering them in, those successions of her face?

But she had reason to be burdened. Both my parents looked at her with such keen eyes that it must have been a strain on her good humor—she was a most good-humored girl—to sustain the pressure of that gaze. My mother was always cautious, maintaining her exemplary trick of perpetual understatement in order to teach Ifat something of the art of moderation. She developed habits that Ifat passionately admired but could not emulate, for Ifat's habits were my father's. From him she learned her stance of wild inquiry, the arrogant angle at which she held her head. It was her gesture of devotion to him, really, the proud position she maintained when—to the complete devastation of domestic serenity—those two wills clashed. It made me groan aloud to think that Papa could not see that Ifat was simply loving him for what he was when she handed back to him, gesture by gesture, his prickling independence of style. But he could not see deeply enough into the lonely work of this fidelity, noticing only with alarm her flaring spirit, so much like his own. "When Ifat learns to love another man, what will happen to it, her habit of fidelity?" I could read written in my mother's eyes. And so there was an even greater tentativeness to Mamma's touch when she sat down at her piano to play a while and then to softly sing.

Oh sisters two, how may we do,
for to preserve this day?
This poor youngling, for whom we sing,
Bye bye, lully, lullay.

I felt it sharply, when Ifat learned to love another man. There were always in her great reserves of devotion to dispense: I did not feel deprived but feared that it would be too expensive to her spirit to utter to my father such a complete good-bye. After having lived for years with his endless eloquence of voice, how could she do it, choose to love a silent man? So I warned her against Javed and the ways he could be alien: "He sees your face," I warned, "and not the spirit that constructs your face." Ifat would not listen. It put a gulf between us in those years before she ran away from home and married him, because my disapproval hurt, making her instinctively hide in order to protect her love. "If anything needs that much protection," I told her, "you know it must be wrong." Then I hated myself for being right, when I saw the quick cloud of pain that I had cast about her eyes. So those years in Lahore were difficult with my disapproval, although even I had to laugh on the night when Javed, prowling round the house in amorous pursuit of Ifat, lay down on Dadi's bed. He was waiting for Ifat in the garden and saw what he thought was an empty bed, only to discover that the tiny curlicue of my Dadi was lying next to him, asleep beneath the stars.

What did he signify to her? For a while I was perplexed, until I slowly saw that rather than at a man, I should be looking at the way Javed signified to Ifat a complete immersion into Pakistan. She was living here for good now, she must have thought, so why not do it well? And what greater gift could she give my father than literally to become the land he had helped to make? He, of course, could never see the touching loyalty of this decision, but then our adulthood would often seem to him betrayal's synonym. He could not countenance her love for a polo-playing army man, a spark about the town, not stopping to consider that Ifat was his child and well designed to match adamant with adamant, iron with iron. Javed's elder brother was in prison at that time—for rape, after a trial of great notoriety—but the more prudence that amassed against him, the more resolution to Ifat's loyalty. "Oh, girl," I groaned to myself in exasperation, "why are you so perishably pretty? Who put such pretty notions in your head?" By this time Ifat was in college at Kinnaird, willing a greater distance between my father and herself in a determination uncannily like his in tone. And then, with perverse aplomb, she chose to enter into the heart of Pakistan in the most un-Pakistani way possible: she ran away from Kinnaird and called home a few days later to say, bravely, "Papa, I'm married." "Congratulations," he replied, put down the phone, and refused to utter her name again for years. Ifat was then nineteen.

Adrift from each familiar she had known, what energies my sister devoted to Pakistan! First she learned how to speak Punjabi and then graduated to the Jehlum dialect, spoken in the region from which Javed's family came. She taught herself the names and stations of a hundred-odd relations, intuiting how each of them would wish to be addressed. She learned more than I will ever know about the history of the army, and then she turned to polo's ins and outs. The game, she discovered, had originated in the valleys of Kaghan where, in place of a ball, the tribes most commonly played with an enemy's head instead: "Oh," said Ifat, digested it, and moved on to something else. She went with her mother-in-law to the family's ancestral village in the Punjab to perform an annual sacrifice of some poor animal—a goat was killed for god and then doled out to the village's poor. Later she discovered that the rite was a traditional atonement, performed on the spot where Javed's great-grandfather had slain his infant daughter, so aggrieved was he to have a female as a child. "Oh!" said Ifat and listened, white as ice. She listened to her father-in-law, the brigadier, a polo-playing man, tell her that he wanted his four sons to be gentlemen, he did not want them to be cads. She listened to all this, and then she taught herself the most significant task of them all. She learned the names of Pakistan.

For never has there been, in modern times, such a Homeric world, where so much value is pinned onto the utterance of name! Entire conversations, entire lives, are devoted to the act of naming people, and in Pakistan the affluent would be totally devoid of talk if they were unable to take names in vain. Caste and all its subclassifications are recreated every day in the structure of a conversation that knows which names to name: "Do you know Puppoo and Lola?" "You mean Bunty's cousins?" "No, Bunty's cousins are Lali and Cheeno, I'm talking about the Shah Nazir family—you know, Dippoo's closest friends." "Oh, of course, I used to meet them all the time at Daisy Aunty's place!" For everyone has a family name and then a diminutive name, so that to learn an ordinary name is not enough— you must also know that Zahid is Podger, and Seema is Nikki, and Rehana is Chunni, and on and on. To each name attaches a tale, and the tales give shape to the day. "Poor Goga, she's so cut up! I think she really misses Chandni quite a lot." "What is the Chandni story, though?" "Darling, all Karachi knows! When Saeed discovered that she was having an affair with Billo, he just couldn't handle it—he had to have her killed!" We had felt too supercilious, in our youth, to bother with this lingo, so it was somewhat of a surprise to hear such names on Ifat's lips. She was permitted to return only after long negotiations: an energetic lady, Aunty Nuri, undertook to mediate between the brigadier and Pip until—under her auspices—a reconciliation of the clans was tautly staged. "I can't stand it," Shahid told me afterward, "when Ifat talks Punjabi or does this Nikki Pikki stuff!" "Well, it must have been hard work," I mused. In any case, I was distracted. For when we met again, how strange I felt to notice that Ifat's beautiful body, which I had missed so much, was now convex with a child.

I wanted to shield her, but I did not have the means. In the pink house on the hill—the brigadier's invention—Ifat was public, praiseworthy for her beauty, while in ours she was treated with a strict formality. My father would never properly forgive her, and my mother's quaintly decorous way sought to extend privacy to Ifat now that she thought her daughter belonged to a different life. So in the end there was no place left where Ifat could return: in each room she was new. "Will no one ever let that girl be at home," I thought, protection spluttering in me like the sulphur smell of a match that flares beyond the call of duty. Ifat watched my face; "It doesn't matter, Sara," she once told me ruefully. "Men live in homes, and women live in bodies." For she was preoccupied with the creature living inside her: I could watch her make a dwelling of her demeanor, a startling place in which to live. My heart was wrenched to see her lying there later, with her infant boy next to her side, red and wrinkled as an infant is after living so long in water! Ifat's eyes smiled at me from her bed, as she lay with her beauty and her discourse and now a baby, too. Your father called you Taimur, child, as in Tamburlaine, a curious appellation for your sweetest disposition, you little infant boy.

What happened, in the war? Javed had been sent to Bangladesh in the era of the emergency. He came back wounded for a month once, and people said that in his impetuous way he had simply shot himself so he could return to look at Ifat's face. "Don't say such things to me, please!" I said. But then the war began, those bitter days for all. The naming games that went on in the drawing rooms of Pakistan now turned their poison outward: it was no longer enough to say, "Do you know Kittoo?"; it was necessary to add, "He died on the Sargodha front," or "Last night Zafar died." I lived with Ifat in the pink house on the hill, sitting with her as those names came tolling in, cold terror in our eyes. During each air raid, the brigadier would stride into the garden barking out commands to the soldiers who were operating the antiaircraft guns installed on the top of his house: gradually it became a practice of us all to trail into the garden after him, gazing up at those atrocious noises in the sky. The war was brief, but the waiting of those days was long, and it was followed only by a longer waiting when, after the fall of Dacca, we discovered that Javed was alive in India, a prisoner of war. Ifat was pregnant again, but before the daughter that she bore could see her father, the child would be almost two.

Ifat put on her bridal clothes the day Javed returned. What festivity went quickening through our house in Lahore, making us wince to contemplate the gravity of her joy. Fawzi took a photograph of Ifat on that day: it is an uncanny image, which almost seems to know what it must represent, the twinning impulses of Ifat's soul. She stands white and erect, glancing down at a diagonal to the tugging of her daughter Alia's hand. She seems tall and finely boned, head bowed in the face of its own beauty, quite grave to be what it must be. Her slenderness is such as to suggest a keen fragility, most poignant to me, so that when the photograph first met my eyes I cried aloud, "I must protect this girl!"

Those were peculiar days in Pakistan, but the country made quick provisions to forget the war in Bangladesh; when two years later the prisoners of that war finally returned, they came back to a world that did not really want to hear the kind of stories they had to tell. One day, standing in the dining room, Javed suddenly began to describe what he had felt during his first killing. I stopped still, and my head swam at the thought of what came next, overwhelming me with images of what he must have seen. My terror asked me, how will Ifat do it, make Javed's mind a human home again and take those stories from his head? That was the most arduous labor of Ifat's life, as she began with great reserve to bring her husband home again. She matched her courage with compassion, working hard to counteract those three years brutalized, that waste of life. It made me hold my breath to see such concentration on her face, to see her biting her lip—the mannerism of her childhood—trying brick by brick to break that prison down. The only way in which she can do it, I thought to myself, is by first learning what that prison was: what anecdotes must fill her evenings now, what intensity of detail? "If anyone can do it," I told my mother, "Ifat can." "Yes," said Mamma, "she is generous in that way—if anybody can . . ." And then we looked away from one another, silent with dismay.

After Javed left the army, they moved to Sargodha, an uninteresting part of the Punjab, where he took to cultivating land and opening a stud farm. By the next time we met Ifat, she could tell us with fine verve every detail of how that farm was run and how the world breeds polo ponies. I could not help laughing at this incongruous linkage: the finesse of Ifat's thought and the breeding of a horse! Still, she made her stories funny, almost as if she enjoyed it all, never talking about the effort of her secret work. She would saunter into our house, with three children now, along with her discourse and her face, making abundant company. "Thank goodness you look like yourself, Ifat." I hugged my welcome. "I could not bear it if you looked horsey." "Me?" said Ifat, drawing up her scorn, "Do I have yokel's hands?" For we wished only to joke with one another now, telling minor stories, only dainty tales. I felt that I owed her the courtesy of silence on her life's score, as though to be unquestioning in my attention would be the deftest way to demonstrate my sympathy. We developed new patterns of conversation, then, in which phrases floated between us in an unsaid context so limpid that it could dazzle me. It caused her dazzling face the least distress, I hoped, to be surrounded by a discretion so complete as to be dazzling. "Always two," I murmured in her direction, "always two." Ifat smiled a little wearily at that and glanced at me. "They told me I was everything," she sighed, "They lied; I am not beauty-proof."

She walked as erectly as ever, through the fierce reclamation of those times. I wondered about the progress of her work, whether or not her manner of making welcome would suffice: could such a will for healing, by ill luck, serve to magnify the bruise's sense that it was just a shoddy bruise? If that were true, more bruising would come—save her, I begged my limpid context, save her from being bruised. But I would be angry in Lahore when company eager over Javed's name brought me tales of wealth and scandal, waiting for my verdict. "You must not say such things about my sister's husband," I said slowly, "It is impolite." For surely it was discourteous, I felt, for them to bring such tales to me, as though some third person could ever understand the nature of Ifat's work. If only you could remain unnoticed, I told her in my mind, then such indignity would not be cast at the flamboyance of your face. Beauty is a whip they should not use, but will, your trouble being that even the crudest eye that looks at you can believe it comprehends. I winced for Ifat, then. "Brave girl," I said, "ignore the world: continue with your task."

I think it was an irritant to the world, her continued merriment. Nor was this pretense: Ifat was good at getting at joy, as the shape of her eyes would often attest. Some of the most festive moments in my life occurred when Ifat simply walked into my room: she would visit on winter afternoons, sitting upstairs in my red room with Tillat and me, the three of us cross-legged upon the bed. And what exclamation of delight we made when the door quietly opened to my mother's touch, bringing her into our midst with a little smile and a pansy in her hand. "I've just been walking in the garden," she murmured absently, "and I found this pansy . . ." It was often her way of starting conversation, to walk into a room with a flower or pebble, simply saying, "Look . . . " "Oh, Mamma, what a beautiful pansy!" we exclaimed, ravished by her, and handed it around. "Yes, it is rather, isn't it," she said, turning to leave, until, "Don't go, Mamma, don't go! Stay and talk to us," we begged.

Those were the moments that Ifat and I had to collect and recollect after Mamma died. It changed the tenor of our talk again, for then our context had no option but to rise weightless, entranced by her remaining aura. Ifat told me at exquisite pace the stories of her soul: a few months earlier, some sickness had made her flee her family and come to stay at home. She would lie on the sofa, sleeping fitfully throughout the day, while Mamma would be reading student papers at a table close at hand. "And when I woke, she'd smile at me," marveled Ifat, as though recounting miracle. "When I awoke, she'd smile!" "But I was angry at her, Ifat," I confessed, "I felt that someone was handing me a relic of her, some rag doll, and I refused to kiss those button eyes," Ifat shook her lovely head: "Poor Sara, you should have come home then . . . " We were silent for a while. "I miss her," Ifat sighed.

"Although," she added, "a woman can't come home." Her face had clouded, then, making me watch intently the way that meaning shadowed itself, came and went around her eyes. "Why, Ifat?" I finally asked. "Oh, home is where your mother is, one; it is when you are mother, two; and in between it's almost as though your spirit must retract . . . ."—she was concentrating now, in the earnest way she concentrated as a child—"your spirit must become a tiny, concentrated little thing, so that your body feels like a spacious place in which to live—is that right, Sara?" she asked me, suddenly tentative. "Perhaps," I said, "perhaps. But when I look at you, Ifat, I am in home's element!" Ifat's two fingers suddenly grasped my wrist. "You know the profit to me, all these years, from your support?" "But Ifat," I said with sudden tears, "to have you as sister is a high honor of my life!" Then we rose and turned to other things, conscious of having uttered all that could be said.

Now it is sweet relief to me to know I need not labor to describe what happened in my mind when Ifat died. I was in surprise. The thickness of event made me a rigid thing, whose thoughts came one by one, as if in pain. I found myself inhabiting a flattened day in which nothing could be two: where is the woman of addition? my mind inquired of me. I could not conceive her body, then, nor tolerate the tales of that body's death, the angle of its face, the bruise upon its neck. What would I not have done, I mused, to keep you from that bruise? But then I felt most vain, most vain. "I did not do enough for your strong heart when doing was open to me," I cried out, "How was I to know we had not years and years? Think of me as the cloth they put around you, some indifferent thing, when you most lithe in all your faith became inflexible!" A curious end for such a moving body, one that, like water, moved most generously in light.

Then commenced keen labor. I was imitating all of them, I knew, my mother's laborious production of her five, my sisters' of their seven (at that stage), so it was their sweat that wet my head, their pushing motion that allowed me to extract, in stifled screams, Ifat from her tales. We picked up our idea of her as though it were an infant, slippery in our hands with birthing fluids, a notion most deserving of warm water. Let us wash the word of murder from her limbs, we said, let us transcribe her into some more seemly idiom. And so with painful labor we placed Ifat's body in a different discourse, words as private and precise as water when water wishes to perform both in and out of light. Let it lie hidden in my eye, I thought, her tiny spirit, buoyant in the excessive salt of that dead sea, so that henceforth too she can direct my gaze, a strange happening, phosphorescent!

Around us, in the city, talk of murder rose like a pestilence, making it a painful act ever to leave the house. My face felt nude, and for the first time in my life I wished I were a woman who could wear a veil, an advertisement of anonymity to mirror all the blankness in my mind. At home I had Shahid and Tillat and Nuz, and we talked and laughed as often as we could, but our hearts were strung with silence. Ifat would like it if we laughed, we knew, and so all of us tried: Shahid rediscovered "Uncle Tom Cobbleigh," his favorite song from childhood, and entertained us for hours with his ingenious adaptations: "Oh, what shall we do with Nuzzi Begum? Pill-popping, pill-popping, pill-popping, pill-popping, and Sara and Farni and all, and Sara and Farni and all." Tillat and I totally disgraced ourselves when one of the mourners who came visiting us, a lady with a hearing aid, warned us that her battery was down and we would have to speak quite loudly. By the third time I had to bellow, "Yes, it is very sad!" to her persistent "What?" Tillat's strength broke down, and we both burst into some of the most uncontrollable laughter that we have ever laughed. Nuz and I noticed that occasionally our visitors would whisper to each other, "That's the half-sister," so we staged some half-sisterly fights for their benefit: I called her short and dark; she called me cold and proud. Then we would take flowers to the cemetery, a companionable thing to do, and when Shahid spread a sheet of roses on the grave, a look of satisfaction crossed his face that I had last seen when I watched him feed his daughter. It brought to mind the most wrenching question of those days: what could we do for Ifat's children?

As the talk of murder settled into irresolution, the rift between my father's house and the brigadier's became complete. Papa insisted that the children belonged with Javed now, that they could only suffer from our influence. "I'm used to thinking more highly of what it means to be loved by me," I answered ruefully. We played with them while we were there, but then they left us for the pink house on the hill, and in our secret minds we all realized that they would, they must, forget. We would not tell one another what we knew, for it seemed the worst disloyalty of all to those children's mother: but what else can happen, our eyes said, once we have all dispersed to various parts of the world? "What can we do, what can we do," the rhythm of my day breathed. So on the morning when they left Lahore, for the pink house on the hill, there was terror in my hands as I held them one by one: "Child's mind, do not forget, I am your mother's sister," my fingers begged. But as they drove away, I turned to see Tillat raise her head in the anguish of such despairing tears that I knew it, then, that they were lost.

Javed has remarried now, and when I visit Pakistan, Ifat's children look at me shyly, at this strange aunt belonging to an era before their lives capsized: their mother's younger sister, older now than their mother was when she was taken from them. In some police station in Lahore a file of an unsolved murder from 1980 lies forgotten, or perhaps completely lost. But we have managed to live with ourselves, it seems, making a habit of loss. "The thought most killing to me," I told Tillat, "is—if Ifat could be asked—how firmly she would swear that we would never let the children go." Tillat winced. "We did not have a choice, Sara. What could we do—live with them in Javed's house after what had been said?" We shivered at the contemplation of that old terrain. "I think Ifat would feel most compassionate for us," Tillat murmured, "you know what she was like . . . compassionate . . . " I shook my head. "But to such an extreme that she would probably have imagined that we would be capable of a most radically compassionate act." "Yes, she was extreme," she said. And, suddenly, we smiled at some moment of Ifat's extremity: we did not need to tell them to each other but let those two moments rise between us like a tiny replication of her aura. It was nearly with us, that astonishing radiance, in the way that something you have dreamed the night before can come flashing in and out of your morning, leaving you astonishing, "What was it that I dreamed?"

I like to imagine that there is a space for improvident angels, the ones who wish to get away from too much light. There, a company of Ifat lie, arms across their foreheads, such an intensely familiar thought that it brings tears of delight to the grave eyes of god.

AMITAV GHOSH (b. 1956)
India

With the success of his first two novels, *Circle of Reason* (1986) and *The Shadow Lines* (1988), Amitav Ghosh has quickly become one of the most well-regarded Indian novelists writing in English. In his highly inventive second novel, Ghosh investigates the stability and integrity of social, geographical, and political boundaries. His most recent book, *In an Antique Land,* was published in 1992. In this excerpt from *The Shadow Lines* a dying mother challenges the narrator's sense of a fluid and changeable reality.

from *The Shadow Lines*

Going Away

I happened to be at home that day, she said. And I know that Nick didn't stop to help Ila. He ran all the way back. He used to run back home from school early those days.

Why?

May plucked out a peepul leaf that was growing out of the brick staircase and fanned herself with it.

I'm not sure, she said. But I think Nick didn't want to be seen with Ila. Ila didn't have any friends in school you see. Perhaps it was just that she was shy. But after she began going to school Nick used to come home much earlier than he used to. Then that day something happened in Ila's class, and I think Nick got to hear of it. He ran back even earlier than usual and went straight up to his room. Mummy asked him what the matter was but he wouldn't tell her. An hour or so later, just when we were beginning to worry about Ila, a policeman brought her back. She was a bit bruised, but otherwise all right. She never told us what happened but she didn't go back to school after that. And then soon after, they left.

I tried then to think of Ila walking back from school alone through the lanes of West Hampstead. I could see her swinging her schoolbag in time with her footsteps, faster and faster, until she was almost running, laughing out loud, so that people turned to smile after her; Ila walking, smiling to herself as I had sometimes seen her, her dimple rippling on her cheek. Ila walking alone in a drizzle under that cold grey sky: Ila who in Calcutta was surrounded by so many relatives and cars and servants that she would never have had to walk so much as the length of the street—and as for alone, why there we were, all of us, I, her relatives, her friends, all waiting to walk with Ila, Ila the sophisticate, who could tell us stories about smart girls and rich boys in far-away countries whose names we had learnt from maps. Ila walking alone because Nick Price was ashamed to be seen by his friends, walking home with an Indian.

You shouldn't think too badly of him, May said. She was pleading with me now: He was very young, and at that age children want everyone to be alike.

Many years later, when my grandmother had been lying in bed for months with what was to prove to be her final illness, one evening, while I was sitting by her bedside, I found myself telling her the story Ila had told me and about the odd little ending that May had added.

That evening, although she was surrounded by oxygen cylinders, bottles of glucose, disposable syringes and all the other paraphernalia of her sickness, she seemed more cheerful than she had been in a long time. When she had heard me out she said: I don't blame the boy. It was Ila's fault. It was her own fault, and Maya's fault and the fault of that half-witted mother of hers. It was bound to happen: anyone can see that. She has no right to be there. She doesn't belong there.

She buried her head in a towel and began to cough. In the two weeks that had passed since I came back from Delhi for my college's summer holidays I had been kept up every night by that hollow echoing cough. After a quarter of an hour the fit left her and she fell back panting, on her pillows. She turned to look at me, with a handkerchief clamped over her mouth. I knew then from the brightness of her eyes, that she was about to go into one of her sudden rages. I rose guiltily from my chair, angry with myself for having told her the story, and tried to calm her.

It doesn't matter Tha'mma, I said, pulling her shawl over her thin, trembling shoulders. It doesn't matter. Lie down now and rest.

Ila shouldn't *be* there, she said, stammering hoarsely. She doesn't belong there. What's she doing in that country?

She's just studying there for a while Tha'mma, I said gently.

At that time Ila was at University College in London, doing a B.A. in history.

But she shouldn't *be* there, my grandmother cried, pushing my hands feebly away.

I leant back in my chair looking helplessly at her. Over the last few months the flesh had wasted slowly away from her face so that the skin on her cheeks hung down now, like dry, brittle leather.

Ila has no right to live there, she said hoarsely. She doesn't belong there. It took those people a long time to build that country; hundreds of years, years and years of war and bloodshed. Everyone who lives there has earned his right to be there with blood: with their brother's blood and their father's blood and their son's blood. They know they're a nation because they've drawn their borders with blood. Hasn't Maya told you how regimental flags hang in all their cathedrals and how all their churches are lined with memorials to men who died in wars, all around the world? War is their religion. That's what it takes to make a country. Once that happens people forget they were born this or that, Muslim or Hindu, Bengali or Punjabi: they become a family born of the same pool of blood. That is what *you* have to achieve for India, don't you see?

I can still see her as though it had happened today, her eyes bloodshot, threads of phlegm hanging from her lips, while she lies ranting in her bed. And yet, when I look at her, lying crumpled in front of me, her white thinning hair matted with her invalid's sweat, my heart fills with love for her—love and that other thing, which is not pity but something else, something the English language knows only in its absence—ruth—a tenderness which is not merely pity and not only love. It comes over me so powerfully that even now I can feel the anger that exploded in my head once when I told Ila what she had said and Ila, drawing on her cigarette, made some offhanded remark about warmongering fascists. I remember how I shouted at her and told her what Tridib had once said: that she was *not* a fascist, she was only a modern middle-class woman—though not wholly, for she would not permit herself the self-deceptions that make up the fantasy world of that kind of person. All she wanted was a middle-class life in which, like the middle classes the world over, she would thrive believing in the unity of nationhood and territory, of self-respect and national power: that was all she wanted—a modern middle-class life, a small thing that history had denied her in its fullness and for which she could never forgive it.

Early next morning my grandmother asked that I be sent to her room. When I sat down beside her I saw that her eyes were bloodshot and her face pale and more strained than ever.

Shall I tell you why Ila lives there? she said, propping herself up on her elbow.

I pleaded with her to lie down, to rest, but she cut me short.

Shall I tell you what Ila's gone there for? she said. She was shivering now, her eyes burning in her face.

She's gone there because she's greedy; she's gone there for money.

I couldn't help smiling then.

Why should she go there for money? I said. Her family has much more money here than they'd ever have over there. She's the only grandchild in the family and you know how rich they are. If she stayed here she would have more money than she could count in a lifetime. And she would have houses and servants and cars too. She has nothing over there. She lives in a tiny room in a house she has to share with five other students; she has to cook and clean and do all kinds of things that a dozen servants would rush to do for her here. . . .

It's not just *money,* my grandmother cried. It's things: it's all the things money can buy—fridges like the one Mrs Sen's son-in law brought back from America, with two doors and a spout that drops ice-cubes into your glass; colour T.V.s and cars, calculators and cameras, all those things you can't get here.

But she doesn't *have* things, I retorted, trying to keep my voice in control. You know that. She has to live on pocket money; she doesn't have the money to buy things like that. Besides, she doesn't want things. She spends her spare time going on demonstrations and acting in radical plays for Indian immigrants in east London. You know that—when she was here last, you asked me yourself: Has Ila become a communist?

She's a greedy little slut, my grandmother said, pounding on the bedclothes with a fist she had not the strength to clench properly. I can't understand why you're defending her. You tell me then, since you know her so well: why *does* she live there, if it's not for the money and the comforts.

By that time I was so angry that I did tell her.

The year before Ila had come to Calcutta in summer, at almost exactly the same time that Robi and I came back from Delhi for the University's summer vacations.

Ila's trip was very sudden. She had made up her mind two days after her college in London closed for the vacations. Then she had rung her father in Bratislava and he had rung his travel agent in London and four days later she was in Calcutta.

It was so sudden that even my parents didn't know.

When the Kalka Mail[1] from Delhi got in at Howrah Station they were waiting, as they always were, under the old clock that no one had ever seen working, on platform nine: my mother in a sea-green sari, flushed with pleasure at the thought of having me back for the summer; my father bustling, looking after our luggage, organising. We dropped Robi at their house in Ballygunge Place, where he was to spend a few days before going off to visit his parents in Darjeeling.

After I had banished my four-month-old college-starved hunger with an hour-long meal, my mother, in her usual anxiously circuitous way was trying to find out what I would like, *really* like to eat for dinner, when my grandmother declared grimly: You'd better forget about his dinner. You're not likely to see him this evening.

Why not? my mother cried, turning to her in alarm. But I've already made . . .

Because, my grandmother said, her eyes boring into mine; because Ila is here.

I waited, not daring to believe what she had said.

Ila's here! said my mother. How do you know?

She rang yesterday, said my grandmother. Queen Victoria had asked her to inquire after my health.

Why didn't you tell us? my mother said.

Because I thought you'd like to have him here for lunch, my grandmother said.

How is she? I asked her. Did she say?

I'm sure she's fine, said my grandmother. Perhaps she's even better than she was when she came here last year—with her hair cut short, like the bristles on a toothbrush, wearing tight trousers like a Free School Street whore.

I wonder why she's come now, my mother said quickly, changing the subject. Why is this heat?

Because, Ila told me an hour later, when we were sitting in her room in their Elgin Road house; this is when I have my holidays too, you know, and besides I haven't been back for a year.

Anyway, she laughed, watching me as I mopped my sweating face with a handkerchief, the heat bothers you much more than it does me.

And of course she was right: the heat hadn't touched her.

She looked younger with her hair cut, boyish in a way, and she was thinner too, her arms were like wands, and the dimple was never quite gone from her cheek. She looked improbably exotic to me, dressed in faded blue jeans and a T shirt—like no girl I had ever seen before except in pictures in American magazines.

There she is, in the green afternoon darkness of that shuttered, high-ceilinged

---

1. A passenger train.

room, not quite sitting, but draped over a leather armchair, her legs thrown over the back so that the top of her jeans have crept away from her T shirt and left the hollow of her stomach glowing in the darkness; her body cradled lazily in the seat, her head flung back over the arm, so that her small pointed breasts have thrust the thin cotton of her T shirt into two gentle points which harden with her breathing, and then swell away again into dark circles, one of them dotted with a tiny black mole. She flops about in the chair, heedless of her body, childlike, and I, bracing the muscles in my thighs to contain the dull, swelling ache in my groin, have to roll over on my stomach and look at a magazine, though that makes the pain much worse, like the throbbing of a torniquet, as though something were about to burst in my balls. I push myself away from her, along the floor, for I cannot let her see me like this, not for shame, but merely to preserve my friendship with her, for I know that between us there lies a chequerboard of relationships in which I have been given the place of a cousin, a favourite perhaps, but still a cousin and nothing more.

The day before Robi was to leave for Darjeeling, we spent a long sleepy day in their house, rolling about in her room, looking for cool spots on the floor, reading and quarrelling. When the afternoon had dragged itself out and the sun had set, Ila threw open the shutters. The sight of the cars inching along the road below seemed to act on her like a tonic.

Come on, she said, tugging at my hand; let's go out somewhere. We can't lie about all day like this. Besides Robi's leaving tomorrow. I think we should give him a party.

Robi stirred torpidly on the floor and dropped the book he had been reading. A party, he said. In this heat?

Yes, said Ila. Let's go somewhere and have fun.

Robi and I exchanged a long, doubtful look.

I haven't got enough money, I said.

I've got money, she laughed. I'll give you a treat.

But where can we go? said Robi.

I'll tell you what, said Ila; let's go to the Grand Hotel. I've heard they have a nightclub there.

What are we going to do in a nightclub? said Robi.

We can drink a few beers, said Ila. And watch the cabaret—that kind of thing.

Drink! cried Robi. In a place like that?

What's the matter, she said sharply. You do drink, don't you? What about that story you were telling me about the send-off you got from your pals in college? You *are* a little hypocrite.

Judgements of that kind came very easily to Ila, because to her morality could only be an absolute. She could understand and admire someone who never ate meat on principle, but a person who was a vegetarian only at home was, to her, the worst kind of hypocrite. She knew that Robi was quite happy to risk expulsion occasionally by smuggling bottles of rum into his college room and drinking the night away with his friends, and because she could not see that he would do those things in college precisely because there was a certain innocence about those exploits in those circumstances, the kind of monasticism which honours the rules of the order in their breach, she could not understand why Robi would feel himself defiled, drinking in a nightclub, surrounded by paunchy men with dark-pouched eyes. She could not understand the real nature of his prudishness because context had no place in her judgements.

It's just petit-bourgeois nastiness, Ila had said to me once about Robi. It's a mystery to me how he's become such a legend in your college: I thought students were meant to be defiant of narrowmindedness. But undergraduates respect muscle I suppose, and he's got plenty of those.

I had been puzzled too when I first discovered how much deference Robi commanded in college. It was hard to understand, for he did not excel particularly in any of the spheres which were held to confer distinction in that milieu: he was not unusually good at sports, just about good enough to keep a place in the college cricket eleven; he was good at his studies but not brilliant; he was not clever, not well-dressed, not talented, nor in any way unlike a dozen others in our college, and yet, without asking for it, barely seeming to notice, he commanded a respect immeasurably greater than the best sportsmen and the most brilliant students.

It took me time to see that this respect was really a tribute to the superhuman simplicity of his view of the world: to the fact that he had no hesitation in making judgments—because there were whole domains of conduct within which he would not admit the possibility of argument—and no fear of defending them, because of his abundant physical courage. Once, for example, there was a great uproar in our college because a student had been expelled for some minor misdeameanour—for asking a girl up to his room for a cup of tea or some such thing. The students' union was unanimous in calling for a strike. But Robi, alone in the whole college, refused to go along with everyone else: he didn't argue or make speeches, he merely refused to attend the union meetings. And when some of the union's leaders threatened to give him a beating, they found to their surprise that he was relieved at the prospect of settling the issue by a straight-forward physical contest. Such was his standing in the college that eventually the leaders gave in and the strike was called off.

Later, I asked him: Why *wouldn't* you join the strike? Tell me, just as a matter of interest.

He wouldn't answer, so I asked him again, and then reluctantly he said: Because a rule's a rule; if you break one you have to be willing to pay the price.

But is it a *good* rule? I asked. He only smiled, and no matter how hard I tried I could not get him to answer my question.

I understood then that he *could not* answer: that his authority grew out of that subterranean realm of judgement which we call Morality, the condition of whose success is that its rulings be always shrouded from argument. I understood why his opinions always prevailed against his peers': because while they had to find their way through a fog of ordinary confusions, in every difficult situation Robi had an intuition which led him directly to what he knew he *ought* to do, even if he did not know why. And they followed him since he, uniquely, was willing to defend those inconvenient, often ridiculous, scruples which they could only too easily be persuaded to forget. That was why they, and I, both admired him and feared him, and that was why his courage, even when it manifested itself physically, was moral in the purest sense.

Come on, enjoy yourself for once, said Ila. You'll be going away soon anyway, so you can forget all about it afterwards.

But why do you want to go to the Grand Hotel? said Robi.

Because it's the poshest place in the city of course, said Ila, tipping her head back. Isn't that the best possible reason?

I don't want to go to a place like that, Robi said.

But once Ila had made up her mind she had to have her way. She bent down in front of him and touched her forehead to his feet.

Please, Robi-kaku, she said. Please, just this once. If you don't like it, we'll leave. I promise.

So we went: Ila resplendent in a silk blouse and a skirt. Robi and I grimly insistent on not changing out of our usual student uniform of kurta[2] and crumpled trousers.

When we reached the entrance of the Grand Hotel and saw the beturbaned doorman's dead-fish eyes flicking disdainfully over us, both Robi and I would have kept on walking, all the way down Chowringhee. But Ila was right behind us, and with a rustle of silk she shepherded us through the corridor, into a chandeliered hall. She led us to the reception counter and in the plummiest of her English accents she asked them to show us the way to the nightclub. Suitably awed, they sent a liveried attendant to show us the way. He led us down another corridor to a large ornate door. He pushed the door open, pocketed Ila's tip, and stood aside, bowing.

We heard the hum of an electric guitar echoing out of the darkness, somewhere inside the cavernous room.

I'm not going in there, said Robi. He pulled his hand out of Ila's; she was sweating.

Oh come on, Ila said in exasperation. Come on, Uncle Robi. You've made your point: we're willing to accept that you're just a poor peasant horrified by the badness of the big city. So now you may as well relax and enjoy yourself.

She took his hand again and he let himself be led in.

It was so dark inside that the waiter had to lead us through the clusters of empty tables with an electric torch. I felt the touch of something moist and strangely furry on my face. Instinctively my arm rose to fight it off. I felt it again, on my forearm, and jumped backwards, knocking over a chair.

What are those things? I cried, my skin tingling. Something touched me.

It's only the decorations sir, said the waiter. He brought us to a halt at an empty table and pulled back a chair for Ila. We sat down, and when our eyes had grown accustomed to the darkness, we saw that every available space was covered with nodding palm fronds. There were catamarans painted on the walls and clusters of coconuts were dangling from the roof. Ila pointed at the band, on a platform beside the dance floor; it consisted of four men in dark suits, bow ties, and straw hats.

---

2. A long, loose shirt.

She giggled: I think it's meant to be a beach.

Clasping her hands she looked at the two of us, smiling. All right, she said, shall we ask for some beer?

I nodded when she turned to me, but Robi said nothing.

Can't you just pretend that you're in college? she said. If it makes you feel less of a hypocrite?

Robi raised his hand abruptly and signalled to the waiter. When the waiter came, he said: Get us three beers please.

He put his hands flat on the table and turned to look at Ila, swivelling his broad, powerful shoulders.

Do your Trotskyite comrades know, he said, how you spend your time when you're not demonstrating for the revolution?

She smiled and tapped his cheek with her forefinger. You can't demonstrate for a revolution stupid, she said. And yes they do know, and they don't care because Trotskyists aren't joyless little clerks like you're getting to be.

She was angry with herself as soon as she said it.

Oh come on Robi, she pleaded. It's your last evening here. Let's not quarrel.

That made Robi angrier still, but as always, when he was really angry, he could not think of anything to say. Then our bottles of beer arrived, and he busied himself pouring them out. When our glasses were full, he raised his and drained half of it in one long swallow. Then he leant back, wiping his mouth, breathing hard, and stared into it.

To my relief, there was a loud roll on the drums and the leader of the band announced into the microphone: Now Ladies and Gentlemen, we have Miss Jennifer here, to sing for you. Please give her a hand.

Miss Jennifer swam out of the darkness, bowing and bobbing; a paper-pale, matronly woman, in a skin-tight crimson sheath covered with silver spangles.

Hi folks: she trilled in a thin, high voice, full of professional gaiety. Hi there! Come on now then, get yourself ready, you all, for a whole bagful of fun.

The spotlights spun, her spangles erupted into flashes of colour and she strutted down to the table next to us.

Now then, she said huskily into the microphone. Who have we got here?

The two middle-aged businessmen who were sitting at the table wriggled in shy delight. She patted their cheeks, but when they stretched their hands out to touch her, she slapped them away and danced out of reach, noisily clicking her tongue.

My, my, she said, looking at them through her eyelashes. Aren't we naughty today?

If she comes here, Robi said into his glass, I'm going to knock her teeth in.

But instead she walked into the middle of the dance floor, flung her arms dramatically outwards, like a diver on a high board, and cried: All right folks—let's dance with Ol' Blue Eyes—let's dance with a stranger tonight.

Yes, gasped Ila, that's it. Let's dance, that'll cheer us up.

Come on, she said, tugging at my hand. Get up, let's dance.

But I was clumsy and self-conscious on my feet at the best of times. And when I looked at the empty expanse of the dance floor, at plump Miss Jennifer swaying in the middle, and the hungry eyes of the businessmen staring at her, I knew that I would never be able to step on to that floor.

No, I said, shaking my head. I couldn't, not here.

She turned away disappointedly. Robi? she said. Wouldn't you like to dance?

I can't dance, he said, raising his head to look at her. And even if I could, I wouldn't in a place like this. I think you should sit down, for you're not going to dance either.

At first she was merely surprised.

I'm not going to dance? she said. Why not?

Because I won't let you, said Robi evenly.

You won't let me? she said. The muscles of her face went slowly rigid.

You won't *let* me? she said. Why, who do you think you are?

Robi folded his arms across his chest. It doesn't matter who I am, he said. I won't let you.

She turned to look at me now, her lips going thin and bloodless. Does he think, she asked me, that I'm one of his college freshers or something? Does he think because he's got a lot of muscles, he can stop *me*? Does he think *I'm* scared of a college bully? Well let's see him stop me.

She kicked her chair back and rose to her feet.

I put out my hand and tugged at her skirt. Ila please don't, I said. You don't know him. Please sit down and let's go home.

She gave my hand a stinging slap. I'm going to find out, she said. Let's see what he does to stop me.

I jumped to my feet and stood in front of her. Ila please, I said. What are you going to do?

She pushed me aside. I'll tell you what I'm going to do, she said. I'm going to go over to those two businessmen over there, and I'm going to ask the thin one to dance with me.

She turned on her heel and walked away.

Pivoting in his chair, Robi watched her walk up to the two businessmen. We saw her smiling at them, then she bent her head gracefully to talk to the thinner of the two, and he started to his feet. We watched as his face creased into a smile and then clouded over with a leering, greedy suspicion. Then she smiled again, and he, nodding eagerly, stepped out to take her hand.

I heard the scrape of Robi's chair and stepped sideways to stop him. He elbowed me away and reached them with three long strides. He caught hold of the neck of Ila's blouse with one hand and wrenched her away from the businessman. Then he opened the palm of his hand and planted it squarely in the middle of the man's chest. Arching his shoulder back, he swivelled, suddenly, with so much force that the man staggered back for a good five feet or so, taking his chair with him.

The singer dropped her microphone and the band froze into a silvery tableau under the spotlight. There was a moment of complete silence. Then, like a reel of film coming unstuck, everyone sprang to life, and a crowd of waiters surrounded us.

The only person who was perfectly calm was Robi. He held his hands open in front of him and said, in a quiet, mild voice: Don't touch me. We'll pay and we'll leave right now, but don't touch me.

He took out his wallet and handed one of the waiters a fifty-rupee note. Then he put his arm around Ila and led us out. The waiters followed us all the way to the pavement.

Ila did not say a word until we had walked as far as the Museum. At the corner she stopped and leant against the wrought-iron railings.

Have you gone mad? she said to Robi, spitting the words through her teeth? What did you think you were doing?

Look, Robi said. It's over now, let's just forget it.

We won't forget it, she said; she was screaming now, but with her voice very low, in that way women have. We will not forget it. Just tell me: what did you think you were doing?

Listen Ila, Robi said, shaking his head. You shouldn't have done what you did. You ought to know that; girls don't behave like that here.

What the fuck do you *mean?* she spat at him. What do you mean 'girls'? I'll do what I bloody well want, when I want and where.

No you won't, he said. Not if I'm around. Girls don't behave like that here.

Why not? she screamed. Why fucking well not?

You can do what you like in England, he said. But here there are certain things you cannot do. That's our culture; that's how we live.

She stared at him, wide-eyed, speechless. Then she spun around to face me. Do you see now? she cried. She bit her lip fiercely and the tears came pouring out of her brimming eyes.

I put my arms around her and pulled her towards me. She rubbed her face into my kurta, sobbing, saying over and over again: Do you see now? Do you understand?—and I uncomprehending, repeated after her: See what? understand what? while trying to stop the flow of her tears with the back of my hand.

Then she pushed me away and waved at a taxi. It stopped, and she darted into it, rolled down the window, and shouted: Do you see now why I've chosen to live in London? Do you see? It's only because I want to be free.

Free of what? I said.

Free of *you!* she shouted back. Free of your bloody culture and free of all of you.

The taxi started moving and I began to run along with it.

You can never be free of me, I shouted through the open window. If I were to die tomorrow you would not be free of me. You cannot be free of me because *I am within you* . . . just as you are within me.

Then the taxi picked up speed and disappeared along Chowringhee.

So that was what I told my grandmother as she lay in her sickbed, glaring at me; I told her that Ila lived in London only because she wanted to be free.

But I knew I had made a mistake the moment I said it; I should have known that she would have nothing but contempt for a freedom that could be bought for the price of an air ticket. For she too had once wanted to be free; she had dreamt of killing for her freedom.

It's not freedom she wants, said my grandmother, her bloodshot eyes glowing in the hollows of her withered face. She wants to be left alone to do what she pleases: that's all that any whore would want. She'll find it easily enough over there; that's what those places have to offer. But that is not what it means to be free.

I got up then and went back to my room. Staring out of my window, at the darkness of the Lake, I saw Ila's face again, as I had seen it that night in the taxi, wet with tears, twisted with anger and hatred, and I thought of how much they all wanted to be free; how they went mad wanting their freedom; I began to wonder whether it was I that was mad because I was happy to be bound: whether I was alone in knowing that I could not live without the clamour of the voices within me.

Ancestral figures from Nias, Sumatra.
Detail of twelve figures in dark brown
wood, tied to bamboo rods by rattan
strips.

SECTION X
Southeast Asia

Southeast Asia—that is, the coastal countries of Vietnam, Cambodia, Thailand, Burma/Myanmar,* and Laos, as well as the archipelago countries of Malaysia, Indonesia, and the Philippines—has long been a cosmopolitan region, with trade connecting its various parts and binding them to more distant nations. Distinctive of the region as a whole is a long history of interaction with expansive world civilizations: Polynesian, Hindu, Islamic, Buddhist, Chinese-Confucian, and European-colonial. When, in the seventeenth century, the Dutch began to build their commercial empire on the basis of trade between Europe and what is now Indonesia, they found the inhabitants well accustomed to dealing with Indian, Persian, Arab, and Chinese traders, many of whom had taken up residence in the towns and received protection from local rulers.

Early visitors often remarked on the cultural singularities of precolonial Southeast Asia. Generally speaking, women enjoyed a far greater degree of autonomy, including economic independence, than did their Chinese or Indian counterparts. Only rarely were states highly centralized. Urban centers were few. For much of the region's history, land was plentiful and labor scarce. Rather than aiming at self-sufficiency in all things, a family or a village would expect to supply many of its needs through trade. As the historian Anthony Reid has observed, these porous and interdependent societies were ill-suited to

*Burma was renamed Myanmar in 1989.

resist the advances of European mercantile monopolies. From the nineteenth century onward, production of a narrow range of raw materials and dependence on a colonial metropole for finished goods were the usual pattern. Aspects of this economic history appear in the short story "The Birth," by Pramoedya Ananta Toer, given here.

As befits a region of intensive trade, the languages of Southeast Asia are many and intermingled. Malay long served as a region-wide common spoken language. Up until the late nineteenth century, much of the literature in this area was written in cosmopolitan languages (such as Chinese, Sanskrit, Pali, or literary Arabic) rather than vernacular ones. The tendency remains: Filipino literature today includes writings in Spanish and English, alongside Tagalog, Cebuano, and dozens of local languages. Indonesia and Malaysia share a common language derived from the earlier Malay. In many areas today the national vernaculars are supplanting older written idioms or tribal languages, but not without encountering resistance.

In its themes and forms, too, Southeast Asian literature reflects a many-layered historical inheritance. The early literatures of Malay and Javanese show much borrowing and adaptation of imported materials, retelling and elaborating on the Indian and Persian epics. The folk theater of Bali still derives its plots from Indian classics such as the *Ramayana* and *Mahabharata*. Hồ Xuân Hu'o'ng's verses make ribald humor out of a venerable Chinese type of poetic allegory. In the colonial period, the European education made available to a small segment of the urban populations gave the novel and spoken theater a place in the new national vernacular literatures. The works of Pramoedya Ananta Toer testify to the power of the Southeast Asian novel—characteristically read as a form of historical commentary—to disturb consensus.

In Thailand, however, the adaptation of foreign literary forms has run a somewhat different course. Unlike its neighbors, Thailand was never colonized by Western powers. The alphabet developed under King Ramkamhaeng in the thirteenth century was not replaced by a romanized system (as were the original Malay and Vietnamese scripts, for instance); as a consequence, modern Thai literature has retained strong links to its past. Poetry, the forms and conventions of which have been developed and refined over six centuries, has remained the most respected and beloved of the literary arts. Although contemporary Thai poets are influenced by the poets of other nations, their principal debt is to the masterpieces of their own poetic tradition. When Thais began to attend European universities in the nineteenth century, they enthusiastically adapted those Western literary forms that appealed to them, especially the short story and the novel. They felt neither pressed to adopt Western literary practices nor reluctant to do so, a dilemma complicating the development of modern vernacular literatures in many of those countries where foreign influences were inescapable in all facets of life. The readings in this section provide a clear indication of the complexity of Southeast Asia's literary relations with the rest of the world.

Historical Background

The civilizations of Southeast Asia evolved largely during the centuries from 200 B.C.E. to 1500 C.E. It was during this period that ethnic groups were formed, reflecting the names of the countries on the mainland—the Burmese, the Thai, the

Laotians, the Khmer (Cambodians), and the Vietnamese. It was also during this period that trade flourished and exposed the region to the formative influences of India, China, and Islam.

With the exception of the Vietnamese, almost all of Southeast Asia experienced over a millennium of Indian or Indianized influence, when Buddhist and Hindu elements mingled with indigenous customs and beliefs to produce new religious and cultural identities. Hundreds of small Indianized states arose over the mainland and throughout the islands, as well as several kingdoms and empires of great territorial expansion and cultural brilliance. Among these were the Dvarati kingdom of the Mon people (second century B.C.E.?–eleventh century C.E.), whose early civilization in Lower Burma and Thailand was instrumental in passing Indianized culture on to later arrivals; the Malay kingdom of Srivijaya on Sumatra (eighth–thirteenth century); the Pagan kingdom of the newly ascendant Burmese (fl. eleventh–thirteenth century); the Khmer empire with its spectacular capital at Angkor (tenth–fifteenth century); the Lan Xang kingdom of the Lao (thirteenth–eighteenth century); and the Ayutthaya kingdom of the Thai (fl. fourteenth–sixteenth century). The Vietnamese, in contrast, were subject to direct or indirect Chinese rule from the second century B.C.E. to the tenth century C.E., and their present culture owes much to Confucian, Taoist, and Buddhist elements from China.

Between the fifth and thirteenth century C.E., Buddhism (whether derived from India, Sri Lanka or China) emerged as the dominant religion on the mainland. The islands, however, are today largely Islamic (with the notable exception of the Indonesian island of Bali, where the pre-Islamic Hindu culture of Java still thrives). Arab trading ships had plied the Indian Ocean and South China Sea from at least the ninth century. Beginning in the thirteenth century, Arab and Indian Muslim traders arrived in greater numbers, and from their settlements Islam mingled with Buddhist and Hindu practices as a third formative cultural factor. Major Muslim states included Majapahit on western Java (fl. thirteenth century), the peninsular states of Malacca (fl. fifteenth century) and Johor (fl. fifteenth–sixteenth century), and the empire of Brunei (fl. sixteenth century). Numerous smaller kingdoms existed, each experiencing its period of preeminence.

The first Europeans to arrive in the region were the Portuguese in the early sixteenth century, followed by the Dutch a century later. Through the eighteenth century, French, Italian, and English settlements were also established. With the rise of European empire-building toward the end of the eighteenth century, the European presence became more domineering. Beginning with Dutch sovereignty over Java in 1759, the entire region except for Thailand came under European colonial rule. The Anglo-Dutch treaty of 1824 formalized the boundaries of British Malaya and Dutch Indonesia, thus bringing the peninsula and thousands of islands – historically home to numerous rival kingdoms – into their present-day formation as two nations. Starting in 1826, three wars captured Burma for the British, who ruled it as a province of India. Cambodia became a French protectorate in 1863, and in 1897 it joined Vietnam and Laos as French Indochina.

Colonization had occurred even earlier in the Philippines, which were claimed by the Spanish in the fifteenth century and held until 1901, when sovereignty passed to the United States as a result of the Spanish-American War. Our knowledge of Philippine history before the Spanish occupation is limited. Although Chinese and Indian traders had certainly visited and even settled portions of the islands, there seems to have been no sustained cultural influence, and

Spanish missionaries were successful in effecting a large-scale conversion to Christianity. The Brunei empire embraced some of the islands at the time of Spanish occupation, and Muslim sultanates in the Philippines continued to resist Spanish rule into the late nineteenth century.

Various political/nationalist liberation movements arose throughout the region in the first decades of the twentieth century. Japanese occupation during World War II decisively interrupted European control, and in the decades following the war, the nations of Southeast Asia gained their independence: the Philippines in 1946, Burma in 1948, Indonesia in 1949 (following a four-year war against the Dutch), and Malaysia in 1957. The reestablishment of French colonial authority in Indochina, successfully negotiated with Laos and Cambodia, met with militant resistance in Vietnam, provoking the first Indochina war (1946–1953). The Geneva Conference, which negotiated the war's end, recognized the independence of all three nations and divided Vietnam temporarily at the seventeenth parallel until national elections could be held. The elections never took place. Instead, backed by the United States, South Vietnam made a bid for independence from the North in the second Indochina War, better known in the United States as the Vietnam War. In 1975 the North claimed victory, and Vietnam was reunified in the following year.

Further Readings

Becker, A. L., ed. *Writing on the Tongue*. Ann Arbor: Center for South and Southeast Asian Studies, 1989.

Benda, Harry J., and John A. Larkin, eds. *The World of Southeast Asia: Selected Historical Readings*. New York: Harper & Row, 1967.

Bowie, Katherine, ed. and trans. *Voices from the Thai Countryside: The Short Stories of Samruam Singh*. Madison: University of Wisconsin Center for Southeast Asian Studies, Monograph 6, 1991.

Durand, Maurice, and Nguyen Tran Huan. *An Introduction to Vietnamese Literature*. Trans. D. M. Hawke. New York: Columbia University Press, 1985.

Kepner, Susan Fulop. *The Lioness in Bloom: Women in Modern Thai Literature*. Berkeley: University of California Press, 1995.

Phillips, Herbert P. *Modern Thai Literature: An Ethnographic Interpretation*. Honolulu: University of Hawaii Press, 1987.

Raffel, Burton. *The Development of Modern Indonesian Poetry*. Albany: State University of New York Press, 1967.

Reid, Anthony. *The Lands Below the Winds*. New Haven: Yale University Press, 1988. Vol. 3 of *Southeast Asia in the Age of Commerce, 1450–1680*.

Treasury of Thai Literature: The Modern Period. Bangkok: The National Identity Board, Office of the Prime Minister, 1988.

NGUYỄN DŨ (1765–1820)
Vietnam

By Nguyễn Dũ's time, Feng Hsiao-ch'ing [Feng Xiaoqing] had already been the subject of several biographies, plays, and fictionalized accounts. The historical Hsiao-ch'ing was an educated young woman from Yangchow, skilled at writing poetry, who became the concubine of a young man from an influential Hangchow family. The young man's first wife was jealous of her talent and beauty, however, and had her removed from the household to an isolated pavilion on the West Lake of Hangchow, where she died, brokenhearted, in 1612. After her death, her rival had her writings burned; only a handful of poems were spared.

Reading Hsiao-ch'ing [Xiaoqing]*

West Lake flower garden: a desert, now.
Alone, at the window, I read through old pages.
A smudge of rouge, a scent of perfume, but
I still weep.
Is there a Fate for books?   5
Why mourn for a half-burned poem?
There is nothing, there is no one to question,
And yet this misery feels like my own.
Ah, in another three hundred years
Will anyone weep, remembering my Fate?   10

HỒ XUÂN HƯƠNG
(NINETEENTH CENTURY)
Vietnam

The four poems by Hồ Xuân Hương presented here show her satirical verve (directed against the clergy, in "A Buddhist Priest") and her metaphorical skill. "A Riddle" and "Night Weaving" exploit the multiple meanings of words and Chinese characters as well as the suggestive qualities of objects. "The Temple of Fragrance," in addition, parodies the conventional style of poetry written to commemorate visits to famous places. In China, the "poem on an object" had

*Translated by Nguyen Ngoc Bich and Burton Raffel.

long been a means of indirect self-expression, a discreet way of conveying the depth of one's feelings; Hồ 's poems on objects reverse that reticent attitude.

A Buddhist Priest*

He's neither Chinese
Nor one of us:
Bald, his clothes unstitched,
He sits behind rows of rice-cake offerings
And in front of six or seven nuns.   5
Now and then he touches a gong,
A bell, cymbals;
He hums, drawls, incants.
Pray hard: You too can be a Superior
And squat, proud, on a lotus.   10

A Riddle†1

My body is white, in shape I am rounded;
Sometimes I float on the surface, sometimes I am under water.
Large or small, the hand that molded me matters little:
I shall always preserve my vermilion heart.

Night Weaving†

When the wick of the lamp is up, everything is all white.
The shuttle flying continually all night penetrates the cloth.
The feet keep pushing down and gently letting up again.
At a stroke the shuttle shoots through, in ecstasy at its own speed.
Broad or narrow, large or small, anything will suit it;   5
Short or long, the shape is always the same.
The weaver-girl who wants to do a good job leaves it to soak a long time;
She waits three autumns before showing its color.2

Translated by Nguyen Ngoc Bich and Burton Raffel.
†*Translated by Maurice Durand, Nguyen Tran Huan, and D. M. Hawke.*

---

1. Title supplied by the editors. The poem describes, without naming it, a Vietnamese sweet called *bánh trôi nùớc*—a nugget of red sugar wrapped in a ball of sticky rice, served in a bowl of syrup. According to the translators, the sweet "represents the woman who remains pure at heart despite having to endure intercourse with men."

2. The translators note that in the original, the word translated as "autumn" puns on another word meaning "joining together, gathering in, receiving."

Anonymous, Angkor Vat, first half of the twelfth century. *Devatā*.

The Temple of Fragrance*

Who could have fashioned this marvel?
The mountain cracks into a wide, hollow cave.
Pious Buddhists struggle to set foot inside,
others gaze at it tirelessly.
Drippings form a sweet streamlet,   5
as sailors on incoming junks bend their heads.
City folk also flock to these springs and woods.
Clever, indeed, the Old Man in Heaven!

PRAMOEDYA ANANTA TOER (b. 1926)

Indonesia

Pramoedya Ananta Toer's father, like the father of the narrator of "The Birth," was in the 1930s the headmaster of a private school sympathetic to the Indonesian nationalist movement. Such schools were discouraged by the Dutch colonial

*Translated by Nguyen Ngoc Bich.

Anonymous, Mandalay (?), c. 1850. *The Disciple Moggallana.* Lacquered and gilt wood. Victoria & Albert Museum.

government through laws that required registration of schools and teachers and subjected the curriculum of a private school to official approval. Parallel to the rise and fall of the school in this story is the popular effort, inspired by Gandhi's self-sufficiency campaigns, to replace imported textiles with village weavings. "The Birth" ends inconclusively; as any Indonesian reader of the story will know, it would take the Japanese invasion of Dutch East India in 1942 to overturn the colonial government and two years of war between 1947 and 1949 to remove it entirely.

The Birth

1

One of the adopted children in our house was a student called Hurip. He had finished government high school in the provincial capital, Semarang. A number of young men, still students, stayed with us too. The older boys often gathered to talk.

Translated by Harry Aveling.

I could not understand many of the things they talked about, and I certainly couldn't understand Hurip when he said, "We need dynamism. Our society is too static. We should have the courage to do something other than being civil servants."

I was curious to find out as much as I could, and often left father's books and desk in a mess. I asked mother about things I couldn't understand. I asked her what Hurip meant. She told me politely that when I was grown up I would understand readily enough.

I worried about it. I asked my friends what he meant and they didn't know. I asked the servant who was seven times as old as I was and she didn't understand either.

Hurip's opinions were respected in our house because he had passed through the Dutch school system. Even mother respected him. It was scarcely surprising that he became the centre of attention and that everyone paid close attention to whatever he said. He dominated every conversation. Mother said he had joined a political party.

I was amazed to hear of this. To me politics meant the police and our whole house hated anything to do with the police.

"Isn't father angry he's joined the police?" I asked.

She smiled at my question. Then explained simply what politics was and told me: "Those who join the parties are the enemies of the police."

I understood a little. I tried to explain it to my friends but they laughed in disbelief. Our servant refused to believe it. I felt surrounded by thick impenetrable walls.

Then came that afternoon. We had washed; the older boys had not yet begun to play chess, study or paint. They sat on a mat around a low table—a desk—and engaged in earnest conversation. I sat behind Hurip, who spoke with great fire: "It must be boring being a civil servant. They go to work at a set time, stay in the office for a set period, go home at a set time, play with their wives and have children at regular intervals. They live like that year after year. Really boring. They dream like donkeys of a bundle of hay, a drink of water and quiet rest. Beautiful thoughts about their next pay rise. Then they jump about like dogs, a pat on the head from their boss and they dream of promotion. They they get scared like rabbits: a frown from the boss and they'll lose their jobs."

The other boys listened carefully. I tried to, but couldn't follow it all. One thing stayed with me: you would get babies if you played with your wife.

Hurip continued about how boring it would be to be a civil servant. "Never any variety," he said. "You need change to be creative. And when the month was safely over, they carried their salaries home looking pleased with themselves, light in the head—and a little flushed. From the middle to the end of the month they sweated because they didn't have enough money. Bills, chits, invoices and pawnshop tickets danced in their heads. And those who never got bored with themselves became solid gold civil servants in the top echelons. Their lives never changed. They just kept having more kids . . ."

This was before the second world war, when the Dutch and their civil service seemed likely to stay forever.

And I still didn't understand what he meant, so I just listened quietly.

After lunch I asked mother if you really got babies by playing with your wife. She didn't answer me. Without changing her expression she ordered me to go and study and to call Hurip on my way. When she saw I still wanted an answer, she said firmly: "Go and study! Don't put it off. There'll always be study until you're grown up. Go on."

And I repeated my question. She was angry. I never saw her uncertain about anything, even the smallest thing—she was always resolute. It was of great value to her in running the house.

I went. And shortly after I heard her calling Hurip. From then on, my adopted brother was more careful when I was around. He would joke noisily with the others and then, when I came, turn the conversation to serious matters.

2

The ordinariness of our smalltown existence suddenly changed. I could not have described it explicitly but I felt it strongly. From the conversations I heard, I found out that there was turmoil among the nobles. And among the merchants. And among the farmers and artisans. Hurip spoke of India and *swadesi*,[1] of the Japanese and of the rise of Asia. He spoke fiercely, as father did when he made his speeches: "From the time of the first kings in the fatherland, the nobles have been the most powerful class in society—power they have wrongly usurped. They claim the right—although no-one admits or practices the right other than themselves—to be called 'lord' by the lower-classes. They try to be contemplative rather than active. They are at peace only because they cannot see what is going on around them. The only thing they are interested in is promotion, prestige and their salary. Sometimes their fine dreams turn into groundless fears: retrenchment, the anger of their superiors, a drop in their salary. But we are organizing. If they don't want to join us, we will sweep them aside."

As usual I couldn't follow all he had to say.

3

Life in our small town was passing through a ferment. A football club was established and soon each part of town had three football clubs of its own. Football clubs grew like mushrooms among the young. Among the nobles there were artistic circles: theatre, shadow-play, classical dance, singing and the

---

1. The Indonesian term for the policy of "self-sufficiency," an element of Gandhi's opposition to British rule in India. Gandhi's followers produced and wore coarse homespun cloth rather than buy imported British finished goods.

traditional *gamelan*.[2] Among the young people there were modern theatre groups and pop orchestras. Father was a patron of several artistic, sporting and social clubs. And mother was patron of a women's club.

Many of the people in our neighborhood joined the police. They reported that the government was strengthening its police forces. But the people still came in droves when Engineer Sukarno[3] came to speak in our town. And they weren't stopped from gathering in their thousands when Doctor Sosrokartono came to visit, and from asking him to turn water into holy water. The head of almost every family came home in great delight with half a bottle of salt water, as if his family's salvation were assured for ever.

In the early morning squads of men would be out running. And almost every Sunday there was a football game. Often the children would line up and sing the popular nationalist song:

> As the sun in the east begins to rise
> Let us stand and go forth in our strength. . .

Father ordered us to join the scouts. And at a grand campfire a line of old men were sworn in as honorary members of the Boy Scouts of Indonesia. Among them, in scout's uniform, was father. The number of scouts quadrupled. Two new troops were formed, one Muslim and one using the medium of Dutch.

Slowly but surely we began to hate the Dutch. And the hate finally spread.

"Don't think Europeans will always be more important than we," father once told mother, happily. I noticed her stomach was slightly full.

Mother enjoyed the taste of the words. I still remember him saying that, although I was only seven. She was holding a book. It was, as I found out ten or eleven years later, a book on the political consequences of the cotton trade. Cotton was an important commodity and a disguised political issue.

She fondly looked at me and then said, while looking at father, "There are other ways of earning a living than working in an office. What do you want to be when you grow up, my son?"

"A farmer!" I exclaimed with delight.

"A farmer?" asked father. I said "yes." Mother continued: "If you really want to be a farmer you can't be lazy like you are now." And she told me about the ranches in the United States, Australia and in the Hawaiian islands.

Her simple words made me eager to hoe the small plot of ground prepared for me. Often she helped me. And once as we planted sweet potato she said hopefully, "The fruit of one's own labour is sweetest, my son. Look! you're starting to sweat. That's good for your blood and your health."

She even told me that one day the highest officials ruling over Indonesia would no longer be Dutch, but our own people. Then, "You're still young. Later,

---

2. A Javanese percussion orchestra.
3. Sukarno (1901–1967; also spelled Soekarno) was president of the indepen-

dent Indonesian Republic from 1945 to 1965.

when you've done with your schooling and like to read big books like your father does, you'll know a lot—and the seed I've planted will bear fruit. As will the labours of those who want to see our own people in control. But you can't understand yet. Do you know what father's doing?"

"He's not home very often," I said interrupting.

"No, he's not. He's still planting for the future—for future decades—and the crop will never be exhausted."

"Never? Sweet potato?"

"Sweet potato. Not the kind you eat. But something you can enjoy when you've grown up. Something better than this. Better for you then than now. And for your friends."

I stopped hoeing and looked at her for a while. Seeing my hoe still, she too stopped and looked at me. "You don't understand," she said regretfully. "One day you'll understand without all the riddles."

I never forgot her words. Or the vitality which gripped our small town.

Hurip no longer talked as much as he had. He was obliged by father to teach in his school, a private school established nine years before I was born. After Hurip came home from school, he slept. In the early evening he corrected his students' work, later he studied. He had no time to sit around talking or to play chess or practice the violin.

Once—I remember—on the afternoon prior to the weekly holiday, a group sat around the study table. I was there, as usual sitting behind Hurip. And in a controlled but firm voice he said: "The government taxes are crippling us. They tax anything and everything. And we all suffer because of it. We have to pay tax for every meter of cloth we buy and every time we walk on the road."

I could understand what he was saying and could imagine how happy people would be if there were no taxes. He finished up: "The Dutch haven't come here to make you all senior civil servants. They've come to take our money away from us in taxes. And if we don't pay and have nothing they can pillage, we have to do forced labour in prison. The *Samin* rebels to the south of us were smart. They refused ever to pay any taxes."

His voice always carried conviction. And that made the other children believe every word he uttered.

The change in attitude became clear when people began to wear *lurik,* a coarse, quickly-fading village-woven striped cloth. Even the nobles wore it. I was not rich, but I had never felt drawn to *lurik* either. Wash it two or three times and the colour was a mess. But father wore pyjamas and shirts made of *lurik.* And one day we all received a set of *lurik* shirts each. My confusion was increased. When Hurip, in the company of the other boys said, "The people in India are wearing *lurik* too, and burning overseas cloth," I said, automatically, "What a pity. If they gave it to me, I'd have it."

Everyone laughed and I fell silent. I realized then how unimportant I was and that I was expected to listen and not to try to make myself heard. Hurip put me on his lap and said; "When you make your own cloth and burn overseas clothing, that's called *swadesi*. It makes work for your own countrymen, and when they work they get the benefits. If you wear foreign clothing, foreigners do the work and they get all the benefits."

I nodded uncomprehendingly. The conversation which I could neither follow nor understand went on until midnight. I slept on the mat and was allowed to stay there until morning when the cold air began to bite my skin.

At that time wearing *lurik* made you a more respected person. I wasn't surprised when mother told an old village woman: "Make me twelve lengths of *lurik*—nicely coloured and well-patterned, for the children."

The cloth had to be for us. Mother ordered none for herself because she disliked wearing it.

The weaver said happily, "Lots of people are wearing *lurik* nowadays."

"It's *swadesi*, dear," mother explained.

"The villagers are starting to use that word," the weaver said. "It's *swadesi*. My neighbours are weaving day and night, just like when I was a kid. And they're starting to plant cotton in their yards. Even the sandalman—he makes sandals out of old tyres—is getting more trade. Every week people come from the co-operatives to buy this many or that many dozen. He's got a lot of people working for him. He used to have just himself. And now he's got fifteen men."

Mother listened delightedly. I still cannot understand why she was so pleased. When the weaver left she said to herself, as she looked at me, "*Swadesi* is bringing industry to the villages. If this can keep going for twenty or thirty years, the little man—" she pointed to the south where a bamboo craftsman lived, "will be well off, not miserable like he is now. He has so many children. Eight. And each basket is only worth a farthing. And it takes a person over half a day to make one."

I heard much about *swadesi* but still do not know how important it was. I was never very interested.

Mother's stomach began to expand. She seldom worked. The weaving equipment she bought stayed in the shed. She had been shown how to use it, and had studied seven more days on her own. But she couldn't bear to weave for more than three hours at a time. Her stomach and wholy body ached, she said. So she usually sat in the rotunda, where she could see the scenery, and read a foreign book. Father was seldom at home. Planting for the future, she said. And when he did come, he always had three or four people with him. Then they talked about things I couldn't understand, stopping occasionally to laugh or to whisper in great earnestness. They spiced their talk with the now common words: *swadesi*, co-operatives, the people's bank, education, mass literacy and indigenous enterprise.

I was pleased to know as much as I did. I never felt guilty listening in the corner. Children in our district were not supposed to do that, but father never forbade me. Once a guest even singled me out and said, half to me, half to father: "He must carry on the work we have begun." I listened harder, hoping for more of such sweet praise.

Father said nothing. He smiled and his thick moustache was stretched a little.

His guests wore *lurik* and sandals made out of old tyres, or were barefooted. Their faces shone with the passion and spirit the *lurik* reflected.

Gradually more and more guests came to our house. Neighbours who were illiterate came to talk with father. And others whom I did not recognize at all, village owls from far away, came to meet him. Then other old men—who were far from illiterate—came and asked to be allowed to follow courses in politics, economics and general studies. And many students who had only finished primary school and then worked for the government or themselves came to undertake teaching or trade courses. My older "brothers" organised it all. Father administered, with a look of victory on his face.

Several weeks later we gained some new furniture: two duplicators, a large box of paper and five typewriters. Our house was suddenly an office. The machines typed all the time and the duplicator spun off lessons for the students.

In the admission register I read: Three hundred new students for the literacy course. Forty to be teachers. Three to learn a trade. Fifty for general studies. Fifteen in the kindergarten and twenty for the English course. Eleven for the Dutch course, all government schoolteachers.

"We're starting," father said to Hurip.

From then on father was the centre of attention in our small town. He was always busy, often away for long periods. The pile of books he had to mark continually increased. Sometimes my older brothers helped him. Mother enjoyed the new situation. Many women came to the house and asked about this and that. And she always accepted the patronage of newly-formed women's groups. She went to the meetings even though her stomach hurt.

Whenever father was home the police came by frequently, looking in from astride their bikes. But they did no more than look. I didn't understand why they did that. When I asked mother why, she explained:

"They like to make sure your father's up to no mischief."

"He's only teaching people how to work, isn't he?"

"They don't want too many of us to understand and be able to read and write as well."

She refused to explain more, even though I kept on asking. I had to be content to wait for a few years until I could understand for myself.

Great changes took place in the family. Industry filled the time which had once been empty and relaxed. When I walked in the streets, people would sometimes say to each other "That's his son." They even asked me to stop and talk about my father and sometimes gave me money. I liked that. I grew to feel that father was an important man in town.

Father came home after teaching and ate with mother. Once he looked sullen and pale. I was helping get the meal ready. Mother asked him "Don't you feel well? You're working too hard."

Father said he didn't feel well.

"You'd better take a week off."

"It's not the work. It's this—we have to be the boss here before we can do what we want. Certainly before we can do anything that will benefit society."

"Explain yourself," she said.

"I've got a letter."

"Go on."

"From the government."

"What about?"

"It's a threat. Or more politely, a reminder. I have to stop everything I'm doing."

Mother looked at him sharply. I left.

I always liked to spread anything I knew. So I told Hurip. He wasn't surprised. His face suddenly tired, like father's. He didn't accept the news as I had expected him to. Disappointedly I sat in the doorway of the kitchen waiting until mother and father had finished eating. And I thought of father's pale, sullen face.

"Aren't you eating with your father?" the servant asked.

I shook my head.

"Why not?"

"Father can't work." I complained and informed at the same time.

"Who's stopped him? No-one would dare. Even the mayor's afraid of him."

I considered that, repeated it to myself to tell others. But his pale, sullen face quickly wiped that thought away. I went quickly to a fifteen-year-old who was in fifth grade. I told him what I had heard from father and mother. He interrupted me: "The inspector and five of his men came when father was teaching us civics."

"Why didn't I see them?"

"Your class had gone home."

I understood now. He continued, "All the books he had printed in Semarang—for the first and second literacy courses—have been confiscated. Over seven thousand of them. It's a shame. He worked hard on them. And the printing was expensive. We had no classes for over three hours. All the teachers were rounded up. We had to wait in our rooms. We watched the police taking the books away. They cut the school's powerlines too. No-one can study at night now."

The rest of the story was irrelevant. Only father's cold, sullen face and the disaster it portended mattered.

When I returned to the dining table they had finished. Mother was asking "And how about the people's bank you put fifty thousand Rupiah into?" He shook his head. The expression contained a greater threat: "Any loss will be ours."

Slowly and deliberately he said "Our only responsibility was that we should make the effort. And we did. If the outcome is other than we hoped, that is none of our business."

Mother agreed, repressing a moan. Then, trying to hide the disappointment she felt, she said "I believe that what you have done will endure. I have prayed for the safe progress and rapid completion of your work. But if evil comes—it is indeed none of our business."

6

From that time on, few people came to our house. Even the school children who usually came to play stayed away. Our house became an island. Mother was more solitary than usual. Hurip regularly sat with a book in his hand, thinking, but never reading. When he realized what he was doing, his eyes returned to the rows of print but focused on nothing. He would sigh and get up and go out of the house. When I went to bed he would still be out.

The number of pupils in the school gradually fell away. A friend whose father was a civil servant told me, "Civil servants with children in non-state schools have no hope of promotion."

In the primary school I attended the numbers dropped from nearly four hundred to eighty-four. The school buildings no longer shone as brightly and nobly as before. They were dark and gloomy.

And once I overheard mother complain to herself as she lay on her bed "How could they relieve them of their duties and position just for being members of a club?" I saw her cry. The tears turned me dumb and I ran away.

One night I woke to hear a hard, cruel voice coming from the room next to mine, Hurip's room: "They're strangling us. I can't bear living in a small town with so many problems."

It was Hurip's voice. The tone was one of extreme anger. I didn't know why he was angry. But the next day he saw father and asked his permission to leave.

He never wrote to us to tell us how he was, where he was staying, whether he was working or studying.

Mother advised me to read as much as Hurip used to: he even took a book to the toilet. After he left his name was often recalled with genuine affection. But he never sent us any news of himself.

As before when he was busy, father was away more and more. Sometimes no-one saw him for three days and nights at a time. He wasn't at school. At home he never read or marked the students' books; he never walked in the garden and he never took us walking in the early morning. He seldom smiled—or even talked, except when it was strictly necessary. It was a swift and extraordinary change. I realised in my own way that something had happened over which neither father nor mother had any control.

When the schoolyard was overgrown with weeds, the gloom and the sullen chill began to lift from his face. He began to teach regularly, although still he often did not come home at night. And one night when he was absent, mother said to me "We made life too easy for the foreigners. They've given us back nothing but trouble and deceit, force and threats, lies and oppression." Her voice was harsh, threatening.

I tried to understand her in my childish way. But couldn't. I didn't understand. It was hopeless. And I didn't dare ask any questions. The memory of the bite in her voice terrified me. I was silent. And it made no difference to her.

"I hope," she continued, this time without the threat, the harshness or the despair; her voice was soft and coaxing, "that you'll study properly, my son. Hurip was clever but the situation was too much for him. He had to run away to forget his disappointment. Your father's clever but he can't do anything. So you have to be cleverer than them both. If you are cleverer—far cleverer than they—you won't fail."

I did not fully understand her. The softness of her voice stirred me but I did not know what I should say. Mother embraced me and kissed my neck. I felt the warmth of her tears. I still did not understand. When she had calmed a little, I asked "Daddy can't work any more but he still keeps going out. Why?"

"He can't forget his students' studies, my dear."

"But there's no electricity and he doesn't come home at night. How can he work then?"

"Your father's a very disappointed man. You cannot possibly understand how disappointed he is. You're still a child and can't feel the disappointment grown-ups can feel. Your father is sad and needs amusement."

The answer stopped any desire in me to ask further. Not just because I didn't understand, but also because the rhythm of her voice terrified me.

When I was a child I often used to wander all over the district. The first place I visited was the market after selling was over, and before the sweepers began their work. I gathered the labels from balls of thread and put them in a box. Many of my friends had hundreds, some even had thousands. Whoever had the most felt the richest—like adults with their coins. The one with the most had pride of place in any conversation. People were reluctant to contradict him because they secretly hoped for some of his labels.

I often saw father gambling at other people's places, sometimes at a Chinese man's place. And I would pass by pretending not to notice. So I found out what mother meant by amusement. But I could never bring my understanding into line with my discovery.

Too I often heard people mocking father for shifting his interests to gambling, away from the various areas of nationalist endeavour. I never said anything. But because of the strong influence of mother's ethical teachings I knew, childishly, how offensive they thought gambling was. I never told her until one day she asked "Have you seen your father anywhere?"

It was late afternoon. I knew father had not come home.

"I saw him . . ."

"Find him. Tell him I asked him to come home."

I found him over his cards. When he saw me coming his expression muddied. But, despite that, I told him mother wanted him to come home. He said "I'll come in a little while."

Shortly after I arrived home he came. Mother did not say much. Nor did he. At night he read a Dutch book. I don't know what it was about. And as I went to sleep I heard mother say to him "You've comforted your grief long enough now."

I didn't hear his answer. Two days and nights passed peacefully. Father went nowhere. He came home from school each day. But he was restless. And then, quite suddenly, he went out. Mother saw him go and said nothing. And when he came home from school and again went out, she let him go. Until one day: "He's been gone four days," mother said from her bed.

I saw an expression of despair pass across her face. And I answered "yes."

"Find a pen and some paper," she ordered.

She wrote, finding it difficult to use the words she wanted. Wrote briefly. Then handed the short letter to me silently and returned to her bed.

"For father?" I asked nervously.

For a long time she said nothing. I watched her anxiously. Finally she nodded. I went. I searched for hours but couldn't find him. The places he usually played in were empty. And each time I went to one of the houses where he played, I was smartly told "Your father's not here."

"Do you know where he is, please?"

"Perhaps at So-and-so's house."

I went to So-and-so's house. He wasn't there either. I walked around the town for four or five hours. Without success. And, remembering how mother had looked, I didn't dare return home. Despondently I sat under a tamarind tree at the edge of the street. I thought of sad things. Very sad things! I don't know why. The confiscation of his books, the failure of the bank, the dwindling number of students, the duplicator sitting useless, the typewriters silent, the schoolyard overgrown with weeds. And the co-operative store at the edge of the city, which I had often visited with him, now closed down. I thought of these. Then the trial plantation in front of our house, which had to be sold to meet the bank's debts and now belonged to the government.

I thought of that. Suddenly I thought of how he looked and the moustache and beard he shaved so seldom recently. They made him look much older. An uncomprehending but deep feeling of despair swept over me. I rested against the tree, and took out the letter. I was afraid to read it, but my curiosity to know anything and everything overcame my fear. So I read it:

> Have you no thought for the child in my womb? Honour him by devoting yourself to Almighty God, so that the child may grow to be wise and virtuous.
> Come home.

If you don't want to come home when you get this letter, pray that I die and take your unborn child with me to the grave.

The letter had no date and no signature. The force of the words was sufficient to drive me to tears. I put the letter back in my trouser pocket, quickly. My dreams returned, more beautiful than ever. The faces suddenly grew dark. Hope vanished, from the land, sea and sky, from other people, from myself.

The letter forced me to get up again and find father. Eventually I found him on the back verandah of a Chinese house. As usual when he was asked to come he looked annoyed. But he took the letter, and read it. Then he said "I'll be home soon," a formula which always made me feel better.

Actually he was always home soon after me. He did not go at once to mother but talked with the children instead. He spoke louder than usual, it seemed to me, so that she would hear him. I don't know what happened between them but he stayed home after that. He helped us with our homework. A week passed.

Three men came. They chatted for ten to fifteen minutes. I prepared light refreshments for them. And as I carried them in, father and mother were talking in her room. I heard her slowly say, "This is the house where all my children except the first were born. I don't care—I don't want it turned into a gambling den. You must think of your children."

I still remember: it was two o'clock. And afterwards he and his guests went to another of our houses, four hundred metres to the north of our residence. It was the first time she had never received his guests. What really surprised me was the way that as soon as father and his guests had left, she got quickly out of bed and ordered the oldest adopted child to buy six loaves of bread.

She went skittishly to the kitchen and made a bread-pudding. She forbade the servant to help. She put in a lot of cinnamon so that it would be sweet. Towards twilight, about six o'clock, four of my brothers and I took it to the men. Father was at first surprised to see so much food but then shouted with pleasure: "Well! Pudding, how nice."

And the guests all laughed, although the white cards were more important than food. They shifted their eyes from their cards to the food and then to the host and shouted with more attention to politeness than was necessary: "How nice."

We went home, not saying a word the whole way.

7

Once, unexpectedly, the weaver came to see mother. I met her too.

"No-one's buying *lurik* anymore," she said. "Everyone wanted it before. Now no-one does. In fact the only ones who want it are the people in villages and they don't have any money. Wouldn't you like to buy some?"

Mother had gently to say 'no': she still had a lot in her cupboards. The woman sighed. She continued: "My neighbour's sandal factory has folded up completely. He's left town to go and be a coolie in the city. And labourers aren't very well off—they're worse than my family."

"I'm afraid *swadesi* is over," mother explained sadly and hollowly. As she spoke her eyes glazed. She used to like talking to villagers. Now she didn't.

The weaver tiredly returned across the river to her village.

No-one spoke very much of *swadesi* anymore. Times had changed. The villagers were sorry that they had put their money into co-operatives and lost the lot. The *swadesi* fever had retreated and vanished. The town returned to its usual quiet ways. Civil servants no longer played out great dramas of nationalism in their heads. They forced themselves back into their routine: going to work, staying in the office for a set period, going home, playing with their wives, sleeping, getting up in the morning again—for a while.

Gambling took over from *swadesi*. Gambling! Gambling! Even small children with two or five cent pieces a day gambled. Cock fighting gained new life and spread rapidly. It was announced in the villages that the government had fifty vacancies for policemen and young men fought for the positions. Other news told of large numbers of men being arrested for gambling, cock fighting, robbery and murder.

Both the duplicators and all the typewriters were put in boxes. Mother explained: "They have to go back to the shop because father can't keep up the payments."

And a few days later men came and took away our furniture. I asked mother where they were taking it but she only shook her head. I fell silent, but later learnt that they had been taken by a man to whom father was in debt. At night she called us and ordered one of us to go and find him. I had to do the cooking with the servant. Two hours later the search for father was declared unsuccessful.

That night the fourth child was safely born: a boy! It screamed lustily.

The next morning, as the sun bathed the earth in its glow, I went to mother's room to see my new brother and to kiss him—the child who was my blood-brother forever. Mother greeted me with a smile. My brother slept on. All signs of suffering were gone from mother's face. At that moment father came, and walked straight into her room. He shouted happily: "It's a boy! He'll be bigger than either of us."

And mother greeted him hollowly, tiredly, forcing herself to speak, full of pride: "He'll get nothing from you. Or from here. Or from this particular cycle of time. He'll do it all by himself."

I left.

8

And with the birth of my brother, *swadesi* breathed its last and left, never to be spoken of again by those it had destroyed. So did the co-operatives and the literacy campaign. And cock fighting and thieving, robbery and murder retreated to the outskirts of the region, to return to the centre occasionally. Ten new policemen were taken on.

Finally everything returned to the way it had been before. Blora was quiet and peaceful. And then the age of the rising sun, slowly advancing, sometimes startling, began to penetrate the darkness of the night.

And life went on as usual.

SHIRLEY GEOK-LIN LIM (b. 1944)
Malaysia/United States

Shirley Geok-lin Lim is a poet, short-story writer, and professor at the University of Santa Barbara, California. Her *Crossing the Peninsula & Other Poems* (1980), the anthology from which the following poems are taken, won the Commonwealth Poetry Prize. Her statement about poetry here is at once lucid and ambivalent.

from *Crossing the Peninsula & Other Poems*

Imagine

Imagine—
a sheet of glass
reflecting nothing
but itself.

No image—   5
all surface
a pure depth.

Still—
words are significations
of things other than.   10

All poetry
necessarily
begins with a lie.

Divorce

While you sat certainly
On your bed, on your sofa,
By your work table, I
Fetched you food, etcetera,

Standing Uma (?), National Museum, Bangkok.

To wait upon your, oh who knows?   5
Love. Each day strung on errands;
Each night, on hands and knees, so
Insistent on duty.

Some of your gifts I keep:
A dress for a birthday,   10
A cloth cat I sleep
With, a pretty purse.
Your battered ring I wear
And again put away.

What stays soonest to hand   15
Is the stuff of two years
Together and the bright
Edges of rare meetings.
My quarrel has little
To do with you. No, not even   20

When I drank a bottle
Of your best whiskey and cried
For mama. (I still cry
But know it is for me.)

Did you not see   25
A frightened child out
Looking for home and father?
You played so well at
The unloving figure,
And I nothing if not   30
A crying child. Separate,
At last, I know
Father will not come,
And if he will, I shall not
Let him in into my home.   35

Silence

Lightly you brush your hand against my hair,
In this gesture, too, careful.
And I, when I hold you, your bare
Chest beating like a clock against my ear,
It is to release you only.   5
Always we take pains to leave each other
Our acre of breathing space. Now that we lie,
For the moment content to lace fingers,
Cheek against cheek, in deep breathing
Together, I forget and speak out; then,   10
Chairs, tables, the wide ceiling
And long glass of the room which keeps
Night out, discomfort suddenly a woman
Caught naked before a strange man.
I come to where I prefer to guess at   15
Silence, that bare and careful quiet.

USSIRI DHAMMACHOTI (b. 1947)
Thailand

Ussiri Dhammachoti, one of Thailand's most famous writers and the editor-in-chief
of *Siam Rath,* the nation's most influential newspaper, has written many stories set

in his seaside hometown. When he was a boy, his father and the fathers of most of his friends were fishermen. In the space of a few years, during the 1960s, the booming commercial fishing industry drove them out of business; by 1981, when "The Dancing Girl" was written, it seemed to Ussiri that the men who had bought the large, expensive new boats, and then hired fisherman to work on them for wages, had come to "own" the very sea itself. This story evokes sweet, painful memories of the years when Ussiri and his friends were young and in love with the prettiest girl in town, and never dreamed that, as men, they would not earn their living from the sea, as their fathers and grandfathers had done before them.

from As If the Sea Could Be Owned

The Dancing Girl

She left her home by the sea when she was very young. She also left an ocean of sadness in the hearts of a multitude of young fishermen, when they learned that she had become the star of a famous *ramwong* dancing troupe.[1] The most beautiful girl in our town had been transformed into a dancing girl, adored by a mob of admirers who hung around the dance floor and begged her to wear the garlands of flowers they vied to bestow on her. We hated it.

The depth of our bitterness and disappointment was reflected in the viciousness with which we soothed our wounded feelings.

"Once, she even asked me for my picture!" said one of the boys. "By now, she's probably thrown it in the toilet." He was particularly wounded, since he had given her not only his picture but a sea-horse he had made into a key-ring.

"Is there any difference between being a *ramwong* dancer and being a whore?" another suggested boldly. We were stunned. "Well, you tell me! Dancing around with men, for money, and—you know how those girls act."

We didn't.

"I don't think a girl like that can know anything about love," I added. "We should just forget her." I was the philosophical one.

"Forget her?" rejoined the one who had opined that *ramwong* dancing was basic whoredom. "Forgetting is too good for her."

Our crowd—that is, my friends from grammar school days, who worked with their fathers on the boats, and I, mysteriously still a student—engaged in long, intimate conversations on the nature of love and friendship, during which we inevitably turned to the subject of our dancing girl and her perfidy. She had been at school with us, she was our age, she had been *one of us*.

Translated by Susan Fulop Kepner.

---

1. The *ramwong* is a stylized folk dance with gestures that evoke classical Thai dancing. In the post–World War II era, troupes of dancers and musicians developed a corrupt form of *ramwong* dancing that they took to temple fairs and other festive occasions in rural areas. Men paid to dance with the *ramwong* girls. During the 1970s and 1980s, these *ramwong* troupes lost popularity, and today they have almost disappeared.

Before she had become a dancing girl, she had been nothing more than a girl who cleaned fish at the docks.

No, that is unfair. She had been the prettiest girl in our town since she was a child. And when she was grown, even the smell of fish and wet, salty air could not detract from her wonderful good looks.

Every morning when the boats reached shore, and the boys had done their chores, they would casually amble down the dock to the brine house, where she worked. They flattered her and showed off, each trying to get the largest share of her attention.

She scraped and washed and gutted fish, then steamed them and sold them in the high-roofed brine house.

I had but one desire: to be near the one who was loveliest of all, loveliest in every part. Even her teeth were lovely, as white and as regular as the whitecaps in the bay on a breezy day. Such was the extent of my madness.

But pursuing her was more difficult for me than for the others. I didn't go fishing with my father, and I had no honest excuse for hanging around the brine house. I solved this problem by developing a passionate, obscure love for the sea. Early each morning, I would wander down to the shore to stare thoughtfully at the waves, and gaze raptly at the horizon, where the sun was about to emerge for yet another day. Having stared and gazed for five or ten minutes, I would casually saunter into the brine house.

If she was leaving to go somewhere, I might discover where she was going. I would follow that graceful, gliding, maddening walk at a careful distance, then run ahead and happen to run into her at her destination.

Perhaps I was a little madder than the rest.

It was a bitter thing to realize that a man had come from a *ramwong* troupe, had talked her into an audition, and had led her away to her new life—and not one of us had known a thing about it until the day we went to the brine house and learned, from others who in no way felt about her as we did, the reason for her absence. She had not confided in a single one of us, or asked our opinion, or even mentioned the matter. It was then that we understood we were nothing to her.

When we thought of a dancer in a *ramwong* troupe, the picture in our minds was of a girl in a skirt so short that when she twirled around, you could see not only her bottom but her actual . . . cheeks. Ordinarily, a girl dancing the *ramwong* had the grace of a sandpiper, smartly dipping and bobbing. But this was not the ordinary *ramwong,* as it would be danced in our town on holidays; this was the *ramwong* of the girls in the professional troupes. It was their job to entice and stir up the men, who would then pay well to dance with them.

We thought of the girl we had known, the girl whose only scent had been the pure, honest smell of fish. How could she do it? How could our own angel of the brine house gyrate in public in front of a crowd of sleazy men whom we knew perfectly well would all be trying to get at her? How could she sway provocatively between colored paper rainbows and flashing lights, on a stage, showing parts of the body that shouldn't be seen in public, with red makeup on her face, her lips, her fingernails?

Eventually, we stopped talking about her, and even thinking about her. Life went on, we grew up. Several years passed. And then, one day, our dancing girl came home.

It was a day when flocks of birds floated on the bay, their pale, sand-colored wings reflecting the soft afternoon sun. She had come home with the fresh, salty winds we called "kite winds," the winds of the southwest monsoon.

There she was, sitting composedly on the bench of a trishaw.[1] When its brakes squealed to a stop, people turned to look.

"I can't believe it!" one of my friends whispered. "Look—she's got a kid!"

We watched her casually, from a distance, as she smiled at the trishaw man and climbed down carefully with a baby on one arm.

The friend who stood beside me that afternoon had a baby son of his own. Almost all of my old crowd had married young, and now had wives and children. Everyone was married except for me, whose mysterious, never-ending education did not allow it.

I was the only one who greeted her, and even dared to start up a conversation.

She had changed greatly, but if she had been living the kind of wild life we had imagined, it didn't show. In fact, she was cleaner, softer, paler, and even better looking than in the old days. Her clothes were fashionable and up-to-date. Definitely, she looked like a stranger; there was nothing about her to suggest our town.

She had married a guitar player. He had got shot in a fight over her. She had picked up her baby and come home, and left the occupation of *ramwong* dancer forever. Her plan, she told me, was to work with her father on his fishing boat.

When I told my friends, they laughed themselves sick.

"With red nail polish," one scoffed.

Several of them suggested that perhaps her plan was to lure the fish into the nets by standing up in the boat and dancing. Others were sure that she had come home for another reason.

"It's obvious. She needs a new husband to support the kid she got from the guitar player."

That seemed reasonable, but most of us thought that she wouldn't last long enough to make that happen.

"In a couple of weeks, she'll be back in the *ramwong*. Work out in a boat? Come on. It's heavy work out there. Can't you see her pulling nets in the rain?"

We all agreed on one thing: somehow, the dancing girl had run out of alternatives, and had had no choice but to come home to the old folks.

Her father's boat was small. He brought his catch home to his wife, who hawked the fish through the streets of town. Everyone had felt sorry for both of them when their daughter went off to her *ramwong* dancing career, caring nothing about their fate.

---

1. Human-powered taxi on three wheels.

Years had passed since she left us. Like the sand and the waves, like the current and the voice of the wind, we and our town might look unchanging, but in fact nothing was quite the same as when she left. Surely, our injured feelings had healed long ago; our love had died.

In their stead were suspicion and mistrust. We knew her, and yet we didn't know her at all, so we felt justified in our mistrust, and suspicion, and contempt.

I could scarcely remember how I once felt about her. I doubted, now, whether the girl had ever had the slightest notion of our madness. What right had any of us to hold a grudge? For that was what our suspicion and mistrust were grounded in. An old grudge. We had loved her, and she hadn't spared a thought for us.

I decided that I, at least, was above old grudges; and yet, when I told the others about her intention of going out with her father in the little fishing boat, and they all laughed, I must admit that I laughed with them. The first day the dancing girl went to sea, the sound of laughter reached far, far out over the Gulf of Thailand.

* * *

My editor frowned.

"Look, this is a perfect story for you. Why can't you fly down there for a couple of days? Here's this woman, all by herself, going out to sea every day, bringing in her catch just like a man. It's incredible! I heard about her while I was down there on vacation. I can't believe you didn't think of this yourself."

I said nothing.

"Come on, you must know her—she's from your town, she's your age. The fishermen down there call her "*Meh Ya Nang,*" which means the guardian spirit of the fleet. It's like a novel. Here she is, a widow with a kid, living with her old mother. She was gorgeous when she was young. She was a *ramwong* dancer in one of those travelling troupes, the star, so what does she do? Her old man gets shot, she quits, goes home to a fishing village, and goes out to sea with her father.

"Look, I *want* this story. You go down there, talk to her, get the details. Ask her everything. How does she feel when she's out there in the middle of the night. Is she cold? Is she lonely? Has she ever been really scared? People will want to know what inspired her to take up her father's work, that kind of thing. How much money she makes. What she does for fun. Does she go the movies? Go to watch the *likay*?[2] What does she think about small-boat fishing as an occupation? And women's rights—whatever you do, don't forget to ask what she thinks about women's rights. Why didn't she remarry? Get her thoughts about sex. And get the name of that boat."

* * *

When her father died, everyone thought that would be the end of the fishing. No woman went out alone, in a small boat, fighting the sea and the wind. And there never had been a new husband. Alone, she cared for her little girl, and her

---

2. Folk drama based on old tales and performed outdoors by itinerant troupes.

old mother. When people asked whether it was not a hard life, she said that she could endure.

And she did endure. She was tough, and as brave as any man. She was the only woman on the whole of the Gulf who went out alone, every night, into the wind, the darkness, the loneliness, and the uncertainty of the sea.

* * *

"The Dancing Girl" was painted in crooked red letters on the bowsprit of the shabby boat.

The fishing boats left town at night. Each evening, when the wind came off the shore, she would start her engine and aim the small boat out into the darkness, standing erect with one hand on the helm, her loose fisherman's clothes snapping in the wind, her hair streaming out behind her.

I did not expect to see any trace of the girl in the brine house, or of the *ramwong* star, and I did not find any. Her skin was dark and coarse. The palms of her hands were hard, and covered with scars. From head to foot, she was dirty, and she didn't smell too good. Her manner was straightforward. She looked strong. There wasn't much about her that was—well, how else can I say it? That was like a woman.

Too embarrassed to tell her what I was doing there, I said that I had come to visit the old crowd. I asked her how things were going.

"Oh, fine," she said, looking straight at me, with what seemed to me a measuring look. "What do you do now?"

"I write. I write things and, uh, I sell them." I figured there was no way I could work it into the conversation gracefully, so I just blurted out, "Would you mind if I took your picture?"

"My picture?" She laughed, and in that moment she seemed shy. "Oo-y! Waste your film for nothing." She looked away shyly, and wiped her hands on her pants, and said, "I still have that picture you gave me."

Yes, it was I who had sent her the picture, and the sea-horse key ring. In the end, she let me take her picture.

My old friends had become the fishermen who called her "Meh Ya Nang." They told me that they were ashamed to remember their unkindness to her, when she first came home. They spoke of her as if she were some miraculous treasure they had discovered offshore. She was theirs. She belonged to them, and to the town.

It was not an easy visit for me. For several years, I had lived far from them, and far from their life. I was a stranger, a foreigner, and worse. The palms of my hands were soft and pale. A little salt water made them peel. Watching the waves offshore made me feel dizzy. The wind stung my eyes. A few hours in the sun gave me a headache, and I worried about malaria.

I was too soft for this place. My old friends endured heat, cold, rain, huge waves and fierce winds to earn a living. And so did this woman, at whom we all *had laughed* when she climbed into a boat with her father on that morning so long ago.

Like the sand and waves, like the current and the voice of the wind, the old town looked pretty much the same, but in fact everything had changed. My friends had changed, I had changed. She, like everything and everyone else, had changed. She was a different dancing girl. But I saw in her another kind of beauty, the quality and permanence of which was so much greater than the beauty I had remembered.

She was like a star far above the dark bay, or a tern floating on the wind; or the color of the sky, or a cloud, all of which, taken together, made the little town by the sea, which is very beautiful, more beautiful still.

Ch'ing Dynasty, eighteenth century. *A Scene from the Romance of the Western Chamber*. Hanging scroll; ink and color on silk. Freer Gallery of Art.

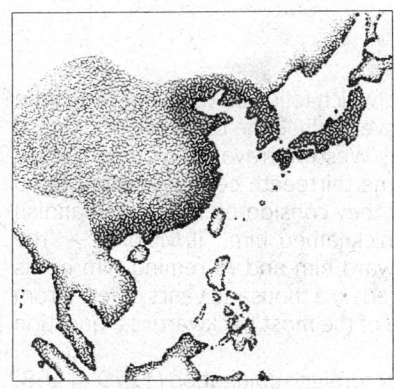

SECTION XI
Modern East Asia

China
Japan
Korea

CHINA

The culture of China strikes Westerners as so old, so venerable, so ancient that the term "modern China" seems almost a contradiction in terms. Western tourists traveling in China, especially in rural areas, experience a sense of time warp—as if they were visiting certain parts of the United States in the 1930s. While most of Western culture is striving to define the *post*-modern, China today remains in a *pre*-modern stage, struggling to become modern. Yet it is in the very tensions of this term, how "modern China"—i.e., the China of today—came to be so very *un*modern, that we must seek for a key to Chinese history.

The irony of it all is that a thousand years ago, China was the most technologically advanced civilization on earth. Many of the symbols of modern life, for better or for worse, were developed in China during the Sung Dynasty (906–1279). Rag paper, paper money, the navigational compass, gunpowder, movable type printing (which existed in China four to five centuries before Gutenberg)—all these were invented or developed in China between the tenth and the thirteenth centuries. These are some of the inventions that, in the words of one Western historian, "were to make possible the advent of modern times in the West."* The legacy of that

*Jacques Gernet, *A History of Chinese Civilization*, trans. J. R. Foster (Cambridge, Eng.: Cambridge University Press, 1985) p. 348.

development was evident in the Yuan Dynasty, which followed the Sung, when the Mongols, under Kublai Khan, took dominion over China. The brilliance of Chinese civilization was what dazzled the most famous Western traveler to China: Marco Polo. Indeed, contemporaries at the end of the thirteenth century found Marco Polo's accounts of China so unbelievable that they considered him an outlandish talespinner, a preposterous braggart: they nicknamed him "Il Milione" — "the Million" both to express their skepticism toward him and to remind him of his tendency toward hyperbole. How China changed, in a thousand years or less, from the most advanced civilization on earth to one of the most backward is a question to challenge the most astute analysts.

During the three and a half centuries under foreign subjugation (1279–1368; 1644–1911), a phenomenon arose that was, until then, unknown to the Chinese. During the Yuan and Ch'ing dynasties, the Chinese elite were, with only a few exceptions, displaced from positions of influence and power. In traditional times the goal of most literati was to serve the country as an official: all scholars strived to pass the multitude of examinations, from county and provincial competitions to imperial tests, that led to the pinnacle: the *chin-shih* (the "advanced scholar degree").* Those who survived this competition were guaranteed appointments as officials in the government. For centuries, this "ladder of success" dictated career paths. As governments changed during certain periods of history, there was the possibility — indeed, the likelihood — that climbing this ladder would not always guarantee a position of power and influence.

This general demotion of power for the literati had the net effect of "vernacularizing" Chinese literature. Its perspective shifted from the refined, reclusive, hermetic stance of the scholar-poet to the earthier, more urbane and sociable viewpoint of the cosmopolite. Philosophical speculations and an obsession with history as a political parable were now increasingly replaced with bemused observations on the comings and goings on of the world. As literature became more demotic, more *of* and *from* if not *by* the people, the emphasis shifted from the single-voiced lyric of the T'ang *shih* or the more feminized, if not feminine Sung *tz'u*, to what Mikhail Bakhtin, the modern Russian literary theorist, would have called the "polyphonic" voices of the vernacular tale.[†]

This tendency toward the vernacular coincided with three factors: increased commercialization, the rise of the merchant or entrepreneurial class, and the growth and development of urban centers. Each of these factors would decisively influence Chinese literature. Increased commercialization enhanced the spread of literature through the sale of printed books, not only as a culture but as a commodity. The motive for disseminating certain kinds of literature could now be material as well as moral profit. The rise of the merchant and entrepreneurial class meant that a greater proportion of the population could aspire to increased social

---

*There were, of course, differences in the examination system from dynasty to dynasty, in terms of content, frequency, and procedures.

[†]It would be foolish to suggest that before the Tang Dynasty, Chinese authors spoke only "classical Chinese," and that afterward they spoke only "vernacular" Chinese. This is, however, the impression that students inevitably get when they look at the curriculum in any university Chinese program— where "traditional" is equated with the "classical" and the contemporary with the "vernacular." Despite the position of pedagogues, the vernacular has always been current and contemporary: what is regarded as classical today, including the *Shih-ching* in China, Dante in Italy, Shakespeare in England, were—in their day—*vernacular*. No one, not even the Greeks or the Romans, spoke a classical language, although there are many ancient texts written in languages that have subsequently come to be regarded as "classic."

status through education. No longer were only the elite and cultured families interested in education: those with the wherewithal could afford to hire scholars as tutors to minister to the educational needs of their children. There was always an ample supply of failed scholars to occupy these positions, but even successful scholars became available during the Yuan and the Ch'ing dynasties, who were displaced by the Mongol Khans and the Manchu aristocrats in the seats of government. The irony is that during the very times when the literati were denied a place of eminence, the *parvenu* classes in Chinese society sought to enhance their social position by employing them as private tutors. Furthermore, the rise of urban centers provided not only an arena for the dissemination of literature as well as an audience and a market for new texts, but also new subject matter. Fiction, always an integral part of traditional literature, now reached a wider audience in print. What had been a coterie phenomenon now became, gradually, a matter of more than scholarly interest.

The effect of all this on literature was telling: more and more, the literati were fascinated with popular culture, the stories that were "performed" in the marketplace (in areas called the *chiao-fang*); the carnivalesque productions that became known as *tsa-chü*, which might be best translated as "variety show," comprising singing, acting, and miming, as well as acrobatics, tumbling, fencing, and vaudeville. There was always some guilt among the literati about indulging in such frivolous diversions, even if many believed, as did Su Tung-p'o (1037–1101), that the colloquial tales recounting historical events taught the young about good and evil. With some rare exceptions, the writing of fiction to divert and entertain was an occupation that the literati would engage in surreptitiously.

With the advent of print, the rise of commercialism, and the swelling numbers of literati who failed to receive official appointment, an audience emerged for narratives that previously could only be heard in person. There was, of course, fiction written before the Sung Dynasty, but this was of two kinds: one was written by scholars and was usually autobiographical or historical; the T'ang *ch'uan-ch'i* exemplified this type. The other type, which survives only in the form of storytellers' notes and prompts, was the oral story that was "composed" extemporaneously by illiterate or semiliterate narrators. In the first group stories were written by the elite for the elite; in the second were oral tales transmitted by word of mouth from generation to generation through the population at large. The "illiterati" were familiar only with the second. The literati, on the other hand, were familiar with both, but they did not consider the oral stories that were the delight of their childhood worthy of the status of "literature."*

What is significant about the developments after the Sung Dynasty is that, with the creation of "reading audiences" — that is, those who could "hear" a story by reading it, the interaction between the elite and the vernacular elements in Chinese culture became more routine. The transition from purely oral stories to readable versions may be traced to the semi-oral genres that have been preserved on paper: from the T'ang *pien-wen* (oral scripts) to the Sung *hua-pen* (story

---

*The distinctions between a literati culture and a vernacular culture may be compared to the predominance in the west of Latin as the scholarly language for over a millennium, and the development of vernacular literatures in the late medieval period. The difference is that while the vernaculars in the West became distinct national languages, each with a separate and unique culture, in China the vernaculars became dialects of the same national culture and national language. Indeed, some Chinese dialects are more different phonetically from each other than, say, Italian is from Spanish.

texts or "prompt-books") to the Ming *p'ing-hua* ("plain language" stories) and *yenyi* (fictionalizations of history).

If in the last thousand years Chinese literature lost something in refinement and elegance, it gained in earthiness, immediacy, and variety. There remains a greater interest in stories for their own sake: in *kung-an* (magistrates' tales, equivalent to our "police stories"), that pique our curiosity and engage the mind; in tales of the supernatural that exercise our fancies and make our hearts shudder; and in timeless characterizations that fire the imagination and captivate the soul. The discourse becomes less elevated and more bawdy; the voices come from different sectors of society; and the cast of characters is more inclusive.

There is a marked conceptual difference between the forms of "literati" literature and the genres of the vernacular. In the vernacular, the language is less elliptical and less deliberately allusive.* The literati forms are integrated, sharply demarcated, with clear beginnings, middles, and ends. Most of the T'ang *ch'uan ch'i*, for example, start off with specific references to a historical period and geographical place, and they end with a definitive conclusion, often reinforced with a moral comment or some historical warrant of authenticity. The T'ang lyric form, the so-called "new style poetry" (*lü-shih*), is perhaps the paradigmatic "literary" form, containing careful balances and symmetries, and exact formal requirements. The vernacular forms, on the other hand, resemble the "loose baggy monsters" that Henry James saw in certain large, disheveled works of fiction. Vernacular forms wander creatively: sometimes in the actual setting of action; sometimes in the imaginary locale separating the natural and the supernatural, as in P'u Sung-ling's (1640–1715) "The Wise Neighbor"; sometimes in the ins-and-outs of a narrative device, as in "The Canary Murders" and Li Ch'ang-chi's (1376–1452) "The Hibiscus Screen"—all included here.

Historical Background

A thousand years ago, the great T'ang Dynasty came to an end, followed by a period of instability during which five dynasties succeeded each other in quick succession over a span of less than sixty years. In some ways this period was to prove a decisive time in Chinese history, a time when the proximity of barbarians to the north and west would henceforth constitute a constant source of pressure to the hegemony of the Chinese over their own territory. In earlier periods, China withstood foreign influence, either by subjugating outsiders militarily and exacting tribute from them or by more subtle methods of "conquest"—that is, by absorbing foreigners so thoroughly in Chinese culture that the threat from the outside was effectively neutralized, a process known in English by the term "Sinicization." After the T'ang Dynasty, however, the threat of "barbarian" invasion was not so effectively parried. For the thousand years after 960, periods of Chinese rule over China alternated with foreign domination. The native Sung rulers (960–1279) were followed by the Mongol rulers of the Yuan Dynasty (1279–1368), and the native Ming (1368–1644) were succeeded by the Manchu rulers of the Ch'ing Dynasty (1644–1911). The two or three generations in the twentieth century since the last emperor can best be characterized as

---

*Of course, some of the contemporary cultural references will seem—inevitably—arcane to the modern reader, but they were not intended to be *recherché* to contemporaries.

"mixed": it is true that China has not been subservient to any foreign power, yet for nearly half of that time it has closed itself off while under the sway of Communism, a distinctly Western ideology. (Mao Tse-tung, of course, followed tradition by trying to Sinicize Marxist ideology in the Maoist version.)

Of course, of all the threats to Chinese hegemony, the most cataclysmic were the humiliations suffered at the hands of the Europeans and the Japanese during the nineteenth century. These included the Opium War (1840–1842), which ended in the surrender of Hong Kong to Great Britain and the opening of key Chinese cities to the sale of opium; the sack of Peking by the French and British in 1860; the Sino-Japanese War (1894–1895); the Boxer Rebellion (1900–1901), for which China had to pay an indemnity of 450 million silver dollars.

Such humiliations convinced the Chinese that in the struggles for wealth and power in the modern world their elitist tradition was no longer viable. It also became painfully obvious that the age-old technique of cultural conquest—their strategy of Sinicization—would no longer work. During the twentieth century, China launched a cycle of reforms that, even as the century comes to a close, has not yet finished. The three-thousand-year-old tradition of imperial rule fell in 1911, and along with it the ancient examination system; a literary revolution was signaled on May 4, 1919, though critical events that radically changed the language occurred at other times as well; in the aftermath of World War II, which for China lasted from 1936 to 1945, the Communists would emerge in 1949, establishing a hegemony that would endure to the present (even when Communism would be repudiated in virtually every other part of the world). The holocaust of the Cultural Revolution of 1966 to 1976, and the brief and tragic insurgencies of the "China spring" at Tienanmen Square in 1989, would not sway China from its traditionalist ways. Through it all, resiliently or intractably—depending on one's point of view—China has remained to friend and foe alike the China of the ages.

These tensions and ambivalences can be seen, if one chooses to look for them, in the literature. They may be found variously in the plea for individualism (a Western bias) in Ping Hsin's feminism; in Lu Hsün's sardonic realism (learned from the Russian writer, Maxim Gorky); in Mao Tse-tung's "revolutionary" fervor, which he nevertheless expressed in the traditional *tz'u* form; in the fiction of Huang Ch'un-ming asking questions about the individual and society, reminiscent of the literature of social criticism, and especially of Ibsen's *An Enemy of the People*. The outbursts of Bei Dao and his cohorts, sanctified by the bloodshed at Tiananmen, are but the most recent expressions of what seems to be a schizophrenic, almost contradictory, desire: to remain, as always, Chinese and to become, after a thousand years, modern once again.

Further Readings

Birch, Cyril, ed., *Stories from a Ming Collection*. New York: Grove Press, 1958.

Chaves, Jonathan, *The Columbia Book of Later Chinese Poetry: Yuan, Ming, and Ch'ing Dynasties (1279–1911)*. New York: Columbia University Press, 1986.

Hsia, C. T., *A History of Modern Chinese Fiction*. New Haven: Yale University Press, 1971.

———. *The Classic Chinese Novel*. New York: Columbia University Press, 1968.

Hsia, C. T., Joseph Lau, and Leo Lee, *Modern Chinese Stories and Novellas, 1919–1949*. New York: Columbia University Press, 1981.

Liu, W. C., and Irving Lo, *Sunflower Splendor: Three Thousand Years of Chinese Poetry.* Bloomington, Ind.: Indiana University Press, 1990.

Ma, Y. W. and Joseph Lau, eds., *Traditional Chinese Stories: Themes and Variations.* New York: Columbia University Press, 1978.

Rolston, David, ed. *How to Read a Chinese Novel.* Princeton: Princeton University Press, 1991.

Saussy, Haun, *The Problem of a Chinese Aesthetics.* Stanford: Stanford University Press, 1993.

Yeh, Michelle, ed. *Anthology of Modern Chinese Poetry.* New Haven: Yale University Press, 1992.

Yeh, Michelle, *Modern Chinese Poetry: Theory and Practice Since 1917.* New Haven: Yale University Press, 1991.

LI CH'ANG-CH'I [LI CHANGQI]
(1376–1452)
China

Li Ch'ang-ch'i was a native of Luling in the province of Liangsi (today the town of Chi-an). After winning his *chin-shih* degree, he was made a high official in Kuanghsi (Kwangxi).

During the early Ming period, tales written in the classical style about miraculous happenings, like those in the T'ang period, returned in fashion with some literati. Leading the vogue was *The New Tales Under the Lamplight* [*Chien-teng hsin-hua*], written by Ch'ü You, a scholar from Hangchou. Emulating Ch'ü's work, Li Ch'ang-ch'i wrote a collection of stories entitled *More Tales Under the Lamplight* [*Chien-teng yü-hua*]. This resurgence of the classical tales represents another link in the tradition that eventually extends to P'u Sung-ling.

In "The Hibiscus Screen" Ts'ui Ying, a scholar-painter, is traveling by boat with his wife Madame Wang to assume the duties of his new position. They are robbed by the boat's crew, and Ts'ui Ying is thrown into the water. Believing her husband dead, Madame Wang escapes and seeks refuge in a nunnery. The reappearance of a picture scroll of a hibiscus painted by Ts'ui Ying, followed by a series of coincidences, eventually leads to the happy reunion of the couple.

from *More Tales Under the Lamplight [Chien-teng yü-hua]*

The Hibiscus Screen

In the Hsin-mao year of the reign of Chih Chêng (1351), there lived in Chên-chou a young man by the name of Ts'ui Ying, who came from a very rich family. Because of his father's services, he had enough pull to get appointed to the post of Town Governor of Yung-chia in the provinces and set out with his wife, whose maiden name was Wang, to take up this office.

The journey took him past the Chui Mountains near Su-chou, where Ts'ui moored his boat in order to pause for a little rest. He had paper money, sacrificial foods, and wine purchased, and sacrificed them to the god in the temple there. Then he held a little banquet with his wife in the boat. But the boat's crew noticed that the drinking vessels were all made of gold or silver and they were at once seized by evil desires. That very night they threw Ts'ui into the water and murdered all the servants and maids. To the lady whose maiden name was Wang the boatman said: "Shall I tell you why you don't have to die too? My younger son has no wife yet. He has gone on toward Hang-chou with my people and will be

Translated by Christopher Levenson from Wolfgang Bauer and Herbert Franke's German translation.

coming back in one or two months' time. Then you will marry him. As you now belong to our family, you need have nothing to fear."

When he had finished speaking, he gathered together all Madame Wang's possessions and addressed her as New Wife. She feigned agreement and forced herself into the role of a housewife who saw to her duties with great circumspection. The skipper was secretly very pleased that he was to have her as a wife for his son, and the more he came to know her, the less strictly he kept watch over her.

So about a month passed and the Mid-Autumn Festival approached. The boat's crew prepared themselves a rich feast with wine and caroused so much that in the end they were all drunk. The young woman waited until they had all sunk into a deep sleep and then, without further ado, she stepped ashore and ran off. After two or three miles she had completely lost her way; all around for as far as the eye could see lay a swampy plain full of reeds and rushes. As she had been brought up in a well-to-do family her tender feet could scarcely bear the exertions of running and wading any longer and she feared that her pursuers would catch up with her. But she summoned all her strength and ran on until at last after a long time the sky in the east gradually became lighter. As she looked around her she noticed buildings in the middle of a copse and hurried over there to find a sanctuary. When she arrived, she found the gate still locked and could vaguely hear the sound of bells and prayers. Shortly afterwards the gate was opened and it turned out that this was a nunnery. Madame Wang entered but when the Abbess asked her the reason for her coming, she did not dare to tell her the full truth but invented the following story:

"I come from Chên-chou. My uncle traveled as an official to Chê-chiang and took the whole family with him. He had scarcely taken up his new office when my husband died and I lived for several years as a widow. Then my uncle gave me in marriage as a second wife to the Town Governor Wei of Yung-chia. His principal wife was cruel and difficult to please, so that I suffered beatings and humiliations of all sorts. Recently her husband was replaced and we traveled down here by ship. So that they could enjoy the moonlight during the Mid-Autumn Festival, I was told to fetch wine goblets for the company. In doing so, a golden goblet accidentally fell from my hands into the river. If the mistress had her way, that would certainly have meant my death, and so I have come here to save my life."

"So you do not dare to return to your boat, and your native country is far from here. However, should you wish to find yourself a new consort we lack a competent go-between. Where will you turn in your desolation?"

The woman said nothing but burst into tears. "I, an old person," the nun continued, "could advise you, but I don't yet know what your esteemed intentions are!"

"If you, my instructress, knew of a place for me, I would willingly suffer even death for it."

"Our house is modest and lies in a riverside wilderness, where no man's way ever strays, where reeds and bamboo are our only neighbors and sea gulls and herons are our friends. But fortunately I have here one or two companions, all of them over fifty, and a few serving sisters who are likewise of a pure and assiduous disposition. It is true that you are still of tender years and have a pretty appearance, but how do you think you are going to survive the blows of fate and the ill-will of the times? Why not renounce love, release yourself from its illusion, and realize that our self represents only a deception? Take the veil and have your hair cut short, come to us and renounce the world. A light meal in the morning, some rice porridge in the evening on the meditation seat under lamps to the honor of the Buddha—thus you would find a sanctuary from the times. Is that not better than to be the favorite of another man? Do you not prefer to accept in this life sacrifices for which you will receive your reward in a coming existence?"

Madame Wang bowed gratefully and said: "This will be my decision." Her hair fell in front of the Buddha and she received the religious name of Hui-yüan, Perfect Insight. As she could not only read and write but also paint, not a year had passed before she had completely mastered the holy texts of the Buddha so that the Abbess treated her with great courtesy. In all matters, whether weighty or trivial, the Abbess would do nothing without the advice of Madame Wang, but despite this she remained of a gentle and friendly disposition, so that she was liked by all. Every day, whether it was hot or cold, she bowed down before the white-robed Bodhisattva Kuan-yin over a hundred times and confessed there what was hidden in the most secret corners of her heart. Then she would retire into her lonely cell and it was only rarely that anyone caught sight of her.

Over a year had passed when a man came on an excursion to the nunnery, remained there for a meatless meal, and then went on again. Next day he returned bringing with him a picture scroll of a hibiscus which he presented to the nunnery. The old Abbess stretched the scroll out on a plain wall screen. When Madame Wang caught sight of the picture, she realized at once that these were the brush strokes of her husband, Ts'ui Ying.

To her question as to where the picture came from, the Abbess replied: "A benefactor has just presented it to us."

Madame Wang asked what his name was, where he lived, and how he earned his living.

"They are Ku A-hsiu and his brothers from this district, who are boatmen by trade. Of course for some years people have been saying that he engages in piracy on the rivers and lakes, but I do not know if that is true."

Madame Wang then asked if he came often.

"Only rarely," was the answer, which relieved her.

Then she took a brush and wrote on the screen:

"In his youth a painter full of the joy of living,
Full of marital love,
He no longer devotes himself to me.
Now I fade away, forsaken.
True, the painted hibiscus
Still exudes freshness and charm.
But how could I think of beauty
When revenge is a matter of life and death?
When the paint has coldly faded
Nothing remains but the deceptive material.
Who takes pity on those who have been forsaken?

The simple screen is my silent companion
In meditation upon mortality.
Snapped are the bonds of our present life,
There remains only the longing to retie them in the next."

This was a song to the melody of "The Genius at the River's Brim." But none of the nuns understood the meaning.

One day it happened that a gentleman by the name of Kuo Ch'ing-ch'un came from the city to the nunnery on some business or other. When he saw the picture and the inscription he was enthusiastic about its perfect beauty, bought the screen, took it home with him, and regarded it as a choice work of art. The previous Censor, Mr. Kao Na-lien, was living in retirement in Su-chou at the time and was a great lover of calligraphy and painting. Kuo Ch'ing-ch'un made him a present of the screen, and the Censor hung it up in his residence, but he did not find the time to inquire more closely about its origins.

One day a young man came into his antechamber hoping to sell four rolls of calligraphy in a running hand. When Mr. Kao inspected them more closely he found that the characters were written in the style of the great master Huai-su and betrayed an altogether unusual clarity and power. On asking who had written them, he received the reply: "These are writing exercises of my own." As the young man, to judge by his appearance, did not seem of humble stock, Kao asked him for his name and origins.

With a sad face the man replied: "My name is Ts'ui Ying and my style Chün-chên; I come from Chên-chou and because of my father's services I received the post of Town Governor of Yung-chia. With my whole household I set out for my official residence, but I was careless and became the victim of an attack by my boatmen. I was thrown into the water and I have never seen my goods and chattels and my wife again. Fortunately, from my earliest childhood I have been used to the water and I dived beneath the waves until I was far enough away and could climb out onto the bank, where, drenched and without a single copper, I found refuge with simple folk. The master of the house was very good to me, gave me a change of clothes, and regaled me with food and wine. Then he gave me some money for the journey and said: 'The fact that you have fallen among thieves is bound to reach the ears of the authorities soon, and so I do not dare to keep you here longer, lest I should become involved in the affair.'

"So I inquired my way into the city and reported everything to the district administration of P'ing-chiang. Meanwhile a year has passed but the investigations have not produced the slightest clue. So I sell manuscripts for my living but I would never presume to give them out to be good calligraphy. I make so bold as to show these clumsy characters to Your Grace for examination."

When Kao heard that, he felt deep sympathy for the young man and said: "As this is how things are with you, there is really no alternative for me but to keep you here as house tutor, to teach my grandchildren to write. Do you agree to this?"

Ts'ui was beside himself with joy, and Mr. Kao invited him to step into the main chambers and to drink with him there. Then Ts'ui suddenly noticed among the wall screens one with a hibiscus and his tears began to flow. When Kao asked him in amazement what the matter was, he replied: "That is one of the pieces that was stolen from me on the boat, and it is one that I painted with my own hands. How does it come to be here?" Then he read the song aloud and said: "That is by my wife."

"How can you tell that?" Kao wanted to know.

"From her handwriting, and also because there is a special meaning hidden in the words. I can tell without a doubt that it comes from my untalented wife."

"If that is so, I will gladly take upon myself the task of making sure that the robbers are taken into custody. But please keep this strictly secret!"

Thereupon he gave Ts'ui lodging in his house and the next day secretly sent for Kuo Ch'ing-ch'un, from whom he discovered that the screen had been bought in the nunnery. At once he got an intermediary to inquire of the nuns from whom they had got the screen, and who had composed the poem on it. Soon the answer arrived: "The screen was presented by A-hsiu from our region, and the verse inscription comes from the nun Hui-yüan."

Immediately Kao sent someone to the Abbess of the nunnery and had her informed: "Mrs. Kao likes reciting the holy texts of the Buddha and has no one to keep her company. She has learned that the nun Hui-yüan has attained complete illumination and would therefore like to have her as an instructress. It is her wish that this request should not be turned down."

The Abbess would not at first give her permission. But Hui-yüan had for some time harbored longings to get outside so that she might perhaps find some opportunity to avenge the injustice she had suffered. Moreover, the Abbess could not very well oppose Mr. Kao's requests.

So the young woman went there and was put up by Mr. Kao in the same room with his wife. One day Mrs. Kao questioned the nun about her origins and past history. Restraining her tears with difficulty, Madame Wang thereupon recounted her whole story and also mentioned the question of the inscription on the hibiscus screen. Then she said: "The robbers cannot be far off. If you report this to your husband, Madame, the criminals can be caught and the old disgrace blotted out, and vengeance will be exacted for my husband. That would be a great favor on your husband's part." She did not, however, know what had happened to her husband since then.

When Mrs. Kao reported all this to her husband and added: "She is cultured and of a modest disposition. She certainly does not come from humble surroundings," Mr. Kao no longer doubted that she was indeed Ts'ui's wife. In his investigations at the robber's residence he also found out at what times he used to appear and disappear, but he still did not dare to set proceedings in motion rashly. On the other hand he got his wife to urge Madame Wang to let her hair grow again and to put on all her old worldly clothing.

Roughly half a year later the Doctor of the First Degree and Inspection Censor Serig Buqa undertook an official visit to the region. Buqa had previously been a subordinate of Mr. Kao's and the latter knew that he was an intelligent and able man. So he informed him of the case and advised him to proceed with a search of the house and an arrest. It turned out then that the document appointing Ts'ui together with all household effects was still at hand. But of Madame Wang there was no trace. When the evildoer was cross-examined about this, he confessed: "I wanted to keep her as a wife for my second son. But I did not keep an eye on her and so she fled from me at the Mid-Autumn Festival in the eighth month. I don't know where she has run away to."

Thereupon Buqa imposed a severe punishment on the criminal and also made sure that Ts'ui was able to take up the post originally intended for him.

When Ts'ui went to take his leave of Mr. Kao before leaving for his new official residence, the latter said: "I have played the go-between for Your Excellency and should like you to take a wife before you depart. There is still time enough for that."

Ts'ui, however, declined with thanks, saying: "My wife for long enough shared poverty and humiliation with me and is now unhappily lost to sight somewhere or other. It is not certain whether she is still alive or has already met her death. If I go alone to my post and pass the years there, Heaven and earth will certainly have pity on me. But if she should still be alive I cannot give up the hope that sometime I will be happily reunited with her. I am deeply moved by your kindness and will not forget it to my dying day. But a second marriage would not be in accord with my wishes."

Kao pretended to be unhappy and said: "Your Excellency's high sense of justice will certainly in due time be blessed by Heaven. How should I wish to trouble you any further? Only allow me, however, before your departure, to prepare a festive meal for you."

The following day the meal took place, attended by all the officials of the provincial administration and all the most notable people of the district without exception. Mr. Kao raised his goblet and greeted those present: "I, an old man, have today newly joined the bonds of this life for Town Governor Ts'ui."

None of the guests understood that. Then Kao had the nun Hui-yüan called. When she entered the room she was none other than Ts'ui's former wife.

The two took each other by the hand, deeply moved, and simply couldn't believe that they had met again until Mr. Kao told them the whole course of events. He also had the hibiscus screen fetched and showed it to the guests. Now they too understood why Kao had spoken of the bonds of the present life, for these words were featured in the poem by Mrs. Ts'ui on the screen and Hui-yüan had been her nunnery name. The whole company was moved to tears and they all praised the unparalleled kindness of Mr. Kao, who presented Ts'ui with a manservant and a maidservant before he set off on his journey.

When the young man's period of office had elapsed, he again passed through Su-chou, but Mr. Kao had in the meantime died. Husband and wife wept for him, as if they had lost their own father, and for three days and nights they offered a sacrifice to his soul at his burial mound in order to give expression to their gratitude before journeying on. Mrs. Ts'ui, moreover, observed a long period of fasting during which she prayed incessantly to the Bodhisattva Kuan-yin.

CHU YÜN-MING [ZHU YUNMING]
(1460–1526)
China

Chu Yün-ming, who is probably better known by his alternate name Chu Chih-shan, was a native of Kiangsu Province. After earning the *chü-jen,* a secondary degree, Chu was made an official of a junior rank, but his reputation as a master of calligraphy and literary composition brought him great prestige.

"A Painting of the Butterfly Dream by the Master Artist Li Tsai" is a poem of philosophical speculation. Like the ancient sage Chuang-tzu, a Taoist philosopher who dreamed he was a butterfly, and when he awoke, could not decide if he was a man dreaming he was a butterfly or a butterfly dreaming he was a man, Chu Yün-ming calls into question the opposition between subjectivity and objectivity. For him, the butterfly and the man and the dream in the painting and his own dream become in a way hardly distinguishable.

In Ming times, *Chü-jen* designated those who had passed the provincial examinations; success on this level usually meant an official appointment.

A Painting of the Butterfly Dream by the Master Artist Li Tsai*

I used to dream of Chuang Tzu;
I read every word in his book.
Day and night I thought of meeting him,
"flitting and fluttering" before my eyes!
But Chuang Tzu cannot come back,   5
the butterfly cannot appear again:
so who put them into this painting?
I see them and feel we're old friends!
If Chuang Tzu could become a butterfly,
why shouldn't a butterfly be able to become me?   10
The dream of a thousand years, here on this paper—
how do I know it is not my own?

SHEN CHOU [SHEN ZHOU] (1427–1509)
China

Shen Chou, a painter-poet of the middle Ming period, came from a distinguished family in Suchow (Suzhou). A native of Kiangsu, he was perhaps one of the most

Translated by Jonathan Chaves.

T'ang Yin, Ming Dynasty. *Lady Pan Holding a Fan*. National Palace Museum, Taiwan.

influential painters of his generation. His poems integrate emotions with scenic details, following the manner of Po Chü-yi, a poet of the T'ang period.

In "A Lady Picking Flowers," the sight of flowers blooming triggers the memory of a woman met last spring. Phrases such as "purple grief, red sorrow" reveal the special aesthetic sensibility of this artist.

A Lady Picking Flowers

Last year we parted as the flowers began to bloom.
Now the flowers bloom again, and you still have not returned.
Purple grief, red sorrow—a hundred thousand kinds,
and the spring wind blows each of them into my hands.

Translated by Jonathan Chaves.

P'U SUNG-LING [PU SONGLING]
(1640–1715)
China

P'u Sung-ling was a native of Shantung Province. He spent most of his life as a private tutor. Despite his literary talents, he had no luck whatsoever in passing the civil service examination and it was not until the age of seventy that he became a senior licentiate (*Kung-sheng,* "a tribute scholar"), i.e., someone invited to serve as an official because of his scholarly or literary accomplishments.

As a writer, P'u Sung-ling was known for his *Uncanny Stories from a Scholar's Studio [Liao-chai chih-yi],* a collection of short stories written in the classical style about the supernatural and the miraculous. He was influenced by the supernatural tales of the T'ang period, but most of his stories were based on what he had heard or collected from others. Despite the title of the book, these "strange tales" actually contain detailed and realistic descriptions of everyday life: even the flower-spirits and fox-fairies appear truly human.

In "The Wise Neighbor," a rich man's wife, Mrs. Chu, is losing the affection of her husband to his concubine. With the counsel of her neighbor, Mrs. Heng, she wins her husband back. The wise neighbor, as the story does not reveal until the very end, turns out to be a fox-spirit, but the depiction of polygamy in traditional Chinese society and the subtleties of human sexual psychology provide a realism that is far from "supernatural."

from *Uncanny Stories from a Scholar's Studio [Liao-chai chih-yi]*

The Wise Neighbor

Hung Ta-yeh was a man of the capital who was married to a girl whose maiden name was Chu, an exceptionally charming and pretty woman, whom he loved as much as she him. After some time Hung took a girl by the name of Pao-tai as his second wife and, although she was not nearly as beautiful as Mrs Chu, the husband preferred the concubine to the wife. This upset Mrs Chu and led to matrimonial quarrels between them. Although Hung did not dare to spend all his nights openly in the concubine's rooms, he nevertheless favoured her in every respect and neglected his wife.

Later Hung moved to another house and thereby became the neighbor of a textile merchant by the name of Ti. Ti's wife, Mrs Hêng by name, of her own accord paid a call on Mrs Chu. Mrs Hêng must have been more than thirty years old by then and was scarcely of even average beauty, but her conversation was so

Translated by Christopher Levenson.

amusing and quick-witted that Mrs Chu at once took a liking to her and paid her a return visit the following day. In doing so she found that Mr Ti also had a younger concubine who was as pretty as she was lovable. But even after Hung had lived with his family for almost half a year next to Mr Ti they never noticed any sign of quarrels or discord in their household. Mr Ti esteemed and loved only his wife Hêng, while the concubine in her 'side chamber' was nothing more than mere decoration.

One day Hung's wife visited her neighbor and asked her: "I always used to think that my husband loved a secondary wife simply because she was a secondary wife, and I wished I could exchange the title of wife for that of secondary wife. But now I know that that cannot be the explanation. How have you managed this? If you would be so kind as to reveal your secret methods, I should like to be your humble pupil."

"Well then, you must simply withdraw into yourself, and repulse your husband for a change. You should keep him waiting the whole day with trivial chit-chat. In the twinkling of an eye, the separation from you will arouse his desires, but you must leave it all to him. Only, when he comes back to you of his own accord, you should not let him have his will. In a month's time I will see what further advice I can give you."

Mrs Chu obeyed these instructions and adorned the girl Pao-tai even more beautifully and even let her husband spend whole nights with her. Likewise she arranged for Mr Hung to take all his meals with the concubine. But as soon as he so much as approached his wife in a friendly way she repulsed him as hard as she could. Mr Hung therefore praised his principal wife everywhere as virtuous. When this had gone on for more than a month Mrs Chu went to call on Mrs Hêng again.

"Well done," said her neighbor. "Now as soon as you get home you must make yourself ugly. Don't wear any more beautiful clothes and don't take any more trouble with your complexion; go among your maids with a dirty face and worn-out shoes, and do housework. After a month you can come to me again."

Mrs Chu followed this advice also, put on threadbare, patched clothes, and deliberately did not keep herself clean any longer. Moreover, she devoted all her time to spinning, without demanding anything more. Thereupon Mr Hung began to take pity on her and instructed Pao-tai to help his wife in her work. Mrs Chu, however, refused all offers of help and scolded the girl and sent her packing.

After a month she paid another visit to Mrs Hêng and received new instructions: "You are really a diligent pupil! In a few days' time it will be the Spring Festival. I will then invite you to admire the beauty of the blossoms in our garden. On this occasion, take off your old clothes and put on the most beautiful and newest gown, shoes, and stockings that you possess and come first to me."

Mrs Chu promised to do this and, when the day of the Festival had come, seated herself in front of her mirror and made herself up most beautifully, just as Mrs Hêng had advised her. When she had finished her toilette she went across to Mrs Hêng, who exclaimed joyfully: "That is just right!" Then her neighbor put her phoenix hair style in order with her own hands, so that you could see your reflection in the gleaming black hair. Moreover, as the cut of the gown was not in the very latest fashion, she opened the seams and altered the gown. She felt too that the shoes were of inelegant shape and fetched from her own wardrobe a pair of not quite finished shoes that the two women then finished together with embroideries. When Mrs Chu had put on the shoes, Mrs Hêng offered her guest a glass of wine before she took her leave and impressed upon her: "Go home now and when your husband has seen you, lock yourself into your room early and retire to bed. If he knocks at your door, pay no attention to it at first. When he has called you three times, you may at most let him in once, and when he seeks your tongue with his mouth, when his hands strive towards your feet, be sparing of your favours. Then after half a month, you must come to me again."

On arriving home, Mrs Chu showed herself in all the glory of her outfit to her husband, who did not tire of looking her up and down and laughed and joked with her as he had never done before. But Mrs Chu said little during the Festival and walked around looking at the garden, with her head propped on her hand and with an expression of indifference on her face. And even before sunset she withdrew to her bedroom, barred the door, and lay down to sleep. Sure enough, Mr Hung came along shortly afterwards and knocked on the door, but Mrs Chu remained lying where she was and did not even rise from the bed, so that Hung had to go away again. The next day exactly the same thing occurred and only on the third day, when Hung began to insist politely, did Mrs Chu say: "As a matter of fact, I've got used to sleeping by myself and don't feel I can put up with such interference again." As the sun sank down towards the west, Mr Hung went into the bedroom where his wife was already seated waiting for him. The lamps were extinguished and both of them climbed into bed. Hung felt as if he were with a young married woman and found the greatest of pleasure in their embraces. He wanted to make an arrangement with her for the following evening also but Mrs Chu said that it was impossible and as a special favour gave him permission to come to her every third day.

A fortnight later she again visited Mrs Hêng. The neighbor locked the door behind her guest and said to her: "From now on, you have the upper hand in the bedroom. But however beautiful you may be, you are not seductive. If your attractiveness were as great as your beauty, you would enjoy favour among men at least equal to that of the famous Hsi-shih."[1]

Then she got Mrs Chu to practise casting glances and said: "Quite wrong! The fault lies in the far corner of your eye." Then Mrs Chu had to practise smiling, but to this too her neighbor said: "Wrong again! Your left cheek is not right yet." Then Mrs Hêng herself cast a few glances that radiated the seductiveness of the damp autumn wave, smiling so winsomely that her regular white teeth were slightly visible. Mrs Chu had to imitate all this a few dozen times before she had approximately caught the knack of it. Then Mrs Hêng said: "Now go home and practise everything exactly with a mirror in your hand. I can't teach you anything more in the way of tactics. As for how you behave in bed, act as the occasion

---

1. Hsi-shih was the Helen of Chinese antiquity (fifth century B.C.), whose beauty was the cause of a state's downfall.

demands and surrender yourself in the way that he likes best. I can't teach you that with mere words."

Mrs Chu went home and acted in every point in accordance with her neighbor's advice. Mr Hung was beside himself with joy and fell heart and soul in love with his wife, so that he feared only one thing—to be repulsed by her. As day was declining he used to smile at her in a friendly way and his steps no longer made their way towards the other woman's chamber. So it went on, day by day, and finally he could no longer be induced to go to the secondary wife. But Mrs Chu treated Pao-tai ever better, and whenever she prepared a supper in her bedroom Pao-tai had to sit with her on the same bed. Mr Hung, however, began to find Pao-tai uglier and uglier and usually sent her away before the end of the meal. On such occasions Mrs Chu played the trick on her husband of going to Pao-tai's room herself and locking herself in there so that the whole night through Hung could find no place where he could satisfy his desires. To add to it all, Pao-tai began to grow resentful of Mr Hung and to grumble about him in front of other people so that Hung got more and more tired of her, lost his temper with her, and even began to beat her. From sorrow at this Pao-tai neglected her toilette and began to go about with poor clothes on, with dirty shoes and tousled hair, so that she hardly looked human any more.

"How have my arts worked?" Mrs Chu's neighbor asked her one day.

"Your method is really wonderful, but although I follow it as your pupil, I don't quite see how it all comes about."

"Have you never heard how it is with such matters? In love, you value whatever is new and find what is old depressing; you throw yourself wholeheartedly into difficult things and despise what is easy. If a husband loves his concubine, it's not because she just happens to be beautiful. It is rather that he finds it delicious to possess her through some unexpected adventure and is happy when he can get together with her only under difficulties. Let someone gorge as he pleases, and he will soon grow sick of the most costly foods—and all the more so when he is just offered groats."

"But why make yourself ugly first before shining out in radiant beauty?"

"If you arrange things so that you attract no glances at all, it's just as good as a long separation. If your husband then sees you again suddenly in all your seductive charm, it's as good as if you were coming to him for the first time. If a poor man is suddenly given meat and millet to eat, he finds that coarse hulled rice is no longer tasty. And if a wife does not casually allow her husband to have everything, the result is that the other woman grows old for him while the wife herself is new, the other woman easy to get while she herself is obtained with difficulty. That, you see, is my method: to become, instead of your husband's main wife, his concubine."

Mrs Chu was extremely pleased and remained subsequently for a number of years her neighbor's intimate friend. One day Mrs Hêng said: "We two like each other as much as if we had but the one body, and I don't want shadows to be cast across your life on my account. For a long time I have often wanted to talk openly to you but I feared that you would mistrust me. Now, however, our ways must part, so I may dare to tell you the truth. You see, I am a fox spirit. In my youth I was unlucky enough to have a stepmother who sold me at the capital. But because my husband treated me so well, I could not bring myself to leave him and our love has lasted up to the present day. But tomorrow my old father will give up his corporeal existence and I must therefore go back to my family and will not return."

Mrs Chu gripped her hands and took her leave sobbing. When she went over again next morning, the whole family next door was in a great commotion, for Mrs Hêng had vanished without a trace.

WANG WEI (SEVENTEENTH CENTURY)
China

Wang Wei was a native of Kiangsu Province. She lost her parents when she was only seven and grew up to be a courtesan in Yangchou. Despite her minimal formal education, she became a poet. She got married, but after the death of her husband, she became a Taoist priestess and went into a nunnery. One of her hobbies was to travel by boat on the waterways of Central China with her library on board, enjoying and writing about the landscape along the river.

"Seeking a Mooring" describes such a moment. The poet's intoxication with the evening's serenity and the rustic beauty is tinged with a traveler's loneliness and melancholy. The piece clearly betrays the influence of earlier nature poets, especially the famous "Nightly Mooring at Maple Bridge" [Feng-ch'iao ye-po] by the T'ang poet Chang Chi.

Seeking a Mooring

A leaf floats in endless space.
A cold wind tears the clouds.
The water flows westward.
The tide pushes upstream.
Beyond the moonlit reeds,   5
In village after village, I hear
The sound of fullers' mallets
Beating the wet clothing
In preparation for winter.
Everywhere crickets cry   10
In the autumn frost.
A traveller's thoughts in the night
Wander in a thousand miles of dreams.

Translated by Kenneth Rexroth and Ling Chung.

The sound of a bell cannot disperse
The sorrows that come   15
In the fifth hour of night.
What place will I remember
From all this journey?
Only still bands of desolate mist
And a single fishing boat.   20

ANONYMOUS (SEVENTEENTH CENTURY)
China

Oral storytelling as a form of public entertainment as well as moral edification has
a long history in China. During the Sung period, storytelling flourished in many
urban centers of the nation, especially those in the lower Yangtze valley. Toward
the end of the Ming Dynasty (1368–1644), there was a revival of such stories,
which led to an ascendance of vernacular literature. Two scholars, Feng
Meng-lung and Ling Meng-ch'u, compiled anthologies of short stories, which are
either based on the Sung *hua-pen* (prompt-books of the storytellers), or creative
writings imitating the storyteller's style. Collected in Feng Meng-lung's *Stories
Ancient and Modern [Ku-chin hsiao-shuo]*, "The Canary Murders" is probably a
retold version of a popular story from the Sung period.

    When the story begins, Shen Hsiu is a young man of leisure. He takes his
canary to the market to show it off. While he is distracted, the bird is stolen. This
leads subsequently to a chain of events, which takes a total of seven lives before
the case is finally solved. The linked narrative structure may remind Western
readers of such works as Arthur Schnitzler's *La Ronde* or Thornton Wilder's *The
Bridge of San Luis Rey*.

from *Stories Ancient and Modern [Ku-chin hsiao-shuo]*

The Canary Murders

A bird it was at the root of the trouble:
Seven lives lost—what a lamentable case!
Note, all of you, this tragic lesson:
Do not let your sons and daughters neglect their home.

It is told how in the year 1121, the third year of the period Hsüan-ho in the reign
of the Emperor Hui-tsung of the great Sung dynasty, a master-weaver named Shen
Yü had his home in the prefecture of Hai-ning, near Hangchow. He lived below

---

Translated by Cyril Birch.

the New North Bridge, outside the Wu-lin Gate. This Shen Yü, styled Pi-hsien, was in a prosperous way of business, and he and his wife, Madam Yen, were devoted to each other. They had an only son, Shen Hsiu, who had reached the age of sixteen but had not yet married. The father made his living solely from weaving silk cloth, but to everyone's surprise Shen Hsiu took no heed of his duty to earn his keep. He devoted himself to pleasure and amusement and spent all his time breeding canaries,[1] and his parents doted on their only child and had no control over him. The neighbours gave him the nickname "Birdie" Shen. Every day at dawn he would take up one of his canaries and hurry off to match it against others in the park of willows inside the city.

This went on day after day, until it came to the end of spring, when the weather is neither too hot nor too cold, when the flowers bloom red and the willows are green. One morning at this time Shen Hsiu got up at the crack of dawn, washed and dressed and ate his breakfast, and made ready a cage, into which he put one matchless canary. This creature was the sort that is found only in heaven and not here below. He took it all over the place to fight, and it had never been defeated. It had won him over a hundred strings of cash, and he doted on it and held it dearer than life itself. He had made a cage for it of gold lacquer, with a brass hook, a green gauze cover, and seed-pot and water-pot of Ko-yao porcelain.[2] This particular morning Shen Hsiu took up the cage and proudly hurried off through the city-gate to match his bird in the willow park. And who would have thought that Shen Hsiu, off on this jaunt of his, was going to his death? Just like

> A pig or a lamb to the slaughter,
> Seeking with every step the road to death.

Shen Hsiu took his bird into the willow park, but he was later than he had thought and the bird-fanciers had dispersed. The place was silent and gloomy, with not a soul about. Shen Hsiu, finding himself alone, hung the bird in its cage on a willow-branch, where it sang for a while. Then, disappointed, he took the cage down again and was just about to go back, when suddenly a bout of pain came surging up from his belly and forced him to his knees.

The fact was that Shen Hsiu was a sufferer from what is known as "dumplings on the heart," or hernia. Every attack sent him into a dead faint. It must have been that he had risen earlier than usual that morning, and then, arriving late to find no one there, he felt disappointed and miserable, so that this time the attack was particularly severe. He collapsed on the ground at the foot of a willow-tree, where he lay unconscious for four whole hours.

---

1. 'Canary' is used purely for the sake of familiarity to represent the bird *hua-mei*. There are in fact several points of resemblance. The *hua-mei* is a member of the oriole family, four–five inches in length, with greyish-yellow plumage and a yellowish-white breast; white markings above the eyes give rise to the name, literally, "painted eyebrows." The male is a singer

and a fighter. The bird is found in North China, wild and as a pet.
2. Ko-yao: "the elder Kilu": term used to describe the work of the Sung potter Chang Sheng-yi, whose kiln was at Lung-ch'üan in Chekiang. The porcelain of Sheng-yi's younger brother, Sheng-erh, was known as Chang-yao ware.

Now, wouldn't you agree that "there is such a thing as coincidence?" This very day a cooper called Chang came walking through the park, his pack on his back, on the way to a job at the Ch'u household. He saw from a distance that there was someone lying at the foot of this tree, and so he came bounding up to the spot, set down his load and had a look. Shen Hsiu's face was a waxy yellow, and he was still in a coma. There was nothing of any value on him, but at one side was the canary in its cage; and the canary chose just this moment to sing away more beautifully than ever. It was a case of "the sight of the treasure provides the motive," and "the plan is born when the man is poorest." Chang thought, "I might work all day for a couple of silver cents. What good would that do me?"

Shen Hsiu must have been doomed to die, for at the sight of Chang the canary began to sing harder than ever. Chang said to himself, "The rest doesn't matter, but this canary alone is worth two or three silver taels at least." So he picked up the cage and was just making off, when to his surprise Shen Hsiu came round. Shen opened his eyes to see Chang picking up the cage. He tried to get up but couldn't. All he could do was cry out, "Where are you off to with my canary, you old blackguard?"

"This little fool has too quick a tongue," Chang thought to himself. "Suppose I take it, and he manages to get up and comes after me—he'll make trouble for me. There's only one thing for it, one way or the other I'm in a mess." So he went to the barrel he had been carrying and took out a curved paring-knife, then turned to Shen Hsiu and struck at him. The knife was sharp and he used all his strength, and Shen Hsiu's head rolled away to one side.

Chang cast panic-stricken glances to left and right, fearful lest someone should have seen him. Then, looking up, he saw that to one side stood a hollow tree. Hurriedly he picked up the head and dropped it into the hollow trunk, returned the knife to the barrel, and hung the bird-cage from his pack. He did not go on to the job at the Ch'u house, but went off like a puff of smoke, through the streets and alleys of the town, looking for somewhere to hide.

Now, how many lives do you think were lost on account of this one live bird? Indeed,

> Private words among men,
> Heard in Heaven like thunder;
> A misdeed in a dark room,
> But the gods have eyes like lightning.

As Chang walked along the thought came to him, "There is a travelling merchant who stays in an inn at Huchou-shu, and I have often seen him buying pets. Why not go there and sell the bird to him?" And he made straight for the suburb past the Wulin Gate.

The evil fate in store must have been determined from a previous existence, for there he saw three merchants with two youths at their heels, five persons all told. They had just packed up their goods to go back, and he met them coming in through the gate. The merchants were all men of the Eastern Capital, Pien-liang (Kaifeng). One of them was called Li Chi, a trader in herbs. He had always had a fancy for canaries, and seeing this lovely bird on the cooper's back he called to

Chang to let him see it. Chang set down his pack. The merchant examined the canary's plumage and eyes, and saw that it was a fine bird. It had a lovely singing-voice, too, and he was delighted with it. "Would you like to sell him?" he asked Chang.

By this time Chang's only concern was to be rid of the evidence. So he said, "How much will you give me, sir?"

The longer Li Chi looked at the bird the more he liked it. "I'll give you a tael of silver," he said.

Chang realized the deal was on. "I don't want to haggle," he said, "It's just that this bird's very precious to me. But give me a little more and you can have him."

Li Chi took out three pieces of silver and weighed them: there was one tael and a fifth. "That's the lot," he said, handing it to Chang.

Chang took the silver, examined it and put it in his wallet. He gave the canary to the merchant and took his leave. "That's a good deed done, getting rid of the evidence," he told himself. He did not go back to his work, but hurried straight home. But still he felt certain misgivings at heart. Indeed,

> The evil-doer fears the wrath of Heaven and earth,
> The swindler dreads discovery by gods and demons.

Chang's home was in fact against the city-wall by the Yung-chin Gate. There was only himself and his wife, they had no children. When his wife saw him coming back, she said, "You haven't used a single splint. Why have you come home so early? What's the trouble?"

Chang said not a word until he had entered the house, taken off his pack and turned back to bolt the door. Then he said, "Come here, wife, I've something to tell you. Today I've been to such-and-such and done such-and-such, and I've come by this ounce and a fifth of silver. I'm giving it to you so that you can enjoy yourself for a while." And the two of them gloated over the money.

But this does not concern us. Let us rather go on to tell how there was no one about in the willow park until late morning, when two peasants carrying loads of manure happened to pass through. The headless corpse blocking their path gave them a fright, and they began to kick up a fuss, quickly rousing the ward-headman and all the citizens of the neighbourhood. The ward submitted the matter to the *hsien*, and the *hsien* to the prefecture, and the next day a coroner and other officers were sent to the willow park to investigate. They found no mark on the body: the only thing wrong was that the head was missing; nor had anyone come forward as plaintiff. The officers made their report to the authorities at the prefecture, who despatched runners to arrest the criminal. Within the city and out in the suburbs, all was thrown into an uproar.

Let us now rather tell how Shen Hsiu's parents, when evening came and he still had not returned, sent people out in every direction to search for him, but without success. When again at dawn searchers were sent into the city, in the vicinity of the inn at Hu-chou-shu they heard a commotion about the headless corpse of a murdered man being found in the willow park. When Shen Hsiu's mother heard of this she thought, "My boy went into the city yesterday to show his canary, and there's still no sign of him. Can it be him?" And at once she cried to her husband, "You must go into the city yourself and make enquiries."

Shen Yü gave a jump when he heard this, and filled with alarm he hurried off to the willow park. There he saw the headless corpse, which, after a careful look at the clothing, he recognized as his own son. He began to wail in a loud voice. "Here is the plaintiff," said the ward headman. "Now all that is missing is the criminal."

Shen Yü went at once to make accusation before the Prefect of Lin-an. "It is my son," he said. "Early yesterday morning he went into the city to show his canary, and he has been murdered, no one knows how or why. Your Highness, I demand justice!"

Runners and detectives were sent from the prefecture throughout the area, with orders to arrest the criminal within ten days. Shen Yü was ordered to prepare a coffin in the willow park to contain the corpse. He went straight home and said to his wife, "It's our son, he's been murdered. But no one knows where the head has been taken. I have made accusation at the prefecture, and they have sent runners out everywhere to arrest the criminal. I've been told to buy a coffin for him. What is best for us to do about it all?"

At this news, Madam Yen began to wail aloud and collapsed to the floor. "If you don't know how she felt inside, first see how she lies there motionless." Indeed,

> Body like the waning moon at cock-crow, half-hidden behind the hills;
> Spirit like a dying lamp at the third watch, the oil already gone.

They proceeded to revive her by forcing hot soup down her throat, and when she came to she said, through her tears, "My boy would never listen to good advice, and now he is dead and we cannot bury him. O my son, so young, and dead in such a grievous manner. Who could have told that in my old age I should be left without support?" All the time she was speaking her tears flowed ceaselessly. She would take neither food nor drink, although her husband used every effort to console her. Somehow or other they got through the next fortnight, without any news. Then Shen Yü and his wife began to discuss the matter. "Our boy would never heed our words, and now this terrible thing has happened and he has been murdered. Nor can the murderer be found. There is nothing we can do about it. But at least it would be something if his corpse could be made whole. Our best plan is to write out a notice and inform people everywhere that if they find the head, so that the corpse can be made whole, they will be rewarded for it."

When the two had come to this decision they promptly wrote out copies of a notice and went out to paste them up all over the city. The notice ran:

> "To all citizens: One thousand strings of cash reward to anyone discovering the whereabouts of the head of Shen Hsiu. Two thousand strings of cash reward to anyone apprehending the murderer."

They informed the prefecture of this, and the authorities issued fresh orders to the runners to arrest the criminal within so many days, and put out an official notice, as follows:

"Official reward of five hundred strings of cash to anyone discovering the whereabouts of the head of Shen Hsiu. One thousand strings of cash reward to anyone apprehending the murderer."

We will leave the town in its ferment of excitement over the notices, and go on to tell how at the foot of the Southern Peak there lived an old pauper whose name was Huang and who was known by the nickname "Old Dog." He was an ignorant man who had spent his life as a chair-coolie. With old age he had lost his sight, and he depended entirely on the support of his two sons, Big Pao and Little Pao. The three of them, father and sons, had neither enough clothes to wear nor enough food to eat. They lived from hand to mouth and their bellies were never full. One day Old Dog Huang called Big Pao and Little Pao to him and said, "I hear talk of some rich man or other call Shen Hsiu, who's been murdered, and his head is missing. And now they're offering a reward, and they say if anyone finds this head, the family will give them a thousand strings of cash and the authorities will give them another five hundred. I've called you together now just to say this: I'm an old man now anyway, and I'm no use, I can't see and I've no money. So I've decided to give you two a chance to make something and enjoy yourselves. Tonight you must cut off my head. Hide it in the water at the edge of the Western Lake, and in a few days it will be unrecognizable. Then you must take it to the prefecture and claim the reward, and altogether you'll get one thousand five hundred strings of cash. It's better than staying on here in misery. It's a very clever scheme, and you mustn't waste any time, because if somebody else gets in first I'll have lost my life for nothing."

This "Old Dog" made this speech because he had given up in despair; moreover, his two sons were very stupid men and understood nothing of the law. Indeed,

> The mouth is the gateway of disaster,
> The tongue is an executioner's knife.
> Keep your mouth shut and your tongue well-hidden,
> And you will live at peace and secure.

The two went outside to discuss the matter. "This is a brilliant idea of our father's," said Little Pao. "Not even a Commander-in-Chief or a Field-Marshal could have thought up a plan like this. It's a very good one, although it's a pity we have to lose Dad."

Big Pao was by nature both cruel and stupid. He said, "He's got to die sooner or later anyway. Why shouldn't we seize this opportunity and do him in? We can dig a pit at the foot of the mountain and bury him, and there'll be no trace, so how can we be found out? This is what they call 'doing it while the water's hot,' and 'leaving no trace.' Men's hearts are governed by Heaven: it wasn't ourselves who forced him to it, he told us to do this of his own accord."

"All right then," said Little Pao, "only we'll not set to work until he's fast asleep."

Having laid their plans, the brothers went bustling off and bought two bottles of wine on credit. They came back to their father, and the three of them got good and drunk and sprawled about all over the place. The two brothers slept right through to the early hours of the morning, when they crept out of bed to watch the old man lying there, snoring. Then Big Pao took a kitchen-knife from in front of the stove, and with one powerful stroke at his father's neck cut his head clean off. Hurriedly they wrapped it in an old garment and hid it in the bed. Then they went off to the foot of the mountain and dug a deep pit. They carried the body there and buried it, and before it was daylight they had hidden the head in the shallow water at the edge of the lake, near the Lotus House at the foot of the Nan-p'ing hills.

A fortnight later they went into the city and looked at the notice. First of all they went to Shen Yü's house to make their report: "The two of us were shrimping yesterday when we saw a human head by the edge of the lake near the Lotus House. We thought it must be your son's head."

"If it really is," said Shen Yü at this, "there is a reward of a thousand strings of cash for you, not a copper short." Then he prepared food and wine for them, and presently they took him straight to the point by the Lotus House at the foot of the Nan-p'ing hills. There they found the head, lightly buried in the mud. When they picked it up and examined it, they found it had been under water so long that the features were bloated and past recognition. But Shen Yü thought, "It must be my son's head. If it isn't how does another head come to be here?"

Shen Yü wrapped the head in a kerchief, and accompanied the two of them straight to the prefecture, where they reported the discovery of Shen Hsiu's head. The Prefect repeatedly questioned the two brothers, who replied, "We saw it when we were shrimping. We don't know anything else about it." Their word was accepted, and they were given the five hundred strings of cash. Then, taking the· head with them, they accompanied Shen Yü to the willow park. They opened the coffin, set the head on the shoulders of the corpse, and nailed the coffin up again. Then Shen Yü took the brothers back to his home. When Madam Yen heard that her son's head had been found she was much happier, and at once set out food and wine to feast the brothers. They received the thousand strings of cash as their reward, and took their leave and returned home. There, they built a house, and bought farming implements and household goods. "We are not going to work as chair-coolies any longer," they said to each other. "We'll work hard at our farming, and we can make a bit extra by gathering firewood from the hillside and selling that."

But this does not concern us. Indeed, "time flew like an arrow" and "days and months passed like a weaver's shuttle." Several months passed unnoticed, and the authorities grew lax and concerned themselves less every day with the affair.

We will say no more of all this, but go on to tell how the time came for Shen Yü, who was a master-weaver for the Eastern Capital, to make a journey there to deliver a consignment of cloth. When all his weavers had completed their quotas he went to the prefecture for the delivery permit, returned home to order his affairs there, and then started out. This journey, just because Shen Yü chanced to see a bird which had belonged to his own family, resulted in the forfeiture of another life. Indeed,

> Take no illegal goods,
> Commit no illegal acts.
> Here above the law will catch you,
> Down below the demons pursue you.

Let us now tell how Shen Yü, on his journey, ate when hungry and drank when thirsty, rested each night and set out again each morning, and after more than one day like this arrived in the Eastern Capital. He delivered each and every bolt of cloth, and collected his permit to return. Then he thought, "I have heard that the sights of the Eastern Capital are unique. Why shouldn't I stroll about for a while? This is an opportunity which doesn't come often." He visited all the historic sites and beauty-spots, the monasteries both Taoist and Buddhist, and all the other celebrated sights. Then he chanced to pass by the gate of the Imperial Aviary. Now, Shen Yü was very fond of pets, and he felt he would like to have a look inside. On distributing a dozen or so cash at the gate he was allowed in to have a look round. All at once he heard a canary singing beautifully. Taking a careful look at it, he realized it was his son's canary which had disappeared. When the canary saw Shen Yü's familiar face it sang louder than ever, and hopped about its cage jerking its head towards him. The sight of the bird reminded Shen Yü of his son. Tears streamed down his face and his heart filled with sorrow. Without reflecting where he was he began to cry out and make an uproar, shouting, "Could such a thing come to pass?"

The guard who was keeper of the Aviary shouted, "Here's a fool who doesn't know the regulations. Where do you think you are, making such a fuss?"

Shen Yü, unable to contain his grief, began to yell louder still, and the guard, fearful of bringing trouble on his own head, found nothing for it but to arrest Shen Yü and have him brought before the Grand Court. The officer of the Grand Court shouted, "Where do you come from, that you dare to enter a part of the palace itself and make a disturbance like this? If you have some grievance, come straight out with it like an honest fellow, and you'll be let off."

So Shen Yü told how his son had gone off to match his canary and had been murdered, the whole story from beginning to end. The officer of the Grand Court was dumbfounded by the story. Then he reflected that the bird had been presented as tribute by a man of the capital, Li Chi; but whoever had dreamt there could be all this business behind it? He sent off runners to arrest Li Chi and bring him to court on the instant. The questioning commenced: "What was your reason for murdering this man's son in Hai-ning, and bringing his canary here as tribute? Make a full and open statement, or you will be punished."

"I went to Hangchow on business," said Li Chi, "and as I was going through the Wu-lin Gate I chanced to see a cooper who had this canary in a cage hanging from his pack. When I heard it singing and saw that it was a fine bird I bought it, for an ounce and a fifth of silver. I brought it back with me; but I did not dare to keep it for myself, because it was such a fine specimen, and so I presented it as tribute for the Emperor's use. I know nothing about any murder."

"Who are you trying to implicate?" said his interrogator. "This canary is concrete evidence. Tell the truth!"

Li Chi pleaded again and again: "It is the truth that I bought it from an old cooper. I know nothing about a murder. How would I dare to make a false statement?"

"This old man you bought it from," went on the interrogating officer, "what was his name and where did he come from? Give me the true facts and I will have him brought in. Then we shall get at the truth, and you will be released."

"I simply bought it from him when I ran into him on the street," said Li Chi. "I really don't know what his name is or where he lives."

The interrogating officer began to abuse him: "You're only trying to confuse the issue. Are you hoping to make someone else pay for this man's life? We must go by the concrete evidence, this canary. This rascal won't confess until he's beaten."

Li Chi was flogged over and over until the flesh was ripped open. He could not bear the pain, and had no alternative but to make up a story that when he saw what a fine bird this canary was he had killed Shen Hsiu and cast his head away. Thereupon Li Chi was committed to the main jail, while the officer of the Grand Court prepared his report for submission to the Emperor. The Imperial rescript ran: "Li Chi was beyond doubt the murderer of Shen Hsiu, the canary being evidence of this. The law requires that he shall be executed." The canary was returned to Shen Yü, who was also given a permit and allowed to return to his home; whilst Li Chi was sent under escort to the execution-ground, and there beheaded. Indeed,

> When the old turtle won't turn tender
> You shift the blame on to the firewood.

At this time, the two merchants who had accompanied Li Chi to Hai-ning on business could hardly keep still for indignation. "How could such an injustice be done," they complained, "when it was plain for all to see that he had bought the canary. We would have pleaded for him, but what could we do? Although we would recognize the man who sold Li Chi the canary, we don't know his name any more than Li did. Moreover he is in Hangchow. We should not have been able to clear Li Chi, and we should have implicated ourselves. How can the truth be brought to light? A man has been executed when he was obviously innocent, and all because of one single bird. The only thing is for us to go to Hangchow, and when we get there, to wring the truth out of this fellow."

Let us say no more of this, but rather tell how Shen Yü packed his baggage, picked up his canary and hurried home, travelling day and night. He reported to his wife: "When I was in the Eastern Capital I succeeded in avenging our son."

"How did that come about?" asked Madam Yen. Shen Yü told her the whole story right through, beginning with his seeing the canary in the Imperial Aviary. When Madam Yen saw the canary she burst out weeping, for the sight of things brings back sad memories; but we will say no more of this. The next day Shen Yü took up the canary again and went to the prefecture to have his permit cancelled, and there he reported all that had happened. "What a lucky coincidence," cried the delighted Prefect. Indeed,

Do nothing of which you need feel ashamed:
Who, throughout time, has been allowed to escape?

And murder, needless to say, is the concern of Heaven, not to be taken lightly. The Prefect dismissed Shen Yü with the words, "Since the criminal has been caught and executed, you may have the coffin cremated." Shen Yü had the coffin cremated and the remains scattered, and we will say no more of this, but go on to tell how of the two merchants who had accompanied Li Chi to Hangchow on that former occasion to sell herbs, one was called Ho and the other Chu. These two got some more herbs together and went straight to Hangchow, to stay in the inn at Hu-chou-shu. They quickly sold up their herbs, then, their hearts filled with a sense of injustice, they went into the city to look for the cooper. They searched all day without finding a trace of him, and returned, weary and dispirited, to the inn to sleep. The next morning they returned to the city, and as luck would have it they chanced to see a man with a cooper's pack. "Tell us, brother," they said, calling to him to stay, "is there another cooper here, an old man who looks like this?" And they described him. "We don't know his name, but perhaps you know him?"

"Gentlemen," said the cooper, "there are only two old men here in the cooper's trade. One is called Li, and lives in Pomegranate Garden Street; the other is called Chang, and he lives by the city-wall on the west side. I don't know which one it is that you want."

The two merchants thanked him and carried their search straight to Pomegranate Garden Street. As it happened, the man named Li was sitting there cutting splints. The two took a look at him, but he was not their man. Then they found the house by the western wall, and coming up to the door they asked if Chang was at home. "No, he isn't" replied Chang's wife. "He's gone out to a job."

The two men turned away again without more ado. It was now early afternoon. They had gone no more than a few hundred yards when they saw in the distance a man carrying a cooper's pack. And this man's fate it was to pay for the life of Shen Hsiu and to clear the name of Li Chi. Indeed, "let mercy and righteousness everywhere prevail, and you will meet with them at every turn of your life; never make an enemy, for when you meet him in a narrow path it is not easy to turn back." Chang was walking south towards his home, and the two men were walking towards the north, so that they met face to face. Chang did not recognize the pair, but they recognized him. They stopped him and asked his name. "My name is Chang." he replied.

"It must be you who live by the western wall," they continued. "That is so," replied Chang. "What do you want of me?"

"We have some things at the inn that need repairing," said the merchants, "and we are looking for an experienced man to do the job. That's why we wanted you. Where are you going now?"

"I'm on my way home," said Chang. The three of them talked as they went along, until they came to Chang's door. "Please sit down and have some tea," said Chang.

But the others replied, "It is getting late. We'll come again tomorrow."

"Then I won't go out tomorrow, but will wait for you here," said Chang.

The two men took their leave of him, but they did not return to the inn: they went straight to the prefecture to inform on him. The court had just begun its evening session, and the two men went straight in and knelt down. They told the whole story of Shen Yü's recognition of the canary and Li Chi's execution, and of Li's earlier meeting with Chang when he bought the canary. "We two are filled with a sense of injustice, and with the desire to avenge Li Chi. We entreat your honour to question Chang thoroughly and to find out how he came by the canary."

"The Shen Hsiu case has been wound up," said the Prefect. "The criminal has been executed—what more remains to be done?"

So the two merchants made an accusation: "The officer of the Grand Court was misled. He took the canary as evidence, but did not look carefully into the details of the case. It is plain for all to see that Li Chi was wrongfully executed. We have 'found injustice in our path,' and are determined to avenge Li Chi. If we were not speaking the truth, how would we dare to make a nuisance of ourselves with this accusation? We beg your honour in your mercy to intervene in this matter."

Observing how earnestly they pleaded, the Prefect at once sent out runners to arrest Chang that very night. It was just like

> Vultures chasing a purple swallow,
> Fierce tigers slavering over a lamb.

That night the men from the court hurried to the western wall. They tied Chang's arms behind his back and delivered him up to the prefecture, where he was committed to the main jail. When court opened the next day, Chang was brought from the jail and forced to his knees. The Prefect said, "What was your reason for murdering Shen Hsiu and making Li Chi pay for it with his life? Today the facts have come to light, and the right must prevail." The Prefect shouted to his men to flog the prisoner, and Chang received thirty strokes to begin with, till his flesh was ripped open and the blood came soaking out. Over and over again he was flogged, but he would not confess.

The merchants and the two youths who had been with them shouted at him: "Although Li Chi is dead, we four are still here, and we were with him when he bought your canary for an ounce and a fifth of silver. Who are you going to put the blame on now? If you say it wasn't you who did it, then tell us where the canary came from. Tell the truth: you can't lie your way out of this, and it's no use trying to make excuses."

But Chang continued to defy them, and at last the Prefect roared at him, "The canary is genuine evidence of the theft, and these four are eye-witnesses. If you still refuse to confess, we'll have the finger-press out and torture you." Terrified, Chang had no choice but to confess everything, how he had stolen the canary and cut off Shen Hsiu's head.

"When you had killed him, where did you put the head?" asked the Prefect.

"I was seized by panic," Chang answered, "and seeing a hollow tree nearby I dropped the head into the hole. Then I picked up the bird and went straight to the Wu-lin Gate. There I happened to come across three merchants, with two youths.

They wanted to buy the canary, and I got an ounce and a fifth of silver for it. I took the money home and spent it, and this is the truth."

The Prefect ordered Chang to make his mark on his deposition, and sent men to summon Shen Yü. Then they all proceeded, with Chang under escort, to the willow park to search for the head. Hundreds of people on the streets, all agog, gathered round and followed them to the willow park to look for it. They found that there was indeed a hollow tree, and when they had sawn it down they gave a shout of excitement, for there inside the trunk was a human head. When they examined it they saw it to be completely unaffected by the passage of time.[3] When Shen Yü saw the head he took a close look and recognized it as that of his son. He cried out in a loud voice and fainted to the ground, remaining unconscious for a long time. Then they wrapped the head in a cloth and returned to the prefecture, with Chang still under escort.

"Now that the head has been found," said the Prefect, "the facts are clear and the guilt established." They put a large wooden cangue round Chang's neck, fettered his hands and feet and dragged him off to the condemned cells, where he was put under close guard. The Prefect then put a question to Shen Yü: "Those two Huang brothers, Big Pao and Little Pao: where did they get that human head, when they came to claim the reward? There is some mystery here. Your son's head has been found now: whose head was that?"

Runners were immediately ordered to bring in the Huang brothers for interrogation. Shen Yü led the runners to the Huangs' house in the southern hills. The two brothers were arrested and brought to court, where they were forced to kneel.

"The murderer of Shen Hsiu has been arrested," the Prefect told them, "and Shen Hsiu's head has been recovered. Who was it that you two conspired together to murder, so that you could claim the reward for his head? Confess or you will be tortured!"

Big Pao and Little Pao were dumbfounded and bewildered and could make no reply. The Prefect, enraged, ordered them to be strung up and flogged, but for a long time they refused to confess. But then they were branded with red-hot irons. This was more than they could bear, and they fainted away. When water was spurted over them and they revived, they saw there was nothing for it but to blurt out the truth. "Seeing that our father was old and sick and miserable," they said, "on an evil impulse we got him drunk and cut off his head. We hid it at the edge of the Western Lake near the Lotus House, and then made up a story to claim the reward."

"Where did you bury your father's body?" asked the Prefect. "At the foot of the Southern Peak," they replied. When the brothers were taken there under escort and the ground was dug, there did indeed prove to be a headless corpse buried at the spot. The two men were taken back to the prefecture and the guards reported: "There is indeed a headless corpse, in a shallow grave in the southern hills."

---

3. Decomposition would not set in, it was believed, until the spirit had departed; the spirit was waiting for the murderer to be brought to justice.

"That such a thing should happen!" said the Prefect. "It is a most abominable crime. If there really are such evil men in this world, I want neither to speak nor hear nor write of them. Let them be flogged to death here and now, and we shall be rid of them; how can this evil deed ever be expiated?" He shouted to his men to flog them without keeping count of the strokes. The two brothers were flogged unconscious and revived again many times, then large cangues were placed on them and they were taken off to the condemned cells to be closely guarded.

Shen Yü and the original plaintiffs returned to their homes to await events, while a report on the wrongful execution of Li Chi was at once submitted in the form of a memorial. The Imperial rescript ordered the Board of Punishments and the Censorate to investigate the conduct of the officer of the Grand Court who had originally questioned Li Chi, and to reduce him to the status of commoner and banish him to Ling-nan (in the southernmost province of Kwangtung). Li Chi was declared to have been innocent and wrongfully convicted. The Imperial sympathy was expressed, and his family was granted once thousand strings of cash in compensation and his descendants exempted from compulsory service. Chang, for premeditated murder for gain and for wronging an innocent man, was to be executed in accordance with the law. In view of the seriousness of the crime, the execution was to be performed by the slow process, with two hundred and forty cuts, and his corpse dismembered. The Huang brothers, convicted of patricide for gain, were both without distinction to be executed by the slow process, with two hundred and forty cuts, their corpses dismembered and their heads publicly exposed as a warning. Indeed,

> Heaven, clear and profound, is not to be deceived,
> Before the design appears to you it is already known.
> Do nothing of which you need feel ashamed:
> Who, throughout time, has been allowed to escape?

When the rescript reached the prefecture, officers and executioners and the rest mounted the three criminals on "wooden mules," and it was broadcast throughout the city that in three days' time they were to be executed by the slow process, their corpses dismembered and their heads publicly exposed as a warning.

When Chang's wife heard that her husband was to be sliced to death she went to the execution-ground in the hope of catching a glimpse of him. Who would have thought it possible?—when the executioners were given the signal to start, they all began to slice their victims, and it was indeed a frightful sight: Chang's wife was frightened out of her wits, and she turned to go, her body bent with grief. But by accident she tripped and fell heavily, injuring her whole body, and when she reached home she died. Indeed,

> Store up good deeds and you will meet with good,
> Store up evil and you will meet with evil.
> If you think about it carefully,
> Things usually turn out right.

TS'AO HSÜEH-CH'IN [CAO XUEQIN]

(1715?–1763?)

China

Ts'ao Chan, better known by his courtesy name Ts'ao Hsüeh-ch'in, was born in an aristocratic family in Nanjing Province. His grandfather was appointed by Emperor K'ang-hsi of the Ch'ing Dynasty to a prominent and lucrative official position. After his grandfather's death, his father was appointed successor, but within a short period the Ts'ao family fell out of favor with the new emperor, and the family's properties were confiscated. Consequently, Ts'ao Hsüeh-ch'in, who once lived in sumptuousness, was reduced to poverty. When he was about forty, he started to write *The Dream of the Red Chamber*. According to a generally accepted theory, he wrote only the first eighty chapters; the last forty were contributed by a scholar named Kao E, who took over the project twenty years after Ts'ao Hsüeh-ch'in's death.

The Dream of the Red Chamber, which describes the prosperity and final ruination of an aristocratic clan, is probably based on events in Ts'ao Hsüeh-ch'in's own family. The main thread running through the novel is the love story of Pao-yü, an unconventional son of the Chia family, and Tai-yü, a delicate and sentimental girl. The love story ends tragically: Tai-yü dies on the day when Pao-yü is made to marry another girl and Pao-yü in bitterness goes away to seek refuge in a Buddhist monastery.

The first chapter of the novel sets the tone for the entire work. The mysterious Taoist's "Forget and Be Free Song," ("We all envy the immortals because they are free"), which is about the restrictions of earthly concerns on human wills and the unpredictability of the vicissitudes of worldly matters, may be taken as the theme song for the novel. Probably hinting at the autobiographical nature of the work, the writer plays on the relationship between reality and fictionality: "When fiction turns into fact, fact turns out to be fiction; /Where illusion becomes reality, reality becomes illusion."

from *The Dream of the Red Chamber*

[Chen Shih-yin meets the Stone of Spiritual Understanding]

When the Goddess Nügua undertook to repair the Dome of Heaven, she fashioned at the Great Mythical Mountain under the Nonesuch Bluff 36,501 pieces of stone, each 120 feet high and 240 feet around. Of these she used only 36,500 and left the remaining piece in the shadow of the Green Meadows Peak. However, the divine hands of Nügua had touched off a spark of life in the Stone

Translated and adapted by Chi-chen Wang.

and endowed it with supernatural powers. It was able to come and go as it pleased and change its size and form at will. But it was not happy because it alone had been rejected by the Goddess, and it was given to sighing over its ill fortune.

As it was thus bemoaning its fate one day, it saw coming toward it a Buddhist monk and a Taoist priest, both of uncommon appearance. They were talking and laughing and, when they reached the shadow of the Peak, they sat down by the side of the Stone and continued their conversation. At first they talked about cloud-wrapped mountains and mist-covered seas and the mysteries of immortal life, but presently they changed the topic of their conversation and spoke of the wealth and luxury and the good things of life in the Red Dust.[1] This stirred the earthly strain in the Stone and aroused in it a desire to experience for itself the pleasures of mortal life. Therefore, it addressed the monk and the priest thus:

"Venerable sirs, forgive me for intruding. I could not help overhearing your conversation and I should like very much to have a taste of the pleasures of the Red Dust of which you spoke. Though I am crude in substance, I am not without some degree of understanding or a sense of gratitude. If you, venerable sirs, would be kind enough to take me for a turn in the Red Dust and let me enjoy for a few years its pleasures and luxuries, I shall be grateful to you for eons to come."

"It is true that the Red Dust has its joys," the two immortals answered with an indulgent smile, "but they are evanescent and illusory. Moreover, there every happiness is spoiled by a certain lack, and all good things are poisoned by the envy and covetousness of other men, so that in the end you will find the pleasure outweighed by sorrow and sadness. We do not advise such a venture."

But the fire of earthly desires, once kindled, could not easily be extinguished. The Stone ignored the warning of the immortals and continued to importune them, until the Buddhist monk said to his companion with a sigh, "We have here another instance of Quiescence giving way to Activity and Non-Existence yielding to Existence." Then turning to the Stone, he said, "We shall take you for a turn in the Red Dust if you insist, but don't blame us if you do not find it to your liking."

"Of course not, of course not," the Stone assured them eagerly.

Then the monk said, "Though you are endowed with some degree of understanding, your substance needs improvement. If we take you into the world the way you are, you will be kicked about and cursed like any ordinary stumbling block. How would you like to be transformed into a substance of quality for your sojourn in the Red Dust and then be restored to your original self afterward?"

The Stone agreed, and thereupon the monk exercised the infinite power of the Law and transformed the Stone into a piece of pure translucent jade, oval in shape and about the size of a pendant. The monk held it on his palm and smiled as he said, "You will be treasured now as a precious object, but you still lack real distinguishing marks. A few characters must be engraved upon you so that everyone who sees you will recognize you as something unique. Only then shall we take you down to some prosperous land, where you will enjoy the advantages

---

1. The mortal world.

of a noble and cultured family and all the pleasures that wealth and position can bring."

The Stone was overjoyed on hearing this and asked what characters were to be engraved upon it and where it was to be taken, but the monk only smiled and said, "Don't ask what and where now; you will know when the time comes." So saying, he tucked the Stone in his sleeve and disappeared with the priest to we know not where.

Nor do we know how many generations or epochs it was afterward that the Taoist of the Great Void passed by the Great Mythical Mountain, the Nonesuch Bluff, and the Green Meadows Peak and came upon the Stone, now restored to its original form and substance. Engraved on it was a long, long story. The Taoist read it from beginning to end and found that it was the self-same Stone that was first carried into the Red Dust and then guided to the Other Shore by the Buddhist of Infinite Space and the Taoist of Boundless Time. The story was that of the Stone itself. The land of its descent, the place of its incarnation, the rise and fall of fortunes, the joys and sorrows of reunion and separation—all these were recorded in detail, together with the trivial affairs of the family, the delicate sentiments of the maidens' chambers, and a number of poems and conundrums which one usually finds in such stories. At the end there was this quatrain:

> Without merits that would entitle me to a place in the blue sky,
> In vain have I lived in the Red Dust for so many years.
> These are the events before my birth and after my death—
> Who will transcribe them and give the world my story?

As the material appeared eminently suited for the beguilement of idle moments and the relief of boredom, the Taoist copied it down from beginning to end and gave it the title of *Transcribed by a Priest*. Later, Wu Yü-feng gave it the title of *Dream of the Red Chamber*, while K'ung Mei-ch'i called it *Precious Mirror of Breeze and Moonlight*. Still later, Ts'ao Hsüeh-ch'in studied it for ten years and revised it five times. He divided it into chapters and then composed an analytical couplet for each. He gave it yet another title, *The Twelve Maidens of Chinling*. He also composed a poem on the novel.

> Pages full of unlikely words,
> Handfuls of hot, bitter tears,
> They call the author a silly fool,
> For they know not what he means.

Finally, when "Chih Yen Chai" made still another copy together with a new set of comments in the year *chia-hsu* (1754), he gave it the more appropriate title, *The Story of the Stone*.

Now that the origin of our story has been explained, the reader may turn to what was actually written on the Stone.

In the southeast there was a city named Soochow. The region around Chang-men, one of the city's principal gates, represented one of the foremost centers of wealth and luxury in the Red Dust. Outside Chang-men there was an ancient temple, nicknamed, because of its shape, the Temple of the Gourd. By the side of this temple there lived a member of the gentry by the name of Chen Shih-yin[2] with his wife, Feng-shih.[3] Although not rich, they were one of the well-to-do and respected families of the district.

Shih-yin was a man who cared nothing for fame or fortune. He devoted his time to planting bamboo and watering flowers, sipping wine and writing verses, much after the fashion of the Taoist sages. But unfortunately he lacked one thing to complete his happiness: he was over fifty years of age and had no son. To comfort his old age he had only a three-year-old daughter named Lotus.

One hot summer day, Shih-yin was reading idly in his study. The book dropped from his languid hand and he fell asleep over his desk. He seemed to have traveled far, to some place that he did not recognize. Suddenly he saw a Buddhist monk and a Taoist priest coming in his direction. The Taoist was speaking.

"I am afraid you shouldn't have taken it upon yourself to interfere with the destiny of the Stone. What are you going to do with it?"

"Rest your anxieties," the monk said. "The Stone is, as a matter of fact, involved in a romance that must be enacted on earth. Far from interfering with fate, I am acting as its instrument."

"So another group of spirits have brought upon themselves the curse of incarnation! Where did this drama originate and where is it to be enacted?"

"It is a very amusing story," the monk answered. "As you know, the Stone has been given to wandering about the universe since it acquired supernatural powers. One day it came to the Palace of Vermilion Clouds of the Goddess of Disillusion- ment. And the Goddess, aware of its unique background and destiny, retained it in her service, conferring upon it the title of the Divine Stone Page. Then one day while roaming along the banks of the Ethereal, it came upon a Crimson Flower growing by the side of the Rock of Three Incarnations. The Stone was struck with the great beauty of the fairy plant and assumed the task of caring for it and feeding it daily with sweet dew. Under this tender care, the Crimson Flower thrived and continued to absorb year after year the cosmic essences of Heaven and Earth until it, too, acquired supernatural qualities and transformed itself into a beautiful fairy goddess. The Goddess manifested, however, a solitary nature and perverse spirit. It was her wont to explore the Realm of Parting Sorrow, to feed upon the Fruit of Unfulfilled Love, and drink from the Fountain of Ineffable Sadness. She was grateful for the care lavished upon her by the Stone and was unhappy because she did not know how to repay it. She used to say to herself, 'I can't pay him back in kind since he has no need of sweet dew. Perhaps I can repay him with my tears, should both of us be sent down to the Red Dust.'

"It was an odd thought but it coincided with the earthly desire of the Stone. The result is that both are to be incarnated, together with a number of other spirits who are in one way or another involved, and all will play their parts in a little drama of the Red Dust."

---

2. Homophone for "true matters concealed."   **3.** "Of the Feng family"; cf. *née* Smith.

"It is an odd story indeed," the Taoist said, "I never heard of such a thing as repaying a debt with tears. I imagine the stories of these creatures will be different from the usual 'breeze and moonlight' school."

"Undoubtedly so," the Buddhist answered. "In stories of famous personalities we are usually accorded only the briefest outline of their careers, together with conventional poems by and about them. We are never given any details of their everyday life, what they eat and drink, what they think and say to one another. As to the stories of breeze and moonlight, they all deal with such obvious things as secret meetings and elopements; none venture to describe the real feelings and sentiments that motivate their heroes and heroines. But I have reason to believe that the stories of these creatures will be different, be they good or bad, of subtle sensibilities or gross intemperance."

"I propose," the Taoist said, "that we go down to the mortal world ourselves when the time comes and save a few that are especially worth saving."

"That is what I am thinking myself," the Buddhist answered. "But we must first take the Stone to the Goddess of Disillusionment and have it registered. We must wait until all the spirits involved have descended before we go ourselves. Only half of them have done so now."

Shih-yin heard every word of the conversation and could not resist the urge to break in at this point. "Greetings, immortal masters. I have heard you speak of things I never heard before and which I only half comprehend. Could you elaborate a bit for the benefit of my obtuse mind and thus point the way to salvation?"

"We cannot, unfortunately, divulge the secrets of Heaven," the two immortals replied. "However, if you remember us when the hour comes, you will be able to escape the fiery pits of Hell."

"If you cannot betray the secrets of Heaven," Shih-yin continued, "perhaps you can show me the Stone of which you spoke?"

"That happens to be within your destiny," the monk replied, as he took the Stone from his sleeve and passed it to Shih-yin. It was the same Stone in the shape of a pendant, clear and translucent, but four characters had been engraved upon it: *T'ung ling pao yü* (Precious Jade of Spiritual Understanding). Before Shih-yin could look at the other side, the monk took it from him, saying, "We have reached the Land of Illusion." Then Shih-yin saw before him a great stone arch, across the top of which were engraved four characters: "Great Void Illusion Land." There was a couplet on the two pillars of the central arch, which read:

When the unreal is taken for the real, then the real becomes unreal;
Where non-existence is taken for existence, then existence becomes non-existence.

The two immortals passed through the archway, but when Shih-yin tried to follow them, he suddenly heard a crash as if the mountains had collapsed and the earth parted asunder. He woke with a start and saw nothing but the bright sun beating down on the courtyard and the broad leaves of the plantain tree casting a cool shade. He had forgotten most of his dream.

Just then, the nurse came up with his daughter Lotus in her arms, and Shih-yin was filled with joy and pride as he observed how pretty and lovable she had grown to be. He took the child from the nurse and played with her a while and then took her to the gate to watch a procession pass by. As he was about to enter the house, he saw a Buddhist monk and a Taoist priest coming toward him. The monk was barefooted and his head mangy; the priest was lame and his hair disheveled. When they came near and saw Shih-yin with his daughter in his arms, the Buddhist suddenly burst out crying and said, "Kind donor, what are you carrying that ill-fated creature for? She will only bring misfortune upon her parents." Shih-yin ignored him, taking him for a beggar trying to attract attention. The monk continued, "Give her to me as a sacrifice to Buddha. Give her to me!" Shih-yin was annoyed and was about to retreat into the house when the monk as suddenly burst out laughing and, pointing at Shih-yin, recited the following lines:

> Love and tender care will be of no avail;
> The water caltrop will be blighted by snow.
> Rejoice not even though it be the Feast of Lanterns,
> For you may sorrow at what follows in its wake.[4]

As Shih-yin wondered at the significance of the poem and what manner of men the monk and his companion were, he heard the priest say, "We need not go on together from here. Let each go his own way. When the time comes I shall wait for you at Mount Pei Mang and go with you to the Land of Illusion and do what must be done."

"Excellent," the monk replied. And before Shih-yin could speak to them, both had vanished.

Shih-yin realized then that these were not common beggars and regretted that he had not been more attentive to them. His thoughts were interrupted by the appearance of Chia Yu-tsun,[5] a graduate in poor circumstances who lived next door to him in the Temple of the Gourd. A native of Huchow and of a good but impoverished family, he was on his way to the Capital for the Examinations when he found himself stranded in Soochow. He made a precarious living by selling calligraphic scrolls and inscriptions.

"What has brought you to the gate?" Yu-tsun said by way of greeting.

"Nothing," Shih-yin answered. "I was just trying to quiet this crying daughter of mine. You have come at an opportune time. Please come in and help me while away the long summer day." The nurse relieved Shih-yin of Lotus. Tea was served in the study, but presently Shih-yin had to excuse himself because of the arrival of another guest. Yu-tsun amused himself by browsing through the books on the shelves. Suddenly he heard a voice outside the window. It was a maid picking flowers in the courtyard. She was not particularly pretty, but there was something about her features and the way she carried herself that set her apart from the common run of bondmaids, and Yu-tsun found himself staring at her. As she

---

4. Example of the kind of conundrum in which the future is forecast. Later, under the name of Fragrant Caltrop, Lotus became the much-abused concubine of the crude and bumptious Hsueh Pan, Hsueh being a homophone for "snow." The signifi-

cance of the last two lines is made clear in the pages immediately following.

5. Homophonous with the first three characters of a four-character phrase meaning "disguised in the idiom of the uncultivated."

finished her task and was about to leave, she happened to look up and their eyes met.

"This must be Chia Yu-tsun whom the master has often spoken of," the maid thought to herself. "He is evidently in poor circumstances, but he does not look like one who would remain poor for very long. The master is right in prophesying a bright future for him." So thinking, she could not help turning her head to steal another glance at Yu-tsun as she walked toward the inner court. On his part, Yu-tsun was pleased with the impression he seemed to have made. "She is not an ordinary maidservant," he said to himself. "She seems to appreciate me when few in the world do."

On the night of the Festival of the Harvest Moon, Yu-tsun found himself alone in his quarters in the Temple of the Gourd. He had not forgotten the maid, and on this festive occasion his thoughts again turned to her. The bright moon stimulated his fancies, and he composed a poem on their meeting. Then he sighed as he thought how far he was from realizing his ambitions and he recited aloud the couplet in which the poet compared himself to a piece of jade waiting to be discovered by someone who recognized its real worth. He was overheard by Shih-yin, who had come in just at the moment.

"I see that you are a man of ambition, Brother Yu-tsun," Shih-yin said.

"Oh, no," Yu-tsun replied with an embarrassed smile. "I was only reciting the lines of a former poet. What has brought you here, Brother Shih-yin?"

"Tonight is the Harvest Moon, the Festival of Reunion," Shih-yin said. "It occurred to me that on this occasion you might feel like honoring me with your company. I have prepared a small measure of wine in my study and should be delighted if you would share it with me."

Yu-tsun readily accepted the invitation and went with Shih-yin to his house. At first, host and guest poured the wine in small cups and sipped it slowly, but as their spirits rose and good cheer mounted, they called for larger cups and drank more freely. The sound of flutes and strings came from every house, and overhead the moon shone in full splendor. Yu-tsun, emboldened by the wine, improvised a poem to the moon, the wonder and admiration of all during its phase of fulfillment.

Shih-yin applauded heartily: "I have always said you are not one to remain in obscurity. Your poem is a portent of better things to come. Let me congratulate you!" He filled another cup for Yu-tsun, and the latter drained it in one draught.

"If you will forgive me for the lack of modesty," Yu-tsun said, "I would like to say that I am not without a degree of competence in the sort of compositions that the Examinations require. I think I have a fair chance of success. But my purse is empty and the Capital far away. I shall never be able to save enough for the journey through the sort of drudgery I have been doing."

"Why have you not spoken of this before?" asked Shih-yin. "I have often thought of this matter but have not presumed to speak of it. The Metropolitan Examinations are coming up next year, and you must go to the Capital to exercise your talents. I shall consider it a great honor if you will allow me to take care of your traveling expenses." He told his servant to go in and get fifty ounces of silver and two suits of winter clothes. "The nineteenth is a propitious day," he said. "You can hire a boat and start your westward journey. Next winter, I am sure I shall have the pleasure of congratulating you on your return."

Yu-tsun accepted the silver and clothes without any pretense at refusing. When Shih-yin sent two letters of introduction to him the next day, the servant brought back the report that Yu-tsun had started on his journey before dawn, leaving word with the temple attendant to thank Shih-yin for his kindness and to tell him that he did not believe in fortunetellers and that he had therefore left without waiting for the nineteenth.

Truly, time passes quickly when the days are uneventful. In a twinkling, the New Year had come and gone, and soon it was the fifteenth of the First Moon, the Feast of Lanterns. As Shih-yin had no inclination for the diversions of the season, he asked his servant Huo Chi[6] to take his daughter to see the fireworks and lantern processions. Having to attend to a trivial but necessary call, the hapless servant left Lotus alone for a moment under the shelter of a gate. When he returned, his charge had disappeared. The servant spent most of the night looking for her and when he realized she must have fallen into the hands of a kidnaper, he too disappeared, not having the courage to face his master and mistress. Shih-yin and his wife were deeply stricken by the loss of their only daughter. Crushed by the burden of their grief, first Shih-yin fell sick and then his wife, so that for a time their days were occupied in consulting physicians and fortunetellers.

Blessing seldom comes in two's, and misfortune rarely comes singly. Two months later, on the fifteenth of the third month, a fire broke out in the Temple of the Gourd. Since wood and bamboo were extensively used for hedges and partitions in that region, the fire was soon out of control and spread to the entire street. Shih-yin's house, being next to the temple, was burned to the ground. He talked things over with his wife and decided they should go to live on their farm. But in the years immediately preceding, flood and drought had followed one another, and gangs of bandits sprang up on every hand. Then came the troops, and between their exactions and the depredations of the bandits, life became all but impossible. Under these circumstances, Shih-yin was glad to take his wife's suggestion to sell their farm and go live with her family.

Now Feng Su, Shih-yin's father-in-law, was a small landowner who had done well. He was not of a generous nature and was none too pleased when his daughter and son-in-law came to him as refugees. Fortunately for Shih-yin, he had some money from the sale of his farm and was able to contribute to the household expenses. But he knew little of financial matters, much less how to drive a bargain. So when he asked Feng Su to invest in some property for him, the latter took advantage of his ignorance and pocketed a good part of the funds. In a year or two, his money was gone, and his father-in-law began to complain about his improvidence, his laziness, and extravagant ways. Shih-yin realized too late that he had thrown himself on the mercy of the wrong man. The long period of illness and misfortune aged Shih-yin rapidly. He took on the appearance of a man approaching the end of his days. He was walking one day on the street, leaning on

---

6. Homophone for "trouble begins."

a cane, when he saw a lame Taoist in hemp sandals and tattered rags coming toward him, chanting this song:

> We all envy the immortals because they are free,
> But fame and fortune we cannot forget.
> Where are the ministers and generals of the past and the present?
> Under neglected graves overgrown with weeds.
>
> We all envy the immortals because they are free,
> But gold and silver we cannot forget.
> All our lives we save and hoard and wish for more,
> When suddenly our eyes are forever closed.
>
> We all envy the immortals because they are free,
> But our precious wives we cannot forget.
> They speak of love and constancy while we live,
> But marry again soon enough after we are dead.
>
> We all envy the immortals because they are free,
> But our sons and grandsons we cannot forget.
> Many there are, of doting parents, from ancient times—
> But how few of the sons are filial and obedient!

After hearing this, Shih-yin went up to the Taoist and asked him, "What are you trying to say? All I can get is 'free' and 'forget.' "

"That's all you need to get," the Taoist answered, laughing. "For if you are free, you'll forget, and if you forget, you'll be free. In other words, to forget is to be free and to be free is to forget. That's why I call my song 'Forget and be free.' "

Now Shih-yin had always been a man of great intuitive understanding. He immediately grasped the purport of the Taoist's enigmatic words. "Would you let me elaborate on your theme?" he asked.

"Please do," the Taoist encouraged, and thereupon Shih-yin recited the following lines:

> Dingy rooms and desert halls
>   Were once filled with insignia of rank.
> Fields choked with weeds and blighted trees
>   Were once scenes of dancing and song.
> While here spiders weave their webs between carved beams
>   There they replace window mats with silken gauze.
> Boast not that you wear your powder and rouge well,
>   But grieve that your temples will soon be covered with frost.
> Tonight a pair of cooing doves under red bridal curtains,
>   Tomorrow a heap of bleached bones like those of yesteryear.
> Chests filled with gold, chests filled with silver—
>   In a twinkling, beggars despised by all.
> One moment we grieve over a short-lived friend,
>   The next we are ourselves overtaken by death.
> Careful as we may be with our sons,
>   We cannot be certain they will not turn bandits and thieves.
> We would all bring up our daughters to be ladies,

But who can say that they will not end up in courtesans' quarters?
Discontent with one's position
  May bring chains upon one's feet.
Yesterday, 'twas the coat because it was not warm enough;
  Today, 'tis the dragon robe because it is too long.
What bustle and confusion, as one set of actors exits and another enters,
  Each taking the illusory for the real.
What stupidity; for in the end, in the end
  One only wears out one's fingers for someone else's trousseau.

"Wonderful! Wonderful!" the Taoist exclaimed, clapping his hands, and Shih-yin relieving the Taoist of the sack he was carrying, said, "Let us be on our way!" And so saying, he went off with the priest.

Shih-yin's wife spared no effort in trying to locate her husband, but how can one find a man who wants to be lost? Fortunately she still had the two maids that she had brought with her from Soochow. With their help she was able to contribute to her own support by sewing and embroidering.

LIU E (1857–1909)
China

A native of Tant'u in Kiangsu Province, Liu E was a mathematician, a physician, and an engineer as well as a writer. As a consequence of his drawing up and executing plans for a water conservatory project on the Yellow River, he was appointed to a prefectship. In 1900, when Peking was under the siege of allied forces of the Western powers, the residents of the capital were starving. Liu succeeded in negotiating with the occupying troops and bought grain from a state granary controlled by the Westerners for the purpose of general relief. That action saved many lives but jeopardized his own: a few years later he was accused of illegally selling state grain and was banished to Sinkiang (Xinjiang), a province in the northwest (Chinese Turkestan) where he died.

As a writer, Liu E is known chiefly for his picaresque and semiautobiographical novel *The Travel Records of Lao-ts'an* [hao-ts'an yu-chi], in which he exposes the many social, economic and political problems of the nation and weeps over the decline of the Ch'ing Empire. But Liu E was also a poet, writing in the classical style. "New Year's Eve" reflects the sorrow and misery of his later years, caused by both social conditions and his personal grievances.

New Year's Eve

The north wind blows, cracking the earth,
in sadness, seeing off the old year.

Translated by Jonathan Chaves.

Ch'i Pai-Shih, *Lamp and Mouse.*

The servant announces we're out of rice,
and a creditor has come, asking for money.
A hungry crow caws in evening snow;
a wild goose cuts through cold mist.   5
This is the way my life is now:
others are even worse off.

(1906)

LU HSÜN [LU XUN] (1881–1936)
China

Chou Shu-jen, who is better known by his pen name Lu Hsün, was a native of
Shaohsing in Chechiang Chekiang Province. During his youth, he went to Japan
to study Western medicine, but he shortly thereafter quit medicine and turned to
literature. He believed that it was the mind, not the body, that he should focus on.
He became engaged in translating Western literature into Chinese, mostly from

Japanese translations. After returning to China in 1909, Lu Hsün quickly emerged as a leading essayist and short story writer. His essays, usually short and pithy, are full of scathing satire and trenchant invectives against his opponents. His short stories were his scalpel for cutting at what he thought to be China's social and cultural tumors. Among his stories, "True Story of Ah Q" and "The Diary of a Madman" have been translated into many languages.

The first two decades of this century witnessed in China the so-called "literary revolution," which climaxed around 1919. The vernacular was finally established as the standard medium for literary writing. At the same time, with countless translations of Western literary works, Chinese literary genres were quickly reforming themselves under Western influence. For the first time, "novels" and "short stories," including those by Lu Hsün, fit well with such generic designations imported from the West.

In "My Old Home" Lu Hsün portrays a poor peasant, Jun-t'u, as seen through the eyes of the narrator, a "master" and an intellectual, who returns to his hometown after a twenty-year absence. The writer deplores the economic plight of the peasants and its negative effect on their moral character, but he is not pessimistic about the future of the Chinese peasantry: "It is just like pathways over the land. For actually there were no paths originally, but when many people traveled one way, a road was made."

My Old Home

Braving the bitter cold, I traveled more than seven hundred miles back to the old home I had left over twenty years before.

It was late winter. As we drew near my former home the day became overcast and a cold wind blew into the cabin of our boat, while all one could see through the chinks in our bamboo awning were a few desolate villages, void of any sign of life, scattered far and near under the somber yellow sky. I could not help feeling depressed.

Ah! Surely this was not the old home I had remembered for the past twenty years?

The old home I remembered was not in the least like this. My old home was much better. But if you asked me to recall its peculiar charm or describe its beauties, I had no clear impression, no words to describe it. And now it seemed this was all there was to it. Then I rationalized the matter to myself, saying: Home was always like this, and although it has not improved, still it is not so depressing as I imagine: it is only my mood that has changed, because I am coming back to the country this time without any illusions.

This time I had come with the sole object of saying goodbye. The old house our clan had lived in for so many years had already been sold to another family, and was to change hands before the end of the year. I had to hurry there before New Year's Day to say goodbye forever to the familiar old compound, and to move my family far from the old home town they knew to the other place where I was making a living.

Translated by Yang Hsien-yi and Gladys Yang.

At dawn on the second day I reached the gateway of my home. Broken stems of withered grass on the roof, trembling in the wind, made it very clear why this old house would inevitably change hands. Several branches of our clan had probably already moved away, so it was unusually quiet. By the time I reached our own house my mother was already at the door to welcome me, and my eight-year-old nephew, Hung-erh, rushed out after her.

Though Mother was delighted, she was also trying to hide a certain feeling of sadness. She told me to sit down, rest, have some tea, and not discuss the business of moving just yet. Hung-erh, who had never seen me before, stood watching me at a distance.

But finally we had to talk about moving. I said that I had already rented a place elsewhere, and I had bought a little furniture. In addition, it would be necessary to sell all the furniture in the house in order to buy more things. Mother agreed, saying that the luggage was nearly all packed, and about half the furniture that could not easily be moved had already been sold. Only it was difficult to collect the money for it.

"You must rest for a day or two, and call on our relatives to pay your respects. Then we can go," said Mother.

"That's fine."

"Then there is Jun-t'u. Each time he comes here he asks about you, and wants very much to see you again. I told him the probable date of your return home, and he may be coming any time."

At this point a strange picture suddenly flashed into my mind: a golden moon suspended in a deep blue sky and beneath it the seashore, planted as far as the eye could see with jade-green watermelons. In their midst a boy of eleven or twelve, wearing a silver necklet and grasping a steel pitchfork in his hand, was thrusting with all his might at a zha[1] which dodged the blow and escaped between his legs.

This boy was Jun-t'u. When I first met him he was just over ten—that was thirty years ago. At that time my father was still alive and the family well off, so I was really a "young master." That year it was our family's turn to take charge of a big ancestral sacrifice, which came around only once in thirty years or more, and so was an important one. In the first month the ancestral images were presented and offerings made, and since the sacrificial vessels were very fine and there was such a crowd of worshippers, it was necessary to guard against theft. Our family had only one part-time laborer. (In our district we divide laborers into three classes. Those who are hired by the day are called dailies; and those who farm their own land and only work for one family at New Year, during festivals, or when rents are being collected are called part-timers.) And since there was so much to be done, he told my father that he would send for his son Jun-t'u to look after the sacrificial vessels.

When my father gave his consent I was overjoyed, because I had long since

---

1. A word invented by Lu Hsün for a kind of animal which most commentators have taken to mean "badger."

heard of Jun-t'u and knew that he was about my own age, born in the intercalary month.[2] When his horoscope was told it was found that of the five elements, the earth element was lacking, so his father called him Jun-t'u, "Intercalary Earth." He could set traps and catch small birds.

I looked forward every day to New Year, for New Year would bring Jun-t'u. At last, one day when the end of the year came, Mother told me that Jun-t'u had come, and I flew to see him. He was standing in the kitchen. He had a round, ruddy face and wore a small felt cap on his head and a gleaming silver necklet around his neck. From this it was obvious that his father doted on him and, fearing he might die, had made a pledge with the gods and Buddhas, using the necklet as a talisman. He was very shy, and I was the only person he was not afraid of. When there was no one else there, he would talk with me, so in a few hours we were close friends.

I don't know what we talked of then, but I remember that Jun-t'u was in high spirits, saying that since he had come to town he had seen many new things.

The next day I wanted him to catch birds.

"I can't do it," he said. "It's only possible after a heavy snowfall. On our sands, after it snows, I sweep clear a patch of ground, prop up a big threshing basket with a short stick, and scatter husks of grain beneath. When the birds come there to eat, I tug on a long, long string tied to the stick, and the birds are caught in the basket. There are all kinds: wild pheasants, woodcocks, wood-pigeons, 'blue-backs' . . ."

Accordingly I really hoped it would snow.

"Just now it's too cold," said Jun-t'u another time, "but you must come to our place in summer. In the daytime we'll go to the seashore to look for shells and 'Buddha hands.' In the evening when dad and I go to see the watermelons, you'll come along too."

"Is it to look out for thieves?"

"No. If passersby are thirsty and pick a watermelon, folk down our way don't consider it stealing. What we have to look out for are badgers, hedgehogs, and *zha*. When under the moonlight you hear the crunching sound made by the *zha* when it bites the melons, then you take your pitchfork and creep stealthily over . . ."

I had no idea then what this thing called *zha* was—and I am not much clearer now for that matter—but somehow I felt it was something like a small dog, and very fierce.

"Don't they bite people?"

"You have a pitchfork. You go across, and when you see it you strike. It's a very cunning creature and will rush toward you and get away between your legs. Its fur is as slippery as oil . . ."

I had never known that all these fresh and exciting things existed: at the seashore there were shells all colors of the rainbow; watermelons were exposed to

---

2. The Chinese lunar calendar reckons three hundred and sixty days to a year, and each month comprises twenty-nine or thirty days, never thirty-one. Hence every few years a thirteenth, or intercalary, month is inserted in the calendar.

such danger, yet all I had known of them before was that they were sold in the fruit and vegetable shop.

"On our shore, when the tide comes in, there are lots of jumping fish, each with two legs like a frog . . ."

Jun-t'u's mind was a treasure house of such strange lore, all of it unknown to my other friends. They were ignorant of all these things and, while Jun-t'u lived by the sea, they like me could see only the four corners of the sky above the high courtyard wall.

Unfortunately, a month after New Year Jun-t'u had to go home. I was so upset I burst into tears and he hid in the kitchen, crying and refusing to come out, until finally his father carried him off. Later he had his father bring me a packet of shells and a few very beautiful feathers, and I sent him presents once or twice, but we never saw each other again.

Now that my mother mentioned him, this childhood memory sprang into life like a flash of lightning, and I seemed to see my beautiful old home. So I answered:

"Fine! And he—how is he?"

"He? Things aren't going very well for him," said Mother. And then, looking out of the door: "Here come those people again. They say they want to buy our furniture: but actually they'll casually walk off with something. I must go and watch them."

Mother stood up and went out. The voices of several women could be heard outside. I called Hung-erh to me and started talking to him, asking him whether he could write, and whether he would be glad to leave.

"Are we going to take the train?"

"Yes, we're going to take the train."

"And a boat?"

"First we'll take a boat."

A strange shrill voice suddenly rang out:

"Looking like this! With such a long moustache!"

I looked up with a start, and saw a woman of about fifty with prominent cheekbones and thin lips standing in front of me. With her hands on her hips, not wearing a skirt but with her trousered legs apart, she seemed just like a thin, spindly-legged compass in a box of geometrical instruments.

I was really startled.

"Don't you know me? Why, I have held you in my arms!"

I was even more taken aback. Fortunately my mother came in just then and broke in:

"He's been away so long, you must excuse his forgetting. You should remember," she said to me, "this is Mrs. Yang from across the road. She has a beancurd shop."

Then, of course, I remembered. When I was a child there was a Mrs. Yang who used to sit nearly all day long in the beancurd shop across the road, and everybody used to call her Beancurd Beauty. She used to powder herself, and her cheekbones were not so prominent then or her lips so thin; besides, she sat there the whole day, so that I had never noticed this resemblance to a compass. In those days people said that, thanks to her, that beancurd shop did a very good business.

But, probably on account of my age, she had made no impression on me, so that later I forgot her entirely. However, the Compass was extremely indignant and looked at me contemptuously, just as one might look at a Frenchman who had never heard of Napoleon or an American who had never heard of Washington. Smiling sarcastically she said:

"You had forgotten? Naturally I am beneath your notice."

"Certainly not . . . . I . . . ." I answered nervously, getting to my feet.

"Then you listen to me, Master Hsün. You have grown rich, and they are too heavy to move, so you can't possibly want these worn-out pieces of furniture anymore. You had better let me take them away. Poor people like us can make use of them."

"I haven't grown rich. I must sell these in order to buy—"

"Oh, come now, you have been made the intendant of a circuit; how can you still say you're not rich? Hah! You can't hide anything from me."

I knew there was nothing I could say, so I kept quiet and just stood still there.

"Come now, really, the more money people have the more miserly they get, and the more miserly they are the more money they get," jabbered the Compass, as she turned away indignantly and walked slowly off, casually picking up a pair of my mother's gloves and stuffing them into her pocket as she left.

After this a number of relatives in the neighborhood came to call. In the intervals between entertaining them I did some packing, and so three or four days passed.

One very cold afternoon, I sat drinking tea after lunch when I was aware of someone coming in, and turned my head to see who it was. At the first glance I gave an involuntary start, hastily stood up, and went over to welcome him.

The newcomer was Jun-t'u. But although I knew at a glance that this was Jun-t'u, it was not the Jun-t'u I remembered. He had grown to twice his former size. His round face, once ruddy, had become sallow and now had deep lines and wrinkles: his eyes too were like his father's, the rims swollen and red. I knew that most peasants who work by the sea and are exposed all day to the wind from the ocean were like this. He wore a shabby felt cap and just a very thin padded jacket, and was shivering from head to foot. He carried a package wrapped in paper and a long pipe. His hands were not the plump red hands I remembered, but coarse and clumsy and chapped, like the bark of a pine tree.

I was delighted, but I didn't know what words to use, so I only said:

"Oh! Jun-t'u—so it's you? . . ."

There were so many things then to talk about that I wanted to spew them out like a string of beads: woodcocks, jumping fish, shells, *zha* . . . But something seemed to hold me back. Everything just swirled around in my head and I couldn't get the words out.

He stood there, joy and sadness both showing on his face. His lips moved, but not a sound did he utter. Finally, assuming a respectful attitude, he said clearly:

"Master!"

I felt a shiver run through me, for I knew then what a lamentably thick wall had grown up between us. Yet I could not say anything.

He turned his head to call:

"Shui-sheng, bow to the master." Then he pulled forward a boy who had been hiding behind his back, and this was just the Jun-t'u of twenty years before, only a little paler and thinner, and he had no silver necklet.

"This is my fifth," he said. "He hasn't had any experience with social occasions, so he's shy and awkward."

Mother came downstairs with Hung-erh, probably after hearing our voices.

"I got your letter some time ago, madam," said Jun-t'u. "I was really so pleased to know the master was coming back."

"Now, why are you so polite? Didn't you consider yourselves brothers in the past?" said Mother gaily. "Why don't you still call him Brother Hsün as you used to?"

"Oh, you are really too . . . What bad manners that would be. I was a child then and didn't understand." As he was speaking Jun-t'u motioned Shui-sheng to come and bow, but the child was shy, and stood stock still behind his father.

"So he is Shui-Sheng? Your fifth?" asked Mother. "We are all strangers, you can't blame him for feeling shy. Hung-erh had better take him out to play."

When Hung-erh heard this he went over to Shui-sheng, and Shui-sheng went out with him, entirely at his ease. Mother asked Jun-t'u to sit down, and after a little hesitation he did so; then, leaning his long pipe against the table, he handed over the paper package, saying:

"In winter there is nothing worth bringing: but these few green beans we dried ourselves, if you will excuse the liberty, sir."

When I asked him how things were with him, he just shook his head.

"In a very bad way. Even my sixth can do a little work, but still we haven't enough to eat . . . and then there is no security . . . all sorts of people want money, there is no fixed rule . . . and the harvests are bad. You grow things, and when you take them to sell you always have to pay several taxes and lose money, while if you don't try to sell, the things will only spoil . . ."

He kept shaking his head: yet, although his face was lined with wrinkles, not one of them moved, just as if he were a stone statue. No doubt he felt intensely bitter, but could not openly express himself. After a pause he took up his pipe and began to smoke in silence.

From her chat with him, Mother learned that he was busy at home and had to go back the next day; and since he had had no lunch, she told him to go to the kitchen and fry some rice for himself.

After he had gone out, Mother and I both shook our heads over his hard life; many children, famines, taxes, soldiers, bandits, officials, and landed gentry, all had been so hard on him that he seemed a wooden image of a man. Mother said that we should offer him all the things we didn't need to take with us, letting him choose for himself.

That afternoon he picked out a number of things: two long tables, four chairs, an incense burner and candlesticks, and a balance. He also asked for all the ashes from the stove (in our region we cook over straw, and the ashes can be used to fertilize sandy soil), saying that when we left he would come to take them away by boat.

That night we talked again, but not of anything serious; and the next morning he went away with Shui-sheng.

After another nine days it was time for us to leave. Jun-t'u came in the morning. Shui-sheng did not come with him—he had just brought a little girl of five to watch the boat. We were very busy all day, and had no time to talk. We also had quite a number of visitors, some to see us off, some to fetch things, and some to do both. It was nearly evening when we left by boat, and by that time everything in the house, however old or shabby, large or small, fine or coarse, had been cleared out.

As we set off, in the dusk, the green mountains on either side of the river became deep blue, receding toward the stern of the boat.

Hung-erh and I, leaning against the cabin window, were both watching the indistinct scene outside, when suddenly he asked:

"Uncle, when shall we go back?"

"Go back? Do you mean that before you've left you want to go back?"

"Well, Shui-sheng has invited me to his home . . ." He opened wide his black eyes, engrossed in thought.

Mother and I both felt rather sad, and so Jun-t'u's name came up again. Mother said that ever since our family started packing up, Mrs. Yang from the beancurd shop had come over every day, and the day before in the ash-heap she had unearthed a dozen bowls and plates, which after some discussion she insisted must have been buried there by Jun-t'u, so that when he came to remove the ashes he could take them home at the same time. After making this discovery Mrs. Yang was very pleased with herself, and flew off taking the dog-teaser with her. (The dog-teaser is used by poultry keepers in our parts. It is a wooden cage inside which food is put, so that hens can stretch their necks in to eat but dogs can only look on furiously.) And it was a marvel, considering the thick-soled shoes on her bound feet, how fast she could run.

I was leaving the old house farther and farther behind, while the hills and rivers of my old home were also receding gradually ever farther in the distance. But I felt no regret. I only felt that all around me was an invisible high wall, cutting me off from others, and this depressed me thoroughly. The vision of that small hero with the silver necklet among the watermelons had formerly been as clear as day, but now it suddenly blurred, adding to my depression.

Mother and Hung-erh fell asleep.

I lay down, listening to the water rippling beneath the boat, and knew that I was going my own way. I thought: although there is such a barrier between Jun-t'u and myself, the children still have much in common, for wasn't Hung-erh thinking of Shui-sheng just now? I hope they will not be like us, that they will not allow a barrier to grow up between them. Then again, I wouldn't want them, because they want to be alike, to have a treadmill existence like mine nor to suffer like Jun-t'u until they become stupefied, nor yet, like others, to lead a cruel life of dissipation. They should have a new life, a life we never experienced.

The thought of hope made me suddenly afraid. When Jun-t'u asked for the incense burner and candlesticks I had laughed at him to myself, to think that he still worshipped idols and could not put them out of his mind. Yet what I now called hope, wasn't it nothing more than an idol I had created myself? The only difference was that what he desired was close at hand, while what I desired was less easily realized.

As I dozed, a stretch of jade-green seashore spread itself before my eyes, and above a round golden moon hung in a deep blue sky. I thought: hope cannot be said to exist, nor can it be said not to exist. It is just like pathways over the land. For actually there were no paths originally, but when many people traveled one way, a road was made.

MAO TSE-TUNG [MAO ZEDONG]
(1893–1976)
China

Mao Tse-tung is known throughout the world as the leader of the Chinese Communist revolution. Born into a well-to-do peasant's family in Hsiang-t'an County in Hunan Province, Mao was trained to be a teacher, but he soon gave up his profession to become a revolutionary. With his political skills and military talents, he rose to leadership of the Communist Party in 1935, a time during which the Red Army was being all but eliminated by the Nationalist government. In 1949 the Chinese Communists led by Mao became strong enough to drive the Nationalists to the island of Taiwan and the People's Republic was founded on the mainland of the nation. In today's China, while Mao is still eulogized for leading the Communist revolution to triumph, he is accused of launching the disastrous Cultural Revolution in 1966, which did not end until after his death ten years later.

Most of Mao's poems conform to the classical *tz'u* tradition. They follow a specific pattern called the *tiao* or "tune," for they were originally set to music. "Loushan Pass" was written in the 1930s, when Mao was leading the Red Army against Nationalist troops. "Tune: 'Spring in [Princess] Ch'in's Garden'" was written in the 1940s as an expression of Mao's ambitions and aspirations as a political leader.

Tune: "Spring in [Princess] Ch'in's Garden"

Northern landscape,
Thousand miles around covered by ice,
Ten thousand miles under snowdrifts.
    On both sides of the Great Wall,
    I see vast wastes;
    Up and down the Great River
    Suddenly the torrents are still; 5

Translated by Eugene Eoyang.

Mountains wind around like silver serpents,
High headlands ramble about like waxen elephants,
On the verge of challenging heaven.   10
    A sunny day is best
    For watching the red against the white:
    Extraordinary enchantment.

The rivers and mountains have this special charm
That inspires countless heroes to great deeds.   15
Pity the First Sovereign and the Martial Emperor
        Had small talent for literature,
And the founding fathers of T'ang and Sung
        Lacked both grace and charm.
In his own generation—favored by heaven—   20
        Genghis Khan
Knew only how to bend the bow, bringing down the great vulture.
    All these are gone now,
To single out the men of high character,
We must look to now; the present.   25

Loushan Pass*

Fierce west wind,
Geese call in the open air, there's frost under the morning moon,
                        frost under the morning moon
        Shattering sounds of horses' hooves
        And of the bugles' wail.   5

Do not say the mountain pass is like steel,
For today we have marched right up to the summit,
                        right up to the summit,
        Atop green hills like the sea,
        Under a dying sun like blood.   10

PING HSIN [BING XIN] (b. 1902)
China

Ping Hsin is the pen name of Hsieh Wan-ying, a poet, essayist, and short-story
writer. She was born in Fuchien Province and her father was an officer in the

*Translated by Eugene Eoyang.

navy. Upon finishing her undergraduate studies at Yenching University in Beijing, she went to the United States to study literature at Wellesley College. In 1926 she received her master's degree and returned to China. Because of her prolific and versatile literary career, Ping Hsin is considered one of the most respected writers of this century in China.

Ping Hsin's career as a writer started during the time that the literary revolution was triumphantly ending. Her first short story appeared in 1919, and two years later she began to publish her short poems. By that time, the classical style of versification with its rigid formal regulations had been largely replaced by the so-called "New Poetry," a vernacular free verse with few restrictions on the rhyme and rhythm. "Deliverance" vividly represents this poetic style.

Deliverance

Moonlight, clear as water,
I pace the ground under a tree
In deep, deep thought.
Deep in thought, I pick up a fallen twig
To tap, with a sigh, my own shadow   5
On the moonlit ground.

Life—
Everybody treats it as a dream,
A blurred dream.
My friend,   10
As you try to find clear lines in the blurred world,
Your life's suffering
Thus begins!

You may treasure life's snow-white robe,
Yet life has to cross   15
The immense sea of darkness.
My friend,
The world does not abandon you,
Why should you abandon the world?

Let life stand alone and noble like a stork,   20
Free as a cloud,
And pure and calm as water,
Even if life were a dream,
Let it be a clear dream.

In deep, deep thought—   25
Deep in thought, I throw away the fallen twig.

Translated by Kai-yu Hsu.

Quietly and calmly I gaze at my shadow
On the moonlit ground.

(1923)

HUANG CH'UN-MING [HUANG CHUNMING] (b. 1939)
Taiwan

Huang Ch'un-ming, a native of I-lan, a small coastal town in northeastern Taiwan, began his higher education at a college in Taipei. After a series of transfers, he ended up graduating from Pingtung Normal College in southern Taiwan. Huang Ch'un-ming is a writer of broad interests and remarkable versatility, but he is first of all a short story writer. During the 1960s as a major contributor to the influential *Literature Quarterly,* Huang was hailed as a representative of *hsiang-t'u wen-hsueh,* the so-called indigenous literature that centers on rural life. In his more recent works, however, Huang has turned his attention more toward urban culture.

"The Drowning of an Old Cat" is a short story that bears the stamp of indigenous literature. Its theme is a typical one in developing nations: the conflict between rural and urban life, between the traditional and the modern. The residents of Clear Spring Village, aroused by Uncle Ah-sheng, attempt to resist the encroachment of urban culture represented by a nearby community where a swimming pool is to be constructed on the village's Dragon-Eye Well. The attempt to prevent the construction has failed, and Uncle Ah-sheng issues a final protest against the ruthless god of modernization by drowning himself in the newly built pool. His death, however, has as little impact as the drowning of an old cat, for children are soon afterward splashing and frolicking in the pool. Echoes of Ibsen's *Enemy of the People* reverberate throughout the story.

The Drowning of an Old Cat

1. THE LAY OF THE LAND

The out-of-the-way county in this story has been designated by the Taiwan provincial government as a developing area. Its urban center is a small town of forty or fifty thousand people. When the town youth are in the presence of people from the outlying countryside, they habitually put on airs of self-importance to show that they are urbanites; the somewhat older people, with their greater understanding of humility, will go no further than to nod their heads with slightly

Translated by Howard Goldblatt.

superior smiles on their faces. People from the countryside cheerfully and loudly tell anyone within earshot stories of their daughters who have married men from town. And even though the ears of the listeners ring with this barrage of talk, they feel it only proper, for were they to have an eligible young daughter, she too would leave the farm and marry a townsman (so they think). Even greater glory comes to someone whose son brings a townswoman back to the farm as his wife, for no matter how their lives together turn out in the end, at least in the beginning there is a great deal of loud, enthusiastic talk.

This urban center is only about seventy or eighty kilometers from the nearest big city, and transportation to and from the city—by train or by car—is extremely convenient. The roads are well traveled every day, for a round trip takes no more than four hours; a person can go to the city, take care of his business, and return home all in the same day. As a result, many big-city fads find their way to this urban center. Miniskirts that come to a point twenty centimeters above the knee are displayed on girls of the town, and go-go dancing is very popular at the parties held by the town's youth. As for their elders, the fear of death has become a fashionable trend, with an emphasis on the beneficial effects self-awareness has on one's health.

Someone had recently discovered a number of young children swimming in a spring in the village of Clear Spring, and before long, men with expanding pot bellies and respectable positions in society got up at the crack of dawn and drove over to Clear Spring Village to soak themselves in the spring. Later, when they discovered that they were able to take in their belts one hole after another, their numbers increased. They were so diligent about coming that not even inclement weather stopped them. After a while, in addition to soaking in the water, they were all able to propel themselves a bit through the water, more or less in the fashion of swimming. Among them were physicians, senior bank officials, lawyers, school principals, assemblymen, businessmen, and many others. Nearly every member of the local Rotary Club participated, except for David and Tom, one of whom had an artificial leg, the other a case of congenital rickets.

Clear Spring Village had gotten its name from a spring the size of two parcels of land that was in the middle of the village and was under the jurisdiction of the local Water Control Board. Actually, if one were to dig a hole three to four or perhaps five to six feet deep anywhere in Clear Spring Village, a bubbling spring of sweet water would rise to the surface in a continuous flow.

The sixty or more households who live here are as pure and simple as the spring water that flows to the surface; there is little difference between them and the unbroken gush of spring water as they diligently till the more than forty parcels of land they own, plus the side of Ku-tzu Hill. There has never been a drought over the farmland here, yet for many years the place has been an impoverished area, which is the prime reason for the people's pure and simple nature. Though no more than two and a half kilometers separate them from the urban center, since the road to town crosses the hill and is fairly steep, and since there is no busline between the two places, the townspeople feel that Clear Spring Village is a great distance away.

2. THE SKY IS FALLING

In the year when the Temple of the Patriarch was erected, a banyan tree had been planted beside it; now that more than sixty years had passed, fully half of the more than four thousand square feet of temple ground lay in the shade of this banyan tree. On the portion of the red-tiled temple roof that stood under the shade day in and day out, year after year, a carpet of deep green moss and grass flourished, while on the other half the aged red tiles were in full, sunlit view. For this reason the people referred to the Clear Spring Village Temple of the Patriarch as the Yin-Yang Temple, or the Temple of Dark and Light. This long process of change was mirrored in Uncle Ah-sheng and four or five other old-timers who lived in the village, as they had grown old watching the gradual change take place. In earlier days they had hitched rides on the back of the oxcart that carried bricks used to build the temple, getting an occasional taste of the carter's whip. Now they were the oldest people in the village, and on every temple festival the duties and activities of the villagers were under the direction of these few men, led by Uncle Ah-sheng.

But temple festivals only came around a few times a year, and during the remaining long days these old timers congregated in one of the temple's siderooms. In the winter they secured the door, each of them carrying a small heater to keep himself warm; in the summertime they swung the door open and availed themselves of the cool breezes that passed through the sideroom and carried up to the heavens the fragrant smoke of incense from the black joss sticks that symbolized the people's devotion. For the most part these men talked of the past, and even though their talk was very repetitious, they never tired of it. With great fondness they recalled those early days when they had struggled with poverty. Memories of the past are always fond ones, and this was especially true for these men in their twilight years for whom only their pasts gave them feelings of pride. For them tomorrow was a big question mark; who could say that tomorrow would not be the day they stopped coming to the temple? This was evident in that last year there had been seven or eight of them, and now, a mere year later, their number had been cut almost in half.

The stone block just inside the door pillar to the left had originally been Uncle T'ien-sung's seat, but it had lost its source of warmth and now just stood there in icy coldness. After T'ien-sung had departed, Uncle Huo-shu selected this seat for his own and sat on it for a single day. That night T'ien-sung appeared at the head of Huo-shu's bed in a dream, angrily demanding the return of his stone-block seat. From that day on, Uncle Huo-shu was bothered by a case of hemorrhoids, until everyone in the village knew about the incident. His hemorrhoids eventually became extremely painful; he took dozens of medications and applied dozens of ointments, but even the generations-old nostrum of the K'un-t'ien family had no effect. Finally he heeded the advice of several old friends and dragged his half-dead body over to T'ien-sung's spirit tablet, where he burned incense and offered his apologies. Uncle Ah-sheng, in his role as eldest among them, stood in front of the spirit tablet and upbraided T'ien-sung: "T'ien-sung, when you were alive you were open-minded, so why have you become such a short-tempered ghost? You and I and Huo-shu and the others are old friends who grew up together in Clear Spring Village from the time we were all wearing pants with split crotches. Now, just because he sat on your stone block, your meanness has brought him to death's doorstep. The fact of the matter is, that stone block doesn't belong to you. Since it's inside the temple, it belongs to the Patriarch. . ." At first many of the startled villagers present paled when they heard this, for it was as though Uncle T'ien-sung were actually there among them accepting Uncle Huo-shu's apologies and being scolded by Uncle Ah-sheng.

Strange as it sounds, within a week Uncle Huo-shu's hemorrhoids inexplicably disappeared. But then two months later he simply up and died. Naturally no one else ever again dared to sit on the stone block, and in the minds of the Clear Spring villagers this stone block had already been given a special name as a warning—hemorrhoid stone.

Only when he had an important matter that required his attention would one of these old-timers willingly miss passing the time of day with the others in the temple sideroom. Their number had diminished to four or five, and when they talked among themselves, no explanation of what was being said was ever needed. Their interests and topics of conversation were entirely compatible. And so, coming to the temple to chat right after lunchtime had become a big part of their lives.

On this particular afternoon, Uncle Cow's Eye, Uncle Earthworm, Uncle Yü-tsai, and Uncle Ah-ch'uan were all there; only Uncle Ah-sheng had not yet arrived. Usually he was the first on the scene, and even if he had to be late, one would think that by three o'clock at least he would have shown up. The others were soon so worried and uncomfortable that they were unable to talk about anything for more than a few moments.

"I hope nothing's happened to him," someone said uneasily.

"I saw him leading his ox out to Grass Canal to graze this morning."

"How could that be? I took my own ox out to Grass Canal this morning and I didn't see him there. But I did see you walking along the canal down to the end."

"Oh, right! That wasn't this morning, it was yesterday," the old-timer said, quickly acknowledging his forgetfulness.

"Could he be sick?"

"I don't think so. He was just fine yesterday. This morning when I was out at Grass Canal with my ox I ran into his eldest daughter-in-law with an armful of clothes she was taking out to wash. She would have told me if he was sick." He paused, then added: "But she didn't say a word, so there can't be anything wrong."

"Well, that's strange! He couldn't have just disappeared, could he?" A momentary smile appeared on Cow's Eye's face, but then faded away as a brief silence fell over the group of men.

"Oh shit, that's right!" Earthworm suddenly blurted out. "Didn't he say just the day before yesterday that he was going into town to find a divinator to select the right date to rebuild his stove? He said that the firewood burned too hot."

"Ah-ha, now I remember!" Ah-ch'uan's lips parted momentarily into a broad grin before he continued: "This old noggin of mine's like a stone in the field—it oughta be thrown away. This morning I bumped into into him by the well just as he was setting out for town."

"Well I'll be damned! Is that the truth?"

"You said it—just another stone in the field!" Uncle Yu-tsai cursed him, half in jest.

"Still, if he went to town to select a date he should have gotten back by now!"

"Do you think he might have dropped dead on some whorehouse bed?" Earthworm asked with growing interest.

"Shit! That'd be the way to go—the old fart."

"You're not so young yourself."

"That's right! I'm saying we're all old farts—right?"

Without Uncle Ah-sheng in their midst it was as though they were missing their leavening agent, so their conversation never really got started. Most of what they had talked about in the past had been subjects he had introduced. As the day grew later they all dozed off in the refreshing cool breeze.

On the magnificent tree that stood near the west sideroom—that large banyan tree—the ripe figs were bright purple, since it was just in the fruit-bearing month of June; the slightest bump sent them falling, splattering as they hit the ground. Beneath the tree there was already a blanket of crushed figs that gave off a sickly sweet, slightly acrid but generally pleasant aroma. A group of lively birds was hopping from branch to branch singing songs that sounded like delicate fingers flowing across piano keys in a musical run. The ripe fruit beat out a rhythmical background as it fell to the ground—*splat, splat*. The twin six-year-old grandsons whom Earthworm had brought along with him each sat astride one of the stone lions at the temple entrance, both of them fast asleep, their arms draped tightly around the lions' necks.

Uncle Ah-sheng was hurrying home from town. His heart felt as though it were burning a hole in his chest, and the faster he tried to make the return trip to Clear Spring, the longer the road seemed, as though there were something deliberately delaying his return. He grumbled to himself along the way: "Won't this be the end of Clear Spring? I won't let them get away with this, I absolutely won't allow it! I'll hurry home and tell the others." He went down the road as fast as he could; after K'un-ch'ih's farm came Mute's farm, followed by Red Turtle's farm. After Red Turtle's farm there was Dragon-Eye Well and Clear Spring's public school. When Uncle Ah-sheng drew up alongside Dragon-Eye, the village's natural spring well, after having made a point of cutting across to take a look at the well and the area surrounding it, he muttered angrily to himself: "If we let the people in town get away with this, it'll be the end of Clear Spring's geography. What a mean, vicious thing to do! This is a matter as great as heaven and earth itself, and they've made up their minds just like that! Damn!" He quickly turned on his heel and ran to the temple.

The moment Uncle Ah-sheng strode into the western sideroom of the Temple of the Patriarch he shouted at the top of his lungs: "Hey! Let's see how long the Demon of Sleep can keep you in his power!"

The men were startled to their senses by this unexpected and unusual shout.

Then when they saw his appearance they knew that something important and inauspicious was in the air; otherwise, that red birthmark on the side of his face would surely not have lost color like that. A quick glance showed that he was so winded that his nostrils could not handle his breathing, and his parted lips were trembling wildly.

"Why the hell do you have to yell so loud?" Earthworm said angrily after having been frightened awake. But when he saw that Ah-sheng's expression was different than usual, he changed his tone to say with growing interest: "We thought you'd wound up in the whorehouse on the other side of town and decided not to come back." He wiped the saliva that had run down the side of his mouth while he was asleep.

"What took you so long?" Ah-ch'uan asked.

Ah-sheng suddenly spread himself out in a bamboo chair, but the moment his back touched the back of the chair he sprang up into a sitting position and said: "We simply cannot allow them to do this—it'll be the end of our Clear Spring." This time he spread open his arms and lay all the way back in the chair, giving the impression of one who had expended his last bit of energy in uttering these few words.

The others just looked at one another until Earthworm said anxiously: "What's going on with you, old man? Since you've brought home some bad news, you'll have to make things clear to us if you want us to share your concern! Isn't that right? All you did was say two words—'the end!'—then just stretched out there. What's happened?"

The several pairs of eyes that had been riveted on Earthworm shifted over to Uncle Ah-sheng, who breathed a long sigh.

"The people in town want to come out and dig up Clear Spring's Dragon-Eye." Everyone froze when they heard this.

"What does that mean?"

"It means that those people who come here every day to swim in our spring have scraped up three hundred thousand dollars to build a swimming pool next to our village well." Ah-sheng looked at the others, who had been stunned just a moment before, only to observe that his revelation had produced no effect at all. Quickly growing irritated, he said: "What's this! Aren't any of you concerned?"

"What's wrong with having a swimming pool?" Ah-ch'uan asked.

"What *isn't* wrong with having a swimming pool? First, it'll ruin our geography here. Have you forgotten that the only reason this Clear Spring of ours is such a terrific place is because we've got Dragon-Eye Well? My grandfather told me so when I was just a boy."

"Sure, everyone knows that. But what difference will it make if they build a swimming pool alongside the well?"

"You see what I'm saying! Cow's Eye, you've got no reason to be angry when people laugh at you for being a fool. Just think! They'll have to draw water for that swimming pool from the well by motor, and if they draw it dry, what are we gonna do with a dried-up well? Won't that be the end of Clear Spring?"

They all looked at one another and nodded their heads.

"That's right," Cow's Eye said. "This is a serious matter."

"Have you all forgotten that year when the big typhoon hit and somebody threw a bale of straw down the well? Don't you remember how the eyes of everyone in the village, young and old, began to hurt as a result? Luckily that time it was only some straw. If it had been balls of thorns[1] probably everybody in Clear Spring would have dropped dead!" Observing that looks of distress were beginning to show on their faces, Ah-sheng began to experience the grim satisfaction he had expected. "You see what I'm saying." Ah-sheng had a habit of prefacing his remarks with this phrase or uttering it whenever he was about to make a positive concluding remark. "How'll we ever be able to put up with a motor in Dragon-Eye?"

"Are you telling us the truth?" Ah-sheng was the focus of attention. As they became convinced that he was telling the absolute truth, a mood of grim concern began to settle upon them. Still they were hoping desperately that the answer might be negative, and it was this hope that had prompted Uncle Earthworm's question.

At this stage Ah-sheng grew decidedly more relaxed, sensing that the heavy burden this news had placed on him was starting to be shared by the others. "Some time ago—just when, I'm not sure," he said, "they tested some of our water and concluded that it was special. The fools! Of course the water from Clear Spring's Dragon-Eye Well is good. We didn't need any stupid tests to tell us that! But just because the water's good doesn't mean they can come and dig a swimming pool!"

"Then we're going to have to fight this all the way," Uncle Yü-tsai said, so greatly aroused that he sprayed saliva onto the others' faces.

Cow's Eye, unflappable as ever, gently wiped the spit off his face and said: "Well, of course we will. We won't stand for this!"

Uncle Yü-tsai also reached up and wiped his face.

"And there's another reason. Rest assured that if the pool opens, the people who come from town to go swimming will be mixing with each other, wearing almost nothing. Who knows what'll be going through their minds? Here in Clear Spring we've always been simple, decent folk, but this could bring ruin to our sons and daughters and corrupt the entire village!"

Ah-sheng noticed the others nodding their heads in silence, so he added: "You see what I'm saying, we've got every reason to fight this."

Just then Ah-ch'uan, in whose heart anger had been building, gave yet another reason: "Not only that, it wouldn't be right to let Dragon-Eye see all those girls and boys with their indecent clothing. The dragon's whole body would grow restless."

"That's right! So now we have three good reasons. Let's think now, are there any more?"

Earthworm jumped angrily to his feet: "What other reasons do we need? With these three it's the same as saying the sky is falling!"

Just then one of his grandsons fell off the stone lion and began to cry. The

---

1. Steel barbs formed in the shape of a ball and used in Taiwanese temples.

timing of the tail-end of Earthworm's comment—"the sky is falling!"—made it seem like a reaction to seeing his grandson fall to the ground.

3. THE FUNDAMENTAL KNOWLEDGE IN DEMOCRACY[2]

Never before had these few old-timers attended one of the village meetings, but on this particular evening they arrived very early at the makeshift meeting grounds at Village Chief Hsieh's grain-drying yard and seated themselves on front-row benches. Everyone in the village knew that they had been waiting impatiently for this evening's meeting, and in fact were anxiously waiting to see whether their opposition to the construction of a swimming pool next to Dragon-Eye Well would have an effect. Consequently, those who came to the meeting were much more enthusiastic than usual. Some families were even represented by several members.

The people responsible for conducting and witnessing the village meeting had still not arrived by the time the meeting site was crowded with villagers; from Village Chief Hsieh's house came the sounds of a local opera on his radio, which had been turned up full blast. Normally so little significance was placed on such meetings by the people who had gathered there this evening that if each household hadn't been required to send a representative to stamp the attendance sheet with a personal seal at the beginning and end of each meeting as proof of attendance, no one would ever show up. It was normally the children who took the heads of household's seals to the meeting, where they simply played the whole time. This satisfied the adults as well as the children, who earned fifty cents for their efforts. But this time it was different. Everyone felt that the meeting was absolutely necessary to solve this problem of theirs, one that had been rapidly growing more pressing each day. Everyone in attendance was emotionally stirred up to the point that the slightest additional stimulus might just turn them into a mob.

Uncle Ah-sheng and the others turned their heads back repeatedly to look at their fellow villagers who were crowding in behind them; their smiles showed that they were pleased by what they saw. Never before had these few men felt as secure as they did on this evening, for at this moment at least, all their fellow villagers were standing beside them in support. The feeling of superiority they had could be likened to someone on a battlefield fearlessly facing the enemy and shouting: "Come on ahead, damn you! Anyone who turns and flees is a son of a bitch!"

Cow's Eye turned to his cronies and said: "Hey, let's not let these youngsters think that we're all over the hill. Tonight we oldtimers can give them a real show." The others nodded their heads simultaneously, determined to do just that.

After the village secretary had raised the flag, he disappeared, following which the village chief also vanished. The meeting had originally been scheduled for

---

2. A book dealing with the procedure of parliamentary rule, written by Dr. Sun Yat-sen.

seven-thirty, and although it was already more than twenty minutes late, you couldn't have told it from the people's faces, for they were all listening with keen interest to the Taiwanese opera radio program. Suddenly, just before eight o'clock, someone turned off the radio, bringing the crowd up short. The village secretary and village chief emerged from the front door of the house, panting as though they had been running. As someone in the crowd yelled that it was time to start the meeting, the village chief got up onto a crate and announced with a slight stammer that it would begin in a moment. He asked everyone to quiet down.

The village secretary kept glancing down the road, and when he finally spotted some figures walking toward them he shouted excitedly: "Here they come! Here they come!" All the villagers turned their attention to the road. Some even stood up, throwing a momentary fright into the approaching people, who stopped in their tracks, surveyed the situation, then slowly began to approach the meeting site. The village chief quickly jumped down from the crate, went over and shook hands all around, then led the people over to the speaker's area.

To the crowd's surprise, even the district chief had shown up, but what made them feel that something highly unusual was afoot was that Constable Liu had brought five unfamiliar policemen with him. As usual, there was a smile on the constable's face, but there were disagreeable looks on the faces of the five policemen. There were in addition three members of the gentry, who wore Western suits and carried paper fans, all nearly identical. It became clear after they were introduced by the village chief that they were special invited guests.

It was eight-thirty by the time the official party was seated; everything this evening was extraordinary, for under normal circumstances the officials were the ones who waited for the villagers to arrive. The village secretary kept his eye on the three gentlemen, and when he saw the fat one nod his head he yelled out at the top of his lungs: "The village meeting will come to order!"

Before the secretary had even requested the chairman to take charge of the meeting, Earthworm nudged Uncle Ah-sheng to get up and have his say. So Uncle Ah-sheng stood up and began to speak in a loud voice: "I have something to say . . ."

Wanting to preserve the decorum of the meeting, the village secretary ignored Uncle Ah-sheng's remark and continued with his parliamentary command in an even louder voice: "The chairman will please take charge!"

When Uncle Ah-sheng saw that he was being ignored by everyone on the platform, he called the village chief by his nickname: "Hey! Gander K'un-tsai, before we begin the meeting, I want you to know that I've got something to say tonight."

Several people began to laugh despite themselves and even the five policemen with tightly set faces smiled briefly. Village Chief Hsieh Ah-k'un turned to look down from the platform at Ah-sheng, giving him an angry and exasperated stare. But Ah-sheng thought that this constituted an unjust rebuke by the village chief, so he continued: "I really do, damn it! I already told you I did!" This elicited another outburst of laughter.

The village secretary quickly walked over and put his mouth up to Ah-sheng's ear; upon being told that the right ear was no good and that he would have to speak into the left one, he whispered to Ah-sheng: "Don't you know that fat guy is a big shot? You shouldn't try to break up the meeting with a lot of funny remarks."

This sort of threat greatly displeased Ah-sheng, so he shouted: "What's this? You call it breaking up the meeting just because I want to say something?"

In obvious embarrassment, the village secretary whispered again into his ear, this time saying very politely: "You've got us all wrong. We want you to talk in a moment, but we're not ready for you yet. I'll tell you when your time comes."

Ah-sheng nodded, but added loudly: "How was I supposed to know it wasn't time to talk yet?" Then he gave Earthworm a jab: "Damn you, it's all your fault 'cause you told me to stand up and talk."

"How was I supposed to know?" Earthworm answered in an equally loud voice.

An argument nearly broke out between the two of them, but the village secretary stepped in quickly to calm them down: "Okay, okay now. Whatever it is you have to say, I'll let you have your turn in a little while."

The whole episode produced a good deal of laughter among the villagers, and each time his actions drew laughter from the crowd, Uncle Ah-sheng turned around to survey the laughing faces to see if the people were still standing by him. Evidently he was encouraged by what he saw, as anyone could tell by his rustic, somewhat foolish manner.

The village chief opened the meeting with a speech in Mandarin that left our old-timers feeling terribly dissatisfied, simply because they didn't understand a word he said. Next the three gentlemen came up and gave speeches, though in the eyes of the oldsters it was nothing more than an unbearable series of gestures. The same thing happened with the district chief and the village chief, and finally even the constable got up and said a few words. Ah-sheng figured he'd have to wait until each of the five policemen had his say before his own turn finally rolled around, so he turned to Earthworm and said in a grudging voice: "Shit! We might sit here until our backs are hunched before our turn to talk comes."

But before too long, just prior to inviting Uncle Ah-sheng up to speak, the village chief recapped in Taiwanese what had been said. He explained that the chief representative had described in detail how all sides concerned had enthusiastically promoted the construction of a swimming pool alongside the well in the interest of developing Clear Spring, and how he hoped that the local people would synchronize their efforts to realize this goal. After the swimming pool was completed, there would be vehicular traffic, the local school would gain independence, and Clear Spring Village would soon prosper. As he finished his announcement, not a single villager below the platform applauded, but when Ah-sheng eventually stood up, he was greeted by a burst of enthusiastic applause. He turned to look at the villagers, then faced the platform and clearly voiced his opinions in a challenging tone:

"I would like you to go back and tell the people in town that Uncle Ah-sheng of Clear Spring says that if they want to go swimming to please go home and take a dip in their bathtubs!"

Not only did this provocative statement produce an outburst of laughter and an almost deafening round of applause, even Uncle Ah-sheng himself was at a loss to understand just where his inspiration had come from. He continued: "Don't be fooled into thinking that Clear Spring is the place for you to build your swimming pool—the water in Clear Spring is for our use in the rice fields, not for you townspeople to take baths in!" The waves of applause increased the pitch of excitement in the old man's words: "The people of Clear Spring have no use for your 'vehicular traffic'—all anyone needs is two good legs. We're concerned only about our fields and our water. As for the lay of the land, Clear Spring is a dragon's head. The village exit leading to town is the mouth of the dragon, and the well beside the school is the eye, which is why we call it Dragon-Eye Well. Ever since the time of our ancestors, the people of Clear Spring have been protected by this dragon, which is why we've been able to live our lives in peace. Now suddenly someone wants to bring harm to our dragon's eye, and the people of Clear Spring are not going to just stand by and let that happen." He turned around. "Isn't that right?" he asked the crowd. They all jumped eagerly to their feet. The people sitting on the platform were shocked by Uncle Ah-sheng's ability to incite the crowd.

Cow's Eye leaned over to Uncle Ah-sheng: "Say, old pal, has the revered Patriarch adopted you as his spokesman?"

"I don't know," Uncle Ah-sheng answered him. "Somehow everything seems as clear as a bell to me."

After the meeting ended, Uncle Ah-sheng was invited by the village chief to his house, where he met several of the special guests in the reception room. The village secretary interpreted what they were saying for his benefit. The chief representative said to Uncle Ah-sheng respectfully: "Old uncle, I sure admire your ability to speak."

"You flatter me. I've never been to school and can't even write the simplest character."

"To be able to speak like that without ever having been to school is even more amazing."

"Don't talk like that. You're embarrassing me," Uncle Ah-sheng said. "I've heard people quote some of the things the master Confucius said, and that's more than enough for my use."

The chief representative then exchanged some words with the people around him, which Uncle Ah-sheng asked the village secretary to interpret for him.

"He's commenting on your speaking ability."

"There's no need for that kind of talk. I'm only being reasonable, taking the truth as I see it and speaking as honestly as I know how. The more you speak common sense, the clearer everything becomes. The truth can stand any test, or as they say, 'true gold fears no fire.' Isn't that right?"

"Old uncle, I want to ask you something, and I hope you'll answer me honestly. Just what is it that makes you so brave, and why do you oppose this matter so strongly? Is someone in the background goading you into doing this?"

"No!" Ah-sheng was angry.

"Then why are you so set against it?"

Uncle Ah-sheng responded without a moment's hesitation, and with considerable pride: "Because I love this piece of land and everything on it."

4. THE FIRST ROUND

On the very day that the Reliable Construction Company erected its sign over the twenty-five-by-fifty-meter swimming-pool site in Clear Spring Village, they ran into trouble, for they were unable to find a single temporary laborer anywhere in the village to dig the hole. On the second day they hired fifty laborers from elsewhere to come and carry off the dirt from the hole.

Uncle Ah-sheng and the others spent the whole of every day at the work site obstructing the construction company workers, until finally the police had to step in and warn them that they were breaking the law. This greatly upset Uncle Ah-sheng. He could not understand why others received the protection of the law for coming and interfering with his and the others' actions, while the righteousness of his behavior was considered illegal.

The old-timers split up, each recruiting a group of men who returned to the construction site with poles and knives. When the laborers saw this turn of events they threw down their carrying poles and baskets and fled from the work site. The group of men Uncle Ah-sheng had brought with him then piled up all the abandoned tools, set a torch to them, and watched them burn. As the flames burned fiercely, the men gathered around the bonfire, the thrill of victory instilling them with a feeling of freshly gained glory. Before long a circle of village women and children formed around them, their admiration causing the men to experience a heroic dignity that showed on their faces.

From the midst of the crowd came some loudly voiced comments by Uncle Ah-sheng: "Since they've fled, well and good. That way they can keep their scrawny hides. We've given them a taste of what the people of Clear Spring can do, now let's see if they dare to come back after this and move even a blade of our grass!"

Just then they heard shouts off in the distance: "Here they come! Here they come!" And before they knew what was happening, a fire engine carrying a dozen or so armed policemen had arrived in their midst. The policemen jumped down from the truck and quickly penetrated into the heart of the crowd, after which they turned and began forcing the people back, scattering them before them. The farmers were disarmed and herded one by one into the fire engine. The whole procedure was carried out with the precision of a military exercise.

After Uncle Ah-sheng got into the fire engine voluntarily, the whole lot of them were delivered to the town's station house. Several of the armed policemen stayed behind to calm down the remaining villagers and smilingly urged everyone to quietly return home.

The village and district chiefs ran from place to place over this incident; the construction company officials said they wanted assurances that this sort of thing wouldn't happen again and guarantees for the safety of the laborers at the work site before they would be willing to work out a settlement.

Late that evening the word came down to release the men, each of whose tightly drawn face showed the effects of the scare he had been given.

The apprehensive mood they were in remained with them even after they had returned to Clear Spring, and their minds were still on the written depositions and fingerprints they had left behind at the station house. They wondered what kind of trouble this might mean for them later on. This somewhat terrifying consideration hit them even harder when they reached home and looked into the faces of their family members. Regret set in, and no matter what thought of Dragon-Eye or, for that matter, of the entire village of Clear Spring came to them, they were powerless to muster the slightest feeling of resistance. In fact, some even lacked the will to resist that was normally hidden in their subconscious.

When they thought of the incident they couldn't imagine how they had gotten so stirred up; all Uncle Ah-sheng had done was sound the call and everyone had joined the charge like a swarm of bees. They could not know how proud Uncle Ah-sheng was that they had dared to throw out their chests and come forth on behalf of Clear Spring.

Although Uncle Ah-sheng had been declared the ringleader of the mob and was kept overnight at the station house, the reassurance he felt in his heart gave him the appearance of a religious soul completely at peace with himself. From the moment he had allowed his actions to be dictated by his ardent love for Clear Spring, he sensed that he had changed somehow, and he no longer considered himself a man devoid of purpose. In fact, this matter had taken on a greater importance than his own life. If he didn't do it, who would? It was as though a kind of faith had attached itself to his body and had thus become personified; somehow others too had the feeling that he was enveloped by a layer of something that shielded him from outside forces. The rustic airs that had always been with him began to fall away, and the gap between him and other people grew to vast proportions. This feeling was shared both by those who knew Uncle Ah-sheng well and by others who had at one time or another had a serious chat with him. But Uncle Ah-sheng was aware only that he spoke altogether differently than before. He was amazed by almost every sentence he uttered. For example, when someone who was sent specifically to change his mind asked what was so good about the water of Clear Spring, a mystical look came to Uncle Ah-sheng's eyes as he said, as if he were in a completely different world: "If you can speak to fish, then you ask that question of the fish in Clear Spring. Otherwise, just take a look at how happy they are and you will get the answer you seek. And it won't be your Uncle Ah-sheng who gave it to you."

The people around Uncle Ah-sheng were just as confused by all of this as he was; the sensitivity with which he felt the changes in himself gradually diminished. The extraordinary mystery of faithful devotion to a belief can cause a man to approach godlike sublimity. This was probably the case with Uncle Ah-sheng—he had already begun the process leading to that plateau where man and God exist together as an apostle.

In the middle of the night Uncle Ah-sheng was taken to a larger room, and the moment he entered he spotted the honored guest from the village meeting of the previous night—the fat man who had been sitting in the middle. Everyone was very polite to Uncle Ah-sheng, inviting him to sit in a rattan chair in front of a table, pouring him a cup of tea, and offering him a cigarette. They wanted to take down his statement, but before they began, the fat man explained to Uncle Ah-sheng that he was not being detained by the police, that they only wanted the "elderly gentleman" to cool down. As far as they were concerned, the whole incident had started out as a simple matter, even though inciting the superstitious masses and nearly turning the whole thing into a violent affair was something the law could not tolerate. But since the "elderly gentleman's" motives were pure, they were willing to turn a major affair into a minor one, and a minor affair into none at all, with the hope that the "elderly gentleman" would go home and enjoy his grandchildren. Uncle Ah-sheng thanked them unenthusiastically and began to answer their questions for the written statement.

"What's your name?"

"Hsü Ah-sheng."

"How old are you?"

"I'm seventy-nine, not counting intercalary years, and I won't live many more."

The others laughed at this comment, and one of them said: "Then you ought to take it easy and enjoy your twilight years. Why bother yourself with matters that don't concern you?"

Uncle Ah-sheng answered him in a very relaxed manner: "For the simple reason that I won't be around too many more years, and if I don't concern myself with such matters now, I won't have the chance to do it later." He suddenly turned very serious as he continued: "Whether a matter concerns a person or not depends on your point of view. And I . . . I don't agree with you."

The man who was taking down the deposition responded nervously: "Why do you oppose the construction of a swimming pool in Clear Spring?"

Uncle Ah-sheng gave the three major reasons, embellishing upon them quite a bit.

"Then why did you organize such a big crowd to disturb the peace?"

"I could hear Clear Spring moaning with each bit of earth those people's hoes took out of her to build the swimming pool, and since I didn't have the power to come to her rescue alone, I had to gather the villagers of Clear Spring around me to stop what was happening."

"Do you realize what sort of criminal act this constitutes?"

"What does that have to do with the geography of our village?"

"I wish you'd just answer my questions. I'll ask you one more time. Do you realize what sort of criminal act this constitutes?"

"No, I don't."

". . ."

". . ."

Uncle Ah-sheng was still full of vigor as dawn broke in the morning and they quietly sent him back to Clear Spring by jeep.

5. OLD MASTER CHEN'S GRANDSON

The construction work proceeded apace, as Uncle Ah-sheng had by now lost the active support of his fellow villagers. His isolation and worries had aged him considerably, and even though his family had tricked him into leaving Clear Spring for Taipei to visit some relatives, owing to his unfamiliarity with flush toilets and a mental block against using them, that night he returned to Clear Spring with a growing pressure in his gut. He entered his home without saying a word and headed straight for the outhouse located in the pigsty.

Several of his old friends had grown very passive over this whole matter, and as he witnessed the work on the swimming pool moving along day by day, he knew that somehow he would have to stop it soon. for even if he managed to stop the work after all the earth had been scooped out, the refilling of the hole alone would be a taxing job. He thought things over, deciding that rather than trying to interfere directly at the work site, he would use the more indirect method of enlisting the aid of a friend. If only he could find someone with some real clout, that would solve all his problems.

But considering Uncle Ah-sheng's circumstances, there could not possibly be any bigwigs with whom he had a personal friendship. Then in the midst of his dilemma, he suddenly thought of County Chief Chen. He could still vividly recall how County Chief Chen had come to Clear Spring during the election campaign, sweating profusely, and had pumped his hand enthusiastically, begging over and over again for his support. He had promised that if he was elected, Ah-sheng could come to him any time with his problems.

One of County Chief Chen's campaign workers had told Uncle Ah-sheng that people who voted for County Chief Chen were folks with insight, for Chen was not a man to make empty promises. So not only did Uncle Ah-sheng vote for Chen, he also urged others to do the same. At the time, he had been genuinely moved that the owner of that plump, delicate hand had been willing to let it be shaken by his coarse, rustic one.

"That's it!" he thought. "Why not go to see County Chief Chen? He once promised me that I could bring him any problems I had. During the Manchu dynasty County Chief Chen's grandfather was known as Old Master Chen, and my grandfather was one of his tenant farmers. In the old days, whenever the provincial governor came to recruit soldiers and collect taxes, my grandfather and my father always volunteered their services as provisional soldiers. All I have to do is go see County Chief Chen and tell him that our family used to be his family's tenant farmers, then he'll be obliged to help." This thought brought a new flicker of hope to Uncle Ah-sheng.

Early the next day he changed into a set of clean clothes and went into town to the county office to look up County Chief Chen.

Only after going to several offices did he finally manage to present himself at the outer office of the county chief, and after surveying the stylish surroundings, he inwardly felt very pleased. The county chief must certainly be a big shot: his office was so hard to find, and was such a solemn place, that he must oversee a lot of people. As long as he gave his approval, anything was possible.

The secretary informed him that since the county chief was in a meeting inside, he should return in the afternoon, but he told her he was willing to wait until the meeting was over; in fact, he was happy to wait, for in his estimation, the harder a person was to see, the greater his stature.

When he finally got in to see the county chief, he gave a deep bow, which, however, was not returned. When the girl had told him in the outer office that he could have no more than ten minutes of the county chief's time, he had experienced some feelings of apprehension. Where should he begin if he hoped to make this matter clear to the county chief in ten minutes' time?

He thought it best to first make the county chief aware of their relationship, so after the county chief asked him to take a seat, he began by saying: "My family, the Hsü's, used to be tenant farmers of Great Master Chen's." He cast a hopeful glance at the county chief's face to see if there was an expression of appreciation, but he merely heard him give a grunt and saw him lower his head to leaf through a tall stack of red-lined official documents. Uncle Ah-sheng lapsed into silence, but the county chief raised his head and urged him to continue with what he had come to say. Yet all the time Uncle Ah-sheng was talking, the county chief's head was buried in the stack of official documents, as he mechanically affixed his seal to one after the other. It was apparent that he didn't even have to read them—there were so many that it took all of his time just to affix his seal on each one.

After Uncle Ah-sheng had mentioned all the important points and was awaiting a reply, the county chief was still hurriedly stamping the documents. As for the matter at hand, the county chief felt that it was a dispute involving land and developers, so he pondered over which agency he should assign to settle the matter—the social services administration, the civil administration, or the construction bureau.

While he was still giving the matter some thought, he rang for his secretary, who then led Uncle Ah-sheng over to the construction bureau.

As things turned out, Uncle Ah-sheng was the butt of a number of jokes in the construction bureau before finally being turned down; since there was no place else he could go, he returned wearily to Clear Spring, his original impression of County Chief Chen now completely shattered.

On the road home, he reflected on what had happened, cursing inwardly: "Damn! So that's Old Master Chen's grandson! Old Master Chen would certainly weep if he knew this."

6. A CAT IS NOT A DOG

After Uncle Ah-sheng lost the support of his fellow villagers, he found he was no longer able to translate his beliefs into action. He gradually lost that religious aura that had surrounded him at the beginning, so that on the day when the swimming pool was completed, he had completely reverted back to his old rustic self.

A great many people were gathered outside the chain fence around the swimming pool watching the splashing and hilarity inside. Many of the local children ran home, raising a big fuss until they were given a dollar to go swimming. Young people who should have been out working in the fields had put their hoes aside and were staring, as though mesmerized, at the bras and short red pants of the swimsuits, their desires aroused. Seeing all of this, Uncle Ah-sheng was greatly troubled. He paced back and forth outside the pool enclosure agonizingly stewing in his own juices. Finally he rushed crazily into the pool area and shouted at the top of his lungs: "If you're gonna take your clothes off, why don't you just go all the way, like this?" With that he stripped right in front of everyone. The young girls were so shocked they scrambled out of the pool shrieking, while the young boys laughed hilariously and applauded. Uncle Ah-sheng bent over at the waist and dove headfirst into the deep end of the pool, even though he didn't even know how to dog-paddle. When he didn't surface right away, the people who were watching no longer thought it was funny. Two girls dove in with a sense of urgency and pulled him to the surface, but they were just a moment too late—all that now remained of Uncle Ah-sheng was his name.

7. THE SOUND OF LAUGHTER

On the day of the funeral, Uncle Ah-sheng's family had requested that the swimming pool be closed down for the day—after all, it had been the cause of his death. The procession with Uncle Ah-sheng's coffin had to pass right by the entrance to the swimming pool, so the manager of the pool had given his consent to drape some black bunting across the entrance. But even before the coffin had passed by, many of the children of Clear Spring, not to be denied, had sneaked into the pool area, and the peals of laughter that accompanied their frolicking in the water poured across the walls like waves.

BEI DAO [PEI TAO] (b. 1949)
China

Bei Tao is the pen name of Chao Chen-k'ai [Zhao Zhenkai], one of the foremost poets that have emerged in the post–Cultural Revolution era in China. Born in Beijing in 1949 just two months before the People's Republic was founded, Bei Tao grew up under Communism. He was sent to one of the nation's best high schools and was expected to be a loyal beneficiary of the system. Disillusioned by the violence and destructiveness of the Cultural Revolution (1966–1976), Bei Tao tried to keep himself aloof from politics by devoting himself to his poetry. Paradoxically, he has found himself involved in the democracy movements since the late seventies.

Indeed, even if he were not a political activist, Bei Tao would still remain a "dissident-poet," for his experiments in poetry defiantly challenged the literary orthodoxy sanctioned by the government. In sharp contrast to the "standard" poetic diction of the poets of the older generation, Bei Tao's poems are often marked by various kinds of oblique imagery and elliptical syntax, which, as critics have pointed out, make his poems a blending of Western modernist poetry on the one hand and classical Chinese verse on the other.

Chords

The grove and I closely
Encircle the small lake
A hand plunges into the water
Rousing swifts from a deep sleep
The wind is all alone   5
The sea is much too far away

When I walk out on city streets
The traffic clangor stops behind a red light
Shadows open like a fan
Footprints twist crookedly   10
The safety island is all alone
The sea is much too far away

Downstairs a blue window
Illumines a group of boys
Who strum a guitar and hum a tune   15
The ends of their cigarettes glow and fade
The stray cat is all alone
The sea is much too far away

When you fall asleep on the beach
The wind pulls up short at your mouth   20
Waves stealthily lap nearby
Shaped in soft curves
The dream is all alone
The sea is much too far away

Declaration

For the martyr Yu Luoke[1]

Perhaps the last moment is here
I haven't left a will

Translated by Fang Dai, Dennis Ding, and Edward Morin.

---

1. Yu Luoke was a young writer accused of violating socialist policy when he argued that social class is not necessarily inherited. He was executed in 1970, about six years before the end of the Cultural Revolution.

Only a pen . . . . to my mother
I'm not a hero
In an era without heroes
I just wanted to be a man

The quiet horizon
Separated the ranks of the living from the dead
I had to choose the sky
And would never kneel on the ground   10
To let executioners look gigantic
So they could block the wind of freedom

Out of starlike bullet holes
A bloody dawn is flowing

Electric Shock

A shapeless person I once met
Shook hands, a painful scream
My hand was burned
And left with scars
Whenever I meet people with a shape   5
And shake hands, a painful scream
Their hands are burned
And left with scars
I dare not shake hands with people anymore
And I always hide my hands behind my back   10
But when I pray
To heaven, I clasp my hands
A painful scream
The deepest place in my heart
Is left with scars   15

JAPAN

Literature obviously partly defines and partly responds to national and international events. A perfect illustration of a continuity that includes change can be
found in the *haikai* style of linked poetry practiced by the best known of Japanese
poets, Matsuo Bashō (1644–1694), a wanderer for much of his life, especially in
the rural areas of northeastern Japan.

No literary genre is more distinctively Japanese than linked poetry in its two forms: *renga* linked poetry and the *haikai*. *Renga* linked poetry grew from play. It later evolved into serious literature by modeling its language on that of court poetry (*waka*), by establishing elaborate canons (rules or code), and by gaining court approval. The canons were necessary because a typical *renga* sequence of 100 stanzas would be composed by three or four poets writing stanzas in rapid alternation. A stanza might be composed, checked, written down, and repeated aloud in less than three minutes.

With such apparent haphazardness went discipline. Each stanza formed a semantic unit with, and only with, its predecessor. There was no meaningful connection—no echo or parallel—with any stanza other than the preceding one (and therefore also the succeeding one). Linked poetry was written on the front and back of folded sheets. The front of the first sheet (stanzas 1–8 of 100, 1–6 of 36) constituted a dignified introduction. On the back of the last sheet (93–100 or 31–36) was a rapid conclusion ("fast close") with a positive ending. The long middle (9–92, 7–30) was a development, the most unstructured and agitated part. Each side (except the last) was to have one moon stanza, and each sheet one flower (or blossom) stanza. The assigned place was the penultimate stanza of a side: 7 and 21 for the first sheet of 100 stanzas. The flower had a position of precedence on the back of a sheet (for example, in stanza 21), and the moon was assigned to stanza 18. These are but the simplest of the rules.

Serious *renga* of earlier periods featured impressive stanzas. Later, variety of impressiveness (a version of the central Japanese aesthetic principle of asymmetry) was sought after. Four degrees of impressiveness were distinguished: design, design-ground, ground-design, ground. Variety in closeness of semantic connection was also sought after, and again four degrees were distinguished: close, close-distant, distant-close, distant. The most esteemed sequences have variety and surprise, and yet a certain inevitability. In the art of stanzaic connection, many a close and ground stanza was better *for the sequence* than the most impressive quality of distant and design.

Each stanza has as its subject one of the seasons or a miscellaneous topic. Each stanza may have a subtopic: love, travel, Buddhism, and so on. Each may have motifs such as people, birds, insects, plants, dwellings, nights, radiant things, peaks, waters, rising or falling things. Diction or conception determines these matters, as does the code. The mention of dusk or the moon implies autumn (unless another season is named). Love involves yearning, not fulfillment. Spring, autumn, and love should run to at least three stanzas. Miscellaneous stanzas appear chiefly in the middle development, where there may be as many, providing that variety of subtopics, impressiveness, and so on, is maintained.

Among the named stanzas, the most important is the *hokku*—the opening stanza. This crucial stanza refers factually to the actual conditions of the scene of meeting. Subsequent stanzas are primarily fictional. As the *renga* form evolved during its history, the opening stanzas were written down or collected, and in the modern era became separate *haiku*.

Haikai was the second version of linked poetry with a good deal of game to it. Its mixture of low with high makes it unstable, difficult. It admitted diction and conceptions deemed "low" by previous poets. Its conceptions are often comic: the lid of a box will not fit, a gate will not close, a hermit will not stay put. But despite such comedy, the *haikai* of a poet such as Matsuo Bashō has fundamental, even religious seriousness. In general, the *haikai* is freer with the *renga* code (love diminishes in importance) but it may also be stricter — for example, requiring the last flower to appear in its assigned place.

The greater *renga* and *haikai* sequences possess controlled variation. They honor the *renga* code, manipulate it, and transform it with originality. In the successful *renga* sequence, a single strong poet exercises a role like that of a conductor. Other able *renga* poets never composed as well as fourteenth-century poet, Ilio Sôgi. Other able *haikai* poets never did so well as a Bashō or Yosa Buson (1716–1783). Sôgi ensured that the beauty of the total sequence predominated. Bashō remarked that he would not boast of overshadowing his followers in composing opening stanzas (*hokku*). But it was only "this old man" who practiced the sequential art fully.

For its spirit and principles, linked poetry is indebted to the sequences and collections of court poetry. It bequeathed its three-part order to nō, the most prestigious Japanese dramatic form. Some critics have gone too far, seeing the principles of linked poetry throughout later literature. But linked poetry is truly Japanese, both in aesthetic spirit and lack of counterparts in other literatures.

Many schoolchildren — inside and outside Japan — have tried their hand at *haiku*, discrete poems of seventeen syllables (in a 5, 7, 5 pattern) in three lines, usually juxtaposing a sound or sight with a phrase suggesting a season or emotion. As contemporary western poets have been discovering, however, linked poetry such as the *renga* or *haikai* is fresher, more challenging, more various in possibilities.

Examples of prose narrative and of modern poetry in this section provide us with a clear idea of the range of tone and the excellence of modern writing. In "Separate ways" Higuchi Ichiyō writes of the friendship between an attractive young woman and an unattractive young man — and of his agony in understanding (as she does not) that the life she is choosing is one of degradation. The author expresses her own concern with great subtlety and sensitivity. Shiga Naoya's brief story "At Kinosaki" is widely considered by Japanese themselves as the acme of short story writing.

Fortunately, one chapter, "A Garden in the Capital," provides a microcosm of *The Sound of the Mountain,* the most appealing and perhaps greatest work by the Nobel laureate Kawabata Yasunari (1899–1972). One of the last selections is a short story which is both Japanese and international. Set in Shanghai, "Yellow Sand" is in part a story of a girl's initiation into adult evil. On the other hand, the author, Hayashi Kyōko, counterpoints that theme with her highly imagistic and even symbolic style.

Of the four modern poets, Yosano Akiko, shares with Ichiyō an attachment to the literature of the past — but of the court rather than the city. She translated *The Tale of Genji* into modern Japanese, and her poetic language is a triumph of revitalizing the classical. Readers will be first struck, however, by the frankness — including the physical sexuality — that revives the ancient convention of the passionate female poet. Two male poets, Hagiwara Sakutarō and Takamura Kōtarō, appear in virtually every Japanese collection of modern poetry. Sakutarō's collection, *Howling at the Moon,* and Kōtarō's *Chieko Poems,* are equally well-known; in fact, along with Akiko's *Tangled Hair,* they are also the best known titles in modern Japanese poetry. The section ends with Tomioka Taeko, who deserves, if any Japanese does, the title of international contemporary poet. Today she chiefly writes short stories, focusing on the concerns of contemporary life in highly industrialized, prosperous societies.

Historical Background

Japan has remained almost continuously a monarchy from prehistoric times. As a consequence, the country has a long history of developing government agencies that have increasingly deprived their monarchs of real power. Rivalry among such groups led to two centuries of bloodshed and chaos, ending about 1600 with rule by a military government, or *bakufu,* dominated by the Tokugawa family. The *bakufu* allowed the impoverished monarchy to continue and divided the rest of society into a new hierarchy: warriors, farmers, artisans, and merchants. By the eighteenth century, Japan became dominated by two urban mercantile centers: Osaka-Kyoto and Edo (today's Tokyo), the largest city in the world at that time.

From the seventeenth century, Japanese began to learn about the West from books — chiefly in Dutch — brought to Japan by traders from Holland. After Japan's forced opening by the United States in the 1860s, the nation turned from the Asian mainland to the West for its model. Victory in the Russo-Japanese War (1904–1905) and alliance with the victorious Allies in World War I led Japan to follow the example of Western imperialism and to colonialize Manchuria, Korea, Taiwan, and portions of the Chinese mainland. After defeat in World War II, the Japanese were determined to excel in economic terms, gaining increasing success in the second half of the twentieth century. Japan's modern era is conventionally dated from the Meiji Restoration of 1868, an event that returned formal power to the monarch and dismantled the shogunate — the system of military rule that had dominated since the twelfth century. The first selections here date from the era immediately preceding the Restoration, a 250-year span (c. 1350–1600) — comprising Japan's Late Middle Ages known alternatively as the Edo period (after the seat of the government, present-day Tokyo) or the Tokugawa era (after the ruling family).

Tokugawa shoguns unified Japan after a century of civil warfare, instituting broad social and political changes to stabilize their new order. Deeply (and justifiably) suspicious of the motives behind the growing European presence in Asia, they decreed a policy of *sakoku,* or national seclusion: Japanese were forbidden to make overseas voyages; Christianity, which had made significant inroads in Japan since its introduction in the mid-sixteenth century, was outlawed; foreign ships were banned from Japanese ports. Only the Dutch and Chinese were permitted to continue trade, and even their presence was confined to a small island near Nagasaki. For over 200 years, Japan was thus almost completely isolated from the outside world.

Internal changes were profound as well. The social hierarchy was reinforced, with the *shogun* (*bakufu* head, commander-in-chief to the monarch, and *de facto* ruler of Japan when he dominated his advisers), *daimyos* (regional land-owning nobles), and *samurai* (warriors) constituting a privileged aristocracy. Domains were redistributed among the *daimyos* in an attempt to create a workable balance of regional and central power. *Daimyos* were further kept under control by what amounted to an official hostage system: periodically their wives, their children and they themselves were required to live in the capital. As time went on, they naturally gave up the ways of the locale of their fiefs for those of Edo. To support its version of social unity, the government turned to neo-Confucianism, which it promoted over the long esteemed Shinto and Buddhism.

Culturally, the Edo period was an important one for Japan. The stabilizing measures of the *bakufu* brought peace, cultural innovations, and increasing although unstable prosperity. By the first decades of the eighteenth century, Edo had become the largest city in the world, with approximately one million inhabitants. Although Japanese society was rigicly organized, it nevertheless underwent fundamental changes. The *samurai*, willfully rough and unlettered at the beginning of the period, transformed themselves over a long peacetime into the most highly cultivated class: elite warriors were also patrons, poets, calligraphers, scholars and connoisseurs. Merchants, theoretically the lowest members of the social order in the Confucian view, increasingly dominated economic life as *samurai* in need of ready money fell in their debt. At first (seventeenth century) centered in the area of the old capital and Osaka and (thereafter) in Edo, the new urban population became audience and authors cf the creative literature of the time. In a country reluctant to give up any form of achievement, the manners and customs of the court and of the aristocracy were gradually adapted by society at large, shaping what we now think of as "traditional" Japanese culture. Reaction to continental philosophy led to a nativist movement, National Studies, to recover and restore what was deemed most fundamentally Japanese in the nation's cultural identity. At the same time, Western influence was not wholly absent: as mentioned earlier, Dutch learning—especially science and technology—was cultivated. To complete the picture, it should be added that the emperor continued to hold court in Kyoto, reigning as a symbol of national unity and continuity.

By the mid-nineteenth century, European attempts to break through Japan's isolation grew more insistent. During the 1840s, British, French, and U.S. warships and a Dutch treaty mission all came to call—and were sent packing. It was not until 1853 that an American naval officer, Commodore Matthew Perry, forced the Japanese to sign the Treaty of Friendship, opening the way for commercial relations. A series of treaties with European powers followed, all of them on unfavorable terms to Japan. Viewing these treaties as a fundamental betrayal to the emperor and to Japan, many already discontented *daimyo* and their *samurai*—encouraged by the court—rebelled, bringing about the downfall of the shogunate in 1867. The following year, the emperor was formally restored to power. In 1869 the court moved to Edo, renamed Tokyo, or Eastern Capital.

Japan assessed its situation with complete clarity: the West had developed economic and military superiority. Furthermore, this superiority was intimately linked to the intellectual and social liberties made possible by the centralized, constitutional nation-states that had emerged during Japan's isolation. The new government reacted swiftly and decisively. By 1890, Japan had a constitution modeled on that of Germany, with a bicameral parliament. Political parties emerged. *Daimyos* surrendered their lands to the crown, which launched a program of private ownership. The rigid social hierarchy was at least officially abolished. A new conscripted military undercut the power of the samurai. Finally, a massive program of industrialization was launched and the goal of universal education announced, leading both to indoctrination and to the world's highest literacy rate.

Japan's new power and ambition were made clear to the world with an unexpected victory in the Sino-Japanese War of 1894–1895. China ceded the island of Taiwan (then called Formosa) together with mainland rights equaling those enjoyed by European colonial powers. Japan's European treaties were soon renegotiated for more equitable arrangements. Europe and the United States were startled into admiration and suspicion by Japan's victory in the Russo-Japanese War in 1905. Western recognition of Japan's interests in Korea and

Manchuria soon followed. Japan formally annexed Korea in 1910. The Versailles Treaty that closed World War I ceded additional Chinese coastal areas to Japan, whose limited participation in the war had been on the side of the Allies.

After the war, Japan experienced many of the same social movements that Western nations did, as the discontents and inequities of raw industrialized capitalism grew more acute. Dissatisfied with liberalism and Westernization, the military began to gather political power, a process facilitated by the difficulties brought on by the world depression that began in 1929. Increasing military dominance and independence led to the takeover of Manchuria in 1931, war with China in 1937, and eventually to Japan's disastrous participation in World War II as an Axis power.

The atomic bombs dropped on Hiroshima and Nagasaki by the United States precipitated Japan's surrender in 1945. Reforms introduced during American occupation after the war were aimed at demilitarization and promoting democracy. Central to these causes was the new Japanese constitution adopted in 1947, which renounced war as a sovereign right and forbade the creation of a standing military. The civil code was also revised to grant women legal parity and suffrage. Economic restructuring, begun under Allied supervision, began to bring prosperity during the 1950s, and Japan's economic vigor since that time has often been the envy of the postwar industrialized world.

A Note on Japanese Names

Names are given here in contemporary style and according to representations of contemporary Japanese pronunciation. Surnames precede given names. Abbreviations are employed according to one modern style: Ariwara Narihira rather than Ariwara no Narihira, which is more, but not entirely, "correct." For Kakinomoto Hitomaro, one could use title, the "no," in the middle, and a modified version of Old Japanese: Kakinomoto no Asomi no Hitomaro; but the shorter version has been chosen here. By convention, some writers are known by the pen name versions of their given names (Bashō) and while others contemporary with them by their (sometimes pseudo-) surnames (Chikamatsu). For modern writers, the tendency has been to use both surname and given name (although one or both might be pen names). Poets, however, are commonly known by the pen name version of a given name. There is no single rule to be followed or style to be adopted. A writer simply adopts one of the accepted practices.

Further Readings

Bowring, Richard. *Murasaki Shikibu: The Tale of Genji*. Cambridge, Eng.: Cambridge University Press, 1988.

Brower, Robert H., and Earl Miner. *Japanese Court Poetry*. Stanford: Stanford University Press, 1961.

Keene, Donald, ed. *Anthology of Japanese Literature*. New York: Grove, 1955.

———. *Modern Japanese Literature*. New York: Grove, 1956.

———. *World Within Walls*. New York: Holt, Rinehart, and Winston, 1976 (premodern, c. 1600–1868).

———. *Dawn to the West*. 2 vols. New York: Holt, Rinehart, and Winston, 1984. Volume 1: *Fiction*; Volume 2: *Poetry, Drama, Criticism* (modern and contemporary).

Miner, Earl. *Introduction to Japanese Court Poetry,* in Brower and Miner, 1961.

Miner, Earl, Hiroko Odagiri, and Robert E. Morrell. *The Princeton Companion to Classical Japanese Literature.* Princeton: Princeton University Press, 1985.

Sato, Hiroaki, trans. *Ten Japanese Poets.* Hanover, NH: Granite, 1973 (modern and contemporary).

Ueda, Makoto. *Modern Japanese Writers and the Nature of Literature.* Stanford: Stanford University Press, 1976.

————. *Bashō and His Interpreters.* Stanford: Stanford University Press, 1992 (selected *hokku,* translated and with commentary from Bashō's time to the present).

MATSUO BASHŌ (1644–1694)
NOZAWA BONCHŌ (d. 1714)
OKADA YASUI (1658–1743)
MUKAI KYORAI (1651–1704)

Japan

Nozawa Bonchō, Okada Yasui, and Mukai Kyorai were challenged by Matsuo Bashō, as they said to "squeeze the juice from our bone marrow" in composing a thirty-six-stanza (*kasen*) *haikai*. Written in 1690, this sequence has been regarded as one of the greatest *haikai* achievements.

At the Tub of Ashes [Akuoke no no Maki]

1 BONCHŌ

> At the tub of ashes
> dripping sounds yield to stillness
> as crickets chirp

Design. No Relation. Autumn. Insects. Products. Waters.
Ashes were kept in a tub outside the house for such uses as scouring or otherwise cleaning kitchen objects. During a dry period the tub ceases to drip. That silence is intensified by the sounds of the crickets. An excellent hokku, open to various development. The insects are named.

2 BASHŌ

> At the tub of ashes
> dripping sounds yield to stillness
> as crickets chirp
> in his lamp the oil grows low
> and autumn brings him early sleep

Design-Ground. Heavy-Light. Autumn. Night. Products.
The scene moves indoors to one who might be listening. As the oil grows low (like the water ceasing to drip), he falls asleep for want of light to make activity possible. Autumn nights are proverbially long, so early sleep means lengthy sleep.

Translated by Earl Miner.

3 YASUI

> In the lamp the oil grows low
> and autumn brings him early sleep
> the floor matting
> freshly laid out in the chamber
> shines in the moonlight

Design. Heavy-Light. Autumn. Residences. Products. Night. Radiance.
The first Moon stanza comes two before its standard place, and the white light streams on the slightly green new mats, a beautiful image.

* * *

8 YASUI

> Galloping for a ride
> he finds his grip cannot restrain
> the young spring stallion
> as there upon Mount Maya
> clouds hang on the lofty peak

Design-Ground. Light-Heavy. Miscellaneous. Peaks.
Yasui slows the action, not just with the clouds hanging but by naming the mountain where they are (near present Kobe). The scene once more opens up, but with a typical haikai modification by clouds obstructing the view. Clouds are a Rising Thing in renga.

9 BONCHŌ

> While there upon Mount Maya
> clouds hang on the lofty peak
> at summer supper
> as he is eating saury minnows
> the breeze brings fragrance

Ground-Design. Light. Summer.
It is a humble scene, apparently close to the sea. The stillness of 9 is slightly altered with the summer breeze.

10 BASHŌ

> At summer supper
> as I am eating saury minnows
> the breeze brings fragrance
> in scratching where the leech had bit
> there is something that feels good

Ground-Design. Light-Heavy. Summer. Insects.
The new scene moves inland from the seashore.

11 YASUI

> In scratching where the leech had bit
> there is something that feels good
> the throes of longing
> are such that she wishes to forget
> on a day free from service

Ground-Design. Light. Miscellaneous. Love.
This is an extreme example of Light relation. The connection lies in the strenuousness of the service from which the woman now has a day or so of respite. The work and the longing had combined to exhaust her. This and the preceding stanza are easily assessed as to connection but in impressiveness may well be thought Design-Ground.

12 KYORAI

> The throes of longing
> are such that she wishes to forget
> on a day free from service
> but her return is demanded
> in a love letter from her lord

Ground-Design. Heavy-Light. Miscellaneous. Love. Persons. Military.
If we follow the interpretation that this recalls the first book of *The Tale of Genji*, the class is Court rather than Military. But this seems much more like various post-court stories and suggests the concubine of a military lord rather than the usual court situation in which the woman waits.

13 BASHŌ

> Her return is demanded
> in a love letter from her lord
> what complacency
> there is in hearing people say
> she is fortune's child

Ground-Design. Light. Miscellaneous. Persons. Products.
This stanza exemplifies a kind of connection that looks Heavy (by juxtaposition) but in fact is Light. It is desirable to have one or two such as these, but too many would disjoint the sequence, as too Heavy a relation would make all seem the same. Lacking personal nouns, the Japanese of this stanza is obscure as to point of view and person described.

14 BONCHŌ

What complacency
there is in hearing people say
that one is fortune's child
and basking in a fine hot bath
each night with the moon in view

Design-Ground. Light-Heavy. Autumn. Night. Radiance.
This second Moon stanza comes in the standard place. Since all Japanese like baths, someone who is specially said to bask in them must be an old person, a person with little work, or a dandy. But the moon each night is appreciated. A fine haikai combination.

15 KYORAI

Basking in a fine hot bath
each night with the moon in view
throughout the town
autumn also hastens on
by vacant buildings

Design-Ground. Heavy-Light. Autumn. Residences. Town.
In this fine, sombre stanza autumn seems to move right through the town past empty buildings that also hasten on — in time. The passage of time is beautifully and sadly evoked.

16 YASUI

Throughout the town
autumn also hastens on
by vacant buildings
all the world offers to our sight
is covered with the moment's dew

Ground. Light-Heavy. Autumn. Evanescence.
In itself, this stanza has only Autumn in common with 15, but Evanescence grows so well out of that stanza as to give some Heaviness of connection. This is the first Ground stanza, and has a certain flat moralizing to it, in preparation for a contrasting Flower stanza. Dew is a Falling Thing in renga.

17 BASHŌ

All the world offers to our sight
is covered with the moment's dew
as cherry blossoms fall
so I have reached the time for robes
that tell of priestly life

Design-Ground. Light-Heavy. Spring. Buddhism. Persons. Clothes. Trees.
Using the religious emblematic status of dew rather than its seasonal emblem of autumn, Bashō moves to spring from autumn, a somewhat violent movement, especially since the flower imagery works so strongly from the beginning of this stanza. This is the proper location for the first Flower stanza. After the positive nature of much earlier, this is very sober for this stanza.

18 BONCHŌ

As cherry blossoms fall
so have I reached the time for robes
that tell of priestly life
in Kiso the pickled greens
taste as if the spring is ending

Design-Ground. Light-Heavy. Spring. Plants.
In 17 it seemed the speaker would become a recluse. Here he is on the road at a named place. Both stanzas regret the passing of an aspect of spring. Japanese pickle many vegetables, but this particular one seems to be a local specialty.

19 YASUI

in Kiso the pickled greens
taste as if the spring is ending
it seems the titmice
fly home northward as they follow
the loom of the mountains

Design-Ground. Heavy-Light. Spring. Birds. Peaks.
It appears to be assumed here that the traveler of 18 is going southwest and the birds are returning northeast—to what was thought their proper home. There are now five stanzas in a row alternating real and figurative motion.

20 KYORAI

It seems the titmice
fly homeward as they follow
the loom of the mountains
the last twig thatching has been bound
to the ridge pole on the cottage roof

Ground-Design. Light. Miscellaneous. Residences. Plants. Peasants.
Kyorai brings the action to rest at a mountain scene (the thatch is of twigs, not straw). Here is a human home in contrast to that for the titmice in 19. But since no human creature is mentioned as present, the scene appears very still. The stanzaic connection continues in the brilliant fashion of what went before, and will go on—with ceaseless variety in what follows.

21 BONCHŌ

The last twig thatching has been bound
to the ridge pole on the cottage roof
the winter sky
has been shaken into disarray
by the northern storm

Design-Ground. Light. Winter.
The mountain atmosphere of 20 associates with the wind blowing from the north here, but
the connection is Light. The stillness of the house in 21 has contrast in the violent sky seen
over a considerable distance.

22 BASHŌ

The winter sky
has been shaken into disarray
by the northern storm
as a welcome to the traveler
the host brings a floor lamp for the night

Ground-Design. Light-Heavy. Miscellaneous. Travel. Prcducts. Radiance.
After enduring the bitter weather of 21, the traveler arrives at lodging to find a considerate
host. The lamp is probably a simple box with apertures for light and air, but the image of its
light is very comforting.

23 KYORAI

To welcome her distant lover
she brought a floor lamp for the night
utterly useless
her vaunted female wisdom
also ends in nothing

Ground. Heavy-Light. Autumn. Love. Persons.
The situation of the woman waiting in vain for a faithless lover is standard, but Kyorai
skillfully uses 22 to his ends. The presence of both Love and Autumn in a Ground stanza is
rather unusual, since they are both subjects of high price. The "also" in the last line means
women's as well as men's wisdom.

24 YASUI

Utterly useless
her vaunted female wisdom
also ends in nothing

> what feelings stir the wanton-flowers
> as the wolf cries out for his mate

Ground-Design. Light-Heavy. Autumn. Love. Animals.
The stag's cries are traditional, but the wolf is so novel as to make impressiveness difficult to judge. Apparently the wolf's male wisdom helps no more here than the woman's in 23, but there seems some comic misogyny in the change to wolves. The flowers are ominaeshi, patrinia, and designate autumn. The conception of the stanza implies a speaker in a Love situation.

25 BASHŌ

> What feelings stir the wanton-flowers
> as the wolf cries out for his mate
> in the moonlit night
> by the reeds upon the hillside
> he guards the royal tomb

Design. Heavy-Light. Autumn. Plants. Night. Radiance. Peaks. Court.
At a desolate site, but brightened with moonlight, the faithful guard waits out autumn and his life, hearing the wolf cry in the wilds. Bashō introduces the third Moon stanza with great effect as the last of three Autumn stanzas but four before its usual place.

26 BONCHŌ

> In the moonlit night
> by the reeds upon the hillside
> he guards the royal tomb
> everybody has neglected
> the well holding brackish water

Ground-Design. Heavy-Light. Miscellaneous. Waters.
The desertion of the scene is intensified. The stanza may imply in connection with 25 that the guard does not use the water, and by itself, that animals do not use it, or that no one at all uses it, stressing the absence of anyone at the scene.

27 YASUI

> Everybody has neglected
> the well holding brackish water
> with his tall stories
> the tale-teller swaggers on
> amusing the hearers

Ground-Design. Light. Miscellaneous. Persons.
This very Light linking uses little more than contrast to connect: between the objective, factual character and dreariness of 26 and the unbelievable tales told with such relish here. We now enter a new stage, the finest of this outstanding sequence.

28 KYORAI

With his tall stories
the tale-teller swaggers on
amusing us listeners
again he brings out with a flourish
the sushi that he thinks so grand

Ground. Light-Heavy. Summer. Town?
The humor is very similar to that in 27, condescending but goodnatured. To compensate, a different person is implied, the impressiveness is changed, and a season is freshly introduced. The old-style sushi — fish pressed on rice — designates summer.

29 BONCHŌ

Again brought out with a flourish
the sushi that is thought so grand
far beyond the dike
the lush green rice plants in the fields
have fresh purity

Design. Light. Summer. Cultivation. Peasants.
The stanza rises in impressiveness over recent ones, freeing itself with a Light relation to 28, but connecting by season and rice plants. This is a very Japanese scene. Here begins the most memorable run of stanzas in this sequence.

30 BASHŌ

Far beyond the dike
the lush green rice plants in the fields
have fresh purity
the precincts of the Kamo shrine
abundant with divinity

Design-Ground. Light-Heavy. Miscellaneous. Shinto.
The prosaic quality of the stanza is a decorum for this kind of simple but, to a Japanese, impressive scene in a named place. Others might find it less impressive. Its connection of the lovely rice in 29 with native divinities is very effective.

31 KYORAI

The precincts of the Kamo Shrine
abundant with divinity
the strolling peddler
loudly calls his wares in shortened names
as he passes by

Ground-Design. Light. Miscellaneous. Persons. Town.
The high tone and peacefulness of 30 are altered. In connection with 30, this suggests a busy market at the entrance to the Kyoto shrine. By itself, it gives the tonal contrast. The back side of the second sheet, and the Fast Close, begin with this stanza.

32 YASUI

The strolling peddler
loudly calls his wares in shortened names
as he passes by
no more than cover from a shower
is human life in ceaseless flux

Design-Ground. Light. Miscellaneous. Evanescence.
The thematic connection with 31 is clear. But the imagery sets it quite apart. Rain is a Falling Thing in renga.

33 BASHŌ

No more than cover from a shower
is this world in ceaseless flux
sleeping at noon
the body of the blue heron
poised in nobility

Design. Light-Heavy. Miscellaneous. Birds.
Again a thematic connection lightened by differing imagery. This symbol of peace and understanding of the Buddhist Law gives surprising stillness. The stipulation of time and place in the sequence no doubt decreases the near sanctity of the image of a bird in water, on one leg, its head under its wing, free from phenomenal flow. The phrase of the first line, Bashō's use of "nobility" elsewhere for religious purposes, and the connection with 32 (and its echo), all contribute to a symbol of religious beauty, of devotion and enlightenment.

34 BONCHŌ

Sleeping at noon
the body of the blue heron
poised in nobility
trickle trickle go the waters
where rushes sway in utter peace

Ground-Design. Heavy-Light. Miscellaneous. Plants. Waters.
The atmosphere of 33 continues, but now there is motion and less dignified language. The imagery associates well with that in 33, but this whole stanza has new
elements.

35 KYORAI

Trickle trickle go the waters
where rushes sway in utter peace
the drooping cherries
have flowered in such loveliness
as fills me utterly

Ground-Design. Light. Spring. Trees.
Only Light relation enables Kyorai to make this stanza the Flower stanza it should
be. He violates decorum by giving a named flower, which does not count in renga or
haikai for a Flower stanza. Bahsō is said to have approved, because of the colloquial
expression *hara ippai,* a bellyful, which has not quite the associations of the image
in English.

36 YASUI

The drooping cherries
have flowered in such loveliness
as fills me utterly
spring glories in the third of months
with dawn's first glowing in the sky.

Design-Ground. Heavy-Light. Spring. Night.
We end with spring at its height, the cherry blossoms cf 35 dimly visible at dawn (a night
word). The "third of months" purposely lowers the tone, stressing the traditional beauty of
spring dawn in a fresh way.

MATSUO BASHŌ (1644–1694)
Japan

For the Japanese, this work is one of the most beloved prose classics. It includes fifty opening stanzas (*hokku*) by Bashō along with many compositions by other writers and rich allusions to a wide range of Japanese and Chinese writing. In the spring of 1689, Matsuo Bashō set out on a journey through Japan—first to the north and then to the west and south. He wanted to visit famous places and to spread the practice of his school of *haikai* linked poetry. He had other motives: to compose *haikai* and to satisfy his restless spirit. He did not return to his house in Edo (Tokyo) for two and a half years.

The Narrow Road deals with the first six months of Bashō's journey. He was accompanied most of this time by a disciple, Iwanami Sora (1650–1711), who kept a diary of detailed unliterary notes and also recorded poetic composition. By comparing his and Bashō's accounts, we can discover when Bashō makes things up. We learn that nearly everything accords with fact, with additions or heightenings. Rightly regarding this as his masterpiece among his "diaries of the road," Bashō kept tinkering with it, leaving it unpublished at the end of his life.

It is now agreed that the work is designed like a linked-poetry sequence. The selection included here provides the stately "Introduction" and "Fast Close." The variety in between corresponds to the long middle "Development," even including some ingenious love stanzas (the prostitutes at Ichiburi), the conspicuous fictional episode. That episode and much else illustrate the principle of "*haikai* change," the shift to a decorum lower than is appropriate to *renga* or court literature.

Through various references, Bashō shows his awareness that he is writing during the five hundredth anniversary of the death of the itinerant poet Monk Saigyo (1118–1190). Various antigovernment political overtones, as described in the Hiraizumi episode, allude to the fact that 500 years have also passed since the death of Minamoto Yoshitsune (d. 1190). Such commentaries grow much longer than the account itself.

from *The Narrow Road Through the Provinces* *[Oku no Hosomichi]*

Opening, Departure, Buddha Gozaemon, Nikkō

The months and days are the wayfarers of the centuries,[1] and as yet another year comes round, it, too, turns traveler. Sailors whose lives float away as they labor on boats, horsemen who encounter old age as they draw the horse around once more

Translated by Earl Miner.

---

1. Echoing the Preface of *Ch'un yeh yen t'ao li tu*, by Li Po (701–762).

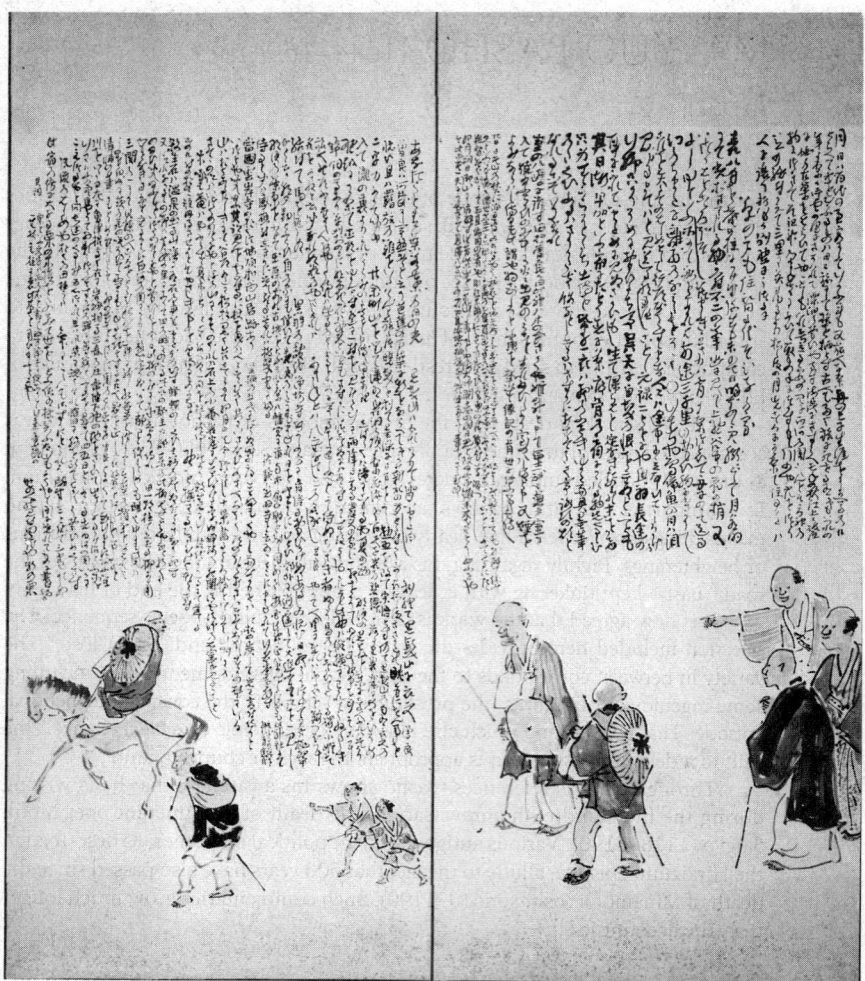

Yosa Buson. *Narrow Road to the Deep North.* 1779. Two panels from a sixfold screen. Yamagata Museum of Art.

by the bit, they also spend their days in travel and make their home in wayfaring. Over the centuries many famous men have met death on the way; and I, too, though I do not know what year it began, have long yielded to the wind like a loosened cloud and, unable to give up my wandering desires, have taken my way along the coast. Last autumn,[2] as I cleaned the old cobwebs from my dilapidated house by the riverside,[3] I found that the year had suddenly drawn to its close. As

---

2. Early autumn of 1688, after returning from travel to Suma and Sarashina.

3. Referring to a residence of some months at his house along the Sumida River in Edo, now Tokyo.

the sky of the new year filled with the haze of spring, I thought of going beyond the Shirakawa Barrier,[4] and so possessed was I by some peripatetic urge that I thought I had an invitation from the god of travelers himself and so became unable to settle down to anything. I mended my underpants, re-corded my rain hat, and took three bits of moxa cautery. I could not put from my mind how lovely the moon must be at Matsushima. I disposed of my property and moved to Sampū's villa.[5]

> My red grasshut,
> Lived in now by another generation,
> Is decked out with dolls.

This and the rest of the first eight stanzas of a *haikai*[6] I left posted on a pillar of my cottage.

The twenty-seventh of the Third Month, the sky at dawn was hazed over, and observing the pale soft light of the moon as it faded from the sky,[7] I looked beyond to where the peak of Mount Fuji rose dimly in the sky, and then nearer at hand from Ueno to Yanaka, wondering when I would again see these cherry blossoms. I felt a heaviness of heart. Everyone with whom I was on close terms assembled the night before I was to leave and saw me off on the boat. As I was landing at a place called Senju, my heart was burdened by the thought of the many miles stretching ahead, and my tears fell over such a parting on the illusory path of this world.

> With spring leaving,
> The birds cry out regret, the fish
> Have tears in their eyes.

That poem marked the beginning of the pilgrimage, but it was difficult to set forth. There were all my friends gathered to see me off and apparently prepared to stand there till they saw the last of my back vanish down the road.

This year, that is to say 1689, the thought suddenly entered my head to go on an aimless wandering through distant provinces. I knew that the sufferings of travel are said to bring a fall of frost to one's head, like snow from a Chinese sky; still, there were places I had heard of but had not yet seen. To live long enough to arrive back home was a happiness I could not rely upon. With thoughts of such kinds occupying my mind, I found that at last I had made my way to the post station of Sōka. The pack of things on my bony, thin shoulders was giving me pain. Setting out with nothing but what I could bear myself, I carried a stout paper raincoat to keep out the chill at night, a cotton kimono, raingear, something in the way of ink and brush—and various things given me as farewell presents and

---

4. Alluding to a poem by Priest Nōin (998–1050), and possibly also to a verse by Li Po.
5. Sampū (1648–1733), proper surname Sugiyama, was a follower of Bashō in poetry.
6. It was common to think of the first eight

stanzas of a *haikai* (as also in the earlier linked verse, *renga*), as comprising the opening unit. They were commonly written on one fold of a sheet of paper.
7. Echoing a passage from the second chapter, "Hahakigi," in *The Tale of Genji*.

therefore difficult to dispose of. It was the traveler's dilemma, knowing them a hindrance and unable to throw them away.

We paid homage at the shrine of the god of Muro no Yashima. Sora,[8] who accompanied me on the journey, explained: "The god enshrined here is called the Flower Blooming Princess and is the same as the deity of Sengen Shrine on Mount Fuji. She was called Muro no Yashima after giving birth to Lord Hohodemi when she had entered into a house without doors and set herself on fire to prove his divinity.[9] It is because of such a background that poets associate smoke with this place." It is also forbidden here to eat the *konoshiro* fish, which smells when overheated, but almost everybody knows the outlines of such stories.

The thirtieth, we are stopping at a place in the foothills of Mount Nikkō. The owner of the inn approached us. "People call me Buddha Gozaemon," he said. "I am honest in all my dealings—people will tell you as much—so spend a night of your travels at ease in my little inn." Had the Buddha appeared, then, in temporary form in this corrupt world of ours, perhaps to save one like myself, a mendicant or pilgrim in the habit of an itinerant priest? If one examined the innkeeper's conduct closely, one would discover no calculation or worldliness, only a thoroughly honest man. He was a kind such as the Confucian *Analects* speak of, with a strength of will and rugged honesty close to the ideal virtue—an admirable purity of disposition.

The first of the Fourth Month, we worshiped at the shrine on this mountain. Long ago the characters used for Mount Nikkō were the "Nikō" meaning "Double Rough," but when the Great Teacher Kūkai set up a temple here, he changed the name to "Nikkō" or "Sun's Radiance." It is not clear whether or not he had foreseen what would be a thousand years later, but now the light of this radiant place reaches everywhere, extending the benefit of the temple to the last corner of the country, assisting all four classes,[10] in the peaceable and prosperous conduct of their affairs. More might be said, but feeling hesitant at such a place, I put aside my brush.

> As all begins afresh,
> On the green leaves, on the young leaves
> The brightness of the sun.

Hard Travel from Iizuka to Iwanuma

From there we went on to Iizuka for lodging. It is a place with hot springs, and so we took accommodation at a place offering such bathing. What we discovered was a dirt-floored room with rice mats spread out. Such a hovel had little appeal. Since

---

8. Sora (1650–1711), surname Iwanami (later Kawai), was a disciple of Bashō, accompanied him on at least one other journey, and kept a record of the present journey, *The Diary of Sora*.

9. A story in the *Kojiki* says that the princess announced her pregnancy after but one night with her husband. To prove it his, she gave birth safely in a closed, burning room; hence the child's name, Hohodemi, "Visible by Firelight."

10. The four classes are those of feudal Japan: soldiers, farmers, artisans, and merchants. Bashō obliquely praises the shogunate.

there was no lamp, either, we had to rely upon the faint light of the sunken hearth to prepare our bedclothes and get to bed. As night came on, thunder rumbled and rain came down in a torrent, leaking from the roof above our beds. To add to it, we were attacked by fleas and mosquitoes. I was unable to sleep and had an attack of colic. I thought that I was about to go under. The short night of the season was at last over, and once again we set out on our travels. The distress of the night still weighed upon me, however, and I felt very low. We engaged a horse and with it we got to the post station of Kōri.

It is not a very reassuring state of affairs to have this illness while the road we must take lies vague and far ahead. Our tour is a pilgrimage through remote back country. I thought of the lack of stability in human affairs and of resigning myself to leaving my body behind in a forsaken area. The thought that I would die halfway on my journey seemed to me the will of heaven, and my spirits revived. In my new mood I stepped along jauntily, and one might say that—as we came to Ōkido in Date—I was dotty.

We passed through the castle towns of Abumizuri and Shiroishi. We had come to the Kasajima Territory and therefore inquired of people where we might find the grave of Fujiwara Sanekata.[11] "The hamlet you can see dimly off to the right," we were told, "is called Minowa, and beyond that lies Kasajima. There you can still find the Kasajima Shrine of the god of travelers and the pampas grass that was a keepsake to Priest Saigyō."[12] The rains of the Fifth Month had set in, however, leaving the side roads all but impassable, and in my weakened condition it was best just to pass through the country, only looking from a distance upon Minowa and Kasajima. The suggestion of raincoats and rainhats[13] was altogether appropriate to this rainy season, and so I wrote:

> Yes, Kasajima—
> Over what foul roads does it lie
> Beneath summer rains?

We stopped overnight at Iwanuma.

Matsushima

The day was close to noon. Hiring a boat, we set out for Matsushima.[14] The distance is about five miles, but we soon landed at Ojima Beach.

What one can say about the place is sure to have little novelty, but Matsushima is the finest beauty spot of Japan and for it there is no need to feel ashamed of a comparison with Lake Tung-t'ing or the West Lake at

---

11. Sanekata, a poet and provincial governor, died in 998 while living in exile from the capital. Bashō feels sympathy and kinship.
12. Alluding to Saigyō's poem on Sanekata, regretting that Sanekata remains only a name in the world, with only withered pampas grass a reminder of him.
13. The mino- of Minowa means a straw rain-

coat, and the kasa- of Kasajima suggests in this context a sedge rainhat.
14. Matsushima is one of the great beauty spots of Japan, a group of islands off the coast from Sendai. Bashō's account is no doubt the best known of writings of visits to the island.

Hangchow, the best that China can offer. The sea comes in from the southeast and over the years has beaten out an inlet over six miles around, and within the arc the tide comes in an eagre as it does at Che-chiang. There were islands beyond counting, some tall ones pointing each its finger toward heaven, and other low ones crawling on their bellies across the sea. Some islands are piled up in two layers, others in three; some on the left stand aloof from each other, others join hands on the right. Some look as if they were children being carried on the back, yet others as if they were being hugged—in the manner in which parents or grandparents fondle their young ones. The needles of the pines are a rich green; the sprays of the trees are blown in a whirl by the sea winds, and yet their lovely twisted forms seem to have been assumed of their own accord. The deep attraction of the place is that of the loveliest face made lovelier.[15] It must have been the special care of the god of hills, Ōyamatsumi, in the remote past of the mighty gods. And who is there that could paint or describe the handiwork of Zōka, the demiurge of heaven and earth?

The island coastline of Ojima juts from the main body of land, an island looking like a peninsula. One can still see the site of the detached temple of the Zen Priest Ungo, along with such other things as the stone he sat upon for meditation.[16] In the shade of the pines there were also one or two priests who had renounced the world, leading the lives of hermits in their grass-thatched huts, above which rose the thin smoke of fires built of pine cones or fallen needles. Of course I do not know them, but their life is appealing. As I approached them, the moon rose, sparkling upon the sea, creating a loveliness different from that in daylight. We went back to the inlet and looked for lodging. Our room was in the upper of two storeys, and we opened our window, enjoying our traveler's sleep in the freshest of breezes, borne upon us with the strangest feeling of delicacy. Sora wrote a poem.

> Here at Matsushima,
> O wood thrush, the plumage of cranes
> Would add to your song.

I decided to be silent as a poet in such a place, but though I intended to go to sleep, I could not. When I left my old hut to set out on this trip, Sodō gave me a Chinese poem on Matsushima and Hara Anteki gave me his *waka* on Matsugaura.[17] Opening my pilgrim's knapsack, I took out these poems for my companions that night. I also had the opening verses by Sampū and those by Dakushi.[18]

---

15. Echoing Su Tung-p'o (1036–1101), *Yin hu-shang ch'u ch'ing hou yü*.

16. Priest Ungo (1582–1658) had gone from the capital (now Kyoto) to a temple supported by the rich Date daimiate. The site must have been abandoned not long before Bashō's visit.

17. Yamaguchi Sodō (1642–1716) was a *hai-kai* poet and Hara Anteki (dates unknown) a physician and *tanka* poet.

18. For Sampū, see n. 5, above; the dates of Nakagawa Dakushi are unknown.

Hiraizumi: Yoshitsune and Heroism

On the twelfth we took Hiraizumi as our aim. With memories of places like the Pine of Anewa or the Bridge of Odae celebrated in many poems, we walked over roads where there were but few tracks, roads used only by hunters and grass-cutters, and so became unable to say which direction lay where, losing our way completely but at last coming out in the harbor town of Ishinomaki. I looked across the waters at Mount Kinka, which Yakamochi had written about for Emperor Shōmu as the blossoming of gold flowers,[19] and I saw in the harbor hundreds of the little boats that ply along the coast, while in the village the houses lay so close as to struggle with each other for room, and above them the smoke from cooking fires spiraled up over an area as far as the eye could see. We had come here with no intention of visiting at all, and now when we sought to rent lodgings we found that there was no one who let them. At last we found a pitiful little place to spend the night, and the next morning we set out once again on random travel over unknown roads. We walked along the embankment of the Kitakami River, getting glimpses from afar of places celebrated in verse—the Sode Ford, the Pasture of Obachi, and the Reed Plain of Mano. Trudging on a road along a lengthy expanse of marshy ground, we found that the countryside weighed heavily upon our feelings. We came to a place called Toima and there spent the night. At last, the next day, we arrived in Hiraizumi. The distance we had covered was more than forty-five miles.

The splendors of the three generations of Hiraizumi[20] now comprise the briefest of dreams, and of the grand façade there are only faint remains stretching out for two and a half miles. Hidehira's castle is now leveled to overgrown fields, and of all the splendors of his past, only Mount Kinkei retains its form. Climbing up to the high ramparts of what had been Yoshitsune's stronghold, one can see below the Kitakami River flowing in a wide stream from the south. The Koromo River pours past the site of loyal Izumi Saburō's castle, then beneath these ramparts, and at last into the Kitakami. The old relics of others like Yasuhira are to be found separated to the west at Koromo Barrier, which controlled the southern approach and probably was meant to protect the area against incursions by the northern tribesmen. Yoshitsune and his brave adherents took refuge in this citadel, but the most famous names claim the world only a little while, and now the level grass covers their traces. What Tu Fu wrote[21] came to my mind—

The country crumbles, but mountains and rivers endure;
A late spring visits the castle, replacing it with
green grasses . . .

---

19. Alluding to a poem by Ōtomo Yakamochi (718–785).
20. The rebellious but splendid court at Hiraizumi was established by Fujiwara Kinohara (d. 1126) in 1094. Its next two generations were those of his descendants: Motohira (d. 1157) and Hidehira (d. 1187). Hidehira's eldest son, Yasuhira

(d. 1189), disregarded his father's charge to support Yoshitsune. His betrayal led the ruthless Yoritomo in turn to destroy him and Hiraizumi in 1189.
21. Bashō adapts lines from "A Spring View" (*Ch'un wang*) by the T'ang poet, Tu Fu (712–770).

and sitting down on my pilgrim's hat I wept over the turns of time.

> The summer grasses:
> The high bravery of men-at-arms,
>   The vestiges of dream.

And by Sora:

> The white hydrangeas—
> One can see in them Kanefusa,
>   Brave when white-haired.[22]

I saw at last with astonishment the wonders of Chūson Temple, of which I had heard before. In one hall there are statues of the three great generations of Hiraizumi, in the other their coffins and three statues of the Buddha. But the seven sacred treasures had been scattered, the jeweled door was broken by the wind, and the gilt pillars were moldered by frost and snow. Yet a place that ought long since to have been utterly reduced and left level under the turf has been enclosed not long ago, and with the roof retiled it withstands the wind and the rain. It is preserved for a time as a remembrance of the past.

> The brightness lasts
> Undimmed by ages of summer rain:
>   The Temple of Light.

Dangerous Places; Penitent Prostitutes at Ichiburi

Today we passed the most trying part of our north-country journey, going through dangerous places with such horrible names as Abandoned Parents, Abandoned Children, Excluded Dog, and Rejected Horse. I was so tired that I searched out a pillow and lay down as soon as I could. Two young women were talking, however, in the next room but one, toward the front of the building. Mingled with their voices was that of an old man, and from what was said I understood that the women were from Niigata in Echigo Province, and that they were prostitutes. They were on their way to worship at the Ise Shrine, and the man had come to see them as far as this barrier at Ichiburi. He would go back to Niigata tomorrow, while they were writing letters and giving him various broken messages to carry back.

The conversation floated to me. "We are as they say waves falling upon the beach, coming to ruin on the shore, expecting no better end than 'fisherwomen' like us ever have. People treat us with disgust, and we fall lower and lower. Each night we are pledged to love a different man. To have to endure such a shameful life, what terrible things must we have done in a previous existence?"

---

22. One of the heroes of the Yoshitsune saga, Kanefusa showed great bravery when Yoshitsune and his family met destruction at Hiraizumi.

I fell to sleep with their words in my ears, and just as we were setting out the next morning, the two women came up to us weeping.

"We don't know what route to take," they said, "and so we are terribly worried about our trip. Our anxiety has made us miserable about what lies ahead, and we wonder, may we follow you—at a distance far enough so we would not embarrass you? Your clothes show that you are priests, and that means you will have pity. The boundless grace of the Buddha can be bestowed even on such as we, so please help our souls to enter his Way." They continued in tears as they spoke.

"I regret it very much," I told them, "but we are not so much traveling anywhere as stopping here and there for periods of time. It would really be better for you if you accompanied ordinary travelers. The favor of the gods should enable you to get to Ise without trouble." With that we set out on our way, but the great pity of their situation troubled me for some time.

> Prostitutes and priest
> Slept under a roof lent a beauty
> By bush clover and moon.[23]

I spoke out the verses to Sora, who set them down in his *Diary*.

Meeting Friends; A Prospect of Ise; Close

The next day, the sixteenth, the sky had cleared, and thinking that I would like to look for the famous little colored clams, I took a boat to the Beach of Iro.[24] It is a passage of about fifteen miles. A man called Tenya Something-or-other went with me, his servants taking an ample provision of lunchboxes and sake flasks.[25] We settled in the boat and set off with a smart wind, arriving in no time at all. On the beach, where there were but few huts of fishermen, there was a pitiable little Nichiren temple. It was there that we sat, and as we drank tea, heating and drinking sake, I felt the particular melancholy of an autumn evening.

> The lonely sadness,
> Exceeding even that of Suma Beach,
> These shores of autumn.

> In intervals of surf,
> The little colored shells are jumbled
> With bush-clover rubbish.[26]

---

23. The flowering bush clover symbolizes the women as the moon does the poet-priest. The poem is esteemed for the kinship, beauty, and pathos it implies Bashō found in the encounter. It is not in Sora's *Diary* and therefore was written later, probably, as the Introduction to this reading suggests, to have a love episode after the manner of a "love-verse" in linked poetry.
24. The clams are those made famous by

Saigyō's poem, *Sankashū, Zoku Kokka Taikan.*
25. Tenya Gorōzaemon (dates unknown) was a *haikai* poet. The passage is actually about four miles.
26. The two poems vary greatly, the first being subjective and allusive to the sadness of Soma Beach (from *The Tale of Genji* and other stories), the second, objective with its image of bits of broken bush-clover mingling with the famous shells.

At my request, Tōsai wrote an outline of the events of the day and left it at the temple.

Rotsū met me as I was going back to Tsuruga Harbor, and from there accompanied me to Mino Province.[27] Our pace quickened by going on horseback, it was not long before we entered the town of Ōgaki, where Sora had arrived from Ise and where Etsujin had also hurried in by horse. We all gathered at Jokō's house. Master Zensen, Keikō and his sons, and many others among my close friends came, by day and by night. They looked upon me as if I had come back from the dead, sympathized with me for the hardships of travel, and rejoiced with me that I had come through. The strain of travel still weighed upon me. But because it was already the sixth of the Ninth Month, I resolved to get on to observe the rare ceremonies at the Great Shrines of Ise.[28] And so, boarding a boat yet again—

> Parting for Futami Bay
> Is like tearing the body from the clam-shell:
> Autumn goes to its end.[29]

HIGUCHI ICHIYŌ (1872–1896)
Japan

Higuchi Ichiyō (whose given name was Natsu) was born to a socially prominent family. After receiving more education than most women, Ichiyō was reduced (with her mother and younger sister) to a grinding poverty not unlike Okyō's in the story given here. Her literary achievement during the last three years of her life earned her attention and praise. Her great work is the novella *Comparing Heights* [*Takekurabe*], completed the year she died of tuberculosis. Ichiyō is a protofeminist who focused on the struggles and miseries of women in her work. As in the writings of many of her successors today, women are presented as suffering literary subjects as well as representatives of all humanity.

Ichiyō discovered in premodern literature the resources for defining what mattered to her. As has been long recognized, Ichiyō's chief literary debt is to the gifted poet and storyteller Ihara Saikaku (1642–1693). The resemblances range from stylistic distinction to an unblinking view of reality.

---

27. The names of a number of Bashō's friends and pupils follow. Yasomura or Inbe Rotsū (1648–1738) was in Bashō's school. Ochi Etsujin (d. *ca.* 1739) was a prominent member of it. Kondō Jōkō entered it in 1687. Tsuda Zensen (dates unknown) belonged, as did also Miyazaki Keikō (d. 1693) and his three sons. As in *haikai* or *renga* linked verse, the passage of time speeds up just before the last verse, a great distance and many people being covered here.

28. The rare ceremonies, which were held every twenty-one years, took place on the tenth and thirteenth of the Ninth Month of 1689.

29. Futami Bay is near the Ise Shrines, but *Futami* may also be taken as shell-body.

"Separate Ways" features the miserable, taunted Kichizō and the gifted and well-liked heroine, Okyō. But a reversal of roles takes place. He feels grief, but she does not as she goes off to be a concubine. It becomes clear to all that she will survive through a cynicism and selfishness she has hitherto not shown. Like Saikaku, Ichiyō realistically portrays human misery with understanding rather than sentimentality.

Separate Ways [Wakare-Michi]

There was someone outside, tapping at her window.

"Okyō? Are you home?"

"Who is it? I'm already in bed," she lied. "Come back in the morning."

"I don't care if you are in bed. Open up! It's me—Kichizō, from the umbrella shop."

"What a bothersome boy you are. Why do you come so late at night? I suppose you want some rice cakes again," she chuckled. "Just a minute. I'm coming."

Okyō, a stylish woman in her early twenties, put her sewing down and hurried into the front hall. Her abundant hair was tied back simply—she was too busy to fuss with it—and over her kimono she wore a long apron and a jacket. She opened the lattice, then the storm door.

"Sorry," Kichizō said as he barged in.

Dwarf, they called him. He was a pugnacious little one. He was sixteen, and he worked as an apprentice at the umbrella shop, but to look at him one would think he was eleven or twelve. He had spindly shoulders and a small face. He was a bright-looking boy, but so short that people teased him and dubbed him "Dwarf."

"Pardon me." He went right for the brazier.

"You won't find enough fire in there to toast any of your rice cakes. Go get some charcoal from the cinder box in the kitchen. You can heat the cakes yourself. I've got to get this done tonight." She took up her sewing again. "The owner of the pawnshop on the corner ordered it to wear on New Year's."

"Hmm. What a waste, on that old baldie. Why don't I wear it first?"

"Don't be ridiculous. Don't you know what they say? 'He who wears another's clothes will never get anywhere in life.' You're a hopeless one, you are. You shouldn't say such things."

"I never did expect to be successful. I'll wear anybody's clothes—it's all the same to me. Remember what you promised once? When your luck changes, you said you'd make me a good kimono. Will you really?" He wasn't joking now.

"If only I could sew you a nice kimono, it would be a happy day. I'd gladly do it. But look at me. I don't have enough money to dress myself properly. I'm sewing to support myself. These aren't gifts I'm making." She smiled at him. "It's a dream, that promise."

"That's all right. I'm not asking for it now. Wait until some good luck comes.

Translated by Robert Lyons Danly.

At least say you will. Don't you want to make me happy? That would be a sight, though, wouldn't it?" The boy had a wistful smile on his face. "Me dressed up in a fancy kimono!"

"And if you succeed first, Kichizō, promise me you'll do the same. That's a pledge I'd like to see come true."

"Don't count on it. I'm not going to succeed."

"How do you know?"

"I know, that's all. Even if someone came along and insisted on helping me, I'd still rather stay where I am. Oiling umbrellas suits me fine. I was born to wear a plain kimono with workman's sleeves[1] and a short band around my waist. To me, all 'good luck' means is squeezing a little money from the change when I'm sent to buy persimmon juice.[2] If I hit the target someday, shooting arrows through a bamboo pole,[3] that's about all the good luck I can hope for. But someone like you, from a good family—why, fortune will come to greet you in a carriage. I don't mean a man's going to come and take you for his mistress, or something. Don't get the wrong idea." He toyed with the fire in the brazier and sighed over his fate.

"It won't be a fine carriage that comes for me. I'll be going to hell in a handcart."[4] Okyō leaned against her yardstick and turned to Kichizō. "I've had so many troubles on my mind, sometimes it feels as if my heart's on fire."

Kichizō went to fetch the charcoal from the kitchen, as he always did.

"Aren't you going to have any rice cakes?"

Okyō shook her head. "No thank you."

"Then I'll go ahead. That old tightwad at the umbrella shop is always complaining. He doesn't know how to treat people properly. I was sorry when the old woman died. *She* was never like that. These new people! I don't talk to any of them. Okyō, what do you think of Hanji at the shop? He's a mean one, isn't he? He's so stuck-up. He's the owner's son, but, you know, I still can't think of him as a future boss. Whenever I have the chance, I like to pick a fight and cut him down to size." Kichizō set the rice cakes on the wire net above the brazier. "Oh, it's hot!" he shouted, blowing on his fingers. "I wonder why it is—you seem almost like a sister to me, Okyō. Are you sure you never had a younger brother?"

"I was an only child. I never had any brothers or sisters."

"So there really is no connection between us. Boy, I'd sure be glad if someone like you would come and tell me she was my sister. I'd hug her so tight . . . After that, I wouldn't care if I died. What was I, born from a piece of wood? I've never run into anyone who was a relative of mine. You don't know how many times I've thought about it: if I'm never, ever going to meet anyone from my own family, I'd be better off dying right now. Wouldn't I? But it's odd. I still want to go on living. I have this funny dream. The few people who've been the least bit kind to me all

---

1. Narrow sleeves (*tsutsu-sode*), the better to work in.
2. Persimmon tannin was used to treat umbrellas.
3. A kind of carnival game in which arrows were blown through a bamboo tube, with a prize for hitting the target.

4. Literally, "Instead of a carriage, it will probably be a cart of fire that comes." Ichiyō plays with the meaning of "hi no kuruma" to pun on "basha." The fiery cart has two meanings: (1) the carriage that drives sinners through hell, and (2) straitened circumstances.

of a sudden turn out to be my mother and father and my brother and sister. And then I think, I want to live a little longer. Maybe if I wait another year, someone will tell me the truth. So I go on oiling umbrellas, even if it doesn't interest me a bit. Do you suppose there's anyone in the world as strange as I am? I don't have a mother or a father, Okyō. How could a child be born without either parent? It makes me pretty odd." He tapped at the rice cakes and decided they were done.

"Don't you have some kind of proof of your identity? A charm with your name on it, for instance?[5] There must be something you have, some clue to your family's whereabouts."

"Nothing. My friends used to tease me. They said I was left underneath a bridge when I was born, so I'd be taken for a beggar's baby. It may be true. Who knows? I may be the child of a tramp. One of those men who pass by in rags every day could be a kinsman. That old crippled lady with one eye who comes begging every morning—for all I know, she could be my mother. I used to wear a lion's mask and do acrobatics in the street," he said dejectedly, "before I worked at the umbrella shop. Okyō, if I were a beggar's boy, you wouldn't have been so nice to me, would you? You wouldn't have given me a second look."

"You shouldn't joke like that, Kichizō. I don't know what kind of people your parents were, but it makes no difference to me. These silly things you're saying—you're not yourself tonight. If I were you, I wouldn't let it bother me. Even if I were the child of an outcast. I'd make something of myself, whether I had any parents or not, no matter who my brothers were. Why are you whining around so?"

"I don't know," he said, staring at the floor. "There's something wrong with me. I don't seem to have any get-up-and-go."

She was dead now, but in the last generation the old woman Omatsu, fat as a *sumō* wrestler, had made a tidy fortune at the umbrella shop. It was a winter's night six years before that she had picked up Kichizō, performing his tumbler's act along the road, as she was returning from a pilgrimage.

"It's all right," she had assured him. "If the master gives us any trouble, we'll worry about it when the time comes. I'll tell him what a poor boy you are, how your companions abandoned you when your feet were too sore to go on walking. Don't worry about it. No one will raise an eyebrow. There's always room for a child or two. Who's going to care if we spread out a few boards for you to sleep on in the kitchen, and give you a little bit to eat? There's no risk in that. Why, even with a formal apprenticeship boys have been known to disappear. It doesn't prevent them from running off with things that don't belong to them. There are all kinds of people in this world. You know what they say: 'You don't know a horse till you ride it.' How can we tell whether we can use you in the shop if we don't give you a try? But listen, if you don't want to go back to that slum of yours, you're going to have to work hard. And learn how things are done. You'll have to make

---

5. "Nishiki no mamori-bukuro": paper charms with a child's name written on them were placed inside a brocade bag and car-ried by the child for good luck and protection. The little charm-bags thus became a means of identification.

up your mind: this is where your home is. You're going to have to work, you know."

And work he did. Today, by himself, Kichizō could treat as many umbrellas as three adults, humming a tune as he went about his business. Seeing this, people would praise the dead lady's foresight: "Granny knew what she was doing."

The old woman, to whom he owed so much, had been dead two years now, and the present owners of the shop and their son Hanji were hard for Kichizō to take. But what was he to do? Even if he didn't like them, he had nowhere else to go. Had not his anger and resentment at them caused his very bones and muscles to contract? "Dwarf! Dwarf!" everybody taunted him. "Eating fish on the anniversary of your parents' death! It serves you right that you're so short. Round and round we go—look at him! The tiny monk who'll never grow!"[6]

In his work, he could take revenge on the sniveling bullies, and he was perfectly ready to answer them with a clenched fist. But his valor sometimes left him. He didn't even know the date of his parents' death, he had no way to observe the yearly abstinences. It made him miserable, and he would throw himself down underneath the umbrellas drying in the yard and push his face against the ground to stifle his tears.

The boy was a little fireball. He had a violence about him that frightened the entire neighborhood. The sleeves of his plain kimono would swing as he flailed his arms, and the smell of oil from the umbrellas followed him through every season. There was no one to calm his temper, and he suffered all the more. If anyone were to show Kichizō a moment's kindness, he knew that he would cling to him and find it hard ever to let go.

In the spring Okyō the seamstress had moved into the neighborhood. With her quick wit, she was soon friendly with everyone. Her landlord was the owner of the umbrella shop, and so she was especially cordial to the members of the shop. "Bring over your mending any time, boys. I don't care what condition it's in. There are so many people at your house, the mistress won't have time to tend to it. I'm always sewing anyway, one more stitch is nothing. Come and visit when you have time. I get lonely living by myself. I like people who speak their minds, and that rambunctious Kichizō—he's one of my favorites. Listen, the next time you lose your temper," she would tell him, "instead of hitting the little white dog at the rice shop, come over to my place. I'll give you my mallet, and you can take out your anger on the fulling block. That way, people won't be so upset with you. And you'll be helping me—it'll do us both good."

In no time Kichizō began to make himself at home. It was "Okyō, this" and Okyō, that" until he had given the other workmen at the shop something new to

---

6. A song from a game that children played, forming a ring around one of their number and chanting, in part:

Mawari no mawari no kobotoke,
Naze sei ga hikui na?
Oya no hi ni aka no mama kutte toto kutte,
Sore ga sei ga hikui na!

Round and round we go, around the little monk.
Why are you so short?
You ate fish and red rice on the day you should have fasted in memory of your parents.
That's why you're so short!

tease him about. "Why, he's the mirror image of the great Chōemon!" they would laugh.[7] "At the River Katsura, Ohan will have to carry *him!* Can't you see the little runt perched on top of her sash for the ride across the river? What a farce!"

Kichizō was not without retort. "If you're so manly, why don't you ever visit Okyō? Which one of you can tell me each day what sweets she's put in the cookie jar? Take the pawnbroker with the bald spot. He's head over heels in love with her, always ordering sewing from her and coming round on one pretext or another, sending her aprons and neckpieces and sashes—trying to win her over. But she's never given him the time of day. Let alone treat him the way she does me! Kichizō from the umbrella shop—*I'm* the one who can go there any hour of the night, and when she hears it's me, she'll open the door in her nightgown. 'You haven't come to see me all day. Did something happen? I've been worried about you.' That's how she greets me. Who else gets treated that way? 'Hulking men are like big trees: not always good supports.[8] Size has nothing to do with it. Look at how the tiny peppercorn is prized.' "[9]

"Listen to him!" they would yell, pelting Kichizō across the back.

But all he did was smile nonchalantly. "Thank you very much." If only he had a little height, no one would dare to tease him. As it was, the disdain he showed them was dismissed as nothing more than the impertinence of a little fool. He was the butt of all their jokes and the gossip they exchanged over tobacco.

On the night of the thirtieth of December, Kichizō was returning home. He had been up the hill to call on a customer with apologies for the late filling of an order. On his way back now he kept his arms folded across his chest and walked briskly, kicking a stone with the tip of his sandal. It rolled to the left and then to the right, and finally Kichizō kicked it into a ditch, chuckling aloud to himself. There was no one around to hear him. The moon above shone brightly on the white winter roads, but the boy was oblivious to the cold. He felt invigorated. He thought he would stop by Okyō's on the way home. As he crossed over to the back street, he was suddenly startled: someone appeared from behind him and covered his eyes. Whoever it was, the person could not keep from laughing.

"Who is it? Come on, who is it?" When he touched the hands held over his eyes, he knew who it was. "Ah, Okyō! I can tell by your snaky fingers.[10] You shouldn't scare people."

Kichizō freed himself and Okyō laughed. "Oh, too bad! I've been discovered."

---

7. An allusion to the puppet play *Katsuragawa Renri no Shigarami* (The River Katsura and the Floodgate of Eternal Love, 1858) by Suga Sensuke. In the play, Chōemon, the head of a draper's shop, is a middle-aged man charged with watching after a fourteen-year-old girl, Ohan, when her father dies; in one scene he carries her across the Katsura River. Here, in an analogy to Kichizō's dependence on Okyō, the roles are reversed: Chōemon rides to safety on Ohan's back.

8. The saying was that great, gawky trees would never make good pillars. Ichiyō alludes to the proverb, "Udo no taiboku hashira ni naranu."

9. This too is based on a proverb: "Sanshō wa kotsubu de mo piriri to karai" (A grain of pepper may be small, but it is very hot).

10. "Koyubi no manushi," so called because the first joint of the finger would bend, but not the second.

Over her usual jacket she was wearing a hood that came down almost to her eyes. She looked smart tonight, Kichizō thought as he surveyed her appearance. "Where've you been? I thought you told me you were too busy even to eat the next few days." The boy did not hide his suspicion. "Were you taking something to a customer?"

"I went to make some of my New Year's calls early," she said innocently.

"You're lying. No one receives greetings on the thirtieth. Where did you go? To your relatives?"

"As a matter of fact, I *am* going to a relative's—to live with a relative I hardly know. Tomorrow I'll be moving. It's so sudden, it probably surprises you. It *is* unexpected, even I feel a little startled. Anyway, you should be happy for me. It's not a bad thing that's happened."

"Really? You're not teasing, are you? You shouldn't scare me like this. If you went away, what would I do for fun? Don't ever joke about such things. You and your nonsense!" He shook his head at her.

"I'm not joking. It's just as you said once—good luck has come riding in a fancy carriage. So I can't very well stay on in a back tenement, can I? Now I'll be able to sew you that kimono, Kichizō."

"I don't want it. When you say 'Good luck has come,' you mean you're going off some place worthless. That's what Hanji said the other day. 'You know Okyō the seamstress?' he said. 'Her uncle—the one who gives rub-downs over by the vegetable market—he's helped her find a new position. She's going into service with some rich family. Or so they say. But it sounds fishy to me—she's too old to learn sewing from some housewife. Somebody's going to set her up. I'm sure of it. She'll be wearing tasseled coats the next time we see her, la-de-da, and her hair all done up in ringlets, like a kept woman. You wait. With a face like hers, you don't think she's about to spend her whole life sewing, do you?' That's what he said. I told him he was full of it, and we had a big fight. But you *are* going to do it, aren't you? You're going off to be someone's mistress!"

"It's not that I want to. I don't have much choice. I suppose I won't be able to see you any more, Kichizō, will I?"

With these few words, Kichizō withered. "I don't know, maybe it's a step up for you, but don't do it. It's not as if you can't make a living with your sewing. The only one you have to feed is yourself. When you're good at your work, why give it up for something so stupid? It's disgusting of you. Don't go through with it. It's not too late to change your mind." The boy was unyielding in his notion of integrity.

"Oh, dear," Okyō sighed. She stopped walking. "Kichizō, I'm sick of all this washing and sewing. Anything would be better. I'm tired of these drab clothes. I'd like to wear a crepe kimono, too, for a change—even if it is tainted."

They were bold words, and yet it didn't sound as if she herself fully comprehended them. "Anyway," she laughed, "come home with me. Hurry up now."

"What! I'm too disgusted. You go ahead," he said, but his long, sad shadow followed after her.

Soon they came to their street. Okyō stopped beneath the window where

Kichizō always tapped for her. "Every night you come and knock at this window. After tomorrow night," she sighed, "I won't be able to hear your voice calling any more. How terrible the world is."

"It's not the world. It's you."

Okyō went in first and lit a lamp. "Kichizō, come get warm," she called when she had the fire in the brazier going.

He stood by the pillar. "No, thanks."

"Aren't you chilly? It won't do to catch a cold."

"I don't care." He looked down at the floor as he spoke. "Leave me alone."

"What's the matter with you? You're acting funny. Is it something I said? If it is, please tell me. When you stand around with a long face like that and won't talk to me, it makes me worry."

"You don't have to worry about anything. This is Kichizō from the umbrella shop you're talking to. I don't need any woman to take care of me." He rubbed his back against the pillar. "How pointless everything turns out. What a life! People are friendly, and then they disappear. It's always the ones I like. Granny at the umbrella shop, and Kinu, the one with short hair, at the dyer's shop. First Granny dies of palsy. Then Kinu goes and throws herself into the well behind the dyer's—she didn't want to marry. Now you're going off. I'm always disappointed in the end. Why should I be surprised, I suppose? What am I but a boy who oils umbrellas? So what if I do the work of a hundred men? I'm not going to win any prizes for it. Morning and night, the only title I ever hear is 'Dwarf' . . . 'Dwarf'! I wonder if I'll ever get any taller. 'All things come to him who waits,'[11] they say, but I wait and wait, and all I get is more unhappiness. Just the day before yesterday I had a fight with Hanji over you. Ha! I was so sure he was wrong. I told him you were the last person rotten enough to go off and do that kind of thing. Not five days have passed, and I have to eat crow. How could I have thought of you as a sister? You, with all your lies and tricks, and your selfishness. This is the last you'll ever see of me. Ever. Thanks for your kindness. Go on and do what you want. From now on, I won't have anything to do with anyone. It's not worth it. Good-by, Okyō."

He went to the front door and began to put his sandals on.

"Kichizō! You're wrong. I'm leaving here, but I'm not abandoning you. You're like my little brother. How can you turn on me?" From behind, she hugged him with all her might. "You're too impatient. You jump to conclusions."

"You mean you're not going to be someone's mistress?" Kichizō turned around.

"It's not the sort of thing anybody wants to do. But it's been decided. You can't change things."

He stared at her with tears in his eyes.

"Take your hands off me, Okyō."

---

11. Literally, "Honey comes to him who
    waits" (Mateba kanro).

YOSANO AKIKO (1878–1942)
Japan

Yosano Akiko was born into a family of respectable confectioners in a mercantile area of Sakai, now part of Osaka. Her husband, Tekkan (1872–1935), was also a poet and once her teacher.

As Higuchi Ichiyō revealed the strong connections between modern and premodern narrative, Yosano Akiko revives the more or less obsolete *tanka* form of court poetry. She does so with a volcanic intensity, no matter what her subject. Her language is sufficiently classical to pose difficulties to readers trained solely in modern Japanese. Akiko well knew, if all her readers did not, her debt to the figures of the past: female court poets such as Ono no Komachi, Lady Ise, Izumi Shikibu, and Princess Shokushi, not to mention male poets such as Fujiwara Teika.

Her creation of poetry was prodigious: more than twenty volumes of *tanka* and a volume devoted to *shi*, free verse or verse of regular prosody but indefinite length. Her most famous collection was undoubtedly *Tangled Hair*, [Midaregami], which presents traditional erotic images such as touch, moisture, untying a sash, as well as hair itself. Ladies of the court took pride in their long hair, which became tangled in the agitation of making love. Akiko's poetic ideal, actual experience (*jikkan*), contributed to her art: neither she nor her readers then or now could miss the conviction with which she asserted her passion.

Other recurrent images and metaphors in Akiko's poems include various domestic details: bathing, clothes and nakedness, breasts, and genitalia, as well as the traditional eroticism of spring. Her Buddhism becomes spiritual enlightenment through love, in fact, Japanese and Western concepts of love differ considerably, although Akiko if anybody transcends them both.

Akiko also confronted political themes in her poems. In one she urges her conscripted younger brother not to participate in the Russo-Japanese War; in another, she violates the taboo against criticism of the monarchy. She lent support to Japan's cause in World War II: perhaps the cause seemed better, or perhaps she had grown more conservatively patriotic. With all her poetic activity, and with the demands of family life and her many children, she still found it possible to demonstrate her bond with classical literature by translating Murasaki Shikibu's *The Tale of Genji*—thereby honoring Japan's greatest author and bringing her to life for modern readers.

from *Tangled Hair [Midaregami]*

[do not ask]

do not ask
if I have any songs
   in me now   slender

Translated by Laurel Rasplica Rodd.

Goyo Hashiguchi. *Woman Combing Her Hair.* 1920.

koto strings without bridges   all
twenty-five echo soundlessly

   in the spring breeze
cherry petals flutter to   earth
   near the many-tiered
pagoda   on the wings of doves
I will write my new poems

   all I've seen are
those green dreams of youth
   thin weightless dreams
ah   forgive me   traveler
I lack the stuff of stories

   the dancing girl
drifts off to sleep   how lovely
   her slumbering face
this morning   aboard the riverboat
of spring   leaving the capital

   spring is short
what is there in life that
   does not decay
I let him caress
these breasts   their vital force

   to punish men
those men of heavy sins
   was I created
with skin clean and pure
with black hair hanging long   30

My Brother, You Must Not Die [Kimi Shinitamō Koto nakare][1]

My young brother, I weep for you.
My brother, you must not die.
You, the last born,
Apple of our parents' eyes.
Did they teach you to hold a sword,   5
Teach you to kill?
Did they nurture you for twenty-four years
And send you to kill and die?

You are to carry on the name
Of a proud old house,   10
Merchants of Sakai.
My brother, you must not die.
Whether the fortress at Port Arthur falls
Or not—what does it matter?
Should it concern you? War is not   15
The tradition of a merchant house.
My brother, you must not die.
Let the Emperor himself go
Off to war.
"Die like beasts,   20
Leaving pools of human blood.
In death is your glory."
If that majestic heart is truly wise,
He cannot have such thoughts.

Ah, my young brother,   25
You must not die in battle.
Since this past autumn, your aged mother,
Widowed,
Has been pathetic in her grief.
Now she's sent her son away and keeps the house alone.   30
Even in this "secure and joyful" reign
Her white hairs increase.

---

1. Written in the 7-5 measure associated with
   song and stage.

Weeping in the shadow of the shop curtain,
Your young bride
Of but ten months—
Have you forgotten her? Do you not yearn for her?   35
Imagine her misery
If you to whom she would turn in sorrow
Were gone.
Oh no, my brother, you must not die.   40

from *Love's Robe* [*Koigoromo*]

[*To raise yet higher*]

To raise yet higher
the *Passions of Spring Dawn* I add
    The Tales of Ise[2]
but they fail to hold as a pillow
tumbling beneath our motions.   5

So. Kamakura,
and here the great Buddha sits
    while *my* Shakamuni
manifests himself in beauty
here in this summer woods.   10

(1905)

from *Collection of Spring Mud* [*Shundeishū*][3]

[*Bear no suspicion*]

Bear no suspicion
that my passion is of a kind
    to be extinguished,
O love you are the man who bestows
upon the skies their twilight hour.

(1911)

Translated by Earl Miner.

---

2. *Passions of Spring Dawn* (*Shunjōshō*) appears to exist only in this poem, whereas *The Tales of Ise* is real enough: see above. The title of the collection, *Love's Robe* (*Koi-*

goromo), is an ancient word imaging love as an enveloping passion.
3. The title of the collection is adapted from Yosa Buson's *Spring Mud Collection of Stanzas* (1727).

TAKAMURA KŌTARŌ (1883–1956)
Japan

Takamura Kōtarō is considered one of the two principal creators of modern Japanese poetry.

After living together for some time, Kōtarō and the artist Naganuma Chieko married in 1915. Their initial happiness and fulfillment did not last and Chieko gradually but increasingly showed signs of mental breakdown: depression, suicidal gestures, schizophrenia. Kōtarō went to the extraordinary lengths to care for his wife, and he tried to hide her wild behavior from the neighborhood.

It remains a mystery how poetry written during such turbulent times could be so readable. *Chieko Poems* (1941) contains twenty-nine free-verse poems of varying length and six *tanka*. Kōtarō also ventured into prose with "Memories of My Dead Wife—The Latter Half of Her Life" [*Kanojo no Hansei—Naki Tsuma no Omoide*]. A poet of free verse who takes both to the ancient form of the *tanka* and to prose clearly is compelled to self-expression. The sheer readability of his poems as well as his great versatility with literary forms—from the *tanka* to free verse to prose—have preserved his rank among Japan's greatest modern poets.

Dream

By that smart mountain cable car with Chieko
I went to peer into the crater of Vesuvius.
The apparent dream fragmented like spice.
Chieko wrapped me with the bursting mist of her twenties.
At the end of the telescope like a slender bamboo tube   5
gaseous fire spurted as from a jet plane.
Mt. Fuji appeared through the telescope.
Something interesting occurred at the bottom and
people swarmed at the bowl edge.
At the foot of Mt. Fuji, Chieko had made a sheaf of seven
     autumn grasses
and threw it deep into the crater of Vesuvius.   10
Chieko was warm, pure, beautiful
and yet full of sensuous charm.
That woman's body burning translucent as mountain water,
she walked clinging to me, treading the crumbling sands.   15
Everywhere the Pompeian stench was suffocating.
Vanished the inharmony of whole being that until yesterday
     existed
and in the autumn fresh mountain hut at 5 a.m. I awoke.

Translated by Hiroaki Sato.

Soliloquy on a Night of Blizzard

Outside, there's a blizzard raging.
The rats stay put, the village
far off, is hushed into sleep
and there's no other soul on the mountain.
I throw a big stump in the fire   5
and it burns splendidly.
My physiology sixty-seven years old,
I think I feel much better now.
As long as that lust is there,
I tell you, doing real work is hard.   10
Art, at bottom, demands such inhumanity.
Total absence of lust of course wouldn't help.
I'd better say, I've known it thoroughly
and now I don't have it.
If Chieko appeared here now   15
she'd simply be all gaiety, and laugh.
What comes out of that harsh inhumanity,
a barely perceptible fragrance, is perhaps
what they call divine—
though I can't be senile.   20

Barren Homecoming

Chieko, so anxious to return,
has come home, dead.
Late in the October night, I sweep
a small corner of the empty studio
and put there Chieko, carefully.   5
Before this single human body
that does not move
I stand, lost.
People set the screens upside down.
People light candles, burn incense.   10
People make up Chieko's face,
And so things get done by themselves.
Day breaks, night comes,
all around there's noisy and gaiety,
the house fills with flowers,   15
it comes to look like someone else's funeral
and before I know it, Chieko is gone.
In the deserted, dark studio I stand alone.
Outside, there's a full bright moon,
or so they say.   20

Metropolis

Into the depth of nature that Chieko longed for
the turning of fate has cast me.
Fate destroyed the living Chieko in the capital
and put me, a child of the capital, here.
Mountains of Iwate are fierce, beautiful, immaculate,   5
surround me, and are without mercy.
Hypocrisy and idleness cannot exist in this soil.
I, like nature, breathless
thrust forward the elemental only.
Chieko who died lives again   10
lives here, lodged in my flesh
and delights in being mingled with river, mountain, grass, tree.
Phenomena of cosmos that generates endless transformation,
rising and falling of generations that forever turn,
all these Chieko receives   15
and I too receive them.
My heart stirring,
what people see as a solitary life in mountain woods,
sitting by the fireplace of my small hut
I consider a metropolis on earth.   20

Two at the Foot of the Mountain

The back mountain of Bandai that splits in two and slopes
glares fiercely at the August sky above.
Its skirts spread out, trail into the distance
and a profusion of pampas grass overwhelms.
Half mad, my wife sits with the grass beneath her   5
and leaning heavily on my arm,
like a small girl cries without ceasing.
—I'll go to pieces pretty soon—
Borne away by the demon of fate that assaults consciousness,
she takes inevitable leave of her soul.   10
Premonition of the inexorable,
—I'll go to pieces pretty soon.—
The mountain wind feels cold to my hands wet with tears.
Wordless, I look intently at the figure of my wife.
Turning to me once more at the border of awareness   15
she clings to me.
Now there is not in the world a means to recover her.
My heart in this moment splits, drops away
and in the sharp silence becomes one with the universe
    that wraps us two.   20

Lemon Elegy

So intensely you had been waiting for the lemon
in the sad white light deathbed
you took that one lemon from my hand
and bit it sharply with your bright teeth.
A fragrance arose in topaz   5
and those heavenly drops of juice
flashed you back to sanity.
Your eyes smiled, blue and transparent.
You grasped my hand, how vigorous you were—
There had been a storm in your throat   10
but just before life was gone
you found again yourself,
all life's love into one moment fallen.
As once you did in the depth of mountains
you did then—let out a great sigh   15
and with it your organs stopped.

Today too I shall put a cool fresh piece of lemon
by the cherry blossoms in front of your photograph.

Invaluable Chieko

Chieko sees what one cannot see,
hears what one cannot hear.

Chieko goes where one cannot go,
does what one cannot do.

Chieko does not see the living me,   5
yearns for the me behind me.

Chieko has cast off the weight of suffering,
has strayed out to the endless desolate zone of beauty.

I persistently hear her call to me, but
Chieko no longer has a ticket to the human world.   10

SHIGA NAOYA (1883–1971)
Japan

Shiga was a cofounder of the literary magazine *Shirakaba* ("White Birches") along
with Mushanokoji Saneatsu, the three Arishima brothers, and others. The school

associated with the magazine is credited with establishing Japanese versions of humanism and naturalism and with introducing impressionism. To a Western observer, that may seem like a strange combination, but the versions are definitely Japanese; in fact, modern Japanese literature is often discussed as a succession of such schools. Different people mean and practice differing things under the same terms. "At Kinosaki," one of Shiga's major works, combines the introspection that the *White Birches* school favored with a highly admired, clean economy of style.

Shiga's works require a redefinition of the term "novel." The Japanese have coined the borrowed word *noberu* for novel, but for what they value as Japanese, they use *shōsetsu*. The term is adapted from the Chinese word *xiaoshuo* ("little talk"), although standard examples run to 120 chapters. *Shōsetsu* sets the modern prose narrative off from the *monogatari,* a courtly story genre from a later period, as well as from varieties of writing from the period between 1600 and 1868. It also distinguishes Shiga from anything in Western literature. These very distinctions are also connections, especially between the *shōsetsu* and basic Japanese aesthetic principles. In short, the term designates modern literary prose narrative (commonly much more factual than the novel) referring in varying degrees to both earlier Japanese narrative and to the Western novel and its assumptions. The *shōsetsu* comes in three lengths (short, medium, and long) and in two supposedly distinct versions (serious and mass-circulated).

Shiga's *shōsetsu* is serious and exemplifies the singular Japanese concept of the *shishōsetsu* (or *watakushishōsetsu*), the "I-*shōsetsu*," to translate half of it back into English. That is, Shiga did go himself to Kinosaki to recuperate from an illness. He did read the biography, observe the bees, etc. We know he did, not simply from other records but because in Japan literature is still thought to be author-dominated and factual—in the absence of contrary evidence. Understanding and appreciation of this brief story is a touchstone to our comprehension of mainstream modern Japanese literature and of enduring Japanese tastes.

At Kinosaki

I went by myself to the hot springs of Tajima-Kinoskai to convalesce after my accident. I had been hit by a train on the Tokyo loop line, and was told by the doctor that there was some slight risk of my developing meningitis where I had been injured on my back. Such a development would surely prove fatal but was, he said, highly unlikely. I would not be wholly out of danger, however, for two or three years; in the meantime, rest and caution were imperative. And so I went on this journey intending to stay for something over three weeks, which would bring me to well over a month since the time of the accident.

My mind was still not quite clear. I had become terribly forgetful. And yet a tranquility such as I had not known in recent years came over me, and I felt at peace. The rice harvest was about to begin; the weather was favorable.

As I had come alone, there was neither the need nor the opportunity to talk with anyone. I spent my days reading and writing or sitting back in a chair set just outside my room looking up at the mountains and down at the people passing by; and I went out for walks. One pleasant walk was to take the road that leads

Translated by William F. Sibley.

gradually upward from town alongside a small stream. Where the stream cuts down around the flank of the mountain, it creates a small pool that is full of brook trout. If you look closely you can also see large river crabs, hairy, resting motionless like stones on the bottom. I would often take this walk before dinner. The thoughts that came to mind in the chill evening air, by the thin blue stream traversing solitary autumn ravines, naturally tended toward the melancholy. Yet, for all my gloomy thoughts, I felt quiet and contented. Many times I though of the accident, of how close I had come to finding myself under the sod of Aoyama: my face cold and blue and stiff, the wounds I had suffered still there and on my back, untreated; the bodies of my grandfather and my mother lying beside me, nothing passing between us. Such were my thoughts. Melancholy though they were, they did not fill me with dread. It would happen some day. When? In the past, whenever I wondered about the "when," I had unconsciously thrust it far into the future. Now I had come to know it could be anytime. I was meant to die right then but did not. Something had not let me die. There was work for me as yet undone. According to a life of Lord Clive that was read at my school, he had been much encouraged by such notions in his later undertakings, and I would have liked to view my own narrow escape in this light. Indeed, I did, in a certain sense. And yet my spirit had grown so unaccountably tranquil. In one way or another, I had become intimate with death.

My room was off by itself on the second floor and so unusually restful by day. When I was tired of reading and writing I would relax in a chair on the balcony. To one side of my room the roof of the inn's entranceway was joined to the building with wooden panels. Beneath the paneling there was apparently a beehive; for there was always, when the weather was clear, a quantity of plump, tiger-striped bees busy at work from morning until close to sundown. Once they had squeezed themselves out through the cracks between the panels, they would drop down onto the roof of the entranceway. There they would use their front legs to make fine adjustments on wings and antennae; then, except for a few that continued to walk about awhile, they would thrust their wings tautly forward and take off with a low buzzing sound. They gathered speed as soon as they were in the air, swarming toward the potted *yatsude* shrubs that had just come into bloom. I idled away much time at the railing of my balcony, entertained by the comings and goings of these bees.

It happens one morning that I discover a dead bee on the roof. Its legs are folded tightly under its belly, its antennae droop lackadaisically over its face. The other bees appear coldly indifferent. They continue to pass close by as they purposefully fly to and from the nest but show no sign of alarm at this spectacle. The bees busily going about their work now seem especially alive. And the one that lies collapsed in their path, rooted to the same spot, I note at intervals, all day long, seems especially dead. The bee remains there for about three days. It is a very tranquil sight to see. It is, to be sure, lonely to look at this solitary corpse on the cold rooftiles after the other bees have returned to the hive at twilight. But it is also thoroughly tranquil.

One night it rained very hard. By morning it was clear; the ground, the foliage, the roof had been washed clean. The bee's body was gone. The others went on buzzing industriously around the hive while the dead one, most likely swept down the rainspout, would now be encased in the mud somewhere below, legs bent, antennae drooping as before. It would remain frozen there until the outside world wrought some new change in its situation. For that matter, it was possible that ants had already come to drag it away. But even that prospect conveyed a sense of great tranquility, in that this bee, which had toiled so furiously, was now utterly still. I felt a kinship with that stillness.

Not long ago, I had written a short story entitled "Han's Crime," in which the principal character kills his wife in a jealous rage, intensified by a strong, almost biological impulse, upon discovering an affair she once engaged in with a friend of his before their marriage. The story I had written centers on Han's motives and reactions; now I wished to rewrite it from the viewpoint of his wife, ending with the tranquility of her lying in the grave after the violence is over. Although I did not, finally, carry through with my resolve to write "The Murdered Wife of Han," the urge to recast the piece into her point of view was very strong—and very unsettling, since it was quite opposite to the outlook on such matters maintained by the hero of a novel I was working on.

One morning after the dead bee had been swept out of sight forever, I left my inn on an excursion to a park at Higashiyama that affords a view of the Maruyama river, where it flows out into the Sea of Japan. Along the way, in front of the spa at Ichinoyu, a small stream flows serenely down the middle of the road toward its confluence with the Maruyama. As I walked down this road, I came across a small crowd of people gathered on a bridge and the adjacent banks. They were peering down into the stream and making quite a commotion, the cause of which, I soon saw, was a large rat that had been thrown into the water.

The rat is swimming frantically in a desperate effort to reach safety. Its neck has been pierced through with a broiling skewer over half a foot long, which protrudes a few inches above the head and below the neck. The rat keeps trying to crawl up onto the stone embankment. Several children and a rickshaman who looks to be about forty begin to hurl rocks in its direction but fail to hit the mark. As the rocks ricochet off the embankment, the crowd roars with laughter. The rat at last manages to gain a foothold in a crack between the stones of the embankment, only to be blocked in its upward progress by the protruding skewer and fall back into the water. The creature resumes its struggle to escape, by whatever means, with a vengeance: this much is clear from its movements, even if one cannot read the expression on its face. In the apparent conviction that, regardless of the piercing skewer, if only it can get away it will be saved, the rat swims back into midstream. The children and the rickshaman throw more rocks, rising warmly to this new challenge. Startled by the rocks, a few ducks that have been foraging by a laundry station at the water's edge extend their necks and stare suspiciously. As the rocks land here and there with a loud splash, the ducks' look of suspicion turns to consternation; necks outstretched, with much quacking they start to work their webbed feet as fast as they will go, and paddle away upstream. I finally lack the stomach to watch the rat's inevitable end.

Afterward, I retained in my mind's eye, with amazing clarity, the image of this creature struggling for all it was worth against its fate of certain death. Once again I felt sad and lonely, but this time I was upset as well. This was surely what dying was like. The suffering that comes before that tranquility I aspired to was frightening. However sympathetic I had come to feel with the silent nothingness that follows death, these strenuous exertions that precede it filled me with fear. Animals have no choice, lacking the recourse of suicide, other than to struggle that way to the bitter end. What would I do, I wondered, if I found myself in a plight similar to the rat's? Would I not behave in the same way? I could not help reflecting that indeed I had approached that state after my accident. I had chosen the hospital myself and supplied directions to those who were helping me; I had insisted that they call ahead lest the proper doctor be unavailable when I arrived and my treatment delayed. I was myself astonished later on to recall how lucidly my mind had focused on a few vital matters when I was in fact partly unconscious—and even though, for all I knew, I was facing a crisis of life and death. Not that I was unaware of the gravity of my situation, but I had gone along inexplicably unscathed by any strong fear of death. I did at length turn to a friend at the hospital and ask him what the doctor had said—would I pull through? And when he replied that my injury was apparently not fatal, I felt a sudden surge of strength. All my tension had given way to elation. But how would I have reacted had I been told it was fatal? I could not be sure. It was quite possible that I would have despaired. And yet, it struck me, at that moment I might well not have been overwhelmed by the fear of death, as one expects the case to be in the abstract. I now imagined that, confronted with the most pessimistic diagnosis, I would nevertheless have persisted in my will to survive and done everything in my power to that end. I would not then have acted so very differently from the rat. And if it were to happen to me again . . . I put it to myself, and decided that even now I was likely to react in more or less the same fashion as the rat had. And so it seemed that my impulse to accept death whenever, however it might come had not had any immediate effect in reality; yet it was just as real to me as the will to survive; and I could only conclude that if, when the time came, my spirit of acceptance were to prevail, well and good, if not, so be it.

One evening some time after this encounter I was leisurely walking up the hill that follows the little stream out of town. Where the road crosses the Sanin Line tracks (just before the tunnel) it suddenly grows steep and narrow, the stream turns into rapids, and the houses disappear. When I reached that point I really meant to turn back but allowed myself to be led on by one prospect after another "just up the road," until I had rounded quite a few bends. The surroundings were cloaked in a pale blue aura, the air was cool enough to produce a slight chill on the skin, the enveloping stillness not so much soothing as vaguely unsettling. There were tall mulberry trees growing along the roadside. On a branch that stretched out over the road from one of the trees on the opposite side, I noticed a single leaf that fluttered constantly in an even, steady rhythm. Without a breath of wind, in the stillness only faintly interrupted by the murmur of the stream, there was this leaf unmistakably flapping back and forth, back and forth. I could scarcely believe my eyes, and was even a little frightened. But my curiosity got the better of me. Just as I went over to investigate from underneath the tree, a breeze came up. Whereupon the leaf ceased to move. It was, I realized, a quite ordinary phenomenon. And I had thought I knew a good deal about such matters!

It was becoming noticeably dark. There was no end to this business of going on "just up the road," I told myself, and firmly decided to turn back. My gaze wandered for a moment toward the stream. On the far bank was a large rock, at least three feet across, that slanted down into the water, and on the rock there was a small black creature—a salamander. It was still wet, its color particularly lustrous. It lay against the sloping rock with its eyes fixed downward on the flowing stream. A trickle of water from its body etched a dark, inch-long mark on the dry surface of the rock. I crouched down to have a clearer look, out of nothing more than idle curiosity. I was no longer disgusted at the sight of salamanders, as I had been at one time. (Among such creatures, the ordinary lizard, of the sort one sees in stone walls and the like, I am rather fond of; geckos I loathe above all things that crawl; and salamanders I don't feel very strongly about one way or the other. Ten years or so ago, it is true, when I was at Ashinoko, I used to see salamanders clustered around the drainpipe of my hotel and think to myself how horrid it would be if I were one of them. I would conjure up the possibility of being reborn as one, until it became a kind of automatic association. But I had long since got over this strange notion.)

Simply out of curiosity, then, I take it into my head to startle the salamander and make it move. I can already picture it wriggling down the rock in its ungainly way. I pick up a stone the size of a small ball which lies at hand and, still in a crouching position, toss it across the stream. It can hardly be said that I have aimed at the salamander, and even if I did, I am much too poor a shot to entertain the possibility of hitting it. I hear the stone knock against the rock then plop down into the stream. Simultaneous with the first sound the salamander appears to hop a few inches to one side. Then its tail arches up in the air. I cannot make out what has happened, it does not at first occur to me that I could have hit it. Slowly and effortlessly the arch of the salamander's tail collapses. At the end of its rigid forelegs braced against the incline of the rock, the toes curl inward, and its whole body flops forward listlessly. Its tail now glued flat against the rock, the salamander does not move a muscle. It is dead.

What a foolish thing I have done, I thought to myself. I kill insects all the time, to be sure, but this was different: to have killed without the slightest intention of doing so was somehow utterly repugnant. I was undeniably the agent, but this had come about through sheer random chance. The salamander's death was in a real sense quite accidental. As I crouched there lost in thought, the world narrowed down to myself and the salamander. From the point of view of this particular creature, I could see the pity of it. At the same time, I felt with equal force the gentle pathos of all living things. By chance I had not died and by chance the salamander had. Moved by the pathos that lay in these realities, I made my way back to the inn along the dark road now barely visible at my feet. When I came within sight of the lights at the edge of town, my thoughts turned to the dead bee. By now it would have been soaked into the ground with the rains we had since had. And the rat—it was not unlikely that its water-logged corpse had been carried downriver with other pieces of refuse and been washed up on the seashore. And here am I, I noted to myself, walking down the road. I knew I ought to be grateful for this fact. Any yet I could not bring myself honestly to exult in it. To be alive and to be dead were not opposite extremes. They were not far apart at all, I felt. It was now quite dark. My eyes could make out nothing but the distant lights. Unaided by sight, my feet moved very haltingly. Only my thoughts moved swiftly, oblivious to the surroundings, confirming me in that sense of my recent experience at which I had already arrived.

I left Kinosaki when my three weeks were up. I have in the end been spared the serious complications which could have developed out of my injury. Or, at least, that of meningitis.

HAGIWARA SAKUTARŌ (1886–1942)
Japan

A vote by critics would elect Hagiwara Sakutarō as Japan's greatest modern poet. In his work Japanese poetry took on a music not heard before, but heard in variations ever since. Earlier free verse had been more or less prose set in separate lines. Sakutarō invented a free prosody (so to speak) and a language that was poetic in the best sense of doing what prose could not. He also transcended the self-pity preoccupying other poets, dealing instead with existential crisis. His best-known collection, *Howling at the Moon,* appeared in 1917, predating T. S. Eliot's *The Waste Land* by five years and having no Ezra Pound to teach Sakutarō verbal economy.

Sakutarō's poems are deceptively simple, becoming more complex the closer one looks. His situations and diminutive plots reveal an intuitive grasp of modernity—which is defined in terms of something lost. Yet even Sakutarō's harshest critics agree that there are deep implications in his poems. There is in him a totally unsentimental version of that yearning that marks Japanese poetry, especially concerning love—a subject he rarely touches on, though some would argue that love is generally implied. Finally, beyond the yearning, but growing from its presence, is an implied other order, a transcendent world.

The titles alone of Sakutarō's major collections are suggestive. *Howling at the Moon* [*Tsuki ni Hoeru, 1917*] is wolf-like, but the moon is humanly sought out and occupies a realm above us. *The Blue Cat* [*Aoneko,* 1923] recalls the work of Picasso and Cézanne, and it anticipates Wallace Stevens' "Man with a Blue Guitar." *Dear Scenes of Home* [*Kyōdo Bōkeishi,* 1926] implies a yearning for what belongs to us but can be reached only by memory. *Ice Land* [*Hyoto,* 1934], which some think his greatest work, grew from a deeply painful divorce, to which the title refers. As these selections make clear, understanding Sakutarō is a strenuous but rewarding experience.

from **Howling at the Moon [Tsuki ni Hoeru, 1917]**

Frog's Death

A frog was killed,
the children made a circle and raised their hands,
all, together,
raised their lovely,
bloody hands,   5
the moon appeared,
on the hill stands a man.
Under his hat, a face.

Chrysanthemum Gone Rancid

The chrysanthemum has gone sour,
the chrysanthemum aches and drips,
a pity what a pity, in early Frost Month,
my platinum hand wilts,
as I sharpen my fingers,   5
hoping to nip the chrysanthemum,
the chrysanthemum lest it be nipped,
in a corner of glittering heaven,
the chrysanthemum is ill,
the rancid chrysanthemum aches.   10

Chair

The person sleeping under the chair,
is he the children of the person who made the grand house?

The Reason the Person Inside Looks Like a Deformed Invalid

I am standing in the shadow of a *lace* curtain,
that is the reason my face looks vague.
I am holding a telescope in my hands,
I am looking through it far into the distance,
I am looking at the woods,   5
where dogs and lambs made of nickel and children with bald heads are walking,
those are the reasons my eyes look *somewhat* smoked over.
I ate too much of the plate of *cabbage* this morning,
and besides this windowglass is very shoddily made,
that is the reason my face looks so excessively distorted.   10

Translated by Hiroaki Sato.

To tell you the truth,
I am healthy, perhaps too healthy,
and yet, why are you staring at me, there?
Why smiling so eerie a smile?
Oh, of course, as for the part of my body below the waist,   15
if you are saying that area isn't *clear,*
that's a somewhat foolish question,
of course, that is, close to this pale window wall,
I am standing inside the house.

The World of Bacteria

Bacteria's legs,
bacteria's mouths,
bacteria's ears,
bacteria's noses,

bacteria are swimming.   5

Some in a person's womb,
some in a clam's intestines,
some in an onion's spherical core,
some in a landscape's center.

Bacteria are swimming.   10

Bacteria's hands grow right and left, crosswise,
the tips of their hands branch out like roots,
from there sharp nails grow,
capillaries and such spread *all over.*

Bacteria are swimming.   15

Where bacteria live their lives,
as if through an invalid's skin,
a vermilion light shines thinly in,
and only that area is faintly visible,
looks truly, truly sorrow-unbearable.   20

Bacteria are swimming.

Spring Night

Things like littlenecks,
things like quahogs,
things like water-fleas,
these organisms, bodies buried in sand,
out of nowhere,   5

hands like silk threads innumerably grow,
hands' slender hairs move as the waves do.
A pity, on this lukewarm spring night,
purling the brine flows,
over the organisms water flows,   10
even the tongues of clams, flickering, looking sad,
as I look around at the distant beach,
along the wet beach path,
a row of invalids, bodies below their waists missing, is walking,
walking unsteadily.   15
Ah, over the hair of those human beings as well,
passes the spring night haze, all over, deeply,
rolling, rolling in,
this white row of waves is ripples.

Daybreak

During the long illness and pain,
spiders have covered his face with webs,
his body below the waist has faded like a shadow,
a bush has grown above his waist,
arms gone rotten,   5
body all over, truly messed up,
oh, today again the moon is out,
the daybreak moon is out,
and in the opaque light like a lantern
a deformed white dog is howling.   10
With eastern clouds near,
in the lonesome road's direction, howling, a dog, you see.

Swimmer

The swimmer's body elongates aslant,
his arms, laid out long side by side, are extended,
the swimmer's heart becomes translucent as a jellyfish,
the swimmer's eyes listening to a temple bell ringing,
the swimmer's soul looks above the water, at the moon.

Fear of the Countryside

I fear the countryside,
fear the rows of rice stalks growing thin and long,
trembling in deserted paddies of the countryside.
Fear the swarms of poor human beings living in dark dwellings.

When sitting on a ridge between paddies,   5
the billow-like weight of soil darkens my heart,
the rotten smell of soil blackens my skin,
winter-withered lonely nature oppresses my life.

The air of the countryside is gloomy and oppressive,
the touch of the countryside is gritty and sickening,   10
when I sometimes think of the countryside,
I'm tormented by the smell of animal skin coarse in *texture*.
I fear the countryside,
the countryside is a pale fever dream.

Sunny Spring

Ah, spring comes from afar, smoky,
under puffy swollen willow buds,
eager to press its gentle lips close,
and suck in a virgin's kiss,
spring comes from afar riding a *rubber*-wheeled rickshaw.   5
In the absent-minded landscape,
the white rickshawman's legs hurry,
but going, going, the wheels turn backward,
gradually the shafts begin to lift away from the ground,
then too, the good passenger is *oddly* unsteady about his waist,   10
all of which looks much too precarious—so saying,
at the least expected moment the spring gives a snow-white yawn.

KAWABATA YASUNARI (1899–1972)
Japan

Kawabata Yasunari still remains Japan's only Nobel laureate in literature (1968). He is considered to be among the modern *shōsetsu* artists ("novelists") who have most deserved such recognition. First is Natsume Sōseki (1867–1916). To many he is the greatest of modern Japanese writers, but his accomplishments cannot be conveyed by a brief selection of writing. The next is Tanizaki Jun'ichirō (1888–1965), whose *Makioka Sisters* is a very great work indeed.

Some think Kawabata's greatest work is *Snow Country* [*Yukiguni*], but we are making a different judgment here. *The Sound of the Mountain* [*Yama no oto*] deals with a family headed by the aging Shingo and his wife, Yasuko. Their daughter, Fusako, comes home with her child after a disastrous marriage. She becomes jealous of Kikuko, her sister-in-law, wife of the war-damaged son, Shūichi. Numerous other important characters are recalled or appear, since the story features the sen-

sations and memories of Shingo, who has heard "the sound of the mountain," signifying his approaching death. The emotional current of the story is that generated by
the respect, transformed sexuality, and love between Shingo and Kikuko.

The selection begins with Fusako taxing her mother's patience by complaining about her father's greater care for Kikuko, who, we learn, has had an abortion.
She does not wish to bear Shūichi a child because she feels his philanderings and
drinking make him an unworthy husband. She upsets everybody concerned
except Fusako by returning to her family to convalesce after the abortion. The
main action of the chapter involves Kikuko's agreeing to come back to Shingo's
home in Kamakura, near Tokyo. Her telephone conversation and rendezvous
with Shingo in gardens where lovers often meet are high points in the work.

The Sound of the Mountain focuses on the dislocations of prewar Japan and
the immediate postwar period before Japan's economic success. Shūichi and
Fusako are spiritual casualties. To Kawabata, Shingo and Kikuko represent what
is enduringly Japanese, at least for the male imagination. In fact, although Kikuko
can be resisted on many grounds, she cannot be resisted as Kawabata's surrogate
for hope in the world, for faith in human beauty and goodness.

Three things are essential for an understanding of Kawabata. The first is his
frequent expression of hope: "Our language is primarily for expressing human
goodness and beauty." Another is his suicide in 1972. The third is that, in the
Japanese view, neither the first nor the second factor is wholly positive or wholly
negative.

The Sound of the Mountain was published not so much serially as in separate
parts. One might say that Kawabata respected plot: he trusted it to take care of
itself. He greatly admired *The Tale of Genji,* Sei Shōnagon's *Pillow Book,* and *renga*
linked poetry. All the chapters in *The Sound of the Mountain* share the spirit of
linked-poetry discipline: like the title of the entire book (*Yama no Oto*), the title
of each chapter consists of two nouns joined by a possessive particle. When
Kawabata finds he has no more to write, he simply stops.

from **The Sound of the Mountain [Yama no Oto]**

A Garden in the Capital

1

Father is a very interesting man, isn't he, Mother?" said Fusako, noisily loading the
dinner dishes onto a tray. "He's more reserved with his daughter than with the girl
who came in from outside."

"Please, Fusako."

"But it's true. If the spinach was overdone, why didn't he come out and say
so? It wasn't as if I'd cooked it to a pulp. You could still see the shape of spinach.
Maybe he should have it done in a hot spring."

"A hot spring?"

"They cook eggs and dumplings in hot springs, don't they? I remember you

Translated by Edward G. Seidensticker.

Kawabata Ryushi. *Music of Spring Trees.*

once gave me something called radium eggs, from somewhere or other, with the whites hard and the yolks soft. And didn't you say they could cook a fine egg at the Squash House in Kyoto?"

"Squash House?"

"Oh, the Gourd House. Every beggar knows that much. I'm just saying you can squash your ideas about good and bad cooking for all the difference they make to me."

Yasuko laughed.

But Fusako went on unsmiling. "If he takes it to a radium spring and watches the time and the temperature very, very closely, he'll be as healthy as Popeye, even without Kikuko to look after him. Myself, I've had enough of all this moping." Pushing herself up from her knees, she went off with the heavy tray. "Dinner doesn't seem to taste the same without a handsome son and a beautiful daughter-in-law."

Shingo looked up. His eyes met Yasuko's. "She does talk."

"Yes. She's been holding back both the talk and the tears because of Kikuko."

"You can't keep children from crying," muttered Shingo.

His mouth was slightly open, as if he meant to say more, but Fusako, staggering off toward the kitchen, spoke first. "It's not the children. It's me. Of course children cry."

They heard her flinging dishes into the sink.

Yasuko half stood up. They heard sniffling in the kitchen.

Rolling her eyes up at Yasuko, Satoko ran off after her mother.

A most unpleasing expression, thought Shingo.

Yasuko put Kuniko on Shingo's knee. "Watch her for a minute," she said, following them to the kitchen.

The baby was soft in his arms. He pulled her close to him. He took her feet in his hand. The hollow of the ankles and the swelling of the calves were also in his hand.

"Does it tickle?" but Kuniko evidently did not think so.

It seemed to Shingo that when Fusako, still a babe in arms, had lain naked, having a change of clothes, and he had tickled her armpits, she had wrinkled her nose and waved her arms at him, but he could not really remember.

Shingo had seldom spoken of what a homely baby she was. To speak of the matter would have been to bring back the image of Yasuko's beautiful sister.

His hope that Fusako would change faces several times before she grew up had not been realized, and the hope itself had faded with the years.

His granddaughter Satoko seemed somewhat better favored than her mother, and there was hope for the baby.

Was he searching for the image of Yasuko's sister even in his grandchildren? The thought made Shingo dislike himself.

And even while disliking himself, he was lost in fantasy: would not the child Kikuko had done away with, his lost grandchild, have been Yasuko's sister, reborn, was she not a beauty refused life in this world? He was even more dissatisfied with himself.

As he loosened his grip on her feet, Kuniko climbed from his knee and started off toward the kitchen. Her arms were bent in front of her, and her legs were unsteady.

"You'll fall, " said Shingo. But the baby had already fallen.

She fell forward and rolled to her side, and for a time did not cry.

The four of them came back into the breakfast room, Satoko clinging to Fusako's sleeve, Yasuko with Kuniko in her arms.

"Father is very absent-minded these days, Mother," said Fusako, wiping the table. "When he was changing clothes this evening, he was quite a sight. He was starting to put on an obi, and he had his kimono and *juban*[1] with the right side pulled over the left. Can you imagine it? I don't suppose he's ever done that before. He must be getting senile."

"I did it once before. I had the right side over the left, and Kikuko said that in Okinawa it didn't matter whether you had the left side or the right side over."

"In Okinawa? I wonder if that's true."

Fusako was scowling again. "Kikuko knows how to please you. That was very clever of her. In Okinawa, was it?"

Shingo controlled his irritation. "The word *juban* comes from Portuguese. I don't know whether they wear the left or the right side on top in Portugal."

"Another piece of information from Kikuko?"

Yasuko sought to intercede. "Father is always putting on summer kimonos inside out."

"There is a difference between accidentally putting a kimono on inside out and standing there like a fool bringing the right side over the left."

"Let Kuniko have a try at putting on a kimono. You can't be sure which side will come out in front."

"It's early for second childhood, Father," said Fusako, unflagging. "Isn't it a little too much, Mother? So his daughter-in-law does go home for a day or two,

---

1. A singlet worn under a kimono.

that's no excuse for losing track of which side of his kimono goes in front. Hasn't it been six months now since his own daughter came home to Mother?"

It was true: six months had passed since that rainy New Year's Eve. There had been no word from her husband, Aihara, nor had Shingo seen Aihara.

"Six months," nodded Yasuko. "Not that there's any relation between that and Kikuko."

"No relation? I think both have some relation to Father."

"You *are* his children. It would be nice if he could find an answer."

Fusako looked down in silence.

"All right, Fusako, now is your chance. Come out with everything. Say what you have to say. You'll feel better. Kikuko is away."

"I was wrong, and I'm not going to complain. But I should think you could eat it even if it didn't come from Kikuko's hands." Fusako was weeping again. "Isn't it the truth? You sit there grimly forcing it down. I'm not happy myself."

"Fusako. You must have all sorts of things to say. When you went to the post office the other day—I imagine it was to mail a letter to Aihara?"

A tremor seemed to pass over Fusako, but she shook her head.

"I decided it had to be Aihara, because I couldn't think of anyone else you'd have any reason to write to." Yasuko's voice was not often so sharp. "Did you send money?"

So Yasuko had been giving Fusako money.

"Where is Aihara?" Shingo looked at Fusako, waiting for an answer. "He doesn't seem to be at home. I've been sending someone around from the office once a month or so to have a look at the place. No, not that so much, really, as to give a little money to his mother. If you were there you might be the one to take care of her."

Yasuko sat open-mouthed. "You send someone from the office?"

"Don't worry. He's someone you can depend on. Someone who doesn't give away secrets or ask questions. If Aihara were there I'd go and talk your problem over, but there's no point in talking to a lame old woman."

"What is Aihara doing?"

"Peddling drugs or something of the sort, it would seem. I imagine he was being used to peddle the stuff, and he moved from drink to drugs."

Yasuko gazed at him in fright. It seemed possible that she was less frightened by the matter of Aihara than by her own husband, who had kept his secret so long.

Shingo went on. "But now it seems that the old woman isn't there either. Someone else is in the place. In other words, Fusako no longer has a house."

"And what about Fusako's things?"

"My chests and trunks have been empty for a long time, Mother."

"I see." Yasuko sighed. "You're an easy target for him and come home with everything you own tied up in one kerchief."

Shingo wondered whether Fusako might know where Aihara was, and whether she might be in communication with him.

And as he looked out at the garden, moving into dusk, he wondered who it was that had been unable to keep Aihara from falling, Fusako or Shingo or Aihara himself. Or perhaps no one at all.

2

Shingo got to the office at about ten to find a note from Tanizaki Eiko.

She wanted to talk to him about the young mistress, and would come again later.

The young mistress could only be Kikuko.

Shingo questioned Iwamura Natsuko, who had replaced Eiko as his secretary.

"What time was Tanizaki here?"

"I had just come in and was dusting the desks. I suppose it would have been a little after eight."

"Did she wait?"

"Yes, for a while."

Shingo disliked the dull, heavy way in which Natsuko said "Yes." Perhaps it had to do with her native dialect.

"Did she see Shuichi?"

"I believe she went away without seeing him."

"Oh?" Shingo was talking to himself. "If it was a little after eight, then. . . ."

Eiko had probably come on her way to work. She would probably come again at noon.

After rereading the note, tiny at the edge of a large sheet of paper, he looked out of the window.

He looked out at the clear sky of the most May-like of May days.

He had seen it from the train. All the passengers looking out had their windows open.

The birds skimming low over the shining stream that marked the limits of Tokyo shone silver themselves. It seemed more than accidental that a red-banded bus should be crossing the bridge to the north.

"In the heavens, a high wind." For no particular reason, he repeated the motto on his counterfeit Ryokan.

"Well!" The Ikegami grove came into view, and he leaned forward as if he meant to jump out. "Maybe the pines aren't in the Ikegami grove at all."

This morning the two pines that stood out above the grove seemed nearer.

Had it been that, in the rains and the spring mists, the perspective had been blurred?

He gazed on, trying to make sure.

He gazed at them every morning, and he thought he would like to go and inspect the site itself.

But though he saw the grove every morning, he had only recently discovered the two pines. He had looked at it absently over the years, knowing that it was the grove of the Ikegami Hommonji Temple.

Today, in the clear May sky, he had discovered that the pine trees did not seem to be in the Ikegami grove at all.

And so he had twice discovered the two pines that leaned toward each other as if about to embrace.

When, last night after dinner, he had told of seeking out Aihara's house and giving modest help to his old mother, the agitated Fusako had fallen silent.

He had felt sorry for her. He thought that he had discovered something in her, but what he had discovered was by no means as clear as the discovery in the Ikegami grove.

Some days earlier, looking out at this same grove, he had questioned Shuichi, and drawn from him the news of Kikuko's abortion.

The pines were no longer just pines. They were entangled with the abortion. Perhaps he would always be reminded of it when he passed them to and from work.

This morning, of course, it had been so again.

On the morning of Shuichi's admission, the pines had melted back into the grove, dim in the wind and rain. This morning, standing apart, associated in his mind with Kikuko's abortion, they somehow looked dirty. Perhaps the weather was too good.

"Even when natural weather is good, human weather is bad," he muttered to himself, somewhat inanely. Turning away from the clear sky framed in the office window, he set about the day's work.

Shortly after noon there was a telephone call from Eiko. Busy with summer clothes, she would not be able to come by today.

"You're so good at it that you're kept busy?"

"Yes." Eiko fell silent.

"You're at the shop?"

"Yes. But Kinu isn't here." The name of Shuichi's woman came out smoothly. "I waited for her to leave."

"Oh?"

"Hello? I'll stop by tomorrow morning."

"Tomorrow morning? At eight again?"

"No. I'll wait for you."

"It's all that pressing?"

"Yes. Well, it is and it isn't. To me it seems pressing. I want to talk to you as soon as I can. I'm rather worked up about it."

"Worked up? About Shuichi?"

"I'll tell you when I see you."

He did not attach much importance to her being "worked up," but he was uneasy that she should so want to talk as to come two days in a row.

The uneasiness increased. At about three he called Kikuko's family house.

The Sagawa maid answered. Music came over the telephone as he waited for Kikuko.

He had not talked to Shuichi of Kikuko since she had gone home to her family. Shuichi seemed anxious to avoid the subject.

And Shingo had avoided going to inquire after Kikuko, because to do so would only have been to give the matter unnecessary emphasis.

Shingo thought that, being what she was, Kikuko would have spoken to her family neither of Kinu nor of the abortion. But he could not be sure.

Kikuko's voice came up from the symphony over the telephone. "Father?" There was affection in it. "I've kept you waiting."

"Hello." A surge of relief swept over him. "And how are you?"

"Oh, I'm fine again. I'm pampering myself."

"Not at all." He found it hard to go on.

"Father," said Kikuko happily. "I want to see you. May I come now?"

"Now? Is it all right?"

"Yes. The quicker I see you the easier it will be for me to go home again."

"I'll be waiting here for you." The music went on. "Hello, hello," Shingo did not want to let her hang up. "That's very good music."

"I forgot to turn it down, didn't I? It's ballet music. *Les Sylphides,* by Chopin. I'll steal it from them and bring it home with me."

"You're coming right away?"

"Yes. But let me think a minute. I don't really want to go to the office."

She suggested that they meet at the Shinjuku Garden.

Shingo laughed, somewhat disconcerted at this proposed rendezvous.

Kikuko seemed to think that she had hit upon a remarkably good idea. "The green will bring you to life."

"The Shinjuku Garden? I've been there exactly once. For some reason or other I went to a dog show there."

"Come and let me show you myself instead." And after her laughter, *Les Sylphides* played on.

3

He went in through the main gate of the Shinjuku Garden.

A notice beside the gate announced that perambulators were available for thirty yen per hour, and straw mats for twenty yen per day and up.

There was an American couple ahead of him. The husband had a little girl in his arms, and the wife was leading a German pointer. There were other people too, all young couples. Only the Americans were walking at an easy pace.

Shingo fell in after them.

To the left of the path, what at first seemed to be a stand of deciduous pines proved to be deodars. When he had come to the dog show, a benefit given by an organization for the prevention of cruelty to animals, he had seen a remarkable stand of deodars; but he could not remember where.

To the right were signs identifying trees and shrubs as Oriental arborvitae and *utsukushimatsu*[2] and the like.

He walked on at his leisure, thinking he would be ahead of Kikuko; but he found her on a bench under a gingko, by the pond to which the path shortly led.

Turning toward him and half rising to her feet, Kikuko bowed.

---

2. A pine, to judge from the name. Not identified in botanical dictionaries.

"You're early. It's still fifteen minutes to half-past four." He looked at his watch.

"I was so pleased when you called that I ran right out of the house." She spoke rapidly. "I can't tell you how pleased I was."

"So you've been waiting? Shouldn't you have on something heavier?"

"I've had this sweater since I was in school." A note of shyness came into her voice. "I don't have any clothes at home anymore. I couldn't very well borrow a kimono from my sister."

Kikuko was the youngest of eight children, and all her sisters were married. It was probably to a sister-in-law that she had reference.

The dark green sweater had short sleeves. It seemed to Shingo that he was seeing her bare arms for the first time this year.

She apologized in a somewhat more formal manner for having gone home to her family.

"Can you come back to Kamakura yet?" he asked softly, not knowing what sort of reply was called for.

"Yes." She nodded simply and quickly. "I've been wanting to come back." The beautiful shoulders moved as she gazed at Shingo. His eye had not caught the exact motion, but a gentle scent came from her to surprise him.

"Did Shuichi go to see you?"

"Yes. But if you hadn't called. . . ."

It would have been difficult for her to go back?

The remark unfinished, Kikuko stepped out of the shade.

The green of the giant trees, so rich as to be almost heavy, seemed to fall upon the slender neck of the retreating figure.

The lake was Japanese, after a fashion. On the little island, his foot on a stone lantern, a foreign soldier was joking with a prostitute. There were other couples on the benches around the lake.

Shingo followed Kikuko out through the trees to the right of the lake. "Enormous," he said, surprised at the vastness of the expanse before them.

"It *has* brought you to life, Father," she said, openly pleased with herself. "I told you it would."

Shingo stopped before a loquat beside the path. He did not immediately go out upon the broad lawn.

"A splendid loquat. It has nothing to get in its way, and it spreads out just as it wants to, all the way to the bottom."

Shingo was deeply moved by the form the tree had taken in free and natural growth.

"Beautiful. Yes—when I came to the dog show there was a row of deodars growing just as they wanted to, spreading as far as they could spread, all the way down to the bottom. I felt like growing with them. I wonder where it was."

"Over in the direction of Shinjuku."

"Yes. I came in from Shinjuku."

"You said on the telephone that you came to look at dogs?"

"There weren't so many of them, but it was a benefit given by the Society for the Prevention of Cruelty to Animals. There were more foreigners than Japanese.

Diplomats and people from the Occupation, I imagine. It was summer. The Indian girls were the most beautiful, all done up in red and blue silk gauzes. There were Indian and American stalls. We didn't have many such affairs in those days."

It had been two or three years before, but Shingo could not remember exactly when.

As he spoke, he moved away from the loquat tree.

"Let's get rid of the *yatsude* at the foot of the cherry. Remind me when you get home."

"I will."

"We've never cut back the cherry. I like it as it is."

"It has all those tiny branches loaded with flowers. We listened to the temple bell when it was in full bloom. Remember? Last month during the festival."

"Such a small thing—it's good of you to remember."

"I'll never forget. And there was the kite."

She came close to him. They walked from the shadow of a great *keyaki*[3] out over the broad lawn.

The vast green expanse set Shingo free.

"You can stretch out. It's like getting out of Japan—I wouldn't have dreamed that there was a place like this right in the middle of Tokyo." He gazed at the distant expanse of green toward Shinjuku.

"They paid a great deal of attention to the vista. It looks even farther off than it is."

"What's a vista?" Kikuko had used the Italian word.

"A line of vision, you might say. See how all the paths and the borders are in gentle curves."

Kikuko had come on a school outing, and her teacher had told them all about the garden. The wide lawn, with trees scattered over it, was in the English fashion, it seemed.

There were few people other than young couples, lying down, sitting up, strolling casually about. There were also children, and schoolgirls in groups of five and six. Shingo was surprised, and somehow thought it inappropriate, that the park should be an Eden for assignations.

Did the scene tell one that the youth of the land had been liberated, just as the imperial garden had been?

No one paid the slightest attention to the two of them as they made their way over the lawn weaving in and out among the couples. Shingo stayed as far from them as he could.

And what would Kikuko be thinking? He was an old man who had brought his young daughter-in-law to the garden, but there was something about the situation that did not rest well with him.

He had not given much thought to the matter when Kikuko had suggested over the telephone that they meet in the Shinjuku Garden, but now that they had come it all seemed very odd.

---

3. *Zelkova serrata*, related to the elms.

Munakata Shiko.
Woman with Hawk.

Shingo was drawn to one particularly high tree out on the lawn.

As he approached, looking up at it, the dignity and the mass of the towering green came grandly down to him, to wash away his and Kikuko's gloom. She had been right to think that the garden would bring him to life.

The tree was what is called in Japan a "lily tree." Coming nearer, he saw that it was in fact three trees. The sign explained that, since the flowers resemble both the lily and the tulip, it is also known as a tulip tree. A fast grower, it came originally from North America. These specimens were about fifty years old.

"Fifty years old? They're younger than I am." Shingo looked up in surprise.

The broad-leafed branches spread out as if to enfold and hide the two of them.

Shingo sat down on a bench, but he felt restless.

Kikuko looked at him, puzzled, as he stood up again.

"Let's go have a look at the flowers over there," he said.

There was a bed of white flowers, fresh in the distance beyond the lawn, about as high as the dipping branches of the tulip tree.

"They had a victory reception here for the generals in the Russo-Japanese War. I was in my teens, still out in the country."

There were trees in grand rows on either side of the flower bed. Shingo chose a bench set among them.

Kikuko stood before him. "I'll come home tomorrow morning. Tell Mother, and see that she doesn't scold me." She sat down beside him.

"Do you have anything you want to say to me first?"

"Say to you? All sorts of things, but. . . ."

4

Shingo waited hopefully the following morning, but Kikuko had not yet come back when he left for the office.

"She said I was to see that you didn't scold her."

"Scold her?" Yasuko's face was bright and happy. "We ought to apologize."

He had said only that he had telephoned Kikuko.

"You have a remarkably strong influence on her." Yasuko saw him to the door. "But that's all right."

Eiko came shortly after he arrived at the office.

"You're prettier," he said affably. "And you brought flowers."

"I can't get away once I'm at the shop, and so I walked around killing time. The florist's was beautiful."

But the expression on her face was solemn as she approached his desk. "Get rid of her," she wrote with her finger on the desk.

"What?" He was startled. "Would you mind leaving us alone for a minute?" he said to Natsuko.

Waiting for Natsuko to go, Eiko found a vase and put three roses in it. She was wearing a slip-on dress that gave her the look of one who worked for a *modiste*. She had put on a little weight, he thought.

"I'm sorry about yesterday." Her manner was strangely tense. "I—coming two days in a row, and all that."

"Have a seat."

"Thank you." She sat with bowed head.

"I'm making you late for work."

"It doesn't matter." Looking up at him, she drew in her breath sharply, as if she were about to weep. "Is it all right to talk to you? I'm boiling over, and I may be a little hysterical."

"Oh?"

"It's about the young mistress." She choked over the words. "I believe she had an abortion."

Shingo did not answer.

How could she have known? Shuichi would hardly have spoken to her of it. But Eiko worked with Shuichi's woman. He braced himself for unpleasantness.

"It's all right for her to have an abortion." Eiko hesitated again.

"Who told you?"

"Shuichi got the hospital money from Kinu."

Shingo felt a tightening in his chest.

"I thought it was outrageous. Really too insulting, too unfeeling. I felt so sorry for the young mistress that I wanted to cry. He gives Kinu money, and so I suppose you can think of it as his money, but it wasn't the right thing to do. He comes from a different class than the rest of us, and he could put together that amount of money any way he pleased. Does being on a different level make it all right for him to do things like that?" She fought to keep her slender shoulders from trembling. "And then there was Kinu, letting him have the money. I couldn't understand her. I was boiling over. I wanted to talk to you even if it meant that I couldn't work with her any more. I know I'm telling you more than I ought to, of course."

"Thank you."

"You were good to me here. I only met the young mistress once, but I liked her." Tears glistened in her eyes. "Have them separate."

"Yes."

She meant Shuichi and Kinu, of course—and yet the remark could also be interpreted as referring to Shuichi and Kikuko.

Into such depths Shuichi had been pushed.

Shingo was astonished at his son's spiritual paralysis and decay, but it seemed to him that he was caught in the same filthy slough. Dark terror swept over him.

Having had her say, Eiko prepared to leave.

"Don't rush off." He sought to detain her, but without enthusiasm.

"I'll come again. Today I'd weep for you and make a fool of myself."

He felt benevolence and a sense of responsibility in her.

He had thought it remarkably indelicate of her to go to work in the same shop as Kinu; but how much worse were Shuichi and Shingo himself.

He gazed absently at the crimson roses Eiko had brought.

Shuichi had said that squeamishness had kept Kikuko from bearing a child "with things as they are now." Was she not being trampled on for her squeamishness?

Unknowing, Kikuko would now be back in Kamakura. He closed his eyes.

ISHIGAKI RIN (b. 1920)

Japan

Ishigaki Rin—having lost her mother very young, and two stepmothers—began writing poetry while still in grammar school. For many years, she worked in a bank, and some of her meditations in prose concern her life there, and the problems of aging women. With other women writers, she began the journal *Dansō* (*Dislocations*), and then wrote extensively: poems, stories, and essays. She could be called a realist in her descriptions of everyday happiness, loneliness, pain, and determination. Her *Collected Poetry* was published in 1971, and then an *Abbreviated Resumé* (1979), *Household Poems* (1981), and *Gentle Words* (1984), as well as prose collection: *Warming my Hands at the Fire* (1980). The following poem, which gave its title to her first collection, is about a kitchen and much more.

The Pan, the Pot, the Fire I Have Before Me

For a long time
these things have always been placed
before us women:

the pan of a reasonable size
suited to the user's strength,   5
the pot in which it's convenient for rice
to begin to swell and shine, grain by grain,
the glow of the fire inherited from time immemorial—
before these there have always been
mothers, grandmothers, and their mothers   10

What measures of love and sincerity
these persons must have poured
into these utensils—
now red carrots,
now black seaweed,   15
now crushed fish

in the kitchen, always accurately
for morning, noon, and evening, preparations have been made
and before the preparations, in a row, there have always been
some pairs of warm knees and hands.   20

Ah without those persons waiting
how could women have gone on
cooking so happily?
their unflagging care,
so daily a service they became unconscious of it.   25

Cooking was mysteriously assigned
to women, as a role,
but I don't think that was unfortunate;
because of that, their knowledge and positions in society
may have lagged behind the times   30
but it isn't too late:
the things we have before us,
the pan and the pot, and the burning fire,

before these familiar things,
let us study government, economy, literature   35
as sincerely
as we cook potatoes and meat.
not for vanity and promotion
but so everyone

Translated by Hiroaki Sato.

may serve all

so everyone may work for love.

40

Roof

The Japanese house has a low roof,
the poorer the house, the lower the roof;
the low roof
weighs on my back.

What makes the weight of the roof?
I walk away ten steps to look:
what's on top of the house
is not the blue of the sky,
but the thickness of blood.

5

What holds me and blocks my way,
what confines my strength in its narrowness
and wastes it

10

my sick father lives on the roof,
my stepmother lives on the roof,
my brothers live on the roof.

The tin roof twangs
when the wind blows,
four hundred square feet at the most,
a gust can easily carry it away—
look, also lying on it,
white radishes, rice,
and the warmth of the bed.

15

20

Bear it, they say;
under the weight of this roof
a woman, her spring darkens,
in the distance, the sun sinks.

25

IBARAGI NORIKO (b. 1926)

Japan

Having initially wanted to be a playwright, Ibaragi Noriko decided, after reading
the poetic anthology Monyōshū from the eighth century, on a career as a poet. She
helped found the poetry journal *Kai* (*Oar*) in 1953, and published the collections
Conversations (1955), *Invisible Mailmen* (1958), and, in memory of her father,

Requiem Poems (1965). Her poems are realistic, energetic, and relatively optimistic. Her prose works (*Clarifying Words,* 1975), and *Travels to Hangul,* 1986), are particularly concerned with language—that of poetry—and with the interest, for a writer, of learning other languages, including Noriko's own study of Korean.

When My Beauty Was at Its Best

When my beauty was at its best
town after town came tumbling down, giving us
glimpses of blue sky stuck up in
the least expected places.

When my beauty was at its best   5
many people around me died
in factories, at sea, on unknown islands, and
I had no chance to make the best of myself.

When my beauty was at its best
I had no young man bringing me lovely presents.   10
All they did was raise their hands in salute, and soon
left for the front, leaving me with nothing more than pure looks.

When my beauty was at its best
I was empty-headed,
I was stubborn-hearted,   15
my limbs were a glossy brown.

When my beauty was at its best
my country was defeated.
"How can that be?"
I strode around the humbled town, my sleeves rolled up.   20

When my beauty was at its best
I heard jazz streaming from the radio,
and I plunged myself as rapturously into its sweet melodies
of when I first knew the forbidden pleasure of smoking.

When my beauty was at its best   25
I was very unhappy
I was very awkward,
I was very, very lonely.
That's why I've decided to live a long time if I can,
like Monsieur Rouault, the dear old man who   30
painted those marvelously beautiful pictures in his old age.
—Yes, in his old age![1]

Translated by James Kirkup.

---

1. Georges Rouault (1871–1958): French Expressionist artist best known for his stained-glass-like religious portraits.

Outrun*

When you feel you've outrun somebody,
without trying to,
or even knowing you were running;
you feel an indefinite loneliness.

One night I outran father,
and cried on a damp pillow without a sound
while he snored, one room over.
And I hate myself for it now.

Hate myself!
I'm not better than he is.

But I outran him,
and like a revelation,
or sword-slash,
it marks a phase of my life.

I wonder if I'll ever give
young friends, nieces, nephews
such a moment.

When you've outrun somebody, you know it.
But if you're outrun, who's to tell you?

HAYASHI KYŌKO (b. 1930)
Japan

Hayashi Kyōko is a writer of prose narrative known for the skill and naturalness with which she interprets the modern Japanese *shōsetsu*, short or long. Kyōko grew up in Shanghai before and during part of World War II. She suffered the calamity of the bombing of Nagasaki and has had a lifetime of aftereffects. She has also lived in the United States. Most of her writing centers on her previous experiences; it is a life that does not allow for contemporary delights.

Like Kawabata Yasunari, Kyōko affirmatively muses on what exists if it might prove moving. Like Shiga Naoya, she writes with spare intensity of what she has seen and thought. Like Higuchi Ichiyō, she finds that defining human life by what women must endure is even more serious than what is anticipated by the central female consciousness of the story. The story included here opens with a haze of yellow sand. Without our noticing when or how, the scene shifts to a human desert whose few flowers are lovingly observed with their inevitable

*Translated by Fukuko Kobayashi.

Yoshida Hiroshi. *Soshu-Suzhou*. 1940. Woodblock print.

withering. Her scenes are unforgettable, fictional or not. Like Ichiyō, she tells a bleak story of human fate best illustrated by what women encounter and endure.

Yellow Sand

As I opened the raindoors, the sky was a brown haze. The morning news explained this as yellow sand.

The dust that rose in the air in the interior of the Chinese continent, having crossed the Yellow Sea and the Korean peninsula on the westerly wind, seems to be blowing over a wide area from Kyushu to the Kantō and Hokuriku districts. The yellow sand borne by the forty kilometer per hour west wind takes one to two days before arriving in Japan. During the long two-day trip, heavier grains drop on the mountains of the Korean peninsula or into the Yellow Sea, and only comparatively light grains reach the Japanese sky.

Even so, almost all the sky above the entire land of Japan, it is reported, is shrouded in smoke, covered by a thick layer of sandy dust, as though wearing a cotton hat. On the day the yellow sand falls, however, there is an odd brightness. The grass field in front of my house and the trees of the surrounding hills are both bright, vaguely hazy like the light we see through frosted glass.

China is where I spent my girlhood. It was Shanghai, China, then called *Shina*. Part of the land which extends from Shanghai rises in the air in a huge cloud of smoke and descends in the air of the interior of Japan. I wanted the feeling of the

Translated by Kyoko Iriye Selden.

dust directly on my skin and went out to the field. Stretching my arms wide, I inhaled deeply. Facing the sky, I shook my head violently a few times like a dog after bathing in water. The moist wind moved across my cheeks. There was the smell of the dirt of the continent reeking in the sun, though perhaps it was just an illusion.

In March, the yellow sand often blew in Shanghai, too. Just like the saying "Yellow dust of ten thousand yards," the yellow dust which starts around Taiyuan near the Gobi Desert sometimes turns the Shanghai sky the color of the earth. Even the Huangpu turns muddy and fuller than usual, and its level starts to rise. In the fields of the suburbs, rape flowers bloom. The sky, the river, and the earth merge in one yellow, and Shanghai enters spring with no distinction between heaven and earth.

Though dust is in the air, the wind is moist and soft to the skin.

In the field, too, the moist warm wind characteristic of the yellow sand days was blowing, just as I expected. In the misty wind that blurred the world, it seemed as though an event which should be called the original picture of my thoughts remained in its pure shape without any finger grease, as it was first perceived in my childhood days. Thinking of going where a richer yellow sand wind blew, I started to walk. The hills that surrounded me on three sides came to an end, and I reached a gentle slope.

Below the slope, I saw the rows of houses in town. Since the town formed a valley, yellow sand, more deeply hued than in the fields and hills, sank smokily to the eaves of the houses. I stopped in the middle of the road. Knotted currents of wind blew from beneath the slope. I closed my eyes and listened to its sound. The wind, slightly trembling as it passed my ears, brought back to me the hush of the rape flower field that I entered with Okiyo-san when I was young.

I first met Okiyo-san in the spring of 1937, the year I entered primary school in Shanghai. She might have been twenty-three or -four. On July 7 of that year, Chinese and Japanese armies clashed near the Marco Polo Bridge, igniting the Sino-Japanese War.

Both Okiyo-san's house and mine were located at the entrance of Hongkou, near the Garden Bridge. Hongkou was in a Shanghai district then under Japanese control. With the Garden Bridge over the Huangpu as the boundary, the international settlement lay across the bridge. It was controlled by England, the United States, and France. This side of the bridge was Hongkou, the Japanese quarter. Okiyo-san's house was a few minutes' walk from mine. In that area, red brick houses of the same style stood in rows. Perhaps because it faced the international settlement across the river, the appearance of the town reflected its influence. The houses were English-style three-story buildings with brown slate roofs. A big rectangular chimney stuck out of each roof, connected to the living room fireplace below. The roof had a bulge which resembled a horse's saddle. Though narrow, there was also an unfenced lawn that one could enter freely from the pavement.

Okiyo-san lived in this house with several prostitutes. Her fellow prostitutes where White Russians, she being the only Japanese. On the eve of the Sino-Japanese war, Shanghai brimmed with Japanese military men, and accordingly, there were brothels all over town. Japanese prostitutes were rare, however. Japanese women entertainers worked at Japanese-owned restaurants under supervision. They were divided into army and navy categories. They were not of course called prostitutes, and I don't know whether monetary transactions took place. Anyway, nobody ever heard of a Japanese woman like Okiyo-san who openly became a prostitute and engaged exclusively in the trade.

In the front of the yard was a street lined with plane trees. Beyond the pavement, the Huangpu flowed in a big curve around the Garden Bridge. Facing the river was a wooden bench for resting. Just across from Okiyo-san's house, too, was a bench. I was fond of sitting on this bench and watching steamers come and go on the river.

That day, after lunch, I sat on the bench watching the boats. People had gathered in front of Okiyo-san's house, which was usually quiet during the day. As I turned back attracted by the noise, I saw that they were coolies. They had probably missed out on longshoreman jobs at the port. In four or five minutes, they formed a human fence of nearly twenty people in front of the house. They were all shouting, looking at her yard.

In a corner of the yard away from the people was an acacia tree. It was the only tree in her yard. A man was leaning against the trunk of that tree. He was the man with rather dark skin seen around this area from time to time in the evening. He was twenty-three or -four, about the same age as Okiyo-san. He wore silken Chinese clothes. The coolies pointed one or two fingers at the man, shouting, "one hundred," "two hundred." The man, his arms crossed, shook his head in a lordly way, grinning. He did not respond. Finding the man adamant, the coolies raised their voices, the numbers increasing little by little by tens and fifteens.

The men seemed to be betting. In Shanghai this was hardly unusual. Whenever people gathered in a circle, there was always a bet going on. Anything would do for a bet. Sometimes it was an ant crawling on the street. Or some crickets in an unglazed pot, whose bottoms they tickled with the tip of a blade of pampas grass to see which could be made to chirp better. Everything that caught their eye became the object of a bet.

It seemed that here too, in front of Okiyo-san's house, betting had started. Interested, I crossed the tree-lined street and, mingling in the crowd, looked for the object of the bet. In the center of the grass was a bamboo couch. The betting seemed to center around that couch, but nothing like a betting object was seen on or near it. All I saw was the spring sun covered with yellow dust shining on the amber skin of the bamboo. A coolie loudly shouted, "Three hundred!" As if on cue, a few others, raising three fingers, shouted, "Three hundred" toward the third-floor window. Then they called "Okiyo!"

One window faced the Huangpu from the third floor. In our house, the third floor was the children's play area. If we jumped up with arms stretched in the garret, we could easily tap the beam, because the roof was low. The room was the size of a ten-mat room, but there was only one window. It was gloomy even during the day. On a fair day, however, it was pleasant: it felt like being inside a goldfish bowl, as the swaying reflection of the river waves made rings on the walls and the roof beam.

Okiyo-san's room was probably the third-floor garret. A blue curtain hung over the closed window. The coolies kept calling, trying to entice her to come down from that window. The man in silk raised both hands to quiet the coolies.

The entrance doorknob turned slowly from inside. The door with a stained glass decoration opened slightly, and Okiyo-san came out as lightly as a small silver carp swimming in and out of river weeds. The coolies became quiet.

Okiyo-san wore a Chinese dress. On ordinary days, she wore a red Hakata-woven undersash over a summer kimono. I saw her in a Chinese dress for the first time. Her hair, too, had a big bulge in front like a visor. She was naked beneath the Chinese dress with a thigh-length slit on the sides. She wore satin Chinese shoes on her bare feet. In comparison with her hairdo neatly finished with oil, her bare skin seemed disarmed. With her smooth, pliant arms hanging naturally, Okiyo-san leaned against the door. The man in silk slowly approached the sofa. Seeing him move, Okiyo-san, too, walked toward the couch. Then she sat on the edge of the couch, legs decorously together. The man sat, too. The moment he sat, he drew her toward him, embracing her waist. He held her with his left arm and pushed her down on the couch. Okiyo-san, pushed down, beat him on the sides with both hands. Five fingers flitting apart, she beat him with an expression which seemed neither jocular nor serious. He clasped one wrist and then the other. He put them together with his hands, then held them with his right hand. After depriving her of the freedom of her hands, he held her legs between his.

Okiyo-san became still. The man also became still. *Wei, wei,* the coolies shouted. While shouting, one of them beat the man on the back with all his strength. At this signal, the man sprang up from the couch. Okiyo-san also sprang up with the same agility.

Swiftly smoothing the wrinkles on her dress, Okiyo-san smiled to the man, curling her red-daisy-colored lips. The man bowed to her, joining his hands in front of his chest.

The coolies clapped frantically. They threw the money, bid from one hundred to two hundred and up, clapping repeatedly. Seeing the copper coins and bills scattered around his feet, the man laughed aloud. Okiyo-san, too, laughed very loudly, beating her belly with her fists.

The bidding seemed to have been on their union: whether the man would attack successfully, or the woman would defend herself to the end. The match had ended quickly, with Okiyo-san the loser.

It was then that I first saw the union of man and woman. I only saw it, without understanding the meaning of the act. The impression was not so strong as to haunt me, but the union accomplished in the sunlight was as refreshing as watching a pair of coupling dragonflies flying over the ears of rice.

The coolies had gone. The man in silk clothes was also no longer there. On the pavement devoid of people, I stood watching Okiyo-san. She stood with her back toward me but apparently felt my eyes on her back, for she turned around. She noticed me. Looking surprised, she asked, "Are you a Japanese child?" I answered, "Yes." "Were you watching?" she asked. "Yes," I answered clearly. Okiyo-san remained silent for a while. Then she said, "I see."

We started to walk toward the bridge. Okiyo-san sat on the bench. I, too, sat down, but not close by. A steamer moved toward the mouth of the river. At high tide, the surface of the river was swelling, as the water rose in a dull sheen. Okiyo-san watched the steamer going against the tide with her eyes narrowed;

then she suddenly asked, "Do you think you could reach home if you added bulwarks of hardwood to that boat, hard as oak?" It would be dangerous, though it wouldn't be impossible to go home that way. But why invite danger when five- or six-thousand-ton-class ferries like the Shanghai and the Nagasaki were plying back and forth between Shanghai and Nagasaki? Once aboard the ferry, she could return to Japan as she wished, even the next day. Why did she think of the near impossibility of secretly returning, purposely choosing a small boat with bulwarks of all the steamers on the Huangpu River?

By setting up an impossible situation, Okiyo-san seemed to be trying to cut off her nostalgia for her country. The reason she had to cut it off probably lay in her past. That past, which forced her to cross the sea to Shanghai as a youth of twenty-three or -four to live away from her female compatriots and among foreigners who fled their countries, was perhaps so harsh as to never again allow her to live in her homeland.

As the days went by, her union disappeared from my memory. However, because she had asked if I thought it was possible to go home, before long I started to think of my country in connection with the end of the flow of the Huangpu River. Yet I knew nothing concrete about how I related to my country or how people lived over there.

Someone seemed to have told my mother. She knew that I had watched the union of bodies. She asked, "Were you watching?" "Yes," I answered. She stared straight into my eyes and asked, "Were you watching till it was over?" "Yes," I answered again. "Shame on her," she said angrily. "Isn't she a Japanese?—exposing herself in front of people; she is a disgrace to our nation." Then she told me that that kind of woman should be forcibly sent home.

This was the feeling of the Japanese adults in town toward Okiyo-san. When living in a foreign country, one was apt to feel that each person represented his or her home country. Since at that time national prestige was important, the Japanese residents especially were strongly self-conscious. Women were even forbidden to go out without socks or stockings. It was thought that Japanese women's skin should not be exposed to foreigners' eyes. My mother, too, went out wearing white *tabi* as though rich. Beggars, robbers, and even poverty were a disgrace to the nation, and were considered grounds for repatriation. This severity was not limited to thoughts about foreigners; they observed one another with an even severer eye. Such words as "traitor" and "repatriation" often characterized their conversation. Even children, when they fought with friends, said, "You'll be repatriated." However, the children did not necessarily realize that they were shouldering the weight of their country.

As extreme expressions became commonplace among adults, the clannish-ness among the Japanese intensified. On the other hand, the public peace of Shanghai was increasingly threatened. A town association was formed for self-defense. A vigilance committee was also organized. When compatriots live in a foreign country, the greatest security is in flocking together.

Okiyo-san, though Japanese, was excluded from the group. She didn't seem to mind too much.

In April, half a month after I saw the union of bodies, I entered primary school. One day, on the way home from school, on the bridge over the creek, I met Okiyo-san. The bridge spanned the Hongkou Creek which separated my house from the school. In the middle of the bridge stood two huts painted green, facing each other. Marine sentinels stood guard there armed with bayonets. Behind one hut a long line of Chinese people had formed on one side of the bridge.

In the summer, cholera raged in Shanghai. All residents, regardless of nationality, had to be immunized. Japanese were supposed either to receive injections at hospitals especially designated for them or to call a doctor to the town association to immunize the entire town. My mother was among those who had received a shot from a doctor at the town association the day before.

Only Chinese people got shots on the bridge or on a street corner. Okiyo-san was standing in the all-Chinese line. In the same Chinese dress as on the day of the union of bodies, she moved one step forward each time the line advanced. In her Chinese dress, she seemed no different from the others. The people before and after her didn't seem to notice any difference. They spoke to Okiyo-san. Yet, although her skin and bone structure were the same as those of the Chinese people, somehow she was different. To me who knew her to be a Japanese, Okiyo-san alone stood out. Okiyo-san looked pitiable to me, shut out by her compatriots and joining the foreigners' line. Going near her, I softly called from behind, "Okiyo-san." She turned back, and as she noticed me, said "Go home quick," with her hand on my school satchel.

"I'll wait for you," I said.

We waited nearly half an hour before it was finally her turn. The army surgeon who stood with his legs apart like a Deva king grabbed her left arm and abruptly stabbed it with a needle without even sterilizing it. Injecting the liquid in a flash of a second, he hurriedly pulled out the needle. The point of the needle seemed to have been worn, for a black drop of blood came out after it was pulled out. "Does it hurt?" I asked. "Huh?" The surgeon inclined his head, and asked Okiyo-san, "Are you a Japanese, too?" Okiyo-san didn't answer. Rubbing the drop of blood into her arm with her palm in the same way as the Chinese did, she started to walk in the opposite direction from home.

Across the bridge and past the primary school, we came to another bridge over the same creek. As we crossed this bridge, we left the Japanese town of Hongkou. There were few houses, few people, and we came to an open field. As we walked further, there were no more houses, only the field extending to the horizon. An asphalt road divided the field. It had been made by the Japanese army in order to carry material to the Chinese interior.

Okiyo-san walked in the middle of the wide road. Rape flowers bloomed all over the field, and here and there amidst the flowers white-walled houses could be seen. These small houses were not for people; they were not even as tall as children. They were only as large as one tatami. The roof of each hut was made of lusterless black slate. Right under the slope, one window was open, the size of a postcard. The white-walled houses were said to be Chinese people's graves. To what class of people these graves belonged, and whether or not this house-like style was limited to the Shanghai area, were unknown. The graves had neither the names of the dead nor the dates of their deaths. All that were there were white-walled graves. They were not formed into clusters like Japanese people's graves; one by one, they stood separately on the spacious earth.

"Come and see," Okiyo-san said from among the rape flowers. I went into the field of blooming rape. As told, I peered into the window of a grave. There were no wooden pieces of a rotten coffin, no bones, no clothes—nothing attached to the dead. Weeds growing high enough to brush the ceiling filled the grave, stretching, their heads together, toward the window opened for the dead. The grass was deeper green than the green of the rape plants bathing in the sun.

"All I see is grass," I said. "That's what man is," said Okiyo-san.

Pressing down the rape flowers with her hands, Okiyo-san sat on the flowers with her legs outstretched. Then she lay back on the flowers, her hands pillowing her head. "The sky's pure yellow," she said. I stood in the flowers, watching the rape field stretching endlessly. The yellow of the flowers spread from around my breast into the sky and blazed as it met the sky at the horizon.

In the yellow color fused without break, the scattered grave windows were black holes. The hollow where Okiyo-san lay also had opened a big black hole in the earth.

The season of the yellow sand being over, Shanghai in July was in summer. Since parting in the field of rape flowers, I hadn't seen Okiyo-san. That we two had lined up in the column for immunization, and that we were in the rape field, my mother knew.

A Japanese neighbor had seen us and alerted her. I had done nothing to be blamed for. But just because Okiyo-san was a prostitute, my mother said, "It's your affair if you become a delinquent." She asked me what we had talked about in the rape flowers. I didn't answer. Suppose I told her, "She said 'That's what man is,' pointing at the weeds in a grave," my mother wouldn't understand, I thought. Only in the light of the spring field where heaven and earth joined, the words made sense.

The activities of anti-Japanese elements increased day by day. In the bustling quarters of Hongkou, an army lieutenant was shot with a pistol in broad daylight from across the street. Since he was shot at close range, the event shook up the Japanese all the more.

M Products where my father worked always ordered its employees' families to leave before an area was exposed to the disasters of war, as was to be the case at the conclusion of the Pacific War. Thanks to their secret information, about the time the family finished evacuating, war inevitably broke out in the area.

Before the skirmish at the Marco Polo Bridge on July 7, employees' families had already been ordered to leave. We were prepared to return to Japan as soon as we could obtain boat tickets. My mother said to me who hadn't seen our country, "It's safe at home; there we won't have to flee as refugees."

Partly owing to the threatening atmosphere, I was forbidden to go out of our yard. That day, too, I was playing with my thumb on the mouth of the sprinkler in a corner of the yard, spraying the water to the street, when I saw Okiyo-san walking. I stopped my water game and went to her. With a red undersash over her summer kimono, she said in a low voice, eyeing the windows of my house, "Would you come and play later? I'll give you biscuits with sugar crystals." Then she asked, "Are you going home?" As I nodded, Okiyo-san, too, nodded a few times, saying, "I see."

It was two hours later, about four o'clock in the afternoon. Okiyo-san hanged herself. Slipping away from my mother, I went to her house on the tree-lined street. A bigger crowd of people than that on the day of the union had formed in front of her house.

A black Municipal Police car was parked along the walkway. This car was, so to speak, a cleaning car: it collected everything including corpses of human babies discarded on the street, sick people on the road, and dead cats and dogs. I went among the coolies so as not to be seen by Japanese neighbors, and looked up at Okiyo-san's window.

"It seems she was found hanging from the beam," I heard a Japanese woman say. "I hear she hanged herself with her undersash," I heard another female voice. "How frightening—undersashes are strong, of course," I heard my mother say from the crowd unexpectedly nearby. I ducked down in the ring of people.

Okiyo-san, it was said, was found dead hanging from the beam of her garret. Its ceiling was low. Okiyo-san was not large, but if she had hanged herself with an undersash dangling from the beam, her toes would have reached the floor. How did she hang herself from the low beam? Listening to the talk of my mother and others, I recalled Okiyo-san's voice when she said she would give me biscuits. Why Okiyo-san, who had made that promise just a while ago, suddenly committed suicide, I couldn't understand. At least when she made that promise, she must have meant to be alive two hours later. If I went to her room, there would be biscuits with sugar crystals ready for me.

I had to see the biscuits wrapped in tissue paper, placed on the table or stored away in the tea cabinet.

The knob of the door decorated with stained glass turned slowly, and a plump, red-haired prostitute opened the door.

The staircase leading upstairs was visible from the entrance. A man in white came downstairs holding a stretcher high. It seemed that his steps didn't harmonize with those of the man behind who held the rear end of the stretcher. The stretcher swayed right and left at each step on the staircase.

Okiyo-san lay with her head toward us. Her hair showed from behind the man in white. She came out on the stretcher to the crowded yard. Neither a white cloth nor a blanket covered her body. Her arms powerless on the stretcher and her head stretched, she was dead. Her body looked longer than when she was alive. On that long body, she wore her familiar summer kimono, her usual undersash around it.

The men in white put Okiyo-san's stretcher directly on the car floor. Then they noisily shut the folding doors. The car with a small iron-grilled window drove off in the still bright summer city, carrying Okiyo-san. The car presently became a black speck and disappeared.

Two days after she hanged herself, our family returned to Japan. There I heard the news of the outbreak of the Sino-Japanese war.

The yellow sand that reached Japan covered the sky all day long. I was restless. I went outside many times and walked to the slope. In the blowing wind, I felt peaceful. I stood on the slope a long while, looking at the sky and the town. At the bottom of the slope in the gathering dusk, several girls were playing.

The yellow sand grew deeper as time passed. In time the sky, the town, and the girls all sank into the yellow sand; dispersed as countless black specks. It resembled the rape flower landscape which I saw with Okiyo-san, but in the landscape at the foot of the slope, the brightness of that day was missing.

KOREA

There is no single East Asian word that corresponds to the Western idea of "modern." Although the use of "modern" as constant novelty has occurred in the past, the notion of "modern" as an age or its use to designate modernity (modernism) is imported from Western tradition and is therefore new.

The invention of "modern" literature in Korea was prompted by unprecedented historical changes imposed by foreign powers: the imposition of unequal treaties, political penetration, economic exploitation, and finally, seizure of the country by Japan in 1910. It required a radical revaluation of the past, the shaping of a new language (the vernacular style that corresponds to living speech), new literary forms, and a new theory of literature. New-style poems, inspired by translations of Western poetry, were written from 1908 on. A poem entitled "From the Sea to Boys" (1908) by Ch'ŏe Namson (1890–1957) is usually considered to be the first of its kind: Ch'ŏe's experiment is marked by varying line lengths, rejection of traditional meter, use of flexible new rhythms and enjambed lines, recurrence of refrains, and the same syllable count in corresponding lines of each stanza. Another example of new-style poems is Han Yongun's (1879–1944) poem, "I Cannot Know," included here.

The selections written before 1945, the end of Japan's occupation, show how modern Korean poets dealt with the issues of nationalism and modernism, and how poets of resistance such as Yun Tongju, who perished in a Japanese prison, voiced sorrow and anger at the destruction of the land. Some of the poets who came of age after the liberation of 1945—especially Hwang Tonggyu—attempted to assimilate elements of Korean history. Their imagination was fired by the events and issues of their time.

Historical Background

During the nineteenth century, Western presence in East Asia grew increasingly insistent. Confident of their material and military superiority and buoyed by a rising tide of nationalism, the countries of the West entered a period of aggressive colonialism. The country that adapted most effectively to the Western challenge was Japan, which after 1868 embarked on a rapid program of modernization (broadly, industrialization along with Western-inspired government, social, and education reforms) that soon fueled its own expansionist ambitions.

Korea initially pursued a policy of national isolation, even resorting to the practice of repelling foreign vessels by force when necessary. In 1876, however, Japan pressured Korea into signing a treaty of friendship and trade. China, apprehensive about the Japanese presence in an area where Chinese influence had traditionally prevailed, sent troops to Korea and began to meddle directly in Korean affairs, first forcing a treaty favorable to Chinese merchants, then mediating a series of treaties with Western powers, all on unfavorable terms to Korea.

Having thus been strong-armed into opening to the West, Korea embarked on its own program of modernization. The financial burden of change, however, fell ultimately on the peasant farmers, who, rallying around a religion known as Tonghak, rebelled in 1894. The Korean government called on Chinese troops to help suppress the uprisings, but Japan used the rebellion as a pretext to send troops as well. Attempts to defuse the situation failed, and longstanding tensions between Japan and China finally erupted into war, with Japan's victory in 1895 securing hegemony in Korea as well as privileges and territories in China.

Japan began immediately to dictate a variety of reforms to Korea, but Japanese involvement in the 1896 assassination of Korea's queen produced a strong backlash, and for a time, aided by western advisors, the Korean government charted a relatively independent course. In 1905, however, Japan's supremacy in Korea was granted international recognition by the treaty that ended the Russo-Japanese War (1904–1905). Korea was forced to declare itself a Japanese protectorate. In 1910 Japan annexed the country outright, and for the next thirty-six years Korea was ruled as the Japanese province of Chosen.

Japanese rule was harsh and exploitative. Modernization continued, especially in transportation and communications, but only for the purpose of improving Japan's industrial base. Koreans were denied political rights and had no administrative power. Opposition parties and movements were routinely suppressed, though after a particularly large resistance movement in 1919 some freedom of the press was granted as a mollifying measure. In 1931 Japan's rule again grew militaristic, and with the outbreak first of the Sino-Japanese War of 1937–1945 and then World War II (1939–1945), Japan openly tried to obliterate Korea as a nation, outlawing publications in Korean, forbidding all study of Korean culture, demanding that Koreans take Japanese names and practice the Shinto religion, and drafting hundreds of thousands of Koreans into the Japanese war effort.

The end of World War II in 1945 found the northern portion of Korea occupied by the Soviet Union and the southern portion by the United States. By the time of the formal Japanese surrender several days later, the Soviet Union had already begun sealing off its half at the thirty-eighth parallel, creating two zones. A four-power, temporary trusteeship was negotiated with a view to eventually reuniting the country in independence, and in 1948 the United Nations called for general elections. Monitored by the UN, the south elected a National Assembly and declared the Republic of Korea. The Soviet Union, however, refused to allow the UN election monitors into the north, sponsoring instead elections from a single list of candidates to create a Communist government, which declared itself the Democratic People's Republic of Korea. Only the southern government was recognized by the UN; only the northern government was recognized by the Soviet Union.

In 1950 the Korean War broke out when North Korean troops launched a full-scale invasion of South Korea. Acting under the banner of the United Nations, U.S. and other forces came to the south's aid, quickly turning the tide against the north. Chinese troops then entered the war on the side of the north, routing the UN forces. The war ended in a stalemate, and the armistice of 1953 redrew the border between north and south almost exactly where it had stood in 1945.

Throughout the Cold War era, relations between North and South Korea remained hostile and unstable. Even such negotiations as those undertaken in the 1970s to reunite families long separated by the country's partition foundered in mutual mistrust. Only recently, with the collapse of the Soviet Union, have reconciliation and reunification come to seem possible and have the first encouraging steps in diplomacy been taken.

Further Readings

Fulton, Bruce, and Ju-chan Fulton, trans. *Words of Farewell: Stories by Korean Women Writers*. Seattle: Seal Press, 1989.

Lee, Ki-baik. *A New History of Korea*. Trans. Edward W. Wagner and Edward J. Shultz. Cambridge: Harvard University Press, 1984.

Lee, Peter H. *The Silence of Love: Twentieth-Century Korean Poetry*. Honolulu: University of Hawaii Press, 1980.

————. *Modern Korean Literature: An Anthology*. Honolulu: University of Hawaii Press, 1990.

————. *Flowers of Fire: Twentieth-Century Korean Stories*. Rev. ed. Honolulu: University of Hawaii Press, 1986.

McCann, David R., ed. *Black Crane: An Anthology of Korean Literature*. Ithaca: Cornell University East Asian Paper 14, 1977.

Suh Jih-moon, trans. *The Rainy Spell and Other Korean Stories*. London: Onyx Press, 1983.

Pronunciation Guide

Chŏng Chiyong (jong jee-yong)
Han Yongun (hahn yong-oon)
Hwang Sunwŏn (hwang soon-won)
Hwang Tonggyu (hwang dong-kyoo)
Kim Sowŏl (kim so-wol)
Pak Mog wŏl (pahk mok-wol)

HAN YONGUN (1879–1944)
YUN TONGJU (1917–1945)
CHŎNG CHIYONG (b. 1903)
SŎ CHŎNGJU (b. 1915)
PAK MOGWŎL (1916–1978)
HWANG TONGGYU (b. 1938)
Korea

Han Yongun was a Buddhist monk-poet who sang of the identity of self and the phenomenal world with the ultimate truth of Emptiness. Particularly sensitive to landscape and the symbolic imagery of travel, he manages to convey an epic feeling even in the depiction of the simplest things. In "A Ferryboat and a Traveler" his images are sharply etched in the reader's consciousness. Chŏng Chiyong was the first genuinely successful poet of Korea, whose work, clear and precise, could be called imagist (usually defined as "an intellectual and emotional complex in an instant of time"). The self dissolves in its apprehension of nature, whose reality is grasped in solitude; in his most celebrated work, *White Deer Lake* (1941), a spiritual pilgrimage takes place, with a final initiation. After studying William Blake and Walt Whitman and converting to Catholicism, Chŏng placed himself in the tradition of East Asian nature poetry, always seen from the viewpoint of the individual. Yun Tongju was a Christian, and a poet of resistance to an enslaved society, who died in a prison in Fukuoka at the age of twenty-eight. He spoke out against the banishment of Koreans from the public sphere and against a tyrannical obliteration of personal integrity. He became a symbol of the national crisis and suffering, and of an affirmation of the self in a time of stress. All these poets stress the actual moment in its immediacy, and the use of tradition renewed by the individual writer. Each gives a different sense of how to survive as a poet in a divided and confused country, and—in occasionally elliptical references and metaphorical allusions—shows the constraints of censorship. Some, like Sŏ Chŏngju and Pak Mogwŏl sought to assimilate tradition through the incorporation of unpoetic words, dialects, and native modes of expression. Some, like Hwang Tonggyu, are determined to bear witness to the age, and yet draw upon a number of Western traditions to enrich their work. All have sought the voice of their own conscience in bearing testimony to the self, within a culture in crisis. The liberation in 1945 opened the way for a reflowering of poetry in its many expressions.

In order to keep the poetry together, we have placed the prose selection at the end of this section.

HAN YONGUN

I Cannot Know

Whose footstep is that paulownia leaf that falls quietly in the windless air, drawing
    a straight wave?

Whose face is that piece of blue sky flickering between ominous black clouds,
    chased by the west wind after a rainy spell?

Whose breath is that unnameable fragrance that brushes by the still sky, born   5
    amid the green moss in the flowerless deep forest and trailing over the ancient
    stupa?

Whose song is that small winding stream gushing from an unknown source and
    breaking against the rocks?

Whose poem is that twilight that adorns the falling day, treading over the   10
    boundless sea with lotus heels and caressing the endless sky with jade hands?

The ash left after burning becomes oil again. For whose night does this feeble
    lantern keep vigil, my heart that never stops burning?

A Ferryboat and a Traveler

I am a ferryboat,
you are a traveler.

You tread on me with muddy feet,
I embrace you and cross the water.
When I embrace you, I can cross deeps, shallow, or rapids.   5

When you don't come, I wait from night to day, exposed to the wind, wet with
    snow and rain.
Once across the water, you never look back at me.
Yet I know you will come sooner or later.
Waiting for you, I grow older day after day.   10

I am a ferryboat,
You are a traveler.

YUN TONGJU

Self-Portrait

I go round the foot of the mountain seeking a lone well by the field, to look into
    it without words.

In the well the moon is bright, clouds flow, sky spreads open, a blue wind blows,
    and there is autumn.

Translated by Peter H. Lee.

A young man is in the well too. Hating him I turn away. But as I go on, I come to   5
    pity him.

When I return and look in the well again, that young man is still there. I start to
    hate him again and turn away. But as I go on, I come to long for him.

In the well the moon is bright, clouds flow, sky spreads open, the blue wind
    blows, autumn reigns, a young man stands there like memory.   10

CHŎNG CHIYONG

Pomegranate*

Coals in the brazier burn lovely as a rose,
Spring night smells of dry burning grass.

I crack a pomegranate that passed a winter
To savor its kernal stones one by one.

O clear recollection, rainbow of new sorrow,   5
Soft and quick as a goldfish.

This fruit mellowed at the last harvest month
When our small story sprouted.

Young girl, frail friend, stealthily
A pair of jade rabbits doze on your bosom.   10

Fingers of a white fish in an ancient lake,
Silver threads tremble, lithe and lonely.

Holding a pomegranate grain against the light,
I dream of a blue sky, Silla's myriad years.[1]

SŎ CHŎNGJU

Beside a Crysanthemum†

To bring one chrysanthemum
to flower, the cuckoo has cried
since spring.

To bring one chrysanthemum to bloom,
thunder has rolled   5
through the black clouds.

*Translated by Peter H. Lee.
†Translated by David R. McCann.

---

1. One of the three ancient Korean kingdoms,
the traditional dates of which are 57 B.C. to
A.D. 935—hence a round number, one
thousand.

Flower, like my sister returning
from distant, youthful byways
of throat-tight longing
to stand by the mirror: 10

for your yellow petals to open,
last night such a frost fell,
and I did not sleep.

PAK MOGWŎL

Wild Peach Blossoms

The stony hill
lapped by purple mist

Quiet
daylong

On such a day
wild peach blossoms   5

In a hillside village
the sounds of water

Clamorous, down the slope,
birds warble, mountain birds   10

A sun-drenched girl
crossing March.

HWANG TONGGYU

Snow Under Martial Law

Ah, those are sick words.
My soles shiver.
I'm determined to become a simple man!
When dry winds,
Daylong,   5
Chase the snow here and there,
In the evening
Every snowflake is muddy—
With sun-shaped sun suddenly down,
My dream shattered,   10
Prostrate on the ground,

Translated by Peter H. Lee.

I wipe away my eyes, nose, and mouth.
Terrifying even to myself,
Am I turning into
Muddy snow   15
Driven about and trampled again?

HWANG SUNWŎN (b. 1915)
Korea

Hwang Sunwŏn, a prizewinning novelist and short-story writer, and a professor
at Kyŏnghŭi University in Seoul, focuses in his works on human loneliness and
interpersonal relations, mediating between realism and lyricism. He is known in
particular for his short stories, which follow a lyrical flow against a backdrop of
natural scenery, and for his insight into the psychology of his characters. He is
concerned with revealing Korean myths and legends as the underpinning of the
Korean character.

Cranes

The northern village lay snug beneath the high, bright autumn sky, near the
border at the Thirty-eighth Parallel. White gourds lay one against the other on the
dirt floor of an empty farmhouse. Any village elders who passed by extinguished
their bamboo pipes first, and the children, too, turned back some distance off.
Their faces were marked with fear.

As a whole, the village showed little damage from the war, but it still did not
seem like the same village Sŏngsam had known as a boy.

At the foot of a chestnut grove on the hill behind the village he stopped and
climbed a chestnut tree. Somewhere far back in his mind he heard the old man
with a wen shout, "You bad boy, climbing up my chestnut tree again!"

The old man must have passed away, for he was not among the few village
elders Sŏngsam had met. Holding onto the trunk of the tree, Sŏngsam gazed up
at the blue sky for a time. Some chestnuts fell to the ground as the dry clusters
opened of their own accord.

A young man stood, his hands bound, before a farmhouse that had been
converted into a Public Peace Police office. He seemed to be a stranger, so
Sŏngsam went up for a closer look. He was stunned: this young man was none
other than his boyhood playmate. Tŏkchae.

Sŏngsam asked the police officer who had come with him from Ch'ŏnt'ae for

Translated by Peter H. Lee.

Kim Young-cheol. *Stillness*.

an explanation. The prisoner was the vice-chairman of the Farmers' Communist League and had just been flushed out of hiding in his own house, Sŏngsam learned.

Sŏngsam sat down on the dirt floor and lit a cigarette.

Tŏkchae was to be escorted to Ch'ŏngdan by one of the peace police.

After a time, Sŏngsam lit a new cigarette from the first and stood up.

"I'll take him with me."

Tŏkchae averted his face and refused to look at Sŏngsam. The two left the village.

Sŏngsam went on smoking, but the tabacco had no flavor. He just kept drawing the smoke in and blowing it out. Then suddenly he thought that Tŏkchae, too, must want a puff. He thought of the days when they had shared dried gourd leaves behind sheltering walls, hidden from the adults' view. But today, how could he offer a cigarette to a fellow like this?

Once, when they were small, he went with Tŏkchae to steal some chestnuts from the old man with the wen. It was Sŏngsam's turn to climb the tree. Suddenly the old man began shouting. Sŏngsam slipped and fell to the ground. He got chestnut burrs all over his bottom, but he kept on running. Only when the two had reached a safe place where the old man could not overtake them did Sŏngsam turn his bottom to Tŏkchae. The burrs hurt so much as they were plucked out that Sŏngsam could not keep tears from welling up in his eyes. Tŏkchae produced a fistful of chestnuts from his pocket and thrust them into Sŏngsam's. . . . Sŏngsam threw away the cigarette he had just lit, and then made up his mind not to light another while he was escorting Tŏkchae.

They reached the pass at the hill where he and Tŏkchae had cut fodder for the cows until Sŏngsam had to move to a spot near Ch'ŏnt'ae, south of the Thirty-eighth Parallel, two years before the liberation.

Sŏngsam felt a sudden surge of anger in spite of himself and shouted, "So how many have you killed?"

For the first time, Tŏkchae cast a quick glance at him and then looked away.

"You! How many have you killed?" he asked again.

Tŏkchae looked at him again and glared. The glare grew intense, and his mouth twitched.

"So you managed to kill quite a few, eh?" Sŏngsam felt his mind clearing itself, as if some obstruction had been removed. "If you were vice-chairman of the Communist League, why didn't you run? You must have been lying low with a secret mission."

Tŏkchae did not reply.

"Speak up. What was your mission?"

Tŏkchae kept walking. Tŏkchae was hiding something, Sŏngsam thought. He wanted to take a good look at him, but Tŏkchae kept his face averted.

Fingering the revolver at his side, Sŏngsam went on: "There's no need to make excuses. You're going to be shot anyway. Why don't you tell the truth here and now?"

"I'm not going to make any excuses. They made me vice-chairman of the League because I was a hardworking farmer, and one of the poorest. If that's a capital offense, so be it. I'm still what I used to be— the only thing I'm good at is tilling the soil." After a short pause, he added, "My old man is bedridden at home. He's been ill almost half a year." Tŏkchae's father was a widower, a poor, hardworking farmer who lived only for his son. Seven years ago his back had given out, and he had contracted a skin disease.

"Are you married?"

"Yes," Tŏkchae replied after a time.

"To whom?"

"Shorty."

"To Shorty?" How interesting! A woman so small and plump that she knew the earth's vastness, but not the sky's height. Such a cold fish! He and Tŏkchae had teased her and made her cry. And Tŏkchae had married her!

"How many kids?"

"The first is arriving this fall, she says."

Sŏngsam had difficulty swallowing a laugh that he was about to let burst forth in spite of himself. Although he had asked how many children Tŏkchae had, he could not help wanting to break out laughing at the thought of the wife sitting there with her huge stomach, one span around. But he realized that this was no time for joking.

"Anyway, it's strange you didn't run away."

"I tried to escape. They said that once the South invaded, not a man would be spared. So all of us between seventeen and forty were taken to the North. I thought of evacuating, even if I had to carry my father on my back. But Father said no. How could we farmers leave the land behind when the crops were ready for harvesting? He grew old on that farm depending on me as the prop and mainstay of the family. I wanted to be with him in his last moments so I could close his eyes with my own hand. Besides, where can farmers like us go, when all we know how to do is live on the land?"

Sŏngsam had had to flee the previous June. At night he had broken the news privately to his father. But his father had said the same thing: Where could a farmer go, leaving all the chores behind? So Sŏngsam had left alone. Roaming about the strange streets and villages in the South, Sŏngsam had been haunted by thoughts of his old parents and the young children, who had been left with all the chores. Fortunately, his family had been safe then, as it was now.

They had crossed over a hill. This time Sŏngsam walked with his face averted. The autumn sun was hot on his forehead. This was an ideal day for the harvest, he thought.

When they reached the foot of the hill, Sŏngsam gradually came to a halt. In the middle of a field he spied a group of cranes that resembled men in white, all bent over. This had been the demilitarized zone along the Thirty-eighth Parallel. The cranes were still living here, as before, though all the people were gone.

Once, when Sŏngsam and Tŏkchae were about twelve, they had set a trap here, without anybody else knowing, and caught a crane, a Tanjŏng crane. They had tied the crane up, even binding its wings, and paid it daily visits, patting its neck and riding on its back. Then one day they overheard the neighbors whispering: someone had come from Seoul with a permit from the governor-general's office to catch cranes as some kind of specimens. Then and there the two boys had dashed off to the field. That they would be found out and punished had no longer mattered; all they cared about was the fate of their crane. Without a moment's delay, still out of breath from running, they untied the crane's feet and wings, but the bird could hardly walk. It must have been weak from having been bound.

The two held the crane up. Then, suddenly, they heard a gunshot. The crane flutter its wings once or twice and then sank back to the ground.

The boys thought their crane had been shot. But the next moment, as another crane from a nearby bush fluttered its wings, the boys' crane stretched its long neck, gave out a whoop, and disappeared into the sky. For a long while the two boys could not tear their eyes away from the blue sky into which their crane had soared.

"Hey, why don't we stop here for a crane hunt?" Sŏngsam said suddenly.

Tŏkchae was dumbfounded.

"I'll make a trap with this rope; you flush a crane over here."

Sŏngsam had untied Tŏkchae's hands and was already crawling through the weeds.

Tŏkchae's face whitened. "You're sure to be shot anyway"—these words flashed through his mind. Any instant a bullet would come flying from Sŏngsam's direction, Tŏkchae thought.

Some paces away, Sŏngsam quickly turned toward him.

"Hey, how come you're standing there like a dummy? Go flush a crane!"

Only then did Tŏkchae understand. He began crawling through the weeds.

A pair of Tanjŏng cranes soared high into the clear blue autumn sky, flapping their huge wings.

Abdel Hadi Al-Gazzar. *The Popular Chorus, or The Theater of Life* (detail). 1948. Oil on cardboard. Museum of Modern Art, Cairo.

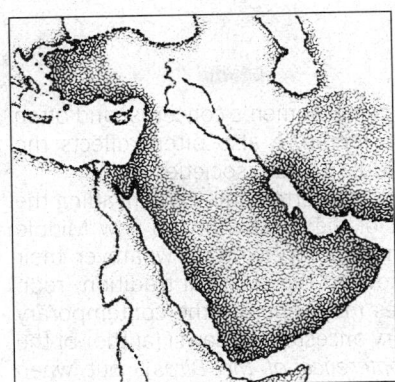

SECTION XII
The Modern Middle East

The modern literatures of Arabic, Persian, and Turkish are intimately tied at once to the modern West and to the cultural and literary heritage that gave birth to them. In the nineteenth and twentieth centuries, Western influence was more than just political. With Western imperialism came new literary genres: the novel and the short story. Poetry, which has always been one of the mainstays of Middle Eastern culture, continues to be promoted and promulgated in a spirit different from that of prose.

With newly found independence, critics could begin to speak of Egyptian literary production versus Syrian, Egyptian versus Sudanese. But in fact, tempting as these national categories might be, the major driving force behind the literary categories has remained linguistic. Modern national literatures have developed in Arabic, Persian, and Turkish; their readers are those, in whichever country, who speak the languages in question. Writers, for example, from one Arab country are read in other countries, whether they live at home or in exile.

In the modern period, more than genres have changed. The female literary voice — in Persian and Turkish as well as in Arabic — is much more important in the contemporary literary production of the Islamic Middle East than it was in the premodern period. The male dominance of most of the classical Islamic literary genres has been replaced by a far greater balance between male and female voices. This is true not only in poetry — where women contributed even in classical times — but also in the novel and short story. With women's writings have come women's concerns, and often feminism. Of course, both male and female literature also often reflects the political and social issues in contemporary Middle Eastern societies.

Metafictional creations and narratives rich in intertextuality are invading the prose of the Middle East, as they have that of the West. But the new Middle Eastern literary experiment is different. Contemporary writers, whatever their religious or political allegiance, are turning toward the classical tradition, redigesting it, redefining it, recasting it. Centuries may separate the contemporary Persian poet Nāder Nāderpour from his literary ancestors Firdawsī (author of the Shāh Nāma) and ᶜAttār (author of *The Conference of the Birds*), but when Nāderpour places allusions to both in one of his poems, he expects his reader to link his or her literary universe intertextually with theirs.

Arabic, Persian, and Turkish are today, as they have been in earlier centuries, the dominant literatures of the Islamic Middle East. Through their close relations with contemporary Western literature, they participate in an emerging world literary culture. At the same time, through their frequently self-conscious relation to their own immense literary inheritance, they add their own distinctive flavor.

Hebrew literature has been written continually, and it is very difficult to determine precisely where a "modern" period might be said to begin, given the vastly differing conditions and sources of influence available to diverse Jewish communities. Hebrew dramas, for instance, were written in Italy and Holland in the seventeenth and eighteenth centuries, while poetry, rhymed prose narrative, and various other forms flourished in Italy, Provence, Greece, the Balkans, North Africa, and Yemen throughout the nineteenth century, and in some cases, into the twentieth century: much of this writing is rooted in the cultural practices of Mediterranean and Islamic civilization. Modern or "new" Hebrew literature in Northern Europe developed within the framework of the Jewish Enlightenment Movement in Germany in the second half of the eighteenth century; subsequently, it developed for more than a century in various Jewish centers within the czarist Russian Empire, where it was affiliated first with the Jewish Russian Enlightenment Movement, and then (from the 1880s) with the new Jewish nationalism, primarily with Zionism. In the twentieth century, due to the fragmentation and eventual destruction of Jewish life in Eastern Europe, its center shifted from Europe to other parts of the world, first and foremost to Palestine, where Hebrew literature played a significant role in the establishment of a new Hebraic culture, but it also developed in the United States as well as in other places. After the foundation of the state of Israel in 1948, Hebrew literature was gradually transformed into an Israeli literature, strongly rooted in the ethos and achievements of earlier Hebrew literature, yet evolving a distinct identity of its own.*

Basically, modern Hebrew literature presumed to be the voice and consciousness of a new, contemporary Jewish culture, a culture that would negotiate a compromise or, better, a synthesis between Judaic cultural particularity and modern "universal" (that is, European, Western) humanistic civilization. In this it purported to break with the "old" Jewish literature—that is, "traditional" literature, which had been based primarily on religious rabbinical and liturgical

*This passage concerning Hebrew literature was contributed by Dan Miron, Columbia University.

principles (in spite of the extensive corpus of medieval poetry dealing with nonliturgical, "mundane" topics). The "new" literature was not out to "destroy" religion, and many of its earlier exponents cannot be described as "secularists." However, from the start it oriented itself toward four new literary and cultural perspectives: Humanistic ideals, the humanistic norm of the good, moral, balanced, and fully realized human being; a concept of literature as "the watchman unto the house of Israel," an institution that replaces the rabbinical authorities as the custodian of the national spiritual well-being—in this perspective, literature is viewed as a modern continuation of Biblical prophecy; a concept of literature bound by the norms of Western aesthetics and poetics; as such, modern Hebrew literature insisted on developing the entire generic spectrum of European literature as well as participating in the major aesthetic-literary movements of the last 300 years: neoclassicism, sentimentalism, romanticism, realism, symbolism and postsymbolist modernistic movements; the notion that Hebrew is the only Jewish language that fosters Jewish cultural continuity (the "new" literature developed strong, "renaissance" type ties with the Bible), while at the same time providing a vehicle for the highest aesthetic-emotive literary expression. Hebrew was to be both the link with the past and the harbinger of the Jewish cultural future, while a Jewish literature written in a European language would eventually assimilate into the non-Jewish national literature of that language, and a literature written in a Jewish "jargon" (like Yiddish) would inevitably focus on the present and lose sight of past and future cultural vistas.

These four parameters or aspects of modern Hebrew literature did not always coexist harmoniously. Indeed, as the defining edges of a cultural matrix they contained built-in dichotomies between didacticism (propaganda) and pure emotive expression or mimetic-descriptive loyalty to "truth" (art); between the individualism asserted by the humanistic ideal of the perfect, happy, and free human being and the collectivism prescribed by nationalistic ideologies; between the assumed sublimity of the Hebrew language and the "lowly" expression necessitated by a realistic rendering of daily life. Thus Hebrew writers had to balance themselves carefully between conflicting "demands" or dimensions of their tradition.

This emergence had to do with the problematic notion of a Hebrew and Jewish "renaissance." On the one hand, the nation as a whole (through Zionism) and the Jewish individual (by asserting his or her individuality as an intellectual and physical being) were seething with a new sense of strength and need for activism. On the other hand, some writers suspected that this new activism would lead, particularly if the Zionist experiment failed, to assimilation and to the "death" of Judaism as a distinct civilization. This tragic notion of a vulnerable, possibly self-defeating "resurrection" of the free Jewish psyche found its most profound expression in the poetry of Chaim Nachman Bialik, the great "national" romantic poet, and in the prose fiction of Shmuel Yosef Agnon, a writer who presumably aimed at relinking the new literature with the religious tradition. Agnon, while pretending to recapitulate the perspective of a traditionalist naive raconteur, actually undermined the norms of the tradition, such as the norm of sanctity achieved by total control of the instincts. In Agnon's "The Tale of the Scribe," a pair of misguided good people, whose life is permeated by traditional Jewish "purity," cannot understand why sexual abstinence and fertility are mutually exclusive—a misunderstanding that brings about tragedy and death.

What Bialik pointed to through his grandiose pathos, Agnon, from the opposite direction, pointed to through his subtle but corrosive ironies.

Modernism seemed for a while to lead Hebrew literature away from the Judaic focus, but the literature bounced back. Uri Tsvi Greenberg, the chief Hebrew expressionist, emerged out of an initial anarchistic and nihilistic phase as, on the one hand, the modern Hebrew existentialist who strives to counterbalance his sense of physical and moral entropy by a new religious experience, and, on the other hand, as the prophet of radical Zionism.

Israeli literature developed both as a continuation of the "new" Hebrew literature and as an autonomous entity. Of the four perspectives of Hebrew literature of the nineteenth and early twentieth centuries, it dropped altogether the fourth one—that of retaining Hebrew as the only Jewish language. It did not choose Hebrew as the language of the future Jewish culture but simply used it as the only spoken idiom and literary language available to its writers. Thus it completely divorced itself from linguistic sublimity, and for the first time in post-biblical literature, made the spoken idiom its chief source of inspiration. Also, for a time at least, Israeli writers presumed that the existence of the Jewish state freed its artists and intellectuals from the eternal role of "The watchman unto the house of Israel" as well as from the pathos that goes with it. They presented variants of the individual experience—love, death, psychic occurrences, the sense of misery and elation—with little or no reference to their "Jewish" ramifications; of course, this had been done earlier by "peripheral" or noncanonic writers. Yehuda Amichai explored the consolations of love in a mundane, noneschatological environment. Nathan Zach focused on entropy and the presence of death. Dalia Ravikovitch wrote convincingly on mental and emotional pain. In their thematics, style, prosody, and structures they gave expression to a new sense of reality—unceremonial, nonprophetic, antieschatological. The Israeli writers of prose fiction (Amos Oz, A.B. Yehoshua, J. Shabtai et al.), who walked in the path established by these poets, developed, from the same principles, the new Israeli novel. However, Jewish continuity asserts itself in Israeli literature as it evolves and grows. It is forced upon Israeli writers by the history of their state, which continuously fights for its very existence, by the internal encounter of different Jewish "tribes" within the Israeli society and perhaps even more dramatically by the realization of the implications of the Holocaust during World War II. Some Israeli writers seek a way of their own to express their sense of Jewish reality and Jewish fate; see, for example, the bitter ironies of confronting Biblical characters and intentions against the stark relief of the Holocaust, as in Dan Pagis's "Footprints," and Amir Gilboa's "Isaac." Others keep marching away from a Judaic identity.

Currently, Israeli literature finds itself at a new crossroads; remarkably diverse and dynamic (with some Palestinians writing in Hebrew and some Jews writing in English or other languages), a distinct and unique Israeli culture has taken root. This is evident in the growing cultural and literary presence and influence of Israel's majority, Jews of Middle Eastern and Mediterranean origin such as the novelists Sami Michael and Eli Amir and the poets Eret Britton, Shelley Elkayam, Amira Hess, and Amir Sami. Here, issues that are quite familiar to readers of many other literatures (such as Arabic, African, African-American, or Latin American), have come to the forefront, particularly questions concerning the intertwining of personal, political, and cultural identity.

Historical Background

The roots of the Ottoman Empire's decline can be traced to its period of greatest dominance. Founded in the fourteenth century by Turkish tribes in Anatolia (southern Turkey), the empire encompassed southeastern Europe and almost all of the world's Arabic-speaking countries by the mid-sixteenth century. In the latter half of the century, Ottoman sultans began to offer trading and legal privileges (known as Capitulations) to European merchants. During the empire's ascendancy, the privileges had little effect. With time, however, these agreements were manipulated by the rapidly developing European nations of the seventeenth and eighteenth centuries in an effort to undermine Ottoman trade and political authority. Regional fragmentation, negligible technical advances, failing economies, and incompetent leadership all weakened the empire, and European powers, both independently and in various alliances, recaptured many Ottoman holdings.

By the early nineteenth century, sultans Selim III (r. 1789–1807) and Mahmud II (r. 1808–1839) began to enact military and administrative reforms that reflected European advancements. More thoroughgoing reforms, referred to as the Tanzimat ("order"), were launched with an 1839 royal decree implementing principles borrowed from European liberalism, including equal rights for all subjects, freedom of trade and travel, and penal reform. While serving to concentrate authority in the shrinking empire's sultanate, the Tanzimat reforms also yielded a constitution in 1876, the first in any Islamic country.

Weathering internal revolts, a nascent Turkish nationalist movement, and the loss of virtually all its European territory, the empire averted dissolution until shortly after defeat in World War I (during which Ottoman Turks in 1915 massacred approximately one million Armenians, ostensibly to quash possible domestic support for Russia). In peace negotiations ratified by the League of Nations in 1922, the Ottomans surrendered their Arab provinces in the Middle East to the Allied nations. The same year, a protracted struggle for independence was led by Mustafa Kemal (1881–1938), a former general known as Ataturk ("Father of the Turks"). The final Ottoman sultan was deposed, and in 1923 the Republic of Turkey was established, with Ataturk serving as president until his death.

Ataturk guided Turkey through an extraordinarily rapid and thorough transformation into a secular, Western-style state. After 1928, Islam no longer functioned as the state religion, religious orders were abolished, and the Latin alphabet replaced Arabic script. Laws and schools followed Western models. Women attained suffrage and the right to hold office. Ataturk proved a powerful, autocratic ruler, suppressing rivals and minority uprisings—notably among the country's Kurdish population—while working to reconfigure a Turkish society based on nationalist solidarity rather than religious precepts.

The Arabic-speaking countries of the former Ottoman Empire were ruled by European imperial powers well into the twentieth century before gaining independence. Nationalist movements of varying intensity and ideological provenance—some secular, others engaging Islamic tradition—characterized the Arab world as it entered the modern period.

Many Arab nationalists looked to the achievements of Egypt and Egyptian president Gamal Abdel Nasser (1918–1970; president 1956–1970). Although nominally ruled by the Ottoman sultanate, Egypt had established significant political independence by the early nineteenth century. Seeking greater control of the Suez Canal—which had been built in 1869, opening a direct route to India and Asia from the Mediterranean—Britain seized control of the country in 1882. A constitutional monarchy under King Fu'ad (r. 1922–1936) was established in 1922, but British supervision continued until a group of military officers led by Nasser toppled the monarchy in 1952 and proclaimed a republic. Under Nasser's guidance, the revolutionary energy of pre-1952 Egypt modulated into an ardent but stable and religiously progressive pan-Arabism. Nasser's popularity skyrocketed following the 1956 Suez Crisis, wherein the military gains of a joint Anglo-French-Israeli attack on Egypt were surrendered after the action was condemned by the United States and the Soviet Union—scoring a significant political victory for Nasser and ending England's imperial ambitions in the Middle East.

Nasser's merger of modernization, social reform, and ethnic pride created a "Nasserist" blueprint for Arab leaders. However, the rout of Egypt (along with Syria and Jordan) by Israel in the Six-Day War of June 1967 abruptly deflated the Egyptian president's stature. For most Arabs, Nasser could no longer be considered champion of the single most potent pan-Arab cause, that of the Palestinians displaced or disfranchised by the establishment of the State of Israel in 1948. Several groups—most notably the Palestine Liberation Organization (PLO), under the leadership of the exiled Palestinian Yasir Arafat (b. 1929)—agitated for the Palestinians after Nasser's demise.

Nasser died in 1970; his successor, the military officer Anwar al-Sadat (1918–1981), negotiated a peace treaty with Israel in 1979 despite vigorous Arab resistance. Sadat was assassinated in 1981 by Islamic religious extremists. Hosni Mubarak, who succeeded Sadat, fought to suppress the efforts of similar militant religionists, as have the leaders of several other Middle Eastern countries. Indeed, an invigorated Islamic devotion, prompted by the problems of urbanization and poverty and a displeasure with Western ideas and practices, demonstrated how a vital Islam may inspire nationalisms that subvert rather than support a regime: a secular state, for many of the devout, defied Islamic law *(shari'a)*. The tensions engendered by competing civic and religious demands sharply (and sometimes alarmingly) focused the problems of modernism in the Middle East.

This ascendant Islamic radicalism has found perhaps its chief inspiration in the Iranian Revolution of 1979. For many Muslims, the revolution represented a long-awaited repudiation of Western ideology and power and a collective spiritual renewal. Like its Arab neighbors to the West, the Persian-speaking Iranians (the nation was called Persia until 1935) had battled European colonizers for several hundred years—dating back to the sixteenth century, when the Portuguese established beachheads along the Persian Gulf. Throughout the early decades of the Qajar Dynasty (1794–1925), Iran suffered territorial losses in the Caucasus to Russia. Later skirmishes with the Afghans elicited British intervention on behalf of Afghanistan. Qajar shahs (sovereigns) attempted Western-style reforms in the manner of the Ottoman Tanzimat, but rejuvenated Shi'ite activism encouraged disfavor with the Qajar dynasts. (Islam's major schism, between Shi'ite and Sunni Muslims, originated in a dispute over the legitimacy of the claim made by Muhammad's son-in-law Ali to sole leadership in the community—a claim Shi'ites support. Most of Islam is comprised of Sunni Muslims.)

Russian and British interest in Iran continued into the twentieth century following the discovery of Iran's vast oil reserves. By treaty, the two countries occupied a neutral Iran during World War I. In the imperial machinations that followed the war, Britain attempted, unsuccessfully, to establish a protectorate, while the Soviet Union withdrew following Iran's recognition of the Russians.

In 1921 Reza Khan, an army officer, led a military coup d'etat; he was named hereditary shah in 1925, founding the Pahlevi Dynasty. Twenty years later he abdicated the throne; his son Muhammad Reza ruled from 1941 to 1979. Muhammad Reza's long reign was marked both by its severity and by economic and social reforms financed through oil exports and substantial U.S. aid. The shah's close affiliation with Western powers and his secularism eventually spurred a backlash: fearing revolution, the shah fled to Egypt in 1978. The Ayatollah Ruhollah Khomeini returned from exile in Paris to establish a theocratic government; an estimated 70,000 dissidents were executed.

In 1980, after several years of border disputes, Iraq invaded Iran, beginning a bloody and debilitating eight-year war that ended in an inconclusive ceasefire brokered by the United Nations.

Modern European Jewish history, on the other hand, derives from the same ferment of ideas and developments that gave birth to modern Europe. The ascendancy in the eighteenth century of capitalism and secular liberalism was premised on new notions of human equality and progress—notions that were best and most explicitly articulated by the thinkers of the Enlightenment, the century's defining Eurpoean intellectual movement.

For the Jews, a people who had been marginalized in the Chirstian world since the Roman Empire and subject to persecutions and legal degradations through most of the Western medieval period and the Renaissance, the emergence of this inchoate, post-Christian humanism promised immense gains. Beginning in revolutionary France in the 1790s (after heated debate), and continuing throughout most of the continent into the mid-nineteenth century, Western Europe's Jewry was gradually emancipated from longstanding anti-Jewish laws and practices, which were known as disabilities.

The dissolution of ghetto life—to which Jewish communities in parts of Europe had been consigned for centuries—and the attendant prospect of assimilation into their native countries radically altered both the daily lives of nineteenth century Jews and the broader trend of Jewish history. Emancipation created the conditions whereby, despite persisting prejudices, Jews rose to prominence in nearly every field of endeavor, including business, science, the arts, and politics. At the same time, the assimilation that underlay these successes predicated a weakening of religious identity and solidarity. Jews had defined and fortified themselves for centuries according to a legal status as an autonomous community as well as a notion of exile, by which they saw themselves as a people apart, waiting in alien countries for a messiah to redeem and ingather them in a promised homeland. The newfound opportunity to participate successfully as citizens of existing countries tempered, when it did not wholly supplant, adherence to the idea of a passive Jewish exceptionalism. Indeed, religious observance declined during the nineteenth century and significant numbers of Jews converted to Christianity.

These issues had engaged leading Jewish intellectuals and scholars since religion and religious history had first come under the scrutiny of eighteenth-century Enlightenment thinkers. The German-Jewish philosopher Moses Mendelssohn (1729–1786), attempted to bridge a universal humanistic rational-ism—which provided new civic and intellectual opportunities for Jews—with the exilic tradition. A Jewish movement committed to European cultural traditions, known as *Haskala* ("Englightenment" in Hebrew), arose around Mendelssohn during his later years in Berlin. While Mendelssohn's teachings fundamentally influenced the development of reform Judaism, most of his immediate followers in *Haskala* would completely assimilate or convert.

In Russia, however, the *Haskala* movement went on to thrive during the mid-nineteenth century. Circumstances in this country did not reflect those of Western Europe. Russia had been traditionally the home of fervent nationalism and anti-Semitism, and when the partitions of Poland in 1772, 1793, and 1795 added one million Jews to the burgeoning country's census (giving Russia about five million Jews in all—by far the largest total of any country and nearly half of the world's Jewry), severe restrictions were placed on the Jews: they were forced to live and work within an impoverished Pale of Settlement, a region in the western provinces. Russian Jews would not gain legal emancipation until 1917.

Following the brutal regime of Tsar Nicholas I (r. 1825–1855), the Russian *Haskala* flourished under the relatively benevolent reign of Alexander II (r. 1855–1881). Yiddish became the vehicle for several literary masterpieces, and a number of writers also began to produce brilliant work in Hebrew—paving the way for the emergence of Hebrew as the chief spoken idiom in Israel. The optimism of the Hebrew renaissance in Russia was chastened by the massacres of Jews in the reactionary backlash that followed the assassination of Alexander in 1881. The government sponsored or allowed these attacks (known as pogroms), and additionally legislated stringent new anti-Jewish laws. As a result, Russian Jews began to emigrate to Western Europe and the United States in large numbers.

Several Russian Jewish intellectuals, bereft of their faith in European culture, now argued that Jews required their own territory in order to live without the threats of violent prejudice and legal sanction. Leo Pinsker (1821–1891), an Odessa physician, appealed to Western European Jews to help secure a home-land for all Jews. Pinsker did not specify Palestine, the Biblical homeland of the Jewish people—an area largely conterminous with present-day Israel. The idea of Jewish settlement in Palestine did, however, reflect an ancient yearning among Jews.

Pinsker's appeal to the Jews of Western Europe proved ineffective, despite the fact that many there were facing new rounds of persecution. In large part a reaction to Jewish progress, the revived animus engaged not merely longstanding religious prejudices but a new pseudo-scientific racial bias. The term "anti-Semitism" was coined around 1880 to describe prejudice against those of Jewish extraction regardless of their religious practice or profession. This new anti-Semitism was manifest most markedly in German racist movements originating in the 1880s and during—and for several years after—the 1894 Dreyfus Affair in France, wherein a French Jewish military officer was falsely accused and convicted of treason.

The Dreyfus case convinced Theodor Herzl (1860–1904), a charismatic Austrian journalist who reported on the case, that anti-Semitism made assimila-tion impossible. In 1895 he began to work to establish a Jewish nation: He organized the movement that came to be known as Zionism, after the hill of Zion in Jerusalem. In 1897 Herzl convened the first World Zionist Congress in Basel, Switzerland, where the movement's purpose was declared: "Zionism seeks to secure for the Jewish people a publicly recognized, legally secured, home in Palestine."

In the meantime, Jewish thinkers in North Africa and the Ottoman Empire saw Jewish political life in relation to the burgeoning independence movements of Serbia and Greece. Their political thought, however, differed radically from European Zionism in that it took into account the local and regional populations and economics. The conditions and circumstances prevailing in most of the Islamic world were quite different due, primarily, to the fact that Islamic law recognized Jews as a legitimate nation, "the people of the Book." Although ostensibly conceived of as a liberation movement for the Jewish people in fact of Europe's oppressive anti-Semitism, European Zionism also developed within the general context of European colonialism with all its attendant attitudes about the "Orient." This has been reflected over the past 100 years on many levels in intra-communal conflicts between European and non-European Jews as well as through Zionist practice and idelogy in relation to the Middle East in general, and Palestinian Arabs in particular.

The growth of Zionism remained intricately connected to the effects of European anti-Semitism on Jewish communities as well as the Western powers' efforts to control the territories of the former Ottoman Empire. Great Britain was persuaded, in 1917, to issue the Balfour Declaration, pledging British help in the creation of a national home for the Jewish people in Palestine. The conflict between native Palestinian Arabs and primarily European Jewish settlers finds its roots in this period, revolving around issues of equitable political representation and economic independence for all the inhabitants of Palestine. As European anti-Semitic ideology and practice reached its conclusion in the ascendancy of the National Socialist (Nazi) party under Adolf Hitler and the systematic slaughter of some six million Jews by the Nazis and their sympathizers during World War II, so did tensions between Arabs and Jews in Palestine increase. Jewish immigation to Palestine rose, and Zionist activity became more violent and urgent, while Arab opposition stiffened. In 1946, the British, unable to resolve these explosive circumstances while battling Zionist paramilitary and terrorist groups, referred the question of Palestine to the United Nations. In November 1947, the United Nations recommended partition.

In response, the Palestinian Arabs, buttressed by reinforcements from neighboring Arab countries, took up arms against the Zionist forces. In Israel's War of Independence, hundreds of Palestinian villages were razed and the largely civilian population found themselves exiled from the new State of Israel, proclaimed on May 14, 1948.

Israel's independence, along with a state of war between its Arab neighbors, put the ancient Jewish communities of the Middle East in a highly precarious position. In most of these countries, Jews had remained a prominent and productive minority since the days of Islamic rule in Spain for the better part of a millennium—with various ups and downs—Jewish civilization flourished in the Middle East, producing an enormous range of literary and other works in Hebrew, Arabic, Judeo-Spanish and other languages.

While Israel has served as a powerful symbol of the hopes and fears of much of world Jewry, its forty-five-year history has been in large part a struggle to justify the nation's existence to the rest of the world. Arab neighbors have considered Israel an illegitimate and unacceptable imperialist presence. Israeli-Arab wars in 1956, 1967, and 1973 exacerbated Arab hostility and frustration—particularly the Six-Day War of 1967, during which Israel annexed and occupied Jordan's West Bank and East Jerusalem, Syria's Golan Heights, and Egypt's Sinai region. (The Sinai was returned to Egypt in the landmark 1979 Egypt-Israel peace treaty known as the Camp David Accords; the other areas are commonly referred to as the Occupied Territories.) In 1975 the United Nations issued a bitterly contested resolution equating Zionism with racism.

Recent years have proven especially turbulent and controversial due to the Palestinian *intifada* ("shaking off"), an uprising in the Occupied Territories that began in December 1987; Israel's severe attempts to suppress the revolt elicited dismay among the nation's critics and some of its supporters, including a number of Israelis. On the other hand, the peace with Egypt, broadening diplomatic relations with such countries as Russia and Japan, and the 1991 repeal of the 1975 U.N. resolution equating Zionism with racism all signify Israel's growing acceptance among the nations of the world. The historic recognition between the State of Israel and the Palestine Liberation Organization in 1993 may begin to unravel some of the highly tangled strands of Jewish/Arab and Israeli/Palestinian relations.

Further Readings

Accad, Evelyne. *Sexuality and War: Literary Marks of the Middle East.* New York: New York University Press, 1990.

Alcalay, Ammiel. *After Jews and Arabs: Remaking Levantine Culture.* Minneapolis: University of Minnesota Press, 1993.

Allen, Roger. *The Arabic Novel: An Historical and Critical Introduction.* Syracuse: Syracuse University Press, 1982.

Carmi, T, ed. *The Penguin Book of Hebrew Verse.* New York: Penguin, 1981.

Levient, Curt, ed. *Masterpieces of Hebrew Literature.* New York: Ktav, 1969.

Malti-Douglas, Fedwa. *Woman's Body, Woman's Word. Gender and Discourse in Arabo-Islamic Writing.* Princeton University Press, 1991.

Pagis, Dan. *Hebrew Poetry of the Middle Ages and the Renaissance.* Berkeley: University of California Press, 1991.

Scheindlin, Raymond. *Wine, Women, and Death: Medieval Hebrew Poems on the Good Life.* Philadelphia: Jewish Publication Society, 1986.

Sharabi, Hisham. *Neopatriarchy: A Theory of Distorted Change in Arab Society.* New York, Oxford University Press, 1988.

Yar Shater, Ehsan, ed. *Persian Literature.* Albany, N.Y.: Bibliotheca Persica, 1988.

SHMUEL YOSEF AGNON (1888–1970)
Galicia/Palestine

Samuel Yosef Agnon was born Samuel Josef Czaczkes in Galicia, a region in today's southeastern Poland and western Ukraine. He received a traditional Jewish education and devoted himself to intensive research of Hasidic stories. In 1907 Agnon emigrated to Palestine. Reintroducing Hebrew styles into a land where writers had been greatly influenced by European trends, Agnon represents, perhaps more than any other author, modern Hebrew fiction in a mixture of realism, romanticism, and irony. *The Bridal Canopy* (1937), *Days of Awe* (1948), *Forever More* (1961), and *Twenty-One Stories* (1970) have all appeared in English. In 1966 Agnon became the first Hebrew writer to be awarded the Nobel Prize for literature.

The Tale of the Scribe

(Dedicated to my wife, Esther)

1

This is the story of Raphael the scribe. Raphael was a righteous and blameless man who copied Torah scrolls, phylacteries, and *mezuzot* in holiness and purity. And any man in the household of Israel who was childless, Mercy deliver us, or whose wife had died, Mercy deliver us, would come to Raphael the scribe and say: "You know, Reb Raphael my brother, what are we and what are our lives? I had indeed hoped that my sons and my sons' sons would come to you to have you write phylacteries for them; but now, alas, I am alone, and my wife, for whom I had thought I would wait long days and years in the upper world, has died and has left me to my sorrows. Perhaps, Reb Raphael my brother, you can undertake to write a Torah scroll under the good guidance of God's hand, and I will compensate you for it. Let us not be lost both in this world and the next, my dear Reb Raphael. Perhaps God will be gracious unto me and the work of your hands will be found acceptable." And Raphael then would sit and write a Torah scroll to give the man and his wife a name and remembrance in the household of Israel.

What may this be likened to? To a man who travels far from his own city, to a place where he is not known, and the watchmen who guard that city find him and ask: "Who are you and where do you live?" If the man is wealthy and a property owner, then as soon as he says I am So-and-so, the son of Thus-and-so, from such-and-such a place, they check the record books and documents, and find out how much he had given to the king's treasury, how much in property taxes he had

Translated by Isaac Franck.

paid, and they welcome him immediately, saying: "Come in, you blessed of God, the entire land is before you, dwell wherever you wish." But if the traveler is an ordinary man, and has neither property nor wealth, then he shows them a document written and signed by officials of his own city, which states that so-and-so is a resident of our city. Then he is permitted to remain and they do not hurry him out.

Likewise, when a man comes to the next world, and the evil angels meet him and ask, "Who are you and where are you from?"; if in his earthly life he had been an upright and blameless man, and left behind him good deeds, or sons busy with Torah and commandments, then these certainly serve as his good advocates. But if he had had none of these then he is lost. However, when Jews come to the synagogue to pray and take a Torah scroll out of the Ark and read from it, if the scroll was written as a memorial for the ascent of this man's soul, then it is immediately known on high that he had been So-and-so, a resident of such-and-such a place, and that is his identification. They then say to him, enter and rest in peace.

Raphael the scribe sat and wrote, and his wife, most blessed among women, the pious Miriam, stayed home and made life pleasant for him in a fine house with fine utensils which she scrubbed and cleaned and purified, so that her husband would do his work in a clean and pure atmosphere. She delighted him with delicate foods and savory beverages, and for Sabbaths and holidays, and sometimes even for the New Moon, she would buy a goose, cook the meat in a pot, or roast it; and Raphael would prepare the quills for writing Torah scrolls, phylacteries, and *mezuzot*. He sat at the Torah and at God's service in holiness and purity, wielding the scribe's pen and fashioning crowns for his Creator.

2

Before we begin telling part of the story itself, let us tell about his way in his holy work. This was his way in holiness:

At midnight he would rise, seat himself on the floor, place ashes on his head, and weep for the destruction of Jerusalem, for the death of the righteous, the burning of the Temple, the length of the exile, the exile of the Divine Presence, the suffering under enslavement, and all sorts of hard and cruel decrees that are inflicted on the people of Israel day in and day out, and for our just Messiah, who is held in iron chains because of the sins of our generation. After that he would study the *Path of Life* and the *Book of Splendor* until the morning light, thus tying together what is proper for the night with what is proper for the day.

In the morning he would go down to the ritual bath and immerse his thin body in the water, then recite the morning prayers, return home and eat a piece of honey cake dipped in brandy, and fortify his weak body with a very light repast. After that he would go back and immerse himself again in the ritual bath, and then turn his heart away from all worldly matters. All day he sat in his house communing with his soul in solitude, completely within the frame of Torah. He did not mingle with other human beings and was thus saved from any of the transgressions between man and man, and remained holy in his speech, thought, and deed, and was spared all temptation and distraction. He sat secluded and isolated and no one was with him except His Name, may He be blessed, and he studied a portion of the Talmud in order to tie together the oral teachings with the written ones, and concentrated on all the sacred meanings hinted at in Scripture. He was careful never to write the Holy Name without first having purified his body. For this reason he often wrote an entire sheet of parchment but left blank the spaces for the Holy Name, and later he wrote the Name in the blank spaces only after having immersed himself again in the purifying ritual bath.

He may thus be likened to a craftsman making a crown for a king: does he not first make the crown and then set into it the diamonds and other precious stones? Thus Raphael sat and wrote, until the beadle came, knocked on the window, and announced that the time had come for the afternoon prayers.

3

How good is a word in its proper time. Having told of his way in his sacred work, let us now note the place of this work.

He lived in a small house close to the big synagogue and to the old House of Study and to other houses of prayer, a few steps from—not to be mentioned in the same breath—the bathhouse which contained the ritual bath. His house was small and low. It had only one room which was divided in the middle by a partition made of boards. On the other side of the partition there was an oven and a range for pots, and between oven and range the pious and modest mistress of his house sat, and she cooked and baked and preserved and wove and knitted and looked to the needs of her home. Children they had none. Because the Holy One, blessed be He, desires the prayers of the righteous, He closed her womb.

When she completes the tasks that a wife is required to perform for her husband, she takes out a used garment and remakes it into clothing for an orphan. She is especially fond of this task because it enables her to sit quietly, to pull thread after thread, and in her thoughts take stock of the world. And in order to avoid doubts, Heaven forfend, about God's ways, and not to complain, Heaven forfend, against Him, she recalls several pious tales of salvation. For example, the story of a childless woman like herself who saved money in a stocking to buy a ruby, which is a proven remedy against childlessness. Then she saw the officials of the Society for Clothing the Naked, and gave them all the money, and in addition sewed clothes for the orphan children. Not many days later her womb was blessed, and out of her came affluent men who served God in comfort.

Or another story about a woman who was making a small prayer shawl for an orphan, and suddenly she felt that the ritual fringes were being pulled and drawn upward, and a fragrance like that of the Garden of Eden was all around her. When she looked up she saw Reb Gadiel, the infant who had been born by virtue of his father's having taught Torah to Jewish children; Reb Gadiel was kissing the ritual fringes she had made, and she heard him say to her: "Know that your deeds are acceptable on high, and that you will yet merit making ritual fringes for your own sons and sons' sons." Not many days later she was rewarded and her womb was blessed, and out of her came righteous, God-fearing good men, taken up with

Torah and God's commandments. And this birth was out of the ordinary, because that woman had been barren by nature.

Thus the pious Miriam sits, drawing thread after thread, and a thread of mercy is drawn and extended on high, and good angels bring up before her various fantasies: for example, that she is preparing a garment for her son who is sitting in his schoolroom and studying Torah.

From time to time she raises her pure eyes toward Raphael, the husband of her youth, who sits on the other side of the partition, near the window, at the clean table covered with a prayer shawl. Also on the other side of the partition there are a wardrobe and a bed. The bed is covered with a colored, clean spread, and the wardrobe contains rolls of parchment and sacred implements. In it her white wedding dress hangs, and in it also earth from the Land of Israel lies hidden away.

Across the top of the room a dark beam stretches from one end of the house to the other. On top of the beam there are a number of sacred books: some new, some old; some thick, some thin; some bound in cured sheepskins and some in a plain binding.

Near the beam, to the right, on the eastern wall, is the embroidered wall-hanging which Miriam had made in her youth at her father's house. It depicts a garden full of fruit trees, with a palace in the garden, and two lions watching over the garden. The lions' faces are turned toward each other, lion facing lion, one tongue reaching out toward the other; and stretching from tongue to tongue there is an inscription in large letters of gold, which says, "The earth is the Lord's and the fullness thereof," as if it were one mighty roar. In each of the four corners of the embroidery there is a square which contains the words: "I have set the Lord always before me."

Facing the east-wall embroidery, on the opposite wall, there is a mirror, and on top of its frame lies a bundle of willow twigs. Every year, on Hoshana Rabbah, Miriam brings home a bundle of the twigs that had been beaten against the prayer lecterns in the synagogue as part of the liturgy. A number of women had already been helped at childbirth by water in which such willow twigs were boiled. Only she herself has never yet made use of that water. The willow twigs continue to wither, and leaf after leaf is shed into the web that the spider has spun over the amulet that is near the bed. Her mother had given her the amulet on her wedding day to help keep away from the house the evil spirits that prevent births.

The amulet is written in the letters of the sacred alphabet but in the tongue of the gentiles, *Yak krova mloda*, etc., meaning, "When the cow is young and healthy why should she not give birth to a calf?" It was written for her mother, peace be upon her, who had been childless for a number of years, by Rabbi Simon of Yaroslav during his stay at the inn operated by her mother. He wrote it at the insistence of several righteous rabbis, while she cooked red borsht and potatoes for them after they had gone without food for three days on their journey to their saintly rabbi, the "seer" of Lublin. And since at that time Rabbi Simon had not yet been ordained, he did not write the amulet in the sacred tongue; but the Hebrew letters in which the amulet was written spelled out the name of the angel in charge of pregnancy, with the Holy Name interwoven among them. Miriam tied the amulet with seven threads from seven veils of seven women from whom had come sons and sons of sons, none of whom had died during the lives of their parents.

From time to time Miriam comes softly to her side of the partition, and stands there letting her pure eyes rest on her husband as he sits at his work in holiness and purity. And if Raphael should interrupt his work and notice her standing there, immediately the pallor leaves her face and a blush takes its place, and she offers him the excuse that she had only come to fetch the Sabbath candlesticks to polish them in honor of the Sabbath. This is the rule of the house. Outside of the house nothing unclean ever appears, because the schoolchildren drive away any dog or pig that may wander into the street. The only animal present is the cat, which was created for the purpose of keeping the house free of mice. Geese and other clean fowl wander around the house. And the birds of heaven, at the time of their migration to the Land of Israel when the Torah portion *ki tavo* is read in the synagogue, and again at the time when they return on Passover to hear the recitation of the Song of Songs in the classroom, sing their own song at his window every morning.

4

Inside the house there is quiet and peace. A feeling like Sabbath rest prevails. And the beauty of the place is reflected in its dwellers. The beloved Miriam's head is always covered by a clean white kerchief knotted below her throat, with its ends resting upon her heart like a dove's wings. Unlike most women she uses no pin in her kerchief so that not even the smallest part of the covered area may become exposed, Heaven forbid. And if her hands were not busy with her work, one might mistakenly think that every day is Sabbath unto the Lord.

At times a poor man comes to the house to ask for alms, or a traveler comes in to have his phylacteries repaired, and they tell Raphael what they had seen and heard in the dispersion of Israel. "What shall we say and what shall we relate, Reb Raphael? If told it would not be believed. In the house of Thus-and-so the scribe, I saw with my own eyes a number of young men sitting day and night writing Torah scrolls, phylacteries, and *mezuzot,* thus making factory work of the sacred Torah. Not only this, but I have heard that another scribe even employs girls to sit and write."

Raphael listens respectfully and replies humbly: "Do not say this, my dear fellow Jew. Why should we slander the people of God? Indeed, we have reason to rejoice that we have reached a time such as this when the Torah is spread so widely that a single scribe for a city is no longer enough."

At times a woman neighbor comes in to consult Miriam on something related to cooking, or to ask when the new month will begin. And if there is a difficult birth in town, someone comes running to her to borrow her willow twigs. The woman says to her: "My dear Miriam, surely you wish to save two human souls, therefore please lend me your willow twigs. Tomorrow, God willing, I shall go from one end of the town to the other end and find other willow twigs to replace these." And Miriam answers with a sigh: "Take the willow twigs, my dear soul, and may they bring good fortune and long life. As for me, I am not worthy of your going to any trouble about me; for myself, what will these willow twigs give or add, even if they were boiled in tears?" And her neighbor replies: "Don't, Miriam, don't, my precious life, let us not give Satan a foothold by complaining. We have a mighty Father in Heaven and His mercies are over all His works. Many barren women have given birth, and children have clung to their breasts. There is a women's prayerbook that has been brought from the Holy Land; nothing I can say matters, but in that book you will discover God's acts and miracles, and in it also you will learn how to entreat God."

When Miriam visits the bathhouse Raphael remains in the House of Study. When she returns home she dresses in fine clothes like a bride on her wedding day, and stands before the mirror. At that moment it seems as if the days of her youth were returning to her. She recalls an inn on a main road, frequented by gentile lords and ladies, and cattle dealers sojourning there, and herself sitting with her father and mother, and with Raphael the husband of her youth. She recalls the crown her mother placed on her head on her wedding day, and at that moment the thought enters her mind to make herself beautiful for her husband. But then she sees reflected in the mirror the east-wall embroidery with its scenes and those two lions with their mouths open; immediately she is startled and shrinks back: "The earth is the Lord's and the fullness thereof."

And when Raphael returns home after the prayers and sees his wife in her true beauty reflected in the mirror, he is immediately attracted to her. He goes toward her to make some pleasing remark. But when he is near her, His Name, may He be blessed, flashes before him out of the mirror. Immediately he stops and recites devoutly and in holiness: "I have set the Lord always before me," and shuts his eyes before the glory and awe of the Name. Both turn away silently. He sits in one corner and studies the *Book of Splendor,* and she sits in another corner reading the women's prayerbook, until sleep invades their eyes. They take the large bucket of water with the large copper fish embossed on its bottom, and wash their hands in preparation for reciting, "Hear, O Israel" before retiring.

5

When hope and patience came to an end and she no longer had the strength to weep and pray for children, she stood before her husband heartbroken and with great humility. Said Raphael to Miriam, "What is your wish, Miriam, and what is your request?" And Miriam replied: "My wish and my request, if I have found favor in my husband's eyes, and if it please my husband to do my wish and fulfill my petition, then let him write a Torah scroll for us also."

At that moment Reb Raphael took Miriam's head and placed it on his knees, then he placed his eyes upon her eyes, his face upon her face, his mouth upon her mouth, and said to her: "Please don't, my daughter, God has not yet withdrawn His mercy from us. We shall surely still behold seed upon the earth." Miriam lowered her eyelids and replied: "May the words of your mouth enter the ears of the Holy One, blessed be He." From then on her hands were busy making a mantle for a Torah scroll, and other sacred implements, as does a woman whose hands are busy making decorative ribbons, sheets, and coverings for the expected newborn baby.

6

"Good fortune is not forever." God chastises those He loves. One Sabbath morning Miriam returned from the synagogue, put down her prayerbook, and, before she was able to remove her outer garment and prepare her heart and soul to greet her husband properly, a sigh escaped from deep within her, she began to feel alternately chilled and hot, her face turned green, her bones began rattling in their joints, and her whole skin sought to escape from her body. She lay down on her bed and remained there and never again rose or left her bed. She had not been inscribed on high for a long life, and was plucked while still in her youth.

Miriam died in the prime of her days and left her husband to his sorrows. She died in the prime of her days and left behind her neither son nor daughter.

7

At the end of the seven days of mourning Raphael the scribe arose, put on his shoes, went to the marketplace, and obtained sheets of parchment, bundles of quills, a string of gallnuts for ink, soft gut-thread for sewing together the sheets of parchment, and set his heart to the writing of a Torah scroll in memory of the soul of his wife whom God had taken away.

What may this be likened to? To a great gardener who raised beautiful plants in his garden, and all the officials who were to see the king would first come to his garden and buy beautiful flowers to take with them. Once the gardener's wife was to see the king, and the gardener said: "All others who visit the king take flowers from my garden. Now that my own wife is to visit the king it is only proper that I go down to my garden and pick flowers for her."

The comparison is clear. Raphael was a great gardener. He planted beautiful Torah scrolls in the world. And whoever was invited to appear before the King—the King over kings of kings, the Holy One, blessed be He—took a Torah scroll with him. And now that Miriam's time had come to appear before the King—the Holy One, blessed be He—Raphael immediately went down to his garden—that is, to his pure and holy table—and picked roses—that is, the letters of the Torah scroll which he wrote—and made a beautiful bouquet—that is, the Torah scroll he had prepared. Thus the work began.

8

Raphael sat and wrote. He wrote his Torah scroll day and night, interrupting the work only for prayers with the congregation and for the recitation of the kaddish.

A prayer shawl was spread over the clean table, its fringes drooping below the table and getting intertwined with the fringes of the little prayer shawl he wore. On the prayer shawl lay a lined sheet of parchment dazzling in its whiteness as the sky itself in its purity.

From morning to evening the quill wrote on the parchment and beautiful black letters glistened and alighted on the parchment as birds upon the snow on the Sabbath when the Song of Moses is read. When he came to the writing of the great and awesome Name he would go down to the ritual bath and immerse himself.

Thus he sat and wrote until he completed the entire Torah scroll.

9

But the doing does not flow as fast as the words. Raphael sat at his toil a long time before he completed the writing of the scroll. His face shrank, his cheeks became hollow, his temples sunken, his eyes larger and larger, as he sat bewildered in the emptiness of his desolate house. Near its hole a mouse plays with a discarded quill, and the cat lies dejectedly on the abandoned oven. A month comes and a month goes, and time sprinkles his earlocks with gray. Raphael prods himself with the sage's saying: "Raphael, Raphael, do not forget death because death will not forget you." Month comes and month goes and there is no action and no work done. The sheet of parchment lies on the table and the quill lies in the sunshine, and the sun's reflection out of the quill shines as the hidden light from among the wings of the celestial creatures. Sunbeams come down to bathe in the scribe's inkwell, and when they depart in order to bid welcome to the shadows of the night, the sheet of parchment lies unchanged.

At times Raphael summoned strength, dipped the pen in ink, and wrote a word, but this did not lead to any more work because his eyes filled with tears. When he sat down to write a single letter in the Torah, immediately his eyes brimmed with tears which rolled down to the parchment.

> In vain do builders build palaces
> If a flooding river sweeps away their foundations;
> In vain do people kindle a memorial candle
> If the orphans extinguish it with their tears.

And when he swallowed his tears and said to himself, Now I will work, now I will write, he would reach such a peak of devout ecstasy that his quill spattered droplets of ink, and he was unable to write even a single letter properly.

It is told of the Rabbi of Zhitomir that he once asked the Rabbi of Berditchev about the biblical verse "And Aaron did so," on which the commentator Rashi, of blessed memory, commented that Aaron did not deviate from God's instructions. This is puzzling; how could it have been otherwise? The Holy One, blessed he He, told Aaron to kindle the lights; would it have been possible for Aaron to deviate? Had God instructed an ordinary man to do this, would that man have deviated? Therefore, what is so praiseworthy about Aaron's not having deviated? However, if the Holy One, blessed be He, had told the Rabbi of Berditchev to kindle the lights, he would surely have felt ecstasy and awe and fervor, and if he tried to kindle them he would spill the oil on the ground, and, because of his awe, would not succeed in kindling them. But Aaron, even though he surely possessed ecstasy and awe and fervor more than any other person, when he came to kindle the lights, he did as God commanded, without any deviation.

That winter it once happened that the bathhouse in Raphael's town was closed down by the authorities because it was near collapse, and when Raphael reached a place in the Torah scroll where the Name had to be written, he could find no bath of purification. He took an ax, went down to the river on the outskirts of the town, broke the ice, immersed himself in the water three times, and returned and wrote the Name with the joy of wondrous fervor. At that moment Raphael attained the merit of discovering the divine secret that before a man is able to rise to the height of joyous fervor he has to be like a man who stands in icy water on a snowy day.

From then on Raphael sat, physically weakened, in the joy of silence, and with emaciated hand he wielded the quill on the parchment until he completed his scroll. The wooden rollers on which the parchment sheets are rolled, and other sacred implements, he made by himself. In this he may be compared to a host who always had guests in his house and had several servants waiting on them. Once he made a feast for the king. Who should properly wait on the king? Surely the host himself.

10

And now let us recall the custom—a custom in Israel is like a law—observed at the completion of the writing of a Torah scroll.

When a scribe is about to complete a scroll, he leaves several verses at the end unfinished, in outlined lettering, in order that any Jew who had not himself had the privilege to fulfill the biblical admonition "And now ye shall write down this song for yourselves" may be afforded the opportunity to come and fill in one of the letters of the Torah. And whoever is so favored takes a pen, dips its tip in ink, and fills in the hollow, outlined letter. Raphael put down his quill, having left several verses in outlined letters, and said to himself: "I shall go and invite a quorum of ten Jews, so that the Torah will not be lonely, and saintly Jews may see and rejoice in the completion of a Torah." He walked over to the mirror to look into it and straighten out his earlocks and his beard in honor of the Torah and in honor of those who would come to rejoice with him.

The mirror was covered with a sheet. From the day of Miriam's death, peace be with her, no one had removed this sign of mourning. Raphael pulled aside the end of the sheet, looked into the mirror, and saw his own face, and the eastwall embroidery across the room, and the scroll he had written, with the hollow, outlined letters at its end. At that moment his soul stirred and he returned to the table, took the quill, and filled in the letters in the scroll he had written in memory of his wife's soul. When he completed the task he rolled up the scroll, raised it high, dancing with great joy, and he leaped and danced and sang in honor of the Torah. Suddenly Raphael stopped, puzzled about the melody he was singing in honor of the completion of the scroll. He felt sure that he had heard this melody before but could not remember where he had heard it. And now, even when he closed his lips the singing of the melody continued by itself. Where had he heard this melody?

11

Having mentioned the melody, I shall not refrain from relating where he had heard it.

It was the evening of the Festival of Rejoicing in the Torah. That evening the rabbi's House of Study was full of bright lights, every light fixture glowing with a radiance from on high. Righteous and saintly Hasidim clothed in white robes of pure silk, with Torah scrolls in their arms, circled the pulpit, dancing with holy fervor, and enjoying the pleasures of the Torah. A number of Hasidim as well as ordinary householders get the privilege of dancing with them, and they cling to the sacred Torah and to those who selflessly obey the Torah, and they forget all anger and all disputes and all kinds of troublesome trivialities. And their young children form an outer circle around them, each child carrying a colored flag, red or green or white or blue, each flag inscribed with letters of gold. On top of each flag is an apple, and on top of each apple a burning candle, and all the candles glow like planets in the mystical "field of sacred apples." And when young boys or girls see their father receive this honor, carrying a Torah scroll in his arms, they immediately jump toward him, grasping the scroll, caressing, embracing, kissing it with their pure lips that have not tasted sin; they clap their hands and sing sweetly, "Happy art thou, O Israel," and their fathers nod their heads toward the children, singing "Ye holy lambs." And the women in the outer lobby feast their eyes on this exalted holiness.

When the seventh round of the procession around the pulpit is reached, the cantor takes a Torah scroll to his bosom and calls out to the youths: "Whoever studies the Torah let him come and take a Torah scroll," and a number of fine youths come and take scrolls in their arms.

Then the cantor calls out again: "The distinguished young man, Raphael, is honored with the honor of the Torah, and with the singing of a beautiful melody."

Raphael came forward, went to the Ark, accepted the scroll from the cantor, and walked at the head of the procession. The elders stood and clapped their hands, adding to the rejoicing. The children stood on the benches chanting aloud "Ye holy lambs" and waving their flags over the heads of the youths. But when Raphael began to sing his melody all hands became still and everyone stood motionless without saying a word. Even the older Hasidim whose saintly way in prayer and in dancing with great fervor is like that of the ancient sage Rabbi Akiba—of whom it is told that when he prayed by himself, his bowing and genuflecting were so fervent that "if when you left him he was in one corner, you found him in another corner at the next moment"—even they restrained themselves with all their might from doing this. They did not lift a hand to clap because of the ecstatic sweetness, even though their hearts were consumed with fire. The women leaned from the windows of the women's gallery, and their heads hung out like a flock of doves lined up on the frieze of a wall.

Raphael held the scroll in his arm, walking in the lead with all the other youths following him in the procession around the pulpit. At that moment a young girl pushed her way through the legs of the dancers, leaped toward Raphael, sank her red lips into the white mantle of the Torah scroll in Raphael's arm, and kept on kissing the scroll and caressing it with her hands. Just then the flag fell out of her hand, and the burning candle dropped on Raphael's clothing.

After the holiday Raphael's father brought an action before the rabbi against the girl's father in the matter of Raphael's robe that had been burned because of the girl. The rabbi, indulging himself in the pleasure of a wise remark, said to the girl's father: "God willing, for their wedding day you will have a new garment made for him." Immediately they brought a decanter of brandy and wrote the betrothal contract. And for Raphael's and Miriam's wedding a new garment was made for him. This is the story of the melody.

And Raphael continues to circle the pulpit, singing sweet melodies. His voice is lovely and sad, numbing the senses but wakening the soul to rise and dance the dance of the Divine Presence. That dance without sound or movement, in which even the earlocks and beard remain motionless, and only the fringes of the prayer shawl drip down to the knees. The house is still, the feet are stilled, and the hands unmoved. The girls come down from the women's gallery to the House of Study to watch the youths dance. The youths continue to circle the pulpit, and the girls reach out with the tips of their fingers toward the Torah scrolls in the hands of the youths.

The sun has set, her last rays shine through the cracks in the shutters, and their light adorns Miriam's white dress. Raphael came toward Miriam and bowed before her with the Torah scroll held in his arm. He could not see her face because she was wrapped in her wedding dress. Silently Raphael stood and wondered where her wedding dress had come from, because he had taken it out of her wardrobe to have a curtain for the Ark made out of it. He walked over to see whether her dress hung there, but when he got there he no longer remembered what he had come for. He stood facing the wardrobe and looked into its black void. Suddenly he noticed the little bag of earth from the Land of Israel. He had placed some of this earth on Miriam's eyes in her grave. Raphael took the little bag of earth in his hand and his heart trembled violently. His hand faltered and the earth spilled to the floor of the house. His heart became agitated as that of a man who stands on sacred soil.

The lamp flickers. Raphael is wrapped in his prayer shawl, a Torah scroll in his arm, and the scroll has a mantle of fine silk on which the name of Miriam the wife of Raphael the scribe is embroidered. The house becomes filled with many Torah scrolls, and many elders dancing. As they dance they neither lift their feet nor bend their knees, but move as if they had no joints. They dance without motion, revolving their bodies, and Miriam stands in the center, her face covered, dancing with her shoulders, her arms raised into the emptiness of the room. She approaches Raphael's scroll. She takes off her veil and covers her face with her hands. Suddenly her hands slide down, her face is uncovered, and her lips cling to the mantle of the Torah scroll in Raphael's arms.

The Holy One, blessed be He, removed His robe of light, and the world stood in silent evening prayer. The lamp flickered and the wick sank into the oil. Suddenly a tongue of flame leaped up and illumined the room. Its light framed the face of Raphael the scribe who sank down with his scroll. His wife's wedding dress was spread out over him and over his scroll.

NAZIM HIKMET [NAZIM HIKMET RON] (1902–1963)
Turkey

Hikmet is without a doubt Turkey's most acclaimed poet, and many of his works have been translated abroad. He introduced free verse, adapted from that of Mayakovski, and also wrote fiction and drama. An exponent of Communist ideology, he died in self-imposed exile in Moscow.

On Victory

Your frightful hands will clutch your wound,
   biting your lips till they bleed
   you shall endure the pain.
Now hope is a shriek
   naked and pitiless   5
And victory
   will be snatched away tooth and nail
    so it will forgive nothing.

The days weigh down,
days bearing tidings of death.   10
The enemy is grim
   cruel
    sly.
Our men are dying in combat
—yet they were so worthy of life—   15
our men are dying

Translated by Talat Sait Halman.

Hamed Nada. Egyptian. *Hassan et Naïma.* Oil on canvas. Musée de l'Institut du Monde Arabe.

—so many of them—
as if they were up in arms
   with songs and banners on a holiday
     so young
       and daring.   20

The days weigh down,
days bearing tidings of death.
With bare hands
   we set the loveliest worlds on fire,
our eyes can no longer weep: 25
we are left a little sad and stiff
   our tears have abandoned us,
that is why
   we no longer know how to forgive.   30

We can only reach our goal
   amid blood-letting
and victory
   will be snatched away tooth and nail
     so it will forgive nothing.   35

My Funeral*

Will my funeral begin down in the courtyard?
How shall you take me there from the third floor?
The elevator will not take a coffin
The stairs are narrow

Perhaps the courtyard will be knee-deep with sunlight and pigeons   5
Perhaps the air will be full of snowflakes and children's cries
Or the asphalt wet with rain
The rubbish bins will be in their usual place

If my face is to be open, as is the local custom
A pigeon may drop something of it, for luck   10
Whether there is a band or no, the children will come
Children love a funeral.

Our kitchen window will stare at me as I go
Our balcony will see me off, waving the laundry
I have been happier than you can think in this courtyard   15
Dear neighbours, I wish you a long and merry life.

NAGUIB MAHFOUZ (b. 1911)
Egypt

As recipient of the 1988 Nobel Prize in literature, Egyptian-born Naguib Mahfouz is the only Arab writer to ever receive the coveted prize. His literary output has been enormous. Mahfouz's fiction has passed through various phases, including the realist and the mystical and, most recently, the metafictional and the postmodern. His novel *Trilogy* won Mahfouz great critical acclaim; some critics even consider it the major contribution that led to his winning the Nobel Prize. "Zaabalawi," a mystical search more than anything else, is considered by many critics and readers to be one of his most finely crafted literary works.

Zaabalawi†

Finally I became convinced that I had to find Sheikh Zaabalawi.
    The first time I had heard of his name had been in a song:

> "What's wrong with the world, O Zaabalawi?
> They've turned it upside down and made it insipid."

*Translated by Nermin Menemencioğlu.
†Translated by Denys Johnson-Davies.

It had been a popular song in my childhood and one day it had occurred to me—in the way children have of asking endless questions—to ask my father about him.

"Who is Zaabalawi, father?"

He had looked at me hesitantly as though doubting my ability to understand the answer. However, he had replied:

"May his blessing descend upon you, he's a true saint of God, a remover of worries and troubles. Were it not for him I would have died miserably—"

In the years that followed I heard him many a time sing the praises of this good saint and speak of the miracles he performed. The days passed and brought with them many illnesses from each one of which I was able, without too much trouble and at a cost I could afford, to find a cure, until I became afflicted with that illness for which no one possesses a remedy. When I had tried everything in vain and was overcome by despair, I remembered by chance what I had heard in my childhood: Why, I asked myself, should I not seek out Sheikh Zaabalawi? I recollected that my father had said that he had made his acquaintance in Khan Gaafar at the house of Sheikh Kamar, one of those sheikhs who practised law in the religious courts, and I therefore took myself off to his house. Wishing to make sure that he was still living there, I made enquiries of a vendor of beans whom I found in the lower part of the house.

"Sheikh Kamar!" he said, looking at me in amazement. "He left the quarter ages ago. They say he's now living in Garden City and has his office in Al-Azhaar Square."

I looked up the office address in the telephone book and immediately set off to the Chamber of Commerce Building, where it was located. On asking to see him I was ushered into a room just as a beautiful woman with a most intoxicating perfume was leaving it. The man received me with a smile and motioned me towards a fine leather-upholstered chair. My feet were conscious of the costly lushness of the carpet despite the thick soles of my shoes. The man wore a lounge suit and was smoking a cigar; his manner of sitting was that of someone well satisfied both with himself and his worldly possessions. The look of warm welcome he gave me left no doubt in my mind that he thought me a prospective client, and I felt acutely embarrassed at encroaching upon his valuable time.

"Welcome!" he said, prompting me to speak.

"I am the son of your old friend Sheikh Ali al-Tatawi," I answered so as to put an end to my equivocal position.

A certain languor was apparent in the glance he cast at me; the languor was not total in that he had not as yet lost all hope in me.

"God rest his soul," he said. "He was a fine man."

The very pain that had driven me to go there now prevailed upon me to stay.

"He told me," I continued, "of a devout saint named Zaabalawi whom he met at Your Honour's. I am in need of him, sir, if he be still in the land of the living."

The languor became firmly entrenched in his eyes and it would have come as no surprise to me if he had shown the door to both me and my father's memory.

"That," he said in the tone of one who has made up his mind to terminate the conversation, "was a very long time ago and I scarcely recall him now."

Rising to my feet so as to put his mind at rest regarding my intention of going, I asked:

"Was he really a saint?"

"We used to regard him as a man of miracles."

"And where could I find him today?" I asked, making another move towards the door.

"To the best of my knowledge he was living in the Birgawi Residence in al-Azhar," and he applied himself to some papers on his desk with a resolute movement that indicated he wouldn't open his mouth again. I bowed my head in thanks, apologized several times for disturbing him and left the office, my head so buzzing with embarrassment that I was oblivious to all sounds around me.

I went to the Birgawi Residence which was situated in a thickly populated quarter. I found that time had so eaten into the building that nothing was left of it save an antiquated façade and a courtyard which, despite it being supposedly in the charge of a caretaker, was being used as a rubbish dump. A small insignificant fellow, a mere prologue to a man, was using the covered entrance as a place for the sale of old books on theology and mysticism.

On my asking him about Zaabalawi, he peered at me through narrow, inflamed eyes and said in amazement:

"Zaabalawi! Good heavens, what a time ago that was! Certainly he used to live in this house when it was livable in, and many was the time he would sit with me talking of bygone days and I would be blessed by his holy presence. Where, though, is Zaabalawi today?"

He shrugged his shoulders sorrowfully and soon left me to attend to an approaching customer. I proceeded to make enquiries of many shopkeepers in the district. While I found that a large number of them had never even heard of him, some, though recalling nostalgically the pleasant times they had spent with him, were ignorant of his present whereabouts, while others openly made fun of him, labelled him a charlatan, and advised me to put myself in the hands of a doctor—as though I had not already done so. I therefore had no alternative but to return disconsolately home.

With the passing of the days like motes in the air my pains grew so severe that I was sure I would not be able to hold out much longer. Once again I fell to wondering about Zaabalawi and clutching at the hopes his venerable name stirred within me. Then it occurred to me to seek the help of the local Sheikh of the district; in fact, I was surprised I hadn't thought of this to begin with. His office was in the nature of a small shop except that it contained a desk and a telephone, and I found him sitting at his desk wearing a jacket over his striped *galabia*.[1] As he did not interrupt his conversation with a man sitting beside him, I stood waiting till the man had gone. He then looked up at me coldly. I told myself that I should win him over by the usual methods, and it wasn't long before I had him cheerfully inviting me to sit down.

---

1. A type of outer robe worn by both men and
   women.

"I'm in need of Sheikh Zaabalawi," I answered his enquiry as to the purpose of my visit.

He gazed at me with the same astonishment as that shown by those I had previously encountered.

"At least," he said, giving me a smile that revealed his gold teeth, "he is still alive. The devil of it is, though, he has no fixed abode. You might well bump into him as you go out of here, on the other hand you might spend days and months in fruitless search of him."

"Even you can't find him!"

"Even I! He's a baffling man, but I thank the Lord that he's still alive!"

He gazed at me intently, and murmured:

"It seems your condition is serious."

"Very!"

"May God come to your aid! But why don't you go about it rationally?"

He spread out a sheet of paper on the desk and drew on it with unexpected speed and skill until he had made a full plan of the district showing all the various quarters, lanes, alleyways, and squares. He looked at it admiringly and said, "These are dwelling-houses, here is the Quarter of the Perfumers, here the Quarter of the Coppersmiths, the Mouski, the Police and Fire Stations. The drawing is your best guide. Look carefully in the cafés, the places where the dervishes perform their rites, the mosques and prayer-rooms, and the Green Gate, for he may well be concealed among the beggars and be indistinguishable from them. Actually, I myself haven't seen him for years, having been somewhat preoccupied with the cares of the world and was only brought back to those most exquisite times of my youth by your enquiry."

I gazed at the map in bewilderment. The telephone rang and he took up the receiver.

"Take it," he told me, generously. "We're at your service."

Folding up the map, I left and wandered off through the quarter, from square to street to alleyway, making enquiries of everyone I felt was familiar with the place. At last the owner of a small establishment for ironing clothes told me:

"Go to the calligrapher Hassanein in Umm al-Ghulam—they were friends."

I went to Umm al-Ghulam where I found old Hassanein working in a deep, narrow shop full of signboards and jars of colour. A strange smell, a mixture of glue and perfume, permeated its every corner. Old Hassanein was squatting on a sheepskin rug in front of a board propped against the wall; in the middle of it he had inscribed the word "Allah" in silver lettering. He was engrossed in embellishing the letters with prodigious care. I stood behind him, fearful to disturb him or break the inspiration that flowed to his masterly hand. When my concern at not interrupting him had lasted some time, he suddenly enquired with unaffected gentleness:

"Yes?"

Realizing that he was aware of my presence, I introduced myself.

"I've been told that Sheikh Zaabalawi is your friend and I'm looking for him," I said.

His hand came to a stop. He scrutinized me in astonishment.

"Zaabalawi! God be praised!" he said with a sigh.

"He is a friend of yours, isn't he?" I asked eagerly.

"He was, once upon a time. A real man of mystery: he'd visit you so often that people would imagine he was your nearest and dearest, then would disappear as though he'd never existed. Yet saints are not to be blamed."

The spark of hope went out with the suddenness of a lamp by a power-cut.

"He was so constantly with me," said the man, "that I felt him to be a part of everything I drew. But where is he today?"

"Perhaps he is still alive?"

"He's alive, without a doubt. He had impeccable taste and it was due to him that I made my most beautiful drawings."

"God knows," I said, in a voice almost stifled by the dead ashes of hope, "that I am in the direst need of him and no one knows better than you of the ailments in respect of which he is sought."

"Yes—yes. May God restore you to health. He is, in truth, as is said of him, a man, and more—"

Smiling broadly, he added: "And his face is possessed of an unforgettable beauty. But where is he?"

Reluctantly I rose to my feet, shook hands and left. I continued on my way eastwards and westwards through the quarter, enquiring about him from everyone who, by reason of age or experience, I felt was likely to help me. Eventually I was informed by a vendor of lupine that he had met him a short while ago at the house of Sheikh Gad, the well-known composer. I went to the musician's house in Tabakshiyya where I found him in a room tastefully furnished in the old style, its walls redolent with history. He was seated on a divan, his famous lute lying beside him, concealing within itself the most beautiful melodies of our age, while from within the house came the sound of pestle and mortar and the clamour of children. I immediately greeted him and introduced myself, and was put at my ease by the unaffected way in which he received me. He did not ask, either in words or gesture, what had brought me, and I did not feel that he even harboured any such curiosity. Amazed at his understanding and kindness, which boded well, I said:

"O Sheikh Gad, I am an admirer of yours and have long been enchanted by the renderings of your songs."

"Thank you," he said with a smile.

"Please excuse my disturbing you," I continued timidly, "but I was told that Zaabalawi was your friend and I am in urgent need of him."

"Zaabalawi!" he said, frowning in concentration. "You need him? God be with you, for who knows, O Zaabalawi, where you are?"

"Doesn't he visit you?" I asked eagerly.

"He visited me some time ago. He might well come now; on the other hand I mightn't see him till death!"

I gave an audible sigh and asked:

"What made him like that?"

He took up his lute. "Such are saints or they would not be saints," he said laughing.

"Do those who need him suffer as I do?"

"Such suffering is part of the cure!"

He took up the plectrum and began plucking soft strains from the strings. Lost in thought, I followed his movements. Then, as though addressing myself, I said:

"So my visit has been in vain!"

He smiled, laying his cheek against the side of the lute.

"God forgive you," he said, "for saying such a thing of a visit that has caused me to know you and you me!"

I was much embarrassed and said apologetically:

"Please forgive me; my feelings of defeat made me forget my manners!"

"Do not give in to defeat. This extraordinary man brings fatigue to all who seek him. It was easy enough with him in the old days when his place of abode was known. Today, though, the world has changed and after having enjoyed a position attained only by potentates, he is now pursued by the police on a charge of false pretences. It is therefore no longer an easy matter to reach him, but have patience and be sure that you will do so."

He raised his head from the lute and skillfully led into the opening bars of a melody. Then he sang:

"I make lavish mention, even though I blame myself,
of those I have loved,
For the words of lovers are my wine."

With a heart that was weary and listless I followed the beauty of the melody and the singing.

"I composed the music to this poem in a single night," he told me when he had finished. "I remember that it was the night of the Lesser Bairam. He was my guest for the whole of that night and the poem was of his choosing. He would sit for a while just where you are, then would get up and play with my children as though he were one of them. Whenever I was overcome by weariness or my inspiration failed me he would punch me playfully in the chest and joke with me, and I would bubble over with melodies and thus I continued working till I finished the most beautiful piece I have ever composed."

"Does he know anything about music?"

"He was the epitome of things musical. He had an extremely beautiful speaking voice and you had only to hear him to want to burst into song. His loftiness of spirit stirred within you—"

"How was it that he cured those diseases before which men are powerless?"

"That is his secret. Maybe you will learn it when you meet him."

But when would that meeting occur? We relapsed into silence and the hubbub of children once more filled the room.

Again, the Sheikh began to sing. He went on repeating the words "and I have a memory of her" in different and beautiful variations until the very walls danced in ecstasy. I expressed my wholehearted admiration and he gave me a smile of thanks. I then got up and asked permission to leave and he accompanied me to the outer door. As I shook him by the hand he said, "I hear that nowadays he frequents the house of Haag Wanas al-Damanhouri. Do you know him?"

I shook my head, a modicum of renewed hope creeping into my heart.

"He is a man of private means," he told me, "who from time to time visits Cairo, putting up at some hotel or other. Every evening, though, he spends at the Negma Bar in Alfi Street."

I waited for nightfall and went to the Negma Bar. I asked a waiter about Hagg Wanas and he pointed to a corner which was semi-secluded because of its position behind a large pillar with mirrors on its four sides. There I saw a man seated alone at a table with a bottle three-quarters empty and another empty one in front of him; there were no snacks or food to be seen and I was sure that I was in the presence of a hardened drinker. He was wearing a loosely flowing silk *galabia* and a carefully wound turban; his legs were stretched out towards the base of the pillar, and as he gazed into the mirror in rapt contentment the sides of his face, rounded and handsome despite the fact that he was approaching old age, were flushed with wine. I approached quietly till I stood but a few feet away from him. He did not turn towards me or give any indication that he was aware of my presence.

"Good evening, Mr. Wanas," I said with amiable friendliness.

He turned towards me abruptly as though my voice had roused him from slumber and glared at me in disapproval. I was about to explain what had brought me to him when he interrupted me in an almost imperative tone of voice which was none the less not devoid of an extraordinary gentleness:

"First, please sit down, and, second, please get drunk!"

I opened my mouth to make my excuses but, stopping up his ears with his fingers, he said:

"Not a word till you do what I say."

I realized that I was in the presence of a capricious drunkard and told myself that I should go along with him at least halfway.

"Would you permit me to ask one question?" I said with a smile, sitting down.

Without removing his hands from his ears he indicated the bottle.

"When engaged in a drinking bout like this I do not allow any conversation between myself and another unless, like me, he is drunk, otherwise the session loses all propriety and mutual comprehension is rendered impossible."

I made a sign indicating that I didn't drink.

"That's your look-out," he said offhandedly. "And that's my condition!"

He filled me a glass which I meekly took and drank. No sooner had it settled in my stomach than it seemed to ignite. I waited patiently till I had grown used to its ferocity, and said:

"It's very strong, and I think the time has come for me to ask you about—"

Once again, however, he put his fingers in his ears.

"I shan't listen to you until you're drunk!"

He filled up my glass for the second time. I glanced at it in trepidation; then, overcoming my innate objection, I drank it down at a gulp. No sooner had it come to rest inside me than I lost all will-power. With the third glass I lost my memory and with the fourth the future vanished. The world turned round about me and I forgot why I had gone there. The man leaned towards me attentively but I saw him—saw everything—as a mere meaningless series of coloured planes. I don't know how long it was before my head sank down on to the arm of the chair and I plunged into deep sleep. During it I had a beautiful dream the like of which I had never experienced. I dreamed that I was in an immense garden surrounded on all sides by luxuriant trees and the sky was nothing but stars seen between the entwined branches, all enfolded in an atmosphere like that of sunset or a sky overcast with cloud. I was lying on a small hummock of jasmine petals which fell upon me like rain, while the lucent spray of a fountain unceasingly sprinkled my head and temples. I was in a state of deep contentedness, of ecstatic serenity. An orchestra of warbling and cooing played in my ear. There was an extraordinary sense of harmony between me and my inner self, and between the two of us and the world, everything being in its rightful place without discord or distortion. In the whole world there was no single reason for speech or movement, for the universe moved in a rapture of ecstasy. This lasted but a short while. When I opened my eyes consciousness struck at me like a policeman's fist and I saw Wanas al-Damanhouri regarding me with concern. In the bar only a few drowsy people were left.

"You have slept deeply," said my companion; "you were obviously hungry for sleep."

I rested my heavy head in the palms of my hands. When I took them away in astonishment and looked down at them I found that they glistened with drops of water.

"My head's wet," I protested.

"Yes, my friend tried to rouse you," he answered quietly.

"Somebody saw me in this state?"

"Don't worry, he is a good man. Have you not heard of Sheikh Zaabalawi?"

"Zaabalawi!" I exclaimed, jumping to my feet.

"Yes," he answered in surprise. "What's wrong?"

"Where is he?"

"I don't know where he is now. He was here and then he left."

I was about to run off in pursuit but found I was more exhausted than I had imagined. Collapsed over the table, I cried out in despair:

"My sole reason for coming to you was to meet him. Help me to catch up with him or send someone after him."

The man called a vendor of prawns and asked him to seek out the Sheikh and bring him back. Then he turned to me.

"I didn't realize you were afflicted. I'm very sorry—"

"You wouldn't let me speak," I said irritably.

"What a pity! He was sitting on this chair beside you the whole time. He was playing with a string of jasmine petals he had round his neck, a gift from one of his admirers, then, taking pity on you, he began to sprinkle some water on your head to bring you round."

"Does he meet you here every night?" I asked, my eyes not leaving the doorway through which the vendor of prawns had left.

"He was with me tonight, last night and the night before that, but before that I hadn't seen him for a month."

"Perhaps he will come tomorrow," I answered with a sigh.

"Perhaps."

"I am willing to give him any money he wants."

Wanas answered sympathetically:

"The strange thing is that he is not open to such temptations, yet he will cure you if you meet him."

"Without charge?"

"Merely on sensing that you love him."

The vendor of prawns returned, having failed in his mission.

I recovered some of my energy and left the bar, albeit unsteadily. At every street corner I called out, "Zaabalawi!" in the vague hope that I would be rewarded with an answering shout. The street boys turned contemptuous eyes on me till I sought refuge in the first available taxi.

The following evening I stayed up with Wanas al-Damanhouri till dawn, but the Sheikh did not put in an appearance. Wanas informed me that he would be going away to the country and wouldn't be returning to Cairo until he'd sold the cotton crop.

I must wait, I told myself; I must train myself to be patient. Let me content myself with having made certain of the existence of Zaabalawi, and even of his affection for me, which encourages me to think that he will be prepared to cure me if a meeting between us takes place.

Sometimes, however, the long delay wearied me. I would become beset by despair and would try to persuade myself to dismiss him from my mind completely. How many weary people in this life know him not or regard him as a mere myth! Why, then, should I torture myself about him in this way?

No sooner, however, did my pains force themselves upon me than I would again begin to think about him, asking myself as to when I would be fortunate enough to meet him. The fact that I ceased to have any news of Wanas and was told he had gone to live abroad did not deflect me from my purpose; the truth of the matter was that I had become fully convinced that I had to find Zaabalawi.

Yes, I have to find Zaabalawi.

AZIZ NESIN (b. 1915)

Turkey

Aziz Nesin is considered to be modern Turkey's leading satirist. His autobiography, *Istanbul Boy* (1977), is a literary masterpiece that chronicles the major social and political changes in Turkey in this century from the alphabet reforms to the introduction of Western dress codes.

from *Istanbul Boy*

The Fire Prayer

One day, before noon, first a little smoke started coming from the third house to the right of ours, then flames spurted forth. The house was on fire. All the neighborhood was alarmed. The houses were of wood and built one next to the other. Our neighbors were carrying their belongings from their homes and piling them on a nearby slope. But we couldn't take our belongings out of our house, because my father prevented it. Though in control of his bad temper, still he was sternly yelling: "Stop! Leave it alone! Don't touch it! Nothing will happen! The fire won't harm us!"

He knelt down on the sheepskin. And, telling his beads, prayed. He was reciting the fire prayer. Fire and flame wouldn't touch the house of he who recited this prayer. Even if every house burned, not one spark could fly onto our old, rotten, wooden house with its dry, warped siding. When my sister couldn't stand it and wanted to smuggle out one or two belongings, my father saw her and yelled. Everyone else was outside, but Father wouldn't leave the house. Hafez rushed in and said, "Come on, Sheyh Efendi; outside!"

Waterman Ahmet Aga came and urged, "Come on, Sheyh Efendi!"

Father, with the belittling smile of one who knows many things, said, "Our house is insured, it won't burn!"

There was no telephone. It was difficult to inform them, so the fire department was late in coming. It was hard, too, for the fire-cart to climb the steep hill. But most difficult was finding water on the Island to put out the fire.

The great, long foundation bolts of the house which was burning grew white-hot, whined through the air like shells, and flew far. It was feared that these fiery bolts would ignite the other houses or the pine trees.

The firemen pumped water on the houses most likely to catch fire. When the burning house collapsed and fell in the flames burned even stronger, and the fire roared louder. But the wind suddenly started to blow in the opposite direction and fanned the flames away from us. Our house had been saved from the fire. Near evening, the fire was completely extinguished. However, the next day until evening, smoke and hot steam rose from the burned pile of rubble.

At the time of the fire, word spread of my father's not leaving the house. The rumor that our house didn't burn because of the prayer he recited, was on everyone's lips. Thus, my father's influence increased.

I would tell Father, "The wind shifted, and that's why our house didn't burn . . ."

And he would say, "True, but who shifted the wind, my son, and why did He shift it?"

Translated by Joseph S. Jacobson.

An Epileptic Woman

Above the road that goes to Ayazma, behind the Navy High School, were two rows of look-alike wooden houses, called the *Beylik Evler* [G.I. quarters]. The Navy High School and Naval Academy teachers—those on duty there—and naval officers used to live in Beylik Evler.

On the first floor of one of these two-story houses lived one of my father's acquaintances, Hasan Usta [Hasan the Master Craftsman]. Hasan Usta was a master boilermaker at the Navy High School. Invariably, he wore dark-blue clothes, a white shirt, black tie and well-shined shoes, the same as worn by the administrators of the Navy High School. He came from Sivas. Short but broad-shouldered, he was a stoutly built man with a large head. Perhaps he appeared short due to the stoutness of his body. Hasan Usta's body was so husky that only if he were two meters tall would his height correspond. He had a son three or four years my senior. He'd given his son, who was uninterested in education and who, at that age, had only been able to finish elementary school with difficulty, to a Greek grocer as an apprentice. The son, like the father, was stout, husky and strong.

Upon the death of the boy's mother, Hasan Usta had married a second time. His second wife was young and beautiful. But the poor woman had epilepsy. At unexpected times, the woman would suffer epileptic seizures. Furthermore, these attacks would last a long time, sometimes even two or three hours. When having these fits, the woman would fall and suffer cuts and bruises. Every day, Hasan Usta went to his job, his son went to the grocery store where he was an apprentice, and no one stayed at home except the woman. Sometimes, upon Hasan Usta's return from work, he'd find his wife there, injured. He'd requested that Father let me stay at their house and visit with his wife during vacation, when I had free time. For this reason, I stayed days, and sometimes nights, at Hasan Usta's house.

My father used to recite prayers for this epileptic woman and try to make her well. Every two or three days, he came to pray over her. He'd also written an amulet for her. It must have been the power of suggestion, but Father's prayers had a positive effect. As the epileptic seizures occurred less frequently, Hasan Usta became filled with hope that his wife would recover. He felt that if my father would pray right at the time the fit came, the woman would be completely cured.

One day, the two of us—Hasan's wife and I—were at the house. I think she was nineteen or twenty years old. I'd never seen her when she had a seizure. That day, while I was talking with her, the woman suddenly threw herself to the floor. Her jaws were locked. Foamy saliva kept drooling from between her teeth. She clenched her fists. All her muscles were taut and she'd become stiff as a board. she lay on the floor in a completely rigid seizure.

I couldn't do a thing. There was no one to call. I couldn't leave the woman in this condition to go tell some one, anyway.

There was an add-on room at the entry of the house, and the woman had fallen down there. I was taking care to see that she didn't roll down the stairs. How long this went on, I don't remember, but it seemed like an awfully long time to me. Soon, the woman began to perspire. Sweat beaded on her forehead. Her hair became soaked in perspiration. Gradually, more foam spilled from her mouth. First she muttered, then began to make unintelligible noises and murmurings. For a time, she convulsed. She tore her smock and ripped her underthings, so that I was ashamed to look at the half-naked woman. I couldn't decide whether I should stay there or leave the house. While I was hesitating, she wet herself. Later, she commenced to weep. She sobbed and sobbed. I thought her weeping was because she had come to and was ashamed at my being with her when she fell into that state. Later on, her husband told my father that every time she came out of her epileptic seizure, she wet and cried.

Then the woman, who'd stopped weeping, got to her feet, and though her gaze was directed at the walls and ceiling, she actually was looking at some indistinguishable point in the distance. She started to talk to people who weren't there and, from time to time, to laugh or yell at them. So, the talk of her speaking with genies and fairies had grown from this. It was also rumored that the woman had married a male genie, or that one was in love with her. Therefore, when she married Hasan Usta, the jealous male genie had made the poor woman this way.

She spoke sweetly with some people who appeared to her and fought with others. I even got scared when she looked right through me and talked with those imaginary people . . . But much later on, I came to the conclusion that the woman only pretended to talk with so-called genies.

The woman spoke for a long time, then sat down, fatigued. To come to her senses took a considerable length of time. She pulled herself together and changed her clothes. She said very little to me and spoke as if in her sleep. Then in the evening, when Hasan Usta came, I left.

My father tried hard to get the woman to tell about those hallucinations, the people she saw and talked to when she had a seizure. It was Father's belief that if she could tell, when she was lucid, what had happened during the seizure, the woman would be saved, but she couldn't remember what she saw or said during the epileptic fit. Some time later, saying that she'd slowly recalled, the woman related a few things. She even spoke of the young man and such.

I listened to the woman a few times when she talked about these things. It seemed to me that there was nothing she remembered from her epileptic state, but due to my father's influence she'd made up a few things to tell. While on the way home with Father, I told him I didn't believe her, that she'd invented something because he insisted. He told me that whether or not she remembered what she said or saw in the seizure was not important, and that even if she did make it up, what she told us was very important.

Another day, while my father was at Hasan Usta's home, the woman had another seizure. He prayed over her while she was in that state, but still she didn't get well.

From the top floor of boilermaker Hasan Usta's house, either the noise of stamping and fighting was heard or (when those noises ceased) the sound of violin playing. The history teacher for the Navy High School and Academy lived on the top floor. This teacher was blind in both eyes. Guided by the arm of a seaman, he went back and forth between home and school. He was a famous historian who'd written history books, especially naval warfare histories. This distinguished historian had three sons. Due to a well-known dread affliction, the three sons, like their father, were going blind. The hereditary disease had been transmitted through the father to the sons. The children weren't blind at birth, but later on, slowly began going blind. Usually, by the twelfth to fifteenth year, blindness was complete. The oldest son had been blind for a long time; the second had become so just recently. The small brother was half-blind. In a few years, he too would be blind like his big brothers. I had never seen them. They didn't go out. All of them knew how to play the violin. In their home on the top floor, they either played the violin or made a rumpus. Probably they roughhoused and wrestled to pass the time. There was no woman in their house.

Hasan Usta's son had an amazing talent. One night, when I stayed at their house, I became acquainted with his "gift." That night, Hasan Usta and his wife had gone visiting. His son was at home, along with a number of his friends. Because I was three or four years younger than they (at that age, three years seems a great difference), they considered me small and unimportant. Hasan Usta's son was slapping his fat stomach with his hand, just like playing a drum, and making music by passing wind. His marching in time with the drum, as if he were in a parade, lasted several minutes. What's further, he could perform this ugly drum solo any time he wanted. His friends laughed themselves silly at his exhibition.

Sex Education

Like all of my generation, I was brought up without any sex education. We received no sex education either indirectly, through movies and books, or directly. My father was a dignified man who didn't make jokes on the subject of sex, even among his friends. I've never, even once, heard him tell a dirty story, nor has he let anyone tell one to him. As a matter of fact, other people told all kinds of those vulgar stories. And although I've heard and learned many anecdotes of this type, I just don't like to tell them myself. (However, among these obscene stories, there are some which are so effective as the shortest means of interpreting political events, that when told with that aim, they are no longer obscene . . .)

My father, who never spoke about the subject of sex, said a few words to me in this regard one day. This was the first and last bit of sex education I had in my childhood:

A retired naval-officer friend of my father's lived in one of the Beylik Evler houses. We were passing by his house on our return from some place, and were going to visit him because he'd suffered a stroke. At his age, a man should never have had a stroke! He was still young. But he hadn't known how to take care of himself. Intelligent people take care of their health. After lamenting his friend, Father mentioned that some men suffered paralytic strokes because they slept too frequently with women. A man should refrain from having excessive sexual relations.

While on the way, Father had explained these things to me, choosing his word and speaking easily, as if the conversation were natural and of no importance. As a matter of fact, in those times, a father's telling his son these things wouldn't be considered natural at all. I really enjoyed my father's indirect counseling. It meant that I'd reached the age where I would now be able to speak about such subjects. I was twelve years old, so my father would consider me a young man from now on, and bring up this subject. Yet I still couldn't talk with Father on this theme, I just listened to him, walking silently beside him . . .

EMILE HABIBY (b. 1921)
Israel

Emile Habiby is an Israeli Palestinian who remained in the state of Israel in 1948. A long-time member of the Israeli Knesset, Habiby was also the head of Israel's Communist Party. Habiby has distinguished himself in his fiction by the fact that each of his literary works brilliantly exploits different literary and narrative techniques. *The Secret Life of Saeed, the Ill-Fated Pessoptimist* (1985), his first novel, put Habiby on the literary map. The work is a tour de force in Arab fiction, displaying a mastery both of the Arabic language and of storytelling. Like much of Habiby's fiction, it describes the plight of the Palestinians in Israel.

from *The Secret Life of Saeed, the Ill-Fated Pessoptimist*

Saeed Claims to Have Met Creatures From Outer Space

In his letter to me, Saeed, the ill-fated Pessoptimist, pleaded. "Please tell my story. It is surely as weird as the story of Moses's staff, the resurrection of Jesus, and the election of the husband of a lady bird to the presidency of the United States.

The fact is I've disappeared. But I'm not dead. I wasn't killed at the border, as some of you imagined. Nor did I join the guerrilla movement, as those who knew my virtue feared. Nor am I rotting long-forgotten in some jail, as your friends may suppose.

Now, now! Patience, please! And don't ask, "Who is this 'Saeed' fellow?" Or, "Since he drew no attention throughout his life, why should we give him any now?"

All right. I know my place. I'm not one of your so-called leaders, someone thought worthy of notice by an elite. What I am, my dear sir, is—the office boy!

Didn't you just break up at that Israeli joke about the lion that sneaked inside the offices of the executive committee of the *Histadrut*, the Labor Union Confederation? First day it ate the director of union organization, but not one of

Translated by Salma Khadra Jayyusi and Trevor Le Gassick.

Parvaneh Etemadi. *Memory (II)*. 1988. Colored pencil on paper.

his colleagues noticed. Next day it devoured the director of Arab affairs, but the rest didn't miss him. So the lion went on roving happily about, munching contentedly. Finally it ate the office boy, and then they caught it right away.

Yep, I'm that office boy, honored friend. So why didn't you notice I'd gone?

No problem. What matters is that my disappearance, for all its weirdness, was something I'd been expecting all my life. Anyway, the miracle did occur, fine sir, and I did indeed meet with creatures from outer space. I'm in their company right now. As I write to you of my fantastic mystery, I'm soaring with them high above you.

Now don't be a skeptic. Don't say the Age of Miracles is past. What makes you always get things upside down?

By those heavenly hosts with whom I abide, I swear this age has got to be the strangest since the destruction of those errant ancestors of ours, the peoples of Aad and Thamood. But we're used to the wonders of today. Why, if our forebears were to arise and hear the radio, see television, and witness a jumbo jet landing at an airport, spitting and roaring in the pitch-black night, they would think us polytheists for sure.

But we're used to these wonders. We don't raise an eyebrow if kings are deposed or if they stay. Brutus is no big deal now, no subject worth writing about. "Et tu Brute," indeed! The Arabs certainly don't say, "Et tu Baybars"; Qutuz, the sultan this hero Baybars murdered, could only, after all, mutter a grunt in Turkish. *And now our great hero Abu Zaid El-Hilaly* bends to kiss royal hands. But the sultans have no cause for concern. "I'm no Qutuz," say the kings. And their slaves repeat, "This is no age for Baybars!"

The moon is closer to us now than are the fig trees of our departed village. You accept all these wonders—why not mine too?

Easy there, easy! Don't press me for more details yet. Everything in its own time. Please don't pester me with questions about my companions, how they look, dress, organize, and think. Oh, it all makes me feel so superior! I now know what you don't. Why shouldn't I put on airs?

As for why they chose me alone of all God's creatures—well, I'm not sure I am the only one ever to meet with them. When I asked them what they would think of my informing you of what has happened to me so that the world might know, they just smiled and said: "We have no objection. But the world won't find out. Your friend won't believe you. You see, all that descends from the sky is not necessarily divinely inspired. This itself is one of your 'miracles.'"

So, although I might not be the only one, I most certainly have been chosen by them. And you too, my fine friend, are chosen as well. I have selected you to relate my weirdest wonder of all. You may well puff with pride.

Why did they choose me? Because I chose them. I spent my whole life searching for them, waiting for them, relying on their protection, until meeting them became inevitable.

You find this peculiar? Never mind. In the so-called Age of Ignorance, before Islam, our ancestors used to form their gods from dates and eat them when in need. Who is more ignorant then, dear sir, I or those who ate their gods?

You might say: "It's better for people to eat their gods than for the gods to eat them."

But I'd respond, "Yes, but their gods were made of dates."

Saeed Reports How His Life in Israel Was All Due to the Munificence of an Ass

Let's start at the beginning. My whole life has been strange, and a strange life can only end strangely. When I asked my extraterrestrial friend why he took me in, he merely replied, "What alternative did you have?"

So when did it all begin?

When I was born again, thanks to an ass.

During the fighting in 1948 they waylaid us and opened fire, shooting my father, may he rest in peace. I escaped because a stray donkey came into the line of fire and they shot it, so it died in place of me. My subsequent life in Israel, then, was really a gift from that unfortunate beast. What value then, honored sir, should we assign to this life of mine?

I consider myself quite remarkable. You've no doubt read of dogs lapping up poisoned water and dying to warn their masters and save their lives. And of horses, too, racing the wind bearing their wounded riders to safety, only to die of exhaustion themselves. But I'm the first man, to my knowledge, to be saved by a mulish donkey, an animal unable either to race the wind or to bark. I truly am remarkable. That must be why the men from outer space chose me.

Tell me, please do, what makes one truly remarkable? Must one be different from all the rest or, indeed, be very much one of them?

You said you never noticed me before. That's because you lack sensitivity, my good friend. How very often you have seen my name in the leading newspapers. Didn't you read of the hundreds imprisoned by Haifa police when that melon exploded in Hanatir Square, now Paris Square? Afterwards every Arab they found in Lower Haifa, pedestrian or on wheels, they put in jail. The papers published the names of everyone notable who was caught, but merely gave general reference to the rest.

The rest—yes, that's me! The papers haven't ignored me. How can you claim not to have heard of me? I truly am remarkable. For no paper with wide coverage, having sources, resources, advertisements, celebrity writers, and a reputation, can ignore me. Those like me are everywhere—towns, villages, bars, everywhere. I am "the rest." I am remarkable indeed!

Saeed Gives His Ancestry

Saeed, the ill-fated Pessoptimist—my name fits my appearance precisely. The Pessoptimist family is truly noble and long established in our land. It traces its origins to a Cypriot girl from Aleppo. Tamerlane, unable to find room for her head in his pyramid of skulls, for all its reported dimensions of 20,000 arms length by 10 high, sent her with one of his lieutenants to Baghdad, where she was to clean herself up and await his return. But she made a fool of the man. They say, and this is a family secret, that this was the cause of the infamous massacre. Anyway, she ran off with a Bedouin of the Tuwaisat tribe named Abjar, of whom a poet has said:

> Abjar, Abjar, son of Abjar,
> Divorced his wife when he couldn't feed her.

He divorced her when he found she had deceived him with Loaf, son of Hunger, from the Jaftlick lowlands, who in turn divorced her in Beersheba. Our forefathers went on divorcing our grandmothers until our journey brought us to a flat and fragrant land at the shore of the sea called Acre, then on to Haifa at the other side of the bay. We continued this practice of divorcing our wives right up until the state was founded.

After the first misfortunes, those of 1948, the members of our great family became scattered, living in all of the Arab countries not yet occupied. And so I have relatives working in the very Arabian Aal Rabi court, with posts in the Bureau of Translation—both from and into Persian, I might add. And I have one who has specialized in lighting the cigarettes of different kings. We also had a captain in Syria, a major in Iraq and a lieutenant-colonel in Lebanon. The last mentioned, however, died of a heart attack when the Intra Bank there, the country's biggest, went bankrupt. The first Arab to be appointed by the government of Israel as head of the Committee for Distribution of Dandelion and Watercress in Upper Galilee is from our family, even though his mother, so they say, was a divorced Circassian girl. And he still claims, so far unsuccessfully, distribution rights for Lower Galilee too. My father, may he rest in peace, did many favors for the state before it was founded. These services of his are known in detail by his good friend Adon (Mr., that is) Safsarsheck, the retired police officer.

After my father fell a martyr on the open road and I was redeemed by the ass, my family took the boat to Acre. When we found that we were in no danger, and that everyone was busy saving their skins, we fled to Lebanon to save ours. And there we sold them to live.

When we had nothing left to sell, I recalled my father's behest to me as he breathed his last, there on the open road. "Go," he had said, "to Mr. Safsarsheck and say to him: 'My father, before his martyrdom, sent you his compliments and asked you to fix me up.' "

And fix me he did.

Saeed Enters Israel for the First Time

I crossed the border into Israel in the car of a doctor affiliated with the Arab Salvation Army. He used to flirt with my sister in his clinic in Haifa. When we emigrated to Tyre, in Lebanon, we found him awaiting us. And when I came to suspect what was going on between him and my sister, he began treating me as his dearest friend. Then his wife began to fancy me.

One day, the doctor asked me, "Can you keep a secret?"

I replied "Like a star over two lovers."

"Then hold your tongue, for my wife won't hold hers."

And so, for my sister's sake, I held mine.

When I revealed to him my desire to sneak into Israel, he promptly volunteered to take me in his car. "It will be better for you to go," he said.

"And for you to," I responded.

"God bless you then," he said.

And my mother did bless us farewell.

We reached Tarshiha just as the sun and the villagers were abandoning it. The Arab guards stopped us. When the doctor showed them his papers, they greeted us warmly. I still felt scared though. But the doctor joked and swore with them, and they laughed and swore back.

In Maaliya we slept. But before dawn I awoke to hear whispering coming from the doctor's bed nearby. I held my breath and made out a woman's voice whispering that her husband would not be awake that early. I told myself that this could not be my sister since she as yet had no husband. So I went contentedly back to sleep.

We lunched at the home of that woman's father in Abu Snan, which was at that time in no-man's-land; that is, it was territory frequented only by spies, cattle merchants, and stray donkeys.

They hired an ass for me and I rode it down to Kufr Yasif. This was in the summer of 1948. And it was riding this donkey as I descended from Abu Snan to Kufr Yasif that I celebrated my twenty-fourth birthday.

They directed me to the headquarters of the military governor. I entered it still riding the donkey. It proudly mounted the three steps at the building's entrance. Soldiers rushed towards me amazed. I shouted, "Safsarsheck, Safsarsheck!"

A fat soldier ran toward me shouting, "I am the military governor, dismount!"

"I am so-and-so, the son of so-and-so," I replied, "and I shall only alight at the door of Mr. Safsarsheck." He swore at me violently but I shouted, "I claim sanctuary with Adon Safsarsheck."

But he merely cursed Mr. Safsarsheck.

So I dismounted from the donkey.

Research on the Origins of the Pessoptimists

When I alighted from the donkey, I found that I was taller than the military governor. I felt much relieved at being bigger than him without the help of the donkey's legs. So I settled comfortably into a chair in the school they had converted into the governor's headquarters. The blackboards were being used as Ping-Pong tables.

There I sat, at ease, thanking God for making me taller than the military governor without the help of the donkey's legs.

That's the way our family is and why we bear the name Pessoptimist. For this word combines two qualities, pessimism and optimism, that have been blended perfectly in the character of all members of our family since our first divorced mother, the Cypriot. It is said that the first to so name us was Tamerlane, following the second massacre of Baghdad. This was when it was reported to him that my first ancestor, Abjar son of Abjar, mounted on his horse outside the city walls, had stared back at the tongues of flame and shouted, "After me, the deluge!"

Take me, for example. I don't differentiate between optimism and pessimism and am quite at a loss as to which of the two characterizes me. When I awake each morning I thank the Lord he did not take my soul during the night. If harm befalls me during the day, I thank Him that it was no worse. So which am I, a pessimist or an optimist?

My mother is also a Pessoptimist. My older brother used to work at the port of Haifa. One day a storm blew up and overturned the crane he was operating, throwing them both onto the rocks and down into the sea. They collected his remains and brought them to us. Neither his head nor his insides could be found. He had been married less than a month and his bride sat weeping and bewailing her hard luck. My mother sat there too, crying silently.

Suddenly my mother became agitated and started beating her hands together. She said hoarsely: "It's best it happened like this and not some other way!"

None of us was surprised at her conclusion except the bride, who was not from our family and therefore did not understand our kind of wisdom. She almost lost her mind and began screaming in my mother's face, "What do you mean, 'some other way'? You ill-fated [this, of course, was the name of my father, may he rest in peace] hag! What worse way could there have been?"

My mother did not appreciate this childish outburst and answered with all the calm assurance of a fortuneteller: "For you to have run off during his life, my girl, to have run away with some other man." One should remember, of course, that my mother knew our family history all too well.

My brother's widow did indeed run off with another man two years later and he turned out to be sterile. When my mother heard that he was so, she repeated her favorite saying, "And why should we not praise God?"

So what are we then? Optimists or pessimists?

EBRÂHÎM GOLESTÂN (b. 1922)

Iran

Ebrâhîm Golestân is an important Iranian writer and filmmaker who has also worked as a translator and a publisher. Among the authors he has translated into Persian are Mark Twain and Ernest Hemingway. He has excelled particularly in the short story in which his sense of form, apparent in "Esmat's Journey," is particularly innovative. He has written a novel as well, *The Secrets of the Haunted Valley's Treasure (Asrâr-e Ganj-e Darra-ye Jenni)*, which he translated himself into English.

Esmat's Journey

She trembled when she reached the courtyard of the shrine. She had been trembling ever since the start of the trip, ever since that night when there had been so many customers and she had been tired and weak and not really up to much and had become sick. And it had ended up in a fight, and she had developed a headache and had started sobbing in the midst of all that uproar. She had been trembling all along the way out of excitement at having made the pilgrimage at all, out of excitement at realizing that she might ultimately reach her goal. And now she had reached it, and she trembled in the courtyard before entering the shrine. She had lost patience and courage, and the entrance hall was so awesome, and the mediating holy glow that would redeem her lay there in the deep dark heart of the tomb. She was impatient. She had forgotten to inquire of anyone as to the proper ways of penitence. She went up the steps of the terraces and, in unconscious reverence, knelt down and wept there on the threshold of the sepulchre.

When she raised her head, her eyes had already grown accustomed to the light, and she felt that everything was washed clean, and that there was no one there except herself. The multitude of people milling around the high-domed sanctuary failed to dispel her solitude. It was as if no human being had ever gone beyond that threshold and that no glance had ever reached the limits of the

Translated by Carter Bryant.

sepulchre and it had remained ever so clean, so untouched, virgin. She had reached it now, and there she was alone, and whoever else there was was nobody but herself; it was she herself alone with the immediate link with being, with the grillwork around the centre of sanctity. And she wept.

Kneeling there, caught in this self-realization, it was as if all the years of her life had become inconsequential, as though it had been some one else's life, as if she had returned to the first day of time. She had come to the realization now that no one had really ever loved her, that never had she loved anyone, that never had she really existed. She put her finger through the bars and stroked the polished hardness of them, searching for the sanctified dust screened from her by the grillwork. She ran her finger along the dust and rubbed the finger over her eyelids. She pressed her lips to the bars, until the pressing kiss turned into a greedy sucking to absorb all that was godly.

"Sister, may your pilgrimage be recompensed." She turned to see a *sayyed*,[1] tall and handsome, eyebrows thick and full, red cheeks, black beard, and velvety eyes gazing upon her with solemn compassion and clemency.

The *sayyed* spoke again, "These tears of yours are pearls, sister." The woman wiped her eyes, brushed the tears from her cheeks, and overwhelmed with awe, bid him hello.

The *sayyed*, whispering a prayer, fixed his heavy, dignified gaze on the the back of his hand and the agate gem of his ring and spoke softly, "Your *chādor*[2] has slipped off your head, sister." And he gave her a moment to replace the *chādor* on her head, and then he said, "Let your good deed be completed, allow me to recite a verse of praise to the *Emām*[3] on your behalf, worthy of your scorched heart." And he began reading in a steady bass voice.

From the moment she had crossed the threshold of the sepulchre, the outside world had faded away, and in her mind nothing had remained of names or faces or features and memory, not even thoughts for the future, nothing but her state of ecstasy. Under the shadow of the *sayyed*'s voice, the world once again came into being, one that was a negation of memories of the past. Memories of nights at the house were swept away, the smell of sweat vanished, and the terrible bath of blood at the end of her anguish. The man whose breath faded away, the man with a heavy body, the man smelling of manure, the man whose manliness under his round gonflated hard stomach was dangling like the last autumn leaf from the hollowed trunk of a tree, breathing in useless desire and unable to reach her. The man with a knife between his shoulders, he who with a single blow of his foot had kicked the door open and entered, crying "Esmat." And when the man who was fucking her, frightened and confused, had jumped up and fled, the man had fallen on her, all covered with blood putting his bloody hands all over her face. And he had pressed his lips to her neck down to her breast, and he had moaned, and she

---

1. A title normally meaning "Sir." Also refers to individuals directly descended from the Prophet Muhammad.
2. The term most common in Iran for a woman's veil or covering.

3. Also written *Imam*. In Sunni Islam, a prayer leader; in Shii Islam, both a general honorific term for a religious leader and the title of the divinely inspired, infallible leader of the Shii community.

had uttered not a sound. And then she had seen that there was a knife, plunged up to the hilt in his back and that there was blood flowing onto her breast. She had remained speechless, and then the man died. She had remained silent, and then gone to sleep beneath the corpse.

Esmat, Esmat. Esmat.

Esmat was moved to tears. The incantation of the professional reader had the odor of rosewater, and brought warmth to her cheeks. She stood between the sepulchre and the *sayyed*. She shut her eyes and silently implored, "Oh *Emām*, forgive me!"

Behind the grillwork of the sepulchre lay the Grave. The *sayyed* broke off his holy words and said, "May God recompense your tears. Amen, by the truth of the God, by the truth of the sanctity of this sepulchre."

"Oh God," said the woman and turned back to look at him. He had noble, affectionate, velvety eyes. Beneath the dome hummed failures and supplications. And people circled the sepulchre with fear, tears, and hope.

"All actions are governed by certain rules," the *sayyed* spoke sternly and gently. "You must learn the rules and rituals of pilgrimage. This sepulchre is dear and holy. Do you know the rules and rituals?"

"No," she said and was afraid lest she had already done something wrong.

"You have to know the right way to do it. Why didn't you ask someone?"

She helplessly said, "I . . . just arrived today. This is the first time I have ever made a pilgrimage."

"May God accept your pilgrimage and bless it. Whereabouts are you from, Sister?"

"I'm just a poor unfortunate . . . from nowhere really."

"No. You mustn't say such things. The home where you dwell is in the state of felicity. This weeping of yours is a sign of a pure heart. Did you make a vow? An oblation?"

"No."

"Eh! Well, first you must make an oblation for yourself, for your children. Promise something to charity."

"What children? I have no one. I am alone."

"Alone? Then who did you come on this pilgrimage with?"

"I am alone."

"Alone is God. Alone! A woman does not travel alone, let alone make a pilgrimage to a holy shrine."

The woman bowed her head and said, "Well, I'm alone. What can I do? I'm alone." Then she said softly, "It's as if all at once the sepulchre had summoned me." And all around them it seemed calm and quiet to her, and she knew that she had found refuge. There was the smell of rosewater.

The *sayyed* spoke kindly to her, "You are certainly a woman of great fortune to have been summoned by the *Emām* himself."

Near them stood a woman, her back to the sepulchre, staring up at the underside of the dome. The *sayyed* spoke softly, "Now it is time to circumambulate the tomb." He nudged the woman forward and followed along close behind, reciting the votive prayer. She could hear him praying behind her as she walked along moving her hands from one bar of the grillwork to another, passing among the other people milling around the sepulchre. The *sayyed,* now walking along beside her, interrupted his prayer with "You are very indebted to His Perfection, the holy *Emām.* You have an obligation to fulfill to Him."

Turning at the first corner of the tomb, the woman said, "How should I? I am so unworthy!"

"Stay here, under the shadow of His Perfection. It is a great glory to serve him here."

"What could I possibly do then?"

"I will show you the rites, myself, with His gracious help. You see, many pilgrims come here. For a day or two, sometimes several days, they stay under His gracious presence." And they passed another corner of the sepulchre. "These pilgrims have needs. They need mending . . . and tending. You will make some money out of it, enough to live on. Whenever your heart is troubled, you can come here to the shrine. It's good business, doing good deeds for people, and you can live the life of a constant pilgrim."

They passed the next turn. "What should I do?" the woman asked. "Come stay with me. My house, my humble little hut is nearby. Here beneath the shadow of the shrine. There are several sisters of the faith dwelling with me there. Pilgrims come there, pilgrims, students and others of the faithful. They have needs."

And they passed the final corner, so the circumambulation was complete. The *sayyed* said, "And for doing your religious duty, you will make quite a comfortable life for yourself. And your actions will be within the sanction of Islam."

The woman stopped. She saw in the gentle caressing of the velvety eyes the luminous acceptance of all her prayers. She beheld the end of her wandering and the achievement of Grace. The *sayyed* spoke with determining kindliness, "I myself will arrange everything for you."

Close by them a woman was moaning before the grillwork of the holy tomb. When the *sayyed* and the woman emerged into the courtyard, it was noon, and the pure, resounding call to prayer of the muezzin sounded through the flapping wing of the pigeons, "Come to your deliverance!"

YASAR KEMAL (b. 1922)
Turkey

Yasar Kemal is the name most familiar to non-Turks when it comes to the modern Turkish novel. Of all Turkish writers, Kemal is the one with the greatest number of works translated into other languages. The translated works include *My Hawk* and *The Wind from the Plain.*

from *Seagull (1981)*

Salih the Gazer

Salih had been waiting in front of the little tavern since noon. The seagull was beside him in its basket, quite frisky now, opening and closing its wings, even the wounded one, tasting the joy of living again, of having eaten its fill.

In the summer months, the children would gather gulls' eggs on the steep crags of Outer Isle and Ocakli Island and sell them to fanciers. Bearded Haydar, the veterinary, was one of those. He could tell at a glance whether an egg was fresh or not and, if he laid hands on a new-laid one he went wild with joy. Then and there, he'd break it open, sniff it blissfully and down it at one go. "Ah, this is the life!" he'd exclaim, wiping his bushy moustache with the back of his hand. "It's all the seas of the world I've swallowed with that one gull's egg. All the seas of the world are coursing in my veins. Ah life! Life in all its plenitude. . ."

He was in the tavern now and showing no sign of getting up and going home. Before him was a large bottle of wine, half empty, and he was talking to a man, asleep with his head on the table. Once in a while the man grunted and lifted a bleary gaze at him. This acted as a spur for Bearded Haydar. "Yes, my friend, indeed you're quite right," he would say and hurry on more quickly than before, shaking the man awake whenever his head fell back onto the table. "This sorrow is going to kill you. Sorrow can destroy a man and it's killing me here, in this godforsaken town. All my studies, all those schools . . . The highest degrees in the sciences of men and animals . . . To end up in this town! Why did I come here? Why did I stay here? It wasn't for the love of a woman, oh no, it was for love of nature, of the sea, of seagulls and their eggs . . . And now I'm dying of sorrow . . . Listen, my friend, everything's dead in me, love, all human feeling. I'm sick of things, sick of everyone. I must kill myself, today, tonight . . . Why should I live, for whom, for what reason? To drag out this miserable existence? Listen, my friend, let this be my last will and testament to you. After I'm dead, throw yourself into the sea and put an end to your life too, the best of ends, at one with the sea! What a beautiful death, aaah!" He grabbed the man's hair. "D'you hear me? My last will and testament . . . You'll kill yourself at sea, d'you understand?" He shook him sharply. "D'you understand?"

The man opened his eyes and stared blankly. "Yes, yes, yes," he mumbled. "I understand." And his head fell back, slam, onto the table.

"Well, I hope you do," Bearded Haydar panted. "AAAh, how I'd like to die at sea too! To become part of the immortal sea, immortalized . . . But I'm afraid, my friend. I'm afraid of the sea." He was shouting suddenly. His voice could be heard all over the marketplace. "Afraid! Afraid. . . Too bad, but I'll have to kill myself in the forest. One day they'll find me gone . . . Who? Someone will surely notice I'm missing. They'll look for me and find me hanging on a tall tree. Not at sea, ah, not at sea . . ."

Salih's hair stood on end. What he'd gathered from all this talk was that the

Translated by Thilda Kemal.

two men inside were bent on taking their lives. The one was going to drown himself, that was sure, but Bearded Haydar was still hesitating, undecided on the kind of death he should choose. What if Salih went to him now, before he killed himself, this man who'd studied all about birds and beasts, and said to him: Look, you love seagull eggs and anyway you'll find a way to kill yourself today. Won't you do a last good deed before you die and mend this baby seagull's wing? If you do, who knows, Allah may give you the courage to kill yourself at sea. You wouldn't be at all afraid and would drown yourself right where it's very deep . . .

The bottle was almost empty now, but Bearded Haydar rambled on, though his tongue seemed to have thickened in his mouth. "A man can have about enough of it all. Hey, my friend, wake up! I'm saying a man can get bored to death in this town, no larger than the palm of my hand. The same sky, the same earth, the same seas with the same white waves, the sun rising there, in the same place every day, the trees never moving, the flowers returning each spring, always, always, never any different . . . And we? Waking, drinking, sleeping, and beginning again the next day and the next and the next . . ." He grabbed the other's hair again. "Isn't that so?"

"Yes, yes" the man said, his head dropping, but Bearded Haydar would not let it go. "Tell me, tell me!" he yelled. "What can a man do in such a world but kill himself? What?"

"Yes, yes . . . Kill himself," the other moaned as he fell asleep once more.

Bearded Haydar got up and blundered to the door, knocking against chairs and tables. He stood in the doorway like a bird holding on with its talons to a sharp crag, its wings fighting against the wind. Suddenly he laughed and pulled his tongue. Salih looked behind him. There was no one. It was at him that Bearded Haydar had pulled his tongue. Salih did the same and also thumbed his nose, to which Haydar promptly reciprocated. Encouraged, Salih crept up to the door where the vet was tottering more dangerously than ever. "Look at this bird," he said as loudly as he dared. "Look, it's a wounded seagull . . ."

Bearded Haydar was trying to focus his gaze. Clutching the door-jamb, he carefully negotiated the three steps and placed his hand heavily on Salih's shoulder. "Who are you?" he said. "Where d'you come from, friend, and where are you going?"

"I'm Salih. They told me you know all about birds and their ailments. This gull's got a broken wing, so I came to you for some medicine."

The veterinary bent down to look, reeling this way and that and making Salih reel too. The he leaned back against the wall and laughed until the tears ran down his face.

After a while he started to walk away, taking a few stumbling steps, then stopping to regain his balance. Salih followed him step by step to the gate of his house and into the yard. Bearded Haydar's face lit up at the sight of an old stunted olive tree with only a few leafless branches on its trunk. He made straight for it and relieved himself. As he was buttoning up his trousers, his face took on a hunted expression. He looked about him in alarm and his eyes rested on Salih.

"Forgive me, effendi," he said, bowing to the ground. "It's just a habit of mine to urinate each evening in this same spot. Only I didn't realize it was still day . . . I'm sorry, very sorry." He took a few cautious steps towards Salih. "You've been following me, effendi. Did I seem to be doing anything suspicious? Let me assure you, effendi, that I committed suicide the very day I was appointed to this town, twenty-seven years ago. Like a stone at the bottom of a well I've been ever since. Thirty years without any political activity whatsoever . . . We belong to a lost generation, effendi, born dead, dead already when we die . . . Ah, but you *have* been following me, effendi! Please go on. It's such an honour for a suicide of thirty years to feel he's important once more. After such an honor I must go inside and blow my brains out . . . But I pity my wife . . . My children too, but my wife most of all . . . She's had to suffer so much from me. It's not easy to bear the burden for thirty years of a man who's committed suicide. And a drunken one at that . . ." He drew nearer to Salih and looked fixedly into his eyes. "A great honor, effendi, you've conferred on me. You've brought me to life after all these years . . . Just as in my student days, when the police used to follow me . . . Ah, what a time it was in Ankara then! All for equality, justice, brotherhood . . . Do you know Dr. Hikmet, effendi? Of course you do, who doesn't? He died only recently in Yugoslavia, and in the presence of Comrade Tito himself . . ." He was talking himself into a fever. Salih hardly understood what he was saying. All he knew was that this man had decided to blow his brains out the minute he entered the house.

Suddenly, Bearded Haydar seized Salih's hand and kissed it noisily. "Thank you, thank you," he said with tears in his eyes. "You've made me so happy, so happy . . ." And he plunged into the house, banging the door. The walls rattled and a woman's scream rent the air. Bearded Haydar was howling too: "Whores, harlots! You've destroyed me. You're all in league in this ignorant town to ruin me. I'll kill you, kill you! See this gun here? And afterwards, I'll hold it to my own mouth and shoot myself . . ."

Smack, whack came the sound of blows raining inside and shrieks from the woman. There was a crash of something breaking and Salih held his breath, waiting for the blast of a gun. Then the door was flung open and he saw a woman rush out, all dishevelled, almost naked in a torn green nightgown. He ran after her. "He's going to kill himself," he cried. "Blow his brains out tonight. He said so to me . . ."

The woman stopped and looked back at Salih. "Don't worry, child," she said softly. "It's been like this for thirty years. I'm just getting out of his way not to get beaten too much."

How strange! She sounded almost amused. Could this be the same woman who'd been screaming for her life only a minute ago? She smiled at Salih and disappeared into a neighboring house.

After a while Bearded Haydar appeared on the threshold, as though nothing had happened. He had combed his hair and straightened his tie, and even changed his soiled trousers for a freshly-pressed pair. He stared at Salih pleasantly enough. Then he saw the seagull in its basket and laughed.

"Its wing is broken," Salih said. "Remember?"

Bearded Haydar peered at the bird and ran a finger over its broken wing. His face changed and wrinkled up as though trying to recall something, but is was no use. "There's nothing doing with this bird," he snapped at last with a look of hatred at Salih. "It'll die. Wounded gulls can't live. Never!" He staggered off, his legs weaving into each other, muttering under his breath. "Why can't I kill myself, why? I've never been able to do anything, anything . . ."

The truth was that Bearded Haydar in all his twenty-seven years in this town had never tended to a single animal. He wouldn't even look at the sick horses, donkeys or goats that were brought to him. Official letters from the administration in Ankara were usually left unanswered, unless some friend obliged, just to save him from further trouble.

Quivering with indignation Salih dashed down the slope after him. "Stop," he said, his voice strangling. "Look here, this bird's full of life. How can you say it'll die?"

Bearded Haydar glared at him. "I say it'll die, and that's that, my greenhorn!"

"You know nothing about it," Salih challenged him. "It would have died long ago if it was going to die . . ."

"That's neither here nor there," the vet retorted. "Once wounded, they always die, these birds."

Salih was at a loss, but not for long. "You killed yourself thirty years ago," he flung at him. "What does a dead man know about a live bird?"

It was Haydar's turn to be baffled. He blinked and cast around, swaying backward and forward as though looking for help. "Hee-hee-hee!" He forced a laugh. "Hee-hee-hee, I'm not really dead. It's inside me I'm dead, inside . . ."

Salih took the seagull in his hands and held it out to him. "Then look! Look at it! Does it seem to be dying?"

But Bearded Haydar felt he couldn't retract now. "It'll die," he repeated stubbornly. "It'll die . . ."

Salih eyed him with scorn. "Go fuck yourself, you!" he cried. "A maniac, that's what you are!" He settled his seagull back into its basket and stalked away. "And you call yourself a vet! Go fuck yourself!"

Everybody in this town, old and young, knew all there was to know about Doctor Yasef, the old Jewish doctor who'd come here as a young man of twenty-five and never left again. After settling in the run-down wooden mansion up on the hill near the windmills, he had sent for his aged father, a famous doctor in Istanbul, to live with him, together with his mother and his two sisters. Then he had married a Greek girl from the town, a graduate of the American College in Istanbul. They had one daughter, but by the time she attained the age of ten, his wife had run off to America, taking the child along with her. Ever since that day she would write one letter a year to the doctor. The letter always came in April and was full of words of love. To tell the truth, Doctor Yasef was perfectly happy with this arrangement. That one single letter kept him content the whole year round and, by the middle of March, he was already preparing himself for it. Every day he would wash and dress up meticulously in elegant suits, starched shirts and bright ties, and with barely suppressed excitement, would direct his steps to the post office. The whole town would hold its breath in expectation and share his joy when the letter arrived at last. As for the doctor, he would shut himself up in his house, not to be seen for days afterwards. Then, one early morning, he would emerge and walk pensively to the seaside, where he would remain standing, wrapped in thought, until the evening shadows fell. Then slowly, with infinite care he'd take the letter out of his pocket and begin to tear it up, making the pieces smaller and smaller and casting them all into the sea, down to the last tiny scrap.

The doctor had carried on his practice until ten years ago, tending to the townfolk and villagers hereabouts, accepting whatever remuneration they were willing to make: money, eggs, chickens, honey, grain, and never exacting a penny from those who couldn't pay. It was said that he had inherited quite a fortune from his father, including houses and apartments in Istanbul. His two sisters had never married and kept house for him. They looked after the garden and read a lot, and at every hour of the day one could hear the sad strains of a piano coming from the mansion.

The doctor had very fixed habits, and Salih knew them very well as did everyone else. His first visit on leaving his house was to the druggist, Fazil Bey, whose pharmacy was open so early that, indeed, some people believed he never closed shop at all. He could be seen at all hours, sitting at a table with a microscope, a balance and little mortars, fussing about with herbs and flowers and powders. If anybody came in with a prescription, he screwed up his face, left the table with ill grace to get the drug and return to his herbs as quickly as he could. But he would always brighten up at the arrival every morning of the doctor. "I'm getting nearer now, doctor," he would cry joyfully. "It won't be long before I find it."

All the year round old people from the mountain villages gathered unusual herbs and flowers to sell to him, and Fazil Bey would sort them out, classify them and pore over them for days. If he should chance upon some kind he'd never seen before, he would rush over to the doctor, wild with excitement, "I've got it, doctor, got it," he'd shout, and the two would put their heads together to try and unravel the mysteries of their new find.

Salih had trailed after the doctor to the pharmacy. Surely, out of so many drugs, something would be found for his seagull's wing . . .

Fazil Bey and the doctor were deep in a long argument over a strange plant that resembled the comb of a cock. With trembling hands they snipped off a piece, sniffed at it, tasted it with the tip of their tongues and then pounded it in a mortar. Outside, white-bearded, slant-eyed villagers sat about on the pavement with baskets and saddle-bags full of herbs, waiting with long-accustomed patience for the two to finish their discussion. The druggist's white smock was spick and span. He changed it every day. His gold-rimmed spectacles rested on the tip of his nose.

"We'll find it, doctor," he said, snuffing at the crushed flower in the mortar. "If it isn't this one, it's the other. There are such a variety of medicinal herbs, infinite really. Why, mother nature yields forth a new one every day, breeding, fertilizing all the time, thousands and thousands."

"How right you are!" Doctor Yasef said, as he rose to go. "If nature were to stop breeding new kinds and only repeated itself, everything would die out. Nature never repeats itself. It creates again and again infinitely."

Fazil Bey's face paled, the spectacles on the tip of his nose trembled and his long wrinkled neck twitched. "But we'll find it, I'm sure we will, sure!" he blurted out quickly, as though something was eluding his grasp. "Tomorrow I'll have analyzed this plant and I'll give you the result."

"Thank you, my dear sir."

"Not at all . . . Pleasure . . . It's all for the good of mankind."

The doctor walked to the door, leaning on his cane, his sparse beard bobbing at the end of his chin, and Fazil Bey accompanied him, still talking. "We'll find it, my honored friend. It's been fifty years now . . . And look! See what a lot of fresh herbs these people have brought me?" He hurried over to an old man, who looked well over eighty, squatting at the foot of the wall. "What have you got for me?" he asked eagerly.

The old man's face broke into a smile. "Such I've brought you, Bey!" he said, very pleased with himself. "I haven't seen the like in all my life."

Fazil Bey drew him up by the hand and embraced him.

The doctor's route after this led him to the honey dealer, Faik Efendi, who raised bees, and there the two of them would sit a while talking to the bees. This, Salih could swear to, and it was as if the bees answered them too.

Salih was beginning to lose patience. "A bunch of crazy people, that's what I'm dealing with," he muttered to himself. If it wasn't for the sake of this poor little wounded bird, he wouldn't have taken a second look at them. Crazy fools . . .

After the bee-man it was the baker, Resul Agha, the doctor went to. And then, just at the call to the noonday prayer, he walked over to the lighthouse and sat on this accustomed rock, the one that was shaped like an armchair, talking away without a break to himself and to whomever came his way.

This was Salih's chance. He settled on a rock opposite the doctor, who greeted him politely and went on with what he was saying. "Such a lot of wars I've seen . . . Cannonballs hurtling right past me, but I wasn't afraid there at Çanakkale, though we hadn't yet heard of the Gazi, Mustafa Kemal Pasha. I fought in the Balkan wars too and on the Caucasian front. Ninety thousand men we lost there, devoured by lice, exterminated by typhus, frozen to death . . . Our Fazil Bey must be a little crazy. Have you ever had the honor of meeting him, sir? . . . I have a daughter, a small child like you, sir. And this little daughter has had six babies by now . . ." He began to laugh, his beard trembling, but there was something sad, almost tearful in his laughter. "Strange, isn't it, sir? My daughter's in America, you know. My wife too. Every year they write to me, inviting me to join them. How can I leave you all, leave my home and country, and go there?" He sprang up and brandished his stick angrily at the sea. "I can't! I'd die the minute I got there. Can a fish live out of water? . . . Don't you believe Fazil Bey, my dear sir, he's an idealist, a great romantic. If nature were to repeat itself, everything would inexorably wear out into nothingness. Have I made myself clear, dear sir? Look at us, can we ever relive a single day that is past? The rose that blooms again each year is not the same as last year's, though it may seem the same to us. See that wave lapping at the shore, it'll only come once, never again. Eternity is a great illusion, sir, and our *friend Fazil Bey a great romantic* . . . Therefore America . . . Do you think my daughter will come to see me? Because I don't want to go anywhere away from here. I'm afraid to. As you will have noticed, sir, I've grown old, and the Lord's will be done sooner or later. I love life, my dear sir . . . If she wants to see her father, why doesn't she come herself? She's my daughter, yes, but at the same time she isn't. She never lived with me that I should regard her as my daughter. Then what is it, why do I welcome those letters I get each year? For the pleasure of having something to wait for . . . And it cannot have escaped your attention, dear sir, that the whole town expects those letters with even more eagerness than me. Now, Cerrah Ali, the magician, that's a man for you! A real creator. Do you know him? He riveted his clear blue eyes on Salih and repeated insistently: "You know him? Cerrah Ali. . . ."

Salih seized on this pause in the doctor's unending discourse. "Yes, yes I know him," he said quickly. "But doctor . . ."

"Yes, my dear sir?"

Salih loved the way the doctor kept calling him "sir." It made him feel ever so confident. "Have you seen this seagull?"

The doctor rose and bent over the basket Salih was holding out. "Very pretty, my dear sir. Beautiful birds, these seagulls, and friendly to men too, the little rascals."

"This one's got a broken wing."

"Oh dear, dear, dear! That's bad . . ."

"Why don't you examine it? You can cure it, you who worked wonders during the war . . ."

Doctor Yasef changed his spectacles, took the baby seagull in his hands and inspected it with meticulous care. He looked at its eyes, fingered its wing, he shook his head dolefully, as though faced with a desperate case. "I'm sorry, sir. What a pity! Quite regrettable . . . Such a lovely bird. But there are two creatures on earth that can never recover from a wound."

"Which are they?" Salih shouted.

"Don't get excited, sir, please calm yourself. I know this is going to be painful for you, but it's the law of nature. The snake is one. It cannot renew its cells after a wound. And the seagull is the other."

Salih glared at the doctor. "D'you mean to tell me that this bird here is going to die?"

Doctor Yasef's beard trembled. His hands flew as he replaced the seagull in its basket and slumped wearily onto his rock.

"Is it going to die? Is it? Is it?" Salih kept repeating. "Isn't there anything we can do?"

The doctor was silent, his face brightening and falling in turn. It was obvious he was trying hard to find something, and Salih began to pity him.

"Hah!" the doctor exclaimed at last. "I've got it . . . Fazil Bey's herbs . . . They've never been of any use, not in fifty years . . . But perhaps . . ." He laid his chin on the knob of his cane and closed his eyes. The hairs of his beard stood out like spines. "Perhaps among those herbs there's one that might cure this seagull's wing. Are gulls and snakes alike? Ah, old age! I can't remember . . . Yes, Fazil Bey's herbs . . . Who knows?"

"Of course, there must be!" Salih cried. "Many, many good herbs . . ."

"But Fazil Bey is a very touchy person. He'd take it ill if I asked him. The best thing is to tackle him yourself when he's in a good mood. In the morning . . ."

"Yes, yes," Salih shouted excitedly. "He even laughs sometimes. I've seen him laughing just like you and me. I can ask him then."

"Well, I wish you every success, my dear sir."

His hopes buoyed up again, Salih looked gratefully at the old doctor. He must do something to thank him, something . . . Suddenly it came to him. He seized the doctor's hand, kissed it three times and touched it to his forehead. "Doctor," he said, and hesitated. Should he? . . . He cleared his throat. "Doctor, if ever those boys do anything to you again . . . Those boys who . . . You know . . . Just let me see them. I'll make them sorry they were ever born. We'll beat the life out of them, Bahri and I."

The doctor's face grew anxious. "Please sir," he begged. "They're my friends. I entreat you, please don't do anything to them."

"Very well," Salih said. "I won't if you don't want me to." But he felt terribly ashamed of himself. Unable to face the doctor another minute, he turned and ran all the way to the market without another look behind him.

The next morning he rose very early and, after feeding his seagull at the seaside, took up his observation post outside the pharmacy. Doctor Yasef had come and gone, and they had winked at each other in secret complicity. A few villagers were waiting too on the pavement with baskets and sacks from which emanated the fresh smell of mountain plants. As the morning progressed Fazil Bey began to brighten up. Now and then he tasted an herb or flower which he was pounding in a mortar and an ineffable look of gladness spread over his face. After a while, as he was sniffing at a flower, he gave a laugh of sheer delight. Salih saw his eyes, mossgreen, full of kindness . . . He decided the moment had come and went in.

"Uncle," he began.

Fazil Bey absentimindedly held out his hand for a prescription. Then, as nothing came he looked up and saw Salih. The boy's insistent gaze fixed on him ever since early morning had disturbed him, mocked him, made him feel small, useless . . . At the sight of him there before him in the pharmacy, he lost his temper and seized the broomstick at his side.

"Out!" he yelled. "Out with you, miserable brat!"

Salih was not quick enough to escape the blow. He only just avoided falling down with the basket and all, and killing his seagull.

"Like leeches, they are these brats, like sticky leeches!" Fazil Bey was foaming at the mouth. "Where have they sprung from, these impudent whippersnappers? What has this town come to?" He lunged out of the pharmacy. "Look at him still standing there!" he screamed. "Look at those eyes, as though he wants to kill me . . ."

Salih turned away slowly, walked past the school and sank onto the steps that led down to the shore. He was almost in tears, but there was still Cerrah Ali, the magician . . .

Cerrah Ali was very old and wise to the ways of this world. Everyone in this town, young and old, had heard tell of his exploits. Long ago, he had been in the habit of walking on a tightrope stretched between Ocakli Island and Olive Island, always choosing a sunny day in April for his stunt. The town would be roused early in the morning to the sound of drums and fifes and pour down to the shore, where Cerrah Ali would be pacing up and down at the foot of the ruined tower on Ocakli Island like a purebred making ready for the race. He was very handsome then, a tall, fair man, and very proud of his prowess too. When the crowd was large enough, he would climb up a ladder to the tightrope, fling his arms out like wings and run quickly across to the other island, a distance of a hundred and fifty to two hundred meters, turn around and walk back in slow tempo this time. Afterwards, until the close of day, he would perform all kinds of acrobatics on the tightrope, standing on one foot, somersaulting, walking on his hands, his legs opening and closing in the air like a pair of scissors, inventing new feats every year, which he displayed first to his own townfolk. It brought him luck. The rest of the year he toured the country, going as far as Arabia and other neighboring lands to make money, but that one spring day in April was set aside for his home town, and indeed it was a day of festivity for all. Ali the magician had many other tricks up his sleeve too, like producing doves from his nose, swallowing flaming swords, stepping barefoot over red-hot coals, winding a boa snake round his neck and thrusting his hand right down its throat . . . All this, and countless other marvels, Ali had learnt when he was a prisoner of war in India. It was said that he could shut himself up in a deep grave and remain there without breathing for forty days. Also there was the magic bonnet he had managed to steal from his Indian master. When he wore it, he became invisible and could travel to wherever he wished in the twinkling of an eye . . .

In time, Ali grew to be very rich. He bought up land and property in the town and all along the Black Sea coast. He had one son called Sultan. No one had ever seen his wife, nor even Sultan in his childhood. He suddenly appeared one day, out of nowhere, a grown-up, handsome young man.

Ah, Ali the magician could have been the richest man in all of Turkey, but for the evil day when the passion for treasure hunting seized him and he sold his lands and houses to go seeking up hill and down vale for long-lost treasures. In the end, when that final blow hit him, he was still rich, with half-a-dozen houses and some land and even those three bays all his own, but nothing like he could have been. Yet, when he embarked on this venture he was full of confidence in his powers of divination and thought he could win over the gods and jinns and supernatural spirits to his cause. Think of it, treasures immeasurable that had belonged to the wealthy Croesus,[1] to Alexander the Great, to King Darius,[2] and to untold kings and potentates, buried in the ground, useless, when so many people on this earth lived in want and poverty . . .

For three years he shut himself up in his house with history books and read and read until he felt he would go crazy if he did not start out at once. Who could blame him? Fourteen thousand ancient cities still lay unexcavated all over Anatolia, and what cities! From Anavarza, to Tarsus, to Misis, Castabala,

---

1. Ancient king known for his wealth and greed.

2. A great conqueror; one of the most important Achaemenid Persian kings.

Hattushash, Troy, Sardis, each one of them crammed with tombs, mausoleums, shrines and who knows what roomfuls of treasures . . .

For a full twenty-five years he pursued his quest, aided by seven companions, digging and delving into tells, unearthing gold coins, ancient statues, and precious stones that he smuggled out of the country with the collusion of a German, five Americans, and two Englishmen. But they were badly duped by the German who gave them forged dollars in exchange for thirty-six Hittite, Phrygian and Greek statues of inestimable value. It was a good thing that Ali had the dollars expertized before using them or they would have been in real trouble. After this, they often had to melt the gold and silver objects they found in order to sell them, because one way or another these illicit antique dealers always found a means of cheating them.

But nothing could discourage Ali. He was thoroughly bewitched by these old cities, the tombstones, the shrines, and lived among them as though they were his own town, making heartfelt offerings to the Hittite tempest god in the ruined shrines just like any citizen of the time, and dressing up like the Greek, Hittite, Roman or Phrygian statues he encountered. On Nemrud Mountain, King Antiochus was his closest companion, and everywhere in those ancient sites, at Yazilikaya, Karatepe, Hattushash, Sakçagöz, Gözlükule, Kültepe, he had friends, statues, reliefs, inscriptions that he loved. He had grown to regard himself as the last monarch of all these kingdoms dead and gone. So immersed was he in the past that he even imagined himself married at times, or in love with old-time queens and goddesses.

The digging would always be done at night, in secret. Sometimes, Ali would take along his son, Sultan, for the youth had grown even more fascinated with the quest than his father, devouring in a few years all the history and archaeology books he could lay his hands on.

One of the places that interested Ali most was Nurhak Mountain in the Çukurova, for it was there, Ali was certain, that Cleopatra's treasure must lie buried. The Egyptian Queen had brought it along with her when she sailed over to Tarsus in her gold-embossed ships to meet her lover, and had stored it away in the palace he built for her on Nurhak Mountain. And when she died there in the Çukurova, her lover had buried her in a sumptuous underground vault on that same mountain. But there were so many ruins on Nurhak . . . Any one of them could be Cleopatra's castle. Poor Ali tried them all and, though he never found Cleopatra's treasure, he was lucky enough to unearth three Hittite statues which he sold to an American colonel at the İncirlik Air Base for a goodly sum in dollars, and genuine ones too.

At Divriği, in the province of Sivas, stands the copper mountain that King Solomon had mined in times of yore. The imprint of his foot can still be seen on a copper rock, and beside it that of Belkis, the Queen of Sheba . . . For many long years Ali explored this mountain, searching for King Solomon's fabulous treasure, made even richer by the gifts the Queen of Sheba had brought. The mountain, reddish, tinged with green in places, exuding an odor of burnt ammoniac, smoked day and night, smoldering as though from some perpetual fire, and there were nights when it glowed like a mass of incandescent coals, shooting blinding sparks into the darkness. Ali and his companions would cast themselves down, prostrate in worship, until the brightness passed away. This, they had learnt to do from the peasants of the region.

Ali had discovered an ancient manuscript inscribed on deerskin, full of information about the mountain and its history, and in it were three maps, all three showing the exact location of the treasure. But the writing was in Armenian, so Ali had his old friend Agop Süleymanian read it out to him. Now, Agop Süleymanian had an irrefutable theory that he was a descendant of King Solomon and that his ancestor's treasure must be buried somewhere here, on this mountain, in the old Armenian homeland of Divriği. The treasure for him would be palpable proof of his theory. He would not touch a single gold coin of it, he promised. All would go to Ali, who deserved it for his life-long exertions to bring to light the historic values of Anatolia. "Indeed I do," Ali would boast. "Think how many old bones have passed through my hands, the bones and skulls of kings and queens and goddesses, of Cleopatra, Alexander the Great, Hattushil, Midas, Mithridates, Hadrianus . . ."

The copper mountain was bare of all vegetation but for three tall trees on its very crest, which nobody dared even to touch, for fear of being caught in a spell. A bright spring sprouted beneath these trees. According to the deerskin manuscript, the treasure lay seven paces below the tree to the east. Dig into the copper rock there, it said, seventeen meters down, and you will uncover the entrance to a passage, on the right wall of which seven hands, three times the size of an ordinary hand are engraved. Do not touch them, but work your way down the passage and ninety-nine paces further, you will come upon thirty-three green serpents on the stone floor. Lift up the first serpent and you will see the mouth to a well wrought with pearl and coral and jade. At the bottom of the well is a palace, the like of which was never seen. Forty spacious rooms, thirty of them filled with gold, diamonds, rubies, all the rarest gems of this earth. But a dragon guards this treasure. It must be killed before you can reach the treasure. For this, you shall recite the ancient Armenian prayer, ten thousand years old . . .

Now, Agop Süleymanian knew this prayer, but he dared not break the age-old proscription and reveal it to anyone. Only the Grand Rabbi could teach this prayer to Ali. He was the only person who, though not Armenian, knew the words and would not be cursed if he taught them to others . . .

All these things Ali did, but it was labor in vain. Sixty-six wells he found, and descended into the bowels of the earth at the cost of the lives of nine of his companions. Many prayers were read, verses from the Koran, from Christian, Jewish, Armenian, and Yezidi liturgies, but the doors to the treasure of King Solomon would not open for him. He even had a book of prayers sent to him by the King of Abyssinia, for who knew but that the Queen of Sheba might not have put some kind of Abyssinian spell on the treasure. For seven days and seven nights he knelt at the foot of the mountain and recited all those prayers. But when they struck their picks and mattocks again, the copper mountain only resounded emptily, boom, boom, boom . . .

In the end Ali lost hope and with an aching heart he gave up the search.

But not Sultan, his son. He persisted. For years he attacked the copper mountain with pickaxes, dynamite, and bombs, splintering, smashing, tearing it apart, hoping against hope, making of his very hopelessness his strength. At last he, too, fled in despair, but the mountain would not let him go. It pursued him wherever he went, a red smoldering mass vomiting its poisonous green, sounding deafeningly even in his sleep, boom, boom, boom … In Priam's celebrated Troy, in Croesus's Sardis, on Antiochus's Nemrud Mountain, in the Lord Abraham's Urfa, wherever Sultan sought refuge, the mountain tracked him down, boom boom boom, even in the Land of Canaan, boom boom boom … It gave him no peace until it had dragged him back again to Divriği.

Sultan was all alone now. He slept on the mountain's crest under the three lofty plane trees by the brightly bubbling spring. And King Solomon appeared to him in a dream, holding the Queen of Sheba by the hand, and at last revealed the magic words to him. After this, Sultan started again with renewed fervor. He found many hands of gold, many serpents, and came upon the well, wrought in pearl and coral and jade. The doors to the forty rooms of the palace opened wide before him and he saw the glittering treasure, the gold, the rubies, the precious stones … But when he stretched his hand out to them, they receded and the doors closed down again. Instead, a seven-headed green dragon stood before him with seven flickering tongues of flame. Seven times it lashed its tail at the mountainside. The hollow copper mountain shook and boomed, seven times.

"Oh son of man," the dragon spoke to him, "give up your quest! This treasure is not for the times you live in. Solomon, the King of Kings, has hidden it away for a day when men will no longer be wicked and cruel, another age of gold. This world is too full of evil and violence. I cannot let you have the treasure." And so saying, it lashed its tail at the mountain again, three times, and vanished.

So Sultan went up to the spring on the summit. He washed and cleansed himself. Then with strong rope he hanged himself on a branch of the middle one of the three plane trees. As he gave up the ghost, the mountain throbbed and shook for seven days and its angry booming was heard as far as Sivas city and the great bazaar in Kayseri.

Cerrah Ali, the magician, heard it too and hastened back to Divriği, only to find Sultan swinging at the end of the rope. "Too late, too late," he lamented. "What have I done! Dead, my only son … All because of me. Immolated to the copper mountain …" He brought him back home, and with great keening and ritual prayers buried him on a hilltop near the town. Everyone mourned for Sultan and the tale of his adventures was told and retold until it became a legend.

Salih had heard it from Ismail the blacksmith, from Skipper Temel and countless others. His feet flew as he climbed the hill to the magician's house, a two-storied wooden structure, its wood blackened by time, its white curtains always tightly drawn. The garden was planted with fruit trees, plums, cherries, peaches, all in full bloom, humming with bees under the warm spring sun. He peeped through the wooden fence, and there was Cerrah Ali himself, half naked, his long white beard reaching to his wrinkled belly, wearing only a pair of blue trousers tucked up to the knees and a red kerchief knotted loosely round his neck. With wild gesticulations, talking aloud to himself, he paced the grass-grown stones of the garden path, stopping now and again, frozen in his tracks, to glare balefully at earth and sky.

How was Salih to tackle this barrel of rumbling wrath? He was still hesitating when he saw Cerrah Ali making for a cherry tree where a large swarm of bees had settled on a bough, blanketing all the flowers. The magician began to seize the bees by the handful and cast them up into the air. Not until he cleaned up the whole bough did he stop, and the bees never stung him at all! Salih was enchanted. So the magician was so powerful he could even cast his spell on bees! Forgetting his fear, he climbed over the fence and faced Cerrah Ali eagerly, the basket with the seagull always in his hand.

Cerrah Ali showed no surprise. "Hello!" he laughed and his white beard shook over his chest. "What's this? Who are you?"

"I'm Salih . . . And you are Cerrah Ali the magician, aren't you?"

"That's right."

"They say you own twenty times a thousand old cities . . . With the title-deed too . . ."

"Yes, but without the title-deeds."

"And the copper mountain?"

"Yes . . ."

"And you can bring back the dead to life?"

Cerrah Ali was silent.

"And fly like a bird in the sky?" Salih was trembling in all his limbs now.

"Don't be afraid," Cerrah Ali said. "You sound like a good sensible boy and if you want the truth, flying's one thing I cannot do."

"But the whole town says that you do."

"I know. Only people like to exaggerate sometimes." The magician tugged at his beard. "Why have you come here?" he asked suddenly.

"My seagull . . . Its wing is broken and no one could mend it in this town, no one. Fazil Bey just chased me away. Everyone says you can cure it." Salih looked up with pleading eyes. "Doctor Yasef sent me to you with his compliments. We all know about your son and grieved for him, me and Bahri and Cemil . . . It was such a pity . . . If only the mountain hadn't closed up against him that one time . . . The snake prince, too, grieved for him . . . If only . . ."

The magician's beard trembled. "Do you love that bird so much?"

"Very, very much," Salih shouted.

"Let me have a look then." Cerrah Ali picked up the gull and stroked it before lifting the wounded wing. His face changed slowly as he looked at Salih and back again at the wing. It was just like that he had been glaring at earth and sky a while ago. He began to mutter to himself too, but Salih could not make out a word of what he was saying. Then it came out quite clearly. "This bird can't ever fly again. This seagull will die . . . It will die . . ."

Salih's ears rang, boom boom, like the copper mountain. His head whirled and his eyes went black. He grabbed the bird from Cerrah Ali's hands and fled blindly down to the sea.

And there he sat, his head in his hands, and in front of him the seagull in its basket was looking at him with bright trusting eyes, lifting its good wing up, longing to fly . . .

YEHUDA AMICHAI (b. 1924)
Germany/Israel

Born in Wurzburg, Germany, Yehuda Amichai moved to Jerusalem with his family in 1936. He has established himself as a poet, novelist, and short-story writer, and was awarded the Israel Prize for poetry in 1982. His books of poetry include *Songs of Jerusalem and Myself* (1973), *Amen* (1977), and *Great Tranquility* (1983). Although much of his poetry deals with war, he does not allow his pain to slide into sentimentality. His novel *Not of This Time, Not of This Place* was published in 1963.

Seven Laments for the War-Dead

1

Mr. Beringer, whose son
fell at the Canal that strangers dug
so ships could cross the desert,
crosses my path at Jaffa Gate.

He has grown very thin, has lost   5
the weight of his son.
That's why he floats so lightly in the alleys
and gets caught in my heart like little twigs
that drift away.

2

As a child he would mash his potatoes   10
to a golden mush.
And then you die.

A living child must be cleaned
when he comes home from playing.
But for a dead man   15
earth and sand are clear water, in which
his body goes on being bathed and purified
forever.

3

The Tomb of the Unknown Soldier
across there. On the enemy's side. A good landmark   20
for gunners of the future.

Translated by Chana Bloch.

Käthe Kollwitz. *Outbreak.* 1903. Lithograph from *Peasants' War.*

Or the war monument in London
at Hyde Park Corner, decorated
like a magnificent cake: yet another soldier
lifting head and rifle,   25
another cannon, another eagle, another
stone angel.

And the whipped cream of a huge marble flag
poured over it all
with an expert hand.   30

But the candied, much-too-red cherries
were already gobbled up
by the glutton of hearts. Amen.

4

I came upon an old zoology textbook,
Brehm, Volume II, *Birds:*
in sweet phrases, an account of the life of the starling,   35
swallow, and thrush. Full of mistakes in an antiquated
Gothic typeface, but full of love, too. "Our feathered
friends." "Migrate from us to the warmer climes."
Nest, speckled egg, soft plumage, nightingale,   40

stork. "The harbingers of spring." The robin,
red-breasted.

Year of publication: 1913, Germany,
on the eve of the war that was to be
the eve of all my wars.   45

My good friend who died in my arms, in
his blood,
on the sands of Ashdod. 1948, June.

Oh my friend,
red-breasted   50

5

Dicky was hit.
Like the water tower at Yad Mordekhai.
Hit. A hole in the belly. Everything
came flooding out.

But he has remained standing like that   55
in the landscape of my memory
like the water tower at Yad Mordekhai.

He fell not far from there,
a little to the north, near Houlayqat.

6

Is all of this   60
sorrow? I don't know.
I stood in the cemetery dressed in
the camouflage clothes of a living man: brown pants
and a shirt yellow as the sun.

Cemeteries are cheap; they don't ask for much.   65
Even the wastebaskets are small, made for holding
tissue paper
that wrapped flowers from the store.
Cemeteries are a polite and disciplined thing.
"I shall never forget you," in French   70
on a little ceramic plaque.
I don't know who it is that won't ever forget:
he's more anonymous than the one who died.

Is all of this sorrow? I guess so.
"May ye find consolation in the building   75
of the homeland." But how long
can you go on building the homeland

and not fall behind in the terrible
three-sided race
between consolation and building and death?   80

Yes, all of this is sorrow. But leave
a little love burning always
like the small bulb in the room of a sleeping baby
that gives him a bit of security and quiet love
though he doesn't know what the light is   85
or where it comes from.

7

Memorial Day for the war-dead: go tack on
the grief of all your losses—
including a woman who left you—
to the grief of losing them; go mix   90
one sorrow with another, like history,
that in its economical way
heaps pain and feast and sacrifice
onto a single day for easy reference.

Oh sweet world, soaked like bread   95
in sweet milk for the terrible
toothless God. "Behind all this,
some great happiness is hiding." No use
crying inside and screaming outside.
Behind all this, some great happiness may   100
be hiding.

Memorial day. Bitter salt, dressed up as
a little girl with flowers.
Ropes are strung out the whole length of the route
for a joint parade: the living and the dead together.   105
Children move with the footsteps of someone else's grief
as if picking their way through broken glass.

The flautist's mouth will stay pursed for many days.
A dead soldier swims among the small heads
with the swimming motions of the dead,   110
with the ancient error the dead have
about the place of the living water.

A flag loses contact with reality and flies away.
A store window decked out with beautiful dresses for women
in blue and white. And everything   115
in three languages: Hebrew, Arabic, and Death.

A great royal beast has been dying all night long
under the jasmine,

with a fixed stare at the world.
A man whose son died in the war   120
walks up the street
like a woman with a dead fetus in her womb.
"Behind all this, some great happiness is hiding."

KHALÎL HÂWÎ (1925–1982)
Lebanon

Khalîl Hâwî earned his doctorate in Arabic literature from Cambridge University
and was a professor of Arabic literature at the American University of Beirut. He
is the author of several collections of poetry and works of criticism. His tragic
suicide in Beirut was an act of political protest against the Israeli invasion of
Lebanon in June 1982.

from *Naked in Exile*

The Cave

And I have come to know how minutes drag their feet
And how they petrify, metamorphose into centuries.
And I've become a cave among the caves on shore;
A night that calloused in the rocks has blotched my brow.
And I have suffered Neptune's[1] steeds to chew the flesh   5
Of my entrails and lose it in the desert of the deep.
I have observed the dread of ships falling headlong
In broken echoes that wail in vain into my depths
And cast upon my eyes a night of flowing locks
Howling into the wind, entreating, falling helplessly.   10

With the retreating sea there settle in my blood
Dead fish, some rotten fruit, some peels; and in the sand
My hand caves in; it folds and carious grows;
The sand-wind riddles through and whistles in its veins.
An old and rusty dagger cuts into my flesh   15

Translated by Adman Haydar and Michael Beard.

---

1. Greco-Roman god of the sea (unless the
   reference here is to the planet).

And leaves a deep impression, but I do not bleed.
Had I but one rebellious vein!
Dear God, how ruthlessly the minutes drag their feet
And how they petrify, metamorphose into centuries.

Behold! Thou hast prevailed,   20
An unawaited guest,
Lavished the choicest quail
And manna on my board,
Hast waited on my cup
With wine unknown to jars,   25
Empowered me to rule
The genie of the caves,
Thou hast imbued my hands
With might to mould my dreams,
Enlivened in the clay   30
What hopes cannot perceive.
Behold! Now nymphs, now gems,
Now lofty palaces;
The wizard strikes his wand:
"Let there be," and there is.   35
The fire flowers, ripens
On my hearth, and spring
Tiptoes and canopies
My room amid the frost;

The sun, returning home,   40
Dispels the polar fog
And, basking in my warmth,
Contented, passes on.
Awaiting its return,
I stir the green ember   45
And fructify our land
With bounty, effortless.

Thou that hast favoured me
With manna and with quail,
Empowered me to rule   50
The genie of the caves,
Imbued my hands with might
To mold and to create,
I have become ashamed
Of my own poverty.   55
For thee I spilled my blood,
Butchered the only vein
In reverential fear

And due expectancy.
Hide not in leaden caves
Out of the range of sight;   60
My eyes are lidless, nailed
To curtained horizons.

And now I'm horrified
Of the sulphurous blaze
Of sudden thunderbolt   65
That blasts into my eyes
Peals of insanity.
I know not who you are.
Damnation rages red
Upon my lips and pain   70
And prayer leave their brand
Upon them and contend.
Shame strips my folded cave
Naked in its exile;
And shall I call for one   75
Who may work wonders yet?
The great magician died
And he will not return.
From the magician's corpse
A tattered rag somehow   80
Evaporates. It grows:
Some sprightly form sets forth
Unfurled and chased along
From road to wayward road.   85

When evening haze prevails
Save your maternal tears;
Entreat me not to say:
"Behind the wasted caves
Behind the barren shores   90
A world of books, a home
A field, a plough, await."
My kingdom is not there.
Omnipotent I rule
The genie of the caves.   95
Manna and quail and wine
Unknown to earthly jars.
What but a hungry cave, a wasted yawning mouth,
A hollow hand that drags and draws the hollow line
Only to wipe it out with slow tepidity?   100
The tedious clock is stopped; its hands are frozen still.
And O! how ruthlessly the minutes drag their feet
And how they petrify, metamorphose into centuries.

SALMA KHADRA JAYYUSI (b. 1926)
Israel/United States

A Palestinian poet and critic, Salma Khadra Jayyusi earned a doctorate from the University of London. She has been a significant influence on the international literary scene partly, because of a massive project of translation of Arabic literature into English that she launched. Publication of her own poetry was curtailed by the June 1967 war. Jayyusi now lives in the United States.

On Visiting the M. D. Anderson[1]

(In memory of Anne Royal, who translated this poem three years before her tragic death in 1985)

I saw you in Houston, waiting for the verdict
to decree life or death for you, one foot rooted
in death row, beating out an even song:
"Drive this death from me, scatter
these thousand seeds of death   5
from my tortured blood, those seeds
that dropped a steel anchor
deep into my heart's heart."

Where, stranger, did the crab monster strike?
Your face pale as bloodless wheat?   10
Where has his stinging tail
plunged into your flesh?
Tomorrow drink the cup of bitterness
and slowly watch the horrors of the battle
you must wage with this beast of many tails: 15
Watch and tire, tire and rest, then fight again, again.

Life here is a dagger: honed and sharp;
Here fellow bodies await the knife—twisted flesh,
half-slit veins, bloodless, dwindling sacks of bones,
chancred, chopped, flayed, hairless . . .   20
(these bald heads the beacons of this battle,
gleaming under the pitiless neon
that glazes their eyes,

Translated by Anne Royal and Charles Doria.

---

1. The famous cancer clinic and hospital in
   Houston, Texas.

grieving eyes whose hopes the beast has wounded,
eyes still brimming with the will to live).   25

For tomorrow, silent stranger, my countryman,
you will drink the bitter worm and the still more bitter cure[2]
soon you will join the ranked heroes,
the legions of those who fight back.
For, yes, you are one more hero,   30
Your body made nothing, drowned in frothing quicklime
Now that that eight-armed demon makes your flesh burst
with alien cells that wall you in,
Jailing you in ransom to death . . .

You are one more hero who dared enter the wolf's lair,   35
selling him slices of your corpse: arm, leg, breast, neck,
letting him rape you head to spine to feet,
Giving him your body to mar
(the way he will my sister
who stands here beside me like a fallen queen).   40
But you will not yield!

You are one more hero who mocked the hyena's slashing laugh
He who tears you to shreds indelibly
But you will fight, fight him in an equal fight.
Life is the terrible sword shall contest   45
death and all his minions.

This is the war that only lovers,
consumed by love of life, will wage.
This is the war that flies
a single banner: "Live or die!"   50
a war where all: captive, victim, warrior—are one,
The enemy the crab tyrant of a thousand claws
a million poisoned cells.

This hollow crab, stranger friend,
where did he sting you?   55
I see you before me possessing that calm
those lambs display who climb
Mount Arafat[3] for their sacrifice.
For you are the best of heroes,
of those who decline the victim's part,   60
You who crossed oceans

---

2. In Arabic it says "the CMF," which is the
medicine given to cancer patients to arrest
metastasis, i.e., chemotherapy. It can cause
great nausea and loss of hair.

3. The mountain near Mecca where the Muslim pilgrimage ends and animals are sacrificed.

to slay the crab within
and then return.

And then return?
I hope
I hope!

YÛSUF IDRÎS (1927–1990)
Egypt

A compatriot of Nawal al-Sa dawi, Yûsuf Idrîs was also trained as a physician (he
and al-Sa dawi were medical students at the same time). Idrîs went on to become
what many consider the Arab world's leading short-story writer. Many of his
earlier short stories are narrative masterpieces. His fiction shows an obsession
with sexuality and its social consequences.

House of Flesh

The ring is beside the lamp. Silence reigns and ears are blinded. In the silence the
finger slides along and slips on the ring. In silence too, the lamp is put out.
Darkness is all around. In the darkness eyes too are blinded.

The widow and her three daughters. The house is a room. The beginning is
silence.

* * *

The widow is tall, fair-skinned, slender, thirty-five years of age. Her daughters too
are tall and full of life. They never take off their flowing clothes which, whether
they be in or out of mourning, are black. The youngest is sixteen, the eldest
twenty. They are ugly, having inherited their father's dark-skinned body, full of
bulges and curves wrongly disposed; from their mother they have taken hardly
anything but her height.

Despite its small size, the room is large enough for them during the daytime;
despite the poverty of it, it is neat and tidy, homely with the touches given to it by
four females. At night their bodies are scattered about like large heaps of warm,
living flesh, some on the bed, some around it, their breathing rising up warm and
restless, sometimes deeply drawn.

Silence has reigned ever since the man died. Two years ago the man died after
a long illness. Mourning ended but the habits of the mourners stayed on, and of
these silence was the most marked, a silence long and interminable, for it was in
truth the silence of waiting. The girls grew up and for long they waited

Translated by Denys Johnson-Davies.

expectantly, but the bridegrooms did not come. What madman will knock at the door of the poor and the ugly, particularly if they happen to be orphans? But hope, of course, is present, for—as the proverb says—even a rotten bean finds some blind person to weigh it out, and every girl can find her better half. Be there poverty, there is always someone who is poorer; be there ugliness, there is always someone uglier. Hopes come true, sometimes come true, with patience.

A silence broken only by the sound of reciting from the Koran; the sound rises up, with dull, unimpassioned monotony. It is being given by a Koranic reciter and the reciter is blind. It is for the soul of the deceased and the appointed time for it never changes: Friday afternoons he comes, raps at the door with his stick, gives himself over to the hand stretched out to him, and squats down on the mat. When he finishes he feels around for his sandals, gives a greeting which no one troubles to answer, and takes himself off. By habit he recites, by habit he takes himself off, and so no one is aware of him.

The silence is permanent. Even the breaking of it by the Friday afternoon recital has become like silence broken by silence. It is permanent like the waiting, like hope, a hope that is meagre yet permanent, which is at least hope. However little a thing may be, there is always something less, and they are not on the look-out for anything more; never do they do so.

Silence goes on till something happens. Friday afternoon comes and the reciter does not come, for to every agreement however long it may last there is an end—and the agreement has come to an end.

Only now the widow and her daughters realize what has occurred: it was not merely that his was the only voice that broke the silence but that he was the only man, be it only once a week, who knocked at the door. Other things too they realized: while it was true that he was poor like them, his clothes were always clean, his sandals always polished, his turban always wound with a precision of which people with sound eyesight were incapable, while his voice was strong, deep and resonant.

The suggestion is broached: Why not renew the agreement, right away? Why not send for him this very moment? If he's busy, so what—waiting's nothing new? Towards sunset he comes and recites, and it is as if he recites for the first time. The suggestion evolves: Why doesn't one of us marry a man who fills the house for us with his voice? He is a bachelor, has never married, has sprouted a sparse moustache and is still young. One word leads to another—after all he too is no doubt looking for some nice girl to marry.

The girls make suggestions and the mother looks into their faces so as to determine to whose lot he shall fall, but the faces turn away, suggesting, merely suggesting, saying things without being explicit. Shall we fast and break that fast with a blind man? They are still dreaming of bridegrooms—and normally bridegrooms are men endowed with sight. Poor things, they do not yet know the world of men; it is impossible for them to understand that eyes do not make a man.

"You marry him, Mother. You marry him,"

"I? Shame on you! And what will people say?"

"Let them say what they like. Whatever they say is better than a house in which there is not the sound of men's voices."

"Marry before you do? Impossible."

"Is it not better that you marry before us so that men's feet may know the way to our house and that we may marry after you. Marry him. Marry him, Mother."

She married him. Their number increased by one and their income increased slightly—and a bigger problem came into being.

It is true that the first night passed with the two of them in their bed, but they did not dare, even accidentally, to draw close to one another. The three girls were asleep but from each one of them was focused a pair of searchlights, aimed unerringly across the space between them: searchlights made up of eyes, of ears, of senses. The girls are grown up; they know; they are aware of things, and by their wakeful presence it is as if the room has been changed into broad daylight. During the day, however, there is no reason for them to stay there, and one after the other they sneak out and do not return till around sunset. They return shy and hesitant, moving a step forward, a step back, until, coming closer, they are amazed, thrown into confusion, are made to hasten their steps by the laughter and guffaws of a man interspersed by the giggling of a woman. It must be their mother who is laughing, also laughing is the man whom previously they had always heard behaving so correctly, so properly. Still laughing, she met them with open arms, her head bared, her hair wet and combed out, and still laughing. Her face, which they had instinctively perceived as nothing but a dead lantern where spiders, like wrinkles, had made their nest, had suddenly filled with light; there it was in front of them as bright as an electric bulb. Her eyes were sparkling; they had come forth and shown themselves, bright with tears of laughter; eyes that had previously sought shelter deep down in their sockets.

The silence vanished, completely disappeared. During dinner, before dinner, and after dinner, there are plenty of jokes and stories, also singing, for he has a beautiful voice when he sings and imitates Umm Kulthoum and Abdul Wahhab; his voice is loud and booming, raucous with happiness.

You have done well, Mother. Tomorrow the laughter will attract men, for men are bait for men.

Yes, daughters. Tomorrow men will come, bridegrooms will make their appearance. Yet the fact is that what most occupied her was not men or bridegrooms but that young man—albeit he was blind, for how often are we blind to people just because they are blind—that strong young man full of robust health and life who had made up for her the years of sickness and failure and premature old age.

The silence vanished as though never to return and the clamour of life pervaded the place. The husband was hers, her legitimate right in accordance with the law of God and His Prophet. What, then, was there to be ashamed about when everything he does is lawful? No longer does she even worry about hiding her secrets or being discreet, and even as night comes and they are all together and bodies and souls are set loose, even as the girls are scattered far apart about the room, knowing and understanding, as though nailed to where they are sleeping, all sounds and breathing aquiver, controlling movements and coughs, suddenly deep sighs issue forth and are themselves stifled by more sighs.

She spent her day doing the washing at the houses of the rich, he his day reciting the Koran at the houses of the poor. At first he did not make it a practice to return to the house at midday, but when the nights grew longer and his hours of sleep less, he began to return at midday to rest his body for a while from the toil of the night that had passed and to prepare himself for the night to come. Once, after they had had their fill of the night, he suddenly asked her what had been the matter with her at midday; why was she talking unrestrainedly now and had maintained such complete silence then, why was she now wearing the ring that was so dear to him, it being the only thing by way of bridal money and gifts the marriage had cost him, while she had not been wearing it then?

She could have risen up in horror and screamed, could have gone mad. He could be killed for this, for what he is saying has only one meaning—and what a strange and repulsive meaning.

A choking lump in the throat stifled all this, stifled her very breathing. She kept silent. With ears that had turned into nostrils, tactile sense and eyes, she began listening, her sole concern being to discover the culprit. For some reason she is sure it is the middle one: in her eyes there is a boldness that even bullets cannot kill. She listens. The breathing of the three girls rises up, deep and warm as if fevered; it groans with yearning, hesitates, is broken, as sinful dreams interrupt it. The disturbed breathing changes to a hissing sound, a hissing like the scorching heat that is spat out by thirsty earth. The lump in the throat sinks down deeper, becomes stuck. What she hears is the breathing of the famished. However much she sharpens her senses she is unable to distinguish between one warm, muffled heap of living flesh and another. All are famished; all scream and groan, and the moaning breathes not with breathing but perhaps with shouts for help, perhaps with entreaties, perhaps with something that is even more.

She immersed herself in her second legitimate pursuit and forgot her first, her daughters. Patience became bitter-tasting, even the mirage of bridegrooms no longer made its appearance. Like someone awakened in terror to some mysterious call, she is suddenly stung into attention: the girls are famished. It is true that food is sinful, but hunger is even more so. There is nothing more sinful than hunger. She knows it. Hunger had known her, had dried up her soul, had sucked at her bones; she knows it, and however sated she is, it is impossible for her to forget its taste.

They are famished, and it was she who used to take the piece of food out of her own mouth in order to feed them; she, the mother, whose sole concern it was feed them even if she herself went hungry. Has she forgotten?

Despite his pressing her to speak, the feeling of choking turned into silence. The mother kept silent and from that moment silence was ever with her.

At breakfast, exactly as she had expected, the middle one was silent—and continued in her silence.

Dinner-time came with the young man happy and blind and enjoying himself, still joking and singing and laughing, and with no one sharing his laughter but the youngest and the eldest.

Patience is protracted, its bitter taste turns to sickness—and still no one shows up.

One day, the eldest one looks at her mother's ring on her finger, expresses her delight in it. The mother's heart beats fast—and beats yet faster as she asks her if she might wear it for a day, just for one single day. In silence she draws it off her finger; in silence the eldest puts it on her own same finger.

At the next dinner-time the eldest one is silent, refuses to utter.

The blind youth is noisy, he sings and he laughs, and only the youngest one joins in with him.

But the youngest one, through patience, through worry, through lack of luck, grows older and begins asking about when her turn will come in the ring game. In silence she achieves her turn.

The ring lies beside the lamp. Silence descends and ears are blinded. In silence the finger whose turn it is stealthily slips on the ring. The lamp is put out: darkness is all-embracing and in the darkness eyes are blinded.

No one remains who is noisy, who tells jokes, who sings, except for the blind young man.

Behind his noisy boisterousness there lurks a desire that almost makes him rebel against the silence and break it to pieces. He too wants to know, wants to know for certain. At first he used to tell himself that it was the nature of women to refuse to stay the same, sometimes radiantly fresh as drops of dew, at other times spent and stale as water in a puddle; sometimes as soft as the touch of rose petals, at other times rough as cactus plants. True, the ring was always there, but it was as if the finger wearing it were a different finger. He all but knows, while they all know for certain, so why does the silence not speak, why does it not utter?

One dinner-time the question sneaks in upon him unawares: What if the silence should utter? What if it should talk?

The mere posing of the question halted the morsel of food in his throat.

From that moment onwards he sought refuge in silence and refused to relinquish it.

In fact it was he who became frightened that sometime by ill chance the silence might be scratched; maybe a word might slip out and the whole edifice of silence come tumbling down—and woe to him should the edifice of silence tumble down!

The strange, different silence in which they all sought refuge.

Intentional silence this time, of which neither poverty nor ugliness nor patient waiting nor despair is the cause.

It is, though, the deepest form of silence, for it is silence agreed upon by the strongest form of agreement—that which is concluded without any agreement.

* * *

The widow and her three daughters.

And the house is a room.

And the new silence.

And the Koran reciter who brought that silence with him, and who with silence set about assuring for himself that she who shared his bed was always his wife, all proper and legitimate, the wearer of his ring. Sometimes she grows younger or older, she is softskinned or rough, slender or fat—it is solely her concern, the concern of those with sight, it is their responsibility alone in that they possess the boon of knowing things for certain; it is they who are capable of distinguishing while the most he can do is to doubt, a doubt which cannot become certainty without the boon of sight and so long as he is deprived of it just so long will he remain deprived of certainty, for he is blind and no moral responsibility attaches to a blind man?

Or does it?

NÂDER NÂDERPOUR (b. 1929)

Iran

One of Iran's most important contemporary poets, Nâder Nâderpour was born into an upper-class Iranian family that always encouraged his literary inclinations. He became involved in politics from an early age and received constant exposure to the West, first through his education in Paris and then through various travels, including to the United States. He now lives in exile in Paris.

40 Sohrāb and Simorgh

I was returning from your grave,
that pure earth which embraced you.
The sky was an azure elegy,
the plain had the color of sorrow and ashes,
in my mind you were an effervescent spring.   5
Underneath that dome which like a green head
had sprung from the middle of the mountain's depths,
on the red brick pavement of the courtyard
which burned continually
    from the fever of the desert sun,   10
water from a pitcher seemed
    to have spilled on the ground.

Translated by Michael Craig Hillman.

Simin Meykadeh. *Gregory No. 2.*
Undated.

Underneath that damp spot, you were hidden,
   your grave had no stone,
you were as nameless as desert flowers.
Ah, Sohrāb! At the beginning of your fruitful youth 15
who knew
that, several breaths after the celebration of spring,
you would bid the world a closed-lipped, eternal adieu?
Who knew 20
that after all that life-heartedness
you would sleep in the dark night
   of the earth's forgetfulness?
Ah, perhaps you yourself were aware of this bad dream.
When I came down from the mountain to the plain, 25
I stood and stared at the horizon.
Birds all with white wings
were writing on that blue slate:
Your pens, o learners of art,
are the stalks of our feathers, 30
our fallen feathers cause your flight.
From that apogee—the bird's path of flight—
to that perigee in the cruel darkness
   of which you slept,
I looked and I saw how wide lay the difference. 35

O, friend! You too were perplexed in this space:
The desire to fly stirred your pen;
you were the power to fly in the thoughts of humankind.

You traced your lineage to two fathers:
on earth, from Sohrāb;   40
in time, from Simorgh.
The accursed name of the son of the invincible Rostam[1]
knocked you to the ground and killed you, o friend,
despite the fact that from another direction
you were the descendant of the firmament's kings,   45
that is to say, of the tribe of the deathless,
that is to say, of the dynasty of dwellers of Qāf Mountain.

One night in a dream, I asked you ironically;
By the way, where is Sohrāb's house?
You pointed to an old poplar   50
and said smiling:
Before you get to the tree,
there is a tree-lined lane greener than a dream of God
and in it love is as blue as feathers of sincerity.
You go to the end of that lane which   55
emerges from behind adolescence.
In the intimate flow of space
you will hear rustling,
you will see a child
having climbed a tall pine tree   60
to pick a baby bird from the nest of light.
And you ask him:
By the way, where is Sohrāb's house?
He will tell you that
from the day of creation   65
I built a house on the other side of night.
And he can bring these signs to your memory
that one night as well, o friend,
you were a guest in this unknown house.
In reply, I told you reproachfully   70
that you came from heaven's eternal solitude
since in your sky-seeing eyes
the picture of the earth's countenance is dark,
that of the effect of time unclear.
You do not talk of the past, the future, or history.   75

---

1. Legendary Sassanian Persian king.

It is not without reason that your words
   are not addressed to me.
You looked at me and answered:
Do not talk to me of past and future—
I am ignorant of temporal divisions.
I have neither a beginning in birth
nor an end in life—
I come from creation's horizons,
I go to the remote climes of eternity.
But my words have always   85
addressed you since that very first day,
from that day when as sperm you were eloquent.

You were right and I knew
that in this startling century
you and I came into the world   90
after and before our turns.
Because of fate's heartlessness I am now upset.
Because of the unfaithfulness of the age
   you were fleeting.

You were going from this to that side of time;   95
your earthly existence
was a pause between two journeys.
It is for this reason that your city
   was other than Kāshān
even though you were of the people of Kāshān.   100

The word death had no dot in your view.
It is for this reason that in life's ledger
you did not consider death a point of conclusion.
It is for this reason that
   when bidding your father farewell   105
your optimistic eyes
saw the world's policemen as all poets,
and the poets you saw possessed
   of the patience of water
with the lightness of light,   110
all of them near the throne of God.
Your eyes had a heavenly vision
because in the religion of love
you were the messenger of gnosticism.

In your eyes, morning   115
was the smile of a cluster of grapes
   as dark as the vineyard.
Life was the first black figs

in the acrid mouth of summer.
And that train which came from the region of dawn   120
took the lily seeds and canary songs
to the shores of eternity.
The wave plundered disturbed false acacia petals
from the river's edge.
You listened to the swallow's minstrelsy   125
   in the heart of the ceiling
and you laughed.

You plucked God's unripe fruit
   with finger tips of desire
from young trees.   130
You saw death as a newborn cancer
at the bottom of flowing water.
Suddenly someone called from afar: Sohrāb!
You leaped up and cried: Where are my shoes:
Then you left the house   135
and with the speed of wind were under the rain.

My troubled dream ended
and in that clear noon
I was returning from your grave,
that pure earth which embraced you.   140
The sky was an azure elegy
the plain had the color of sadness and ashes.
For a few moments on the horizons of imagination
I saw you and I began to weep,
you saw me and you were smiling.   145

(Late Winter 1984, Paris)

DAN PAGIS (1930–1986)
Romania/Ukraine/Palestine

Like Paul Celan, the celebrated and tragic poet who wrote a selection, given in the
Modern Europe section, Dan Pagis was born in Radantz, Bukovina (Western
Ukraine and Northeastern Romania). Interned in a concentration camp in the
Ukraine, he escaped in 1944 and immigrated into Palestine in 1946. Pagis was a
pioneer scholar of medieval and Renaissance Hebrew literature. He also broke
new ground in revealing to Israeli readers the inner world of a Holocaust
survivor.

Footprints

From heaven to the heaven of heavens to the heaven of night.

—Yannai

Against my will
I was continued by this cloud: restless, gray,
trying to forget in the horizon, which always receded

Hail falling hard,
like the chatter of teeth: 5
refugee pellets pushing eagerly
into their own destruction

In another sector
clouds not yet identified.
Searchlights that set up   10
giant crosses of light
for the victim.
Unloading of cattle-cars.

Afterwards the letters fly up,
after the flying letters mud   15
hurries, snuffs, covers for a time

It's true, I was a mistake, I was forgotten
in the sealed car, my body tied up
in the sack of life

Here's the pocket where I found bread,   20
sweet crumbs, all from the same world

Maybe there's a window here—if you don't mind,
look near that body, maybe you can open up
a bit. That reminds me
(pardon me) of the joke about the two Jews   25
in the train, they were traveling to
Say something more; talk.
Can I pass from my body and onwards—
        *

From heaven to the heaven of heavens to the heaven of night
long convoys of smoke   30

The new seraphim who haven't yet understood,
prisoners of hope, astray in the empty freedom,
suspicious as always: how to exploit

Translated by Stephen Mitchell.

this sudden vacuum, maybe
the double citizenship will help,   35
the old passport,
maybe the cloud? what's new in the cloud,
here too of course
they take bribes. And between us: the biggest bills
are still nicely hidden away, sewn   40
between the soles—
but the shoes have been piled up below:
a great gaping heap

Convoys of smoke. Sometimes
someone breaks away,   45
recognizes me for some reason, calls my name.
And I put on a pleasant face, try to remember:
who else
who

Without any right to remember, I remember   50
a man screaming in a corner, bayonets rising
to fulfill their role
in him

Without any right to remember. What else
was there? Already I'm not afraid   55
that I might say

without any connection at all:
there was heart, blue from excessive winter,
and a lamp, round, blue, kind-hearted.
But the kerosene disappears with the blood, the flame flickers—   60

Yes, before I forget:
the rain stole across some border, so did I,
on forbidden escape-routes, with forbidden hope,
we both passed the mouth of the pits

Maybe now   65
I'm looking in that rain
for the scarlet thread

Where to begin?
I don't even know how to ask.
Too many tongues are mixed in my mouth. But   70
at the crossing of these winds,
very diligent, I immerse myself
in the laws of heavenly grammar; I am learning

the declensions and ascensions of
silence.

> *Who has given you the right to jest?*
> *What is above you you already know.*
> *You meant to ask about what is within you,*
> *what is abysmally through you.*
> *How is it that you did not see?*

But I didn't know I was alive.
From the heaven of heavens to the heaven of night
angels rushed, sometimes one of them
would look back, see me, shrug his shoulders,
continue from my body and onwards
    *

Frozen and burst, clotted,
scarred,
charred, choked.

If it has been ordained that I pull out of here,
I'll try to descend rung by rung,
I hold on to each one, carefully—
but there is no end to the ladder, and already
no time. All I can still do is fall
into the world

And on my way back
my eyes hint to me:
you have been, what more did you want to see?
Close us and see:
you are the darkness, you are the sign.

And my throat says to me:
if you are still alive, give me an opening, I
must praise.

And my upside-down head is faithful to me,
and my hands hold me tight:
I am falling   falling
from heaven to the heaven of heavens to the heaven of night
    *

Well then: a world.
The gray is reconciled by the blue.
In the gate of this cloud, already a turquoise
innocence, perhaps light green. Already sleep.
Heavens renew themselves, try out their wings, see me

and run for their lives. I no longer wonder.
The gate bursts open:
a lake
void   void   pure of reflections   115

Over there,
in that arched blue, on the edge of the air,
I once lived. My window was fragile.
Maybe what remained of me
were little gliders that hadn't grown up: 120
they still repeat themselves in still-clouds, glide,
slice the moment
    (not to remember now, not to remember)

And before I arrive
    (now to stretch out to the end, to stretch out)   125
already awake, spread to the tips of my wings,
against my will I feel that, very near,
inside, imprisoned by hopes, there flickers
this ball of the earth,
scarred, covered with footprints.   130

ADUNIS (b. 1930)

Syria/Lebanon

Adunis is the pen name of the Syrian poet, ʿAlî Ahmad Saʿîd, who studied and
lived extensively in Beirut. He now resides in Paris. Adunis is one of the most
influential, though controversial, living Arab poets, part of whose influence is due
to his authorship of critical works on Arabic poetics. Adunis founded and runs
the highly respected magazine *Mawâqif*. His work is known for its combination
of modernism and syncretism.

This Is My Name

I

Where does the master of sadness drouse?
How does he carry his eyes?

Translated by Adnan Haydar.

My sky is strangled,
My shoulders sag,
And earth is a helmet   5
Filled with sand and straw.
Distraught, I run
A swallow wraps me
I rise
(Its breast aflame)   10
I rise
Open a window—
Verdant fields.
I am the conqueror;
Earth is a game   15
A horse enters the clouds.
Trees in love come out,
A branch shakes me,
Water gushes out;
Gone is people's time,   20
I have begun.

My face is orbits;
In light there is a revolution;
In its flares
A village wakes me up;   25
Silence is shattered—
Hold me, O creator of exhaustion,
Give me swings,
Test me,
I am the rock,   30
The quest, and the question
In absence of feast and fireplace;
I am the ghost,
Standing guard in the chasm of the city
While people sleep.   35
I enter the snares of light,
Pure like violence
Shining like ostentation,
Light—
My limbs are lightning,   40
My limbs are sculptured winds;
My bones do not taste of a crown
Or of silver;
I am no king,
My blood is the exodus of the sky   45
My eyes are birds.

It is said your skin is thorn,
Then die.
Let my sky yellow in your skin.
It is said your skin is an eon
That settles in the depth of the dream.   50

Let the spears of eternal chaos be born;
Between us there is a chasm of collapse,
And my voice is the delirium of the conqueror
When he breaks the crutch of songs   55
And uproots the alphabet . . .
This is the age of death;
And yet
Each death subsumes an Arab death.
Days fall in its fields.   60
Like the stems of the aging cedars;
It is the swan song of a bird
In a blazing forest.

II

That's how I loved a tent
And made the sand in the lashes,   65
Trees that rain;
Made the desert a cloud.
I said: This broken urn
is a vanquished nation,
This space   70
A stye,
These eyes
Pits:
I said: madness—
A planet hiding in a tree.   75

I will see the raven's face
In the profile of my country,
And I will call
This book a shroud,
This city carrion;   80
And I will call
The trees of Damascus mourning birds,
(After such naming, a flower or a song
may be born)
And I will call   85
The moon of the desert a palm tree—
Perhaps the earth will wake up,
Become a child or a child's dream.

NATHAN ZACH (b. 1930)
Germany/Israel

Nathan Zach was born in Berlin, and moved to Palestine with his family at the age of 5. He has translated Frisch, Brecht, and Durrenmatt from German and has been widely influential as an editor and critic in re-evaluating contemporary Hebrew poetry. He is a poet, the author of *Against Parting* (1967), and the co-editor of *The Burning Bush: Poems from Modern Israel* (1977).

Harvest Month

Harvest month. A full moon
Rounds out the pain of earth.
A gleam of springtide floats
To the verge of shadow and falls.
Evening. Like evening now in a land   5
Breathing crows' poison, thinking of
Lovers on a night which darkness stars, raising a cypress
With strange longings. A man's song in his blood cells, the thought
He thinks in his image, waking with evening
To his name like death   10
Embedded in his body like
Heat in rumpled pillows.

Give Me What the Tree Has

Give me what the tree has and what it won't lose
and give me the power to lose what the tree has.
The faint tracings the wind makes in the darkness of a summer night
and the darkness which has neither trace nor shape.
Give me the shapes I once had and have no more   5
the strength to think that they've been lost. Give me
an eye stronger than what it sees and a hand
harder than what it seeks. Let me inherit
you without receiving anything that's not past
the moment I receive it. Give me the power to come near,   10
without fear, precisely to what I'm not meant
to hold dear, let me come near.

Translated by Warren Bargad and Stanley F. Chyet.

NAWAL AL-SA DAWI (b. 1931)
Egypt

Nawal al-Sa dawi is a physician and the author of important feminist studies as well as numerous short stories and novels. She has achieved visibility in the West mainly because of her outspoken views on such issues as women's sexuality and the practice of clitoridectomy. She received her medical degree in 1955 and has practiced in the areas of gynecology, family medicine, thoracic surgery, and psychiatry. The selection included here is the first chapter of *Memoirs of a Female Physician* [*Mudhakkirat tabiba*], a novel first published in 1965. It chronicles the development of a female physician, from her childhood and medical education through her adult years to the age of thirty. Although the life described in this book is not that of the author, the crossing of the genre of action with that of autobiography gives the text much of its immediacy.

from *Memoirs of a Female Physician* [*Mudhakkirat tabiba*]

Growing Up Female in Egypt

The struggle between me and my femininity began very early . . . before my femininity sprouted and before I knew anything about myself, my sex, or my origin . . . indeed, before I knew what hollow had enclosed me before I was tossed out into this wide world.

All that I knew at that time was that I was a girl, as I heard from my mother. A girl!

And there was only one meaning for the word "girl" in my mind . . . that I was not a boy . . . I was not like my brother . . .

My brother cuts his hair and leaves it free, he does not comb it, but as for me, my hair grows longer and longer. My mother combs it twice a day, chains it in braids, and imprisons its ends in ribbons . . .

My brother wakes up and leaves his bed as it is, but I, I have to make my bed and his as well.

My brother goes out in the street to play, without permission from my mother or my father, and returns at any time . . . but I, I do not go out without permission.

My brother takes a bigger piece of meat than mine, eats quickly, and drinks the soup with an audible sound, yet my mother does not say anything to him . . .

As for me . . .! I am a girl! I must watch my every movement . . . I must hide my desire for food and so I eat slowly and drink soup without a sound . . .

My brother plays . . . jumps . . . turns somersaults . . . but I, whenever I sit and

Translated by Fedwa Malti-Douglas.

Afaf Arafat. *Orange Picking*. 1975. Oil on canvas.

the dress rides up a centimeter on my thighs, my mother throws a sharp, wounding glance at me, and I hide my shame and impurity . . . .

Shame and impurity!

Everything in me is shame and impurity, though I am a child of nine years!

I felt sorry for myself.

I closed the door of my room on myself and sat crying alone . . .

The first tears of my life were not shed because I failed in school or because I broke something expensive . . . but because I was a girl!

I cried over my femininity before I knew it . . .

I opened my eyes on the world with enmity between myself and my nature.

I bounded down the steps three at a time to get to the street before I finished counting to ten . . .

My brother and his friends, sons and daughters of the neighbors, are waiting for me to play cops and robbers . . . I have received permission from my mother to go out . . . I love to play! I love to run as fast as I can . . . I feel an overflowing happiness whenever I move my head, my arms, or my legs in the air . . . and I run in great bounds, hindered only by the weight of my body, which the earth draws to itself . . .

Why did God not make me a bird so I could fly like a dove, but instead made me a girl? It seemed to me that God preferred birds to girls . . .

But my brother does not fly . . .

This fact comforted me a bit . . . I felt that boys, despite their wide freedom, were incapable, like me, of flying . . . and I began to always search for the areas of weakness in men to console me for the weakness that my femininity imposed on me.

I do not know what happened to me while I was jumping . . . I felt a violent shiver running through my body and a dizziness in my head . . . Then I saw something red!

"What is this?"

I was extremely alarmed, I stopped playing, mounted the stairs to my house, and locked myself in the bathroom to search secretly for the explanation of this grave event . . .

But I did not understand anything . . . And I thought that this might be a sudden illness that had stricken me . . . So I went in terror to ask my mother . . .

I saw my mother laughing happily . . . I was amazed that my mother could confront this hideous sickness with such a broad smile . . .

My mother saw my surprise and confusion and took me by the hand to my room, where she told me women's bloody story . . .

I stayed in my room for four days in a row, not having the courage to face my brother, or my father, or even the servant boy.

They have all certainly become aware of my shame and impurity . . . My mother has undoubtedly betrayed my new secret . . . I closed the door on myself to explain this strange phenomenon to myself . . . Was there no other way for girls to mature, other than this unclean way? Is it possible for a person to live for days under the control of his tyrannical, involuntary muscles? God undoubtedly hates girls, so he tarnished them all with this shame . . .

I felt that God had sided with boys in everything . . .

I got up from my bed, dragging my oppressive existence, and looked in the mirror . . . What is this?

Two small protrusions had grown on my chest!

Oh! If only I could die!

What is this strange body that surprises me every day with a new shame that increases my weakness and my withdrawal into myself?!

I wonder what else will grow on my body tomorrow? Or, I wonder through what other new symptom my tyrannical femininity will erupt!

I hated my femininity . . .

I felt that it was chains . . . chains of my own blood that bind me to the bed so that I am unable to run and jump . . . chains from within my own body . . . that shackle me in fetters of shame and disgrace so that I withdraw within myself, hiding my dejected existence . . .

I no longer ran . . . And I no longer played . . .

These two protrusions on my chest are getting bigger and they quiver whenever I walk . . .

I stood sadly with my tall, slender frame, hiding my chest with my arms, and watched, with sorrow, my brother and his companions playing . . .

I grew . . . I outgrew my brother, though he was older than I . . . I outgrew the other children, so I withdrew from them and sat by myself thinking . . .

My childhood came to an end . . . a short, breathlessly fast childhood . . . No sooner did I experience it then it slipped away and left me a mature woman's body carrying within it a ten-year-old child . . .

I saw the eyes and teeth of the doorkeeper shining in the middle of his coal-black face . . . He approached me while I was sitting by myself on his wooden bench, following my brother and his friends with my eyes, while they ran and jumped . . .

I felt the rough edge of his *galabeyya*[1] touching my leg and I smelled the strange odor of his garments, so I moved away with disgust; but he drew near me again and I tried to hide my fear from him by watching my brother and his companions playing, but I felt his rough, coarse fingers groping around my thighs and ascending under my clothing! . . .

I got up in terror and quickly ran away from him . . .

This repulsive black man is also staring at my femininity?!

And I ran until I entered the house . . . . My mother asked me the reason for my alarm . . . But I could not say anything to her . . . Perhaps I was afraid or ashamed, or both . . . Or perhaps I thought that she would reprimand me and that there would not be between us that affection that would make me tell her my secrets . . .

I no longer went out in the street . . . And I no longer sat on the wooden bench . . .

I fled from those strange, rough-voiced and mustached beings that they call men . . . and I created a special world for myself designed by my imagination . . . and I made myself the god of this world, and I made men into weak, ignorant creatures charged with serving me . . .

I sat in my world on my high throne arranging the dolls on the chairs and placing the boys on the ground, and I would tell stories to myself . . .

No one disturbed my life alone with my imagination and my dolls except my mother . . . with her many orders that never ended . . . the house and kitchen chores . . . the ugly, limited world of women, from which emanated the odor of garlic and onion.

No sooner would I escape to my small world than my mother would drag me to the kitchen, saying, "Your future lies in marriage . . . You have to learn to cook . . . Your future lies in marriage . . . Marriage! Marriage!"

That loathsome word that my mother repeated every day until I hated it . . . And I never heard it without imagining in front of me a man with a big belly inside of which was a table of food . . .

In my mind, I connected the smell of the kitchen with the smell of a husband . . .

And I hated the word "husband" and I hated the smell of food.

My old grandmother remained silent amidst the chatter and looked at my chest . . . . I saw her worn eyes contemplating the two new protruding buds and weighing them . . . . Then I saw her whispering something to my mother . . .

---

1. Galabeyya, overdress or robe.

I heard my mother say to me: "Wear the light-blue dress so that you can come in and greet the guest who is with your father in the salon . . ."

I smelled the odor of conspiracy in the air . . .

I used to greet most of my father's friends and serve them coffee . . . And sometimes I would sit with them and listen to my father while he told them about my success in school, and I would feel happy and sense that my father, by recognizing my intelligence, was freeing me from the gloomy world of women, from which emanated the odor of onion and marriage . . .

But why the light-blue dress? That new dress that I hate . . . On the front of it was a strange pleat that rested on my breasts and increased their prominence . . .

My mother looked at me searchingly . . . She said, "Where is the light-blue dress?"

I answered angrily: "I will never wear it!" . . . She saw the stirrings of rebellion in my eyes, looked at me sadly, and said, "Then smooth over your eyebrows . . ."

But I did not look at her . . . And before opening the salon door to enter, I ran my fingers through my eyebrows, mussing them up . . .

I greeted my father's friend and sat down . . . I saw a strange, frightful face with a relentless, scrutinizing gaze that resembled that of my grandmother . . .

My father said, "She is first in her class this year in junior high school . . ."

I did not see any expression of admiration in the man's eyes at these words . . . . But I saw his scrutinizing glances hover around my body and settle finally on my chest. So I stood up in terror and left the room, running as though a demon were chasing me . . .

My mother and my grandmother met me at the door with a passionate anxiety and said in one breath, "My God! . . . What have you done?"

I uttered a single shriek in their faces, ran to my room, and locked myself in . . . Then I went to the mirror to look at my chest . . .

I hated them! Those two protrusions! Those two small pieces of flesh that circumscribed my future! I wished that I could tear them from my chest with a sharp knife!

But I could not . . . I could only hide them . . . compress them with a thick corset to flatten them . . .

This long, heavy hair . . . that I carry on top of my head everywhere . . . It hampers me every morning, burdens me in the bath, and burns my neck in the summer . . .

Why is it not short, free, like my brother's hair? He does not carry it on top of his head, nor does it hamper him or burden him.

But my mother rules over my life, my future, and my body, even down to the locks of my hair . . .

Why . . .?

Because she gave birth to me? But what is her merit in having given birth to me? She pursued her normal life like any other woman, and then I came along without any act of will on her part in one of her moments of happiness . . . I came without her knowing me . . . without her choosing me . . . and without my choosing her . . .

I was imposed on her as a daughter and she was imposed on me as a mother . . .

Is it possible for someone to love a being who has been imposed on her? And, if my mother loved me despite herself, instinctively, then what virtue is there in this love? And is she thus superior to the cat who, at times, loves her kittens, but, at other times, devours them?

Is not my mother's harsh treatment more painful to me than if she were to devour me?!

And if my mother loved me with a true love whose aim was my happiness and not hers, then why are all her orders and desires in contradiction with my comfort and happiness?!

Can she love me while putting chains every day on my feet, on my hands, and around my neck?

For the first time in my life, I went out of the house without asking permission from my mother . . .

I walked in the street, and the challenge had given me a kind of power, but my heart was beating from fear . . .

I saw a sign that said "Ladies' Hairdresser". . .

I hesitated for an instant and then went in . . .

I watched the locks of my hair twisting between the blades of the sharp scissors and then falling to the ground . . .

Are these the locks that my mother spoke of as woman's crown and throne? Does woman's crown fall to the ground like this, in a single moment of decisiveness? I felt great contempt for women . . . I saw with my own eyes that they believed in worthless things of no value . . . And this contempt for them gave me a new strength that permitted me to go home with a firm step, and I was able to stand up before my mother with my short hair.

My mother uttered one loud scream and gave me a sharp slap on the face . . Then more and more slaps followed . . . while I remained standing . . .

As though I had become frozen . . . as though the challenge had made of me a force that nothing could shake . . . as though my victory over my mother had made of me a hard substance that did not feel the slaps . . .

My mother's hand would crash against my face and then fall back from it, as though it had crashed into granite . . .

How is that I did not cry? I was the one who would be made to cry by a single shout or a light slap.

But my tears did not fall . . . My eyes were wide open, looking into my mother's eyes boldly and strongly . . .

My mother continued to slap me . . . then she collapsed on the couch, sitting, repeating in a daze: "She has gone crazy!"

I pitied her when I saw her face sink in defeat and weakness. I felt a strong desire to hug her, kiss her, and cry between her arms . . . to say to her: "Reason does not lie in my always obeying you . . ."

But I pulled my eyes away from hers so that she would not be aware that I had witnessed her defeat, and I ran to my room . . .

I looked in the mirror and smiled over my short hair and the flash of victory in my eyes . . .

I knew for the first time in my life what victory was like . . . Fear leads only to defeat . . . and victory can only be won through courage.

The fear that I used to feel toward my mother left me . . . That great halo that made me dread her fell from her . . . I felt that she was an ordinary woman . . . And her slaps, which were the strongest things she possessed, I no longer feared . . . because they no longer hurt me . . .

I hated the house except for my study . . . I loved school except for the home economics class . . . I loved the days of the week except for Friday . . .

I participated in all the school activities . . . I joined the acting club, the speech club, the athletics club, the music club, and the drawing club . . . But this was not enough for me; instead, I got together with some of my girlfriends and I created a club called the Friendship Club . . . Why did I choose the word "friendship"? I did not know . . . but I felt that deep within me was a great longing for friendship . . . for a great big friendship that nothing could satisfy . . . for vast groups of people who would keep me company, speak to me, listen to me, and go off with me to heaven . . .

I did not believe that any achievement would suffice me . . . it would not extinguish the fire burning in my soul . . . I hated the repeated, monotonous lessons . . . I used to read the material once . . . once only . . . I felt that repetition would suffocate me . . . kill me . . . I wanted something new . . . new . . . always . . .

I was not aware of him when he entered my room and when he stood beside me while I sat reading my book until he said, "Wouldn't you like to relax a little?"

I had been reading for a long time and felt tired. So I smiled and said, "I would like to take a walk outside."

"Put on your coat and let's go."

I put on my coat quickly and ran to him . . . I was on the point of putting my hand in his so we could run together, as we used to do when we were children, but my eyes fastened on his and I suddenly remembered the long years I had not played and during which my feet had forgotten how to run and had grown accustomed to walking slowly like adults . . . So I put my hands in my coat and set out slowly beside him . . .

I hear him say, "You have grown."

"And you also."

"Do you remember the days when we used to play together?"

"You always used to beat me at running."

"And you always used to win at marbles."

We laughed a long time . . . A lot of air entered my chest and it invigorated me, making me feel that I was recovering some of my lost childhood . . .

He said, "I want to run a race with you."

I said confidently, "I will beat you."

He said, "Let's see . . .!"

We drew line of the ground . . . and stood next to each other . . . He yelled out: "One . . . two . . . three . . ." And we took off running the course . . .

I was about to reach the finish line before him, but he grabbed me by my clothing from behind so I stumbled and fell to the ground, and he fell next to me . . . I lifted my eyes to him, breathless, and I saw him gazing at me with a strange look that made the blood rise to my face . . . Then I saw his arm reach for my waist . . . and he whispered in my ear with a rough voice, "I will kiss you."

My whole being shook with a violent, strange shudder and I wished for an instant—it flashed through my senses like lightning—that his arm would reach further and embrace me strongly . . . strongly . . . But my strange secret desire, emerging from my hidden depths, changed into an intense anger . . .

But my anger increased his persistence, and he grabbed me with an iron hand . . . I do not know where the strength came from that made me push his arm far away from me, and lift up my hand and then let it fall on his face in one violent slap . . .

I tossed around my bed confused . . . Strange feelings flood my being . . . and many phantoms pass before me . . . But one vision lingers before my eyes . . .

My cousin lying on the ground next to me with his arms almost wrapped around my waist and his strange glances piercing my head . . .

I closed my eyes to float with my specter, who began to move his arm until it wound strongly around my waist . . . and he moved his lips until they touched mine and pressed upon them with force . . .

I hid my head under the covers . . .

Am I sincere?! This hand of mine that rose and slapped him is the very same hand that trembles in his imaginary hand?!

I wrapped the covers tightly around my head to shut out this strange illusion, but it slipped under the covers to me . . . So I put the pillow on my head and I pressed it with all my strength to smother that stubborn specter . . . and I kept pressing on my head until sleep smothered me . . .

I opened my eyes in the morning, when the sunlight had dispersed the darkness with all the ghosts that lurked in it . . .

I opened the window . . . The invigorating air entered my chest and it destroyed the remnants clinging to my vision from the delusions of the night . . .

I smiled scornfully at my inner self, this cowardly self that shakes out of fear of me when I am awake and then sneaks into my bed in the dark and fills the bed, surrounding me with specters and illusions!

I finished my secondary studies and I was first in my class . . . Then I sat thinking: What course do I follow?

What course can I follow since I hate my femininity, detest my nature, and disown my body?!

None but denial . . . challenge . . . resistance!

I will deny my femininity . . . I will challenge my nature . . . I will resist all the desires of my body . . .

I will prove to my mother and grandmother that I am not a woman like them . . . I will never spend my life in the kitchen peeling onions and garlic . . . I will never devote my life to a husband who eats and eats . . .

I will prove to my mother that I am smarter than my brother, than man, than all men . . . and that I am capable of doing all that my father does, and still more . . . .

[NOTE: I would like to thank Dr. Nawal al-Saᶜ dawi and Dr. Sherif Hetata for reading and commenting on the translation. Responsibility for the text and the title of the selection, however, is my own.]

SALÂH ᶜABD AL-SABÛR (1931–1981)
Egypt

The Egyptian Salâh ᶜAbd al-Sabûr was one of the Arab world's leading poets and dramatists. Educated in Cairo, ᶜAbd al-Sabûr edited *al-Kâtib,* an important literary journal. He was Undersecretary of State for Culture and Director of the National Library and General Egyptian Book Organization at the time of his death. Like Adunis (and some other influential Arab poets), ᶜAbd al-Sabûr also wrote critical works.

Dreams of the Ancient Knight

If only we were the two boughs of a tree
The sun would nourish our roots together
And together, dawn would water us with dew
Then we would be tinted with blossoming verdure
When we grew long we would link our arms   5
In the spring don many-hued garments
In the autumn cast them off, baring our bodies
And bathe in the winter, warmed by our affection

If only we were two waves on the seashore
Pure of sand and shell   10
Crowned with an ingot of light and foam
Out reins grasped by the current
Driving us on together, from cradle to grave
With dancing, humming gait
A gentle cloud imbibes us   15

Translated by Mounah A. Khouri and Hamid Algar.

And melts in the breath of a sweet and tender sun
Then again we are twin waves
Our reins grasped by the current
In an eternal cycle
From sea to sky   20
From sky to sea.

If only we were two neighboring stars
Rising from the same lofty point
Setting behind the same cloud
Shedding light on solitary lovers and wayfarers   25
To the lands of love and passion
And on the wakeful sorrowers holding fast to their beloved's pact
When fortune sets, o my love
Decline will overtake us
Our long passion will be extinguished with us   30
God casting us along the stream-beds of paradise like two pearls among pebbles
An angel might see us as he trod his path
And stoop down, his eye caught by our purity
Lift us up and rub us on his cloak, amazed at our luster
And then cast us back into the limpid crossroads   35

If only we were the wings of a gentle, tender
Seagull, never leaving the strait
Hovering over the ship's wake
Giving the sailor tidings of arrival
Awakening desire for loved ones and for home   40
His beak nourished by the breeze
Drinking from the perspiration of the clouds

Whenever the marine night descends it encloses us together . . . . together
Then the gull sleeps on the sail of an ancient ship
In company with the sailors stricken by homesickness   45
They see his fear and confusion
From the singing and the poetry
And the blowing on the horn

If only we
If only   50
If only we, and o the cruelty of "if only"
O my enchantress if we prefaced our words with wishes
But we
O the cruelty of "but we"
For it proclaims in its intricate twisting letters   55
That we reject the traces time has left upon our souls
We wish we could remove them
We wish we could forget them
We wish we could return them to the womb of life

But I o my enchantress am a crippled experimenter   60
On the edge of a world heaving with confusion and decay
A world devoid of beauty
Which granted me darkness and gloom
When dropped onto it at the dawn of childhood

I was once in bygone days   65
O my enchantress a steadfast warrior, a heroic knight
Before my heart was trodden underfoot
Before sun and frost lashed me
That you might humble my lofty splendor
I used to dwell in unending spring—what a spring   70

When I wept my weeping would convulse me
And I would wish, on hearing the laments
Of the wretched and the weak
That I could nourish them from my grieving heart
I would wish seeing the miserable and perplexed   75
Wandering in the gloom
That their perdition could set me aflame, that I could shed light
I was carefree when I laughed as if a brook
Whose pure face shows an image of the stars

What befell the heroic knight?   80
His heart was plucked out and he took to flight dropping the reins
The vanguards of his dreams were shattered
O you who guide my steps on the path of guileless tears
O you who guide my steps on the path of guileless laughter
Peace be upon you   85
Peace be upon you
I offer you the experience and skill bestowed on me by the world
In return for a single day of innocence
No it is only you who can make me again the ancient knight
Without any payment   90
Without any reckoning of profit and loss

I see you serene my love as if you had matured apart from time
Whenever we meet my love I know we will part
And I will remain standing in a void
Would that your tender love had not returned me to chastity   95
Then we would know love like the two branches of a tree
Two neighboring stars

Twin waves
The wings of a gentle sea-gull
Then we would not part   100
A road brings us together again
A road brings us together again

SEVIM BURAK (1931–1983)
Turkey

Sevim Burak—a novelist, short-story writer, and playwright—was born in Istanbul and studied in a German high school. Her life involved much traveling and she lived extensively in Africa. Her writings include *The African Dance,* a collection of short stories, and *His Master's Voice,* a play.

The Window

For the last two days I've been waiting for the woman who lives across the street to commit suicide.

> She may not do it;
> I don't know what she has on her mind.
> She may have a secret design.
> It's been exactly two days.
> I keep going from one window to the other—if I could stop my window-watching I could be free.
> I keep going from one window to the other.

Rabab Nim. Untitled. 1985. Oil on wood.

Translated by Nilüfer Miyanoğlu Reddy.

The woman is walking on that high terrace with quick, slippery steps.

She's going to the dangerous edges of the terrace.

She's climbing over the parapet and making the clothesline tighter.

I can't be sure. I have an idea that she deliberately started playing this game because she knows that I'm spying on her from behind the window.

She keeps leaning from her waist, down toward Streetcar Avenue; she looks down, then shakes her head as if she's saying "no."

Because of this I suppose that she doesn't want to die.

I still can't be sure.

I haven't entertained any hopes for years.

As though I'm about to start a new diary, I raise my head off and on and I look at the woman.

And she is looking at me.

She understands what I'm thinking about.

Because of this she's sore at me.

She's very worried.

Neither of us is feeling good.

She's waiting for the smallest sign from me to jump down; she'll do anything for me, as if I were the one who brought her into this world and she would like me to see her die. But I'm not controlling anything from behind my curtain with the red roses—I don't feel like meddling in her affairs.

I don't want

    to save her or

      to stop her . . .

Whatever I can see—I can grab—FROM HER LIFE is enough for me; I make a tiny hole in the middle of my curtain—so she can't see me—and I observe HER. One of her feet is completely covered with a white bandage; I think about how the bandage would suddenly become red. I think about how her body would fall onto Streetcar Avenue with a big thud and cover the whole avenue, stopping the passers-by. In a magical couple of seconds her body would become sacred and it would grow bigger and everything would end happily.

She is thinking of the same things.

She looks at Streetcar Avenue and smiles.

The smile becomes softer around her mouth and expands; this is the first time I have seen an inward smile grow so big. I imagine that one could only smile like this when one is thinking about one's own death—the woman is showing her love for her own dead body lying on the ground. I have no objection to her jumping off the terrace or out the window. On the contrary: to me this seems like reasonable behavior. Soon her body would be broken into pieces; she would tell her friends: "See, you didn't know me . . ."; she would bare her secret, covered parts to those gathered around to watch her die, and she would make the parts of her face, hands and knees quiver with passion. Everybody would run to see this uncovering—they would only be able to take it for a few minutes but they would never forget it . . .

I look at the empty buses rolling down Streetcar Avenue in a different way; I have a notion that there must be a reason for their traveling without passengers.

Then I imagine putting some of my acquaintances in front of the buses one by one; then I push a man I don't know at all in front of a bus—he's wearing a long black coat all the way down to his ankles—his height keeps changing; then I push a woman just out of the hairdresser's with the head of a sheep; then I push a lot of people with goats', cows' and foxes' heads in front of the buses; they are bewildered, they act in an unnatural manner; obviously they had not thought that their ends would be like this . . . they become thousands of feet and run away. Cats' paws, rabbits' feet, roosters' claws—my own feet . . .

I finally see the white-bandaged leg, covered up to the knee. I suspect that the bandage will be removed, and underneath I'll see some truth that I've been searching for for a long time. My whole being is shaken by the quivering pink flesh of a wound not yet healed and bones not yet set. I think about how all the bones in each part of my own body support me and keep me in good shape.

The woman starts walking with the bandaged leg on the wall of the terrace—the distance from where she started her first steps to the end of the wall seems very long to me. I think about how something always gets longer and slows down before its demise.

She lifts one of her feet

A stone will fall down

It has nothing to do with the woman

The woman will throw herself down as though she's doing something unimportant.

She totters, standing on one foot

At that moment, an unexpected person, a man carrying a gigantic tumor, appears at the bottom of the street; he comes running and enters the scene at the last minute. I say that's all for today, for tomorrow there will be others—important and unfamiliar ones.

The woman opens her arms as if she wants to fly.

I can see her left eye.

As well as I can see from the hole in the curtain, she seems to be saying, "How about you doing this job?" She gives me a hostile look. What if she gives up the idea of jumping? What if all these things I have planned turn out to be dreams? Then I would lose my peace of mind, I would be devastated.

The woman looks haughtily at my window; she's saying, "I'm here."

She hops on her bandaged leg.

She goes backward and runs like a butting ram toward my window; she makes fun of me; I wish the wall under her feet would collapse. But the wall is strong and holds onto the woman's feet.

Nevertheless she should have died.

I knew where and when this should happen better than she does.

I come out from behind the curtain and call her:

"Do it, jump," I say.

I also motion with my hand.

She rocks her body without leaving her place.

Her heavy body is divided in two by the thin line of the wall.

Just then someone opens a window in one of the apartments below; someone else cries "Hermine."

There are intermittent sounds of kicking.

There are crying sounds reaching upstairs.

The sounds of imploring are heard.

The sounds come up to the terrace.

I see the woman for the first time—

Without lies

Without a curtain

She appears in front of the window like a puppet moved by strings.

Her mouth is distorted; she's saying things that are incomprehensible and she wants me to help her. Two fat women are hanging onto her arms; she's not able to free herself from them.

She's defeated and defenseless.

They shake her and slap her to make her talk.

She keeps looking at me.

What does she want from me?

They take her away like that.

They will make her scream again.

In the dining room

In the kitchen

In the storage room

Tomorrow she will go up to the terrace to hang the laundry.

I will see her face again

Her freckled arms

Her laundry

Her clotheslines

She will look at my window and say, "I've become wiser."

For days I've been choosing the most beautiful death for her among the innumerable deaths that occupy my mind.

I've been looking at

the crowds

the bell towers

the streets

and I'm feeling moved

I exaggerate my loneliness in front of the window because of her . . . .

I'VE HAD NO HOPES WHATSOEVER

I'VE TRIED EVERYTHING FOR MYSELF

I keep holding the edge of the curtain and putting it behind the armchair but it doesn't stay there and goes back and closes. I again put it behind the armchair and wait for it to go back to its place. I GET USED TO IT. I keep saying PERHAPS THIS IS THE MEANING OF EVERYTHING. For the first time I am afraid of disappointment and of being defeated. Then I see no REASON why I should run away from it. IT HAS TO HAPPEN . . . I come near the edge of the curtain.

The hand of the curtain's edge touches my hand.

I turn my eyes away from the curtain.

curtains turn purple. My sleepless bed, my heavy wardrobe, my...
stuck, motionless. WHAT SHALL I DO NOW?
I SHOULD HIDE MY HAND SOME PLACE
I hang around my feelings, fine as hair, I'm like a spider, face to face with the
flowers of death. IT'S GETTING DARK.
WHAT SHALL I DO NOW?
Should I bring the salt shaker in here?
The table is not going to be set—it is useless
It is O.K. if I don't bring it in
Maybe it is not O.K.
I don't know
I recollect some thoughts
I spread over the house like a huge stain
The buses travel from Galatasaray to Tünel
Purple-ribboned fragments of life come out of the flower market.
The roses of death
The white lilies
The orphan girl students in 1890 in their Sainte Pulchérie uniforms and
ridiculous hats . . .
At the twilight hour posters with strange smiles appear in the street of death;
the ever-growing crowd advances with a strange rustling sound. THE MAN IN
THE GREEN HAT IS AMONG THEM.
He keeps taking his hat off and waving it
He says come down and join us
I lean toward the darkness, bending all the way from my waist; I start to fall
with a great noise and I crash into a thousand pieces.

ALIFA RIFAT (b. 1930)

Egypt

Alifa Rifat, primarily a short-story writer, has remained an elusive figure on the
Arabic literary scene. She is well educated in the Islamic religious tradition and
her fiction shows great concern with sexuality and women's role.

My World of the Unknown

There are many mysteries in life, unseen powers in the universe, worlds other than
our own, hidden links and radiations that draw creatures together and whose

Translated by Denys Johnson-Davies.

A HOUSE

AN AVENUE

A CLOUD

A MAN IN A GREEN HAT

The man in the green hat walks on the avenue in the same direction as the
cloud. I say this is the man who ran away. THIS IS THE MAN WHO RAN AWAY
from deep sleep, rusty staircases, windows and doorbells.

I LOOK AT THE HOUSE

I SAY THIS IS THE HOUSE

THIS IS THE ROOM

THIS IS THE HOUSE WHERE THE WOMAN HANGED HERSELF

THIS IS THE CHAIR

THIS IS THE TABLE

THIS IS THE AVENUE

THESE ARE THE CHILDREN

THE SAME CHILDREN

Then I look at my diary and think all these are lies; that I drew THE MAN IN
THE GREEN HAT myself to deceive myself; that THE MAN IN THE GREEN HAT
knows this and passes by my window to deceive me

I THINK THAT

THE CLOUD IS NOT THE CLOUD

THE AVENUE IS NOT THE AVENUE

THE HOUSE IS NOT THE HOUSE

AND THE MAN IN THE GREEN HAT

IS NOT THE MAN IN THE GREEN HAT

FROM THE DIARY

I cross out

The cloud

The house

The avenue

The man in the green hat

I think I can always play a game like this all by myself and spoil it; The Man
in The Green Hat too can play this game; the woman across the street and all sorts
of people can play and spoil all sorts of games.

The woman's mouth is distorted

She looks at me with empty and impassive eyes.

She says, "Help me."

I don't know how to perform certain acts

It's getting dark

I'm a little fearful in the shadow of death. The roses on the

effect is interacting. They may merge or be incompatible, and perhaps the day will come when science will find a method for connecting up these worlds in the same way as it has made it possible to voyage to other planets. Who knows?

Yet one of these other worlds I have explored; I have lived in it and been linked with its creatures through the bond of love. I used to pass with amazing speed between this tangible world of ours and another invisible earth, mixing in the two worlds on one and the same day, as though living it twice over.

When entering into the world of my love, and being summoned and yielding to its call, no one around me would be aware of what was happening to me. All that occurred was that I would be overcome by something resembling a state of languor and would go off into a semi-sleep. Nothing about me would change except that I would become very silent and withdrawn, though I am normally a person who is talkative and eager to go out into the world of people. I would yearn to be on my own, would long for the moment of surrender as I prepared myself for answering the call.

Love had its beginning when an order came through for my husband to be transferred to a quiet country town and, being too busy with his work, delegated to me the task of going to this town to choose suitable accommodation prior to his taking up the new appointment. He cabled one of his subordinates named Kamil and asked him to meet me at the station and to assist me.

I took the early morning train. The images of a dream I had had that night came to me as I looked out at the vast fields and gauged the distances between the towns through which the train passed and reckoned how far it was between the new town in which we were fated to live and beloved Cairo.

The images of the dream kept reappearing to me, forcing themselves upon my mind: images of a small white house surrounded by a garden with bushes bearing yellow flowers, a house lying on the edge of a broad canal in which were swans and tall sailing boats. I kept on wondering at my dream and trying to analyse it. Perhaps it was some secret wish I had had, or maybe the echo of some image that my unconscious had stored up and was chewing over.

As the train arrived at its destination, I awoke from my thoughts. I found Kamil awaiting me. We set out in his car, passing through the local *souk*. I gazed at the mounds of fruit with delight, chatting away happily with Kamil. When we emerged from the *souk* we found ourselves on the bank of the Mansoura canal, a canal on which swans swam and sailing boats moved to and fro. I kept staring at them with uneasy longing. Kamil directed the driver to the residential buildings the governorate had put up for housing government employees. While gazing at the opposite bank a large boat with a great fluttering sail glided past. Behind it could be seen a white house that had a garden with trees with yellow flowers and that lay on its own amidst vast fields. I shouted out in confusion, overcome by the feeling that I had been here before.

"Go to that house," I called to the driver. Kamil leapt up objecting vehemently: "No, no,—no one lives in that house. The best thing is to go to the employees' buildings."

I shouted insistently, like someone hypnotized: "I must have a look at that house." "All right," he said. "You won't like it, though—it's old and needs repairing." Giving in to my wish, he ordered the driver to make his way there.

At the garden door we found a young woman, spare and of fair complexion. A fat child with ragged clothes encircled her neck with his burly legs. In a strange silence, she stood as though nailed to the ground, barring the door with her hands and looking at us with doltish enquiry.

I took a sweet from my bag and handed it to the boy. He snatched it eagerly, tightening his grip in her neck with his podgy, mud-bespattered feet so that her face became flushed from his high-spirited embrace. A half-smile showed on her tightly-closed lips. Taking courage, I addressed her in a friendly tone: "I'd like to see over this house." She braced her hands resolutely against the door. "No," she said quite simply. I turned helplessly to Kamil, who went up to her and pushed her violently in the chest so that she staggered back. "Don't you realize," he shouted at her, "that this is the director's wife? Off with you!"

Lowering her head so that the child all but slipped from her, she walked off dejectedly to the canal bank where she lay down on the ground, put the child on her lap, and rested her head in her hands in silent submission.

Moved by pity, I remonstrated: "There's no reason to be so rough, Mr. Kamil. Who is the woman?" "Some mad woman," he said with a shrug of his shoulders, "who's a stranger to the town. Out of kindness the owner of this house put her in charge of it until someone should come along to live in it."

With increased interest I said: "Will he be asking a high rent for it?" "Not at all," he said with an enigmatic smile. "He'd welcome anyone taking it over. There are no restrictions and the rent is modest—no more than four pounds."

I was beside myself with joy. Who in these days can find somewhere to live for such an amount? I rushed through the door into the house with Kamil behind me and went over the rooms: five spacious rooms with wooden floors, with a pleasant hall, modern lavatory, and a beautifully roomy kitchen with a large verandah overlooking vast pistachio-green fields of generously watered rice. A breeze, limpid and cool, blew, playing with the tips of the crop and making the delicate leaves move in continuous dancing waves.

I went back to the first room with its spacious balcony overlooking the road and revealing the other bank of the canal where, along its strand, extended the houses of the town. Kamil pointed out to me a building facing the house on the other side. "That's where we work," he said, "and behind it is where the children's schools are."

"Thanks be to God," I said joyfully. "It means that everything is within easy reach of this house—and the souk's nearby too." "Yes," he said, "and the fishermen will knock at your door to show you the fresh fish they've caught in their nets. But the house needs painting and re-doing, also there are all sorts of rumours about it—the people around here believe in djinn and spirits."

"This house is going to be my home," I said with determination. "Its low rent will make up for whatever we may have to spend on re-doing it. You'll see what this house will look like when I get the garden arranged. As for the story about djinn and spirits, just leave them to us—we're more spirited than them."

We laughed at my joke as we left the house. On my way to the station we agreed about the repairs that needed doing to the house. Directly I reached Cairo I cabled my husband to send the furniture from the town we had been living in, specifying a suitable date to fit in with the completion of the repairs and the house being ready for occupation.

On the date fixed I once again set off and found that all my wishes had been carried out and that the house was pleasantly spruce with its rooms painted a cheerful orange tinge, the floors well polished and the garden tidied up and made into small flowerbeds.

I took possession of the keys and Kamil went off to attend to his business, having put a chair on the front balcony for me to sit on while I awaited the arrival of the furniture van. I stretched out contentedly in the chair and gazed at the two banks with their towering trees like two rows of guards between which passed the boats with their lofty sails, while around them glided a male swan heading a flotilla of females. Halfway across the canal he turned and flirted with them, one after the other, like a sultan amidst his harem.

Relaxed, I closed my eyes. I projected myself into the future and pictured to myself the enjoyment I would have in this house after it had been put in order and the garden fixed up. I awoke to the touch of clammy fingers shaking me by the shoulders.

I started and found myself staring at the fair-complexioned woman with her child squatting on her shoulders as she stood erect in front of me staring at me in silence. "What do you want?" I said to her sharply. "How did you get in?" "I got in with this," she said simply, revealing a key between her fingers.

I snatched the key from her hand as I loudly rebuked her: "Give it here. We have rented the house and you have no right to come into it like this." "I have a lot of other keys," she answered briefly. "And what," I said to her, "do you want of this house?" "I want to stay on in it and for you to go," she said. I laughed in amazement at her words as I asked myself: Is she really mad? Finally I said impatiently: "Listen here, I'm not leaving here and you're not entering this house unless I wish it. My husband is coming with the children, and the furniture is on the way. He'll be arriving in a little while and we'll be living here for such period of time as my husband is required to work in this town."

She looked at me in a daze. For a long time she was silent, then she said: "All right, your husband will stay with me and you can go." Despite my utter astonishment I felt pity for her. "I'll allow you to stay on with us for the little boy's sake," I said to her gently, "until you find yourself another place. If you'd like to help me with the housework I'll pay you what you ask."

Shaking her head, she said with strange emphasis: "I'm not a servant. I'm Aneesa." "You're not staying here," I said to her coldly, rising to my feet. Collecting all my courage and emulating Kamil's determination when he rebuked her, I began pushing her in the chest as I caught hold of the young boy's hand. "Get out of here and don't come near this house," I shouted at her. "Let me have all the keys. I'll not let go of your child till you've given them all to me."

With a set face that did not flicker she put her hand to her bosom and took out a ring on which were several keys, which she dropped into my hand. I released my grip on the young boy. Supporting him on her shoulders, she started to leave. Regretting my harshness, I took out several piastres from my bag and placed them in the boy's hand. With the same silence and stiffness she wrested the piastres from the boy's hand and gave them back to me. Then she went straight out. Bolting the door this time, I sat down, tense and upset, to wait.

My husband arrived, then the furniture, and for several days I occupied myself with putting the house in order. My husband was busy with his work and the children occupied themselves with making new friends and I completely forgot about Aneesa, that is until my husband returned one night wringing his hands with fury: "This woman Aneesa, can you imagine that since we came to live in this house she's been hanging around it every night. Tonight she was so crazy she blocked my way and suggested I should send you off so that she might live with me. The woman's gone completely off her head about this house and I'm afraid she might do something to the children or assault you."

Joking with him and masking the jealousy that raged within me, I said: "And what is there for you to get angry about? She's a fair and attractive enough woman—a blessing brought to your very doorstep!" With a sneer he took up the telephone, muttering: "May God look after her!"

He contacted the police and asked them to come and take her away. When I heard the sound of the police van coming I ran to the window and saw them taking her off. The poor woman did not resist, did not object, but submitted with a gentle sadness that as usual with her aroused one's pity. Yet, when she saw me standing in tears and watching her, she turned to me and, pointing to the wall of the house, called out: "I'll leave her to you." "Who?" I shouted. "Who, Aneesa?" Once again pointing at the bottom of the house, she said: "Her."

The van took her off and I spent a sleepless night. No sooner did day come than I hurried to the garden to examine my plants and to walk round the house and carefully inspect its walls. All I found were some cracks, the house being old, and I laughed at the frivolous thought that came to me: Could, for example, there be jewels buried here, as told in fairy tales?

Who could "she" be? What was the secret of this house? Who was Aneesa and was she really mad? Where were she and her son living? So great did my concern for Aneesa become that I began pressing my husband with questions until he brought me news of her. The police had learnt that she was the wife of a well-to-do teacher living in a nearby town. One night he had caught her in an act of infidelity, and in fear she had fled with her son and had settled here, no one knowing why she had betaken herself to this particular house. However, the owner of the house had been good enough to allow her to put up in it until someone should come to live in it, while some kind person had intervened on her behalf to have her name included among those receiving monthly allowances from the Ministry of Social Affairs. There were many rumours that cast doubt upon her conduct: people passing by her house at night would hear her conversing with unknown persons. Her madness took the form of a predilection for silence and isolation from people during the daytime as she wandered about in a dream world. After the police had persuaded them to take her in to safeguard the good repute of her family, she was returned to her relatives.

The days passed and the story of Aneesa was lost in oblivion. Winter came and with it heavy downpours of rain. The vegetation in my garden flourished though the castor-oil plants withered and their yellow flowers fell. I came to find pleasure in sitting out on the kitchen balcony looking at my flowers and vegetables and enjoying the belts of sunbeams that lay between the clouds and lavished my balcony with warmth and light.

One sunny morning my attention was drawn to the limb of a nearby tree whose branches curved up gracefully despite its having dried up and its dark bark being cracked. My gaze was attracted by something twisting and turning along the tip of a branch: bands of yellow and others of red, intermingled with bands of black, were creeping forward. It was a long, smooth tube, at its end a small striped head with two bright, wary eyes.

The snake curled round on itself in spiral rings, then tautened its body and moved forward. The sight gripped me; I felt terror turning my blood cold and freezing my limbs.

My senses were numbed, my soul intoxicated with a strange elation at the exciting beauty of the snake. I was rooted to the spot, wavering between two thoughts that contended in my mind at one and the same time: should I snatch up some implement from the kitchen and kill the snake, or should I enjoy the rare moment of beauty that had been afforded me?

As though the snake had read what was passing through my mind, it raised its head, tilting it to right and left in thrilling coquetry. Then, by means of two tiny fangs like pearls, and a golden tongue like a twig of *arak* wood, it smiled at me and fastened its eyes on mine in one fleeting, commanding glance. The thought of killing left me. I felt a current, a radiation from its eyes that penetrated to my heart ordering me to stay where I was. A warning against continuing to sit out there in front of it surged inside me, but my attraction to it paralysed my limbs and I did not move. I kept on watching it, utterly entranced and captivated. Like a bashful virgin being lavished with compliments, it tried to conceal its pride in its beauty, and, having made certain of captivating its lover, the snake coyly twisted round and gently, gracefully glided away until swallowed up by a crack in the wall. Could the snake be the "she" that Aneesa had referred to on the day of her departure?

At last I rose from my place, overwhelmed by the feeling that I was on the brink of a new world, a new destiny, or rather, if you wish, the threshold of a new love. I threw myself onto the bed in a dreamlike state, unaware of the passage of time. No sooner, though, did I hear my husband's voice and the children with their clatter as they returned at noon than I regained my sense of being a human being, wary and frightened about itself, determined about the existence and continuance of its species. Without intending to I called out: "A snake—there's a snake in the house."

My husband took up the telephone and some men came and searched the house. I pointed out to them the crack into which the snake had disappeared, though racked with a feeling of remorse at being guilty of betrayal. For here I was denouncing the beloved, inviting people against it after it had felt safe with me.

The men found no trace of the snake. They burned some wormwood and fumigated the hole but without result. Then my husband summoned Sheikh

Farid, Sheikh of the Rifa'iyya order in the town, who went on chanting verses from the Qur'an as he tapped the ground with his stick. He then asked to speak to me alone and said:

"Madam, the sovereign of the house has sought you out and what you saw is no snake, rather it is one of the monarchs of the earth—may God make your words pleasant to them—who has appeared to you in the form of a snake. Here in this house there are many holes of snakes, but they are of the non-poisonous kind. They inhabit houses and go and come as they please. What you saw, though, is something else."

"I don't believe a word of it," I said, stupefied. "This is nonsense. I know that the djinn[1] are creatures that actually exist, but they are not in touch with our world, there is no contact between them and the world of humans."

With an enigmatic smile he said: "My child, the Prophet went out to them and read the Qur'an to them in their country. Some of them are virtuous and some of them are Muslims, and how do you know there is no contact between us and them? Let your prayer be 'O Lord, increase me in knowledge.' and do not be nervous. Your purity of spirit, your translucence of soul have opened to you doors that will take you to other worlds known only to their Creator. Do not be afraid. Even if you should find her one night sleeping in your bed, do not be alarmed but talk to her with all politeness and friendliness."

"That's enough of all that, Sheikh Farid. Thank you," I said, alarmed, and he left us.

We went on discussing the matter. "Let's be practical," suggested my husband, "and stop all the cracks at the bottom of the outside walls and put wire-mesh over the windows, also paint wormwood all round the garden fence."

We set about putting into effect what we had agreed. I, though, no longer dared to go out onto the balconies. I neglected my garden and stopped wandering about in it. Generally I would spend my free time in bed. I changed to being someone who liked to sit around lazily and was disinclined to mix with people; those diversions and recreations that previously used to tempt me no longer gave me any pleasure. All I wanted was to stretch myself out and drowse. In bewilderment I asked myself: Could it be that I was in love? But how could I love a snake? Or could she really be one of the daughters of the monarchs of the djinn? I would awake from my musings to find that I had been wandering in my thoughts and recalling to mind how magnificent she was. And what is the secret of her beauty? I would ask myself. Was it that I was fascinated by her multi-coloured, supple body? Or was it that I had been dazzled by that intelligent, commanding way she had of looking at me? Or could it be the sleek way she had of gliding along, so excitingly dangerous, that had captivated me?

Excitingly dangerous! No doubt it was this excitement that had stirred my feelings and awakened my love, for did they not make films to excite and frighten? There was no doubt but that the secret of my passion for her, my preoccupation

---

1. In Moslem legend, a spirit capable of assuming human or animal form and exercising supernatural influence.

with her, was due to the excitement that had aroused, through intense fear, desire within myself; an excitement that was sufficiently strong to drive the blood hotly through my veins whenever the memory of her came to me, thrusting the blood in bursts that made my heart beat wildly, my limbs limp. And so, throwing myself down in a pleasurable state of torpor, my craving for her would be awakened and I would wish for her coil-like touch, her graceful gliding motion.

And yet I fell to wondering how union could come about, how craving be quenched, the delights of the body be realized, between a woman and a snake. And did she, I wondered, love me and want me as I loved her? An idea would obtrude itself upon me sometimes: did Cleopatra, the very legend of love, have sexual intercourse with her serpent after having given up sleeping with men, having wearied of amorous adventures with them so that her sated instincts were no longer moved other than by the excitement of fear, her senses no longer aroused other than by bites from a snake? And the last of her lovers had been a viper that had destroyed her.

I came to live in a state of continuous torment, for a strange feeling of longing scorched my body and rent my senses, while my circumstances obliged me to carry out the duties and responsibilities that had been placed on me as the wife of a man who occupied an important position in the small town, he and his family being objects of attention and his house a Kaaba for those seeking favours; also as a mother who must look after her children and concern herself with every detail of their lives so as to exercise control over them; there was also the house and its chores, this house that was inhabited by the mysterious lover who lived in a world other than mine. How, I wondered, was union between us to be achieved? Was wishing for this love a sin or was there nothing to reproach myself about?

And as my self-questioning increased so did my yearning, my curiosity, my desire. Was the snake from the world of reptiles or from the djinn? When would the meeting be? Was she, I wondered, aware of me and would she return out of pity for my consuming passion?

One stormy morning with the rain pouring down so hard that I could hear the drops rattling on the window pane, I lit the stove and lay down in bed between the covers seeking refuge from an agonizing trembling that racked my yearning body which, ablaze with unquenchable desire, called out for relief.

I heard a faint rustling sound coming from the corner of the wall right beside my bed. I looked down and kept my eyes fixed on one of the holes in the wall, which I found was slowly, very slowly, expanding. Closing my eyes, my heart raced with joy and my body throbbed with mounting desire as there dawned in me the hope of an encounter. I lay back in submission to what was to be. No longer did I care whether love was coming from the world of reptiles or from that of the djinn, sovereigns of the world. Even were this love to mean my destruction, my desire for it was greater.

I heard a hissing noise that drew nearer, then it changed to a gentle whispering in my ear, calling to me: "I am love, O enchantress. I showed you my home in your sleep; I called to you to my kingdom when your soul was dozing on the horizon of dreams, so come, my sweet beloved, come and let us explore the depths of the azure sea of pleasure. There, in the chamber of coral, amidst cool, shady rocks where reigns deep, restful silence lies our bed, lined with soft, bright green damask, inlaid with pearls newly wrenched from their shells. Come, let me sleep with you as I have slept with beautiful women and have given them bliss. Come, let me prise out your pearl from its shell that I may polish it and bring forth its splendour. Come to where no one will find us, where no one will see us, for the eyes of swimming creatures are innocent and will not heed what we do nor understand what we say. Down there lies repose, lies a cure for all your yearnings and ills. Come, without fear or dread, for no creature will reach us in our hidden world, and only the eye of God alone will see us; He alone will know what we are about and He will watch over us."

I began to be intoxicated by the soft musical whisperings. I felt her cool and soft and smooth, her coldness producing a painful convulsion in my body and hurting me to the point of terror. I felt her as she slipped between the covers, then her two tiny fangs, like two pearls, began to caress my body; arriving at my thighs, the golden tongue, like an *arak* twig, inserted its pronged tip between them and began sipping and exhaling; sipping the poisons of my desire and exhaling the nectar of my ecstasy, till my whole body tingled and started to shake in sharp, painful, rapturous spasms—and all the while the tenderest of words were whispered to me as I confided to her all my longings.

At last the cool touch withdrew, leaving me exhausted. I went into a deep slumber to awake at noon full of energy, all of me a joyful burgeoning to life. Curiosity and a desire to know who it was seized me again. I looked at the corner of the wall and found that the hole was wide open. Once again I was overcome by fear. I pointed out the crack to my husband, unable to utter, although terror had once again awakened in me passionate desire. My husband filled up the crack with cement and went to sleep.

Morning came and everyone went out. I finished my housework and began roaming around the rooms in boredom, battling against the desire to surrender myself to sleep. I sat in the hallway and suddenly she appeared before me, gentle as an angel, white as day, softly undulating and flexing herself, calling to me in her bewitching whisper: "Bride of mine, I called you and brought you to my home. I have wedded you, so there is no sin in our love, nothing to reproach yourself about. I am the guardian of the house, and I hold sway over the snakes and vipers that inhabit it, so come and I shall show you where they live. Have no fear so long as we are together. You and I are in accord. Bring a container with water and I shall place my fingers over your hand and we shall recite together some verses from the Qur'an, then we shall sprinkle it in the places from which they emerge and shall thus close the doors on them, and it shall be a pact between us that your hands will not do harm to them."

"Then you are one of the monarchs of the djinn?" I asked eagerly. "Why do you not bring me treasures and riches as we hear about in fables when a human takes as sister her companion among the djinn?"

She laughed at my words, shaking her golden hair that was like dazzling threads of light. She whispered to me, coquettishly: "How greedy is mankind! Are not the pleasures of the body enough? Were I to come to you with wealth we would both die consumed by fire."

"No, no," I called out in alarm. "God forbid that I should ask for unlawful wealth. I merely asked it of you as a test, that it might be positive proof that I am not imagining things and living in dreams."

She said: "And do intelligent humans have to have something tangible as evidence? By God, do you not believe in His ability to create worlds and living beings? Do you not know that you have an existence in worlds other than that of matter and the transitory? Fine, since you ask for proof, come close to me and my caresses will put vitality back into your limbs. You will retain your youth. I shall give you abiding youth and the delights of love—and they are more precious than wealth in the world of man. How many fortunes have women spent in quest of them? As for me I shall feed from the poisons of your desire, the exhalations of your burning passion, for that is my nourishment and through it I live."

"I thought that your union with me was for love, not for nourishment and the perpetuation of youth and vigour," I said in amazement.

"And is sex anything but food for the body and an interaction in union and love?" she said. "Is it not this that makes human beings happy and is the secret of feeling joy and elation?"

She stretched out her radiant hand to my body, passing over it like the sun's rays and discharging into it warmth and a sensation of languor.

"I am ill," I said. "I am ill. I am ill," I kept on repeating. When he heard me my husband brought the doctor, who said: "High blood pressure, heart trouble, nervous depression." Having prescribed various medicaments he left. The stupidity of doctors! My doctor did not know that he was describing the symptoms of love, did not even know it was from love I was suffering. Yet I knew my illness and the secret of my cure. I showed my husband the enlarged hole in the wall and once again he stopped it up. We then carried the bed to another corner.

After some days had passed I found another hole alongside my bed. My beloved came and whispered to me: "Why are you so coy and flee from me, my bride? Is it fear of your being rebuffed or is it from aversion? Are you not happy with our being together? Why do you want for us to be apart?"

"I am in agony," I whispered back. "Your love is so intense and the desire to enjoy you so consuming. I am frightened I shall feel that I am tumbling down into a bottomless pit and being destroyed."

"My beloved," she said. "I shall only appear to you in beauty's most immaculate form."

"But it is natural for you to be a man," I said in a precipitate outburst, "seeing that you are so determined to have a love affair with me."

"Perfect beauty is to be found only in woman," she said, "so yield to me and I shall let you taste undreamed of happiness; I shall guide you to worlds possessed of such beauty as you have never imagined."

She stretched out her fingers to caress me, while her delicate mouth sucked in the poisons of my desire and exhaled the nectar of my ecstasy, carrying me off into a trance of delicious happiness.

After that we began the most pleasurable of love affairs, wandering together in worlds and living on horizons of dazzling beauty, a world fashioned of jewels,

in worlds and living on horizons of dazzling beauty, a world fashioned of jewels, a world whose every moment was radiant with light and formed a thousand shapes, a thousand colours.

As for the opening in the wall, I no longer took any notice. I no longer complained of feeling ill, in fact there burned within me abounding vitality. Sometimes I would bring a handful of wormwood and, by way of jest, would stop up the crack, just as the beloved teases her lover and closes the window in his face that, ablaze with desire for her, he may hasten to the door. After that I would sit for a long time and enjoy watching the wormwood powder being scattered in spiral rings by unseen puffs of wind. Then I would throw myself down on the bed and wait.

For months I immersed myself in my world, no longer calculating time or counting the days, until one morning my husband went out on the balcony lying behind our favoured wall alongside the bed. After a while I heard him utter a cry of alarm. We all hurried out to find him holding a stick, with a black, ugly snake almost two metres long, lying at his feet.

I cried out with a sorrow whose claws clutched at my heart so that it began to beat wildly. With crazed fury I shouted at my husband: "Why have you broken the pact and killed it? What harm has it done?" How cruel is man! He lets no creature live in peace.

I spent the night sorrowful and apprehensive. My lover came to me and embraced me more passionately than ever. I whispered to her imploringly: "Be kind, beloved. Are you angry with me or sad because of me?"

"It is farewell," she said. "You have broken the pact and have betrayed one of my subjects, so you must both depart from this house, for only love lives in it."

In the morning I packed up so that we might move to one of the employees' buildings, leaving the house in which I had learnt of love and enjoyed incomparable pleasures.

I still live in memory and in hope. I crave for the house and miss my secret love. Who knows, perhaps one day my beloved will call me. Who really knows?

FORUGH FARROKHZÂD (1935–1967)
Iran

Iran's leading woman poet, Forugh Farrokhzâd died tragically in a car accident when she was in her thirties and at the height her poetic career. She lived quite unconventionally, had an affair with Ebrâhim Golestân, the filmmaker and writer, and attempted suicide. Her most influential collection of poems is *Another Birth*, which has been translated into several languages.

My Lover

With that naked, shameless body
my lover stands on his legs like death.
Restless diagonal lines trace his rebel limbs in their solid designs.

My lover looks as if he comes from forgotten generations,
as if in the depths of his eyes,   5
A Tartar[1] is constantly waiting to ambush a horseman,
as if in the flash of his teeth
there is a barbarian enthralled by the warm blood of the prey.

Like nature,
my lover has an unavoidably frank meaning.   10
In conquering me, he confirms
the candid law of power.
He is savagely free
like a healthy instinct deep in an uninhabited island.
He cleans the dust of the street from his shoes   15
with pieces torn from Majnun's[2] tent.

My lover was a stranger
from the beginning of his existence
like a god in a Nepalese temple.

He is a man from centuries past,   20
a reminder of beauty's authenticity.

In his own atmosphere,
like the smell of a child,
he constantly awakens innocent memories.
Like a joyous folk song, he is full of roughness and nakedness.   25

He truly loves life's atoms, earth's particles,
the sorrows of humanity, the pure sorrows.

He truly loves a village garden path,
a tree, a dish of ice-cream, a clothesline.

My lover is a simple person   30
a simple person whom I
in this ominous strange land
have hidden like the last trace of a great religion
in the thicket of my breasts.

(1959?)

Translated by Michael Craig Hillman.

---

1. Central Asian nomadic people.   2. Famous Arab lover; symbol of unsuccessful love.

The Poet's Reading of "Another Birth"
Forugh Farrokhzâd and Karim Emami

My whole being is a dark chant
which will carry you
perpetuating you
to the dawn of eternal growths and blossomings
in this chant I sighed you sighed   5
in this chant
I grafted you to the tree to the water to the fire.

Life is perhaps
a long street through which a woman holding a basket
   passes every day   10

life is perhaps
a rope with which a man hangs himself from a branch
life is perhaps a child returning home from school.

Life is perhaps lighting up a cigarette
in the narcotic repose between two love-makings   15
or the absent gaze of a passerby
who takes off his hat to another passerby
with a meaningless smile and a good morning.
Life is perhaps that enclosed moment
when my gaze destroys itself in the pupil of your eyes   20
and it is in the feeling
which I will put into the Moon's impression
   and the Night's perception.

In a room as big as loneliness
my heart   25
which is as big as love
looks at the simple pretexts of its happiness
at the beautiful decay of flowers in the vase
at the sapling you planted in our garden
and the song of canaries   30
which sing to the size of a window.

Ah
this is my lot
this is my lot
my lot is   35
a sky which is taken away at the drop of a curtain
my lot is going down a flight of disused stairs
to regain something amid putrefaction and nostalgia
my lot is a sad promenade in the garden of memories
and dying in the grief of a voice which tells me   40

I love
your hands.

I will plant my hands in the garden
I will grow   I know   I know   I know
and swallows will lay eggs
in the hollow of my ink-stained hands.

I shall wear
a pair of twin cherries as ear-rings
and I shall put dahlia petals on my finger-nails
there is an alley
where the boys who were in love with me
still loiter with the same unkempt hair
    thin necks and bony legs
and think of the innocent smiles of a little girl
who was blown away by the wind one night.

There is an alley
which my heart has stolen
    from the streets of my childhood.
The journey of a form along the line of time
inseminating the line of time with the form
a form conscious of an image
coming back from a feast in a mirror.

And it is in this way
that someone dies
and someone lives on.

No fisherman shall ever find a pearl in a small brook
    which empties into a pool.

I know a sad little fairy
who lives in an ocean
and ever so softly
plays her heart into a magic flute
a sad little fairy
who dies with one kiss each night
and is reborn with one kiss each dawn.

[Garden Conquered]

The crow
that flew over us
and dove into the troubled thoughts of a vagrant cloud
whose cry, like a short spear, streaked across the horizon
will carry news of us to the town.

45

50

55

60

65

70

5

Everyone knows
everyone knows
through that cold and sulking crevice
You and I gazed at the garden
and from that coy and distant branch
picked the apple.

Everyone fears
everyone fears
yet you and I joined the water, the mirror, and the lamp
and did not fear.

It is not a matter of a weak bond between two names
on the old pages of a registry.
It is a matter of my charmed hair
and the burning peonies of your kisses
and the mutinous intimacy of our bodies
and our nakedness glittering
like fish scales in water
it is a matter of the little fountain's silver song
sung at dawn.

We asked, one night
in the green, flowing forest
of the wild hares,
in the anxious, cold-blooded sea
of the pearl-filled shells,
in the strange, haughty mountain,
of the eagles
"What is to be done?"

Everyone knows
everyone knows
we found our way into the cold and silent repose
of Simorghs
we found truth in the little garden
in the bashful look of a nameless flower
and eternity in the never ending moment when two suns gaze
at each other.

It is not a matter of fearful whispers in the dark
It is a matter of daylight, open windows, and fresh air,
and an oven where useless things are burnt,
and an earth pregnant with a new crop.
It is a matter of birth, completion, and pride.
It is a matter of our amorous hands
connecting the nights
with perfume's messages of breeze and light.

Come to the meadow
come to the large meadow
and call me from behind acacia blossom's breath
like a deer calling its mate.

The curtains are overflowing with a hidden spite
and innocent white doves
from the heights of their white towers
gaze at the earth below.

DALIA [DALYAH] RAVIKOVITCH

(b. 1936)

Israel

Born in Ramat Gan, Palestine (now Israel), Ravikowitch has been writing poetry since about 1954. She taught high school from 1959 to 1963 and has written children's stories as well as stories for adults. Her work published outside Israel can be found in *The New Israeli Writers: Short Stories of the First Generation* (1969) and *A Dress of Fire* (1976).

A Hard Winter

The wick shook in the candle flame,
and before it glory vanished
it was lapped in sadness.

Rain and sun ruled by turns; in the house
we were afraid to think
what would become of us.

The bushes reddened at their hearts
and the pond hid away.
Each of us was sunk in himself alone.

But for a moment, distracted,
I saw
how people are cut off from this world

Translated by Chana and Ariel Bloch.

like trees struck by lightning,
heavy with flesh and sinew,
the wet branches trampled like dead grass.   15

The shutter was damaged, the walls thin.
Rain and sun, by turns, rode over us
with iron wheels.

All the plants were intent
on themselves alone.   20
This time I never thought I'd survive.

A Dress of Fire

You know, she said, they made you
a dress of fire.
Remember how Jason's wife burned in her dress?
It was Medea, she said, Medea did that to her.
You've got to be careful, she said,   5
they made you a dress that glows
like an ember, that burns like coals.

Are you going to wear it, she said, don't wear it.
It's not the wind whistling, it's the poison
seeping in.
You're not even a princess, what can you do to Medea?   10
Can't you tell one sound from another, she said,
it's not the wind whistling.

Remember, I told her, that time when I was six?
They shampooed my hair and I went out into the street.
The smell of shampoo trailed after me like a cloud.   15
Then I got sick from the wind and the rain.
I didn't know a thing about reading Greek tragedies,
but the smell of the perfume spread
and I was very sick.   20
Now I can see it's an unnatural perfume.

What will happen to you now, she said,
they made you a burning dress.
They made me a burning dress, I said. I know.
So why are you standing there, she said,   25
you've got to be careful.
You know what a burning dress is, don't you?

I know, I said, but I don't know
how to be careful.
The smell of that perfume confuses me.   30

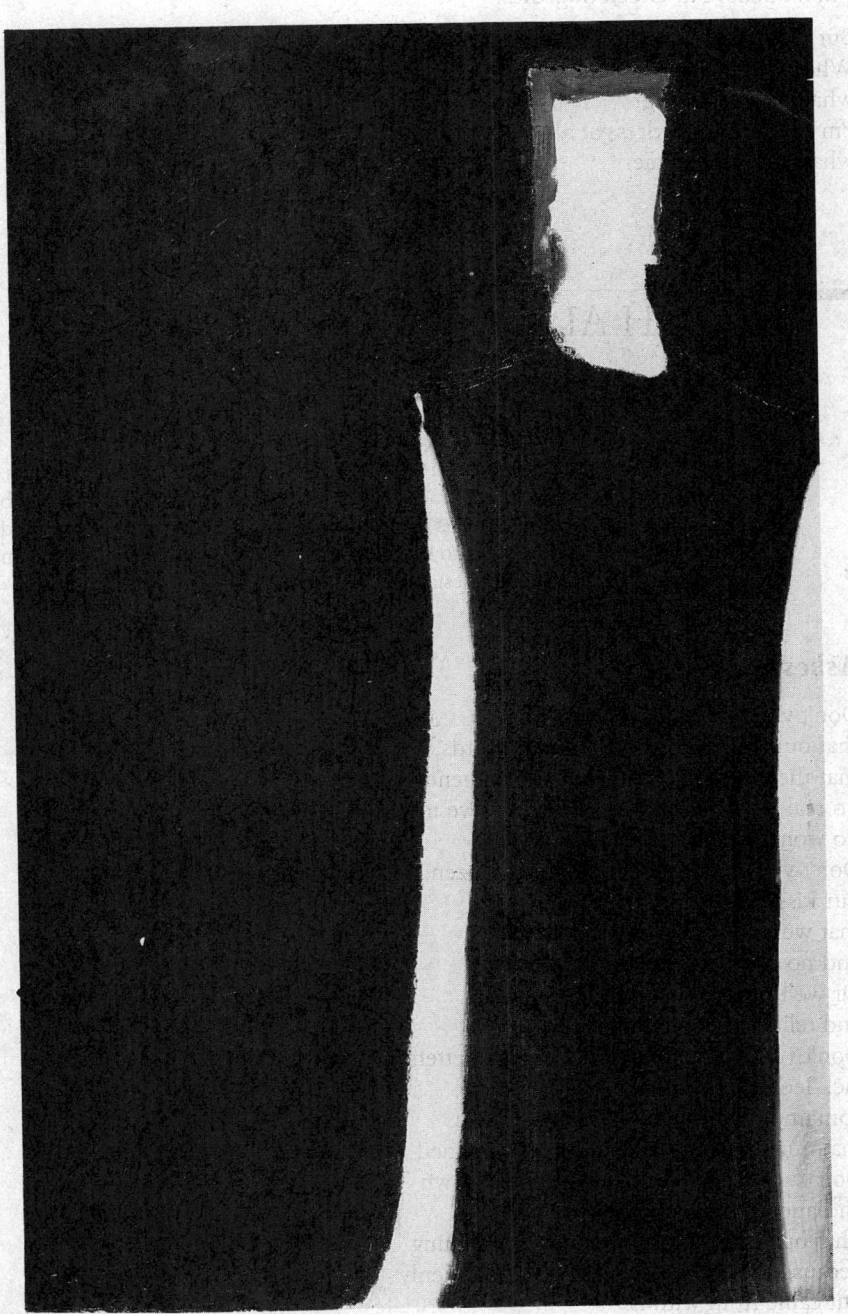

Michael Gross. *Woman in Black*. 1963. Oil on canvas.

I said to her, No one has to agree with me,
I don't believe in Greek tragedies.

But the dress, she said, the dress is on fire.
What are you saying, I shouted,
what are you saying?   35
I'm not wearing a dress at all,
what's burning is me.

SAMÎH AL-QÂSIM (b. 1939)
Israel

Samîh Al-Qâsim is rightly considered to be one of the leading Palestinian poets. He worked as a teacher in an Israeli public school but was fired from his job because of his political beliefs. His opinions as well as his poems have generated much controversy and have led to his imprisonment and house arrest. Al-Qâsim is also a playwright, seeking to establish a Palestinian theater.

Ashes

Don't you feel we have lost so much
that our "great" love is now only words,
that there's no more yearning, no urgency,
no real joy in our hearts, and when we meet
no wonder in our eyes?   5
Don't you feel our encounters are frozen,
our kisses cold,
that we've lost the fervor of contact
and now merely exchange polite talk?
Or we forget to meet at all   10
and tell false excuses . . .
Don't you feel that our brief hurried letters
lack feeling and spirit,
contain no whispers or dreams of love,
that our responses are slow and burdened . . .   15
Don't you feel a world has tumbled down
and another arisen?
That our end will be bitter and frightening
because the end did not fall on us suddenly
but came from within?   20

Translated by Sharif Elmusa and Naomi Shihab Nye.

MAHMÛD DARWÎSH (b. 1942)
Israel/France/Tunisia

Mahmûd Darwîsh is probably the name most Westerners associate with Palestinian poetry. Darwîsh was a member of the Israeli Communist Party and was imprisoned and placed under house arrest while still living in Israel. He left Israel in 1971 and went to Beirut, but eventually left for Paris and Tunis, where he now lives. Darwîsh's poetry has been set to music. He is considered the foremost poetic voice of the Palestinian struggle.

Pride and Fury*

O homeland! O eagle,
Plunging, through the bars of my cell,
Your fiery beak in my eyes!
All I possess in the presence of death
Is pride and fury.   5
I have willed that my heart be planted as a tree,
That my forehead become an abode for skylarks.
O eagle,
I am unworthy of your lofty wing,
I prefer a crown of flame.   10
O homeland!
We were born and raised in your wound,
And ate the fruit of your trees,
To witness the birth of your daybreak.
O eagle unjustly languishing in chains,   15
O legendary death which once was sought,
Your fiery beak is still plunged in my eye,
Like a sword of flame.
Unworthy of your lofty wing,
All I possess in the presence of death   20
Is pride and fury.

EREZ BITTON (b. 1942)
Algeria/Israel

Erez Bitton was born in Oran, Algeria, and immigrated to Israel in 1948; he now lives in Tel Aviv. A social worker and psychologist, he has devoted himself more

*Translated by Mournah A. Khouri and Hamid Algar.

fully to literary activities in recent years. He is one of the first poets to popularize
Middle Eastern themes in Israeli poetry, by using Moroccan-Arabic dialect, and
performing his work to traditional musical accompaniment. He is the editor of
Aperion, a literary journal founded in the early 1980s, and dedicated to creating
a forum for Mediterranean and Middle Eastern intellectuals and visual artists. He
has been the chairman of the Israeli Writer's Union. This is one of the many
poems in which Bitton explores the experience of his own blindness—as a result
of a childhood accident—in relation to cultural and societal issues.

*Families at a School for the Blind in Jerusalem**

And us kids at the school for the blind in Jerusalem,
seven kids would grab another kid
and tell him
you be our father
and tell her
you be our mother,   5
the body of one kid stumbling upon the body of another,
an apparent encounter
to gather warmth,
at least as far as meets the eye.   10
And making families, families,
and calling one kid: Father Shalom
and another, Mother Shoshannah,
and the girl I used to call my sister my sister Rachel
and the boy my brother my brother Yossi   15
that's how we'd make make-believe families
us kids at the school for the blind in Jerusalem.

HANÂN AL-SHAYKH (b. 1945)
Lebanon

Hanân al-Shaykh began writing fiction while working as a journalist with the
daily newspaper *al-Nahâr* in Beirut. She then moved to the Persian Gulf and from
there to London. She has published novels and short stories and is a force in
contemporary Arabic literature. Her novel *The Story of Zahra* [*Hikâyat Zahra*] is
a powerful narrative of the Lebanese civil war

Translated by Ammiel Alcalay.

Nazir Naba'a. *Lover of the Son*. 1967. Acrylic oil on canvas.

A Girl Called Apple

Apple had not married. She was almost forty and she had not yet married. Her dark skin was not the reason; many girls with her color had married. Nor was it her name. That is the least important matter in marriage, and anyhow oasis girls are sometimes called by the names of fruit: her girl friend Banana had married last year.

Fate? Accident? Or Apple's obstinacy which had refused and continued to refuse to raise the wedding flag on the roof? Even though its hoisting upon the occasion of the girl's first menses was customary in the oasis. But Apple had refused. She had begged and cried, hiding her face, saying to her father, "Daddy, please don't. I don't want it." Her mother had thought that Apple was embarrassed that everyone—old and young in the oasis—should learn that she had reached womanhood. So she shook her head at her husband, who understood and left Apple alone.

A month later when the matter was forgotten, her father was about to plant the red flag in an earth-filled container. But Apple ran up to him, begging him with tears streaming from her eyes, "Daddy, I don't want it." And he didn't understand. He asked her in obvious confusion, "You mean that you don't want to get married?" And when she answered, he did not understand what she meant despite the fact that he heard her say, "I want to get married, but I don't want the flag." And her weeping increased. Her father clapped his hands together and repeated, "There is no power and no strength save in God Almighty." How was it

Translated by Miriam Cooke.

possible? Her grandmother, her mother, all her aunts, and every woman born in this oasis had been married by means of the flag. The importance of raising the flag had not been explained to them, but they knew as well as they knew their own faces that the flag was probably the only way to get married. Indeed, this oasis was the only one that had not relied on the services of a matchmaker for generations— in fact, not from the time of Hind,[1] who separated more than she brought together, and who used to describe every bride as a model of virtue, every groom as the moon of his age, a cavalier. The girl was said to be an enchanting dark-skinned innocent and the groom owned ten camels. The families would agree quickly to these descriptions, and Hind would swear solemnly that this was the truth. And on the wedding night the screams could be heard. Moreover, many strangers came to this oasis. They would halt their caravans, letting their camels drink for a couple of hours. Surely the idea of marriage would not occur to anyone in such a short period, and yet the flags fluttering above the roofs would tickle the men's hearts, enticing them to marry in this oasis.

Apple refused the red flag, although her father had tried to plant it in some sand in a can whose shiny surface rust had dulled. He tried to hoist the flag without her knowing. But Apple did not let the night pass with the stars guarding her flag. She pulled it down, and then she knelt and kissed her father's feet, weeping and saying, "I don't want it." Her father could not understand the secret of her refusal, but believed that an evil fortune had chosen his daughter, Apple, to be this generation's oasis spinster.

Scandal tried to whisper to her mother, but how? For Apple, like all the girls of the oasis, never left her home, day or night. And if ever these girls did leave their homes, they would be enveloped in abayas, their faces covered and accompanied by someone. Days passed and Apple continued to help her father dye the sheep skins at home, bringing water from the well, sweeping and cooking. Then she sat at her loom and with her woolen threads wove a carpet of camel hair. She thought about herself and wondered why it was that she refused despite her ardent desire to get married and to have a house of her own. And she loved children. She wanted to have lots of them. When she had really asked herself the reason, she discovered that the answer was easy: she was mortified at the thought of the flag and its fluttering on the roof. When she said this to her father, his wrinkles smoothed out and his hopes rose as he replied with the solution which had occurred to him quickly. Without further ado he got up and set off to plant the flag on the roof of the house of her bachelor uncle, after saying to her happily, "Rejoice, for whoever knocks at your uncle's door will be sent here." And to her amazement she found herself refusing adamantly. She was surprised by her refusal, especially since the red flag, the one that was used for the under-twenties, was about to pass her by; the blue one was good until age thirty, and then finally came the yellow one. Apple thought: "God willing, I shall marry under the shadow of the blue flag."

But she did not. The days passed, never to return, and the blue flag was about

---

1. A woman's name.

to disappear with her years. And Apple refused to let the flag flutter above the roof. And whenever she passed by the mud houses of the oasis and saw the colored flags playing with the breeze, she laughed to herself and said, "Crazy, stupid women." And yet Apple envied the bride when she dyed her hands with henna in preparation for the wedding, choking whenever she saw her sitting like a princess and surrounded by singing and dancing in her honor. Whenever she heard the cry of the newborn babe she would run to the house, pick up the infant, put antimony in its eyes, and bathe it in oil, wishing that it were of her own flesh and blood.

The red flag flew away, and then the blue one, as she jumped past thirty. And although Apple shrugged her shoulders as though she did not care, she began to know depression and dogged patience. She had never before found herself grumbling about helping her father and doing the housework. She sat behind her loom, pulling the threads through and tying them nervously in annoyance. She kept asking herself, "Why do I refuse marriage? Despite my longing for a husband to be the crown on my head, and for children to skip around me. I am hiding the beautiful clothes and the turquoise stones and the heavy rugs until the day of my marriage." She turned and saw the shadow of a date branch on the wall of the living room. She saw her mother's dress next to the prayer garment, and suddenly she was filled with tenderness for everything she saw, and she felt that this time she had found the answer. And she said out loud, "I don't want to leave this oasis." And she hurried to her father and said, "I don't want to leave you or the oasis." And her father's wrinkles smoothed out and he felt much better: "May you never leave my sight, Apple. If the man who marries you is a stranger to the oasis, I shall give him three camels and I shall build you a house in our oasis." He got up and, leaning under the bed, dragged out a palm leaf basket that Apple had made. When part of the yellow flag appeared, Apple ran to her father and kissed his hands, weeping and crying, and her head was almost rent from her body to fling itself against the walls. And she sighed and wept for herself because she had refused, because she could not control her obstinacy. The following day after a sleepless night, she compelled herself to accept, and she hurried to tell her father the news, having seen with pity the grief and sorrow which had inscribed themselves in his wrinkles. But no sooner had she seen the yellow flag in her father's trembling hand than she fell to his feet, once again begging his pardon and again refusing the flag.

Apple changed as though the black sickness had hit her. She began to frown much more, becoming thin and sad. She was annoyed by her mother when she wished her good morning and by her father when he wished her good evening. But she never let her annoyance cross the bridge to her inside.

One evening she was holding the thread in her hand and was asking herself the question that she had thought about every moment of her life when she held her breath and heaved a deep sigh. And this time she grasped the true answer and it was so simple: the flag might well flutter for months on end, and no one might come. I would be like mutton or old dates for sale. And she found herself for the first time coming to grips with her fear: "Maybe no one will come. And everyone in the oasis will see the flag wherever they go, and they will feel so sorry for me because I am unsalable merchandise." Again she blamed herself, defeated: "But why was this simple, clear reason so hard to find before age forty?" Apple found herself leaning under the bed and carefully dragging out the basket, making sure not to wake up her mother. She took out the flag that no house in the oasis needed, and she climbed the stairs up to the roof while her mother and father and the oasis were sound asleep. And this after everyone was sure that marriage had passed Apple by forever, because it would not be long before even the yellow flag would be gone, and then no one would open the path of marriage to her. Indeed, it was felt that this was already the case.

In the starlight Apple raised her face to the heavens and called upon God to be her witness. Then she knelt and fixed the flag in the container, thinking all the while that the oasis was small, that there were few men and that there was no matchmaker. She went downstairs and, sighing, sat down to await a knock at the door.

NASRÎN ETTEHÂD (b. 1945)
Iran

Nasrîn Ettehâd is the pseudonym of an Iranian woman writer. After attending school in Germany, she returned to Iran. Politically active, she first returned to her country at the outset of the Iranian revolution in 1979 only to flee in 1982. She is currently a social worker in a refugee camp in Austria. Her literary activity has consisted primarily of translation of Western works into Persian.

A Veil with Tiny Aster Flowers

I first saw her at a party. A middle-aged woman, looking neat, fashionable, and energetic. She had no reservations about mingling with men, showing no sign of uneasiness or inadequacy in their company. She was working with one of the political organizations, independently of her husband, as I gathered from her remarks.

A few months later I saw her again at a friend's house. I didn't recognize her. She was wearing a veil with tiny aster flowers, which she took off upon arriving. She acted fidgety, and her watchful, green eyes moved about anxiously. There was no one but my friend and me in the house.

I knew that her husband had left the country, his life being in danger. She may have insisted, too. And now she was left behind with three children, the oldest of whom had been wounded by a bullet in a demonstration or a direct confrontation with the police.

She said, "I'm looking for a place to stay. I'm living in a janitor's house now,

Translated by Soraya Paknayar Sullivan.

doing his housework. He's acting as if I were his official servant. He expects me to cook for him every day, and if I leave the house he screams at me. My daughter screams at me, too. She says it was I who chose to live a life like this, not she."

I was in the same boat myself, having no place to stay. My friend could not put up both of us. She left as nervously as she had arrived. I thought, "If a revolutionary guard noticed her anxious eyes, she would be in trouble."

I heard a few weeks later that she had taken a bottle of sleeping pills, hired a taxi, and asked the driver to drive her around the city. She must not have been able to find a better deathbed. Or perhaps she had not wished her children to watch her die. Whether the story is true, I don't know. I only know that she no longer lives.

The story that follows is the reiterative account of the life of another woman wearing a veil with tiny aster flowers, another woman with anxious eyes. I have made no changes, except of proper names, in this story that she told me.

"I was five years old when we moved to Tehran from the village. I had three sisters and no brother. My father was out of work for a couple of years, mainly because no one wanted to hire an illiterate man.

"We lived in poverty-stricken southern Tehran. My mother worked and supported us, but she made very little money; so little that my parents couldn't even afford to buy books and other school supplies for their children.

"When my older sister turned thirteen, my parents married her off. Being passionately in love with school, I managed to finish grammar school in spite of my family's financial difficulties. I was about thirteen, and just out of school, when I started looking for work. I used all my resources and asked everyone I knew to help me. Soon, I got a job as a teacher in a grade school. It was a private school and the salaries were low; nevertheless, my salary paid for most of my family's expenses. I taught for two years, and when I was sixteen, I met my husband.

"Mostafa and I knew each other for two years, occasionally talking to each other, mostly about political issues. I had no particular ideological tendency, but I did wonder why, if there were a God, He made people suffer so much. No evening passed in our house without agitation and quarrels. I often talked to Mostafa about what troubled my mind. And I was very curious.

"Two years later I married Mostafa. My mother prohibited me from working as soon as I got engaged. She said, 'Now that you're engaged you should stay home.' But she was wrong, because the other teachers in our school continued teaching and were hired as regular teachers later on, receiving higher salaries.

"Mostafa was a worker. His wages were very low when we first got married. We couldn't afford to rent a room for ourselves, so we lived with his brother's family. His brother had eight children, and his house comprised one room and a kitchen. We didn't encounter any major problems, since we got along very well. We lived in their kitchen for about six months, until we could afford to rent a room of our own.

"It was 1972. We had just settled down when Mostafa was arrested. I was in my third month of pregnancy. For the first six months of his prison term, he wasn't allowed any visitors. We went to the prison, and, like the families of the 'regular prisoners,' looked at them from a distance. Sometimes we went to the

Redress of Grievances Office of the military and protested. The university students used to gather there and ask us questions and we explained our situation to them. One time they went on a hunger strike for thirteen days.

"While Mostafa served his prison sentence, I stayed at my brother-in-law's house. My parents were afraid of getting involved and didn't approve of Mostafa's political activities.

"My time had come. I knew a doctor who worked at the Russian Hospital. He had treated me before when I had a miscarriage. He took three hundred *tomans* from me and said, 'Come to the hospital when the pains start. We will admit you then and you can stay until the baby arrives.' But he disappeared from that hospital before I had my baby.

"I was admitted to the hospital and went through a difficult labor. They had to use forceps to deliver the baby. When I was ready to leave the hospital, they asked for seven thousand *tomans*. I didn't have anywhere near that amount. I told them they could keep my baby and me both, since I had no place to go. They decided to release me, knowing that they really would get stuck with me.

"The baby was six months old when Mostafa was released from prison. No one was willing to give him employment because he belonged to an 'Organization' referred to as 'Saka.' Eventually someone hired him, offering him minimal wages. Mostafa was a technician, but he was paid only six hundred *tomans* a month. It was not enough; at the rate the rent, food, and clothing expenses went, that amount could not bring any balance to our lives. It was a tough time, and on top of it all, a good chunk of the money had to go for bottle feeding the baby.

"We were forced to rent a single room again. We found a cheap room for two hundred *tomans* a month. The walls were half-way damp. Later, we found out that our room had been a bathroom, but we couldn't afford to get something more decent; so we struggled through. The baby got sick with bronchitis, because of the dampness. He couldn't breathe. We didn't have a family physician so we took him to a public clinic where my husband's insurance paid the expenses. They admitted him to the clinic and opened his throat right away. Three or four holes, to give him artificial respiration. My baby died after three days. He was two years old. We moved out of our room right after his death. Mostafa had two full time jobs; both day and night shifts. He came home to rest between his two jobs for an hour or so. Those were irksome days. We were determined to save enough money and cut all unnecessary expenses, and we were able to put down thirty thousand *tomans* on a house. It was on the south side of Tehran; more accurately on the outskirts of the city limits.

"Mostafa continued working with the 'Organization' after the revolution. I also participated in some activities in relation to his duties. I took part in all the demonstrations against the Islamic Republic. Even when Mostafa was busy, or working at his job, I took the children along and joined the demonstrators. I had all four of them, then. Kaveh, my youngest son, was very little.

"In the year 1982, on a holiday, Mostafa was arrested, carrying a bag full of newspapers. He was detained in the Civil Court No—. The same day I took all my children along and went to the court. I caused such a ruckus they let him go. I didn't want him to stay there long enough for them to look into his past records.

I was very good at figuring those things out. But after that incident they kept harassing him. He had a car and they had identified it. Every time something happened in our neighborhood, my husband would have to prove his noninvolvement to the authorities. Once the Mujahedeen's [1] leaflet was distributed in our neighborhood and they had suspected Mostafa. They arrested him on his way home and detained him for twelve hours. They let him go after comparing his handwriting with the one on the leaflet. Once they went to his work place and dragged him into a car and interrogated him. They threatened him; they wanted names of a few people. He didn't give them any names. They sentenced him to death right there in the car. But later they let him go.

"We were constantly molested, both by government agents and by some of our neighbors who had painted the slogan on our building, 'Death to Communists.' They had told my children that we were anti-revolutionaries, non-Hezbollahis, i.e. the fanatic members of the Party of God.

"One day we went out with the children for a walk. We decided to visit Mostafa's brother afterwards. Someone came to his house looking for us, to tell us that it wasn't wise to return to our house that night. We asked, 'What for?' 'Someone has given them your names,' he answered. We didn't go. Mostafa decided to take the next day off. A week later I went back to see what was going on. The neighbors came to visit, asking me where I'd been.

"I said, 'My mother-in-law was ill and she has passed away. I came to get my black garments. We're going to the funeral.'

"We stayed at my brother-in-law's and other relatives' houses for three weeks. After three weeks a revolutionary guard came looking for us. My brother-in-law didn't want to tell us at first, but he changed his mind later and said, 'He came after you.' Mostafa said after the guard left, 'We've got to leave.' Kaveh was asleep. I picked him up, got the other children ready, and we left for my mother's house.

"My mother was upset; not because we wanted to stay with her, but because she felt we were living a miserable life. We stayed with her for two days. Then the word came that we had to leave because they had my mother's address, too. Mostafa went underground after he left my mother's house, and I moved on to stay with other relatives.

"The first two months were very tough on me. Everywhere I went, I encountered strange looks, as if they were telling me, 'You may stay for an hour, but not longer!' I could sense these things. They were afraid. . . Some of my relatives were harsh on my children; they beat them in front of me. It's difficult for a mother to watch her children get beaten. Under these circumstances, we couldn't stay anywhere. I came to prefer the streets over the relatives' houses.

"One morning I took the children and we walked all the way to my sister's house. Her house was very far, on the way to the city of Saveh. We arrived in the evening. My brother-in-law became uncomfortable when he saw us. He said, 'You may stay here overnight, but you have to leave early in the morning! I will be held

---

1. Fighters for the faith, who carry on the
   jihad.

responsible for this!' My brother-in-law was a fanatic Hezbollahi. . . I had only gone to his house out of desperation. My children were feeling uneasy. They shrank into a corner and stared at me. I told my brother-in-law, 'What've we done to deserve treatment like this . . .? Why is everyone treating us as if we were criminals?'

"We stayed there overnight and left the next morning crying. I was insulted . . . Since that day, we took to the streets every day, as a matter of course. The children were smeared with dirt and their heels were callused from excessive walking. My foot was also wounded and bled. Sometimes we sat on a bench in a park. I would buy something for the children and they ate there. As for myself, I had lost my appetite altogether. At night we went to stay with our distant relatives who knew nothing about our situation. Often, we left early in the morning with empty stomachs and walked all day without having eaten anything. Once I made an arrangement with my mother to see her on a street corner. My sister came, too. We went to a restaurant. I said spontaneously, 'I wish they would let us sleep here at night.' My mother cried helplessly and said, 'You're that desperate?'

"What could I do? Everywhere I went I got the message that I wasn't welcome. I wished I could sit on a restaurant chair, like that day, with all my children around me. I wished that I were by myself, but what could I do with four children? Some people told me that the guards knew we had four children; that we could be easily spotted. They told me that I shouldn't be walking the streets with my children. But what was I supposed to do? How could I leave them with someone else? The poor kids were suffering tremendously. People advised me to be watchful, to avoid the areas where the guards hung out, to be quiet, to avoid passing the guards' headquarters, the Komiteh. My children would get nervous when they heard these comments. Women are at a disadvantage in situations like these. A man could go to all kinds of places and sleep on the streets, but a woman! Especially one with four children!

"After two months we received a message from Mostafa saying that we could go home; that it was safe now. He had made sure that they didn't know I was involved in any activities. I was reluctant to go. Although staying on the streets had made me miserable, I preferred tolerating this hardship over returning to our house. I was afraid the guards would come take my children away. I had heard they sometimes took the children and the wives hostages.

"On the way to my house I had a strange feeling, as if I were about to go crazy. When we got to our street and got out of the car, I suddenly started crying. I was going home without my husband. The children had been crying continuously. At night they pleaded for their father. The youngest one was particularly fond of him. He suffered the most during this period. He would go stand in the alley and watch the neighbors come home. Then he would come home and say, 'Everyone else's father came home; but my father didn't come. Why?' I would say, 'If he came, the guards would arrest him and take him away.' Then he would calm down a bit.

"Our neighbors' reactions to us changed drastically. They would come and ask us if we needed anything. If one of my children got sick, they would take him to a doctor and offer to help us when we needed help. They had developed affection and respect for us. I had told them Mostafa's mother was dead, but they had found out what we had actually gone through. They knew that Mostafa had been forced to go underground.

"Our neighborhood was mostly occupied by families of workers. But by this time most of them had turned against the government. Among the neighbors living on our side of the alley there were two Hezbollahi families; out of forty-four.

"But the guards continued harassing us. At night, at about two in the morning, they would ring our doorbell. I was unable to sleep at night. I just stayed awake, as I was constantly worried that they'd show up any time. I knew that the person they had arrested didn't know me, since I did my work independently from Mostafa. But I was afraid of being taken hostage. Once, in the middle of the night, someone rang our doorbell mercilessly. Keyvan jumped from his sleep so suddenly I thought he would lose his mind. I didn't open the door. I asked who it was; no one answered. I went to the rooftop to look; I didn't see anyone. This happened frequently at night, and everywhere I went I was tailed. Every now and then I went to my brother-in-law's house to let them know we were all right, that they hadn't come for us. The school children molested my son Kavoos. They had made an older boy, one who had fallen behind the rest of the children, sit next to Kavoos and constantly ask him where his father was. Kavoos would get mad and tell him that it was none of his business.

"Kaveh would shrink back to a corner all day and cry. At night he kept asking about his father, calling his name. He was three and a half years old then.

"The children saw their father twice during the six months Mostafa was in hiding. We tried to visit him four times, but twice we were followed, so we didn't go. Kaveh was shocked the first time he saw his father. He was laughing and crying simultaneously. He hadn't seen his father for a long time, and Mostafa had let his beard grow. Kaveh was naturally confused. He could recognize his father's voice but not his face. He thought they had arrested his father and that this man was his friend. (A few minutes before, when asked who he missed most in Iran, he had said, 'My father.' He was slightly mixed up.)

"Once, after we had visited Mostafa, my mother, who wanted to test whether Kaveh was tight-lipped, bought him a lot of chocolate, candy, and pastry and said, 'Did you see your father, Kaveh? If you tell the truth, I'll give you all of these!' Kaveh said, 'No.' My mother kept showing him the baits, making him frustrated. Finally he started crying and said, 'No! Leave me alone! I didn't see him!'

"We had asked him not to tell anybody that he had seen his father, and we said that if he did, they would take his father away and kill him. This request had stuck in his mind for a long time. After our escape from Iran, one day when we were at a motel in the city of Van, Kaveh woke up and didn't see his father. He started crying and repeated, 'They've arrested my father, they've arrested my father!' I told him, 'Don't worry! We're in Turkey now. Your father has gone out to buy something and will return soon!' But Kaveh kept on crying until his father came back. He was very fond of him and when it came to his father, he was very difficult to deal with. My hair turned gray during those six months. Mostafa was a good father and the children missed him. I thought if he wasn't kind to them they would even welcome his absence, like most children who have strict fathers. But Mostafa treated them kindly and he is still the best father they could dream of.

I don't mean to give him too much credit. Sometimes I lost my temper with my children, but he didn't.

"Finally, we decided that we couldn't go on like that forever. The neighbors knew the truth, the children were restless and frustrated, and most importantly, Mostafa knew a lot of people and was afraid he might talk if arrested and tortured. In fact, it was not just to save our own lives that we decided to leave the country. We didn't want to risk any of Mostafa's friends' lives. . . Anyway, we made all the preparations; and our friends helped, too, to get us out.

"We were not able to sell any of our belongings. Our house was under surveillance twenty-four hours a day. We only brought the clothes we were in. We set off at the end of November of 1983.

"One of my sons went to school in the mornings. I had received directions to tell my son that he should not return home on that day, and instead should wait on the street corner. My oldest son went to school in the afternoons. I was to tell him to leave the house at the usual time and, instead of going to school, to join his younger brother. I was to take the two young ones along and leave after my oldest son. They asked me to come up with a story to tell anyone who happened to see me leave. I was instructed not to take anything with me. 'Only wear as much as you can, but don't carry any bags,' they said.

"We followed the instructions that afternoon. I held my sons' hands and left the house. A Hezbollahi woman in our neighborhood stopped me and asked, 'Where are you off to?' I answered, 'I'm going to the city to see a doctor.' Luckily Kaveh's eyes were slightly red and inflamed. That settled it. We kept backtracking and changing our route to make sure no one was following us. Then we entered a building with two entrances. I entered through one entrance, took my veil off, changed my appearance and exited from the other door. A car was waiting for us there. We got in and took off. Mostafa was in the car, too. We drove to the bus station, bought our tickets and went to city A. From there we went to city B in Van. We arrived in a village at night and were given a room next to a stable to sleep in. We were ordered not to leave the room, lest the villagers see us. The children had to 'go to the bathroom' in the same room. They moved us from there in the middle of the night. We walked for about three hours; then they brought horses for us. It was very cold and we were all trembling. We didn't have sufficient clothing. We continued these rides for six days. We rode in the daytime and slept at night in one of the villages on our way. The children rode on horses, too. Each sat next to a guide. Once Kaveh almost froze to death. We wrapped him in a blanket. The guide was trying to rearrange his seat and put him down for a minute on the snow. Suddenly Kaveh started to cry. His feet were numb. His father rubbed his feet until they regained their senses. We were worried that the children might get ill, for we had not been able to bring any medicine or extra clothing for them. Nothing.

"In Kurdistan, they provided us with Kurdish outfits. After we crossed the border, they brought a car and took us to the city of Van. On the way there, our car was inspected once.

"We stayed in Van for thirty-eight days. We took a small room with two beds in the Aslan Hotel. (The room wasn't even half the size of this one. I don't know if you have seen the rooms in that hotel.) They were very dirty. We were miserable. Lice had attacked all my children and we didn't have extra clothes to replace their dirty ones. Our financial situation was hopeless. As we hadn't been able to sell our furniture, our friends had put up the resources for us: one hundred fifty thousand *tomans* went for travel expenses and thirty thousand *tomans* we had with us. We had to make this money stretch for an unknown period of time. We went through an extremely tough time. All six of us slept on the two beds.

"Then we came to Istanbul. We had to make two beds do there, too, since the rooms were so expensive. Then our friends in Germany sent us plane tickets, and here we are!

"The children were really calm throughout the entire trip. They wanted to behave their best to impress their father. When we were in Iran, I sometimes told them, 'Your father is planning to go abroad but we have to stay in Iran.' The children would say, 'No, we want to be with our father.' I would then say, 'How am I supposed to take four children along? What if we were caught on the way and got arrested, what then, would you still like to go?' They would say, 'Yes, we want to be where our father is.' They did not complain at all; not a word. Our co-travelers were amazed. So was I, because the children had really drained me before the trip. This was why the trip had actually been a relief to me, to the extent that I tolerated the freezing weather and the other hardships without much difficulty. God knows what I went through—during these six months. Hearing it is an entirely different matter. Our lives consisted of little more than that. Sheer misery and vagrancy. It is safe to say that our troubles are mostly over now. But the ones who've stayed behind. . ."

cA'ISHA ARNA'ÛT (b. 1946)
Syria/France

cA'isha Arna'ût was born in Damascus and now lives in Paris. She worked for many years as an elementary school teacher and was actively involved in artistic projects involving young children. She has published several collections of poetry and has also written short stories.

[It troubles me]

It troubles me
that water is colorless
air is tasteless

Translated by Kamal Boullata.

the hymen
is without tears.   5

The tenderness of thorns
    their perpetual renewal
Wounds me:
The neighing of extinct beasts
    in my blood   10
The scream of demons
    dead under the trees
    of remote shores.

I lay my rough palms
    over a man's foot   15
    a passing stranger
And bless my children
    coming forth with the wind
Penetrating through time.

SHELLEY ELKAYAM (b. 1955)
Israel

Shelley Elkayam's work filters biblical language through a Sephardi/Oriental
political and cultural consciousness that sees Middle Eastern Jews as native to the
region and the need for Israel to integrate itself among the other Middle Eastern
and Mediterranean cultures of its neighbors. In the poem included here, Elkayam
ranges from the diction and vocabulary of the Song of Songs to the language of
covenant and commandment found in the Pentateuch; she also expands the
possibilities of the biblical text by approaching it from a woman's perspective, to
the point—as in this poem—of switching the gender of the poem's persona.

Poem

YES INDEED I'LL ANSWER GOD

And this is the judgement.
I will ever be what I now am inscribing letters in light.
A small letter as a sign in a crown of light.
Peace unto the crown.   5
Peace unto the King and the Queen and peace, peace unto the Escort.

Translated by Ammiel Alcalay.

Don't take it to heart.
Wind hovers over the deep
and space is laid out between the lines from sentence
to sentence like   10
chess: black and white.
Like on a park bench: a sitting king's falling.
A parable, my beloved readers:
the garden's a song
and the architect's checkmate.   15

And whoever wants to come to the garden—
arise
and enter.

Bless this breach.
Peace to Yeshurun.   20
Welcome, Lord's favour.
And Bless the Name, naturally, day by day in Mahaneh Yehudah.[1]

All kidding aside.
Believe me, the Gates of Grace are already open.

Right now, this minute, today and forever,   25
and this song a witness between you and me
alive this instant, all, like they say,
with love and awe and completion.

Please don't worry.
For right before your very eyes what's written   30
is written. And that's a fact.

To everything there is a season and this is the time
since that's how song goes—
a pillar of fire:
intransitory.   35

And whatever is distinct has intention—
in other words, perfection within perfection.
Whatever you decide.
I'm with you.

As for me.   40
And I took it upon myself for the sake of the song so
indeed I'll come back to God.

---

1. Mahaneh Yehudah ("The Camps of Juda")
   is a popular Middle Eastern market in West
   Jerusalem.

And I gave my word
to grow to the scent of a blossom of light.
To be kindled by the right aroma.   45
To be
Amen.

Truly, simply, with love.

And whoever is bound
and finds himself in the garden,   50
finds himself
in the garden:
sing to him.
Come, my pleasantly tied,
unlace yourself in the palm   55
of my hand
the man among you who is fine and tender.
Now, since I was reminded, I remember now.
My blood my soul my heart and will are one.
One—regardless.   60
You are one.
One now.

Enough.
This is judgement.
And I take the verdict upon myself   65
at its word.

Therefore, for the sake of the liberty you gained:
All ceremonies of the covenant
are memorial.
In Remembrance, of course.   70
Like a garden bell. Accordingly, say,
I forgive my father for doing things without questioning my desires.
Look, after all, the ledger's open.
Ceremonial testaments inscribed in the body.
A man and his covenant   75
carved in his form.

Accept this, take it upon yourself
and look at the voice
how
suddenly the body's stone.   80
The body suddenly ape.
    Ape.
The body suddenly blossoms.
At once the body's at the Gates of Grace,
and someone utters—live, now   85

And who
ever wishes to enter the garden
arise
in fragrance
whoever among you is a man of fine and tender   90
scent.

Helen Sebidi. *Mother Africa*. 1988.
Pastel and collage on paper.

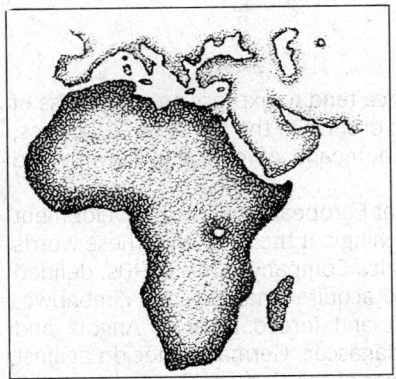

SECTION XIII
Modern Africa

The map of Africa looks like a giant question mark fattened by enormous tracts of land. It is a continent of countless paradoxes: the largest desert in the world (the Sahara, 7,000 miles long and 1,200 miles wide); three of the world's longest rivers (Nile, Congo, Niger); a huge river (Okavango) emptying its waters into a seemingly uninhabitable desert (Kalahari); the longest-lived state in human history (Pharaonic Egypt, 4000–300 B.C.) and societies who still today have no need for rulers; very high and very low standards of living; 1200 distinct languages in use today, though not the 2000 estimated for a century ago; centuries of exploitation and forced export of treasures, foods, and human beings, along with a highly developed sense of how people should treat one another. All of these paradoxes bring up many questions, but four things are definitely known. First, humanity began in Africa. The researches of paleontologists have established that *Homo sapiens* came into existence in what is now Kenya and Tanzania. Second, generalizations about Africa, even by the most sympathetic anthropologists, reflect a tiny corner of the continent and a large portion of the observer's mentality. Third, of all the world's regions, Africa has produced one of the most verbal art, nearly all of it for immediate consumption through live performance. Such literary traditions often depend heavily on many generations of oral performance, and modern novelists or poets are likely to be keenly aware of their village predecessors, either drawing from or avoiding their example.

Fourth, both oral and written literature in Africa tend to express an awareness of the place of human interaction in the cosmic order. On the social level, poetics, performance, and publication function as a means of critically viewing and evaluating human life.

Southern Africa typifies the history of what Europeans call their development of the continent. "We will leave them with nothing but the air." With these words Cecil Rhodes, bullyboy of the British South Africa Company in the 1890s, defined colonial policy as the British headed north to acquire what is today Zimbabwe, Zambia, and Malawi. Portuguese land-theft and forced labor in Angola and Mozambique, the French plantocracy in Madagascar, German genocide against the Herero in Namibia, and the Dutch takeover of the Cape of Good Hope—the southwest coast of South Africa—in 1652 and the eventual settlement of the interior with slave labor were no different. The only thing European colonialism developed for Africans in Southern Africa was underdevelopment—the reduction to peasant status and vast farm- and mine-labor reserves of what had been well-adapted African societies of hunter-gatherers, herdsmen and farmers with a complex culture and social organization—enriching the European metropolis and the white settlers in the process.

With its introduction of a market economy integrated into the markets of the developing European world system, colonialism shattered Southern Africa. With commercialized settler ranches and farms, mining with investment from the largest conglomerations of capital in the world, and the trade, transportation, finance, and governmental structures of taxation and regulation of the African population that all this entailed, Europeans built on African labor the present regional political economy of urban (largely white) prosperity and rural (entirely black) underdevelopment. It was a structure of power that was also gendered, built on male dominance. The political independence of all the British and Portuguese colonies and protectorates by 1980, and the apparent success of the struggle for African rule in Namibia and South Africa, have not yet altered this fundamental maldistribution of power and wealth in the region.

Moreover, an official culture of white racism has blanketed Southern Africa like smog for three centuries. From the point of view of the average African, "Western Civilization," as Agostinho Neto described it in a famous poem, has been a disaster. But Africans had the cultural strength to resist, to negotiate, and to survive against all odds. In the rich oral tradition and, from 1850 on, in the literary tradition as well, Southern African cultural production reaches very far back into the poetry and ceremonies of the Khoi and San peoples who were the original inhabitants, and into the praise-poems, story cycles, music, and dance-theater of the peoples speaking Bantu languages, who settled from the north well over a thousand years ago. As the African National Congress (ANC), Congress of South African Trade Unions (COSATU), and others negotiate with the regime in power for majority rule in South Africa, there is a sense throughout the region—dominated as it is by the apartheid ("separateness") metropolis—of a decisive historical moment. The present moment will be decisive for culture, for a new regime of gender and race, as well as for political economy. Although there remain great odds to be overcome, this may be the time for a new literature and a new nation in South Africa, whose effects will be felt throughout the region.

This region has had a spectacularly turbulent history in the last two centuries, and it is not surprising that its literature has the tone of crisis. Nineteenth-century upheavals within African societies (especially Zulu expansion after 1818), and the advance of colonial power after 1836, leading to the formation of the white Union of South Africa in 1910, set the stage for the victory of apartheid in the 1950s, and white South African dominance of the region. Yet the three-way struggle among world capital, local white rule, and African self-determination was not ended by apartheid. The economic sanctions applied by most of the world against South Africa in the 1980s, and the rise of black popular mobilization (whose history is continuous since the ANC was founded in 1912), have forced the settler state to negotiate a more acceptable form of capitalist nonracial democracy. As this new phase has unfolded in South Africa, it has interacted with pressures for democratization and social reform elsewhere in the region, with results for the whole continent that cannot be foreseen.

A human value that has been asserted in literature throughout Africa is interdependence—the belief that other people are important. Africans have lived for centuries in close face-to-face societies that are both the audience and the subject for literary expression. Countless proverbs reinforce this idea: "In the dark, hold on to one another by the robe"; "Even the dead like to be many"; and (quoting an ant) "Nothing's better than a swarming crowd." Folktales reunite a stolen bride with her parents and husband; they restore riches not to only the finder but to a whole community.

Because so much African literature is created and performed for live audiences, a few oral texts are included in this section. The principal fact about African systems of verbal art is the capacity that performers have developed for remodeling and adaptation. Especially when cultures and languages come into contact, poets and reciters sense a creative potential in the convergence. Proverbs are learned and reused, riddles are transmitted, and folktales are remodeled in accordance with local values. This capacity for mixing and remaking, fostered by African cultures, is visible, for example, in all the variant forms of a single folktale.

Interdependence is heard, too, in African music, where leader and chorus are, in the words of the ethnomusicologist Alan Lomax, in his *Folk Song Style and Culture*:

> singing without letup in exciting rhythmic relationship to each other. Not only does this way of making music open up tremendous choral possibilities for Africans, but one is tempted to compare it to the way in which actions of the village chief are embedded in the reactions of his tribal council and his fellow villagers.

Performing the Mwindo epic in Zaire, the bard and his collaborators receive gifts and praises from the crowd, who are an essential part of the performance. Posing riddles to their younger brothers and sisters, African children sharpen their intelligence through metaphor. Listening to myths of the origin of death or the acquisition of necessities like rice, African audiences must acknowledge the importance of gods and deities.

Along with interdependence, modern African literatures have been marked by less optimistic themes. The hypocrisies inherent in the colonial system, the opposition between traditional and modern systems of value, the differences that separate village life and city life, the varieties of religious experience in a continent where Christianity and Islam have only recently begun their conflict with traditional religion, doubts about the viability of African cultures in the modern world, the disillusionments of the era after independence, and the painfulness of exile—all these can be heard in African literature today. Some of the themes

presented in this section include the role of women and the prospects for their
liberation, the emergence of new class affiliations, the struggle for freedom, and
the magnetic force of the city, which draws rural families away from their
traditions. The literary discovery of the African past includes both fictional
reconstructions and research into the inherited traditions of the epic and folk
song. Difficult as it sometimes is for Europeans and North Americans to tolerate
the anger or bitterness in postcolonial writing, a greater understanding of the
sensibilities of the oppressed is essential to the liberation of all peoples everywhere.

If the performers of oral literature depend so much on their audiences, what
resources has the novelist, dramatist, or poet? Four language stocks exist in Africa
(apart from the Malagasy language of Madagascar, which is Malayo-Polynesian):
the "click" languages of the south; the Afro-Asiatic of the north; the Savanna-
Sahara from the bend of the Niger to the Indian Ocean; and the Niger-Congo
(which covers the largest area of all). Written literatures in Swahili (east coast) and
Hausa (Nigeria) demonstrate that if there is an audience and if there is literacy,
literature will be produced.

The language in which most African literature has been produced is Arabic,
English, French, Swahili, Portuguese, and Afrikaans. Writers disagree as much
about what language is appropriate for African literature as about anything else.
In the multilingual region of East Africa, four countries have each instituted an
African language as their official *lingua franca:* Somalia (Somali), Ethiopia
(Amharic), Tanzania (Kiswahili), and the Sudan (Arabic). Madagascar has done the
same, thus committing itself to bilingualism for international relations. These
political decisions urge writers toward an official language. Other countries like
Kenya, Zimbabwe, and Nigeria, where English is the official language, still show
the linguistic impress of British colonization.

But to say naively, "We all speak the same language," whether in postcolonial Africa or France, is to make a political statement. Concepts of language and
dialect are far more the product of cultural politics than of purely linguistic factors.
In Africa, language is not a single system; it is what the Russian critic M. M.
Bakhtin called "multi-speechedness." Most Africans are bilingual or trilingual.
The linguistic consciousness of the folktale teller or the writer, therefore, is
sociohistorically ordained to be a multiple consciousness.

A writer's decision about language is also a decision among various possible
audiences and modes of publication. If intellectuals or novelists turn away from
the French or English of postcolonial Dakar or Nairobi to the Wolof or Gikuyu of
rural life, what audience can they expect in a situation where many people cannot
read? The answer of the East African novelist Ngugi wa Thiong'o, who decided to
find his audience among his own Gikuyu people, was to write dramas such as *I Will
Marry When I Want* [*Ngahika Ndeenda,* 1982], which could reach people
immediately. Other writers and critics defend the use of international languages.
Poetry, prose, and drama in French or English have been produced by writers of
international stature: Wole Soyinka, Chinua Achebe, Ngugi wa Thiong'o, Léopold
Sédar Senghor, Nadine Gordimer, Sembène Ousmane. Those languages, of
course, became African property through the political dominance of France and
Britain and their occupation of African and other countries.

The writings selected here do not, of course, simply reflect either history or a
writer's dependence on oral sources, but they do evoke major currents that have
swept through Africa's history and consciousness. This literature may best be

understood through the thinking of those who have analyzed colonial and racist culture and the process of decolonization. The African-American writer and educator W. E. B. Du Bois, for instance, wrote in *The Souls of Black Folk* (1903) of the "double consciousness" that people of color live with in a society with a color bar, being aware both of their own experience and of how that experience is "othered" by whites with power over them. Many of the bitter contrasts and psychological conflicts of African writing could be seen as a result of double consciousness; interestingly, the same worldview also produces much of the irony, humor and self-confidence (the "signifying") in these poems and stories.

Frantz Fanon, a psychoanalyst from Martinique who joined the Algerian revolution, spoke in *The Wretched of the Earth* (1961) of the sharp "Manichaean" division between colonizer and colonized, of the "nervous condition" or psychological instability colonial power produces in the colonized mind, and of the violent necessity to uproot this colonized condition. He illuminates, certainly, the directly political writing here that enacts clashes between African and European on the terrain of class, gender, and race. But Fanon's thinking applies equally to the literature of private life, where "the decolonization of the mind" (in the phrase of Ngugi wa Thiong'o) takes place, at the level of the ability to break the silence and speak out, or to complete the rites of passage to adult identity. Fanon's ideas have also been extended by some African women writers to depict the struggles of women of color with colonial and traditional forms of patriarchal power in home, school, work, and politics.

On "race" itself, inevitably foregrounded in much African work, these writers have many complex and differing views. Some tend, like Fanon in "The Fact of Blackness," to see race—nothing in itself, scientifically and rationally a pure *fiction*—as nevertheless historically the overriding *fact*. Others like Du Bois tend to deconstruct "race" as an ideological invention, a category produced out of social interaction according to rules designed to enforce the interests of the racial group in power and destined to disappear in a democratic, that is, a *non*racial, society.

There is a related debate over the concept of the nation and the politics of national identity. Postindependence writers in Malawi or Zimbabwe, for instance, often criticize the identification of the nation with the state-class, suggesting that the nation is rather the poorest of its citizens. The "New Nation" theories of many in the South African movement (e.g., Njabulo Ndebele and Lauretta Ngcobo) would now identify what is important in this literature as that which begins to imagine radically new forms of national culture. One challenging approach to these texts would therefore be to ask whether and how they help to construct such a new, decolonized, postracist, feminist, democratic, multiethnic culture—for Africans.

Finally, such questions about the philosophical or ethical bearing of African literature are also crisscrossed by questions about its form, style, and aesthetic principles. It is remarkable, for example, how much a literature one would have thought bound to protest narratives and stark realism is in fact devoted to parable, dream, fable, and prophecy, often between the naturalistic lines; in many cases the greatest realists are the wildest utopians. The influence of orality on the print literature, and its survivals in contemporary urban oral performance art, are everywhere extraordinary. In the case of English, the language itself bends and twists into new syntactic and semantic shapes under the pressure of urban black "double consciousness" or rural vernacular speech. The figure and role of the artist preoccupy several of the writers here, calling up traditional African views of the poet as teacher, social critic, and custodian of history, spirituality, and culture, as well as many international trends in art. Perhaps the varied aesthetics of this literature, like its ethics and its politics, is best understood as a kind of coming-to-voice whose full, rich timbre will only become audible in a happier time.

* * *

The three countries of North Africa—Morocco, Algeria, and Tunisia—known in Arabic as the Maghreb, which France controlled until Algeria finally won its independence in 1962, have a specific colonial history. Close to France geographically, yet fiercely independent owing to their ancient Islamic culture with its highly developed scriptural tradition on the one hand, and their pre-Islamic, Berber tribal cultures with their rich oral traditions on the other, the peoples of the Maghreb nonetheless learned the colonizer's language, only to use it to de-colonize themselves. Although Memmi and Fanon predicted the disappearance of Maghrebian literature in French with independence, such has not been the case. On the contrary, Francophone North African literature is flourishing. The Moroc-can novelist Tahar Ben Jelloun has won the Prix Goncourt, France's most prestigious prize for literature. The selections here include three Algerian writers whose projects could not be more different, and who therefore give some sense of the range of Maghrebian literature in French, particularly since independence in the 1950s and 1960s. Algeria, especially, has produced a large and fascinating corpus, much of it embroidering on the long, painful war of independence from France. In 1954, when the war against the French began, there were one million French people living in Algeria, and nine million indigenous Algerians. It was only after eight violent years of fighting that French President Charles de Gaulle agreed to independence for Algeria.

The colonial history of North Africa had a deep and lasting influence on the literary production of the region. Unlike their cousins in Eastern Africa, many North African writers had to bear the burden of linguistic imperialism. French was and remains the major literary medium for many of North Africa's most prominent writers and intellectuals.

The last few decades, however, have seen a movement toward Arabization. This, interestingly enough, has been coupled with the intense cultural and religious pull of the Islamist ("revivalist") movement that promotes pride in the Arabic language and literary heritage. Of course, the extent and influence of the Arabic medium varies from country to country.

Historical Background

Modern African history may be traced to the Berlin West African Conference of 1884–1885, wherein European imperial powers negotiated agreements among themselves that made the near-total colonization of Africa a certain conclu-sion. Europe's interest in Africa was not new: commerce had quickly followed the exploratory voyages of Portuguese mariners along the coast of the continent in the fifteenth century. The Portuguese sacked the lavish Swahili emporiums on the East African coast but initiated profitable trade, first in gold and later in slaves, on the central west coast. The Dutch, British, and French followed shortly thereafter.

With the colonization of the lands of the New World the slave trade became enormous. Offering cotton, firearms, metalware and cheap textiles, Europeans redirected and vastly expanded existing inter-African slave systems. The wealth of great polities like the Ashanti empire and the kingdom of Dahomey (in present-day Ghana, Benin, and Nigeria, respectively), as well as a number of Niger delta cities, was founded on this new economy. Beginning in the late eighteenth century, a heavy Indian Ocean slave trade emerged as well, overseen by the Portuguese on the Mozambique coast and by Arab merchants among the Swahili further north, most profitably in Zanzibar.

Europe's exchange with Africa remained coastal until the nineteenth century. While Islam made inroads along the Nile valley into the Sudan and across medieval trans-Saharan trade routes into the savannas south of the desert, the dislocations of coastal societies engendered by slavery generally did not affect the pastoral cultures of hunters, food-gatherers, and subsistence farmers—with the notable exception of the Great Lakes region of the east. Explorers began to trace river and slave raiding routes into the interior, however, and were followed by missionaries and traders. In the north, France invaded Algeria in 1830; in the south, Dutch farmers, or Boers, who had first settled at Cape of Good Hope in the seventeenth century, dispossessed and enslaved Khoi- and Bantu-speaking peoples as they steadily enlarged their holdings.

Despite significant governmental ambivalence, European imperial activity in Africa gained a fantastic momentum by the 1880s. National rivalries, the promise of huge new markets and resources that would engage the abundant capitalist energy of industrial Europe, and the achievements of magnate-adventurers like Britain's Cecil Rhodes and George Goldie all precipitated "the scramble for Africa," as the *fin-de-siècle* imperialist enterprise came to be called, as well as the racist ideologies that undergirded this enterprise.

The Berlin conference divided the continent among the major colonial powers. Over the next forty years, Great Britain, France, Germany, Portugal, and Italy—along with King Leopold II of Belgium, who seized the Congo—invaded and annexed the territories they had claimed in European conference rooms. The authors whose work is represented here come from Algeria, Morocco, Madagascar, and Senegal, all occupied by France; Kenya, Uganda, Malawi, Ghana, and Nigeria, occupied by Britain (Germany lost Tanzania in World War I); Angola, a Portuguese colony; South Africa, originally a British colony and later an independent nation ruled by Dutch descendants.

The civilizations subjugated by Europe were exceptionally diverse and numerous. Tribe, the traditional designation of groupings of Africans, belies both the variety and structural and moral sophistication of African societies.

The unifying characteristics of most of these societies—including clan-and-lineage social systems and preindustrial, low-producing, usually subsistence economies—made Africans vulnerable to the invasions of modern armies, the predations of European commerce, and the degradations of colonial administration. At the same time, although much of Africa was partitioned without violence, a number of African nations vigorously if unsuccessfully resisted colonization. Just as Ottoman Arabs had defied the French in Algeria between 1830 and 1847, Samori Touré in the Western Sudan (today's Guinea, Mali, and Côte d'Ivorie) resisted with great tenacity the colonial armies of France during the last two decades of the century. Prolonged struggles emerged throughout the continent, including the resistance of the Islamic Mahdi in Eastern Sudan against the British, the successful defense of Ethiopia by Menelik II against Italy, and the Boer-British conflicts in South Africa. This last antagonism climaxed in the Boer War (1899–1902), which ended with an English military victory but also in territorial concessions that led to Boer independence in 1910, when the Union of South Africa was established.

Colonial rule was not monolithic. The differences between the "indirect rule" of the British—whose administration often engaged the agency of local African leaders and customs—and the more centralized, assimilationist imperatives of French and Portuguese governance blurred in practice, however. Ultimately, all colonial experience shared a central fact: the devastating effects of the imposition of a new political and social economy—the modern western economy—upon a premodern populace.

The colonial powers and their agents implemented the new industries of this economy without any attempt to integrate these industries with traditional structures. Economic development, frequently supervised by enormous private conglomerates, was almost wholly oriented toward the provision of export goods. Moreover, colonies were under constant pressure to pay for their own administration, a circumstance that demanded extremely high rates of production. To meet the demand, new plantations and mines—such as the Belgian rubber trade in the Congo and the British diamond and gold cartels in South Africa—violently exploited masses of forced laborers. Additionally, a system of labor taxes forced African men either to leave their villages and work for European firms or to pay stiff levies. The ensuing creation of a migrant labor population—made larger by a new and growing need among Africans for money—crippled and impoverished village community and family life. At the same time, race codes, known as "color bars," prevented the new generations of African workers from assuming any but the most arduous and menial jobs.

In regions with significant settler populations—Kenya, Southern Rhodesia (now Zimbabwe), and South Africa in particular—landholding laws forced native populations off most arable lands. By 1936, for instance, nearly 90 percent of South Africa was reserved for white settlers. "Pass laws" restricted movement. Violent animosities arose between African groups that had peacefully coexisted as land dispossession overthrew traditional habitation patterns—falsely supporting the racist myth that Africans were warring savages who would be "civilized" by their European "benefactors."

Conditions were better in the western regions—especially in the Gold Coast (modern Ghana)—which had a longer history of trade with Europe and only a small settler presence. By the outbreak of World War II in 1939, though, political and economic inertia characterized almost all colonial rule. Nationalist sentiments that had been percolating for several years began to find a voice among Arab dissidents in the north, among African workers, particularly miners in South Africa, and among the few Africans who had been educated during the European possession.

The events of World War II brought these inchoate nationalisms—movements for independence within the frontiers that had been constructed by the imperial powers—to the forefront of African life. Massive urbanization was prompted by the industrial demands of the war effort, creating intensifying centers of unrest and political agitation. The war itself, a struggle for freedom and national self-determination, naturally fostered a climate of nationalist ardor. These developments engaged traditions of political independence—manifest during the modern era in resistance to invasion and revolt under colonial rule—to produce powerful insurgencies across the continent. By 1945, at the sixth Pan-African Congress, figures like Kwame Nkrumah (later president of Ghana) and Jomo Kenyatta (later president of Kenya) championed independence as well as the need for African unity.

The pace of the independence movements was extraordinarily rapid; constitutional concessions by the French and British did not appreciably slow it. In 1952 a group of military officers led by Gamal Abdel Nasser toppled the Farouk monarchy in 1952 and proclaimed a republic. These events proved a watershed: Morocco, Tunisia, and the Sudan all gained independence in 1956. Algeria, a settler colony, undertook an armed revolt in 1954 and achieved its independence from France in 1962 at the cost of one million lives.

More than forty-five African states have since become independent as well, beginning with Ghana, under Nkrumah's guidance, in 1957. As in Algeria, settler colonies waged the most contentious and violent independence struggles. Kenya's emergence as a republic in 1963 followed a decade of bloody conflicts between the British government and Kikuyu rebels—most notably in the Mau Mau uprisings and reprisals of the early 1950s. The white minority government of Southern Rhodesia declared independence as Rhodesia in 1965; internal warfare and international sanctions eventually forced recognition of a majority government in 1980, at which time the country took the name Zimbabwe. Additionally, after years of guerrilla warfare, Mozambique and Angola gained their independence from Portugal in 1975.

The subsequent progress of the new states of Africa was everywhere beset with difficulties. The colonial structures inherited by the first leaders of state remained wholly inadequate to address the overwhelming challenges that modernity had posed to Africa. Even the wealthiest nations continued to depend on European aid and imports, accumulating vast debt and failing to develop domestic economies. The combination of largely uncritical public support, the failure of established models, and political degeneration led to single party systems guided by charismatic figures who increasingly concentrated the power of their regimes. Popular upheavals, socialist experiments, violence, and military coups followed, and by the mid-1960s a sense of crisis again pervaded much of the continent. Political instability was exacerbated by the interference of the United States and the Soviet Union during the course of their Cold War maneuvers.

The problems and promise of modern Africa are reflected in the recent history of the Republic of South Africa. After more than eighty years of repressive and racist minority white rule, codified as a system of governance known as apartheid in 1948, a reformist government took power in 1989. It has undertaken the dismantling of the apartheid system and in 1990 freed Nelson Mandela, the vastly popular leader of the African National Congress, after more than twenty-seven years of imprisonment.

With few exceptions, African nations entered the 1990s seeking new approaches to meet the most elementary needs of their citizens—as well as the broader and more perilous problems of famine and drought, overpopulation, and the AIDS epidemic.

Further Readings

Andrzejewski, B. W., et al., eds. *Literature in African Languages*. Cambridge: Cambridge University Press, 1988.

Barnett, Ursula A. *A Vision of Order: A Study of Black South African Literature in English (1914–1980)*. Amherst: University of Massachusetts Press, 1983.

Burton, Richard. *First Footsteps in East Africa*. 2 vols. London: Tylston and Edwards, 1894, repr. New York: Prager, 1966; New York: Dover, 1987.

Calame-Griaule, Genevieve. *Words and the Dogon World*. Trans. Deirdre LaPin. Philadelphia: Institute for the Study of Human Issues, 1987.

Campschreur, Willem, and Joost Divendal, eds. *Culture in Another South Africa*. New York: Olive Branch, 1989.

Coplan, David B. *In Township Tonight! South Africa's Black City Music and Theatre*. New York: Longman, 1985.

Davidson, Basil, *African Civilization Revisited from Antiquity to Modern Times*. Trenton: Africa World Press, 1991.

Finnegan, Ruth. *Oral Literature in Africa*. Oxford: Clarendon Press, 1970.

Horne, Alistair. *A Savage War of Peace: Algeria. 1954–1962*. London: Penguin Books, 1977.

Iliffe, John. *The African Poor: A History*. Cambridge: Cambridge University Press, 1987.

Kavanagh, Robert. *Theatre and Cultural Struggle in South Africa*. London: Zed Books, 1985.

Kaye, Jacqueline, and Abdelhamid Zoubir. *The Ambiguous Compromise: Language, Literature, and National Identity in Algeria and Morocco*. New York: Routledge, 1990.

Kenyatta, Jomo. *Facing Mount Kenya*. New York: Vintage Books, 1965.

Killam, G. D. *The Writing of East and Central Africa*. London: Heinemann, 1984.

Memmi, Albert. *The Colonizer and the Colonized*. Boston: Beacon Press, 1965.

Monego, Joan. *Maghrebian Literature in French*. Boston: Twayne, 1984.

Ogot, B. A., ed. *Zamani: A Survey of East African History*. Nairobi: Longmans and East African Publishing House, 1974.

Omond, Roger. *The Apartheid Handbook: A Guide to South Africa's Everyday Racial Policies*. Harmondsworth, Eng.: Penguin, 1986.

Ranger, Terence O. "The Invention of Tradition in Colonial Africa." *The Invention of Tradition*. Eric Hobsbawn and Terence Ranger, eds. Cambridge: Cambridge University Press, 1983.

Scheub, Harold. *African Oral Narratives, Proverbs, Riddles, Poetry and Song*. Boston: G. K. Hall, 1977.

———. "A Review of African Oral Traditions and Literature." *African Studies Review* 28. 2–3 (June-September 1985): 1–72.

Shillington, Kevin. *History of Southern Africa*. New York: Longman, 1987.

Vansina, Jan. *Oral Tradition as History*. Madison: University of Wisconsin Press, 1985.

Zell, Hans M., et al. *A New Reader's Guide to African Literature*. New York: Africana Publishing Company, 1983.

KHOI PEOPLE

This oral poem from the Khoi people (shepherds and hunters who were the original inhabitants of the Cape region) is part story, part charm recited to ensure the sun's return. God, represented in the figure of a woman gathering food, collects the light of the Milky Way for human use. The rhythmic repetitions ("he piles them . . . piles them up . . . piles them into her pot, piles them up") carry the startling energy of the metaphors on a stream of sound; this sort of word play and rich texture is typical of oral art, which is anything but simple. The poem's sudden reversals of fortune, so keyed to changes in weather, reflect the life of centuries of hunting and pastoral cultures in the dry savanna of much of Southern Africa: life is either up or down, a sudden darkening or an overflowing of light.

Song for the Sun that Disappeared Behind the Rainclouds*

The fire darkens, the wood turns black.
The flame extinguishes, misfortune upon us.
God sets out in search of the sun.
The rainbow sparkles in his hand,
the bow of the divine hunter.   5
He has heard the lamentations of his children.
He walks along the milky way, he collects the stars.
With quick arms he piles them into a basket
piles them up with quick arms
like a woman who collects lizards   10
and piles them into her pot, piles them up
until the pot overflows with lizards
until the basket overflows with light.

VAI PEOPLE OF LIBERIA

The Vai people of Liberia invented their own system of writing in the nineteenth century or earlier, but not for tales like "The Wax Doll." As with most agricultural peoples, one of their principal arts is oral performance. This tale typifies live

Translated by Ulli Beier.

performances of African folktales, proverbs, riddles, and folksongs. Conventional opening and closing phrases, innumerable varieties of repetition, and recurrent plots and characters are found in such tales. Verbal art in Africa perfectly illustrates the Roman poet Horace's notion that poetry teaches and pleases at the same time. Amusing as it is, the tale can be seen as helping to preserve old ways. Trickster, a character familiar to any audience, and also common in Western literature, is rewarded in tale after tale for his antisocial behavior. Those tales raise questions about the relative importance of strength and wit. But can trickster always get away with violating social norms? No, say his fellow animals, who give him his comeuppance by destroying him—in this tale. In others, he will come back to life. Thus does fiction communicate a truth about society and its values, which do not need to be stated as "morals." African-American tarbaby stories derive from this widely popular plot, which was brought to the New World in the memories of thousands of slaves.

The Wax Doll

It was the farm season, and everybody was making plantations, first in the low marshes and then on the highland or in the mountainous regions—all except Spider, who was said to have been at the time very ill. Everybody in the town turned out to work but Spider. From the time the bushes were cut down and burnt to the time when the rice began to ripen, Spider lay in bed ailing.

When the rice was fully ripe and the people started to gather it, Spider's case became serious. It was thought he would die. But just before dying, he asked the people, when he was dead, to bury his body in some large rice farm.

Spider then died, and his body was accordingly interred in his uncle's largest farm.

Every morning after the burial, when the people came out to the farm, they found that either rice or some other article had been stolen during the previous night. This went on every night for a week. Several attempts were made to lay hands on the thief, but without success. There was no one who could guess who the thief was.

The people then went to a diviner to seek his priestly advice, or, if possible, to have the culprit described to them. The priest, however, told them to go and make a wax doll in the shape of a young girl, and to place it near the corner of the kitchen. In the morning, on their return, they would find that the burglar had been caught.

As the shades of night gradually fell, the disheartened laborers began to retire from their daily toil. There was a perfect stillness—all the farmers had gone home—and, when it was nearly midnight, Spider crept out easily from his grave, and went into the kitchen on a hunt for rice. His search was a quick one, he got everything he needed, and he commenced cooking some food. When the blaze became brighter, he looked around for a spoon with which to stir the rice, and his eyes suddenly fell on the beautiful young initiate (the doll is meant to resemble a schoolgirl in puberty) standing in the corner.

Translated by Harold Scheub.

Ibanehe Djilatendo. Zaire. *Deux Chasseurs*. 1931. Watercolor on paper.

Spider laughed, and said, "Are you watching me burn my hands without coming to my assistance?"

Spider was puzzled because the initiate did not reply. He dropped the spoon on the ground, and stepped up boldly to her and put his left hand on her shoulder.

The pots began to boil, and Spider made several attempts to go and look at his food, but the initiate refused to let him go—he was stuck to the wax.

Spider got vexed, and started to curse and swear. He told the initiate that if she did not speak or allow him to go and look after his pots, he would slap, kick, and knock her all over her face.

A deep silence ensued for a quarter of an hour. The initiate did not speak, nor did she release him.

It was now almost day—the rice in the pot had burned to cinders—and there was Spider, hanging with his hands, feet, and teeth stuck on to the beeswax coating of the initiate. When it was day, and the people came to their farms, they found old Spider hanging. They yelled and shouted at him, and some of them poured oil on him and set his body on fire. Spider was burned to cinders, and his ashes were thrown into his old grave.

YORUBA PEOPLE OF NIGERIA

A thoroughly urban, proud, assertive people, the Yoruba of Nigeria have attracted the attention of Europeans for centuries through their extraordinary art, monarchic society, and highly developed religion. They inhabit densely populated

southwestern Nigeria and eastern Benin; the slave trade brought them also to
Cuba and Brazil.

According to traditional Yoruba marriage rituals, a substantial price must be
paid for a bride, to compensate the bride's family for the loss of her labor. A bridal
chant is a specialized form of *oriki,* or praise-poetry; other forms eulogize
persons, animals, or deities. The speaker in "Rárà Iyawó," a slender beauty,
thanks her parents, describes her future husband, praises her town and lineage,
and expresses the hope that her bridal home will be hospitable to her.

Rárà Iyawó

When I was coming to the world
My mother, I brought 1400 cowries' worth of kola
When I was coming to the world
My mother, I brought 1200 cowries' worth of kola
Not because of death, not because of disease   5
Because of co-wives in this world,
The ones that bring their enmity from heaven.
Whatever co-wife I may chance to have,
Child of the Okin people, may she be a mother to me,
May good luck attend me today.   10

I was sitting quietly at home
I was staying quietly in my house
"The owner of good teeth inherits laughter"
It was he who said I should come and be his partner.
May good luck attend me today.   15

My mother did me proud, to my great satisfaction
She didn't let me go begging for cloth from abusive people
She didn't let me go begging for gowns from the scurrilous
I'm wearing this cloth that I like very much
She didn't let me go through the town dressed in *kijipa* [coarse cotton cloth]   20
May good luck attend me today.

Today I want to salute our town
He is a senior man, offspring of Oyo
Offspring of Oyo people, I want to salute our town.
Where might our home be?   25
And where might the home of my father be?
Oyo is our home
Oyo is the home of my father.
How many bushfowl
Are there in our Oyo?   30
There are only three bushfowl
In our Oyo.

Translated by Karin Barber.

One said "Let's sit, let's sit,"
One said "Let's fly, let's fly,"
One said, "Let's whirr off and go to Ale-Oyun."   35
The first time round
I made a little farm
A little tiny farm at Ale-Oyun
Locusts came as if in jest
Locusts ate my farm up.   40
The second time around
I made another little farm
A little tiny farm at Ale-Oyun
Locusts came as if in jest
Locusts ate my farm up.   45
I took my case to the palace of Ale-Oyun.
Ale-Oyun said I was in the wrong.
I said why?
He said, "When the locusts have no farm and no river,
What do you expect the locusts to eat?"   50

. . .

Money and children, I say they should go with me
I say if that is not the way, if that is not the house
I'll quickly turn and go another way.
I took my calabash and went to Oyo town
The prince of Oyo took the calabash from off my head.   55
I said, Sir, excuse me, why did you do that?
He said it's because I am a slender beauty
I have a neck worthy to wear blue *segi* beads
May good luck attend me today.

JEAN-JOSEPH RABÉARIVELO

(1901–1937)

Madagascar; Malagasy/French

Jean-Joseph Rabéarivelo came from the unique confluence of cultures in Madagascar: Indonesian, Indian, Arabo-Persian, and French. He expressed perfectly the variability of his island culture, and he was influenced by European romanticism, and Baudelaire. He took opium and lived from one crisis to the next, but at the same time he researched, collected, and translated Malagasy oral poetry. His own poems are written in a traditional dense, private, and dreamlike style, but with a passion, true to tradition, for conforming to old styles and making beautiful sounds. "Cactus" rests on a single conceit, the analogy between a leper's hand and the fleshy shape of succulents. From this nightmarish image, the cactus grows to personify spirits of the arid region, also representing the nocturnal creativity of poem and dream.

Cactus

This multitude of melted hands
   still offering flowers to the blue,
   this multitude of hands without fingers
   that the wind can't move:
   hidden water rises in their seamless palms,   5
   I'm told, to satisfy the thirst of
   a thousand cattle
   and the nomad tribes
   that wander to the limits of the South.

Hands without fingers sprung from streams,   10
Melted hands that stand against the blue.

Here,
   when the City's flanks were still as green
   as moonlight leaping in the forests,
   when goats still grazed the hills of Iarive,   15
   it was on the steep forbidding rocks
   they stood to guard their source,
   these lepers decked in flowers.

Penetrate the grotto that they spring from
   to know the sickness that afflicts them   20
   —its origin more nebulous than night,
   more distant than the dawn—
   but you will know no more than I:
   blood from the earth, sweat from the stone,
   and sperm from the wind   25
   have run together in these palms,
   dissolved their fingers
   and set golden flowers in their place.

I know a child
   a prince still in God's realm   30
   who'd add:
   "And Destiny, taking pity on these lepers
   told them to plant flowers
   and to keep their sources
   far from cruel men."   35

Translated by John Reed and Clive Wake.

BIRAGO DIOP (b. 1906)
Senegal; French

Birago Diop, a Senegalese veterinarian, has rewritten the oral folktales of the *griot** Amaduo Koumga Ngom, into literary texts. The allegorical characters in "Truth and Falsehood" represent universal human tendencies, while Fène-Falsehood's success reworks the West African trickster theme of the cleverness necessary for survival.

Truth and Falsehood

Fène-Falsehood had grown big and learnt much. But there were many things that he still did not know, amongst others that man—and woman even less—bears no resemblance to the good Lord. So he took umbrage, and thought himself hard done by, every time he heard anyone say, 'The good Lord loves Truth!' And he heard it very often. It is true that some people said that Truth and Falsehood were as like as two peas, but the majority stated that Truth and Falsehood were like night and day. That is why, when one day he set out on a journey with Deug-Truth, Fène-Falsehood said to his travelling companion,

"You are the one whom the Lord loves, you are the one whom people no doubt prefer, so it is you who must do the talking wherever we go. For if I were recognised we should be very badly received."

They set out early one morning and walked for a long time. At midday they entered the first house in the village which they had reached. After the exchange of greetings they had to ask before being given anything to drink. Then the mistress of the house gave them some luke-warm water, which would have made an ostrich vomit, in a calabash of doubtful cleanliness. She showed no signs of giving them anything to eat, although a pot full of rice was boiling at the entrance to the hut. The travellers lay down in the shade of a baobab in the middle of the courtyard and waited for the good Lord, that is to say luck and the return of the master of the house. The latter came back at twilight and asked for food for himself and the strangers.

"I've nothing ready yet," said the woman, who could not have devoured the contents of the pot unaided.

The husband flew into a great rage, not only on his own account, although he was famished after spending the whole day working in the fields under the blazing sun, but because of his unknown guests, who had been left with empty bellies, and whom he had not been able to honour as any self-respecting master of a house should do. He asked:

Translated by Dorothy S. Blair.
*A West African reciter of traditional poetry and history.

"Is this the action of a good wife? Is this the action of a generous woman? Is this a good housewife?"

Fène-Falsehood, as agreed, prudently said nothing, but Deug-Truth could not keep silent. She answered frankly that a woman worthy of the name of mistress of the house might have been more hospitable to strangers, and ought always to have food prepared for her husband's return.

Then the woman flew into a furious rage and, threatening to arouse the whole village, ordered her husband to throw out of her house these impertinent strangers, who interfered with the way she ran her home and took it upon themselves to give her advice; otherwise she would return to her parents on the spot. So the poor husband, who could not see himself managing without a wife (even a bad housekeeper) and without any cooking, all on account of two passing strangers, whom he had never seen before and whom he would probably never see again in his life, was forced to tell the travellers to be on their way. Did they not remember that even if life was not all *couscous* it did nevertheless need some softening? Did they have to be so ill-bred as to say things so crudely?

So Deug and Fène continued their journey which had begun so inauspiciously. They walked for a long time till they reached a village where they found some children busy sharing a fat bull which they had just slaughtered. On entering the house of the village head-man, they saw some children saying to him,

"Here is your share," and they gave him the head and the feet of the animal.

Now, since time immemorial, since N'Diadiane n'Diaye, in every village inhabited by man, it is the head-man who distributes the meat, and chooses his own share—the best.

"Who do you think commands here, in this village?" the head-man asked the travellers.

Fène-Falsehood prudently kept silent and did not open his mouth; Deug-Truth was obliged, as agreed, to give her opinion:

"To all appearances," she said, "it is these children."

"You are most insolent!" cried the old man in a fury. "Leave this village! Go, go immediately, or you will never leave it again! Begone, begone!"

As they went, Fène said to Deug,

"The results have not been brilliant so far, and I am not sure that they will be any better if I leave you in charge of our affairs any longer. So from now on I am going to look after both of us. I am beginning to think that even if the good Lord loves you, man does not appreciate you very much."

Not knowing how they would be received in the village they were now approaching, from which came cries and lamentations, Deug and Fène stopped at the well before calling at any dwelling, and were quenching their thirst when a woman came along, all in tears.

"What is the meaning of these cries and tears?" asked Deug-Truth.

"Alas!" said the woman (who was a slave), "our favourite queen, the youngest of the king's wives, died yesterday, and the king is so heart-sore that he wants to kill himself so that he may join the woman who was the fairest and most gracious of his wives."

"And is that the sole cause of so much lamentation?" asked Fène-Falsehood.

"Go and tell the king that there is at the well a stranger who can bring back to life people who have even been dead for a long time."

The slave went off and returned a minute later accompanied by an old man who led the travellers into a fine hut, where they found a whole roasted sheep and two calabashes full of *couscous*.

"My master brings you here," said the old man, "and bids you rest after your long journey. He bids you wait and he will send for you before long."

The next day an even more copious meal was brought before the strangers and the day after the same thing happened. But Fène pretended to be angry and impatient; he said to the messengers,

"Go, tell your king that I have no time to waste here, and that I shall continue on my way if he has no need of me."

An old man returned to say,

"The king is asking for you." Fène followed him, leaving Deug in the hut.

"First, what do you desire as a reward for what you are about to do?" asked the king, when he came before him.

"What can you offer me?" replied Fène-Falsehood.

"I will give you one hundred things from all that I possess in this land."

"That will not satisfy me," Fène reckoned.

"Then you yourself say what you desire," suggested the king.

"I desire the half of all that you possess."

The king agreed.

Fène had a hut built above the grave of the favourite and went in alone, armed with a hoe. He could be heard puffing and panting; then, after a long time, he began to talk, softly at first, then in a loud voice as if he were arguing with several persons. At length he came out of the hut and stood with his back pressed firmly against the door.

"Things are getting very complicated," he said to the king. "I have dug up the grave, and woken up your wife, but scarcely had she returned to life and was about to emerge from beneath the ground, than your father woke up too and seized her by the feet, saying to me, 'Leave this woman alone. What can she give you? Whereas if *I* return to earth, I will give you my son's whole fortune.' He had barely finished making me this proposition, than *his* father emerged in his turn and offered me all his goods and half the property of his son. Your grandfather was elbowed out of the way by your father's grandfather, who offered me your property, your father's property, his son's property and the half of his own fortune. Scarcely had he finished speaking than *his* father arrived, so that your ancestors and the forebears of your ancestors are all now at the exit of your wife's grave."

King Bour looked at his advisers, and the notables looked at the king. The stranger was quite right when he'd said that things were in a mess. Bour gazed at Fène-Falsehood, and the old men looked at him. What was to be done?

"To help you out of your dilemma, and to avoid too difficult a choice," said Fène-Falsehood, "just give me an idea of whom I should bring back, your wife or your father?"

"My wife!" cried the king, who loved the favourite more than ever. He had always been afraid of the late king, and had in fact precipitated his death with the assistance of the notables of the land.

"Naturally, naturally!" replied Fène-Falsehood. "Only you see, your father did offer me double what you promised me just now."

Bour turned towards his advisers, and the advisers gazed at him and at the stranger. The price was high, and what good would it do the king to see his beloved wife again if he were deprived of all his goods? Would he still be king? Fène guessed the thoughts of the king and of his notables.

"Unless," he said, "unless you give me, for leaving your wife where she is at present, what you promised me to bring her back."

"That is certainly the best and most reasonable thing to do!" replied the notables in chorus, remembering how they had helped to get rid of the old king.

"What do you say, Bour?" asked Fène-Falsehood.

"Oh well, let my father, my father's father, and their father's fathers remain where they are, and my wife likewise," said the king.

And so it was that Fène-Falsehood received half the king's goods for bringing no one back from the other world, while the king himself soon forgot his favourite and took another wife.

LÉOPOLD SÉDAR SENGHOR (b. 1906)
Senegal; French

Léopold Sédar Senghor was the first African poet writing in French to win acclaim. As a founder of the *Négritude* movement in the 1930s, he reaffirmed the dignity of black people around the world. As the first president of the Republic of Senegal (1960–1980) and a member of the Académie Française, Senghor expressed his hopes for the universal reconciliation of all races. "Black Woman" extols a beauty that had been disparaged by the racist attitudes of colonialism. In "Prayer to the Masks," Senghor celebrates, from the African side, the art objects that had revitalized European art in the early twentieth century.

Black Woman

Naked woman, black woman
Dressed in your color that is life, in your form that is beauty!
I grew up in your shadow. The softness of your hands
Shielded my eyes and now at the height of Summer and Noon,
From the crest of a charred hilltop I discover you, Promised Land   5
And your beauty strikes my heart like an eagle's lightning flash.

Translated by Melvin Dixon.

Naked woman, dark woman
Ripe fruit with firm flesh, dark raptures of black wine,
Mouth that gives music to my mouth
Savanna of clear horizons, savanna quivering to the fervent caress   10

Of the East Wind, sculptured tom-tom, stretched drumskin
Moaning under the hands of the conqueror
Your deep contralto voice is the spiritual song of the Beloved.

Naked woman, dark woman
Oil no breeze can ripple, oil soothing the thighs   15
Of athletes and the thighs of the princes of Mali
Gazelle with celestial limbs, pearls are stars
Upon the night of your skin. Delight of the mind's riddles,
The reflections of red gold from your shimmering skin
In the shade of your hair, my despair   20
Lightens in the close suns of your eyes.

Naked woman, black woman
I sing your passing beauty and fix it for all Eternity
before jealous Fate reduces you to ashes to nourish the roots of life.

Prayer to the Masks

Masks! O Masks!
Black mask, red mask, you white-and-black masks
Masks of the four cardinal points where the Spirit blows
I greet you in silence!
And you, not the least of all, Ancestor with the lion head.   5
You keep this place safe from women's laughter
And any wry, profane smiles
You exude the immortal air where I inhale
The breath of my Fathers.
Masks with faces without masks, stripped of every dimple   10
And every wrinkle
You created this portrait, my face leaning

On an altar of blank paper
And in your image, listen to me!
The Africa of empires is dying—it is the agony   15
Of a sorrowful princess
And Europe, too, tied to us at the navel.
Fix your steady eyes on your oppressed children
Who give their lives like the poor man his last garment.
Let us answer "present" at the rebirth of the World   20
As white flour cannot rise without the leaven.
Who else will teach rhythm to the world
Deadened by machines and cannons?

Who will sound the shout of joy at daybreak to wake orphans and the dead?
Tell me, who will bring back the memory of life   25
To the man of gutted hopes?
They call us men of cotton, coffee, and oil
They call us men of death.
But we are men of dance, whose feet get stronger
As we pound upon firm ground.   30

ELISABETH EYBERS (b. 1915)
South Africa/Holland

One of the first important poets writing in the Afrikaans language, Eybers was a member of the *Dertigers* (writers of the 1930s), a group with modernist tendencies, open to poetic developments outside Africa. From her first collection of poems, *Confession in the Twilight* (1936), through a later selection, *The Quiet Adventure* (1948), and her more recent *Balance* (1962), *Shelter* (1968), and *Cross or Coin* (1973), her poetry has been celebrated for its reflective irony. After the advent of apartheid in 1948, Eybers left South Africa to settle in Holland, one of the first Afrikaner writers to choose self-exile for political reasons. These poems bear witness to her perception of a woman's strength and of a poet's ecstasy; they portray a quiet and essential loneliness.

Narrative

A woman grew, with waiting, over-quiet.
The earth along its spiralled path was spun
through many a day and night, now green, now dun;
at times she laughed, and then, at times, she cried.
The years went by. By turns she woke and slept   5
through the long hours of night, but every day
she went, as women go, her casual way,
and no one knew what patient tryst she kept.
Hope and despair tread their alternate round
and merge into acceptance, till at length   10
the years have only quietness in store.
And so at last the narrative has found
in her its happy end; this tranquil strength
is better than the thing she's waiting for.

Translated by Elisabeth Eybers.

Emily Dickinson

"Essential oils are wrung:
The attar from the rose
Is not expressed by suns alone,
It is the gift of screws"
Emily Dickinson

That knowledge which the ruthless screws distil
she could not weigh against the easy truth
that's cheap and readily negotiable:
as time went on, her days grew more aloof.
The years proved meagre as they came and went;   5
her narrow, ardent love, commodity
that found no market, still remained unspent:
yearning, forsakenness and ecstasy.
She climbed the scaffolding of loneliness
not to escape from living, but to gain   10
a perilous glimpse into the universe;
and tunnelled down into the mind's dark mine,
through tortuous shafts descending to obtain
its flawless fragments, glittering, crystalline.

GABRIEL OKARA (b. 1921)
Nigeria; English

Gabriel Okara was educated in Nigeria and the United States. He has worked as
a print and broadcast journalist, in print and on the radio, and he is the author
of a poetic novel of social concern, *The Voice*, in which he makes Ijaw culture
accessible to readers of English, as he does in his poetry. In "You Laughed and
Laughed and Laughed," which is addressed to a Westerner, he challenges
hypocritical attitudes about Africa.

from **The Fisherman's Invocation**

You Laughed and Laughed and Laughed

In your ears my song
is motor car misfiring
stopping with a choking cough;
and you laughed and laughed and laughed.

In your eyes my ante-
natal walk was inhuman, passing
your "omnivorous understanding"
and you laughed and laughed and laughed.   5

You laughed at my song,
you laughed at my walk.   10

Then I danced my magic dance
to the rhythm of talking drums pleading, but you shut your
eyes and laughed and laughed and laughed.

And then I opened my mystic
inside wide like   15
the sky, instead you entered your
car and laughed and laughed and laughed.

You laughed at my dance,
you laughed at my inside.

You laughed and laughed and laughed.   20
But your laughter was ice-block
laughter and it froze your inside froze
your voice froze your ears
froze your eyes and froze your tongue.

And now it's my turn to laugh;   25
but my laughter is not
ice-block laughter. For I
know not cars, know not ice-blocks.

My laughter is the fire
of the eye of the sky, the fire   30
of the earth, the fire of the air,
the fire of the seas and the
rivers fishes animals trees
and it thawed your inside,
thawed your voice, thawed your   35
ears, thawed your eyes and
thawed your tongue.

So a meek wonder held
your shadow and you whispered:
"Why so?"   40
And I answered:
"Because my fathers and I
are owned by the living
warmth of the earth
through our naked feet."   45

NADINE GORDIMER (b. 1923)
South Africa; English

Nadine Gordimer, an English-speaking white South African writer, was awarded the Nobel Prize in 1991. To readers all over the world, for nearly forty years this novelist has represented the possibility that white conscience and action may help erase racism from her country. Avoiding an overt political tone, her fiction explores the inner worlds and interactions of female and male, black and white, making the linkage of public and private, personal and political, her major theme. Though Gordimer is avowedly no feminist (she considers white feminism unthinkable in a racist society), many readers think that novels such as *Burger's Daughter* and *July's People* are deeply feminist in effect.

A Lion on the Freeway, from *A Soldier's Embrace*, captures a fragment of a middle-aged white woman's consciousness in a moment between sleep and waking. In the narrator's mind, the remembered sounds of zoo lions, boat foghorns, black dock workers' chants, and people making love all fuse with the actually heard sound of a truck on the new freeway. The pattern of sounds in the story presents a contrast between a private life of love, intimacy, travel, and leisure and a public world of tension, anguish, strikes, and imprisonment. At the end the African lion, symbolizing the black freedom struggle, reaches powerfully into the night musings of this suburban white woman.

from *A Soldier's Embrace*

A Lion on the Freeway

Open up!
Open up!
What hammered on the door of sleep?
Who's that?

Anyone who lives within a mile of the zoo hears lions on summer nights. A tourist could be fooled. Africa already; at last; even though he went to bed in yet another metropole.

Just before light, when it's supposed to be darkest, the body's at its lowest ebb and in the hospital on the hill old people die—the night opens, a Black Hole between stars, and from it comes a deep panting. Very distant and at once very close, right in the ear, for the sound of breath is always intimate. It grows and grows, deeper, faster, more rasping, until a great groan, a rising groan lifts out of the curved bars of the cage and hangs above the whole city—

And then drops back, sinks away, becomes panting again.

Wait for it; it will fall so quiet, hardly more than a faint roughness snagging the air in the ear's chambers. Just when it seems to have sunk between strophe and antistrophe, a breath is taken and it gasps once; pauses, sustaining the night as a singer holds a note. And begins once more. The panting reaches up up up down down down to that awe-ful groan—

Open up!
Open up!
Open your legs.

In the geriatric wards where lights are burning they take the tubes out of noses and the saline-drip needles out of arms and draw the sheets to cover faces. I pull the sheet over my head. I can smell my own breath caught there. It's very late; it's much too early to be awake. Sometimes the rubber tyres of the milk truck rolled over our sleep. You turned . . .

Roar is not the word. Children learn not to hear for themselves, doing exercises in the selection of verbs at primary school: 'Complete these sentences: The cat ...s The dog ...s The lion ...s.' Whoever decided that had never listened to the real thing. The verb is onomatopoeically incorrect just as the heraldic beasts drawn by thirteenth- and fourteenth-century engravers at second hand from the observations of early explorers are anatomically wrong. Roar is not the the word for the sound of great chaps sucking in and out the small hours.

The zoo lions do not utter during the day. They yawn; wait for their ready-slaughtered kill to be tossed at them; keep their unused claws sheathed in huge harmless pads on which top-heavy, untidy heads rest (the visualized lion is always a maned male), gazing through lid-slats with what zoo visitors think of in sentimental prurience as yearning.

Or once we were near the Baltic and the leviathan hooted from the night fog at sea. But would I dare to open my mouth now? Could I trust my breath to be sweet, these stale nights?

It's only on warm summer nights that the lions are restless. What they're seeing when they gaze during the day is nothing, their eyes are open but they don't see us—you can tell that when the lens of the pupil suddenly shutters at the close swoop of one of the popcorn-begging pigeons through the bars of the cage. Otherwise the eye remains blank, registering nothing. The lions were born in the zoo (for a few brief weeks the cubs are on show to the public, children may hold them in their arms). They know nothing but the zoo; they are not expressing our yearnings. It's only on certain nights that their muscles flex and they begin to pant, their flanks heave as if they had been running through the dark night while other creatures shrank from their path, their jaws hang tense and wet as saliva flows as if in response to a scent of prey, at last they heave up their too-big heads, heavy, heavy heads, and out it comes. Out over the suburbs. A dreadful straining of the bowels to deliver itself: a groan that hangs above the houses in a low-lying cloud of smog and anguish.

O Jack, O Jack, O Jack, oh—I heard it once through a hotel wall. Was alone and listened. Covers drawn over my head and knees drawn up to my fists. Eyes strained wide open. Sleep again!—my command. *sleep again.*

It must be because of the new freeway that they are not heard so often lately. It passes its five-lane lasso close by, drawing in the valley between the zoo and the houses on the ridge. There is traffic there very late, too early. Trucks. Tankers, getting a start before daylight. The rising spray of rubber spinning friction on tarmac is part of the quality of city silence; after a time you don't hear much beyond it. But sometimes—perhaps it's because of a breeze. Even on a still summer night there must be some sort of breeze opening up towards morning. Not enough to stir the curtains, a current of air has brought, small, clear and distant, right into the ear, the sound of panting.

Or perhaps the neat whisky after dinner. The rule is don't drink after dinner. A metabolic switch trips in the brain: open up.

Who's that?

A truck of potatoes going through traffic lights quaked us sixteen flights up.

Slack with sleep, I was impaled in the early hours. You grew like a tree and lifted the pavements; everything rose, cracked, and split free.

Who's that?

Or something read in the paper . . . Yes. Last night—this night—in the City Late, front page, there were the black strikers in the streets, dockers with sticks and knobkerries. A thick prancing black centipede with thousands of waving legs advancing. The panting grows louder, it could be in the garden or under the window; there comes that pause, that slump of breath. Wait for it: waiting for it. Prance, advance, over the carefully-tended please keep off the grass. They went all through a city not far from this one, their steps are so rhythmical, waving sticks (no spears any more, no guns yet); they can cover any distance, in time. Shops and houses closed against them while they passed. And the cry that came from them as they approached—that groan straining, the rut of freedom bending the bars of the cage, he's delivered himself of it, it's as close as if he's out on the freeway now, bewildered, finding his way, turning his splendid head at last to claim what he's never seen, the country where he's king.

AGOSTINHO NETO (1922–1979)
Angola; Portuguese

Agostinho Neto was born in Catete, Angola, and died of cancer in Moscow in 1979. A medical doctor by profession, he led his country in its war of independence from Portugal, becoming its first president. He was associated with the student center Casa dos Estudiantes do Imperio in Lisbon, which published many African poets before closing in the 1960s. Neto, who wrote in Portuguese, protested the brutality of Portuguese colonialism and celebrated black brotherhood, part of the *Négritude* consciousness. To an African who faced the rape of his land and his soul by Westerners, Western civilization was anything but admirable. In this poem we see the effects of colonialism on an African laborer who lives in poverty and ill health and is exhausted by excessive physical work. For him, death is a relief from the horror of Western civilization.

Western Civilisation*

Sheets of tin nailed to posts
driven in the ground
make up the house.

Some rags complete
the intimate landscape.   5

The sun slanting through cracks
welcomes the owner

After twelve hours of slave
labour.

breaking rock   10
shifting rock
breaking rock
shifting rock
fair weather
wet weather   15
breaking rock
shifting rock

Old age comes early

a mat on dark nights
is enough when he dies   20
gratefully
of hunger.

SEMBÈNE OUSMANE (b. 1923)
Senegal; French

Sembène Ousmane served in the French army and worked in a variety of jobs—fisherman, mechanic, Marseilles dockworker, and union organizer—before taking up writing and film. Writing in French, Ousmane often literally

*Translated by Margaret Dickinson.

translates Wolof (the dominant language in Senegal) and Arabic terms that convey a multilingual effect. "Love in Sandy Lane" (1962) represents a deliberately simplified view of his native Senegal that forces the reader to think back over the story. The love of young people, which had reinforced a sense of community among the inhabitants of Sandy Lane, is thwarted by a system of arranged marriage. The subsequent degeneration of the neighborhood symbolizes the malaise into which such a system has precipitated a whole country. The reader is left to wonder if this apparently simple allegory is all there is to the story.

Love in Sandy Lane

It had no street sign, but everyone knew it as Sandy Lane. It was short—no more than two hundred yards long—and started at the charming villa "Mariame Ba," which blocked the far end, and came out on to the main street which ran right through the district.

It had got its name from a great number of things.

Opposite the entrance to Sandy Lane the villa "Mariame Ba" stood proud and spruce, painted yellow and blue. Amid the collection of decrepit old shacks, it had a manorial aspect; its greyish windows disclosed three rooms, each covered from floor to ceiling with photographs, some in glass frames. After *timis*, the sunset prayer, El Hadj Mar usually climbed on to the terrace overlooking the street. Below him was spread the jumble of rooftops, some flat, some pointed, the straw huts and the shacks. The inhabitants of Sandy Lane might have seemed very proud of "their villa." But deep down, each of them nursed a feeling of animosity towards the old employee of the late colonial administration, who from his lofty perch openly pried on their every action.

First in the lane, going down on the right, was Pourogne's shack, which leaned outwards and was shored up by three beams firmly embedded in the sand; the bottom planks were crumbling away and had been patched up with pieces of galvanized iron, and the red paint had faded in the sun. Then came the public fountain which had been condemned. (It was whispered in the district that this was due to the inhabitant's obstinacy towards government policy; for everyone except El Hadj Mar, so it was said, had voted "No" in the 1958 referendum.[1] So because of their rebellious character they were obliged to go elsewhere for water.) Next came Yaye Hady's compound, which was fenced round with bamboo wattle; in order to be considered a member of the Sandy Lane community, Yaye Hady had blocked up the old entrance giving on to the main street and had made a new one on the Sandy Lane side. Adjacent to him was the Niang's M'bar. The Niang family still carried on the goldsmith's craft handed down to them by their forbears, and by their love of this delicate work had greatly contributed to the fame of the lane. Their female clientele came from all parts of the town. The eldest Niang, a big fellow with a large behind, had a jolly face and the cavernous eyes of the old,

Translated by Len Ortyen.

---

1. Whether or not to become independent of France.

without eyebrows or lashes; he sat outside his workshop and gave interminable *salamalics*[2] to everyone coming out into the lane, except to El Hadj Mar. Then there was Salif's carpenter's shop; he was a wiry, very dark man, most amusing when so inclined, but a tireless singer. The people of Sandy Lane became worried if he was silent. That is why, when Salif's voice was no longer heard, it was said that "the Sandy Lane people" were in a bad way. And last of all on the right-hand side, adjoining the villa "Mariame Ba," was the big shack housing the family of old Maissa. He was a very devout man who never went out without his beads.

On the left-hand side of the lane was the mother-house of Granny Aita; the brick base was crumbling away and was riddled with holes into which the hens and ducks vanished. Three tall, pliable filos served as a refuge for the *catiocatios*. As soon as it was dusk, these weaver-birds filled the air with their "catio-catio" calls, hence their name. Their textile-nests looked like dangling black balls in the gathering darkness. Next came Mavdo's patch; he was the charcoal merchant, and a black dune as high as a hut spilled over from the patch. Then came the Youth Club, a hut with "Palais de l'ONU" (UNO Palace) chalked above the door. A few dozen young men met there, most of them out of work through no fault of their own. Through the door could be seen piles of old magazines, emblems of many nations and pictures of Heads of State and leaders of political parties all over the world. When the young men were tired of discussions they drowned their passion for politics in Moorish tea. Last of all, at an angle to the villa "Mariame Ba," was an unfinished building intended long ago for a policeman. When evening came, children went and relieved themselves among the heaps of bricks still lying around, as though it was the most natural thing in the world.

Such was the outward appearance, the material aspect, of Sandy Lane. It was nothing to write home about. But the people who lived there harboured a different kind of wealth, which had brought renown to this part of the town.

Once a week all the housewives got together to clean the lane. Early in the morning they all lined up in front of their doorways on both sides of the lane; they would bend down, little brush in hand, as though about to begin a dance. The two lines advanced and met in the middle, where, as if working to music, they divided into little groups and swept towards the main street like rippling waves. Then they dug a hole and buried all the rubbish. The lane was made of very fine sand which did not crunch underfoot. It was because of this rather exaggerated cleanliness that the inhabitants proudly allowed people from neighbouring streets to organize drum sessions in their lane, and the faithful there celebrated the birth of the Prophet.

It was a peaceful little lane, and the only one in the town to have such diverse and yet united characters living in it. However, a very common incident, too common at the present time, put an end to this state of affairs . . . . The people of Sandy Lane were not scandalmongers, but—and this was the cause of the trouble—neither did they confide in one another.

---

2. An Islamic greeting (in Arabic), given in a local setting; as a plural noun, greetings in general.

In Sandy Lane there lived a girl, Kine, who was El Hadj Mar's eldest daughter by his second wife. Her beauty was talked about all over the town. Her physical charms were a favourite subject for the songs of the youths who frequented the "Palais de l'ONU." When she returned from market, her calabash on her slightly tilted head, her graceful neck curved a little and her smooth, velvety shoulders showing above the wide neck of her muslin *boubou*, her walk so stately, the people of Sandy Lane—especially the men—turned and teased her; and she smiled back, showing her regular little white teeth.

Nothing was a secret in Sandy Lane; but no one ever talked of it, that was all. Everyone knew that Kine's heart beat only for Yoro, the old charcoal-merchant's son. Yoro was a shy young man, but he also played the kora. Sometimes he left the shelter of the "Palais de l'ONU" and plucked up his courage to go and strum his kora beneath the windows of the villa "Mariame Ba." When he and Kine happened to come face to face, or when their eyes met, there was a pleasant rush of blood, a warm, sweet rush of blood, in both of them; it rose from their toes and ran through their veins, giving them a warm sensation, warmer than anything else.

The people of Sandy Lane were simple or naive and they liked these two youngsters; and as this love reminded them of their own, they seemed to bless it by a conspiratorial silence. They thought quite simply that if two people loved one another, nothing could be strong enough to stand in their way.

Secretly—though the Sandy Lane folk were not very talkative—they were preparing to celebrate the wedding in their own fashion. All of them, men and women, said to Kine whenever she passed by, "How's Yoro?"

And to Yoro they said, "How's Kine?"

When Yoro came home from work at midday and at six o'clock, as soon as he reached Pourogne's shop he would look towards the villa. He scanned all the windows; and Kine, knowing it was the time for him to return, would be standing at one of the windows. And all Sandy Lane having discovered the young couple's secret, their way of greeting and communicating with each other, as soon as Yoro entered the lane a swarm of eyes instantly turned in the direction of the villa. They were very discreet, though, the lane's inhabitants. They never said very much. In the end the two turtle-doves gave up this deaf-and-dumb language; and in the evenings, after the last prayer, when everybody had come to sit outside and the night was draped in its starry robe, Yoro would sit in a fold of darkness and strum his kora while Kine, sitting with her parents in front of the villa, would let her thoughts run on.

Sandy Lane was well known. It was often mentioned in the songs of griots, for El Hadj Mar, a generous man, frequently invited story-tellers into his house. The tale of the mute love of Kine and Yoro went from mouth to mouth. Yet neither of them had gone beyond stealing shy glances, blinking, or sounding the quivering notes of the kora.

One day people saw mature men who occupied prominent positions in the country arriving in Sandy Lane. Among them was more than one Minister, several Chief Secretaries and other personalities. They all went to El Hadj Mar's house, where they spent the whole day feasting and drinking to excess. And they returned several times. Every week holes were dug in front of the villa and soon whole sheep could be seen roasting on spits over a wood fire. There were always official cars parked at the entrance to Sandy Lane; big, luxurious cars.

The regulars of the "Palais de l'ONU" felt frustrated; they supported Yoro. The other people, experienced observers as they were, muttered indignantly. Every day now, at midday and at six, their eyes remained firmly fixed on the ground; and the strumming of the kora was no longer heard in the evening. A month went by, a funereal silence settled on the lane—and Yoro had disappeared. Three months later, Kine was seen no more. (I was told that after the disappearance of the lovers, two trees were planted—a male and a female.) But since these happenings, Sandy Lane has ceased to be the pride of the district; the rubbish piles up, and the women throw their slops outside the villa "Mariame Ba." These people who formerly never uttered an oath have become foul-mouthed. The young men leave to live elsewhere. No longer are religious chants heard in the lane, and the drums throb no more . . .

Sandy Lane has become the saddest place in the world.

And as I walked around Dakar I wondered if the whole town was not under this curse.

DAVID DIOP (1927–1960)
France/Senegal; French

David Diop, of Senegalese and Cameroonian parentage, and born in Senegal, was educated in France. He spent most of his life in Paris, where he envisaged through poetry a newly liberated Africa. Believing that Francophone African literature had no future and that African literature should glorify its own past, he went to teach in West Africa for two years, until his sudden death in an airplane crash. Like his other poems, "Close to You" expresses his solidarity with all African peoples and his dream of a future based on social justice.

Close to You

Close to you I have regained my name
My name long hidden beneath that salt of distances
I have regained eyes no longer veiled by fevers
And your laugh like a flame making holes in the dark
Has given Africa back to me beyond the snows of yesterday   5
Ten years my love
And mornings of illusion and wreckage of ideas
And sleep peopled with alcohol

Translated by Simon Mpondo and Frank Jones.

Ten years and the breath of the world has poured its pain upon me
Pain that loads the present with the flavor of tomorrows   10
And makes of love an immeasurable river
Close to you I have regained the memory of my blood
And necklaces of laughter around the days
Days that sparkle with joys renewed.

JOHN MUNONYE (b. 1929)
Nigeria; English

John Munonye, an Igbo from Nigeria, is a teacher and educational administrator. He writes of the moral dilemmas facing societies like the Igbo, torn between Christianity, modern technology, and traditional values. He focuses on how people adjust and on what conflicts result when, as in Munonye's novels, the foreign institutions draw a person inexorably away from old ways. "Pack Pack Pack," which is set during the Nigerian civil war (1966–1969), reveals the traditionalist mentality of an old man who resists the message to "pack" up and leave, despite being surrounded by destruction.

Pack Pack Pack

He had on several occasions heard about people in flight—men and women, young and old, all moving in a sombre stream, hastily away from their homes, to unknown destinations. He would listen in silence, like an old man he was. However, his twitching eyelids often betrayed his deep emotion.

And now, the crisis was on him . . .

Pack Pack Pack! . . . Enemy machine-gun was sounding, ordering everyone in the village to move out before it was too late.

"Dede, it sounds so near," gasped Lolo, his wife.

"Does it?"

"Yes. Some say it is from Morube village."

"Morube which is our neighbour?"

"Yes. And people are moving." Her voice was cracked. Her eyes had an unusual lustre.

"So we too should move?"

He folded his hands across his chest. He tucked his legs underneath his chair . . .

"Dede, we're packing."

"I see!" And he walked away on her.

He went to the forehouse, which was a small, roomless hut. Two legs of wood were smouldering end to end there on the floor. He sat facing the fire, and definitely backing the dwelling house, which was another way of letting Lolo and the rest of his family know he wasn't interested in their plans for departure.

He picked up the family idol which was mounted on a tripod at a corner of the hut. He stood transfixed as he contemplated the idol. His countenance was grave and his cheeks were creased. As head of the family by direct descent, it was his duty and privilege to preserve the idol, and to communicate through it with the spirits of the ancestors.

Boom!

The ground vibrated and the atmosphere shook and the sky seemed to tremble. The shrill, hysterical cries rose everywhere; they were urging one another to make haste and run away.

Lolo came into the forehouse panting.

"Dede, we are ready."

"What for, my sister? Where to?" he wondered.

"I say we are ready."

Pack Pack Pack! . . .

He sat tight in his seat, shaking his head.

"I believe you are insane," she charged him with fury. "I will not talk to you again."

"Women!"

She was not longer there.

He looked round the room; then, he looked out, at the plot of land directly before the hut, specially at two plants of nearly equal heights that grew close together. Those plants marked his father Lamazu's grave—Lamazu, the notable warrior who was killed in one of the frequent battles with neighbouring Morube. But they recovered his body and brought it home, and gave it a hero's burial, and his name went into songs, and he became a model for courage. All that had happened many years ago, before things began to change the way they did. Indeed, things were different now. Wars were fought differently—so much so that people whom you owed no debt and with whom you had never disputed any piece of land, or chieftancy title, or a bride, came all the way, from far, far, far places, to drive you from your home.

Pack Pack Pack! . . .

Boom! . . . Boom boom boom! . . . Boom!

Smoke and confusion; cries of despair.

He saw Lolo, and the six children leaving the compound, each clutching at one object or the other, or carrying them on their heads. So that's all your packing? he thought to himself.

"Father, let's go," called Chieke who was the youngest child.

"Oh, you have your rattle in your hand?" he evaded.

"Yes. When I shake it you will play your lyre and people will begin to dance."

Another sound of guns put an end to their conversation.

Soon Lolo came again.

"We are leaving; stay here and die." With that, her eyes brimmed over.

"You can go, my sister," said he, slowly, coolly. "I'll stay. How many years more has Dede in this world?" He stopped abruptly and began to beat his chest with his fist. "To leave my house and go to die in a strange land?" His legs trembled in his bitter defiance. "It will never happen. Please go; and take good care of the children."

"My lyre, where are you?" He rose, stretched, looked around.

He went into the living house, took the lyre, and returned to the forehouse. He sat down again, this time close to the idol. Like the idol, the instrument now in his hand had come to him from his father.

He plucked at the metal prongs with the tips of his fingers, gently, deftly. Soon, he began to sing. His voice was deep and smooth.

Come rain come sun
The ground will never move
The leaves may wither and the springs may dry up
Yet the ground will never never move.

Along the stretch of road leading from his compound, scores of people were moving. It was like a flood after a heavy rain when tributaries converge from side paths. They were carrying or dragging along with them all sorts of objects in addition to domestic animals, especially the tame goat and the companionable dog.

Pack Pack Pack! . . .

Boom! . . . Boom! . . .

Continuous hissing sound! Up in the air! . . . It was advancing—roaring, ringing, racing, tearing the heavens apart. Everybody had escaped into the bush. The road was empty. Dede merely blinked with spite, and drew his chair forward, towards the idol.

A rocket flying out of the plane moments later exploded a good distance behind his compound, starting its own column of smoke. He laughed. Which house was that smoking a pipe this cold afternoon? He asked the question aloud.

That was that, he thought. Machine-gun artillery, then a war plane. What next?

Nobody in the land had believed it would ever come to this. For well over a year now, the enemy had been halted a good distance away, from where they would often fire their shell. And nearly everybody had got quite used to their shelling, except that the sound almost made one deaf. But who bothered about deafness so long as the soldiers themselves never arrived?

Stories had it that the advancing soldiers were terrible beings: tall and fearsome, dark-skinned, tattooed, unsmiling. The more gifted story-tellers around (one of them claimed to have heard from someone who had sat close to an important officer's mouth) told about how the enemy soldiers destroyed everything that moved, including human beings, by shooting non-stop and at random for days on end.

Any moment from now, they would arrive in Odukano. They had broken through the defense at last and were advancing without much resistance. There was confusion everywhere. Yes, the confusion had reached Odukano. Men and women of Odukano were now in flight. Except Dede.

He cleared his throat and sniffed. The weather had turned dull and chilly once again. Remembering his snuffbox, he sobbed with the pain of deprivation. It was over a month since he last had snuff. Tobacco had become so expensive that a leaf cost two whole pounds, and five-shillings worth of snuff could not last one a single night. Who had five shillings for tobacco alone?

He went out of the compound, into the nearby farmland.

Yet, tobacco was just one thing. Meat was another. Lack of meat, they said, was responsible for the disease which gave people cannon legs, and which some called Kwashiokor.[1] Then, salt . . . And no peace of mind . . . And the ears would never rest . . . What type of life was it? . . . But the ground was there; the ground would never move.

The farm was in deep-green bloom. Yam vines had climbed up the props with vigour. Maize plants held out their fruits like arms in a happy salute. It was no surprise. This had been the family's favourite soil fed with compound sweepings from year to year and from generation to generation.

He gathered some straying tendrils, handling them with affection and care, and yet frowning at them like the delinquents they were.

An awareness of his solitary state struck him when he stepped on some dry leaves and the sound bounced over a wide area. But he merely paused for a while; then, bracing himself, he cleared his throat. A squirrel scurrying past halted right before him. *You call yourself a man and yet you want to go after me—to go after a squirrel like me? Why not go after those men who are coming to drive you out of your home?* Its cheeks appeared bloated with contempt. Dede turned round and walked away.

From behind a row of cocoyam plants, a voice asked: "What are you doing there?"

He rallied swiftly and gave a sob of ordinary surprise.

"It's you I'm asking." The soldier had already drawn his gun, ready to shoot. And now, he began to advance.

No; he would not shoot, otherwise he would not have bothered to advance. Wasn't he a pitiable sight—all rags, eyes sunken, mud-stained, like a creature just excavated from the ground and from the region of death. Somebody's son!

"I can see you speak my own language, my son," Dede ventured.

"Answer me or I'll shoot," the soldier threatened, his voice quivering with what seemed like weariness and exhaustion. "What are you doing here?"

"Guarding my own house."

"Your house?"

"Yes, my son; Dede's own house. And my father's And my father's father's."

The soldier looked right and left; then, he lowered his gun.

Four more emerged from the bush adjoining the farm.

The soldier gave a salute.

They said many things in English which Dede could not understand. Then they turned to him again.

"Old man, tell us everything about yourself," demanded the one who had no visible tear in his dress and who looked like their leader.

---

1. A childhood disease resulting from malnutrition.

"Like what, my son?"

"You are here spying for the enemy, collecting information for them."

Pack Pack Pack! . . .

The interval was sufficient for Dede to regain his self-control.

"That cannot be, my son." He shook his head too.

"We'll soon find out." He reverted to English: "Go inside, boys. And take good care of yourselves."

Two climbed over the compound wall, while two others entered by the entrance door.

"I hope they will find something to eat."

"Is that what it's all about?"

There was no reply.

Some time passed.

"I want to return to my house."

The soldier watched as Dede went towards the entrance door with long confident strides, very composed, and looking much younger from behind. Then, he followed.

They came to the door.

"Don't you want to go out and see what is happening in the village?"

He halted, turned. "What else is happening other than death and destruction?"

They entered the forehouse. He sat down, facing the tripod with the idol. And he cast stealthy glances at the knife on the roof rafter.

"You have never seen any of their soldiers, I believe. Why don't you go out and see them?" the soldier spoke.

No reply.

"Why hide here? Go out and see what they look like. After all, you're an old man and they don't touch the old."

He cut a line in the air before him with his hand, thereby erecting a barrier between himself and the evil words that were coming out of the other's lips.

"Proverbs of the young!"

"Why do you say that?"

"I was talking to myself, my son. Proverbs of the young are like bags made of banana leaves, in that they puncture before they are put to use."

The other gazed with incomprehension.

"My son, Dede is a good man." He shook his head, dismally. "I only wish I still had the strength in me."

"Why?"

Again, he pounded his chest with his fist. "I would fight and fight." He rose, drew the knife from the rafter and brushed it hard on the mud-earth floor, and flashed it in the air in an impressive style. "Even now, I would fight them with this knife."

"Let's go into the yard together," the soldier now proposed. So easily, he had been reassured: they were not being trapped into the compound, into danger, by an enemy agent. "We want to see what we can liberate from there," he told himself in English.

Even so, he thought that the place might still be dangerous. It was unusual to go in after so brief and so friendly, and almost pious, interrogation. But he and his men badly wanted something to eat; they could take the risk.

Then, with long sticks they stabbed the ground here and there. They stabbed harder wherever the ground undulated or there were signs of fresh earth, at times aiding the probe with their feet.

They all looked sad, even hostile. There was no trace anywhere of the first harvest of yams which must have been buried for preservation in the earth. Yam was indeed what they wanted most—yam, the king among crops which had become so rare with so many mouths consuming what a few hands produced.

"We want yam," the leader declared in a good-natured way.

Dede smiled with compassion. *Son of a fellow man.* "Good thing you spoke the way you did. Your gun could never have got even a single tuber out of Dede."

He led them to a most improbable spot, a level ground behind the rear wall where he had buried well over forty yams.

Pack Pack Pack! . . .

It sounded feeble, Dede thought. But the soldiers who knew better pronounced that there was cunning in it.

"We're going," their leader said.

"Why?" He was genuinely worried. He had begun to like their company, including their coarse manners and their appetite for food.

They stood slinging some yams down their necks and forearms and covering them with the remains of their shirts.

"That low sound is only a trick," he heard in a whisper.

"Yes?"

Pack pack pack! . . .

"Very close!"

Silence followed.

"If they get here, don't tell them about our visit."

"Tfia!" he swore, and shrugged.

Turning, he found that he was now alone. They had escaped like spirits. He gave a deep groan.

Dark, laden clouds went sweeping across.

It was evening. It began to pour with rain. It rained for a long time. The trees twisted. Flood water flowing through open spaces coursed down with speed to the same direction in which the villagers had fled.

He rekindled the fire, drew his seat closer. He rubbed at his ankles from time to time, distributing the heat full circle.

Night came suddenly, succeeding the rain.

He was hungry and had not realized that until now. He went out, behind the rear wall, dug up a medium-sized tuber and returned to the forehouse. He put the tuber in the fire to roast. Leaning backward in his chair and holding his head with his hand, he stared into the open where it was pitch dark.

The smouldering wood, sometimes cracking and sometimes giving out a brief, gentle flame, managed to illumine the insides of the hut. Then a big flame burst out. This caught him unprepared, fully relaxed to a point of nudity. Smiling, he threw his cloth quickly over his exposed groin.

Everywhere was silent, except for the hissing of insects which only gave the silence a tense, throbbing essence. Dede thought about many things . . . Then he thought about his family. He knew where they ought to be . . . It was in the church building at Nembo. That was where the kindred had agreed to move to, should danger come from the north. And indeed, danger did come from the north. Nembo was a considerable distance off. They should be safe there . . . Lolo would be there with her anger . . . Chieke would be holding his rattle.

He ate the yam hot. He drank it down with clean, cold water from the rain.

Sleep came on him heavily, but soon petered out into brief and shallow instalments. The night's chill contracted his muscles and bit into his bones, and he was compelled to stamp his feet on the ground from time to time.

When dawn came, it took him unawares. He jerked his body and rubbed his palm over his eyes, bringing his senses back to the reality of his position. He looked round. They were still there—he could see them even in the faint light of early dawn: the idol on the tripod, the lyre, and the knife; then, the grave of his father; finally, himself. He smiled and cried: "Ah!"

He picked up the knife and went out.

Pack pack pack! . . .

The bush close by stirred.

A figure emerged. It was a dark, very dark, shape, carrying a gun, wearing a helmet, the face hardly visible, the clothes blending with the vegetation in the still imperfect light.

"Yes, come here!" He pointed with his rather short gun. "Come here, I say!" And he advanced.

"Welcome, my son," Dede greeted in his own tongue.

"Come!" he ordered again, still in English.

He swallowed.

Two more bodies came out. The three said something in a language which was foreign and yet not English. Then, they advanced towards him, within a few yards.

Dede mustered all the strength and will-power left in him for the supreme and final act of manly courage, and of self-defense, and was about to rear.

"Drop that knife! Quick!" It was in his own tongue.

Silence intervened.

"Drop it at once. Drop!"

"Father, you are very lucky," the boy said with a cool, touching voice. "Had you delayed for a second, you would have been shot through the heart."

"Are the three of you of our own side?" he asked.

"Yes and no."

"How?"

"This way: I am but these two are not."

"So they are our enemy?"

"We all are of one country," he explained. "These soldiers belong to a pacification company of the federal army. They will do you no harm; instead, they will look after you and your family. Come on now, send for your kinsmen; let them come out of hiding and they will be well cared for."

He gave along, mystifying sob. Then he said:

"Please, my son, tell me one thing."

"Yes, ask it."

He hesitated. "What about you?"

"What?"

He changed. "When will this thing end?"

Two good years passed before he was in a position to tell the story to friends and relatives among whom Lolo was no more. They were assembled in the forehouse, with the overfill in the open front yard.

Some remarked that he was just lucky—no more, and then went on to remind him about the wise proverbial coward who would run away in good time from the scene of battle so as to be able to relate how the brave ones had died fighting. But some said his survival was all the work of the spirits of the fathers whom he had refused to desert even at very grave personal risk. Replying, Dede urged all of them to accept the simple fact that he was still alive only because he did not leave his home.

He picked up his lyre. He sang as he played. Some joined in.

Come rain come sun
The ground will never never . . .

KATEB YACINE (1929–1989)
Algeria; French/Arabic

Kateb Yacine is the father of the postcolonial Maghrebian Francophone novel. Kateb (he ironically inverted his name to read surname first, the way it had to appear on all French civil documents) came of age during the first anticolonial riots at Sétif, Algeria, in 1945, which were brutally repressed by the French. After World War II, the first stirrings toward national independence were felt throughout North Africa. Kateb's first novel, *Nedjma,* published in 1956, elicited comparisons to William Faulkner and was hailed as a major event on the French literary scene. Espousing an Arabic, circular notion of time, the novel is deeply embedded in the mythic origins of the Algerian people. The heroine, whose name means star, is the enigmatic love object of all in the novel and has been read as an allegorical figure for colonized Algeria. The obsessive character of Nedjma was already the source for Kateb's early poetry, and he claims her as the matrix for his creativity. The theme of war and its brutal disruption of a people's heritage is always interwoven with that of impossible love in his work. In the 1970s, Kateb stopped writing in French and chose instead to express his political engagement by creating an agit-prop theater that he developed in dialectal Arabic, moving his troupe from village to village.

As a young high school student in the town of Sétif, Kateb was imprisoned after the violent anticolonial riots of May 8, 1945. He claimed that in prison he discovered the two things most dear to him: "poetry and revolution." Kateb's literary output, highly poetic in its constellations of images, has thus always been linked to his political engagement for the cause of Algerian self-determination. Added to these concerns was an impossible, life-long love for his cousin, who becomes the Nedjma of his famous novel. Nedjma functions as a pole, magnetizing experience and poetic figures. As a love object, she mediates between the rude present and the mythologized past, the nomadism of the ancestral Berber tribe, and their belonging to a modern Islamic culture; but her enigmatic presence always signals death as well as love.

In the prose poem "The Deserter," Kateb imagines the exile and wandering of a man who has deserted—his war? his homeland?—but also who feels deserted by some hope or promise: "our mother has bravely mutilated us." Tortured, he seeks out his fellows, yet is condemned to a kind of existential freedom.

The Deserter

To Geneviève Serreau

Cast into freedom in darkest night, he wanders, halting at some trifle. In the shadow of the country of death, all the superstitions rain down upon him. But the birds of prey can only move him to tears, those messengers of the Incorruptible with whom he mingles behind the trees doubly complicitous, to whom he clings, and for whom he finally substitutes himself, leaving at last. He wanders, fading out like an occult science. His provisional migration has no other end, and the rebellious forest repulses him—unfit to do each other violence, they have concluded the pact of the deserter and the forest.

Embarked in another world, with a blasphematory cap, a moustache at half-mast, badly shaved through his incurable optimism, he wanders in the dark night. Not knowing how to read, at the mercy of scribes, not knowing his way around in the forces of order, he is wandering in the dark night, and all the superstitions rain down upon him. Great town of Europe! Saturday evening in the bustle, humping his back like an ox returning from the watering trough, he who used to pray now wanders in freedom in the dark night. He scarcely belongs.

He wanders in the dark night, less naked
But stronger than anyone thought
Hedgehog off the track in the forest he carries within himself
He seems to have lost his head, he is playing with his muscles
In the forest he carries within himself
Unless, his head held high? Unless a centipede

Translated by Mary Ann Caws and Ronnie Scharfman.

Taking unlikely twists?
So much vulnerable vitality makes an impression
And he feigns his agony, for his life is hard
He wanders in freedom in the dark night.

The town seemed empty. At last some unknown man made a gesture, a deserter also. Deserters all, either because curiosity has pitched us in the laps of the witches, or because another imprudence leads us to jail.

And so as not to recognize us at the hours of the sacrifice, our mother has bravely mutilated us.

Clouds
All badly slaughtered!
And those winters huddled
In the grotto's depths,
Those arduous dreams
To our summers that have never been,
Those deserts of squall.

Let's take a lizard, face-to-face with his tail, in the torments of division; banished from his hole, he wants to take refuge in himself, with or without his tail; when this is done, his wanderlust will bring him back among you, dragons and chameleons whose shed skins are lying on his road, as if he had never tired of resting on the remains of your childhood. So it is he anguishes, renounces the sun, this lizard who was once grave and thoughtful. So it is he is present at your twilight and sets you trembling when he slithers into your sheets. He does not want to die without warming up some other corpses. Some real deserter's madness! He has come from too far off for you to have followed him. And he's no missionary. All the superstitions rain down upon him. He's not through changing, and his life is hard. He is still wandering in freedom in the dark night, in the torments of division. He is still wandering in freedom like some ancestor. Like an old ideal. And it is like this that he judges, the deserter, and like this that he rules.

Nedjma: The poem or the sword

We had prepared two glasses of blood
Nedjma opened her eyes among the trees

A lute was frothing the plains into gardens
Black as a blood that had drunk the sun
I had Nedjma under my cool heart breathed in layers of precious flesh   5
Nedjma since we have been dreaming many stars have followed our trail. . .
I had foreseen you immortal like air and the unknown
And now you are dying and I am perishing and you cannot ask me to weep. . .
Where Nedjma are those dry nights we used to carry them on our back to shelter
    other slumbers!   10

Translated by Mary Ann Caws.

The fountain where the saints revived the *bendir* drums
The mosque to think white smooth as silk chiffon
The sea blowing on our faces by the moons hung in the water like rounds of
    frosted skin. . .
It was this poem of Arabia Nedjma that we had to keep!

Nedjma I have taught you a mighty DIWAN[1] yet my voice falters
    I am forlorn in music I cast your heart away but it returns decomposed
And yet we were named in epic we traversed the land of lament we followed the
    mourners laughing behind the Nile. . .
Now Algiers separates us a siren deafens us a windlass quietly uproots your
    beauty
Nedjma the charm may have passed yet your water abounds under my respectful
    gaze!

And the mosques were crumbling under the lances of the sun. . .
And the emirs gave presents to the people it was the end of Ramadan
    Ramadan
The mornings rose from the hottest of the hills a fragrant rain exposed the belly of
    the cactus
Nedjma held my racehorse by its harness sketching crystals in the sand
I said Nedjma the sand is full of our imprints gorged with gold!
The nomads are watching us their cries pierce our words like bubbles
We will no longer see the palm trees push toward the tender hail of the stars
Nedjma the cameleers are far and the last stage is to the North!
Nedjma pulled on the harness I saddled a dromedary power of the ages.

When I lost the Andalusian woman, I could say nothing I was dying under her
    breath I needed the time to name her
The palmtrees were weeping on my head I could have left the child for the fo-
    liage
But Nedjma was sleeping still immortal and I thought I touched her troubling
    breasts
It was in Bone in the bright time of jujubes Nedjma had opened immense palm
    groves for me
Nedjma was sleeping like a ship love was bleeding under her unmoving heart
Nedjma open your legendary eyes time is passing I shall die in seven and seven
    years be not inhuman!
Dig deeper into the deepest basins it is there she flows when her eyes close the
    nights like traps
Knife my dreams like snakes or bear me into Nedjma's sleep I cannot stand this
    solitude!

15

---

1. A collection of poems in Persian or Arabic;
   a series of poems by one author.

Love and Work*

Love and work take too much night, and the lover awakens as worker, holding
tightly in his arms the night, the vast night escaping. Why can't we work in
bed, or sleep upon the table!

GRACE OGOT (b. 1930)
Kenya; English

Grace Ogot, Kenya's first well-known woman writer, writes in English. She reflects,
albeit subtly and indirectly, the concerns of feminists around the world. In Africa
as everywhere else, the women's liberation movement, despite setbacks, has
emerged as a powerful agent of social and cultural change. There has been a surge
in feminist journalism, research, history, religious movements, music, creative
writing, and criticism. Ogot looks at the effect on one woman of the continuance of
old customs. The Luo people depicted in "The Rain Came" are not concerned, of
course, with feminism, or with European colonialists or British-dominated government. They follow traditional patterns even when these threaten the life of Oganda,
the chief's only daughter. "The thread between life and eternity," Ogot has said, "is
very narrow." Oganda, for her part, is such a good Luo that she is willing to sacrifice
herself for the sake of her people, in accordance with ancestral precedent, but in
accordance too with a tragic sacrificial pattern found in much of the world's
literature. "There are more tragic incidents in life than there are comic ones," the
author has written. The reader is left with the unanswered question whether escape
with a husband is really a solution to the doubts raised by this destructive but
time-honored custom of female sacrifice.

from **Land Without Thunder**

The Rain Came

The chief was still far from the gate when his daughter Oganda saw him. She ran to
meet him. Breathlessly she asked her father, "What is the news, great Chief?
Everyone in the village is anxiously waiting to hear when it will rain." Labong'o held
out his hands for his daughter but he did not say a word. Puzzled by her father's cold
attitude Oganda ran back to the village to warn the others that the chief was back.

The atmosphere in the village was tense and confused. Everyone moved
aimlessly and fussed in the yard without actually doing any work. A young woman
whispered to her co-wife, "If they have not solved this rain business today, the
chief will crack." They had watched him getting thinner and thinner as the people

*Translated by Mary Ann Caws and Ronnie Scharfman.

kept on pestering him. "Out cattle lie dying in the fields," they reported. "Soon it will be our children and then ourselves. Tell us what to do to save our lives, oh great Chief." So the chief had daily prayed with the Almighty through the ancestors to deliver them from their distress.

Instead of calling the family together and giving them the news immediately, Labong'o went to his own hut, a sign that he was not to be disturbed. Having replaced the shutter, he sat in the dimly-lit hut to contemplate.

It was no longer a question of being the chief of hunger-stricken people that weighed Labong'o's heart. It was the life of his only daughter that was at stake. At the time when Oganda came to meet him, he saw the glittering chain shining around her waist. The prophecy was complete. "It is Oganda, Oganda, my only daughter, who must die so young." Labong'o burst into tears before finishing the sentence. The chief must not weep. Society had declared him the bravest of men. But Labong'o did not care any more. He assumed the position of a simple father and wept bitterly. He loved his people, the Luo, but what were the Luo for him without Oganda? Her life had bought a new life in Labong'o's world and he ruled better than he could remember. How would the spirit of the village survive his beautiful daughter? "There are so many homes and so many parents who have daughters. Why choose this one? She is all I have." Labong'o spoke as if the ancestors were there in the hut and he could see them face to face. Perhaps they were there, warning him to remember his promise on the day he was enthroned when he said aloud, before the elders, "I will lay down life, if necessary, and the life of my household, to save this tribe from the hands of the enemy." "Deny! Deny!" he could hear the voice of his forefathers mocking him.

When Labong'o was consecrated chief he was only a young man. Unlike his father, he ruled for many years with only one wife. But people rebuked him because his only wife did not bear him a daughter. He married a second, a third, and a fourth wife. But they all gave birth to male children. When Labong'o married a fifth wife, she bore him a daughter. They called her Oganda, meaning "beans," because her skin was very fair. Out of Labong'o's twenty children, Oganda was the only girl. Though she was the chief's favourite, her mother's co-wives swallowed their jealous feelings and showered her with love. After all, they said, Oganda was a female child whose days in the royal family were numbered. She would soon marry at a tender age and leave the enviable position to someone else.

Never in his life had he been faced with such an impossible decision. Refusing to yield to the rainmaker's request would mean sacrificing the whole tribe, putting the interests of the individual above those of the society. More than that. It would mean disobeying the ancestors, and most probably wiping the Luo people from the surface of the earth. On the other hand, to let Oganda die as a ransom for the people would permanently cripple Labong'o spiritually. He knew he would never be the same chief again.

The words of Ndithi, the medicine man, still echoed in his ears. "Podho, the ancestor of the Luo, appeared to me in a dream last night, and he asked me to speak to the chief and the people," Ndithi had said to the gathering of tribesmen. "A young woman who has not known a man must die so that the country may have rain. While Podho was still talking to me, I saw a young woman standing at the lakeside, her hands raised, above her head. Her skin was as fair as the skin of young deer in the wilderness. Her tall slender figure stood like a lonely reed at the river bank. Her sleepy eyes wore a sad look like that of a bereaved mother. She wore a gold ring on her left ear, and a glittering brass chain around her waist. As I still marvelled at the beauty of this young woman, Podho told me, 'Out of all the women in this land, we have chosen this one. Let her offer herself a sacrifice to the lake monster! And on that day, the rain will come down in torrents. Let everyone stay at home on that day, lest he be carried away by the floods.' "

Outside there was a strange stillness, except for the thirsty birds that sang lazily on the dying trees. The blinding mid-day heat had forced the people to retire to their huts. Not far away from the chief's hut, two guards were snoring away quietly. Labong'o removed his crown and the large eagle-head that hung loosely on his shoulders. He left the hut, and instead of asking Nyabog'o the messenger to beat the drum, he went straight and beat it himself. In no time the whole household had assembled under the siala tree where he usually addressed them. He told Oganda to wait a while in her grandmother's hut.

When Labong'o stood to address his household, his voice was hoarse and the tears choked him. He started to speak, but words refused to leave his lips. His wives and sons knew there was great danger. Perhaps their enemies had declared war on them. Labong'o's eyes were red, and they could see he had been weeping. At last he told them. "One whom we love and treasure must be taken away from us. Oganda is to die." Labong'o's voice was so faint that he could not hear it himself. But he continued, "The ancestors have chosen her to be offered as a sacrifice to the lake monster in order that we may have rain."

They were completely stunned. As a confused murmur broke out, Oganda's mother fainted and was carried off to her own hut. But the other people rejoiced. They danced around singing and chanting, "Oganda is the lucky one to die for the people. If it is to save the people, let Oganda go."

In her grandmother's hut Oganda wondered what the whole family were discussing about her that she could not hear. Her grandmother's hut was well away from the chief's court and, much as she strained her ears, she could not hear what they were saying. "It must be marriage," she concluded. It was an accepted custom for the family to discuss their daughter's future marriage behind her back. A faint smile played on Oganda's lips as she thought of the several young men who swallowed saliva at the mere mention of her name.

There was Kech, the son of a neighbouring clan elder. Kech was very handsome. He had sweet, meek eyes and a roaring laughter. He would make a wonderful father, Oganda thought. But they would not be a good match. Kech was a bit too short to be her husband. It would humiliate her to have to look down at Kech each time she spoke to him. Then she thought of Dimo, the tall young man who already distinguished himself as a brave warrior and an outstanding wrestler. Dimo adored Oganda, but Oganda thought he would make a cruel husband, always quarrelling and ready to fight. No, she did not like him. Oganda fingered the glittering chain on her waist as she thought of Osinda. A long time ago when she was quite young Osinda had given her that chain, and instead of wearing it around her neck several times, she wore it round her waist where it could stay permanently. She heard her heart pounding so loudly as she thought of him. She whispered, "Let it be you they are discussing, Osinda the lovely one. Come now and take me away. . . ."

The lean figure in the doorway startled Oganda who was rapt in thought about the man she loved. "You have frightened me, Grandma," said Oganda laughing. "Tell me, is it my marriage you were discussing? You can take it from me that I won't marry any of them." A smile played on her lips again. She was coaxing the old lady to tell her quickly, to tell her they were pleased with Osinda.

In the open space outside the excited relatives were dancing and singing. They were coming to the hut now, each carrying a gift to put at Oganda's feet. As their singing got nearer Oganda was able to hear what they were saying: "If it is to save the people, if it is to give us rain, let Oganda go. Let Oganda die for her people, and for her ancestors." Was she mad to think that they were singing about her? How could she die? She found the lean figure of her grandmother barring the door. She could not get out. The look on her grandmother's face warned her that there was danger around the corner. "Mother, it is not marriage then?" Oganda asked urgently. She suddenly felt panicky like a mouse cornered by a hungry cat. Forgetting that there was only one door in the hut Oganda fought desperately to find another exit. She must fight for her life. But there was none.

She closed her eyes, leapt like a wild tiger through the door, knocking her grandmother flat to the ground. There outside in mourning garments Labong'o stood motionless, his hands folded at the back. He held his daughter's hand and led her away from the excited crowd to the little red-painted hut where her mother was resting. Here he broke the news officially to his daughter.

For a long time the three souls who loved one another dearly sat in darkness. It was no good speaking. And even if they tried, the words could not have come out. In the past they had been like three cooking stones, sharing their burdens. Taking Oganda away from them would leave two useless stones which would not hold a cooking-pot.

News that the beautiful daughter of the chief was to be sacrificed to give the people rain spread across the country like wind. At sunset the chief's village was full of relatives and friends who had come to congratulate Oganda. Many more were on their way coming, carrying their gifts. They would dance till morning to keep her company. And in the morning they would prepare her a big farewell feast. All these relatives thought it a great honour to be selected by the spirits to die, in order that the society may live. "Oganda's name will always remain a living name among us," they boasted.

But was it maternal love that prevented Minya from rejoicing with the other women? Was it the memory of the agony and pain of child-birth that made her feel so sorrowful? Or was it the deep warmth and understanding that passes between a suckling babe and her mother that made Oganda part of her life, her flesh? Of course it was an honour, a great honour, for her daughter to be chosen to die for the country. But what could she gain once her only daughter was blown away by the wind? There were so many other women in the land, why choose her daughter, her only child! Had human life any meaning at all—other women had houses full of children while she, Minya, had to lose her only child!

In the cloudless sky the moon shone brightly, and the numerous stars glittered with a bewitching beauty. The dancers of all age-groups assembled to dance before Oganda, who sat close to her mother, sobbing quietly. All these years she had been with her people she thought she understood them. But now she discovered that she was a stranger among them. If they loved her as they had always professed why were they not making any attempt to save her? Did her people really understand what it felt like to die young? Unable to restrain her emotions any longer, she sobbed loudly as her age-group got up to dance. They were young and beautiful, and very soon they would marry and have their own children. They would have husbands to love and little huts for themselves. They would have reached maturity. Oganda touched the chain around her waist as she thought of Osinda. She wished Osinda was there too, among her friends. "Perhaps he is ill," she thought gravely. The chain comforted Oganda—she would die with it around her waist and wear it in the underground world.

In the morning a big feast was prepared for Oganda. The women prepared many different tasty dishes so that she could pick and choose. "People don't eat after death," they said. Delicious though the food looked, Oganda touched none of it. Let the happy people eat. She contented herself with sips of water from a little calabash.

The time for her departure was drawing near, and each minute was precious. It was a day's journey to the lake. She was to walk all night, passing through the great forest. But nothing could touch her, not even the denizens of the forest. She was already anointed with sacred oil. From the time Oganda received the sad news she had expected Osinda to appear any moment. But he was not there. A relative told her that Osinda was away on a private visit. Oganda realised that she would never see her beloved again.

In the afternoon the whole village stood at the gate to say good-bye and to see her for the last time. Her mother wept on her neck for a long time. The great chief in a mourning skin came to the gate bare-footed, and mingled with the people—a simple father in grief. He took off his wrist bracelet and put it on his daughter's wrist saying, "You will always live among us. The spirit of our forefathers is with you."

Tongue-tied and unbelieving Oganda stood there before the people. She had nothing to say. She looked at her home once more. She could hear her heart beating so painfully within her. All her childhood plans were coming to an end. She felt like a flower nipped in the bud never to enjoy the morning dew again. She looked at her weeping mother, and whispered, "Whenever you want to see me, always look at the sunset. I will be there."

Oganda turned southwards to start her trek to the lake. Her parents, relatives, friends and admirers stood at the gate and watched her go.

Her beautiful slender figure grew smaller and smaller till she mingled with the thin dry trees in the forest. As Oganda walked the lonely path that wound its way in the wilderness, she sang a song, and her own voice kept her company.

"The ancestors have said Oganda must die
The daughter of the chief must be sacrificed,
When the lake monster feeds on my flesh.
The people will have rain.
Yes, the rain will come down in torrents.

And the floods will wash away the sandy beaches
When the daughter of the chief dies in the lake.
My age-group has consented
My parents have consented
So have my friends and relatives.
Let Oganda die to give us rain.
My age-group are young and ripe,
Ripe for womanhood and motherhood
But Oganda must die young;
Oganda must sleep with the ancestors.
Yes, rain will come down in torrents."

The red rays of the setting sun embraced Oganda, and she looked like a burning candle in the wilderness.

The people who came to hear her sad song were touched by her beauty. But they all said the same thing: "If it is to save the people, if it is to give us rain, then be not afraid. Your name will forever live among us."

At midnight Oganda was tired and weary. She could walk no more. She sat under a big tree, and having sipped water from her calabash, she rested her head on the tree trunk and slept.

When Oganda woke up in the morning the sun was high in the sky. After walking for many hours, she reached the *tong'*, a strip of land that separated the inhabited part of the country from the sacred place (*kar lamo*). No layman could enter this place and come out alive—only those who had direct contact with the spirits and the Almighty were allowed to enter this holy of holies. But Oganda had to pass through this sacred land on her way to the lake, which she had to reach at sunset.

A large crowd gathered to see her for the last time. Her voice was now hoarse and painful, but there was no need to worry any more. Soon she would not have to sing. The crowd looked at Oganda sympathetically, mumbling words she could not hear. But none of them pleaded for life. As Oganda opened the gate, a child, a young child, broke loose from the crowd, and ran towards her. The child took a small earring from her sweaty hands and gave it to Oganda saying, "When you reach the world of the dead, give this earring to my sister. She died last week. She forgot this ring." Oganda, taken aback by the strange request, took the little ring, and handed her precious water and food to the child. She did not need them now. Oganda did not know whether to laugh or cry. She had heard mourners sending their love to their sweethearts, long dead, but this idea of sending gifts was new to her.

Oganda held her breath as she crossed the barrier to enter the sacred land. She looked appealingly at the crowd, but there was no response. Their minds were too preoccupied with their own survival. Rain was the precious medicine they were longing for, and the sooner Oganda could get to her destination the better.

A strange feeling possessed Oganda as she picked her way in the sacred land. There were strange noises that often startled her, and her first reaction was to take to her heels. But she remembered that she had to fulfil the wish of her people. She was exhausted, but the path was still winding. Then suddenly the path ended on sandy land. The water had retreated miles away from the shore leaving a wide stretch of sand. Beyond this was the vast expanse of water.

Oganda felt afraid. She wanted to picture the size and shape of the monster, but fear would not let her. The society did not talk about it, nor did the crying children who were silenced by the mention of its name. The sun was still up, but it was no longer hot. For a long time Oganda walked ankle-deep in the sand. She was exhausted and longed desperately for her calabash of water. As she moved on, she had a strange feeling that something was following her. Was it the monster? Her hair stood erect, and a cold paralysing feeling ran along her spine. She looked behind, sideways and in front, but there was nothing, except a cloud of dust.

Oganda pulled up and hurried but the feeling did not leave her, and her whole body became saturated with perspiration.

The sun was going down fast and the lake shore seemed to move along with it.

Oganda started to run. She must be at the lake before sunset. As she ran she heard a noise coming from behind. She looked back sharply, and something resembling a moving bush was frantically running after her. It was about to catch up with her.

Oganda ran with all her strength. She was now determined to throw herself into the water even before sunset. She did not look back, but the creature was upon her. She made an effort to cry out, as in a nightmare, but she could not hear her own voice. The creature caught up with Oganda. In the utter confusion, as Oganda came face with the unidentified creature, a strong hand grabbed her. But she fell flat on the sand and fainted.

When the lake breeze brought her back to consciousness, a man was bending over her. ". . . . .!" Oganda opened her mouth to speak, but she had lost her voice. She swallowed a mouthful of water poured into her mouth by the stranger.

"Osinda, Osinda! Please let me die. Let me run, the sun is going down. Let me die, let them have rain." Osinda fondled the glittering chain around Oganda's waist and wiped the tears from her face.

"We must escape quickly to the unknown land." Osinda said urgently. "We must run away from the wrath of the ancestors and the retaliation of the monster."

"But the curse is upon me, Osinda, I am no good to you any more. And moreover the eyes of the ancestors will follow us everywhere and bad luck will befall us. Nor can we escape from the monster."

Oganda broke loose, afraid to escape, but Osinda grabbed her hands again.

"Listen to me, Oganda! Listen! Here are two coats!" He then covered the whole of Oganda's body, except her eyes, with a leafy attire made from the twigs of *Bwombwe*.[1] "These will protect us from the eyes of the ancestors and the wrath of the monster. Now let us run out of here." He held Oganda's hand and they ran from the sacred land, avoiding the path that Oganda had followed.

The bush was thick, and the long grass entangled their feet as they ran. Halfway through the sacred land they stopped and looked back. The sun was almost touching the surface of the water. They were frightened. They continued to run, now faster, to avoid the sinking sun.

---

1. An East African plant.

"Have faith, Oganda—that thing will not reach us."

When they reached the barrier and looked behind them trembling, only a tip of the sun could be seen above the water's surface.

"It is gone! It is gone!" Oganda wept, hiding her face in her hands.

"Weep not, daughter of the chief. Let us run, let us escape."

There was a bright lightning. They looked up, frightened. Above them black furious clouds started to gather. They began to run. Then the thunder roared, and the rain came down in torrents.

MAZISI KUNENE (b. 1930)
South Africa; Zulu/English

Mazisi Kunene, who writes in Zulu and English, was an officer of the African National Congress after his exile in 1959 and later became a university professor in the United States. His epic poem, *Emperor Shaka the Great,* revolves around the hero Shaka, the greatest of the Zulu warrior-kings. The poem preserves traditional symbols like the gourd, processions, libations, and invocation of ancestors, while at the same time broadening its audience through the author's own translation of the work into English. The "Dirge of the Palm Race" which mourns Shaka's death in 1828, takes up the praise-poem genre, still alive orally, and highlights the function of the praise-singer. Parallelisms, long lines, and chanting rhythms all transpose oral devices into written poetry. Its Africa-centered outlook makes no reference to European settlers, who are notable only for their possession of firearms. The vigor of precolonial life challenges the automatic assumptions of Eurocentric modernity. Shaka's stature stands for fallen heroes such as Steve Bantu Biko, leader of the Black Consciousness Movement in South Africa from the mid 1960's to the late 1970's, and Albert John Luthuli, a Zulu chief and president of the African National Congress, advocate of non-violence and passive resistance to the apartheid laws. He won the Nobel Prize in 1960 and wrote an autobiography called *Let My People Go* (1962).

from *Emperor Shaka the Great*

Dirge of the Palm Race[1]

The great cloud opens: the mountain has fallen.
Silence hangs on to the shoulders of the heavens.
The thunderbolts travel making the skies tremble.

---

1. The Zulu nation, formed by Shaka from many clans.

The flashes of lightning haunt our earth with destruction.
"The mountain has fallen, the earth's centre quivers."   5
Great Protectors, Beautiful Ones, Forefathers, come!
Run into the semi-circle of the wind and carry the child.
Take him with both arms and utter these words:
"It is us who planted the sacred word
It is us who accompany you into the night.   10
We have summoned you with our songs and epics.
Our home awaits you with an eternal feast.
All the Beautiful Ones have begun to sing their anthem"
Our nation is like the wind—it will go on and on forever!

Great ocean throw the white wave   15
And let the feet of the hero be seen on the sand.
Through the mirror of the silent lake
Let us see the eyes of the Forefathers.
Let us watch the Ancestors with their children.
Let the generations hereafter say in their song: 20
"It is not I alone who was chosen by the gods
The children of the Palm Race multiply.
In the eternal spring there is the song of the morning."
Here is the mountain of Ngoye, Son of Gumede,[2]
It is rising to touch the sky   25
And the lips of generations speak in her womb,
For whatever we do in the name of the Forefathers is eternal.

The whirlwinds shall not uproot it from the ground
Until we enter the centre of the earth . . .
Nandi,[3] daughter of Bhebhe, is it you who approaches?   30
Touch then the wound with your fingers
Tell my child he must listen to you,
He must listen to the Ancestors as they sing the song.
Here they come! Dingiswayo,[4] son of Jobe: "Bayede!"[5]
Mbikwane,[6] voice of the gentle rain: "Bayede!"   35
Mgobhozi,[7] brother of the sacred mountain: "Bayede!"
The Ancestors are bringing the emblem of the black beads.

At the grounds of Bulawayo people are frightened of the night
Shaka! They are shouting your name they are calling you,
Their hands are heavy like iron on their heads: 40
"The mountain has fallen, the earth trembles."
The wind carries the voices of the women

---

2. A Zulu ancestor.
3. Mother of Shaka and a political figure in her
   own right.
4. King of the Mthethwa, the most powerful
   clan before Shaka's nation-building.

5. A Zulu royal salute: "Bring the enemies, we
   are ready to fight them."
6. Uncle of Dingiswayo, and Shaka's governor
   over the white settlement of Port Natal.
7. One of Shaka's generals.

The wound is tended by women, the wound is dark.
"Our child is dead, our sun breathes the final agony."
Have you ever heard the wailing voices of women?   45
The women came first before us!
The women tell us when our calabash shall be swallowed by the night,
The women hear first the crying of the infant.
"Our child is dead, the Ancestors have come."
They summon the rain, they speak through the opening: 50
"We have arrived. We have come to take the child.
Whoever was last to speak against him shall follow us,
He shall be judged among the Forefathers;
They shall tie him with a rope and bury him!"
They know best, they were here at the beginning of time.   55

They saw the procession of elephants to the mountain.
We must do their bidding and put the stone on the cairn,[8]
We must raise the grain basket and scatter the seeds.
Summer will come and envelop the earth.
When all the enemies have died   60
And their bodies are reeked through with worms,
Those who are born from his plant shall honour him!
They shall fill the gourd with water to make the sacred mark.
They shall arrive at the feast at the crack of dawn,
They shall listen to the epics of the Forefathers.   65
Because they are older than our children
They shall ask them to tell us the truth:
"After the Mourning-of-the-Circling-Vultures
There shall be the Feast of Return.
Your children shall dance on the ancient grounds.   70
The earth itself shall yield, opening its lakes,
People shall drink and sing the song."

Great Ancestral Forefathers because you are older than us
Accompany us into the night,
Tell us the tale while our trembling eyes follow the path;   75
Let us learn to speak the language of poets.
Beautiful Ones! Restless-feet-of-the-morning, come!
Touch our shoulders and wake the ram from sleep;
Give us the courage of the river.
He who is like an Ancestral Spirit cannot be stabbed.   80
He is like the stars of the milky way as they climb the heavens
He is like the rain that falls on the heads of the ripening plants
He is the forest that keeps secret our legends.

---

8. A pile of stones, a marker.

He is an Ancestral Spirit; he cannot be stabbed.
Even now they sing his song. They call his name.   85
They dance in the arena listening to the echoes of his epics
Till the end of time—they shall sing of him.
Till the end of time his shield shall shelter the hero from the winds,
And his children shall rise like locusts.
They shall scatter the dust of our enemies,   90
They shall make our earth free for the Palm Race.

OKOT P'BITEK (1931–1982)
Uganda; Acoli/English

Okot p'Bitek was a product of the interaction of Acoli language and custom and
British government and education. He wrote in both Acoli, his mother tongue,
and English. His form of social and political commitment, in contrast to that of
Ngugi wa Thiong'o or Grace Ogot, was to cultivate an interest in oral literature
and traditional religion among his own people and the related Luo. His writing
uses an English version of traditional Acoli style, "based," he has said, "primarily
on the traditional, I think, but one is bound to be influenced by friends, enemies,
school, etc., so it becomes all mixed." *Song of Lawino* (1966), written first in Acoli,
is a dramatic monologue in which Lawino, a traditional wife, laments that her
husband, Ocol, is attracted to new ways and a Westernized woman, Clementine
(Tina for short), "who speaks English." As folktale characters personify qualities
or attitudes larger than themselves, so these two women represent polarities of
traditionalism and modernization within the emerging nation of Uganda. Ocol,
speaking for the Africa of modernization, is given a chance to rebut in a sequel,
Song of Ocol, but the poet's affection for tradition looms large.

from **Song of Lawino**

The Graceful Giraffe Cannot Become a Monkey

My husband tells me
I have no ideas
Of modern beauty.
He says
I have stuck   5
To old fashioned hair styles.

It is true
I cannot do my hair
As white women do.

Baule group, Akan peoples. Ivory Coast. Female figure with snake. c. 1960. Paint on wood.

Listen,
My father comes from Payira,
My mother is a woman of Koc!
I am a true Acoli
I am not a half-caste
I am not a slave girl;
My father was not brought home
Be the spear
My mother was not exchanged
For a basket of millet.

Ask me what beauty is
To the Acoli
And I will tell you;
I will show it to you
If you give me a chance!

You once saw me,
You saw my hair style
And you admired it,
And the boys loved it.
At the arena
Boys surrounded me
And fought for me.

My mother taught me
Acoli hair fashions;
Which fits the kind
Of hair of the Acoli,
And the occasion   35

Listen,
Ostrich plumes differ
From chicken feathers,

He says   40
I am stupid and very backward,
That my hair style
Makes him sick
Because I am dirty.

A monkey's tail   45
Is different from that of the giraffe,
The crocodile's skin
Is not like the guinea fowl's,
And the hippo is naked, and hairless.

The hair of the Acoli   50
Is different from that of the Arabs;
The Indians' hair
Resembles the tail of the horse;
It is like sisal strings
And needs to be cut   55
With scissors.
It is black,
And is different from that of white women.

A white woman's hair
Is soft like silk;   60
It is light
And brownish like
That of the brown monkey,
And is very different from mine.
A black woman's hair   65
Is thick and curly;
It is true
Ring-worm sometimes eats up
A little girl's hair
And this is terrible;   70
But when hot porridge
Is put on the head
And the dance is held
Under the sausage-fruit tree
And the youths have sung   75

You, Ring-worm,
Who is eating Duka's hair
Here is your porridge.

Then the girl's hair
Beings to grow again
And the girl is pleased.

80

No-one, except wizards
And women who poison others
Leaves her hair untrimmed!
And the men

85

Do not leave their chins
To grow bushy
Like the lion's neck,
Like the chin
Of a billy goat,

90

So that they look
Like wild beasts.
They put hot ash
On the hair
Below the belly button

95

And pluck it up,
And they pluck the hair on their face
And the hair of the armpits.

When death has occurred
Women leave their hair uncombed!

100

They remove all beads
And necklaces,
Because they are mourning
Because of sorrows.
The woman who adorns herself

105

When others are wailing
Is the killer!
She comes to the funeral
To congratulate herself.

When you go to dance

110

You adorn yourself for the dance,
If your string-skirt
Is ochre-red
You do your hair
With ochre,

115

And you smear your body
With red oil
And you are beautifully red all over!
If you put on a black string-skirt

You do your hair with *akuku*[1]   120
Your body shines with simsim oil
And the tattoos on your chest
And on your back
Glitter in the evening sun.
And the healthy sweat   125
On your bosom
Is like the glassy fruits of *ocuga*.

Young girls
Whose breasts are just emerging
Smear *shea* butter on their bodies,   130
The beautiful oil from Labworomor.

The aroma is wonderful
And their white teeth sparkle
As they sing
And dance fast   135
Among the dancers
Like small fish
In a shallow stream.

Butter from cows' milk
Or the fat from edible rats   140
Is cooked together with *lakura*
Or *atika*;
You smear it on your body today
And the aroma
Lasts until the next day.   145

And when you balance on your head
A beautiful water pot
Or a new basket
Or a long-necked jar
Full of honey,   150
Your long neck
Resembles the *alwiri* spear.

And as you walk along the pathway
On both sides
The *obiya* grasses are flowering   155
And the *pollok* blossoms
And the wild white lilies

---

1. This selection contains many names of
   plants for which there are no English equivalents.

Are shouting silently
To the bees and butterflies!

And as the fragrance   160
Of the ripe wild berries
Hooks the insects and little birds,
As the fishermen hook the fish
And pull them up mercilessly,

The young men   165
From the surrounding villages,
And from across many streams,
They come from beyond the hills
And the wide plains,
They surround you   170
And bite off their ears
Like jackals.

And when you go
To the well
Or into the freshly burnt woodlands   175
To collect the red *oceyu,*
Or to cut *oduggu* shrubs,
You find them
Lurking in the shades
Like the leopardess with cubs.   180

Ocol tells me
That I like dirt.
He says
Shea butter causes
Skin diseases.   185

He says, Acoli adornments
Are old fashioned and unhealthy.
He says I soil his white shirt
If I touch him,
My husband treats me   190
As if I am suffering from
The "Don't touch me" disease!

He says that I make his bedsheets dirty
And his bed smelly.
Ocol says   195
I look extremely ugly
When I am fully adorned
For the dance!

When I walk past my husband
He hisses like a wounded *ororo* snake   200

Choking with vengeance.
He has vowed
That he will never touch
My hands again.
My husband   205
Is in love with Tina
The woman with the large head;
Ocol dies for Clementine
Ocol never sleeps
For the beautiful one   210
Who has read!

When the beautiful one
With whom I share my husband
Returns from cooking her hair
She resembles   215
A chicken
That has fallen into a pond;
Her hair looks
Like the python's discarded skin.

They cook their hair   220
With hot iron
And pull it hard
So that it may grow long.
Then they rope the hair
On wooden pens   225
Like a billy goat
Brought for the sacrifice
Struggling to free itself.

They fry their hair
In boiling oil   230
As if it were locusts,
And the hair sizzles
It cries aloud in sharp pain
As it is pulled and stretched.
And the vigorous and healthy hair   235
Curly, springy and thick
That glistens in the sunshine
Is left listless and dead
Like the elephant grass
Scorched brown by the fierce   240
February sun.
It lies lifeless
Like the sad and dying banana leaves
On a hot and windless afternoon.

The beautiful woman
With whom I share my husband
Smears black shoe polish
On her hair
To blacken it
And to make it shine,
She washes her hair
With black ink;

But the thick undergrowth
Rejects the shoe polish
And the ink
And it remains untouched
Yellowish, greyish
Like the hair of the grey monkey.

There is much water
In my husband's house
Cold water and hot water.
You twist a cross-like handle
And water gushes out
Hot and steaming
Like the urine
Of the elephant.

You twist another cross-like handle;
It is cold water,
Clean like the cooling fresh waters
From the streams
Of Lututuru hills.

But the woman
With whom I share my husband
Does not wash her head;
The head of the beautiful one
Smells like rats
That have fallen into the fireplace.

And she uses
Powerful perfumes
To overcome the strange smells,
As they treat a pregnant coffin!
And the different smells
Wrestle with one another
And the smell of the shoe polish
Mingles with them.

Clementine has many headkerchiefs,
Beautiful headkerchiefs of many colours.

245

250

255

260

265

270

275

280

285

She ties one on her head
And it covers up
The rot inside;

She ties the knot
On her forehead

Ocol, my friend
Look at my skin
It is smooth and black.   295
And my boy friend
Who plays the *nanga*
Sings praises to it.

I am proud of the hair
With which I was born
And as no white woman   300
Wishes to do her hair
Like mine,
Because she is proud
Of the hair with which she was born,
And arranges the edges   305
With much care
So that it covers
Her ears
As well as the bold forehead
That jumps sparks   310
When lightning has splashed,
And hurls back sunlight
More powerfully than a mirror!

Sometimes she wears
The hair of some dead woman   315
Of some white woman
Who died long ago
And she goes with it
To the dance!
Which witchcraft!   320

Shamelessly, she dances
Holding the shoulder of my husband,
The hair of a dead woman
On her head
The body of the dead woman   325
Decaying in the tomb!

One night
The ghost of the dead woman
Pulled away her hair
From the head of the wizard   330

And the beautiful one
Fell down
And shook with shame
She shook   335
As if the angry ghost
Of the white woman
Had entered her head.

I have no wish
To look like a white woman.   340

No leopard
Would change into a hyena,
And the crested crane
Would hate to be changed
Into the bold-headed,   345
Dung-eating vulture,
The long-necked and graceful giraffe
Cannot become a monkey.

Let no one
Uproot the Pumpkin.   350

FLORA NWAPA (b. 1931)
Nigeria; English

Flora Nwapa, the first Nigerian woman novelist, gives voice to a woman's perspective on the recurrent African literary theme of young people moving away from rural areas and renouncing traditional beliefs and values. She is the author of *Efuru, Idu,* and *Never Again* as well as the recent *One is Enough* (1992), and *Wives at War and Other Stories* (1992). The young woman in "This Is Lagos" has left her Igbo village to stay with her aunt in Lagos, Africa's largest city. Gradually, as we see her through the eyes of her mother and her aunt, she becomes absorbed into the impersonal urban life that ignores traditional family ties and obligations.

from This Is Lagos *and Other Stories*

This Is Lagos

"They say Lagos men do not just chase women, they snatch them," Soha's mother told her on the eve of her departure to Lagos. "So my daughter be careful. My sister will take care of you. You should help her with her housework and her children, just as you have been doing here."

Soha was fond of her aunt. She called her Mama Eze. Eze was her aunt's first son. And Mama Eze called Soha my sister's daughter. She too was fond of Soha whom she looked after when she was a little girl.

Soha was a sweet girl. She was just twenty when she came to Lagos. She was not beautiful in the real sense of the word. But she was very pretty and charming. She was full of life. She pretended that she knew her mind, and showed a confidence rare in a girl who had all her education in a village.

Her aunt and her family lived in Shomolu in the outskirts of Lagos. There was a primary school nearby, and it was in the school that her uncle by marriage got her a teaching job. Soha did not like teaching, but there was no other job, and so, like so many teachers, the job was just a stepping stone.

In the morning before she went to school, Soha saw that her aunt's children, five in all, were well prepared for school. She would see that they had their baths, wore their uniforms, and looked neat and tidy. Then she prepared their breakfast, and before seven each morning, the children were ready to go to school.

Everybody in the 'yard' thought how dutiful Soha was. Her aunt's husband who was a quiet man praised Soha, and told his wife that she was a good girl. Her aunt was proud of her. Since she came to stay with them, her aunt had had time for relaxation, she did less housework, and paid more attention to her trade, which was selling bread.

For some time, everything went well with them. But Mama Eze did not like the way Soha refused to go on holiday when the school closed at the end of the first term. She was surprised when Soha told her that she did not want to go home to see her mother, despite the fact that her mother had been ill, and was recovering.

"Why don't you want to go home, my sister's daughter?"

"Who will look after the children if I go home?" she asked.

Mama Eze did not like the tone of Soha's voice. "Who had been looking after the children before you came, my sister's daughter? Your mother wants you to come home. You know how fond she is of you. I don't want her to think that I prevented you from coming home."

"She won't think so. I shall go during the Christmas holiday. This is a short holiday, only three weeks. And the roads. Remember what Lagos-Onitsha road is like." But she did not go home during the Christmas holiday either.

It was that argument that sort of did the trick. Mama Eze remembered the accident she witnessed not long ago. She was returning from the market, a huge load on her head, when, just in a flash it happened. It was a huge tipper-lorry and a Volkswagen car. She saw blood, and bodies, and the wreck of the Volkswagen. She covered her face with her hands. When she opened them, she looked the other way, and what did she see, a human tongue on the ground.

When she returned home, she told her husband. She swore that from thenceforth she would travel home by train.

She did not suggest going home by train to her niece. Soha had long rejected that idea. She did not see the sanity of it all. Why should a man in Lagos, wishing to go to Port Harcourt decide to go up to Kaduna in the North first, then down south to Port Harcourt, and to take three days and three nights doing the journey he would do in a few hours if he were travelling by road.

One Saturday, during the holiday a brand new car stopped in front of the big 'yard.' The children in the 'yard' including Mama Eze's children trooped out to have a closer look. A young man stepped out of the car and asked one of the children whether Soha lived there. "Yes, sister Soha lives here. Let me go and call her for you," Eze said, and ran into the house.

Soha was powdering her face when Eze pushed open the door and announced, "Sister Soha, a man is asking for you. He came in a car, a brand new car. I have not seen that car before. Come and see him. He wants you." Eze held her hand and began dragging her to the sitting room. "No Eze, ask him to sit down in the sitting room and wait for me," Soha said quietly to Eze. Eze dropped her hand and ran outside again. "She is coming. She says I should ask you to sit down in the sitting room and wait for her," he said to the man. The man followed him to the sitting room.

The children stood admiring the car. "It is a Volkswagen," one said. "How can that be a Volkswagen? It is a Peugeot," another said. "Can't you people see? It is a Record," yet another child said. They were coming close now. Some were touching the body of the car and leaving their dirty fingerprints on it when Eze came out again and drove them out. "Let me see who says he is strong, dare come near this car." He planted himself in front of the car, looking bigger than he really was.

"Does the car belong to Eze's father?" a child asked.

"No. It belongs to sister Soha's friend," one of Eze's brothers replied without hesitation.

"I thought it belonged to your father," the same child said again.

"Keep quiet. Can't my father buy a car?" Eze shouted standing menacingly in front of the child.

Soha was still in front of the mirror admiring herself. She was not in a hurry at all. Her mother had told her that she should never show a man that she was anxious about him. She should rather keep him waiting as long as she wished. She was wearing one of the dresses she sewed for herself when she was at home. She suddenly thought of changing it. But she changed her mind, and instead came out. She was looking very shy as she took the outstretched hand of the man who had come to visit her.

"Are you ready?"

"For . . ."

"We are going to Kingsway Stores."

"Kingsway Stores?"

"Of course. But we discussed it last night, and you asked me to come at nine thirty," the man said looking at his watch.

"I am sorry. But I can't go again."

"You can't go?"

"No."

"Why?"

"Can't I change my mind?"

"Of course you can," the man said quietly a little surprised.

"I am going then."

"Already?"

"Yes."

"Don't you work on Saturdays?"

"No."

"Go well then," Soha said.

"When am I seeing you again?"

"I don't know. I have no car."

"Let's go to the cinema tonight."

"No, my mother will kill me."

"Your aunt."

"Yes. She is my mother. You said you will buy something for me today."

"Let's go to the Kingsway Stores then. I don't know how to buy things for women."

"Don't you buy things for your wife?"

"I told you, I have no wife." Soha laughed long and loud. The man watched her.

"Who are you deceiving? Please go to your wife and don't bother me. Lagos men, I know Lagos men."

"How many of them do you know?" She did not answer. She rather rolled her eyes and shifted in the chair in which she sat.

"I am going," he said standing up.

"Don't go now," she said. They heard the horn of a car.

"That's my car," he said.

"So?"

"The children are playing with the horn."

"So?"

"You are exasperating! I like you all the same. Let's go to this shopping, Soha. What is wrong with you? You are so stubborn."

"No, I won't go. I shall go next Saturday. I did not tell Mama Eze."

"You said you would."

"So I said."

He got up. It did not seem to him that there would be an end to this conversation.

"You are going?"

"I am going."

"Wait, I'll come with you." He breathed in and breathed out again.

"Go and change then."

"Change. Don't you like my dress?"

"I like it, but change into a better dress."

"I have no other dress. I might as well stay. You are ashamed of me."

"You have started again."

"I won't go again. How dare you say that my dress is not respectable. Well, maybe you will buy dresses for me before I go out with you." He put his hand in his back pocket and brought out his wallet. He pressed a five pound note in her hand. She smiled and they went out.

"Eze, you have been watching his car?" Soha said.

Eze nodded. He dipped into his pocket and gave Eze a shilling.

Eze jumped with joy.

"We watched with him," the other children chorused.

"Yes. They watched with him," Soha said. He brought out another shilling and gave to them. Then he drove away.

Mama Eze did not know about the young man who visited Soha. Soha warned the children not to tell their parents. But it was obvious to her that Soha had secrets. It was easy for a mother of five children who had watched so many girls growing up in the 'yard' to know when they were involved in men. At first, she thought of asking Soha, but she thought better of it until one day when Soha told her she was going to the shops and did not come back until late in the evening. She called her in.

"Where did you go, my sister's daughter?"

"I told you I went to the shops."

"Many people went to the shops from this 'yard', but they returned long before you."

"Well, we did not go the same shops," Soha said. Mama Eze did not like the way Soha talked to her. She smiled. "Soha," she called her. That was the first time Mama Eze called her by her name. "Soha," she called again. "This is Lagos. Lagos is different from home. Lagos is big. You must be careful here. You are a mere child. Lagos men are too deep for you. Don't think you are clever. You are not. You can never be cleverer than a Lagos man. I am older than you are, so take my advice."

Soha said nothing. She did not give a thought to what her aunt told her. But that night, Mama Eze did not sleep well. She told her husband. "You worry yourself unnecessarily. Didn't she tell you before she went to the shops?"

"She did."

"Well then?"

"Well then," Mama Eze echoed mockingly. "Well then. Go on speaking English, 'well then'. When something happens to Soha now, you will stay there. This is the time you should do something."

"Why are you talking like that, Mama Eze? What has the girl done? She is such a nice girl. She doesn't go out. She has been helping you with your housework. You yourself say so."

Mama Eze said nothing to him any more. One evening when Soha returned from school, she asked her aunt if she would allow her to go to the cinema. Her aunt clapped her hands in excitement, and rushed out of the room. "Mama Bisi, come out and hear what Soha is saying."

Mama Bisi who was her neighbour came out. "What did she say?" she asked clasping her chest. She was afraid.

"Soha, my sister's daughter, wants to go to the cinema." Mama Bisi hissed. "Is that all? You are excited because she has told you today. What about the other nights she has been going?"

"Other nights? Other nights?"

"Go and sit down *Ojari*. You don't know what you are saying. Soha, your sister's daughter, has been going out with different men for a long time now. You don't even see the dresses she wears, and the shoes. Do they look like the dresses a girl like her would wear?"

Mama Eze said nothing. Soha said nothing. "When Papa Eze returns, ask him whether you can go to the cinema," Mama Eze finally said after looking at her niece for a long time.

It wasn't long after this that Soha came to her aunt and told her that she wanted to move to a hostel.

"To a hostel, my sister's daughter. Who will pay for you?"

"I receive a salary."

"I see. I know you receive a salary. Those of us who have never received salaries in our lives know about salaries. But why now? Why do you want to leave us now? Don't you like my home any more? Is it too small for you? Or too humble? Are you ashamed of entertaining your friends here?"

"I want to start reading again. That's why I want to move to a hostel. It will be more convenient for me there."

"That is true. When you sing well, the dancer dances well. I understand my sister's daughter. I have to tell my husband and my sister. You mother said you should stay with me. It is only reasonable that I tell her that you are leaving me to go to a hostel. What hostel is that by the way?"

"The one at Ajagba Street."

"I see."

When Soha went to school, Mama Eze went over to Mama Bisi and told her what Soha said. "I have told you," Mama Bisi said. "Soha is not a better girl. Do you know the kind of girls who live in that hostel at Ajagba street? Rotten girls who will never marry. No man will bring them into his home and call them wives. You know that my sister who is at Abeokuta whom I went to see last week?"

"Yes, I know her. Iyabo."

"That's right. Iyabo. One of her friends who stayed in that hostel, nearly took Iyabo there. I stopped it. As soon as I heard it, I went to her mother at Abeokuta and told her. She came down, and both of us went to her. After talking to her, she changed her mind. So that's the place Soha wants to go and live. I no tell you, they say to go Lagos no hard, na return. Soha will be lost if she goes there."

Mama Eze returned home one evening from the market and was told that Soha had not been home from school. She put down her basket of unsold bread and sat down. "Didn't she tell you where she went?" she asked Eze. Eze shook his head. "And where is your father?" Mama Eze asked Eze.

"He has gone out."

"Where has he gone?"

"I don't know."

"You don't know. Every question, you don't know. Do you think you are still a child? Let me have some water quickly." Eze brought the water. Then Eze's father returned.

"They say Soha has not returned home," Mama Eze said to her husband.

"So Eze told me."

"And you went out, because Soha is not your sister. If Soha were your sister you would have been hysterical."

Then Mama Bisi came in, and sat down. She had heard of course.

"Eze, why not tell them the truth?" Mama Bisi said. Eze said nothing.

"Eze, so you know where Soha went?" Mama Eze asked. "I don't know," Eze protested vehemently.

"You helped Soha with her box. I saw you," Mama Bisi accused.

She did not see Eze do this, but what she said was true. Mama Eze and her husband were confused.

"Mama Bisi, please, tell me what you know."

"Ask your son there. He knows everything. He knows where Soha went."

"I don't know. You are lying, Mama Bisi." Mama Eze got up and slapped Eze's face. "How dare you, how dare you say that Mama Bisi is lying, you, you good-for-nothing child."

"Ewo, Mama Eze, that will do. If you slap the boy again, you'll have it hot."

"Jo don't quarrel," Mama Bisi begged. She went over to Papa Eze. "Please don't. But Eze, you are a bad child. Why are you hiding evil? A child like you behaving in this way."

Eze knew a lot. He helped Soha pack her things, and it was the gentleman with the car who took Soha away. Soha told him not to breathe a word to anybody. She also told him that she and her husband would come in the night to see his parents.

As they were wondering what to do, Eze slipped out. He was the only one who heard the sound of the car. He had grown to like Soha's friend since the day he watched his car for him. And he had also had many rides in his car as well, for anywhere Soha's friend saw Eze, he stopped to give him a lift, and he had enjoyed this very much.

Soha and the gentleman stepped out of the car, Soha leading the way. Mama Eze, Mama Bisi and Papa Eze stared at them. Soha and her friend stood. They stared at them.

"Can we sit down?" Soha asked as she sat down. The gentleman stood.

"Sit down," Papa Eze said. He sat down.

None found words. Soha's gentleman was completely lost.

"Is Soha living with you?" Papa Eze asked after a long time.

"Yes," he said.

"In fact we were married a month ago," Soha said.

"No," Mama Eze shouted. "You, you married to my sister's daughter. Impossible. You are going to be 'un-married.' Do you hear? Mama Bisi, is that what they do here?"

"This is Lagos. Anything can happen here," Mama Bisi said. Then she turned to the gentleman and spoke in Yoruba to him. It was only Papa Eze who did not understand.

"It is true, Papa Eze. They are married. What is this country turning into? Soha, you, you who left home only yesterday to come to Lagos, you are married, married to a Lagos man, without telling anybody. It is a slight and nothing else. What do I know? I didn't go to school. If I had gone to school, you wouldn't have treated me in this way."

"So you pregnated her," Mama Bisi said to Soha's husband in Yoruba. He did not immediately reply. Soha's heart missed a beat. "So it is showing already," she said to herself. Mama Bisi smiled bitterly. "You children. You think you can deceive us. I have seven children."

"What is your name?" Mama Bisi asked Soha's husband in Yoruba.

"Ibikunle," he replied.

"Ibikunle, we don't marry like this in the place where we come from . . ." Mama Eze did not finish.

"Even in the place where he comes from *kpa kpa*," Mama Bisi interrupted. "It is Lagos. When they come to Lagos they forget their home background. Imagine coming here to say they are married. Where in the world do they do this sort of thing?"

"You hear, Mr. Ibikunle, we don't marry like that in my home," Mama Eze said "Home people will not regard you as married. This is unheard of. And you tell me this is what the white people do. So when white people wish to marry, they don't seek the consent of their parents, they don't even inform them. My sister's daughter," she turned to Soha, "you have not done well. You have rewarded me with evil. Why did you not take me into confidence? Am I not married? Is marriage a sin? Will I prevent you from marrying? Isn't it the prayer of every woman?"

"It is enough Mama Eze," Mama Bisi said. "And besides . . ."

"You women talk too much. Mr Ibikunle has acted like a gentleman. What if he had run away after pregnating Soha. What would you do?"

"Hear what my husband is saying. I don't blame you. What am I saying? Aren't you a man. Aren't all men the same? Mr. Ibikunle, take your wife to your house, and get ready to go home to see your father and mother-in-law. I'll help you with the preparations."

Husband and wife went home. Mama Eze went home and told Soha's parents what had happened. A whole year passed. Mr. Ibikunle did not have the courage, or was it the money to travel to Soha's home to present himself to Soha's parents as their son-in-law.

NGUGI WA THIONG'O (b. 1938)
Kenya; English

Ngugi wa Thiong'o, East Africa's leading English-language novelist and play-wright, is also one of Africa's leading literary dissidents. Educated at the British-model Makerere College in Uganda and the University of Leeds in Northern England, Ngugi has rejected these Western influences as having been pernicious for Africa. His fiction and drama, inevitably influenced by European models, reflect the passionate disillusionment of a generation, in Kenya and elsewhere, that heard the promise of popular revolution offered before independence and saw it afterward corrupted by the emergence of new elites and exploiters. Ngugi calls for socialist revolution. His detention as a political prisoner by the Kenya government from 1977 to 1978 brought international protest. "Minutes of Glory" and "National Identity and Imperialist Domination" capture typical African themes—gender, class, and rural/urban inequities.

In "Minutes of Glory," a short story concerning a woman's decision to act for herself, cultural conflict begins in her preference for a European Christian name over her Gikuyu name. Hopeless about bettering herself, she has internalized the oppression of her own people. She fails to respect herself until she finds courage to reject the bar owner. Then her newfound self-assertion confronts and is defeated by the male-dominated social and legal system. She distrusts Nyagūthiī (and all other women) until the two find a mutual understanding and respect.

Ngugi puts the debate about modern Africa's problems in a new context in "National Identity and Imperialist Domination," an essay written in 1982. In his earlier essays, he advocated "a completely socialized economy, collectively owned and controlled by the people," the "elimination of all exploitative forces," and a consequent "complete and total liberation of the people." Here, he notices and criticizes in African literature a tendency to pit rural against urban and tradition against modernization. Enlarging the scope of the debate, Ngugi asserts imperialism to be the principal force acting on the peoples of developing countries. He presents this argument so forcefully that the reader begins to wonder why Africans have been so willing to accept foreign goods, tastes, and customs, why strong, loving, cooperative people have so devalued themselves.

from *Secret Lives and Other Stories*

Minutes of Glory

Her name was Wanjiru. But she liked better her Christian one, Beatrice. It sounded more pure and more beautiful. Not that she was ugly; but she could not be called beautiful either. Her body, dark and full fleshed, had the form, yes, but it was as if it waited to be filled by the spirit. She worked in beer halls where sons of women came to drown their inner lives in beer cans and froth. Nobody seemed to notice her. Except, perhaps, when a proprietor or an impatient customer called out her name, Beatrice; then other customers would raise their heads briefly, a few seconds, as if to behold the bearer of such a beautiful name, but not finding anybody there, they would resume their drinking, their ribald jokes, their laughter and play with the other serving girls. She was like a wounded bird in flight: a forced landing now and then but nevertheless wobbling from place to place so that she would variously be found in Alaska, Paradise, The Modern, Thome and other beer-halls all over Limuru. Sometimes it was because an irate proprietor found she was not attracting enough customers; he would sack her without notice and without a salary. She would wobble to the next bar. But sometimes she was simply tired of nesting in one place, a daily witness of familiar scenes; girls even more decidedly ugly than she were fought over by numerous claimants at closing hours. What do they have that I don't have? She would ask herself, depressed. She longed for a bar-kingdom where she would be at least one of the rulers, where petitioners would bring their gifts of beer, frustrated smiles and often curses that hid more lust and love than hate.

She left Limuru town proper and tried the mushrooming townlets around. She worked at Ngarariga, Kamiritho, Rironi and even Tiekunu and everywhere the story was the same. Oh, yes, occasionally she would get a client; but none cared for her as she would have liked, none really wanted her enough to fight over her. She was always a hard-up customer's last resort. No make-believe even, not for her that sweet pretence that men indulged in after their fifth bottle of Tusker. The following night or during a pay-day, the same client would pretend not to know her; he would be trying his money-power over girls who already had more than a fair share of admirers.

She resented this. She saw in every girl a rival and adopted a sullen attitude. Nyagũthĩ especially was the thorn that always pricked her wounded flesh. Nyagũthĩ, arrogant and aloof, but men always in her courtyard; Nyagũthĩ, fighting with men, and to her they would bring propitiating gifts which she accepted as of right. Nyagũthĩ could look bored, impatient, or downright contemptuous and still men would cling to her as if they enjoyed being whipped with biting words, curled lips and the indifferent eyes of a free woman. Nyagũthĩ was also a bird in flight, never really able to settle in one place, but in her case it was because she hungered for change and excitement: new faces and new territories for her conquest. Beatrice resented her very shadow. She saw in her the girl she would have liked to be, a girl who was both totally immersed in and yet completely above the underworld of bar violence and sex. Wherever Beatrice went the long shadow of Nyagũthĩ would sooner or later follow her.

She fled Limuru for Ilmorog in Chiri District. Ilmorog had once been a ghost village, but had been resurrected to life by that legendary woman, Nyang'endo, to whom every pop group had paid their tribute. It was of her that the young dancing Muthuu and Muchun g' wa[1] sang:

> When I left Nairobi for Ilmorog
> Never did I know
> I would bear this wonder-child mine
> Nyang'endo.[2]

As a result, Ilmorog was always seen as a town of hope where the weary and the down-trodden would find their rest and fresh water. But again Nyagũthĩ followed her.

She found that Ilmorog, despite the legend, despite the songs and dances, was not different from Limuru. She tried various tricks. Clothes? But even here she never earned enough to buy herself glittering robes. What was seventy-five shillings a month without house allowance, *posho,* without salaried boy-friends? By that time, Ambi had reached Ilmorog, and Beatrice thought that this would be the answer. Had she not, in Limuru, seen girls blacker than herself transformed overnight from ugly sins into white stars by a touch of skin-lightening creams? And men would ogle them, would even talk with exaggerated pride of their

---

1. A pop music group.   2. A fictional character.

newborn girl friends. Men were strange creatures, Beatrice thought in moments of searching analysis. They talked heatedly against Ambi, Butone, Firesnow, Moonsnow,[3] wigs, straightened hair; but they always went for a girl with an Ambi-lightened skin and head covered with a wig made in imitation of European or Indian hair. Beatrice never tried to find the root cause of this black self-hatred, she simply accepted the contradiction and applied herself to Ambi with a vengeance. She had to rub out her black shame. But even Ambi she could not afford in abundance; she could only apply it to her face and to her arms so that her legs and her neck retained their blackness. Besides there were parts of her face she could not readily reach—behind the ears and above eyelashes, for instance—and these were a constant source of shame and irritation to her Ambi-self.

She would always remember this Ambi period as one of her deepest humiliation before her later minutes of glory. She worked in Ilmorog Starlight Bar and Lodging. Nyagūthiī, with her bangled hands, her huge earrings, served behind the counter. The owner was a good Christian soul who regularly went to church and paid all his dues to *Harambee*[4] projects. Pot-belly. Grey hairs. Soft-spoken. A respectable family man, well known in Ilmorog. Hardworking even, for he would not leave the bar until the closing hours, or more precisely, until Nyagūthiī left. He had no eyes for any other girl; he hung around her, and surreptitiously brought her gifts of clothes without receiving gratitude in kind. Only the promise. Only the hope for tomorrow. Other girls he gave eighty shillings a month. Nyagūthiī had a room to herself. Nyagūthiī woke up whenever she liked to take the stock. But Beatrice and the other girls had to wake up at five or so, make tea for the lodgers, clean up the bar and wash dishes and glasses. Then they would hang around the bar in shifts until two o'clock when they would go for a small break. At five o'clock, they had to be in again, ready for customers whom they would now serve with frothy beers and smiles until twelve o'clock or for as long as there were customers thirsty for more Tuskers and Pilsners. What often galled Beatrice, although in her case it did not matter one way or another, was the owner's insistence that the girls should sleep in Starlight. They would otherwise be late for work, he said. But what he really wanted was for the girls to use their bodies to attract more lodgers in Starlight. Most of the girls, led by Nyagūthiī, defied the rule and bribed the watchman to let them out and in. They wanted to meet their regular or one-night boy-friends in places where they would be free and where they would be treated as not just barmaids. Beatrice always slept in. Her occasional one-night patrons wanted to spend the minimum. Came a night when the owner, refused by Nyagūthiī, approached her. He started by finding fault with her work; he called her names, then as suddenly he started praising her, although in a grudging almost contemptuous manner. He grabbed her, struggled with her, potbelly, grey hairs, and everything. Beatrice felt an unusual revulsion for the man. She could not, she would not bring herself to accept that which had so recently been cast aside by Nyagūthiī. My God, she wept inside, what does

---

3. Beauty creams for skin bleaching.
4. A slogan meaning "let us all do it together"; coined by Jomo Kenyatta (1893–1978),

first president of Kenya, to promote self-help projects.

Nyagūthiĩ have that I don't have? The man now humiliated himself before her. He implored. He promised her gifts. But she would not yield. That night she too defied the rule. She jumped through a window; she sought a bed in another bar and only came back at six. The proprietor called her in front of all the others and dismissed her. But Beatrice was rather surprised at herself.

She stayed a month without a job. She lived from room to room at the capricious mercy of the other girls. She did not have the heart to leave Ilmorog and start all over again in a new town. The wound hurt. She was tired of wandering. She stopped using Ambi. No money. She looked at herself in the mirror. She had so aged, hardly a year after she had fallen from grace. Why then was she scrupulous, she would ask herself. But somehow she had a horror of soliciting lovers or directly bartering her body for hard cash. What she wanted was decent work and a man or several men who cared for her. Perhaps she took that need for a man, for a home and for a child with her to bed. Perhaps it was this genuine need that scared off men who wanted other things from barmaids. She wept late at nights and remembered home. At such moments, her mother's village in Nyeri seemed the sweetest place on God's earth. She would invest the life of her peasant mother and father with romantic illusions of immeasurable peace and harmony. She longed to go back home to see them. But how could she go back with empty hands? In any case the place was now a distant landscape in the memory. Her life was here in the bar among this crowd of lost strangers. Fallen from grace, fallen from grace. She was part of a generation which would never again be one with the soil, the crops, the wind and the moon. Not for them that whispering in dark hedges, not for her that dance and love-making under the glare of the moon, with the hills of TumuTumu rising to touch the sky. She remembered that girl from her home village who, despite a life of apparent glamour being the kept mistress of one rich man after another in Limuru, had gassed herself to death. This generation was not awed by the mystery of death, just as it was callous to the mystery of life; for how many unmarried mothers had thrown their babies into latrines rather than lose that glamour? The girl's death became the subject of jokes. She had gone metric[5] without pains, they said. Thereafter, for a week, Beatrice thought of going metric. But she could not bring herself to do it.

She wanted love; she wanted life.

A new bar was opened in Ilmorog. Treetop Bar, Lodging and Restaurant. Why Treetop, Beatrice could not understand unless because it was a storied building: tea-shop on the ground floor and beer-shop in a room at the top. The rest were rooms for five-minute or one-night lodgers. The owner was a retired civil servant but one who still played at politics. He was enormously wealthy with business sites and enterprises in every major town in Kenya. Big shots from all over the country came to his bar. Big men in Mercedes. Big men in their Bentleys. Big men in their Jaguars and Daimlers. Big men with uniformed chauffeurs drowsing with boredom in cars waiting outside. There were others not so big who came to pay respects to the great. They talked politics mostly. And about their work. Gossip

---

5. She died.

was rife. Didn't you know? Indeed so and so has been promoted. Really? And so and so has been sacked. Embezzlement of public funds. So foolish you know. Not clever about it at all. They argued, they quarrelled, sometimes they fought it out with fists, especially during the elections campaign. The only point on which they were all agreed was that the Luo community[6] was the root cause of all the trouble in Kenya; that intellectuals and University students were living in an ivory tower of privilege and arrogance; that Kiambu had more than a lion's share of developments; that men from Nyeri and Muranga had acquired all the big business in Nairobi and were even encroaching on Chiri District; that African workers, especially those on the farms, were lazy and jealous of 'us' who had sweated ourselves to sudden prosperity. Otherwise each would hymn his own praises or return compliments. Occasionally in moments of drunken ebullience and self-praise, one would order two rounds of beer for each man present in the bar. Even the poor from Ilmorog would come to Treetop to dine at the gates of the *nouveaux riches*.

Here Beatrice got a job as a sweeper and bedmaker. Here for a few weeks she felt closer to greatness. Now she made beds for men she had previously known as names. She watched how even the poor tried to drink and act big in front of the big. But soon fate caught up with her. Girls flocked to Treetop from other bars. Girls she had known at Limuru, girls she had known at Ilmorog. And most had attached themselves to one or several big men, often playing a hide-and-not-to-be-found game with their numerous lovers. And Nyagūthiī was there behind the counter, with the eyes of the rich and the poor fixed on her. And she, with her big eyes, bangled hands and earrings maintained the same air of bored indifference. Beatrice as a sweeper and bedmaker became even more invisible. Girls who had fallen into good fortune looked down upon her.

She fought life with dreams. In between putting clean sheets on beds that had just witnessed a five-minute struggle that ended in a half-strangled cry and a pool, she would stand by the window and watch the cars and the chauffeurs, so that soon she knew all the owners by the number plates of their cars and the uniforms of their chauffeurs. She dreamt of lovers who would come for her in sleek Mercedes sports cars made for two. She saw herself linking hands with such a lover, walking in the streets of Nairobi and Mombasa, tapping the ground with high heels, quick, quick short steps. And suddenly she would stop in front of a display glass window, exclaiming at the same time; Oh darling, won't you buy me those . . .? Those what, he would ask, affecting anger. Those stockings, darling. It was as an owner of several stockings, ladderless and holeless, that she thought of her well-being. Never again would she mend torn things. Never, never, never. Do you understand? Never. She was next the proud owner of different coloured wigs, blonde wigs, brunette wigs, redhead wigs, Afro wigs, wigs, wigs, all the wigs in the world. Only then would the whole earth sing hallelujah to the one Beatrice. At such moments, she would feel exalted, lifted out of her murky self, no longer a floor sweeper and bedmaker for a five-minute instant love, but Beatrice, descen-

---

6. One of the major ethnic groups in Kenya.

dant of Wangu Makeri[7] who made men tremble with desire at her naked body bathed in moonlight, daughter of Nyang'endo, the founder of modern Ilmorog, of whom they often sang that she had worked several lovers into impotence.

Then she noticed him and he was the opposite of the lover of her dreams. He came one Saturday afternoon driving a big five-ton lorry. He carefully parked it beside the Benzes, the Jaguars and the Daimlers, not as a lorry, but as one of those sleek cream-bodied frames, so proud of it he seemed to be. He dressed in a baggy grey suit over which he wore a heavy khaki military overcoat. He removed the overcoat, folded it with care, and put it in the front seat. He locked all the doors, dusted himself a little, then walked round the lorry as if inspecting it for damage. A few steps before he entered Treetop, he turned round for a final glance at his lorry dwarfing the other things. At Treetops he sat in a corner and, with a rather loud defiant voice, ordered a Kenya one. He drank it with relish, looking around at the same time for a face he might recognize. He indeed did recognize one of the big ones and he immediately ordered for him a quarter bottle of Vat 69. This was accepted with a bare nod of the head and a patronizing smile; but when he tried to follow his generosity with a conversation, he was firmly ignored. He froze, sank into his Muratina. But only for a time. He tried again: he was met with frowning faces. More pathetic were his attempts to join in jokes; he would laugh rather too loudly, which would make the big ones stop, leaving him in the air alone. Later in the evening he stood up, counted several crisp hundred shilling notes and handed them to Nyagūthiī behind the counter ostensibly for safekeeping. People whispered; murmured; a few laughed, rather derisively, though they were rather impressed. But this act did not win him immediate recognition. He staggered towards room no. 7 which he had hired. Beatrice brought him the keys. He glanced at her, briefly, then lost all interest.

Thereafter he came every Saturday. At five when most of the big shots were already seated. He repeated the same ritual, except the money act, and always met with defeat. He nearly always sat in the same corner and always rented room 7. Beatrice grew to anticipate his visits and, without being conscious of it, kept the room ready for him. Often after he had been badly humiliated by the big company, he would detain Beatrice and talk to her, or rather he talked to himself in her presence. For him, it had been a life of struggles. He had never been to school although getting an education had been his ambition. He never had a chance. His father was a squatter in the European settled area in the Rift Valley. That meant a lot in those colonial days. It meant among other things a man and his children were doomed to a future of sweat and toil for the white devils and their children. He had joined the freedom struggle and like the others had been sent to detention. He came from detention the same as his mother had brought him to this world. Nothing. With independence he found he did not possess the kind of education which would have placed him in one of the vacancies at the top. He started as a charcoal burner, then a butcher, gradually working his own way

---

7. A woman who was made a chief by the British colonialists. The men taunted her and told her she had to dance naked or seminaked like the male chiefs. She did. She has now become a legendary powerful woman of the past.

to become a big transporter of vegetables and potatoes from the Rift Valley and Chiri districts to Nairobi. He was proud of his achievement. But he resented that others, who had climbed to their present wealth through loans and a subsidized education, would not recognize his like. He would rumble on like this, dwelling on education he would never have, and talking of better chances for his children. Then he would carefully count the money, put it under the pillow, and then dismiss Beatrice. Occasionally he would buy her a beer but he was clearly suspicious of women whom he saw as money-eaters of men. He had not yet married.

One night he slept with her. In the morning he scratched for a twenty shilling note and gave it to her. She accepted the money with an odd feeling of guilt. He did this for several weeks. She did not mind the money. It was useful. But he paid for her body as he would pay for a bag of potatoes or a sack of cabbages. With the one pound, he had paid for her services as a listener, a vessel of his complaints against those above, and as a one-night receptacle of his man's burden. She was becoming bored with his ego, with his stories that never varied in content, but somehow, in him, deep inside, she felt that something had been there, a fire, a seed, a flower which was being smothered. In him she saw a fellow victim and looked forward to his visits. She too longed to talk to someone. She too longed to confide in a human being who would understand.

And she did it one Saturday night, suddenly interrupting the story of his difficult climb to the top. She did not know why she did it. Maybe it was the rain outside. It was softly drumming the corrugated iron sheets, bringing with the drumming a warm and drowsy indifference. He would listen. He had to listen. She came from Karatina in Nyeri. Her two brothers had been gunned down by the British soldiers. Another one had died in detention. She was, so to speak, an only child. Her parents were poor. But they worked hard on their bare strip of land and managed to pay her fees in primary school. For the first six years she had worked hard. In the seventh year, she must have relaxed a little. She did not pass with a good grade. Of course she knew many with similar grades who had been called to good government secondary schools. She knew a few others with lesser grades who had gone to very top schools on the strength of their connections. But she was not called to any high school with reasonable fees. Her parents could not afford fees in a Harambee school. And she would not hear of repeating standard seven.[8] She stayed at home with her parents. Occasionally she would help them in the shamba and with house chores. But imagine: for the past six years she had led a life with a different rhythm from that of her parents. Life in the village was dull. She would often go to Karatina and to Nyeri in search of work. In every office, they would ask her the same questions: what work do you want? What do you know? Can you type? Can you take shorthand? She was desperate. It was in Nyeri, drinking Fanta in a shop, tears in her eyes, that she met a young man in a dark suit and sun-glasses. He saw her plight and talked to her. He came from Nairobi. Looking for work? That's easy; in a big city there would be no difficulty

---

8. The highest grade in intermediate school.

with jobs. He would certainly help. Transport? He had a car—a cream-white Peugeot. Heaven. It was a beautiful ride, with the promise of dawn. Nairobi. He drove her to Terrace Bar. They drank beer and talked about Nairobi. Through the window she could see the neon-lit city and knew that here was hope. That night she gave herself to him, with the promise of dawn making her feel light and gay. She had a very deep sleep. When she woke in the morning, the man in the cream-white Peugeot was not there. She never saw him again. That's how she had started the life of a barmaid. And for one and a half years now she had not been once to see her parents. Beatrice started weeping. Huge sobs of self-pity. Her humiliation and constant flight were fresh in her mind. She had never been able to take to bar culture, she always thought that something better would come her way. But she was trapped, it was the only life she now knew, although she had never really learnt all its laws and norms. Again she heaved out and in, tears tossing out with every sob. Then suddenly she froze. Her sobbing was arrested in the air. The man had long covered himself. His snores were huge and unmistakable.

She felt a strange hollowness. Then a bile of bitterness spilt inside her. She wanted to cry at her new failure. She had met several men who had treated her cruelly, who had laughed at her scruples, at what they thought was an ill-disguised attempt at innocence. She had accepted. But not this, Lord, not this. Was this man not a fellow victim? Had he not, Saturday after Saturday, unburdened himself to her? He had paid for her human services; he had paid away his responsibility with his bottle of Tuskers and hard cash in the morning. Her innermost turmoil had been his lullaby. And suddenly something in her snapped. All the anger of a year and a half, all the bitterness against her humiliation were now directed at this man.

What she did later had the mechanical precision of an experienced hand.

She touched his eyes. He was sound asleep. She raised his head. She let it fall. Her tearless eyes were now cold and set. She removed the pillow from under him. She rummaged through it. She took out his money. She counted five crisp pink notes. She put the money inside her brassiere.

She went out of room no. 7. Outside it was still raining. She did not want to go to her usual place. She could not now stand the tiny cupboard room or the superior chatter of her roommate. She walked through mud and rain. She found herself walking towards Nyagūthiī's room. She knocked at the door. At first she had no response. Then she heard Nyagūthiī's sleepy voice above the drumming rain.

"Who is that?"

"It is me. Please open."

"Who?"

"Beatrice."

"At this hour of the night?"

"Please."

Lights were put on. Bolts unfastened. The door opened. Beatrice stepped inside. She and Nyagūthiī stood there face to face. Nyagūthiī was in a see-through nightdress: on her shoulders she had a green pullover.

"Beatrice, is there anything wrong?" She at last asked, a note of concern in her voice.

"Can I rest here for a while? I am tired. And I want to talk to you." Beatrice's voice carried assurance and power.

"But what has happened?"

"I only want to ask you a question, Nyagūthiī."

They were still standing. Then, without a word, they both sat on the bed.

"Why did you leave home, Nyagūthiī?" Beatrice asked. Another silent moment. Nyagūthiī seemed to be thinking about the question. Beatrice waited. Nyagūthiī's voice when at last it came was slightly tremulous, unsteady.

"It is a long story, Beatrice. My father and mother were fairly wealthy. They were also good Christians. We lived under regulations. You must never walk with the heathen. You must not attend their pagan customs—dances and circumcision rites, for instance. There were rules about what, how and when to eat. You must even walk like a Christian lady. You must never be seen with boys. Rules, rules all the way. One day instead of returning home from school, I and another girl from a similar home ran away to Eastleigh. I have never been home once this last four years. That's all."

Another silence. Then they looked at one another in mutual recognition.

"One more question, Nyagūthiī. You need not answer it. But I have always thought that you hated me, you despised me."

"No, no, Beatrice, I have never hated you. I have never hated anybody. It is just that nothing interests me. Even men do not move me now. Yet I want, I need instant excitement. I need the attention of those false flattering eyes to make me feel myself, myself. But you, you seemed above all this—somehow you had something inside you that I did not have."

Beatrice tried to hold her tears with difficulty.

Early the next day, she boarded a bus bound for Nairobi. She walked down Bazaar street looking at the shops. Then down Government Road, right into Kenyatta Avenue, and Kimathi street. She went into a shop near Hussein Suleman's street and bought several stockings. She put on a pair. She next bought herself a new dress. Again she changed into it. In a Bata Shoeshop, she bought high heeled shoes, put them on and discarded her old flat ones. On to an Akamba[9] kiosk, and she fitted herself with earrings. She went to a mirror and looked at her new self. Suddenly she felt enormous hunger as if she had been hungry all her life. She hesitated in front of Moti Mahal. Then she walked on, eventually entering Fransae. There was a glint in her eyes that made men's eyes turn to her. This thrilled her. She chose a table in a corner and ordered Indian curry. A man left his table and joined her. She looked at him. Her eyes were merry. He was dressed in a dark suit and his eyes spoke of lust. He bought her a drink. He tried to engage her in conversation. But she ate in silence. He put his hand under the table and felt her knees. She let him do it. The hand went up and up her thigh. Then suddenly

---

9. Another major ethnic group in Kenya.

she left her unfinished food and her untouched drink and walked out. She felt good. He followed her. She knew this without once turning her eyes. He walked beside her for a few yards. She smiled at herself but did not look at him. He lost his confidence. She left him standing sheepishly looking at a glass window outside Gino's. In the bus back to Ilmorog, men gave her seats. She accepted this as of right. At Treetops bar she went straight to the counter. The usual crowd of big men was there. Their conversations stopped for a few seconds at her entry. Their lascivious eyes were turned to her. The girls stared at her. Even Nyagūthiī could not maintain her bored indifference. Beatrice bought them drinks. The manager came to her, rather unsure. He tried a conversation. Why had she left work? Where had she been? Would she like to work in the bar, helping Nyagūthiī behind the counter? Now and then? A barmaid brought her a note. A certain big shot wanted to know if she would join their table. More notes came from different big quarters with the one question; would she be free tonight? A trip to Nairobi even. She did not leave her place at the counter. But she accepted their drinks as of right. She felt a new power, confidence even.

She took out a shilling, put it in the slot and the juke box boomed with the voice of Robinson Mwangi singing Hūnyū wa Mashambani. He sang of those despised girls who worked on farms and contrasted them with urban girls. Then she played a Kamaru and a D.K. Men wanted to dance with her. She ignored them, but enjoyed their flutter around her. She twisted her hips to the sound of yet another D.K. Her body was free. She was free. She sucked in the excitement and tension in the air.

Then suddenly at around six, the man with the five-ton Lorry stormed into the bar. This time he had on his military overcoat. Behind him was a policeman. He looked around. Everybody's eyes were raised to him. But Beatrice went on swaying her hips. At first he could not recognize Beatrice in the girl celebrating her few minutes of glory by the juke box. Then he shouted in triumph. "That is the girl! Thief! Thief!"

People melted back to their seats. The policeman went and handcuffed her. She did not resist. Only at the door she turned her head and spat. Then she went out followed by the policeman.

In the bar the stunned silence broke into hilarious laughter when someone made a joke about sweetened robbery without violence. They discussed her. Some said she should have been beaten. Others talked contemptuously about 'these bar girls.' Yet others talked with a concern noticeable in unbelieving shakes of their heads about the rising rate of crime. Shouldn't the Hanging Bill be extended to all thefts of property? And without anybody being aware of it the man with the five-ton lorry had become a hero. They now surrounded him with questions and demanded the whole story. Some even bought him drinks. More remarkable, they listened, their attentive silence punctuated by appreciative laughter. The averted threat to property had temporarily knit them into one family. And the man, accepted for the first time, told the story with relish.

But behind the counter Nyagūthiī wept.

National Identity and Imperialist Domination:

THE CRISIS OF CULTURE IN AFRICA TODAY[1]

The crisis of culture in Africa (and the developing world) has too often been seen in terms of a conflict between tradition and modernity; the rural and the urban; and the clash of values consequently engendered by that dichotomy. In this schema, the urban (industry, technology, electronics, etc.) is identified with modernity; the rural (subsistence agriculture, economic backwardness, etc.) with tradition. But ironically the same modernity is supposed to evoke images of fast changes, instability, human isolation while tradition evokes contrary images of peace, stability, and communal existence. Rampant urbanization and industrialization are seen as destroying a harmony of values embodied in tradition whose repository is the rural community. Thus the false glitter of the electronic culture is seen as luring an unwary youth away from the stability of communal life in a rural village into the chaos and loneliness of life in the big city.

It is all there in written literature. The peasant who follows the mirage of prosperity and happiness in the big city only to find the opposite is a familiar character in many a novel from the developing world. What often is not stated is that such a character is actually escaping from the hell of rural poverty and misery into the hades of urban poverty and misery, in both cases brought about by ruthless exploitation, internal and external. But even where this is stated, the schema of rural/urban dichotomy as the basis of analysis of the problems of culture in developing countries remains, and the crisis of culture is still seen in terms of a conflict between tradition and modernity.

Two misleading assumptions underlie the schema.

Firstly, modern industry, science and technology are seen as being in opposition to tradition and peasant cultures. The destruction of tradition or aspects of tradition and peasant culture is seen as necessarily evil. Within this false schema the beauty of rural culture rests on a foundation of poverty and abject want. But in fact modern science and technology, if organized, owned and controlled differently, could make possible a total economic transformation of the countryside and the construction of a whole people's culture on a structure of prosperity instead of on that of backwardness. Moreover, far from destroying tradition, modern technology (e.g. video, cinema, television, radio) should make it possible to actually reclaim the positive aspects of tradition and peasant cultures which are withering away under the pressures of the economic exploitation. Africa, for instance, has a rich tradition of oral literature. The narrative was often accompanied by mime and song. With video, film and television, it is now possible to reclaim this tradition through an integration of the visual image (e.g. animated cartoons), the voice and the music. The same is true in theater. African

---

1. This is a revised and abbreviated version of a paper written for UNESCO, and subse-   quently read in London, Oxford, Uppsala, Stockholm, and elsewhere.

peasant theater relied heavily on song, dance and mime, and these can now be permanently captured on the screen. Thus not only is it possible to use modern science and technology to democratize access to this heritage—more people can be told the tale at the same time—but even more crucial, it is possible to use it to integrate the cultures of the different nationalities within the geographic state into a national whole. Through video, T.V. or cinema, the tales from the different nationalities become mutually accessible and comprehensible.

The second misleading assumption is that the rural and the urban are two self-contained islands and a character from one to the other is actually walking across two unlinked entities. But in fact the two are a creation of each other. The urban is a creation of the rural as much as the rural is a creation of the urban. The peasants had to be alienated from the soil and be driven into towns, that is, they had to be proletarianized before the modern city could be born. But where under feudal and semifeudal systems the town was under the sway of the countryside, the modern city which emerged with capitalism, the city of gold, became the master of the rural out of which it had been born and bred. Marx and Engels wrote of 19th century Europe:

> The bourgeoisie has subjected the country to the rule of the towns. It has created enormous cities, has greatly increased the urban population as compared with the rural, and has thus rescued a considerable part of the population from the idiocy of rural life. Just as it has made the country dependent upon towns, so it has made barbarian and semibarbarian countries dependent on the civilized ones, nations of peasants on nations of bourgeoisie, the East on the West.

With the evolution of capitalism into the higher stage of imperialism, the rural and urban sectors of "the nations of peasants" became even more subjected to the rule of "the nations of bourgeoisie," and with what results? The subject nations—that is the majority of the population—were reduced to the idiocy of both urban and rural life.

This economic and political subjection of "the nations of peasants" to "the nations of bourgeoisie" is the heart of the matter when discussing cultural problems of the developing countries. For economic and political dependence are bound to be reflected in culture.

But by posing the problems of culture in the developing world in terms of a conflict between the rural and the urban, thus concentrating on secondary contradictions, the real issues behind the crisis are avoided. What are the real forces behind the modernity and tradition, the urban and the rural? Viewed in a historical perspective, the whole problem (modernity, tradition, rural, urban, etc.) brings us face to face with the inescapable fact: the all encompassing impact of imperialism on third world peoples and the national struggles which that very impact has generated.

The developing world, with its economic, political and cultural backwardness, its massive poverty, illiteracy and disease, is a creation of imperialism in its colonial and neocolonial stages. The developing world can in fact be defined as all those countries in Asia, Africa and Latin America which have been underdeveloped by imperialism, those countries whose economy, politics and culture have been and continue to be dominated by Western imperialist nations, in essence meaning the subjection of the whole population of the dominated countries to the ruling bourgeois classes of the dominating nations. Marx and Engels wrote:

> The bourgeoisie by the rapid development of all instruments of production, by the immensely facilitated means of communication, draws all, even the most barbarian, nations into civilization. The cheap prices of its commodities are the heavy artillery with which it batters down all Chinese walls, with which it forces the barbarians intensely obstinate hatred of foreigners to capitulate. It compels all nations, on pain of extinction to adopt the bourgeois mode of production; it compels them to introduce what it calls civilization into the midst, i.e. to become bourgeois themselves. In a word, it creates a world after its own image.

A world after its own image: this it tried to achieve not only through economic exploitation and political subjugation but more importantly, through cultural domination. Economic and political control have never been possible without a mental control. Thus the robbery of a peoples' wealth was accompanied by a repressive political colonial rule enforced by the gun and the boot and also a programmed attempt to destroy people's dances, songs, literature, religions, languages, while imposing the conqueror's languages, literature, education and religion.

The colonial system could not of course hold cultural captive the entire population. That would have been an achievement unparalleled in history. But they had an achievement of a sort which is now proving so fatal to real development in Africa. They created a colonial elite. In his introduction to Frantz Fanon's classic. *The Wretched of the Earth,* Jean-Paul Sartre has aptly and ably described the process of creating a colonial elite in the image of the Western bourgeois:

> They picked out promising adolescents; they branded them, as with red-hot iron, with the principles of Western culture; they stuffed their mouths full of high-sounding phrases, grand glutinous words that stuck to their teeth. After a short stay in the mother country they were sent home, white-washed. These walking lies had nothing to say to their brothers; they only echoed. From Paris, from London, from Amsterdam we would utter the words "Parthenon! Brotherhood!" and somewhere in Asia or Africa lips would open ". . . Parthenon . . . Brotherhood!"

This elite saw the world, they perceived themselves and the possibilities opened out to them, with glasses "Made in Europe" and which were now permanently glued to their eyes.

But the process created its opposite: the economic, political and cultural struggle for national independence and total liberation. This resulted in some sort of independence with the elite manufactured in Europe a la Sartre's description inheriting the state with one dictum signed at the end of Constitutional Conferences: don't change the colonial economic structures of dependence! On the cultural level, in the colonies and neocolonies there grew two cultures in mortal conflict: foreign imperialist; national and patriotic. And so, out of the different nationalities often inhabiting one geographic state, there emerged a people's literature, music, dance, theater, art in fierce struggle against foreign imperialist literature, music, dance, theater, art imposed on colonies, semicolonies, and neocolonies. Thus the major contradiction in the third world is between national identity and imperialist domination.

This to me is still the real and fundamental conflict of cultures: viz. a national patriotic culture arising out of and getting its character from the struggle against imperialism. Other contradictions, between the urban and the rural, the modern and the traditional, and between the different nationalities are secondary and they can only be properly appreciated within the context of the larger basic contradiction.

In this conflict, the national tries to find roots in the traditions mostly kept alive by the peasantry in the forms of their songs, poems, theater and dances. The foreign imperialist culture tries to build strongholds in the cities where it parades itself as modernity and progress. Thus this crucial struggle between the national and foreign is deliberately made to appear as a conflict between the rural and the urban or between tradition and modernity.

This is not an accident. The impoverished exploited peasantry with its oral heritage lives in the countryside. But the native bourgeoisie through whom imperialism works resides in the city. It controls the state instruments of coercion, persuasion and propaganda. In their state theaters, cinemas, television and radio stations, they mostly allow only reactionary foreign programs. They champion the cause of imperialism which they present as "modern and national" while in the countryside they pay lip service to peasant cultures by championing irrelevant traditionalism emptied of all meaningful dynamic content, a petrified museum culture for the amusement of state guests and tourists.

But even in these towns and cities, new cultures are emerging out of that struggle for total liberation from imperialism. This can be clearly seen in the poetry and songs and theatre among workers in the urban areas of the developing world. It is a fighting culture, and though fusing different elements, it is in basic harmony with the resistance culture of the countryside. The urban and the rural struggles are actually in basic harmony in their opposition to exploitation and domination by an alliance of a servile native ruling class and imperialism. Thus the worker and the peasant are the basis and creators of truly modern cultures in the developing world because all through the colonial and neocolonial stages they have resisted being branded with the red-hot irons of Western bourgeois values and outlook. These worker/peasant cultures are national in character and are in basic conflict with all forms of foreign domination.

This real conflict of cultures in Africa between imperialism and resistance is rapidly moving toward a crisis. This is because so many of the ruling regimes in the developing world are committed to both nurturing, promoting and encouraging foreign reactionary cultures while at the same time actively suppressing any genuine progressive national initiatives.

MUBARAK RABI (b. 1935)
Morocco

A native of Casablanca, Rabi studied philosophy at Muhammad V University in Rabat, Morocco. Although he writes both poetry and fiction, it has been his fiction that has placed for him in the limelight. He has received several prizes for both his short stories and his novel, *The Good Ones*.

Zinah

By God Almighty, it would be much better to kill oneself. By God Almighty it would be; but he fears Zinah's commentary, referring to him as "Poor empty-headed Haddan, the deformed," and besides, he would never then be able to marry her.

It is not his fault he is deformed; God alone is perfect. (He is deformed on the upper part a little and on the lower part too.) Despite his condition, he fell in love with her; his love inspired him to call her Zinah[1] while the rest of God's creatures in the village use her real name, ʿArabiyya, daughter of the *faqih*,[2] Si Nasir.

He went to her father in Masida, not to ask him for her hand—he certainly was no fool although they claim he is, but to ask for a charm to attract his beloved. He offered as fee a basket of warm eggs which he removed from under his old mother's only hen.

(*You understand, Mother, that your son is impatient for Zinah, so why be so angry with him?*)

The *faqih* asked for her name, but Haddan the deformed stuttered, refusing to divulge it. He was no fool, no matter what people said. Could he have uttered, "*Faqih* Si Nasir, write me words which will make your beloved daughter fall in love with me?" He could only give the *faqih* the first initial of her name.

"Oh, the first letter, the first letter, Sir, blessed be the letter, Si Nasir."

"Say it, say the name, Haddan, may God bless you."

"It is ʿA'—the first letter of her name, master *Faqih*."

The *faqih* wrote the first letter and stopped, staring at the paper as if he had discovered something strange. . . . Had he figured it out? God have mercy! How could he recognize his daughter from just the first letter of her name? The *Faqih* stared at Haddan's morose, frightened face and anguished posture, leaning to the left as if ready to run away. Now the *Faqih* seemed to be trembling himself, almost strongly. Oh miserable, distorted Haddan. You'd better run away. He certainly recognized the name! The *Faqih* gradually gathered his composure, with conscious effort. He spat around him, then invoked God's help and blessing and recited the Kursi verse and other such prescribed verses from the Qur'an. Then he grasped the anxious Haddan and, trying to persuade him to sit down, said, "Sit down, my son, sit down."

Again the *Faqih* recited the Kursi verse and his features relaxed. Haddan too felt more at east. Rejoice Haddan, the *Faqih* knows and accepts!

Translated by Aida Bamia and Naomi Shihab Nye.

---

1. The word *zinah* means beautiful.
2. A Qur'an reciter, or a man learned in Islamic studies. The word can also point to some powers of divination associated with a *faqih*.

The *Faqih* whispered, "Oh my God, the infidel has conquered your soul, Haddan."

What could Haddan do if the *Faqih*, rightly or wrongly, had guessed the wrong obsession when he stammered as he was about to mention her simple initial? It would not be the *Faqih*'s fault, either, if he pursued a natural logic, realizing Haddan's passion by simple deduction: since Haddan the distorted was unable to pronounce her name, her initial was ᶜA, and he looked so pathetic, all this could lead to only one person, the unbeliever, she whose name should never be mentioned[3]. . . . In the Name of God, the Merciful, the Compassionate. Haddan's neck swayed, bent by the amulet attached to it by a black woolen thread. He leapt to her side as she was returning from the water wheel.

"Good morning to you, Zinah!"

She stiffened in surprise. "I won't bid you good morning, distorted and unlucky man."

His long stature quivered, losing its tentative balance, but he did not fall to the ground. He said, "You ought to be ashamed of yourself, Zinah, you ought to." Was he guilty because he had fallen in love with you? Because he was deformed and you were well-built? Because he was Fatna's son, still living with her in the same hut? Was he at fault because all they possessed was a single cow tied to the large cactus tree? But she was expected to calve in two months time and then they would have an abundance of butter and milk. It is for *your* sake, Zinah, daughter of the *Faqih* Si Nasir, that I deprived a chicken of the hatch and left it angry, its feathers ruffled! While *your* house is full of blessings. But poor Haddan's intention is to be your husband—that is, with the help of your father's amulet.

Haddan swayed like a drunkard at her side. Smiling, he thought, "The amulet is around my neck, my heart is filled with love for her, and patience solves most problems." He called out his secret name for her, "Zinah!"

"May you be deprived of all good, you twisted owl-owner." (By God Almighty it would be better for me to die, kill myself, and get it over with. Is it my fault if my hut has been surrounded by thorny cactus trees since the days of my great-grandfather? I can't help it if the ill-omened owl[4] happens to like our place and stays, appearing there mornings and evenings, facing the hut. By God I will deal with this owl. One of us has to go.) With his eyes he followed a dark spot flying far off in the sky. As it shrank he slapped one hand against the other, like a person washing his hands after a difficult job. Before entering his hut to rest, and feeling much more cheerful, he gazed at a gap in the dense growth of cactus trees. It looked as if a gun had shot through a strong citadel.

(He was musing. . . . You know, Mother, you who have understanding and knowledge, how hard it is to hear my Zinah calling me, "The Owl Man"! The cactus tree will spread until it fills in the breach. What is important is that the ill-omened bird has now lost its favored place and will look for another resting stop. One would be ready to cut off anything, even one's head, in order to escape the owl's gaze.)

---

3. He is speaking here of an evil spirit that the *faqih* thinks has entered Haddan's soul.

4. In Arab society the owl is regarded as a bird of ill omens.

"Good morning to you, Zinah!"

He was quivering and jumping at her side, on the road she walked daily.

"Is it you again?"

(But the amulet was hanging on his neck, love was in his heart, and patience eventually pays well.)

"Yes, it is me again."

"How is your mother, Fatna, the poor woman?"

(Joy, Haddan! Haven't you just begun to see results?!)

"We are all fine, Zinah. The owl has left the place. I jumped at it and surprised it."

She walked with swinging gait, laughing as if delighted by this achievement. (He mused, Do you see, Haddan? Do you see, Mother. You are the one who understands.)

"Zinah, let me carry the jug." (He was musing, Where do you find this sudden glibness and good manners? May none of your bones burn, hand of Si Nasir!)

It was not his fault that he swayed as usual and lost his balance. Some of the water in the jug splashed onto him, and onto Zinah. But she reclaimed the jug, laughingly saying, "Let's leave it on my head, Haddan."

(Do you see how kind she is, Haddan? Didn't you just hear the most beautiful voice and enjoy the most soothing fragrance. By God Almighty, even if Zinah asked him to die, he would do it, happily.)

Was it his fault if, upon his jubilant return home, he found the owl quietly standing on top of his hut? It was on the very top of the top, over the *shashiya*.[5] Haddan froze at the sight of it.

He mused. . . . Now what? My frightened mother told me to leave the creature in peace; its own God had given it the right to be here. But how could your son bear to hear Zinah say to him, "Ha, the owl is nesting over the *shashiya* of your hut!"

Hardly knowing if what he was doing was right or wrong, Haddan crawled around the hut searching for a long strand of dwarf palm. He gripped it, looped it over the hut, and twisted it around the *shashiya,* forming a trap. When the bird returned and alighted, Haddan pulled the strands and knotted them tightly in his hand. He went out to see the owl struggling blindly on the ground. Haddan reached the finest point of his plan when he poured petrol on the struggling bird. He lit the fuel while still gripping the ends of the palm. The owl was burning before his own eyes. Now Zinah would have nothing to say, except that he was deformed, a characteristic he admitted.

By God, it would be better to kill oneself.

Well then, Mother, you are lamenting and angry. But it is not my fault if the palm burnt first and I lost hold over it, and the bird was still able to fly, burning, to land on the roof of the hut, still in flames. All this was happening while your poor son Haddan was slapping his cheeks and calling for help, "My fire! My fire! Oh Mother, see this hut, I burnt it with my own hands!" It would be better for me

---

5. A textile that covers the roof of a hut.

to kill myself than hear Zinah tell me tomorrow, "Go on your way, ill-fated man, deformed owner of a burnt hut."

Well, was it his fault if he did not own any reeds or straw or any animal to slaughter so he could gather people to help him build a new hut? Was it his fault if he needed to use his brain more than he ever had before? All that he wanted was to meet Zinah, or ᶜArabiyya, one morning, and walk beside her, tall and proud, and say, blushing: "Good morning to you, Zinah."

She would swing her hips and reply, "Good morning to you, mightiest of men. . . . how lovely you are, owner of a new hut!"

WOLE SOYINKA (b. 1935)
Nigeria; English

Wole Soyinka, a Nigerian poet and dramatist, educated at the Universities of Ibadan and Leeds, awarded the Nobel Prize for literature in 1986, reveals in his plays the profound influence of Yoruba traditions and settings. Following his imprisonment (1967–69) during the Nigerian civil war, Soyinka exiled himself in Europe for five years, returning to Nigeria in 1975. His drama *Death and the King's Horseman,* complex and powerful, is based on an actual event. Soyinka has warned against interpreting the play as a simple clash of cultures. His primary concern is to dramatize the Yoruba worldview, to reveal its internal coherence, and to demonstrate its understanding of the human condition. According to Yoruba belief, acceptance of death by the King's Horseman will ensure an orderly transition between the world of the living, the world of the dead, and the world of the not-yet-born. Tragedy results when this act is prevented by the District Officer.

Other celebrated writings include his plays *The Lion and the Jewel* (1962) and *A Play of Giants* (1984), his poems *A Shuttle in the Crypt* (1972) (originally called *Poems from Prison,* 1969), his novels *The Interpreters* (1965), and *Season of Anomy,* and his autobiography, *Aké: The Years of Childhood* (1981).

Death and the King's Horseman

[This play is based on events which took place in Oyo, ancient Yoruba city of Nigeria, in 1946. That year, the lives of Elesin (Olori Elesin), his son, and the Colonial District Officer intertwined with the disastrous results set out in the play. The changes I have made are in matters of detail, sequence and of course characterisation. The action has also been set back two or three years while the war was still on, for minor reasons of dramaturgy.

The factual account still exists in the archives of the British Colonial Administration. It has already inspired a fine play in Yoruba (Oba Wàjà) by Duro Ladipo. It has also misbegotten a film by some German television company.

The bane of themes of this genre is that they are no sooner employed creatively than they acquire the facile tag of "clash of cultures," a prejudicial label which, quite apart from its frequent misapplication, presupposes a potential equality *in every given situation* of the alien culture and the indigenous, on the actual soil of the latter. (In the area of misapplication, the overseas prize for illiteracy and mental conditioning undoubtedly goes to the blurb-writer for the American edition of my novel *Season of Anomy* who unblushingly declares that this work portrays the "clash between old values and new ways, between western methods and African traditions"!) It is thanks to this kind of perverse mentality that I find it necessary to caution the would-be producer of this play against a sadly familiar reductionist tendency, and to direct his vision instead to the far more difficult and risky task of eliciting the play's threnodic[1] essence.

One of the more obvious alternative structures of the play would be to make the District Officer the victim of a cruel dilemma. This is not to my taste and it is not by chance that I have avoided dialogue or situation which would encourage this. No attempt should be made in production to suggest it. The Colonial Factor is an incident, a catalytic incident merely. The confrontation in the play is largely metaphysical, contained in the human vehicle which is Elesin and the universe of the Yoruba mind—the world of the living, the dead and the unborn, and the numinous[2] passage which links all: transition. *Death and the King's Horseman* can be full realised only through an evocation of music from the abyss of transition.—W. S.]

Characters

PRAISE-SINGER

ELESIN, *Horseman of the King*

IYALOJA, *"Mother" of the market*

SIMON PILKINGS, *District Officer*

JANE PILKINGS, *his wife*

SERJEANT AMUSA

JOSEPH, *houseboy to the Pilkingses*

BRIDE

H.R.H. THE PRINCE

THE RESIDENT

AIDE-DE-CAMP

OLUNDE, *eldest son of Elesin*

DRUMMERS, WOMEN, YOUNG GIRLS, DANCERS AT THE BALL

The play should run without an interval. For rapid scene changes, one adjustable outline set is very appropriate.

[Note to this edition: Certain Yoruba words which appear in italics in the text are explained in a brief glossary at the end.]

1

A passage through a market in its closing stages. The stalls are being emptied, mats folded. A few women pass through on their way home, loaded with baskets. On a cloth-stand, bolts of cloth are taken down, display pieces folded and piled on a tray. Elesin Oba enters along a passage before the market, pursued by his drummers and praise-singers. He is a man of enormous vitality, speaks, dances and sings with that infectious enjoyment of life which accompanies all his actions.

PRAISE-SINGER: Elesin! Elesin Oba! Howu! What tryst is this the cockerel[3] goes to keep with such haste that he must leave his tail behind?

---

1. Resembling a song of lamentation for the dead.

2. Filled with a sense of the presence of divinity.

3. A male domestic fowl.

Yoruba peoples. Nigeria. Divination cup. Nineteenth to twentieth century. Wood.

ELESIN: [Slows down a bit, laughing.] A tryst where the cockerel needs no adornment.

PRAISE-SINGER: O-oh, you hear that my companions? That's the way the world goes. Because the man approaches a brand-new bride he forgets the long faithful mother of his children.

ELESIN: When the horse sniffs the stable does he not strain at the bridle? The market is the long-suffering home of my spirit and the women are packing up to go. That Esu-harrassed day slipped into the stewpot while we feasted. We ate it up with the rest of the meat. I have neglected my women.

PRAISE-SINGER: We know all that. Still it's no reason for shedding your tail on this day of all days. I know the women will cover you in damask and *alari* but when the wind blows cold from behind, that's when the fowl knows his true friends.

ELESIN: Olohun-iyo!

PRAISE-SINGER: Are you sure there will be one like me on the other side?

ELESIN: Olohun-iyo!

PRAISE-SINGER: Far be it for me to belittle the dwellers of that place but, a man is either born to his art or he isn't. And I don't know for certain that you'll meet my father, so who is going to sing these deeds in accents that will pierce the deafness of the ancient ones. I have prepared my going—just tell me: Olohun-iyo, I need you on this journey and I shall be behind you.

ELESIN: You're like a jealous wife. Stay close to me, but only on this side. My fame, my honour are legacies to the living; stay behind and let the world sip its honey from your lips.

PRAISE-SINGER: Your name will be like the sweet berry a child places under his tongue to sweeten the passage of food. The world will never spit it out.

ELESIN: Come then. This market is my roost. When I come among the women I am a chicken with a hundred mothers. I become a monarch whose palace is built with tenderness and beauty.

PRAISE-SINGER: They love to spoil you but beware. The hands of women also weaken the unwary.

ELESIN: This night I'll lay my head upon their lap and go to sleep. This night I'll touch feet with their feet in a dance that is no longer of this earth. But the smell of their flesh, their sweat, the smell of indigo on their cloth, this is the last air I wish to breathe as I go to meet my great fore-bears.

PRAISE-SINGER: In their time the world was never tilted from its groove, it shall not be in yours.

ELESIN: The gods have said No.

PRAISE-SINGER: In their time the great wars came and went, the little wars came and went; the white slavers came and went, they took away the heart of our race, they bore away the mind and muscle of our race. The city fell and was rebuilt; the city fell and our people trudged through mountain and forest to found a new home but—Elesin Oba do you hear me?

ELESIN: I hear your voice Olohun-iyo.

PRAISE-SINGER: Our world was never wrenched from its true course.

ELESIN: The gods have said No.

PRAISE-SINGER: There is only one home to the life of a river-mussel; there is only one home to the life of a tortoise; there is only one shell to the soul of man; there is only one world to the spirit of our race. If that world leaves its course and smashes on boulders of the great void, whose world will give us shelter?

ELESIN: It did not in the time of my forebears, it shall not in mine.

PRAISE-SINGER: The cockerel must not be seen without his feathers.

ELESIN: Nor will the Not-I bird be much longer without his nest.

PRAISE-SINGER: [Stopped in his lyric stride.] The Not-I bird, Elesin?

ELESIN: I said, the Not-I bird.

PRAISE-SINGER: All respect to our elders but, is there really such a bird?

ELESIN: What! Could it be that he failed to knock on your door?

PRAISE-SINGER: [Smiling.] Elesin's riddles are not merely the nut in the kernel that breaks human teeth; he also buries the kernel in hot embers and dares a man's fingers to draw it out.

ELESIN: I am sure he called on you. Olohun-iyo. Did you hide in the loft and push out the servant to tell him you were out?

[Elesin executes a brief, half-taunting dance. The drummer moves in and draws a rhythm out of his steps. Elesin dances towards the market-place as he chants the story of the Not-I bird, his voice changing dexterously to mimic his characters. He performs like a born raconteur, infecting his retinue with his humour and energy. More women arrive during his recital, including Iyaloja.]

Death came calling.
Who does not know his rasp of reeds?
A twilight whisper in the leaves before
The great araba falls? Did you hear it?
Not I! swears the farmer. He snaps
His fingers round his head, abandons
A hard-worn harvest and begins

A rapid dialogue with his legs.

"Not I," shouts the fearless hunter, "but—
It's getting dark, and this night-lamp
Has leaked out all its oil. I think
It's best to go home and resume my hunt
Another day." But now he pauses, suddenly
Lets out a wail: "Oh foolish mouth, calling
Down a curse on your own head! Your lamp
Has leaked out all its oil, has it?"
Forwards or backwards now he dare not move.
To search for leaves and make *etutu*
On that spot? Or race home to the safety
Of his hearth? Ten market-days have passed
My friends, and still he's rooted there
Rigid as the plinth[4] of Orayan.

The mouth of the courtesan barely
Opened wide enough to take a ha' penny *robo*
When she wailed: "Not I." All dressed she was
To call upon my friend the Chief Tax Officer.
But now she sends her go-between instead:
"Tell him I'm ill: my period has come suddenly
But not—I hope—my time."
Why is the pupil crying?
His hapless head was made to taste
The knuckles of my friend the Mallam:
"If you were then reciting the Koran
Would you have ears for idle noises
Darkening the trees, you child of ill omen?"
He shuts down school before its time
Runs home and rings himself with amulets.

And take my good kinsman, Ifawomi.
His hands were like a carver's, strong
And true, I saw them
Tremble like wet wings of a fowl

---

4. The lowest member of a base.

One day he cast his time-smoothed *opele*
Across the divination board. And all because
The suppliant looked him in the eye and asked,
"Did you hear that whisper in the leaves?"
"Not I," was his reply: "perhaps I'm growing deaf—
Good-day." And Ifa spoke no more that day
The priests locked fast his doors,

Sealed up his leaking roof—but wait!
This sudden care was not for Fawomi
But for Osanyin, courier-bird of Ifa's
Heart of wisdom, I did not know a kite
Was hovering in the sky
And Ifa now a twittering chicken in
The blood of Fawomi the Mother Hen.

Ah, but I must not forget my evening
Courier from the abundant palm, whose groan
Became Not I, as he constipated down
A wayside bush. He wonders if Elegbara
Has tricked his buttocks to discharge
Against a sacred grove. Hear him
Mutter spells to ward off penalties
For an abomination he did not intend.
If any here
Stumbles on a gourd of wine, fermenting
Near the road, and nearby hears a stream
Of spells issuing from a crouching form.
Brother to a *sigidi*, bring home my wine,
Tell my tapper I have ejected
Fear from home and farm. Assure him,
All is well.

PRAISE-SINGER: In your time we do not doubt the peace of farmstead and home,
the peace of road and hearth, we do not doubt the peace of the forest.

ELESIN: There was fear in the forest too.
Not-I was lately heard even in the lair
Of beasts. The hyena cackled loud Not I,
The civet twitched his fiery tail and glared:
Not I. Not-I became the answering-name
Of the restless bird, that little one
Whom Death found nesting in the leaves
When whisper of his coming ran
Before him on the wind. Not-I
Has long abandoned home. This same dawn
I heard him twitter in the gods' abode.
Ah, companions of this living world
What a thing this is, that even those

           We call immortal
           Should fear to die.

IYALOJA: But you, husband of multitudes?

ELESIN: I, when that Not-I bird perched
           Upon my roof, bade him seek his nest again,
           Safe, without care or fear. I unrolled
           My welcome mat for him to see. Not-I
           Flew happily away, you'll hear his voice
           No more in this lifetime—You all know
           What I am.

PRAISE-SINGER: That rock which turns its open lodes
           Into the path of lightning. A gay
           Thoroughbred whose stride disdains
           To falter though an adder reared
           Suddenly in his path.

ELESIN: My rein is loosened.
           I am master of my Fate. When the hour comes
           Watch me dance along the narrowing path
           Glazed by the soles of my great precursors.
           My soul is eager. I shall not turn aside.

WOMEN: You will not delay?

ELESIN: Where the storm pleases, and when, it directs
           The giants of the forest. When friendship summons
           Is when the true comrade goes.

WOMEN: Nothing will hold you back?

ELESIN: Nothing. What! Has no one told you yet?
           I go to keep my friend and master company.
           Who says the mouth does not believe in
           "No, I have chewed all that before?" I say I have.
           The world is not a constant honey-pot.
           Where I found little I made do with little.
           Where there was plenty I gorged myself.
           My master's hands and mine have always
           Dipped together and, home or sacred feast,
           The bowl was beaten bronze, the meats
           So succulent our teeth accused us of neglect.
           We shard the choicest of the season's
           Harvest of yams. How my friend would read
           Desire in my eyes before I knew the cause—
           However rare, however precious, it was mine.

WOMEN: The town, the very land was yours.

ELESIN: The world was mine. Our joint hands
           Raised houseposts of trust that withstood
           The siege of envy and the termites of time.
           But the twilight hour brings bats and rodents—
           Shall I yield them cause to foul the rafters?

PRAISE-SINGER: Elesin Oba! Are you not that man who
             Looked out of doors that stormy day
             The god of luck limped by, drenched
             To the very lice that held
             His rags together? You took pity upon
             His sores and wished him fortune.
             Fortune was footloose this dawn, he replied,
             Till you trapped him in a heartfelt wish
             That now returns to you. Elesin Oba!
             I say you are that man who
             Chanced upon the calabash of honour
             You thought it was palm wine and
             Drained its contents to the final drop.

ELESIN: Life has an end. A life that will outlive
             Fame and friendship begs another name.
             What elder takes his tongue to his plate,
             Licks it clean of every crumb? He will encounter
             Silence when he calls on children to fulfill
             The smallest errand! Life is honour.
             It ends when honour ends.

WOMEN: We know you for a man of honour.

ELESIN: Stop! Enough of that!

WOMEN: *[Puzzled, they whisper among themselves, turning mostly to Iyaloja.]* What
        is it? Did we say something to give offence? Have we slighted him in
        some way?

ELESIN: Enough of that sound I say. Let me hear no more in that vein. I've heard
        enough.

IYALOJA: We must have said something wrong. *[Comes forward a little.]* Elesin
        Oba, we ask forgiveness before you speak.

ELESIN: I am bitterly offended.

IYALOJA: Our unworthiness has betrayed us. All we can do is ask your forgiveness.
        Correct us like a kind father.

ELESIN: This day of all days . . .

IYALOJA: It does not bear thinking. If we offend you now we have mortified the
        gods. We offend heaven itself. Father of us all, tell us where we went
        astray. *[She kneels, the other women follow.]*

ELESIN: Are you not ashamed? Even a tear-veiled
             Eye preserves its function of sight.
             Because my mind was raised to horizons
             Even the boldest man lowers his gaze
             In thinking of, must my body here
             Be taken for a vagrant's?

IYALOJA: Horseman of the King, I am more baffled than ever.

PRAISE-SINGER: The strictest father unbends his brow when the child is penitent,
        Elesin. When time is short, we do not spend it prolonging the riddle.
        Their shoulders are bowed with the weight of fear lest they have marred

your day beyond repair. Speak now in plain words and let us pursue the
ailment to the home of remedies.

ELESIN: Words are cheap. "We know you for
A man of honour." Well tell me, is this how
A man of honour should be seen?
Are these not the same clothes in which
I came among you a full half-hour ago?

*[He roars with laughter and the women, relieved, rise and rush into stalls to
fetch rich cloths.]*

WOMAN: The gods are kind. A fault soon remedied is soon forgiven. Elesin Oba,
even as we match our words with deed, let your heart forgive us
completely.

ELESIN: You who are breath and giver of my being
How shall I dare refuse you forgiveness
Even if the offence were real.

IYALOJA: *[Dancing round him. Sings.]*
He forgives us. He forgives us.
What a fearful thing it is when
The voyager sets forth
But a curse remains behind.

WOMEN: For a while we truly feared
Our hands had wrenched the world adrift
In emptiness.

IYALOJA: Richly, richly, robe him richly
The cloth of honour is *alari*
Sanyan is the band of friendship
Boa-skin makes slippers of esteem.

WOMEN: For a while we truly feared
Our hands had wrenched the world adrift
In emptiness.

PRAISE-SINGER: He who must, must voyage forth
The world will not roll backwards
It is he who must, with one
Great gesture overtake the world.

WOMEN: For a while we truly feared
Our hands had wrenched the world
In emptiness.

PRAISE-SINGER: The gourd you bear is not for shirking.
The gourd is not for setting down
At the first crossroad of wayside grove.
Only one river may know its contents

WOMEN: We shall all meet at the great market
We shall all meet at the great market
He who goes early takes the best bargains
But we shall meet, the resume our banter.

[Elesin stands resplendent in rich clothes, cap, shawl, etc. His sash is of a bright red alari *cloth. The women dance round him. Suddenly, his attention is caught by an object off-stage.]*

ELESIN: The world I know is good.

WOMEN: We know you'll leave it so.

ELESIN: The world I know is the bounty
Of hives after bees have swarmed.
No goodness teems with such open hands
Even in the dreams of deities.

WOMEN: And we know you'll leave it so.

ELESIN: I was born to keep it so. A hive
Is never known to wander. An anthill
Does not desert its roots. We cannot see
The still great womb of the world—
No man beholds his mother's womb—
Yet who denies it's there? Coiled
To the naval of the world is that
Endless cord that links us all
To the great origin. If I lose my way
The trailing cord will bring me to the roots.

WOMEN: The world is in your hands.

[The earlier distraction, a beautiful young girl, comes along the passage through which Elesin first made his entry.]

ELESIN: I embrace it. And let me tell you, women—
I like this farewell that the world designed,
Unless my eyes deceive me, unless
We are already parted, the world and I,
And all that breeds desire is lodged
Among our tireless ancestors. Tell me friends,
Am I still earthed in that beloved market
Of my youth? Or could it be my will
Has outleapt the conscious act and I have come
Among the great departed?

PRAISE-SINGER: Elesin-Oba why do your eyes roll like a bushrat who sees his fate like his father's spirit, mirrored in the eye of a snake? And all these questions! You're standing on the same earth you've always stood upon. This voice you hear is mine, Oluhun-iyo, not that of an acolyte in heaven.

ELESIN: How can that be? In all my life
As Horseman of the King, the juiciest
Fruit on every tree was mine. I saw,
I touched, I wooed, rarely was the answer No.
The honour of my place, the veneration I
Received in the eye of man or woman
Prospered my suit and
Played havoc with my sleeping hours.

And they tell me my eyes were a hawk
In perpetual hunger. Split an iroko tree
In two, hide a woman's beauty in its heartwood
And seal it up again—Elesin, journeying by,
Would make his camp beside that tree
Of all the shades in the forest.

PRAISE-SINGER: Who would deny your reputation, snake-on-the-loose in dark
passages of the market! Bed-bug who wages war on the mat and receives
the thanks of the vanquished! When caught with his bride's own sister he
protested—but I was only prostrating myself to her as becomes a grateful
in-law. Hunter who carries his powder-horn on the hips and fires
crouching or standing! Warrior who never makes that excuse of the
whining coward—but how can I go to battle without my trousers?—
trouserless or shirtless it's all one to him. Oka-rearing-from-a-
camouflage-of-leaves, before he strikes the victim is already prone! Once
they told him, Howu, a stallion does not feed on the grass beneath him:
he replied, true, but surely he can roll on it!

WOMEN: Ba-a-a-ba O!

PRAISE-SINGER: Ah, but listen yet. You know there is the leaf-nibbling grub and
there is the cola-chewing beetle; the leaf-nibbling grub lives on the leaf,
the cola-chewing beetle lives in the colanut. Don't we know what our
man feeds on when we find him cocooned in a woman's wrapper?

ELESIN: Enough, enough, you all have cause
To know me well. But, if you say this earth
Is still the same as gave birth to those songs,
Tell me who was that goddess through whose lips
I saw the ivory pebbles of Oya's river-bed.
Iyaloja, who is she? I saw her enter
Your stall; all your daughters I know well.
No, not even Ogun-of-the-farm toiling
Dawn till dusk on his tuber patch
Not even Ogun with the finest hoe he ever
Forged at the anvil could have shaped
That rise of buttocks, not though he had
The richest earth between his fingers.
Her wrapper was no disguise
For thighs whose ripples shamed the river's
Coils around the hills of Ilesi. Her eyes
Were new-laid eggs glowing in the dark.
Her skin . . .

IYALOJA: Elesin Oba . . .

ELESIN: What! Where do you all say I am?

IYALOJA: Still among the living.

ELESIN: And that radiance which so suddenly
Lit up this market I could boast
I knew so well?

IYALOJA: Has one step already in her husband's home. She is betrothed.
ELESIN: [Irritated.] Why do you tell me that?

[Iyaloja falls silent. The women shuffle uneasily.]

IYALOJA: Not because we dare give you offence Elesin. Today is your day and the
         whole world is yours. Still, even those who leave town to make a new
         dwelling elsewhere like to be remembered by what they leave behind.
ELESIN: Who does not seek to be remembered?
         Memory is Master of Death, the chink
         In his armour of conceit. I shall leave
         That which makes my going the sheerest
         Dream of an afternoon. Should voyagers
         Not travel light? Let the considerate traveller
         Shed, of his excessive load, all
         That may benefit the living.
WOMEN: [Relieved.] Ah Elesin Oba, we knew you for a man of honour.
ELESIN: Then honour me. I deserve a bed of honour to lie upon.
IYALOJA: The best is yours. We know you for a man of honour. You are not one who
         eats and leaves nothing on his plate for children. Did you not say it your-
         self? Not one who blights the happiness of others for a moment's pleasure.
ELESIN: Who speaks of pleasure? O women, listen!
         Pleasure palls. Our acts should have meaning.
         The sap of the plantain never dries.
         You have seen the young shoot swelling
         Even as the parent stalk begins to wither.
         Women, let my going be likened to
         The twilight hour of the plantain.
WOMEN: What does he mean Iyaloja? This language is the language of our elders,
         we do not fully grasp it.
IYALOJA: I dare not understand you yet Elesin.
ELESIN: All you who stand before the spirit that dares
         The opening of the last door of passage,
         Dare to rid my going to regrets! My wish
         Transcends the blotting out of thought
         In one mere moment's tremor of the senses.
         Do me credit. And do me honour.
         I am girded for the route beyond
         Burdens of waste and longing.
         Then let me travel light. Let
         Seed that will not serve the stomach
         On the way remain behind. Let it take root
         In the earth of my choice, in this earth
         I leave behind.
IYALOJA: [Turns to women.] The voice I hear is already touched by the waiting
         fingers of our departed. I dare not refuse.
WOMAN: But Iyaloja . . . .

IYALOJA: The matter is no longer in our hands.

WOMAN: But she is betrothed to your own son. Tell him.

IYALOJA: My son's wish is mine. I did the asking for him, the loss can be remedied. But who will remedy the blight of closed hands on the day when all should be openness and light? Tell him, you say! You wish that I burden him with knowledge that will sour his wish and lay regrets on the last moments of his mind. You pray to him who is your intercessor to the other world—don't set this world adrift in your own time; would you rather it was my hand whose sacrilege wrenched it loose?

WOMAN: Not many men will brave the curse of a dispossessed husband.

IYALOJA: Only the curses of the departed are to be feared. The claims of one whose foot is on the threshold of their abode surpasses even the claims of blood. It is impiety even to place hindrances in their ways.

ELESIN: What do my mothers say? Shall I step
Burdened into the unknown?

IYALOJA: Not we, but the very earth says No. The sap in the plantain does not dry. Let grain that will not feed the voyager at his passage drop here and take root as he steps beyond this earth and us. Oh you who fill the home from hearth to threshold with the voices of children, you who now bestride the hidden gulf and pause to draw the right foot across and into the resting-home of the great forebears, it is good that your loins be drained into the earth we know, that your last strength be ploughed back into the womb that gave you being.

PRAISE-SINGER: Iyaloja, mother of multitudes in the teeming market of the world, how your wisdom transfigures you!

IYALOJA: [Smiling broadly, completely reconciled.] Elesin, even at the narrow end of the passage I know you will look back and sigh a last regret for the flesh that flashed past your spirit in flight. You always had a restless eye. Your choice has my blessing. [To the women.] Take the good news to our daughter and make her ready. [Some women go off.]

ELESIN: Your eyes were clouded at first.

IYALOJA: Not for long. It is those who stand at the gateway of the great change to whose cry we must pay heed. And then, think of this—it makes the mind tremble. The fruit of such a union is rare. It will be neither of this world nor of the next. Nor of the one behind us. As if the timelessness of the ancestor world and the unborn have joined spirits to wring an issue of the elusive being of passage . . . . Elesin!

ELESIN: I am here. What is it?

IYALOJA: Did you hear all I said just now?

ELESIN: Yes.

IYALOJA: The living must eat and drink. When the moment comes, don't turn the food to rodents' droppings in their mouth. Don't let them taste the ashes of the world when they step out at dawn to breathe the morning dew.

ELESIN: This doubt is unworthy of you Iyaloja.

IYALOJA: Eating the awusa nut is not so difficult as drinking water afterwards.

ELESIN: The waters of the bitter stream are honey to a man
Whose tongue has savoured all.

IYALOJA: No one knows when the ants desert their home; they leave the mound intact. The swallow is never seen to peck holes in its nest when it is time to move with the season. There are always throngs of humanity behind the leave-taker. The rain should not come through the roof for them, the wind must not blow through the walls at night.

ELESIN: I refuse to take offence.

IYALOJA: You wish to travel light. Well, the earth is yours. But be sure the seed you leave in it attracts no curse.

ELESIN: You really mistake my person Iyaloja.

IYALOJA: I said nothing. Now we must go prepare your bridal chamber. Then these same hands will lay your shrouds.

ELESIN: [*Exasperated.*]: Must you be so blunt? [*Recovers.*] Well, weave your shrouds, but let the fingers of my bride seal my eyelids with earth and wash my body.

IYALOJA: Prepare yourself Elesin.

[*She gets up to leave. At that moment the women return, leading the Bride. Elesin's face glows with pleasure. He flicks the sleeves of his agbada with renewed confidence and steps forward to meet the group. As the girl kneels before Iyaloja, lights fade out on the scene.*]

2

The verandah of the District Officer's bungalow. A tango is playing from an old hand-cranked gramophone and, glimpsed through the wide windows and doors which open onto the fore-stage verandah are the shapes of Simon Pilkings and his wife, Jane, tangoing in and out of shadows in the living-room. They are wearing what is immediately apparent as some form of fancy-dress. The dance goes on for some moments and then the figure of a "Native Administration" policeman emerges and climbs up the steps onto the verandah. He peeps through and observes the dancing couple, reacting with what is obviously a long-standing bewilderment. He stiffens suddenly, his expression changes to one of disbelief and horror. In his excitement he upsets a flowerpot and attracts the attention of the couple, They stop dancing.

PILKINGS: Is there anyone out there?

JANE: I'll turn off the gramophone.

PILKINGS: [*Approaching the verandah.*] I'm sure I heard something fall over. [*The constable retreats slowly, open-mouthed as Pilkings approaches the verandah.*] Oh it's you Amusa. Why didn't you just knock instead of knocking things over?

AMUSA: [*Stammers badly and points a shaky finger at his dress.*] Mista Pirinkin . . . Mista Pirinkin . . .

PILKINGS: What is the matter with you?

JANE: [*Emerging.*] Who is it dear? Oh, Amusa . . .

PILKINGS: Yes, it's Amusa, and acting most strangely.

AMUSA: [*His attention now transferred to Mrs Pilkings.*] Mammadam . . . you too!

PILKINGS: What the hell is the matter with you man!

JANE: Your costume darling. Our fancy dress.

PILKINGS: Oh, hell, I'd forgotten all about that. *[Lifts the face mask over his head showing his face. His wife follows suit.]*

JANE: I think you've shocked his big pagan heart bless him.

PILKINGS: Nonsense, he's a Moslem. Come on Amusa, you don't believe in all this nonsense do you? I thought you were a good Moslem.

AMUSA: Mista Pirinkin, I beg you sir, what you think you do with that dress? It belong to dead cult, not for human being.

PILKINGS: Oh Amusa, what a let down you are. I swear by you at the club you know—thank God for Amusa, he doesn't believe in any mumbo-jumbo. And now look at you!

AMUSA: Mista Pirinkin, I beg you, take it off. Is not good for man like you to touch that cloth.

PILKINGS: Well, I've got it on. And what's more Jane and I have bet on it we're taking first prize at the ball. Now, if you can just pull yourself together and tell me what you wanted to see me about . . .

AMUSA: Sir, I cannot talk this matter to you in that dress. I no fit.

PILKINGS: What's that rubbish again?

JANE: He is dead earnest too Simon. I think you'll have to handle this delicately.

PILKINGS: Delicately my . . .! Look here Amusa, I think this little joke has gone far enough hm? Let's have some sense. You seem to forget that you are a police officer in the service of His Majesty's Government. I order you to report your business at once or face disciplinary action.

AMUSA: Sir, it is a matter of death. How can man talk against death to person in uniform of death? Is like talking against government to person in uniform of police. Please sir, I go and come back.

PILKINGS: *[Roars.]* Now! *[Amusa switches his gaze to the ceiling suddenly, remains mute.]*

JANE: Oh Amusa, what is there to be scared of in the costume? You saw it confiscated last month from those *egungun* men who were creating trouble in town. You helped arrest the cult leaders yourself—if the juju didn't harm you at the time how could it possibly harm you now? And merely by looking at it?

AMUSA: *[Without looking down.]* Madam, I arrest the ringleaders who make trouble but me I no touch *egungun*. That *egungun* inself, I no touch. And I no abuse 'am. I arrest ringleader but I treat *egungun* with respect.

PILKINGS: It's hopeless. We'll merely end up missing the best part of the ball. When they get this way there is nothing you can do. It's simply hammering against a brick wall. Write your report or whatever it is on that pad Amusa and take yourself out of here. Come on Jane. We only upset his delicate sensibilities by remaining here.

[Amusa waits for them to leave, then writes in the notebook, somewhat laboriously. Drumming from the direction of the town wells up. Amusa listens, makes a movement as if he wants to recall Pilkings but changes his mind. Completes his note and goes. A few moments later Pilkings emerges, picks up the pad and reads.]

PILKINGS: Jane!

JANE: *[From the bedroom.]* Coming darling. Nearly ready.

PILKINGS: Never mind being ready, just listen to this.

JANE: What is it?

PILKINGS: Amusa's report. Listen. "I have to report that it come to my information that one prominent chief, namely, the Elesin Oba, is to commit death tonight as a result of native custom. Because this is criminal offence I await further instruction at charge office. Sergeant Amusa."

[Jane comes out onto the verandah while he is reading.]

JANE: Did I hear you say commit death?

PILKINGS: Obviously he means murder.

JANE: You mean a ritual murder?

PILKINGS: Must be. You think you've stamped it all out but it's always lurking under the surface somewhere.

JANE: Oh. Does it mean we are not getting to the ball at all?

PILKINGS: No-o. I'll have the man arrested. Everyone remotely involved. In any case there may be nothing to it. Just rumours.

JANE: Really? I thought you found Amusa's rumours generally reliable.

PILKINGS: That's true enough. But who knows what may have been giving him the scare lately. Look at his conduct tonight.

JANE: *[Laughing.]* You have to admit he had his own peculiar logic. *[Deepens her voice.]* How can man talk against death to person in uniform of death? *[Laughs.]* Anyway, you can't go into the police station dressed like that.

PILKINGS: I'll send Joseph with instructions. Damn it, what a confounded nuisance!

JANE: But don't you think you should talk first to the man, Simon?

PILKINGS: Do you want to go to the ball or not?

JANE: Darling, why are you getting rattled? I was only trying to be intelligent. It seems hardly fair just to lock up a man—and a chief at that—simply on the er . . . what is that legal word again?—uncorroborated word of a sergeant.

PILKINGS: Well, that's easily decided. Joseph!

JOSEPH: *[From within.]* Yes master.

PILKINGS: You're quite right of course. I am getting rattled. Probably the effect of those bloody drums. Do you hear how they go on and on?

JANE: I wondered when you'd notice. Do you suppose it has something to do with this affair?

PILKINGS: Who knows? They always find an excuse for making a noise . . . *[Thoughtfully.]* Even so . . .

JANE: Yes Simon?

PILKINGS: It's different Jane. I don't think I've heard this particular—sound— before. Something unsettling about it.

JANE: I thought all bush drumming sounded the same.

PILKINGS: Don't tease me now Jane. This may be serious.

JANE: I'm sorry. *[Get's up and throws her arms around his neck. Kisses him. The houseboy enters, retreats and knocks.]*

PILKINGS: *[Wearily.]* Oh, come in Joseph! I don't know where you pick up all these elephantine notions of tact. Come over here.

JOSEPH: Sir?

PILKINGS: Joseph, are you a Christian or not?

JOSEPH: Yessir.

PILKINGS: Does seeing me in this outfit bother you?

JOSEPH: No sir, it has no power.

PILKINGS: Thank God for some sanity at last. Now Joseph, answer me on the honour of a Christian—what is supposed to be going on in town tonight?

JOSEPH: Tonight sir? You mean that chief who is going to kill himself?

PILKINGS: What?

JANE: What do you mean, kill himself?

PILKINGS: You do mean he is going to kill somebody don't you?

JOSEPH: No master. He will not kill anybody and no one will kill him. He will simply die.

JANE: But why Joseph?

JOSEPH: It is native law and custom. The King die last month. Tonight is his burial. But before they can bury him, the Elesin must die so as to accompany him to heaven.

PILKINGS: I seem to be fated to clash more often with that man than with any of the other chiefs.

JOSEPH: He is the King's Chief Horseman.

PILKINGS: *[In a resigned way.]* I know.

JANE: Simon, what's the matter?

PILKINGS: It would have to be him!

JANE: Who is he?

PILKINGS: Don't you remember? He's that chief with whom I had a scrap some three or four years ago. I helped his son get to a medical school in England, remember? He fought tooth and nail to prevent it.

JANE: Oh now I remember. He was that very sensitive young man. What was his name again?

PILKINGS: Olunde. Haven't replied to his last letter come to think of it. The old pagan wanted him to stay and carry on some family tradition or the other. Honestly I couldn't understand the fuss he made. I literally had to help the boy escape from close confinement and load him onto the next boat. A most intelligent boy, really bright.

JANE: I rather thought he was much too sensitive you know. The kind of person you feel should be a poet munching rose petals in Bloomsbury.

PILKINGS: Well, he's going to make a first-class doctor. His mind is set on that. And as long as he wants my help he is welcome to it.

JANE: *[After a pause.]* Simon.

PILKINGS: Yes?

JANE: This boy, he was his eldest son wasn't he?

PILKINGS: I'm not sure. Who could tell with that old ram?

JANE: Do you know, Joseph?

JOSEPH: Oh yes madam. He was the eldest son. That's why Elesin cursed master good and proper. The eldest son is not supposed to travel away from the land.

JANE: *[Giggling.]* Is that true Simon? Did he really curse you good and proper?

PILKINGS: By all accounts I should be dead by now.

JOSEPH: Oh no, master is white man. And good Christian. Black man juju can't touch master.

JANE: If he was his eldest, it means that he would be the Elesin to the next king. It's a family thing isn't it Joseph?

JOSEPH: Yes madam. And if this Elesin had died before the King, his eldest son must take his place.

JANE: That would explain why the old chief was so mad you took the boy away.

PILKINGS: Well it makes me all the more happy I did.

JANE: I wonder if he knew.

PILKINGS: Who? Oh, you mean Olunde?

JANE: Yes. Was that why he was so determined to get away? I wouldn't stay if I knew I was trapped in such a horrible custom.

PILKINGS: *[Thoughtfully.]* No, I don't think he knew. At least he gave no indication. But you couldn't really tell with him. He was rather close you know, quite unlike most of them. Didn't give much away, not even to me.

JANE: Aren't they all rather close, Simon?

PILKINGS: These natives here? Good gracious. They'll open their mouths and yap with you about their family secrets before you can stop them. Only the other day . . .

JANE: But Simon, do they really give anything away? I mean, anything that really counts. This affair for instance, we didn't know they still practised that custom did we?

PILKINGS: Ye-e-es, I suppose you're right there. Sly, devious bastards.

JOSEPH: *[Stiffly.]* Can I go now master? I have to clean the kitchen.

PILKINGS: What? Oh, you can go. Forgot you were still here.

[Joseph goes.]

JANE: Simon, you really must watch your language. Bastard isn't just a simple swear-word in these parts, you know.

PILKINGS: Look, just when did you become a social anthropologist, that's what I'd like to know.

JANE: I'm not claiming to know anything. I just happen to have overheard quarrels among the servants. That's how I know they consider it a smear.

PILKINGS: I thought the extended family system took care of all that. Elastic family, no bastards.

JANE: *[Shrugs.]* Have it your own way. *[Awkward silence. The drumming increases in volume. Jane gets up suddenly, restless.]* That drumming Simon, do you think it might really be connected with this ritual? It's been going on all evening.

PILKINGS: Let's ask our native guide. Joseph! Just a minute Joseph. *[Joseph re-enters.]* What's the drumming about?

JOSEPH: I don't know master.

PILKINGS: What do you mean you don't know? It's only two years since your conversion. Don't tell me all that holy water nonsense also wiped out your tribal memory.

JOSEPH: *[Visibly shocked.]* Master!

JANE: Now you've done it.

PILKINGS: What have I done now?

JANE: Never mind. Listen Joseph, just tell me this. Is that drumming connected with dying or anything of that nature?

JOSEPH: Madam, this is what I am trying to say: I am not sure. It sounds like the death of a great chief and then, it sounds like the wedding of a great chief. It really mix me up.

PILKINGS: Oh get back to the kitchen. A fat lot of help you are.

JOSEPH: Yes master. *[Goes.]*

JANE: Simon . . .

PILKINGS: All right, all right. I'm in no mood for preaching.

JANE: It isn't my preaching you have to worry about, it's the preaching of the missionaries who preceded you here. When they make converts they really convert them. Calling holy water nonsense to our Joseph is really like insulting the Virgin Mary before a Roman Catholic. He's going to hand in his notice tomorrow you mark my word.

PILKINGS: Now you're being ridiculous.

JANE: Am I? What are you willing to bet that tomorrow we are going to be without a steward-boy? Did you see his face?

PILKINGS: I am more concerned about whether or not we will be one native chief short by tomorrow. Christ! Just listen to those drums. *[He strides up and down, undecided.]*

JANE: *[Getting up.]* I'll change and make up some supper.

PILKINGS: What's that?

JANE: Simon, it's obvious we have to miss this ball.

PILKINGS: Nonsense. It's the first bit of real fun the European club has managed to organise for over a year. I'm damned if I'm gong to miss it. And it is a rather special occasion. Doesn't happen every day.

JANE: You know this business has to be stopped Simon. And you are the only man who can do it.

PILKINGS: I don't have to stop anything. If they want to throw themselves off the top of a cliff or poison themselves for the sake of some barbaric custom what is that to me? If it were ritual murder or something like that I'd be duty-bound to do something. I can't keep an eye on all the potential suicides in this province. And as for that man—believe me it's good riddance.

JANE: *[Laughs.]* I know you better than that Simon. You are going to have to do something to stop it—after you've finished blustering.

PILKINGS: *[Shouts after her.]* And suppose after all it's only a wedding. I'd look a proper fool if I interrupted a chief on his honeymoon, wouldn't I? *[Resumes his angry stride, slows down.]* Ah well, who can tell what those chiefs actually do on their honeymoon anyway? *[He takes up the pad and scribbles rapidly on it.]* Joseph! Joseph! Joseph! *[Some moments later Joseph puts in a sulky appearance.]* Did you hear me call you? Why the hell didn't you answer?

JOSEPH: I didn't hear master.

PILKINGS: You didn't hear me! How come you are here then?

JOSEPH: [Stubbornly.] I didn't hear master.

PILKINGS: [Controls himself with an effort.] We'll talk about it in the morning. I want
you to take this note directly to Sergeant Amusa. You'll find him at the
charge office. Get on your bicycle and race there with it. I expect you
back in twenty minutes exactly. Twenty minutes, is that clear?

JOSEPH: Yes master. [Going.]

PILKINGS: Oh er . . . Joseph.

JOSEPH: Yes master?

PILKINGS: [Between gritted teeth.] Er . . . forget what I said just now. The holy water
is not nonsense. I was talking nonsense.

JOSEPH: Yes master. [Goes.]

JANE: [Pokes her head round the door.] Have you found him?

PILKINGS: Found who?

JANE: Joseph. Weren't you shouting for him?

PILKINGS: Oh yes, he turned up finally.

JANE: You sounded desperate. What was it all about?

PILKINGS: Oh nothing. I just wanted to apologise to him. Assure him that the holy
water isn't really nonsense.

JANE: Oh? And how did he take it?

PILKINGS: Who the hell gives a damn! I had a sudden vision of our Very Reverend
Macfarlane drafting another letter of complaint to the Resident about my
unchristian language towards his parishioners.

JANE: Oh I think he's given up on you by now.

PILKINGS: Don't be too sure. And anyway, I wanted to make sure Joseph didn't
'lose' my note on the way. He looked sufficiently full of the holy crusade
to do some such thing.

JANE: If you've finished exaggerating, come and have something to eat.

PILKINGS: No, put it all way. We can still get to the ball.

JANE: Simon . . .

PILKINGS: Get your costume back on. Nothing to worry about. I've instructed
Amusa to arrest the man and lock him up.

JANE: But that station is hardly secure Simon. He'll soon get his friends to help
him escape.

PILKINGS: A-ah, that's where I have out-thought you. I'm not having him put in
the station cell. Amusa will bring him right here and lock him up in my
study. And he'll stay with him till we get back. No one will dare come
here to incite him to anything.

JANE: How clever of you darling. I'll get ready.

PILKINGS: Hey.

JANE: Yes darling.

PILKINGS: I have a surprise for you. I was going to keep it until we actually got to
the ball.

JANE: What is it?

PILKINGS: You know the Prince is on a tour of the colonies don't you? Well, he docked in the capital only this morning but he is already at the Residency. He is going to grace the ball with his presence later tonight.

JANE: Simon! Not really.

PILKINGS: Yes he is. He's been invited to give away the prizes and he has agreed. You must admit old Engleton is the best Club Secretary we ever had. Quick off the mark that lad.

JANE: But how thrilling.

PILKINGS: The other provincials are going to be damned envious.

JANE: I wonder what he'll come as.

PILKINGS: Oh I don't know. As a coat-of-arms perhaps. Anyway it won't be anything to touch this.

JANE: Well that's lucky. If we are to be presented I won't have to start looking for a pair of gloves. It's all sewn on.

PILKINGS: [Laughing.] Quite right. Trust a woman to think of that. Come on, let's get going.

JANE: [Rushing off.] Won't be a second. [Stops.] Now I see why you've been so edgy all evening. I thought you weren't handling this affair with your usual brilliance—to begin with that is.

PILKINGS: [His mood is much improved.] Shut up woman and get your things on.

JANE: Alright boss, coming.

[Pilkings suddenly begins to hum the tango to which they were dancing before. Starts to execute a few practice steps. Lights fade.]

3

A swelling, agitated hum of women's voices rises immediately in the background. The lights come on and we see the frontage of a converted cloth stall in the market. The floor leading up to the entrance is covered in rich velvets and woven cloth. The women come on stage, borne backwards by the determined progress of Sergeant Amusa and his two constables who already have their batons out and use them as a pressure against the women. At the edge of the cloth-covered floor however the women take a determined stand and block all further progress of the men. They begin to tease them mercilessly.

AMUSA: I am tell you women for last time to commot my road. I am here on official business.

WOMAN: Official business you white man's eunuch? Official business is taking place where you want to go and it's a business you wouldn't understand.

WOMAN: [Makes a quick tug at the constable's baton.] That doesn't fool anyone you know. It's the one you carry under your government knickers that counts. [She bends low as if to peep under the baggy shorts. The embarrassed constable quickly puts his knees together. The women roar.]

WOMAN: You mean there is nothing there at all?

WOMAN: Oh there was something. You know that handbell which the whiteman uses to summon his servants . . . ?

AMUSA: [He manages to preserve some dignity throughout.] I hope you women know that interfering with officer in execution of his duty is criminal offence.

WOMAN: Interfere? He says we're interfering with him. You foolish man we're telling you there's nothing there to interfere with.

AMUSA: I am order you now to clear the road.

WOMAN: What road? The one your father built?

WOMAN: You are a Policeman not so? Then you know what they call trespassing in court. Or—[Pointing to the cloth-lined steps.]—do you think that kind of road is built for every kind of feet.

WOMAN: Go back and tell the white man who sent you to come himself.

AMUSA: If I go I will come back with reinforcement. And we will all return carrying weapons.

WOMAN: Oh, now I understand. Before they can put on those knickers the white man first cuts off their weapons.

WOMAN: What a check! You mean you come here to show power to women and you don't even have a weapon.

AMUSA: [Shouting above the laughter.] For the last time I warn you women to clear the road.

WOMAN: To where?

AMUSA: To that hut. I know he dey dere.

WOMAN: Who?

AMUSA: The chief who call himself Elesin Oba.

WOMAN: You ignorant man. It is not he who calls himself Elesin Oba, it is his blood that says it. As it called out to his father before him and will to his son after him. And that is in spite of everything your white man can do.

WOMAN: Is it not the same ocean that washes this land and the white man's land? Tell your white man he can hide our son away as long as he likes. When the time comes for him, the same ocean will bring him back.

AMUSA: The government say dat kin' ting must stop.

WOMAN: Who will stop it? You? Tonight our husband and father will prove himself greater than the laws of strangers.

AMUSA: I tell you nobody go prove anyting tonight or anytime. Is ignorant and criminal to prove dat kin' prove.

IYALOJA: [Entering, from the hut. She is accompanied by a group of young girls who have been attending the Bride.] What is it Amusa? Why do you come here to disturb the happiness of others.

AMUSA: Madame Iyaloja, I glad you come. You know me. I no like trouble but duty is duty. I am here to arrest Elesin for criminal intent. Tell these women to stop obstructing me in the performance of my duty.

IYALOJA: And you? What gives you the right to obstruct our leader of men in the performance of his duty.

AMUSA: What kin' duty be dat one Iyaloja.

IYALOJA: What kin' duty? What kin' duty does a man have to his new bride?

AMUSA: [Bewildered, looks at the women and at the entrance to the hut.] Iyaloja, is it wedding you call dis kin' ting?

IYALOJA: You have wives haven't you? Whatever the white man has done to you he hasn't stopped you having wives. And if he has, at least he is married. If you don't know what a marriage is, go and ask him to tell you.

AMUSA: This no to wedding.

IYALOJA: And ask him at the same time what he would have done if anyone had
come to disturb him on his wedding night.

AMUSA: Iyaloja, I say dis no to wedding.

IYALOJA: You want to look inside the bridal chamber? You want to see for yourself
how a man cuts the virgin knot?

AMUSA: Madam . . .

WOMAN: Perhaps his wives are still waiting for him to learn.

AMUSA: Iyaloja, make you tell dese women make den no insult me again. If I hear
dat kin' indult once more . . .

GIRL: [Pushing her way through.] You will do what?

GIRL: He's out of his mind. It's our mothers you're talking to, do you know that?
Not to any illiterate villager you can bully and terrorise. How dare you
intrude here anyway?

GIRL: What a cheek, what impertinence!

GIRL: You've treated them too gently. Now let them see what it is to tamper with
the mothers of this market.

GIRLS: Your betters dare not enter the market when the women say no!

GIRL: Haven't you learnt that yet, you jester in khaki and starch?

IYALOJA: Daughters . . .

GIRL: No no Iyaloja, leave us to deal with him. He no longer knows his mother,
we'll teach him.

[With a sudden movement they snatch the batons of the two constables. They
begin to hem them in.]

GIRL: What next? We have your batons? What next? What are you going to do?

[With equally swift movements they knock off their hats.]

GIRL: Move if you dare. We have your hats, what will you do about it? Didn't the
white man teach you to take off your hats before women?

IYALOJA: It's a wedding night. It's a night of joy for us. Peace . . .

GIRL: Not for him. Who asked him here?

GIRL: Does he dare go to the Residency without an invitation?

GIRL: Not even where the servants eat the left-overs.

GIRLS: [In turn. In an "English" accent.] Well well it's Mister Amusa. Were you
invited? [Play-acting to one another. The older women encourage them with
their titters.]

- Your invitation card please?
- Who are you? Have we been introduced?
- And who did you say you were?
- Sorry, I didn't quite catch your name.
- May I take your hat?
- If you insist. May I take yours? [Exchanging the policeman's hats.]
- How very kind of you.
- Not at all. Won't you sit down?
- After you.
- Oh no.

- *I insist.*
- *You're most gracious.*
- *And how do you find the place?*
- *The natives are alright.*
- *Friendly?*
- *Tractable.*
- *Not a teeny-weeny bit restless?*
- *Well, a teeny-weeny bit restless.*
- *One might even say, difficult?*
- *Indeed one might be tempted to say, difficult.*
- *But you do manage to cope?*
- *Yes indeed I do. I have a rather faithful ox called Amusa.*
- *He's loyal?*
- *Absolutely.*
- *Lay down his life for you what?*
- *Without a moment's thought.*
- *Had one like that once. Trust him with my life.*
- *Mostly of course they are liars.*
- *Never known a native tell the truth.*
- *Does it get rather close around here?*
- *It's mild for this time of the year.*
- *But the rains may still come.*
- *They are late this year aren't they?*
- *They are keeping African time.*
- *Ha ha ha ha*
- *Ha ha ha ha*
- *The humidity is what gets me.*
- *It used to be whisky.*
- *Ha ha ha ha*
- *Ha ha ha ha*
- *What's your handicap old chap?*
- *Is there racing by golly?*
- *Splendid golf course, you'll like it.*
- *I'm beginning to like it already.*
- *And a European club, exclusive.*
- *You've kept the flag flying.*
- *We do our best for the old country.*
- *It's a pleasure to serve.*
- *Another whisky old chap?*
- *You are indeed too too kind.*
- *Not at all sir. Where is that boy? [With a sudden bellow.] Sergeant!*

AMUSA: *[Snaps to attention.]* Yessir!

> *[The women collapse with laughter.]*

GIRL: Take your men out of here.

AMUSA: *[Realising the trick, he rages from loss of face.]* I'm give you warning . . .

GIRL: Alright then. Off with his knickers! *[They surge slowly forward.]*

IYALOJA: Daughters, please.

AMUSA: *[Squaring himself for defence.]* The first woman wey touch me . . .

IYALOJA: My children, I beg of you . . .

GIRL: Then tell him to leave this market. This is the home of our mothers. We don't want the eater of white left-overs at the feast their hands have prepared.

IYALOJA: You heard them Amusa. You had better go.

GIRLS: Now!

AMUSA: *[Commencing his retreat.]* We dey go now, but make you no say we no warn you.

GIRL: Now!

GIRL: Before we read the riot act—you should know all about that.

AMUSA: Make we go. *[They depart, more precipitately.]*

[The women strike their palms across in the gesture of wonder.]

WOMEN: Do they teach you all that at school?

WOMAN: And to think I nearly kept Apinke away from the place.

WOMAN: Did you hear them? Did you see how they mimicked the white man?

WOMAN: The voices exactly. Hey, there are wonders in this world!

IYALOJA: Well, our elders have said it: Dada may be weak, but he has a younger sibling who is truly fearless.

WOMAN: The next time the white man shows his face in this market I will set Wuraola on his tail.

[A woman bursts into song and dance of euphoria—"Tani l'awa o l'ogbeja? Kayi! A l'ogbeja. Omo Kekere l'ogbeja."[5] The rest of the women join in, some placing the girls on their back like infants, other dancing round them. The dance becomes general, mounting in excitement. Elesin appears, in wrapper only. In his hands a white velvet cloth folded loosely as if it held some delicate object. He cries out.]

ELESIN: Oh you mothers of beautiful brides! *[The dancing stops. They turn and see him, and the object in his hands. Iyaloja approaches and gently takes the cloth from him.]* Take it. It is no mere virgin stain, but the union of life and the seeds of passage. My vital flow, the last from this flesh is intermingled with the promise of future life. All is prepared. Listen! *[A steady drum-beat from the distance.]* Yes. It is nearly time. The King's dog has been killed. The King's favourite horse is about to follow his master. My brother chiefs know their task and perform it well. *[He listens again.]*

[The Bride emerges, stands shyly by the door. He turns to her.]

Our marriage is not yet wholly fulfilled. When earth and passage wed, the consummation is complete only when there are grains of earth on the eyelids of passage. Stay by me till then. My faithful drummers, do me

---

5. "Who says we haven't a defender? Silence! We have our defenders. Little children are our champions."

your last service. This is where I have chosen to do my leave-taking, in this heart of life, this hive which contains the swarm of the world in its small compass. This is where I have known love and laughter away from the palace. Even the richest food cloys when eaten days on end; in the market, nothing ever cloys. Listen. *[They listen to the drums.]* They have begun to seek out the heart of the King's favourite horse. Soon it will ride in its bolt of raffia with the dog at its feet. Together they will ride on the shoulders of the King's grooms through the pulse centres of the town. They know it is here I shall await them. I have told them. *[His eyes appear to cloud. He passes his hand over them as if to clear his sight. He gives a faint smile.]* It promises well; just then I felt my spirit's eagerness. The kite makes for wide spaces and the wind creeps up behind its tail; can the kite say less than—thank you, the quicker the better? But wait a while my spirit. Wait. Wait for the coming of the courier of the King. Do you know friends, the horse is born to this one destiny, to bear the burden that is man upon its back. Except for this night, this night alone when the spotless stallion will ride in triumph on the back of man. In the time of my father I witnessed the strange sight. Perhaps tonight also I shall see it for the last time. If they arrive before the drums beat for me, I shall tell him to let the Alafin know I follow swiftly. If they come after the drums have sounded, why then, all is well for I have gone ahead. Our spirits shall fall in step along the great passage. *[He listens to the drums. He seems again to be falling into a state of semi-hypnosis; his eyes scan the sky but it is in a kind of daze. His voice is a little breathless.]* The moon has fed, a glow from its full stomach fills the sky and air, but I cannot tell where is that gateway through which I must pass. My faithful friends, let our feet touch together this last time, lead me into the other market with sounds that cover my skin with down yet make my limbs strike earth like a thoroughbred. Dear mothers, let me dance into the passage even as I have lived beneath your roofs. *[He comes down progressively among them. They make away for him, the drummers playing. His dance is one of solemn, regal motions, each gesture of the body is made with a solemn finality. The women join him, their steps a somewhat more fluid version of his. Beneath the Praise-Singer's exhortations the women dirge 'Alę lę lę, swo mi lǫ'.]*

PRAISE-SINGER: Elesin Alafin, can you hear my voice?

ELESIN: Faintly, my friend, faintly.

PRAISE-SINGER: Elesin Alafin, can you hear my call?

ELESIN: Faintly my king, faintly.

PRAISE-SINGER: Is your memory sound Elesin?
    Shall my voice be a blade of grass and
    Tickle the armpit of the past?

ELESIN: My memory needs no prodding but
    What do you wish to say to me?

PRAISE-SINGER: Only what has been spoken. Only what concerns
    The dying wish of the father of all.

ELESIN: It is buried like seed-yam in my mind.

This is the season for quick rains, the harvest
Is this moment due for gathering.

PRAISE-SINGER: If you cannot come, I said, swear
You'll tell my favourite horse. I shall
Ride on through the gates alone.

ELESIN: Elesin's message will be read
Only when his loyal heart no longer beats.

PRAISE-SINGER: If you cannot come Elesin, tell my dog.
I cannot stay the keeper too long
At the gate.

ELESIN: A dog does not outrun the hand
That feeds it meat. A horse that throws its rider
Slows down to a stop. Elesin Alafin
Trusts no beasts with messages between
A king and his companion.

PRAISE-SINGER: If you get lost my dog will track
The hidden path to me.

ELESIN: The seven-way crossroads confuses
Only the stranger. The Horseman of the King
Was born in the recesses of the house.

PRAISE-SINGER: I know the wickedness of men. If there is
Weight on the loose end of your sash, such weight
As no mere man can shift; if your sash is earthed
By evil minds who mean to part us at the last . . .

ELESIN: My sash is of the deep purple *alari;*
It is no tethering-rope. The elephant
Trails no tethering-rope; that king
It not yet crowned who will peg an elephant—
Not even you my friend and King.

PRAISE-SINGER: And yet this fear will not depart from me
The darkness of this new abode is deep
Will your human eyes suffice?

ELESIN: In a night which falls before our eyes
However deep, we do not miss our way.

PRAISE-SINGER: Shall I now not acknowledge I have stood
Where wonders met their end? The elephant deserves
Better than that we say "I have caught
A glimpse of something." If we see the tamer
Of the forest let us say plainly, we have seen
An elephant.

ELESIN: [*His voice is drowsy.*]
I have freed myself of earth and now
It's getting dark. Strange voices guide my feet.

PRAISE-SINGER: The river is never so high that the eyes
Of a fish are covered. The night is not so dark
That the albino fails to find his way. A child

Returning homewards craves no leading by the hand.
Gracefully does the mask regain his grove at the end of day . . .
Gracefully. Gracefully does the mask dance
Homeward at the end of day, gracefully . . .

[Elesin's trance appears to be deepening, his steps heavier.]

IYALOJA: It is the death of war that kills the valiant,
Death of water is how the swimmer goes
It is the death of markets that kills the trader
And death of indecision takes the idle away
The trade of the cutlass blunts its edge
And the beautiful die the death of beauty.
It takes an Elesin to die the death of death . . .
Only Elesin . . . dies the unknowable death of death . . .
Gracefully, gracefully does the horseman regain
The stables at the end of day, gracefully . . .

PRAISE-SINGER: How shall I tell what my eyes have seen? The Horseman gallops on
before the courier, how shall I tell what my eyes have seen? He says a dog
may be confused by new scents of beings he never dreamt of, so he must
precede the dog to heaven. He says a horse may stumble on strange
boulders and be lamed, so he races on before the horse to heaven. It is
best, he says, to trust no messenger who may falter at the outer gate; oh
how shall I tell what my ears have heard? But do you hear me still Elesin,
do you hear your faithful one?

*[Elesin in his motions appear to feel for a direction of sound, subtly, but he
only sinks deeper into his trance-dance.]*

Elesin Alafin, I no longer sense your flesh. The drums are changing now
but you have gone far ahead of the world. It is not yet noon in heaven;
let those who claim it is begin their own journey home. So why must you
rush like an impatient bride: why do you race to desert your Olohun-iyo?

*[Elesin is now sunk fully deep in his trance, there is no longer sign of any
awareness of his surroundings.]*

Does the deep voice of *gbedu* cover you then, like the passage of royal
elephants? Those drums that brook no rivals, have they blocked the
passage to your ears that my voice passes into wind, a mere leaf floating
in the night? Is your flesh lightened Elesin, is that lump of earth I slid
between your slippers to keep you longer slowly sifting from your feet?
Are the drums on the other side now tuning skin to skin with ours in
osugbo? Are there sounds there I cannot hear, do footsteps surround you
which pound the earth like *gbedu*, roll like thunder round the dome of
the world? Is the darkness gathering in your head Elesin? Is there now a
streak of light at the end of the passage, a light I dare not look upon?
Does it reveal whose voices we often heard, whose touches we often felt,
whose wisdoms come suddenly into the mind when the wisest have

shaken their heads and murmured; It cannot be done? Elesin Alafin, don't think I do not know why your lips are heavy, why your limbs are drowsy as palm oil in the cold of harmattan. I would call you back but when the elephant heads for the jungle, the tail is too small a handhold for the hunter that would pull him back. The sun that heads for the sea no longer heeds the prayers of the farmer. When the river begins to taste the salt of the ocean, we no longer know what deity to call on, the river-god or Olokun. No arrow flies back to the string, the child does not return through the same passage that gave it birth. Elesin Oba, can you hear me at all? Your eyelids are glazed like a courtesan's, is it that you see the dark groom and master of life? And will you see my father? Will you tell him that I stayed with you to the last? Will my voice ring in your ears awhile, will you remember Olohun-iyo even if the music on the other side surpasses his mortal craft? But will they know you over there? Have they eyes to gauge your worth, have they the heart to love you, will they know what thoroughbred prances towards them in caparisons of honour? If they do not Elesin, if any there cuts your yam with a small knife, or pours you wine in a small calabash, turn back and return to welcoming hands. If the world were not greater than the wishes of Olohun-iyo, I would not let you go . . .

[*He appears to break down. Elesin dances on, completely in a trance. The dirge wells up louder and stronger. Elesin's dance does not lose its elasticity but his gestures become, if possible, even more weighty. Lights fade slowly on the scene.*]

4

A Masque. The front side of the stage is part of a wide corridor around the great hall of the Residency extending beyond vision into the rear and wings. It is redolent of the tawdry decadence of a far-flung but key imperial frontier. The couples in a variety of fancy-dress are ranged around the walls, gazing in the same direction. The guest-of-honour is about to make an appearance. A portion of the local police brass band with its white conductor is just visible. At last, the entrance of Royalty. The band plays "Rule Britannia," badly, beginning long before he is visible. The couples bow and curtsey as he passes by them. Both he and his companions are dressed in seventeenth century European costume. Following behind are the Resident and his partner similarly attired. As they gain the end of the hall where the orchestra dais begins the music comes to an end. The Prince bows to the guests. The band strikes up a Viennese waltz and the Prince formally opens the floor. Several bars later the Resident and his companion follow suit. Others follow in appropriate pecking order. The orchestra's waltz rendition is not of the highest musical standard.

Some time later the Prince dances again into view and is settled into a corner by the Resident who then proceeds to select couples as they dance past for introduction, sometimes threading his way through the dancers to tap the lucky couple on the shoulder. Desperate efforts from many to ensure that they are recognised in spite of, perhaps, their costume. The ritual of introduction soon takes in Pilkings and his wife. The Prince is quite fascinated by their costume and they demonstrate the adaptations they have made to it, pulling down the mask to demonstrate how the egungun normally appears, then showing the various press-button controls they have innovated for the face flaps, the sleeves, etc. They demonstrate the dance steps and the guttural sounds made by the egungun, harrass other dancers in the hall, Mrs Pilkings playing the 'restrainer' to Pilkings' manic darts. Everyone is highly entertained, the Royal Party especially who lead the applause.

At this point a liveried footman comes in with a note on a salver and is intercepted almost absent-mindedly by the Resident who takes the note and reads it. After polite coughs he succeeds in excusing the Pilkingses from the Prince and takes them aside. The Prince considerately offers the Resident's wife his hand and dancing is resumed.

On their way out the Resident gives an order to his Aide-de-Camp. They come into the side corridor where the Resident hands the note to Pilkings.

RESIDENT: As you see it says "emergency" on the outside. I took the liberty of opening it because His Highness was obviously enjoying the entertainment. I didn't want to interrupt unless really necessary.

PILKINGS: Yes, yes of course sir.

RESIDENT: Is it really as bad as it says? What's it all about?

PILKINGS: Some strange custom they have sir. It seems because the King is dead some important chief has to commit suicide.

RESIDENT: The King? Isn't it the same one who died nearly a month ago?

PILKINGS: Yes sir.

RESIDENT: Haven't they buried him yet?

PILKINGS: They take their time about these things sir. The pre-burial ceremonies last nearly thirty days. It seems tonight is the final night.

RESIDENT: But what has it got to do with the market women? Why are they rioting? We've waived that troublesome tax haven't we?

PILKINGS: We don't quite know that they are exactly rioting yet sir. Sergeant Amusa is sometimes prone to exaggerations.

RESIDENT: He sounds desperate enough. That comes out even in his rather quaint grammar. Where is the man anyway? I asked my aide-de-camp to bring him here.

PILKINGS: They are probably looking in the wrong verandah. I'll fetch him myself.

RESIDENT: No no you stay here. Let your wife go and look for them. Do you mind my dear . . . ?

JANE: Certainly not, your Excellency. *[Goes.]*

RESIDENT: You should have kept me informed Pilkings. You realise how disastrous it would have been if things had erupted while His Highness was here.

PILKINGS: I wasn't aware of the whole business until tonight sir.

RESIDENT: Nose to the ground Pilkings, nose to the ground. If we all let these little things slip past us where would the empire be eh? Tell me that. Where would we all be?

PILKINGS: *[Low voice.]* Sleeping peacefully at home I bet.

RESIDENT: What did you say Pilkings?

PILKINGS: It won't happen again sir.

RESIDENT: It mustn't Pilkings. It mustn't. Where is that damned sergeant? I ought to get back to His Highness as quickly as possible and offer him some plausible explanation for my rather abrupt conduct. Can you think of one Pilkings?

PILKINGS: You could tell him the truth sir.

RESIDENT: I could? No no no no Pilkings, that would never do. What! Go and tell him there is a riot just two miles away from him? This is supposed to be a secure colony of His Majesty, Pilkings.

PILKINGS: Yes sir.

RESIDENT: Ah, there they are. No, these are not our native police. Are these the ring-leaders of the riot?

PILKINGS: Sir, these are my police officers.

RESIDENT: Oh, I beg your pardon officers. You do look a little . . . I say, isn't there something missing in their uniform? I think they used to have some rather colourful sashes. If I remember rightly I recommended them myself in my young days in the service. A bit of colour always appeals to the natives, yes, I remember putting that in my report. Well well well, where are we? Make your report man.

PILKINGS: [*Moves close to Amusa, between his teeth.*] And let's have no more superstitious nonsense from you Amusa or I'll throw you in the guardroom for a month and feed you pork!

RESIDENT: What's that? What has pork to do with it?

PILKINGS: Sir, I was just warning him to be brief. I'm sure you are most anxious to hear his report.

RESIDENT: Yes yes yes of course. Come on man, speak up. Hey, didn't we give them some colourful fez hats with all those wavy things, yes, pink tassells . . .

PILKINGS: Sir, I think if he was permitted to make his report we might find that he lost his hat in the riot.

RESIDENT: Ah yes indeed. I'd better tell His Highness that. Lost his hat in the riot, ha ha. He'll probably say well, as long as he didn't lose his head. [*Chuckles to himself.*] Don't forget to send me a report first thing in the morning young Pilkings.

PILKINGS: No sir.

RESIDENT: And whatever you do, don't let things get out of hand. Keep a cool head and—nose to the ground Pilkings. [*Wanders off in the general direction of the hall.*]

PILKINGS: Yes sir.

AIDE-DE-CAMP: Would you be needing me sir?

PILKINGS: No thanks Bob. I think His Excellency's need of you is greater than ours.

AIDE-DE-CAMP: We have a detachment of soldiers from the capital sir. They accompanied His Highness up here.

PILKINGS: I doubt if it will come to that but, thanks, I'll bear it in mind. Oh, could you send an orderly with my cloak.

AIDE-DE-CAMP: Very good sir. [*Goes.*]

PILKINGS: Now Sergeant.

AMUSA: Sir . . . [*Makes an effort, stops dead. Eyes to the ceiling.*]

PILKINGS: Oh, not again.

AMUSA: I cannot against death to dead cult. This dress get power of dead.

PILKINGS: Alright, let's go. You are relieved of all further duty Amusa. Report to me first thing in the morning.

JANE: Shall I come Simon?

PILKINGS: No, there's no need for that. If I can get back later I will. Otherwise get Bob to bring you home.

JANE: Be careful Simon . . . I mean, be clever.

PILKINGS: Sure I will. You two, come with me. [*As he turns to go, the clock in the Residency begins to chime. Pilkings looks at his watch then turns, horror-stricken, to stare at his wife. The same thought clearly occurs to her. He swallows hard. An orderly brings his cloak.*] It's midnight. I had no idea it was that late.

JANE: But surely . . . they don't count the hours the way we do. The moon, or something . . .

PILKINGS: I am . . . not so sure.

[*He turns and breaks into a sudden run. The two constables follow, also at a run. Amusa, who has kept his eyes on the ceiling throughout waits until the last of the footsteps has faded out of hearing. He salutes suddenly, but without once looking in the direction of the woman.*]

AMUSA: Goodnight madam.

JANE: Oh. [*She hesitates.*] Amusa . . . [*He goes off without seeming to have heard.*] Poor Simon . . . [*A figure emerges from the shadows, a young black man dressed in a sober western suit. He peeps into the hall, trying to make out the figures of the dancers.*] Who is that?

OLUNDE: [*Emerging into the light.*] I didn't mean to startle you madam. I am looking for the District Officer.

JANE: Wait a minute . . . don't I know you? Yes, you are Olunde, the young man who . . .

OLUNDE: Mrs Pilkings! How fortunate. I came here to look for your husband.

JANE: Olunde! Let's look at you. What a fine young man you've become. Grand but solemn. Good God, when did you return? Simon never said a word. But you do look well Olunde. Really!

OLUNDE: You are . . . well, you look quite well yourself Mrs Pilkings. From what little I can see of you.

JANE: Oh, this. It's caused quite a stir I assure you, and not all of it very pleasant. You are not shocked I hope?

OLUNDE: Why should I be? But don't you find it rather hot in there? Your skin must find it difficult to breathe.

JANE: Well, it is a little hot I must confess, but it's all in a good cause.

OLUNDE: What cause Mrs Pilkings?

JANE: All this. The ball. And His Highness being here in person and all that.

OLUNDE: [*Mildly.*] And that is the good cause for which you desecrate an ancestral mask?

JANE: Oh, so you are shocked after all. How disappointing.

OLUNDE: No I am not shocked Mrs Pilkings. You forget that I have now spent four years among your people. I discovered that you have no respect for what you do not understand.

JANE: Oh. So you've returned with a chip on your shoulder. That's a pity Olunde. I am sorry.

[*An uncomfortable silence follows.*]

I take it then that you did not find your stay in England altogether edifying.

OLUNDE: I don't say that. I found your people quite admirable in many ways, their conduct and courage in this war for instance.

JANE: Ah yes the war. Here of course it is all rather remote. From time to time we have a black-out drill just to remind us that there is a war on. And the rare convoy passes through on its way somewhere or on manoeuvres. Mind you there is the occasional bit of excitement like that ship that was blown up in the harbour.

OLUNDE: Here? Do you mean through enemy action?

JANE: Oh no, the war hasn't come that close. The captain did it himself. I don't quite understand it really. Simon tried to explain. The ship had to be blown up because it had become dangerous to the other ships, even to the city itself. Hundreds of the coastal population would have died.

OLUNDE: Maybe it was loaded with ammunition and had caught fire. Or some of those lethal gases they've been experimenting on.

JANE: Something like that. The captain blew himself up with it. Deliberately. Simon said someone had to remain on board to light the fuse.

OLUNDE: It must have been a very short fuse.

JANE: [Shrugs.] I don't know much about it. Only that there was no other way to save lives. No time to devise anything else. The captain took the decision and carried it out.

OLUNDE: Yes . . . I quite believe it. I met men like that in England.

JANE: Oh just look at me! Fancy welcoming you back with such morbid news. Stale too. It was at least six months ago.

OLUNDE: I don't find it morbid at all. I find it rather inspiring. It is an affirmative commentary on life.

JANE: What is?

OLUNDE: That captain's self-sacrifice.

JANE: Nonsense. Life should never be thrown deliberately away.

OLUNDE: And the innocent people round the harbour?

JANE: Oh, how does one know? The whole thing was probably exaggerated anyway.

OLUNDE: That was a risk the captain couldn't take. But please Mrs Pilkings, do you think you could find your husband for me? I have to talk to him.

JANE: Simon? Oh. [As she recollects for the first time the full significance of Olunde's presence.] Simon is . . . there is a little problem in town. He was sent for. But . . . when did you arrive? Does Simon know you're here?

OLUNDE: [Suddenly earnest.] I need your help Mrs Pilkings. I've always found you somewhat more understanding than your husband. Please find him for me and when you do, you must help me talk to him.

JANE: I'm afraid I don't quite . . . follow you. Have you seen my husband already?

OLUNDE: I went to your house. Your houseboy told me you were here. [He smiles.] He even told me how I would recognise you and Mr Pilkings.

JANE: Then you must know what my husband is trying to do for you.

OLUNDE: For me?

JANE: For you. For your people. And to think he didn't even know you were coming back! But how do you happen to be here? Only this evening we

were talking about you. We thought you were still four thousand miles
away.

OLUNDE: I was sent a cable.

JANE: A cable? Who did? Simon? The business of your father didn't begin till
tonight.

OLUNDE: A relation sent it weeks ago, and it said nothing about my father. All it
said was, Our King is dead. But I knew I had to return home at once so
as to bury my father. I understood that.

JANE: Well, thank God you don't have to go through that agony. Simon is going
to stop it.

OLUNDE: That's why I want to see him. He's wasting his time. And since he has
been so helpful to me I don't want him to incur the enmity of our people.
Especially over nothing.

JANE: *[Sits down open-mouthed.]* You . . . you Olunde!

OLUNDE: Mrs Pilkings, I came home to bury my father. As soon as I heard the
news I booked my passage home. In fact we were fortunate. We travelled
in the same convoy as your Prince, so we had excellent protection.

JANE: But you don't think your father is also entitled to whatever protection is
available to him?

OLUNDE: How can I make you understand? He *has* protection. No one can
undertake what he does tonight without the deepest protection the mind
can conceive. What can you offer him in place of his peace of mind, in
place of the honour and veneration of his own people? What would you
think of your Prince if he had refused to accept the risk of losing his life
on this voyage? This . . . showing-the-flag tour of colonial possessions.

JANE: I see. So it isn't just medicine you studied in England.

OLUNDE: Yet another error into which your people fall. You believe that everything which appears to make sense was learnt from you.

JANE: Not so fast Olunde. You have learnt to argue I can tell that, but I never said
you made sense. However cleverly you try to put it, it is still a barbaric
custom. It is even worse—it's feudal! The king dies and a chieftain must
be buried with him. How feudalistic can you get!

OLUNDE: *[Waves his hand towards the background. The Prince is dancing past
again—to a different step—and all the guests are bowing and curtseying as he
passes.]* And this? Even in the midst of a devastating war, look at that.
What name would you give to that?

JANE: Therapy, British style. The preservation of sanity in the midst of chaos.

OLUNDE: Others would call it decadence. However, it doesn't really interest me. You
white races know how to survive; I've seen proof of that. By all logical and
natural laws this war should end with all the white races wiping out one
another, wiping out their so-called civilisation for all time and reverting to
a state of primitivism the like of which has so far only existed in your
imagination when you thought of us. I thought all that at the beginning.
Then I slowly realised that your greatest art is the art of survival. But at least
have the humility to let others survive in their own way.

JANE: Through ritual suicide?

OLUNDE: Is that worse than mass suicide? Mrs Pilkings, what do you call what those young men are sent to do by their generals in this war? Of course you have also mastered the art of calling things by names which don't remotely describe them.

JANE: You talk! You people with your long-winded, roundabout way of making conversation.

OLUNDE: Mrs Pilkings, whatever we do, we never suggest that a thing is the opposite of what it really is. In your newsreels I heard defeats, thorough, murderous defeats described as strategic victories. No wait, it wasn't just on your newsreels. Don't forget I was attached to hospitals all the time. Hordes of your wounded passed through those wards. I spoke to them. I spent long evenings by their bedside while they spoke terrible truths of the realities of that war. I know now how history is made.

JANE: But surely, in a war of this nature, for the morale of the nation you must expect . . .

OLUNDE: That a disaster beyond human reckoning be spoken of as a triumph? No. I mean, is there no mourning in the home of the bereaved that such blasphemy is permitted?

JANE: [After a moment's pause.] Perhaps I can understand you now. The time we picked for you was not really one for seeing us at our best.

OLUNDE: Don't think it was just the war. Before that even started I had plenty of time to study your people. I saw nothing, finally, that gave you the right to pass judgment on other peoples and their ways. Nothing at all.

JANE: [Hesitantly.] Was it the . . . colour thing? I know there is some discrimination.

OLUNDE: Don't make it so simple, Mrs Pilkings. You make it sound as if when I left, I took nothing at all with me.

JANE: Yes . . . and to tell the truth, only this evening, Simon and I agreed that we never really knew what you left with.

OLUNDE: Neither did I. But I found out over there. I am grateful to your country for that. And I will never give it up.

JANE: Olunde, please . . . promise me something. Whatever you do, don't throw away what you have started to do. You want to be a doctor. My husband and I believe you will make an excellent one, sympathetic and competent. Don't let anything make you throw away your training.

OLUNDE: [Genuinely surprised.] Of course not. What a strange idea. I intend to return and complete my training. Once the burial of my father is over.

JANE: Oh, please . . . !

OLUNDE: Listen! Come outside. You can't hear anything against that music.

JANE: What is it?

OLUNDE: The drums. Can you hear the change? Listen.

[The drums come over, still distant but more distinct. There is a change of rhythm, it rises to a crescendo and then, suddenly, it is cut off. After a silence, a new beat begins, slow and resonant.]

There. It's all over.

JANE: You mean he's . . .

OLUNDE: Yes Mrs Pilkings, my father is dead. His will-power has always been enormous; I know he is dead.

JANE: *[Screams.]* How can you be so callous! So unfeeling! You announce your father's own death like a surgeon looking down on some strange . . . stranger's body! You're just a savage like all the rest.

AIDE-DE-CAMP: *[Rushing out.]* Mrs Pilkings. Mrs Pilkings. *[She breaks down, sobbing.]* Are you alright, Mrs Pilkings?

OLUNDE: She'll be alright. *[Turns to go.]*

AIDE-DE-CAMP: Who are you? And who the hell asked your opinion?

OLUNDE: You're quite right, nobody. *[Going.]*

AIDE-DE-CAMP: What the hell! Did you hear me ask you who you were?

OLUNDE: I have business to attend to.

AIDE-DE-CAMP: I'll give you business in a moment you impudent nigger. Answer my question!

OLUNDE: I have a funeral to arrange. Excuse me. *[Going.]*

AIDE-DE-CAMP: I said stop! Orderly!

JANE: No no, don't do that. I'm alright. And for heaven's sake don't act so foolishly. He's a family friend.

AIDE-DE-CAMP: Well he'd better learn to answer civil questions when he's asked them. These natives put a suit on and they get high opinions of themselves.

OLUNDE: Can I go now?

JANE: No no don't go. I must talk to you. I'm sorry about what I said.

OLUNDE: It's nothing Mrs Pilkings. And I'm really anxious to go. I couldn't see my father before, it's forbidden for me, his heir and successor to set eyes on him from the moment of the king's death. But now . . . . I would like to touch his body while it is still warm.

JANE: You will. I promise I shan't keep you long. Only, I couldn't possibly let you go like that. Bob, please excuse us.

AIDE-DE-CAMP: If you're sure . . .

JANE: Of course I'm sure. Something happened to upset me just then, but I'm alright now. Really.

[The Aide-de-Camp goes, somewhat reluctantly.]

OLUNDE: I mustn't stay long.

JANE: Please, I promise not to keep you. It's just that . . . . oh you saw yourself what happens to one in this place. The Resident's man thought he was being helpful, that's the way we all react. But I can't go in among that crowd just now and if I stay by myself somebody will come looking for me. Please, just say something for a few moments and then you can go. Just so I can recover myself.

OLUNDE: What do you want me to say?

JANE: Your calm acceptance for instance, can you explain that? It was so unnatural. I don't understand that at all. I feel a need to understand all I can.

OLUNDE: But you explained it yourself. My medical training perhaps. I have seen death too often. And the soldiers who returned from the front, they died on our hands all the time.

JANE: No. It has to be more than that. I feel it has to do with the many things we don't really grasp about your people. At least you can explain.

OLUNDE: All these things are part of it. And anyway, my father has been dead in my mind for nearly a month. Ever since I learnt of the King's death. I've lived with my bereavement so long now that I cannot think of him alive. On that journey on the boat, I kept my mind on my duties as the one who must perform the rites over his body. I went through it all again and again in my mind as he himself had taught me. I didn't want to do anything wrong, something which might jeopardise the welfare of my people.

JANE: But he had disowned you. When you left he swore publicly you were no longer his son.

OLUNDE: I told you, he was a man of tremendous will. Sometimes that's another way of saying stubborn. But among our people, you don't disown a child just like that. Even if I had died before him I would still be buried like his eldest son. But it's time for me to go.

JANE: Thank you. I feel calmer. Don't let me keep you from your duties.

OLUNDE: Goodnight Mrs Pilkings.

JANE: Welcome home. [She holds out her hand. As he takes it footsteps are heard approaching the drive. A short while later a woman's sobbing is also heard.]

PILKINGS: [Off.] Keep them here till I get back. [He strides into view, reacts at the sight of Olunde but turns to his wife.] Thank goodness you're still here.

JANE: Simon, what happened?

PILKINGS: Later Jane, please. Is Bob still here?

JANE: Yes, I think so. I'm sure he must be.

PILKINGS: Try and get him out here as quietly as you can. Tell him it's urgent.

JANE: Of course. Oh Simon, you remember . . .

PILKINGS: Yes yes. I can see who it is. Get Bob out here. [She runs off.] At first I thought I was seeing a ghost.

OLUNDE: Mr Pilkings, I appreciate what you tried to do. I want you to believe that. I can only tell you it would have been a terrible calamity if you'd succeeded.

PILKINGS: [Opens his mouth several times, shuts it.] You . . . said what?

OLUNDE: A calamity for us, the entire people.

PILKINGS: [Sighs.] I see. Hm.

OLUNDE: And now I must go. I must see him before he turns cold.

PILKINGS: Oh ah . . . em . . . but this is a shock to see you. I mean er thinking all this while you were in England and thanking God for that.

OLUNDE: I came on the mail boat. We travelled in the Prince's convoy.

PILKINGS: Ah yes, a-ah, hm . . . er well . . .

OLUNDE: Goodnight. I can see you are shocked by the whole business. But you must know by now there are things you cannot understand—or help.

PILKINGS: Yes. Just a minute. There are armed policemen that way and they have instructions to let no one pass. I suggest you wait a little. I'll er . . . yes, I'll give you an escort.

OLUNDE: That's very kind of you. But do you think it could be quickly arranged.

PILKINGS: Of course. In fact, yes, what I'll do is send Bob over with some men to the er . . . place. You can go with them. Here he comes now. Excuse me a minute.

AIDE-DE-CAMP: Anything wrong sir?

PILKINGS: [Takes him to one side.] Listen Bob, that cellar in the disused annexe of the Residency, you know, where the slaves were stored before being taken down to the coast . . .

AIDE-DE-CAMP: Oh yes, we use it as a storeroom for broken furniture.

PILKINGS: But it's still got the bars on it?

AIDE-DE-CAMP: Oh yes, they are quite intact.

PILKINGS: Get the keys please. I'll explain later. And I want a strong guard over the Residency tonight.

AIDE-DE-CAMP: We have that already. The detachment from the coast . . .

PILKINGS: No, I don't want them at the gates of the Residency. I want you to deploy them at the bottom of the hill, a long way from the main hall so they can deal with any situation long before the sound carries to the house.

AIDE-DE-CAMP: Yes of course.

PILKINGS: I don't want His Highness alarmed.

AIDE-DE-CAMP: You think the riot will spread here?

PILKINGS: It's unlikely but I don't want to take a chance. I made them believe I was going to lock the man up in my house, which was what I had planned to do in the first place. They are probably assailing it by now. I took a roundabout-route here so I don't think there is any danger at all. At least not before dawn. Nobody is to leave the premises of course—the native employees I mean. They'll soon smell something is up and they can't keep their mouths shut.

AIDE-DE-CAMP: I'll give instructions at once.

PILKINGS: I'll take the prisoner down myself. Two policemen will stay with him throughout the night. Inside the cell.

AIDE-DE-CAMP: Right sir. [Salutes and goes off at the double.]

PILKINGS: Jane. Bob is coming back in a moment with a detachment. Until he gets back please stay with Olunde. [He makes an extra warning gesture with his eyes.]

OLUNDE: Please Mr Pilkings . . .

PILKINGS: I hate to be stuffy old son, but we have a crisis on our hands. It has to do with your father's affair if you must know. And it happens also at a time when we have His Highness here. I am responsible for security so you'll simply have to do as I say. I hope that's understood. [Marches off quickly, in the direction from which he made his first appearance.]

OLUNDE: What's going on? All this can't be just because he failed to stop my father killing himself.

JANE: I honestly don't know. Could it have sparked off a riot?

OLUNDE: No. If he'd succeeded that would be more likely to start the riot. Perhaps there were other factors involved. Was there a chieftancy dispute?

JANE: None that I know of.

ELESIN: [*An animal bellow from off.*] Leave me alone! Is it not enough that you have covered me in shame! White man, take your hands from my body!

[*Olunde stands frozen on the spot. Jane understanding at last, tries to move him.*]

JANE: Let's go in. It's getting chilly out here.

PILKINGS: [*Off.*] Carry him.

ELESIN: Give me back the name you have taken away from me you ghost from the land of the nameless!

PILKINGS: Carry him! I can't have a disturbance here. Quickly! stuff up his mouth.

JANE: Oh God! Let's go in. Please Olunde. [*Olunde does not move.*]

ELESIN: Take your albino's hand from me you . . .

[*Sounds of a struggle. His voice chokes as he is gagged.*]

OLUNDE: [*Quietly.*] That was my father's voice.

JANE: Oh you poor orphan, what have you come home to?

[*There is a sudden explosion of rage from off-stage and powerful steps come running up the drive.*]

PILKINGS: You bloody fools, after him!

[*Immediately Elesin, in handcuffs, comes pounding in the direction of Jane and Olunde, followed some moments afterwards by Pilkings and the constables. Elesin confronted by the seeming statue of his son, stops dead. Olunde stares above his head into the distance. The constables try to grab him. Jane screams at them.*]

JANE: Leave him alone! Simon, tell them to leave him alone.

PILKINGS: All right, stand aside you. [*Shrugs.*] Maybe just as well. It might help to calm him down.

[*For several moments they hold the same position. Elesin moves a few steps forward, almost as if he's still in doubt.*]

ELESIN: Olunde? [*He moves his head, inspecting him from side to side.*] Olunde! [*He collapses slowly at Olunde's feet.*] Oh son, don't let the sight of your father turn you blind!

OLUNDE: [*He moves for the first time since he heard his voice, brings his head slowly down to look on him.*] I have no father, eater of left-overs.

[*He walks slowly down the way his father had run. Light fades out on Elesin, sobbing into the ground.*]

5

A wide iron-barred gate stretches almost the whole width of the cell in which Elesin is imprisoned. His wrists are encased in thick iron bracelets, chained together; he stands against the bars, looking out. Seated on the ground to one side on the outside is his recent bride, her eyes bent perpetually to the ground. Figures of the two guards can be seen deeper inside the cell, alert to every movement Elesin makes. Pilkings now in a police officer's *uniform enters noiselessly, observes him for a while. Then he coughs ostentatiously and approaches. Leans against the bars near a corner, his back to Elesin. He is obviously trying to fall in mood with him. Some moments' silence.*

PILKINGS: You seem fascinated by the moon.

ELESIN: *[After a pause.]* Yes, ghostly one. Your twin-brother up there engages my thoughts.

PILKINGS: It is a beautiful night.

ELESIN: Is that so?

PILKINGS: The light on the leaves, the peace of the night . . .

ELESIN: The night is not at peace, District Officer.

PILKINGS: No? I would have said it was. You know, quiet . . .

ELESIN: And does quiet mean peace for you?

PILKINGS: Well, nearly the same thing. Naturally there is a subtle difference . . .

ELESIN: The night is not at peace ghostly one. The world is not at peace. You have shattered the peace of the world for ever. There is no sleep in the world tonight.

PILKINGS: It is still a good bargain if the world should lose one night's sleep as the price of saving a man's life.

ELESIN: You did not save my life District Officer. You destroyed it.

PILKINGS: Now come on . . .

ELESIN: And not merely my life but the lives of many. The end of the night's work is not over. Neither this year nor the next will see it. If I wished you well, I would pray that you do not stay long enough on our land to see the disaster you have brought upon us.

PILKINGS: Well, I did my duty as I saw it. I have no regrets.

ELESIN: No. The regrets of life always come later.

[Some moments' pause.]

You are waiting for dawn white man. I hear you saying to yourself: only so many hours until dawn and then the danger is over. All I must do is keep him alive tonight. You don't quite understand it all but you know that tonight is when what ought to be must be brought about. I shall ease your mind even more, ghostly one. It is not an entire night but a moment of the night, and that moment is past. The moon was my messenger and guide. When it reached a certain gateway in the sky, it touched that moment for which my whole life has been spent in blessings. Even I do not know the gateway. I have stood here and scanned the sky for a glimpse of that door but, I cannot see it. Human eyes are useless for a search of this nature. But in the house of *osugbo*, those who keep watch through this spirit recognised the moment, they sent word to me through the voice of our sacred drums to prepare myself. I heard them and I shed all thoughts of earth. I began to follow the moon to the abode of gods . . . servant of the white king, that was when you entered my chosen place of departure on feet of desecration.

PILKINGS: I'm sorry, but we all see our duty differently.

ELESIN: I no longer blame you. You stole from me my firstborn, sent him to your country so you could turn him into something in your own image. Did you plan it all beforehand? There are moments when it seems part of a larger plan. He who must follow my footsteps is taken from me, sent across the ocean. Then, in my turn, I am stopped from fulfilling my destiny. Did you think it all out before, this plan to push our world from its course and sever the cord that links us to the great origin?

PILKINGS: You don't really believe that. Anyway, if that was my intention with your son, I appear to have failed.

ELESIN: You did not fail in the main thing ghostly one. We know the roof covers the rafters, the cloth covers blemishes; who would have known that the white skin covered our future, preventing us from seeing the death our enemies had prepared for us. The world is set adrift and its inhabitants are lost. Around them, there is nothing but emptiness.

PILKINGS: Your son does not take so gloomy a view.

ELESIN: Are you dreaming now white man? Were you not present at my reunion of shame? Did you not see when the world reversed itself and the father fell before his son, asking forgiveness?

PILKINGS: That was in the heat of the moment. I spoke to him and . . . if you want to know, he wishes he could cut out his tongue for uttering the words he did.

ELESIN: No. What he said must never be unsaid. The contempt of my own son rescued something of my shame at your hands. You may have stopped me in my duty but I know now that I did give birth to a son. Once I mistrusted him for seeking the companionship of those my spirit knew as enemies of our race. Now I understand. One should seek to obtain the secrets of his enemies. He will avenge my shame, white one. His spirit will destroy you and yours.

PILKINGS: That kind of talk is hardly called for. If you don't want my consolation . . .

ELESIN: No white man, I do not want your consolation.

PILKINGS: As you wish. Your son anyway, sends his consolation. He asks your forgiveness. When I asked him not to despise you his reply was: I cannot judge him, and if I cannot judge him, I cannot despise him. He wants to come to you to say goodbye and to receive your blessing.

ELESIN: Goodbye? Is he returning to your land?

PILKINGS: Don't you think that's the most sensible thing for him to do? I advised him to leave at once, before dawn, and he agrees that is the right course of action.

ELESIN: Yes, it is best. And even if I did not think so, I have lost the father's place of honour. My voice is broken.

PILKINGS: Your son honours you. If he didn't he would not ask your blessing.

ELESIN: No. Even a thoroughbred is not without pity for the turf he strikes with his hoof. When is he coming?

PILKINGS: As soon as the town is a little quieter. I advised it.

ELESIN: Yes white man, I am sure you advised it. You advise all our lives although on the authority of what gods, I do not know.

PILKINGS: *[Opens his mouth to reply, then appears to change his mind. Turns to go. Hesitates and stops again.]* Before I leave you, may I ask just one thing of you?

ELESIN: I am listening.

PILKINGS: I wish to ask you to search the quiet of your heart and tell me—do you not find great contradictions in the wisdom of your own race?

ELESIN: Make yourself clear, white one.

PILKINGS: I have lived among you long enough to learn a saying or two. One came to my mind tonight when I stepped into the market and saw what was going on. You were surrounded by those who egged you on with song and praises. I thought, are these not the same people who say: the elder grimly approaches heaven and you ask him to bear your greetings yonder; do you really think he makes the journey willingly? After that, I did not hesitate.

[A pause. Elesin sighs. Before he can speak a sound of running feet is heard.]

JANE: *[Off.]* Simon! Simon!

PILKINGS: What on earth . . . ! *[Runs off.]*

[Elesin turns to his new wife, gazes on her for some moments.]

ELESIN: My young bride, did you hear the ghostly one? You sit and sob in your silent heart but say nothing to all this. First I blamed the white man, then I blamed my gods for deserting me. Now I feel I want to blame you for the mystery of the sapping of my will. But blame is a strange peace offering for a man to bring a world he has deeply wronged, and to its innocent dwellers. Oh little mother, I have taken countless women in my life but you were more than a desire of the flesh. I needed you as the abyss across which my body must be drawn, I filled it with earth and dropped my seed in it at the moment of preparedness for my crossing. You were the final gift of the living to their emissary to the land of the ancestors, and perhaps your warmth and youth brought new insights of this world to me and turned my feet leaden on this side of the abyss. For I confess to you, daughter, my weakness came not merely from the abomination of the white man who came violently into my fading presence, there was also a weight of longing on my earth-held limbs. I would have shaken it off, already my foot had begun to lift but then, the white ghost entered and all was defiled.

[Approaching voices of Pilkings and his wife.]

JANE: Oh Simon, you will let her in won't you?

PILKINGS: I really wish you'd stop interfering.

[They come in view. Jane is in a dressing-gown. Pilkings is holding a note to which he refers from time to time.]

JANE: Good gracious, I didn't initiate this. I was sleeping quietly, or trying to anyway, when the servant brought it. It's not my fault if one can't sleep undisturbed even in the Residency.

PILKINGS: He'd have done the same if we were sleeping at home so don't sidetrack the issue. He knows he can get round you or he wouldn't send you the petition in the first place.

JANE: Be fair Simon. After all he was thinking of your own interests. He is grateful you know, you seem to forget that. He feels he owes you something.

PILKINGS: I just wish they'd leave this man alone tonight, that's all.

JANE: Trust him Simon. He's pledged his word it will all go peacefully.

PILKINGS: Yes, and that's the other thing. I don't like being threatened.

JANE: Threatened? [Takes the note.] I didn't spot any threat.

PILKINGS: It's there. Veiled, but it's there. The only way to prevent serious rioting tomorrow—what's a cheek!

JANE: I don't think he's threatening you Simon.

PILKINGS: He's picked up the idiom alright. Wouldn't surprise me if he's been mixing with commies or anarchists over there. The phrasing sounds too good to be true. Damn! If only the Prince hadn't picked this time for his visit.

JANE: Well, even so Simon, what have you got to lose? You don't want a riot on your hands, not with the Prince here.

PILKINGS: [Going up to Elesin.] Let's see what he has to say. Chief Elesin, there is yet another person who wants to see you. As she is not a next-of-kin I don't really feel obliged to let her in. But your son sent a note with her, so it's up to you.

ELESIN: I know who that must be. So she found out your hiding place. Well, it was not difficult. My stench of shame is so strong, it requires no hunter's dog to follow it.

PILKINGS: If you don't want to see her, just say so and I'll send her packing.

ELESIN: Why should I not want to see her? Let her come. I have no more holes in my rag of shame. All is laid bare.

PILKINGS: I'll bring her in. [Goes off.]

JANE: [Hesitates, then goes to Elesin.] Please, try and understand. Everything my husband did was for the best.

ELESIN: [He gives her a long strange stare, as if he is trying to understand who she is.] You are the wife of the District Officer?

JANE: Yes. My name, is Jane.

ELESIN: That is my wife sitting down there. You notice how still and silent she sits? My business is with your husband.

[Pilkings returns with Iyaloja.]

PILKINGS: Here she is. Now first I want your word of honour that you will try nothing foolish.

ELESIN: Honour? White one, did you say you wanted my word of honour?

PILKINGS: I know you to be an honourable man. Give me your word of honour you will receive nothing from her.

ELESIN: But I am sure you have searched her clothing as you would never dare touch your own mother. And there are these two lizards of yours who roll their eyes even when I scratch.

PILKINGS: And I shall be sitting on that tree trunk watching even how you blink.

Just the same I want your word that you will not let her pass anything to you.

ELESIN: You have my honour already. It is locked up in that desk in which you will put away your report of this night's events. Even the honour of my people you have taken already; it is tied together with those papers of treachery which make you masters in this land.

PILKINGS: Alright. I am trying to make things easy but if you must bring in politics we'll have to do it the hard way. Madam, I want you to remain along this line and move no nearer to that cell door. Guards! [*They spring to attention.*] If she moves beyond this point, blow your whistle. Come on Jane. [*They go off.*]

IYALOJA: How boldly the lizard struts before the pigeon when it was the eagle itself he promised us he would confront.

ELESIN: I don't ask you to take pity on me Iyaloja. You have a message for me or you would not have come. Even if it is the curses of the world, I shall listen.

IYALOJA: You made so bold with the servant of the white king who took your side against death. I must tell your brother chiefs when I return how bravely you waged war against him. Especially with words.

ELESIN: I more than deserve your scorn.

IYALOJA: [*With sudden anger.*] I warned you, if you must leave a seed behind, be sure it is not tainted with the curses of the world. Who are you to open a new life when you dared not open the door to a new existence? I say who are you to make so bold? [*The Bride sobs and Iyaloja notices her. Her contempt noticeably increases as she turns back to Elesin.*] Oh you self-vaunted stem of the plantain, how hollow it all proves. The pith is gone in the parent stem, so how will it prove with the new shoot? How will it go with that earth that bears it? Who are you to bring this abomination on us!

ELESIN: My powers deserted me. My charms, my spells, even my voice lacked strength when I made to summon the powers that would lead me over the last measure of earth into the land of the fleshless. You saw it, Iyaloja. You saw me struggle to retrieve my will from the power of the stranger whose shadow fell across the doorway and left me floundering and blundering in a maze I had never before encountered. My senses were numbed when the touch of cold iron came upon my wrists. I could do nothing to save myself.

IYALOJA: You have betrayed us. We fed your sweetmeats such as we hoped awaited you on the other side. But you said No, I must eat the world's left-overs. We said you were the hunter who brought the quarry down; to you belonged the vital portions of the game. No, you said, I am the hunter's dog and I shall eat the entrails of the game and the faeces of the hunter. We said you were the hunter returning home in triumph, a slain buffalo pressing down on his neck; you said wait, I first must turn up this cricket hole with my toes. We said yours was the doorway at which we first spy the tapper when he comes down from the tree, yours was the blessing of the twilight wine, the purl that brings night spirits out of doors to steal their portion before the light of day. We said yours was the body of wine whose burden shakes the tapper like a sudden gust on his perch. You said, No, I am content to lick the dregs from each calabash when the drinkers are done. We said, the dew on earth's surface was for you to wash your feet along the slopes of honour. You said No, I shall step in the vomit of cats and the droppings of mice; I shall fight them for the left-overs of the world.

ELESIN: Enough Iyaloja, enough.

IYALOJA: We called you leader and oh, how you led us on. What we have no intention of eating should not be held to the nose.

ELESIN: Enough, enough. My shame is heavy enough.

IYALOJA: Wait, I came with a burden.

ELESIN: You have more than discharged it.

IYALOJA: I wish I could pity you.

ELESIN: I need neither your pity nor the pity of the world. I need understanding. Even I need to understand. You were present at my defeat. You were part of the beginnings. You brought about the renewal of my tie to earth, you helped in the binding of the cord.

IYALOJA: I gave you warning. The river which fills up before our eyes does not sweep us away in its flood.

ELESIN: What were warnings beside the moist contact of living earth between my fingers? What were warnings beside the renewal of famished embers lodged eternally in the heart of man. But even that, even if it over-whelmed one with a thousandfold temptations to linger a little while, a man could overcome it. It is when the alien hand pollutes the source of will, when a stranger force of violence shatters the mind's calm resolu-tion, this is when a man is made to commit the awful treachery of relief, commit in his thought the unspeakable blasphemy of seeing the hand of the gods in this alien rupture of his world. I know it was this thought that killed me, sapped my powers and turned me into an infant in the hands of unnamable strangers. I made to utter my spells anew but my tongue merely rattled in my mouth. I fingered hidden charms and the contact was damp; there was no spark left to sever the life-strings that should stretch from every finger-tip. My will was squelched in the spittle of an alien race, and all because I had committed this blasphemy of thought— that there might be the hand of the gods in a stranger's intervention.

IYALOJA: Explain it how you will, I hope it brings you peace of mind. The bush-rat fled his rightful cause, reached the market and set up a lamentation. "Please save me!"—are these fitting words to hear from an ancestral mask? "There's a wild beast at my heels" is not becoming language from a hunter.

ELESIN: May the world forgive me.

IYALOJA: I came with a burden I said. It approaches the gates which are so well guarded by those jackals whose spittle will from this day on be your food and drink. But first, tell me, you who were once Elesin Oba, tell me, you who know so well the cycle of the plantain: is it the parent shoot which withers to give sap to the younger or, does your wisdom see it running the other way?

ELESIN: I don't see your meaning Iyaloja?

IYALOJA: Did I ask you for a meaning? I asked a question. Whose trunk withers to give sap to the other? The parent shoot or the younger?

ELESIN: The parent.

IYALOJA: Ah. So you do know that. There are sights in this world which say different Elesin. There are some who choose to reverse this cycle of our being. Oh you emptied bark that the world once saluted for a pith-laden being, shall I tell you what the gods have claimed of you?

[In her agitation she steps beyond the line indicated by Pilkings and the air is rent by piercing whistles. The two Guards also leap forward and place safe-guarding hands on Elesin. Iyaloja stops, astonished. Pilkings comes racing in, followed by Jane.]

PILKINGS: What is it? Did they try something?

GUARD: She stepped beyond the line.

ELESIN: [In a broken voice.] Let her alone. She meant no harm.

IYALOJA: Oh Elesin, see what you've become. Once you had no need to open your mouth in explanation because evil-smelling goats, itchy of hand and foot had lost their senses. And it was a brave man indeed who dared lay hands on you because Iyaloja stepped from one side of the earth onto another. Now look at the spectacle of your life. I grieve for you.

PILKINGS: I think you'd better leave. I doubt you have done him much good by coming here. I shall make sure you are not allowed to see him again. In any case we are moving him to a different place before dawn, so don't bother to come back.

IYALOJA: We foresaw that. Hence the burden I trudged here to lay beside your gates.

PILKINGS: What was that you said?

IYALOJA: Didn't our son explain? Ask that one. He knows what it is. At least we hope the man we once knew as Elesin remembers the lesser oaths he need not break.

PILKINGS: Do you know what she is talking about?

ELESIN: Go to the gates, ghostly one. Whatever you find there, bring it to me.

IYALOJA: Not yet. It drags behind me on the slow, weary feet of women. Slow as it is Elesin, it has long overtaken you. It rides ahead of your laggard will.

PILKINGS: What is she saying now? Christ! Must your people forever speak in riddles?

ELESIN: It will come white man, it will come. Tell your men at the gates to let it through.

PILKINGS: [Dubiously.] I'll have to see what it is.

IYALOJA: You will. [Passionately.] But this is one oath he cannot shirk. White one, you have a king here, a visitor from your land. We know of his presence here. Tell me, were he to die would you leave his spirit roaming restlessly on the surface of earth? Would you bury him here among those you consider less than human? In your land have you no ceremonies of the dead?

PILKINGS: Yes. But we don't make our chiefs commit suicide to keep him company.

IYALOJA: Child, I have not come to help your understanding. *[Points to Elesin.]* This is the man whose weakened understanding holds us in bondage to you. But ask him if you wish. He knows the meaning of a king's passage; he was not born yesterday. He knows the peril to the race when our dead father, who goes as intermediary, waits and waits and knows he is betrayed. He knows when the narrow gate was opened and he knows it will not stay for laggards who drag their feet in dung and vomit, whose lips are reeking of the left-overs of lesser men. He knows he has condemned our king to wander in the void of evil with beings who are enemies of life.

PILKINGS: Yes er . . . but look here . . .

IYALOJA: What we ask is little enough. Let him release our King so he can ride on homewards alone. The messenger is on his way on the backs of women. Let him send word through the heart that is folded up within the bolt. It is the least of all his oaths, it is the easiest fulfilled.

[The Aide-de-Camp runs in.]

PILKINGS: Bob?

AIDE-DE-CAMP: Sir, there's a group of women chanting up the hill.

PILKINGS: *[Rounding on Iyaloja.]* If you people want trouble . . .

JANE: Simon, I think that's what Olunde referred to in his letter.

PILKINGS: He knows damned well I can't have a crowd here! Damn it, I explained the delicacy of my position to him. I think it's about time I got him out of town. Bob, send a car and two or three soldiers to bring him in. I think the sooner he takes his leave of his father and gets out the better.

IYALOJA: Save your labour white one. If it is the father of your prisoner you want, Olunde, he who until this night we knew as Elesin's son, he comes soon himself to take his leave. He has sent the women ahead, so let them in.

[Pilkings remains undecided.]

AIDE-DE-CAMP: What do we do about the invasion? We can still stop them far from here.

PILKINGS: What do they look like?

AIDE-DE-CAMP: They're not many. And they seem quite peaceful.

PILKINGS: No men?

AIDE-DE-CAMP: Mm, two or three at the most.

JANE: Honestly, Simon, I'd trust Olunde. I don't think he'll deceive you about their intentions.

PILKINGS: He'd better not. Alright, let them in Bob. Warn them to control themselves. Then hurry Olunde here. Make sure he brings his baggage because I'm not returning him into town.

AIDE-DE-CAMP: Very good sir. *[Goes.]*

PILKINGS: *[To Iyaloja.]* I hope you understand that if anything goes wrong it will be on your head. My men have orders to shoot at the first sign of trouble.

IYALOJA: To prevent one death you will actually make other deaths? Ah, great is the wisdom of the white race. But have no fear. Your Prince will sleep peacefully. So at long last will ours. We will disturb you no further, servant of the white king. Just let Elesin fulfil his oath and we will retire home and pay homage to our King.

JANE: I believe her Simon, don't you?

PILKINGS: Maybe.

ELESIN: Have no fear ghostly one. I have a message to send my King and then you have nothing more to fear.

IYALOJA: Olunde would have done it. The chiefs asked him to speak the words but he said no, not while you lived.

ELESIN: Even from the depths to which my spirit has sunk, I find some joy that this little has been left to me.

[The women enter, intoning the dirge 'Alę lę lę' and swaying from side to side. On their shoulders is borne a longish object roughly like a cylindrical bolt, covered in cloth. They set it down on the spot where Iyaloja had stood earlier, and form a semi-circle round it. The Praise-singer and Drummer stand on the inside of the semi-circle but the drum is not used at all. The Drummer intones under the Praise-singer's invocations.]

PILKINGS: *[As they enter.]* What is that?

IYALOJA: The burden you have made white one, but we bring it in peace.

PILKINGS: I said *what* is it?

ELESIN: White man, you must let me out. I have a duty to perform.

PILKINGS: I most certainly will not.

ELESIN: There lies the courier of my King. Let me out so I can perform what is demanded of me.

PILKINGS: You'll do what you need to do from inside there or not at all. I've gone as far as I intend to with this business.

ELESIN: The worshipper who lights a candle in your church to bear a message to his god bows his head and speaks in a whisper to the flame. Have I not seen it ghostly one? His voice does not ring out to the world. Mine are no words for anyone's ears. They are not words even for the bearers of this load. They are words I must speak secretly, even as my father whispered them in my ears and I in the ears of my first-born. I cannot shout them to the wind and the open night-sky.

JANE: Simon . . .

PILKINGS: Don't interfere. Please!

IYALOJA: They have slain the favourite horse of the king and slain his dog. They have borne them from pulse to pulse centre of the land receiving prayers for their king. But the rider has chosen to stay behind. Is it too much to ask that he speak his heart to heart of the waiting courier? *[Pilkings turns his back on her.]* So be it. Elesin Oba, you see how even the mere leavings are denied you. *[She gestures to the Praise-singer.]*

PRAISE-SINGER: Elesin Oba! I call you by that name only this last time. Remember
when I said, if you cannot come, tell my horse. [Pause.] What? I cannot
hear you? I said, if you cannot come, whisper in the ears of my horse. Is
your tongue severed from the roots Elesin? I can hear no response. I said,
if there are boulders you cannot climb, mount my horse's back, this
spotless black stallion, he'll bring you over them. [Pauses.] Elesin Oba,
once you had a tongue that darted like a drummer's stick. I said, if you
get lost my dog will track a path to me. My memory fails me but I think
you replied: My feet have found the path, Alafin.

[The dirge rises and falls.]

I said at the last, if evil hands hold you back, just tell my horse there is
weight on the hem of your smock. I dare not wait too long.

[The dirge rises and falls.]

There lies the swiftest ever messenger of a king, so set me free with the
errand of your heart. There lie the head and heart of the favourite of the
gods, whisper in his ears. Oh my companion, if you had followed when
you should, we would not say that the horse preceded its rider. If you
had followed when it was time, we would not say the dog has raced
beyond and left his master behind. If you had raised your will to cut the
thread of life at the summons of the drums, we would not say your mere
shadow fell across the gateway and took its owner's place at the banquet.
But the hunter, laden with a slain buffalo, stayed to root in the cricket's
hole with his toes. What now is left? If there is a dearth of bats, the pigeon
must serve us for the offering. Speak the words over your shadow which
must now serve in your place.

ELESIN: I cannot approach. Take off the cloth. I shall speak my message from heart
to heart of silence.

IYALOJA: [Moves forward and removes the covering.] Your courier Elesin, cast your
eyes on the favoured companion of the King.

[Rolled up in the mat, his head and feet showing at either end is the body of
Olunde.]

There lies the honour of your household and of our race. Because he
could not bear to let honour fly out of doors, he stopped it with his life.
The son has proved the father Elesin, and there is nothing left in your
mouth to gnash but infant gums.

PRAISE-SINGER: Elesin, we placed the reins of the world in your hands yet you
watched it plunge over the edge of the bitter precipice. You sat with folded
arms while evil strangers tilted the world from its course and crashed it
beyond the edge of emptiness—you muttered, there is little that one man
can do, you left us floundering in a blind future. Your heir has taken the
burden on himself. What the end will be, we are not gods to tell. But this
young shoot has poured its sap into the parent stalk, and we know this is
not the way of life. Our world is tumbling in the void of strangers, Elesin.

[Elesin has stood rock-still, his knuckles taut on the bars, his eyes glued to the body of his son. The stillness seizes and paralyses everyone, including Pilkings who has turned to look. Suddenly Elesin flings one arm round his neck, once, and with the loop of the chain, strangles himself in a swift, decisive pull. The guards rush forward to stop him but they are only in time to let his body down. Pilkings has leapt to the door at the same time and struggles with the lock. He rushes within, fumbles with the handcuffs and unlocks them, raises the body to a sitting position while he tries to give resuscitation. The women continue their dirge, unmoved by the sudden event.]

IYALOJA: Why do you strain yourself? Why do you labour at tasks for which no one, not even the man lying there would give you thanks? He is gone at last into the passage but oh, how late it all is. His son will feast on the meat and throw him bones. The passage is clogged with droppings from the King's stallion; he will arrive all stained in dung.

PILKINGS: *[In a tired voice.]* Was this what you wanted?

IYALOJA: No child, it is what you brought to be, you who play with strangers' lives, who even usurp the vestments of our dead, yet believe that the stain of death will not cling to you. The gods demanded only the old expired plantain but you cut down the sap-laden shoot to feed your pride. There is your board, filled to overflowing. Feast on it. *[She screams at him suddenly, seeing that Pilkings is about to close Elesin's staring eyes.]* Let him alone! However sunk he was in debt he is no pauper's carrion abandoned on the road. Since when have strangers donned clothes of indigo before the bereaved cries out his loss?

[She turns to the Bride who has remained motionless throughout.]

Child.

[The girl takes up a little earth, walks calmly into the cell and closes Elesin's eyes. She then pours some earth over each eyelid and comes out again.]

Now forget the dead, forget even the living. Turn your mind only to the unborn.

[She goes off, accompanied by the Bride. The dirge rises in volume and the women continue their sway. Lights fade to a black-out.]

GLOSSARY

agbada	a type of clothing
Alafin	the title of a Yoruba ruler
alari	a rich, woven cloth, brightly coloured
egungun	ancestral masquerade
etutu	placatory rites or medicine
gbedu	a deep-timbred royal drum
opele	string of beads used in Ifa divination
osugbo	secret "executive" cult of the Yoruba; its meeting place

robo	a delicacy made from crushed melon seeds, fried in tiny balls
sanyan	a richly valued woven cloth
sigidi	a squat, carved figure, endowed with the powers of an incubus

ASSIA DJÉBAR (b. 1936)
Algeria/France; French

Algerian women—veiled, cloistered in their domesticity, silenced by their Islamic culture and their illiteracy—have only recently begun to write, and only in French if they were from enlightened families who sent them to the Francophone schools. Assia Djébar, Algeria's most famous contemporary woman writer, first published *La Soif* in 1957, in the midst of the 1954–1962 Algerian War. Her struggles as a woman writer and filmmaker viewing history from a specifically feminist point of view in a traditionally patriarchal society give a special dimension to her writing. "Ramadan Day" is taken from a collection of short stories and essays written between 1958 and 1970, and entitled, after the famous painting by Eugène Delacroix, *Women of Algiers in Their Apartment.* It deals with Djébar's pressing concerns: the relationship of the Algerian woman to her traditional, religious, cloistered past; her role in the Algerian War; her relations with her Arab sisters and the men in her life—father, husband, son; and finally, her position in postindependence Algeria. In "Ramadan Day" women gather, as is the Muslim custom during the month-long fasting period, to keep each other company, telling stories until the one meal permitted each evening. In this small gem the writer weaves personal, political, and generational conflicts into a text and culture where women are still struggling to speak their minds. Djébar concentrates on dialogue here, stressing the need for women to voice their opinions in Algeria today.

from **Women of Algiers in Their Apartment**

Ramadan Day

The time grows longer on fast days, the houses grow deep, the shade grows translucent and the body languid.

"How the seasons fly," Lla Fatouma began.

"How fasting flies!" Nadjia hummed.

"You'll see how it feels in the winter! Soft and tender as wool, the winter Ramadan[1]"—and Lla Fatouma, heavy and imposing, started her housework again.

Translated by Mary Ann Caws and Ronnie Scharfman.

---

1. The ninth month of the Muslim year, during which the faithful fast daily, between sunrise and sunset.

"I remember"—murmured Houria, the eldest of the girls—"when I began at ten, yes . . . it was winter."

"No, fall," the second one corrected her.—"The oranges were still green, I'm sure of it. I was eight and one day I fasted, one day I didn't."

Nfissa contemplated her sisters without saying anything. Their father had gone out, Lla Fatouma was now praying in a corner of the big living room, while Nfissa was piling up the sheep skins that had been used for their naps. The others were busy, but in a disordered way due to the change of housekeeping habits in these first days of Ramadan.

The time grows longer, the houses grow deep, the shade grows translucid and the body languid: again, Nfissa's mind analyzes, then wanders about negligent among its memories—formerly, in the same season, she and Nadjia who were impatient to begin fasting (when would they finally get permission? The family refused to wake them up in the middle of the night for the strengthening meal.) Once upon a time, just yesterday . . .

Yesterday, Nfissa was in prison . . . Ramadan among truly sequestered women, that French prison where they had been grouped, six "rebels"—so they said—who were going to be judged.

They had begun their fast happy as ascetics: exile and chains became immaterial, a deliverance from the body that turns around in the cell but suddenly no longer bumping into the walls; two French women arrested in the same network had joined the Islamic observance and, in spite of the dreariness of the soup at twilight, how the respite stretched out beyond the gray hours, how the vigil song, in spite of the guard, seemed to cross the sea, to rejoin the mountains of the fatherland!

"The first Ramadan without any suffering!" murmured Lla Fatouma, going back to her kitchen.

"It's still all wrapped up in it though!" Houria moaned quietly.

Only Nfissa, who was pretending to read, heard this. She looked up at their eldest sister: twenty-eight and already a widow. "If at least he had left me a child, a son who could remind me of his face!" she had complained for months.

"To raise a child without a man around, you can't imagine the difficulties!" the mother replied. "You are young. God will bring you a new husband, God will fill your house with a harvest of little angels!"

"God willing!" the others responded in chorus. From the kitchen, the smell of grilled pepper.

"Four o'clock already!" . . . Still two hours of patience!

"I haven't felt hungry or thirsty!" Nadjia exclaimed, spinning about. She suddenly felt she was in some festival, turned on the radio, and gave a little dance step.

"To fast in the middle of laughter and joy!" she declared, in mock gaiety "My fast will count double!"

Houria had gone into a wash of nostalgia. Nfissa looked hard and long at her younger sister: nineteen, her eyes lit with pride, so thin it was almost disturbing.

"You should be making less noise!" she warned, half-smiling indulgently. "Houria remembers!"

"Me too, I remember! You may have been in prison, but so have I, right here, in this house you find so marvelous."

Nadjia's voice grew harsh: she sprang up, gave a sharp little laugh, and stopped still, confronting Nfissa, ready for another quarrel.

"You're not going to start that again!"—grumbled Nfissa, going back to her reading.

"If you get angry, well then, your fast won't count at all!" Lla Fatouma's jovial voice broke in from the kitchen doorway.

Her arms were bare: she had pulled off her organdy blouse, and was now wearing nothing but an undershirt decorated in the old-fashioned way. She had been kneading the dough for some cookies and pink with the effort, went out to wash her hands in the courtyard basin. The household became a kingdom of women, since their father was not coming home until sunset, a few minutes before the mueddin's[2] song was to come through the vine-branches and the languorous jasmine. The village mosque was nearby.

At her mother's words, Nadjia shrugged her shoulders sadly, unable to do anything about it. Lla Fatouma had understood without having heard the exchange: during the last two years of the war, Nadjia's father had made her interrupt her studies. Nadjia, since independence, had been wanting to resume them, to go to town and work, to be a teacher or a student, it didn't matter, but to work: a family drama was brewing.

'Ramadan brings a truce to everything bitter! A dark heart will never gain remission . . . ," Lla Fatouma murmured to herself when she came back.

She crossed the room, put her blouse back on with the slow gestures of a queen, and then returned to her cooking. At the breaking of the fast, Nfissa and Nadjia were waiting in front of the low table laden with dishes for the others, including their father, to finish their twilight prayer. The meal took place almost in silence because of the presence of the father, who, right after the coffee, left to participate in a religious wake. Then some women neighbors came for a visit, chirping in the courtyard, pulling down sails and veils, sitting down sighing on the sofas.

"During those seven years of war," one of them began, "everyone stayed home!". . .

"With our daughter in enemy hands, how could we have the heart to drink coffee?" another exclaimed, speaking to Nfissa, then embracing and blessing her.

Nadjia greeted the women, exchanging the interminable formulas of politeness with them, and then went out silently. To Nfissa, who came to bring her back in vain:

"No!" she protested. "Gossiping, gorging on cakes, filling yourself up waiting for tomorrow, is it for that there was mourning and blood? No, I won't settle for it . . . Me,"—and her voice choked with tears—"I believed, don't you see, that all that would change, that something else would come, that. . . ." Nadjia burst into tears, buried her face in her pillow on her same childhood bed.

Nfissa went out without responding.

"If we could at least forget!"—said one old woman who had lost her two sons

---

2. Also *muezzin;* a Muslim functionary who
    calls the faithful to prayer from the minaret
    of a mosque.

in the war, interrupting the conversation. "We could get back the Ramadans we used to have, the serenity we had!"

A silence came upon the room, uncertain, imbued with regrets.

"Fortunate are the martyrs of the faith!" . . . Lla Fatouma said gravely, coming back in with a teapot in her hand.

The fragrance of the mint wafted out to the courtyard thick with night, and Houria went out to dry her tears.

NABILE FARÈS (b. 1941)
Algeria/France; French

Nabile Farès is truly a son of the Algerian War (1954–1962). Radicalized by the struggle against colonialism and then, in the late 1960s and early 1970s, discouraged by the abuses and failures of the National Liberation Front government that took power after independence, Farès chose exile in Spain and France. But his growing corpus of highly poetic works—even his novels, which are like those of Kateb Yacine—is profoundly rooted in the culture of his origins, Arabian and Berber, that of the Kabyle region of northern Algeria. His work constitutes an on-going dialogue between archaic and modern, traditional oral culture with its myths, proverbs, and songs, and contemporary European literary forms, particularly the novel. The poem "The ( ) Writing Against All Silence" appeared in the prestigious French Journal *Europe,* in a special volume devoted to Algerian literature in 1976. By this time, Farès had already written four major novels dealing with the upheavals of the Algerian War. In this moving, disturbing poem, he makes use of polyphonic devices, inscribing multiple voices in the poem through graphic indications, such as quotation marks and italics, as a way of mediating between the narrator's personal, individual experience of loss and wound, and a collective memory of both pride and struggle. The purpose of evoking the pains and promises of resistance in this stream-of-consciousness way is to project both writer and people beyond the tragic martyrdom of "the brother" toward a meaningful solidarity where a future community can be constructed. The disrupted narrative, the moving back and forth among past, present, and future, the theme of the war and death, the rural imagery, are all characteristics of Farès's literary concerns.

from *The ( ) Writing Against All Silence*

II

[There were meetings without end, meetings upon meetings]

There were meetings without end, meetings upon meetings just about everywhere in the buildings the countrysides and the fields. Meetings which wanted to say

Translated by Mary Ann Caws and Ronnie Scharfman.

Baya. *Women Carrying Vessels*. 1966. Gouache on paper. Musée de l'Institut du Monde Arabe.

everything at a fell swoop for so much time (that's it) there-was-so-much-time to catch up with on long races

and then
a great leap
not into emptiness
but into the world the word and the song
a great leap of tenderness and desires
the brother gave up his life
what he had
what he had—in sum nothing
or his life: exactly
everything he had and that he gave—
his life—
the brother gave up his life
naively
naively
generously as if
he were giving nothing
but his coat or nothing
or his life—the brother

—that is to say
that after a certain
time

                    like a worm
                    the petty bourgeoisie
                    came to life
                    advantage
                    in the . . . revolution.—
        —that is to say
                really to say
        after a certain
        but
        (already) a bout of
        anger or
        from the effects of
        anger
        for the lands where
        man and the fields become together freshly then the

countrysides open
        the countrysides want to come to the other side of the
harvest Faces of the people Workers of the lands demanding claiming
requiring what it is owed
        its pleasure its ecstasy the land which lasts in exiles
dreams and detours.
        So the Power
        the one who says he is the Power
        for how could he not be the Power?
        the Power says
        because of the land which
        is moving accuse
        speak denounce: power says
        Agrarian Revolution
        Revolution to Bring About
        A Revolution to Bring About . . .

III

[So my brother]

So my brother
the oldest the most the
one who haunted the village
and who was to die there
alone
far from himself
and from us . . .
brother.
                for the others-his
                to speak sing shout

and sometimes flee run fly
so He in the veiled retreat speech where
we are working speech where
we are living
   alike
   in the
   fire of desiring
   dazzling
      love (death-life).
We,
   values
     and
shadows
       running through
          the sayable
  in
   the
    gesture
     of
      living.

ARTHUR NORTJE (1942–1970)
South Africa; English

Arthur Nortje, a young suicide and a casualty of "the isolation of exile," was a brilliant black South African poet and scholar whose promise can be seen in his posthumous volume *Dead Roots* (1973). What Nortje said of famous exiles of an older generation—Peter Abrahams, Es'kia Mphahlele, Dennis Brutus—is also true of himself: "the blond/colossus vomits its indigestible/black stepchildren like autotoxins" ("Autopsy," 1966). He was a poet of sad inwardness and Baudelairean spleen, a fierce outsider in the British poetic climate, like Sylvia Plath, for whom he wrote two poems. Although he wrote despairingly of his teacher and friend Dennis Brutus that "the luminous tongue in the black world / has infinite possibilities no longer," the end of his "Native's Letter," a poem of 1970, suggests that Nortje even in exile saw value in the sharp witnessing of poetry: "some of us must storm the castles / some define the happening." Reciting the names of nineteenth-century warriors—Adam Kok, Shaka, Hendrik Witbooi—this text is, like his others, a passionate identification with the South African struggle. "At Lansdowne Bridge," written in Cape Town in 1964 and included here, is a delicate act of "defining the happening," bridging the text of graffiti and the writer of poems, who "holds" the political act in the "spidery light" of that action at a distance which is art, and most poignantly art in prison, art in exile.

from **Dead Roots**

At Lansdowne Bridge

After the whoosh of doors slid shut
at Lansdowne Bridge I swim in echoes.
Who fouled the wall O people?
FREE THE DETAINEES someone wrote there.

Black letters large as life stare you   5
hard by day in the black face;
above the kikuye grass[1] to the sandflats
goes the boorish clang-clang of railways.

Darkness neutralizes the request
till dawn falls golden and sweet,   10
though a sudden truck by night
cornering, holds it in spidery light.

(Cape Town, May 1964)

Native's letter

Habitable planets are unknown or too
far away from us to be
of consequence. To be of
value to his homeland must the wanderer
not weep by northern waters, but love   5
his own bitter clay
roaming through the hard cities, tough
himself as coffin nails.

Harping on the nettles of his melancholy,
keening on the blue strings of the blood,   10
he will delve into mythologies perhaps
call up spirits through the night.

Or carry memories apocryphal
of Tshaka, Hendrik Witbooi, Adam Kok,[1]
of the Xhosa nation's dream[2]   15
as he moonlights in another country:

At Lansdowne Bridge

1. A type of sharp-bladed grass.

Native's Letter

1. Tshaka: The military genius who built the
early 19th-century Zulu state. Hendrik
Witbooi: leader of the Nama people of
Namibia against the German colonial army

in 1905. Adam Kok: founder of the Griqua
community, a frontier people of mixed race
who remained independent 1795–1880.

2. The prophecy of the princess Nongqause,
which in 1856–57 led many Xhosa to destroy their crops and cattle, as a magical act
to bring victory in battle.

but he shall also have
cycles of history
outnumbering the guns of supremacy.

Now and wherever he arrives   20
extending feelers into foreign scenes
exploring times and lives,
equally may he stand and laugh,
explode with a paper bag of poems,
burst upon a million televisions   25
with a face as in a Karsh photograph,
slave voluntarily in some siberia
to earn the salt of victory.

Darksome, whoever dies
in the malaise of my dear land   30
remember me at swim,
the moving waters spilling through my eyes:
and let no amnesia
attack at fire hour:
for some of us must storm the castles   35
some define the happening.

                                        Toronto, May 1970

MONGANE WALLY SEROTE (b. 1944)
South Africa; English

Mongane Wally Serote gives direct poetic voice to the Black Consciousness
movement, led by Steve Bantu Biko, which swept up black students and
intellectuals in South Africa from the mid-1960s to the late 1970s. It is a black
voice directed to black readers in a spirit of mobilization for black unity against
racism. Although Serote is today working again with the African National
Congress, at that time he had made a clean break with the nonracial policy of the
old ANC and with the passive resistance or "protest" politics it shared with the
nationalist Pan-African Congress (PAC). His aim, along with other *Staffrider*
writers like Ndebele, Mattera, Sepamla, Douts, Gwala and Banoobhai, was black
self-determination and self-representation. "My Brothers in the Streets" delivers
an intense appeal for black unity against the divisiveness of sexism.

My Brothers in the Streets
Oh you black boys,
You thin shadows who emerge like a chill in the night,

You whose heart-tearing footsteps sound in the night,
My brothers in the streets,
Who holiday in jails,   5
Who rest in hospitals,
Who smile at insults,
Who fear the whites,
Oh you black boys,
You horde-waters[1] that sweep over black pastures,   10
You bloody bodies that dodge bullets,
My brothers in the streets,
Who booze and listen to records,
Who've tasted rape of mothers and sisters,
Who take alms from white hands,   15
Who grab bread from black mouths,
Oh you black boys,
Who spill blood as easy as saying 'Voetsek'[2]
Listen!
Come my black brothers in the streets,   20
Listen,
It's black women who are crying.

MUHAMMAD ZAFZÂF (b. 1945)

Morocco

Muhammad Zafzâf studied at Muhammad V University in Rabat. He is considered by most critics to be one of the most outstanding Moroccan authors writing in Arabic. Primarily known for his novels and short stories, Zafzâf has nevertheless written dramatic works and criticism. His novels include *The Woman and the Rose* and *Graves in the Water*.

Men and Mules

That day the collected all the mules of the village.

"Why the mules, particularly?" we asked ourselves. But then they came back and rounded up all the donkeys as well. And no one was able to know why they had gathered all the mules and donkeys, for they, and they alone, had the answer.

Translated by Lena Jayyusi and Thomas G. Ezzy.

1. Both a "horde" (invading force) and
   floodwaters.

2. Get lost!

Late that night our mules and donkeys returned to us. As they arrived a trumpet blared, and we awoke in panic. We discovered that behind our own donkeys and mules was a line of other donkeys and mules, and that behind them was a line of barefoot men—people like us, who had come from other villages in the plain.

And behind them came armed soldiers. Of these, there were only a handful, that could be counted on the tips of one's fingers. They singled out the young men among us.

"Put your hands above your heads!" they said. "And don't try to make any noise by scraping your shoes on the ground!"

This was a rather silly thing for them to say, since not one of us had any shoes to wear, not even slippers, in fact.

Yet, one of the foreigners struck me with the butt of his rifle and insisted: "Got that? No shoe-scraping!"

Feeling still heavy with sleep, I bent my head to see if I might actually have come into a pair of shoes. He hit me again. I straightened out and woke up. He passed on behind me and harangued the others, perhaps with the same warning.

The ground was cold. Because it had been raining there were small puddles beneath our feet. As the mules and donkeys filed falteringly by, we could hear the squishing of their hooves, and every so often water would spatter under our *jilbabs*[1] and up to our thighs. This felt chilly, for at the time we owned no trousers—neither of the European nor of the baggy Moroccan types. Our bodies winced, but we stayed shivering where we stood. We could not even budge because the slightest stir might provoke a rifle shot.

For a while we remained standing among the puddles. Then, they pushed all the women and children and old people into the huts. To the rest of us they said, in an Arabic that was hard to understand:

"Each of you is to take charge of a mule. Do you see those mountains? We will split up into smaller groups and rendezvous there. If any one of you makes one false move—or gives us any kind of trouble—then, one single bullet will take care of him!"

I was certain that none of us would make the slightest move, so the warning did not seemed called for. Or, perhaps it was: one of us might make a wrong move unawares. And, as a result, one single bullet would take care of him. . . .

Though we did not know it at the time, the mules were loaded with arms—each was carrying two cannons, in fact, and it had been decided that we would all have to climb those rugged hills. No one could ride his mule except for the foreigners, who were to march behind and guard us in case someone tried to escape and hide among the thick trees that grew in various places. I was sure that none of us would dare such a thing, especially since the weather was chilly and rain was threatening to fall any minute. And besides, what could any of us hope to do against these foreigners, with their rifles and pistols?

We walked in a single column, each behind a mule. The mules were not close

---

1. Also jellaba or djellaba; a long gown, sometimes woven, worn by men and women in
   North Africa.

together but spaced, with intervals between them. The foreigners had taken part of the mules on another road. I did not know whether friends of mine from our village had gone with that group because we were not allowed to turn our heads either to the left or to the right. What we had to do was look straight ahead of us and keep walking behind our mules towards those mountains. As to what the mules were carrying, it was none of our business to know: it was only later that we found out about the cannons, the big iron chains, and the rest of it.

And as to where we were going, and why, that also we found out later on. . . . Some of the tribes had risen in revolt against the authorities, and these weapons were to be used to put down their uprising. This had not been as easy as one might think: so far, the foreigners had not been able to make their way across any of the valleys without being ambushed from behind the rocks. One night, after a battle in the mountains in which the tribes had beaten the foreigners, these latter, in the belief that we too had been there shooting at them from above and behind, had descended on our village, bent on avenging their honour. They had killed a good number among us, slashing open the bellies of pregnant women to remove the embryos, and then they had completely withdrawn and not come back again.

Until today. Now here they were, pointing their rifles at our backs and chests. There were both whites and blacks among them. The blacks, it was said, were Muslims like us, who prayed and fasted and gave alms. We did not find this too surprising, since it was a well-known fact that there were Muslims in the foreigners' army. . . .

As we walked, we kept expecting that the sun would rise soon. When it didn't, we began to suspect that the time was not close to daybreak, as we'd thought, but closer to midnight instead. The cold was biting and the wind was strong, and the wolf-like howls of animals came to us from the valleys. There was no light, and the dark was intense; we could not see the mountains, but we could visualise them. We had to bear the cold and keep pace with all the others. Occasionally a cursed mule or donkey would stop, and one of us would get the blame. I would hear the grunting of a mule and then hear the sound of a hard blow. I would imagine the blow falling on a man's back, but, whenever a man did not cry out, it was safe to assume a mule had got it that time.

We had heard that those tribes had rebelled again, but we had not been certain of anything, since we lived in the plain. There had been rumours that some of our men, despite tight security, had actually gone to join the tribes in the mountains and were there now fighting beside them. I wondered why they should have accepted any of us even though we had never in our lives had any experience in the use of arms. . . .

"Walk, Bourkabi!" said a foreigner behind me. His Arabic was so clear that I suspected he was not a foreigner at all. (Later we learned that some of the officers were Algerian, though their fair and ruddy complexions made them look like foreigners.)

For fear he would strike me, I hurried to catch up with my mule, who had started running despite the weight of his load. Other mules were not doing this, and I had no idea what had got into mine. Nevertheless, I took hold of his tail and let him pull me along with him.

We could hear the growls of distant dogs, which grew louder until their echoes reverberated everywhere. The darkness deepened, so that I could not make out the outlines of the other mules. I felt very tired, and envied the foreigners their privilege of following us on muleback. I thought of running away, but how could I? They could have flushed me out of anywhere, even my mother's womb. . . .

At last the mules began to work their way up the slopes, and deep fatigue came over all of us. I held on tighter to my mule's tail and felt he was dragging me along. I realised that if it hadn't been for this, I would not have been able to make the climb, especially after such a long walk. . . .

It seemed clear that the foreigners intended to surprise the tribespeople in their sleep, and then do to them what they had done to us before: slaughter and dismember them, skin them and tan their hides. I did not believe that they would succeed, however, because the tribespeople were armed, while we had not been. . . .

As the mules kept climbing, I could feel an intense cold rise up from the ground, seep under my *jilbab,* and spread into my belly, my chest, and the whole of my body. To top it off, rain began to fall—slowly at first, then hard and strong. Mules began to lose each other beneath the sheets of rain. They stumbled and almost fell beneath the weight of their loads.

The order came for us to stop. At first we thought it was because they had taken pity on us, for most of us were wearing clothes that could not protect them from the cold and rain. I was one of the lucky ones because I was wearing a *jilbab,* and I thought of those who had on only shirt-dresses. How could they bear this damnable weather?

Mules and men, we huddled beneath a great overhanging rock. Up and down the column, other teams were doing the same thing. We could not see them, but we learned of it later on. The rains poured down so heavily that the mules began to whimper. One of the foreigners chose a well-protected spot, lit a cigarette, and began to smoke it. Someone approached him and began to speak to him. We ourselves had no right to speak, and we heard that person tell us:

"The Sholouh want to kill every last one of you. But we will not give them the chance to!"

The man was a Moroccan, then, who spoke the foreigners' language fluently. I wondered where he had learned it. For all I knew, he might even have been one of the Sholouh, but the foreigners had been able to turn him into another kind of person—into a foreigner like themselves. . . .

I thought of sitting down, but I was afraid of the foreigner. They had forbidden us to sit. Two mules began to move and stamp the ground with their hooves. My mother, God rest her soul, had once told me that if a mule cut a groove in the ground with its heel, this meant that one of your relatives was dead. I became afraid that death had snatched one of my family. . . .

My *jilbab* was now clinging to my body, and still the foreigner took no pity on us. I pressed close to the mule, but it moved away from me. The Moroccan returned to the foreigner and spoke to him in his own language. The foreigner leapt to his feet.

"Get ready, all of you," the soldier told us. "We have not been able to take them by surprise the way we wanted to."

How could we prepare ourselves to kill our brothers in Faith, I wondered; moreover, we had no training in the use of arms. . . .

The soldier walked hurriedly into the darkness until we could no longer see him. At the same time, the foreigner in charge of us began to wheel around and jabber at us in his own language. I wondered if he had gone mad. He shouted in my face, gave me a hard shove, and gestured towards the mule. I saw my neighbor shivering with cold. He was someone I knew. There were six men in our group, aside from the foreigner.

When I showed no sign of understanding what he said, the foreigner came back and said, "Cochon!" (I found out later this means "pig".) He gave me a sharp slap and a kick in the belly. I felt pain but kept silent. The rain was still pouring savagely. At last he ordered us to continue our ascent, one mule after another and a man behind each.

In the dark we came upon a small hut with no light showing and its door open. With his rifle at the ready, the foreigner approached it and told one of us to enter and bring out whoever was inside. When the man came out and reported that the hut was empty of any trace of humans, the foreigner did not believe him, so he pointed a flashlight inside the hut. All of us could see there was no one inside. Then he ordered us to continue climbing.

Exhausted, we walked on. Then suddenly we heard rifle shots. The mules became recalcitrant. They grunted, brayed, then stopped in their tracks.

The tribespeople were on the alert then. The foreigner ordered us to beat the mules so we could get going, but none of us had a stick. We began to hit them with our hands, but they did not budge. The shots stopped, then rang out again. The reports resonated from the valleys and mountains, came to us mixed with the wind and the rain. From out of the dark two other soldiers joined us and began beating the mules with their rifle butts. With reluctance, the mules began to move. Their task accomplished, the soldiers headed back to where they'd come from. It seemed to me I heard one of them stumble and fall to the ground. The shooting intensified, and I became afraid for myself.

The foreigner told us to walk close to the rocks for cover. No sooner had he spoken than a volley of bullets whizzed over our heads. I saw something gushing out of my mule's body. It was blood. He had been hit, whether by one or many bullets I could not tell. I used him as a shield, and could hear the foreigner moaning. The other mules scattered in the dark and pressed up against boulders.

There was no sign of the rest of the men. I was certain they had all got away. Nearby, the foreigner was stretched out beneath a small jutting rock. He was wounded. He fired a few shots, until pain overwhelmed him. I drew back a few steps from him, but he ordered me to stop where I was. I did not understand his Arabic at first, but I stood as he aimed his rifle at my chest. Then he let it fall. I reached out into the mule's saddlebag, which was close to me. When my hand touched a piece of light metal, I pulled it out and hid it behind my back.

In his pain, the foreigner was screaming into the downpour, "Get back here, Cochon! Where are your friends? Come closer!"

There was no sign of my companions who had escaped with their lives. Even the mules—except for mine and another one further up—had disappeared under the hail of bullets and rain. I started to draw near him in the dark. I felt an anger that had no limits. The blood boiled in my head. The piece of metal trembled in my hand; I wanted to pounce on him with it, but I hesitated. Slowly, I began to move backwards. The mule had moved lower down the slope.

Once again the foreigner ordered me to stop and come closer. This time he did not point his rifle at me right from the start. Then as he did, I heard him give a loud scream. Obviously, another bullet had struck him. I began to quake with fear that perhaps a stray bullet might hit me. I threw the piece of metal down. Ignoring his orders, I found myself running downhill. Then I stumbled into a mule stretched out in the road. I fell to the ground. Bullets were still whizzing through the air, coming from somewhere or other. In my panic I stood up and ran, with no idea of where I was going.

"Halt!" called a voice, this time in the Sholouh tongue. When I kept going, a shot was fired at me. I stopped. A man wearing a short *jilbab* and a *barnous*[2] sprang on me. Another man joined him.

"Are you with them, traitor?" asked the first man.

"No, by God! I'm not a foreigner! They took us by force! I don't even know how to use a gun!"

"Be quiet!"

"They slaughtered us! Then they took our mules. . . ."

"Let him go," the second man said. "He's not one of them."

But the first man paid no attention. He grabbed me, led me to a small tree, and tied me to its trunk. I offered no resistance.

"Stay here until we come back!" he said.

But they did not come back. Who knows, perhaps they were killed?

By the time the sun came up, I could no longer hear the whine of bullets. I tried to figure out where I was but could not. The whole place was enfolded in silence; the rain had stopped falling and the ground was wet. With great difficulty I untied my knots and made off, exhausted, looking for a path that would lead me back to my village.

In that battle, the tribes had captured the cannons, the arms—everything, even the mules. And despite the fact that they are Moroccans, like us, and Muslims, they have still not, to this day, returned our mules to us.

B. KOJO LAING (b. 1946)
Ghana/Scotland; English

B. Kojo Laing was educated in Scotland. He has been a school principal and a novelist (*Search Sweet Country*, 1986; *Woman of the Airplanes*, 1988) as well as a

---

2. Also burnoose, a hooded cloak worn by Arabs.

Hezbon Owiti. *Goodbye*. 1968. Linocut.

poet. "Godhorse," reflecting the influence of Christianity on contemporary Ghana, satirizes the hypocritical words of a church preaching racial hatred.

Godhorse

The horse with birds on its mane, doubt on its tail . . .
doubt about the flies being whisked north or south . . .
crawled out of the relieved horizon, in
a burst of dung part-coloured with kente.[1]
And the angle at which the horse bisected the hills,   5
made it easy for the old man with the square body
to jump up its decorated left flank, leaving
half his age behind as his bones came down like a pounder.
Galloping was a definition of time, more
for the man, less for the horse   10
whose high brown snorting would be framed
if only there were strong hands,
if only the ancestors would jump the centuries.
Now a woman raised her right breast on the right flank

---

1. A woven cloth of blue, gold, and red, which
   was the mark of royalty in Ghana.

of this horse of wonder, this horse   15
with a mane maimed by the limiting beauty of birds.
Mansa's whole body shook—O god of soft thunder!—
as the old man stretched his lust across horse flesh,
trying to speed through the geography of tails, but
suddenly meeting ghana   20
                half-way up the horse instead; suddenly
seeing bishops and fetish priests
so that his reverence gently covered his lust, true
the religious men wanted to bless the impudent hooves, but
the horse threw off angels with a burst of shank, with   25
the old man kneeling on the saddle and begging Mansa for love,
as her breasts shook in incense.
Since the sun and moon were
                in a simultaneous sky,
Mansa watched half a country hang on half a horse,   30
                watched the old man's smiles and rejected
                each one,
throwing the most outrageous one under the hardest hoof.

Pound your laughter, pound your world!
Rejection was no different, even when mixed with speed,   35
old man's nails were digging into horse country,
old man's knees were shaking the shanks
                of a suddenly stationary stallion:
horse hair was full of brown regret,
                was full of the morality of not galloping   40
when the country was sagging with the speed of time.
But let horse dung salute accra!
Let the blue moon burst over a clear gallop!
Let them rise against the unwanted pity of the horse ethics!
We want the african touch, neighed the horse, for   45
it desperately loved Mansa's thigh pressing against it. But
old man shouted the horse on. Onnnn!
For the half of ghana that was missing
                was merely the gaps in his old teeth,
                was merely the spatial side of galloping.   50
On! Human flesh orbits horse flesh!
Old man falls from flank to flank,
bouncing across a withering country, shivering
under the weight of horse decrees
                that Mansa carried on behalf of the   55
                authorities.
On! with the most moral horse in the world, for its
thighs did not return the pressure of Mansa's thighs, for

after all the universe was a stilled gallop,   60
    was an old man crawling away from a
     cantering, crazy life,
    was a contradictory shank shaking.
As Mansa fell off at last by the tune of a distant highlife,
the horse snorted for other women, the
   horse . . . its morality lost in its speed at last . . .   65
     threw off the old man.
Man, poor, old: he died with a smile before he hit the ground:
    and under him were the crushed birds, O God,
    carrying their expanding beauty still, still.

KOFI ANYIDOHO (b. 1947)
Ghana; English

Kofi Anyidoho, a poet and university professor, expresses a deep rootedness in
his Ewe culture. "Festival of Hopes," written in 1975, transposes into poetry an
Ewe cleansing rite that reaffirms tradition and its underlying balance.

Festival of Hopes

3rd Cock-crow
In the centre, where the midnight libation still lay in dregs,
a pointed peg broke through the soil, stood a foot above the Earth.
Upon
this peg, a needle perched.   5
Upon
that needle, a calabash came and sat.
Inside
this calabash, there was a void.
Then the Clan appeared.   10
Around the grounds they threw a ring,
their jaws still locked in a 7-day communion with Silence.
One by one,
Man by man
they stepped into the ring, bowed.   15
Publicly, silently, they shed their private fears
draining their secret cares
into that big brown calabash, container of the Clan's tears.

Noon   20
A step away from the calabash of public fears
Earth cracked and produced a neck without a head;
the neck rose and revealed a body slightly pregnant;
the body produced no legs: on a flat bottom it sat:
a gourd.   25
Inside
that gourd, there was a void.
Again the Clan came
Around the gourd, they wove a ring,
their teeth still clenched in a cruel gruelling duel with Life.   30
Two by two
Man and wife
Widow with orphan
they hopped into the ring, bowed.
Quietly, openly, they poured out their secret toils,   35
draining their private sweat
into the deep brown gourd pregnant with the Clan's broils.

Dusk
3 steps from the calabash of tears and gourd of toils
the Earth pushed up a hearth.   40
Into
this hearth, dried wood piled up.
Upon
that pile, a pot installed herself
Inside   45
this iron pot, there was a void.
Screaming and shrieking and groaning and moaning,
armed with muscle bone and nerve,
eyes swimming in flooded passions of souls possessed,
the Clan rushed, charged, stopped.   50
In the gathering dusk of that festive eve,
each clansman gnashed his teeth
              and bit his lips
        and vomited blood
              into   55
        the void which filled that pot.
Upon no signal, the chant began—low, heavy, nostalgic:
a terrible valediction offered in memoriam to a suspended
    millennium
Echoes, they say, fly fast to closed chapters of life,   60
stirring frozen heartbeats of older worlds.
The chants rose deep, mingling with
re-awakened rhythms of *atrikpui* and *adzogbo*,
bringing vigorous memories of

mortalised heroes   65
and
ethnic vendettas.
The rhythms boiled to a frenzy, driving
Clansmen crazy with re-juvenated glories of
               younger worlds.   70

A clap of clouds, a shaft of light
and a distraught meteor struck the pile of wood,
inflaming the hearth, the flames engulfing the pot of blood,
flooding the festive grounds with a glory
made hoary by crazed shadows of dazed clansmen   75
each wrestling with his mortal self in
a jubilant desperation to evoke the second self.
The flames made a triple leap and grabbed
the gourd of sweat and calabash of tears.
Excitement seized an old clansman—he tossed   80
himself above the flames and landed neat
               in the pot of boiling blood.
He died chanting an ancient song of Life
The Clan forgot the chorus.
But they jumped and danced,   85
embracing and shaking hands,
       watching the flames
       dwindling into
       a pencil
       of smoke   90
       which
       shot
       in-
       to
       higher realms, laden with   95
       evaporated impurities for symbolic
       purification in distilleries of Destiny.

                          27 January–11 April 1975

ZOË WICOMB (b. 1948)
South Africa/England; English

Born in Cape Province, Zoë Wicomb returned to South Africa in 1991 from
teaching in England to lecture at the University of the Western Cape. She writes

in English. *You Can't Get Lost in Cape Town* (1987) is a subtly shaped group of linked stories tracing the coming of age of Frieda Shenton, a girl of mixed ancestry in Cape Province. The title story comes midway in the book and ends the section on Frieda's college education. A powerful, painful treatment of its abortion theme, the story is even more concerned with questions of power and subjectivity, of how a woman's body is regulated by the apartheid state, with its laws against abortion and interracial sex, and by the patriarchal assumptions of religion, fathers, and male lovers. Frieda's stream of consciousness shows her negotiating a response ("For once I do not plead and capitulate; I find it quite easy to ignore these men"). She must deal with the problem of identity as a woman of color with a white lover ("At Cape Point where the oceans meet and part. The Indian and the Atlantic, fighting for their separate identities"). The story is open-ended and provocative; it relies on "the stealthy negotiation of race and gender" which Wicomb refers to in her article "To Hear the Variety of Discourses" (1990). She will have much to contribute to that analysis in these times of fundamental questions for South African culture.

from You Can't Get Lost in Cape Town

You Can't Get Lost in Cape Town

In my right hand resting on the base of my handbag I clutch a brown leather purse. My knuckles ride to and fro, rubbing against the lining . . . surely cardboard . . . and I am surprised that the material has not revealed itself to me before. I have worn this bag for months. I would have said with a dismissive wave of the hand, "Felt, that is what the base of this bag is lined with."

Then, Michael had said, "It looks cheap, unsightly," and lowering his voice to my look of surprise, "Can't you tell?" But he was speaking of the exterior, the way it looks.

The purse fits neatly into the palm of my hand. A man's purse. The handbag gapes. With my elbow I press it against my hip but that will not avert suspicion. The bus is moving fast, too fast, surely exceeding the speed limit, so that I bob on my seat and my grip on the purse tightens as the springs suck at my womb, slurping it down through the plush of the red upholstery. I press my buttocks into the seat to ease the discomfort.

I should count out the fare for the conductor. Perhaps not; he is still at the front of the bus. We are now travelling through Rondelbosch so that he will be fully occupied with white passengers at the front. Women with blue-rinsed heads tilted will go on telling their stories while fishing leisurely for their coins and just lengthen a vowel to tide over the moment of paying their fares.

"Don't be so anxious," Michael said. "It will be all right." I withdrew the hand he tried to pat.

I have always been anxious and things are not all right, things may never be all right again. I must not cry. My eyes travel to and fro along the grooves of the floor. I do not look at the faces that surround me but I believe that they are lifted speculatively at me. Is someone constructing a history for this hand resting foolishly in a gaping handbag? Do these faces expect me to whip out an amputated stump dripping with blood? Do they wince at the thought of a hand, cold and waxen, left on the pavement where it was severed? I draw my hand out of the bag and shake my fingers ostentatiously. No point in inviting conjecture, in attracting attention. The bus brakes loudly to conceal the sound of breath drawn in sharply at the exhibited hand.

Two women pant like dogs as they swing themselves on to the bus. The conductor has already pressed the bell and they propel their bodies expertly along the swaying aisle. They fall into seats opposite me—one fat, the other thin—and simultaneously pull off the starched servants' caps which they scrunch into their laps. They light cigarettes and I bite my lip. Would I have to vomit into this bag with its cardboard lining? I wish I had brought a plastic bag; this bag is empty save for the purse. I breathe deeply to stem the nausea that rises to meet the curling bands of smoke and fix on the bulging bags they grip between their feet. They make no attempt to get their fares ready; they surely misjudge the intentions of the conductor. He knows that they will get off at Mowbray to catch the Golden Arrow buses to the townships.[1] He will not allow them to avoid paying; not he who presses the button with such promptness.

I watch him at the front of the bus. His right thumb strums an impatient jingle on the silver levers, the leather bag is cradled in the hand into which the coins tumble. He chants a barely audible accompaniment to the clatter of coins, a recitation of the newly decimalised currency. Like times tables at school and I see the fingers grow soft, bending boyish as they strum an ink-stained abacus; the boy learning to count, leaning earnestly with propped elbows over a desk. And I find the image unaccountably sad and tears are about to well up when I hear an impatient empty clatter of thumb-play on the coin dispenser as he demands, "All fares please," from a sleepy white youth. My hand flies into my handbag once again and I take out the purse. A man's leather purse.

Michael too is boyish. His hair falls in a straight blond fringe into his eyes. When he considers a reply he wipes it away impatiently, as if the hair impedes thought. I cannot imagine this purse ever having belonged to him. It is small, U-shaped and devoid of ornament, therefore a man's purse. It has an extending tongue that could be tucked into the mouth or be threaded through the narrow band across the base of the U. I take out the smallest note stuffed into this plump purse, a five-rand note. Why had I not thought about the busfare? The conductor will be angry if my note should exhaust his supply of coins although the leather bag would have a concealed pouch for notes. But this thought does not comfort me. I feel angry with Michael. He has probably never travelled by bus. How would he know of the fear of missing the unfamiliar stop, the fear of keeping an impatient conductor waiting, the fear of saying fluently, "Seventeen cents please," when you are not sure of the fare and produce a five-rand note? But this is my journey and I must not expect Michael to take responsibility for everything. Or rather, I cannot

---

1. Segregated black districts outside the cities.

expect Michael to take responsibility for more than half the things. Michael is scrupulous about this division; I am not always sure of how to arrive at half. I was never good at arithmetic, especially this instant mental arithmetic that is sprung on me.

How foolish I must look sitting here clutching my five-rand note. I slip it back into the purse and turn to the solidity of the smoking women. They have still made no attempt to find their fares. The bus is going fast and I am surprised that we have not yet reached Mowbray. Perhaps I am mistaken, perhaps we have already passed Mowbray and the women are going to Sea Point to serve a nightshift at the Pavilion.

Marge, Aunt Trudie's eldest daughter, works as a waitress at the Pavilion but she is rarely mentioned in our family. "A disgrace," they say. "She should know better than to go with white men."

"Poor whites," Aunt Trudie hisses. "She can't even find a nice rich man to go steady with. Such a pretty girl too. I won't have her back in this house. There's no place in this house for a girl who's been used by white trash."

Her eyes flash as she spits out a cherished vision of a blond young man sitting on her new vinyl sofa to whom she serves gingerbeer and *koeksisters*,[2] because it is not against the law to have a respectable drink in a Coloured home. "Mrs Holman," he would say, "Mrs Holman, this is the best gingerbeer I've had for years."

The family do not know of Michael even though he is a steady young man who would sit out such a Sunday afternoon with infinite grace. I wince at the thought of Father creaking in a suit and the unconcealed pleasure in Michael's successful academic career.

Perhaps this is Mowbray after all. The building that zooms past on the right seems familiar. I ought to know it but I am lost, hopelessly lost, and as my mind gropes for recognition I feel a feathery flutter in my womb, so slight I cannot be sure, and again, so soft, the brush of a butterfly, and under cover of my handbag I spread my left hand to hold my belly. The shaft of light falling across my shoulder, travelling this route with me, is the eye of God. God will never forgive me.

I must anchor my mind to the words of the women on the long seat opposite me. But they fall silent as if to protect their secrets from me. One of them bends down heavily, holding on to the jaws of her shopping bag as if to relieve pressure on her spine, and I submit to the ache of my own by swaying gently while I protect my belly with both hands. But having eyed the contents of her full bag carefully, her hand becomes the beak of a bird dipping purposefully into the left-hand corner and rises triumphantly with a brown paper bag on which grease has oozed light-sucking patterns. She opens the bag and her friend looks on in silence. Three chunks of cooked chicken lie on a piece of greaseproof paper. She deftly halves a piece and passes it to her thin friend. The women munch in silence, their mouths glossy with pleasure.

---

2. Doughnuts.

"These are for the children," she says, her mouth still full as she wraps the rest up and places it carelessly at the top of the bag.

"It's the spiced chicken recipe you told me about." She nudges her friend. "*Lekker*[3] hey!"

The friend frowns and says, "I like to taste a bit more cardamom. It's nice to find a whole cardamom in the food and crush it between your teeth. A cardamom seed will never give up all its flavour to the pot. You'll still find it there in the chewing."

I note the gaps in her teeth and fear for the slipping through of cardamom seeds. The girls at school who had their two top incisors extracted in a fashion that raged through Cape Town said that it was better for kissing. Then I, fat and innocent, nodded. How would I have known the demands of kissing?

The large woman refuses to be thwarted by criticism of her cooking. The chicken stimulates a story so that she twitches with an irrepressible desire to tell.

"To think," she finally bursts out, "that I cook them this nice surprise and say what you like, spiced chicken can make any mouth water. Just think, it was yesterday when I say to that one as she stands with her hands on her hips against the stove saying, 'I don't know what to give them today, I've just got too much organising to do to bother with food.' And I say, feeling sorry for her, I say, 'Don't you worry about a thing, Marram, just leave it all in cook's hands (wouldn't it be nice to work for really grand people where you cook and do nothing else, no bladdy scrubbing and shopping and all that) . . . in cook's hands,' I said," and she crows merrily before reciting: "And I'll dish up a surprise / For Master Georgie's blue eyes.

"That's Miss Lucy's young man. He was coming last night. Engaged, you know. Well there I was on my feet all day starching linen, making roeties and spiced lentils and sweet potato and all the lekker things you must mos have with cardamom chicken. And what do you think she says?"

She pauses and lifts her face as if expecting a reply, but the other stares grimly ahead. Undefeated she continues, "She says to me, Tiena, because she can't keep out of my pots, you know, always opening my lids and sniffing like a *brakhond*,[4] she says, 'Tiena,' and waits for me to say, 'Yes Marram,' so I know she has a wicked plan up her sleeve and I look her straight in the eye. She smile that one, always smile to put me off the track, and she say looking into the fridge, 'You can have this nice bean soup for your dinner so I can have the remains of the chicken tomorrow when you're off.' So I say to her, 'That's what I had for lunch today,' and she say to me, 'Yes I know but me and Miss Lucy will be on our own for dinner tomorrow,' and she pull a face, 'Ugh, how I hate reheated food.' Then she draws up her shoulders as if to say, That's that."

"Cheek hey! And it was a great big fowl." She nudges her friend. "You know for yourself how much better food tastes the next day when the spices are drawn right into the meat and anyway you just switch on the electric and there's no

---

3. Nice.   4. A mongrel dog.

chopping and crying over onions, you just wait for the pot to dance on the stove. Of course she wouldn't know about that. Anyway, a cheek, that's what I call it, so before I even dished up the chicken for the table, I took this," and she points triumphantly to her bag, "and to hell with them."

The thin one opens her mouth, once, twice, winding herself up to speak.

"They never notice anyway. There's so much food in their pantries, in the fridge and on the tables; they don't know what's there and what isn't." The other looks pityingly at her.

"Don't you believe that. My marram was as cross as a bear by the time I brought in the pudding, a very nice apricot ice it was, but she didn't even look at it. She know it was a healthy grown fowl and she count one leg, and she know what's going on. She know right away. Didn't even say, 'Thank you Tiena.' She won't speak to me for days but what can she do?" Her voice softens into genuine sympathy for her madam's dilemma.

"She'll just have to speak to me." And she mimics, putting on a stern horse face. " 'We'll want dinner by seven tonight,' then 'Tiena the curtains need washing,' then, 'Please, Tiena, will you fix this zip for me, I've got absolutely nothing else to wear today.' And so on the third day she'll smile and think she's smiling forgiveness at me."

She straightens her face. "No," she sighs, "the more you have, the more you have to keep your head and count and check up because you know you won't notice or remember. No, if you got a lot you must keep snaps in your mind of the insides of all the cupboards. And every day, click, click, new snaps of the larder. That's why that one is so tired, always thinking, always reciting to herself the lists of what's in the cupboards. I never know what's in my cupboard at home but I know my Sammie's a thieving bastard, can't keep his hands in his pockets."

The thin woman stares out of the window as if she had heard it all before. She has finished her chicken while the other, with all the talking, still holds a half-eaten drumstick daintily in her right hand. Her eyes rove over the shopping bag and she licks her fingers abstractedly as she stares out of the window.

"Lekker hey!" the large one repeats, "the children will have such a party."

"Did Master George enjoy it?" the other asks.

"Oh he's a gentleman all right. Shouted after me, 'Well done, Tiena. When we're married we'll have to steal you from madam.' Dressed to kill he was, such a smart young man, you know. Mind you, so's Miss Lucy. Not a prettier girl in our avenue and the best-dressed too. But then she has mos to be smart to keep her man. Been on the pill for nearly a year now; I shouldn't wonder if he don't feel funny about the white wedding. Ooh, you must see her blush over the pictures of the wedding gowns, so pure and innocent she think I can't read the packet. 'Get me my headache pills out of that drawer Tiena,' she say sometimes when I take her cup of cocoa at night. But she play her cards right with Master George; she have to cause who'd have what another man has pushed to the side of his plate. A bay leaf and a bone!" and moved by the alliteration the image materialises in her hand. "Like this bone," and she waves it under the nose of the other who starts. I wonder whether with guilt, fear or a debilitating desire for more chicken.

"This bone," she repeats grimly, "picked bare and only wanted by a dog." Her friend recovers and deliberately misunderstands, "Or like yesterday's bean soup, but we women mos know that food put aside and left to stand till tomorrow always has a better flavour. Men don't know that hey. They should get down to some cooking and find out a thing or two."

But the other is not deterred. "A bone," she insists, waving her visual aid, "a bone."

It is true that her bone is a matt grey that betrays no trace of the meat or fat that only a minute ago adhered to it. Master George's bone would certainly look nothing like that when he pushes it aside. With his fork he would coax off the fibres ready to fall from the bone. Then he would turn over the whole, deftly, using a knife, and frown at the sinewy meat clinging to the joint before pushing it aside towards the discarded bits of skin.

This bone, it is true, will not tempt anyone. A dog might want to bury it only for a silly game of hide and seek.

The large woman waves the bone as if it would burst into prophecy. My eyes follow the movement until the bone blurs and emerges as the Cross where the head of Jesus lolls sadly, his lovely feet anointed by sad hands, folded together under the driven nail. Look, Mamma says, look at those eyes molten with love and pain, the body curved with suffering for our sins, and together we weep for the beauty and sadness of Jesus in his white loincloth. The Roman soldiers stand grimly erect in their tunics, their spears gleam in the light, their dark beards are clipped and their lips curl. At midday Judas turns his face to the fading sun and bays, howls like a dog for its return as the darkness grows around him and swallows him whole with the money still jingling in the folds of his saffron robes. In a concealed leather purse, a pouch devoid of ornament.

The buildings on this side of the road grow taller but oh, I do not know where I am and I think of asking the woman, the thin one, but when I look up the stern one's eyes already rest on me while the bone in her hand points idly at the advertisement just above my head. My hands, still cradling my belly, slide guiltily down my thighs and fall on my knees. But the foetus betrays me with another flutter, a sigh. I have heard of books flying off the laps of gentle mothers-to-be as their foetuses lash out. I will not be bullied. I jump up and press the bell.

There are voices behind me. The large woman's "Oi, I say" thunders over the conductor's cross "Tickets please." I will not speak to anyone. Shall I throw myself on the grooved floor of this bus and with knees drawn up, hands over my head, wait for my demise? I do not in any case expect to be alive tomorrow. But I must resist; I must harden my heart against the sad, complaining eyes of Jesus.

"I say, Miss," she shouts and her tone sounds familiar. Her voice compels like the insistence of Father's guttural commands. But the conductor's hand falls on my shoulder, the barrel of his ticket dispenser digs into my ribs, the buttons of his uniform gleam as I dip into my bag for my purse. Then the large woman spills out of her seat as she leans forward. Her friend, reconciled, holds the bar of an arm across her as she leans forward shouting, "Here, I say, your purse." I try to look grateful. Her eyes blaze with scorn as she proclaims to the bus, "Stupid these young people. Dress to kill maybe, but still so stupid."

She is right. Not about my clothes, of course, and I check to see what I am wearing. I have not been alerted to my own stupidity before. No doubt I will sail through my final examinations at the end of this year and still not know how I dared to pluck a fluttering foetus out of my womb. That is if I survive to-night.

I sit on the steps of this large building and squint up at the marble facade. My elbows rest on my knees flung comfortably apart. I ought to know where I am; it is clearly a public building of some importance. For the first time I long for the *veld*[5] of my childhood. There the red sand rolls for miles, and if you stand on the *koppie*[6] behind the house the landmarks blaze their permanence: the river points downward, runs its dry course from north to south; the *geelbos*[7] crowds its banks in near straight lines. On either side of the path winding westward plump little buttocks of cacti squat as if lifting the skirts to pee, and the swollen fingers of *vygies*[8] burst in clusters out of the stone, pointing the way. In the veld you can always find your way home.

I am anxious about meeting Michael. We have planned this so carefully for the rush hour when people storming home crossly will not notice us together in the crush.

"It's simple," Michael said. "The bus carries along the main roads through the suburbs to the City, and as you reach the Post Office you get off and I'll be there to meet you. At five."

A look at my anxious face compelled him to say, "You can't get lost in Cape Town. There," and he pointed over his shoulder, "is Table Mountain and there is Devil's Peak and there Lion's Head, so how in heaven's name could you get lost?" The words shot out unexpectedly, like the fine arc of brown spittle from between the teeth of an old man who no longer savours the tobacco he has been chewing all day. There are, I suppose, things that even a loved one cannot over-look.

Am I a loved one?

I ought to rise from these steps and walk towards the City. Fortunately I always take the precaution of setting out early, so that I should still be in time to meet Michael who will drive me along de Waal Drive into the slopes of Table Mountain where Mrs. Coetzee waits with her tongs.

Am I a loved one? No. I am dull, ugly and bad-tempered. My hair has grown greasy, I am forgetful and I have no sense of direction. Michael, he has long since stopped loving me. He watched me hugging the lavatory bowl, retching, and recoiled at my first display of bad temper. There is a faraway look in his eyes as he plans his retreat. But he is well brought up, honourable. When the first doubts gripped the corners of his mouth, he grinned madly and said, "We must marry," showing a row of perfect teeth.

---

5. Open country.
6. A small hill.

7. A type of bush.
8. Figlike succulents.

"There are laws against that," I said unnecessarily.

But gripped by the idyll of an English landscape of painted greens, he saw my head once more held high, my lettuce-luscious skirts crisp on a camomile lawn and the willow drooping over the red mouth of a suckling infant.

"Come on," he urged. "Don't do it. We'll get to England and marry. It will work out all right," and betraying the source of his vision, "and we'll be happy for ever, thousands of miles from all this mess."

I would have explained if I could. But I could not account for this vision: the slow shower of ashes over yards of diaphanous tulle, the moth wings tucked back with delight as their tongues whisked the froth of white lace. For two years I have loved Michael, have wanted to marry him. Duped by a dream I merely shook my head.

"But you love babies, you want babies some time or other, so why not accept God's holy plan? Anyway, you're a Christian and you believe it's a sin, don't you?"

God is not a good listener. Like Father, he expects obedience and withdraws peevishly if his demands are not met. Explanations of my point of view infuriate him so that he quivers with silent rage. For once I do not plead and capitulate; I find it quite easy to ignore these men.

"You're not even listening," Michael accused. "I don't know how you can do it." There is revulsion in his voice.

For two short years I have adored Michael.

Once, perched perilously on the rocks, we laughed fondly at the thought of a child. At Cape Point where the oceans meet and part. The Indian and the Atlantic, fighting for their separate identities, roared and thrashed fiercely so that we huddled together, his hand on my belly. It is said that if you shut one eye and focus the other carefully, the line separating the two oceans may rear drunkenly but remains ever clear and hair-fine. But I did not look. In the mischievous wind I struggled with the flapping ends of a scarf I tried to wrap around my hair. Later that day on the silver sands of a deserted beach he wrote solemnly: Will you marry me? and my trembling fingers traced a huge heart around the words. Ahead the sun danced on the waves, flecking them with gold.

I wrote a poem about that day and showed Michael. "Surely that was not what *Logiesbaai*[9] was about," he frowned, and read aloud the lines about warriors charging out of the sea, *assegais*[10] gleaming in the sun, the beat of tom-toms riding the waters, the throb in the carious cavities of rocks.

"It's good," he said, nodding thoughtfully, "I like the title, 'Love at Logiesbaai (Whites Only),' though I expect much of the subtlety escapes me. Sounds good," he encouraged, "you should write more often."

I flushed. I wrote poems all the time. And he was wrong; it was not a good poem. It was puzzling and I wondered why I had shown him this poem that did not even make sense to me. I tore it into little bits.

---

9. The name of a beach.　　　　10. Spears.

Love, love, love, I sigh as I shake each ankle in turn and examine the swelling.

Michael's hair falls boyishly over his eyes. His eyes narrow merrily when he smiles and the left corner of his mouth shoots up so that the row of teeth forms a queer diagonal line above his chin. He flicks his head so that the fringe of hair lifts from his eyes for a second, then falls, so fast, like the tongue of a lizard retracted at the very moment of exposure.

"We'll find somewhere," he would say, "a place where we'd be quite alone." This country is vast and he has an instinctive sense of direction. He discovers the armpits of valleys that invite us into their shadows. Dangerous climbs led by the roar of the sea take us to blue bays into which we drop from impossible cliffs. The sun lowers herself on to us. We do not fear the police with their torches. They come only by night in search of offenders. We have the immunity of love. They cannot find us because they do not know we exist. One day they will find out about lovers who steal whole days, round as globes.

There has always been a terrible thrill in that thought.

I ease my feet back into my shoes and the tears splash on to my dress with such wanton abandon that I cannot believe they are mine. From the punctured globes of stolen days these fragments sag and squint. I hold, hold these pictures I have summoned. I will not recognise them for much longer.

With tilted head I watch the shoes and sawn-off legs ascend and descend the marble steps, altering course to avoid me. Perhaps someone will ask the police to remove me.

Love, love, love, I sigh. Another flutter in my womb. I think of moth wings struggling against a window pane and I rise.

The smell of sea unfurls towards me as I approach Adderley Street. There is no wind but the brine hangs in an atomised mist, silver over a thwarted sun. In answer to my hunger, Wellingtons looms on my left. The dried-fruit palace which I cannot resist. The artificial light dries my tears, makes me blink, and the trays of fruit, of Cape sunlight twice trapped, shimmer and threaten to burst out of their forms. Rows of pineapple are the infinite divisions of the sun, the cores lost in the amber discs of mebos[11] arranged in arcs. Prunes are the wrinkled backs of aged goggas[12] beside the bloodshot eyes of cherries. Dark green figs sit pertly on their bottoms peeping over trays. And I too am not myself, hoping for refuge in a metaphor that will contain it all. I buy the figs and mebos. Desire is a Tsafendas tapeworm[13] in my belly that cannot be satisfied and as I pop the first fig into my mouth I feel the danger fountain with the jets of saliva. Will I stop at one death?

I have walked too far along this road and must turn back to the Post Office. I break into a trot as I see Michael in the distance, drumming with his nails on the side of the car. His sunburnt elbow juts out of the window. He taps with anxiety or impatience and I grow cold with fear as I jump into the passenger seat and say merrily, "Let's go," as if we are setting off for a picnic.

---

11. Salted dried apricots.
12. Insects.

13. An intestinal parasite.

Michael will wait in the car on the next street. She had said that it would take only ten minutes. He takes my hand and so prevents me from getting out. Perhaps he thinks that I will bolt, run off into the mountain, revert to savagery. His hand is heavy on my forearm and his eyes are those of a wounded dog, pale with pain.

"It will be all right." I try to comfort and wonder whether he hears his own voice in mine. My voice is thin, a tinsel thread that springs out of my mouth and flutters straight out of the window.

"I must go." I lift the heavy hand off my forearm and it falls inertly across the gearstick.

The room is dark. The curtains are drawn and a lace-shaded electric light casts shadows in the corners of the rectangle. The doorway in which I stand divides the room into sleeping and eating quarters. On the left there is a table against which a servant girl leans, her eyes fixed on the blank wall ahead. On the right a middle-aged white woman rises with a hostess smile from a divan which serves as sofa, and pats the single pink-flowered cushion to assert homeliness. There is a narrow dark wardrobe in the corner.

I say haltingly, "You are expecting me. I spoke to you on the telephone yesterday. Sally Smit." I can see no telephone in the room. She frowns.

"You're not Coloured, are you?" It is an absurd question. I look at my brown arms that I have kept folded across my chest, and watch the gooseflesh sprout. Her eyes are fixed on me. Is she blind? How will she perform the operation with such defective sight? Then I realise: the educated voice, the accent has blinded her. I have drunk deeply of Michael, swallowed his voice as I drank from his tongue. Has he swallowed mine? I do not think so.

I say "No," and wait for all the cockerels in Cape Town to crow simultaneously. Instead the servant starts from her trance and stares at me with undisguised admiration.

"Good," the woman smiles, showing yellow teeth. "One must check nowadays. These Coloured girls, you know, are very forward, terrible types. What do they think of me, as if I would do every Tom, Dick and Harry. Not me you know; this is a respectable concern and I try to help decent women, educated you know. No, you can trust me. No Coloured girl's ever been on this sofa."

The girl coughs, winks at me and turns to stir a pot simmering on a primus stove on the table. The smell of offal[14] escapes from the pot and nausea rises in my throat, feeding the fear. I would like to run but my feet are lashed with fear to the linoleum. Only my eyes move, across the room where she pulls a newspaper from a wad wedged between the wall and the wardrobe. She spreads the paper on the divan and smooths with her hand while the girl shuts the door and turns the key. A cat crawls lazily from under the table and stares at me until the green jewels of its eyes shrink to crystal points.

She points me to the sofa. From behind the wardrobe she pulls her instrument and holds it against the baby-pink crimplene[15] of her skirt.

---

14. The parts (tail, feet, etc.) of a slaughtered animal often thrown away.

15. Cheap nylon fabric.

"Down, shut your eyes now," she says as I raise my head to look. Their movements are carefully orchestrated, the manoeuvres practised. Their eyes signal and they move. The girl stations herself by my head and her mistress moves to my feet. She pushes my knees apart and whips out her instrument from a pocket. A piece of plastic tubing dangles for a second. My knees jerk and my mouth opens wide but they are in control. A brown hand falls on my mouth and smothers the cry; the white hands wrench the knees apart and she hisses, "Don't you dare. Do you want the bladdy police here? I'll kill you if you scream."

The brown hand over my mouth relaxes. She looks into my face and says, "She won't." I am a child who needs reassurance. I am surprised by the softness of her voice. The brown hand moves along the side of my face and pushes back my hair. I long to hold the other hand; I do not care what happens below. A black line of terror separates it from my torso. Blood spurts from between my legs and for a second the two halves of my body make contact through the pain.

So it is done. Deflowered by yellow hands wielding a catheter. Fear and hypocrisy, mine, my deserts spread in a dark stain on the newspaper.

"OK," she says, "get yourself decent." I dress and wait for her to explain. "You go home now and wait for the birth. Do you have a pad?"

I shake my head uncomprehendingly. Her face tightens for a moment but then she smiles and pulls a sanitary towel out of the wardrobe.

"Won't cost you anything lovey." She does not try to conceal the glow of her generosity. She holds out her hand and I place the purse in her palm. She counts, satisfied, but I wave away the purse which she reluctantly puts on the table.

"You're a good girl," she says and puts both hands on my shoulders. I hold my breath; I will not inhale the foetid air from the mouth of this my grotesque bridegroom with yellow teeth. She plants the kiss of complicity on my cheek and I turn to go, repelled by her touch. But have I the right to be fastidious? I cannot deny feeling grateful, so that I turn back to claim the purse after all. The girl winks at me. The purse fits snugly in my hand; there would be no point in giving it back to Michael.

Michael's face is drawn with fear. He is as ignorant of the process as I am. I am brisk, efficient and rattle off the plan. "It'll happen tonight so I'll go home and wait and call you in the morning. By then it will be all over." He looks relieved.

He drives me right to the door and my landlady waves merrily from the stoep[16] where she sits with her embroidery among the potted ferns.

"Don't look," she says anxiously. "It's a present for you, for your trousseau,"[17] and smiling slyly, "I can tell when a couple just can't wait any longer. There's no catching me out, you know."

Tonight in her room next to mine she will turn in her chaste bed, tracing the tendrils from pink and orange flowers, searching for the needle lost in endless folds of white linen.

---

16. A small veranda at the entrance to a building.

17. A bride's clothes, houselinens, etc.

Semi-detached houses with red-polished stoeps line the west side of Trevelyan Road. On the east is the Cape Flats line where electric trains rattle reliably according to timetable. Trevelyan Road runs into the elbow of a severely curved Main Road which nevertheless has all the amenities one would expect: butcher, baker, hairdresser, chemist, library, liquor store. There is a fish and chips shop on that corner, on the funny bone of that elbow, and by the side, strictly speaking in Trevelyan Road, a dustbin leans against the trunk of a young palm tree. A newspaper parcel dropped into this dustbin would absorb the vinegary smell of discarded fish and chips wrappings in no time.

The wrapped parcel settles in the bin. I do not know what has happened to God. He is fastidious. He fled at the moment that I smoothed the wet black hair before wrapping it up. I do not think he will come back. It is 6 a.m. Light pricks at the shroud of Table Mountain. The streets are deserted and, relieved, I remember that the next train will pass at precisely 6.22.

NJABULO S. NDEBELE (b. 1948)
South Africa; English

Njabulo S. Ndebele, a poet and writer of short stories and cultural criticism, has been called the most influential figure in South African literary studies today. He is president of the Congress of South African Writers (COSAW) and rector of the University of the North. He writes in English. His poetry concerning the movement of the Black Consciousness (1970s), his *Fools and Other Stories* (1984), and his critical and theoretical essays have redefined the way South Africans think of their new multiracial culture in the making. Ndebele argues for a confident, bold, experimental rethinking and remaking of literature and culture at the hands of the majority. He also calls for an exploration of the resources of language, history, and social organization that the people have already developed, and for the dismantling of the authority of the old settler culture. "Death of a Son" (1987), like his earlier stories, moves beyond protest politics. For example, Buntu's first impulse to challenge the police when they remove his son's body is only machismo. The real issue lies rather between Buntu and his wife, the narrator of the story. Questions of gender role and gender hierarchy arise, as does a feminist point of view. The story also attends to issues of class formation, as this couple rethinks their dreams of upward mobility.

Death of a Son

At last we got the body. Wednesday. Just enough time for a Saturday funeral. We were exhausted. Empty. The funeral still ahead of us. We had to find the strength

Patrick Holo. *Desperate*. Linocut
on paper.

to grieve. There had been no time for grief, really. Only much bewilderment and confusion. Now grief. For isn't grief the awareness of loss?

That is why when we finally got the body, Buntu said: "Do you realize our son is dead?" I realized. Our awareness of the death of our first and only child had been displaced completely by the effort to get his body. Even the horrible events that caused the death: we did not think of them, as such. Instead, the numbing drift of things took over our minds: the pleas, letters to be written, telephone calls to be made, telegrams to be dispatched, lawyers to consult, "influential" people to "get in touch with," undertakers to be contacted, so much walking and driving. That is what suddenly mattered: the irksome details that blur the goal (no matter how terrible it is), each detail becoming a door which, once unlocked, revealed yet another door. Without being aware of it, we were distracted by the smell of the skunk and not by what the skunk had done.

We realized something too, Buntu and I, that during the two-week effort to get our son's body, we had drifted apart. For the first time in our marriage, our presence to each other had become a matter of habit. He was there. He'll be there. And I'll be there. But when Buntu said: "Do you realize our son is dead?" he uttered a thought that suddenly brought us together again. It was as if the return of the body of our son was also our coming together. For it was only at that moment that we really began to grieve; as if our lungs had suddenly begun to take in air when just before, we were beginning to suffocate. Something with meaning began to emerge.

We realized. We realized that something else had been happening to us, adding to the terrible events. Yes, we had drifted apart. Yet, our estrangement, just at that moment when we should have been together, seemed disturbingly comforting to me. I was comforted in a manner I did not quite understand.

The problem was that I had known all along that we would have to buy the body anyway. I had known all along. Things would end that way. And when things turned out that way, Buntu could not look me in the eye. For he had said: "Over my dead body! Over my dead body!" as soon as we knew we would be required to pay the police or the government for the release of the body of our child.

"Over my dead body! Over my dead body!" Buntu kept on saying.

Finally, we bought the body. We have the receipt. The police insisted we take it. That way, they would be "protected." It's the law, they said.

I suppose we could have got the body earlier. At first I was confused, for one is supposed to take comfort in the heroism of one's man. Yet, inwardly, I could draw no comfort from his outburst. It seemed hasty. What sense was there to it when all I wanted was the body of my child? What would happen if, as events unfolded, it became clear that Buntu would not give up his life? What would happen? What would happen to him? To me?

For the greater part of two weeks, all of Buntu's efforts, together with friends, relatives, lawyers and the newspapers, were to secure the release of the child's body without the humiliation of having to pay for it. A "fundamental principle."

Why was it difficult for me to see the wisdom of the principle? The worst thing, I suppose, was worrying about what the police may have been doing to the body of my child. How they may have been busy prying it open "to determine the cause of death"?

Would I want to look at the body when we finally got it? To see further mutilations in addition to the "cause of death"? What kind of mother would not want to look at the body of her child? people will ask. Some will say: "It's grief." She is too grief-stricken.

"But still . . . ," they will say. And the elderly among them may say: "Young people are strange."

But how can they know? It was not that I would not want to see the body of my child, but that I was too afraid to confront the horrors of my own imagination. I was haunted by the thought of how useless it had been to have created something. What had been the point of it all? This body filling up with a child. The child steadily growing into something that could be seen and felt. Moving, as it always did, at that time of day when I was all alone at home waiting for it. What had been the point of it all?

How can they know that the mutilation to determine "the cause of death" ripped my own body? Can they think of a womb feeling hunted? Disgorged?

And the milk that I still carried. What about it? What had been the point of it all?

Even Buntu did not seem to sense that that principle, the "fundamental principle," was something too intangible for me at that moment, something that

I desperately wanted should assume the form of my child's body. He still seemed far from ever knowing.

I remember one Saturday morning early in our courtship, as Buntu and I walked hand-in-hand through town, window-shopping. We cannot even be said to have been window-shopping, for we were aware of very little that was not ourselves. Everything in those windows was merely an excuse for words to pass between us.

We came across three girls sitting on the pavement, sharing a packet of fish and chips after they had just bought it from a nearby Portuguese cafe. Buntu said: "I want fish and chips too." I said: "So seeing is desire." I said: "My man is greedy!" We laughed. I still remember how he tightened his grip on my hand. The strength of it!

Just then, two white boys coming in the opposite direction suddenly rushed at the girls, and, without warning, one of them kicked the packet of fish and chips out of the hands of the girl who was holding it. The second boy kicked away the rest of what remained in the packet. The girl stood up, shaking her hand as if to throw off the pain in it. Then she pressed it under her armpit as if to squeeze the pain out of it. Meanwhile, the two boys went on their way laughing. The fish and chips lay scattered on the pavement and on the street like stranded boats on a river that had gone dry.

"Just let them do that to you!" said Buntu, tightening once more his grip on my hand as we passed on like sheep that had seen many of their own in the flock picked out for slaughter. We would note the event and wait for our turn. I remember I looked at Buntu, and saw his face was somewhat glum. There seemed no connection between that face and the words of reassurance just uttered. For a while, we went on quietly. It was then that I noticed his grip had grown somewhat limp. Somewhat reluctant. Having lost its self-assurance, it seemed to have been holding on because it had to, not because of a confident sense of possession.

It was not to be long before his words were tested. How could fate work this way, giving to words meanings and intentions they did not carry when they were uttered? I saw that day, how the language of love could so easily be trampled underfoot, or scattered like fish and chips on the pavement, and left stranded and abandoned like boats in a river that suddenly went dry. Never again was love to be confirmed with words. The world around us was too hostile for vows of love. At any moment, the vows could be subjected to the stress of proof. And love died. For words of love need not be tested.

On that day, Buntu and I began our silence. We talked and laughed, of course, but we stopped short of words that would demand proof of action. Buntu knew. He knew the vulnerability of words. And so he sought to obliterate words with acts that seemed to promise redemption.

On that day, as we continued with our walk in town, that Saturday morning, coming up towards us from the opposite direction, was a burly Boer[1] walking with

---

1. A farmer; the term for an Afrikaner.

his wife and two children. They approached Buntu and me with an ominously determined advance. Buntu attempted to pull me out of the way, but I never had a chance. The Boer shoved me out of the way, as if clearing a path for his family. I remember, I almost crashed into a nearby fashion display window. I remember, I glanced at the family walking away, the mother and the father each dragging a child. It was for one of those children that I had been cleared away. I remember, also, that as my tears came out, blurring the Boer family and everything else, I saw and felt deeply what was inside of me: a desire to be avenged.

But nothing happened. All I heard was Buntu say: "The dog!" At that very moment, I felt my own hurt vanish like a wisp of smoke. And as my hurt vanished, it was replaced, instead, by a tormenting desire to sacrifice myself for Buntu. Was it something about the powerlessness of the curse and the desperation with which it had been made? The filling of stunned silence with an utterance? Surely it ate into him, revealing how incapable he was of meeting the call of his words.

And so it was, that that afternoon, back in the township, left to ourselves at Buntu's home, I gave in to him for the first time. Or should I say I offered myself to him? Perhaps from some vague sense of wanting to heal something in him? Anyway, we were never to talk about that event. Never. We buried it alive deep inside of me that afternoon. Would it ever be exhumed? All I vaguely felt and knew was that I had the keys to the vault. That was three years ago, a year before we married.

The cause of death? One evening I returned home from work, particularly tired after I had been covering more shootings by the police in the East Rand. Then I had hurried back to the office in Johannesburg to piece together on my typewriter the violent scenes of the day, and then to file my report to meet the deadline. It was late when I returned home, and when I got there, I found a crowd of people in the yard. They were those who could not get inside. I panicked. What had happened? I did not ask those who were outside, being desperate to get into the house. They gave way easily when they recognized me.

Then I heard my mother's voice. Her cry rose well above the noise. It turned into a scream when she saw me. "What is it, mother?" I asked, embracing her out of a vaguely despairing sense of terror. But she pushed me away with an hysterical violence that astounded me.

"What misery have I brought you, my child?" she cried. At that point, many women in the room began to cry too. Soon, there was much wailing in the room, and then all over the house. The sound of it! The anguish! Understanding, yet eager for knowledge, I became desperate. I had to hold onto something. The desire to embrace my mother no longer had anything to do with comforting her; for whatever she had done, whatever its magnitude, had become inconsequential. I needed to embrace her for all the anguish that tied everyone in the house into a knot. I wanted to be part of that knot, yet I wanted to know what had brought it about.

Eventually, we found each other, my mother and I, and clasped each other tightly. When I finally released her, I looked around at the neighbors and suddenly had a vision of how that anguish had to be turned into a simmering kind of indignation. The kind of indignation that had to be kept at bay only because there was a higher purpose at that moment: the sharing of concern.

Slowly and with a calmness that surprised me, I began to gather the details of what had happened. Instinctively, I seemed to have been gathering notes for a news report.

It happened during the day, when the soldiers and the police that had been patrolling the township in their Casspirs[2] began to shoot in the streets at random. Need I describe what I did not see? How did the child come to die just at that moment when the police and the soldiers began to shoot at random, at any house, at any moving thing? That was how one of our windows was shattered by a bullet. And that was when my mother, who looked after her grandchild when we were away at work, panicked. She picked up the child and ran to the neighbors. It was only when she entered the neighbor's house that she noticed the wetness of the blanket that covered the child she held to her chest as she ran for the sanctuary of neighbors. She had looked at her unaccountably bloody hand, then she noted the still bundle in her arms, and began at that moment to blame herself for the death of her grandchild . . . .

Later, the police, on yet another round of shooting, found people gathered at our house. They stormed in, saw what had happened. At first, they dragged my mother out, threatening to take her away unless she agreed not to say what had happened. But then they returned and, instead, took the body of the child away. By what freak of logic did they hope that by this act their carnage would never be discovered?

That evening, I looked at Buntu closely. He appeared suddenly to have grown older. We stood alone in an embrace in our bedroom. I noticed, when I kissed his face, how his once lean face had grown suddenly puffy.

At that moment, I felt the familiar impulse come upon me once more, the impulse I always felt when I sensed that Buntu was in some kind of danger, the impulse to yield something of myself to him. He wore the look of someone struggling to gain control of something. Yet, it was clear he was far from controlling anything. I knew that look. Had seen it many times. It came at those times when I sensed that he faced a wave that was infinitely stronger than he, that it would certainly sweep him away, but that he had to seem to be struggling. I pressed myself tightly to him as if to vanish into him; as if only the two of us could stand up to the wave.

"Don't worry," he said. "Don't worry. I'll do everything in my power to right this wrong. Everything. Even if it means suing the police!" We went silent.

I knew that silence. But I knew something else at that moment: that I had to find a way of disengaging myself from the embrace.

Suing the police? I listened to Buntu outlining his plans. "Legal counsel.

---

2. An armored vehicle.

That's what we need," he said. "I know some people in Pretoria," he said. As he spoke, I felt the warmth of intimacy between us cooling. When he finished, it was cold. I disengaged from his embrace slowly, yet purposefully. Why had Buntu spoken?

Later, he was to speak again, when all his plans had failed to work: "Over my dead body! Over my dead body!"

He sealed my lips. I would wait for him to feel and yield one day to all the realities of misfortune.

Ours was a home, it could be said. It seemed a perfect life for a young couple: I, a reporter; Buntu, a personnel officer at an American factory manufacturing farming implements. He had traveled to the United States and returned with a mind fired with dreams. We dreamed together. Much time we spent, Buntu and I, trying to make a perfect home. The occasions are numerous on which we paged through *Femina, Fair Lady, Cosmopolitan, Home Garden, Car,* as if somehow we were going to surround our lives with the glossiness in the magazines. Indeed, much of our time was spent window-shopping through the magazines. This time, it was different from the window-shopping we did that Saturday when we courted. This time our minds were consumed by the things we saw and dreamed of owning: the furniture, the fridge, TV, videocassette recorders, washing machines, even a vacuum cleaner and every other imaginable thing that would ensure a comfortable modern life.

Especially when I was pregnant. What is it that Buntu did not buy, then? And when the boy was born, Buntu changed the car. A family, he would say, must travel comfortably.

The boy became the center of Buntu's life. Even before he was born, Buntu had already started making inquiries at white private schools. That was where he would send his son, the bearer of his name.

Dreams! It is amazing how the horrible findings of my newspaper reports often vanished before the glossy magazines of our dreams, how I easily forgot that the glossy images were concocted out of the keys of typewriters, made by writers whose business was to sell dreams at the very moment that death pervaded the land. So powerful are words and pictures that even their makers often believe in them.

Buntu's ordeal was long. So it seemed. He would get up early every morning to follow up the previous day's leads regarding the body of our son. I wanted to go with him, but each time I prepared to go he would shake his head.

"It's my task," he would say. But every evening he returned, empty-handed, while with each day that passed and we did not know where the body of my child was, I grew restive and hostile in a manner that gave me much pain. Yet Buntu always felt compelled to give a report on each day's events. I never asked for it. I suppose it was his way of dealing with my silence.

One day he would say: "The lawyers have issued a court order that the body be produced. The writ of *habeas corpus*."

On another day he would say: "We have petitioned the Minister of Justice."

On yet another he would say: "I was supposed to meet the Chief Security

Officer. Waited the whole day. At the end of the day they said I would see him tomorrow if he was not going to be too busy. They are stalling."

Then he would say: "The newspapers, especially yours, are raising the hue and cry. The government is bound to be embarrassed. It's a matter of time."

And so it went on. Every morning he got up and left. Sometimes alone, sometimes with friends. He always left to bear the failure alone.

How much did I care about lawyers, petitions and Chief Security Officers? A lot. The problem was that whenever Buntu spoke about his efforts, I heard only his words. I felt in him the disguised hesitancy of someone who wanted reassurance without asking for it. I saw someone who got up every morning and left not to look for results, but to search for something he could only have found with me.

And each time he returned, I gave my speech to my eyes. And he answered without my having parted my lips. As a result, I sensed, for the first time in my life, a terrible power in me that could make him do anything. And he would never ever be able to deal with that power as long as he did not silence my eyes and call for my voice.

And so, he had to prove himself. And while he left each morning, I learned to be brutally silent. Could he prove himself without me? Could he? Then I got to know, those days, what I'd always wanted from him. I got to know why I have always drawn him into me whenever I sensed his vulnerability.

I wanted him to be free to fear. Wasn't there greater strength that way? Had he ever lived with his own feelings? And the stress of life in this land: didn't it call out for men to be heroes? And should they live up to it even though the details of the war to be fought may often be blurred? They should.

Yet it is precisely for that reason that I often found Buntu's thoughts lacking in strength. They lacked the experience of strife that could only come from a humbling acceptance of fear and then, only then, the need to fight it.

Me? In a way, I have always been free to fear. The prerogative of being a girl. It was always expected of me to scream when a spider crawled across the ceiling. It was known I would jump onto a chair whenever a mouse blundered into the room.

Then, once more, the Casspirs came. A few days before we got the body back, I was at home with my mother when we heard the great roar of truck engines. There was much running and shouting in the streets. I saw them, as I've always seen them on my assignments: the Casspirs. On five occasions they ran down our street at great speed, hurling tear-gas canisters at random. On the fourth occasion, they got our house. The canister shattered another window and filled the house with the terrible pungent choking smoke that I had got to know so well. We ran out of the house gasping for fresh air.

So, this was how my child was killed? Could they have been the same soldiers? Now hardened to their tasks? Or were they new ones being hardened to their tasks? Did they drive away laughing? Clearing paths for their families? What paths?

And was this our home? It couldn't be. It had to be a little bird's nest waiting to be plundered by a predator bird. There seemed no sense to the wedding pictures on the walls, the graduation pictures, birthday pictures, pictures of relatives, and paintings of lush landscapes. There seemed no sense any- more to what seemed recognizably human in our house. It took only a random swoop to obliterate personal worth, to blot out any value there may have been to the past. In desperation, we began to live only for the moment. I do feel hunted.

It was on the night of the tear gas that Buntu came home, saw what had happened, and broke down in tears. They had long been in the coming . . .

My own tears welled out too. How much did we have to cry to refloat stranded boats? I was sure they would float again.

A few nights later, on the night of the funeral, exhausted, I lay on my bed, listening to the last of the mourners leaving. Slowly, I became conscious of returning to the world. Something came back after it seemed not to have been there for ages. It came as a surprise, as a reminder that we will always live around what will happen. The sun will rise and set, and the ants will do their endless work, until one day the clouds turn gray and rain falls, and even in the township, the ants will fly out into the sky. Come what may.

My moon came, in a heavy surge of blood. And, after such a long time, I remembered the thing Buntu and I had buried in me. I felt it as if it had just entered. I felt it again as it floated away on the surge. I would be ready for another month. Ready as always, each and every month, for new beginnings.

And Buntu? I'll be with him, now. Always. Without our knowing, all the trying events had prepared for us new beginnings. Shall we not prevail?

JEREMY CRONIN (b. 1949)
South Africa; English

Jeremy Cronin was a lecturer at the University of Cape Town when he was arrested in 1976 as an African National Congress militant and served seven years in prison (joining Dennis Brutus and many other South African writers who have been "inside"). His prize-winning book of poems *Inside* was published in 1983. "To Learn How to Speak," written from the perspective of a white English- speaking observer, points to a new conception of South African culture. The radical politics of language implied by the poem, espoused by the ANC policy on language, speaks to issues raised in East Africa by Ngugi wa Thiong'o: a truly multiracial (or nonracial) culture, Cronin says, requires a multilingual people. In this poem language carries desire, for knowledge and acknowledgment of another's subjectivity, face to face with the voice that speaks the "cow-skinned vowel," the "suffix of their aches," the "syllables born in tin shacks,"and the "low chant" of the miners' political will. Cronin's poem gives those outside South Africa a glimpse of how white people might, with longing and difficulty, begin to secede from white supremacy.

To Learn How to Speak

To learn how to speak
With the voices of the land,
To parse the speech in its rivers,
To catch in the inarticulate grunt,
Stammer, call, cry, babble, tongue's knot   5
A sense of the stoneness of these stones
From which all words are cut.
To trace with the tongue wagon-trails
Saying the suffix of their aches in -kuil, -pan, -fontein,[1]
In watery names that confirm   10
The dryness of their ways.
To visit the places of occlusion, or the lick
in a vlei-bank[2] dawn.
To bury my mouth in the pit of your arm,
In that planetarium,   15
Pectoral beginning to the nub of time
Down there close to the water-table, to feel
The full moon as it drums
At the back of my throat
Its cow-skinned vowel.   20
To write a poem with words like:
I'm telling you,
Stompie, stickfast,[3] golovan,
Songololo, just boombang,[4] just
To understand the least inflections,   25
To voice without swallowing
Syllables born in tin shacks, or catch
the 5.15 ikwata bust fife
Chwannisberg train,[5] to reach
the low chant of the mine gang's   30
Mineral glow of our people's unbreakable resolve.

To learn how to speak
With the voices of this land.

---

1. The endings -kuil (pool), -pan (flat place),
   and -fontein (fountain) are common in Afrikaans place-names.
2. A small inland pond.

3. A stompie is a cigarette butt, or a short
   person; a stickfast is a flea.
4. A songololo is a millipede; a boombang is
   something quick and sudden.
5. A train going to Johannesburg.

INGRID DE KOK (b. 1951)
South Africa; English

Ingrid de Kok lectures at the University of Cape Town. Her book of poems *Familiar Ground* (1987) explores South African territory from the vantage point of a younger white feminist generation that, along the same lines as Nadine Gordimer and others, dreams of a common language. She works for a nonracial solidarity described in "Small Passing" as "the place of the mothers." The poem is a clear-eyed testing of the difficulty of genuine solidarity; the poet knows her "suffering is white" even as she angrily rejects its dismissal by a white man, and even as she hopes some black women can find it in their hearts not to ignore that suffering too.

from *Familiar Ground*

Small Passing

For a woman whose baby died stillborn, and who was told by a man to stop mourning, "because the trials and horrors suffered daily by black women in this country are more significant than the loss of one white child."

1

In this country you may not
suffer the death of your stillborn,
remember the last push into shadow and silence,
the useless wires and cords on your stomach,
the nurse's face, the walls, the afterbirth in a basin.   5
Do not touch your breasts
still full of purpose.
Do not circle the house,
pack, unpack the small clothes.
Do not lie awake at night hearing   10
the doctor say "It was just as well"
and "You can have another."
In this country you may not
mourn small passings.

See: the newspaper boy in the rain   15
will sleep tonight in a doorway.
The woman in the busline
may next month be on a train
to a place not her own.

My children are dying too
Look at them:
How dull their eyes
How slow their walk and the turning
Of their heads
Nothing for them to eat
Can you hear?
They are crying.

I spit at the sun
Shining on me
Blazing everyday
I am waiting for the rain to come
And I cannot plow this beautiful piece of earth.
Here I am: unemployed

I
the unemployed
I am here but invisible.
Preacher-man pray for the rain to come

White collars
In your chrome and brown armchairs
Please brighten up this thinning light
I am appealing to you oppressors
To free
Freedom from the tree.

My face
Buried with anger and sorrow
My stomach
Filled with hatred and pain
I behave like a lunatic
My kids are dying—
Malnutrition, kwashiokor[1]
There is nothing growing here
And the animals have died.

10

15

20

25

30

35

40

---

1. This childhood disease results from malnutrition.

All I hear now
Is the wind at night
It whirls around
Spelling the agony of a death
I'm dying.

45

(Curries Fountain Stadium, May Day 1985)

Paula Modersohn-Becker. *Self-portrait with Camellia Branch*. 1906–1907. Museum Folkwang, Essen.

SECTION XIV
Modern Europe

This period in Europe is marked by political upheaval, massive international conflict, and rapid social change: the French Revolution of 1789, the failed liberal revolution of 1848, the two world wars, the heyday and decline of colonialism, the spread of industrialism and of universal suffrage, the emancipation of women, the Russian Revolution of 1917, and the move toward the creation of the European Community. Scientific rationality of the kind that emerged into prominence in the seventeenth century is applied now to the organization of human societies, the development of myth and religion, the history of language, and the structure of the human mind itself.

In art and literature, all kinds of schools, genres, and tendencies suddenly proliferate. Included in this section is a sampling of the characteristic tensions, uncertainties, and excitement of the period, beginning in the eighteenth century with the Enlightenment—an age of progress and understanding—and moving to the birth of romanticism at the beginning of the nineteenth century, with its emphasis on the individual consciousness engaged in heroic tanglings with Fate. The late nineteenth century introduced symbolism, relying on suggestion and the unstated, while the turn of the twentieth century championed the supremacy of facts with the arrival of realism and naturalism. The early twentieth century opened a fresh age of experimentation, with the visual and verbal innovations of the cubists, and the noisy iconoclastic dada and futurist movements—

including the Italian-born Frenchman Guillaume Apollinaire, the Romanian Tristan Tzara, and the Italian Filippo Tommaso Marinetti—leading to André Breton's more optimistic surrealist movement in the 1920s, combining reason and the imagination, and a whole new range of expression across the entire literary spectrum, including lyric poetry, the minimalist novel, and the theater of the absurd. This is an age of -isms and avant-gardes, of the paradoxical clash of alienation and commitment. The complexities and contradictions of these 200 years in Western Europe are shown here in the vastly differing perspectives taken on the same thing, as, for example, the ways in which Keats, Rilke, and Cavafy offer quite separate ways of recalling and reexperiencing antiquity. Voltaire's plea for a tolerant and enlightened humanism may be set against the despair of the victims of political repression. Overall, a few often overlapping features of European literature seem to stand out in particular during this time: irony, experiment, the will to inclusiveness, and the cult of extremity or excess.

Irony penetrates or provides many of the conceptions, styles, and strategies of writers and thinkers as different from one another as Swift, Voltaire, Baudelaire, Kafka, and Beckett. Radical experimentation takes place in both form and psychology, as the literary artist creates and manipulates mood and mode. Free verse, attention-calling visual poetry, and new demands for different rhythms mark the poetry and manifestos of Apollinaire, Tzara, and Marinetti, at times mingled with a lyric consciousness that makes avant-garde writing of this epoch a heady mixture. The free indirect style of reflection in Virginia Woolf's and James Joyce's later writings, along with the automatic writing experiments of the surrealists are of special note among the formal innovations of the age. These new, sometimes technical and rhetorical effects summon novel kinds of awareness in the reader, who is often called upon to participate in the actual workings of the languages of fiction, lyricism, or fantasy. The imaginative musing of Sławomir Mrozek and Wolfgang Hildesheimer, and the eccentric styling of writers like Isak Dinesen in her "Gothic" manner and Samuel Beckett in his "minimalist" one push the creative energy to its limits.

Extremity and excess mark this age, even to an obsession with death: Paul Celan's "Death Fugue" responds to the Holocaust, in which human destructiveness has exploded on a scarcely intelligible scale. To some extent, the literary imagination in our time is simply disempowered by the carnage of the battlefield, by the Holocaust, and the determination of oppressors, so that silence seems to be, for certain writers, the only appropriate response, as in the final selection here by Bella Akhatovna Akhmadulina. But there are at least two ways in which the literature of the time is seen as effective reaction to these disasters. Certain writers bear witness directly or indirectly to the public catastrophes of the age, as in the works of Akhmatova, Tsvetayeva, and Mandelstam, Sachs and Celan; the impact of the terrible ironies of moral choices and their results in time of crisis makes itself felt in the existential writings of Sartre. Other writers deliberately enact destructiveness and its particular pleasures in their own texts. Gerard Manley Hopkins is an extreme case of the self torn between despair, guilt, and self-denial on the one hand, and the admiration of religious grandeur and natural beauty on the other: he, along with Baudelaire and Beckett, provide, in however anguished a form, the basis for a new aesthetics.

It is an age of contradictions, in which a concern with extreme violence plays against the more optimistic concerns: for example, in the new view of the human subject in Rilke, Celan, Breton, and Woolf, where its intense consciousness permits a fluctuation of psychological states. Although this is a period in which the literary imagination is often drawn to the brink of its own collapse, the crucial sense of the extreme motivates the parallel and vastly resourceful attack on conventional sense-making procedures that occurs in late Mallarmé, Joyce, Beckett, and Sarraute.

Included here are not just the grand and apocalyptic, the ironic and the experimental, but also work in the realist and naturalist modes: Pardo Bazán, Tolstoy, Ibsen Chekhov. In the lyric tradition of poetry, bearing its thoughtful witness from the romantics down to our days we see Droste-Hülshoff, Hölderlin, Keats, Leopardi, Hugo, Yeats, Rilke, Machado, Lorca, and Szymborska. Autobiographical reflections, such as those of Simone de Beauvoir on her own aging, show the other side of the reflective gaze upon the world: the self-examination that invites readers to reflect in their turn on past, present, and ongoing things.

Historical Background

Many ideas we now take for granted first gained a foothold during a period known variously as the Age of Reason, the Enlightenment, and the neoclassical period. Although it was once common to think of the Age of Reason as falling neatly between two revolutions—the English of 1688 and the French of 1789—historians now locate its origins much earlier, in the humanism of the sixteenth century Renaissance as well as in the rational and empirical methods that underlay the discoveries of the Scientific Revolution and the ideas of such thinkers as Locke, Bacon, and Descartes. By the eighteenth century, the legacy of these thinkers had paved the way for the intellectual and cultural movement known as the Enlightenment. From this period come the ideas that government should rest with the consent of the governed, that the life of citizens should be free of state interference, and that all human beings are created equal. More fundamentally, Enlightenment thinkers argued that human nature was essentially good and that happiness is a proper aim of human life. Armed with a belief in mathematical reasoning, scientific methods, and skepticism toward received ideas and traditional theology, eighteenth-century thinkers envisioned their age as one of illumination and amelioration, a period when human reason could bring about the individual's greater understanding and moral behavior as well as unlimited societal progress and reform. Accompanying such momentous changes in the minds of Europeans were new political and social developments. The period between 1700 and 1789 saw the augmented political power of a few great states, particularly France and Great Britain, followed by Prussia, Austria, Russia, and the Netherlands; migration from rural to urban areas, principally in England and France; and the rise of the middle class to political and cultural prominence, along with the end of the great age of kings and the gradual replacement of absolutist rule with enlightened despotism. The latter was particularly marked in Prussia and Austria, as well as in France, where Louis XV struggled to maintain Louis XIV's power and prestige at court.

Now in this enlightened world where tolerance and moderation were supposed to rule, public life took precedence over the private one, and philosophers, economists and novelists alike turned their attention to society and a citizen's proper place in it. During this period, the French language dominated much of the literature and replaced Latin as the language of diplomacy, scholarship, and trade. The *philosophes* associated with the *Encyclopédie,* the optimistic compendium of knowledge directed by Denis Diderot, sought to enforce real reforms, but they bypassed women's rights as well as those of slaves in the colonies; throughout this period women remained subordinate to men.

For all its talk of reform, the Enlightenment provided less action in the real world than the period between 1760 and 1830, when three revolutions profoundly altered not only the European mind but also the political, economic, and social structure of Europe. The American Revolution provided a visible alternative to monarchy in the idea of a government of and by the people. Along with the French Revolution, the American Revolution led to beliefs basic to Western political life—namely, that constitutions should spell out the laws of the state while identifying basic human liberties. The expansion of civil and natural rights throughout the modern period is a natural outgrowth of these revolutions. The Industrial Revolution made possible the dominance of industrialism over agriculture as the economic staple of the state. It fostered a classical economics in which a laissez-faire policy was seen as irretrievably linked to capitalism and continuous industrial expansion. Led by Great Britain, it was fueled by the investment of capital, lenient trade laws, technological advances that began in the coal and iron ore industries and quickly spread, and, finally, population increases that began in the late eighteenth century and extended into the nineteenth. Between 1750 and 1800, the populations of many countries doubled, providing avid consumer markets and a large labor force, which came to be known as the working class, organized by employers who brought workers together, often in squalid working conditions, to maximize production. Transportation networks flourished—in particular railroads and steam shipping—enabling producers to transport finished goods to far-off markets and to move raw materials. The resulting societal changes included a decline in the autonomy of the worker and the speeding up of work, with machines often setting the pace; the employment of women and children in work settings often dangerous; the development of a work ethic among the middle class; the decline of the family as a production unit; and the establishment of a more rigid work-home dichotomy.

The most visible and shattering of the revolutions occurred in neither American nor Britain but in France, where it would have an enormous impact on the mind and geography of modern Europe. More than any other event, the French Revolution of 1789 signaled a turning from the past, with its hierarchies, entrenched patronage systems, and unhurried rate of change, marking the increasing power of the bourgeoisie and a resurgent aristocracy over a financially beleagred monarchy. Developments came to a head in 1789, when the Estates-General, called by Louis XVI, instituted a parliamentary system in which the third estate—comprised largely of an urban middle class—declared itself the National Assembly, true representatives of the people with power over the two other estates, the nobles and the clergy. Devoted to liberty, equality, and fraternity, the Assembly closed the door on royal despotism and introduced a representative government in the form of a limited, constitutional monarchy much like England's. By 1792, the fragile balance had unraveled, with radical reformers suspending the 1791 constitution, executing the king, and founding the French Republic. A wide range of reforms was instituted, from the decimal system and mass military conscription to voting rights for all males, including Jews and blacks, the abolition of the slave trade, and an open educational system. Such radical reforms were met with alarm by groups within France as well as by other countries, and the new

Republic soon faced civil war and invasions from abroad. These events led to a period of suppression known as the Reign of Terror (1793–1794), in which suspected enemies of the revolution were executed. In 1799 the post-Revolutionary government was overthrown by Napoleon, whose regime produced a period of relative internal stability and colonial expansion, translating many Enlightenment principles into reality. In addition to stabilizing the economy, revamping France's educational system, and promoting religious freedom, he instituted a series of rational legal principles in the form of the Napoleonic Code, incorporating various revolutionary-era reforms, including the abolition of serf-dom and guilds, and a centralized bureaucracy in which talent, not birthright, was rewarded. Despite Napoleon's defeat at Waterloo in 1815 and the moves of other European countries to restrict radical reforms, the spirit of Napoleonic reform endured.

The revolutions of the late eighteenth century shattered the aristocracy's monopoly of power and paved the way for an age of the bourgeoisie, in which a prosperous middle class exercised political and cultural power, and in which the lower classes, yet to share in the wealth of a newly modernized society, would press for equality and reforms. Two forces in particular underlay the events of nineteenth century Europe. The first was liberalism, with its ideas of religious toleration, free speech, a laissez-faire economics that allowed wealth to be accumulated in massive amounts. There was also a growing belief in the values of middle class life—hard work, social mobility, thrift, and a well-earned modesty. The other prime force was nationalism, with its idea that the common language and life of a nation took precedence over mere class divisions. During the period between 1871 and 1914, Europe experienced a period of tranquility that tended to obscure the rampant nationalism and growing militarism underlying it. Imperi-alism, motivated by a desire to tap new financial markets and provide increased revenues, spawned colonization, the spread of Western technologies, and exploi-tation, particularly in Africa as well as in Indochina. By 1914, conflicts arising from both increasing nationalism and intractable domestic problems erupted in World War I, with Russia, France, and Great Britain on one side, and Germany and Austria-Hungary on the other. By 1917—the date of the Russian Revolution with its all-important furtherance of the ideas of communism and socialism—the United States had joined the Allied cause. The war lasted four years and resulted in ten million casualties. The period between the two world wars, marked by boom times, soon gave way to depression and political crises in the United States as well as in Germany. By 1939, only twenty years after the Versailles Treaty ended World War I, most of the new democracies—from Germany and Austria-Hungary to Russia, Italy, Spain, and Romania—had become totalitarian, and the problems ostensibly settled by the Versailles Treaty were once again surfacing. The precari-ous peace established by the treaty was broken in 1939 when Germany, under Adolf Hitler, marched into Poland. France and Great Britain promptly responded by declaring war. When the war finally ended in 1945 with the atomic bombing of Japan by the United States, the world had witnessed some of the most inhuman examples of human depravity and suffering, not only in the death camps where thousands of Jews were sent to their deaths but also in the aftermath of the bombings of Hiroshima and Nagasaki.

At the moment of the two most destructive wars in history there emerged a mass society in which the middle class had effectively challenged the political and cultural ascendancy of the bourgeoisie in much the same way that the bourgeoisie had repudiated the power of the aristocracy in the previous century. Paired with such shifts in power was a growing revulsion—on the part of artists and intellectuals—toward a mass culture grounded in what was perceived as the naive and outmoded fiction of "social progress." In some sense, it was World War I itself that had stymied the future, clouded ideas of a rational, unified, and progressive Europe, and questioned the liberal social tenets of the past. Such skepticism was not entirely new. Nineteenth century writers as diverse as Arnold, Ruskin, Nietzsche, Flaubert, and Baudelaire attacked the smugness and banality of middle class society, repudiated a past marked by an unjustified belief in both "progress" and positivistic thinking, and questioned the belief in the moral underpinnings not only of the individual but of society as well. By the twentieth century such goals had become more pronounced. The aim of art was, as Ezra Pound remarked, to "make it new," and the first decades of the twentieth century spawned a number of diverse movements dedicated to radical stylistic experimentation. There arose a deep philosophical skepticism about what could be known, and, ultimately, about the nineteenth century belief that language as we had come to think of it could provide a specific and faithful measure of the objective world.

The anxious postwar period was characterized by an essentially bipolar balance of power, regulated by a Cold War policy that pitted the democratic, free enterprise system of the West against the state planning and collectivist mentality of the Soviet Union. Such policies remained in effect until the late 1970s when a loosening of pressures, or détente, set in, marked by arms reduction treaties and a gradual end of the Cold War. The end of the bipolar world view has coincided with the spiraling power of American mass culture forms, from movies to television to T-shirts, and the rise of an increasingly global and democratic culture, a culture that has all but extinguished native cultures, according to some critics. A more optimistic view holds that this global mentality transcends the boundaries of a single continent to embrace the ideas, beliefs, cultural productions, and customs of many different groups, men and women, members of all races, and inhabitants of many countries—even as it preserves national differences.

Further Readings

Abrams, M. H. *The Mirror and the Lamp: Romantic Theory and the Critical Tradition*. New York: Oxford University Press, 1953.

Aldridge, Alfred O. *Voltaire and the Century of Light*. Princeton: Princeton University Press, 1975.

Alter, Robert. *The Pleasures of Reading in an Ideological Age*. New York: Simon and Schuster, 1989.

Auerbach, Eric. *Mimesis*. Princeton: Princeton University Press, 1953.

Brooks, Cleanth. *Understanding Fiction*. New York: Appleton-Century Crofts, 1959.

Burger, Peter. *Theory of the Avant-Garde*. Manchester: Manchester University Press, 1984.

Frank, Joseph. *The Widening Gyre: Crisis and Mastery in Modern Literature*. Bloomington: Indiana University Press, 1968.

Girard, René. *Deceit, Desire, and the Novel: Self and Other in Literary Structure*. Trans. Yvonne Freccero. Baltimore: Johns Hopkins University Press, 1965.

Guillen, Claudio. *Literature as System: Essays Toward the Theory of Literary History*. Princeton: Princeton University Press, 1971.

Hamburger, Michael. *The Truth of Poetry: Tensions in Modern Poetry from Baudelaire to the Nineteen-Sixties*. New York: Harcourt, Brace and World, 1969.

Jameson, Fredric. *The Political Unconscious: Narrative as a Socially Symbolic Act*. Ithaca: Cornell University Press, 1981.

Johnson, Barbara. *The Critical Difference: Essays in the Contemporary Rhetoric of Reading*. Baltimore: Johns Hopkins University Press, 1981.

Moi, Toril. *Sexual-Textual Politics*. New York: Methuen, 1985.

Praz, Mario. *The Romantic Agony*. New York: Meridian Books, 1956.

Symons, Arthur. *The Symbolist Movement in Literature*. New York: Haskell House, 1971.

Vickery, John B., ed. *Myth and Literature: Contemporary Theory and Practice*. Lincoln: University of Nebraska Press, 1966. (repr. Bison Books, 1971)

Williams, Raymond. *Culture and Society: 1780–1950*. Garden City: Doubleday, 1960.

JONATHAN SWIFT (1667–1745)
Ireland/England

After some years in England, learning a great deal about politics, and writing *The Tale of a Tub* (1704), a ridicule of religious extremism, as well as producing *The Examiner* (1710), a Tory newspaper, Swift was ordained a priest in the Anglican Church and became dean of Saint Patrick's Cathedral in Dublin, where he had been born (of English parents) and educated. Throughout his life, he was involved in political and religious controversy and was recognized in his own lifetime as a master of satiric writing, and poet. His best-known work is *Gulliver's Travels* (1726). *A Modest Proposal*, published in 1729, is a savage commentary on the poverty prevalent in Ireland as a result of repressive English rule. He puts forward a "solution"; the result is a ghastly satire on the plans to correct injustice.

A Modest Proposal

FOR PREVENTING THE CHILDREN OF POOR PEOPLE IN IRELAND FROM BEING A BURDEN TO THEIR PARENTS OR COUNTRY, AND FOR MAKING THEM BENEFICIAL TO THE PUBLIC

It is a melancholy object to those who walk through this great town or travel in the country, when they see the streets, the roads, and cabin doors, crowded with beggars of the female sex, followed by three, four, or six children, all in rags and importuning every passenger for an alms. These mothers, instead of being able to work for their honest livelihood, are forced to employ all their time in strolling to beg sustenance for their helpless infants, who, as they grow up, either turn thieves for want of work, or leave their dear native country to fight for the Pretender[1] in Spain, or sell themselves to the Barbadoes.

I think it is agreed by all parties that this prodigious number of children in the arms, or on the backs, or at the heels of their mothers, and frequently of their fathers, is in the present deplorable state of the kingdom a very great additional grievance; and therefore whoever could find out a fair, cheap, and easy method of making these children sound, useful members of the commonwealth would deserve so well of the public as to have his statue set up for a preserver of the nation.

But my intention is very far from being confined to provide only for the children of professed beggars; it is of a much greater extent, and shall take in the whole number of infants at a certain age who are born of parents in effect as little able to support them as those who demand our charity in the streets.

---

[1]. The son of James II, the "pretender" or claimant to England's throne, to whom many Irishmen in exile were faithful. They sold their work for passage overseas.

As to my own part, having turned my thoughts for many years upon this important subject, and maturely weighed the several schemes of other projectors,[2] I have always found them grossly mistaken in this computation. It is true, a child just dropped from its dam may be supported by her milk for a solar year, with little other nourishment; at most not above the value of two shillings, which the mother may certainly get, or the value in scraps, by her lawful occupation of begging; and it is exactly at one year old that I propose to provide for them in such a manner as instead of being a charge upon their parents or the parish, or wanting food and raiment for the rest of their lives, they shall on the contrary contribute to the feeding, and partly to the clothing, of many thousands.

There is likewise another great advantage in my scheme, that it will prevent those voluntary abortions, and that horrid practice of women murdering their bastard children, alas! too frequent among us! sacrificing the poor innocent babes I doubt more to avoid the expense than the shame, which would move tears and pity in the most savage and inhuman breast.

The number of souls in this kingdom being usually reckoned one million and a half, of these I calculate there may be about 200,000 couple whose wives are breeders; from which number I subtract 30,000 couple who are able to maintain their own children (although I apprehend there cannot be so many, under the present distress of the kingdom); but this being granted, there will remain 170,000 breeders. I again subtract 50,000 for those women who miscarry, or whose children die by accident or disease within the year. There only remain 120,000 children of poor parents annually born. The question therefore is, how this number shall be reared and provided for? which, as I have already said, under the present situation of affairs, is utterly impossible by all the methods hitherto proposed. For we can neither employ them in handicraft or agriculture; we neither build houses (I mean in the country) nor cultivate land; they can very seldom pick up a livelihood by stealing, till they arrive at six years old, except where they are of towardly parts; although I confess they learn the rudiments much earlier; during which time they can, however, be properly looked upon only as probationers, as I have been informed by a principal gentleman in the county of Cavan, who protested to me that he never knew above one or two instances under the age of six, even in a part of the kingdom so renowned for the quickest proficiency in that art.

I am assured by our merchants that a boy or a girl before twelve years old is no salable commodity: and even when they come to this age they will not yield above three pounds, or three pounds and a half a crown at most, on the exchange; which cannot turn to account either to the parents or kingdom, the charge of nutriment and rags having been at least four times that value.

I shall now therefore humbly propose my own thoughts, which I hope will not be liable to the least objection.

I have been assured by a very knowing American of my acquaintance in London that a young healthy child well nursed is at a year old a most delicious,

---

2. Projectors of theoretical solutions, like this one.

nourishing, and wholesome food, whether stewed, roasted, baked, or boiled; and I make no doubt that it will equally serve in a fricassee or a ragout.

I do therefore humbly offer it to public consideration that of the hundred and twenty thousand children already computed, twenty thousand may be reserved for breed, whereof only one-fourth part to be males; which is more than we allow to sheep, black cattle, or swine; and my reason is that these children are seldom the fruits of marriage, a circumstance not much regarded by our savages; therefore one male will be sufficient to serve four females. That the remaining hundred thousand may, at a year old, be offered in sale to the persons of quality and fortune through the kingdom; always advising the mother to let them suck plentifully in the last month, so as to render them plump and fat for a good table. A child will make two dishes at an entertainment for friends; and when the family dines alone, the fore or hind quarter will make a reasonable dish, and seasoned with a little pepper or salt will be very good boiled on the fourth day, especially in winter.

I have reckoned upon a medium that a child just born will weigh twelve pounds, and in a solar year, if tolerably nursed, will increase to twenty-eight pounds.

I grant this food will be somewhat dear, and therefore very proper for landlords, who, as they have already devoured most of the parents, seem to have the best title to the children.

Infant's flesh will be in season throughout the year, but more plentifully in March, and a little before and after: for we are told by a grave author, an eminent French physician, that fish being a prolific diet, there are more children born in Roman Catholic countries about nine months after Lent than at any other season: therefore, reckoning a year after Lent, the markets will be more glutted than usual, because the number of popish infants is at least three to one in this kingdom: and therefore it will have one other collateral advantage, by lessening the number of papists among us.

I have already computed the charge of nursing a beggar's child (in which list I reckon all cottagers, laborers, and four-fifths of the farmers) to be about two shillings per annum, rags included: and I believe no gentleman would repine to give ten shillings for the carcass of a good fat child, which, as I have said, will make four dishes of excellent nutritive meat, when he has only some particular friend or his own family to dine with him. Thus the squire will learn to be a good landlord and grow popular among his tenants: the mother will have eight shillings net profit and be fit for work till she produces another child.

Those who are more thrifty (as I must confess the times require) may flay the carcass; the skin of which artificially dressed will make admirable gloves for ladies and summer boots for fine gentlemen.

As to our city of Dublin, shambles[3] may be appointed for this purpose in the most convenient parts of it, and butchers we may be assured will not be wanting; although I rather recommend buying the children alive and dressing them hot from the knife as we do roasting pigs.

---

3. Slaughterhouses.

A very worthy person, a true lover of his country, and whose virtues I highly esteem, was lately pleased, in discoursing on this matter, to offer a refinement upon my scheme. He said that many gentlemen of this kingdom, having of late destroyed their deer, he conceived that the want of venison might be well supplied by the bodies of young lads and maidens, not exceeding fourteen years of age nor under twelve; so great a number of both sexes in every country being now ready to starve for want of work and service; and these to be disposed of by their parents, if alive, or otherwise by their nearest relations. But with due deference to so excellent a friend and so deserving a patriot, I cannot be altogether in his sentiments; for as to the males, my American acquaintance assured me from frequent experience that their flesh was generally tough and lean, like that of our schoolboys, by continual exercise, and their taste disagreeable; and to fatten them would not answer the charge. Then as to the females, it would, I think with humble submission, be a loss to the public, because they soon would become breeders themselves; and besides, it is not improbable that some scrupulous people might be apt to censure such a practice (although indeed very unjustly) as a little bordering upon cruelty; which I confess, hath always been with me the strongest objection against my project, how well soever intended.

But in order to justify my friend, he confessed that this expedient was put into his head by the famous Psalmanazar,[4] a native of the island Formosa, who came from thence to London above twenty years ago, and in conversation told my friend that in his country when any young person happened to be put to death, the executioner sold the carcass to persons of quality as a prime dainty; and that in his time the body of a plump girl of fifteen, who was crucified for an attempt to poison the emperor, was sold to his Imperial Majesty's prime minister of state, and other great mandarins of the court, in joints from the gibbet, at four hundred crowns. Neither indeed can I deny that if the same use were made of several plump young girls in this town, who without one single coat to their fortunes cannot stir abroad without a chair, and appear at the playhouse and assemblies in foreign fineries which they never will pay for, the kingdom would not be the worse.

Some persons of a desponding spirit are in great concern about that great number of poor people who are aged, diseased, or maimed, and I have been desired to employ my thoughts what course may be taken to ease the nation of so grievous an encumbrance. But I am not in the least pain upon that matter, because it is very well known that they are every day dying and rotting by cold and famine, and filth and vermin, as fast as can be reasonably expected. And as to the younger laborers, they are now in almost as hopeful a condition. They cannot get work, and consequently pine away for want of nourishment to a degree that if at any time they are accidentally hired to common labor, they have not strength to perform it; and thus the country and themselves are happily delivered from the evils to come.

I have too long digressed, and therefore shall return to my subject. I think the

---

4. Really a Frenchman, who passed himself off as Formosan, recounting these delightful instances of cannibal customs in a foreign land.

advantages by the proposal which I have made are obvious and many, as well as of the highest importance.

For first, as I have already observed, it would greatly lessen the number of papists, with whom we are yearly overrun, being the principal breeders of the nation, as well as our most dangerous enemies; and who stay at home on purpose to deliver the kingdom to the pretender, hoping to take their advantage by the absence of so many good protestants, who have chosen rather to leave their country than stay at home and pay tithes against their conscience to an episocopal curate.

Secondly, the poorer tenants will have something valuable of their own, which by law may be made liable to distress,[5] and help to pay their landlord's rent; their corn and cattle being already seized, and money a thing unknown.

Thirdly, whereas the maintenance of a hundred thousand children, from two years old and upwards, cannot be computed at less than ten shilling a piece per annum, the nation's stock will be thereby increased fifty thousand pounds per annum, beside the profit of a new dish introduced to the tables of all gentlemen of fortune in the kingdom, who have any refinement in taste. And the money will circulate among ourselves, the goods being entirely of our growth and manufacture.

Fourthly, the constant breeders, beside the gain of eight shillings sterling per annum by the sale of their children, will be rid of the charge of maintaining them after the first year.

Fifthly, this food would likewise bring great custom to taverns: where the vintners will certainly be so prudent as to procure the best receipts for dressing it to perfection, and consequently have their houses frequented by all the fine gentlemen, who justly value themselves upon their knowledge in good eating; and a skillful cook, who understands how to oblige his guests, will contrive to make it as expensive as they please.

Sixthly, this would be a great inducement to marriage, which all wise nations have either encouraged by rewards or enforced by laws and penalties. It would increase the care and tenderness of mothers toward their children, when they were sure of a settlement for life to the poor babes, provided in some sort by the public, to their annual profit instead of expense. We should see an honest emulation among the married women, which of them could bring the fattest child to the market. Men would become as fond of their wives during the time of their pregnancy as they are now of their mares in foal, their cows in calf, or sows when they are ready to farrow; nor offer to beat or kick them (as is too frequent a practice) for fear of a miscarriage.

Many other advantages might be enumerated. For instance, the addition of some thousand carcasses in our exportation of barreled beef, the propagation of swine's flesh, and improvement in the art of making good bacon, so much wanted among us by the great destruction of pigs, too frequent at our tables; which are no way comparable in taste or magnificence to a well-grown, fat yearling child, which

---

5. The takeover of land to pay debts.

roasted whole will make a considerable figure at a lord mayor's feast, or any other public entertainment. But this and many others I omit, being studious of brevity.

Supposing that one thousand families in this city would be constant customers for infants' flesh, besides others who might have it at merry-meetings, particularly weddings and christenings. I compute that Dublin would take off annually about twenty thousand carcasses; and the rest of the kingdom (where probably they will be sold somewhat cheaper) the remaining eighty thousand.

I can think of no one objection that will possibly be raised against this proposal, unless it should be urged that the number of people will be thereby much lessened in the kingdom. This I freely own, and it was indeed one principal design in offering it to the world. I desire the reader will observe that I calculate my remedy for this one individual kingdom of Ireland, and for no other that ever was, is, or, I think, ever can be upon earth. Therefore let no man talk to me of other expedients: of taxing our absentees at five shillings a pound; of using neither clothes nor household furniture, except what is of our own growth and manufacture; of utterly rejecting the materials and instruments that promote foreign luxury; of curing the expensiveness of pride, vanity, idleness, and gaming in our women; of introducing a vein of parsimony, prudence, and temperance: of learning to love our country in the want of which we differ even from LAPLANDERS and the inhabitants of TOPINAMBOO; of quitting our animosities and factions, nor acting any longer like the Jews, who were murdering one another at the very moment their city was taken; of being a little cautious not to sell our country and conscience for nothing; of teaching landlords to have at least one degree of mercy toward their tenants; lastly, of putting a spirit of honesty, industry, and skill into our shop-keepers; who, if a resolution could now be taken to buy only our native goods, would immediately unite to cheat and exact upon us in the price, the measure, and the goodness, nor could ever yet be brought to make one fair proposal of just dealing, though often and earnestly invited to it.

Therefore, I repeat, let no man talk to me of these and the like expedients, till he has at least some glimpse of hope that there will be ever some hearty and sincere attempt to put them in practice.

But as to myself, having been wearied out for many years with offering vain, idle, visionary thoughts, and at length utterly despairing of success, I fortunately fell upon this proposal: which, as it is wholly new, so it has something solid and real, of no expense and little trouble, full in our own power, and whereby we can incur no danger in disobliging ENGLAND. For this kind of commodity will not bear exportation, the flesh being of too tender a consistence to admit a long continuance in a salt, although perhaps I could name a country which would be glad to eat up our whole nation without it.[6]

After all, I am not so violently bent upon my own opinion as to reject any offer proposed by wise men, which shall be found equally innocent, cheap, easy, and effectual. But before something of that kind shall be advanced in contradiction to my scheme, and offering a better, I desire the author or authors will be

---

6. He could have named England, specifically.

pleased maturely to consider two points. First, as things now stand, how they will be able to find food and raiment for an hundred thousand useless mouths and backs. And secondly, there being a round million of creatures in human figure throughout this kingdom, whose sole subsistence put into a common stock would leave them in debt two millions of pounds sterling, adding those who are beggars by profession to the bulk of farmers, cottagers, and laborers, with their wives and children who are beggars in effect; I desire those politicians who dislike my overture, and may perhaps be so bold to attempt an answer, that they will first ask the parents of these mortals whether they would not at this day think it a great happiness to have been sold for food at a year old in the manner I prescribe, and thereby have avoided such a perpetual sense of misfortunes as they have since gone through by the oppression of landlords, the impossibility of paying rent without money or trade, the want of common sustenance, with neither house nor clothes to cover them from the inclemencies of the weather, and the most inevitable prospect of entailing the like or greater miseries upon their breed forever.

I profess, in the sincerity of my heart, that I have not the least personal interest in endeavoring to promote this necessary work, having no other motive than the public good of my country, by advancing our trade, providing for infants, relieving the poor, and giving some pleasure to the rich. I have no children by which I can propose to get a single penny, the youngest being nine years old, and my wife past childbearing.

VOLTAIRE [FRANÇOIS-MARIE AROUET] (1694–1778)
France

Because of his biting wit, Voltaire got into trouble early, insulting the Chevalier de Rohan, whose lackeys beat him up; he was imprisoned, then exiled to England, where he spent three years, meeting Pope and Swift, Locke and Newton, whose ideas he propagated in France upon his return. His *Philosophical Letters* (1734) were condemned by the French government; many of his works were controversial, especially his diatribes against the Roman Catholic Church and Calvinism. Voltaire was one of the first cultural critics in the modern sense. He wrote stories, plays, and poems, literary and philosophic criticism, and was an active polemicist for the application of enlightened reason to human affairs. *Candide* (1759) is a hilarious satire on idealism, specifically on the German philosopher Gottfried Leibniz, whose conception of order in the universe ungraspable by the human mind is reduced to the saying "Everything is for the best in this best of all possible worlds." Voltaire's work has much in common with the bitterly comic satire of Jonathan Swift.

Candide or Optimism

Translated from the German of Dr. Ralph[1] . . . with the additions found in the Doctor's pocket when he died at Minden in the Year of Our Lord 1759

1

HOW CANDIDE WAS BROUGHT UP IN A FINE CASTLE, AND HOW HE WAS EXPELLED THEREFROM

In Westphalia, in the castle of My Lord the Baron of Thunder-ten-tronckh, there was a young man whom nature had endowed with the gentlest of characters. His face bespoke his soul. His judgment was rather sound and his mind of the simplest; this is the reason, I think, why he was named Candide. The old servants of the house suspected that he was the son of My Lord the Baron's sister and of a good and honorable gentlemen of the neighborhood whom that lady never would marry because he could prove only seventy-one quarterings[2] and the rest of his genealogical tree had been lost by the injuries of time.

My Lord the Baron was one of the most powerful lords in Westphalia, for his castle had a door and windows. His great hall was even adorned with a piece of tapestry. All the dogs of his stable yards formed a pack of hounds when necessary; his grooms were his huntsmen; the village vicar was his Grand Almoner. They all called him My Lord, and they laughed at the stories he told.

My Lady the Baroness, who weighed about three hundred and fifty pounds, attracted very great consideration by that fact, and did the honors of the house with a dignity that made her even more respectable. Her daughter Cunégonde, aged seventeen, was rosy-complexioned, fresh, plump, appetizing. The Baron's son appeared in all respects worthy of his father. The tutor Pangloss[3] was the oracle of the house, and little Candide listened to his lessons with all the candor of his age and character.

Pangloss taught metaphysico-theologo-cosmolo-nigology.[4] He proved admirably that there is no effect without a cause and that, in this best of all possible worlds,[5] My Lord the Baron's castle was the finest of castles, and My Lady the best of all possible Baronesses.

"It is demonstrated," he said, "that things cannot be otherwise, for, everything being made for an end, everything is necessarily for the best end. Note that noses were made to wear spectacles, and so we have spectacles. Legs were visibly

Translated by Donald M. Frame.

1. For some weeks after its publication Voltaire denied authorship of *Candide*, as he often did with works potentially dangerous to himself.
2. Divisions on a coat of arms indicating degrees of nobility. Sixty-four was considered the maximum.
3. From the Greek: "all tongue."

4. The "-nigo-" suggests the French *nigaud*, "booby."
5. The systematic optimism ridiculed throughout *Candide* is a caricature of that of Leibniz (1646–1716), popularized by Alexander Pope in his *Essay on Man* (1733–1734), and systematized by Christian Wolff (1679–1754).

instituted to be breeched, and we have breeches. Stones were formed to be cut and to make into castles; so My Lord has a very handsome castle; the greatest baron in the province should be the best housed; and, pigs being made to be eaten, we eat pork all year round: consequently, those who have asserted that all is well have said a foolish thing; they should have said that all is for the best."

Candide listened attentively and believed innocently; for he thought Mademoiselle Cunégonde extremely beautiful, though he never made bold to tell her so. He concluded that after the happiness of being born Baron of Thunder-ten-tronckh, the second degree of happiness was to be Mademoiselle Cunégonde; the third, to see her every day; and the fourth, to listen to Doctor Pangloss, the greatest philosopher in the province and consequently in the whole world.

One day Cunégonde, walking near the castle in the little wood they called The Park, saw in the bushes Doctor Pangloss giving a lesson in experimental physics to her mother's chambermaid, a very pretty and very docile little brunette. Since Mademoiselle Cunégonde had much inclination for the sciences, she observed breathlessly the repeated experiments of which she was a witness; she clearly saw the Doctor's sufficient reason, the effects and the causes, and returned home all agitated, all pensive, all filled with the desire to be learned, thinking that she might well be the sufficient reason of young Candide, who might equally well be hers.

She met Candide on the way back to the castle, and blushed; Candide blushed too; she said good morning to him in a faltering voice; and Candide spoke to her without knowing what he was saying. The next day, after dinner, as everyone was leaving the table, Cunégonde and Candide found themselves behind a screen; Cunégonde dropped her handkerchief, Candide picked it up, she innocently took his hand, the young man innocently kissed the young lady's hand with a very special vivacity, sensibility, and grace; their lips met, their eyes glowed, their knees trembled, their hands wandered. My Lord the Baron of Thunder-ten-tronckh passed near the screen and, seeing this cause and this effect, expelled Candide from the castle with great kicks in the behind; Cunégonde swooned; she was slapped in the face by My Lady the Baroness as soon as she had come to herself; and all was in consternation in the finest and most agreeable of all possible castles.

2

WHAT BECAME OF CANDIDE AMONG THE BULGARIANS[6]

Candide, expelled from the earthly paradise, walked for a long time without knowing where, weeping, raising his eyes to heaven, turning them often toward the finest of castles, which enclosed the most beautiful of future Baronesses; he lay down to sleep without supper in the midst of the fields between two furrows; the

---

6. Voltaire chose this name to represent the Prussians of Frederick the Great because he had reason to think that Frederick was a pederast and because the French *bougre,* like the English "bugger," comes from *Bulgare* (Bulgarian). Note the treatment of the Baron's son in Chapter 4 and his adventures narrated in Chapters 15 and 28.

snow was falling in flat flakes. The next day Candide, frozen, dragged himself toward the neighboring town, which was named Valdberghoff-trarbk-dikdorff, with no money, dying of hunger and fatigue. He stopped sadly at the door of an inn. Two men dressed in blue noticed him.

"Comrade," said one, "there's a very well-built young man, and he's of the right height."

They advanced toward Candide and very civilly invited him to dinner.

"Gentlemen," said Candide with charming modesty, "you do me great honor, but I haven't the money to pay my bill."

"Ah, sir," said one of the men in blue, "persons of your figure and merit never pay for anything; aren't you five feet five?"

"Yes, gentlemen, that is my height," he said with a bow.

"Ah, sir, sit down to table; not only will we pay your expenses, but we will never allow a man like you to lack money; men are made only to help one another."

"You are right," said Candide. "That is what Monsieur Pangloss always told me, and I clearly see that all is for the best."

They urge him to accept a few crowns, he takes them and wants to make out a promissory note; they want none, they all sit down to table.

"Don't you love tenderly . . . ?"

"Oh yes," he replied, "I love Mademoiselle Cunégonde tenderly."

"No," said one of the gentlemen, "we are asking you whether you do not tenderly love the King of the Bulgarians."

"Not at all," he said, "for I have never seen him."

"What! He is the most charming of Kings, and you must drink his health."

"Oh! most gladly, gentlemen"; and he drinks.

"That is sufficient," they say to him, "you are now the prop, the support, the defender, the hero of the Bulgarians; your fortune is made, and your glory is assured."

They immediately put irons on his legs and they take him to the regiment. They make him turn right, turn left, raise the ramrod, return the ramrod, take aim, fire, march on the double, and they give him thirty strokes with a stick; the next day he drills a little less badly and he gets only twenty strokes; the day after they give him only ten, and he is regarded as a prodigy by his comrades.

Candide, completely stupefied, could not yet understand too well how he was a hero. He took it into his head one fine spring day to go for a stroll, walking straight ahead, believing that it was a privilege of the race of humans, as of the race of animals, to use their legs as they please.[7] He had not gone two leagues when up came four other heroes, six feet tall; they overtake him, they bind him, they put him in a dungeon. He was asked, juridically, which he liked better, to be beaten thirty-six times by the whole regiment, or to receive twelve lead bullets at once in his brain. In vain he told them that the will is free and that he wanted neither of

---

7. This whole chapter satirizes the drillmaster-
ship of Frederick the Great. The desertion is
suggested by Voltaire's memory of a
Frenchman named Courtilz, whose release
from prison into a hospital Voltaire had
procured from Frederick.

these; he had to make a choice. By virtue of the gift of God that is called *liberty*, he decided to run the gantlet thirty-six times; he did it twice. The regiment was made up of two thousand men. That gave him four thousand strokes of the ramrod, which laid open his muscles and nerves the nape of his neck to his rump. As they were about to proceed to the third run, Candide, at the end of his rope, asked them as a favor to be kind enough to smash in his head; he obtained this favor. They bandage his eyes; they make him kneel; at that moment the King of the Bulgarians passes, inquires about the victim's crime; and since this King was a man of great genius, he understood, from all he learned about Candide, that this was a young metaphysician very ignorant of the ways of this world, and he granted him his pardon with a clemency that will be praised in all newspapers and in all ages. A worthy surgeon cured Candide in three weeks with the emollients prescribed by Dioscorides. He already had a little bit of skin, and could walk, when the King of the Bulgarians gave battle to the King of the Abarians.[8]

3

HOW CANDIDE ESCAPED FROM AMONG THE BULGARIANS, AND WHAT BECAME OF HIM

Nothing could be so beautiful, so smart, so brilliant, so well drilled as the two armies. Trumpets, fifes, oboes, drums, cannons formed a harmony such as was never heard even in hell. First the cannons felled about six thousand men on each side; then the musketry removed from the best of worlds some nine or ten thousand scoundrels who infected its surface. The bayonet also was the sufficient reason for the death of some thousands of men. The whole might well amount to about thirty thousand souls. Candide, trembling like a philosopher, hid himself as best he could during this heroic butchery.

Finally, while both kings were having *Te Deums* sung, each in his own camp, he decided to go reason elsewhere about effects and causes. He passed over heaps of dead and dying and first reached a neighboring village; it was in ashes; it was an Abarian village which the Bulgarians had burned in accordance with the rules of international law. Here, old men riddled with wounds watched their wives die, with their throats cut, holding their children to their bleeding breasts; there, girls, disemboweled after satisfying the natural needs of a few heroes, were gasping their last sighs; others, half-burned, screamed to be given the *coup de grâce*. Brains were spattered over the ground beside severed arms and legs.

Candide fled full speed to another village; it belonged to some Bulgarians, and the Abarian heroes had treated it in the same way. Candide, still treading on quivering limbs or through ruins, arrived at last outside the theater of war, carrying a few small provisions in his knapsack, and never forgetting Mademoiselle Cunégonde. His provisions ran out when he was in Holland; but having heard that everyone in that country was rich, and that they were Christians, he

---

8. This name, which designates a Scythian tribe, represents the French, who were in-volved in the Seven Years' War (1756–1763) opposite the Prussians.

had no doubt that he would be treated as well as he had been in the castle of My Lord the Baron before he had been expelled from it on account of the lovely eyes of Mademoiselle Cunégonde.

He asked alms of several grave personages, who all replied that if he continued that practice he would be shut up in a house of correction to teach him how to live.

He then addressed a man who had just talked about charity for one solid hour unaided in a large assembly. This orator, looking askance at him, said to him: "What brings you here? Are you here for the good cause?"

"There is no effect without a cause," replied Candide modestly, "everything is linked by necessity and arranged for the best. It was necessary for me to be expelled from the presence of Mademoiselle Cunégonde and to run the gantlet, and now to beg my bread until I can earn it; all this could not happen differently."

"My friend," said the orator to him, "do you believe that the Pope is antichrist?"

"I had never heard that before," replied Candide; "but whether he is or not, I have no bread."

"You do not deserve to eat any," said the other. "Hence, scoundrel; hence, wretch; never come near me again in your life."

The orator's wife, who had put her head out the window, seeing a man who doubted that the Pope was antichrist, poured out on his head a full . . . O Heavens! to what excess is religious zeal carried in ladies!

A man who had not been baptized, a good Anabaptist[9] named Jacques, saw the cruel and ignominious treatment accorded to one of his brethren, a two-footed featherless creature with a soul;[10] he took him home, cleaned him up, gave him some bread and some beer, made him a present of two florins, and even volunteered to teach him to work in his factories of Persian cloth that is made in Holland. Candide, wanting to fall prostrate at his feet, cried:

"Doctor Pangloss was certainly right to tell me that all is for the best in this world, for I am infinitely more touched by your extreme generosity than by the harshness of that gentleman in the black coat and of my lady his wife."

The next day on a walk he met a beggar all covered with sores, his eyes dull as death, the end of his nose eaten away, his mouth awry, his teeth black, talking out of his throat, tormented with a violent cough, and spitting out a tooth at each spasm.

4

HOW CANDIDE MET HIS OLD PHILOSOPHY TEACHER, DOCTOR PANGLOSS, AND WHAT HAPPENED

Candide, moved even more by compassion than by horror, gave this frightful beggar the two florins he had received from his honest Anabaptist Jacques. The

---

9. Member of a Christian sect that rejected infant baptism in favor of baptism on confession of faith.

10. The phrase goes back to Plato's so-called *Definitions*.

phantom gazed fixedly at him, shed tears, and threw his arms around his neck. Candide recoiled in terror.

"Alas!" said the wretch to the other wretch, "don't you recognize your dear Pangloss any more?"

"What do I hear? You, my dear master! You in this horrible state! Why, what misfortune has happened to you? Why are you no longer in the finest of castles? What has become of Mademoiselle Cunégonde, the pearl of young ladies, the masterpiece of nature?"

"I am exhausted," said Pangloss.

Immediately Candide took him into the Anabaptist's stable, where he had him eat a little bread; and when Pangloss had recovered: "Well," he said, "Cunégonde?"

"She is dead," the other replied.

Candide swooned at these words; his friend restored him to his senses with a little bad vinegar that happened to be in the stable. Candide opened his eyes.

"Cunégonde is dead! Ah, best of worlds, where are you? But what illness did she die of? Could it have been for having seen me expelled with great kicks from the fine castle of My Lord, her father?"

"No," said Pangloss, "she was disemboweled by Bulgarian soldiers after being raped as much as anyone can be; they smashed in the head of My Lord the Baron, who tried to defend her; My Lady the Baroness was cut to pieces; my poor pupil was treated precisely like his sister; and as for the castle, not a stone is left standing upon another, not a barn, not a sheep, not a duck, not a tree; but we have been well avenged, for the Abarians did as much in a neighboring barony that belonged to a Bulgarian lord."

At this account Candide swooned again; but having come back to his senses and said all that was appropriate, he inquired about the cause and effect, the sufficient reason, which had put Pangloss in such a piteous state.

"Alas!" said Pangloss, "it is love; love, the consoler of the human race, the preserver of the universe, the soul of all emotional beings, tender love."

"Alas!" said Candide, "I have known this love, this sovereign of hearts, this soul of our soul; all it has ever brought me was one kiss and twenty kicks in the ass. How could this beautiful cause produce in you so abominable an effect?"

Pangloss answered in these terms:

"O my dear Candide! You knew Paquette, that pretty attendant upon our august Baroness; I tasted in her arms the delights of paradise, which produced these torments of hell by which you see me devoured; she was infected and she may have died of it. Paquette had received this present from a very learned Franciscan, who had gone back to the source; for he had got it from an old countess, who had received it from a cavalry captain, who owed it to a marquise, who had it from a page, who had received it from a Jesuit, who as a novice had got it in a direct line from one of the companions of Christopher Columbus. For my part I shall give it to no one, for I am dying."

"O Pangloss!" exclaimed Candide, "that is a strange genealogy! Wasn't the devil the root of it?"

"Not at all," replied the great man. "It was an indispensable thing in the best of

Syphilis causes people to become sterile but there's chocolate and cochineal so everything is O.K.

worlds, a necessary ingredient; for if Columbus had not caught, in an island in America, this disease which poisons the source of generation, which often even prevents generation, and which is obviously opposed to the great purpose of nature, we would not have either chocolate or cochineal. It should also be noted that to this day this malady is peculiar to us in our continent, like religious controversy. The Turks, the Indians, the Persians, the Chinese, the Siamese, the Japanese are not yet acquainted with it; but there is sufficient reason for their making its acquaintance, in their turn, within a few centuries. Meanwhile it has made marvelous progress among us, and especially in those great armies composed of decent, well-brought-up mercenaries, which decide the destiny of states; one may confidently assert that when thirty thousand men fight a pitched battle against an equal number of troops, there are about twenty thousand on each side with the pox."

"That is admirable," said Candide, "but we must get you cured."

"How can I be?" said Pangloss. "I haven't a sou, my friend; and in the whole area of this globe you cannot be bled or given an enema without paying, or without someone paying for you."

This last speech made up Candide's mind; he went and threw himself at the feet of his charitable Anabaptist Jacques and painted him such a touching picture of the state to which his friend was reduced that the good man had no hesitation in taking in Doctor Pangloss; he had him cured at his own expense. In the cure Pangloss lost only one eye and one ear. He wrote a good hand and knew arithmetic perfectly. The Anabaptist Jacques made him his bookkeeper.

Two months later, having to go to Lisbon on business, he took his two philosophers on his ship with him. Pangloss explained to him how everything was for the very best. Jacques was not of this opinion.

"Surely," he said, "men must have corrupted nature a little, for they were not born wolves, and they have become wolves; God gave them neither twenty-four-pounder cannon nor bayonets, and they have made bayonets and cannon to destroy one another. I could put bankruptcies into account, and the justice which seizes the goods of the bankrupt to defraud their creditors of them."

"All that was indispensable," replied the one-eyed Doctor, "and private misfortunes make up the general good; so that the more private misfortunes there are, the more all is well."

While he was reasoning, the air darkened, the winds blew from the four corners of the world, and the ship was assaulted by the most horrible tempest in sight of the port of Lisbon.

5

TEMPEST, SHIPWRECK, EARTHQUAKE, AND WHAT HAPPENED TO DOCTOR PANGLOSS, CANDIDE, AND THE ANABAPTIST JACQUES

Half the passengers, weakened, nearly dying of those inconceivable tortures that the rolling of a ship imparts to the nerves and all the humors of a body tossed in opposite directions, had not even the strength to worry about the danger. The other half were uttering screams and prayers; the sails were torn, the masts shattered, the vessel split open. Those who could worked, no one co-operated, no one commanded. The Anabaptist was helping a little with the work; he was on the main deck; a frenzied sailor struck him a hard blow and stretched him on the planks, but got such a jolt from the blow he gave him that he fell out of the ship headfirst. He was caught on a piece of broken mast and remained dangling from it. The good Jacques runs to his aid, helps him to climb back up, and by this effort is flung headfirst into the sea in full view of the sailor, who lets him perish without even deigning to look at him. Candide approaches, sees his benefactor come up again for a moment and then be swallowed up forever. He wants to throw himself into the sea after him; the philosopher Pangloss stops him, proving to him that the Lisbon roads had been formed expressly for this Anabaptist to be drowned in. While he was proving this a priori, the ship splits open and everyone perishes with the exception of Pangloss, Candide, and that brute of a sailor who had drowned the virtuous Anabaptist; the scoundrel swam successfully ashore and Pangloss and Candide were carried there on a plank.

When they had recovered themselves a little, they walked toward Lisbon; they had a little money left, with which they hoped to be saved from hunger after escaping from the tempest.

Hardly have they set foot in the city, weeping over the death of their benefactor, when they feel the earth tremble under their feet; the sea rises boiling in the port and shatters the vessels that are at anchor.[11] Whirlwinds of flame and ashes cover the streets and public squares, the houses crumble, the roofs are tumbled down upon the foundations, and the foundations disintegrate; thirty thousand inhabitants of every age and of either sex are crushed beneath the ruins. Said the sailor, whistling and swearing: "There'll be something to pick up here." Said Pangloss: "What can be the sufficient reason for this phenomenon?" "It is the end of the world," exclaimed Candide.

The sailor runs headlong into the midst of the debris, braves death to find money, finds some, seizes it, gets drunk, and when he has slept it off buys the favors of the first girl of good will he meets upon the ruins of demolished houses and in the midst of the dying and the dead. Pangloss meanwhile was tugging at his sleeve: "My friend," he said, "this is not good, you are departing from universal reason, you are choosing your time badly."

" 'Sblood and zounds!" the other replied. "I am a sailor, and born in Batavia; I have stamped on the crucifix four times on four trips to Japan;[12] you certainly picked the right man, you and your universal reason!"

Candide has been wounded by some splinters of stone; he was stretched out in the street and covered with debris. He said to Pangloss: "Alas! get me a little wine and oil, I am dying."

---

11. The Lisbon earthquake and fire (November 1, 1755), which killed over 30,000 people and reduced the city to ruins, led Voltaire to make strong attacks on philosophical optimism, especially in his *Poem*

on the Lisbon Disaster (written in 1755) and in *Candide*.

12. To discourage trade with the Christians, the Japanese required European merchants to stamp on the cross as a sign of rejection of Christianity.

"This earthquake is not a new thing," replied Pangloss. "The town of Lima suffered the same shocks in America last year; same causes, same effects; there is certainly a vein of sulfur underground from Lima to Lisbon."

"Nothing is more probable," said Candide, "but for the love of God, a little oil and wine."

"What do you mean, probable?" replied the philosopher. "I maintain that the matter is proved." Candide lost consciousness, and Pangloss brought him a little water from a neighboring fountain.

The next day, having found a few victuals as they slipped through the ruins, they restored their strength a bit. Then they worked like the rest to relieve the inhabitants who had escaped death. A few citizens whom they had helped gave them as good a dinner as could be provided in such a disaster. True, the meal was sad, the guests watered their bread with their tears; but Pangloss consoled them by assuring them that things could not be otherwise.

"For," he said, "all this is for the very best. For if there is a volcano in Lisbon, it could not be anywhere else. For it is impossible that things should not be where they are. For all is well."

A little dark man, a familiar of the Inquisition, who was beside him, spoke up politely and said: "Apparently the gentleman does not believe in original sin; *for,* if all is for the best, then there has been neither fall nor punishment."

"I very humbly beg Your Excellency's pardon," replied Pangloss still more politely, "for the fall of man and the curse necessarily entered into the best of possible worlds."

"Then the gentleman does not believe in free will?" said the familiar.

"Your Excellency will excuse me," said Pangloss; "free will can coexist with absolute necessity, for it was necessary that we should be free; for after all, predetermined will . . ."

Pangloss was in the middle of his sentence when the familiar gave a nod to his armed attendant, who was pouring him out some port, or Oporto, wine.

6

HOW THEY HELD A FINE AUTO-DA-FÉ TO PREVENT EARTHQUAKES, AND HOW CANDIDE WAS FLOGGED

After the earthquake, which had destroyed three-quarters of Lisbon, the country's wise men had found no more efficacious means of preventing total ruin than to give the people a fine auto-da-fé;[13] it was decided by the University of Coimbra that the spectacle of a few persons burned by a slow fire in great ceremony is an infallible secret for keeping the earth from quaking.

They had consequently seized a Biscayan convicted of having married his godchild's godmother, and two Portuguese who when eating a chicken had taken

---

13. From the Portuguese, "act of the faith": the ceremony attendant to a judgment by the Inquisition; hence the burning of heretics as a result of such a judgment.

out the bacon;[14] after dinner they came and bound Doctor Pangloss and his disciple Candide, the one for having spoken, and the other for having listened with an air of approbation, both were taken separately into extremely cool apartments in which one was never bothered by the sun;[15] a week later they were each clad in a sanbenito,[16] and their heads were adorned with paper miters; Candide's miter and sanbenito were painted with flames upside down and with devils that had neither tails nor claws; but Pangloss's devils wore claws and tails, and his flames were right side up.

Thus dressed, they marched in procession and heard a very pathetic sermon followed by some beautiful music in a droning plain song. Candide was flogged in time to the singing, the Biscayan and the two men who wouldn't eat the bacon were burned, and Pangloss was hanged although this is not the custom. On the same day the earth quaked again with a fearful crash.

Candide, terrified, dumfounded, bewildered, bleeding and quivering all over, said to himself:

"If this is the best of all possible worlds, then what are the others? I could let it pass if I had only been flogged, that happened also with the Bulgarians; but, O my dear Pangloss, greatest of philosophers, was it necessary that I see you hanged without knowing why! O my dear Anabaptist, best of men, was it necessary that you be drowned in the port! O Mademoiselle Cunégonde, pearl of young ladies, was it necessary that your belly be slit open!"

He was going back, barely supporting himself, preached at, flogged, absolved and blessed, when an old woman accosted him and said: "My son, take courage, follow me."

7

HOW AN OLD WOMAN TOOK CARE OF CANDIDE, AND HOW HE RECOVERED THAT WHICH HE LOVED

Candide did not take courage, but he followed the old woman into a hovel; she gave him a jar of ointment to rub on and left him food and drink; she showed him a fairly clean little bed; beside the bed there was a suit of clothes.

"Eat, drink, sleep," she said, "and may Our Lady of Atocha, My Lord Saint Anthony of Padua, and My Lord Saint James of Compostela take care of you. I shall come back tomorrow."

Candide, still astounded at all he had seen, at all he had suffered, and even more at the old woman's charity, tried to kiss her hand.

"It is not my hand you should kiss," said the old woman. "I shall come back tomorrow. Rub yourself with ointment, eat, and sleep."

Candide for all his misfortunes ate and slept. The next day the old woman

---

14. Thus showing that they were Jews still secretly faithful to Judaism.
15. Prison cells.

16. A yellow robe worn by heretics condemned to the stake by the Inquisition.

brings him some breakfast, examines his back, rubs it herself with ointment; later she brings him dinner; she returns toward evening and brings supper. The day after, she again performed the same ceremonies.

"Who are you?" Candide kept asking her. "Who has inspired you with such kindness? How can I possibly thank you?"

The good woman never made any answer; she returned toward evening and brought no supper. "Come with me," she said, "and don't say a word."

She takes him by the arm and walks with him into the country for about a quarter of a mile; they arrive at an isolated house surrounded with gardens and canals. The old woman knocks on a little door. It is opened; she takes Candide by a hidden staircase into a gilded boudoir, leaves him on a brocaded sofa, closes the door, and goes away. Candide thought he was dreaming and considered his whole life as a sinister dream and the present moment as a sweet dream.

The old woman soon reappeared; she was supporting with difficulty a trembling woman of majestic stature, gleaming with precious stones and covered with a veil. "Remove that veil," said the old woman to Candide. The young man approaches, he lifts the veil with a timid hand. What a moment! What a surprise! He thinks he sees Mademoiselle Cunégonde, he did indeed see her, it was she herself. His strength fails him, he cannot utter a word, he falls at her feet. Cunégonde falls on the sofa. The old woman plies them copiously with aromatic spirits; they regain their senses, they speak to each other; at first it is only disconnected words, questions and answers at cross purposes, sighs, tears, cries. The old woman recommends that they make less noise, and leaves them by themselves.

"What! Is it you?" said Candide. 'You are alive! I find you again here in Portugal! Then you were not raped? Your belly was not slit open, as the philosopher Pangloss had assured me?"

"Oh yes," said the fair Cunégonde, "but people do not always die of those two accidents."

"But were your father and mother killed?"

" 'Tis only too true," said Cunégonde, weeping.

"And your brother?"

"My brother was killed too."

"And why are you in Portugal, and how did you learn I was here, and by what strange adventure did you have me brought to this house?"

"I will tell you all that," replied the lady; "but first you must tell me everything that has happened to you since the innocent kiss that you gave me and the kicks that you received."

Candide obeyed her with profound respect; and though he was dumfounded, though his voice was weak and trembling, though his spine still hurt a little, he told her in the most naïve manner all that he had undergone since the moment of their separation. Cunégonde kept raising her eyes to heaven; she shed tears at the death of the good Anabaptist and of Pangloss; after which she spoke in these terms to Candide, who did not miss a word and devoured her with his eyes.

8

CUNÉGONDE'S STORY

"I was in bed and fast asleep when it pleased Heaven to send the Bulgarians to our fine castle of Thunder-ten-tronckh; they slaughtered my father and brother and cut my mother into pieces. A big Bulgarian six feet tall, seeing that I had lost consciousness at the sight of this, set about raping me; this brought me to, I regained my senses, I screamed, I struggled, I bit, I scratched, I tried to tear that big Bulgarian's eyes out, not knowing that all that was happening in my father's castle was a matter of custom; the brute stabbed me with a knife in the left side and I still bear the mark." "Alas! I certainly hope I shall see it," said the naïve Candide. "You shall see it," said Cunégonde, "but let me go on." "Go on," said Candide.

She took up the thread of her story thus:

"A Bulgarian captain came in, he saw me all bleeding, and the soldier did not disturb himself. The captain grew angry at the lack of respect this brute showed him, and killed him upon my body. Then he had my wounds dressed and took me to his quarters as a prisoner of war. I laundered the few shirts he had, I did his cooking; he found me very pretty, I must admit; and I shall not deny that he was very well built and had soft white skin; for the rest little wit, little philosophy; it was easy to see that he had not been brought up by Doctor Pangloss. After three months, having lost all his money as well as his taste for me, he sold me to a Jew named Don Issachar, who traded in Holland and Portugal and had a passionate love of women. This Jew grew much attached to my person but could not triumph over it; I resisted him better than I did the Bulgarian soldier. A person of honor may have been raped once, but her virtue gains strength from it. The Jew, to tame me, brought me to this country house that you see. I had thought until then that there was nothing on earth so splendid as the castle of Thunder-ten-tronckh. I was undeceived.

"The Grand Inquisitor noticed me one day at Mass; he eyed me a great deal, and sent word to me that he had secret affairs to speak to me about. I was taken to his palace, I informed him of my birth; he pointed out to me how much it was beneath my rank to belong to an Israelite. On his behalf it was proposed to Don Issachar to yield me to His Lordship. Don Issachar, who is the court banker and a man of influence, would do no such thing. The Inquisitor threatened him with an auto-da-fé. Finally my Jew, intimidated, made a bargain by which the house and I would belong to them both in common, the Jew would have Monday, Wednesday, and the Sabbath day for him, and the Inquisitor would have the other days of the week. This agreement has lasted for six months. It has not been without quarrels, for it has often been undecided whether the night between Saturday and Sunday belongs to the old law or the new. For my part, thus far I have resisted them both, and I think that is the reason why I have still been loved.

"Finally, to turn aside the scourge of earthquakes and to intimidate Don

Issachar, My Lord the Inquisitor was pleased to celebrate an auto-da-fé. He did me the honor of inviting me. I had a very good seat; they served the ladies with refreshments between the Mass and the execution. Truly I was seized with horror on seeing them burn those two Jews and that worthy Biscayan who had married the godmother of his godchild; but what was my surprise, my fright, my distress, when I saw, in a sanbenito and under a miter, a face resembling that of Pangloss! I rubbed my eyes, I looked attentively, I saw him hanged; I fell into a faint; hardly was I regaining my senses when I saw you stripped stark naked; that was the height of horror, consternation, grief, despair. I will tell you truthfully that your skin is even whiter and more perfectly rosy than that of my Bulgarian captain. This sight redoubled all the feelings that crushed me, that devoured me. I cried out, I tried to say 'Stop, barbarians!' but my voice failed me, and my cries would have been useless. When you had been well flogged, I said: 'How can it be that the charming Candide and the wise Pangloss are in Lisbon, one to receive a hundred lashes, and the other to be hanged by order of My Lord the Inquisitor, whose dearly beloved I am? Then Pangloss deceived me most cruelly when he told me that all is for the very best.'

"Agitated, bewildered, now beside myself and now ready to die of faintness, I had my mind filled with the massacre of my father, mother, and brother, the insolence of my horrid Bulgarian soldier, the stab he gave me, my slavery, my work as a cook, my Bulgarian captain, my horrid Don Issachar, my abominable Inquisitor, the hanging of Doctor Pangloss, that long *miserere* in droning plain song during which they were whipping you, and above all the kiss I gave you behind a screen the day I saw you for the last time. I praised God, who was bringing you back to me through so many trials. I charged my old woman to take care of you and to bring you here as soon as she could. She has carried out my commission very well; I have enjoyed the inexpressible pleasure of seeing you again, hearing you, speaking to you. You must be ravenously hungry; my appetite is good; let's begin with supper."

So they both sit down to table, and after supper resume their places on that handsome sofa that has been already mentioned; they were there when Señor Don Issachar, one of the masters of the house, arrived. It was the Sabbath day. He was coming to enjoy his rights and expound his tender love.

9

WHAT HAPPENED TO CUNÉGONDE, CANDIDE, THE GRAND INQUISITOR, AND A JEW

This Issachar was the most choleric Hebrew ever seen in Israel since the Babylonian captivity.

"What!" he said. "Bitch of a Galilean, My Lord the Inquisitor isn't enough? This scoundrel must share with me too?"

So saying, he draws a long dagger which he always carried and, not thinking that his adversary was armed, throws himself upon Candide; but our good

Westphalian had received a fine sword from the old woman together with the suit. He draws his sword, although he had a very gentle character, and stretches out the Israelite stone dead on the floor at the feet of the fair Cunégonde.

"Holy virgin!" she cried, "what is to become of us? A man killed in my house! If the law comes, we are lost."

"If Pangloss had not been hanged," said Candide, "he would give us good advice in this extremity, for he was a great philosopher. Failing him, let us consult the old woman."

She was very prudent, and was beginning to state her advice, when another little door opened. It was one hour after midnight, it was the beginning of Sunday. That day belonged to My Lord the Inquisitor. He came in and saw the flogged Candide sword in hand, a dead man stretched on the floor, Cunégonde terrified, and the old woman giving advice.

Here is what went on in that moment in Candide's soul, and how he reasoned: "If this holy man calls for help, he will have me burned without fail; he may do as much to Cunégonde; he has had me pitilessly whipped; he is my rival; I have started killing, there is no hesitating."

This reasoning was clear-cut and swift, and without giving the Inquisitor the time to recover from his surprise, he pierces him through and through and tosses him beside the Jew.

"Now here's another one," said Cunégonde; "there is no more chance of pardon; we are excommunicated, our last hour is come. How could you, who were born so mild, manage to kill one Jew and one Inquisitor in two minutes?"

"My fair lady," replied Candide, "when a man is in love, jealous, and whipped by the Inquisition, he is out of his mind."

The old woman then spoke up and said: "There are three Andalusian horses in the stable with their saddles and bridles; let the brave Candide prepare them; My Lady has moidores[17] and diamonds; let us mount quickly, although I can ride on only one buttock, and let us go to Cádiz; the weather could not be finer, and it is a great pleasure to travel in the cool of the night."

Immediately, Candide saddles the three horses. Cunégonde, the old woman, and he do thirty miles at one stretch. While they were riding away, the Holy Hermandad[18] arrives in the house; they bury His Lordship in a beautiful church and they toss Don Issachar on the dump.

Candide, Cunégonde, and the old woman were already in the little town of Avacena in the midst of the mountains of the Sierra Morena; and they were talking as follows in an inn.

---

17. A gold coin of Portugal and Brazil.
18. The Holy Brotherhood, an association formed in Spain with a police force to track down criminals.

10

IN WHAT DISTRESS CANDIDE, CUNÉGONDE, AND THE OLD WOMAN ARRIVE AT CÁDIZ; AND ABOUT THEIR EMBARKATION

"Now who can have stolen my pistoles[19] and my diamonds?" said Cunégonde, weeping. "What shall we live on? What shall we do? Where shall we find Inquisitors and Jews to give me others?"

"Alas!" said the old woman. "I strongly suspect a reverend Franciscan father who slept in the same inn with us yesterday at Badajoz; God keep me from forming a rash judgment, but he came into our room twice and he left long before us."

"Alas!" said Candide, "the good Pangloss had often proved to me that the goods of the earth are common to all men, that each has an equal right to them. That Franciscan, according to these principles, should certainly have left us enough to complete our trip. Have you nothing at all left then, my fair Cunégonde?"

"Not a maravedi,"[20] said she. "What should we do?" said Candide. "Let's sell one of the horses," said the old woman. "I'll ride on the crupper behind my lady, although I can ride on only one buttock, and we will get to Cádiz."

In the same hostelry there was a Benedictine prior; he bought the horse at a bargain. Candide, Cunégonde, and the old woman passed through Lucena, Chillas, Lebrixa, and at last reached Cádiz. There a fleet was being equipped and troops assembled to bring to terms the reverend Jesuit Fathers in Paraguay, who were accused of causing one of their tribes, near the town of San Sacramento, to revolt against the kings of Spain and Portugal.[21] Candide, having served with the Bulgarians, performed the Bulgarian drill before the general of the little army with so much grace, celerity, skill, pride, and agility, that they gave him an infantry company to command. Here he is a captain; he embarks with Mademoiselle Cunégonde, the old woman, two valets, and the two Andalusian horses that had belonged to His Lordship the Grand Inquisitor of Portugal.

During the whole crossing they reasoned a great deal about the philosophy of poor Pangloss.

"We are going to another universe," said Candide; "no doubt it is in that one that all is well. For it must be admitted that one might groan a little over what happens in the physical and the moral domain in ours."

"I love you with all my heart," said Cunégonde, "but my soul is still frightened by what I have seen, what I have undergone."

"All will be well," replied Candide; "the sea of this new world is already better than the seas of our Europe; it is calmer, the winds are more constant. It is certainly the new world that is the best of possible universes."

---

19. A Spanish gold coin.
20. A small Spanish copper coin.

21. This revolt occurred in 1756.

"God grant it," said Cunégonde; "but I have been so horribly unhappy in mine that my heart is almost closed to hope."

"You complain," the old woman said to them. "Alas! You have not undergone misfortunes such as mine."

Cunégonde almost burst out laughing, and thought this good woman very comical to claim to be more unfortunate than herself.

"Alas!" she said to her, "my dear woman, unless you have been raped by two Bulgarians, been stabbed twice in the belly, had two of your castles demolished and two mothers and two fathers slaughtered before your eyes, and seen two of your beloveds flogged in an auto-da-fé, I don't see that you can outdo me; plus the fact that I was born a Baroness with seventy-two quarterings, and now I have been a cook."

"My Lady," replied the old woman, "you do not know my birth, and if I showed you my bottom you would not speak as you do and you would suspend your judgment."

This speech aroused extreme curiosity in the minds of Cunégonde and Candide. The old woman spoke to them in these terms.

11

THE OLD WOMAN'S STORY

"My eyes were not always bloodshot and red-rimmed; my nose did not always touch my chin, and I was not always a servant. I am the daughter of Pope Urban X and the Princess of Palestrina.[22] Until the age of fourteen I was brought up in a palace to which all the castles of your German barons would not have served as stables, and one of my dresses was worth more than all the magnificence of Westphalia. I grew in beauty, graces, and talents, in the midst of pleasures, respect, and hopes. Already I inspired love, my bosom was forming; and what a bosom! White, firm, sculptured like that of the Venus de' Medici. And what eyes! What eyelids! What black eyebrows! What flames shone in my two irises and dimmed the glistening of the stars, as the neighborhood poets used to tell me. The women who dressed and undressed me fell into ecstasies when they looked at me in front and behind, and all the men would have liked to be in their place.

"I was betrothed to a sovereign prince of Massa-Carrara. What a prince! As handsome as I, formed of sweetness and charms, agleam with wit and afire with love. I loved him as one loves for the first time, with idolatrous frenzy. The nuptials were prepared. The pomp, the magnificence were unheard of; there were continual festivities, tournaments, comic operas, and all Italy composed for me sonnets not one of which was passable.

"The moment of my happiness was at hand when an old marquise who had been my prince's mistress invited him to have some chocolate at her house. He died in less than two hours of frightful convulsions. But that is only a trifle. My

---

22. Author's posthumous note: "Observe the author's extreme discretion. There has been up to now no Pope named Urban X. The author fears to assign a bastard daughter to a known Pope. What circumspection! What delicacy of conscience!"

mother, in despair, yet much less afflicted than I, decided to tear herself away for a time from such a fateful place. She had a very beautiful estate near Gaeta.[23] We embarked on a local galley, gilded like the altar of St. Peter's in Rome. Suddenly a pirate from Salé[24] swoops down on us and boards us. Our soldiers defended themselves like soldiers of the Pope; they all fell on their knees, throwing away their arms, and begging the pirates for absolution in *articulo mortis*.[25]

"Immediately they stripped them naked as monkeys, and my mother too, our ladies of honor too, and me too. The diligence with which those gentlemen undress people is a wonderful thing. But what surprised me more was that they put their fingers in a place in all of us where we women ordinarily admit only the nozzle of a syringe. This ceremony seemed quite strange to me; that is how one judges of everything when one has never been out of one's country. I soon learned that this was to see whether we had not hidden some diamonds there; it is a custom established from time immemorial among the civilized nations that roam the seas. I learned that My Lords the religious Knights of Malta never fail to do this when they capture Turkish men and women; it is a rule of international law that has never been broken.

"I shall not tell you how hard it is for a young princess to be taken to Morocco as a slave with her mother. You can imagine well enough all that we had to suffer in the pirate ship. My mother was still very beautiful; our ladies of honor, our mere chambermaids had more charms than can be found in all Africa. As for me, I was ravishing, I was beauty and grace itself, and I was a virgin. I was not so for long: that flower that had been reserved for the handsome Prince of Massa-Carrara was ravished from me by the pirate captain. He was an abominable Negro who yet thought he was doing me much honor. Indeed My Lady the Princess of Palestrina and I had to be very strong to endure all we underwent until we arrived in Morocco. But let's go on; these are things so common that they are not worth speaking of.

"Morocco was swimming in blood when we arrived. Fifty sons of the Emperor Muley Ismael each had a faction; which produced in effect fifty civil wars, of blacks against blacks, blacks against tans, tans against tans, mulattoes against mulattoes. It was a continual carnage over the whole extent of the empire.

"Hardly had we landed when some blacks, of a faction hostile to that of my pirate, came up to take his booty from him. After the diamonds and the gold, we were the most precious thing he had. I was witness to a combat such as you never see in your European climates. The blood of the northern peoples is not ardent enough. They are not mad about women to the point that is common in Africa. It seems as though your Europeans have milk in their veins; it is vitriol, it is fire that flows in those of the inhabitants of Mount Atlas and the neighboring countries. They fought with the fury of the lions, tigers, and snakes of the country to see who should have us. One Moor seized my mother by the right arm, my captain's lieutenant held her back by the left arm; a Moorish soldier took her by one leg, one

---

23. An Italian port northwest of Naples.
24. A Moroccan port on the Atlantic near Rabat, once a headquarters for pirates.

25. At the point of death.

of our pirates held her by the other. In a moment nearly all our girls found themselves pulled in this way by four soldiers. My captain kept me hidden behind him. He had his scimitar in hand, and was killing everything that opposed his rage. Finally I saw all our Italian women and my mother torn, cut, massacred by the monsters who were fighting over them. My fellow captives, those who had captured them, soldiers, sailors, blacks, tans, whites, mulattoes, and finally my captain—all were killed, and I remained dying on a heap of dead. Similar scenes were taking place, as everyone knows, over an area of more than three hundred square leagues, without anyone failing to say the five prayers a day ordained by Mohammed.

"I extricated myself with great difficulty from the press of so many heaped-up bleeding corpses, and I dragged myself beneath a big orange tree at the edge of a nearby stream; there I fell down from fright, weariness, horror, despair, and hunger. Soon afterward my exhausted senses gave themselves up to a sleep that was more like a swoon than a rest. I was in this state of weakness and insensibility, between life and death, when I felt something pressing on me and moving on my body. I opened my eyes and saw a white man of good appearance who was sighing and muttering between his teeth: *'O che sciagura d'essere senza coglioni!'* "[26]

12

CONTINUATION OF THE OLD WOMAN'S MISFORTUNES

"Astounded and delighted to hear the language of my homeland, and no less surprised at the words this man was uttering, I replied that there were worse misfortunes than the one he was complaining of. I informed him in a few words of the horrors I had suffered, and I fell back into a faint. He took me into a neighboring house, had me put to bed and given food, served me, consoled me, flattered me, told me he had never seen anything as beautiful as I and that he had never so much regretted what no one could restore to him.

" 'I was born in Naples,' he told me; 'there they caponize two or three thousand boys every year; some die of it, others acquire a voice more beautiful than a woman's, others go and govern states. This operation was performed on me with great success, and I was a musician in the chapel of My Lady the Princess of Palestrina.'

" 'Of my mother!' I cried out.

" 'Of your mother!' he exclaimed, weeping. 'What! Can you be that young princess that I brought up until the age of six, and who already then promised to be as beautiful as you are?'

" 'I am indeed; my mother is four hundred yards from here, cut into quarters under a heap of dead.'

"I told him everything that had happened to me; he too told me his adventures, and informed me that he had been sent by a Christian power to the

---

26. "Oh, what an affliction to be without testicles!"

King of Morocco to conclude a treaty with that monarch by which he would be furnished with gunpowder, cannon, and ships to help him to exterminate the commerce of the other Christians. 'My mission is performed,' this honest eunuch said; 'I am going to embark at Ceuta and I will take you back to Italy. *Ma che sciagura d'essere senza coglioni!'*

"I thanked him with tears of emotion, and instead of taking me to Italy he conducted me to Algiers and sold me to the Dey of that province. Hardly was I sold when that plague which has spread all over Africa, Asia, and Europe broke out furiously in Algiers. You have seen earthquakes; but, My Lady, have you ever had the plague?"

"Never," replied the Baroness.

"If you had had it," the old woman went on, "you would admit that it is far worse than an earthquake. It is very common in Africa; I was struck with it. Imagine what a situation for the daughter of a Pope, aged fifteen, who in three months' time had undergone poverty and slavery, had been raped almost every day, had seen her mother cut into quarters, had endured hunger and war, and was now dying of the plague in Algiers. However, I did not die of it; but my eunuch and the Dey and almost all the seraglio of Algiers perished.

"When the first ravages of this frightful plague were over, the Dey's slaves were sold. A merchant bought me and took me to Tunis. He sold me to another merchant, who resold me at Tripoli; from Tripoli I was resold to Alexandria, from Alexandria resold to Smyrna, from Smyrna to Constantinople. I finally belonged to an Aga of the Janizaries,[27] who was soon ordered to go and defend Azov against the Russians who were besieging it.

"The Aga, who was a very gallant man, took his whole seraglio with him and lodged us in a little fort on the Maeotian Marsh,[28] guarded by two black eunuchs and twenty soldiers. They killed a prodigious number of Russians, but these repaid us with interest. Azov was put to fire and sword, and there was no pardon for sex nor for age; nothing remained but our little fort; the enemy tried to take us by famine. The twenty Janizaries had sworn never to surrender. The extremities of hunger to which they were reduced forced them to eat our two eunuchs, for fear of violating their oath. A few days later they resolved to eat the women.

"We had with us a very pious and very compassionate imam,[29] who preached them a fine sermon by which he persuaded them not to kill us completely. 'Just cut off one buttock from each of these ladies,' he said, 'you will make very good cheer; if you have to come back, you will have as much again in a few days; heaven will be pleased with you for so charitable an action, and you will be rescued.'

"He had great eloquence; he persuaded them. They performed this horrible operation on us. The imam applied to us the same balm that they put on children who have just been circumcised. We were all at the point of death.

"Scarcely had the Janizaries eaten the meal we had furnished them when the Russians arrived in flat-bottomed boats; not one Janizary escaped. The Russians paid no attention to the state we were in. There are French surgeons everywhere;

---

27. A high officer of the guards of the Turkish Sultan.

28. Ancient name for the Sea of Azov.
29. A Mohammedan priest.

one of them, who was very skillful, took care of us; he cured us; and I shall remember all my life that when my wounds were fully closed, he made propositions to me. For the rest, he told us all to console ourselves; he assured us that the same sort of thing had happened in many sieges and that it was a law of war.

"As soon as my companions could walk, they were sent to Moscow. I fell to the lot of a Boyar,[30] who made me his gardener and gave me twenty lashes a day. But when this lord was broken on the wheel two years later with some thirty other Boyars for some petty fuss at court, I profited by this adventure; I fled; I crossed the whole of Russia; I was long a servant in an inn at Riga, then at Rostock, at Wismar, at Leipzig, Cassel, Utrecht, Leyden, the Hague, Rotterdam; I have grown old in misery and opprobrium, having only half a backside, always remembering that I was the daughter of a Pope; a hundred times I wanted to kill myself, but I still loved life. This ridiculous foible is perhaps one of our most disastrous inclinations. For is there anything more stupid than to want to bear continually a burden that we always want to throw to the ground? To regard our being with horror, and to cling to our being? In fine, to caress the serpent that devours us until it has eaten up our heart?

"I have seen, in the countries that fate has driven me through and in the inns where I have served, a prodigious number of persons who loathed their existence; but I have seen only twelve who voluntarily put an end to their misery: three Negroes, four Englishmen, four Genevans, and a German professor named Robeck.[31] I ended up by being a servant to the Jew Don Issachar; he put me in your service, my fair young lady; I have attached myself to your destiny, and I have been more occupied with your adventures than with mine. I would never even have spoken to you of my misfortunes if you had not piqued me a little and if it were not customary on shipboard to tell stories to conquer boredom. In short, My Lady, I have experience, I know the world; have some fun, get each passenger to tell you his story; and if there is a single one who has not often cursed his life, who has not often said to himself that he was the unhappiest of men, throw me into the sea headfirst."

Everyone is miserable at some pt. in their life.

13

HOW CANDIDE WAS OBLIGED TO PART FROM THE FAIR CUNÉGONDE AND THE OLD WOMAN

The fair Cunégonde, having heard the old woman's story, showed her all the courtesy due to a person of her rank and merit. She accepted the proposition and got all the passengers one after the other to tell her their adventures; Candide and she admitted that the old woman was right.

"It is a great pity," said Candide, "that the wise Pangloss was hanged contrary to custom in an auto-da-fé; he would tell us wonderful things about the physical

---

30. Russian nobleman.
31. Author of theses on the folly of loving life, who drowned himself in 1739 at the age of sixty-seven.

evil and the moral evil that cover earth and sea, and I would feel strong enough to dare to offer him; respectfully, a few objections."

As each one was telling his story the vessel moved on. They landed in Buenos Aires. Cunégonde, Captain Candide, and the old woman called on the governor, Don Fernando d'Ibaraa y Figueora y Mascarenes y Lampourdos y Souza. This lord had the pride befitting a man who bore so many names. He spoke to men with the noblest disdain, bearing his nose so high, raising his voice so pitilessly, assuming so imposing a tone, affecting so lofty a bearing, that all who addressed him were tempted to give him a beating. He loved women with a frenzy. Cunégonde seemed to him the most beautiful thing he had ever seen. The first thing he did was ask if she were not the Captain's wife. The air with which he asked this question alarmed Candide; he did not dare say she was his wife because in fact she was not; he did not dare say she was his sister, because she was not that either; and although this diplomatic lie was once very fashionable among the ancients[32] and might be useful to the moderns, his soul was too pure to be disloyal to the truth. "Mademoiselle Cunégonde," he said, "is to do me the honor of marrying me, and we beseech Your Excellency to deign to perform our wedding ceremony."

Don Fernando d'Ibaraa y Figueora y Mascarenes y Lampourdos y Souza, twirling his mustache, smiled bitterly and ordered Captain Candide to go pass his company in review. Candide obeyed; the governor remained with Mademoiselle Cunégonde. He declared his passion to her, protested that the next day he would marry her publicly in church, or otherwise, as it might please her charms. Cunégonde asked him for a quarter of an hour to collect herself, to consult the old woman, and to make up her mind.

The old woman said to Cunégonde:

"My Lady, you have seventy-two quarterings and not a penny; it depends on you alone to be the wife of the greatest lord in South America, who has a very handsome mustache; is it for you to pride yourself on an invincible fidelity? You have been raped by the Bulgarians; a Jew and an Inquisitor have enjoyed your good graces. Misfortunes confer rights. I admit that if I were in your place, I would have no scruple over marrying My Lord the Governor and making the fortune of Captain Candide."

While the old woman was speaking with all the prudence that age and experience give, a little vessel was seen to enter the port; it brought an alcaide and some alguazils,[33] and here is what had happened.

The old woman had guessed correctly that it was a long-sleeved Franciscan who stole Cunégonde's money and jewels in the town of Badajoz when she was fleeing in haste with Candide. This monk tried to sell some of the precious stones to a jeweler. The merchant recognized them as belonging to the Grand Inquisitor. The Franciscan, before being hanged, admitted that he had stolen them; he indicated the persons and the route they were taking. The flight of Cunégonde

---

32. A reference to Abraham and Sarah (Genesis 12:12–13 and again 20:2–3) and to Isaac and Rebekah (Genesis 26:7–9).

33. A municipal officer and some police officers.

and Candide was already known. They were followed to Cádiz; with no loss of time a ship was sent in pursuit of them. The ship was already in the port of Buenos Aires. The rumor spread that an alcaide was about to land and that they were pursuing the murderers of His Lordship the Grand Inquisitor. The prudent old woman saw in an instant all that was to be done.

"You cannot flee," she said to Cunégonde, "and you have nothing to fear; it was not you that killed His Lordship; besides, the governor, who loves you, will not allow you to be maltreated; stay."

She immediately ran to Candide. "Flee," she said, "or you're going to be burned within an hour." There was not a moment to lose; but how could he part with Cunégonde, and where was he to take refuge?

14

HOW CANDIDE AND CACAMBO WERE RECEIVED BY THE JESUITS IN PARAGUAY

Candide had brought from Cádiz a valet of a type often found on the coasts of Spain and in the colonies. He was one-quarter Spanish, born of a half-breed in Tucuman;[34] he had been a choirboy, sacristan, sailor, monk, merchant's representative, soldier, lackey. His name was Cacambo, and he loved his master very much, because his master was a very good man. He saddled the two Andalusian horses as fast as possible.

"Come, master, let us take the old woman's advice, leave, and run for it without looking behind us."

Candide shed tears. "O my dear Cunégonde! Must I abandon you just when My Lord the Governor is going to perform our marriage! Cunégonde, brought here from so far, what will become of you?"

"She will get along as best she can," said Cacambo; "women are never at a loss; God looks after them; let's run for it."

"Where are you taking me? Where are we going? What shall we do without Cunégonde?" said Candide.

"By St. James of Compostela," said Cacambo, "you were going to make war on the Jesuits; let's make war for them; I know the roads well enough, I will take you to their kingdom, they will be delighted to have a captain who can drill Bulgarian style, you will make a prodigious fortune; when you don't get your due in one world you find it in another. It is a very great pleasure to see and do new things."

"Then you have already been in Paraguay?" said Candide.

"Oh yes indeed," said Cacambo, "I was a servant in the College of the Assumption, and I know the government of *Los Padres*[35] as well as I know the streets of Cádiz. It is an admirable thing, this government. The kingdom is already more than three hundred leagues in diameter; it is divided into thirty provinces; *Los Padres* have everything and the people nothing; it is the masterpiece of reason

---

34. A province in northern Argentina.   35. "The Fathers," i.e., the Jesuits.

and justice. For my part, I know nothing so divine as *Los Padres,* who here make war on the King of Spain and the King of Portugal, and who in Europe confess those Kings; who here kill Spaniards, and in Madrid send them to heaven; this enchants me; let's get on; you are going to be the happiest of men. What pleasure *Los Padres* will have when they learn that a captain is coming to them who knows the Bulgarian drill!"

As soon as they had reached the first barrier, Cacambo told the outpost that a captain asked to speak to My Lord the Commandant. They went to notify the main guard. A Paraguayan officer ran to the feet of the Commandant to impart the news to him. First Candide and Cacambo were disarmed; their two Andalusian horses were seized. The two strangers were brought in between two ranks of soldiers; the Commandant was at the end, three-cornered hat on head, gown tucked up, sword at side, and a half-pike in hand. He made a sign; and immediately twenty-four soldiers surround the two newcomers. A sergeant tells them that they must wait, that the Commandant cannot speak to them, that the Reverend Provincial Father does not permit any Spaniard to open his mouth except in his presence or to remain more than three hours in the country.

"And where is the Reverend Provincial Father?" said Cacambo.

"He is at the parade after having said Mass," replied the sergeant, "and you will not be able to kiss his spurs until three hours from now."

"But," said Cacambo, "the captain, who is dying of hunger as I am, is not a Spaniard, he is a German; mightn't we have breakfast while waiting for His Reverence?"

The sergeant immediately went and reported this statement to the Commandant.

"Praise God!" said this lord. "Since he is a German I can speak to him; let him be brought to my arbor."

Candide was taken immediately into a leafy bower adorned with a very pretty colonnade in green and gold marble and with trellises which enclosed parrots, two kinds of hummingbirds, guinea fowl, and all the rarest of birds. An excellent breakfast stood prepared in vessels of gold; and while the Paraguayans ate corn out of wooden bowls in the open fields in the blaze of the sun, the Reverend Father Commandant entered the arbor.

He was a very handsome young man, full-faced, rather white-skinned, high-colored, with arched eyebrows, keen eyes, red ears, vermilion lips, his manner proud, but with a pride that was neither that of a Spaniard nor that of a Jesuit. Candide and Cacambo were given back their arms, which had been taken from them, as well as their two Andalusian horses; Cacambo fed them oats near the arbor and kept his eye constantly on them for fear of a surprise.

Candide first kissed the hem of the Commandant's robe, then they sat down to table.

"So you are a German?" the Jesuit said to him in that language.

"Yes, Reverend Father," said Candide.

Each one, as he pronounced these words, looked at the other with extreme surprise and an emotion which they could not master.

"And what part of Germany are you from?" said the Jesuit.

"From the filthy province of Westphalia," said Candide; "I was born in the castle of Thunder-ten-tronckh."

"Heavens! Is it possible!" cried the Commandant.

"What a miracle!" cried Candide.

"Can it be you?" said the Commandant.

"That is not possible," said Candide. They both fall over backwards, they embrace, they shed torrents of tears.

"What! Can that be you, Reverend Father? You, the brother of the fair Cunégonde! You, who were killed by the Bulgarians! You, the son of My Lord the Baron! You a Jesuit in Paraguay! I must admit that this world is a strange thing. O Pangloss! Pangloss! How happy you would be if you had not been hanged!"

The Commandant sent away the Negro slaves and the Paraguayans who were serving drink in rock-crystal goblets. He thanked God and St. Ignatius a thousand times; he clasped Candide in his arms; their faces were bathed in tears.

"You would be even more astounded, more touched, more beside yourself," said Candide, "if I told you that Mademoiselle Cunégonde your sister, whom you thought disemboweled, is in full health."

"Where?"

"In your neighborhood, with My Lord the Governor of Buenos Aires; and I was coming to make war on you."

Each word they uttered in this long conversation piled prodigy upon prodigy. Their whole souls flew from their tongues, listened in their ears, sparkled in their eyes. Since they were Germans, they stayed long at table, waiting for the Reverend Father Provincial; and the Commandant spoke thus to his dear Candide.

15

HOW CANDIDE KILLED THE BROTHER OF HIS DEAR CUNÉGONDE

"All my life I shall have present in my memory the horrible day when I saw my father and mother killed and my sister raped. When the Bulgarians were withdrawn, that adorable sister was not found, and my mother, my father, and I, two serving girls and three little boys who had all been slaughtered were put into a cart to be taken and buried in a Jesuit chapel two leagues from the castle of my forefathers. A Jesuit threw holy water on us; it was horribly salt; a few drops got into my eyes; the father noticed a tiny movement in my eyelid; he put his hand on my heart and felt it beating; I was rescued, and after three weeks it was as if nothing had happened. You know, my dear Candide, that I was very pretty, I became even more so; so the Reverend Father Kroust,[36] superior of

---

36. Father Antoine Kroust, Jesuit, rector at Colmar from 1753 to 1763, hostile to Voltaire and the *philosophes*.

the house, conceived the most tender friendship for me; he gave me the dress of a novice; some time later I was sent to Rome. The Father General needed some young German Jesuit recruits. The sovereigns of Paraguay receive as few Spanish Jesuits as they can; they prefer foreigners, since they feel more their masters. I was judged fit by the Reverend Father General to go and labor in this vineyard. We set out, a Pole, a Tyrolese, and I. On arriving, I was honored with a subdeaconate and a lieutenancy; today I am a colonel and priest. We shall give the King of Spain's troops a vigorous reception; I warrant you they will be excommunicated and beaten. Providence sends you here to second us. But is it really true that my dear sister Cunégonde is in the neighborhood with the Governor of Buenos Aires?"

Candide assured him on his oath that nothing could be truer. Their tears began to flow again.

The Baron seemed unable to tire of embracing Candide; he kept calling him his brother, his savior.

"Ah!" he said, "my dear Candide, perhaps we can enter the city together as conquerors and regain my sister Cunégonde."

"That is all I wish for," said Candide; "for I was counting on marrying her, and I still hope to."

"You, insolent wretch!" replied the Baron. "You would have the impudence to marry my sister who has seventy-two quarterings! I am amazed at your effrontery in daring to speak to me of so rash a plan!"

Candide, petrified at such a speech, replied: "Reverend Father, all the quarterings in the world have nothing to do with it; I have saved your sister from the arms of a Jew and an Inquisitor; she has obligations enough toward me, she wants to marry me; Doctor Pangloss always told me that men are equal, and certainly I shall marry her."

"We'll see about that, you scoundrel!" said the Jesuit Baron of Thunder-ten-tronckh, and at the same time he struck him a great blow on the face with the flat of his sword. That same instant Candide drew his own and thrust it up to the hilt in the Jesuit Baron's belly; but as he drew it out all smoking he began to weep: "Alas! Good Lord!" he said. "I have killed my former master, my friend, my brother-in-law; I am the kindest man in the world, and here I am killing three men already, and two of the three are priests."

Cacambo, who was standing watch at the door to the arbor, ran up.

"There is nothing left for us but to sell our lives dear," said his master to him. "No doubt they will be coming into the arbor, we must die arms in hand."

Cacambo, who had seen the likes of this before, did not lose his head; he took the Jesuit robe worn by the Baron, put it over Candide's body, gave him the dead man's square bonnet, and got him to mount his horse. All this was done in the twinkling of an eye. "Let's gallop, master. Every one will take you for a Jesuit on his way to give orders, and we will have passed the frontiers before they can come after us."

He was already in flight as he uttered these words, and shouted in Spanish: "Make way, make way for the Reverend Father Colonel."

The Oreillons found this speech very reasonable; they deputized two notables to go with all diligence and find out the truth; the two deputies acquitted themselves of their commission like intelligent men and soon returned bearing good news. The Oreillons untied their two prisoners, paid them all sorts of courtesies, offered them girls, gave them refreshments, and conducted them all the way to the confines of their states, shouting joyfully: "He's not a Jesuit, he's not a Jesuit!"

Candide could not tire of wondering at the reason for this deliverance. "What a race!" he said. "What men! What customs! If I had not had the good fortune of giving a great sword thrust through the body of Mademoiselle Cunégonde's brother, I would have been eaten without mercy. But after all, the pure state of nature is good, since these people, instead of eating me, offered me a thousand courtesies as soon as they learned that I was not a Jesuit."

17

ARRIVAL OF CANDIDE AND HIS VALET IN THE COUNTRY OF ELDORADO,[39] AND WHAT THEY SAW THERE

When they were at the frontiers of the Oreillons, Cacambo said to Candide: "You see, this hemisphere is no better than the other; take my word for it, let's go back to Europe by the shortest route."

"How can we go back there?" said Candide. "And where could we go? If I go to my own country, the Bulgarians and Abarians are slaughtering everyone; if I go back to Portugal I am burned; if we stay in this country we run the risk at any moment of being put on the spit. But how can one bring oneself to leave the part of the world where Mademoiselle Cunégonde lives?"

"Let's turn toward Cayenne," said Cacambo; "there we will find Frenchmen; they go all over the world; they may help us; perhaps God will have pity on us."

It was not easy to go to Cayenne. They knew about what direction they had to go; but mountains, rivers, precipices, brigands, savages, were terrible obstacles on all sides. Their horses died of fatigue; their provisions were used up. For a whole month they lived on wild fruits, and at last found themselves by a little river bordered with coconut trees, which supported their lives and hopes.

Cacambo, who always gave as good advice as the old woman, said to Candide: "We are at the end of our rope, we have walked far enough; I see an empty canoe on the bank, let us fill it with coconuts, cast ourselves into this little bark, and drift with the current; a river always leads to some inhabited spot. If we do not find pleasant things, at least we shall find new things."

"Let's go," said Candide, "let us recommend ourselves to Providence."

They drifted a few leagues between banks now flowery, now barren, now smooth, now rugged. The river kept getting wider; finally it disappeared under an arch of frightful rocks that rose to the heavens. The two travelers had the

---

39. "The Golden (Country)," which a lieutenant of Pizarro claimed to have discovered.

hardihood to abandon themselves to the waters underneath this arch. The river, at this point narrowed, carried them along with horrible rapidity and noise. After twenty-four hours they saw daylight again, but their canoe smashed on the reefs. They had to drag themselves from rock to rock for a whole league; finally they discovered an immense horizon bordered by inaccessible mountains. The country was cultivated for pleasure as well as for need; everywhere the useful was attractive. The roads were covered, or rather adorned, with carriages brilliant in form and material, bearing men and women of singular beauty, and drawn rapidly by big red sheep which in swiftness surpassed the finest horses of Andalusia, Tetuan,[40] and Meknes.[41]

"All the same," said Candide, "here is a country that is better than Westphalia." With Cacambo he set foot on land near the first village he came upon. A few village children covered with badly torn gold brocade were playing quoits at the entrance to the village. Our two men from the other world watched them with enjoyment. Their quoits were rather wide round pieces, yellow, red, and green, which shone with singular brilliance. The travelers took a notion to pick up a few of them; they were gold, emerald, and rubies, the least of which would have been the greatest ornament of the Mogul's throne.

"No doubt," said Cacambo, "these children are the sons of the King of the country playing quoits."

The village schoolmaster appeared at that moment, to call them back to school. "That," said Candide, "is the tutor of the royal family."

The little beggars immediately left their game, leaving on the ground their quoits and everything they had been playing with. Candide picks them up, runs to the tutor, and humbly presents them to him, giving him to understand by signs that Their Royal Highnesses had forgotten their gold and their precious stones. The village schoolmaster, smiling, threw them on the ground, looked at Candide's face for a moment with much surprise, and continued on his way.

The travelers did not fail to pick up the gold, the rubies, and the emeralds. "Where are we?" exclaimed Candide. "Kings' children must be well brought up in this country, since they teach them to despise gold and jewels." Cacambo was as surprised as Candide. Finally they approached the first house in the village. It was built like a European palace. A crowd of people was bustling at the door, and even more inside the house. You could hear very pleasant music and smell a delicious odor of cooking. Cacambo approached the door and heard them speaking Peruvian; it was his mother tongue; for everyone knows that Cacambo was born in Tucuman in a village where only that language was known. "I will serve as your interpreter," he said to Candide; "let's go in, this is an inn."

Instantly two boys and two girls of the hostelry, dressed in cloth of gold, their hair bound up with ribbons, invited them to sit at the host's table. They served four soups each garnished with two parrots, a boiled condor that weighed two hundred pounds, two roast monkeys of excellent flavor; three hundred colibri hummingbirds on one platter and six hundred other hummingbirds on another;

---

40. A town in Morocco.   41. A town in Morocco.

exquisite stews, delicious pastries; all this on platters of a sort of rock crystal. The boys and girls of the inn poured several liquors made of sugar cane.

The guests were for the most part merchants and coachmen, all of the greatest politeness, who asked Cacambo many questions with the most circumspect discretion and who answered his in a wholly satisfactory manner.

When the meal was over, Cacambo, like Candide, thought to pay his bill full well by throwing on the host's table two of those big gold pieces that he had picked up; the host and hostess burst out laughing and held their sides for quite a while. Finally they recovered themselves.

"Gentlemen," said the host, "we can easily see that you are foreigners; we are not accustomed to see any. Pardon us if we began to laugh when you offered us in payment the pebbles of our highroads. No doubt you have none of this country's money, but it is not necessary to have any in order to dine here. All the hostelries established for the convenience of commerce are paid for by the government. You had a bad meal here because this is a poor village; but everywhere else you will be received as you deserve to be."

Cacambo explained to Candide all the host's remarks, and Candide listened to them with the same amazement and the same bewilderment with which his friend Cacambo reported them. "What kind of a country is this, then," they said to each other, "unknown to the rest of the world, and where all nature is of a sort so different from ours? Probably this is the country where all is well; for there absolutely must be one of that sort. And no matter what Doctor Pangloss said about it, I often noticed that all was pretty bad in Westphalia."

18

WHAT THEY SAW IN THE LAND OF ELDORADO

Cacambo manifested all his curiosity to his host; the host said to him: "I am very ignorant, and I get along all right that way; but we have here an old man who has retired from the court, who is the most learned man in the kingdom and the most communicative." Immediately he took Cacambo to the old man. Candide was now playing only second fiddle and going along with his valet. They entered a house that was very simple, for the door was only of silver and the paneling in the apartments only of gold, but wrought with so much taste that the richest paneling did not eclipse it. True, the antechamber was encrusted only with rubies and emeralds, but the order in which everything was arranged fully made up for this extreme simplicity.

The old man received the two foreigners on a sofa stuffed with hummingbird feathers, and had them served liquors in diamond vases; after which he satisfied their curiosity in these terms:

"I am a hundred and seventy-two years old, and I learned from my late father, equerry to the King, of the astounding revolutions in Peru that he had witnessed. The kingdom we are in is the ancient homeland of the Incas, who left it very imprudently to go and subjugate part of the world, and who were finally destroyed by the Spaniards.

"The princes of their family who remained in their native country were wiser; they ordained, with the consent of the nation, that no inhabitant should ever leave our little kingdom; and that is what has preserved our innocence and happiness for us. The Spaniards gained some confused knowledge of this country; they called it El Dorado; and an Englishman named Lord Raleigh even came near it about a hundred years ago; but since we are surrounded by inaccessible rocks and precipices, we have up to now always been sheltered from the rapacity of the nations of Europe, who have an inconceivable rage for the pebbles and mud of our land, and who would kill us all to the last man to get some."

The conversation was long; it bore on the form of government, customs, women, public spectacles, arts. Finally Candide, who always had a taste for metaphysics, had Cacambo ask whether there was a religion in the country.

The old man blushed a little. "What," he said, "can you doubt it? Do you take us for ingrates?" Cacambo humbly asked what was the religion of Eldorado. The old man blushed again.

"Can there be two religions?" he said. "We have, I think, the religion of everyone; we worship God from morning till evening."

"Do you worship only one single God?" said Cacambo, who was still serving as interpreter for Candide's doubts.

"It appears," said the old man, "that there are not two, or three or four. I must admit that the people of your world ask very singular questions."

Candide could not tire of having this good old man questioned; he wanted to know how they prayed to God in Eldorado.

"We do not pray to him," said the good and respectable sage; "we have nothing to ask him for; he has given us all we need, we thank him without ceasing."

Candide had a curiosity to see some priests; he asked where they were. The good old man smiled.

"My friends," he said, "we are all priests; the King and all the heads of families solemnly sing hymns of thanksgiving every morning, and five or six thousand musicians accompany them."

"What! you have no monks to teach, to dispute, to govern, to intrigue, and to have people burned who are not of their opinion?"

"We would have to be crazy," said the old man; "we are all of the same opinion, and we do not understand what you mean with your monks."

At all these remarks Candide remained in ecstasy and said to himself:

"This is very different from Westphalia and the castle of My Lord the Baron; if our friend Pangloss had seen Eldorado, he would no longer have said that the castle of Thunder-ten-tronckh was the best thing on earth; travel is certainly necessary."

After this long conversation, the good old man had a carriage harnessed with six sheep and gave the two travelers twelve of his servants to take them to court. "Excuse me," he said to them, "if my age deprives me of the honor of accompanying you. The King will receive you in a way that will not leave you discontented, and you will doubtless pardon the customs of the country if there are some that displease you."

Candide and Cacambo climbed into the carriage, the six sheep flew, and in less than four hours they arrived at the King's palace, situated at one end of the capital. The portal was two hundred and twenty feet high and a hundred wide; it is impossible to describe what material it was. It is easy to see what prodigious superiority it must have had over those pebbles and sand that we call gold and precious stones.

Twenty beautiful girls of the watch received Candide and Cacambo as they got out of the carriage, took them to the baths, dressed them in robes woven from hummingbird down; after which the men and women grand officers of the crown took them to His Majesty's apartment between two files of a thousand musicians each, according to the ordinary custom. When they approached the throne room, Cacambo asked one grand officer how they should go about saluting His Majesty: whether you crawled on your knees or on your belly, whether you put your hands on your head or on your backside, whether you licked the dust of the room, in short what the ceremony was.

"The custom," said the grand officer, "is to embrace the King and kiss him on both cheeks."

Candide and Cacambo threw their arms around the neck of His Majesty, who received them with all the grace imaginable and politely asked them to supper.

While waiting, they were shown the town, the public buildings rising to the clouds, the market places adorned with a thousand columns, the fountains of pure water, those of rose water, and those of cane-sugar liquors, which flowed continually in great squares paved with a kind of precious stone which gave off a perfume like that of cloves and cinnamon.

Candide asked to see the law courts; they told him that there were none and that people never went to law. He inquired whether there were prisons, and they told him no. What surprised him even more and pleased him most was the Palace of Sciences, in which he saw a great gallery two thousand paces long all full of instruments for mathematics and physics.

After spending all afternoon touring about the thousandth part of the city, they were taken back to the King's palace; Candide sat down to table with His Majesty, his valet Cacambo, and several ladies. Never was better cheer made, and never had a man more wit at supper than His Majesty. Cacambo explained the King's witty remarks to Candide, and even when translated they still appeared witty. Of all that astounded Candide this was not what astounded him least.

They stayed a month in this hospitable place. Candide never stopped saying to Cacambo:

"It is true, my friend, once again, that the castle where I was born is not worth the country where we are now; but after all, Mademoiselle Cunégonde is not here, and no doubt you have some mistress in Europe. If we stay here, we shall only be like the others, whereas if we return to our own world with just twelve sheep laden with the pebbles of Eldorado, we shall be richer than all the Kings put together, we shall have no more Inquisitors to fear, and we shall easily be able to recover Mademoiselle Cunégonde."

Cacambo liked this idea; people are so fond of running about, showing off before the folks at home, and parading what they have seen on their travels, that

Candide is corruptable.

the two happy men resolved to be so no longer and to ask His Majesty for leave to go.

"You are doing a foolish thing," the King said to them. "I know that my country is not much; but when a person is reasonably well off somewhere he should stay there. I certainly have no right to detain foreigners; that is a tyranny that does not exist either in our customs or in our laws; all men are free; leave when you will, but the way out is very difficult. It is impossible to go back up the rapid river on which by a miracle you came here and which runs under arches of rock. The mountains that surround my whole kingdom are ten thousand feet high and as perpendicular as walls; they are each more than ten leagues wide, you can descend them only by way of precipices. However, since you absolutely want to leave, I am going to give orders to the directors of machinery to make a machine that can transport you comfortably. When you have been taken to the other side of the mountains, no one will be able to accompany you farther; for my subjects have made a vow never to go beyond the mountain walls, and they are too wise to break their vow. Ask of me anything else you like."

"We ask of Your Majesty," said Cacambo, "only a few sheep loaded with victuals, pebbles, and some of the country's mud."

The King laughed. "I do not understand," he said, "the taste your people of Europe have for our yellow mud; but take as much as you want, and much good may it do you."

He immediately gave orders to his engineers to make a machine to hoist these two extraordinary men out of the kingdom. Three thousand good physicists worked on it; it was ready in two weeks and cost no more than twenty million pounds sterling in the money of the country. They put Candide and Cacambo on the machine; there were two big red sheep saddled and bridled to serve them as mounts when they had crossed the mountains; twenty pack sheep laden with victuals, thirty bearing presents of the most curious products of the country, and fifty laden with gold, precious stones, and diamonds. The King embraced the two wanderers tenderly.

A fine spectacle was their departure and the ingenious manner in which they and their sheep were hoisted to the top of the mountains. The physicists took leave of them after setting them down safely, and Candide was left with no other desire and object than to go and present his sheep to Mademoiselle Cunégonde.

"We have enough," he said, "to pay the Governor of Buenos Aires, if Mademoiselle Cunégonde can be ransomed. Let us head for Cayenne and take ship, and then we shall see what kingdom we can buy."

19

WHAT HAPPENED TO THEM IN SURINAM, AND HOW CANDIDE MADE THE ACQUAINTANCE OF MARTIN

Our two travelers' first day was rather pleasant. They were encouraged by the idea of finding themselves possessors of more treasures than Asia, Europe, and Africa could assemble. Candide in transport wrote Cunégonde's name on the trees. On the second day two of their sheep got stuck in marshes and went down with their loads; two other sheep died of fatigue a few days later; seven or eight then died of hunger in a desert; a few days later some others fell from precipices. Finally, after a hundred days of travel, they had only two sheep left.

Candide said to Cacambo: "My friend, you see how perishable are the riches of this world; there is nothing solid but virtue and the happiness of seeing Mademoiselle Cunégonde again."

"I admit it," said Cacambo, "but we still have two sheep left with more treasures than the King of Spain will ever have, and I see in the distance a town that I suspect is Surinam, which belongs to the Dutch. We are at the end of our troubles and the beginning of our happiness."

As they approached the town they met a Negro stretched on the ground, with only half his clothes left, that is to say a pair of blue cloth shorts; the poor man had his left leg and his right hand missing. "Oh, good Lord!" said Candide to him in Dutch. "What are you doing there, my friend, in that horrible state I see you in?"

"I am waiting for my master Monsieur Vanderdendur, the famous merchant," the Negro replied.

"Was it Monsieur Vanderdendur," said Candide, "who treated you this way?"

"Yes, sir," said the Negro, "it is the custom. They give us a pair of cloth shorts twice a year for all our clothing. When we work in the sugar mills and we catch our finger in the millstone, they cut off our hand; when we try to run away, they cut off a leg; both things have happened to me.[42] It is at this price that you eat sugar in Europe. However, when my mother sold me for ten patacóns[43] on the Guinea coast, she said to me: 'My dear child, bless our fetishes, worship them always, they will make you live happily; you have the honor to be a slave to our lords the whites and thereby you are making the fortune of your father and mother.' Alas! I don't know if I made their fortune, but they didn't make mine. Dogs, monkeys, parrots are a thousand times less miserable than we are. The Dutch fetishes who converted me tell me every Sunday that we are all, whites and blacks, children of Adam. I am no genealogist, but if those preachers are telling the truth, we are all second cousins. Now you must admit that no one could treat his relatives in a more horrible way."

"O Pangloss!" exclaimed Candide, "you had not guessed this abomination; this does it, at last I shall have to renounce your optimism."

"What is optimism?" said Cacambo.

"Alas," said Candide, "it is the mania of maintaining that all is well when we are miserable!" And he shed tears as he looked at his Negro, and he entered Surinam weeping.

The first thing they inquired about was whether there was not some ship in the port that could be sent to Buenos Aires. The man they addressed proved to be a Spanish ship's captain, who offered to make an honest bargain with them. He

---

42. It was actually in French-owned Santo Domingo that the penalty for escaping was the removal of an arm and a leg.

43. Patacon (or pataca), a Portuguese and Brazilian silver coin.

arranged to meet them at an inn. Candide and the faithful Cacambo went and waited for him there with their two sheep.

Candide, whose heart was on his lips, told the Spaniard all his adventures and admitted to him that he wanted to carry off Mademoiselle Cunégonde.

"I shall take good care not to take you to Buenos Aires," said the captain. "I would be hanged and you too. The fair Cunégonde is His Lordship's favorite mistress."

This was a bolt from the blue for Candide; he wept for a long time; finally he drew Cacambo aside.

"My dear friend," he said to him, "here is what you must do. We each have in our pockets five or six millions worth of diamonds; you are cleverer than I; go get Mademoiselle Cunégonde in Buenos Aires. If the Governor makes any difficulties, give him a million; if he still doesn't give in, give him two; you haven't killed an Inquisitor, they won't suspect you. I will fit out another ship; I will go to Venice and wait for you; it is a free country where there is nothing to fear either from Bulgarians, or Abarians, or Jews, or Inquisitors."

Cacambo applauded this wise resolution. He was in despair at parting from a good master who had become his intimate friend; but the pleasure of being useful to him overcame the grief of leaving him. They embraced, shedding tears. Candide recommended to him not to forget the good old woman. Cacambo left that very day. He was a very good man, this Cacambo.

Candide stayed on some time in Surinam and waited for another captain to be willing to take him to Italy, him and the two sheep he had left. He took servants and bought everything he needed for a long voyage. At last Monsieur Vanderdendur, master of a big ship, came to see him.

"How much do you want," he asked this man, "to take me straight to Venice, me, my men, my baggage, and the two sheep you see here?" The captain agreed to ten thousand piasters.[44] Candide did not hesitate.

"Oho!" said the prudent Vanderdendur to himself, "this foreigner gives ten thousand piasters right away! He must be very rich." Then, returning a moment later, he signified that he could not sail for less than twenty thousand. "Very well, you shall have them," said Candide.

"Whew!" said the merchant softly to himself, "this man gives twenty thousand piasters as easily as ten thousand." He came back again and said that he could not take him to Venice for less than thirty thousand piasters. "Then you shall have thirty thousand," said Candide.

"Oho!" said the Dutch merchant to himself again, "thirty thousand piasters means nothing to this man; no doubt the two sheep are carrying immense treasures; let's not insist any further; let's get the thirty thousand piasters paid first, and then we shall see."

Candide sold two little diamonds the smaller of which was worth more than all the money the captain was asking. He paid him in advance. The two sheep were

---

44. A coin, usually silver, of Turkey and
    Egypt, also used to signify the Spanish
    peso.

put aboard. Candide was following in a little boat to join the ship in the roads; the captain seizes his chance, sets sail, weighs anchor; the wind favors him. Candide, bewildered and stupefied, soon loses sight of him. "Alas!" he cried, "that's a trick worthy of the Old World." He returns to shore sunk in grief, for after all he had lost enough to make the fortune of twenty monarchs.

He goes to see the Dutch judge; and since he was somewhat upset, he knocks roughly on the door; he enters, expounds his adventure, and exclaims a little louder than was fitting. The judge began by making him pay ten thousand piasters for the noise he had made. Then he listened to him patiently, promised to look into his affair as soon as the merchant had returned, and charged him another ten thousand piasters for the costs of the hearing.

This procedure completed Candide's despair; true, he had endured misfortunes a thousand times more painful; but the cold-bloodedness of the judge, and of the captain by whom he had been robbed, inflamed his bile and plunged him into a black melancholy. The wickedness of men appeared to his mind in all its ugliness; he fed only on sad ideas.

Finally when a French ship was on the point of leaving for Bordeaux, since he had no more sheep laden with diamonds to put on board, he hired a cabin at a proper price and let it be known in the town that he would pay the passage and food and two thousand piasters to a decent man who would like to make the voyage with him, on condition that this man should be the most disgusted with his lot, and the most unfortunate in the province.

A throng of aspirants presented themselves that a fleet could not have held. Candide, wanting to choose among the most promising, picked out about twenty persons who seemed to him sociable enough and who all claimed to deserve the preference. He assembled them in his inn and gave them supper on condition that each would take an oath to tell his story faithfully; promising to choose the one who should seem to him the most to be pitied and the most discontented with his lot for the best reasons, and to give the others rewards.

The session lasted until four in the morning. Candide, as he listened to all their adventures, remembered what the old woman had said to him on the way to Buenos Aires, and the wager she had made that there was no one on the ship to whom very great misfortunes had not happened. At each adventure that was told him he thought of Pangloss.

"That Pangloss," said he, "would be much embarrassed to try to prove his system. I wish he were here. Certainly if all is well it is in Eldorado and not in the rest of the world."

Finally he made up his mind in favor of a poor scholar who had worked ten years for the booksellers in Amsterdam.[45] He judged that there was no occupation in the world that a man should be more disgusted with.

This scholar, moveover, who was a good man, had been robbed by his wife, beaten by his son, and abandoned by his daughter, who had eloped with a

---

45. Because of French censorship, Dutch freedom of the press, and the lack of international copyright laws, many French books were published piratically in Holland. Voltaire, among others, had suffered much from this pirating.

Portuguese. He had just been deprived of a small job on which he lived, and the preachers of Surinam were persecuting him because they took him for a Socinian.[46] It must be admitted that the others were at least as unfortunate as he; but Candide hoped that the scholar would allay his boredom on the voyage. All his other rivals considered that Candide was doing them a great injustice, but he appeased them by giving them each a hundred piasters.

20

WHAT HAPPENED TO CANDIDE AND MARTIN AT SEA

So the old scholar, whose name was Martin, embarked with Candide for Bordeaux. Both had seen much, and suffered much; and if the ship had been scheduled to set sail from Surinam to Japan by the Cape of Good Hope, they would have had enough to say about moral and physical evil to last the whole voyage.

However, Candide had one great advantage over Martin: he still hoped to see Mademoiselle Cunégonde again, and Martin had nothing to hope for; furthermore, he had gold and diamonds; and though he had lost a hundred big red sheep laden with the greatest treasures on earth, though he still had the knavery of the Dutch captain on his mind, nevertheless, when he thought about what he had left in his pockets, and when he talked about Cunégonde, especially toward the end of a meal, he still leaned toward the system of Pangloss.

"But you, Monsieur Martin," he said to the scholar, "what do you think of all that? What is your idea about moral and physical evil?"

"Sir," replied Martin, "my priests accused me of being a Socinian; but the truth of the matter is that I am a Manichean."[47]

"You are making fun of me," said Candide, "there are no more Manicheans in the world."

"There's me," said Martin; "I don't know what to do about it, but I cannot think any other way."

"You must be full of the devil," said Candide.

"He takes so much part in the affairs of this world," said Martin, "that I might well be full of him, just like everything else; but I must admit that when I cast my eyes over this globe, or rather over this globule, I think that God has abandoned it to some maleficent being—always excepting Eldorado. I have hardly seen a town that did not desire the ruin of the neighboring town, never a family that did not want to exterminate some other family. Everywhere the weak loathe the powerful before whom they crawl, and the powerful treat them like flocks whose wool and flesh are for sale. A million regimented assassins, ranging from one end of Europe to the other, practice murder and brigandage with discipline to earn their bread, because there is no more honest occupation; and in the towns that

---

46. A religious rationalist, denying the Trinity and the personality of Christ.
47. A follower of Mani or Manicheus, a third-century Persian who believed in two nearly equal forces, of good and of evil. The sect flourished in St. Augustine's time.

seem to enjoy peace and where the arts flourish, men are devoured with more envy, cares, and anxieties than the scourges suffered by a town besieged. Secret griefs are even more cruel than public miseries. In a word, I have seen so much, and undergone so much, that I am a Manichean."

"Yet there is some good," said Candide.

"That may be," said Martin, "but I do not know it."

In the midst of this dispute they heard the sound of cannon. The noise redoubles each moment. Everyone takes his spyglass. They see two ships fighting about three miles away. The wind brought them both so near the French ship that they had the pleasure of seeing the combat quite at their ease. Finally one of the two ships sent the other a broadside so low and so accurate as to sink it. Candide and Martin distinctly saw a hundred men on the main deck of the sinking ship; they all raised their hands to heaven and uttered frightful screams; in a moment all was swallowed up.

"Well," said Marin, "that is how men treat each other."

"It is true," said Candide, "that there is something diabolical in this affair."

So saying, he spied something bright red swimming near his ship. They launched the ship's boat to see what it could be; it was one of his sheep. Candide felt more joy on finding this sheep again than he had felt grief on losing a hundred all laden with big diamonds from Eldorado.

The French captain soon perceived that the captain of the ship that sank the other was a Spaniard and that the captain of the ship that sank was a Dutch pirate; he was the very one who had robbed Candide. The immense riches that this scoundrel had stolen were buried with him in the sea, and nothing but one sheep was saved.

"You see," said Candide to Martin, "that crime is sometimes punished; that rascal of a Dutch captain met the fate he deserved."

"Yes," said Martin, "but was it necessary that the passengers on his ship should perish also? God punished that knave, the devil drowned the others."

Meanwhile the French ship and the Spaniard continued on their way, and Candide continued his conversations with Martin. They argued for two weeks without stopping, and after two weeks they were as far advanced as the first day. But after all they were talking, they were exchanging ideas, they were consoling each other. Candide kept stroking his sheep. "Since I have found you again," he said, "I may well find Cunégonde again."

21

CANDIDE AND MARTIN APPROACH THE COAST OF FRANCE, REASONING

At last they sighted the coast of France.

"Have you ever been in France, Monsieur Martin?" said Candide.

"Yes," said Martin, "I have been through several provinces. There are some where half the inhabitants are crazy, some where they are too tricky, others where they are usually rather gentle and rather stupid; others where they try to be witty;

and in all of them the principal occupation is making love, the second talking slander, and the third talking nonsense."

"But, Monsieur Martin, have you seen Paris?"

"Yes, I have seen Paris; it is like all those kinds, it's a chaos, it's a crowd in which everyone seeks pleasure and in which almost no one finds it, at least so it appeared to me. I did not stay there long; on arrival I was robbed of all I had by pickpockets at the Saint-Germain fair. I was taken for a thief myself and I was in prison for a week; after which I became a printer's proofreader to earn enough to return on foot to Holland. I came to know the writing rabble, the intriguing rabble, and the convulsionary[48] rabble. They say there are some very polite persons in that city; I am willing to believe it."

"For my part, I have no curiosity to see France," said Candide. "You can easily guess that when a man has spent a month in Eldorado, he does not care about seeing anything else on earth, except Mademoiselle Cunégonde; I am going to wait for her in Venice; we will cross France on our way to Italy; won't you come along with me?"

"Very gladly," said Martin. "They say that Venice is good only for Venetian nobles, but that nevertheless they receive foreigners very well when they have a lot of money; I have none, you have, I will follow you anywhere."

"By the way," said Candide, "do you think that the earth was originally a sea, as we are assured in that big book[49] that belongs to the ship's captain?"

"I believe nothing of the sort," said Martin, "any more than all the daydreams that people have been trying to sell us for some time now."

"But then to what end was this world formed?" said Candide.

"To drive us mad," replied Martin.

"Aren't you quite astonished," Candide continued, "at the love of those two girls in the country of the Oreillons for those two monkeys, the adventure with whom I told you?"

"Not at all," said Martin, "I don't see what is strange about that passion; I have seen so many extraordinary things that there is nothing extraordinary left."

"Do you think," said Candide, "that men have always massacred each other as they do today, always been liars, cheats, faithbreakers, ingrates, brigands, weaklings, rovers, cowards, enviers, gluttons, drunkards, misers, self-seekers, carnivores, calumniators, debauchees, fanatics, hypocrites, and fools?"

"Do you think," said Martin, "that sparrow hawks have always eaten pigeons when they found any?"

"Yes, no doubt," said Candide.

"Well," said Martin, "if sparrow hawks have always had the same character, why do you expect men to have changed theirs?"

"Oh!" said Candide, "there's a big difference, for free will . . . ."

Reasoning thus, they arrived at Bordeaux.

---

48. Manifestations of religious ecstasy or mania, like those of the Holy Rollers today. The Jansenists were noted for them.

49. The "big book" presumably is the Bible; the theory had recently been advanced again in Buffon's *Théorie de la terre* (1749).

22

WHAT HAPPENED TO CANDIDE AND MARTIN IN FRANCE

Candide stopped in Bordeaux only as long as it took to sell a few pebbles from Eldorado and to provide himself with a good two-seated chaise; for he now could not do without his philosopher Martin; only he was very sorry to part with his sheep, which he left to the Bordeaux Academy of Science, which proposed, as the subject of that year's competition, to find out why this sheep's wool was red; and the prize was awarded to a scholar from the north, who proved by A plus B, minus C, divided by Z, that the sheep must be red and die of sheep pox.

Meanwhile all the travelers that Candide met in the inns on the road said to him: "We are going to Paris." This general eagerness finally gave him a hankering to see this capital; it was not much of a detour off the road to Venice.

He entered by the Faubourg Saint-Marceau[50] and thought he was in the ugliest village in Westphalia.

Hardly was Candide in his inn when he was attacked by a slight illness caused by his fatigue. Since he had an enormous diamond on his finger and a prodigiously heavy strongbox had been observed in his baggage, he immediately had at his side two doctors he had not called, some intimate friends who did not leave him, and two pious ladies heating up his broths.

Martin said: "I remember having been sick in Paris too on my first trip; I was very poor, so I had neither friends, nor pious ladies, nor doctors; and I got well."

However, by dint of medicines and bloodlettings, Candide's illness became serious. A neighborhood priest came and asked him gently for a note payable to the bearer in the next world.[51] Candide wanted no part of it; the pious ladies assured him that it was a new fashion. Candide replied that he was not a man of fashion. Martin wanted to throw the priest out the window. The cleric swore that Candide should not be buried.[52] Martin swore that he would bury the cleric if he continued to bother them. The quarrel grew heated; Martin took him by the shoulders and pushed him out roughly, which caused a great scandal which led in turn to a legal report.

Candide got well, and during his convalescence he had very good company to supper with him. They gambled for high stakes. Candide was quite amazed that he never got any aces, and Martin was not amazed at this at all.

Among those who did the honors of the town for him was a little abbé from Périgord, one of those eager people, always alert, always obliging, brazen, fawning, complaisant, who lie in wait for strangers passing through, tell them the history of the town's scandals, and offer them pleasures at any price. This man first took Candide and Martin to the theater. They were playing a new tragedy. Candide found himself seated next to some wits. This did not keep him from

---

50. In Voltaire's time an ugly, dirty suburb.
51. A reference to the *billets de confession* required from 1746 on, on pain of refusal of absolution and the sacraments.

52. That is, buried in consecrated ground. See note 56.

weeping at certain perfectly played scenes. One of the reasoners beside him said to him during an intermission:

"You are very wrong to weep, for that actress is very bad, the actor playing opposite her even worse, the play is even worse than the actors: the author doesn't know a word of Arabic, and yet the scene is in Arabia; and besides, he is a man who doesn't believe in innate ideas;[53] tomorrow I will bring you twenty pamphlets against him."

"Sir,[54] how many plays do you have in France?" said Candide to the abbé, who replied: "Five or six thousand."

"That's a lot," said Candide. "How many of them are good?"

"Fifteen or sixteen," replied the other.

"That's a lot," said Martin.

Candide was very pleased with an actress who played Queen Elizabeth in a rather dull tragedy that is sometimes performed.[55]

"I like this actress very much," he said to Martin; "she reminds me of Mademoiselle Cunégonde; I would very much like to pay her my respects."

The abbé from Périgord offered to take him to meet her. Candide, brought up in Germany, asked what the proper etiquette was, and how they treated queens of England in France.

"You have to make a distinction," said the abbé. "In the provinces they take them to a tavern, in Paris they respect them when they are beautiful and throw them on the dump when they are dead."

"Queens on the dump!" said Candide.

"Yes, really," said Martin; "the abbé is right; I was in Paris when Mademoiselle Monime[56] passed on, as they say, from this life to the next; she was refused what those people call the honors of burial, that is to say, of rotting with all the beggars of the district in an ugly cemetery; alone of her troupe, she was buried at the corner of the Rue de Bourgogne; which must have pained her extremely, for she had a very noble mind."

"That was very impolite," said Candide.

"What do you expect?" said Martin. "These people are made that way. Imagine all possible contradictions and incompatibilities, you will see them in the government, the tribunals, the churches, the entertainments of this queer nation."

"Is it true that people are always laughing in Paris?" said Candide.

"Yes," said the abbé, "but it is with rage in their hearts; for here people complain about everything with great bursts of laughter, and they even perform the most detestable actions with a laugh."

"Who," said Candide, "is that fat pig who was telling me so many bad things

---

53. Voltaire followed Locke's view of the mind at birth as a blank slate, rather than Descartes' theory of innate ideas.

54. Here begins a long passage added by Voltaire in 1761. See note 67.

55. Presumably Thomas Corneille, *Le Comte d'Essex*.

56. Adrienne Lecouvreur (1690–1730), a distinguished actress who made her debut at the Comédie Française as Monime in Racine's *Mithridate*. Being an actress, at her death she was refused burial in consecrated ground.

about the play at which I wept so much and about the actors who gave me such pleasure?"

"He is a living disease," replied the abbé, "who makes his living by saying bad things about all plays and all books; he hates anyone who succeeds, as eunuchs hate those who can enjoy sex; he is one of those serpents of literature who feed on filth and venom; he is a foliferous pamphleteer. . . . ."

"What do you mean by a foliferous pamphleteer?" said Candide.

"A producer of scribbled leaves," said the abbé, "a Fréron."[57]

That is how Candide, Martin, and the Perigordian were talking on the staircase as they watched people file out after the play.

"Although I am very eager to see Mademoiselle Cunégonde again," said Candide, "still I would like to have supper with Mademoiselle Clairon,[58] for she seemed admirable to me."

The abbé was not the man to approach Mademoiselle Clairon, for she saw only good company. "She is engaged for this evening," he said, "but I shall have the honor of taking you to the house of a lady of quality, and there you will come to know Paris as if you had been here four years."

Candide, who was naturally curious, let himself be taken to the lady's house, at the far end of the Faubourg Saint-Honoré;[59] they were busy playing faro; twelve sad punters[60] each held a small hand of cards, the foolish register of their misfortunes. A deep silence reigned, pallor sat on the punters' foreheads, anxiety on that of the banker; and the lady of the house, seated beside this pitiless banker, watched with a lynx's eyes all the underhand plays for double stakes or for three straight wins to pay seven times, for which each player turned up the corner of his cards;[61] she had them turned back down with severe but polite attention, and did not show any anger for fear of losing her customers; the lady called herself the Marquise de Parolignac.[62] Her daughter, aged fifteen, was one of the punters, and tipped her off with a wink to the cheating of those who were trying to repair the cruelties of fortune. The abbé from Périgord, Candide, and Martin entered, no one got up, greeted them, or looked at them; all were deeply preoccupied with their cards.

"My Lady the Baroness of Thunder-ten-tronckh was more civil," said Candide.

However, the abbé got the ear of the Marquise, who half rose, honored Candide with a gracious smile and Martin with a truly noble nod; she saw to it that a seat and a hand of cards were given to Candide, who lost fifty thousand francs in two deals; after which they had supper most gaily, and everyone was astounded

---

57. Elie Fréron (1719–1776), publisher of the *Année Littéraire,* enemy of Voltaire and the *philosophes* and a favorite target for Voltaire's wit.

58. A celebrated actress who played leading roles in many of Voltaire's plays.

59. An aristocratic quarter of Paris.

60. Faro is played by an unlimited number of punters against the banker.

61. To mark that he was making this bet— illegally, however.

62. From *paroli,* the doubled stakes alluded to above, and the *-gnac* ending common in the southwest of France, a great source of impoverished and spurious nobility.

that Candide was not moved by his loss; the lackeys said to one another in their lackey language: "He must be some English Milord."

The supper was like most suppers in Paris; first a silence; then a noise of undistinguishable words; then jokes, most of them insipid, false news, bad reasoning, a little politics, and a lot of slander; there was even some talk about new books.

"Have you seen," said the abbé from Périgord, "the novel by a certain Gauchat,[63] Doctor of Theology?"

"Yes," replied one of the guests, "but I could not finish it. We have a host of nonsensical writings, but all of them together do not approach the nonsensicality of Gauchat, Doctor of Theology; I am so surfeited with this immense number of detestable books that inundate us that I have taken to punting at faro. . . ."

"What about the *Mélanges* by Archdeacon Trublet?[64] What do you say about them?" said the abbé.

"Oh!" said Madame de Parolignac, "what a tedious mortal! How assiduously he tells you what everybody knows! How ponderously he discusses what is not worth being noted lightly! With what absence of wit he appropriates the wit of others! How he spoils what he plunders! How he disgusts me! But he will not disgust me any more; it is enough to have read a few pages by the Archdeacon."

There was a learned man of taste at table who supported what the Marquise said. They talked of tragedies next; the lady asked why there were tragedies that were sometimes played and that could not be read. The man of taste explained very well how a play could have some interest and almost no merit; he proved in a few words that it was not enough to bring on one or two of those situations that you find in all novels and that always beguile the spectators, but that you have to be new without being bizarre, often sublime, and always natural, know the human heart and make it speak, be a great poet without letting any character in the play appear to be a poet, know the language perfectly, speak it with purity, with continual harmony, without ever rhyming at the expense of the sense.

"Anyone," he added, "who does not observe all these rules may compose one or two tragedies that win applause at the theater, but he will never be ranked among good writers; there are very few good tragedies; some are idyls in well-written and well-rhymed dialogue, other are political arguments that put you to sleep, or repulsive amplifications; still other are the dreams of enthusiasts, in a barbarous style; interrupted speeches, long apostrophes to the gods—because the author does not know how to speak to men—false maxims, bombastic commonplaces."

Candide listened attentively to this speech and formed a fine impression of the speaker; and since the Marquise had taken care to place him next to her, he got her ear and took the liberty of asking her who was that man who spoke so well.

"He is a learned man," said the lady, "who does not play faro and whom the abbé sometimes brings to supper with me; he is a perfect connoisseur of tragedies

---

63. Gabriel Gauchat (1709–1774 or 1779), enemy of Voltaire and the Encyclopedists.
64. Nicholas-Charles-Joseph Trublet (1697–1770), bitter critic of Voltaire and the *Encyclopédie*, author of *Essais de littérature*.

and books, and he has written a tragedy that was hissed and a book of which only one copy, which he dedicated to me, was ever seen outside his publisher's store."

"What a great man!" said Candide. "He is another Pangloss."

Then, turning toward him, he said to him:

"Sir, no doubt you think that all is for the best in the physical world and in the moral, and that nothing could have been otherwise?"

"I, sir," replied the scholar, "I think nothing of the sort; I think that everything goes awry with us, that no one knows his rank or his job or what he is doing or what he should do, and that except for supper, which is rather gay and where there seems to be a good deal of agreement, all the rest of the time is spent in senseless quarrels: Jansenists[65] against Molinists,[66] lawyers against churchmen, men of letters against men of letters, courtiers against courtiers, financiers against the people, wives against husbands, relatives against relatives—it's an eternal war."

Candide replied: "I have seen worse; but a sage, who has since had the misfortune to be hanged, taught me that all this is wonderful: these are shadows in a beautiful picture."

"Your hanged man was making fun of everybody," said Martin; "your shadows are horrible stains."

"It is men who make the stains," said Candide, "and they can't help it."

"Then it isn't their fault," said Martin.

Most of the gamblers, who understood nothing of this kind of talk, were drinking; and Martin talked theory with the scholar, and Candide told the lady of the house part of his adventures.

After supper the Marquise took Candide into her boudoir and sat him down on a sofa.

"Well," she said to him, "so you are still madly in love with Mademoiselle Cunégonde of Thunder-ten-tronckh!"

"Yes, Madame," answered Candide.

The Marquise replied to him with a tender smile: "You answer me like a young man from Westphalia; a Frenchman would have said to me: 'It is true that I have been in love with Mademoiselle Cunégonde, but when I see you, Madame, I fear I no longer love her.'"

"Alas! Madame," said Candide, "I will answer as you wish."

"Your passion for her," said the Marquise, "began when you picked up her handkerchief; I want you to pick up my garter."

"With all my heart," said Candide, and he picked it up.

---

65. A Christian sect stressing predestination and asceticism, founded by Cornelius Jansen or Jansenius (1585–1638), Dutch Bishop of Ypres, author of the *Augustinus,* (1640). It spread rapidly and widely in France, notably through the efforts of Saint-Cyran and Arnauld, and established its center near Paris in the religious community of Port-Royal. Opposed violently by the Sorbonne and the Jesuits, persecuted by Louis XIV, and condemned by Pope Clement XI in 1713, Jansenism still retained some strength in France until about the mid-eighteenth century.

66. Jesuits, from the name of Luis Molina (1535–1600), Spanish Jesuit, author of a widely influential theory reconciling predestination with free will.

"But I want you to put it back on me," said the lady, and Candide put it back on her.

"You see," said the lady, "you are a foreigner; I sometimes make my Parisian lovers languish for two weeks, but I give myself to you on the very first night, because one must do the honors of one's country to a young man from Westphalia."

The beauty, having perceived two enormous diamonds on her young foreigner's two hands, praised them so sincerely that they passed from Candide's fingers to the fingers of the Marquise.

When Candide went home with his Perigordian abbé, he felt some remorse at having been unfaithful to Mademoiselle Cunégonde; the abbé took part in his grief; he had got only a small share of the fifty thousand francs lost at gambling by Candide and of the value of the two brilliants half given, half extorted from him. His plan was to make all the profit he could from the advantages that his acquaintance with Candide might procure him. He talked to him a lot about Cunégonde, and Candide told him that he would certainly beg that fair lady's pardon for his infidelity when he saw her in Venice.

The Perigordian redoubled his courtesies and attentions, and took a tender interest in everything Candide said, everything he did, everything he wanted to do.[67]

"So you have a rendezvous in Venice, sir?" he said.

"Yes, Mr. Abbé," said Candide; "I absolutely must go and find Mademoiselle Cunégonde."

Then, led on by the pleasure of talking about the one he loved, he related, as was his custom, a part of his adventures with that illustrious lady of Westphalia.

"I suppose," said the abbé, "that Mademoiselle Cunégonde has a great deal of wit and writes charming letters?"

"I have never received any from her," said Candide, "for you must realize that having been expelled from the castle for love of her, I could not write her; that soon afterward I learned that she was dead, then I found her again, and then lost her; and that I have sent her a dispatch by special messenger two thousand five hundred leagues from here and am awaiting her reply."

The abbé listened attentively and seemed at bit thoughtful. He soon took leave of the two foreigners after embracing them tenderly. The next day Candide, on waking, received a letter couched in these terms:

"Sir, my very dear lover, I have been ill in this city for a week; now I learn that you are here. I would fly into you arms if I could move. I heard that you had passed through Bordeaux, I left the faithful Cacambo and the old woman there, and they are to follow me soon. The Governor of Buenos Aires took everything, but I still have your heart. Come, your presence will restore me to life or make me die of pleasure."

This charming letter, this unhoped-for letter, transported Candide with inexpressible joy; and the illness of his dear Cunégonde overwhelmed him with

---

67. Here ends the addition of 1761 that began
   at note 54.

grief. Torn between these two feelings, he takes his gold and his diamonds and has himself driven with Martin to the hotel where Mademoiselle Cunégonde was staying. He enters, trembling with emotion; his heart beats, his voice sobs; he wants to open the bed curtains, he wants to have a light brought.

"Don't do anything of the sort," says the waiting maid, "light is the death of her"; and promptly she closes the curtains again.

"My dear Cunégonde," says Candide, weeping, "how are you feeling? If you cannot see me, at least speak to me."

"She cannot speak," says the maid.

The lady then stretches out of the bed a plump hand which Candide waters at length with his tears and which he then fills with diamonds, leaving a bag full of gold on the armchair.

In the midst of these transports a police officer arrives followed by the Perigordian abbé and a squad.

"So these are those two suspicious foreigners?" he says.

He immediately has them arrested and orders his bravoes to drag them off to prison.

"This is not how they treat travelers in Eldorado," says Candide.

"I am more of a Manichean than ever," says Martin.

"But, sir, where are you taking us?" says Candide.

"To a deep dungeon," says the police officer.

Martin, having regained his coolness, decided that the lady who claimed to be Cunégonde was a fraud, the abbé from Périgord a fraud who had taken advantage of Candide's innocence as fast as he could, and the police officer another fraud of whom they could easily get rid.

Rather than expose himself to the processes of justice, Candide, enlightened by Martin's advice and moreover still impatient to see the real Mademoiselle Cunégonde again, suggests to the police officer three little diamonds worth about three thousand pistoles each.

"Ah, sir," says the man with the ivory baton, "even had you committed all the crimes imaginable, you are the finest man in the world. Three diamonds! Each worth three thousand pistoles! Sir, I would let myself by killed for you, instead of taking you to a dungeon. They arrest all foreigners here, but let me take care of things; I have a brother at Dieppe in Normandy, I'm going to take you there; and if you have an extra diamond to give him, he will take care of you just as I am doing myself."

"And why do they arrest all foreigners?" said Candide.

The abbé from Périgord then spoke up and said: "It is because a tramp from the region of Atrebatum[68] listened to foolish talk; this alone made him commit a parricide, not like that of May, 1610, but like that of December, 1594,[69] and like

---

68. Latin name for Arras, home of Damiens, who attempted to assassinate Louis XV in 1757.

69. Two attempts on the life of Henry IV were the unsuccessful one by Châtel in 1594 and the successful one by Ravaillac in 1610.

many others committed in other years and other months by other tramps who had listened to foolish talk."

The police officer then explained what it was all about.

"Oh, the monsters!" exclaimed Candide. "What! Such horrors in a nation that dances and sings! Can I not depart at once out of this country where monkeys incite tigers? I have seen bears in my country; I have seen men only in Eldorado. In the name of God, Mr. Officer, take me to Venice, where I am to await Mademoiselle Cunégonde."

"I can take you only to Lower Normandy," said the officer.

Immediately he has his chains taken off, says he has made a mistake, sends his men away, and takes Candide and Martin to Dieppe and leaves them in the hands of his brother. There was a little Dutch ship in the roads. The Norman, having with the help of three other diamonds become the most obliging of men, embarks Candide and his men on the ship, which was about to set sail for Portsmouth in England. It was not the way to Venice; but Candide thought he was delivered from hell, and fully intended to get back on the way to Venice at the first opportunity.

23

CANDIDE AND MARTIN GO TO THE COAST OF ENGLAND; WHAT THEY SEE THERE

"O Pangloss, Pangloss! O Martin, Martin! O my dear Cunégonde! What sort of a world is this?" said Candide on the Dutch ship.

"Something very mad and very abominable," replied Martin.

"You know England; are they as mad there as in France?"

"It's another kind of madness," said Martin. "You know that these two nations are at war over a few acres of snow out around Canada, and that they are spending on that fine war much more than all of Canada is worth. As for telling you precisely whether there are more people who need to be locked up in one country than another, that is something that my poor lights do not allow me to do. I only know that in general the people we are on our way to see are very gloomy."

While chatting thus, they arrived at Portsmouth; a multitude of people covered the shore and looked attentively at a rather fat man who was on his knees, his eyes bandaged, on the main deck of one of the ships of the fleet; four soldiers posted facing this man shot three bullets each into his skull as peacefully as can be, and the whole assemblage went back home extremely satisfied.

"What in the world is all this?" said Candide. "And what demon is exercising his domination everywhere?" He asked who was that fat man who had just been ceremoniously killed.

"An admiral,"[70] was the reply.

---

70. Admiral Byng of England was executed on March 14, 1757, after a court-martial, for losing a naval battle to the French the year before. Voltaire had tried in vain to intervene to save his life.

"And why kill this admiral?"

"Because," he was told, "he did not get enough people killed; he gave battle to a French admiral, and they decided that he was not close enough to him."

"But," said Candide, "the French admiral was as far from the English admiral as he was from him!"

"That is incontestable," was the reply; "but in this country it is a good thing to kill an admiral from time to time to encourage the others."

Candide was so stunned and so shocked at what he saw and what he heard that he would not even set foot on land, and made his bargain with the Dutch captain (even if he were to rob him like the one in Surinam) to take him to Venice without delay.

Two days later the captain was ready. They sailed along the coast of France. They passed in sight of Lisbon, and Candide shuddered. They entered the Strait[71] and the Mediterranean. Finally they landed in Venice. "God be praised," said Candide, embracing Martin, "here is where I shall see the fair Cunégonde again. I count on Cacambo as on myself. All is well, all goes well, all goes as well as it possibly could."

24

PAQUETTE AND FRIAR GIROFLÉE

As soon as he was in Venice, he had a search made for Cacambo in all the taverns, all the cafés, and among all the ladies of pleasure, and did not find him. Every day he sent to investigate all the ships and boats: no news of Cacambo.

"What!" he said to Martin. "I have had time to cross from Surinam to Bordeaux, to go from Bordeaux to Paris, from Paris to Dieppe, from Dieppe to Portsmouth, to skirt the coasts of Portugal and Spain, to cross the whole Mediterranean, to spend a few months in Venice, and the fair Cunégonde has not arrived! Instead of her I have met only a tricky wench and an abbé from Périgord! Cunégonde is beyond doubt dead, there is nothing left for me to do but die. Ah! it would have been better to remain in the paradise of Eldorado than to return to this accursed Europe. How right you are, my dear Martin! All is but illusion and calamity."

He fell into a black melancholy and took no part in the opera à la mode or the other diversions of the carnival; not one lady caused him the least temptation. Martin said to him:

"Truly you are very simple to imagine that a half-breed valet who has five or six million in his pockets will go find your mistress at the end of the world and bring her to you in Venice. He will take her for himself if he finds her. If he does not find her, he will take another. I advise you to forget your valet Cacambo and your mistress Cunégonde."

Martin was not consoling. Candide's melancholy increased, and Martin never

---

71. Of Gibraltar.

stopped proving to him that there was little virtue and little happiness on earth, except perhaps in Eldorado, where no one could go.

While arguing about this important matter and waiting for Cunégonde, Candide noticed a young Theatine[72] monk in the Piazza San Marco arm-in-arm with a girl. The Theatine looked fresh, plump, vigorous; his eyes were brilliant, his manner assured, his head erect, his bearing proud. The girl was very pretty and was singing; she looked lovingly at her Theatine, and from time to time pinched his plump cheeks.

"You will admit to me at least," said Candide to Martin, "that these people are happy; up to now I have found, in all the habitable earth except Eldorado, nothing but unfortunates; but as for that girl and that Theatine, I wager they are very happy creatures."

"I wager they're not," said Martin.

"We have only to ask them to dinner," said Candide, "and you'll see whether I'm wrong."

Immediately he accosts them, pays them his compliments, and invites them to come to his inn and eat macaroni, Lombardy partridges, and caviar, and drink Montepulciano, Lacryma Christi, Cyprus and Samos wine. The lady blushed, the Theatine accepted the invitation, and the girl followed him, looking at Candide with eyes full of surprise and confusion and dimmed with a few tears. Hardly had she entered Candide's room when she said to him: "What! Monsieur Candide no longer recognizes Paquette!"

At these words Candide, who had not looked at her with any attention until then, because he was preoccupied only with Cunégonde, said to her:

"Alas! my poor child, so it was you who put Doctor Pangloss in the fine state in which I saw him?"

"Alas! sir, I myself," said Paquette; "I see that you are informed about everything. I learned about the frightful misfortunes that happened to the whole household of My Lady the Baroness and to the fair Cunégonde. I swear to you that my destiny has been hardly less sad. I was very innocent when you knew me. A Franciscan who was my confessor easily seduced me. The consequences were frightful; I was obliged to leave the castle a little while after My Lord the Baron had sent you away with great kicks in the backside. If a famous doctor had not taken pity on me I would have died. For some time out of gratitude I was that doctor's mistress. His wife, who was madly jealous, used to beat me pitilessly every day, she was a fury. This doctor was the ugliest of all men, and I the unhappiest of all creatures at being beaten continually because of a man I did not love. You know, sir, how dangerous it is for a shrewish woman to be a doctor's wife. This man, outraged at his wife's ways, one day gave her, to cure her of a little cold, a medicine so efficacious that she died of it in two hours' time in horrible convulsions. My lady's relatives brought a criminal suit against the gentleman; he took flight, and I was put in prison. My innocence would not have saved me if I had not been rather pretty. The judge turned me loose on condition that he would succeed the

---

72. A member of a Catholic order founded in
    1524 to combat Protestantism.

doctor. I was soon supplemented by a rival, tossed out with no compensation, and obliged to continue this abominable occupation which seems so amusing to you men and which for us is but an abyss of misery. I went to Venice to practice the profession. Ah! sir, if you could imagine what it is to be obliged to caress indiscriminately an old merchant, a lawyer, a monk, a gondolier, an abbé; to be exposed to every insult, every outrage; to be often reduced to borrowing a skirt in order to go have it lifted by some disgusting man; to be robbed by one of what you have earned with the other; to be forced by the officers of the law to buy protection, and to have in prospect nothing but a frightful old age, a hospital, and a dunghill—you would conclude that I am one of the unhappiest creatures in the world."

Thus Paquette opened her heart to the good Candide in a private room in the presence of Martin, who said to Candide:

"You see, I have already won half my wager."

Friar Giroflée had remained in the dining room and was having a drink while waiting for dinner.

"But," said Candide to Paquette, "you looked so gay, so happy, when I met you, you were singing, you were caressing the Theatine with natural complaisance; you seemed to me as happy as you claim to be unfortunate."

"Ah! sir," replied Paquette, "that is still another of the miseries of the trade. Yesterday I was robbed and beaten by an officer, and today I have to appear in a good humor to please a monk"

Candide had enough, he admitted that Martin was right. They sat down to table with Paquette and the Theatine; the meal was rather entertaining; and toward the end they talked to each other with some frankness.

"Father," said Candide to the monk, "you seem to me to enjoy a destiny that everyone must envy; the flower of health shines on your face,[73] your physiognomy bespeaks happiness, you have a very pretty girl for your recreation, and you seem very content with your condition as a Theatine."

"Faith, sir," said Friar Giroflée, "I wish all Theatines were at the bottom of the sea. I have been tempted a hundred times to set fire to the monastery and go turn Turk. My parents forced me at the age of fifteen to put on this detestable robe, in order to leave a greater fortune to an accursed older brother whom God confound! Jealousy, discord, rage inhabit the monastery. It is true, I have preached a few bad sermons that have brought me in a little money, half of which the prior steals from me; the rest serves me to keep girls; but when I go back to the monastery in the evening I am ready to smash my head against the dormitory walls; and all my colleagues are in the same state."

Martin, turning toward Candide with his customary coolness, said to him: "Well! Haven't I won the whole wager?"

Candide gave two thousand piasters to Paquette and a thousand piasters to Friar Giroflée. "I warrant you," he said, "with this they will be happy."

---

73. In French, the monk's name means *gilly-flower* or *wallflower*, while that of Paquette means *daisy*.

"I don't believe it in the very least," said Martin; "perhaps with these piasters you will make them much unhappier yet."

"That will be as it may," said Candide. "But one thing consoles me: I see that we often find people again whom we never thought to find; it may well be that having met up with my red sheep and Paquette, I shall also meet Cunégonde again."

"I hope," said Martin, "that she may someday be the making of your happiness; but that is something I strongly doubt."

"You are very hard," said Candide.

"That's because I have lived," said Martin.

"But look at these gondoliers," said Candide. "Aren't they always singing?"

"You don't see them at home, with their wives and their brats of children," said Martin. "The Doge has his troubles, the gondoliers have theirs. It is true that taken all in all the lot of a gondolier is preferable to that of a doge; but I think the difference is so slight that it is not worth examining."

"They speak," said Candide, "of Senator Pococurante,[74] who lives in that handsome palace on the Brenta, and who receives foreigners rather well. They claim he is a man who has never known grief."

"I would like to see so rare a species," said Martin.

Candide immediately sent to ask Lord Pococurante for permission to come to see him the next day.

25

Essential to this book.

VISIT TO THE VENETIAN NOBLEMAN, LORD POCOCURANTE

Candide and Martin took a gondola onto the Brenta and arrived at the palace of the noble Pococurante. The gardens were well conceived and adorned with handsome marble statues; the architecture of the palace was fine. The master of the house, a man of sixty, very rich, received the two sightseers very politely but with very little enthusiasm, which disconcerted Candide and did not displease Martin.

First two pretty, neatly dressed girls served chocolate, well prepared with whipped cream. Candide could not refrain from praising them for their beauty, their grace, and their skill.

"They are pretty good creatures," said Senator Pococurante; "I sometimes take them to bed with me, for I am very tired of the town ladies, their coquetries, their jealousies, their quarrels, their humors, their pettinesses, their pride, their follies, and the sonnets one must compose on order for them; but after all, these two girls are beginning to bore me a lot."

Candide, walking after breakfast in a long gallery, was surprised by the beauty of the pictures. He asked what master had painted the first two.

"They are by Raphael," said the senator; "I bought them a few years ago at a

---

74. From the Italian: "caring little."

very high price out of vanity; they say they are the finest things in Italy, but I do not like them at all; their color has become very dark; the figures are not rounded enough and do not stand out enough; the draperies are not at all like cloth. In a word, no matter what they say, I do not find in them a true imitation of nature. I will like a picture only when I think I am seeing nature itself; and there are none of that kind. I have many pictures, but I no longer look at them."

While waiting for dinner, Pococurante had a concerto played for him. Candide found the music delightful.

"That noise," said Pococurante, "can be entertaining for half an hour, but if it lasts longer, it tires everyone, though no one dares admit it. Music today is merely the art of executing difficult things; and in the long run what is merely difficult is not pleasing. Perhaps I would like opera better, if they had not found the secret of making it a monster that revolts me. Let those who wish go to see bad tragedies set to music, where the scenes are composed only to bring in very clumsily two or three ridiculous songs which show off an actress's vocal cords. Let those who will, or who can, swoon with pleasure at seeing a eunuch hum the part of Caesar or Cato and tread the boards awkwardly. As for me, it has been a long time since I gave up these trivialities, which today are the glory of Italy and for which sovereigns pay so dear."

Candide argued a little, but with discretion. Martin was entirely in agreement with the senator.

They sat down to table, and after an excellent dinner they went into the library. Candide, seeing a magnificently bound Homer, praised the Illustrissimo for his good taste.

"That," he said, "is a book that was the delight of the great Pangloss, the best philosopher in Germany."

"It is no delight to me," said Pococurante coldly. "Once I was made to believe I took pleasure in reading it.[75] But that continual repetition of combats that are all alike, those gods that are always active and never do anything decisive, that Helen who is the subject of the war and who has hardly any part in the action, that Troy which is always besieged and never taken—all that caused me the most deadly boredom. I have sometimes asked learned men whether they were as bored as I was in reading it. All the sincere ones admitted to me that the book fell out of their hands, but that you always had to have it in your library, like an ancient monument, or like those rusty coins which cannot be used in commerce."

"Your Excellency does not think the same thing about Virgil?" said Candide.

"I admit," said Pococurante, "that the second, fourth, and sixth books of his *Aeneid* are excellent; but as for his pious Aeneas and strong Cloanthes and faithful Achates and little Ascanius and the imbecile King Latinus and middle-class Amata and insipid Lavinia, I do not believe there is anything so frigid or more disagreeable. I prefer Tasso and the fantastic fairy tales of Ariosto."

---

75. Pococurante's opinions are not to be taken for Voltaire's, but they often express Voltaire's sense of the weaknesses of the great. Virgil was generally much preferred to Homer until the nineteenth century. Ariosto and Tasso were favorites of Voltaire's.

"Might I venture to ask you, sir," said Candide, "if you do not take great pleasure in reading Horace?"

"There are some maxims in him," said Pococurante, "that can profit a man of the world, and which, being compressed into energetic verses, engrave themselves the more easily on the memory. But I care very little about his journey to Brundisium or his description of a bad dinner, or the ruffians' quarrel between someone named Pupilus,[76] whose words, he said, were full of pus, and another whose words were vinegar. I have read only with extreme disgust his gross verses against old women and against witches; and I do not see what merit there can be in telling his friend Maecenas that if he is placed by him among the lyric poets he will strike the stars with his lofty brow. Fools admire everything in a noted author. I read only for myself, I like only what I have use for."

Candide, who had been brought up never to judge anything for himself, was greatly astonished at what he heard, and Martin considered Pococurante's way of thinking rather reasonable.

"Oh, here is a Cicero," said Candide. "Now as for that great man, I suppose you never tire of reading him?"

"I never read him," replied the Venetian. "What do I care whether he pleaded for Rabirius or for Cluentius? I have quite enough with the cases that I judge; I would have made out better with his philosophical works, but when I saw that he doubted everything, I concluded that I knew as much about it as he did, and that I did not need help from anyone in order to be ignorant."

"Ah, there are eighty volumes of proceedings of an Academy of Sciences," exclaimed Martin; "there may be something good there."

"There would be," said Pococurante, "if a single one of the authors of that rubbish had invented even the art of making pins; but in all those volumes there is nothing but empty systems and not a single useful thing."

"What a lot of plays I see here," said Candide, "in Italian, Spanish, and French!"

"Yes," said the senator, "there are three thousand of them and not three dozen good ones. As for these collections of sermons, which all together are not worth one page of Seneca, and all these great volumes of theology, you may well suppose that I never open them, not I nor anyone else."

Martin noticed some shelves loaded with English books. "I suppose," he said, "a republican must enjoy most of those works written with so much freedom."

"Yes," replied Pococurante, "it is fine to write what you think; that is the privilege of man. In all this Italy of ours people write only what they do not think; those who inhabit the land of the Caesars and the Antonines dare not have an idea without the permission of a Dominican.[77] I would be glad of the freedom that inspires English geniuses, if passion and factionalism did not corrupt all that is estimable in that precious freedom."

---

76. Should be Rupilius. See *Satires*, I, vii.

77. The Inquisition was in the hands of the Dominicans.

Candide, noticing a Milton,[78] asked him if he did not regard that author as a great man.

"Who?" said Pococurante. "That barbarian who writes a long commentary on the first chapter of Genesis in ten books of harsh verses? That crude imitator of the Greeks, who disfigures the Creation and who, whereas Moses represents the eternal Being as producing the world by the word. has the Messiah take a great compass from a cupboard in Heaven to trace out his work? I should esteem the man who spoiled Tasso's Hell and Devil, who disguises Lucifer now as a toad, now as a pygmy, who has him repeat the same remarks a hundred times, who has him argue about theology, who, imitating in all seriousness the comical invention of firearms in Ariosto, has the devils fire cannon in Heaven? Not I, nor anyone in Italy has been able to enjoy all these sad eccentricities; and the marriage of Sin and Death, and the snakes that Sin gives birth to, make any man vomit who has a little delicacy of taste; and his long description of a hospital is good only for a gravedigger. This obscure, bizarre, and disgusting poem was despised at its birth; I treat it today as it was treated in its own country by its contemporaries. Besides, I say what I think, and I worry very little whether others think as I do."

Candide was distressed by these remarks. He respected Homer, and he rather liked Milton.

"Alas!" he whispered to Martin. "I'm very much afraid that this man may have a sovereign contempt for our German poets."

"There would be no great harm in that," said Martin.

"Oh, what a superior man!" said Candide under his breath. "What a great genius this Pococurante is! Nothing can please him."

After they had thus passed all the books in review, they went down into the garden. Candide praised all its beauties.

"I know of nothing in such bad taste," said the master; "we have nothing but trifles here; but tomorrow I am going to have one planted on a nobler plan."

When the two sight-seers had taken leave of His Excellency, Candide said to Martin: "Well now, you will agree that there is the happiest of all men; for he is above everything he posesses."

"Don't you see," said Martin, "that he is disgusted with everything he possesses? Plato said a long time ago that the best stomachs are not those which refuse all food."

"But," said Candide, "isn't there pleasure in criticizing everything, in sensing defects where other men think they see beauties?"

"That is to say," retorted Martin, "that there is pleasure in taking no pleasure?"

"Oh well!" said Candide, "then there is no one happy except me—when I see Mademoiselle Cunégonde again."

"It is always a good thing to hope," said Martin.

However, the days, the weeks passed by; Cacambo still did not come back,

---

78. Voltaire had much admiration for Milton, as he did for Shakespeare, but as time passed he became more and more critical of what he considered the barbarism of both.

and Candide was so sunk in his sorrow that he did not even notice that Paquette and Friar Giroflée had not so much as come to thank him.

26

OF A SUPPER THAT CANDIDE AND MARTIN HAD WITH SIX FOREIGNERS, AND WHO THESE WERE

One evening when Candide, followed by Martin, was going to sit down to table with the foreigners who were staying in the same hotel, a man with a soot-colored face came up to him from behind and, taking him by the arm, said: "Be ready to leave with us, do not fail."

He turns around and sees Cacambo. Only the sight of Cunégonde could have astounded and pleased him more. He was on the point of going mad with joy. He embraced his dear friend.

"Then doubtless Cunégonde is here? Where is she? Take me to her, let me die of joy with her."

"Cunégonde is not here," said Cacambo, "she is in Constantinople."

"Oh heavens! In Constantinople! But were she in China, I fly to her, let's go."

"We will leave after supper," said Cacambo; "I cannot tell you any more; I am a slave, my master is waiting for me, I must go and serve him at table. Don't say a word; have supper and be ready."

Candide, torn between joy and sorrow, charmed to see his faithful agent again, astounded to see him a slave, full of the idea of recovering his mistress, his heart agitated and his mind topsy-turvy, sat down to table with Martin, who observed all these adventures imperturbably, and with six foreigners who had come to spend the Carnival in Venice.

Cacambo, who was pouring drink for one of these six foreigners, got his master's ear toward the end of the meal and said to him: "Sire, Your Majesty will leave when you wish, the vessel is ready." Having said these words he went out.

The guests, astonished, looked at each other without uttering a single word, when another servant, coming up to his master, said to him: "Sire, Your Majesty's chaise is in Padua, and the boat is ready." The master made a sign, and the servant left.

All the guests looked at each other again, and the general surprise redoubled. A third valet, also approaching a third foreigner, said to him: "Sire, believe me, Your Majesty must not remain here any longer; I am going to prepare everything." And immediately he disappeared.

By now Candide and Martin had no doubt that this was a Carnival masquerade. A fourth servant said to the fourth master: "Your Majesty will leave when you please," and went out like the others. The fifth valet said as much to the fifth master. But the sixth valet spoke differently to the sixth foreigner who was sitting with Candide; he said to him: "Faith, Sire, they won't give Your Majesty credit any more, nor me either; and we could well be locked up tonight, you and me; I am going to see to my own affairs; farewell."

All the servants having disappeared, the six foreigners, Candide, and Martin remained in deep silence. Finally Candide broke it:

"Gentlemen," he said, "this is a singular jest. Why are you all kings? For myself, I admit that neither Martin nor I am."

Cacambo's master then spoke up gravely and said in Italian: "I am not jesting, my name is Ahmed III.[79] I was Grand Sultan for several years; I dethroned my brother; my nephew dethroned me; my viziers[80] had their heads cut off; I am ending my days in the old seraglio. My nephew, the Grand Sultan Mahmud, allows me to travel sometimes for my health, and I have come to spend the Carnival in Venice."

A young man who was next to Ahmed spoke after him and said: "My name is Ivan; I was Emperor of all the Russias; I was dethroned in my cradle; my father and mother were locked up; I was brought up in prison; I sometimes have permission to travel, accompanied by those who guard me, and I have come to spend the Carnival in Venice."

The third said: "I am Charles Edward, King of England; my father ceded me his rights to the kingdom. I fought to maintain them; they tore the hearts out of eight hundred of my supporters and dashed them in their faces. I was put in prison; I am going to Rome to pay a visit to the King my father, who is dethroned like my grandfather and me; and I have come to spend the Carnival in Venice."

The fourth took the floor and said: "I am King of the Poles; the fortunes of war have deprived me of my hereditary states; my father underwent the same reverses; I resign myself to Providence like Sultan Ahmed, Emperor Ivan, and King Charles Edward, whom God give long life; and I have come to spend the Carnival in Venice."

The fifth said: "I too am King of the Poles; I have lost my kingdom twice; but Providence has given me another state[81] in which I have done more good than all the kings of the Sarmatians together have ever been able to do on the banks of the Vistula; I too resign myself to Providence; and I have come to spend the Carnival in Venice."

It remained for the sixth monarch to speak. "Gentlemen," said he, "I am not as great a lord as you; but even so I have been a King like anyone else. I am Theodore; I was elected King of Corsica; I have been called Your Majesty, and at present I am hardly called Sir. I have coined money, and I do not have a penny; I have had two secretaries of state, and I have scarcely a valet. I was once on a throne, and I was in prison for a long time in London, on the straw. I am much afraid I shall be treated the same way here, although I have come, like Your Majesties, to spend the Carnival in Venice."

The five other Kings listened to this speech with noble compassion. Each of

---

79. All these kings are real.
80. A high Mohammedan executive or judicial officer.
81. Stanislas Leszczynski (1677–1766), father of the Queen of France, abdicated the throne of Poland in 1736, was made Duke of Lorraine, and did much good in and around Lunéville. The Sarmatians are the Slavs.

them gave King Theodore twenty sequins to get clothes and shirts; and Candide presented him with a diamond worth two thousand sequins. "Who is this man," said the five Kings, "who is in a position to give a hundred times as much as each of us, and who gives it? Are you a King too, sir?"

"No, gentlemen, and I have no desire to be."[82]

At the moment when they were leaving the table, there arrived in the same hotel four Most Serene Highnesses, who had also lost their states by the fortunes of war, and who were coming to spend the rest of the Carnival in Venice. But Candide did not even take note of these newcomers; he was preoccupied only with going to find his dear Cunégonde in Constantinople.

27

CANDIDE'S VOYAGE TO CONSTANTINOPLE

The faithful Cacambo had already obtained an agreement with the Turkish captain who was about to take Sultan Ahmed back to Constantinople that he would take Candide and Martin on his ship. Both came on board after having prostrated themselves before his miserable Highness. On the way, Candide said to Martin:

"But those were six dethroned Kings that we had supper with, and besides, among those six Kings there was one to whom I gave alms. Maybe there are many other princes still more unfortunate. As for me, I have lost only a hundred sheep, and I am flying to Cunégonde's arms. My dear Martin, once again, Pangloss was right, all is well."

"I hope so," said Martin.

"But," said Candide, "that was a most implausible adventure we had in Venice. No one ever saw or heard of six dethroned Kings having supper together in an inn."

"That is no more extraordinary," said Martin, "than most of the things that have happened to us. It is very common for Kings to be dethroned; and as for the honor we had in having supper with them, it is a thing that does not deserve our attention. What does it matter whom you sup with, provided you make good cheer?"[83]

Scarcely was Candide in the ship when he threw his arms around the neck of his former valet, his friend Cacambo.

"Well," he said, "what is Cunégonde doing? Is she still a prodigy of beauty? Does she still love me? How is she? No doubt you bought her a palace in Constantinople?"

---

82. These three sentences (from " 'Who is this man' " on) are the final form that Voltaire intended, replacing the following: " 'Who is this ordinary citizen,' said the five Kings, 'who is in a position to give a hundred times as much as each of us, and who gives it?' "

83. This passage, from "it is a thing" on, is another change intended by Voltaire (cf. note 82) to replace this: " 'it is a trifle that does not deserve our attention.' "

"My dear master," replied Cacambo, "Cunégonde is washing dishes on the banks of Propontis[84] for a prince who has very few dishes; she is a slave in the household of a former sovereign named Ragotsky,[85] to whom the Grand Turk gives three crowns a day in his refuge; but what is much sadder is that she has lost her beauty and become horribly ugly."

"Ah! beautiful or ugly," said Candide, "I am an honorable man, and my duty is to love her always. But how can she be reduced to so abject a state with the five or six millions you brought her?"

"Well," said Cacambo, "did I not have to give two millions to Señor Don Fernando d'Ibaraa y Figueora y Mascarenes y Lampourdos y Souza, Governor of Buenos Aires, for permission to take Mademoiselle Cunégonde back? And did not a pirate bravely despoil us of all the rest? And did not that pirate take us to Cape Matapan, to Milo, to Nicaria, to Samos, to Petra, to the Dardanelles, to Marmora, to Scutari? Cunégonde and the old woman are servants with that prince I spoke to you about, and I am a slave of the dethroned Sultan."

"What a chain of frightful calamities one after another!" said Candide. "But after all, I still have a few diamonds. I shall easily deliver Cunégonde. It is a great pity that she has become so ugly."

Then, turning toward Martin, he said: "Which one do you think is the most to be pitied, Emperor Ahmed, Emperor Ivan, King Charles Edward, or I?"

"I know nothing about that," said Martin; "I would have to be inside your hearts to know."

"Ah!" said Candide, "if Pangloss were here, he would know and would tell us."

"I do not know," said Martin, "with what scales your Pangloss could have weighed the misfortunes of men and estimated their sorrows. All I presume is that there are millions of men on earth a hundred times more to be pitied than King Charles Edward, Emperor Ivan, and Sultan Ahmed."

"That might well be," said Candide.

They arrived in a few days in the Bosporus. Candide began by buying back Cacambo at a very high price; and without wasting time he flung himself into a galley with his companions to go to the shores of Propontis and find Cunégonde, however ugly she might be.

In the convict crew there were two galley slaves who rowed very badly, and from time to time the Levantine captain applied a few strokes of a bull's pizzle to their bare shoulders; Candide, from a natural impulse, looked at them more attentively than at the other galley slaves and went up to them in pity. Some features of their disfigured faces seemed to him to have some resemblance to Pangloss and to that hapless Jesuit, the Baron, Mademoiselle Cunégonde's brother. This idea touched and saddened him. He looked at them even more attentively. "Truly," he said to Cacambo, "if I had not seen Doctor Pangloss

---

84. The Sea of Marmora, between the Bosporus and the Dardanelles.

85. A former prince of Transylvania.

hanged, and if I had not had the misfortune to kill the Baron, I would think it is they that are rowing in this galley."

At the names "Baron" and "Pangloss" the two convicts uttered a loud cry, sat still on their bench, and dropped their oars. The Levantine captain ran up to them, and the lashes with the bull's pizzle redoubled.

"Stop, stop, my lord," cried Candide, "I will give you as much money as you want."

"What! It's Candide!" said one of the convicts.

"What! It's Candide!" said the other.

"Is it a dream?" said Candide. "Am I really awake? Am I in this galley? Is that My Lord the Baron, whom I killed? Is that Doctor Pangloss, whom I saw hanged?"

"It is indeed, it is indeed," they replied.

"What! Is this that great philosopher?" said Martin.

"Oh! Master Levantine Captain," said Candide, "how much money do you want for the ransom of My Lord of Thunder-ten-tronckh, one of the first barons of the Empire, and for Monsieur Pangloss, the most profound metaphysician of Germany?"

"Dog of a Christian," replied the Levantine captain, "since these two dogs of Christian convicts are barons and metaphysicians, which is no doubt a great dignity in their country, you shall give me fifty thousand sequins for them."

"You shall have them, sir; take me back like a flash to Constantinople, and you shall be paid on the spot. But no, take me to Mademoiselle Cunégonde."

The Levantine captain, at Candide's first offer, had already turned his prow toward the city, and he was making the oarsmen row faster than a bird cleaves the air.

Candide embraced the Baron and Pangloss a hundred times. "And how is it that I did not kill you, my dear Baron? And my dear Pangloss, how is it that you are alive after being hanged? And why are you both in the galleys in Turkey?"

"Is it really true that my dear sister is in this country?" said the Baron.

"Yes," replied Cacambo.

"So I see my dear Candide again," exclaimed Pangloss.

Candide introduced Martin and Cacambo to them. They all embraced, they all talked at once. The galley flew, they were already in the port. They sent for a Jew, to whom Candide sold for fifty thousand sequins a diamond of the value of a hundred thousand, and who swore to him by Abraham that he could not give any more. Candide immediately paid the ransom of the Baron and Pangloss. The latter threw himself at the feet of his liberator and bathed them with tears; the other thanked him with a nod and promised to repay him the money at the first opportunity. "But is it really possible that my sister is in Turkey?" he said.

"Nothing is so possible," retorted Cacambo, "since she is scouring dishes for a prince of Transylvania."

Immediately they sent for two Jews; Candide sold some more diamonds; and they all set out again in another galley to go and deliver Cunégonde.

28

WHAT HAPPENED TO CANDIDE, CUNÉGONDE, PANGLOSS, MARTIN, ET AL.

"Once again, pardon," said Candide to the Baron, "pardon me, Reverend Father, for having given you a great sword thrust through the body."

"Let's say no more about it," said the Baron; "I was a little too hasty, I admit; but since you want to know by what chance you saw me in the galleys, I will tell you. After being cured of my wound by the brother apothecary of the College, I was attacked and carried off by a party of Spaniards; they put me in prison in Buenos Aires at the time when my sister had just left. I asked to return to the Father General in Rome, I was named to go to Constantinople and serve as almoner with My Lord the Ambassador of France. Not a week after I had taken up my duties, I met, toward evening, a very attractive ichoglan.[86] It was very hot; the young man wanted to bathe; I took the opportunity to bathe too. I did not know that it was a capital crime for a Christian to be found stark naked with a young Moslem. A cadi[87] had me given a hundred strokes on the soles of my feet and condemned me to the galleys. I do not think a more horrible injustice has ever been done. But I would certainly like to know why my sister is in the kitchen of a sovereign of Transylvania who is a refugee among the Turks."

"But you, my dear Pangloss," said Candide, "how can it be that I see you again?"

"It is true," said Pangloss, "that you saw me hanged; naturally I was supposed to be burned; but you remember there was a heavy downpour just when they were going to cook me; the storm was so violent that they despaired of lighting the fire; I was hanged because they could do no better; a surgeon bought my body, took me home, and dissected me. First he made a cross-shaped incision in me from the navel to the clavicle. No one could have been worse hanged than I had been. The Holy Inquisition's Executor of High Operations, who was a subdeacon, did indeed burn people marvelously, but he was not accustomed to hanging them; the rope was wet and slipped badly, it became knotted; in short, I was still breathing. The cross-shaped incision made me utter such a loud scream that my surgeon fell over backward and, thinking that he was dissecting the devil, he fled, half-dead from fear, and he fell again on the staircase as he fled. His wife came running from a nearby room at the noise; she saw me stretched out on the table with my cross-shaped incision; she was even more afraid than her husband, fled, and fell over him. When they had recovered a little, I heard the surgeon's wife say to the surgeon: 'My dear, what are you thinking of, dissecting a heretic? Don't you know that the devil is always in those people? I am going quickly to get a priest to exorcise him.'

"I shuddered at these words and collected the little strength I had left to call

---

86. Page to the Sultan.   87. A minor Mohammedan judge or magistrate.

out: 'Have pity on me!' Finally the Portuguese barber[88] grew bolder; he sewed up my skin; his wife even took care of me; in two weeks I was on my feet. The barber found me a job and made me lackey to a knight of Malta who was going to Venice; but as this master had no money to pay me, I entered the service of a Venetian merchant and followed him to Constantinople.

"One day I took a notion to enter a mosque; there was no one there but an old imam and a very pretty young devotee who was saying her prayers. Her bosom was fully uncovered; between her breasts she had a beautiful bouquet of tulips, roses, anemones, buttercups, hyacinths, and yellow primroses; she dropped her bouquet; I picked it up, and I replaced it for her with the most respectful eagerness. I was so long in replacing it for her that the imam grew angry, and, seeing that I was a Christian, called for help. I was taken before the cadi, who had me given a hundred strokes on the soles of the feet and sent me to the galleys. I was chained precisely in the same galley and on the same bench as My Lord the Baron. In this galley there were four young men from Marseilles, five Neapolitan priests, and two monks from Corfu, who told us that similar adventures occurred every day. My Lord the Baron claimed that he had suffered a greater injustice than I; for my part I claimed that it was much more permissible to replace a bouquet on a woman's bosom than to be stark naked with an ichoglan. We were arguing unceasingly and receiving twenty strokes a day of the bull's pizzle, when the concatenation of the events of this universe brought you into our galley and you ransomed us."

"Well, my dear Pangloss," said Candide, "when you were hanged, dissected, racked with blows, and rowing in the galleys, did you still think that all was for the very best?"

"I am still of my first opinion," replied Pangloss; "for after all I am a philosopher, it is not fitting for me to recant, for Leibniz cannot be wrong; and besides, pre-established harmony is the finest thing in the world, like the plenum and subtle matter."

29

HOW CANDIDE FOUND CUNÉGONDE AND THE OLD WOMAN AGAIN

While Candide, the Baron, Pangloss, Martin, and Cacambo were relating their adventures, reasoning on the contingent or noncontingent events of this universe, arguing about effects and causes, moral and physical evil, free will and necessity, and the consolations that may be experienced when one is in the galleys in Turkey, they landed on the shore of Propontis at the house of the prince of Transylvania. The first objects that met their eyes were Cunégonde and the old woman, who were spreading out towels on lines to dry.

The Baron paled at this sight. The tender lover Candide, on seeing his fair Cunégonde dark-skinned, eyes bloodshot, flat-bosomed, cheeks wrinkled, arms

---

88. The surgeon.

red and rough, recoiled three steps in horror, and then advanced out of good manners. She embraced Candide and her brother; they embraced the old woman; Candide ransomed them both.

There was a little farm in the neighborhood; the old woman proposed to Candide that he buy it while waiting for the entire group to enjoy a better destiny. Cunégonde did not know that she had grown ugly, no one had told her so; she reminded Candide of his promises in so positive a tone that the good Candide did not refuse her. So he notified the Baron that he was going to marry his sister.

"I shall never endure," said the Baron, "such baseness on her part and such insolence on yours; no one shall ever reproach me with that infamy; my sister's children would not be able to enter the chapters[89] of Germany. No, never shall my sister marry anyone but a baron of the Empire."

Cunégonde threw herself at his feet and bathed them with tears; he was inflexible.

"You maddest of madmen," said Candide, "I rescued you from the galleys, I paid your ransom, I paid your sister's too; she was washing dishes here, she is ugly, I am kind enough to make her my wife, and you still presume to oppose it; I would kill you again if I heeded my anger."

"You may kill me again," said the Baron, "but you shall not marry my sister while I am alive."

30

CONCLUSION

At the bottom of his heart, Candide had no desire to marry Cunégonde. But the Baron's extreme impertinence determined him to clinch the marriage, and Cunégonde urged him on so eagerly that he could not retract. He consulted Pangloss, Martin, and the faithful Cacambo. Pangloss composed a fine memoir by which he proved that the Baron had no rights over his sister, and that according to all the laws of the Empire she could make a left-handed marriage[90] with Candide. Martin's judgment was to throw the Baron in the sea; Cacambo decided that he should be returned to the Levantine captain and put back in the galleys, after which he would be sent by the first ship to the Father General in Rome. The plan was considered very good; the old woman approved it; they said nothing about it to his sister; for a little money the thing was carried out, and they had the pleasure of trapping a Jesuit and punishing the pride of a German Baron.

It was quite natural to imagine that after so many disasters Candide, married to his mistress and living with the philosopher Pangloss, the philosopher Martin, the prudent Cacambo, and the old woman, moreover having brought back so many diamonds from the land of the ancient Incas, would lead the most pleasant life in the world. But he was so cheated by the Jews[91] that he had nothing left but

---

89. Knightly assemblies.
90. A morganatic marriage, giving no equality to the party of lower rank.

91. Voltaire had suffered financial losses from the bankruptcies of Jewish bankers.

his little farm; his wife, becoming uglier every day, became shrewish and intolerable; the old woman was an invalid and was even more bad-humored than Cunégonde. Cacambo, who worked in the garden and who went and sold vegetables at Constantinople, was worn out with work and cursed his destiny. Pangloss was in despair at not shining in some university in Germany. As for Martin, he was firmly persuaded that a man is equally badly off anywhere; he took things patiently.

Candide, Martin, and Pangloss sometimes argued about metaphysics and morality. They often saw passing under the windows of the farm boats loaded with effendis,[92] pashas,[93] and cadis who were being sent into exile at Lemnos, Mitylene, and Erzerum. They saw other cadis arriving, other pashas, other effendis, who took the place of the exiles and were exiled in their turn. They saw properly impaled heads on their way to be presented to the Sublime Porte.[94] These sights redoubled their discourses; and when they were not arguing, the boredom was so excessive that one day the old woman dared to say to them:

"I would like to know which is worse—to be raped a hundred times by Negro pirates, have a buttock cut off, run the gantlet among the Bulgarians, be flogged and hanged in an auto-da-fé, be dissected, row in the galleys, in short to undergo all the miseries we have all been through—or to stay here doing nothing?"

"It's a great question," said Candide.

These remarks engendered new reflections, and Martin above all concluded that man was born to live in the convulsions of anxiety or the lethargy of boredom. Candide did not agree, but he asserted nothing. Pangloss admitted that he had always suffered horribly; but having once maintained that everything was wonderful, he still maintained it and believed not a bit of it.

One thing completely confirmed Martin in his detestable principles, made Candide hesitate more than ever, and embarrassed Pangloss: one day they saw coming to their farm Paquette and Friar Giroflée, who were in the utmost misery; they had very quickly gone through their three thousand piasters, had parted, made it up, quarreled, been put in prison, escaped, and finally Friar Giroflée had turned Turk. Paquette continued to ply her trade everywhere, and no longer earned anything at it.

"I had quite foreseen," said Martin to Candide, "that your presents would soon be dissipated and would only make them more miserable. You and Cacambo were once glutted with millions of piasters, and you are no happier than Friar Giroflée and Paquette."

"Aha!" said Pangloss to Paquette, "so heaven brings you back among us here, my poor child! Do you realize that you cost me the end of my nose, an eye, and an ear? Look at you now! Ah! What a world is this!"

This new adventure led them to philosophize more than ever.

In the neighborhood there was a very famous dervish who was considered the best philosopher in Turkey; they went to consult him; Pangloss was the

---

92. Turkish title of respect used especially of state officials.
93. A Turkish governor or military leader.

94. Originally, the gate of the Sultan's palace, where justice was once administered; hence, his government.

spokesman and said to him: "Master, we have come to ask you to tell us why such a strange animal as man was ever created."

"What are you meddling in?" said the dervish. "Is that your business?"

"But, Reverend Father," said Candide, "there is a horrible amount of evil on earth."

"What does it matter," said the dervish, "whether there is evil or good? When His Highness sends a ship to Egypt, is he bothered about whether the mice in the ship are comfortable or not?"

"Then what should we do?" said Pangloss.

"Hold your tongue," said the dervish.

"I flattered myself," said Pangloss, "that you and I would reason a bit together about effects and causes, the best of all possible worlds, the origin of evil, the nature of the soul, and pre-established harmony." At these words the dervish shut the door in their faces.

During this conversation the news had gone round that in Constantinople they had just strangled two viziers of the Divan[95] and the mufti[96] and impaled several of their friends. This catastrophe caused a great stir everywhere for a few hours. Pangloss, Candide, and Martin, returning to the little farm, came upon a good old man enjoying the fresh air by his door under a bower of orange trees. Pangloss, whose curiosity was as great as his love of reasoning, asked him the name of the mufti who had just been strangled.

"I know nothing about it," replied the good man, "and I have never known the name of any mufti or any vizier. I am entirely ignorant of the adventure that you are telling me about; I presume that in general those who meddle with public affairs sometimes perish miserably, and that they deserve it; but I never inquire what is going on in Constantinople; I content myself with sending there for sale the fruits of the garden that I cultivate."

Having said these words, he had the strangers come into his house; his two daughters and his two sons presented them with several kinds of sherbets which they made themselves, Turkish cream flavored with candied citron peel, oranges, lemons, limes, pineapples, pistachios, and Mocha coffee that had not been mixed with the bad coffee from Batavia and the West Indies. After which the two daughters of this Moslem perfumed the beards of Candide, Pangloss, and Martin.

"You must have a vast and magnificent estate?" said Candide to the Turk.

"I have only twenty acres," replied the Turk; "I cultivate them with my children; work keeps away three great evils: boredom, vice, and need."

As Candide went back to his farm, he reflected deeply on the Turk's remarks. He said to Pangloss and Martin: "That good old man seems to me to have made himself a life far preferable to that of the six Kings with whom we had the honor of having supper."

"Great eminence," said Pangloss, "is very dangerous, according to the report of all philosophers. For after all Eglon,[97] King of the Moabites, was assassinated

---

95. Turkish council of state.
96. An official expounder of Mohammedan law.

97. For this first group, of Old Testament rulers, see Judges 3, II Samuel 18, and I and II Kings.

by Ehud; Absalom was hanged by his hair and pierced with three darts; King Nadab son of Jeroboam was killed by Baasha, King Elah by Zimri, Ahaziah by Jehu, Athaliah by Jehoiada; Kings Jehoiakim, Jeconiah, and Zedekiah became slaves. You know how Croesus perished, Astyages, Darius, Dionysius of Syracuse, Pyrrhus, Perseus, Hannibal, Jugurtha, Ariovistus, Caesar, Pompey, Nero, Otho, Vitellius, Domitian, Richard II of England, Edward II, Henry VI, Richard III, Mary Stuart, Charles I, the three Henrys of France, the Emperor Henry IV? You know . . ."

"I also know," said Candide, "that we must cultivate our garden."

"You are right," said Pangloss, "for when man was put in the Garden of Eden, he was put there *ut operaretur eum,* to work; which proves that man was not born for rest."

"Let us work without reasoning," said Martin, "it is the only way to make life endurable."

All the little society entered into this laudable plan; each one began to exercise his talents. The little piece of land produced much. True, Cunégonde was very ugly; but she became an excellent pastry cook; Paquette embroidered; the old woman took care of the linen. No one, not even Friar Giroflée, failed to perform some service; he was a very good carpenter, and even became an honorable man; and Pangloss sometimes said to Candide: "All events are linked together in the best of all possible worlds; for after all, if you had not been expelled from a fine castle with great kicks in the backside for love of Mademoiselle Cunégonde, if you had not been subjected to the Inquisition, if you had not traveled about America on foot, if you had not given the Baron a great blow with your sword, if you had not lost all your sheep from the good country of Eldorado, you would not be here eating candied citrons and pistachios."

"That is well said," replied Candide, "but we must cultivate our garden."

Philosophy is fine, but work is happiness.

FRIEDRICH HÖLDERLIN (1770–1843)
Germany

One of the great German lyric and philosophic poets, Friedrich Hölderlin tried to bridge the gap between the optimistic philosophy of the eighteenth-century Enlightenment and the new, uncertain, and as yet undefined world of the nineteenth century that followed on the upheaval, terrors, and possibilities of the French Revolution. The disharmony of life was his great theme, his own life was unhappy and poverty-stricken, and his poetic career lasted only a decade. His *Hyperion or a Hermit in Greece* (1797–99) is one of the seminal works for romanticism. His heroine "Diotima" was a married woman, Suzette Gontard, his love for whom was partially responsible, it is thought, for his onset of madness. He showed symptoms of mental decline from 1802, and from 1806 until his death in 1843 he was confined as insane. But even in his madness he occasionally

Caspar David Friedrich. *Moonrise over the Sea*. 1822. Oil on canvas. Staatliche Museen, Berlin.

produced small lyrics of strange but surpassing beauty. The poems included here were written when he was at the height of his powers.

Half of Life

With its yellow pears
And wild roses everywhere
The shore hangs in the lake,
O gracious swans,
And drunk with kisses   5
You dip your heads
In the sobering holy water.

Ah, where will I find
Flowers, come winter,
And where the sunshine   10
And shade of the earth?
Walls stand cold
And speechless, in the wind
The weathervanes creak.

Translated by Burton Pike.

*Home**

And no one knows

Meanwhile let me roam
And pick wild berries
To quiet my love for you
Upon your paths, O Earth   5

   Here where
  and the thorns of roses
And sweet lindens cast their fragrance
Beside the beeches, at noon, when the pale rye
Rustles with the growth of slender stalks,   10
Their ears bowed to the side
Like autumn, but beneath the high
Vault of oaks, as I muse
And question the sky, the sound of bells
I know well   15
From afar rings golden at the hour
Of reawakening birds. So it goes.

JOHN KEATS (1795–1821)
England

From a humble background, John Keats was to develop rapidly into one of the
great English lyric poets before he was cut down by tuberculosis at the age of
twenty-six. His great theme is the overflowing abundance of the physical world
and its phenomena, including art, which create mystery and wonder in the mind
that contemplates them. The "Ode on a Grecian Urn" presents the unsolvable
puzzle of an ancient work of art, a decorated object whose "message" is
undecipherable to the modern mind but "dost tease us out of thought" as the
modern mind contemplates the rich echoes of the urn (and of the past). "To
Autumn," in which the season is personified as an allegorical female figure sitting
amid her fruitfulness, is one of the most sensuous mood-poems in English.

Ode on a Grecian Urn

Thou still unravished bride of quietness,
   Thou foster-child of silence and slow time,

---

*Translated by Richard Sieburth.

Sylvan[1] historian, who canst thus express
  A flowery tale more sweetly than our rhyme:
What leaf-fringed legend haunts about thy shape
    Of deities or of mortals, or of both,
      In Tempe or the dales of Arcady?[2]
    What men or gods are these? What maidens loth?
What mad pursuit? What struggle to escape?
    What pipes and timbrels? What wild ecstasy?

Heard melodies are sweet, but those unheard
  Are sweeter; therefore, ye soft pipes, play on;
Not to the sensual ear, but, more endeared,
  Pipe to the spirit ditties of no tone:
Fair youth, beneath the trees, thou canst not leave
  Thy song, nor ever can those trees be bare;
    Bold lover, never, never canst thou kiss,
Though winning near the goal—yet, do not grieve;
    She cannot fade; though thou hast not thy bliss,
  For ever wilt thou love, and she be fair!

Ah, happy, happy boughs! that cannot shed
  Your leaves, nor ever bid the Spring adieu;
And, happy melodist, unwearièd,
  For ever piping songs for ever new;
More happy love! more happy, happy love!
  For ever warm and still to be enjoyed,
    For ever panting, and for ever young;
All breathing human passion far above,
  That leaves a heart high-sorrowful and cloyed,
    A burning forehead, and a parching tongue.

Who are these coming to the sacrifice?
  To what green altar, O mysterious priest,
Lead'st thou that heifer lowing at the skies,
  And all her silken flanks with garlands drest?
What little town by river or sea shore,
  Or mountain-built with peaceful citadel,
    Is emptied of this folk, this pious morn?
And, little town, thy streets for evermore
  Will silent be; and not a soul to tell
    Why thou art desolate, can e'er return.

O Attic[3] shape! Fair attitude! with brede[4]
  Of marble men and maidens overwrought,
With forest branches and the trodden weed;

---

1. Of the woods.
2. By tradition, perfect pastoral landscapes.
3. Greek, generally Athenian.
4. A braid, or anything interwoven.

Thou, silent form, dost tease us out of thought
As doth eternity: Cold Pastoral!   45
   When old age shall this generation waste,
     Thou shalt remain, in midst of other woe
Than ours, a friend to man, to whom thou say'st,
   "Beauty is truth, truth beauty,"—that is all
     Ye know on earth, and all ye need to know.   50

To Autumn

Season of mists and mellow fruitfulness,
   Close bosom-friend of the maturing sun;
Conspiring with him how to load and bless
   With fruit the vines that round the thatch-eves run;
To bend with apples the moss'd cottage-trees,   5
   And fill all fruit with ripeness to the core;
     To swell the gourd, and plump the hazel shells
With a sweet kernel; to set budding more,
   And still more, later flowers for the bees,
     Until they think warm days will never cease,   10
      For Summer has o'er-brimm'd their clammy cells.

Who hath not seen thee oft amid thy store?
   Sometimes whoever seeks abroad may find
Thee sitting careless on a granary floor,
   Thy hair soft-lifted by the winnowing wind;[1]   15
Or on a half-reap'd furrow sound asleep,
   Drows'd with the fume of poppies, while thy hook[2]
     Spares the next swath and all its twined flowers:
And sometimes like a gleaner thou dost keep
   Steady thy laden head across a brook;   20
   Or by a cyder-press, with patient look,
     Thou watchest the last oozings hours by hours.

Where are the songs of Spring? Ay, where are they?
   Think not of them, thou hast thy music too,—
While barred clouds bloom the soft-dying day,   25
   And touch the stubble-plains with rosy hue;
Then in a wailful choir the small gnats mourn
   Among the river sallows,[3] borne aloft
     Or sinking as the light wind lives or dies;
And full-grown lambs loud bleat from hilly bourn;[4]   30
   Hedge-crickets sing; and now with treble soft

---

1. Blowing off the chaff from the grain.
2. Sickle.

3. Willows, with their branches low-reaching.
4. Field.

The red-breast whistles from a garden-croft;[5]
And gathering swallows twitter in the skies.

ANNETTE VON DROSTE-HÜLSHOFF (1797–1848)
Germany

Born to a noble Westphalian family, the versatile and spirited Annette von Droste-Hülshoff wrote often in her poems of being stifled because she was a woman in a man's world. Some of her poems show a woman yearning for the freedom to be herself; others have a strange twist to them. She is particularly known for her ballads combining natural scenes from her homeland with compact narrative, for her religious nature, evident in her collection *The Spiritual Year,* (1851), and for her sense of mystery, as in *The Jews' Beech Tree* (1842). Her pessimistic and peculiar vision of nature is sometimes attributed to her poor eyesight. But, as she says here, "my one need is to observe" and she is never afraid of lifting and lighting up her eyes "to all / that I have done and thought." That is true seeing, embodied in this poem. Her poetry has the ring of the modern.

The Last Day of the Year (New Year's Eve)

The year at its turn,
the whirring thread unrolls.

One hour more, the last today,
and what was living time is scrolls
of dust dropping into a grave.
I wait in stern   5

silence, O deep night!
Is there an open eye?
Time, your flowing passage shakes
these walls. I shiver, my   10
one need is to observe. Night wakes
in solitude. I light

Translated by Willis Barnstone.

5. Small field near a house.

my eyes to all
that I have done and thought.
All that was in my head and heart   15
now stands like sullen rot
at Heaven's door. Victory in part—
the rest a fall

into dark wind
whipping my house! Yes, this year   20
will shatter and ride on the wings
of storm; not breathe under the clear
light of stars like quiet things.
You, child of sin,

has there not been   25
a hollow, secret quiver each
day in your savage chest,
as the polar winds reach
across the stones, breaking, possessed
with slow and in-   30

sistent rage? Now my lamp
is about to die; the wick
greedily sucks the last drop of oil.
Is my life like smoke lick-
ing the oil? Will death's cave uncoil   35
before me black, damp?

My life breaks down
somewhere in the circle of
this year. Long have I known
decay. Yet my heart in love   40
glows under the huge stone
of passion. I frown,

sweating in deep
fear, my hands, forehead wet.
Why? Is there a moist star   45
burning through clouds? Is it
the star of love, with far
light, dim from fear, a steep

booming note. Do you hear?
Again! Song for the dead!   50
The bell shakes in its mouth.
O Lord, on my knees I spread
my arms, and from my drouth
beg mercy. Dead is the year!

GIACOMO LEOPARDI (1798–1837)
Italy

The life of Count Giacomo Leopardi, a self-taught prodigy with a spinal deformation who was always in poor health, was outwardly unhappy and uneventful, but he led an inner life of great intensity; his disability did not prevent him from becoming Italy's greatest poet since the Renaissance. Leopardi's overwhelming melancholy is in tune with his unshakable belief in a nature hostile to humanity and forever opposed to human happiness. No matter how keen his pessimism, he believed, like a true romantic, no less strongly in imagination and inspiration. His pessimism is treated philosophically in his aphorisms (*Thoughts,* 1834–37); his most famous works are the *Songs* (1836) and the *Moral Essays* (1824). The critic Patrick Creagh has called Leopardi "as passionate and sensitive as Keats, but as learned and tough-minded as Milton."

The Infinite*

I've always liked this lonely hill
crowned with a thicket cutting from view
so great a part of the far horizon.
Sitting and gazing out, I can imagine
interminable spaces beyond, supernatural   5
silences, and that profound calm
in which the heart comes near
to terror. And as I hear
the wind flutter the branches around me,
I weigh its voice against that infinite   10
silence; and summon up Eternity,
the dead seasons, and the present one
alive with sound. And so in this Immensity
my thoughts drown; and I find how sweet
it is to shipwreck in that sea.

VICTOR HUGO (1802–1885)
France/Channel Islands

Leader of the French romantic movement, Victor Hugo was a novelist, dramatist, poet, artist, and public personality, his production and fame bigger than life. Like

*Translated by William Jay Smith.

the writer Chateaubriand, whom he greatly admired, Hugo was greatly involved in political life. He served as a peer under the monarchy of Louis Philippe, then transferred his loyalty to the republicans and, upon the establishment of the Second Empire, went into exile in the Channel Islands, returning upon its overthrow. The preface to his drama *Cromwell* (1827) became the manifesto of romanticism in France; some of his poetry—for example, *Twilight Songs* (1835)—present the poet as prophet, whereas the *Contemplations* of 1856 place him in a more reflective stance. Hugo also wrote great melodramas. Two of them, *Hernani* (1830) and *The King Has Fun* (1832), were set to music by Verdi, the latter as *Rigoletto*. Hugo's stature was unquestionable: asked who was the greatest French poet ever, André Gide responded "Victor Hugo, alas!"

Mors*

I saw that reaper. She was in her field.
With long steps she passed and took her harvest,
A black skeleton letting the twilight go by.
All seemed to shrink back trembling in the shadows;
You could watch the flickering of her scythe.   5
And the victors under their triumphal arches
Fell; into a desert she changed Babylon,
Thrones into scaffolds and scaffolds into thrones,
Children were birds and roses turned to rot,
Gold turned to ashes, mothers' eyes to streams.   10
And the women were crying: "Where, where is our child?
If it was only for death, why give it life?"
High and low, the earth was one lament.
From wretched pallets bony fingers stretched cut;
Bitter wind whispered in the countless shrouds;   15
Throngs despairing under the somber scythe
Seemed a flock fleeing cold into the dark.
All she trod was horror, grief, and night.
Behind her, his forehead bathed in gentle flames,
An angel carried a sheaf of souls, and smiled.   20

March 1854

June Nights†

Summertime: after day has fled, the plain
Strewn with flowers gives off a heady scent;
Eyes closed, ears half-open to every sound
You drowse in a translucent slumber.

Translated by Patricia Terry and Mary Ann Caws.
†*Translated by Mary Ann Caws.*

The stars seem more intense, the shade more sweet;   5
A hazy half-light tints the eternal dome;
And mild pale dawn, in wait for its hour,
Lingers nightlong near the edge of the sky.

CHARLES BAUDELAIRE (1821–1867)
France

A genius, a dandy, and a "poète manudit," Baudelaire was prey to financial misery, drug addiction, and violent depression. When his adored mother remarried, after his father's death, his detested stepfather, le général Aupick, became the target of his hatred and obsession. Baudelaire died aphasiac at forty-six, able only to pronounce the syllable—"Cre"—as in an oath or a prayer, and unable to recognize himself in a mirror. A major poet spanning the romantic and the symbolist traditions, Charles Baudelaire is also known as the French translator of Edgar Allan Poe, for whose great reputation in France he is responsible. In *The Flowers of Evil* (1857), poems of erotic celebration of his white and black muses (Madame Sabatier and Jeanne Duval) are interwoven with those of utter tedium, distress, and "spleen," a vivid form of *ennui*. This attitude is one of the characteristic features of the romantic temperament, showing the individual as the passive prey of overwhelming gloom. The prose poem "Windows" from *Paris Spleen: Little Poems in Prose* celebrates the mystery of what is not known over the more prosaic everyday evidence, this mystery a characteristic of symbolism, in which suggestion takes the place of statement. The window is a frequent image for all the symbolists, whether the view leads out or in.

Spleen (III) [I'm like the king]

I'm like the king of a rainy country, rich
but helpless, decrepit though still a young man
who scorns his fawning tutors, wastes his time
on dogs and other animals, and has no fun;
nothing distracts him, neither hawk nor hound   5
nor subjects starving at the palace gate.
His favorite fool's obscenities fall flat
—the royal invalid is not amused—
and ladies in waiting for a princely nod
no longer dress indecently enough   10
to win a smile from this young skeleton.
The bed of state becomes a stately tomb.

Translated by Richard Howard.

The alchemist who brews him gold has failed
to purge the impure substance from his soul,
and baths of blood, Rome's legacy recalled
by certain barons in their failing days,
are useless to revive this sickly flesh
through which no blood but brackish Lethe[1] seeps.

15

Spleen (IV) [When skies are low]*

When skies are low and heavy as a lid
over the mind tormented by disgust,
and hidden in the gloom the sun pours down
on us a daylight dingier than the dark;

when earth becomes a trickling dungeon where
Trust like a bat keeps lunging through the air,
beating tentative wings along the walls
and bumping its head against the rotten beams;

5

when rain falls straight from unrelenting clouds,
forging the bars of some enormous jail,
and silent hordes of obscene spiders spin
their webs across the basements of our brains;

10

then all at once the raging bells break loose,
hurling to heaven their awful caterwaul,
like homeless ghosts with no one left to haunt
whimpering their endless grievances.

15

—And giant hearses, without dirge or drums,
parade at half-step in my soul, where Hope,
defeated, weeps, and the oppressor Dread
plants his black flag on my assenting skull.

20

Windows†

Looking from outside into an open window one never sees as much as when one
looks through a closed window. There is nothing more profound, more mysterious, more pregnant, more insidious, more dazzling than a window lighted by a
single candle. What one can see out in the sunlight is always less interesting than

*Translated by Richard Howard.
†Translated by Louise Varèse.

---

1. The river of forgetfulness, in which by
legend all the living must lose their memory
before crossing to Hades.

what goes on behind a windowpane. In that black or luminous square life lives, life dreams, life suffers.

Across the ocean of roofs I can see a middle-aged woman, her face already lined, who is forever bending over something and who never goes out. Out of her face, her dress, and her gestures, out of practically nothing at all, I have made up this woman's story, or rather legend, and sometimes I tell it to myself and weep.

If it had been an old man I could have made up his just as well.

And I go to bed proud to have lived and to have suffered in some one besides myself.

Perhaps you will say "Are you sure that your story is the real one?" But what does it matter what reality is outside myself, so long as it has helped me to live, to feel that I am, and what I am?

HENRIK IBSEN (1828–1906)
Norway

After his middle-class family suffered a financial reverse in his youth, Henrik Ibsen did an apprenticeship with a druggist and studied medicine before going towards the theatre. He was appointed manager and official playwright of Belgium's New National Theatre. He later lived in Italy and Germany, before returning to Norway. His plays include the verse dramas *Brand* (1886) and *Peer Gynt* (1867), and the study of marriage called *A Doll's House* (1879), the sociological drama An *Enemy of the People* (1882), and *Hedda Gabler* (1890), the story of a modern woman. Along with Sophocles' *Antigone* and Racine's *Phaedra*—both included in the first volume of this reader: *Antiquity to Early Modern*—*Hedda Gabler* might be seen as one of a trilogy of plays, from three very different nations and time periods, wherein the heroine represents a unique wilfulness and a violent opposition to social customs with her extreme desires and action. In his introduction to the Modern Library edition of Ibsen's plays, H. L. Mencken describes Hedda Gabler as "a neurotic and lascivious woman"—and this play as one in which Ibsen "fashioned a thumping drama out of the oldest, shoddiest materials" of the French melodramatists Scribe, Feuillet, Sardou, Meilhac, and Halévy, proving himself "a dramatist first and last, and not a windy evangelist and reformer, and that he could meet any other dramatist, however skilful, on equal terms, and dispose of him neatly and completely." Hedda's entrapment in an impossible situation—and her talent for boring herself and destroying others—might have had no other outcome than this: it is up to the audience to see and then, if they choose, to judge. Ibsen is preaching no cause here. *Hedda Gabler* is not, he says, in a reflection on the play, about problems; he wanted only "to depict human beings, human emotions, and human destinies, upon a groundwork of certain of the social conditions and principles of the present day."

Hedda Gabler

Characters

JØRGEN TESMAN, *University Research Fellow in History of Civilization*

HEDDA, *his wife*

MISS JULIANE TESMAN, *his aunt*

MRS ELVSTED

JUDGE BRACK

EILERT LØVBORG

BERTE, *the Tesmans' maid*

SCENE

The Tesmans' villa in a fashionable residential section of the town.

Act I

A spacious, handsome, tastefully furnished room. Dark décor. In the rear, a wide doorway with open portieres. Beyond is a smaller room, furnished in the same style as the front room. A door, right, leads to the front hall. Left, French doors, with portieres drawn aside, through which can be seen a part of a roofed verandah and trees with autumn foliage. Front center, an oval table covered with a cloth. Chairs around it. Front right, a wide, dark, porcelain stove, a high-backed easy chair, a footstool with a pillow, and two ottomans. In the corner far right, a sofa and a small, round table. Front left, a sofa, set out from the wall. Far left, beyond the French doors, an upright piano. On both sides of the doorway, rear center, whatnots with knick-knacks. Against the rear wall of the inner room, a sofa, and in front of it a table and two chairs. Above the sofa, a portrait of a handsome, elderly man in general's uniform. Over the table hangs a lamp with milky white glass. There are several bouquets of flowers, in vases and glasses, in various places in the front room. Others are lying on the tables. Thick carpets on the floors of both rooms. The morning sun is shining through the French doors.

Miss Juliane Tesman, with hat and parasol, enters right, followed by Berte, who carries a bouquet of flowers wrapped in paper. Miss Tesman is a nice-looking woman of 65, of pleasant mien, neatly but not expensively dressed in a gray suit. Berte is a middle-aged servant girl, of rather plain and countrified appearance.

MISS TESMAN: [*Stops inside the door, listens, says in a low voice.*] On my word—I don't think they are even up yet!

BERTE: [*Also softly.*] That's what I told you, miss. When you think how late the steamer got in last night. And afterwards—! Goodness!—all the stuff she wanted unpacked before she turned in.

MISS TESMAN: Well—just let them sleep. But fresh morning air—*that* we can give them when they come in here. [*Goes and opens the French doors wide.*]

BERTE: [*By the table, lost, still holding the flowers.*] Please, miss—I just don't see a bit of space anywhere! I think I'd better put these over here. [*Puts the flowers down on the piano.*]

MISS TESMAN: Well, well my dear Berte. So you've got yourself a new mistress now. The good Lord knows it was hard for me to let you go.

BERTE: [*Near tears*] What about me, then, miss! What shall I say? I who have served you and Miss Rina all these blessed years.

MISS TESMAN: We shall just have to make the best of it, Berte. There's nothing else

Translated by Otto Reinert.

to do. Jørgen can't do without you, you know. He just can't. You've looked after him ever since he was a little boy.

BERTE: Yes, but miss—I'm ever so worried about leaving Miss Rina. The poor dear lying there all helpless. With that new girl and all! She'll never learn how to make things nice and comfortable for an invalid.

MISS TESMAN: Oh yes, you'll see, I'll teach her. And of course, you know, I'll do most of it myself. So don't worry yourself about my poor sister, Berte.

BERTE: Yes, but there's another thing, too, miss. I'm scared I won't be able to suit young Mrs. Tesman.

MISS TESMAN: Oh, well. Good heavens. So there is a thing or two—Right at first—

BERTE: For I believe she's ever so particular.

MISS TESMAN: Can you wonder? General Gabler's daughter? Just think of the kind of life she was used to when the General was alive. Do you remember when she rode by with her father? That long black riding habit she wore? And the feather in her hat?

BERTE: Oh, I remember, all right. But I'll be blessed if I ever thought she and the young master would make a pair of it.

MISS TESMAN: Nor did I. By the way, while I think of it, Berte. Jørgen has a new title now. From now on you must refer to him as "the Doctor."

BERTE: Yes, the young mistress said something about that, too, last night. Soon as they were inside the door. Then it's really so, miss?

MISS TESMAN: It certainly is. Just think, Berte—they have made him a doctor abroad. During the trip, you know. I hadn't heard a thing about it till last night on the pier.

BERTE: Well, I daresay he could be anything he put his mind to, *he* could—smart as *he* is. But I must say I'd never thought he'd turn to doctoring people, too.

MISS TESMAN: Oh, that's not the kind of doctor he is [*Nods significantly.*] And as far as that is concerned, there is no telling but pretty soon you may have to call him something grander yet.

BERTE: You don't say! What might that be miss?

MISS TESMAN: [*Smiles.*] Wouldn't you like to know! [*Moved.*] Ah yes, indeed—! If only dear Jochum could see from his grave what has become of his little boy! [*Looking around.*] But look, Berte—what's this for? Why have you taken off all the slip covers?

BERTE: She told me to. Said she can't stand slip covers on chairs.

MISS TESMAN: Do you think they mean to make this their everyday living room, then?

BERTE: It sure sounded that way. Mrs. Tesman did, I mean. For he—the doctor—he didn't say anything.

[*Jørgen Tesman enters from the right side of the inner room. He is humming to himself. He carries an open, empty suitcase. He is of medium height, youthful-looking, thirty-three years old, somewhat stoutish. Round, open, cheerful face. Blond hair and beard. He wears glasses and is dressed in a comfortable, rather casual suit.*]

MISS TESMAN: Good morning, good morning, Jørgen!

TESMAN: [*In the doorway.*] Auntie! Dearest Aunt Julle! [*Comes forward and shakes her hand.*] All the way out here—as early as this! Hm?

MISS TESMAN: Well—I just had to drop in for a moment. To see how you are getting along, you know.

TESMAN: Even though you haven't had a good night's sleep.

MISS TESMAN: Oh, that doesn't matter at all.

TESMAN: But you did get home from the pier all right, I hope. Hm?

MISS TESMAN: Oh yes, certainly I did, thank you. The Judge was kind enough to see me all the way to my door.

TESMAN: We were so sorry we couldn't give you a ride in our carriage. But you saw for yourself—all the boxes Hedda had.

MISS TESMAN: Yes, she certainly brought quite a collection.

BERTE: [*To Tesman.*] Should I go and ask Mrs. Tesman if there's anything I can help her with?

TESMAN: No, thank you, Berte—you'd better not. She said she'll ring if she wants you.

BERTE: [*Going right.*] Well, all right.

TESMAN: But, look—you might take the suitcase with you.

BERTE: [*Takes it.*] I'll put it in the attic.

[*Exits right.*]

TESMAN: Just think, Auntie—that whole suitcase was brimful of copies of old documents. You wouldn't believe me if I told you all the things I have collected from libraries and archives all over. Quaint old items nobody has known anything about.

MISS TESMAN: Well, no, Jørgen. I'm sure you haven't wasted your time on your honeymoon.

TESMAN: No, I think I may say I have not. But take your hat off, Auntie—for goodness' sake. Here! Let me untie the ribbon for you. Hm?

MISS TESMAN: [*While he does so.*] Ah. God forgive me, if this isn't just as if you were still at home with us!

TESMAN: [*Inspecting the hat.*] My, what a fine-looking hat you've got yourself!

MISS TESMAN: I bought it for Hedda's sake.

TESMAN: For Hedda's sake? Hm?

MISS TESMAN: So she won't need to feel ashamed of me if we ever go out together.

TESMAN: [*Patting her cheek.*] If you don't think of everything, Auntie! [*Puts the hat down on a chair by the table.*] And now—over here to the sofa—we'll just sit and chat for a while till Hedda comes.

[*They seat themselves. She places her parasol in the corner by the sofa.*]

MISS TESMAN: [*Takes both his hands in hers and gazes at him.*] What a blessing it is to have you back again, Jørgen, big as life! You—Jochum's little boy!

TESMAN: For me, too, Aunt Julle. To see you again. For you have been both father and mother to me.

MISS TESMAN: Ah, yes—don't you think I know you'll always keep a spot in your heart for these two old aunts of yours!

TESMAN: So Aunt Rina isn't any better, hm?

MISS TESMAN: Oh no. We mustn't look for improvement in her case, poor dear. She is lying there just as she has been all these years. Just the same, may the good Lord keep her for me a long time yet! For else I just wouldn't know what to do with myself, Jørgen. Especially now, when I don't have you to look after any more.

TESMAN: [*Pats her back.*] There, there, now!

MISS TESMAN: [*Changing tone.*] And to think that you are a married man, Jørgen! And that you were the one to walk off with Hedda Gabler. The lovely Hedda Gabler. Just think! As many admirers as she had!

TESMAN: [*Hums a little, smiles contentedly.*] Yes, I daresay I have quite a few good friends here in town who'd gladly be in my shoes, hm?

MISS TESMAN: And such a lovely, long honeymoon you had! More than five—almost six months!

TESMAN: Well, you know—for me it has been a kind of study tour as well. All the collections I had to go through. And the books I had to read!

MISS TESMAN: Yes, I suppose. [*More confidentially, her voice lowered a little.*] But listen, Jørgen—haven't you got something—something special to tell me?

TESMAN: About the trip?

MISS TESMAN: Yes.

TESMAN: No—I don't know of anything besides what I wrote in my letters. They gave me a doctor's degree down there—but I told you that last night; I'm sure I did.

MISS TESMAN: Well, yes, that sort of thing—What I mean is—don't you have certain—certain—expectations?

TESMAN: Expectations?

MISS TESMAN: Ah for goodness' sake, Jørgen! I am your old Auntie, after all!

TESMAN: Certainly I have expectations.

MISS TESMAN: Well!!

TESMAN: I fully expect to be made a professor one of these days.

MISS TESMAN: Professor—oh yes—

TESMAN: I may even say I am quite certain of it. But dear Aunt Julle—you know this just as well as I do!

MISS TESMAN: [*Laughing a little*]. Of course I do. You're quite right. [*Changing topic.*] But we were talking about the trip. It must have cost a great deal of money—hm, Jørgen?

TESMAN: Well, now; you know that large stipend went quite a long way.

MISS TESMAN: I just don't see how you made it do for both of you, though.

TESMAN: No, I suppose that's not so easy to understand, hm?

MISS TESMAN: Particularly with a lady along. For I have always heard that is ever so much more expensive.

TESMAN: Well, yes, naturally. That *is* rather more expensive. But Hedda had to have this trip, Auntie! She really had to. Nothing less would do.

MISS TESMAN: No, I daresay. For a wedding journey is quite the thing these days. But now tell me—have you had a chance to look around here yet?

TESMAN: I certainly have. I have been up and about ever since dawn.

MISS TESMAN: And what do you think of it all?

TESMAN: Delightful! Perfectly delightful! The only thing is I don't see what we are going to do with the two empty rooms between the second sitting room in there and Hedda's bedroom.

MISS TESMAN: [*With a chuckle.*] Oh my dear Jørgen—you may find them useful enough—when the time comes!

TESMAN: Of course, you're right, Auntie! As my library expands, hm?

MISS TESMAN: Quite so, my dear boy. It was your library I was thinking of.

TESMAN: But I'm really most happy on Hedda's behalf. For you know, before we were engaged she used to say she wouldn't care to live anywhere but in Secretary Falk's house.

MISS TESMAN: Yes, just think—wasn't that a lucky coincidence, that it was up for sale right after you had left?

TESMAN: Yes, Aunt Julle. We've certainly been lucky. Hm?

MISS TESMAN: But it will be expensive, my dear Jørgen. Terribly expensive—all this.

TESMAN: [*Looks at her, a bit crestfallen.*] Yes, I daresay it will, Auntie.

MISS TESMAN: Heavens, yes!

TESMAN: How much, do you think? Roughly. Hm?

MISS TESMAN: No, I couldn't possibly say till all the bills arrive.

TESMAN: Well, anyway, Judge Brack managed to get very reasonable terms for us. He said so himself in a letter to Hedda.

MISS TESMAN: Yes, and I won't have you uneasy on that account, Jørgen. Besides, I have given security for the furniture and the carpets.

TESMAN: Security? You? But dear Aunt Julle—what kind of security could you give?

MISS TESMAN: The annuity.

TESMAN: [*Jumps up.*] What! Your and Aunt Rina's annuity?

MISS TESMAN: Yes. I didn't know what else to do, you see.

TESMAN: [*Standing before her.*] But are you clear out of your mind, Auntie! That annuity—that's all the two of you have to live on!

MISS TESMAN: Oh well, there's nothing to get so excited about, I'm sure. It's all just a matter of form, you now. That's what the Judge said, too. For he was kind enough to arrange the whole thing for me. Just a matter of form—those were his words.

TESMAN: That's all very well. Still——

MISS TESMAN: For now you'll have your own salary, you know. And, goodness— what if we do have a few expenses—Help out a bit right at first—? That would only be a joy for us—

TESMAN: Oh, Auntie! When will you ever stop making sacrifices for my sake!

MISS TESMAN: [*Gets up, puts her hands on his shoulders.*] But what other happiness do I have in this world than being able to smooth your way a little, my own dear boy? You, who haven't had either father or mother to lean on?

And now the goal is in sight, Jørgen. Things may have looked black at times. But heaven be praised: you're on top now!

TESMAN: Yes, it's really quite remarkable the way things have worked out.

MISS TESMAN: Yes—and those who were against you—who tried to block your way—now they are tasting defeat. They are down, Jørgen! He, the most dangerous of them all, his fall was the greatest! He made his bed, and now he is lying in it—poor, lost wretch that he is!

TESMAN: Have you had any news about Eilert? Since I went away, I mean?

MISS TESMAN: Just that he is supposed to have published a new book.

TESMAN: What! Eilert Løvborg? Recently? Hm?

MISS TESMAN: That's what they say. But I wonder if there can be much to it. What do you think? Ah—but when *your* new book comes, that will be something quite different, Jørgen! What is it going to be about?

TESMAN: It will deal with the domestic industries of Brabant during the Middle Ages.

MISS TESMAN: Just think—being able to write about something like that!

TESMAN: But as far as that is concerned, it may be quite some time before it is ready. I have all these collections to put in order first, you see.

MISS TESMAN: Yes, collecting and putting things in order—you certainly know how to do that. In that you are you father's son.

TESMAN: Well, I must say I am looking forward to getting started. Particularly now, that I've got my own delightful home to work in.

MISS TESMAN: And most of all now that you have the one your heart desired, dear Jørgen.

TESMAN: [*Embracing her.*] Oh yes, yes, Aunt Julle! Hedda—she is the most wonderful part of it all! [*Looks toward the doorway.*] There—I think she is coming now, hm?

[*Hedda enters from the left side of the inner room. She is twenty-nine years old. Both features and figure are noble and elegant. Pale, ivory complexion. Steel-gray eyes, expressive of cold, clear calm. Beautiful brown hair, though not particularly ample. She is dressed in a tasteful, rather loose-fitting morning costume.*]

MISS TESMAN: [*Going toward her.*] Good morning, my dear Hedda! A very happy morning to you!

HEDDA: [*Giving her hand.*] Good morning, dear Miss Tesman! So early a call? That is most kind.

MISS TESMAN: [*Seems slightly embarrassed.*] And—has the little lady of the house slept well the first night in her new home?

HEDDA: Passably, thank you.

TESMAN: [*Laughs.*] Passably! You are a good one, Hedda! You were sleeping like a log when I got up.

HEDDA: Fortunately. And then, of course, Miss Tesman, it always takes time to get used to new surroundings. That has to come gradually. [*Looks left.*] Oh dear. The maid has left the verandah doors wide open. There's a veritable flood of sunlight in here.

MISS TESMAN: [*Toward the doors.*] Well, then, we'll just close them.

HEDDA: No, no, not that. Tesman, dear, please pull the curtains. That will give a softer light.

TESMAN: [*Over by the French doors.*] Yes, dear. There, now! Now you have both shade and fresh air, Hedda.

HEDDA: We certainly can use some air in here. Such loads of flowers—But, Miss Tesman, please—won't you be seated?

MISS TESMAN: No thanks. I just wanted to see if everything was all right—and so it is, thank goodness. I had better get back to Rina. I know she is waiting for me, poor thing.

TESMAN: Be sure to give her my love, Auntie. And tell her I'll be around to see her later today.

MISS TESMAN: I'll certainly do that!—Oh my! I almost forgot! [*Searches the pocket of her dress.*] I have something for you, Jørgen. Here.

TESMAN: What's that, Auntie? Hm?

MISS TESMAN: [*Pulls out a flat parcel wrapped in newspaper and gives it to him.*] Here you are, dear.

TESMAN: [*Opens the parcel.*] Well, well, well! So you took care of them for me, Aunt Julle! Hedda! Now, isn't that sweet, hm?

HEDDA: [*By the whatnot, right.*] If you'd tell me what it is—

TESMAN: My old slippers! *You* know!

HEDDA: Oh really? I remember you often talked about them on the trip.

TESMAN: Yes, for I missed them so. [*Walks over to her.*] Here—now you can see what they're like, Hedda.

HEDDA: [*Crosses toward stove.*] Thanks. I don't know that I really care.

TESMAN: [*Following.*] Just think—Aunt Rina embroidered these slippers for me. Ill as she was. You can't imagine how many memories they hold for me!

HEDDA: [*By the table.*] Hardly for me.

MISS TESMAN: That's true, you know, Jørgen.

TESMAN: Yes, but—I just thought that now that she's one of the family—

HEDDA: [*Interrupting.*] I don't think we'll get on with that maid, Tesman.

MISS TESMAN: Not get on with Berte?

TESMAN: Whatever makes you say that, dear? Hm?

HEDDA: [*Points.*] Look—she has left her old hat on the chair over there.

TESMAN: [*Appalled, drops the slippers.*] But Hedda—!

HEDDA: What if somebody were to come and see it!

TESMAN: No, no, Hedda—that's Aunt Julle's hat!

HEDDA: Oh?

MISS TESMAN: [*Picking up the hat.*] Yes, indeed it is. And it isn't old either, my dear young lady.

HEDDA: I really didn't look that closely—

MISS TESMAN: [*Tying the ribbons.*] I want you to know that this is the first time I have it on my head. On my word it is!

TESMAN: And very handsome it is, too. Really a splendid-looking hat!

MISS TESMAN: Oh, I don't know that it is anything so special, Jørgen. [*Looks around.*] My parasol—? Ah, here it is. [*Picks it up.*] For that is mine, too. [*Mutters.*] Not Berte's.

TESMAN: New hat and new parasol! What do you think of that, Hedda!

HEDDA: Very nice indeed.

TESMAN: Yes, don't you think so? Hm? But, Auntie, take a good look at Hedda before you leave. See how pretty and blooming she looks.

MISS TESMAN: Dear me, Jørgen; that's nothing new. Hedda has been lovely all her days.

[*She nods and walks right.*]

TESMAN: [*Following.*] Yes, but have you noticed how full-figured and healthy she looks after the trip? How she has filled out?

HEDDA: [*Crossing.*] Oh—stop it!

MISS TESMAN: [*Halts, turns around.*] Filled out?

TESMAN: Yes, Aunt Julle. You can't see it so well now when she wears that dress. But I, who have the opportunity—

HEDDA: [*By the French doors, impatiently.*] Oh, you have no opportunity at all!

TESMAN: It must be the mountain air in Tyrol.

HEDDA: [*Curtly interrupting.*] I am just as I was when I left.

TESMAN: Yes, so you say. I just don't think you're right. What do you think, Auntie?

MISS TESMAN: [*Has folded her hands, gazes at Hedda.*] Lovely—lovely—lovely! that is what Hedda is. [*Goes over to her, inclines her head forward with both her hands, and kisses her hair.*] God bless and keep Hedda Tesman. For Jørgen's sake.

HEDDA: [*Gently freeing herself.*] There, *there,* Now let me go.

MISS TESMAN: [*In quiet emotion.*] Every single day I'll be over and see you two.

TESMAN: Yes, please do, Auntie. Hm?

MISS TESMAN: Goodbye, goodbye!

[*She leaves through door, right. Tesman sees her out. The door remains ajar. Tesman is heard repeating his greetings for Aunt Rina and his thanks for the slippers. In the meantime, Hedda paces up and down, raises her arms, clenching her fists, as in quiet rage. Opens the curtains by the French doors and stands looking out. In a few moments, Tesman re-enters and closes the door behind him.*]

TESMAN: [*Picking up the slippers.*] What are you looking at, Hedda?

HEDDA: [*Once again calm and controlled.*] Just the leaves. They are so yellow. And so withered.

TESMAN: [*Wrapping the slippers in their paper, putting the parcel down on the table.*] Well, you know—we're in September now.

HEDDA: [*Again restless.*] Yes—just think. We are already in—September.

TESMAN: Don't you think Aunt Julle acted strange, Hedda? Almost solemn. I wonder why. Hm?

HEDDA: I hardly know her, you see. Isn't she often like that?

TESMAN: Not the way she was today.

HEDDA: [*Turning away from the French doors.*] Do you think she minded that business with the hat?

TESMAN: Oh, I don't think so. Not much. Perhaps a little bit right at the moment—

HEDDA: Well, I'm sorry, but I must say it strikes me as very odd—putting her hat down here in the living room. One just doesn't do that.

TESMAN: Well, you may be sure Aunt Julle won't ever do it again.

HEDDA: Anyway, I'll make it up to her, somehow.

TESMAN: Oh yes, Hedda; if only you would!

HEDDA: When you go over there today, why don't you ask her over for tonight?

TESMAN: I'll certainly do that. And then there is one other thing you could do that she'd appreciate ever so much.

HEDDA: What?

TESMAN: If you could just bring yourself to call her Auntie. For my sake, Hedda, hm?

HEDDA: No, Tesman, no. You really mustn't ask me to do that. I have already told you I won't. I'll try to call her Aunt Juliane. That will have to do.

TESMAN: All right, if you say so. I just thought that now that you're in the family—

HEDDA: Hmmm—I don't know about that—

[*She walks toward the doorway.*]

TESMAN: [*After a brief pause.*] Anything the matter, Hedda? Hm?

HEDDA: I'm just looking at my old piano. It doesn't quite go with the other furniture in here.

TESMAN: As soon as I get my first pay check we'll have it traded in.

HEDDA: No—I don't want to do that. I want to keep it. But let's put it in this inner room and get another one for out here. Whenever it's convenient, I mean.

TESMAN: [*A little taken back.*] Well—yes—we could do that—

HEDDA: [*Picks up the bouquet from the piano.*] These flowers weren't here last night.

TESMAN: I suppose Aunt Julle brought them for you.

HEDDA: [*Looking at the flowers.*] There's a card here. [*Takes it out and reads.*] "Will be back later." Can you guess who it's from?

TESMAN: No. Who? Hm?

HEDDA: Thea Elvsted.

TESMAN: No, really? Mrs. Elvsted! Miss Rysing that was.

HEDDA: That's right. The one with that irritating head of hair she used to show off with. An old flame of yours, I understand.

TESMAN: [*Laughs.*] Well, now—that didn't last long! Anyway, that was before I knew you, Hedda. Just think—her being in town.

HEDDA: Strange, that she'd call on us. I have hardly seen her since we went to school together.

TESMAN: As far as that goes, I haven't seen her either for—God knows how long. I don't see how she can stand living in that out-of-the-way place. Hm?

HEDDA: [*Suddenly struck by a thought.*] Listen, Tesman—isn't it some place near
there that he lives—what's his name—Eilert Løvborg?

TESMAN: Yes, that's right. He is up there, too.

[*Berte enters right.*]

BERTE: Ma'am, she's here again, that lady who brought those flowers a while back.
[*Pointing.*] The flowers you're holding in your hand, ma'am.

HEDDA: Ah, she is? Well, show her in, please.

[*Berte opens the door for Mrs. Elvsted and exits. Mrs. Elvsted is of slight build,
with a pretty, soft face. Her eyes are light blue, large, round, rather
prominent, of a timid and querying expression. Her hair is strikingly light in
color, almost whitish, and unusually rich and wavy. She is a couple of years
younger than Hedda. She is dressed in a dark visiting dress, tasteful, but not
quite in the most recent fashion.*]

HEDDA: [*Walks toward her. Friendly.*] Good morning, my dear Mrs. Elvsted. How
very nice to see you again.

MRS. ELVSTED: [*Nervous, trying not to show it.*] Well, yes, it is quite some time since
we met.

TESMAN: [*Shaking hands.*] And we, too. Hm?

HEDDA: Thank you for your lovely flowers—

MRS. ELVSTED: Please, don't—I would have come here yesterday afternoon. But I
was told you were still traveling—

TESMAN: You've just arrived in town, hm?

MRS. ELVSTED: I got here yesterday, at noon. Oh, I was quite desperate when I
learned you weren't home.

HEDDA: Desperate? But why?

TESMAN: But my dear Mrs. Rysing—I mean Mrs. Elvsted—

HEDDA: There is nothing wrong, I hope?

MRS. ELVSTED: Yes there is. And I don't know a single soul other than you that I can
turn to here.

HEDDA: [*Putting the flowers down on the table.*] Come—let's sit down here on the
sofa.

MRS. ELVSTED: Oh, I'm in no mood to sit!

HEDDA: Of course you are. Come on. [*She pulls Mrs. Elvsted over to the sofa and sits
down next to her.*]

TESMAN: Well, now Mrs.—? Exactly what—?

HEDDA: Has something—special happened at home?

MRS. ELVSTED: Well, yes—and no. Oh, but I am so afraid you are going to
misunderstand!

HEDDA: In that case, it seems to me you ought to tell us exactly what has
happened, Mrs. Elvsted.

TESMAN: After all, that's why you are here. Hm?

MRS. ELVSTED: Yes, yes, of course. Well, then, maybe you already know—Eilert
Løvborg is in town.

HEDDA: Is Løvborg—!

TESMAN: No! You don't say! Just think, Hedda—Løvborg's back!

HEDDA: All right. I can hear.

MRS. ELVSTED: He has been here a week already. Imagine—a whole week! In this dangerous place. Alone! With all that bad company around.

HEDDA: But my dear Mrs. Elvsted—why is he a concern of yours?

MRS. ELVSTED: [*With an apprehensive look at her, says quickly.*] He tutored the children.

HEDDA: Your children?

MRS. ELVSTED: My husband's. I don't have any.

HEDDA: In other words, your stepchildren.

MRS. ELVSTED: Yes.

TESMAN: [*With some hesitation.*] But was he—I don't quite know how to put this—was he sufficiently—regular—in his way of life to be thus employed? Hm?

MRS. ELVSTED: For the last two years, there hasn't been a thing to object to in his conduct.

TESMAN: No, really? Just think, Hedda!

HEDDA: I hear.

MRS. ELVSTED: Not the least little bit, I assure you! Not in any respect. And yet—knowing he's here—in the big city—And with all that money, too! I'm scared to death

TESMAN: But in that case, why didn't he remain with you and your husband? Hm?

MRS. ELVSTED: After his book came out, he was too restless to stay.

TESMAN: Ah yes, that's right. Aunt Julle said he has published a new book.

MRS. ELVSTED: Yes, a big new book, about the course of civilization in general. It came out about two weeks ago. And since it has had such big sales and been discussed so much and made such a big splash—

TESMAN: It has, has it? I suppose this is something he has had lying around from better days?

MRS. ELVSTED: You mean from earlier?

TESMAN: Yes.

MRS. ELVSTED: No; it's all been written since he came to stay with us. During this last year.

TESMAN: Well, now! That's very good news, Hedda! Just think!

MRS. ELVSTED: Yes, if it only would last!

HEDDA: Have you seen him since you came to town?

MRS. ELVSTED: No, not yet. I had a great deal of trouble finding his address. But this morning I finally tracked him down.

HEDDA: [*Looks searchingly at her.*] Isn't it rather odd that your husband—hm—

MRS. ELVSTED: [*With a nervous start.*] My husband! What about him?

HEDDA: That he sends you to town on such an errand? That he doesn't go and look after his friend himself?

MRS. ELVSTED: Oh, no, no—my husband doesn't have time for things like that. Besides, I have some—some shopping to do, anyway.

HEDDA: [*With a slight smile.*] Well, in that case, of course—

MRS. ELVSTED: [*Getting up, restlessly.*] And now I beg of you, Mr. Tesman—won't you please receive Eilert Løvborg nicely if he calls on you? And I am sure he will. After all—Such good friends as you two used to be. And then you both do the same kind of work—the same studies, as far as I know.

TESMAN: We used to, at any rate.

MRS. ELVSTED: Yes. And that's why I implore you to please, please, try to keep an eye on him—you too. You'll do that, Mr. Tesman, won't you? Promise?

TESMAN: With the greatest pleasure, Mrs. Rysing.

HEDDA: Elvsted.

TESMAN: I'll gladly do as much for Eilert as I possibly can. You may certainly count on that.

MRS. ELVSTED: Oh, how good and kind you are! [*Clasps his hands.*] Thank you, thank you! [*Nervously.*] You see, my husband is so very fond of him.

HEDDA: [*Getting up.*] You ought to write him a note, Tesman. Maybe he won't come without an invitation.

TESMAN: Yes, I suppose that would be the right thing to do, Hedda. Hm?

HEDDA: The sooner the better. Right away I think.

MRS. ELVSTED: [*Pleadingly.*] If only you would!

TESMAN: I'll write this minute. Do you have his address, Mrs.—Mrs. Elvsted?

MRS. ELVSTED: Yes. [*Pulls a slip of paper from her bag and gives it to him.*] Here it is.

TESMAN: Very good. Well, then, if you'll excuse me—[*Looks around.*] By the way—the slippers? Ah, here we are. [*Leaving with the parcel.*]

HEDDA: Be sure you write a nice, warm, friendly letter, Tesman. And a long one, too.

TESMAN: Certainly, certainly.

MRS. ELVSTED: But not a word that it is I who—!

TESMAN: No, that goes without saying, I should think. Hm? [*Goes out right through inner room.*]

HEDDA: [*Goes over to Mrs. Elvsted, smiles, says in a low voice.*] There! We've just killed two birds with one stone.

MRS. ELVSTED: What do you mean?

HEDDA: Didn't you see I wanted him out of the room?

MRS. ELVSTED: Yes, to write that letter—

HEDDA: And to speak to you alone.

MRS. ELVSTED: [*Flustered.*] About the same thing?

HEDDA: Exactly.

MRS. ELVSTED: [*Anxious.*] But there *is* nothing more, Mrs. Tesman! Really, there isn't!

HEDDA: Oh yes, there is. There is considerably more. I can see that much. Over here—We are going to have a real, nice, confidential talk, you and I. [*She forces Mrs. Elvsted down in the easy chair and seats herself on one of the ottomans.*]

MRS. ELVSTED: [*Worried, looks at her watch.*] But my dear Mrs. Tesman—I had really thought I would be on my way now.

HEDDA: Oh, I am sure there is no rush. Now, then. Tell me about yourself. How are things at home?

MRS. ELVSTED: That is just what I don't want to talk about.

HEDDA: But to me—! After all, we are old schoolmates.

MRS. ELVSTED: But you were a year ahead of me. And I used to be so scared of you!

HEDDA: Scared of me?

MRS. ELVSTED: Terribly. For when we met on the stairs, you always ruffled my hair.

HEDDA: Did I really?

MRS. ELVSTED: Yes. And once you said you were going to burn it off.

HEDDA: Oh, but you know—I wasn't serious!

MRS. ELVSTED: No, but I was such a silly, then. Anyway. Afterwards we drifted far apart. Our circles are so very different, you know.

HEDDA: All the more reason for getting close again. Listen. In school we called each other by our first names.

MRS. ELVSTED: Oh I'm sure you're wrong—

HEDDA: I'm sure I'm not! I remember it quite clearly. And now we want to be open with one another, just the way we used to. [*Moves the ottoman closer.*] There now! [*Kisses her cheek.*] You call me Hedda.

MRS. ELVSTED: [*Seizes her hands.*] Oh, you are so good and kind! I'm not used to that

HEDDA: There, there! And I'll call you my dear Thora, just as in the old days.

MRS. ELVSTED: My name is Thea.

HEDDA: So it is. Of course. I meant Thea. [*Looks at her with compassion.*] So you're not much used to goodness and kindness, Thea? Not in your own home?

MRS. ELVSTED: If I even had a home! But I don't. I never have had one.

HEDDA: [*Looks at her for a moment.*] I thought there might be something like this.

MRS. ELVSTED: [*Helplessly, looking straight ahead.*] Yes—yes—yes—

HEDDA: I am not sure if I quite remember—Didn't you first come to your husband as his housekeeper?

MRS. ELVSTED: I was really hired as governess. But his wife—his first wife—was ailing already then and was practically bedridden. So I had to take charge of the household as well.

HEDDA: But in the end you became his wife.

MRS. ELVSTED: [*Dully.*] So I did.

HEDDA: Let's see. How long ago is that?

MRS. ELVSTED: Since my marriage?

HEDDA: Yes.

MRS. ELVSTED: About five years.

HEDDA: Right. It must be that long.

MRS. ELVSTED: Oh, those five years! Or mostly the last two or three! Oh, Mrs. Tesman—if you could just imagine!

HEDDA: [*Slaps her hand lightly.*] Mrs. Tesman? Shame on you!

MRS. ELVSTED: Oh yes, all right; I'll try. Yes—if you could just—conceive—understand—

HEDDA: [*Casually.*] And Eilert Løvborg has been living near you for some three years or so, hasn't he?

MRS. ELVSTED: [*Looks at her uncertainly.*] Eilert Løvborg? Yes—he has.

HEDDA: Did you know him before? Here in town?

MRS. ELVSTED: Hardly at all. That is, of course I did in a way. I mean, I knew *of* him.

HEDDA: But up there—You saw a great deal of him; did you?

MRS. ELVSTED: Yes, he came over to us every day. He was supposed to tutor the children, you see. For I just couldn't do it all by myself.

HEDDA: Of course not. And your husband—? I suppose he travels quite a bit.

MRS. ELVSTED: Well, yes, Mrs. Tes—Hedda—as a public magistrate, you know, he very often has to travel all over his district.

HEDDA: [*Leaning against the armrest on the easy chair.*] Thea—poor, sweet Thea—now you have to tell me everything—just as it is.

MRS. ELVSTED: You'd better ask me, then.

HEDDA: How *is* your husband, Thea? I mean—you know—*really*? To be with. What kind of person is he? Is he good to you?

MRS. ELVSTED: [*Evasively.*] I believe he thinks he does everything for the best.

HEDDA: But isn't he altogether too old for you? He is more than twenty years older, isn't he?

MRS. ELVSTED: [*With irritation.*] Yes, there is that, too. But there isn't just one thing. Every single little thing about him repels me! We don't have a thought in common, he and I. Not a thing in the world!

HEDDA: But isn't he fond of you all the same? I mean in his own way?

MRS. ELVSTED: I don't know. I think I am just useful to him. And I don't use much money. I am inexpensive.

HEDDA: That is foolish of you.

MRS. ELVSTED: [*Shakes her head.*] Can't be changed. Not with him. I don't think he cares for anybody much except himself. Perhaps the children a little.

HEDDA: And Eilert Løvborg, Thea.

MRS. ELVSTED: [*Looks at her.*] Eilert Løvborg? What makes you think that?

HEDDA: Well, it seems to me that when he sends you all the way to town to look after him—[*With an almost imperceptible smile.*] Besides, you said so yourself. To Tesman.

MRS. ELVSTED: [*With a nervous twitch.*] Did I? I suppose I did. [*With a muted outburst.*] No! I might as well tell you now as later. For it's bound to come out, anyway.

HEDDA: But my dear Thea—?

MRS. ELVSTED: All right. My husband doesn't know I've gone!

HEDDA: What! He doesn't know?

MRS. ELVSTED: He wasn't even home. He's away again. Oh, I just couldn't take it any longer, Hedda! It had become utterly impossible. All alone as I was.

HEDDA: So what did you do?

MRS. ELVSTED: I packed some of my things. Just the most necessary. Without telling anybody. And left.

HEDDA: Just like that?

MRS. ELVSTED: Yes. And took the next train to town.

HEDDA: But dearest Thea—how did you dare to do a thing like that!

MRS. ELVSTED: [*Rises, walks.*] What else could I do?

HEDDA: But what do you think your husband will say when you go back?

MRS. ELVSTED: [*By the table; looks at her.*] Go back to him?

HEDDA: Yes!

MRS. ELVSTED: I'll never go back.

HEDDA: [*Rises, approaches her slowly.*] So you have really, seriously—left every-thing?

MRS. ELVSTED: Yes. It seemed to me there was nothing else I could do.

HEDDA: And quite openly, too.

MRS. ELVSTED: You can't keep a thing like that secret, anyway.

HEDDA: But what do you think people will say, Thea?

MRS. ELVSTED: In God's name, let them say whatever they like. [*Sits down on the sofa, dully tired.*] For I have only done what I had to do.

HEDDA: [*After a brief silence.*] And what do you plan to do with yourself? What sort of work will you do?

MRS. ELVSTED: I don't know yet. I only know I have to live where Eilert Løvborg is. If I am to live at all.

HEDDA: [*Moves a chair from the table closer to Mrs. Elvsted, sits down, strokes her hands.*] Thea—tell me. How did this—this friendship between you and Eilert Løvborg—how did it begin?

MRS. ELVSTED: Oh, it grew little by little. I got some sort of power over him.

HEDDA: Oh?

MRS. ELVSTED: He dropped his old ways. Not because I asked him to. I never dared to do that. But I think he must have noticed how I felt about that kind of life. So he changed.

HEDDA: [*Quickly suppresses a cynical smile.*] So you have—rehabilitated him, as they say. Haven't you, Thea?

MRS. ELVSTED: At least, that's what *he* says. On the other hand, he has turned me into a real human being. Taught me to think—and understand—all sorts of things.

HEDDA: Maybe he tutored you, too?

MRS. ELVSTED: No, not tutored exactly. But he talked to me. About so many, many things. And then came that lovely, lovely time when I could share his work with him. He let me help him!

HEDDA: He did?

MRS. ELVSTED: Yes! Whatever he wrote, he wanted us to be together about it.

HEDDA: Just like two good comrades.

MRS. ELVSTED: [*With animation.*] Comrades!—that's it! Imagine, Hedda—that's just what he called it, too. Oh, I really ought to feel so happy. But I can't. For you see, I don't know if it will last.

HEDDA: You don't trust him any more than that?

MRS. ELVSTED: [*Heavily.*] The shadow of a woman stands between Eilert Løvborg and me.

HEDDA: [*Tensely, looks at her.*] Who?

MRS. ELVSTED: I don't know. Somebody or other from—his past. I don't think he has ever really forgotten her.

HEDDA: What has he told you about it?

MRS. ELVSTED: He has mentioned it only once—just casually.

HEDDA: And what did he say?

MRS. ELVSTED: He said that when they parted she was going to kill him with a gun.

HEDDA: [*Cold, controlled.*] Oh, nonsense. People don't do that sort of thing here.

MRS. ELVSTED: No, I know. And that is why I think it must be that red-headed
  singer he used to—

HEDDA: Yes, I suppose so.

MRS. ELVSTED: For I remember people said she carried a loaded gun.

HEDDA: Well, then I'm sure it's she.

MRS. ELVSTED: [*Wringing her hands.*] Yes, but just think, Hedda—now I hear that
  she—that singer—that she's here in town again, too! Oh, I'm just
  desperate—!

HEDDA: [*With a glance toward the inner room.*] Shhh; Here's Tesman. [*Rises and
  whispers.*] Not a word about all this to anybody, Thea!

MRS. ELVSTED: [*Jumps up.*] No, no. For God's sake—!

[*Tesman, carrying a letter, enters from the right side of the inner room.*]

TESMAN: There, now—here's the missive, all ready to go!

HEDDA: Good. But I believe Mrs. Elvsted wants to be on her way. Wait a moment.
  I'll see you to the garden gate.

TESMAN: Say, Hedda—do you think Berte could take care of this?

HEDDA: [*Takes the letter.*] I'll tell her. [*Berte enter right.*]

BERTE: Judge Brack is here and wants to know if you're receiving.

HEDDA: Yes, ask the Judge please to come in. And—here—drop this in a mailbox,
  will you?

BERTE: [*Takes the letter.*] Yes, ma'am.

[*She opens the door for Judge Brack and exits. The Judge is forty-five years of
age. Rather thickset, but well-built and with brisk, athletic movements.
Roundish face, aristocratic profile. His hair is short, still almost completely
black, very neatly dressed. Lively, sparkling eyes. Thick eyebrows and
mustache with cut-off points. He is dressed in an elegant suit, a trifle youthful
for his age. He wears pince-nez glasses, attached to a string, and lets them
drop from time to time.*]

JUDGE BRACK: [*Hat in hand, salutes.*] May one pay one's respects as early as this?

HEDDA: One certainly may.

TESMAN: [*Shaking his hand.*] You are always welcome. [*Introducing.*] Judge Brack—
  Miss Rysing—

HEDDA: [*Groans.*]

BRACK: [*Bowing.*] Delighted!

HEDDA: [*Looks at him, laughs.*] How nice it is to see you in daylight, Judge!

BRACK: You find me changed, perhaps?

HEDDA: A bit younger, I think.

BRACK: Much obliged.

TESMAN: But what do you think of Hedda? Hm? Did you ever see her in such
  bloom? She positively—

HEDDA: Will you please leave me out of this? You had better thank the Judge for all the trouble he has taken.

BRACK: Oh, nonsense. It's been a pleasure.

HEDDA: Yes, you are indeed a faithful soul. But my friend here is dying to be off. Don't leave, Judge. I'll be back in a minute.

[*Mutual goodbyes. Mrs. Elvsted and Hedda exit, right.*]

BRACK: Well now—your wife—is she tolerably satisfied?

TESMAN: Yes, indeed, and we really can't thank you enough. That is, I understand there will have to be some slight changes made here and there. And there are still a few things—just a few trifles—we'll have to get.

BRACK: Oh? Really?

TESMAN: But we certainly don't want to bother you with that. Hedda said she's going to take care of it herself. But do sit down, hm?

BRACK: Thanks. Maybe just for a moment—[*Sits down by the table.*] There's one thing I'd like to talk to you about, my dear Tesman.

TESMAN: Oh? Ah, I see. [*Sits down.*] I suppose it's the serious part of the festivities that's beginning now. Hm?

BRACK: Oh—there's no great rush as far as the money is concerned. Though I must say I wish we could have established ourselves a trifle more economically.

TESMAN: Out of the question, my dear fellow! Remember, it's all for Hedda! You, who know her so well—! After all, I couldn't put her up like any little middle-class housewife—

BRACK: No. I suppose—That's just it.

TESMAN: Besides—fortunately—it can't be long now before I receive my appointment.

BRACK: Well, you know—things like that have a way of hanging fire.

TESMAN: Perhaps you have heard something? Something definite? Hm?

BRACK: No, nothing certain—[*Interrupting himself.*] But that reminds me. I have some news for you.

TESMAN: Oh?

BRACK: Your old friend Eilert Løvborg is back in town.

TESMAN: I know that already.

BRACK: So? Who told you?

TESMAN: The lady who just left.

BRACK: I see. What did you say her name was again? I didn't quite catch—

TESMAN: Mrs. Elvsted.

BRACK: Ah yes—the Commissioner's wife. Yes, it's up in her part of the country that Løvborg has been staying, too.

TESMAN: And just think. I am so glad to hear it. He is quite respectable again.

BRACK: Yes, so they say.

TESMAN: And he has published a new book, hm?

BRACK: Oh yes.

TESMAN: Which is making quite a stir.

BRACK: Quite an unusual stir.

TESMAN: Just think! Isn't that just wonderful! He—with his remarkable gifts. And I was so sure he'd gone under for good.

BRACK: That seems to have been the general opinion.

TESMAN: What I don't understand, though, is what he is going to do with himself. What sort of living can he make? Hm?

[*During the last remark Hedda re-enters, right.*]

HEDDA: [*To Brack, with a scornful little laugh.*] Tesman is forever worrying about how people are going to make a living.

TESMAN: Well, you see, we are talking about poor Eilert Løvborg, Hedda.

HEDDA: [*With a quick look at him.*] You are? [*Sits down in the easy chair by the stove and asks casually.*] What is the matter with him?

TESMAN: Well, you see, I believe he's run through his inheritance a long time ago. And I don't suppose he can write a new book every year. Hm? So I really must ask how he is going to make out.

BRACK: Maybe I could help you answer that.

TESMAN: Yes?

BRACK: Remember, he has relatives with considerable influence.

TESMAN: Ah—unfortunately, those relatives have washed their hands of him long ago.

BRACK: Just the same, they used to call him the hope of the family.

TESMAN: Yes, before! But he has ruined all that.

HEDDA: Who knows? [*With a little smile.*] I hear the Elvsteds have rehabilitated him.

BRACK: And then this book—

TESMAN: Well, I certainly hope they will help him to find something or other. I just wrote him a letter. Hedda, dear, I asked him to come out here tonight.

BRACK: Oh dear, I am sorry. Don't you remember—you're supposed to come to my little stag dinner tonight? You accepted last night on the pier, you know.

HEDDA: Had you forgotten, Tesman?

TESMAN: So I had.

BRACK: Oh well. I'm sure he won't come, so it doesn't really make any difference.

TESMAN: Why is that? Hm?

BRACK: [*Gets up somewhat hesitantly, rests his hands on the back of the chair.*] Dear Tesman—and you, too, Mrs. Tesman—I cannot in good conscience let you remain in ignorance of something, which—which—

TESMAN: Something to do with Eilert?

BRACK: With both you and him.

TESMAN: But my dear Judge, do speak!

BRACK: You must be prepared to find that your appointment will not come through as soon as you hope and expect.

TESMAN: [*Jumps up, nervously.*] Something's happened? Hm?

BRACK: It may conceivably be made contingent upon the result of a competition.

TESMAN: Competition! Just think, Hedda!

HEDDA: [*Leaning farther back in her chair.*] Ah—I see, I see—!

TESMAN: But with whom? Don't tell me with—?

BRACK: Precisely. With Eilert Løvborg.

TESMAN: [*Claps his hands together.*] No, no! This can't be. It is unthinkable! Quite impossible! Hm?

BRACK: All the same, that's the way it may turn out.

TESMAN: No, but Judge, this would amount to the most incredible callousness toward me! [*Waving his arms.*] For just think—I'm a married man! We married on the strength of these prospects, Hedda and I. Got ourselves deep in debt. Borrowed money from Aunt Julle, too. After all, I had practically been promised the post, you know. Hm?

BRACK: Well, well. I daresay you'll get it in the end. If only after a competition.

HEDDA: [*Motionless in her chair.*] Just think, Tesman. It will be like a kind of contest.

TESMAN: But dearest Hedda, how can you be so unconcerned!

HEDDA: [*Still without moving.*] I'm not at all unconcerned. I'm dying to see who wins.

BRACK: In any case, Mrs. Tesman, I'm glad you know the situation for what it is. I mean—before you proceed to make the little additional purchases I understand you threaten us with.

HEDDA: This makes no difference as far as that is concerned.

BRACK: Really? Well, in that case, of course—Goodbye! [*To Tesman.*] I'll pick you up on my afternoon walk.

TESMAN: What? Oh yes, yes, of course. I'm sorry; I'm just all confused.

HEDDA: [*Without getting up, gives her hand.*] Goodbye, Judge. Come back soon.

BRACK: Thanks. Goodbye, goodbye.

TESMAN: [*Sees him to the door.*] Goodbye, my dear Judge. You really must excuse me—

[*Judge Brack exits, right.*]

TESMAN: [*Pacing the floor.*] Oh, Hedda, Hedda! One should never venture into fairyland. Hm?

HEDDA: [*Looks at him, smiles.*] Do *you* do that?

TESMAN: Well, yes—it can't be denied—it is most venturesome of me to rush into marriage and set up a home on the strength of mere prospects.

HEDDA: Well, maybe you're right.

TESMAN: Anyway—we do have our own nice, comfortable home, now. Just think, Hedda—the very home both of us dreamed about. Set our hearts on, I may almost say. Hm?

HEDDA: [*Rises, slowly, tired.*] The agreement was that we were to maintain a certain position—entertain—

TESMAN: Don't I know it! Dearest Hedda—I have been so looking forward to seeing you as hostess in a select circle! Hm? Well, well, well! In the meantime, we'll just have to be content with one another. See Aunt Julle once in a while. Nothing more. And you were meant for such a different kind of life, altogether!

HEDDA: I suppose a footman is completely out of the question.

TESMAN: I'm afraid so. Under the circumstances, you see—we couldn't possibly—

HEDDA: And as for getting my own riding horse—

TESMAN: [*Aghast.*] Riding horse!

HEDDA: I suppose I mustn't even think of that.

TESMAN: Good heavens, no! That goes without saying, I hope!

HEDDA: [*Walking.*] Well—at least I have one thing to amuse myself with in the meantime.

TESMAN: [*Overjoyed.*] Oh thank goodness for that! And what *is* that, Hedda, Hm?

HEDDA: [*In the doorway, looks at him with suppressed scorn.*] My guns—Jørgen!

TESMAN: [*In fear.*] Your guns!

HEDDA: [*With cold eyes.*] General Gabler's guns.

[*She exits left, through the inner room.*]

TESMAN: [*Runs to the doorway, calls after her.*] But Hedda! Good gracious! Hedda, dear! Please don't touch those dangerous things! For my sake, Hedda! Hm?

Act II

The same room at the Tesmans'. The piano has been moved out and replaced by an elegant little writing desk. A small table has been placed near the sofa, left. Most of the flowers have been removed. Mrs. Elvsted's bouquet is on the big table front center. Afternoon.

Hedda, dressed to receive callers, is alone. She is standing near the open French doors loading a revolver. Its mate is lying in an open case on the desk.

HEDDA: [*Looking down into the garden, calls.*] Hello there, Judge! Welcome back!

JUDGE BRACK: [*Off-stage.*] Thanks, Mrs. Tesman!

HEDDA: [*Raises the gun, sights.*] Now I am going to shoot you, Judge Brack!

BRACK: [*Calls off-stage.*] No—no—no! Don't point the gun at me like that!

HEDDA: That's what you get for sneaking in at the back door! [*Fires.*]

BRACK: [*Closer.*] Are you out of your mind—!

HEDDA: Oh dear—did I hit you?

BRACK: [*Still off-stage.*] Stop that nonsense!

HEDDA: Come on in, then.

[*Judge Brack, dressed for dinner, enters left. He carries a light overcoat over his arm.*]

BRACK: Dammit! Do you still fool around with that thing? What are you shooting at, anyway?

HEDDA: Oh—just firing off into blue air.

BRACK: [*Gently but firmly taking the gun away from her.*] With your permission, Mrs. Tesman. [*Looks at it.*] Ah yes, I remember this gun very well. [*Looks around.*] Where is the case? Ah, here we are. [*Puts the gun in the case and closes it.*] That's enough of that silliness for today.

HEDDA: But in the name of heaven, what do you expect me to do with myself?

BRACK: No callers?

HEDDA: [*Closing the French doors.*] Not a soul. All my close friends are still out of town, it seems.

BRACK: And Tesman is out, too, perhaps?

HEDDA: [*By the desk, puts the gun case in a drawer.*] Yes. He took off for the aunts' right after lunch. He didn't expect you so early.

BRACK: I should have thought of that. That was stupid of me.

HEDDA: [*Turns her head, looks at him.*] Why stupid?

BRACK: I would have come a little—sooner.

HEDDA: [*Crossing.*] If you had, you wouldn't have found anybody home. For I have been in my room ever since lunch, changing my clothes.

BRACK: And isn't there the tiniest little opening in the door for negotiations?

HEDDA: You forgot to provide one.

BRACK: Another stupidity.

HEDDA: So we'll have to stay in here. And wait. For I don't think Tesman will be back for some time.

BRACK: By all means. I'll be very patient.

[*Hedda sits on the sofa in the corner. Brack puts his overcoat over the back of the nearest chair and sits down, keeping his hat in his hand. Brief silence. They look at one another.*]

HEDDA: Well?

BRACK: [*In the same tone.*] Well?

HEDDA: I said it first.

BRACK: [*Leans forward a little.*] All right. Let's have a nice little chat, Mrs. Tesman.

HEDDA: [*Leans back.*] Don't you think it's an eternity since last time we talked? I don't count last night and this morning. That was nothing.

BRACK: You mean—just the two of us?

HEDDA: Something like that.

BRACK: There hasn't been a day I haven't wished you were back again.

HEDDA: My feelings, exactly.

BRACK: Yours? Really, Mrs. Tesman? And I have been assuming you were having such a wonderful time.

HEDDA: I'd say!

BRACK: All Tesman's letters said so.

HEDDA: Oh yes, he! He's happy just poking through old collections of books. And copying old parchments—or whatever they are.

BRACK: [*With a touch of malice.*] Well, that's his calling, you know. Partly, anyway.

HEDDA: Yes, so it is. And in that case I suppose—But I! Oh, Judge! You've no idea how bored I've been.

BRACK: [*With sympathy.*] Really? You're serious?

HEDDA: Surely you can understand that? For a whole half year never to see anyone who knows even a little bit about our circle? And talks our language?

BRACK: Yes, I think I would find that trying, too.

HEDDA: And then the most unbearable thing of all—

BRACK: Well?

HEDDA: —everlastingly to be in the company of the same person—

BRACK: [*Nods in agreement.*] Both early and late—yes. I can imagine—at all possible times—

HEDDA: I said everlastingly.

BRACK: All right. Still, it seems to me that with as excellent a person as our Tesman, it ought to be possible—

HEDDA: My dear Judge—Tesman is a specialist.

BRACK: Granted.

HEDDA: And specialists are not at all entertaining travel companions. Not in the long run, at any rate.

BRACK: Not even—the specialist—one happens to love?

HEDDA: Bah! That nauseating word!

BRACK: [*Puzzled.*] Really, now, Mrs. Tesman—?

HEDDA: [*Half laughing, half annoyed.*] You ought to try it some time! Listening to talk about the history of civilization, early and late—

BRACK: Everlastingly—

HEDDA: All right. And then the business about the domestic industry in the Middle Ages—! That's the ghastliest part of it all!

BRACK: [*Looking searchingly at her.*] But in that case—tell me—how I am to explain—?

HEDDA: That Jørgen Tesman and I made a pair of it, you mean?

BRACK: If you want to put it that way—yes.

HEDDA: Come now. Do you really find that so strange?

BRACK: Both yes and no—Mrs. Tesman.

HEDDA: I had danced myself tired, my dear judge. My season was over—[*Gives a slight start.*] No, no—I don't really mean that. Won't think it, either!

BRACK: Nor do you have the slightest reason to, I am sure.

HEDDA: Oh—as far as reason is concerned—[*Looks at him as if trying to read his mind.*] And, after all, Jørgen Tesman must be said to be a most proper young man in all respects.

BRACK: Both proper and substantial. Most certainly.

HEDDA: And one can't say there is anything exactly comical about him. Do you think there is?

BRACK: Comical? No—o. I wouldn't say that—

HEDDA: All right, then. And he is a most assiduous collector. Nobody can deny that. I think it is perfectly possible he may go quite far, after all.

BRACK: [*Looks at her rather uncertainly.*] I assumed that you, like everybody else, were convinced that he will in time become an exceptionally eminent man?

HEDDA: [*With a weary expression.*] Yes, I was. And then, you see—there he was, wanting so desperately to be allowed to provide for me—I don't know why I shouldn't have accepted?

BRACK: No, certainly. From that point of view—

HEDDA: For you know, Judge, that was considerably more than my other admirers were willing to do.

BRACK: [*Laughs.*] Well! Of course I can't answer for all the others. But as far as

I am concerned, I have always had a certain degree of—respect for the bonds of matrimony. You know—as a general proposition, Mrs. Tesman.

HEDDA: [*Lightly.*] Well, I never really counted very heavily on *you*—

BRACK: All I want is a nice, confidential circle, in which I can be of service, both in deed and in counsel. Be allowed to come and go like a true and trusted friend—

HEDDA: You mean, of the master of the house—?

BRACK: [*With a slight bow.*] To be perfectly frank—rather of the mistress. But by all means—the master, too, of course. Do you know, that kind of—shall I say, triangular?—relationship can really be a great comfort to all parties involved.

HEDDA: Yes, many were the times I missed a second travel companion. To be twosome in the compartment—brrr!

BRACK: Fortunately, the wedding trip is over.

HEDDA: [*Shakes her head.*] There's a long journey ahead. I've just arrived at a station on the way.

BRACK: Well, at the station one gets out and moves around a bit, Mrs. Tesman.

HEDDA: I never get out.

BRACK: Really?

HEDDA: No. For there's always someone around, who—

BRACK: [*Laughs.*]—looks at one's legs; is that it?

HEDDA: Exactly.

BRACK: Oh well, really, now—

HEDDA: [*With a silencing gesture.*] I won't have it! Rather stay in my seat—once I'm seated. Twosome and all.

BRACK: But what if a third party were to join the couple?

HEDDA: Well, now—*that* would be something altogether different!

BRACK: A proven, understanding friend—

HEDDA: —entertaining in all sorts of lively ways—

BRACK: —and not at all a specialist!

HEDDA: [*With audible breath.*] Yes, that would indeed be a comfort.

BRACK: [*Hearing the front door open, looking at her.*] The triangle is complete.

HEDDA: [*Half aloud.*] And the train goes on.

[*Tesman, in gray walking suit and soft hat, enters, right. He carries a pile of paperbound books under his arm. Others are stuffed in his pockets.*]

TESMAN: [*Walks up to the table in front of the corner sofa.*] Puuhh—! Quite some load to carry, all this—and in this heat, too. [*Puts the books down.*] I am positively perspiring, Hedda. Well, well. So you're here already, my dear Judge. Hm? And Berte didn't tell me.

BRACK: [*Rises.*] I came through the garden.

HEDDA: What are all those books?

TESMAN: [*Leafing through some of them.*] Just some new publications in my special field.

HEDDA: Special field, hm?

BRACK: Ah yes—professional publications, Mrs. Tesman. [*He and Hedda exchange knowing smiles.*]

HEDDA: Do you still need more books?

TESMAN: Yes, my dear. There is no such thing as having too many books in one's special field. One has to keep up with what is being written and published, you know.

HEDDA: I suppose.

TESMAN: [*Searching among the books.*] And look. Here is Eilert Løvborg's new book, too. [*Offers it to her.*] Want to take a look at it, Hedda? Hm?

HEDDA: No—thanks just the same. Or perhaps later.

TESMAN: I glanced at it on my way home.

BRACK: And what do you think of it? As a specialist yourself?

TESMAN: It is remarkable for its sobriety. He never wrote like that before. [*Gathers up all the books.*] I just want to take these into my study. I am so much looking forward to cutting them open! And then I'll change. [*To Brack.*] I assume there's no rush to be off, is there?

BRACK: Not at all. We have plenty of time.

TESMAN: In that case, I think I'll indulge myself a little. [*On his way out with the books he halts in the doorway and turns.*] That's right, Hedda—Aunt Julle won't be out to see you tonight, after all.

HEDDA: No? Is it that business with the hat, do you think?

TESMAN: Oh, no—not at all. How can you believe a thing like that about Aunt Julle! Just think! No, it's Aunt Rina. She's feeling very poorly.

HEDDA: Isn't she always?

TESMAN: Yes, but it's especially bad today, poor thing.

HEDDA: Well, in that case I suppose she ought to stay home. I shall have to put up with it; that's all.

TESMAN: And you have no idea how perfectly delighted Aunt Julle was, even so. Because of how splendid you look after the trip, Hedda!

HEDDA: [*Half aloud, rising.*] Oh, these everlasting aunts!

TESMAN: Hm?

HEDDA: [*Walks over to the French doors.*] Nothing.

TESMAN: No? All right, Well, excuse me.

[*Exits right, through inner room.*]

BRACK: What is this about a hat?

HEDDA: Oh, something with Miss Tesman this morning. She had put her hat down on the chair over there. [*Looks at him, smiles.*] So I pretended to think it was the maid's.

BRACK: [*Shakes his head.*] But my dear Mrs. Tesman—how could you do a thing like that! And to that excellent old lady, too!

HEDDA: [*Nervously pacing the floor.*] Well, you see—something just takes hold of me at times. And then I can't help myself—[*Throws herself down in the easy chair near the stove.*] Oh I can't explain it even to myself.

BRACK: [*Behind her chair.*] You aren't really happy—that's the trouble.

HEDDA: [*Staring into space.*] I don't know any reason why I should be. Do you?

BRACK: Well, yes—partly because you've got the home you've always wanted.

HEDDA: [*Looks up at him and laughs.*] So you too believe that story about my great desire?

BRACK: You mean, there is nothing to it?

HEDDA: Well, yes; there is *something* to it.

BRACK: Well?

HEDDA: There is this much to it, that last summer I used Tesman to see me home from evening parties.

BRACK: Unfortunately—my route was in quite a different direction.

HEDDA: True. You walked other roads last summer.

BRACK: [*Laughs.*] Shame on you, Mrs. Tesman! So, all right—you and Tesman—?

HEDDA: One evening we passed by here. And Tesman, poor thing, was practically turning himself into knots trying to find something to talk about. So I felt sorry for all that erudition—

BRACK: [*With a doubting smile.*] You did? Hm—

HEDDA: I really did. So, just to help him out of his misery, I happened to say that I'd like to live in this house.

BRACK: Just that?

HEDDA: That was all—*that* evening.

BRACK: But afterwards—?

HEDDA: Yes, my frivolity had consequences, Judge.

BRACK: Unfortunately—that's often the way with frivolities. It happens to all of us, Mrs. Tesman.

HEDDA: Thanks! So in our common enthusiasm for Mr. Secretary Falk's villa Tesman and I found each other, you see! The result was engagement and wedding and honeymoon abroad and all the rest of it. Well, yes, my dear Judge—I've made my bed—I almost said.

BRACK: But this is priceless! And you didn't really care for the house at all?

HEDDA: Certainly not.

BRACK: Not even now? After all, we've set up quite a comfortable home for you here, haven't we?

HEDDA: Oh—it seems to me I smell lavender and rose sachets in all the rooms. But maybe that's a smell Aunt Julle brought with her.

BRACK: [*Laughs.*] My guess is rather the late lamented Secretary's wife.

HEDDA: It smells of mortality, whoever it is. Like corsages—the next day. [*Clasps her hands behind her neck, leans back, looks at him.*] Judge, you have no idea how dreadfully bored I'll be—out here.

BRACK: But don't you think life may hold some task for you, too, Mrs. Tesman?

HEDDA: A task? With any kind of appeal?

BRACK: Preferably that, of course.

HEDDA: Heaven knows what kind of task that might be. There are times when I wonder if—[*Interrupts herself.*] No; I'm sure that wouldn't work, either.

BRACK: Who knows? Tell me.

HEDDA: It has occurred to me that maybe I could get Tesman to enter politics.

BRACK: [*Laughs.*] Tesman! No, really—I must confess that—politics doesn't strike me as being exactly Tesman's line.

HEDDA: I agree. But suppose I were to prevail on him, all the same?

BRACK: What satisfaction could you possibly find in that? If he can't succeed—why do you want him even to try?

HEDDA: Because I am bored, I tell you! [*After a brief pause.*] So you think it's quite out of the question that Tesman could ever become prime minister?

BRACK: Well, you see, Mrs. Tesman—to do that he'd first of all have to be a fairly wealthy man.

HEDDA: [*Getting up, impatiently.*] Yes! There we are! These shabby circumstances I've married into! [*Crosses the floor.*] That's what makes life so mean. So outright ludicrous! For that's what it is, you know.

BRACK: Personally I believe something else is to blame.

HEDDA: What?

BRACK: You've never been through anything that's really stirred you.

HEDDA: Something serious, you mean?

BRACK: If you like. But maybe it's coming now.

HEDDA: [*With a toss of her head.*] You are thinking of that silly old professorship! That's Tesman's business. I refuse to give it a thought.

BRACK: As you wish. But now—to put it in the grand style—now when a solemn challenge of responsibility will be posed? Demands made on you? [*Smiles.*] New demands, Mrs. Tesman.

HEDDA: [*Angry.*] Quiet! You'll never see anything of the kind.

BRACK: [*Cautiously.*] We'll talk about this a year from now—on the outside.

HEDDA: [*Curtly.*] I'm not made for that sort of thing, Judge! No demands for me!

BRACK: But surely you, like most women, are made for a duty, which—

HEDDA: [*Over by the French doors.*] Oh, do be quiet! Often it seems to me there's only one thing in the world that I am made for.

BRACK: [*Coming close.*] And may I ask what that is?

HEDDA: [*Looking out.*] To be bored to death. Now you know. [*Turns, looks toward the inner room, laughs.*] Just as I thought. Here comes the professor.

BRACK: [*Warningly, in a low voice.*] Steady now, Mrs. Tesman!

[*Tesman, dressed for a party, carrying his hat and gloves, enters from the right side of the inner room.*]

TESMAN: Hedda, any word yet from Eilert Løvborg that he isn't coming, hm?

HEDDA: No.

TESMAN: In that case, I wouldn't be a bit surprised if we have him here in a few minutes.

BRACK: You really think he'll come?

TESMAN: I am almost certain he will. For I'm sure it's only idle gossip what you told me this morning.

BRACK: Oh?

TESMAN: Anyway, that's what Aunt Julle said. She doesn't for a moment believe he'll stand in my way. Just think!

BRACK: I'm very glad to hear that.

TESMAN: [*Puts his hat and his gloves down on a chair, right.*] But you must let me wait for him as long as possible.

BRACK: By all means. We have plenty of time. Nobody will arrive at my place before seven—seven-thirty, or so.

TESMAN: And in the meantime we can keep Hedda company. Take our time. Hm?

HEDDA: [*Carrying Brack's hat and coat over to the sofa in the corner.*] And if worst comes to worst, Mr. Løvborg can stay here with me.

BRACK: [*Trying to take the things away from her.*] Let me, Mrs. Tesman—What do you mean—"if worst comes to worst?"

HEDDA: If he doesn't want to go with you and Tesman.

TESMAN: [*Looks dubiously at her.*] But, dearest Hedda—do you think that will quite do? He staying here with you? Hm? Remember, Aunt Julle won't be here.

HEDDA: No, but Mrs. Elvsted will. The three of us will have a cup of tea together.

TESMAN: Oh yes; *that* will be perfectly all right!

BRACK: [*With a smile.*] And perhaps the wiser course of action for him.

HEDDA: What do you mean?

BRACK: Begging your pardon, Mrs. Tesman—you've often enough looked askance at my little stag dinners. It's been your opinion that only men of the firmest principles ought to attend.

HEDDA: I should think Mr. Løvborg is firm-principled enough now. A reformed sinner—

[*Berte appears in door, right.*]

BERTE: Ma'am—there's a gentleman here who asks if—

HEDDA: Show him in, please.

TESMAN: [*Softly.*] I'm sure it's he! Just think!

[*Eilert Løvborg enters right. He is slim, gaunt. Of Tesman's age, but he looks older and somewhat dissipated. Brown hair and beard. Pale, longish face, reddish spots on the cheekbones. Dressed for visiting in elegant, black, brand-new suit. He carries a silk hat and dark gloves in his hand. He remains near the door, makes a quick bow. He appears a little embarrassed.*]

TESMAN: [*Goes over to him, shakes his hand.*] My dear Eilert—at last we meet again!

EILERT LØVBORG: [*Subdued voice.*] Thanks for your note, Jørgen! [*Approaching Hedda.*] Am I allowed to shake your hand, too, Mrs. Tesman?

HEDDA: [*Accepting his proffered hand.*] I am very glad to see you, Mr. Løvborg. [*With a gesture.*] I don't know if you two gentlemen—

LØVBORG: [*With a slight bow.*] Judge Brack, I believe.

BRACK: [*Also bowing slightly.*] Certainly. Some years ago—

TESMAN: [*To Løvborg, both hands on his shoulders.*] And now I want you to feel quite at home here, Eilert! Isn't that right, Hedda? For you plan to stay here in town, I understand. Hm?

LØVBORG: Yes, I do.

TESMAN: Perfectly reasonable. Listen—I just got hold of your new book, but I haven't had a chance to read it yet.

LØVBORG: You may save yourself the trouble.

TESMAN: Why do you say that?

LØVBORG: There's not much to it.

TESMAN: Just think—you saying that!

BRACK: Nevertheless, people seem to have very good things to say about it.

LØVBORG: That's exactly why I wrote it—so everybody would like it.

BRACK: Very wise of you.

TESMAN: Yes, but Eilert—

LØVBORG: For I am trying to rebuild my position. Start all over again.

TESMAN: [*With some embarrassment.*] Yes, I suppose you are, aren't you? Hm?

LØVBORG: [*Smiles, puts his hat down, pulls a parcel out of his pocket.*] When *this* appears—Jørgen Tesman—this you must read. For this is the real thing. This is me.

TESMAN: Oh really? And what is it?

LØVBORG: The continuation.

TESMAN: Continuation? Of what?

LØVBORG: Of this book.

TESMAN: Of the new book?

LØVBORG: Of course.

TESMAN: But Eilert—you've carried the story all the way up to the present!

LØVBORG: So I have. And this is about the future.

TESMAN: The future! But, heavens—we don't know a thing about the future!

LØVBORG: No, we don't. But there are a couple of things to be said about it all the same. [*Unwraps the parcel.*] Here, let me show you—

TESMAN: But that's not your handwriting.

LØVBORG: I have dictated it. [*Leafs through portions of the manuscript.*] It's in two parts. The first is about the forces that will shape the civilization of the future. And the second [*Riffling through more pages.*]—about the course that future civilization will take.

TESMAN: How remarkable! It would never occur to me to write anything like that.

HEDDA: [*Over by the French doors, her fingers drumming the pane.*] Hmm—No—

LØVBORG: [*Replacing the manuscript in its wrappings and putting it down on the table.*] I brought it along, for I thought maybe I'd read parts of it aloud to you this evening.

TESMAN: That's very good of you, Eilert. But this evening—? [*Looks at Brack.*] I'm not quite sure how to arrange that—

LØVBORG: Some other time, then. There's no hurry.

BRACK: You see, Mr. Løvborg, there's a little get-together over at my house tonight. Mainly for Tesman, you know—

LØVBORG: [*Looking for his hat.*] In that case, I certainly won't—

BRACK: No, listen. Won't you do me the pleasure to join us?

LØVBORG: [*Firmly.*] No, I won't. But thanks all the same.

BRACK: Oh come on! Why don't you do that? We'll be a small, select circle. And I think I can promise you a fairly lively evening, as Hed—as Mrs. Tesman would say.

LØVBORG: I don't doubt that. Nevertheless—

BRACK: And you may bring your manuscript along and read aloud to Tesman over at my house. I have plenty of room.

TESMAN: Just think, Eilert! Wouldn't that be nice, hm?

HEDDA: [*Intervening.*] But can't you see that Mr. Løvborg doesn't want to? I'm sure he would rather stay here and have supper with me.

LØVBORG: [*Looks at her.*] With you, Mrs. Tesman?

HEDDA: And with Mrs. Elvsted.

LØVBORG: Oh—! [*Casually.*] I ran into her at noon today.

HEDDA: Oh? Well she'll be here tonight. So you see your presence is really required, Mr. Løvborg. Otherwise she won't have anybody to see her home.

LØVBORG: True. All right, then, Mrs. Tesman—I'll stay, thank you.

HEDDA: Good. I'll just tell the maid. [*She rings for Berte over by the door, right.*]

[*Berte appears just off-stage. Hedda talks with her in a low voice, points toward the inner room. Berte nods and exits.*]

TESMAN: [*While Hedda and Berte are talking, to Løvborg.*] Tell me, Eilert—is it this new subject—about the future— is that what you plan to lecture on?

LØVBORG: Yes.

TESMAN: For the bookseller told me you have announced a lecture series for this fall.

LØVBORG: Yes. I have. I hope you won't mind too much.

TESMAN: Of course not! But—

LØVBORG: For of course I realized it is rather awkward for you.

TESMAN: [*Unhappily.*] Oh well—I certainly can't expect—that just for my sake—

LØVBORG: But I will wait till you receive your appointment.

TESMAN: Wait? But—but—but—you mean you aren't going to compete with me? Hm?

LØVBORG: No. Just triumph over you. In people's opinion.

TESMAN: Oh, for goodness' sake! Then Aunt Julle was right, after all! I knew it all the time. Hedda! Do you hear that! Just think—Eilert Løvborg isn't going to stand in our way after all.

HEDDA: [*Tersely.*] Our! I have nothing to do with this. [*She walks into the inner room, where Berte is bringing in a tray with decanters and glasses. Hedda nods her approval and comes forward again.*]

TESMAN: [*During the foregoing business.*] How about that, Judge? What do you say to this? Hm?

BRACK: I say that moral victory and all that—hm—may be glorious enough and beautiful enough—

TESMAN: Oh, I agree. All the same—

HEDDA: [*Looks at Tesman with a cold smile.*] You look as if the lightning had hit you.

TESMAN: Well, I am—pretty much—I really believe—

BRACK: After all, Mrs. Tesman, that was quite a thunderstorm that just passed over.

HEDDA: [*Points to the inner room.*] How about a glass of cold punch, gentlemen?

BRACK: [*Looks at his watch.*] A stirrup cup. Not a bad idea.

TESMAN: Splendid, Hedda. Perfectly splendid. In such a light-hearted mood as I am now—

HEDDA: Please. You, too, Mr. Løvborg.

LØVBORG: [*With a gesture of refusal.*] No, thanks. Really. Nothing for me.

BRACK: Good heavens, man! Cold punch isn't poison, you know!

LØVBORG: Perhaps not for everybody.

HEDDA: I'll keep Mr. Løvborg company in the meantime.

TESMAN: All right, Hedda. You do that.

> [*He and Brack go into the inner room, sit down, drink punch, smoke cigarettes, and engage in lively conversation during the next scene. Eilert Løvborg remains standing near the stove. Hedda walks over to the desk.*]

HEDDA: [*Her voice a little louder than usual.*] I'll show you some pictures, if you like. You see—Tesman and I, we took a trip through Tyrol on our way back.

> [*She brings an album over to the table by the sofa. She sits down in the far corner of the sofa. Løvborg approaches, stops, looks at her. He takes a chair and sits down at her left, his back toward the inner room.*]

HEDDA: [*Opens the album.*] Do you see these mountains, Mr. Løvborg? They are the Ortler group. Tesman has written their name below. Here it is: "The Ortler group near Meran."

LØVBORG: [*Has looked steadily at her all this time. Says slowly.*] Hedda—Gabler!

HEDDA: [*With a quick glance sideways.*] Not that! Shhh!

LØVBORG: [*Again.*] Hedda Gabler!

HEDDA: [*Looking at the album.*] Yes, that used to be my name. When—when we two knew each other.

LØVBORG: And so from now on—for the whole rest of my life—I must get used to never again saying Hedda Gabler.

HEDDA: [*Still occupied with the album.*] Yes, you must. And you might as well start right now. The sooner the better, I think.

LØVBORG: [*With indignation.*] Hedda Gabler married? And married to—Jørgen Tesman!

HEDDA: Yes—that's the way it goes.

LØVBORG: Oh, Hedda, Hedda—how could you throw yourself away like that!

HEDDA: [*With a fierce glance at him.*] What's this? I won't have any of that!

LØVBORG: What do you mean?

> [*Tesman enters from the inner room.*]

HEDDA: [*Hears him coming and remarks casually.*] And this here, Mr. Løvborg, this is from somewhere in the Ampezzo valley. Just look at those peaks over there. [*With a kindly look at Tesman.*] What did you say those peaks were called, dear?

TESMAN: Let me see. Oh, they—they are the Dolomites.

HEDDA: Right. Those are the Dolomites, Mr. Løvborg.

TESMAN: Hedda, I thought I'd just ask you if you don't want me to bring you some
   punch, after all? For you, anyway? Hm?

HEDDA: Well, yes; thanks. And a couple of cookies, maybe.

TESMAN: No cigarettes?

HEDDA: No.

TESMAN: All right.

   *[He returns to the inner room, then turns right. Brack is in there, keeping an
   eye on Hedda and Løvborg from time to time.]*

LØVBORG: *[Still in a low voice.]* Answer me, Hedda. How could you do a thing like
   that?

HEDDA: *[Apparently engrossed in the album.]* If you keep on using my first name I
   won't talk to you.

LØVBORG: Not even when we're alone?

HEDDA: No. You may think it, but you must not say it.

LØVBORG: I see. It offends your love for—Jørgen Tesman.

HEDDA: *[Glances at him, smiles.]* Love? That's a good one!

LØVBORG: Not love, then.

HEDDA: But no infidelities, either! I won't have it.

LØVBORG: Hedda—answer me just this one thing—

HEDDA: Shhh!

   [Tesman enters with a tray from the inner room.]

TESMAN: Here! Here are the goodies. *[Puts the tray down.]*

HEDDA: Why don't you get Berte to do it?

TESMAN: *[Pouring punch.]* Because I think it's so much fun waiting on you, Hedda.

HEDDA: But you've filled both glasses. And Mr. Løvborg didn't want any—

TESMAN: I know, but Mrs. Elvsted will soon be here, won't she?

HEDDA: That's right. So she will.

TESMAN: Had you forgotten about her? Hm?

HEDDA: We've been so busy looking at this. *[Shows him a picture.]* Remember this
   little village?

TESMAN: That's the one just below the Brenner Pass, isn't it? We spent the night
   there—

HEDDA: —and ran into that lively crowd of summer guests.

TESMAN: Right! Just think—if we only could have had you with us, Eilert! Oh
   well.

   *[Returns to the inner room, sits down, and resumes his conversation with
   Brack.]*

LØVBORG: Just tell me this, Hedda—

HEDDA: What?

LØVBORG: Wasn't there love in your feelings for me, either? Not a touch—not a
   shimmer of love? Wasn't there?

HEDDA: I wonder. To me, we seemed to be simply two good comrades. Two close
   friends. *[Smiles.]* You, particularly, were very frank.

LØVBORG: You wanted it that way.

HEDDA: And yet—when I think back upon it now, there was something beautiful, something thrilling, something brave, I think, about the secret frankness—that comradeship that not a single soul so much as suspected.

LØVBORG: Yes, wasn't there, Hedda? Wasn't there? When I called on your father in the afternoons—And the General sat by the window with his newspapers—his back turned—

HEDDA: And we two on the sofa in the corner—

LØVBORG: —always with the same illustrated magazine—

HEDDA: —for want of an album, yes—

LØVBORG: Yes, Hedda—and then when I confessed to you—! Told you all about myself, things the others didn't know. Sat and told you about all my orgies by day and night. Dissipation day in and day out! Oh, Hedda—what sort of power in you was it that forced me to tell you things like that?

HEDDA: You think there was some power in me?

LØVBORG: How else can I explain it? And all those veiled questions you asked—

HEDDA: —which you understood so perfectly well—

LØVBORG: That you could ask such questions as that! With such complete frankness!

HEDDA: *Veiled,* if you please.

LØVBORG: But frankly all the same. All about—that!

HEDDA: And to think that you answered, Mr. Løvborg!

LØVBORG: Yes, that's just what I can't understand—now, afterwards. But tell me, Hedda; wasn't love at the bottom of our whole relationship? Didn't you feel some kind of urge to—purify me—when I came to you in confession? Wasn't that it?

HEDDA: No, not quite.

LØVBORG: Then what made you do it?

HEDDA: Do you find it so very strange that a young girl—when she can do so, without anyone knowing—

LØVBORG: Yes—?

HEDDA: —that she wants to take a peek into a world which—

LØVBORG: —which—?

HEDDA: —she is not supposed to know anything about?

LØVBORG: So that was it!

HEDDA: That, too. That, too—I think—

LØVBORG: Companionship in the lust for life. But why couldn't *that* at least have continued?

HEDDA: That was your own fault.

LØVBORG: You were the one who broke off.

HEDDA: Yes, when reality threatened to enter our relationship. Shame on you, Eilert Løvborg! How could you want to do a thing like that to your frank and trusting comrade!

LØVBORG: [*Clenching his hands.*] Oh, why didn't you do it! Why didn't you shoot me down, as you said you would!

HEDDA: Because I'm scared of scandal.

LØVBORG: Yes, Hedda. You are really a coward.

HEDDA: A terrible coward. [*Changing her tone.*] But that was your good luck, wasn't it? And now the Elvsteds have healed your broken heart very nicely.

LØVBORG: I know what Thea has told you.

HEDDA: Perhaps you have told her about us?

LØVBORG: Not a word. She is too stupid to understand.

HEDDA: Stupid?

LØVBORG: In things like that.

HEDDA: And I'm a coward. [*Leans forward, without looking in his eyes, whispers.*] But now I am going to confess something to *you*.

LØVBORG: [*Tense.*] What?

HEDDA: That I didn't dare to shoot—

LØVBORG: Yes—?

HEDDA: —that was not the worst of my cowardice that night.

LØVBORG: [*Looks at her a moment, understands, whispers passionately.*] Oh, Hedda! Hedda Gabler! Now I being to see what was behind the companionship! You and I! So it *was* your lust for life—!

HEDDA: [*In a low voice, with an angry glance.*] Take care! Don't you believe that!

[*Darkness is falling. The door, right, is opened, and Berte enters.*]

HEDDA: [*Closing the album, calls out, smiling.*] At last! So there you are, dearest Thea! Come in!

[*Mrs. Elvsted enters. She is dressed for a party. Berte exits, closing the door behind her.*]

HEDDA: [*In the sofa, reaching out for Mrs. Elvsted.*] Sweetest Thea, you have no idea how I've waited for you.

[*In passing, Mrs. Elvsted exchanges quick greetings with Tesman and Brack in the inner room. She walks up to the table and shakes Hedda's hand. Eilert Løvborg rises. He and Mrs. Elvsted greet one another with a silent nod.*]

MRS. ELVSTED: Maybe I ought to go in and say hello to your husband?

HEDDA: No, never mind that. Let them be. They're soon leaving, anyway.

MRS. ELVSTED: Leaving?

HEDDA: They're off to a spree.

MRS. ELVSTED: [*Quickly, to Løvborg.*] Not you?

LØVBORG: No.

HEDDA: Mr. Løvborg stays here with us.

MRS. ELVSTED: [*Pulls up a chair, is about to sit down next to Løvborg.*] Oh, how wonderful it is to be here!

HEDDA: Oh no, little Thea. Not that. Not there. Over here by me, please. I want to be in the middle.

MRS. ELVSTED: Just as you like. [*She walks in front of the table and seats herself on the sofa, on Hedda's right. Løvborg sits down again on his chair.*]

LØVBORG: [*After a brief pause, to Hedda.*] Isn't she lovely to look at?

HEDDA: [*Gently stroking her hair.*] Just to look at?

LØVBORG: Yes. For you see—she and I—we are real comrades. We have absolute faith in one another. And we can talk together in full freedom.

HEDDA: Unveiled, Mr. Løvborg?

LØVBORG: Well—

MRS. ELVSTED: [*In a low voice, clinging to Hedda.*] Oh, I am so happy, Hedda! For just think—he says I have inspired him, too!

HEDDA: [*Looks at her with a smile.*] No, really! He says that?

LØVBORG: And she has such courage, Mrs. Tesman! Such courage of action.

MRS. ELVSTED: Oh, my God—courage—! I!

LØVBORG: Infinite courage—when it concerns the comrade.

HEDDA: Yes, courage—if one only had that.

LØVBORG: What then?

HEDDA: Then maybe life would be tolerable, after all. [*Changing her tone.*] But now, dearest Thea, you want a glass of nice, cold punch.

MRS. ELVSTED: No, thanks. I never drink things like that.

HEDDA: Then what about you, Mr. Løvborg?

LØVBORG: Thanks. Nothing for me, either.

MRS. ELVSTED: No, nothing for him, either.

HEDDA: [*Looks firmly at him.*] If I say so?

LØVBORG: Makes no difference.

HEDDA: [*Laughs.*] Poor me! So I have no power over you at all. Is that it?

LØVBORG: Not in that respect.

HEDDA: Seriously, though; I really think you should. For your own sake.

MRS. ELVSTED: No, but Hedda—!

LØVBORG: Why so?

HEDDA: Or rather for people's sake.

LØVBORG: Oh?

HEDDA: For else they might think you don't really trust yourself—That you lack self-confidence—

MRS. ELVSTED: [*Softly.*] Don't, Hedda!

LØVBORG: People may think whatever they like for all I care—for the time being.

MRS. ELVSTED: [*Happy.*] Exactly!

HEDDA: I could easily tell from watching Judge Brack just now.

LØVBORG: Tell what?

HEDDA: He smiled so contemptuously when you didn't dare to join them in there.

LØVBORG: Didn't I dare to! It's just that I'd much rather stay here and talk with you!

MRS. ELVSTED: But that's only natural, Hedda.

HEDDA: The Judge had no way of knowing that. And I also noticed he smiled and looked at Tesman when you didn't dare to go to his silly old party.

LØVBORG: Didn't dare! Are you saying I didn't dare?

HEDDA: *I* am not. But that's how Judge Brack understood it.

LØVBORG: Let him.

HEDDA: So you're not going?

LØVBORG: I'm staying here with you and Thea.

MRS. ELVSTED: Of course, he is, Hedda!

HEDDA: [*Smiles, nods approvingly.*] That's what I call firm foundations. Principled forever; that's the way a man ought to be! [*Turning to Mrs. Elvsted, stroking her cheek.*] What did I tell you this morning—when you came here, quite beside yourself—?

LØVBORG: [*Puzzled.*] Beside herself?

MRS. ELVSTED: [*In terror.*] Hedda—Hedda—don't!

HEDDA: Now do you see? There was no need at all for that mortal fear of yours—[*Interrupting herself.*] There, now! Now we can all three relax and enjoy ourselves.

LØVBORG: [*Startled.*] What's all this, Mrs. Tesman?

MRS. ELVSTED: Oh, God, Hedda—what are you saying? What are you doing?

HEDDA: Please be quiet. That horrible Judge is looking at you.

LØVBORG: In mortal fear? So that's it. For my sake.

MRS. ELVSTED: [*Softly, wailing.*] Oh, Hedda—if you only knew how utterly miserable you have made me!

LØVBORG: [*Stares at her for a moment. His face is distorted.*] So that was the comrade's happy confidence in me!

MRS. ELVSTED: Oh, my dearest friend—listen to me first—!

LØVBORG: [*Picks up one of the glasses of punch, raises it, says hoarsely.*] Here's to you, Thea! [*Empties the glass, puts it down, picks up the other one.*]

MRS. ELVSTED: [*Softly.*] Hedda, Hedda—why did you want to do this?

HEDDA: Want to! I! Are you mad?

LØVBORG: And here's to you, too, Mrs. Tesman! Thanks for telling me the truth. Long live the truth! [*He drains the glass and is about to fill it again.*]

HEDDA: [*Restrains him.*] That's enough for now. Remember you are going to a party.

MRS. ELVSTED: No, no, no!

HEDDA: Shhh! They are looking at you.

LØVBORG: [*Puts his glass down.*] Listen, Thea—tell me the truth—

MRS. ELVSTED: I will, I will!

LØVBORG: Did your husband know you were coming after me?

MRS. ELVSTED: [*Wringing her hands.*] Oh, Hedda—do you hear what he's asking?

LØVBORG: Did the two of you agree that you were to come here and look after me? Maybe it was his idea, even? Did he send you? Ah, I know what it was—he missed me in the office, didn't he? Or was it at the card table?

MRS. ELVSTED: [*Softly, in agony.*] Oh, Løvborg, Løvborg!

LØVBORG: [*Grabs a glass and is about to fill it.*] Here's to the old Commissioner, too!

HEDDA: [*Stops him.*] No more now. You're supposed to read aloud for Tesman tonight—remember?

LØVBORG: [*Calm, again, puts the glass down.*] This was silly of me, Thea. I'm sorry. To take it this way. Please, don't be angry with me. You'll see—both you and all those others—that even if I have been down—! With your help, Thea—dear comrade.

MRS. ELVSTED: [*Beaming.*] Oh, thank God—!

> [*In the meantime, Brack has looked at his watch. He and Tesman get up and come forward.*]

BRACK: [*Picking up his coat and hat.*] Well, Mrs. Tesman; our time is up.

HEDDA: I suppose it is.

LØVBORG: [*Rising.*] Mine, too, Judge.

MRS. ELVSTED: [*Softly, pleadingly.*] Oh, Løvborg—don't do it!

HEDDA: [*Pinches her arm.*] They can hear you!

MRS. ELVSTED: [*With a soft exclamation.*] Ouch!

LØVBORG: [*To Brack.*] You were good enough to ask me—

BRACK: So you're coming, after all?

LØVBORG: If I may.

BRACK: I'm delighted.

LØVBORG: [*Picks up his manuscript and says to Tesman.*] For there are a couple of things here I'd like to show you before I send it off.

TESMAN: Just think! Isn't that nice! But—dearest Hedda—? In that case, how are you going to get Mrs. Elvsted home? Hm?

HEDDA: We'll manage some how.

LØVBORG: [*Looking at the two women.*] Mrs. Elvsted? I'll be back to pick her up, of course. [*Coming closer.*] About ten o'clock, Mrs. Tesman? Is that convenient?

HEDDA: Certainly. That will be fine.

TESMAN: Then everything is nice and settled. But don't expect me that early, Hedda.

HEDDA: You just stay as long as—as long as you want, dear.

MRS. ELVSTED: [*In secret fear.*] I'll be waiting for you here, then, Mr. Løvborg.

LØVBORG: [*Hat in hand.*] Of course, Mrs. Elvsted.

BRACK: All aboard the pleasure train, gentlemen! I hope we'll have a lively evening—as a certain fair lady would say.

HEDDA: Ah—if only the fair lady could be present. Invisible.

BRACK: Why invisible?

HEDDA: To listen to some of your unadulterated liveliness, Judge.

BRACK: [*Laughs.*] I shouldn't advise the fair lady to do that!

TESMAN: [*Also laughing.*] You're a good one, Hedda! Just think!

BRACK: Well—good night, ladies!

LØVBORG: [*With a bow.*] Till about ten, then.

> [*Brack, Løvborg, and Tesman go out, right. At the same time Berte enters from the inner room with a lighted lamp, which she places on the table, front center. She goes out the same way.*]

MRS. ELVSTED: [*Has risen and paces restlessly up and down.*] Hedda, Hedda—how do you think all this will end?

HEDDA: At ten o'clock he'll be here. I see him already. With vine leaves in his hair. Flushed and confident.

MRS. ELVSTED: I only hope you're right.

HEDDA: For then, you see, he'll have mastered himself. And be a free man for all the days of his life.

MRS. ELVSTED: Dear God—how I hope you are right! That he comes back like that.

HEDDA: That is the way he will come. Not any other way. [*Rises and goes closer to Mrs. Elvsted.*] You may doubt as long as you like. I believe in him. And now we'll see—

MRS. ELVSTED: There is something behind all this, Hedda. Some hidden purpose.

HEDDA: Yes, there is! For once in my life I want to have power over a human destiny.

MRS. ELVSTED: But don't you already?

HEDDA: I don't and I never have.

MRS. ELVSTED: But your husband—?

HEDDA: You think that's worth the trouble? Of, if you knew how poor I am! And you got to be so rich! [*Embraces her passionately.*] I think I'll have to burn your hair off, after all!

MRS. ELVSTED: Let me go! Let me go! You scare me, Hedda!

BERTE: [*In the doorway.*] Supper is served, ma'am.

HEDDA: Good. We're coming.

MRS. ELVSTED: No, no, no! I'd rather go home by myself! Right now!

HEDDA: Nonsense! You'll have your cup of tea first, you little silly. And then—at ten o'clock—Eilert Løvborg comes—with vine leaves in his hair! [*She almost pulls Mrs. Elvsted toward the doorway.*]

Act III

The same room at the Tesmans'. The doorway and the French windows both have their portieres closed. The lamp, turned half down, is still on the table. The stove is open. Some dying embers can be seen.

    Mrs. Elvsted, wrapped in a big shawl, is in the easy chair near the stove, her feet on a footstool. Hedda, also dressed, is lying on the sofa, covered by a blanket.

MRS. ELVSTED: [*After a while suddenly sits up, listens anxiously; then she wearily sinks back in her chair, whimpers softly.*] Oh my God, my God—not yet!

    [*Berte enters cautiously, right, carrying a letter.*]

MRS. ELVSTED: [*Turns and whispers tensely.*] Well—has anybody been here?

BERTE: [*In a low voice.*] Yes. Just now there was a girl with this letter.

MRS. ELVSTED: [*Quickly, reaches for it.*] A letter! Give it to me!

BERTE: No, ma'am. It's for the Doctor.

MRS. ELVSTED: I see.

BERTE: Miss Tesman's maid brought it. I'll leave it here on the table.

MRS. ELVSTED: All right.

BERTE: [*Puts the letter down.*] I'd better put out the lamp. It just reeks.

MRS. ELVSTED: Yes, do that. It must be daylight soon, anyway.

BERTE: [*Putting out the lamp.*] It's light already, ma'am.

MRS. ELVSTED: Light already! And still not back!

BERTE: No, so help us. Not that I didn't expect as much—

MRS. ELVSTED: You did?

BERTE: Yes, when I saw a certain character was back in town. Taking off with them. We sure heard enough about him in the old days!

MRS. ELVSTED: Not so loud. You are waking up Mrs. Tesman.

BERTE: [Looks toward the sofa, sighs.] God forbid!—Let her sleep, poor thing. Do you want me to get the fire going again?

MRS. ELVSTED: Not on my account, thank you.

BERTE: All right; I won't then. [Exits quietly right.]

HEDDA: [Awakened by the closing door.] What's that?

MRS. ELVSTED: Just the maid.

HEDDA: [Looks around.] Why in here—? Oh, I remember! [Sits up, rubs her eyes, stretches.] What time is it, Thea?

MRS. ELVSTED: [Looks at her watch.] Past seven.

HEDDA: When did Tesman get home?

MRS. ELVSTED: He didn't.

HEDDA: Not home yet!

MRS. ELVSTED: [Getting up.] Nobody's come.

HEDDA: And we who waited till four!

MRS. ELVSTED: [Wringing her hands.] And how we waited!

HEDDA: [Her hand covering a yawn.] We—ll. We could have saved ourselves that trouble.

MRS. ELVSTED: Did you get any sleep at all?

HEDDA: Yes, I slept pretty well, I think. Didn't you?

MRS. ELVSTED: Not a wink. I just couldn't, Hedda! It was just impossible.

HEDDA: [Rises, walks over to her.] Well, now! There's nothing to worry about, for heaven's sake. I know exactly what's happened.

MRS. ELVSTED: Then tell me please. Where do you think they are?

HEDDA: Well, first of all, I'm sure they were terribly late leaving the Judge's—

MRS. ELVSTED: Dear yes. I'm sure you're right. Still—

HEDDA: —and so Tesman didn't want to wake us up in the middle of the night. [Laughs.] Maybe he didn't want us to see him, either—after a party like that.

MRS. ELVSTED: But where do you think he has gone?

HEDDA: To the aunts', of course. His old room is still there, all ready for him.

MRS. ELVSTED: No, he can't be there. Just a few minutes ago there came a letter for him from Miss Tesman. It's over there.

HEDDA: Oh? [Looks at the envelope.] So it is—Auntie Julle herself. In that case, I suppose he's still at Brack's. And there's Eilert Løvborg, too—reading aloud, with vine leaves in his hair.

MRS. ELVSTED: Oh Hedda—you're only saying things you don't believe yourself.

HEDDA: My, what a little imbecile you really are, Thea!

MRS. ELVSTED: Yes, I suppose I am.

HEDDA: And you look dead tired, too.

MRS. ELVSTED: I am dead tired.

HEDDA: Why don't you do as I say. Go into my room and lie down.

MRS. ELVSTED: No, no—I wouldn't be able to go to sleep, anyway.

HEDDA: Of course, you would.

MRS. ELVSTED: And your husband is bound to be home any minute now. And I have to know right away.

HEDDA: I'll let you know as soon as he gets here.

MRS. ELVSTED: You promise me that, Hedda?

HEDDA: I do. You just go to sleep.

MRS. ELVSTED: Thanks. At least I'll try. [*Exits through inner room.*]

[*Hedda goes to the French doors, opens the portieres. The room is now in full daylight. She picks up a little hand mirror from the desk, looks at herself, smooths her hair. Walks over to door, rings the bell for the maid. Berte presently appears.*]

BERTE: You want something, ma'am?

HEDDA: Yes. You'll have to start the fire again. I'm cold.

BERTE: Yes, ma'am! I'll get it warm in no time. [*Rakes the embers together and puts in another piece of wood. Then she suddenly listens.*] There's the doorbell, ma'am.

HEDDA: All right. See who it is. I'll take care of the stove myself.

BERTE: You'll have a nice blaze going in a minute. [*Exits right.*]

[*Hedda kneels on the footstool and puts in more pieces of wood. Presently Tesman enters, right. He looks tired and somber. He tiptoes toward the doorway and is about to disappear between the portieres.*]

HEDDA: [*By the stove, without looking up.*] Good morning.

TESMAN: [*Turning.*] Hedda! [*Comes closer.*] For heaven's sake—you up already! Hm?

HEDDA: Yes, I got up very early this morning.

TESMAN: And I was so sure you'd still be sound asleep! Just think!

HEDDA: Not so loud. Mrs. Elvsted is asleep in my room.

TESMAN: Mrs. Elvsted stayed here all night?

HEDDA: Yes. Nobody came for her, you know.

TESMAN: No, I suppose—

HEDDA: [*Closes the stove, rises.*] Well, did you have a good time at the Judge's?

TESMAN: Were you worried about me? Hm?

HEDDA: I'd never dream of worrying about you. I asked if you had a good time.

TESMAN: Yes, indeed. Nice for a change, anyway. But I think I liked it best early in the evening. For then Eilert read to me. Just think—we were more than an hour early! And Brack, of course, had things to see to. So Eilert read.

HEDDA: [*Sits down at the right side of the table.*] So? Tell me all about it.

TESMAN: [*Sits down on an ottoman near the stove.*] Oh Hedda, you'll never believe what a book that will be! It must be just the most remarkable thing ever written! Just think!

HEDDA: Yes, but I don't really care about that—

TESMAN: I must tell you, Hedda—I have a confession to make. As he was reading—something ugly came over me—

HEDDA: Ugly?

TESMAN: I sat there envying Eilert for being able to write like that! Just think, Hedda!

HEDDA: All right. I'm thinking!

TESMAN: And yet, with all his gifts—he's incorrigible, after all.

HEDDA: I suppose you mean he has more courage for life than the rest of you?

TESMAN: No, no—I don't mean that. I mean he's incapable of exercising moderation in his pleasures.

HEDDA: What happened—in the end?

TESMAN: Well—I would call it a bacchanal, Hedda.

HEDDA: Did he have vine leaves in his hair?

TESMAN: Vine leaves? No, I didn't notice any vine leaves. But he gave a long, muddled speech in honor of the woman who had inspired him in his work. Those were his words.

HEDDA: Did he say her name?

TESMAN: No, he didn't. But I'm sure it must be Mrs. Elvsted. You just wait and see if I'm not right!

HEDDA: And where did you and he part company?

TESMAN: On the way back to town. We left—the last of us did—at the same time. And Brack came along, too, to get some fresh air. Then we decided we'd better see Eilert home. You see, he had had altogether too much to drink!

HEDDA: I can imagine.

TESMAN: But then the strangest thing of all happened, Hedda! Or maybe I should say the saddest. I'm almost ashamed—on Eilert's behalf—even talking about it.

HEDDA: Well—?

TESMAN: You see, on the way back I happened to be behind the others a little. Just for a minute or two—you know—

HEDDA: All right, all right—!

TESMAN: And when I hurried to catch up with them, can you guess what I found by the roadside? Hm?

HEDDA: How can I possibly—?

TESMAN: You mustn't tell this is to a living soul, Hedda! Do you hear! Promise me that, for Eilert's sake. [*Pulls a parcel out of his coat pocket.*] Just think—I found this!

HEDDA: Isn't that what he had with him here yesterday?

TESMAN: Yes! It's his whole, precious, irreplaceable manuscript! And he had dropped it—just like that! Without even noticing! Just think, Hedda! Isn't that awfully sad?

HEDDA: But why didn't you give it back to him?

TESMAN: In the condition he was in! Dear—I just didn't dare to.

HEDDA: And you didn't tell any of the others that you had found it, either?

TESMAN: Of course not. I didn't want to, for Eilert's sake—don't you see?

HEDDA: So nobody knows that you have Eilert Løvborg's papers?

TESMAN: Nobody. And nobody must know, either.

HEDDA: And what did you and he talk about afterwards?

TESMAN: I didn't have a chance to talk to him at all after that. For when we came into town, he and a couple of the others simply vanished. Just think!

HEDDA: Oh? I expect they took him home.

TESMAN: I suppose that must be it. And Brack took off on his own, too.

HEDDA: And what have you been doing with yourself since then?

TESMAN: Well, you see, I and some of the others went home with one of the younger fellows and had a cup of early morning coffee. Or night coffee maybe, rather. Hm? And now, after I've rested a bit and poor Eilert's had some sleep, I'll take this back to him.

HEDDA: [*Reaches for the parcel.*] No—don't do that! Not right away, I mean. Let me look at it first.

TESMAN: Dearest Hedda—honestly, I just don't dare to.

HEDDA: Don't you dare to?

TESMAN: No, for I'm sure you realize how utterly desperate he'll be when he wakes up and finds that the manuscript is gone. For he hasn't got a copy, you know. He said so himself.

HEDDA: [*Looks searchingly at him.*] But can't a thing like that be written over again?

TESMAN: Hardly. I really don't think so. For, you see—the inspiration—

HEDDA: Yes, I daresay that's the main thing. [*Casually.*] By the way, here's a letter for you.

TESMAN: Imagine!

HEDDA: [*Gives it to him.*] It came early this morning.

TESMAN: It's from Aunt Julle, Hedda! I wonder what it can be. [*Puts the manuscript down on the other ottoman, opens the letter, skims the content, jumps up.*] Oh Hedda! She says here that poor Aunt Rina is dying!

HEDDA: You know we had to expect that.

TESMAN: And if I want to see her again I had better hurry. I'll rush over right away.

HEDDA: [*Suppressing a smile.*] You'll rush?

TESMAN: Dearest Hedda of mine—if only you could bring yourself to come along! Hm?

HEDDA: [*Rises, weary, with an air of refusal.*] No, no. You mustn't ask me that. I don't want to look at death and disease. I want to be free from all that's ugly.

TESMAN: Well, all right—[*Rushing around.*] My hat? My coat? Oh—out here in the hall. I just hope I won't be too late, Hedda. Hm?

HEDDA: Oh I'm sure that if you rush—

[*Berte appears in the door, right.*]

BERTE: Judge Brack is here and wants to know if he may see you.

TESMAN: At this hour! No, no. I can't possibly see him now!

HEDDA: But I can. [*To Berte.*] Tell the Judge please to come in.

[*Berte exits.*]

HEDDA: [*With a quick whisper.*] Tesman! The package! [*She grabs it from the ottoman.*]

TESMAN: Yes! Give it to me!

HEDDA: No, no. I'll hide it for you till later.

> [*She walks over to the desk and sticks the parcel among the books on the shelf. In his hurry Tesman is having difficulties getting his gloves on. Judge Brack enters right.*]

HEDDA: [*Nods to him.*] If you aren't an early bird—

BRACK: Yes, don't you think so? [*To Tesman.*] You're going out, too?

TESMAN: Yes, I must go and see the aunts. Just think, the invalid—she's dying!

BRACK: Oh, I'm terribly sorry! In that case, don't let me keep you. At such a moment—

TESMAN: Yes, I really must run. Goodbye, goodbye. [*Hurries out, right.*]

HEDDA: [*Approaching Brack.*] It appears that things were quite lively last night over at your house.

BRACK: Indeed, Mrs. Tesman—I didn't get to bed at all.

HEDDA: You didn't either?

BRACK: As you see. But tell me—what has Tesman told you about the night's adventures?

HEDDA: Just some tiresome story about having coffee with somebody some-place—

BRACK: I believe I know all about that coffee. Eilert Løvborg wasn't one of them, was he?

HEDDA: No, they had taken him home first.

BRACK: Tesman, too?

HEDDA: No. Some of the others, he said.

BRACK: [*Smiles.*] Jørgen Tesman is really an ingenuous soul, you know.

HEDDA: He certainly is. But why do you say that? Is there something more to all this?

BRACK: Yes, there is.

HEDDA: Well! In that case, why don't we make ourselves comfortable, Judge. You'll tell your story better, too.

> [*She sits down at the left side of the table, Brack near her at the adjacent side.*]

HEDDA: All right?

BRACK: For reasons of my own I wanted to keep track of my guests' movements last night. Or, rather—some of my guests.

HEDDA: Eilert Løvborg was one of them, perhaps?

BRACK: As a matter of fact—he was.

HEDDA: Now you are really making me curious.

BRACK: Do you know where he and a couple of the others spent the rest of the night, Mrs. Tesman?

HEDDA: No—tell me. If it is at all tellable.

BRACK: Oh, certainly it can be told. They turned up at an exceptionally gay early morning gathering.

HEDDA: Of the lively kind?

BRACK: The very liveliest.

HEDDA: A little more about this, Judge.

BRACK: Løvborg had been invited beforehand. I knew all about that. But he had declined. He is a reformed character, you know.

HEDDA: As of his stay with the Elvsteds—yes. But he went after all?

BRACK: Well, yes, you see, Mrs. Tesman—unfortunately, the spirit moved him over at my house last evening.

HEDDA: Yes, I understand he became inspired.

BRACK: Quite violently inspired. And that, I gather, must have changed his mind. You know, we men don't always have as much integrity as we ought to have.

HEDDA: Oh I'm sure you're an exception, Judge Brack. But about Løvborg—?

BRACK: To make a long story short—he ended up at Miss Diana's establishment.

HEDDA: Miss Diana's?

BRACK: She was the hostess at this gathering—a select circle of intimate friends, male and female.

HEDDA: Is she a redhead, by any chance?

BRACK: That's correct.

HEDDA: And a singer—of sorts?

BRACK: Yes—that, too. And a mighty huntress—of men, Mrs. Tesman. You seem to have heard of her. Eilert Løvborg used to be one of her most devoted protectors in his more affluent days.

HEDDA: And how did it all end?

BRACK: Not in a very friendly fashion, apparently. It seems that after the tenderest reception Miss Diana resorted to brute force—

HEDDA: Against Løvborg?

BRACK: Yes. He accused her or her woman friends of having stolen something of his. Said his wallet was gone. And other things, too. In brief, he's supposed to have started a pretty wicked row.

HEDDA: With what results?

BRACK: Nothing less than a general free-for-all—men and women both. Fortunately, the police stepped in—

HEDDA: The police—!

BRACK: Yes. I'm afraid this will be an expensive escapade for Eilert Løvborg, crazy fool that he is.

HEDDA: Well!

BRACK: It appears that he made quite violent objection—struck an officer in the ear and tore his coat. So they had to take him along.

HEDDA: How do you know all this?

BRACK: From the police.

HEDDA: [*Staring straight ahead.*] So that's how it was. No vine leaves in his hair.

BRACK: Vine leaves, Mrs. Tesman?

HEDDA: [*Changing her tone.*] But tell me, Judge Brack—why did you keep such a close watch on Eilert Løvborg?

BRACK: Well—for one thing, it is obviously of some concern to me if he testifies that he came straight from my party.

HEDDA: So you think there will be an investigation?

BRACK: Naturally. But I suppose that doesn't really matter too much. However, as a friend of the house I considered it my duty to give you and Tesman a full account of his night-time exploits.

HEDDA: Yes, but why?

BRACK: Because I very strongly suspect that he intends to use you as a kind of screen.

HEDDA: Really! Why do you think that?

BRACK: Oh, come now, Mrs. Tesman! We can use our eyes, can't we? This Mrs. Elvsted—she isn't leaving town right away, you know.

HEDDA: Well, even if there should be something going on between those two, I'd think there would be plenty of other places they could meet.

BRACK: But no home. After last night, every possible respectable house will once again close its doors to Eilert Løvborg.

HEDDA: And so should mine, you mean?

BRACK: Yes. I admit I would find it more than embarrassing if the gentleman were to become a daily guest here, Mrs. Tesman. If he, as an outsider—a highly dispensable outsider—if he were to intrude himself—

HEDDA: —into the triangle?

BRACK: Precisely. It would amount to homelessness for me.

HEDDA: [Smiling.] Sole cock-o'-the-walk—so, that's your goal, is it, Judge?

BRACK: [Nods slowly, lowers his voice.] Yes. That is my goal. And for that I will fight with every means at my disposal.

HEDDA: [Her smile fading.] You're really a dangerous person, you know—when you come right down to it.

BRACK: You think so?

HEDDA: Yes. I am beginning to think so now. And I must say I am exceedingly glad you don't have any kind of hold on me.

BRACK: [With a noncommital laugh.] Well, well, Mrs. Tesman! Maybe there is something to what you are saying, at that. Who knows what I might do if I did.

HEDDA: Really, now, Judge Brack! Are you threatening me?

BRACK: [Rising.]—Nonsense! For the triangle, you see—is best maintained on a voluntary basis.

HEDDA: My sentiments, exactly.

BRACK: Well, I have said what I came to say. And now I should get back to town. Goodbye, Mrs. Tesman! [Walks toward the French doors.]

HEDDA: [Rises.] You're going through the garden?

BRACK: Yes. For me that's a short cut.

HEDDA: Yes, and then it's a back way.

BRACK: Quite true. I have nothing against back ways. There are times when they are most intriguing.

HEDDA: You mean when real ammunition is used?

BRACK: [Already in the door, laughs back at her.] Oh good heavens! I don't suppose one shoots one's tame roosters!

HEDDA: [Laughs also.] No—not if one has only one—!

[They nod to each other, both still laughing. He leaves. She closes the door behind him. For a few moments she remains by the door, quite serious now, looking into the garden. Then she walks over to the doorway and opens the portieres wide enough to look into the inner room. Walks to the desk, pulls Løvborg's manuscript from the bookshelf and is about to read in it when Berte's voice, very loud, is heard from the hall, right. Hedda turns around, listens. She hurriedly puts the manuscript into the drawer of the desk and puts the key down on its top. Eilert Løvborg, wearing his coat and with his hat in his hand, flings open the door, right. He looks somewhat confused and excited.]

LØVBORG: *[Turned toward the invisible Berte in the hall.]* And I say I must! You can't stop me!

[He closes the door, turns, sees Hedda, immediately controls himself, greets her.]

HEDDA: *[By the desk.]* Well, well, Mr. Løvborg—aren't you a trifle late coming for Thea?

LØVBORG: Or a trifle early for calling on you. I apologize.

HEDDA: How do you know she is still here?

LØVBORG: The people she is staying with told me she's been gone all night.

HEDDA: *[Walks over to the table.]* Did they seem—strange—when they told you that?

LØVBORG: *[Puzzled.]* Strange?

HEDDA: I mean, did they seem to find it a little—unusual?

LØVBORG: *[Suddenly understands.]* Ah, I see what you mean! Of course! I'm dragging her down with me. But as a matter of fact, I didn't notice anything. I suppose Tesman isn't up yet?

HEDDA: I—I don't think so—

LØVBORG: When did he get home?

HEDDA: Very late.

LØVBORG: Did he tell you anything?

HEDDA: Yes, he said you'd all had quite a time over at Brack's.

LØVBORG: Just that?

HEDDA: I think so. But I was so awfully sleepy—

[Mrs. Elvsted enters through portieres in the rear.]

MRS. ELVSTED: *[Toward him.]* Oh, Løvborg! At last!

LØVBORG: Yes, at last. And too late.

MRS. ELVSTED: *[In fear.]* What is too late?

LØVBORG: Everything is too late now. It's all over with me.

MRS. ELVSTED: Oh no, no! Don't say things like that!

LØVBORG: You'll say the same yourself when you hear—

MRS. ELVSTED: I don't want to hear—!

HEDDA: Maybe you'd rather talk with her alone? I'll leave.

LØVBORG: No, stay—you, too. I beg you to.

MRS. ELVSTED: But I don't want to listen, do you hear?

LØVBORG: It isn't last night I want to talk about.

MRS. ELVSTED: What about then?

LØVBORG: We'll have to part, Thea.

MRS. ELVSTED: Part!

HEDDA: [*Involuntarily.*] I knew it!

LØVBORG: For I don't need you any more.

MRS. ELVSTED: And you can stand there and tell me a thing like that! Don't need me! Why can't I help you the way I did before? Aren't we going to keep on working together?

LØVBORG: I don't intend to work any more.

MRS. ELVSTED: [*Giving up.*] What am I going to do with my life, then?

LØVBORG: You'll have to try to live your life as if you'd never known me.

MRS. ELVSTED: But I can't do that!

LØVBORG: Try, Thea. Go back home.

MRS. ELVSTED: [*Agitated.*] Never again! Where you are I want to be! And you can't chase me away just like that. I want to stay right here! Be with you when the book appears.

HEDDA: [*In a tense whisper.*] Ah—yes—the book!

LØVBORG: [*Looks at her.*] My book—and Thea's. For that's what it is.

MRS. ELVSTED: That's what I feel, too. And that's why I have the right to be with you when it comes out. I want to see all the honor and all the fame you'll get. And the joy—I want to share the joy, too.

LØVBORG: Thea, our book is never going to come out.

HEDDA: Ah!

MRS. ELVSTED: It won't!

LØVBORG: *Can't* ever appear.

MRS. ELVSTED: [*With fearful suspicion.*] Løvborg, what have you done with the manuscript?

HEDDA: [*Watching him tensely.*] Yes—what about the manuscript?

MRS. ELVSTED: Where is it?

LØVBORG: Oh Thea—please, don't ask me about that!

MRS. ELVSTED: Yes, yes—I want to be told! I have the right to know—right now!

LØVBORG: All right. I've torn it to pieces.

MRS. ELVSTED: [*Screams.*] Oh, no! No!

HEDDA: [*Involuntarily.*] But that's not—!

LØVBORG: [*Looks at her.*] Not true, you think?

HEDDA: [*Composing herself.*] Well, of course, if you say so. You should know. It just sounds so—so unbelievable.

LØVBORG: All the same, it's true.

MRS. ELVSTED: [*Hands clenched.*] Oh God—oh God, Hedda. He has torn his own work to pieces!

LØVBORG: I have torn my whole life to pieces, so why not my life's work as well?

MRS. ELVSTED: And that's what you did last night?

LØVBORG: Yes, I tell you! In a thousand pieces. And scattered them in the fjord. Far out—where the water is clean and salty. Let them drift there,

with wind and current. Then they'll sink. Deep, deep down. Like me,
Thea.

MRS. ELVSTED: Do you know, Løvborg—this thing you've done to the book—all
the rest of my life I'll think of it as killing a little child.

LØVBORG: You are right. It is like murdering a child.

MRS. ELVSTED: But then, how could you? For the child was mine, too!

HEDDA: [*Almost soundlessly.*] The child—

MRS. ELVSTED: [*With a deep sigh.*] So it's all over. I'll go now, Hedda.

HEDDA: But you aren't leaving town?

MRS. ELVSTED: Oh, I don't know myself what I'll do. There's only darkness before
me.

[*Exits, right.*]

HEDDA: [*Waits for a moment.*] Aren't you going to see her home, Mr. Løvborg?

LØVBORG: I? Through the streets? Letting people see her with me?

HEDDA: Of course, I don't know what else may have happened last night. But is it
really so absolutely irreparable—?

LØVBORG: Last night is not the end of it. That I know. And yet, I don't really care
for that kind of life any more. Not again. She has broken all the courage
for life and all the defiance that was in me.

HEDDA: [*Staring ahead.*] So that sweet little goose has had her hand in a human
destiny. [*Looks at him.*] But that you could be so heartless, even so!

LØVBORG: Don't tell me I was heartless!

HEDDA: To ruin everything that's given her soul and mind meaning for such a
long, long time! You don't call that heartless!

LØVBORG: Hedda—to you I can tell the truth.

HEDDA: The truth?

LØVBORG: But first promise me—give me your word you'll never let Thea know
what I'm going to tell you now.

HEDDA: You have it.

LØVBORG: All right. It isn't true what I just told her.

HEDDA: About the manuscript?

LØVBORG: Yes. I have not torn it up. Not thrown it in the sea, either.

HEDDA: But then—where is it?

LØVBORG: I've destroyed it just the same. Really, I have, Hedda!

HEDDA: I don't understand.

LØVBORG: Thea said that what I had done seemed to her like murdering a child.

HEDDA: Yes—she did.

LØVBORG: But killing a child, that's not the worst thing a father can do to it.

HEDDA: No?

LØVBORG: No. And the worst is what I don't want Thea to know.

HEDDA: What *is* the worst?

LØVBORG: Hedda—suppose a man, say, early in the morning, after a stupid,
drunken night—suppose he comes home to his child's mother and says:
Listen, I've been in such and such a place. I've been here—and I've been
there. And I had our child with me. In all those places. And the child is

lost. Gone. Vanished! I'll be damned if I know where it is. Who's got hold of it—

HEDDA: Yes—but when all is said and done—it is only a book, you know.

LØVBORG: Thea's pure soul was in that book.

HEDDA: I realize that.

LØVBORG: Then you surely also realize that she and I can have no future together.

HEDDA: Where do you go from here?

LØVBORG: Nowhere. Just finish everything off. The sooner the better.

HEDDA: [*A step closer.*] Listen—Eilert Løvborg—Couldn't you make sure it's done beautifully?

LØVBORG: Beautifully? [*Smiles.*] With vine leaves in the hair, as you used to say.

HEDDA: Oh no. I don't believe in vine leaves any more. But still beautifully! For once. Goodbye. Go now. And don't come back.

LØVBORG: Goodbye, Mrs. Tesman. Give my regards to Jørgen Tesman. [*He is about to leave.*]

HEDDA: Wait! I want to give you something—a remembrance. [*Goes to the desk, opens the drawer, takes out the gun case. Returns to Løvborg with one of the revolvers.*]

LØVBORG: The gun? That's the remembrance?

HEDDA: [*Nods slowly.*] Do you recognize it? It was pointed at you once.

LØVBORG: You should have used it then.

HEDDA: Take it! *You* use it.

LØVBORG: [*Pockets the gun.*] Thanks!

HEDDA: And beautifully, Eilert Løvborg! That's all I ask!

LØVBORG: Goodbye, Hedda Gabler.

[*Exits, right.*]

[*Hedda listens by the door for a moment. Then she crosses to the desk, takes out the manuscript, glances inside the cover, pulls some of the pages halfway out and looks at them. Carries the whole manuscript over to the chair by the stove. She sits down with the parcel in her lap. After a moment she opens the stove and then the manuscript.*]

HEDDA: [*Throws a bundle of sheets into the fire, whispers.*] Now I'm burning your child, Thea. You—curlyhead! [*Throws more sheets in.*] Your and Eilert Løvborg's child. [*Throws all the rest of the manuscript into the stove.*] I am burning—I am burning your child.

The same rooms at the Tesmans'. Evening. The front room is dark. The inner room is lighted by the ceiling lamp over the table. Portieres cover the French doors.

Hedda, in black, is walking up and down in the dark of the front room. She goes into the inner room, turning left in the doorway. She is heard playing a few bars on the piano. She reappears and comes forward again. Berte enters from the right side of the inner room. She carries a lighted lamp, which she puts down on the table in front of the corner sofa. Her eyes show signs of weeping; she wears black ribbons on her uniform. She exits quietly, right. Hedda goes over to the French windows, looks between the portieres into the dark. Presently Miss Tesman, in mourning, with hat and veil, enters, right. Hedda walks over to meet her, gives her her hand.

MISS TESMAN: Yes, my dearest Hedda—here you see me in my garb of grief. For now at last my poor sister has fought her fight to the end.

HEDDA: I already know—as you see. Tesman sent word.

MISS TESMAN: Yes, he promised he'd do that. But I thought that to you, Hedda—here in the house of life—I really ought to bring the tidings of death myself.

HEDDA: That is very kind of you.

MISS TESMAN: Ah, but Rina shouldn't have died just now. There should be no mourning in Hedda's house at this time.

HEDDA: [*Changing the topic.*] I understand she had a very quiet end.

MISS TESMAN: Oh so beautiful, so peaceful! She left us so quietly! And then the unspeakable happiness of seeing Jørgen one more time! To say goodbye to him to her heart's content! Isn't he back yet?

HEDDA: No. He wrote I mustn't expect him back very soon. But do sit down.

MISS TESMAN: No—no, thanks, my dear, blessed Hedda. Not that I wouldn't like to. But I don't have much time. I must go back and prepare her as best I can. I want her to look right pretty when she goes into her grave.

HEDDA: Is there anything I can help you with?

MISS TESMAN: I won't have you as much as think of it! That's not for Hedda Tesman to lend a hand to. Or lend thoughts to, either. Not now, of all times!

HEDDA: Oh—thoughts! We can't always control our thoughts—

MISS TESMAN: [*Still preoccupied.*] Ah yes—such is life. At home we're making a shroud for Rina. And here, too, there'll be sewing to do soon, I expect. But of quite different kind, thank God!

[*Tesman, enters, right.*]

HEDDA: So finally you're back!

TESMAN: You here, Aunt Julle? With Hedda? Just think!

MISS TESMAN: I am just about to leave, Jørgen dear. Well—did you do all the things you promised me you'd do?

TESMAN: No, I'm afraid I forgot half of them, Auntie. I'd better run in again tomorrow. I'm all confused today. I can't seem to keep my thoughts together.

MISS TESMAN: But dearest Jørgen—you mustn't take it this way!

TESMAN: Oh, I mustn't? How do you mean?

MISS TESMAN: You ought to be joyful in the midst of your sorrow. Glad for what's happened. The way I am.

TESMAN: Oh yes, of course. You're thinking of Aunt Rina.

HEDDA: You're going to feel lonely now, Miss Tesman.

MISS TESMAN: The first few days, yes. But I hope that won't last long. Dear Rina's little parlor won't be empty for long, if I can help it!

TESMAN: Oh? And who do you want to move in there, hm?

MISS TESMAN: Ah—it's not very hard to find some poor soul who needs nursing and comfort.

HEDDA: And you really want to take on such a burden all over again?

MISS TESMAN: Heavens! God forgive you, child—burden? It has not been a burden to me.

HEDDA: Still—a stranger, who—

MISS TESMAN: Oh, it's easy to make friends with sick people. And I sorely need something to live for, I, too. Well, the Lord be praised, maybe soon there'll be a thing or two an old aunt can turn her hand to here.

HEDDA: Please, don't let our affairs worry you—

TESMAN: Yes, just think—how lovely it would be for the three of us, if only—

HEDDA: If only—?

TESMAN: [*Uneasy.*] Oh, nothing, I daresay it will all work out. Let's hope it will, hm?

MISS TESMAN: Well, well. I can see that you two have something to talk about. [*With a smile.*] And perhaps Hedda has something to tell *you*, Jørgen! Goodbye! I'm going home to Rina, now. [*Turns around in the door.*] Dear, dear—how strange to think—! Now Rina is both with me and with Jochum!

TESMAN: Yes, just think, Aunt Julle! Hm?

[*Miss Tesman exits, right.*]

HEDDA: [*Coldly scrutinizing Tesman.*] I wouldn't be at all surprised if you are not more affected by this death than she is.

TESMAN: Oh, it isn't just Aunt Rina's death, Hedda. It's Eilert I worry about.

HEDDA: [*Quickly.*] Any news about him?

TESMAN: I went over to his room this afternoon to tell him the manuscript is safe.

HEDDA: Well? And didn't you see him?

TESMAN: No. He wasn't home. But I ran into Mrs. Elvsted and she told me he'd been here early this morning.

HEDDA: Yes, right after you'd left.

TESMAN: And he said he'd torn up the manuscript? Did he really say that?

HEDDA: Yes. So he claimed.

TESMAN: But dear God—in that case he really must have been out of his mind! So I assume you didn't give it to him either, hm, Hedda?

HEDDA: No. He didn't get it.

TESMAN: But you told him we had it, of course?

HEDDA: No [*Quickly.*] Did you tell Mrs. Elvsted?

TESMAN: No, I didn't want to. But you ought to have told him, Hedda. Just think—what if he does something rash—something to hurt himself! Give me the manuscript, Hedda! I want to rush down to him with it right this minute. Where is it?

HEDDA: [*Cold, motionless, one arm resting on the chair.*] I haven't got it any more.

TESMAN: You haven't got it! What do you mean by that?

HEDDA: I burned it—the whole thing.

TESMAN: [*Jumps up.*] Burned it! Burned Eilert's book!

HEDDA: Don't shout. The maid might hear you.

TESMAN: Burned it? But good God—no, no, no!—This can't be—!

HEDDA: It is, all the same.

TESMAN: But do you realize what you've done, Hedda? It's illegal! Willful destruction of lost property! You just ask Judge Brack! He'll tell you!

HEDDA: You'd better not talk about this to anyone—the Judge or anybody else.

TESMAN: But how could you do a thing like that! I never heard anything like it! What came over you? What can possibly have been going on in your head? Answer me! Hm?

HEDDA: [Suppresses an almost imperceptible smile.] I did it for your sake, Jørgen.

TESMAN: For my sake!

HEDDA: When you came back this morning and told me he had read aloud to you—

TESMAN: Yes, Yes! What then?

HEDDA: You confessed you were jealous of him for having written such a book.

TESMAN: But good gracious—! I didn't mean it as seriously as all that!

HEDDA: All the same. I couldn't stand the thought that somebody else was to overshadow you.

TESMAN: [In an outburst of mingled doubt and joy.] Hedda—oh Hedda! Is it true what you're saying! But—but—but—I never knew you loved me like that! Just think!

HEDDA: In that case, I might as well tell you—that—just at this time—[Breaks off, vehemently]. No, no! You can ask Aunt Julle. She'll tell you.

TESMAN: I almost think I know what you mean, Hedda! [Claps his hands.] For goodness' sake! Can that really be so! Hm?

HEDDA: Don't shout so! The maid can hear you.

TESMAN: [Laughing with exuberant joy.] The maid! Well, if you don't take the prize, Hedda! The maid—but that's Berte! I'm going to tell Berte myself this very minute!

HEDDA: [Her hands clenched in despair.] Oh I'll die—I'll die, in all this!

TESMAN: In what, Hedda? Hm?

HEDDA: [Cold and composed.] In all this—ludicrousness, Jørgen.

TESMAN: Ludicrous? That I'm so happy? Still—maybe I oughtn't to tell Berte, after all.

HEDDA: Oh, go ahead. What difference does it make.

TESMAN: No, not yet. But on my word—Aunt Julle must be told. And that you've started to call me "Jørgen," too! Just think! She'll be ever so happy—Aunt Julle will!

HEDDA: Even when you tell her that I have burned Eilert Løvborg's papers?

TESMAN: No, oh no! That's true! That about the manuscript—nobody must know about that. But to think that you'd burn for me, Hedda—I certainly want to tell *that* to Aunt Julle! I wonder now—is that sort of thing usual with young wives, hm?

HEDDA: Why don't you ask Aunt Julle about that, too.

TESMAN: I shall—I certainly shall, when I get the chance. [Looks uneasy and disturbed again.] But the manuscript! Good God—I don't dare to think what this is going to do to poor Eilert!

[Mrs. Elvsted, dressed as on her first visit, wearing hat and coat, enters, right.]

MRS. ELVSTED: *[Gives a hurried greeting, is obviously upset.]* Oh Hedda, you must forgive me for coming here again!

HEDDA: What has happened, Thea?

TESMAN: Something to do with Eilert Løvborg again? Hm?

MRS. ELVSTED: Yes, yes—I'm so terribly afraid something's happened to him.

HEDDA: *[Seizing her arm.]* Ah—you think so?

TESMAN: Oh dear—why do you think that, Mrs. Elvsted?

MRS. ELVSTED: I heard them talking about him in the boarding house, just as I came in. And people are saying the most incredible things about him today.

TESMAN: Yes, imagine! I heard that, too! And I can testify that he went straight home to bed! Just think!

HEDDA: And what did they say in the boarding house?

MRS. ELVSTED: Oh, I didn't find out anything. Either they didn't know any details or—They all became silent when they saw me. And I didn't dare to ask.

TESMAN: *[Pacing the floor uneasily.]* We'll just have to hope—to hope that you heard wrong, Mrs. Elvsted!

MRS. ELVSTED: No, no. I'm sure it was he they were talking about. And somebody said something about the hospital or—

TESMAN: The hospital—!

HEDDA: Surely, that can't be so!

MRS. ELVSTED: I got so terribly frightened! So I went up to his room and asked for him there.

HEDDA: Could you bring yourself to do that, Thea?

MRS. ELVSTED: What else could I do? For I felt I just couldn't stand the uncertainty any longer.

TESMAN: But I suppose you didn't find him in, either, did you? Hm?

MRS. ELVSTED: No. And the people there didn't know anything about him. He hadn't been home since yesterday afternoon, they said.

TESMAN: Yesterday! Just think! How could they say that!

MRS. ELVSTED: I don't know what else *to* think—something bad must have happened to him!

TESMAN: Hedda, dear—? What if I were to walk down town and ask for him at several places—?

HEDDA: No, no—don't you go and get mixed up in all this.

[Judge Brack, hat in hand, enters through the door, right, which Berte opens and closes for him. He looks serious and greets the others in silence.]

TESMAN: So here you are, Judge, hm?

BRACK: Yes. I had to see you this evening.

TESMAN: I can see you have got Aunt Julle's message.

BRACK: That, too—yes.

TESMAN: Isn't it sad, though?

BRACK: Well, my dear Tesman—that depends on how you look at it.

TESMAN: [*Looks at him uncertainly.*] Has something else happened?

BRACK: Yes.

HEDDA: [*Tense.*] Something sad, Judge Brack?

BRACK: That, too, depends on how you look at it, Mrs. Tesman.

MRS. ELVSTED: [*Bursting out.*] Oh, I'm sure it has something to do with Eilert Løvborg!

BRACK: [*Looks at her for a moment.*] Why do you think that, Mrs. Elvsted? Maybe you already know something—?

MRS. ELVSTED: [*Confused.*] No, no; not at all. It's just—

TESMAN: For heaven's sake, Brack, out with it!

BRACK: [*Shrugging his shoulders.*] Well—unfortunately, Eilert Løvborg's in the hospital. Dying.

MRS. ELVSTED: [*Screams.*] Oh God, oh God!

TESMAN: In the hospital! And dying!

HEDDA: [*Without thinking.*] So soon—!

MRS. ELVSTED: [*Wailing.*] And we didn't even part as friends, Hedda!

HEDDA: [*Whispers.*] Thea, Thea—for heaven's sake—!

MRS. ELVSTED: [*Paying no attention to her.*] I want to see him! I want to see him alive!

BRACK: Won't do you any good, Mrs. Elvsted. Nobody can see him.

MRS. ELVSTED: Then tell me what's happened to him! What?

TESMAN: For, surely, he hasn't himself—!

HEDDA: I'm sure he has.

TESMAN: Hedda! How can you—!

BRACK: [*Observing her all this time.*] I am sorry to say that your guess is absolutely correct, Mrs. Tesman.

MRS. ELVSTED: Oh, how awful!

TESMAN: Did it himself? Just think!

HEDDA: Shot himself!

BRACK: Right again, Mrs. Tesman.

MRS. ELVSTED: [*Trying to pull herself together.*] When did this happen, Judge?

BRACK: This afternoon. Between three and four.

TESMAN: But dear me—where can he have done a thing like that? Hm?

BRACK: [*A little uncertain.*] Where? Well—I suppose in his room. I don't really know—

MRS. ELVSTED: No, it can't have been there. For I was up there sometime between six and seven.

BRACK: Well, then, some other place. I really can't say. All I know is that he was found. He had shot himself—in the chest.

MRS. ELVSTED: Oh, how horrible to think! That he was to end like that!

HEDDA: [*To Brack.*] In the chest?

BRACK: Yes—as I just told you.

HEDDA: Not the temple?

BRACK: In the chest, Mrs. Tesman.

HEDDA: Well, well—the chest is a good place, too.

BRACK: How is that, Mrs. Tesman?

HEDDA: [*Turning aside.*] Oh—nothing.

TESMAN: And you say the wound is fatal? Hm?

BRACK: No doubt about it—absolutely fatal. He's probably dead already.

MRS. ELVSTED: Yes, yes! I feel you're right! It's over! It's all over! Oh, Hedda!

TESMAN: But tell me—how do *you* know all this?

BRACK: [*Tersely.*] A man on the force told me. One I had some business with.

HEDDA: [*Loudly.*] At last a deed!

TESMAN: [*Appalled.*] Oh dear—what are you saying, Hedda!

HEDDA: I am saying there is beauty in this.

BRACK: Well, now—Mrs. Tesman—

TESMAN: Beauty—! Just think!

MRS. ELVSTED: Oh, Hedda—how can you talk about beauty in a thing like this!

HEDDA: Eilert Løvborg has settled this account with himself. He has had the courage to do—what had to be done.

MRS. ELVSTED: But you mustn't believe it happened that way! He did it when he was not himself!

TESMAN: In despair! That's how!

HEDDA: He did not. I am certain of that.

MRS. ELVSTED: Yes he did! He was not himself! That's the way he tore up the book, too!

BRACK: [*Puzzled.*] The book? You mean the manuscript? Has he torn it up?

MRS. ELVSTED: Yes, last night.

TESMAN: [*Whispers.*] Oh, Hedda—we'll never get clear of all this!

BRACK: That is strange.

TESMAN: [*Walking the floor.*] To think that this was to be the end of Eilert! Not to leave behind him anything that would have preserved his name—

MRS. ELVSTED: Oh, if only it could be put together again!

TESMAN: Yes, if only it could. I don't know what I wouldn't give—

MRS. ELVSTED: Maybe it can, Mr. Tesman.

TESMAN: What do you mean?

MRS. ELVSTED: [*Searching her dress pocket.*] Look. I have kept these little slips he dictated from.

HEDDA: [*A step closer.*] Ah—!

TESMAN: You've kept them, Mrs. Elvsted? Hm?

MRS. ELVSTED: Yes. Here they are. I took them with me when I left. And I've had them in my pocket ever since—

TESMAN: Please, let me see—

MRS. ELVSTED: [*Gives him a pile of small paper slips.*] But it's in such a mess. Without any kind of system or order—!

TESMAN: But just think if we could make sense out of them, all the same! Perhaps if we helped each other—

MRS. ELVSTED: Oh yes! Let's try, anyway!

TESMAN: It will work! It *has* to work! I'll stake my whole life on this!

HEDDA: You, Jørgen? Your life?

TESMAN: Yes, or at any rate all the time I can set aside. My own collections can wait. Hedda, you understand—don't you? Hm? This is something I owe Eilert's memory.

HEDDA: Maybe so.

TESMAN: And now, my dear Mrs. Elvsted, we want to get to work. Good heavens, there's no point brooding over what's happened. Hm? We'll just have to acquire sufficient peace of mind to—

MRS. ELVSTED: All right, Mr. Tesman. I'll try to do my best.

TESMAN: Very well, then, Come over here. Let's look at these slips right away. Where can we sit? Here? No, it's better in the other room. If you'll excuse us, Judge! Come along, Mrs. Elvsted.

MRS. ELVSTED: Oh dear God—if only it were possible—!

[*Tesman and Mrs. Elvsted go into the inner room. She takes off her hat and coat. Both sit down at the table under the hanging lamp and absorb themselves in eager study of the slips. Hedda walks over toward the stove and sits down in the easy chair. After a while, Brack walks over to her.*]

HEDDA: [*In a low voice.*] Ah, Judge—what a liberation there is in this thing with Eilert Løvborg!

BRACK: Liberation, Mrs. Tesman? Well, yes, for him perhaps one may say there was liberation of a kind—

HEDDA: I mean for me. There is liberation in knowing that there is such a thing in the world as an act of free courage. Something which becomes beautiful by its very nature.

BRACK: [*Smiles.*] Well—dear Mrs. Tesman—

HEDDA: Oh I know what you're going to say! For you see—you really are a kind of specialist, too!

BRACK: [*Looks at her fixedly.*] Eilert Løvborg has meant more to you than perhaps you're willing to admit, even to yourself. Or am I wrong?

HEDDA: I won't answer such questions. All I know is that Eilert Løvborg had the courage to live his own life. And then now—this—magnificence! The beauty of it! Having the strength and the will to get up and leave life's feast—so early—

BRACK: Believe me, Mrs. Tesman, this pains me, but I see it is necessary that I destroy a pretty illusion—

HEDDA: An illusion?

BRACK: Which could not have been maintained very long, anyway.

HEDDA: And what is that?

BRACK: He didn't shoot himself—of his own free will.

HEDDA: Not of his own—!

BRACK: No. To tell the truth, the circumstances of Eilert Løvborg's death aren't exactly what I said they were.

HEDDA: [*Tense.*] You've held something back? What?

BRACK: For the sake of poor Mrs. Elvsted I used a few euphemisms.

HEDDA: What?

BRACK: First—he is already dead.

HEDDA: In the hospital.

BRACK: Yes. And without regaining consciousness.

HEDDA: What else haven't you told?

BRACK: The fact that it did not happen in his room.

HEDDA: Well, does that really make much difference?

BRACK: Some. You see—Eilert Løvborg was found shot in Miss Diana's bedroom.

HEDDA: [*Is about to jump up, but sinks back.*] That's impossible, Judge Brack! He can't have been there again today!

BRACK: He was there this afternoon. He came to claim something he said they had taken from him. Spoke some gibberish about a lost child—

HEDDA: So that's why—!

BRACK: I thought maybe he meant his manuscript. But now I hear he has destroyed that himself. So I suppose it must have been something else.

HEDDA: I suppose. So it was there—so they found him there?

BRACK: Yes. With a fired gun in his pocket. Mortally wounded.

HEDDA: Yes—in the chest.

BRACK: No—in the guts.

HEDDA: [*Looks at him with an expression of disgust.*] That, too! What is this curse that turns everything I touch into something ludicrous and low!

BRACK: There is something else, Mrs. Tesman. Something I'd call—nasty.

HEDDA: And what is that?

BRACK: The gun they found—

HEDDA: [*Breathless.*] What about it?

BRACK: He must have stolen it.

HEDDA: [*Jumps up.*] Stolen! That's not true! He didn't!

BRACK: Anything else is impossible. He *must* have stolen it.—Shhh!

[*Tesman and Mrs. Elvsted have risen from the table and come forward into the front room.*]

TESMAN: [*With papers in both hands.*] D'you know, Hedda—you can hardly see in there with that lamp! Just think!

HEDDA: I am thinking.

TESMAN: I wonder if you'd let us use your desk, hm?

HEDDA: Certainly, if you like. [*Adds quickly.*] Wait a minute, though! Let me clear it off a bit first.

TESMAN: Ah, there's no need for that, Hedda. There's plenty of room.

HEDDA: No, no. I want to straighten it up. Carry all this in here. I'll put it on top of the piano for the time being.

[*She has pulled an object, covered by note paper, out of the bookcase. She puts several other sheets of paper on top of it and carries the whole pile into the left part of the inner room. Tesman puts the papers down on the desk and moves the lamp from the corner table over to the desk. He and Mrs. Elvsted sit down and resume their work. Hedda returns.*]

HEDDA: [*Behind Mrs. Elvsted's chair, softly ruffling her hair.*] Well, little Thea—how is Eilert Løvborg's memorial coming along?

MRS. ELVSTED: [*Looks up at her, discouraged.*] Oh God—I'm sure it's going to be terribly hard to make anything out of all this.

TESMAN: But we have to. We just don't have a choice. And putting other people's papers in order—that's just the thing for me.

[*Hedda walks over to the stove and sits down on one of the ottomans. Brack stands over her, leaning on the easy chair.*]

HEDDA: [*Whispers.*] What were you saying about the gun?

BRACK: [*Also softly.*] That he must have stolen it.

HEDDA: Why, necessarily?

BRACK: Because any other explanation ought to be out of the question, Mrs. Tesman.

HEDDA: Oh?

BRACK: [*Looks at her for a moment.*] Eilert Løvborg was here this morning, of course. Isn't that so?

HEDDA: Yes.

BRACK: Were you alone with him?

HEDDA: Yes, for a while.

BRACK: You didn't leave the room while he was here?

HEDDA: No.

BRACK: Think. Not at all? Not even for a moment?

HEDDA: Well—maybe just for a moment—out in the hall.

BRACK: And where was the gun case?

HEDDA: Down in the—

BRACK: Mrs. Tesman?

HEDDA: On the desk.

BRACK: Have you looked to see if both guns are still there?

HEDDA: No.

BRACK: You needn't bother. I saw the gun they found on Løvborg, and I knew it immediately. From yesterday—and from earlier occasions, too.

HEDDA: Perhaps you have it?

BRACK: No, the police do.

HEDDA: What are the police going to do with it?

BRACK: Try to find the owner.

HEDDA: Do you think they will?

BRACK: [*Leans over her, whispers.*] No, Hedda Gabler—not as long as I keep quiet.

HEDDA: [*With a hunted look.*] And if you don't.

BRACK: [*Shrugs his shoulders.*] Of course, there's always the chance that the gun was stolen.

HEDDA: [*Firmly.*] I'd rather die!

BRACK: [*Smiles.*] People *say* things like that. They don't *do* them.

HEDDA: [*Without answering.*] And if the gun was not stolen—and if they find the owner—then what happens?

BRACK: Well, Hedda—then comes the scandal!

HEDDA: The scandal!

BRACK: Yes—the scandal. That you are so afraid of. You will of course be required to testify. Both you and Miss Diana. Obviously, she'll have to explain how the whole thing happened. Whether it was accident or homicide. Did he try to pull the gun out of his pocket to threaten her? And did it fire accidentally? Or did she grab the gun away from him, shoot him, and put it back in his pocket? She might just possibly have done that. She's a pretty tough girl—Miss Diana.

HEDDA: But this whole disgusting affair has nothing to do with me.

BRACK: Quite so. But you'll have to answer the question: Why did you give Eilert Løvborg the gun? And what inferences will be drawn from the fact that you did?

HEDDA: [*Lowers her head.*] That's true. I hadn't thought of that.

TESMAN: Well—luckily, there's nothing to worry about as long as I don't say anything.

HEDDA: [*Looks up at him.*] So then I'm in your power, Judge. From now on you can do anything you like with me.

BRACK: [*In an even softer whisper.*] Dearest Hedda—believe me, I'll not misuse my position

HEDDA: In your power, all the same. Dependent on your will. Servant to your demands. Not free. Not free! [*Rises suddenly.*] No—I can't stand that thought! Never!

BRACK: [*Looks at her, half mockingly.*] Most people submit to the inevitable.

HEDDA: [*Returning his glance.*] Perhaps. [*Walks over to the desk. Suppresses a smile and mimics Tesman's way of speaking.*] Well? Do you think you can do it, Jørgen? Hm?

TESMAN: Lord knows, Hedda. Anyway, I can already see it will take months.

HEDDA: [*Still mimicking.*] Just think! [*Runs her hands lightly through Mrs. Elvsted's hair.*] Doesn't this seem strange to you. Thea? Sitting here with Tesman—just the way you used to with Eilert Løvborg?

MRS. ELVSTED: Oh dear—if only I could inspire your husband, too!

HEDDA: Oh, I'm sure that will come—in time.

TESMAN: Well, yes—do you know, Hedda? I really think I begin to feel something of the kind. But why don't you go and talk to the Judge again.

HEDDA: Isn't there anything you two can use me for?

TESMAN: No, not a thing, dear. [*Turns around.*] From now on, you must be good enough to keep Hedda company, my dear Judge!

BRACK: [*Glancing at Hedda.*] I'll be only too delighted.

HEDDA: Thank you. I'm tired tonight. I think I'll go and lie down for a while on the sofa in there.

TESMAN: Yes, you do that, dear; why don't you? Hm?

[*Hedda goes into the inner room, closes the portieres behind her. Brief pause. Suddenly, she is heard playing a frenzied dance tune on the piano.*]

MRS. ELVSTED: [*Jumps up.*] Oh God! What's that!

TESMAN: [*Running to the doorway.*] But dearest Hedda—you mustn't play dance music tonight, for goodness' sake! Think of Aunt Rina! And Eilert, too!

HEDDA: [*Peeks in from between the portieres.*] And Aunt Julle. And everybody. I'll be quiet.

[*She pulls the portieres shut again.*]

TESMAN: [*Back at the desk.*] I don't think it's good for her to see us at such a melancholy task. I'll tell you what, Mrs. Elvsted. You move in with Aunt Julle, and then I'll come over in the evenings. Then we can sit and work over there. Hm?

MRS. ELVSTED: Maybe that would be better—

HEDDA: [*From the inner room.*] I hear every word you're saying, Tesman. And how am I going to spend my evenings?

TESMAN: [*Busy with the papers.*] Oh, I'm sure Judge Brack will be good enough to come out and see you, anyway.

BRACK: [*In the easy chair, calls out gaily.*] Every single night, as far as I'm concerned, Mrs. Tesman! I'm sure we're going to have a lovely time, you and I!

HEDDA: [*Loud and clear.*] Yes, don't you think that would be nice, Judge Brack? You—sole cock-o'-the-walk—

A shot is heard from the inner room. Tesman, Mrs. Elvsted, and Judge Brack all jump up.]

TESMAN: There she is, fooling with those guns again.

[*He pulls the portieres apart and runs inside. Mrs. Elvsted also. Hedda, lifeless, is lying on the sofa. Cries and confusion. Berte, flustered, enters, right.*]

TESMAN: [*Shouts to Brack.*] She's shot herself! In the temple! Just think!

BRACK: [*Half stunned in the easy chair.*] But, merciful God—! People don't *do* things like that!

LEO TOLSTOY (1828–1910)

Russia

Born on the family estate of Yasnaya Polyana south of Moscow, Tolstoy lost his mother at 2 and his father at 9; he was happily brought up by his aunts, a childhood recounted in an autobiographical trilogy (*Childhood*, 1852; *Boyhood*, 1854, and *Youth*, 1857). Originally intending to study oriental languages, he enrolled in the University of Kazan, but abandoned them. In the army from 1851–54, he served in the Caucasus and Sevastopol, and then returned to his estate and involved himself in the education of the children of the peasants, travelling several times to Europe to study European educational methods.

Staunchly antiromantic, Tolstoy was passionately attached to the reality of life and created memorable characters in his fiction, notably in *War and Peace* (1869) and *Anna Karenina* (1876), two of the greatest and most influential European novels. Following his famous midlife "conversion," he renounced the art of high society—which he had known in St. Petersburg as a celebrated author—as false, vainglorious, and inadequate to the task of communicating the important values of life and truth to all people. He called upon art to be as simple, accessible, and powerful as folk art or mythology, and he himself began to write what he called "stories for the people." "God Sees the Truth but Waits" (1872) is one of the series of tales that appeal because of their narrative power and resonate with the force of parables and moral *exempla*.

God Sees the Truth but Waits

I

In the town of Vladímir lived a young merchant named Iván Dmítrich Aksënov. He had two shops and a house of his own.

Aksënov was a handsome, fair-haired, curly-headed fellow, full of fun and very fond of singing. When quite a young man he had been given to drink and was riotous when he had had too much, but after he married he gave up drinking except now and then.

One summer Aksënov was going to the Nízhny Fair, and as he bade good-bye to his family his wife said to him, "Iván Dmítrich, do not start to-day; I have had a bad dream about you."

Aksënov laughed, and said, "You are afraid that when I get to the fair I shall go on the spree."

His wife replied: "I do not know what I am afraid of; all I know is that I had a bad dream. I dreamt you returned from the town, and when you took off your cap I saw that your hair was quite grey."

Aksënov laughed. "That's a lucky sign," said he. "See if I don't sell out all my goods and bring you some presents from the fair."

So he said good-bye to his family and drove away.

When he had travelled half-way, he met a merchant whom he knew, and they put up at the same inn for the night. They had some tea together and then went to bed in adjoining rooms.

It was not Aksënov's habit to sleep late, and wishing to travel while it was still cool, he aroused his driver before dawn and told him to put in the horses.

Then he made his way across to the landlord of the inn (who lived in a cottage at the back), paid his bill, and continued his journey.

When he had gone about twenty-five miles he stopped for the horses to be fed. Aksënov rested awhile in the passage of the inn, then he stepped out into the porch and, ordering a samovar to be heated, got out his guitar and began to play.

Translated by Louise and Aylmer Maude.

Suddenly a *trôyka*[1] drove up with tinkling bells, and an official alighted, followed by two soldiers. He came to Aksënov and began to question him, asking him who he was and whence he came. Aksënov answered him fully and said, "Won't you have some tea with me?" But the official went on cross-questioning him and asking him, "Where did you spend last night? Were you alone, or with a fellow-merchant? Did you see the other merchant this morning? Why did you leave the inn before dawn?"

Aksënov wondered why he was asked all these questions, but he described all that had happened, and then added, "Why do you cross-question me as if I were a thief or a robber? I am travelling on business of my own, and there is no need to question me."

Then the official, calling the soldiers, said, "I am the police-officer of this district, and I question you because the merchant with whom you spent last night has been found with his throat cut. We must search your things."

They entered the house. The soldiers and the police-officer unstrapped Aksënov's luggage and searched it. Suddenly the officer drew a knife out of a bag, crying, "Whose knife is this?"

Aksënov looked, and seeing a blood-stained knife taken from his bag, he was frightened.

"How is it there is blood on this knife?"

Aksënov tried to answer but could hardly utter a word and only stammered: "I don't know—not mine."

Then the police-officer said, "This morning the merchant was found in bed with his throat cut. You are the only person who could have done it. The house was locked from inside, and no one else was there. Here is this blood-stained knife in your bag, and your face and manner betray you! Tell me how you killed him and how much money you stole?"

Aksënov swore he had not done it; that he had not seen the merchant after they had had tea together; that he had no money except eight thousand rubles of his own, and that the knife was not his. But his voice was broken, his face pale, and he trembled with fear as though he were guilty.

The police-officer ordered the soldiers to bind Aksënov and to put him in the cart. As they tied his feet together and flung him into the cart, Aksënov crossed himself and wept. His money and goods were taken from him, and he was sent to the nearest town and imprisoned there. Enquiries as to his character were made in Vladímir. The merchants and other inhabitants of that town said that in former days he used to drink and waste his time but that he was a good man. Then the trial came on: he was charged with murdering a merchant from Ryazán and robbing him of twenty thousand rubles.

His wife was in despair and did not know what to believe. Her children were all quite small; one was a baby at the breast. Taking them all with her, she went to the town where her husband was in gaol. At first she was not allowed to see him, but, after much begging, she obtained permission from the officials and was

---

1. A vehicle drawn by three horses abreast.

taken to him. When she saw her husband in prison-dress and in chains, shut up with thieves and criminals, she fell down and did not come to her senses for a long time. Then she drew her children to her, and sat down near him. She told him of things at home and asked about what had happened to him. He told her all, and she asked, "What can we do now?"

"We must petition the Tsar not to let an innocent man perish."

His wife told him that she had sent a petition to the Tsar but that it had not been accepted.

Aksënov did not reply but only looked downcast.

Then his wife said, "It was not for nothing I dreamt your hair had turned grey. You remember? You should not have started that day." And passing her fingers through his hair she said: "Ványa dearest tell your wife the truth; was it not you who did it?"

"So you, too, suspect me!" said Aksënov, and, hiding his face in his hands, he began to weep. Then a soldier came to say that the wife and children must go away, and Aksënov said good-bye to his family for the last time.

When they were gone, Aksënov recalled what had been said, and when he remembered that his wife also had suspected him, he said to himself, "It seems that only God can know the truth; it is to Him alone we must appeal and from Him alone expect mercy."

And Aksënov wrote no more petitions, gave up all hope, and only prayed to God.

Aksënov was condemned to be flogged and sent to the mines. So he was flogged with a knout, and when the wounds caused by the knout were healed, he was driven to Siberia with other convicts.

For twenty-six years Aksënov lived as a convict in Siberia. His hair turned white as snow, and his beard grew long, thin, and grey. All his mirth went; he stooped; he walked slowly, spoke little, and never laughed, but he often prayed.

In prison Aksënov learnt to make boots, and earned a little money, with which he bought *The Lives of the Saints*. He read this book when it was light enough in the prison; and on Sundays in the prison-church he read the epistle and sang in the choir, for his voice was still good.

The prison authorities liked Aksënov for his meekness, and his fellow-prisoners respected him: they called him "Grandfather," and "The Saint." When they wanted to petition the prison authorities about anything, they always made Aksënov their spokesman, and when there were quarrels among the prisoners they came to him to put things right and to judge the matter.

No news reached Aksënov from his home, and he did not even know if his wife and children were still alive.

One day a fresh gang of convicts came to the prison. In the evening the old prisoners collected round the new ones and asked them what towns or villages they came from, and what they were sentenced for. Among the rest Aksënov sat down near the new-comers, and listened with downcast air to what was said.

One of the new convicts, a tall, strong man of sixty, with a closely-cropped grey beard, was telling the others what he had been arrested for.

"Well, friends," he said, "I only took a horse that was tied to a sledge, and I was arrested and accused of stealing. I said I had only taken it to get home quicker, and had then let it go; besides, the driver was a personal friend of mine. So I said, 'It's all right.' 'No,' said they, 'you stole it.' But how or where I stole it they could not say. I once really did something wrong and ought by rights to have come here long ago, but that time I was not found out. Now I have been sent here for nothing at all. . . . Eh, but it's lies I'm telling you; I've been to Siberia before, but I did not stay long."

"Where are you from?" asked some one.

"From Vladímir. My family are of that town. My name is Makár, and they also call me Semënich."

Aksënov raised his head and said: "Tell me, Semënich, do you know anything of the merchants Aksënov, of Vladímir? Are they still alive?"

"Know them? Of course, I do. The Aksënovs are rich, though their father is in Siberia: a sinner like ourselves, it seems! As for you, Gran'dad, how did you come here?"

Aksënov did not like to speak of his misfortune. He only sighed, and said, "For my sins I have been in prison these twenty-six years."

"What sins?" asked Makár Semënich.

But Aksënov only said, "Well, well—I must have deserved it!" He would have said no more, but his companions told the new-comer how Aksënov came to be in Siberia: how some one had killed a merchant and had put a knife among Aksënov's things, and he had been unjustly condemned.

When Makár Semënich heard this he looked at Aksënov, slapped his own knee, and exclaimed, "Well, this is wonderful! Really wonderful! But how old you've grown, Gran'dad!"

The others asked him why he was so surprised, and where he had seen Aksënov before; but Makár Semënich did not reply. He only said: "It's wonderful that we should meet here, lads!"

These words made Aksënov wonder whether this man knew who had killed the merchant; so he said, "Perhaps, Semënich, you have heard of that affair, or maybe you've seen me before?"

"How could I help hearing? The world's full of rumours. But it's long ago, and I've forgotten what I heard."

"Perhaps you heard who killed the merchant?" asked Aksënov.

Makár Semënich laughed, and replied, "It must have been him in whose bag the knife was found! If some one else hid the knife there—'He's not a thief till he's caught,' as the saying is. How could any one put a knife into your bag while it was under your head? It would surely have woke you up?"

When Aksënov heard these words he felt sure this was the man who had killed the merchant. He rose and went away. All that night Aksënov lay awake. He felt terribly unhappy; and all sorts of images rose in his mind. There was the image of his wife as she was when he parted from her to go to the fair. He saw her as if she were present; her face and her eyes rose before him, he heard her speak and laugh. Then he saw his children, quite little, as they were at that time: one with a little cloak on, another at his mother's breast. And then he remembered himself as he used to be—young and merry. He remembered how he sat playing the guitar in the porch of the inn where he was arrested, and how free from care he had been. He saw in his mind the place where he was flogged, the executioner, and the people standing around; the chains, the convicts, all the twenty-six years of his prison life, and his premature old age. The thought of it all made him so wretched that he was ready to kill himself.

"And it's all that villain's doing!" thought Aksënov. And his anger was so great against Makár Semënich that he longed for vengeance, even if he himself should perish for it. He kept saying prayers all night but could get no peace. During the day he did not go near Makár Semënich nor even look at him.

A fortnight passed in this way. Aksënov could not sleep at nights and was so miserable that he did not know what to do.

One night as he was walking about the prison he noticed some earth that came rolling out from under one of the shelves on which the prisoners slept. He stopped to see what it was. Suddenly Makár Semënich crept out from under the shelf, and looked up at Aksënov with frightened face. Aksënov tried to pass without looking at him, but Makár seized his hand and told him that he had dug a hole under the wall, getting rid of the earth by putting it into his high boots and emptying it out every day on the road when the prisoners were driven to their work.

"Just you keep quiet, old man, and you shall get out too. If you blab they'll flog the life out of me, but I will kill you first."

Aksënov trembled with anger as he looked at his enemy. He drew his hand away, saying, "I have no wish to escape, and you have no need to kill me; you killed me long ago! As to telling of you—I may do so or not, as God shall direct."

Next day, when the convicts were led out to work, the convoy soldiers noticed that one or other of the prisoners emptied some earth out of his boots. The prison was searched and the tunnel found. The Governor came and questioned all the prisoners to find out who had dug the hole. They all denied any knowledge of it. Those who knew would not betray Makár Semënich, knowing he would be flogged almost to death. At last the Governor turned to Aksënov, whom he knew to be a just man, and said: "You are a truthful old man; tell me, before God, who dug the hole?"

Makár Semënich stood as if he were quite unconcerned, looking at the Governor and not so much as glancing at Aksënov. Aksënov's lips and hands trembled, and for a long time he could not utter a word. He thought, "Why should I screen him who ruined my life? Let him pay for what I have suffered. But if I tell, they will probably flog the life out of him, and maybe I suspect him wrongly. And, after all, what good would it be to me?"

"Well, old man," repeated the Governor, "tell us the truth: who has been digging under the wall?"

Aksënov glanced at Makár Semënich and said, "I cannot say, your honour. It is not God's will that I should tell! Do what you like with me; I am in your hands."

However much the Governor tried, Aksënov would say no more, and so the matter had to be left.

That night, when Aksënov was lying on his bed and just beginning to doze, some one came quietly and sat down on his bed. He peered through the darkness and recognized Makár.

"What more do you want of me?" asked Aksënov. "Why have you come here?"

Makár Semënich was silent. So Aksënov sat up and said, "What do you want? Go away or I will call the guard!"

Makár Semënich bent close over Aksënov, and whispered, "Iván Dmítrich, forgive me!"

"What for?" asked Aksënov.

"It was I who killed the merchant and hid the knife among your things. I meant to kill you too, but I heard a noise outside; so I hid the knife in your bag and escaped through the window."

Aksënov was silent and did not know what to say. Makár Semënich slid off the bed-shelf and knelt upon the ground. "Iván Dmítrich," said he, "forgive me! For the love of God, forgive me! I will confess that it was I who killed the merchant, and you will be released and can go to your home."

"It is easy for you to talk," said Aksënov, "but I have suffered for you these twenty-six years. Where could I go to now? My wife is dead, and my children have forgotten me. I have nowhere to go. . . ."

Makár Semënich did not rise but beat his head on the floor. "Iván Dmítrich, forgive me!" he cried. "When they flogged me with the knout it was not so hard to bear as it is to see you now . . . yet you had pity on me and did not tell. For Christ's sake forgive me, wretch that I am!" And he began to sob.

When Aksënov heard him sobbing he, too, began to weep.

"God will forgive you!" said he. "Maybe I am a hundred times worse than you." And at these words his heart grew light and the longing for home left him. He no longer had any desire to leave the prison but only hoped for his last hour to come.

In spite of what Aksënov had said, Makár Semënich confessed his guilt. But when the order for his release came, Aksënov was already dead.

STÉPHANE MALLARMÉ (1842–1898)
France

The central and most "modern" figure of the movement of suggestion and ambivalence known as symbolism, Stéphane Mallarmé was heavily influenced by Baudelaire and Poe. Gathered around Mallarmé in his celebrated Tuesdays on the *rue de Rome* were all the young symbolists; he would muse aloud for them and himself. He made his living by teaching English in a *lycée*, and his translation of a talk by the artist James Abbott McNeill Whistler and his commentaries on the letters of the English alphabet remain as curious witnesses to the intricacy of his mind, in part a musical one. When Debussy said he understood Mallarmé had set *The Afternoon of a Faun* [*L'après-Midi d'un Faune*, 1876] to music, the poet replied he had already done that. For Mallarmé, true existence takes place in the mind, which has its own theatrical presentations that become increasingly elaborate in his later poems. Early writings such as "Sea Breeze," a poem of longing and nostalgia dedicated to the idea of voyage, suggest the allure of the ideal as opposed to ordinary reality, seen as less profitable for the imaginative mind. Mallarmé's later poetry and prose express absence as superior to presence and silence as preferable to speech, taking an oblique form: in his "Crisis in Verse" he famously defines the rose, a central image in symbolist poetry, as that which is "absent from every bouquet."

Will New and Alive the Beautiful Today[*]

Will new and alive the beautiful today
Shatter with a blow of drunken wing
This hard lake, forgotten, haunted under rime[1]
By the transparent glacier, flights unflown!

A swan of long ago remembers now that he,   5
Magnificent but lost to hope, is doomed
For having failed to sing the realms of life
When the ennui of sterile winter gleamed.

His neck will shake off the white torment space
Inflicts upon the bird for his denial,   10
But not this horror, plumage trapped in ice.

Phantom by brilliance captive to this place,
Immobile, he assumes disdain's cold dream,
Which, in his useless exile, robes the Swan.

Sea Breeze[†]

Alas, the flesh is sad, and I've read all the books.
Oh if I could escape! the birds are drunk
With being amid the unknown foam and skies!
Nothing, not the old gardens reflected in our eyes,
Will hold me now I have dipped into the sea   5
Oh nights! nor the desert brightness of my lamp
On the empty paper guarded by its white,
Nor the young mother, her baby at her breast.
I won't stay! Steamer under your swaying masts,
Weigh anchor for a nature far away!   10
Boredom, victim of the cruelest hopes,
Still puts its trust in absolute farewells!

---

[*]*Translated by Patricia Terry and Maurice Z. Shroder.*
[†]*Translated by Patricia Terry and Mary Ann Caws.*

---

1. Frost.

And, perhaps, the masts, summoning the storms,
Will be those which a wind bends over lost
Ships bereft of masts, of masts, and fertile isles,   15
But, oh my heart, do you hear the sailors' song?

from **Crisis in Verse**

[Each soul is a melody]*

. . . Each soul is a melody to be picked up again, and everyone's flute or viola exists
for that.

I sense the true possibility finally imminent, not just of expressing yourself
but modulating yourself as you choose.

Languages are imperfect since among the many, the supreme one is lacking.
Thinking is writing without accessories, or whispering; but because the immortal
word is still silent, the diversity of mortal tongues keeps us all from uttering the
word which would otherwise have one unique rendering, in substance truth itself
. . . *Only,* we must understand, *poetry would not exist;* philosophically, verse is
superior, making up for what languages lack.

. . .

The pure work implies the disappearance of the poet as speaker, yielding the
initiative to words now mobilized by the shock of their difference; they sparkle in
reciprocal reflections, a virtual stream of fireworks over jewels, restoring perceptible
breath to the lyric impulse, or the enthusiastic personal direction of the sentence.

. . .

Why transpose a fact of nature into its almost complete and vibratory play within
the word unless there issues forth from it a pure notion, free of any needless
concrete reminder?

I say: a flower! and beyond the oblivion to which my voice relegates any
shape other than the chalice, there arises musically, delicate as the idea itself, the
one absent from every bouquet.

GERARD MANLEY HOPKINS
(1844–1889)
England; died in Wales

Gerard Manley Hopkins, one of the leading Victorian poets, trained at Oxford
with Benjamin Jowett, the scholar and translator of Plato, and Walter Pater, the

*Translated by Mary Ann Caws.

aesthetician (*Studies in the History of the Renaissance,* 1873) and author (*Marius the Epicurean,* 1885). He converted to Catholicism in 1866, and was ordained as a Jesuit priest in 1868, a vocation that was to cause him to destroy much of his own writing. What remains was not published during his lifetime, but it is now seen as the radiant and heartrending testimony to a soul struggling with God and with its own despair. The so-called "Terrible Sonnets," from which "I Wake and Feel the Fell of Dark" is taken, are indeed terrible in their feeling of truth and their blinding inwardness. These sonnets were written in Wales, in whose penetrating dampness Hopkins underwent a dark night of the soul in these "black hours"; they are among the most heartrending outcries ever written: "I see / The lost are like this . . . ." Hopkins was greatly influenced by Saint Thomas Aquinas, upon whose thought some of his sermons are based. His emphasis on "insight" and "inscape" (or the seeing into the inward form of things) was part of his intense and exalted way of perceiving the universe: "The Windhover," "God's Grandeur," and "Pied Beauty" celebrate the way things verbal and visual merge, heightened in the excited vision bestowed by God on those who care to see. Hopkins' "sprung rhythm" with its elliptical phrasing and compound metaphor, its strongly scanned and forced pulsation, is the perfect highly concentrated form for this vision. Torn between these two sides of his nature, exalting and despairing, he speaks through his anguish believable to present-day readers, and to their own doubleness.

[I Wake and Feel the Fell of Dark]

I wake and feel the fell[1] of dark, not day.
What hours, O what black hours we have spent
This night! what sights you, heart, saw; ways you went!
And more must, in yet longer light's delay.

With witness I speak this. But where I say   5
Hours I mean years, mean life. And my lament
Is cries countless, cries like dead letters sent
To dearest him that lives alas! away.

I am gall, I am heartburn. God's most deep decree
Bitter would have me taste: my taste was me;   10
Bones built in me, flesh filled, blood brimmed the curse.

Selfyeast of spirit a dull dough sours. I see
The lost are like this, and their scourge to be
As I am mine, their sweating selves, but worse.

(1885)

---

1. The word has several meanings: bitterness; the hide of an animal; or fierce, associated with "fall."

The Windhover

To Christ Our Lord

I caught this morning morning's minion,[1] king-
    dom of daylight's dauphin, dapple-dawn-drawn Falcon, in his riding
    Of the rolling level underneath him steady air, and striding
High there, how he rung upon the rein of a wimpling[2] wing
In his ecstasy! then off, off forth on swing,   5
    As a skate's heel sweeps smooth on a bow-bend: the hurl and gliding
    Rebuffed the big wind. My heart in hiding
Stirred for a bird,—the achieve of, the mastery of the thing!

Brute beauty and valour and act, oh, air, pride, plume, here
    Buckle![3] AND the fire that breaks from thee then, a billion   10
Times told lovelier, more dangerous, O my chevalier![4]

    No wonder of it: shéer plód makes plough down sillion
Shine, and blue-bleak embers, ah my dear,
    Fall, gall themselves, and gash gold-vermilion.

                                   (1877 1918)

God's Grandeur

The world is charged with the grandeur of God.
    It will flame out, like shining from shook foil;
    It gathers to a greatness, like the ooze of oil
Crushed.[1] Why do men then now not reck his rod?
Generations have trod, have trod, have trod;   5
    And all is seared with trade; bleared, smeared with toil;
    And wears man's smudge and shares man's smell: the soil
Is bare now, nor can foot feel, being shod.

And for all this, nature is never spent;
    There lives the dearest freshness deep down things;   10
And though the last lights off the black West went
    Oh, morning, at the brown brink eastward, springs—
Because the Holy Ghost over the bent
    World broods with warm breast and with ah! bright wings.

The Windhover

1. A favorite person.
2. Rippling.
3. To connect (as with a belt), but also to give

way: the *tension* of the contrary meanings is
the point.
4. Lord.

God's Grandeur

1. As olives are.

Pied[1] Beauty

Glory be to God for dappled things—
  For skies of couple-colour as a brinded[2] cow;
    For rose-moles all in stipple upon trout that swim;
Fresh-firecoal chestnut-falls; finches' wings;
  Landscape plotted and pieced—fold, fallow and plough;[3]   5
    And áll trádes, their gear and tackle and trim.
All things counter,[4] original, spare, strange;
  Whatever is fickle, freckled (who knows how?)
    With swift, slow; sweet, sour; adazzle, dim;
He fathers-forth whose beauty is past change: 10
    Praise him.

                                    (1877 1918)

FRIEDRICH NIETZSCHE (1844–1900)
Germany/Switzerland

The son of a minister, Friedrich Nietzsche studied classics at the University of Bonn and was appointed to the chair of classical philosophy at the University of Basel in 1869, a position he had to abandon in 1879 because of trouble with his eyes and his nerves. A controversial philosopher, writer, and philologist, he was greatly influenced by the pessimistic philosophy of Arthur Schopenhauer (1788–1860), particularly in his early writings like *The Birth of Tragedy* (1872). Nietzsche presents the dichotomy between the serenity of Apollonian culture and the flood of unrestrained feeling and music in the Dionysian. It is in this work that his idolization of the composer Richard Wagner is first apparent. The aphorisms of *Human, All-Too-Human* (1878) and its appendix, *Mixed Opinions and Maxims* (1879), through *The Gay Science* (1882), sparkle with genius, and contain in their brief intensities much of the essence of his always impassioned thought, at once romantic and existentialist. One of Nietzsche's most crucial creations is the figure of Zarathustra, and the antirational, antichrist "superman" ("Ubermensch"): *Thus Spake Zarathustra* (1892). In 1889, Nietzsche went mad, and remained so until his death.

---

1. One of Hopkins' favorite words: two or more colors patched together.
2. Streaked.

3. Three uses of the land—to fold in the seed, to lie fallow, and to be ploughed.
4. Opposed to the ordinary.

from Human, All-Too-Human

[Higher culture is necessarily misunderstood]

Higher culture is necessarily misunderstood. He who has but two strings on his instrument—like the scholars who, in addition to the urge for knowledge, have only the religious urge, instilled by education—does not understand those who can play on more strings. It is of the essence of the higher, multi-stringed culture that it is always misinterpreted by the lower culture—as happens, for example, when art is considered a disguised form of religion. Indeed, people who are only religious understand even science as a search of the religious feeling, just as deaf-mutes do not know what music is, if it is not visible movement.

[The most dangerous party member]

The most dangerous party member. In every party there is one member who, by his all-too-devout pronouncement of the party principles, provokes the others to apostasy.

[Why one contradicts]

Why one contradicts. One often contradicts an opinion when it is really only the tone in which it has been presented that is unsympathetic.

[Marriage as a long conversation]

Marriage as a long conversation. When marrying, one should ask oneself this question: Do you believe that you will be able to converse well with this woman into your old age? Everything else in marriage is transitory, but the most time during the association belongs to conversation.

[And to say it once more]

And to say it once more. Public opinions—private lazinesses.

[Enemies of truth]

Enemies of truth. Convictions are more dangerous enemies of truth than lies.

Translated by Walter Kaufmann.

[The value of insipid opponents.]

The value of insipid opponents. At times one remains faithful to a cause only because its opponents do not cease to be insipid.

[Not suitable as a party member]

Not suitable as a party member. Whoever thinks much is not suitable as a party member: he soon thinks himself right through the party.

[On the whole, scientific methods]

On the whole, scientific methods are at least as important as any other result of research: for it is upon the insight into method that the scientific spirit depends: and if these methods were lost, then all the results of science could not prevent a renewed triumph of superstition and nonsense. Clever people may learn as much as they wish of the results of science—still one will always notice in their conversation, and especially in their hypotheses, that they lack the scientific spirit; they do not have that instinctive mistrust of the aberrations of thought which through long training are deeply rooted in the soul of every scientific person. They are content to find any hypothesis at all concerning some matter; then they are all fire and flame for it and think that is enough. To have an opinion means for them to fanaticize for it and thenceforth to press it to their hearts as a conviction. If something is unexplained, they grow hot over the first notion that comes into their heads and looks like an explanation—which results progressively in the worst consequences, especially in the sphere of politics. For that reason everyone should now study at least one science from the bottom up: then he will know what method means and how important is the utmost circumspection. . . .

from Mixed Opinions and Maxims

[Dissipation]

Dissipation. The mother of dissipation is not joy but joylessness.

["Love"]

"Love." The most subtle artifice that distinguishes Christianity from other religions is a word: it speaks of *love*. Thus it became the lyrical religion (whereas in both their other creations the Semites presented the world with heroic-epic religions). There is something so ambiguous and suggestive about the word love, something that speaks to memory and to hope, that even the lowest intelligence and the coldest heart still feel something of the glimmer of this word. The cleverest woman and the most vulgar man recall the relatively least selfish moments of their whole

life, even if Eros has taken only a low flight with them; and for those countless ones who miss love, whether from their parents or their children or their beloved, and especially for people with sublimated sexuality, Christianity has always been a find.

[Readers of aphorisms]

Readers of aphorisms. The worst readers of aphorisms are the author's friends if they are intent on guessing back from the general to the particular instance to which the aphorism owes its origin; for with such pot-peeking they reduce the author's whole effort to nothing; so that they deservedly gain, not a philosophic outlook or instruction, but—at best, or at worst—nothing more than the satisfaction of vulgar curiosity.

[Sign of rank]

Sign of rank. All poets and writers who are in love with the superlative want more than they are capable of.

[Jokes]

Jokes. A joke is the epigram on the death of a feeling.

[Humaneness in friendship and mastership]

Humaneness in friendship and mastership. "If thou wilt go toward morning, then I will go toward evening": to feel this way is a high sign of humaneness in a closer association: without this feeling, every friendship, every discipleship and pupil-ship, becomes at one time or another hypocrisy.

[Way to a Christian virtue]

Way to a Christian virtue. Learning from one's enemies is the best way toward loving them; for it makes us grateful to them.

[Every philosophy]

Every philosophy is the philosophy of some stage of life. The stage of life at which a philosopher found his doctrine reverberates through it; he cannot prevent this, however far above time and hour he may feel. Thus Schopenhauer's philosophy remains the reflection of ardent and melancholy *youth*—it is no way of thinking for older people. And Plato's philosophy recalls the middle thirties, when a cold and a hot torrent often roar toward each other, so that a mist and tender little clouds form—and under favorable circumstances and the rays of the sun, an enchanting rainbow.

[Unfaithfulness, a condition of mastership]

Unfaithfulness, a condition of mastership. Nothing avails: every master has but one disciple, and that one becomes unfaithful to him, for he too is destined for mastership.

GUY DE MAUPASSANT (1850–1893)
France

The son of an ancient Norman family, Guy de Maupassant became known by 1880 as the most brilliant of the circle around Émile Zola (1840–1902). He died in a sanatorium. With Gustave Flaubert as his teacher, Guy de Maupassant paid great attention to the details of his short stories and novels. He is thought of as a naturalist and known for giving a highly ironic twist to most of what he wrote. The frustrations and turns of such stories as "The Necklace" and the novels *A Life* (*Une vie,* 1883) and *Pierre et Jean* (1888) make generally somber stuff for the reader. "An Old Man" presents a picture at once compassionate and gently mocking, like most of his portraits.

An Old Man

All the newspapers had carried this advertisement:

> The new spa at Rondelis offers all the advantages desirable for a lengthy stay or even for permanent residence. Its ferruginous waters, recognized as the best in the world for countering all impurities of the blood, also seem to possess special qualities calculated to prolong human life. This remarkable circumstance may be due in part to the exceptional situation of the little town, which lies in a mountainous region, in the middle of a forest of firs. The fact remains that for several centuries it has been noted for cases of extraordinary longevity.

And the public came along in droves.

One morning the doctor in charge of the springs was asked to call on a newcomer, Monsieur Daron, who had arrived a few days before and had rented a charming villa on the edge of the forest. He was a little old man of eighty-six, still quite sprightly, wiry, healthy and active, who went to infinite pains to conceal his age.

Translated by Roger Colet.

He offered the doctor a seat and started questioning him straight away.

"Doctor," he said, "if I am in good health, it is thanks to careful living. Though not very old, I have already attained a respectable age, yet I keep free of all illnesses and indispositions, even the slightest malaises, by means of careful living. It is said that the climate here is very good for the health. I am perfectly prepared to believe it, but before settling down here I want proof. I am therefore going to ask you to come and see me once a week to give me the following information in detail.

"First of all I wish to have a complete, absolutely complete, list of all the inhabitants of the town and the surrounding area who are over eighty years old. I also need a few physical and physiological details regarding each of them. I wish to know their professions, their way of life, their habits. Every time one of those people dies you will be good enough to inform me, giving me the precise cause of death and describing the circumstances."

Then he added graciously, "I hope, Doctor, that we shall become good friends," and held out his wrinkled little hand. The doctor shook it, promising him his devoted co-operation.

Monsieur Daron had always had an obsessive fear of death. He had deprived himself of nearly all the pleasures of this world because they were dangerous, and whenever anyone expressed surprise that he should not drink wine—wine, that purveyor of dreams and gaiety—he would reply in a voice in which a note of fear could be detected: "I value my life." And he stressed the word *my,* as if that life, *his* life, possessed some special distinction. He put into that *my* such a difference between his life and other people's lives that any rejoinder was out of the question.

For that matter he had a very special way of stressing the possessive pronouns designating parts of his person and even things which belonged to him. When he said "my eyes, my legs, my arms, my hands," it was quite obvious that there must be no mistake about this: those organs were not at all like other people's. But where this distinction was particularly noticeable was in his references to his doctor. When he said "my doctor," one would have thought that that doctor belonged to him and nobody else, destined for him alone, to attend to his illnesses and to nothing else, and that he was superior to all the other doctors in the world, without exception.

He had never regarded other men as anything but puppets of a sort, created to fill up an empty world. He divided them into two classes: those he greeted because some chance had put him in contact with them, and those he did not greet. But both these categories of individuals were equally insignificant in his eyes.

However, beginning with the day when the Rondelis doctor brought him the list of the seventeen inhabitants of the town who were over eighty, he felt a new interest awaken in his heart, an unfamiliar solicitude for these old people whom he was going to see fall by the wayside one by one. He had no desire to make their acquaintance, but he formed a very clear idea of their persons, and when the doctor dined with him, every Thursday, he spoke only of them. "Well, doctor," he would say, "and how is Joseph Poincot today? We left him feeling a little ill last week." And when the doctor had given him the patient's bill of health, Monsieur Daron would suggest changes in his diet, experiments, methods of treatment which he might later apply to himself if they had succeeded with the others. Those seventeen old people provided him with an experimental field from which he learnt many a lesson.

One evening the doctor announced as he came in: "Rosalie Tournel has died."

Monsieur Daron gave a start and immediately asked, "What of?"

"Of a chill."

The little old man gave a sigh of relief. Then he said, "She was too fat, too heavy, she must have eaten too much. When I get to her age I'll be more careful about my weight." [He was two years older than Rosalie Tournel, but he claimed to be only seventy.]

A few months later it was the turn of Henri Brissot. Monsieur Daron was very upset. This time it was a man, and a thin man at that, within three months of his own age, and careful about his health. He did not dare to ask any questions, but waited anxiously for the doctor to give him some details.

"Oh, so he died just like that, all of a sudden," he said. "But he was perfectly all right last week. He must have done something silly, I suppose, Doctor?"

The doctor, who was enjoying himself, replied: "I don't think so. His children told me he had been very careful."

Then, unable to contain himself any longer, and filled with fear, Monsieur Daron asked: "But . . . but . . . what did he die of, then?"

"Of pleurisy."

The little old man clapped his dry hands in sheer joy.

"I told you so! I told you he had done something silly. You don't get pleurisy for nothing. He must have gone out for a breath of air after his dinner and the cold must have gone to his chest. Pleurisy! Why, that's an accident, not an illness. Only fools die of pleurisy."

And he ate his dinner in high spirits, talking about those who were left.

"There are only fifteen of them now, but they are all hale and hearty, aren't they? The whole of life is like that: the weakest go first; people who live beyond thirty have a good chance of reaching sixty; those who pass sixty often get to eighty; and those who pass eighty nearly always live to be a hundred, because they are the fittest, toughest and most sensible of all."

Another two disappeared during the year, one of dysentery and the other of a choking fit. Monsieur Daron was highly amused by the death of the former and concluded that he must have eaten something stimulating the day before.

"Dysentery is the disease of careless people. Dammit all, Doctor, you ought to have watched over his diet."

As for the man who had been carried off by a choking fit, his death could only be due to a heart condition which had hitherto gone unnoticed.

But one evening the doctor announced the decease of Paul Timonet, a sort of mummy of whom it had been hoped to make a centenarian and an advertisement for the spa.

When Monsieur Daron asked, as usual: "What did he die of?" the doctor replied, "Bless me, I really don't know."

"What do you mean, you don't know. A doctor always knows. Hadn't he some organic lesion?"

The doctor shook his head.

"No none."

"Possibly some infection of the liver or the kidneys?"

"No, they were quite sound."

"Did you check whether the stomach was functioning properly? A stroke is often caused by poor digestion."

"There was no stroke."

Monsieur Daron, very perplexed, said excitedly: "Look, he must have died of something! What do you think it was?"

The doctor threw up his hands.

"I've no idea, no idea at all. He died because he died, that's all."

Then Monsieur Daron, in a voice full of emotion, asked: "Exactly how old was that one? I can't remember."

"Eighty-nine."

And the little old man, at once incredulous and reassured, exclaimed: "Eighty-nine! So whatever it was, it wasn't old age. . . ."

EMILIA PARDO BAZÁN (1852–1921)
Spain

The most famous short-story writer of the nineteenth century in Spain, Emilia Pardo Bazán was made a countess for her work but was never admitted to the Academia de la Lengua, presumably because she was a woman. Closely following the naturalism of Émile Zola—an advanced form of realism—she championed the writing of Pérez Galdos and other Spanish realists, even claiming that the proper characteristic of Spanish literature was always "more realist than anything else." Her novel *The Paths of Ulloa* (1886) with its depiction of the Galician countryside and the degeneration of an aristocratic Galician family, was an enormous success, as were her stories. Zola was to become irritated by her "misrepresentation" of his theories. Her writing scandalized her husband, and they separated, after which she enjoyed a highly colorful lifestyle. She also wrote plays and many critical studies, and she edited the *Nuevo Teatro Critico* (1891–1893): her works are collected in more than forty volumes. Her articles for various Latin American periodicals are still being assembled for republication. The terrible irony of "The Revolver" is reminiscent of Maupassant at his grimmest.

The Revolver

In a burst of confidence, one of those provoked by the familiarity and companionship of bathing resorts, the woman suffering from heart trouble told me about her

Translated by Angel Flores.

illness, with all the details of choking, violent palpitations, dizziness, fainting spells, and collapses, in which one sees the final hour approach. . . . As she spoke, I looked her over carefully. She was a woman of about thirty-five or thirty-six, maimed by suffering; at least I thought so, but, on closer scrutiny, I began to suspect that there was something more than the physical in her ruin. As a matter of fact, she spoke and expressed herself like someone who had suffered a good deal, and I know that the ills of the body, when not of imminent gravity, are usually not enough to produce such a wasting away, such extreme dejection. And, noting how the broad leaves of the plane tree, touched with carmine by the artistic hand of autumn, fell to the ground majestically and lay stretched out like severed hands, I remarked, in order to gain her confidence, on the passing of all life, the melancholy of the transitoriness of everything . . . .

"Nothing is anything," she answered, understanding at once that not curiosity but compassion was beckoning at the gates of her spirit. "Nothing is anything . . . unless we ourselves convert that nothing into something. Would to God we could see everything, always, with the slight but sad emotion produced in us by the fall of this foliage on the sand."

The sickly flush of her cheeks deepened, and then I realized that she had probably been very beautiful, although her beauty was effaced and gone, like the colors of a fine picture over which is passed cotton saturated with alcohol. Her blond, silky hair showed traces of ash, premature gray hair. Her features had withered away; her complexion especially revealed those disturbances of the blood which are slow poisonings, decompositions of the organism. Her soft blue eyes, veined with black, must have once been attractive, but now they were disfigured by something worse than age; a kind of aberration, which at certain moments lent them the glitter of blindness.

We grew silent; but my way of contemplating her expressed my pity so plainly that she, sighing for a chance to unburden her heavy heart, made up her mind, and stopping from time to time to breathe and and regain her strength, she told me the strange story.

"When I married, I was very much in love. . . . My husband was, compared to me, advanced in years; he was bordering on forty, and I was only nineteen. My temperament was gay and lively; I retained a childlike disposition, and when he was not home I would devote my time to singing, playing the piano, chatting and laughing with girl-friends who came to see me and envied me my happiness, my brilliant marriage, my devoted husband, and my brilliant social position.

"This lasted a year—the wonderful year of the honeymoon. The following spring, on our wedding anniversary, I began to notice that Reinaldo's disposition was changing. He was often in a gloomy mood, and, without my knowing the cause, he spoke to me harshly, and had outbursts of anger. But it was not long before I understood the origins of his transformation: Reinaldo had conceived a violent, irrational jealousy, a jealousy without object or cause, which, for that very reason, was doubly cruel and difficult to cure.

"If we went out together, he was watchful lest people stare at me or tell me, in passing, one of those silly things people say to young women; if he went out alone, he was suspicious of what I was doing in the house, and of the people who came to see me; if I went out alone, his suspicions and suppositions were even more defamatory. . . .

"If I proposed, pleadingly, that we stay home together, he was watchful of my saddened expression, of my supposed boredom, of my work, of an instant when, passing in front of the window, I happened to look outside . . . He was watchful, above all, when he noticed that my birdlike disposition, my good, childlike humor, had disappeared, and that on many afternoons, when I turned on the lights, he found my skin shining with the damp, ardent trace of tears. Deprived of my innocent amusements, now separated from my friends and relatives, and from my own family, because Reinaldo interpreted as teacherous artifices the desire to communicate and look at faces other than his, I often wept, and did not respond to Reinaldo's transports of passion with the sweet abandonment of earlier times.

"One day, after one of the usual bitter scenes, my husband said:

"Flora, I may be a madman, but I am not a fool. I have alienated your love, and although perhaps you would not have thought of deceiving me, in the future, without being able to remedy it, you would. Now I shall never again be your beloved. The swallows that have left do not return. But because, unfortunately, I love you more each day, and love you without peace, with eagerness and fever, I wish to point out that I have thought of a way which will prevent questions, quarrels, or tears between us—and once and for all you will know what our future will be."

"Speaking thus, he took me by the arm and led me toward the bedroom.

"I went trembling; cruel presentiments froze me. Reinaldo opened the drawer of the small inlaid cabinet where he kept tobacco, a watch, and handkerchiefs and showed me a large revolver, a sinister weapon.

"'Here,' he said, 'is your guarantee that in the future your life will be peaceful and pleasant. I shall never again demand an accounting of how you spend your time, or of your friends, or of your amusements. You are free, free as the air. But the day I see something that wounds me to the quick . . . that day, I swear by my mother! Without complaints or scenes, or the slightest sign that I am displeased, oh no, not that! I will get up quietly at night, take the weapon, put it to your temple and you will wake up in eternity. Now you have been warned. . . .'

"As for me, I was in a daze, unconscious. It was necessary to send for the doctor, inasmuch as the fainting spell lasted. When I recovered consciousness and remembered, the convulsion took place. I must point out that I have a mortal fear of firearms; a younger brother of mine died of an accidental shot. My eyes, staring wildly, would not leave the drawer of the cabinet that held the revolver.

"I could not doubt, from Reinaldo's tone and the look on his face, that he was prepared to carry out his threat, and knowing also how easily his imagination grew confused, I began to consider myself as dead. As a matter of fact, Reinaldo kept his promise, and left me complete mistress of myself, without directing the slightest censure my way, or showing, even by a look, that he was opposed to any of my wishes or disapproved of my actions; but this itself frightened me, because it indicated the strength and tyranny of a resolute will . . . and, victim of a terror which every day grew more profound, I remained motionless, not daring to take a step. I would always see the steely reflection of the gun barrel.

"At night, insomnia kept my eyes open, and I imagined I felt the metallic cold of a steel circle on my temple; or if I got to sleep, I woke up startled with palpitations that made my heart seem to leap from my breast, because I dreamed that an awful report was ripping apart the bones of my skull and blowing my brains out, dashing them against the wall . . . And this lasted four years, four years without a single peaceful moment, when I never took a step without fearing that that step might give rise to tragedy."

"And how did that horrible situation end?" I asked, in order to bring her story to a close, because I saw her gasping for breath.

"It ended . . . . with Reinaldo, who was thrown by a horse, and had some internal injury, being killed on the spot.

"Then, and only then, I knew that I still loved him, and I mourned him quite sincerely, although he was my executioner, and a systematic one at that!"

"And did you pick up the revolver to throw it out the window?"

"You'll see," she murmured. "Something rather extraordinary happened. I sent Reinaldo's manservant to remove the revolver from my room, because in my dreams I continued to see the shot and feel the chill on my temple. . . . And after he carried out the order, the manservant came to tell me: 'Señora, there was no cause for alarm. . . . This revolver wasn't loaded.'

" 'It wasn't loaded'"

" 'No, Señora, and it looks to me as though it never was . . . As a matter of fact, the poor master never got around to buying the cartridges. Why, I would even ask him at times if he wanted me to go to the gunsmith's and get them, but he didn't answer, and then he never spoke of the matter again.' "

"And so," added the sufferer from heart disease, "an unloaded revolver shot me, not in the head, but in the center of my heart, and believe me when I tell you that, in spite of digitalis and baths and all the remedies, the bullet is unsparing. . . ."

ANTON PAVLOVICH CHEKHOV
(1860–1904)
Russia

Anton Chekhov, born in Taganrog in the south of Russia, was the grandson of an ex-serf who had purchased his freedom. He enrolled in the School of Medicine at the University of Moscow, and began writing humorous sketches to finance his medical studies, and he continued writing together with the practice of medicine for the rest of his life. Eventually he published in a leading St. Petersburg daily; but his tuberculosis, which declared itself while he was still a student, obliged him to move to the milder climate of Yalta by 1898, where he met with the writers Maxim Gorky and Count Leo Tolstoy. Chekhov's stories and dramatic masterpieces mark a turning point in world literature from the direct event-centered narratives of realism to an impressionistic, evocative style of storytelling on the threshold of symbolism and modernism. His genius has been described as the capacity to capture the quotidian in what has been called a "slice of life." His principal theme, around which "Enemies" turns, is the inability of humans to communicate with each other.

Enemies

Between nine and ten on a dark September evening the only son of the district doctor, Kirilov, a child of six, called Andrey, died of diphtheria. Just as the doctor's wife sank on her knees by the dead child's bedside and was overwhelmed by the first rush of despair there came a sharp ring at the bell in the entry.

All the servants had been sent out of the house that morning on account of the diphtheria. Kirilov went to open the door just as he was, without his coat on, with his waistcoat unbuttoned, without wiping his wet face or his hands which were scalded with carbolic. It was dark in the entry and nothing could be distinguished in the man who came in but medium height, a white scarf, and a large, extremely pale face, so pale as its entrance seemed to make the passage lighter.

"Is the doctor at home?" the newcomer asked quickly.

"I am at home," answered Kirilov. "What do you want?"

"Oh, it's you? I am very glad," said the stranger in a tone of relief, and he began feeling in the dark for the doctor's hand, found it and squeezed it tightly in his own. "I am very . . . very glad! We are acquainted. My name is Abogin, and I had the honour of meeting you in the summer at Gnutchev's. I am very glad I have found you at home. . . . For God's sake don't refuse to come back with me at once. . . . My wife has been taken dangerously ill. . . . And the carriage is waiting. . . ."

From the voice and gestures of the speaker it could be seen that he was in a state of great excitement. Like a man terrified by a house on fire or a mad dog, he could hardly restrain his rapid breathing and spoke quickly in a shaking voice, and there was a note of sincerity and childish alarm in his voice. As people always do who are frightened and overwhelmed, he spoke in brief, jerky sentences and uttered a great many unnecessary, irrelevant words.

"I was afraid I might not find you in," he went on. "I was in a perfect agony as I drove here. Put on your things and let us go, for God's sake. . . . This is how it happened. Alexandr Semyonovitch Paptchinsky, whom you know, came to see me. . . . We talked a little then we sat down to tea; suddenly my wife cried out, clutched at her heart, and fell back on her chair. We carried her to bed and . . . and I rubbed her forehead with ammonia and sprinkled her with water . . . she lay as though she were dead . . . I am afraid it is aneurism. . . . Come along . . . her father died of aneurism."

Kirilov listened and said nothing, as though he did not understand Russian.

When Abogin mentioned again Paptchinsky and his wife's father and once more began feeling in the dark for his hand the doctor shook his head and said apathetically, dragging out each word:

Translated by Constance Garnett.

"Excuse me, I cannot come . . . my son died . . . five minutes ago!"

"Is it possible!" whispered Abogin, stepping back a pace. "My God, at what an unlucky moment I have come! A wonderfully unhappy day . . . wonderfully. What a coincidence. . . . It's as though it was on purpose!"

Abogin took hold of the door-handle and bowed his head. He was evidently hesitating and did not know what to do—whether to go away or to continue entreating the doctor.

"Listen," he said fervently, catching hold of Kirilov's sleeve. "I well understand your position! God is my witness that I am ashamed of attempting at such a moment to intrude on your attention, but what am I to do? Only think, to whom can I go? There is no other doctor here, you know. For God's sake come! I am not asking you for myself. . . . I am not the patient!"

A silence followed. Kirilov turned his back on Abogin, stood still a moment, and slowly walked into the drawing-room. Judging from his unsteady, mechanical step, from the attention with which he set straight the fluffy shade on the unlighted lamp in the drawing-room and glanced into a thick book lying on the table, at that instant he had no intention, no desire, was thinking of nothing and most likely did not remember that there was a stranger in the entry. The twilight and stillness of the drawing-room seemed to increase his numbness. Going out of the drawing-room into his study he raised his right foot higher than was necessary, and felt for the doorposts with his hands, and as he did so there was an air of perplexity about his whole figure as though he were in somebody else's house, or were drunk for the first time in this life and were now abandoning himself with surprise to the new sensation. A broad streak of light stretched across the bookcase on one wall of the study; this light came together with the close, heavy smell of carbolic and ether from the door into the bedroom, which stood a little way open. . . . The doctor sank into a low chair in front of the table; for a minute he stared drowsily at his books, which lay with the light on them, then got up and went into the bedroom.

Here in the bedroom reigned a dead silence. Everything to the smallest detail was eloquent of the storm that had been passed through, of exhaustion, and everything was at rest. A candle standing among a crowd of bottles, boxes, and pots on a stool and a big lamp on the chest of drawers threw a brilliant light over all the room. On the bed under the window lay a boy with open eyes and a look of wonder on his face. He did not move, but his open eyes seemed every moment growing darker and sinking further into his head. The mother was kneeling by the bed with her arms on his body and her head hidden in the bedclothes. Like the child, she did not stir; but what throbbing life was suggested in the curves of her body and in her arms! She leaned against the bed with all her being, pressing against it greedily with all her might, as though she were afraid of disturbing the peaceful and comfortable attitude she had found at last for her exhausted body. The bedclothes, the rags and bowls, the splashes of water on the floor, the little paint-brushes and spoons thrown down here and there, the white bottle of lime water, the very air, heavy and stifling—were all hushed and seemed plunged in repose.

The doctor stopped close to his wife, thrust his hands in his trouser pockets, and slanting his head on one side fixed his eyes on his son. His face bore an expression of indifference, and only from the drops that glittered on his beard it could be seen that he had just been crying.

That repellent horror which is thought of when we speak of death was absent from the room. In the numbness of everything, in the mother's attitude, in the indifference on the doctor's face there was something that attracted and touched the heart, that subtle, almost elusive beauty of human sorrow which men will not for a long time learn to understand and describe, and which it seems only music can convey. There was a feeling of beauty, too, in the austere stillness. Kirilov and his wife were silent and not weeping, as though besides the bitterness of their loss they were conscious, too, of all the tragedy of their position; just as once their youth had passed away, so now together with this boy their right to have children had gone for ever to all eternity! The doctor was forty-four, his hair was grey and he looked like an old man; his faded and invalid wife was thirty-five. Andrey was not merely the only child, but the last child.

In contrast to his wife the doctor belonged to the class of people who at times of spiritual suffering feel a craving for movement. After standing for five minutes by his wife, he walked, raising his right foot high, from the bedroom into the little room which was half filled up by a big sofa; from there he went into the kitchen. After wandering by the stove and the cook's bed he bent down and went by a little door into the passage.

There he saw again the white scarf and the white face.

"At last," sighed Abogin, reaching towards the door-handle. "Let us go, please."

The doctor started, glanced at him, and remembered. . . .

"Why, I have told you already that I can't go!" he said, growing more animated. "How strange!"

"Doctor, I am not a stone, I fully understand your position . . . . I feel for you," Abogin said in an imploring voice, laying his hand on his scarf. "But I am not asking you for myself. My wife is dying. If you had heard that cry, if you had seen her face, you would understand my pertinacity. My God, I thought you had gone to get ready! Doctor, time is precious. Let us go, I entreat you."

"I cannot go," said Kirilov emphatically, and he took a step into the drawing-room.

Abogin followed him and caught hold of his sleeve.

"You are in sorrow, I understand. But I'm not asking you to a case of toothache, or to a consultation, but to save a human life!" he went on entreating like a beggar. "Life comes before any personal sorrow! Come, I ask for courage, for heroism! For the love of humanity!"

"*Humanity*—that cuts both ways," Kirilov said irritably. "In the name of humanity I beg you not to take me. And how queer it is, really! I can hardly stand and you talk to me about humanity! I am fit for nothing just now. . . . Nothing will induce me to go, and I can't leave my wife alone. No, no. . . ."

Kirilov waved his hands and staggered back.

"And . . . and don't ask me," he went on in a tone of alarm. "Excuse me. By No. XIII of the regulations I am obliged to go and you have the right to drag me by

my collar . . . drag me if you like, but . . . I am not fit . . . I can't even speak
. . . excuse me."

"There is no need to take that tone to me, doctor!" said Abogin, again taking
the doctor by his sleeve. "What do I care about No. XIII! To force you against your
will I have no right whatever. If you will, come; if you will not—God forgive you;
but I am not appealing to your will, but to your feelings. A young woman is dying.
You were just speaking of the death of your son. Who should understand my
horror if not you?"

Abogin's voice quivered with emotion; that quiver and his tone were far more
persuasive than his words. Abogin was sincere, but it was remarkable that
whatever he said his words sounded stilted, soulless, and inappropriately flowery,
and even seemed an outrage on the atmosphere of the doctor's home and on the
woman who was somewhere dying. He felt this himself, and so, afraid of not being
understood, did his utmost to put softness and tenderness into his voice so that
the sincerity of his tone might prevail if his words did not. As a rule, however fine
and deep a phrase may be, it only affects the indifferent, and cannot fully satisfy
those who are happy or unhappy; that is why dumbness is most often the highest
expression of happiness of unhappiness; lovers understand each other better
when they are silent, and a fervent, passionate speech delivered by the grave only
touches outsiders, while to the widow and children of the dead man it seems cold
and trivial.

Kirilov stood in silence. When Abogin uttered a few more phrases concerning
the noble calling of a doctor, self-sacrifice, and so on, the doctor asked sullenly:
"Is it far?"

"Something like eight or nine miles. I have capital horses, doctor! I give you
my word of honour that I will get you there and back in an hour. Only one hour."

These words had more effect on Kirilov than the appeals to humanity or the
noble calling of the doctor. He thought a moment and said with a sigh: "Very well,
let us go!"

He went rapidly with a more certain step to his study, and afterwards came
back in a long frock-coat. Abogin, greatly relieved, fidgeted round him and
scraped with his feet as he helped him on with his overcoat, and went out of the
house with him.

It was dark out of doors, though lighter than in the entry. The tall, stooping
figure of the doctor, with his long, narrow beard and aquiline nose, stood out
distinctly in the darkness. Abogin's big head and the little student's cap that barely
covered it could be seen now as well as his pale face. The scarf showed white only
in front, behind it was hidden by his long hair.

"Believe me, I know how to appreciate your generosity," Abogin muttered as
he helped the doctor into the carriage. "We shall get there quickly. Drive as fast as
you can, Luka, there's a good fellow! Please!"

The coachman drove rapidly. At first there was a row of indistinct buildings
that stretched alongside the hospital yard; it was dark everywhere except for a
bright light from a window that gleamed through the fence into the furthest part
of the yard while three windows of the upper storey of the hospital looked paler
than the surrounding air. Then the carriage drove into dense shadow; here there

was the smell of dampness and mushrooms, and the sound of rustling trees; the crows, awakened by the noise of the wheels, stirred among the foliage and uttered prolonged plaintive cries as though they knew the doctor's son was dead and that Abogin's wife was ill. Then came glimpses of separate trees, of bushes; a pond, on which great black shadows were slumbering, gleamed with a sullen light—and the carriage rolled over a smooth level ground. The clamour of the crows sounded dimly far away and soon ceased altogether.

Kirilov and Abogin were silent almost all the way. Only once Abogin heaved a deep sigh and muttered:

"It's an agonizing state! One never loves those who are near one so much as when one is in danger of losing them."

And when the carriage slowly drove over the river, Kirilov started all at once as though the splash of the water had frightened him, and made a movement.

"Listen—let me go," he said miserably. "I'll come to you later, I must just send my assistant to my wife. She is alone, you know!"

Abogin did not speak. The carriage swaying from side to side and crunching over the stones drove up the sandy bank and rolled on its way. Kirilov moved restlessly and looked about him in misery. Behind them in the dim light of the stars the road could be seen and the riverside willows vanishing into the darkness. On the right lay a plain as uniform and as boundless as the sky; here and there in the distance, probably on the peat marshes, dim lights were glimmering. On the left, parallel with the road, ran a hill tufted with small bushes, and above the hill stood motionless a big, red half-moon, slightly veiled with mist and encircled by tiny clouds, which seemed to be looking round at it from all sides and watching that it did not go away.

In all nature there seemed to be a feeling of hopelessness and pain. The earth, like a ruined woman sitting alone in the dark room and trying not to think of the past, was brooding over memories of spring and summer and apathetically waiting for the inevitable winter. Wherever one looked, on all sides, nature seemed like a dark, infinitely deep, cold pit from which neither Kirilov nor Abogin nor the red half-moon could escape. . . .

The nearer the carriage got to its goal the more impatient Abogin became. He kept moving, leaping up, looking over the coachman's shoulder. And when at last the carriage stopped before the entrance, which was elegantly curtained with striped linen, and when he looked at the lighted windows of the second storey there was an audible catch in his breath.

"If anything happens . . . I shall not survive it," he said, going into the hall with the doctor, and rubbing his hands in agitation. "But there is no commotion, so everything must be going well, so far," he added, listening in the stillness.

There was no sound in the hall of steps or voices and all the house seemed asleep in spite of the lighted windows. Now the doctor and Abogin, who till then had been in darkness, could see each other clearly. The doctor was tall and stooped, was untidily dressed and not good-looking. There was an unpleasantly harsh, morose, and unfriendly look about his lips, thick as a negro's, his aquiline nose, and listless, apathetic eyes. His unkempt head and sunken temples, the premature greyness of his long, narrow beard through which his chin was visible, the pale grey hue of his skin and his careless, uncouth manners—the harshness of all this was suggestive of years of poverty, of ill fortune, of weariness with life and with men. Looking at his frigid figure one could hardly believe that this man had a wife, that he was capable of weeping over his child. Abogin presented a very different appearance. He was a thick-set, sturdy-looking, fair man with a big head and large, soft features; he was elegantly dressed in the very latest fashion. In his carriage, his closely buttoned coat, his long hair, and his face there was a suggestion of something generous, leonine; he walked with his head erect and his chest squared, he spoke in an agreeable baritone, and there was a shade of refined almost feminine elegance in the manner in which he took off his scarf and smoothed his hair. Even his paleness and the childlike terror with which he looked up at the stairs as he took off his coat did not detract from his dignity nor diminish the air of sleekness, health, and aplomb which characterized his whole figure.

"There is nobody and no sound," he said going up the stairs. "There is no commotion. God grant all is well."

He led the doctor through the hall into a big drawing-room where there was a black piano and a chandelier in a white cover; from there they both went into a very snug, pretty little drawing-room full of agreeable, rosy twilight.

"Well, sit down here, doctor, and I . . . will be back directly. I will go and have a look and prepare them."

Kirilov was left alone. The luxury of the drawing-room, the agreeably subdued light and his own presence in the stranger's unfamiliar house, which had something of the character of an adventure, did not apparently affect him. He sat in a low chair and scrutinized his hands, which were burnt with carbolic. He only caught a passing glimpse of the bright red lamp-shade and the violoncello case, and glancing in the direction where the clock was ticking he noticed a stuffed wolf as substantial and sleek-looking as Abogin himself.

It was quiet. . . . Somewhere far away in the adjoining rooms someone uttered a loud exclamation:

"Ah!" There was a clang of a glass door, probably of a cupboard, and again all was still. After waiting five minutes Kirilov left off scrutinizing his hands and raised his eyes to the door by which Abogin had vanished.

In the doorway stood Abogin, but he was not the same as when he had gone out. The look of sleekness and refined elegance had disappeared—his face, his hands, his attitude were contorted by a revolting expression of something between horror and agonizing physical pain. His nose, his lips, his moustache, all his features were moving and seemed trying to tear themselves from his face, his eyes looked as though they were laughing with agony. . . .

Abogin took a heavy stride into the drawing-room, bent forward, moaned, and shook his fists.

"She has deceived me," he cried, with a strong emphasis on the second syllable of the verb. "Deceived me, gone away. She fell ill and sent me for the doctor only to run away with that clown Paptchinsky! My God!"

Abogin took a heavy step towards the doctor, held out his soft white fists in his face, and shaking them went on yelling:

"Gone away! Deceived me! But why this deception? My God! My God! What need of this dirty, scoundrelly trick, this diabolical, snakish farce? What have I done to her? Gone away!"

Tears gushed from his eyes. He turned on one foot and began pacing up and down the drawing-room. Now in his short coat, his fashionable narrow trousers which made his legs look disproportionately slim, with his big head and long mane he was extremely like a lion. A gleam of curiosity came into the apathetic face of the doctor. He got up and looked at Abogin.

"Excuse me, where is the patient?" he said.

"The patient! The patient!" cried Abogin, laughing, crying, and still brandishing his fists. "She is not ill, but accursed! The baseness! The vileness! The devil himself could not have imagined anything more loathsome! She sent me off that she might run away with a buffoon, a dull-witted clown, an Alphonse! Oh God, better she had died! I cannot bear it! I cannot bear it!"

The doctor drew himself up. His eyes blinked and filled with tears, his narrow beard began moving to right and to left together with his jaw.

"Allow me to ask what's the meaning of this?" he asked, looking round him with curiosity. "My child is dead, my wife is in grief alone in the whole house. . . . I myself can scarcely stand up, I have not slept for three nights. . . . And here I am forced to play a part in some vulgar farce, to play the part of a stage property! I don't . . . don't understand it."

Abogin unclenched one first, flung a crumpled note on the floor, and stamped on it as though it were an insect he wanted to crush.

"And I didn't see, didn't understand," he said through clenched teeth, brandishing one first before his face with an expression as though some one had trodden on his corns. "I did not notice that he came every day! I did not notice that he came today in a closed carriage! What did he come in a closed carriage for? And I did not see it! Noodle!"

"I don't understand . . ." muttered the doctor. "Why, what's the meaning of it? Why, it's an outrage on personal dignity, a mockery of human suffering! It's incredible. . . . It's the first time in my life I have had such an experience!"

With the dull surprise of a man who has only just realized that he has been bitterly insulted the doctor shrugged his shoulders, flung wide his arms, and not knowing what to do or to say sank helplessly into a chair.

"If you have ceased to love me and love another—so be it; but why this deceit, why this vulgar, treacherous trick?" Abogin said in a tearful voice. "What is the object of it? And what is there to justify it? And what have I done to you? Listen, doctor," he said hotly, going up to Kirilov. "You have been the involuntary witness of my misfortune and I am not going to conceal the truth from you. I swear that I loved the woman, loved her devotedly, like a slave! I have sacrificed everything for her; I have quarrelled with my own people, I have given up the service and music, I have forgiven her what I could not have forgiven my own mother or sister. . . . I have never looked askance at her. . . . I have never gainsaid her in anything. Why this deception? I do not demand love, but why this loathsome duplicity? If she did not love me, why did she not say so openly, honestly, especially as she knows my views on the subject? . . ."

With tears in his eyes, trembling all over, Abogin opened his heart to the doctor with perfect sincerity. He spoke warmly, pressing both hands on his heart, exposing the secrets of his private life without the faintest hesitation, and even seemed to be glad that at last these secrets were no longer pent up in his breast. If he had talked in this way for an hour or two, and opened his heart, he would undoubtedly have felt better. Who knows, if the doctor had listened to him and had sympathized with him like a friend, he might perhaps, as often happens, have reconciled himself to his trouble without protest, without doing anything needless and absurd. . . . But what happened was quite different. While Abogin was speaking the outraged doctor perceptibly changed. The indifference and wonder on his face gradually gave way to an expression of bitter resentment, indignation, and anger. The features of his face became even harsher, coarser, and more unpleasant. When Abogin held out before his eyes the photograph of a young woman with a handsome face as cold and expressionless as a nun's and asked him whether, looking at that face, one could conceive that it was capable of duplicity, the doctor suddenly flew out, and with flashing eyes said, rudely rapping out each word:

"What are you telling me all this for? I have no desire to hear it! I have no desire to!" he shouted and brought his fist down on the table. "I don't want your vulgar secrets! Damnation take them! Don't dare to tell me of such vulgar doings! Do you consider that I have not been insulted enough already? That I am a flunkey whom you can insult without restraint? Is that it?"

Abogin staggered back from Kirilov and stared at him in amazement.

"Why did you bring me here?" the doctor went on, his beard quivering. "If you are so puffed up with good living that you go and get married and then act a farce like this, how do I come in? What have I to do with your love affairs? Leave me in peace! Go on squeezing money out of the poor in your gentlemanly way. Make a display of humane ideas, play (the doctor looked sideways at the violoncello case) play the bassoon and the trombone, grow as fat as capons, but don't dare to insult personal dignity! If you cannot respect it, you might at least spare it your attention!"

"Excuse me, what does all this mean?" Abogin asked, flushing red.

"It means that it's base and low to play with people like this! I am a doctor; you look upon doctors and people generally who work and don't stink of perfume and prostitution as your menials and *mauvais ton*[1]; well, you may look upon them so, but no one has given you the right to treat a man who is suffering as a stage property!"

"How dare you say that to me!" Abogin said quietly, and his face began working again, and this time unmistakably from anger.

"No, how dared you, knowing of my sorrow, bring me here to listen to these vulgarities!" shouted the doctor, and he again banged on the table with his fist. "Who has given you the right to make a mockery of another man's sorrow?"

"You have taken leave of your senses," shouted Abogin. "It is ungenerous. I am intensely unhappy myself and . . . and . . . ."

---

1. Crude.

"Unhappy!" said the doctor, with a smile of contempt. "Don't utter that word, it does not concern you. The spendthrift who cannot raise a loan calls himself unhappy, too. The capon, sluggish from over-feeding, is unhappy, too. Worthless people!"

"Sir, you forget yourself," shrieked Abogin. "For saying things like that . . . people are thrashed! Do you understand?"

Abogin hurriedly felt in his side pocket, pulled out a pocket-book, and extracting two notes flung them on the table.

"Here is the fee for your visit." he said, his nostrils dilating. "You are paid."

"How dare you offer me money?" shouted the doctor and he brushed the notes off the table onto the floor. "An insult cannot be paid for in money!"

Abogin and the doctor stood face to face, and in their wrath continued flinging undeserved insults at each other. I believe that never in their lives, even in delirium, had they uttered so much that was unjust, cruel, and absurd. The egoism of the unhappy was conspicuous in both. The unhappy are egoistic, spiteful, unjust, cruel, and less capable of understanding each other than fools. Unhappiness does not bring people together but draws them apart, and even where one would fancy people should be united by the similarity of their sorrow, far more injustice and cruelty is generated than in comparatively placid surroundings.

"Kindly let me go home!" shouted the doctor, breathing hard.

Abogin rang the bell sharply. When no one came to answer the bell he rang again and angrily flung the bell on the floor; it fell on the carpet with a muffled sound, and uttered a plaintive note as though at the point of death. A footman came in.

"Where have you been hiding yourself, the devil take you?" His master flew at him, clenching his fists. "Where were you just now? Go and tell them to bring the victoria round for this gentleman, and order the closed carriage to be got ready for me. Stay," he cried as the footman turned to go out. "I won't have a single traitor in the house by to-morrow! Away with you all! I will engage fresh servants! Reptiles!"

Abogin and the doctor remained in silence waiting for the carriage. The first regained his expression of sleekness and his refined elegance. He paced up and down the room, tossed his head elegantly, and was evidently meditating on something. His anger had not cooled, but he tried to appear not to notice his enemy. . . . The doctor stood, leaning with one hand on the edge of the table, and looked at Abogin with that profound and somewhat cynical, ugly contempt only to be found in the eyes of sorrow and indigence when they are confronted with well-nourished comfort and elegance.

When a little later the doctor got into the victoria and drove off there was still a look of contempt in his eyes. It was dark, much darker than it had been an hour before. The red half-moon had sunk behind the hill and the clouds that had been guarding it lay in dark patches near the stars. The carriage with red lamps rattled along the road and soon overtook the doctor. It was Abogin driving off to protest, to do absurd things. . . .

All the way home the doctor thought not of his wife, nor of his Andrey, but of Abogin and the people in the house he had just left. His thoughts were unjust and inhumanly cruel. He condemned Abogin and his wife and Paptchinsky and all who lived in rosy, subdued light among sweet perfumes, and all the way home he hated and despised them till his head ached. And a firm conviction concerning those people took shape in his mind.

Time will pass and Kirilov's sorrow will pass, but that conviction, unjust and unworthy of the human heart, will not pass, but will remain in the doctor's mind to the grave.

CONSTANTINE CAVAFY (1863–1933)
Egypt; Greek

One of the great modern European poets, Constantine Cavafy had an international upbringing and international literary interests. Technically a Greek citizen, although he visited Athens only a few times, he spent most of his life as a civil servant in Alexandria, the ancient Egyptian city where he was born. At home in English and French, an admirer of T. S. Eliot and a friend of E. M. Forster, Cavafy was the most original and influential poet writing in the Greek language in this century. He also gave a new lift to Greek poetic language: his poetry combines formal and informal styles, Hellenistic expressions, and ironic tone. He writes of his homosexual experiences with directness and candor. In "Ithaka," a poem named after the Greek island that was Odysseus's home, Cavafy presents an internalized "instruction" to an Odysseus-like voyager who will see the world and carry the image of home with him wherever he goes.

Ithaka

As you set out for Ithaka
hope your road is a long one,
full of adventure, full of discovery.
Laistrygonians,[1] Cyclops,[2]
angry Poseidon[3]—don't be afraid of them:
you'll never find things like that on your way
as long as you keep your thoughts raised high,

5

Translated by Edmund Keeley and Philip Sherrard.

---

1. The Laistrygonians were giant cannibals whom some of Odysseus's party meets ashore (in Book 10 of the *Odyssey*) on the way back from Troy. The huge daughter of their king invites them to meet her father, who promptly crushes them to bits. Odysseus, learning this, pulls up his anchor and sets sail, but the giants throw boulders down at those of his ships that are too slow-moving.
2. A giant with one eye in the middle of his forehead.
3. The Greek god of the sea; Neptune in Roman mythology.

as long as a rare excitement
stirs your spirit and your body.
Laistrygonians, Cyclops,   10
wild Poseidon—you won't encounter them
unless you bring them along inside your soul,
unless your soul sets them up in front of you.

Hope your road is a long one.
May there be many summer mornings when,   15
with what pleasure, what joy,
you enter harbours you're seeing for the first time;
may you stop at Phoenician trading stations
to buy fine things,
mother of pearl and coral, amber and ebony,   20
sensual perfume of every kind—
as many sensual perfumes as you can;
and may you visit many Egyptian cities
to learn and go on learning from their scholars.

Keep Ithaka always in your mind.   25
Arriving there is what you're destined for.
But don't hurry the journey at all.
Better if it lasts for years,
so you're old by the time you reach the island,
wealthy with all you've gained on the way,   30
not expecting Ithaka to make you rich.

Ithaka gave you the marvellous journey.
Without her you wouldn't have set out.
She has nothing left to give you now.

And if you find her poor, Ithaka won't have fooled you.   35
Wise as you will have become, so full of experience,
you'll have understood by then what these Ithakas mean.

WILLIAM BUTLER YEATS (1865–1939)
Ireland

The son of the painter John Butler Yeats, William Butler Yeats studied painting for three years. In London, he was a founding member of the Pre-Raphaelite Rhymer's Club, under the sway of "pure" poetry and the cult of Walter Pater. Upon his return to Ireland, Yeats became a leader of the Irish Renaissance and a lifelong passionate admirer of its heroine, Maud Gonne. With Lady Gregory and

George Moore, he founded the Abbey Theatre in 1899, and wrote many of his plays for it. Under Ezra Pound's influence, he wrote ritualistic, symbolic dramas like the Japanese Nō plays. He was awarded the Nobel Prize in 1923. An Irish nationalist and a major figure in the Irish Literary Renaissance at the beginning of the twentieth century, William Butler Yeats was above all a symbolist, whose attachment to Irish tradition and legends provided him with the material for his poetry. Heavily steeped in mysticism, his haunting songs to the imaginative possibilities of the poetic mind have been immensely influential on subsequent English-language poetry. "The Lover Tells of the Rose in His Heart" is a heartrending lament on the passing of time, invoked in the traditional image of the rose (recurrent in symbolist poetry) and its evanescent loveliness. "Leda and the Swan" invokes the myth of the beloved beauty who was visited by Zeus in the form of a swan, but it also harks back to the Trojan War and other violent events: the god who loves the mortal swoops her up, impregnates her, and lets her drop; she will give birth to a legend, to Helen of Troy, to the death of the Greek leader Agamemnon, and to the future. "Sailing to Byzantium" opposes the stylized and undying representations of oriental art to the natural and sensual realization of what lives and dies, more freely and with less craft; art wins out over life, sacrificed to the golden bird and its song, of which the poem sings in its turn.

The Lake Isle of Innisfree

I will arise and go now, and go to Innisfree,
And a small cabin build there, of clay and wattles made:
Nine bean-rows will I have there, a hive for the honeybee,
And live alone in the bee-loud glade.

And I shall have some peace there, for peace comes dropping slow, 5
Dropping from the veils of the morning to where the cricket sings;
There midnight's all a glimmer, and noon a purple glow,
And evening full of the linnet's wings.

I will arise and go now, for always night and day
I hear lake water lapping with low sounds by the shore;
While I stand on the roadway, or on the pavements grey, 10
I hear it in the deep heart's core.

The Lover Tells of the Rose in His Heart

All things uncomely and broken, all things worn out and old,
The cry of a child by the roadway, the creak of a lumbering cart,
The heavy steps of the ploughman, splashing the wintry mould,
Are wronging your image that blossoms a rose in the deeps of my heart.

The wrong of unshapely things is a wrong too great to be told; 5
I hunger to build them anew and sit on a green knoll apart,
With the earth and the sky and the water, re-made, like a casket of gold
For my dreams of your image that blossoms a rose in the deeps of my heart.

Leda and the Swan

A sudden blow: the great wings beating still
Above the staggering girl, her thighs caressed
By the dark webs, her nape caught in his bill,
He holds her helpless breast upon his breast.

How can those terrified vague fingers push   5
The feathered glory from her loosening thighs?
And how can body, laid in that white rush,
But feel the strange heart beating where it lies?

A shudder in the loins engenders there
The broken wall, the burning roof and tower   10
And Agamemnon dead.

                  Being so caught up,
So mastered by the brute blood of the air,
Did she put on his knowledge with his power
Before the indifferent beak could let her drop?   15

Sailing to Byzantium

I

That is no country for old men. The young
In one another's arms, birds in the trees
—Those dying generations—at their song,
The salmon-falls, the mackerel-crowded seas,
Fish, flesh, or fowl, commend all summer long   5
Whatever is begotton, born, and dies.
Caught in that sensual music all neglect
Monuments of unageing intellect.

II

An aged man is but a paltry thing,
A tattered coat upon a stick, unless   10
Soul clap its hands and sing, and louder sing
For every tatter in its mortal dress,
Nor is there singing school but studying
Monuments of its own magnificence;
And therefore I have sailed the seas and come   15
To the holy city of Byzantium.

III

O sages standing in God's holy fire
As in the gold mosaic of a wall,
Come from the holy fire, perne in a gyre,[1]
And be the singing-masters of my soul.
Consume my heart away; sick with desire   20
And fastened to a dying animal
It knows not what it is; and gather me
Into the artifice of eternity.

IV

Once out of nature I shall never take
My bodily form from any natural thing,   25
But such a form as Grecian goldsmiths make
Of hammered gold and gold enamelling
To keep a drowsy Emperor awake;
Or set upon a golden bough to sing
To lords and ladies of Byzantium   30
Of what is past, or passing, or to come.

(1927)

RAINER MARIA RILKE (1875–1926)
Austro-Hungarian Empire; German

Born in Prague to German-speaking parents, Rainer Maria Rilke was sent to
military academies, then to the University of Prague. In the artists' colony of
Worpswede outside of Bremen, he met and married the sculptor Clara Westhoff,
whom he abandoned with their child when he left for Paris, where he served as
Rodin's secretary and wrote poetry in French. He returned to Germany during
the war, and after 1919, lived in Switzerland, where he died of blood poisoning
after being pricked by a rose thorn.

   The greatest modern poet in the German language, Rilke also wrote one of
the twentieth century's most influential novels, *The Notebooks of Malte Laurids
Brigge* (1910). Although he wrote much poetry that was religiously inspired—
some of it by Slavic mysticism—his best work combines a modern scientific
precision of observation and statement with the lyric virtuosity of Goethe and the

---

1. The sages are invited to move in a spiral (as
   thread around a bobbin—"pirn"), into the
   gyres or cycles of history.

metaphysical questioning of Hölderlin. His major poetic achievements are the *Book of Pictures* (1902–1906), the *New Poems* (1907–1908), *The Duino Elegies* (1912–1922) and *The Sonnets to Orpheus* (1922). The early "Autumn Day" has the sweet-sad nostalgic tone of Hölderlin and other French and German romantics; a tone that permeates much of this major poetry. "Archaic Torso of Apollo," from the *New Poems,* in the form of a Petrarchan sonnet, shows the quantum leap of energy that results from an observer's intense observation of an unpolished and broken work of art, a statue. The "unicorn" poem from *The Sonnets to Orpheus* combines all the diverse hopes held out by legend, religion, love, and poetry into a lyric statement of possibility that goes past them all.

from The Sonnets to Orpheus

[Oh this is the animal that never was]

II, 4

Oh this is the animal that never was.
They hadn't seen one; but just the same, they loved
its graceful movements, and the way it stood
looking at them calmly, with clear eyes.

It had not *been*. But for them, it appeared   5
in all its purity. They left space enough.
And in the space hollowed out by their love
it stood up all at once and didn't need

existence. They nourished it, not with grain,
but with the mere possibility of being.   10
And finally this gave it so much power

that from its forehead a horn grew. One horn.
It drew near to a virgin, white, gleaming—
and was, inside the mirror and in her.

from The Book of Pictures

Autumn Day

Lord: it is time. The huge summer has gone by.
Now overlap the sundials with your shadows,
and on the meadows let the wind go free.

Command the fruits to swell on tree and vine;   5
grant them a few more warm transparent days,
urge them on to fulfillment then, and press
the final sweetness into the heavy wine.

Translated by Stephen Mitchell.

Whoever has no house now, will never have one.
Whoever is alone will stay alone,
will sit, read, write long letters through the evening,   10
and wander on the boulevards, up and down,
restlessly, while the dry leaves are blowing.

from **New Poems**

Archaic Torso of Apollo[1]

We cannot know his legendary head
with eyes like ripening fruit. And yet his torso
is still suffused with brilliance from inside,
like a lamp, in which his gaze, now turned to low,

gleams in all its power. Otherwise   5
the curved breast could not dazzle you so, nor could
a smile run through the placid hips and thighs
to that dark center where procreation flared.

Otherwise this stone would seem defaced
beneath the translucent cascade of the shoulders   10
and would not glisten like a wild beast's fur:

would not, from all the borders of itself,
burst like a star: for here there is no place
that does not see you. You must change your life.

ANTONIO MACHADO (1873–1939)
Spain/France

Born in Andalusia, a landscape sensible in his early poetry, Machado traveled to
Paris in 1899, studied with the French philosopher Henri Bergson, and met the
French symbolist and modernist poets—among them, Ruben Dario—to whom
his own writing was sympathetic. He spent most of his life in Castile, and was
considered a major poet both of Castile and Andalusia, and one of the leading
poets of the Generation of '98; his best-known collection is *Campos de Castilla*
(1912–1917). *Loyal to the Republic*, he left Spain after the fall of Catalonia in the

---

1. Inspired by the fifth-century *Torso of a
   Youth* from Miletis (a Greek colony on
   coast of Asia Minor); Apollo represents the
   ideal male youth. Archaic here signifies that
   period of ancient Greek art (c. 630–480
   B.C.E.) just before the classical period.

Civil War and died in Collioure, a tiny French town of painters. His descriptions of the somber Castilian landscape in "Naked Is the Earth" are inescapably powerful as is "The Crime Was in Granada," his elegy for the death—at the hands of the Spanish Militia—of Federico García Lorca.

Naked Is the Earth

Naked is the earth,
and the soul howls to the pale horizon
like a hungry she-wolf. Poet, what do you seek
in the sunset?

Bitter walking, for the road   5
weighs upon the heart. The frozen wind
and coming night, and the bitterness
of distance! On the white road

a few stiff trees blacken;
in the distant mountains there is gold   10
and blood. The sun is dead. Poet, what do you seek
in the sunset?

The Crime Was in Granada

I

He was seen walking between rifles
down a long street,
coming upon the cold field
which still held stars of early dawn.
They killed Federico   5
when daylight came.
The squad of executioners
dared not look upon his face.
All had shut their eyes.
They prayed: Not even God can save you!   10
Dead fell Federico—
blood on his forehead and lead in his entrails.
. . . . Oh, that the crime was in Granada.
Let all know it! Poor Granada! In his Granada!

Translated by Willis Barnstone.

II

The Poet and Death

He was seen walking alone with her,   15
without fear of her scythe.
The sun was already on the towers; hammers
on the anvils, anvils and anvils of the forges.
Federico spoke,
flirting with death. She listened.   20
"Because the clapping of your dry palms
sounded yesterday in my verse, companion,
and you gave ice to my song and the edge
of your silver sickle to my tragedy,
I will sing you the flesh you do not have,   25
the eyes you lack,
the hair the wind was ruffling,
the red lips where they kissed you.
Today as before, gypsy, my death,
how good it is alone with you   30
in these winds of Granada, my Granada!"

III

He was seen walking . . .
        My friends, build
of stone and dream in the Alhambra,
a tomb for the poet,   35
over a fountain where water weeps
and says eternally:
The crime was in Granada, in his Granada!

FILIPPO TOMMASO MARINETTI

(1876–1944)

Italy

Filippo Tommaso Marinetti was born in Alexandria, Egypt, and died in Bellagio.
Rich, energetic, and a superb organizer, he was the scourge of the ritualistic and
the academic sides of Italian cultural life from the time he broadcast his First
Manifesto in 1909. The founder of Italian furturism, Marinetti was on the side of
Mussolini and on the side of war: he loved its noise and its violence, and he

wanted for his own work the same energy and intensity as that conveyed on the battleground; all the Italian Futurists participated in the First World War. Boccioni and Sant' Elia were killed, and Marinetti and Russolo were wounded. Marinetti's position was clear: burn the libraries and all the books; down with culture; murder the moonshine and all sentimentality. He praised the rapid— particularly the automobile—and detested anything slow, sweet, or sacred. Art should be, he thought, quick and stimulating, the opposite of boring. "The New Religion-Morality of Speed" is a manifesto sounding loud, an intellectual/sensual explosion exemplifying the Italian Futurist movement, highly attractive to Tristan Tzara, whose Dada manifestos owe it a great deal, and to Guillaume Apollinaire, who was himself to write an upbeat and peculiar Futurist manifesto. Other Futurist eulogies to speed, like that of Velimir Khlebnikov, were to determine the course of avant-garde poetry in Russia.

The New Religion-Morality of Speed
Futurist Manifesto Published in the First Number of *L'Italia Futurista*
May 11, 1916

In my First Manifesto (February 20, 1909) I declared: the magnificence of the world has been enriched by a new beauty, *the beauty of speed*. Following dynamic art, the new religion-morality of speed is born this Futurist year from our great liberating war. Christian morality served to develop man's inner life. Today it has lost its reason for existing, because it has been emptied of all divinity.

Christian morality defended the physiological structure of man from the excesses of sensuality. It moderated his instincts and balanced them. The *Futurist morality* will defend man from the decay caused by slowness, by memory, by analysis, by repose and habit. Human energy centupled by speed will master Time and Space.

Man began by despising the isochronal, cadenced rhythm, identical with the rhythm of his own stride, of the great rivers. Man envied the rhythm of torrents, like that of a horse's gallop. Man mastered horse, elephant, and camel to display his divine authority through an increase in speed. He made friends with the most docile animals, captured the rebellious animals, and fed himself with the eatable animals. From space man stole electricity and then the liquid fuels, to make new allies for himself in the motors. Man shaped the metals he had conquered and made flexible with fire, to ally himself with his fuels and electricity. He thereby assembled an army of slaves, dangerous and hostile but sufficiently domesticated to carry him swiftly over the curves of the earth.

Tortuous paths, roads that follow the indolence of streams and wind along the spines and uneven bellies of mountains, these are the laws of the earth. Never straight lines; always arabesques and zigzags. Speed finally gives to human life one of the characteristics of divinity: *the straight line*.

The opaque Danube under its muddy tunic, its attention turned on its inner

Translated by R. W. Flint and Arthur A. Coppotelli.

Luigi Russolo. *Dynamisme d'une automobile.* 1911. Musée National d'Art Moderne, Paris.

life full of fat libidinous fecund fish, runs murmuring between the high implacable banks of its mountains as if within the immense central corridor of the earth, a convent split open by the swift wheels of the constellations. How long will this shuffling stream allow an automobile, barking like a crazy fox terrier, to pass it at top speed? I hope to see the day when the Danube will run in a straight line at 300 kilometers an hour.

One must persecute, lash, torture all those who sin against speed.

Grave guilt of the passéist cities where the sun settles in, slows down, and never moves again. Who can believe that the sun will go away tonight? Nonsense! Impossible! It has been domiciled here. Squares, lakes of stagnant fire. Streets, rivers of lazy fire. No one can pass, for the moment. You can't escape! An inundation of sun. You would need a refrigerated boat or a diving suit of ice to cross that fire. Dig in. A despotism, a police raid of light, about to arrest the rebels in their blazons of coolness and speed. A solar state of siege. Woe to the body that leaves home. A sledgehammer blow on the head. Finished. Solar guillotine over every door. Woe to the thought that leaves its skull. Two, three, four leaden notes will fall on it from the ruined bell tower. In the house, sultrily, a madness of nostalgic flies. A stir of thighs and sweaty memories.

Criminal slowness of Sunday crowds and the Venetian lagoons.

Speed, having as its essence the intuitive synthesis of every force in movement, is naturally *pure.* Slowness, having as its essence the rational analysis of every exhaustion in repose, is naturally *unclean.* After the destruction of the antique good and the antique evil, we create a new good, speed, and a new evil, slowness.

Speed = synthesis of every courage in action. Aggressive and warlike.

Slowness = analysis of every stagnant prudence. Passive and pacifistic.

Speed = scorn of obstacles, desire for the new and unexplored. Modernity, hygiene.

Slowness = arrest, ecstasy, immobile adoration of obstacles, nostalgia for the already seen, idealization of exhaustion and rest, pessimism about the unexplored. Rancid romanticism of the wild, wandering poet and long-haired, bespectacled dirty philosopher.

If prayer means communication with the divinity, running at high speed is a prayer. Holiness of wheels and rails. One must kneel on the tracks to pray to the divine velocity. One must kneel before the whirling speed of a gyroscope compass: 20,000 revolutions per minute, the highest mechanical speed reached by man. One must snatch from the stars the secret of their stupefying, incomprehensible speed. Then let us join the great celestial battles, vie with the star 1830 Groombridge that flies at 241 km. a second, with Arthur that flies at 413 km. a second. Invisible mathematical artillery. Wars in which the stars, being both missiles and artillery, match their speeds to escape from a greater star or to strike a smaller one. Our male saints are the numberless corpuscles that penetrate our atmosphere at an average velocity of 42,000 meters a second. Our female saints are the light and electromagnetic waves at 3×10^{10} meters a second.

The intoxication of great speeds in cars is nothing but the joy of feeling oneself fused with the only *divinity*. Sportsmen are the first catechumens of this religion. Forthcoming destruction of houses and cities, to make way for great meeting places for cars and planes.

GUILLAUME APOLLINAIRE (1880–1918)
Italy/France; French

Guillaume Apollinaire, born in Italy as Wilhelm Apollinaris de Kostrowitski, an illegitimate child, said to be related to a Pope, met Alfred Jarry in Paris in 1898 and was attracted to the idea of a synthesis in the arts. He was a cocelebrator of the adventurous New Spirit ("L'esprit nouveau") with other avant-gardists; the poem "Always" bears witness to this preoccupation, with its insistence on openness. He wants to include many new things in poetry: the reading aloud of newspapers, tapping on your cheeks to make a hollow sound, and the transcription of anything you hear around you, recorded in his "conversation poems." Associated both with "simultaneism," an attitude of celebration of many things happening at once, and with cubism, allied as he was with Picasso and Braque, and with the poets Pierre Reverdy, Blaise Cendrans, and Max Jacob, Apollinaire wrote an influential study of *The Cubist Painters: Aesthetic Meditations*, (1913). He is beloved above all for poems such as the epic "Zone" and "The Farewell," included here, with their intense lyric feeling: they come from his inebriating collection *Alcools,* originally called *Eau-de-vie,* named after not just strong alcohols but literally "the water of life." "Always" and "The Pretty Red-Head" are both the poetic equivalent of a manifesto, which tries to bridge tradition and adventure but finally celebrate the "new spirit" without looking back. Apollinaire's greatest poems bear witness to the warmth of his personality as they do to his adventurous spirit. In order to enlist in the war, he adopted French nationality. He had admired war as a spectacle—as Marinetti had for its noise. He was wounded, but died of Spanish fever at the time of the armistice.

from Alcohols

The Farewell

I picked this fragile sprig of heather
Autumn has died long since remember
Never again shall we see one another
Odor of time sprig of heather
Remember I await our life together   5

from Calligrams

The Pretty Red-Head

Behold me before all a man of good sense
Knowing life and of death what a living man can know
Having experienced the griefs and the joys of love
Having been able to assert his ideas on occasion
Knowing several languages   5
Having travelled a good bit
Having seen the war in the Artillery and Infantry
Wounded in the head trepanned under chloroform
Having lost his best friends in that frightful struggle
I know of the old and of the new as much as one man alone can know of them   10
And without being uneasy today about this war
Between us and for us my friends
I pronounce judgement on this long quarrel of tradition and innovation
            Of Order and Adventure

You whose mouths are made in the image of God's   15
            Mouths which are order itself

Be indulgent when you compare us
To those who have been the perfection of order
We who seek everywhere for adventure

We are not your enemies   20
We wish to offer you vast and strange domains

Translated by Roger Shattuck.

Where flowering mystery offers itself to whoever wishes to pick it
There are new fires there and colors never yet seen
A thousand imponderable phantasms
To which reality must be given   25
We would explore goodness a vast country where everything is silent
There is also time which one can banish or call back
Pity us who fight always in the front lines
Of the limitless and of the future
Pity our errors pity our sins   30
Behold the return of summer season of violence
And my youth died like the spring
O Sun it is the time for flaming Judgement
      And I wait
To follow for ever the sweet noble form   35
It assumes in order that I may love it alone
It comes and it attracts me as a magnet does the needle
    It looks for all the world just like
    My redhead darling my beloved

Her hair is really gold you'd say   40
A flash of lightning which endures
Or flames which dance a proud pavane
In roses as they slowly fade

But laugh laugh long at me
Men from anywhere above all men of this place   45
for there are so many things I dare not tell you
So many things you will not let me say
Have pity on me

JAMES JOYCE (1882–1941)
Ireland

Son of an always impoverished civil servant and extremely pious mother, James
Joyce was educated at Jesuit schools in Ireland. In 1902 he left Dublin, but the
language and topography of Ireland marked all his work, as did his early
Catholicism. With Nora Barnacle and their two children, he wandered around
Europe (Paris, Rome, Trieste, and Zurich), his eyesight constantly deteriorating
and his funds constantly depleted, doing clerical work and teaching languages as
long as he could. His books were banned, and his daughter had to be
institutionalized. Joyce is one of the great wordsmiths of literature in English; his
beautiful early collection of stories *Dubliners* (1914), from which "Araby" is

Valerio Adami. *Ritratto di James Joyce.*

taken, was followed in 1916 by the autobiographical novel *A Portrait of the Artist as a Young Man* and in 1922 by his most famous novel, *Ulysses,* which was banned in the United States until 1933. *Finnegans Wake,* pursuing in experimental language the nocturnal dreams and waking of a single character who is at the same time the whole human race, appeared in 1939. "Araby" is a sensitive story of an adolescent boy's love, its mood conveyed by the sharply etched sights and sounds of Dublin.

from **Dubliners**

Araby

North Richmond Street, being blind, was a quiet street except at the hour when the Christian Brothers' School set the boys free. An uninhabited house of two storeys stood at the blind end, detached from its neighbors in a square ground. The other houses of the street, conscious of decent lives within them, gazed at one another with brown imperturbable faces.

The former tenant of our house, a priest, had died in the back drawing-room. Air, musty from having been long enclosed, hung in all the rooms, and the waste room behind the kitchen was littered with old useless papers. Among these I found a few paper-covered books, the pages of which were curled and damp: *The Abbot,* by Walter Scott, *The Devout Communicant* and *The Memoirs of Vidocq.* I liked the last best because its leaves were yellow. The wild garden behind the house contained a central apple-tree and a few straggling bushes under one of which I found the late tenant's rusty bicycle-pump. He had been a very charitable priest;

in his will he had left all his money to institutions and the furniture of his house to his sister.

When the short days of winter came dusk fell before we had well eaten our dinners. When we met in the street the house had grown sombre. The space of sky above us was the colour of ever-changing violet and towards it the lamps of the street lifted their feeble lanterns. The cold air stung us and we played till our bodies glowed. Our shouts echoed in the silent street. The career of our play brought us through the dark muddy lanes behind the houses where we ran the gauntlet of the rough tribes from the cottages, to the back doors of the dark dripping gardens where odours arose from the ashpits, to the dark odorous stables where a coachman smoothed and combed the horse or shook music from the buckled harness. When we returned to the street light from the kitchen windows had filled the areas. If my uncle was seen turning the corner we hid in the shadow until we had seen him safely housed. Or if Mangan's sister came out on the doorstep to call her brother in to his tea we watched her from our shadow peer up and down the street. We waited to see whether she would remain or go in and, if she remained, we left our shadow and walked up to Mangan's steps resignedly. She was waiting for us, her figure defined by the light from the half-opened door. Her brother always teased her before he obeyed and I stood by the railings looking at her. Her dress swung as she moved her body and the soft rope of her hair tossed from side to side.

Every morning I lay on the floor in the front parlour watching the door. The blind was pulled down to within an inch of the sash so that I could not be seen. When she came out on the doorstep my heart leaped. I ran to the hall, seized my books and followed her. I kept her brown figure always in my eye and, when we came near the point at which our ways diverged, I quickened my pace and passed her. This happened morning after morning. I had never spoke to her, except for a few casual words, and yet her name was like a summons to all my foolish blood.

Her image accompanied me even in places the most hostile to romance. On Saturday evenings when my aunt went marketing I had to go to carry some of the parcels. We walked through the flaring streets, jostled by drunken men and bargaining women, amid the curses of labourers, the shrill litanies of shop-boys who stood on guard by the barrels of pigs' cheeks, the nasal chanting of street-singers, who sang a *come-all-you* about O'Donovan Rossa, or a ballad about the troubles in our native land. These noises converged in a single sensation of life for me: I imagined that I bore my chalice safely through a throng of foes. Her name sprang to my lips at moments in strange prayers and praises which I myself did not understand. My eyes were often full of tears (I could not tell why) and at times a flood from my heart seemed to pour itself out into my bosom. I thought little of the future. I did not know whether I would ever speak to her or not, or, if I spoke to her, how I could tell her of my confused adoration. But my body was like a harp and her words and gestures were like fingers running upon the wires.

One evening I went into the back drawing-room in which the priest had died. It was a dark rainy evening and there was no sound in the house. Through one of the broken panes I heard the rain impinge upon the earth, the fine incessant needles of water playing in the sodden beds. Some distant lamp or lighted window gleamed below me. I was thankful that I could see so little. All my senses seemed to desire to veil themselves and, feeling that I was about to slip from them, I pressed the palms of my hands together until they trembled, murmuring: *"O love! O love!"* many times.

At last she spoke to me. When she addressed the first words to me I was so confused that I did not know what to answer. She asked me was I going to *Araby*. I forgot whether I answered yes or no. It would be a splendid bazaar, she said she would love to go.

"And why can't you?" I asked.

While she spoke she turned a silver bracelet round and round her wrist. She could not go, she said, because there would be a retreat that week in her convent. Her brother and two other boys were fighting for their caps and I was alone at the railings. She held one of the spikes, bowing her head towards me. The light from the lamp opposite our door caught the white curve of her neck, lit up her hair that rested there and, falling, lit up the hand upon the railing. It fell over one side of her dress and caught the white border of a petticoat, just visible as she stood at ease.

"It's well for you," she said.

"If I go," I said, "I will bring you something."

What innumerable follies laid waste my waking and sleeping thoughts after that evening! I wished to annihilate the tedious intervening days. I chafed against the work of school. At night in my bedroom and by day in the classroom her image came between me and the page I strove to read. The syllables of the word *Araby* were called to me through the silence in which my soul luxuriated and cast an Eastern enchantment over me. I asked for leave to go the bazaar on Saturday night. My aunt was surprised and hoped it was not some Freemason affair. I answered few questions in class. I watched my master's face pass from amiability to sternness; he hoped I was not beginning to idle. I could not call my wandering thoughts together. I had hardly any patience with the serious work of life which, now that it stood between me and my desire, seemed to me child's play, ugly monotonous child's play.

On Saturday morning I reminded my uncle that I wished to go to the bazaar in the evening. He was fussing at the hallstand, looking for the hat-brush, and answered me curtly:

"Yes, boy, I know."

As he was in the hall I could not go into the front parlour and lie at the window. I felt the house in bad humor and walked slowly towards the school. The air was pitilessly raw and already my heart misgave me.

When I came home to dinner my uncle had not yet been home. Still it was early. I sat staring at the clock for some time and, when its ticking began to irritate me, I left the room. I mounted the staircase and gained the upper part of the house. The high cold empty gloomy rooms liberated me and I went from room to room singing. From the front window I saw my companions playing below in the street. Their cries reached me weakened and indistinct and, leaning my forehead against the cool glass, I looked over at the dark house where she lived. I may have stood there for an hour, seeing nothing but the brown-clad figure cast by my imagination, touched discreetly by the lamplight at the curved neck, at the hand upon the railings and at the border below the dress.

When I came downstairs again I found Mrs. Mercer sitting at the fire. She was an old garrulous woman, a pawnbroker's widow, who collected used stamps for some pious purpose. I had to endure the gossip of the tea-table. The meal was prolonged beyond an hour and still my uncle did not come. Mrs. Mercer stood up to go: she was sorry she couldn't wait any longer, but it was after eight o'clock and she did not like to be out late, as the night air was bad for her. When she had gone I began to walk up and down the room, clenching my fists. My aunt said:

"I'm afraid you may put off your bazaar for this night of Our Lord."

At nine o'clock I heard my uncle's latchkey in the halldoor. I heard him talking to himself and heard the hallstand rocking when it had received the weight of his overcoat. I could interpret these signs. When he was midway through his dinner I asked him to give the money to go to the bazaar. He had forgotten.

"The people are in bed and after their first sleep now," he said.

I did not smile. My aunt said to him energetically:

"Can't you give him the money and let him go? You've kept him late enough as it is."

My uncle said he was very sorry he had forgotten. He said he believed in the old saying: "All work and no play makes Jack a dull boy." He asked me where I was going and, when I had told him a second time he asked me did I know *The Arab's Farewell to his Steed*. When I left the kitchen he was about to recite the opening lines of the piece to my aunt.

I held a florin tightly in my hand as I strode down Buckingham Street towards the station. The sight of the streets thronged with buyers and glaring with gas recalled to me the purpose of my journey. I took my seat in a third-class carriage of a deserted train. After an intolerable delay the train moved out of the station slowly. It crept onward among ruinous houses and over the twinkling river. At Westland Row Station a crowd of people pressed to the carriage doors; but the porters moved them back, saying that it was a special train for the bazaar. I remained alone in the bare carriage. In a few minutes the train drew up beside an improvised wooden platform. I passed out on to the road and saw by the lighted dial of a clock that it was ten minutes to ten. In front of me was a large building which displayed the magical name.

I could not find any sixpenny entrance and, fearing that the bazaar would be closed, I passed in quickly through a turnstile, handing a shilling to a weary-looking man. I found myself in a big hall girdled at half its height by a gallery. Nearly all the stalls were closed and the greater part of the hall was in darkness. I recognised a silence like that which pervades a church after a service. I walked into the centre of the bazaar timidly. A few people were gathered about the stalls which were still open. Before a curtain, over which the words *Café Chantant* were written in coloured lamps, two men were counting money on a salver. I listened to the fall of the coins.

Remembering with difficulty why I had come I went over to one of the stalls and examined porcelain vases and flowered tea-sets. At the door of the stall a young lady was talking and laughing with two young gentlemen. I remarked their English accents and listened vaguely to their conversation.

"O, I never said such a thing!"

"O, but you did!"

"O, but I didn't!"

"Didn't she say that?"

"Yes, I heard her."

"O, there's a . . . . fib!"

Observing me the young lady came over and asked me did I wish to buy anything. The tone of her voice was not encouraging; she seemed to have spoken to me out of a sense of duty. I looked humbly at the great jars that stood like eastern guards at either side of the dark entrance to the stall and murmured:

"No, thank you."

The young lady changed the position of one of the vases and went back to the two young men. They began to talk of the same subject. Once or twice the young lady glanced at me over her shoulder.

I lingered before her stall, though I knew my stay was useless, to make my interest in her wares seem the more real. Then I turned away slowly and walked down the middle of the bazaar. I allowed the two pennies to fall against the sixpence in my pocket. I heard a voice call from one end of the gallery that the light was out. The upper part of the hall was now completely dark.

Gazing up into the darkness I saw myself as a creature driven and derided by vanity; and my eyes burned with anguish and anger.

VIRGINIA WOOLF (1882–1941)
England

A novelist and critic, whose writing is crucially significant for contemporary feminism, Virginia Stephen was the daughter of the philosopher Sir Leslie Stephen, who is portrayed in perhaps her most famous novel *To the Lighthouse* (1927). She lost her mother, stepmother and half-sister when very young, and her beloved brother not much later. In 1912, she married the critic and writer Leonard Woolf, and they set up the Hogarth Press in 1917. She and her sister Vanessa—who married Clive Bell and lived with Duncan Grant, another painter—together with the historian Lytton Strachey and the art critic Roger Fry, were the heart of the Bloomsbury group. After being plagued all her life by bouts of madness, Virginia Woolf drowned herself so as to spare Leonard further grief.

From her more approachable early work, such as *Mrs. Dalloway* (1925), to later works such as her major epic and poetic novel *The Waves* (1931), Woolf's experiments with forms of thinking unfold like waves themselves, showing an entirely new way of conceiving the universe sensitively. Woolf was also a staunch defender of women's rights to equal consideration with men (*Three Guineas*,

1938, a pamphlet about women's education and place), and to a space private to themselves (*A Room of One's Own,* 1929). "Kew Gardens" of (1919) traces the mental meanderings, the feeling and seeing "stream-of-consciousness" frequent in the modern novel. Her writing here is impressionistic in the strong sense of the word. Eudora Welty speaks movingly of Virginia Woolf and her importance for us: "That beautiful mind! That was the thing. Lucid, passionate, independent, acute, proudly and incessantly nourished, eccentric for honorable reasons, sensitive for every reason, it has marked us forever."*

"Professions for Women," an essay against the Victorian concept of the constantly-nourishing never-complaining woman, or the Angel in the House, is based on a speech given in London in 1931. It is one of Woolf's most influential statements.

Kew Gardens

From the oval-shaped flower-bed there rose perhaps a hundred stalks spreading into heart-shaped or tongue-shaped leaves half way up and unfurling at the tip red or blue or yellow petals, marked with spots of colour raised upon the surface; and from the red, blue or yellow gloom of the throat emerged a straight bar, rough with gold dust and slightly clubbed at the end. The petals were voluminous enough to be stirred by the summer breeze, and when they moved, the red, blue and yellow lights passed one over the other, staining an inch of the brown earth beneath with a spot of the most intricate colour. The light fell either upon the smooth grey back of a pebble, or the shell of a snail with its brown circular veins, or, falling into a raindrop, it expanded with such intensity of red, blue and yellow the thin walls of water that one expected them to burst and disappear. Instead, the drop was left in a second silver grey once more, and the light now settled upon the flesh of a leaf, revealing the branching thread of fibre beneath the surface, and again it moved on and spread its illumination in the vast green spaces beneath the dome of the heart-shaped and tongue-shaped leaves. Then the breeze stirred rather more briskly overhead and the colour was flashed into the air above, into the eyes of the men and women who walk in Kew Gardens in July.

The figures of these men and women straggled past the flower-bed with a curiously irregular movement not unlike that of the white and blue butterflies who crossed the turf in zig-zag flights from bed to bed. The man was about six inches in front of the woman, strolling carelessly, while she bore on with greater purpose, only turning her head now and then to see that the children were not too far behind. The man kept this distance in front of the woman purposely, though perhaps unconsciously, for he wanted to go on with his thoughts.

"Fifteen years ago I came here with Lily," he thought. "We sat somewhere over there by a lake, and I begged her to marry me all through the hot afternoon. How the dragon-fly kept circling round us: how clearly I see the dragon-fly and her shoe with the square silver buckle at the toe. All the time I spoke I saw her shoe and when it moved impatiently I knew without looking up what she was going to say: the whole of her seemed to be in her shoe. And my love, my desire, were in the dragon-fly; for

---

*Eudora Welty, introduction, *To the Lighthouse,* by Virginia Woolf (New York: Harcourt Brace, 1991), vii.

Vanessa Bell. *Virginia Woolf*. 1912. National Portrait Gallery, London.

some reason I thought that if it settled there, on that leaf, the broad one with the red flower in the middle of it, if the dragon-fly settled on the leaf she would say 'Yes' at once. But the dragon-fly went round and round: it never settled anywhere—of course not, happily not, or I shouldn't be walking here with Eleanor and the children—Tell me, Eleanor, d'you ever think of the past?"

"Why do you ask, Simon?"

"Because I've been thinking of the past. I've been thinking of Lily, the woman I might have married . . . . Well, why are you silent? Do you mind my thinking of the past?"

'Why should I mind, Simon? Doesn't one always think of the past, in a garden with men and women lying under the trees? Aren't they one's past, all that remains of it, those men and women, those ghosts lying under the trees, ... one's happiness, one's reality?'

"For me, a square silver shoe-buckle and a dragon fly—"

"For me, a kiss. Imagine six little girls sitting before their easels twenty years ago. down by the side of a lake, painting the water-lilies, the first red water-lilies I'd ever seen. And suddenly a kiss, there on the back of my neck. And my hand shook all the afternoon so that I couldn't paint. I took out my watch and marked the hour when I would allow myself to think of the kiss for five minutes only—it was so precious—the kiss of an old grey-haired woman with a wart on her nose, the mother of all my kisses all my life. Come Caroline, come Hubert."

They walked on past the flower-bed, now walking four abreast, and soon diminished in size among the trees and looked half transparent as the sunlight and shade swam over their backs in large trembling irregular patches.

In the oval flower-bed the snail, whose shell had been stained red, blue and yellow for the space of two minutes or so, now appeared to be moving very slightly in its shell, and next began to labour over the crumbs of loose earth which broke away and rolled down as it passed over them. It appeared to have a definite goal in front of it, differing in this respect from the singular high-stepping angular green insect who attempted to cross in front of it, and waited for a second with its antennae trembling as if in deliberation, and then stepped off as rapidly and strangely in the opposite direction. Brown cliffs with deep green lakes in the hollows, flat blade-like trees that waved from root to tip, round boulders of grey stone, vast crumpled surfaces of a thin crackling texture—all these objects lay across the snail's progress between one stalk and another to his goal. Before he had decided whether to circumvent the arched tent of a dead leaf or to breast it there came past the bed the feet of other human beings.

This time they were both men. The younger of the two wore an expression of perhaps unnatural calm; he raised his eyes and fixed them very steadily in front of him while his companion spoke, and directly his companion had done speaking he looked on the ground again and sometimes opened his lips only after a long pause and sometimes did not open them at all. The elder man had a curiously uneven and shaky method of walking, jerking his hand forward and throwing up his head abruptly, rather in the manner of an impatient carriage horse tired of waiting outside a house; but in the man these gestures were irresolute and pointless. He talked almost incessantly; he smiled to himself and again began to talk, as if the smile had been an answer. He was talking about spirits—the spirits of the dead, who, according to him, were even now telling him all sorts of odd things about their experiences in Heaven.

"Heaven was known to the ancients as Thessaly, William, and now, with this war, the spirit matter is rolling between the hills like thunder." He paused, seemed to listen, smiled, jerked his head and continued:—

"You have a small electric battery and a piece of rubber to insulate the wire—isolate?—insulate?—well, we'll skip the details, no good going into details that wouldn't be understood—and in short the little machine stands in any convenient position by the head of the bed, we will say, on a neat mahogany stand. All arrangements being properly fixed by workmen under my direction, the widow applies her ear and summons the spirit by sign as agreed. Women! Widows! Women in black—"

Here he seemed to have caught sight of a woman's dress in the distance, which in the shade looked a purple black. He took off his hat, placed his hand upon his heart, and hurried towards her muttering and gesticulating feverishly. But William caught him by the sleeve and touched a flower with the top of his walking-stick in order to divert the old man's attention. After looking at it for a moment in some confusion the old man bent his ear to it and seemed to answer a voice speaking from it, for he began talking about the forests of Uruguay which he had visited hundreds of years ago in company with the most beautiful young woman in Europe. He could be heard murmuring about forests of Uruguay blanketed with the wax petals of tropical roses, nightingales, sea beaches, mermaids and women drowned at sea, as he suffered himself to be moved on by

William, upon whose face the look of stoical patience grew slowly deeper and deeper.

Following his steps so closely as to be slightly puzzled by his gestures came two elderly women of the lower middle class, one stout and ponderous, the other rosy-cheeked and nimble. Like most people of their station they were frankly fascinated by any signs of eccentricity betokening a disordered brain, especially in the well-to-do; but they were too far off to be certain whether the gestures were merely eccentric or genuinely mad. After they had scrutinised the old man's back in silence for a moment and given each other a queer, sly look, they went on energetically piecing together their very complicated dialogue:

"Nell, Bert, Lot, Cess, Phil, Pa, he says, I says, she says, I says, I says, I says—"
"My Bert, Sis, Bill, Grandad, the old man, sugar,

Sugar, flour, kippers, greens
Sugar, sugar, sugar."

The ponderous woman looked through the pattern of falling words at the flowers standing cool, firm and upright in the earth, with a curious expression. She saw them as a sleeper waking from a heavy sleep sees a brass candlestick reflecting the light in an unfamiliar way, and closes his eyes and opens them, and seeing the brass candlestick again, finally starts broad awake and stares at the candlestick with all his powers. So the heavy woman came to a standstill opposite the oval-shaped flower-bed, and ceased even to pretend to listen to what the other woman was saying. She stood there letting the words fall over her, swaying the top part of her body slowly backwards and forwards, looking at the flowers. Then she suggested that they should find a seat and have their tea.

The snail had now considered every possible method of reaching his goal without going round the dead leaf or climbing over it. Let alone the effort needed for climbing a leaf, he was doubtful whether the thin texture which vibrated with such an alarming crackle when touched even by the tip of his horns would bear his weight; and this determined him finally to creep beneath it, for there was a point where the leaf curved high enough from the ground to admit him. He had just inserted his head in the opening and was taking stock of the high brown roof and was getting used to the cool brown light when two other people came past outside on the turf. This time they were both young, a young man and a young woman. They were both in the prime of youth, or even in that season which precedes the prime of youth, the season before the smooth pink folds of the flower have burst their gummy case, when the wings of the butterfly, though fully grown, are motionless in the sun.

"Lucky it isn't Friday," he observed.
"Why? D'you believe in luck?"
"They make you pay sixpence on Friday."
"What's sixpence anyway? Isn't it worth sixpence?"
"What's 'it'—what do you mean by 'it'?"
"O anything—I mean—you know what I mean."
Long pauses came between each of these remarks: they were uttered in toneless and monotonous voices. The couple stood still on the edge of the

flower-bed, and together pressed the end of her parasol deep down into the soft earth. The action and the fact that his hand rested on the top of hers expressed their feelings in a strange way, as these short insignificant words also expressed something, words with short wings for their heavy body of meaning, inadequate to carry them far and thus alighting awkwardly upon the very common objects that surrounded them and were to their inexperienced touch so massive: but who knows (so they thought as they pressed the parasol into the earth) what precipices aren't concealed in them, or what slopes of ice don't shine in the sun on the other side? Who knows? Who has ever seen this before? Even when she wondered what sort of tea they gave you at Kew, he felt that something loomed up behind her words, and stood vast and solid behind them; and the mist very slowly rose and uncovered—O Heavens,—what were those shapes?—little white tables, and waitresses who looked first at her and then at him; and there was a bill that he would pay with a real two shilling piece, and it was real, all real, he assured himself, fingering the coin in his pocket, real to everyone except to him and to her; even to him it began to seem real; and then—but it was too exciting to stand and think any longer, and he pulled the parasol out of the earth with a jerk and was impatient to find the place where one had tea with other people, like other people.

"Come along, Trissie; it's time we had our tea."

"Wherever *does* one have one's tea?" she asked with the oddest thrill of excitement in her voice, looking vaguely round and letting herself be drawn on down the grass path, trailing her parasol, turning her head this way and that way, forgetting her tea, wishing to go down there and then down there, remembering orchids and cranes among wild flowers, a Chinese pagoda and a crimson-crested bird; but he bore her on.

Thus one couple after another with much the same irregular and aimless movement passed the flower-bed and were enveloped in layer after layer of green-blue vapour, in which at first their bodies had substance and a dash of colour, but later both substance and colour dissolved in the green-blue atmosphere. How hot it was! So hot that even the thrush chose to hop, like a mechanical bird, in the shadow of the flowers, with long pauses between one movement and the next; instead of rambling vaguely the white butterflies danced once above another, making with their white shifting flakes the outline of a shattered marble column above the tallest flowers; the glass roofs of the palm house shone as if a whole market full of shiny green umbrellas had opened in the sun; and in the drone of the aeroplane the voice of the summer sky murmured its fierce soul. Yellow and black, pink and snow white, shapes of all these colours, men, women and children, were spotted for a second upon the horizon, and then, seeing the breadth of yellow that lay upon the grass, they wavered and sought shade beneath the trees, dissolving like drops of water in the yellow and green atmosphere, staining it faintly with red and blue. It seemed as if all gross and heavy bodies had sunk down in the heat motionless and lay huddled upon the ground, but their voices went wavering from them as if they were flames lolling from the thick waxen bodies of candles. Voices, yes, voices, wordless voices, breaking the silence suddenly with such depth of contentment, such passion of desire, or, in the voices of children, such freshness of surprise; breaking the silence? But there was no silence; all the time the motor omnibuses were turning their wheels and changing their gear; like a vast nest of Chinese boxes all of wrought steel turning ceaselessly one within another the city murmured; on the top of which the voices cried aloud and the petals of myriads of flowers flashed their colours into the air.

Professions for Women

When your secretary invited me to come here, she told me that your Society is concerned with the employment of women and she suggested that I might tell you something about my own professional experiences. It is true I am a woman; it is true I am employed; but what professional experiences have I had? It is difficult to say. My profession is literature; and in that profession there are fewer experiences for women than in any other, with the exception of the stage—fewer, I mean, that are peculiar to women. For the road was cut many years ago—by Fanny Burney, by Aphra Behn, by Harriet Martineau, by Jane Austen, by George Eliot—many famous women, and many more unknown and forgotten, have been before me, making the path smooth, and regulating my steps. Thus, when I came to write, there were very few material obstacles in my way. Writing was a reputable and harmless occupation. The family peace was not broken by the scratching of a pen. No demand was made upon the family purse. For ten and sixpence one can buy paper enough to write all the plays of Shakespeare—if one has a mind that way. Pianos and models, Paris, Vienna and Berlin, masters and mistresses, are not needed by a writer. The cheapness of writing paper is, of course, the reason why women have succeeded as writers before they have succeeded in the other professions.

But to tell you my story—it is a simple one. You have only got to figure to yourselves a girl in a bedroom with a pen in her hand. She had only to move that pen from left to right—from ten o'clock to one. Then it occurred to her to do what is simple and cheap enough after all—to slip a few of those pages into an envelope, fix a penny stamp in the corner, and drop the envelope into the red box at the corner. It was thus that I became a journalist; and my effort was rewarded on the first day of the following month—a very glorious day it was for me—by a letter from an editor containing a cheque for one pound ten shillings and sixpence. But to show you how little I deserve to be called a professional woman, how little I know of the struggles and difficulties of such lives, I have to admit that instead of spending that sum upon bread and butter, rent, shoes and stockings, or butcher's bills, I went out and bought a cat—a beautiful cat, a Persian cat, which very soon involved me in bitter disputes with my neighbours.

What could be easier than to write articles and to buy Persian cats with the profits? But wait a moment. Articles have to be about something. Mine, I seem to remember, was about a novel by a famous man. And while I was writing this review, I discovered that if I were going to review books I should need to do battle with a certain phantom. And the phantom was a woman, and when I came to know her better I called her after the heroine of a famous poem, The Angel in the

House. It was she who used to come between me and my paper when I was writing reviews. It was she who bothered me and wasted my time and so tormented me that at last I killed her. You who come of a younger and happier generation may not have heard of her—you may not know what I mean by the Angel in the House. I will describe her as shortly as I can. She was intensely sympathetic. She was immensely charming. She was utterly unselfish. She excelled in the difficult arts of family life. She sacrificed herself daily. If there was chicken, she took the leg; if there was a draught she sat in it—in short she was so constituted that she never had a mind or a wish of her own, but preferred to sympathize always with the minds and wishes of others. Above all—I need not say it—she was pure. Her purity was supposed to be her chief beauty—her blushes, her great grace. In those days—the last of Queen Victoria—every house had its Angel. And when I came to write I encountered her with the very first words. The shadow of her wings fell on my page; I heard the rustling of her skirts in the room. Directly, that is to say, I took my pen in my hand to review that novel by a famous man, she slipped behind me and whispered: 'My dear, you are a young woman. You are writing about a book that has been written by a man. Be sympathetic; be tender; flatter; deceive; use all the arts and wiles of our sex. Never let anybody guess that you have a mind of your own. Above all, be pure.' And she made as if to guide my pen. I now record the one act for which I take some credit to myself, though the credit rightly belongs to some excellent ancestors of mine who left me a certain sum of money—shall we say five hundred pounds a year?—so that it was not necessary for me to depend solely on charm for my living. I turned upon her and caught her by the throat. I did my best to kill her. My excuse, if I were to be had up in a court of law, would be that I acted in self-defence. Had I not killed her she would have killed me. She would have plucked the heart out of my writing. For, as I found, directly I put pen to paper, you cannot review even a novel without having a mind of your own, without expressing what you think to be the truth about human relations, morality, sex. And all these questions, according to the Angel of the House, cannot be dealt with freely and openly by women; they must charm, they must conciliate, they must—to put it bluntly—tell lies if they are to succeed. Thus, whenever I felt the shadow of her wing or the radiance of her halo upon my page, I took up the inkpot and flung it at her. She died hard. Her fictitious nature was of great assistance to her. It is far harder to kill a phantom than a reality. She was always creeping back when I thought I had despatched her. Though I flatter myself that I killed her in the end, the struggle was severe; it took much time that had better have been spent upon learning Greek grammar; or in roaming the world in search of adventures. But it was a real experience; it was an experience that was found to befall all women writers at that time. Killing the Angel in the House was part of the occupation of a woman writer.

But to continue my story. The Angel was dead; what then remained? You may say that what remained was a simple and common object—a young woman in a bedroom with an inkpot. In other words, now that she had rid herself of falsehood, that young woman had only to be herself. Ah, but what is 'herself'? I mean, what is a woman? I assure you, I do not know. I do not believe that you know. I do not believe that anybody can know until she has expressed herself in all the arts and professions open to human skill. That indeed is one of the reasons why I have come here—out of respect for you, who are in process of showing us by your experiments what a woman is, who are in process of providing us, by your failures and successes, with that extremely important piece of information.

But to continue the story of my professional experiences. I made one pound ten and six by my first review; and I bought a Persian cat with the proceeds. Then I grew ambitious. A Persian cat is all very well, I said; but a Persian cat is not enough. I must have a motor car. And it was thus that I became a novelist—for it is a very strange thing that people will give you a motor car if you will tell them a story. It is a still stranger thing that there is nothing so delightful in the world as telling stories. It is far pleasanter than writing reviews of famous novels. And yet, if I am to obey your secretary and tell you my professional experiences as a novelist, I must tell you about a very strange experience that befell me as a novelist. And to understand it you must try first to imagine a novelist's state of mind. I hope I am not giving away professional secrets if I say that a novelist's chief desire is to be as unconscious as possible. He has to induce in himself a state of perpetual lethargy. He wants life to proceed with the utmost quiet and regularity. He wants to see the same faces, to read the same books, to do the same things day after day, month after month, while he is writing, so that nothing may break the illusion in which he is living—so that nothing may disturb or disquiet the mysterious nosings about, feelings round, darts, dashes and sudden discoveries of that very shy and illusive spirit, the imagination. I suspect that this state is the same both for men and women. Be that as it may, I want you to imagine me writing a novel in a state of trance. I want you to figure to yourselves a girl sitting with a pen in her hand, which for minutes, and indeed for hours, she never dips into the inkpot. The image that comes to my mind when I think of this girl is the image of a fisherman lying sunk in dreams on the verge of a deep lake with a rod held out over the water. She was letting her imagination sweep unchecked round every rock and cranny of the world that lies submerged in the depths of our unconscious being. Now came the experience, the experience that I believe to be far commoner with women writers than with men. The line raced through the girl's fingers. Her imagination had rushed away. It had sought the pools, the depths, the dark places where the largest fish slumber. And then there was a smash. There was an explosion. There was foam and confusion. The imagination had dashed itself against something hard. The girl was roused from her dream. She was indeed in a state of the most acute and difficult distress. To speak without figure she had thought of something, something about the body, about the passions which it was unfitting for her as a woman to say. Men, her reason told her, would be shocked. The consciousness of what men will say of a woman who speaks the truth about her passions had roused her from her artist's state of unconsciousness. She could write no more. The trance was over. Her imagination could work no longer. This I believe to be a very common experience with women writers—they are impeded by the extreme conventionality of the other sex. For though men sensibly allow themselves great freedom in these respects, I doubt that they realize or can control the extreme severity with which they condemn such freedom in women.

These then were two very genuine experiences of my own. These were two of the adventures of my professional life. The first—killing the Angel in the House—I think I solved. She died. But the second, telling the truth about my own experiences as a body, I do not think I solved. I doubt that any woman has solved it yet. The obstacles against her are still immensely powerful—and yet they are very difficult to define. Outwardly, what is simpler than to write books? Outwardly, what obstacles are there for a woman rather than for a man? Inwardly, I think, the case is very different; she has still many ghosts to fight, many prejudices to overcome. Indeed it will be a long time still, I think, before a woman can sit down to write a book without finding a phantom to be slain, a rock to be dashed against. And if this is so in literature, the freest of all professions for women, how is it in the new professions which you are now for the first time entering?

Those are the questions that I should like, had I time, to ask you. And indeed, if I have laid stress upon these professional experiences of mine, it is because I believe that they are, though in different forms, yours also. Even when the path is nominally open—when there is nothing to prevent a woman from being a doctor, a lawyer, a civil servant—there are many phantoms and obstacles, as I believe, looming in her way. To discuss and define them is I think of great value and importance; for thus only can the labour be shared, the difficulties be solved. But besides this, it is necessary also to discuss the ends and the aims for which we are fighting, for which we are doing battle with these formidable obstacles. Those aims cannot be taken for granted; they must be perpetually questioned and examined. The whole position, as I see it—here in this hall surrounded by women practising for the first time in history I know not how many different professions—is one of extraordinary interest and importance. You have won rooms of your own in the house hitherto exclusively owned by men. You are able, though not without great labour and effort, to pay the rent. You are earning your five hundred pounds a year. But this freedom is only a beginning; the room is your own, but it is still bare. It has to be furnished; it has to be decorated; it has to be shared. How are you going to furnish it, how are you going to decorate it? With whom are you going to share it, and upon what terms? These, I think are questions of the utmost importance and interest. For the first time in history you are able to ask them; for the first time you are able to decide for yourselves what the answers should be. Willingly would I stay and discuss those questions and answers—but not tonight. My time is up; and I must cease.

FRANZ KAFKA (1883–1924)
Czechoslovakia/German
Austro-Hungarian Empire

Born in the German-Jewish enclave of Prague, to a well-to-do businessman, Franz Kafka was always unhappy: in a letter never delivered, he blamed his father for his lack of self-confidence and unending feeling of guilt. He died of tuberculosis, leaving all his writing to his friend Max Brod, asking he destroy everything. (The poet Stéphane Mallarmé left the same instructions to his heirs: neither instruction was obeyed.) One of Kafka's contemporaries called him "the unicorn in the forest of modern literature." Author of three novels (*Amerika, The Trial,* and *The Castle*), all unfinished, and of numerous stories and parables, Kafka has haunted the modern imagination as has perhaps no other writer. He was a master at fusing the comic and tragic extremes of life in compelling and unforgettable images. *Alice in Wonderland* was one of his favorite books, and he admired the films of Charlie Chaplin, as well as the novels of Dickens and Dostoyevsky. *The Metamorphosis,* which has fascinated generations of readers, is horrendously convincing in its details and feeling; like a nightmare, it is both realistic and fantastic. The reader is made to share—ironically, through Gregor's own consciousness—in the intense discomfort of his family, and its final relief.

The Metamorphosis

I

When Gregor Samsa woke up one morning from unsettling dreams, he found himself changed in his bed into a monstrous vermin. He was lying on his back as hard as armor plate, and when he lifted his head a little, he saw his vaulted brown belly, sectioned by arch-shaped ribs, to whose dome the cover, about to slide off completely, could barely cling. His many legs, pitifully thin compared with the size of the rest of him, were waving helplessly before his eyes.

"What's happened to me?" he thought. It was no dream. His room, a regular human room, only a little on the small side, lay quiet between the four familiar walls. Over the table, on which an unpacked line of fabric samples was all spread out—Samsa was a traveling salesman—hung the picture which he had recently cut out of a glossy magazine and lodged in a pretty gilt frame. It showed a lady done up in a fur hat and a fur boa, sitting upright and raising up against the viewer a heavy fur muff in which her whole forearm had disappeared.

Gregor's eyes then turned to the window, and the overcast weather—he could hear raindrops hitting against the metal window ledge—completely depressed him. "How about going back to sleep for a few minutes and forgetting all this nonsense," he thought, but that was completely impracticable, since he was used to sleeping on his right side and in his present state could not get into that position. No matter how hard he threw himself onto his right side, he always rocked onto his back again. He must have tried it a hundred times, closing his eyes so as not to have to see his squirming legs, and stopped only when he began to feel a slight, dull pain in his side, which he had never felt before.

"Oh God," he thought, "what a grueling job I've picked. Day in, day out—on the road. The upset of doing business is much worse than the actual business in the home office, and besides, I've got the torture of traveling, worrying about changing trains, eating miserable food at all hours, constantly seeing new faces, no

Translated by Stanley Corngold.

relationships that last or get more intimate. To the devil with it all!" He felt a slight itching up on top of his belly; shoved himself slowly on his back closer to the bedpost, so as to be able to lift his head better; found the itchy spot, studded with small white dots which he had no idea what to make of; and wanted to touch the spot with one of his legs but immediately pulled it back, for the contact sent a cold shiver through him.

He slid back again into his original position. "This getting up so early," he thought, "makes anyone a complete idiot. Human beings have to have their sleep. Other traveling salesmen live like harem women. For instance, when I go back to the hotel before lunch to write up the business I've done, these gentlemen are just having breakfast. That's all I'd have to try with my boss; I'd be fired on the spot. Anyway, who knows if that wouldn't be a very good thing for me. If I didn't hold back for my parents' sake, I would have quit long ago, I would have marched up to the boss and spoken my piece from the bottom of my heart. He would have fallen off the desk! It is funny, too, the way he sits on the desk and talks down from the heights to the employees, especially when they have to come right up close on account of the boss's being hard of hearing. Well, I haven't given up hope completely; once I've gotten the money together to pay off my parents' debt to him—that will probably take another five or six years—I'm going to do it without fail. Then I'm going to make the big break. But for the time being I'd better get up, since my train leaves at five."

And he looked over at the alarm clock, which was ticking on the chest of drawers. "God Almighty!" he thought. It was six-thirty, the hands were quietly moving forward, it was actually past the half-hour, it was already nearly a quarter to. Could it be that the alarm hadn't gone off? You could see from the bed that it was set correctly for four o'clock; it certainly had gone off, too. Yes, but was it possible to sleep quietly through a ringing that made the furniture shake? Well, he certainly hadn't slept quietly, but probably all the more soundly for that. But what should he do now? The next train left at seven o'clock; to make it, he would have to hurry like a madman, and the line of samples wasn't packed yet, and he himself didn't feel especially fresh and ready to march around. And even if he did make the train, he could not avoid getting it from the boss, because the messenger boy had been waiting at the five-o'clock train and would have long ago reported his not showing up. He was a tool of the boss, without brains or backbone. What if he were to say he was sick? But that would be extremely embarrassing and suspicious because during his five years with the firm Gregor had not been sick even once. The boss would be sure to come with the health-insurance doctor, blame his parents for their lazy son, and cut off all excuses by quoting the health-insurance doctor, for whom the world consisted of people who were completely healthy but afraid to work. And, besides, in this case would he be so very wrong? In fact, Gregor felt fine, with the exception of his drowsiness, which was really unnecessary after sleeping so late, and he even had a ravenous appetite.

Just as he was thinking all this over at top speed, without being able to decide to get out of bed—the alarm clock had just struck a quarter to seven—he heard a cautious knocking at the door next to the head of his bed. "Gregor," someone called—it was his mother—"it's a quarter to seven. Didn't you want to catch the train?" What a soft voice! Gregor was shocked to hear his own voice answering, unmistakably his own voice, true, but in which, as if from below, an insistent distressed chirping intruded, which left the clarity of his words intact only for a moment really, before so badly garbling them as they carried that no one could be sure if he had heard right. Gregor had wanted to answer in detail and to explain everything, but, given the circumstances, confined himself to saying, "Yes, yes, thanks, Mother, I'm just getting up." The wooden door must have prevented the change in Gregor's voice from being noticed outside, because his mother was satisfied with this explanation and shuffled off. But their little exchange had made the rest of the family aware that, contrary to expectations, Gregor was still in the house, and already his father was knocking on one of the side doors, feebly but with this fist. "Gregor, Gregor," he called, "what's going on?" And after a little while he called again in a deeper, warning voice, "Gregor! Gregor!" At the other side door, however, his sister moaned gently, "Gregor? Is something the matter with you? Do you want anything?" Toward both sides Gregor answered: "I'm all ready," and made an effort, by meticulous pronunciation and by inserting long pauses between individual words, to eliminate everything from his voice that might betray him. His father went back to his breakfast, but his sister whispered, "Gregor, open up, I'm pleading with you." But Gregor had absolutely no intention of opening the door and complimented himself instead on the precaution he had adopted from his business trips, of locking all the doors during the night even at home.

First of all he wanted to get up quietly, without any excitement; get dressed; and the main thing, have breakfast, and only then think about what to do next, for he saw clearly that in bed he would never think things through to a rational conclusion. He remembered how even in the past he had often felt some kind of slight pain, possibly caused by lying in an uncomfortable position, which, when he got up, turned out to be purely imaginary, and he was eager to see how today's fantasy would gradually fade away. That the change in his voice was nothing more than the first sign of a bad cold, an occupational ailment of the traveling salesman, he had no doubt in the least.

It was very easy to throw off the cover; all he had to do was puff himself up a little, and it fell off by itself. But after this, things got difficult, especially since he was so unusually broad. He would have needed hands and arms to lift himself up, but instead of that he had only his numerous little legs, which were in every different kind of perpetual motion and which, besides, he could not control. If he wanted to bend one, the first thing that happened was that it stretched itself out; and if he finally succeeded in getting this leg to do what he wanted, all the others in the meantime, as if set free, began to work in the most intensely painful agitation. "Just don't stay in bed being useless," Gregor said to himself.

First he tried to get out of bed with the lower part of his body, but this lower part—which by the way he had not seen yet and which he could not form a clear picture of—proved too difficult to budge; it was taking so long; and when finally, almost out of his mind, he lunged forward with all his force, without caring, he had picked the wrong direction and slammed himself violently against the lower bedpost, and the searing pain he felt taught him that exactly the lower part of his body was, for the moment anyway, the most sensitive.

He therefore tried to get the upper part of his body out of bed first and warily turned his head toward the edge of the bed. This worked easily, and in spite of its width and weight, the mass of his body finally followed, slowly, the movement of his head. But when at last he stuck his head over the edge of the bed into the air, he got too scared to continue any further, since if he finally let himself fall in this position, it would be a miracle if he didn't injure his head. And just now he had better not for the life of him lose consciousness; he would rather stay in bed.

But when, once again, after the same exertion, he lay in his original position, sighing, and again watched his little legs struggling, if possible more fiercely, with each other and saw no way of bringing peace and order into this mindless motion, he again told himself that it was impossible for him to stay in bed and that the most rational thing was to make any sacrifice for even the smallest hope of freeing himself from the bed. But at the same time he did not forget to remind himself occasionally that thinking things over calmly—indeed, as calmly as possible—was much better than jumping to desperate decisions. At such moments he fixed his eyes as sharply as possible on the window, but unfortunately there was little confidence and cheer to be gotten from the view of the morning fog, which shrouded even the other side of the narrow street. "Seven o'clock already," he said to himself as the alarm clock struck again, "seven o'clock already and still such a fog." And for a little while he lay quietly, breathing shallowly, as if expecting perhaps, from the complete silence the return of things to the way they really and naturally were.

But then he said to himself, "Before it strikes a quarter past seven, I must be completely out of bed without fail. Anyway, by that time someone from the firm will be here to find out where I am, since the office opens before seven." And now he started rocking the complete length of his body out of the bed with a smooth rhythm. If he let himself topple out of bed in this way, his head, which on falling he planned to lift up sharply, would presumably remain unharmed. His back seemed to be hard; nothing was likely to happen to it when it fell onto the carpet. His biggest misgiving came from his concern about the loud crash that was bound to occur and would probably create, if not terror, at least anxiety behind all the doors. But that would have to be risked.

When Gregor's body already projected halfway out of bed—the new method was more of a game than a struggle, he only had to keep on rocking and jerking himself along—he thought how simple everything would be if he could get some help. Two strong persons—he thought of his father and the maid—would have been completely sufficient; they would only have had to shove their arms under his arched back, in this way scoop him off the bed, bend down with their burden, and then just be careful and patient while he managed to swing himself down onto the floor, where his little legs would hopefully acquire some purpose. Well, leaving out the fact that the doors were locked, should he really call for help? In spite of all his miseries, he could not repress a smile at this thought.

He was already so far along that when he rocked more strongly he could hardly keep his balance, and very soon he would have to commit himself, because in five minutes it would be a quarter past seven—when the doorbell rang. "It's someone from the firm," he said to himself and almost froze, while his little legs only danced more quickly. For a moment everything remained quiet. "They're not going to answer," Gregor said to himself, captivated by some senseless hope. But then, of course, the maid went to the door as usual with her firm stride and opened up. Gregor only had to hear the visitor's first word of greeting to know who it was—the office manager himself. Why was only Gregor condemned to work for a firm where at the slightest omission they immediately suspected the worst? Were all employees louts without exception, wasn't there a single loyal, dedicated worker among them who, when he had not fully utilized a few hours of the morning for the firm, was driven half-mad by pangs of conscience and was actually unable to get out of bed? Really, wouldn't it have been enough to send one of the apprentices to find out—if this prying were absolutely necessary—did the manager himself have to come, and did the whole innocent family have to be shown in this way that the investigation of this suspicious affair could be entrusted only to the intellect of the manager? And more as a result of the excitement produced in Gregor by these thoughts than as a result of any real decision, he swung himself out of bed with all his might. There was a loud thump, but it was not a real crash. The fall was broken a little by the carpet, and Gregor's back was more elastic than he had thought, which explained the not very noticeable muffled sound. Only he had not held his head carefully enough and hit it; he turned it and rubbed it on the carpet in anger and pain.

"Something fell in there," said the manager in the room on the left. Gregor tried to imagine whether something like what had happened to him today could one day happen even to the manager; you really had to grant the possibility. But, as if in rude reply to this question, the manager took a few decisive steps in the next room and made his patent leather boots creak. From the room on the right his sister whispered, to inform Gregor, "Gregor, the manager is here" "I know," Gregor said to himself; but he did not dare raise his voice enough for his sister to hear.

"Gregor," his father now said from the room on the left, "The manager has come and wants to be informed why you didn't catch the early train. We don't know what we should say to him. Besides, he wants to speak to you personally. So please open the door. He will certainly be so kind as to excuse the disorder of the room." "Good morning, Mr. Samsa," the manager called in a friendly voice. "There's something the matter with him," his mother said to the manager while his father was still at the door, talking. "Believe me, sir, there's something the matter with him. Otherwise how would Gregor have missed a train? That boy has nothing on his mind but the business. It's almost begun to rile me that he never goes out nights. He's been back in the city for eight days now, but every night he's been home. He sits there with us at the table, quietly reading the paper or studying timetables. It's already a distraction for him when he's busy working with his fretsaw. For instance, in the span of two or three evenings he carved a little frame. You'll be amazed how pretty it is; it's hanging inside his room. You'll see it right away when Gregor opens the door. You know, I'm glad that you've come, sir. We would never have gotten Gregor to open the door by ourselves; he's so stubborn. And there's certainly something wrong with him, even though he said this morning there wasn't." "I'm coming right away," said Gregor slowly and deliberately, not moving in order not to miss a word of the conversation. "I haven't any other explanation myself," said the manager. "I hope it's nothing serious. On the other hand, I must say that we businessmen—fortunately or unfortunately, whichever you prefer—very often simply have to overcome a slight indisposition for business reasons." "So can the manager come in now?" asked his father, impatient, and knocked on the door again. "No," said Gregor. In the room on the left there was an embarrassing silence; in the room on the right his sister began to sob.

Why didn't his sister go in to the others? She had probably just got out of bed and not even started to get dressed. Then what was she crying about? Because he didn't get up and didn't let the manager in, because he was in danger of losing his job, and because then the boss would start hounding his parents about the old debts? For the time being, certainly, her worries were unnecessary. Gregor was still here and hadn't the slightest intention of letting the family down. True, at the moment he was lying on the carpet, and no one knowing his condition could seriously have expected him to let the manager in. But just because of this slight discourtesy, for which an appropriate excuse would easily be found later on, Gregor could not simply be dismissed. And to Gregor it seemed much more sensible to leave him alone now than to bother him with crying and persuasion. But it was just the uncertainty that was tormenting the others and excused their behavior.

"Mr. Samsa," the manager now called, raising his voice, "what's the matter? You barricade yourself in your room, answer only 'yes' and 'no,' cause your parents serious, unnecessary worry, and you neglect—I mention this only in passing—your duties to the firm in a really shocking manner. I am speaking here in the name of your parents and of your employer and ask you in all seriousness for an immediate, clear explanation. I'm amazed, amazed. I thought I knew you to be a quiet, reasonable person, and now you suddenly seem to want to start strutting about, flaunting strange whims. The head of the firm did suggest to me this morning a possible explanation for your tardiness—it concerned the cash payments recently entrusted to you—but really, I practically gave my word of honor that this explanation could not be right. But now, seeing your incomprehensible obstinacy, I am about to lose even the slightest desire to stick up for you in any way at all. And your job is not the most secure. Originally I intended to tell you all this in private, but since you make me waste my time here for nothing, I don't see why your parents shouldn't hear too. Your performance of late his been very unsatisfactory; I know it is not the best season for doing business, we all recognize that; but a season for not doing any business, there is no such thing, Mr. Samsa, such a thing cannot be tolerated."

"But sir," cried Gregor, beside himself, in his excitement forgetting everything else, "I'm just opening up, in a minute. A slight indisposition, a dizzy spell, prevented me from getting up. I'm still in bed. But I already feel fine again. I'm just getting out of bed. Just be patient for a minute! I'm not as well as I thought yet. But really I'm fine. How something like this could just take a person by surprise! Only last night I was fine, my parents can tell you, or wait, last night I already had a slight premonition. They must have been able to tell by looking at me. Why didn't I report it to the office! But you always think that you'll get over a sickness without staying home. Sir! Spare my parents! There's no basis for any of the accusations that you're making against me now; no one has ever said a word to me about them. Perhaps you haven't seen the last orders I sent in. Anyway, I'm still going on the road with the eight o'clock train; these few hours of rest have done me good. Don't let me keep you, sir. I'll be at the office myself right away, and be so kind as to tell them this, and give my respects to the head of the firm."

And while Gregor hastily blurted all this out, hardly knowing what he was saying, he had easily approached the chest of drawers, probably as a result of the practice he had already gotten in bed, and now he tried to raise himself up against it. He actually intended to open the door, actually present himself and speak to the manager; he was eager to find out what the others, who were now so anxious to see him, would say at the sight of him. If they were shocked, then Gregor had no further responsibility and could be calm. But if they took everything calmly, then he, too, had no reason to get excited and could, if he hurried, actually be at the station by eight o'clock. At first he slid off the polished chest of drawers a few times, but at last, giving himself a final push, he stood upright; he no longer paid any attention to the pains in his abdomen, no matter how much they were burning. Now he let himself fall against the back of a nearby chair, clinging to its slats with his little legs. But by doing this he had gotten control of himself and fell silent, since he could now listen to what the manager was saying.

"Did you understand a word?" the manager was asking his parents. "He isn't trying to make fools of us, is he?" "My God," cried his mother, already in tears, "maybe he's seriously ill, and here we are, torturing him. Grete! Grete!" she then cried. "Mother?" called his sister from the other side. They communicated by way of Gregor's room. "Go to the doctor's immediately. Gregor is sick. Hurry, get the doctor. Did you just hear Gregor talking?" "That was the voice of an animal," said the manager, in a tone conspicuously soft compared with the mother's yelling. "Anna!" "Anna!" the father called through the foyer into the kitchen, clapping his hands, "get a locksmith right away!" And already the two girls were running with rustling skirts through the foyer—how could his sister have gotten dressed so quickly?—and tearing open the door to the apartment. The door could not be heard slamming; they had probably left it open, as is the custom in homes where a great misfortune has occurred.

But Gregor had become much calmer. It was true that they no longer understood his words, though they had seemed clear enough to him, clearer than before, probably because his ear had grown accustomed to them. But still, the others now believed that there was something the matter with him and were ready to help him. The assurance and confidence with which the first measures had been taken did him good. He felt integrated into human society once again and hoped for marvelous, amazing feats from both the doctor and the locksmith, without really distinguishing sharply between them. In order to make his voice as clear as possible for the crucial discussions that were approaching, he cleared his throat a little—taking pains, of course, to do so in a very muffled manner, since this noise, too, might sound different from human coughing, a thing he no longer trusted himself to decide. In the next room, meanwhile, everything had become completely still. Perhaps his parents were sitting at the table with the manager, whispering; perhaps they were all leaning against the door and listening.

Gregor slowly lugged himself toward the door, pushing the chair in front of him, then let go of it, threw himself against the door, held himself upright against it—the pads on the bottom of his little legs exuded a little sticky substance—and for a moment rested there from the exertion. But then he got started turning the key in the lock with his mouth. Unfortunately it seemed that he had no real teeth—what was he supposed to grip the key with?—but in compensation his jaws, of course, were very strong; with their help he actually got the key moving and paid no attention to the fact that he was undoubtedly hurting himself in some way, for a brown liquid came out of his mouth, flowed over the key, and dripped onto the floor. "Listen," said the manager in the next room, "he's turning the key." This was great encouragement to Gregor; but everyone should have cheered him on, his father and mother too. "Go, Gregor," they should have called, "keep going, at the lock, harder, harder!"And in the delusion that they were all following his efforts with suspense, he clamped his jaws madly on the key with all the strength he could muster. Depending on the progress of the key, he danced around the lock; holding himself upright only by his mouth, he clung to the key, as the situation demanded, or pressed it down again with the whole weight of his body. The clearer click of the lock as it finally snapped back literally woke Gregor up. With a sigh of relief he said to himself, "So I didn't need the locksmith after all," and laid his head down on the handle in order to open wide one wing of the double doors.

Since he had to use this method of opening the door, it was really opened very wide while he himself was still invisible. He first had to edge slowly around the one wing of the door, and do so very carefully if he was not to fall flat on his back just before entering. He was still busy with this difficult maneuver and had no time to pay attention to anything else when he heard the manager burst out with a loud "Oh!"—it sounded like a rush of wind—and now he could see him, standing closest to the door, his hand pressed over his open mouth, slowly backing away, as if repulsed by an invisible, unrelenting force. His mother—in spite of the manager's presence she stood with her hair still unbraided from the night, sticking out in all directions—first looked at his father with her hands clasped, then took two steps toward Gregor, and sank down in the midst of her skirts spreading out around her, her face completely hidden on her breast. With a hostile expression his father clenched his fist, as if to drive Gregor back into his room, then looked uncertainly around the living room, shielded his eyes with his hands, and sobbed with heaves of his powerful chest.

Now Gregor did not enter the room after all but leaned against the inside of the firmly bolted wing of the door, so that only half his body was visible and his head above it, cocked to one side and peeping out at the others. In the meantime it had grown much lighter; across the street one could see clearly a section of the endless, grayish-black building opposite—it was a hospital—with its regular windows starkly piercing the façade; the rain was still coming down, but only in large, separately visible drops that were also pelting the ground literally one at a time. The breakfast dishes were laid out lavishly on the table, since for his father breakfast was the most important meal of the day, which he would prolong for hours while reading various newspapers. On the wall directly opposite hung a photograph of Gregor from his army days, in a lieutenant's uniform, his hand on his sword, a carefree smile on his lips, demanding respect for his bearing and his rank. The door to the foyer was open, and since the front door was open too, it was possible to see out onto the landing and the top of the stairs going down.

"Well," said Gregor—and he was thoroughly aware of being the only one who had kept calm—"I'll get dressed right away, pack up my samples, and go. Will you. will you please let me go? Now, sir, you see, I'm not stubborn and I'm willing to work; traveling is a hardship, but without it I couldn't live. Where are you going, sir? To the office? Yes? Will you give an honest report of everything? A man might find for a moment that he was unable to work, but that's exactly the right time to remember his past accomplishments and to consider that later on, when the obstacle has been removed, he's bound to work all the harder and more efficiently. I'm under so many obligations to the head of the firm, as you know very well. Besided, I also have my parents and my sister to worry about. I'm in a tight spot, but I'll also work my way out again. Don't make things harder for me than they already are. Stick up for me in the office, please. Traveling salesmen aren't well liked there, I know. People think they make a fortune leading the gay life. No one has any particular reason to rectify this prejudice. But you, sir, you have a better perspective on things than the rest of the office, an even better perspective, just between the two of us, than the head of the firm himself, who in his capacity as owner easily lets his judgment be swayed against an employee. And you also know very well that the traveling salesman, who is out of the office practically the whole year round, can so easily become the victim of gossip, coincidences, and unfounded accusations, against which he's completely unable to defend himself, since in most cases he knows nothing at all about them except when he returns exhausted from a trip, and back home gets to suffer on his own person the grim consequences, which can no longer be traced back to their causes. Sir. don't go away without a word to tell me you think I'm at least partly right!"

But at Gregor's first words the manager had already turned away and with curled lip looked back at Gregor only over his twitching shoulder. And during Gregor's speech he did not stand still for a minute but, without letting Gregor out of his sight, backed toward the door, yet very gradually, as if there were some secret prohibition against leaving the room. He was already in the foyer, and from the sudden movement with which he took his last step from the living room, one might have thought he had just burned the sole of his foot. In the foyer, however, he stretched his right hand far out toward the staircase, as if nothing less than an unearthly deliverance were awaiting him there.

Gregor realized that he must on no account let the manger go away in this mood if his position in the firm were not to be jeopardized in the extreme. His parents did not understand this too well; in the course of the years they had formed the conviction that Gregor was set for life in this firm; and furthermore, they were so preoccupied with their immediate troubles that they had lost all consideration for the future. But Gregor had this forethought. The manager must be detained, calmed down, convinced, and finally won over; Gregor's and the family's future depended on it! If only his sister had been there! She was perceptive; she had already begun to cry when Gregor was still lying calmly on his back. And certainly the manager, this ladies' man, would have listened to her; she would have shut the front door and in the foyer talked him out of his scare. But his sister was not there, Gregor had to handle the situation himself. And without stopping to realize that he had no idea what his new faculties of movement were, and without stopping to realize either that his speech had possibly—indeed, probably—not been understood again, he let go of the wing of the door; he shoved himself through the opening, intending to go to the manager, who was already on the landing, ridiculously holding onto the banisters with both hands; but groping for support, Gregor immediately fell down with a little cry onto his numerous little legs. This had hardly happened when for the first time that morning he had a feeling of physical well-being; his little legs were on firm ground; they obeyed him completely, as he noted to his joy; they even strained to carry him away wherever he wanted to go; and he already believed that final recovery from all his sufferings was imminent. But at that very moment, as he lay on the floor rocking with repressed motion, not far from his mother and just opposite her, she, who had seemed so completely self-absorbed, all at once jumped up, her arms stretched wide, her fingers spread, and cried, "Help, for God's sake, help!" held her head bent as if to see Gregor better, but inconsistently darted madly backward instead; had forgotten that the table laden with the breakfast dishes stood behind her; sat down on it hastily, as if her thoughts were elsewhere, when she reached it; and did not seem to notice at all that near her the big coffeepot had been knocked over and coffee was pouring in a steady stream onto the rug.

"Mother, Mother," said Gregor softly and looked up at her. For a minute the manager had completely slipped his mind; on the other hand at the sight of the spilling coffee he could not resist snapping his jaws several times in the air. At this his mother screamed once more, fled from the table, and fell into the arms of his father, who came rushing up to her. But Gregor had no time now for his parents; the manager was already on the stairs; with his chin on the banister, he was taking a last look back. Gregor was off to a running start, to be as sure as possible of catching up with him; the manager must have suspected something like this, for he leaped down several steps and disappeared; but still he shouted "Agh," and the sound carried through the whole staircase. Unfortunately the manager's flight now seemed to confuse his father completely, who had been relatively calm until now, for instead of running after the manager himself, or at least not hindering Gregor in his pursuit, he seized in his right hand the manager's cane, which had been left behind on a chair with his hat and overcoat, picked up in his left hand a heavy newspaper from the table, and stamping his feet, started brandishing the cane and the newspaper to drive Gregor back into his room. No plea of Gregor's helped, no plea was even understood; however humbly he might turn his head, his father merely stamped his feet more forcefully. Across the room his mother had thrown open a window in spite of the cool weather, and leaning out, she buried her face, far outside the window, in her hands. Between the alley and the staircase a strong draft was created, the window curtains blew in, the newspapers on the table rustled, single sheets fluttered across the floor. Pitilessly his father came on, hissing like a wild man. Now Gregor had not had any practice at all walking in reverse, it was really very slow going. If Gregor had only been allowed to turn around, he could have gotten into his room right away, but he was afraid to make his father impatient by this time-consuming gyration, and at any minute the cane in his father's hand threatened to come down on his back or his head with a deadly blow. Finally, however, Gregor had no choice, for he noticed with horror that in reverse he could not even keep going in one direction; and so, incessantly throwing uneasy side-glances at his father, he began to turn around as quickly as possible, in reality turning only very slowly. Perhaps his father realized his good intentions, for he did not interfere with him; instead, he even now and then directed the maneuver from afar with the tip of his cane. If only his father did not keep making this intolerable hissing sound! It made Gregor lose his head completely. He had almost finished the turn when—his mind continually on this hissing—he made a mistake and even started turning back around to his original position. But when he had at last successfully managed to get his head in front of the opened door, it turned out that his body was too broad to get through as it was. Of course in his father's present state of mind it did not even remotely occur to him to open the other wing of the door in order to give Gregor enough room to pass through. He had only the fixed idea that Gregor must return to his room as quickly as possible. He would never have allowed the complicated preliminaries Gregor needed to go through in order to stand up on one end and perhaps in this way fit through the door. Instead he drove Gregor on, as if there were no obstacle, with exceptional loudness; the voice behind Gregor did not sound like that of only a single father; now this was really no joke any more, and Gregor forced himself—come what may—into the doorway. One side of his body rose up, he lay lop-sided in the opening, one of his flanks was scraped raw, ugly blotches marred the white door, soon he got stuck and could not have budged any more by himself, his little legs on one side dangled tremblingly in midair, those on the other were painfully crushed against the floor—when from behind his father gave him a hard shove, which was truly his salvation, and bleeding profusely, he flew far into his room. The door was slammed shut with the cane, then at last everything was quiet.

II

It was already dusk when Gregor awoke from his deep, comalike sleep. Even if he had not been disturbed, he would certainly not have woken up much later, for he felt that he had rested and slept long enough, but it seemed to him that a hurried step and a cautious shutting of the door leading to the foyer had awakened him. The light of the electric street-lamps lay in pallid streaks on the ceiling and on the upper parts of the furniture, but underneath, where Gregor was, it was dark. Groping clumsily with his antennae, which he was only now beginning to appreciate, he slowly dragged himself toward the door to see what had been happening there. His left side felt like one single long, unpleasantly tautening scar, and he actually had to limp on his two rows of legs. Besides, one little leg had been seriously injured in the course of the morning's events—it was almost a miracle that only one had been injured—and dragged along lifelessly.

Only after he got to the door did he notice what had really attracted him—the smell of something to eat. For there stood a bowl filled with fresh milk, in which small slices of white bread were floating. He could almost have laughed for joy, since he was even hungrier than he had been in the morning, and he immediately dipped his head into the milk, almost to over his eyes. But he soon drew it back again in disappointment; not only because he had difficulty eating on account of the soreness in his left side—and he could eat only if his whole panting body cooperated—but because he didn't like the milk at all, although it used to be his favorite drink, and that was certainly why his sister had put it in the room; in fact, he turned away from the bowl almost with repulsion and crawled back to the middle of the room.

In the living room, as Gregor saw through the crack in the door, the gas had been lit, but while at this hour of the day his father was in the habit of reading the afternoon newspaper in a loud voice to his mother and sometimes to his sister too, now there wasn't a sound. Well, perhaps this custom of reading aloud, which his sister was always telling him and writing him about, had recently been discontinued altogether. But in all the other rooms too it was just as still, although the apartment certainly was not empty. "What a quiet life the family has been leading," Gregor said to himself, and while he stared rigidly in front of him into the darkness, he felt very proud that he had been able to provide such a life in so nice an apartment for his parents and his sister. But what now if all the peace, the comfort, the contentment were to come to a horrible end? In order not to get involved in such thoughts, Gregor decided to keep moving, and he crawled up and down the room.

During the long evening first one of the side doors and then the other was opened a small crack and quickly shut again; someone had probably had the urge to come in and then had had second thoughts. Gregor now settled into position right by the living-room door, determined somehow to get the hesitating visitor to come in, or a least to find out who it might be; but the door was not opened again, and Gregor waited in vain. In the morning, when the doors had been locked, everyone had wanted to come in; now that he had opened one of the doors and the others had evidently been opened during the day, no one came in, and now the keys were even inserted on the outside.

It was late at night when the light finally went out in the living room, and now it was easy for Gregor to tell that his parents and his sister had stayed up so long, since, as he could distinctly hear, all three were now retiring on tiptoe. Certainly no one would come in to Gregor until the morning; and so he had ample time to consider undisturbed how best to rearrange his life. But the empty high-ceilinged room in which he was forced to lie flat on the floor made him nervous, without his being able to tell why—since it was, after all, the room in which he had lived for the past five years—and turning half unconsciously and not without a slight feeling of shame, he scuttled under the couch where, although his back was a little crushed and he could not raise his head any more, he immediately felt very comfortable and was only sorry that his body was too wide to go completely under the couch.

There he stayed the whole night, which he spent partly in a sleepy trance, from which hunger pangs kept waking him with a start, partly in worries and vague hopes, all of which, however, led to the conclusion that for the time being he would have to lie low and, by being patient and showing his family every possible consideration, help them bear the inconvenience which he simply had to cause them in his present condition.

Early in the morning—it was still almost night—Gregor had the opportunity of testing the strength of the resolutions he had just made, for his sister, almost fully dressed, opened the door from the foyer and looked in eagerly. She did not see him right away, but when she caught sight of him under the couch—God, he had to be somewhere, he couldn't just fly away—she became so frightened that she lost control of herself and slammed the door shut again. But, as if she felt sorry for her behavior, she immediately opened the door again and came in on tiptoe, as if she were visiting someone seriously ill or perhaps even a stranger. Gregor had pushed his head forward just to the edge of the couch and was watching her. Would she notice that he had left the milk standing, and not because he hadn't been hungry, and would she bring in a dish of something he'd like better? If she were not going to do it of her own free will, he would rather starve than call it to her attention, although, really, he felt an enormous urge to shoot out from under the couch, throw himself at his sister's feet, and beg her for something good to eat. But his sister noticed at once, to her astonishment, that the bowl was still full, only a little milk was spilled around it; she picked it up immediately—not with her bare hands, of course, but with a rag—and carried it out. Gregor was extremely curious to know what she would bring him instead, and he racked his brains on the subject. But he would never have been able to guess what his sister, in the goodness of her heart, actually did. To find out his likes and dislikes, she brought him a wide assortment of things, all spread out on an old newspaper: old, half-rotten vegetables; bones left over from the evening meal, caked with congealed white sauce; some raisins and almonds; a piece of cheese, which two days before Gregor had declared inedible; a plain slice of bread, a slice of bread and butter, and one with butter and salt. In addition to all this she put down some water in the bowl apparently permanently earmarked for Gregor's use. And out of a sense of delicacy, since she knew that Gregor would not eat in front of her, she left hurriedly and even turned the key, just so that Gregor should know that he might make himself as comfortable as he wanted. Gregor's legs began whirring now that he was going to eat. Besides, his bruises must have completely healed, since he no longer felt any handicap, and marveling at this he thought how, over a month ago, he had cut his finger very slightly with a knife and how this wound was still hurting him only the day before yesterday. "Have I become less sensitive?" he thought, already sucking greedily at the cheese, which had immediately and forcibly attracted him ahead of all the other dishes. One right after the other, and with eyes streaming with tears of contentment, he devoured the cheese, the vegetables, and the sauce; the fresh foods, on the other hand, he did not care for; he couldn't even stand their smell and even dragged the things he wanted to eat a bit further away. He had finished with everything long since and was just lying lazily at the same spot when his sister slowly turned the key as a sign for him to withdraw. That immediately startled him, although he was almost asleep, and he scuttled under the couch again. But it took great self-control for him to stay under the couch even for the short time his sister was in the room, since his body had become a little bloated from the heavy meal, and in his cramped position he could hardly breathe. In between slight attacks of suffocation he watched with bulging eyes as his unsuspecting sister took a broom and swept up, not only his leavings, but even the foods which Gregor had left completely untouched—as if they too were no longer usable—and dumping everything hastily into a pail, which she covered with a wooden lid, she carried everything out. She had hardly turned her back when Gregor came out from under the couch, stretching and puffing himself up.

This, then, was the way Gregor was fed each day, once in the morning, when his parents and the maid were still asleep, and a second time in the afternoon after everyone had had dinner, for then his parents took a short nap again, and the maid could be sent out by his sister on some errand. Certainly they did not want him to starve either, but perhaps they would not have been able to stand knowing any more about his meals than from hearsay, or perhaps his sister wanted to spare them even what was possibly only a minor torment, for really, they were suffering enough as it was.

Gregor could not find out what excuses had been made to get rid of the doctor and the locksmith on that first morning, for since the others could not understand what he said, it did not occur to any of them, not even to his sister, that he could understand what they said, and so he had to be satisfied, when his sister was in the room, with only occasionally hearing her sighs and appeals to the saints. It was only later, when she had begun to get used to everything—there could never, of course, be any question of a complete adjustment—that Gregor sometimes caught a remark which was meant to be friendly or could be interpreted as such. "Oh, he liked what he had today," she would say when Gregor had tucked away a good helping, and in the opposite case, which gradually occurred more and more frequently, she used to say, almost sadly, "He's left everything again."

But if Gregor could not get any news directly, he overheard a great deal from the neighboring rooms, and as soon as he heard voices, he would immediately run to the door concerned and press his whole body against it. Especially in the early days, there was no conversation that was not somehow about him, if only implicitly. For two whole days there were family consultations at every mealtime about how they should cope; this was also the topic of discussion between meals, for at least two members of the family were always at home, since no one probably wanted to stay home alone and it was impossible to leave the apartment completely empty. Besides, on the very first day the maid—it was not completely clear what and how much she knew of what had happened—had begged his mother on bended knees to dismiss her immediately; and when she said goodbye a quarter of an hour later, she thanked them in tears for the dismissal, as if for the greatest favor that had ever been done to her in this house, and made a solemn vow, without anyone asking her for it, not to give anything away to anyone.

Now his sister, working with her mother, had to do the cooking too; of course that did not cause her much trouble, since they hardly ate anything. Gregor was always hearing one of them pleading in vain with one of the others to eat and getting no answer except, "Thanks, I've had enough," or something similar. They did not seem to drink anything either. His sister often asked her father if he wanted any beer and gladly offered to go out for it herself; and when he did not answer, she said, in order to remove any hesitation on his part, that she could also send the janitor's wife to get it, but then his father finally answered with a definite "No," and that was the end of that.

In the course of the very first day his father explained the family's financial situation and prospects to both the mother and the sister. From time to time he got up from the table to get some kind of receipt or notebook out of the little strongbox he had rescued from the collapse of his business five years before. Gregor heard him open the complicated lock and secure it again after taking out what he had been looking for. These explanations by his father were to some extent the first pleasant news Gregor had heard since his imprisonment. He had always believed that his father had not been able to save a penny from the business, at least his father had never told him anything to the contrary, and Gregor, for his part, had never asked him any questions. In those days Gregor's sole concern had been to do everything in his power to make the family forget as quickly as possible the business disaster which had plunged everyone into a state of total despair. And so he had begun to work with special ardor and had risen almost overnight from stock clerk to traveling salesman, which of course had opened up very different money-making possibilities, and in no time his successes on the job were transformed, by means of commissions, into hard cash that could be plunked down on the table at home in front of his astonished and delighted family. Those had been wonderful times, and they had never returned, as least not with the same glory, although later on Gregor earned enough money to meet the expenses of the entire family and actually did so. They had just gotten used to it, the family as well as Gregor, the money was received with thanks and given with pleasure, but no special feeling of warmth went with it any more. Only his sister had remained close to Gregor, and it was his secret plan that she who, unlike him, loved music and could play the violin movingly, should be sent next year to the Conservatory, regardless of the great expense involved, which could surely be made up for in some other way. Often during Gregor's short stays in the city, the Conservatory would come up in his conversations with his sister, but always merely as a beautiful dream which was not supposed to come true, and his parents were not happy to hear even these innocent allusions; but Gregor had very concrete idea on the subject and he intended solemnly to announce his plan on Christmas Eve.

Thoughts like these, completely useless in his present state, went through his head as he stood glued to the door, listening. Sometimes out of general exhaustion he could not listen any more and let his head bump carelessly against the door, but immediately pulled it back again, for even the slight noise he made by doing this had been heard in the next room and made them all lapse into silence. "What's he carrying on about in there now?" said his father after a while, obviously turning toward the door, and only then would the interrupted conversation gradually be resumed.

Gregor now learned in a thorough way—for his father was in the habit of often repeating himself in his explanations, partly because he himself had not dealt with these matters for a long time, partly, too, because his mother did not understand everything the first time around—that in spite of all their misfortunes a bit of capital, a very little bit, certainly, was still intact from the old days, which in the meantime had increased a little through the untouched interest. But besides that, the money Gregor had brought home every month—he had kept only a few dollars for himself—had never been completely used up and had accumulated into a tidy principal. Behind his door Gregor nodded emphatically, delighted at this unexpected foresight and thrift. Of course he actually could have paid off more of his father's debt to the boss with this extra money, and the day on which he could have gotten rid of his job would have been much closer, but now things were undoubtedly better the way his father had arranged them.

Now this money was by no means enough to let the family live off the interest; the principal was perhaps enough to support the family for one year, or at the most two, but that was all there was. So it was just a sum that really should not be touched and that had to be put away for a rainy day; but the money to live on would have to be earned. Now his father was still healthy, certainly, but he was an old man who had not worked for the past five years and who in any case could not be expected to undertake too much; during these five years, which were the first vacation of his hard-working yet unsuccessful life, he had gained a lot of weight and as a result had become fairly sluggish. And was his old mother now supposed to go out and earn money, when she suffered from asthma, when a walk through the apartment was already an ordeal for her, and when she spent every other day lying on the sofa under the open window, gasping for breath? And was his sister now supposed to work—who for all her seventeen years was still a child and whom it would be such a pity to deprive of the life she had led until now, which had consisted of wearing pretty clothes, sleeping late, helping in the house, enjoying a few modest amusements, and above all playing the violin? At first, whenever the conversation turned to the necessity of earning money, Gregor would let go of the door and throw himself down on the cool leather sofa which stood beside it, for he felt hot with shame and grief.

Often he lay there the whole long night through, not sleeping a wink and only scrabbling on the leather for hours on end. Or, not balking at the huge effort of pushing an armchair to the window, he would crawl up to the window sill and, propped up in the chair, lean against the window, evidently in some sort of remembrance of the feeling of freedom he used to have from looking out the window. For, in fact, from day to day he saw things even a short distance away less and less distinctly; the hospital opposite, which he used to curse because he saw so much of it, was now completely beyond his range of vision, and if he had not been positive that he was living in Charlotte Street—a quiet but still very much a city street—he might have believed that he was looking out of his window into a desert where the gray sky and the gray earth were indistinguishably fused. It took his observant sister only twice to notice that his armchair was standing by the window for her to push the chair back to the same place by the window each time she had finished cleaning the room, and from then on she even left the inside casement of the window open.

If Gregor had only been able to speak to his sister and thank her for everything she had to do for him, he could have accepted her services more easily; as it was, they caused him pain. Of course his sister tried to ease the embarrassment of the whole situation as much as possible, and as time went on, she naturally managed it better and better, but in time Gregor, too, saw things much more clearly. Even the way she came in was terrible for him. Hardly had she entered the room than she would run straight to the window without taking time to close the door—though she was usually so careful to spare everyone the sight of Gregor's room—then tear open the casements with eager hands, almost as if she were suffocating, and remain for a little while at the window even in the coldest weather, breathing deeply. With this racing and crashing she frightened Gregor twice a day; the whole time he cowered under the couch, and yet he knew very well that she would certainly have spared him this if only she had found it possible to stand being in a room with him with the window closed.

One time—it must have been a month since Gregor's metamorphosis, and there was certainly no particular reason any more for his sister to be astonished at Gregor's appearance—she came a little earlier than usual and caught Gregor still looking out the window, immobile and so in an excellent position to be terrifying. It would not have surprised Gregor if she had not come in, because his position prevented her from immediately opening the window, but not only did she not come in, she even sprang back and locked the door; a stranger might easily have thought that Gregor had been lying in wait for her, wanting to bite her. Of course Gregor immediately hid under the couch, but he had to wait until noon before his sister came again, and she seemed much more uneasy than usual. He realized from this that the sight of him was still repulsive to her and was bound to remain repulsive to her in the future, and that she probably had to overcome a lot of resistance not to run away at the sight of even the small part of his body that jutted out from under the couch. So, to spare her even this sight, one day he carried the sheet on his back to the couch—the job took four hours—and arranged it in such a way that he was now completely covered up and his sister could not see him even when she stooped. If she had considered this sheet unnecessary, then of course she could have removed it, for it was clear enough that it could not be for his own pleasure that Gregor shut himself off altogether, but she left the sheet the way it was, and Gregor thought that he had even caught a grateful look when one time he cautiously lifted the sheet a little with his head in order to see how his sister was taking the new arrangement.

During the first two weeks, his parents could not bring themselves to come in to him, and often he heard them say how much they appreciated his sister's work, whereas until now they had frequently been annoyed with her because she had struck them as being a little useless. But now both of them, his father and his mother, often waited outside Gregor's room while his sister straightened it up, and as soon as she came out she had to tell them in great detail how the room looked, what Gregor had eaten, how he had behaved this time, and whether he had perhaps shown a little improvement. His mother, incidentally, began relatively soon to want to visit Gregor, but his father and his sister at first held her back with reasonable arguments to which Gregor listened very attentively and of which he wholeheartedly approved. But later she had to be restrained by force, and then when she cried out, "Let me go to Gregor, he is my unfortunate boy! Don't you understand that I have to go to him?" Gregor thought that it might be a good idea after all if his mother did come in, not every day of course, but perhaps once a week; she could still do everything much better than his sister, who, for all her courage, was still only a child and in the final analysis had perhaps taken on such a difficult assignment only out of childish flightiness.

Gregor's desire to see his mother was soon fulfilled. During the day Gregor did not want to show himself at the window, if only out of consideration for his parents, but he couldn't crawl very far on his few square yards of floor space, either; he could hardly put up with just lying still even at night; eating soon stopped giving him the slightest pleasure, so, as a distraction, he adopted the habit of crawling crisscross over the walls and the ceiling. He especially liked hanging from the ceiling; it was completely different from lying on the floor; one could breathe more freely; a faint swinging sensation went through the body; and in the almost happy absent-mindedness which Gregor felt up there, it could happen to his own surprise that he let go and plopped onto the floor. But now, of course, he had much better control of his body than before and did not hurt himself even from such a big drop. His sister immediately noticed the new entertainment Gregor had discovered for himself—after all, he left behind traces of his sticky substance wherever he crawled—and so she got it into her head to make it possible for Gregor to crawl on an altogether wider scale by taking out the furniture which stood in his way—mainly the chest of drawers and the desk. But she was not able to do this by herself; she did not dare ask her father for help; the maid would certainly not have helped her, for although this girl, who was about sixteen, was bravely sticking it out after the previous cook had left, she had asked for the favor of locking herself in the kitchen at all times and of only opening the door on special request. So there was nothing left for his sister to do except to get her mother one day when her father was out. And his mother did come, with exclamations of excited joy, but she grew silent at the door of Gregor's room. First his sister looked to see, of course, that everything in the room was in order; only then did she let her mother come in. Hurrying as fast as he could, Gregor had pulled the sheet down lower still and pleated it more tightly—it really looked just like a sheet accidentally thrown over the couch. This time Gregor also refrained from spying from under the sheet; he renounced seeing his mother for the time being and was simply happy that she had come after all. "Come on, you can't see him," his sister said, evidently leading her mother in by the hand. Now Gregor could hear the two frail women moving the old chest of drawers—heavy for anyone—from its place and his sister insisting on doing the harder part of the job herself, ignoring the warnings of her mother, who was afraid that she would overexert herself. It went on for a long time. After struggling for a good quarter of an hour, his mother said that they had better leave the chest where it was, because, in the first place, it was too heavy, they would not finished before his father came, and with the chest in the middle of the room, Gregor would be completely barricaded; and, in the second place, it was not at all certain that they were doing Gregor a favor by removing his furniture. To her the opposite seemed to be the case; the sight of the bare wall was heart-breaking; and why shouldn't Gregor also have the same feeling, since he had been used to his furniture for so long and would feel abandoned in the empty room. "And doesn't it look," his mother concluded very softly—in fact she had been almost whispering the whole time, as if she wanted to avoid letting Gregor, whose exact whereabouts she did not know, hear even the sound of her voice, for she was convinced that he did not understand the words—"and doesn't it look as if by removing his furniture we were showing him that we have given up all hope of his getting better and are leaving him to his own devices without any consideration? I think the best thing would be to try to keep the room exactly the way it was before, so that when Gregor comes back to us again, he'll find everything unchanged and can forget all the more easily what's happened in the meantime."

When he heard his mother's words, Gregor realized that the monotony of family life, combined with the fact that not a soul had addressed a word directly to him, must have addled his brain in the course of the past two months, for he could not explain to himself in any other way how in all seriousness he could have been anxious to have his room cleared out. Had he really wanted to have his warm room, comfortably fitted with furniture that had always been in the family, changed into a cave, in which, of course, he would be able to crawl around unhampered in all directions but at the cost of simultaneously, rapidly, and totally forgetting his human past? Even now he had been on the verge of forgetting, and only his mother's voice, which he had not heard for so long, had shaken him up. Nothing should be removed; everything had to stay; he could not do without the beneficial influence of the furniture on his state of mind; and if the furniture prevented him from carrying on this senseless crawling around, then that was no loss but rather a great advantage.

But his sister unfortunately had a different opinion; she had become accustomed, certainly not entirely without justification, to adopt with her parents the role of the particularly well-qualified expert whenever Gregor's affairs were being discussed; and so her mother's advice was now sufficient reason for her to insist, not only on the removal of the chest of drawers and the desk, which was all she had been planning at first, but also on the removal of all the furniture with the exception of the indispensable couch. Of course it was not only childish defiance and the self-confidence she had recently acquired so unexpectedly and at such a cost that led her to make this demand; she had in fact noticed that Gregor needed plenty of room to crawl around in; and on the other hand, as best she could tell, he never used the furniture at all. Perhaps, however, the romantic enthusiasm of girls her age, which seeks to indulge itself at every opportunity, played a part, by tempting her to make Gregor's situation even more terrifying in order that she might do even more for him. Into a room in which Gregor ruled the bare walls all alone, no human being beside Grete was ever likely to set foot.

And so she did not let herself be swerved from her decision by her mother, who, besides, from the sheer anxiety of being in Gregor's room, seemed unsure of herself, soon grew silent, and helped her daughter as best she could to get the chest of drawers out of the room. Well, in a pinch Gregor could do without the chest, but the desk had to stay. And hardly had the women left the room with the chest, squeezing against it and groaning, than Gregor stuck his head out from under the couch to see how he could feel his way into the situation as considerately as possible. But unfortunately it had to be his mother who came back first, while in the next room Grete was clasping the chest and rocking it back and forth by herself, without of course budging it from the spot. His mother, however, was not used to the sight of Gregor, he could have made her ill, and so Gregor, frightened, scuttled in reverse to the far end of the couch but could not stop the sheet from shifting a little at the front. That was enough to put his mother on the alert. She stopped, stood still for a moment, and then went back to Grete.

Although Gregor told himself over and over again that nothing special was happening, only a few pieces of furniture were being moved, he soon had to admit that this coming and going of the women, their little calls to each other, the scraping of the furniture along the floor had the effect on him of a great turmoil swelling on all sides, and as much as he tucked in his head and his legs and shrank until his belly touched the floor, he was forced to admit that he would not be able to stand it much longer. They were clearing out his room; depriving him of everything that he loved; they had already carried away the chest of drawers, in which he kept the fretsaw and other tools; were now budging the desk firmly embedded in the floor, the desk he had done his homework on when he was a student at business college, in high school, yes, even in public school—now he really had no more time to examine the good intentions of the two women, whose existence, besides, he had almost forgotten, for they were so exhausted that they were working in silence, and one could hear only the heavy shuffling of their feet.

And so he broke out—the women were just leaning against the desk in the next room to catch their breath for a minute—changed his course four times, he really didn't know what to salvage first, then he saw hanging conspicuously on the wall, which was otherwise bare already, the picture of the lady all dressed in furs, hurriedly crawled up on it and pressed himself against the glass, which gave a good surface to stick to and soothed his hot belly. At least no one would take away this picture, while Gregor completely covered it up. He turned his head toward the living-room door to watch the women when they returned.

They had not given themselves much of a rest and were already coming back; Grete had put her arm around her mother and was practically carrying her. "So what should we take now?" said Grete and looked around. At that her eyes met Gregor's as he clung to the wall. Probably only because of her mother's presence she kept her self-control, bent her head down to her mother to keep her from looking around, and said, though in a quavering and thoughtless voice: "Come, we'd better go back into the living room for a minute." Grete's intent was clear to Gregor, she wanted to bring his mother into safety and then chase him down from the wall. Well, just let her try! He squatted on his picture and would not give it up. He would rather fly in Grete's face.

But Grete's words had now made her mother really anxious; she stepped to one side, caught sight of the gigantic brown blotch on the flowered wallpaper, and before it really dawned on her that what she saw was Gregor, cried in a hoarse, bawling voice: "Oh, God, Oh, God!"; and as if giving up completely, she fell with outstretched arms across the couch and did not stir. "You, Gregor!" cried his sister with raised fist and piercing eyes. These were the first words she had addressed directly to him since his metamorphosis. She ran into the next room to get some kind of spirits to revive her mother; Gregor wanted to help too—there was time to rescue the picture—but he was stuck to the glass and had to tear himself loose by force; then he too ran into the next room, as if he could give his sister some sort of advice, as in the old days; but then had to stand behind her doing nothing while she rummaged among various little bottles; moreover, when she turned around she was startled, a bottle fell on the floor and broke, a splinter of glass wounded Gregor in the face, some kind of corrosive medicine flowed around him; now without waiting any longer, Grete grabbed as many little bottles as she could carry and ran with them inside to her mother; she slammed the door behind her with her foot. Now Gregor was cut off from his mother, who was perhaps near death through his fault; he could not dare open the door if he did not want to chase away his sister, who had to stay with his mother; now there was nothing for him to do except wait; and tormented by self-reproaches and worry, he began to crawl, crawled over everything, walls, furniture and ceiling, and finally in desperation, as the whole room was beginning to spin, fell down onto the middle of the big table.

A short time passed; Gregor lay there prostrate; all around, things were quiet, perhaps that was a good sign. Then the doorbell rang. The maid, of course, was locked up in her kitchen and so Grete had to answer the door. His father had come home. "What's happened?" were his first words; Grete's appearance must have told him everything. Grete answered in a muffled voice, her face was obviously pressed against her father's chest; "Mother fainted, but she's better now. Gregor's broken out." "I knew it," his father said. "I kept telling you, but you women don't want to listen." It was clear to Gregor that his father had put the worst interpretation on Grete's all-too-brief announcement and assumed that Gregor was guilty of some outrage. Therefore Gregor now had to try to calm his father down, since he had neither the time nor the ability to enlighten him. And so he fled to the door of his room and pressed himself against it for his father to see, as soon as he came into the foyer, that Gregor had the best intentions of returning to his room immediately and that it was not necessary to drive him back; if only the door were opened for him, he would disappear at once.

But his father was in no mood to notice such subtleties; "Ah!" he cried as he entered, in a tone that sounded as if he were at once furious and glad. Gregor turned his head away from the door and lifted it toward his father. He had not really imagined his father looking like this, as he stood in front of him now; admittedly Gregor had been too absorbed recently in his newfangled crawling to bother as much as before about events in the rest of the house and should really have been prepared to find some changes. And yet, and yet—was this still his father? Was this the same man who in the old days used to lie wearily buried in bed when Gregor left on a business trip; who greeted him on his return in the evening, sitting in his bathrobe in the armchair, who actually had difficulty getting to his feet but as sign of joy only lifted up his arms; and who, on the rare occasions when the whole family went out for a walk, on a few Sundays in June and on the major holidays, used to shuffle along with great effort between Gregor and his mother, who were slow walkers themselves, always a little more slowly than they, wrapped in his old overcoat, always carefully planting down his crutch-handled cane, and, when he wanted to say something, nearly always stood still and assembled his escort around him? Now, however, he was holding himself very erect, dressed in a tight-fitting blue uniform with gold buttons, the kind worn by messengers at banking concerns; above the high stiff collar of the jacket his heavy chin protruded; under his bushy eyebrows his black eyes darted bright, piercing glances; his usually rumpled white hair was combed flat, with a scrupulously exact, gleaming part. He threw his cap—which was adorned with a gold monogram, probably that of a bank—in an arc across the entire room onto the couch, and with the tails of his long uniform jacket slapped back, his hands in his pants pockets, went for Gregor with a sullen look on his face. He probably did not know himself what he had in mind; still he lifted his feet unusually high off the floor, and Gregor staggered at the gigantic size of the soles of his boots. But he did not linger over this, he had known right from the first day of his new life that his father considered only the strictest treatment called for in dealing with him. And so he ran ahead of his father, stopped when his father stood still, and scooted ahead again when his father made even the slightest movement. In this way they made more than one tour of the room, without anything decisive happening; in fact the whole movement did not even have the appearance of a chase because of its slow tempo. So Gregor kept to the floor for the time being, especially since he was afraid that his father might interpret a flight onto the walls or the ceiling as a piece of particular nastiness. Of course Gregor had to admit that he would not be able to keep up even this running for long, for whenever his father took one step, Gregor had to execute countless movements. He was already beginning to feel winded, just as in the old days he had not had very reliable lungs. As he now staggered around, hardly keeping his eyes open in order to gather all his strength for the running; in his obtuseness not thinking of any escape other than by running; and having almost forgotten that the walls were at his disposal, though here of course they were blocked up with elaborately carved furniture full of notches and points—at that moment a lightly flung object hit the floor right near him and rolled in front of him. It was an apple; a second one came flying right after it; Gregor stopped dead with fear; further running was useless, for his father was determined to bombard him. He had filled his pockets from the fruit bowl on the buffet and was now pitching one apple after another, for the time being without taking good aim. These little red apples rolled around on the floor as if electrified, clicking into each other. One apple, thrown weakly, grazed Gregor's back and slid off harmlessly. But the very next one that came flying after it literally forced its way into Gregor's back; Gregor tried to drag himself away, as if the startling, unbelievable pain might disappear with a change of place; but he felt nailed to the spot and stretched out his body in a complete confusion of all his senses. With his last glance he saw the door of his room burst open, as his mother rushed out ahead of his screaming sister, in her chemise, for his sister had partly undressed her while she was unconscious in order to let her breathe more freely; saw his mother run up to his father and on the way her unfastened petticoats slide to the floor one by one; and saw as, stumbling over the skirts, she forced herself onto his father, and embracing him, in complete union with him—but now Gregor's sight went dim—her hands clasping his father's neck, begged for Gregor's life.

III

Gregor's serious wound, from which he suffered for over a month—the apple reminded imbedded in his flesh as a visible souvenir since no one dared to remove it—seemed to have reminded even his father that Gregor was a member of the family, in spite of his present pathetic and repulsive shape, who could not be treated as an enemy; that, on the contrary, it was the commandment of family duty to swallow their disgust and endure him, endure him and nothing more.

And now, although Gregor had lost some of his mobility probably for good because of his wound, and although for the time being he needed long, long minutes to get across his room, like an old war veteran—crawling above ground was out of the question—for this deterioration of his situation he was granted compensation which in his view was entirely satisfactory; every day around dusk the living-room door—which he was in the habit of watching closely for an hour or two beforehand—was opened, so that, lying in the darkness of his room, invisible from the living room, he could see the whole family sitting at the table under the lamp and could listen to their conversation, as it were with general permission; and so it was completely different from before.

Of course these were no longer the animated conversations of the old days, which Gregor used to remember with a certain nostalgia in small hotel rooms when he'd had to throw himself wearily into the damp bedding. Now things were mostly very quiet. Soon after supper his father would fall asleep in his armchair; his mother and sister would caution each other to be quiet; his mother, bent low under the light, sewed delicate lingerie for a clothing store; his sister, who had taken a job as a salesgirl, was learning shorthand and French in the evenings in order to attain a better position some time in the future. Sometimes his father woke up, and as if he had absolutely no idea that he had been asleep, said to his mother, "Look how long you're sewing again today!" and went right back to sleep, while mother and sister smiled wearily at each other.

With a kind of perverse obstinacy his father refused to take off his official uniform even in the house; and while his robe hung uselessly on the clothes hook, his father dozed, completely dressed, in his chair, as if he were always ready for duty and were waiting even here for the voice of his superior. As a result his uniform, which had not been new to start with, began to get dirty in spite of all the mother's and sister's care, and Gregor would often stare all evening long at this garment, covered with stains and gleaming with its constantly polished gold buttons, in which the old man slept most uncomfortably and yet peacefully.

As soon as the clock struck ten, his mother tried to awaken his father with soft encouraging words and then persuade him to go to bed, for this was no place to sleep properly, and his father badly needed his sleep, since he had to be at work at six o'clock. But with the obstinacy that had possessed him ever since he had become a messenger, he always insisted on staying at the table a little longer, although he invariably fell asleep and then could be persuaded only with the greatest effort to exchange his armchair for bed. However much mother and sister might pounce on him with little admonitions, he would slowly shake his head for a quarter of an hour at a time, keeping his eyes closed, and would not get up. Gregor's mother plucked him by the sleeves, whispered blandishments into his ear, his sister dropped her homework in order to help her mother, but all this was of no use. He only sank deeper into his armchair. Not until the women lifted him up under his arms did he open his eyes, look alternately at mother and sister, and usually say, "What a life. So this is the peace of my old age." And leaning on the two women, he would get up laboriously, as if he were the greatest weight on himself, and let the women lead him to the door, where, shrugging them off, he would proceed independently, while Gregor's mother threw down her sewing and his sister her pen as quickly as possible so as to run after his father and be of further assistance.

Who in this overworked and exhausted family had time to worry about Gregor any more than was absolutely necessary? The household was stinted more and more; now the maid was let go after all; a gigantic bony cleaning woman with white hair fluttering about her head came mornings and evenings to do the heaviest work; his mother took care of everything else, along with all her sewing. It even happened that various pieces of family jewelry, which in the old days his mother and sister had been overjoyed to wear at parties and celebrations, were sold, as Gregor found out one evening from the general discussion of the prices they had fetched. But the biggest complaint was always that they could not give up the apartment, which was much too big for their present needs, since no one could figure out how Gregor was supposed to be moved. But Gregor understood easily that it was not only consideration for him which prevented their moving, for he could easily have been transported in a suitable crate with a few air holes; what mainly prevented the family from moving was their complete hopelessness and the thought that they had been struck by a misfortune as none of their relatives and acquaintances had ever been hit. What the world demands of poor people they did to the utmost of their ability; his father brought breakfast for the minor officials at the bank, his mother sacrificed herself to the underwear of strangers, his sister ran back and forth behind the counter at the request of the customers; but for anything more than this they did not have the strength. And the wound in Gregor's back began to hurt anew when mother and sister, after getting his father to bed, now came back, dropped their work, pulled their chairs close to each other and sat cheek to cheek; when his mother, pointing to Gregor's room, said, "Close that door, Grete"; and when Gregor was back in darkness, while in the other room the women mingled their tears or stared dry-eyed at the table.

Gregor spent the days and nights almost entirely without sleep. Sometimes he thought that the next time the door opened he would take charge of the family's affairs again, just as he had done in the old days; after this long while there again appeared in his thoughts the boss and the manager, the salemen and the trainees, the handyman who was so dense, two or three friends from other firms, a chambermaid in a provincial hotel—a happy fleeting memory—a cashier in a millinery store, whom he had courted earnestly but too slowly—they all appeared, intermingled with strangers or people he had already forgotten; but instead of helping him and his family, they were all inaccessible, and he was glad when they faded away. At other times he was in no mood to worry about his family, he was completely filled with rage at his miserable treatment, and although he could not imagine anything that would pique his appetite, he still made plans for getting into the pantry to take what was coming to him, even if he wasn't hungry. No longer considering what she could do to give Gregor a special treat, his sister, before running to business every morning and afternoon, hurriedly shoved any old food into Gregor's room with her foot; and in the evening, regardless of whether the food had only been toyed with or—the most usual case—had been left completely untouched, she swept it out with a swish of the broom. The cleaning up of Gregor's room, which she now always did in the evenings, could not be done more hastily. Streaks of dirt ran along the walls, fluffs of dust and filth lay here and there on the floor. At first, whenever his sister came in, Gregor would place himself in those corners which were particularly offending, meaning by his position in a sense to reproach her. But he could probably have stayed there for weeks without his sister's showing any improvement; she must have seen the dirt as clearly as he did, but she had just decided to leave it. At the same time she made sure—with an irritableness that was completely new to her and which had in fact infected the whole family—that the cleaning of Gregor's room remain her province. One time his mother had submitted Gregor's room to a major housecleaning, which she managed only after employing a couple of pails of water—all this dampness, of course, irritated Gregor too and he lay prostrate, sour and immobile, on the couch—but his mother's punishment was not long in coming. For hardly had his sister noticed the difference in Gregor's room that evening than, deeply insulted, she ran into the living room and, in spite of her mother's imploringly uplifted hands, burst out in a fit of crying, which his parents—his father had naturally been startled out of his armchair—at first watched in helpless amazement; until they too got going; turning to the right, his father blamed his mother for not letting his sister clean Gregor's room; but turning to the left, he screamed at his sister that she would never again be allowed to clean Gregor's room; while his mother tried to drag his father, who was out of his mind with excitement, into the bedroom; his sister, shaken with sobs, hammered the table with her small fists, and Gregor hissed loudly with rage because it did not occur to any of them to close the door and spare him such a scene and a row.

But even if his sister, exhausted from her work at the store, had gotten fed up with taking care of Gregor as she used to, it was not necessary at all for his mother to take her place and still Gregor did not have to be neglected. For now the cleaning woman was there. This old widow, who thanks to her strong bony frame had probably survived the worst in a long life, was not really repelled by Gregor. Without being in the least inquisitive, she had once accidentally opened the door of Gregor's room, and at the sight of Gregor—who, completely taken by surprise, began to race back and forth although no one was chasing him—she had remained standing, with her hands folded on her stomach, marveling. From that time on she never failed to open the door a crack every morning and every evening and peek in hurriedly at Gregor. In the beginning she also used to call him over to her with words she probably considered friendly, like, "Come over here for a minute, you old dung beetle!" or "Look at the old dung beetle!" To forms of address like these Gregor would not respond but remained immobile where he was, as if the door had not been opened. If only they had given this cleaning woman orders to clean up his room every day, instead of letting her disturb him uselessly whenever the mood took her. Once, early in the morning—heavy rain, perhaps already a sign of approaching spring, was beating on the window panes—Gregor was so exasperated when the cleaning woman started in again with her phrases that he turned on her, of course slowly and decrepitly, as if to attack. But the cleaning woman, instead of getting frightened, simply lifted up high a chair near the door, and as she stood there with her mouth wide open, her intention was clearly to shut her mouth only when the chair in her hand came crashing down on Gregor's back. "So, is that all there is?" she asked when Gregor turned around again, and she quietly put the chair back in the corner.

Gregor now hardly ate anything anymore. Only when he accidentally passed the food laid out for him would he take a bite into his mouth just for fun, hold it in for hours, and then mostly spit it out again. At first he thought that his grief at the state of his room kept him off food, but it was the very changes in his room to which he quickly became adjusted. His family had gotten into the habit of putting in this room things for which they could not find any other place, and now there were plenty of these, since one of the rooms in the apartment had been rented to three boarders. These serious gentlemen—all three had long beards, as Gregor was able to register once through a crack in the door—were obsessed with neatness, not only in their room, but since they had, after all, moved in here, throughout the entire household and especially in the kitchen. They could not stand useless, let alone dirty junk. Besides, they had brought along most of their own household goods. For this reason many things had become superfluous, and though they certainly weren't salable, on the other hand they could not just be thrown out. All these things migrated into Gregor's room. Likewise the ash can and the garbage can from the kitchen. Whatever was not being used at the moment was just flung into Gregor's room by the cleaning woman, who was always in a big hurry; fortunately Gregor generally saw only the object involved and the hand that held it. Maybe the cleaning woman intended to reclaim the things as soon as she had a chance or else to throw out everything together in one fell swoop, but in fact they would have remained lying wherever they had been thrown in the first place if Gregor had not squeezed through the junk and set it in motion, at first from necessity, because otherwise there would have been no room to crawl in, but later with growing pleasure, although after such excursions, tired to death and sad, he did not budge again for hours.

Since the roomers sometimes also had their supper at home in the common living room, the living-room door remained closed on certain evenings, but Gregor found it very easy to give up the open door, for on many evenings when it was opened he had not taken advantage of it, but instead, without the family's noticing, had lain in the darkest corner of his room. But once the cleaning woman had left the living-room door slightly open, and it also remained opened a little when the roomers came in in the evening and the lamp was lit. They sat down at the head of the table where in the old days his father, his mother, and Gregor had eaten, unfolded their napkins, and picked up their knives and forks. At once his mother appeared in the doorway with a platter of meat, and just behind her came his sister with a platter piled high with potatoes. A thick vapor steamed up from the food. The roomers bent over the platters set in front of them as if to examine them before eating, and in fact the one who sat in the middle, and who seemed to be regarded by the other two as an authority, cut into a piece of meat while it was still on the platter, evidently to find out whether it was tender enough or whether it should perhaps be sent back to the kitchen. He was satisfied, and mother and sister, who had been watching anxiously, sighed with relief and began to smile.

The family itself ate in the kitchen. Nevertheless, before going into the kitchen, his father came into this room and, bowing once, cap in hand, made a turn around the table. The roomers rose as one man and mumbled something into their beards. When they were alone again, they ate in almost complete silence. It seemed strange to Gregor that among all the different noises of eating he kept picking up the sound of their chewing teeth, as if this were a sign to Gregor that you needed teeth to eat with and that even with the best make of toothless jaws you couldn't do a thing. "I'm hungry enough," Gregor said to himself, full of grief, "but not for these things. Look how these roomers are gorging themselves, and I'm dying!"

On this same evening—Gregor could not remember having heard the violin during the whole time—the sound of violin playing came from the kitchen. The roomers had already finished their evening meal, the one in the middle had taken out a newspaper, given each of the two others a page, and now, leaning back, they read and smoked. When the violin began to play, they became attentive, got up, and went on tiptoe to the door leading to the foyer, where they stood in a huddle. They must have been heard in the kitchen, for his father called, "Perhaps the playing bothers you, gentlemen? It can be stopped right away." "On the contrary," said the middle roomer. "Wouldn't the young lady like to come in to us and play in here where it's much roomier and more comfortable?" "Oh, certainly," called Gregor's father, as if he were the violinist. The boarders went back into the room and waited. Soon Gregor's father came in with the music stand, his mother with the sheet music, and his sister with the violin. Calmly his sister got everything ready for playing; his parents—who had never rented out rooms before and therefore behaved toward the roomers with excessive politeness—did not even dare sit down on their own chairs; his father leaned against the door, his right hand inserted between two buttons of his uniform coat, which he kept closed; but his mother was offered a chair by one of the roomers, and since she left the chair where the roomer just happened to put it, she sat in a corner to one side.

His sister began to play. Father and mother, from either side, attentively followed the movements of her hands. Attracted by the playing, Gregor had dared to come out a little further and already had his head in the living room. It hardly surprised him that lately he was showing so little consideration for the others; once such consideration had been his greatest pride. And yet he would never have had better reason to keep hidden; for now, because of the dust which lay all over his room and blew around at the slightest movement, he too was completely covered with dust; he dragged around with him on his back and along his sides fluff and hairs and scraps of food; his indifference to everything was much too deep for him to have gotten on his back and scrubbed himself clean against the carpet, as once he had done several times a day. And in spite of his state, he was not ashamed to inch out a little farther on the immaculate living-room floor.

Admittedly no one paid any attention to him. The family was completely absorbed by the violin-playing; the roomers, on the other hand, who at first had stationed themselves, hands in pockets, much too close behind his sister's music stand, so that they could all have followed the score, which certainly must have upset his sister, soon withdrew to the window, talking to each other in an undertone, their heads lowered, where they remained, anxiously watched by his father. It now seemed only too obvious that they were disappointed in their expectation of hearing beautiful or entertaining violin-playing, had had enough of the whole performance, and continued to let their peace be disturbed only out of politeness. Especially the way they all blew the cigar smoke out of the nose and mouth toward the ceiling suggested great nervousness. And yet his sister was playing so beautifully. Her face was inclined to one side, sadly and probingly her eyes followed the lines of music. Gregor crawled forward a little farther, holding his head close to the floor, so that it might be possible to catch her eye. Was he an animal, that music could move him so? He felt as if the way to the unknown nourishment he longed for were coming to light. He was determined to force himself on until he reached his sister, to pluck at her skirt, and to let her know in this way that she should bring her violin into his room, for no one here appreciated her playing the way he would appreciate it. He would never again let her out of his room—at least not for as long as he lived; for once, his nightmarish looks would be of use to him; he would be at all the doors of his room at the same time and hiss and spit at the aggressors; his sister, however, should not be forced to stay with him, but would do so of her own free will; she should sit next to him on the couch, bending her ear down to him, and then he would confide to her that he had had the firm intention of sending her to the Conservatory, and that, if the catastrophe had not intervened, he would have announced this to everyone last Christmas—certainly Christmas had come and gone?—without taking notice of any objections. After this declaration his sister would burst into tears of emotion, and Gregor would raise himself up to her shoulder and kiss her on the neck which, ever since she started going out to work, she kept bare, without a ribbon or collar.

"Mr. Samsa!" the middle roomer called to Gregor's father and without wasting another word pointed his index finger at Gregor, who was slowly moving forward. The violin stopped, the middle roomer smiled first at his friends, shaking his head, and then looked at Gregor again. Rather than driving Gregor out, his father seemed to consider it more urgent to start by soothing the roomers although they were not at all upset, and Gregor seemed to be entertaining them more than the violin-playing. He rushed over to them and tried with outstretched arms to drive them into their room and at the same time with his body to block their view of

Gregor. Now they actually did get a little angry—it was not clear whether because of his father's behavior or because of their dawning realization of having had without knowing it such a next door neighbor as Gregor. They demanded explanations from his father; in their turn they raised their arms, plucked excitedly at their beards, and, dragging their feet, backed off toward their room. In the meantime his sister had overcome the abstracted mood into which she had fallen after her playing had been so suddenly interrupted; and all at once, after holding violin and bow for a while in her slackly hanging hands and continuing to follow the score as if she were still playing, she pulled herself together, laid the instrument on the lap of her mother—who was still sitting in her chair, fighting for breath, her lungs violently heaving—and ran into the next room, which the roomers, under pressure from her father, were nearing more quickly than before. One could see the covers and bolsters on the beds, obeying his sister's practiced hands, fly up and arrange themselves. Before the boarders had reached the room, she had finished turning down the beds and had slipped out. Her father seemed once again to be gripped by his perverse obstinacy to such a degree that he completely forgot any respect still due his tenants. He drove them on and kept on driving until, already at the bedroom door, the middle boarder stamped his foot thunderingly and thus brought him to a standstill. "I herewith declare," he said raising his hand and casting his eyes around for Gregor's mother and sister too, "that in view of the disgusting conditions prevailing in this apartment and family"—here he spat curtly and decisively on the floor—"I give notice as of now. Of course I won't pay a cent for the days I have been living here, either; on the contrary, I shall consider taking some sort of action against you with claims that—believe me—will be easy to substantiate." He stopped and looked straight in front of him, as if he were expecting something. And in fact his two friends at once chimed in with the words, "We too give notice as of now." Thereupon he grabbed the door knob and slammed the door with a bang.

Gregor's father, his hands groping, staggered to his armchair and collapsed into it; it looked as if he were stretching himself out for his usual evening nap, but the heavy drooping of his head, as if it had lost all support, showed that he was certainly not asleep. All this time Gregor had lain quietly at the spot where the roomers had surprised him. His disappointment at the failure of his plan—but perhaps also the weakness caused by so much fasting—made it impossible for him to move. He was afraid with some certainty that in the very next moment a general debacle would burst over him, and he waited. He was not even startled by the violin as it slipped from under his mother's trembling fingers and fell off her lap with a reverberating clang.

"My dear parents," said his sister and by way of an introduction pounded her hand on the table, "things can't go on like this. Maybe you don't realize it, but I do. I won't pronounce the name of my brother in front of this monster, and so all I say is: we have to try to get rid of it. We've done everything humanly possible to take care of it and to put up with it; I don't think anyone can blame us in the least."

"She's absolutely right," said his father to himself. His mother, who still could not catch her breath, began to cough dully behind her hand, a wild look in her eyes.

His sister rushed over to his mother and held her forehead. His father seemed to have been led by Grete's words to more definite thoughts, had sat up, was playing with the cap of his uniform among the plates which were still lying on the table from the roomers' supper, and from time to time looked at Gregor's motionless form.

"We must try to get rid of it," his sister now said exclusively to her father, since her mother was coughing too hard to hear anything. "It will be the death of you two, I can see it coming. People who already have to work as hard as we do can't put up with this constant torture at home, too. I can't stand it anymore either." And she broke out crying so bitterly that her tears poured down onto her mother's face, which she wiped off with mechanical movements of her hand.

"Child," said her father kindly and with unusual understanding, "but what can we do?"

Gregor's sister only shrugged her shoulders as a sign of the bewildered mood that had now gripped her as she cried, in contrast with her earlier confidence.

"If he could understand us," said her father, half questioning; in the midst of her crying Gregor's sister waved her hand violently as a sign that that was out of the question.

"If he could understand us," his father repeated and by closing his eyes, absorbed his daughter's conviction of the impossibility of the idea, "then maybe we could come to an agreement with him. But the way things are————"

"It has to go," cried his sister. "That's the only answer, Father. You just have to try to get rid of the idea that it's Gregor. Believing it for so long, that is our real misfortune. But how can it be Gregor? If it were Gregor, he would have realized long ago that it isn't possible for human beings to live with such a creature, and he would have gone away of his own free will. Then we wouldn't have a brother, but we'd be able to go on living and honor his memory. But as things are, this animal persecutes us, drives the roomers away, obviously wants to occupy the whole apartment and for us to sleep in the gutter. Look, Father," she suddenly shrieked, "he's starting in again!" And in a fit of terror that was completely incomprehensible to Gregor, his sister abandoned even her mother, literally shoved herself off from her chair, as if she would rather sacrifice her mother than stay near Gregor, and rushed behind her father, who, upset only by her behavior, also stood up and half-lifted his arms in front of her as if to protect her.

But Gregor had absolutely no intention of frightening anyone, let alone his sister. He had only begun to turn around in order to trek back to his room; certainly his movements did look peculiar, since his ailing condition made him help the complicated turning maneuver along with his head, which he lifted up many times and knocked against the floor. He stopped and looked around. His good intention seemed to have been recognized; it had only been a momentary scare. Now they all watched him, silent and sad. His mother lay in her armchair, her legs stretched out and pressed together, her eyes almost closing from exhaustion; his father and his sister sat side by side, his sister had put her arm around her father's neck.

Now maybe they'll let me turn around, Gregor thought and began his labors again. He could not repress his panting from the exertion, and from time to time he had to rest. Otherwise no one harassed him, he was left completely on his own. When he had completed the turn, he immediately began to crawl back in a straight line. He was astonished at the great distance separating him from his room and could not understand at all how, given his weakness, he had covered the same distance a little while ago almost without realizing it. Constantly intent only on rapid crawling, he hardly noticed that not a word, not an exclamation from his family interrupted him. Only when he was already in the doorway did he turn his head—not completely, for he felt his neck stiffening; nevertheless he still saw that behind him nothing had changed except that his sister had gotten up. His last glance ranged over his mother, who was now fast asleep.

He was hardly inside his room when the door was hurriedly slammed shut, firmly bolted, and locked. Gregor was so frightened at the sudden noise behind him that his little legs gave way under him. It was his sister who had been in such a hurry. She had been standing up straight, ready and waiting, then she had leaped forward nimbly, Gregor had not even heard her coming, and she cried "Finally!" to her parents as she turned the key in the lock.

"And now?" Gregor asked himself, looking around in the darkness. He soon made the discovery that he could no longer move at all. It did not surprise him; rather, it seemed unnatural that until now he had actually been able to propel himself on these thin little legs. Otherwise he felt relatively comfortable. He had pains, of course, throughout his whole body, but it seemed to him that they were gradually getting fainter and fainter and would finally go away altogether. The rotten apple in his back and the inflamed area around it, which were completely covered with fluffy dust, already hardly bothered him. He thought back on his family with deep emotion and love. His conviction that he would have to disappear was, if possible, even firmer than his sister's. He remained in this state of empty and peaceful reflection until the tower clock struck three in the morning. He still saw that outside the window everything was beginning to grow light. Then, without his consent, his head sank down to the floor, and from his nostrils streamed his last weak breath.

When early in the morning the cleaning woman came—in sheer energy and impatience she would slam all the doors so hard although she had often been asked not to, that once she had arrived, quiet sleep was no longer possible anywhere in the apartment—she did not at first find anything out of the ordinary on paying Gregor her usual short visit. She thought that he was deliberately lying motionless, pretending that his feelings were hurt; she credited him with unlimited intelligence. Because she happened to be holding the long broom, she tried from the doorway to tickle Gregor with it. When this too produced no results, she became annoyed and jabbed Gregor a little, and only when she had shoved him without any resistance to another spot did she begin to take notice. When she quickly became aware of the true state of things, she opened her eyes wide, whistled softly, but did not dawdle; instead, she tore open the door of the bedroom and shouted at the top of her voice into the darkness: "Come and have a look, it's croaked; it's lying there, dead as a doornail!"

The couple Mr. and Mrs. Samsa sat up in their marriage bed and had a struggle overcoming their shock at the cleaning woman before they could finally grasp her message. But then Mr. and Mrs. Samsa hastily scrambled out of bed, each on his side, Mr. Samsa threw the blanket around his shoulders, Mrs. Samsa came out in nothing but her nightgown; dressed this way, they entered Gregor's room. In the meantime the door of the living room had also opened, where Grete had been sleeping since the roomers had moved in; she was fully dressed, as if she had not been asleep at all; and her pale face seemed to confirm this. "Dead?" said Mrs. Samsa and looked inquiringly at the cleaning woman, although she could scrutinize everything for herself and could recognize the truth even without scrutiny. "I'll say," said the cleaning woman, and to prove it she pushed Gregor's corpse with her broom a good distance sideways. Mrs. Samsa made a movement as if to hold the broom back but did not do it. "Well," said Mr. Samsa, "now we can thank God!" He crossed himself, and the three women followed his example. Grete, who never took her eyes off the corpse, said, "Just look how thin he was. Of course he didn't eat anything for such a long time. The food came out again just the way it went in." As a matter of fact, Gregor's body was completely flat and dry; this was obvious now for the first time, really, since the body was no longer raised up by his little legs and nothing else distracted the eye.

"Come in with us for a little while, Grete," said Mrs. Samsa with a melancholy smile, and Grete, not without looking back at the corpse, followed her parents into their bedroom. The cleaning woman shut the door and opened the window wide. Although it was early in the morning, there was already some mildness mixed in with the fresh air. After all, it was already the end of March.

The three boarders came out of their room and looked around in astonishment for their breakfast; they had been forgotten. "Where's breakfast?" the middle roomer grumpily asked the cleaning woman. But she put her finger to her lips and then hastily and silently beckoned the boarders to follow her into Gregor's room. They came willingly and then stood, their hands in the pockets of their somewhat shabby jackets, in the now already very bright room, surrounding Gregor's corpse.

At that point the bedroom door opened, and Mr. Samsa appeared in his uniform, his wife on one arm, his daughter on the other. They all looked as if they had been crying; from time to time Grete pressed her face against her father's sleeve.

"Leave my house immediately," said Mr. Samsa and pointed to the door, without letting go of the women. "What do you mean by that?" said the middle roomer, somewhat nonplussed, and smiled with a sugary smile. The two others held their hands behind their back and incessantly rubbed them together, as if in joyful anticipation of a big argument, which could only turn out in their favor. "I mean just what I say," answered Mr. Samsa and with his two companions marched in a straight line toward the roomer. At first the roomer stood still and looked at the floor, as if the thoughts inside his head were fitting themselves together in a new order. "So, we'll go, then," he said and looked up at Mr. Samsa as if, suddenly overcome by a fit of humility, he were asking for further permission even for this decision. Mr. Samsa merely nodded briefly several times, his eyes wide open. Thereupon the roomer actually went immediately into the foyer, taking long strides; his two friends had already been listening for a while, their hands completely still, and now they went hopping right after him, as if afraid that Mr. Samsa might get into the foyer ahead of them and interrupt the contact with their leader. In the foyer all three took their hats from the coatrack, pulled their canes from the umbrella stand, bowed silently, and left the apartment. In a suspicious mood which proved completely unfounded, Mr. Samsa led the two women out onto the landing; leaning over the banister, they watched the three roomers slowly but steadily going down the long flight of stairs, disappearing on each landing at a particular turn of the stairway and a few moments later emerging again; the farther down they got, the more the Samsa family's interest in them wore off, and when a butcher's boy with a carrier on his head came climbing up the stairs with a proud bearing, toward them and then up on past them, Mr. Samsa and the women quickly left the banister and all went back, as if relieved, into their apartment.

They decided to spend this day resting and going for a walk; they not only deserved a break in their work, they absolutely needed one. And so they sat down at the table and wrote three letters of excuse, Mr. Samsa to the management of the bank, Mrs. Samsa to her employer, and Grete to the store owner. While they were writing, the cleaning woman came in to say that she was going, since her morning's work was done. The three letter writers at first simply nodded without looking up, but as the cleaning woman still kept lingering, they looked up, annoyed. "Well?" asked Mr. Samsa. The cleaning woman stood smiling in the doorway, as if she had some great good news to announce to the family but would do so only if she were thoroughly questioned. The little ostrich feather which stood almost upright on her hat and which had irritated Mr. Samsa the whole time she had been with them swayed lightly in all directions. "What do you want?" asked Mrs. Samsa, who inspired the most respect in the cleaning woman. "Well," the cleaning woman answered, and for good-natured laughter could not immediately go on, "look, you don't have to worry about getting rid of the stuff next door. It's already been taken care of." Mrs. Samsa and Grete bent down over their letters, as if to continue writing; Mr. Samsa, who noticed that the cleaning woman was now about to start describing everything in detail, stopped her with a firmly outstretched hand. But since she was not going to be permitted to tell her story, she remembered that she was in a great hurry, cried, obviously insulted, "So long, everyone," whirled around wildly, and left the apartment with a terrible slamming of doors.

"We'll fire her tonight," said Mr. Samsa, but did not get an answer from either his wife or his daughter, for the cleaning woman seemed to have ruined their barely regained peace of mind. They got up, went to the window, and stayed there, holding each other tight. Mr. Samsa turned around in his chair toward them and watched them quietly for a while. Then he called, "Come on now, come over here. Stop brooding over the past. And have a little consideration for me, too." The women obeyed him at once, hurried over to him, fondled him, and quickly finished their letters.

Then all three of them left the apartment together, something they had not done in months, and took the trolley into the open country on the outskirts of the city. The car, in which they were the only passengers, was completely filled with warm sunshine. Leaning back comfortably in their seats, they discussed their prospects for the time to come, and it seemed on closer examination that these weren't bad at all, for all three positions—about which they had never really asked one another in any detail—were exceedingly advantageous and especially promising for the future. The greatest immediate improvement in their situation would come easily, of course, from a change in apartments; they would now take a smaller and cheaper apartment, but one better situated and in every way simpler to manage than the old one, which Gregor had picked for them. While they were talking in this vein, it occurred almost simultaneously to Mr. and Mrs. Samsa, as they watched their daughter getting livelier and livelier, that lately, in spite of all the troubles which had turned her cheeks pale, she had blossomed into a good-looking, shapely girl. Growing quieter and communicating almost unconsciously through glances, they thought that it would soon be time, too, to find her a good husband. And it was like a confirmation of their new dreams and good intentions when at the end of the ride their daughter got up first and stretched her young body.

VELEMIR VLADIMIROVICH KHLEBNIKOV

(1885–1922)

Russia

The futurist Khlebnikov invented poetic techniques to instill new life into Russian poetry. Mayakovsky called him "the Columbus of new poetic continents." But he loved old Slavic culture to the point of changing his given name (Viktor) to Velemir. His eulogy of speed and of the locomotive, associated with youth and futurism, and his rejection of the slow-moving past associated with what has gone by link him to Filippo Tommaso Marinetti, Guillaume Apollinaire, and Tristan Tzara. His 1916 diatribe against the past, "Subjects for Discussion," has the frenetic appeal of the latter's Dada manifestos of 1917 and writings from the same period about poetry and life as they hurtle by.

Subjects for Discussion

"Alloo, Alloo, Martians!"

1. How can we free ourselves from being dominated by people from the past who still retain a shadow of power in the world of space, without soiling ourselves by coming into contact with their lives (we can use the soap of word-creation), and leave them to drown in the destiny they have earned for themselves, that of

Translated by Paul Schmidt.

malicious termites? We are fated to fight with *rhythm and time* for our right to be free from the filthy habits of people from past centuries, and to win that right.

2. How can we free the speeding locomotive of the younger generation from the insolent freight train of the older generation, hitched on without our permission?

Old ones! You are holding back the fast advance of humanity, you are preventing the boiling locomotive of youth from crossing the mountain that lies in its path. We have broken the locks and see what your freight cars contain: tombstones for the young.

You've hooked your earthling wagon to our star, our locomotive and its defiant whistle, hoping for a free ride!

ISAK DINESEN [KAREN BLIXEN]
(1885–1962)

Denmark/Kenya

Isak Dinesen, pseudonym of Karen Christence Dinesen, Baroness Blixen-Finecke, was married to her cousin Baron Blixen in 1914. That year the couple set off for Africa, where they owned and operated a coffee plantation. Dinesen's life in Kenya through 1931 forms the basis of *Out of Africa* (1937), a work that took on cult status and was made into a film in 1985. During the German occupation of Denmark, she wrote, under the pseudonym Pierre Andrézel, an attack on the occupiers in 1944, translated in 1947 as *The Angelic Avengers*. Her *Seven Gothic Tales* (1934) and *Last Tales* (1957), from which "The Blank Page" is taken, reveal a kinship with a tradition both mystical and lyric. This story combines the power of suggestion with the sure atmosphere of the consummate storyteller.

from *Last Tales*

The Blank Page

By the ancient city gate sat an old coffee-brown, black-veiled woman who made her living by telling stories.

She said:

"You want a tale, sweet lady and gentleman? Indeed I have told many tales, one more than a thousand, since that time when I first let young men tell me, myself, tales of a red rose, two smooth lily buds, and four silky, supple, deadly entwining snakes. It was my mother's mother, the black-eyed dancer, the often-embraced, who in the end—wrinkled like a winter apple and crouching beneath the mercy of the veil—took upon herself to teach me the art of story-telling. Her own mother's mother had taught it to her, and both were better story-tellers than I am. But that, by now, is of no consequence, since to the people they and I have become one, and I am most highly honored because I have told stories for two hundred years."

Now if she is well paid and in good spirits, she will go on.

"With my grandmother," she said, "I went through a hard school. 'Be loyal to the story,' the old hag would say to me. 'Be eternally and unswervingly loyal to the story.' 'Why must I be that, Grandmother?' I asked her. 'Am I to furnish you with reasons, baggage?' she cried. 'And you mean to be a story-teller! Why, you are to become a story-teller, and I shall give you my reasons! Hear then: Where the story-teller is loyal, eternally and unswervingly loyal to the story, there, in the end, silence will speak. Where the story has been betrayed, silence is but emptiness. But we, the faithful, when we have spoken our last word, will hear the voice of silence. Whether a small snotty lass understands it or not.'

"Who then," she continues, "tells a finer tale than any of us? Silence does. And where does one read a deeper tale than upon the most perfectly printed page of the most precious book? Upon the blank page. When a royal and gallant pen, in the moment of its highest inspiration, has written down its tale with the rarest ink of all—where, then, may one read a still deeper, sweeter, merrier and more cruel tale than that? Upon the blank page."

The old beldame[1] for a while says nothing, only giggles a little and munches with her toothless mouth.

"We," she says at last, "the old women who tell stories, we know the story of the blank page. But we are somewhat averse to telling it, for it might well, among the uninitiated, weaken our own credit. All the same, I am going to make an exception with you, my sweet and pretty lady and gentleman of the generous hearts. I shall tell it to you."

High up in the blue mountains of Portugal there stands an old convent for sisters of the Carmelite order, which is an illustrious and austere order. In ancient times the convent was rich, the sisters were all noble ladies, and miracles took place there. But during the centuries highborn ladies grew less keen on fasting and prayer, the great dowries flowed scantily into the treasury of the convent, and today the few portionless and humble sisters live in but one wing of the vast crumbling structure, which looks as if it longed to become one with the gray rock itself. Yet they are still a blithe and active sisterhood. They take much pleasure in their holy meditations, and will busy themselves joyfully with that one particular task which did once, long, long ago, obtain for the convent a unique and strange privilege: they grow the finest flax and manufacture the most exquisite linen of Portugal.

The long field below the convent is plowed with gentle-eyed, milk-white bullocks, and the seed is skillfully sown out by labor-hardened virginal hands with mold under the nails. At the time when the flax field flowers, the whole valley becomes air-blue, the very color of the apron which the blessed virgin put on to

---

1. An old woman, hag.

go out and collect eggs within St. Anne's poultry yard, the moment before the Archangel Gabriel in mighty wing-strokes lowered himself onto the threshold of the house, and while high, high up a dove, neck-feathers raised and wings vibrating, stood like a small clear silver star in the sky. During this month the villagers many miles round raise their eyes to the flax field and ask one another: "Has the convent been lifted into heaven? Or have our good little sisters succeeded in pulling down heaven to them?"

Later in due course the flax is pulled, scutched and hackled; thereafter the delicate thread is spun, and the linen woven, and at the very end the fabric is laid out on the grass to bleach, and is watered time after time, until one may believe that snow has fallen round the convent walls. All this work is gone through with precision and piety and with such sprinklings and litanies as are the secret of the convent. For these reasons the linen, baled high on the backs of small gray donkeys and sent out through the convent gate, downwards and ever downwards to the towns, is a flower-white, smooth and dainty as was my own little foot when, fourteen years old, I had washed it in the brook to go to a dance in the village.

Diligence, dear Master and Mistress, is a good thing, and religion is a good thing, but the very first germ of a story will come from some mystical place outside the story itself. Thus does the linen of the Convento Velho draw its true virtue from the fact that the very first linseed was brought home from the Holy Land itself by a crusader.

In the Bible, people who can read may learn about the lands of Lecha and Maresha, where flax is grown. I myself cannot read, and have never seen this book of which so much is spoken. But my grandmother's grandmother as a little girl was the pet of an old Jewish rabbi, and the learning she received from him has been kept and passed on in our family. So you will read, in the book of Joshua, of how Achsah the daughter of Caleb lighted from her ass and cried unto her father: "Give me a blessing! For thou hast now given me land; give me also the blessing of springs of water!" And he gave her the upper springs and the nether springs. And in the fields of Lecha and Maresha lived, later on, the families of them that wrought the finest linen of all. Our Portuguese crusader, whose own ancestors had once been great linen weavers of Tomar, as he rode through these same fields was struck by the quality of the flax, and so tied a bag of seeds to the pommel of his saddle.

From this circumstance originated the first privilege of the convent, which was to procure bridal sheets for all the young princesses of the royal house.

I will inform you, dear lady and gentleman, that in the country of Portugal in very old and noble families a venerable custom has been observed. On the morning after the wedding of a daughter of the house, and before the morning gift had yet been handed over, the Chamberlain or High Steward from a balcony of the palace would hang out the sheet of the night and would solemnly proclaim: *Virginem eam tenemus*—"we declare her to have been a virgin." Such a sheet was never afterwards washed or again lain on.

This time-honored custom was nowhere more strictly upheld than within the royal house itself, and it has there subsisted till within living memory.

Now for many hundred years the convent in the mountains, in appreciation of the excellent quality of the linen delivered, has held its second high privilege: that of receiving back that central piece of the snow-white sheet which bore witness to the honor of a royal bride.

In the tall main wing of the convent, which overlooks an immense landscape of hills and valleys, there is a long gallery with a black-and-white marble floor. On the walls of the gallery, side by side, hangs a long row of heavy, gilt frames, each of them adorned with a coroneted plate of pure gold, on which is engraved the name of a princess: Donna Christina, Donna Ines, Donna Jacintha Lenora, Donna Maria. And each of these frames encloses a square cut from a royal wedding sheet.

Within the faded markings of the canvases people of some imagination and sensibility may read all the signs of the zodiac: the Scales, the Scorpion, the Lion, the Twins. Or they may there find pictures from their own world of ideas: a rose, a heart, a sword—or even a heart pierced through with a sword.

In days of old it would occur that a long, stately, richly colored procession wound its way through the stone-gray mountain scenery, upwards to the convent. Princesses of Portugal, who were now queens or queen dowagers of foreign countries, Archduchesses, or Electresses, with their splendid retinue, proceeded here on a pilgrimage which was by nature both sacred and secretly gay. From the flax field upwards the road rises steeply; the royal lady would have to descend from her coach to be carried this last bit of the way in a palanquin presented to the convent for the very same purpose.

Later on, up to our own day, it has come to pass—as it comes to pass when a sheet of paper is being burnt, that after all other sparks have run along the edge and died away, one last clear little spark will appear and hurry along after them—that a very old highborn spinster undertakes the journey to Convento Velho. She has once, a long long time ago, been playmate, friend and maid-of-honor to a young princess of Portugal. As she makes her way to the convent she looks round to see the view widen to all sides. Within the building a sister conducts her to the gallery and to the plate bearing the name of the princess she has once served, and there takes leave of her, aware of her wish to be alone.

Slowly, slowly a row of recollections passes through the small, venerable, skull-like head under its mantilla of black lace, and it nods to them in amicable recognition. The loyal friend and confidante looks back upon the young bride's elevated married life with the elected royal consort. She takes stock of happy events and disappointments—coronations and jubilees, court intrigues and wars, the birth of heirs to the throne, the alliances of younger generations of princes and princesses, the rise or decline of dynasties. The old lady will remember how once, from the markings on the canvas, omens were drawn; now she will be able to compare the fulfillment to the omen, sighing a little and smiling a little. Each separate canvas with its coroneted name-plate has a story to tell, and each has been set up in loyalty to the story.

But in the midst of the long row there hangs a canvas which differs from the others. The frame of it is as fine and as heavy as any, and as proudly as any carries the golden plate with the royal crown. But on this one plate no name is inscribed, and the linen within the frame is snow-white from corner to corner, a blank page.

I beg of you, you good people who want to hear stories told: look at this page, and recognize the wisdom of my grandmother and of all old story-telling women!

For with what eternal and unswerving loyalty has not this canvas been inserted in the row! The story-tellers themselves before it draw their veils over their faces and are dumb. Because the royal papa and mama who once ordered this canvas to be framed and hung up, had they not had the tradition of loyalty in their blood, might have left it out.

It is in front of this piece of pure white linen that the old princesses of Portugal—worldly wise, dutiful, long-suffering queens, wives and mothers—and their noble old playmates, bridesmaids and maids-of-honor have most often stood still.

It is in front of the blank page that old and young nuns, with the Mother Abbess herself, sink into deepest thought.

ANNA AKHMATOVA (1888–1966)
Russia

Anna Akhmatova was born near Odessa and began to publish her poetry in Paris in 1907, in the journal *Sirius* run by the poet Nikolai Gumilyov (1886–1921), whom she married in 1910. She returned to Petersburg to study literature; with Gumilyov and with poet Osip Mandelstam, she formed the Russian literary movement of acmeism or Adamism, which advocated extreme precision and detail. She divorced Gumilyov in 1918, withdrew from literary circles and after 1922 fell silent for a long stretch. She was expelled from the Union of Soviet writers in 1946 and rehabilitated in 1964. The Russian public took Akhmatova to its heart, although she was denied the right to publish. One of the major modern poets, she moved Russian poetry beyond the formulas of symbolism. "Requiem 1935–1940," not published in its entirety in Russia until 1987, is an autobiographical account of her experiences during the purges when her lover and her son were both arrested. Akhmatova's lyric voice is noted for its intensely personal, often colloquial quality, and her verse is unique in resurrecting the syntax and style of the Old Church Slavonic language and folklore, in combination with the clear and precise lines of her modernist aesthetic.

Requiem 1935–1940

No foreign sky protected me,
no stranger's wing shielded my face,

Translated by Stanley Kunitz and Max Hayward.

N. I. Altman. *Anna Akhmatova*. 1914. Oil on canvas.

I stand as witness to the common lot,
survivor of that time, that place.
                        —1961

Instead of a Preface

In the terrible years of the Yezhov[1] terror I spent seventeen months waiting in line outside the prison in Leningrad. One day somebody in the crowd identified me. Standing behind me was a woman, with lips blue from the cold, who had, of course, never heard me called by name before. Now she started out of the torpor common to us all and asked me in a whisper (everyone whispered there):
        "Can you describe this?"
        And I said: "I can."
        Then something like a smile passed fleetingly over what had once been her face.

                        —Leningrad, 1 April 1957

---

1. Yezhov was head of the NKVD (later the KGB or secret police) at the height of the terror, from 1936 to 1938. The Black Mar-

ias were black vehicles they used to round up prisoners.

Dedication

Such grief might make the mountains stoop,
reverse the waters where they flow,
but cannot burst these ponderous bolts
that block us from the prison cells
crowded with mortal woe. . . .   5
For some the wind can freshly blow,
for some the sunlight fade at ease,
but we, made partners in our dread,
hear but the grating of the keys,
and heavy-booted soldiers' tread   10
As if for early mass, we rose
and each day walked the wilderness,
trudging through silent street and square,
to congregate, less live than dead.
The sun declined, the Neva[2] blurred,   15
and hope sang always from afar
Whose sentence is decreed? . . . That moan,
that sudden spurt of woman's tears,
shows one distinguished from the rest,
as if they'd knocked her to the ground   20
and wrenched the heart out of her breast,
then let her go, reeling alone.
Where are they now, my nameless friends
from those two years I spent in hell?
What specters mock them now, amid   25
the fury of Siberian snows,
or in the blighted circle of the moon?
To them I cry, Hail and Farewell!
                                   —March 1940

Prologue

That was a time when only the dead
could smile, delivered from their wars,
and the sign, the soul, of Leningrad
dangled outside its prison-house;
and the regiments of the condemned,   5
herded in the railroad-yards,
shrank from the engine's whistle-song
whose burden went, "Away, pariahs!"
The stars of death stood over us.
And Russia, guiltless, beloved, writhed   10

---

2. A river flowing to the Baltic Sea, connected
   by a system of canals with the Volga River
   and the White Sea.

under the crunch of bloodstained boots,
under the wheels of Black Marias

1

At dawn they came and took you away.
You were my dead: I walked behind.
In the dark room children cried,
the holy candle gasped for air.
Your lips were chill from the ikon's kiss,   5
sweat bloomed on your brow—those deathly flowers!
Like the wives of Peter's troopers[3] in Red Square
I'll stand and howl under the Kremlin towers.
                                        —1935

2

Quietly flows the quiet Don;[4]
into my house slips the yellow moon.

It leaps the sill, with its cap askew,
and balks at a shadow, that yellow moon.

This woman is sick to her marrow-bone,   5
this woman is utterly alone,

with husband dead, with son away
in jail. Pray for me. Pray.

3

Not, not mine: it's somebody else's wound.
I could never have borne it. So take the thing
that happened, hide it, stick it in the ground.
Whisk the lamps away . . .
                              Night.

4

They should have shown you—mocker,
delight of your friends, hearts' thief,
naughtiest girl of Pushkin's[5] town

---

3. The Streltzy, literally, his musketeers. Peter the Great (1672–1725), Emperor and Tzar of Russia, had these semifree troops executed, not trusting them.
4. A river linked with the Volga by canal. The Don Cossacks, from a settlement along the river, were used to suppress uprisings and sided with the White Russians.
5. Aleksandr Sergeyevich Pushkin (1799–1837), Russian poet and prose writer, author of *Eugene Onegin*. *The Bronze Horseman* (1833) glorifies Peter the Great.

this picture of your fated years,
as under the glowering wall you stand,
shabby, three hundredth in the line,
clutching a parcel in your hand,
and the New Year's ice scorched by your tears.
See there the prison poplar bending!
No sound. No sound. Yet how many
innocent lives are ending. . . .

5

For seventeen months I have cried aloud,
calling you back to your lair.
I hurled myself at the hangman's foot.
You are my son, changed into nightmare.
Confusion occupies the world.
and I am powerless to tell
somebody brute from something human,
or on what day the word spells, "Kill!"
Nothing is left but dusty flowers,
the tinkling thurible, and tracks
that lead to nowhere. Night of stone,
whose bright enormous star
stares me straight in the eyes,
promising death, ah soon!

6

The weeks fly out of mind,
I doubt that it occurred:
how into your prison, child,
the white nights, blazing, stared;
and still, as I draw breath,
they fix their buzzard eyes
on what the high cross shows,
this body of your death.

7

The Sentence

The word dropped like a stone
on my still living breast.
Confess: I was prepared,
am somehow ready for the test.

So much to do today:
kill memory, kill pain,

turn heart into a stone,
and yet prepare to live again.

Not quite. Hot summer's feast
brings rumors of carouse.
How long have I foreseen
this brilliant day, this empty house?

—Summer, 1939

8

To Death

You will come in any case—so why not now?
How long I wait and wait. The bad times fall.
I have put out the light and opened the door
for you, because you are simple and magical.
Assume, then, any form that suits your wish,
take aim, and blast at me with poisoned shot,
or strangle me like an efficient mugger,
or else infect me—typhus be my lot—
or spring out of the fairytale you wrote,
the one we're sick of hearing, day and night,
where the blue hatband marches up the stairs,
led by the janitor, pale with fright.
It's all the same to me. The Yenisei swirls,
the North Star shines, as it will shine forever;
and the blue lustre of my loved one's eyes
is clouded over by the final horror.

—The House on the Fontanka,
19 August 1939

9

Already madness lifts its wing
to cover half my soul.
That taste of opiate wine!
Lure of the dark valley!

Now everything is clear.
I admit my defeat. The tongue
of my ravings in my ear
is the tongue of a stranger.

No use to fall down on my knees
and beg for mercy's sake.
Nothing I counted mine, out of my life,
is mine to take:

not my son's terrible eyes,
not the elaborate stone flower
of grief, not the day of the storm,   15
not the trial of the visiting hour,

not the dear coolness of his hands,
not the lime trees' agitated shade,
not the thin cricket-sound
of consolation's parting word.   20
                          —4 May 1940

10
Crucifixion

*"Do not weep for me, Mother,
when I am in my grave."*

I

A choir of angels glorified the hour,
the vault of heaven was dissolved in fire.
"Father, why hast Thou forsaken me?
Mother, I beg you, do not weep for me. . . ."

II

Mary Magdalene[6] beat her breasts and sobbed,
His dear disciple, stone-faced, stared.
His mother stood apart. No other looked
into her secret eyes. Nobody dared.
                          —1940–1943

Epilogue
I

I have learned how faces fall to bone,
how under the eyelids terror lurks,
how suffering inscribes on cheeks
the hard lines of its cuneiform texts,
how glossy black or ash-fair locks
turn overnight to tarnished silver,   5
how smiles fade on submissive lips,
and fear quavers in a dry titter.

---

6. A Christian saint, by legend a repentant
   prostitute, washing Jesus's feet and present
   at his crucifixion and entombment.

And I pray not for myself alone . . .
for all who stood outside the jail,
in bitter cold or summer's blaze,
with me under that blind red wall.   10

II

Remembrance hour returns with the turning year.
I see, I hear, I touch you drawing near:

the one we tried to help to the sentry's booth,
and who no longer walks this precious earth,

and that one who would toss her pretty mane   5
and say, "It's just like coming home again."

I want to name the names of all that host,
but they snatched up the list, and now it's lost.

I've woven them a garment that's prepared
out of poor words, those that I overheard,   10

and will hold fast to every word and glance
all of my days, even in new mischance,

and if a gag should blind my tortured mouth,
through which a hundred million people shout,

then let them pray for me, as I do pray   15
for them, this eve of my remembrance day.

And if my country ever should assent
to casting in my name a monument,

I should be proud to have my memory graced,
but only if the monument be placed   20

not near the sea on which my eyes first opened—
my last link with the sea has long been broken—

nor in the Tsar's garden near the sacred stump,
where a grieved shadow hunts my body's warmth,

but here, where I endured three hundred hours   25
in line before the implacable iron bars.

Because even in blissful death I fear
to lose the clangor of the Black Marias,

to lose the banging of that odious gate
and the old crone howling like a wounded beast.   30

And from my motionless bronze-lidded sockets
may the melting snow, like teardrops, slowly trickle,

and a prison dove coo somewhere, over and over,
as the ships sail softly down the flowing Neva.

—March 1940

OSIP EMILYEVICH MANDELSTAM

(1891–1938)

Russia

One of the great poets associated with the acmeist school (1910–1917), as were
Anna Akhmatova and Nikolai Gumilyov, Osip Mandelstam is noted for his
concision and classically precise poetry, especially the collections *Stone* (1913) and
Tristia (1932). His arrest in 1933 or 1934 during the purges, and subsequent death
in a concentration camp are recounted in Nadezhd Mandelstam's celebrated *Hope
Against Hope*. The taut intelligent melancholy of these poems about Homer,
Akhmatova, and himself resounds through these superb translations.

[Insomnia]

Insomnia. Homer. Taut sails.
I've read to the middle of the list of ships:
the strung-out flock, the stream of cranes
that once rose above Hellas.

Flight of cranes crossing strange borders,   5
leaders drenched with the foam of the gods,
where are you sailing? What would Troy be to you,
men of Achaea, without Helen?

The sea—Homer—it's all moved by love. But to whom
shall I listen? No sound now from Homer,   10
and the black sea roars like a speech
and thunders up the bed.

1915

To Anna Akhmatova

Keep my words forever for their aftertaste of misfortune and smoke,
their tar of mutual tolerance, honest tar of work.
Sweet and black should be the water of Novgorod wells
to reflect the seven fins of the Christmas star.

Translated by Clarence Brown and W. S. Merwin.

And in return, father, friend, rough helper, I
the unrecognized brother, outlawed from the people's family,
promise to fit the beam-cages tight to the wells
so the Tartars can lower the princes in tubs, for torture.

O ancient headsman's blocks, keep on loving me!
Players in the garden seem to aim at death, and hit nine-pins.
I walk through my life aiming like that, in my iron shirt
(why not?) and I'll find an old beheading axe in the woods.

Khmelnitskaya. 3 May 1931

[What street is this?]

—What street is this?
—Mandelstam Street.
—What the hell kind of name is that?
No matter which way you turn it
it comes out crooked.

—He wasn't a straight-edge exactly.
His morals resembled no lily.
And that's why this street (or rather,
to be honest, this sewer)
was given the name
of that Mandelstam.

Voronezh. April 1935

NELLY SACHS (1891–1970)
Germany

Born in Berlin to upper middle-class Jewish parents, Nelly Sachs was well educated in the arts: as a child, she wanted to become a dancer, and her poetry is marked by a dancer's rhythmic longing to overcome gravity. She stayed outside the currents of the literary avant-garde. Fleeing from Nazism to exile in Sweden in 1940, she discovered the resources of Judaism and Christian mysticism. Her family died in Nazi concentration camps, and her unrhymed poems *In the Dwellings of Death* (1947) recount the horrors of the Holocaust. Her later poems such as *And No One Knows Where to Go* (1957), and *O the Chimneys* (1967), form one enormous cycle, responding to what she felt was her responsibility, thanks to her survival and her deepening religious sense, to bear witness to the suffering of her people, calling upon the healing power of poetry. In 1966 she shared the Nobel Prize in literature with S. J. Agnon.

A "Line like/living hair," as it ties death to love, manages, through the felt intensity of its longing, to convey a presence, however tremulous.

Georg Baselitz. *Der Brückechor*. 1983. Oil on canvas.

Line Like

Line like
living hair
drawn
deathnightobscured
from you
to me.   5
Reined in
outside
I bend
thirstily
to kiss the end of all distances.   10

Evening
throws the springboard
of night over the redness
lengthens your promontory
and hesitant I place my foot   15
on the trembling string
of my death already begun.

But such is love—

Translated by Michael Hamburger.

MARINA TSVETAYEVA (1892–1941)
Russia

From an upperclass family in which her father was an art historian, Marina
Tsvetayeva was a linguist and an acclaimed poet. Having been on the side of the
White Russians during the Russian Revolution, Tsvetayeva left in 1922 to join her
husband Sergey Efron in Berlin. They later moved to Prague and then in 1925 to
Paris where she wrote her memoirs and criticism. She suffered increasing
isolation from impoverishment and criticism by the other emigrés for her defense
of the Soviet poets Vladimir Mayakovsky and Boris Pasternak. When her
daughter and husband, who had been denounced as a Soviet spy, returned to
Russia in 1937, she returned also in 1939. But her poetry could not be published
in the Soviet Union. Her sister and her daughter were both imprisoned, her
husband was shot as an enemy of the people and her son was killed on the war
front in 1941. Evacuated from Moscow to the Tatar Autonomous Republic,
where she was totally alone and near starvation, she hanged herself in Elabuga.
Tsvetayeva's poetry—intense and unforgiving, elliptical and inventive—is a
poet's poetry. Of her, Boris Pasternak once said, "She was the best of us." Both
poems included here mingle passion, despair, and bitter irony with the certainty
of some black Hell or raging pain replacing everything once finely-clothed and
shared, now forever lost.

We Shall Not Escape Hell

We shall not escape Hell, my passionate
sisters, we shall drink black resins—
we who sang our praises to the Lord
with every one of our sinews, even the finest.

we did not lean over cradles or   5
spinning wheels at night, and now we are
carried off by an unsteady boat
under the skirts of a sleeveless cloak,

we dressed every morning in
fine Chinese silk, and we would   10
sing our paradisal songs at
the fire of the robbers' camp,

slovenly needlewomen (all
our sewing came apart), dancers,
players upon pipes: we have been   15
the queens of the whole world!

Translated by Elaine Feinstein.

Natalya Goncharova. *Angels over a City*. 1914. Lithograph from a portfolio, *Mystical Images of War*.

first scarcely covered by rags,
then with constellations in our hair, in
gaol and at feasts we have
bartered away heaven.

in starry nights, in the apple
orchards of Paradise.
—Gentle girls, my beloved sisters,
we shall certainly find ourselves in Hell!

from **Poem of the End**

[*Rain. A heavy mane*]

Rain. A heavy mane
in our eyes. Hills.
We have passed the suburbs,
we are out of town.

The town is there, but not
for us: only a stepmother.
There's nowhere further to go.
This is the end of the road.

Translated by Paul Schmidt.

A field. A fence.
Brother and sister we stand.   10
Life is a suburb,
build out of town.

Oh, it's a lost
cause, gentlemen,
it's suburbs everywhere.   15
Whatever became of the town?

The rain tears and rages.
We stand and tear apart.
In the last three months   20
this is all we've shared.

God even wanted
to borrow from Job.
It didn't work.
We're out of town.

Out of town. Understand?   25
Outside! Beyond the walls.
Life is a place where no one
can live: a Jewish quarter.

It's a hundred times better
being the Wandering Jew.   30
For all but reptiles
life is a Jewish

Pogrom.[1] Only converts survive,
Judases of all faiths.
Go live in leper colonies,   35
in hell. Anywhere. Only leave

Life. Life wants converts
only, sheep for butchers.
I trample on my right-to-life   40
certificate.

Vengeance for the Star of David!
For jumbles of bodies!
Isn't it entrancing that the Jews
simply didn't want to live?

---

1. Originally, "riot," but now refers to attacks
   on Jews in Russia or Russia-related countries.

This ghetto of the Elect. A wall,
a ditch. Expect no mercy.
In this most Christian of worlds
all poets are Jews.   45

EUGENIO MONTALE (1896–1981)
Italy

Eugenio Montale worked as an editor, and later became Chief Librarian of the
Gabinetto Vieusseux in Florence. With the publication of his first collection of
poems *Cuttlefish Bones* in 1916, he was accepted as one of the major modern
poets, who, along with Giuseppe Ungaretti, was responsible for crafting the new
Italian poetry. As he himself said of the Ligurian landscape for his work, "it is
most universal." His language mingles universal and specific terms, informal style
and scientific terms, and it manages to bestow an entirely new life on the objects
it deals with, seeing them close up and making them intense and real for the
reader, and yet imbued with moral sense: nowhere is this clearer than "In the
Park" with its magnolias and poplars, its laughter and uncomfortable love. In
"The Sunflower" he writes, "Bring me that flower, impassioned of the light," and
both the flower and the world seem newly luminous. As he writes in "The Lemon
Trees," we have the sense of a thread we might somehow untangle, even in "the
pain of living," on the way to some truth. Montale's poetry remains suggestive
and deliberately ambiguous, rather than clear; layers build on layers of meaning.
In 1975 Montale received the Nobel Prize for literature.

In the Park

In the magnolia's ever
stricter shade, at one
puff from a blowgun
the dart grazes me and is gone.

It was like a leaf let fall   5
by the poplar a gust of wind
uncolors—perhaps a hand
roving through green from afar.

A laughter not my own
pierces through hoary branches   10
into my breast, a thrill
shakes me, stabs my veins,

Translated by James Merrill.

and I laugh with you on the warped
wheel of shade, I stretch out
discharged of myself on the sharp   15
protruding roots, and needle

your face with bits of straw. . . .

TRISTAN TZARA (1896–1963)
Romania/Switzerland/France

Tristan Tzara, pen name of Samuel Rosenfeld, was born in Romania and wrote his
early poems in Romanian. Part of the delight of his texts, from the earliest poems
influenced by African art and language to the later poems, is his original use of
French; he kept lists of the words new to him that he planned to use, and did. Tzara
was a founder, together with poet Hugo Ball and artist Jean (Hans) Arp of the
joyously and angrily nihilist dada movement, which gave its first demonstrations in
1916 at the Cabaret Voltaire in Zurich. The dadaists went on at that time to upset
the bourgeoisie of Switzerland and subsequently in Paris, where they were joined
by André Breton, Louis Aragon, and Philippe Soupault. The word *dada* was found
at random in a dictionary, according to one story about the group's founding; it
means "hobby horse" and it is also one of the first words said by a baby. The
negative energy of dada and its proponents is felt in alternate waves with the more
positive proclamations of the surrealist movement, started in Paris in 1923, after
dada, in the words of Tzara, "commits suicide." Tzara himself went on after his early
poetry in Romanian and his dada texts to write the epic poem *Approximate Man*
(1925–1931). Tzara's "Note on Art," from the first issue of the journal *DADA* in
1917, stressed the act of seeing in its most luminous simplicity. His "Proclamation
Without Pretention of 1918," a dada document like a poetic manifesto, makes more
noise, while his moving elegy to Apollinaire ("The Death of Guillaume Apollinaire"
of 1918) bears witness to his innate poetic sense. The poetry Tzara wrote in the
1940s was typified by an uncomplicated line and vision, like that of the prose poem
of 1955 "The Horse," included here. To some extent this change in style occurred
because of Tzara's political involvement with the Communist Party, which
demanded more "intelligible" writing than the noisy early texts.

from *Of Our Birds*

The Death of Guillaume Apollinaire

we know nothing
we knew nothing of grief

Translated by Mary Ann Caws.

the bitter season of cold
              digs long furrows in our muscles

he would have preferred the joy of victory
      wise under calm sorrows   caged
                    unable to do anything at all
              if snow fell upward
if the sun rose to meet us during the night
              to warm us
    and trees hung with their crown upside down
             —unique teardrop—
   if birds were here with us to contemplate themselves
in the tranquil lake above our heads

       WE COULD UNDERSTAND
        death would be a beautiful long voyage
and an unlimited vacation from the flesh of structures and of
bones

Proclamation Without Pretention

Art goes to sleep for the birth of a new world
"ART"—a *parrot word*—replaced by **DADA**
PLESIAUSAURUS, or handkerchief
The talent WHICH YOU CAN LEARN *makes the poet a*
   druggist **TODAY** *criticism balances no longer launches resemblances*
Hypertrophic painters hyperestheticized and hypnotized by
   the hyancinths of muezzins of hypocritical appearance
CONSOLIDATE THE EXACT HARVEST OF
   CALCULATIONS
HYPERDROME OF IMMORTAL GUARANTEES: *There is no importance*
   there is no transparency or apparency
MUSICIANS BREAK YOUR BLIND INSTRUMENTS on the
   stage
The **SYRINGE** *is only for my understanding.* **I am writing**
   because it is as natural as pissing as being sick
Art needs an operation
Art is a **PRETENTION** heated in the TIMIDITY of the urinary
basin, **Hysteria** born in the **Studio**

We are seeking **upright pure sober unique** strength we are
seeking **NOTHING** we affirm the **VITALITY** of
   each instant the anti-philosophy of **Spontaneous** acrobatics
In this moment I hate the man who whispers before
   intermission—eau de cologne—bitter theater. CHEERY WIND.
IF EVERYBODY SAYS THE OPPOSITE IT IS BECAUSE THEY ARE RIGHT.
Prepare the geyser actions of our blood—submarine formation

of transchromatic airplanes, cellular metals numbered in the
leap of images
                  above the regulations of the
BEAUTIFUL and its control
**It is not for the runts who are still worshipping
their navel**

from **Miennes (Mine)**

The Horse

It is true that I believed in the immense privilege of living. Each step amplified in
me old but always mobile adorations. It was a tree, the night, whole forests of
roads, or the sky and its troubled life, certainly the sun.

One day I saw solitude. At the top of hill, a horse, alone, immobile, was planted
in an arrested universe. So my love, suspended in time, gathered to itself in one instant its petrified memory. Life and death completed each other, all doors open to
possible prolongations. For once, without sharing in the meaning of things, I saw.
I isolated my vision, enlarging its borders infinitely. I left for later the concern of seeing what one was to see. But who could maintain that the promises had been kept?

Note on Art

Art is at present the only construction complete unto itself, about which nothing
more can be said; it is such richness, vitality, sense, wisdom. Understanding,
seeing. Describing a flower: relative poetry more or less paper flower. Seeing.

Until the intimate vibrations of the last cell of a brain-god-mathematics are
discovered along with the explanation of primary astronomies, that is the essence,
impossibility will always be described with the logical elements of continual
contradiction, that swamp of stars and of useless bells. Toads of cold lanterns,
squashed flat against the descriptive sense of a red belly. What is written on art is
an educational work and in that sense it can be justified. We want to make men
realize afresh that the one unique fraternity exists in the moment of intensity when
the beautiful and life itself are concentrated on the height of a wire rising toward
a burst of light, a blue trembling linked to the earth by our magnetic gazes
covering the peaks with snow. The miracle. I open my heart to creation.

Many are the artists who no longer seek solutions in the object and in its relations with the external; they are cosmic or primary, decided, simple, wise, serious.

The diversity of today's artists gathers the fountain's spray into a great crystal freedom. And their efforts create new clear organisms, in a world of purity,
with the help of transparencies and the constructive materiality of a simple image
as it forms. They continue the tradition: the past and its evolution push them
slowly snakelike toward the interior, direct consequences far beyond surfaces and
reality.

ANDRÉ BRETON (1896–1966)
France

André Breton was born in Tinchebray-sur-Orne, a small Breton village, and did his military service in a psychiatric unit in Nantes. Influenced by his association with dadaists such as the poet Tristan Tzara, and after his break with dada, beginning in 1921, André Breton founded the surrealist movement, which aimed at giving the dream and the irrational equal footing with reason—as seen in his poetic novel *Nadja* (1928) and his major treatise-texts *Communicating Vessels* (1932) and *Mad Love* (1937)—and at mingling night and day, and the two sides of human experience, by having contrary impulses and phenomena seen at a juncture he called "the sublime point." Some of the irony of dadaists can be seen in early prose poems such as "Less time." Surrealism's exaltation of emotion, together with its belief in multiple possibilities for the human spirit, gives it a more positive outlook than dada's deliberate nihilism. The two last poems given here illustrate that conviction: the first, an oneiric meditation beginning with the word "dreaming," ends with a vision of unity, like the great poem of unity and poetic faith appropriately entitled "Vigilance."

from **Soluble Fish**

[*Less time*]

Less time than it takes to say it, fewer tears than it takes to die; I've taken count of everything, there you have it. I've made a census of the stones; they are numerous as my fingers and some others; I've handed out some pamphlets to the plants, but not all were willing to accept. I've kept company with music for a second only and no longer know what to think of suicide, for if I want to leave myself, the exit is on this side and, I add perversely, the entrance, the re-entrance on the other. Now you see what you're left with. Hours, grief, I don't keep a reasonable check of them; I'm alone, I look out the window; there are no passersby, or rather, no one *passes*. You don't know this man? It's Mr. Same. May I introduce Madam Madam? And their children. Then I turn my back on my steps, my steps turn back too, but I don't know exactly what on. I consult a schedule; all the names of towns have been replaced by names of people who have been quite close to me. Shall I go to A, return to B, change at X? Yes, of course I'll change at X. Provided I don't miss my connection with boredom! There we are: boredom, the lovely parallels, ah! how lovely are parallels under the perpendicularity of God.

Translated by Mary Ann Caws and Matthew Caws.

[Dreaming I see you]

Dreaming I see you infinitely superposed upon yourself
You are seated on the high coral stool
Before your mirror still in its first quarter
Two fingers on the water wing of the comb
And at the same time   5
You return from your travels you are the last to linger in the grotto
Streaming with sparkles
You do not recognize me
You are lying on the bed you awaken or you fall asleep
You awaken where you fell asleep or elsewhere   10
You are naked the elderberry ball bounces once more
A thousand elderberry balls drone above you
So light that at every instant unknown to you
Your breath your blood are saved from the wild trickery of the air
You cross the street the cars rushing toward you are now nothing but their shadow   15
And the same
Child
Caught in a bellows of spangles
You are skipping rope
Until at the top of the invisible stair there appears   20
The only green butterfly haunting the Asian summits
I caress all that you were
In all that must still be you
I listen as your countless arms
Melodiously slither   25
Single snake in all the trees
Your arms in whose center turns the crystal of the compass[1]
My living fountain of Shiva[2]

Vigilance

In Paris the Tour Saint-Jacques swaying
Like a sunflower
Sometimes knocks against the Seine its shadow glides quiet

Translated by Mary Ann Caws.

---

1. *La rose des vents:* Literally, "the rose of winds"—that is, the design on the dial of a mariner's compass showing the thirty-two rhumbs or directions.
2. Shiva, one of the principal gods of Hinduism, identified with the Vedic god Rudra and, as such, the god of destruction. He is worshipped in the form of the *lingam*, or symbolic phallus. As a yoga he is portrayed as seated deep in meditation, holding a trident, a snake coiled around his neck, his body smeared with ashes, and his hair long and matted. As Nataraja, Lord of the Cosmic Dance, he is depicted with four arms, bearing various emblems, and dancing, with one foot on a prostrate demon.

among the tugs
Just then on tiptoe in my sleep
I head for the room where I am lying
And set fire to it
To keep nothing of the consent wrung from me
The furniture gives way to animals who gaze at me like brothers
Lions their manes consume the chairs
Sharks their white bellies drink the last quiver of the sheets
At the hour of love and blue eyelids
I see myself burning now I see that solemn nest of nothings
Once my body
Probed by the patient beaks of birds
When it is finished I enter invisible in the ark
Ignoring life's passersby whose shuffling steps you hear far off
I see the ridges of sun
Through the hawthorn of rain
I hear human linen tear like a great leaf
Under the nails of absence and presence in collusion
All the looms are withering just a piece of perfumed lace remains
A perfect breast-shaped shell
I touch nothing but the heart of things I hold the thread

FEDERICO GARCÍA LORCA (1898–1936)
Spain

Federico García Lorca was born near Granada, and began the study of law, but abandoned it for literature. In Madrid he encountered the surrealists Salvador Dali and Luis Buñuel, and was associated with the Generation of 1927, which included the poets Jorge Guillén, Rafael Alberti, Luis Cernuda, Vicente Aleixandre, and Pedro Salinas. Spain's most famous modern poet, García Lorca represents Spanish literature at its highest point perhaps since the time of Cervantes and Lope de Vega. From his early rendering of traditional Andalusian gypsy ballads [Romancero Gitano] to the haunting vision of The Poet in New York, García Lorca always combines the power of repetitive, obsessive folk melody with a radically new vision. He became a martyr of Franco's government in Spain, murdered by the Falangist Civil Guard during the Spanish Civil War, probably because of his radical views: see Antonio Machado's lament for Lorca earlier in this section, "The Crime Was in Granada," p. 2105.

His poetry and his starkly rendered plays—among them Blood Wedding and The House of Bernarda Alba—effectively combine symbolism and surrealism. The poems included here are from The Poet in New York and his book of ballads.

from **The Poet in New York**

The Dawn

The New York dawn has
four columns of mud
and a hurricane of black doves
that paddle in putrescent waters.

The New York dawn grieves
along the immense stairways,
seeking amidst the groins
spikenards of fine-drawn anguish.

The dawn comes and no one receives it in his mouth,
for there no morn or hope is possible.
Occasionally, coins in furious swarms
perforate and devour abandoned children.

The first to come out understand in their bones
that there will be no paradise nor amours stripped of leaves:
they know they are going to the mud of figures and laws,
to artless games, to fruitless sweat.

The light is buried under chains and noises
in impudent challenge of rootless science.
Through the suburbs sleepless people stagger,
as though just delivered from a shipwreck of blood.

from **Gypsy Ballads**

Somnambule Ballad

Green, how much I want you green.
Green wind. Green branches.
The ship upon the sea
and the horse in the mountain.
With the shadow on her waist
she dreams on her balcony,
green flesh, hair of green,
and eyes of cold silver.
Green, how much I want you green.
Beneath the gypsy moon,
all things look at her
but she cannot see them.

Translated by Stephen Spender and J. L. Gili.

Green, how much I want you green.
Great stars of white frost
come with the fish of darkness
that opens the road of dawn.
The fig tree rubs the wind
with the sandpaper of its branches,
and the mountain, a filching cat,
bristles its bitter aloes.

15

20

NATHALIE SARRAUTE (b. 1902)
Russia/France

Growing up between Russia and France, Nathalie Sarraute finally settled in Paris, where she trained and practiced law, after studying history at Oxford and sociology in Berlin. Her *Age of Suspicion* (1956) was the first theoretization of the French "New Novel," advocating a "new realism" based on the human psyche, demanding a different kind of writing that permitted the reader to participate in what she terms extraordinary "profusion of sensations, of images, of feelings, of memories . . . which no interior language expresses." This peculiar profusion is best seen in *Tropisms* (1939), a work named after the scientific term indicating a reaction to stimuli, like a plant turning toward light; these texts are investigations of "the small, rapid, and sometimes very complex dramas concealed beneath our actions, our gestures, the words we speak, our avowed and clear feelings." The brief chapters are the most celebrated examples of this new form as it conveys these subtle psychological shifts and transformations.

from *Tropisms*

[In the afternoon they went out together]

In the afternoon they went out together, led the life that women lead. And what an extraordinary life it was! They went to "tearooms," ate cakes, which they picked out daintily, in a slightly greedy manner: chocolate éclairs, "babas," and tarts.

All about them was a chirping aviary, warm and gaily lighted and decorated. They remained there, seated, pressed close together around their little tables, talking.

There was a current of excitement and bustle about them, a slight disquiet filled with joy, the memory of a difficult choice, concerning which they were still

Translated by Maria Jolas.

not certain (would it go with the blue and grey outfit? Why of course, it would be perfect), the prospect of this metamorphosis, of this sudden enhancement of their personality, of this glamour.

They, they, they, they, always they, voracious, chirping, dainty.

Their faces seemed to be stiff with a sort of inner tension, their indifferent eyes skimmed lightly over the aspect, the mask of things, weighed it for a short second (was it pretty or ugly?) then let it drop. And their make-up gave them a hard brilliancy, a lifeless freshness.

They went to tea-rooms. They remained sitting there for hours, while entire afternoons slipped by. They talked: "They have awful scenes, disputes about nothing at all. I must say that he's the one I feel sorry for in it all. How much? Oh, at least two millions. And if only what she inherited from her Aunt Josephine . . . No . . . How could it? He won't marry her. What he needs is a good housewife, he doesn't realise it himself. Certainly not, I mean it. What he needs is a good housewife . . . Housewife . . . Housewife . . ." They had always heard it said, they knew it: the sentiments, love, life, these were their domain. It belonged to them.

And they talked and talked, repeating the same things, going over them, then going over them again, from one side then from the other, kneading and kneading them, continually rolling between their fingers this unsatisfactory, mean substance that they had extracted from their lives (what they called "life," their domain), kneading it, pulling it, rolling it until it ceased to form anything between their fingers but a little pile, a little grey pellet.

[They could be seen walking in front of the shop-windows]

They could be seen walking in front of the shop-windows, the upper part of their bodies very erect, slightly thrust forward, their stiff legs a bit apart, and their small feet, arched above their very high heels, knocking hard against the pavement.

With their handbags under their arms, their gauntlet gloves, their little regulation "bibis" at just the right angle on their heads, their long, stiff lashes set in bulging lids, their hard eyes, they trotted along in front of the shop-windows, stopped all of a sudden, ferreted about with an avid, knowing look.

Very valiantly, for they had great powers of endurance, they had been hunting in all the shops for a "little sport suit," in heavy tweed with a pattern, "a sort of little pattern, I can see it perfectly, with little grey and blue checks . . . Oh! you haven't any? Where can I get it?" and they had resumed their hunt.

That little blue suit . . . that little grey suit . . . their wide-stretched eyes ferreted about in search of it . . . Little by little it took stronger hold of them, it engrossed them imperatively, became indispensable, became an end in itself, they no longer knew why, but which they felt obliged to achieve at any cost.

Bravely they went trotting about, climbed four or five flights of dark stairs (nothing could stop them now) "to firms that specialised in English tweeds, where you were sure to find it" and, a bit annoyed, they were beginning to grow weary, (they were about to lose heart), they begged: "No, no, no, you know perfectly what I mean, with sort of little checks, and diagonal stripes . . . No, that's not it, that's not it at all . . . Oh dear! you haven't got it? Where on earth am I going to find it? I've looked everywhere . . . Oh, there, perhaps? You think so? Very well, I'll go there . . . Good-bye . . . Yes, of course, I'm extremely sorry, yes I'll come again . . ."; and they smiled nevertheless, pleasantly, well-bred, having been well trained, during the many years when they were still hunting with their mothers, to figure out how to "dress on nothing," "because a young girl needs so many things, in any case, and you have to know how to manage."

[They were rarely to be seen]

They were rarely to be seen, they remained buried in their apartments, shut up in their dark rooms, watching and waiting.

They telephoned to one another, ferreted about, called back again, seized upon the slightest indication, the slightest sign.

Some of them took delight in cutting out the newspaper advertisement according to which his mother was looking for a seamstress to sew by the day.

They remembered everything, they kept jealous watch; holding hands in a tight ring, they surrounded him.

Their humble brotherhood, with its half-obliterated, dimmed faces, stood about him in a circle.

And when they saw him crawling shamefacedly to try and slip in among them, they quickly lowered their entwined hands, and crouching down all together around him, they fixed upon him their empty, dogged eyes, they smiled their slightly childish smile.

JEAN-PAUL SARTRE (1905–1980)
France

Jean-Paul Sartre was born and educated in Paris. After studying philosophy in Germany in 1933 and 1934 with Edmund Husserl and Martin Heidegger, Sartre became a highly influential critic and philosopher and the founder of the politico-literary review *Les Temps Modernes* in 1945. He achieved fame as a novelist (*Nausea*, 1938) and a playwright with a message. *The Flies* (1943), which focused on the German occupation of France, is a call by a thinker to thoughtful action. Existentialism, the movement that he founded, is a positive vision of the way we can remake ourselves through our choice of commitment (*engagement*). In 1964 Sartre refused the Nobel Prize, believing that to accept such a tribute would undermine his own view and that of the public of his political commitment. Sartre often examined the ambiguities and complexities of human behavior under personal and political stress. The novella *Dirty Hands*, the play *No Exit*, and the short story "The Wall" are among the most celebrated examples of his writings (from 1939) about the problems of moral conduct, collective and individual, reaching a point of excruciation in the latter story.

The Wall

They pushed us into a big white room and I began to blink because the light hurt my eyes. Then I saw a table and four men behind the table, civilians, looking over the papers. They had bunched another group of prisoners in the back and we had to cross the whole room to join them. There were several I knew and some others who must have been foreigners. The two in front of me were blond with round skulls; they looked alike. I suppose they were French. The smaller one kept hitching up his pants; nerves.

It lasted about three hours; I was dizzy and my head was empty; but the room was well heated and I found that pleasant enough: for the past 24 hours we hadn't stopped shivering. The guards brought the prisoners up to the table, one after the other. The four men asked each one his name and occupation. Most of the time they didn't go any further—or they would simply ask a question here and there: "Did you have anything to do with the sabotage of munitions?" Or "Where were you the morning of the 9th and what were you doing?" They didn't listen to the answers or at least didn't seem to. They were quiet for a moment and then looking straight in front of them began to write. They asked Tom if it were true he was in the International Brigade; Tom couldn't tell them otherwise because of the papers they found in his coat. They didn't ask Juan anything but they wrote for a long time after he told him his name.

"My brother José is the anarchist," Juan said, "you know he isn't here any more. I don't belong to any party, I never had anything to do with politics."

They didn't answer. Juan went on, "I haven't done anything. I don't want to pay for somebody else."

His lips trembled. A guard shut him up and took him away. It was my turn.

"Your name is Pablo Ibbieta?"

"Yes."

The man looked at the papers and asked me, "Where's Ramon Gris?"

"I don't know."

"You hid him in your house from the 6th to the 19th."

"No."

They wrote for a minute and then the guards took me out. In the corridor Tom and Juan were waiting between two guards. We started walking. Tom asked one of the guards, "So?"

"So what?" the guard said.

"Was that the cross-examination or the sentence?"

"Sentence," the guard said.

Translated by Lloyd Alexander.

"What are they going to do with us?"

The guard answered dryly, "Sentence will be read in your cell."

As a matter of fact, our cell was one of the hospital cellars. It was terrifically cold there because of the drafts. We shivered all night and it wasn't much better during the day. I had spent the previous five days in a cell in a monastery, a sort of hole in the wall that must have dated from the middle ages: since there were a lot of prisoners and not much room, they locked us up anywhere. I didn't miss my cell; I hadn't suffered too much from the cold but I was alone; after a long time it gets irritating. In the cellar I had company. Juan hardly ever spoke: he was afraid and he was too young to have anything to say. But Tom was a good talker and he knew Spanish well.

There was a bench in the cellar and four mats. When they took us back we sat and waited in silence. After a long moment, Tom said, "We're screwed."

"I think so too," I said, "but I don't think they'll do anything to the kid."

"They don't have a thing against him," said Tom. "He's the brother of a militiaman and that's all."

I looked at Juan: he didn't seem to hear. Tom went on, "You know what they do in Saragossa? They lay the men down on the road and run over them with trucks. A Moroccan deserter told us that. They said it was to save ammunition."

"It doesn't save gas," I said.

I was annoyed at Tom: he shouldn't have said that.

"Then there's officers walking along the road," he went on, "supervising it all. They stick their hands in their pockets and smoke cigarettes. You think they finish off the guys? Hell no. They let them scream. Sometimes for an hour. The Moroccan said he damned near puked the first time."

"I don't believe they'll do that here," I said. "Unless they're really short on ammunition."

Day was coming in through four airholes and a round opening, they had made in the ceiling on the left, and you could see the sky through it. Through this hole, usually closed by a trap, they unloaded coal into the cellar. Just below the hole there was a big pile of coal dust; it had been used to heat the hospital but since the beginning of the war the patients were evacuated and the coal stayed there, unused; sometimes it even got rained on because they had forgotten to close the trap.

Tom began to shiver. "Good Jesus Christ, I'm cold," he said. "Here it goes again."

He got up and began to do exercises. At each movement his shirt opened on his chest, white and hairy. He lay on his back, raised his legs in the air and bicycled. I saw his great rump trembling. Tom was husky but he had too much fat. I thought how rifle bullets or the sharp points of bayonets would soon be sunk into this mass of tender flesh as in a lump of butter. It wouldn't have made me feel like that if he'd been thin.

I wasn't exactly cold, but I couldn't feel my arms and shoulders any more. Sometimes I had the impression I was missing something and began to look around for my coat and then suddenly remembered they hadn't given me a coat. It was rather uncomfortable. They took our clothes and gave them to their soldiers leaving us only our shirts—and those canvas pants that hospital patients wear in the middle of summer. After a while Tom got up and sat next to me, breathing heavily.

"Warmer?"

"Good Christ, no. But I'm out of wind."

Around eight o'clock in the evening a major came in with two *falangistas*. He had a sheet of paper in his hand. He asked the guard, "What are the names of those three?"

"Steinbock, Ibbieta and Mirbal," the guard said.

The major put on his eyeglasses and scanned the list: "Steinbock . . . Steinbock . . . oh yes . . . you are sentenced to death. You will be shot tomorrow morning." He went on looking. "The other two as well."

"That's not possible," Juan said. "Not me."

The major looked at him amazed. "What's your name?"

"Juan Mirbal," he said.

"Well, your name is there," said the major. "You're sentenced."

"I didn't do anything," Juan said.

The major shrugged his shoulders and turned to Tom and me.

"You're Basque?"

"Nobody is Basque."

He looked annoyed. "They told me there were three Basques. I'm not going to waste my time running after them. Then naturally you don't want a priest?"

We didn't even answer.

He said, "A Belgian doctor is coming shortly. He is authorized to spend the night with you." He made a military salute and left.

"What did I tell you," Tom said. "We get it."

"Yes," I said, "it's a rotten deal for the kid."

I said that to be decent but I didn't like the kid. His face was too thin and fear and suffering had disfigured it, twisting all his features. Three days before he was a smart sort of kid, not too bad; but now he looked like an old fairy and I thought how he'd never be young again, even if they were to let him go. It wouldn't have been too hard to have a little pity for him but pity disgusts me, or rather it horrifies me. He hadn't said anything more but he had turned grey; his face and hands were both grey. He sat down again and looked at the ground with round eyes. Tom was good hearted, he wanted to take his arm, but the kid tore himself away violently and made a face.

"Let him alone," I said in a low voice, "you can see he's going to blubber."

Tom obeyed regretfully; he would have liked to comfort the kid, it would have passed his time and he wouldn't have been tempted to think about himself. But it annoyed me: I'd never thought about death because I never had any reason to, but now the reason was here and there was nothing to do but think about it.

Tom began to talk. "So you think you've knocked guys off, do you?" he asked me. I didn't answer. He began explaining to me that he had knocked off six since the beginning of August; he didn't realize the situation and I could tell he didn't *want* to realize it. I hadn't quite realized it myself, I wondered if it hurt much, I thought of bullets, I imagined their burning hail through my body. All that was beside the real question; but I was calm: we had all night to understand. After a while Tom stopped talking and I watched him out of the corner of my eye; I saw he too had turned grey and he looked rotten; I told myself "Now it starts." It was almost dark, a dim glow filtered through the airholes and the pile of coal and made a big stain beneath the spot of sky; I could already see a star through the hole in the ceiling: the night would be pure and icy.

The door opened and two guards came in, followed by a blond man in a tan uniform. He saluted us. "I am the doctor," he said. "I have authorization to help you in these trying hours."

He had an agreeable and distinguished voice. I said, "What do you want here?"

"I am at your disposal. I shall do all I can to make your last moments less difficult."

"What did you come here for? There are others, the hospital's full of them."

"I was sent here," he answered with a vague look. "Ah! Would you like to smoke?" he added hurriedly, "I have cigarettes and even cigars."

He offered us English cigarettes and *puros,* but we refused. I looked him in the eyes and he seemed irritated. I said to him, "You aren't here on an errand of mercy. Besides, I know you. I saw you with the fascists in the barracks yard the day I was arrested."

I was going to continue, but something surprising suddenly happened to me; the presence of this doctor no longer interested me. Generally when I'm on somebody I don't let go. But the desire to talk left me completely; I shrugged and turned my eyes away. A little later I raised my head; he was watching me curiously. The guards were sitting on a mat. Pedro, the tall thin one, was twiddling his thumbs, the other shook his head from time to time to keep from falling asleep.

"Do you want a light?" Pedro suddenly asked the doctor. The other nodded "Yes": I think he was about as smart as a log, but he surely wasn't bad. Looking in his cold blue eyes it seemed to me that his only sin was lack of imagination. Pedro went out and came back with an oil lamp which he set on the corner of the bench. It gave a bad light but it was better than nothing: they had left us in the dark the night before. For a long time I watched the circle of light the lamp made on the ceiling. I was fascinated. Then suddenly I woke up, the circle of light disappeared and I felt myself crushed under an enormous weight. It was not the thought of death, or fear; it was nameless. My cheeks burned and my head ached.

I shook myself and looked at my two friends. Tom had hidden his face in his hands. I could only see the fat white nape of his neck. Little Juan was the worst, his mouth was open and his nostrils trembled. The doctor went to him and put his hand on his shoulder to comfort him: but his eyes stayed cold. Then I saw the Belgian's hand drop stealthily along Juan's arm, down to the wrist. Juan paid no attention. The Belgian took his wrist between three fingers, distractedly, the same time drawing back a little and turning his back to me. But I leaned backward and saw him take a watch from his pocket and look at it for a moment, never letting go of the wrist. After a minute he let the hand fall inert and went and leaned his back against the wall, then, as if he suddenly remembered something very important which had to be jotted down on the spot, he took a notebook from his pocket and wrote a few lines. "Bastard," I thought angrily, "let him come and take my pulse. I'll shove my fist in his rotten face."

He didn't come but I felt him watching me. I raised my head and returned his look. Impersonally, he said to me, "Doesn't it seem cold to you here?" He looked cold, he was blue.

"I'm not cold," I told him.

He never took his hard eyes off me. Suddenly I understood and my hands went to my face: I was drenched in sweat. In this cellar, in the midst of winter, in the midst of drafts, I was sweating. I ran my hands through my hair, gummed together with perspiration; at the same time I saw my shirt was damp and sticking to my skin: I had been dripping for an hour and hadn't felt it. But that swine of a Belgian hadn't missed a thing; he had seen the drops rolling down my cheeks and thought: this is the manifestation of an almost pathological state of terror; and he had felt normal and proud of being alive because he was cold. I wanted to stand up and smash his face but no sooner had I made the slightest gesture than my rage and shame were wiped out; I fell back on the bench with indifference.

I satisfied myself by rubbing my neck with my handkerchief because now I felt the sweat dropping from my hair onto my neck and it was unpleasant. I soon gave up rubbing, it was useless; my handkerchief was already soaked and I was still sweating. My buttocks were sweating too and my damp trousers were glued to the bench.

Suddenly Juan spoke. "You're a doctor?"

"Yes," the Belgian said.

"Does it hurt . . . very long?"

"Huh? When . . .? Oh, no," the Belgian said paternally. "Not at all. It's over quickly." He acted as though he were calming a cash customer.

"But I . . . they told me . . . sometimes they have to fire twice."

"Sometimes," the Belgian said, nodding. "It may happen that the first volley reaches no vital organs."

"Then they have to reload their rifles and aim all over again?" He thought for a moment and then added hoarsely, "That takes time!"

He had a terrible fear of suffering, it was all he thought about: it was his age. I never thought much about it and it wasn't fear of suffering that made me sweat.

I got up and walked to the pile of coal dust. Tom jumped up and threw me a hateful look: I had annoyed him because my shoes squeaked. I wondered if my face looked as frightened as his: I saw he was sweating too. The sky was superb, no light filtered into the dark corner and I had only to raise my head to see the Big Dipper. But it wasn't like it had been: the night before I could see a great piece of sky from my monastery cell and each hour of the day brought me a different memory. Morning, when the sky was a hard, light blue, I thought of beaches on the Atlantic; at noon I saw the sun and I remembered a bar in Seville where I drank *manzanilla* and ate olives and anchovies; afternoons I was in the shade and I thought of the deep shadow which spreads over half a bull-ring leaving the other half shimmering in sunlight; it was really hard to see the whole world reflected in the sky like that. But now I could watch the sky as much as I pleased, it no longer evoked anything in me. I liked that better. I came back and sat near Tom. A long moment passed.

Tom began speaking in a low voice. He had to talk, without that he wouldn't have been able to recognize himself in his own mind. I thought he was talking to me but he wasn't looking at me. He was undoubtedly afraid to see me as I was, grey and sweating: we were alike and worse than mirrors of each other. He watched the Belgian, the living.

"Do you understand?" he said. "I don't understand."

I began to speak in a low voice too. I watched the Belgian. "Why? What's the matter?"

"Something is going to happen to us that I can't understand."

There was a strange smell about Tom. It seemed to me I was more sensitive than usual to odors. I grinned. "You'll understand in a while."

"It isn't clear," he said obstinately. "I want to be brave but first I have to know. . . . Listen, they're going to take us into the courtyard. Good. They're going to stand up in front of us. How many?"

"I don't know. Five or eight. Not more."

"All right. There'll be eight. Someone'll holler 'aim!' and I'll see eight rifles looking at me. I'll think how I'd like to get inside the wall, I'll push against it with my back . . . with every ounce of strength I have, but the wall will stay, like in a nightmare. I can imagine all that. If you only knew how well I can imagine it."

"All right, all right!" I said, "I can imagine it too."

"It must hurt like hell. You know, they aim at the eyes and mouth to disfigure you," he added mechanically. "I can feel the wounds already; I've had pains in my head and in my neck for the past hour. Not real pains. Worse. This is what I'm going to feel tomorrow morning. And then what?"

I well understood what he meant but I didn't want to act as if I did. I had pains too, pains in my body like a crowd of tiny scars. I couldn't get used to it. But I was like him, I attached no importance to it. "After," I said, "you'll be pushing up daisies."

He began to talk to himself: he never stopped watching the Belgian. The Belgian didn't seem to be listening. I knew what he had come to do; he wasn't interested in what we thought; he came to watch our bodies, bodies dying in agony while yet alive.

"It's like a nightmare," Tom was saying. "You want to think something, you always have the impression that it's all right, that you're going to understand and then it slips, it escapes you and fades away. I tell myself there will be nothing afterwards. But I don't understand what it means. Sometimes I almost can . . . and then it fades away and I start thinking about the pains again, bullets, explosions. I'm a materialist, I swear it to you; I'm not going crazy. But something's the matter. I see my corpse; that's not hard but *I'm* the one who sees it, with *my* eyes. I've got to think . . . think that I won't see anything any more and the world will go on for the others. We aren't made to think that, Pablo. Believe me: I've already stayed up a whole night waiting for something. But this isn't the same: this will creep up behind us, Pablo, and we won't be able to prepare for it."

"Shut up," I said. "Do you want me to call a priest?"

He didn't answer. I had already noticed he had the tendency to act like a prophet and call me Pablo, speaking in a toneless voice. I didn't like that: but it seems all the Irish are that way. I had the vague impression he smelled of urine. Fundamentally, I hadn't much sympathy for Tom and I didn't see why, under the pretext of dying together, I should have any more. It would have been different with some others. With Ramon Gris, for example. But I felt alone between Tom and Juan. I liked that better, anyhow: with Ramon I might have been more deeply moved. But I was terribly hard just then and I wanted to stay hard.

He kept on chewing his words, with something like distraction. He certainly talked to keep himself from thinking. He smelled of urine like an old prostate case. Naturally, I agreed with him, I could have said everything he said: it isn't *natural* to die. And since I was going to die, nothing seemed natural to me, not this pile of coal dust, or the bench, or Pedro's ugly face. Only it didn't please me to think the same things as Tom. And I knew that, all through the night, every five minutes, we would keep on thinking things at the same time. I looked at him sideways and for the first time he seemed strange to me: he wore death on his face. My pride was wounded: for the past 24 hours I had lived next to Tom, I had listened to him, I had spoken to him and I knew we had nothing in common. And now we looked as much alike as twin brothers, simply because we were going to die together. Tom took my hand without looking at me.

"Pablo, I wonder . . . I wonder if it's really true that everything ends."

I took my hand away and said, "Look between your feet, you pig."

There was a big puddle between his feet and drops fell from his pants-leg.

"What is it?" he asked, frightened.

"You're pissing in your pants," I told him.

"It isn't true," he said furiously. "I'm not pissing. I don't feel anything."

The Belgian approached us. He asked with false solicitude, "Do you feel ill?"

Tom did not answer. The Belgian looked at the puddle and said nothing.

"I don't know what it is," Tom said ferociously. "But I'm not afraid. I swear I'm not afraid."

The Belgian did not answer. Tom got up and went to piss in a corner. He came back buttoning his fly, and sat down without a word. The Belgian was taking notes.

All three of us watched him because he was alive. He had the motions of a living human being, the cares of a living human being; he shivered in the cellar the way the living are supposed to shiver; he had an obedient, well-fed body. The rest of us hardly felt ours—not in the same way anyhow. I wanted to feel my pants between my legs but I didn't dare; I watched the Belgian, balancing on his legs, master of his muscles, someone who could think about tomorrow. There we were, three bloodless shadows; we watched him and we sucked his life like vampires.

Finally he went over to little Juan. Did he want to feel his neck for some professional motive or was he obeying an impulse of charity? If he was acting by charity it was the only time during the whole night.

He caressed Juan's head and neck. The kid let himself be handled, his eyes never leaving him, then suddenly, he seized the hand and looked at it strangely. He held the Belgian's hand between his own two hands and there was nothing pleasant about them, two grey pincers gripping this fat and reddish hand. I suspected what was going to happen and Tom must have suspected it too: but the Belgian didn't see a thing, he smiled paternally. After a moment the kid brought the fat red hand to his mouth and tried to bite it. The Belgian pulled away quickly and stumbled back against the wall. For a second he looked at us with horror, he must have suddenly understood that we were not men like him. I began to laugh and one of the guards jumped up. The other was asleep, his wide-open eyes were blank.

I felt relaxed and over-excited at the same time. I didn't want to think any more about what would happen at dawn, at death. It made no sense. I only found words of emptiness. But as soon as I tried to think of anything else I saw rifle barrels pointing at me. Perhaps I lived through my execution twenty times; once I even thought it was for good: I must have slept a minute. They were dragging me to the wall and I was struggling; I was asking for mercy. I woke up with a start and looked at the Belgian: I was afraid I might have cried out in my sleep. But he was stroking his moustache, he hadn't noticed anything. If I had wanted to, I think I could have slept a while; I had been awake for 48 hours. I was at the end of my rope. But I didn't want to lose two hours of life: they would come to wake me up at dawn, I would follow them, stupefied with sleep and I would have croaked without so much as an "Oof!"; I didn't want that, I didn't want to die like an animal, I wanted to understand. Then I was afraid of having nightmares. I got up, walked back and forth, and, to change my ideas, I began to think about my past life. A crowd of memories came back to me pell-mell. There were good and bad ones—or at least I called them that *before*. There were faces and incidents. I saw the face of a little *novillero* who was gored in Valencia during the *Feria,* the face of one of my uncles, the face of Ramon Gris. I remembered my whole life: how I was out of work for three months in 1926, how I almost starved to death. I remembered a night I spent on a bench in Granada: I hadn't eaten for three days. I was angry, I didn't want to die. That made me smile. How madly I ran after happiness, after women, after liberty. Why? I wanted to free Spain, I admired Pi y Margall, I joined the anarchist movement, I spoke in public meetings: I took everything as seriously as if I were immortal.

At that moment I felt that I had my whole life in front of me and I thought, "It's a damned lie." It was worth nothing because it was finished. I wondered how I'd been able to walk, to laugh with the girls: I wouldn't have moved so much as my little finger if I had only imagined I would die like this. My life was in front of me, shut, closed, like a bag and yet everything inside of it was unfinished. For an instant I tried to judge it. I wanted to tell myself, this is a beautiful life. But I couldn't pass judgment on it; it was only a sketch; I had spent my time counterfeiting eternity, I had understood nothing. I missed nothing: there were so many things I could have missed, the taste of *manzanilla* or the baths I took in summer in a little creek near Cadiz; but death had disenchanted everything.

The Belgian suddenly had a bright idea. "My friends," he told us, "I will undertake—if the military administration will allow it—to send a message for you, a souvenir to those who love you. . . ."

Tom mumbled, "I don't have anybody."

I said nothing. Tom waited an instant then looked at me with curiosity. "You don't have anything to say to Concha?"

"No."

I hated this tender complicity: it was my own fault, I had talked about Concha the night before, I should have controlled myself. I was with her for a year. Last night I would have given an arm to see her again for five minutes. That was why I talked about her, it was stronger than I was. Now I had no more desire to see her, I had nothing more to say to her. I would not even have wanted to hold her in my arms: my body filled me with horror because it was grey and sweating—and I wasn't sure that her body didn't fill me with horror. Concha would cry when she found out I was dead, she would have no taste for life for months afterward. But I was still the one who was going to die. I thought of her soft, beautiful eyes. When she looked at me something passed from her to me. But I knew it was over: if she looked at me *now* the look would stay in her eyes, it wouldn't reach me. I was alone.

Tom was alone too but not in the same way. Sitting cross-legged, he had begun to stare at the bench with a sort of smile, he looked amazed. He put out his hand and touched the wood cautiously as if he were afraid of breaking something, then drew back his hand quickly and shuddered. If I had been Tom I wouldn't have amused myself by touching the bench; this was some more Irish nonsense, but I too found that objects had a funny look: they were more obliterated, less dense than usual. It was enough for me to look at the bench, the lamp, the pile of coal dust, to feel that I was going to die. Naturally I couldn't think clearly about my death but I saw it everywhere, on things, in the way things fell back and kept their distance, discreetly, as people who speak quietly at the bedside of a dying man. It was *his* death which Tom had just touched on the bench.

In the state I was in, if someone had come and told me I could go home quietly, that they would leave me my life whole, it would have left me cold: several hours or several years of waiting is all the same when you have lost the illusion of being eternal. I clung to nothing, in a way I was calm. But it was a horrible calm—because of my body; my body, I saw with its eyes, I heard with its ears, but it was no longer me; it sweated and trembled by itself and I didn't recognize it any more. I had to touch it and look at it to find out what was happening, as if it were the body of someone else. At times I could still feel it, I felt sinkings, and fallings, as when you're in a plane taking a nose dive, or I felt my heart beating. But that didn't reassure me. Everything that came from my body was all cockeyed. Most of the time it was quiet and I felt no more than a sort of weight, a filthy presence against me; I had the impression of being tied to an enormous vermin. Once I felt my pants and I felt they were damp; I didn't know whether it was sweat or urine, but I went to piss on the coal pile as a precaution.

The Belgian took out his watch, looked at it. He said, "It is three-thirty."

Bastard! He must have done it on purpose. Tom jumped; he hadn't noticed time was running out; night surrounded us like a shapeless, somber mass, I couldn't even remember that it had begun.

Little Juan began to cry. He wrung his hands, pleaded, "I don't want to die. I don't want to die."

He ran across the whole cellar waving his arms in the air then fell sobbing on one of the mats. Tom watched him with mournful eyes, without the slightest desire to console him. Because it wasn't worth the trouble: the kid made more noise than we did, but he was less touched: he was like a sick man who defends himself against illness by fever. It's much more serious when there isn't any fever.

He wept: I could clearly see he was pitying himself; he wasn't thinking about death. For one second, one single second, I wanted to weep myself, to weep with pity for myself. But the opposite happened: I glanced at the kid, I saw his thin sobbing shoulders and felt inhuman: I could pity neither the others nor myself. I said to myself, "I want to die cleanly."

Tom had gotten up, he placed himself just under the round opening and began to watch for daylight. I was determined to die cleanly and I only thought of that. But ever since the doctor told us the time, I felt time flying, flowing away drop by drop.

It was still dark when I heard Tom's voice: 'Do you hear them?'

Men were marching in the courtyard.

"Yes."

"What the hell are they doing? They can't shoot in the dark."

After a while we heard no more. I said to Tom, "It's day."

Pedro got up, yawning, and came to blow out the lamp. He said to his buddy, "Cold as hell."

The cellar was all grey. We heard shots in the distance.

"It's starting," I told Tom. "They must do it in the court in the rear."

Tom asked the doctor for a cigarette. I didn't want one; I didn't want cigarettes or alcohol. From that moment on they didn't stop firing.

"Do you realize what's happening?" Tom said.

He wanted to add something but kept quiet, watching the door. The door opened and a lieutenant came in with four soldiers. Tom dropped his cigarette.

"Steinbock?"

Tom didn't answer. Pedro pointed him out

"Juan Mirbal?"

"On the mat."

"Get up," the lieutenant said.

Juan did not move. Two soldiers took him under the arms and set him on his feet. But he fell as soon as they released him.

The soldiers hesitated.

"He's not the first sick one," said the lieutenant. "You two carry him; they'll fix it up down there."

He turned to Tom. "Let's go."

Tom went out between two soldiers. Two others followed, carrying the kid by the armpits. He hadn't fainted; his eyes were wide open and tears ran down his cheeks. When I wanted to go out the lieutenant stopped me.

"You Ibbieta?"

"Yes."

"You wait here, they'll come for you later."

They left. The Belgian and the two jailers left too, I was alone. I did not understand what was happening to me but I would have liked it better if they had gotten it over with right away. I heard shots at almost regular intervals; I shook with each one of them. I wanted to scream and tear out my hair. But I gritted my teeth and and pushed my hands in my pockets because I wanted to stay clean.

After an hour they came to get me and led me to the first floor, to a small room that smelt of cigars and where the heat was stifling. There were two officers sitting smoking in the armchairs, papers on their knees.

"You're Ibbieta?"

"Yes."

"Where is Ramon Gris?"

"I don't know."

The one questioning me was short and fat. His eyes were hard behind his glasses. He said to me, "Come here."

I went to him. He got up and took my arms, staring at me with a look that should have pushed me into the earth. At the same time he pinched my biceps with all his might. It wasn't to hurt me, it was only a game: he wanted to dominate me. He also thought he had to blow his stinking breath square in my face. We stayed for a moment like that, and I almost felt like laughing. It takes a lot to intimidate a man who is going to die; it didn't work. He pushed me back violently and sat down again. He said, "It's his life against yours. You can have yours if you tell us where he is."

These men dolled up with their riding crops and boots were still going to die. A little later than I, but not too much. They busied themselves looking for names in their crumpled papers, they ran after other men to imprison or suppress them; they had opinions on the future of Spain and on other subjects. Their little activities seemed shocking and burlesqued to me; I couldn't put myself in their place, I thought they were insane. The little man was still looking at me, whipping his boots with the riding crop. All his gestures were calculated to give him the look of a live and ferocious beast.

"So? You understand?"

"I don't know where Gris is," I answered. "I thought he was in Madrid."

The other officer raised his pale hand indolently. This indolence was also calculated. I saw through all their little schemes and I was stupefied to find there were men who amused themselves that way.

"You have a quarter of an hour to think it over," he said slowly. "Take him to the laundry, bring him back in fifteen minutes. If he still refuses he will be executed on the spot."

They knew what they were doing: I had passed the night in waiting; then they had made me wait an hour in the cellar while they shot Tom and Juan and now they were locking me up in the laundry; they must have prepared their game the night before. They told themselves that nerves eventually wear out and they hoped to get me that way.

They were badly mistaken. In the laundry I sat on a stool because I felt very weak and I began to think. But not about their proposition. Of course I knew where Gris was; he was hiding with his cousins, four kilometers from the city. I also knew that I would not reveal his hiding place unless they tortured me (but they didn't seem to be thinking about that). All that was perfectly regulated, definite and in no way interested me. Only I would have liked to understand the reasons for my conduct. I would rather die than give up Gris. Why? I didn't like Ramon Gris any more. My friendship for him had died a little while before dawn at the same time as my love for Concha, at the same time as my desire to live. Undoubtedly I thought highly of him: he was tough. But it was not for this reason that I consented to die in his place; his life had no more value than mine; no life had value. They were going to slap a man up against a wall and shoot at him till he died, whether it was I or Gris or somebody else made no difference. I knew he was more useful than I to the cause of Spain but I thought to hell with Spain and anarchy; nothing was important. Yet I was there, I could save my skin and give up Gris and I refused to do it. I found that somehow comic; it was obstinacy. I thought, "I must be stubborn!" And a droll sort of gaiety spread over me.

They came for me and brought me back to the two officers. A rat ran out from under my feet and that amused me. I turned to one of the *falangistas* and said, "Did you see the rat?"

He didn't answer. He was very sober, he took himself seriously. I wanted to laugh but I held myself back because I was afraid that once I got started I wouldn't be able to stop. The *falangista* had a moustache. I said to him again, "You ought to shave off your moustache, idiot." I thought it funny that he would let the hairs of his living being invade his face. He kicked me without great conviction and I kept quiet.

"Well," said the fat officer, "have you thought about it?"

I looked at them with curiosity, as insects of a very rare species. I told them, "I know where he is. He is hidden in the cemetery. In a vault or in the gravediggers' shack."

It was a farce. I wanted to see them stand up, buckle their belts and give orders busily.

They jumped to their feet. "Let's go. Molés, go get fifteen men from Lieutenant Lopez. You," the fat man said, "I'll let you off if you're telling the truth, but it'll cost you plenty if you're making monkeys out of us."

They left in a great clatter and I waited peacefully under the guard of *falangistas*. From time to time I smiled, thinking about the spectacle they would make. I felt stunned and malicious. I imagined them lifting up tombstones, opening the doors of the vaults one by one. I represented this situation to myself as if I had been someone else: this prisoner obstinately playing the hero, these grim *falangistas* with their moustaches and their men in uniform running among the graves; it was irresistibly funny. After half an hour the little fat man came back alone. I thought he had come to give the orders to execute me. The others must have stayed in the cemetery.

The officer looked at me. He didn't look at all sheepish. "Take him into the big courtyard with the others," he said. "After the military operations a regular court will decide what happens to him."

"Then they're not . . . not going to shoot me . . .?"

"Not now, anyway. What happens afterwards is none of my business."

I still didn't understand. I asked, "But why . . .?"

He shrugged his shoulders without answering and the soldiers took me away. In the big courtyard there were about a hundred prisoners, women, children and a few old men. I began walking around the central grass-plot, I was stupefied. At noon they let us eat in the mess hall. Two or three people questioned me. I must have known them, but I didn't answer: I didn't even know where I was.

Around evening they pushed about ten new prisoners into the court. I recognized Garcia, the baker. He said, "What damned luck you have! I didn't think I'd see you alive."

"They sentenced me to death," I said, "and then they changed their minds. I don't know why."

"They arrested me at two o'clock," Garcia said.

"Why?" Garcia had nothing to do with politics.

"I don't know," he said. "They arrest everybody who doesn't think the way they do." He lowered his voice. "They got Gris."

I began to tremble. "When?"

"This morning. He messed it up. He left his cousin's on Tuesday because they had an argument. There were plenty of people to hide him but he didn't want to owe anything to anybody. He said, 'I'd go and hide in Ibbieta's place, but they got him, so I'll go hide in the cemetery.'"

"In the cemetery?"

"Yes. What a fool. Of course they went by there this morning, that was sure to happen. They found him in the gravediggers' shack. He shot at them and they got him."

"In the cemetery!"

Everything began to spin and I found myself sitting on the ground: I laughed so hard I cried.

SAMUEL BECKETT (1906–1989)
Ireland/France

Samuel Beckett, born in Ireland like James Joyce, his close friend, settled in Paris in 1937; he lived in France for much of his life and wrote most of his works after 1939 in French, and then translated them into English. One of the masters of language, Beckett paradoxically regards silence as the ultimate but unreachable goal toward which art strives. Beckett's works typically show us people stuck in inexplicable, or at any rate unexplained, situations, with language—in all its uncertainty as their only link to a world that eludes them. Beckett is best known for his play *Waiting for Godot* (1952) and his novels *Watt* (written in 1944, published in 1953), and the superb trilogy, *Malloy, Malone Dies,* and *The Unnamable* (1951–1953). He was awarded the Nobel Prize in 1969. "A Piece of Monologue" is one of Beckett's late minimalist plays, luminous in a small space.

Samuel Beckett.

A Piece of Monologue

Written in English for actor David Warrilow in 1979 and performed by him in New York in 1980. First published by *Kenyon Review* in 1979.

Curtain.
Faint diffuse light.
Speaker stands well off centre downstage audience left.
White hair, white nightgown, white socks.
Two metres to his left, same level, same height, standard lamp,
skull-sized white globe, faintly lit.
Just visible extreme right, same level, white foot of pallet bed.
Ten seconds before speech begins.
Thirty seconds before end of speech lamplight begins to fail.
Lamp out. Speaker, globe, foot of pallet, barely visible
in diffuse light.
Ten seconds.
Curtain.

SPEAKER: Birth was the death of him. Again. Words are few. Dying too. Birth was the death of him. Ghastly grinning ever since. Up at the lid to come. In cradle and crib. At suck first fiasco. With the first totters. From mammy to nanny and back. All the way. Bandied back and forth. So ghastly grinning on. From funeral to funeral. To now. This night. Two and a half billion seconds. Again. Two and a half billion seconds. Hard to believe so few. From funeral to funeral. Funerals of . . . he all but said of loved ones. Thirty thousand nights. Hard to believe so few. Born dead of night. Sun long sunk behind the larches. New needles turning green. In the room dark gaining. Till faint light from standard lamp. Wick turned low. And now. This night. Up at nightfall. Every nightfall. Faint light in room. Whence unknown. None from window. No. Next to none. No such thing as none. Gropes to window and stares out. Stands there staring out. Stock still staring out. Nothing stirring in that black vast. Gropes back in the end to where the lamp is standing. Was standing. When last went out. Loose matches in right-hand pocket. Strikes one on his buttock the way his father taught him. Takes off milk white globe and sets it down. Match goes out. Strikes a second as before. Takes off chimney. Smoke-clouded. Holds it in left hand. Match goes out. Strikes a third as before and sets it to wick. Puts back chimney. Match goes out. Puts back globe. Turns wick low. Backs away to edge of light and turns to face east. Blank wall. So nightly. Up. Socks. Nightgown. Window. Lamp. Backs away to edge of light and stands facing blank wall. Covered with pictures once. Pictures of . . . he all but said of loved ones. Unframed. Unglazed. Pinned to wall with drawing-pins. All shapes and sizes. Down one after another. Gone. Torn to shreds and scattered. Strewn all over the floor. Not at one sweep. No sudden fit of . . . no word. Ripped from the wall and torn to shreds one by one. Over the years. Years of nights. Nothing on the wall now but the pins. Not all. Some out with the wrench. Some still pinning a shred. So stands there facing blank wall. Dying on. No more no less. No. Less. Less to die. Ever less. Like light at nightfall. Stands there facing east. Blank pinpocked surface once white in shadow. Could once name them all. There was father. That grey void. There mother. That other. There together. Smiling. Wedding day. There all three. That grey blot. There alone. He alone. So on. Not now. Forgotten. All gone so long. Gone. Ripped off and torn to shreds. Scattered all over the floor. Swept out of the way under the bed and left. Thousand shreds under the bed with the dust and spiders. All the . . . he all but said the loved ones. Stands there facing the wall staring beyond. Nothing there either. Nothing stirring there either. Nothing stirring anywhere. Nothing to be seen anywhere. Nothing to be heard anywhere. Room once full of sounds. Faint sounds. Whence unknown. Fewer and fainter as time wore on. Nights wore on. None now. No. No such thing as none. Rain some nights still slant against the panes. Or dropping gentle on the place beneath. Even now. Lamp smoking though wick turned low. Strange. Faint smoke issuing through vent in globe. Low ceiling stained by night after night of this. Dark shapeless blot on surface elsewhere white. Once white. Stands facing wall after the various motions described. That is up at nightfall and into gown and socks. No. In them already. In them all night. All day. All day and night. Up at nightfall in gown and socks and after a moment to get his bearings gropes to window. Faint light in room. Unutterably faint. Whence unknown. Stands stock still staring out. Into black vast. Nothing there. Nothing stirring. That he can see. Hear. Dwells thus as if unable to move again. Or no will left to move again. Not enough will left to move again. Turns in the end and gropes to where he knows the lamp is standing. Thinks he knows. Was last standing. When last went out. Match one as described for globe. Two for chimney. Three for wick. Chimney and globe back on. Turns wick low. Backs away to edge of light and turns to face wall. East. Still as the lamp by his side. Gown and socks white to take faint light. Once white. Hair white to take faint light. Foot of pallet just visible edge of frame. Once white to take faint light. Stands there staring beyond. Nothing. Empty dark. Till first word always the same. Night after night the same. Birth. Then slow fade up of a faint form. Out of the dark. A window. Looking west. Sun long sunk behind the larches. Light dying. Soon none left to die. No. No such thing as no light. Starless moonless heaven. Dies on to dawn and never dies. There in the dark that window. Night slowly falling. Eyes to the small pane gaze at that first night. Turn from it in the end to face the darkened room. There in the end slowly a faint hand. Holding aloft a lighted spill.[1] In the light of spill faintly the hand and milkwhite globe. Then second hand. In light of spill. Takes off globe and disappears. Reappears empty. Takes off chimney. Two hands and chimney in light of spill. Spill to wick. Chimney back on. Hand with spill disappears. Second hand disappears. Chimney alone in gloom. Hand reappears with globe. Globe back on. Turns wick low. Disappears. Pale globe alone in gloom. Glimmer of brass bedrail. Fade. Birth the death of him. That nevoid smile. Thirty thousand nights. Stands at edge of lamplight staring beyond. Into dark whole again. Window gone. Hands gone. Light gone. Gone. Again and again. Again and again gone. Till dark slowly parts again. Grey light. Rain pelting. Umbrellas round a grave. Seen from above. Streaming black canopies. Black ditch beneath. Rain bubbling in the black mud. Empty for the moment. That place beneath. Which . . . he all but said which loved one? Thirty seconds. To add to the two and a half billion odd. Then fade. Dark whole again. Blest dark. No. No such thing as whole. Stands staring beyond half hearing what he's saying. He? The words falling from his mouth. Making do with his mouth. Lights lamp as described. Backs away to edge of light and turns to face wall. Stares beyond into dark. Waits for first word always the same. It gathers in his mouth. Parts lips and thrusts tongue forward. Birth. Parts the dark. Slowly the window. That first night. The room. The spill. The hands. The lamp. The gleam of brass. Fade. Gone. Again and again. Again and again gone. Mouth agape. A cry. Stifled by nasal. Dark parts. Grey light. Rain pelting. Streaming umbrellas. Ditch. Bubbling black mud. Coffin out of frame. Whose? Fade. Gone. Move on to other matters. Try to move on. To other matters. How far from wall? Head almost touching. As at window. Eyes glued to pane staring out. Nothing stirring. Black vast. Stands there stock still staring out as if unable to move again. Or gone the will to move again. Gone. Faint cry in his ear. Mouth agape. Closed with hiss of breath. Lips joined. Feel soft touch of lip on lip. Lip lipping lip. Then parted by cry as before. Where is he now? Back at window staring out. Eyes glued to pane. As if looking his last. Turns away at last and

---

gropes through faint unaccountable light to unseen lamp. White gown moving through that gloom. Once white. Lights and moves to face wall as described. Head almost touching. Stands there staring beyond waiting for first word. It gathers in his mouth. Birth. Parts lips and thrusts tongue between them. Tip of tongue. Feel soft touch of tongue on lips. Of lips on tongue. Fade up in outer dark of window. Stare beyond through rift in dark to other dark. Further dark. Sun long sunk behind the larches. Nothing stirring. Nothing faintly stirring. Stock still eyes glued to pane. As if looking his last. At that first night. Of thirty thousand odd. Turn away in the end to darkened room. Where soon to be. This night to be. Spill. Hands. Lamp. Gleam of brass. Pale globe alone in gloom. Brass bedrail catching light. Thirty seconds. To swell the two and a half billion odd. Fade. Gone. Cry. Snuffed with breath of nostrils. Again and again. Again and again gone. Till whose grave? Which . . . he all but said which loved one's? He? Black ditch in pelting rain. Way out through the grey rift in dark. Seen from on high. Streaming canopies. Bubbling black mud. Coffin on its way. Loved one . . . he all but said loved one on his way. Her way. Thirty seconds. Fade. Gone. Stands there staring beyond. Into dark whole again. No. No such thing as whole. Head almost touching wall. White hair catching light. White gown. White socks. White foot of pallet edge of frame stage left. Once white. Least . . . give and head rests on wall. But no. Stock still head haught staring beyond. Nothing stirring. Faintly stirring. Thirty thousand nights of ghosts beyond. Beyond that black beyond. Ghost light. Ghost nights. Ghost rooms. Ghost graves. Ghost . . . he all but said ghost loved ones. Waiting on the rip word. Stands there staring beyond at that black veil lips quivering to half-heard words. Treating of other matters. Trying to treat of other matters. Till half hears there are no other matters. Never were other matters. Never two matters. Never but the one matter. The dead and gone. The dying and the going. From the word go. The word begone. Such as the light going now. Beginning to go. In the room. Where else? Unnoticed by him staring beyond. The globe alone. Not the other. The unaccountable. From nowhere. On all sides nowhere. Unutterably faint. The globe alone. Alone gone.

VARLAM [TIKHONOVICH] SHALAMOV (1907–1982)
Russia

Shalamov was arrested in 1937 during the Stalinist purges, in part for having praised the Russian émigré Ivan Bunin, the novelist and short-story writer who left Russia for France in 1918 and was the first Russian to win the Nobel Prize in literature (1933). Shalamov was sent to the Kolyma labor camps, where he remained for seventeen years. He was released in the 1950s and permitted to publish his poems. "In the Night" is one of a series of stories he wrote about the labor camp. These were circulated secretly and then appeared in French in 1969 and in English in 1980 as *Kolyma Tales*. Shalamov had to denounce their publication, but their effect was searing.

from **Kolyma Tales**

In the Night

Supper was over. Slowly Glebov licked the bowl and brushed the bread crumbs methodically from the table into his left palm. Without swallowing, he felt each miniature fragment of bread in his mouth coated greedily with a thick layer of saliva. Glebov couldn't have said whether it tasted good or not. Taste was an entirely different thing, not worthy to be compared with this passionate sensation that made all else recede into oblivion. Glebov was in no hurry to swallow; the bread itself melted in his mouth and quickly vanished.

Bagretsov's cavernous, gleaming eyes stared into Glebov's mouth without interruption. None of them had enough will power to take his eyes from food disappearing in another's mouth. Glebov swallowed his saliva, and Bagretsov immediately shifted his gaze to the horizon—to the large orange moon crawling out onto the sky.

"It's time," said Bagretsov. Slowly they set out along a path leading to a large rock and climbed up onto a small terrace encircling the hill. Although the sun had just set, cold had already settled into the rocks that in the daytime burned the soles of feet that were bare inside the rubber galoshes. Glebov buttoned his quilted jacket. Walking provided no warmth.

"Is it much farther?" he asked in a whisper.

"Some way," Bagretsov answered quietly.

They sat down to rest. They had nothing to say or even think of—everything was clear and simple. In a flat area at the end of the terrace were mounds of stone dug from the ground and drying moss that had been ripped from its bed.

"I could have handled this myself," Bagretsov smiled wryly. "But it's more cheerful work if there are two of us. Then, too I figured you were an old friend. . . ."

They had both been brought on the same ship the previous year.

Bagretsov stopped: "Get down or they'll see us."

They lay down and began to toss the stones to the side. None of the rocks was too big for two men to lift since the people who had heaped them up that morning were no stronger than Glebov.

Bagretsov swore quietly. He had cut his finger and the blood was flowing. He sprinkled sand on the wound, ripped a piece of wadding from his jacket, and pressed it against the cut, but the blood wouldn't stop.

"Poor coagulation," Glebov said indifferently.

"Are you a doctor?" asked Bagretsov, sucking the wound.

Translated by John Glad.

Glebov remained silent. The time when he had been a doctor seemed very far away. Had it ever existed? Too often the world beyond the mountains and seas seemed unreal, like something out of a dream. Real were the minute, the hour, the day—from reveille to the end of work. He never guessed further, nor did he have the strength to guess. Nor did anyone else.

He didn't know the past of the people who surrounded him and didn't want to know. But then, if tomorrow Bagretsov were to declare himself a doctor of philosophy or a marshal of aviation, Glebov would believe him without a second thought. Had he himself really been a doctor? Not only the habit of judgment was lost, but even the habit of observation. Glebov watched Bagretsov suck the blood from his finger but said nothing. The circumstance slid across his consciousness, but he couldn't find or even seek within himself the will to answer. The consciousness that remained to him—the consciousness that was perhaps no longer human—had too few facets and was now directed toward one goal only, that of removing the stones as quickly as possible.

"Is it deep?" Glebov asked when they stopped to rest.

"How can it be deep?" Bagretsov replied.

And Glebov realized his question was absurd, that of course the hole couldn't be deep.

"Here he is," Bagretsov said. He reached out to touch a human toe. The big toe peered out from under the rocks and was perfectly visible in the moonlight. The toe was different from Glebov's and Bagretsov's toes—but not in that it was lifeless and stiff; there was very little difference in this regard. The nail of the dead toe was clipped, and the toe itself was fuller and softer than Glebov's. They quickly tossed aside the remaining stones heaped over the body.

"He's a young one," Bagretsov said.

Together the two of them dragged the corpse from the grave.

"He's so big and healthy," Glebov said, panting.

"If he weren't so fattened up," Bagretsov said, "they would have buried him the way they bury us, and there would have been no reason for us to come here today."

They straightened out the corpse and pulled off the shirt.

"You know, the shorts are like new," Bagretsov said with satisfaction.

Glebov hid the underwear under his jacket.

"Better to wear it," Bagretsov said.

"No, I don't want to," Glebov muttered.

They put the corpse back in the grave and heaped it over with rocks.

The blue light of the rising moon fell on the rocks and the scant forest of the taiga, revealing each projecting rock, each tree in a peculiar fashion, different from the way they looked by day. Everything seemed real but different than in the daytime. It was as if the world had a second face, a nocturnal face.

The dead man's underwear was warm under Glebov's jacket and no longer seemed alien.

"I need a smoke," Glebov said in a dreamlike fashion.

"Tomorrow you'll get your smoke."

"Bagretsov smiled. Tomorrow they would sell the underwear, trade it for bread, maybe even get some tobacco. . . .

SIMONE DE BEAUVOIR (1908–1986)
France

After receiving her degree in philosophy from the University of Paris in 1929, Simone de Beauvoir taught in secondary schools until 1943, after which she devoted herself to writing. Her fiction exemplifies the problems of existentialism—the belief that our daily life and the problems of existence and how we resolve them finally make our essential nature. As a figure, a writer, and a thinker, she remains of major interest for today's feminists in France and throughout the world. Her emotional and working relationship with Jean-Paul Sartre, starting in 1929 and lasting to his death, in no way precluded her relation to other men or his to other women. It is rather their intellectual life as a couple and their political involvement in radical causes that has seized the imagination of many women.

She was a celebrated novelist: *The Blood of Others*, (1945) and *The Mandarins*, (1954) in particular, and a philosopher and essayist: *The Second Sex*, (1949), are her best-known works. In de Beauvoir's memories of her childhood and then of her life as a grown woman, she is able to express with clarity and emotional force her relationship with her mother (*A Very Easy Death*, 1964) and with Sartre (*Adieu: A Farewell to Sartre*, 1984). We give here the end of the second volume of her autobiography, *The Force of Circumstance*, (1965), with its bitter realization: "how much I was gypped." Her life goes on from there, but in keeping with her attitude of ambivalence on many issues (see the *Ethics of Ambiguity*, 1947), this lucid despair in her self-examination remains representative of her nature and her times, as it is of ours.

from *The Force of Circumstance*

[To grow old]

To grow old is to set limits on oneself, to shrink. I have fought always not to let them label me; but I have not been able to prevent the years from enmeshing me. I shall live for a long time in this little landscape where my life has come to rest. I shall remain faithful to the old friendships; my stock of memories, even if there are some additions still to come, will stay as it is now. I have written certain books, not others. And at this point, suddenly, I feel strangely disconcerted. I have lived stretched out toward the future, and now I am recapitulating, looking back over the past. It's as though the present somehow got left out. For years I thought my work still lay ahead, and now I find it is behind me: there was no moment when it took place. It's a bit like the number in mathematics which has no place in either of the two series it separates. I was learning all the time so that one day I could put my store of knowledge to good use. I have forgotten an enormous amount, and for all that still floats on the surface of my memory I can see no possible use. As I retrace the story of my past, it seems as though I was always just approaching or just beyond something that never actually was accomplished. Only my emotions seem to have given me the experience of fulfillment.

Translated by Richard Howard.

The writer nevertheless has the good fortune to be able to escape his own petri-
faction at the moments when he is writing. Every time I start on a new book, I am
a beginner again. I doubt myself, I grow discouraged, all the work accomplished in
the past is as though it never was, my first drafts are so shapeless that it seems impossible to go on with the attempt at all, right up until the moment—always imperceptible, there, too, there is a break—when it has become impossible not to finish
it. Each page, each sentence, makes a fresh demand on the powers of invention and
requires an unprecedented choice. Creation is adventure, it is youth and liberty.

But then, once my worktable is left behind, time past closes its ranks behind
me. I have other things that I must think; suddenly, I collide again with my age.
That ultramature woman is my contemporary. I recognize that young girl's face
belatedly lingering amid the withered features. That hoary-headed gentleman,
who looks like one of my great-uncles, tells me with a smile that we used to play
together in the gardens of the Luxembourg. "You remind me of my mother," I am
told by a woman of about thirty or so. At every turn the truth jumps out at me, and
I find it hard to understand by what trick it manages to attack me thus from the
outside when it lives inside me all the time.

Old age. From a distance you take it to be an institution; but they are all
young, these people who suddenly find that they are old. One day I said to myself:
"I'm forty!" By the time I recovered from the shock of that discovery I had reached
fifty. The stupor that seized me then has not left me yet.

I can't get around to believing it. When I read in print Simone de Beauvoir,
it is a young woman they are telling me about, and who happens to be me. Often
in my sleep I dream that in a dream I'm fifty-four, I wake and find I'm only thirty.
"What a terrible nightmare I had!" says the young woman who thinks she's awake.
Sometimes, too, just before I come back to reality, a giant beast settles on my
breast: "It's true! It's my nightmare of being more than fifty that's come true!" How
is it that time, which has no form nor substance, can crush me with so huge a
weight that I can no longer breathe? How can something that doesn't exist, the
future, so implacably calculated its course? My seventy-second birthday is now as
close as the Liberation Day that happened yesterday.

To convince myself of this, I have but to stand and face my mirror. I thought,
one day when I was forty: "Deep in that looking glass, old age is watching and
waiting for me; and it's inevitable, one day she'll get me." She's got me now. I often
stop, flabbergasted, at the sight of this incredible thing that serves me as a face. I
understand La Castiglione, who had every mirror smashed. I had the impression
once of caring very little what sort of figure I cut. In much the same way, people
who enjoy good health and always have enough to eat never give their stomachs
a thought. While I was able to look at my face without displeasure I gave it no
thought, it could look after itself. The wheel eventually stops. I loathe my
appearance now: the eyebrows slipping down toward the eyes, the bags underneath, the excessive fullness of the cheeks, and that air of sadness around the
mouth that wrinkles always bring. Perhaps the people I pass in the street see
merely a woman in her fifties who simply looks her age, no more, no less. But
when I look, I see my face as it was, attacked by the pox of time for which there
is no cure.

My heart too has been infected by it. I have lost my old power to separate the shadows from the light, to pay the price of the tornadoes and still make sure I had the radiance of clear skies between. My powers of revolt are dimmed now by the imminence of my end and the fatality of the deteriorations that troop before it; but my joys have paled as well. Death is no longer a brutal event in the far distance; it haunts my sleep. Awake, I sense its shadow between the world and me: it has already begun. That is what I had never foreseen: it begins early and it erodes. Perhaps it will finish its task without much pain, everything having been stripped from me so completely that this presence I have so longed to retain, my own, will one day not be present anywhere, not be, and allow itself to be swept away with indifference. One after the other, thread by thread, they have been worn through, the bonds that hold me to this earth, and they are giving way now, or soon will.

Yes, the moment has come to say: Never again! It is not I who am saying good-bye to all those things I once enjoyed, it is they who are leaving me; the mountain paths disdain my feet. Never again shall I collapse, drunk with fatigue, into the smell of hay. Never again shall I slide down through the solitary morning snows. Never again a man. Now, not my body alone but my imagination too has accepted that. In spite of everything, it's strange not to be a body any more. There are moments when the oddness of it, because it's so definitive, chills my blood. But what hurts more than all these deprivations is never feeling any new desires: they wither before they can be born in this rarefied climate I inhabit now. Once, the days slipped by with no sense of haste. I was going even faster than they, drawn into the future by all my plans. Now, the hours are all too short as they whirl me on in the last furious gallop to the tomb. I try not to think: In ten years, in a year. Memories grow thin, myths crack and peel, projects rot in the bud; I am here, and around me circumstances. If this silence is to last, how long it seems, my short future!

And what threats it includes! The only thing that can happen now at the same time new and important is misfortune. Either I shall see Sartre dead, or I shall die before him. It is appalling not to be there to console someone for the pain you cause by leaving him. It is appalling that he should abandon you and then not speak to you again. Unless I am blessed by a most improbable piece of good fortune, one of these fates is to be mine. Sometimes I want to finish it all quickly so as to shorten the dread of waiting.

Yet I loathe the thought of annihilating myself quite as much now as I ever did. I think with sadness of all the books I've read, all the places I've seen, all the knowledge I've amassed and that will be no more. All the music, all the paintings, all the culture, so many places: and suddenly nothing. They made no honey, those things, they can provide no one with any nourishment. At the most, if my books are still read, the reader will think: There wasn't much she didn't see! But that unique sum of things, the experience that I lived, with all its order and its randomness—the Opera of Peking,[1] the arena of Huelva, the *candomblé* in Bahía, the dunes of El-Oued, Wabansia Avenue, the dawns in Provence, Tiryns, Castro

---

1. The names recalled here in a rush represent various memories of places: Huelva is a harbor of Andalusia in southwestern Spain; Bahía is a state in eastern Brazil; and Tiryns is the site of an anciet city in the Peloponnesus.

talking to five hundred thousand Cubans, a sulphur sky over a sea of clouds, the purple holly, the white nights of Leningrad, the bells of the Liberation, an orange moon over the Piraeus, a red sun rising over the desert, Torcello, Rome, all the things I've talked about, others I have left unspoken—there is no place where it will live again. If it had at least enriched the earth; if it had given birth to . . . what? A hill? A rocket? But no. Nothing will have taken place, I can still see the hedge of hazel trees flurried by the wind and the promises with which I fed my beating heart while I stood gazing at the gold mine at my feet: a whole life to live. The promises have all been kept. And yet, turning an incredulous gaze toward that young and credulous girl, I realize with stupor how much I was gypped.

June 1960–March 1963

ALBERT CAMUS (1913–1960)
Algeria/France

Like Simone de Beauvoir and Jean-Paul Sartre, Albert Camus is associated with the movement called existentialism. Camus left his native Algeria, where he had been a journalist for France, in 1940, but he remained haunted by that land, by its landscape of desert and sun, and by his own ill health from tuberculosis. *The Stranger* (1942), his widely read portrait of a man alienated from society by a series of absurd events, takes up the themes of exile and return to Algeria. A similar theme permeates the lyric and moving "Return to Tipasa" (1953). Camus quarrelled publicly with Sartre, whose journal *Les Temps Modernes* condemned Camus's essay *The Rebel* (1951) because it made revolution an ethical rather than a political concept. In 1957 Camus won the Nobel Prize. Adulated by the youth of his day, he was popular writer of plays and novels until his death in an automobile accident in 1960.

Return to Tipasa

You sailed away from your father's dwelling
With your heart on fire, Medea! And you passed
Between the rocky gates of the seas;
And now you sleep on a foreign shore.

Medea

For five days the rain had been falling unceasingly on Algiers, finally drenching the sea itself. From the heights of an apparently inexhaustible sky, unending sheets of rain, so thick they were viscous, crashed into the gulf. Soft and gray like

Translated by Ellen Fitzroy Kennedy.

a great sponge, the sea heaved in the shapeless bay. But the surface of the water seemed almost motionless beneath the steady rain. At long intervals, however, a broad and imperceptible movement raised a murky cloud of steam from the sea and rolled it into the harbor, below a circle of soaking boulevards. The town itself, its white walls running with damp, gave off another cloud of steam that billowed out to meet the first. Whichever way you turned you seemed to be breathing water, you could drink the very air.

Looking at this drowned sea, seeing in December an Algiers that was still for me the city of summers, I walked about and waited. I had fled from the night of Europe, from a winter of faces. But even the town of summers was emptied of its laughter, offering me only hunched and streaming backs. In the evening, in the fiercely lit cafés where I sought refuge, I read my age on faces I recognized without knowing their names. All I knew was that these men had been young when I was, and that now they were young no longer.

I stayed on, though, without any clear idea of what I was waiting for, except, perhaps, the moment when I could go back to Tipasa. It is certainly a great folly, and one that is almost always punished, to go back to the places of one's youth, to want to relive at forty the things one loved or greatly enjoyed at twenty. But I was aware of this folly. I had already been back to Tipasa once, not long after those war years that marked for me the end of my youth. I hoped, I think, to rediscover there a liberty I was unable to forget. Here, more than twenty years ago, I had spent whole mornings wandering among the ruins, breathing the scent of absinthe, warming myself against the the stones, discovering the tiny, short-lived roses that survive in springtime. Only at noon, when even the crickets are silenced by the heat, would I flee from the avid blaze of an all-consuming light. Sometimes, at night, I would sleep open-eyed beneath a sky flowing with stars. I was alive at those moments. Fifteen years later, I found my ruins again. A few steps from the first waves, I followed the streets of the forgotten city across the fields covered with bitter trees; and, on the hills overlooking the bay, could still caress their pillars, which were the color of bread. But now the ruins were surrounded by barbed wire, and could be reached only through official entrances. It was also forbidden, for reasons sanctioned, it would seem, by morality, to walk there after dark; by day, one would meet an official guard. That morning, doubtless by chance, it was raining across the whole sweep of the ruins.

Bewildered, walking through the lonely, rainsoaked countryside, I tried at least to recover the strength that has so far never failed me, that helps me to accept what is, once I have realized I cannot change it. I could not, of course, travel backward through time and restore to this world the face I had loved, which had disappeared in a single day a long time before. On the second of September, 1939, I did not go to Greece, as I had planned. Instead, the war enveloped us, then Greece itself. This distance, these years separating the warm ruins from the barbed wire, were also within me, as I stood that day staring at tombs filled with black water or beneath the dripping tamarisk trees. Raised above all in the spectacle of a beauty that was my only wealth, I had begun in plenty. The barbed wire came later—I mean tyrannies, war, policings, the time of revolt. We had had to come to terms with night: the beauty of daytime was only a memory. And in this muddy Tipasa, even the memory was growing dim. No room now for beauty, fullness, or youth! In the light cast by the flames, the world had suddenly shown its wrinkles and its afflictions, old and new. It had suddenly grown old, and we had too. I knew the ardor I had come in search of could only be roused in someone not expecting it. There is no love without a little innocence. Where was innocence? Empires were crumbling, men and nations were tearing at one another's throats; our mouths were dirtied. Innocent at first without knowing it, now we were unintentionally guilty: the more we knew, the greater the mystery. This is why we busied ourselves, oh mockery, with morality. Frail in spirit, I dreamed of virtue! In the days of innocence, I did not know morality existed. Now I knew it did, and could not live up to it. On the promontory I had loved in former days, between the drenched pillars of the ruined temple, I seemed to be walking behind someone whose footsteps I could still hear on the tombstones and mosaics, but whom I would never catch up with again. I went back to Paris, and stayed for some years before returning home again.

During all these years, however, I had a vague feeling of missing something. Once you have had the chance to love intensely, your life is spent in search of the same light and the same ardor. To give up beauty and the sensual happiness that comes with it and devote one's self exclusively to unhappiness requires a nobility I lack. But, after all, nothing is true that compels us to make it exclusive. Isolated beauty ends in grimaces, solitary justice in oppression. Anyone who seeks to serve the one to the exclusion of the other serves no one, not even himself, and in the end is doubly the servant of injustice. A day comes when, because we have been inflexible, nothing amazes us anymore, everything is known, and our life is spent in starting again. It is a time of exile, dry lives, dead souls. To come back to life, we need grace, a homeland, or to forget ourselves. On certain mornings, as we turn a corner, an exquisite dew falls on our heart and then vanishes. But the freshness lingers, and this, always, is what the heart needs. I had to come back once again.

And, in Algiers a second time, still walking under the same downpour that I felt had not stopped since what I thought was my final departure, in the midst of this immense melancholy smelling of rain and sea, in spite of the misty sky, the sight of people's backs fleeing beneath the deluge, the cafés whose sulphurous light decomposed everyone's face, I persisted in my hopes. Anyway, didn't I know that rain in Algiers, although it looks as if it would go on forever, nonetheless does stop suddenly, like the rivers in my country that swell to a flood in two hours, devastate acres of land, and dry up again in an instant? One evening, in fact, the rain stopped. I waited still one more night. A liquid morning rose, dazzling, over the pure sea. Form the sky, fresh as a rose, washed and rewashed by the waters, reduced by each successive laundering to its most delicate and clearest texture, a quivering light fell, endowing each house, each tree, with a palpable shape and a magic newness. The earth must have risen in just such a light the morning the world was born. Once again I set out for Tipasa.

There is not a single one of these sixty-nine kilometers of highway that is not filled for me with memories and sensations. A violent childhood, adolescent daydreams to the hum of the bus's engines, mornings, the freshness of young girls, beaches, young muscles always tensed, the slight anguish that the evening brings to a sixteen-year-old heart, the desire to live, glory, and always the same sky, for

The secret I am looking for is buried in a valley of olive trees, beneath the grass and cold violets, around an old house that smells of vines. For more than twenty years I have wandered over this valley, and over others like it, questioning dumb goatherds, knocking at the door of empty ruins. Sometimes, when the first star shines in a still, clear sky, beneath a rain of delicate light, I have thought that I knew. I did know, in fact. Perhaps I still know. But no one is interested in this secret, doubtless I myself do not desire it, and I cannot cut myself off from my own people. I live with my family, who believe they reign over rich and hideous cities, built of stones and mists. Day and night it raises its voice, and everything yields beneath it while it bows down to nothing: it is deaf to all secrets. Its power sustains me and yet bores me, and I come to be weary of its cries. But its unhappiness is my own, we are of the same blood. I too am sick and am I not a noisy accomplice who has cried out among the stones? Thus I try to forget, I march through our cities of iron and fire, I smile bravely at the night, I welcome the storms, I will be faithful. In fact, I have forgotten: henceforth, I shall be deaf and active. But perhaps one day, when we are ready to die of ignorance and exhaustion, I shall be able to renounce our shrieking tombs, to go and lie down in the valley, under the unchanging light, and learn for one last time what I know.

1953

PAUL CELAN [PAUL ANTSCHEL]
(1920–1970)
Romania; German

Paul Celan was born into an assimilated but religiously observant German-Jewish family in the eastern part of the recently dissolved Austro-Hungarian Empire. Celan's family was exterminated by the Nazis and Romanian fascists in 1940; he escaped deportation but was sent to forced labor. In 1945 he made his way to Bucharest, in 1947 to Vienna, and in 1948 to Paris, where he taught and became friends with many leading French writers. He committed suicide in 1970. In a letter to him, the German poet Nelly Sachs addressed him as "Paul Celan, . . . blessed by Bach and Hölderlin, blessed by the Hasidim." Celan was a poet of the Holocaust generation, and the Holocaust haunts his poetry, as it does his most famous poem, "Death Fugue." His enigmatic poetic language, profound and moving, resists interpretation and is so packed with echoes that it almost defies translation. In "Death Fugue," the final address to "your hair," as it is directly said to the victims, picks up on centuries of lyric evocation and invocation of female beauty in its fullest sensuality and inevitable fading; here the catastrophe contained in that image is at once simple and overwhelming, a dramatic, inescapable, eternal loss.

Death Fugue

Black milk of dawn we drink it at dusk
we drink it at noon and at daybreak we drink it at night

Translated by Joachim Neugroschel.

Erik Wengelin. *The Potato Thief Is Being Punished.* Nationalmuseet/ The Museum of Denmark's Fight for Freedom 1940–1945.

we drink and we drink
we are digging a grave in the air there's room for us all
A man lives in the house he plays with the serpents he writes   5
he writes when it darkens to Germany your golden hair Margarete
he writes it and steps outside and the stars all aglisten he whistles for
                  his hounds
he whistles for his Jews he has them dig a grave in the earth
he commands us to play for the dance   10

Black milk of dawn we drink you at night
we drink you at daybreak and noon we drink you at dusk
we drink and we drink
A man lives in the house he plays with the serpents he writes
he writes when it darkens to Germany your golden hair Margarete   15
Your ashen hair Shulamite we are digging a grave in the air there's
                  room for us all

He shouts cut deeper in the earth to some the rest of you sing and
                  play
he reaches for the iron in his belt he heaves it his eyes are blue   20
make your spades cut deeper the rest of you play for the dance

Black milk of dawn we drink you at night
we drink you at noon and at daybreak we drink you at dusk
we drink and we drink

a man lives in the house your golden hair Margarete   25
your ashen hair Shulamite he plays with the serpents

He shouts play death more sweetly death is a master from Germany
he shouts play the violins darker you'll rise as smoke in the air
then you'll have a grave in the clouds there's room for you all

Black milk of dawn we drink you at night   30
we drink you at noon death is a master from Germany
we drink you at dusk and at daybreak we drink and we drink you
death is a master from Germany his eye is blue
he shoots you with bullets of lead his aim is true
a man lives in the house your golden hair Margarete   35
he sets his hounds on us he gives us a grave in the air
he plays with the serpents and dreams death is a master from
                                                         Germany

your golden hair Margarete
your ashen hair Shulamite   40

WISŁAWA SZYMBORSKA (b. 1923)
Poland

A major contemporary Polish poet, Wisława Szymborska is associated with the
avant-garde. Author of the collection *Every Incident* (1972), she writes of her own
work that she "borrows words weighed down with pathos, and then tries to make
them appear light." Her great themes are prodigality and unpredictability of
nature, as opposed to mankind the spoiler, and the theme of loss. Poetry, she
says, has "the power of preserving." The vivid details in her poems cohere around
one central vision, with its own emotional focus, as in these three recent works,
the prose poem about Job (see the *Book of Job* included in the first part of this
Reader), the poem about the complicated nature of woman, and the much-
quoted "poem of apology," a reflection on language and the self.

A Tale Retold

Job, afflicted in body and possessions, curses his fate as a man. That is great
poetry. His friends come to him and, rending their mantles, probe Job's guiltiness
before the Lord. Job cries out that he has been a righteous man. Job does not know
wherefore the Lord has smitten him. Job does not want to speak with them. Job

Translated by Magnus J. Krynski and Robert A. Maguire.

wants to speak with the Lord. The Lord appears riding the chariot of a whirlwind. Unto that man, open to the very bone, He praises His own creation: the heavens, the seas, the earth and the beasts. And especially Behemoth, and in particular Leviathan, pride-inspiring monsters. That is great poetry. Job listens—the Lord does not speak to the point, for the Lord does not wish to speak to the point. Hence Job makes haste to abase himself before the Lord. Now events follow swiftly. Job regains his asses and his camels, his oxen and his sheep, all increased twofold. The grinning skull begins to take on flesh. And Job assents. Job resigns himself. Job does not want to spoil a masterwork.

Portrait of a Woman

She must be willing to please.
To change so that nothing should change.
It's easy, impossible, hard, worth trying.
Her eyes are if need be now deep blue, now gray,
dark, playful, filled for no reason with tears.   5
She sleeps with him like some chance acquaintance, like his one and only.
She will bear him four children, no children, one.
Naive yet giving the best advice.
Weak yet lifting the weightiest burdens.
Has no head on her shoulders but will have.   10
Reads Jaspers and ladies' magazines.
Doesn't know what this screw is for and will build a bridge.
Young, as usual young, as always still young.
Holds in her hands a sparrow with a broken wing,
her own money for a journey long and distant,   15
a meat-cleaver, poultice, and a shot of vodka.
Where is she running so, isn't she tired?
Not at all, just a bit, very much, doesn't matter.
Either she loves him or has made up her mind to.
For better, for worse, and for heaven's sake.   20

Under a Certain Little Star

I apologize to coincidence for calling it necessity.
I apologize to necessity just in case I'm mistaken.
Let happiness be not angry that I take it as my own.
Let the dead not remember they scarcely smoulder in my memory.
I apologize to time for the muchness of the world overlooked per second.   5
I apologize to old love for regarding the new as the first.
Forgive me, far-off wars, for bringing flowers home.
Forgive me, open wounds, for pricking my finger.
I apologize to those who cry out of the depths for the minuet-record.
I apologize to people at railway stations for sleeping at five in the morning.   10

Pardon me, hounded hope, for laughing now and again.
Pardon me, deserts, for not rushing up with a spoonful of water.
And you, O falcon, the same these many years, in that same cage,
forever staring motionless at that self-same spot,
absolve me, even though you are but a stuffed bird.   15
I apologize to the cut-down tree for the table's four legs.
I apologize to big questions for small answers.
O Truth, do not pay me too much heed.
O Solemnity, be magnanimous unto me.
Endure, mystery of existence, that I pluck out the threads of your train.   20
Accuse me not, O soul, of possessing you but seldom.
I apologize to everything that I cannot be everywhere.
I apologize to everyone that I cannot be every man and woman.
I know that as long as I live nothing can justify me,
because I myself am an obstacle to myself.   25
Take it not amiss, O speech, that I borrow weighty words,
and later try hard to make them seem light.

SŁAWOMIR MROZEK (b. 1930)
Poland

Polish dramatist and short-story writer Sławomir Mrozek is known for his satiric
vision. His plays *Emigres* (1950) and *The Policeman* (1956), were highly
successful, as was his masterpiece, the play *Tango* (1964), which presents the
unusual picture of revolutionary parents with a conservative son, killed by the
lover of his mother. His surrealist vision is clear in *The Elephant,* a collection of
brilliant and absurd short pieces, some gentler in appearance, and some prickly
like "The Swan."

from *The Elephant*

The Swan

In the park was a lake. On the lake lived a swan. It was the chief attraction of the
park. One day the swan disappeared. It had been stolen by hooligans.

The department of Municipal Gardens procured a new swan. A special guard
was appointed to protect the bird from it predecessor's fate.

The post was given to a little old man who had been lonely for years. When

Translated by Konrad Syrop.

he took up his job evenings were already beginning to turn chilly. The park was deserted. While patrolling the lake the old man kept an eye on the swan, but sometimes he allowed himself a glance at the stars. He was cold. It would be lovely, he thought, to look in at the small restaurant near the park. He started in that direction but remembered the swan. Someone might steal the bird while he was away. He would lose his job. The idea had to be given up.

But the bitter cold kept on nagging at him, increasing his loneliness. In the end he decided to go to the restaurant and take the swan with him. Even should someone come to the park, while they were away, to breathe in the beauty of nature he would not notice the absence of the swan immediately. It was a starlit, but moonless, night and they would be back shortly.

They went.

In the restaurant they were greeted by a comforting wave of warm air carrying delicious smells of frying food. The old man put the swan on a chair at the opposite side of the table and sat down. In this way he could watch his charge while consuming a modest meal. To warm himself he also ordered a small glass of vodka.

When he was eating a dish of mutton, and enjoying it hugely, he noticed that the swan was gazing at him unhappily. The old man felt sorry for the bird. Under the swan's reproachful eyes he lost all desire for food. Then he had an idea. He called the waiter and ordered a roll and some hot beer with sugar. Dipping the roll in the beer he fed the swan and the bird quickly regained its good humour. After the meal, satisfied and refreshed, they both returned to their posts.

The next evening was even colder. On that occasion the stars seemed uncommonly bright and the old guard felt each of them as an ice-cold nail driven into his warm but lonely heart. However, he resisted the temptation to visit the restaurant once more.

In the centre of the lake the swan appeared, its white feathers glowing gently in the starlight.

The thought of any living creature being in contact with water on that bitterly cold evening made the old man shiver. Poor swan, he deserved a better fate. The guard was sure that the bird would welcome some warmth and food.

So he took the swan under his arm and carried it to the restaurant.

Another cold evening came and filled the old man with gloom. This time he was determined not to visit the restaurant because, the night before, after their return, the swan had danced and sung in a most peculiar fashion.

So he sat by the edge of the lake in the empty cold park and observed the sky. Suddenly he felt that someone was tugging at his trousers. It was the swan asking for something. They went.

A month later both the guard and the swan were dismissed by the authorities. The swan had been observed reeling about in the water, in broad daylight too. A mother, who had brought her small children to the park to see the swan, complained to the authorities, of course purely out of consideration for the young.

Even in the most modest position its holder must have some moral principles.

BELLA AKHATOVNA AKHMADULINA (b. 1937)

Russia

One of the followers of Boris Pasternak and of Marina Tsvetayeva, Bella Akhatovna Akhmadulina—who was married to two prominent writers, first to Yevgeny Yevtushenko and then to Yuri Nagibin, is a poet, a novelist, and a filmwriter, particularly known for her writing in a fantastic vein. Her poems range from quite short and direct, to longer and more involved; they may be cast informally and deal with unconventional topics, from catching a cold to buying a soft drink—quite unlike the Russian formal tradition, although many of her poems are influenced by Acmeism. Her long poems, like "My Geneaology" (1964), are noted for their excursion into symbolist-style fantasy, evoking a contemporary present that remains veiled by the bizarre and the mysterious. Some of the later works are collected in *Fever and Other Poems*, a 1969 translation of *Oznob* (1968). Her path as a poet constituted one long struggle with the sensation of suffocating muteness, a condition shared by her fellow artists and poets during the oppressive years of Stalin's rule, the great writers practicing what Isaac Babel termed "the new genre of silence." She was a contributor to the 1979 anthology *Metropol*, whose suppression occasioned a widespread protest. Read in the light of the philosopher and music critic Theodor Adorno's comment about the difficulty of writing poetry after Auschwitz, this poem has a particular resonance in a country where so many were silenced.

Goodbye

And in conclusion I'll say—
goodbye. Don't commit yourself to love.
I'm breaking down. Or going up
to a high degree of madness.

How did you love?—you tasted 5
disasters. That's not the question.
How did you love?—you ruined.
but you ruined so clumsily.

The cruelty of a mistake, oh, for
you there's no forgiveness. My body's alive, 10
and wanders, sees the world,
but everything's gone out of me.

My head still manages a little work.
But my hands fall slack,
and in a flock, obliquely, 15
my senses leave me.

Translated by Barbara Einzig.

Autumn*

Not working, not breathing,
the beehive sweetens and dies.
the autumn deepens, the soul
ripens and grows round;

drawn into the turning color of fruit,
cast out of the idle blossoms.
Work is long and dull in autumn,
the word is heavy.

More and more heavily, day by day,
nature weighs down the mind.

A laziness like wisdom
overshadows the mouth with silence.

Even a child, riding along,
cycling into white shafts of light,
suddenly will look up
with a pale, clear sadness.

Silence†

Who was it that took away my voice?
The black wound he left in my throat
Can't even cry.

March is at work under the snow
And the birds of my throat are dead,
Their gardens turning into dictionaries.

I beg my lips to sing.
I beg the lips of the snowfall.
Of the cliff and the bush to sing.

Between my lips, the round shape
Of the air in my mouth.
Because I can say nothing.

I'll try anything
For the trees in the snow.
I breathe. I swing my arms. I lie.

From this sudden silence,
Like death, that loved
The names of all words,
You raise me now in song.

*Translated by Barbara Einzig and Daniel Halpern.
†Translated by Daniel Halpern.

Diego Rivera. *Flower Day*. Oil on canvas.
Los Angeles County Museum of Art.

SECTION XV
The Americas

Latin America
The Caribbean
The United States
Canada

Latin America

It is a commonplace of European literary history that literature as an autonomous system of free, imaginative creation does not fully come into existence until the late eighteenth century. According to this view, as the middle classes created an array of social institutions (coffeehouses and clubs, reading societies, lending libraries, journals, and newspapers) that became self-sufficient (i.e., independent of the court and aristocratic patrons) through their own market system, there emerged the idea of the literary work as an inner-directed form in which (aesthetic) value inhered, free from all determinants, including the particular mental and moral development of the reader. In a discussion of Gottfried August Bürger's poems, for example, the critic Friedrich Schiller argued that "the first indispensable requirement for the perfection of a poem is that it must possess an absolute inner value which is in no way dependent on the varying powers of comprehension of its readers."[1]

In Latin America something resembling this autonomous status for letters did not appear until the

1. Friedrich Schiller, *Sammtliche Werke*, vol. 19, eds. Otto Guntter and Georg Witkowski (Leipzig, Germany: 1925, 232–233).

end of the nineteenth century, challenged every bit of the way since then by mass cultural forms like the contemporary telenovela and by popular semiliterary, semipolitical genres like the *testimonio*.[2] However, back in the early colonial period, dramatic, poetic, and narrative forms of writing were an essential part of the political and economic project of colonization; they were thus "externally motivated." Writing conformed generally to the epic or evangelizing modes: on the one hand, the chronicles of the Indies, in which the conquistadors and some official historians sought recognition for their feats as a means to gain titles, posts, and land grants, or on the other hand, works written by the clergy for the Christianization of the native peoples. Theatrical forms, often in Indian languages, were adapted specifically to persuade the Indians to adopt the colonizers' faith. In connection with this use of writing, in fact, the novel was prohibited by law in 1532 and again in 1543 from being imported from Europe or being published in the colonies. It was felt by the clergy, who constituted the majority of writers, that its fictitious character might confuse the native peoples into thinking that the stories told in the sacred scriptures were similar in nature. In any case, even those novels that made it into the colonies found a very limited public.

This public increased gradually as the literate functionaries or *letrados,* as Uruguayan critic Angel Rama calls them,[3] were recruited into the administration of church and empire from new or previously excluded social groups. An example of new groups are the *mestizos* (people of mixed ancestry, usually Indian and European), who rapidly became a large middle sector between Indians and Spaniards. To an extent, the new *letrados* engaged in cooptation, in the sense that they managed cultural exchange between dominant and subordinate groups in ways that reduced tensions for the benefit of the status quo. Nevertheless, hitherto subordinated groups were able to add their voices to the chorus that is national culture. Of course, as long as some groups remained illiterate or were radically excluded because they were deemed too backward or otherwise unprepared to participate, they did not have the opportunity to inflect the melody.

This sketch of the social role of *letrados* is especially evident in the colonial period. In the first place, whatever authority indigenous peoples had among themselves was not recognized by the conquerors and colonizers, who virtually destroyed the native cultures, at least in their grander expressions (architecture, religious statuary and oratory, imperial celebrations, etc.), replacing them with Ibero-Christian forms. Hernán Cortés, conqueror of Mexico, destroyed the Aztecs' idols and replaced them with crosses, provoking the ire of Father Bartolomé de Las Casas (1474–1566), famous for his defense of the Indians. Nevertheless, even Las Casas accepted the legitimacy of a "kinder, gentler" evangelization of native peoples. Although he took the Indians' side, he argued that it was foolish to destroy material idols without first "eradicat[ing] idols from the heart of the

---

2. In Latin America it is useful to distinguish between forms produced by the culture industry (radio, television, mass magazines, etc.) and forms created by people's cultural practices (oratory, song, dance, theater, and other types of performance that constitute religious and cultural events such as feasts, holidays, get-togethers, etc.). Although it is evident that the difference between these two dimensions is reciprocally being blurred, it still remains true that some forms, regardless of how affected they are by mass culture, are created or recreated from the perspective of people's everyday needs.

3. Angel Rama, *La ciudad letrada* (Hanover, N.H.: Ediciones del Norte, 1985).

idolater . . . by means of constant, diligent and long-lasting indoctrination."[4] In other words, the colonized should be made to adopt the ways of the colonizers through cultural exchange, the specialty of the *letrados*.

It is not necessary to insist on this point with respect to the conquest and the early colonial period. The selections from Las Casas, Guamán Poma de Ayala, and the Inca Garcilaso de la Vega, included in the first volume of this book, all bear witness to the role of the *letrados*, a class to which these writers belong, in managing the relationship between Indians and Europeans through religious, historical, or cultural legitimation. Later in the colonial period, the obstacles put in the way of those with lesser authority is again evident in the silencing of Sor Juana Inés de la Cruz (Mexico, 1651–1695), the first truly modern Latin American literary voice. Sor Juana was not free to cultivate her philosophical and literary talents because she was a woman. She entered the sisterhood as a means to release herself from the constraints of marriage and family life. As a nun, however, she came under the authority of the church hierarchy, whose function it was to maintain the status quo.

If *mestizos* and even some indigenous figures were able to gain entry to the ranks of the *letrados*, it would take women writers until the twentieth century to achieve the same, and then at the cost of struggling, alienating family and friends, even challenging hierarchy when necessary, although often having to back down and accept defeat. Such conditions were still encountered by the women who, finally, entered literary history in their own right and not as exceptional tokens. There are, of course, outstanding women writers in both the eighteenth century and the nineteenth—the mystic Sor Francisca Josefa del Castillo y Guevara (Colombia, 1671–1742), the novelists Gertrudis Gomez de Avollaneda (Cuba, 1814–1873), Juana Manuela Gorriti (Argentina, 1818–1892), and Clorinda Matto de Turner (Peru, 1854–1909)—but it is not until the 1950s and 1960s, and especially with the subsequent advance of feminism, that women are taken seriously in literary history and criticism. The obvious point is that it takes social authority to gain access to institutions such as the university, the publishing industry, newspapers and journals, and so on, precisely the places in which history is recorded and literary canons are devised. The literary public sphere idealized by Schiller and other late eighteenth- and early nineteenth-century writers is in reality comprised of institutions that function as arbiters of cultural value.

At first, as in the case of Delmira Agustini (Uruguay, 1886–1914) and Gabriela Mistral (Chile, 1889–1957), women writers were accorded a place in the "honorary sepulchers" and "elegant pantheons"—as Sor Juana ironically calls the institutions where literary works are canonized—only if their work could be perceived as "feminine," that is, as conforming to such themes as love of nature and humanity, maternity, and "fantasized" eroticism. (One literary historian prefers to think that Agustini's sensuality was "more imagined and cerebral than really experienced.")[5] Such notions of femininity were dealt with in several ways—for example, by taking them seriously and elaborating an aesthetic around feminine experience, as does Mistral in an essay in which she attributes the origin of poetic musicality to a mother's "verbal rockings" or lullabies. Alfonsina Storni

---

4. Bartolomé de Las Casas, *History of the Indies*, trans. and ed. Andree M. Collard (New York: Harper and Row, 1971) 232.

5. Orlando Gomez-Gil, *Historia crítica de la literatura hispanoamericana* (New York: Holt, Rinehart, and Winston, 1968) 482.

(Argentina, 1892–1938), on the other hand, directly confronts and defuses the pretensions of male poets who create the image of woman as silent, chaste, and passive. When the Chilean poet Pablo Neruda (1904–1973) wrote, in *Twenty Love Poems and a Song of Despair* (1924), "I like you when you are silent because you seem to be absent," Storni's "The Deceit," (1925) responded: "I look at you silently, with my sweet smile / and when you get excited, I think: not too fast / it's not you who deceives me but my own dream."[6]

Other writers, like Rosario Castellanos (Mexico, 1925–1974) and Rosario Ferré (Puerto Rico, b. 1942), reject the stereotypes even while seeking to create a new aesthetic that transcends, on the one hand, mythifications of femininity and, on the other, forms of resistance to masculine authority at the expense of self-injury. The point is elaborated in Castellanos's play *The Eternal Feminine* (1975), in which she pokes holes in the mythification of women who have responded to their oppression within the limitations imposed by patriarchy: "It's not good enough to imitate the models proposed for us that are answers to circumstances other than our own. It isn't even enough to discover who we are. We have to invent ourselves."[7]

"To invent ourselves." If there is one phrase that might characterize many (though certainly not all) of the different traditions of Latin American literature, it is this one. The very act of independence in the early nineteenth century, with its mix of enlightenment ideas of progress and romantic self-realization, as well as the many revolutionary movements that succeeded it right down to the present, can be seen as attempts at self-invention. Historically, literature played perhaps the most important part of this endeavor. José Joaquín Fernández de Lizardi (Mexico, 1776–1827), Latin America's first novelist, employed the picaresque genre in his satires of corrupt colonial authority at the very moment of its demise. Inventing the new independent country of Mexico required a thoroughgoing exorcism of all the flaws of the preceding regime. Fernández de Lizardi was also fundamental in the establishment of a critical, albeit precarious, public sphere as the founder of several newspapers and journals.

Andrés Bello (Venezuela, 1781–1865) took the project of self-invention even further, arguing that Latin America would not have real independence until it consolidated an independent culture, especially a literary culture. He meant by that the creation of new expressive forms not modeled on those of Europe. Bello, the prototypical statesman-intellectual who initiated a long line of descendants right down to the present in such figures as Octavio Paz (Mexico, b. 1914) and Ernesto Cardenal (Nicaragua, b. 1925), designed a totally original grammar for American Spanish that broke with the custom of patterning linguistic structure after the classical languages. He also set forth a new historiography in which European theories would have no modeling role. He argued that history must be grounded in a series of events and social and natural structures that, unlike the European case, had not been recorded yet in Latin America. Consequently, philosophical notions of history had to take a back seat to the historical particularity grounded in narratives of local life and customs. The literature of

6. Alfonsina Storni, *Ocre* (Buenos Aires: Agenica de Librerías y Publicaciones, 1925) 49.
7. Rosario Castellanos, "The Eternal Feminine," trans. Diane E. Marting and Betty Tyree Osiek, *A Rosario Castellanos Reader:*

An Anthology of Her Poetry, Short Fiction, Essays, and Drama, ed. Maureen Ahern (Austin: University of Texas Press, 1988) 356.

customs of the period and the emerging novel form—both represented in this volume by Clorinda Matto de Turner—could only contribute to this self-invention.

Not all projects for creating a new civilization were positive, if we judge them from our own current democratic perspective. Domingo F. Sarmiento (Argentina, 1811–1888) sought to modernize his country, and by extension the rest of Latin America, by eradicating native peoples and the Spanish stock and replacing them with northern Europeans, who had, he emphasized, created the prosperous giant to the north. Why, he argued, could not Argentina progress in the same way? Sarmiento eventually became president and put his plan into operation.

From the late 1880s through the first two decades of the twentieth century, all of Latin America underwent rapid modernization, that is, industrialization of manufactures in the cities and of agriculture in the countryside. New metropolises arose: Buenos Aires, São Paulo, Havana, Mexico City, and other capital cities. But rather than being a mirror image of the United States or England—which was Sarmiento's aspiration—this development was highly uneven, concentrating large masses of poor workers and displaced peasants in urban centers and thus adding to backwardness. One similarity with the industrialized north was the concentration of immense wealth in small commercial and landowning groups: the renowned rubber, coffee, cocoa, copper, and tin barons.

It is against this background that the two literary movements most expressive of the will to self-invention were generated: late nineteenth-century Spanish-American *modernismo* and the avant-garde movements of the second and third decades of the twentieth century (which, to help confuse the student of literary history, were also called *modernismo* in Brazil). The relative stabilization of political matters in some of these countries and the newly accumulated wealth contributed to opening up new public spheres in which literature was no longer wedded to politics; instead, literature began its entry into the then nascent commodity market, which split it into two discursive systems, one for high culture—poetry, novel, essay, serious drama—and one for the masses—pulp fiction, romances, "yellow" (i.e., sensational) journalism, and popular theater. Needless to say, in an age in which value was thought to reside in the ideal reaches of high culture, the writers canonized by literary history cultivated the poetic arts, with a premium placed on French models. This new bond would enable Latin American culture to make its final break with its old metropolitan parent cultures.

Modernismo, under the leadership of the Nicaraguan Rubén Darío (1867–1916), was also a turning point in Latin American literature, in that it was the first movement that was not based in national culture. Darío himself was an exemplary cosmopolitan intellectual who was no doubt more at home in the great metropolises of Santiago, Buenos Aires, Madrid, or Paris than in his native Nicaragua. *Modernismo,* then, was a continental phenomenon, and Darío was received by his followers with open arms wherever he went. He was also the exemplary modern writer, usually of middle class extraction, who without his own resources and without the philanthropic patrons of former times, unwillingly had to professionalize—that is, to turn to bureaucratic, diplomatic, educational, and journalistic employ to earn his keep. These livelihoods, of course, only added to the cosmopolitan sweep of his lifestyle and his aesthetics. If Baudelaire was the *flaneur* of the city, Darío was the new globetrotter, for in this period of rapid modernization, culture had become highly mobile and the poet or the chronicler needed to move with the flow.

Logically, as Latin America modernized it generated a highly aestheticized literature to safeguard against the menacing materialism that, according to intellectuals like José Martí (Cuba, 1853–1895) and José Enrique Rodó (Uruguay, 1872–1917), corroded the soul of the north. The Spanish-American War (1898), of course, had a lot to do with this rejection of Yankee ways, an attitude that has survived into the present as the United States has repeatedly intervened in affairs internal to Latin America.

Isolated from the rest of Latin America by language and geographical barriers, Brazil's cultural movements did not have to make constant reference to the threat of the United States. The avant-garde movement in Brazil, known also as *modernismo*, emerged as a project to create a new nation. Like the historical avant-gardes of Europe (cubism, dadaism, surrealism, etc.) and their Spanish-American variants, *modernismo* broke with the past and endeavored to create a "new man." A bit more interesting in this regard than its Spanish-American cousins, Brazilian *modernismo*, especially in the persons of Mário de Andrade (1893–1945) and Oswald de Andrade (1890–1954; no relation) pretended to "cannibalize" cultural resources, no matter where they originated, digest them, and create a new cultural matrix. The movement had an enormous impact, so much so that even the dictator Getúlio Vargas who took power in the 1930s, considered it the point of origin for his nationalist program. After all, the *modernistas* urged the rejection of imported products, both commercial and cultural, and their production for exportation under a program of national construction.

Mário de Andrade's quasimythic "rhapsodic" novel, *Macunaíma,* sought to create an image of Brazil that did not yet exist in the culture. In this immense country with many distinct regions, there was not at the time a cultural form that linked all the parts. By using the rhapsodic technique, literally "stitching together" heterogeneous elements, de Andrade created a poetic unity, and through it an alluring image of the "nation." In other parts of Latin America, there were similar attempts to create a new national consciousness through avant-garde techniques. The Nicaraguan *Vanguardia* movement, which was an important precursor to the Sandinista poetics of Ernesto Cardenal, also sought to piece together a national culture from indigenous and traditional as well as some modern elements. In other countries such as Mexico and Cuba, the indigenous or African-based popular cultures also significantly influenced the avant-garde. The Mexican muralists (Diego Rivera, Rufino Tamayo, and Alfredo Siqueiros) used cubist and other avant-gardist techniques to "piece in" the diverse elements of the new "national-popular" culture they were helping to create.

These avant-garde experiments were important precedents for "marvelous" or "magic realism," which in Latin America is created from a popular base with a predominantly Indian or African inflection. Although the imperial civilizations were destroyed and the African slaves uprooted from their homelands, their cultures continued to evolve according to a "logic" transmitted through everyday practices. If the high cultural forms were destroyed, the styles of moving, dressing, dancing, singing, and praying were still informed by an ethos quite different from European modes of conduct. The resulting cultural forms therefore have built into them a tension between Western rationality and a mytho-logic, to paraphrase the anthropologist Claude Lévi-Strauss, based in different world views. This is evident in marvelous realism, for from the popular viewpoint all the unusual or impossible or supernatural events that occur in the eye of the Western mind are quite normal. Alejo Carpentier (Cuba, 1904–1980), who coined this phrase for the Latin

American context in the preface to the novel *The Kingdom of This World* (1949), noted that Europeans had to resort to "artificial" avant-gardist techniques to produce a means of expression different from their own rationalized forms, whereas Latin Americans lived this difference "naturally." According to Carpentier, the Latin Americans' world is imbued with all kinds of forces and presences that belie Western science and narrative realism. To a degree, this is another version of the above-mentioned Latin American aestheticism that is believed to differentiate the "spiritual" southerners from the "materialist" northerners.

Not all Latin American writers, of course, subscribe to an avant-gardist or a marvelous-realist aesthetic. Latin America has a very rich social realist literature that pretends to depict injustices in order to raise the consciousness of citizens and incites them to seek redress. Often this literature is written from a nationalist perspective, as in the "novel of the earth" and the "Indianist" novels written between the 1920s and the 1940s. In a different vein, ex–avant-gardist Jorge Luis Borges (Argentina, 1899–1986) wrote many of his stories or *Ficciones* as spoofs on the avant-garde desire to create "new realities." "Tlön, Uqbar, Orbis Tertius," included in this volume, is such a story.

On the other hand, many writers have reconciled all of these contrasting aesthetics. In his novel *One Hundred Years of Solitude* (1967), Gabriel García Márquez (Colombia, b. 1928) employs some avant-gardist techniques, is an exemplar of marvelous realism, and depicts and denounces the brutal massacre of workers on a banana plantation owned by a U.S. company.

Throughout the 1960s avant-gardism again inspired a new generation of writers to attempt to forge a new Latin American language as a means to invent their "true identity." Carlos Fuentes, for example, in a very influential essay in *The New Hispano-American Novel* (1969), defined the dilemma as follows:

> If we Hispano-Americans are capable of creating our own model of progress [as compared to Western technocratic models], then our language is the only vehicle that can give form, propose goals, establish priorities, elaborate critiques of a given way of life: of saying everything that cannot be said in any other way. I believe that in Spanish America there are novels being written and to be written which, when such a consciousness is attained, will provide the necessary instruments to drink the waters and the fruits of our true identity.[8]

From the mid-1970s, however, the influence of avant-gardist aesthetics has been on the wane. Literary history was no longer to be construed according to one overriding aesthetic. Fiction and poetry became quite heterogeneous in comparison with the 1960s. It seems that since then it is acceptable to write in any style; the narrative realism condemned by avant-gardist experimentalists survives in the new historical novel, while the sonnet and other classical forms rejected by iconoclasts like Vicente Huidobro (Chile, 1893–1948) are cultivated by younger poets. At the same time, a new and more popular aesthetic emerged in the *testimonio* or testimonial narrative, in which a professional writer or an anthropologist collaborates with a person from a modest background to narrate a life story that illuminates history in ways that official history and literary fiction cannot. The emphasis here is no longer the creation of a "new language" that conveys the

---

8. Carlos Fuentes, *La nueva novela hispanoamericana* (Mexico: Joaquín Mortiz, 1969) 98.

"truth" of Latin Americanness, nor the creation of a national identity that appeals to most groups. Rather, it lets us hear the voices of those who have been excluded from such an identity. Often, the *testimonio* has precise political motivations, as does the one by Rigoberta Menchú (Guatemala, b. 1961) included in this volume.

The overall picture, then, as far as Latin American literary history is concerned, far exceeds any notion of autonomous, "inner-directed" literary forms. Moreover, literature no longer has the same status as it did previously. Literary critics are as comfortable writing on soap operas or music videos as they are on, say, the novel of the Mexican revolution. Literature itself has gotten ever closer to mass culture. *Testimonio*, on the other hand, has provided the poor and subordinated, even the illiterate, with access to legitimacy within aesthetic public spheres, once the exclusive domain of high art and literature. In point of fact, there are no longer any hard-and-fast axioms on what is valid literature. Even nonliterature, whatever that is—remember Borges's postmodern statement in "Tlön, Uqbar, Orbis Tertius" on the implosion of life into literature—fits the bill.

Historical Background

What we refer to as Latin America incorporates an enormously diverse set of cultures within South America, Central America, Mexico, and the Caribbean. While the disparate ways of life found across such a vast area may appear to have little in common, the decisive historical event for all of Latin America is the same: the colonial activities of Spain and Portugal beginning at the end of the fifteenth century.

Throughout the region, the European incursion left an indelible legacy. The indigenous population (called Indians by Christopher Columbus upon the mistaken belief that he had found the coveted sea route to Asia) was either enslaved or subjected to a harsh system of forced labor, and intense efforts were made to convert them to Christianity. Colonizers altered the ecology of Latin America by introducing European agriculture and livestock, and they remade its racial character, both by importing African slaves and by setting into motion a proliferation of mixed unions among Indians, Africans, and Europeans. While ultimate authority was vested in European hands, colonialism spawned a class of American-born Spaniards and Portuguese, called Creoles, among whom was concentrated local political and economic control.

The ascendancy of the Bourbon royal family to the Spanish throne in the eighteenth century marked an era of change for Spain's colonies. The economy of Spanish America had grown increasingly inefficient because of widespread corruption among large landowners and colonial governors, an unwieldy bureaucracy, abuses of Indian labor, and the domination of trade by a small group of Spanish merchants. Beginning with Philip V in 1700, and culminating with the reign of Charles III (1759–1788), the Bourbons promulgated reforms in colonial administration, not with the intention of encouraging self-government, but rather to revive the flagging economy. Inspired in part by the European intellectual movement known as the Enlightenment, a basic tenet of which was that science and rational inquiry should be applied to improve social conditions, the Bourbons expanded productivity by several means. They removed restrictions on trade (while preserving Spain's monopoly), reinvigorated silver mining in Peru and

Mexico, and decentralized political authority by increasing the number of governmental districts.

Although the Bourbons restored financial health to the empire, the bulk of the population remained mired in poverty, illiteracy, and near if not actual slavery. The Creoles, on the other hand, were greatly enriched, and their growing economic power exacerbated their resentment against Spain's absolute rule, engendering a number of Creole-led insurrections that prefigured nineteenth-century independence movements. The frequency and vehemence of popular uprisings also intensified toward the end of the century, the most notable of which was the failed revolt in Peru during the 1780s led by José Gabriel Tupac Amaru, a champion of Indian liberation who took his name from Topa Amaru, an Incan ruler defeated by Spain in the sixteenth century.

Conditions during the eighteenth century were similar in Brazil, which had come under Portuguese control by treaty and papal decree early in the colonial period. Corruption and inefficiency plagued the colony, and its sugarcane, tobacco, mining, and cattle-raising enterprises were based upon the labor of slaves, many of whom were imported from Africa. Although African slavery played a much larger role in Brazil than it did anywhere else, intermittent disruptions in the slave trade by Dutch piracy led to large expeditions in search of Indian replacements. Brazil's present southern and western borders are in fact mainly the result of a series of these expeditions between the 1740s and 1780s.

Alarmed by the French Revolution in 1789, the Spanish monarchy veered sharply away from its reformist outlook and attempted to supress the rationalist ideas emanating from both France and the newly independent United States. Creole leaders, emboldened after French forces led by Napoléon occupied Spain in 1808, attempted to seize power in 1810 in Venezuela, Argentina, Chile, and Colombia. It was not until the 1824 defeat of the Spanish army in Peru, however, that the wars of independence were successfully completed. Simón Bolívar of Venezuela, an inspirational figure imbued with the liberal ethos of the Enlightenment, directed the campaigns in northern South America, where he was instrumental in liberating Colombia, Venezuela, and Ecuador between 1818 and 1821. In Argentina a Creole junta declared independence in 1816, and, under the leadership of José de San Martín, helped liberate Chile and Peru.

The route to independence was somewhat different in Brazil and Mexico. Escaping France's 1808 invasion of Portugal, the Portuguese court fled to Brazil, where it liberalized colonial policies and opened trade with countries other than Portugal. In 1820, however, a revolution in Portugal threatened to reverse these measures, and Brazilian Creoles convinced Dom Pedro (the heir to Portugal's throne) to defy the revolutionary parliament. Dom Pedro refused to return to Portugal and was named the constitutional emperor of Brazil in 1822. Contrary to events in Spanish America, Brazilian independence was thus achieved with relatively little warfare. It was, however, largely an affair of the Creole elite that failed to address the socioeconomic inequities to which most of the population was subjected, as was also the case in most of Spanish America.

Only in Mexico did the drive for independence take on the character of a genuine social transformation in which the Indian and *mestizo* masses played a significant role. In its early stages, the revolt was led during the 1810s by Miguel Hidalgo and the *mestizo* José María Morelos, two priests intent on eliminating slavery and returning land to the Indians. Opposed to such radical changes, independence-minded Creoles withheld their support and both priests were captured and killed by the Spanish. After years of fighting, the movement was close to defeat until the 1820 revolution in Spain prompted an alliance between Creoles and Agustín de Iturbide, a military officer who had previously defended Spain's colonial supremacy. After declaring Mexico's independence in 1821, Iturbide ruled as emperor for only a few months before being replaced by a Creole-led republic.

Following independence, the new nations of Latin America experienced several tumultuous decades during which most of its people remained the disempowered subjects of authoritarian regimes while two factions among the elite quarreled over the form of government. A federal system modeled on the United States, limiting presidential power and guaranteeing individual rights, was promoted by urban intellectuals. The *caudillos*, military officers who were in most cases also large landowners, sought to create highly centralized governments allied with the Catholic Church. With the exception of Chile, where civilian rule was established during the 1820s, much of Latin America was dominated by violent *caudillos*, who were often successful at enlisting the support of such rural *mestizo* groups as the Argentine *gauchos* (cowboys) and their Venezuelan counterpart, the *llaneros*.

In the latter half of the nineteenth century, these violent political conflicts gave way to efforts to improve national economies. Facilitated by an influx of foreign capital, especially from the United States and Great Britain, mining was modernized, and agriculture was transformed from a subsistence activity into a large-scale export business. These developments, most prominent in Argentina, Brazil, Mexico, and Central America, inaugurated a marked economic dependency on Europe and the United States. Many Latin-American governments encouraged immigration from Europe at this time in order to meet the booming labor demand that accompanied this commercial reorientation. Between the 1850s and World War I, several million immigrants, mostly from Italy, Spain, Portugal, and Germany, settled primarily in Argentina, Uruguay, and Brazil. As a consequence, Buenos Aires (the Argentine capital) and Montevideo (Uruguay's capital) took on a pronounced European character that they retain to this day. While rural life continued to prevail in nations with large Indian populations—including Bolivia, Ecuador, and much of Central America—the years leading up to World War I were a period of intense urbanization for most of the other republics.

In spite of technological improvements and commercial gains throughout the region, most Latin Americans entered the twentieth century under the constraint of still-rigid socioeconomic hierarchies. Indeed, it was not until 1888 that Brazil outlawed slavery, and its monarchy was not replaced by a republic until 1889. Shortly before World War I, the United States became an important political factor, especially in the form of President Theodore Roosevelt's interventionist "big stick" policy. In addition to less naked exertions of its influence, the repeated use of U.S. military power in Central America and the Caribbean bred a great deal of antagonism that was ultimately reflected in the failure of many Latin American nations to endorse the Allied cause in World War I. By contrast, support for the Allies in World War II was virtually unanimous (except for Fascist-leaning Argentina), in part because of the Good Neighbor Policy established by the United States during the 1930s to eschew further military intervention in Latin America.

Between the two world wars, six nations—Brazil, Argentina, Uruguay, Chile, Mexico, and Costa Rica—distinguished themselves from the rest of the region by making large strides in economic development, social reforms, and political stability. (In the 1960s Venezuela made similar progress.) State intervention in commerce, legal protection for workers, and a degree of social mobility character-ized this period. In addition, the eclipse of European hegemony coupled with a dislike for the United States fostered a new nationalism among both intellectuals and business managers.

Following World War II, the general trend in Latin America has been toward industrialization, a second wave of urban growth, the decline of agriculture, the institutionalization of a democratic electoral process, and sporadic efforts at agrarian reform (most notably in Mexico, Cuba, Chile, and, most recently, by the leftist Sandinista regime of Nicaragua). In spite of backlashes against the Roman Catholic Church in the late nineteenth and early twentieth centuries, the Church has remained a vital force in Latin America (where the population is overwhelm-ingly Catholic), and in recent decades it has become increasingly active on behalf of the marginalized poor.

Further Readings

Albuquerque, Severino João. *Violent Acts: A Study of Contemporary Latin American Theatre*. Detroit: Wayne State University Press, 1991.

Beverly, John and Zimmerman, Marc. *Literature and Politics in the Central American Revolutions*. Austin: University of Texas Press, 1990.

Collier, Simon, Blakemore, Harold and Skidmore, Thomas E., eds. *The Cambridge Encyclo-pedia of Latin America and the Caribbean*. Cambridge: Cambridge University Press, 1985.

Franco, Jean. *Spanish American Literature since Independence*. New York: Barnes and Noble, 1973.

García, J.E., ed. *Philosophy and Literature in Latin America*. New York: SUNY Press, 1989.

González, Mike and Treecc, David. *The Gathering of Voices: The Twentieth-Century Poetry of Latin America*. London: Verso, 1992.

Kirkpatrick, Gwen. *The Dissonant Legacy of Modernismo*. Berkeley: University of California Press, 1989.

Meyer, Doris. *Lives on the Line: The Testimony of Contemporary Latin American Authors*. Berkeley: University of California Press, 1988.

Sommer, Doris. *Foundational Fictions: The National Romances of Latin America*. Berkeley: University of California Press, 1991.

Stern, Irwin, ed. *Dictionary of Brazilian Literature*. New York: Greenwood Press, 1988.

Weiss, Judith. *Latin American Popular Theatre: The First Five Centuries*. Albuquerque: University of New Mexico Press, 1993.

Wilson, Jason. *An A-Z of Modern Latin American Literature in Translation*. London: Institute of Latin American Studies, 1990.

Yúdice, George, Franco, Jean and Flores, Juan, eds. *On Edge: The Crisis of Contemporay Latin American Culture*. Minneapolis: University of Minnesota Press, 1992.

SOR JUANA INÉS DE LA CRUZ
(1651–1695)

Mexico

Sor Juana Inés de la Cruz is without a doubt the most important writer of the colonial period. Born into a noble Mexican family, she decided to become a nun at the age of sixteen, this being the only means available for women to pursue their intellectual and artistic interests. As a nun, she lived a continual tension between her religious obligations and her literary vocation. In fact, after writing a critique (*The Athenagóric Letter*, 1690) of the ideas of Father Antonio Vieira, a famous Jesuit preacher, she was urged by the Bishop of Puebla to abandon secular writing despite her extraordinary talents. Sor Juana's *Response to Sor Philotea de la Cruz* (1691) is an eloquent defense of the rights of women and an important autobiographical essay.

Sor Juana is best known as a writer for her lyric poetry, which is derived from the classics of the Spanish Baroque, especially Luis de Góngora, but also Francisco de Quevedo and Pedro Calderón de la Barca, whom she rivals and perhaps surpasses in the construction of elaborate conceits, multiple paradoxes, and highly complex metaphors, as in the two sonnets selected here, which use familiar Baroque imagery and shifting concepts in a complex metaphysical and psychological reflection. According to Octavio Paz, she initiates in Hispanic letters a new form of subjectivity akin to Descartes' doubting and rational ego.

To Her Portrait

This coloured counterfeit that thou beholdest,
vainglorious with the excellencies of art,
is, in fallacious syllogisms of colour,
nought but a cunning dupery of sense;

this in which flattery has undertaken
to extenuate the hideousness of years,
and, vanquishing the outrages of time,
to triumph o'er oblivion and old age,   5

is an empty artifice of care,
is a fragile flower in the wind,
is a paltry sanctuary from fate,   10

is a foolish sorry labour lost,
is conquest doomed to perish and, well taken,
is corpse and dust, shadow and nothingness.

Translated by Samuel Beckett.

Alcino, What Is This . . .*

Alcino, what is this; Do you permit
wild jealousy to mar your prudent care?
Your furious extremes assume the air
of madness worse than any frenzied fit.

In what did I offend you that you grieve?   5
Or why do you condemn love's influence
as traitorous? For to make pretense
that you can keep its beauty is naive.

The ownership of any temporal thing
is temporal. Its nature you abuse   10
when to its constancy you try to cling.

Your error or your ignorance I accuse.
If fortune comes with love as offering,
you may not own it; you may only use.

CLORINDA MATTO DE TURNER

(1854–1909)

Peru

Clorinda Matto de Turner, who married an English doctor at age 19 and went to live on his ranch in Peru, began writing stories and essays under various pseudonyms. Like Fernández de Lizardi, she is a social critic, belonging to a generation of novelists that had perfected realist techniques while maintaining the critical emphasis that characterizes most of Latin American literature. At the age of twenty-two she was already the head of the newspaper *El Recreo del Cuzco* and later the editor of *La Bolsa de Arequipa*. Her novel *Birds Without a Nest* (1889) is the best nineteenth-century fictional treatment of the plight of Indians. The church and the state objected to it because of its vehement indictment of their class ally, the landed oligarchy. She was excommunicated, and attacked so violently that she was forced into exile in Argentina, where she died. The novel constitutes a major stepping-stone from the romantic idealization of Indians in the earlier part of the century to the social realist and "protest" novel of the twentieth century.

"What a Decree!" is one of her *tradiciones* or *traditions*, a blend of history, legend, and narrative of customs deriving from the romantic period but transformed by her into an often humorous critique of the oppression of the Indians.

*Translated by Pauline Cook.

What a Decree!

(To the director and owner of the newspaper "La Bolsa," Señor Francisco Ibanez.)

On the twenty-fourth day of September in 1601 the galleon *Petate* set sail from Cádiz with a crew of 132 men under the command of don Gasco Nuno Guzman, in the direction of the rich lands of Peru, Manila, and the Ladrones Islands, subsequently named the Marianas.

The *Petate* brought a portion of the wares ordered by the Viceroy don Luis de Velasco for barter in the Spanish colonies; part of the cargo consisted of eight crates of eyeglasses.

After a weary crossing racked by stormy weather and a lack of drinking water, in which the sailors paid homage to two chickens that daily left their two corral fruits, in Palma's phrasing, the galleon reached the port of Callao.[1]

On December 12, 1602, there arrived in Cuzco a chest containing four royal decrees and the news that the *infanta* doña Ana had been born in Valladolid on September 22, 1601, which all Cuzco was to celebrate with fireworks, bullfights and tollings of the little bell at the church of Santo Domingo, the only one to be heard here in those days.

The four decrees contained in the chest, or postbox as we say more pompously nowadays, were not without interest and consequently we shall remark upon them: one was for the faithful executors of Cuzco to make a visit to the los Molinos, taking weights and measurements for three leagues all around; another was to pay the Town Council lawyer his salary; the third commanded that the allotted Indians be used for service in the plaza, sixteen of them destined to work as bakers; and the fourth related to the system of jurisdiction of the Corregidores.[2] All of this was duly entered on page 144 of the Book of Decrees.

Another curious document that came in that post was an announcement to the Town Council, the Judiciary, and the Regiment, that our dear Viceroy was sending to Cuzco the eight crates of eyeglasses that came from Cádiz on the *Petate*, with an order to sell them as quickly as possible.

Don Gabriel Paniagua de Loaiza immediately sent messengers to fetch those crates since, in this as on other occasions, the master's whims would be paid for by the sweat of the Indian, who compensated by his swiftness of foot for the lack of railroads that were to expand commerce in the nineteenth century.[3]

Thanks to the Indian the crates of eyeglasses made it to Cuzco and all that was needed was to find a quick way of disposing of several thousand of them, quite useless instruments if we are to judge by the quality of vision of our forebears.

Translated by George Yúdice.

---

1. The reference is to Ricardo Palma (Peru, 1833–1919), creator of the romantic genre of the *tradicion*, of which "What a Decree!" is an example.
2. Archaic name for magistrates.
3. The pun "Paniagua," literally *pan* [bread] *i* [and] *agua* [water], is no doubt meant to convey the idea that those who live under this master do so on "bread and water." [Translator's note]

Unfortunately, it is a fact that the conquistadors found two kinds of mine that abounded in Peru and that made for easy exploitation: mines with precious metals enclosed in the bosom of the earth and those *speaking* mines that were counted with each *mita* or labor draft. That's exactly what these poor Indians were, producers of big fortunes for their *patrón* [boss], and harvesters of ingratitude and opprobrium for themselves, for as a historian of our day explains, the magistrates and vice-governors demanded that they buy dispensable things as if they were the most necessary: "they would sell worn out mules, spoiled grains, rancid wine for three or four times more than if they were of excellent quality. They had no other right than to be the targets of what the authorities wanted to sell. Based on this principle, Magistrate Paniagua ordered all the Indians from beyond the mountains to attend in festive garb the mass that was to be celebrated in all parts of his jurisdiction for the health of the Queen Mother who had given her vassals a princess like the infanta doña Ana.

The Indians obeyed without the slightest reaction and on the indicated day it was impossible to see in the Magistry of Cuzco even one of them who was not wearing glasses, thus submitting to the mortification that glass produces in those with good sight.

On the other hand, the decree produced a good many doubloons[4] that went into reinforcing the crates in which the eyeglasses had arrived.

What a decree!

Don Gabriel had no doubt become the Viceroy's *Panioro* rather than his Paniagua.[5]

Where might we look for a don Gabriel to sign the order for all the Indians to buy a copy of our *traditions* and thus reinforce our pockets?

GABRIELA MISTRAL (1889–1957)
Chile

Born Lucila Godoy Alcayaga in a small town in a northern province of Chile, Gabriela Mistral, an autodidact, became the most active Latin American educator of her time, designing curricula in several countries and occupying an important post at the United Nations. Despite her continental renown and having been in 1945 the first Latin American author to be awarded the Nobel Prize, Mistral's poetry and writing have been overshadowed by avant-gardist and politico-nationalist criteria determining who are the "best" or more "characteristic" writers of Latin America. That so much of her work seemed "simplistic" in

---

4. Gold coin used in Spain and Spanish America.
5. The pun on Paniagua is now elaborated such that don Gabriel not only represents

"bread and water" for the Indians but, also, *pan* [bread] *i* [and] *oro* [gold] for the Viceroy. [Translator's note]

contrast to the avant-garde ("simplistic" being a term used by most critics), and that many of her themes were drawn from motherhood and beneficent nature, puts her at a disadvantage with those poets who expected to find the answers to existence and the means to human freedom in their poetry. More recent critics have pointed out that women writers in the early decades of this century tended to explore such themes as human rights and the equality of men and women, and such topics as maternity and love relationships not because they were inherently "feminine" but because those were the important issues in the public spheres in which women participated.

"Colophon in the Guise of an Alibi" is a rarely commented on manifesto found at the end of her book of poetry *Tenderness* (1924), which has provoked increasing interest among feminists. In it Mistral makes the argument that the source of poetry is provided by the "hummings," "verbal rockings," or lullabies that women produce as they rock their children to sleep. This is a feminine version of Paul Valéry's notion that poetry is born of bodily rhythms; but the rhythms of the lullabies are anchored in a maternal body. Mistral also makes the argument that these lullabies do not really serve the instrumental purpose of putting children to sleep, but rather that they are creative in and of themselves as the means by which women cultivate an ethical freedom through communication with the self.

from Tenderness

Colophon in the Guise of an Alibi[1]

Once upon a time, in Lima, I spoke of the significance of the Lullaby genre *as something with which a mother treats herself and not the child, who cannot understand*. . . .

And now I must digress, upon my Editor's request, on the birth of these Lullabies, because any first utterance, even that of animals or the industry of words, has significance for people . . .

It is woman who most sings in this world, and yet so infrequently does she appear as a creator in the History of Music that she traverses it with her lips sealed. I have always been intrigued by our sterility in producing and disciplining rhythms in song, especially in view of the fact that we Creoles live surrounded by rhythms, which even a child can grasp and mold in compositions. Why is it that we women have dared to write poetry and not music? Why have we opted for the word, a more serious expressive mode, laden as it is with concepts, and thus not of our own realm?

Meandering about in our aridity for musical composition, I came upon the island of the Lullaby. Surely the first cooings, those of folklore, which are musical, came from humble women ignorant of the melodic arts and sciences. The first

Translated by George Yúdice.

---

1. Literally, "Colophon with the face of an excuse"—The present title is, however, the one now current.

Eves began by silently rocking their children, on their knees or in the cradle; later they realized that slumber comes when the back and forth movement has a murmuring accompaniment; a humming which need be no more than a closed-lipped drone.

But soon the mother got the desire to address words to the child and to herself. After all, we mothers cannot be still for long, even if much is made of our supposed passivity; and much less can we be silent for years. The mother sought and found a way of speaking with herself while rocking her child, and more so by babbling with it, with herself, and with the night, which is also "a living being."

The Lullaby is thus the mother's daily and nightly conversation with herself, with the child, and with Gaia, visible in the daytime and audible at night.

The sick who couldn't fall asleep, or those campers who have spent the night staring at the stars, and the women who know what it's like to wait up for their husbands or brothers, all those who know what a vigil is know full well that the night is a plural and active person. "The night is legion," says the Devil in the Gospel. Perhaps we fool ourselves into thinking that light multiplies things and that night joins them all. The truth is that the darkness, that ambiguous, enormous fruit, breaks apart into murmuring shadows. In enlarging everything, the night stretches the slightest noise and swells the smallest objects, thus enriching the shadows. The mother who stays up, then, shares this subterranean world that frightens her with its false immensity and fertilizes her fancy with its numerous mysteries.

Woman not only hears her child breathe; she also feels the earth matriarch teeming with progeny. Finally she puts to sleep the child of her flesh, those of the matriarch, and then herself, for the drone ultimately fells the singer. . . .

This mother, with her Hindu goddess-like multiple mouths, tells in her Lullaby of her daily labors; she weaves and unravels dreams for what lies ahead for her child; she makes little jokes about the little one; she seriously entrusts it to God and in jest to the fairies; she frightens it with make-believe threats and sets its mind at ease before it has a chance to believe them. The lyrics of the Lullaby go from the sublimely funny to the pathetically ridiculous, zig-zagging between play and agony, jokes and anxiety. (I confess that the "murmurings" I like the most are the most disjointed, precisely because logic has the slightest part to play on their out-of-tune drum-rolls.)

The repertoire of Lullabies has changed very little in America. It is very likely that the Creole population never created any and that it has gone on singing for centuries those borrowed from Spain, humming tatters of Andalusian and Castilian lays, which are truly verbal wonders. We women have perhaps spun a few phrases with the ancestral threads or embroidered a few Creole flourishes on the original cloth.

Our grandmothers breastfed us, our mothers too, thank God; but then came a siege of corporal motherhood, both in terms of the number of children borne as well as the refusal of mothers to suckle, to be the "fig tree of milk" of the fairy tales.

Who, then, is going to sing these songs? The governess, salaried employee, will repeat the ones she knows; another's child does not move her to invent them as a result of an overdose of love or less still on the high of happiness. And the Lullaby is no less than the second milk of the suckling mother. It is like milk by dint of its long thread, its sweet taste and the warmth of the inner body. Consequently, the mother who does not give her its breast, who does not feel its weight on her lap, who does not coo it to sleep in the daytime or at night, how can she possibly hum a "berceuse"? How can she break into a suite of sweet sayings mixed with lively frolicking? The best lullaby singer will always be the mother-source, the mother who lets her child drink from her for a good two years, time enough to gild the act with custom, to mature it to the point of gushing with the juices of poetry.

A Spanish colleague once made fun of the Creole endeavors to force popular poetry, to provoke its birth by sheer force of will, or rather by abortion. I listened to her intently: Spaniards always have the right to speak about the language they bequeathed to us and whose handle they still hold in their right hand, that is, in the most experienced one. But, what will they have us do? Many things Spanish are no longer of use to us in this world of peoples, habits, birds and plants at odds with the Peninsular. We may still be their clients in matters of language, but there are many who want to take full possession of the outside trappings of this New World. The enterprise to invent may be grotesque but so is that of repeating from A to Z what the Nina, the Pinta, and the Santa María brought us. Someday I shall have to answer my colleague on the *tremendous conflict between being faithful and being unfaithful in matters of verbal colonialism.*

These songs are very distant from the folkloric compositions which are my fancy, and I know it full well as I know my cheerless hairstyle and the disarray of my clothes.

Those who are up on the trials and tribulations of our colonial languages . . . only they can explain fully the failure of our children's literature. They are no doubt sure, as am I, that folklore is *par excellence* the literature of children and that cultures in which it is lacking will master the genre very late.

The honest poet knows where she failed and confesses it. I, besides knowing it, declare that outside of two or three fortunate pieces included in this book, the rest are a stale "moulage," next to the firm flesh of the popular songs.

My poor, crippled compositions were born to invite a musician to make them run. I wrote them in part in remembrance of the hummings of my childhood that I liked so much and also in part to serve the emotional needs of other women. The poet is an unraveller of knots and love, without words, is a knot, an asphyxiation.

In the matter of finding winged feet, these Lullabies have not been too unfortunate and have even had a stroke of luck. Mexicans, Chileans, and Argentines, who surpass the fingers of both hands, offered them their decisive aid. And they were so honored and even transformed. The music of these tunes, of these "nanas," "vidalitas," is all glorious body and the flesh adds nothing; it is not words that give them life; their blood and their nourishment do not come from their lyrics. Music has such a precedence over lyrics that the latter should grovel at the former's feet. (By not disdaining these texts, our Creole music will have to gallop over such foolish and tacky words.)

As I was saying, I know my defects and the errors of each of my *verbal rockings*, and yet I have offered them and do so now, even though the more complex and labored ones should have been cremated as unfortunate abortions. Once again I assume, knowingly, the drawbacks of our verbal *mestizaje*. . . . I belong to that group of ill-fated ones who were born when there is no longer Patriarchy or the Middle Ages; I am one of those who bears contorted and irregular organs, face and expression on account of this racial grafting; I count myself among the progeny of that twisted thing which is called racial experience, or better yet, *racial violence*.

I go on writing "hummings" with long pauses; perhaps I shall die putting myself to sleep, having become my own mother, like the old women who rave with their eyes fixed on their useless lap, or like the child of the Japanese poet who wanted to put to sleep his own song before he himself fell asleep. . . .

They may have been of use to no one, and yet I'd go on writing them. Perhaps because my life has been hard I have always blessed sleep and I deem it the greatest divine grace. In sleep I have had the happiest and cheerful home, my true fatherland, my sweetest planet. There are no meadows so spacious, or so walkable or so delicate that can match it.

Some fragments of these Lullabies—perhaps one or two inspired lines— provide me with a door to my secret homeland, they open a crack in existence or the trapdoor of escape. The point in the music at which the child steals off and leaves the mother singing uselessly, I know this last step very well: in this or that word, the child and I turn around and escape, cast off the world, fall in our flight as if it were a cape that got in the way. . . .

With this digression I should like to say that I have not forgotten the "hummings" I heard when I was two: I still fall asleep on a vague maternal support, often moving on the bridge of my mother's or my own straggling words to the great dark lap of the Divine Mother who, from the other side, takes hold of me as if I were a bruised seaweed, buffeted the whole day long, who now returns to her.

ALFONSINA STORNI (1892–1938)
Argentina

Alfonsina Storni, of a humble background like Gabriela Mistral, began her career as a teacher and an office worker, eventually becoming one of Argentina's most popular columnists, particularly among women. As in Mistral's case, too, literary history has not served her very well. If "simplicity" is the adjective applied to the Chilean poet, critics have frequently explained Storni's poetry and her rebellious attitude as a means of compensating for an inferiority complex deriving from her social status, her correlative lack of education, and her supposed ugliness. Jorge Luis Borges and other avant-gardists were particularly hostile to her, apparently misconstruing her feminist activism (she was a suffragette) for penis envy. A careful reading of her poetry, however, demonstrates that she had a very sophisticated aesthetic, particularly in relation to desire and imagination. Her aesthetic challenged the desire projected in the work of the most heralded poets of her time, Borges and Pablo Neruda. "You Want Me White" parodies the absurd ways in which women are construed in male poetry. It is tempting to read "I Am Going to Sleep" as related to Storni's own suicide.

You Want Me White

You'd like me to be white as dawn,
You'd like me to be made of foam,
You wish I were mother of pearl,
A lily
Chaste above all others.   5
Of delicate perfume.
A closed bud.

Not one ray of the moon
Should have filtered me,
Not one daisy   10
Should have called me sister.
You want me to be snowy,
You want me to be white,
You want me to be like dawn.

You who have held all the wineglasses   15
In your hand,
Your lips stained purple
With fruit and honey
You who in the banquet
Crowned with young vines   20
Made toasts with your flesh to Bacchus.
You who in the gardens
Black with Deceit
Dressed in red
Ran to your Ruin   25

You who keep your skeleton
Well preserved, intact,
I don't know yet
Through what miracles
You want to make me white   30
(God forgive you),
You want to make me chaste

Translated by Marion Freeman and Mary Crow.

(God forgive you),
You want to make me like dawn!

Run away to the woods;   35
Go to the mountain;
Wash your mouth;
Get to know the wet earth
With your hands;
Feed your body   40
With bitter roots;
Drink from the rocks;
Sleep on the white frost;
Renew your tissue
With the salt of rocks and water;   45
Talk to the birds
And get up at dawn
And when your flesh
Has returned to you,
And when you have put   50
Your soul back into it,
Your soul which was left entangled
In all the bedrooms,
Then, my good man,
Ask me to be white,   55
Ask me to be snowy,
Ask me to be chaste.

I Am Going to Sleep (Suicide Poem)

Teeth of flowers, hairnet of dew,
hands of herbs, you, perfect wet nurse,
prepare the earthly sheets for me
and the down quilt of weeded moss.

I am going to sleep, my nurse, put me to bed.   5
Set a lamp at my headboard;
a constellation; whatever you like;
all are good: lower it a bit.

Leave me alone; you heart he buds breaking through . . .
a celestial foot rocks you from above   10
and a bird traces a pattern for you

so you'll forget . . . Thank you. Oh, one request:
if he telephones again
tell him not to keep trying, for I have left . . .

Translated by Aliki Barnstone and Willis Barnstone.

MÁRIO DE ANDRADE (1893–1945)
Brazil

The most important writer of the first half of this century, Mário de Andrade was also a literary critic and theorist, a professor of music history at the Conservatory of São Paulo, the director of the Cultural Institute at the University of Rio de Janeiro, and a noted folklorist. Together with Oswald de Andrade (1890–1954), who was no relation, he was a founder and principal figure of *modernismo*, Brazil's most important avant-garde movement. His "Extremely Interesting Preface," *Hallucinated City,* [1922], is a call to free Brazilian poetry from the literary conventions not only of the symbolists and Parnassians but also of the more institutionalized avant-garde movements like Italian futurism. His greatest claim to fame, however, is his "prose rhapsody" *Macunaíma* (1928), an epic collage of mythic, popular, and literary motifs from native and African-based Brazilian folk culture as well as European traditions, arranged, as in a rhapsody, on the basis not of plot but of the thematic and "chromatic" affinities among them. The work is subtitled *Hero Without Character,* and the wanderings of the antihero Macunaíma throughout Brazil provide a trajectory that brings together, as in a patchwork quilt, the many different elements from which a national identity might be constructed. Such a construction, in fact, was the chief merit of modernismo, which, in its other memorable manifesto, *Manifesto Antropofágico* by Oswald de Andrade, "cannibalized" all cultural forms and digested them so as to become a new entity. This is evident in the selected excerpt, which could be titled "If a straw, a match, or a cigarette," a parody of the creation myths of the Amazon Indians. Besides the evident parody, this "myth" comically reconciles the major industrial transformation which Brazil was beginning to undergo with the premodern character of the vast majority of its cities, towns, and rural areas. It is a spoof of modernization, always the utopian lure and unreachable horizon of Brazilian society.

from *Macunaíma*

[If a straw, a match, or a cigarette]

Macunaíma took out a tortoise-shell cigarette case made in Pará by Antônio de Rosáric, offered homemade stogies of wina bark to the boy and the girl, lit one match for them and another for himself; then, after brushing off the mosquitoes, he began to tell a tale. The night passed quickly like this, and the listeners did not become vexed by the monotonous whistle with which the tinamou marks every passing hour of darkness.

The story he told went like this:

"In times gone by, my young friends, the motorcar was not the mechanical *contraption it is today,* but a golden-brown jaguar. His name was Palauá, and he

Translated by E. A. Goodland.

lived in the great What's-its-name Forest. One day Palauá spoke to his eyes and said, 'Go to the seashore, O my pair of green eyes, quickly, quickly, quickly!'

"The pair of eyes went, and the golden-brown jaguar stayed where he was, sightless. But he lifted his muzzle to sniff the breeze, and scented that Aimalá-Pódole, the Father of the Fresh-water Sharks, was swimming there off the beach, so he cried, 'Come back from the seashore, O my pair of green eyes, quickly, quickly, quickly!'

"The eyes came back and Palauá could see again. A very fierce black puma was passing by and said to Palauá, 'What were you doing, cousin?'

" 'I was sending my eyes to look at the sea.'

" 'Is that a good idea?'

" 'It's a dog's trick!'

" 'Send my eyes too, cousin!'

" 'I won't send yours, because Aimalá-Pódole is swimming there off shore. He is the Father of the Fresh-water Sharks.'

" 'Send them or I'll gobble you up, cousin!'

"So Palauá spoke thus: 'Go to the seashore, O yellow eyes of my cousin the puma. Quickly, quickly, quickly!'

"The eyes went, and the black puma stayed there, blind. Aimalá-Pódole was there off the seashore and pounced on the black puma's eyes and swallowed them. Palauá had surmised this would happen, since the scent of the Father of the Fresh-water Sharks was so strong. He moved off, intending to escape, but the black puma, who was most ferocious, sensed his movement and said to the golden-brown jaguar, 'Just a minute, cousin!'

" 'Sorry, I can't stay. I have to go and hunt up some dinner for my children, cousin. Be seeing you another day!'

" 'First tell my eyes to come back, cousin, I've had my fill of darkness.'

"Palauá shouted, 'Come back from the seashore, O yellow eyes of my cousin the puma, quickly, quickly, quickly!'

"But the eyes did not come back, and the black puma burst into a fury. 'Now I'm going to gobble you up, cousin!' he roared, and he charged after the golden-brown jaguar. A father and mother of a row broke out in that forest. The songbirds were shriveled up with fright, and the night drew a deep breath and swooned. This is why, when it is daytime above the forest canopy, it is still as dark as night on the ground in the midst of the forest; a poor fellow can hardly see to walk.

"When Palauá had run a league and a half he began to tire and looked back. The black puma was close behind. Going on, Palauá came to a hill called Ibiraçoaba, and there he came across an enormous anvil that had once belonged to Afonso Sardinha's foundry at the beginning of industrial life in Brazil. Near the anvil were four forgotten wheels. Palauá lashed these wheels to his feet so that he could glide along with far less effort and, as they say, let go forrard and aft and careered away in a headlong rush. What a hellish row there was! The jaguar swallowed up a league and a half in no time, but the puma soon narrowed the lead. They made such a hideous din that the songbirds shriveled up to almost nothing with fright, and the darkness grew so intense that nobody could see to walk. Yet even this hubbub was pierced by the shrill keening of the nighthawk.

The nighthawk, my young friends, is the Father of the Night, and he was lamenting the plight of his daughter.

"Palauá was stricken by hunger. The puma didn't feel it, but Palauá could hardly keep going like this with his belly sticking to his backbone. However, he kept going, and sometime later, when he was crossing the sandbar at Boipeba, where the impish moonlight yuwarri lives, he saw an old motorboat engine lying there, so he swallowed it whole. The engine had no sooner sunk into the jaguar's empty belly than he was able to summon a fresh burst of energy and sped on. He did another league and a half before looking back. There was the puma, almost on top of him. The darkness was deeper than usual because the grief of the night had cast gloom over everything; this caused the jaguar to have a terrible crash into a fence on a small hill, missing death only by the skin of his teeth. Running along, he caught two fireflies and held them in his mouth to light the way. As soon as he had covered another league and a half, he looked around again; the black puma was close behind. He was able to follow because the golden-brown jaguar's scent was very strong, and blindness had given the puma the nose of a retriever. While he was running, Palauá swallowed a pint of castor oil, picked up a can of that essence called gasoline and poured it into his bladder, whereupon he went *boom-boom-boom!*, just like a mule farting. The row was such that it drowned the ghostly crash of broken plates coming from the Clashing Stones of Whistle Hill.

The black puma had become confused by his blindness and inability to pick out his cousin's scent from the fumes. Palauá ran a good way farther, and looked back. He could no longer see the puma, nor could he run anymore, as steam was blowing out of his nostrils due to overheating. Palauá had arrived at a large banana plantation alongside a tract of swamp near the port of Santos. He went down and poured swamp water into his nostrils until he had cooled off. Then he cut a big leaf from a fig banana, and draping it over his head like a hood, he hid himself and went to sleep. The black puma, who was very ferocious, passed right by him; the jaguar didn't let out a peep and the puma went on, unaware of his cousin.

"The jaguar never quite shook off the fright he had, and always kept close to him all those things that had helped him escape. Ever afterward he went around with wheels on his feet, a motor in his belly, a dose of oil in his gullet, water in his snout, gas up his backside, two fireflies in his mouth, and covered by a banana-leaf hood; all ready to roar off—*bam-bam!*—in an instant. To begin with, he found himself in trouble with the great swarm of taxi ants he had trodden on. They found their way into his sleek pelt and bit his ear—*wow!*—and he howled to high heaven. After that, to disguise himself still further, he took a strange name; he called himself an automobile contraption. Because he had drunk stagnant water from the swamp, Palauá had a seizure making him very ill. Automobiles can have seizures too, my young friends, causing a lot of trouble to the owner.

"They say that later on the golden-brown jaguar produced an enormous number of children. Some being masculine and others feminine explains why people call some cars by girls' names, such as Mercedes or Princess, and others by boys' names, such as Morris, Austin or Bentley.

"And that's the end of this story."

Macunaíma stopped. The young couple wept with emotion.

JORGE LUIS BORGES (1899–1986)
Argentina

While other children played with toys, Jorge Luis Borges played with books. At the age of seven, he translated a work by Oscar Wilde for his father, who was a professor of English literature. Educated in a French school in Geneva during World War I, Borges taught himself German, traveled throughout Europe, and was partly responsible for initiating *Ultraismo,* the most important Spanish avant-garde movement, in Madrid. Once back in Buenos Aires, he attempted to make good on the *Ultraista* tenet of creating radically new realities and a "new man" in *The Magnitude of My Hope,* [*El tamano de mi esperanza,* 1926] and *Fervor of Buenos Aires* (1932). By the late 1930s however, Borges's philosophical explorations, especially in idealism, led him to find the avant-gardist goal naive. He then turned to fiction, in which he subjected avant-gardist pretensions to a merciless irony, first in a series of apocryphal book reviews that became the form that many of his best-known short stories would take, such as "Pierre Menard, Author of the *Quixote*" (1939). Metaphysical discussions, often cast into a detective fiction format as in "The Garden of Forking Paths," included in *Ficciones* [Fictions] [1944], became the concern of stories that otherwise have no plots. The most important of these metaphysical discussions have to do with the relationship that language bears to reality and whether there can be a truly original author. This latter question is dealt with in "The Circular Ruins" (included in *Ficciones*) in which a man dreams another man into existence only to realize that he too is being dreamt by someone who in turn is being dreamt by someone else, and so on to infinity. God, then, is an author who has precursors and epigones or imitative followers, a mere point in an infinite series known as Literature. In "Tlön, Uqbar, Orbis Tertius" (also included in *Ficciones*), Borges works through more completely than elsewhere the relationship of author to language and of language to reality. The old avant-gardist idea that man can invent new realities through literature becomes a joke and a nightmare, as the plans of a secret society to create a fantastic country eventually culminate in an idealist world in which science and the language it depends on (nouns to name facts) are invalidated. And yet this world impacts upon our own to the point that simulacra (copies without originals) replace reality. The result, then, is not the invention of a "new" reality but the implosion of reality itself, an artistic act that, according to John Barth and others, has provoked the emergence of postmodern literature.

from *Ficciones*

Tlön, Uqbar, Orbis Tertius

I owe the discovery of Uqbar to the conjunction of a mirror and an encyclopedia. The unnerving mirror hung at the end of a corridor in a villa on Calle Goana, in

Translated by Alastair Reid.

Ramos Mejía; the misleading encyclopedia goes by the name of *The Anglo-American Cyclopaedia* (New York, 1917), and is a literal if inadequate reprint of the 1902 *Encyclopaedia Britannica*. The whole affair happened some five years ago. Bioy Casares had dined with me that night and talked to us at length about a great scheme for writing a novel in the first person, using a narrator who omitted or corrupted what happened and who ran into various contradictions, so that only a handful of readers, a very small handful, would be able to decipher the horrible or banal reality behind the novel. From the far end of the corridor, the mirror was watching us; and we discovered, with the inevitability of discoveries made late at night, that mirrors have something grotesque about them. Then Bioy Casares recalled that one of the heresiarchs of Uqbar had stated that mirrors and copulation are abominable, since they both multiply the numbers of man. I asked him the source of that memorable sentence, and he replied that it was recorded in the *Anglo-American Cyclopaedia,* in its article on Uqbar. It so happened that the villa (which we had rented furnished) possessed a copy of that work. In the final pages of Volume XLVI, we ran across an article on Upsala; in the beginning of Volume XLVII, we found one on Ural-Altaic languages; but not one word on Uqbar. A little put out, Bioy consulted the index volumes. In vain he tried every possible spelling—Ukbar, Ucbar, Ooqbar, Ookbar, Oukbahr. . . . Before leaving, he informed me it was a region in either Iraq or Asia Minor. I must say that I acknowledged this a little uneasily. I supposed that this undocumented country and its anonymous heresiarch had been deliberately invented by Bioy out of modesty, to substantiate a phrase. A futile examination of one of the atlases of Justus Perthes strengthened my doubt.

On the following day, Bioy telephoned me from Buenos Aires. He told me that he had in front of him the article on Uqbar, in Volume XLVI of the encyclopedia. It did not specify the name of the heresiarch, but it did note his doctrine, in words almost identical to the ones he had repeated to me, though, I would say, inferior from a literary point of view. He had remembered: "Copulation and mirrors are abominable." The text of the encyclopedia read: "For one of those gnostics, the visible universe was an illusion or, more precisely, a sophism. Mirrors and fatherhood are abominable because they multiply it and extend it." I said, in all sincerity, that I would like to see that article. A few days later, he brought it. This surprised me, because the scrupulous cartographic index of Ritter's *Erdkunde* completely failed to mention the name of Uqbar.

The volume which Bioy brought was indeed Volume XLVI of *The Anglo-American Cyclopaedia*. On the title page and spine, the alphabetical key was the same as in our copy, but instead of 917 pages, it had 921. These four additional pages consisted of the article on Uqbar—not accounted for by the alphabetical cipher, as the reader will have noticed. We ascertained afterwards that there was no other difference between the two volumes. Both, as I think I pointed out, are reprints of the tenth *Encyclopaedia Britannica*. Bioy had acquired his copy in one of a number of book sales.

We read the article with some care. The passage remembered by Bioy was perhaps the only startling one. The rest seemed probable enough, very much in keeping with the general tone of the work and, naturally, a little dull. Reading it over, we discovered, beneath the superficial authority of the prose, a fundamental vagueness. Of the fourteen names mentioned in the geographical section, we recognized only three—Khurasan, Armenia, and Erzurum—and they were dragged into the text in a strangely ambiguous way. Among the historical names, we recognized only one, that of the imposter, Smerdis the Magian, and it was invoked in a rather metaphorical sense. The notes appeared to fix precisely the frontiers of Uqbar, but the points of reference were all, vaguely enough, rivers and craters and mountain chains in that same region. We read, for instance, that the southern frontier is defined by the lowlands of Tsai Haldun and the Axa delta, and that wild horses flourish in the islands of that delta. This, at the top of page 918. In the historical section (page 920), we gathered that, just after the religious persecutions of the thirteenth century, the orthodox sought refuge in the islands, where their obelisks have survived, and where it is a common enough occurrence to dig up one of their stone mirrors. The language and literature section was brief. There was one notable characteristic: it remarked that the literature of Uqbar was fantastic in character, and that its epics and legends never referred to reality, but to the two imaginary regions of Mlejnas and Tlön. . . . The bibliography listed four volumes, which we have not yet come across, even although the third—Silas Haslam: *History of the Land Called Uqbar,* 1874—appears in the library catalogues of Bernard Quaritch. The first, *Lesbare und lesenswerthe Bemerkungen über das Land Ukkbar in Klein-Asien,* is dated 1641, and is a work of Johann Valentin Andreä. The fact is significant; a couple of years later I ran across that name accidentally in the thirteenth volume of De Quincey's *Writings,* and I knew that it was the name of a German theologian who, at the beginning of the seventeenth century, described the imaginary community of Rosae Crucis—the community which was later founded by others in imitation of the one he had preconceived.

That night, we visited the National Library. Fruitlessly we exhausted atlases, catalogues, yearbooks of geographical societies, memoirs of travelers and historians—nobody had ever been in Uqbar. Neither did the general index of Bioy's encyclopedia show the name. The following day, Carlos Mastronardi, to whom I had referred the whole business, caught sight, in a Corrientes and Talcahuano bookshop, of the black and gold bindings of *The Anglo-American Cyclopaedia.* . . . He went in and looked up Volume XLVI. Naturally, there was not the slightest mention of Uqbar.

II

Some small fading memory of one Herbert Ashe, an engineer for the southern railroads, hangs on in the hotel in Androgué, between the luscious honeysuckle and the illusory depths of the mirrors. In life, he suffered from a sense of unreality, as do so many Englishmen; dead, he is not even the ghostly creature he was then. He was tall and languid; his limp squared beard had once been red. He was, I understand, a widower, and childless. Every so many years, he went to England to visit—judging by the photographs he showed us—a sundial and some oak trees. My father and he had cemented (the verb is excessive) one of those English friendships which begin by avoiding intimacies and eventually eliminate speech altogether. They used to exchange books and periodicals; they would beat one another at chess, without saying a word. . . . I remember him in the corridor of the hotel, a mathematics textbook in his hand, gazing now and again at the passing colors of the sky. One afternoon, we discussed the duodecimal numerical system (in which twelve is written 10). Ashe said that as a matter of fact, he was transcribing some duodecimal tables, I forget which, into sexagesimals (in which sixty is written 10), adding that this work had been commissioned by a Norwegian in Rio Grande do Sul. We had known him for eight years and he had never mentioned having stayed in that part of the country. . . . We spoke of rural life, of *capangas,* of the Brazilian etymology of the word *gaucho* (which some old people in the east still pronounce *gaúcho*), and nothing more was said—God forgive me—of duodecimal functions. In September, 1937 (we ourselves were not at the hotel at the time), Herbert Ashe died of an aneurysmal rupture. Some days before, he had received from Brazil a stamped, registered package. It was a book, an octavo volume. Ashe left it in the bar where, months later, I found it. I began to leaf through it and felt a sudden curious lightheadedness, which I will not go into, since this is the story, not of my particular emotions, but of Uqbar and Tlön and Orbis Tertius. In the Islamic world, there is one night, called the Night of Nights, on which the secret gates of the sky open wide and the water in the water jugs tastes sweeter; if those gates were to open, I would not feel what I felt that afternoon. The book was written in English, and had 1001 pages. On the yellow leather spine, and again on the title page, I read these words: *A First Encyclopaedia of Tlön.* Volume XI. Hlaer to Jangr. There was nothing to indicate either date or place of origin. On the first page and on a sheet of silk paper covering one of the colored engravings there was a blue oval stamp with the inscription: ORBIS TERTIUS. It was two years since I had discovered, in a volume of a pirated encyclopedia, a brief description of a false country; now, chance was showing me something much more valuable, something to be reckoned with. Now, I had in my hands a substantial fragment of the complete history of an unknown planet, with its architecture and its playing cards, its mythological terrors and the sound of its dialects, its emperors and its oceans, its minerals, its birds, and its fishes, its algebra and its fire, its theological and metaphysical arguments, all clearly stated, coherent, without any apparent dogmatic intention or parodic undertone.

The eleventh volume of which I speak refers to both subsequent and preceding volumes. Néstor Ibarra, in an article (in the *N.R.F.*), now a classic, has denied the existence of those corollary volumes; Ezequiel Martínez Estrada and Drieu La Rochelle have, I think, succeeded in refuting this doubt. The fact is that, up until now, the most patient investigations have proved fruitless. We have turned the libraries of Europe, North and South America upside down—in vain. Alfonso Reyes, bored with the tedium of this minor detective work, proposes that we all take on the task of reconstructing the missing volumes, many and vast as they were: *ex ungue leonem.* He calculates, half seriously, that one generation of Tlönists would be enough. This bold estimate brings us back to the basic problem: who were the people who had invented Tlön? The plural is unavoidable, because we have unanimously rejected the idea of a single creator, some transcendental

Leibnitz working in modest obscurity. We conjecture that this "brave new world" was the work of a secret society of astronomers, biologists, engineers, metaphysicians, poets, chemists, mathematicians, moralists, painters and geometricians, all under the supervision of an unknown genius. There are plenty of individuals who have mastered these various disciplines without having any facility for invention, far less for submitting that inventiveness to a strict, systematic plan. This plan is so vast that each individual contribution to it is infinitesimal. To begin with, Tlön was thought to be nothing more than a chaos, a free and irresponsible work of the imagination; now it was clear that it is a complete cosmos, and that the strict laws which govern it have been carefully formulated, albeit provisionally. It is enough to note that the apparent contradictions in the eleventh volume are the basis for proving the existence of the others, so lucid and clear is the scheme maintained in it. The popular magazines have publicized, with pardonable zeal, the zoology and topography of Tlön. I think, however, that its transparent tigers and its towers of blood scarcely deserve the unwavering attention of *all* men. I should like to take some little time to deal with its conception of the universe.

Hume remarked once and for all that the arguments of Berkeley were not only thoroughly unanswerable but thoroughly unconvincing. This dictum is emphatically true as it applies to our world; but it falls down completely in Tlön. The nations of that planet are congenitally idealist. Their language, with its derivatives—religion, literature, and metaphysics—presupposes idealism. For them, the world is not a concurrence of objects in space, but a heterogeneous series of independent acts. It is serial and temporal, but not spatial. There are no nouns in the hypothetical *Ursprache* of Tlön, which is the source of the living language and the dialects; there are impersonal verbs qualified by monosyllabic suffixes or prefixes which have the force of adverbs. For example, there is no word corresponding to the noun *moon*, but there is a verb *to moon* or *to moondle*. *The moon rose over the sea* would be written *hlör u fang axaxaxas mlö*, or, to put it in order: *upward beyond the constant flow there was moondling*. (Xul Solar translates it succinctly: *upward, behind the onstreaming it mooned*.)

The previous passage refers to the languages of the southern hemisphere. In those of the northern hemisphere (the eleventh volume has little information on its *Ursprache*), the basic unit is not the verb, but the monosyllabic adjective. Nouns are formed by an accumulation of adjectives. One does not say moon; one says *airy-clear over dark-round* or *orange-faint-of-sky* or some other accumulation. In the chosen example, the mass of adjectives corresponds to a real object. The happening is completely fortuitous. In the literature of this hemisphere (as in the lesser world of Meinong), ideal objects abound, invoked and dissolved momentarily, according to poetic necessity. Sometimes, the faintest simultaneousness brings them about. There are objects made up of two sense elements, one visual, the other auditory—the color of a sunrise and the distant call of a bird. Other objects are made up of many elements—the sun, the water against the swimmer's chest, the vague quivering pink which one sees when the eyes are closed, the feeling of being swept away by a river or by sleep. These second degree objects can be combined with others; using certain abbreviations, the process is practically an infinite one. There are famous poems made up of one enormous word, a word which in truth forms a poetic *object,* the creation of the writer. The fact that no one believes that nouns refer to an actual reality means, paradoxically enough, that there is no limit to the numbers of them. The languages of the northern hemisphere of Tlön include all the names in Indo-European languages—plus a great many others.

It is no exaggeration to state that in the classical culture of Tlön, there is only one discipline, that of psychology. All others are subordinated to it. I have remarked that the men of that planet conceive of the universe as a series of mental processes, whose unfolding is to be understood only as a time sequence. Spinoza attributes to the inexhaustibly divine in man the qualities of extension and of thinking. In Tlön, nobody would understand the juxtaposition of the first, which is only characteristic of certain states of being, with the second, which is a perfect synonym for the cosmos. To put it another way—they do not conceive of the spatial as everlasting in time. The perception of a cloud of smoke on the horizon and, later, of the countryside on fire and, later, of a half-extinguished cigar which caused the conflagration would be considered an example of the association of ideas.

This monism, or extreme idealism, completely invalidates science. To explain or to judge an event is to identify or unite it with another one. In Tlön, such connection is a later stage in the mind of the observer, which can in no way affect or illuminate the earlier stage. Each state of mind is irreducible. The mere act of giving it a name, that is of classifying it, implies a falsification of it. From all this, it would be possible to deduce that there is no science in Tlön, let alone rational thought. The paradox, however, is that sciences exist, in countless number. In philosophy, the same thing happens as happens with the nouns in the northern hemisphere. The fact that any philosophical system is bound in advance to be a dialectical game, a *Philosophie des Als Ob,* means that systems abound, unbelievable systems, beautifully constructed or else sensational in effect. The metaphysicians of Tlön are not looking for truth, nor even for an approximation of it; they are after a kind of amazement. They consider metaphysics a branch of fantastic literature. They know that a system is nothing more than the subordination of all the aspects of the universe to some one of them. Even the phrase "all the aspects" can be rejected, since it presupposes the impossible inclusion of the present moment, and of past moments. Even so, the plural, "past moments" is inadmissable, since it supposes another impossible operation. . . . One of the schools in Tlön has reached the point of denying time. It reasons that the present is undefined, that the future has no other reality than as present hope, that the past is no more than present memory.[1] Another school declares that the *whole of time* has already happened and that our life is a vague memory or dim reflection, doubtless false and fragmented, of an irrevocable process. Another school has it that the history of the universe, which contains the history of our lives and the most tenuous details of them, is the handwriting produced by a minor god in order to

---

1. Russell (*The Analysis of Mind,* 1921, page 159) conjectures that our planet was created a few moments ago, and provided with a humanity which "remembers" an illusory past.

communicate with a demon. Another maintains that the universe is comparable to those code systems in which not all the symbols have meaning, and in which only that which happens every three hundredth night is true. Another believes that, while we are asleep here, we are awake somewhere else, and that thus every man is two men.

Among the doctrines of Tlön, none has occasioned greater scandal than the doctrine of materialism. Some thinkers have formulated it with less clarity than zeal, as one might put forward a paradox. To clarify the general understanding of this unlikely thesis, one eleventh century[2] heresiarch offered the parable of nine copper coins, which enjoyed in Tlön the same noisy reputation as did the Eleatic paradoxes of Zeno in their day. There are many versions of this "feat of specious reasoning" which vary the number of coins and the number of discoveries. Here is the commonest:

> On Tuesday, X ventures along a deserted road and loses nine copper coins. On Thursday, Y finds on the road four coins, somewhat rusted by Wednesday's rain. On Friday, Z comes across three coins on the road. On Friday morning, X finds two coins in the corridor of his house. [The heresiarch is trying to deduce from this story the reality, that is, the continuity, of the nine recovered coins.] It is absurd, he states, to suppose that four of the coins have not existed between Tuesday and Thursday, three between Tuesday and Friday afternoon, and two between Tuesday and Friday morning. It is logical to assume that they *have* existed, albeit in some secret way, in a manner whose understanding is concealed from men, in every moment, in all three places.

The language of Tlön is by its nature resistant to the formulation of this paradox; most people do not understand it. At first, the defenders of common sense confined themselves to denying the truth of the anecdote. They declared that it was a verbal fallacy, based on the reckless use of two neological expressions, not substantiated by common usage, and contrary to the laws of strict thought— the verbs *to find* and *to lose* entail a *petitio principii,* since they presuppose that the first nine coins and the second are identical. They recalled that any noun—*man, money, Thursday, Wednesday, rain*—has only metaphorical value. They denied the misleading detail "somewhat rusted by Wednesday's rain," since it assumes what must be demonstrated—the continuing existence of the four coins between Thursday and Tuesday. They explained that equality is one thing and identity another, and formulated a kind of *reductio ad absurdum,* the hypothetical case of nine men who, on nine successive nights, suffer a violent pain. Would it not be ridiculous, they asked, to claim that this pain is the same one each time?[3] They said that the heresiarch was motivated mainly by the blasphemous intention of attributing the divine category of *being* to some ordinary coins; and that sometimes he was denying plurality, at other times not. They argued thus: that if

---

2. A century, in accordance with the duodecimal system, signifies a period of one hundred and forty-four years.
3. Nowadays, one of the churches of Tlön maintains platonically that such and such a pain, such and such a greenish-yellow color, such and such a temperature, such and such a sound etc., make up the only reality there is. All men, in the climactic instant of coitus, are the same man. All men who repeat one line of Shakespeare *are* William Shakespeare.

equality entails identity, it would have to be admitted at the same time that the nine coins are only one coin.

Amazingly enough, these refutations were not conclusive. After the problem had been stated and restated for a hundred years, one thinker no less brilliant than the heresiarch himself, but in the orthodox tradition, advanced a most daring hypothesis. This felicitous supposition declared that there is only one Individual, and that this indivisible Individual is every one of the separate beings in the universe, and that those beings are the instruments and masks of divinity itself. X is Y and is Z. Z finds three coins because he remembers that X lost them. X finds only two in the corridor because he remembers that the others have been recovered. . . . The eleventh volume gives us to understand that there were three principal reasons which led to the complete victory of this pantheistic idealism. First, it repudiated solipsism. Second, it made possible the retention of a psychological basis for the sciences. Third, it permitted the cult of the gods to be retained. Schopenhauer, the passionate and clear-headed Schopenhauer, advanced a very similar theory in the first volume of his *Parerga und Paralipomena*.

The geometry of Tlön has two somewhat distinct systems, a visual one and a tactile one. The latter system corresponds to our geometry; they consider it inferior to the former. The foundation of visual geometry is the surface, not the point. This system rejects the principle of parallelism, and states that, as man moves about, he alters the forms which surround him. The arithmetical system is based on the idea of indefinite numbers. It emphasizes the importance of the concepts *greater* and *lesser,* which our mathematicians symbolize as $>$ and $<$. It states that the operation of counting modifies quantities and changes them from indefinites into definites. The fact that several individuals counting the same quantity arrive at the same result is, say their psychologists, an example of the association of ideas or the good use of memory. We already know that in Tlön the source of all-knowing is single and eternal.

In literary matters too, the dominant notion is that everything is the work of one single author. Books are rarely signed. The concept of plagiarism does not exist; it has been established that all books are the work of one single writer, who is timeless and anonymous. Criticism is prone to invent authors. A critic will choose two dissimilar works—the *Tao Tê Ching* and *The Thousand and One Nights,* let us say—and attribute them to the same writer, and then with all probity explore the psychology of this interesting *homme de lettres.* . . .

The books themselves are also odd. Works of fiction are based on a single plot, which runs through every imaginable permutation. Works of natural philosophy invariably include thesis and antithesis, the strict pro and con of a theory. A book which does not include its opposite, or "counter-book," is considered incomplete.

Centuries and centuries of idealism have not failed to influence reality. In the very oldest regions of Tlön, it is not an uncommon occurrence for lost objects to be duplicated. Two people are looking for a pencil; the first one finds it and says nothing; the second finds a second pencil, no less real, but more in keeping with his expectation. These secondary objects are called *hrönir* and, even though awkward in form, are a little larger than the originals. Until recently, the *hrönir* were the accidental children of absent-mindedness and forgetfulness. It seems improbable that the methodical production of them has been going on for almost a hundred years, but so it is stated in the eleventh volume. The first attempts were fruitless. Nevertheless, the *modus operandi* is worthy of note. The director of one of the state prisons announced to the convicts that in an ancient river bed certain tombs were to be found, and promised freedom to any prisoner who made an important discovery. In the months preceding the excavation, printed photographs of what was to be found were shown the prisoners. The first attempt proved that hope and zeal could be inhibiting; a week of work with shovel and pick succeeded in unearthing no *hrön* other than a rusty wheel, postdating the experiment. This was kept a secret, and the experiment was later repeated in four colleges. In three of them the failure was almost complete; in the fourth (the director of which died by chance during the initial excavation), the students dug up—or produced—a gold mask, an archaic sword, two or three earthenware urns, and the moldered mutilated torso of a king with an inscription on his breast which has so far not been deciphered. Thus was discovered the unfitness of witnesses who were aware of the experimental nature of the search. . . . Mass investigations produced objects which contradicted one another; now, individual projects, as far as possible spontaneous, are preferred. The methodical development of *hrönir,* states the eleventh volume, has been of enormous service to archaeologists. It has allowed them to question and even to modify the past, which nowadays is no less malleable or obedient than the future. One curious fact: the *hrönir* of the second and third degree—that is, the *hrönir* derived from another *hrön,* and the *hrönir* derived from the *hrön* of a *hrön*—exaggerate the flaws of the original; those of the fifth degree are almost uniform; those of the ninth can be confused with those of the second; and those of the eleventh degree have a purity of form which the originals do not possess. The process is a recurrent one; a *hrön* of the twelfth degree begins to deteriorate in quality. Stranger and more perfect than any *hrön* is sometimes the *ur,* which is a thing produced by suggestion, an object brought into being by hope. The great gold mask I mentioned previously is a distinguished example.

Things duplicate themselves in Tlön. They tend at the same time to efface themselves, to lose their detail when people forget them. The classic example is that of a stone threshold which lasted as long as it was visited by a beggar, and which faded from sight on his death. Occasionally, a few birds, a horse perhaps, have saved the ruins of an amphitheater. (1940. *Salto Oriental.*)

Postscript. 1947. I reprint the foregoing article just as it appeared in the *Anthology of Fantastic Literature, 1940,* omitting no more than some figures of speech, and a kind of burlesque summing up, which now strikes me as frivolous. So many things have happened since that date. . . . I will confine myself to putting them down.

In March, 1941, a manuscript letter by Gunnar Erfjord came to light in a volume of Hinton, which had belonged to Herbert Ashe. The envelope bore the postmark of Ouro Preto. The letter cleared up entirely the mystery of Tlön. The text of it confirmed Martínez Estrada's thesis. The elaborate story began one night in Lucerne or London, in the early seventeenth century. A benevolent secret society (which counted Dalgarno and, later, George Berkeley among its members) came together to invent a country. The first tentative plan gave prominence to "hermetic studies," philanthropy, and the cabala. Andreä's curious book dates from that first period. At the end of some years of conventicles and premature syntheses, they realized that a single generation was not long enough in which to define a country. They made a resolution that each one of the master-scholars involved should elect a disciple to carry on the work. That hereditary arrangement prevailed; and after a hiatus of two centuries, the persecuted brotherhood reappeared in America. About 1824, in Memphis, Tennessee, one of the members had a conversation with the millionaire ascetic, Ezra Buckley. Buckley listened with some disdain as the other man talked, and then burst out laughing at the modesty of the project. He declared that in America it was absurd to invent a country, and proposed the invention of a whole planet. To this gigantic idea, he added another, born of his own nihilism[4]—that of keeping the enormous project a secret. The twenty volumes of the *Encyclopaedia Britannica* were then in circulation; Buckley suggested a systematic encyclopedia of the imaginary planet. He would leave the society his mountain ranges with their gold fields, his navigable rivers, his prairies where bull and bison roamed, his Negroes, his brothels, and his dollars, on one condition: "The work will have no truck with the imposter Jesus Christ." Buckley did not believe in God, but nevertheless wished to demonstrate to the nonexistent God that mortal men were capable of conceiving a world. Buckley was poisoned in Baton Rouge in 1828; in 1914, the society forwarded to its collaborators, three hundred in number, the final volume of the *First Encyclopaedia of Tlön*. The edition was secret; the forty volumes which comprised it (the work was vaster than any previously undertaken by men) were to be the basis for another work, more detailed, and this time written, not in English, but in some one of the languages of Tlön. This review of an illusory world was called, provisionally, *Orbis Tertius,* and one of its minor demiurges was Herbert Ashe, whether as an agent of Gunnar Erfjord, or as a full associate, I do not know. The fact that he received a copy of the eleventh volume would favor the second view. But what about the others? About 1942, events began to speed up. I recall with distinct clarity one of the first, and I seem to have felt something of its premonitory character. It occurred in an apartment on the Calle Laprida, facing a high open balcony which looked to the west. From Poitiers, the Princess of Faucigny Lucinge had received her silver table service. Out of the recesses of a crate, stamped all over with international markings, fine immobile pieces were emerging—silver plate from Utrecht and Paris, with hard heraldic fauna, a samovar. Amongst them, trembling faintly, just perceptibly, like a sleeping bird, was a magnetic compass. It shivered mysteriously. The princess did not recognize it. The blue needle longed for magnetic north. The metal case was concave. The letters on the dial corresponded to those of one of the alphabets of Tlön. Such was the first intrusion of the fantastic world into the real one. A disturbing accident

---

4. Buckley was a freethinker, a fatalist, and an apologist for slavery.

brought it about that I was also witness to the second. It happened some months afterward, in a grocery store belonging to a Brazilian, in Cuchilla Negra. Amorim and I were on our way back from Sant'Anna. A sudden rising of the Tacuarembó river compelled us to test (and to suffer patiently) the rudimentary hospitality of the general store. The grocer set up some creaking cots for us in a large room, cluttered with barrels and wineskins. We went to bed, but were kept from sleeping until dawn by the drunkenness of an invisible neighbor, who alternated between shouting indecipherable abuse and singing snatches of *milongas,* or rather, snatches of the same *milonga.* As might be supposed, we attributed this insistent uproar to the fiery rum of the proprietor. . . . At dawn, the man lay dead in the corridor. The coarseness of his voice had deceived us; he was a young boy. In his delirium, he had spilled a few coins and a shining metal cone, of the diameter of a die, from his heavy gaucho belt. A serving lad tried to pick up this cone—in vain. It was scarcely possible for a man to lift it. I held it in my hand for some minutes. I remember that it was intolerably heavy, and that after putting it down, its oppression remained. I also remember the precise circle it marked in my flesh. This manifestation of an object which was so tiny and at the same time so heavy left me with an unpleasant sense of abhorrence and fear. A countryman proposed that it be thrown into the rushing river. Amorim acquired it for a few pesos. No one knew anything of the dead man, only that "he came from the frontier." Those small and extremely heavy cones, made of a metal which does not exist in this world, are images of divinity in certain religions in Tlön.

Here I conclude the personal part of my narrative. The rest, when it is not in their hopes or their fears, is at least in the memories of all my readers. It is enough to recall or to mention subsequent events, in as few words as possible; that concave basin which is the collective memory will furnish the wherewithal to enrich or amplify them. About 1944, a reporter from the Nashville, Tennessee, *American* uncovered, in a Memphis library, the forty volumes of the *First Encyclopaedia of Tlön.* Even now it is uncertain whether this discovery was accidental, or whether the directors of the still nebulous *Orbis Tertius* condoned it. The second alternative is more likely. Some of the more improbable features of the eleventh volume (for example, the multiplying of the *hrönir*) had been either removed or modified in the Memphis copy. It is reasonable to suppose that these erasures were in keeping with the plan of projecting a world which would not be too incompatible with the real world. The dissemination of objects from Tlön throughout various countries would complement that plan. . . .[5] The fact is that the international press overwhelmingly hailed the "find." Manuals, anthologies, summaries, literal versions, authorized reprints, and pirated editions of the Master Work of Man poured and continue to pour out into the world. Almost immediately, reality gave ground on more than one point. The truth is that it hankered to give ground. Ten years ago, any symmetrical system whatsoever which gave the appearance of order—dialectical materialism, anti-Semitism,

---

5. There remains, naturally, the problem of the *matter* of which some of these objects consisted.

Nazism—was enough to fascinate men. Why not fall under the spell of Tlön and submit to the minute and vast evidence of an ordered planet? Useless to reply that reality, too, is ordered. It may be so, but in accordance with divine laws—I translate: inhuman laws—which we will never completely perceive. Tlön may be a labyrinth, but it is a labyrinth plotted by men, a labyrinth destined to be deciphered by men.

Contact with Tlön and the ways of Tlön have disintegrated this world. Captivated by its discipline, humanity forgets and goes on forgetting that it is the discipline of chess players, not of angels. Now, the conjectural "primitive language" of Tlön has found its way into the schools. Now, the teaching of its harmonious history, full of stirring episodes, has obliterated the history which dominated my childhood. Now, in all memories, a fictitious past occupies the place of any other. We know nothing about it with any certainty, not even that it is false. Numismatics, pharmacology and archaeology have been revised. I gather that biology and mathematics are awaiting their avatar. . . . A scattered dynasty of solitaries has changed the face of the world. Its task continues. If our foresight is not mistaken, a hundred years from now someone will discover the hundred volumes of the *Second Encyclopaedia of Tlön*.

Then, English, French, and mere Spanish will disappear from this planet. The world will be Tlön. I take no notice. I go on revising, in the quiet of the days in the hotel at Androgué, a tentative translation into Spanish, in the style of Quevedo, which I do not intend to see published, of Sir Thomas Browne's *Urn Burial*.

PABLO NERUDA (1904–1973)
Chile

Born Ricardo Eliecer Neftalí Reyes in a southern Chilean town to working class parents, Pablo Neruda took as his pseudonym the surname of Jan Neruda, a nineteenth-century Czech writer. Having already won a prize for young poets, Neruda published *Twenty Love Poems and a Song of Despair* (1924), which transformed him almost overnight into Chile's most popular poet, especially among young people. His experiences as a diplomat in the East (Burma in 1927; Sri Lanka in 1928; Jakarta in 1930; Singapore in 1931) had a great impact on him and on his poetry. Cut off from other Spanish speakers and feeling quite alien to both Eastern life and the ways of the ruling British, he sought relief in sex and drugs and turned to poetry as a means of coming to terms with his alienation. By the time of his return to Chile in 1932, he had elaborated a completely new poetic in relation not only to his previous work but to that of poetic tradition in Spanish. In *Residence on Earth* (I, 1933; II, 1935; III, 1947), he takes avant-garde experiments with chance and the subconscious to a different plane in which he tries to work through what we might call a metaphysics of matter. His images go beyond traditional metaphor as they give body and shape to time (as a concrete disintegration) in relation to the elements and to the poet's own consciousness. In the 1940s Neruda rejected the solipsism of *Residencia* and espoused a poetry of political commitment to the socialist cause against fascism, nazism, and capitalist imperialism. On his way home from a diplomatic stint in Mexico, he stopped off in Peru to visit the ancient Inca site of Machu Picchu, which inspired his next book, *General Song* [1950], of which "The Heights of Macchu Picchu" (he added a "c" to Machu) is the best-known canto. As in his earlier poetry, the poet plunges into *materia,* the stony residence of generations of oppressed Indians ("I plunged a turbulent and tender hand / to the most secret organs of the earth"), putting his voice at the service of their redemption: "I come to speak for your dead mouths." In this way he resolves his earlier metaphysical concerns with his current political commitments.

Neruda was awarded the Nobel Prize in 1971. Two years later the military, which had just overthrown President Salvador Allende, broke into his home, where he was undergoing a painful and costly treatment for cancer. Neruda died of a heart attack.

from **The Heights of Macchu Picchu**

I

[*From air to air*]

From air to air, like an empty net,
dredging through streets and ambient atmosphere, I came
lavish, at autumn's coronation, with the leaves'
proffer of currency and—between spring and wheat ears—
that which a boundless love, caught in a gauntlet fall,   5
grants us like a long-fingered moon.

(Days of live radiance in discordant
bodies: steels converted
to the silence of acid:
nights disentangled to the ultimate flour,   10
assaulted stamens of the nuptial land.)

Someone waiting for me among the violins
met with a world like a buried tower
sinking its spiral below the layered leaves
color of raucous sulphur: 15
and lower yet, in a vein of gold,
like a sword in a scabbard of meteors,
I plunged a turbulent and tender hand
to the most secret organs of the earth.

Leaning my forehead through unfathomed waves   20
I sank, a single drop, within a sleep of sulphur
where, like a blind man, I retraced the jasmine
of our exhausted human spring.

Translated by Nathaniel Tarn.

Machu Picchu, Peru. Photograph by Roloff Beny.

II

[How many times in wintry city streets]

How many times in wintry city streets, or in
a bus, a boat at dusk, or in the denser solitude
of festive nights, drenched in the sound
of bells and shadows, in the very lair of human pleasure,
have I wanted to pause and look for the eternal, unfathomable   5
truth's filament I'd fingered once in stone, or in the flash a kiss released.

· · ·

I could only grasp a cluster of faces or masks
thrown down like rings of hollow gold,
like scarecrow clothes, daughters of rabid autumn
shaking the stunted tree of the frightened races.   10

I had no place in which my hand could rest—
no place running like harnessed water,
firm as a nugget of anthracite or crystal—
responding, hot or cold, to my open hand.

What was man? In what layer of his humdrum conversation,   15
among his shops and sirens—in which of his metallic movements
lived on imperishably the quality of life?

IV

[Irresistible death invited me]

Irresistible death invited me many times:
it was like salt occulted in the waves
and what its invisible fragrance suggested
was fragments of wrecks and heights
or vast structures of wind and snowdrift.   5

I had come to the cut of the blade, the narrowest
channel in air, the shroud of field and stone,
the interstellar void of ultimate steps
and the awesome spiral way:
though not through wave on wave do you attain us, vast sea of death,   10
but rather like a gallop of twilight,
the comprehensive mathematics of the dark.

You never came to scrabble in our pockets,
you could not pay a visit without a scarlet mantle,
an early carpet hush enclosed in silence,   15
a heritage of tears, enshrined or buried here.

I could not love within each man a tree
with its remaindered autumns on its back (leaves falling in their thousands),
all these false deaths and all these resurrections,
sans earth, sans depths: 20
I wished to swim in the most ample lives,
the widest estuaries,
and when, little by little, man came denying me
closing his paths and doors so that I could not touch
his wounded inexistence with my divining fingers,   25
I came by other ways, through streets, river by river,
city by city, one bed after another,
forcing my brackish semblance through a wilderness
till in the last of hovels, lacking all light and fire,
bread, stone and silence, I paced at last alone,   30
dying of my own death.

X

[Stone within stone]

Stone within stone, and man, where was he?
Air within air, and man, where was he?
Time within time, and man, where was he?
Were you also the shattered fragment
of indecision, of hollow eagle   5

which, through the streets of today, in the old tracks,
through the leaves of accumulated autumns,
goes pounding at the soul into the tomb?
Poor hand, poor foot, and poor, dear life . . .
The days of unraveled light   10
in you, familiar rain
falling on feast-day banderillas,
did they grant, petal by petal, their dark nourishment
to such an empty mouth?
     Famine, coral of mankind,   15
hunger, secret plant, root of the woodcutters,
famine, did your jagged reef dart up
to those high, side-slipping towers?

I question you, salt of the highways,
show me the trowel; allow me, architecture,   20
to fret stone stamens with a little stick,
climb all the steps of air into the emptiness,
scrape the intestine until I touch mankind.
Macchu Picchu, did you lift
stone above stone on a groundwork of rags?   25
coal upon coal and, at the bottom, tears?
fire-crested gold, and in that gold, the bloat
dispenser of this blood?

Let me have back the slave you buried here!
Wrench from these lands the stale bread   30
of the poor, prove me the tatters
on the serf, point out his window.
Tell me how he slept when alive,
whether he snored,
his mouth agape like a dark scar   35
worn by fatigue into the wall.
That wall, that wall! If each stone floor
weighed down his sleep, and if he fell
beneath them, as if beneath a moon, with all that sleep!

Ancient America, bride in her veil of sea,   40
your fingers also,
from the jungle's edges to the rare height of gods,
under the nuptial banners of light and reverence,
blending with thunder from the drums and lances,
your fingers, your fingers also—   45
that bore the rose in mind and hairline of the cold,
the blood-drenched breast of the new crops translated
into the radiant weave of matter and adamantine hollows—
with them, with them, buried America, were you in that great depth,
the bilious gut, hoarding the eagle hunger?   50

XII

[Arise to birth with me]

Arise to birth with me, my brother.

Give me your hand out of the depths
sown by your sorrows.
You will not return from these stone fastnesses.
You will not emerge from subterranean time.
Your rasping voice will not come back,   5
nor your pierced eyes rise from their sockets.

Look at me from the depths of the earth,
tiller of fields, weaver, reticent shepherd,
groom of totemic guanacos,   10
mason high on your treacherous scaffolding,
iceman of Andean tears,
jeweler with crushed fingers,
farmer anxious among his seedlings,
potter wasted among his clays—   15
bring to the cup of this new life
your ancient buried sorrows.
Show me your blood and your furrow;
say to me: here I was scourged
because a gem was dull or because the earth   20
failed to give up in time its tithe of corn or stone.
Point out to me the rock on which you stumbled,
the wood they used to crucify your body.
Strike the old flints
to kindle ancient lamps, light up the whips   25
glued to your wounds throughout the centuries
and light the axes gleaming with your blood.

I come to speak for your dead mouths.

Throughout the earth
let dead lips congregate,   30
out of the depths spin this long night to me
as if I rode at anchor here with you.

And tell me everything, tell chain by chain,
and link by link, and step by step;
sharpen the knives you kept hidden away,   35
thrust them into my breast, into my hands,
like a torrent of sunbursts,
an Amazon of buried jaguars,
and leave me cry: hours, days and years,
blind ages, stellar centuries.   40

And give me silence, give me water, hope.

Give me the struggle, the iron, the volcanoes.

Let bodies cling like magnets to my body.

Come quickly to my veins and to my mouth.

Speak through my speech, and through my blood.   45

JULIO CORTÁZAR (1914–1984)
Argentina

Julio Cortázar was born in Brussels; in 1920, his family moved back to Argentina. Cortázar may be characterized as an "internal" exile, although he voluntarily left his country for Paris in 1951 during the regime of Juan Perón. He worked there as a translator for UNESCO, and accepted French citizenship in 1981. Traditionally, Paris is the aspired-to metropolis for Latin American intellectuals and artists; in Cortázar's case, however, it is the "other side" from which his creativity continually drew its energy. Already in his early writings (*Bestiary,* 1951; *End of the Game,* 1956; *The Winners,* 1959; *Cronopios and Famas,* 1963), surrealism offered him a model for the irrational desire to experience the "other side" of language, for what can be thought when the security of given structures and conventions is abandoned. This desire evolves into the existentialist vacillation that characterizes his masterpiece *Hopscotch* (1963), wavering from the one side to the other, from Paris to Buenos Aires. The vacillation seems to be resolved in the political stances he takes in *Someone Is Walking Around Here* (1977) and *Manual for Manuel* (1973). But his last works—*We Love Glenda So Much,* 1981; *Inopportune Times* (1983)—put into question, again, the possibility of collapsing language with one's desire for resolutions.

In "Axolotl" the narrator gets so fascinated by the objects of his observation—the salamanders or, in Nahautl, "axolotl"—that his consciousness—and with it the ability to use personal pronouns—is transformed. This fantastic transformation is the process that Cortázar attempts to convey through an ingenious use of pronouns and other grammatical categories. The vacillation, however, is ever present. The reader does not know how the transformation took place, if it is imagined or not, if the narrator is mad, or if such things do in fact happen, and if they do, how it is that the story can get narrated.

Axolotl

There was a time when I thought a great deal about the axolotls. I went to see them in the aquarium at the Jardin des Plantes and stayed for hours watching them, observing their immobility, their faint movements. Now I am an axolotl.

Translated by Paul Blackburn.

I got to them by chance one spring morning when Paris was spreading its peacock tail after a wintry Lent. I was heading down the boulevard Port-Royal, then I took Saint-Marcel and L'Hôpital and saw green among all that grey and remembered the lions. I was friend of the lions and panthers, but had never gone into the dark, humid building that was the aquarium. I left my bike against the gratings and went to look at the tulips. The lions were sad and ugly and my panther was asleep. I decided on the aquarium, looked obliquely at banal fish until, unexpectedly, I hit it off with the axolotls. I stayed watching them for an hour and left, unable to think of anything else.

In the library at Sainte-Geneviève, I consulted a dictionary and learned that axolotls are the larval stage (provided with gills) of a species of salamander of the genus Ambystoma. That they were Mexican I knew already by looking at them and their little pink Aztec faces and the placard at the top of the tank. I read that specimens of them had been found in Africa capable of living on dry land during the periods of drought, and continuing their life under water when the rainy season came. I found their Spanish name, *ajolote,* and the mention that they were edible, and that their oil was used (no longer used, it said) like cod-liver oil.

I didn't care to look up any of the specialized works, but the next day I went back to the Jardin des Plantes. I began to go every morning, morning and afternoon some days. The aquarium guard smiled perplexedly taking my ticket. I would lean up against the iron bar in front of the tanks and set to watching them. There's nothing strange in this, because after the first minute I knew that we were linked, that something infinitely lost and distant kept pulling us together. It had been enough to detain me that first morning in front of the sheet of glass where some bubbles rose through the water. The axolotls huddled on the wretched narrow (only I can know how narrow and wretched) floor of moss and stone in the tank. There were nine specimens, and the majority pressed their heads against the glass, looking with their eyes of gold at whoever came near them. Disconcerted, almost ashamed, I felt it a lewdness to be peering at these silent and immobile figures heaped at the bottom of the tank. Mentally I isolated one, situated on the right and somewhat apart from the others, to study it better. I saw a rosy little body, translucent (I thought of those Chinese figurines of milky glass), looking like a small lizard about six inches long, ending in a fish's tail of extraordinary delicacy, the most sensitive part of our body. Along the back ran a transparent fin which joined with the tail, but what obsessed me was the feet, of the slenderest nicety, ending in tiny fingers with minutely human nails. And then I discovered its eyes, its face. Inexpressive features, with no other trait save the eyes, two orifices, like brooches, wholly of transparent gold, lacking any life but looking, letting themselves be penetrated by my look, which seemed to travel past the golden level and lose itself in a diaphanous interior mystery. A very slender black halo ringed the eye and etched it onto the pink flesh, onto the rosy stone of the head, vaguely triangular, but with curved and irregular sides which gave it a total likeness to a statuette corroded by time. The mouth was masked by the triangular plane of the face, its considerable size would be guessed only in profile; in front a delicate crevice barely slit the lifeless stone. On both sides of the head where the ears should have been, there grew three tiny sprigs red as coral, a vegetal outgrowth, the gills, I suppose. And they were the only thing quick about it; every ten or fifteen seconds the sprigs pricked up stiffly and again subsided. Once in a while a foot would barely move, I saw the diminutive toes poise mildly on the moss. It's that we don't enjoy moving a lot, and the tank is so cramped—we barely move in any direction and we're hitting one of the others with our tail or our head—difficulties arise, fights, tiredness. The time feels like it's less if we stay quietly.

It was their quietness that made me lean toward them fascinated the first time I saw the axolotls. Obscurely I seemed to understand their secret will, to abolish space and time with an indifferent immobility. I knew better later; the gill contraction, the tentative reckoning of the delicate feet on the stones, the abrupt swimming (some of them swim with a simple undulation of the body) proved to me that they were capable of escaping that mineral lethargy in which they spent whole hours. Above all else, their eyes obsessed me. In the standing tanks on either side of them, different fishes showed me the simple stupidity of their handsome eyes so similar to our own. The eyes of the axolotls spoke to me of the presence of a different life, of another way of seeing. Glueing my face to the glass (the guard would cough fussily once in a while), I tried to see better those diminutive golden points, that entrance to the infinitely slow and remote world of these rosy creatures. It was useless to tap with one finger on the glass directly in front of their faces; they never gave the least reaction. The golden eyes continued burning with their soft, terrible light; they continued looking at me from an unfathomable depth which made me dizzy.

And nevertheless they were close. I knew it before this, before being an axolotl. I learned it the day I came near them for the first time. The anthropomorphic features of a monkey reveal the reverse of what most people believe, the distance that is traveled from them to us. The absolute lack of similarity between axolotls and human beings proved to me that my recognition was valid, that I was not propping myself up with easy analogies. Only the little hands . . . But an eft, the common newt, has such hands also, and we are not at all alike. I think it was the axolotls' heads, that triangular pink shape with the tiny eyes of gold. That looked and knew. That laid the claim. They were not *animals*.

It would seem easy, almost obvious, to fall into mythology. I began seeing in the axolotls a metamorphosis which did not succeed in revoking a mysterious humanity. I imagined them aware, slaves of their bodies, condemned infinitely to the silence of the abyss, to a hopeless meditation. Their blind gaze, the diminutive gold disc without expression and nonetheless terribly shining, went through me like a message: "Save us, save us." I caught myself mumbling words of advice, conveying childish hopes. They continued to look at me, immobile; from time to time the rosy branches of the gills stiffened. In that instant I felt a muted pain; perhaps they were seeing me, attracting my strength to penetrate into the impenetrable thing of their lives. They were not human beings, but I had found in no animal such a profound relation with myself. The axolotls were like witnesses of something, and at times like horrible judges. I felt ignoble in front of them; there was such a terrifying purity in those transparent eyes. They were larvas, but larva means disguise and also phantom. Behind those Aztec faces, without expression but of an implacable cruelty, what semblance was awaiting its hour?

I was afraid of them. I think that had it not been for feeling the proximity of other visitors and the guard, I would not have been bold enough to remain alone with them. "You eat them alive with your eyes, hey," the guard said, laughing; he likely thought I was a little cracked. What he didn't notice was that it was they devouring me slowly with their eyes, in a cannibalism of gold. At any distance from the aquarium, I had only to think of them, it was as though I were being affected from a distance. It got to the point that I was going every day, and at night I thought of them immobile in the darkness, slowly putting a hand out which immediately encountered another. Perhaps their eyes could see in the dead of night, and for them the day continued indefinitely. The eyes of axolotls have no lids.

I know now that there was nothing strange, that that had to occur. Leaning over in front of the tank each morning, the recognition was greater. They were suffering, every fiber of my body reached toward that stifled pain, that stiff torment at the bottom of the tank. They were lying in wait for something, a remote dominion destroyed, an age of liberty when the world had been that of the axolotls. Not possible that such a terrible expression which was attaining the overthrow of that forced blankness on their stone faces should carry any message other than one of pain, proof of that eternal sentence, of that liquid hell they were undergoing. Hopelessly, I wanted to prove to myself that my own sensibility was projecting a nonexistent consciousness upon the axolotls. They and I knew. So there was nothing strange in what happened. My face was pressed against the glass of the aquarium, my eyes were attempting once more to penetrate the mystery of those eyes of gold without iris, without pupil. I saw from very close up the face of an axolotl immobile next to the glass. No transition and no surprise. I saw my face against the glass, I saw it on the outside of the tank, I saw it on the other side of the glass. Then my face drew back and I understood.

Only one thing was strange: to go on thinking as usual, to know. To realize that was, for the first moment, like the horror of a man buried alive awaking to his fate. Outside, my face came close to the glass again, I saw my mouth, the lips compressed with the effort of understanding the axolotls. I was an axolotl and now I knew instantly that no understanding was possible. He was outside the aquarium, his thinking was a thinking outside the tank. Recognizing him, being him himself, I was an axolotl and in my world. The horror began—I learned in the same moment—of believing myself prisoner in the body of an axolotl, metamorphosed into him with my human mind intact, buried alive in an axolotl, condemned to move lucidly among unconscious creatures. But that stopped when a foot just grazed my face, when I moved just a little to one side and saw an axolotl next to me who was looking at me, and understood that he knew also, no communication possible, but very clearly. Or I was also in him, or all of us were thinking humanlike, incapable of expression, limited to the golden splendor of our eyes looking at the face of the man pressed against the aquarium.

He returned many times, but he comes less often now. Weeks pass without his showing up. I saw him yesterday, he looked at me for a long time and left briskly. It seemed to me that he was not so much interested in us any more, that he was coming out of habit. Since the only thing I do is think, I could think about him a lot. It occurs to me that at the beginning we continued to communicate, that he felt more than ever one with the mystery which was claiming him. But the bridges were broken between him and me, because what was his obsession is now an axolotl, alien to his human life. I think that at the beginning I was capable of returning to him in a certain way—ah, only in a certain way—and of keeping awake his desire to know us better. I am an axolotl for good now, and if I think like a man it's only because every axolotl thinks like a man inside his rosy stone semblance. I believe that all this succeeded in communicating something to him in those first days, when I was still he. And in this final solitude to which he no longer comes, I console myself by thinking that perhaps he is going to write a story about us, that, believing he's making up a story, he's going to write all this about axolotls.

OCTAVIO PAZ (b. 1914)
Mexico

Octavio Paz received the Nobel Prize in 1990. Together with Vicente Huidobro and Pablo Neruda, Paz is a writer of long poems with transcendental pretensions (*Sun Stone,* 1958; *Blanco,* 1967). However, he is also Latin America's best essayist, ranging from explorations of the Mexican character to universal, Latin American, and Mexican literary history, art, politics, and the contradictions of modernity. Paz's poetic origins, like Huidobro's and Neruda's, lie in the avant-garde, especially surrealism. Like them and as had some of the surrealists in earlier times, he became a communist at the time of the Spanish Civil War and the antifascist struggle, an affiliation that he renounced when Stalin was unmasked; he has vigorously combatted that ideology ever since. In 1968, after twenty-five years in the diplomatic service, he resigned his post as ambassador to India to protest the Mexican government's suppression of a student-worker demonstration.

It might be said that throughout his poetic career, Paz has held to one fundamental tenet of surrealism and his interpretation of Eastern philosophy (like Neruda, he also served in the diplomatic corps in the East): the reconciliation of opposites (time and space, life and death, past and future, self and other, solitude and community, silence and speech, the profane and the sacred, yin and yang, East and West) through the poetic/metaphysical "leap." For Paz, as argued in *The Bow and the Lyre* (1956), *The Signs in Rotation* (1965), *The Children of the Mire* (1974) and many other essays, poetry is more than verse; it is the very embodiment of the transhistorical: "Poetry is our only resource against rectilinear time, against progress" (*Alternating Current,* 1967). Poetry, then, is more than time, it is the plenitude of existence in which "all meanings coexist." In "The Dialectic of Solitude," poetry, like myth, love, and the *fiesta,* manifests the ever present "indivisible unity" which is obscured by the ordinary divisions of modern rationality.

from **The Labyrinth of Solitude: Life and Thought in Mexico**

The Dialectic of Solitude

Solitude—the feeling and knowledge that one is alone, alienated from the world and oneself—is not an exclusively Mexican characteristic. All men, at some moment in their lives, feel themselves to be alone. And they are. To live is to be separated from what we were in order to approach what we are going to be in the mysterious future. Solitude is the profoundest fact of the human condition. Man is the only being who knows he is alone, and the only one who seeks out another. His nature—if that word can be used in reference to man, who has "invented" himself by saying "No" to nature—consists in his longing to realize himself in another. Man is nostalgia and a search for communion. Therefore, when he is aware of himself he is aware of his lack of another, that is, of his solitude.

The foetus is at one with the world around it; it is pure brute life, unconscious of itself. When we are born we break the ties that joined us to the blind life we lived in the maternal womb, where there is no gap between desire and satisfaction. We sense the change as separation and loss, as abandonment, as a fall into a strange or hostile atmosphere. Later this primitive sense of loss becomes a feeling of solitude, and still later it becomes awareness: we are condemned to live alone, but also to transcend our solitude, to re-establish the bonds that united us with life in a paradisiac past. All our forces strive to abolish our solitude. Hence the feeling that we are alone has a double significance: on the one hand it is self-awareness, and on the other it is a longing to escape from ourselves. Solitude—the very condition of our lives—appears to us as a test and a purgation, at the conclusion of which our anguish and instability will vanish. At the exit from the labyrinth of solitude we will find reunion (which is repose and happiness), and plenitude, and harmony with the world.

Popular language reflects this dualism by identifying solitude with suffering. The pangs of love are pangs of solitude. Communion and solitude are opposite and complementary. The redemptive power of solitude clarifies our obscure but vivid sense of guilt: the solitary man is "forsaken by the hand of God." Solitude is both a sentence and an expiation. It is a punishment but it is also a promise that our exile will end. All human life is pervaded by this dialectic.

Death and birth are solitary experiences. We are born alone and we die alone. When we are expelled from the maternal womb, we begin the painful struggle that finally ends in death. Does death mean a return to the life that precedes life? Does it mean to relive that prenatal life in which rest and motion, day and night, time and eternity are not opposites? Does dying mean to cease existing as a being and finally, definitively, to be? Is death the truest kind of life? Is birth death, and is death birth? We do not know. But although we do not know, our whole being strives to escape the opposites that torment us. Everything—self-awareness, time,

Translated by Lysander Kemp.

reason, customs, habits—tends to make us exiles from life, but at the same time everything impels us to return, to descend to the creative womb from which we were cast out. What we ask of love (which, being desire, is a hunger for communion, a will to fall and to die as well as to be reborn) is that it give us a bit of true life, of true death. We do not ask it for happiness or repose, but simply for an instant of that full life in which opposites vanish, in which life and death, time and eternity are united. In some obscure way we realize that life and death are but two phases—antagonistic but complementary—of a single reality. Creation and destruction become one in the act of love, and during a fraction of a second man has a glimpse of a more perfect state of being.

In our world, love is an almost inaccessible experience. Everything is against it: morals, classes, laws, races and the very lovers themselves. Woman has always been for man the "other," his opposite and complement. If one part of our being longs to unite itself with her, another part—equally imperious—rejects and excludes her. Woman is an object, sometimes precious, sometimes harmful, but always different. By converting her into an object and by subjecting her to the deformations which his interests, his vanity, his anguish and his very love dictate, man changes her into an instrument, a means of obtaining understanding and pleasure, a way of achieving survival. Woman is an idol, a goddess, a mother, a witch or a muse, as Simone de Beauvoir has said, but she can never be her own self. Thus our erotic relationships are vitiated at the outset, are poisoned at the root. A phantasm comes between us, and this phantasm is her image, the image we have made of her and in which she clothes herself. When we reach out to touch her, we cannot even touch unthinking flesh, because this docile, servile vision of a surrendering body always intrudes. And the same thing happens to her: she can only conceive of herself as an object, as something "other." She is never her own mistress. Her being is divided between what she really is and what she imagines she is, and this image has been dictated to her by her family, class, school, friends, religion and lover. She never expresses her femininity because it always manifests itself in forms men have invented for her. Love is not a "natural" thing. It is something human, the most human trait of all. Something that we have made ourselves and that is not found in nature. Something that we create—and destroy—every day.

These are not the only obstacles standing between love and ourselves. Love is a choice . . . perhaps a free choosing of our destiny, a sudden discovery of the most secret and fateful part of our being. But the choosing of love is impossible in our society. In one of his finest books—*Mad Love*[1]—Breton has said that two prohibitions restrict it from the very outset: social disapproval and the Christian idea of sin. To realize itself, love must violate the laws of our world. It is scandalous and disorderly, a transgression committed by two stars that break out in their predestined orbits and rush together in the midst of space. The romantic

---

1. *L'amour Jou*, 1937. Translated as *Mad Love*, tr. Mary Ann Caws. Lincoln: University of Nebraska Press, 1987. (Editor's note)

conception of love, which implies a breaking away and a catastrophe, is the only one we know today because everything in our society prevents love from being a free choice.

Women are imprisoned in the image masculine society has imposed on them; therefore, if they attempt a free choice it must be a kind of jail break. Lovers say that "love has transformed her, it has made her a different person." And they are right. Love changes a woman completely. If she dares to love, if she dares to be herself, she has to destroy the image in which the world has imprisoned her.

* * *

Society denies the nature of love by conceiving of it as a stable union whose purpose is to beget and raise children. It identifies it, that is, with marriage. Every transgression against this rule is punished, the severity of the punishment depending on the time and place. (In Mexico the punishment is often fatal if the transgressor is a woman, because—like all Hispanic peoples—we have two sets of morals: one for the "señor," another for women, children and the poor.) The protection given to marriage would be justifiable if society permitted free choice. Since it does not, it should accept the fact that marriage is not the supreme realization of love, but rather a legal, social and economic form whose purposes are different from love's. The stability of the family depends upon marriage, which becomes a mere protection for society with no other object but the reproducing of that same society. Hence marriage is by nature profoundly conservative. To attack it is to attack the very bases of society. And love, for the same reason, is an antisocial act, though not deliberately so. Whenever it succeeds in realizing itself, it breaks up a marriage and transforms it into what society does not want it to be: a revelation of two solitary beings who create their own world, a world that rejects society's lies, abolishes time and work, and declares itself to be self-sufficient. It is hardly strange, then, that society should punish love and its testimony—poetry— with equal malevolence, condemning them to the confused, clandestine world of the forbidden, the absurd, the abnormal. Nor it is strange that both love and poetry explode in strange, pure form: a scandal, a crime, a poem.

* * *

The dualism inherent in every society, and which every society tries to resolve by transforming itself into a community, expresses itself today in many ways: good and evil, permission and taboo, the ideal and the real, the rational and the irrational, beauty and ugliness, dreams and vigils, poverty and wealth, bourgeoisie and proletariat, innocence and knowledge, imagination and reason. By an irresistible movement of its own being, society attempts to overcome this dualism and to convert its hostile, solitary components into a harmonious whole. But modern society attempts to do this by suppressing the dialectic of solitude, which alone can make love possible. Industrial societies, regardless of their differing "ideologies," politics and economics, strive to change qualitative—that is, human—differences into quantitative uniformity. The methods of mass production are also applied to morality, art and the emotions. Contradictions and exceptions are eliminated, and this results in the closing off of our access to the profoundest experience life can offer us, that of discovering reality as a oneness in which opposites agree. The new powers prohibit solitude by fiat . . . and thus they also prohibit love, a clandestine and heroic form of communion. Defending love has always been a dangerous, antisocial activity. Now it is even beginning to be revolutionary. The problem of love in our world reveals how the dialectic of solitude, in its deepest manifestation, is frustrated by society. Our social life prevents almost every possibility of achieving true erotic communion.

* * *

The dual significance of solitude—a break with one world and an attempt to create another—can be seen in our conception of heroes, saints and redeemers. Myth, biography, history and poetry describe a period of withdrawal and solitude—almost always during early youth—preceding a return to the world and to action. These are years of preparation and study, but above all they are years of sacrifice and penitence, of self-examination, of expiation and purification. Arnold Toynbee gives many illustrations of this idea: the myth of Plato's cave, the lives of St. Paul, Buddha, Mahomet, Machiavelli, Dante. And all of us in our own lives, and within our limitations, have lived in solitude and retirement, in order to purify ourselves and then return to the world.

The dialectic of solitude—"the twofold motion of withdrawal-and-return," to use Toynbee's words—is clearly revealed in the history of every people. Perhaps the ancient societies, less complex than ours, are better illustrations of this double motion.

It is not difficult to imagine the extent to which solitude is a dangerous and terrifying condition for the persons we refer to—complacently and inaccurately— as "primitives." In archaic societies, a complex and rigid system of prohibitions, rules and rituals protects the individual from solitude. The group is the only source of health. The solitary man is an invalid, a dead branch that must be lopped off and burned, for society as a whole is endangered if one of its components becomes ill. Repetition of secular beliefs and formulas assures not only the permanence of the group but also its unity and cohesion; while religious ritual, and the constant presence of the dead, create a center of relationships which restrict independent action, thus protecting the individual from solitude and the group from dissolution.

* * *

Despite all these safeguards, the group is not immune to dispersion. Anything can break it up: wars, religious schisms, changes in the systems of production, conquests. . . . As soon as the group is divided, each of its fragments is faced with a drastic new situation. When the source of health—the old, closed society—is destroyed, solitude is no longer merely a threat or an accident; it is a condition, the basic and ultimate condition. And it leads to a sense of sin—not a sin resulting from the violation of some rule, but rather one that forms a part of their nature. Or, to be more precise, one that now *is* their nature. Solitude and original sin become one and the same. Also, health and communion again become synonymous, but are located in a remote past. They constitute the golden age, an era which preceded history and to which we could perhaps return if we broke out of time's prison. When we acquire a sense of sin, we also grow aware of our need for redemption and a redeemer.

A new mythology and a new religion are then created. The new society—unlike the old—is open and fluid, since it is made up of exiles. The fact of having been born within the group no longer assures a man that he belongs: he has to be worthy of belonging. Prayer begins to take the place of magic formulas, and initiation rites put more and more emphasis on purification. The idea of redemption fosters religious speculation, theology, asceticism and mysticism. Sacrifice and communion cease to be totem feasts (if that is what they actually were) and become means of entering the new society. A god—almost always a god who is also a son, a descendant of ancient creation-gods—dies and is resurrected at fixed periods. He is a fertility god but he is also a redeemer, and his sacrifice is a pledge that the group is an earthly prefiguration of the perfect society awaiting us on the other side of death. These hopes concerning the next life are in part a nostalgic longing for the old society. A return to the golden age is implicit in the promise of salvation.

* * *

Several related ideas make the labyrinth one of the most fertile and meaningful mythical symbols: the talisman or other object, capable of restoring health or freedom to the people, at the center of a sacred area; the hero or saint who, after doing penance and performing the rites of expiation, enters the labyrinth or enchanted palace; and the hero's return either to save or redeem his city or to found a new one. In the Perseus myth the mystical elements are almost invisible, but in that of the Holy Grail asceticism and mysticism are closely related: sin, which causes sterility in the lands and subjects of the Fisher King; purification rites; spiritual combat; and, finally, grace—that is, communion.

We have been expelled from the center of the world and are condemned to search for it through jungles and deserts or in the underground mazes of the labyrinth. Also, there was a time when time was not succession and transition, but rather the perpetual source of a fixed present in which all times, past and future, were contained. When man was exiled from that eternity in which all times were one, he entered chronometric time and became a prisoner of the clock and the calendar. As soon as time was divided up into yesterday, today and tomorrow, into hours, minutes and seconds, man ceased to be one with time, ceased to coincide with the flow of reality. When one says, "at this moment," the moment has already passed. These spatial measurements of time separate man from reality—which is a continuous present—and turn all the presences in which reality manifests itself, as Bergson said, into phantasms.

If we consider the nature of these two opposing ideas, it becomes clear that chronometric time is a homogeneous succession lacking all particularity. It is always the same, always indifferent to pleasure or pain. Mythological time, on the other hand, is impregnated with all the particulars of our lives: it is as long as eternity or as short as a breath, ominous or propitious, fecund or sterile. This idea allows for the existence of a number of varying times. Life and time coalesce to form a single whole, an indivisible unity. To the Aztecs, time was associated with space, and each day with one of the cardinal points. The same can be said of any religious calendar. A fiesta is more than a date or anniversary. It does not celebrate an event: it *reproduces* it. Chronometric time is destroyed and the eternal present—for a brief but immeasurable period—is reinstated. The fiesta becomes the creator of time; repetition becomes conception. The golden age returns. . . . Every poem we read is a re-creation, that is, a ceremonial ritual, a fiesta.

The theater and the epic are also fiestas. In theatrical performances and in the reciting of poetry, ordinary time ceases to operate and is replaced by original time. Thanks to participation, this mythical time—father of all the times that mask reality—coincides with our inner, subjective time. Man, the prisoner of succession, breaks out of his invisible jail and enters living time: his subjective life becomes identical with exterior time, because this has ceased to be a spatial measurement and has changed into a source, a spring, in the absolute present, endlessly re-creating itself. Myths and fiestas, whether secular or religious, permit man to emerge from his solitude and become one with creation. Therefore myth—disguised, obscure, hidden—reappears in almost all our acts and intervenes decisively in our history: it opens the doors of communion.

Contemporary man has rationalized the myths, but he has not been able to destroy them. Many of our scientific truths, like the majority of our moral, political and philosophical conceptions, are only new ways of expressing tendencies that were embodied earlier in mythical forms. The rational language of our day can barely hide the ancient myths behind it. Utopias—especially modern political utopias (despite their rationalistic disguises)—are violently concentrated expressions of the tendency that causes every society to imagine a golden age from which the social group was exiled and to which man will return on the Day of Days. Modern fiestas—political meetings, parades, demonstrations and other ritual acts—prefigure the advent of that day of redemption. Everyone hopes society will return to its original freedom, and man to his primitive purity. Then time will cease to torment us with doubts, with the necessity of choosing between good and evil, the just and the unjust, the real and the imaginary. The kingdom of the fixed present, of perpetual communion, will be re-established. Reality will tear off its masks, and at last we will be able to know both it and our fellow men.

Every moribund or sterile society attempts to save itself by creating a redemption myth which is also a fertility myth, a creation myth. Solitude and sin are resolved in communion and fertility. The society we live in today has also created its myth. The sterility of the bourgeois world will end in suicide or a new form of creative participation. This is the "theme of our times," in Ortega y Gasset's phrase; it is the substance of our dreams and the meaning of our acts.

Modern man likes to pretend that his thinking is wide-awake. But this wide-awake thinking has led us into the mazes of a nightmare in which the torture chambers are endlessly repeated in the mirrors of reason. When we emerge, perhaps we will realize that we have been dreaming with our eyes open, and that the dreams of reason are intolerable. And then, perhaps, we will begin to dream once more with our eyes closed.

ROSARIO CASTELLANOS (1925–1974)

Mexico

Although born in Mexico City, Rosario Castellanos spent her youth in the southern state of Chiapas, whose indigenous population became a focus of her writing and political interests. She attended the National University in Mexico City where she formed part of the group of writers known as the "Generation of 1950." She worked as a journalist and a researcher at the National Indigenous Institute in Mexico City. After teaching at several universities in the United States, she returned to the National University to accept an appointment in comparative literature. She wrote twelve books of poetry, two novels, three volumes of short stories, several books of essays and criticism, and a posthumously published satirical play entitled *The Eternal Feminine*. Much of her writing addresses the exploitation and oppression of poor, uneducated Indians and of women kept in their place by the dominant ideology of machismo. Her best known works include the novels *The Nine Guardians* (1957) and *Occupation of Darkness [Oficio de tinieblas,* 1958], the short story collection *Family Album* (1971) and a book of poetry entitled *Poetry Is Not You* (1971), a play on one of the canonical works of Hispanic letters by the nineteenth century romantic poet Gustavo Adolfo Becquer. Her poems seek to invert the images of woman that man has projected and to affirm her own creative and imaginative power. She is especially critical of women, real and fictional, who, like Anna Karenina, Madame Bovary, Sor Juana, and Emily Dickinson, do harm to themselves in the search for their own freedom: "There must be another way . . . / Another way to be human and free / Another way to be."

Metamorphosis of the Sorceress

(For Remedios Varo)[1]

Being born, issuing from the mother like the river
that tumbling, thrusting foreign matter, propels
its volume to the end without seeing the sky,
the tree on the bank,
or giving a loving polish to the pebble in its belly.   5

We call our living vertigo,
devouring whirlpool, algae that traps

Translated by Maureen Ahern.

---

1. Remedios Varo, 1913–1963, surrealist painter born in Spain who immigrated to Mexico in 1941. Varo's paintings are distinctive for their cosmic visions of feminine figures among whimsical beings and objects that make up the creative forces that propel the universe.

whatever tries to rise to the surface.
Between the roaring and its extinction
there is only turbid mire, dark fish, and ceaseless pulse.   10

So it is for all of us who flow
into the sea before achieving an identity.

For all of us. Not for her. She too was made of water
and lingered in reflected eddies.

What forms we glimpse through her transparency!   15
Endless corridors, desolate palaces,
complex machinery
transforming the universe
into beauty, into order, into shining laws.
Woman, spinning bolls of light, weaving   20
nets to catch the stars.

Woman, holding her masks, playing at self-deception
and deceiving others,
but when she saw her own true face
it was a flower of pale   25
withered petals; love, absence, and death.
On its corolla
a faint scar.

Because of all she knew she was obedient and sad
and when she departed down that street   30
—the one she knew so well—of good-byes,
beautiful creatures came out to bid her farewell,
the ones she had rescued from chaos, shadow, and
contradiction and made live
in the magic atmosphere her spirit created.   35

CLARICE LISPECTOR (1925–1977)
Ukraine/Brazil

The Ukrainian born Brazilian novelist Clarice Lispector was trained as a lawyer.
She married a diplomat, and lived most of her life abroad. She is best known on
the international scene for the story on which the Brazilian film *The Hour of the
Star* is based and the French writer Hélenè Cixous's feminist interpretations,
especially of *The Passion According to G.H.* (1964).* Unlike Brazil's better known

*Reading with Clarice Lispector, tr. Verena Andermatt Conley (Minneapolis: University of Minnesota
Press, 1990).

novelists (e.g., Jorge Amado), Lispector does not revel in local color or questions of national identity. Her work is, rather, more abstract and psychological. Lispector's characters, like those of Julio Cortázar, live in a state of disorientation, incapable of establishing a balance between reality and their own imaginations. This disjunction is conveyed lucidly in the grammatical disruptions of their styles. However, while Cortázar resolves the problem by raising it to the realm of the fantastic, Lispector remains, like Kafka, anchored in the concreteness of the strange and, like Sartre, caught in the depths of existential anguish. In other words, there are no external forces that can save Lispector's characters from their struggles with the desires that compel them to question the ties—familial, religious, social, etc.—that endow their lives with an arbitrary and artificial significance. This questioning generally manifests itself involuntarily and is experienced as *nausea,* the felt proof, as in Sartre's *Nausea,* that one exists. In "The Dinner" the narrator is overcome by nausea as he is drawn into and prevented from understanding what the old diner might be conveying. In fact, the diner is just going through the motions of an everyday act that has nothing unusual about it. It is in the consciousness of the narrator that the drama unfolds and reaches its climax as nausea: "My eyes were burning and the brightness was intense and persistent. I felt gripped by the heaving ecstasy of nausea. Everything seemed to loom large and dangerous." It is as if the narrator were willing the old man to choke on his food and have a heart attack. But when it is evident that things have been occurring all along in their customary banality, the narrator sinks back into his own powerlessness. The capacity to bring on the strangeness is not totally in his control and depends upon the presence of another who is amenable, at least temporarily, to serving as the object onto which he can project his own desires.

The Dinner

He came into the restaurant late. No doubt he had been detained until then over important business. His appearance suggested a man in his sixties, tall, corpulent, with grey hair, bushy eyebrows, and powerful hands. On one finger the ring symbolizing his power. He sat down, broad and solid.

I lost sight of him, and, as I ate, I glanced once more at the thin woman in a large hat. She was laughing with her mouth full and her dark eyes sparkled.

Just as I was lifting the fork to my mouth, I saw him. There he sat with his eyes shut, mechanically chewing his bread with obvious pleasure, both his fists clenched on the table. I went on eating and watching him. The waiter set out the plates on the table cloth, but the elderly gentleman remained with his eyes closed. As the waiter made some livelier gesture, he opened his eyes so abruptly that their movement simultaneously communicated with his enormous hands and a fork dropped on the floor. The waiter murmured words of reassurance as he bent down to retrieve it, but the man offered no comment. Now fully awake, he was suddenly turning his meat from one side to another, examining it vehemently, the tip of his tongue showing, prodding the steak with the back of his fork, almost sniffing at it, his mouth already in action. And he began to cut the meat with a vigorous movement which involved his whole body and seemed quite superfluous. After a short pause, he lifted a piece

Translated by Giovanni Pontiero.

of meat to a certain height, level with his face, and, as if required to catch it in flight, he snatched it with one swift movement of his head. I looked down at my plate. When I looked up again, he was completely absorbed in enjoying his dinner, chewing with open mouth and licking his teeth with his tongue, his gaze fixed on the ceiling light. I was about to cut myself another piece of meat when I saw him come to a complete halt.

And as if he could bear it no longer—but what?—he quickly grabbed his napkin and dabbed round his eyes with his hairy hands. I stopped to watch. His body breathed with difficulty and appeared to swell. Finally, he lowered his napkin from his face and stared numbly into space. He panted, opening and closing his eyelids in a startling manner, and, carefully wiping his eyes, he slowly chewed the rest of the food still in his mouth.

A second later, however, he seemed revived and once more impenetrable: he seized a forkful of salad with his entire frame and ate with his head leaning forward, the line of his jaw giving an impression of disdain, the oil moistening his lips. He then paused for a moment, dried his eyes again, briefly swung his head—and another forkful of lettuce and meat was caught in mid-air.

He called to the passing waiter, "This is not the wine I ordered."

Exactly the tone of voice I would have expected of him: a voice that invited no rejoinder, and I saw that no one could ever do anything for him. Except obey.

The waiter courteously withdrew, carrying the bottle. But suddenly the elderly gentleman stiffened once more as if his chest were constricted by some obstruction. His mighty strength was suddenly frustrated. He waited . . . until the hunger seemed to assault him and he began to chew heartily again, his eyebrows furrowed in a frown. I had already started to eat slowly, slightly nauseated without knowing why, taking part in something I could not understand. Suddenly he started to shake from head to foot, raised his napkin to his eyes and pressed them with a brutality which enthralled me. With a certain decisiveness, I put my fork down on my plate, as I, too, experienced an unbearable choking in my throat, and I felt furious and forced into submission. But the elderly gentleman did not pause for long, holding his napkin to his eyes. This time, when he unhurriedly removed it, his pupils were extremely relaxed and tired, and before he could dry them—I saw something. I saw a tear.

I leaned over my meat, lost. When I finally managed to confront him from the depths of my pallid face, I observed that he, too, was leaning forward, his elbows resting on the table, his head between his hands. And obviously he could bear it no longer. His bushy eyebrows were touching. His food must have lodged just below his throat under the stress of his emotion, for when he was able to continue, he made a visible effort to swallow, dabbing his forehead with his napkin. I could bear it no longer, the meat on my plate was raw . . . and I really could not bear it another minute. But he—he was eating.

The waiter brought a bottle in a bucket of ice. I noted every detail without being capable of discrimination. The bottle was different, the waiter in tails, and the light haloed the robust head of Pluto which was now moving with curiosity, greedy and attentive. For a second the waiter obliterated my view of the elderly gentleman and I could only see his black coattails hovering over the table as he poured red wine into the glass and waited with ardent eyes—because here was surely a man who would tip generously, one of those elderly gentlemen who still command attention . . . and power. The elderly gentleman, who now seemed larger, confidently took a sip, lowered his glass, and sourly considered the taste in his mouth. He compressed his lips and smacked them with distaste, as if the good were also intolerable. I waited, the waiter waited, and we both leaned forward in suspense. Finally he made a grimace of approval. The waiter curved his shiny head in submission to the man's words of thanks and went off with lowered head, while I sighed with relief.

He now mingled gulps of wine with the meat in his great mouth and his false teeth ponderously chewed while I observed him . . . in vain. Nothing more happened. The restaurant appeared to radiate with renewed intensity under the tinkling of glass and cutlery; in the brightly lit dome of the room the whispered conversations rose and fell in gentle waves; the woman in the large hat smiled with half-closed eyes, looking slender and beautiful as the waiter carefully poured the wine into her glass. But now he was making another gesture.

With a ponderous hairy hand, in the palm of which destiny had drawn such lines, he made a pensive gesture; it expressed, in mime, as much as it could, yet alas I failed to understand. And, as if he could no longer go on, he put down his fork on his plate. This time you let yourself be caught, old man. He sat there breathing heavily and visibly weary. He then held his glass of wine and drank with his eyes closed, in sonorous resurrection. My eyes were burning and the brightness was intense and persistent. I felt gripped by the heaving ecstasy of nausea. Everything seemed to loom large and dangerous. The slender woman, appearing ever more beautiful, shivered gravely among the lights.

He finished eating, his face drained of expression. He shut his eyes and distended his jaws. I tried to take advantage of this moment in which he no longer had his own face, in order to discover something at last. But it was useless. The great apparition before me meant nothing to me . . . regal, cruel and blind. What I wanted to confront directly, on account of the extraordinary strength of the elderly gentleman, ceased to exist at that moment. He refused to yield.

The dessert arrived, a melted cream, and I registered surprise at the decadence of his choice. He ate slowly, lifted a spoonful to his mouth and watched the creamy liquid trickle. He swallowed the lot, despite making a grimace and, now grown and nourished, he pushed away his plate. No longer hungry, the great horse rested his head on one hand. The first clear sign began to appear. The old child-eater was deep in meditation. With a pale expression I saw him raise his napkin to his mouth. I imagined that I could hear him sobbing, but we both kept silent in the center of the room. Perhaps he had eaten too quickly. Because, despite everything, you hadn't lost your hunger, eh? I provoked him with irony, rage, and exhaustion. But he was visibly collapsing. His expression was now crestfallen and imbecilic, and he was swaying his head from one side to another—from one side to the other, unable to control himself any longer, his mouth tightly drawn, his eyes shut as he swayed to and fro—the patriarch was crying to himself.

Rage choked me. I saw him put on his spectacles and become much older. As he counted his change, his teeth pushed his chin forward, surrendering for a moment to the kindness of old age. Even I, so intently was I studying him, did not notice him take out his money to pay, nor see him examine the bill, nor the waiter return with the change.

Finally he removed his spectacles, clicked his teeth and dried his eyes, making futile and painful grimaces. He passed his broad hand through his grey hair, smoothing it down with authority. Then he stood up, steadying himself on the edge of the table with his vigorous hands. And there, suddenly deprived of any support, he seemed less mighty, although still enormous and capable of stabbing any one of us present. Powerless to act, I watched him putting on his hat and adjusting his tie in the mirror. He then crossed the brightness of the room and disappeared.

But I am still a man.

When I have been betrayed and slaughtered, when someone has gone away forever, or I have lost the best of my possessions, or when I have learned that I am about to die—I do not eat. I have not yet attained this power, this edifice, this ruin. I push away my plate, I reject the meat and its blood.

GABRIEL GARCÍA MÁRQUEZ (b. 1928)
Colombia

Gabriel García Márquez, the novelist and short-story writer, left Colombia in 1950 on assignment to Europe as a newspaper reporter, and has spent much of his life outside his country, to whose people and myths he seems to feel all the closer. The most widely read author of the "boom" in Latin American fiction, García Márquez was awarded the Nobel Prize in 1982. His major work, *One Hundred Years of Solitude* (1967), has sold more copies than any novel ever written in Latin America and has been translated into more then twenty languages. García Márquez's literary style developed principally from two contrasting sources: journalism, which he has practiced all his life, and the marvelous legends and tales told to him by his grandparents. A third, more literary, influence is the work of Faulkner, Woolf, and Kafka, which were the preferred writers of the "Group of Barranquilla" (a Caribbean coastal city) to which he belonged. In his early fiction, *Leafstorm* (1955), *No One Writes to the Colonel* (1961), and *Big Mama's Funeral* (1962), he had already invented the magical town of Macondo and several of the characters that were integrated into the allegorical genealogy of Macondo-Latin America in *One Hundred Years of Solitude*, which tells the prehistory of Macondo. It spans a series of events lived through by the dynastic family of the Buendías: foundation, civil wars, and modernization (i.e., capitalist exploitation and economic dependency). The intrusion of foreigners and modernity are eliminated by a flood that washes them away and returns Macondo to its beginnings, not to a paradise lost but to fiction. A member of the Buendia family deciphers a parchment written in Sanskrit that tells the entire story of the family and of Macondo. History, then, completes the fiction.

García Márquez has written many other highly regarded novels, including

The Autumn of the Patriarch (1975), Chronicle of a Death Foretold (1980), Love in the Time of Cholera (1985), and The General in His Labyrinth (1989). The selection here, "Big Mama's Funeral," is very much like the novels of the sixties and seventies, which treat the effects of political power on history. In this particular respect, although García Márquez's fiction shares several features with the major works of "marvelous realism," it parts company with them by situating the marvelous not in some essential native magic but, rather, in the exercise of power.

from No One Writes to the Colonel and Other Stories

Big Mama's Funeral

This is, for all the world's unbelievers, the true account of Big Mama, absolute sovereign of the Kingdom of Macondo, who lived for ninety-two years, and died in the odor of sanctity one Tuesday last September, and whose funeral was attended by the Pope.

Now that the nation, which was shaken to its vitals, has recovered its balance; now that the bagpipers of San Jacinto, the smugglers of Guajira, the rice planters of Sinú, the prostitutes of Caucamayal, the wizards of Sierpe, and the banana workers of Aracataca have folded up their tents to recover from the exhausting vigil and have regained their serenity, and the President of the Republic and his Ministers and all those who represented the public and supernatural powers on the most magnificent funeral occasion recorded in the annals of history have regained control of their estates; now that the Holy Pontiff has risen up to Heaven in body and soul; and now that it is impossible to walk around in Macondo because of the empty bottles, the cigarette butts, the gnawed bones, the cans and rags and excrement that the crowd which came to the burial left behind; now is the time to lean a stool against the front door and relate from the beginning the details of this national commotion, before the historians have a chance to get at it.

Fourteen weeks ago, after endless nights of poultices, mustard plasters, and leeches, and weak with the delirium of her death agony, Big Mama ordered them to seat her in her old rattan rocker so she could express her last wishes. It was the only thing she needed to do before she died. That morning, with the intervention of Father Anthony Isabel, she had put the affairs of her soul in order, and now she needed only to put her worldly affairs in order with her nine nieces and nephews, her sole heirs, who were standing around her bed. The priest, talking to himself and on the verge of his hundredth birthday, stayed in the room. Ten men had been needed to take him up to Big Mama's bedroom, and it was decided that he should stay there so they should not have to take him down and then take him up again at the last minute.

Nicanor, the eldest nephew, gigantic and savage, dressed in khaki and spurred boots, with a .38-caliber long-barreled revolver holstered under his shirt, went to look for the notary. The enormous two-story mansion, fragrant from

Translated by J. S. Bernstein.

molasses and oregano, with its dark apartments crammed with chests and the odds and ends of four generations turned to dust, had become paralyzed since the week before, in expectation of that moment. In the long central hall, with hooks on the walls where in another time butchered pigs had been hung and deer were slaughtered on sleepy August Sundays, the peons were sleeping on farm equipment and bags of salt, awaiting the order to saddle the mules to spread the bad news to the four corners of the huge hacienda. The rest of the family was in the living room. The women were limp, exhausted by the inheritance proceedings and lack of sleep; they kept a strict mourning which was the culmination of countless accumulated mournings. Big Mama's matriarchal rigidity had surrounded her fortune and her name with a sacramental fence, within which uncles married the daughters of their nieces, and the cousins married their aunts, and brothers their sisters-in-law, until an intricate mesh of consanguinity was formed, which turned procreation into a vicious circle. Only Magdalena, the youngest of the nieces, managed to escape it. Terrified by hallucinations, she made Father Anthony Isabel exorcise her, shaved her head, and renounced the glories and vanities of the world in the novitiate of the Mission District.

On the margin of the official family, and in exercise of the *jus primae noctis*, the males had fertilized ranches, byways, and settlements with an entire bastard line, which circulated among the servants without surnames, as godchildren, employees, favorites, and protégés of Big Mama.

The imminence of her death stirred the exhausting expectation. The dying woman's voice, accustomed to homage and obedience, was no louder than a bass organ pipe in the closed room, but it echoed in the most far-flung corners of the hacienda. No one was indifferent to this death. During this century, Big Mama had been Macondo's center of gravity, as had her brothers, her parents, and the parents of her parents in the past, in a dominance which covered two centuries. The town was founded on her surname. No one knew the origin, or the limits or the real value of her estate, but everyone was used to believing that Big Mama was the owner of the waters, running and still, of rain and drought, and of the district's roads, telegraph poles, leap years, and heat waves, and that she had furthermore a hereditary right over life and property. When she sat on her balcony in the cool afternoon air, with all the weight of her belly and authority squeezed into her old rattan rocker, she seemed, in truth, infinitely rich and powerful, the richest and most powerful matron in the world.

It had not occurred to anyone to think that Big Mama was mortal, except the members of her tribe, and Big Mama herself, prodded by the senile premonitions of Father Anthony Isabel. But she believed that she would live more than a hundred years, as did her maternal grandmother, who in the War of 1885 confronted a patrol of Colonel Aureliano Buendía's, barricaded in the kitchen of the hacienda. Only in April of this year did Big Mama realize that God would not grant her the privilege of personally liquidating, in an open skirmish, a horde of Federalist Masons.

During the first week of pain, the family doctor maintained her with mustard plasters and woolen stockings. He was a hereditary doctor, a graduate of Montpellier, hostile by philosophical conviction to the progress of his science, whom Big Mama had accorded the lifetime privilege of preventing the establish-ment in Macondo of any other doctors. At one time he covered the town on horseback, visiting the doleful, sick people at dusk, and Nature had accorded him the privilege of being the father of many another's children. But arthritis kept him stiff-jointed in bed, and he ended up attending to his patients without calling on them, by means of suppositions, messengers, and errands. Summoned by Big Mama, he crossed the plaza in his pajamas, leaning on two canes, and he installed himself in the sick woman's bedroom. Only when he realized that Big Mama was dying did he order a chest with porcelain jars labeled in Latin brought, and for three weeks he besmeared the dying woman inside and out with all sorts of academic salves, magnificent stimulants, and masterful suppositories. Then he applied bloated toads to the site of her pain, and leaches to her kidneys, until the early morning of that day when he had to face the dilemma of either having her bled by the barber or exorcised by Father Anthony Isabel.

Nicanor sent for the priest. His ten best men carried him from the parish house to Big Mama's bedroom, seated on a creaking willow rocker, under the mildewed canopy reserved for great occasions. The little bell of the Viaticum in the warm September dawn was the first notification to the inhabitants of Macondo. When the sun rose, the little plaza in front of Big Mama's house looked like a country fair.

It was like a memory of another era. Until she was seventy, Big Mama used to celebrate her birthday with the most prolonged and tumultuous carnivals within memory. Demijohns of rum were placed at the townspeople's disposal, cattle were sacrificed in the public plaza, and a band installed on top of a table played for three days without stopping. Under the dusty almond trees, where, in the first week of the century, Colonel Aureliano Buendía's troops had camped, stalls were set up which sold banana liquor, rolls, blood puddings, chopped fried meat, meat pies, sausage, yucca breads, crullers, buns, corn breads, puff pastes, *longanizas,* tripes, coconut nougats, rum toddies, along with all sorts of trifles, gewgaws, trinkets, and knicknacks, and cockfights and lottery tickets. In the midst of the confusion of the agitated mob, prints and scapularies with Big Mama's likeness were sold.

The festivities used to begin two days before and end on the day of her birthday, with the thunder of fireworks and a family dance at Big Mama's house. The carefully chosen guests and the legitimate members of the family, generously attended by the bastard line, danced to the beat of the old pianola which was equipped with the rolls most in style. Big Mama presided over the party from the rear of the hall in an easy chair with linen pillows, imparting discreet instructions with her right hand, adorned with rings on all her fingers. On that night the coming year's marriages were arranged, at times in complicity with the lovers, but almost always counseled by her own inspiration. To finish off the jubilation, Big Mama went out to the balcony, which was decorated with diadems and Japanese lanterns, and threw coins to the crowd.

That tradition had been interrupted, in part because of the successive mournings of the family and in part because of the political instability of the last few years. The new generations only heard stories of those splendid celebrations.

They never managed to see Big Mama at High Mass, fanned by some functionary of the Civil Authority, enjoying the privilege of not kneeling, even at the moment of the elevation, so as not to ruin her Dutch-flounced skirt and her starched cambric petticoats. The old people remembered, like a hallucination out of their youth, the two hundred yards of matting which were laid down from the manorial house to the main altar the afternoon on which Maria del Rosario Castañeda y Montero attended her father's funeral and returned along the matted street endowed with a new and radiant dignity, turned into Big Mama at the age of twenty-two. That medieval vision belonged then not only to the family's past but also to the nation's past. Ever more indistinct and remote, hardly visible on her balcony, stifled by the geraniums on hot afternoons, Big Mama was melting into her own legend. Her authority was exercised through Nicanor. The tacit promise existed, formulated by tradition, that the day Big Mama sealed her will the heirs would declare three nights of public merrymaking. But at the same time it was known that she had decided not to express her last wishes until a few hours before dying, and no one thought seriously about the possibility that Big Mama was mortal. Only this morning, awakened by the tinkling of the Viaticum, did the inhabitants of Macondo become convinced not only that Big Mama was mortal but also that she was dying.

Her hour had come. Seeing her in her linen bed, debaubed with aloes up to her ears, under the dust-laden canopy of Oriental crêpe, one could hardly make out any life in the thin respiration of her matriarchal breasts. Big Mama, who until she was fifty rejected the most passionate suitors, and who was well enough endowed by Nature to suckle her whole issue all by herself, was dying a virgin and childless. At the moment of extreme unction, Father Anthony Isabel had to ask for help in order to apply the oils to the palms of her hands, for since the beginning of her death throes Big Mama had had her fists closed. The attendance of the nieces was useless. In the struggle, for the first time in a week, the dying woman pressed against her chest the hand bejeweled with precious stones and fixed her colorless look on the nieces, saying, "Highway robbers." Then she saw Father Anthony Isabel in his liturgical habit and the acolyte with the sacramental implements, and with calm conviction she murmured, "I am dying." Then she took off the ring with the great diamond and gave it to Magdalena, the novice, to whom it belonged since she was the youngest heir. That was the end of a tradition: Magdalena had renounced her inheritance in favor of the Church.

At dawn Big Mama asked to be left alone with Nicanor to impart her last instructions. For half an hour, in perfect command of her faculties, she asked about the conduct of her affairs. She gave special instructions about the disposition of her body, and finally concerned herself with the wake. "You have to keep your eyes open," she said. "Keep everything of value under lock and key, because many people come to wakes only to steal." A moment later, alone with the priest, she made an extravagant confession, sincere and detailed, and later on took Communion in the presence of her nieces and nephews. It was then that she asked them to seat her in her rattan rocker so that she could express her last wishes.

Nicanor had prepared, on twenty-four folios written in a very clear hand, a scrupulous account of her possessions. Breathing calmly, with the doctor and

Father Anthony Isabel as witnesses, Big Mama dictated to the notary the list of her property, the supreme and unique source of her grandeur and authority. Reduced to its true proportions, the real estate was limited to three districts, awarded by Royal Decree at the founding of the Colony; with the passage of time, by dint of intricate marriages of convenience, they had accumulated under the control of Big Mama. In that unworked territory, without definite borders, which comprised five townships and in which not one single grain had ever been sown at the expense of the proprietors, three hundred and fifty-two families lived as tenant farmers. Every year, on the eve of her name day, Big Mama exercised the only act of control which prevented the lands from reverting to the state: the collection of rent. Seated on the back porch of her house, she personally received the payment for the right to live on her lands, as for more than a century her ancestors had received it from the ancestors of the tenants. When the three-day collection was over, the patio was crammed with pigs, turkeys, and chickens, and with the tithes and first fruits of the land which were deposited there as gifts. In reality, that was the only harvest the family ever collected from a territory which had been dead since its beginnings, and which was calculated on first examination at a hundred thousand hectares. But historical circumstances had brought it about that within those boundaries the six towns of Macondo district should grow and prosper, even the county seat, so that no person who lived in a house had any property rights other than those which pertained to the house itself, since the land belonged to Big Mama, and the rent was paid to her, just as the government had to pay her for the use the citizens made of the streets.

On the outskirts of the settlements, a number of animals, never counted and even less looked after, roamed, branded on the hindquarters with the shape of a padlock. This hereditary brand, which more out of disorder than out of quantity had become familiar on distant districts where the scattered cattle, dying of thirst, strayed in summer, was one of the most solid supports of the legend. For reasons which no one had bothered to explain, the extensive stables of the house had progressively emptied since the last civil war, and lately sugar-cane presses, milking parlors, and a rice mill had been installed in them.

Aside from the items enumerated, she mentioned in her will the existence of three containers of gold coins buried somewhere in the house during the War of Independence, which had not been found after periodic and laborious excavations. Along with the right to continue the exploitation of the rented land, and to receive the tithes and first fruits and all sorts of extraordinary donations, the heirs received a chart kept up from generation to generation, and perfected by each generation, which facilitated the finding of the buried treasure.

Big Mama needed three hours to enumerate her earthly possessions. In the stifling bedroom, the voice of the dying woman seemed to dignify in its place each thing named. When she affixed her trembling signature, and the witnesses affixed theirs below, a secret tremor shook the hearts of the crowds which were beginning to gather in front of the house, in the shade of the dusty almond trees of the plaza.

The only thing lacking then was the detailed listing of her immaterial possessions. Making a supreme effort—the same kind that her forebears made before they died to assure the dominance of their line—Big Mama raised herself up on her monumental buttocks, and in a domineering and sincere voice, lost in her memories, dictated to the notary this list of her invisible estate:

The wealth of the subsoil, the territorial waters, the colors of the flag, national sovereignty, the traditional parties, the rights of man, civil rights, the nation's leadership, the right of appeal, Congressional hearings, letters of recommendation, historical records, free elections, beauty queens, transcendental speeches, huge demonstrations, distinguished young ladies, proper gentlemen, punctilious military men, His Illustrious Eminence, the Supreme Court, goods whose importation was forbidden, liberal ladies, the meat problem, the purity of the language, setting a good example, the free but responsible press, the Athens of South America, public opinion, the lessons of democracy, Christian morality, the shortage of foreign exchange, the right of asylum, the Communist menace, the ship of state, the high cost of living, republican traditions, the underprivileged classes, statements of political support.

She didn't manage to finish. The laborious enumeration cut off her last breath. Drowning in the pandemonium of abstract formulas which for two centuries had constituted the moral justification of the family's power, Big Mama emitted a loud belch and expired.

That afternoon the inhabitants of the distant and somber capital saw the picture of a twenty-year-old woman on the first page of the extra editions, and thought that it was a new beauty queen. Big Mama lived again the momentary youth of her photograph, enlarged to four columns and with needed retouching, her abundant hair caught up atop her skull with an ivory comb and a diadem on her lace collar. That image, captured by a street photographer who passed through Macondo at the beginning of the century, and kept in the newspaper's morgue for many years in the section of unidentified persons, was destined to endure in the memory of future generations. In the dilapidated buses, in the elevators at the Ministries, and in the dismal tearooms hung with pale decorations, people whispered with veneration and respect about the dead personage in her sultry, malarial region, whose name was unknown in the rest of the country a few hours before—before it had been sanctified by the printed word. A fine drizzle covered the passers-by with misgiving and mist. All the church bells tolled for the dead. The President of the Republic, taken by surprise by the news when on his way to the commencement exercises for the new cadets, suggested to the War Minister, in a note in his own hand on the back of the telegram, that he conclude his speech with a minute of silent homage to Big Mama.

The social order had been brushed by death. The President of the Republic himself, who was affected by urban feelings as if they reached him through a purifying filter, managed to perceive from his car in a momentary but to a certain extent brutal vision the silent consternation of the city. Only a few low cafés remained open; the Metropolitan Cathedral was readied for nine days of funeral rites. At the National Capitol, where the beggars wrapped in newspapers slept in the shelter of the Doric columns and the silent statues of dead Presidents, the lights of Congress were lit. When the President entered his office, moved by the vision of the capital in mourning, his Ministers were waiting for him dressed in funereal garb, standing, paler and more solemn than usual.

The events of that night and the following ones would later be identified as a historic lesson. Not only because of the Christian spirit which inspired the most lofty personages of public power, but also because of the abnegation with which dissimilar interests and conflicting judgments were conciliated in the common goal of burying the illustrious body. For many years Big Mama had guaranteed the social peace and political harmony of her empire, by virtue of the three trunks full of forged electoral certificates which formed part of her secret estate. The men in her service, her protégés and tenants, elder and younger, exercised not only their own rights of suffrage but also those of electors dead for a century. She exercised the priority of traditional power over transitory authority, the predominance of class over the common people, the transcendence of divine wisdom over human improvisation. In times of peace, her dominant will approved and disapproved canonries, benefices, and sinecures, and watched over the welfare of her associates, even if she had to resort to clandestine maneuvers or election fraud in order to obtain it. In troubled times, Big Mama contributed secretly for weapons for her partisans, but came to the aid of her victims in public. That patriotic zeal guaranteed the highest honors for her.

The President of the Republic had not needed to consult with his advisers in order to weigh the gravity of his responsibility. Between the Palace reception hall and the little paved patio which had served the viceroys as a *cochère,* there was an interior garden of dark cypresses where a Portuguese monk had hanged himself out of love in the last days of the Colony. Despite his noisy coterie of bemedaled officials, the President could not suppress a slight tremor of uncertainty when he passed that spot after dusk. But that night his trembling had the strength of a premonition. Then the full awareness of his historical destiny dawned on him, and he decreed nine days of national mourning, and posthumous honors for Big Mama at the rank befitting a heroine who had died for the fatherland on the field of battle. As he expressed it in the dramatic address which he delivered that morning to his compatriots over the national radio and television network, the Nation's Leader trusted that the funeral rites for Big Mama would set a new example for the world.

Such a noble aim was to collide nevertheless with certain grave inconveniences. The judicial structure of the country, built by remote ancestors of Big Mama, was not prepared for events such as those which began to occur. Wise Doctors of Law, certified alchemists of the statutes, plunged into hermeneutics and syllogisms in search of the formula which would permit the President of the Republic to attend the funeral. The upper strata of politics, the clergy, the financiers lived through entire days of alarm. In the vast semicircle of Congress, rarefied by a century of abstract legislation, amid oil paintings of National Heroes and busts of Greek thinkers, the vocation of Big Mama reached unheard-of proportions, while her body filled with bubbles in the harsh Macondo September. For the first time, people spoke of her and conceived of her without her rattan rocker, her afternoon stupors, and her mustard plasters, and they saw her ageless and pure, distilled by legend.

Interminable hours were filled with words, words, words, which resounded throughout the Republic, made prestigious by the spokesmen of the printed word.

Until, endowed with a sense of reality in that assembly of aseptic lawgivers, the historic blahblahblah was interrupted by the reminder that Big Mama's corpse awaited their decision at 104° in the shade. No one batted an eye in the face of that eruption of common sense in the pure atmosphere of the written law. Orders were issued to embalm the cadaver, while formulas were adduced, viewpoints were reconciled, or constitutional amendments were made to permit the President to attend the burial.

So much had been said that the discussions crossed the borders, traversed the ocean, and blew like an omen through the pontifical apartments at Castel Gandolfo. Recovered from the drowsiness of the torpid days of August, the Supreme Pontiff was at the window watching the lake where the divers were searching for the head of a decapitated young girl. For the last few weeks, the evening newspapers had been concerned with nothing else, and the Supreme Pontiff could not be indifferent to an enigma located such a short distance from his summer residence. But that evening, in an unforeseen substitution, the newspapers changed the photographs of the possible victims for that of one single twenty-year-old woman, marked off with black margins. "Big Mama," exclaimed the Supreme Pontiff, recognizing instantly the hazy daguerreotype which many years before had been offered to him on the occasion of his ascent to the Throne of Saint Peter. "Big Mama," exclaimed in chorus the members of the College of Cardinals in their private apartments, and for the third time in twenty centuries there was an hour of confusion, chagrin, and bustle in the limitless empire of Christendom, until the Supreme Pontiff was installed in his long black limousine en route to Big Mama's fantastic and far-off funeral.

The shining peach orchards were left behind, the Via Appia Antica with warm movie stars tanning on terraces without as yet having heard any news of the commotion, and then the somber promontory of Castel Sant' Angelo on the edge of the Tiber. At dusk the resonant pealing of St. Peter's Basilica mingled with the cracked tinklings of Macondo. Inside his stifling tent across the tangled reeds and the silent bogs which marked the boundary between the Roman Empire and the ranches of Big Mama, the Supreme Pontiff heard the uproar of the monkeys agitated all night long by the passing of the crowds. On his nocturnal itinerary, the canoe had been filled with bags of yucca, stalks of green bananas, and crates of chickens, and with men and women who abandoned their customary pursuits to try their luck at selling things at Big Mama's funeral. His Holiness suffered that night, for the first time in the history of the Church, from the fever of insomnia and the torment of the mosquitoes. But the marvelous dawn over the Great Old Woman's domains, the primeval vision of the balsam apple and the iguana, erased from his memory the suffering of his trip and compensated him for his sacrifice.

Nicanor had been awakened by three knocks at the door which announced the imminent arrival of His Holiness. Death had taken possession of the house. Inspired by successive and urgent Presidential addresses, by the feverish controversies which had been silenced but continued to be heard by means of conventional symbols, men and congregations the world over dropped everything and with their presence filled the dark hallways, the jammed passageways, the stifling attics; and those who arrived later climbed up on the low walls around the church, the palisades, vantage points, timberwork, and parapets, where they accommodated themselves as best they could. In the central hall, Big Mama's cadaver lay mummifying while it waited for the momentous decisions contained in a quivering mound of telegrams. Weakened by their weeping, the nine nephews sat the wake beside the body in an ecstasy of reciprocal surveillance.

And still the universe was to prolong the waiting for many more days. In the city-council hall, fitted out with four leather stools, a jug of purified water, and a burdock hammock, the Supreme Pontiff suffered from a perspiring insomnia, diverting himself by reading memorials and administrative orders in the lengthy, stifling nights. During the day, he distributed Italian candy to the children who approached to see him through the window, and lunched beneath the hibiscus arbor with Father Anthony Isabel, and occasionally with Nicanor. Thus he lived for interminable weeks and months which were protracted by the waiting and the heat, until the day Father Pastrana appeared with his drummer in the middle of the plaza and read the proclamation of the decision. It was declared that Public Order was disturbed, ratatatat, and that the President of the Republic, ratatatat, had in his power the extraordinary prerogatives, ratatatat, which permitted him to attend Big Mama's funeral, ratatatat, tatatat, tatat, tatat.

The great day had arrived. In the streets crowded with carts, hawkers of fried foods, and lottery stalls, and men with snakes wrapped around their necks who peddled a balm which would definitively cure erysipelas and guarantee eternal life; in the mottled little plaza where the crowds had set up their tents and unrolled their sleeping mats, dapper archers cleared the Authorities' way. There they were, awaiting the supreme moment: the washerwomen of San Jorge, the pearl fishers from Cabo de la Vela, the fishermen from Ciénaga, the shrimp fishermen from Tasajera, the sorcerers from Mojajara, the salt miners from Manaure, the accordionists from Valledupar, the fine horsemen of Ayapel, the ragtag musicians from San Pelayo, the cock breeders from La Cueva, the improvisers from Sábanas de Bolívar, the dandies from Rebolo, the oarsmen of the Magdalena, the shysters from Monpox, in addition to those enumerated at the beginning of this chronicle, and many others. Even the veterans of Colonel Aureliano Buendía's camp—the Duke of Marlborough at their head, with the pomp of his furs and tiger's claws and teeth—overcame their centenarian hatred of Big Mama and those of her line and came to the funeral to ask the President of the Republic for the payment of their veterans' pensions which they had been waiting for for sixty years.

A little before eleven the delirious crowd which was sweltering in the sun, held back by an imperturbable élite force of warriors decked out in embellished jackets and filigreed morions[1], emitted a powerful roar of jubilation. Dignified, solemn in their cutaways and top hats, the President of the Republic and his Ministers, the delegations from Parliament, the Supreme Court, the Council of State, the traditional parties and the clergy, and representatives of Banking,

---

1. Crested metal helmet, worn by soldiers in
   the Seventeenth- and Eighteenth-centuries.

Commerce, and Industry made their appearance around the corner of the telegraph office. Bald and chubby, the old and ailing President of the Republic paraded before the astonished eyes of the crowds who had seen him inaugurated without knowing who he was and who only now could give a true account of his existence. Among the archbishops enfeebled by the gravity of their ministry, and the military men with robust chests armored with medals, the Leader of the Nation exuded the unmistakable air of power.

In the second rank, in a serene array of mourning crêpe, paraded the national queens of all things that have been or ever will be. Stripped of their earthly splendor for the first time, they marched by, preceded by the universal queen: the soybean queen, the green-squash queen, the banana queen, the meal yucca queen, the guava queen, the coconut queen, the kidney-bean queen, the 255-mile-long-string-of-iguana-eggs queen, and all the others who are omitted so as not to make this account interminable.

In her coffin draped in purple, separated from reality by eight copper turnbuckles, Big Mama was at that moment too absorbed in her formaldehyde eternity to realize the magnitude of her grandeur. All the splendor which she had dreamed of on the balcony of her house during her heat-induced insomnia was fulfilled by those forty-eight glorious hours during which all the symbols of the age paid homage to her memory. The Supreme Pontiff himself, whom she in her delirium imagined floating above the gardens of the Vatican in a resplendent carriage, conquered the heat with a plaited palm fan, and honored with his Supreme Dignity the greatest funeral in the world.

Dazzled by the show of power, the common people did not discern the covetous bustling which occurred on the rooftree of the house when agreement was imposed on the town grandees' wrangling and the catafalque was taken into the street on the shoulders of the grandest of them all. No one saw the vigilant shadow of the buzzards which followed the cortege through the sweltering little streets of Macondo, nor did they notice that as the grandees passed they left a pestilential train of garbage in the street. No one noticed that the nephews, godchildren, servants, and protégés of Big Mama closed the doors as soon as the body was taken out, and dismantled the doors, pulled the nails out of the planks, and dug up the foundations to divide up the house. The only thing which was not missed by anyone amid the noise of that funeral was the thunderous sigh of relief which the crowd let loose when fourteen days of supplications, exaltations, and dithyrambs were over, and the tomb was sealed with a lead plinth. Some of those present were sufficiently aware as to understand that they were witnessing the birth of a new era. Now the Supreme Pontiff could ascend to Heaven in body and soul, his mission on earth fulfilled, and the President of the Republic could sit down and govern according to his good judgment, and the queens of all things that have been or ever will be could marry and be happy and conceive and give birth to many sons, and the common people could set up their tents where they damn well pleased in the limitless domains of Big Mama, because the only one who could oppose them *and had sufficient* power to do so had begun to rot *beneath a lead* plinth. The only thing left then was for someone to lean a stool against the doorway to tell this story, lesson and example for future generations, so that not one of the world's disbelievers would be left who did not know the story of Big Mama, because tomorrow, Wednesday, the garbage men will come and will sweep up the garbage from her funeral, forever and ever.

ISABEL FRAIRE (b. 1934)
Mexico

After studying philosophy at the National University in Mexico City, Isabel Fraire began to publish poems, reviews, and articles of criticism, and became a member of the editorial board of the *Revista Mexicana de literatura*. She has translated English language poetry, including that of Ezra Pound, into Spanish, and her own works have been translated into English: *Fifteen Poems of Isabel Fraire* (1959) and *Only This Light* (1969). The power of the poem included here is derived from its combination of surrealist imagery and a pseudological framework: "If . . . then. . . ."

[If night takes the form of a whale]

if night takes the form of a whale and
    devours everything obliterating the image from memory
and you fall in time losing even
    the track of your name
  leaving in space traces   5
    of shadow over shadow
eyeless night keeps silent
    silence without hearing
it is only an enormous scar
and everything insists on persistent movement   10
    useless withered leaves
      in a blind well

then
a sequence of nothingness
the end and beginning   15
are tied and untied by absent-minded fingers
    I spin and spin toward my death
    and I desire nothing
dreams have been erased from my eyes
    the world from my hands   20

Translated by Thomas Hoeksema.

balancing on a stain of earth
seizing my death in a root

I write
    night takes the form of a whale
        that devours everything
           endlessly

25

ESTEBAN MONTEJO (1858?–1966), MIGUEL BARNET (b. 1940)
Cuba

Esteban Montejo was born under slavery and lived through all the events that make up Cuba's history up to the revolution of 1959 and beyond. Montejo, who had a reputation for storytelling and who at 105 would not live much longer, was sought out by anthropologist Miguel Barnet. Barnet wanted to record that history "from within and below," to "fill in certain gaps" through ethnography, as he says in his introduction. He also says that "Esteban became the real author of this book," for he "forced me to write down everything he said" and it is his vision of the world—that of a black plantation worker—that comes through. Montejo's view of the world and his storytelling style belong in literary history, for it is from such a base that some of Latin America's greatest literature, particularly the works of marvelous realism, has emerged.

Miguel Barnet, trained as an anthropologist, has sought to get beyond the limitations of, on the one hand, scientifically informed ethnography and, on the other, the fictionalized documentary novel. Barnet adopted the recording methods employed in *Children of Sanchez* by the American "anthropologist of poverty" Oscar Lewis (1914–1970) but crafted Montejo's materials as if he were writing a novel. Barnet does not impose a sociological plan on the exposition of events; instead he works as a medium for Montejo's own style and world view. In other words, as he says in his introduction, he "paraphrases a good deal of what was told [to him]," for a word-for-word transcription "would have been confusing and repetitive." Barnet "kept the story within fixed time-limits, not being concerned to recreate the period in minute detail of time and place." He coined the term "testimonial novel" for this new hybrid genre that made it possible for nonprofessionals to have access to a larger cultural public sphere. (Testimonial writing, or *testimonio* as it is commonly known in Spanish, was officially recognized in 1971 as a genre by the Casa de las Americas, an institute in Havana that awards an annual literary prize to the best *testimonio*.) Barnet has written three other testimonial novels: *Song of Rachel* (1967), *The Galician* (1983), and [*La vida real,*] *Real Life,* the last of which attempts to offer a more authentic or real "Vida" than Oscar Lewis's eponymous book.

from *The Autobiography of a Runaway Slave*

[Ma Lucía, the great storyteller]

What the old men enjoyed most was telling jokes and stories. They told stories all the time, morning, noon and night, they were at it constantly. There were so many stories that it was often difficult to keep track of them, you go so muddled up. I always pretended to be listening, but to be honest, by the end it was all whirling round in my head. There were three or four African elders at Ariosa. There was a difference between the Africans and the Creoles. The various Africans understood each other, but the Creoles hardly ever understood the Africans. They used to listen to them singing, but they didn't understand them. I got on all right with them because I spent my whole life listening to them. They were fond of me, too.

I still remember Ma Lucía. I first met her outside Ariosa, I don't recall whether it was at Remedios or Zulueta, but in any case I met her again long afterwards at Santa Clara, when I went there to a fiesta. I got on well with Ma Lucía. She was a black-skinned Negress, rather tall, a Lucumi by birth. After I got to know her she devoted most of her time to *santería*. She had a big collection of godchildren, being so well-known. Ma Lucía was a great story-teller. She spent hours ironing her clothes, her white costume and cambric blouse, out of vanity, and she wore her hair in a piled-up style which you never see nowadays. She said it was African. She made sweets and *amalá*[1] which she sold in the streets and in the plantation town when she did the rounds, and she made a lot of money.

She finally bought herself a house in Santa Clara after the war, which she left to a daughter. One day she called me and said, "You're a good, quiet man, I'm going to tell you something," and she began telling me all sorts of African stories. Unfortunately, almost all the stories and things I hear get muddled in my memory, and I don't know whether I'm talking about an elephant or a mouse. Old age does this to you. There are some things I remember clearly, but old age is old age, and it isn't given you for pleasure.

The point is, Ma Lucía started telling me about African customs which I never saw here, and nor did she either, which is why they were in her memory. She told me that in her country all the men ever did was fell trees, while the women had to clear the ground and bring in the food, and then cook meals for the family, which was very big. She said her own family was bigger than a slave settlement. I suppose this is because in Africa women give birth every year. I once saw a photograph of Africa, and all the women had swollen bellies and bare tits. I don't recall seeing such a spectacle in Cuba. Certainly it was quite different in the barracoons—the women there wore layers of clothes and covered their breasts. Well, not to wander too far from Ma Lucía, what she said about the elephants was very strange; whenever she saw one of those circuses which went from village to village, with elephants and monkeys, she would say, "Look, Creole, you don't

Translated by Jocasta Innes.

---

1. Corn-flour with pork.

know what an elephant is! Those aren't elephants you see in the circus, elephants in my country are much higher, high as a palm-tree heart." I was struck dumb. It really did seem a bit much to me, especially when she went on to say that in her country elephants weighed five or six hundred pounds. We boys couldn't help laughing at that, though we didn't let on to her. A lot of her stories were lies, but some might have been true. Well, let's say I thought they were lies, though the others thought they were the truth. Heaven help anyone who tried to tell one of those old women she was wrong!

I remember the story of the tortoise and the toad; she must have told it to me a hundred times. The tortoise and the toad had this big feud going for years, and the toad used to deceive the tortoise because he was frightened of her and thought she was stronger than him. One day the toad got hold of a big bowl of food and presented it to the tortoise, setting it down right under her nose, almost in her mouth. When the tortoise saw the bowl she took a fancy to it and gobbled it so fast she choked. It never even crossed her mind that the toad had put it there for a reason. She was very simple-minded, and so it was easy to trick her. After that, feeling full and satisfied, she started wandering through the forest in search of the toad, who had hidden himself in a cave. When the toad saw her in the distance, he called out, "Here I am, tortoise, look." She looked but couldn't see him, and after a while she got tired and went away till she came across a heap of dry straw and lay down to sleep. The toad seized her while she was asleep and poisoned her by peeing over her, and she didn't even wake up because she had eaten so heavily. The moral of this story is that people shouldn't be greedy, and you should trust no one. An enemy might offer you a meal merely to trick you.

Ma Lucía went on telling me about the toad. She was afraid of toads because, she said, they had a fatal poison in their veins instead of blood. The proof of this is that when you harm one by hitting it with a stick or a stone, it will follow you and poison you through the mouth or the nose, usually the mouth, because nearly everyone sleeps with their mouth open.

She told me that tigers were treacherous animals who climbed trees so as to be able to spring down on to men's backs and kill them. But they would seize women by their parts and force them to do dirty things with them, like the orang-outangs. But the orang-outangs were worse. According to Ma Lucía an orang-outang could tell a woman by her smell and capture her quite easily, so she couldn't even move. All monkeys are like that, like men with tails, but dumb.

Monkeys often fall in love with women. There have been cases like this in Cuba. I heard of two women of rich families who slept with monkeys, two sisters. One of them came from Santa Clara. I don't remember much about the other one, but she must have had children, because I saw monkeys lording it about in her house. I had to go along there one day, I can't remember why, and there was this monkey sitting in a chair in the doorway. That's why I think that the elders were sometimes speaking the truth—it was just that we had not seen these things for ourselves, so we either disbelieved them or laughed at them. Today, after so many years, I find myself thinking about all this again, and to tell the truth, I am coming to the conclusion that the African was a wise man in all matters. Some people say they were no better than monkeys off the trees—there's always some bloody white going round saying things like that—but having known them, I think differently. They weren't the least bit like animals. They taught me many things without being able to read or write—customs, which are more important than knowledge: to be polite, not to meddle in other people's affairs, to speak softly, to be respectful and religious, to work hard. They used to say, "Water falls on the arum plant but it never gets wet," which was a warning to me not to get involved in arguments. They advised me to listen and take note so as to be able to stick up for myself, but not to talk too much. A person who talks too much ties himself in knots. Lots of people put their foot in it simply because they let their tongues run away with them.

ROSARIO FERRÉ (b. 1942)
Puerto Rico

Rosario Ferré has been a student and critic of literature since the time of her undergraduate and graduate studies in Puerto Rico and the United States. She began her own literary career in the 1970s as editor of the magazine *Zona de carga,* in which her first story, "The Youngest Doll," included here, was published and later included in the volume *Pandora's Papers,* (1976). She has also published a book of poetry, *Fables of the Bled Heron,* (1982) several collections of essays, among them *Eros Besieged,* (1980) and *Colloquy of the Bitches,* (1990), a novel, *Damned Love,* (1986) and literary criticism and children's stories.

Brought up in an upper-class family, Ferré's work has largely been a critique of traditional cultural myths and taboos, especially those pertaining to women. "The Youngest Doll" is about the women of an impoverished but aristocratic landowning family. As the daughters are married off, an old spinster aunt, with a peculiar leg wound, makes dolls in their image. When the youngest of the girls marries an exploitative physician seeking to raise his social standing, the doll replaces her and takes revenge on her behalf for her husband's abuse. The doll also takes revenge on behalf of the aunt. It was her wound that enabled the young physician's father to make a fortune in the first place; since he never cured her, he could go on charging her for his services.

from *Pandora's Papers*

The Youngest Doll

Early in the morning the maiden aunt took her rocking chair out onto the porch facing the cane fields, as she always did whenever she woke up with the urge to make a doll. As a young woman, she had often bathed in the river, but one day when

Translated by Diana Vélez and Rosario Ferré.

Frida Kahlo. *Self-Portrait with Thorn Necklace and Humming-bird*. 1940. University of Texas at Austin.

the heavy rains had fed the dragontail current, she had a soft feeling of melting snow in the marrow of her bones. With her head nestled among the black rocks' reverberations, she could hear the slamming of salty foam on the beach rolled up with the sound of waves, and she suddenly thought that her hair had poured out to sea at last. At that very moment, she felt a sharp bite in her calf. Screaming, she was pulled out of the water and, writhing in pain, was taken home on a stretcher.

The doctor who examined her assured her it was nothing, that she had probably been bitten by an angry river prawn. But days passed and the scab wouldn't heal. A month later the doctor concluded that the prawn had worked its way into the soft flesh of her calf and had nestled there to grow. He prescribed a mustard plaster so that the heat would force it out. The aunt spent a whole week with her leg covered with mustard from thigh to ankle, but when the treatment was over, they found that the ulcer had grown even larger and that it was covered with a slimy, stonelike substance that couldn't be removed without endangering the whole leg. She then resigned herself to living with the prawn permanently curled up in her calf.

She had been very beautiful, but the prawn hidden under the long, gauzy folds of her skirt stripped her of all vanity. She locked herself up in her house, refusing to see any suitors. At first she devoted herself entirely to bringing up her sister's children, dragging her enormous leg around the house quite nimbly. In those days, the family was nearly ruined; they lived surrounded by a past that was breaking up around them with the same impassive musicality with which the dining room chandelier crumbled on the frayed linen cloth of the dining room table. Her nieces adored her. She would comb their hair, bathe and feed them, and

Frida Kahlo. *Self-Portrait with Cropped Hair.* 1940. Oil on canvas. Museum of Modern Art, New York.

when she read them stories, they would sit around her and furtively lift the starched ruffle of her skirt so as to sniff the aroma of ripe sweetsop that oozed from her leg when it was at rest.

As the girls grew up, the aunt devoted herself to making dolls for them to play with. At first they were just plain dolls, with cotton stuffing from the gourd tree and stray buttons sewn on for eyes. As time passed, though, she began to refine her craft, gaining the respect and admiration of the whole family. The birth of a doll was always cause for a ritual celebration, which explains why it never occurred to the aunt to sell them for profit, even when the girls had grown up and the family was beginning to fall into need. The aunt had continued to increase the size of the dolls so that their height and other measurements conformed to those of each of the girls. There were nine of them, and the aunt made one doll for each per year, so it became necessary to set aside a room for the dolls alone. When the eldest turned eighteen there were one hundred and twenty-six dolls of all ages in the room. Opening the door gave the impression of entering a dovecote, or the ballroom in the Czarina's palace, or a warehouse in which someone had spread out a row of tobacco leaves to dry. But the aunt did not enter the room for any of these pleasures. Instead, she would unlatch the door and gently pick up each doll, murmuring a lullaby as she rocked it: "This is how you were when you were a year old, this is you at two, and like this at three," measuring out each year of their lives against the hollow they left in her arms.

The day the eldest had turned ten, the aunt sat down in her rocking chair facing the cane fields and never got up again. She would rock away entire days on the porch, watching the patterns of rain shift in the cane fields, coming out of her stupor only when the doctor paid a visit or whenever she awoke with the desire to make a doll. Then she would call out so that everyone in the house would come and help her. On that day, one could see the hired help making repeated trips to town like cheerful Inca messengers, bringing wax, porcelain clay, lace, needles, spools of thread of every color. While these preparations were taking place, the aunt would call the niece she had dreamt about the night before into her room and take her measurements. Then she would make a wax mask of the child's face, covering it with plaster on both sides, like a living face wrapped in two dead ones. She would draw out an endless flaxen thread of melted wax through a pinpoint on its chin. The porcelain of the hands and face was always translucent; it had an ivory tint to it that formed a great contrast with the curled whiteness of the bisque faces. For the body, the aunt would send out to the garden for twenty glossy gourds. She would hold them in one hand, and with an expert twist of her knife, would slice them up against the railing of the balcony, so that the sun and breeze would dry out the cottony *guano* brains. After a few days, she would scrape off the dried fluff with a teaspoon and, with infinite patience, feed it into the doll's mouth.

The only items the aunt would agree to use that were not made by her were the glass eyeballs. They were mailed to her from Europe in all colors, but the aunt considered them useless until she had left them submerged at the bottom of the stream for a few days, so that they could learn to recognize the slightest stirring of the prawns' antennae. Only then would she carefully rinse them in ammonia water and place them, glossy as gems and nestled in a bed of cotton, at the bottom of one of her Dutch cookie tins. The dolls were always dressed in the same way, even though the girls were growing up. She would dress the younger ones in Swiss embroidery and the older ones in silk *guipure*, and on each of their heads she would tie the same bow, wide and white and trembling like the breast of a dove.

The girls began to marry and leave home. On their wedding day, the aunt would give each of them their last doll, kissing them on the forehead and telling them with a smile, "Here is your Easter Sunday." She would reassure the grooms by explaining to them that the doll was merely a sentimental ornament, of the kind that people used to place on the lid of grand pianos in the old days. From the porch, the aunt would watch the girls walk down the staircase for the last time. They would carry a modest checkered cardboard suitcase in one hand, the other hand slipped around the waist of the exuberant doll made in their image and likeness, still wearing the same old-fashioned kid slippers and gloves, and with Valenciennes bloomers barely showing under their snowy, embroidered skirts. But the hands and faces of these new dolls looked less transparent than those of the old: they had the consistency of skim milk. This difference concealed a more subtle one: the wedding doll was never stuffed with cotton but filled with honey.

All the older girls had married and only the youngest was left at home when the doctor paid his monthly visit to the aunt, bringing along his son who had just returned from studying medicine up north. The young man lifted the starched ruffle of the aunt's skirt and looked intently at the huge, swollen ulcer which oozed a perfumed sperm from the tip of its greenish scales. He pulled out his stethoscope and listened to her carefully. The aunt thought he was listening for the breathing of the prawn to see if it was still alive, and she fondly lifted his hand and placed it on the spot where he could feel the constant movement of the creature's antennae. The young man released the ruffle and looked fixedly at his father. "You could have cured this from the start," he told him. "That's true," his father answered, "but I just wanted you to come and see the prawn that has been paying for your education these twenty years."

From then on it was the young doctor who visited the old aunt every month. His interest in the youngest was evident from the start, so the aunt was able to begin her last doll in plenty of time. He would always show up wearing a pair of brightly polished shoes, a starched collar, and an ostentatious tiepin of extravagantly poor taste. After examining the aunt, he would sit in the parlor, lean his paper silhouette against the oval frame of the chair and, each time, hand the youngest an identical bouquet of purple forget-me-nots. She would offer him ginger cookies, taking the bouquet squeamishly with the tips of her fingers as if she were handling a sea urchin turned inside out. She made up her mind to marry him because she was intrigued by his sleepy profile and also because she was deathly curious to see what the dolphin flesh was like.

On her wedding day, as she was about to leave the house, the youngest was surprised to find that the doll her aunt had given her as a wedding present was warm. As she slipped her arm around its waist, she looked at it curiously, but she quickly forgot about it, so amazed was she at the excellence of its craft. The doll's face and hands were made of the most delicate Mikado porcelain. In the doll's half-open and slightly sad smile, she recognized her full set of baby teeth. There was also another notable detail: the aunt had embedded her diamond eardrops inside the doll's pupils.

The young doctor took her on to live in town, in a square house that made one think of a cement block. Each day he made her sit out on the balcony, so that passersby would be sure to see that he had married into high society. Motionless inside her cubicle of heat, the youngest began to suspect that it wasn't only her husband's silhouette that was made of paper, but his soul as well. Her suspicions were soon confirmed. One day, he pried out the doll's eyes with a tip of his scalpel and pawned them for a fancy gold pocket watch with a long embossed chain. From then on the doll remained seated on the lid of the grand piano, but with her gaze modestly lowered.

A few months later, the doctor noticed the doll was missing from her usual place and asked the youngest what she'd done with it. A sisterhood of pious ladies had offered him a healthy sum for the porcelain hands and face, which they thought would be perfect for the image of the Veronica in the next Lenten procession. The youngest answered that the ants had at last discovered the doll was filled with honey and, streaming over the piano, had devoured it in a single night. "Since its hands and face were of Mikado porcelain," she said, "they must have thought they were made of sugar and at this very moment they are most likely wearing down their teeth, gnawing furiously at its fingers and eyelids in some underground burrow." That night the doctor dug up all the ground around the house, to no avail.

As the years passed, the doctor became a millionaire. He had slowly acquired the whole town as his clientele, people who didn't mind paying exorbitant fees in order to see a genuine member of the extinct sugar cane aristocracy up close. The youngest went on sitting in her rocking chair on the balcony, motionless in her muslin and lace, and always with lowered eyelids. Whenever her husband's patients, draped with necklaces and feathers and carrying elaborate canes, would seat themselves beside her, shaking their self-satisfied rolls of flesh with a jingling of coins, they would notice a strange scent that would involuntarily remind them of a slowly oozing sweetsop. They would then feel an uncomfortable urge to rub their hand together as though they were paws.

There was only one thing missing from the doctor's otherwise perfect happiness. He noticed that although he was aging, the youngest still kept that same firm porcelained skin she had had when he would call on her at the big house on the plantation. One night he decided to go into her bedroom to watch her as she slept. He noticed that her chest wasn't moving. He gently placed his stethoscope over her heart and heard a distant swish of water. Then the doll lifted her eyelids, and out of the empty sockets of her eyes came the frenzied antennae of all those prawns.

RIGOBERTA MENCHÚ (b. 1961)
Guatemala

Rigoberta Menchú is a human rights activist in Guatemala, who won the Nobel Peace Prize in 1992. Although organized and edited like Esteban Montejo's *testimonio, I . . . Rigoberta Menchú. An Indian Woman in Guatemala* was not crafted as a novel by the social scientist Elisabeth Burgos-Debray. Two points of comparison and contrast can be made with the Montejo-Barnet collaboration. First, Menchú, like Montejo, became the "author" of the book, but she also went beyond Montejo in prompting the transcriber to tell things in a way that conveyed her very specific political vision. Second, the book does not aim to fill in the gaps in Guatemala's history but, rather, to persuade the reader to intervene politically and economically in the future of the country. The book was not written for a national audience but for the international community interested in this future and others like it. It is similar in purpose (but certainly not vision), then, to one of the founding texts of nineteenth century post-independence Latin American literature: the Argentinian Domingo Faustino Sarmiento's *Facundo* (1845), written in opposition to the dictatorship of Juan Manuel de Rosas. The book, however, is much richer than its immediate purpose; it is politically motivated but it also conveys alternative vision to that of the dominant classes of Guatemala and of professional writers. This vision includes, for example, the religious nature of Indian life, the ceremonies that accompany birth, and the progressive initiation of children into the history of the group, its ancestors, and their *nahual* or "spirit double," the being correspondent to their material one. Mayan cosmology as presented by Menchú sees humankind as integral to nature, although this is not a static relation since it adapts to historical circumstances. The fact that Mayan culture is based on a dialogical relationship with earth and

have on Earth. But as Christians, we have understood that being a Christian means refusing to accept all the injustices which are committed against our people, refusing to accept the discrimination committed against a humble people who barely know what eating meat is but who are treated worse than horses. We've learned all this by watching what has happened in our lives. This awakening of the Indians didn't come, of course, from one day to the next, because Catholic Action and other religions and the system itself have all tried to keep us where we were. But I think that unless a religion springs from within the people themselves, it is a weapon of the system. So, naturally, it wasn't at all difficult for our community to understand all this and the reasons for us to defend ourselves, because this is the reality we live.

As I was saying, for us the Bible is our main weapon. It has shown us the way. Perhaps those who call themselves Christians but who are really only Christians in theory, won't understand why we give the Bible the meaning we do. But that's because they haven't lived as we have. And also perhaps because they can't analyse it. I can assure you that any one of my community, even though he's illiterate and has to have it read to him and translated into his language, can learn many lessons from it, because he has no difficulty understanding what reality is and what the difference is between the paradise up above, in Heaven, and the reality of our people here on Earth. We do this because we feel it is the duty of Christians to create the kingdom of God on Earth among our brothers. This kingdom will exist only when we all have enough to eat, when our children, brothers, parents don't have to die from hunger and malnutrition. That will be the "Glory," a Kingdom for we who have never known it. I'm only talking about the Catholic church in general terms because, in fact, many priests came to our region and were anti-communists, but nevertheless understood that the people weren't communists but hungry; not communists, but exploited by the system. And they joined our people's struggle too, they opted for the life we Indians live. Of course many priests call themselves Christians when they're only defending their own petty interests and they keep themselves apart from the people so as not to endanger these interests. All the better for us, because we know very well that we don't need a king in a palace but a brother who lives with us. We don't need a leader to show us where God is, to say whether he exists or not, because, through our own conception of God, we know there is a God and that, as the father of us all, he does not wish even one of his children to die, or be unhappy, or have no joy in life. We believe that, when we started using the Bible, when we began studying it in terms of our reality, it was because we found in it a document to guide us. It's not that the document itself brings about the change, it's more that each one of us learns to understand his reality and wants to devote himself to others. More than anything else, it was a form of learning for us. Perhaps if we'd had other means to learn, things would have been different. But we understood that any element in nature can change man when he is ready for change. We believe the Bible is a necessary weapon for our people. Today I can say that it is a struggle which cannot be stopped. Neither the governments nor imperialism can stop it because it is a struggle of hunger and poverty. Neither the government nor imperialism can say: "Don't be hungry," when we are all dying of hunger.

natural or oral inspiration by male writers in her own society, it is only within the last twenty-five or so years that women have begun to produce written literature on an important scale in the French Caribbean. Almost thirty-five years separate Schwarz-Bart's novel and Césaire's great poem, during which time the former French colonies gained in 1946 the ambiguous status of "departments," something like new states, with their residents having all the rights and privileges of French citizens. Once a certain civic status was guaranteed, other issues of identity began to surface. One of these issues was bilingualism. If Césaire's goal was to inflect the French language so that it would reflect his *"moi-nègre,"* if his method was to use all the classical learning at his disposal to insert subversively the flora and fauna of his native land in their most esoteric nomenclature, Schwarz-Bart seems to be coming at literary bilingualism from another angle. Since one of the other keystones of colonial policy was to devalue native languages—Creole in the Antilles, dialectal Arabic, local patois, and tribal languages in the Maghreb—in favor of the universal language that was French, the problem of writing in French for the colonized subject was obviously a complex one. Is writing in the other's language not, by definition, an alienated gesture? In the case of Schwarz-Bart, the ease with which her narrator and the *"petit peuple,"* the rural peasantry who populate her novel, express their natural folk wisdom and oral culture has to do with the author's Creolization of French. Without much lexical intervention of actual Creole vocabulary into the French, she has translated turns of phrase—particularly proverbs, sayings, and dictums—often maintaining Creole syntax, so that we actually seem to "hear" the Creole through the French. The novel's unique language accounts in part for its great success and charm, and confers upon it an authenticity that has not been degraded into mere folkloric nostalgia for a lost culture. Schwarz-Bart prefigured the current cultural movement in the French Caribbean by defining its "Creolity."

Historical Background

The history of the Caribbean cannot be considered apart from its geographical situation in the heart of the Caribbean Sea, its discovery and annexation by various colonial powers from 1492 onward, and a complex demographic canvas in which various races, cultures, and classes have become inseparable. The long history of colonization and subsequent partitioning by the Spanish, French, Dutch, British, and Danish that followed Columbus's discovery of the New World has to be set against another history: the virtual disappearance of the three principal pre-Columbian Indian groups—the Ciboney, the Carib, and the Arawak—under the strains of European slavery, disease, and cultural shock.

What we refer to as the Caribbean is actually an island chain that extends for over 2,000 miles from Cuba to the northern coast of South America and to countries on the Central and South American mainlands—Belize, Guyana, Suriname, and French Guiana. The archipelago branches into the Lesser and Greater Antilles, with the latter containing Cuba, Jamaica, Haiti, the Dominican Republic, and Puerto Rico. The Lesser Antilles, a double arc of islands, begins to the east and the south of the Virgin Islands and stretches from Saint Kitts to Grenada, with the outer arc running from Anguilla to Barbados. Scattered on the edges of the Greater and Lesser Antilles are the Bahamas, Trinidad, and Tobago, as well as numerous smaller islands.

Not surprisingly, these islands have proved fertile grounds for an intricate amalgam of races[2], cultures, and class divisions. Although blacks, whites, and mulattoes are found in roughly equal numbers throughout the West Indies, ethnic breakdown varies widely from island to island. Although many have a predominantly — but not necessarily a majority — black population, in some areas such as Cuba and Puerto Rico, whites make up 70 percent of the population, and in others, such as the Dominican Republic, mulattoes comprise 75 percent of the population.

Such diversity has produced cultures in which inherited colonial tongues compete against native languages, and where it is not unusual to find more than one language spoken in a single household. In addition to languages such as English, French, Spanish, and Dutch, a number of non-European immigrants have brought other languages into the amalgam, the most prominent ones being Chinese, Urdu, and Hindi. Equally important has been the development of Creole variants of the various European languages. Many of these languages have become the common spoken language of the people. In Aruba, Papiamento, a Spanish-Portuguese-Dutch-English Creole is spoken. English Creole has flowered in the former British colonies, particularly in Jamaica where Creole often weaves in and out with standard English in novels, poems, and plays and on radio broadcasts, and the "Creole movement" in the French Caribbean is standardizing the written language so that it is taught in the schools and used in all forms of cultural production. Nonetheless, in many instances, standard English or French is still a class marker that communicates not only one's education, but ultimately one's social status.

The history of resistance to colonialism goes back as far as the sixteenth and seventeenth centuries, but the first successful revolution against colonial rule began in 1791 in Haiti, when slaves, after a series of rebellions, successfully revolted against the French. By 1794, the French were forced to abolish slavery in order to maintain control, and by 1804, after years of bloody rebellion, the former colony of Saint-Domingue gained its independence. Haiti, as the new country was known, was the first black republic in the Americas. By 1807 Britain had abolished the slave trade and then granted full emancipation in 1838, with the Dutch following suit in 1863. While such changes were taking place, Cuba, on the other hand, was cultivating its sugar trade around a slave-plantation system and full emancipation did not arrive in Cuba until 1886.

Somewhat surprisingly, emancipation did not bring about an end to inequality and ultimately posed less of a threat to the existing social order than slave owners at first feared. Nevertheless, emancipated slaves were allowed to migrate, market their labor, squat on other's lands, and buy property. In Haiti, Jamaica, and the Windward Islands especially, a new and reconstituted peasant force began taking shape. But because the most arable land was already confined to plantations, many of the emancipated were forced to remain as plantation workers or else migrate to Central America or the United States. The result was, then, largely a continuation of the plantation system, overseen by the white colonial powers, and systematically working to suppress democracy and economic and racial equality. The region's demographic complexity and the various

---

2. Definitions and concepts of race vary from place to place throughout the region. Labels such as black, white, and mulatto are used differently across different areas.

socia hierarchies erected around race have been added to, at various times, by the influx of Chinese indentured immigration to Cuba, East Indian immigration to Trinidad and Jamaica, as well as the arrival of Portuguese, Syrian, and Lebanese populations.

The single most important factor in the changing status of the people of the Caribbean was not emancipation but decolonization. By World War II, most West Indian islands had begun decolonization in one way or another, with some islands incorporated by the colonial powers as was the case with the French Antilles; and, with some islands more or less loosely associated with the colonial powers as was the case with the Dutch Antilles. Nevertheless, the end of World War II in 1945 saw only three West Indian states with full independence—Haiti, the Dominican Republic, and Cuba—and these countries, moreover, were on the brink of dictatorship. A number of the islands under British rule—Montserrat, Anguilla, the British Virgin Islands, the Cayman Islands—have remained dependencies and have expressed little desire to attain full independence.

Despite decolonization, full sovereignty for much of the Caribbean has been hard to achieve, with much of the region still dependent on foreign countries for capital and technology, as well as effective transport for Caribbean export products such as petroleum, sugar, and iron ore. Divestiture of Caribbean holdings by a number of European firms has led in some places to increasing local control of the economy, and the general program of a period of decolonization carried out in the region has sometimes led to the implementation of largely democratic governments in which the people of the Caribbean have played an increasingly important political and social role.

Further Readings

Arnold, A. James. *Modernism and Négritude: The Poetry and Poetics of Aimé Césaire.* Cambridge: Harvard University Press, 1981.

Baugh, Edward, ed. *Critics on Caribbean Literature.* New York: St. Martin's Press, 1978.

Brown, Lloyd. *West Indian Poetry.* London: Heinemann, 1984.

Clarke, Sebastian. *Jah Music: The Evolution of Popular Jamaican Song.* London: Heinemann, 1980.

Cudjoe, Selwyn, ed. *Caribbean Women Writers.* Wellesley, Mass: Calaloux and University of Massachusetts Press, 1990.

Dance, Daryl Cumber, ed. *Fifty Caribbean Writers: A Bio-Bibliographical Critical Sourcebook.* Westport, Conn: Greenwood Press, 1986.

Dash, J. M. *Literature and Ideology in Haiti 1915–1961.* Totowa: Barnes, 1981.

———. *Haiti and the United States: National Stereotypes and the Literary Imagination.* New York: St. Martin's Press, 1988.

Davies, Carol Boyce, and Elaine Savory Fido, eds. *Out of the Kumbla: Caribbean Women and Literature.* Trenton, NJ: Africa World Press, 1990.

Fanon, Frantz. *Black Skin, White Masks.* New York: Grove Press, 1967.

Glissant, Edouard. *Discourse: Selected Essays.* Charlottesville: University Press of Virginia, 1989.

James, C. L. R. *The Black Jacobins.* New York: Vintage, 1963.

King, Bruce, ed. *West Indian Literature.* London: Macmillan, 1979.

Knight, Franklin W., and Colin A. Palmer. *The Modern Caribbean*. Chapel Hill: University of North Carolina Press, 1989.

Ramchand, Kenneth. *The West Indian Novel and Its Background*. 2nd. ed. London: Heinemann, 1983.

Rigaud, Milo. *Secrets of Voodoo*. San Francisco: City Lights Books, 1985.

Roberts, Peter A. *West Indians and Their Language*. Cambridge: Cambridge University Press, 1988.

Scharfman, Ronnie. *Engagement and the Language of the Subject in the Poetry of Aimé Césaire*. Gainesville: University of Florida Press, 1987.

Sunshine, Catherine A. *The Caribbean: Survival, Struggle and Sovereignty*. Boston: Epica/South End Press, 1988.

Trouillot, Michel-Rolph. *Haiti: State Against Nation*. New York: Monthly Review Press, 1990.

AIMÉ CÉSAIRE (b. 1913)
Martinique; French

Aimé Césaire's now classic poem, *Notebook of a Return to the Native Land,* first appeared in an obscure journal in Paris in 1939, on the eve of the young poet's return to Martinique after his student years at France's prestigious École Normale Supérieure. In it the poet confronts the racial alienation of the colonized Black Antillean from a personal and collective point of view. In a dizzyingly dramatic style that, contrasting verse and prose, both echoes and transforms the late nineteenth-century French poetic heritage of Rimbaud and Lautréamont, Césaire deepens his exploration of the suffering of an entire community, which he figures as impoverished and humiliated, by going back into its past history until he reaches the unhealable wound of slavery. The past remembered and articulated can then be surpassed and a new identity, which Césaire calls "négritude," achieved. Dense with the rage of revolt and the hope of humanism, Césaire's poetic project led to political engagement. Since 1945 he has held the dual posts of mayor of Fort-de-France, the Martiniqan capital, and representative from Martinique to the French National Assembly.

The passages included here from the poem stage a kind of descent into hell for the poet who seeks to be the spokesman of his people but must first throw off his grandiosity in order to accept the painful, shameful reality of the black Antillean's poverty, misery, and passivity, all residues of his slave past. Taking inventory of the suffering and oppression around him, he comes to terms with all the wretched of the earth, understanding his identification with those children of slaves the world over. The poetic resurrection of Toussant L'Ouverture, the hero of the 1791 Haitian uprising, constitutes a first step toward giving positive value to that traumatic past. Accepting his solidarity with, rather than his alienation from, his people, allows the poetic voice of the poem to articulate a definition of *négritude*—a dynamic concept, rooted in emphasizing the values of community and living in harmony with the cosmos. This is opposed to the technological advances of the colonizing Europeans, whose inventions only serve the destructive ends of domination and exploitation.

Finally, reconciled with self and world, the poet prays for the strength to construct, to create, to represent his people, and to transcend racial hatred toward universal justice. These themes are a constant throughout Césaire's career as poet, essayist, playwright, and even statesman. We see two different stagings of these issues in the poems "Lost Body" and "Seism."

from *Notebook of a Return to the Native Land*

[Descent into Hell]

To go away. My heart was pounding with emphatic generosities. To go away . . . I would arrive sleek and young in this land of mine and I would say to this land

Translated by Clayton Eshleman and Annette Smith.

whose loam is part of my flesh: "I have wandered for a long time and I am coming back to the deserted hideousness of your sores."

I would go to this land of mine and I would say to it: "Embrace me without fear. . . . And if all I can do is speak, it is for you I shall speak."

And again I would say:

"My mouth shall be the mouth of those calamities that have no mouth, my voice the freedom of those who break down in the solitary confinement of despair."

And on the way I would say to myself:

"And above all, my body as well as my soul, beware of assuming the sterile attitude of a spectator, for life is not a spectacle, a sea of miseries is not a proscenium, a man screaming is not a dancing bear . . ."

And behold here I am!

Once again this life hobbling before me, what am I saying life, *this death,* this death without sense or piety, this death that so pathetically falls short of greatness, the dazzling pettiness of this death, this death hobbling from pettiness to pettiness: these shovelfuls of petty greeds over the conquistador; these shovelfuls of petty flunkies over the great savage, these shovelfuls of petty souls over the three-souled Carib.

and all these deaths futile

absurdities under the splashing of my open conscience

tragic futilities lit up by this single noctiluca

and I alone, sudden stage of these wee hours when the apocalypse of monsters cavorts then,

capsized, hushes.

warm election of cinders, of ruins and collapses

—One more thing! only one, but please make it only one: I have no right to measure life by my sooty finger span; to reduce myself to this little ellipsoidal nothing trembling four fingers above the line, I a man, to so overturn creation, that I include myself between latitude and longitude!

At the end of the wee hours,

the male thirst and the desire stubborn,

here I am, severed from the cool oases of brotherhood

this so modest nothing bristles with hard splinters

this too safe horizon is startled like a jailer.

Your last triumph, tenacious crow of Treason.

What is mine, these few thousand deathbearers who mill in the calabash of an island and mine too, the archipelago arched with an anguished desire to negate itself, as if from maternal anxiety to protect this impossibly delicate tenuity separating one America from another: and these loins which secrete for Europe the hearty liquor of a Gulf Stream, and one of the two slopes of incandescence between which the Equator tightropewalks toward Europe. And my nonfence island, its brave audacity standing at the stern of this Polynesia, before it. Guadeloupe, split in two down its dorsal line and equal in poverty to us, Haiti

where negritude rose for the first time and stated that it believed in its humanity
and the funny little tail of Florida where the strangulation of a nigger is being
completed, and Africa gigantically caterpillaring up to the Hispanic foot of Europe
it nakedness where Death scythes widely.

And I say to myself Bordeaux and Nantes and Liverpool and New York and
San Francisco

not an inch of this world devoid of my fingerprint
and my calcaneum on the spines of skyscrapers and my filth in the glitter of gems!
Who can boast of being better off than I? Virginia.   5
Tennessee. Georgia. Alabama
monstrous putrefactions of stymied
revolts
marshes of putrid blood
trumpets absurdly muted   10
land red, sanguineous, consanguineous land.

What is mine also: a little
cell in the Jura,
a little cell, the snow lines it with white bars
the snow is a jailer mounting   15
guard before a prison

What is mine
a lonely man imprisoned in
whiteness
a lonely man defying the white   20
screams of white death
(TOUSSAINT, TOUSSAINT L'OUVERTURE)

a man who mesmerizes
the white hawk of white death
a man alone in the sterile   25
sea of white sand
a coon grown old standing up to
the waters of the sky
Death traces a shining circle
above this man   30
death stars softly above his head
death breathes, crazed, in the ripened
cane field of his arms
death gallops in the prison like
a white horse   35
death gleams in the dark like the
eyes of a cat
death hiccups like water under the Keys
death is a struck bird

death wanes
death flickers
death is a very shy patyura[1]
death expires in a white pool
of silence.
Swellings of night in the four corners
of this dawn
convulsions of congealed death
tenacious fate
screams erect from mute earth
the splendor of this blood will it not burst open?
oh friendly light
oh fresh source of light
those who have invented neither powder nor compass
those who could harness neither steam nor electricity
those who explored neither the seas nor the sky but those
without whom the earth would not be the earth
gibbosity[2] all the more beneficent as the bare earth even more earth.
silo where that which is earthiest about earth ferments and ripens
my negritude is not a stone, its deafness hurled against the clamor of the day
my negritude is not a leukoma of dead liquid over the earth's dead eye
my negritude is neither tower nor cathedral
it takes root in the red flesh of the soil
it takes root in the ardent flesh of the sky
it breaks through the opaque prostration with its upright patience

Eia[3] for the royal Cailcedra![4]
Eia for those who have never invented anything
for those who never explored anything
for those who never conquered anything

but yield, captivated, to the essence of all things
ignorant of surfaces but captivated by the motion of all things
indifferent to conquering, but playing the game of the world
truly the eldest sons of the world
porous to all the breathing of the world
fraternal locus for all the breathing of the world
drainless channel for all the water of the world
spark of the sacred fire of the world
flesh of the world's flesh pulsating with the very motion of the world!
    Tepid dawn of ancestral virtues

40
45
50
55
60
65
70
75

---

1. A small marsupial found in the forests of
   South America.
2. A hump or swelling.

3. Ancient Greek interjection signifying
   "Come on," or "Courage."
4. A majestic tree of the African savannah; it
   does not exist in the Caribbean.

Blood! Blood! all our blood aroused by the male heart of the sun
those who know about the femininity of the moon's oily body
the reconciled exultation of antelope and star
those whose survival travels in the germination of grass!
Eia perfect circle of the world, enclosed concordance!

Hear the white world
horribly weary from its immense efforts
its stiff joints crack under the hard stars
hear its blue steel rigidity pierce the mystic flesh
its deceptive victories tout its defeats
hear the grandiose alibis of its pitiful stumblings

Pity for our omniscient and native conquerors!

Eia for grief and its udders of reincarnated tears
for those who have never explored anything
for those who have never conquered anything

Eia for joy
Eia for love
Eia for grief and its udders of reincarnated tears

and here at the end of these wee hours is my virile prayer that I hear neither the
        laughter nor the
screams, my eyes fixed on this town which I prophesy, beautiful,

grant me the savage faith of the sorcerer
grant my hands power to mold
grant my soul the sword's temper
I won't flinch. Make my head into a figurehead
and as for me, my heart, do not make me into a father nor a brother,
nor a son, but into the father, the brother, the son,
nor a husband, but the lover of this unique people.

Make me resist any vanity, but espouse its genius as the fist the extended arm!

Make me a steward of its blood
make me trustee of its resentment
make me into a man for the ending
make me into a man for the beginning
make me into a man of meditation
but also make me into a man of germination

make me into the executor of these lofty works
the time has come to gird one's loins like a brave man—

But in doing so, my heart, preserve me from all hatred
do not make me into that man of hatred for whom I feel only hatred
for entrenched as I am in this unique race

you still know my tyrannical love
you know that it is not from hatred of other races   120
that I demand a digger for this unique race
that what I want
is for universal hunger
for universal thirst

to summon it to generate,   125
free at last, from its intimate closeness
the succulence of fruit.

And be the tree of our hands!
it turns, for all, the wounds cut
in its trunk   130
the soil works for all
and toward the branches a headiness of fragrant precipitation.

But before stepping on the shores of future orchards
grant that I deserve those on their belt of sea
grant me my heart while awaiting the earth   135
grant me on the ocean sterile
but somewhere caressed by the promise of the clew-line
grant me on this diverse ocean
the obstinacy of the fierce pirogue
and its marine vigor.   140

Lost Body

I who Krakatoa[1]
I who everything better than a monsoon
I who open chest
I who Laelaps[2]
I who bleat better than a cloaca   5
I who outside the musical scale
I who Zambezi[3] or frantic or rhombos or cannibal
I would like to be more and more humble and more lowly
always more serious without vertigo or vestige
to the point of losing myself falling   10
into the live semolina[4] of a well-opened earth
Outside in lieu of atmosphere there'd be a beautiful haze no dirt in it

---

1. An Indonesian volcano that erupted in
   1883, killing 30,000 people.
2. According to Greek mythology, a wind with
   canine features, or a hurricane.
3. A river in Africa.
4. An image of a living grain—i.e., the earth's
   fertility.

each drop of water forming a sun there
whose name the same for all things
would be DELICIOUS TOTAL ENCOUNTER   15
so that one would no longer know what goes by
—a star or a hope
or a petal from the flamboyant tree
or an underwater retreat
raced across by the flaming torches of aurelian jellyfish   20
Then I imagine life would flood my whole being
better still I would feel it touching me or biting me
lying down I would see the finally free odors come to me
like merciful hands
finding their way   25
to sway their long hair in me
longer than this past that I cannot reach
Things stand back make room among you
room for my repose carrying in waves
my frightening crest of anchor-like roots   30
looking for a place to take hold
Things I probe I probe
me the street-porter I am root-porter
and I bear down and I force and I arcane
    I omphale⁵   35
Ah who leads me back toward the harpoons
    I am very weak
I hiss yes I hiss very ancient things
as serpents do as do cavernous things
I whoa lie down wind   40
and against my unstable and fresh muzzle
against my eroded face
press your cold face of ravaged laughter
The wind alas I will continue to hear it
nigger nigger nigger from the depths   45
of the timeless sky
a little less loud than today
but still too loud
and this crazed howling of dogs and horses
which it thrusts at our forever fugitive heels   50
but I in turn in the air
shall rise a scream so violent
that I shall splatter the whole sky

---

5. A neologism of Césaire's signifying "to take
root." Constructed from *omphalos*, a Greek
word meaning "navel." Also, in Greek mythology: related to the queen of Lydia, to
whom Heracles is enslaved.

and with my branches torn to shreds
and with the insolent jet of my wounded and solemn bole   55

    I shall command the islands to be

Seism[1]*

so many huge sections of dreams
so many parts of intimate homelands
                    collapsed
fallen empty and the soiled sonorous slipstream of the idea
and the two of us? what two?   5
Roughly the history of the family surviving the disaster:
"in the old grass snake smell of our blood we were fleeing
the valley, the village was after us its roaring stone lions on our heels."
Sleep, sick sleep, sick awakening of the heart
yours over mine chipped crockery piled up in the pitching trough of meridians   10
To try words? Rubbing them to conjure up the unformed as nocturnal insects rub
    their maddening
  wing covers?
Caught caught caught outside the lie caught
caught caught caught
      forbeten pushed along   15
     along nothing
except for the poorly read abrupt persistence of
our true names, our miraculous names
until now in the reserve of a supine
oblivion.   20

RENÉ DEPESTRE (b. 1926)
Haiti/France; French

The French- and Creole-speaking island of Haiti gained its independence from France in 1804 following the French Revolution, but for political, social, racial, and economic reasons it has never, tragically, been able to constitute itself as a democratic republic. Its problems situate it within the parameters of the postcolonial Francophone world. Haiti's literary output since the early nineteenth century has been tremendous. René Depestre, a poet, an essayist, and, recently, a novelist, was born in Jacmel, Haiti. Self-exiled from François Duvalier's dictatorship and now living in France, he is the contemporary

*Translated by Clayton Eshleman and Annette Smith.

---

1. An earthquake.

embodiment of the Haitian paradox. He cannot live in his native land for political reasons, being a *persona non grata*. Yet his entire imaginative world and all of his literary output are nourished by his native culture.

In "The Last Degree of Exile" Depestre takes up the theme of the wandering imposed on the politically exiled poet who nonetheless always writes of his homeland, even if he believes his beloved no longer awaits him.

from In a State of Poetry

The Last Degree of Exile*

A wandering Haitian, I rip apart
(tears in my eyes) my eternal
temporary resident card.
Once again from west to east
with a loyal dog's timid steps   5
my life tries to recapture
its besieged poet's roots.
Traveler with bags
full of tenderness and derision,
I go to eat the blue flower: 10
the lotus which reduces my country
to an airport baggage claim.
In my tropical Ithaca
Penelope no longer awaits my reddest blood:
each night with her body she reweaves   15
the joyous work of the night before.

EDWARD KAMAU BRATHWAITE

(b. 1930)

Barbados

Born in Barbados, Edward Kamau Brathwaite studied history at Cambridge University. He lived for seven years in Ghana, where he had an opportunity to study firsthand the African roots of Caribbean culture. Although Brathwaite's work encompasses the entire scope of Caribbean history, it is especially concerned with the African heritage of the region and its predominantly African-based creole adaptations in language and music. His collection of poems, *The Arrivants: A New World Trilogy* (1973) is an epic account of the African diaspora in the Americas.

---

*Translated by Paul Farmer and Haun Saussy.

"Vèvè," a poem from *Islands*, the last book of the trilogy, suggests a ritual of spiritual repossession, the gathering up of the fragmented and repressed parts of Afro-Caribbean identity in order to achieve a new vision of possibility in an alien land. The *vèvè* is a symbolic drawing made on the ground with chalk or flour by a priest before the beginning of a vodun ceremony. The poem begins as a response to the failure of a carnival masquerade, and evokes the image of the poet as fisherman-priest, who merges both Christian and African symbols of redemption.

from **Islands**

Vèvè

1

But on the beach
the fisherman's net is completed;
the fine webs fell softly,

sand shifting under his walking;
the water is ready;   5
twined spray through the air

and the seine holds the sun
and the line in his hand
tightens steady.

The net drifted downward,   10
through tides and reversals
of shell-clinking water,

through time and the hopes
that were drowned in the deep
sleeping sound of the bay.   15

The fan sifted slowly
through cobwebs of light
catching softly the moons of his green
spreading opening day

2

And so the black eye travels to the brink of vision
but not yet;
hold back the fishnet's fling of morning; unloose the sugarcane;

my spattered breast must undertake one more incision;   5
cut, carve, dissect
the merchant's pound of flesh, the soldier's pawn
of violence, the preacher's hymn of pain.

The black eye travels to the brink of vision:
look, the fields are wet,   10
the sea sits gentle on the dawn
of sand; but voices fill the green with hurricane.

And yet it is what happens
it is what happens
when they fall: 15

conquerors, helmets, plumes,
unloosened knots
of blood, dried river beds of iron,
rust;

it is the bird that sings,   20
the green that wavers, wavers, wins
the slave rebellion of the rot
of dust

that matters;
it is this that glitters   25
in the salt
lagoon,

that crusts the coral
with foundation stone,
that stirs the resurrection   30
out of Tacky's[1] bones.

3

So on this ground,
write;
within the sound
of this white limestone *vèvè,*

talk
of the empty roads,   5
vessels of your head,
claypots, shards, ruins.

And on this sailing ground,
sprinkled with rum, bitten   10
with the tenor of your open wound,
walk

---

1. An African leader of a slave revolt that took
   place in 1760 on the island of Jamaica.

walk
the hooves will come, welcomed
by drumbeats, into your ridden head;　　　　　　　　　　　　15
and the horse, cheval of the dead,
charade of *la mort*,

tongued with the wind
possession of the fire
possession of the dust　　　　　　　　　　　　　　　　　20
sundered from your bone
plundered from my breast

by ice, by chain, by sword, by the east wind,
surrenders up to you the graven Word
carved from Olodumare[2]　　　　　　　　　　　　　　　25
from Ogun of Alare, from Ogun of Onire
from Shango broom of thunder and Damballa Grand Chemin.

For on this ground
trampled with the bull's swathe of whips
where the slave at the crossroads was a red anthill　　　　30
eaten by moonbeams, by the holy ghosts
of his wounds

the Word becomes
again a god and walks among us;
look, here are his rags,　　　　　　　　　　　　　　　35
here is his crutch and his satchel
of dreams; here is his hoe and his rude implements

on this ground
on this broken ground.

SIMONE SCHWARZ-BART (b. 1938)
Guadeloupe; French

Born in France, Simone Schwarz-Bart accompanied her mother to Guadeloupe
for the first time when she was three years old. In spite of having lived in Europe
and Africa for many years, her major preoccupation is the articulation of a creole
voice. With her husband, André Schwarz-Bart, she wrote *A Dish of Pork with*

---

2. The supreme god of the Yoruba people of
West Africa; Ogun is the Yoruba and Afro-
Caribbean god of iron and invention;

Shango is the god of thunder; Damballa is
the Afro-Haitian god of Dahomean origin,
whose sign is the rainbow-serpent.

Green Bananas (1967). In 1983, her mythic narrative Ti-Jean the Horizon appeared; her play My Lovely Captain dates from 1987. In Simone Schwarz-Bart's first novel, The Bridge of Beyond (1972), the Guadeloupean author chooses to portray a female protagonist who is empowered in life by her capacity to inscribe herself into a maternal lineage of family women who not only have survived in a harsh world of poverty, bad luck, and destructive men, but have also triumphed.

The selection included here, from the delightful opening pages of the novel, traces the heroine Télumée's matriarchal lineage back several generations, lauding the women of the Logandour family—Minerva, Toussine, and Victory—as they battle in poverty and pain to endure and triumph, sometimes even over madness and death. They are powerful, positive women endowed with pride and, although great believers in love, used to managing in the absence of stable men. In the French Caribbean, women have always been storytellers, but rarely, until recently, writers. Relegated to the domestic domain of oral culture, their literary output has been slight. We should therefore not underestimate the psychic function of the protagonist's capacity to "tell her story" here, nor, in particular, that of the female role models who preceded her. But the exceptional quality of the novel resides in the lyrical grace of its language, the poetic evocation, in French, of the rural Creole world, and the daily lives of women in that world, which is often cruel and unjust. This woman's narrative celebrates human dignity.

from *The Bridge of Beyond*

[My People]

A man's country may be cramped or vast according to the size of his heart. I've never found my country too small, though that isn't to say my heart is great. And if I could choose it's here in Guadeloupe that I'd be born again, suffer and die. Yet not long back my ancestors were slaves on this volcanic, hurricane-swept, mosquito-ridden, nasty-minded island. But I didn't come into the world to weigh the world's woe. I prefer to dream, on and on, standing in my garden, just like any other old woman of my age, till death comes and takes me as I dream, me and all my joy.

When I was a child my mother, Victory, often talked to me about my grandmother Toussine. She spoke of her with fervour and veneration: Toussine, she'd say, was a woman who helped you hold your head up, and people with this gift are rare. My mother's reverence for Toussine was such I came to regard her as some mythical being not of this world, so that for me she was legendary even while still alive.

I got into the habit of calling her, as men called her, Queen Without a Name. But her maiden name had been Toussine Lougandor.

. . .

Her mother was Minerva, a fortunate woman freed by the abolition of slavery from a master notorious for cruelty and caprice. After the abolition Minerva

Translated by Barbara Bray.

wandered in search of a refuge far from the plantation and its vagaries, and she came to rest at L'Abandonnée. Some runaway slaves came there afterwards, and a village grew up. The wanderers seeking refuge were countless, and many would not settle anywhere permanently for fear the old days might return. One Negro from Dominica vanished as soon as he learned he had sired a child, and those in L'Abandonnée whom Minerva had scorned now laughed at her swollen belly. But when dark-skinned Xango took on the shame of my great-grandmother Minerva, the laughter stopped dead, and those who had been amusing themselves at others' misfortunes choked on their own bile. Little Toussine came into the world, and Xango loved her as if she were his own. As the child grew, shooting up as gracefully as a sugar cane, she became the light of his eyes, the blood in his veins, the air in his lungs. Thus through the love and respect lavished on her by Xango, Minerva, now long dead, could walk without shame along the main street of the hamlet, head high, back arched, arms akimbo, and foul breath turned from her to blow over better pastures. And so life began for young Toussine, as delicately as dawn on a clear day.

They lived in a hamlet swept alternately by winds from the land and winds from the sea. A steep road ran along by cliffs and wastelands, leading, it seemed, to nothing human. And that was why it was called the deserted village, L'Abandonnée. At certain times everyone there would be filled with dread, like travellers lost in a strange land. Still young and strong, always dressed in a worker's overall, Minerva had a glossy, light mahogany skin and black eyes brimming over with kindness. She had an unshakable faith in life. When things went wrong she would say that nothing, no one, would ever wear out the soul God had chosen out for her and put in her body. All the year round she fertilized vanilla, picked coffee, hoed the banana groves, and weeded the rows of sweet potatoes. And her daughter Toussine was no more given to dreaming than she. Almost as soon as she woke the child would make herself useful sweeping, gathering fruit, peeling vegetables. In the afternoon she would go to the forest to collect leaves for the rabbits, and sometimes the whim would take her to kneel in the shade of the mahoganies and look for the flat brightly coloured seeds that are made into necklaces. When she came back with a huge pile of greenstuff on her head, Xango delighted to see her with leaves hanging down over her face, and would fling both arms in the air and shout: "Hate me, so long as you love Toussine. Pinch me till you draw blood, but don't touch so much as the hem of her robe." And he would laugh and cry just to look at the radiant, frank-faced child whose features were said to be like those of the Negro from Dominica, whom he would have liked to meet once, just to see. But as yet she was not in full bloom. It was when she was fifteen that she stood out from all the other girls with the unexpected grace of a red canna growing on a mountain, so that the old folk said she in herself was the youth of L'Abandonnée.

There was also in L'Abandonnée at that time a young fisherman called Jeremiah who filled one's soul with the same radiance. But he paid no attention to girls, to whom his friends used to say, laughing, "When Jeremiah falls in love it will be with a mermaid." But this didn't make him any less handsome, and the girls' hearts shriveled up with vexation. He was nineteen and already the best fisherman in Caret cove. Where on earth did he get those hauls of vivaneaux, tazars, and blue balarous?[1] Nowhere but from beneath his boat, the *Headwind,* in which he used to go off forever, from morn till night and night till morn; all he lived for was hearing the sound of the waves in his ears and feeling the tradewinds caressing his face. Such was Jeremiah when Toussine was for everyone a red canna growing on a high mountain.

On windless days when the sea was dead calm Jeremiah would go into the forest to cut the lianas[2] he made into lobster pots. One afternoon when he left the beach for this purpose, Toussine appeared in his path, right in the middle of a wood. She was wearing one of her mother's old dresses that came down to her ankles, and with her heap of greenstuff coming down over her eyes and hiding her face, she looked as if she didn't know where she was going. The young man asked her. "Is this L'Abandonnée's latest fashion in donkeys?" She threw down her burden looked at him, and said in surprise, almost in tears: "A girl just goes to collect greenstuff from the forest, and here I am, insulted." With that, she burst out laughing and scampered off into the shadow. It was then Jeremiah was caught in the finest lobster pot he ever saw. When he got back from his excursion his friends noticed he looked absentminded, but they did not ask any questions. Real fishermen, those who have taken the sea for their native country, often have that lost look. So his friends just thought dry land didn't agree with Jeremiah, and that his natural element was the water. But they sang a different tune in the days that followed, when they saw Jeremiah neglecting the *Headwind,* deserting her and leaving her high and dry on the beach. Consulting among themselves, they came to the conclusion he must be under the spell of the Guiablesse, the most wicked of spirits, the woman with the cloven hoof who feeds exclusively on your desire to live, and whose charms drive you sooner or later to suicide. They asked him if he hadn't met someone that ill-fated day when he went up into the forest. Eventually Jeremiah confessed: "The only Guiablesse I met that day," he said, "is called Toussine—Xango's Toussine." Then they said, chuckling, "Oh, so that's it! Now we see. But it's not such a problem as you might think; if you want our opinion there are no prince's daughters in L'Abandonnée that we know of. Fortunately we're only a pack of Negroes all in the same boat, without any fathers and mothers before God. Here everyone is everyone's else's equal, and none of our women can boast of having three eyes or two tourmalines sleeping in the hollow of her thighs. True, you'll say *she* isn't like all the others, the women you see everywhere, like lizards, protected by the very insipidity of their flesh. We answer: Jeremiah, you say well, as usual. For we too have eyes, and when Toussine brushes against our pupils our sight is refreshed. All these words to say just one thing, friend: Beautiful as she is, the girl is like you, and when you appear with her in the street you will be a good match for her. One more thing. When you go to tell her parents of your intentions, remember we don't have any cannibals here, and Xango and Minerva won't eat you."

---

1. Various types of local Caribbean fish; the names are left in Creole.

2. Creeping vines found in the tropics and jungles.

Then they left Jeremiah to himself, so that he could make his decision like a man.

Thank God for my friends, thought Jeremiah the day he went to see Toussine's parents, dressed as usual and carrying a fine catch of pink crabs. As soon as they opened the door he told them he loved Toussine, and they asked him right in, without even consulting the young lady. Their behaviour gave the impression they knew all about Jeremiah, what he did in life on land and sea, and that he was in a position to take a wife, have children, and bring up a family. It was the beginning of one of those warm Guadeloupe afternoons, lit up at the end by the arrival of Toussine with a tray spread with an embroidered cloth, with vermouth for the men and sapodilla syrup for the weaker sex. When Jeremiah left, Minerva told him the door of the cottage would be open to him day and night from now on, and he knew he could consider the vermouth and the invitation as marking definite victory: for in the case of such a choice morsel as Toussine it isn't usual for people to fall on someone's neck the first time of asking, as if they were trying to get rid of a beast that had something wrong with it. That evening, to celebrate this triumph, Jeremiah and his friends decided to go night fishing, and they brought back so much fish their expedition was long remembered in L'Abandonnée. But they had enjoyed catching those coulirous[3] too much to sell them on the beach, so they gave them away, and that too remained in everyone's memory. At noon that day the men, with glasses of rum in their hands, threw out their chests with satisfaction, tapped them three times, and exulted: "In spite of all, the race of men is not dead." The women shook their heads and whispered, "What one does a thousand undo." "But in the meanwhile," said one of them, as if reluctantly, "it does spread a little hope." And the sated tongues went full tilt, while inside Jeremiah's head the sound of the waves had started up again.

Jeremiah came every afternoon. He was treated not as a suitor but rather as if he were Toussine's brother, the son Minerva and Xango had never had. No acid had eaten into the young man's soul, and my poor great-grandmother couldn't take her eyes off him. Gay by temperament, she was doubly gay to see this scrap of her own country, the man sent by St. Anthony in person especially for her daughter. In the overflowing of her joy she would sometimes tease her. "I hope you're fond of fish, Miss Toussine. Come along, you lucky girl, and I'll teach you to make a court-bouillon that'll make Jeremiah lick the fingers of both hands, polite as he is." Then she would hold out her wide yellow skirt and sing to her daughter:

"I want a fisherman for a husband
To catch me fine sea bream

I don't know if you know
But I want a fisherman

O oar before, he pleases me
O oar behind, I die."

---

3. A local Caribbean fish.

But Toussine scarely listened. Since Jeremiah had taken to spending his afternoons with her his image danced continually in her mind's eye, and she spent the whole day admiring the one she loved, unsuspected, as she thought, by all the world. She looked at his figure and saw it was slim and supple. She looked at his fingers and saw they were nimble and slender, like coconut leaves in the wind. She gazed into his eyes, and her body was filled with a great peace. But what she liked best of all about the man St. Anthony had sent her was the satiny, iridescent skin like the juicy flesh of certain mauve coco plums, so delicious under one's teeth. Minerva with her song about the fisherman knew very well how her daughter passed her time, but she still sang and danced just for the pleasure of seeing Toussine go on dreaming.

Here, as everywhere else, reality was not made up entirely of laughing and singing, dancing and dreaming: for one ray of sun on one cottage there was a whole village still in the shade. All through the preparations for the wedding, L'Abandonnée remained full of the same surliness, the same typical human desire to bring the level of the world down a peg, the same heavy malice weighing down on the chambers of the heart. The breeze blowing over Minerva's cottage embittered the women, made them more unaccountable than ever, fierce, fanciful, always ready with some new shrewishness. "What I say is, Toussine's more for ornament than for use. Beauty's got no market value. The main thing is not getting married, but sticking together year in year out," said one. "They're laughing now, but after laughter come tears, and three months from now Minerva's happy band will find itself with six eyes to cry with," said another. The most savage of all were those living with a man on a temporary basis. They grudged in advance the scrap of gold that was going to gleam on her finger, they wondered if she really possessed some unique and exceptional quality, some virtue or merit so great it elicited marriage. And to console themselves and soothe a deep-seated resentment, they would come right up to Minerva's cottage at dusk and mutter, with a kind of savage frenzy, incantations like:

> Married today
> Divorced tomorrow
> But Mrs just the same.

Minerva knew these women had nothing in their lives but a few planks balanced on four stones and a procession of men over their bellies. For these lost Negresses, marriage was the greatest and perhaps the only dignity. But when she couldn't stand hearing them any longer, Minerva would plant her hands on her hips and shout: "I'm not the only one with a daughter, my fine windbags, and I wish yours the same you wish my Toussine. For, under the sun, the saying has never gone unfulfilled. All they that take the sword shall perish with the sword." Then she would go inside and shut the doors and let the mad bitches yelp.

On the day of the wedding all the village paths were swept and decorated as for the local feast day. Xango and Minerva's cottage was surrounded by huts of woven coconut palm. The one reserved for the bridal couple was a great bouquet of hibiscus, mignonette, and orange blossom—the scent was intoxicating. Rows of tables stretched as far as the eye could see, and you were offered whatever drink you were thirsty for, whatever meat would tickle your palate. There was meat of pig, sheep, and cattle, and even poultry served in the liquor it was cooked in. Blood pudding rose up in shining coils; tiered cakes were weighed down with lacy frosting; every kind of water ice melted before your eyes—custard-apple, water-lemon, coconut. But for the Negroes of L'Abandonnée all this was nothing without some music, and when they saw the three bands, one for quadrilles[4] and mazurkas,[5] one for the fashionable beguine,[6] and the traditional combination of drum, wind instruments, and horn, then they knew they'd really have something worth talking about at least once in their lives. And this assuaged the hearts swollen with jealousy. For three days everyone left behind hills and plateaus, troubles and indignities of every kind, to relax, dance, and salute the bridal couple, going to and fro before them in the flower-decked tent, congratulating Toussine on her luck and Jeremiah on his best of luck. It was impossible to count how many mouths uttered the word luck, for that was the theme they decided to adopt for telling their descendants, in later years, of the wedding of Toussine and Jeremiah.

* * *

The years flowed over it all, and Toussine was still the same dragonfly with shimmering blue wings, Jeremiah still the same glossy-coated sea dog. He continued to go out alone, never bringing back an empty boat, however niggardly the sea. Scandalmongers said he used witchcraft and had a spirit go out fishing in his stead when no one else was about. But in fact his only secret was his enormous patience. When the fish would not bite at all, he dived for lambis. If there were no lambis, he put out long rods with hooks or live crabs to tempt the octopi. He knew the sea as the hunter knows the forest. When the wind had gone and the boat was hauled up on the shore, he would make for his little cottage, pour the money he'd earned into his wife's lap, and have a snack as he waited for the sun to abate. Then the two of them would go to tend their garden. While he dug, she would mark out the rows; while he burned weeds, she would sow. And the sudden dusk of the islands would come down over them, and Jeremiah would take advantage of the deepening dark to have a little hors d'oeuvre of his wife's body, there on the ground, murmuring all sorts of foolishness to her, as on the very first day. "I still don't know what it is I like best about you—one day it's your eyes, the next your woodland laugh, another your hair, and the day after the lightness of your step; another, the beauty spot on your temple, and then the day after that the grains of rice I glimpse when you smile at me." And to this air on the mandolin, Toussine, trembling with delight, would reply with a cool, rough little air on the flute: "My dear, anyone just seeing you in the street would give you the host without asking you to go to confession, but you're a dangerous man, and you'd have buried me long ago if people ever died of happiness." Then they would go indoors and

---

4. A square dance for four couples.
5. A dance of Polish origin, incorporating a slide and a hop to the side.

6. A popular dance of the islands.

Jeremiah would address the evening, casting a last look over the fields: "How can one help loving a garden?"

Their prosperity began with a grass path shaded by coconut palms and kept up as beautifully as if it led to a castle. In fact it led to a little wooden house with two rooms, a thatched roof, and a floor supported on four large cornerstones. There was a hut for cooking in, three blackened stones for a hearth, and a covered tank so that Toussine could do her washing without having to go and gossip with the neighbours by the river. As the women did their washing they would pick quarrels to give zest to the work, comparing their respective fates and filling their hearts with bitterness and rancour. Meanwhile Toussine's linen would be boiling away in a pan in the back yard, and she took advantage of every minute to make her house more attractive. Right in front of the door she'd planted a huge bed of Indian poppies, which flowered all year round. To the right there was an orange tree with hummingbirds and to the left clumps of Congo cane from which she used to cut pieces to give to her daughters, Eloisine and Meranee, for their tea. She would go to and fro amid all this in a sort of permanent joy and richness, as if Indian poppies, Congo canes, hummingbirds, and orange trees were enough to fill a woman's heart with complete satisfaction. And because of the richness and joy she felt in return for so little, people envied and hated her. She could withdraw at will into the recesses of her own soul, but she was reserved, not disillusioned. And because she bloomed like that, in solitude, she was also accused of being an aristocrat stuck-up. Late every Sunday evening she would walk through the village on Jeremiah's arm to look at the place and the people and the animals just before they disappeared in the darkness. She was happy, herself part of all that spectacle, that close and familiar universe. She came to be the thorn in some people's flesh, the delight of others, and because she had a distant manner they thought she put on aristocratic airs.

After the grass path came a veranda, which surrounded the little house, giving constant cool and shade if you moved the bench according to the time of day. Then there were the two windows back and front, real windows with slatted shutters, so that you could close the door and shut yourself safely away from spirits and still breathe in the scents of evening. But the true sign of their prosperity was the bed they inherited from Minerva and Xango. It was a vast thing of locust wood with tall head posts and three mattresses, which took up the entire bedroom. Toussine used to put vetiver roots under the mattresses, and citronella leaves, so that whenever anyone lay down there were all sorts of delicious scents: the children said it was a magic bed. It was a great object of curiosity in that poor village, where everyone else still slept on old clothes laid down on the floor at night, carefully folded up in the morning, and spread in the sun to get rid of the fleas. People would come and weigh up the grass path, the real windows with slatted shutters, the bed with its oval-panelled headboard lording it beyond the open door, and the red-bordered counterpane, which seemed an additional insult. And some of the women would say with a touch of bitterness, "Who do they take themselves for, these wealthy Negroes? Toussine and Jeremiah, with their two-roomed house, their wooden veranda, their slatted shutters, and their bed with three mattresses and red borders—do they think all these things make them white?"

Later on Toussine also had a satin scarf, a broad necklace of gold and silver alloy, garnet earrings, and high-vamped slippers she wore twice a year, on Ash Wednesday and Christmas Day. And as the wave showed no sign of flagging, the time came when the other Negroes were no longer surprised, and talked about other things, other people, other pains and other wonders. They had got used to the prosperity as they had got used to their own poverty. The subject of Toussine and wealthy Negroes was a thing of the past; it had all become quite ordinary.

Woe to him who laughs once and gets into the habit, for the wickedness of life is limitless: if it gives you your heart's desire with one hand, it is only to trample on you with both feet and let loose on you that madwoman bad luck, who seizes and rends you and scatters your flesh to the crows.

Eloisine and Meranee, twins, were ten years old when luck forsook their mother Toussine. A school had just opened in the village, and a teacher came twice a week to teach the children their letters in exchange for a few pennyworth of foodstuff. One evening as they were learning their alphabet, Meranee said her sister had all the light and told her to move the lamp to the middle of the table. And so just one little word gave bad luck an opening. "Have it all, then!" said Eloisine, giving the light an angry shove. It was over in an instant: the china lamp was in pieces and the burning oil was spreading all over Meranee's legs and shoulders and hair. A living torch flew out into the darkness, and the evening breeze howled around it, fanning the flames. Toussine caught up a blanket and ran after the child, shouting to her to stand still, but she rushed madly hither and thither, leaving a luminous track behind her like a falling star. In the end she collapsed, and Toussine wrapped her in the blanket, picked her up, and went back toward the house, which was still burning. Jeremiah comforted Eloisine, and they all sat in the middle of their beautiful path, on the damp grass of evening, watching their sweat, their life, their joy, go up in flames. A big crowd had gathered: the Negroes stood there fascinated, dazzled by the magnitude of the disaster. They stared at the flames lighting up the sky, shifting from foot to foot, in two minds—they felt an impulse to pity, and yet saw the catastrophe as poetic justice. It made them forget their own fate and compare the cruelty of this misfortune with the ordinariness of their own. At any rate, it's one thing that won't happen to us, they said.

Meranee's suffering was terrible. Her body was one great wound attracting more and more flies as it decayed. Toussine, her eyes empty of all expression, fanned them away, put on soothing oil, and grew hoarse calling on death, which, being no doubt occupied elsewhere, refused to come. If anyone offered to replace Toussine at the bedside for a while, she would say, smiling gently: "Don't worry about me. However heavy a woman's breasts, her chest is always strong enough to carry them." She spent seventeen days and seventeen nights cajoling death, and then, ill luck having gone elsewhere, Meranee expired. Life went on as before, but without one vestige of heart left, like a flea feasting on your last drop of blood, delighting in leaving you senseless and sore, cursing heaven and earth and the womb that conceived you.

Against sorrow and the vanity of things, there is and will always be human fantasy. It was thanks to the fantasy of a white man that Toussine and Jeremiah found a roof. He was a Creole called Colbert Lanony, who in the old days just after the abolition of slavery had fallen in love with a strange and fascinating young Negress. Cast out by his own people, he had sought refuge in a desolate and inaccessible wasteland far from the eyes that looked askance at his love. Nothing remained of all that now but some fine blocks of stone mouldering away in the wilderness, colonnades, worm-eaten ceilings, and tiles bearing witness still to the past and to an outlawed white man's fancy for a Negress. To those who were surprised to find a house like that in such a place, the local people got into the habit of saying, "It's L'Abandonnée," and the name later came to be used for the hamlet itself. Only one room on the first floor was habitable, a sort of closet, where the window openings were covered with sheets of cardboard. When it rained the water trickled through a hole in the roof into a bucket, and at night the ground floor was the resort of toads, frogs, and bats. But none of this seemed to bother Toussine, who had gone to live there like a body without a soul, indifferent to such details. As was the custom, she was visited there the first nine evenings by all the people of the village, who came to pay their respects to the dead and to keep the living company. Toussine did not weep or complain, but sat upright on a bench in a corner as if every breath of air were poison. People did not want to desert a ship like Toussine, but the sight of her was so unbearable they cut the ceremony short, just coming in, greeting her, and leaving, full of pitying kindness, thinking she was lost forever.

The leaf that falls into the pond does not rot the same day, and Toussine's sorrow only grew worse with time, fulfilling all the gloomy predictions. At first Jeremiah still went to sea three times a week, but then only twice, then once, then not at all. The house looked as deserted as ever, as if there were no one living there. Toussine never left the room with the cardboard windows, and Jeremiah collected their food from the woods around—purslane, scurvy grass, pink maxanga bananas. Before, the women going to market used to take a path that led by the ruined house; it was a shortcut to the main road and Basse-Terre, where they sold their wares. But now they were afraid, and they made a big detour through the forest rather than go near the pig-headed Toussine, who didn't speak, wouldn't even answer, but just sat staring into space, a bag of bones as good as dead. Every so often, when the conversation came around to her and Jeremiah and little Eloisine, a man would shin up a tree, peer towards the house, and report that it was still the same; nothing had changed, nothing had moved.

Three years went by before people began to talk about them again. As usual, a man climbed a tree and looked towards the ruins; but this time he didn't say anything, and showed no sign of coming down. When questioned he only signed for someone else to come up and look. It was the second man who announced that Toussine, the little stranded boat, the woman thought to be lost forever, had come out of her cardboard tower and was taking a little walk outside in the sun.

Glad as they were at this news, the Negroes still waited, hesitating to rejoice outright until the kid was safely caught and tethered and they were sure they hadn't sharpened their knives for nothing. And as they looked, this is what they saw: Toussine was cutting down the weeds around the ruined house. She shivered a moment, went in, then came out again almost at once and began to cut down brushwood and scrub with the furious energy of a woman with something urgent to do and not a minute to lose.

From that day on the place began to be a little less desolate and the market women went back to using the shortcut to Basse-Terre. Toussine had taken her family into prison with her, and now she brought them back to life again. First Eloisine was seen in the village again, as slight and brittle as a straw. Next poor Jeremiah came down to the beach, filled his eyes with the sea and stood staring, fascinated, then went back smiling up the hill as in the days when the song of the waves sounded in his head. It could be seen plainly written across his brow that he would go back to sea again. Toussine put curtains up at the windows, and planted Indian poppies around the ruin, Angola peas, root vegetables, and clumps of Congo cane for Eloisine. And then one day she planted the pip of a hummingbird orange. But the Negroes did not rejoice yet. They still watched and waited, from a distance. They thought of the old Toussine, in rags, and compared her with the Toussine of today—not a woman, for what is a woman? Nothing at all, they said, whereas Toussine was a bit of the world, a whole country, a plume of a Negress, the ship, sail, and wind, for she had not made a habit of sorrow. Then Toussine's belly swelled and burst and the child was called Victory. And then the Negroes did rejoice. On the day of the christening they came to Toussine and said:

"In the days of your silks and jewels we called you Queen Toussine. We were not far wrong, for you are truly a queen. But now, with your Victory, you may boast that you have put us in a quandary. We have tried and tried to think of a name for you, but in vain, for there isn't one that will do. And so from now on we shall call you 'Queen Without a Name!' "

And they ate, drank, and were merry, and from that day forth my grandmother was called the Queen Without a Name.

Queen Without a Name went on living in L'Abandonnée with her two daughters, Eloisine and my mother, Victory, until my grandfather died. Then, when her daughters came to have the wombs of women, she left them to steer the course of their lives under their own sail. She wanted to go away from the house where her fisher husband had loved and cherished her and kept her safe in her affliction, when her hair was unkempt and her dress in rags. She longed for solitude, so she had a little hut built in a place called Fond-Zombi, which was said to be very wild. An old childhood friend of hers, a famous witch called Ma Cia, lived nearby, and Toussine hoped she would put her in touch with Jeremiah. So Toussine lived in the woods, and came very seldom to L'Abandonnée.

BOB MARLEY (1945–1981),
CARLTON BARRETT (1950–1987),
LEON COGIL (b. 1945)
Jamaica

Bob Marley was born in Jamaica in 1945. He grew up in Trench Town, one of the poorest districts of Kingston. Before his death from cancer at the age of thirty-six, Marley achieved international fame as a reggae musician and lyric writer. The Rastafarian-inspired vision of his music expresses concern for the injustices suffered by the poor and faith in spiritual transcendence.[1]

The songs included here are an example of the socially conscious popular culture of the Anglophone Caribbean. The first, "Them Belly Full" was written by Carlton Barrett, a member of Bob Marley's band, along with Leon Cogil, in the early seventies. The lyrics are a reggae version of Louise Bennett's poem "Dutty Tough," which in Jamaican Creole means "hard ground" and is a reference to the proverb "De rain a fall but de dutty tough" (The rain has fallen but the ground is still hard). "Duppy Conqueror" was written by the singer himself.

Them Belly Full

Na-Na-Na-Na-Na-Na-Na-Na-Na;
Na-Na-Na-Na-Na-Na-Na-Na-Na;
Na-Na-Na-Na-Na-Na-Na-Na-Na;
Na-Na-Na-Na-Na-Na-Na-Na-Na.

Them belly full but we hungry.   5
A hungry mob is a angry mob.
A rain a-fall but the dirt it tough;
A pot a-cook but the food no' nough.
You're gonna dance to Jah music, dance.
We're gonna dance to Jah music, dance.   10
Forget your troubles and dance.
Forget your sorrow and dance.
Forget your sickness and dance.
Forget your weakness and dance.
Cost of living get so high,   15
Rich and poor, they start a cry.
Now the weak must get strong.
They say, "Oh, what a tribulation."

---

1. Rastafarianism is a religious movement that originated in Jamaica in the 1930s, whose adherents believe in the divinity of the late Haile Selassie, former emperor of Ethiopia. Rastafarians reject Western values and regard Africa as the Promised Land.

Them belly full but we hungry.
A hungry mob is a angry mob.   20
A rain a-fall but the dirt it tough;
A pot a-cook but the food no 'nough.
We're gonna chuck to Jah music,
     chuckin'
We're chuckin' to Jah music,   25
     we're chuckin'.

A belly full but them hungry.
A angry mob is a angry mob.
A rain a-fall but the dirt it tough;
A pot a-cook but the food no 'nough.   30

A angry man is a angry man.
A rain a-fall but the dirt it tough;
A pot a-cook but the food no 'nough.

(*Repeat*)

A angry mob is a angry mob.

Duppy[1] Conqueror

Yes me friend
We de a street again[2]
Yes me friend (me good friend)
Dem say we're free again

The bars could not hold me   5
Force could not control me, now
They try to keep me down
But Jah put I around[3]

Yes, I've been accused (many a times)
And wrongly abused, now   10
But through the powers of the most-high
They've got to turn me loose

Don't try to cold[4] me up on this bridge, now
I've got to reach Mount Zion—the highest region
So if you're a bull-bucker,[5]   15
Let me tell you this—I'm a Duppy Conqueror

(*Repeat first verse*)

---

1. Ghost.
2. In the street.
3. God helped me.

4. Mixture of cold and hold: stop.
5. Who can ride a bull, powerful.

(Repeat fourth verse)

Yes me friend
Dem say we're free again
Yes me friend
Dem set de a street again[6]

20

LORNA GOODISON (b. 1947)
Jamaica

Lorna Goodison, poet, short-story writer, and painter, belongs to the new group of Caribbean women writers whose work began to appear in the early 1980s. Goodison has published three books of poetry—*Tamarind Season* (1980), *I am Becoming My Mother* (1986), *Heartease* (1988)—and a collection of stories, *Baby Mother and the King of the Swords* (1990). Her poetry and fiction express the feelings of women, their inner conflicts, doubts, and desires. She writes in a powerful personal voice that rarely gives in to bitterness or despair. In "Mother the Great Stones Got to Move" she invokes the spirit of the mother, a strong presence in her work, as a powerful agent of social change, whose compassion and sense of justice can remove the obstacles that block memories of the past and dreams of the future.

Mother the Great Stones Got to Move

Mother, one stone is wedged across the hole in our history
and sealed with blood wax.
In this hole is our side of the story, exact figures,
headcounts, burial artefacts, documents, lists, maps
showing our way up through the stars; lockets of brass   5
containing all textures of hair clippings.
It is the half that has never been told, some of us
must tell it.

Mother there is the stone on the hearts of some women and men
something like an onyx, cabochon cut   10
which hung on the wearer seeds bad dreams, speaking for the small
dreamers of this earth, plagued with nightmares, yearning
for healing dreams
We want that stone to move.

---

6. They have gone to the street again.

Upon an evening like this mother, when one year is making way   15
for another, in a ceremony attended by a show of silver stars,
mothers see the moon, milk-fed, herself a nursing mother
and we think of our children and the stones upon their future
and we want these stones to move.

For the year going out came in fat at first   20
but towards the harvest it grew lean.
And many mouth corners gathered white
and another kind of poison, powdered white
was brought in to replace what was green.
And death sells it with one hand   25
and with the other death palms a gun
then death, gets death's picture
in the papers asking,
'Where does all this death come from?'
Mother, stones are pillows   30
for the homeless sleep on concrete sheets.
Stone flavours soup, stone is now meat
the hard-hearted giving our children
stones to eat.

Mother the great stones over mankind got to move.   35
It's been ten thousand years we've been watching them now
from various points in the universe.
From the time of our birth as points of light
in the eternal coiled workings of the cosmos.
Roll away stone of poisoned powders come   40
to blot out the hope of our young.
Move stone of sacrificial lives we breed
to feed up tribalistic economic machines.
From across the pathway to mount morning
site of the rose quartz fountain   45
brimming anise and star water
bright fragrant for our children's future.

Mother these great stones got to move.

RAMABAI ESPINET (b. 1948)
Trinidad/Canada

Born in Trinidad in 1948, Ramabai Espinet, of Indian heritage, now lives and works in Canada, where she does research in literature and women's studies. She is

Mural in Port-au-Prince, Haiti, showing an angel lancing a Tonton Macoute.

actively involved in the women's movement in both the Caribbean and Canada. Her essays and poetry have been published in a number of journals, and she is the editor of *Creation Fire* (1990), an anthology of poetry by Caribbean women. Although a number of male writers—most notably V. S. Naipaul, Samuel Selvon, and Neil Bissoondath, all East Indians from Trinidad—have written about the Indo-Caribbean experience, there has been an absence of Indian women writers until quite recently. First brought to the Caribbean as indentured laborers in the mid-nineteenth century, people of Indian and Pakistani descent constitute at least half of the population of Trinidad and Guyana. The multiple voices of Espinet's narrative represent the sense of dislocation, gender oppression, and ethnic bias experienced by Indo-Caribbean women, but these voices also indicate their resistance to the cultural traditions and social forces that would silence them.

Barred: Trinidad 1987

I put a chair against the door of the room last night. Jammed it securely to the edge where the crib met the wall so that if the key turned in the lock and the door was pushed forward, a horrible grating noise would begin and I would wake up.

All of this because I lost my keys a few days ago. That and my wallet. All of my life I have flirted with the fantasy of losing these two things—a fantasy of being locked out and thrown absolutely upon my own primary resources. I remember standing above the Hastings Bridge in Vancouver, many years ago, high over the cold water and suddenly finding myself possessed by the mad urge to fling all valuables down. The valuables were pretty meager: a bit of makeup, a few dollars, the key to a shabby room in a little hotel. But what would I have done without them?

And that impulse has resurfaced over and over. All at once it happens without my consciously trying. All night long I hear a key turning in the lock downstairs, heavy footfalls on the stairs—an intruder confident and careless—what does this mean? And if someone has been dogging my footsteps and now possesses my keys, not to mention my wallet, what will I do when he appears?

I have no idea, but under my bed I keep a tin of insect repellent which I am told is good for spraying in their eyes. I also possess an old walking stick, a rape alarm with a light on it, and some candles and matches. Otherwise, there's only paper. Nothing much for a thief.

And, in between the waiting and his forced entry, I might die before the night is out of nerve-racking loneliness and anguish. All of my loves, fights, anxieties, and fears have crystallized into this mournful night where I am reduced to a purple jellyfish-like consistency. I can't sleep. And then I rise and throw open the doors to my balcony high above the ground. I look up at the peaks of the Northern Range—Morne Wash and El Tucuche. Unto the hills around do I lift up my longing eyes. Only I have no idea what I'm longing for, or if I do, it's still only an apprehension of something. I'm trying to approach closure, which for me is a completion of the whatever which is necessary for living and which remains like a door perpetually, uneasily, left ajar.

The mango tree is heavily fruited at this time of the year. I think: this is the land that spawned me, far from the continent of my origin. Can an island be someone's real home, I wonder? My ancestral roots are far from here and I don't even know, really, what they are.

I am Indian, plain and simple, not East nor West, just an Indian. I live in the West. My travel across the water to this land has not been easy and many a time I have squatted in the dirt of this or that lepayed hut, a few coins knotted in the corner of my ohrni,[1] waiting, waiting—waiting to make the next move. There is fear, poverty, and sometimes a heavy hand striking at night. The enemy waits outside. Who is the enemy? Is it rum? The boy I married turns into a strange man who hits and curses at night. I bear much and one night I squat in the dirt waiting, the night black and quiet with only frogs singing in the bush where we live. I hear him coming home, drunk again, falling and cursing. The baby sleeping, the night quiet quiet. It is dark. I should move to go and light the lamp. But I don't move, I stay crouching on the dirt. After he is inside the house and stumbling around, then I follow and light the lamp. He is hungry.

"Way de food?"

He is enraged. I move to warm up the food and suddenly a cuff connects. And then he is deadly accurate—all over my head and breasts. The baby wakes and starts to cry.

I fall near the chulhah[2] and he kicks me as I fall. I see him move towards the bedroom door mashing up everything on the way—a green-and-orange-flowered

---

1. A headshawl worn by married Indian women.

2. A clay fireplace used for cooking.

wedding lemonade set, a vision pot, and a blue and red plaque. His voice is deep and menacing, his boot heavy.

"Ah go kill dat chile tonight. Ah go dash out she focking brains. All yuh think is joke! All ah all yuh think I sorf. Well, tonight we go see. All ah all yuh go see."

The night dark and is only me and he and the baby in all this bush. He reach the bed and then he fall down near it. Where he going? Where the arse he think he going? He getting up, then he fall again straight on the new Slumberking. The springs start creaking again, he getting up. The baby bawling now and he getting up . . .

The cutlass by the fire, I chop some wood up this evening to cook the food. He on the bed and quick quick I chop him two, three times, me ain't know how hard. He give a lil sound and then he stop quiet. Me ain't really know how much time I chop he. He ain't get chance to touch the baby yet. I snatch she up and go outside and sit down in the middle of the road. No car don't come up here this hour. Is only high bush around. It getting cold but I can't move at all. All I could do is to rock the baby. And she, she sleeping. Light coming. I walk up the road—three mile-post up—and call my brother-in-law. He come back to the house with me. They say the man dead.

All around us the cane fires are burning—rising and falling, smoke and soot. Nothing on earth has the live sugar smell of burning cane. And when the cane-sugar boils in the vats the smell is like all the holidays rolled into one fragrant ball—amber and crystalline on the outside and full of honeyed liquid in the center. We bought those balls at Ramdillah, later corrected to Ramleela. Which one is right, what the books now say or what we uttered in the peasant newness of this settlement? We are lost here, have not found the words to utter our newness, our strangeness, our unfound being. Our clothes are strange, our food is strange, our names are strange. And it is not possible for anyone to coax or help us. Our utterance can only come roaring out of our mouths when it is ready, set, and can go.

It has not been a happy arrival and we are still so morbid. There is a weed-killer sold to gardeners on this island. It is labelled gramoxone but everyone knows it as Indian tonic. The suicide tonic.

Indians ain't have no backbone, no stamina. You ain't see how at the slightest sign of stress they does run and drink Indian tonic? (Boy meets and loves girl but the arranged marriage gets in the way. Boy and girl drink GRAMAZONE and perish together—desire literally burning a hole through their bowels.) Indians ain't fraid to die. They does kill easy too. Is because they believe in reincarnation, don't doubt it. If you look in the hospitals is mostly Indians you go see. They there for accident, chopping, and poor guts. Is all the dhal and bhaji[3] they does eat. And all the time the bitches and them have all kinda money hide up and save up. Yuh see all them saddhu[4] and babu[5] all yuh see walking the streets. Them is

---

3. *Dhal* are yellow split peas; *bhaji* is a spinach-like vegetable.
4. A Hindu ascetic who usually belongs to a

lower caste and therefore cannot become a pundit or priest.
5. A term used to refer to an Indian man.

millionaires, man, millionaires. How yuh think Indians have so much business in this country? Them controlling the business community, you know, is only me and you stupid enough to think is white people. We born yesterday, we can't see what in front we eye. Them controlling ninety-five percent of the business in this country. They smart too bad. And all they children does do in school is study, study. I went to school with plenty Cramlal Booksingh and them yuh hear. And when they can't get in the good schools they does bribe man, bribe. Even in university they does buy the test paper. Is true they don't have no big job and money but them people low, they ain't bong for that.[6] They ain't know how to live, they don't even spend money on food. Is only dhal and bhaji day and night.

After the birth of the second child there was no money in the house. Dass was working at a sweet-drink factory up on the main road, and one day they fired all the workers. Then he got a part-time end at the curry factory. But the little end never came home. He said it wasn't enough. He started to drink and gamble in the recreation club. We lived in the back in a low wooden house and I din't know how to manage. I couldn't cook good enough to sell and I had two children to mind.

One morning I got up. Dass had gone for the day already. He had forgotten a full pack of Anchor cigarettes on the table. And right where the window faced the road, I put an empty Klim tin,[7] and two empty condensed milk tins turned upside down on either side of the Klim tin. Then I placed the pack of Anchor on the Klim tin. It wasn't long before a man came and bought the packet of cigarettes. He was my first customer. He was a tall thin Negro gentleman and I think he was a teacher. He said good morning before he bought the cigarettes and thank you when he left. I was nineteen years old. I bought two potatoes with the money to eat with roti[8] for dinner. I didn't have to buy flour so I bought some sweeties with the change and put that in an empty bottle in the window. A Creole woman down the road showed me how to make sugar-cakes and tamarind balls.

Some time after Dass helped me to build a wooden counter just underneath the window. Later we put up a Coca-Cola sign, a Solo[9] sign, and a newspaper sign. People came and bought in my little parlor. And only when Dass and his brother saw how I was making my way, they put together and we started the shop.

Outside now, the rain is pouring. Rain on a galvanized iron roof is the sweetest sound on earth. And when you lie with someone under the sheets in a safe bed while rain pelts down on the roof above, there is no other experience on earth like that. A crystal clear morning after the rain—dewfall, rainfall, footfalls of love. It is Sunday morning. I have lived through the long night.

---

6. A Trinidadian expression meaning "they don't need that."
7. A brand of powdered milk.
8. A kind of bread.
9. A soft drink.

JAMAICA KINCAID (b. 1949)
Antigua/United States

Jamaica Kincaid left Antigua at age sixteen to go to school in the United States, where she later became a freelance writer. When she joined the staff of *The New Yorker* in 1974, she began writing many of the stories that would appear in her critically acclaimed *At the Bottom of the River* (1983). In addition to her two semiautobiographical novels, *Annie John* (1985) and *Lucy* (1990), she has published *A Small Place* (1988), a brilliant essay about the impact of colonialism and tourism on her native Antigua. Kincaid's fiction deals with the complex psychological bonds between mothers and daughters. The following monologue, with its insistent litany of rules and prohibitions, suggests the source of her heroines' ambivalence toward their mothers and their confusion about what it means to become a woman.

from *At the Bottom of the River*

Girl

Wash the white clothes on Monday and put them on the stone heap; wash the color clothes on Tuesday and put them on the clothesline to dry; don't walk barehead in the hot sun; cook pumpkin fritters in very hot sweet oil; soak your little cloths right after you take them off; when buying cotton to make yourself a nice blouse, be sure that it doesn't have gum on it, because that way it won't hold up well after a wash; soak salt fish overnight before you cook it; is it true that you sing benna[1] in Sunday school?; always eat your food in such a way that it won't turn someone else's stomach; on Sundays try to walk like a lady and not like the slut you are so bent on becoming; don't sing benna in Sunday school; you mustn't speak to wharf-rat boys, not even to give directions; don't eat fruits on the street—flies will follow you; *but I don't sing benna on Sundays at all and never in Sunday school*; this is how to sew on a button; this is how to make a button-hole for the button you have just sewed on; this how to hem a dress when you see the hem coming down and so to prevent yourself from looking like the slut I know you are so bent on becoming; this is how you iron your father's khaki shirt so that it doesn't have a crease; this is how you iron your father's khaki pants so that they don't have a crease; this is how you grow okra—far from the house, because okra tree harbors red ants; when you are growing dasheen, make sure it gets plenty of water or else it makes your throat itch when you are eating it; this is how you sweep a corner; this is how you sweep a whole house; this is how you sweep a yard; this is how you smile to someone you don't like too much; this is how you smile to someone you don't like at all; this is how you smile to someone you like completely; this is how you set a table for tea; this is how you set a table for dinner;

---

1. To sing popular songs.

this is how you set a table for dinner with an important guest; this is how you set a table for lunch; this is how you set a table for breakfast; this is how to behave in the presence of men who don't know you very well, and this way they won't recognize immediately the slut I have warned you against becoming; be sure to wash every day, even if it is with your own spit; don't squat down to play marbles—you are not a boy, you know; don't pick people's flowers—you might catch something; don't throw stones at blackbirds, because it might not be a blackbird at all; this is how to make a bread pudding; this is how to make doukona;[2] this is how to make pepper pot; this is how to make a good medicine for a cold; this is how to make a good medicine to throw away a child before it even becomes a child; this is how to catch a fish; this is how to throw back a fish you don't like, and that way something bad won't fall on you; this is how to bully a man; this is how a man bullies you; this is how to love a man, and if this doesn't work there are other ways, and if they don't work don't feel too bad about giving up; this is how to spit up in the air if you feel like it, and this is how to move quick so that it doesn't fall on you; this how to make ends meet; always squeeze bread to make sure it's fresh; *but what if the baker won't let me feel the bread?*; you mean to say that after all you are really going to be the kind of woman who the baker won't let near the bread?

THE UNITED STATES

The United States is an experiment and, like all experiments, exists in possibility: that a nation can be founded and flourish on an idea, the idea of liberty. As Garry Wills has most recently and gracefully phrased it, "Americans are intellectually autochthonous, having no pedigree except that of the idea."[1] The experiment continues, conducted and observed, unusually, by its subjects. Self-examination and constant questioning of results are intrinsic to the process. We affect ourselves and the progress of the experiment by what we note. The notes comprise our literature. The laboratory is the mind of its makers; the field, at first the imagining of a place that must be becomes that portion of the new world dedicating itself "to the proposition that all men are created equal." Yet, America began with enslavement, while escaping one kind, imposing another.

Long before the idea of America was conceived, the continent bred and nurtured generations who knew and preserved the sacred balance of nature that

---

Girl

2. A spicy pudding.

The United States

1. Garry Wills, *Lincoln at Gettysburg: The Words that Remade America* (New York: Simon and Schuster, 1992) 86.

later colonists would brutally ignore. There are at present 271 Native American languages being spoken by a population that makes up approximately one half of one percent of the current total population of North America. Imagining the number of languages spoken before the European settlement, when Native American tribes made up one hundred percent of the population, is chilling. Languages such as Penobscot, Muscogee, Navajo, Omaha, and Yup'ik are as different from one another as Mandarin Chinese and Italian. That the songs and prayers and stories of these different tribes are uniformly phrased in English, as are the songs, prayers and stories of every other group that comes to participate in the experiment, provokes troubling questions about language and identity.

Thomas Jefferson's thought of what America could be like circled these questions, as is evidenced by his proposal that the national language be Classical Greek, so that at least all would start on the common footing of learning a language not in currency and so new for the new nation. The additional accidental features of Classical Greek—its numerous verb tenses and forms, its complex yet resilent syntax—would also have allowed, to his mind, greater and more various possibilities of expression, somewhat closer in spirit to the plurality offered in the many Native American languages. As Wallace Stevens would note 150 years later, "His soil is man's intelligence." The magnitude and diversity of nature and climate on the continent, if nothing else, called and calls for something more than what the language belonging to a large rocky island in the North Sea could provide. The newly arrived colonizers had no words to describe the vast and frightening frontiers they faced. Nearly 400 years after Columbus's landing, with the frontier still a "wild, ruinous waste," to the descendents of the good Puritans, Walt Whitman was still searching: "One wants new words in writing about these plains, and all the inland American West—the terms *far, large, vast, &c.,* are insufficient." Nature here was ever-present, a miracle and a mirror. Against this monumental background, human beings placed themselves or were placed by others to found a nation. The record of what they found is only very partially represented by the selections offered here.

For Columbus and the later colonizers, the thought of what America would be like preceded the actual experiences that prompted later reflection and recording. The tension between the idea of the thing and the thing itself is the thread we follow through its amazing and disturbing history. Jefferson provided the clew on which to secure the thread to find our way through the labyrinth of the American experience: that we are creatures of "nature and of nature's God." The minotaur devouring our children is, of course, slavery, miscegenated from freedom's rape of the real.

The strongest voices remind us of "nature and nature's God." The storytelling and singing of the Native American tribes spin filaments of the sacred web that holds all life together, from stones to stars. The ring chants of the African-Americans insinuate themselves into calls and responses and polyrhythmic structures in poems, stories, novels, and plays that urge our participation in what is beyond ourselves. Such traces of powerful oral traditions—the tales of the Native American tribal groups repeating the belief that community is not only human but made up of all living things, and the many testimonials to the African sense of the word *Nommo* as an active creative force—offer the possibility of closing the circle opened in the early East with the Vedic hymns and the celebration of nature. America could become the bridge between East and West, ancient and modern if we listen to these voices and to those others who have also learned to attend to nature's clues. Heeding these reverses the priority that reason, ideals, and principles have exercised. It seems that we have begun to cross the bridge as we read writers such as Li-Young Lee and Hisaye Yamamoto.

The work of writers like Ralph Waldo Emerson, Henry David Thoreau, Frederick Douglass, Zora Neale Hurston, and the others represented in this section reveals their understanding of both the uses and abuses of idealisms. American writers, products or subjects of democracy, the "dream of reason," have been particularly sensitive to the nightmarish distortions of "rationalists, wearing square hats, . . .think[ing] in square rooms."[2] Nature, human nature, cannot be penned.

The writers represented here are keenly alert to how words hunt and trap and can kill. Balancing this awareness, most also implicitly realize the pointed accuracy of Emerson's observation that "The sentence is the unit of democracy," that effective political action begins with the power of words, that one does not have a voice unless one can speak. Their struggle has been to find words that would suffice to express something living. This is abundantly clear in Frederick Douglass's work, for example. Writing was an enormous privilege for early African-Americans. In many Southern slave states, it was illegal for slaves even to know how to read and write, since it was obvious to the slaveowners that literacy gave the slave the power to communicate his or her plight to a wide audience. Those few who learned to write saw it as a means of expressing not only the self as an individual but also the self as part of a community. Writing for most African-American writers, then, has been both a personal and communal act. Even if some writers wanted to see themselves only as individuals, they were inevitably seen as black and therefore inferior. As a result, much of African-American writing has been strongly related to movements for social change—the Abolitionist Movement of the nineteenth century, the Social Protest Movement of the 1930s, the Civil Rights and Black Power movements of the 1960s, the Feminist Movement of the 1970s. Thus the literature has sometimes been denigrated by the use of the term "political," as if all literary practices, whether they are from Europe, Asia, or the United States, were not related to a social context.

The strongest writers have been attentive, too, to the voices of the past, acknowledging, as the novelist and critic Robert Penn Warren put it, that:

> any true self is not only the result of a vital relation with a community but is also a development in time, and if there is no past there can be no self.
>
> Furthermore, a society with no sense of the past, with no sense of the human role as significant not merely in experiencing history but in creating it can have no sense of destiny. And what kind of society is it that has no sense of destiny and no sense of self?[3]

Walt Whitman, breaking a sentence to add an all-important note to the opening entry of his *Specimen Days,* observed that "The war of attempted secession has, of course, been the distinguishing event of my time . . . the middle range of the Nineteenth century in the New World: a strange, unloosen'd, wondrous time." Is it a rhetorical question to ask what we can add to that "distinguishing event"? We have engaged in other wars, each one more horrifying in its special way, but we

---

2. Wallace Stevens, *The Collected Poems* (New York: Knopf, 1987) 75.

3. *Democracy and Poetry: The 1974 Jefferson* *Lecture in the Humanities.* (Cambridge, Mass., London, England: Harvard University Press, 1975).

have not finished the struggle with the issues of that war. The selections collected here foreground this.

In our time, the last range of the twentieth century, "pluralism" has become "multiculturalism," but the sins of the fathers are still visited on their children. Still, the inheritors and inhabitants of the dream of reason have not forgotten Socrates's observations that the unexamined life is not worth living. And our strongest writers have not let us forget that we are men and women "made out of words." It is, then, most important that we take full responsibility for them, become, in Emerson's words, human beings "thinking" rather than containers or receivers of others' thoughts. The words of the writers set down here prompt that active thinking.

Deeper sometimes than thought, certain stories and songs, such as those of the Native Americans, have the power to create, to restore, and to heal. Active and interactive, the living word continues the world. As Leslie Silko writes in *Ceremony:*

> I will tell you something about stories.
> (He said)
> They aren't just entertainment.
> Don't be fooled.
> They are all we have, you see,
> all we have to fight off
> illness and death.
>
> You don't have anything
> if you don't have the stories.

The many tribal peoples of this continent continue to believe that stories and songs ensure the survival of a people. It must be so.

Historical Background

The origins of the United States lie in the European colonization of North America during the early decades of the seventeenth century. Driven by their search for new sources of profit and a western route to the Far East, English merchants financed expeditions that led to the first permanent settlements in Jamestown, Virginia, in 1607 and Plymouth, Massachusetts, in 1620. Although the Dutch challenged English hegemony in the region by founding New Netherlands in 1624, the British regained preeminence by capturing the colony forty years later, when they renamed it New York.

Religious ideals were central to many of the early colonies. Maryland was originally conceived in the 1630s as a refuge for English Catholics, and Pennsylvania was organized along Quaker principles in 1681 by William Penn (1644–1718). In terms of its impact on national culture, however, the most significant development was the formation of two Massachusetts colonies by English Puritans. On Cape Cod, a small group of Puritans known as Pilgrims, separatists from the Church of England, founded Plymouth Plantation. A much larger group of Puritans committed to reforming the English Church established the Massachusetts Bay Colony at Salem in 1630. Two other New England colonies, Connecticut and Rhode Island, were created in the 1640s by Puritans unhappy with the religious orthodoxy of Massachusetts Bay.

The Puritans were radical Protestants at odds with the Church of England (and its ally, the English monarchy) because of their conviction that its rituals and ecclesiastical hierarchy were inconsistent with tenets of the Protestant Reformation, the sixteenth-century religious revolt against the Catholic Church that emphasized self-scrutiny and the reading of Scripture. Because Puritans tended to view their struggle in terms of God's conflict with Satan, those who came to New England interpreted their migration as divinely inspired. Thus they likened themselves to the biblical Israelites, America to the Promised Land, and their colonies to the "New Jerusalem." This religious sense of mission reverberates throughout much of U.S. history, and writers to this day continue to examine the influence of the Puritan frame of mind upon the American psyche.

Clerical domination of political affairs, most marked in New England, declined toward the end of the seventeenth century. In their place developed an elite class of merchants and lawyers, and, in the southern colonies (Virginia, Maryland, the Carolinas, and Georgia), wealthy cotton and tobacco planters, who tended to hold more authority than the royal British governors. African slaves, scarcely present during the seventeenth century, swelled the population of southern regions in the mid-eighteenth century, becoming the mainstay of the plantation economy. Another alteration in the population stemmed from a surge of European immigration during the first half of the eighteenth century, bringing hundreds of thousands of Germans, Irish, and Scotch-Irish to the colonies. This influx helped push the frontier westward; in the process, control over much of the land was wrested away from the Indians, the indigenous inhabitants of North America.

Colonial antagonism toward British rule during the eighteenth century culminated in the War of Independence (1775–1782). In addition to resentment over taxation, the revolt was fed by a subtle but potent factor: an emerging nationalism that engaged ideals of rustic simplicity, innocence, and personal independence. Fueled by the image of America as an idyllic land unfettered by authority—which had wide currency since the earliest years of colonization—this notion of national identity prefigured the nonconformist, individualistic tenor of nineteenth-century America.

Colonial leaders responded to British interventions in provincial affairs during the 1760s and 1770s by affirming, at the First Continental Congress (1774), the autonomy of colonial legislatures and by limiting trade with England. Most delegates to the First and Second Congresses (1775) were opposed to independence, but the 1775 battle between the Massachusetts militia and British troops at Lexington and Concord, and the publication of *Common Sense* (1776), Thomas Paine's (1737–1809) widely read revolutionary pamphlet, turned popular opinion against reconciliation with England. On behalf of the Congress, Thomas Jefferson (1743–1826), a liberal Virginia landowner who would become the third president of the United States, drafted the Declaration of Independence (adopted July 4, 1776), a document that founded the republic upon the Enlightenment ideals of equality and natural rights.

The protracted military struggle against Britain, waged internationally and involving French, Dutch, and Spanish forces on the victorious American side, was settled by the 1783 Treaty of Paris. Delegates to the Constitutional Convention (1787) adopted a bold plan for a powerful federal government based on the separation of powers between an executive, a two-chambered legislature, and a judiciary. After much debate, and the inclusion of the Bill of Rights, which guaranteed a range of civil rights, including freedom of religion and expression, the Constitution was ratified by most states in 1788. In 1789 George Washington (1732–1799), who had commanded American forces against the British, was elected the nation's first president.

Beginning with Jefferson's presidency (1800–1808), the United States pursued an aggressive policy of westward expansion, doubling its area by purchasing the vast Louisiana Territory from France in 1803. Settlement of western regions surged between 1820 and 1860, fed by an ascendant nationalism, the construction of roads and railroads, a burgeoning economy, and the migration of millions of Europeans. This turbulent era, which gave birth to the notion that it was the republic's "manifest destiny" to extend its border to the Pacific Ocean, was also marked by a wave of reform movements, promoting such causes as women's rights, temperance, labor, and the elimination of slavery. Expansion and reform collided as abolitionists (opponents of slavery) sought to prohibit slavery in the newly created western states. Tensions over slavery, inflamed by the Mexican War (1846–1848)—through which the United States acquired the California and New Mexico territories—eventually erupted into war in 1861 when six southern states (Alabama, South Carolina, Mississippi, Louisiana, Florida, and Georgia, joined later by others, including Virginia and Texas), seceded from the nation and formed the Confederate States of America.

The Civil War (1861–1865) was a bitter, costly struggle that had far-reaching consequences for the nation. Slavery had been in conflict with American egalitarianism since the republic's inception (the Constitution defined slaves as "three-fifths" of a person), but it was not until the 1820s, when it was outlawed in Northern states and simultaneously came to dominate the Southern cotton economy, that it began to foment deep political division. Suffused through much of Southern society, the racist conviction that African-Americans were innately inferior was shared by many northerners as well. Although President Abraham Lincoln (1809–1865), leader of the Union forces of the North, is popularly known as the liberator of the slaves, during the early stages of the war he subordinated his personal objection to slavery to the goal of reunifying the nation. In 1862, however, he issued the Emancipation Proclamation, freeing all slaves, in part because he believed it would aid the military conquest of the Confederacy.

Following the 1865 Union victory, the South—ravaged by the war—entered a period of turmoil known as Reconstruction in which most southerners resisted black empowerment, sometimes through the violent activities of organizations like the Ku Klux Klan, created shortly after the war. Although the Thirteenth Amendment (1865) to the Constitution had abolished slavery, and the Fourteenth (1866) had guaranteed "equal protection" to all Americans, African-Americans continued to face severe obstacles that actually worsened in the 1890s when southern states adopted "Jim Crow" laws, disfranchising African-Americans and institutionalizing segregational practices that were not overturned until the 1950s and 1960s.

In the decades following the Civil War, the United States underwent a profound metamorphosis. The frontier disappeared, industry proliferated, and millions of immigrants from southern and eastern Europe streamed into the nation's rapidly growing cities. Technological breakthroughs—including the invention of the automobile, telephone, and electric light—facilitated the expansion of the economy, and a new class of powerful, charismatic business leaders emerged.

The country's expanding economic power propelled it into world politics by the turn of the century, when it embarked on a number of imperial ventures, including the acquisition of Puerto Rico and the Philippines (1898), military interventions in Latin America, and the construction of the Panama Canal. Although President Woodrow Wilson (1856–1924) endeavored to remain neutral in World War I, America's eventual entry into the war in 1917, along with Wilson's prominent role in the subsequent peace negotiations, and his centrality to the creation of the League of Nations all helped establish the United States as a global power.

A commercial boom after the war accompanied a questioning of traditional values, seemingly hollow after the brutality and degradation of the war. Under the influence of a flourishing youth culture, the 1920s (known as the Jazz Age) were marked by a literary and artistic outpouring, and by striking changes in the role of women, who won the right to vote in 1920. The decade also brought reactions to social liberalization, including a resurgence of xenophobia and the prohibition of alcoholic beverages. The Great Depression of 1929, and the ensuing years of economic crisis, were met with President Franklin D. Roosevelt's controversial recovery plan, the New Deal, which relied on an unprecedented degree of federal involvement in the economy.

Although the United States had withdrawn into an isolationist mood after World War I, it was ultimately pulled into World War II when the Japanese attacked Pearl Harbor in 1941, and it was instrumental in defeating the German-led Axis forces in Europe. The conclusion of the war left America and the Soviet Union the preeminent global powers, and the postwar decades were dominated by political competition and periodic confrontations between them known as the Cold War.

American society since World War II has been shaped by suburban growth, an economic expansion that subsided in the 1970s, political divisiveness over the Vietnam War, the increasing presence of women in professional and political life, and—despite great strides achieved by the Civil Rights Movement during the 1950s and 1960s—the persistence of racial antagonisms.

Further Readings

Bercovitch, Sacvan. *The Puritan Origins of the American Self*. New Haven: Yale University Press, 1975.

Cameron, Sharon. *The Corporeal Self: Allegories of the Body in Melville and Hawthorne*. Baltimore: Johns Hopkins University Press, 1981.

Cavell, Stanley. *The Senses of Walden*. New York: Viking Press, 1972.

Costello, Bonnie. *Marianne Moore: Imaginary Possessions*. Cambridge, Mass: Harvard University Press, 1981.

Dictionary of Literary Biography, Vols. 33, 38, and 51. Detroit: Gale Research, 1984.

Dijkstra, Bram. *The Hieroglyphics of New Speech*. Princeton: Princeton University Press, 1969.

Draper, James R., ed. *Black Literature Criticism. 4 vols*. Detroit: Gale Research, 1992.

Howe, Susan. *My Emily Dickinson*. Berkeley: North Atlantic Books, 1985.

Kazin, Alfred. *An American Procession*. New York: Knopf, 1984.

———. *A Writer's America: Landscape in Literature*. New York: A. A. Knopf, 1988.

King-kok Cheung, "Asian American Literature," in *Benet's Reader's Encyclopedia of American Literature*. New York: HarperCollins.

Levin, Harry. *The Power of Blackness*. New York: Knopf, 1980.

Mariani, Paul. *William Carlos Williams*. New York: McGraw-Hill, 1981.

Miller, J. Hillis. *Hawthorne and History: Defacing It*. Cambridge, Mass.: Basil Blackwell, 1991.

Poirer, Richard. *A World Elsewhere: The Place of Style in American Literature*. New York: Oxford University Press, 1966.

———. *Poetry and Pragmatism*. Cambridge: Harvard University Press, 1992.

Rowe, J. C. *Through the Custom-House: Nineteenth-Century American Fiction and Modern Theory*. Baltimore: Johns Hopkins University Press, 1982.

Smith, Valerie, ed. *African American Writers*. New York: Scribner's, 1991.

Sturtevant, William C., ed. *Handbook of North American Indians*. 20 vols. projected. Washington: Smithsonian Institution. 1978–.
Vol. 4 (1988): *History of Indian-White Relations*. Wilcomb E. Washburn, ed.
Vol. 5 (1984): *Arctic*. David Damas, ed.
Vol. 6 (1981): *Subarctic*. June Helm, ed.
Vol. 7 (1990): *Northwest*. Wayne Suttles, ed.
Vol. 8 (1978): *California*. Robert F. Heizer, ed.
Vol. 9 (1979): *Southwest*. Alfonso Ortiz, ed.
Vol. 10 (1983): *Southwest*. Alfonso Ortiz, ed.
Vol. 11 (1986): *Great Basin*. Warren L. D'Azevedo, ed.
Vol. 15 (1978): *Northeast*. Bruce G. Trigger, ed.

Tanner, Tony. *Scenes of Nature, Signs of Men*. New York: Cambridge University Press, 1987.

Todorov, Tsvetan. *The Conquest of America. Perceiving the Other*. New York: Harper & Row, 1983.

Tompkins, Jane. *Sensational Designs*. New York: Oxford University Press, 1985.

Vendler, Helen. *The Music of What Happens: Poems, Poets, Critics*. Cambridge: Harvard University Press, 1988.

ANNE BRADSTREET (c. 1612–1672)
United States

Cultural sophistication and political involvement marked the life of Anne Bradstreet from her childhood in Northampton, England—where her father was a financial officer in the household of a Puritan nobleman eventually prosecuted by Charles I—through her adulthood as mother of eight and wife of a man who was, at different times, secretary to the Bay Company of the Massachusetts Bay Colony, its deputy governor, and in 1645 its governor; with the restoration of the monarchy in England in 1661, Simon Bradstreet traveled there to renegotiate the charter of the Bay Company. Anne Bradstreet's experience is a metaphor for the Puritan errand into the wilderness. She crossed in 1630, with her husband, Simon Bradstreet, and her parents on the same ship with Governor John Winthrop and found that her heart "rose" in horror when she first saw the "wild, the ruinous waste" of America's shore; she was sixteen, weak in health, and already married for two years—the Old World's conventions bridged her passage to the New. Reared to wear the Puritan habit of mind, she never stopped examining her life in an attempt to discover the divine harmony and sing her part in it through her poems.

The Author to Her Book

Thou ill-formed offspring of my feeble brain,
Who after birth didst by my side remain,
Til snatched from thence by friends, less wise than true,
Who thee abroad, exposed to public view,
Made thee in rags, halting to th' press to trudge,   5
Where errors were not lessened (all may judge).
At thy return my blushing was not small,
My rambling brat (in print) should mother call,
I cast thee by as one unfit for light,
Thy visage was so irksome in my sight;   10
Yet being mine own, at length affection would
Thy blemishes amend, if so I could:
I washed thy face, but more defects I saw,
And rubbing off a spot still made a flaw.
I stretched thy joints to make thee even feet,   15
Yet still thou run'st more hobbling than is meet;
In better dress to trim thee was my mind,
But nought save homespun cloth i' th' house I find.
In this array 'mongst vulgars may'st thou roam.
In critic's hands beware thou dost not come,   20
And take thy way where yet thou art not known;
If for thy father asked, say thou hadst none;

And for thy mother, she alas is poor,
Which caused her thus to send thee out of door.

PHILLIS WHEATLEY (1753–1784)

Born along the Gambia River in West Africa, in what is now Gambia, Phillis
Wheatley was captured by slaves at the age of seven and brought to New
England. She was bought by Susanna and John Wheatley, who quickly recog-
nized her remarkable faculty with language. Her *Poems on Various Subjects,
Religious and Moral* (London, 1773), the first book to be published by an African
American and primarily occasional poems, is a tour de force in the poetic style of
the day and earned her much recognition in the United States and England.
Although Wheatley was maligned for many generations for her apparent
wholehearted acceptance of slavery, contemporary African-American poets such
as Alice Walker and June Jordan have demonstrated the complexity of Wheatley's
context and how she used irony and metaphor to express her longing for
freedom. Constrained by her situation, Wheatley is emblematic of many
African-American writers who had to code their work carefully in order to write
and to be published. She died early, in poverty and obscurity.

On Being Brought from Africa to America

'Twas mercy brought me from my *Pagan* land,
Taught my benighted soul to understand
That there's a God, that there's a *Saviour* too:
Once I redemption neither sought nor knew.
Some view our sable race with scornful eye,
"Their colour is a diabolic die."
Remember, *Christians, Negros,* black as *Cain,*
May be refin'd, and join th' angelic train.

5

ANONYMOUS (EARLY NINETEENTH CENTURY)
United States

The people known as the Iroquois were made up of the Mohawk, Seneca,
Oneida, Onondaga, and Cayuga nations. The Five Nations were joined, in the

early nineteenth century, by the Tuscarora of North Carolina, thus becoming the Six Nations. These inhabitants of the eastern Woodlands were speakers of the Algonquian language group, and it was some unidentified Algonquian word that early French explorers seized upon to coin the term *Iroquois*.

Warfare was an important element of Iroquois cultural experience and it was in response to the terrible consequences of ongoing wars that the League or Confederacy of the Five Nations was founded sometime in the late fifteenth century by a man named Hiawatha. According to Iroquois legend, having lost all of his daughters in war, Hiawatha, in a rage of grief and despair, went off by himself into the forest where he encountered a supernatural being named Deganawidah, the Peacemaker. Deganawidah comforted Hiawatha and taught him Rituals of Condolence which were to be the core of a new creed, the Good News of Peace and Power. Thus, the cultural ideal of peace was established, and, while war continued as a central reality of Iroquois life, at least there were now ritual means of comforting the bereaved—and an ongoing hope for more lasting peace.

The selections below are from William Fenton's edition of *Parker on the Iroquois* (Syracuse: Syracuse University Press, 1968). Arthur C. Parker was himself an Iroquois who contributed to the study of his people's legends and history, in the early twentieth century. Atotarho was a particularly powerful and evil Onondaga chief who opposed Hiawatha initially, and was eventually won over by him to the ideal of peace. What is said of the Onondaga lords or principal persons would be largely true of the practices observed by other members of the Iroquois League.

Instructions for the Iroquois Confederation

I am Dekanawidah, and with the Five Nations confederate lords I plant the Tree of the Great Peace. . . . I name the tree the Tree of the Great Long Leaves. Under the shade of this Tree of the Great Peace we spread the soft white feather down of the globe thistle as seats for you, Atotarho, and your cousin lords. There shall you sit and watch the council fire of the confederacy of the Five Nations. Roots have spread out from the Tree, and the name of these roots is the Great White Roots of Peace. If any man of any nation shall show a desire to obey the laws of the Great Peace, they shall trace the roots to their source, and they shall be welcomed to take shelter beneath the Tree of the Long Leaves. The smoke of the confederate council fire shall pierce the sky so that all nations may discover the central council fire of the Great Peace. I, Dekanawidah, and the confederate lords now uproot the tallest pine tree and into the cavity thereby made we cast all weapons of war. Into the depth of the earth, down into the deep underearth currents of water flowing into unknown regions; we cast all weapons of war. We bury them from sight forever and plant again the Tree.

* * *

We do now crown you with the sacred emblem of the antlers, the sign of your lordship. You shall now become a mentor of the people of the Five Nations. The thickness of your skin will be seven spans, for you will be proof against anger, offensive action, and criticism. With endless patience you shall carry out your duty, and your firmness shall be tempered with compassion for your people.

Neither anger nor fear shall find lodgment in your mind, and all your words and actions shall be tempered with calm deliberation. In all your official acts, self-interest shall be cast aside. You shall look and listen to the welfare of the whole people, and have always in view, not only the present but the coming generations—the unborn of the future Nation.

* * *

The Onondaga lords shall open each council by expressing their gratitude to their cousin lords, and greeting them, and they shall make an address and offer thanks to the earth where men dwell, to the streams of water, the pools, the springs, the lakes, to the maize and the fruits, to the medicinal herbs and the trees, to the forest trees for their usefulness, to the animals that serve as food and who offer their pelts as clothing, to the great winds and the lesser winds, to the Thunderers, and the Sun, the mighty warrior, to the moon, to the messengers of the Great Spirit who dwells in the skies above, who gives all things useful to men, who is the source and the ruler of health and life.

Then shall the Onondaga lords declare the council open.

ANONYMOUS (MID-NINETEENTH CENTURY)
United States

Spirituals, or sorrow songs as they are sometimes called, are a body of communal oral literature created by Africans enslaved in America. Influenced by African rhythms and concepts, spirituals also draw from the Bible and from the Book of Common Prayer, even as they are rooted in the everyday lives of slaves. Spirituals are a truly American art, for they are the result of the forced union of African and European concepts.

A major theme in spirituals is the longing for a mother, reflecting not only a longing for mothers who were sometimes sold away from their children but also a longing for the motherland left behind. Another equally pervasive theme is the desire for freedom that slaves expressed through their use of the biblical story of Moses liberating the Israelites from Egypt. By using biblical stories, slaves could protest their condition in a form to which their Christian masters could hardly object. The spirituals are both an expression of the slave's emotions and a protest against their condition.

Go Down, Moses

Go down, Moses,
Way down in Egyptland
Tell old Pharaoh
To let my people go.

When Israel was in Egyptland   5
Let my people go
Oppressed so hard they could not stand
Let my people go.

Go down, Moses,
Way down in Egyptland   10
Tell old Pharaoh
"Let my people go."

"Thus saith the Lord," bold Moses said,
"Let my people go;
If not I'll smite your first-born dead   15
Let my people go.

"No more shall they in bondage toil,
Let my people go;
Let them come out with Egypt's spoil,
Let my people go."   20

The Lord told Moses what to do
Let my people go;
To lead the children of Israel through,
Let my people go.

Go down, Moses,   25
Way down in Egyptland,
Tell old Pharaoh,
"Let my people go!"

RALPH WALDO EMERSON (1803–1882)

Emerson was born in Boston into an old New England family of ministers; his father was the liberal minister of the First Church in Boston, holding beliefs later to be formulated as Unitarianism. Emerson attended the Boston Latin School, Harvard and then its Divinity School, and became minister of the Second Church in Boston until he was relieved of his duties for not wishing to administer the sacraments. He toured Europe and returned to a career as lecturer, essayist, and poet, delivering occasional guest sermons. He was linked with the Transcendentalists (especially Margaret Fuller and Henry David Thoreau). Called "The Sage of Concord," Emerson was revered as the most original philosopher of his time. His *Journals* provide some insight into the relation between his consciousness—the development of which can be followed in his *Essays* (1841 and 1844) or experiments in thinking—and his ongoing life. Here he stores up what matters to him.

Walt Whitman said of Emerson's work that it "set his simmering mind to boil." The careful reader of Emerson will understand why. Emerson quizzed all words, all sounds. Aware that all institutions are imprisoning, he charged his sentences to break out of themselves constantly to represent more adequately nature's incessant motion.

from Journals

[September 6, 1833: My Book About Nature]

Fair fine wind, still in the Channel—off the coast of Ireland but not in sight of land. This morning 37 sail in sight.

I like my book about nature & wish I knew where & how I ought to live. God will show me. I am glad to be on my way home yet not so glad as others & my way to the bottom I could find perchance with less regret for I think it would not hurt me, that is the ducking or drowning.

[November–December 1833: This Book Is My Savings Bank]

This Book is my Savings Bank. I grow richer because I have somewhere to deposit my earnings; and fractions are worth more to me because corresponding fractions are waiting here that shall be made integers by their addition.

[from November 15, 1834: Hail to the Quiet Fields]

Hail to the quiet fields of my fathers! Not wholly unattended by supernatural friendship & favor let me come hither. Bless my purposes as they are simple & virtuous. . . . Henceforth I design not to utter any speech, poem, or book that is not entirely & peculiarly my work. I will say at Public Lectures & the like, those things which I have meditated for their own sake & not for the first time with a view to that occasion. If otherwise you select a new subject & labor to make a good appearance on the appointed day, it is so much lost time to you & lost time to your hearer. It is a parenthesis in your genuine life. You are your own dupe. & for the sake of conciliating your audience you have failed to edify them & winning their ear you have really lost their love and gratitude.

[May 26, 1837: The One Universal Mind]

Who shall define to me an Individual? I behold with awe & delight many illustrations of the One Universal Mind. I see my being imbedded in it. As a plant in the earth so I grow in God. I am only a form of him. He is the soul of Me. I can even with a mountainous aspiring say, *I am God,* by transferring my *Me* out of the flimsy & unclean precincts of my body, my fortunes, my private will, & meekly retiring upon the holy austerities of the Just & the Loving—upon the secret fountains of Nature. That thin & difficult ether, I also can breathe. The mortal lungs & nostrils burst & shrivel, but the soul itself needeth no organs—it is all element & all organ. Yet why not always so? How came the Individual thus armed & impassioned to parricide, thus murderously inclined ever to traverse & kill the divine life? Ah wicked Manichee![1] Into that dim problem I cannot enter. A believer in Unity, a seer of Unity, I yet behold two.

I behold; I bask in beauty; I await; I wonder; Where is my Godhead now? This is the Male & Female principle in Nature. One Man, male & female created he him. Hard as it is to describe God, it is harder to describe the Individual.

A certain wandering light comes to me which I instantly perceive to be the Cause of Causes. It transcends all proving. It is itself the ground of being; and I see that it is not one & I another, but this is the life of my life. That is one fact, then; that in certain moments I have known that I existed directly from God, and am, as it were, his organ. And in my ultimate consciousness Am He. Then, secondly, the contradictory fact is familiar, that I am a surprised spectator & learner of all my life. This is the habitual posture of the mind—beholding. But whenever the day dawns, the great day of truth on the soul, it comes with awful invitation to me to accept it, to blend with its aurora.

Cannot I conceive the Universe without a contradiction?

[from October 26, 1838: An Original Genius]

Every word, every striking word that occurs in the pages of an original genius will provoke attack & be the subject of twenty pamphlets & a hundred paragraphs. Should he be so duped as to stop & listen? Rather, let him know that the page he writes today will contain a new subject for the pamphleteers, & that which he writes tomorrow, more. Let him not be misled to give it any more than the notice due from him, viz. just that which it had in his first page, before the controversy. The exaggeration of the notice is right for them, false for him. Every word that he quite naturally writes is as prodigious & offensive. So write on, & by & by will come a reader and an age that will justify all your context. Do not even look behind. Leave that bone for them to pick & welcome.

Let me study & work contentedly & faithfully, I do not remember my critics. I forget them—I depart from them by every step I take. If I think then of them, it is a bad sign. . . .

[May 28, 1839: The New Individual]

There is no history: There is only Biography. The attempt to perpetuate, to fix a thought or principle, fails continually. You can only live for yourself: Your action is good only whilst it is alive—whilst it is in you. The awkward imitation of it by

---

1. Manichean: one who follows the dualistic religious philosophy taught by the Persian prophet Manes (c. third century B.C.).

your child or your disciple, is not a repetition of it, is not the same thing but another thing. The new individual must work out the whole problem of science, letters, & theology for himself, can owe his fathers nothing. There is no history; only biography.

NATHANIEL HAWTHORNE (1804–1864)
United States

Born in Salem, Massachusetts, to the old New England family of Hathornes—he changed the spelling as a young man—Hawthorne lost his merchant seaman father from yellow fever when he was four, and early developed habits of solitude. After attending Bowdoin College, he had, as he wrote to Longfellow, to do something "sensible for a living," which he did for journals at first. By the time of *The Scarlet Letter* (1850), he was counted as a major American author; his friendship with Herman Melville, begun shortly afterwards, was of capital importance for both men. Hawthorne became the United States consul in Liverpool from 1853–1857, and after a stay in Italy (which provided the material for *The Marble Faun*), he returned to New England and died, probably of a brain tumor.

Troubling reminders of our hidden states characterize Nathaniel Hawthorne's fictions. Henry James brilliantly noted "Hawthorne's catlike faculty of seeing in the dark." His *Twice-Told Tales* (1837) show his obsession with seventeenth century Puritanism: More than any other American writer, he grappled with the Puritan habit of mind, unfolding and exposing for public attention the consequences of regularly examining one's conscience and setting down a record. A descendant of two judges active in the persecution, first, of Quakers in the 1650s, then of witches in the Salem trials of the 1690s, Hawthorne was uncomfortably familiar with the sense of common guilt. In "The Minister's Black Veil: A Parable," this intense consciousness of guilt is made vivid by the haunting image of the title. The heavy psychological and physical atmosphere of brooding—like the veil—will not lift.

from *Twice-Told Tales*

The Minister's Black Veil: A Parable[1]

The sexton stood in the porch of Milford meeting-house, pulling busily at the bell-rope. The old people of the village came stooping along the street. Children,

---

1. Another clergyman in New England, Mr. Joseph Moody, of York, Maine, who died about eighty years since, made himself remarkable by the same eccentricity that is here related of the Reverend Mr. Hooper. In his case, however, the symbol had a different import. In early life he had accidentally killed a beloved friend; and from that day till the hour of his own death, he hid his face from men. [Hawthorne's note]

with bright faces, tripped merrily beside their parents, or mimicked a graver gait, in the conscious dignity of their Sunday clothes. Spruce bachelors looked sidelong at the pretty maidens, and fancied that the Sabbath sunshine made them prettier than on week days. When the throng had mostly streamed into the porch, the sexton began to toll the bell, keeping his eye on the Reverend Mr. Hooper's door. The first glimpse of the clergyman's figure was the signal for the bell to cease its summons.

"But what has good Parson Hooper got upon his face?" cried the sexton in astonishment.

All within hearing immediately turned about, and beheld the semblance of Mr. Hooper, pacing slowly his meditative way towards the meeting-house. With one accord they started, expressing more wonder than if some strange minister were coming to dust the cushions of Mr. Hopper's pulpit.

"Are you sure it is our parson?" inquired Goodman Gray of the sexton.

"Of a certainty it is good Mr. Hooper," replied the sexton. "He was to have exchanged pulpits with Parson Shute, of Westbury; but Parson Shute sent to excuse himself yesterday, being to preach a funeral sermon."

The cause of so much amazement may appear sufficiently slight. Mr. Hooper, a gentlemanly person, of about thirty, though still a bachelor, was dressed with due clerical neatness, as if a careful wife had starched his band, and brushed the weekly dust from his Sunday's garb. There was but one thing remarkable in his appearance. Swathed about his forehead, and hanging down over his face, so low as to be shaken by his breath, Mr. Hooper had on a black veil. On a nearer view it seemed to consist of two folds of crape, which entirely concealed his features, except the mouth and chin, but probably did not intercept his sight, further than to give a darkened aspect of all living and inanimate things. With this gloomy shade before him, good Mr. Hooper walked onward, at a slow and quiet pace, stooping somewhat, and looking on the ground, as is customary with abstracted men, yet nodding kindly to those of his parishioners who still waited on the meeting-house steps. But so wonder-struck were they that his greeting hardly met with a return.

"I can't really feel as if good Mr. Hooper's face was behind that piece of crape," said the sexton.

"I don't like it," muttered an old woman, as she hobbled into the meeting-house. "He has changed himself into something awful, only by hiding his face."

"Our parson has gone mad!" cried Goodman Gray, following him across the threshold.

A rumor of some unaccountable phenomenon had preceded Mr. Hooper into the meeting-house, and set all the congregation astir. Few could refrain from twisting their heads towards the door; many stood upright, and turned directly about; while several little boys clambered upon the seats, and came down again with a terrible racket. There was a general bustle, a rustling of the women's gowns and shuffling of the men's feet, greatly at variance with that hushed repose which should attend the entrance of the minister. But Mr. Hooper appeared not to notice the perturbation of his people. He entered with an almost noiseless step, bent his head mildly to the pews on each side, and bowed as he passed his oldest parishioner, a white-haired great grandsire, who occupied an arm-chair in the centre of the aisle. It was strange to observe how slowly this venerable man became conscious of something singular in the appearance of his pastor. He seemed not fully to partake of the prevailing wonder, till Mr. Hooper had ascended the stairs, and showed himself in the pulpit, face to face with his congregation, except for the black veil. That mysterious emblem was never once withdrawn. It shook with his measured breath, as he gave out the psalm; it threw its obscurity between him and the holy page, as he read the Scriptures; and while he prayed, the veil lay heavily on his uplifted countenance. Did he seek to hide it from the dread Being whom he was addressing?

Such was the effect of this simple piece of crape, that more than one woman of delicate nerves was forced to leave the meeting-house. Yet perhaps the pale-faced congregation was almost as fearful a sight to the minister, as his black veil to them.

Mr. Hooper had the reputation of a good preacher, but not an energetic one: he strove to win his people heavenward by mild, persuasive influences, rather than to drive them thither by the thunders of the Word. The sermon which he now delivered was marked by the same characteristics of style and manner as the general series of his pulpit oratory. But there was something, either in the sentiment of the discourse itself, or in the imagination of the auditors, which made it greatly the most powerful effort that they had ever heard from their pastor's lips. It was tinged, rather than more darkly than usual, with the gentle gloom of Mr. Hooper's temperament. The subject had reference to secret sin, and those sad mysteries which we hide from our nearest and dearest, and would fain conceal from our own consciousness, even forgetting that the Omniscient can detect them. A subtle power was breathed into his words. Each member of the congregation, the most innocent girl, and the man of hardened breast, felt as if the preacher had crept upon them, behind his awful veil, and discovered their hoarded iniquity of deed or thought. Many spread their clasped hands on their bosoms. There was nothing terrible in what Mr. Hooper said, at least, no violence; and yet, with every tremor of his melancholy voice, the hearers quaked. An unsought pathos came hand in hand with awe. So sensible were the audience of some unwonted attribute in their minister, that they longed for a breath of wind to blow aside the veil, almost believing that a stranger's visage would be discovered, though the form, gesture, and voice were those of Mr. Hooper.

At the close of the services, the people hurried out with indecorous confusion, eager to communicate their pent-up amazement, and conscious of lighter spirits the moment they lost sight of the black veil. Some gathered in little circles, huddled closely together, with their mouths all whispering in the centre; some went homeward alone, wrapt in silent meditation; some talked loudly, and profaned the Sabbath day with ostentatious laughter. A few shook their sagacious heads, intimating that they could penetrate the mystery; while one or two affirmed that there was no mystery at all, but only that Mr. Hooper's eyes were so weakened by the midnight lamp, as to require a shade. After a brief interval, forth came good Mr. Hooper also, in the rear of his flock. Turning his veiled face from one group to another, he paid due reverence to the hoary heads, saluted the middle aged with kind dignity as their friend and spiritual guide, greeted the young with mingled authority and love, and laid his hands on the little children, to bless them. Such was always his custom on the Sabbath day. Strange and bewildered looks repaid him for his courtesy. None, as on former occasions, aspired to the honor of walking by their pastor's side. Old Squire Saunders, doubtless by an accidental lapse of memory, neglected to invite Mr. Hooper to his table, where the good clergyman had been wont to bless the food, almost every Sunday since his settlement. He returned, therefore, to the parsonage, and, at the moment of closing the door, was observed to look back upon the people, all of whom had their eyes fixed upon the minister. A sad smile gleamed faintly from beneath the black veil, and flickered about his mouth, glimmering as he disappeared.

"How strange," said a lady, "that a simple black veil, such as any woman might wear on her bonnet, should become such a terrible thing on Mr. Hooper's face!"

"Something must surely be amiss with Mr. Hooper's intellects," observed her husband, the physician of the village. "But the strangest part of the affair is the effect of this vagary, even on a sober-minded man like myself. The black veil, though it covers only our pastor's face, throws its influence over his whole person, and makes him ghostlike from head to foot. Do you not feel it so?"

"Truly do I," replied the lady; "and I would not be alone with him for the world. I wonder he is not afraid to be alone with himself!"

"Men sometimes are so," said her husband.

The afternoon service was attended with similar circumstances. At its conclusion, the bell tolled for the funeral of a young lady. The relatives and friends were assembled in the house, and the more distant acquaintances stood about the door, speaking of the good qualities of the deceased, when their talk was interrupted by the appearance of Mr. Hooper, still covered with his black veil. It was now an appropriate emblem. The clergyman stepped into the room where the corpse was laid, and bent over the coffin, to take a last farewell of his deceased parishioner. As he stooped, the veil hung straight down from his forehead, so that, if her eyelids had not been closed forever, the dead maiden might have seen his face. Could Mr. Hooper be fearful of her glance, that he so hastily caught back the black veil? A person who watched the interview between the dead and living, scrupled not to affirm, that, at the instant when the clergyman's features were disclosed, the corpse had slightly shuddered, rustling the shroud and muslin cap, though the countenance retained the composure of death. A superstitious old woman was the only witness of this prodigy. From the coffin Mr. Hooper passed into the chamber of the mourners, and thence to the head of the staircase, to make the funeral prayer. It was a tender and heart-dissolving prayer, full of sorrow, yet so imbued with celestial hopes, that the music of a heavenly harp, swept by the fingers of the dead, seemed faintly to be heard among the saddest accents of the minister. The people trembled, though they but darkly understood him when he prayed that they, and himself, and all of mortal race, might be ready, as he trusted this young maiden had been, for the dreadful hour that should snatch the veil from their faces. The bearers went heavily forth, and the mourners followed, saddening all the street, with the dead before them, and Mr. Hooper in his black veil behind.

_____ool back?" said one in the procession to his partner.

"Why do yo'____," replied she, "that the minister and the maiden's spirit were
"I had an ha'd."
walking ____ had _at the same moment," said the other.

"___night, ____e handsomest couple in Milford village were to be joined in
_____. Thou'_ reckoned a melancholy man, Mr. Hooper had a placid
____fulness f_r such occasions, which often excited a sympathetic smile where
_____lier merr_ment would have been thrown away. There was no quality of his
_disposition which made him more beloved than this. The company at the
wedding awaited his arrival with impatience, trusting that the strange awe, which
had gathered over him throughout the day, would now be dispelled. But such was
not the result. When Mr. Hooper came, the first thing that their eyes rested on was
the same horrible black veil, which had added deeper gloom to the funeral, and
could portend nothing but evil to the wedding. Such was its immediate effect on
the guests that a cloud seemed to have rolled duskily from beneath the black
crape, and dimmed the light of the candles. The bridal pair stood up before the
minister. But the bride's cold fingers quivered in the tremulous hand of the
bridegroom, and her deathlike paleness caused a whisper that the maiden who
had been buried a few hours before was come from her grave to be married. If ever
another wedding were so dismal, it was that famous one where they tolled the
wedding knell. After performing the ceremony, Mr. Hooper raised a glass of wine
to his lips, wishing happiness to the new-married couple in a strain of mild
pleasantry that ought to have brightened the features of the guests, like a cheerful
gleam from the hearth. At that instant, catching a glimpse of his figure in the
looking-glass, the black veil involved his own spirit in the horror with which it
overwhelmed all others. His frame shuddered, his lips grew white, he spilt the
untasted wine upon the carpet, and rushed forth into the darkness. For the Earth,
too, had on her Black Veil.

The next day, the whole village of Milford talked of little else than Parson
Hooper's black veil. That, and the mystery concealed behind it, supplied a topic
for discussion between acquaintances meeting in the street, and good women
gossiping at their open windows. It was the first item of news that the
tavern-keeper told to his guests. The children babbled of it on their way to school.
One imitative little imp covered his face with an old black handkerchief, thereby
so affrighting his playmates that the panic seized himself, and he well-nigh lost his
wits by his own waggery.

It was remarkable that all of the busybodies and impertinent people in the
parish, not one ventured to put the plain question to Mr. Hooper, wherefore he
did this thing. Hitherto, whenever there appeared the slightest call for such
interference, he had never lacked advisers, nor shown himself averse to be guided
by their judgment. If he erred at all, it was by so painful a degree of self-distrust,
that even the mildest censure would lead him to consider an indifferent action as
a crime. Yet, though so well acquainted with this amiable weakness, no individual
among his parishioners chose to make the black veil a subject of friendly
remonstrance. There was a feeling of dread, neither plainly confessed nor carefully
concealed, which caused each to shift the responsibility upon another, till at

length it was found expedient to send a deputation of the church, in order to deal with Mr. Hooper about the mystery, before it should grow into a scandal. Never did an embassy so ill discharge its duties. The minister received them with friendly courtesy, but became silent, after they were seated, leaving to his visitors the whole burden of introducing their important business. The topic, it might be supposed, was obvious enough. There was the black veil swathed around Mr. Hooper's forehead, and concealing every feature above his placid mouth, on which, at times, they could perceive the glimmering of a melancholy smile. But that piece of crape, to their imagination, seemed to hang down before his heart, the symbol of a fearful secret between him and them. Were the veil but cast aside, they might speak freely of it, but not till then. Thus they sat a considerable time, speechless, confused, and shrinking uneasily from Mr. Hooper's eye, which they felt to be fixed upon them with an invisible glance. Finally, the deputies returned abashed to their constituents, pronouncing the matter too weighty to be handled, except by a council of the churches, if, indeed, it might not require a general synod.

But there was one person in the village unappalled by the awe with which the black veil had impressed all beside herself. When the deputies returned without an explanation, or even venturing to demand one, she, with the calm energy of her character, determined to chase away the strange cloud that appeared to be settling round Mr. Hooper, every moment more darkly than before. As his plighted wife, it should be her privilege to know what the black veil concealed. At the minister's first visit, therefore, she entered upon the subject with a direct simplicity, which made the task easier both for him and her. After he had seated himself, she fixed her eyes steadfastly upon the veil, but could discern nothing of the dreadful gloom that had so overawed the multitude: it was but a double fold of crape, hanging down from his forehead to his mouth, and slightly stirring with his breath.

"No," said she aloud, and smiling, "there is nothing terrible in this piece of crape, except that it hides a face which I am always glad to look upon. Come, good sir, let the sun shine from behind the cloud. First lay aside your black veil: then tell me why you put it on."

Mr. Hooper's smile glimmered faintly.

"There is an hour to come," said he, "when all of us shall cast aside our veils. Take it not amiss, beloved friend, if I wear this piece of crape till then."

"Your words are a mystery, too," returned the young lady. "Take away the veil from them, at least."

"Elizabeth, I will," said he, "so far as my vow may suffer me. Know, then, this veil is a type and a symbol, and I am bound to wear it ever, both in light and darkness, in solitude and before the gaze of multitudes, and as with strangers, so with my familiar friends. No mortal eye will see it withdrawn. This dismal shade must separate me from the world: even you, Elizabeth, can never come behind it!"

"What grievous affliction hath befallen you," she earnestly inquired, "that you should thus darken your eyes forever?"

"If it be a sign of mourning," replied Mr. Hooper, "I, perhaps, like most other mortals, have sorrows dark enough to be typified by a black veil."

"But what if the world will not believe that it is the type of an innocent sorrow?" urged Elizabeth. "Beloved and respected as you are, there may be whispers that you hide your face under the consciousness of secret sin. For the sake of your holy office, do away this scandal!"

The color rose into her cheeks as she intimated the nature of the rumors that were already abroad in the village. But Mr. Hooper's mildness did not forsake him. He even smiled again—that same sad smile, which always appeared like a faint glimmering of light, proceeding from the obscurity beneath the veil.

"If I hide my face for sorrow, there is cause enough," he merely replied; "and if I cover it for secret sin, what mortal might not do the same?"

And with this gentle, but unconquerable obstinacy did he resist all her entreaties. At length Elizabeth sat silent. For a few moments she appeared lost in thought, considering, probably, what new methods might be tried to withdraw her lover from so dark a fantasy, which, if it had no other meaning, was perhaps a symptom of mental disease. Though of a firmer character than his own, the tears rolled down her cheeks. But, in an instant, as it were, a new feeling took the place of sorrow: her eyes were fixed insensibly on the black veil, when, like a sudden twilight in the air, its terrors fell around her. She arose, and stood trembling before him.

"And do you feel it then, at last?" said he mournfully.

She made no reply, but covered her eyes with her hand, and turned to leave the room. He rushed forward and caught her arm.

"Have patience with me, Elizabeth!" cried he, passionately. "Do not desert me, though this veil must be between us here on earth. Be mine, and hereafter there shall be no veil over my face, no darkness between our souls! It is but a mortal veil—it is not for eternity! O! you know now how lonely I am, and how frightened, to be alone behind my black veil. Do not leave me in this miserable obscurity forever!"

"Lift the veil but once, and look me in the face," said she.

"Never! It cannot be!" replied Mr. Hooper.

"Then farewell!" said Elizabeth.

She withdrew her arm from his grasp, and slowly departed, pausing at the door, to give one long shuddering gaze, that seemed almost to penetrate the mystery of the black veil. But, even amid his grief, Mr. Hooper smiled to think that only a material emblem had separated him from happiness, though the horrors, which it shadowed forth, must be drawn darkly between the fondest of lovers.

From that time no attempts were made to remove Mr. Hooper's black veil, or, by a direct appeal, to discover the secret which it was supposed to hide. By persons who claimed a superiority to popular prejudice, it was reckoned merely an eccentric whim, such as often mingles with the sober actions of men otherwise rational, and tinges them all with its own semblance of insanity. But with the multitude, good Mr. Hooper was irreparably a bugbear. He could not walk the street with any peace of mind, so conscious was he that the gentle and timid would turn aside to avoid him, and that others would make it a point of hardihood to throw themselves in his way. The impertinence of the latter class compelled him to give up his customary walk at sunset to the burial ground; for when he leaned pensively over the gate, there would always be faces behind the gravestones, peeping at his black veil. A fable went the rounds that the stare of the dead people drove him thence. It grieved him, to the very depth of his kind heart, to observe how the children fled from his approach, breaking up their merriest sports, while his melancholy figure was yet afar off. Their instinctive dread caused him to feel more strongly than aught else, that a preternatural horror was interwoven with the threads of the black crape. In truth, his own antipathy to the veil was known to be so great, that he never willingly passed before a mirror, nor stopped to drink at a still fountain, lest, in its peaceful bosom, he should be affrighted by himself. This was what gave plausibility to the whispers, that Mr. Hooper's conscience tortured him for some great crime too horrible to be entirely concealed, or otherwise than so obscurely intimated. Thus, from beneath the black veil, there rolled a cloud into the sunshine, an ambiguity of sin or sorrow, which enveloped the poor minister, so that love or sympathy could never reach him. It was said that ghost and fiend consorted with him there. With self-shudderings and outward terrors, he walked continually in its shadow, groping darkly within his own soul, or gazing through a medium that saddened the whole world. Even the lawless wind, it was believed, respected his dreadful secret, and never blew aside the veil. But still good Mr. Hooper sadly smiled at the pale visages of the worldly throng as he passed by.

Among all its bad influences, the black veil had the one desirable effect, of making its wearer a very efficient clergyman. By the aid of his mysterious emblem—for there was no other apparent cause—he became a man of awful power over souls that were in agony for sin. His converts always regarded him with a dread peculiar to themselves, affirming, though but figuratively, that, before he brought them to celestial light, they had been with him behind the black veil. Its gloom, indeed, enabled him to sympathize with all dark affections. Dying sinners cried aloud for Mr. Hooper, and would not yield their breath till he appeared; though ever, as he stooped to whisper consolation, they shuddered at the veiled face so near their own. Such were the terrors of the black veil, even when Death had bared his visage! Strangers came long distances to attend service at his church, with the mere idle purpose of gazing at his figure, because it was forbidden them to behold his face. But many were made to quake ere they departed! Once, during Governor Belcher's administration, Mr. Hooper was appointed to preach the election sermon. Covered with his black veil, he stood before the chief magistrate, the council, and the representatives, and wrought so deep an impression, that the legislative measures of that year were characterized by all the gloom and piety of our earliest ancestral sway.

In this manner Mr. Hooper spent a long life, irreproachable in outward act, yet shrouded in dismal suspicions; kind and loving, though unloved, and dimly feared; a man apart from men, shunned in their health and joy, but ever summoned to their aid in mortal anguish. As years wore on, shedding their snows above his sable veil, he acquired a name throughout the New England churches, and they called him Father Hooper. Nearly all his parishioners, who were of mature age when he was settled, had been borne away by many a funeral: he had one congregation in the church, and a more crowded one in the churchyard; and having wrought so late into the evening, and done his work so well, it was now good Father Hooper's turn to rest.

Several persons were visible by the shaded candlelight, in the death chamber of the old clergyman. Natural connections he had none. But there was the decorously grave, though unmoved physician, seeking only to mitigate the last pangs of the patient whom he could not save. There were the deacons, and other eminently pious members of his church. There, also, was the Reverend Mr. Clark, of Westbury, a young and zealous divine, who had ridden in haste to pray by the bedside of the expiring minister. There was the nurse, no hired handmaiden of death, but one whose calm affection had endured thus long in secrecy, in solitude, amid the chill of age, and would not perish, even at the dying hour. Who, but Elizabeth! And there lay the hoary head of good Father Hooper upon the death pillow, with the black veil still swathed about his brow, and reaching down over his face, so that each more difficult gasp of his faint breath caused it to stir. All through life that piece of crape had hung between him and the world: it had separated him from cheerful brotherhood and woman's love, and kept him in that saddest of all prisons, his own heart; and still it lay upon his face, as if to deepen the gloom of his darksome chamber, and shade him from the sunshine of eternity.

For some time previous, his mind had been confused, wavering doubtfully between the past and the present, and hovering forward, as it were, at intervals, into the indistinctness of the world to come. There had been feverish turns, which tossed him from side to side, and wore away what little strength he had. But in his most convulsive struggles, and in the wildest vagaries of his intellect, when no other thought retained its sober influence, he still showed an awful solicitude lest the black veil should slip aside. Even if his bewildered soul could have forgotten, there was a faithful woman at this pillow, who, with averted eyes, would have covered that aged face, which she had last beheld in the comeliness of manhood. At length the death-stricken old man lay quietly in the torpor of mental and bodily exhaustion, with an imperceptible pulse, and breath that grew fainter and fainter, except when a long, deep, and irregular inspiration seemed to prelude the flight of his spirit.

The minister of Westbury approached the bedside.

"Venerable Father Hooper," said he, "the moment of your release is at hand. Are you ready for the lifting of the veil that shuts in time from eternity?"

Father Hooper at first replied merely by a feeble motion of his head; then, apprehensive, perhaps, that his meaning might be doubted, he exerted himself to speak.

"Yea," said he, in faint accents, "my soul hath a patient weariness until that veil be lifted."

"And is it fitting," resumed the Reverend Mr. Clark, "that a man so given to prayer, of such a blameless example, holy in deed and thought, so far as mortal judgment may pronounce; is it fitting that a father in the church should leave a shadow on his memory, that may seem to blacken a life so pure? I pray you, my venerable brother, let not this thing be! Suffer us to be gladdened by your triumphant aspect as you go to your reward. Before the veil of eternity be lifted, let me cast aside this black veil from your face!"

And thus speaking, the Reverend Mr. Clark bent forward to reveal the mystery of so many years. But, exerting a sudden energy, that made all the beholders stand aghast, Father Hooper snatched both his hands from beneath the bedclothes, and pressed them strongly on the black veil, resolute to struggle, if the minister of Westbury would contend with a dying man.

"Never!" cried the veiled clergyman. "On earth, never!"

"Dark old man!" exclaimed the affrighted minister, "with what horrible crime upon your soul are you now passing to the judgment?"

Father Hooper's breath heaved; it rattled in his throat; but, with a mighty effort, grasping forward with his hands, he caught hold of life, and held it back till he should speak. He even raised himself in bed; and there he sat, shivering with the arms of death around him, while the black veil hung down, awful, at that last moment, in the gathered terrors of a lifetime. And yet the faint, sad smile, so often there, now seemed to glimmer from its obscurity, and linger on Father Hooper's lips.

"Why do you tremble at me alone?" cried he, turning his veiled face round the circle of pale spectators. "Tremble also at each other! Have men avoided me, and women shown no pity, and children screamed and fled, only for my black veil? What, but the mystery which it obscurely typifies, has made this piece of crape so awful? When the friend shows his inmost heart to his friend; the lover to his best beloved; when man does not vainly shrink from the eye of his Creator, loathsomely treasuring up the secret of his sin; then deem me a monster, for the symbol beneath which I have lived, and die! I look around me, and, lo! on every visage a Black Veil!"

While his auditors shrank from one another, in mutual affright, Father Hooper fell back upon his pillow, a veiled corpse, with a faint smile lingering on the lips. Still veiled, they laid him in his coffin, and a veiled corpse they bore him to the grave. The grass of many years has sprung up and withered on that grave, the burial stone is moss-grown, and good Mr. Hooper's face is dust; but awful is still the thought that it mouldered beneath the Black Veil!

MARGARET FULLER (1810–1850)
United States

Henry James until his death felt himself haunted by Margaret Fuller's ghost whispering to him about what he called the central issue of the modern period, "the woman question." He had first heard of her when as a boy of eight, traveling with his father on a steamer from Albany, someone told Henry James, Sr., of the tragic drowning of Fuller, together with her husband and infant son, off the coast of Long Island (on July 19, 1850); they were returning from Italy, where Fuller had been at work covering the revolution. Soon after her death, Ralph Waldo

Emerson confided to his journal, "I have lost in her my audience." But neither Emerson nor the rest of her male contemporaries were comfortable acknowledging the power of her effect, even though she was more active than they in editing *The Dial,* their standard-setting journal of intellectual excellence. Horace Greeley did, however, recognize her talent; he made her the first woman newspaper reporter for his New York *Daily Tribune,* and supported all her future efforts as a writer. It was in New York in 1845 that *Woman in the Nineteenth Century* first appeared, scandalizing the public with its revolutionary views on the relationship between men and women. She had already antagonized many of the men of her period by her scholarship, critical acumen, and determined feminism.

from Woman in the Nineteenth Century

[Freedom as a Right, Not a Concession]

Knowing that there exists in the minds of men a tone of feeling toward women as toward slaves, such as is expressed in the common phrase, "Tell that to women and children"; that the infinite soul can only work through them in already ascertained limits; that the gift of reason, Man's highest prerogative, is allotted to them in much lower degree; that they must be kept from mischief and melancholy by being constantly engaged in active labor, which is to be furnished and directed by those better able to think, &c., &c.,—we need not multiply instances, for who can review the experience of last week without recalling words which imply, whether in jest or earnest, these views, or views like these,—knowing this, can we wonder that many reformers think that measures are not likely to be taken in behalf of women, unless their wishes could be publicly represented by women?

"That can never be necessary," cry the other side.

"All men are privately influenced by women; each has his wife, sister, or female friends, and is too much biased by these relations to fail of representing their interests; and, if this is not enough, let them propose and enforce their wishes with the pen. The beauty of home would be destroyed, the delicacy of the sex be violated, the dignity of halls of legislation degraded, by an attempt to introduce them there. Such duties are inconsistent with those of a mother"; and then we have ludicrous pictures of ladies in hysterics at the polls, and senate-chambers filled with cradles.

But if, in reply, we admit as truth that Woman seems destined by nature rather for the inner circle, we must add that the arrangements of civilized life have not been, as yet, such as to secure it to her. Her circle, if the duller, is not the quieter. If kept from "excitement," she is not from drudgery. Not only the Indian squaw carries the burdens of the camp, but the favorites of Louis XIV accompany him in his journeys, and the washerwoman stands at her tub, and carries home her work at all seasons, and in all states of health. Those who think the physical circumstances of Woman would make a part in the affairs of national government unsuitable, are by no means those who think it impossible for negresses to endure field-work, even during pregnancy, or for sempstresses to go through their killing labors.

As to the use of the pen, there was quite as much opposition to Woman's possessing herself of that help to free agency as there is now to her seizing on the rostrum or the desk; and she is likely to draw, from a permission to plead her cause that way, opposite inferences to what might be wished by those who now grant it.

As to the possibility of her filling with grace and dignity any such position, we should think those who had seen the great actresses, and heard the Quaker preachers of modern times, would not doubt that Woman can express publicly the fulness of thought and creation, without losing any of the peculiar beauty of her sex. What can pollute and tarnish is to act thus from any motive except that something needs to be said or done. Woman could take part in the processions, the songs, the dances of old religion; no one fancied her delicacy was impaired by appearing in public for such a cause.

As to her home, she is not likely to leave it more than she now does for balls, theatres, meetings for promoting missions, revival meetings, and others to which she flies, in hope of an animation for her existence commensurate with what she sees enjoyed by men. Governors of ladies'-fairs are no less engrossed by such a charge, than the governor of a state by his; presidents of Washingtonian societies no less away from home than presidents of conventions. If men look straitly to it, they will find that, unless their lives are domestic, those of the women will not be. A house is no home unless it contain food and fire for the mind as well as for the body. The female Greek, of our day, is as much in the street as the male to cry, "What news?" We doubt not it was the same in Athens of old. The women, shut out from the market-place, made up for it at the religious festivals. For human beings are not so constituted that they can live without expansion. If they do not get it in one way, they must in another, or perish.

As to men's representing women fairly at present, while we hear from men who owe to their wives not only all that is comfortable or graceful, but all that is wise, in the arrangement of their lives, the frequent remark, "You cannot reason with a woman,"—when from those of delicacy, nobleness, and poetic culture, falls the contemptuous phrase "women and children," and that in no light sally of the hour, but in works intended to give a permanent statement of the best experiences,—when not one man, in the million, shall I say? no, not in the hundred million, can rise above the belief that Woman was made *for Man*,—when such traits as these are daily forced upon the attention, can we feel that Man will always do justice to the interests of Woman? Can we think that he takes a sufficiently discerning and religious view of her office and destiny *ever* to do her justice, except when prompted by sentiment,—accidentally or transiently, that is, for the sentiment will vary according to the relations in which he is placed? The lover, the poet, the artist, are likely to view her nobly. The father and the philosopher have some chance of liberality; the man of the world, the legislator for expediency, none.

Under these circumstances, without attaching importance, in themselves, to the changes demanded by the champions of Woman, we hail them as signs of the times. We would have every arbitrary barrier thrown down. We would have every path laid open to Woman as freely as to Man. Were this done, and a slight temporary fermentation allowed to subside, we should see crystallizations more pure and of more various beauty. We believe the divine energy would pervade nature to a degree unknown in the history of former ages, and that no discordant collision, but a ravishing harmony of the spheres, would ensue.

Yet, then and only then will mankind be ripe for this, when inward and outward freedom for Woman as much as for Man shall be acknowledged as a *right*, not yielded as a concession. As the friend of the negro assumes that one man cannot by right hold another in bondage, so should the friend of Woman assume that Man cannot by right lay even well-meant restrictions on Woman. If the negro be a soul, if the woman be a soul, apparelled in flesh, to one Master only are they accountable. There is but one law for souls, and, if there is to be an interpreter of it, he must come not as man, or son of man, but as son of God.

Were thought and feeling once so far elevated that Man should esteem himself the brother and friend, but nowise the lord and tutor, of Woman,—were he really bound with her in equal worship,—arrangements as to function and employment would be of no consequence. What Woman needs is not as a woman to act or rule, but as a nature to grow, as an intellect to discern, as a soul to live freely and unimpeded, to unfold such powers as were given her when we left our common home. If fewer talents were given her, yet if allowed the free and full employment of these, so that she may render back to the giver his own with usury, she will not complain; nay, I dare to say she will bless and rejoice in her earthly birth-place, her earthly lot. Let us consider what obstructions impeded this good era, and what signs give reason to hope that it draws near.

FREDERICK DOUGLASS (1817–1895)
United States

Recognized during his lifetime as the great African-American statesman of the nineteenth century, Frederick Douglass was born Frederick Augustus Washington Bailey to a slave woman and a white man in Maryland. Realizing the power of literacy, Fred Bailey educated himself secretly, since it was illegal for a slave to learn to read. In 1838 he escaped to the North and changed his name to Douglass. By 1845 he had become the most prominent black abolitionist, due to his masterful oratory and brilliant writing. As founder and editor of the influential abolitionist paper *The North Star*, Douglass was a scathing critic of racial inequality. Later in his life he had many prestigious political positions, the last of which was U.S. consul general to the Republic of Haiti.

Douglass is best known for his authoritative slave narrative and autobiographies: *The Narrative of the Life of Frederick Douglass, an American Slave, Written by Himself* (1945), *My Bondage and My Freedom* (1855), and *The Life and Times of Frederick Douglass* (1881). Because they could not write, many ex-slaves told their narratives to whites who wrote them down, thus affecting what the

Jacob Lawrence. *Frederick Douglass Series No. 21.* 1938–1939. Tempera on hardboard. Hampton University Museum.

narrators were willing to tell and how their stories were framed. Douglass's ability to write his own narrative resulted both in his rendering of his interior life and his ironic denunciation of slavery, as demonstrated by his account of his resistance to his master, Edward Covey's attempt to "break" him. Douglass was not only a legendary activist; he was also a major planter of the seeds that would develop into a unique literary tradition.

from *Narrative of the Life of Frederick Douglass, an American Slave, Written by Himself*

[Life with Mr. Covey]

I left Master Thomas's house, and went to live with Mr. Covey, on the 1st of January, 1833. I was now, for the first time in my life, a field hand. In my new employment, I found myself even more awkward than a country boy appeared to be in a large city. I had been at my new home but one week before Mr. Covey gave me a very severe whipping, cutting my back causing the blood to run, and raising ridges on my flesh as large as my little finger. The details of this affair are as follows: Mr. Covey sent me, very early in the morning of one of our coldest days in the month of January, to the woods, to get a load of wood. He gave me a team of unbroken oxen. He told me which was the in-hand ox, and which the off-hand one. He then tied the end of a large rope around the horns of the in-hand ox, and gave me the other end of it, and told me, if the oxen started to run, that I must hold on upon the rope. I had never driven oxen before, and of course I was very awkward. I, however, succeeded in getting to the edge of the woods with little difficulty; but I had got a very few rods into the woods, when the oxen took fright, and started full tilt, carrying the cart against trees, and over stumps, in the most frightful manner. I expected every moment that my brains would be dashed out against the trees. After running thus for a considerable distance, they finally upset the cart, dashing it with great force against a tree, and threw themselves into a dense thicket. How I escaped death, I do not know. There I was, entirely alone, in a thick wood, in a place new to me. My cart was upset and shattered, my oxen were entangled among the young trees, and there was none to help me. After a long spell of effort, I succeeded in getting my cart righted, my oxen disentangled, and again yoked to the cart. I now proceeded with my team to the place where I had, the day before, been chopping wood, and loaded my cart pretty heavily, thinking in this way to tame my oxen. I then proceeded on my way home. I had now consumed one half of the day. I got out of the woods safely, and now felt out of danger. I stopped my oxen to open the woods gate; and just as I did so, before I could get hold of my ox-rope, the oxen again started, rushed through the gate, catching it between the wheel and the body of the cart, tearing it to pieces, and coming within a few inches of crushing me against the gate-post. Thus twice, in one short day, I escaped death by the merest chance. On my return, I told Mr. Covey what had happened, and how it happened. He ordered me to return to the woods again immediately. I did so, and he followed on after me. Just as I got into the woods, he came up and told me to stop my cart, and that he would teach me how to trifle away my time, and break gates. He then went to a large gum-tree, and with his axe cut three large switches, and, after trimming them up neatly with his pocket-knife, he ordered me to take off my clothes. I made him no answer, but stood with my clothes on. He repeated his order. I still made him no answer, nor did I move to strip myself. Upon this he rushed at me with the fierceness of a tiger, tore off my clothes, and lashed me till he had worn out his switches, cutting me so savagely as to leave the marks visible for a long time after. This whipping was the first of a number just like it, and for similar offences.

I lived with Mr. Covey one year. During the first six months, of that year, scarce a week passed without his whipping me. I was seldom free from a sore back. My awkwardness was almost always his excuse for whipping me. We were worked fully up to the point of endurance. Long before day we were up, our horses fed, and by the first approach of day we were off to the field with our hoes and ploughing teams. Mr. Covey gave us enough to eat, but scarce time to eat it. We were often less than five minutes taking our meals. We were often in the field from the first approach of day till its last lingering ray had left us; and at saving-fodder time, midnight often caught us in the field binding blades.

Covey would be out with us. The way he used to stand it, was this. He would spend the most of his afternoons in bed. He would then come out fresh in the evening, ready to urge us on with his words, example, and frequently with the whip. Mr. Covey was one of the few slaveholders who could and did work with his hands. He was a hard-working man. He knew by himself just what a man or a boy could do. There was no deceiving him. His work went on in his absence almost as well as in his presence; and he had the faculty of making us feel that he was ever present with us. This he did by surprising us. He seldom approached the spot where we were at work openly, if he could do it secretly. He always aimed at taking us by surprise. Such was his cunning, that we used to call him, among ourselves, "the snake." When we were at work in the cornfield, he would sometimes crawl on his hands and knees to avoid detection, and all at once he would rise nearly in our midst, and scream out, "Ha, ha! Come, come! Dash on, dash on!" This being his mode of attack, it was never safe to stop a single minute. His comings were like a thief in the night. He appeared to us as being ever at hand. He was under every tree, behind every stump, in every bush, and at every window, on the plantation. He would sometimes mount his horse, as if bound to St. Michael's, a distance of seven miles, and in half an hour afterwards you would see him coiled up in the corner of the woodfence, watching every motion of the slaves. He would, for this purpose, leave his horse tied up in the woods. Again, he would sometimes walk up to us, and give us orders as though he was upon the point of starting on a long journey, turn his back upon us, and make as though he was going to the house to get ready; and, before he would get half way thither, he would turn short and crawl into a fence-corner, or behind some tree, and there watch us till the going down of the sun.

Mr. Covey's *forte* consisted in his power to deceive. His life was devoted to planning and perpetrating the grossest deceptions. Every thing he possessed in the shape of learning or religion, he made conform to his disposition to deceive. He seemed to think himself equal to deceiving the Almighty. He would make a short prayer in the morning, and a long prayer at night; and, strange as it may seem, few men would at times appear more devotional than he. The exercises of his family devotions were always commenced with singing; and, as he was a very poor singer himself, the duty of raising the hymn generally came upon me. He would read his hymn, and nod at me to commence. I would at times do so; at others, I would not. My non-compliance would almost always produce much confusion. To show himself independent of me, he would start and stagger through with his hymn in the most discordant manner. In this state of mind, he prayed with more than ordinary spirit. Poor man! such was his disposition, and success at deceiving, I do verily believe that he sometimes deceived himself into the solemn belief, that he was a sincere worshipper of the most high God; and this, too, at a time when he may be said to have been guilty of compelling his woman slave to commit the sin of adultery. The facts in the case are these: Mr. Covey was a poor man; he was just commencing in life; he was only able to buy one slave; and, shocking as is the fact, he bought her, as he said, for a *breeder*. This woman was named Caroline. Mr. Covey bought her from Mr. Thomas Lowe, about six miles from St. Michael's. She was a large, able-bodied woman, about twenty years old. She had already given birth to one child, which proved her to be just what he wanted. After buying her, he hired a married man of Mr. Samuel Harrison, to live with him one year; and him he used to fasten up with her every night! The result was, that, at the end of the year, the miserable woman gave birth to twins. At this result Mr. Covey seemed to be highly pleased, both with the man and the wretched woman. Such was his joy, and that of his wife, that nothing they could do for Caroline during her confinement was too good, or too hard, to be done. The children were regarded as being quite an addition to his wealth.

If at any one time of my life more than another, I was made to drink the bitterest dregs of slavery, that time was during the first six months of my stay with Mr. Covey. We worked in all weathers. It was never too hot or too cold; it could never rain, blow hail, or snow, too hard for us to work in the field. Work, work, work, was scarcely more the order of the day than of the night. The longest days were too short for him, and the shortest nights too long for him. I was somewhat unmanageable when I first went there, but a few months of this discipline tamed me. Mr. Covey succeeded in breaking me. I was broken in body, soul, and spirit. My natural elasticity was crushed, my intellect languished, the disposition to read departed, the cheerful spark that lingered about my eye died; the dark night of slavery closed in upon me; and behold a man transformed into a brute!

Sunday was my only leisure time. I spent this in a sort of beast-like stupor, between sleep and wake, under some large tree. At times I would rise up, a flash of energetic freedom would dart through my soul, accompanied with a faint beam of hope, that flickered for a moment, and then vanished. I sank down again, mourning over my wretched condition. I was sometimes prompted to take my life, and that of Covey, but was prevented by a combination of hope and fear. My sufferings on this plantation seem now like a dream rather than a stern reality.

Our house stood within a few rods of the Chesapeake Bay, whose broad bosom was ever white with sails from every quarter of the habitable globe. Those beautiful vessels, robed in purest white, so delightful to the eye of freemen, were to me so many shrouded ghosts, to terrify and torment me with thoughts of my wretched condition. I have often, in the deep stillness of a summer's Sabbath, stood all alone upon the lofty banks of that noble bay, and traced, with saddened heart and tearful eye, the countless number of sails moving off to the mighty ocean. The sight of these always affected me powerfully. My thoughts would compel utterance; and there, with no audience but the Almighty, I would pour out my soul's complaint, in my rude way, with an apostrophe to the moving multitude of ships:—

"You are loosed from your moorings, and are free; I am fast in my chains, and am a slave! You move merrily before the gentle gale, and I sadly before the bloody whip! You are freedom's swift-winged angels, that fly round the world; I am confined in bands of iron! O that I were free! O, that I were on one of your gallant decks, and under your protecting wing! Alas! betwixt me and you, the turbid waters roll. Go on, go on. O that I could also go! Could I but swim! If I could fly! O, why was I born a man, of whom to make a brute! The glad ship is gone; she hides in the dim distance. I am left in the hottest hell of unending slavery. O God, save me! God, deliver me! Let me be free! Is there any God? Why am I a slave? I will run away. I will not stand it. Get caught, or get clear, I'll try it. I had as well die with ague as the fever. I have only one life to lose. I had as well be killed running as die standing. Only think of it; one hundred miles straight north, and I am free! Try it? Yes! God helping me, I will. It cannot be that I shall live and die a slave. I will take to the water. This very bay shall yet bear me into freedom. The steamboats steered in a northeast course from North Point. I will do the same; and when I get to the head of the bay, I will turn my canoe adrift, and walk straight through Delaware into Pennsylvania. When I get there, I shall not be required to have a pass; I can travel without being disturbed. Let but the first opportunity offer, and, come what will, I am off. Meanwhile, I will try to bear up under the yoke. I am not the only slave in the world. Why should I fret? I can bear as much as any of them. Besides, I am but a boy, and all boys are bound to some one. It may be that my misery in slavery will only increase my happiness when I get free. There is a better day coming."

Thus I used to think, and thus I used to speak to myself; goaded almost to madness at one moment, and at the next reconciling myself to my wretched lot.

I have already intimated that my condition was much worse, during the first six months of my stay at Mr. Covey's, than in the last six. The circumstances leading to the change in Mr. Covey's course toward me form an epoch in my humble history. You have seen how a man was made a slave; you shall see how a slave was made a man. On one of the hottest days of the month of August, 1833, Bill Smith, William Hughes, a slave numbed Eli, and myself, were engaged in fanning wheat. Hughes was clearing the fanned wheat from before the fan, Eli was turning, Smith was feeding, and I was carrying wheat to the fan. The work was simple, requiring strength rather than intellect; yet, to one entirely unused to such work, it came very hard. About three o'clock of that day, I broke down; my strength failed me; I was seized with a violent aching of the head, attended with extreme dizziness; I trembled in every limb. Finding what was coming, I nerved myself up, feeling it would never do to stop work. I stood as long as I could stagger to the hopper with grain. When I could stand no longer, I fell, and felt as if held down by an immense weight. The fan of course stopped; every one had his own work to do; and no one could do the work of the other, and have his own go on at the same time.

Mr. Covey was at the house, about one hundred yards from the treading-yard where we were fanning. On hearing the fan stop, he left immediately, and came to the spot where we were. He hastily inquired what the matter was. Bill answered that I was sick, and there was no one to bring wheat to the fan. I had by this time crawled away under the side of the post and rail-fence by which the yard was enclosed, hoping to find relief by getting out of the sun. He then asked where I was. He was told by one of the hands. He came to the spot, and, after looking at me awhile, asked me what was the matter. I told him as well as I could, for I scarce had strength to speak. He then gave me a savage kick in the side, and told me to get up. I tried to do so, but fell back in the attempt. He gave me another kick, and again told me to rise. I again tried, and succeeded in gaining my feet; but, stooping to get the tub with which I was feeding the fan, I again staggered and fell. While down in this situation, Mr. Covey took up the hickory slat with which Hughes had been striking off the half-bushel measure, and with it gave me a heavy blow upon the head, making a large wound, and the blood ran freely; and with this again told me to get up. I made no effort to comply, having now made up my mind to let him do his worst. In a short time after receiving this blow, my head grew better. Mr. Covey had now left me to my fate. At this moment I resolved, for the first time, to go to my master, enter a complaint, and ask his protection. In order to [do] this,

I must that afternoon walk several miles; and this, under the circumstances, was truly a severe undertaking. I was exceedingly feeble; made so as much by the kicks and blows which I received, as by the severe fit of sickness to which I had been subjected. I, however, watched my chance, while Covey was looking in an opposite direction, and started for St. Michael's. I succeeded in getting a considerable distance on my way to the woods, when Covey discovered me, and called after me to come back, threatening what he would do if I did not come. I disregarded both his calls and his threats, and made my way to the woods as fast as my feeble state would allow; and thinking I might be overhauled by him if I kept the road, I walked through the woods, keeping far enough from the road to avoid detection, and near enough to prevent losing my way. I had not gone far before my little strength again failed me. I could go no farther. I fell down, and lay for a considerable time. The blood was yet oozing from the wound on my head. For a time I thought I should bleed to death; and think now that I should have done so, but that the blood so matted my hair as to stop the wound. After lying there about three quarters of an hour, I nerved myself up again, and started on my way, through bogs and briers, barefooted and bareheaded, tearing my feet sometimes at nearly every step; and after a journey of about seven miles, occupying some five hours to perform it, I arrived at master's store. I then presented an appearance enough to affect any but a heart of iron. From the crown of my head to my feet, I was covered with blood. My hair was all clotted with dust and blood; my shirt was stiff with blood. My legs and feet were torn in sundry places with briers and thorns, and were also covered with blood. I suppose I looked like a man who had escaped a den of wild beasts, and barely escaped them. In this state I appeared before my master, humbly entreating him to interpose his authority for my protection. I told him all the circumstances as well as I could, and it seemed, as I spoke, at times to affect him. He would then walk the floor, and seek to justify Covey by saying he expected I deserved it. He asked me what I wanted. I told him, to let me get a new home; that as sure as I lived with Mr. Covey again, I should live with but to die with him; that Covey would surely kill me; he was in a fair way for it. Master Thomas ridiculed the idea that there was any danger of Mr. Covey's killing me, and said that he knew Mr. Covey; that he was a good man, and that he could not think of taking me from him; that, should he do so, he would lose the whole year's wages; that I belonged to Mr. Covey for one year, and that I must go back to him, come what might; and that I must not trouble him with any more stories, or that he would himself *get hold of me*. After threatening me thus, he gave me a very large dose of salts, telling me that I might remain in St. Michael's that night, (it being quite late,) but that I must be off back to Mr. Covey's early in the morning; and that if I did not, he would *get hold of me*, which meant that he would whip me. I remained all night, and, according to his orders, I started off to Covey's in the morning, (Saturday morning,) wearied in body and broken in spirit. I got no supper that night, or breakfast that morning. I reached Covey's about nine o'clock; and just as I was getting over the fence that divided Mrs. Kemp's fields from ours, out ran Covey with his cowskin, to give me another whipping. Before he could reach me, I succeeded in getting to the cornfield; and as the corn was very high, it afforded me the means of hiding. He seemed very angry, and searched for me a long time. My behavior was altogether unaccountable. He finally gave up the chase, thinking, I suppose, that I must come home for something to eat; he would give himself no further trouble in looking for me. I spent that day mostly in the woods, having the alternative before me,—to go home and be whipped to death, or stay in the woods and be starved to death. That night, I fell in with Sandy Jenkins, a slave with whom I was somewhat acquainted. Sandy had a free wife who lived about four miles from Mr. Covey's; and it being Saturday, he was on his way to see her. I told him my circumstances, and he very kindly invited me to go home with him. I went home with him, and talked this whole matter over, and got his advice as to what course it was best for me to pursue. I found Sandy an old adviser. He told me, with great solemnity, I must go back to Covey; but that before I went, I must go with him into another part of the woods, where there was a certain *root,* which, if I would take some of it with me, carrying it *always on my right side,* would render it impossible for Mr. Covey, or any other white man, to whip me. He said he had carried it for years; and since he had done so, he had never received a blow, and never expected to while he carried it. I at first rejected the idea, that the simple carrying of a root in my pocket would have any such effect as he had said, and was not disposed to take it; but Sandy impressed the necessity with much earnestness, telling me it could do no harm, if it did no good. To please him, I at length took the root, and, according to his direction, carried it upon my right side. This was Sunday morning. I immediately started for home; and upon entering the yard gate, out came Mr. Covey on his way to meeting. He spoke to me very kindly, made me drive the pigs from a lot near by, and passed on towards the church. Now, this singular conduct of Mr. Covey really made me begin to think that there was something in the *root* which Sandy had given me; and had it been on any other day than Sunday, I could have attributed the conduct to no other cause than the influence of that root; and as it was, I was half inclined to think the *root* to be something more than I at first had taken it to be. All went well till Monday morning. On this morning, the virtue of the *root* was fully tested. Long before daylight, I was called to go and rub, curry, and feed, the horses. I obeyed, and was glad to obey. But whilst thus engaged, whilst in the act of throwing down some blades from the loft, Mr. Covey entered the stable with a long rope; and just as I was half out of the loft, he caught hold of my legs, and was about tying me. As soon as I found what he was up to, I gave a sudden spring, and as I did so, he holding to my legs, I was brought sprawling on the stable floor. Mr. Covey seemed now to think he had me, and could do what he pleased; but at this moment—from whence came the spirit I don't know—I resolved to fight; and, suiting my action to the resolution, I seized Covey hard by the throat; and as I did so, I rose. He held on to me, and I to him. My resistance was so entirely unexpected, that Covey seemed taken all aback. He trembled like a leaf. This gave me assurance, and I held him uneasy, causing the blood to run where I touched him with the ends of my fingers. Mr. Covey soon called out to Hughes for help. Hughes came, and, while Covey held me, attempted to tie my right hand. While he was in the act of doing so, I watched my chance, and gave him a heavy kick close under the ribs. This kick fairly sickened Hughes, so that he left me in the hands of Mr. Covey. This kick had the effect of not only weakening

Hughes, but Covey also. When he saw Hughes bending over with pain, his courage quailed. He asked me if I meant to persist in my resistance. I told him I did, come what might; that he had used me like a brute for six months, and that I was determined to be used so no longer. With that, he strove to drag me to a stick that was lying just out of the stable door. He meant to knock me down. But just as he was leaning over to get the stick, I seized him with both hands by his collar, and brought him by a sudden snatch to the ground. By this time, Bill came. Covey called upon him for assistance. Bill wanted to know what he could do. Covey said, "Take hold of him, take hold of him!" Bill said his master hired him out to work, and not to help to whip me; so he left Covey and myself to fight our own battle out. We were at it for nearly two hours. Covey at length let me go, puffing and blowing at a great rate, saying that if I had not resisted, he would not have whipped me half so much. The truth was, that he had not whipped me at all. I considered him as getting entirely the worst end of the bargain; for he had drawn no blood from me, but I had from him. The whole six months afterwards, that I spent with Mr. Covey, he never laid the weight of his finger upon me in anger. He would occasionally say, he didn't want to get hold of me again. "No," thought I, "you need not; for you will come off worse than you did before."

This battle with Mr. Covey was the turning-point in my career as a slave. It rekindled the few expiring embers of freedom, and revived within me a sense of my own manhood. It recalled the departed self-confidence, and inspired me again with a determination to be free. The gratification afforded by the triumph was a full compensation for whatever else might follow, even death itself. He only can understand the deep satisfaction which I experienced, who has himself repelled by force the bloody arm of slavery. I felt as I never felt before. It was a glorious resurrection, from the tomb of slavery, to the heaven of freedom. My long-crushed spirit rose, cowardice departed, bold defiance took its place; and I now resolved that, however long I might remain a slave in form, the day had passed forever when I could be a slave in fact. I did not hesitate to let it be known of me, that the white man who expected to succeed in whipping, must also succeed in killing me.

HENRY DAVID THOREAU (1817–1862)
United States

Thoreau lived almost his entire life in Concord, Massachusetts, where he was born in a shopkeeper's family. After graduation from Harvard, where he was influenced by the Transcendentalist movement, he taught school, wrote occasional pieces, and lectured. He was briefly incarcerated in the Concord jail for refusing to pay his poll tax, protesting against the Mexican War (which he and his fellow abolitionists saw as a pretense for extending slavery). This led to his essay

"Resistance to Civil Government" of 1849 (later called "Civil Disobedience"), a seminal text for nonviolent resistance in the twentieth century.

Attentive to roots of all kinds, Thoreau knew that the word *economy* traces its roots to householding—from the Greek word *oikos*, meaning house, dwelling; hence, his two-year experiment at Walden Pond to learn how to inhabit America's nature as a native might have. Thoreau's style—often self-consciously Emersonian—is so demanding and his sense of shaped form so central to understanding the various works he fashioned out of the raw material of his journals that it is unfair to their integrity to extract what would present itself as a "representative" sampling. Instead, the following journal entry is offered because it expresses so directly the foundation of Thoreau's delicately rigorous project. Thoreau himself felt that the journal's advantage over *Walden* or *A Week on the Concord and Merrimack Rivers* was that it followed the "organic," spontaneous form of his relationship to nature, while the other titled works were composed with an audience in mind.

from Journals

[March 5, 1858: Language of the Indians]

How little I know of that *arbor-vitae* when I have learned only what science can tell me! It is but a word. It is not a *tree* of *life*. But there are twenty words for the tree and its different parts which the Indian gave, which are not in our botanies, which imply a more practical and vital science. He used it every day. He was well acquainted with its wood, and its bark, and its leaves. No science does more than arrange what knowledge we have of any class of objects. But, generally speaking, how much more conversant was the Indian with any wild animal or plant than we are, and in his language is implied all that intimacy, as much as ours is expressed in our language. How many words in his language about a moose, or birch bark, and the like! The Indian stood nearer to wild nature than we. The wildest and noblest quadrupeds, even the largest fresh-water fishes, some of the wildest and noblest birds and the fairest flowers have actually receded as *we* advanced, and we have but the most distant knowledge of them. A rumor has come down to us that the skin of a lion was seen and his roar heard here by an early settler. But there was a race here that slept on his skin. It was a new light when my guide gave me Indian names for things for which I had only scientific ones before. In proportion as I understood the language, I saw them from a new point of view.

A dictionary of the Indian language reveals another and wholly new life to us. Look at the word "canoe," and see what a story it tells of outdoor life, with the names of all its parts and modes of using it, as our words describing the different parts and seats of a coach—with the difference in practical knowledge between him who rides and him who walks; or at the word "wigwam," and see how close it brings you to the ground; or "Indian corn," and see which race was most familiar with it. It reveals to me a life within a life, or rather a life without a life, as it were threading the woods between our towns still, and yet we can never tread in its trail. The Indian's earthly life was as far off from us as heaven is.

HERMAN MELVILLE (1819–1891)
United States

Herman Melville was born to a distinguished family in New York. While his forebears played significant historical roles, Herman Melville's immediate family experienced economic hardship. His father died just as the young Herman was coming into manhood; he was never himself a successful provider for his own family. After his father's death, he dropped out of the Albany Academy in 1832, taught school, and then lived a sailor's life from 1839 to 1843, when he returned to settle. He moved with his growing family to the Berkshires in Massachusetts, where he farmed and wrote in several veins: his tales of adventure and metaphysics and his gloomy brilliant *Pierre, or, The Ambiguities* (1852), a commercial failure, as *Moby Dick* had been. Melville sounded the depths of physical and spiritual experience. At sea ourselves in the vastness of *Moby Dick* (1851), we often overlook, in discussions of Melville, the importance of his hard, practical education on board whalers, living with a native tribe in the Marquesas Islands, as a mutineer in a Tahitian prison, as a naive naturalist on Tahiti, Eimeo, and Honolulu. Melville himself dated his life from the beginning of his twenty-fifth year, when he began to reflect on what these episodes meant to him. Melville seems to have had a sense of himself as a half-breed of sorts even before his exposure to South Pacific populations alerted him to sympathies he could not have anticipated. Like Dickens, he had an intense sensitivity to the plight of the impoverished and the miserable. In this "blessed" new world, he exposes with blasting satire the actual misery of the least and the hypocrisy of moralizing attitudes.

Poor Man's Pudding and Rich Man's Crumbs

"You see," said Poet Blandmour, enthusiastically—as some forty years ago we walked along the road in a soft, moist snow-fall, toward the end of March—"you see, my friend, that the blessed almoner, Nature, is in all things beneficent; and not only so, but considerate in her charities, as any discreet human philanthropist might be. This snow, now, which seems so unseasonable, is in fact just what a poor husbandman needs. Rightly in this soft March snow, falling just before seed-time, rightly is it called 'Poor Man's Manure.' Distilling from kind heaven upon the soil, by a gentle penetration it nourishes every clod, ridge, and furrow. To the poor farmer it is as good as the rich farmer's farm-yard enrichments. And the poor man has no trouble to spread it, while the rich man has to spread his."

"Perhaps so," said I, without equal enthusiasm, brushing some of the damp flakes from my chest. "It may be as you say, dear Blandmour. But tell me, how is it that the wind drives yonder drifts of 'Poor Man's Manure' off poor Coulter's two-acre patch here, and piles it up yonder on rich Squire Teamster's twenty-acre field?"

"Ah! to be sure—yes—well; Coulter's field, I suppose, is sufficiently moist without further moistenings. Enough is as good as a feast, you know."

"Yes," replied I, "of this sort of damp fare," shaking another shower of the damp flakes from my person. "But tell me, this warm spring-snow may answer very well, as you say; but how is it with the cold cold snows of the long, long winters here?"

"Why, do you not remember the words of the Psalmist?
—'The Lord giveth snow like wool;' meaning not only that snow is white as wool, but warm, too, as wool. For the only reason, as I take it, that wool is comfortable, is because air is entangled, and therefore warmed among its fibres. Just so, then, take the temperature of a December field when covered with this snow-fleece, and you will no doubt find it several degrees above that of the air. So, you see, the winter's snow *itself* is beneficent; under the pretense of frost—a sort of gruff philanthropist—actually warming the earth, which afterward is to be fertilizingly moistened by these gentle flakes of March."

"I like to hear you talk, dear Blandmour; and, guided by your benevolent heart, can only wish to poor Coulter plenty of this 'Poor man's Manure.' "

"But that is not all," said Blandmour, eagerly. "Did you never hear of the 'Poor Man's Eye-water?' "

"Never."

"Take this soft March snow, melt it, and bottle it. It keeps pure as alcohol. The very best thing in the world for weak eyes. I have a whole demijohn of it myself. But the poorest man, afflicted in his eyes, can freely help himself to this same all-bountiful remedy. Now, what a kind provision is that!"

"Then 'Poor Man's Manure' is 'Poor Man's Eye-water' too?"

"Exactly. And what could be more economically contrived? One thing answering two ends—ends so very distinct."

"Very distinct, indeed."

"Ah! that is your way. Making sport of earnest. But never mind. We have been talking of snow; but common rain-water—such as falls all the year round—is still more kindly. Not to speak of its known fertilizing quality as to fields, consider it in one of its minor lights. Pray, did you ever hear of a 'Poor Man's Egg?' "

"Never. What is that, now?"

"Why, in making some culinary preparations of meal and flour, where eggs are recommended in the receipt-book, a substitute for the eggs may be had in a cup of cold rain-water, which acts as leaven. And so a cup of cold rain-water thus used is called by housewives a 'Poor Man's Egg.' And many rich men's housekeepers sometimes use it."

"But only when they are out of hen's eggs, I presume, dear Blandmour. But your talk is—I sincerely say it—most agreeable to me. Talk on."

"Then there's 'Poor Man's Plaster' for wounds and other bodily harms; an alleviative and curative, compounded of simple, natural things; and so, being very cheap, is accessible to the poorest of sufferers. Rich men often use 'Poor Man's Plaster.' "

"But not without the judicious advice of a fee'd physician, dear Blandmour."

"Doubtless, they first consult the physician; but that may be an unnecessary precaution."

"Perhaps so. I do not gainsay it. Go on."

"Well, then, did you ever eat of a 'Poor Man's Pudding'?"

"I never so much as heard of it before."

"Indeed! Well, now you shall eat of one; and you shall eat it, too, as made, unprompted, by a poor man's wife, and you shall eat it at a poor man's table, and in a poor man's house. Come now, and if after this eating, you do not say that a 'Poor Man's Pudding' is as relishable as a rich man's, I will give up the point altogether; which briefly is: that, through kind Nature, the poor, out of their very poverty, extract comfort."

Not to narrate any more of our conversations upon this subject (for we had several—I being at that time the guest of Blandmour in the country, for the benefit of my health, suffice it that, acting upon Blandmour's hint, I introduced myself into Coulter's house on a wet Monday noon (for the snow had thawed), under the innocent pretense of craving a pedestrian's rest and refreshment for an hour or two.

I was greeted, not without much embarrassment—owing, I suppose, to my dress—but still with unaffected and honest kindness. Dame Coulter was just leaving the wash-tub to get ready her one o'clock meal against her good man's return from a deep wood about a mile distant among the hills, where he was chopping by day's-work—seventy-five cents per day—and found himself. The washing being done outside the main building, under an infirm-looking old shed, the dame stood upon a half-rotten, soaked board to protect her feet, as well as might be, from the penetrating damp of the bare ground; hence she looked pale and chill. But her paleness had still another and more secret cause—the paleness of a mother to be. A quiet, fathomless heart-trouble, too, couched beneath the mild, resigned blue of her soft and wife-like eye. But she smiled upon me, as apologizing for the unavoidable disorder of a Monday and a washing-day, and, conducting me into the kitchen, set me down in the best seat it had—an old-fashioned chair of an enfeebled constitution.

I thanked her; and sat rubbing my hands before the ineffectual low fire, and—unobservantly as I could—glancing now and then about the room, while the good woman, throwing on more sticks, said she was sorry the room was no warmer. Something more she said, too—not repiningly, however—of the fuel, as old and damp; picked-up sticks in Squire Teamster's forest, where her husband was chopping the sappy logs of the living tree for the Squire's fires. It needed not her remark, whatever it was, to convince me of the inferior quality of the sticks; some being quite mossy and toad-stooled with long lying bedded among the accumulated dead leaves of many autumns. They made a sad hissing, and vain spluttering enough.

"You must rest yourself here till dinner-time, at least," said the dame; "what I have you are heartily welcome to."

I thanked her again, and begged her not to heed my presence in the least, but go on with her usual affairs.

I was struck by the aspect of the room. The house was old, and constitutionally damp. The window-sills had beads of exuded dampness upon them. The shriveled sashes shook in their frames, and the green panes of glass were clouded with the long thaw. On some little errand the dame passed into an adjoining chamber, leaving the door partly open. The floor of that room was carpetless, as the kitchen's was. Nothing but bare necessaries were about me; and those not of the best sort. Not a print on the wall; but an old volume of Dodridge lay on the smoked chimney-shelf.

"You must have walked a long way, sir; you sigh so with weariness."

"No, I am not nigh so weary as yourself, I dare say."

"Oh, but I am accustomed to that; *you* are not, I should think," and her soft, sad blue eye ran over my dress. "But I must sweep these shavings away; husband made him a new axe-helve this morning before sunrise, and I have been so busy washing, that I have had no time to clear up. But now they are just the thing I want for the fire. They'd be much better though, were they not so green."

Now if Blandmour were here, thought I to myself, he would call those green shavings "Poor Man's Matches," or "Poor Man's Tinder," or some pleasant name of that sort.

"I do not know," said the good woman, turning round to me again—as she stirred among her pots on the smoky fire—"I do not know how you will like our pudding. It is only rice, milk, and salt boiled together."

"Ah, what they call 'Poor Man's Pudding,' I suppose you mean."

A quick flush, half resentful, passed over her face.

"*We* do not call it so, sir," she said, and was silent.

Upbraiding myself for my inadvertence, I could not but again think to myself what Blandmour would have said, had he heard those words and seen that flush.

At last a slow, heavy footfall was heard; then a scraping at the door, and another voice said, "Come wife; come, come—I must be back again in a jiff—if you say I *must* take all my meals at home, you must be speedy; because the Squire—Good day, sir," he exclaimed, now first catching sight of me as he entered the room. He turned toward his wife, inquiringly, and stood stock-still, while the moisture oozed from his patched boots to the floor.

"This gentleman stops here awhile to rest and refresh: he will take dinner with us, too. All will be ready now in a trice; so sit down on the bench, husband, and be patient, I pray. You see, sir," she continued, turning to me, "William there wants, of mornings, to carry a cold meal into the woods with him, to save the long one o'clock walk across the fields to and fro. But I won't let him. A warm dinner is more than pay for the long walk."

"I don't know about that," said William, shaking his head. "I have often debated in my mind whether it really paid. There's not much odds, either way, between a wet walk after hard work, and a wet dinner before it. But I like to oblige a good wife like Martha. And you know, sir, that women will have their whimsies."

"I wish they all had as kind whimsies as your wife has," said I.

"Well, I've heard that some women ain't all maple-sugar; but, content with dear Martha, I don't know much about others."

"You find rare wisdom in the woods," mused I.

"Now, husband, if you ain't too tired, just lend a hand to draw the table out."

"Nay," said I, "let him rest, and let me help."

"No," said William, rising.

"Sit still," said his wife to me.

The table set, in due time we all found ourselves with plates before us.

"You see what we have," said Coulter—"salt pork, rye-bread, and pudding. Let me help you. I got this pork of the Squire; some of his last year's pork, which he let me have on account. It isn't quite so sweet as this year's would be; but I find it hearty enough to work on, and that's all I eat for. Only let the rheumatiz and other sicknesses keep clear of me, and I ask no flavors or favors from any. But you don't eat of the pork!"

"I see," said the wife, gently and gravely, "that the gentleman knows the difference between this year's and last year's pork. But perhaps he will like the pudding."

I summoned up all my self-control, and smilingly assented to the proposition of the pudding, without by my looks casting any reflections upon the pork. But, to tell the truth, it was quite impossible for me (not being ravenous, but only a little hungry at the time) to eat of the latter. It had a yellowish crust all round it, and was rather rankish, I thought, to the taste. I observed, too, that the dame did not eat of it, though she suffered some to be put on her plate and pretended to be busy with it when Coulter looked that way. But she ate of the rye-bread, and so did I.

"Now, then, for the pudding," said Coulter. "Quick, wife; the Squire sits in his sitting-room window, looking far out across the fields. His time-piece is true."

"He don't play the spy on you, does he?" said I.

"Oh no!—I don't say that. He's a good enough man. He gives me work. But he's particular. Wife, help the gentleman. You see, sir, if I lose the Squire's work, what will become of—" and, with a look for which I honored humanity, with sly significance he glanced toward his wife; then, a little changing his voice, instantly continued—"that fine horse I am going to buy."

WALT WHITMAN (1819–1892)

United States

Walt Whitman's family moved from a farmland in West Hills, New York, to Brooklyn, where he went to public school and studied printing, a trade he practiced from 1840 to 1845 in New York City. He edited newspapers, wrote for popular magazines, and was a reporter. His *Leaves of Grass,* which would have many versions and editions (from 1855 to 1892), was saluted by Emerson and praised in England, where William Rossetti published selections. In 1873–4, he suffered a paralyzing stroke and lost his mother; he was never completely to recover. But in his house in Camden, New Jersey—bought with the sales of the poems, given extra publicity from the attacks on them in Boston—he was visited by celebrities, especially from England, and continued to work on his poetry and his self-education, calm and cheerful of disposition until his death. In his willingness to accept and celebrate the contradictions in himself, Whitman became America's voice. He intended *Leaves of Grass* to be a "new Bible" for a secularized democracy. He wanted his audiences to be moved by intoning his words as if they were prayers that he had made out of their own: "A perfect writer would make words sing, dance, kiss, do the male and female act, bear children . . . do anything that man or woman or the natural powers can do." Reared as a Quaker, Whitman lived and worked to kindle the inner light that shines sometimes at its brightest in community. During the Civil War, Whitman served as a volunteer nurse and wound-dresser. This experience marked him as no other. As he noted in *Specimen Days,* where what he witnessed is painfully yet beautifully set down, "The war of attempted secession has, of course, been the distinguishing event of my time." Reading aloud "Crossing Brooklyn Ferry" is the strongest evidence of the success of Whitman's project.

from *Leaves of Grass*

Crossing Brooklyn Ferry

1

Flood-tide below me! I see you face to face!
Clouds of the west—sun there half an hour high—I see you also face to face.
Crowds of men and women attired in the usual costumes, how curious you are to me!
On the ferry-boats the hundreds and hundreds that cross, returning home, are more curious to me than you suppose,
And you that shall cross from shore to shore years hence are more to me, and 5
    more in my meditations, than you might suppose.

2

The impalpable sustenance of me from all things at all hours of the day,
The simple, compact, well-join'd scheme, myself disintegrated, every one disintegrated yet part of the scheme,
The similitudes of the past and those of the future,
The glories strung like beads on my smallest sights and hearings, on the walk in the street and the passage over the river,
The current rushing so swiftly and swimming with me far away, 10
The others that are to follow me, the ties between me and them,
The certainty of others, the life, love, sight, hearing of others.

Others will enter the gates of the ferry and cross from shore to shore,
Others will watch the run of the flood-tide,
Others will see the shipping of Manhattan north and west, and the heights of 15
    Brooklyn to the south and east,
Others will see the islands large and small;
Fifty years hence, others will see them as they cross, the sun half an hour high,

A hundred years hence, or ever so many hundred years hence, others will see them,
Will enjoy the sunset, the pouring-in of the flood-tide, the falling-back to the sea
    of the ebb-tide.

3

It avails not, time nor place—distance avails not,   20
I am with you, you men and women of a generation, or ever so many generations
    hence,
Just as you feel when you look on the river and sky, so I felt,
Just as any of you is one of a living crowd, I was one of a crowd,
Just as you are refresh'd by the gladness of the river and the bright flow, I was
    refresh'd,
Just as you stand and lean on the rail, yet hurry with the swift current, I stood yet   25
    was hurried,
Just as you look on the numberless masts of ships and the thick-stemm'd pipes of
    steamboats, I look'd.

I too many and many a time cross'd the river of old,
Watched the Twelfth-month sea-gulls, saw them high in the air floating with
    motionless wings, oscillating their bodies,
Saw how the glistening yellow lit up parts of their bodies and left the rest in strong
    shadow,
Saw the slow-wheeling circles and the gradual edging toward the south,   30
Saw the reflection of the summer sky in the water,
Had my eyes dazzled by the shimmering track of beams,
Look'd at the fine centrifugal spokes of light round the shape of my head in the
    sunlit water,
Look'd on the haze on the hills southward and south-westward,
Look'd on the vapor as it flew in fleeces tinged with violet,   35
Look'd toward the lower bay to notice the vessels arriving,
Saw their approach, saw aboard those that were near me,
Saw the white sails of schooners and sloops, saw the ships at anchor,
The sailors at work in the rigging or out astride the spars,
The round masts, the swinging motion of the hulls, the slender serpentine   40
    pennants,
The large and small steamers in motion, the pilots in their pilot-houses,
The white wake left by the passage, the quick tremulous whirl of the wheels,
The flags of all nations, the falling of them at sunset,
The scallop-edged waves in the twilight, the ladled cups, the frolicsome crests and
    glistening,
The stretch afar growing dimmer and dimmer, the gray walls of the granite   45
    storehouses by the docks,
On the river the shadowy group, the big steam-tug closely flank'd on each side by
    the barges, the hay-boat, the belated lighter,
On the neighboring shore the fires from the foundry chimneys burning high and
    glaringly into the night,

Casting their flicker of black contrasted with wild red and yellow light over the
    tops of houses, and down into the clefts of streets.

4

These and all else were to me the same as they are to you,
I loved well those cities, loved well the stately and rapid river,   50
The men and women I saw were all near to me,
Others the same—others who look back on me because I look'd forward to them,
(The time will come, though I stop here to-day and to-night.)

5

What is it then between us?
What is the count of the scores or hundreds of years between us?   55

Whatever it is, it avails not—distance avails not, and place avails not,
I too lived, Brooklyn of ample hills was mine,
I too walk'd the streets of Manhattan island, and bathed in the waters around it,
I too felt the curious abrupt questionings stir within me,
In the day among crowds of people sometimes they came upon me,   60
In my walks home late at night or as I lay in my bed they came upon me,
I too had been struck from the float forever held in solution,
I too had receiv'd identity by my body,
That I was I knew was of my body, and what I should be I knew I should be of my
    body.

6

It is not upon you alone the dark patches fall,   65
The dark threw its patches down upon me also,
The best I had done seem'd to me blank and suspicious,
My great thoughts as I supposed them, were they not in reality meagre?
Nor is it you alone who know what it is to be evil,   70
I am he who knew what it was to be evil,
I too knotted the old knot of contrariety,
Blabb'd, blush'd, resented, lied, stole, grudg'd,
Had guile, anger, lust, hot wishes I dared not speak,
Was wayward, vain, greedy, shallow, sly, cowardly, malignant,
The wolf, the snake, the hog, not wanting in me,   75
The cheating look, the frivolous word, the adulterous wish, not wanting,
Refusals, hates, postponements, meanness, laziness, none of these wanting,
Was one with the rest, the days and haps of the rest,
Was call'd by my nighest name by clear loud voices of young men as they saw me
    approaching or passing,

Felt their arms on my neck as I stood, or the negligent leaning of their flesh against   80
    me as I sat,
Saw many I loved in the street or ferry-boat or public assembly, yet never told
    them a word,
Lived the same life with the rest, the same old laughing, gnawing, sleeping,
Play'd the part that still looks back on the actor or actress,
The same old role, the role that is what we make it, as great as we like,
Or as small as we like, or both great and small.   85

7

Closer yet I approach you,
What thought you have of me now, I had as much of you—I laid in my stores in
    advance,
I consider'd long and seriously of you before you were born.

Who was to know what should come home to me?
Who knows but I am enjoying this?   90
Who knows, for all the distance, but I am as good as looking at you now, for all
    you cannot see me?

8

Ah, what can ever be more stately and admirable to me than mast-hemm'd
    Manhattan?
River and sunset and scallop-edg'd waves of flood-tide?
The sea-gulls oscillating their bodies, the hay-boat in the twilight, and the belated
    lighter?
What gods can exceed these that clasp me by the hand, and with voices I love call   95
    me promptly and loudly by my nighest name as I approach?
What is more subtle than this which ties me to the woman or man that looks in
    my face?
Which fuses me into you now, and pours my meaning into you?

We understand then do we not?
What I promis'd without mentioning it, have you not accepted?   100
What the study could not teach—what the preaching could not accomplish is
    accomplish'd, is it not?

9

Flow on, river! flow with the flood-tide, and ebb with the ebb-tide!
Frolic on, crested and scallop-edg'd waves!
Gorgeous clouds of the sunset! drench with your splendor me, or the men and
    women generations after me!
Cross from shore to shore, countless crowds of passengers!
Stand up, tall masts of Mannahatta! stand up, beautiful hills of Brooklyn!   105

Throb, baffled and curious brain! throw out questions and answers!
Suspend here and everywhere, eternal float of solution!
Gaze, loving and thirsting eyes, in the house or street or public assembly!
Sound out, voices of young men! loudly and musically call me by my nighest   110
    name!
Live, old life! play the part that looks back on the actor or actress!
Play the old role, the role that is great or small according as one makes it!
Consider, you who peruse me, whether I may not in unknown ways be looking
    upon you;
Be firm, rail over the river, to support those who lean idly, yet haste with the
    hasting current;
Fly on, sea-birds! fly sideways, or wheel in large circles high in the air;   115
Receive the summer sky, you water, and faithfully hold it till all downcast eyes
    have time to take it from you!
Diverge, fine spokes of light, from the shape of my head, or any one's head, in the
    sunlit water!
Come on, ships from the lower bay! pass up or down, white-sail'd schooners,
    sloops, lighters!
Flaunt away, flags of all nations! be duly lower'd at sunset!
Burn high your fires, foundry chimneys! cast black shadows at nightfall! cast red   120
    and yellow light over the tops of the houses!
Appearances, now or henceforth, indicate what you are,
You necessary film, continue to envelop the soul,
About my body for me, and your body for you, be hung our divinest aromas,
Thrive, cities—bring your freight, bring your shows, ample and sufficient rivers,
Expand, being than which none else is perhaps more spiritual,   125
Keep your places, objects than which none else is more lasting.

You have waited, you always wait, you dumb, beautiful ministers,
We receive you with free sense at last, and are insatiate henceforward,
Not you any more shall be able to foil us, or withhold yourselves from us,
We use you, and do not cast you aside—we plant you permanently within us,   130
We fathom you not—we love you—there is perfection in you also,
You furnish your parts toward eternity,
Great or small, you furnish your parts toward the soul.

EMILY DICKINSON (1830–1886)
United States

As a child Emily Dickinson loved to read the dictionary. Later in her life she wrote
poems that offered odd new definitions. Reared as a good Protestant, she also

knew hymns by heart and delighted in perusing Christian emblem books with their allegorical pictures and texts. Her father and grandfather, actively involved in education in Amherst, Massachusetts, never discouraged her bookishness. She was, perhaps too early, exposed to the illnesses and deaths of close relations. She remained preoccupied with death throughout her life, as is evident in her poetry. Having abandoned the comforting beliefs of orthodox Christianity, Dickinson filled the shells of hymns lingering in her mind's ear with challenging riddles. Her spirit is adamant, purely American.

It was not until 1955 that all Dickinson's known poetry was published, and not until 1982 that her own arrangement of her poems was made known; the poems total nearly 2000.

[There's a certain Slant of light]

There's a certain Slant of light,
Winter Afternoons—
That oppresses, like the Heft
Of Cathedral Tunes—

Heavenly Hurt, it gives us—   5
We can find no scar,
But internal difference,
Where the Meanings, are—

None may teach it—Any—
'Tis the Seal Despair—   10
An imperial affliction
Sent us of the Air—

When it comes, the Landscape listens—
Shadows—hold their breath—
When it goes, 'tis like the Distance   15
On the look of Death—

[This is my letter to the World]

This is my letter to the World
That never wrote to Me—
The simple News that Nature told—
With tender Majesty

Her Message is committed   5
To Hands I cannot see—
For love of Her—Sweet—countrymen—
Judge tenderly—of Me

[Pain—has an Element of Blank]

Pain—has an Element of Blank—
It cannot recollect
When it begun—or if there were
A time when it was not—

It has no Future—but itself—   5
Its Infinite contain[1]
Its Past—enlightened to perceive
New Periods—of Pain.

[I dwell in Possibility]

I dwell in Possibility—
A fairer House than Prose—
More numerous of Windows—
Superior—for Doors—

Of Chambers as the Cedars—   5
Impregnable of Eye—
And for an Everlasting Roof
The Gambrels of the Sky—

Of Visitors—the fairest—
For Occupation—This—   10
The spreading wide my narrow Hands
To gather Paradise—

[Tell all the Truth but tell it slant]

Tell all the Truth but tell it slant—
Success in Circuit lies
Too bright for our infirm Delight
The Truth's superb surprise

As Lightning to the Children eased   5
With explanation kind
The Truth must dazzle gradually
Or every man be blind—

---

1. In one version, the line reads: "Its infinite
   realms contain"—thus the plural verb.

Joseph Cornell. *Toward the Blue Peninsula: For Emily Dickinson.* 1951–1952. Box construction. The Pace Gallery. © The Joseph and Robert Cornell Memorial Foundation.

[To make a prairie it takes a clover and one bee]

To make a prairie it takes a clover and one bee,
One clover, and a bee,
And revery.
The revery alone will do,
If bees are few.

MARK TWAIN [SAMUEL LANGHORNE CLEMENS] (1835–1910)

Called the "Lincoln of our literature" by William Dean Howells, Mark Twain walked among his readers, grabbed their collars and made them listen, spellbound. His words and characters speak with the simple majesty of the actual. He braided regional dialects, pinned them fast with sharp wit. He claimed that his early experience as a printer's devil, setting all manner of texts, taught him all he needed to know about style. Fulfilling his boyhood longing to captain a riverboat completed his education. Like Herman Melville's *Moby Dick,* or Walt Whitman's *Leaves of Grass,* Twain's masterpiece, *Huckleberry Finn,* did not win contemporary approval. Subsequent generations, however, have concurred with Ernest Hemingway who in 1935 noted, "It's the best book we've had." "The War Prayer," published fifteen years after Twain's death, concisely presents the mordant seriousness behind Twain's grin.

The War Prayer

It was a time of great and exalting excitement. The country was up in arms, the war was on, in every breast burned the holy fire of patriotism; the drums were beating, the bands playing, the toy pistols popping, the bunched firecrackers hissing and spluttering; on every hand and far down the receding and fading spread of roofs and balconies a fluttering wilderness of flags flashed in the sun; daily the young volunteers marched down the wide avenue gay and fine in their new uniforms, the proud fathers and mothers and sisters and sweethearts cheering them with voices choked with happy emotion as they swung by; nightly the packed mass meetings listened, panting, to patriot oratory which stirred the deepest deeps of their hearts, and which they interrupted at briefest intervals with cyclones of applause, the tears running down their cheeks the while; in the churches the pastors preached devotion to flag and country, and invoked the God of Battles, beseeching His aid in our good cause in outpouring of fervid eloquence which moved every listener. It was indeed a glad and gracious time, and the half dozen rash spirits that ventured to disapprove of the war and cast a doubt upon its righteousness straightway got such a stern and angry warning that for their personal safety's sake they quickly shrank out of sight and offended no more in that way.

Sunday morning came—next day the battalions would leave for the front; the church was filled; the volunteers were there, their young faces alight with martial dreams—visions of the stern advance, the gathering momentum, the rushing charge, the flashing sabers, the flight of the foe, the tumult, the enveloping smoke, the fierce pursuit, the surrender!—them home from the war, bronzed heroes, welcomed, adored, submerged in golden seas of glory! With the volunteers sat their dear ones, proud, happy, and envied by the neighbors and friends who had no sons and brothers to send forth to the field of honor, there to win for the flag, or, failing, die the noblest of noble deaths. The service proceeded; a war chapter from the Old Testament was read; the first prayer was said; it was followed by an organ burst that shook the building, and with one impulse the house rose, with glowing eyes and beating hearts, and poured out that tremendous invocation—

"God the all-terrible! Thou who ordainest,

"Thunder thy clarion and lightning thy sword!"[1]

Then came the "long" prayer. None could remember the like of it for passionate pleading and moving and beautiful language. The burden of its supplication was, that an ever-merciful and benignant Father of us all would watch over our noble young soldiers, and aid, comfort, and encourage them in

---

1. An Episcopal hymn by Henry Fothergill Chorley (1808–1872), music by Alexis Lyon (1799–1870); the first line usually reads: "God the Omnipotent! King who ordainest."

their patriotic work; bless them, shield them in the day of battle and the hour of peril, bear them in His mighty hand, make them strong and confident, invincible in the bloody onset; help them to crush the foe, grant to them and to their flag and country imperishable honor and glory—

An aged stranger entered and moved with slow and noiseless step up the main aisle, his eyes fixed upon the minister, his long body clothed in a robe that reached to his feet, his head bare, his white hair descending in a frothy cataract to his shoulders, his seamy face unnaturally pale, pale even to ghastliness. With all eyes following him and wondering, he made his silent way; without pausing, he ascended to the preacher's side and stood there, waiting. With shut lids the preacher, unconscious of his presence, continued his moving prayer, and at last finished it with the words, uttered in fervent appeal, "Bless our arms, grant us the victory, O Lord our God, Father and Protector of our land and flag!"

The stranger touched his arm, motioned him to step aside—which the startled minister did—and took his place. During some moments he surveyed the spellbound audience with solemn eyes, in which burned an uncanny light; then in a deep voice he said:

"I come from the Throne—bearing a message from Almighty God!" The words smote the house with a shock; if the stranger perceived it he gave no attention. "He has heard the prayer of His servant your shepherd, and will grant it if such shall be your desire after I, His messenger, shall have explained to you its import—that is to say, its full import. For it is like unto many of the prayers of men, in that it asks for more than he who utters it is aware of—except he pause and think.

"God's servant and yours has prayed his prayer. Has he paused and taken thought? Is it one prayer? No, it is two—one uttered, the other not. Both have reached the ear of Him Who heareth all supplications, the spoken and the unspoken. Ponder this—keep it in mind. If you would beseech a blessing upon yourself, beware! lest without intent you invoke a curse upon a neighbor at the same time. If you pray for the blessing of rain upon your crop which needs it, by that act you are possibly praying for a curse upon some neighbor's crop which may not need rain and can be injured by it.

"You have heard your servant's prayer—the uttered part of it. I am commissioned of God to put into words the other part of it—that part which the pastor—and also you in your hearts—fervently prayed silently. And ignorantly and unthinkingly? God grant that it was so! You heard these words: 'Grant us the victory, O Lord our God!' That is sufficient. The *whole* of the uttered prayer is compact into those pregnant words. Elaborations were not necessary. When you have prayed for victory you have prayed for many unmentioned results which follow victory—*must* follow it, cannot help but follow it. Upon the listening spirit of God the Father fell also the unspoken part of the prayer. He commandeth me to put it into words. Listen!

"O Lord our Father, our young patriots, idols of our hearts, go forth to battle—be Thou near them! With them—in spirit—we also go forth from the sweet peace of our beloved firesides to smite the foe. O Lord our God, help us to tear their soldiers to bloody shreds with our shells; help us to cover their smiling fields with the pale forms of their patriot dead; help us to drown the thunder of the guns with the shrieks of their wounded, writhing in pain; help us to lay waste their humble homes with a hurricane of fire; help us to wring the hearts of their unoffending widows with unavailing grief; help us to turn them out roofless with their little children to wander unfriended the wastes of their desolated land in rags and hunger and thirst, sports of the sun flames of summer and the icy winds of winter, broken in spirit, worn with travail, imploring Thee for the refuge of the grave and denied it—for our sakes who adore Thee, Lord, blast their hopes, blight their lives, protract their bitter pilgrimage, make heavy their steps, water their way with their tears, stain the white snow with the blood of their wounded feet! We ask it, in the spirit of love, of Him Who is the Source of Love, and Who is the ever-faithful refuge and friend of all that are sore beset and seek His aid with humble and contrite hearts. Amen."

(*After a pause.*) "Ye have prayed it; if ye still desire it, speak! The messenger of the Most High waits."

It was believed afterward that the man was a lunatic, because there was no sense in what he said.

ZORA NEALE HURSTON (1891–1960)
United States

Zora Neale Hurston was born and grew up in Eatonville, Florida, an all-black township whose cultural practices were decidedly African-American. Unlike many of her literary contemporaries of the Harlem Renaissance as well as the 1940s, Hurston did not perceive of blackness as a tragic state—the theme of her essay, "How It Feels to Be Colored Me." She loved the complexity of African-American culture—its speech patterns, storytelling, rituals, philosophical approaches. Her *Mules and Men* (1935), the first book of folklore by an African-American, emphasizes her recurrent themes, the complexity and vitality of African-American folklore and speech, as well as the roles of women in that culture. These qualities reached their finest portrayal in her now acknowledged classic *Their Eyes Were Watching God* (1937)

Hurston's works were neglected for many years, partly because the norms of African-American literature emphasized racism and its pathological effects on blacks, rather than African-American culture as a wholesome phenomenon, and partly because of Hurston's woman-centered focus in many of her works. Due to the explosion of African-American women's literary studies in the 1970s, and specifically because of the efforts of the writer Alice Walker, Hurston's novels, collections of folklore, short stories, and essays, and her autobiography are now well known. They have deeply influenced many American writers and readers.

How It Feels to Be Colored Me

I am colored but I offer nothing in the way of extenuating circumstances except the fact that I am the only Negro in the United States whose grandfather on the mother's side was *not* an Indian chief.

Elizabeth Catlett. *Cartas (Letters)*. 1986. Lithograph.

I remember the very day that I became colored. Up to my thirteenth year I lived in the little Negro town of Eatonville, Florida. It is exclusively a colored town. The only white people I knew passed through the town going to or coming from Orlando. The native whites rode dusty horses, and the Northern tourists chugged down the sandy village road in automobiles. The town knew the Southerners and never stopped cane chewing when they passed. But the Northerners were something else again. They were peered at cautiously from behind curtains by the timid. The more venturesome would come out on the porch to watch them go past and got just as much pleasure out of the tourists as the tourists got out of the village.

The front porch might seem a daring place for the rest of the town, but it was a gallery seat for me. My favorite place was atop the gate-post. Proscenium box for a born first-nighter. Not only did I enjoy the show, but I didn't mind the actors knowing that I liked it. I usually spoke to them in passing. I'd wave at them and when they returned my salute, I would say something like this: "Howdy-do-well-I-thank-you-where-you-goin'?" Usually automobile or the horse paused at this, and after a queer exchange of compliments, I would probably "go a piece of the way" with them, as we say in farthest Florida. If one of my family happened to come to the front in time to see me, of course negotiations would be rudely broken off. But even so, it is clear that I was the first "welcome-to-our-state" Floridian, and I hope the Miami Chamber of Commerce will please take notice.

During this period, white people differed from colored to me only in that they rode through town and never lived there. They liked to hear me "speak pieces" and sing and wanted to see me dance the parse-me-la, and gave me generously of their small silver for doing these things, which seemed strange to me for I wanted to do them so much that I needed bribing to stop. Only they didn't know it. The colored people gave no dimes. They deplored any joyful tendencies in me, but I was their Zora nevertheless. I belonged to them, to the nearby hotels, to the county—everybody's Zora.

But changes came in the family when I was thirteen, and I was sent to school in Jacksonville. I left Eatonville, the town of the oleanders, as Zora. When I disembarked from the river-boat at Jacksonville, she was no more. It seemed that I had suffered a sea change. I was not Zora of Orange County any more, I was now a little colored girl. I found it out in certain ways. In my heart as well as in the mirror, I became a fast brown—warranted not to rub nor run.

But I am not tragically colored. There is no great sorrow dammed up in my soul, nor lurking behind my eyes. I do not mind at all. I do not belong to the sobbing school of Negrohood who hold that nature somehow has given them a lowdown dirty deal and whose feelings are all hurt about it. Even in the helter-skelter skirmish that is my life, I have seen that the world is to the strong regardless of a little pigmentation more or less. No, I do not weep at the world—I am too busy sharpening my oyster knife.

Someone is always at my elbow reminding me that I am the granddaughter of slaves. It fails to register depression with me. Slavery is sixty years in the past. The operation was successful and the patient is doing well, thank you. The terrible struggle that made me an American out of a potential slave said "On the line!" The Reconstruction said "Get set!"; and the generation before said "Go!" I am off to a flying start and I must not halt in the stretch to look behind and weep. Slavery is the price I paid for civilization, and the choice was not with me. It is a bully adventure and worth all that I have paid through my ancestors for it. No one on earth ever had a greater chance for glory. The world to be won and nothing to be lost. It is thrilling to think—to know that for any act of mine, I shall get twice as much praise or twice as much blame. It is quite exciting to hold the center of the national stage, with the spectators not knowing whether to laugh or to weep.

The position of my white neighbor is much more difficult. No brown specter pulls up a chair beside me when I sit down to eat. No dark ghost thrusts its leg against mine in bed. The game of keeping what one has is never so exciting as the game of getting.

I do not always feel colored. Even now I often achieve the unconscious Zora of Eatonville before the Hegira. I feel most colored when I am thrown against a sharp white background.

For instance at Barnard, "Beside the waters of the Hudson," I feel my race. Among the thousand white persons, I am a dark rock surged upon, and overswept, but through it all, I remain myself. When covered by the waters, I am; and the ebb but reveals me again.

Sometimes it is the other way around. A white person is set down in our midst, but the contrast is just as sharp for me. For instance, when I sit in the drafty basement that is The New World Cabaret with a white person, my color comes. We enter chatting about any little nothing that we have in common and are seated by the jazz waiters. In the abrupt way that jazz orchestras have, this one plunges into a number. It loses no time in circumlocutions, but gets right down to business. It constricts the thorax and splits the heart with its tempo and narcotic harmonies. This orchestra grows rambunctious, rears on its hind legs and attacks the tonal veil with primitive fury, rending it, clawing it until it breaks through to the jungle beyond. I follow those heathen—follow them exultingly. I dance wildly inside myself; I yell within, I whoop; I shake my assegai above my head, I hurl it true to the mark *yeeeeooww!* I am in the jungle and living in the jungle way. My face is painted red and yellow and my body is painted blue. My pulse is throbbing like a war drum. I want to slaughter something—give pain, give death to what, I do not know. But the piece ends. The men of the orchestra wipe their lips and rest their fingers. I creep back slowly to the veneer we call civilization with the last tone and find the white friend sitting motionless in his seat, smoking calmly.

"Good music they have here," he remarks, drumming the table with his fingertips.

Music. The great blobs of purple and red emotion have not touched him. He has only heard what I felt. He is far away and I see him but dimly across the ocean and the continent that have fallen between us. He is so pale with his whiteness then and I am *so* colored.

At certain times I have no race, I am *me*. When I set my hat at a certain angle and saunter down Seventh Avenue, Harlem City, feeling as snooty as the lions in front of the Forty-Second Street Library, for instance. So far as my feelings are concerned, Peggy Hopkins Joyce on the Boule Mich with her gorgeous raiment, stately carriage, knees knocking together in a most aristocratic manner, has nothing on me. The cosmic Zora emerges. I belong to no race nor time. I am the eternal feminine with its string of beads.

I have no separate feeling about being an American citizen and colored. I am merely a fragment of the Great Soul that surges within the boundaries. My country, right or wrong.

Sometimes, I feel discriminated against, but it does not make me angry. It merely astonishes me. How *can* any deny themselves the pleasure of my company? It's beyond me.

But in the main, I feel like a brown bag of miscellany propped against a wall. Against a wall in company with other bags, white, red and yellow. Pour out the contents, and there is discovered a jumble of small things priceless and worthless. A first-water diamond, an empty spool, bits of broken glass, lengths of string, a key to a door long since crumbled away, a rusty knife-blade, old shoes saved for a road that never was and never will be, a nail bent under the weight of things too heavy for any nail, a dried flower or two still a little fragrant. In your hand is the brown bag. On the ground before you is the jumble it held—so much like the jumble in the bags, could they be emptied, that all might be dumped in a single heap and the bags refilled without altering the content of any greatly. A bit of colored glass more or less would not matter. Perhaps that is how the Great Stuffer of Bags filled them in the first place—who knows?

BLACK ELK (1863–1950)
United States

Black Elk was a Oglala Sioux priest and warrior from the Teton river region in Northwest Montana, who survived the battles of Little Big Horn and Wounded Knee. His memoirs were recorded by the anthropologist John G. Niehardt in *Black Elk Speaks* (1932). The Great Vision begins with the grandfathers speaking and continues with this lyric and visionary meditation.

from *Black Elk Speaks*

The Great Vision: [Breaking camp]

I entered the village, riding, with the four horse troops behind me—the blacks, the whites, the sorrels, and the buckskins; and the place was filled with moaning and with mourning for the dead. The wind was blowing from the south like fever, and when I looked around I saw that in nearly every tepee the women and the children and the men lay dying with the dead.

So I rode around the circle of the village, looking in upon the sick and dead, and I felt like crying as I rode. But when I looked behind me, all the women and the children and the men were getting up and coming forth with happy faces.

And a Voice said: "Beyond, they have given you the center of the nation's hoop to make it live."

So I rode to the center of the village, with the horse troops in their quarters round about me, and there the people gathered. And the Voice said: "Give them now the flowering stick that they may flourish, and the sacred pipe that they may know the power that is peace, and the wing of the white giant that they may have endurance and face all winds with courage."

So I took the bright red stick and at the center of the nation's hoop I thrust it in the earth. As it touched the earth it leaped mightily in my hand and was a waga chun, the rustling tree,[1] very tall and full of leafy branches and of all birds singing. And beneath it all the animals were mingling with the people like relatives and making happy cries. The women raised their tremolo of joy, and the men shouted all together: "Here we shall raise our children and be as little chickens under the mother sheo's[2] wing."

Then I heard the white wind blowing gently through the tree and singing there, and from the east the sacred pipe came flying on its eagle wings, and stopped before me there beneath the tree, spreading deep peace around it.

As told to John G. Niehardt.

---

1. The cottonwood.

2. Prairie hen.

Then the daybreak star was rising, and a Voice said: "It shall be a relative to them; and who shall see it, shall see much more, for thence comes wisdom; and those who do not see it shall be dark." And all the people raised their faces to the east, and the star's light fell upon them, and all the dogs barked loudly and the horses whinnied.

Then when the many little voices ceased, the great Voice said: "Behold the circle of the nation's hoop, for it is holy, being endless, and thus all powers shall be one power in the people without end. Now they shall break camp and go forth upon the red road, and your Grandfathers shall walk with them." So the people broke camp and took the good road with the white wing on their faces, and the order of their going was like this:

First, the black horse riders with the cup of water; and the white horse riders with the white wing and the sacred herb; and the sorrel riders with the holy pipe; and the buckskins with the flowering stick. And after these the little children and the youths and maidens followed in a band.

Second, came the tribe's four chieftains, and their band was all young men and women.

Third, the nation's four advisers leading men and women neither young nor old.

Fourth, the old men hobbling with their canes and looking to the earth.

Fifth, old women hobbling with their canes and looking to the earth.

Sixth, myself all alone upon the bay with the bow and arrows that the First Grandfather gave me. But I was not the last; for when I looked behind me there were ghosts of people like a trailing fog as far as I could see—grandfathers of grandfathers and grandmothers of grandmothers without number. And over these a great Voice—the Voice that was the South—lived, and I could feel it silent.

And as we went the Voice behind me said: "Behold a good nation walking in a sacred manner in a good land!"

Then I looked up and saw that there were four ascents ahead, and these were generations I should know. Now we were on the first ascent, and all the land was green. And as the long line climbed, all the old men and women raised their hands, palms forward, to the far sky yonder and began to croon a song together, and the sky ahead was filled with clouds of baby faces.

When we came to the end of the first ascent we camped in the sacred circle as before, and in the center stood the holy tree, and still the land about us was all green.

Then we started on the second ascent, marching as before, and still the land was green, but it was getting steeper. And as I looked ahead, the people changed into elks and bison and all four-footed beings and even into fowls, all walking in a sacred manner on the good red road together. And I myself was a spotted eagle soaring over them. But just before we stopped to camp at the end of that ascent, all the marching animals grew restless and afraid that they were not what they had been, and began sending forth voices of trouble, calling to their chiefs. And when they camped at the end of that ascent, I looked down and saw that leaves were falling from the holy tree.

And the Voice said: "Behold your nation, and remember what your Six Grandfathers gave you, for thenceforth your people walk in difficulties."

Then the people broke camp again, and saw the black road before them towards where the sun goes down, and black clouds coming yonder; and they did not want to go but could not stay. And as they walked the third ascent, all the animals and fowls that were the people ran here and there, for each one seemed to have his own little vision that he followed and his own rules; and all over the universe I could hear the winds at war like wild beasts fighting.[3]

W. E. B. DuBOIS (1868–1963)
United States

Probably the most significant African-American intellectual of the twentieth century, William Edward Burghardt DuBois was born in Great Barrington, Massachusetts. He grew up in a practically white environment, yet he vigorously devoted his long life to the liberation of African-Americans. Educated at Fisk University, Berlin University, and Harvard University, where he was the first black to earn a Ph.D., DuBois published many major scholarly works and poems, as well as five novels, and hundreds of essays and journalistic pieces. A founder of the Niagara Movement (1905–1909), and the National Association for the Advancement of Colored People (NAACP), he was also a leading figure in the Harlem Renaissance, a high point in African-American culture and art in the 1920's, including Countee Cullen, Claude McKay, Zora Neale Hurston, James Weldon Johnson, and Langston Hughes. He became a vocal Communist in the 1930s and was persecuted during the McCarthy period. He was a proponent of African liberation movements in the 1950s, and in 1961 emigrated to Ghana, where he died in 1963. His often-quoted statement "The problem of the twentieth century is the problem of the color line" has unfortunately proved to be prophecy.

The Souls of Black Folk (1903) is the best known of his tremendous number of publications, and it has had a lasting effect on twentieth-century African-American history, sociology, and literature. Comprised of historical, sociological, fictional, and personal essays, this work was influenced by DuBois's experiences with black farmers while he was a student at Fisk University, as well as by the German concept of the *Volk*, which he encountered in his studies in Berlin. This duality marks the entire volume. The motif of psychological homelessness has been a major theme in African-American thought. DuBois was one of the first to articulate it in haunting musical prose.

---

3. At this point Black Elk remarked: "I think we are near that place now, and I am afraid something very bad is going to happen all over the world." He could not read and knew nothing of world affairs.

from **The Souls of Black Folk**

I
Of Our Spiritual Strivings

O water, voice of my heart, crying in the sand,
  All night long crying with a mournful cry,
As I lie and listen, and cannot understand
    The voice of my heart in my side or the voice of the sea,
  O water, crying for rest, is it I, is it I?
  All night long the water is crying to me.

Unresting water, there shall never be rest
  Till the last moon droop and the last tide fail,
And the fire of the end begin to burn in the west;
    And the heart shall be weary and wonder and cry like the sea,
  All life long crying without avail,
    As the water all night long is crying to me.

Arthur Symons

Between me and the other world there is ever an unasked question: unasked by some through feelings of delicacy; by others through the difficulty of rightly framing it. All, nevertheless, flutter round it. They approach me in a half-hesitant sort of way, eye me curiously or compassionately, and then, instead of saying directly, How does it feel to be a problem? they say, I know an excellent colored man in my town; or, I fought at Mechanicsville; or, Do not these Southern outrages make your blood boil? At these I smile, or am interested, or reduce the boiling to a simmer, as the occasion may require. To the real question, How does it feel to be a problem? I answer seldom a word.

And yet, being a problem is a strange experience,—peculiar even for one who has never been anything else, save perhaps in babyhood and in Europe. It is in the early days of rollicking boyhood that the revelation first bursts upon one, all in a day, as it were. I remember well when the shadow swept across me. I was a little thing, away up in the hills of New England, where the dark Housatonic winds between Hoosac and Taghkanic to the sea. In a wee wooden schoolhouse, something put it into the boys' and girls' heads to buy gorgeous visiting-cards— ten cents a package—and exchange. The exchange was merry, till one girl, a tall newcomer, refused my card,—refused it peremptorily, with a glance. Then it dawned upon me with a certain suddenness that I was different from the others; or like, mayhap, in heart and life and longing, but shut out from their world by a vast veil. I had thereafter no desire to tear down that veil, to creep through; I held all beyond it in common contempt, and lived above it in a region of blue sky and great wandering shadows. That sky was bluest when I could beat my mates at examination-time, or beat them at a foot-race, or even beat their stringy heads.

Alas, with the years all this fine contempt began to fade; for the worlds I longed for, and all their dazzling opportunities, were theirs, not mine. But they should not keep these prizes, I said; some, all, I would wrest from them. Just how I would do it I could never decide: by reading law, by healing the sick, by telling the wonderful tales that swam in my head,—some way. With other black boys the strife was not fiercely sunny: their youth shrunk into tasteless sycophancy, or into silent hatred of the pale world about them and mocking distrust of everything white; or wasted itself in a bitter cry, Why did God make me an outcast and a stranger in mine own house? The shades of the prison-house closed round about us all: walls strait and stubborn to the whitest, but relentlessly narrow, tall, and unscalable to sons of night who must plod darkly on in resignation, or beat unavailing palms against the stone, or steadily, half hopelessly, watch the streak of blue above.

After the Egyptian and Indian, the Greek and Roman, the Teuton and Mongolian, the Negro is a sort of seventh son, born with a veil, and gifted with second-sight in this American world,—a world which yields him no true self-consciousness, but only lets him see himself through the revelation of the other world. It is a peculiar sensation, this double-consciousness, this sense of always looking at one's self through the eyes of others, of measuring one's soul by the tape of a world that looks on in amused contempt and pity. One ever feels his twoness,—an American, a Negro; two souls, two thoughts, two unreconciled strivings; two warring ideals in one dark body, whose dogged strength alone keeps it from being torn asunder.

The history of the American Negro is the history of this strife—this longing to attain self-conscious manhood, to merge his double self into a better and truer self. In this merging he wishes neither of the older selves to be lost. He would not Africanize America, for America has too much to teach the world and Africa. He would not bleach his Negro soul in a flood of white Americanism, for he knows that Negro blood has a message for the world. He simply wishes to make it possible for a man to be both a Negro and an American, without being cursed and spit upon by his fellows, without having the doors of Opportunity closed roughly in his face.

This, then, is the end of his striving: to be a co-worker in the kingdom of culture, to escape both death and isolation, to husband and use his best powers and his latent genius. These powers of body and mind have in the past been strangely wasted, dispersed, or forgotten. The shadow of a mighty Negro past flits through the tale of Ethiopia the Shadowy and of Egypt the Sphinx. Throughout history, the powers of single black men flash here and there like falling stars, and die sometimes before the world has rightly gauged their brightness. Here in America, in the few days since Emancipation, the black man's turning hither and thither in hesitant and doubtful striving has often made his very strength to lose effectiveness, to seem like absence of power, like weakness. And yet it is not weakness,—it is the contradiction of double aims. The double-aimed struggle of the black artisan—on the one hand to escape white contempt for a nation of mere hewers of wood and drawers of water, and on the other hand to plough and nail and dig for a poverty-stricken horde—could only result in making him a poor craftsman, for he had but half a heart in either cause. By the poverty and ignorance of his people, the Negro minister or doctor was tempted toward quackery and demagogy; and by the criticism of the other world, toward ideals that made him ashamed of his lowly tasks. The would-be black *savant* was confronted by the paradox that the knowledge his people needed was a twice-told tale to his white neighbors, while the knowledge which would teach the white world was Greek to his own flesh and blood. The innate love of harmony and beauty that set the ruder souls of his people a-dancing and a-singing raised but confusion and doubt in the soul of the black artist; for the beauty revealed to him was the soul-beauty of a race which his larger audience despised, and he could not articulate the message of another people. This waste of double aims, this seeking to satisfy two unreconciled ideals, has wrought sad havoc with the courage and faith and deeds of ten thousand thousand people,—has sent them often wooing false gods and invoking false means of salvation, and at times has even seemed about to make them ashamed of themselves.

Away back in the days of bondage they thought to see in one divine event the end of all doubt and disappointment; few men ever worshipped Freedom with half such unquestioning faith as did the American Negro for two centuries. To him, so far as he thought and dreamed, slavery was indeed the sum of all villainies, the cause of all sorrow, the root of all prejudice; Emancipation was the key to a promised land of sweeter beauty than ever stretched before the eyes of wearied Israelites. In song and exhortation swelled one refrain—Liberty; in his tears and curses the God he implored had Freedom in his right hand. At last it came,—suddenly, fearfully, like a dream. With one wild carnival of blood and passion came the message in his own plaintive cadences:—

> "Shout, O children!
> Shout, you're free!
> For God has bought your liberty!"

Years have passed away since then,—ten, twenty, forty; forty years of national life, forty years of renewal and development, and yet the swarthy spectre sits in its accustomed seat at the Nation's feast. In vain do we cry to this our vastest social problem:—

> "Take any shape but that, and my firm nerves
> Shall never tremble!"

The Nation has not yet found peace from its sins; the freedman has not yet found in freedom his promised land. Whatever of good may have come in these years of change, the shadow of a deep disappointment rests upon the Negro people,—a disappointment all the more bitter because the unattained ideal was unbounded save by the simple ignorance of a lowly people.

The first decade was merely a prolongation of the vain search for freedom, the boon that seemed ever barely to elude their grasp,—like a tantalizing will-o'-the-wisp, maddening and misleading the headless host. The holocaust of war, the terrors of the Ku-Klux Klan, the lies of carpet-baggers, the disorganization of industry, and the contradictory advice of friends and foes, left the bewildered serf with no new watch-word beyond the old cry for freedom. As the time flew, however, he began to grasp a new idea. The ideal of liberty demanded for its attainment powerful means, and these the Fifteenth Amendment gave him. The ballot, which before he had looked upon as a visible sign of freedom, he now regarded as the chief means of gaining and perfecting the liberty with which war had partially endowed him. And why not? Had not votes made war and emancipated millions? Had not votes enfranchised the freedmen? Was anything impossible to a power that had done all this? A million black men started with renewed zeal to vote themselves into the kingdom. So the decade flew away, the revolution of 1876 came, and left the half-free serf weary, wondering, but still inspired. Slowly but steadily, in the following years, a new vision began gradually to replace the dream of political power,—a powerful movement, the rise of another ideal to guide the unguided, another pillar of fire by night after a clouded day. It was the ideal of "book-learning"; the curiosity, born of compulsory ignorance, to know and test the power of the cabalistic letters of the white man, the longing to know. Here at last seemed to have been discovered the mountain path to Canaan; longer than the highway of Emancipation and law, steep and rugged, but straight, leading to heights high enough to overlook life.

Up the new path the advance guard toiled, slowly, heavily, doggedly; only those who have watched and guided the faltering feet, the misty minds, the dull understandings, of the dark pupils of these schools know how faithfully, how piteously, this people strove to learn. It was weary work. The cold statistician wrote down the inches of progress here and there, noted also where here and there a foot had slipped or someone had fallen. To the tired climbers, the horizon was ever dark, the mists were often cold, the Canaan was always dim and far away. If, however, the visits disclosed as yet no goal, no resting-place, little but flattery and criticism, the journey at least gave leisure for reflection and self-examination; it changed the child of Emancipation to the youth with dawning self-consciousness, self-realization, self-respect. In those sombre forests of his striving his own soul rose before him, and he saw himself,—darkly as through a veil; and yet he saw in himself some faint revelation of his power, of his mission. He began to have a dim feeling that, to attain his place in the world, he must be himself, and not another. For the first time he sought to analyze the burden he bore upon his back, that dead-weight of social degradation partially masked behind a half-named Negro problem. He felt his poverty; without a cent, without a home, without land, tools, or savings, he had entered into competition with rich, landed, skilled neighbors. To be a poor man is hard, but to be a poor race in a land of dollars is the very bottom of hardships. He felt the weight of his ignorance,—not simply of letters, but of life, of business, of the humanities; the accumulated sloth and shirking and awkwardness of decades and centuries shackled his hands and feet. Nor was his burden all poverty and ignorance. The red stain of bastardy, which two centuries of systematic legal defilement of Negro women had stamped upon his race, meant not only the loss of ancient African chastity, but also the hereditary weight of a mass of corruption from white adulterers, threatening almost the obliteration of the Negro home.

A people thus handicapped ought not to be asked to race with the world, but rather allowed to give all its time and thought to its own social problems. But alas! while sociologists gleefully count his bastards and his prostitutes, the very soul of the toiling, sweating black man is darkened by the shadow of a vast despair. Men call the shadow prejudice, and learnedly explain it as the natural defence of culture against barbarism, learning against ignorance, purity against crime, the "higher" against the "lower" races. To which the Negro cries Amen! and swears that to so much of this strange prejudice as is founded on just homage to civilization, culture, righteousness, and progress, he humbly bows and meekly does obeisance. But before that nameless prejudice that leaps beyond all this he stands helpless, dismayed, and well-nigh speechless; before that personal disre-spect and mockery, the ridicule and systematic humiliation, the distortion of fact and wanton license of fancy, the cynical ignoring of the better and the boisterous welcoming of the worse, the all-pervading desire to inculcate disdain for everything black, from Toussaint to the devil,—before this there rises a sickening despair that would disarm and discourage any nation save that black host to whom "discouragement" is an unwritten word.

But the facing of so vast a prejudice could not but bring the inevitable self-questioning, a self-disparagement, and lowering of ideals which ever accom-pany repression and breed in an atmosphere of contempt and hate. Whisperings and portents came borne upon the four winds: Lo! we are diseased and dying, cried the dark hosts; we cannot write, our voting is vain; what need of education, since we must always cook and serve? And the Nation echoed and enforced this self-criticism, saying: Be content to be servants, and nothing more; what need of higher culture for half-men? Away with the black man's ballot, by force or fraud,—and behold the suicide of a race! Nevertheless, out of the evil came something of good,—the more careful adjustment of education to real life, the clearer perception of the Negroes' social responsibilities, and the sobering realization of the meaning of progress.

So dawned the time of *Sturm und Drang*: storm and stress today rocks our little boat on the mad waters of the world-sea; there is within and without the sound of conflict, the burning of body and rending of soul; inspiration strives with doubt, and faith with vain questionings. The bright ideals of the past,—physical freedom, political power, the training of brains and the training of hands,—all these in turn have waxed and waned, until even the last grows dim and overcast. Are they all wrong,—all false? No, not that, but each alone was over-simple and incomplete,—the dreams of a credulous race-childhood, or the fond imaginings of the other world which does not know and does not want to know our power. To be really true, all these ideals must be melted and welded into one. The training of the schools we need to-day more than ever,—the training of deft hands, quick eyes and ears, and above all the broader, deeper, higher culture of gifted minds and pure hearts. The power of the ballot we need in sheer self-defence,—else what shall save us from a second slavery? Freedom, too, the long-sought, we still seek,—the freedom of life and limb, the freedom to work and think, the freedom to love and aspire. Work, culture, liberty,—all these we need, not singly but together, not successively but together, each growing and aiding each, and all striving toward that vaster ideal that swims before the Negro people, the ideal of human brotherhood, gained through the unifying ideal of Race; the ideal of fostering and developing the traits and talents of the Negro, not in opposition to or contempt for other races, but rather in large conformity to the greater ideals of the American Republic, in order that some day on American soil two world-races may give each to each those characteristics both so sadly lack. We the darker ones come even now not altogether empty-handed: there are to-day no truer exponents of the pure human spirit of the Declaration of Independence than the American Negroes; there is no true American music but the wild sweet melodies of the Negro slave; the American fairy tales and folklore are Indian and African; and, all in all, we black men seem the sole oasis of simple faith and reverence in a dusty desert of dollars and smartness. Will America be poorer if she replace her brutal dyspeptic blundering with light-hearted but determined Negro humility? or her coarse and cruel wit with loving jovial good-humor? or her vulgar music with the soul of the Sorrow Songs?

Merely a concrete test of the underlying principles of the great republic is the Negro Problem, and the spiritual striving of the freedmen's sons is the travail of souls whose burden is almost beyond the measure of their strength, but who bear it in the name of an historic race, in the name of this land of their fathers' fathers, and in the name of human opportunity.

And now what I have briefly sketched in large outline let me on coming pages tell again in many ways, with loving emphasis and deeper detail, that men may listen to the striving in the souls of black folk.

WILLA CATHER (1873–1947)
United States

Willa Cather was born in Virginia, moved with her family to Nebraska when she was nine, attended the state university in Lincoln, and became a journalist, editor, and then, after 1911, a full-time writer. Living in Pittsburgh and New York, she continued to write of Nebraska, as in *O Pioneers!* (1913) and *My Antonia* (1918), stories of the farming frontier. An unfinished novel was destroyed after her death by Edith Lewis, her longtime companion. Cather was wisely recognized by Wallace Stevens in the 1930s to be one of America's finest novelists. The poet, supremely sensitive to the sound of words, especially appreciated her gift for capturing the different varieties of American speech, each embodying its own history of coming to the new continent and moving in or across it. "The Enchanted Bluff" captures Cather's tactile sense of landscape, another aspect of her magisterial style. Fortunate in having experienced the newness of the frontier, Cather also preserved in her writing what seems an indigenous apprehension of the sacred. It is not only her characters who utter words; for her, light, rock, night, and stars have their own vocabularies. This early story holds these secrets.

The Enchanted Bluff

We had our swim before sundown, and while we were cooking our supper the oblique rays of light made a dazzling glare on the white sand about us. The translucent red ball itself sank behind the brown stretches of corn field as we sat down to eat, and the warm layer of air that had rested over the water and our clean sand-bar grew fresher and smelled of the rank ironweed and sunflowers growing on the flatter shore. The river was brown and sluggish, like any other of the half-dozen streams that water the Nebraska corn lands. On one shore was an irregular line of bald clay bluffs where a few scrub-oaks with thick trunks and flat, twisted tops threw light shadows on the long grass. The western shore was low and level, with corn fields that stretched to the sky-line, and all along the water's edge were little sandy coves and beaches where slim cottonwoods and willow saplings flickered.

The turbulence of the river in springtime discouraged milling, and, beyond keeping the old red bridge in repair, the busy farmers did not concern themselves with the stream; so the Sandtown boys were left in undisputed possession. In the autumn we hunted quail through the miles of stubble and fodder land along the flat shore, and, after the winter skating season was over and the ice had gone out, the spring freshets and flooded bottoms gave us our great excitement of the year. The channel was never the same for two successive seasons. Every spring the swollen stream undermined a bluff to the east, or bit out a few acres of corn field to the west and whirled the soil away to deposit it in spumy mud banks somewhere else. When the water fell low in midsummer, new sand-bars were thus exposed to dry and whiten in the August sun. Sometimes these were banked so firmly that the fury of the next freshet failed to unseat them; the little willow seedlings emerged triumphantly from the yellow froth, broke into spring leaf, shot up into summer growth, and with their mesh of roots bound together the moist sand beneath them against the batterings of another April. Here and there a cottonwood soon glittered among them, quivering in the low current of air that, even on breathless days when the dust hung like smoke above the wagon road, trembled along the face of the water.

It was on such an island, in the third summer of its yellow green, that we built our watch-fire; not in the thicket of dancing willow wands, but on the level terrace of fine sand which had been added that spring; a little new bit of world, beautifully ridged with ripple marks, and strewn with the tiny skeletons of turtles and fish, all as white and dry as if they had been expertly cured. We had been careful not to mar the freshness of the place, although we often swam to it on summer evenings and lay on the sand to rest.

This was our last watch-fire of the year, and there were reasons why I should remember it better than any of the others. Next week the other boys were to file back to their old places in the Sandtown High School, but I was to go up to the Divide to teach my first country school in the Norwegian district. I was already homesick at the thought of quitting the boys with whom I had always played; of leaving the river, and going up into a windy plain that was all windmills and corn fields and big pastures; where there was nothing wilful or unmanageable in the landscape, no new islands, and no chance of unfamiliar birds—such as often followed the watercourses.

Other boys came and went and used the river for fishing or skating, but we six were sworn to the spirit of the stream, and we were friends mainly because of the river. There were the two Hassler boys, Fritz and Otto, sons of the little German tailor. They were they youngest of us; ragged boys of ten and twelve, with sunburned hair, weather-stained faces, and pale blue eyes. Otto, the elder, was the best mathematician in school, and clever at his books, but he always dropped out in the spring term as if the river could not get on without him. He and Fritz caught the fat, horned catfish and sold them about the town, and they lived so much in the water that they were as brown and sandy as the river itself.

There was Percy Pound, a fat, freckled boy with chubby cheeks, who took half a dozen boys' storypapers and was always being kept in for reading detective stories behind his desk. There was Tip Smith, destined by his freckles and red hair to be the buffoon in all our games, though he walked like a timid little old man and had a funny, cracked laugh. Tip worked hard in his father's grocery store every afternoon, and swept it out before school in the morning. Even his recreations were laborious. He collected cigarette cards and tin tobacco-tags indefatigably, and would sit for hours humped up over a snarling little scroll-saw which he kept in his attic. His dearest possessions were some little pill-bottles that purported to contain grains of wheat from the Holy Land, water from the Jordan and the Dead Sea, and earth from the Mount of Olives. His father had bought these dull things from a Baptist missionary who peddled them, and Tip seemed to derive great satisfaction from their remote origin.

The tall boy was Arthur Adams. He had fine hazel eyes that were almost too reflective and sympathetic for a boy, and such a pleasant voice that we all loved to hear him read aloud. Even when he had to read poetry aloud at school, no one ever thought of laughing. To be sure, he was not at school very much of the time. He was seventeen and should have finished the High School the year before, but he was always off somewhere with his gun. Arthur's mother was dead, and his father, who was feverishly absorbed in promoting schemes, wanted to send the boy away to school and get him off his hands; but Arthur always begged off for another year and promised to study. I remember him as a tall, brown boy with an intelligent face, always lounging among a lot of us little fellows, laughing at us oftener than with us, but such a soft, satisfied laugh that we felt rather flattered when we provoked it. In after-years people said that Arthur had been given to evil ways even as a lad, and it is true that we often saw him with the gambler's sons and with old Spanish Fanny's boy, but if he learned anything ugly in their company he never betrayed it to us. We would have followed Arthur anywhere, and I am bound to say that he led us into no worse places than the cat-tail marshes and the stubble fields. These, then, were the boys who camped with me that summer night upon the sand-bar.

After we finished our supper we beat the willow thicket for driftwood. By the time we had collected enough, night had fallen, and the pungent, weedy smell from the shore increased with the coolness. We threw ourselves down about the fire and made another futile effort to show Percy Pound the Little Dipper. We had tried it often before, but he could never be got past the big one.

"You see those three big stars just below the handle, with the bright one in the middle?" said Otto Hassler; "that's Orion's belt, and the bright one is the clasp." I crawled behind Otto's shoulder and sighted up his arm to the star that seemed perched upon the tip of his steady forefinger. The Hassler boys did seine-fishing at night, and they knew a good many stars.

Percy gave up the Little Dipper and lay back on the sand, his hands clasped under his head, "I can see the North Star," he announced, contentedly, pointing toward it with his big toe. "Anyone might get lost and need to know that."

We all looked up at it.

"How do you suppose Columbus felt when his compass didn't point north any more?" Tip asked.

Otto shook his head. "My father says that there was another North Star once, and that maybe this one won't last always. I wonder what would happen to us down here if anything went wrong with it?"

Arthur chuckled. "I wouldn't worry, Ott. Nothing's apt to happen to it in your time. Look at the Milky Way! There must be lots of good dead Indians."

We lay back and looked, meditating, at the dark cover of the world. The gurgle of the water had become heavier. We had often noticed a mutinous, complaining note in it at night, quite different from its cheerful daytime chuckle, and seeming like the voice of a much deeper and more powerful stream. Our water had always these two moods: the one of sunny complaisance, the other of inconsolable, passionate regret.

"Queer how the stars are all in sort of diagrams," remarked Otto. "You could do most any proposition in geometry with 'em. They always look as if they meant something. Some folks say everybody's fortune is all written out in the stars, don't they?"

"They believe so in the old country," Fritz affirmed.

But Arthur only laughed at him. "You're thinking of Napoleon, Fritzey. He had a star that went out when he began to lose battles. I guess the stars don't keep any close tally on Sandtown folks."

We were speculating on how many times we could count a hundred before the evening star went down behind the corn fields, when someone cried, "There comes the moon, and it's as big as a cart wheel!"

We all jumped up to greet it as it swam over the bluffs behind us. It came up like a galleon in full sail; an enormous, barbaric thing, red as an angry heathen god.

"When the moon came up red like that, the Aztecs used to sacrifice their prisoners on the temple top," Percy announced.

"Go on, Perce. You got that out of *Golden Days*.[1] Do you believe that, Arthur?" I appealed.

---

1. *Golden Days for Boys and Girls* (1880–1907) was a weekly journal of serialized fiction, published by James Elverson.

Arthur answered, quite seriously: "Like as not. The moon was one of their gods. When my father was in Mexico City he saw the stone where they used to sacrifice their prisoners."

As we dropped down by the fire again some one asked whether the Mound-Builders were older than the Aztecs. When we once got upon the Mound-Builders we never willingly got away from them, and we were still conjecturing when we heard a loud splash in the water.

"Must have been a big cat jumping," said Fritz. "They do sometimes. They must see bugs in the dark. Look what a track the moon makes!"

There was a long, silvery streak on the water, and where the current fretted over a big log it boiled up like gold pieces.

"Suppose there ever *was* any gold hid away in this old river?" Fritz asked. He lay like a little brown Indian, close to the fire, his chin on his hand and his bare feet in the air. His brother laughed at him, but Arthur took his suggestion seriously.

"Some of the Spaniards thought there was gold up here somewhere. Seven cities chuck full of gold, they had it, and Coronado and his men came up to hunt it. The Spaniards were all over this country once."

Percy looked interested. "Was that before the Mormons went through?"

We all laughed at this.

"Long enough before. Before the Pilgrim Fathers, Perce. Maybe they came along this very river. They always followed the watercourses."

"I wonder where this river really does begin?" Tip mused. That was an old and a favorite mystery which the map did not clearly explain. On the map the little black line stopped somewhere in western Kansas; but since rivers generally rose in mountains, it was only reasonable to suppose that ours came from the Rockies. Its destination, we knew, was the Missouri, and the Hassler boys always maintained that we could embark at Sandtown in floodtime, follow our noses, and eventually arrive at New Orleans. Now they took up their old argument. "If us boys had grit enough to try it, it wouldn't take no time to get to Kansas City and St. Joe."

We began to talk about the places we wanted to go to. The Hassler boys wanted to see the stock-yards in Kansas City, and Percy wanted to see a big store in Chicago. Arthur was interlocutor and did not betray himself.

"Now it's your turn, Tip."

Tip rolled over on his elbow and poked the fire, and his eyes looked shyly out of his queer, tight little face. "My place is awful far away. My Uncle Bill told me about it."

Tip's Uncle Bill was a wanderer, bitten with mining fever, who had drifted into Sandtown with a broken arm, and when it was well had drifted out again.

"Where is it?"

"Aw, it's down in New Mexico somewheres. There aren't no railroads or anything. You have to go on mules, and you run out of water before you get there and have to drink canned tomatoes."

"Well, go on, kid. What's it like when you do get there?"

Tip sat up and excitedly began his story.

"There's a big red rock there that goes right up out of the sand for about nine hundred feet. The country's flat all around it, and this here rock goes up all by itself, like a monument. They call it the Enchanted Bluff down there, because no white man has ever been on top of it. The sides are smooth rock, and straight up, like a wall. The Indians say that hundreds of years ago, before the Spaniards came, there was a village away up there in the air. The tribe that lived there had some sort of steps, made out of wood and bark, hung down over the face of the bluff, and the braves went down to hunt and carried water up in big jars swung on their backs. They kept a big supply of water and dried meat up there, and never went down except to hunt. They were a peaceful tribe that made cloth and pottery, and they went up there to get out of the wars. You see, they could pick off any war party that tried to get up their little steps. The Indians say they were a handsome people, and they had some sort of queer religion. Uncle Bill thinks they were Cliff-Dwellers who had got into trouble and left home. They weren't fighters, anyhow.

"One time the braves were down hunting and an awful storm came up—a kind of waterspout—and when they got back to their rock they found their little staircase had been all broken to pieces, and only a few steps were left hanging away up in the air. While they were camped at the foot of the rock, wondering what to do, a war party from the north came along and massacred 'em to a man, with all the old folks and women looking on from the rock. Then the war party went on south and left the village to get down the best way they could. Of course they never got down. They starved to death up there, and when the war party came back on their way north, they could hear the children crying from the edge of the bluff where they had crawled out, but they didn't see a sign of a grown Indian, and nobody has ever been up there since."

We exclaimed at this dolorous legend and sat up.

"There couldn't have been many people up there," Percy demurred. "How big is the top, Tip?"

"Oh, pretty big. Big enough so that the rock doesn't look nearly as tall as it is. The top's bigger than the base. The bluff is sort of worn away for several hundred feet up. That's one reason it's so hard to climb."

I asked how the Indians go up, in the first place.

"Nobody knows how they got up or when. A hunting party came along once and saw that there was a town up there, and that was all."

Otto rubbed his chin and looked thoughtful. "Of course there must be some way to get up there. Couldn't people get a rope over someway and pull a ladder up?"

Tip's little eyes were shining with excitement. "I know a way. Me and Uncle Bill talked it all over. There's a kind of rocket that would take a rope over—life-savers use 'em—and then you could hoist a rope-ladder and peg it down at the bottom and make it tight with guy-ropes on the other side. I'm going to climb that there bluff, and I've got it all planned out."

Fritz asked what he expected to find when he got up there.

"Bones, maybe, or the ruins of their town, or pottery, or some of their idols. There might be 'most anything up there. Anyhow, I want to see."

"Sure nobody else has been up there, Tip?" Arthur asked.

"Dead sure. Hardly anybody ever goes down there. Some hunters tried to cut steps in the rock once, but they didn't get higher than a man can reach. The Bluff's all red granite, and Uncle Bill thinks it's a boulder the glaciers left. It's a queer place, anyhow. Nothing but cactus and desert for hundreds of miles, and yet right under the Bluff there's good water and plenty of grass. That's why the bison used to go down there."

Suddenly we heard a scream above our fire, and jumped up to see a dark, slim bird floating southward far above us—a whooping-crane, we knew by her cry and her long neck. We ran to the edge of the island, hoping we might see her alight, but she wavered southward along the rivercourse until we lost her. The Hassler boys declared that by the look of the heavens it must be after midnight, so we threw more wood on our fire, put on our jackets, and curled down in the warm sand. Several of us pretended to doze, but I fancy we were really thinking about Tip's Bluff and the extinct people. Over in the wood the ring-doves were calling mournfully to one another, and once we heard a dog bark, far away. "Somebody getting into old Tommy's melon patch," Fritz murmured sleepily, but nobody answered him. By and by Percy spoke out of the shadows.

"Say, Tip, when you go down there will you take me with you?"

"Maybe."

"Suppose one of us beats you down there, Tip?"

"Whoever gets to the Bluff first has got to promise to tell the rest of us exactly what he finds," remarked one of the Hassler boys, and to this we all readily assented.

Somewhat reassured, I dropped off to sleep. I must have dreamed about a race for the Bluff, for I awoke in a kind of fear that other people were getting ahead of me and that I was losing my chance. I sat up in my damp clothes and looked at the other boys, who lay tumbled in uneasy attitudes about the dead fire. It was still dark, but the sky was blue with the last wonderful azure of night. The stars glistened like crystal globes, and trembled as if they shone through a depth of clear water. Even as I watched, they began to pale and the sky brightened. Day came suddenly, almost instantaneously. I turned for another look at the blue night, and it was gone. Everywhere the birds began to call, and all manner of little insects began to chirp and hop about in the willows. A breeze sprang up from the west and brought the heavy smell of ripened corn. The boys rolled over and shook themselves. We stripped and plunged into the river just as the sun came up over the windy bluffs.

When I came home to Sandtown at Christmas time, we skated out to our island and talked over the whole project of the Enchanted Bluff, renewing our resolution to find it.

Although that was twenty years ago, none of us have ever climbed the Enchanted Bluff. Percy Pound is a stockbroker in Kansas City and will go nowhere that his red touring-car cannot carry him. Otto Hassler went on the railroad and lost his foot braking; after which he and Fritz succeeded their father as the town tailors.

Arthur sat about the sleepy little town all his life—he died before he was twenty-five. The last time I saw him, when I was home on one of my college vacations, he was sitting in a steamer-chair under a cottonwood tree in the little yard behind one of the two Sandtown saloons. He was very untidy and his hand was not steady, but when he rose, unabashed, to greet me, his eyes were as clear and warm as ever. When I had talked with him for an hour and heard him laugh again, I wondered how it was that when Nature had taken such pains with a man, from his hands to the arch of his long foot, she had ever lost him in Sandtown. He joked about Tip Smith's Bluff, and declared he was going down there just as soon as the weather got cooler; he thought the Grand Canyon might be worth while, too.

I was perfectly sure when I left him that he would never get beyond the high plank fence and the comfortable shade of the cottonwood. And, indeed, it was under that very tree that he died one summer morning.

Tip Smith still talks about going to New Mexico. He married a slatternly, unthrifty country girl, has been much tied to a perambulator, and has grown stooped and gray from irregular meals and broken sleep. But the worst of his difficulties are now over, and he has, as he says, come into easy water. When I was last in Sandtown I walked home with him late one moonlight night, after he had balanced his cash and shut up his store. We took the long way around and sat down on the schoolhouse steps, and between us we quite revived the romance of the lone red rock and the extinct people. Tip insists that he still means to go down there, but he thinks now he will wait until his boy Bert is old enough to go with him. Bert has been let into the story, and thinks of nothing but the Enchanted Bluff.

GERTRUDE STEIN (1874–1946)
United States

Gertrude Stein, the novelist, playwright, and essayist, was born into a German-Jewish family in Allegheny, Pennsylvania, who then moved to Oakland, California; both parents died during her adolescence. She studied psychology at Harvard (Radcliffe) and medicine at Johns Hopkins, then turned to writing. With her brother Leo, she set up house at 27 rue de Fleurus in Paris, where her collection of Cézannes, Matisse, and Picassos was celebrated. Alice B. Toklas moved to Paris in 1909 to become Stein's lifelong companion. During World War I, Stein drove her Ford for the American Fund for the French wounded. Widely recognized as an important modernist writer, she toured America, lecturing in 1934–5. During the Vichy period, the couple took refuge in the countryside, returning to Paris at the liberation; Stein died there of cancer in 1946.

Stein's "An Indian Boy" exemplifies both her formal stylistic contribution to modernism and the thoughtful disturbance behind it. Stein, as an attentive student of William James, understood why James considered himself Ralph Waldo Emerson's spiritual son. Stein practiced language as a doctor practices medicine; trained in medicine herself, she translated what she had learned, transforming words into cures. She knew that we are made out of the words we use; her project was to make her readers self-conscious about language, to feel the beat of strong emotions in repetitions, the change of moods in variations, the confusion in twisting syntax. Her acknowledged and unacknowledged influence is immense. Preserving the health of a kind of Marx Brothers' skepticism even on her deathbed, she rallied to ask, "What is the answer?" and, there being no reply, added, "In that case, what is the question?"

An Indian Boy

It happens to be here.

Black and white and red all over.

One little Indian two little Indian three little Indian boys five little four little three little two little one little Indian boy.

They were all anxious to go. I accidentally met some one else. I said to him, where have you been. And he said I have been. And I said to him and what were your experiences. And he answered they do not understand the proper use of violets. Violets and mimosa, these can please.

Another instance of the thing I mean is this. They were in the midst of excitement and she was there and she was not representative. In this way no mistake can be made.

And an Indian boy.

Five Indians as we said we know how to say five Indians as we said. We are amused when we say who is abused as we say.

An Indian boy in Mexico.

An Indian boy in India.

An Indian boy in America.

An Indian Boy in Russia.

Also an Indian boy in Georgia.

An Indian boy in Italy.

An Indian boy in India.

An Indian boy in Africa.

An Indian boy in America.

An Indian boy and individuals and close answers.

She said a big fig and she said they had Jocelyn.

An Indian boy in India in America in Africa in Georgia in Italy and in Asia.
An an Indian boy and individuals and close answers.

AN INDIAN BOY.

An Indian boy was said to be red.
He leaves no doubt as to this.
An Indian boy is said to be red and he leaves no one in doubt of this.
An Indian boy says he is red and so no one has any doubt of this.
An Indian boy or is he red and is there any doubt of this.
If an Indian boy can naturally be an inhabitant is there any doubt of it.
An Indian boy being an inhabitant is there any doubt about it.

By naturally being an Indian boy and an inhabitant may one say that may be he is but we doubt it.

An explanation of the situation as to an Indian boy being an inhabitant leads to the expression of doubt of this on the part of these who do doubt this.

An Indian boy is an inhabitant of this place and he has no doubt about it.

Dawson Johnston Librarian. What is gentle. To gentle. To be gentle.

AN INDIAN BOY.

Can the first one see me.
Can the second one see me.
Can the third one see me.
Can the fifth one see me.
Can the fourth one see me.
Can the third one see me.
Can the second one see me.
Can the first one see me.

When I see them and they see me I say to them that I see them and that they see me.

An Indian boy can very nearly see to this. An Indian boy can very nearly come to see to this. An Indian boy can be very nearly said to have seen to this.

An Indian boy nearly an Indian boy and very nearly an Indian boy. When I say all this I remember that choice.

An Indian boy can say what to say.

And an Indian boy can say what does he say.

He says he needs to say he needs to be able to say what he can say.

An Indian boy can say what he says and he says that there is a singular relief in two daughters. A singular relief in two daughters. In their relief he was not disappointed.

When he sees he sees to it that they are celebrated to-day.

An Indian boy can be satisfied.

An Indian boy can be satisfied and by the outcropping of a central hill. He can be satisfied.

If you mean to be reconciled if you mean to be altogether reconciled can they say another may another may ask a question eight times and nine times.

ROBERT FROST (1874–1963)
United States

Reared in New England, Robert Frost was introduced to the poetry of William Wordsworth and Ralph Waldo Emerson by his mother, a devotee of the Swedish mystic Emanuel Swedenborg, whose intuitive insights mixed with the observation of nature were a great influence on his poetry. Like Gertrude Stein, Frost was a student of William James. Frost went to Harvard University specifically to study psychology with him; James was on leave, but Frost enrolled in the course taught from the pioneering *Principles of Psychology* in the shortened form James designed for college classes. Later in his career, Frost himself taught psychology using James's text at a secondary school for boys. "After Apple-Picking" is a prime example of how the poet used words, grammar, and syntax as psychological tools. And as the American critic Richard Poirier has observed, while the poem is a "dream vision," it "proposes that only labor can penetrate to the essential facts of natural life"—the essence of James's principles, a key insight into living.

After Apple-Picking

My long two-pointed ladder's sticking through a tree
Toward heaven still,
And there's a barrel that I didn't fill
Beside it, and there may be two or three
Apples I didn't pick upon some bough.   5
But I am done with apple-picking now.
Essence of winter sleep is on the night,
The scent of apples: I am drowsing off.
I cannot rub the strangeness from my sight
I got from looking through a pane of glass   10
I skimmed this morning from the drinking trough.
And held against the world of hoary grass.
It melted, and I let it fall and break.
But I was well
Upon my way to sleep before it fell,   15
And I could tell
What form my dreaming was about to take.
Magnified apples appear and disappear,
Stem end and blossom end,
And every fleck of russet showing clear.   20
My instep arch not only keeps the ache,
It keeps the pressure of a ladder-round.
I feel the ladder sway as the boughs bend.

And I keep hearing from the cellar bin
The rumbling sound   25
Of load on load of apples coming in.
For I have had too much
Of apple-picking: I am overtired
Of the great harvest I myself desired.
There were ten thousand thousand fruit to touch,   30
Cherish in hand, lift down, and not let fall.
For all
That struck the earth,
No matter if not bruised or spiked with stubble,
Went surely to the cider-apple heap   35
As of no worth.
One can see what will trouble
This sleep of mine, whatever sleep it is.
Were he not gone,
The woodchuck could say whether it's like his   40
Long sleep, as I describe its coming on,
Or just some human sleep.

1914

WALLACE STEVENS (1879–1955)
United States

Wallace Stevens wanted his biography to say only that he was a lawyer and lived
in Hartford: he walked to his office, and traveled mostly in his mind. Like Walt
Whitman, Stevens believed that his *whole work* would serve generations of
readers as the Bible once had, like "a missal found in the mud" of the
decaying/fertile soil of America. Stevens belongs in the rank with Gertrude Stein
and Robert Frost as another who keenly apprehended the revolutionary import
of Ralph Waldo Emerson and his heir, William James. Stevens's poetry is
thinking about thinking. But it never lets us forget, in the sound of his words, that
thinking is feeling. Stevens's poems tempt us like forbidden fruit to fall into
thinking ourselves.

   These two poems about death are chosen as examples of Stevens's ability to
adopt different stances on the most vital subjects. "Sunday Morning" is based on
the experience of Stevens's mother in her bedroom awaiting her "gentle, delicate"
death against a background of Christian belief and meditation on life's meaning.

In a letter of 1928, he says of this poem that it is "an expression of paganism" of which he was not conscious while writing it.

The Emperor of Ice-Cream

Call the roller of big cigars,
The muscular one, and bid him whip
In kitchen cups concupiscent[1] curds.
Let the wenches dawdle in such dress
As they are used to wear, and let the boys   5
Bring flowers in last month's newspapers.
Let be be finale of seem.
The only emperor is the emperor of ice-cream.

Take from the dresser of deal,
Lacking the three glass knobs, that sheet   10
On which she embroidered fantails once
And spread it so as to cover her face.
If her horny feet protrude, they come
To show how cold she is, and dumb.
Let the lamp affix its beam.   15
The only emperor is the emperor of ice-cream.

Sunday Morning

I

Complacencies of the peignoir, and late
Coffee and oranges in a sunny chair,
And the green freedom of a cockatoo
Upon a rug mingle to dissipate
The holy hush of ancient sacrifice.   5
She dreams a little, and she feels the dark
Encroachment of that old catastrophe,
As a calm darkens among water-lights.
The pungent oranges and bright, green wings
Seem things in some procession of the dead,   10
Winding across wide water, without sound.
The day is like wide water, without sound,
Stilled for the passing of her dreaming feet
Over the seas, to silent Palestine,
Dominion of the blood and sepulchre.   15

---

1. Strongly desirous, usually in a sexual sense.

II

Why should she give her bounty to the dead?
What is divinity if it can come
Only in silent shadows and in dreams?
Shall she not find in comforts of the sun,
In pungent fruit and bright, green wings, or else   20
In any balm or beauty of the earth,
Things to be cherished like the thought of heaven?
Divinity must live within herself:
Passions of rain, or moods in falling snow;
Grievings in loneliness, or unsubdued   25
Elations when the forest blooms; gusty
Emotions on wet roads on autumn nights;
All pleasures and all pains, remembering
The bough of summer and the winter branch.
These are the measures destined for her soul.   30

III

Jove in the clouds had his inhuman birth.
No mother suckled him, no sweet land gave
Large-mannered motions to his mythy mind.
He moved among us, as a muttering king,
Magnificent, would move among his hinds,   35
Until our blood, commingling, virginal,
With heaven, brought such requital to desire
The very hinds discerned it, in a star.
Shall our blood fail? Or shall it come to be
The blood of paradise? And shall the earth   40
Seem all of paradise that we shall know?
The sky will be much friendlier then than now,
A part of labor and a part of pain,
And next in glory to enduring love,
Not this dividing and indifferent blue.   45

IV

She says, "I am content when wakened birds,
Before they fly, test the reality
Of misty fields, by their sweet questionings;
But when the birds are gone, and their warm fields
Return no more, where, then, is paradise?"   50
There is not any haunt of prophecy,
Nor any old chimera of the grave,

Neither the golden underground, nor isle
Melodious, where spirits gat them home,
Nor visionary south, nor cloudy palm   55
Remote on heaven's hill, that has endured
As April's green endures; or will endure
Like her remembrance of awakened birds,
Or her desire for June and evening, tipped
By the consummation of the swallow's wings.   60

V

She says, "But in contentment I still feel
The need of some imperishable bliss."
Death is the mother of beauty; hence from her,
Alone, shall come fulfilment to our dreams
And our desires. Although she strews the leaves   65
Of sure obliteration on our paths,
The path sick sorrow took, the many paths
Where triumph rang its brassy phrase, or love
Whispered a little out of tenderness,
She makes the willow shiver in the sun   70
For maidens who were wont to sit and gaze
Upon the grass, relinquished to their feet.
She causes boys to pile new plums and pears
On disregarded plate.[1] The maidens taste
And stray impassioned in the littering leaves.   75

VI

Is there no change of death in paradise?
Does ripe fruit never fall? Or do the boughs
Hang always heavy in that perfect sky,
Unchanging, yet so like our perishing earth,
With rivers like our own that seek for seas   80
They never find, the same receding shores
That never touch with inarticulate pang?
Why set the pear upon those river-banks
Or spice the shores with odors of the plum?

---

1. In a letter, Stevens describes this "plate" as the silver-plated dishes used by the family, and continues: "Disregarded refers to the disuse into which things fall that have been possessed for a long time. I mean, therefore, that death releases and renews. What the old have come to disregard, the young inherit and make use of." (*Selected Letters.* New York: A.A. Knopf, 1966, p. 183).

Alas, that they should wear our colors there,   85
The silken weavings of our afternoons,
And pick the strings of our insipid lutes!
Death is the mother of beauty, mystical,
Within whose burning bosom we devise
Our earthly mothers waiting, sleeplessly.   90

VII

Supple and turbulent, a ring of men
Shall chant in orgy on a summer morn
Their boisterous devotion to the sun,
Not as a god, but as a god might be,
Naked among them, like a savage source.   95
Their chant shall be a chant of paradise,
Out of their blood, returning to the sky;
And in their chant shall enter, voice by voice,
The windy lake wherein their lord delights,
The trees, like serafin, and echoing hills,   100
That choir among themselves long afterward.
They shall know well the heavenly fellowship
Of men that perish and of summer morn.
And whence they came and whither thay shall go
The dew upon their feet shall manifest.[2]   105

VIII

She hears, upon that water without sound,
A voice that cries, "The tomb in Palestine
Is not the porch of spirits lingering.
It is the grave of Jesus, where he lay."
We live in an old chaos of the sun,   110
Or old dependency of day and night,
Or island solitude, unsponsored, free,
Of that wide water, inescapable.
Deer walk upon our mountains, and the quail
Whistle about us their spontaneous cries;   115
Sweet berries ripen in the wilderness;
And, in the isolation of the sky,
At evening, casual flocks of pigeons make

---

2. Stevens comments on this line that it refers
   to life as "fugitive as dew upon the feet" of
   men dancing. (*Selected Letters*, p. 250).

Ambiguous undulations as they sink,
Downward to darkness, on extended wings.   120

1923

WILLIAM CARLOS WILLIAMS
(1883–1963)
United States

William Carlos Williams was a practicing obstetrician. He delivered words into
the world as well as children. Each one was new and he made it cry out. A
contemporary of Wallace Stevens, Marianne Moore, and Ezra Pound, he stressed
the importance of making a purely American language, washed clean of Old
World residues. Throughout his lifetime he argued this in various ways with
Stevens, who took the opposing position, that the words we use carry their own
histories and ourselves along with them. The clear lines of "The Red Wheelbar-
row" fit as well into the complex condensation in one instant of time of the
movement called "Imagism" as into the concrete emphasis on the thing perceived
called "Objectivism"; "so much" and more depends on the clarity of this one
simple sight. The sight of the circling dancers in one of Williams' *Pictures from
Brueghel* makes a noisy poem in the round for a joyful response to a great artist
by a great poet.

The Red Wheelbarrow

so much depends
upon

a red wheel
barrow

glazed with rain
water

beside the white
chickens.

The Dance

In Brueghel's great picture, The Kermess,
the dancers go round, they go round and

around, the squeal and the blare and the
tweedle of bagpipes, a bugle and fiddles
tipping their bellies (round as the thick-   5
sided glasses whose wash they impound)
their hips and their bellies off balance
to turn them. Kicking and rolling about
the Fair Grounds, swinging their butts, those
shanks must be sound to bear up under such   10
rollicking measures, prance as they dance
in Breughel's great picture, The Kermess.

MARIANNE MOORE (1887–1972)
United States

Marianne Moore, who moved early from Missouri to Pennsylvania, was a student
and then a teacher at Bryn Mawr Collge there. From age 30 until her death in
New York City, where she was associated with a group of writers and artists
including William Carlos Williams, Wallace Stevens, Mina Loy, and Marsden
Hartley. Marianne Moore's exquisite facility with words is evident as much in her
reviews and criticism as it is in her poems. An intuitive detective of poetic
intelligence, Moore pinpointed in her perspicacious evaluations of her contemporaries' writing the motives for metaphor hidden from most. Her regular
contributions to *The Dial* (under her editorship from 1924 to 1929) and to other
leading periodicals shaped the cultural sensibility of her time, much in the same
way as Edmund Wilson's perceptions. Moore's acuity is at its sharpest in poems
like the two represented here. Her readers are cajoled into recreating a natural
history of thinking to follow the clues she so deftly left.

The Mind Is an Enchanting Thing

is an enchanted thing
  like the glaze on a
katydid-wing
    subdivided by sun
    till the nettings are legion.
Like Gieseking playing Scarlatti;[1]   5

---

1. The German pianist Walter Gieseking (1895–1956) was widely acclaimed for his interpretations of the works of Italian com- poser Domenico Scarlatti, whose chromatic harmonies of seventeenth-century operas anticipated both Mozart and Schubert.

like the apteryx-awl[2]
   as a beak, or the
kiwi's rain-shawl
     of haired feathers, the mind
     feeling its way as though blind,
walks along with its eyes on the ground.

It has memory's ear
   that can hear without
having to hear.   15
     Like the gyroscope's fall,
     truly unequivocal
because trued by regnant certainty,

it is a power of
   strong enchantment. It   20
is like the dove-
     neck animated by
     sun; it is memory's eye;
it's conscientious inconsistency.

It tears off the veil; tears
   the temptation, the
mist the heart wears,   25
     from its eyes—if the heart
     has a face; it takes apart
dejection. It's fire in the dove-neck's   30

iridescence; in the
   inconsistencies
of Scarlatti.
     Unconfusion submits
     its confusion to proof; it's   35
not a Herod's oath that cannot change.

What Are Years?

  What is our innocence,
what is our guilt? All are
   naked, none is safe. And whence
is courage: the unanswered question,
the resolute doubt—   5
dumbly calling, deafly listening—that
is misfortune, even death,

---

2. The apteryx, or kiwi bird, has a long,
   pointed bill (like an awl) and cannot fly.

And the light crept up between the shutters
And you heard the sparrows in the gutters,
You had such a vision of the street
As the street hardly understands;
Sitting along the bed's edge, where   35
You curled the papers from your hair,
Or clasped the yellow soles of feet
In the palms of both soiled hands.

4

His soul stretched tight across the skies
That fade behind a city block,
Or trampled by insistent feet   40
At four and five and six o'clock;
And short square fingers stuffing pipes,
And evening newspapers, and eyes
Assured of certain certainties,   45
The conscience of a blackened street
Impatient to assume the world.

I am moved by fancies that are curled
Around these images, and cling:
The notion of some infinitely gentle   50
Infinitely suffering thing.

Wipe your hand across your mouth, and laugh;
The worlds revolve like ancient women
Gathering fuel in vacant lots.

The Love Song of J. Alfred Prufrock

S'io credesse che mia risposta fosse
A persona che mai tornasse al mondo,
Questa fiamma staria senza piu scosse,
Ma perciocche giammai di questo fondo
Non torno vivo alcun, s'i'odo il vero,
Senza tema d'infamia it rispondo.[1]

Let us go then, you and I,
When the evening is spread out against the sky
Like a patient etherised upon a table;

---

1. Dante's *Inferno*, XXVII, 61–66: "If I thought
   that my reply were to be to someone who
   would ever return to the world, this flame
   would be still, without further motion. But
   since no one has ever returned alive from
   this depth, if what I hear is true, I answer
   you without fear of shame."

Let us go, through certain half-deserted streets,
The muttering retreats   5
Of restless nights in one-night cheap hotels
And sawdust restaurants with oyster-shells:
Streets that follow like a tedious argument
Of insidious intent
To lead you to an overwhelming question. . .   10
Oh, do not ask, "What is it?"
Let us go and make our visit.

    In the room the women come and go
Talking of Michelangelo.

    The yellow fog that rubs its back upon the window-panes,   15
The yellow smoke that rubs its muzzle on the window-panes,
Licked its tongue into the corners of the evening,
Lingered upon the pools that stand in drains,
Let fall upon its back the soot that falls from chimneys,
Slipped by the terrace, made a sudden leap,   20
And seeing that it was a soft October night,
Curled once about the house, and fell asleep.

    And indeed there will be time
For the yellow smoke that slides along the street,
Rubbing its back upon the window-panes;
There will be time, there will be time   25
To prepare a face to meet the faces that you meet;
There will be time to murder and create,
And time for all the works and days[2] of hands
That lift and drop a question on your plate;   30
Time for you and time for me,
And time yet for a hundred indecisions,
And for a hundred visions and revisions,
Before the taking of a toast and tea.

    In the room the women come and go   35
Talking of Michelangelo.

    And indeed there will be time
To wonder, "Do I dare?" and, "Do I dare?"
Time to turn back and descend the stair,
With a bald spot in the middle of my hair—   40
(They will say: "How his hair is growing thin!")
My morning coat, my collar mounting firmly to the chin,
My necktie rich and modest, but asserted by a simple pin—

---

2. The Greek poet Hesiod (eighth century
   B.C.E.) wrote *Works and Days*, a georgic
   poem concerning rural life.

(They will say: "But how his arms and legs are thin!")
Do I dare
Disturb the universe?
In a minute there is time
For decisions and revisions which a minute will reverse.

    For I have known them all already, known them all—
Have known the evenings, mornings, afternoons,
I have measured out my life with coffee spoons;
I know the voices dying with a dying fall
Beneath the music from a farther room.
    So how should I presume?

    And I have known the eyes already, known them all—
The eyes that fix you in a formulated phrase,
And when I am formulated, sprawling on a pin,
When I am pinned and wriggling on the wall,
Then how should I begin
To spit out all the butt-ends of my days and ways?
    And how should I presume?

    And I have known the arms already, known them all—
Arms that are braceleted and white and bare
(But in the lamplight, downed with light brown hair!)
Is it perfume from a dress
That makes me so digress?
Arms that lie along a table, or wrap about a shawl.
    And should I then presume?
    And how should I begin?

. . .

    Shall I say, I have gone at dusk through narrow streets
And watched the smoke that rises from the pipes
Of lonely men in shirt-sleeves, leaning out of windows?. . .

    I should have been a pair of ragged claws
Scuttling across the floors of silent seas.

. . .

    And the afternoon, the evening, sleeps so peacefully!
Smoothed by long fingers,
Asleep . . . tired . . . or it malingers,
Stretched on the floor, here beside you and me.
Should I, after tea and cakes and ices,
Have the strength to force the moment to its crisis?
But though I have wept and fasted, wept and prayed,
Though I have seen my head (grown slightly bald) brought in upon a platter,[3]

45

50

55

60

65

70

75

80

---

3. The head of John the Baptist was delivered
   on a platter to Salome (Matthew 14:1–11).

I am no prophet—and here's no great matter;
I have seen the moment of my greatness flicker,
And I have seen the eternal Footman hold my coat, and snicker,   85
And in short, I was afraid.

    And would it have been worth it, after all,
After the cups, the marmalade, the tea.
Among the porcelain, among some talk of you and me,
Would it have been worth while,   90
To have bitten off the matter with a smile,
To have squeezed the universe into a ball
To roll it toward some overwhelming question,
To say: "I am Lazarus, come from the dead,[4]
Come back to tell you all, I shall tell you all"—   95
If one, settling a pillow by her head,
    Should say: "That is not what I meant at all.
    That is not it, at all."

       . . .

    And would it have been worth it, after all,
Would it have been worth while,   100
After the sunsets and the dooryards and the sprinkled streets,
After the novels, after the teacups, after the skirts that trail along the floor—
And this, and so much more?—
It is impossible to say just what I mean!
But as if a magic lantern threw the nerves in patterns on a screen: 105
Would it have been worth while
If one, settling a pillow or throwing off a shawl,
And turning toward the window, would say:
    "That is not it at all,
    That is not what I meant, at all."   110

       . . .

No! I am not Prince Hamlet, nor was meant to be;
Am an attendant lord, one that will do
To swell a progress,[5] start a scene or two,
Advise the prince; no doubt, an easy tool,
Deferential, glad to be of use,   115
Politic, cautious, and meticulous;
Full of high sentence, but a bit obtuse;
At times, indeed, almost ridiculous—
Almost, at times, the Fool.

    I grow old . . . I grow old . . .   120
I shall wear the bottoms of my trousers rolled.

---

4. Lazarus was raised from the dead by Jesus (John 11: 1–44).

5. A royal court procession.

Shall I part my hair behind? Do I dare to eat a peach?
I shall wear white flannel trousers, and walk upon the beach.
I have heard the mermaids singing, each to each.

I do not think that they will sing to me.   125

I have seen them riding seaward on the waves
Combing the white hair of the waves blown back
When the wind blows the water white and black.

We have lingered in the chambers of the sea
By sea-girls wreathed with seaweed red and brown   130
Till human voices wake us, and we drown.

ERNEST HEMINGWAY (1899–1961)
United States

Ernest Hemingway's training in raw facts began in his childhood in Oak Park,
Illinois. His father was a physician and a hunter, and the boy learned of life and
death with him. He gave his son his first fishing rod at age two and his first gun
at ten. In 1928, when Hemingway was twenty-nine, his father committed suicide.
Hemingway's wordskill was sharpened by his years of work as a reporter of one
kind or another, on the Kansas City *Star* to begin with, then the Toronto *Star*.
Admiring and emulating Twain and Stein, Hemingway developed a style that has
itself been imitated probably more than that of any other American writer. He
spent a crucial time in Paris, associated with Gertrude Stein and Ezra Pound (*A
Moveable Feast*) and in Spain (*For Whom the Bell Tolls,* 1940). He committed
suicide with one of his shotguns, the barrel in his mouth, in 1961, "unable to
stand things."

"Indian Camp" is one of the short stories Gertrude Stein thought marked the
young Hemingway's mastery. Its pristine brutality is the product of intense
experience and an attentiveness to language like that a hunter exercises in
stalking prey.

Indian Camp

At the lake shore there was another rowboat drawn up. The two Indians stood
waiting.

Nick and his father got in the stern of the boat and the Indians shoved it
off and one of them got in to row. Uncle George sat in the stern of the camp
rowboat. The young Indian shoved the camp boat off and got in to row Uncle
George.

The two boats started off in the dark. Nick heard the oarlocks of the other boat quite a way ahead of them in the mist. The Indians rowed with quick choppy strokes. Nick lay back with his father's arm around him. It was cold on the water. The Indian who was rowing them was working very hard, but the other boat moved further ahead in the mist all the time.

"Where are we going, Dad?" Nick asked.

"Over to the Indian camp. There is an Indian lady very sick."

"Oh," said Nick.

Across the bay they found the other boat beached. Uncle George was smoking a cigar in the dark. The young Indian pulled the boat way up on the beach. Uncle George gave both the Indians cigars.

They walked up from the beach through a meadow that was soaking wet with dew, following the young Indian who carried a lantern. Then they went into the woods and followed a trail that led to the logging road that ran back into the hills. It was much lighter on the logging road as the timber was cut away on both sides. The young Indian stopped and blew out his lantern and they all walked on along the road.

They came around a bend and a dog came out barking. Ahead were the lights of the shanties where the Indian bark-peelers lived. More dogs rushed out at them. The two Indians sent them back to the shanties. In the shanty nearest the road there was a light in the window. An old woman stood in the doorway holding a lamp.

Inside on a wooden bunk lay a young Indian woman. She had been trying to have her baby for two days. All the old women in the camp had been helping her. The men had moved off up the road to sit in the dark and smoke out of range of the noise she made. She screamed just as Nick and the two Indians followed his father and Uncle George into the shanty. She lay in the lower bunk, very big under a quilt. Her head was turned to one side. In the upper bunk was her husband. He had cut his foot very badly with an ax three days before. He was smoking a pipe. The room smelled very bad.

Nick's father ordered some water to be put on the stove, and while it was heating he spoke to Nick.

"This lady is going to have a baby, Nick," he said.

"I know," said Nick.

"You don't know," said his father. "Listen to me. What she is going through is called being in labor. The baby wants to be born and she wants it to be born. All her muscles are trying to get the baby born. That is what is happening when she screams."

"I see," Nick said.

Just then the woman cried out.

"Oh, Daddy, can't you give her something to make her stop screaming?" asked Nick.

"No. I haven't any anaesthetic," his father said. "But her screams are not important. I don't hear them because they are not important."

The husband in the upper bunk rolled over against the wall.

The woman in the kitchen motioned to the doctor that the water was hot. Nick's father went into the kitchen and poured about half of the water out of the big kettle into a basin. Into the water left in the kettle he put several things he unwrapped from a handkerchief.

"Those must boil," he said, and began to scrub his hands in the basin of hot water with a cake of soap he had brought from the camp. Nick watched his father's hands scrubbing each other with the soap. While his father washed his hands very carefully and thoroughly, he talked.

"You see, Nick, babies are supposed to be born head first but sometimes they're not. When they're not they make a lot of trouble for everybody. Maybe I'll have to operate on this lady. We'll know in a little while."

When he was satisfied with his hands he went in and went to work.

"Pull back that quilt, will you, George?" he said. "I'd rather not touch it."

Later when he started to operate Uncle George and three Indian men held the woman still. She bit Uncle George on the arm and Uncle George said, "Damn squaw bitch!" and the young Indian who had rowed Uncle George over laughed at him. Nick held the basin for his father. It all took a long time. His father picked the baby up and slapped it to make it breathe and handed it to the old woman.

"See, it's a boy, Nick," he said. "How do you like being an interne?"

Nick said, "All right." He was looking away so as not to see what his father was doing.

"There. That gets it," said his father and put something into the basin. Nick didn't look at it.

"Now," his father said, "there's some stitches to put in. You can watch this or not, Nick, just as you like. I'm going to sew up the incision I made."

Nick did not watch. His curiosity had been gone for a long time.

His father finished and stood up. Uncle George and the three Indian men stood up. Nick put the basin out in the kitchen.

Uncle George looked at his arm. The young Indian smiled reminiscently.

"I'll put some peroxide on that, George," the doctor said. He bent over the Indian woman. She was quiet now and her eyes were closed. She looked very pale. She did not know what had become of the baby or anything.

"I'll be back in the morning," the doctor said, standing up. "The nurse should be here from St. Ignace by noon and she'll bring everything we need."

He was feeling exalted and talkative as football players are in the dressing room after a game.

"That's one for the medical journal, George," he said. "Doing a Caesarian with a jack-knife and sewing it up with nine-foot, tapered gut leaders."

Uncle George was standing against the wall, looking at his arm.

"Oh, you're a great man, all right," he said.

"Ought to have a look at the proud father. They're usually the worst sufferers in these little affairs," the doctor said. "I must say he took it all pretty quietly."

He pulled back the blanket from the Indian's head. His hand came away wet. He mounted on the edge of the lower bunk with the lamp in one hand and looked in. The Indian lay with his face toward the wall. His throat had been cut from ear to ear. The blood had flowed down into a pool where his body sagged the bunk. His head rested on his left arm. The open razor lay, edge up, in the blankets.

"Take Nick out of the shanty, George," the doctor said.

There was no need of that. Nick, standing in the door of the kitchen, had a good view of the upper bunk when his father, the lamp in one hand, tipped the Indian's head back.

It was just beginning to be daylight when they walked along the logging road back toward the lake.

"I'm terribly sorry I brought you along, Nickie," said his father, all his post-operative exhilaration gone. "It was an awful mess to put you through."

"Do ladies always have such a hard time having babies?" Nick asked.

"No, that was very, very exceptional."

"Why did he kill himself, Daddy?"

"I don't know, Nick. He couldn't stand things, I guess."

"Do many men kill themselves, Daddy?"

"Not very many, Nick."

"Do many women?"

"Hardly ever."

"Don't they ever?"

"Oh, yes. They do sometimes."

"Daddy?"

"Yes."

"Where did Uncle George go?"

"He'll turn up all right."

"Is dying hard, Daddy?"

"No, I think it's pretty easy, Nick. It all depends."

They were seated in the boat. Nick in the stern, his father rowing. The sun was coming up over the hills. A bass jumped, making a circle in the water. Nick trailed his hand in the water. It felt warm in the sharp chill of the morning.

In the early morning on the lake sitting in the stern of the boat with his father rowing, he felt quite sure that he would never die.

LANGSTON HUGHES (1902–1967)
United States

Often called "the poet laureate of the Negro Race," James Langston Hughes was born in Joplin, Missouri. Raised by his maternal grandmother, whose two husbands had been leading black abolitionists, Langston learned early on about political activism. Influenced by the poets Walt Whitman, Carl Sandburg, Paul Laurence Dunbar, and W. E. B. DuBois, he wrote "The Negro Speaks of Rivers" within a year after graduating from high school. An active figure in the Harlem Renaissance, in 1926 Hughes published his first poetry collection, *The Weary Blues,* possibly the first American writing to transform blues and jazz into poetic forms.

From that time on Hughes became internationally known for his portrayals of black people's culture and struggles throughout the world in deceptively simple but innovative folk forms. His travels to the Caribbean, Latin America, and Africa in the 1920s helped to create links among the poets who would develop the *négritude* movement with its emphasis on black literary culture. A socialist in the 1930s, he traveled to the Soviet Union and China, where he related the struggles of African-Americans to a larger world transformation. From the 1940s to the 1960s, he encouraged younger African-American writers like Lorraine Hansberry, Gwendolyn Brooks, and Alice Walker.

At the time of his death, Hughes had published five collections of poetry, two books of stories, two novels, two autobiographies, the popular newspaper series "The Simple Stories" (based on the character Jesse B. Semple or "Simple"), several children's books, and five plays. With Arna Bontemps, he also edited many anthologies on black folk culture. A struggling writer for most of his life, Hughes produced a remarkable body of writing devoted to the common man, particularly African-Americans, in poetic forms that have indelibly transformed American literature.

The Negro Speaks of Rivers

I've known rivers:
I've known rivers ancient as the world and older than the
   flow of human blood in human veins.

My soul has grown deep like the rivers.

I bathed in the Euphrates when dawns were young.   5
I built my hut near the Congo and it lulled me to sleep.
I looked upon the Nile and raised the pyramids above it.
I heard the singing of the Mississippi when Abe Lincoln
   went down to New Orleans, and I've seen its muddy
   bosom turn all golden in the sunset.   10

I've known rivers:
Ancient, dusky rivers.

My soul has grown deep like the rivers.

LOUIS (LITTLECOON) OLIVER

(b. 1904)

United States

A fullblood Muskogee/Creek Indian, Louis Littlecoon Oliver was born in 1904, in Koweta Town, in what was to become (three years later) the state of

Oklahoma. Orphaned as a child, raised by his grandmother and his aunts, he went through government schools until the fifth grade, eventually managing, on his own, to matriculate into the high school at Bacone College, from which he graduated in 1926. Wandering the country, fishing and hunting along the banks of the Illinois River, tending his vegetable gardens, stomp-dancing, singing and praying the old prayers and songs, Oliver nonetheless felt, as he puts it, "a void in my life." It was then, as he says, that it dawned on him "to leave something in writing of my heritage in the Native American sense." Having been impressed, as far back as high school, by some of the English and American poets, he decided to try his own hand at written verse. The result has been a body of poems and stories of great power and interest.

Empty Kettle

I do not waste what is wild
I only take what my cup
   can hold.
When the black kettle gapes
   empty   5
and children eat roasted acorns
   only,
it is time to rise-up early
   take no drink—eat no food
   sing the song of the hunter.   10
I see the Buck—I chant
I chant the deer chant:
   "He-hebah-Ah-kay-kee-no!"
My arrow, no woman has ever touched,
   finds its mark.   15
I open the way for the blood to pour
   back to Mother Earth
     the debt I owe.
My soul rises—rapturous
   and I sing a different song,   20
     I sing,
     I sing.

RICHARD WRIGHT (1908–1960)
United States

One of the most influential of African-American writers, Richard Wright was born in Natchez, Mississippi, where he knew extreme hunger and intense racism, themes that would dominate his writings. At the age of nineteen he moved to Chicago, where his involvement in the John Reed Club gave him the intellectual space to develop his writing and to study philosophy, psychology, sociology, and literature. Communist philosophy influenced his early poems, *Uncle Tom's Children* (1938), and his novel *Native Son* (1941), which challenged the sexual taboos at the heart of American racism. *Black Boy* (1945), his first autobiography, some of which covers his schooling in the South, is a realistic account of the psychological effects of the hunger and racism Wright experienced in his childhood and is related to his illustrated essay book, *Twelve Million Voices, a Folk History of the Negro in the U.S.* (1941).

In 1947 Wright and his white wife, Ellen, moved to Paris, partly to escape American discrimination. His life there influenced his work in that he became increasingly involved in the conflicts between the West and the developing countries. From 1947 until his death in 1960, he wrote four novels, another collection of short stories, three collections of essays, and the autobiographical sequel to *Black Boy,* called *American Hunger,* published seventeen years after his death. Wright changed the African-American literary tradition with his powerful psychological protest fiction and his intensely political essays to the extent that the period of the 1940s is often called the Age of Wright.

from **Black Boy**

[Looking for a job]

Summer again. The old problem of hunting for a job. I told the woman for whom I was working, a Mrs. Bibbs, that I needed an all-day job that would pay me enough money to buy clothes and books for the next school term. She took the matter up with her husband, who was a foreman in a sawmill.

"So you want to work in the mill, hunh?" he asked.

"Yes, sir."

He came to me and put his hands under my arms and lifted me from the floor, as though I were a bundle of feathers.

"You're too light for our work," he said.

"But maybe I could do *something* there," I said.

"That's the problem," he said soberly. "The work's heavy and dangerous." He was silent and I knew that he considered the matter closed. That was the way things were between whites and blacks in the South; many of the most important things were never openly said; they were understated and left to seep through to one. I, in turn, said nothing; but I did not leave the room; my standing silent was a way of asking him to reconsider, telling him that I wanted ever so much to try for a job in his mill. "All right," he said finally. "Come to the mill in the morning. I'll see what I can do. But I don't think that you'll like it."

I was at the mill at dawn the next morning and saw men lifting huge logs with tackle blocks. There were scores of buzzing steel saws biting into green wood with loud whines.

"Watch out!" somebody yelled.

I looked around and saw a black man pointing above my head; I glanced up.

A log was swinging toward me. I scrambled out of its path. The black man came to my side.

"What do you want here, boy?"

"Mr. Bibbs, the foreman, told me to look around. I'm looking for a job." I said.

The man gazed at me intently.

"I wouldn't try for this if I was you," he said. "If you know this game, all right. But this is dangerous stuff for the guy that's green." He held up his right hand from which three fingers were missing. "See?"

I nodded and left.

Empty days. Long days. Bright hot days. The sun heated the pavements until they felt like the top of an oven. I spent the mornings hunting for jobs and I read during the afternoons. One morning I was walking toward the center of town and passed the home of a classmate, Ned Greenley. He was sitting on his porch, looking glum.

"Hello, Ned. What's new?" I asked.

"You've heard, haven't you?" he asked.

"About what?"

"My brother, Bob?"

"No, what happened?"

Ned began to weep softly.

"They killed him," he managed to say.

"The white folks?" I asked in a whisper, guessing.

He sobbed his answer. Bob was dead; I had met him only a few times, but I felt that I had known him through his brother.

"What happened?"

"Th-they t-took him in a c-car . . . Out on a c-country road . . . "Th-they shot h-him," Ned whimpered.

I had heard that Bob was working at one of the hotels in town.

"Why?"

"Th-they said he was fooling with a white prostitute there in the hotel," Ned said.

Inside of me my world crashed and my body felt heavy. I stood looking down the quiet, sun-filled street. Bob had been caught by the white death, the threat of which hung over every male black in the South. I had heard whispered tales of black boys having sex relations with white prostitutes in the hotels in town, but I had never paid any close attention to them; now those tales came home to me in the form of the death of a man I knew.

I did not search for a job that day; I returned home and sat on my porch too, and stared. What I had heard altered the look of the world, induced in me a temporary paralysis of will and impulse. The penalty of death awaited me if I made a false move and I wondered if it was worth-while to make any move at all. The things that influenced my conduct as a Negro did not have to happen to me directly; I needed but to hear of them to feel their full effects in the deepest layers of my consciousness. Indeed, the white brutality that I had not seen was a more effective control of my behavior than that which I knew. The actual experience would have let me see the realistic outlines of what was really happening, but as long as it remained something terrible and yet remote, something whose horror and blood might descend upon me at any moment, I was compelled to give my entire imagination over to it, an act which blocked the springs of thought and feeling in me, creating a sense of distance between me and the world in which I lived.

A few days later I sought out the editor of the local Negro newspaper and found that he could not hire me. I had doubts now about my being able to enter school that fall. The empty days of summer rolled on. Whenever I met my classmates they would tell me about the jobs they had found, how some of them had left town to work in summer resorts in the North. Why did they not tell me of these jobs? I demanded of them. They said that they simply had not thought of it, and as I heard the words fall from their lips my sense of isolation became doubly acute. But, after all, what would make them think of me in connection with jobs when for years I had encountered them only casually in the classroom? I had had no association with them; the religious home in which I lived, my mush-and-lard-gravy poverty had cut me off from the normal processes of the lives of black boys my own age.

One afternoon I made a discovery in the home that stunned me. I was talking to my cousin, Maggie, who was a few months younger than I, when Uncle Tom entered the room. He paused, stared at me with silent hostility, then called his daughter. I gave the matter no thought. A few moments later I rose from my chair, where I had been reading, and was on my way down the hall when I heard Uncle Tom scolding his daughter. I caught a few phrases:

"Do you want me to break your neck? Didn't I tell you to stay away from him? That boy's a dangerous fool, I tell you! Then why don't you keep away from him? And make the other children keep away from him? Ask me no questions, but do as I tell you! Keep away from him, or I'll skin you!"

And I could hear my cousin's whimpering replies. My throat grew tight with anger. I wanted to rush into the room and demand an explanation, but I held still. How long had this been going on? I thought back over the time since Uncle Tom and his family had moved into the house, and I was filled with dismay as I recalled that on scarcely any occasion had any of his children ever been alone with me. Be careful now, I told myself; don't see what isn't there . . . But no matter how carefully I weighed my memories, I could recall no innocent intimacy, no games, no playing, none of the association that usually exists between young people living in the same house. Then suddenly I was reliving that early morning when I had held Uncle Tom at bay with my razors. Though I must have seemed brutal and desperate to him, I have never thought of myself as being so, and now I was appalled at how I was regarded. It was a flash of insight which revealed to me the true nature of my relations with my family, an insight which altered the entire course of my life. I was now definitely decided upon leaving home. But I would remain until the ninth grade term had ended. There were many days when I spoke to no one in the home except my mother. My life was falling to pieces and I was acutely aware of it. I was poised for flight, but I was waiting for some event, some word, some act, some circumstance to furnish the impetus.

I returned to my job at Mrs. Bibbs's and bought my schoolbooks; my clothing remained little better than rags. Luckily the studies in the ninth—my last year at school—were light; and, during a part of the term the teacher turned over the class to my supervision, an honor that helped me emotionally and made me hope faintly. It was even hinted that, if I kept my grades high, it would be possible for me to teach in the city school system.

During that winter my brother came home from Chicago; I was glad to see him, though we were strangers. But it was not long before I felt that the affection shown him by the family was far greater than that which I had ever had from them. Slowly my brother grew openly critical of me, taking his cue from those about him, and it hurt. My loneliness became organic. I felt walled in and I grew irritable. I associated less and less with my classmates, for their talk was now full of the schools they planned to attend when the term was over. The cold days dragged mechanically: up early and to my job, splitting wood, carrying coal, sweeping floors, then off to school and boredom.

The school term ended. I was selected as valedictorian of my class and assigned to write a paper to be delivered at one of the public auditoriums. One morning the principal summoned me to his office.

"Well, Richard Wright, here's your speech," he said with smooth bluntness and shoved a stack of stapled sheets across his desk.

"What speech?" I asked as I picked up the papers.

"The speech you're to say the night of graduation," he said.

"But, professor, I've written my speech already," I said.

He laughed, confidently, indulgently.

"Listen, boy, you're going to speak to both *white* and colored people that night. What can you alone think of saying to them? You have no experience . . ."

I burned.

"I know that I'm not educated, professor," I said. "But the people are coming to hear the students, and I won't make a speech that you've written."

He leaned back in his chair and looked at me in surprise.

"You know, we've never had a boy in this school like you before," he said. "You've had your way around here. Just how you managed to do it, I don't know. But, listen, take this speech and say it. I know what's best for you. You can't afford to just say *anything* before those white people that night." He paused and added meaningfully: "The superintendent of schools will be there; you're in a position to make a good impression on him. I've been a principal for more years than you are old, boy. I've seen many a boy and girl graduate from this school, and none of them was too proud to recite a speech I wrote for them."

I had to make up my mind quickly; I was faced with a matter of principle. I wanted to graduate, but I did not want to make a public speech that was not my own.

"Professor, I'm going to say my own speech that night," I said.

He grew angry.

"You're just a young, hotheaded fool," he said. He toyed with a pencil and looked up at me. "Suppose you don't graduate?"

"But I passed my examinations," I said.

"Look, mister," he shot at me, "I'm the man who says who passes at this school."

I was so astonished that my body jerked. I had gone to this school for two years and I had never suspected what kind of man the principal was; it simply had never occurred to me to wonder about him.

"Then I don't graduate," I said flatly.

I turned to leave.

"Say, you. Come here," he called.

I turned and faced him; he was smiling at me in a remote, superior sort of way.

"You know, I'm glad I talked to you," he said. "I was seriously thinking of placing you in the school system, teaching. But, now, I don't think that you'll fit."

He was tempting me, baiting me; this was the technique that snared black young minds into supporting the southern way of life.

"Look, professor, I may never get a chance to go to school again," I said. "But I like to do things right."

"What do you mean?"

"I've no money. I'm going to work. Now, this ninth-grade diploma isn't going to help me much in life. I'm not bitter about it; it's not your fault. But I'm just not going to do things this way."

"Have you talked to anybody about this?" he asked me.

"No, why?"

"Are you sure?"

"This is the first I've heard of it, professor," I said, amazed again.

"You haven't talked to any white people about this?"

"No, sir!"

"I just wanted to know," he said.

My amazement increased; the man was afraid now for his job!

"Professor, you don't understand me." I smiled.

"You're just a young, hot fool," he said, confident again. "Wake up, boy. Learn the world you're living in. You're smart and I know what you're after. I've kept closer track of you than you think. I know your relatives. Now, if you play safe," he smiled and winked, "I'll help you to go to school, to college."

"I want to learn, professor," I told him. "But there are some things I don't want to know."

"Good-bye," he said.

I went home, hurt but determined. I had been talking to a "bought" man and he had tried to "buy" me. I felt that I had been dealing with something unclean. That night Griggs, a boy who had gone through many classes with me, came to the house.

"Look, Dick, you're throwing away your future here in Jackson," he said. "Go to the principal, talk to him, take his speech and say it. I'm saying the one he wrote. So why can't you? What the hell? What can you lose?"

"No," I said.

"Why?"

"I know only a hell of a little, but my speech is going to reflect that," I said.

"Then you're going to blacklisted for teaching jobs," he said.

"Who the hell said I was going to teach?" I asked.

"God, but you've got a will," he said.

"It's not will. I just don't want to do things that way," I said.

He left. Two days later Uncle Tom came to me. I knew that the principal had called him in.

"I hear that the principal wants you to say a speech which you've rejected," he said.

"Yes, sir. That's right," I said.

"May I read the speech you've written?" he asked.

"Certainly," I said, giving him my manuscript.

"And may I see the one that the principal wrote?"

I gave him the principal's speech too. He went to his room and read them. I sat quiet, waiting. He returned.

"The principal's speech is the better speech," he said.

"I don't doubt it," I replied. "But why did they ask me to write a speech if I can't deliver it?"

"Would you let me work on your speech?" he asked.

"No, sir."

"Now, look, Richard, this is your future . . ."

"Uncle Tom, I don't care to discuss this with you," I said.

He stared at me, then left. The principal's speech was simpler and clearer than mine, but it did not say anything; mine was cloudy, but it said what I wanted to say. What could I do? I had half a mind not to show up at the graduation exercises. I was hating my environment more each day. As soon as school was over, I would get a job, save money, and leave.

Griggs, who had accepted a speech written by the principal, came to my house each day and we went off into the woods to practice orating; day in and day out we spoke to the trees, to the creeks, frightening the birds, making the cows in the pastures stare at us in fear. I memorized my speech so thoroughly that I could have recited it in my sleep.

The news of my clash with the principal had spread through the class and the students became openly critical of me.

"Richard, you're a fool. You're throwing away every chance you've got. If they had known the kind of fool boy you are, they would never have made you valedictorian," they said.

I gritted my teeth and kept my mouth shut, but my rage was mounting by the hour. My classmates, motivated by a desire to "save" me, pestered me until I all but reached the breaking point. In the end, the principal had to caution them to let me alone, for fear I would throw up the sponge and walk out.

I had one more problem to settle before I could make my speech. I was the only boy in my class wearing short pants and I was grimly determined to leave school in long pants. Was I not going to work? Would I not be on my own? When my desire for long pants became known at home, yet another storm shook the house.

"You're trying to go too fast," my mother said.

'You're nothing but a child," Uncle Tom pronounced.

"He's beside himself," Granny said.

I served notice that I was making my own decisions from then on. I borrowed money from Mrs. Bibbs, my employer, made a down payment on a pearl-gray suit. If I could not pay for it, I would take the damn thing back after graduation.

On the night of graduation I was nervous and tense; I rose and faced the audience and my speech rolled out. When my voice stopped there was some applause. I did not care if they liked it or not; I was through. Immediately, even before I left the platform, I tried to shunt all memory of the event from me. A few of my classmates managed to shake my hand as I pushed toward the door, seeking the street. Somebody invited me to a party and I did not accept. I did not want to see any of them again. I walked home, saying to myself: The hell with it! With almost seventeen years of baffled living behind me, I faced the world in 1925.

EUDORA WELTY (b. 1909)
United States

Eudora Welty's father was a midwesterner; she studied at the University of Wisconsin and the Columbia School of Business, yet she chose to make her home in Jackson Mississippi, the setting for most of her fiction, and made herself part of the movement known as the Southern Renaissance. Her novels *Delta Wedding* (1946) and *Losing Battles* (1970), among others, and her autobiography *One Writer's Beginnings* (1984) represent Southern speech and a wide vision. Eudora Welty's language is enlivened by questions we can neither escape nor answer— questions that are our very nature. The selection here perfectly depicts the imperfect that is our paradise. With its subtle variations on the mythic parable grounded in the homely details of Miss Lark's habits, this story provokes an uneasiness appropriate to an uncertain century. At the same time, Welty's words, like the Southern landscape that sinews them, nourish us. Her metaphors are powerful, her insights keen. Her stylish achievement is to have interwoven lyrical and elegiac elements into the short-story form while preserving the paradoxical edge that marks its prime examples.

A Curtain of Green

Every day one summer in Larkin's Hill, it rained a little. The rain was a regular thing, and would come about two o'clock in the afternoon.

One day, almost as late as five o'clock, the sun was still shining. It seemed almost to spin in a tiny groove in the polished sky, and down below, in the trees along the street and in the rows of flower gardens in the town, every leaf reflected the sun from a hardness like a mirror surface. Nearly all the women sat in the windows of their houses, fanning and sighing, waiting for the rain.

Mrs. Larkin's garden was a large, densely grown plot running downhill behind the small white house where she lived alone now, since the death of her husband. The sun and the rain that beat down so heavily that summer had not kept her from working there daily. Now the intense light like a tweezers picked out her clumsy, small figure in its old pair of men's overalls rolled up at the sleeves and trousers, separated it from the thick leaves, and made it look strange and yellow as she worked with a hoe—over-vigorous, disreputable, and heedless.

Within its border of hedge, high like a wall, and visible only from the upstairs windows of the neighbors, this slanting, tangled garden, more and more over-abundant and confusing, must have become so familiar to Mrs. Larkin that quite possibly by now she was unable to conceive of any other place. Since the accident in which her husband was killed, she had never once been seen anywhere else. Every morning she might be observed walking slowly, almost timidly, out of the white house, wearing a pair of the untidy overalls, often with her hair streaming and tangled where she had neglected to comb it. She would wander about for a little while at first, uncertainly, deep among the plants and wet with their dew, and yet not quite putting out her hand to touch anything. And then a sort of sturdiness would possess her—stabilize her; she would stand still for a moment, as if a blindfold were being removed; and then she would kneel in the flowers and begin to work.

She worked without stopping, almost invisibly, submerged all day among the thick, irregular, sloping beds of plants. The servant would call her at dinnertime, and she would obey; but it was not until it was completely dark that she would truthfully give up her labor and with a drooping, submissive walk appear at the house, slowly opening the small low door at the back. Even the rain would bring only a pause to her. She would move to the shelter of the pear tree, which in mid-April hung heavily almost to the ground in brilliant full leaf, in the center of the garden.

It might seem that the extreme fertility of her garden formed at once a preoccupation and a challenge to Mrs. Larkin. Only by ceaseless activity could she cope with the rich blackness of this soil. Only by cutting, separating, thinning and tying back in the clumps of flowers and bushes and vines could she have kept them from overreaching their boundaries and multiplying out of all reason. The daily summer rains could only increase her vigilance and her already excessive energy. And yet, Mrs. Larkin rarely cut, separated, tied back. . . . To a certain extent, she seemed not to seek for order, but to allow an over-flowering, as if she consciously ventured forever a little farther, a little deeper, into her life in the garden.

She planted every kind of flower that she could find or order from a catalogue—planted thickly and hastily, without stopping to think, without any regard for the ideas that her neighbors might elect in their club as to what constituted an appropriate vista, or an effect of restfulness, or even harmony of color. Just to what end Mrs. Larkin worked so strenuously in her garden, her neighbors could not see. She certainly never sent a single one of her fine flowers to any of them. They might get sick and die, and she would never send a flower. And if she thought of *beauty* at all (they regarded her stained overalls, now almost of a color with the leaves), she certainly did not strive for it in her garden. It was impossible to enjoy looking at such a place. To the neighbors gazing down from their upstairs windows it had the appearance of a sort of jungle, in which the slight, heedless form of its owner daily lost itself.

At first, after the death of Mr. Larkin—for whose father, after all, the town had been named—they had called upon the widow with decent frequency. But she had not appreciated it, they said to one another. Now, occasionally, they looked down from their bedroom windows as they brushed studiously at their hair in the morning; they found her place in the garden, as they might have run their fingers toward a city on a map of a foreign country, located her from their distance almost in curiosity, and then forgot her.

Early that morning they had heard whistling in the Larkin garden. They had recognized Jamey's tune, and had seen him kneeling in the flowers at Mrs. Larkin's side. He was only the colored boy who worked in the neighborhood by the day. Even Jamey, it was said, Mrs. Larkin would tolerate only now and then. . . .

Throughout the afternoon she had raised her head at intervals to see how fast he was getting along in his transplanting. She had to make him finish before it began to rain. She was busy with the hoe, clearing one of the last patches of uncultivated ground for some new shrubs. She bent under the sunlight, chopping in blunt, rapid, tireless strokes. Once she raised her head far back to stare at the flashing sky. Her eyes were dull and puckered, as if from long impatience of bewilderment. Her mouth was a sharp line. People said she never spoke.

But memory tightened about her easily, without any prelude of warning or even despair. She would see promptly, as if a curtain had been jerked quite unceremoniously away from a little scene, the front porch of the white house, the shady street in front, and the blue automobile in which her husband approached, driving home from work. It was a summer day, a day from the summer before. In the freedom of gaily turning her head, a motion she was now forced by memory to repeat as she hoed the ground, she could see again the tree that was going to fall. There had been no warning. But there was the enormous tree, the fragrant chinaberry tree, suddenly tilting, dark and slow like a cloud, leaning down to her husband. From her place on the front porch she had spoken in a soft voice to him, never so intimate as at that moment, "You can't be hurt." But the tree had fallen, had struck the car exactly so as to crush him to death. She had waited there on the porch for a time afterward, not moving at all—in a sort of recollection—as if to reach under and bring out from obliteration her protective words and to try them once again . . . so as to change the whole happening. It was accident that was incredible, when her love for her husband was keeping him safe.

She continued to hoe the breaking ground, to beat down the juicy weeds. Presently she became aware that hers was the only motion to continue in the whole slackened place. There was no wind at all now. The cries of the birds had hushed. The sun seemed clamped to the side of the sky. Everything had stopped once again, the stillness had mesmerized the stems of the plants, and all the leaves went suddenly into thickness. The shadow of the pear tree in the center of the garden lay callous on the ground. Across the yard, Jamey knelt, motionless.

"Jamey!" she called angrily.

But her voice hardly carried in the dense garden. She felt all at once terrified, as though her loneliness had been pointed out by some outside force whose finger parted the hedge. She drew her hand for an instant to her breast. An obscure fluttering there frightened her, as though the force babbled to her, The bird that flies within your heart could not divide this cloudy air. . . . She stared without expression at the garden. She was clinging to the hoe, and she stared across the green leaves toward Jamey.

A look of docility in the Negro's back as he knelt in the plants began to infuriate her. She started to walk toward him, dragging the hoe vaguely through the flowers behind her. She forced herself to look at him, and noticed him closely for the first time—the way he looked like a child. As he turned his head a little to one side and negligently stirred the dirt with his yellow finger, she saw, with a sort of helpless suspicion and hunger, a soft, rather deprecating smile on his face; he was lost in some impossible dream of his own while he was transplanting the little shoots. He was not even whistling; even that sound was gone.

She walked nearer to him—he must have been deaf!—almost stealthily bearing down upon his laxity and his absorption, as if that glimpse of the side of his face, that turned-away smile, were a teasing, innocent, flickering and beautiful vision—some mirage to her strained and wandering eyes.

Yet a feeling of stricture, of a responding hopelessness almost approaching ferocity, grew with alarming quickness about her. When she was directly behind him she stood quite still for a moment, in the queer sheathed manner she had before beginning her gardening in the morning. Then she raised the hoe above her head; the clumsy sleeves both fell back, exposing the thin, unsunburned whiteness of her arms, the shocking fact of their youth.

She gripped the handle tightly, tightly, as though convinced that the wood of the handle could feel, and that all her strength could indent its surface with pain. The head of Jamey, bent there below her, seemed witless, terrifying, wonderful, almost inaccessible to her, and yet in its explicit nearness meant surely for destruction, with its clustered hot wooly hair, its intricate, glistening ears, its small brown branching streams of sweat, the bowed head holding so obviously and so fatally its ridiculous dream.

Such a head she could strike off, intentionally, so deeply did she know, from the effect of a man's danger and death, its cause in oblivion; and so helpless was she, too helpless to defy the workings of accident, of life and death, of unaccountability. . . . Life and death, she thought, gripping the heavy hoe, life and death, which now meant nothing to her but which she was compelled continually to wield with both her hands, ceaselessly asking, Was it not possible to compensate? to punish? to protest? Pale darkness turned for a moment through the sunlight, like a narrow leaf blown through the garden in a wind.

In that moment, the rain came. The first drop touched her upraised arm. Small, close sounds and coolness touched her.

Sighing, Mrs. Larkin lowered the hoe to the ground and laid it carefully among the growing plants. She stood still where she was, close to Jamey, and listened to the rain falling. It was so gentle. It was so full—the sound of the end of waiting.

In the light from the rain, different from sunlight, everything appeared to gleam unreflecting from within itself in its quiet arcade of identity. The green of the small zinnia shoots was very pure, almost burning. One by one, as the rain reached them, all the individual little plants shone out, and then the branching vines. The pear tree gave a soft rushing noise, like the wings of a bird alighting. She could sense behind her, as if a lamp were lighted in the night, the signal-like whiteness of the house. Then Jamey, as if in the shock of realizing the rain had come, turned his full face toward her, questions and delight intensifying his smile, gathering up his aroused, stretching body. He stammered some disconnected words, shyly.

She did not answer Jamey or move at all. She would not feel anything now except the rain falling. She listened for its scattered soft drops between Jamey's words, its quiet touching of the spears of the iris leaves, and a clear sound like a bell as it began to fall into a pitcher the cook had set on the doorstep.

Finally, Jamey stood there quietly, as if waiting for his money, with his hand trying to brush his confusion away from before his face. The rain fell steadily. A wind of deep wet fragrance beat against her.

Then as if it had swelled and broken over a daily levee, tenderness tore and spun through her sagging body.

It has come, she thought senselessly, her head lifting and her eyes looking without understanding at the sky which had begun to move, to fold nearer in softening, dissolving clouds. It was almost dark. Soon the loud and gentle night of rain would come. It would pound upon the steep roof of the white house. Within, she would lie in her bed and hear the rain. On and on it would fall, beat and fall. The day's work would be over in the garden. She would lie in bed, her arms tired at her sides and in motionless peace: against that which was inexhaustible, there was no defense.

Then Mrs. Larkin sank in one motion down into the flowers and lay there, fainting and streaked with rain. Her face was fully upturned, down among the plants, with the hair beaten away from her forehead and her open eyes closing at once when the rain touched them. Slowly her lips began to part. She seemed to move slightly, in the sad adjustment of a sleeper.

Jamey ran jumping and crouching about her, drawing in his breath alternately at the flowers breaking under his feet and at the shapeless, passive figure on the ground. Then he became quiet, and stood back at a little distance and looked in awe at the unknowing face, white and rested under its bombardment. He remembered how something had filled him with stillness when he felt her standing there behind him looking down at him, and he would not have turned around at that moment for anything in the world. He remembered all the while the oblivious crash of the windows next door being shut when the rain started. . . . But now, in this unseen place, it was he who stood looking at poor Mrs. Larkin.

He bent down and in a horrified, piteous, beseeching voice he began to call her name until she stirred.

"Miss Lark'! Miss Lark'!"
Then he jumped nimbly to his feet and ran out of the garden.

ELIZABETH BISHOP (1911–1979)
United States

Elizabeth Bishop was herself a kind of Robinson Crusoe, repeatedly forced to explore new islands. Semiorphaned as a very young girl, she was sent to relatives in Massachusetts and Nova Scotia. Eventually she went to Vassar—she belonged to the class Mary McCarthy described in *The Group*—then lived in Key West before moving on to France, Mexico, and Brazil. In the last years of her life she returned to the United States and taught at Harvard. Bishop mapped her soul as if it were itself an as yet undiscovered island. In her searching and setting down her record, she placed herself in line with Henry David Thoreau, Emily Dickinson, Wallace Stevens, and Marianne Moore. The poetic meditation "Crusoe in England" comes from her final collection, *Geography III* of 1976 and is convincing proof of her status as a major poet.

Crusoe in England

A new volcano has erupted,
the papers say, and last week I was reading
where some ship saw an island being born:
at first a breath of steam, ten miles away;
and then a black fleck—basalt, probably—   5
rose in the mate's binoculars
and caught on the horizon like a fly.
They named it. But my poor old island's still
un-rediscovered, un-renamable.
None of the books has ever got it right.   10

Well, I had fifty-two
miserable, small volcanoes I could climb
with a few slithery strides—
volcanoes dead as ash heaps.
I used to sit on the edge of the highest one   15
and count the others standing up,
naked and leaden, with their heads blown off.
I'd think that if they were the size
I thought volcanoes should be, then I had
become a giant;   20

and if I had become a giant,
I couldn't bear to think what size
the goats and turtles were,
or the gulls, or the over-lapping rollers
—a glittering hexagon of rollers   25
closing and closing in, but never quite,
glittering and glittering, though the sky
was mostly overcast.

My island seemed to be
a sort of cloud-dump. All the hemisphere's   30
left-over clouds arrived and hung
above the craters—their parched throats
were hot to touch.
Was that why it rained so much?
And why sometimes the whole place hissed?   35
The turtles lumbered by, high-domed,
hissing like teakettles.

(And I'd have given years, or taken a few,
for any sort of kettle, or course.)
The folds of lava, running out to sea,   40
would hiss. I'd turn. And then they'd prove
to be more turtles.

The beaches were all lava, variegated,
black, red, and white, and gray;
the marbled colors made a fine display   45
And I had waterspouts. Oh,
half a dozen at a time, far out,
they'd come and go, advancing and retreating,
their heads in cloud, their feet in moving patches
of scuffed-up white.   50
Glass chimneys, flexible, attenuated,
sacerdotal[1] beings of glass . . . I watched
the water spiral up in them like smoke.
Beautiful, yes, but not much company.

I often gave way to self-pity.   55
"Do I deserve this? I suppose I must.
I wouldn't be here otherwise. Was there
a moment when I actually chose this?
I don't remember, but there could have been."
What's wrong about self-pity, anyway?   60

---

1. Priestly.

With my legs dangling down familiarly
over a crater's edge, I told myself
"Pity should begin at home." So the more
pity I felt, the more I felt at home.

The sun set in the sea; the same odd sun   65
rose from the sea,
and there was one of it and one of me.
The island had one kind of everything:
one tree snail, a bright violet-blue
with a thin shell, crept over everything,   70
over the one variety of tree,
a sooty, scrub affair.
Snail shells lay under these in drifts
and, at a distance,
you'd swear that they were beds of irises.   75
There was one kind of berry, a dark red.
I tried it, one by one, and hours apart.
Sub-acid, and not bad, no ill effects;
and so I made home-brew. I'd drink
the awful, fizzy, stinging stuff   80
that went straight to my head
and play my home-made flute
(I think it had the weirdest scale on earth)
and, dizzy, whoop and dance among the goats.
Home-made, home-made! But aren't we all?   85
I felt a deep affection for
the smallest of my island industries.
No, not exactly, since the smallest was
a miserable philosophy.

Because I didn't know enough.   90
Why didn't I know enough of something?
Greek drama or astronomy? The books
I'd read were full of blanks;
the poems—well, I tried
reciting to my iris-beds,
"They flash upon that inward eye,   95
which is the bliss . . ." The bliss of what?[2]
One of the first things that I did
when I got back was look it up.

---

2. From William Wordsworth's "Daffodils;"
   the quotation continues: "the bliss of solitude."

The island smelled of goat and guano.   100
The goats were white, so were the gulls,
and both too tame, or else they thought
I was a goat, too, or a gull.
Baa, baa, baa and *shriek, shriek, shriek,*
baa . . . shriek . . . baa . . . I still can't shake   105
them from my ears; they're hurting now.
The questioning shrieks, the equivocal replies
over a ground of hissing rain
and hissing, ambulating turtles
got on my nerves.   110

When all the gulls flew up at once, they sounded
like a big tree in a strong wind, its leaves.
I'd shut my eyes and think about a tree,
an oak, say, with real shade, somewhere.
I'd heard of cattle getting island-sick.   115
I thought the goats were.
One billy-goat would stand on the volcano
I'd christened *Mont d'Espoir*[3] or *Mount Despair*
(I'd time enough to play with names),
and bleat and bleat, and sniff the air.   120
I'd grab his beard and look at him.

His pupils, horizontal, narrowed up
and expressed nothing, or a little malice.
I got so tired of the very colors!
One day I dyed a baby goat bright red   125
with my red berries, just to see
something a little different.
And then his mother wouldn't recognize him.

Dreams were the worst. Of course I dreamed of food
and love, but they were pleasant rather   130
than otherwise. But then I'd dream of things
like slitting a baby's throat, mistaking it
for a baby goat. I'd have
nightmares of other islands
stretching away from mine, infinities   135
of islands, islands spawning islands,
like frogs' eggs turning into polliwogs
of islands, knowing that I had to live
on each and every one, eventually,

---

3. The French translates as "Mount Hope."

for ages, registering their flora, 140
their fauna, their geography.

Just when I thought I couldn't stand it
another minute longer, Friday came.
(Accounts of that have everything all wrong.)
Friday was nice. 145
Friday was nice, and we were friends.
If only he had been a woman!
I wanted to propagate my kind,
and so did he, I think, poor boy.
He'd pet the baby goats sometimes, 150
and race with them, or carry one around.
—Pretty to watch; he had a pretty body.
And then one day they came and took us off.

Now I live here, another island,
that doesn't seem like one, but who decides? 155
My blood was full of them; my brain
bred islands. But that archipelago
has petered out. I'm old.
I'm bored, too, drinking my real tea,
surrounded by uninteresting lumber. 160
The knife there on the shelf—
it reeked of meaning, like a crucifix.
It lived. How many years did I
beg it, implore it, not to break?

I knew each nick and scratch by heart, 165
the bluish blade, the broken tip,
the lines of wood-grain on the handle . . .
Now it won't look at me at all.
The living soul has dribbled away.
My eyes rest on it and pass on. 170

The local museum's asked me to
leave everything to them:
the flute, the knife, the shrivelled shoes,
my shedding goatskin trousers
(moths have got in the fur), 175
the parasol that took me such a time
remembering the way the ribs should go.
It still will work but, folded up,
looks like a plucked and skinny fowl.
How can anyone want such things? 180
—And Friday, my dear Friday, died of measles
seventeen years ago come March.
1976

GWENDOLYN BROOKS (b. 1917)
United States

Born in Chicago to working-class parents who encouraged her writing, Gwendolyn Brooks is possibly the most honored African-American poet and was the
first to receive a Pulitizer Prize, awarded for her poem *Annie Allen* (1949). Since
1945 Brooks has published many volumes of poetry, some of which are for
children; a novella, *Maud Martha* (1953); and an autobiography, *Report from Part
I* (1972). In 1968, she succeeded Carl Sandburg as the poet laureate of Illinois,
a fitting honor since a major theme in her poetry is the value and wonder of
ordinary people, many of whom live in the black communities of Chicago.
Known for her remarkable ability to mesh African-American folk forms such as
the blues with European forms such as the sonnet, Brooks's poetry is about both
the political as well as the personal interior lives of African-Americans.

The Chicago Defender Sends a Man to Little Rock

Fall, 1957

In Little Rock the people bear
Babes, and comb and part their hair
And watch the want ads, put repair
To roof and latch. While wheat toast burns
A woman waters multiferns.   5

Time upholds or overturns
The many, tight, and small concerns.

In Little Rock the people sing
Sunday hymns like anything,
Through Sunday pomp and polishing.   10

And after testament and tunes,
Some soften Sunday afternoons
With lemon tea and Lorna Doones.

I forecast
And I believe   15
Come Christmas Little Rock will cleave
To Christmas tree and trifle, weave,
From laugh and tinsel, texture fast.

In Little Rock is baseball; Barcarolle.
That hotness in July . . . the uniformed figures raw and implacable   20

And not intellectual,
Batting the hotness or clawing the suffering dust.
The Open Air Concert, on the special twilight green. . . .
When Beethoven is brutal or whispers to lady-like air.
Blanket-sitters are solemn, as Johann troubles to lean   25
To tell them what to mean. . . .

There is love, too, in Little Rock. Soft women softly
Opening themselves in kindness,
Or, pitying one's blindness,
Awaiting one's pleasure   30
In azure
Glory with anguished rose at the root. . . .
To wash away old semi-discomfitures.
They re-teach purple and unsullen blue.
The wispy soils go. And uncertain   35
Half-havings have they clarified to sures.

In Little Rock they know
Not answering the telephone is a way of rejecting life,
That it is our business to be bothered, is our business
To cherish bores or boredom, be polite   40
To lies and love and many-faceted fuzziness.

I scratch my head, massage the hate-I-had.
I blink across my prim and pencilled pad.
The saga I was sent for is not down.
Because there is a puzzle in this town.   45
The biggest News I do not dare
Telegraph to the Editor's chair:
"They are like people everywhere."

The angry Editor would reply
In hundred harryings of Why.   50

And true, they are hurling spittle, rock,
Garbage and fruit in Little Rock.
And I saw coiling storm a-writhe
On bright madonnas. And a scythe
Of men harassing brownish girls.   55
(The bows and barrettes in the curls
And braids declined away from joy.)

I saw a bleeding brownish boy. . . .

The lariat lynch-wish deplored.

The loveliest lynchee was our Lord.   60

HISAYE YAMAMOTO (b. 1921)
United States

Hisaye Yamamoto was born in Redondo Beach, California. Much of her work is intimately connected with the events of her own life. "Seventeen Syllables"—her most widely anthologized piece—is the story of her mother, though all the details are invented.

Most Japanese immigrants came to the United States between 1885 and 1924, the first waves consisting mainly of single young men. Some arranged their marriages by means of an exchange of photographs across the Pacific. Hence a large number of Japanese "picture brides" came to this country after the turn of the century to meet bridegrooms they had never seen in person.

Yamamoto persistently explores the relationship between *issei* (first-generation) men and women and between *issei* and their children, or *nisei*. In "Seventeen Syllables" Mr. Hayashi is preoccupied with survival in the New World, while his wife is concerned with haiku, and also with her tie to Japan. Class differences further complicate the relationship between husband and wife. The generational gap between Rosie and her parents, on the other hand, is aggravated by language barriers and disparate cultural values. Seen through the startled eyes of Rosie, who must come to grips with her maternal legacy even as she is experiencing her first romance, the mother's story reverberates ominously.

Seventeen Syllables

The first Rosie knew that her mother had taken to writing poems was one evening when she finished one and read it aloud for her daughter's approval. It was about cats, and Rosie pretended to understand it thoroughly and appreciate it no end, partly because she hesitated to disillusion her mother about the quantity and quality of Japanese she had learned in all the years now that she had been going to Japanese school every Sunday (and Wednesday, too, in the summer). Even so, her mother must have been skeptical about the depth of Rosie's understanding, because she explained afterwards about the kind of poem she was trying to write.

See, Rosie, she said, it was a *haiku,* poem in which she must pack all her meaning into seventeen syllables only, which were divided into three lines of five, seven, and five syllables. In the one she had just read, she had tried to capture the charm of a kitten, as well as comment on the superstition that owning a cat of three colors meant good luck.

"Yes, yes, I understand. How utterly lovely," Rosie said, and her mother, either satisfied or seeing through the deception and resigned, went back to composing.

The truth was that Rosie was lazy; English lay ready on the tongue but Japanese had to be searched for and examined, and even then put forth tentatively (probably to meet with laughter). It was so much easier to say yes, yes, even when one meant no, no. Besides, this was what was in her mind to say: I was looking through one of your magazines from Japan last night, Mother, and towards the back I found some *haiku* in English that delighted me. There was one that made me giggle off and on until I fell asleep—

> It is morning, and lo!
> I lie awake, comme il faut,
> sighing for some dough.

Now, how to reach her mother, how to communicate the melancholy song? Rosie knew formal Japanese by fits and starts, her mother had even less English, no French. It was much more possible to say yes, yes.

It developed that her mother was writing the *haiku* for a daily newspaper, the *Mainichi Shimbun,* that was published in San Francisco. Los Angeles, to be sure, was closer to the farming community in which the Hayashi family lived and several Japanese vernaculars were printed there, but Rosie's parents said they preferred the tone of the northern paper. Once a week, the *Mainichi* would have a section devoted to *haiku,* and her mother became an extravagant contributor, taking for herself the blossoming pen name, Ume Hanazono.

So Rosie and her father lived for awhile with two women, her mother and Ume Hanazono. Her mother (Tome Hayashi by name) kept house, cooked, washed, and, along with her husband and the Carrascos, the Mexican family hired for the harvest, did her ample share of picking tomatoes out in the sweltering fields and boxing them in tidy strata in the cool packing shed. Ume Hanazono, who came to life after the dinner dishes were done, was an earnest, muttering stranger who often neglected speaking when spoken to and stayed busy at the parlor table as late as midnight scribbling with pencil on scratch paper or carefully copying characters on good paper with her fat, pale green Parker.

The new interest had some repercussions on the household routine. Before, Rosie had been accustomed to her parents and herself taking their hot baths early and going to bed almost immediately afterwards, unless her parents challenged each other to a game of flower cards or unless company dropped in. Now if her father wanted to play cards, he had to resort to solitaire (at which he always cheated fearlessly), and if a group of friends came over, it was bound to contain someone who was also writing *haiku,* and the small assemblage would be split in two, her father entertaining the non-literary members and her mother comparing ecstatic notes with the visiting poet.

If they went out, it was more of the same thing. But Ume Hanazono's life span, even for a poet's, was very brief—perhaps three months at most.

One night they went over to see the Hayano family in the neighboring town to the west, an adventure both painful and attractive to Rosie. It was attractive because there were four Hayano girls, all lovely and each one named after a season of the year (Haru, Natsu, Aki, Fuyu), painful because something had been wrong with Mrs. Hayano ever since the birth of her first child. Rosie would sometimes watch Mrs. Hayano, reputed to have been the belle of her native village, making her way about a room, stooped, slowly shuffling, violently trembling (*always* trembling), and she would be reminded that this woman, in this same condition, had carried and given issue to three babies. She would look wonderingly at Mr. Hayano, handsome, tall, and strong, and she would look at her four pretty friends. But it was not a matter she could come to any decision about.

On this visit, however, Mrs. Hayano sat all evening in the rocker, as motionless and unobtrusive as it was possible for her to be, and Rosie found the greater part of the evening practically anaesthetic. Too, Rosie spent most of it in the girls' room, because Haru, the garrulous one, said almost as soon as the bows and other greetings were over, "Oh, you must see my new coat!"

It was a pale plaid of grey, sand, and blue, with an enormous collar, and Rosie, seeing nothing special in it, said, "Gee, how nice."

"Nice?" said Haru, indignantly. "Is that all you can say about it? It's gorgeous! And so cheap, too. Only seventeen-ninety-eight, because it was a sale. The saleslady said it was twenty-five dollars regular."

"Gee," said Rosie. Natsu, who never said much and when she said anything said it shyly, fingered the coat covetously and Haru pulled it away.

"Mine," she said, putting it on. She minced in the aisle between the two large beds and smiled happily. "Let's see how your mother likes it."

She broke into the front room and the adult conversation and went to stand in front of Rosie's mother, while the rest watched from the door. Rosie's mother was properly envious. "May I inherit it when you're through with it?"

Haru, pleased, giggled and said yes, she could, but Natsu reminded gravely from the door, "You promised me, Haru."

Everyone laughed but Natsu, who shamefacedly retreated into the bedroom. Haru came in laughing, taking off the coat. "We were only kidding, Natsu," she said. "Here, you try it on now."

After Natsu buttoned herself into the coat, inspected herself solemnly in the bureau mirror, and reluctantly shed it, Rosie, Aki, and Fuyu got their turns, and Fuyu, who was eight, drowned in it while her sisters and Rosie doubled up in amusement. They all went into the front room later, because Haru's mother quaveringly called to her to fix the tea and rice cakes and open a can of sliced peaches for everybody. Rosie noticed that her mother and Mr. Hayano were talking together at the little table—they were discussing a *haiku* that Mr. Hayano was planning to send to the *Mainichi*, while her father was sitting at one end of the sofa looking through a copy of *Life*, the new picture magazine. Occasionally, her father would comment on a photograph, holding it toward Mrs. Hayano and speaking to her as he always did—loudly, as though he thought someone such as she must surely be at least a trifle deaf also.

The five girls had their refreshments at the kitchen table, and it was while Rosie was showing the sisters her trick of swallowing peach slices without chewing (she chased each slipper crescent down with a swig of tea) that her father brought his empty teacup and untouched saucer to the sink and said, "Come on, Rosie, we're going home now."

"Already?" asked Rosie.

"Work tomorrow," he said.

He sounded irritated, and Rosie, puzzled, gulped one last yellow slice and stood up to go, while the sisters began protesting, as was their wont.

"We have to get up at five-thirty," he told them, going into the front room quickly, so that they did not have their usual chance to hang onto his hands and plead for an extension of time.

Rosie, following, saw that her mother and Mr. Hayano were sipping tea and still talking together, while Mrs. Hayano concentrated, quivering, on raising the handleless Japanese cup to her lips with both her hands and lowering it back to her lap. Her father, saying nothing, went out the door, onto the bright porch, and down the steps. Her mother looked up and asked, "Where is he going?"

"Where is he going?" Rosie said. "He said we were going home now."

"Going home?" Her mother looked with embarrassment at Mr. Hayano and his absorbed wife and then forced a smile. "He must be tired," she said.

Haru was not giving up yet. "May Rosie stay overnight?" she asked, and Natsu, Aki, and Fuyu came to reinforce their sister's plea by helping her make a circle around Rosie's mother. Rosie, for once having no desire to stay, was relieved when her mother, apologizing to the perturbed Mr. and Mrs. Hayano for her father's abruptness at the same time, managed to shake her head no at the quartet, kindly but adamant, so that they broke their circle and let her go.

Rosie's father looked ahead into the windshield as the two joined him. "I'm sorry," her mother said. "You must be tired." Her father, stepping on the starter, said nothing. "You know how I get when it's *haiku*," she continued. "I forget what time it is." He only grunted.

As they rode homeward silently, Rosie, sitting between, felt a rush of hate for both—for her mother for begging, for her father for denying her mother. I wish this old Ford would crash, right now, she thought, then immediately, no, no, I wish my father would laugh, but it was too late: already the vision had passed through her mind of the green pick-up crumpled in the dark against one of the mighty eucalyptus trees they were just riding past, of the three contorted, bleeding bodies, one of them hers.

Rosie ran between two patches of tomatoes, her heart working more rambunctiously than she had ever known it to. How lucky it was that Aunt Taka and Uncle Gimpachi had come tonight, though, how very lucky. Otherwise she might not have really kept her half-promise to meet Jesus Carrasco. Jesus was going to be a senior in September at the same school she went to, and his parents were the ones helping with the tomatoes this year. She and Jesus, who hardly remembered seeing each other at Cleveland High where there were so many other people and two whole grades between them, had become great friends this summer—he always had a joke for her when he periodically drove the loaded pick-up up from the fields to the shed where she was usually sorting while her mother and father did the packing, and they laughed a great deal together over infinitesimal repartee during the afternoon break for chilled watermelon or ice cream in the shade of the shed.

What she enjoyed most was racing him to see who could finish picking a double row first. He, who could work faster, would tease her by slowing down until she thought she would surely pass him this time, then speeding up furiously to leave her several sprawling vines behind. Once he had made her screech hideously by crossing over, while her back was turned, to place atop the tomatoes in her green-stained bucket a truly monstrous, pale green worm (it had looked more like an infant snake). And it was when they had finished a contest this morning, after she had pantingly pointed a green finger at the immature tomatoes evident in the lugs at the end of his row and he had returned the accusation (with justice), that he had startlingly brought up the matter of their possibly meeting outside the range of both their parents' dubious eyes.

"What for?" she had asked.

"I've got a secret I want to tell you," he said.

"Tell me now," she demanded.

"It won't be ready till tonight," he said.

She laughed. "Tell me tomorrow then."

"It'll be gone tomorrow," he threatened.

"Well, for seven hakes, what is it?" she had asked, more than twice, and when he had suggested that the packing shed would be an appropriate place to find out, she had cautiously answered maybe. She had not been certain she was going to keep the appointment until the arrival of mother's sister and her husband. Their coming seemed a sort of signal of permission, of grace, and she had definitely made up her mind to lie and leave as she was bowing them welcome.

So as soon as everyone appeared settled back for the evening, she announced loudly that she was going to the privy outside. "I'm going to the *benjo!*" and slipped out the door. And now that she was actually on her way, her heart pumped in such an undisciplined way that she could hear it with her ears. It's because I'm running, she told herself, slowing to a walk. The shed was up ahead, one more patch away, in the middle of the fields. Its bulk, looming in the dimness, took on a sinisterness that was funny when Rosie reminded herself that it was only a wooden frame with a canvas roof and three canvas walls that made a slapping noise on breezy days.

Jesus was sitting on the narrow plank that was the sorting platform and she went around to the other side and jumped backwards to seat herself on the rim of a packing stand. "Well, tell me," she said without greeting, thinking her voice sounded reassuringly familiar.

"I saw you coming out the door," Jesus said. "I heard you running part of the way, too."

"Uh-huh," Rosie said. "Now tell me the secret."

"I was afraid you wouldn't come," he said.

Rosie delved around on the chicken-wire bottom of the stall for number two tomatoes, ripe, which she was sitting beside, and came up with a left-over that felt edible. She bit into it and began sucking out the pulp and seeds. "I'm here," she pointed out.

"Rosie, are you sorry you came?"

"Sorry? What for?" she said. "You said you were going to tell me something."

"I will, I will," Jesus said, but his voice contained disappointment, and Rosie fleetingly felt the older of the two, realizing a brand new power which vanished without category under her recognition.

"I have to go back in a minute," she said. "My aunt and uncle are here from Wintersburg. I told them I was going to the privy."

Jesus laughed. "You funny thing," he said. "You slay me!"

"Just because you have a bathroom *inside*," Rosie said. "Come on, tell me."

Chuckling, Jesus came around to lean on the stand facing her. They still could not see each other very clearly, but Rosie noticed that Jesus became very sober again as he took the hollow tomato from her hand and dropped it back into the stall. When he took hold of her empty hand, she could find no words to protest; her vocabulary had become distressingly constricted and she thought desperately that all that remained intact now was yes and no and oh, and even these few sounds would not easily out. Thus, kissed by Jesus, Rosie fell for the first time entirely victim to a helplessness delectable beyond speech. But the terrible, beautiful sensation lasted no more than a second, and the reality of Jesus' lips and tongue and teeth and hands made her pull away with such strength that she nearly tumbled.

Rosie stopped running as she approached the lights from the windows of home. How long since she had left? She could not guess, but gasping yet, she went to the privy in back and locked herself in. Her own breathing deafened her in the dark, close space, and she sat and waited until she could hear at last the nightly calling of the frogs and crickets. Even then, all she could think to say was oh, my, and the pressure of Jesus' face against her face would not leave.

No one had missed her in the parlor, however, and Rosie walked in and through quickly, announcing that she was next going to take a bath. "Your father's in the bathhouse," her mother said, and Rosie, in her room, recalled that she had not seen him when she entered. There had been only Aunt Taka and Uncle Gimpachi with her mother at the table, drinking tea. She got her robe and straw sandals and crossed the parlor again to go outside. Her mother was telling them about the *haiku* competition in the *Mainichi* and the poem she had entered.

Rosie met her father coming out of the bathhouse. "Are you through, Father?" she asked. "I was going to ask you to scrub my back."

"Scrub your own back," he said shortly, going toward the main house.

"What have I done now?" she yelled after him. She suddenly felt like doing a lot of yelling. But he did not answer, and she went into the bathhouse. Turning on the dangling light, she removed her denims and T shirt and threw them in the big carton for dirty clothes standing next to the washing machine. Her other things she took with her into the bath compartment to wash after her bath. After she had scooped a basin of hot water from the square wooden tub, she sat on the grey cement of the floor and soaped herself at exaggerated leisure, singing "Red Sails in the Sunset" at the top of her voice and using da-da-da where she suspected her words. Then, standing up, still singing, for she was possessed by the notion that any attempt now to analyze would result in spoilage and she believed that the

larger her volume the less she would be able to hear herself think, she obtained
more hot water and poured it on until she was free of lather. Only then did she
allow herself to step into the steaming vat, one leg first, then the remainder of her
body inch by inch until the water no longer stung and she could move around at
will.

She took a long time soaking, afterwards remembering to go around outside
to stoke the embers of the tin-lined fireplace beneath the tub and to throw on a
few more sticks so that the water might keep its heat for her mother, and when she
finally returned to the parlor, she found her mother still talking *haiku* with her
aunt and uncle, the three of them on another round of tea. Her father was nowhere
in sight.

At Japanese school the next day (Wednesday, it was), Rosie was grave and
giddy by turns. Preoccupied at her desk in the row for students on Book Eight, she
made up for it at recess by performing wild mimicry for the benefit of her friend
Chizuko. She held her nose and whined a witticism or two in what she considered
was the manner of Fred Allen; she assumed intoxication and a British accent to go
over the climax of the Rudy Vallee recording of the pub conversation about
William Ewart Gladstone; she was the child Shirley Temple piping, "On the Good
Ship Lollipop"; she was the gentleman soprano of the Four Inkspots trilling, "If I
Didn't Care." And she felt reasonably satisfied when Chizuko wept and gasped.
"Oh, Rosie, you ought to be in the movies!"

Her father came after her at noon, bringing her sandwiches of minced ham
and two nectarines to eat while she rode, so that she could pitch right into the
sorting when they got home. The lugs were piling up, he said, and the ripe
tomatoes in them would probably have to be taken to the cannery tomorrow if
they were not ready for the produce haulers tonight. "This heat's not doing them
any good. And we've got no time for a break today."

If *was* hot, probably the hottest day of the year, and Rosie's blouse stuck
damply to her back even under the protection of the canvas. But she worked as
efficiently as a flawless machine and kept the stalls heaped, with one part of her
mind listening in to the parental murmuring about the heat and the tomatoes and
with another part planning the exact words she would say to Jesus when he drove
up with the first load of the afternoon. But when at last she saw that the pick-up
was coming, her hands went berserk and the tomatoes started falling in the wrong
stalls, and her father said, "Hey, hey! Rosie, watch what you're doing!"

"Well, I have to go to the *benjo*," she said, hiding panic.

"Go in the weeds over there," he said, only half-joking.

"Oh, Father!" she protested.

"Oh, go on home," her mother said. "We'll make out for awhile."

In the privy Rosie peered through a knothole toward the fields, watching as
much as she could of Jesus. Happily she thought she saw him look in the direction
of the house from time to time before he finished unloading and went back toward
the patch where his mother and father worked. As she was heading for the shed,
a very presentable black car purred up the dirt driveway to the house and its driver
motioned to her. Was this the Hayashi home, he wanted to know. She nodded.

Was she a Hayashi? Yes, she said, thinking that he was a good-looking man. He got out of the car with a huge, flat package and she saw that he warmly wore a business suit. "I have something here for your mother then," he said, in a more elegant Japanese than she was used to.

She told him where her mother was and he came along with her, patting his face with an immaculate white handkerchief and saying something about the coolness of San Francisco. To her surprised mother and father, he bowed and introduced himself as, among other things, the *haiku* editor of the *Mainichi Shimbun,* saying that since he had been coming as far as Los Angeles anyway, he had decided to bring her the first prize she had won in the recent contest.

"First prize?" her mother echoed, believing and not believing, pleased and overwhelmed. Handed the package with a bow, she bobbed her head up and down numerous times to express her utter gratitude.

"It is nothing much," he added, "but I hope it will serve as a token of our great appreciation for your contributions and our great admiration of your considerable talent."

"I am not worthy," she said, falling easily into his style. "It is I who should make some sign of my humble thanks for being permitted to contribute."

"No, no, to the contrary," he said, bowing again.

But Rosie's mother insisted, and then saying that she knew she was being unorthodox, she asked if she might open the package because her curiosity was so great. Certainly she might. In fact, he would like her reaction to it, for personally, it was one of his favorite *Hiroshiges.*

Rosie thought it was a pleasant picture, which looked to have been sketched with delicate quickness. There were pink clouds, containing some graceful calligraphy, and a sea that was a pale blue except at the edges, containing four sampans with indications of people in them. Pines edged the water and on the far-off beach there was a cluster of thatched huts towered over by pin-dotted mountains of grey and blue. The frame was scalloped and gilt.

After Rosie's mother pronounced it without peer and somewhat prodded her father into nodding agreement, she said Mr. Kuroda must at least have a cup of tea after coming all this way, and although Mr. Kuroda did not want to impose, he soon agreed that a cup of tea would be refreshing and went along with her to the house, carrying the picture for her.

"Ha, your mother's crazy!" Rosie's father said, and Rosie laughed uneasily as she resumed judgment on the tomatoes. She had emptied six lugs when he broke into an imaginary conversation with Jesus to tell her to go and remind her mother of the tomatoes, and she went slowly.

Mr. Kuroda was in his shirtsleeves expounding some *haiku* theory as he munched a rice cake, and her mother was rapt. Abashed in the great man's presence, Rosie stood next to her mother's chair until her mother looked up inquiringly, and then she started to whisper the message, but her mother pushed her gently away and reproached, "You are not being very polite to our guest."

"Father says the tomatoes . . ." Rosie said aloud, smiling foolishly.

"Tell him I shall only be a minute," her mother said, speaking the language of Mr. Kuroda.

When Rosie carried the reply to her father, he did not seem to hear and she said again, "Mother says she'll be back in a minute."

"All right, all right," he nodded, and they worked again in silence. But suddenly, her father uttered an incredible noise, exactly like the cork of a bottle popping, and the next Rosie knew, he was stalking angrily toward the house, almost running in fact, and she chased after him crying, "Father! Father! What are you going to do?"

He stopped long enough to order her back to the shed. "Never mind!" he shouted. "Get on with the sorting!"

And from the place in the fields where she stood, frightened and vacillating, Rosie saw her father enter the house. Soon Mr. Kuroda came out alone, putting on his coat. Mr. Kuroda got into his car and backed out down the driveway onto the highway. Next her father emerged, also alone, something in his arms (it was the picture, she realized), and, going over to the bathhouse woodpile, he threw the picture on the ground and picked up the axe. Smashing the picture, glass and all (she heard the explosion faintly), he reached over for the kerosene that was used to encourage the bath fire and poured it over the wreckage. I am dreaming, Rosie said to herself, I am dreaming, but her father, having made sure that his act of cremation was irrevocable, was even then returning to the fields.

Rosie ran past him and toward the house. What had become of her mother? She burst into the parlor and found her mother at the back window watching the dying fire. They watched together until there remained only a feeble smoke under the blazing sun. Her mother was very calm.

"Do you know why I married your father?" she said without turning.

"No," said Rosie. It was the most frightening question she had ever been called upon to answer. Don't tell me now, she wanted to say, tell me tomorrow, tell me next week, don't tell me today. But she knew she would be told now, that the telling would combine with the other violence of the hot afternoon to level her life, her world to the very ground.

It was like a story out of the magazines illustrated in sepia, which she had consumed so greedily for a period until the information had somehow reached her that those wretchedly unhappy autobiographies, offered to her as the testimonials of living men and women, were largely inventions: Her mother, at nineteen, had come to America and married her father as an alternative to suicide.

At eighteen she had been in love with the first son of one of the well-to-do families in her village. The two had met whenever and wherever they could, secretly, because it would not have done for his family to see him favor her—her father had no money; he was a drunkard and a gambler besides. She had learned she was with child; an excellent match had already been arranged for her lover. Despised by her family, she had given premature birth to a stillborn son, who would be seventeen now. Her family did not turn her out, but she could no longer project herself in any direction without refreshing in them the memory of her indiscretion. She wrote to Aunt Taka, her favorite sister in America, threatening to kill herself if Aunt Taka would not send for her. Aunt Taka hastily arranged a marriage with a young man of whom she knew, but lately arrived from Japan, a young man of simple mind, it was said, but of kindly heart. The young man was never told why his unseen betrothed was so eager to hasten the day of meeting.

The story was told perfectly, with neither groping for words nor untoward passion. It was as though her mother had memorized it by heart, reciting it to herself so many times over that its nagging vileness had long since gone.

"I had a brother then?" Rosie asked, for this was what seemed to matter now; she would think about the other later, she assured herself, pushing back the illumination which threatened all that darkness that had hitherto been merely mysterious or even glamorous. "A half-brother?"

"Yes."

"I would have liked a brother," she said.

Suddenly, her mother knelt on the floor and took her by the wrists. "Rosie," she said urgently, "Promise me you will never marry!" Shocked more by the request than the revelation, Rosie stared at her mother's face. Jesus, Jesus, she called silently, not certain whether she was invoking the help of the son of the Carrascos or of God, until there returned sweetly the memory of Jesus' hand, how it had touched her and where. Still her mother waited for an answer, holding her wrists so tightly that her hands were going numb. She tried to pull free. Promise, her mother whispered fiercely, promise. Yes, yes, I promise, Rosie said. But for an instant she turned away, and her mother, hearing the familiar glib agreement, released her. Oh, you, you, you, her eyes and twisted mouth said, you fool. Rosie, covering her face, began at last to cry, and the embrace and consoling hand came much later than she expected.

JAMES BALDWIN (1924–1987)
United States

Born in Harlem to poor migrants from the South, James Baldwin was strongly affected by his early years in Harlem where he attended DeWitt Clinton High School, by his stepfather's bitterness, and by the imagery and language of the black church. From the 1950s on, Baldwin was as well known a public figure as he was a writer. His essay collections, especially *Notes of a Native Son* (1955) and *The Fire Next Time* (1963), are passionate fusions of reflections on his own life and on African-American culture as well as analyses of American racism. Although encouraged in the 1950s by Richard Wright, Baldwin disagreed with the view of black literature as primarily a protest vehicle, and in his early novels and plays attempted to portray the complexity of African-American life. By the 1960s, however, Baldwin's work became more focused on protest in response to America's resistance to social change. Although he did not consider himself a writer focusing on his homosexuality, Baldwin would also explore that aspect of his life, in essays and in novels, such as *Giovanni's Room* (1956) and *Another Country* (1962). Baldwin's novels, short stories, collections of plays, and essay collections are marked by his belief in the redemptive power of love, a point of

Norman Lewis. *Madonna*. 1939.
Oil on canvas.

view that enraged many militant black writers of the 1960s. Nonetheless, in 1987 more than 5000 people attended his funeral in New York and he was eulogized by major African-American writers—by Maya Angelou and Amiri Baraka, and by Toni Morrison who stated that James Baldwin had given African-American writers "a language within which to dwell."

This letter keeps the rhythms of speech, and its warmth: it is about "accepting, with love."

from *The Fire Next Time*

[My Dungeon Shook]

Dear James:

I have begun this letter five times and torn it up five times. I keep seeing your face, which is also the face of your father and my brother. Like him, you are tough, dark, vulnerable, moody—with a very definite tendency to sound truculent because you want no one to think you are soft. You may be like your grandfather in this, I don't know, but certainly both you and your father resemble him very much physically. Well, he is dead, he never saw you, and he had a terrible life; he was defeated long before he died because, at the bottom of his heart, he really believed what white people said about him. This is one of the reasons that he became so holy. I am sure that your father has told you something about all that. Neither you nor your father exhibit any tendency towards holiness: you really *are* of another era, part of what happened when the Negro left the land and came into what the late E. Franklin Frazier called "the cities of destruction." You can only be destroyed by believing that you really are what the white world calls a *nigger*. I tell you this because I love you, and please don't you ever forget it.

I have known both of you all your lives, have carried your Daddy in my arms and on my shoulders, kissed and spanked him and watched him learn to walk. I don't know if you've known anybody from that far back; if you've loved anybody that long, first as an infant, then as a child, then as a man, you gain a strange perspective on time and human pain and effort. Other people cannot see what I see whenever I look into your father's face, for behind your father's face as it is today are all those other faces which were his. Let him laugh and I see a cellar your father does not remember and a house he does not remember and I hear in his present laughter his laughter as a child. Let him curse and I remember him falling down the cellar steps, and howling, and I remember, with pain, his tears, which my hand or your grandmother's so easily wiped away. But no one's hand can wipe away those tears he sheds invisibly today, which one hears in his laughter and in his speech and in his songs. I know what the world has done to my brother and how narrowly he has survived it. And I know, which is much worse, and this is the crime of which I accuse my country and my countrymen, and for which neither I nor time nor history will ever forgive them, that they have destroyed and are destroying hundreds of thousands of lives and do not know it and do not want to know it. One can be, indeed one must strive to become, tough and philosophical concerning destruction and death, for this is what most of mankind has been best at since we have heard of man. (But remember: *most* of mankind is not *all* of mankind.) But it is not permissible that the authors of devastation should also be innocent. It is the innocence which constitutes the crime.

Now, my dear namesake, these innocent and well-meaning people, your countrymen, have caused you to be born under conditions not very far removed from those described for us by Charles Dickens in the London of more than a hundred years ago. (I hear the chorus of the innocents screaming, "No! This is not true! How *bitter* you are!"—but I am writing this letter to *you,* to try to tell you something about how to handle *them,* for most of them do not yet really know that you exist. I *know* the conditions under which you were born, for I was there. Your countrymen were *not* there, and haven't made it yet. Your grandmother was also there, and no one has ever accused her of being bitter. I suggest that the innocents check with her. She isn't hard to find. Your countrymen don't know that *she* exists, either, though she has been working for them all their lives.)

Well, you were born, here you came, something like fourteen years ago; and though your father and mother and grandmother, looking about the streets through which they were carrying you, staring at the walls into which they brought you, had every reason to be heavyhearted, yet they were not. For here you were, Big James, named for me—you were a big baby, I was not—here you were: to be loved. To be loved, baby, hard, at once, and forever, to strengthen you against the loveless world. Remember that: I know how black it looks today, for you. It looked bad that day, too, yes, we were trembling. We have not stopped trembling yet, but if we had not loved each other none of us would have survived.

And now you must survive because we love you, and for the sake of your children and your children's children.

This innocent country set you down in a ghetto in which, in fact, it intended that you should perish. Let me spell out precisely what I mean by that, for the heart of the matter is here, and the root of my dispute with my country. You were born where you were born and faced the future that you faced because you were black and *for no other reason*. The limits of your ambition were, thus, expected to be set forever. You were born into a society which spelled out with brutal clarity, and in as many ways as possible, that you were a worthless human being. You were not expected to aspire to excellence: you were expected to make peace with mediocrity. Wherever you have turned, James, in your short time on this earth, you have been told where you could go and what you could do (and *how* you could do it) and where you could live and whom you could marry. I know your countrymen do not agree with me about this, and I hear them saying, "You exaggerate." They do not know Harlem, and I do. So do you. Take no one's word for anything, including mine—but trust your experience. Know whence you came. If you know whence you came, there is really no limit to where you can go. The details and symbols of your life have been deliberately constructed to make you believe what white people say about you. Please try to remember that what they believe, as well as what they do and cause you to endure, does not testify to your inferiority but to their inhumanity and fear. Please try to be clear, dear James, through the storm which rages about your youthful head today, about the reality which lies behind the words *acceptance* and *integration*. There is no reason for you to try to become like white people and there is no basis whatever for their impertinent assumption that *they* must accept *you*. The really terrible thing, old buddy, is that *you* must accept *them*. And I mean that very seriously. You must accept them and accept them with love. For these innocent people have no other hope. They are, in effect, still trapped in a history which they do not understand, and until they understand it, they cannot be released from it. They have had to believe for many years, and for innumerable reasons, that black men are inferior to white men. Many of them, indeed, know better, but, as you will discover, people find it very difficult to act on what they know. To act is to be committed, and to be committed is to be in danger. In this case, the danger, in the minds of most white Americans, is the loss of their identity. Try to imagine how you would feel if you woke up one morning to find the sun shining and all the stars aflame. You would be frightened because it is out of the order of nature. Any upheaval in the universe is terrifying because it so profoundly attacks one's sense of one's own reality. Well, the black man has functioned in the white man's world as a fixed star, as an immovable pillar: and as he moves out of his place, heaven and earth are shaken to their foundations. You, don't be afraid. I said that it was intended that you should perish in the ghetto, perish by never being allowed to go behind the white man's definitions, by never being allowed to spell your proper name. You have, and many of us have, defeated this intention; and, by a terrible law, a terrible paradox, those innocents who believed that your imprisonment made them safe are losing their grasp of reality. But these men are your brothers—your lost, younger brothers. And if the word *integration* means anything, this is what it means: that we, with love, shall force our brothers to see themselves as they are, to cease fleeing from reality and begin to change it. For this is your home, my friend, do not be driven from it; great men have done great things here, and will again, and we can make America what America must become. It will be hard, James, but you come from sturdy, peasant stock, men who picked cotton and dammed rivers and built railroads, and, in the teeth of the most terrifying odds, achieved an unassailable and monumental dignity. You come from a long line of great poets, some of the greatest poets since Homer. One of them said, *The very time I thought I was lost, My dungeon shook and my chains fell off.*

You know, and I know, that the country is celebrating one hundred years of freedom one hundred years too soon. We cannot be free until they are free. God bless you, James, and Godspeed.

Your uncle,
James

JAMES MERRILL (b. 1926)
United States

From *Water Street* (1962) to *Late Settings* (1985) and *The Inner Room* (1988), James Merrill's poetry makes, as he says, a kind of formal dwelling "out of the life lived, out of the love spent." Creating this space "windless, compact, and sunny," intertextually and metaphorically woven with the created spaces and echoes of other poets and times, his own voice, sometimes distant, sometimes intimate, manages to address the topic of pain with a resonance unique in American poetry. "Farewell Performance" is taken from the anthology called *Poets for Life: Seventy-Six Poets Respond to AIDS.*

from *Poets for Life: Seventy-Six Poets Respond to AIDS*

Farewell Performance

Art. It cures affliction. As lights go down and
Maestro lifts his wands, the unfailing sea change
starts within us. Limber alembics once more
make of the common

lot a pure, brief gold. At the end our bravos   5
call them back, sweat-soldered and leotarded,
back, again back—anything not to face the
fact that it's over.

You are gone. You'd caught like a cold their airy
lust for essence. Now, in the furnace parched to   10

ten or twelve light handfuls, a mortal gravel
sifted through fingers,

coarse, yet grayly glimmering sublimate of
palace days, Strauss, Sidney, the lover's plaintive
Can't we just be friends? which your breakfast phone call   15
clothed in amusement,

this is what we paddled a neighbor's dinghy
out to scatter—Peter who grasped the buoy,
I who held the box underwater, freeing
all it contained. Past   20

sunny, fluent soundings that gruel of selfhood
taking manlike shape for one last jete on
ghostly—wait, ah!—point into darkness vanished.
High up, a gull's wings

clapped. The house lights (always supposing, caro,   25
Earth remains your house) at their brightest set the
scene for good: true colors, the sun-warm hand to
cover my wet one. . . .

Back they come. How you would have loved it. We in
turn have risen. Pity and terror done with,   30
programs furled, lips parted, we jostle forward
eager to hail them,

more, to join the troupe—will a friend enroll us
one fine day? Strange, though. For up close their magic
self-destructs. Pale, dripping, with downcast eyes they've   35
seen where it led you.

JOHN ASHBERY (b. 1927)
United States

John Ashbery, educated at Deerfield Academy, Harvard, Columbia, and New
York University, was a Fulbright Fellow and then an art critic in Paris. He was
executive editor of *Art News,* and then taught at Brooklyn College before moving
to Bard College. Certainly the most demanding living poet in the United States,
Ashbery etches the mind's landscape like a verbal Rembrandt who has learned to
work with film. At first, we are not quite sure of what we are seeing. Chiaroscuro
effects tease cubist perspectives. Familiar, funny objects turned this way and that
become serious, sometimes sinister. Ashbery's early experience growing up on a

farm in New York state grounded his later education in highly polished capitals. The result is most clearly seen in a poem like "Farm Implements and Rutabagas in a Landscape." There is something so "down home" married to something so "way out" about Ashbery. He is deeply American.

Farm Implements and Rutabagas in a Landscape

The first of the undecoded messages read: "Popeye sits in thunder,
Unthought of. From that shoebox of an apartment,
From livid curtain's hue, a tangram[1] emerges: a country."
Meanwhile the Sea Hag was relaxing on a green couch: "How pleasant
To spend one's vacation *en la casa de Popeye*,"[2] she scratched   5
Her cleft chin's solitary hair. She remembered spinach

And was going to ask Wimpy if he had bought any spinach.
"M'love," he intercepted, "the plains are decked out in thunder
Today, and it shall be as you wish." He scratched
The part of his head under his hat. The apartment   10
Seemed to grow smaller. "But what if no pleasant
Inspiration plunge us now to the stars? *For this is my country*."

Suddenly they remembered how it was cheaper in the country.
Wimpy was thoughtfully cutting open a number 2 can of spinach
When the door opened and Swee'pea crept in. "How pleasant!"   15
But Swee'pea looked morose. A note was pinned to his bib. "Thunder
And tears are unavailing," it read. "Henceforth shall Popeye's apartment
Be but remembered space, toxic or salubrious, whole or scratched."

Olive came hurtling through the window; its geraniums scratched
Her long thigh. "I have news!" she gasped. "Popeye, forced as you know
  to flee the country   20
One musty gusty evening, by the schemes of his wizened, duplicate father, jealous
  of the apartment
And all that it contains, myself and spinach
In particular, heaves bolts of loving thunder
At his own astonished becoming, rupturing the pleasant   25

Arpeggio[3] of our years. No more shall pleasant
Rays of the sun refresh your sense of growing old, nor the scratched
Tree-trunks and mossy foliage, only immaculate darkness and thunder."

---

1. A Chinese puzzle made by dividing a
   square into five triangles, a rhomboid, and
   a square; the purpose of the game is the
   recombination of these shapes into suggestive new figures

2. I.e., in Popeye's house.
3. The playing of the notes of a chord in
   succession (rather than simultaneously).

She grabbed Swee'pea. "I'm taking the brat to the country."   30
"But you can't do that—he hasn't even finished his spinach,"
Urged the Sea Hag, looking fearfully around at the apartment.

But Olive was already out of earshot. Now the apartment
Succumbed to a strange new hush. "Actually it's quite pleasant
Here," thought the Sea Hag. "If this is all we need fear from spinach   35
Then I don't mind so much. Perhaps we could invite Alice the Goon over"—she
    scratched
One dug pensively—"but Wimpy is such a country
Bumpkin, always burping like that." Minute at first, the thunder

Soon filled the apartment. It was domestic thunder,   40
The color of spinach. Popeye chuckled and scratched
His balls: it sure was pleasant to spend a day in the country.

IMAMU AMIRI BARAKA [FORMERLY EVERETT LEROI JONES] (b. 1934)

United States

Born Everett LeRoi Jones in Newark, New Jersey, and first known as a beat poet
in the 1950s, Amiri Baraka is the writer most associated with the militant Black
Arts Movement of the 1960s. Baraka's poetic journey parallels the enormous
changes that have taken place in black writing during the last four decades. In
1961 his trip to the newly socialist country of Cuba would change his view of the
black artist, who, he then came to believe, should be a major catalyst for social
change. His controversial play *The Dutchman* (1964) is a confrontational work
about the artist's role in political struggle.

The assassination of Malcolm X in 1965 marked a turning point in his life,
as was symbolized by his changing his name to Imamu Amiri Baraka; this poem
"for black hearts" expresses in clear terms Baraka's admiration of and love for
Malcolm X. Baraka became the most visible black nationalist writer of the late
1960s. By 1974, after an intense decade of literary and social activism, he became
disillusioned with Black Nationalism because of its narrowness and aligned
himself with the socialism of developing countries. His many works—poetry
collections, collections of plays, a novel, a short-story collection, and nonfiction
works on poetry, music, and politics, as well as his autobiography—have secured
Baraka's place in twentieth-century American literature as one of its most
avant-garde and original political writers.

A Poem for Black Hearts

For Malcolm's eyes, when they broke
the face of some dumb white man. For
Malcolm's hands raised to bless us
all black and strong in his image
of ourselves, For Malcolm's words   5
fire darts, the victor's tireless
thrusts, words hung above the world
change as it may, he said it, and
For this he was killed, for saying,
and feeling, and being/ change, all   10
collected hot in his heart, For Malcolm's
heart, raising us above our filthy cities,
for his stride, and his beat, and his address
to the grey monsters of the world, For Malcolm's
pleas for your dignity, black men, for your life,   15
black man, for the filling of your minds
with righteousness. For all of him dead and
gone and vanished from us, and all of him which
clings to our speech black god of our time.
For all of him, and all of yourself, look up,   20
black man, quit stuttering and shuffling, look up,
black man, quit whining and stooping, for all of him.
For Great Malcolm a prince of the earth, let nothing in us rest
until we avenge ourselves for his death, stupid animals
that killed him, let us never breathe a pure breath if   25
we fail, and white men call us faggots till the end of
the earth.

AUDRE LORDE (1934–1992)
United States

Born Audrey Lorde in Harlem to Caribbean immigrants, Audre Lorde was the
most celebrated contemporary black feminist lesbian poet and essayist. In her
work she emphasizes the creative possibilities of recognizing differences as a
positive dynamic by insisting on her various identities as a necessity for her
wholeness of self. Her volumes of poetry, especially *The Black Unicorn* (1978), are
grounded in the complex spiritual and political tradition of women, even while
voicing feminist protest. Her biomythography," *ZAMI: A New Spelling of My Name*

(1982), is the first autobiographical narrative of an African-American lesbian, while her essay collections, especially *Sister Outsider* (1984), have been major contributions to feminist theory and political thought.

A Litany for Survival

For those of us who live at the shoreline
standing upon the constant edges of decision
crucial and alone
for those of us who cannot indulge
the passing dreams of choice   5
who love in doorways coming and going
in the hours between dawns
looking inward and outward
at once before and after
seeking a now that can breed   10
futures
like bread in our children's mouths
so their dreams will not reflect
the death of ours:

For those of us   15
who were imprinted with fear
like a faint line in the center of our foreheads
learning to be afraid with our mother's milk
for by this weapon
this illusion of some safety to be found   20
the heavy-footed hoped to silence us
For all of us
this instant and this triumph
We were never meant to survive.

And when the sun rises we are afraid   25
it might not remain
when the sun sets we are afraid
it might not rise in the morning
when our stomachs are full we are afraid
of indigestion   30
when our stomachs are empty we are afraid
we may never eat again
when we are loved we are afraid
love will vanish
when we are alone we are afraid   35
love will never return
and when we speak we are afraid
our words will not be heard

nor welcomed
but when we are silent   40
we are still afraid.

So it is better to speak
remembering
we were never meant to survive

N. SCOTT MOMADAY (b. 1934)
United States

A member of the Kiowa tribe, N. Scott Momaday [Tsoai-talee] grew up on reservations in the Southwest and was educated at the University of New Mexico and Stanford. He has taught at Berkeley, Stanford, and the University of Arizona. Momaday won the Pulitzer Prize in 1968 for his novel, *House Made of Dawn*. The selection presented here, an excerpt from *The Way to Rainy Mountain*, is an autobiographical story that celebrates the emergence of the Kiowa people onto the southern Great Plains where their culture flourished during the eighteenth century. The are now located in Oklahoma.

Momaday juxtaposes his memory of the death of his beloved grandmother with the death of a particular form of Kiowa culture. The story acknowledges that the grandmother has passed on, that a particular moment of Kiowa history has passed, yet all remains living and continues in Momaday's memory. Memory is alive and exists undeniably in the present. This is a classic piece of American literature.

from *The Way to Rainy Mountain*

[Continuance of a Kiowa Culture]

A single knoll rises out of the plain in Oklahoma, north and west of the Wichita Range. For my people, the Kiowas, it is an old landmark, and they gave it the name Rainy Mountain. The hardest weather in the world is there. Winter brings blizzards, hot tornadic winds arise in the spring, and in summer the prairie is an anvil's edge. The grass turns brittle and brown, and it cracks beneath your feet. There are green belts along the rivers and creeks, linear groves of hickory and pecan, willow and witch hazel. At a distance in July or August the steaming foliage seems almost to writhe in fire. Great green and yellow grasshoppers are everywhere in the tall grass, popping up like corn to sting the flesh, and tortoises crawl about on the red earth, going nowhere in the plenty of time. Loneliness is an aspect of the land. All things in the plain are isolate, there is no confusion of objects in the eye, but *one* hill or *one* tree or *one* man. To look upon that landscape in the early morning, with the sun at your back, is to lose the sense of proportion. Your imagination comes to life, and this, you think, is where Creation was begun.

I returned to Rainy Mountain in July. My grandmother had died in the spring, and I wanted to be at her grave. She had lived to be very old and at last infirm. Her only living daughter was with her when she died, and I was told that in death her face was that of a child.

I like to think of her as a child. When she was born, the Kiowas were living that last great moment of their history. For more than a hundred years they had controlled the open range from the Smoky Hill River to the Red, from the headwaters of the Canadian to the fork of the Arkansas and Cimarron. In alliance with the Comanches, they had ruled the whole of the southern Plains. War was their sacred business, and they were among the finest horsemen the world has ever known. But warfare for the Kiowas was preeminently a matter of disposition rather than of survival, and they never understood the grim, unrelenting advance of the U.S. Cavalry. When at last, divided and ill-provisioned, they were driven onto the Staked Plains in the cold rains of autumn, they fell into panic. In Palo Duro Canyon they abandoned their crucial stores to pillage and had nothing then but their lives. In order to save themselves, they surrendered to the soldiers at Fort Sill and were imprisoned in the old stone corral that now stands as a military museum. My grandmother was spared the humiliation of those high gray walls by eight or ten years, but she must have known from birth the affliction of defeat, the dark brooding of old warriors.

Her name was Aho, and she belonged to the last culture to evolve in North America. Her forebears came down from the high country in western Montana nearly three centuries ago. They were a mountain people, a mysterious tribe of hunters whose language has never been positively classified in any major group. In the late seventeenth century they began a long migration to the south and east. It was a journey toward the dawn, and it led to a golden age. Along the way the Kiowas were befriended by the Crows, who gave them the culture and religion of the Plains. They acquired horses, and their ancient nomadic spirit was suddenly free of the ground. They acquired Tai-me, the sacred Sun Dance doll, from that moment the object and symbol of their worship, and so shared in the divinity of the sun. Not least, they acquired the sense of destiny, therefore courage and pride. When they entered upon the southern Plains they had been transformed. No longer were they slaves to the simple necessity of survival; they were a lordly and dangerous society of fighters and thieves, hunters and priests of the sun. According to their origin myth, they entered the world through a hollow log. From one point of view, their migration was the fruit of an old prophecy, for indeed they emerged from a sunless world.

Although my grandmother lived out her long life in the shadow of Rainy Mountain, the immense landscape of the continental interior lay like memory in her blood. She could tell of the Crows, whom she had never seen, and of the Black Hills, where she had never been. I wanted to see in reality what she had seen more perfectly in the mind's eye, and travelled fifteen hundred miles to begin my pilgrimage.

Yellowstone, it seemed to me, was the top of the world, a region of deep lakes and dark timber, canyons and waterfalls. But, beautiful as it is, one might have the sense of confinement there. The skyline in all directions is close at hand, the high wall of the woods and deep cleavages of shade. There is a perfect freedom in the mountains, but it belongs to the eagle and the elk, the badger and the bear. The Kiowas reckoned their stature by the distance they could see, and they were bent and blind in the wilderness.

Descending eastward, the highland meadows are a stairway to the plain. In July the inland slope of the Rockies is luxuriant with flax and buckwheat, stonecrop and larkspur. The earth unfolds and the limit of the land recedes. Clusters of trees, and animals grazing far in the distance, cause the vision to reach away and wonder to build upon the mind. The sun follows a longer course in the day, and the sky is immense beyond all comparison. The great billowing clouds that sail upon it are shadows that move upon the grain like water, dividing light. Farther down, in the land of the Crows and Blackfeet, the plain is yellow. Sweet clover takes hold of the hills and bends upon itself to cover and seal the soil. There the Kiowas paused on their way; they had come to the place where they must change their lives. The sun is at home on the plains. Precisely there does it have the certain character of a god. When the Kiowas came to the land of the Crows, they could see the dark lees of the hills at dawn across the Bighorn River, the profusion of light on the grain shelves, the oldest deity ranging after the solstices. Not yet would they veer southward to the caldron of the land that lay below; they must wean their blood from the northern winter and hold the mountains a while longer in their view. They bore Tai-me in procession to the east.

A dark mist lay over the Black Hills, and the land was like iron. At the top of a ridge I caught sight of Devil's Tower upthrust against the gray sky as if in the birth of time the core of the earth had broken through its crust and the motion of the world was begun. There are things in nature that engender an awful quiet in the heart of man; Devil's Tower is one of them. Two centuries ago, because they could not do otherwise, the Kiowas made a legend at the base of the rock. My grandmother said:

> Eight children were there at play, seven sisters and their brother. Suddenly the boy was struck dumb; he trembled and began to run upon his hands and feet. His fingers became claws, and his body was covered with fur. Directly there was a bear where the boy had been. The sisters were terrified; they ran, and the bear after them. They came to the stump of a great tree, and the tree spoke to them. It bade them climb upon it, and as they did so it began to rise into the air. The bear came to kill them, but they were just beyond its reach. It reared against the tree and scored the bark all around with its claws. The seven sisters were borne into the sky, and they became the stars of the Big Dipper.

From that moment, and so long as the legend lives, the Kiowas have kinsmen in the night sky. Whatever they were in the mountains, they could be no more. However tenuous their well-being, however much they had suffered and would suffer again, they had found a way out of the wilderness.

My grandmother had a reverence for the sun, a holy regard that now is all but gone out of mankind. There was a wariness in her, and an ancient awe. She was a Christian in her later years, but she had come a long way about, and she never forgot her birthright. As a child she had been to the Sun Dances; she had taken part in those annual rites, and by them she had learned the restoration of her people in the presence of Tai-me. She was about seven when the last Kiowa Sun Dance was held in 1887 on the Washita River above Rainy Mountain Creek. The buffalo were gone. In order to consummate the ancient sacrifice—to impale the head of a buffalo bull upon the medicine tree—a delegation of old men journeyed into Texas, there to beg and barter for an animal from the Goodnight herd. She was ten when the Kiowas came together for the last time as a living Sun Dance culture. They could find no buffalo; they had to hang an old hide from the sacred tree. Before the dance could begin, a company of soldiers rode out from Fort Sill under orders to disperse the tribe. Forbidden without cause the essential act of their faith, having seen the wild herds slaughtered and left to rot upon the ground, the Kiowas backed away forever from the medicine tree. That was July 20, 1890, at the great bend of the Washita. My grandmother was there. Without bitterness, and for as long as she lived, she bore a vision of deicide.

Now that I can have her only in memory, I see my grandmother in the several postures that were peculiar to her: standing at the wood stove on a winter morning and turning meat in a great iron skillet; sitting at the south window, bent above her beadwork, and afterwards, when her vision failed, looking down for a long time into the fold of her hands; going out upon a cane, very slowly as she did when the weight of age came upon her; praying. I remember her most often at prayer. She made long, rambling prayers out of suffering and hope, having seen many things. I was never sure that I had the right to hear, so exclusive were they of all mere custom and company. The last time I saw her she prayed standing by the side of her bed at night, naked to the waist, the light of a kerosene lamp moving upon her dark skin. Her long, black hair, always drawn and braided in the day, lay upon her shoulders and against her breasts like a shawl. I do not speak Kiowa, and I never understood her prayers, but there was something inherently sad in the sound, some merest hesitation upon the syllables of sorrow. She began in a high and descending pitch, exhausting her breath to silence; then again and again—and always the same intensity of effort, of something that is, and is not, like urgency in the human voice. Transported so in the dancing light among the shadows of her room, she seemed beyond the reach of time. But that was illusion; I think I knew then that I should not see her again.

Houses are like sentinels in the plain, old keepers of the weather watch. There, in a very little while, wood takes on the appearance of great age. All colors wear soon away in the wind and rain, and then the wood is burned gray and the grain appears and the nails turn red with rust. The windowpanes are black and opaque; you imagine there is nothing within, and indeed there are many ghosts, bones given up to the land. They stand here and there against the sky, and you approach them for a longer time than you expect. They belong in the distance; it is their domain.

Once there was a lot of sound in my grandmother's house, a lot of coming and going, feasting and talk. The summers there were full of excitement and reunion. The Kiowas are a summer people; they abide the cold and keep to themselves, but when the season turns and the land becomes warm and vital they cannot hold still; an old love of going returns upon them. The aged visitors who came to my grandmother's house when I was a child were made of lean and leather, and they bore themselves upright. They wore great black hats and bright ample shirts that shook in the wind. They rubbed fat upon their hair and wound their braids with strips of colored cloth. Some of them painted their faces and carried the scars of old and cherished enmities. They were an old council of warlords, come to remind and be reminded of who they were. Their wives and daughters served them well. The women might indulge themselves; gossip was at once the mark and compensation of their servitude. They made loud and elaborate talk among themselves, full of jest and gesture, fright and false alarm. They went abroad in fringed and flowered shawls, bright beadwork and German silver. They were at home in the kitchen, and they prepared meals that were banquets.

There were frequent prayer meetings, and great nocturnal feasts. When I was a child I played with my cousins outside, where the lamplight fell upon the ground and the singing of the old people rose up around us and carried away into the darkness. There were a lot of good things to eat, a lot of laughter and surprise. And afterwards, when the quiet returned, I lay down with my grandmother and could hear the frogs away by the river and feel the motion of the air.

Now there is a funeral silence in the rooms, the endless wake of some final word. The walls have closed in upon my grandmother's house. When I returned to it in mourning, I saw for the first time in my life how small it was. It was late at night, and there was a white moon, nearly full. I sat for a long time on the stone steps by the kitchen door. From there I could see out across the land; I could see the long row of trees by the creek, the low light upon the rolling plains, and the stars of the Big Dipper. Once I looked at the moon and caught sight of a strange thing. A cricket had perched upon the handrail, only a few inches away from me. My line of vision was such that the creature filled the moon like a fossil. It had gone there, I thought, to live and die, for there, of all places, was its small definition made whole and eternal. A warm wind rose up and purled like the longing within me.

The next morning I awoke at dawn and went out on the dirt road to Rainy Mountain. It was already hot, and the grasshoppers began to fill the air. Still, it was early in the morning, and the birds sang out of the shadows. The long yellow grass on the mountain shone in the bright light, and a scissortail hied above the land. There, where it ought to be, at the end of a long and legendary way, was my grandmother's grave. Here and there on the dark stones were ancestral names. Looking back once, I saw the mountain and came away.

JUNE JORDAN (b. 1936)
United States

Born in Harlem to Jamaican immigrants, June Jordan grew up in Bedford-Stuyvesant, New York, where she began writing poetry at the age of seven. In the

1960s she was intensely involved in the Civil Rights Movement as a teacher, journalist, and poet. A major advocate of black English as a valuable linguistic system and teaching tool, Jordan has written many books focused on black children. She has also been involved in creating designs for healthy urban involvement, for which she won the Prix de Rome in 1970. An activist in the women's movement and in international movements, as well as in contemporary struggles for racial justice, she is known for her lyrical political poetry and essays. Jordan's poetry and essay collections, children's books, and plays are charged by her belief that the political is intimate, the personal is political, and poetry is for the people.

In Memoriam: Martin Luther King, Jr.

I

honey people murder mercy U.S.A.
the milkland turn to monsters teach
to kill to violate pull down destroy
the weakly freedom growing fruit
from being born   5

America

tomorrow yesterday rip rape
exacerbate despoil disfigure
crazy running threat the
deadly thrall   10
appall belief dispel
the wildlife burn the breast
the onward tongue
the outward hand
deform the normal rainy   15
riot sunshine shelter wreck
of darkness derogate
delimit blank
explode deprive
assassinate and batten up   20
like bullets fatten up
the raving greed
reactivate a springtime
terrorizing

death by men by more   25
than you or I can

STOP

II

They sleep who know a regulated place
or pulse or tide or changing sky
according to some universal   30
stage direction obvious
like shorewashed shells

we share an afternoon of mourning
in between no next predictable
except for wild reversal hearse rehearsal   35
bleach the blacklong lunging
ritual of fright insanity and more
deplorable abortion
more and
more   40

SUSAN HOWE (b. 1937)
United States

In the tradition of Jonathan Edwards, Ralph Waldo Emerson, and Emily Dickinson,
Susan Howe works at the edges of meaning, getting underneath the fabric of our
habits of mind. Equally attuned to history and the sound of words, she exposes the
mythology of mythologies and prophesies' clarity to those who attend. Reading her
we realize how much of what we have always seen we had never seen before. The
poems included here reflect the "more than rational" distortion of language calling
attention to itself and its presentation, as in the upside-down lines of "As if all
history were a progress," upon which *reflection* it ironically mis-reflects.

[As if all history were a progress]

As if all history were a progress
ɯᴉɥ ʇuoɹɐ oʇ ƃuᴉɯoɔ sɐʍ əɥS
    A single thread of narrative
sʇɥƃnoɥʇ ʎɥɔɹɐuɐ ƃuoɹʇspɐəɥ
    Actual world nothing ideal   5

    ssəlǝɯɐu sᴉ əɥs ɹəʇəԀ uI
    The nets were not torn

The Gospel did not grasp

[*Rough messenger Trust*]

Rough messenger Trust

I studious am

Would never have stumbled
on the paved road

What is that law   5

You have your names

To do and to settle
Spirit of Conviction

Who wounded the earth

Out of the way of Night   10
no reason to count

Crying out testimony

Paths of righteousness
Love may be a stumbling

out on the great meadows   15
Prose is unknown

You have your names

I have not read them
Coming from a remote field
abandoned to me   20

ISHMAEL REED (b. 1938)
United States

Born in Chattanooga, Tennessee, and now living in Oakland, California, Ishmael Reed is considered by many critics to be the most prominent satirist of African-American letters. In his novels, poetry collections, essay collections, and plays, Reed makes fun of our most sacred beliefs, especially in relation to history, race, and sex, even as he challenges the literary conventions of the African-American tradition. His novels critique our received views of history—e.g., the Harlem Renaissance in *Mumbo Jumbo,* the antebellum plantation in *Flight to Canada*—through his use of collage, cartoon, and irony. Though some have called him the Black Postmodernist Writer, Reed considers himself a "neo hoodooist," his term for the outrageous non-Western stance he and other like-minded artists have taken.

Reed has been a major promoter of literature by people of color. Besides editing many anthologies, he helped to found the Before Columbus Foundation, which publishes and honors what he calls the "real American writing." Since he is immersed in African-American musical forms, it is not surprising that some of his work has been set in musical contexts. His poem "The Wardrobe Master of Paradise" was set to music and sung by the African-American folk singer Taj Mahal.

The Wardrobe Master of Paradise

He pins the hems of Angels and
He dresses them to kill
He has no time for fashion
No money's in His till
You won't see Him in Paris   5
or in a New York store
He's the wardrobe master
of Paradise; He keeps right
on His toes

He works from ancient patterns   10
He doesn't mind they bore
His models have no measurements
His buyers never roar
He never cares to gossip
He works right on the floor   15
He's the wardrobe master
of Paradise; He keeps right
on His toes

The evil cities burn to
a crisp, from where His   20
clients go; their eyes
are blood red carnage, their
purpose never fluffed,
His customers total seven
they have no time to pose   25
He's the wardrobe master
of Paradise; He keeps right
on His toes

He does not sweat the phony
trends, or fashions dumb   30
decree; His style is always
chic and in, He never takes
a fee
In Vogue or Glamour or Harper's
Bazaar; He's never written up   35
He's the wardrobe master

of Paradise; He keeps right
on His toes

The ups and downs of Commerce
His shop will not effect;
the whims of a fickle market
the trifles of jet-sets
The society editor would
rather die than ask Him for
a tip; He sews uninterrupted   45
He isn't one for quips
His light burns in the pit-black night
I've never seen Him doze
He's the wardrobe master
of Paradise; He keeps right   50
on His toes

SIMON J. ORTIZ (b. 1941)
United States

Simon J. Ortiz is a native of Acoma Pueblo. He is a poet, short fiction writer, essayist and screenwriter, the author of several works, including *Going For the Rain* (1976), *A Good Journey* (1977), and most recently *Woven Stone* (1992), a collected works. As a major, influential Native American writer, he eloquently expresses the living story of his people, a story often marred by social, political, and economic conflicts with Anglo American society. Yet, like Native American oral tradition, he always stresses the possibility of vision and hope through creative struggle and resistance. The story included here blends old and new as well as oral and written traditions. This telling reveals cultural collisions and combinations. The traditional pueblo opening of this story gives way to Rainy's "Onesa Ponsa Time." The network of family is expressed in words that combine Spanish and the Keresan language of the Acoma Pueblo.

There are voices within voices here, voices of the past, present, and future. The ancient intertwines with fresh events of the day. This story is really about continuance, a seasonal existence. Things are never over; there is ongoing life after the fall.

from **A Good Journey**

[And there is always one more story]

And there is always one more story. My mother was telling this one. It must be an old story but this time she heard a woman telling it at one of those Sunday meetings. The woman was telling about her grandson who was telling the story

which was told to him by somebody else. All these voices telling the story,
including the voices in the story—yes, it must be an old one.

One time,
(or like Rainy[1] said, "You're sposed to say, 'Onesa ponsa time,' Daddy")

there were some Quail Women grinding corn.
Tsuushki—Coyote Lady[2]—was with them.

She was   5

grinding u-uuhshtyah—juniper berries.
I don't know why she wasn't grinding corn too—
that's just in the story.

It was a hot, hot day, very hot,
and the Quail Women got thirsty,   10
and they decided to go get some water to drink.
They said,
            "Let's go for a drink of water,
and let's take along our beloved comadre."[3]
So they said, "Comadre, let's all go   15
and get some water to drink."
            "Shrow-uh,"

Coyote said.

The water was in a little cistern[4]
at the top of a tall rock pinnacle   20
which stands southeast of Acu.[5]

They walked

over there but they had to fly to get to the top.
The Quail Women looked at Tsuushki who couldn't fly
to the top because she had no feathers,   25
            and they felt

very sorry and sad for Tsuuschki.

So they decided, "Let us give shracomadre
some of our feathers."

            The Quail Woman said that   30
and they took some feathers out of themselves
and stuck them on Coyote.
            And then they all flew
to the top of the pinnacle where the water was.
They all drank their fill and Coyote   35
was the last to drink.

---

1. Ortiz's daughter, Rainy Dawn.
2. A coyote is a creature whose appetites are always greater than what is available; a trickster.
3. From the Spanish *comadre*, meaning god-mother.

4. Natural sandstone tanks or hollows that capture rain water. They are the only water source on top of the many rock mesas, such as the one where Acoma Pueblo is located.
5. Acoma Pueblo.

                    While she was drinking
from the cistern, on her hands and knees,
the Quail Women decided to play a trick, a joke
on Coyote Lady.   40
                    They said,
"Let's take the feathers from our comadre
and leave her here."
                    "All right," they all agreed,
and they did that, and they all left.   45

When Tsuushki had drunk her fill of water
and was ready to descend the pinnacle,
she found that she could not
because she had no feathers to fly with anymore.
She felt very bad,   50
                    and she sat down,
                                        wondering
what to do.
The rock pinnacle was too high up
to jump down off of.   55

But, pretty soon,
                    Kahmaasquu Baba—
Spider Grandmother[6]—came climbing over the edge
of the pinnacle to drink water also.
And Coyote thought to herself,   60
                                Aha,
I will ask my Grandmother to help me off.
She is always a wonderful helpful person.

So Coyote asked,
"Dya-ow Kahmaasquu, do you think you could help me   65
descend this pinnacle? You are always such a
wonderful helpful person."

And Spider Grandmother said,
                                "Why yes,
beloved one, I will help you.   70
Climb into my basket."
                    She pointed at a basket
tied at the end of her rope.
                    And then
she said, "But I must ask you one thing.   75
While I am letting you down,

---

6. Spider Woman weaves the world into exis-   that of a world weaver in many pueblo
   tence with her web of stories. Her role is a   traditions.

you must not look up, not once,
not even just a little bit.
                        For if you do,
I will drop you,
And that is quite a long ways down."   80

"Oh, don't worry about that, Dyaa-ow,
I won't look up. I'm not that kind of person,"
Coyote promised.
                "All right then,"   85
Spider said, "Climb in
And I will let you down."

The basket began to descend,
                        down
                                and   90
                                        down,

BUT on the way down,
                        Coyote looked up
(At this point, the voice telling the story
is that of the boy who said,   95
                "But Tsuushki
looked up and saw her butt!")
and Spider Grandmother dropped the basket
and Coyote went crashing down.

Well, at this point, the story ends but,   100
as you know, it also goes on.
                        Well, sometime later,
the Shuuwimuu Guiguikuutchah—
Skeleton Fixer—came along.
He saw a scatter of bones at the foot of the pinnacle.   105
Skeleton Fixer said,
                "Oh look,
some poor beloved one must have died.
I wonder who it may be?"
                        The bones   110
were drying white in the sun, lying around.
And Skeleton Fixer said,
                        "I think I will put
the bones together
and find out and he will live again."   115

And he joined the bones together,
                                very carefully,
and when he had finished doing that,
he danced around them while he sang,

"Shuuwimuu shuuwimuu chuchukuu
Shuuwimuu shuuwimuu chuchukuu
Bah Bah."
     (which is to say)
Skeleton skeleton join together
Skeleton skeleton join together
Bah Bah.
     And the skeleton bones did,
and the skeleton jumped up,
and it was Coyote.

"Ah kumeh, Tsuushkitruda," Skeleton Fixer said.
Oh, it's just you Coyote—I thought
it was someone else.
And as Coyote ran away,
Skeleton Fixer called after her,
                "Nahkeh-eh,
bah aihatih eyownih trudrai-nah!"
Go ahead and go, may you get crushed
by a falling rock somewhere!

ALICE WALKER (b. 1944)
United States

Alice Walker was born in Eatonton, Georgia, to parents who were sharecroppers. As a participant in the 1960s in the Civil Rights Movement and as a pioneer in the International Women's Movement, she experienced the effects of political and literary movements on societal and personal change.

    A prolific writer, Walker has published novels, short stories, poetry, essays, and children's books. She is the first African-American woman to receive the Pulitzer Prize for Fiction, for her novel *The Color Purple* (1982), on which the controversial film of the same name was based. In all her work she illuminates the creativity of women, particularly African-Americans, even as she protests the restrictions of their societal conditions.

    In "In Search of Our Mothers' Gardens," which was first published in *MS* magazine in 1975, Walker articulates the neglected creative legacy of ordinary African-American women like her mother and shows how their expressions were artistic forms. Walker uses their forms, such as quilting for example, as the bases for her own literary forms. In this essay Walker also explores the literary history of those few African-American women who were able to publish. Her reinterpretation of this history—especially of the poetry of Phillis Wheatley, the first published African-American writer, and of the centrality of Zora Neale

Hurston—was a major influence in African-American women's literary and critical studies, which developed in the 1970s.

In Search of Our Mothers' Gardens

I described her own nature and temperament. Told how they needed a larger life for their expression. . . . I pointed out that in lieu of proper channels, her emotions had overflowed into paths that dissipated them. I talked, beautifully I thought, about an art that would be born, an art that would open the way for women the likes of her. I asked her to hope, and build up an inner life against the coming of that day. . . . I sang, with a strange quiver in my voice, a promise song.

—*Jean Toomer, "Avey,"*
CANE

The poet speaking to a prostitute who falls asleep while he's talking—

When the poet Jean Toomer walked through the South in the early twenties, he discovered a curious thing: black women whose spirituality was so intense, so deep, so *unconscious,* that they were themselves unaware of the richness they held. They stumbled blindly through their lives: creatures so abused and mutilated in body, so dimmed and confused by pain, that they considered themselves unworthy even of hope. In the selfless abstractions their bodies became to the men who used them, they became more than "sexual objects," more even than mere women: they became "Saints." Instead of being perceived as whole persons, their bodies became shrines: what was thought to be their minds became temples suitable for worship. These crazy Saints stared out at the world, wildly, like lunatics—or quietly, like suicides; and the "God" that was in their gaze was as mute as a great stone.

Who were these Saints? These crazy, loony, pitiful women?

Some of them, without a doubt, were our mothers and grandmothers.

In the still heat of the post-Reconstruction South, this is how they seemed to Jean Toomer: exquisite butterflies trapped in an evil honey, toiling away their lives in an era, a century, that did not acknowledge them, except as "the *mule* of the world." They dreamed dreams that no one knew—not even themselves, in any coherent fashion—and saw visions no one could understand. They wandered or sat about the countryside crooning lullabies to ghosts, and drawing the mother of Christ in charcoal on courthouse walls.

They forced their minds to desert their bodies and their striving spirits sought to rise, like frail whirlwinds from the hard red clay. And when those frail whirlwinds fell, in scattered particles, upon the ground, no one mourned. Instead, men lit candles to celebrate the emptiness that remained, as people do who enter a beautiful but vacant space to resurrect a God.

Our mothers and grandmothers, some of them moving to music not yet written. And they waited.

They waited for a day when the unknown thing that was in them would be made known; but guessed, somehow in their darkness, that on the day of their revelation they would be long dead. Therefore to Toomer they walked, and even ran, in slow motion. For they were going nowhere immediate, and the future was not yet within their grasp. And men took our mothers and grandmothers, "but got no pleasure from it." So complex was their passion and their calm.

To Toomer, they lay vacant and fallow as autumn fields, with harvest time never in sight: and he saw them enter loveless marriages, without joy; and become prostitutes, without resistance; and become mothers of children, without fulfillment.

For these grandmothers and mothers of ours were not Saints, but Artists; driven to a numb and bleeding madness by the springs of creativity in them for which there was no release. They were Creators, who lived lives of spiritual waste, because they were so rich in spirituality—which is the basis of Art—that the strain of enduring their unused and unwanted talent drove them insane. Throwing away this spirituality was their pathetic attempt to lighten the soul to a weight their work-worn, sexually abused bodies could bear.

What did it mean for a black woman to be an artist in our grandmothers' time? In our great-grandmothers' day? It is a question with an answer cruel enough to stop the blood.

Did you have a genius of a great-great-grandmother who died under some ignorant and depraved white overseer's lash? Or was she required to bake biscuits for a lazy backwater tramp, when she cried out in her soul to paint watercolors of sunsets, or the rain falling on the green and peaceful pasturelands? Or was her body broken and forced to bear children (who were more often than not sold away from her)—eight, ten, fifteen, twenty children—when her one joy was the thought of modeling heroic figures of rebellion, in stone or clay?

How was the creativity of the black woman kept alive, year after year and century after century, when for most of the years black people have been in America, it was a punishable crime for a black person to read or write? And the freedom to paint, to sculpt, to expand the mind with action did not exist. Consider, if you can bear to imagine it, what might have been the result if singing, too, had been forbidden by law. Listen to the voices of Bessie Smith, Billie Holiday, Nina Simone, Roberta Flack, and Aretha Franklin, among others, and imagine those voices muzzled for life. Then you may begin to comprehend the lives of our "crazy," "Sainted" mothers and grandmothers. The agony of the lives of women who might have been Poets, Novelists, Essayists, and Short-Story Writers (over a period of centuries), who died with their real gifts stifled within them.

And, if this were the end of the story, we would have cause to cry out in my paraphrase of Okot p'Bitek's great poem:

O, my clanswomen
Let us all cry together!
Come,
Let us mourn the death of our mother,
The death of a Queen
The ash that was produced
By a great fire!

O, this homestead is utterly dead
Close the gates
With *lacari* thorns,
For our mother
The creator of the Stool is lost!
And all the young women
Have perished in the wilderness!

But this is not the end of the story, for all the young women—our mothers and grandmothers, *ourselves*—have not perished in the wilderness. And if we ask ourselves why, and search for and find the answer, we will know beyond all efforts to erase it from our minds, just exactly who, and of what, we black American women are.

One example, perhaps the most pathetic, most misunderstood one, can provide a backdrop for our mothers' work: Phillis Wheatley, a slave in the 1700s.

Virginia Woolf, in her book *A Room of One's Own,* wrote that in order for a woman to write fiction she must have two things, certainly: a room of her own (with key and lock) and enough money to support herself.

What then are we to make of Phillis Wheatley, a slave, who owned not even herself? This sickly, frail black girl who required a servant of her own at times—her health was so precarious—and who, had she been white, would have been easily considered the intellectual superior of all the women and most of the men in the society of her day.

Virginia Woolf wrote further, speaking of course not of our Phillis, that "any woman born with a great gift in the sixteenth century [insert "eighteenth century," insert "black woman," insert "born or made a slave"] would certainly have gone crazed, shot herself, or ended her days in some lonely cottage outside the village, half witch, half wizard [insert "Saint"], feared and mocked at. For it needs little skill and psychology to be sure that a highly gifted girl who had tried to use her gift for poetry would have been so thwarted and hindered by contrary instincts [add "chains, guns, the lash, the ownership of one's body by someone else, submission to an alien religion"], that she must have lost her health and sanity to a certainty."

The key words, as they relate to Phillis, are "contrary instincts." For when we read the poetry of Phillis Wheatley—as when we read the novels of Nella Larsen or the oddly false-sounding autobiography of that freest of all black women writers, Zora Hurston—evidence of "contrary instincts" is everywhere. Her loyalties were completely divided, as was, without question, her mind.

But how could this be otherwise? Captured at seven, a slave of wealthy, doting whites who instilled in her the "savagery" of the Africa they "rescued" her from . . . one wonders if she was even able to remember her homeland as she had known it, or as it really was.

Yet, because she did try to use her gift for poetry in a world that made her a slave, she was "so thwarted and hindered by . . . contrary instincts, that she . . . lost her health. . . ." In the last years of her brief life, burdened not only with the need to express her gift but also with a penniless, friendless "freedom" and several small children for whom she was forced to do strenuous work to feed, she lost her health, certainly. Suffering from malnutrition and neglect and who knows what mental agonies, Phillis Wheatley died.

So torn by "contrary instincts" was black, kidnapped, enslaved Phillis that her description of "the Goddess"—as she poetically called the Liberty she did not have—is ironically, cruelly humorous. And, in fact, has held Phillis up to ridicule for more than a century. It is usually read prior to hanging Phillis's memory as that of a fool. She wrote:

> The Goddess comes, she moves divinely fair,
> Olive and laurel binds her *golden* hair.
> Wherever shines this native of the skies,
> Unnumber'd charms and recent graces rise. [My italics]

It is obvious that Phillis, the slave, combed the "Goddess's" hair every morning; prior, perhaps, to bringing in the milk, or fixing her mistress's lunch. She took her imagery from the one thing she saw elevated above all others.

With the benefit of hindsight we ask, "How could she?"

But at last, Phillis, we understand. No more snickering when your stiff, struggling, ambivalent lines are forced on us. We know now that you were not an idiot or a traitor; only a sickly little black girl, snatched from your home and country and made a slave, a woman who still struggled to sing the song that was your gift, although in a land of barbarians who praised you for your bewildered tongue. It is not so much what you sang, as that you kept alive, in so many of our ancestors, *the notion of song.*

Black women are called, in the folklore that so aptly identifies one's status in society, "the *mule* of the world," because we have been handed the burdens that everyone else—*everyone* else—refused to carry. We have also been called "Matriarchs," "Superwomen," and "Mean and Evil Bitches." Not to mention "Castraters" and "Sapphire's Mama." When we have pleaded for understanding, our character has been distorted; when we have asked for simple caring, we have been handed empty inspirational appellations, then stuck in the farthest corner. When we have asked for love, we have been given children. In short, even our plainer gifts, our labors of fidelity and love, have been knocked down our throats. To be an artist and a black woman, even today, lowers our status in many respects, rather than raises it: and yet, artists we will be.

Therefore we must fearlessly pull out of ourselves and look at and identify with our lives the living creativity some of our great-grandmothers were not allowed to know. I stress *some* of them because it is well known that the majority of our great-grandmothers knew, even without "knowing" it, the reality of their spirituality, even if they didn't recognize it beyond what happened in the singing at church—and they never had any intention of giving it up.

How they did it—those millions of black women who were not Phillis Wheatley, or Lucy Terry or Frances Harper or Zora Hurston or Nella Larsen or Bessie Smith; or Elizabeth Catlett, or Katherine Dunham, either—brings me to the title of this essay, "In Search of Our Mothers' Gardens," which is a personal account that is yet shared, in its theme and its meaning, by all of us. I found, while thinking about the far-reaching world of the creative black woman, that often the truest answer to a question that really matters can be found very close.

In the late 1920s my mother ran away from home to marry my father. Marriage, if not running away, was expected of seventeen-year-old girls. By the time she was twenty, she had two children and was pregnant with a third. Five children later, I was born. And this is how I came to know my mother: she seemed a large, soft, loving-eyed woman who was rarely impatient in our home. Her quick, violent temper was on view only a few times a year, when she battled with the white landlord who had the misfortune to suggest to her that her children did not need to go to school.

She made all the clothes we wore, even my brothers' overalls. She made all the towels and sheets we used. She spent the summers canning vegetables and fruits. She spent the winter evenings making quilts enough to cover all our beds.

During the "working" day, she labored beside—not behind—my father in the fields. Her day began before sunup, and did not end until late at night. There was never a moment for her to sit down, undisturbed, to unravel her own private thoughts; never a time free from interruption—by work or the noisy inquiries of her many children. And yet, it is to my mother—and all our mothers who were not famous—that I went in search of the secret of what has fed that muzzled and often mutilated, but vibrant, creative spirit that the black woman has inherited, and that pops out in wild and unlikely places to this day.

But when, you will ask, did my overworked mother have time to know or care about feeding the creative spirit?

The answer is so simple that many of us have spent years discovering it. We have constantly looked high, when we should have looked high—and low.

For example: in the Smithsonian Institution in Washington, D.C., there hangs a quilt unlike any other in the world. In fanciful, inspired, and yet simple and identifiable figures, it portrays the story of the Crucifixion. It is considered rare, beyond price. Though it follows no known pattern of quilt-making, and though it is made of bits and pieces of worthless rags, it is obviously the work of a person of powerful imagination and deep spiritual feeling. Below this quilt I saw a note that says it was made by "an anonymous Black woman in Alabama, a hundred years ago."

If we could locate this "anonymous" black woman from Alabama, she would turn out to be one of our grandmothers—an artist who left her mark in the only materials she could afford, and in the only medium her position in society allowed her to use.

As Virginia Woolf wrote further, in *A Room of One's Own*:

> Yet genius of a sort must have existed among women as it must have existed among the working class. [Change this to "slaves" and "the wives and daughters of sharecroppers."] Now and again an Emily Brontë or a Robert Burns [change this to "a Zora Hurston or a Richard Wright"] blazes out and proves its presence. But certainly it never got itself on to paper. When, however, one reads of a witch being ducked, of a woman possessed by devils [or "Sainthood"], of a wise woman selling herbs [our root workers], or even a very remarkable man who had

a mother, then I think we are on the track of a lost novelist, a suppressed poet, of some mute and inglorious Jane Austen. . . . Indeed, I would venture to guess that Anon, who wrote so many poems without signing them, was often a woman. . .

And so our mothers and grandmothers have, more often than not anonymously, handed on the creative spark, the seed of the flower they themselves never hoped to see: or like a sealed letter they could not plainly read.

And so it is, certainly, with my own mother. Unlike "Ma" Rainey's songs, which retained their creator's name even while blasting forth from Bessie Smith's mouth, no song or poem will bear my mother's name. Yet so many of the stories that I write, that we all write, are my mother's stories. Only recently did I fully realize this: that through years of listening to my mother's stories of her life, I have absorbed not only the stories themselves, but something of the manner in which she spoke, something of the urgency that involves the knowledge that her stories—like her life—must be recorded. It is probably for this reason that so much of what I have written is about characters whose counterparts in real life are so much older than I am.

But the telling of these stories, which came from my mother's lips as naturally as breathing, was not the only way my mother showed herself as an artist. For stories, too, were subject to being distracted, to dying without conclusion. Dinners must be started, and cotton must be gathered before the big rains. The artist that was and is my mother showed itself to me only after many years. This is what I finally noticed:

Like Mem, a character in *The Third Life of Grange Copeland,* my mother adorned with flowers whatever shabby house we were forced to live in. And not just your typical straggly country stand of zinnias, either. She planted ambitious gardens—and still does—with over fifty different varieties of plants that bloom profusely from early March until late November. Before she left home for the fields, she watered her flowers, chopped up the grass, and laid out new beds. When she returned from the fields she might divide clumps of bulbs, dig a cold pit, uproot and replant roses, or prune branches from her taller bushes or trees—until night came and it was too dark to see.

Whatever she planted grew as if by magic, and her fame as a grower of flowers spread over three counties. Because of her creativity with her flowers, even my memories of poverty are seen through a screen of blooms—sunflowers, petunias, roses, dahlias, forsythia, spirea, delphiniums, verbena . . . and on and on.

And I remember people coming to my mother's yard to be given cuttings from her flowers; I hear again the praise showered on her because whatever rocky soil she landed on, she turned into a garden. A garden so brilliant with colors, so original in its design, so magnificent with life and creativity, that to this day people drive by our house in Georgia—perfect strangers and imperfect strangers—and ask to stand or walk among my mother's art.

I notice that it is only when my mother is working in her flowers that she is radiant, almost to the point of being invisible—except as Creator: hand and eye. She is involved in work her soul must have. Ordering the universe in the image of her personal conception of Beauty.

Her face, as she prepares the Art that is her gift, is a legacy of respect she leaves to me, for all that illuminates and cherishes life. She has handed down respect for the possibilities—and the will to grasp them.

For her, so hindered and intruded upon in so many ways, being an artist has still been a daily part of her life. This ability to hold on, even in very simple ways, is work black women have done for a very long time.

This poem is not enough, but it is something, for the woman who literally covered the holes in our walls with sunflowers:

> They were women then
> My mama's generation
> Husky of voice—Stout of
> Step
> With fists as well as
> Hands
> How they battered down
> Doors
> And ironed
> Starched white
> Shirts
> How they led
> Armies
> Headragged Generals
> Across mined
> Fields
> Booby-trapped
> Kitchens
> To discover books
> Desks
> A place for us
> How they knew what we
> *Must* know
> Without knowing a page
> Of it
> Themselves.

Guided by my heritage of a love of beauty and a respect for strength—in search of my mother's garden, I found my own.

And perhaps in Africa over two hundred years ago, there was just such a mother, perhaps she painted vivid and daring decorations in oranges and yellows and greens on the walls of her hut; perhaps she sang—in a voice like Roberta Flack's—*sweetly* over the compounds of her village; perhaps she wove the most stunning mats or told the most ingenious stories of all the village storytellers. Perhaps she was herself a poet—though only her daughter's name is signed to the poems that we know.

Perhaps Phillis Wheatley's mother was also an artist.

Perhaps in more than Phillis Wheatley's biological life is her mother's signature made clear.

GLORIA ANZALDÚA (b. 1946)
United States

Gloria Anzaldúa is a Chicano lesbian-feminist writer, whose autobiographical *Borderlands/La Frontera: The New Mestiza* (1987) written in Spanish and English, speaks of her experience in a bilingual community. "We Call Them Greasers," published in an anthology of gay and lesbian poetry, is a bitter attack on intolerance of otherness.

We Call Them Greasers

I found them here when I came.
They were growing corn in their small *ranchos*
raising cattle, horses
smelling of woodsmoke and sweat.
They knew their betters: 5
took off their hats
placed them over their hearts,
lowered their eyes in my presence.

Weren't interested in bettering themselves,
why they didn't even own the land but shared it.   10
Wasn't hard to drive them off,
cowards, they were, no backbone.
I showed 'em a piece of paper with some writing
tole 'em they owed taxes
had to pay right away or be gone by *mañana*.   15
By the time me and my men had waved
that same piece of paper to all the families
it was all frayed at the ends.

Some loaded their chickens children wives and pigs
into rickety wagons, pans and tools dangling   20
clanging from all sides.
Couldn't take their cattle—
during the night my boys had frightened them off.
Oh, there were a few troublemakers
who claimed we were the intruders.   25
Some even had land grants
and appealed to the courts.
It was a laughing stock
them not even knowing English.
Still some refused to budge,   30

even after we burned them out.
And the women—well I remember one in particular.
She lay under me whimpering.
I plowed into her hard
kept thrusting and thrusting   35
felt him watching from the mesquite tree
heard him keening like a wild animal
in that instant I felt such contempt for her
round face and beady black eyes like an Indian's.
Afterwards I sat on her face until   40
her arms stopped flailing.
didn't want to waste a bullet on her.
The boys wouldn't look me in the eyes.
I walked up to where I had tied her man to the tree
and spat in his face. Lynch him, I told the boys.   45

LESLIE SILKO (b. 1948)
United States

Leslie Marmon Silko was brought up on the Laguna Pueblo Reservation, where her family has lived for generations. *Laguna Woman: Poems* (1974) was her first book, followed by a novel *Ceremony* (1977), *Storyteller* (1981), a storytelling event, the novel *Alamanac of the Dead* (1991) and her recent self-published *Sacred Water* (1993). She is also a muralist and has begun her own press in the mountains west of Tucson, Arizona. She teaches at the University of Arizona. "Lullaby" is set in a Navajo community not far from Laguna Pueblo. The Navajo, or the Dineh, one of the largest tribes in North America, are known for their skill in weaving and raising sheep. Tuberculosis was epidemic and swept the region several times during the late nineteenth and early twentieth century. Many of the people were hospitalized; many died. A lullaby is a song to sing children to sleep, but here the lullaby functions as a song to be sung over a patient to restore balance in his or her life and in the lives of all people. The past interacts with the present: time is eternal and ever moving.

from *Storyteller*

Lullaby

The sun had gone down but the snow in the wind gave off its own light. It came in thick tufts like new wool—washed before the weaver spins it. Ayah reached out for it like her own babies had, and she smiled when she remembered how she had laughed at them. She was an old woman now, and her life had become memories. She sat down with her back against the wide cottonwood tree, feeling the rough bark on her back bones; she faced east and listened to the wind and snow sing a high-pitched Yeibechei[1] song. Out of the wind she felt warmer, and she could watch the wide fluffy snow fill in her tracks, steadily, until the direction she had come from was gone. By the light of the snow she could see the dark outline of the big arroyo[2] a few feet away. She was sitting on the edge of Cebolleta Creek, where in the springtime the thin cows would graze on grass already chewed flat to the ground. In the wide deep creek bed where only a trickle of water flowed in the summer, the skinny cows would wander, looking for new grass along winding paths splashed with manure.

Ayah pulled the old Army blanket over her head like a shawl. Jimmie's blanket—the one he had sent to her. That was a long time ago and the green wool was faded, and it was unraveling on the edges. She did not want to think about Jimmie. So she thought about the weaving and the way her mother had done it. On the tall wooden loom set into the sand under a tamarack tree for shade. She could see it clearly. She had been only a little girl when her grandma gave her the wooden combs to pull the twigs and burrs from the raw, freshly washed wool. And while she combed the wool, her grandma sat beside her, spinning a silvery, strand of yarn around the smooth cedar spindle. Her mother worked at the loom with yarns dyed bright yellow and red and gold. She watched them dye the yarn in boiling black pots full of beeweed petals, juniper berries, and sage. The blankets her mother made were soft and woven so tight that rain rolled off them like birds' feathers. Ayah remembered sleeping warm on cold windy nights, wrapped in her mother's blankets on the hogan's[3] sandy floor.

The snow drifted now, with the northwest wind hurling it in gusts. It drifted up around her black overshoes—old ones with little metal buckles. She smiled at the snow which was trying to cover her little by little. She could remember when they had no black rubber overshoes; only the high buckskin leggings that they wrapped over their elkhide moccasins. If the snow was dry or frozen, a person could walk all day and not get wet; and in the evenings the beams of the ceiling would hang with lengths of pale buckskin leggings, drying out slowly.

She felt peaceful remembering. She didn't feel cold any more. Jimmie's blanket seemed warmer than it had ever been. And she could remember the morning he was born. She could remember whispering to her mother, who was sleeping on the other side of the hogan, to tell her it was time now. She did not want to wake the others. The second time she called to her, her mother stood up and pulled on her shoes; she knew. They walked to the old stone hogan together, Ayah walking a step behind her mother. She waited alone, learning the rhythms of the pains while her mother went to call the old woman to help them. The

---

1. Masked dancers who become deities during a Navajo Nightway Ceremony conducted to restore balance.

2. A watercourse, usually dry until there is rain.

3. A traditional Navajo home, with the doorway to the east. The site of daily living and ceremonies.

morning was already warm even before dawn and Ayah smelled the bee flowers blooming and the young willow growing at the springs. She could remember that so clearly, but his birth merged into the births of the other children and to her it became all the same birth. They named him for the summer morning and in English they called him Jimmie.

It wasn't like Jimmie died. He just never came back, and one day a dark blue sedan with white writing on its doors pulled up in front of the boxcar shack where the rancher let the Indians live. A man in a khaki uniform trimmed in gold gave them a yellow piece of paper and told them that Jimmie was dead. He said the Army would try to get the body back and then it would be shipped to them; but it wasn't likely because the helicopter had burned after it crashed. All of this was told to Chato because he could understand English. She stood inside the doorway holding the baby while Chato listened. Chato spoke English like a white man and he spoke Spanish too. He was taller than the white man and he stood straighter too. Chato didn't explain why; he just told the military man they could keep the body if they found it. The white man looked bewildered; he nodded his head and he left. Then Chato looked at her and shook his head, and then he told her, "Jimmie isn't coming home anymore," and when he spoke, he used the words to speak of the dead. She didn't cry then, but she hurt inside with anger. And she mourned him as the years passed, when a horse fell with Chato and broke his leg, and the white rancher told them he wouldn't pay Chato until he could work again. She mourned Jimmie because he would have worked for his father then; he would have saddled the big bay horse and ridden the fence lines each day, with wire cutters and heavy gloves, fixing the breaks in the barbed wire and putting the stray cattle back inside again.

She mourned him after the white doctors came to take Danny and Ella away. She was at the shack alone that day they came. It was back in the days before they hired Navajo women to go with them as interpreters. She recognized one of the doctors. She had seen him at the children's clinic at Cañoncito about a month ago. They were wearing khaki uniforms and they waved papers at her and a black ball-point pen, trying to make her understand their English words. She was frightened by the way they looked at the children, like the lizard watches the fly. Danny was swinging on the tire swing on the elm tree behind the rancher's house, and Ella was toddling around the front door, dragging the broomstick horse Chato made for her. Ayah could see they wanted her to sign the papers, and Chato had taught her to sign her name. It was something she was proud of. She only wanted them to go, and to take their eyes away from her children.

She took the pen from the man without looking at his face and she signed the papers in three different places he pointed to. She stared at the ground by their feet and waited for them to leave. But they stood there and began to point and gesture at the children. Danny stopped swinging. Ayah could see his fear. She moved suddenly and grabbed Ella into her arms; the child squirmed, trying to get back to her toys. Ayah ran with the baby toward Danny; she screamed for him to run and then she grabbed him around his chest and carried him too. She ran south into the foothills of juniper trees and black lava rock. Behind her she heard the doctors running, but they had been taken by surprise, and as the hills became steeper and the cholla cactus were thicker, they stopped. When she reached the top of the hill, she stopped to listen in case they were circling around her. But in a few minutes she heard a car engine start and they drove away. The children had been too surprised to cry while she ran with them. Danny was shaking and Ella's little fingers were gripping Ayah's blouse.

She stayed up in the hills for the rest of the day, sitting on a black lava boulder in the sunshine where she could see for miles all around her. The sky was light blue and cloudless, and it was warm for late April. The sun warmth relaxed her and took the fear and anger away. She lay back on the rock and watched the sky. It seemed to her that she could walk into the sky, stepping through clouds endlessly. Danny played with little pebbles and stones, pretending they were birds eggs and then little rabbits. Ella sat at her feet and dropped fistfuls of dirt into the breeze, watching the dust and particles of sand intently. Ayah watched a hawk soar high above them, dark wings gliding; hunting or only watching, she did not know. The hawk was patient and he circled all afternoon before he disappeared around the high volcanic peak the Mexicans called Guadalupe.

Late in the afternoon, Ayah looked down at the gray boxcar shack with the paint all peeled from the wood; the stove pipe on the roof was rusted and crooked. The fire she had built that morning in the oil drum stove had burned out. Ella was asleep in her lap now and Danny sat close to her, complaining that he was hungry; he asked when they would go to the house. "We will stay up here until your father comes," she told him, "because those white men were chasing us." The boy remembered then and he nodded at her silently.

If Jimmie had been there he could have read those papers and explained to her what they said. Ayah would have known then, never to sign them. The doctors came back the next day and they brought a BIA[4] policeman with them. They told Chato they had her signature and that was all they needed Except for the kids. She listened to Chato sullenly; she hated him when he told her it was the old woman who died in the winter, spitting blood; it was her old grandma who had given the children this disease. "They don't spit blood," she said coldly. "The whites lie." She held Ella and Danny close to her, ready to run to the hills again. "I want a medicine man first," she said to Chato, not looking at him. He shook his head. "It's too late now. The policeman is with them. You signed the paper." His voice was gentle.

It was worse than if they had died: to lose the children and to know that somewhere, in a place called Colorado, in a place full of sick and dying strangers, her children were without her. There had been babies that died soon after they were born, and one that died before he could walk. She had carried them herself, up to the boulders and great pieces of the cliff that long ago crashed down from Long Mesa; she laid them in the crevices of sandstone and buried them in fine brown sand with round quartz pebbles that washed down the hills in the rain. She had endured it because they had been with her. But she could not bear this pain. She did not sleep for a long time after they took her children. She stayed on the hill where they had fled the first time, and she slept rolled up in the blanket Jimmie had sent her. She carried the pain in her belly and it was fed by everything

---

4. The Bureau of Indian Affairs.

she saw: the blue sky of their last day together and the dust and pebbles they played with; the swing in the elm tree and broomstick horse choked life from her. The pain filled her stomach and there was no room for food or for her lungs to fill with air. The air and the food would have been theirs.

She hated Chato, not because he let the policeman and doctors put the screaming children in the government car, but because he had taught her to sign her name. Because it was like the old ones always told her about learning their language or any of their ways: it endangered you. She slept alone on the hill until the middle of November when the first snows came. Then she made a bed for herself where the children had slept. She did not lie down beside Chato again until many years later, when he was sick and shivering and only her body could keep him warm. The illness came after the white rancher told Chato he was too old to work for him anymore, and Chato and his old woman should be out of the shack by the next afternoon because the rancher had hired new people to work there. That had satisfied her. To see how the white man repaid Chato's years of loyalty and work. All of Chato's fine-sounding English talk didn't change things.

It snowed steadily and the luminous light from the snow gradually diminished into the darkness. Somewhere in Cebolleta a dog barked and other village dogs joined with it. Ayah looked in the direction she had come, from the bar where Chato was buying the wine. Sometimes he told her to go on ahead and wait; and then he never came. And when she finally went back looking for him, she would find him passed out at the bottom of the wooden steps to Azzie's Bar. All the wine would be gone and most of the money too, from the pale blue check that came to them once a month in a government envelope. It was then that she would look at his face and his hands, scarred by ropes and the barbed wire of all those years, and she would think, this man is a stranger; for forty years she had smiled at him and cooked his food, but he remained a stranger. She stood up again, with the snow almost to her knees, and she walked back to find Chato.

It was hard to walk in the deep snow and she felt the air burn in her lungs. She stopped a short distance from the bar to rest and readjust the blanket. But this time he wasn't waiting for her on the bottom step with his old Stetson hat pulled down and his shoulders hunched up in his long wool overcoat.

She was careful not to slip on the wooden steps. When she pushed the door open, warm air and cigarette smoke hit her face. She looked around slowly and deliberately, in every corner, in every dark place that the old man might find to sleep. The bar owner didn't like Indians in there, especially Navajos, but he let Chato come in because he could talk Spanish like he was one of them. The men at the bar stared at her, and the bartender saw that she left the door open wide. Snowflakes were flying inside like moths and melting into a puddle on the oiled wood floor. He motioned to her to close the door, but she did not see him. She held herself straight and walked across the room slowly, searching the room with every step. The snow in her hair melted and she could feel it on her forehead. At the far corner of the room, she saw red flames at the mica window of the old stove door; she looked behind the stove just to make sure. The bar got quiet except for the Spanish polka music playing on the jukebox. She stood by the stove and shook the snow from her blanket and held it near the stove to dry. The wet wool smell reminded her of new-born goats in early March, brought inside to warm near the fire. She felt calm.

In past years they would have told her to get out. But her hair was white now and her face was wrinkled. They looked at her like she was a spider crawling slowly across the room. They were afraid; she could feel the fear. She looked at their faces steadily. The reminded her of the first time the white people brought her children back to her that winter. Danny had been shy and hid behind the thin white woman who brought them. And the baby had not known her until Ayah took her into her arms, and then Ella had nuzzled close to her as she had when she was nursing. The blonde woman was nervous and kept looking at a dainty gold watch on her wrist. She sat on the bench near the small window and watched the dark snow clouds gather around the mountains; she was worrying about the unpaved road. She was frightened by what she saw inside too: the strips of venison drying on a rope across the ceiling and the children jabbering excitedly in a language she did not know. So they stayed for only a few hours. Ayah watched the government car disappear down the road and she knew they were already being weaned from these lava hills and from this sky. The last time they came was in early June, and Ella stared at her the way the men in the bar were now staring. Ayah did not try to pick her up; she smiled at her instead and spoke cheerfully to Danny. When he tried to answer her, he could not seem to remember and he spoke English words with the Navajo. But he gave her a scrap of paper that he had found somewhere and carried in his pocket; it was folded in half, and he shyly looked up at her and said it was a bird. She asked Chato if they were home for good this time. He spoke to the white woman and she shook her head. "How much longer?" he asked, and she said she didn't know; but Chato saw how she stared at the boxcar shack. Ayah turned away then. She did not say good-bye.

She felt satisfied that the men in the bar feared her. Maybe it was her face and the way she held her mouth with teeth clenched tight, like there was nothing anyone could do to her now. She walked north down the road, searching for the old man. She did this because she had the blanket, and there would be no place for him except with her and the blanket in the old adobe barn near the arroyo. They always slept there when they came to Cebolleta. If the money and the wine were gone, she would be relieved because then they could go home again; back to the old hogan with a dirt roof and rock walls where she herself had been born. And the next day the old man could go back to the few sheep they still had, to follow along behind them, guiding them, into dry sandy arroyos where sparse grass grew. She knew he did not like walking behind old ewes when for so many years he rode big quarter horses and worked with cattle. But she wasn't sorry for him; he should have known all along what would happen.

There had not been enough rain for their garden in five years; and that was when Chato finally hitched a ride into the town and brought back brown boxes of rice and sugar and big tin cans of welfare peaches. After that, at the first of the month they went to Cebolleta to ask the postmaster for the check; and then Chato would go to the bar and cash it. They did this as they planted the garden every

May, not because anything would survive the summer dust, but because it was time to do this. The journey passed the days that smelled silent and dry like the caves above the canyon with yellow painted buffaloes on their walls.

He was walking along the pavement when she found him. He did not stop or turn around when he heard her behind him. She walked beside him and she noticed how slowly he moved now. He smelled strong of woodsmoke and urine. Lately he had been forgetting. Sometimes he called her by his sister's name and she had been gone for a long time. Once she had found him wandering on the road to the white man's ranch, and she asked him why he was going that way; he laughed at her and said, "You know they can't run that ranch without me," and he walked on determined, limping on the leg that had been crushed many years before. Now he looked at her curiously, as if for the first time, but he kept shuffling along, moving slowly along the side of the highway. His gray hair had grown long and spread out on the shoulders of the long overcoat. He wore the old felt hat pulled down over his ears. His boots were worn out at the toes and he had stuffed pieces of an old red shirt in the holes. The rags made his feet look like little animals up to their ears in snow. She laughed at his feet; the snow muffled the sound of her laugh. He stopped and looked at her again. The wind had quit blowing and the snow was falling straight down; the southeast sky was beginning to clear and Ayah could see a star.

"Let's rest awhile," she said to him. They walked away from the road and up the slope to the giant boulders that had tumbled down from the red sandrock mesa throughout the centuries of rainstorms and earth tremors. In a place where the boulders shut out the wind, they sat down with their backs against the rock. She offered half of the blanket to him and they sat wrapped together.

The storm passed swiftly. The clouds moved east. They were massive and full, crowding together across the sky. She watched them with the feeling of horses—steely blue-gray horses startled across the sky. The powerful haunches pushed into the distances and the tail hairs streamed white mist behind them. The sky cleared. Ayah saw that there was nothing between her and the stars. The light was crystalline. There was no shimmer, no distortion through earth haze. She breathed the clarity of the night sky; she smelled the purity of the half moon and the stars. He was lying on his side with his knees pulled up near his belly for warmth. His eyes were closed now, and in the light from the stars and the moon, he looked young again.

She could see it descend out of the night sky: an icy stillness from the edge of the thin moon. She recognized the freezing. It came gradually, sinking snowflake by snowflake until the crust was heavy and deep. It had the strength of the stars in Orion, and its journey was endless. Ayah knew that with the wine he would sleep. He would not feel it. She tucked the blanket around him, remembering how it was when Ella had been with her; and she felt the rush so big inside her heart for the babies. And she sang the only song she knew to sing for babies. She could not remember if she had ever sung it to her children, but she knew that her grandmother had sung it and her mother had sung it:

The earth is your mother,
she holds you.

The sky is your father,
  he protects you.
Sleep,
sleep.
Rainbow is your sister,
  she loves you.
The winds are your brothers,
  they sing to you.
Sleep,
sleep.
We are together always
We are together always
There never was a time
when this
was not so.

MELVIN DIXON (1950–1992)
United States

Winner of the Richard Wright Award for *Black World* magazine in 1974, equally at home in French and English, Melvin Dixon taught at Queens College of the City University of New York until he died an early death from AIDS. As well as writing widely on the slave narrative, Dixon was a published poet (*Change of Territory*, 1983 and many individual poems in leading magazines), as well as a translator of contemporary African-American theater. This poem comes from the anthology *Poets for Life: Seventy-Six Poets Respond to AIDS*.

Heartbeats

Work out. Ten laps.
Chin ups. Look good.

Steam room. Dress warm.
Call home. Fresh air.

Eat right. Rest well.
Sweetheart. Safe sex.

Sore throat. Long flu.
Hard nodes. Beware.

Test blood. Count cells.
Reds thin. Whites low.

Dress warm. Eat well.
Short breath. Fatigue.

Night sweats. Dry cough.
Loose stools. Weight loss.

Get mad. Fight back. 15
Call home. Rest well.

Don't cry. Take charge.
No sex. Eat right.

Call home. Talk slow.
Chin up. No air. 20

Arms wide. Nodes hard.
Cough dry. Hold on.

Mouth wide. Drink this.
Breathe in. Breathe out.

No air. Breathe in. 25
Breathe in. No air.

Black out. White rooms.
Head hot. Feet cold.

No work. Eat right.
CAT scan. Chin up. 30

Breathe in. Breathe out.
No air. No air.

Thin blood. Sore lungs.
Mouth dry. Mind gone.

Six months? Three weeks? 35
Can't eat. No air.

Today? Tonight?
It waits. For me.

Sweet heart. Don't stop.
Breathe in. Breathe out. 40

JOY HARJO (b. 1951)
United States

Born in Oklahoma and a member of the Creek tribe, Joy Harjo attended the
University of New Mexico and the Iowa Writer's Workshop, and now teaches at

the University of New Mexico. Her poetry collections include *The Last Song* (1975), *What Room Drove Me to This?* (1980), *She Had Some Horses* (1983), and *In Mad Love and War* (1990). She is also a musician and plays saxophone with her band, Poetic Justice. "Deer Dancer" is a meeting place for genres: it is storytelling mixed with poetry. It also includes an excerpt of a lyric from a popular country western song, as well as references to contemporary culture (such as the Led Zeppelin song "Stairway to Heaven" and a book of poetry by poet Jorie Graham, *The End of Beauty*). The figure of the Deer Woman is central. In many stories told in and around the Creek Nation she represents transformation. The deer sacrifices herself for the people, so that they may live.

"Eagle Poem" is a prayer that serves as a blessing for all who hear or read it. It takes on the shape of the eagle's flight as it blesses all who take part in its vision. It was influenced by a Navajo song that asks that beauty surround all our acts.

Deer Dancer

Nearly everyone had left that bar in the middle of winter except the hardcore. It was the coldest night of the year, every place shut down but not us. Of course we noticed when she came in. We were Indian ruins. She was the end of beauty. No one knew her, the stranger whose tribe we recognized, her family related to deer, if that's who she was, a people accustomed to hearing songs in pine trees, and making them hearts.

The woman inside the woman who was to dance naked in the bar of misfits blew deer magic. Henry Jack, who could not survive a sober day, thought she was Buffalo Calf Woman[1] come back, passed out, his head by the toilet. All night he dreamed a dream he could not say. The next day he borrowed money, went home, and sent back the money I lent. Now that's a miracle. Some people see vision in a burned tortilla, some in the face of a woman.

This is the bar of broken survivors, the club of shotgun, knife wound, of poison by culture. We who were taught not to stare drank our beer. The players gossiped down their cues. Someone put a quarter in the jukebox to relive despair. Richard's wife dove to kill her. We had to hold her back, empty her pockets of knives and diaper pins, buy her two beers to keep her still, while Richard secretly bought the beauty a drink.

How do I say it? In this language there are no words for how the real world collapses. I could say it in my own and the sacred mounds would come into focus, but I couldn't take it in this dingy envelope. So I look at the stars in this strange city, frozen to the back of the sky, the only promises that ever make sense.

My brother-in-law hung out with white people, went to law school with a perfect record, quit. Says you can keep your laws, your words. And practiced law on the

---

1. A beloved spirit of the Sioux people who brought them the sacred pipe.

street with his hands. He jimmied to the proverbial dream girl, the face of the moon, while the players racked a new game. He bragged to us, he told her magic words and that's when she broke, became human. But we all heard his bar voice crack:

What's a girl like you doing in a place like this?

That's what I'd like to know, what are we all doing in a place like this?

You would know she could hear only what she wanted to; don't we all? Left the drink of betrayal Richard bought her, at the bar. What was she on? We all wanted some. Put a quarter in the juke. We all take risks stepping into this air. Our ceremonies didn't predict this. Or we expected more.

I had to tell you this, for the baby inside the girl sealed up with a lick of hope and swimming into praise of nations. This is not a rooming house, but a dream of winter falls and the deer who portrayed the relatives of strangers. The way back is deer breath on icy windows.

The next dance none of us predicted. She borrowed a chair for the stairway to heaven and stood on a table of names. And danced in the room of children without shoes.

You picked a fine time to leave me, Lucille.
With four hungry children and a crop in the field.

And then she took off her clothes. She shook loose memory, waltzed with the empty lover we'd all become.

She was the myth slipped down through dreamtime. The promise of feast we all knew was coming. The deer who crossed through knots of a curse to find us. She was no slouch, and neither were we, watching.

The music ended. And so does the story. I wasn't there. But I imagined her like this, not a stained red dress with tape on her heels but the deer who entered our dream in white dawn, breathed mist into pine trees, her fawn a blessing of meat, the ancestors who never left.

from **In Mad Love and War**

Eagle Poem

To pray you open your whole self
To sky, to earth, to sun, to moon
To one whole voice that is you.

And know there is more
That you can't see, can't hear,   5
Can't know except in moments
Steadily growing, and in languages
That aren't always sound but other
Circles of motion.
Like eagle that Sunday morning   10
Over Salt River.[1] Circled in blue sky
In wind, swept our hearts clean
With sacred wings.
We see you, see ourselves and know
That we must take the utmost care   15
And kindness in all things.
Breathe in, knowing we are made of
All this, and breathe, knowing
We are truly blessed because we
Were born, and die soon within a   20
True circle of motion,
Like eagle rounding out the morning
Inside us.
We pray that it will be done
In beauty.   25
In beauty.

LOUISE ERDRICH (b. 1954)
United States

Louise Erdrich, of mixed heritage—French, Chippewa, and German—grew up
on reservations in North Dakota and Minnesota. She is a poet (*Jacklight*, 1984),
short-story writer, and novelist (*Love Medicine* 1984, *The Beet Queen*, 1986,
Tracks, 1988).

For native peoples, hunting is a very complex endeavor, as we infer from the
poem "Jacklight." The deer has to be enticed to the hunter; this was often done
through songs and prayer. Tribal customs vary. The deer was seen as a sacrifice
so that people might live. A jacklight is a light used to attract the animals to the
hunter who bears the light, putting the hunter at an unfair advantage. This poem
relies on the play between the hunter and the hunted. We are left to wonder if the
hunters call the deer, or if the deer attract the hunters?

---

1. The Salt River Indian Reservation near
Phoenix, Arizona.

Jacklight

The same Chippewa word is used both
for flirting and hunting game while
another Chippewa word connotes both
using force in intercourse and also
killing a bear with one's bare hands.

—DUNNING 1959

We have come to the edge of the woods,
out of brown grass where we slept, unseen,
out of knotted twigs, out of leaves creaked shut,
out of hiding.

At first the light wavered, glancing over us.   5
Then it clenched to a fist of light that pointed,
searched out, divided us.
Each took the beams like direct blows the heart answers.
Each of us moved forward alone.

We have come to the edge of the woods,   10
drawn out of ourselves by this night sun,
this battery of polarized acids,
that outshines the moon.

We smell them behind it
but they are faceless, invisible.   15
We smell the raw steel of their gun barrels,
mink oil on leather, their tongues of sour barley.
We smell their mother buried chin-deep in wet dirt.

We smell their fathers with scoured knuckles,
teeth cracked from hot marrow.   20
We smell their sisters of crushed dogwood, bruised apples,
of fractured cups and concussions of burnt hooks.

We smell their breath steaming lightly behind the jacklight.
We smell the itch underneath the caked guts on their clothes.
We smell their minds like silver hammers   25
cocked back, held in readiness
for the first of us to step into the open.

We have come to the edge of the woods,
out of brown grass where we slept, unseen,
out of leaves creaked shut, out of our hiding.   30
We have come here too long.

It is their turn now,
their turn to follow us. Listen,

they put down their equipment.
It is useless in the tall brush.   35
And now they take the first steps, not knowing
how deep the woods are and lightless.
How deep the woods are.

LI-YOUNG LEE (b. 1957)
Indonesia/United States

Li-Young Lee was born to Chinese parents in 1957 in Jakarta, Indonesia. His
father was a political prisoner under Sukarno's presidency. The family fled
Indonesia in 1959 and eventually settled in America in 1964. This moving poem
takes us from the collective meal of a living family to a single death, somehow
absorbed into a landscape beyond sorrow and solitude.

Eating Together

In the steamer is the trout
seasoned with slivers of ginger,
two sprigs of green onion, and sesame oil.
We shall eat it with rice for lunch,
brothers, sisters, my mother who will   5
taste the sweetest meat of the head,
holding it between her fingers
deftly, the way my father did
weeks ago. Then he lay down
to sleep like a snow-covered road   10
winding through pines older than him,
without any travelers, and lonely for no one.

CANADA

The problem for the Canadian literary imagination derives from Canada's colonial
history. Literature since the Renaissance must be tied to a national territory

whose mark of identity is language. Canadians writing in English break this chain of nation, language, literature. "Canadian Literature" is a contradiction in terms: to be acknowledged as "good" writers, Canadians must follow the norms of writing in England or more recently, the United States. To be recognized as authentically "Canadian," however, they must break these norms by writing "differently." Writing in Canada in English began in 1583, produced by European explorers whose letters, journals, log books, narratives, petitions, and exhortations to authorities in London turned the imperial gaze comparatively and evaluatively on the Canadian land, estimating its potential economic resources for the imperial power. Following the conquest of French territories (Acadia or the Maritimes in 1713, Quebec in 1759), English-speaking settlers extended this scrutiny to the land's potential for agriculture, to reproduce English culture either as a landed aristocracy for "gentlemen" or as transformed into a democracy through free land grants to all. Tension between these two forms of social organization was heightened by the arrival of United Empire Loyalists in the 1780s after the American Revolution. Both effectively destroyed an indigenous population with vital oral literatures in many languages.

Initially, the emphasis was on "factual" literary genres, works of history, geography, and natural science. Some of the literary forms of exploration and settlement developed as an experiment of the imagination, notably journals, letters and diaries, which became literary sketches, epistolary novels, or pastoral poetry. Written within conflicting institutional codes, those of the imperial center and of what it had colonized, literature in Canada began in the eighteenth and nineteenth centuries to represent this difference thematically by focusing on the rugged Canadian climate and landscape that marked it as a "northern" nation distinct from England and the United States. At the beginning of the twentieth century, with the impetus of literary modernism from Europe, the focus shifted to the shaping power of art, without abandoning the land, as a primary theme of imagist and symbolist poetry and of realistic fiction. In contemporary writing, "Canadian" *difference* is inscribed in language, ambiguous and unstable, undermining all meaning and identity. Lack of identity is read as the sign of Canadianness. Paradoxically, this sense of unidentity is possible because of developments in the literary institution since the centenary of the Canadian Confederation in 1967 that have resulted in the constitution of Canadian Literature as an academic field and a body of texts taught in high schools and universities. Young poets today encounter their predecessors within a history of literature in Canada and no longer situate themselves exclusively in relation to British and American literatures.

The contradiction of a "national" literature is further compounded for many writing in Canada, a settler colony, in that they write in a language other than English or by translating a variety of cultures into English. Canada is an officially bilingual country, with literatures in French and in English. There is also a body of writing by indigenous peoples that, emerging from the colonial archive where it was first transcribed and mediated by administrators in their own terms, constitutes a rapidly expanding body of contemporary writing of resistance or decolonization. Canada also has a policy of official "multiculturalism" that encourages immigrants from many countries of Africa, South America, Asia, and Europe to retain their cultures, though generally not their languages, which remain unofficial. Canadian literary discourse has thus developed between cultures, between languages.

While they inhabit the same physical spaces, the literatures of French and English Canada have followed different cultural paths. French Canadian writers have long been conscious of belonging to what is now termed a "distinct society," a French-speaking (or "Francophone") culture with roots in France and in French Catholicism but located within a North America dominated by a largely Anglo-Protestant tradition. To write in French in this context has been an act of self-definition, on an individual and collective level. In the nineteenth century, as in the turbulent and creative "Quiet Revolution" era of the 1960s. Quiet — in the sense of non-violent — French Canadian writers have been conscious of the role they play in affirming their cultural identity by ensuring the continuing vitality of the French language, although the terms in which this identity has been defined have changed over the years.

As in English Canada, the first works written in Quebec were the product of explorers and missionaries, who marveled at the flora and fauna of a new land and recorded their efforts to convert and educate the native peoples. After a century and a half of settlement by French farmers and fur traders, the vast territory of New France was given over to the British following their military victory on the Plains of Abraham in 1759. The subsequent enforced submission of French North America to British rule disrupted a nascent literary tradition that had been closely linked to France, and the separation from the "mother country" was exacerbated by the French Revolution of 1789, which shocked a French-Canadian population largely respectful of the French monarchy and devoted to the Catholic Church.

Both physically and ideologically distanced from France in the nineteenth century, French Canadians had strong reasons for developing a literary tradition of their own. Many early Quebec writers, encouraged by a clerically dominated literary establishment preoccupied with the problem of French cultural survival, directed their energies toward recreating the French Canadian past, while urban centers saw the formation of a number of literary groups who attempted to define a new, distinctively national literature while retaining their ties to the literature of France. In general, the literature of nineteenth and early twentieth-century Quebec reflected and at times actively promoted the values of a society that saw itself as rural and rooted in tradition.

By the end of World War II, however, writers like Anne Hébert, whose work is included here, and Gabrielle Roy began spontaneously to challenge the traditional structures, both social and literary, that would finally succumb to the sweeping cultural changes of the 1960s. Roy's *The Tin Flute* was, in 1945, the first major Quebec novel to take Montreal as its setting, and Hébert's story "The Torrent" offered an allegorical reading of the collapse of the old rural ideal. The decade of the Quiet Revolution saw an exceptional burst of literary creativity in Quebec, as writers actively sought to define a new national identity that was symbolized by the growing use of the term "Québécois" to replace the older "French Canadian." The poetry of Gaston Miron played a major role in defining this nationalistically-oriented literature, designed to be communicated to a large public and firmly anchored in the linguistic and physical reality of Quebec. As the earliest Quebec literary works had incorporated a rich oral tradition of songs and legends, the writing of the 1960s went back to oral sources, particularly in the work of the popular *chansonniers,* like Gilles Vigneault, who "sang the country." In their effort to create a literary idiom marked distinctively as Québécois, writers often attempted to reproduce the language spoken by the people around them, a project which had a major impact on the theater in the creative use of the

Montreal dialect known as *joual*. This effort to reproduce spoken language was taken up by Francophone writers in other parts of Canada, most notably by the Acadian novelist and playwright Antonine Maillet, who claims the heritage of a long line of storytellers as she recreates the French spoken on the New Brunswick seacoast.

Contemporary writing in Francophone Canada, and particularly in Quebec, has moved beyond questions of identity to address the many and various concerns of modern literatures. The Quebec literary tradition has opened itself to the voices of women who, in the project defined by the feminist poet Nicole Brossard, are consciously "writing in the feminine," as well as to the work of recent arrivals from Europe, the Caribbean, and the Middle East. In the process, contemporary writers are giving new and expanded meaning to the term *Québécois*.

Historical Background

The territories that make up present-day Canada were first settled by the North American Indians and the Inuit (Eskimo). Indians migrated over the Bering Strait from Asia during the last Ice Age and gradually fanned out to people both American continents. The Inuit, a distinct people, populated the arctic and subarctic regions.

The first European visitors to the continent were the Norse, whose ships evidently reached Newfoundland around 1000 C.E. Lasting settlements were not established, however, and the voyage passed into legend, confirmed by archeology only in modern times. The Basques, French and Portuguese fished off Newfoundland in the late fifteenth century. In 1497, Henry Cabot, sailing for England, reached the Canadian coast, landing most probably on Newfoundland. In 1535 and 1536, Jacques Cartier explored the Gulf of Saint Lawrence and ventured up the Saint Lawrence River as far as present-day Montreal, claiming the lands along these waters for France.

Permanent French presence began in the next century, with the founding of Port Royal (present-day Annapolis Royal) in Acadia (the region of Canada centered in Nova Scotia) in 1605 and Quebec in 1608. Over the next century, French explorers, trappers, traders, and missionaries pushed far into the interior, while settlers built up the corridor of the Saint Lawrence River and the thriving towns of Montreal, Trois-Rivières, and Quebec. Following Sir Humphrey Gilbert's 1583 settlement in Newfoundland, west county merchants established a settlement under British royal charter at Conception Bay in 1610. Settlement was slow and discontinuous because of harassment of winter residents by the fishing admirals who held royal authority.

French and British interests in North America clashed from early on. The English colony of Virginia raided Acadia in 1613. In 1629 Quebec fell briefly to the English and Acadia was claimed by Scotland (hence present-day Nova Scotia, or "New Scotland"). In 1670 the Hudson's Bay Company, chartered by England, laid claim to all lands draining into Hudson Bay, boldly challenging French expansion to the north.

From 1689 on, French and British warfare was almost constant, with colonial wars often echoing larger European conflicts. Thus the War of the Spanish Succession (1701–1714) in Europe ignited Queen Anne's War (1702–1713) in

America. British victory secured the Hudson Bay and forced the French to cede Acadia and Newfoundland. The War of Austrian Succession in Europe had its American echo in King George's War (1744–1748), which saw French and British skirmishes at points of tension throughout the colonies. British displeasure at French expansion south from the Great Lakes into the Ohio valley precipitated the French and Indian War (1754–1763) and its European counterpart, the Seven Years War. While early victories fell to the French, the tide soon turned in favor of the British, with the capture of Quebec in 1759 following the famous Battle of the Plains of Abraham serving as the decisive moment. The Treaty of Paris that concluded the war stripped France of all American territories except for a few small islands, and Canada passed to British control.

The task of making British rule palatable to a largely French population was a delicate one. With the Quebec Act of 1774, Britain extended tolerance to the Roman Catholic church, enabled Catholics to hold office, restored French civil law, and recognized French as an official language. Such measures tacitly assumed continuing French dominance in the area. The American Revolution, however, forced thousands of British loyalists (known as the United Empire Loyalists) to seek refuge in Canada; they were easily absorbed in the Maritime region, which had been British since 1713—French speaking Acadians had been expelled in 1755 when war was imminent ("Le Grand dérangement," The Expulsion of the Acadians). In 1784, loyalist settlers were welcomed in Nova Scotia and New Brunswick. Farther west, however, loyalist discontents under French civil law prompted the Constitutional Act of 1791, which divided the dominion of Quebec into Upper Canada, primarily English-speaking (roughly present-day Ontario) and Lower Canada, primarily French (roughly present-day Quebec), each with its own government.

In the early decades of the nineteenth century, expansion, prosperity, and a new wave of immigrants—largely Irish and Scottish—fueled a movement for more democratic government. Reforms proceeded peaceably in the Maritimes, but entrenched colonial powers and a worsening of French/English antagonisms led to rebellions in the Canadas in 1837. Anxious not to lose its remaining North American colonies, Britain responded by reuniting the two Canadas as Canada Province in 1841. Although the union did not succeed in subsuming French separatism into a new sense of Canadian identity, accompanying administrative reforms did lead toward greater autonomy, and responsible government was recognized by the Crown in Nova Scotia and Canada by 1848. In the 1860s, the long-discussed idea of Confederation gained momentum, and in 1867 the British North America Act united the colonies of Nova Scotia, New Brunswick, and Canada (divided now into the provinces of Quebec and Ontario) as the Dominion of Canada.

Over the course of the nineteenth century, Canada expanded to embrace almost all of British North America. In 1869 the Dominion purchased Rupert's Land—the holdings of the Hudson's Bay Company. From the southern portion, the province of Manitoba was organized and added to the confederation in 1870. The colony of British Columbia joined the following year, and Prince Edward Island joined in 1873. The transcontinental railroad completed in 1885 provided a corridor for settlement of the Canadian West to the Rockies, and in 1905 Alberta and Saskatchewan were organized and added to the union. Newfoundland maintained the longest independent existence, joining Canada only in 1949.

Despite the insistence on French and English parity in the British North America Act of 1867, which essentially served as Canada's constitution until 1982, events regularly rekindled old grievances between English- and French-speaking populations. The formation of Manitoba, Alberta, and Saskatchewan was accomplished after open conflict with a French-speaking and Métis population. Struggle, sometimes as fierce as in 1892, over the use of French in schools, continued for a century. Some French schooling was provided for, but nowhere was the dual system of Quebec fully replicated. Canada's allegiance to the British Crown, first as a British colony and subsequently as a member of the British Commonwealth, also proved divisive, especially during the conscription systems that were enacted by overwhelmingly English governments during the last years of each of the two world wars.

The province of Quebec in particular came to embody a paradox. Historically French, it became the most populous, industrialized, and wealthy portion of Canada. Yet its economic power was concentrated almost exclusively in the hands of an English-speaking minority. Conservative leadership, closely allied to the Catholic Church, dominated political life in Quebec through the 1950s—a particularly stifling period known as "The Great Darkness"—and continued to encourage American and English-Canadian development. Opposition grew steadily, however, and with the election of a Liberal government in 1960, Quebec entered a decade of reform known as the Quiet Revolution, which fostered the resurgence of a determinedly French spirit and culture. Quebec's insistence on constitutional recognition of its "special status" as a French province has been at the center of recent Constitutional debates which have also concerned the claims to greater self government of the "First Nations" or native peoples (North American Indian and Inuit) in relation to the "Founding Nations," (French and English), that may ultimately redefine the nature of the Canadian federation.

Further Readings

Blodgett, E. D. *Configuration: Essays on the Canadian Literatures*. Toronto: Essays in Canadian Writing, 1982.

Cagnon, Maurice. *The French Novel of Quebec*. Boston: Twayne Publishers, 1986.

Davidson, Arnold E, ed. *Studies on Canadian Literature*. New York: Modern Language Association, 1990.

Godard, Barbara, ed. *Gynocritics/Gynocritiques: Feminist Approaches to Canadian and Quebec Women Writers*. Toronto: Essays in Canadian Writing, 1987.

Hutcheon, Linda. *The Canadian Postmodern: A Study of Contemporary English-Canadian Fiction*. Toronto: Oxford University Press, 1988.

Lewis, Paula Gilbert, ed. *Traditionalism, Nationalism, and Feminism: Women Writers of Quebec*. Westport, Conn.: Greenwood Press, 1985.

Linteau, Paul-André, René Durocher, Jean-Claude Robert, and Francois Ricard. *Quebec Since 1930*, trans. Robert Chodos and Ellen Gennaise. Toronto: James Lorimer, 1991.

New, W. H. *A History of Canadian Literature*. London: Macmillan, 1989.

———, ed. *Literary History of Canada*, vol. 4, Toronto: University of Toronto Press, 1989.

———, ed. *Dictionary of Literary Biography: Canadian Writers*, vols. 53, 60, 68, and 99. Detroit: Gale, 1986–1990.

Shek, Ben-Z. *French-Canadian and Quebecois Novels*. Toronto: Oxford University Press, 1991.

Smart, Patricia. *Writing in the Father's House: The Emergence of the Feminine in the Quebec Literary Tradition*. Toronto: University of Toronto Press, 1991.

Weiss, Jonathan, *French-Canadian Theater*. Boston: Twayne Publishers, 1986.

CHARLES G. D. ROBERTS (1860–1943)
Canada

Sir Charles George Doyles Roberts was both a poet and a fiction writer, the first Canadian to be knighted for his contribution to Canadian letters. The "Golden Age of Canadian poetry" began with his *Orion and Other Poems* (1880). "The Winter Fields" from *Songs of the Common Day and Ave* (1893) is part of a sonnet cycle. Drawing on the Greek pastoral tradition, William Wordworth's concern for the common agricultural worker, and Ralph Waldo Emerson's fusion of man and nature in the oversoul, Roberts cleared a path for the generation of "Confederation Poets" with their classical form and their subject matter of nature, love, or philosophy, and was called the "Father of Canadian Literature." This sonnet is an example of the "lyrics of earth" dominant in the last decades of the nineteenth century valued by critics as the first "objective" poetic descriptions of the Canadian landscape, careful selection of concrete detail, and control of tone and form. In this, it successfully negotiated the contradiction of writing Canadian difference within a traditional English literary form. "The Winter Fields" is characteristic of his work, with its bleak landscape, devoid of human presence, its pensive melancholy reinforced by the imitative harmony of monosyllables and harsh sibilants mimicking driving sleet. The contrast between the hard frozen land and the language of the octave and the promise of sun, growth, and liquid syllables of the sestet succinctly images the theme of the buried life or inhibited imagination whose ecstatic fulfillment is as yet a "germ" awaiting development under summer's sun.

from *Songs of the Common Day and Ave*

The Winter Fields

Winds here, and sleet, and frost that bites like steel.
   The low bleak hill rounds under the low sky.
   Naked of flock and fold the fallows lie,
Thin streaked with meagre drift. The gusts reveal
By fits the dim grey snakes of fence, that steal   5
   Through the white dusk. The hill-foot poplars sigh,
   While storm and death with winter trample by,
And the iron fields ring sharp, and blind lights reel.
Yet in the lonely ridges, wrenched with pain,
   Harsh solitary hillocks, bound and dumb,   10
Grave glebes[1] close-lipped beneath the scourge and chain.

---

1. Plots of uncultivated land, usually belonging to or sold to support a church.

Emily Carr. *Winter Moonlight.* 1909. Oil on canvas. Glenbow Museum, Calgary, Alberta.

Lurks hid the germ of ecstasy—the sum
Of life that waits on summer, till the rain
   Whisper in April and the crocus come.
                                        1890

PAULINE JOHNSON (TEKAHIONWAKE) (1862–1913)
Canada

Although Pauline Johnson (Tekahionwake), a Mohawk poet, also wrote meditative lyrics about dreaming in a landscape or paddling her canoe. She is noted for her stage performances of dramatic monologues like "Ojistoh." Dressed in native garb, she drew attention to the problem of exclusion faced by a Native woman moving between cultures. In this poem, the cultural conflict is distanced in time and place in a captivity narrative of a Mohawk woman caught by enemy Hurons. Tribal warfare between these two peoples in the seventeenth century was exacerbated by the British and French struggle over North America: the Mohawks of the Iroquois Confederacy were British allies who came north to

Canada as United Empire Loyalists after the American Revolution. Historical material from the oral tradition is the basis of the poem, developed in the frame of romantic love from European literary genres. The ambivalence of the woman mediating between cultures is framed in the love/revenge motif of murder. There is also a tension between speech used dramatically and stilted "poetic" diction constrained by regular meter and rhyming couplets.

Ojistoh

I Am Ojistoh, I am she, the wife
Of him whose name breathes bravery and life
And courage to the tribe that calls him chief.
I am Ojistoh,[1] his white star, and he
Is land, and lake, and sky—and soul to me.   5

Ah! but they hated him, those Huron braves,
Him who had flung their warriors into graves,
Him who had crushed them underneath his heel,
Whose arm was iron, and whose heart was steel
To all—save me, Ojistoh, chosen wife   10
Of my great Mohawk, white star of his life.

Ah! but they hated him, and councilled long
With subtle witchcraft how to work him wrong;
How to avenge their dead, and strike him where
His pride was highest, and his fame most fair.   15
Their hearts grew weak as women at his name:
They dared no war-path since my Mohawk came
With ashen bow, and flinten arrow-head
To pierce their craven bodies; but their dead
Must be avenged. Avenged? They dared not walk   20
In day and meet his deadly tomahawk;
They dared not face his fearless scalping knife;
So—Niyoh![2]—then they thought of me, his wife.

O! evil, evil face of them they sent
With evil Huron speech: "Would I consent   25
To take of wealth? be queen of all their tribe?
Have wampum ermine?" Back I flung the bribe
Into their teeth, and said, "While I have life
Know this—Ojistoh is the Mohawk's wife."

---

1. Character's name, meaning white star.   2. The name for god in Mohawk.

Wah! how we struggled! But their arms were strong.   30
They flung me on their pony's back, with thong
Round ankle, wrist, and shoulder. Then upleapt
The one I hated most: his eye he swept
Over my misery, and sneering said,
"Thus, fair Ojistoh, we avenge our dead."   35

And we two rode, rode as a sea wind-chased,
I, bound with buckskin to his hated waist,
He, sneering, laughing, jeering, while he lashed
The horse to foam, as on and on we dashed.
Plunging through creek and river, bush and trail,   40
On, on we galloped like a northern gale.
At last, his distant Huron fires aflame
We saw, and nearer, nearer still we came.

I, bound behind him in the captive's place,
Scarcely could see the outline of his face.   45
I smiled, and laid my cheek against his back:
"Loose thou my hands," I said. "This pace let slack.
Forget we now that thou and I are foes.
I like thee well, and wish to clasp thee close;
I like the courage of thine eye and brow;   50
I like thee better than my Mohawk now."

He cut the cords; we ceased our maddened haste
I wound my arms about his tawny waist;
My hand crept up the buckskin of his belt;
His knife hilt in my burning palm I felt;   55
One hand caressed his cheek, the other drew
The weapon softly—"I love you, love you,"
I whispered, "love you as my life."
And—buried in his back his scalping knife.

Ha! how I rode, rode as a sea wind-chased,   60
Mad with sudden freedom, mad with haste,
Back to my Mohawk and my home. I lashed
That horse to foam, as on and on I dashed.
Plunging thro' creek and river, bush and trail,
On, on I galloped like a northern gale.   65
And then my distant Mohawk's fires aflame
I saw, as nearer, nearer still I came,
My hands all wet, stained with a life's red dye,
But pure my soul, pure as those stars on high—
"My Mohawk's pure white star, Ojistoh, still am I."   70

ANNE HÉBERT (b. 1916)
Canada; French

Anne Hébert is known as a poet, novelist, and playwright. She was born and raised near Quebec, and educated in her home, because of her ill health. Her volumes of poems include *Dreams in Suspension* (1942) and *The Tombs of Kings* (1953).

Some of her writing deals with the contemporary reality of Quebec, where long-repressed desires for change were threatening the traditional social order. Several of Hébert's works have their roots in Quebec history: in *Kamouraska* (1970), her best-known novel (made into a film by director Claude Jutra), she reconstructs the life of a nineteenth-century woman whose story embodies Hébert's recurrent themes of imprisonment and liberating desire. In her poetry, as in the poetic prose of her novels and plays, Hébert transforms the simple objects and events of daily life into a strange and mysterious world of her own creation. So "Bread Is Born" makes of a "pure ancient act" the symbol of our work and life.

Bread Is Born

How do you make bread talk, this old treasure all wrapped
up in its strictures like a winter tree, anchored so that
its nakedness is set off against the see-through day?

If I lock myself up in the darkroom of my mind's eye
with this everlasting name stamped there, and if I importune   5
the old flat syllable to yield its shifting images

what I hear are a thousand blind and bitter animals thumping
against the door, servile pack of hounds, slack and submissive in their mangy pelts, who've been chomping on words
like grass since the dawn of time.   10

But a clean sweep of space stretches out for the poet,
an open field of wilderness and want, while on the far
side of the horizon time breaks open and the taste of
bread, salt, water sprouts like flat blue stones under the
sea. It's always like this, the age-old hunger.   15

Suddenly the hunger flows forth, it kneels on the ground,
it plants its round heart there in the shape of deep sleep.

O that long first night, face pressed against the cracked
earth, listening, taking the blood's pulse, all dream
banished, all movement arrested, all attention swelling to   20
love's tip.

Translated by Maxine Kumin.

The raw stubble pokes out of the land. An underground
source tells its green head of hair to break through.
The earth's belly bares its flowers and fruits in the
great noon sun.   25

The sky dusts itself blue; our stained hands flush with
the fields are like great fresh poppies.
All the shapes and colors that are called up from the
earth rise on the upbeat like a visible exhaled breath.

The land throbs and bleats. Its wool grows white under   30
the summer's jarring glare, the sour cicada song.

The millstones with their porous rough grains have the
muffled ardor of huge looking glasses condemned to reflect
nothing.

All they can do is serve in the shadows, be heavy and   35
dark, hard and grating so as to shatter the heart of
the harvest, grind it to dust, to a stifling dry downpour.

It makes living flowers of these odd, pointy beach shells.
The seafaring sun crystallizes them in a bright spray. The
kernels open at once for us, singing, giving up their true,   40
well-crafted forms.

After that, we will sleek the milky dough, make it lie out
in its flat torpor, becalmed, still lacking breath where
it sleeps like a little pond.

And what if by chance the wind should rise? What if   45
our souls should give themselves up entirely? What if
their nights were clotted with roots, what if great holes
were bored in their days?

Even so, this bitter teaspoonful will outlast us, will
outlast all those who come after us. Crushed like October   50
leaves to release their musky smell, it will thrive in the
guise of yeast.

In the reek of roasted flesh, on the blackened stone, in
the midst of all this disorderly feasting, see how a pure
ancient act shines forth in the primal night. See how   55
that slow ripening of crust and dough heart begins while
Patience sits on the rim of the fire.

And nothing may touch its silence until morning.

Under the ashes which unmake themselves like a bed, watch
the round loaves and the square loaves puff up. Feel their   60
deep animal heat and the elusive heart perfectly centered
like a captive bird.

Oh, we live again! Day begins again at the skyline!
God can be born in His turn, a pale child to be put on
the cross in his season. Our work has already risen   65
brown and pungent with good smell.

We offer Him some bread for his hunger.

And in time we will sleep, heavy creatures, witness to
the festival and the drunkenness that morning catches us
in. And daylight straddles the world.   70

GASTON MIRON (b. 1928)
Canada; French

Gaston Miron was a guiding force of the new Quebec poetry of the 1950s and
1960s, focused on the reality of Quebec and the effort to locate and name a
collective identity. Rejecting the ideal of solitary creation, Miron played an active
role in the numerous collective projects of the era, helping to found the important
Hexagon publishing house in 1953 and participating in the direction of political
and literary journals. His poems and those of others of his generation were often
read aloud at public gatherings. In Miron's work, the poet's personal drama is
identified with the collective struggle of the Quebec people.

October

The man of the hour has the face of a scourged Christ
and you, Land of Quebec, Mother Courage
in your long march you are swollen
with our painful infectious dreams
with the uncounted wasting of bodies and souls   5

upland back there I was born
your son in the old grated mountains of the north
I hurt and ache with the bite of birth
while in my arms my youth blushes

here are my knees so that men may forgive us   10
we have allowed our fathers' spirit to be degraded
we have allowed the word's splendor to be debased
till we were ashamed and hating ourselves in our brothers

Translated by Marc Plourde.

we didn't know how to bind our suffering's roots
to the universal pain in each man hollowed out 15

I will join my burning companions whose struggle
breaks and shares the bread of our common lot
in the quicksand huddles of grief

we will make you, Land of Quebec
a bed of resurrections 20
and a thousand lightning metamorphoses
of our leavens from which the future shall rise
and of our wills which will concede nothing
men shall hear your pulse beating through history
this is us winding through the October autumn 25
the russet sound of roe-deer in the sunlight
this is our future, clear
              and committed

ANTONINE MAILLET (b. 1929)
Canada; French

Antonine Maillet has given new life to Acadian literature and to its language.
Rewriting the history of her people in her prize-winning novel *Pélagie-la
Charrette* (1979), she emphasizes not the Acadians' deportation and dispersal by
the British in 1755 but rather their triumphant return to the Canadian Maritime
Provinces and their survival as a French-speaking people. Drawing on the oral
forms through which the Acadian tradition had been kept alive, Maillet's novels
and plays are populated by clever and courageous characters who survive against
impossible odds of poverty and the hostility of the surrounding culture. The
following story concerns two vivid characters, whose story is told by a third, no
less colorful. La Sagouine, who appears here, is the celebrated subject of a
dramatic monologue where she speaks for her people in the vivid language
characteristic of the New Brunswick seacoast.

Two Saints

I often used to go around to Sarah's to get my fortune read; not so much to learn
about my own life as about hers. For this Sarah was one of your fortune-tellers
who likes to chat and between club and diamond spin you a yarn and drop an
opinion or two and rummage around in family history. She knew your Great-

Translated by Philip Stratford.

Uncle Jaddus, she did, the one who had the one girl and then eleven boys . . . eleven boys, Great God yes, one on top of another. Ah! they really knew how to do things in those days! And she knew the old sorcerer from Rivière à Hache, the one who could just as well burn you a church right down to the ground as go bury himself stark naked in the middle of a field of wild mustard not a hundred feet from the graveyard. Ah yes, they were something else again, that race of devils was, and you can only hope that on the Other Side there'll be some kind of a Good Lord to look after them . . . And then she knew the Sagouine young, too.

I was afraid Sarah would start talking about something else as she sat there shuffling the cards, so I pounced on the ace of spades when it dropped all hot from her fondling fingers.

"So you knew the Sagouine young, did you?"

"Knew her young and knew her old, aye, and then too the wee bit in between when a person's, as you might say, astraddle life like a cow's back."

And Sarah let spurt from her throat and eyes that big laugh she got from her father who held it himself from a line of ancestors who reached this land jumping across the ice-floes in the bay. Was it the thought of a Sagouine astride a cow's back that set off her laughter, or was she already thinking of something else?

"I knew the Sagouine at the time of her squabble with La Sainte," she says to me. "And that was something, that was. Too bad you missed that."

The old witch was making my mouth water. To think I'd lived so close by and missed it all.

But little by little I got the whole story or what was left of it as Sarah unravelled her ragged memories.

Once a week back in those prosperous times the Sagouine used to open up her stall of old rags and hand-me-down clothes which she sold at bargain prices, though her customers bargained for them just the same, for the pleasure of it. Because it would have been an insult to everyone, and to the Sagouine in particular, to step up and pay cash without bartering, like the bigwigs. No, where the Sagouine comes from you call each other names and haggle and it's all part of the business.

You haggled over the prices but also over the quality of the goods, though nobody was the least in the dark as to where they came from. They could have told you with their eyes shut that was the banker's shirt or the doctor's coat on the back of Henri Big-Belly or Francis Motté.

But don't you go thinking that the Sagouine was a thief. No, she was a beggar. Yes, she begged, as is the right of any poor slave of the Good Lord who never got more out of belonging to the Church than three drops of water at baptism and a slap at confirmation. It was all to the honour of her bump of business acumen then if, from the fruits of her begging on behalf of the shivering poor of the parish, she managed to mount a small trade that allowed her to live with respect and dignity.

That's about how the Sagouine saw things anyway, and the way La Sainte began to see them too one fine day without letting on to anyone.

The entry of La Sainte on the rag market was the hardest blow the Sagouine ever received in her life. Up till then the Catounes and Pitounes of the place had gladly disputed with the Sagouine another commercial activity which on occasion, by necessity, she also practised. But the Sagouine was of an age to understand that in that particular trade there was room for a little competition. Whereas in business, the success of the one is the bankruptcy of the other. That much the Sagouine knew. And it wasn't long before the facts began to bear this out.

Day by day she saw La Sainte adding more and more orange crates to her stand and filling them up with bundles of old clothes. And she was forced to watch, powerless, as business boomed for this brazen upstart who didn't even deign to begin at the bottom of the ladder like everyone else with socks and underwear.

No, right off the bat the hussy was dealing in coats and dresses as if to the manner born. And next breath making so bold as to move right into hats! Yes Ma'am, hats, if you please! And no one there but could recognize the feathers of Dominique's wife's bonnet and the vicar's fur hat. And O Sweet Holy Mother of God! A fox! A fox piece, I tell you! If that isn't a shame to stoop to selling foxes to the poor likes of us who haven't ever even slept in a feather bed yet. A fox! The Sagouine choked on it. It was just too much this time, really too much. And she closed up shop and went down to the shore to mull things over.

Had to find a way to put that big cow back in her place. But the Sagouine saw straight away that it wouldn't be easy. How to get under the skin of a woman who had sworn off all the sins of the flesh for so long? She didn't drink, the old bat, didn't smoke, or dance, or go gallivanting around either, naturally, saint that she was. La Sainte? Phooey! The Sagouine didn't have much book learning but she wasn't born yesterday either, and she judged there was plenty of grimacing under that guise of saintliness. Prissy stuck-up plaster saint paddling in holy water, the Sagouine exclaimed with a roar of laughter.

Then she sobered up. A saint who goes around stealing other folks' business deserves the same treatment . . . But how do you set about stealing somebody's saintliness? Sitting there, feet buried in the sand and head bowed with heavy thoughts, the Sagouine lifted her eyes and saw a heron pass by with his long beak stuck onto his long neck. Along he strode, disdainful and superb, waggling his precious behind with the dignified air of someone on their way to sing vespers. The Sagouine contemplated this shore-bird an instant, then leaping up and yanking her feet out of the sand, let out a tremendous "Hah!" and lit out for the church.

You might have assumed that the Sagouine's first steps in the paths of sanctity would be difficult and gauche. That would be to misjudge a woman who from force of circumstance had been obliged to change her profession at least seven or eight times in her life. And besides, churches were something she knew a little about after all. For years now she had scrubbed out the sisters' chapel and the floor of the parish hall.

So she took to her new *métier* with the same flair as to the others, throwing herself into it heart and soul, belly and guts. As she used to say, either you're a saint or you're not, and the Sagouine was never one to do things by halves. She fitted herself out with a Sunday missal, two hymn books, and the usual array of medals, rosaries and scapulars guaranteed to ward off sickness, bad weather and unrepentant death. She gave up smoking, ceased to chew, quit swearing—yes by the Dear Lord Jesus Christ she did—and even abstained from sounding off from door to door about the conduct of her worst enemy, La Sainte. It was the most sudden and total metamorphosis ever seen on this stretch of coast since the time of the great rains.

It was La Sainte who was the most amazed. The most outraged. For here was someone filching the only thing that was truly hers, stealing her paradise, from her who had renounced the things of this world. It was an insult to God and his saints and a rank injustice to someone who had never missed a First Friday or Sunday Vespers or Public Prayers, Prayers with three rosaries one after the other, interspersed with intentions that La Sainte improvised as the spirit moved her for the dying, the sinners and the renegades of the parish. This time she'd cook up a prayer there'd be no mistaking for the intention of those pushy barbarians who figure they can take over other people's paradises just like that. She'd put that rag-seller back in her place, she would!
. . . But poor La Sainte didn't have a chance to put anyone in their place since her own, there in the front pew as prayer leader, had already been taken. Though she couldn't believe her eyes she was forced to admit that it was really the Sagouine up there at the lectern announcing the intention for the first decade of the rosary: "Let us pray," she declaimed, "that the men of this parish heretofore see fit to do their duty. Our Father who art in Heaven . . ."

So that's how the Sagouine got her business back, for La Sainte understood that she would have to choose between earth and heaven. She chose heaven and left the earth to the Sagouine who, the next day, sold her medals and her scapular along with her socks and coats and underwear.

And that's the story Sarah told me in bits and pieces as she ran her long fingers between heart and spade, laughing her big white-toothed laugh and shuffling her memories with the deck.

ALICE MUNRO (b. 1931)
Canada

Alice Munro, a novelist and short-story writer, places her semi-autobiographical fiction in Jubilee, an invented small town in southern Ontario, which figures in

I had talked about marrying him. This was clear as day to me, and I opened my mouth to say whatever would make it clear to him, and I saw that he knew it all already; this was what he knew, that I had somehow met his good offerings with my deceitful offerings, whether I knew it or not, matching my complexity and play-acting to his true intent.

You think you're too good for it.

"Say you'll do it then!" His dark, amiable but secretive face broken by rage, a helpless sense of insult. I was ashamed of this insult but had to cling to it, because it was only my differences, my reservations, my life. I thought of him kicking and kicking that man in front of the Porterfield beer parlor. I had thought I wanted to know about him but I hadn't really, I had never really wanted his secrets or his violence or himself taken out of the context of that peculiar and magical and, it seemed now, possibly fatal game.

Suppose in a dream you jumped willingly into a hole and laughed while people threw soft tickling grass on you, then understood when your mouth and eyes were covered up that it was no game at all, or if it was, it was a game that required you to be buried alive. I fought underwater exactly as you would fight in such a dream, with a feeling of desperation that was not quite immediate, that had to work upward through layers of incredulity. Yet I thought that he might drown me. I really thought that. I thought that I was fighting for my life.

When he let me come up again he tried the conventional baptizing position, bending me backwards from the waist, and this was a mistake. I was able to kick him low in the belly—not in the genitals though I would not have cared, I did not know or care where I kicked—and these kicks were strong enough to make him lose his hold and stagger a bit and I got away. As soon as there was a yard of water between us the absurdity and horror of our fight became plain and it could not be resumed. He did not come towards me. I walked slowly, safely out of the water which at this time of year was not much more than armpit-deep, anywhere. I was shaking, gasping, drinking air.

I dressed at once in the shelter of the truck, with difficulty making my legs go through the legs of my shorts, trying to hold my breath to steady myself, so I could do up the buttons of my blouse.

Garnet called me.

"I'll give you a ride home."

"I want to walk."

"I'll come and pick you up Monday night."

I didn't answer. I guessed this was said for courtesy. He would not come. If we had been older we would certainly have hung on, haggled over the price of reconciliation, explained and justified and perhaps forgiven, and carried this into the future with us, but as it was we were close enough to childhood to believe in the absolute seriousness and finality of some fights, unforgivability of some blows. We had seen in each other what we could not bear, and we had no idea that people do see that, and go on, and hate and fight and try to kill each other, various ways, then love some more.

I started walking along the track that led to the road and after awhile walking calmed me down and strengthened me; my legs were not so terribly weak. I walked down the Third Concession, which came out at the Cemetery Road. I had about three and a half miles to walk altogether.

I cut through the cemetery. It was getting dark. August was as far away from midsummer as April, a fact always hard to remember. I saw a boy and girl—I could not make out who they were—lying on the clipped grass over by the Mundy mausoleum, on whose dark cement walls Naomi and I had once written an epitaph that we had made up, and thought wicked and hilarious, and that I could no longer fully remember:

> Here lies the bodies of lots of Mundys
> Who died from peeing in their soup on Sundays—

I looked at these lovers lying on the graveyard grass without envy or curiosity. As I walked on into Jubilee I repossessed the world. Trees, houses, fences, streets, came back to me, in their own sober and familiar shapes. Unconnected to the life of love, uncolored by love, the world resumes its own, its natural and callous importance. This is first a blow, then an odd consolation. And already I felt my old self—my old devious, ironic, isolated self—beginning to breathe again and stretch and settle, though all around it my body clung cracked and bewildered, in the stupid pain of loss.

My mother was already in bed. When I had failed to win the scholarship, something she had never questioned—her hopes of the future, through her children—had collapsed. She was faced with the possibility that Owen and I would do nothing and become nothing after all, that we were mediocre, or infected with the dreaded, proud, sacred perversity of my father's family. There was Owen, living out on the Flats Road, saying "turrible" and "drownded" and using Uncle Benny's grammar, saying he wanted to quit school. There was I going out with Garnet French and refusing to talk about it, and not getting the scholarship.

"You will have to do what you want," she said bitterly.

But was that so easy to know? I went out to the kitchen, turned on the light, and made myself a big mixture of fried potatoes and onions and tomatoes and eggs, which I ate greedily and somberly out of the pan, standing up. I was free and I was not free. I was relieved and I was desolate. Suppose, then, I had never wakened up? Suppose I had let myself lie down and be baptized in the Wawanash River?

I entertained this possibility off and on, as if it still existed—along with the leafy shade and waterstains in his house, and the bounty of my lover's body—for many years.

He did not come on Monday. I waited to see if he would. I combed my hair and waited, classically, behind the curtains in our front room. I did not know what I would do if he came; the ache of wanting to see his truck, his face, swallowed up everything else. I thought of walking past the Baptist Church, to see if the truck was there. If I had done that, if it had been there, I might have walked on inside, rigid as a sleepwalker. I did get as far as our veranda. I was crying, I noticed, whimpering in a monotonous rhythm the way children do to celebrate a hurt. I turned around, went back into the hall to look in the dim mirror at my twisted wet face. Without diminishment of pain I observed myself; I was amazed to think that the person suffering was me, for it was not me at all; I was watching. I was watching, I was suffering. I said into the mirror a line from Tennyson, from my mother's *Complete Tennyson* that was a present from her old teacher, Miss Rush. I said it with absolute sincerity, absolute irony. *He cometh not, she said.*

From "Mariana," one of the silliest poems I had ever read. It made my tears flow harder. Watching myself still, I went back to the kitchen and made a cup of coffee and brought it into the dining room where the city paper was still lying on the table. My mother had torn the crossword out and taken it up to bed. I opened it up at the want ads, and got a pencil, so I could circle any job that seemed possible. I made myself understand what I was reading, and after some time I felt a mild, sensible gratitude for these printed words, these strange possibilities. Cities existed; telephone operators were wanted; the future could be furnished without love or scholarships. Now at last without fantasies or self-deception, cut off from the mistakes and confusion of the past, grave and simple, carrying a small suitcase, getting on a bus, like girls in movies leaving home, convents, lovers, I supposed I would get started on my real life.

Garnet French, Garnet French, Garnet French.
Real life.

JOY KOGAWA (b. 1935)
Canada

This selection from the novel *Obasan* (1981) is an example of "historiographic metafiction" (fiction that examines the nature of the distinction between "fact" and "fiction"). This novel interweaves historical documents from newspapers, archives, letters, and diaries of the author's family, relating to the internment of the Japanese-Canadians during World War II, with lyric passages, prose poems, meditating on loss and mourning for a mother killed after the nuclear holocaust at Nagasaki, Japan, whose silence has left her daughter Naomi Nakane (the narrator) bereft. These extracts are found near the conclusion, when Naomi at last learns the secret of her mother's silence. From Aunt Emily, Naomi receives documentary records that incite her to protest; from Aunt Obasan she learns through the words of a Chinese poet that silence may be a form of love, not punishment. A vision of divine indifference to violence, contends with the aesthetic consolation of Buddhist ritual promising regeneration. Political activism, spiritual enlightenment—the novel oscillates between the two seemingly incompatible voices, encompassing both.

from *Obasan*

[Naomi learns the secret of her mother's silence]

There is a folder in Aunt Emily's package containing only one newspaper clipping and an index card with the words "Facts about evacuees in Alberta." The newspaper clipping has a photograph of one family, all smiles, standing around a pile of beets. The caption reads: "Grinning and Happy."

> Find Jap Evacuees Best Beet Workers
> Lethbridge, Alberta, Jan. 22.
>   Japanese evacuees from British Columbia supplied the labour for 65% of Alberta's sugar beet acreage last year, Phil Baker, of Lethbridge, president of the Alberta Sugar Beet Growers' Association, stated today.
>   "They played an important part in producing our all-time record crop of 363,000 tons of beets in 1945," he added.
>   Mr. Baker explained Japanese evacuees worked 19,500 acres of beets and German prisoners of war worked 5,000 acres. The labour for the remaining 5,500 acres of Alberta's 30,000 acres of sugar beets was provided by farmers and their families. Some of the heaviest beet yields last year came from farms employing Japanese evacuees.
>   Generally speaking, Japanese evacuees have developed into most efficient beet workers, many of them being better than the transient workers who cared for beets in southern Alberta before Pearl Harbor. . . .[1]

Facts about evacuees in Alberta? The fact is I never got used to it and I cannot, I cannot bear the memory. There are some nightmares from which there is no waking, only deeper and deeper sleep.

There is a word for it. Hardship. The hardship is so pervasive, so inescapable, so thorough it's a noose around my chest and I cannot move any more. All the oil in my joints has drained out and I have been invaded by dust and grit from the fields and mud is in my bone marrow. I can't move any more. My fingernails are black from scratching the scorching day and there is no escape.

Aunt Emily, are you a surgeon cutting at my scalp with your folders and your filing cards and your insistence on knowing all? The memory drains down the sides of my face, but it isn't enough, is it? It's your hands in my abdomen, pulling the growth from the lining of my walls, but bring back the anaesthetist turn on the ether clamp down the gas mask bring on the chloroform when will this operation be over Aunt Em?

Is it so bad?

Yes.

Do I really mind?

Yes, I mind. I mind everything. Even the flies. The flies and flies and flies from the cows in the barn and the manure pile—all the black flies that curtain the windows, and Obasan with a wad of toilet paper, spish, then with her bare hands as well, grabbing them and their shocking white eggs and the mosquitoes mixed there with the other insect corpses around the base of the gas lamp.

---

1. Naval base in Hawaii where the American fleet was bombed by the Japanese in December 1941, bringing the United States into World War II on the side of the British and Canadians.

It's the chicken coop "house" we live in that I mind. The uninsulated unbelievable thin-as-a-cotton-dress hovel never before inhabited in winter by human beings. In summer it's a heat trap, an incubator, a dry sauna from which there is no relief. In winter the icicles drip down the inside of the windows and the ice is thicker than bricks at the ledge. The only place that is warm is by the coal stove where we rotate like chickens on a spit and the feet are so cold they stop registering. We eat cloves of roasted garlic on winter nights to warm up.

It's the bedbugs and my having to sleep on the table to escape the nightly attack, and the welts over our bodies. And all the swamp bugs and the dust. It's Obasan uselessly packing all the cracks with rags. And the muddy water from the irrigation ditch which we strain and settle and boil, and the tiny carcasses of water creatures at the bottom of the cup. It's walking in winter to the reservoir and keeping the hole open with the axe and dragging up the water in pails and lugging it back and sometimes the water spills down your boots and your feet are red and itchy for days. And it's everybody taking a bath in the round galvanized tub, then Obasan washing clothes in the water after and standing outside hanging the clothes in the freezing weather where everything instantly stiffens on the line.

Or it's standing in the beet field under the maddening sun, standing with my black head a sun-trap even though it's covered, and lying down in the ditch, faint, and the nausea in waves and the cold sweat, and getting up and tackling the next row. The whole field is an oven and there's not a tree within walking distance. We are tiny as insects crawling along the grill and there is no protection anywhere. The eyes are lidded against the dust and the air cracks the skin, the lips crack, Stephen's flutes crack and there is no energy to sing any more anyway.

It's standing in the field and staring out at the heat waves that waver and shimmer like see-through curtains over the brown clods and over the tiny distant bodies of Stephen and Uncle and Obasan miles away across the field day after day and not even wondering how this has come about.

There she is, Obasan, wearing Uncle's shirt over a pair of dark baggy trousers, her head covered by a straw hat that is held on by a white cloth tied under her chin. She is moving like a tiny earth cloud over the hard clay clods. Her hoe moves rhythmically up down up down, tiny as a toothpick. And over there, Uncle pauses to straighten his back, his hands on his hips. And Stephen farther behind, so tiny I can barely see him.

It's hard, Aunt Emily, with my hoe, the blade getting dull and mud-caked as I slash out the Canada thistle, dandelions, crab grass, and other nameless non-beet plants, then on my knees, pulling out the extra beets from the cluster, leaving just one to mature, then three hand spans to the next plant, whack whack, and down on my knees again, pull, flick flick, and on to the end of the long long row and the next and the next and it will never be done thinning and weeding and weeding and weeding. It's so hard and so hot that my tear glands burn out.

And then it's cold. The lumps of clay mud stick on my gumboots and weight my legs and the skin under the boots beneath the knees at the level of the calves grows red and hard and itchy from the flap flap of the boots and the fine hairs on my legs grow coarse there and ugly.

I mind growing ugly.

I mind the harvest time and the hands and the wrists bound in rags to keep the wrists from breaking open. I lift the heavy mud-clotted beets out of the ground with the hook like an eagle's beak, thick and heavy as a nail attached to the top of the sugar-beet knife. Thwack. Into the beet and yank from the shoulder till it's out of the ground dragging the surrounding mud with it. Then crack two beets together till most of the mud drops off and splat, the knife slices into the beet scalp and the green top is tossed into one pile, the beets heaved onto another, one more one more one more down the icy line. I cannot tell about this time, Aunt Emily. The body will not tell.

We are surrounded by a horizon of denim-blue sky with clouds clear as spilled milk that turn pink at sunset. Pink I hear is the colour of llama's milk. I wouldn't know. The clouds are the shape of our new prison walls—untouchable, impersonal, random.

There are no other people in the entire world. We work together all day. At night we eat and sleep. We hardly talk any more. The boxes we brought from Slocan are not unpacked. The King George/Queen Elizabeth mugs stay muffled in the *Vancouver Daily Province*. The cameraphone does not sing. Obasan wraps layers of cloth around her feet and her torn sweater hangs unmended over her sagging dress.

Down the miles we are obedient as machines in this odd ballet without accompaniment of flute or song.

"Grinning and happy" and all smiles standing around a pile of beets? That is one telling. It's not how it was.

I can't remember when Uncle stopped talking about going back. It may have been the first year after the ghost towns, or the next year, or the year after that.

In 1948, three years after our exile from our place of exile, I am twelve years old and Stephen is fifteen. We are still here in Granton, Alberta, still here on the Barker farm, attending school except in thinning season or harvest time.

"Bar Japs for Another Year from Going Back to B.C." says a newspaper clipping from the *Toronto Star*, written by Borden Spears.

> Tues. March 16, 1948
>
> Nearly 20,000 Canadian citizens will be deprived for another year of one of the fundamental rights of citizenship, the House of Commons decreed last night. They are the Canadians of Japanese origin who were expelled from British Columbia in 1941 and are still debarred from returning to their homes.
>
> Led by Angus MacInnis of Vancouver, CCF[2] members made a vain but valiant effort to have the last restriction on the freedom of Japanese Canadians removed at once. The attempt was eloquently supported by David Croll (Lib. Toronto Spadina) and three Liberals[3] declared themselves in opposition to the government.
>
> They were branded, however, as theorists, visionary idealists, purists, talkers of academic nonsense, weepers of crocodile tears. By a standing vote, 73 to 23, the House

---

2. Co-operative Commonwealth Federation, the name of the Canadian social democratic party from 1932 to 1961.
3. Canadian political party of the center. Grew

out of Clear Grits and Reformers of the Canadas (1840–1860) to become the dominant federal party in the House of Commons in Ottawa in the twentieth century.

decided that for another year no Japanese Canadian may enter British Columbia without an RCMP[4] permit, and those now in the interior may not return to the coastal area.

Defenders of the restrictions denied they were motivated by racial considerations. But in nearly four hours of increasingly bitter debate, there was no direct answer to the blunt question posed by Mr. MacInnis: If the national security is no longer in danger, what is the reason for curtailing the freedom of Canadian citizens? There was even, from Tom Reid (Lib. New Westminster) this statement: "As long as I have breath in my body I will keep fighting in this House of Commons to see that the heritage which belongs to Canadians should be returned to the white people."

Maj. Gen. G. R. Pearkes (PC[5] Nanaimo) suggested there would be "crimes of revenge" if the exiles were permitted to return home now. In war, he said, the innocent suffer with the guilty; there was still hatred among the white people of B.C. and he thought the government was wise in in giving the old sores another year to heal.

Another year? Which year should we choose for *our* healing? Restrictions against us are removed on April Fool's Day, 1949. But the "old sores" remain. In time the wounds will close and the scabs drop off the healing skin. Till then, I can read these newspaper clippings, I can tell myself the facts. I can remember since Aunt Emily insists that I must and release the flood gates one by one. I can cry for the flutes that have cracked in the dryness and cry for the people who no longer sing. I can cry for Obasan who has turned to stone. But what then? Uncle does not rise up and return to his boats. Dead bones do not take on flesh.

What is done, Aunt Emily, is done, is it not? And no doubt it will all happen again, over and over with different faces and names, variations on the same theme.

"Nothing but the lowest motives of greed, selfishness and hatred have been brought forward to defend these disgraceful Orders," the *Globe and Mail* noted. Greed, selfishness, and hatred remain as constant as the human condition, do they not? Or are you thinking that through lobbying and legislation, speech-making and story-telling, we can extricate ourselves from our foolish ways? Is there evidence for optimism?

* * *

Exhaustion. Since the Barker's departure, both Obasan and I have been dozing in the living-room. It's almost seven. Aunt Emily and Stephen should be here by now. I hope they've eaten—I haven't thought about supper. There's Uncle's last loaf of everlasting stone bread, but neither of us is hungry.

I was having a nightmare just now. Something about stairs. Ah yes, and a courtyard. That's it. Stairs leading into a courtyard and the place of the dead. It wasn't at all a "fine and private place," that home beyond the grave. They were all there—my parents, the grandparents, and Obasan as well, small as a child. She was intent on being near me at the top of the stairs. And of course, there were soldiers. Always, I dream of soldiers eager for murder, their weapons ready. We die again and again. In my dreams, we are never safe enough.

---

4. Royal Canadian Mounted Police, formed in the 1870s to police the Northwest on horseback. Today they carry out security and intelligence work, narcotics law enforcement, commercial fraud enforcement, etc. on a federal basis across Canada as well as assuming the functions of provincial police for all provinces except Ontario and Quebec.

5. Progressive Conservative, a conservative or right wing Canadian political party.

In the courtyard, a flower ceremony was underway, like the one in my dream yesterday morning. Mother stood in the centre. In her mouth she held a knotted string stem, like the twine and string of Obasan's ball which she keeps in the pantry. From the stem hung a rose, red as a heart. I moved towards her from the top of the stairs, a cloud falling to earth, heavy and full of rain.

Was it then that the nightmare began? The skin of the air became close and dense, a formless hair vest. Up from a valley there rose a dark cloud—a great cape. It was the Grand Inquisitor[6] descending over us, the top of his head a shiny skin cap. With his large hands he was prying open my mother's lips, prying open my eyes.

I fell and cried out. I woke into the room where Obasan sleeps, her skin-coloured mouth open—a small dry cave of a mouth. How unlike my mother's young heart-shaped mouth in my dream, her fingers deftly moving the long thread from knot to knot, drawing the flower closer to her lips.

Once I came across two ideographs for the word "love." The first contained the root words "heart" and "hand" and "action"—love as hands and heart in action together. The other ideograph, for "passionate love," was formed of "heart," "to tell," and "a long thread."

The dance ceremony of the dead was a slow courtly telling, the heart declaring a long thread knotted to Obasan's twine, knotted to Aunt Emily's package. Why I wonder as she danced her love should I find myself unable to breathe? The Grand Inquisitor was carnivorous and full of murder. His demand to know was both a judgement and a refusal to hear. The more he questioned her, the more he was her accuser and murderer. The more he killed her, the deeper her silence became. What the Grand Inquisitor has never learned is that the avenues of speech are the avenues of silence. To hear my mother, to attend her speech, to attend the sound of stone, he must first become silent. Only when he enters her abandonment will he be released from his own.

How the Grand Inquisitor gnaws at my bones. At the age of questioning my mother disappeared. Why, I have asked ever since, did she not write? Why, I ask now, must I know? Did I doubt her love? Am I her accuser?

> Did you not know that people hide their love
> Like a flower that seems too precious to be picked?

the Chinese poet Wu-ti asked.

My mother hid her love, but hidden in life does she speak through dream?

Her tale is a rose with a tangled stem. All this questioning, this clawing at her grave, is an unseemly thing. Let the inquisition rest tonight. In the week of my Uncle's departure, let there be peace.

Obasan stirs and lifts her head, rubbing her eyes. She feels for the glasses dangling on her chest and attempts to get up. The rubber loops at the end of the

---

6. From Dostoyevsky's *The Brothers Karama-zov* (1880); this figure appears in Ivan Karamazov's dream involving a debate with the devil over the meaning of human suffering.

chain that fit around the glasses are frayed and replaced by safety pins. When she has her glasses on she picks up the slippery blue pages from the coffee table and begins reading again.

ROCH CARRIER (b. 1937)
Canada; French

Roch Carrier is known for his comic portrayals of Quebec's cultural conflicts. In his best-known novel, *La Guerre, Yes Sir!* (1968) he offers a burlesque treatment of mutual incomprehension between English-speaking soldiers and Francophone Quebec villagers, against the dark background of World War II. His humor takes a gentler tone in short stories like "The Hockey Sweater," filled with childhood memories, where societal conflicts are played out on the hockey rink. But in this depiction of a mother's helplessness before an Anglophone businessman and of a child's rebellion against the village priest, Carrier offers a far-reaching analysis of life in pre–"Quiet Revolution" Quebec.

The Hockey Sweater

The winters of my childhood were long, long seasons. We lived in three places—the school, the church and the skating rink—but our real life was on the skating-rink. Real battles were won on the skating-rink. Real strength appeared on the skating-rink. The real leaders showed themselves on the skating-rink. School was a sort of punishment. Parents always want to punish children and school is their most natural way of punishing us. However, school was also a quiet place where we could prepare for the next hockey game, lay out our next strategies. As for church, we found there the tranquillity of God: there we forgot school and dreamed about the next hockey game. Through our daydreams it might happen that we would recite a prayer: we would ask God to help us play as well as Maurice Richard.[1]

We all wore the same uniform as he, the red white and blue uniform of the Montreal Canadiens, the best hockey team in the world; we all combed our hair in the same style as Maurice Richard, and to keep it in place we used a sort of glue—a great deal of glue. We laced our skates like Maurice Richard, we taped our sticks like Maurice Richard. We cut all his pictures out of the papers. Truly, we knew everything about him.

Translated by Sheila Fischman.

---

1. A well-known hockey player for the Montreal Canadiens.

On the ice, when the referee blew his whistle the two teams would rush at the puck; we were five Maurice Richards taking it away from five other Maurice Richards; we were ten players, all of us wearing with the same blazing enthusiasm the uniform of the Montreal Canadiens. On our backs, we all wore the famous number 9.

One day, my Montreal Canadiens sweater had become too small; then it got torn and had holes in it. My mother said: 'If you wear that old sweater people are going to think we're poor!' Then she did what she did whenever we needed new clothes. She started to leaf through the catalogue the Eaton company sent us in the mail every year. My mother was proud. She didn't want to buy our clothes at the general store; the only things that were good enough for us were the latest styles from Eaton's catalogue.[2] My mother didn't like the order forms included with the catalogue; they were written in English and she didn't understand a word of it. To order my hockey sweater, she did as she usually did; she took out her writing paper and wrote in her gentle schoolteacher's hand: 'Cher Monsieur Eaton, Would you be kind enough to send me a Canadiens' sweater for my son who is ten years old and a little too tall for his age and Docteur Robitaille thinks he's a little too thin? I'm sending you three dollars and please send me what's left if there's anything left. I hope your wrapping will be better than last time.'

Monsieur Eaton was quick to answer my mother's letter. Two weeks later we received the sweater. That day I had one of the greatest disappointments of my life! I would even say that on that day I experienced a very great sorrow. Instead of the red, white and blue Montreal Canadiens sweater, Monsieur Eaton had sent us a blue and white sweater with a maple leaf on the front—the sweater of the Toronto Maple Leafs.[3] I'd always worn the red, white and blue Montreal Canadiens sweater; all my friends wore the red, white and blue sweater; never had anyone in my village ever worn the Toronto sweater, never had we even seen a Toronto Maple Leafs sweater. Besides, the Toronto team was regularly trounced by the triumphant Canadiens. With tears in my eyes, I found the strength to say:

'I'll never wear that uniform.'

'My boy, first you're going to try it on! If you make up your mind about things before you try, my boy, you won't go very far in this life.'

My mother had pulled the blue and white Toronto Maple Leafs sweater over my shoulders and already my arms were inside the sleeves. She pulled the sweater down and carefully smoothed all the creases in the abominable maple leaf on which, right in the middle of my chest, were written the words 'Toronto Maple Leafs.' I wept.

'I'll never wear it.'

'Why not? This sweater fits you . . . like a glove.'

'Maurice Richard would never put it on his back.'

---

2. A large Canadian department store, with catalog sales.

3. The maple leaf is also the symbol of Canada (as opposed to the fleur-de-lis of Quebec).

'You aren't Maurice Richard. Anyway, it isn't what's on your back that counts, it's what you've got inside your head.'

'You'll never put it in my head to wear a Toronto Maple Leafs sweater.'

My mother sighed in despair and explained to me:

'If you don't keep this sweater which fits you perfectly I'll have to write to Monsieur Eaton and explain that you don't want to wear the Toronto sweater. Monsieur Eaton's an *Anglais*[4]; he'll be insulted because he likes the Maple Leafs. And if he's insulted do you think he'll be in a hurry to answer us? Spring will be here and you won't have played a single game, just because you didn't want to wear that perfectly nice blue sweater.'

So I was obliged to wear the Maple Leafs sweater. When I arrived on the rink, all the Maurice Richards in red, white and blue came up, one by one, to take a look. When the referee blew his whistle I went to take my usual position. The captain came and warned me I'd be better to stay on the forward line. A few minutes later the second line was called; I jumped onto the ice. The Maple Leafs sweater weighed on my shoulders like a mountain. The captain came and told me to wait; he'd need me later, on defense. By the third period I still hadn't played; one of the defensemen was hit in the nose with a stick and it was bleeding. I jumped on the ice: my moment had come! The referee blew his whistle; he gave me a penalty. He claimed I'd jumped on the ice when there were already five players. That was too much! It was unfair! It was persecution! It was because of my blue sweater! I struck my stick against the ice so hard it broke. Relieved, I bent down to pick up the debris. As I straightened up I saw the young vicar, on skates, before me.

'My child,' he said, 'just because you're wearing a new Toronto Maple Leafs sweater unlike the others, it doesn't mean you're going to make the laws[5] around here. A proper young man doesn't lose his temper. Now take off your skates and go to the church and ask God to forgive you.'

Wearing my Maple Leafs sweater I went to the church, where I prayed to God; I asked him to send, as quickly as possible, moths that would eat up my Toronto Maple Leafs sweater.

MARGARET ATWOOD (b. 1939)
Canada

Margaret Atwood is a celebrated Canadian novelist, poet, and critic, is the author of *Lady Oracle* (1976) and *The Handmaid's Tale* (1986). "This Is a Photograph of

---

4. English-speaking Canadians.
5. The vicar's words suggest the legal conflict between provincial and federal legal au-

thority, which has been a source of contention between Quebec and the federal government.

Me," from *The Circle Game* (1966), is typical of Atwood's themes and style—
particularly the interconnections of landscape, language, text, and body—which
have influenced many younger Canadian poets. This poem stages the schizophrenia Atwood identifies in the "progressive insanities" of pioneers such as Susanna
Moodie (see Atwood's *Journals of Susanna Moodie*, 1970), as well as a fear of
the wilderness and a search for aesthetic strategies of containment, self-defeating
ultimately in their generation of psychic disorder. The drowned poet motif relates to a theme Atwood considers dominant in Canadian literature, "survival"
in a hostile environment: see her novel *Surfacing* (1972). Woman seen as nature
is also a common Canadian motif, she notes, a development of the "female
gothic."

"Journey to the Interior" is a further and more complex example of these
motifs: keeping and losing hang in poetic balance, forever here wherever we
are.

This Is a Photograph of Me

It was taken some time ago.
At first it seems to be
a smeared
print: blurred lines and grey flecks
blended with the paper;   5

then, as you scan
it, you see in the left-hand corner
a thing that is like a branch: part of a tree
(balsam or spruce) emerging
and, to the right, halfway up   10
what ought to be a gentle
slope, a small frame house.

In the background there is a lake,
and beyond that, some low hills.

(The photograph was taken   15
the day after I drowned.

I am in the lake, in the center
of the picture, just under the surface.

It is difficult to say where
precisely, or to say   20
how large or small I am:
the effect of water
on light is a distortion

but if you look long enough,
eventually
you will be able to see me.)   25

Journey to the Interior

There are similarities
I notice: that the hills
which the eyes make flat as a wall, welded
together, open as I move
to let me through; become   5
endless as prairies; that the trees
grow spindly, have their roots
often in swamps; that this is a poor country;
that a cliff is not known
as rough except by hand, and is   10
therefore inaccessible. Mostly
that travel is not the easy going

from point to point, a dotted
line on a map, location
plotted on a square surface   15
but that I move surrounded by a tangle
of branches, a net of air and alternate
light and dark, at all times;
that there are no destinations
apart from this.   20

There are differences
of course: the lack of reliable charts;
more important, the distraction of small details:
your shoe among the brambles under the chair
where it shouldn't be; lucent   25
white mushrooms and a paring knife
on the kitchen table; a sentence
crossing my path, sodden as a fallen log
I'm sure I passed yesterday
                                        (have I been   30
walking in circles again?)

but mostly the danger:
many have been here, but only
some have returned safely.

A compass is useless: also
trying to take directions
from the movements of the sun,
which are erratic;
and words here are as pointless   35
as calling in a vacant
wilderness.
        Whatever I do I must   40
keep my head. I know
it is easier for me to lose my way
forever here, than in other landscapes   45

ANNHARTE (MARIE BAKER) (b. 1942)
Canada

In "An Account of Tourist Terrorism" (1991), from *Being on the Moon,* the
Anishanabe poet Annharte adapts traditional indigenous material to poetic
modes. She also writes sharply satiric or parodistic verse attacking the dominant white culture's appropriation of Native peoples, as in this poem where
the narrative of exploration—in the contemporary mode of "discovery"
as "tourism," the means whereby European culture has "othered" Natives—
is turned back against the dominant culture. The clash of meaning between
cultures is figured here in the "ghostwriting" or trace of absent history
("what is history"?) to be filled in by a viewer knowing the code. Knowing
nothing of Native culture, they defile a sacred site, and introduce "plastic
tomahawks." The strength of her writing lies in its compelling images: history as
"used pampers."

An Account of Tourist Terrorism

History is just used pampers on the
grave of Sitting Bull[1] at Yankton but
because of crushed beer cans, obvious

---

1. Sitting Bull (Ta-tanka I-yotank) was a Sioux
chief born in buffalo country around 1834;
he died at Standing Rock, North Dakota, in
1890. The well-known Native warrior lived
in South Saskatchewan for a number of
years after the Battle of Little Big Horn.

Lakota[2] visitors to this historic site
know what is under the earth, the lake,   5
the black cook who died the same day.
McLaughlin buried both in the fort
with quicklime to foul up those Mobridge
businessmen's rendezvous with the right
bones to connect to make one skeleton.   10
What is history and what did happen
is a deeper question than tourists
dumping dollars in an empty memorial.
The words not written on the plaque or
between the lines are ghostwritten graffiti.   15
Glow in the dark instructions if you dare
to landfill history, deposit postcards,
return artifacts, souvenirs and the clutter
of plastic tomahawks buried in our minds.
Indian raids are nothing in comparison.   20
Tourist terrorism is ceremony without fuss,
and who takes the bother stops desecration.

b. p. NICHOL (1944–1988)
Canada

A concrete and sound poet, b. p. Nichol focuses on the materiality of language in his more "conventional" writing, particularly his continuing poem, *The Martyrology* (volumes 1–7, 1971–1990). Developing arbitrary compositional methods for this life-writing, the passing hours that serve as a frame for notation, on the model of the medieval book of religious meditations and the Japanese *utanikki* (poetic journal), this poem explicitly focuses on the poet's life in writing as a becoming, punning here on the multiple meanings of biology, genealogy, geology, etymology, and martyrology, the line of language constructing relations of sounds in a life sentence, grammar or poet's lifeline. Breaking language into elements smaller than semantic units in an effort to renew our perception of it, Nichol's poetics focuses on the construction of personal, national, identity in/as language.

So his grammar can be, in these hours of the grammar trilogy, his own grandma, just as his "graphy" or writing is both that of his existence (bio) and his place (geo), and the end is only the beginning, in this zippy text of proliferation and life.

---

2. A Sioux group.

from **The Book of Hours**

Hour 20

THE GRAMMAR TRILOGY—Hours 20, 21, & 22
Hour 20:
12:35 to 1:35 a.m.

bio ⎫
geo ⎭ graphy

       writing a self
           a country

landscape a can be in

          clOud
          clud

             (or, as in that poem i never published
             (not knowing the etymology):

          CLOUD
            O
            O
            O
          STONE

             too much the clod to see it then
             (ear to the earth))

grammar, grandma. now
in your 97th year
you've outlived most of them
—a husband
—two daughters
—a son
—only my mother & your other son left
the rest of us
grandchildren, great & great great grandchildren,
you feel further & further away from
we become less real
the longer your life becomes

family

     bio ⎫
     geo ⎭ logos

tonight
misreading my notes
mistake the time
miswrite this hour

lo $\begin{cases} \text{gos} \\ \text{cal} \end{cases}$

miss writing?

con $\begin{cases} \text{fusion} \\ \text{nection} \end{cases}$

I$\{$ con $\{$ O $\{$ graphy

IO[1] (inventor of the 5 vowels)
sister of Phoroneus[2]
(variously Bran,[3] Barn, Brennus, etc.
reincarnated as a crow)

(all this out of the con graphy
(the fusion which is the nection) the
bio geo)

we
of grandma, ma,
me & Sarah[4]

beING
  INGwe

(founder of the English tribes
inventor of the runic alphabet)

the continuous presence
the contiguous present

---

1. Io, a figure in Greek mythology, was the sister of Phoroneus and priestess of Hera. She was pursued by Zeus in the form of a cloud. He changed her into a white heifer and set Hermes to free her from Hera. Tortured by Hera with a gadfly, Io fled across the world to Egypt where Zeus restored her to human form and she gave birth to a son Epaphus. Later she was confused with Isis, the Egyptian goddess.
2. The brother of Io and father of Niobe, the first mortal woman loved by Zeus, who gave birth to Argos, founder of the city of that name.
3. A figure of Celtic mythology; Bran the Blessed, one of the children of Lyr, was a giant possessing a cauldron of life; he was also a skilled harpist and poet, Saint Brennan whose purported adventures crossing the Atlantic in a tiny boat was the subject of the first section of *The Martyrology Book 6*.
4. The poet's daughter.

ethereal earth eel

out of rhythm
pattern

CON $\left\{\begin{array}{l}\text{fusion}\\\text{nection}\end{array}\right.$ (a gain)

AM BIG!
u ity?

i-i-i-i
o my sombre era o

(line thru history)

bi
etym
gene $\left.\right\}$ OLOGY
martyr
ge

or all a G
(which is my birth'd A
September 30th being G's beginning
11th month in the Bethluisnion[5]

grammar
:the relations of words in
a sentence

she is my grammar
her name is Agnes[6]

sent m's
sent n's

m art
yr all a G

---

5. "Beth" is the second letter of the Hebrew
alphabet: the term "bethluisnion" is taken
from Robert Graves' *The White Goddess*.

6. The poet's grandmother.

```
what i thot was endin/g
            beginin/g
            writin/g

        in g   we
```

Davida Allen. *Death of My Father, II.*
1983. Oil on canvas.

SECTION XVI
Australia and New Zealand

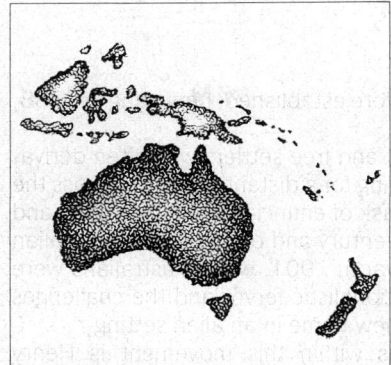

The Australian literary tradition can be said to have begun during the last Ice Age, with the arrival on the continent of Aboriginal peoples perhaps as long as 60,000 years ago. Aboriginal beliefs, coupled with environmental conditions unfavorable to the establishment of permanent agricultural settlements, account for the fact that Aborigines continued to live as peripatetic hunter-gatherers. They never developed a written language but instead preserved their history and traditions through a rich, orally transmitted culture of myth. These myths reveal a conception of life that sees a single order of being embracing godlike ancestral beings, humans, flora, fauna, and features of the landscape. The Aboriginal vision has been an atemporal and metamorphic one in which all forms of creation continually shift into others. This view of reality is reflected in the myth of "Eingana the Mother," while the Maori and Tahitian myths that follow it reflect a different understanding, one in which creation produces order, stability, and separate, discrete beings.

For our purposes, white settlement of Australia may be dated from January 26, 1788, when a shipload of British convicts arrived at Sydney Cove and raised England's flag over mainland Australia. Having recently lost the American colonies as a dumping ground for social and political undesirables, England decided to shift this function to the east coast of Australia, which James Cook had claimed for the Crown in 1770. Penal colonies were therefore established, beginning in 1788, along that coast and in Tasmania.

Early literature produced both by convict and free settlers was often derivative of its British models and expressed a longing for a distant "Home" across the seas. But it soon began to grapple with the task of enunciating the new land and its experience. By the end of the nineteenth century and on the eve of Australian independence, which was to come without war in 1901, white Australians were producing a literature that reflected both nationalistic fervor and the challenges inherent in locating, naming, and claiming a new home in an alien setting.

Among the most representative figures within this movement is Henry Lawson. In his work, pride in what is distinctively Australian, especially the "bush" or "outback," is tempered by awareness that the land demands terrible accommodations as the price of survival. Against overwhelming environmental odds, men band together in the hallowed Australian institution of "mateship." But like the land, mateship has its ambiguities, which Lawson explores in a "sketch" that becomes a parable.

The Australian tendency to romanticize bush life is also questioned by Judith Wright's use in her poem, "South of My Days," of bush tales of deprivation, resignation, and hard won half-successes. On the other hand, Gwen Harwood's "Estuary" suggests that austere surroundings can promote a clarity of perception which renews the present as it shapes and authorizes a future. Both poems make the point that in Australian literature, the investigation of relationship to land and environment is also an investigation of self and identity as these are constructed within that environment. "The Screaming Potato," short story by Nobel Prize-winner Patrick White, extends that investigation to include the relationship to personal and cultural history.

Further developments in the Australian handling of the theme of place and culture are indicated by Peter Carey's story, "Report on the Shadow Industry." Carey's futuristic fable sees that land as menaced by rampant consumerism and other spurious promises imported from overseas. Carey wonders if Australia remains at least the cultural colony of the West, especially of the United States.

New Zealand literature is also concerned with colonialism and the clash of cultures. New Zealand's history is like Australia's (as well as that of the United States, Canada, South America, and elsewhere) in that it chronicles white colonization of the land, violent conflict with and displacement of an indigenous (here, the Maori) population, and the attempt by both cultures to claim or reclaim physical, emotional, spiritual, and cognitive space. New Zealand's history differs from that of Australia, however, in that most of New Zealand's settlers came voluntarily. In addition, official annexation by Britain and the securing of national autonomy occurred about fifty years later in New Zealand than in Australia.

Like the Aborigines, the Maori (who arrived in New Zealand from East Polynesia about 800 C.E.) sustained their history, myths, and cultural practices through an oral tradition and did not develop written language until after the European invasion. Written Maori dates only from about 1815, and spoken Maori had so declined in use by the later twentieth century that an Act of Parliament was deemed necessary in 1987 to recognize the tongue as an official language in New Zealand, to confer the right to use it in certain situations, and to establish a Maori Language Commission to preserve it from extinction.

In New Zealand then, as elsewhere, language has served as one of the colonizers' most effective weapons in suppressing the indigenous population and in silencing resistance. Such strategic uses of language are recognized in "A Way of Talking" a short story by Patricia Grace, a contemporary Maori writer.

White or *Pakeha* writers in New Zealand have also been concerned with issues of place, cultural identity, and the role of language in producing these. Like white Australian writers, they have had to make their peace with a sometimes inimical environment by using language born and bred in other, very different climes. Two of the results of this effort—by what are arguably New Zealand's two best-known writers—are represented here: Katherine Mansfield's "The Woman at the Store" and Frank Sargeson's "The Making of a New Zealander."

Mansfield's elected exile from her New Zealand homeland (she spent much of her short life in England and Europe) makes her effort to come to terms with place at once more pressing and more difficult. In this disturbing story, written well before New Zealand gained its independence, she reexamines colonial stereotypes of New Zealanders and their land by rewriting the literary forms conventionally used to convey them.

Sargeson has most often been identified with the nationalist and "social realist" tradition that dominated New Zealand literature in the mid-twentieth century. But he also seems very contemporary in his demand for reader complicity in the making of meaning. In the story included here, this demand is enjoined by the text's open-endedness: its suggestion that New Zealanders are never made but always only in the making.

The most recent selection from New Zealand literature comes from Janet Frame. Although her story, "You Are Now Entering the Human Heart," is set in the United States, it concerns the terror of confronting the unfamiliar, an experience that white New Zealand settlers shared with Australia's settlers and with Frame's fictional Philadelphia schoolteacher. The story is also concerned with abuses of power and with the mechanisms by which the human heart itself can be colonized.

This group of selections from Australia and New Zealand thus provides a sense of what is and has been happening in this recent frontier of world literature. These texts will begin to suggest the complexities and paradoxes of the process through which nations and peoples locate themselves as products of place, culture, heritage, and language.

Historical Background

Historical records are intriguingly inconclusive on the subject of the earliest contacts with Australia. Both Chinese and Arab records mention a southern land that may be Australia. The spread of Islam though the Southeast Asian archipelagos beginning in the thirteenth century brought Arab ships to within a few hundred miles of Australia, and it is not difficult to imagine that an unexpected wind or current could have carried them the rest of the way. Claims that Chinese astronomers made observations from Australia in the sixth century B.C.E. have been neither proved nor disproved, but Chinese ships probably did visit in the fifteenth century. Aboriginal culture patterns stand as evidence of contact with Indonesia and New Guinea before the arrival of Europeans. European maps of the sixteenth century, meanwhile, show a southern land mass called "Jave la Grande" that may represent Australia.

Beginning with a series of Dutch expeditions in the first half of the seventeenth century, the situation becomes clearer. In the 1640s, Abel Janszoon

Tasman explored the coast of New Zealand (which he named for the Dutch province of Zeeland), the north coast of Australia (which he named New Holland), and the Australian island that now bears his name, Tasmania. British interest succeeded Dutch, culminating with the three voyages of James Cook, who claimed New Zealand and the east coast of Australia (which he named New South Wales) for Britain.

The first shipment of British colonists—some 730 convicts and 250 free persons—settled in 1788 in Sydney Cove, the site of present-day Sydney. In 1817 the name Australia, meaning "southern land," was officially adopted, and in the 1820s Britain extended possession to the entire continent. By 1830 some 58,000 convicts—almost all of them men—had been moved to Australia, where they were employed by the government or assigned to enterprises begun by free settlers. By 1868, when the practice was ended in favor of free migration, the continent had received about 160,000 convicts.

The decades between 1830 and 1860 comprised a period of rapid change. The colonies of Western Australia, South Australia, Victoria, and Queensland were established, and responsible self-government was recognized by the British Crown in all but the first. The discovery of gold, silver, and copper brought the first economic boom, and sheep farming became the mainstay industry it has remained to this day. With the possibility of wealth, Australia's image changed from a land of exile to one of opportunity. The resulting colonial push inland had disastrous consequences for the Aborigines, giving the lie to official British colonial policy, which supposedly safeguarded their rights and accorded them the benefits of British subjects. From 1860 to 1900, the colonies followed individual though largely parallel paths, with increasing democracy culminating in their federation as states in the independent Commonwealth of Australia in 1901.

Colonization did not begin in New Zealand until 1840. Before then, the islands served largely as outposts for the nascent Australian whaling industry. French, American, and British deep-sea whalers also used New Zealand as a way station, and a number of small bay-whaling settlements grew up along the coastline. Traders and missionaries followed, with the result that the Maori were drawn into the new economy and, by midcentury, largely converted to Christianity.

The treaty that placed New Zealand under British sovereignty in 1840 guaranteed the Maori full possession of the land, with the understanding that the British government would buy it from them piecemeal. Unscrupulous private buyers and the rapid pace of settlement quickly soured relations between the Maori and the British, however, and warfare over land continued until 1870. The Native Land Act of 1862 legalized transactions between the Maori and private buyers, and by the end of the nineteenth century the Maori had lost most of their best land.

Although scandalous treatment of indigenous populations during the century of settlement spawned problems that persist today, Australia and New Zealand were notably liberal and advanced in social legislation for their own societies. By the end of the nineteenth century, both had passed social security measures, experienced widespread unionization, and granted women the vote.

In the twentieth century, Australia and New Zealand supported Britain dutifully and even willingly in both world wars, each time suffering heavy losses. World War I served as a sort of coming of age for the two dominions. In the League of Nations, formed after the war, both countries demanded and received their own seats, claiming for the first time a relatively independent voice in international affairs. The Statute of Westminster conferred full independence on New Zealand in 1931, although it was not implemented there until 1947.

World War II saw a further shift in attitudes. Fighting in the Pacific threatened Australia and New Zealand directly (as fighting in Europe during the first war had not). The two countries emerged with a closer relationship to the United States, whose involvement in the Pacific theater was decisive, and an active concern for the political and economic future of the Pacific Rim, where their destinies now clearly lay.

Two factors in particular influenced the character of Australia during the postwar decades. One was widespread affluence, which created a consumer culture and welcomed a large percentage of the population to the middle class. The other was a diversification of Australian society—hitherto almost entirely British in origin—through large-scale immigration from all over Europe. In 1973 restrictions on Asian immigration in place since the beginning of the century were loosened, and the whites-only society of Australia tentatively began to embrace racial diversity. Multiculturalism and its tensions have since become a central political issue.

The experience of the Aborigines and the Maori and their place in contemporary society remain troubling issues. Although a small minority of Aborigines live on reserves in some approximation of traditional culture, the vast majority are racially mixed and increasingly Australian-European in look and manner. Yet their acceptance into society has been slowed by custom and lingering prejudice. Heavy-handed postwar policies aimed at assimilation have given way recently to demands from increasingly vocal and organized part-Aboriginal groups for integration, which would emphasize Aboriginal ancestry as a mark of special distinction within Australian society. Similar failures in New Zealand's official policy gave rise over the 1970s and 1980s to a Maori nationalist movement. Self-determination, land rights, and the preservation of Maori culture and language are central issues. The movement's fundamental claims are that the 1840 Treaty of Waitangi was never intended to confer sovereignty over the Maori people, and that its terms were not honored by the British.

Further Readings

Clark, Manning. *A Short History of Australia*. Rev. ed. New York: New American Library, 1969.

Evans, Patrick. *The Penguin History of New Zealand Literature*. Auckland: Penguin, 1990.

Godwin, Ken. *A History of Australian Literature*. New York: St. Martin's, 1986.

Green, H. M. *A History of Australian Literature*. 2 vols. Sydney: Angus and Robertson, 1961; rev. by Dorothy Green, 1984.

Hankin, Cherry, ed. *Critical Essays on the New Zealand Novel*. Auckland: Heinemann Educational Books, 1976.

———. *Critical Essays on the New Zealand Short Story*. Auckland: Heinemann Educational Books, 1982.

Healy, J. J. *Literature and the Aborigine in Australia*. St. Lucia: University of Queensland Press, 1978.

Hergenhan, Laurie, et al., eds. *The Penguin New Literary History of Australia*. Ringwood: Penguin Australia, 1988.

Hidden, Norman, and Amy Hollins, eds. *Many People, Many Voices: Poetry from the English Speaking World*. London: Hutchinson, 1978.

Hughes, Robert. *The Fatal Shore: The Epic of Australia's Founding*. New York: Knopf, 1987.

Jones, Joseph, and Joanna Jones. *New Zealand Fiction*. Twayne's World Authors Series. Boston: Twayne, 1984.

Molony, John. *The Penguin Bicentennial History of Australia*. Ringwood: Viking, 1987.

Oliver, W. H., ed. *The Oxford History of New Zealand*. Wellington, New Zealand: Oxford University Press, 1981.

Quartermaine, Peter, ed. *Diversity Itself: Essays in Australian Arts and Culture*. Exeter: University of Exeter, 1986.

Robinson, Roland. *Aboriginal Myths and Legends*. Melbourne: Sun Books, 1977.

Ross, Robert L. *Australian Literary Criticism—1945-1988: An Annotated Bibliography*. New York: Garland, 1989.

Shoemaker, Adam. *Black Words, White Page: Aboriginal Literature 1929–1988*. St. Lucia: University of Queensland Press, 1989.

Simms, Norman. *Silence and Invisibility: A Study of the Literatures of the Pacific, Australia, and New Zealand*. Washington: Three Continents Press, 1986.

————. *Points of Contact: Essays on Cultural Interactions and Interpenetrations*. New York: Pace University Press, 1990.

Sturm, Terry, ed. *The Oxford History of New Zealand Literature in English*. Auckland: Oxford University Press, 1991.

Wilde, William, H., Joy Hooton, and Barry Andrews. *The Oxford Companion to Australian Literature*. Melbourne: Oxford University Press, 1985.

RINJEIRA OF THE DJAUAN TRIBE OF ABORIGINALS OF THE NORTHERN TERRITORY

Australia

Non-Aboriginal Australians have come to know the creation time of Aboriginal mythology as "the Dreamtime." The designation is a useful one, in that it hints at the nonlinearity and fertile illogicality of the Dreamtime myths. Like dreams, the myths proceed according to rules of their own (or of the unconscious), with utter disregard for causal connection and chronological sequence. In "Eingana the Mother," a story related by Rinjeira of the Djauan tribe of Aboriginals in Australia's Northern Territory, creation exists even before Eingana creates it. Moreover, one form of creation can easily and atemporally metamorphose into another. "Blackfellows" become birds and animals, for example, and ancestral beings like Eingana herself may evolve into features of the landscape. In addition, one creative force engenders another. Eingana, whose androgyny is forced upon her when the old man Barraiya takes a spear to her phallic body and thus provides her with a vagina, will eventually give birth to the Rainbow Serpent, a more immediately androgynous source of fertility with a huge currency in Aboriginal mythology. Finally, the Dreamtime is not viewed as forever lost in a mythic past. Like a dream, it can recur, invading and enriching the present, so that creation and metamorphosis become ongoing processes. The connections and interdependence suggested in this tale—between past and present, human and animal, animate and inanimate, sacred and profane—not only define life, but constitute it for the Aboriginal consciousness.

Eingana the Mother

That first time, the creation time, we call Bieingana. The first being we call Eingana. We call Eingana our Mother. Eingana made everything: water, rocks, trees, blackfellows: she made all the birds, flying-foxes, kangaroos and emus. Everything Eingana had inside herself in that first time.

Eingana is snake. She swallowed all the blackfellows. She took them, inside herself, down under the water. Eingana came out, she was big with everything inside her. She came out of Gaieingung, the big water-hole near Bamboo Creek. Eingana was rolling about, every way, on the ground. She was groaning and calling out. She was making a big noise with all the blackfellows, everything, inside her belly.

One old-man named Barraiya had been travelling a long way. All the way he had heard Eingana crying out, rolling about and moaning. Barraiya sneaked up.

Told by Rinjeira to Roland Robinson.

He saw Eingana. He saw the big snake rolling and twisting about, moaning and calling out. Barraiya hooked up his stone-spear. He watched the big snake. He saw where he must spear her. Barraiya speared her underneath, near the anus. All blood came out of that spear-wound and all the blackfellows came out after the blood.

Kandagun the dingo[1] chased after all those blackfellows. He chased after them and split them up into different tribes and languages. When Kandagun chased the blackfellows, some flew away as birds, some bounded away as kangaroos, some raced away as emus, some became flying-foxes, porcupines, snakes, everything, to get away from Kandagun.

That first time, before Barraiya speared Eingana, nothing and no one could be born as they are now. Eingana had to spew everything out of her mouth. Blackfellows had to spew everything. Children could not be born as they are now. That is why Barraiya had to spear Eingana.

The old-man Barraiya had been travelling from the east across to the west. After he speared Eingana, the old-man went back to his place Barraiyawim. There he painted himself on a rock. He turned into the blue-winged kookaburra.

Eingana made the big Boolmoon River, she made the Flying-Fox River and the Roper River. Every river she made. We have water now. That's why we are alive.

Eingana made Bolong the Rainbow-Snake. . . .

No one can see Eingana. She stays in the middle water. She has a hole there. In the rain-time, when the flood-water comes, Eingana floats along on the flood water. She stands up and looks out at the country. . . She lets every kind of life, belonging to her, go. When the flood-water goes down Eingana goes back to her camp again. She comes back no more. No matter cold weather or hot weather, she does not come out. Next rain-time she comes out and lets go everything that belongs to her: snakes, birds, dingoes, kangaroos, blackfellows, everything. . .

If Eingana died, everything would die. There would be no more kangaroos, birds, blackfellows, anything. There would be no more water, everything would die.

MAORI PEOPLE OF NEW ZEALAND
New Zealand

This is a creation story from the Maori people of New Zealand, whose culture derives not from the Australian Aborigines, but from Polynesia (from which the

---

1. A wild dog, native to Australia.

first Maoris, or moa bird hunters, migrated in about 800 C.E.). Connections will be seen between this story and the Tahitian myth "Tangaroa Maker of All Things," which follows; in fact, the Tangaroa of that story is introduced here as one of the sons of Papatuanuku, the Earth Mother, and Ranginui, the Sky Father. Notice that while the Australian Aboriginal myth emphasizes the connectedness and interrelatedness of all things, this tale of Papatuanuku stresses the importance of separation and independence to the creative process. Tanemahuta, the god of fertility, forests, and birds, cannot exercise his function until space is made between his embracing parents, a space that provides scope for, and allows light to shine upon, his activities and those of his brothers. Here, specific and differentiated creation seems to disrupt the primal totality, as imaged in the quiescent, androgynous embrace of the first parents.

Papatuanuku, The Earth Mother

Papatuanuku, the earth mother, was born from Te Po, the darkness, the night, the unknown. Ranginui, the sky father, descended and took her as his wife. In the darkness of Te Po, they had seventy children, all male, who crawled and crouched between the bodies of their parents. At length, the offspring became tired of darkness and decided to lift their father, Rangi, up from their mother, Papa, so that light could bring some benefits. First Rongomatane tried to separate his parents, then Tangaroa, then Haumiatiketike, then Tumatauenga. All were unsuccessful. Finally, Tanemahuta pushed his feet on Rangi and his head against Papa and forced them apart. Tumatauenga cut the arms off the parents and caused the blood of Ranginui to flow into the heavens (sunsets) and the blood of Papatuanuku to flow into the soil (red ochre). Both were desperately unhappy at the actions of their children and began weeping unceasingly.

Their sons then turned Papa over so that she could not see her beloved Rangi nor could she be seen by him. Ranginui was placed even higher up on toko (poles) of light by Tane and so the primal parents were separated forever.

In the bottom portion of the image on pg. 2558, the symbolic wooden pegs of equal length are shaped to represent the particular attribute and nature of the godly beings. From left to right they are Tumatauenga, the god who represents man and war, standing erect; Tawhirimatea, the god of winds and storms, with his corkscrew shape; Tanemahuta, the fertiliser and god of forests and birds, with the semi-circular bend signifying growth; Tangaroa, the god of the sea, his shape representing waves; Rongomatane, the god of kumara[1] and cultivated foods, with gentle wave lines showing the mounds raised by kumara while growing; Haumiatiketike, the god of fern root and uncultivated food, with three semi-circles placed on the length of the peg representing the irregular and twisted form of the fern root.

Told by Patricia Grace.

---

1. Sweet potato, a staple of the traditional Maori diet.

Robyn Kahukiwa. *Paptuanuku, the Earth Mother.*

COOK ISLANDS PEOPLE (1400)
New Zealand

This selection is a Maori folktale told in the Cook Islands of New Zealand and in Papau New Guinea, a creation myth both witty and wise. This rendering dates from 1400—although time in the open ocean has a more fluid quality than elsewhere—and takes on new meaning with the increased importance given to Polynesia around 1985. Immensely popular, "Tangaroa: Maker of All Things" is a creation myth, now widely used in the schools and on television.

Tangaroa is depicted here as less violent, for example, than the Hawaiian Pele, goddess of fire and uproar associated with the volcano. Some speculate that this may be a relatively late myth, in a shift toward monotheism, perhaps due to the influence of whites. In any case, this wonderful tale is generated from itself, expanding and growing from the "shell round like an egg."

Tangaroa: Maker of All Things

For a long time Tangaroa lived within a shell that was round like an egg and revolved in a continual, dark void. There was no sun, no moon, no land nor

Told to an anonymous teller.

mountain, nor water (salt or fresh). There was no man, no fowl nor dog, nor any other living thing.

After a great time Tangaroa flicked his shell, making it crack and fall apart, and stepped forth upon it.

"Who is above there?" he called out, "Who is below there?"

No voice replied.

He spoke again. "Who is in front there? Who is behind?"

Still no voice answered.

Then Tangaroa said, "O rock, crawl here!" But no rock existed to crawl to him.

"O sand, crawl here!" he ordered. There was no sand.

Tangaroa, angry because he was not obeyed, overturned his shell and raised it up to form a dome for the sky. He named it Rumia, which means, "Overturned."

After a time great Tangaroa, wearied from being confined, stepped out from another shell that covered him; from it he created rock and sand.

He took his backbone and made a mountain range; his ribs became the ridges that ascend it. His innards turned into broad floating clouds, and his flesh, the fatness of the earth. His arms and legs became the strength of the earth; his fingernails and toenails became the scales and shells of fishes in the sea. Of his feathers he made trees and shrubs and plants to clothe the land; of his guts he made lobsters, shrimps, and eels for the streams and for the sea.

Tangaroa's blood became hot and floated away to make the redness of the sky, and rainbows, and all that is red. But the head of Tangaroa remained sacred and intact—the same head upon the body that remained.

Tangaroa called for gods. It was only later that he called for man, when Tu was with him.

As Tangaroa had shells, so has everything a shell, although no one can name all of the shells in this world. The sky is a shell of endless space, where the gods placed the sun, the moon, the constellations, and the other stars. The land is a shell to the stones, and water, and plants that spring from it. The shell of male and female is woman, since it is from her that each comes forth.

Tangaroa was master of everything that is. From him everything expanded and grew.

HENRY LAWSON (1867–1922)
Australia

At the turn of the twentieth century, Australia was winning its political independence from England, whose colony it had been for more than one hundred years. In this period of nationalistic fervor, writers like Henry Lawson and A. B. ("Banjo") Paterson (who wrote Australia's unofficial national anthem,

"Waltzing Matilda") celebrated things they thought were uniquely Australian, especially the lives of the hardy men who drove cattle, sheared sheep, and battled a hostile environment in the bush or "outback" regions of the country. The bushman's life was thought to embody a quintessentially Australian ethos characterized by egalitarianism, independence, self-reliance, competence in meeting challenges, and "mateship" (a camaraderie with and unswerving devotion to one's companions or mates). But even as they chronicled and sometimes sentimentalized mateship and others aspects of bush existence, the best of these writers observed certain ambiguities as well. As you read this sketch of what befalls two mates, ask yourself whether either has behaved as a true friend to the other. What *are* the demands and responsibilities of friendship? Are these determined by the environment in which the relationship exists?

A Sketch of Mateship[1]

Bill and Jim, professional shearers, were coming into Bourke[2] from the Queensland side. They were horsemen and had two pack-horses. At the last camp before Bourke Jim's pack-horse got disgusted and homesick during the night and started back for the place where he was foaled. Jim was little more than a newchum[3]-Jackeroo,[4] he was no Bushman[5] and generally got lost when he went down the next gully. Bill was a Bushman, so it was decided that he should go back to look for the horse.

Now Bill was going to sell his pack-horse, a well-bred mare, in Bourke, and he was anxious to get her into the yards before the horse sales were over; this was to be the last day of the sales. Jim was the best "barracker"[6] of the two; he had great imagination; he was a very entertaining story-teller and conversationalist in social life, and a glib and a most impressive liar in business, so it was decided that he should hurry on into Bourke with the mare and sell her for Bill. Seven pounds, reserve.

Next day Bill turned up with the missing horse and saw Jim standing against a verandah post of the "Carriers' Arms," with his hat down over his eyes, and thoughtfully spitting in the dust. Bill rode over to him.

"Ullo, Jim."

" 'Ullo, Bill. I see you got him."

"Yes, I got him."

Pause.

"Where'd yer find him?"

" 'Bout ten mile back. Near Ford's Bridge. He was just feedin' along."

Pause. Jim shifted his feet and spat in the dust.

---

1. The fellowship of working partners or companions, always men.
2. A town on the Darling River in New South Wales.
3. Someone newly arrived in the country or situation; an inexperienced novice.
4. A gentleman working on a station to gain

experience he can use later as a manager or owner.
5. Someone experienced in the bush or outback country.
6. A fast talker; someone who loudly supports his point of view.

"Well," said Bill at last. "How did you get on, Jim?"

"Oh, all right," said Jim. "I sold the mare."

"That's right," said Bill. "How much did she fetch?"

"Eight quid;" then, rousing himself a little and showing some emotion, "An' I could 'a' got ten quid for her if I hadn't been a dam' fool."

"Oh, that's good enough," said Bill.

"I could 'a' got ten quid if I'd 'a' waited."

"Well, it's no use cryin'. Eight quid is good enough. Did you get the stuff?"

"Oh, yes. They parted all right. If I hadn't been such a dam' fool an' rushed it, there was a feller that would 'a' given ten quid for that mare."

"Well, don't break yer back about it," said Bill. "Eight is good enough."

"Yes. But I could 'a' got ten," said Bill, languidly, putting his hand in his pocket.

Pause. Bill sat waiting for him to hand over the money; but Jim withdrew his hand empty, stretched, and said—

"Ah, well, Bill, I done it in. Lend us a couple o' notes."

Jim had been drinking and gambling all night and he'd lost the eight pounds as well as his own money.

Bill didn't explode. What was the use? He should have known that Jim wasn't to be trusted with money in town. It was he who had been the fool. He sighed and lent Jim a pound, and they went in to have a drink.

Now it strikes me that if this had happened in a civilized country (like England) Bill would have had Jim arrested and jailed for larceny as a bailee, or embezzlement, or whatever it was. And would Bill or Jim or the world have been any better for it?

KATHERINE MANSFIELD (1888–1923)
New Zealand

The short story writer Katherine Mansfield [Kathleen Mansfield Murry] was born as Kathleen Beauchamp in New Zealand. After a number of unhappy lesbian and other affairs, she married a musician whom she abandoned on their wedding night. When she married John Middleton Murry in 1918, she was already ill with tuberculosis. They collaborated on work for little magazines and the *Athenaum*. She is the author of many well-known stories, including "The Garden Party," and was a friend of Virginia Woolf and D. H. Lawrence. Like Henry Lawson's "A Sketch of Mateship," "The Woman at the Store" is a story about "outback" life, although the bush here is that of New Zealand rather than Australia. It is also a mystery story, but one in which the mystery's solution is to be found less in discovering who did what to whom than in understanding why. The narrator, apparently a woman traveling with her brother Jo and his friend Hin, arrives at a dilapidated store on what used to be a stage line, expecting to find Hin's old pal and his pretty wife, a former barmaid from a coastal town. Instead they find only a deranged hag and her odd daughter, both suspicious, terrified, and obviously concealing some awful secret about the woman's husband. The story is full of gothic elements: the terrible secret, the dark, stormy night, the general atmosphere of gloom, decay, deceit, and insanity. But unlike many gothic tales, this one does not end with life affirmed and the terror neutralized. The "romance" between Jo and the woman at the store is viewed as cheap and opportunistic on both sides, and a potential threat to Jo's well-being. Furthermore, although the mystery is certainly solved, order has not been restored as it usually is by the close of mystery stories: justice has not been and will not be done. Who or what is to blame for the fact that these people have abandoned their allegiance to some of the premises upon which "civilization" is supposed to be built? What role do environment and circumstances play? Do the answers to these questions have anything to say about the task of forging an identity in a lonely, strange, and frightening place?

The Woman at the Store

All that day the heat was terrible. The wind blew close to the ground—it rooted among the tussock grass—slithered along the road, so that the white pumice dust swirled in our faces—settled and sifted over us and was like a dry-skin itching for growth on our bodies. The horses stumbled along, coughing and chuffing. The pack horse was sick—with a big, open sore rubbed under the belly. Now and again she stopped short, threw back her head, looked at us as though she were going to cry, and whinnied. Hundreds of larks shrilled—the sky was slate colour, and the sound of the larks reminded me of slate pencils scraping over its surface. There was nothing to be seen but wave after wave of tussock grass—patched with purple orchids and manuka bushes covered with thick spider webs.

Jo rode ahead. He wore a blue galatea shirt, corduroy trousers and riding boots. A white handkerchief, spotted with red—it looked as though his nose had been bleeding on it—knotted round his throat. Wisps of white hair straggled from under his wideawake[1]—his moustache and eyebrows were called white—he slouched in the saddle—grunting. Not once that day had he sung "I don't care, for don't you see, my wife's mother was in front of me!". . . It was the first day we had been without it for a month, and now there seemed something uncanny in his silence. Hin rode beside me—white as a clown, his black eyes glittered, and he kept shooting out his tongue and moistening his lips. He was dressed in a Jaeger vest[2]—a pair of blue duck trousers, fastened round the waist with a plaited leather belt. We had hardly spoken since dawn. At noon we had lunched off fly biscuits and apricots by the side of a swampy creek.

"My stomach feels like the crop of a hen," said Jo. "Now then, Hin, you're the bright boy of the party—where's this 'ere store you kep' on talking about? 'Oh, yes,' you says, 'I know a fine store, with a paddock for the horses an' a creek runnin' through, owned by a friend of mine who'll give yer a bottle of whisky

---

1. A soft felt hat with a broad brim and low crown.   2. A vest typically worn by a hunter.

Anne Rice. *Portrait of Katherine Mansfield*. National Art Gallery of New Zealand.

before 'e shakes hands with yer.' I'd like ter see that place—merely as a matter of curiosity—not that I'd ever doubt yer word—as yer know very well—*but*. . . ."

Hin laughed. "Don't forget there's a woman too, Jo, with blue eyes and yellow hair, who'll promise you something else before she shakes hands with you. Put that in your pipe and smoke it."

"The heat's making you balmy," said Jo. But he dug his knees into his horse. We shambled on. I half fell asleep, and had a sort of uneasy dream that the horses were not moving forward at all—then that I was on a rocking horse, and my old mother was scolding me for raising such a fearful dust from the drawing-room carpet. "You've entirely worn off the pattern of the carpet," I heard her saying, and she gave the reins a tug. I snivelled and woke to find Hin leaning over me, maliciously smiling.

"That was a case of all but," said he, "I just caught you. What's up, been bye-bye?"

"No!" I raised my head. "Thank the Lord we're arriving somewhere."

We were on the brow of the hill, and below us there was a whare[3] roofed in with corrugated iron. It stood in a garden, rather far back from the road—a big paddock opposite, and a creek and a clump of young willow trees. A thin line of blue smoke stood up straight from the chimney of the whare, and as I looked, a woman came out, followed by a child and a sheep dog—the woman carrying what appeared to me a black stick. She made frantic gestures at us. The horses put on

---

3. A Maori hut or native dwelling.

a final spurt, Jo took off his wideawake, shouted, threw out his chest, and began singing, "I don't care, for don't you see. . . ." The sun pushed through the pale clouds and shed a vivid light over the scene. It gleamed on the woman's yellow hair, over her flapping pinafore and the rifle she was carrying. The child hid behind her, and the yellow dog, a mangy beast, scuttled back into the whare, his tail between his legs. We drew rein and dismounted.

"Hallo," screamed the woman. "I thought you was three 'awks. My kid comes runnin' in ter me. 'Mumma,' says she, 'there's three brown things comin' over the 'ill,' says she. An' I comes out smart. I can tell yer. They'll be 'awks, I says to her. Oh, the 'awks about 'ere, yer wouldn't believe."

The "kid" gave us the benefit of one eye from behind the woman's pinafore—then retired again.

"Where's your old man," asked Hin.

The woman blinked rapidly, screwing up her face.

"Away shearing." Bin away a month. I suppose yer not goin' to stop, are yer? There's a storm comin' up."

"You bet we are," said Jo. "So you're on your lonely, missis?"

She stood, pleating the frills of her pinafore, and glancing from one to the other of us, like a hungry bird. I smiled at the thought of how Hin had pulled Jo's leg about her. Certainly her eyes were blue, and what hair she had was yellow, but ugly. She was a figure of fun. Looking at her, you felt there was nothing but sticks and wires under that pinafore—her front teeth were knocked out, she had red pulpy hands, and wore on her feet a pair of dirty "Bluchers."[4]

"I'll go and turn out the horses," said Hin. "Got any embrocation? Poi's rubbed herself to hell!"

"Arf a mo!" The woman stood silent a moment, her nostrils expanding as she breathed. Then she shouted violently, "I'd rather you didn't stop—you *can't* and there's the end of it. I don't let out that paddock any more. You'll have to go on; I ain't got nothing!"

"Well, I'm blest!" said Jo, heavily. He pulled me aside. "Gone a bit off 'er dot," he whispered, "too much alone, *you know*," very significantly. "Turn the sympathetic tap on 'her, she'll come round all right."

But there was no need—she had come round by herself.

"Stop if yer like!" she muttered, shrugging her shoulders. To me—"I'll give yer the embrocation if yer come along."

"Right-o, I'll take it down to them." We walked together up the garden path. It was planted on both sides with cabbages. They smelled like stale dishwater. Of flowers there were double poppies and sweet-williams. One little patch was divided off by pawa shells—presumably it belonged to the child—for she ran from her mother and began to grub in it with a broken clothes peg. The yellow dog lay across the door step, biting fleas; the woman kicked him away.

"Gar-r, get away, you beast . . . the place ain't tidy, I 'aven't 'ad time ter fix things to-day—been ironing. Come right in."

---

4. Strong leather half-boots.

It was a large room, the walls plastered with old pages of English periodicals. Queen Victoria's Jubilee[5] appeared to be the most recent number—a table with an ironing board and wash tub on it—some wooden forms—a black horsehair sofa, and some broken cane chairs pushed against the walls. The mantelpiece above the stove was draped in pink paper, further ornamented with dried grasses and ferns and a coloured print of Richard Seddon.[6] There were four doors—one, judging from the smell, let into the "store," one on the "back yard," through the third I saw the bedroom. Flies buzzed in circles round the ceiling, and treacle papers[7] and bundles of dried clover were pinned to the window curtains. I was alone in the room—she had gone into the store for the embrocation. I heard her stamping about and muttering to herself: "I got some, now where did I put that bottle? . . . It's behind the pickles . . . no, it ain't." I cleared a place on the table and sat there, swinging my legs. Down in the paddock I could hear Jo singing and the sound of hammer strokes as Hin drove in the tent poles. It was sunset. There is no twilight to our New Zealand days, but a curious half-hour when everything appears grotesque—it frightens—as though the savage spirit of the country walked abroad and sneered at what it saw. Sitting alone in the hideous room I grew afraid. The woman next door was a long time finding that stuff. What was she doing in there? Once I thought I heard her bang her hands down on the counter, and once she half moaned, turning it into a cough and clearing her throat. I wanted to shout "Buck up," but I kept silent.

"Good Lord, what a life!" I thought, "Imagine being here day in, day out, with that rat of a child and a mangy dog. Imagine bothering about ironing—*mad*, of course she's mad! Wonder how long she's been here—wonder if I could get her to talk."

At that moment she poked her head round the door.

"Wot was it yer wanted," she asked.

"Embrocation."

"Oh, I forgot, I got it, it was in front of the pickle jars."

She handed me the bottle.

"My, you do look tired, you do! Shall I knock yer up a few scones for supper? There's some tongue in the store, too, and I'll cook yer a cabbage if you fancy it."

"Right-o." I smiled at her. "Come down to the paddock and bring the kid for tea."

She shook her head, pursing up her mouth.

"Oh, no. I don't fancy it. I'll send the kid down with the things and a billy[8] of milk. Shall I knock up a few extry scones to take with you ter-morrow?"

"Thanks."

She came and stood by the door.

"How old is the kid?"

---

5. The 1887 commemoration in England of fifty years of Queen Victoria's reign.

6. New Zealand's Prime Minister, 1893–1906; "The Woman at the Store" was written in 1911.

7. Sticky papers for catching flies.

8. A pail or can, often used for boiling water for tea.

"Six—come next Christmas. I 'ad a bit of trouble with 'er one way an' another. I 'adn't any milk till a month after she was born and she sickened like a cow."

"She's not like you—takes after her father?" Just as the woman had shouted her refusal at us before, she shouted at me then.

"No, she don't; she's the dead spit of me. Any fool could see that. Come on in now, Els, you stop messing in the dirt."

I met Jo climbing over the paddock fence.

"What's the old bitch got in the store?" he asked.

"Don't know—didn't look."

"Well, of all the fools. Hin's slanging you. What have you been doing all the time?"

"She couldn't find this stuff. Oh, my shakes, you are smart!"

Jo had washed, combed his wet hair in a line across his forehead, and buttoned a coat over his shirt. He grinned.

Hin snatched the embrocation from me. I went to the end of the paddock where the willows grew and bathed in the creek. The water was clear and soft as oil. Along the edges held by the grass and rushes, white foam tumbled and bubbled. I lay in the water and looked up at the trees that were still a moment, then quivered lightly, and again were still. The air smelt of rain. I forgot about the woman and the kid until I came back to the tent. Hin lay by the fire, watching the billy boil.

I asked where Jo was and if the kid had brought our supper.

"Pooh," said Hin, rolling over and looking up at the sky. "Didn't you see how Jo had been tittivating—he said to me before he went up to the whare, 'Dang it! she'll look better by night light—at any rate, my buck, she's female flesh!' "

"You had Jo about her looks—you had me, too."

"No—look here. I can't make it out. It's four years since I came past this way, and I stopped here two days. The husband was a pal of mine once, down the West Coast—a fine, big chap, with a voice on him like a trombone. She'd been barmaid down the Coast—as pretty as a wax doll. The coach used to come this way then once a fortnight, that was before they opened the railway up Napier[9] way, and she had no end of time! Told me once in a confidential moment that she knew one hundred and twenty-five different ways of kissing!"

"Oh, go on, Hin! She isn't the same woman!"

"Course she is. . . . I can't make it out. What I think is the old man's cleared out and left her: that's all my eye about shearing. Sweet life! The only people who come through now are Maoris and sundowners!"[10]

Through the dark we saw the gleam of the kid's pinafore. She trailed over to us with a basket in her hand, the milk billy in the other. I unpacked the basket, the child standing by.

"Come over here," said Hin, snapping his fingers at her.

She went, the lamp from the inside of the tent cast a bright light over her. A

9. A town on the east coast of New Zealand's North Island.
10. Tramps or itinerants, ostensibly seeking work, who arrive at a property too late in the day to do any but in time to draw rations.

mean, undersized brat, with whitish hair, and weak eyes. She stood, legs apart and her stomach protruding.

"What do you do all day?" asked Hin.

She scraped out one ear with her little finger, looked at the result and said—"Draw."

"Huh! What do you draw?—leave your ears alone."

"Pictures."

"What on?"

"Bits of butter paper an' a pencil of my Mumma's."

"Boh! What a lot of words at one time!" Hin rolled his eyes at her. "Baa-lambs and moo-cows?"

"No, everything. I'll draw all of you when you're gone, and your horses and the tent, and that one"—she pointed to me "with no clothes on in the creek. I looked at her where she wouldn't see me from."

"Thanks very much! How ripping of you," said Hin. "Where's Dad?"

The kid pouted. "I won't tell you because I don't like yer face!" She started operations on the other ear.

"Here," I said. "Take the basket, get along home and tell the other man supper's ready."

"I don't want to."

"I'll give you a box on the ear if you don't," said Hin, savagely.

"Hie! I'll tell Mumma. I'll tell Mumma"—the kid fled.

We ate until we were full and had arrived at the smoke stage before Jo came back, very flushed and jaunty, a whisky bottle in his hand.

" 'Ave a drink—you two!" he shouted, carrying off matters with a high hand. " 'Ere, shove along the cups."

"One hundred and twenty-five different ways," I murmured to Hin.

"What's that? Oh! stow it!" said Jo. "Why 'ave you always got your knife into me. You gas like a kid at a Sunday School beano.[11] She wants us to go up there to-night, and have a comfortable chat. I"—he waved his hand airily—"I got 'er round."

"Trust you for that," laughed Hin. "But did she tell you where the old man's got to?"

Jo looked up. "Shearing! You 'eard 'er, you fool!"

The woman had fixed up the room, even to a light bouquet of sweet-williams on the table. She and I sat one side of the table, Joe and Hin the other. An oil lamp was set between us, the whisky bottle and glasses, and a jug of water. The kid knelt against one of the forms, drawing on butter paper. I wondered, grimly, if she was attempting the creek episode. But Jo had been right about night time. The woman's hair was tumbled—two red spots burned in her cheeks—her eyes shone—and we knew that they were kissing feet under the table. She had changed the blue pinafore for a white calico dressing jacket and a black skirt—the kid was decorated to the extent of a blue sateen hair ribbon. In the stifling room with the

---

11. A bean feast, or ceremonial dinner.

flies buzzing against the ceiling and dropping on to the table—we got slowly drunk.

"Now listen to me," shouted the woman, banging her fist on the table. "It's six years since I was married, and four miscarriages. I says to 'im, I says, what do you think I'm doin' up 'ere? If you was back at the Coast, I'd 'ave you lynched for child murder. Over and over I tells 'im—you've broken my spirit and spoiled my looks, and wot for—that's wot I'm driving at." She clutched her head with her hands and stared round at us. Speaking rapidly, "Oh, some days—an' months of them I 'ear them two words knockin' inside me all the time—'Wot for,' but sometimes I'll be cooking the spuds an' I lifts the lid off to give 'em a prong and I 'ears, quite sudden again, 'Wot for.' Oh! I don't mean only the spuds and the kid—I mean—I mean," she hiccoughed—"you know what I mean, Mr Jo."

"I know," said Jo, scratching his head.

"Trouble with me is," she leaned across the table, "he left me too much alone. When the coach stopped coming, sometimes he'd go away days, sometimes he'd go away weeks, and leave me ter look after the store. Back 'e'd come—pleased as Punch. 'Oh, 'allow,' 'e'd say. 'Ow are you gettin' on. Come and give us a kiss.' Sometimes I'd turn a bit nasty, and then 'e'd go off again, and if I took it all right, 'e'd wait till 'e could twist me round 'is finger, then 'e'd say, 'Well, so long, I'm off,' and do you think I could keep 'im?—not me!"

"Mumma," bleated the kid, "I made a picture of them on the 'ill, an' you an' me, an' the dog down below."

"Shut your mouth," said the woman.

A vivid flash of lightning played over the room—we heard the mutter of thunder.

"Good thing that's broke loose," said Jo. "I've 'ad it in me 'ead for three days."

"Where's your old man now?" asked Hin slowly.

The woman blubbered and dropped her head on to the table. "Hin, 'e's gone shearin' and left me alone again," she wailed.

" 'Ere, look out for the glasses," said Jo. "Cheer-o, 'ave another drop. No good cryin' over spilt 'usbands! You Hin, you blasted cuckoo!"

"Mr Jo," said the woman, drying her eyes on her jacket frill, "you're a gent, an' if I was a secret woman, I'd place any confidence in your 'ands. I don't mind if I do 'ave a glass on that."

Every moment the lightning grew more vivid and the thunder sounded nearer. Hin and I were silent—the kid never moved from her bench. She poked her tongue out and blew on it as she drew.

"It's the loneliness," said the woman, addressing Jo—he made sheep's eyes at her—"and bein' shut up 'ere like a broody 'en." He reached his hand across the table and held hers, and though the position looked most uncomfortable when they wanted to pass the water and whiskey, their hands stuck together as though glued. I pushed back my chair and went over to the kid, who immediately sat flat down on her artistic achievements and made a face at me.

"You're not to look," said she.

"Oh, come on, don't be so nasty!" Hin came over to us, and we were just drunk enough to wheedle the kid into showing us. And those drawings of hers were extraordinary and repulsively vulgar. The creations of a lunatic with a lunatic's cleverness. There was no doubt about it, the kid's mind was diseased. While she showed them to us, she worked herself up into a mad excitement, laughing and trembling, and shooting out her arms.

"Mumma," she yelled. "Now I'm going to draw them what you told me I never was to—now I am."

The woman rushed from the table and beat the child's head with the flat of her hand.

"I'll smack you with yer clothes turned up if yer dare say that again," she bawled.

Jo was too drunk to notice, but Hin caught her by the arm. The kid did not utter a cry. She drifted over to the window and began picking flies from the treacle paper.

We returned to the table—Hin and I sitting one side, the woman and Jo, touching shoulders, the other. We listened to the thunder, saying stupidly, "That was a near one," "There it goes again," and Jo, with a heavy hit, "Now we're off," "Steady on the brake," until rain began to fall, sharp as cannon shot on the iron roof.

"You'd better doss[12] here for the night," said the woman.

"That's right," assented Jo, evidently in the know about this move.

"Bring up yer things from the tent. You two can doss in the store along with the kid—she's used to sleep in there and won't mind you."

"O, Mumma, I never did," interrupted the kid.

"Shut yer lies! An' Mr Jo can 'ave this room."

It sounded a ridiculous arrangement, but it was useless to attempt to cross them, they were too far gone. While the woman sketched the plan of action, Jo sat, abnormally solemn and red, his eyes bulging, and pulled at his moustache.

"Give us a lantern," said Hin. "I'll go down to the paddock." We two went together. Rain whipped in our faces, the land was as light as though a bush fire was raging—we behaved like two children let loose in the thick of an adventure—laughed and shouted to each other, and came back to the whare to find the kid already bedded in the counter of the store. The woman brought us a lamp. Jo took his bundle from Hin, the door was shut.

"Good-night all," shouted Jo.

Hin and I sat on two sacks of potatoes. For the life of us we could not stop laughing. Strings of onions and half-hams dangled from the ceiling—wherever we looked there were advertisements for "Camp Coffee" and tinned meats. We pointed at them, tried to read them aloud—overcome with laughter and hiccoughs. The kid in the counter stared at us. She threw off her blanket and scrambled to the floor where she stood in her grey flannel night gown, rubbing one leg against the other. We paid no attention to her.

"Wot are you laughing at," she said, uneasily.

"You!" shouted Hin, "the red tribe of you, my child."

---

12. Sleep.

She flew into a rage and beat herself with her hands. "I won't be laughed at, you curs—you." He swooped down upon the child and swung her on to the counter.

"Go to sleep, Miss Smarty—or make a drawing—here's a pencil—you can use Mumma's account book."

Through the rain we heard Jo creak over the boarding of the next room—the sound of a door being opened—then shut to.

"It's the loneliness," whispered Hin.

"One hundred and twenty-five different ways—alas! my poor brother!"

The kid tore out a page and flung it at me.

"There you are," she said. "Now I done it ter spite Mumma for shutting me up 'ere with you two. I done the one she told me I never ought to. I done the one she told me she'd shoot me if I did. Don't care! Don't care!"

The kid had drawn the picture of the woman shooting at a man with a rook rifle and then digging a hole to bury him in.

She jumped off the counter and squirmed about on the floor biting her nails.

Hin and I sat till dawn with the drawing beside us. The rain ceased, the little kid fell asleep, breathing loudly. We got up, stole out of the whare, down into the paddock. White clouds floated over a pink sky—a chill wind blew; the air smelled of wet grass. Just as we swung into the saddle, Jo came out of the whare—he motioned to us to ride on.

"I'll pick you up later," he shouted.

A bend in the road, and the whole place disappeared.

FRANK SARGESON (1903–1982)
New Zealand

Sargeson's fiction has often been viewed as central to a realistic tradition in New Zealand literature, a tradition seen as a response to and departure from the tradition founded by New Zealand's first great fiction writer, Katherine Mansfield. When compared with Mansfield's work, Sargeson's was judged to be sterner, more masculine, more socially aware, and more evocative of a New Zealand recognizable to readers. In "The Making of a New Zealander" however, Sargeson seems to call the very existence of "reality" into question. Like many of the works in this section, it deals with the difficulties of forging an identity in a new, strange, and sometimes hostile environment. As the narrator reflects upon the hardships faced by two Dalmatian immigrants as they try to establish an orchard, we realize that putting down healthy, nourishing roots in new soil is a long, hard process for people, as it is for apple and pine trees. At what point will the Dalmatians become New Zealanders, the story asks. *Is* there such a thing as a New Zealander, or are cultural and national identity never fully achieved but always precarious and "in the making"? Do the clothes we wear, the places we live, and the labels by which we choose to name ourselves ever add up to a "real" identity? Do such questions assume more urgency in a land as young as New Zealand, which was still achieving the full sovereignty that came in 1947, even as Sargeson was writing this story?

The Making of a New Zealander

When I called at that farm they promised me a job for two months so I took it on, but it turned out to be tough going. The boss was all right, I didn't mind him at all, and most days he'd just settle down by the fire and get busy with his crochet. It was real nice to see him looking happy and contented as he sat there with his ball of wool.

But this story is not about a cocky[1] who used to sit in front of the fire and do crochet. I'm not saying I haven't got a story about him, but I'll have to be getting round to it another time.

Yes, the boss was all right, it was his missis that was the trouble. Some people say, never work for a woman, women'll never listen to reason. But that's not my experience. Use your block and in no time you'll be unlucky if you don't have them eating out of your hand.

But this time I was unlucky. This Mrs Crump was a real tough one. She and the boss ran a market garden besides the cows. She'd tie a flour-bag over her head, get into gumboots, and not counting the time she put in in the house, she'd do about twelve hours a day, and she had me doing the same. Not that I minded all that much. The best of working on the land is that you're not always wishing it was time to knock off. Nor thinking of pay-day, either, particularly if there isn't a pub handy. I'm not going to explain. If you don't believe me, try it yourself and see.

But twelve hours a day, every day. I'll admit I used to get tired. Mrs Crump would see I was done in and tell me to stop working, and that was just what I was waiting for her to do. But there'd be a look in her eye. She'd say that I wasn't built for hard work, but she wasn't surprised because she'd never met a man she couldn't work to a standstill. Well, after she'd said that I'd just go on working, and if I was feeling cheeky I'd tell her I didn't mind giving her a run for her money. And before those two months were up I was feeling cheeky pretty often. Once she got going about my wages and everything else she had to pay out. She couldn't keep the wolf from the door, she said. Well then, I said, if you can't you'll just have to keep the door shut.

Now I'm running on ahead so I'd better break off again, because this isn't just a no-account story about how I began to get cheeky and put wisecracks across Mrs

---

1. A farmer with a small holding, often with a reputation for stinginess and for exploiting hired help.

Crump. It's not about Mrs Crump, she only comes into it. I'm not saying I haven't got a story about her too, but it's another one I'll be getting round to another time.

What I want to tell is about how I sat on a hillside one evening and talked with a man. That's all, just a summer evening and a talk with a man on a hillside. Maybe there's nothing in it and maybe there is.

The man was one of two young Dallies who ran an orchard up at the back of Mrs Crump's place. These two had come out from Dalmatia and put some money down on the land, not much, just enough to give them the chance to start working the land. They were still paying off and would be for a good many years. There was a shed where they could live, and to begin with they took it in turns to go out and work for the money they needed to live and buy trees.

All that was some years before I turned up. The Dallies had worked hard, but it wasn't all plain sailing. They had about twenty-five acres, but it sloped away from the sun. They'd planted pines for shelter, but your shelter has to make a lot of growth before it's any use on land with a good slope to the south. And it was poor land, just an inch or two of dark soil on top of clay. You could tell it was poor from the tea-tree, which made no growth after it was a few feet high. Apples do best on land like that, so it was apple-trees the Dallies had mainly gone in for.

Of course Mrs Crump gossiped to me about all this. When I was there the Dallies weren't keeping a cow, so she was letting them have milk at half the town price. She didn't mind doing that much for them, she said, they worked so hard. And my last job each day was to take a billy[2] up to the back fence. I'd collect an empty billy that'd be hanging on a hook, and I'd always consider going on and having a yarn with the Dallies. It wasn't far across to their shed but it would be getting dark, I'd be feeling like my tea so I'd tell myself I'd go over another time.

Then one evening the billy wasn't on the hook and I went on over, but the door was shut and there was no one about. The dog went for me but he never had a show. He'd had distemper, he couldn't move his hind legs and just had to pull himself along. I had a look round but there wasn't much to see, just two flannels and a towel hanging on the line, and a few empty barrels splashed with bluestone. Close to the shed there were grape vines growing on wires, then the trees began. They were carrying a lot of fruit and looked fine and healthy, but just a bit too healthy I thought. You could tell from the growth that the Dallies had put on a lot of fertilizer. For a while I waited about, kidding to the dog until he wagged his tail, then I went back.

The next day one of the Dallies brought the billy over but I didn't see him. When we were milking Mrs Crump told me. He was the one called Nick, and the evening before he'd had to take his mate[3] into hospital. He'd had a spill off his bike and broken some ribs and his collar-bone. Mrs Crump thought perhaps there'd been some drinking, she said they made wine. Anyhow Nick was upset. If his mate died, he said, he would die too. He'd have nothing left, nothing. And how could he work and live there by himself when his mate was lying all broken up in the

---

2. A tin pail or bucket with a handle.

3. A man's male friend, companion, or partner.

hospital? Every afternoon he would leave off working and ride into town to see his mate.

There's a pal for you, Mrs Crump said.

Well, up at the fence the billy would always be on the hook, but if Nick was in town seeing his cobber[4] I'd think it would be no use going over. Then one evening he was just coming across with the billy so I went over to meet him. We greeted each other, and I think we both felt a bit shy. He was small and dark, almost black, and his flannel and denims were pretty far gone the same as mine were. I gave him my tin and told him to roll a cigarette, and when he lit up he went cross-eyed. I noticed that, and I saw too that there was a sort of sadness on his face.

I asked him how his cobber was, and he said he was good.

In two days he will be here, he said. You could see he was excited about it and his face didn't look so sad. In two weeks, he said, it will be just as if it never happened.

That's great, I said, and we sat down and smoked.

How's the dog? I said.

He is getting better too, Nick said.

He whistled, and the dog pulled himself over to us by his front paws and put his chin on Nick's leg, and somehow with the dog there it was easier to talk.

I asked Nick about his trees and he said they were all right, but there were too many diseases.

Too much quick manure, I said.

He said yes, but what could they do? It would take a long time to make the soil deep and sweet like it was in the part of Dalmatia he came from. Out here everybody wanted money quick, so they put on the manure. It was money, money, all the time. But he and his mate never had any. Everything they got they had to pay out, and if the black-spot got among the apples they had to pay out more than they got. Then one of them had to go out and try for a job.

It's the manure that gives you the black-spot, I said.

Sometimes I think it is God, Nick said.

Well, maybe you're right, I said, but what about the grapes?

On no, Nick said, they grow, yes. But they are not sweet. To make wine we must put in sugar. In Dalmatia it is not done. Never.

Yes, I said, but you don't go back to Dalmatia.

Oh, he said, now I am a New Zealander.

No, I said, but your children will be.

I have no children and I will never marry, Nick said.

No? I said, then your cobber will.

He will never marry either, Nick said.

Why? I said, there are plenty of Dalmatian girls out here. I bet you could get New Zealand girls too.

But Nick only said no no no no no.

If you were in Dalmatia I bet you'd be married, I said.

---

4. Same as "mate"; a friend.

But I am not in Dalmatia, Nick said, now I am a New Zealander. In New Zealand everybody says they cannot afford to get married.

Yes, I said, that's what they say. But it's all wrong.

Yes, Nick said, it is all wrong. Because it is all wrong I am a Communist.

Good, I said. Well, I thought, spoil a good peasant and you might as well go the whole hog.

I bet you don't tell Mrs Crump you're a Communist, I said.

Oh no, Nick said, she would never be a Communist.

No fear, I said.

I will tell you about Mrs Crump, Nick said. She should go to Dalmatia. In Dalmatia our women wear bags on their heads just like her, and she would be happy there.

Yes, I said, I believe you're right. But Nick, I said, I thought you'd be a Catholic.

No, Nick said. It is all lies. In Dalmatia they say that Christ was born when there was snow on the ground in Palestine. But now I have read in a book there is no snow in Palestine. So now I know that they tell lies.

So you're a Communist instead, I said.

Yes, I am a Communist, Nick said. But what is the good of that? I am born too soon, eh? What do you think?

Maybe, I said.

You too, Nick said. You think that you and me are born too soon? What do you think?

He said it over and over, and I couldn't look him in the face. It had too much of that sadness . . . . I mightn't have put it the way Nick had, I mightn't have said I was born too soon, but Nick knew what he was talking about. Nick and I were sitting on the hillside and Nick was saying he was a New Zealander, but he knew he wasn't a New Zealander. And he knew he wasn't a Dalmatian any more.

He knew he wasn't anything any more.

Listen, Nick said, do you drink wine?

Yes, I said.

Then to-morrow night you come up here and we will drink wine, Nick said.

Yes, I said, that's O.K. with me.

There is only to-morrow night, Nick said, then my mate will be here. We will drink a lot of wine, I have plenty and we will get very, very drunk. Oh, heaps drunk.

Yes, I said. Sure thing.

To-morrow night, he said.

He got up and I got up, he just waved his hand at me and walked off. He picked the dog up under his arm and walked off, and I just stood there and watched him go.

But it turned out I never went up to Nick's place. When I was having my tea that evening Mrs Crump told me about how a woman she knew had worked too hard and dropped dead with heart failure. But there's nothing wrong with my heart, she said.

No, I said, except that maybe it's not in the right place.

Of course it must have sounded like one of my wisecracks, but I was thinking of Dalmatia.

Anyhow Mrs Crump said she'd stood enough from me, so when I'd finished my tea I could go.

I wasn't sorry. I stood on the road and wondered if I'd go up to Nick's place, but instead I walked into town, and for a few days I never left off drinking.

I wanted to get Nick out of my mind. He knew what he was talking about, but maybe it's best for a man to hang on.

PATRICK WHITE (1912–1990)
Australia

Winner of the Nobel Prize for Literature in 1973, Patrick White enjoys a wider international reputation than does any other writer Australia has yet produced. In part, his reputation derives from his willingness to confront the big questions: about the meaning and direction of life; about God; about personal, social, and national identities; about individual and societal guilt and redemption. In some of his best novels—such as *The Tree of Man* (1955), *Voss* (1957), and *A Fringe of Leaves* (1976)—White sends his protagonists on journeys into the literal and metaphorical interior of Australia, in search of a way to realize their fullest human potential. In "The Screaming Potato," an aged narrator reflects upon the inevitable damage to the self and others inflicted during such journeys.

The Screaming Potato

It has been said she peels an economical potato. Seven children she had to bring up after he defected. I have seen her holding a skinned potato perhaps admiring her artistry or wondering whether to gouge the eyes. Perhaps she should leave them. A certain amount of flesh would disappear with the gouging.

This was a long time ago. We have all done a fair bit of gouging since then, in the name of morality and justice. As I stand waiting for the WALK sign, the screams of the punished and the avengers flicker along Castlereagh.[1]

Again on the escalators, whether up or down (don't touch the rail, God knows what you'll catch) the screams bump and waver, swell, fade completely before the momentum of a life we're supposed to be living, perhaps some of us actually are.

I would like to believe in the myth that we grow wiser with age. In a sense my disbelief is wisdom. Those of a middle generation, if charitable or sentimental,

---

1. A street in Sydney, Australia.

subscribe to the wisdom myth, while the callous see us as dispensable objects, like broken furniture or dead flowers. For the young we scarcely exist unless we are unavoidable members of the same family, farting, slobbering, perpetually mislaying teeth and bifocals. Some may Christian Science their disgust if they see death as a handout, then if the act is delayed, remember the gouging they have suffered in the past.

Some of us become vegans[2] to atone for the soft cruelties we've inflicted on our fellow animals: parents, children, lovers, friends, though our eyes continue to conceal knives ready for strangers we pass in the street if they don't recognise our right of way.

Prayer and vegies ought to help towards atonement. But don't. There is the chopping to be done. Memories rise to the surface as we hear the whimper of a frivolous lettuce, the hoarse-voiced protest of slivered parsnip, screaming of the naked potato in its pot of tumbled water. So how can an altruist demonstrate his sincerity? Could we perhaps exist on air till the day we are returned to earth, the bed in which potatoes faintly stir as they prepare sightless eyes for birth?

O Lord, dispel our dreams, of murders we did not commit—or did we?

JUDITH WRIGHT (b. 1915)
Australia

Judith Arundell Wright, an Australian poet, critic, and short story writer, deals with her country's landscape and its people's relationships. *The Generations of Men* (1959) depicts the pioneer life of her grandparents when they first settled in Australia. Her poetry is collected in *The Double Tree* (1978). Like several of the works included here from Australian and New Zealand writers, "South of My Days" recognizes the hardships and challenges inherent in settling, claiming, and negotiating a new land. The narrator, in recounting the stories told by "old Dan" around a winter's fire, transports the reader to times of drought and blizzard, times when death came casually and unannounced to animals and their caretakers, and times when one's fellows were often as great a threat as the elements. Simultaneously, however, these retold tales of privation and danger provide the comfort of community by connecting the narrator not only to Dan but to a past that has produced the sense of home and self she claims in the present. Notice that the single "day" of the poem's first line has become plural by the end of the poem. In time—as in space—the poet has extended her reach, embracing and naturalizing more and more of her "blood's country."

---

2. Vegetarians.

South of My Days

South of my day's circle, part of my blood's country,
rises that tableland, high delicate outline
of bony slopes wincing under the winter,
low trees blue-leaved and olive, outcropping granite—
clean, lean, hungry country. The creek's leaf-silenced,   5
willow-choked, the slope a tangle of medlar and crabapple
branching over and under, blotched with a green lichen;
and the old cottage lurches in for shelter.

O cold the black-frost night. The walls draw in to the warmth
and the old roof cracks its joints; the slung kettle   10
hisses a leak on the fire. Hardly to be believed that summer
will turn up again some day in a wave of rambler roses,
thrust its hot face in here to tell another yarn—
a story old Dan can spin into a blanket against the winter.
Seventy years of stories he clutches round his bones.   15
Seventy summers are hived in him like old honey.

Droving that year, Charleville to the Hunter,[1]
nineteen-one it was, and the drought beginning;
sixty head left at the McIntyre, the mud around them
hardened like iron; and the yellow boy died   20
in the sulky ahead with the gear, but the horse went on,
stopped at the Sandy Camp and waited in the evening.
It was the flies we seen first, swarming like bees.
Came to the Hunter, three hundred head of a thousand—
cruel to keep them alive—and the river was dust.   25

Or mustering up in the Bogongs in the autumn
when the blizzards came early. Brought them down; we brought them
down, what aren't there yet. Or driving for Cobb's[2] on the run
up from Tamworth—Thunderbolt at the top of Hungry Hill,
and I give him a wink. I wouldn't wait long, Fred,   30
not if I was you; the troopers are just behind,
coming for that job at the Hillgrove. He went like a luny,
him on his big black horse.

       Oh, they slide and they vanish
as he shuffles the years like a pack of conjuror's cards.   35

---

1. These are the first of a series of names of
   towns, rivers, mountains, and other geographic features with which Wright evokes
   the New England region of New South
   Wales, north of Sydney.
2. Cobb and Company was Australia's most
   famous pioneering coach company,
   founded by four Americans shortly after the
   Australian Gold Rush began in 1851. By the
   1880s Cobb had become a loose federation
   of transport firms whose coaches traversed
   the country from north to south. Coaches
   were often held up and robbed by bandits
   known as "bushrangers," one of whom is
   the "Fred" of this poem.

True or not, it's all the same; and the frost on the roof
cracks like a whip, and the back-log breaks into ash.
Wake, old man. This is winter, and the yarns are over.
No one is listening.
        South of my days' circle   40
I know it dark against the stars, the high lean country
full of old stories that still go walking in my sleep.

GWEN HARWOOD (b. 1920)
Australia

"Estuary" is set in Tasmania, where Harwood has lived since 1945. The natural
and human worlds, and within these, the realms of the physical and the spiritual,
are seen to harmonize in a song which "renew[s] the world." Images of change
and process—some positive, some painful—are presented in terms of musical
motifs. They are notes and chords struck in an ongoing hymn to the cyclical and
interdependent nature of existence. Here Australian nature, while remaining
austere, soothes and comforts more than it confronts. The reader is left to ask
what reassurance does the poet take from the "benediction" of light? What is it
that she must remember?

Estuary

(To Rex Hobcroft)[1]

Wind crosshatches shallow water.
Paddocks rest in the sea's arm.
Swamphens race through spiky grass.
A wire fence leans, a crazy stave
with sticks for barlines, wind for song.   5
Over us, interweaving light
with air and substance, ride the gulls.

Words in our undemanding speech
hover and blend with things observed.

---

1. A friend of Gwen Harwood's who was an
   important influence in her life at the time
   this poem was written.

Syllables flow in the tide's pulse.   10
My earliest memory turns in air:
Eclipse. Cocks crow, as if at sunset;
Grandmother, holding a smoked glass,
says to me, *"Look. Remember this."*

Over the goldbrown sand my children   15
run in the wind. The sky's immense
with spring's new radiance. Far from here,
lying close to the final darkness,
a great-grandmother lives and suffers,
still praising life: another morning   20
on earth, cockcrow and changing light.

Over the skeleton of thought
mind builds a skin of human texture.
The eye's part of another eye
that guides it through the maze of light.   25
A line becomes a firm horizon.
All's as it was in the beginning.
Obscuring symbols melt away.

"Remember this." I will remember
this quiet in which the questioning mind   30
allows reality to enter
its gateway as a friend, unchallenged,
to rest as a friend may, without speaking;
light falling like a benediction
on moments that renew the world.   35

JANET FRAME (b. 1924)
New Zealand

Janet Paterson Frame, the New Zealand novelist and poet, is familiar to many
from the autobiographical film *An Angel at My Table*. Her novels include *Owls Do
Cry* (1957), a rendering of New Zealand village life, and *Living in the Maniototo*
(1979). *The Pocket Mirror* (1967) is a collection of poems. Although "You Are
Now Entering the Human Heart" takes place in Philadelphia, it concerns a
universal experience, one that would have been as familiar to New Zealander
Janet Frame as it is to most of us. The story is about confronting the fear of the
unknown and about what happens when one fails to meet that challenge. It is also
a story about power and about who gets to wield it. The snake handler at the
Natural Science Museum misuses his power over Miss Aitcheson to torture and

humiliate her in front of her pupils. Does he do so deliberately? Does it matter whether or not his actions are calculated to have the effects they do? Might Miss Aitcheson be right not to be lulled into a sense of calm and confidence in this situation? In an irony that Frame fully intends, the narrator, who hasn't time to tour the giant model of a human heart, has actually penetrated the depths of the human heart as she witnesses Miss Aitcheson's encounter with the snake and its keeper. The story's first paragraph suggests that opening one's heart to people always invites danger and damage. However, a fearful, barricaded heart like Miss Aitcheson's may not provide much safety either.

You Are Now Entering the Human Heart

I looked at the notice. I wondered if I had time before my train left Philadelphia for Baltimore in one hour. That heart, ceiling-high, occupied one corner of the large exhibition hall, and from wherever you stood in the hall you could hear its beating, *thum-thump-thum-thump*. It was a popular exhibit, and sometimes, when there were too many children about, the entrance had to be roped off, as the children loved to race up and down the blood vessels and match their cries to the heart's beating. I could see that the heart had already been punished for the day—the floor of the blood vessel was worn and dusty, the chamber walls were covered with marks, and the notice "You Are Now Taking the Path of a Blood Cell Through the Human Heart," hung askew. I wanted to see more of the Franklin Institute and the Natural Science Museum across the street, but a journey through the human heart would be fascinating. Did I have time?

Later. First, I would go across the street to the Hall of North America, among the bear and the bison, and catch up on American flora and fauna.

I made my way to the Hall. More children, sitting in rows on canvas chairs. An elementary class from a city school, under the control of an elderly teacher. A museum attendant holding a basket, and all eyes gazing at the basket.

"Oh," I said. "Is this a private lesson? Is it all right for me to be here?"

The attendant was brisk. "Surely. We're having a lesson in snake-handling," he said. "It's something new. Get the children young and teach them that every snake they meet is not to be killed. People seem to think that every snake has to be knocked on the head. So we're getting them young and teaching them."

"May I watch?" I said.

"Surely. This is a common grass snake. No harm, no harm at all. Teach the children to learn the feel of them, to lose their fear."

He turned to the teacher. "Now, Miss—Mrs—" he said.

"Miss Aitcheson."

He lowered his voice. "The best way to get through to the children is to start with teacher," he said to Miss Aitcheson. "If they see you're not afraid, then they won't be."

She must be near retiring age, I thought. A city woman. Never handled a snake in her life. Her face was pale. She just managed to drag the fear from her eyes to some place in their depths, where it lurked like a dark stain. Surely the attendant and the children noticed?

"It's harmless," the attendant said. He'd been working with snakes for years.

Miss Aitcheson, I thought again. A city woman born and bred. All snakes were creatures to kill, to be protected from, alike the rattler, the copperhead, king snake, grass snake—venom and victims. Were there not places in the South where you couldn't go into the streets for fear of the rattlesnakes?

Her eyes faced the lighted exit. I saw her fear. The exit light blinked, hooded. The children, none of whom had ever touched a live snake, were sitting hushed, waiting for the drama to begin; one or two looked afraid as the attendant withdrew a green snake about three feet long from the basket and with a swift movement, before the teacher could protest, draped it around her neck and stepped back, admiring and satisfied.

"There," he said to the class. "Your teacher has a snake around her neck and she's not afraid."

Miss Aitcheson stood rigid; she seemed to be holding her breath.

"Teacher's not afraid, are you?" the attendant persisted. He leaned forward, pronouncing judgement on her, while she suddenly jerked her head and lifted her hands in panic to get rid of the snake. Then, seeing the children watching her, she whispered, "No, I'm not afraid. Of course not." She looked around her.

"Of course not," she repeated sharply.

I could see her defeat and helplessness. The attendant seemed unaware, as if his perception had grown a reptilian covering. What did she care for the campaign for the preservation and welfare of copperheads and rattlers and common grass snakes? What did she care about someday walking through the woods or the desert and deciding between killing a snake and setting it free, as if there would be time to decide, when her journey to and from school in downtown Philadelphia held enough danger to occupy her? In two years or so, she'd retire and be in that apartment by herself and no doorman, and everyone knew what happened then, and how she'd be afraid to answer the door and to walk after dark and carry her pocketbook in the street. There was enough to think about without learning to handle and love the snakes, harmless and otherwise, by having them draped around her neck for everyone, including the children—most of all the children—to witness the outbreak of her fear.

"See, Miss Aitcheson's touching the snake. She's not afraid of it at all."

As everyone watched, she touched the snake. Her fingers recoiled. She touched it again.

"See, she's not afraid. Miss Aitcheson can stand there with a beautiful snake around her neck and touch it and stroke it and not be afraid."

The faces of the children were full of admiration for the teacher's bravery, and yet there was a cruelly persistent tension; they were waiting, waiting.

"We have to learn to love snakes," the attendant said. "Would someone like to come out and stroke teacher's snake?"

Silence.

One shamefaced boy came forward. He stood petrified in front of the teacher.

"Touch it," the attendant urged. "It's a friendly snake. Teacher's wearing it around her neck and she's not afraid."

The boy darted his hand forward, rested it lightly on the snake, and immediately withdrew his hand. Then he ran back to his seat. The children shrieked with glee.

"He's afraid," someone said. "He's afraid of the snake."

The attendant soothed. "We have to get used to them, you know. Grownups are not afraid of them, but we can understand that when you're small you might be afraid, and that's why we want you to learn to love them. Isn't that right, Miss Aitcheson? Isn't that right? Now who else is going to be brave enough to touch teacher's snake?"

Two girls came out. They stood hand in hand side by side and stared at the snake and then at Miss Aitcheson.

I wondered when the torture would end. The two little girls did not touch the snake, but they smiled at it and spoke to it and Miss Aitcheson smiled at them and whispered how brave they were.

"Just a minute," the attendant said. "There's really no need to be brave. It's not a question of bravery. The snake is *harmless,* absolutely *harmless.* Where's the bravery when the snake is harmless?"

Suddenly the snake moved around to face Miss Aitcheson and thrust its flat head toward her cheek. She gave a scream, flung up her hands, and tore the snake from her throat and threw it on the floor, and, rushing across the room, she collapsed into a small canvas chair beside the Bear Cabinet and started to cry.

I didn't feel I should watch any longer. Some of the children began to laugh, some to cry. The attendant picked up the snake and nursed it. Miss Aitcheson, recovering, sat helplessly exposed by the small piece of useless torture. It was not her fault she was city-bred, her eyes tried to tell us. She looked at the children, trying in some way to force their admiration and respect; they were shut against her. She was evicted from them and from herself and even from her own fear-infested tomorrow, because she could not promise to love and preserve what she feared. She had nowhere, at that moment, but the small canvas chair by the Bear Cabinet of the Natural Science Museum.

I looked at my watch. If I hurried, I would catch the train from Thirtieth Street. There would be no time to make the journey through the human heart. I hurried out of the museum. It was freezing cold. The icebreakers would be at work on the Delaware and the Susquehanna; the mist would have risen by the time I arrived home. Yes, I would just catch the train from Thirtieth Street. The journey through the human heart would have to wait until some other time.

PATRICIA GRACE (b. 1937)
New Zealand

Since language is one of the most powerful tools we have for constructing a version of reality, our "way of talking" is also a way of defining ourselves and our world. Strategic uses of language have always figured among the weaponry of colonizing powers, because words alone can do much to put and confine people "in their place." For example, in "A Way of Talking" we see how the white woman Jane uses the word "Maori" to signify, and thereby to maintain, a class of nameless, faceless, interchangeable people who do manual labor for the *Pakehas* (whites). The fact that she does not feel the need to name the Maoris as individuals suggests that she and her culture need not treat them as individuals either. Moreover, the *Pakehas* are not the only ones guilty of such dismissive essentializing. As the narrator tells her sister Rose, the Maoris themselves abet this system of oppression. They often see *Pakehas* not as separate people but as a dangerous class marked by its untrustworthiness. But if words and the way they are used can stereotype, they can also individualize. Grace insists that we notice the richness of Nanny's "lovely way . . . of talking" when she applies the metaphorizing practices of her Maori tongue to her adopted English. We also see that Rose's linguistic versatility—her ability to make herself heard within a number of different discourse communities—empowers her in important ways. Thus Nanny's and Rose's ways of talking may hint at avenues out of the ghetto of language.

A Way of Talking

Rose came back yesterday; we went down to the bus to meet her. She's just the same as ever Rose. Talks all the time flat out and makes us laugh with her way of talking. On the way home we kept saying, "E. Rohe, you're just the same as ever." It's good having my sister back and knowing she hasn't changed. Rose is the hard-case one in the family, the kamakama[1] one, and the one with the brains.

Last night we stayed up talking till all hours, even Dad and Nanny who usually go to bed after tea. Rose made us laugh telling about the people she knows, and taking off professor this and professor that from varsity. Nanny, Mum and I had tears running down from laughing; e ta Rose we laughed all night.

At last Nanny got out of her chair and said, "Time for sleeping. The mouths steal the time of the eyes." That's the lovely way she has of talking, Nanny, when she speaks in English. So we went to bed and Rose and I kept our mouths going for another hour or so before falling asleep.

This morning I said to Rose that we'd better go and get her measured for the dress up at Mrs Frazer's. Rose wanted to wait a day or two but I reminded her the wedding was only two weeks away and that Mrs Frazer had three frocks to finish.

"Who's Mrs Frazer anyway," she asked. Then I remembered Rose hadn't met these neighbours though they'd been in the district a few years. Rose had been away at school.

"She's a dressmaker," I looked for words. "She's nice."

---

1. Entertaining, lively, friendly, likable.

"What sort of nice?" asked Rose.

"Rose, don't you say anything funny when we go up there," I said. I know Rose, she's smart. "Don't you get smart." I'm older than Rose but she's the one that speaks out when something doesn't please her. Mum used to say, Rohe you've got the brains but you look to your sister for the sense. I started to feel funny about taking Rose up to Jane Frazer's because Jane often says the wrong thing without knowing.

We got our work done, had a bath and changed, and when Dad came back from the shed we took the station-wagon to drive over to Jane's. Before we left we called out to Mum, "Don't forget to make us a Maori bread for when we get back."

"What's wrong your own hands," Mum said, but she was only joking. Always when one of us comes home one of the first things she does is make a big Maori bread.

Rose made a good impression with her kamakama ways, and Jane's two nuisance kids took a liking to her straight away. They kept jumping up and down on the sofa to get Rose's attention and I kept thinking what a waste of a good sofa it was, what a waste of a good house for those two nuisance things. I hope when I have kids they won't be so hoha.[2]

I was pleased about Jane and Rose. Jane was asking Rose all sorts of questions about her life in Auckland.[3] About varsity and did Rose join in the marches and demonstrations. Then they went on to talking about fashions and social life in the city, and Jane seemed deeply interested. Almost as though she was jealous of Rose and the way she lived, as though she felt Rose had something better than a lovely house and clothes and everything she needed to make life good for her. I was pleased to see that Jane liked my sister so much, and proud of my sister and her entertaining and friendly ways.

Jane made up a cup of coffee when she'd finished measuring Rose for the frock, then packed the two kids outside with a piece of chocolate cake each. We were sitting having coffee when we heard a truck turn in at the bottom of Frazers' drive.

Jane said, "That's Alan. He's been down the road getting the Maoris for scrub cutting."

I felt my face get hot. I was angry. At the same time I was hoping Rose would let the remark pass. I tried hard to think of something to say to cover Jane's words though I'd hardly said a thing all morning. But my tongue seemed to thicken and all I could think of was Rohe don't.

Rose was calm. Not all red and flustered like me. She took a big pull on the cigarette she had lit, squinted her eyes up and blew the smoke out gently. I knew something was coming.

"Don't they have names?"

"What. Who?" Jane was surprised and her face was getting pink.

---

2. Rowdy, noisy, undisciplined.

3. A major city on the northernmost of the two islands that constitute New Zealand.

"The people from down the road whom your husband is employing to cut scrub." Rose the stink thing, she was talking all Pakehafied.[4]

"I don't know any of their names."

I was glaring at Rose because I wanted her to stop but she was avoiding my looks and pretending to concentrate on her cigarette.

"Do they know yours?"

"Mine?"

"Your name."

"Well . . . Yes."

"Yet you have never bothered to find out their names or to wonder whether or not they have any."

The silence seemed to hang around in my head for ages and ages. Then I think Jane muttered something about difficulty, but that touchy sister of mine stood up and said, "Come on Hera." And I with my red face and shut mouth followed her out to the station wagon without a goodbye or anything.

I was so wild with Rose. I was wild. I was determined to blow her up about what she had done, I was determined. But now that we were alone together I couldn't think what to say. Instead I felt an awful big sulk coming on. It has always been my trouble, sulking. Whenever I don't feel sure about something I go into a big fat sulk. We had a teacher at school who used to say to some of us girls, "Speak, don't sulk." She's say, "You only sulk because you haven't learned how and when to say your minds."

She was right that teacher, yet here I am a young woman about to be married and haven't learned yet how to get the words out. Dad used to say to me, "Look out girlie, you'll stand on your lip."

At last I said, "Rose, you're a stink thing." Tears were on the way. "Gee Rohe, you made me embarrassed." Then Rose said, "Don't worry Honey she's got a thick hide."

These words of Rose's took me by surprise and I realised something about Rose then. What she said made all my anger go away and I felt very sad because it's not our way of talking to each other. Usually we'd say, "Never mind Sis," if we wanted something to be forgotten. But when Rose said, "Don't worry Honey she's got a thick hide," it made her seem a lot older than me, and tougher, and as though she knew much more than me about the world. It made me realise too that underneath her jolly and forthright ways Rose is very hurt. I remembered back to when we were both little and Rose used to play up at school if she didn't like the teacher. She'd get smart and I used to be ashamed and tell Mum on her when we got home, because although she had the brains I was always the well behaved one.

Rose was speaking to me in a new way now. It made me feel sorry for her and for myself. All my life I had been sitting back and letting her do the objecting. Not only me, but Mum and Dad and the rest of the family too. All of us

---

4. In the manner of a *Pakeha*, a white or
   non-Maori person.

too scared to make known when we had been hurt or slighted. And how can the likes of Jane know when we go round pretending all is well. How can Jane know us?

But then I tried to put another thought into words. I said to Rose, "We do it too. We say, 'the Pakeha doctor,' or 'the Pakeha at the post office,' and sometimes we mean it in a bad way."

"Except that we talk like this to each other only. It's not so much what is said, but when and where and in whose presence. Besides, you and I don't speak in this way now, not since we were little. It's the older ones: Mum, Dad, Nanny who have this habit."

Then Rose said something else. "Jane Frazer will still want to be your friend and mine in spite of my embarrassing her today; we're in the fashion."

"What do you mean?"

"It's fashionable for a Pakeha to have a Maori for a friend." Suddenly Rose grinned. Then I heard Jane's voice coming out of that Rohe's mouth and felt a grin of my own coming. "I have friends who are Maoris. They're lovely people. The eldest girl was married recently and I did the frocks. The other girl is at varsity. They're all so *friendly* and so *natural* and their house is absolutely *spotless*."

I stopped the wagon in the drive and when we'd got out Rose started strutting up the path. I saw Jane's way of walking and felt a giggle coming on. Rose walked up Mum's scrubbed steps, "Absolutely spotless." She left her shoes in the porch and bounced into the kitchen. "What did I tell you? Absolutely spotless. And a friendly natural woman taking new bread from the oven."

Mum looked at Rose then at me. "What have you two been up to? Rohe I hope you behaved yourself at that Pakeha place?" But Rose was setting the table. At the sight of Mum's bread she'd forgotten all about Jane and the events of the morning.

When Dad, Heke, and Matiu came in for lunch, Rose, Mum, Nanny and I were already into the bread and the big bowl of hot corn.

"E ta," Dad said. "Let your hardworking father and your two hardworking brothers starve. Eat up."

"The bread's terrible. You men better go down to the shop and get you a shop bread, " said Rose.

"Be the day," said Heke.

"Come on my fat Rohe. Move over and make room for your Daddy. Come on my baby shift over."

Dad squeezed himself round behind the table next to Rose. He picked up the bread Rose had buttered for herself and started eating. "The bread's terrible all right," he said. Then Mat and Heke started going on about how awful the corn was and who cooked it and who grew it, who watered it all summer and who pulled out the weeds.

So I joined in the carryings on and forgot about Rose and Jane for the meantime. But I'm not leaving it at that. I'll find some way of letting Rose know I understand and I know it will be difficult for me because I'm not clever the way she is. I can't say things the same and I've never learnt to stick up for myself.

But my sister won't have to be alone again. I'll let her know that.

PETER CAREY (b. 1943)
Australia

Colonial imperialism can be exercised and experienced both politically and culturally. Although political domination of Australia by the British ended in 1901, when Australia became an independent commonwealth, British and later American culture continued to provide the standards against which Australians judged their own. The resultant tendency to dismiss all things indigenously Australian as second-rate when compared to products and practices of America, England, and Europe was memorably described by Australian critic A. A. Phillips as a "cultural cringe." It is this cringe that has brought the shadow industry from America to Australia in Carey's surrealistic fable. Fables are stories told to point out a moral, and the moral of this tale seems to be that shadows are evil, deceptive, and dangerous. But what *are* these shadows? Are they the false promises of happiness that materialism holds out to us? Are they images of ideal selves that the culture projects for us? Do they represent all the mechanisms we use to avoid the real? Remember that a shadow shows us only the outline of the body it reflects and that it guarantees the absence of that body. Where the shadow is, the real cannot be. Yet the story's last section suggests there may be possibilities for good as well as evil in these phenomena. Self-consciously examining his enterprise as storyteller, as do so many contemporary writers in Australia and elsewhere, Carey's narrator names his own production as another shadow: one cast by absent beauty and deepening mystery.

Report on the Shadow Industry

1

My friend S. went to live in America ten years ago and I still have the letter he wrote me when he first arrived, wherein he describes the shadow factories that were springing up on the west coast and the effects they were having on that society. "You see people in dark glasses wandering around the supermarkets at 2 A.M. There are great boxes all along the aisles, some as expensive as fifty dollars but most of them only five. There's always Muzak. It gives me the shits more than the shadows. The people don't look at one another. They come to browse through the boxes of shadows although the packets give no indication of what's inside. It really depresses me to think of people going out at two in the morning because they need to try their luck with a shadow. Last week I was in a supermarket near Topanga[1] and I saw an old negro tear the end off a shadow box. He was arrested almost immediately."

A strange letter ten years ago but it accurately describes scenes that have since become common in this country. Yesterday I drove in from the airport past shadow factory after shadow factory, large faceless buildings gleaming in the sun, their secrets guarded by ex-policemen with alsatian dogs.

The shadow factories have huge chimneys that reach far into the sky, chimneys which billow forth smoke of different, brilliant colours. It is said by some of my more cynical friends that the smoke has nothing to do with any manufacturing process and is merely a trick, fake evidence that technological miracles are being performed within the factories. The popular belief is that the smoke sometimes contains the most powerful shadows of all, those that are too large and powerful to be packaged. It is a common sight to see old women standing for hours outside the factories, staring into the smoke.

There are a few who say the smoke is dangerous because of carcinogenic chemicals used in the manufacture of shadows. Others argue that the shadow is a natural product and by its very nature chemically pure. They point to the advantages of the smoke: the beautifully coloured patterns in the clouds which serve as a reminder of the happiness to be obtained from a fully realized shadow. There may be some merit in this last argument, for on cloudy days the skies above our city are a wondrous sight, full of blues and vermilions and brilliant greens which pick out strange patterns and shapes in the clouds.

Others say that the clouds now contain the dreadful beauty of the apocalypse.

2

The shadows are packaged in large, lavish boxes which are printed with abstract designs in many colours. The Bureau of Statistics reveals that the average householder spends 25 per cent of his income on these expensive goods and that this percentage increases as the income decreases.

There are those who say that the shadows are bad for people, promising an impossible happiness that can never be realized and thus detracting from the very real beauties of nature and life. But there are others who argue that the shadows have always been with us in one form or another and that the packaged shadow is necessary for mental health in an advanced technological society. There is, however, research to indicate that the high suicide rate in advanced countries is connected with the popularity of shadows and that there is a direct statistical correlation between shadow sales and suicide rates. This has been explained by those who hold that the shadows are merely mirrors to the soul and that the man who stares into a shadow box sees only himself, and what beauty he finds there is

---

1. A town in California.

his own beauty and what despair he experiences is born of the poverty of his spirit.

3

I visited my mother at Christmas. She lives alone with her dogs in a poor part of town. Knowing her weakness for shadows I brought her several of the more expensive varieties which she retired to examine in the privacy of the shadow room.

She stayed in the room for such a long time that I became worried and knocked on the door. She came out almost immediately. When I saw her face I knew the shadows had not been good ones.

"I'm sorry," I said, but she kissed me quickly and began to tell me about a neighbour who had won the lottery.

I myself know, only too well, the disappointments of shadow boxes for I also have a weakness in that direction. For me it is something of a guilty secret, something that would not be approved of by my clever friends.

I saw J. in the street. She teaches at the university.

"Ah-hah," she said knowingly, tapping the bulky parcel I had hidden under my coat. I know she will make capital of this discovery, a little piece of gossip to use at the dinner parties she is so fond of. Yet I suspect that she too has a weakness for shadows. She confessed as much to me some years ago during that strange misunderstanding she still likes to call "Our Affair." It was she who hinted at the feeling of emptiness, that awful despair that comes when one has failed to grasp the shadow.

4

My own father left home because of something he had seen in a box of shadows. It wasn't an expensive box, either, quite the opposite—a little surprise my mother had bought with the money left over from her housekeeping. He opened it after dinner one Friday night and he was gone before I came down to breakfast on the Saturday. He left a note which my mother only showed me very recently. My father was not good with words and had trouble communicating what he had seen: "Words Cannot Express It What I feel Because of The Things I Saw In The Box Of Shadows You Bought Me."

5

My own feelings about the shadows are ambivalent, to say the least. For here I have manufactured one more: elusive, unsatisfactory, hinting at greater beauties and more profound mysteries that exist somewhere before the beginning and somewhere after the end.

Jacob Lawrence. *Funeral Sermon*. 1946.
Gouache and casein on paper.

SECTION XVII
Oral Literature Today

Although people living in modern Western cultures might never suspect it, writing is a relatively recent invention in the history of our species. If we map its discovery onto a calendar modified to represent the whole panorama of human history, writing emerges late on the thirty-first of December, New Year's Eve. What is more, the invention of printing comes even later, and the advent of mass market textbooks and paperbacks to reach and support a mass readership just a few minutes before midnight. Such a stark situation begs the question of just how our ancestors were transacting their cultural business for the first eleven months and thirty days of our existence.

Nor is yesterday's emergence of writing, print, and "literary literature" only a historical matter. As we move into the twenty-first century, the vast majority of the world's peoples still operate without letters in all or most of their daily activities. Of the tens of thousands of cultures that have inhabited the earth, only about a hundred have ever used writing extensively enough to develop a literature; about eighty of those are still functioning. The reality is that, whether we take the long view from our origins or a wide-angle perspective on the present situation, the written literature we cherish as central to the human condition is an exceedingly rare, almost statistically negligible, phenomenon.

Some idea of the extent to which we focus on that minuscule body of material is apparent even in the title of this section. As many have noted, "oral literature" is, strictly speaking, a contradiction in terms: at the root of the English word "literature" lies the Latin word "letter." We press an inappropriate word into service simply because our standard way of conceiving of verbal art has become so entrenched. In English, as in many other modern languages, there is no longer any neutral term for what we designate by "literature." Before the Battle of Hastings (1066), English had a plethora of such words; in Anglo-Saxon one could speak of a work like *Beowulf* as a *gied* ("tale"), a *sang* ("song"), or even a *word* (not a dictionary item but a unit of utterance large or small). With writing, this kind of terminology eventually becomes rhetorical or simply obsolete, and the "lettered" concept becomes a cultural given whose specialized meaning is forgotten.

Using the designation "literature" obscures another important aspect of the works that are the subject of this chapter: their traditional nature. Verbal art created and transmitted orally, without the media of writing or print, depends upon a tradition of person-to-person, face-to-face performance that lasts only as long as people are willing to maintain a continuous human chain of expression. In this respect oral *tradition,* as these forms are more accurately designated, is intimately tied to cultural dynamics; its tremendous variety of genres, for example, far wider than the repertoire of more narrowly focused literary genres, betokens the wider range of cultural functions verbal art is licensed to perform. Whereas most modern societies have split off the concerns of history, philosophy, law, custom, and the rest into disciplines whose transactions are conducted mainly through the circulation of documents, most other cultures have always subsumed these concerns in active, complex oral traditions. Even though we make the compromise of using the title "Oral Literature Today," then, we should be aware of both its contradictions and its exclusivity in relation to the actual nature of the materials it names.

The general task of this section, in short, is to point toward what lies beneath the iceberg's tip, the vast and multifarious digest of oral literature that dwarfs all existing written literature. In order to emphasize how crucial a role these unwritten traditions continue to play in modern societies, even as in some quarters literacy becomes electronic, "Oral Literature Today" will concentrate on those oral traditions still alive and well in most parts of the world. What remains of ancient, medieval, and other premodern traditions — and we should not forget that almost everything from those first 364 days of the year has perished — is sampled in the various regional selections. Likewise, the works in this section can reflect only an iota of the enormous "text" of oral traditions from our own time, not only because of limitations of space but also because much remains untranslated and most remains uncollected.

The other examples are drawn from traditions on five continents. From India comes the epic performance of the Pābūjī story, a narrative poem that like numerous oral genres utilizes many media in its presentation. The Jewish folktale tradition that dates from at least medieval times but is still flourishing in Israel gives us the instructive and entertaining "Cast Your Bread Upon the Waters," and the Brother Peter tales told in Guatemala in both Spanish and the Mayan language of Kaqchikel make their first appearance in print in this volume. Two shorter forms, each with multiple examples, are the intensely lyrical *hainteny* from Madagascar and the archetypal, culturally reinforcing Arab women's songs from Israel and the West Bank. In order to confront the range of forms and functions that this medium can assume, there is a particular focus on the spectrum of oral tradition within the South Slavic culture, itself ethnically mixed. Although no one area or tradition can ever be said, without qualification, to be typical, the South Slavic (former Yugoslavian) genres sampled here do illustrate several types of verbal expression common to many other areas worldwide: graveside lament, magical charms, lyric poetry, and epic poetry. By reading these specimens in a collective context, it should be possible to gain an overall sense of what it means to speak of oral literature not as the literary medium we know but as an informing cultural enterprise. The collection is rounded out with some reminders that oral tradition has pride of place even in the highly literate United States: Native American stories and songs from the Zuni, Pima, Chippewa, and Havasupai peoples, an African-American proverb and folk sermon, and a Jack tale from a folk teller in Kentucky.

Additional selections of oral literature may be found in this book, primarily in the sections on the Early Americas, Africa, Australia, and New Zealand. In consulting these and other instances, it is well to remember that just as all national or ethnic literatures begin with oral tradition, so oral tradition encounters the media of writing and eventually print in myriad different scenarios. Not only can orality and literacy coexist in the same culture, each with its own communicative responsibilities, but they can even constitute parts of the same individual's expressive repertoire. Then, too, some of these scenarios will be ''transitional,'' with relatively brief periods during which writers and readers will continue to use the oral traditional code before other codes arise to take its place. The key feature as one moves from one culture to another is variability; conceiving of oral literature as a limitless spectrum of forms — an international panoply of genres and functions in an equal diversity of cultural contexts — will prove the soundest approach.

The very heterogeneity of even this small collection should thus make a simple but far-reaching point: that oral tradition is perhaps the most multicultural of ''literatures.'' Like Proteus, the ancient Greek god, whose survival depended on his ability to keep changing and adapting within limits, oral literature lives by recreating itself, by generating itself anew in different situations. What follows is an attempt to glimpse Proteus by pinning him down to a few of his shapes.

Further Readings

Bauman, Richard. *Verbal Art as Performance*. Prospect Heights, Ill.: Waveland Press, 1984.

Foley, John Miles. *The Theory of Oral Composition: History and Methodology*. Bloomington: Indiana University Press, 1988.

———. *Immanent Art*. Bloomington: Indiana University Press, 1991.

Lord, Albert Bates. *The Singer of Tales*. Cambridge, Mass: Harvard University Press, 1960.

Parry, Milman. *The Making of Homeric Verse*. Oxford: Clarendon Press, 1971.

THE RAJASTHAN PEOPLE
Northwestern India

Recorded in Jodhpur in 1976 by John D. Smith, this unique performance of *The Epic of Pābūjī* told by Parbū Bhopo lasted a total of thirty-six hours and reached approximately 4040 lines. Like many of the longer traditional oral forms worldwide, it is seldom if ever performed at "full length"; since the bard and audience share a deep and lifelong experience of the larger story, single episodes can serve both as an evening's central focus and an index to the untold (but immanent) tale as a whole. The performance consists of two major parts or modes, the sung *gāv* and the declaimed, loosely metrical *arthāv*; Smith has translated only the *arthāv* sections, which in fact constitute the principal medium for the epic. Like the other bards in this tradition, Parbū sang and declaimed the story of the hero-deity Pābūjī in front of an elaborate cloth-painting, called a *par*, that presents a digest of Pābūjī's life and times and serves as an epic "map" for the performance. Pointing at times to the visual analog to his orally delivered narrative, Parbū located the fleeting moment of the story and its (partial) performance in the tangible space of the *par* and thus against the permanence and entirety of the epic tale it symbolized. "The Episode of Pushkar" describes Pābūjī's trek to Pushkar for a ritual bath, and his rewarding of Gogo for saving him from injury.

from **The Epic of Pābūjī**

The Episode of Pushkar

(Pābūjī said,) Cãdo my chieftain, make swift speed;
quickly adorn Kesar Kālamī for me to ride!
Cãdo my chieftain, tomorrow morning is the full-moon day of the
month of Kātakī;
we shall take our first bath (of the new half-month) on the steps of   5
Pushkar Lake.
Cãdo my chieftain, make swift speed;
quickly adorn Kesar Kālamī!
Have diamonds and fine pearls threaded in her mane;
have diamonds and fine pearls fastened to her hindquarters!   10
Attach the mare Kesar's chain-linked red bridle;
fasten on the mare's shining, Pāṭan-conquering stirrups!' [Scene 9]
Pābūjī arose with a toss of his saffron robe;
Pābūjī commanded the mare Kesar Kālamī to be brought into his
presence.   15
Pābūjī put his hand on her black mane;
(placing his other) hand on the saddle, he swiftly mounted.

Told by Parbū Bhopo; recorded in 1976 and translated by John D. Smith.

Pābūjī mounted the mare Kesar;
as he mounted, his seven leading warriors conversed with him.
The Hindu king set out as starry midnight passed; 20
he set out and went straight to Pushkar.
It was past midnight, shining with stars;
Pābūjī shone on the road as midnight passed.
The teams of horses travelled along in throngs;
Kesar Kālamī stepped with a strut. 25
Once or twice Pābūjī halted overnight on the road;
at the third halt he removed the stirrups from his feet at Pushkar.
O Pābūjī, pale dawn came in the land;
at the break of day he removed the stirrups from his feet in Pushkar.
Pābūjī stood at the *ghāṭ*[1] of Pushkar; 30
O lord, bowing low he made obeisance to Pushkar;
he made entreaty to the palely rising spotless Sun.
Bowing low Pābūjī made obeisance to Pushkar;
he made entreaty to the rising Sun.
O Pābūjī, on the western steps were encamped the numerous company 35
of the Cauhāns;
Lord Pābūjī pitched his tents on the northern steps.
On the western steps were bathing the numerous company of the
Cauhāns;
O lord, Lord Pābūjī bathed on the northern steps. 40
Lord Pābūjī, as you bathed your foot slipped;
as (Pābūjī's) feet stumbled, Gogo (Cauhān) seized him with his hand.
(Pābūjī said,) "O righteous Gogo, where is your house and home?
Of which king are you called eldest (son and) crown prince?"
[Scene 11] 45
(Gogo answered,) "O Pābūjī, Naravāṇo (village near) Sāmbhar is my
house and home;
I am called the eldest son of King Pītalde."
(Pābūjī said,) "O righteous Gogo, shake out your robe and hold it out
far by its hem;[2] 50
I shall shower you with wealth as the customary gift of the Rāṭhoṛs."
(Gogo replied,) "Pābūjī, shower wealth on your Cāraṇs and Bhāṭs,[3]
O lord, marry me to the eldest daughter of the Rāṭhoṛs!"
(Pābūjī said,) "O righteous Gogo, do not speak the name of the girl
Kelam![4] 55
Gogo, I cannot look at the face of an advancing woman nor at the back
of a retreating woman;
O righteous Gogo, I have no dealings with girls;
O lord, there is no daughter in Pābūjī's palace."

---

1. A bathing-place.
2. I.e. form it into a capacious bag.

3. Court-poets and genealogists.
4. Daughter of Pābūjī's brother Būṛo.

THE SEPHARDIC PEOPLE
Morocco/The Balkans/The Middle East; Judeo-Spanish

The Sephardim are Spanish-speaking Jews who were exiled from Spain in 1492 and took refuge in Morocco and in the Balkan and Near Eastern lands controlled by the Turkish Ottoman Empire. These Spanish Jews took with them into exile a rich body of oral literature—narrative ballads, lyric songs, folktales, riddles, proverbs—very similar to the oral repertoire of Christian and Muslim Spaniards at the end of the Middle Ages. To this medieval Spanish heritage, the Sephardim subsequently added numerous other texts learned from the North African, Balkan, and Near Eastern peoples among whom they settled after their exile. The Judeo-Spanish ballads are particularly interesting for comparative purposes, inasmuch as numerous early Spanish ballads embodying the same narrative types have been preserved in fifteenth-and sixteenth-century manuscripts and printed broadsides copied and published in Spain. Included here are two examples of Judeo-Spanish ballads or *romances*.

"Crossing the Red Sea," which is about Moses leading the people of Israel across the Red Sea, is interesting for several reasons. Curiously enough, there are relatively few Sephardic oral poems in ballad meter concerning biblical subjects. This one is sung in several different Judeo-Spanish communities in Greece and Turkey, but it is also known in certain towns in northeastern Portugal, where Crypto-Jews have been practicing a secret form of Judaism for the last 500 years, ever since they were forced into hiding for fear of the Inquisition. The text translated here was sung for Samuel G. Armistead and Joseph H. Silverman by an informant from Marmara, Turkey, in 1958.

Though the Sephardic ballads have been sung for 500 years by Jewish singers in lands far distant from the Iberian Peninsula, the Judeo-Spanish repertoire still retains numerous Christian elements that originated in the predominantly Christian society of late medieval Spain. "The Beauty in Church" is a ballad about a beautiful lady going to attend mass. She is so radiantly beautiful that the priest is overwhelmed and cannot continue reading the service. This ballad—like many ballads—has a very complex life history. It was originally part of a Greek narrative song. The Catalans, from eastern Spain, occupied Greece during the fourteenth century. During that time, the episode of the beautiful lady going to church was adapted into Catalan and taken back to Catalonia, from where it subsequently spread to southern France and to every region of the Iberian Peninsula. In 1492, when the Jews were forced into exile, they took the Spanish ballad with them and, when they settled in Greece, returned it to its original Greek homeland. The text translated here was sung for S. G. Armistead and J. H. Silverman by an informant from Salonika, Greece, in 1957.

Crossing the Red Sea

When the people of Israel   went out singing from Egypt,
with women and with children,   they went out singing songs.

Sung by an anonymous singer; translated by Samuel G. Armistead and J. H. Silverman.

Some carried the kindling   and some the kneaded dough.
The men carried the children,   in their arms and by the hand.
The women carried the gold,   which was lightest of all.   5
Moses turned his face   to see how far they'd come.
He saw Pharaoh coming onward,   with a scarlet banner.
"Where have you brought us, Moses,   to die in these fields,
to die without burial   or to drown in the sea?"
"Do not be frightened, Jews,   and do not lose patience.   10
Pray to God on high   and I will do my part."
So many were the prayers,   that they rose to God on high.
A voice came out of the heavens,   calling on Moses there:
"Come here, Moses, my son,   and do as I command.
Take this rod, Moses,   take this rod in your hand.   15
Cleave the sea in twelve passages   and save your people from harm."
The Jews went passing over   and the Egyptians drowned.
Pharaoh alone remained,   hanging by his neck.
Let us contemplate the wonders   wrought by God on high.
He is one; there is no other;   He is Lord of all the world.   20

The Beauty in Church

Three ladies go to mass,   to mass to say their prayers.
One is my betrothed,   the dearest one to me. Oh, my lord!
One is my betrothed,   the dearest one to me.
She's wearing many pleated skirts,   a waistcoat of finest cloth. Oh, my lord!
Her head is a round citron;   her hair is golden thread.   5
Whenever she combs it,   it glistens in the the sun. Oh, my lord!
Whenever she combs it,   it glistens in the sun.
Her red cheeks are apples,   apples from Skopje. Oh, my lord!
Her little teeth, so tiny,   are made of ivory.
In her little mouth, so tiny,   a rosebud wouldn't fit. Oh, my lord!   10
In her little mouth, so tiny,   a rosebud wouldn't fit.
Her eyebrows, finely arched,   are an archer's taut bow. Oh, my lord!
The priest, at his readings,   stopped reading his mass.
"Read on, little priest, read on,   I've not come here for you.
I've come for the king's son,   for I'm dying of love."   15

THE JEWISH PEOPLE
Israel; Hebrew

Like many Jewish folktales, "Cast Your Bread Upon the Waters" has a long and
varied history, appearing in medieval literary sources and still circulating today

Marc Chagall. *Over Vitbesk*. 1915–1920. Oil on canvas. Museum of Modern Art, New York.

in contemporary oral tradition. As an oral genre, these tales have traveled with Jewish communities throughout Europe, the Middle East, and parts of Asia and North Africa, serving the intertwining purposes of entertainment, instruction, religious commentary, and history. Because of this geographical and cultural diversity, and also because of the diversity of religious beliefs represented, the folktales as a whole present a tremendous variety of concerns, often contradictory or at least oblique to one another, that cannot be reduced to a single system or set of ideas. Their greatest collector, Micha Joseph bin Gorion (1903–1987), assembled (almost entirely from printed sources) a six-volume edition of folktales, *Mimekor Yisrael,* that has been published in Hebrew, German, and English. The example presented here knits together proverbial expressions from Ecclesiastes, Isaiah, and the sage Ben Sira through the use of a framing device common to international folklore—a father's dying instructions to his son—and the theme of a human's knowledge of animal languages. The result is a traditional narrative vehicle that incorporates the wisdom of sacred texts.

from **Mimekor Yisrael**
Cast Your Bread upon the Waters

A certain man used to teach his son every day the words of Ecclesiastes (11:1): "Cast your bread upon the waters, for you shall find it after many days." In due course the man died, and the young man remembered his father's words. He used to take bread every day and throw it into the sea.

Told by an anonymous teller; translated by I. M. Lask.

On one occasion Elijah, whom it is good to mention, met him in the form of an old man and asked him what he was doing. He answered: "My father ordered me to cast my bread into the water." "Yet surely you have learned," said Elijah, "when you cast your bread upon the water, that bread is like salt. Just as bread cannot be eaten without salt, so the world cannot exist without bread." So from that time on he used to take only a piece of bread every day and went to the river and threw it into the water.

There was a certain fish at that place which used to eat the bread, and it did so every day until it grew very big and distressed the other fishes in that place. At last all the fish in the sea gathered and went to Leviathan and said to him: "Your majesty, there is a certain fish which has grown very big so that we cannot live together with him, and he is so strong that he eats twenty or more of us every day." When he heard this, Leviathan sent for him, saying: "These live out at sea and have not grown so much, yet you have grown so large at the sea's edge. How is that?" "Indeed," answered the fish, "it is because a certain man fetches me a piece of bread every day and I eat it morning and noon; and in the morning I eat twenty fish and in the evening thirty."

"Why do you eat your companions?" asked Leviathan, and he answered: "Because they come to me and I consume them; and the words of the Prophet Isaiah (58:7) apply to them: 'And do not disregard your own flesh.' " "Go," said Leviathan, "and fetch that man to me." "Tomorrow," answered the fish.

He went at once and dug beneath the spot where the young man used to come, and he made a tunnel there, and placed his mouth in that tunnel. Next day the young man came as usual and wished to stand in that spot, but fell into the water. The fish opened its mouth and swallowed him up and carried him away through the sea to Leviathan, who said: "Spit him out." He spat him out of his mouth, and the man fell into the mouth of Leviathan, who said to him: "My son, why have you cast your bread into the water?" and he answered: "Because my father taught me from childhood that I should cast my bread upon the waters."

And what did Leviathan do then? He released him from his mouth, kissed him and taught him seventy languages and the whole Torah, and flung him a distance of three hundred leagues onto the dry land. He fell in a spot where human foot had never trodden. Lying there exhausted, he raised his eyes and saw two ravens flying above him. One of them said to the other: "My father, see whether that man is alive or dead." The father replied: "My son, I do not know." "I shall go down," said the son, "and eat his eyes because I enjoy picking out the eyes of human beings." But his father said: "My son, do not go down in case he is alive." The son insisted: "I shall go down and pick out his eyes," and down he flew.

This man understood what they had been saying to one another, and when the raven settled on his forehead he seized him by the legs. At once the raven cawed to his father: "Father, father, the Lord has delivered me into his hands and I cannot rise." When his father heard this, he croaked and wept and said: "Alas for my son!" And he cried: "You, human being, let my son go! May it be His will that you understand my language! Rise and dig down where you are standing, and you will find the treasures of Solomon, king of Israel."

He let the raven go at once and dug down and found the treasures of

Solomon, with many jewels and pearls, so that he and his sons after him remained wealthy. It was of him that Ben Sira said: "Offer your bread and your table and give to whomever may come."

THE ARABIC AND PALESTINIAN PEOPLE
Israel/West Bank; Arabic

The Arab world has long been and still is everywhere alive with oral tradition—in pre-Islamic classical poetry, the recitation of the sacred Qur'an (Koran), Bedouin oral lyric, the multinational epic tradition of *Sirat Bani Hilal*, and not least the delicately fashioned lyric songs performed by Arab and Palestinian women in Israel and the West Bank. Collected by Mishael Caspi during the 1980s, these poems fall into three categories: bridal songs, lullabies, and lamentations (one example of each is presented below). Each genre draws its style and motifs from a long tradition of oral song, and yet each is undergoing significant change as the modern world enters more and more into that tradition. Taken individually, they express the wonder, humor, beauty, hope, and anxiety that accompany various crucial moments and rites of passage; taken as a whole, they present the strong and eloquent contrapuntal voice of women in this society. "Bridal Song" is a song performed for the bride by a woman in the groom's family; "Lullaby" is a mother's lullaby to her son; and "Lament" is a woman's lament for her deceased mate.

Bridal Song [O you who are seated in the high and noble place]

O you who are seated in the high and noble place
Like a princess you sway cradled by the breeze

O you who are seated in the high place
Like the gazelle you are seated in beauty

Like the full moon your round face shines   5
Like the moon in the month's first night

When your hair is tied with lace
You are like the moon carved in the middle of the month

And when your hair flows free
You are like the moon rising in the night   10

Performed by anonymous singers, collected c. 1980s; translated by Mishael Maswari Caspi and Julia Ann Blessing.

You who are seated in the high exalted place
You sit in majesty with the honorable ones

Your fingers eloquent with strength and grace
Move like a pen in the judge's hand

Lullaby [I want to sing to my son]

I want to sing to my son,
Maybe he will appreciate my singing.
I want to sing him a song,
Perhaps when he hears it he will sleep.
I caress him and sing,   5
Maybe the beloved one will sleep.
I cradle him on my chest.
With a blanket I cover him.
O my son if you are hungry,
I will satisfy you[1] from my heart.   10
And if you are thirsty my son,
I will quench your thirst with water from my eyes.
When you bury me don't cry.
Do not be sad at my sadness,
Keep the smile on your lips,   15
And the happiness in your heart.

Lament [Because of you I lost my heart]

Because of you I lost my heart
And my raven hair eclipsed to white
Our sooty clothes don't suit anyone
In the name of the prophet, we long for the beloved
Ah! cries like camels howling for the day of separation   5
My family has forsaken me and my friends abandoned me
I wander between loneliness and my neighbor's wall
My evil neighbor has deserted me
O shining star, testify that I am miserable
The Christians imprisoned me for the land of Rome   10
O shining star, testify that I am destitute
The Christians imprisoned me for the land of Sham[2]
O shining star, guide me to my beloveds
O scribe, write in the margins
Greetings to the resting place of our beloveds   15
I am in one place and they are in another

---

1. Literally, "I will feed you."   2. The Arabic name for Syria.

And in my heart a fire is burning
O scribe, cease your writing (inscriptions)
We are separating and shall not meet again
O scribe, write slowly, slowly   20
I sat in the heat while others sat in the shade
O camel rider, take me with you my beloved
I am sad, even as I smile
Do not think that my smile conveys happiness
I smile even though my heart is bleeding   25
I vow in the name of God, who for us created poultry
The separation of lovers is more painful than that of flesh and soul

THE MALAGASY PEOPLE (1830–1950)
Madagascar; Malagasy

Hainteny—variously translated as "wise words," "caprice," and "life, breath"—stand
out among an impressive array of oral genres that were the exclusive form of
Malagasy literature until well into the nineteenth century. They are a highly
traditional form of lyric poetry most often devoted to matters of love (both
optimistic and pessimistic, with the full range of emotions involved), but they are
also concerned with themes of good and evil, natural rhythms and processes, and
social relations. They are usually fifteen lines or less and follow a metrical system of
stresses rather than syllable-counting; originally a Malaysian form, they closely
resemble the Indonesian *pantun* in terms of lyric focus, density of metaphor, and
allusive technique. Available evidence indicates that *hainteny* have come to be
employed as exchanges in stylized poetic dispute, although this seems not to have
been their original performance context. Leonard Fox's translations draw from
collections made as early as the 1830s and as recently as the middle of the twentieth
century. The five examples given here are from sections Fox labels Pride ["I am not
the winter that dulls"], Wisdom and Foolishness [" 'I laid my eggs,' said the bird"],
Separation and Abandonment ["Tell the clouds to wait"], Prayers and Imprecations
["What does blame resemble?"], and Death ["Fruit desired"].

from *Haiteny*

Pride [I am not the winter that dulls]

I am not the winter that dulls
or the spring that wearies.

Told by anonymous tellers; translated by Leonard Fox.

For only those who do not love are dull,
those unable to arouse desire, weary.

Wisdom and Foolishness ["I laid my eggs," said the bird]

"I laid my eggs," said the bird,
"there, in a tall tree;
the tree was blown down by the wind;
the wind was stopped by a promontory;
the promontory was bored through by a rat;   5
the rat was eaten by a dog;
the dog was flogged by a man;
the man was overcome by a spear;
the spear was overpowered by a rock;
the rock was passed over by water;   10
the water was walked in by a little bird."

Separation and Abandonment [Tell the clouds to wait]

Tell the clouds to wait,
for the wind is subsiding.
Tell the lake to forget,
for the birds will no longer come there to sleep.
It is bad to forget suddenly,   5
it is good to forget gradually.

Prayers and Imprecations [What does blame resemble?]

What does blame resemble?
It resembles the wind:
I have heard its name, but I have not seen its face.
But what does blame resemble?
It is not heaped up like the clouds;   5
it does not lie on its back like the hills;
it is not the passing man, to whom is said, "Enter the house;"
it is not the visitor, to whom is said, "Return;"
it is not the seated man, to whom is said, "May I pass?"
But it resembles the slippery path: 10
he who is not careful falls.
A rock at the side of the road:
he who does not see it trips.
A deep abyss:
he who looks at it becomes dizzy   15
and it kills him when he falls.

Like the freezing cold:
unseen, it numbs.
May it be removed!
Removed in the morning, may it have no meal!   20
Removed in the evening, may it have no bed!
Removed in the summer, may the floods take it!
Removed in the winter, may it be burned with the grass!
Above, let it not press down;
below, let it not be revived: 25
on two sides, let it not crush;
in front, let it not be able to stop;
behind, let it not be able to pursue!

Death [Fruit desired]

Fruit desired,
bananas sought:
even if a ghost passes and an obstacle is overcome,
they will not be put aside,
but will be eaten.   5
Those who sicken from eating what they love
and die from what they desire
say nothing,
are not distressed;
they are content,   10
free from regret,
for they are like young crocodiles swallowed by their mother
and consumed by the belly that bore them,
if they die for what they love.

ONEGA PEOPLE (TENTH or ELEVENTH CENTURY C.E.)

Russia

This 1022-line *bylina,* or epic narrative, sung by T. G. Riabinin at about age eighty and written down from oral performance by A. F. Hilferding in the summer of 1871, exemplifies the Russian, pan-Slavic, and probably Indo-European tale of the Returning Hero, best known to modern readers as the story of the *Odyssey.* The *bylina* arose in the tenth or eleventh century and was spread initially by wandering minstrels (*skomoroxi*). It has survived to the present day (though now in diminished form, due in large part to the social and political upheaval since the mid-1930s in the former Soviet Union). Dobrynya, the Odysseus figure and hero of this tale, seems to have had a historical prototype dating from about the eleventh century, but his skills at battle, his considerable verbal dexterity, and his extraordinary musical talent are as much the characteristics of the timeless and international Returning Hero as of any individual in a single tradition. The selections given here include the opening, with the classic challenge and acceptance; the doves' notifying of Dobrynya of his wife Nastasia's impending remarriage; Dobrynya's testing of his mother by appearing in disguise and posing a riddle; and the hero's final ruse of impersonating a marvelously gifted minstrel and cleverly revealing his identity to Nastasia.

Dobrynya and Vasily Kazimirov

Prince Vladimir of the capital city Kiev
Gave a feast, a banquet, honoring
Many princes and all the boyars,
All the strong and mighty Russian warriors
And the far-famed and bold Amazons.   5
At the feast of honor Vladimir paced back and forth and said:
"Oh my princes and boyars,
Strong and mighty Russian warriors!
I have been in debt to King Botiyan Botiyanov
In the faraway lands of the Saracens   10
From long ago until today.
I have been in debt to the sovereign for twelve years,
For twelve years and a half.
Who is there for me to send to deliver tribute due
For twelve years and a half   15
To king Botiyan Botiyanov—
Twelve swans, twelve gyrfalcons,
And a letter of obligation?"
All the warriors at table fell silent,
All fell silent, became quiet.   20
The warriors at table sought refuge:
The great hid behind the lesser,
The lesser hid behind the least,
And from the least in rank there was no response.
Then from behind the oaken tables,   25
From behind the surrounding benches,
Stepped forth old Permin son of Ivan.
Permin began to walk through the hall,
And he said to Vladimir:
"Prince Vladimir of the capital city Kiev!   30
Permit me, sovereign, to have my say.
I know who to send to go

Told by Trofim Grigorevich Riabinin, c. 1792–1885; translated by Patricia Arant.

To the faraway lands of the Saracens—
Send young Vasily Kazimirov.
Young Vasily Kazimirov   35
Will deliver the tribute due for twelve years,
For twelve years and a half."
Then Prince Vladimir of the capital city Kiev
Quickly walked through the great hall,
Took a cup in his white hands,   40
Poured a cup of green wine,
Not a small amount but a bucket full,
Diluted it with fermented honey,
And offered it to Vasily Kazimirov.
Young Vasily Kazimirov   45
Quickly jumped to his nimble feet,
Took the cup from the prince in his white hands,
Took the cup in one hand,
And drained the cup dry with a single swallow.
Vasily stood on his feet, not staggering,   50
And talked with the prince, not confounded.
He spoke to Prince Vladimir,
Said the following to the prince:
"Oh Prince Vladimir of the capital city Kiev!
I shall go to the faraway lands of the Saracens,   55
I shall take the tribute due for twelve years,
For twelve years and a half,
Only give me as companion
My brother with whom I have exchanged crosses—
Young Dobrynya Nikitich."   60
Then Prince Vladimir of the capital city Kiev
Walked through the great hall.
Vladimir took the cup in his white hands,
Vladimir poured a cup of green wine,
Not a small amount but a bucket full,   65
Diluted it with fermented honey,
And offered it to young Dobrynya.
Young Dobrynya Nikitich
Quickly jumped to his nimble feet,
Took the cup in his white hands   70
From Prince Vladimir,
Held the cup in one hand
And drained the cup dry with a single swallow.
Dobrynya stood on his feet, not staggering,
And talked with the prince, not confounded: 75
"Prince Vladimir of the capital city Kiev!
Permit me, sovereign, to have my say.
I shall go with Vasily as his companion,

I shall take the tribute due for twelve years,
For twelve years and a half,
Only give us as companion
My brother with whom I have exchanged crosses—
Young Ivan Dubrovich.
Ivan is the one who will saddle the horses,
Ivan is the one who will unsaddle them,
The one who will tether and untether them."
Then Prince Vladimir of the capital city Kiev
Walked through the great hall.
Vladimir took the cup in his white hands,
Poured a cup of green wine,
Not a small amount but a bucket full,
And offered it to Ivan Dubrovich.
Ivan Dubrovich jumped to his nimble feet,
Took the cup in his white hands,
Held the prince's cup in one hand,
And drained the cup dry with a single swallow.
Ivan stood on his feet, not staggering,
Ivan said, not confounded:
"Prince Vladimir of the capital city Kiev!
Permit me, sovereign, to have my say.
I shall go as companion with Vasily
And with young Dobrynya Nikitich.
I shall take the tribute due for twelve years,
For twelve years and a half."

But at that moment, at that time,
A dove and its mate flew up,
And the doves sat on a dry oak branch.
On the dry oak branch the dove and its mate began to coo:
"O young Dobrynya!
You are sleeping in your tent, resting awhile,
And you know not of the ill luck that has befallen you:
Your young wife Nastasia Mikulichna
Is getting married to a warrior,
To the far-famed Alyosha Popovich."
Young Dobrynya Nikitich
Quickly jumped to his nimble feet,
Quickly saddled his good steed,
Quickly mounted his good steed,
Quickly rode across the wide and open plain
To the far-famed capital city Kiev.
Dobrynya Nikitich arrived
At his far-famed wide courtyard,
Stopped his heroic steed

80

85

90

95

100

105

110

115

120

At the porch with a railing,
Tied him with a silken rope
To a silver ring,
And he himself went into his white stone palace,
Went through it into his great hall,
In search of his mother.
His mother was seated and sad,
Was weeping bitter tears.

And young Dobrynya Nikitich
Quickly bowed to her and said:
"Oh honorable widow Mamelfa Timofeevna!
Yesterday Dobrynya and I parted
On the far-famed wide and open plain:
Dobrynya set out for Tsargrad
And sent me to the capital city Kiev,
And he ordered me to come to your wide courtyard,
Ordered me to enter your palace
And tell you that young Dobrynya orders you,
Orders you to go down to the deep cellar
And bring his silken slippers,
Orders you to bring his minstrel's clothing,
Orders you to bring his gusli made of maple wood.
And he ordered me to go to the feast of honor,
To Prince Vladimir,
To Prince Alyosha Popovich,
And to the young princess, Nastasia Mikulichna."
And the honorable widow Mamelfa Timofeevna
Wept bitterly.
The widow said the following:
"Even a peasant from the country could not have found out from the Holy Spirit,
Could not have found out about Dobrynya's silken slippers,
Could not have found out about his minstrel's clothing,
Could not have found out about his gusli made of maple wood."
So she quickly took her gilded keys,
Quickly went down to the deep cellar,
Brought the silken slippers,
Brought the minstrel's clothing,
Brought the gusli made of maple wood,
And gave them to the peasant from the country.
The peasant from the country said:
"Oh honorable widow Mamelfa Timofeevna!
Dobrynya and I grew up together:
Dobrynya and I ate together,
Learned to read and write together:
Wore each other's clothing."

125

130

135

140

145

150

155

160

165

Then the peasant from the country
Put on the silken slippers,
Put on the minstrel's clothing,
Took the gusli made of maple wood in his white hands.
Dobrynya's slippers fit his feet,
And the minstrel's clothing
Of Dobrynya fit him.
Then Dobrynya set out for the feast of honor.

Then the minstrel said the following:
"Oh Prince Vladimir of the capital city Kiev!
Allow me to pour a cup of green wine
And offer it to the young princess,
Nastasia Mikulichna."
He took the cup in his white hands,
Poured a cup of green wine,
Not a small amount but a bucket full,
And diluted it with fermented honey.
And he dropped a golden ring in it,
Dropped it in the cup,
And offered it to Nastasia Mikulichna.
And he said to her the following:
"Oh young princess,
Young Nastasia Mikulichna!
Drink from your cup of green wine."
Young Nastasia Mikulichna
Quickly jumped to her nimble feet,
Took the cup in her white hands
And put it to her sweet lips.
Then the minstrel said to her the following:
"Young Nastasia Mikulichna!
If you want good news, then drain the cup dry."
Young Nastasia Mikulichna
Was not a stupid woman:
She drained the cup dry,
And to her sweet lips
Rolled the golden ring.
She shook the ring out on the oaken table,
Looked at the golden ring,
The ring which she had exchanged in betrothal
In the Church of God, her Mother,
And then put the cup on the oaken table.
Bracing her powerful arms,
Nastasia leaped across the oaken table
And said the following:
"Oh, light of my life, my beloved mate,

170

175

180

185

190

195

200

205

210

Young Dobrynya Nikitich!
A woman's hair is long, but she is short of wisdom.   215
I did not obey the orders of a hero:
married the far-famed warrior,
Alyosha Popovich."
Then young Dobrynya Nikitich
Quickly jumped to his nimble feet,   220
Took Alyosha by his yellow curls,
Threw Alyosha against the brick floor,
Took out his riding whip,
And began to lash Alyosha with the whip.
And Dobrynya said the following: 225
"You tried to take a wife from a husband still living!"
Then Prince Vladimir began to intercede
For Alyosha Popovich:
"Oh young Dobrynya Nikitich!
Forgive us for this unwise act."   230
And young Dobrynya said:
"Oh far-famed Prince Vladimir of the capital city Kiev!
You yourself were matchmaker for Alyosha,
And Opraxia was matchmaker for Nastasia.
You mistreat your own wife and even torment her,   235
And now you have given another man's wife in marriage."
The young Dobrynya Nikitich
Took Nastasia Mikulichna
By her white hands,
Took her by her golden fingers,   240
Led her into his palace,
Led her into his great hall,
Led her again to the marriage bed.

THE SOUTH SLAVIC PEOPLES
Former Yugoslavia (Bosnia, Serbia); Serbo-Croatian

Recorded in 1815 from a performance by the blind singer Filip Višnjić, this rendition of *The Death of Kraljević Marko* is one of the jewels of the classic collection made by Vuk Karadžić, the nineteenth-century ethnographer and linguist who published nine volumes of oral poetry, reformed both the Latin and Cyrillic alphabets, and compiled the major dictionary of the language. Steeped in the Christian tradition of epic singing, which fostered shorter versions of some of the same tales told in the Moslem tradition, Višnjić was well enough known to make his living as an itinerant bard traveling throughout Bosnia. This particular song relates the demise of the most famous hero in the Christian tradition, Prince Marko, an obstreperous, iconoclastic figure whose historical prototype was apparently a minor Turkish vassal who died at the Battle of Rovine in 1395. In other poems this same hero bluntly challenges the tsar whom he must serve as a mercenary, contests other great heroes (not always honorably), and in the role of "underdog" generally embodies the struggle of the Serbian people under the Ottoman Turkish yoke. Within this performance Višnjić plays on Marko's storied relationship to his faithful horse and comrade Šarac, and uniquely reverses certain traditional heroic patterns (arming for battle, preparing one's horse), in order to dramatize the finality of Marko's "last battle."

The Death of Kraljević Marko

Kraljević Marko arose early
On a Sunday before the bright sun,
On Mount Urvina beside the sea.
While Marko was on Urvina,
Šarac began to stumble,   5
To stumble and to shed tears.
Marko was very troubled over this,
And Marko spoke to Šarac:
"Dear Šarac, my dear stalwart!
It's been one hundred sixty years   10
Since I took up with you,
And you never tripped anywhere;
Now today you begin to stumble,
To stumble and to shed tears:
God knows this does not bode well!   15
It will sometime be on our heads,
On either mine or yours!"
As Marko was speaking these words,
A vila from Mount Urvina hailed him,
And called out to Kraljević Marko: 20
"Bloodbrother, Kraljević Marko,
Do you know, brother, why your horse stumbled?—
Šarac is mourning you, his master,
Because you two will soon be parted."
But Marko announced to the vila: 25
"White vila, curse your throat!
If I were parted from Šarac,
And passed through the land and towns,
And searched from east to west,

Told by Filip Višnjić c. 1760–1830; translated by John Miles Foley.

I could find no better horse than Šarac,
Nor could he hope for a better hero than I!
I did not expect to be parted from Šarac
While my head was on my shoulders."
But the white vila responded to him:
"Bloodbrother, Kraljević Marko,
No one will take Šarac from you,
Nor are you fated to die, Marko,
By means of a hero or a sharp saber,
By means of a mace or a war-lance:
You need fear no hero on earth;
But, wretched Marko, you shall die
At the hand of God, the old executioner.
If you do not believe me,
When you go to the top of the mountain,
You will look around from left to right,
Catch sight of two slim fir-trees
Which tower over the entire mountain,
Draping the peak in a green-leaf tapestry:
Between them is a spring of water,
There you will turn Šarac around,
Dismount the horse, tie him to the fir,
Bend down over the spring, over the water,
And you will be looking at your own face;
Then you will see when you will die."
Marko took the vila's advice:
When he came to the top of the mountain,
He looked around from left to right,
Caught sight of two slim fir-trees
Which towered over the entire mountain,
Draping the peak in a green-leaf tapestry:
There Marko turned Šarac around,
Dismounted the horse, tied him to the fir;
He bent down over the spring, over the water,
In the water he was looking at his own face:
And when Marko looked at his own face,
Marko saw when he would die;
He shed tears, then he spoke:
"O lying world, my beautiful flower!
Beautiful you were, and I have walked but little,
Just a little, three hundred years!
The time has come for me to change worlds."
Then Kraljević Marko drew it out,
Drew out his saber from his belt,
And he went to his horse Šarac,
Cut off Šarac's head with the saber,

30

35

40

45

50

55

60

65

70

75

So that Šarac would not fall into Turkish hands,
Not perform service for the Turks,
Not carry water or copper vessels.
And when Marko had beheaded Šarac,
He buried his horse Šarac,   80
Šarac better than his brother Andrija;
He broke his sharp saber in four pieces,
So that the saber would not fall into Turkish hands,
So that the Turks could not gloat over it
As if it were left to them by Marko,   85
So that the Christians would not curse Marko.
And when Marko had broken the sharp saber,
He smashed his war-lance into seven pieces,
Then he threw them among the fir-branches;
Marko took his spiked mace,   90
He took it in his right hand,
Then he cast it from Mount Urvina
And into the sea, into the deep sea.
Then Marko called after the mace:
"When my mace issues forth from the sea,   95
Then let another such hero be born!"
When Marko had destroyed his arms,
He pulled a writing-box from his belt,
And from his pocket a clean sheet of paper;
Kraljević Marko wrote a letter: 100
"Whoever comes to Mount Urvina
To the cold spring between the fir-trees,
And there finds the hero Marko,
Let him know that Marko is dead!
Alongside Marko are three belts of riches,   105
Such riches, all golden ducats!
And I bless one belt for him
If he will bury my body;
Let the second belt adorn the churches;
The third belt to the lame and the blind: 110
Let the blind walk about the world,
Let them sing about and celebrate Marko!"
When Marko had decorated the letter,
He tied the letter on a fir-branch,
Where it could be seen from the road;   115
He cast the gold writing-box into the spring;
Marko took off his green cloak,
Laid it on the grass under the fir-tree,
Made the sign of the cross, sat on the cloak,
Pulled his sable cap down over his eyes;   120
He lay down, he did not get back up.

The dead Marko was near the spring
From one day to the next for a week of days:
Whoever passed by on the wide road,
And caught sight of Kraljević Marko,   125
Thought to a man that Marko was sleeping there.
And so veered far around him,
For fear that he would be roused.
Where there is fortune, there is also misfortune;
Where misfortune, also fortune: 130
And now all good fortune brought
The abbot Vaso of Svetogorac
From the white church of Vilindar,
With his novice Isaiah.
When the abbot caught sight of Marko,   135
He reached for the deacon with his right hand:
"Move softly, son, don't rouse him!—
For Marko is ill-tempered waking from a dream,
And he may kill us both."
Looking on while Marko slept, the monk   140
Caught sight of the letter above Marko,
He studied the letter in front of him:—
The letter said that this was Marko, dead.
Then the monk dismounted from his horse,
And took hold of the hero Marko,   145
But Marko had long since passed away.
Abbot Vaso shed tears,
For he sorrowed deeply over Marko;
He unbuckled the three belts of riches,
Unbuckled them, and buckled them on himself.   150
Abbot Vaso thought and thought
Where he might bury the dead Marko;
He thought and thought, then he made his decision:
He tied the dead Marko on his horse,
Then he bore him to the sea's shore,   155
Sat beside the dead Marko on a galley,
Took him straight to Mount Sveta,
Took him to the church below Vilindar,
Bore him into the church at Vilindar;
He read for Marko a service for the dead,   160
Sang a requiem for his body on earth
In the midst of the white church at Vilindar;
And then the old man buried Marko,
But he fixed no sign above him,
So that Marko's grave would not be known,   165
So that his enemies would not take revenge.

Ivan Generalić. *Taking a Nap.*
1968. Oil on glass.

ANONYMOUS MOTHER OF MILORAD

Recorded by Joel Halpern in 1962, this performance of graveside lament (*tužbalica, kukanje*) memorializes the death of a young man who, along with several friends, was killed by lightning as he returned home from a Saint Peter's Day Fair across a swampy region known as The Marshes. His mother has turned to the culturally approved ritual of a formal mourning song, composed extemporaneously and exclusively by women in the eight-syllable line of the women's songs and the charms, to express her grief over his cruel and sudden departure from life. Women customarily lament in public, at the gravesite, often with other females from the village community; periodically recurring visits also entail preparation of an elaborate meal, which friends and relatives are meant to consume as part of the ritual.

Graveside Lament for Milorad

Good morning, young men,
Oj, where are you this early morn?
Early morn, where did you spend it?
For we had so hoped
That you didn't reach here,
And we had so hoped

5

Sung by the mother of Milorad; translated by Barbara Kerewksy-Halpern.

That our Mile[1] was late [getting home].
Dear luck, we all hoped.
Where your mother embraces a stone,
A sad stone, [already] seven years.   10
At your house, my Mićane,
All quietly sit, without girls
   or little children.
I can't [go on], I lack the strength,
   I lack the heart.   15
You dug out my heart,
Dug out and carried [it] off.
But then to see an even worse grief,
Flashing lightning unexpected.
A great, Mile, a great sorrow,   20
For that Mile brought us grief
Because you brought [it] upon yourself.
If only we had not had sorrow
From this accursed war;
We had just begun to get settled again.   25
But then to see an even worse grief,
Another grief unexpected.
Oj Mićane, my hero,
Speak out, my happiness!
Look, your sister has come.   30
"My beauty," she says,
"I want, mother, to see [where my brother lies]."
You, Miško, did not stay at home
At the hearth, your hearth.
Darinka[2] looks after the house for you   35
And [after] your grieving parents.
Your sister has come to beg you
To give her in turn your blessing.
Here some letters[3] are destroyed;
Who destroyed this?   40
May God destroy his luck
As [He destroyed] you, my Mićane!
Your name [seems] destroyed
And it's a sorrow, son, to me
And for our young people.   45
The young people lead the *kolo*.
They permitted and saw

---

1. The young man being mourned, Milorad, is
   also addressed by various other forms of his
   name—Mile, Mićane, and Miško—and by
   the diminutive of an unrelated name, Suljo.

2. Milorad's (surviving) sister.
3. The "letters" are those on Milorad's grave-
   stone.

That the letters are destroyed.
Woe is me, my Mićane,
Who destroyed the letters?   50
Woe is me, my joy Miško,
But the officials told us
That they will repair this.
I, poor one, did not know,
That it was so much destroyed.   55
But Darinka says to me,
"It isn't, mother, all that much but just a little
And [some] letters are fainter [than others]."
Milorad, my wonderful joy,
This hot sun is burning,   60
But for you it is not hot.
Your youth is destroyed,
And the branch cut off.
And Miško I want to ask you:
Has Peko[4] arrived [there]?   65
Does his wound ache terribly?
Tell me, householder, household head—
Have his orphans remained?
Have your companions, Miško,
Returned to their homes?   70
Did the Poleksić young man
Die? Woe to his mother!
O my Suljo, my "live wire"!
Into The Marshes, suffering,
Into icy dark water,   75
The "live wire" is killed!

WOMEN'S SONGS

The poems included here are examples of so-called "women's" or lyric songs; as
one of a number of South Slavic oral genres practiced chiefly or exclusively by
women, the *ženske pjesme* consist mainly of shorter, nonnarrative poetry—
frequently in eight-syllable lines as opposed to the ten-syllable lines of most
men's genres—that customarily treats matters of love, marriage, and familial
relationships. Collected by fieldworkers Milman Parry and Albert Lord in the
mid-1930s, the four lyrics illustrate typical themes of romantic longing, male and
female attitudes toward the opposite sex, and disappointment and frustration in
romance.

---

4. Another young man from the village who
died prematurely.

Kazimir Malevich. *Taking in the Rye.* 1912. Oil on canvas.

[Blow, blow cold wind]

Blow, blow cold wind!
Come to me, beloved,
Into my white dwelling!
Bring your white horse with you,
And tie him to a branch of the rose tree.   5
Let the rose envelope him in its fragrance,
And let his spirit be filled with longing.

[Thirty maids sat embroidering]

Thirty maids sat embroidering
In a white tower in Lipnik.
At their head was Fata Čengić.
"Swear to me, my thirty maids!
Cast not a glance upon heroic men,   5
For they are changeable and unfaithful.
When one kisses you, he says: 'I shall marry you, my sweet.'

Sung by Halimo Hrvo, Fata Šaković, Hajrija Šaković, and H. Š. and Almasa Zvizdić; translated by Albert B. Lord.

But when he has embraced you, it is: 'Wait until autumn!'
Winter comes, and summer passes.
You know, sisters, it was not long ago 10
That Ljubović came from Nevesinje.
He tricked me and kissed my lips.
'Wait for me until autumn, my sweet!'
Then he went off to Stambol.[1]
A brief note came from Stambol: 15
'Return to me the ring I gave you!
Return to me my countless treasures!
Return to me my silk and satin!'
Beg Ljubović, you lowly cur!
Return their former loveliness to my lips, 20
And I shall give to you your countless treasures."

[I sleep not, I doze not, nor do I dream]

I sleep not, I doze not, nor do I dream,
But all day I am sad and shed tears.
At every bird that flies by, I weep,
And from every traveler who happens by, I ask:
"Oh traveler, oh wanderer, have you seen my loved one?" 5
"If I had seen him, how would I know him?"
"It's easy to know him, for he's a great hero:
His eyes are black, his beard is dark, and he is wondrous tall."

[By Sarajevo, there's a green garden]

By Sarajevo, there's a green garden,
In that garden there's a well of cold water,
By the well, a marble stone,
On the stone, an aged vase,
In the vase three flowers bloomed. 5
Were you to give me the three flowers from that garden,
A wallflower, a carnation, a red rose,
I'd not take the wallflower, nor the carnation, but the red rose.
Were you to give me three girls to kiss,
Ema, Fatima, and Hajrija,[2] 10
I'd not take Ema, nor Fatima, but Hajrija!

---

1. The modern name for Stambol is Istanbul.
2. This song, which epitomizes Hajrija as the fairest of all, was sung by Hajrija Šaković and Almasa Zvizdić.

MAGICAL CHARMS OR SPELLS (BAJANJE)

The magical charms or spells (*bajanje*) are performed exclusively by postmeno-
pausal women, who pass them on as a dowry to prepubertal female family
members. Conjurers use this form of "white magic" to cure a variety of physical
and mental ills, among them the set of nine skin diseases that they also identify
as "winds" (presumably because the maladies are believed to be wind-borne).
Collected by John Foley and Barbara Halpern in July 1975, this particular
performance was shaped to counteract the "red wind," which designates the
streptococcus infection known to modern Western medicine as erysipelas, but
the same pattern can be modified by color to treat eight additional diseases
(jaundice [yellow] and anthrax [black], for example). As a genre jealously
guarded by its practitioners, *bajanje* illustrates how verbal art in oral tradition can
command a practical and important cultural function.

Against the Red Wind

Out of there comes the red man,
The red man, the red mouth,
The red arms, the red legs,
The red mane, the red hooves.

As he comes, so he approaches,   5
He lifts out the disease immediately;

He carries it off and carries it away,
Across the sea without delay—

Where the cat doesn't meow,
Where the pig doesn't grunt,   10
Where the sheep don't bleat,
Where the goats don't low,
Where the priest doesn't come,

Where the cross isn't borne,
So that ritual bread isn't broken,   15
So that candles aren't lit.

Banish the disease into the field,
Banish the disease into the sea,
Banish the disease under a stone;
You have no place here!   20

Out of there comes the red cow,
She gave birth to a red calf.
She provided red milk.

Performed by Desanka Matijašević; translated by John Miles Foley and Barbara Kerewsky-Halpern.

Out of there comes the red hen,
She leads nine red chicks,   25
She fell upon a red dung-heap,
She gathered up red worms.

And she carried it off across the sea,
Across the sea without delay.

Banish the illness into the field,   30
Banish the illness into the sea,
Banish the illness;
You have no place here!

—[Let (name) remain][1]
Light(ly) as a feather,   35
Pure as silver,
Mild as mother's milk.

Out of there comes Ugimir.[2]
Kill the disease, kill it!
Out of there comes Stanimir.[2]   40
Halt the disease, halt it!
Out of there comes Persa.[2]
Stop the disease, stop it!

Ten, nine, eight, seven,
Six, five, four, three, two, one.   45

Into the wolf's four legs, and fifth the tail,
From my speaking may there be a cure!

THE KAQCHIKEL MAYAN PEOPLE
Guatemala; Kaqchikel (Maya)

"And Then Along Came a Lizard . . ." is one of the most popular of a thriving
tradition of folktales about Brother Peter (Hermano Pedro), an oral genre that
circulates in both Spanish and Kaqchikel, a Mayan language. The central figure

---

1. The person seeking the cure is named between these lines.
2. These three artificial proper names image
   the charm's desired action: Ugimir = Kill

[the disease] + peace, Stanimir = Halt +
peace, Persa = Stop (in shortened form) +
peace.

in this tradition, Brother Peter (d. 1667), is remembered in two kinds of tales: those describing miraculous events that occurred during his lifetime and others devoted to more recently accomplished miracles attributed to his intervention. The Roman Catholic Church is now in the final stages of canonizing Peter as a saint. Between 1989 and 1991, a team of four fieldworkers, headed by Jane Frances Morrissey, recorded an extensive body of Brother Peter tales, heretofore known only to the indigenous population of Guatemala. The selection given here, "And Then Along Came a Lizard," in which Peter typically aids the poor and the sick through miraculous means, is presented as they transcribed and translated the performance, with lines established by pauses and breath-groups, complete with repetitions, hesitations, and interruptions, and with spaces (both within and between lines) marking various lengths of pause. The performance lasted about forty minutes in the original Kaqchikel and was attended by Morrissey and Rafael Coyote Tun, a native speaker and member of the community. The storyteller, Nicolás Murcia, is a Kaqchikel Mayan priest and devout Christian who was blinded in his mid-thirties in an accident associated with his work as a baker. He was more than seventy when he performed this version of the tale.

And Then Along Came a Lizard . . .

Then
along came a little
they say that a lizard crossed his path
"Wait there little sister lizard, wait there" and that's how he made the little lizard
    stop   5
she stopped   her dewlap inflated and she stopped   the little lizard stopped
they say he said to her: "Well   today you'll come along with me"
they say that he took out a good-sized piece of paper from his sack   wrapped her
    up in the paper and put her in his sack
they say he said "Now everything is all set"   10
just a little lizard
so he went to a store
he asked for a loan   let's say two thousand   three thousand but in those days
    three thousand was a lot of money
a lot   15
really
because the cost of living was cheaper then   everything was cheaper
he asked for two or three thousand
then he said "do me a favor   lend me some . . . some . . . two thousand
and   20
I'll give you as a pawn this little creature"
he showed him the little creature   she was all covered with gold
Ah!   and she moved to and fro

Told by Nicolás Murcia; translated by Jane Frances Morrissey and Christine Canales.

people thought that the creature could produce gold

then   25

since the . . . the storekeepers carefully calculated her worth according to the gold
    standard of the time

then   one of them said to him

"don't leave it with me   it's worth too much

Ay! all the goods in my wonderful store   my whole house and this place   30

are worth nothing in comparison with this little creature

I can't

I can't buy it

the little creature is worth a lot

a lot" so he said to him   ha! ha! ha!   35

"then go to such and such a store"   and he went to that store

and when he got there

he said to the storekeeper

"well   I've come

to ask you a favor   lend me some two thousand and I'll return it in . . . in two   40

years time"

"what guarantee will you give me?"   Peter put his hand in his sack   pulled out
    the little lizard

they say that he unwrapped her and showed her to him

"Ah! we can't match what that's worth   45

even if we took everything that you see here

I still can't cover the value of this little creature"

"what advice can you give me?"

"we'd advise you to go to this bank

or to that store which has its own bank and has money in the bank   so go there"   50

[knock   knock   knock]

so he did go to the bank to talk to them

"how much money do you want?"

"I want . . ." he asked for two *arrobas*[1]   "I want two *arrobas*"

"Ah! but two *arrobas* won't do the job   what size is the building that you're   55
building?"

"so many meters long and so many wide"

"Ah! you want a lot of money"   "well   yes"

"what guarantee can you give?   what surety can you give?"

well   once again Peter put his hand in the sack   he took out the little lizard   of   60
    pure gold the little creature   and showed her to him   "Ah!

that's good"

---

1. A measure of weight, approximately equal
   to five kilograms. Here it presumably
   means an *arroba* of gold.

"how many hundred-weights do you want for her?" they asked him
well   there's still hope because they asked him how many hundreds of pounds he
        wanted   65
"well   how many can you give me?" he said
"we give . . . we will give you half a truckload"   who knows if it's true   also if at
        that time they measured by truckloads and not by sackfuls
"we'll give you half a truckload   that's what we'll give you"
that's the way they tell it   that's what I've heard well   70
"well   if you do me this favor   in three years time
if . . . if I've got the money   I'll return the money
I'll return it"   and then
they say that he gave her to them as a guarantee
"with great pleasure"   because they realized right away   75
that this little creature . . . this little creature
was not just any little creature
so they went to get the truck and they filled grain sacks with money   with a lot
        of money   well that's what I heard   who knows if it's true or
somewhat exaggerated   I don't know but that's what they told me   80
they put the money in the truck
"we can also take you with us"   and he said to them "that's fine"
they loaded the money without . . . without even weighing it
they gave him the money in grain sacks
that they tied and turned over to him   into his very own hands   they took the   85
        little creature and left her where they kept the money
and at daybreak
there was more money   and the next day   even more and the third day   wow!

they say . . . who knows how much money did that little creature produce
yes   that's another miracle   90
who knows how much money the little creature made
then
they gave him the money   so he took it
Ah! and with the money   he carried out his plan   well
he called on the bricklayers   95
    [Rafael] the workers
    [Nicolás] the workers   and other laborers
    the architects   to construct the building
the masterbuilders
and that way they began building a . . . a big hospital well   100
a big building
there was money
but it wasn't until the third time   that they built it so   except that . . . except that
        it collapsed in the
    [Rafael] earthquake   105
    [Nicolás] earthquake

because the first time   they built a regular sized ward later they enlarged it
volunteers came   they came to him from everywhere more than fifty men and
    they worked   day after day they worked
that way the work went on   that way they did it and he was happy   110
because there was money   there was money
they looked for a secretary   a treasurer   and board members   he looked for
    them for . . .
so that they helped him and in this way more and more work got done
and so it was that when they were half way   115
half done with the building
the money
stayed the same
all that they'd been given had not decreased because long ago everything was
    cheaper   the amount of money went on unchanged   120
    [Rafael] he didn't spend much
    [Nicolás] he didn't spend much
then
the building went forward and he was happy
with all that he was doing   he went to the bricklayers' well   125
the carpenter and he ordered the doors
the windows
the beds
and the benches
and when they were about to finish the walls   they raised the roof   130
so then   he bought everything they needed   the lamina and other things
he bought   he had enough money
enough money to spend
    [Rafael] Yes they gave him a lot of money
    [Nicolás] He took a lot of money he got a lot of money   135
    [Rafael] He got a lot?
    [Nicolás] Well   yes
then
I don't know if it was two or three years   how many years they took to build the
    building   140
he finished the building
when it was finished he put aside a little money
and they say he said "Ah! my little creature is sad"
he said "she is sad"
then   145
only a . . . a little money he set aside since there was just a little left to be done   he
    put aside a little
and he hired another truck
and went to return the borrowed money
    [Rafael] Ah! he went to return it   150
    [Nicolás] but they say that the bank didn't want to take it

[Rafael] they didn't want to take it?
[Nicolás] no   they didn't want to take it
[Rafael] because it seemed to them preferable to have the little creature
[Nicolás] that's it   a live creature that makes money is worth more than the   155
    money itself
"spend it" [they said]   "Ah! I feel sorry for the little creature"   they say that he
    said
"she's fine here" they say that they said to him
"you can see she's just fine here" they said to him   160

then
"Ah! it's just that I feel sorry for the poor little creature that I left behind
and she did me a favor   now   here I give you the money" "Ah! but you didn't
    spend any of the money"   "of course I did
I took such and such an amount"   165
"Ah! that's not how it was
but leave the money then"   Pedro gave them the same amount he had borrowed
the same amount
he didn't spend much of the money
then   170
they unloaded the money and deposited it in the safe of the bank
then   they looked for the little creature but they say that they didn't want to
    return it
"sell her to us   how many sackfuls of money do you want for her?
sell her to us"   175
"it was only a favor   only a favor I asked her for"
and he said   "now that she has done what I had asked and everything's
    fine   that's enough"   the Ladinos gave her to him halfheartedly
so it was that he finished the building
then he took the little creature   afterward . . . afterward   180
he wrapped it in paper   he took her and left the money
then
he took . . . he took with him the little creature and then   when he arrived   he
    kissed her over and over again "Ay! I thank God   thanks be to you Lord
You helped me and this little creature now helped me   185
now go then   my lovely one"   Hermano Pedro went to the spot from where he
    had taken her
he unwrapped her   he let her go and   trrrrrr
she went again to the hill
the little lizard left   190
so he had kept his promise
well   yes
so it is   so it is   this is all I know about Hermano Pedro.

NATIVE AMERICAN PEOPLE
United States

THE ZUNI PEOPLE

"Coyote and Junco," narrated by Andrew Peynetsa when he was in his mid-sixties and recorded by Dennis Tedlock between 1964 and 1966, illustrates the Zuni Pueblo tradition of *telapnaawe* (tales). Presented here in the ethnopoetic transcription devised by Tedlock, the tale is coded as an oral performance: poetic lines were determined by pauses in narration, centered dots indicate longer pauses, capitals mark increased volume, and smaller print signals decreased volume. It is intended to be reperformed aloud by the reader. The principal characters are Coyote, a trickster figure throughout southwest Native American traditions who can show great cleverness or (as here) great foolishness, and Junco, the relatively common bird whose song attracts the attention and envy of Coyote. As do many stories in this tradition, "Coyote and Junco" portrays and caricatures animal behaviors and physical features as part of a humorous byplay.

Coyote and Junco

SON'AHCHI.
           LO——NG A
  SONTI   GO
                   •

AT STANDING ARROWS
OLD LADY JUNCO HAD HER HOME
and COYOTE
Coyote was there at Sitting Rock with his children.
He was with his children
and Old Lady Junco
was winnowing.
Pigweed
and tumbleweed, she was winnowing these.
With her basket
she winnowed these by tossing them in the air.
She was tossing them in the air
   while Coyote
Coyote
was going around hunting, going around hunting for his children there
when he came to where Junco was winnowing.

Told by Andrew Peynetsa; translated by Dennis Tedlock.

"What are you DOING?" that's what he asked her. "Well, I'm winnowing," she said.
"What are you winnowing?" he said. "Well

•

pigweed and tumbleweed"
    that's what she told him.
    "Indeed.
What's that you're saying?" "Well, this is my winnowing song," she said.
"NOW SING IT FOR ME
so that I
may sing it for my children," he said.
Old Lady Junco
sang for Coyote:
    YUUWA^{HINA} YUUWA^{HINA}
    YUUWA^{HINA} YUUWA^{HINA}
        YU^{HINA}   YU^{HINA}
    (blowing) PFFF PFFF
        YU^{HINA}   YU^{HINA}
    (blowing) PFFF PFFF
That's what she said.
"YES, NOW I
can go, I'll sing it to my children."
Coyote went on to Oak Arroyo, and when he got there
    MOURNING DOVES FLEW UP
and he lost his song.
He went back:
(muttering) "Quick! sing for me, some mourning doves made me
lose my song," he said.
Again she sang for him.
He learned the song and went on.
He went through a field there
and broke through a gopher hole.
Again he lost his song.
Again, he came for the third time
to ask for it.
Again she sang for him.
He went on for the third time, and when he came to Oak Arroyo
BLACKBIRDS FLEW UP and again he lost his song.
He was coming for the fourth time
when Old Lady Junco said to herself, (tight) "Oh here you come
but I won't sing," that's what she said.
She looked for a round rock.
When she found a round rock, she
dressed it with her Junco shirt, she put her basket of seeds with the Junco rock.
(tight) "As for you, go right ahead and ask."
    Junco went inside her house.
Coyote was coming for the fourth time.

When he came:
"Quick! sing it for me, I lost the song again, come on,"
   that's what he told her.
Junco said nothing.
"Quick!" that's what he told her, but she didn't speak.
"ONE," he said.
"The fourth time I
speak, if you haven't sung, I'll bite you," that's what he told her.
•

"Second time, TWO," he said.
"Quick sing for me," he said.
She didn't sing. "THREE. I'll count ONCE MORE," he said.
•

Coyote said, "QUICK SING," that's what he told her.
She didn't sing.
Junco had left her shirt for Coyote.
He bit the Junco, CRUNCH, he bit the round rock.
Right here (*points to molars*) he knocked out the teeth, the rows of teeth in back.
(*tight*) "So now I've really done it to you." "AY! AY!" that's what he said.
THE PRAIRIE WOLF WENT BACK TO HIS CHILDREN, and by the time he got
   back there his children were dead.
Because this was lived long ago, Coyote has no teeth here
   (*points to molars*). LEE————SEMKONIKYA. (*laughs*)

THE PIMA PEOPLE

> "Oriole Songs" are taken from a set of forty-seven songs, sung by the Pima singer Vincent Joseph to the anthropologist Donald Bahr, when Joseph was in his seventies. They are songs about songs, and about the finding of them, and, finally, about the opportunities for the singing of such songs dying out, so that even the marks will be rubbed away. According to Bahr, they resemble the Oriental haiku in their spareness and in their intention: to keep things of a brief duration. The oriole takes the dreamer on a trip, singing these songs to him. The transcription here includes a prose statement made by Joseph before each song.

from *Oriole Songs*

[*Look, from here he reaches Black Water*]

9

Look, from here he reaches Black Water[1] where he says, "Women spring out from Black Water. And they run to us, all crowned with cattail leaves they come running. Green dragon-flies sit on them," sounds this Black Water [song]:

Told and sung by Vincent Joseph; transcribed by Donald Bahr.

---

1. A village on the Gila River Reservation,
   named for the nearby pond.

Black Water lies,
From which women jump out,
Run up to us,
All crowned with cattail leaves
Clung with green dragon-flies.

[Look, and then behind the (Gila) river]

10

Look, and then behind the [Gila] river is White Pinched [Mountain]. "From inside a shining wind [should be "rainbow"] jumps," as it says. Another mountain also stands. "On top it [wind] stops," this songs says. It [mountain] is called Grey Hill. Over that way [from Joseph's house] it stands:

White Pinched,
White Pinched
From which a shining rainbow comes out and, spinning,
Stops atop Grey Hill.

[So he says and then reaches]

11

So he says and then reaches what is Zigzag Connected [Mountain]. "Zigzag mountains so connected. On top he rests. There alongside, a black cloud zigzags. He likes it and watches," thus this sounds:

Zigzag Connected,
On top I pause.
There beside me
A black cloud floating zigzagged,
Pleasant for watching.

[Then (he comes) this way to what is called Red Split (Mountain)]

12

Then [he comes] this way to what is called Red Split [Mountain] where "inside a song sounds." He circles behind, but can't enter because, they say, it's a devil's house. "Yet what can I do to enter? In there are many songs to learn," it sounds:

Red Split,
Red Split.
Inside songs sound
And do me ill.
I circle behind,
Oh, what can I do?
Now, enter,
Then, know many songs.

[Then in this direction stands]

13

Then in this direction stands, where stands the Long Grey [Mountain]. It says, "Long Grey below sings. Companion [Coyote] runs toward it, and has a reed flute. He runs and runs, then dances toward me, then hoots and tells songs with me," thus sounds our companion:

Long Grey beneath sing.
Companion runs near,
Then runs up,
Then dances to me,
Then hoots
And tells songs with me.

[Then afterward he reaches Split]

14

Then afterward he reaches Split, Remainder Split [Mountain].[2] He says, "[from] inside, a shining wind comes out." It's an oriole bird that takes him there. "No one sings, no one knows," sounds this Split song:

Split Remainder,
Split Remainder
From which a shining rainbow comes out.
Oriole bird leads me there
And I enter.
No one sings,
No one knows.

[Look, and this says that they will stop singing]

46

Look, and this says that they will stop singing. "And we stop singing. On top of our sitting place, our scrapers [instruments] lie. With song marks marked on them they lie," says this one:

And now we stop singing and scatter.
Here on our seats our poor scraping sticks lie,
With song-marks marked as they lie.

[Well, and one comes on top which is the very end]

47

Well, and one comes on top which is the very end, which says, "And we stop singing, go [away] in various directions. Here at our singing place a wind jumps out. It runs back and forth. People's

---

2. A large mountain near Apache Junction, Arizona; called Superstition Mountain in English. Pima-Papagos say there are petrified people on top of it.

traces—since they have stepped and it shows—peoples' traces it erases. They [traces] won't remain after the wind has run," it says. Well, thus he ends:

And now we stop singing and scatter.
Wind springs from our singing-place,
Runs back and forth,
Erasing the marks of people.
There's nothing left at the end.

THE CHIPPEWA PEOPLE

Frances Densmore, the translator of the songs included here, was born in Red Wing, Minnesota, in 1867. At an early age she made a life's work of her interest in Native American music, from her first publication for the Bureau of American Ethnology of the Smithsonian Institution in 1907, to subsequent publications on Chippewa, Teton Sioux, Mandan, Northern Ute, Papago, Yaqui, Nootka, Quileute, and Seminole music. She died in Red Wing in 1957.

Working among the Minnesota Chippewa, Densmore attempted to provide, in her words, a "phonograph record, analysis, and field notes," together with attention to "the personality of the [individual] singer." Her introduction to volume 1 of *Chippewa Music* (Bureau of American Ethnology, Bulletins 45 and 53, Washington: Government Printing Office, 1910 and 1913), from which these songs are taken, speaks of the history, instrumentation, and tonality of Chippewa music, and includes, for the *Mide'* songs she would record, an extended account of the Mide' or "Grand Medicine" society cf the Chippewa. This is a society concerned with healing and with "power" of medicine, and we need to keep this functional dimension of the songs in mind.

Some of Densmore's songs have been published in a variety of earlier anthologies, although without the music. We have given the musical notation to two songs as a reminder to the reader that these are not just songs in the sense of lyrical or imagist verse, but words to be rhythmically and tonally pronounced, to be *sung* to the accompaniment of a drum.

The Sioux Women Gather Up Their Wounded

WORDS

Oma'mikweg'	the Sioux women
paba'made'mowûg'	pass to and fro wailing
ona'djida'bamawûn'	as they gather up
o'dinini'miwûn	their wounded men
ani'mûde'mûwûg'	the voice of their weeping comes back
	to us

Sung by Odjib'we; translated by Frances Densmore.

The Approach of the Storm*

Densmore, *Chippewa Music,* I, 1910 (BAE, Bulletin 45)

WORDS

Abitû'	From the half
Gicĭguñ'	Of the sky
Ebigwĕn'	That which lives there
Kabide'bwewiduñ'	Is coming, and makes a noise

I Am Walking†

Densmore, *Chippewa Music,* 1910 (BAE, Bulletin 45)

*Sung by Ga'gandac'; translated by Frances Densmore.
†Sung by Maiñ'ǎns.

WORDS

Dabi'nawa'	Toward calm and shady places
Nin'dinose'	I am walking
Mûk'ade'wakûm īg	On the earth

Analysis.—The rhythm of this song is so irregular as to make it difficult of transcription. The tempo is rapid and the accents are slight.

"There Are Spirits"

WORDS

Nigĭgwa'niwĭñ	At Otter Tail
Ea'	There
Manido'	Are spirits
Wenènikan'	Who is this, my Mīde' brother,
Niwawida'bima'	That I am sitting with?

In his dream the singer is sitting with the manido' at Otter Tail.

SONG PICTURE NO. 94. The two figures represent Mīde' manido', or spirits. The animal was said to be a "lion," also a "large cat with horns." A similar figure was drawn on the Mīde' drum used during the ceremony for Nigan'ĭbĭnes'.

Densmore, *Chippewa Music*, 1910 (BAE, Bulletin 45)

They Think Me Unworthy

WORDS

Nin'danawe'nimigog	They think me unworthy
Nikàn'ûg	My Mīde' brethren
Nucke'ekundeg'	But look and see
Niwĭ'gĭwam'	The length of my wigwam

SONG PICTURE NO. 95. The oblong represents the Mīde'wīgan: the two larger figures are manido' and the smaller ones members of the Mīde'wĭwĭn.

Densmore, *Chippewa Music*, 1910 (BAE, Bulletin 45)

Sung by Gegwe'djiwe'bĭnûñ' ("Trial-thrower")

The Water Birds Will Alight*

WORDS

Kegĕt'	Surely
Inda'bunisin'dangûg'	Upon the whole length of my form
Bīnes'iwug'	⎱ The water birds will alight
Ekwa'yaweyán'	⎰

Densmore, *Chippewa Music,* 1910 (BAE, Bulletin 45)

SONG PICTURE NO. 96. The Mĭde'wĭnĭ'nĭ is represented in his own form and also in the form of a fish, upon which the water birds alight. Ability to attract water animals is greatly desired by members of the Mĭde'wĭwĭn.

THE HAVASUPAI PEOPLE

Throughout their history, the Havasupai people have been stewards of a lush tributary of the Grand Canyon in what we now call Arizona. Their name for themselves, which may be translated as "People of the Blue/Green Water," refers to the stream that runs through their canyon, bringing life to the harsh high desert. Almost all Havasupai are proficient in their traditional language; most do not speak English until they reach school age. Their songs and stories express love of their homeland. Stories and songs are performed by all members of the community. Traditional medicine men (shamans) use stories and songs as part of their healing rituals. Leanne Hinton writes: "Dan Hanna learned this song from Mark Hanna, a shaman. Although it is a medicine song, it is not necessarily sung by a medicine man. It can be sung by someone who is ill and wants to cure himself. Many people had these personal medicine songs in the old days, and some people still do. Like the medicine man's songs, a personal medicine song is received through a dream from a spirit. The song goes into rich descriptions of Havasu Canyon. At the end, the song refers to some boulders which lie in a certain place, which, when one lies down on them absorb sickness. The word *bay gjama,* which is translated as 'an illness,' is more correctly either an illness or an accident, and really refers to a straying from the rightful road, the development of a disharmony with nature,"— which is the definition of illness. (The song text was transcribed and translated from the Havasupai Indian language into English in the 1960s.)

Medicine Song†

Singing		Translation	Speaking
Máte genájuwa	he' heye	The land we were given	('mat
Hmáte genájuwa	he' mm	The land we were given	gnaajva)

---

*Sung by Gegwe'djiwe'bīnûñ'.

†Sung by Dan Hanna; translated by Leanne Hinton.

Singing		*Translation*	*Speaking*
Vá geyóvuwa	he' heye	It is right here	(va gyova)
Vá geyóvuwa	he' heye	It is right here	
'Áwe yuhwátiga	he' heye	Red rock	('wii
'Áwe yuhwátiga	he' heyem	Red rock	hwatga) 5
Ñá oséemega	he' heye	Streaked with brown	(ñaa
Ñá oséemega	he' heye	Streaked with brown	seemga)
Ñá om gyájvga	he' heye	Shooting up high	(ñvgyajvga)
Ñá om vgyájevega	he' hemm	Shooting up high	10
'áwam sigávoga	he' heye	All around our home	('wa
'wámje sigávoga	he' heyem	All around our home	sgavoga)
Wé yiwáthuga	he' heye	Red rock	('wii
Wé yiwáthiga	he' heye	Red rock	hwatega)
Ñá om mgyávoga	he' mm	Shooting up high	(nvgyajvga) 15
Thá giyóhuwa	he' heye	It is right here	(tha gyova)
Ñévo ñibúvguge	he' heye	Down at the source	(ñvu
Hábag ñiyújuwa	he' heye	A spring will always be there	ñbuvgge)
			(haabag
			nyuj)
Ñá guwfjuvuwo	he' heyem	It is ours	(na gwiijva)
Ñá guwfjuwo	he' mm	It is ours	20
Hé ñiyúmowe	he' heye	Since a long time ago	(ga
Gávo ńyúmowe	he' heye	Since a long time ago	vuñyum)
'Máte ñuwfjuwa	he' heye	In the land that is ours	('mat
Ñévo ñitúvume	he' heye	Moving right down the center	ñwiijva)
Só 'ugwáthuga	he' heye	Bright blue-green	(suuw-
Vám jimísevga	he' hemm	There moves a line	gwatga) 25
Nó 'iyúhuwa	he' heye	This is what I'm thinking	(ña yuha)
Ñá 'iyúhuwa	he' heyem	This is what I'm thinking	
'Á giyúyuwo	he' heye	At the edge of the water	(ham
Hámes'e'ívtevga	he' heye	Cattails appear	s'ivtvga) 30

Singing	Translation		Speaking
'áme si'ívtevga	he' heye	Cattails appear	(suuw-
Só'ogwátuwa	he' heyem	Bright blue-green	gwatga)
'Ám buwámbuga	he' heye	All around the water	(ham
Ñá 'iyúwuwa	he' heye	This is what I'm thinking	vwamvga)
			(ña yuha)
'Á gejúyiwo	he' heyem	At the edge of the water	(ha gyuuyo) 35
'Á 'amálega	he' heyem	Water foam forming	(ha 'malga)
'Á 'amálega	he' heyem	Water foam forming	
'Á gejúyiwo	he' heyem	At the edge of the water	
Gwáyyve	he' heye	Swirl, swirling	(thgwayv
gwáyvuga			thgwayvga)
Gwáyve	he' heyem	Swirl, swirling	
gwáyvuga			40
'Á gejúyiwo	he' heyem	At the edge of the water	(ha gyuuyo)
'Á gejúyiwo	he' heyem	At the edge of the water	
Má gwanóvjiga	he' heye	Silt layers forming	('mat
Mát gwanóvjiga	he' eyem	Silt layers forming	gwanvjga)
'Á gejúyiwo	he' heye	At the edge of the water	(sgwin
			sgwinga) 45
Máthgwinathgwínega	he' heye	Ripple, rippling	
Máthgwinathgwínega	he' heye	Ripple, rippling	(ña yuha)
Ñá iyúwawa	he' mm	This is what I'm thinking	
Ñá iyúhuwa	he' heya	This is what I'm thinking	(ha gbadga)
Háge 'abádiga	he' heye	Water-walking beetles	50
Ágeyabádiga	he' heyem	Water-walking beetles	(ha javme)
Há ñijáwome	he' heyem	On top of the water	
Ñévo jiháyviga	he' heye	Spreading out	(ñvu
Ñá iyíwuwa	he' heyem	This is what I'm thinking	jhayvga)
			(ña yuha)
'Ámesegwáthuga	he' heye	Water grasses growing	(hams-
Hámesegwáthega	he' heye	Water grasses growing	gwathga) 55
Shó'ogwáthuga	he' heye	Bright blue-green	(suuw-
Shó'ogwáthuga	he' heyem	Bright blue-green	gwatga)

Singing		Translation	Speaking
Singing		*Translation*	*Speaking*
Há ñiyálowe	he' heye	Under the water	(ha ñyaala)
Há ñiyálowe	he' heye	Under the water	60
Mágnognóvoga	he' heye	Wave, waving	(gnov
Mágnognóvoga	he' heye	Wave, waving	gnovga)
Ñá'iyúhuwa	he' heye	This is what I'm thinking	(ña yuha)
Ñá'iyúhuwa	he'hmm	This is what I'm thinking	
Há ñiyálowe	he' heye	Under the water	(ha ñyaala) 65
Há jwáiga	he' heye	Water pebbles	(ha jwayga)
Ñévo jiqvújega	he' heye	Tiny little ones	(ñvu
Géjijávuwa	he' heye	Spreading out over them	jqayvjga)
			(gjjavva)
Vóñijávume	he' heye	Spreading out over them	
Há'eñihájiva	he' heye	Our drinking water	(ha ñhajva) 70
'Á jimhévgowa	he' heyem	The water is gliding	(ha
Máłe megtávoge	he' heye	Toward the north	jmhevga)
			('mał
			mgłavge)
'Ó teyávoga	he' heye	On in that direction	(vu łyavge)
Thá thelávuma	he' heyem	And then it is gone	(tha
			thlavm)
Ña 'iyúhuwa	he' heye	This is what I'm thinking	(ña yuha) 75
Ña 'iyúhuwa	he' heyem	This is what I'm thinking	
Thág ño'evó'oga	he' heye	Here we arrive	(thag
Thág ño'evó'oga	he' heyem	Here we arrive	ñ'voga)
Báyovgijámoha	he' heye	An illness	(bay gjama)
Báyogijámoha	he' heye	An illness	80
Thá vuwámuga	he' heye	I sit down	(thag
Thá vuwámuga	he' heyem	I sit down	vwamg)
Gwéwe 'eswáduga	he' heye	I sing myself a song	(gwe
Gwéwe 'eswáduga	he' heyem	I sing myself a song	'swaadga)
Ñá 'iyúhuwa	he' heye	This is what I'm thinking	(ña yuha) 85
Ñá 'iyúhuwa	he' heye	This is what I'm thinking	
'Ágwe simájuwa	he' heye	A medicine spirit	(gwe
'Ágwe simájuwa	he' mm	A medicine spirit	smaaje)

Singing		*Translation*	*Speaking*
Bá qetheyévuwa	he' heye	A shaman	('ba
Bá qetheyévuwa	he' heye	A shaman	gthiyeva) 90
Vá'aluwíñuga	he' heye	I am the same as him	(vlwiivga)
Vá'aluwíñuga	he'hmm	I am the same as him	
Báyo gijámuha	he' heye	An illness	(bay gjama)
Báyo gijámuga	he' heye	An illness	
Há buwámuga	he' heye	I sit down	(thag
Há buwámuga	he' hmm	I sit down	vwamg) 95
'Ágwe weswáduga	he' heye	I sing myself a song	(gwe
'Ágwe weswáduga	he' heye	I sing myself a song	'swaadga)
'Ágwe 'asiñiga	he' heyem	The things I have named	(gwe
'Ágwe 'asíñiga	he' heyem	The things I have named	'siiñga) 100
'Aɫe nemáguga	he' heye	I leave them behind	('ɫnmagga)
'Aɫenemáguga	he' heye	I leave them behind	
Nó 'iyúhuwa	he' heye	This is what I'm thinking	(ña yuha)
Nó 'iyúhuwa	he' mm	This is what I'm thinking	
Thág ño'ovóga	he' heye	There we arrive	(thag
Thág ño'ovóga	he' heye	There we arrive	ñ'vóga) 105
Thám jovibájuga	he' heyem	We are leaving the canyon	(tham jo
Thám jo wibájuga	he' heye	We are leaving the canyon	jbajga)
Máɫoódwova	he' heye	Out on the rim	('mat
Máɫoódwova	he' mm	Out on the rim	ɫ'odva) 110
Gwé ñiháɫowa	he' heye	Horses that are mine	(gwe ñhaɫ)
Gwé ñiháɫowa	he' heye	Horses that are mine	
Nó 'uwávowo	he' heye	The place where they roam	(ñowavo)
Ño'uwávowo	he' heyem	The place where they roam	
Ñwá 'ajóqowa	he' heyem	Is there at the junipers	(ñwa 'joq) 115
Jóqa havíɫega	he' heyem	Where the junipers are straight	('joq hvitga)
Ñabiñáboga	he' heye	And low and low	(ñab ñabga)
Vú 'ayóhowa	he' heye	They are right here	(vu gyoha)

Singing		*Translation*	*Speaking*	
Gwé ñihátove	he' heye	Horses that are mine	(gwe ñhaŧ)	
Thám jejebúvuvga	he' heye	Are gathered right there	(tham jjbugvga)	120
Ñó 'iyúhuwa	he' heye	This is what I'm thinking	(ña yuha)	
Ñó 'iyúhuwa	he' heyem	This is what I'm thinking		
Thág ño'evówoga	he' heye	Here we arrive	(thag ñ'voga)	
Thág ño'evówoga	he' heyem	Here we arrive		
Yá hawíniga	he' heye	We swing back	(siihwinga)	125
Yá hawíniga	he' hmm	We swing back		
'Áwe gewéyiwo	he' heye	Descending the rocks again	('wii gweeyi)	
'Áwe gewéyiwo	he' heyem	Descending the rocks again		
'Áwe gethílŧewa	he' heye	White rock	('wii gthilŧva)	
Ña'usémuga				
	he' heye	Streaked with brown	(ñaa seemga)	130
'Ó ñibóvuvga	he' heyem	Down at the source	(vu ñbuvvga)	
Hábav ñiyújuwa				
	he' heyem	A spring will always be there	(haabag ñyuj)	
'Ágwe ñigethátemwa	he' heye	The spring that heals	(gwe ñgthaajme)	
Ná geyóhuwa	he' heye	It is right there	(ñgyoha)	
Gá geyóhowa	he' heyem	It is right there	(gwe ñhata)	135
Gwé'e ñihátowa	he' heye	Horses that are mine		
Únihájuve	he' heye	They drink the water	(vu ñhajva)	
Gá geyóhowa	he' hemm	That is right there	(ga gyoha)	
'Áwe gethílŧega	he' heye	White rock	('wii gthilŧga)	
Ná vusémuga	he' heyem	Streaked with brown	(ñaa seemga)	140
Ñam gyávuga	he' heye	Shooting up high	(ñvgyávga)	
Thá thiyóvuwa	he' heye	It is right there	(tha gyova)	
Ñívu vetóvume	he' heyem	Moving down the center	(ñvu vŧuvme)	
Gwé'e ñihátuwa				
	he'mm	Horses that are mine	(gwe ñhata)	
Ñóviñájuwo	he' heye	There is their trail	(ññáaje)	145
Ñóviñájuwo	he' heye	There is their trail		

Singing		Translation	Speaking
'Ágwe gathávuga	he' heye	The color of dust	(gwe
'Ágwe gathávuga	he' heyem	The color of dust	gthavga)
Ó eye'óyvuga	he' heye	Zig-zagging	(vu
Májyo yi'úyvuga	he' heye	Zig-zagging	ŧs'uuyvga)
Vógse vuwávuga	he' heyem	It leads to the source	(buge
Vógse vuwávuga	he' heyem	It leads to the source	vwavga)

150

THE APPALACHIAN PEOPLE
United States

"Raglif Jaglif Tetartlif Pole" exemplifies the strong and very old cluster of "Jack tales," originally a Scots-Irish oral tradition, that continues to thrive throughout Appalachia today, especially in the Smoky Mountains of North Carolina, where Ray Hicks, from Beech Mountain, "tells" Jack tales regularly. The teller of this Jack tale, Leonard Roberts, was born in a log house at the head of Toler Creek in Floyd County, Kentucky, where in 1950 he heard this tale from his aunt, Columbia Roberts. He went on to earn a Ph.D. in English and Folklore at the University of Kentucky, and often told Jack tales as parts of public lectures and performances. In addition to understanding the tradition's overall importance as evidence of an ongoing oral tradition in the United States, we should also observe this particular story's adherence to the international tale-type of "The Girl as Helper in the Hero's Flight." McCarthy's notes indicate that "the storyteller sat quietly through the generally understated performance, but his voice was remarkably expressive in quality, pitch, and pace." One striking feature of the performance as transcribed is the relatively frequent address of the listening audience, a typical feature of oral narrative in many cultures. Drawn-out words or phrases are indicated with hyphens (w-a-y) and audience laughter with bracketed exclamation points; the collector has reconstructed and inserted in brackets the few sentences that were lost during the changing of the tape.

Raglif Jaglif Tetartlif Pole

And so once upon a time, / not my time, not your time, but once upon a time, / there's an old man and woman who lived back in the mountains, / a-n-d they had

---

Told by Leonard Roberts; recorded in 1980 by William McCarthy.

Ray Hicks. *Teller of Jack Tales*. Beech Mountain, N.C. 1988.

a pretty good family, / but most of 'em had jumped up and married and left, / and had only Jack at home. / Old Jack was a pretty fine good little old boy when he was growing up.

By the time he was age thirteen, / he was going down the creek, / and down the forks of the creek, / the old schoolhouse there, / a-n-d—on a Sunday afternoon— / and he was a gambling down there with the boys. / And his father and his mother they come and they threaten what they was going to do [!!!!] / for going down there and a-getting into meanness.

Jack never minded it. / He just went on down there anyway. / And he gambled with those boys and played, / pitching sticks and rocks, / and jumping rail fences. /

And finally one day he was down there, / and Jack felt awfully lucky, / because he won nearly everything, nearly all those boys had around there. / And he was feeling pretty good. / (He was just about fourteen years old.) / W-e-l-l, / first thing he knew some man stepped in a booth there. / And he begin to banter with Jack and says, / "Ah, Jack, I'll have to play you some."

A-h-h-h, Jack felt lucky. / He just played him a few hands, / and shot a few dice. / Won everything the old man had. / Well, that old man said, "Now Jack, / I'll tell you now what I've got. / I've got a very pretty daughter. / Now I'll bet you my daughter against everything you've got / on the next turn of our dice." / (Would you've took that up?) [!!!!]

Jack was just a little old chunk of a boy, you know. / Barely raised up. / Well, he felt lucky and he decided he'd play. /

Ay, he played and he played,
and he played rather skillfully,

and he won that old man's daughter. / Well, the boys got to shaming him and sharping their fingers at him. / And he got to backing off and quarreling with 'em. / And the first thing you know, he looked around, / and that old man was gone.

/ Well, he didn't know where that girl was. / Now the boys was fussing at him so much, / just made him determined to set out and see if he could find her.

W-e-l-l, he put a little budget on his back, / and he set out.

> And d-a-y-s passed,
> and nights passed,
> and weeks passed,
> and months passed,
> and he travelled along the road.

And he couldn't find any hide or hair / of that old man. / And after he's gone for nearly six months, / w-a-y off in a faraway land, / he's decided he'd better come back home, / and give her up. / Maybe he can find another pretty girl.

But just as he was turning back it was getting dark, / and he began to look for a place to stay all night. / And there was just what he was looking, what he was looking for—big old house back on the hill, / on the rise of the land there. / And he just went right up there and he just knocked on the door.

Well, he knocked two or three times. / Pretty soon here the door cracked open. / Here come a fellow out, / and Jack took a look at him. / It was that old fellow.

Said, "A-i-n'-t you that man I / won that girl off of?" [!!!!]

That old man said, "Well, all right, if you're Jack. [!!!!] / I guess you are."

So Jack said, "Well, where is she, here? / I want to see her." / (Wanted to see if she was pretty or not.) / That old man said, "Oh no, I, I can't do that. [!!!!] / No. / Go on in and have supper with us and stay all night."

Well, Jack had been looking for a place to stay all night. / And so Jack said, "Oh, well, I don't care if I do." / He went ahead in. / And pretty soon the old woman had the, had dinner ready. / And a very great old big l-o-n-g table, looked like it was twenty feet long, and just covered all around it with the most a-pretty girls. / And Jack just felt at home. [!!!!!!!!]

So he sat down on one side, and he started eating. / And, time he got his hunger a little bit stayed, / he looked over there and saw a pretty girl right across from him. / And he kept eyeing her through most of that dinner. / And that old man kept watching him and hurrying him up a little. / Well, finally they all did get through, and all went in, went off to their rooms, and so forth. / So he just put Jack down there on a pallet, / and had the room by himself right there. /

Well, next morning Jack waked up bright and early. / Nice sunshiny morning. / And he went out on the porch / and pretty soon here come that old man.

Jack said, "O-h now, which one's mine? / I'm going to take her home today."

"Naah." / That old man started shaking his head. / "Augh, Jack, I don't believe you won that hand from me fair back yonder."

Jack said, "Oh yes, I—I played you fair."

Said, "O-h, you didn't uhh, / but I've got another little job, like to see you do. / And *then,* you can take the girl."

"Well," Jack said, "well, what is it?"

"Well," the old man said, "well now, down there's my big old barn. / It's got

fifty stalls in it, / and my horses, / and hasn't been cleaned out in seven years."
[!!!!!!] / He threw down an old bent-up shovel and down a big new shovel and
says, / "Now you have that barn cleaned out / neat as a pin / when I get back or I'll
cut your head off tonight."

Before Jack could fuss much he looked around and he was gone again. / Well,
Jack began to scratch his head, / but there wasn't nothing he could do / except
look over those shovels and decide which one'd work. / (Which one would you
have taken?) [!!!!!] / Well, there's that old bent-up shovel. / (You know, they're sort
of turned up on the ends, / where you've shoveled a lot on 'em.) / So he just got
that big new fine, fine new shovel, about number, number eight, I guess. / And he
went on down there to those—to that barn. /

> And then he got in there.
> And he got in the stall and he started shoveling,
> started shoveling.
> And every time he'd shovel out a shovelful,
> a couple more'd jump back in.

And he worked that-a-way up in the afternoon. / And he couldn't clean out but
one or two stalls. / Well he came back out and he was just sitting there, looking
at that barn, / looking up toward that house, / and he was wondering how he was
going to save his head.

Well, about the time he looked up toward the house a time or two, / he saw
a—looked like a girl coming down that way. / Here she come just a sailing down
through there, / just kind of perky / and smarty. / And she came down there and
said, "What! What are you doing down here, Jack?"

"Oh," Jack said, "It wouldn't do any good to tell you."

"Oh, go ahead and tell me. / Won't do any harm."

"Well, that old man sent me down here to clean out this barn. / Get it cleaned
out tonight or he'll cut my head off. / And I can't shovel out but one or two stalls
full."

She looked at him, and said, / "Well, which one of those shovels are you
using?"

"Well," he said, "I'm using that *good* shovel."

"Well," she said, "you take that old shovel in that'n's place."

Well, Jack just picked up that old shovel, / and he went in there, / and it just
took about two or three shovels to clean out one stall, / shoveling it out.

> He just went all around through there,
> shoveling it out,
> shoveling it out,
> and he got 'em all cleaned out.

And he came over there / and that girl was waiting for him / and they had about
an hour there to spark and court [!!!!!!!!] / before they had to go back to the house.
/ Well they was a-starting back up the lane there, / going along and this and that,
/ just as close together as they could get, you know. / (He was on one side of the

road and she was on the other side.) [!!!!!!] / And the old man came in. / And he came right to 'em and stopped 'em.

Said, "How'd you get along today, Jack?"

"Why," Jack says, "I got along just fine."

"Did you really clean my barn out?"

Jack says, "Yeah, I cleaned it out as clean as a pin." / The old man looked and saw the girl slipping to get away. / He says, [*gruffly*] "Somebody's been helping you. / I'll get you yet!" / He was just about to jump on Jack.

But Jack, of course, got out of the side of the way, and went and hid around, and went and hid around behind the house. / Waited there to just about suppertime before he showed himself. / But he finally came down, and he went in / and there they all ganged around the table / eating and talking and chatting. / And Jack kept looking over there, and there was that same girl again, / over there, / and he'd wink at her a time or two. / And they talked a little bit louder, and so forth, and finally / the old man noticed 'em, till they was nearly all through. / And he sent 'em all to bed again. / Put Jack in his pallet over there on the floor. / Well, Jack slept good that night, / and he got up and went out on the porch. / Nice sunshiny morning. / Just raring to go, / and the old man came out.

Jack says, "Which one's mine, and I'll go right now?"

The old man said, "A-h-h, Jack, / you're not winning 'em fair. [!!!!!!] / I got one more little job, like to see you do."

Jack said, "Like to know what that is."

"Well," the old man said, / "now you've got my barn cleaned out, / way back here in these mountains is my big fine horses. / And the leader of my big fine herd of horses is named old Raglif Jaglif Tetartlif Pole. / You go back there and you get all those horses and get 'em down here and put 'em in that barn / tonight or I'll cut your head off."

Then he threw out a little old halter there / and a big fine bridle / and he disappeared.

Jack began to look 'em over.

"Now, which one to use?" [!!!!!]

Well, he'd heard about that old big horse, / and it looked like that little old halter wouldn't hold a calf.

Well, he just grabbed up that big new bridle and he took right up that hill.
And he saw that herd of horses and began to run, run through them.
And there's old Raglif Jaglif was a leading 'em across hillside to hillside.
And run 'em right a-w-a-y up in the afternoon and couldn't catch a one.

Well he just had to come back down there to the barn, / where he was. / Sit down. / Sitting there worrying about his head. [!!!!!!] / And he saw the girl coming up that-a-way. / Time she got up there, and her walking, her tossing her head, / he knew who it was. / He's going a time trying to resist her and she came up behind him.

"H-e-y, whattaya say there?"

"Oh-h, it doesn't do any good to tell you."

"Go ahead and tell me. / Won't do any harm." [!!!!!] /

Jack said, [*teary voice*] "Oh-h, well, / he sent me out here to catch his herd of horses. / And I can't get old Raglif Jaglif to take the bridle at all. / 'Bout run me to death. / Said he's gonna cut my head off."

She said, "Which one of those bridles are you using?" [!!!!!]

"Why, I got the big *new* bridle."

"Oh, take this old bridle and go back there and see what happens."

Why, Jack, he just grabbed up that halter / and he ran up there. / And run on up on through that big herd of horses. / And he held it out and old Raglif Jaglif just saw it down there / and put his head through, / put his head in that old halter.

Jack jumped up on his back / and grabbed a-hold of his mane, and started riding him out of there. / And of course all the rest just followed, / and they just came right on down there. / Jack just filed 'em all in the barn, / filled up all those fifty stalls, / and buttoned the doors. / Came on back out, and / had about an hour or two there to court a little bit. [!!!!!]

So he started sparking the girl, / and talking 'bout this 'n that, / t'other thing. / Finally, looks like it was getting late enough for them to go toward the house, / and they met that old man.

He came a roaring out, / and he said, "How'd you get along today, Jack?"

Jack, of course, said, "I got along just fine."

"You got all my horses in that barn?"

"Heh-heh, got 'em everyone in the stalls / and the doors buttoned."

The girl kept on going, of course.

"Oh-h, somebody's helping you, and I'm going to catch you in it yet!" / Jack had to run this time to get out behind the house. / Waited till supper was nearly over before he went in. / Sat down and got eating. / And the girl over there, / nearly through, / she kept looking at him / and talking to him. / He tried to keep his head down and eat. / Finally, it's all over, / and went back to his pallet again.

Next morning, of course, / you know this was the third time: / something's got to happen. [!!!!!!!!] / He was out there. / Sunny and nice. / Pretty soon, here come that old man.

Jack said, "Now, which one is mine, cause I wanna take her?"

Man said, "A-h-h, nah, nah. / You're not, / you're not winning my girl fair. / But I'll tell you what. / I've got one more job. / If you can do it, / you can have her."

Jack was getting hard and didn't want to be passive. / But he said, "All right then. / What is it?"

"Well," he said, "now down here, this body of water here you see, that's the Red Sea. / And w-a-y o-u-t in the middle of the Red Sea is a little island. / And *on* that i-s-land is a big old tree—it's five hundred feet to the first limb. / Just above that limb is a big eagle's nest, / full of eggs and I haven't got those eggs to be gathered in seven years. / You go and get those eggs and have them here tonight or I'll cut your head off." / Then he pointed down there to that old canoe-like thing and a pretty big boat / and he disappeared. / (Take a drink of water. [!!!!!!!!] / Now which one's you going to take?)

Well, I'll tell you, he got in that old thing, he got in that old thing, and it was so, it was so darn leaky, / so full of water, it went up under the water. / He had to wade out of there. / Jack couldn't get away from shore. / So he just had to get back out and sit down. / Who should come down that way? [!!!!] / That pretty girl.

"What are you doing down here, Jack?"

"Oh, wouldn't do any good to tell you."

"Go ahead and tell me. / Won't do any harm."

"Well, that old man / put out these boats, / these boats here. / I need to take my choice. / Go a-c-r-o-s-s the Red Sea: here's an island. / Walk b-a-c-k in that island till I see a crooked tree five hundred feet high. / In the top of that tree is an eagle's nest with eggs. / I'm supposed to have 'em here tonight or he'll cut my head off."

She said, "Now, which one of those boats you trying to use?"

He said, "Well, I got in this *good* boat."

"Why," she says, "get out and get in this old boat and then see what happens."

Well, he got in there / and sat down and started paddling. / And that boat just started a-sizzling and a-singing through the water. / And it 'as a-flying. / And pretty soon it was just run up on the sand, / on an island over there. / Well, he just stepped out, / and the girl stepped out, / and they started walking along on that island.

Wasn't much of a road there, / but they were pretty close together. / He was on one side and she's on the other. / They kept going / and as they kept on going that tree kept on looking higher. / Looked like it was a-growing. / Of course, he kept on *looking*.

Finally, he just stopped, says / "I don't see how in the world I'm going to get to the top of that tree."

"Well," she said, "just come along, / come along, / and I'll, I'll think of a way."

By the time they got up there it was so tall he just couldn't see the top of it. He said, "I don't know how to do it."

She said, "Well, / I guess I'll have to help you. / I've learned a little magic from this old man. / He's been teaching us there for years, / teaching us to do things. / So I'm going to help you this time. / You do everything I tell you, / or you'll fail." / She just, she just pulled off her fingers. / Like that! / Pulled 'em all off.

"Now you take *all* of these, / and they're just like little staubs. / And you stick one in the tree and it'll stick there / and you stick another up there. / And you step on one, step on the other one, and the other one. / If you keep pulling 'em up behind you, / you can go to the top of this tree."

(Would you try that?) [!!!!!]

Well, Jack said, "Well, I'll just— / I'll just have to try it."

So he took 'em and he started stepping. / Put 'em up there, and he got a hold of 'em. / He was pretty stout—Jack. / Keeps on going. / Thinking about coming down any moment. / But pretty soon he looked down: he was so darn far up he may as well go ahead. [!!!] / So he just kept on a-going, / kept on a-going, / kept on a-going. / Pretty soon he was so far up there, could see a-l-l a-r-o-u-n-d, / almost to his land back where he'd come from. / Finally, he just stuck his head up above this first limb / and there's that eagle's nest. / And so he just gathered up the eggs now, / rather carefully, / and put them in his bosom carefully.

He was tired coming down. / Didn't crush the eggs, though. / Just kept on coming. / Took him about two hours to go up. / He's coming down a little faster. / Kept on coming, / kept on coming. / Finally, he got to the ground about four hours later. / He's just about give out.

And the girl was there, talking to him and saying, "You did fine, you did fine. / You all right. / Now give my fingers back."

He climbed back up. [!!!] / They were stuck on there, you see. / And after he went back on up the tree, / finally he came down and found them all, but one missing.

Jack looked up the tree and said, "I'm sorry about that." [!!!!!!!!!] / "Looks like I've left one in the top of that tree" [!!!!!!!!] / "Oh," she said, "don't never mind. / You can't go back up after it." / Says, "Well, yeah, let's go ahead this way. / Of course now, we're gonna have a big masquerade dinner tonight. / Going to have it in that new barn. / Sort of ceremony." / Says, "When we're dancing about, we're gonna be in costumes. / And if you ever happen to see somebody throw a hand out from under a jacket, / where you see one arm with a finger missing, / then you'll know who it is when you pick to dance."

Jack thought that was an awful good idea. / Said, "All right."

So they went walking along, / walking along. / Finally, they came to the boat again. / Jack got in and gave it a little dip of the paddle / and ZIIIP! / they went across and back up on shore. / And they got out, / put the boats up.

Getting pretty dark by now. / A little bit late. / And here, by the time they got started / towards the house, / here comes that old man. / Oh, he was so mad he looked like he was going to cloud up and rain. [!!!!!!]

He said to Jack, "How'd you get along today, Jack?"

"Oh, got along just fine."

"You got my eagle's eggs? Yes?"

"I got your eagle's eggs." / Started to pull 'em out of his hat and give 'em to that old man. / Made him so mad he just started slapping 'em against the ground.

The girl by this time had disappeared.

The old man said, "I see, / somebody's been helping you all along. / And I'm gonna cut your head off TONIGHT!"

Jack had to hurry and run away / and get out behind the house before he got his head cut off. / He waited out there till nearly dusky dark / before he came in and had a little bite of supper. / By that time they're all in their costumes going down toward the barn.

Well, he followed 'em on down there. / Well, when he got in there,

there was the barn litened up nice,
and the hall litened up,
and a room big enough to have dances in.
There was music and making noise
before the square dances begin,
and swinging, and reels, and jigs, and things. [?]

And Jack just walking all around among them— / he couldn't tell one from another. / And he kept on watching rather careful. / All at once he saw somebody's skirt make a little tremble, / and a hand came out from under it, / and he saw a finger missing.

So he kept dancing around until he finally got her by herself. / Started dancing with her. / And they got to talking.

And Jack said, "You know that man, / he's gonna cut off my head tonight."

The girl said, "Well, now, I wonder what are you gonna do?"

Jack said, "Only thing I can do is to try to run away from here. / Would you go with me, sweetheart?" [!!!]

First time he's ever called her that. [!!!!!!!!]

Course, she said, "Well, now, all right. / If you, if you can catch that horse, / why I'll, I'll, I'll run away with you."

And so they made it up just right there. / And so they sashayed around a little bit more until they got around up on the side, / and they came out of one of those stalls / and went out the front / and went on as fast as they could walk towards the house. / Well, Jack got old Raglif Jaglif, / put that old bridle on him. / And the girl ran in the house, / got her a little budget of clothes, / and picked up some money, / and other things, / and came out there. /

Jack got on that horse, and bounced her up behind him, / and they r-o-d-e away clear out of that kingdom as hard as they could go. / On through the night and way up the next day / before they slowed down and began to look around where they were. / Well, they was going trotting along there feeling pretty good. / And looking this way, and this way. / And finally once Jack looked back.

He said, "Hey, I can see something like a little speck of dust way back on the road yonder."

And the girl said, "Well, you keep watching it and see if you can tell what it is?"

Well, after a while, about half an hour there, / Jack looked back again. / He said, "Looks like that old man riding up on a big horse, just about as fast as us."

["Well," the girl said, "you lean forward, / and look in that horse's right ear."

Well, he peeped in there, and said, / "I can't see anything in there, / just a little stick."]

"Well," she said, "you take that little stick / in your right hand, and throw it over your right shoulder. / And you say:

> 'GOOD roads before us,
> And briars and grapevines behind us.' "

Well, Jack just reached in there and he got it out and he *threw* it over his right shoulder:

> "GOOD roads before us,
> And briars and grapevines behind us."

And he just kept watching it.

> And just as soon as it hit the ground it made a little slew up there,
> and little patch of briar.
> Pretty soon a big clump of briar.
> Pretty soon a big field of briar.
> And pretty soon it just spread out A-L-L over EVERY-where.

And he kept watching, and saw that old man ride in there, / ride into those briars, and get all tangled up.

> But then when he turned to the front,

> the r-o-a-d stretched out like a highway.
> And they just r-o-d-e on like the wind
> on old Raglif Jaglif Tetartlif Pole.
> O-n through the night and w-a-y up the next day
> before they slowed that horse down.

And they went ambling along and Jack got to looking around, looking at the timber. / He could tell the names of trees and so forth. / Had a batch to do to get back on in his territory.

It was about the time they got the old horse slowed down, he looked back. / He says, "Uh-ohh, / I see a little speck of dust back yonder again."

But she said, "You keep watching it, / see if you can tell what it is."

Well, they rode on a piece longer, and Jack looked back. / He said, "That's that old man. / He's got out of that briar patch and he's riding down after us."

"Well," the girl said, "look in that horse's right—" *left ear* is what she said.

Well, he peeped in there, / and said, "I can't see anything in there / unless it's a drop of water."

"Well," she said, "you take that drop of water and throw it over your left shoulder / and say:

> 'GOOD road before us,
> And the Red Sea behind us.' "

Well, he just *flipped* that over his left shoulder:

> "GOOD road before us,
> And the Red Sea behind us."

And just as soon as that drop of water hit the ground

> it made a little pool there
> and made a little puddle
> and then a little pond
> and then a little brook.
> And pretty soon it made a w-h-o-l-e sea.

And they saw that old man go riding in there, / right out of sight into that brook and into that water [!!!!!!]
Soon as Jack looked around back to the front,

> there was that r-o-a-d just laid out like a highway.
> And they just r-o-d-e on like the wind
> on old Raglif Jaglif Tetartlif Pole.

Time they looked up again, / next day, after they'd rode all day and all night, / Jack began to recognize his, his territory. / Began to see these little strips of field here and little corn patches. / Looked like he was getting pretty close home. / So he began to talk with the girl, / telling her how he'd been away for about a year, and he didn't know what they was going to do to him when he got back.

Then the girl began to pout a little bit.

Jack said, "What's the matter, darling?"

She said, "I don't want you to stop home. / I want you to ride ahead a way and marry me."

Jack said, "Now, I don't know whether that is natural or not. You know [*chuckling*], I want to stop and see my folks, tell them where I, where I've been."

And she kept on, she kept on trying to persuade him. / And finally she said, "Well, now I'll let you stop. / And you stay for awhile. / But you're not to let any of them, let anybody hug your neck or kiss you, / cause if you do, why you'll forget me. / Maybe I'll have to go back home."

Jack said, "*I'll not.* / I'll just stay here awhile and talk with them. / I won't let 'em do anything to me."

And so she said, "All right, go ahead."

Well, she stayed out there on the horse / and Jack got down and went in / toward the house and they began to yell, / saying "H-e-r-e comes Jack," / till his father came out with a big stick. [!!!!!!!] / And his mother kept on saying, "Come on. Jack. Jack's back home." / The others came around him, / and Jack kept pushing 'em away, / pushing 'em away. / They didn't know what was the matter with him.

Finally, his little black dog came running out, / just a barking and yelping, "Yip, yip!" / and bounced up on his knee here, / and bounced a-way up here, / and licked his lips. / And Jack just grabbed up all them hugs, / and grabbed his father and mother and began to hug 'em.

And pretty soon they had him just a-hanging on and a-carrying on into the house. / And they sat in there talking and talking.

And there was the girl out there. / And he hadn't come and he hadn't come. / So she knew what'd happened— / he'd let one of them kiss him or something, / and he'd forgot her. / So she just rode old Raglif Jaglif across the fields and roads, there / and got her a job around there in a household / for a while.

Well, / Jack— / finally they all called him a great hero, / been gone away so long, / telling all kinds of big yarns. / Girls go to swarming around him so bad, / he did completely forget that other girl. / So he and another girl got sort of thick. / Talking about marrying. / Finally they just norated around the countryside / he was going to marry, / next Friday morning, / at the church house, / forks of the roads.

Well, by the time that time was coming, / the news had reached around the countryside, / and the girl had heard it. / And she realized this was maybe the last time she could / use her magic and bring him back. / So she made three magic boxes. / And Friday morning she put them on old Raglif Jaglif's mane / and she got up behind, / up on the horse, / she got up on the horse, / and rode down, / across the road.

People were gathering 'round the church. / There were wagons and mule teams / and people walking. / After she saw some people in the church she went up to the door, / she, she went up to the door, / and looked in. / Looked like a man standing up there, / with some pretty clothes on, / had a book in his hand. / There were some girls and little boys there. / She tried—climbed up the stairs into the front of the door. / And preacher was there, lining 'em up. / He looked like he was gonna start reading from that book. / And she threw down one of her magic boxes.

It broke open. / And the people watching it. / A rooster and a hen just flew out, popped out of that box. / Rooster pecked the hen. / Hen called out [*very fast, high-pitched, and unintelligible*]: / "Cack-caaaa. You forgot about me cleaning out that barn that hadn't been cleaned out in seven years, or off come your head at n-i-g-h-t!" / [!!!!!!]

Jack didn't know what in the world that was. / Looked back there, was turned around. / And preacher said, "Jack, come on over here now. / Stand right here. [!!!!] / Got to get started reading the ceremony." / Jack stood back over there. / The man put the girl [the bride] back beside Jack.

And the girl saw what was happening, / and she threw in another magic box. / It burst open, and the rooster and hen popped out. / Rooster pecked the hen. / The hen called out [*almost as fast, high-pitched, and slurred*]: / "Cack-caaaa. You forgot about me catching the wild horses, hadn't been caught in seven years, or off come your head at n-i-g-h-t!"

(Did you catch on yet?) / Jack looked back there and he turned around, / moved around a little bit. / Yep, and the preacher said, "Here, Jack, stand back over here." / [!!!!!!!]

Then the girl popped down another box. / It popped open and a rooster and a hen popped out. / Rooster pecked the hen. / Hen took her time, and says: /

"Cack-caaaa. You forgot about me getting these eagle eggs, hadn't been got in seven years, or off come your head at n-i-g-h-t!" [!!!!]

So Jack understood it, / the girl understood it, / and nearly everybody understood what it was. / Jack looked back there and saw that beautiful girl that he'd had those long escapes with. / He just told the preacher, said, "You take the bride and get her back home, if you will, please." [!!!!!!!]

And he walked down to that girl / and he pushed her out the door, / and they ran to that horse, / and Jack got up on that horse / and bounced the girl up behind him / and they just r-o-d-e away from there, / on through two or three county seats, / before they slowed down.

At one county seat they stopped. / Jack got a pair of licenses there. / And he got the minister there to marry them. / And they settled down on the outskirts of that little village. / And they lived pretty happily there. / Had about six children, last time I went by.

AFRICAN-AMERICAN PROVERB
United States

As in many cultures, African-Americans use proverbs to pose solutions to recurrent problems and to understand contemporary events and behaviors by measuring them against a traditional, socially approved standard. Perhaps the most plastic of all oral genres in their inherent variety of applications, proverbs collectively provide a way of viewing the world from a perspective deeper than that of any individual and wider than that of any particular place or time. They also tend to be international in their distribution, with many examples found in geographically distant areas. The example given here, "A Hard Head Makes a Soft Behind," was collected by Prahlad Folly within his own family in Hanover County in Virginia. It includes folk explanations by his mother (Jean Folly) and great-grandmother (Clara Abrams) that shed light on the social implications related to the proverb.

A Hard Head Makes a Soft Behind

Jean: *Oh Lord, I don't know if children started that or not, but the old folks used to tell us that if they was trying to correct you, and you were going to do it anyway. They'd just warn you by saying, "A hard head make a soft tail."*

Collected by Prahlad Folly.

Granny: *Don't use that much. I used to hear mamma say it, especially if you act bully. She didn't only say that to us but she would say it to any child if he didn't listen to her. Like Sarah's children across the road, or John would come here. [These are community members who are now adults who were frequently at my great-great-grandmother's, playing in the yard with other children.] But you know, you can't say it to people's children of this day. You wouldn't dare.*

This proverbial phrase refers of course, to the common practice of spanking children as a disciplinary measure, "soft tail" describing the child's rear end after such punishment.

Both my mother and grandmother indicated that it is used only in reference to children, never adults. Even though I have no children, I still use it metaphorically to describe people of my generation when they are acting hard-headed.

AFRICAN-AMERICAN SERMON
United States

Some of the strongest and most central of African-American oral traditions, such as gospel singing, stem from the communities formed within and supported by the various African-American Protestant churches throughout the country. In areas such as the Midwest, the South, and the Southwest, another oral genre, the folk sermon, is often delivered as part of the regular service. Such sermons demonstrate the same kind of patterning and performance features found in other genres and other traditions, and they have great power to move their congregations or audiences, who participate actively with periodic vocal responses to the preacher. An intense, rhythmic, extemporaneous idiom typifies this oral form. Martin Luther King's memorable Washington Monument Address of 1963 draws on the oral tradition of African-American sermons; although it was intended for an audience far beyond any single congregation and aimed at issues not directly within the religious arena, the medium that it employs brought with it a powerful traditional rhetoric.

DR. MARTIN LUTHER KING, JR. (1915–1984)

from *Washington Monument Address*

[Let freedom ring]

So let freedom ring from the prodigious hilltops of New Hampshire.
Let freedom ring from the mighty mountains of New York.
Let freedom ring from the heightening Alleghenies of Pennsylvania.
Let freedom ring from the snow-capped Rockies of Colorado.

Let freedom ring from the curvaceous slopes of California.
But not only that.
Let freedom ring from Stone Mountain of Georgia.
Let freedom ring from Lookout Mountain of Tennessee.
Let freedom ring from every hill and molehill of Mississippi, from every
    mountainside, let freedom ring.
And when we allow freedom to ring . . . .

Martin Ramirez. Untitled. Mixed media on paper. c. 1953.

SECTION XVIII
Writing Across Boundaries

The principal aim of this concluding section is to provide a context, from a wide variety of different writings across the globe, for making sense of the idea of world literature today. The Irish poet Seamus Heaney has written that "If it is one of the functions of poetry to write place into existence, another of its functions is to unwrite it" (*The Place of Writing*). This notion of unwriting (or rewriting) "place" furnishes a useful way into discussing the contemporary meaning and condition of world literature. Viewed globally, much of the literature of our own time is inextricable from the huge disruptions to the sense of "place"—variously understood on a spectrum from the physical to the cultural—which the later twentieth century has witnessed.

The chief preoccupation here is with aspects and consequences of the crossing of borders and the blurring of boundaries, in terms of languages, cultures, and national literatures. Some of these writers are or have been exiled or self-exiled, thus crossing lateral borders; some import other techniques, forms, or themes across their own borders. The major social contexts for this phenomenon are two-fold; political and cultural/technological. First, much contemporary literature can be read in relation to the modern world-scale experience of colonialism and imperialism and their so-called postcolonial and neo-colonial aftermaths. In this regard, particular importance is attached to the global spread of certain languages—above all English, French, and Spanish—as a consequence of the colonial histories. Any statement about the relevance of the idea of world literature today must reflect those histories, as the story of a cataclysmic epoch that has left few native or national cultures intact.

Second, a great deal of contemporary writing takes place in the context of a general globalization of many aspects of cultural production and transmission, with the transmission in part building on old colonial trade patterns and in part reflecting entirely new (and often improvised) cultural connections. Technology has played an important role in these developments. The modern information explosion, along with vastly increased possibilities for travel and all forms of cultural exchange, has exerted a profound influence on what is written today as well as on how, where, and by whom large portions of modern literature are read.

Moreover, even as external borders have become more fluid, internal borders have become more and more visible, at times tragically in modes of civil war and acute social conflict, at other times in a positive vein as the recovery and assertion of formerly repressed minority voices. Contemporary literature responds to these complexities with a new, at times paradoxical, mixture of heightened cosmopolitanism and accentuated awareness of rootedness.

These processes have raised complex issues of identity and belonging, often expressed ambivalently across a range of feelings from loss, anxiety, and menace to, more optimistically, a sense of new creative possibilities. The overall subject of "border-crossing" thus combines many disparate elements: painful experiences of dispossession along with an expansion of horizons and a multiplication of artistic potential.

The authors in this section come from all over the world: Angola, Argentina, Great Britain, Canada, China, Cuba, India, Ireland, Italy, Jamaica, Japan, Martinique, Nigeria, Palestine, the Philippines, Poland, Russia, Saint Lucia, Trinidad, and the United States. It is in the very nature of the relation of many of these writers to the sense of place that at different times, or indeed simultaneously, they actually "belong" to two or more different countries or regions. To illustrate something of this diversity, a variety of texts have been selected from a variety of genres (poetry, short story, excerpts from novels and autobiography), in modes of comedy, tragedy, and irony of many kinds. The selections span the postwar era, from a 1945 poem by Vladimir Nabokov to selections from Derek Walcott's 1990 *Omeros* — a selection that refers back to Homer's *Odyssey* in the first volume of The HarperCollins World Reader.

Many of these texts address the engagement of the writer with the conflicts and possibilities presented by multiple languages and by differing literary idioms and traditions. Closely linked to issues of linguistic change and expression are the many kinds of unsettlement and new beginnings, individual and collective, voluntary and involuntary, that modern writers have known: exile, emigration, diaspora, travel, and wandering. While the overall scope of the section is worldwide, the selections also have a recurrent focus in encounters between the "New World" (or worlds) and the "Old World." This is vividly illustrated through the texts of those writers who came to the United States in the wake of the dislocations of the wars during the first half of the century and through the texts of a number of Caribbean writers who have lived and worked abroad. As can be seen from these selections, the contemporary cultures of the Americas are taking part in an unprecedented worldwide circulation and interchange of ideas, people, and artistic creation.

KADYA MOLODOVSKY (1894–1975)
Russia [resident of United States]

Kadya Molodovsky was active in progressive Yiddish literary and political circles in New York in the years before and after World War II. Like a number of poems in this section, "White Night" uses the imagery of an ocean voyage to describe her departure both from the Old World and from its cultural traditions, while affirming her ongoing ties to those traditions.

White Night

White night, my painful joy,
your light is brighter than the dawn.
A white ship is sailing from East Broadway[1]
where I see no sail by day.

A quiet star hands me a ticket   5
open for all the seas.
I put on my time-worn jacket
and entrust myself to the night.

Where are you taking me, ship?
Who charted us on this course?   10
The hieroglyphs of the map escape me,
and the arrows of your compass.

I am the one who sees and does not see.
I go along on your deck of secrets,
squeeze shut my baggage on the wreath of sorrows   15
from all my plucked-out homes.

—Pack in all my blackened pots,
their split lids, the chipped crockeries,
pack in my chaos with its gold-encrusted buttons
since chaos will always be in fashion.   20

—Pack the letter stamped *Unknown at This Address*—
vanished addresses that sear my eyes,
postmarked with more than years and days;
sucked into my bones and marrow.

—Pack up my shadow that weighs more than my body,   25
that comes along with its endless exhortations.

Translated by Adrienne Rich.

---

1. A street running through the Lower East
   Side of Manhattan, home to many poor
   immigrants.

Weekdays or holidays, time of flowers or withering,
my shadow is with me, muttering its troubles.

Find me a place of honey cakes and sweetness
where angels and children picnic together
(this is the dream I love best of all),
Where the sacred wine fizzes in bottles.   30

Let me have one sip, here on East Broadway,
for the sake of those old Jews crying in the dark.
I cry my heretic's tears with them,   35
their sobbing is my sobbing.

I'm a difficult passenger, my ship
is packed with the heavy horns, the *shofars*[2] of grief.
Tighten the sails of night as far as you can,
for the daylight cannot carry me.   40

Take me somewhere to a place of rest,
of goats in belled hats playing on trombones—
to the Almighty's fresh white sheets
where the hunter's shadow cannot fall.

Take me. . . . Yes, take me. . . . But you know best   45
where the sea calmly opens its blue road.
I'm wearier than your oldest tower;
somewhere I've left my heart aside.

VLADIMIR NABOKOV (1899–1977)
Russia [resident of United States and Switzerland]

Vladimir Nabokov was born into an aristocratic Russian family which lost their
estates and went into exile after the Russian Revolution of 1917. After living in
Europe, where he wrote several novels and plays in Russian, Nabokov emigrated
to the United States in 1940 and began writing in English. He became an
American citizen in 1945. He taught Russian literature at Cornell University from
1948–1959, when he moved to Switzerland. The success of his novel *Lolita*
(1955) freed him to write full time. His novel *Pale Fire* (1962) is a cutting and
hilarious satire on the pedantry of academic scholarship; "An Evening of Russian
Poetry," written in 1945, looks back with humor and melancholy to the native

---

2. A ram's horn trumpet, blown to herald the
Jewish New Year and the end of the days of
mourning.

language he had foresworn, and to the memories and the reality that its sounds
and its literary conventions still hold.

An Evening of Russian Poetry

*". . . seems to be the best train. Miss Ethel Winter of the Department of English will meet you at
the station and . . ."*

From a letter addressed to the visiting speaker.

The subject chosen for tonight's discussion
is everywhere, though often incomplete:
when their basaltic banks become too steep,
most rivers use a kind of rapid Russian,
and so do children talking in their sleep.   5
My little helper at the magic lantern,
insert that slide and let the colored beam
project my name or any such like phantom
in Slavic characters upon the screen.
The other way, the other way. I thank you.   10

On mellow hills the Greek, as you remember,
fashioned his alphabet from cranes in flight;
his arrows crossed the sunset, then the night.
Our simple skyline and a taste for timber,
the influence of hives and conifers,   15
reshaped the arrows and the borrowed birds.
Yes, Sylvia?

      "Why do you speak of words
when all we want is knowledge nicely browned?"

Because all hangs together—shape and sound,   20
heather and honey, vessel and content.
Not only rainbows—every line is bent,
and skulls and seeds and all good worlds are round,
like Russian verse, like our colossal vowels:
those painted eggs, those glossy pitcher flowers   25
that swallow whole a golden bumblebee,
those shells that hold a thimble and the sea.
Next question.

      "Is your prosody like ours?"

Well, Emmy, our pentameter[1] may seem   30
to foreign ears as if it could not rouse

---

1. A five-beat line of poetry, made up of five
   two-syllable "feet" (*iambus*); from the Latin
   word *iambus*.

the limp iambus from its pyrrhic[2] dream.
But close your eyes and listen to the line.
The melody unwinds; the middle word
is marvelously long and serpentine: 35
you hear one beat, but you have also heard
the shadow of another, then the third
touches the gong, and then the fourth one sighs.

It makes a very fascinating noise;
it opens slowly, like a grayish rose   40
in pedagogic films of long ago.

The rhyme is the line's birthday, as you know,
and there are certain customary twins
in Russian as in other tongues. For instance,
love automatically rhymes with blood,   45
nature with liberty, sadness with distance,
humane with everlasting, prince with mud,
moon with a multitude of words, but sun
and song and wind and life and death with none.

Beyond the seas where I have lost a scepter,   50
I hear the neighing of my dappled nouns,
soft participles coming down the steps,
treading on leaves, trailing their rustling gowns,
and liquid verbs in *ahla* and in *ili*,[3]
Aonian grottoes, nights in the Altai,   55
black pools of sound with "l"s for water lilies.
The empty glass I touched is tinkling still,
but now 'tis covered by a hand and dies.

"Trees? Animals? Your favorite precious stone?"

The birch tree, Cynthia, the fir tree, Joan.   60
Like a small caterpillar on its thread,
my heart keeps dangling from a leaf long dead
but hanging still, and still I see the slender
white birch that stands on tiptoe in the wind,
and firs beginning where the garden ends,   65
the evening ember glowing through their cinders.

Among the animals that haunt our verse,
that bird of bards, regale of night, comes first:
scores of locutions mimicking its throat

---

2. Technical name for a metrical foot of two
   unstressed syllables; better known in the
   phrase "Pyrrhic victory," named for a Greek

king who won a battle with such heavy
losses that he later lost the war.
3. I.e., verbs built around those sounds.

render its every whistling, bubbling, bursting, 70
flutelike or cuckoolike or ghostlike note.
But lapidary[4] epithets are few;
we do not deal in universal rubies.
The angle and the glitter are subdued;
our riches lie concealed. We never liked 75
the jeweler's window in the rainy night.

My back is Argus-eyed.[5] I live in danger.
False shadows turn to track me as I pass
and, wearing beards, disguised as secret agents,
creep in to blot the freshly written page 80
and read the blotter in the looking glass.
And in the dark, under my bedroom window,
until, with a chill whir and shiver, day
presses its starter, warily they linger
or silently approach the door and ring 85
the bell of memory and run away.

Let me allude, before the spell is broken,
to Pushkin,[6] rocking in his coach on long
and lonely roads: he dozed, then he awoke,
undid the collar of his traveling cloak, 90
and yawned, and listened to the driver's song.
Amorphous sallow bushes called *rakeety*,
enormous clouds above an endless plain,
songline and skyline endlessly repeated,
the smell of grass and leather in the rain. 95
And then the sob, the syncope (Nekrasov!),[7]
the panting syllables that climb and climb,
obsessively repetitive and rasping,
dearer to some than any other rhyme.
And lovers meeting in a tangled garden, 100
dreaming of mankind, of untrammeled life,
mingling their longings in the moonlit garden,
where trees and hearts are larger than in life.
This passion for expansion you may follow
throughout our poetry. We want the mole 105
to be a lynx or turn into a swallow
by some sublime mutation of the soul.
But to unneeded symbols consecrated,

---

4. Gemlike.
5. In Greek myth, Argus was a hundred-eyed giant.
6. The Russian poet Alexsandr Pushkin (1799–1837).
7. The Russian poet Viktor Nakrasov (1821–1878).

escorted by a vaguely infantile
path for bare feet, our roads were always fated   110
to lead into the silence of exile.

Had I had more time tonight I would unfold
the whole amazing story—*neighuklúzhe,*
nevynossímo[8]—but I have to go.

What did I say under my breath? I spoke   115
to a blind songbird hidden in a hat,
safe from my thumbs and from the eggs I broke
into the gibus[9] brimming with their yolk.

And now I must remind you in conclusion,
that I am followed everywhere and that   120
space is collapsible, although the bounty
of memory is often incomplete:
once in a dusty place in Mora County
(half town, half desert, dump mound and mesquite)
and once in West Virginia (a muddy   125
red road between an orchard and a veil
of tepid rain) it came, that sudden shudder,
a Russian something that I could inhale
but could not see. Some rapid words were uttered—
and then the child slept on, the door was shut.   130

The conjurer collects his poor belongings—
the colored handkerchief, the magic rope,
the double-bottomed rhymes, the cage, the song.
You tell him of the passes you detected.
The mystery remains intact. The check   135
comes forward in its smiling envelope.

"How would you say 'delightful talk' in Russian?"
"How would you say 'good night'?"

      Oh, that would be:
Bezónnitza, tvoy vzor oonýl i stráshen;   140
lubóv moyá, ostóopnika prostée.
(Insomnia, your stare is dull and ashen,
my love, forgive me this apostasy.[10])

---

8. Ridiculous, unbearable.   10. The abandoning of one's faith.
9. A collapsible hat worn to the opera.

JORGE LUIS BORGES (1899–1986)
Argentina [resident of Mexico]

The Argentinean writer Jorge Luis Borges, a poet and essayist, is especially known for his enigmatic short fictions, often dealing with problems of language and identity and drawing on traditions from many ages and areas of the world. His images of the labyrinth and the fantastic library have had—as have many of his writings—an enormous influence on contemporary writing. Borges gradually lost his eyesight and had to dictate his work. "The Web" was written not long before his death in 1986.

The Web

Which of my cities
am I doomed to die in?
Geneva,
where revelation reached me
from Virgil and Tacitus[1]   5
(certainly not from Calvin)?[2]
Montevideo,
where Luis Melián Lafinur,
blind and heavy with years,
died among the archives   10
of that impartial
history of Uruguay
he never wrote:
Nara,
where in a Japanese inn   15
I slept on the floor
and dreamed the terrible
image of the Buddha
I had touched without seeing
but saw in my dream?[3]   20
Buenos Aires,
where I verge on being a foreigner?
Austin, Texas,
where my mother and I
in the autumn of '61   25

Translated by Alastair Reid.

---

1. The Roman poet Vergil (70–19 B.C.E.); the
   Roman historian Tacitus (55–117 C.E.).

2. The Geneva-based Protestant theologian
   John Calvin (1509–1564).
3. Borges went blind in 1955.

discovered America?
What language
am I doomed to die in?
The Spanish my ancestors used
to call for the charge, or to play *truco*?[4]   30
The English of the Bible
my grandmother read from
at the edges of the desert?
What time will it happen?
In the dove-colored twilight   35
when color drains away,
or in the twilight of the crow
when night abstracts and simplifies
all visible things?
Or at an inconsequential moment—   40
two in the afternoon?
These questions are
digressions that stem not from fear
but from impatient hope.
They form part of the fateful web   45
of cause and effect
that no man can foresee,
nor any god.

NICOLÁS GUILLÉN (1902–1989)
Cuba

Nicolás Guillén is best known for his Afro-Cuban "sound poetry" where sounds can take precedence over sense. Of mixed black-white ancestry, Guillén served as the director of the Folklore Archive in Havana. Several intellectual and artistic strains converge in his work: a general discontent with Western civilization, perhaps best expressed in the German philosopher Oswald Spengler's *The Decline of the West* (1918); the avant-garde movements of the early twentieth century, which formed part of this discontent, particularly the surrealists, who delved into the subconscious life of so-called "primitive" peoples, and the dadaists, who experimented with nonsense sounds and rhythms in an attempt to take thought beyond the postulates of Western rationality; the Spanish poets of the Generation of 1927, especially Federico García Lorca, who had discovered a non-Western ethos in gypsy folklore and who visited Cuba in 1931; Fernando

---

4. A kind of billiards.

Ortiz's and Lydia Cabrera's anthropological research into Afro-Cuban daily life and folklore, particularly *santería*, the Yoruba-derived popular religion related to Haitian Voodoo and Brazilian Candomble; and communism's advocacy of the oppressed. Guillén forms part of a general turn in the Caribbean toward Afro-Antillian culture (for example, the Puerto Rican Luis Pales Matos, and later the Martiniqan Aimé Césaire), but critics have seen in him the most authentic of the *negrista* poets, perhaps because of his greater insistence on criticizing the injustices done to blacks. Nevertheless, his early poems share with Pales Matos and others the tendency to exoticize and sexualize black people, emphasizing their rhythm, their corporeality, and their black Spanish, as in *Motifs of the Son* (*Motivos de son,* 1930) and *Songoro Cosongo* (1931). (The *son* is an Afro-Cuban musical genre.) In his later work Guillén focuses more and more on social issues, integrating his critique of black oppression with a Marxist critique of imperialism, as in *The Total Son* (*El son entero,* 1947) and *West Indies Limited* (1934), from which "My Last Name" is taken. Guillén's goal is to create a more integrally human poetic vision.

My Last Name

A FAMILY ELEGY

I

Ever since school
and even before . . . Since the dawn, when I was
barely a patch of sleep and wailing,
since then
I have been told my name. A password   5
that I might speak with stars.
Your name is, you shall be called . . .
And then they handed me
this you see here written on my card,
this I put at the foot of all my poems: 10
thirteen letters
that I carry on my shoulders through the street,
that are with me always, no matter where I go.
Are you sure it is my name?
Have you got all my particulars?   15
Do you already know my navigable blood,
my geography full of dark mountains,
of deep and bitter valleys
that are not on the maps?
Perhaps you have visited my chasms,   20

Translated by Robert Márquez.

Frida Kahlo. *Self-Portrait on the Border Between Mexico and the United States.*
1932.

my subterranean galleries
with great moist rocks,
islands jutting out of black puddles,
where I feel the pure rush
of ancient waters   25
falling from my proud heart
with a sound that's fresh and deep
to a place of flaming trees,
acrobatic monkeys,
legislative parrots and snakes?   30
Does all my skin (I should have said),
does all my skin come from that Spanish marble?
My frightening voice too,
the harsh cry in my throat?
Are all my bones from there?   35
My roots and the roots
of my roots and also
these dark branches swayed by dreams

and these flowers blooming on my forehead
and this sap embittering my bark?   40

Are you certain?
Is there nothing more than this that you have written,
than this which you have stamped
with the seal of anger?
(Oh, I should have asked!)   45
Well then, I ask you now:
Don't you see these drums in my eyes?
Don't you see these drums, tightened and
beaten with two dried-up tears?
Don't I have, perhaps,   50
a nocturnal grandfather
with a great black scar
(darker still than his skin)
a great scar made by a whip?
Have I not, then,   55
a grandfather who's Mandingo, Dahoman, Congolese?
What is his name? Oh, yes, give me his name!
Andrés? Francisco? Amable?
How do you say Andrés in Congolese?
How have you always said   60
Francisco in Dahoman?
In Mandingo, how do you say Amable?
No? Were they, then, other names?
The last name then!
Do you know my other last name, the one that comes   65
to me from that enormous land, the captured,
bloody last name, that came across the sea
in chains, which came in chains across the sea?

Ah, you can't remember it!
You have dissolved it in immemorial ink.   70
You stole it from a poor, defenseless Black.
You hid it, thinking that I would
lower my eyes in shame.
Thank you!
I am grateful to you!   75
Noble people, thanks!
Merci!
Merci bien!
Merci beaucoup!
But no . . . Can you believe it? No.   80
I am clean.
My voice sparkles like newly polished metal.

Look at my shield: it has a baobab,
it has a rhinoceros and a spear.
I am also the grandson,   85
great grandson,
great great grandson of a slave.
(Let the master be ashamed.)
Am I Yelofe?
Nicolás Yelofe, perhaps?   90
Or Nicolás Bakongo?
Maybe Guillén Banguila?
Or Kumbá?
Perhaps Guillén Kumbá?
Or Kongué?   95
Could I be Guillén Kongué?
Oh, who knows!
What a riddle in the waters!

II

I feel immense night fall
on profound beasts,   100
on innocent castigated souls;
but also on ready voices,
which steal suns from the sky,
the brightest suns,
to decorate combatant blood.   105
From some flaming land pierced through
by the great equatorial arrow,
I know there will come distant cousins,
my ancestral anguish cast upon the winds;
I know there will come portions of my veins,   110
my ancestral blood,
with calloused feet bending frightened grasses;
I know there will come men whose lives are green,
my ancestral jungle,
with their pain open like a cross and their breasts red with flames.   115

Having never met, we will know each other by the hunger,
by the tuberculosis and the syphilis,
by the sweat bought in a black market,
by the fragments of chain
still clinging to the skin;   120
having never met we will know each other
by the dream-full eyes
and even by the rock-hard insults
the quadrumanes of ink and paper

spit at us each day.   125
What can it matter, then?
(What does it matter now!)
Ah, my little name
of thirteen letters?
Or the Mandingo, Bantu,   130
Yoruba, Dahoman name
of the sad grandfather drowned
in notary's ink.
Good friends, what does it matter?
Oh, yes, good friends   135
come look at my name!
My name without end,
made up of endless names;
my name, foreign,
free and mine, foreign and yours,   140
foreign and free as the air.

CZESŁAW MILOSZ (b. 1911)
Poland [resident of United States]

Czesław Milosz was born in 1911 in Lithuania; his family emigrated to Poland,
where he achieved prominence as one of that country's major poets. After World
War II he settled in California, where he became a professor at Berkeley. He
received the Nobel Prize in literature in 1980. This poem describes a childhood
dream that encapsulates the dangers of emigration and seems to foreshadow his
later arrival in California.

Fear-Dream (1918)

Orsha[1] is a bad station. In Orsha a train risks stopping for days.
Thus perhaps in Orsha I, six years old, got lost
And the repatriation train was starting, about to leave me behind.
Forever. As if I grasped that I would have been somebody else,
A poet of another language, of a different fate.   5
As if I guessed my end at the shores of Kolyma[2]

Translated by Czesław Milosz and Robert Hass.

1. A city in Belorussia, on the Dnieper River.   2. Siberian location of Soviet prison camps.

Where the bottom of the sea is white with human skulls.
And a great dread visited me then,
The one destined to be the mother of all my fears.

A trembling of the small before the great. Before the Empire.   10
Which constantly marches westward, armed with bows, lariats,[3] rifles,
Riding in a troika, pummeling the driver's back,
Or in a jeep, wearing fur hats, with a file full of conquered countries.
And I just flee, for a hundred, three hundred years,
On the ice, swimming across, by day, by night, and on and on.   15
Abandoning by my river a punctured cuirass[4] and a coffer with king's grants.
Beyond the Dnieper, then the Niemen, then the Bug and the Vistula.[5]

Finally I arrive in a city of high houses and long streets
And am oppressed by fear, for I am just a villager
Who only pretends to follow what they discuss so shrewdly   20
And tries to hide from them his shame, his defeat.

Who will feed me there, as I walk in the cloudy dawn
With small change in my pocket, for one coffee, no more?
A refugee from fictitious States, who will want me here?

Stony walls, indifferent walls, bitter walls.   25
By order of their reason, not my reason.
Now accept it. Don't kick. You are not going to flee any further.

Berkeley, 1985

AIMÉ CÉSAIRE (b. 1913)
Martinique [resident of France]

Aimé Césaire was educated in Paris, where he and Léopold Senghor developed the concept of *négritude,* a movement designed to restore black people's precolonial African identity; he also became friends with the French surrealists and used their techniques in his poetry and plays. He returned to Martinique in the 1940s and became head of the Martiniqar Progressive Party. "Word" is from a cycle of poems called *The Lost Body [Corps Perdu],* published with illustrations by Picasso.

---

3. A rope used for catching horses.   5. Rivers in Russia and Poland.
4. A piece of armor that protects the torso.

from **The Lost Body**

Word

Among me

from myself
to myself
outside any constellation
clenched in my hands only 5
the rare hiccup of an ultimate raving spasm
keep vibrating word

I will have luck outside the labyrinth

longer wider keep vibrating
in tighter and tighter waves 10
in a lasso to catch me
in a rope to hang me
and let me be nailed by all the arrows
and their bitterest curare[1]
to the beautiful center-stake of very cool stars 15

vibrate
vibrate you very essence of the dark
in a wing in a throat from so much perishing
the word nigger
sprung fully armed from the howling 20
of a poisonous flower
the word nigger
all filthy with parasites
the word nigger
loaded with roaming bandits 25

with screaming mothers
crying children
the word nigger
a sizzling of flesh and horny matter
burning, acrid 30
the word nigger
like the sun bleeding from its claw
onto the sidewalk of clouds
the word nigger
like the last laugh calved by innocence 35
between the tiger's fangs
and as the word sun is
     a cracking of bullets

Translated by Clayton Eshleman and Annette Smith.

---

1. A poison derived from tropical plants.

and the word night
   a ripping of taffeta   40
the word nigger
     dense, right?
from the thunder of a summer
    appropriated by
        incredulous liberties   45

LOUISE BENNETT (b. 1919)
Jamaica [ex-resident of England and the United States]

Louise Bennett is a poet and a popular entertainer. After studying at the Royal Academy of Dramatic Art in London, she had a show on the BBC in London, and directed a folk musical in the United States before returning to Jamaica. She had begun writing and performing her dialect poems in high school, and published her *Verses in Jamaican Dialect* (1942); in 1966, she published her *Jamaica Labrish*. Her recordings appear under her stage name, "Miss Lou." "Colonization in Reverse" is a humorous but also serious account of postwar Jamaican immigration to Great Britain, described as a reverse form of colonization. It also turns the tables on standard literary English by the use of Jamaican dialect.

Colonization in Reverse

What a joyful news, Miss Mattie;
Ah feel like me heart gwine burs—
Jamaica people colonizin
Englan in reverse.

By de hundred, by de tousan,   5
From country an from town,
By de ship-load, by de plane-load,
Jamaica is Englan boun.

Dem a pour out a Jamaica;
Everybody future plan   10
Is fi get a big-time job
An settle in de motherlan.

What a islan! What a people!
Man an woman, ole an young
Jussa pack dem bag an baggage   15
An tun history upside dung!

Some people doan like travel,
Bit fi show dem loyalty
Dem all a open up cheap-fare-
To-Englan agency;   20

An week by week dem shippin off
Dem countryman like fire
Fi immigrate an populate
De seat a de Empire.

Oonoo[1] se how life is funny,   25
Oonoo see de tunabout?
Jamaica live fi box bread
Out a English people mout.[2]

For when dem catch a Englan
An start play dem different role   30
Some will settle down to work
An some will settle fi de dole.

Jane seh de dole is not too bad
Because dey payin she
Two pounds a week fi seek a job   35
Dat suit her dignity.

Me seh Jane will never fine work
At de rate how she dah look
For all day she stay pon Aunt Fan couch
An read love-story book.   40

What a devilment a Englan!
Dem face war an brave de worse;
But ah wonderin how dem gwine stan
Colonizin in reverse.

GABRIEL OKARA (b. 1921)
Nigeria [resident of United States]

Gabriel Okara, a Nigerian poet and novelist, wrote "The Snow Flakes Sail Gently
Down" to describe a memory of Africa. It takes the form of a dream that is also
symbolically a statement of attachment to threatened "roots."

---

1. You.   2. Mouth.

The Snow Flakes Sail Gently Down

The snow flakes sail gently
down from the misty eye of the sky
and fall lightly lightly on the
winter-weary elms. And the branches,
winter-stripped and nude, slowly   5
with the weight of the weightless snow
bow like grief-stricken mourners
as white funeral cloth is slowly
unrolled over deathless earth.
And dead sleep stealthily from the   10
heater rose and closed my eyes with
the touch of silk cotton on water falling.

Then I dreamed a dream
in my dead sleep. But I dreamed
not of earth dying and elms a vigil   15
keeping. I dreamed of birds, black
birds flying in my inside, nesting
and hatching on oil palms bearing suns
for fruits and with roots denting the
uprooters' spades. And I dreamed the   20
uprooters tired and limp, leaning on my roots—
their abandoned roots—
and the oil palms gave them each a sun.

But on their palms
they balanced the blinding orbs   25
and frowned with schisms on their
brows—for the suns reached not
the brightness of gold!
Then I awoke. I awoke
to the silently falling snow   30
and bent-backed elms bowing and
swaying to the winter wind like
white-robed Moslems salaaming[1] at evening
prayer, and the earth lying inscrutable
like the face of a god in a shrine.   35

---

1. Bowing in prayer to Allah.

ANTONIO JACINTO (b. 1924)
West Central Africa [resident of Angola]

Antonio Jacinto was born in Angola, at that time a Portuguese colony in West Central Africa. He was a pioneer in the movement of cultural nationalism that led to a protracted armed struggle against the Portuguese and eventual independence in 1975. Imprisoned in Portugal as a militant, he escaped in 1973 and served in the new government after 1975. "Poem of Alienation" was published in 1961.

Poem of Alienation

This is not yet my poem
the poem of my soul and of my blood
no
I still lack knowledge and power to write my poem
the great poem I feel already turning in me   5

My poem wanders aimlessly
in the bush or in the city
in the voice of the wind
in the surge of the sea
in the Aspect and the Being   10

My poem steps outside
wrapped in showy cloths
selling itself
selling
    "lemons, buy my le-e-e-emons"   15

My poem runs through the streets
with a putrid cloth pad on its head
offering itself
offering
    "mackerel, sardine, sprats
    fine fish, fine fi-i-i-sh . . ."   20

My poem trudges the streets
"here J'urnal" "Dai-i-i-ly"
and no newspaper yet carries my poem

Translated by Michael Wolfers.

Jose Orozco. *The Subway*. Oil on canvas. Museum of Modern Art. New York. 1928.

My poem goes into the cafés   25
"lott'ry draw-a tomorra lott'ry draw-a-tomorra"
and the draw of my poem
wheel as it wheels
whirl as it whirls
never changes   30
   "lott'ry draw-a tomorra
   lott'ry draw-a tomorra"

My poem comes from the township
on Saturdays bring the washing
on Mondays take the washing   35
on Saturdays surrender the washing and surrender self
on Mondays surrender self and take the washing

My poem is in the suffering
of the laundress's daughter
shyly   40
in the closed room
of a worthless boss idling
to build up an appetite for the violation

My poem is the prostitute
in the township at the broken door of her hut   45

> *"hurry hurry*
> *pay your money*
> *come and sleep with me"*

My poem lightheartedly plays at ball
in a crowd where everyone is a servant
and shouts
> *"offside goal goal"*

My poem is a contract worker
goes to the coffee fields to work
the contract is a burden
that is hard to load
> *"contract wor-r-r-ker"*

My poem walks barefoot in the street

My poem loads sacks in the port
fills holds
empties holds
and finds strength in singing
> *"tué tué tué trr*
> *arrimbium puim puim"*

My poem goes tied in ropes
met a policeman
paid a fine, the boss
forgot to sign the pass
goes on the roadwork
with hair shorn
> *"head shaved*
> *chicken braised*
> *o Zé"*

a goad that weighs
a whip that plays

My poem goes to market works in the kitchen
goes to the workbench
fills the tavern and the gaol
is poor ragged and dirty
lives in benighted ignorance
my poem knows nothing of itself
nor how to plead

My poem was made to give itself
to surrender itself
without asking for anything

50

55

60

65

70

75

80

85

But my poem is not fatalist
my poem is a poem that already wants
and already knows
my poem is I-white
mounted on me-black   90
riding through life.

YÜ KWANG-CHUNG (b. 1928)
China [resident of Taiwan]

Yü Kwang-chung was born in Nanking, China, in 1928. When the Communists
came to power in 1949, his family emigrated to the United States. He has taught
English and Chinese literature at universities in Taiwan, Hong Kong, and the
United States, and he now lives and teaches in Taiwan. He has published many
volumes of prose and poetry, and he is well-known to readers in Taiwan, Hong
Kong, and mainland China. "When I Am Dead," written in 1966, describes his
effort to recover his lost homeland in memory and through study of maps.

When I Am Dead

When I am dead, lay me down between the Yangtze
And the Yellow River[1] and pillow my head
On China, white hair against black soil,
Most beautiful, O most maternal of lands,
And I will sleep my soundest taking   5
The whole mainland for my cradle, lulled
By the mother-hum that rises on both sides
From the great rivers, two long, long songs
That on and on flow forever to the East.
This the world's most indulgent roomiest bed   10
Where, content, a heart pauses to rest
And recalls how, of a Michigan winter night,
A youth from China used to keep
Intense watch towards the East, trying
To pierce his look through darkness for the dawn   15
Of China. So with hungry eyes he devoured

Translated by Yü Kwang-chung.

---

1. The Yangtze and Yellow rivers flow through
   central China.

The map, eyes for seventeen years starved
For a glimpse of home, and, like a new weaned child,
He drank with one wild gulp rivers and lakes
From the mouth of the Yangtze all the way up   20
To Poyang and Tungting and to Koko Nor.[2]

DEREK WALCOTT (b. 1930)
Saint Lucia [former resident of United States]

Derek Walcott was born on the Caribbean island of Saint Lucia in 1930; he was
educated and worked there and in Trinidad and Jamaica as a journalist and
dramatist. He later became a professor at Boston University. *Omeros,* published
in 1990, is a book-length narrative poem centered on a fisherman named Achille,
whose boat carries him back to his ancestral home on the coast of West Africa.
The poem resonates with echoes of Homer's heroes Achilles and Odysseus. The
selections included here show Walcott's use of shifting perspective among several
characters: Seven Seas, a blind fisherman who may be one of several manifestations of Homer; Antigone, a young Greek woman whom the narrator meets;
Helen, a beautiful young woman looking for work at a seaside bar; and her
former employers, a retired British army major, Dennis Plunkett, and his wife,
Maud. In 1992, he won the Nobel Prize.

from *Omeros*

[*Seven Seas rose in the half-dark to make coffee*]

Seven Seas rose in the half-dark to make coffee.
Sunrise was heating the ring of the horizon
and clouds were rising like loaves. By the heat of the

glowing iron rose he slid the saucepan's base on-
to the ring and anchored it there. The saucepan shook   5
from the weight of water in it, then it settled.

His kettle leaked. He groped for the tin chair and took
his place near the saucepan to hear when it bubbled.
It would boil but not scream like a bosun's[1] whistle

When I Am Dead
2. Lakes along the Yangtze; Koko Nor is near
Tibet.

Omeros
1. Man in charge of a boat's crew.

to let him know it was ready. He heard the dog's   10
morning whine under the boards of the house, its tail
thudding to be let in, but he envied the pirogues[2]

already miles out at sea. Then he heard the first breeze
washing the sea-almond's wares; last night there had been
a full moon white as his plate. He saw with his ears.   15

He warmed with the roofs as the sun began to climb.
Since the disease had obliterated vision,
when the sunset shook the sea's hand for the last time—

and an inward darkness grew where the moon and sun
indistinctly altered—he moved by a sixth sense,   20
like the moon without an hour or second hand,

wiped clean as the plate that he now began to rinse
while the saucepan bubbled; blindness was not the end.
It was not a palm-tree's dial on the noon sand.

He could feel the sunlight creeping over his wrists.   25
The sunlight moved like a cat along the palings
of a sandy street; he felt it unclench the fists

of the breadfruit tree in his yard, run the railings
of the short iron bridge like a harp, its racing
stick rippling with the river; he saw the lagoon   30

behind the church, and in it, stuck like a basin,
the rusting enamel image of the full moon.
He lowered the ring to sunset under the pan.

The dog scratched at the kitchen door for him to open
but he made it wait. He drummed the kitchen table   35
with his fingers. Two blackbirds quarrelled at breakfast.

Except for one hand he sat as still as marble,
with his egg-white eyes, fingers recounting the past
of another sea, measured by the stroking oars.

O open this day with the conch's moan, Omeros,   40
as you did in my boyhood, when I was a noun
gently exhaled from the palate of the sunrise.

A lizard on the sea-wall darted its question
at the waking sea, and a net of golden moss
brightened the reef, which the sails of their far canoes   45

---

2. Canoes.

avoided. Only in you, across centuries
of the sea's parchment atlas, can I catch the noise
of the surf lines wandering like the shambling fleece

of the lighthouse's flock, that Cyclops[3] whose blind eye
shut from the sunlight. Then the canoes were galleys   50
over which a frigate sawed its scythed wings slowly.

In you the seeds of grey almonds guessed a tree's shape,
and the grape leaves rusted like serrated islands,
and the blind lighthouse, sensing the edge of a cape,

paused like a giant, a marble cloud in its hands,   55
to hurl its boulder that splashed into phosphorous
stars; then a black fisherman, his stubbled chin coarse

as a dry sea-urchin's, hoisted his flour-sack
sail on its bamboo spar, and scanned the opening line
of our epic horizon; now I can look back   60

to rocks that see their own feet when light nets the waves,
as the dugouts set out with ebony captains,
since it was your light that startled our sunlit wharves

where schooners swayed idly, moored to their cold capstans.
A wind turns the harbour's pages back to the voice   65
that hummed in the vase of a girl's throat: "Omeros."

"O-meros," she laughed. "That's what we call him in Greek,"
stroking the small bust with its boxer's broken nose,
and I thought of Seven Seas sitting near the reek

of drying fishnets, listening to the shallow's noise.   70
I said: "Homer and Virg are New England farmers,
and the winged horse guards their gas-station, you're right."

I felt the foam head watching as I stroked an arm, as
cold as its marble, then the shoulders in winter light
in the studio attic. I said, "Omeros,"   75

and O was the conch-shell's invocation, mer was
both mother and sea in our Antillean patois,
os, a grey bone, and the white surf as it crashes

and spreads its sibilant collar on a lace shore.
Omeros was the crunch of dry leaves, and the washes   80
that echoed from a cave-mouth when the tide has ebbed.

---

3. The one-eyed monster blinded by Odysseus.

The name stayed in my mouth. I saw how light was webbed
on her Asian cheeks, defined her eyes with a black
almond's outline, as Antigone turned and said:

"I'm tired of America, it's time for me to go back   85
to Greece. I miss my islands." I write, it returns—
the way she turned and shook out the back gust of hair.

I saw how the surf printed its lace in patterns
on the shore of her neck, then the lowering shallows
of silk swirled at her ankles, like surf without noise,   90

and felt that another cold bust, not hers, but yours
saw this with stone almonds for eyes, its broken nose
turning away, as the rustling silk agrees.

But if it could read between the lines of her floor
like a white-hot deck uncaulked by Antillean heat,   95
to the shadows in its hold, its nostrils might flare

at the stench from manacled ankles, the coffled[4] feet
scraping like leaves, and perhaps the inculpable marble
would have turned its white seeds away, to widen

the bow of its mouth at the horror under her table,   100
from the lyre of her armchair draped with its white chiton,[5]
to do what the past always does: suffer, and stare.

She lay calm as a port, and a cloud covered her
with my shadow; then a prow with painted eyes
slowly emerged from the fragrant rain of black hair.   105

And I heard a hollow moan exhaled from a vase,
not for kings floundering in lances of rain; the prose
of abrupt fishermen cursing over canoes.

[I sat on the white terrace]

I sat on the white terrace waiting for the cheque.
Our waiter, in a black bow-tie, plunged through the sand   110
between the full deck-chairs, bouncing to discotheque

music from the speakers, a tray sailed in one hand.
The tourists revolved, grilling their backs in their noon
barbecue. The waiter was having a hard time

---

4. Linked by chains.   5. Ancient Greek tunic.

with his leather soles. They kept sliding down a dune,
but his tray teetered without spilling gin-and-lime
on a scorched back. He was determined to meet the   115

beach's demands, like a Lawrence of St. Lucia,[6]
except that he was trudging towards a litre
of self-conscious champagne. Like any born loser   120

he soon kicked the bucket. He rested his tray down,
wiped the sand from the ice-cubes, then plunked the cubes in
the bucket, then the bottle; after this was done,

he seemed ready to help the wife stuff her boobs in
her halter, while her husband sat boiling with rage   125
like a towelled sheik. Then Lawrence frowned at a mirage.

That was when I turned with him towards the village,
and saw, through the caging wires of the noon sky,
a beach with its padding panther; now the mirage

dissolved to a woman with a madras head-tie,   130
but the head proud, although it was looking for work.
I felt like standing in homage to a beauty

that left, like a ship, widening eyes in its wake.
"Who the hell is that?" a tourist near my table
asked a waitress. The waitress said, "She? She too proud!"   135

As the carved lids of the unimaginable
ebony mask unwrapped from its cotton-wool cloud,
the waitress sneered, "Helen." And all the rest followed.

[How fast it fades! Maud thought]

How fast it fades! Maud[7] thought; the enamelled sky,
the gilded palms, the bars like altars of raffia,   140
even for that Madonna bathing her baby

with his little shrimp thing! One day the Mafia
will spin these islands round like roulette. What use is
Dennis's devotion when their own ministers

cash in on casinos with their old excuses   145
of more jobs? Their future felt as sinister as
that of that ebony girl in her yellow dress.

---

6. A reference to "Lawrence of Arabia," the British adventurer and writer T. E. Lawrence (1888–1935).

7. In this section, Helen is seen through the eyes of Maud and Dennis Plunkett, British army retirees who have settled on Saint Lucia.

"There's our trouble," Maud muttered into her glass. In
a gust that leant the triangular sails of the
surfers, Plunkett saw the pride of Helen passing   150

in the same yellow frock Maud had altered for her.
"She looks better in it"—Maud smiled—"but the girl lies
so much, and she stole. What'll happen to her life?"

"God knows," said Plunkett, following the butterfly's
yellow-panelled wings that once belonged to his wife,   155
the black V of the velvet back, near the shallows.

Her head was lowered; she seemed to drift like a waif,
not like the arrogant servant that ruled their house.
It was at that moment that he felt a duty

towards her hopelessness, something to redress   160
(he punned relentlessly) that desolate beauty
so like her island's. He drained the foaming Guinness.

Seychelles.[8] Seashells. One more. In the olive saucer,
the dry stones were piling up, their green pith sucked dry.
Got what we took from them, yes sir! Quick, because the   165

Empire was ebbing. He watched the silhouette
of his wife, her fine profile set in an oval
ivory cloud, like a Victorian locket,

as when, under crossed swords, she lifted the lace veil.
The flag then was sliding down from the hill-stations   170
of the Upper Punjab,[9] like a collapsing sail;

an elephant folded its knees, its striations
wrinkling like the tea-pavilions after the Raj,
whose ebbing surf lifted the coastlines of nations

as lacy as Helen's shift. In the noon's mirage   175
the golden palms shook their tassels, Eden's Egypt[10]
sank in the tinted sand. The Giza pyramids

darkened with the sharpening Pitons,[11] as Achille shipped
both oars like rifles. Clouds of delivered Muslims
foamed into the caves of mosques, and honour and glory   180

---

8. A group of islands in the Indian Ocean; a
   British colony.
9. A region in northern India, divided between India and Pakistan upon the end of
   British colonial rule (the Raj) in 1947.
10. A play on the Garden of Eden and on the

name of Sir Anthony Eden, the British
prime minister under whom Britain lost
control of the Suez Canal and its remaining influence over Egypt in 1957.
11. Two cone-shaped mountains overlooking
the harbor.

faded like crested brandies. Then remorseful hymns
soared in the stone-webbed Abbey. *Memento mori*[12]
in the drumbeat of Remembrance Day.[13] Pigeons whirr

over Trafalgar.[14] Helen needed a history,
that was the pity that Plunkett felt towards her.   185
Not his, but her story. Not theirs, but Helen's war.

The name, with its historic hallucination,
brightened the beach; the butterfly, to Plunkett's joy,
twinkling from myrmidon[15] to myrmidon, from one

sprawled tourist to another. Her village was Troy,   190
its smoke obscuring soldiers fallen in battle.
Then her unclouding face, her breasts were its Pitons,

the palms' rusted lances swirled in the death-rattle
of the gargling shoal; for her Gaul and Briton
had mounted fort and redoubt,[16] the ruined barracks   195

with its bushy tunnel and its penile[17] cannon;
for her cedars fell in green sunrise to the axe.
His mind drifted with the smoke of his reverie

out to the channel. Lawrence arrived. He said:
"I changing shift, Major. Major?" Maud tapped his knee.   200
"Dennis. The bill." But the bill had never been paid.

Not to that housemaid swinging a plastic sandal
by the noon sea, in a dress that she had to steal.
Wars. Wars thin like sea-smoke, but their dead were real.

He smiled at the mythical hallucination   205
that went with the name's shadow; the island was once
named Helen; its Homeric association

rose like smoke from a siege; the Battle of the Saints
was launched with that sound, from what was the "Gibraltar
of the Caribbean," after thirteen treaties   210

while she changed prayers often as knees at an altar,
till between French and British her final peace
was signed at Versailles.[18] All of this came to his mind

---

12. Remembrances of death.
13. The British equivalent of Veterans Day.
14. Cape near Gibraltar where the British navy
    defeated Napoleon's fleet in 1805.
15. Warriors allied with Achilles in the Trojan
    War.

16. A fortification.
17. Penis-shaped.
18. This 1814 treaty settled Saint Lucia's
    status as a British colony, which it re-
    mained until 1967.

as Lawrence came staggering up the terrace
with the cheque finally, and that treaty was signed;   215
the paper was crossed by the shadow of her face

as it was at Versailles, two centuries before,
by the shade of Admiral Rodney's[19] gathering force;
a lion-headed island remembering war,

its crouched flanks tawny with drought, and on its ridge, grass   220
stirred like its mane. For a while he watched the waiter
move through the white iron shields of the white terrace.

In the village Olympiad, on St. Peter's Day,
he served as official starter with a flare-gun
borrowed from the manager of the marina.   225

It wasn't Aegean. They climbed no Parthenon
to be laurelled. The depot faced their arena,
the sea's amphitheatre. When one wore a crown—

victor ludorum[20]—no one knew what it meant, or
cared to be told. The Latin syllables would drown   230
in the clapping dialect of the crowd. Hector

would win, or Achille by a hair; but everyone
knew as the crossing ovals of their thighs would soar
in jumps down the cheering aisle, or their marathon

six times round the village, that the true bounty was   235
Helen, not a shield nor the ham saved for Christmas;
as one slid down the greased pole to factional roars.

V.S. NAIPAUL (b. 1932)
Trinidad [resident of England]

V. S. Naipaul was educated at Oxford and has lived in England ever since. His
many books include both novels and reports of life in many parts of the world.
In the selection included here from *Prologue to an Autobiography,* he describes his
own experience as an Asian from the Caribbean trying to find himself as a young
writer in England.

---

19. A British admiral who captured Saint Lu-   20. "Winner of the games."
    cia from the French in 1762.

from Prologue to an Autobiography, "Finding the Center"

[Becoming a Writer]

It is now nearly thirty years since, in a BBC[1] room in London, on an old BBC typewriter, and on smooth, "non-rustle" BBC script paper, I wrote the first sentence of my first publishable book. I was some three months short of my twenty-third birthday. I had left Oxford ten months before, and was living in London, trying to keep afloat and, in between, hoping to alleviate my anxiety but always only adding to it, trying to get started as a writer.

At Oxford I had been supported by a Trinidad government scholarship. In London I was on my own. The only money I got—eight guineas a week, less "deductions"—came from the BBC Caribbean Service. My only piece of luck in the past year, and even in the past two years, had been to get a part-time job editing and presenting a weekly literary program for the Caribbean.

The Caribbean Service was on the second floor of what had been the Langham Hotel, opposite Broadcasting House. On this floor the BBC had set aside a room for people like me, "freelances"—to me then not a word suggesting freedom and valor, but suggesting only people on the fringe of a mighty enterprise, a depressed and suppliant class: I would have given a lot to be "staff."

The freelances' room didn't encourage thoughts of radio glory; it was strictly for the production of little scripts. Something of the hotel atmosphere remained: in the great Victorian-Edwardian days of the Langham Hotel (it was mentioned in at least one Sherlock Holmes story), the freelances' room might have been a pantry. It was at the back of the heavy brick building, and gloomy when the ceiling lights were turned off. It wasn't cheerful when the lights were on: ocher walls with a pea-green dado, the gloss paint tarnished; a radiator below the window, with grit on the sill; two or three chairs, a telephone, two tables, and two old standard typewriters.

It was in that Victorian-Edwardian gloom, and at one of those typewriters, that late one afternoon, without having any idea where I was going, and not perhaps intending to type to the end of the page, I wrote: *Every morning when he got up Hat would sit on the banister of his back verandah and shout across, "What happening there, Bogart?"*

That was a Port of Spain[2] memory. It seemed to come from far back, but it was only eleven or twelve years old. It came from the time when we—various branches of my mother's family—were living in Port of Spain, in a house that belonged to my mother's mother. We were country people, Indians, culturally still Hindus, and this move to Port of Spain was in the nature of a migration: from the Hindu and Indian countryside to the white-negro-mulatto town. (At that time in Trinidad *black,* used by a non-black, was a word of insult; *negro* was—and remains—a polite word.)

Hat was our neighbor on the street. He wasn't negro or mulatto. But we

---

1. The British Broadcasting Corporation.　　2. The capital of Trinidad.

thought of him as halfway there. He was a Port of Spain Indian. The Port of Spain Indians—there were pockets of them—had no country roots, were individuals, hardly a community, and were separate from us for an additional reason: many of them were Madrassis, descendants of South Indians, not Hindi-speaking, and not people of caste. We didn't see in them any of our formalities or restrictions; and though we lived raggedly ourselves (and were far too numerous for the house), we thought of the other Indians in the street only as street people.

That shout of "Bogart!" was in more than one way a shout from the street. And, to add to the incongruity, it was addressed to someone in our yard: a young man, very quiet, yet another person connected in some way with my mother's family. He had come not long before from the country and was living in the separate one-room building at the back of our yard.

*   *   *

The connection of Bogart with my mother's family was unusual. At the turn of the century Bogart's father and my mother's father had traveled out together from India as indentured immigrants. At some time during the long and frightening journey they had sworn a bond of brotherhood; that was the bond that was being honored by their descendants.

Bogart's people were from the Punjab, and handsome. The two brothers we had got to know were ambitious men, rising in white-collar jobs. One was a teacher; the other (who had passed through the servant room) was a weekend sportsman who, in the cricket season, regularly got his name in the paper. Bogart didn't have the education or the ambition of his brothers; it wasn't clear what he did for a living. He was placid, without any pronounced character, detached, and in that crowded yard oddly solitary.

Once he went away. When he came back, some weeks or months later, it was said that he had been "working on a ship." Port of Spain was a colonial port, and we thought of sailors as very rough, the dregs. So this business of working on a ship—though it suggested money as well as luck, for the jobs were not easy to come by—also held suggestions of danger. It was something for the reckless and the bohemian. But it must have suited Bogart, because after a time he went away—disappeared—again.

There was a story this time that he had gone to Venezuela. He came back; but I had no memory of his return. His adventures—if he had had any—remained unknown to me. I believe I was told that the first time he had gone away, to work on the ship, he had worked as a cook. But that might have been a story I made up myself. All that I knew of Bogart while he lived in the servant room was what, as a child, I saw from a distance. He and his comings and goings were part of the confusion and haphazardness and crowd of that time.

I saw a little more of him four or five years later. The war was over. The American base at the end of the street was closed. The buildings were pulled down, and the local contractor, who knew someone in our family, gave us the run of the place for a few days, to pick up what timber we wanted. My mother's extended family was breaking up into its component parts; we were all leaving my grandmother's house. My father had bought a house of his own; I used timber from the old American base to make a new front gate. Soon I had got the Trinidad government scholarship that was to take me to Oxford.

* * *

The time then came for me to go to England. I left Bogart in Carenage.[3] And that was where he had continued to live in my memory, faintly, never a figure in the foreground; the man who had worked on a ship, then gone to Venezuela, sitting placidly ever after at his sewing machine, below my sign, in his little concrete house-and-shop.

That was Bogart's story, as I knew it. And—after all our migrations within Trinidad, after my own trip to England and my time at Oxford—that was all the story I had in mind when—after two failed attempts at novels—I sat at the typewriter in the freelances' room in the Langham Hotel, to try once more to be a writer. And luck was with me that afternoon. *Every morning when he got up Hat would sit on the banister of his back verandah and shout across, "What happening there, Bogart?"* Luck was with me, because that first sentence was so direct, so uncluttered, so without complications, that it provoked the sentence that was to follow. *Bogart would turn in his bed and mumble softly, so that no one heard, "What happening there, Hat?"*

The first sentence was true. The second was invention. But together—to me, the writer—they had done something extraordinary. Though they had left out everything—the setting, the historical time, the racial and social complexities of the people concerned—they had suggested it all; they had created the world of the street. And together, as sentences, words, they had set up a rhythm, a speed, which dictated all that was to follow.

* * *

I had written a book, and I felt it to be real. That had been my ambition for years, and an urgent ambition for the past year. And I suppose that if the book had had some response outside the freelances' room I might have been a little more secure in my talent, and my later approach to writing would have been calmer; it is just possible.

But I knew only anxiety. The publisher that Andrew Salkey took the book to sent no reply for three months (the book remained unpublished for four years). And—by now one long year out of Oxford—I was trying to write another, and discovering that to have written a book was not to be a writer. Looking for a new book, a new narrative, episodes, I found myself as uncertain, and as pretending to be a writer, as I had been before I had written the story of Bogart.

To be a writer, I thought, was to have the conviction that one could go on. I didn't have that conviction. And even when the new book had been written I didn't think of myself as a writer. I thought I should wait until I had written three. And when, a year after writing the second, I had written the third, I thought I should wait until I had written six. On official forms I described myself as a "broadcaster," thinking the word nondescript, suitable to someone from the freelances' room; until a BBC man, "staff," told me it was boastful.

---

3. A village near Port of Spain.

So I became "writer." Though to myself an unassuageable anxiety still attached to the word, and I was still, for its sake, practicing magic. I never bought paper to write on. I preferred to use "borrowed," non-rustle BBC paper; it seemed more casual, less likely to attract failure. I never numbered my pages, for fear of not getting to the end. (This drew the only comment Ernest Eytle made about my writing. Sitting idly at his typewriter one day in the freelances' room, he read some of my pages, apparently with good will. Then, weightily, he said, "I'll tell you what you should do with this." I waited. He said, "You should number the pages. In case they get mixed up.") And on the finished manuscripts of my first four books—half a million words—I never with my own hand typed or wrote my name. I always asked someone else to do that for me. Such anxiety; such ambition.

The ways of my fantasy, the process of creation, remained mysterious to me. For everything that was false or didn't work and had to be discarded, I felt that I alone was responsible. For everything that seemed right I felt I had only been a vessel. There was the recurring element of luck, or so it seemed to me. True, and saving, knowledge of my subject—beginning with Bogart's street—always seemed to come during the writing.

This element of luck isn't so mysterious to me now. As diarists and letter writers repeatedly prove, any attempt at narrative can give value to an experience which might otherwise evaporate away. When I began to write about Bogart's street I began to sink into a tract of experience I hadn't before contemplated as a writer. This blindness might seem extraordinary in someone who wanted so much to be a writer. Half a writer's work, though, is the discovery of his subject. And a problem for me was that my life had been varied, full of upheavals and moves: from my grandmother's Hindu house in the country, still close to the rituals and social ways of village India; to Port of Spain, the negro and G.I. life of its streets, the other, ordered life of my colonial English school, which was called Queen's Royal College; and then Oxford, London, and the freelances' room at the BBC. Trying to make a beginning as a writer, I didn't know where to focus.

In England I was also a colonial. Out of the stresses of that, and out of my worship of the name of writer, I had without knowing it fallen into the error of thinking of writing as a kind of display. My very particularity—which was the subject sitting on my shoulder—had been encumbering me.

The English or French writer of my age had grown up in a world that was more or less explained. He wrote against a background of knowledge. I couldn't be a writer in the same way, because to be a colonial, as I was, was to be spared knowledge. It was to live in an intellectually restricted world; it was to accept those restrictions. And the restrictions could become attractive.

Every morning when he got up Hat would sit on the banister of his back verandah and shout across, "What happening there, Bogart?" That was a good place to begin. But I couldn't stay there. My anxiety constantly to prove myself as a writer, the need to write another book and then another, led me away.

There was much in that call of "Bogart!" that had to be examined. It was spoken by a Port of Spain Indian, a descendant of nineteenth-century indentured immigrants from South India; and Bogart was linked in a special Hindu way with my mother's family. So there was a migration from India to be considered, a migration within the British Empire. There was my Hindu family, with its fading memories of India; there was India itself. And there was Trinidad, with its past of slavery, its mixed population, its racial antagonisms, and its changing political life; once part of Venezuela and the Spanish Empire, now English-speaking, with the American base and an open-air cinema at the end of Bogart's street. And just across the Gulf of Paria was Venezuela, the sixteenth-century land of El Dorado, now a country of dictators, but drawing Bogart out of his servant room with its promise of Spanish sexual adventure and the promise of a job in its oil fields.

And there was my own presence in England, writing: the career wasn't possible in Trinidad, a small, mainly agricultural colony; my vision of the world couldn't exclude that important fact.

So step by step, book by book, though seeking each time only to write another book, I eased myself into knowledge. To write was to learn. Beginning a book, I always felt I was in possession of all the facts about myself; at the end I was always surprised. The book before always turned out to have been written by a man with incomplete knowledge. And the very first, the one begun in the freelances' room, seemed to have been written by an innocent, a man at the beginning of knowledge both about himself and about the writing career that had been his ambition from childhood.

EPIFANIO SAN JUAN (b. 1938)
Philippines [resident of United States]

Epifanio San Juan is a Philippine poet who became a professor in California after receiving his doctorate from Harvard University. "Voyages" speaks of travel and exile without reference to any specific place but with echoes of Homer's Odysseus.

Voyages

To exile I ride on the bountiful surf. And foam-flowers of her dreams gather to
  waylay my anchors.

Roots shall burst the shell. Burnt roots.

She wanders. Sunk in glaciers.

Plough. Siren-song.[1]   5

---

1. Odysseus had to resist the Sirens, mermaids
   who tempted sailors to shipwreck by singing enchanting songs.

Anonymous. *A ship on the high seas*. Borobudur, Ancient Indonesia.
Bas-relief on stone, n.d.

And seeds flower sibylwise[2] to wake the sleeping oracles of desire. Woven.
  Until nets swing against the rocks of her breast-hulls.

Weeds leagues-long, moored by tides and horned nightmares! She summons
  her wild albatross!

Yield to the sargasso[3] of her murmurings.   10

FADWA TUQAN (b. 1917)
Palestine [resident of West Bank]

Fadwa Tuqan is a Palestinian poet born in Nablus, whose work became
increasingly political as the Arab-Israeli conflict intensified; her books *I Found It*
(1957) and *Give Us Love* (1960) and *In Front of the Closed Door* (1967) deal with
the struggle and sufferings of the Palestinians. The poem presented here crosses
borders both in the sense of interweaving the private and the public and in
reaching across barriers of separation imposed by hatred and violence. This
poem is taken from her *Nightmare in Daylight* of 1974.

---

2. The sibyls were prophetesses consulted by   3. Floating beds of seaweed.
   the Greeks and Romans.

To Etan*

An Israeli Child
From the Kibbutz Ma'oz Hayim
He falls
under the star that branches
a wild tree in his hands   5
a web woven with the threads of steel stretching walls of blood
around The Dream.
He is caught.
Opening his eyes
Etan, the child, asks,   10
"How long do we have to watch over this land?"

And time deformed
dragged in khaki, bypasses him
through flames and smoke
sorrows and death.   15
If only the Star could foretell the truth.
Etan, my child
Like the harbor that is drowning
I can see you drown
through the lie   20
The bloated dream is a sinking load.
I am afraid for you, my child
to have to grow up in this web of things
to be gradually stripped of
    your human heart and face   25
you could fall again, my child
    and fall
        and fall
            fading into a fathomless end.

SEAMUS HEANEY (b. 1939)

Northern Ireland (resident of the Republic of Ireland)

"Exposure" is the concluding poem of Seamus Heaney's 1975 collection *North*. The poet speaks of himself as an "inner emigré," signifying both a mental state and a political condition; against the background of the "troubles" in Northern

---

*Translated by Kamal Boullata.

Ireland—the ongoing strife between Catholics and Protestants in the wake of centuries of British colonial rule—Heaney raises the question of the complex relationship between poetry and politics.

from *North*

Exposure

It is December in Wicklow[1]:
Alders dripping, birches
Inheriting the last light,
The ash tree cold to look at.

A comet that was lost   5
Should be visible at sunset,
Those million tons of light
Like a glimmer of haws and rose-hips,

And I sometimes see a falling star.
If I could come on meteorite!   10
Instead I walk through damp leaves,
Husks, the spent flukes of autumn,

Imagining a hero
On some muddy compound,
His gift like a slingstone   15
Whirled for the desperate.

How did I end up like this?
I often think of my friends'
Beautiful prismatic counselling
And the anvil brains of some who hate me   20

As I sit weighing and weighing
My responsible *tristia*.[2]
For what? For the ear? For the people?
For what is said behind-backs?

Rain comes down through the alders,   25
Its low conducive voices
Mutter about let-downs and erosions
And yet each drop recalls

The diamond absolutes.
I am neither internee nor informer;   30
An inner émigré, grown long-haired
And thoughtful; a wood-kerne[3]

---

1. A rural county in southeastern Ireland.   3. An Irish peasant or foot soldier.
2. Sorrows; the title of a poem by Ovid.

Escaped from the massacre,
Taking protective colouring
From bole and bark, feeling   35
Every wind that blows;

Who, blowing up these sparks
For their meagre heat, have missed
The once-in-a-lifetime portent,
The comet's pulsing rose.   40

SALMAN RUSHDIE (b. 1947)
Pakistan [resident of England]

Born in Bombay, Salman Rushdie grew up in India and Pakistan before settling
in England. He achieved international prominence with *Midnight's Children*
(1981), of which the opening pages are given here. The novel, overflowing with
plots and subplots, is both a satiric history of India from the end of British rule
in 1947 through the rise of Indira Gandhi and also a meditation on the nature of
storytelling itself.

from *Midnight's Children*

The Perforated Sheet

I was born in the city of Bombay . . . once upon a time. No, that won't do, there's
no getting away from the date: I was born in Doctor Narlikar's Nursing Home on
August 15th, 1947. And the time? The time matters, too. Well then: at night. No,
it's important to be more . . . On the stroke of midnight, as a matter of fact.
Clock-hands joined palms in respectful greeting as I came. Oh, spell it out, spell
it out: at the precise instant of India's arrival at independence, I tumbled forth into
the world. There were gasps. And, outside the window, fireworks and crowds. A
few seconds later, my father broke his big toe; but his accident was a mere trifle
when set beside what had befallen me in the benighted moment, because thanks
to the occult tyrannies of those blandly saluting clocks I had been mysteriously
handcuffed to history, my destinies indissolubly chained to those of my country.
For the next three decades, there was to be no escape. Soothsayers had prophesied
me, newspapers celebrated my arrival, politicos ratified my authenticity. I was left
entirely without a say in the matter. I, Saleem Sinai, later variously called
Snotnose, Stainface, Baldy, Sniffer, Buddha and even Piece-of-the-Moon, had
become heavily embroiled in Fate—at the best of times a dangerous sort of
involvement. And I couldn't even wipe my own nose at the time.

Now, however, time (having no further use for me) is running out. I will soon be thirty-one years old. Perhaps. If my crumbling, over-used body permits. But I have no hope of saving my life, nor can I count on having even a thousand nights and a night. I must work fast, faster than Scheherazade,[1] if I am to end up meaning—yes, meaning—something. I admit it: above all things, I fear absurdity.

And there are so many stories to tell, too many, such an excess of intertwined lives events miracles places rumors, so dense a commingling of the improbable and the mundane! I have been a swallower of lives; and to know me, just the one of me, you'll have to swallow the lot as well. Consumed multitudes are jostling and shoving inside me; and guided only by the memory of a large white bedsheet with a roughly circular hole some seven inches in diameter cut into the centre, clutching at the dream of that holey, mutilated square of linen, which is my talisman, my open-sesame, I must commence the business of remaking my life from the point at which it really began, some thirty-two years before anything as obvious, as *present,* as my clock-ridden, crime-stained birth.

(The sheet, incidentally, is stained too, with three drops of old, faded redness. As the Quran tells us: *Recite, in the name of the Lord thy Creator, who created Man from clots of blood.*)

One Kashmiri[2] morning in the early spring of 1915, my grandfather Aadam Aziz hit his nose against a frost-hardened tussock[3] of earth while attempting to pray. Three drops of blood plopped out of his left nostril, hardened instantly in the brittle air and lay before his eyes on the prayer-mat, transformed into rubies. Lurching back until he knelt with his head once more upright, he found that the tears which had sprung to his eyes had solidified, too; and at that moment, as he brushed diamonds contemptuously from his lashes, he resolved never again to kiss earth for any god or man. This decision, however, made a hole in him, a vacancy in a vital inner chamber, leaving him vulnerable to women and history. Unaware of this at first, despite his recently completed medical training, he stood up, rolled the prayer-mat into a thick cheroot, and holding it under his right arm surveyed the valley through clear, diamond-free eyes.

The world was new again. After a winter's gestation in its eggshell of ice, the valley had beaked its way out into the open, moist and yellow. The new grass bided its time underground; the mountains were retreating to their hill-stations for the warm season. (In the winter, when the valley shrank under the ice, the mountains closed in and snarled like angry jaws around the city on the lake.)

In those days the radio mast had not been built and the temple of Sankara Acharya, a little black blister on a khaki hill, still dominated the streets and lake of Srinagar.[4] In those days there was no army camp at the lakeside, no endless snakes of camouflaged trucks and jeeps clogged the narrow mountain roads, no soldiers hid behind the crests of the mountains past Baramulla and Gulmarg. In those days travellers were not shot as spies of they took photographs of bridges, and apart from the Englishmen's houseboats on the lake, the valley had hardly

---

1. The storytelling heroine of *The Thousand and One Nights.*
2. Kashmir is a region in northern India.
3. A thick clump.
4. Summer capital of the region.

changed since the Mughal Empire,[5] for all its springtime renewals; but my grandfather's eyes—which were, like the rest of him, twenty-five years old—saw things differently . . . and his nose had started to itch.

To reveal the secret of my grandfather's altered vision: he had spent five years, five springs, away from home. (The tussock of earth, crucial though its presence was as it crouched under a chance wrinkle of the prayer-mat, was at bottom no more than a catalyst.) Now, returning, he saw through travelled eyes. Instead of the beauty of the tiny valley circled by giant teeth, he noticed the narrowness, the proximity of the horizon; and felt sad, to be at home and feel so utterly enclosed. He also felt—inexplicably—as though the old place resented this educated, stethoscoped return. Beneath the winter ice, it had been coldly neutral, but now there was no doubt: the years in Germany had returned him to a hostile environment. Many years later, when the hole inside him had been clogged up with hate, and he came to sacrifice himself at the shrine of the black stone god in the temple on the hill, he would try and recall his childhood springs in Paradise, the way it was before travel and tussocks and army tanks messed everything up.

On the morning when the valley, gloved in a prayer-mat, punched him on the nose, he had been trying, absurdly, to pretend that nothing had changed. So he had risen in the bitter cold of four-fifteen, washed himself in the prescribed fashion, dressed and put on his father's astrakhan cap;[6] after which he had carried the rolled cheroot of the prayer-mat into the small lakeside garden in front of their old dark house and unrolled it over the waiting tussock. The ground felt deceptively soft under his feet and made him simultaneously uncertain and unwary. "In the Name of God, the Compassionate, the Merciful . . ."—the exordium,[7] spoken with hands joined before him like a book, comforted a part of him, made another, larger part feel uneasy—". . . Praise be to Allah, Lord of the Creation . . ."—but now Heidelberg invaded his head; here was Ingrid, briefly his Ingrid, her face scorning-him for this Mecca-turned parroting: here, their friends Oskar and Ilse Lubin the anarchists, mocking his prayer with their anti-ideologies—". . . The Compassionate, the Merciful, King of the Last Judgment! . . ."—Heidelberg, in which, along with medicine and politics, he learned that India—like radium—had been "discovered" by the Europeans: even Oskar was filled with admiration for Vasco da Gama,[8] and this was what finally separated Aadam Aziz from his friends, this belief of theirs that he was somehow the invention of their ancestors—". . . You alone we worship, and You alone we pray for help . . ."—so here he was, despite their presence in his head, attempting to re-unite himself with an earlier self which ignored their influence but knew everything it ought to have known, about submission for example, about what he was doing now, as his hands, guided by old memories, fluttered upwards, thumbs pressed to ears, fingers spread, as he sank to his knees—". . . Guide us to the straight path. The path of those whom You have favoured . . ."—But it was no good, he was caught in a strange middle ground, trapped between belief and disbelief, and

---

5. Islamic empire in northern India from the sixteenth to the mid-eighteenth century.
6. A lambs-wool cap.
7. Opening section.

8. Portuguese explorer (c. 1469–1524) who discovered the sea route around Africa to India.

this was only a charade after all—". . . Not of those who have incurred Your wrath. Nor of those who have gone astray." My grandfather bent his forehead towards the earth. Forward he bent, and the earth, prayer-mat-covered, curved up towards him. And now it was the tussock's time. At one and the same time a rebuke from Ilse-Oskar-Ingrid-Heidelberg as well as valley-and-God, it smote him upon the point of the nose. Three drops fell. There were rubies and diamonds. And my grandfather, lurching upright, made a resolve. Stood. Rolled cheroot. Stared across the lake. And was knocked forever into that middle place, unable to worship a God in whose existence he could not wholly disbelieve. Permanent alteration: a hole.

The young, newly-qualified Doctor Aadam Aziz stood facing the springtime lake, sniffing the whiffs of change; while his back (which was extremely straight) was turned upon yet more changes. His father had had a stroke in his absence abroad, and his mother had kept it a secret. His mother's voice, whispering stoically: ". . . *Because your studies were too important, son.*" This mother, who had spent her life housebound, in purdah,[9] had suddenly found enormous strength and gone out to run the small gemstone business (turquoises, rubies, diamonds) which had put Aadam through medical college, with the help of a scholarship; so he returned to find the seemingly immutable order of his family turned upside down, his mother going out to work while his father sat hidden behind the veil which the stroke had dropped over his brain . . . in a wooden chair, in a darkened room, he sat and made bird-noises. Thirty different species of birds visited him and sat on the sill outside his shuttered window conversing about this and that. He seemed happy enough.

(. . . And already I can see the repetitions beginning; because didn't my grandmother also find enormous . . . and the stroke, too, was not the only . . . and the Brass Monkey had her birds . . . and the curse begins already, and we haven't even got to the noses yet!)

The lake was no longer frozen over. The thaw had come rapidly, as usual; many of the small boats, the shikaras, had been caught napping, which was also normal. But while these sluggards slept on, on dry land, snoring peacefully beside their owners, the oldest boat was up at the crack as old folk often are, and was therefore the first craft to move across the unfrozen lake. Tai's shikara . . . this, too, was customary.

Watch how the old boatman, Tai, makes good time through the misty water, standing stooped over at the back of his craft! How his oar, a wooden heart on a yellow stick, drives jerkily through the weeds! In these parts he's considered very odd because he rows standing up . . . among other reasons. Tai, bringing an urgent summons to Doctor Aziz, is about to set history in motion . . . while Aadam, looking down into the water, recalls what Tai taught him years ago: "The ice is always waiting, Aadam baba, just under the water's skin." Aadam's eyes are a clear blue, the astonishing blue of mountain sky, which has a habit of dripping into the pupils of Kashmiri men; they have not forgotten how to look. They see—there! like the skeleton of a ghost, just beneath the surface of Lake Dal!—the delicate

---

9. The seclusion of women from public view.

tracery, the intricate crisscross of colorless lines, the cold waiting veins of the future. His German years, which have blurred so much else, haven't deprived him of the gift of seeing Tai's gift. He looks up, sees the approaching V of Tai's boat, waves a greeting. Tai's arm rises—but this is a command. "Wait!" My grandfather waits; and during this hiatus, as he experiences the last peace of his life, a muddy, ominous sort of peace, I had better get round to describing him.

Keeping out of my voice the natural envy of the ugly man for the strikingly impressive, I record that Doctor Aziz was a tall man. Pressed flat against a wall of his family home, he measured twenty-five bricks (a brick for each year of his life), or just over six foot two. A strong man also. His beard was thick and red—and annoyed his mother, who said only Hajis, men who had made the pilgrimage to Mecca, should grow red beards. His hair, however, was rather darker. His sky-eyes you know about. Ingrid had said, "They went mad with the colors when they made your face." But the central feature of my grandfather's anatomy was neither color nor height, neither strength of arm nor straightness of back. There it was, reflected in the water, undulating like a mad plantain in the centre of his face . . . Aadam Aziz, waiting for Tai, watches his rippling nose. It would have dominated less dramatic faces than his easily; even on him, it is what one sees first and remembers longest. "A cyranose,"[10] Ilse Lubin said, and Oskar added, "A proboscissimus." Ingrid announced, "You could cross a river on that nose." (Its bridge was wide.)

My grandfather's nose: nostrils flaring, curvaceous as dancers. Between them swells the nose's triumphal arch, first up and out, then down and under, sweeping in to his upper lip with a superb and at present red-tipped flick. An easy nose to hit a tussock with. I wish to place on record my gratitude to this mighty organ—if not for it, who would ever have believed me to be truly my mother's son, my grandfather's grandson?—this colossal apparatus which was to be my birthright, too. Doctor Aziz's nose—comparable only to the trunk of the elephant-headed god Ganesh—established incontrovertibly his right to be a patriarch. It was Tai who taught him that, too. When young Aadam was barely past puberty the dilapidated boatman said, "That's a nose to start a family on, my princeling. There'd be no mistaking whose brood they were. Mughal Emperors would have given their right hands for noses like that one. There are dynasties waiting inside it."—and here Tai lapsed into coarseness—"like snot."

On Aadam Aziz, the nose assumed a patriarchal aspect. On my mother, it looked noble and a little long-suffering; on my aunt Emerald, snobbish; on my aunt Alia, intellectual; on my uncle Hanif it was the organ of an unsuccessful genius; my uncle Mustapha made it a second-rater's sniffer, the Brass Monkey escaped it completely; but on me—on me, it was something else again. But I mustn't reveal all my secrets at once.

---

10. A play on the name of Cyrano de Bergerac,
a seventeenth-century French writer and
soldier, famous for his large nose.

MIRTA YÁÑEZ (b. 1947)
Cuba

Mirta Yáñez was born in Havana 1947. After completing her studies in Spanish language and literature in 1970, she won a prize for poetry for *Visits* [*Las visitas*], published the following year. She has taught Spanish-American literature and has collaborated on and authored many publications both within and outside of Cuba. Her interests include children's literature and cultural history and she has been director of the Department of Cultural Activities in the University Extension service. "We Blacks All Drink Coffee" ["*Todos los Negros tomamos Café*"], which won honorable mention in a short story competition in Cuba, illustrates how self-knowledge grows with an awareness of the choices entailed in crossing racial boundaries.

We Blacks All Drink Coffee

Tell me with what flowers
you greased your plough
so the fragrant land
smells of spikenard?

> *José Martí*

She says that I don't even know how to wash my own clothes and yet I want to go off. What is a mother's child going to do in a place like that? Just imagine what my grandmother would say if she knew, if she were to rise from the grave and see what the apple of her eye wanted to get into. It's a good thing she is dead, because if she weren't . . . There's a lot of talk about irresponsible mothers. But not about her.

And so my mother goes grumbling on and on from the end of the corridor where she has gone to take refuge so that her voice will be lost, will slip in between the furniture, so the neighbours will not hear one word sounding louder than another, what would they think of this family, of this child of fifteen wanting to go off to pick coffee?

Things were different in her time. What would a well brought up girl be doing in the middle of the bush? Who would have thought of such a thing? Going where there are so many dangers. At least that's what the books say. Right into the heart of a titanic forest, a girl from a good family. Luckily there are no wild animals in this country.

For my mother the only safe place is my room with its four walls, a roof, a floor of the most ordinary sort. And not even then is it completely worthy of her confidence.

Translated by Claudette Williams.

What do I care about the neighbours? But she does. And she closes the windows so that the argument will not go beyond this castle which is the protective shell of my family life. And when the room is the way she would have it, like the cell of a cloistered nun, she rushes forward from the other side of the corridor, she claps her hands. She shouts carefully. I am what is known as a girl who was given everything she ever wanted. If I asked for a flying bird, a flying bird I would get. Now look how ungrateful I was.

She says I think of no one but myself. I don't think of anyone, she says. One of my grandmothers is in the grave. If I insist on going off I'll be sending the other one to the edge of the grave. With a sudden collapse. All the catastrophes that could occur because of my pigheadedness. As the eldest, who has led a very sheltered life I should accept my responsibilities. The blood pressure of grand-mothers and aunts can fall precipitously because of a *brigadista* who picks coffee.

There are so many dangers out in the country. My mother does not have a list on hand. A paper which she could unfurl from her chest like a banner, a string of familiar words, the first of which would be diseases. Who is going to look after you? When something goes wrong with your lungs I am the one, she is the one, who will be responsible for you. A daughter at death's door for the rest of her life, kept in a room with its windows closed to keep the early morning dew from coming in and the reproaches from going out, a daughter without any vital signs, without a will of her own, how wonderful. Withering away like a flower, filled with remorse to her last gasp for the folly of her adolescence. A trip to the coffee fields, and then a heroine dependent on the charity of a self-denying mother, always at her post with a load of comments such as, "it happened just as I warned you," "listen when you're told, or you'll never grow old," "that's what you get for disobeying your mother who wants the best for you," for ever and ever. What more could she want?

In the mountains where they pick coffee, or so she has heard, she has never seen it with her own eyes, eyes the worms will soon be picking at thanks to all this heartbreak, the mountains are slippery and treacherous. They slip from under the feet and leave the *brigadistas* hanging in mid-air, from a branch. The plants of the red and green coffee beans are like waves sweeping over a little girl of fifteen who knows nothing of life.

And if afterwards her period, her menstruation, is one, two months late, what will the family think of this child who has risked losing her honour going to do voluntary work? For though it is not actually said, honour is not something you can touch, or see, it is only something you lose. And where will they look for her, where will they go, where would they complain? She will not be the first to have left home a good little girl and to have returned, at best, pregnant. And then, how awful it would be. The whole family having turned its back on her; the neighbours revelling in the gossip; the little girl the talk of the town.

What argument can counter this? How can I know in August if my period will be right on time in October, in December and in all the months to come? What guarantee can I give my mother that I will safeguard the family's precious honour? What a strange agreement to have to sign just to go to pick coffee. Breaking my back at work for forty-five days, and still having to make sure that all my functions are in place, with every gland responding on time. No defect in my body to provoke the anger of such a decent family as mine. Having to contend with the suspicious glances of my mother's fearsome neighbours. What a way to screw up someone's life, I tell myself.

And who knows if the coffee–picking mightn't turn your head so much that you even fall in love with a Negro, she says in a powerless rage.

You know what it means to be a nice white girl. As white as the paper daisy that my mother is crushing nervously between her hands in my birthday photograph, its yellow heart overflowing with innocence. For a white girl must receive maximum care, must be brought up according to all the rules of good health and hygiene. She cannot go alone out onto the street. She must go with her father to the movies. She goes to school holding her mother's hand. She must not play with others. And never, never get into mischief.

How times change.

You are, I am, she says, the one who stands to lose. If my mother would only let me explain to her. If only there were some way of getting out of her head those visions which she is hurling at me from every corner of the room, as she moves about, her voice louder and fiercer with every minute. In this room of white people living together as a family. Where the ancestors have most certainly been white. Where I tell her, who knows what kind of blood anyone has? That in the mother country, there had been dark-skinned Moors for centuries, no-one can avoid it. That those who do not have the Congo in them somewhere . . .[1]

My mother raises her hands to her bosom so as not to hear me, so as not to let another sentence in. So as to separate me from her breath. So as not to listen to me saying I am not a white paper daisy which she keeps between perfumed handkerchiefs. What's the point? What if I fall in love with a Negro? This is important, I learn for the first time in my life. The colours, shades, the tones of voice which show me for what I am, within these four walls, in the bush I am going to, or on the street corner, this little lily-white girl, carefully watching a man with his fly shamelessly open.

Still clasping her breast, my mother retreats along the corridor, saying, "do as you think best."

ALOOTOOK IPELLIE (b. 1951)
Canada

Alootook Ipellie, an Inuit Eskimo poet, explores with passion and humor the experience of fractured identity in a country already divided by language (Inuit, English, French) and culture.

---

1. There is a popular saying that all Cubans have some African ancestry.

Innukjuakjuk. *Female Owl*. Stone-cut. Cape Dorset, 1960.

Walking Both Sides of an Invisible Border

It is never easy
Walking with an invisible border
Separating my left and right foot

I feel like an illegitimate child
Forsaken by my parents
At least I can claim innocence
Since I did not ask to come
Into this world

Walking on both sides of this
Invisible Border
Each and every day
And for the rest of my life
Is like having been
Sentenced to a torture chamber
Without having committed a crime

Understanding the history of humanity
I am not the least surprised
This is happening to me
A non-entity

During this population explosion
In a minuscule world   20

I did not ask to be born an Inuk
Nor did I ask to be forced
To learn an alien culture
With an alien language   25
But I lucked out on fate
Which I am unable to undo

I have resorted to fancy dancing
In order to survive each day
No wonder I have earned   30
The dubious reputation of being
The world's premiere choreographer
Of distinctive dance steps
That allow me to avoid
Potential personal paranoia   35
On both sides of this invisible border

Sometimes this border becomes so wide
That I am unable to take another step
My feet being too far apart
When my crotch begins to tear apart   40
I am forced to invent
A brand new dance step
The premiere choreographer
Saving the day once more

Destiny acted itself out   45
Deciding for me where I would come from
And what I would become

So I am left to fend for myself
Walking in two different worlds
Trying my best to make sense   50
Of two opposing cultures
Which are unable to integrate
Lest they swallow one another whole

Each and every day
Is a fighting day   55
A war of raw nerves
And to show for my efforts
I have a fair share of wins and losses

When will all this end
This senseless battle
Between my left and right foot

When will the invisible border
Cease to be

Afterword:
A Note on Translation
by Jorge Luis Borges

No problem is more essential to literature and its small mysteries than translation. A lapse of memory spurred by vanity, the fear of divulging mental processes that we can guess to be perilously pedestrian, the attempt to maintain an incalculable reserve of mystery—all cast a veil over the alleged original. Translation, in contrast, seems destined to illustrate aesthetic debates. The model to be imitated is a visible text, and the translator is not free to follow the unfathomable labyrinths of past projects or to accept the sudden temptation of an easy solution. Bertrand Russell defined an external object as a circular system radiating many possible impressions. Given the incalculable repercussions of words, the same could be said about a text, whose translations become a partial and precious document of the changes it inevitably suffers. What are the many renderings of the *Iliad*—from Chapman's to Magnien's—if not different perspectives of a mutable fact, if not a long experimental lottery of omissions and emphases? (Changing languages is not necessary for this deliberate juggling of interpretations, which can occur within a single literature.) To assume that all recombinations of elements are necessarily inferior to their original form is to assume that draft 9 is necessarily inferior to draft H—since every text is a draft. The notion of a "definitive text" belongs to religion or perhaps merely to exhaustion.

Our superstition that translations are inferior—reinforced by the age-old Italian adage *traduttore traditore*—is the result of our naïveté: all great works that we turn to time and again seem unalterable and definitive. Hume identified our habitual idea of causality with the experience of temporal succession. Thus a good film seen a second time seems even better; we tend to take repetitions for absolutes. Our first reading of famous books is really the second, since we already know them. The cliché "rereading the classics" turns out to be an unwitting truth. But how can we know now whether the statement "In a place of La Mancha, whose name I don't care to remember, there lived not long ago a nobleman who kept a lance and shield, a greyhound, and a skinny old nag" actually proceeded from divine inspiration? I only know that any modifications would be sacrilegious and that I could not conceive of another beginning for *Don Quixote*. Cervantes, however, probably dispensed with such a frivolous superstition and may not have recognized this paragraph. I, in contrast, can only reject any divergence. Since Spanish is my native language, the *Quixote* is to me an unchanging monument, with no possible variations except those furnished by the editor, the bookbinder, and the compositor. But the *Odyssey,* thanks to my opportune ignorance of Greek, is a library of works in prose and verse, from Chapman's couplets to Andrew Lang's "authorized version" or from Berard's classic French drama and Morris's lively saga to Samuel Butler's ironic bourgeois novel. I mention mostly English names because English writers have always gravitated toward this epic of the sea, and their many versions of the *Odyssey* would be enough to illustrate the history of their literature. But the rich and even contradictory variety of this library is not attributable solely to the evolution of the English language, to the original's grand proportions, or to the deviations and diverse capacities of the translators. The main cause is the impossibility of knowing what belonged to the poet and what belonged to the language. To this fortunate impossibility we owe so many possible versions, all of them sincere, genuine, and divergent.

I do not know of a more controversial issue than the Homeric adjectives. Recurrent expressions such as "the divine Patroclus," "the nourishing earth," "the wine-dark sea," "the uncloven-hoofed horses," "the moist ways," "the dark blood," "the dear knees" stir our hearts at unexpected moments. At one point, there is mention of "rich noblemen who drink of the black waters of the Aesopos"; at another, a tragic king who, "unhappy in lovely Thebes, governed the Cadmeans by the gods' fatal decree." Alexander Pope, whose lavish translation we shall scrutinize later, believed that all these immutable epithets were liturgical in character. Rémy de Gourmont, in his long essay on style, writes that though they must have been enchanting at one time, they are no longer so. I, however, suspect that these standard epithets were what prepositions still are today: modest and obligatory sounds used to join certain words and on which no originality can be exercised. We know, for example, that the correct way to get somewhere is *on* foot and not *with* foot, just as the blind bard knew that the adjective to describe Patroclus was "divine." Neither usage is motivated by aesthetic reasons. I offer these conjectures with humble sobriety: our only certainty is that we cannot separate what belongs to the author from what belongs to the language. When we read in the seventeenth-century playwright Agustín Moreto (if we must read Agustín Moreto) the phrase "Pues en casa tan compuestas/¿Qué hacen todo el santo día?" 'What do these prim ladies do at home the whole damn day?' we know that the day's unholiness belongs to the language and not to the writer. Where Homer's accents lie, however, we can never know.

For a lyrical or elegiac poet, this uncertainty of ours regarding authorial intentions could be devastating, but not so for the conscientious narrator of vast plots. The deeds of the *Iliad* and the *Odyssey* more than survive, even though Achilles and Ulysses have disappeared, as have what Homer had in mind by choosing them and what he really thought of them. The present state of his works resembles a complex equation that delineates precise relations among unknown quantities. What a treasure trove for the translator! Browning's most famous poem, *The Ring and the Book,* consists of ten detailed accounts of a single crime, given by each of those involved. The work's variety derives entirely from the characters, not from the actions, and offers contrasts almost as intense and unfathomable as those among ten just versions of Homer.

The magnificent Newman-Arnold debate (1861–62), more significant than either of its participants, laboriously depicted the two main ways to translate. Newman defended the literal retention of all verbal singularities; Arnold argued for the literary, severe elimination of details that would distract or detain the reader and for the subordination of the ever-unpredictable Homer in each line to the essential or conventional Homer, whose forthright syntax flows and whose ideas are noble yet plain. Arnold's method provides the harmonious pleasures of uniformity; Newman's, continual little surprises.

Let us consider the various destinies of a single passage from Homer, concerning Achilles's son Neoptolemus. Ulysses relays the events to the ghost of Achilles in the city of the Cimmerians, on the night without end (*Odyssey* 11). Buckley's literal version goes like this:

> But when we had sacked the lofty city of Priam, having his share and excellent reward, he embarked unhurt on a ship, neither stricken with the sharp brass, nor wounded hand to hand, as oftentimes happens in war; for Mars confusedly raves.

Here is another literal as well as archaic rendition, by Butcher and Lang:

> But after we had sacked the steep city of Priam, he embarked unscathed with his share of the spoil, and with a noble prize; he was not smitten with the sharp spear, and got no wound in close fight: and many such chances there be in war, for Ares rageth confusedly.

Cowper, in 1791:

At length when we had sack'd the lofty town
Of Priam, laden with abundant spoils
He safe embark'd, neither by spear or shaft
Aught hurt, or in close fight by faulchion's edge
As oft in war befalls, where wounds are dealt
Promiscuous, at the will of fiery Mars.

Pope's 1725 version:

And when the Gods our arms with conquest crown'd,
When Troy's proud bulwarks smok'd upon the ground,
Greece to reward her soldier's gallant toils
Heap'd high his navy with unnumber'd spoils.
* Thus great in glory from the din of war*
Safe he return'd, without one hostile scar:
Tho' spears in iron tempests rain'd around,
Yet innocent they play'd, and guiltless of a wound.

George Chapman, in 1614:

*   In the event,*
High Troy depopulate, he made ascent
To his fair ship, with prise and treasure store
Safe; and no touch away with him he bore

Of far-off-hurl'd lance, or of close-fought sword,
Whose wounds for favours war doth oft afford,
Which he (though sought) miss'd in war's closest wage.
In close fights Mars doth never fight, but rage.

And finally Butler's 1900 version:

> Yet when we had sacked the city of Priam he got his handsome share of the prize money and went on board (such is the fortune of war) without a wound upon him, neither from a thrown spear nor in close combat, for the rage of Mars is a matter of great chance.

The first two—the literal versions—could move us for a variety of reasons: the reverential reference to the sacking of the city; the naive statement that one gets hurt in war; the infinite disorders of combat suddenly embodied in a single, raging god. Other, lesser pleasures are also at work: in one of the texts I have reproduced, the charming pleonasm "embarked on a ship" and, in the other, the unnecessary conjunction in "*and* many such chances there be in war." The third version, Cowper's, is the most innocuous of all since it is completely literal, as far as Miltonic verse permits.

Pope's rendering is extraordinary. His luxuriant language (like Góngora's) can be distinguished by its persistent and excessive use of superlatives. For example, the hero's lone black ship becomes a fleet. Continuously subjected to this law of amplification, all the lines of Pope's text fall into two grand categories: undiluted oratory, as in "And when the Gods our arms with conquest crown'd," or visual representation, as in "When Troy's proud bulwarks smok'd upon the ground." Speeches and spectacles: this is Pope. Chapman's fiery version is also spectacular, but his mode is lyrical, not oratorical. Butler, in contrast, reveals his determination to evade all opportunities for the visual and to turn Homer's text into a sober series of news items.

Which of these many translations is faithful? the reader might ask. I repeat: none or all of them. If fidelity implies conveying Homer's inventions and the bygone people and days that the poet portrayed, none of the versions can succeed for us but all would for a tenth-century Greek. If fidelity means preserving the effects Homer intended, any one of the above might serve, except for the literal ones, whose virtue lies in their departure from current poetic practices. It is not out of the question, then, that Butler's sedate version could be the most faithful.

Appendix A:
World Map, Antiquity to
the Early Modern World

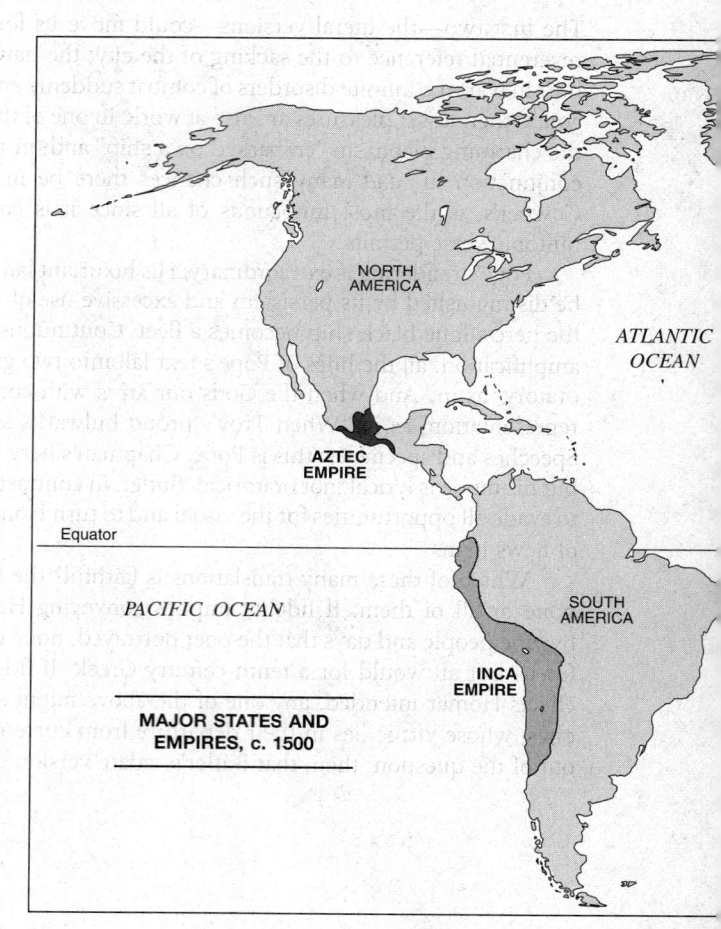

NORTH
AMERICA

ATLANTIC
OCEAN

AZTEC
EMPIRE

Equator

PACIFIC OCEAN

SOUTH
AMERICA

INCA
EMPIRE

MAJOR STATES AND
EMPIRES, c. 1500

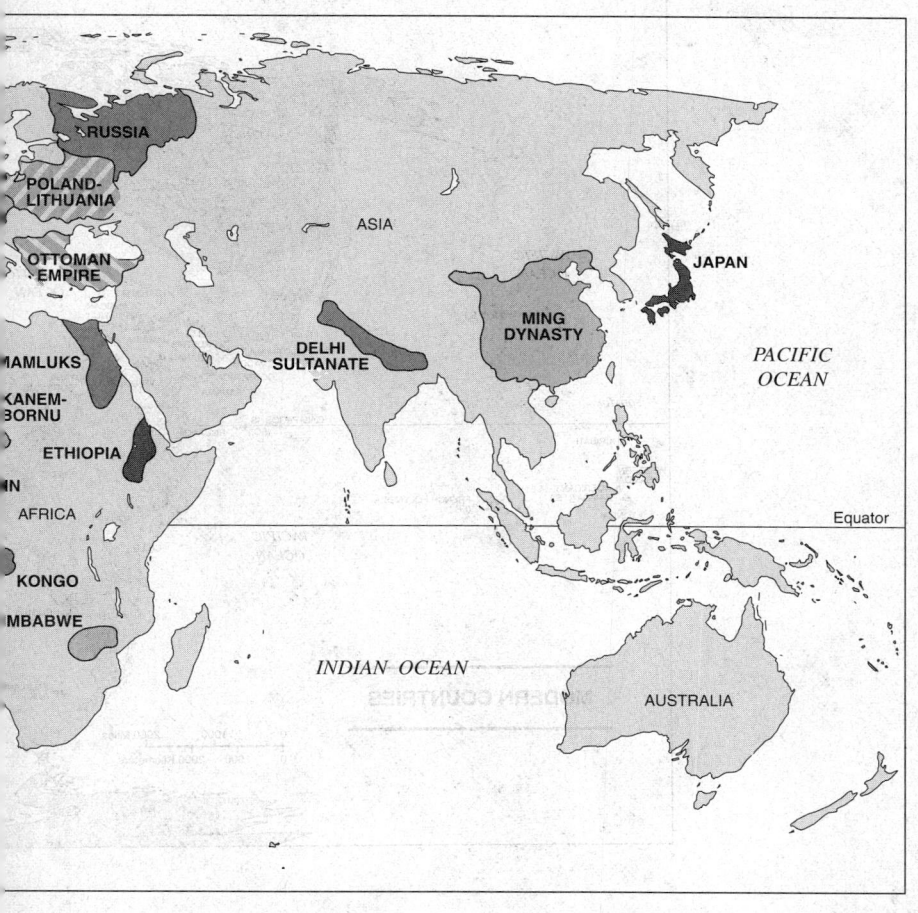

RUSSIA

POLAND-
LITHUANIA

OTTOMAN
EMPIRE

MAMLUKS

KANEM-
BORNU

ETHIOPIA

AFRICA

KONGO

MBABWE

ASIA

DELHI
SULTANATE

MING
DYNASTY

JAPAN

PACIFIC
OCEAN

Equator

INDIAN OCEAN

AUSTRALIA

World Map,
The Modern World

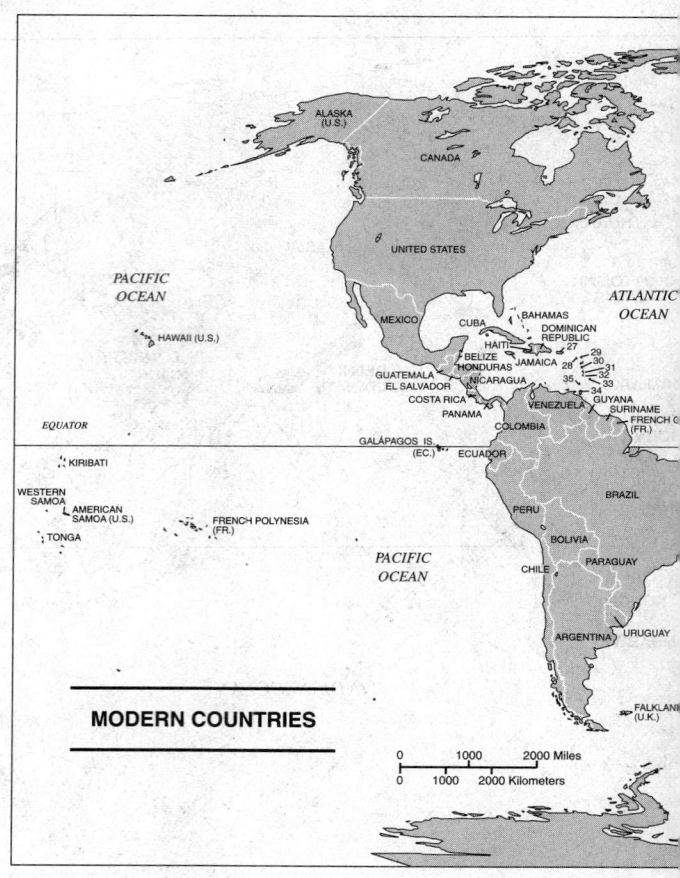

MODERN COUNTRIES

ALASKA
(U.S.)

CANADA

UNITED STATES

PACIFIC
OCEAN

HAWAII (U.S.)

MEXICO

ATLANTIC
OCEAN

BAHAMAS
CUBA
DOMINICAN
REPUBLIC
HAITI
27
BELIZE
29
HONDURAS
JAMAICA 28
30 31
GUATEMALA
32 33
EL SALVADOR
NICARAGUA
35 34
COSTA RICA
GUYANA
VENEZUELA
SURINAME
PANAMA
FRENCH G
COLOMBIA
(FR.)

EQUATOR

GALÁPAGOS IS.
(EC.)
ECUADOR

KIRIBATI

BRAZIL

WESTERN
SAMOA

AMERICAN
SAMOA (U.S.)

FRENCH POLYNESIA
(FR.)

PERU

TONGA

BOLIVIA

PACIFIC
OCEAN

CHILE
PARAGUAY

ARGENTINA
URUGUAY

FALKLAND
(U.K.)

0   1000   2000 Miles
0   1000   2000 Kilometers

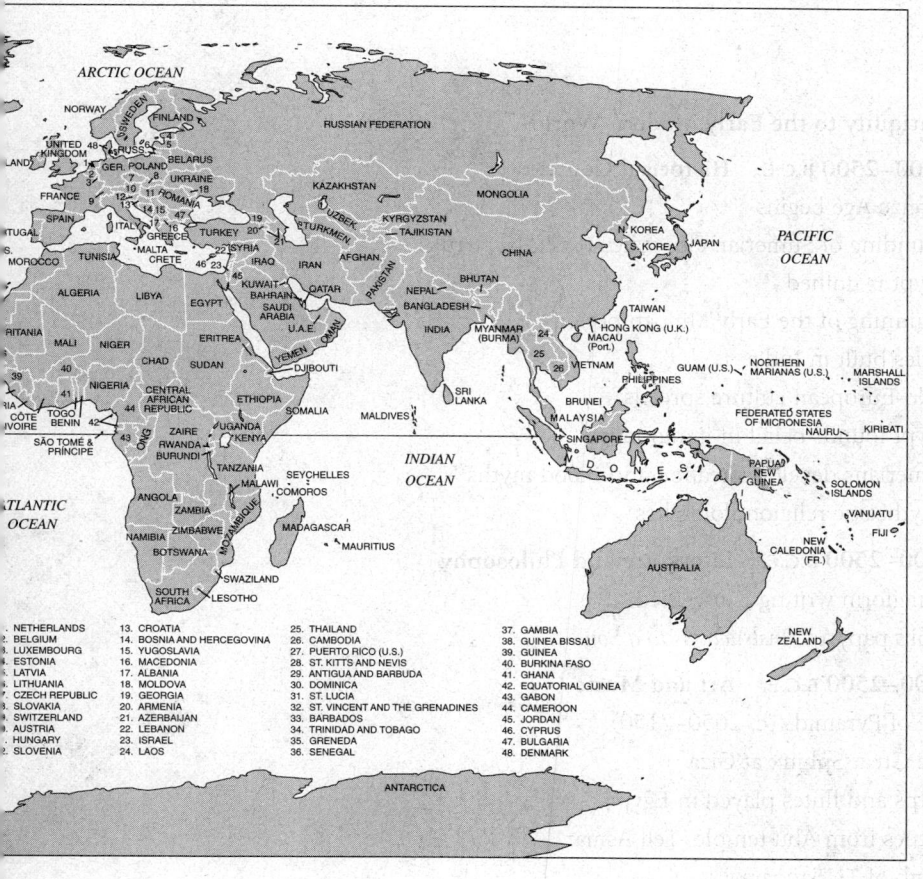

Appendix B: Comparative Chronology of World Cultures

Antiquity to the Early Modern World

4000–2500 B.C.E.   **Historical Context**

Bronze Age begins

Founding of Sumerian city-states (Kish, Ur, Uruk)

Egypt is unified

Beginning of the Early Minoan period

Cities built in India

Indo-European culture spreads

Egypt founds belief in immortality

Sumerians develop Creation and Flood myths

Polytheistic religion flourishes

4000–2500 B.C.E.   **Literature and Philosophy**

Cuneiform writing is invented

Pepi's papyrus, *Instructions to a Son*

4000–2500 B.C.E.   **Art and Music**

Age of Pyramids (c. 2650–2150)

The Great Sphinx at Giza

Harps and flutes played in Egypt

Statues from Abu temple, Tell Asmar

Tomb of Ti, Saqqara

2500–1500 B.C.E.   **Historical Context**

Akkadian and Babylonian Empires

Elamite Dynasty of Awan (c. 2500–2180)

Old and Middle Kingdoms in Egypt

Hsia Dynasty in China

Hyskos invasions

Aryan invasions

Mycenean culture begins

Expansion of trade

Hittites use horses, wheeled carts

Hittites institute monogamy

Patriarchy of Abraham

Semites settle Palestine

Mythical King Tangun founds Old Korea (2333)

Mathematics, medical science founded

2500–1500 B.C.E.   **Literature and Philosophy**

Book of the Dead, Egypt

Code of Hammurabi, Mesopotamia

Epic of Gilgamesh, Sumerian

Shih-ching, or *Book of Odes* (composed between 2205 and 600)

2500–1500 B.C.E.   **Art and Music**

Minoan frescoes

Palace of Knossos constructed on Crete

Snake goddess, Crete

Stele of Hammurabi

Tomb of Tutankhamen

Ziggurat of Ur

Stonehenge, England

Chinese music employs five-tone scale

Painted pottery produced by Chinese

1500–1000 B.C.E.   **Historical Context**

Iron Age begins

New Kingdom in Egypt (1575–1200)

Traditional date for sack of Troy (c. 1184)

Akhnaten introduces monotheism: Eighteenth Dynasty

Destruction of Palace of Knossos

Hebrews emphasize patriarchy

Hebrew Exodus, Moses and the Covenant

Early Assyrian Empire

Fall of Hittites

Babylon defeats the Elamites (1128–1105)

Growth of influence of the Egyptian priesthood

The flourishing of the Levantine trading states

Egypt invaded by the Sea Peoples

Beginning of Greek "Dark Age" (1100–800)

1500–1000 B.C.E.   Literature and Philosophy

Writing of early books of the Bible

Phoenicians develop alphabet

I Ching, or *Book of Changes*, ascribed to Wên Wang (c. 1200)

1500–1000 B.C.E.   Art and Music

Temple of Karnak built in Egypt

Reliefs from Nineveh and Nimrud

Hera from Samos

1000–600 B.C.E.   Historical Context

Sargon II founds Khorsabad

Hebrew kingdoms of David and Solomon

The age of the Hebrew Prophets

Early Greek "tyrants"

Phoenicians found Carthage (814)

Traditional date for the founding of Rome (753)

Jimmu, first Japanese monarch (legendary), begins rule (660)

Hinduism: challenges to Brahmanism by ascetic groups

First Olympic Games in honor of Zeus

Founding of the Greek *polis*

Beginning of the Vedic period

Fall of Assyria

Fall of Israel

Assyrian water clock invented

Zoroaster, founder of the Persian religion (630–553)

1000–600 B.C.E.   Literature and Philosophy

Homer and the Greek epics: the *Iliad* and the *Odyssey*

Hesiod, *Works and Days; Theogony*

Beginnings of lyric poetry in Greece: Archilochus

Earliest Chinese poem: *Book of Songs*

1000–600 B.C.E.   Art and Music

First Doric columns

Building of the Assyrian Palaces

Seven-string lyre in use

Chinese brush and ink painting

Gold vessels, jewelry made in Northern Europe

600–400 B.C.E.   **Historical Context**

Rise of the Persian Empire

Solon of Athens (640–560)

Nedbuchadnezzar II of Babylon (605–562)

Babylonian Captivity of the Jews (586)

Persian conquests of Babylon and Egypt

Founding of the Roman Republic

Cyrus the Great's Rule (553–529)

Cambyses' rule (529–522)

Militarized society founded in Sparta under code of Lycurgus

Vedic period ends

Darius I's rule (522–485)

Persian Wars (499–479)

Rise of Etruscan culture

Greek expansion under Pericles (498–427)

Peloponnesian War (431–404)

Teachings of Buddha and Confucius

Zoroastrianism in Persia

Medical advances of Hippocrates

Life of Socrates

Teachings of Lao-tzu: Taoism (400–300)

600–400 B.C.E.   **Literature and Philosophy**

Birth of Greek tragedy

Aesop's *Fables* (c. 620–560)

Lao-tzu, *Tao-te Ching* (c. 600)

Birth of Greek comedy

Herodotus, *History of the Persian Wars*

Thucydides, *History of the Peloponnesian War*

Poetry of Sappho of Lesbos

Analects, books of Confucius's sayings (fifth to fourth century)

Sophocles, *Antigone* (c. 450)

Hippocrates, *Aphorisms* (c. 415)

Euripides, *The Bacchae* (408)

600–400 B.C.E. **Art and Music**

Pindar, Greek musician and poet (520–447)

Hanging Gardens of Babylon constructed

Classical Greek pottery flourishes

Theater of Dionysus in Athens (493)

Building of the Parthenon (447–432)

400–200 B.C.E. **Historical Context**

Philip of Macedon

Plato (427–347) becomes student of Socrates

Alexander the Great (356–323)

Aetolian and Achaean Leagues

Fall of the Persian Empire

First Illyrian War

Italy unified under Roman conquest (272)

First Punic War (264–241)

Second Punic War (219–201)

Rise of the Mauryan Dynasty in India

End of Chavin Civilization in Latin America

Rise of Ch'in Dynasty, East Asia

400–200 B.C.E. **Literature and Philosophy**

Bhagavad Gita (c. 500–200)

Plato, *Dialogues* (399–347)

Mahabharata, Indian epic, begun

Aristotle (384–322), *The Rhetoric; Constitution of Athens: The Poetics* (335–322)

Writings of Mencius (372–?), defender of Confucianism, named the Second Holy One

Xenophon, *Anabasis* (371)

Ch'ü Yüan, Chinese poet (343–277)

Greek new comedy: Menander, Philemon

Plautus, found of Roman Comedy, *Amphitryon*

Stoicism (Zeno, Epicurus)

Cynic School (Diogenes, Antisthenes)

Cyrenaic School (hedonists)

Appolonius of Rhodes, *Argonautica* (c. 295–215)

The Laws of Manu, sacred Buddhist text (c. 200)

400–200 B.C.E.   Art and Music

Early Hellenistic art

Praxiteles, Greek sculptor (400–330)

Etruscan actors give first theatrical performance in Rome (365)

Corinthian columns appear (c. 350)

Aristotle's musical theory (340)

Sun Temple at Teotihuacan, Mexico (300)

Completion of Colossus of Rhodes (c. 275)

Great Wall of China built (215)

200–1 B.C.E.   Historical Context

Mauryan decline; rise of Shunga Dynasty (185–30)

Revolt of the Maccabees (167)

Third Punic War (149–146)

Greece comes under control of Rome (147)

Rome conquers North Africa

Destruction of Carthage (146)

Age of Wu Ti, East Asia

Nok civilization at height in Africa

Reforms of the Gracchi

Spartacus's slave revolt (71)

Caesar's dictatorship in Rome (46–44)

Augustus begins reign (27)

Marius and Sulla

Forming of Triumvirates

Kushan Invasion, South Asia

Cleopatra VII, Egypt's last queen

200–1 B.C.E.   Literature and Philosophy

Terence, Roman playwright, *Andria* (167)

Catullus, Rome poet (87–54)

Lucretius, *De rerum natura* (60)

Cicero, *De oratore* (55)

Horace, *Satires* (35–29)

Vergil, *Aeneid* (29–19)

Livy, Titus, Roman historian

200–1 B.C.E.   Art and Music

Venus of Milo, sculpture (140)

Victory (Nike) of Samothrace

Vitruvius, *De architectura* (90)

Laocoön, marble sculpture (38)

1–200 C.E.   Historical Context

Age of Augustus (30 B.C.E.–14 C.E.)

Birth of Christ

Conquest of Britain (43–51)

Roman Empire reaches its greatest extent

Nero's persecution of the Christians (64)

Sack of Jerusalem (70)

Indian envoy to Emperor Trajan of Rome (100)

Decline of Kushans, South Asia

Rise of Christianity

Bar-Kokba Rebellion of the Hebrew leader against Rome under Hadrian (132–135)

1–200 C.E.   Literature and Philosophy

Seneca, Roman dramatist and philosopher (4 B.C.E.–65 C.E.)

Ovid, *Metamorphoses* (5)

Julius Caesar, *Commentaries on the Civil War* (45)

Petronius, *Satyricon* (c. 100)

Juvenal, *Satires* (c. 100)

Tacitus, *Historiae* (117)

Apuleius, *The Golden Ass* (c. 155)

Marcus Aurelius, *Meditations* (c. 170–180)

1–200 C.E.   Art and Music

Roman Pantheon built (118–125)

Oldest Mayan monuments (c. 164)

Colosseum, Rome

Column of Trajan, Rome

200–400 C.E.   Historical Context

Neoplatonism, led by Plotinus (205–270)

Period of disorder in Roman Empire (235–284)

Reign of Constantine: Christianity becomes state religion

Diocletian's reforms (285–305)

Constantinople becomes new seat of Roman Empire (331)

Theodosius (379–395)

Monastic orders begin

Fall of Han Dynasty

Rise of Mayan culture

Christianity brought to Ethiopia

Rise of Gupta rule in South Asia

200–400 C.E. Literature and Philosophy

Replacement of scrolls by books begins

Kalidasa, *Sakuntala,* Sanskrit drama (220)

Avesta, Zoroastrian holy text (c. 300–400)

Saint Augustine, *The Confessions* (397–401)

200–400 C.E. Art and Music

Baths of Caracalla built (212–217)

Church of Saint Peter's built in Rome (325)

Saint Ambrose introduces the singing of hymns (386)

400–600 C.E. Historical Context

Decline of western Roman Empire

Alaric's sack of Rome (410)

Pope Leo I (440–461)

Founding of Venice (452)

Germanic invasions

Rise of Attila the Hun

Collapse of Gupta Rule

Silk monopoly maintained by Byzantine Empire

Vandals sack Rome (455)

End of first schism; Western and Eastern Churches reconcile (484)

Mayan urban civilization flourishes in southern Mexico

Corpus juris civilis founded

Emperor Wu-ti embraces Buddhism, brings the religion to central China (517)

Age of Justinian the Great, Byzantine Emperor (527–565)

Death of the legendary King Arthur (537)

Outbreaks of plague (542–594)

Spread of Buddhism into Japan (552)

Czechs settle in Bohemia

Beginning of alchemy, search for the Philosopher's Stone

400–600 C.E.   Literature and Philosophy

Proclus, chief representative of later Neo-Platonism (410–485)

St. Augustine, *The City of God* (411)

Cassiodorus, Roman scholar (490–583)

Aryabhata, Hindu astronomer and mathematician, compiles his manual of astronomy (517)

Priscian, *Institutiones grammaticae* (520)

Boethius, Roman scholar, *The Consolation of Philosophy* (c. 523)

400–600 C.E.   Art and Music

Boethius introduces Greek system of musical notation to Western music (521)

Sophia Basilica, Constantinople, completed (537)

Golden Era of Byzantine art (c. 550)

600–800 C.E.   Historical Context

Muhammad's Vision (610); rise of Islam

Muslims go to Ghana and Sudan

Early Abbasids

Roots of Sunni-Shi'ite division

T'ang Dynasty in East Asia

Muslims manufacture paper

Free Byzantine peasantry established

End of barbarian invasions in Western Europe

Flowering of Korean civilization

Buddhism becomes state religion in Tibet (632)

Arabs attack North Africa (670)

Clovis III becomes king of united Franks (691)

Muslims defeated at Poitiers, ending their westward advance (732)

Water wheels drive mills throughout Europe

Saint Boniface, Benedictine monk, foe of heathen Germanic beliefs

Iconoclastic Controversy divides Byzantine Church

600–800 C.E.   Literature and Philosophy

Bana, Hindu poet, *Kadambari, Harsacarita* (600–650)

Printing of books in China

Lyric poetry of T'ang Dynasty promotes Chinese language

Muhammad, the Koran (c. 660)

Li Po, Chinese poet (701–762)

Tu Fu, Chinese poet (713–770)

The Book of Kells, Latin gospels in Irish (760)

600–800 C.E.   Art and Music

Classic Buddha figures produced in Bihar, northern India

Production of Chinese porcelain (620)

Pueblo period in southwestern North America

Stone churches replace wooden structures in England (700)

Gregorian liturgical music in Europe (750)

Earliest Japanese prints (779)

800–1000 C.E.   Historical Context

Empire of Charlemagne, crowned First Holy Roman Emperor by Pope Leo III (800)

Birth of feudal social structure

Commercial expansion of the Muslim world

Decline of Byzantine peasant class

Unification of England by Anglo-Saxons

Period of Viking invasions

City of Machu Picchu, Peru (800)

Decline of the Mayan Empire: Last Mayan inscriptions (879)

Rise of the Sung Dynasty

Slavic tribes migrate into territories around the Oder

Iconoclastic Debate continues in Eastern Empire

Magyars carry out raids in Germany, Italy

Fatimid Dynasty in North Africa

Hugh Capet, King of France (987–996)

Poles converted to Christianity under first ruler, Mieczyslaw I

800–1000 C.E.   Literature and Philosophy

Lady Ise, Japanese lyric poet (877–940)

The Anglo-Saxon Chronicle (c. 891–924)

The Thousand and One Nights, Arabian tales (begun 900)

Roswitha of Gandersheim, German nun, playwright (935–c. 1000)

Great Master Kyunyô, Korea, Eleven Devotional Poems (965–967)

Murasaki Shikibu, The Tale of Genji (c. 1000)

Beowulf, heroic poem in Old English (1000)

Firdawsi, Persian poet, *Shâh Nâma* (c. 1000)

Al-Mutanabbi, master poet of Abbasid period in Islam (c. tenth century)

Abū Al-Kindi, Arabian philosopher (c. ninth century)

al-Fārābi, Muslim philosopher (c. tenth century)

800–1000 C.E.   Art and Music

Poetry sung to musical accompaniment, court of Charlemagne (800)

Chandi Loro Jonggrang, Prambanam, Java constructed (c. 800)

1000–1200 C.E.   Historical Context

Rise of feudal society

Norman Conquest (1066)

Seljuk Turks defeat Byzantines (1071)

The Crusades (First Crusade, 1095)

Revival of cities

Birth of Genghis Khan, founder of Mongol Empire (1155)

Schism between Byzantine and Roman Churches

Thomas à Becket murdered at Canterbury (1170)

Guild System established

Kamakura Shogunate in East Asia

Spiritual center of Judaism moves to Spain

Climax of Mayan culture in Yucatan

First universities founded; rise of scholasticism

Decline in the social position of women

China perfects the use of gunpowder

Widespread fear of Apocalypse, Last Judgment

1000–1200 C.E.   Literature and Philosophy

Avicenna, Arabian philosopher, physician (980–1037)

Sun Tung Po, Chinese poet (1036–1101)

The Mabinogion, Welsh tales (1050)

Peter Abelard, French philosopher, theologian (1079–1142)

Song of Roland, French heroic poem (1100)

First miracle play recorded, Dunstable, England (1110)

The Rubaiyat, Omar Khayyam, Persian poet, scientist (d. 1123)

Averroes, Arabian scholar, philosopher (b. 1126)

Poema del Cid, Spanish heroic poem (c. 1140)

Chrétien de Troyes, court poet of France (1144–1190)

Wolfram von Eschenbach, German poet (1172–1220)

The Nibelungenlied (1191–1204)

The Njal Saga, Icelandic saga (c. 1300)

1000–1200 C.E. Art and Music

Kuo Hsi, Chinese painter (1020–c. 1090)

Polyphonic singing replaces Gregorian Chant (1050)

Marcabru, Provençal troubadour (1137–1150)

Bertrand de Born, English troubadour (1140–1215)

Building of Angkor Wat (1150)

Hsia Kuei, Chinese painter (1180–1230)

Ma Yüan, Chinese painter (1190–1224)

Construction of Chartres Cathedral begun (1194)

1200–1400 C.E. Historical Context

Early population growth, later decimated by famine, Black Death

Later Crusades

Rise of Mali Empire, Kliwa (c. 1200–1450)

Islam begins to replace Indian religions (1200)

New techniques in warfare: longbow and crossbow

Latin Empire in Constantinople (1204)

Founding of Delhi Sultanate (1206)

Madjapahit kingdom dominant in Malaysia

Opening of European embassy in China

Reign of Saint Louis (1214–1270)

Magna Carta (1215)

Period of Hōjō rule in Japan (1219–1333)

Mongol invasions of Russia (1223), China (1211–1215), Japan (1274)

Travels of Marco Polo (1254–1324)

Founding of the Sorbonne in Paris (1254)

End of the Crusades (1291)

Height of Swahili (east African) city-states (c. 1300–1500)

"Babylonian Captivity" of papacy (1309–1376)

Ashikaga Period in Japan (1336–1568)

Hundred Years' War begins (1337–1453)

Founding of Yuan Dynasty

Rise of the Aztecs

Siamese invasion of Cambodia, collapse of Khmer Empire (1350–1460)

Rise of the Ottoman Turks

Great Interregnum

Inquisition

Founding of Li Dynasty in Korea (1392)

1200–1400 C.E.   Literature and Philosophy

Wang Shih-fu, *Hsi Hsiang Chi*, Chinese play (c. 1200)

Wolfram von Eschenbach, *Parzival* (1203)

Gottfried von Strassburg, *Tristan* (1210)

Roger Bacon, English philosopher, scientist (1214–1294)

Sonnet form developed in Italian poetry (1221)

Sumer is icumen in, probably earliest English round (1225)

The Romance of the Rose, Guillaume de Lorris; continued by Jean de Meun (1227)

Sa'di, *The Gulistān*, Arabian tales (c. 1240)

Kuan Han-ch'ing, "father of Chinese drama" (c. 1245–c. 1322)

Summa theologica (1273), Thomas Aquinas, theologian, philosopher (1225–1274)

Moses de Leon, *Zohar*, foundation of Jewish mysticism (1275)

Dante Alighieri, *La Vita Nuova* (1290); *The Divine Comedy* (1307)

Le Jeu D'Adam, anonymous, miracle play (c. 1300)

Hafiz, Persian poet (1300–1388)

Beginnings of *renga* poetry in Japan (c. 1300)

Tale of the Heike, anonymous, Japanese prose narrative (1310)

Liu Chi, Chinese poet (1311–1375)

Giovanni Boccaccio, *The Decameron* (1353)

The Elder Edda (late thirteenth century)

Development of Japanese Nō drama

Fang Hsiao-Ju, Chinese scholar (1357–1402)

Petrarch, *Canzonieri* (1366)

Geoffrey Chaucer, *The Canterbury Tales* (1387–1400)

1200–1400 C.E.   Art and Music

Gothic period

Jesters first appear in European courts (1202)

Tannhauser, German poet, Minnesinger (1205–1270)

Great Amida Buddha, bronze sculpture, Kamakura period in Japan (1253)

Giotto, Italian painter (1266–1337)

Appearance of *jongleurs*, professional musical entertainers, France (1300)

"Bards" flourish in Ireland

Kumano Mandala, hanging scroll, Japan (c. 1300)

Building of Aztec capital, Tenochtitlan (c. 1325)

Mastersinger movement, Germany (1350)

Guillaume de Machaut, *Mass for Four Voices* (1364)

1400–1600 C.E.   Historical Context

Renaissance in Europe

Jan Hus (1415), Joan of Arc (1431), burned at stake

Torquemada, Grand Inquisitor (1420–1498)

Gutenberg invents the printing press (1450)

Savonarola, Italian religious reformer (1452–1498)

Hundred Years' War ends (1453)

Constantinople falls to the Ottoman Turks (1453)

Voyages of discovery to the New World

Expeditions of Cheng Ho

Wars of the Roses (1455, beginning)

Unification of Japan by Hideyoshi

Birth of Guru Nanak, founder of Sikhism (1469)

Decline of Mali

Nicolaus Copernicus's new astronomy (1473–1543)

Rise of Incas, followed by wars of the conquistadors against Aztecs and Incas

Martin Luther begins the Protestant Reformation (1517)

Haussa Confederation, led by Kebbi, dominant power east of the Niger in Africa (1517)

Reign of Suleiman the Great (1520–1566)

The sack of Rome (1527)

The Council of Trent (1545–1564)

Rise of Muscovy

Age of Akbar, Mogul Emperor of India (1556–1605)

The Battle of Lepanto (1571)

Spain unified

Recovery of the French monarchy

Tudor Dynasty in England

Empire of Kanem at height in Africa (1571–1603)

Massacre of French Protestants (1572)

Akbar's conquest of Gujarat gives him access to the sea (1572)

Revolution in warfare: cannon and muskets

Defeat of the Spanish Armada (1588)

Under Hideyoshi, Japan invades Korea, is rebuffed by Chinese (1592–1597)
Persians defeat Uzbeks (1597)

1400–1600 C.E.   Literature and Philosophy

Shih Nai-an, *Shui Hu Chuan* (c. 1400)

Yü Chiao Li, Chinese novel, anonymous (c. 1400)

Nesimi, Turkish poet (c. 1400)

François Villon, French poet (1431–?)

Pico de Mirandola, Italian humanist (1463–1494)

Thomas More, English statesman, humanist (1478–1535)

Marguerite de Navarre, French author (1492–1549)

Erh Tou Mei, or *Twice Flowering Plum Trees,* anonymous (c. 1500–1600)

Fuzūli, Turkish poet (c. 1500)

Hwang Chini, Korean woman poet (1506–1544)

Garcia Rodriguez de Montalvo, *Amadis de Gaula* (1508)

Desiderius Erasmus, Dutch humanist, *The Praise of Folly* (1509)

Everyman, anonymous, English morality play (1510)

Niccolò Machiavelli, Italian politician, playwright, *The Prince* (1513)

Ch'in P'ing Mei, Chinese novel, attributed to Wang Shih-chêng (1526–1593)

Baldassare Castiglione, *The Book of the Courtier* (1527)

François Rabelais, *Gargantua* and *Pantagruel* (1532–1564)

Tulsi Das, Hindu poet (1532–1623)

Michel de Montaigne, French essayist (1533–1592)

Miguel de Cervantes, Spanish novelist (1547–1616)

Lazarillo de Tormes, anonymous (1554)

Lope de Vega, Spanish dramatist (1562–1635)

John Donne, English metaphysical poet (1572–1631)

Li Shih-Chên, *Materia Medica* (1578)

Galileo, *De Motu,* on the behavior of falling bodies (1590)

Sir Philip Sidney, *The Defense of Poesie* (posthumous, 1595)

1400–1600 C.E.   Art and Music

Jan van Eyck, Dutch painter (c. 1390–1441)

Masaccio, Italian painter (1401–1428)

Donatello, Italian sculptor of *David* (1408), *Saint John* (1408)

Fillippo Brunelleschi, *Rules of Perspective* (1412)

Great Temple of the Dragon completed, Peking (1420)

Florence Cathedral completed (1434)

Sandro Botticelli, Italian painter (1444–1510)

Josquin des Prés, Dutch composer (1450–1521)

Hieronymus Bosch, Dutch painter (1450–1516)

Leonardo da Vinci, Italian painter, sculptor, inventor (1452–1519)

Albrecht Dürer, German artist (1471–1528)

Michelangelo, Italian sculptor, painter, architect, poet (1475–1564)

Titian, Italian painter (1477–1510)

Ch'en Shun, Chinese painter (1483–1544)

Alberti, *De re aedificatoria* (1485)

Ballet first presented at Italian courts (1490)

Benvenuto Cellini, Italian goldsmith, sculptor (1500–1571)

Jacopo Tintoretto, Italian painter (1518–1594)

Pieter Brueghel the Elder, Dutch painter (1520–1569)

Beginnings of kabuki theater in Japan

Ch'iu Ying, Chinese painter (1522–1560)

Palestrina, Italian composer (1525–1594)

Puppet theater combined with narration in Japan (1596–1614)

Cathedral of Saint Basil, Moscow, built (1554–1560)

1600–1715 C.E.   Historical Context

Decline of European aristocracy

Giordano Bruno burned at stake in Rome for heresy (1600)

Founding of Tokugawa family Shogunate in Japan (1603)

Death of Akbar (1605)

Guy Fawkes's Gunpowder Plot (1605)

Galileo discovers Jupiter's moons (1609)

Stuart dynasty

Richelieu's France

Tobacco planted in Virginia (1612)

Peak of Safavid culture, Middle East

Japan's expulsion of Westerners

Religious wars: Thirty Years' War in Germany (1618–1648)

The founding of the French Academy (1634)

English Civil War (1642–1646)

Dutch settle in western Africa

Beginning of African slave trade to North America

Glorious Revolution in England (1688): constitutional monarchy

Fall of Ming Dynasty, replaced by Manchu Dynasty (1644)

Jamestown, Quebec colonized

Ali Bey declares himself bey of Tunis (1650)

Salem witch trials (1692)

Age of Louis XIV in France

Growth of literacy

War of the Spanish Succession (1701–1713)

Chūshingura Incident, Japan (1703)

Peter the Great lays foundations of Petersburg (1703)

Hussein ibn Ali founds Husseinite dynasty in Tunis (1705)

Advances in astronomy by Kepler, Brahe

Beginning of Sikh militancy (1708)

1600–1715 C.E. Literature and Philosophy

Shakespeare's *Hamlet* (1600); *The Tempest* (1611)

Hung Lou Mêng, or *The Dream of the Red Chamber,* anonymous (c. late 1600s)

Chin Ku Ch'i Kuan, or *Marvellous Tales, Ancient and Modern,* anonymous (c. 1600s)

P'u Sung-Ling, *Liao Chai Chih I,* or *Strange Stories* (c. 1600s)

Cervantes, *Don Quixote,* Part I published (1605)

Pierre Corneille, French dramatist (1606–1684)

Francis Bacon, *Novum Organum* (1620)

Francisco Gomez de Quevedo, *Los Suenos* (1627)

Baruch Spinoza, Dutch philosopher (1632–1677)

Pedro Calderon de la Barca, *Life Is a Dream* (1636)

René Descartes, *Discourse on Method* (1637)

Bashô, poet of Japanese haiku (1644–1694)

Anne Bradstreet, *The Tenth Muse Lately Sprung Up in America* (1650)

Thomas Hobbes, *Leviathan* (1651)

Molière, *Tartuffe* (1664)

La Rochfoucauld, *The Maxims* (1665)

Racine, *Andromaque* (1667)

John Milton, *Paradise Lost* (1667–1674)

Wali, Urdu poet (1668–1744)

Blaise Pascal, *Pensées* (1670)

Chikamatsu Monzaemon, Japan's foremost kabuki playwright (flourished in 1670s)

John Bunyan, *Pilgrim's Progress* (1675)

Newtonian physics: *Principia Mathematica* (1687)

John Locke, *An Essay on Toleration* (1689)

1600–1715 C.E. Art and Music

Baroque period

Ninsei, Japanese potter (1596–1660)

Kano Tannyu, Japanese artist (1602–1674)

Founding of Globe Theater

Claudio Monteverdi, *Orfeo*, opera (1607)

El Greco, Rubens, Van Dyck, Velasquez, Rembrandt dominate painting

Building of Taj Mahal (1628–1650)

Molière founds *Illustre Théatre* in Paris (1643)

Ogata Korin, Japanese artist (1658–1716)

Building of Versailles Palace (begun 1662)

Birth of Italian commedia dell'arte companies (1670)

Hua Yen, Chinese painter (1682–c. 1762)

1715–1750 C.E. Historical Context

First phase of Industrial Revolution

Reign of Louis XV: "Ancien Regime" in France (1715–1774)

Peter the Great's modernization efforts in Russia

British military campaign against India

South Sea Bubble (1720)

War of the Polish Succession (1733)

English repeal of witchcraft laws (1736)

Safavid Dynasty ends

Nadir Shah reigns in Iran (1736–1747)

War of the Austrian Succession (1740–1748)

Reign of Frederick the Great (1740–1786)

China invades Tibet (1751)

Lisbon earthquake kills 30,000 people (1755)

Walpole's Ministry in England

Hapsburg-Bourbon Alliance

Voltaire joins court of Frederick the Great

1715–1750 C.E. Literature and Philosophy

Age of Enlightenment

Founding of literary salons

Takedo Izumo, kabuki playwright (1691–1756)

Daniel Defoe, *Robinson Crusoe* (1719)

Khwāja Mir Dard, Sufi poet (1720–1784)

Mir Taqi Mir, Urdu poet (1724–1808)

Jonathan Swift, *Gulliver's Travels* (1726)

Samuel Richardson, *Pamela* (1740); *Clarissa* (1748)

David Hume, *An Enquiry Concerning Human Understanding* (1748)

Henry Fielding, *Tom Jones* (1749)

Thomas Gray, *Elegy Written in a Country Churchyard* (1750)

Denis Diderot, *Encyclopedia* (1751–1772)

Phyllis Wheatley, *Poems on Various Subjects* (1773)

Immanuel Kant, *Critique of Pure Reason* (1781)

1715–1750 C.E.   Art and Music

Rococo style: Watteau, Boucher, Fragonard

Hogarth, Gainsborough, Reynolds dominate English art

Johann Sebastian Bach, German composer (1685–1750)

Suzuki Harunobu, Japanese painter (1718–1770)

Covent Garden Opera House, London, opened (1732)

Maruyama Okyo, Japanese artist (1733–1795)

Handel's *Messiah* (1742)

Kitagawa Utamaro, Japanese painter (1753–1806)

Wolfgang Amadeus Mozart, Austrian composer (1756–1791)

The Modern World

1750–1815 C.E.   Historical Context

Seven Years' War (1756–1763)

American Revolution (1775–1783)

Rice Riots in Edo, Japan (1787)

Russo-Turkish War (1787–1792)

Establishment of first penal colonies in Australia (1788)

French Revolution (1789)

Haitian War of Independence (1791–1804)

China invades Nepal (1792)

First French Republic established (1792)

Reign of Terror in France (1793–1794)

Invention of the telegraph (1794)

Irish Rebellion (1798)

Napoléon Bonaparte's coup (1799)

"Black War" between settlers and Aborigines in Australia (1799)

Qajar Dynasty in Middle East

British occupation of Ceylon, Cape Colony

Napoleonic Code established (1804)

Holy Roman Empire ends (1806)

British abolition of the slave trade (1807)

Peninsular War in Spain (1808)

War of 1812; Battle of New Orleans

French abolition of the slave trade (1815)

Ecuador and Paraguay free from Spanish rule

1750–1815 C.E.   Literature and Philosophy

Early romanticism

Ts'ao Hsüeh-ch'in, *The Dream of the Red Chamber* (c. 1755)

Voltaire, *Candide* (1759)

Immanuel Kant, *Critique of Practical Reason* (1788)

William Blake, *Songs of Innocence* (1789); *Songs of Experience* (1794)

Marquis de Sade, *Justine* (1791)

James Boswell, *The Life of Samuel Johnson, LL.D.* (1791)

Mary Wollstonecraft, *Vindication of the Rights of Women* (1792)

Thomas Paine, *The Age of Reason* (1794–1796)

Friedrich Hölderlin, *Hyperion* (1797–1799)

William Wordsworth, *Tintern Abbey* (1798)

Samuel Taylor Coleridge, *The Rime of the Ancient Mariner* (1798)

Novalis, *Heinrich von Ofterdingen* (1799); *Hymns to the Night* (1800)

Maria Edgeworth, *Castle Rackrent* (1800)

Georg Hegel, *Phenomenologie des Geistes* (1807)

Goethe, *Faust,* Part I (1808)

Heinrich von Kleist, *Michael Kohlhaas* (1810)

Lord Byron, *Childe Harold's Pilgrimage* (1812–1818)

Jane Austen, *Pride and Prejudice* (1813)

Sir Walter Scott, *Waverly* (1814)

1750–1815 C.E.   Art and Music

Early romanticism

Neoclassical revival

Painters: David, Goya, Turner, Gericault

Katsushika Hokusai, Japanese painter (1760–1849)

Mozart, *Don Giovanni* (1787)

The waltz fashionable in England (1791)

The Louvre becomes national art gallery (1793)

Ludwig von Beethoven, *Symphony No. 1 in C Major* (1799–1800)

1815–1840 C.E.   Historical Context

Napoléon defeated at Battle of Waterloo (1815)

Spread of industrialization to European Continent

Egyptian forces conquer the Sudan (1820–1822)

Greek War of Independence (1821–1829)

Liberia established (1822)

First locomotive (1825)

Decembrist Revolt put down in Russia (1825)

Slavery abolished in Mexico (1829)

Age of Metternich

1830 Revolution in Paris

Nat Turner's Rebellion (1830)

1832 Reform Bill

Spanish Inquisition officially ended (1834)

Bengali Renaissance

Independence for Mexico and Brazil

Zulu expansion, South Africa

Simon Bolivar's campaigns

First Opium War between Britain and China (1839–1842)

1815–1840 C.E.   Literature and Philosophy

John Keats, *Endymion* (1818)

Sir Walter Scott, *Rob Roy* (1818); *Ivanhoe* (1820)

Arthur Schopenhauer, *Die Welt als Wille und Vorstellung* (1819)

Shelley, *Prometheus Unbound* (1820)

Pushkin, *Eugene Onegin* (1822–1832)

Alessandro Manzoni, *I promessi sposi* (1825)

Honoré de Balzac begins his *La Comédie humaine* (1830)

Stendhal, *Le Rouge et le Noir* (1830)

Victor Hugo, *Notre Dame de Paris* (1831)

Alfred Tennyson, *The Lady of Shalott* (1833)

George Sand, *Lélia* (1833)

Adam Mickiewicz, *Pan Tadeusz* (1834)

George Büchner, *Dantons Tod* (1835)

Thomas Carlyle, *Sartor Resartus* (1836)

Edgar Allan Poe, *The Fall of the House of Usher* (1839)

Mikhail Lermontov, *A Hero of Our Times* (1840)

Charles Dickens, *Bleak House* (1852)

1815–1840 C.E. Art and Music

Painters: Delacroix, Ingres, Constable, Ando Hiroshige

Nigerian Yoruba sculptures discovered at Benin (c. early 1800s)

Prado Musem, Madrid, founded (1818)

Ludwig von Beethoven, *Ninth Symphony* (1824)

Beginning of realist landscape painting in Germany

Frédéric Chopin, *Twelve Etudes, Op. 10* (1833)

Nelson's Column erected in London (1840)

1840–1870 C.E. Historical Context

Karl Marx and Friedrich Engels, *The Communist Manifesto* (1848)

Abolition of slavery in the French Caribbean (1848)

Resignation of Metternich (1848)

Golden Age of British capitalism (1850–1873)

Crimean War (1853–1856)

Perry's mission to Japan (1854)

Indian mutiny against British rule (1857–1858)

Charles Darwin, *On the Origin of Species by Means of Natural Selection* (1859)

Meiji Restoration in Japan

Building of the Suez Canal (1859–1869)

American Civil War, abolition of slavery (1860–1864)

Russia emancipates the serfs (1861)

Austro-Prussian War (1866)

Foundation of the independent Dominion of Canada (1867)

Suffrage extended in Great Britain (1867)

End of transportation of convicts to Australia (1868)

Franco-Prussian War (1870–1871)

Unification of Germany (1871)

Napoléon III: Second French Empire

1840–1870 C.E. Literature and Philosophy

Nikolai Gogol, *Dead Souls* (1842)

Giacomo Leopardi, *Canti* (1845)

Charlotte Brontë, *Jane Eyre* (1847)

Emily Brontë, *Wuthering Heights* (1847)

Emily Dickinson begins to write her poetry (1850–1855)

Herman Melville, *Moby Dick* (1851)

Ivan Turgenev, *A Sportsman's Sketches* (1852)

Harriet Beecher Stowe, *Uncle Tom's Cabin* (1852)

Henry David Thoreau, *Walden, or Life in the Woods* (1854)

Walt Whitman, *Leaves of Grass* (1855)

Gustave Flaubert, *Madame Bovary* (1856–1857)

Anthony Trollope, *Barchester Towers* (1857)

Charles Baudelaire, *Les Fleurs du Mal* (1857)

Victor Hugo, *Les Misérables* (1862)

John Stuart Mill, *Utilitarianism* (1863)

Leo Tolstoy, *War and Peace* (1864–1869)

Fyodor Dostoyevsky, *Crime and Punishment* (1866)

Louisa May Alcott, *Little Women* (1868)

1840–1870 C.E.   Art and Music

Neo-Gothic style in architecture

Painters: Courbet, Whistler, Manet, Degas

Richard Wagner, *Der Ring des Nibelungen* (1847–1853); *Tristan und Isolde* (1865)

Jean François Millet, *The Sower* (1850)

Guiseppe Verdi, *Il Trovatore, La Traviata* performed in Venice (1853)

Haussmann begins reconstruction of Paris (1853)

Gounod's opera *Faust*, performed in Paris (1859)

Wagner's opera *Tannhäuser* creates scandal in Paris (1861)

1870–1900 C.E.   Historical Context

Worldwide economic depression

Second phase of the Industrial Revolution

Age of Bismarck (1862–1890)

Third Republic in France (1870–1940)

Paris Commune (1871)

Invention of the telephone (1876), lightbulb (1880)

First nationalist movement in Egypt, led by Ahmed Arabi (1881)

Boulanger Crisis (1887)

Dreyfus Affair (1894)

War between China and Japan (1894–1895)
Spanish-American War (1898)
Boer War (1899–1902)
Shintoism reinstated in Japan (1990)
Feudalism ends in Japan
Populism and Nihilism influential in Russia
Socialist parties formed
Imperialism at its peak
Exploration, colonization of Africa

1870–1900 C.E.   Literature and Philosophy

Charles Darwin, *Origin of Species* (1859); *The Descent of Man* (1871)
George Eliot (Mary Ann Evans), *Middlemarch* (1871); *Daniel Deronda* (1874)
Émile Zola, *Les Rougon-Macquart* series (1871–1893)
Friedrich Nietzsche, *The Birth of Tragedy* from the *Spirit of Music* (1872)
Arthur Rimbaud, *Une saison en enfer* (1873)
Leo Tolstoy, *Anna Karenina* (1873)
Walter Pater, *The Renaissance* (1873)
Paul Verlaine, *Romances sans paroles* (1874)
Stéphane Mallarmé, *L'Après-midi d'un faune* (1876)
Thomas Hardy, *The Return of the Native* (1878)
Henrik Ibsen, *A Doll's House* (1879)
Fyodor Dostoyevsky, *The Brothers Karamazov* (1880)
Henry James, *Portrait of a Lady* (1881)
Friedrich Nietzsche, *Also Sprach Zarathustra* (1883)
Mark Twain, *Huckleberry Finn* (1884)
Karl Marx's *Das Kapital* published in English (1886)
Emilia Pardo Bazán, *Los Pazos de Ulloa* (1886)
Naturalism: Zola, Dreiser, Gorky, Hauptmann
Symbolism: Mallarmé, Verlaine, Huysmans, Maeterlinck
August Strindberg, *The Father* (1887)
Oscar Wilde, *The Picture of Dorian Gray* (1890)
Henryk Sienkiewicz, *Quo Vadis?* (1896)
Kate Chopin, *The Awakening* (1899)
Joseph Conrad, *Lord Jim* (1900)
Sigmund Freud, *The Interpretation of Dreams* (1900)
Joaquin María Machado de Assis, *Dom Casmurro* (1900)

1870–1900 C.E. Art and Music

Impressionisim: Cézanne, Renoir, Monet, Seurat, Pissarro, Whistler (*Nocturne in Black and Gold,* 1874)

Bedrich Smetana, *Ma Vlast,* symphonic poems (1874)

Auguste Rodin, *The Age of Bronze,* sculpture (1877)

Pyotr Ilyich Tchaikovsky, *Eugen Onegin,* opera (1879)

Cologne Cathedral completed (1248–1880)

Johannes Brahms, *Symphony No. 3 in F Major* (1884)

Expressionism: Van Gogh (*The Sunflowers,* 1888), Gauguin, Munch, Barlach, Ensor

Art Nouveau: Beardsley, Wilde, Gaudi; *Judenstil* (Germany): Klimt, van der Velde

Symbolism: Moreau, Redon, Rops

Gustave Mahler, *Symphony No. 1* (1891)

Toulouse-Lautrec's music hall posters first appear (1891)

Puccini's opera *La Bohème* performed in Turin (1896)

1900–1930 C.E. Historical Context

Boxer Rebellion in China (1900–1903)

Invention of the airplane (1903)

Japanese victory over Russia (1904–1905)

Albert Einstein's theory of relativity (1905)

Algeciras Conference gives France and Spain control over reforming of Morocco (1906)

Muslim League formed (1906)

Mexican Revolution (1910)

Fall of Manchu Dynasty in China (1911)

Marcus Garvey founds the black nationalist movement (1911)

Sinking of the *Titanic* (1912)

Sigmund Freud, *Totem and Taboo* (1913)

World War I (1914–1918)

Opening of the Panama Canal (1914)

C. G. Jung, *Psychology of the Unconscious* (1916)

Russian Revolution (1917)

British Empire's broadest extension

Creation of Germany's Weimar Republic

Early stages of Nazism, Fascism

Amritsar Massacre in India (1919)

Forming of League of Nations (1919)

Irish Free State (1922)

Gandhi initiates campaigns of passive resistance

Stock market crash (1929)

Suffragette movement

Increasing numbers of women in the work force

1900–1930 C.E. Literature and Philosophy

Rabindranath Tagore, Bengali poet (1861–1941)

Muhammed Iqbal, Indian poet, philosopher (1877–1938)

Premchand (pseudonym of Dhanpat Rai Srivastav), author of stories and novels in Urdu and Hindi (1880–1936)

Lu Hsun, Chinese literary theorist and short-story writer (1881–1936)

Thomas Mann, *Buddenbrooks* (1901); *Death in Venice* (1913); *The Magic Mountain* (1924)

Joseph Conrad, *Heart of Darkness* (1902)

André Gide, *The Immoralist* (1902); *The Counterfeiters* (1926); Nobel Prize (1947)

Maxim Gorky, *The Lower Depths* (1902)

Anton Chekhov, *Three Sisters* (1902)

George Bernard Shaw, *Man and Superman* (1903); Nobel Prize (1925)

Abbey Theatre founded in Dublin (1904)

Henry James, *The Golden Bowl* (1904)

Attila Jozef, Hungarian poet (1905–1937)

Henri Bergson, *L'Evolution créatrice* (1907); Nobel Prize (1927)

Jacques Roumain, Haitian novelist and poet (1907–1944)

Gertrude Stein, *Three Lives* (1908)

Andrey Bely, *Petersburg* (1913)

Guillaume Apollinaire, *Alcools* (1913)

Marcel Proust, *A la recherche du temps perdu* (1913–1927)

James Joyce, *Portrait of the Artist as a Young Man* (1916); *Ulysses* (1922)

Saratchandra Chatterji, *Srikanta* (1917–1933)

Shiga Naoya, *At Kinosaki* (1917)

Aleksander Blok, *The Twelve* (1918)

Tristan Tzara, *Dada Manifestos* (1918)

Willa Cather, *My Antonia* (1918)

William Butler Yeats, *The Wild Swans at Coole* (1919); Nobel Prize (1923)

Colette, *Chéri* (1920)

Sinclair Lewis, *Main Street* (1920); Nobel Prize (1930)

Paul Valéry, *Le Cimitière marin* (1920)

Edith Wharton, *The Age of Innocence* (1920)

D. H. Lawrence, *Women in Love* (1921)

Rainer Maria Rilke, *Sonnets to Orpheus* (1922); *Duino Elegies* (1923)

Italo Svevo, *La conscienza di Zeno* (1923)

André Breton, *First Surrealist Manifesto* (1924)

Virginia Woolf, *Mrs. Dalloway* (1925)

Franz Kafka, *The Trial* (1925)

F. Scott Fitzgerald, *The Great Gatsby* (1925)

Ezra Pound, *Cantos* (1925–1948)

Ernest Hemingway, *The Sun Also Rises* (1926); Nobel Prize (1954)

T. S. Eliot, *The Waste Land* (1927); *Ash Wednesday* (1930)

Hermann Hesse, *Steppenwolf* (1927); Nobel Prize (1946)

Margaret Radclyffe Hall, *The Well of Loneliness* (1928)

Bertolt Brecht, *The Three-Penny Opera* (1928)

William Faulkner, *The Sound and the Fury* (1929); Nobel Prize (1949)

Generation of '98 (Spain): Machado, Vallé-Inclan, Unamuno

Dadism: Tzara, Huelsenbeck, Ball

Surrealism: Breton, Char, Éluard, Desnos, Soupault

1900–1930 C.E.   Art and Music

Henri Matisse (1869–1954)

Picasso, *Les Demoiselles d'Avignon* (1907)

Opening of cabarets

Futurism: Marinetti, Boccioni, Balla

Cubism: Picasso, Léger, Gris, Braque

Der Blaue Reiter: Kandinsky, Marc

Dadism: Arp, Hannah Hoch

Surrealism: Ernst, Man Ray, Buñuel

Meta Warrick Fuller, *Ethiopia Awakening,* sculpture (1914)

Harlem Renaissance (1919–1932)

Constantin Brancusi, *Bird in Space* (1919)

Walter Gropius founds the Bauhaus in Weimar, Germany (1919)

Evolution of jazz: Scott Joplin, Jelly Roll Morton

Advent of cinema

Isadora Duncan rises to fame in dance

Sergei Diaghilev's *Ballet Russe*

Schoenberg, Stravinsky, Berg, Bartok revolutionize Western music

Les Six: Milhaud, Honegger, Poulenc, Auric, Durey, Tagliaferre

Georgia O'Keeffe, *Black Cross* (1929)

Revival of classical dance forms in India

1930–1960 C.E.   **Historical Context**

Great Depression

Gandhi's Salt March (1930)

Rise of Hitler, Mussolini

World War II, defeat of Fascism (1939–1945)

Destruction, rebuilding, remapping of Europe

United Nations created (1945)

Advent of the Nuclear Age: Hiroshima, Nagasaki (1945)

Shintoism abolished in Japan (1945)

Stalinist period, satellite states in Eastern Europe

Postcolonial period begins: independence for India, Pakistan, Ghana, Morocco, Tunisia

Peron Era in Argentina (1946–1955)

Gandhi assassinated (1948)

Apartheid introduced in South Africa (1948)

Israeli statehood (1948)

Berlin blockade and airlift (1948–1949)

China becomes Communist state (1949)

Korean War (1950–1953)

Eisenhower presidency (1953–1960)

Execution of the Rosenbergs (1953)

Nasser's Revolution in Egypt (1954)

French defeat in Indochina (1954)

The Untouchability (Offences) Act of 1955: official end to caste system discrimination in India

Polish, Hungarian uprisings (1956)

Forming of Common Market (1957)

Battle of Algiers (1957)

Fidel Castro overthrows Batista in Cuba (1959)

Congo gains independence, with Joseph Kassavubu as president, Patrice Lummumba as premier (1960)

The Cold War

Institution of complex intelligence networks: CIA, KGB

McCarthyism in U.S.: Era of the Blacklist

Space Race, Sputnik

Growth of mass media, advertising

1930–1960 C.E.   Literature and Philosophy

Existentialism: Sartre, de Beauvoir

Absurdism: Camus, Ionesco, Beckett

Beat Generation: Allen Ginsberg, Jack Kerouac, LeRoi Jones

Angry Young Men: John Osborne, Harold Pinter, Paul Sillitoe

Ya-tzu Liu, Chinese poet and historian (1881–1936)

H. D. (Hilda Doolittle), American imagist poet (1886–1961)

Abulqasim Lahuti, Persian and Tajik poet (1887–1957)

Sufi Abdul Haq Beitāb (1888–1969); poet laureate of Afghanistan (1942)

Henry Miller, American novelist, painter (1891–1980)

Nazim Hikmet, Turkish poet, playwright (1902–1963)

Buzurg Alavi, Iranian novelist (b. 1907)

Faiz Ahmed Faiz, Pakistani poet (b. 1912)

Virginia Woolf, *The Waves* (1931)

Pearl Buck, *The Good Earth* (1931); Nobel Prize (1938)

Eugene O'Neill, *Mourning Becomes Electra* (1931); Nobel Prize (1936)

Aldous Huxley, *Brave New World* (1932)

Gertrude Stein, *The Autobiography of Alice B. Toklas* (1933)

John Maynard Keynes, *The General Theory of Employment, Interest, and Money* (1936)

Zora Neale Hurston, *Their Eyes Were Watching God* (1937)

Jean-Paul Sartre, *La Nausée* (1937)

Lao She, *Lo-t'o Lsiang-tzu* (1938)

Kin-Hak, *Tik Tonle Sap* (1939)

James Joyce, *Finnegans Wake* (1939)

Tawfig Awwād, *Al-Raghif* (1939)

Nathalie Sarraute, *Tropismes* (1939)

Richard Wright, *Native Son* (1940)

Albert Camus, *L'Étranger* (1942); Nobel Prize (1957)

T. S. Eliot, *Four Quartets* (1942); Nobel Prize (1948)

Sartre, *L'Être et le Néant* (1943)

The Diary of Anne Frank, published 1947

Thomas Mann, *Doktor Faustus* (1947)

W. H. Auden, *The Age of Anxiety* (1948)

Simone de Beauvoir, *The Second Sex* (1949–1950)

George Orwell, *Nineteen Eighty-Four* (1949)

Arthur Miller, *Death of a Salesman* (1949)

Ezra Pound, *Seventy Cantos* (1950)

Carson McCullers, *The Ballad of the Sad Café* (1951)

Robert Frost, *Complete Poems* (1951)

J. D. Salinger, *The Catcher in the Rye* (1951)

Ralph Ellison, *The Invisible Man* (1952)

Dylan Thomas, *Collected Poems* (1952)

Samuel Beckett, *Waiting for Godot* (1952); Nobel Prize (1969)

Marianne Moore, *Collected Poems* (1952)

Ludwig Wittgenstein, *Philosophical Investigations* (1953)

Amos Tutuola, *The Palm-Wine Drunkard* (1953)

James Baldwin, *Go Tell It on the Mountain* (1953)

Wisława Szymborska, *Pytania zadawane sobie* (1954)

Wallace Stevens, *Collected Poems* (1954)

Allen Ginsberg, *Howl* (1955–1956)

Jean Genet, *The Balcony,* (1955)

Najib Mahfūz, *Al-Thulāthiyya (Cairo Trilogy)* (1956–1957); Nobel Prize (1988)

Jack Kerouac, *On the Road* (1957)

Czesław Milosz, *Traktat poetycki* (1957); Nobel Prize (1980)

Assia Djebar, *La Soif* (1957)

Chinua Achebe, *Things Fall Apart* (1958)

Boris Pasternak, *Doctor Zhivago* (1958)

Eugene Ionesco, *Rhinocéros* (1959)

Yukio Mishima, *The Temple of the Golden Pavilion* (1959)

Gunter Grass, *The Tin Drum* (1959)

1930–1960 C.E. Art and Music

Swing Era: Louis Armstrong, Duke Ellington, Count Basie, Benny Goodman

Be-Bop Movement: Charlie Parker, Dizzy Gillespie, Miles Davis, Thelonius Monk

African-American Blues: Bessie Smith, Alberta Hunter, Big Mamma Thornton, Billie Holiday, Lightnin' Hopkins, B. B. King

Abstract Expressionism: Pollock, De Kooning, Rothko, Motherwell

Joseph Cornell's boxes

Masters of photography: Brassai, Stieglitz, Margaret Bourke-White

Film as art form: Chaplin, Lang, Flahery, Eisenstein, Renoir, Cocteau, Welles, de Sica, Fellini, Bergman, Wajda

Revolution in architecture, design: Mies van der Rohe, Gropius, Wright, Saarinen

Frida Kahlo, painter of images of rage and pain (1907–1954)

Amrita Sher-Gil, Indian painter (1912–1941)

George Gershwin, *Porgy and Bess,* opera (1935)

Piet Mondrian, *Composition in Red and Blue,* (1936)

Pablo Picasso, *Guernica* (1937)

Dimitri Shostakovich writes his *Symphony No. 7* during siege of Leningrad (1941)

Isami Noguchi, *Contoured Playground* (1941); *Kouras* Scultpures (1945)

Kurt Weill, *Lost in the Stars* (1949)

Mexican muralists Diego Rivera, Clemente Orozco

Guggenheim Museum, designed by Frank Lloyd Wright, opens in New York City (1958)

Revival of Indian art, led by Ananda Coomaraswamy

1960–present   Historical Context

Berlin Wall constructed (1961)

Cuban Missile Crisis (1962)

National Liberation Movements: Castro, Allende, Ho Chi Minh

Civil Rights Movement: Martin Luther King, Malcolm X, Jesse Jackson

Pope John XXIII, Second Vatican Council (1962)

Vietnam War (1962–1973)

Israeli-Arab Wars

Sexual Revolution

Feminist Movement

Indira Gandhi's Era in India (1966–1977)

Gay Rights Movement

American astronaut lands on moon (1969)

Third World a growing force

Overpopulation, food shortages, ecological threat

Islamic resurgence; fundamentalism of Khomeini

Christian fundamentalist revival in U.S.

Oil embargo, power of OPEC (1970s)

Nixon's China diplomacy (1972)

Watergate Scandal, Resignation of Nixon (1974)

Increased nuclear tensions during Reagan Era; arms race

Russian stalemate in Afghanistan

AIDS, new global plague

Gorbachev: Glasnost, Perestroika, dismantling of the postwar Soviet state (1989)

Chinese Democracy Movement

Tiananmen Square Massacre (1989)

Dalai Lama of Tibet awarded Nobel peace prize (1989)

Civil War in Northern Ireland

Close of Cold War Era

Demolition of the Berlin Wall (1990)

Reunification of Germany

Vaclav Havel, playwright, becomes president of Czechoslovakia

Independence for Eastern European nations

Failed military coup in Russia, Yeltsin replaces Gorbachev

Persian Gulf War: Saddam Hussein forced to yield Kuwait

New European Economic Partnership

Trade War between Japan and U.S.

World converts to multinational corporate structure

Age of the personal computer

TV evangelism

1960–present   Literature and Philosophy

Derek Walcott, *In a Green Night: Poems 1948–1960*; Nobel Prize

V. S. Naipaul, *A House for Mr. Biswas* (1961)

Frantz Fanon, *The Wretched of the Earth* (1961)

Juan Carlos Onetti, *The Shipyard* (1961)

Alexander Solzhenitsyn, *One Day in the Life of Ivan Denisovich* (1962); Nobel Prize (1970)

Jorge Luis Borges, *Labyrinths* (1962)

Edward Albee, *Who's Afraid of Virginia Woolf?* (1962)

Stevie Smith, *Selected Poems* (1962)

James Baldwin, *Another Country* (1962)

Yehuda Amichai, *Collected Poems* (1963)

Carlos Fuentes, *The Death of Artemio Cruz* (1964)

Kōbō Abe, *The Woman in the Dunes* (1964)

LeRoi Jones, *Dutchman* (1964)

Anna Akhmatova, *Requiem* (1964)

Mao Tse-tung, *Quotations of Chairman Mao* (1966)

Shmuel Yosef Agnon wins Nobel Prize for literature (1966)

Gabriel García Márquez, *One Hundred Years of Solitude* (1967); Nobel Prize (1982)

The French *nouveau roman*: Sarraute, Robbe-Grillet, Butor

Yasunari Kawabata, Nobel Prize for literature (1968)

Yasar Kemal, *They Burn the Thistles* (1969)

Vladimir Nabokov, *Ada* (1969)

Elizabeth Bishop, *Complete Poems* (1969)

Eudora Welty, *Losing Battles* (1970)

Juan Goytisolo, *Count Julian* (1970)

Maya Angelou, *I Know Why the Caged Bird Sings* (1970)

Sylvia Plath, *The Bell Jar* (1971)

Pablo Neruda wins Nobel Prize (1971)

Thomas Pynchon, *Gravity's Rainbow* (1973)

Patrick White, *The Eye of the Storm* (1973); Nobel Prize (1973)

Isaac Bashevis Singer, *A Crown of Feathers* (1974); Nobel Prize (1978)

Ruth Prawer Jhabvala, *Heat and Dust* (1975)

Wole Soyinka, *Death and the King's Horseman* (1975); Nobel Prize (1986)

Athold Fugard, *Sizwe Banzi is Dead* (1975)

William Gaddis, *J R* (1976)

Alex Haley, *Roots* (1976)

Salman Rushdie, *Midnight's Children* (1981)

Dennis Brutus, *Salutes and Censures* (1982)

Alice Walker, *The Color Purple* (1982)

Isabel Allende, *The House of the Spirits* (1982)

Jamaica Kincaid, *Annie John* (1983)

Mark Mathabane, *Kaffir Boy* (1986)

Toni Morrison, *Beloved* (1988)

1960–present   Art and Music

Music of protest: Joan Baez, Bob Dylan, Phil Ochs, Arlo Guthrie

Rock 'n roll crosses national borders: Elvis Presley, the Beatles

Soul music: James Brown, Otis Redding, Ray Charles, Aretha Franklin

Bob Marley's reggae gives the Third World its voice

African music becomes international: Sonny Adé, Y'oussu n'Dour, Hugh Masekela, Odetta, Dudu Pukwana, Olatunji

South American jazz evolves: Machito, Gato Barbieri, Mongo Santamaria, Celia Cruz

Aleatory music, minimalism: Cage, Stockhausen, Glass

Rudolph Nureyev, Martha Graham, Mikhail Baryshnikov

New Wave Cinema: Resnais, Truffaut, Godard, Cassavetes, Antonioni

Revival of German cinema: Herzog, Fassbinder, Wenders

Asian cinema: Satyagit Ray, Kurasawa, Ito, Itami

Emergence of Black film: Melvin van Peebles, Spike Lee, John Singleton

Popular music influenced by film scores spreads in India, Pakistan

Turkey and the Arab nations adopt forms of popular music

Pop Art: Andy Warhol, Robert Rauschenberg, Keith Haring

1960s: Allen Kaprow initiates the Happening

Performance art: Vito Acconci, Karen Finley, Laurie Anderson, Charlotte Moorman

Draping of public monuments: Christo

Self-begetting media icon: Madonna defines the 1980s

Appendix C:
Reading and Writing
About World Literature

According to advice offered by English novelist Virginia Woolf, you should read with a pencil in hand. Jotting down the thoughts that crowd in upon you as you read helps you to fix—for a while—some of your responses to a work. For it is the mysterious property of sensations, impressions, and thoughts that they dart about in your mind and, sometimes, disappear. Woolf compares the evanescent quality of thought to a fishing line let down in a stream:

> Thought—to call it by a prouder name than it deserved—had let its line down into the stream. It swayed, minute after minute, hither and thither among the reflections and the weeds, letting the water lift it and sink it, until—you know the little tug—the sudden conglomeration of an idea at the end of one's line. (*A Room of One's Own*)

It is important to recognize this gathering of thoughts, this tug of an idea at the end of your line, and to record your early responses to a work, both personal and cultural.

You should read knowing that you are reading with others. Not only are you having a dialogue with an author, someone who writes in a particular time and place, but you are also having a conversation with the cultures represented in *The HarperCollins World Reader,* and, eventually, with the other students in your class. Your curiosity and desire to know about other people and places should propel you into the readings even though you will sometimes feel a strangeness in encountering unfamiliar names and places. Read on. An effort of the imagination is necessary to enter other people's lives and stories, as well as to understand the different responses of other readers in your class who will have a kaleidoscope of views on culture, language, religion, class, race, ethnicity, gender, and sex. Though you read alone, silently, in a private space, you discover that you are always also reading with others as you explore different values and cultures. For example, in reading the Islamic writer Ibn Hazm's eleventh century tales of love in *The Dove's Neckring* (*Towq al-Hamama*), you might be shocked to read stories of the pursuit of "slave-girls" who grow up in the houses of wealthy families. You discover through reading that slavery is a part of Arab culture in the eleventh century, but you also discover the independence in the slave-girl's position as the narrator pursues the sixteen-year-old girl and finds her "far more glamorous in her refusals and rejections" of him, as he describes an experience of unrequited love.

You might debate the value and discussion of womanly and manly beauty in this same Islamic epic. The beauty of the slave girl is described:

> She had a wonderful complexion which she always kept closely veiled. . . . For women are as aromatic herbs, which if not well tended soon lose their fragrance; they are as edifices which, if not constantly cared for quickly fall into ruin. Therefore, it has been said that manly beauty is the truer, the more solidly established, and of higher excellence since it can endure, and that without shelter, onslaughts the merest fraction of which would transform the loveliness of a woman's face beyond recognition: such enemies as the burning heat of noonday, the scorching wind of the desert, every air of heaven, and all the changing moods of the seasons. (Section V, Early and Classical Middle East)

Since the body has different meanings in different cultures, how does each culture teach its women and men to "tend" their bodies? Islamic culture may teach its women to "veil" their bodies; Chinese culture may promote "foot-binding" in a particular period to enhance the daintiness of women's feet; American culture may encourage "thinness" as an aspect of women's beauty. What Islamic culture may see as the "enemy"—"the burning heat of noonday"—may be another culture's "obsession"—suntanning of the body.

Such personal and cultural responses to other literatures grow out of your past reading experiences and your personal and social experiences, and may become the basis for a paper at a later stage of writing. You will quickly follow along from the early moments of your understanding of a text to see and see again, shape and reshape your interpretations and writing about the text as you think about it and discuss it with others. Early thoughts, feelings, and questions may very well control the later phases of writing about a work, and you should preserve these responses.

Your early observations may be recorded in three ways. First, you might want to highlight certain words or write comments in your book. Preserve your sudden sympathy for a character or your feeling of being bothered by an unfamiliar word or your feelings of difference as you read by commenting in the margins or between the lines of your text. Highlight certain words or passages that need further reflection; use question marks to note ambiguities or puzzles; draw arrows to relate different parts of a work. For example, notations on the poem, "Walking Both Sides of an Invisible Border" (stanzas five and six), by Alootook Ipellie, an Eskimo born in Canada, might look like this:

Remind me of Ruth in the Bible "amidst the alien corn."

I did not ask to be born an Inuk   *What?*
Nor did I ask to be forced
To learn an alien culture   *Repeats the word "alien"*
With an alien language
But I lucked out on fate
Which I am unable to undo.
I have resorted to fancy dancing   *Images of dancing*
In order to survive each day
No wonder I have earned
The dubious reputation of being
The world's premier choreographer
Of distinctive dance steps

> *That allow me to avoid*
> *Potential personal paranoia*   Three "*p's*"
> *On both sides of this invisible border*

A second way of recording early responses to a work is to keep a reading notebook, what Ann Berthoff calls a "dialectical notebook." In such a notebook, the facing pages are in dialogue with one another. On the left-hand page, you write your initial impressions of a work or copy out sentences or passages that interest you. You may find a particular sentence puzzling; you may fasten on a certain character; you may be intrigued by the description of a place or you may have a strong feeling of anger. Jot down your impressions and feelings and set the notebook aside. Later, on the right-hand page, explore these impressions further, reflecting upon, questioning, and explaining remarks you made on the left-hand page. On the right-hand page, you will, in effect, be taking notes on your notes, and transforming your first impressions into new understandings. Some observations will remain relevant; some can be ignored. A "dialectical notebook" page on Alootook Ipellie's poem might look like the notes illustrated here.

Initial impressions, copied sentences and passages	Reflections, explanations, interpretations
I remember the pictures of igloos, Eskimos in parkas, fishing through a hole in the ice in my elementary school social studies book. Do Eskimos or Inuits still live in this way? Why are certain Eskimos called "Inuits." Does the word have a meaning? Another language?	Looked up Inuit in the encyclopedia but only found information on the word "Eskimo" which is of Algonquin origin and has the "pejorative meaning of eater of raw flesh." I know little about different kinds of Eskimos. The images I have are stereotypes— oversimplified views of a group of people.

A third method of recording your responses involves generating a list of questions, contradictions, ambiguities, or puzzles that come to mind as you read a work. Such questions would be reconsidered at a later stage of writing, and one or two of them might even grow into a definite subject of research for a paper. Here is a potential list of questions that you might have after reading Alootook Ipellie's poem:

Who is speaking in this poem? Is it Ipellie himself or an Inuk he created?

Why does he feel so bad about himself? Being made to feel like an "illegitimate child" or someone "sent to a torture chamber/without having committed a crime" suggests a strong sense of injustice.

Who is it that is "forcing" him to learn an alien culture? Headnote mentions French and English, but what do I know about the historical situation of Eskimos in Canada?

Why are there so many images of feet and dancing? And lines and borders?

In this first stage of reading and writing, you are actively trying to make sense of the world of Alootook Ipellie by recording the flux of your impressions, questionings, comparisons, and judgments. Writing down your impressions keeps you alert to the meanings that you are making and remaking as you read. And writing helps you to fix meaning—for a while—because once your thoughts are written down you can look at them and then look at them again. Whatever method you choose—highlighting, jotting in a book, keeping a reading notebook, or listing questions that a work provokes—you are creating, reflecting, judging, and comparing meanings from the very moment you begin to read, and you may always reconsider, change, and remake your meanings. Thoughts flutter away but writing stays.

Reading with a pencil in hand will remind you of the relationship between reading and writing. At this early stage, you move from one spot in the text to another, stressing nothing in particular, simply recording the conversation between you, the author, and the work. This, after all, is thinking. Reading, writing, and thinking are intertwined as the French literary critic Gérard Genette says: "The text is that Moebius strip in which the side of writing and the side of reading, ceaselessly turn and cross over, in which writing is constantly read, in which reading is constantly written and inscribed" (*Figures*, 70). As a reader, you enter into such interplays of reading and writing that ceaselessly turn and cross over.

But reading and writing remain in some sense unfinished until completed by others. You work from your responses and feelings outward to other stages that involve you in reading with others. Robert Scholes, an educator and literary critic, identifies three levels:

LEVEL 1: READING

LEVEL 2: INTERPRETATION

LEVEL 3: CRITICISM

These levels of reading take you beyond your inner dialogue that is largely private: the way in which you represented your thinking to yourself in your notebook or jottings or lists of questions as suggested earlier. In discussion with your classmates and your instructor, and maybe even other literary critics, certain initial ideas may be discarded; others will survive.

As meanings evolve, they are shaped and reshaped, and eventually prepared for an audience. It is thus important "how" you move back and forth from early notebook jottings about your reading to more formal discussion and writing for an audience. For example, while reading "Walking Both Sides of the Border" (in Section XVIII Writing Across Boundaries), you may have informally jotted in your notebook:

> *Inuit in this poem being oppressed and physically tortured by somebody. Evidence in the line "having been sentenced to a Torture chamber."*

In discussion, a classmate might point out that Ipellie uses the word "like" before this clause—"like having been sentenced to a torture chamber"—forcing you to concede that Ipellie is here using a comparison (simile) to a torture chamber to convey how the Inuk feels. You realize he has not been physically tortured, and that you read the line too literally. Discussion then might lead you to revise an initial impression as you come into agreement with your classmate on the literal meaning of what you have read. Not all "readings" are equally valid. Sometimes then you must grapple with someone else to establish "what happens" in a poem or story when it is not straightforward or clear. As a reader, you fill in gaps, relate parts of a work to each other, figure out the characters: in short, you make sense of it. This is the literal level of "reading."

On the second level of interpretation, you will discuss the "meaning" of what you have read with others and with your classmates and instructor. You may have noted in the margins of your book that the image of "a border" recurs in the first few stanzas of the poem:

> The Inuk is "Walking with an invisible border" and later "Walking on both sides of an invisible border." Who is making these borders "that become so wide" that he is unable to take another step? Who is creating these difficulties and making him paranoid?

A classmate interested in dancing, may perceive something different in the poem. She might jot down all the passages that mention "feet," "steps," "dancing." The meaning of the poem may reside for her in the Inuk's coping strategies, his "fancy dancing" and refusal to be a victim of opposing cultural forces—in this case, the Inuk and the English. You, on the other hand, may be more sensitive to the Inuk's complaints, his sense of oppression and "paranoia" about his social and historical circumstances. Each of you finds different yet compatible meanings based on your personal and cultural sensitivities and experiences.

The third level of reading, "criticism," involves you in discriminating further by comparing and judging works, and sometimes, the opinions of others. You move beyond the analysis of one text—its events and meanings—to compare texts of two or more authors, cultures, or historical periods in *The HarperCollins World Reader*. You might examine who is speaking in the Ipellie poem, Ipellie himself or a lyric "I," and compare him to the *griot* who chants an epic in the West African culture. In *The Oral Epic of Askia Mohammed*, a sixteenth-century epic by the Songhay People (in Section VI, Africa: The Epic Tradition), we might compare the *griot* known in Songhay as *jésere*, and in English poetry as a "bard" or, later, a "poet." The first English version of this sixteenth-century West African epic appears in *The HarperCollins World Reader*, and was chanted again according to oral traditions in Mali in Saga, Niger, in 1980 and 1981. The tale relates how every time Kassaye, the sister of the threatened ruler, Si, delivers a baby, it is killed by Si, because it has been foretold by the "seers" that his throne will be taken from him by one of his sister's children. The tale of jealousy and power is told over and over again in Mali. Does this *griot* speak for a whole community? How does his role compare with that of the "poet," Ipellie? Does he speak for the community of Inuks in the same way as the Mali epic poet?

What is the difference in the way that you "hear" these two poems? As you experience the Mali epic, you notice that there are unusual repetitions in certain lines. For example, Si is still king, and his sister Kassaye knows that he will continue to kill any child she has; in fact, he has already killed seven of them. She waits to see whether anything will change:

> While Kassaye remained like that
> Until, until, until, until one day, much later, in the middle of the night
> A man came who was wearing beautiful clothes.

The repetition of the word "until" creates for us a sense of Kassaye's waiting: it rhythmically marks the passage of time, "until, until, until, until one day, much later." This repetition reveals the oral dimension of this epic that is chanted in the Mali culture. Reminding us of the oral origins of all poetry, we note, nevertheless, that much English and American poetry today appeals to the eye and not the ear, as it formerly did in Old English epics such as *Beowulf*.

You may have noticed that each time a point has been advanced about world literature here, the thesis is supported with quotations from the texts in *The HarperCollins World Reader*. As you write, the "evidence" you assemble in support of your positions is quotations or paraphrases from the text. Such a practice in writing a paper for the humanities is different from the practice of writing, for example, for the disciplines of psychology or chemistry. The social and physical sciences require citations of case studies or statistics or experiments as evidence in an argument. In the humanities, reading, jottings, rereadings, underlinings, writing, and rewriting provide the evidence you need to write a more formal paper at a later stage.

Reading, writing, and thinking are intertwined. You see that all of these processes are tempered by the realization that you bring your own personal and cultural experiences to any work, and impressions registered are shaped by your memories as well as your growing stock of cultural associations. Samuel Johnson once observed that "the two most engaging powers of any author are, 'to make new things familiar and familiar things new.'" Many selections in a reader marked by cultural, chronological, and geographical diversity will appear to be concerned with strange and "new things," rather than "familiar things," but as you read, you will recognize ways in which the writers have carried out both aims identified by Johnson. On one level, the customs and values of different cultures will become somewhat more familiar; at the same time, certain aspects of your own culture that you have come to take for granted may take on a different meaning and reshape your previous convictions and outlook.

Virtually all works of literature have certain elements in common, whether or not they are written in another language and at a different time. One important aspect of any text is the *point of view* from which it was written. The point of view is the author's dominant focus, from which he or she projects the story, poem, or essay. Sometimes the point of view is so clear it is taken for granted. For instance, when Alootook Ipellie writes, "I feel like an illegitimate child/Forsaken by my parents," readers presume that they are hearing the voice of the poet himself. In the Korean poem "A Ferryboat and a Traveler," by Han Yongun, which begins, "I am a ferryboat, you are a traveler," it is clear that the poet has decided to assume the *persona* of a ferryboat. Alternatively, in "Evening Faces," from the Japanese novel *The Tale of Genji,* written by Murasaki Shikibu, an aristocratic eleventh-century Japanese lady, the viewpoint is third-person. The author is sharing the thoughts of a single major character, the young Buddhist nobleman Prince Genji. The selection begins, "On his way from court to pay one of his calls at Rokujō, Genji stopped to inquire after his old nurse." Had the viewpoint suddenly shifted, and the story continued, "the old nurse was wondering if some tea would help her headache, and trying to decide if she was able to make the journey next day to visit her sister, with whom she had shared her childhood in the country," the reader might be confused; the interest in Prince Genji generated up to that point would be diluted. The viewpoint character must be consistent, supplying the emotion, conflict, and suspense of the work of literature; the reader identifies with the viewpoint and infers the message of the work through the reaction of this character.

The point of view is a necessary staple in all works of literature, though there may be variations in the way the point of view is worked out. For instance, sometimes a speaker in the first person is actually looking back at an earlier period of his or her life. This is the case, for instance, in *Narrative of the Life of Frederick Douglass, an American Slave, Written by Himself* (in Section XV, The Americas sections).

At other times, a work is written in the present, with such an immediacy that the reader seems to be peering over the shoulder of the writer watching the act of composition. This is the case with Vladimir Nabokov's "An Evening of Russian Poetry" (in "Writing Across Boundaries"). The author addresses several audiences: the group of people gathered for his lecture, the person (presumably a student) helping him project slides, the student (Sylvia) who interrupts with a question, and the reader. The larger framework of the lecture embraces two smaller designs: the mechanical difficulty of projecting the slide correctly (i.e., making the visual image conform to the chosen word), and the pedagogical problem posed by Sylvia, who begs for easy packaged knowledge instead of complex linguistic theory.

> The subject chosen for tonight's discussion
> is everywhere, though often incomplete:
> when their basaltic banks become too steep,
> most rivers use a kind of rapid Russian,
> and so do children talking in their sleep.
> My little helper at the magic lantern,
> insert that slide and let the colored beam
> project my name or any such like phantom
> in Slavic characters upon the screen.
> The other way, the other way. I thank you.
>
> On mellow hills the Greek, as you remember,
> fashioned his alphabet from cranes in flight;
> his arrows crossed the sunset, then the night.
> Our simple skyline and a taste for timber,
> the influence of hives and conifers,
> reshaped the arrows and the borrowed birds.
> Yes, Sylvia?
>
> *"Why do you speak of words*
> *when all we want is knowledge nicely browned?"*
>
> Because all hangs together—shape and sound,
> heather and honey, vessel and content.

Within his larger address to the audience, he speaks to the person (presumably a student) inserting slides for him, while, at the same time he seems to be pondering the transitory nature of his own name and, possibly, his message. The slide has apparently been shown reversed or upside-down; he breaks off to ask the person to correct it. He continues his lecture, but interrupts himself to respond to a member of the audience, who has apparently raised her hand: "Yes, Sylvia?" He answers her question as to why "words" are significant, incorporating his reply within his lecture, addressing Sylvia, the audience, and the reader. "Content," or meaning, and the "vessel," or words, cannot be separated, for "all hangs together."

The point of view is only one element that might be considered a common denominator of virtually all literary works of art. Other factors you need to keep in mind are structure and diction, as well as metaphor, irony, symbolism, and other rhetorical devices. Above all, focus on the author's message; grasp the meaning of the piece of writing.

You have been writing since you began reading, making notations in your text and keeping a notebook to remind you of your initial impressions, reflections, and interpretations. At some point, however, you will need to incorporate these fragmentary notes into a public, formal essay.

You will find it helpful to tackle your essay by stages. Students who hastily scribble a paper at three A.M. rarely produce a piece of writing of which they can be proud. The steps in writing most students find useful are these: *invention, drafting,* and *revision.* If you can space out these steps, allowing periods of time away from your writing, results will be far better. The subconscious part of your mind will go on working on the material even though you are doing something else; often you return to it with renewed energy and new ideas.

Invention

"I don't know how to get started," students often say. Several rhetorical techniques may help you as you cast around for initial ideas. Read over your book jottings and your notebook, and then try one or more of these strategies.

Freewriting

Freewriting may be the easiest way to release your powers of invention and discovery. Without devising any sort of outline or plan, force yourself simply to begin writing about a text you have read and to keep writing for five minutes. Do not lift your pen or pencil; just keep writing. Let your mind wander back to the act of reading the text, and give free rein to the associations you gathered. (The reason you should keep writing and not let yourself reread what you have is so that you will not begin editing what you have; that task is reserved for a later stage.) You do not need to write complete sentences, just phrases or vague ideas. Jot down anything that made a strong impression.

As a sample text for freewriting, consider the first five paragraphs of the short story "We Blacks All Drink Coffee" by the Cuban writer Mirta Yañez (included in Section XVIII, Writing Across Boundaries):

> She says that I don't even know how to wash my own clothes and yet I want to go off. What is a mother's child going to do in a place like that? Just imagine what my grandmother would say if she knew, if she were to rise from the grave and see what the apple of her eye wanted to get into. It's a good thing she is dead, because if she weren't . . . . There's a lot of talk about irresponsible mothers. But not about her.
>
> And so my mother goes grumbling on and on from the end of the corridor where she has gone to take refuge so that her voice will be lost, will slip in between the furniture, so the neighbours will not hear one word sounding louder than another, what would they think of this family, of this child of fifteen wanting to go off to pick coffee?
>
> Things were different in her time. What would a well brought up girl be doing in the middle of the bush? Who would have thought of such a thing? Going where there are so many dangers. At least that's what the books say. Right into the heart of a titanic forest, a girl from a good family. Luckily there are no wild animals in this country.

For my mother the only safe place is my room with its four walls, a roof, a floor of the most ordinary sort. And not even then is it completely worthy of her confidence.

What do I care about the neighbours? But she does. And she closes the windows so that the argument will not go beyond this castle which is the protective shell of my family life. And when the room is the way she would like it, like the cell of a cloistered nun, she rushes forward from the other side of the corridor, she claps her hands. She shouts carefully. I am what is known as a girl who was given everything she ever wanted. If I asked for a flying bird, a flying bird I would get. Now look how ungrateful I was.

Here is what freewriting might look like for the above passage:

girl 15 wants to pick coffee beans   mother won't let her   she is too nice neighbors might criticize   she is like flying bird   does she hate mother   picking beans is first job   she is too sheltered   what dangers does the mother mean grandmother would have been shocked   wants to hide girl in room   home equals castle   girl given everything

Clustering

You could take the same five paragraphs and try another strategy. Write each of your main ideas in the center of a piece of blank paper and circle it. Then "cluster" supporting ideas around it, each with relevant quotations, details, and key words. Making such a diagram will allow you to visualize the way the various pieces of your research or your argument fit together.

Your clustering might look like the diagram shown below.

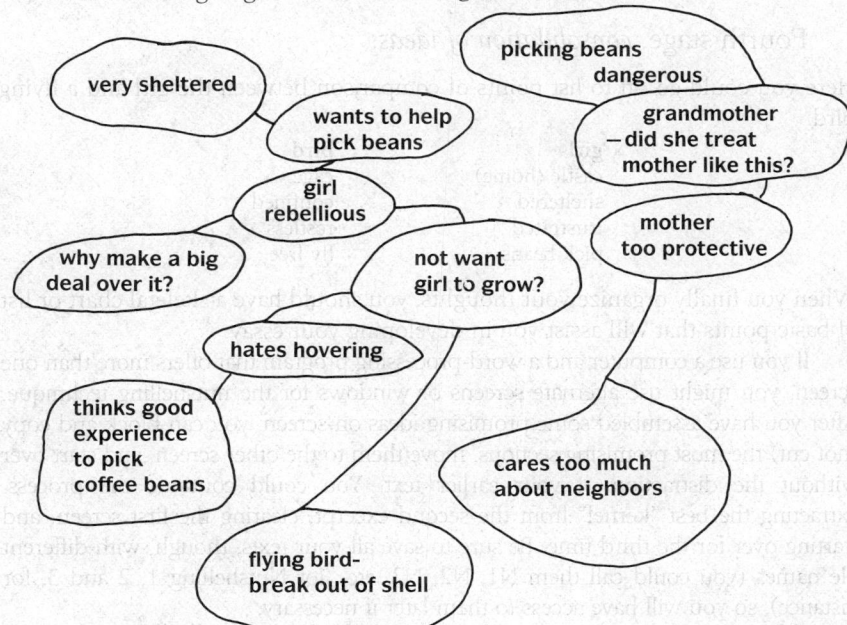

Nutshelling

Nutshelling, sometimes called *looping,* is when you record your thoughts as they come for a few minutes, as you did in freewriting; this process may also be called brainstorming. Then you extract the best idea from what you have, draw a line, and start again with that phrase or sentence. You keep extracting the "kernel" or nucleus of the text and putting it in a new context. Many students find it difficult to narrow a subject and arrive at a workable thesis. This procedure can be very helpful in channeling your initial impressions and shaping them into an argument. Nutshelling might also work well for "We Blacks All Drink Coffee:"

First stage of nutshelling, *freewriting or brainstorming:*

> The girl wants to pick beans in coffee field but her mother objects because she can't even wash her own clothes and is not independent yet and has been given everything she ever wanted even a flying bird if she had wanted one; mother says her grandmother would have been shocked ancestry matters to mother but not to girl it seems like that anyway

Second stage, *first extract or loop:*

> Mother overprotective; she smothers girl who wants to be independent which is good girl wants to be a bird and go free in the fields and break out of the cage not have a bird but be a bird etc.

Third stage, *second extract or loop:*

> Symbol of the bird is good as image of independence which is what girl seems to want maybe that comparison would work

Fourth stage, *consolidation of ideas:*

Here you could go on to list points of comparison between the girl and a flying bird:

girl	bird
castle (home)	cage
sheltered	confined
frustrated	restless
pick beans	fly free

When you finally organize your thoughts, you should have a skeletal chart or list of basic points that will assist you in developing your essay.

If you use a computer and a word-processing program that offers more than one screen, you might use alternate screens or windows for the nutshelling technique. After you have assembled some promising ideas on-screen, you can block and copy (not cut) the most promising sections, move them to the other screen, and start over without the distraction of your earlier text. You could continue the process, extracting the best "kernel" from the second excerpt, clearing the first screen, and starting over for the third time. Be sure to save all your texts, though, with different file names (you could call them N1, N2, N3, etc., for Nutshelling 1, 2 and 3, for instance), so you will have access to them later if necessary.

Cubing

Cubing is a technique offering a way of swiftly considering a subject from six points of view, and is a useful preventive if you tend to be locked into a single way of looking at a subject. If you shift points of view every three to five minutes, your perspective is continually renewed. In cubing, you imagine your subject as a solid block, or cube. Then, for three to five minutes each, carry out the following steps:

> *Describe it*
>
> *Compare it*
>
> *Analyze it*
>
> *Associate it*
>
> *Apply it*
>
> *Argue for/against it*

The quick shift from one perspective to another makes cubing work. If you consider the Yañez story as a solid block, your cubing might look like this:

Describe it: girl wants to pick beans; argues with mother.

Compare it: girl like bird, impatient in cage at home, wants to be independent

Analyze it: girl wants new ways; mother wants old ways; conflict between generations

Associate it: similar to me in high school when I wanted to be free to go out, do things; I can understand girl; who cares what neighbors and ancestors think?

Apply it: could be applied to essay on theme of innocence and experience or to essay on other cultures.

Argue for/against it: I basically agree with the girl in wanting to try new experiences and expand her thinking; the mother should realize the world has changed now; she should trust her daughter not to disgrace the family

Any of these techniques may assist you in collecting your thoughts on a particular text.

Drafting

The next step is to write your first draft. If you are writing on the Yañez story and have carried out the preceding brainstorming techniques, it is likely that by now you might have decided on a single topic that interests you, such as the conflict between generations, the depiction of racial prejudice (undercut by the title, which implies that all Cubans have African blood, inherited from their Spanish/Moorish ancestry), the interplay of color emblems in the story (white, black, yellow, red, green), or the concept of family honor as it pertains to the treatment of daughters among the Cuban upper classes.

Now, you need to develop a thesis, as opposed to a topic. A topic is the overall subject, a rough label, but your thesis expresses your argument and is a vital part of your essay. It should set forth an explicit argument about the text to which you are responding and should be the nucleus of the introductory paragraph. This paragraph should provide a general context within which you can develop your ideas. It should not only make your thesis clear but also provide a transition to the body of the paper. It should be proportional in size to the total length of the paper.

A useful test of a thesis is whether you can convert it into a satisfactory title. The following two titles fail to suggest an argument based on the Yañez story:

> "Working in the Coffee Fields"

(This title is too vague; also the girl does not actually work in the fields.)

> "The Family's Influence on a Young Cuban Girl"

(This title is better, but it does not suggest the import of the story.)

A third title, which implies the theme of the story, is better formulated:

> "Leaving the Nest: The Empowerment of the Heroine in Yañez'
> 'We Blacks All Drink Coffee' "

A possible thesis might be the following:

> The narrator realizes that she is rapidly becoming an adult with choices of her own to make regarding her conduct, yet, at the same time, she perceives that she can never completely escape her upbringing, with its implicit familial obligations. The girl's wish to escape from her childhood is shown by the symbol of the "flying bird." If she had wanted to own a "flying bird," she would have been given one; she was very spoiled. But if she wants to *be* a "flying bird," she is constricted.

Your paper must contain examples and evidence such as the following to support your ideas:

To show she is becoming an adult:

> From the "vision" of her mother's hysterical reaction and her final remark, "do as you think best," the girl judges that she has finally been perceived as an adult, but one with responsibility to herself and her family.

To show that the symbol of a bird leaving a nest is relevant:

> The symbol of the "flying bird" works in two ways in the story: to show the girl's original imprisonment in her cage-like room in the family "castle" or home, and to show her final liberation.

You may find some of the selections in *The HarperCollins World Reader* puzzling, because they deal not only with systems of religious and philosophical thought that are foreign to you but also with habits of daily life that lie outside your immediate experience. For instance, some of the selections from Japanese literature depict subtle criteria of taste and judgment, profoundly meaningful within the social hierarchy, that may seem insignificant to you. The continual sending of poems in *The Tale of Genji* and *The Tale of the Heike* (in Section III, East Asia: Early and Middle Period) is an example. A cultivated man or woman (not just a young lover) was expected to be a close observer, sensitive to the transience of the human condition, and to express his reflections in poetry that was controlled and veiled, not spontaneous and emotional. Matters you might consider trivial, such as the color of writing paper and the quality of handwriting, were actually subjects of very serious scrutiny and were the measure of a person's fastidiousness (in itself a quality you may not consider of primary consequence). As you read, you will note many other differences—in manners, food, dress, and other matters. It may particularly surprise you to read, in "Housewife," by the Indian writer Ismat Chugtai, that the bride Lajo, a former prostitute, despises the pants, or *churidar pyjamas,* her husband Mirza insists on her wearing. She calls them the "devil's intestines" and much prefers a loose skirt, the *lehnga.* A skirt, rather than the traditional pants, symbolizes the freedom she has had before marriage and before being under the control of her husband.

You may find it difficult to tailor your writing to a given audience, assuming you need to shape it to please your instructor, your tutor, your college newspaper editor, or a prospective employer. You should realize, though, that your primary audience is actually yourself. All writing is a form of self-discovery, and it is in writing about a text that you formulate your ideas and begin to sort out your thoughts. You, in fact, collaborate with other readers to become your own teacher as you shape a written response to a text through successive drafts.

Revision

When an essay you have considered your best effort is returned by your instructor with suggestions for revisions, you may feel disheartened. Try, though, to regard the comments as supportive feedback, a good opportunity to enlarge your knowledge of writing and to refine the structure, style, and content of the essay. Feedback from other students, or "peer response," is an invaluable source of insight into your writing. Some instructors build mini-workshops into their courses, with small groups of students reading each other's papers, in order to encourage peer response. Workshops in class may not be feasible for most literature courses, but you might wish to organize informal support group sessions with classmates to try out ideas and exchange preliminary drafts. It has been said that revision is not a finite third stage of writing, but a continual, ongoing process of the "re-vision" of a text; you "re-see" it as you work. Each "re-vision" leads to further changes and improvement.

You might highlight the best sections (those with the clearest ideas), using a colored marker; underline those which are doubtful; then cross through the fuzzy or badly written parts. Begin again, with the clearest idea and the arguments and illustrations related to it. If a paper is not to be revised, make sure you understand the comments so that you can apply them to your future writing. The entire process of revision is made far easier if you can use a computer.

In a sense, reading and writing complement each other. Reading with the aim of describing your reaction to a text—that is, writing about it—heightens your sensitivity to it. Writing, or interpreting, illuminates your reading and is an important component in your assimilation of a piece of writing. Both processes make possible the understanding of a work as part of a global cultural paradigm— unified by themes common to the human condition, yet richly varied in its subtexts and individual motifs. Your acuity as both reader and writer will be sharpened, and your perceptions enlarged, as you enter into dialogue with the diverse works in *The HarperCollins World Reader*.

Comparative Table of Contents by Theme

The Comparative Table of Contents by Theme is a representative grouping of poems, epics, stories, plays, and essays in *The HarperCollins World Reader* that shows how various themes are treated across different cultures, regions, and times. In no sense complete, this alternative table of contents serves as a beginning exploration in the comparative mode, a way to explore, and—in some cases—deviate from, literary expectations.

The alphabetized headings consist of a mixture of cross-cultural genres and selections grouped together around a similar theme. For example, the solemn theme of death may juxtapose a short story from India—Premchand's "The Shroud," for example—with Paul Celan's poem "The Death Fugue," a haunting account of the Holocaust.

From such a central focus, literary themes may be taught across cultures and genres so that, for example, concern about identity described in Yun Tongju's poem, "Self-Portrait" can be compared with Frank Sargeson's short story "The Making of a New Zealander," and Alootook Ipellie's "Walking Both Sides of an Invisible Border."

Thematic groupings give the reader a rough idea as to what notions seem to be of particular significance in certain times and places. Thus reflections on racial hatred, for example, can be examined from the Middle Eastern, African, and Latin American perspectives.

Comparing and contrasting these crosscultural themes will encourage thinking in the comparative mode while at the same time opening a gateway to further investigation of world literature selections.

Age and Aging

Ovid, from the *Amores,* Ancient Mediterranean World, sect. I

Li Po, "The River Merchant's Wife: A Letter," East Asia (China), sect. III

From *The Early Royal Anthologies,* Ono no Komachi, East Asia (Japan), sect. III

Sŏng Hon, [The Mountain Is Silent], East Asia (Korea), sect. III

Hŏ Nansŏrhŏn, "A Woman's Sorrow," East Asia (Korea), sect. III

William Shakespeare, *The Tempest,* Early Modern Europe, sect. VII

Creation and Creation Myths

Crimes Against Humanity and Racial Hatred

Death

Deceit and Greed

Desire and Longing

Enlightenment and Justice

Erotic Love and Sexuality

Evil

Food and Drink

Madness and Folly

Poverty

Po Chü-yi, "Bitter Cold, Living in the Village," "An Old Charcoal Seller," East Asia (China), sect. III

Yamanoue Okura, from the *Man'Yōshū,* Modern Japan, sect. III

Simone de Beauvoir, [To Grow Old], from *The Force of Circumstance,* Modern Europe, sect. XIV

Varlam Shalamov, "In the Night," Modern Europe, sect. XIV

Joy Kogawa, [Naomi learns the secret of her mother's silence], from *Obasan,* the Americas (Canada), sect. XV

Reality and Illusion

Lucius Apuleius, from *The Golden Ass,* Ancient Mediterranean World, sect. I

Anonymous, from *The Thousand and One Nights,* Early and Classical Middle East, sect. V

Ts'ao Hsüeh-chi'n, [Chen Shih-yin meets the Stone of Spiritual Understanding], from *The Dream of the Red Chamber,* Modern East Asia (China), sect. XI

Voltaire, *Candide,* Modern Europe, sect. XIV

Jorge Luis Borges, "Tlön, Uqbar, Orbis Tertius," the Americas (Latin America), sect. XV

Julio Cortazar, "Axolotl," the Americas (Latin America), sect. XV

Frank Sargeson, "The Making of a New Zealander," Australia and New Zealand, sect. XVI

Religion

Lucretius, from *On the Nature of Things,* Ancient Mediterranean World, sect. I

From the Bible, *The Gospel According to Luke,* and *The Acts of the Apostles,* Ancient Mediterranean World, sect. I

Lao Tzu, from the *Tao-Te Ching,* East Asia (China), sect. III

Yamanoue Okura, from the *Man'Yōshū,* East Asia (Japan) sect. III

Murasaki Shikibu, "Evening Faces," from *The Tale of Genji,* East Asia (Japan) sect. III

Anonymous, from *The Tale of the Heike,* East Asia (Japan), sect. III

Kwangdŏk, "Prayer to Amitāyus," East Asia (Korea), sect. III

Saint Augustine, from the *Confessions,* Medieval Europe, sect. IV

Dante Alighieri, from *The Divine Comedy,* Medieval Europe, sect. IV

Alcuin, "The Nightingale," Medieval Europe, sect. IV

François Villon, "Hanged Men," Medieval Europe, sect. IV

From the Qu'ran, "The Darkening," "Joseph," Early and Classical Middle East, sect. V

Renewal and Redemption

Wisdom, Knowledge, and Morality

Art from Around the World

Ma He-chih, Chinese, active twelfth century C.E. Colors on silk. Palace Museum, Beijing. See Section III, East Asia: Early and Middle Periods.

Attributed to Takayoshi, Japanese, Heian period, twelfth century C.E. *The Emperor Playing* Go. Illustration for *The Tale of Genji*. Colors on paper. Tokugawa Art Museum, Nagoya. See *The Tale of Genji*, Section III, East Asia: Early and Middle Periods.

Orcagna [Andrea di Cione], Italian, active c. 1343 C.E.; d. c. 1368. *The Last Judgment: Inferno.* Fresco, twisted columns and fragments. Museo dell'Opera di Santa Croce, Florence. See *The Divine Comedy,* Section IV, Medieval Europe.

Anonymous, French, thirteenth century C.E. manuscript. Illustration for *Renard the Fox* 1174–1205, the farewell scene between Renard the Fox setting off for the King's court, and his son. Bibliothèque Nationale, Paris. See *Renard the Fox,* Section IV, Medieval Europe.

Anonymous, thirteenth century C.E. *Bayad playing the 'ud before Riyad.* Manuscript illustration. Vatican Library, Rome. See Section V, Early and Classical Middle East.

Anonymous, n.d., Arabic. Frontispiece to the *Assemblies
Magāmat* of Al-Hariri. Manuscript illustration. Nationalbibli-
othek, Vienna. See *The Maqāmat,* Section V, Early and
Classical Middle East.

Anonymous, Turcoman, 899–1495. *The Conference of the Birds*. Bodleian Library, Oxford. See *The Conference of the Birds*, Section V, Early and Classical Middle East.

Anonymous, Persian, c. 1515 C.E. *Majnum in the Wilderness*. India Office
Library, London. See Section V, Early and Classical Middle East.

Painter A, Persian, c. 1525–1530 C.E., *Rustam's Fourth Course: He Cleves a Witch*. (Like the demons of the Turcoman album.) The Metropolitan Museum of Art. See *The Shāh Nāma.* See Section V, Early and Classical Middle East.

Michelangelo Buonarroti, Italian, 1510. *The Fall of Man*. Ceiling, Sistine Chapel, the Vatican. See "To Giovanni, the one from Pistoia on Painting the Vault of the Sistine Chapel." See Section VII, Early Modern Europe.

Anonymous, n. d., California Indian Culture. Chumash Rock
Painting, Cuyama. See Section VIII, The Early Americas.

Art from Around the World

Modern East Asia: Japan. Attributed to Tosa Mitsutada. *Giant Snowball*, from an episode in *The Tale of Genji* by Murasaki Shikibu. Eighteenth century. Ink, colors, and gold on paper.

Istanbul, Turkey. Modern Middle East. Halil Dikmen. *The Peasant Women*. c. 1963. Oil.

Morocco. Modern Africa. Chaibla. *Village of Chtouka.* 1982. Oil on canvas.

Russia. Modern Europe. Kasimir Malevich. *Suprematist Painting*. After 1920. Oil on canvas.

United States. The Americas. Georgia O'Keeffe. *Black Cross, New Mexico*. 1929. Oil on canvas.

Latin America. The Americas. Mixtec Art. *Two-headed Serpent.* Turquoise mosaic.

Milingimbi, Australia. Australia and New Zealand. Australian bark painting of rock pythons. The black ovals surrounded by white dots are stringy-bark flowers floating on the surface of the sacred waterhole.

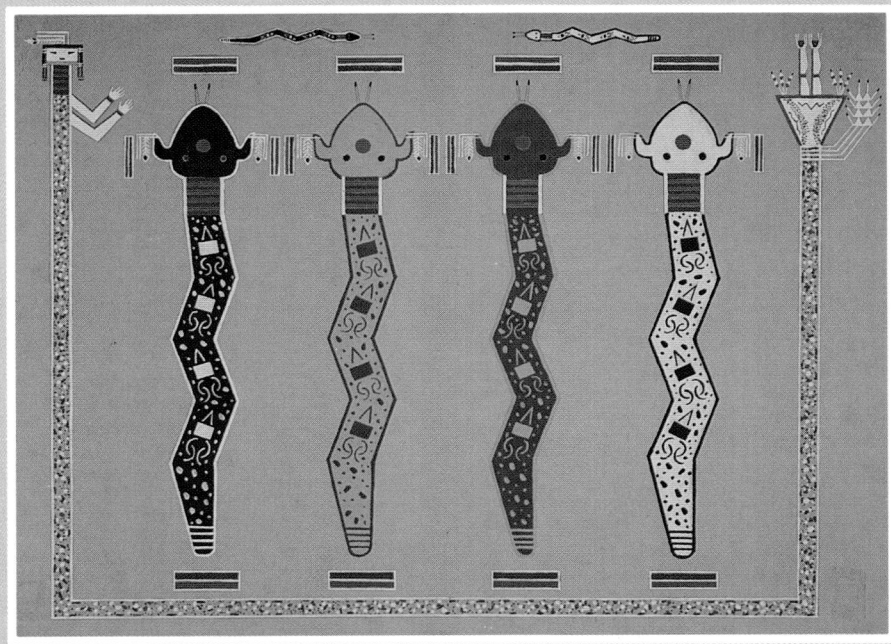

United States. The Americas. *Crooked Big Snakes*. Sand painting from Black Mountain, Arizona. Collected by Laura Adams Armer, repainted by Lloyd Moylan, 1929. From "Beautyway," a Navajo ceremony. (These four crooked horned Big Snakes are black (darkness); yellow (evening light); blue (sky); white (dawn). The short bars below them, in the shape of rainbows, are their means of travel, and those above them are their speech and breath. This sandpainting can also be made showing human figures with quivers on their shoulders, bows in their left hands, and arrows in their right hands.)

Canada. The Americas. Jack Bush. *Red Sky, White Suns*. 1952. Watercolor and pencil.

Youth and Childhood

Credits

Photo Credits

Unless otherwise acknowledged, all photographs are the property of Scott Foresman. P. v: Hirmer Fotoarchiv, Munich; P. 115: Reproduced by permission of Dr. Leonard Gorelick; P. 228: Alinari/Art Resource, NY; P. 287: Hirmer Fotoarchiv, Munich; P. 316: Hirmer Fotoarchiv, Munich; P. 486: Courtesy Indian Museum, Calcutta; P. 549: Photo courtesy of Phaidon Press Ltd., from THE LIFE OF THE BUDDHA by Anil de Silva-Vigier, 1955; P. 557: The Baltimore Museum of Art: Museum Purchase (Julius Levy Memorial Fund); P. 581: The Nelson-Atkins Museum of Art, Kansas City, Missouri (Purchase: Nelson Trust) 50–20; P. 600: National Museum of Korea, Seoul; P. 655: Honolulu Academy of Arts, Purchase, 1954; P. 661: Denman Waldo Ross Collection/Courtesy, Museum of Fine Arts, Boston; P. 712: Itsukushima Jinja Jomotsukan, Hiroshima; P. 716: Gotoh Museum, Tokyo; P. 786: From KOREA: TRADITION AND TRANSFORMATION by Andrew C. Nahm. Courtesy Andrew C. Nahm; P. 790: Rylands Library, Manchester, England; P. 815: From Hildegard of Bingen, SCIVIAS, Otto Müller Verlag, Salzburg, 1954; P. 861: Bibliothèque Nationale, Paris; P. 892: Staatliche Museen Preussischer Kulturbesitz, Kupferstichkabinett, Berlin; P. 903: National Portrait Gallery, London; P. 930: Reproduced by kind permission of the Trustees of the Chester Beatty Library, Dublin; P. 947: Reproduced by kind permission of the Trustees of the Chester Beatty Library, Dublin; P. 1046: The Metropolitan Museum of Art, New York; P. 1058: Photo Documentation Française; P. 1078: Alinari/Art Resource, NY; P. 1097: Alinari/Art Resource, NY; P. 1102: Alinari/Art Resource, NY; P. 1126: Bayerische Staatsbibliothek, Munich; P. 1142: Bibliotheek der Rijksuniversiteit, Utrecht; P. 1276: George Holton/Photo Researchers; P. 1278: Drawing reproduced by permission of Michael D. Coe and Courtesy of the Grolier Club, New York; P. 1290: Neg. No. 326909, Courtesy Department Library Services/American Museum of Natural History; P. 1300: Instituto Nacional de Antropologia e Historia, Mexico; P. 1319: Roloff Beny/ National Archives of Canada (PA189391); P. 1337: From THE ROCK PAINTINGS OF THE CHUMASH: A STUDY OF A CALIFORNIA INDIAN CULTURE, written and illustrated by Campbell Grant. University of California Press, Berkeley and Los Angeles, 1965. Plate 17. P. 1342: University of Texas at Austin/Harry Ransom Humanities Research Center; P. 1406: Rijksmuseum voor Volkenkunde, Leiden; P. 1413: Colorphoto Hans Hinz; P. 1414: Courtesy of the Board of Trustees of the Victoria & Albert Museum; P. 1428: Colorphoto Hans Hinz; P. 1436: Freer Gallery of Art, The Smithsonian Institution, Wash., DC; P. 1450: National Palace Museum, Taipei, Taiwan, Republic of China; P. 1479: From CH'I PAI SHIH by T. C. Lai. University of Washington Press, 1973; P. 1526: Yamagata

Museum of Art; P. 1543: Courtesy Ronin Gallery, New York City; P. 1561: Courtesy of Hugo Munsterberg; P. 1569: Courtesy of Hugo Munsterberg; P. 1576: American Photo Library, Tokyo; P. 1592: From CONTEMPORARY KOREAN PAINTING, Asian Humanities Press, Berkeley, 1979; P. 1596: From: ABDEL HADI AL-GAZZAR: AN EGYPTIAN PAINTER. © Dar al-Mustaqbal al-Arabi, Cairo; P. 1619: Institut du Monde Arabe, Paris; P. 1634: Lazard Corporation; P. 1657: Staatliche Museen Preussischer Kulturbesitz, Kupferstichkabinett, Berlin; P. 1671: Jordan National Gallery of Fine Arts, Amman; P. 1683: Jordan National Gallery of Fine Arts, Amman; P. 1693: Jordan National Gallery of Fine Arts, Amman; P. 1715: Courtesy of Michael Gross; P. 1719: Jordan National Gallery of Fine Arts, Amman; P. 1734: Courtesy of Helen Sebidi. From RESISTANCE ART IN SOUTH AFRICA by Sue Williamson; P. 1747: Courtesy of Iwalewa Haus, Bayreuth University; P. 1789: Private Collection/Photograph by Jeffrey Ploskonka; P. 1824: Courtesy of Michel Cohen; P. 1876: Institut du Monde Arabe, Paris; P. 1887: M. Wolford/Mbari Art; P. 1904: Courtesy of Patrick Holo. From RESISTANCE ART IN SOUTH AFRICA by Sue Williamson; P. 1918: Museum Folkwang Essen; P. 1998: Staatliche Museen Preussischer Kulturbesitz, Nationalgalerie, Berlin; P. 2108: Musée National d'Art Moderne, Paris; P. 2112: Collection Christine and Jacques Dupin. Photo: Galerie Lelong, Paris; P. 2118: National Portrait Gallery, London; P. 2165: The Granger Collection, New York; P. 2174: Private Collection, Photo Courtesy Michael Werner Gallery, New York and Cologne; P. 2176: From WOMEN ARTISTS OF RUSSIA'S NEW AGE by M. Yablonskaya, edited by Anthony Parton. Thames and Hudson, 1990; P. 2202: UPI/Bettmann; P. 2215: Nationalmuseet/The Museum of Denmark's Fight for Freedom 1940–1945; P. 2222: Los Angeles County Museum of Art, Los Angeles County Fund; P. 2260: Roloff Beny/National Archives of Canada (PA189392); P. 2298: University of Texas at Austin/Harry Ransom Humanities Research Center; P. 2299: Frida Kahlo, SELF-PORTRAIT WITH CROPPED HAIR. 1940. Oil on canvas, 15-3/4 × 11″. The Museum of Modern Art, New York. Gift of Edgar Kaufmann, Jr.; P. 2338: Pablo Butcher; P. 2371: Hampton University Museum, Hampton, Virginia; P. 2392: Joseph Cornell, TOWARD THE BLUE PENINSULA: FOR EMILY DICKINSON, 1951–52 box construction 14-1/2 × 10-1/4 × 5-1/2″ © The Joseph and Robert Cornell Memorial Foundation. Photograph by Ellen Page Wilson. Courtesy of The Pace Gallery; P. 2396: Kenkeleba House, Inc.; P. 2466: Kenkeleba House, Inc.; P. 2517: Courtesy of Glenbow Collection, Calgary, Alberta, Canada; P. 2548: Private Collection; P. 2558: Courtesy of Robyn Kahukiwa; P. 2563: National Art Gallery of New Zealand; P. 2590: Jacob Lawrence, FUNERAL SERMON, 1946. Courtesy The Brooklyn Museum, Anonymous Gift (48.24); P. 2598: Marc Chagall, OVER VITEBSK. 1915–20 (after a painting of 1914). Oil on canvas, 26-3/8 × 36-1/2″ The Museum of Modern Art, New York. Acquired through the Lillie P. Bliss Bequest; P. 2615: From THE MAGIC WORLD OF IVAN GENERALIC by Nebojsa Tomasevic. Rizzoli International Publications, Inc., 1976; P. 2618: Stedelijk Museum, Amsterdam; P. 2642: Jon Wilmeshen; P. 2656: Photo by William H. Bengstson, Courtesy of the Phyllis Kind Galleries, Chicago and New York. Private Collection; P. 2668: Courtesy of Christie's; P. 2678: Jose Orozco, THE SUBWAY. (1928). Oil on canvas, 16-1/8 × 22-1/8″. The Museum of Modern Art, New York. Gift of Abby Aldrich Rockefeller; P. 2694: A. J. Bernet Kempers; P. 2705: From: ARTS OF THE ESKIMO: PRINTS by Patrick Furneaux and Leo Rosshandler. Barre Publishers, 1975. © 1975 by Signum Press Limited, Montreal.

COLOR INSERT 1

1(T): Palace Museum, Beijing; 1(B): The Tokugawa Art Museum, Nagoya; 2(T): Scala/Art Resource, NY; 2(B): Bibliothèque Nationale, Paris; 3 Foto Biblioteca Vaticana; 4: Osterreichische Nationalbibliothek, Vienna; 5: Bodleian Library, Oxford, MS. Elliott

246, folio 25 verso; 6: India Office Library/The British Library; 7(T): The Metropolitan Museum of Art, Gift of Arthur A. Houghton, Jr., 1970, (1970.301.17); 7(B): Scala/Art Resource, NY; 8: From THE ROCK PAINTINGS OF THE CHUMASH: A STUDY OF A CALIFORNIA INDIAN CULTURE, written and illustrated by Campbell Grant. University of California Press, Berkeley and Los Angeles, 1965. Plate 29.

COLOR INSERT 2
1: The Metropolitan Museum of Art, Gift of Mary L. Cassilly, 1894 (94.18.1ff); 2: Istanbul Museum of Painting and Sculpture; 3: Institut du Monde Arabe, Paris; 4: Stedelijk Museum, Amsterdam; 5: Georgia O'Keeffe, American, 1887–1986, BLACK CROSS, NEW MEXICO, oil on canvas, 1929, 99 × 77.2 cm, Art Institute Purchase Fund, 1943.95, photograph © 1993, The Art Institute of Chicago. All Rights Reserved; 6(T): Courtesy of the Trustees of the British Museum; 6(B): Australian Museum, Sydney; 7: Courtesy of the Wheelwright Museum of the American Indian (P10A#5); 8: Reproduced by permission and under copyright of the Estate of Jack Bush.

Text Credits

Excerpts from DON QUIXOTE by Miguel de Cervantes Saavedra, translated by J.M. Cohen (Penguin Classics, 1950). Copyright 1950 by J.M. Cohen. Reprinted by permission of Penguin Books Ltd.; "The ardour and the odour and dark wonder" from THE SONNETS OF PETRARCH translated by Joseph Auslander. Reprinted by permission of Random House, Inc.; Excerpt from THE HEPTAMERON by Marguerite de Navarre, translated by P.A. Chilton (Penguin Classics, 1988). Copyright © P.A. Chilton, 1984. Reprinted by permission of Penguin Books Ltd.; THE BACCHAE OF EURIPIDES translated by C.K. Williams. Copyright © 1990 by C.K. Williams. Reprinted by permission of Farrar, Straus & Grioux, Inc.; "Friend, if I found you charming" translated by William Paden from ROMANCE PHILOLOGY, Vol. 35, No. 1, August 1981, pp. 172–173. Copyright © 1981 by the Regents of the University of California. Reprinted by permission; Excerpts from "The Songs of Songs" from THE JERUSALEM BIBLE by Alexander Jones, ed. Copyright © 1966 by Darton, Longman & Todd, Ltd. and Doubleday, a division of Bantam, Doubleday, Dell Publishing Group, Inc. Used by permission of Doubleday, a division of Bantam Doubleday Dell Publishing Group, Inc.; Excerpt from FIFTEEN ODES OF HORACE translated by Cedric Whitman. Cambridge University Press, 1980. Reprinted by permission; Excerpts from POPOL VUH: THE MAYAN BOOK OF THE DAWN OF LIFE translated by Dennis Tedlock. Copyright © 1985 by Dennis Tedlock. Reprinted by permission of Simon & Schuster, Inc.; Adapted from JAPANESE COURT POETRY by Robert H. Brower and Earl Miner with the permission of the publishers, Stanford University Press. Copyright © 1961 by the Board of Trustees of the Leland Stanford Junior University; From LETTER TO A KING by Felipe Huaman Poma de Ayala, translated by Christopher Dilke. Reprinted by permission of A. P. Watt Ltd. on behalf of The Estate of Christopher Dilke; "I Cease Not," "Light in Darkness," "O Ask Not," From FIFTY POEMS OF HAFIZ, by Arthur J. Arberry. Copyright © 1970 by Cambridge University Press. Reprinted with the permission of Cambridge University Press; "The Descent of Ishtar to the Underworld," reprinted from MYTHS FROM MESOPOTAMIA, translated by Stephanie Dalley by permission of Oxford University Press. Copyright © 1989 by Stephanie Dalley; From THE TALE OF GENJI by Murasaki Shikibu, translated by Edward G. Seidensticker. Copyright © 1976 by Edward G.

by Peter Godman. Copyright © 1985 by Peter Godman. Published in the United States by the University of Oklahoma Press. Reprinted by permission; Reprinted with the permission of Macmillan Publishing Company from THE SONG OF ROLAND by Patricia Terry. Copyright © 1965 by Macmillan Publishing Company; From DANTE'S INFERNO by Tom Phillips. Copyright © 1985 Thames and Hudson Ltd. Reprinted by permission of the publisher; "The Wolf and the Lamb" from MARIE DE FRANCE, FABLES, translated by Harriet Spiegel. Reprinted by permission of the University of Toronto Press; "The Seafarer" by Ezra Pound: PERSONAE. Copyright 1926 by Ezra Pound. Reprinted by permission of New Directions Publishing Corporation; Excerpts from THE NIBELUNGENLIED translated by A.T. Hatto (Penguin Classics, Revised edition 1969). Copyright © 1965, 1969 by A.T. Hatto. Reprinted by permission of Penguin Books Ltd.; Excerpts from BEOWULF translated by David Wright (Penguin classics, 1957). Copyright © 1957 by David Wright. Reprinted by permission of Penguin Books Ltd.; Excerpts from TRISTAN by Gottfried Von Strassburg, translated by A.T. Hatto (Penguin Classics, 1960). Copyright © 1960 by A.T. Hatto. Reprinted by permission of Penguin Books Ltd.; Excerpts from CONFESSIONS by Saint Augustine, translated by R.S. Pine-Coffin (Penguin Classics, 1961). Copyright © 1961 by R.S. Pine-Coffin. Reprinted by permission; Excerpt from THE CONSOLATION OF PHILOS-OPHY by Boethius, translated by V.E. Watts (Penguin Classics, 1969). Copyright © 1969 by V.E. Watts. Reprinted by permission of Penguin Books Ltd.; Excerpts from PARZIVAL by Wolfram von Eschenbach, translated by Helen Mustard and Charles Passage. Copyright © 1961 by Helen M. Mustard and Charles E. Passage. Reprinted by permission of Vintage Books, a division of Random House, Inc.; From THE COMPLETE ROMANCES OF CHRÉTIEN DE TROYES, translated by David Staines. Copyright © 1990 by Indiana University Press. Reprinted by permission; Excerpts from THE LIFE OF SAINT TERESA OF AVILA translated by David Lewis. Reprinted by permission of Burns & Oates Ltd.; Notes that accompany "The Tempest" from THE COMPLETE WORKS OF SHAKESPEARE 4th ed. ed. by David Bevington. Copyright © 1992 by HarperCollins Publishers Inc.; "Phaedra" by Jean Racine, from PHAEDRA AND OTHER PLAYS by Jean Racine, translated by John Cairncross. Copyright © 1963, 1970 by John Cairncross. Reprinted by permission of Penguin Books Ltd.; Excerpts from THE BOOK OF THE CITY OF LADIES by Christine de Pizan, translated by Earl Jeffrey Richards. Copyright © 1982 by Persea Books, Inc. Reprinted by permission of Persea Books, Inc.; Excerpts from THE JOURNAL OF CHRISTOPHER COLUMBUS translated by Cecil Jane; Poems 58, 61 and 63 from THE BAMBOO GROVE: AN INTRODUCTION TO SIJO translated by Richard Rutt. Copyright © 1971 The Regents of the University of California. Reprinted by permission; Poems from THE COMPLETE POETRY OF MICHELANGELO, trans-lated by Sidney Alexander. Copyright © 1991 by Ohio University Press. Reprinted by permission; "Gudrun's Lament" from POEMS OF THE ELDER EDDA, translated by Patricia Terry. Copyright © 1990 by the University of Pennsylvania Press. Reprinted by permission; "The Nightingale" by Alcuin from POETRY OF THE CAROLINGIAN RENAISSANCE, by Peter Godman. Published by the University of Oklahoma Press. Reprinted by permission; Excerpts reprinted from ROYAL COMMENTARIES OF THE INCAS AND GENERAL HISTORY OF PERU by Garcilaso de la Vega, El Inca, translated by Harold V. Livermore. Copyright © 1966. By permission of The University of Texas Press; "Restless Night" by Tu Fu from CHINESE LYRICISM translated by Burton Watson. Reprinted by permission of Columbia University Press; "Softly the West Wind Blows" from MEDIEVAL LATIN LYRICS, translated by Helen Waddell. Reprinted by permission of Constables Publishers and Mary Martin; Sonnets: "O Heavenly Father; after wasted days," "She used to let her golden hair fly free," "Life hurries on, a frantic

Index of Titles, Authors, and First Lines of Poetry

Page numbers in italics indicate the location of bibliographic headnotes.